CHILDRENS

THE
PENGUIN
CANADIAN
DICTIONARY

Edited by
THOMAS M. PAIKEDAY

A Penguin Books Canada/Copp Clark Pitman Book

Copyright © 1990, Thomas M. Paikeday

Published jointly by Penguin Books Canada Ltd., 2801 John Street, Markham, Ontario, Canada L3R 1B4 and Copp Clark Pitman Ltd., 2775 Matheson Blvd. East, Mississauga, Ontario, Canada L4W 4P7.

ISBN 0-7730-5007-8

Editing: Maggie Goh, Rubicon Publishing Inc.
Cover Design: David Schembri Design Associates Inc.
Typesetting: Compeer Typographic Services Ltd.
Printing and Binding: John Deyell, Co.

Canadian Cataloguing in Publication Data

Main entry under title:

The Penguin Canadian dictionary

ISBN 0-7730-5007-8

1. English language – Dictionaries. 2. Canadianisms (English) – Dictionaries.* I. Paikeday, Thomas M.

PEI625.P46   1990   423   C87-094891-1

Printed and Bound in Canada

1 2 3 4 5 5007-8 94 93 92 91 90

To
Annie

ABBREVIATIONS

adj.	adjective	interj.	interjection
adv.	adverb	masc.	masculine
art.	article	n.	noun
Brit.	British	neut.	neuter
Cdn.	Canadian	part.	participle
comp.	comparative	pers.	person
conj.	conjunction	pl.	plural
def.	definition	pp.	past participle
e.g.	for example	pres.	present
esp.	especially	pron.	pronoun
etc.	et cetera	pt.	past tense
fem.	feminine	sing.	singular
i.e.	that is	superl.	superlative
indef.	indefinite	v.	verb
indic.	indicative	viz.	namely

PREFACE

This is a dictionary with a new dimension and several new features.

While traditional dictionaries list and define chiefly words, phrases, and idioms, *The Penguin Canadian Dictionary* enters also what are known among linguists as *collocations,* or phrases in which words normally combine with one another in idiomatic English. As the Firthian linguistic dicta go, "Words are known by the company they keep" or "Words of a feather flock together."

Words of a Feather

It is this collocational feature of the language that makes some groups of words idiomatic English and others unidiomatic. Thus, we might say "He has been here a good while" but not " . . . a considerable while," although it is quite grammatical to use "considerable," which is also what *good* means in that collocation; "little" and "short" are other words that collocate with "while." Again, we might say "She is good at *or* in manual work," but not " . . . good *with* manual work."

Structures such as "a good while," "the common good," and "durable goods" are called lexical collocations (combinations of lexical or content words with the keyword) and structures such as "good at *or* in manual work," "good with her hands," and "to come to no good" are called grammatical collocations (combinations of the keyword with grammar words such as prepositions and particles).

Collocations should not be confused with idioms such as **to hold good** (meaning "to be true"), **as good as** (=almost), and **have the goods on someone** (=know something bad about a person that others don't) which, unlike collocations, are expressions peculiar to the language and which, as idioms, convey a meaning that is more than the meaning of the sum of their constituent words. Idioms have traditionally been entered and shown in boldface in English dictionaries.

The uses of entering collocations in a general-purpose dictionary are twofold: (a) They help the dictionary user locate a specific usage he or she has encountered in reading, speech, etc. by being able to identify it, in context and structure, with the collocations listed in the dictionary, and thus to find the appropriate meaning; (b) They show the user the idiomatic ways of using the words being looked up because oftentimes one goes to a dictionary not simply to find the meaning of a word in abstract terms, but to check exactly how that word is used.

If, for instance, the user wants to know what is meant by saying "Joe boasts a large household," there is a similar sentence in the dictionary that tells you that Joe merely takes pride in a large household. Other sentences show the user that Joe would be bragging if he were to "boast *about* or *of* his large household" or "boast *that* he has a large household."

Traditionally, it was thought that only foreign and second-language learners of English needed such help with the language. The so-called "native speaker" was supposed to be inerrant in linguistic matters, as in Noam Chomsky's famous dictum, "The sentences generated will have to be acceptable to the native speaker" (*Syntactic Structures,* 1957). This lexicographer recently had occasion to invite Chomsky and 40 other linguists, philosophers, psychologists, and lexicographers to explain the meaning of this much-abused term, which they graciously did; their collected observations have been published in the format of a quasi-Socratic but thoroughly entertaining dialogue entitled *The Native Speaker Is Dead!* (1985). The book has been reviewed by linguists worldwide, but, like the participants, the reviewers have nothing to say in defence of Chomsky, the protagonist and main contributor to the discussion.

This clarification of the term *native speaker,* however, is without prejudice to the nonjudgmental use of it, as in "Cory is a native speaker of Tagalog," with no implied warranties about Cory's ability to judge the grammaticality and acceptability of a Tagalog sentence, her linguistic expertise probably being in Spanish or English.

A scandalous case of the failure of the "native speaker" is freshman English, which is notorious for bloopers such as the following culled from history essays handed in at the University of Alberta and at McMaster University:

"During the Middle Ages everybody was middle aged. Middle Evil society was made up of monks, lords, and surfs. After a revival of infantile commerce slowly creeped into Europe, merchants appeared. They roamed from town to town exposing themselves and organized big fairies in the countryside. [etc.]" (*Britannica 1984 Book of the Year*).

Recent studies such as *Literacy in Canada: Research Report* (Southam, 1987) should also be an eye-opener for us in this regard.

Even English users who consider themselves experts in the language are sometimes at a loss for a good dictionary when they want to find out, for example, whether they are experts "at," "in," "of," or "on" the subject in question (grammatical collocations), wherever their expertise happens to "be," "rest," "repose," "remain," "sit," "lie," or "lay"! (lexical collocations).

Users of this dictionary should have attained what is generally understood as the primary-school level (Grade 6) of English-language proficiency. With only this as the minimum requirement, *The Penguin Canadian Dictionary* is offered to all Canadian users of English without distinction of native speaker and foreigner, learner and expert. We are all learners of some aspect or other of the language, even if it happens to be our mother tongue, and will continue to be so all life long.

The Baby and the Bathwater

Another feature based on linguistic principles that sets this dictionary apart from others is our defining method which relies on examples of usage rather than on abstract definitions.

As I have explained in a recent review article in *American Speech* ("Revolutionizing Dictionaries," Winter 1989), the procedure traditionally followed in compiling a dictionary is as follows:

Suppose one is defining the entry word **consider.** First, one collects citations of usage of the word excerpted from various sources, then sorts them into groups according to the sense distinctions one perceives, and then proceeds, using all the art and skill at one's command, to craft definitions that give the word's meanings in abstract terms of genus and differentiae, as "**reviewer:** a person [genus] who reviews [differentia]." The abstract definitions are often fleshed out with illustrative phrases and sentences, either based on the citations, sometimes the actual quotations themselves, or conjured up by the lexicographer transported to the appropriate realm or context. The more "unabridged" a dictionary is, the larger is the number of definitions and the amount of illustrative material included.

The citations selected as illustrative of the various meanings of **consider** may read like this: 1. *The old gentleman considered him attentively* – Edith Wharton. 2. *We consider thrift essential.* 3. *Consider how serious your position is.* 4. *He considered her every wish.* 5. *His works are well considered abroad.* 6. *I consider it's best that he left when he did.* 7. *to consider a trade-in on a car.* 8. *to consider a leader to be unwise.* 9. *[He] paused a moment to consider.* 10. *Before she could consider what to do, her husband came in* – Thomas Hardy.

The above sentences are actually taken from *Webster's Third New International Dictionary,* the leader of the unabridged dictionary market. However, when the original dictionary gets more and more abridged in various daughter editions, illustrative material is the first to be discarded, definitions being saved as much as possible. In this lexicographer's view, this is like throwing out the baby and saving the bathwater when the crunch comes,

although perhaps, in Merriam-Webster's view, it may be the baby that is being saved and not the bathwater. The vital question is whether the pulse of the language can be felt in the part that is saved. Are definitions abstracted from reality more meaningful to a dictionary user than meaning in its natural habitat?

Consider the vestiges of meaning left of the original entry from *Webster's Third* for the word **consider** in the smallest of the Merriam line, *The Merriam-Webster Dictionary,* which claims on its cover to be "the world's best-selling dictionary."

consider . . . 1: THINK, PONDER 2: HEED, REGARD 3: JUDGE, BELIEVE

I would consider the above a useless string of synonyms when the actual needs of a dictionary user are taken into account. The Explanatory Notes says that the given meanings are not exactly synonyms (which could serve as apologies for definitions) but "synonymous cross-references" indicating "that a definition at the entry cross-referred to can be substituted as a definition for the entry or the sense in which the cross-reference appears." This is no great help. Defining by synonyms and leading the dictionary users on a merry chase from one synonym to another only lands them in a morass of meanings.

A Morass of Meanings

Consider the case of a user named Pedro who is tossing in his bed at night after a hard day's work on an assembly line. He is worried by a memo leaked to him that says, "Fire every man Jack and consider Pedro for another job." Pedro knows Jack, but happens not to know what *consider* means, the full context also being unknown. And there is no one at hand for Pedro to consult. He reaches for his poor man's Webster for help, but all the help he receives is to be told in effect that he is to be "thought, pondered, heeded, regarded, judged, believed" (take your pick) for another job, probably a triple risk, as the grouping of the definitions would seem to indicate. It would have been more reassuring for Pedro if he could have got the message, in the actual language of his peers if possible, that the boss was going to think about offering him another job.

Even sophisticated dictionary users will find abstract definitions such as the above somewhat confusing. To prove this, as part of a written test of lexicographical aptitude, I recently had over 70 teachers and professors of English who had applied for jobs as dictionary consultants match the six synonyms from the small Merriam-Webster with the ten sentences from the Unabridged. I thought it logical to expect that since the daughter is derived from its mother, the matchings would show some correspondences. However, the result was all sorts of permutations and combinations of definitions and illustrative sentences with absolutely no pattern to them, which, I think, gives the lie to this kind of lexicography.

The futility of such dictionary-making has been exposed by psychologist George Miller and his associates (*Contextual Enrichment by Videodisc,* Princeton, 1988)

in their study of how children learn words. They have announced that "children can write better sentences when they are given a model sentence employing the word than when they are given a definition of the word." They quote the experience of a seventh-grade teacher who asked her class to look up the word *chaste* and use it in a sentence. What they found in *Webster's New Student Dictionary* (Merriam-Webster, 1974) was:

> **chaste** *adj.* 1: innocent of unlawful intercourse. 2: CELIBATE 3: pure in thought and act: MODEST 4: pure or severe in design or expression.

Some of the sentences the students wrote were "The milk was chaste," "The plates were chaste after much use," and "The amoeba is a chaste animal."

Miller and his associates observed that when a word the children looked up was familiar, they had no problem writing an acceptable sentence using it. When the word was unfamiliar, however, the definitions seemed to serve no useful purpose!

It is a commonplace that language is acquired in the normal and natural course by listening and imitation. The child who is exposed to his or her peers speaking a particular language and to books and the media using that language absorbs its basic vocabulary and grammar by an almost passive process, without anyone having to teach it in formal and abstract terms. A seventh grader, for example, who happens to hear the word *chaste* in a TV report that says, "The Pope has pleaded with adolescents to remain chaste until marriage" (if the meaning is not obvious from the context itself) is not going to be helped by being given a list of other words like "innocent, celibate, pure, modest," etc. grouped under four numbers.

An actual "utterance," in the linguistic sense, is always more telling than an abstraction. Even an off-duty lexicographer, if asked what a word such as *celibate* means, would tend to start off with, "You know, as in 'a celibate nun or priest'" and then go on to explain it if necessary, although his dictionary has to give the more formal and studied statement: "one who stays unmarried, especially by religious vow." It is actual speech and writing that exist in reality, formal definitions being abstractions of the lexicographical mind. And a formula such as "**equine:** of, relating to, or resembling a horse or the horse family" is simply dead horse, with no pulse beating in it. We think it much better, therefore, since definitions will remain a necessary evil, to be content with short comprehensive definitions of words, such as "having to do with horses," and supplement them with contextual phrases, collocations, or illustrative sentences to complete the meaning.

The contextual or collocational method is best illustrated with a definition that calls for a distinction between synonymous words. (The following discussion is based on a paper given to the Lexicography Group of the Modern Language Association, New Orleans, 1988). Take, for example, the word *condition* as distinguished from *state* in the general sense of "a mode of existence." The Websters, as in the "variorum" collection below, have two

abstract definitions (Nos. 3 and 4) for what we consider basically one meaning (*Penguin Canadian*, No. 2).

VARIORUM WEBSTER

condition *n.* **1 conditions** *pl.* external or existing circumstances: *Conditions were right for a takeover.* **2** rank or social position. **3** a state of readiness or physical fitness: *getting in condition for the tournament.* **4** state of health: *He was reported to be in critical condition.* **5** a premise upon which the fulfillment of an agreement depends: STIPULATION. **6** in a will, contract, etc., a provision allowing for modification upon the occurrence of some uncertain future event; also, the event. **7** something essential to the appearance or occurrence of something else: PREREQUISITE, as an environmental requirement: *Available oxygen is an essential condition for animal life.* **8** anything essential to the existence or occurrence of something else; prerequisite: *Hard work is a condition of success.* **9 on condition that** provided that; if. **10** an ailment or disease: *My uncle has a heart condition.*

NOTE: The definitions above have been collated without overlapping from the following dictionaries. Def. 1: *Collins English Dictionary,* 1986. 2 & 3: *American Heritage Dictionary,* 1982. 4: *Random House Dictionary,* 1987. 5 & 7: *Webster's Ninth New Collegiate Dictionary,* 1983. 6: *Funk & Wagnalls Canadian College Dictionary.* 8 & 9: *Webster's New World Dictionary,* 1988. 10: *Gage Canadian Dictionary,* 1983. "Webster" is used in the generic sense of "an American English dictionary," names such as Collins, Random House, and Funk & Wagnalls notwithstanding, because all of these are Websterian in their analysis of meaning and defining method. They are also American in origin, including the two titles with "Canadian" in them. Thus, the worthy *Funk & Wagnalls* (which was this lexicographer's first North American flame in the heyday of its virginity in the 1960s) is a patchplated version of the original work which was taken out of the U.S. market in 1974. Canadian entries prepared by the late Prof. Walter S. Avis of Kingston in the 1960s have been patched in. The Gage dictionary is more Canadian because it has been revised and reset in Canada (1966, 1983) with Avis also as the main contributor of Canadianisms (*vide* his pioneering work *Dictionary of Canadianisms,* Gage, 1967) although it too remains substantially the same as its American original. Thus, if you consider an entry such as **consider,** the only difference between the Gage and its parent, *Thorndike-Barnhart High School Dictionary* (1965), is that the latter has the sentence "We consider Shakespeare a great poet" which Gage has replaced with "We consider E. J. Pratt a great Canadian poet."

In our view, what really defines *condition* and distinguishes it from *state* are not the Webster abstractions "a state of readiness or physical fitness" and "a state of health," but the concrete examples that may be given to illustrate the abstract meaning of the word, as the following:

> *a motor in good running condition; in bad, excellent, operating, poor, terrible condition; a patient in critical, fair, good, satisfactory, serious, stable condition; He's either* **in** *or* **out of condition** (= physically fit or unfit) *for a marathon.*

Placing the word in context not only defines it but distinguishes it from *state.* The acid test is whether the language will still remain idiomatic if "state" is substituted for "condition" in the above locations – "a motor in good running state"[?], etc. Substitutability of definition for the word to be defined has been used in traditional lexiocography as a test of good defining, but this applies only to the abstract world of words, not to language as it actually exists. Each word exists as a distinct entity with its own denotations, connotations, usage levels, ranges of applicability, etc.

In most contexts of everyday use, no two words may be substitutable for each other, even if they are identical twins. It is like Ada and Ida having different measurements, habits, temperaments, preferences for breakfast foods, etc. The word *car,* for example, may be substitutable for *automobile* in collocation with "dealer," "insurance," "manufacture," "repair," and "sales," but *car* collocates better than *automobile* does with "armoured," "getaway," "police," "sports," etc. and *automobile* goes better than *car* with "association," "industry," "production," "safety," etc. Moreover, *automobile* is free of the denotational baggage of *car,* as in "cable car," "cattle car," "dining car," "elevator car," etc.

Another advantage of the new lexicography is that definitions can be made so down-to-earth and precise that there will be no need for so-called "synonym notes" which traditional dictionaries provide in the effort to make themselves clear, the definitions themselves being too abstract to bring out essential meaning distinctions. Thus, in the case of *condition* v. *state,* two of the Websters say the words are "often interchangeable" and "largely interchangeable" which is clearly incorrect because one doesn't say "a sad condition of affairs," "solid, liquid, and gaseous conditions of matter," etc. Another Webster says, " 'State' is the general word, often with no concrete implications or material relationships . . . 'Condition' carries an implication of a relationship to causes and circumstances." A fourth synonym note says " 'State' is the general word . . . more often referring to the circumstances in which a person or thing exists or to his (its) nature or form at a certain time: *The state of the world today should interest every serious person.*" The use of "today" in this sentence has the shoehorn effect of forcing the desired distinction, but many good users of the language may want to give it short shrift in the form "The condition of the world should interest every serious person."

Atomization of Meaning

In our view, a word such as *condition* need not be atomized into ten abstractions when three or four will do. Providing synonym notes is indulging in "rhetoric" (not the province of a dictionary), but if a dictionary does provide synonym notes, then all the bases or numbered definitions established by the atomization should be covered. In the present instance, in our analysis, the essential distinction between *condition* and *state* is that *condition* refers to a mode of existence perceived as changeable, whereas *state* (true to its etymology) refers to a steady mode of existence, as in "steady state." The rest are the nuances of actual usage which are better illustrated than defined. And usage, as Horace laid down in his *Ars Poetica,* is the "jus et norma loquendi," the rule and law of language.

Another test of whether ten definitions are really necessary to bring out the meanings of *condition* is how actual users fare when faced with such a plethora of abstractions. Recently, 20 would-be lexicographers were given 20 sentences excerpted from the Toronto *Globe & Mail* in which *condition* was used. The candidates were asked to match the sentences with one or more of the 10 Webster definitions.

To take just Definition Nos. 7 and 8, the sentence judged the most appropriate to No. 7 was, "While substantial resources go into research on arms control and disarmament, the other conditions of stable, peaceful competition between the superpowers appear to attract less attention" (6 votes), closely followed by "The conditions were more advantageous to skiers in the late seeds, including Johnson, who started 21st" (5 votes). The sentence judged the most appropriate to Definition No. 8 was, "Perhaps the trial judge could make it a condition of their [kirpans] being worn in the courtroom that they be blunted and dulled?" (13 votes). The other votes of the testees were distributed haphazardly among the other definitions with absolutely no pattern to them.

Of the three sentences that garnered the most votes, the first and second are totally inappropriate to Definition No. 7 because they clearly illustrate No. 1, defined as "external or existing circumstances." The third sentence is also quite inappropriate to No. 8 because it is an illustration of No. 7. The key to the confusion between Nos. 7 and 8 is that there is no real meaning distinction between them ("Oxygen is an essential condition for animal life" and "Hard work is a condition of success"). The distinction is purely structural, a distinction that hinges on the use of "for" in one case and "of" in the other. Yet, all the candidates (who were the cream of a crop of about 300 applicants) had been misled by the dictionaries instead of being helped. Thus, the Websters had served no useful purpose in the simple task of decoding of meaning (the primary purpose of a dictionary), encoding (constructing a sentence employing the word in a specific sense as defined in the dictionary, as in the Princeton study by George Miller and associates, cited earlier) being the bigger problem for the dictionary user.

The Emperor's New Clothes

Another area in which we have tried to bring lexicography down to earth from the clouds of abstraction is pronunciation. Early in our research on this subject we were aware of the problems of using either the traditional diacritical system of representing English sounds or the International Phonetic Alphabet. An experienced and practical-minded teacher, Professor Richard H. J. Monk of the University of Victoria, put it bluntly in 1967: "After 17 years of teaching in the schools of British Columbia and 11 at a university, I have yet to find a student who can make intelligent use of the vowel systems or pronunciation keys as they appear in most dictionaries." This observation has since been confirmed by almost every educator we checked it with.

However, in spite of Prof. Monk's pointing out that the emperor has no clothes, the general influence of academe proved too strong at that time. In the first Canadian dictionary I worked on (*Gage Canadian Dictionary,* 1966), contractual obligations to the parent dictionary gave us no choice but to use the Thorndike-Barnhart diacritical system without changing even an iota, as in the case of the symbol "i," whether a macron placed over it to symbolize the "long i" could appear with or without the dot. In the first dictionary compiled in Canada using American materials but with no dictation from the U.S. and no royalties owing (*The Winston Dictionary of Canadian English,* 1969), we used IPA, chiefly in consideration of Francophone needs as perceived at the time, but in its Elementary Edition published in 1975, we used both IPA and a new diacritical system adapted to the sounds of Canadian English, this time as a partial reversion or accommodation to the traditionalist school.

It was only in *The New York Times Everyday Dictionary* (Times Books, 1982) that we were able to break free of the constraints of scholastic and traditional practices and opt for a "phonetic" (as popularly understood) style of representing English sounds. When our teacher consultants were polled on the subject and a field-test carried out using high school students from coast to coast, the response was overwhelming. The teachers were unanimous in their opinion that a pronunciation respelling that involves no learning of another set of symbols constituting an abstract system that has no basis in real life is a godsend to students who have a problem learning to read and write their mother tongue.

As for dictionary users from other language backgrounds, we believe that once they have attained the primary-school level of speaking and reading English, our standardized spelling-based system should pose no special problems. It should be easier for them to read English directly than through another system of symbols used to interpret the English sounds. As for those who have not attained that level of English, a direct aural-oral method of teaching pronunciation rather than IPA seems indicated. IPA should be reserved for purely scholarly uses, especially as a tool for the comparative study of the phonetics of various languages.

In our spelling-based system, the primary-school or Grade 6 level of speaking and reading supposes familiarity with about 500 of the most frequently occurring words of English and their pronunciations. A child who knows how to read *and* should have no problem with the sounds of *ant;* the question of accentuation does not even arise. But a word like *aunt* calls for respelling as (ANT) or (AHNT). A child who knows how to read *ah* should have no problem with the latter respelling. **Ant·hill** composed of **ant** and **hill** should pose no problem either, not even of accentuation, because anyone who reads English at the Grade 6 level knows that in words of more than one syllable, the English habit is to stress the initial syllable. Only exceptions to this basic rule of accentuation like **ac·cept** (ac·SEPT), words in which the sound is different from the spelling as in **ac·tive** (AC·tiv), and polysyllabic words like **ab·ra·ca·dab·ruh** (ab·ruh·cuh·DAB·ruh) need to be re-

spelled using a systematized form of English spelling. The question of secondary stresses is largely academic in the context of sentence stresses and how words are actually uttered in everyday English. Students of words in isolation or in the abstract as well as those studying the full pattern of English sounds have resources other than a dictionary meant for daily use in the home, school, and office.

A more detailed explanation of our pronunciation system is given in the User's Guide.

Our Scope and Coverage

The database of this dictionary (which can generate about 20 million citations) was started in Mississauga in 1973 as a manual file in the traditional manner. We were the first to tap electronic databases for lexicographical evidence when vast computerized databases of well-edited current English such as Info Globe and Mead's Nexis came on the scene in the late 1970s.

Entries have been selected on the basis of frequency of occurrence in current English using lexical and grammatical criteria, especially the combinability of entry words with other words in current English. Many purely encyclopedic entries have been omitted in order to do justice to the basic idiom of the language. However, special attention has been paid to the new vocabulary of contemporary North American English that has not yet found its way into the major dictionaries.

Hundreds of such new words and expressions have been researched and entered in *The Penguin Canadian Dictionary.* Such are: *blowout* (slang sense), *cellular phone, cocooning, compact disc, corporate culture, crack cocaine, date rape, deep pocket, downstream* (business sense), *glasnost, heli-ski, hypertext, ice* (drug), *infomercial, leveraged buyout, lifestyle advertising, loose cannon, negative option, nouvelle cuisine, people meter, perestroika, pinstriper, poison pill, prohibitive favourite, to rain on someone's parade, rap music, risk arbitrage, sizzle without the steak, spin doctor, stonewashed, surrogate mother, to take a company private/public, it goes/comes with the territory, user-friendly,* (computer) *virus, yuppie, zipping and zapping* (commercials).

The Penguin Canadian Dictionary is being offered to students and the general public as a Canadian alternative to the midsize Websters (and as a supplementary volume to the larger ones) which dominate the North American market. As a one-man project undertaken as a labour of love, it is a first attempt to practise the principles set out above.

A real change would come about and dictionaries would become more useful and user-friendly only with an English dictionary based on the new principles that matches the leaders of the market in size and scope. We have tried to show the way with this modest volume; it is up to others to achieve the goal.

THOMAS M. PAIKEDAY

ACKNOWLEDGMENTS

My sincerest thanks to the publishers for coming up with the winning contract on this dictionary, in particular to Morton Mint, President of Penguin Books Canada (now President of Penguin U.S.A.), Sandra Hargreaves who succeeded him, and Stephen J. Mills, President of Copp Clark Pitman, who has supported the school edition. I am also grateful to the publishers' editorial, production, publicity, promotional, and sales staffs and to Maggie Goh who helped me debug the manuscript with special attention to socially sensitive matters such as feminism.

On the professional side, I am indebted to the following teachers of English for collectively reviewing the first draft of the manuscript, especially to Elizabeth Doktor whose painstaking and thorough reading of the entire dictionary from the educational point of view has been of great help to me. Some of them also tested out the dictionary in their classrooms.

Sister Jessica A. Bell, SSA, M.A., M.Ed., Tempo School, Edmonton, Alberta

Helen J. Brown, B.A., Burnaby School District, British Columbia.

G. Fred Browning, M.A., B.Ed., Wallaceburg District Secondary School, Ontario.

Maureen Clarke, M.A., Ph.D., University of Toronto.

Donald Clement, M.A., Sheridan College, Brampton, Ontario

Laura Cowan, M.A., Protestant School Board of Greater Montreal, Quebec

Dale Daniels, B.A., North York Board of Education, Ontario

Elizabeth Doktor, M.A., M.Sc.Ed., Educator, Edmonton, Alberta

Robert Eagan, M.A., M.L.S., University of Waterloo, Ontario

Patricia Edlund, Etobicoke Board of Education, Ontario

Ruth Green, B.A., North York Board of Education, Ontario

Jacquie Hunt, M.A., Philemon Wright High School, Hull, Quebec

Kathleen McAuley, B.A., I.E. Weldon Secondary School, Lindsay, Ontario

Frank M. McCormick, B.A., M.Ed., Vancouver School Board, British Columbia

G. Wesley McCullough, B.A., West Hill Secondary School, Owen Sound, Ontario

John Nause, M.A., B.Ed., Ph.D., Yarmouth Consolidated Memorial High School, Nova Scotia

Prof. N. Parker-Jervis, M.A., University of Alberta

Heather Shiffman, B.A., B.Ed., Associated Hebrew Schools, Toronto.

Prof. Murray G. Wanamaker, M.A., Ph.D., University of Manitoba

Lynn Watt, B.A., York Board of Education, Toronto

William J. Young, B.A., Saskatoon Region Community College, Saskatchewan

Special thanks are due to the following educators and experts for occasional help and advice at various stages of the project: Ronald J. Baker, O.C.; John Robert Colombo; Thomas G. Davies; Terry K. Pratt; John Willinsky.

The following teachers and editors have been of help as consultants at the beginning of the work on this dictionary by answering questionnaires: Esmond Bassarath, Kirkland Lake, Ontario . . . Cliff Bell-Smith, Guelph, Ontario . . . Ronald Doumouchelle, Windsor, Ontario . . . Margaret Dunsdon, Toronto . . . Georgia Elston, Lakefield, Ontario . . . Gerda Fermand, Waterloo, Ontario . . . Sylvie Henderson, Don Mills, Ontario . . . Margaret L. Jones, Victoria, B.C. . . . Peter M. Laws, Toronto . . . Larry MacDonald, Ottawa . . . Lynton H. Martin, Pierrefonds, Quebec . . . Anne Montagnes, Toronto.

During the research phase of the project (1982 – 1986), the following professors and teachers answered a detailed questionnaire, conducted fieldwork with the help of their students, and a considerable number reviewed and commented on my *New York Times Everyday Dictionary* (Times Books, 1982). The present dictionary has gained much in practical value to its potential users by the contributions of these teachers of English:

Eileen Adee, Medford Senior High School, Medford, OR . . . Paul Aldridge, Cardinal Gibbons High School, Ft. Lauderdale, FL . . . Peggy Anatol, Lynwood High School, Lynwood, CA . . . William Annis, Silverthorn Collegiate Institute, Toronto, ON, . . . Carmen Aran, Anchorage, AK . . . Billy Bailey, Fleming County High School, Flemingsburg, KY . . . Dennise M. Bartelo, Plymouth State College, Plymouth, NH . . . Nancy Baxer, Temple University, Tokyo, JAPAN . . . Marvin A. Bell, Benton Community School District, Van Horne, IA . . . James D. Benson, York University, Toronto, ON . . . Anne Flaxman Berlin, Chicago, IL . . . Christopher M. Bower, Montoursville Area High School, Montoursville, PA . . . Jo Anne R. Bryant, Auburn University, Auburn, AL . . . Lin Changlu, Sichuan Institute of Foreign Languages, Chongqing, CHINA . . . Victoria Clayton, Queens College, Flushing, NY . . . Burdette Connell, Southern High School, Durham, NC . . . Liam D. Cowan, St. Vincent's Seminary High School, Montebello, CA . . . Ellen F. Garschick, Georgetown University, Washington, DC . . . Lucille Gigante Fischer, Astronaut High School, Titusville, FL . . . Ruben Friedman, Farmingdale Senior High School, Farmingdale, NY . . . Leo Furey, St. Stephen's High School, Stephenville, NF . . . Marjorie Gann, West Highlands School, Amherst, NS . . . Cynthia Garner, Somerset High School, Somerset, KY . . . J. Edward Gates, Indiana State University, Terre Haute, IN . . . Sarah G. George, The Bridge International School, Babson Park, FL . . . Georgia C. Greaney, The Kinkaid School, Houston, TX . . . Roberta M. Gunderson, Fairborn High School, Fairborn, OH . . . Juanita Hallford, Shiloh High School, Lithonia, GA . . . Barbara Hamaker, Southwestern Senior High School, Baltimore, MD . . . Donna Hart, Willington Community Schools, Willington, MI . . . Steven F. Havill, Grants High School, Grants, NM . . . Margaret R. Haygood, University of Maryland, Princess Anne, MD . . . Kay Renee Hensley, Lincoln County High School, Stanford, KY . . . David J. Hibbs, Morgan Park Academy, Chicago, IL . . . Russell K. Hively, R5 School District, Neosho, MO . . . Irvin Howard, California State College, San Bernardino, CA . . . Alyce Hunter, Dunellen High School, Dunellen, NJ . . . Mary Lou Jellen, St. Mary's Academy, Milwaukee, WI . . . Michael A. Kelly, International Airports Projects, Jeddah, SAUDI ARABIA . . . Elaine R. Koerber, Hartford High School, White River Jct., VT . . . Sharon Lasseter, The Robert F. Monroe High School, Quincy, FL . . . Barbara Leigh Laurain, Timothy Edwards School, South Windsor, CT . . . Sister M. Lillian Lazarick, RSM, Notre Dame Convent, Lawrenceville, NJ . . . Judy B. Lee, Deep Creek High School, Chesapeake, VA . . . Dorothy W. Lodge, Ashley Junior High School, Gastonia, NC . . . William R. Martin, George Mason University, Fairfax, VA . . . George D. Masters, The Fox Lane High School, Bedford, NY . . .

Gary L. McLaughlin, Port Angeles Senior High School, Port Angeles, WA . . . Lourdes Mordini, Knox High School, Knox, IN . . . William Musella, Seabury Hall, Makawao, HI . . . Diane Nahas, Aviation High School, Long Island City, NY . . . David Nungesser, Watkins Memorial High School, Pataskala, OH . . . Margaret G. Phillips, Ridgeley, WV . . . Paul Rich, Ministry of Education, Doha, QATAR . . . Patrice D. Robinson, Percy L. Julian High School, Chicago, IL . . . Anne-Marie Sampon, Beaver Dam, WI . . . Louise Scarborough, Valliant High School, Valliant, OK . . . Linda Schink, Windsor Junior High School, Imperial, MO . . . Irene M. Schou, American Falls High School, American Falls, ID . . . Mary Singer, St. Anselm College, Manchester, NH . . . Robert L. Steinruck, Manheim Township High School, Lancaster, PA . . . Richard A. Strugala, Middlesex County College, Edison, NJ . . . Christine Swanberg, Northern Illinois University, DeKalb, IL . . . Anne G. Taylor, Tishomingo Attendance Center, Tishomingo, MS . . . Marie G. Wong, Dallas Independent School District, Dallas, TX . . . Fred R. Yancey, Trout Lake School, Trout Lake, WA.

Other Resources

As a pioneering work that systematically lists word combinations, Morton Benson's *The BBI Combinatory Dictionary of English* (John Benjamins, 1986) has been of great use to us. I appreciate Prof. Benson's encouraging us to use his book.

The main component of our database has been the Toronto *Globe & Mail,* especially its on-line edition started in 1977 and Info Globe on CD-ROM, 1985, both of them world leaders in their respective fields. I am particularly grateful to Ian Hembery, Rick Noble, Carol Marble, and Phil Faughnan for their services in regard to the CD-ROM version of the newspaper.

In drawing upon the print media for evidence of contemporary vocabulary and usage, we have tried to avoid quotations and the use of phraseology of an original nature that carries the writer's signature or trademark. Our policy has been to fashion our own illustrative phrases and sentences in succinct form, based on current English as reflected in well-edited books, periodicals, and the testimony of qualified informants.

Trademarks

We have tried our best to research words suspected of being trademarks and label them as such wherever necessary. However, neither the presence nor the absence of such labelling should be taken as affecting the legal status of any trademark.

THOMAS M. PAIKEDAY

USER'S GUIDE

As a user-friendly reference book, *The Penguin Canadian Dictionary* is designed for use without explanatory notes, pronunciation keys, and such aids. The user should be able to pick up the dictionary "cold" and find the desired information if it is within the scope of the book. However, a few tips on some of the special features of this dictionary are offered below.

I. HOW TO FIND AN ENTRY

The alphabetical order is the same as generally used in all North American dictionaries.

(a) MAIN ENTRIES are the **boldfaced** headwords that start each paragraph. They will be found in strict alphabetical order.

(b) SUBENTRIES are the ones shown **boldfaced** inside the paragraphs. They are mainly of three kinds: (1) inflected forms such as **babies, children, happier, happiest, writes, writing, wrote,** and **written;** (2) phrases and idioms such as **take care of, diamond in the rough,** and **come across;** (3) undefined derivatives such as **amiably, childhood,** and **rosiness.**

(c) COLLOCATIONS are a new feature of this dictionary. As fully explained in the Preface, these are phrases in which words normally combine with one another in good English. Such phrases are included among the illustrative material in italics following a colon.

Collocations are of two kinds. "Lexical" collocations show which *other* words may be used with the headword. Examples are "a labour of love, blind love, platonic love, undying love, unrequited love," etc.

"Grammatical" collocations show *how* other words combine with the headword using grammar words such as prepositions and particles – "in," "away," "upon," "a," "the," and such uninflected forms. Examples of grammatical collocations are "the love for *or* love of one's family, I love to go on dates, He loves watching TV," etc.

Thus, "labour of love," not "effort of love," is the right expression because the word that is normally used with "love" to express the intended meaning is "labour." Again, one may correctly say either "I love to go on dates" or "I love going on dates," "He loves to watch TV" or "loves watching TV," as shown by the collocational sentences given under **love.**

(d) KEYWORDS. Subentries and collocations should be looked for under their keywords, as in the following listing.

SUBENTRIES & COLLOCATIONS	KEYWORD (HEADWORD)
amiably	amiable
babies	baby
cagiest	cagey
children	child
childhood	child
come across	come
don't hold your breath	hold / breath
double whammy	whammy
for love or for money	love / money
hamburger with the works	works
hand in the till	till
inflated ego	inflated / ego
moving violation	move / violation
objective test	objective

organic architecture	organic
out of tune	tune
point of no return	point
sagged	sag
thematic	theme
too close for comfort	close / comfort
written	write

Sometimes it is difficult to determine which word in a phrase is the keyword since dictionary users differ in their perceptions of keywords. Moreover, some phrases belong under more than one headword because of their meaning or structure. As a user-friendly book, this dictionary lists most such phrases, especially collocations such as "don't hold your breath," "for love or for money," and "inflated ego," under both keywords. To get the full meaning of such a phrase, it may be useful to look up the phrase under both of its keywords.

Noun phrases such as *inflated ego* and *moving violation* should be looked up first under their first elements, **inflated** and **moving** respectively. The more fixed of such phrases as well as verbal, adjectival, and other phrases that are more idioms than collocations (e.g. **with kid gloves** and **go one better**) are shown boldfaced under their main keywords. The second entry of a collocation or idiom (namely, under its alternative keyword) is normally in italics as part of the illustrative material. Thus, **on the spur of the moment,** which is a subentry under **spur,** is repeated in italics under **moment.**

BRIEFLY: It is best to look up any word or phrase first as a main entry in its strict alphabetical place, as **limited** which is between **limit** and **limo** or **maid of honour** which is between **maid-in-waiting** and **maidservant.** Next, in the case of a phrase, check its first component among the boldfaced items included under it as headword, as **married quarters** which is under the main entry **married.** Finally, check the phrase under the other suspected keywords, as **no way, shape, or form** which is under **shape** rather than **no** or **way.**

II. SYLLABICATION

Syllabication is shown for a word at its first entry as a headword. No syllabication is shown for hyphenated words like **capital-intensive** and open compounds like **capital city.** Their syllabication should be looked up under their component words.

III. PRONUNCIATION

(a) BASIC SOUNDS. The user of this dictionary is assumed to have attained the primary-school (Grade 6) level of reading and speaking English and have acquired a familiarity with the basic sound and spelling patterns of English, as in about 500 of the most common words of the language. No pronunciation is indicated for sounds whose spelling is such that only one pronunciation is normally possible. Such are:

The vowel sounds of: *at, sail, lake, air, bed, day, big, deep, deer, hide, bye, fire, on, cause, law, more, bone, oh, how, our, boy, oil, ah, but, poor, cure, uh, burn.*

The initial consonant sounds of: *bad, can, chair, dog, fat, go, ghost, guess, guy, hat, just, keep, lake, make, name, page, quick, red, same, take, the, thin, very, wait, what, yes, zoo.*

Vowel sounds in certain phonetic contexts or positions: (1) words ending in *-oal, -old, -olk, -olt* have the long "o" or diphthong; (2) words ending in *-ew, -ool, -oon, -oop, -oose, -ooth, -ude, -uke, -ume, -ute* have long vowels, with the exception of *wool;* (3) words and syllables ending in *-ee, -o,* and *-oo* are long or diphthongized.

These and other rules of English pronunciation are taken as implicitly known to users of English who have reached the primary-school level of proficiency in reading and speaking.

(b) ACCENTUATION. Several levels of stress may be noted in English words when they are studied in isolation.

Thus, **com·mu·ni·ty** could be analysed as having its stresses distributed on the basis of relative force in this order of syllables: 3-1-4-2. In actual speech, however, one rarely hears a stress placed on the second syllable. Even careful news readers on the networks seem to put it, if anywhere, on the first syllable.

In **com·mu·ni·ca·tion,** the main stress is supposed to be on the fourth syllable, but it is frequently placed on the second. Sentence stress is partly to blame for this variation between what the academic experts say and how the language is actually spoken.

Most dictionaries routinely indicate a primary and a secondary stress for words of three syllables or more, as in **ac·cen·tu·ate** which is shown with a primary stress on the second syllable and a secondary stress on the last.

This dictionary uses a more simplified system of accentuation.

(c) TO READ THE PRONUNCIATIONS

1. A stressed syllable is shown in capital letters.

2. A word of two syllables is assumed to have its stress on the first syllable if it is left unmarked for stress. Thus, **milk·shake,** which is not given a pronunciation, should be stressed as (MILK·shake).

3. In polysyllabic words, only the main stress is normally indicated, secondary stresses being considered variable, depending on sentence stress.

A secondary stress, however, is sometimes shown in capital letters when there are more than two syllables preceding the main stress and the syllable with the greater stress may be in doubt.

Thus, **u·til·i·tar·i·an** (yoo·TIL·uh·TAIR·ee·un) is shown with the second syllable in capitals as well as the fourth syllable. This kind of double-stressing is normally not required when all but one of the syllables have neutral vowels, as in **et·y·mo·log·i·cal** (et·uh·muh·LOJ·uh·cul), in which only the first syllable has a full vowel and which therefore is the only syllable that may be pronounced with a secondary stress. The fullness of the vowel should give the syllable any stress that is required for good enunciation.

When there are two stresses of more or less equal force in a word, both stressed syllables are shown in capitals, as in **penny-wise** (PEN·ee·WIZE) and **pound-foolish** (POUND·FOO·lish).

4. The letter group (uh) always stands for the unstressed neutral vowel, as in the first syllable of **a·bove** (uh·BUV), the middle syllable of **syl·la·ble** (SIL·uh·bul), and the last syllable of **i·de·a** (eye·DEE·uh).

Letter groups with (u) plus another consonant, as in **ob·tain** (ub·TAIN), **ran·dom** (RAN·dum), **rang·er** (RAIN·jur), **ray·ment** (RAY·munt), etc. are also normally pronounced with a neutral vowel if they are not shown stressed. Exceptions would be

when a syllable becomes more prominent or gets a secondary stress because of its existence as a separate word. Thus, the second syllable of **do·nut** (DOH·nut) could be pronounced either with a neutral sound or as if it rhymed with **nut.** But the second syllable of **rib·bon** (RIB·un) cannot rhyme with **bun** because "-bon" is not a word or word element.

5. The letter group (zh) is used for the sound of the "s" in *measure, usual, vision,* etc.; the sound of "g" in *beige, regime,* etc.; the sound of "j" in *joual;* and the sound of "z" in *azure.*

6. All other pronunciations should be read using the most common English sounds of the syllables used in the respelling. Thus, **live·long** (LIV·long), **live·ly** (LIVE·lee), **rind** (RINED), etc.

7. When an alternative pronunciation or the pronunciation of a derivative is shown in abbreviated form, as in **Sat·ur·day** (SAT·ur·dee, -day) and **mil·i·tar·i·ly** (-TAIR·uh·lee), the full pronunciation should be read from the previous pronunciation or that of the previous word. Thus, (-day) should be completed as (SAT·ur·day) and **mil·i·tar·i·ly** should be read (MIL·uh·TAIR·uh·lee) based on the previous word **mil·i·tar·y** (MIL·uh·tair·ee). As indicated above, the relative force between the stresses of the first and third syllables of a word like **mil·i·tar·i·ly** is of mainly academic importance.

IV. MEANING

(a) KINDS OF DEFINITIONS

This dictionary has five kinds of definitions:

1. Formal definitions

Most of the formal definitions are of the following type:

ice cream *n.* a frozen dessert of sweetened and flavoured cream.

2. Informal definitions

Note how **classmate** and **classroom** are included in the fourth definition of **class:**

class . . . 4 a group of students, or **class·mates,** instructed together, usually in the same room, or **class·room.**

Formal definitions would have been:

"**class·mate** *n.* a student instructed together with others of the same class."

"**class·room** *n.* a room in which a group of students are instructed together."

When there is sufficient information in the definition of one entry (**class** in the above example) to supply the meaning of another word that is closely connected with it, a formal entry and definition are not provided.

3. Meaning in context

Sometimes an entry is defined in the context provided by an illustrative phrase or sentence, as in the following definition of **fun:**

fun *n.* amusement or what provides amusement; sport: *Skating is fun; We had a lot of fun skating; Children throw snowballs* **for fun** *or* **in fun;** *Guy likes to* **poke fun at** *or* **make fun of** *Cora's walk; The rain spoiled the fun; Life is not all* **fun and games.**

Note how **fun and games, for fun, in fun, poke fun at,** and **make fun of** have been defined in actual contexts of usage. This is how words are learned in real life. No one needs a formal definition of **fun and games** that may read like "activity of a playful or lighthearted kind." Few dictionaries can afford the space to define expressions like **fun and games.** Every child who reads the entry for **fun** given above would understand what **fun and games** means.

4. Meaning by paraphrase

Sometimes a paraphrase is given in parentheses right where a word may call for explanation of its precise meaning, as in the following definition of **whirl:**

— v. swing round and round rapidly and continuously, as leaves caught in the wind or a car gone out of control: *Dancing couples whirled about the room; He whirled her away in his new sports car; Her head whirled* (= She felt dizzy), *and she passed out.*

The illustrative sentences given after the formal definition of **whirl** get more and more complicated. The first sentence gives the literal meaning which is adequately covered by the formal definition. The second sentence is somewhat figurative, but its meaning is not hard to guess. But the third sentence ("Her head whirled") might make someone who doesn't know its meaning wonder about what was happening to the lady's head. The meaning given in brackets should settle any such doubt.

5. Meaning by illustration

After a word has been formally defined and illustrated in one part of speech, it is often unnecessary to give a formal definition of the same meaning in a different part of speech. Note how the *adj.* subentry **round-trip** follows the noun definition without requiring a formal definition saying "having to do with a round trip:"

round trip *n.* a trip to and back from a place.
— **round-trip** *adj.: a round-trip fare, ticket.*

(b) DECODING AND ENCODING

This dictionary helps the user not only to find the meanings of words and phrases (decoding) but also to construct sentences using them (encoding).

For instance, here are two sentences containing the word *root* which you may want to look up in the dictionary for their exact meanings:

Jack is rooting for a solution; Jill is rooting for her school team.

You know enough grammar to identify *rooting* as a verb. So, since *rooting* is not a main entry, you go to the section of the headword **root** that begins with " — *v.*" Soon you locate two sentences that look similar to the ones you have in hand: *"Pigs root for potatoes"* and *"Let's root for the home team."* From the definitions under which the sentences are given, you gather that Jack is *searching* for a solution and Jill is *cheering* for her school team.

For encoding, suppose you are not sure exactly how to use the word *root* referring to someone having settled down in a country. You can recognize and understand *root* in the usage you have in mind when you hear it in speech or see it in print, but it is not part of your active vocabulary. So you turn to the entry for **root.** There you see these sentences: *"Plants* **strike** *or* **take root** *in the soil; We have* **struck root** *or* **roots** (= settled down) *in Canada."* This should tell you that *strike* (not *put down, send, take,* etc.) is the word that goes with "root" in the usage in question and either "root" or "roots" would be correct. With this information, you should be able to use the word *root* with confidence; you only have to pattern your sentence after the one given in the dictionary.

V. GRAMMAR AND USAGE

(a) SYNTAX

The syntax of the words entered in this dictionary can be studied almost exhaustively by examining the illustrative material given under each entry in italics. Since the natural process of learning a language is by listening and imitation of the speech heard around us, no attempt is made in this dictionary to set out the grammar of words in formal terms except for the labelling of categories of words and brief notes about their usage enclosed within parentheses.

Those interested in formal grammar, however, can find the information they want by examining the illustrative examples. Thus, the examples given under the entry for **consider** should yield the grammatical information about the word shown in parentheses below.

They considered her application [transitive use]
. . . took time to consider [intransitive use]
They considered it carefully, favourably [two collocating adverbs]
. . . considered her qualified, intelligent, a genius [object of verb may be a participle, adjective, or noun used with definite article]
They had considered him (to be) not promotable [noun plus adjective as object, with optional "to be"]
They considered her (as a candidate) for his job [object: noun plus prepositional phrase]
. . . considered her as his replacement [object: noun plus noun used with "as"]
He considered resigning, his alternatives, where to go [three kinds of verb objects: "-ing" form; noun; "where" clause]
*They said he had done a good job, **all things considered*** [an idiom and how it is used]
*He had done a good job, **considering*** [another verbal idiom, used with implied object]
*. . . an especially good job **considering** his inexperience, considering that he was inexperienced* [how the idiom is used followed by noun or noun clause]
*That was their **considered** opinion* [a fixed form of the headword used as participial adj.]

(b) PARTS OF SPEECH

The part of speech of each entry word is given using the abbreviations listed on page iv. The following two points should also be kept in mind:

1. The labelling of a headword as a particular part of speech does not extend to modified uses of it in the same entry. Thus, in the entry **consider** above, strictly speaking, the boldfaced subentry **considering** as in "considering his inexperience" may be parsed as a preposition. **Considered** as in "their considered opinion" is really used as an adjective. The point to remember is that these usages are included under the entry labelled "verb" based on their meaning, not their grammatical form or function. The prepositional and adjectival uses are participial forms of **consider** that have the same basic meaning as the verb.

2. The ***adj.*** label often includes modifiers, as *love* in "love children, love letter, love triangle" and *mock* in "mock battle, parliament, turtle soup." Such modifiers do not have all the properties of adjectives such as degrees of comparison and the use of an intensifier such as *very* or *quite* before it, as do full adjectives like *good* and *exciting*. You could NOT say, for example, that "This turtle soup is very mock" or "My mom makes mocker turtle soups than yours."

The modifier ***adj.*** label is normally used when there is more than one such example following a noun definition.

(c) CONTRASTIVE EXAMPLES

Note the following sets of illustrative examples:

notwithstanding: *The party went on, notwithstanding the lateness of the hour. The party went on, notwithstanding the hour was late. The lateness of the hour notwithstanding, the party went on.*

taboo: *To Muslims, food is taboo before sunset during Ramadan. A taboo is placed on eating before sunset. Eating before sunset during Ramadan is under a rigid taboo. Eating before sunset is tabooed.*

sake: *For our **children's sake**, please stop arguing. **For the sake of** our children, please stop arguing. Please stop arguing, **for goodness sake**.* [for added force] ***For Heaven's sake**, please stop arguing. I'm saying this for both our sakes, for your sake and mine. Let's not **argue for arguing's sake*** (=because we like to argue). *Let's suppose, **for argument's sake*** (= as a starting point), *that life does exist on Mars.*

It may look as though your user-friendly dictionary is repeating itself. But our purpose is merely to illustrate various parts of speech and usages of the same word using sentences with minimal change of meaning so as to bring out grammatical and usage differences contrastively.

VI. MISCELLANEOUS MECHANICS

(a) USE OF PARENTHESES

Besides obvious purposes like enclosing pronunciation respellings, parentheses are used in special ways as listed below:

1. To give brief definitions within illustrative examples, as in the definition of **dollar for dollar** below. Sometimes the brief definition is preceded by a label such as *Slang for* and *Informal for* as in the second sentence:

dol·lar (DOLL·ur) *n.* the basic money unit in Canada, the U.S., Australia, and other countries: *Dollar for dollar* (= considering prices), *this car is second to none; Everyone likes **dollars** (Informal for money).*

Sometimes a brief definition or explanation in italics is run on with the rest of the sentence in italics if it can be done without a break in the syntax, as in the examples below:

*An **educated guess** (based on some knowledge of the facts) is likely to be right.*

*Marsupials are **pouched** animals (that have a pouch).*

The parentheses are not dispensed with because, strictly speaking, what is in parentheses is redundant when you consider the meaning of **educated guess** and **pouched** respectively.

2. To telescope two definitions into one as in the following:

East Asian *n. & adj.* (a person) of or from the region comprising eastern China, Japan, North and South Korea, Taiwan, and nearby islands.

Here the noun definition should be read as "a person of or from . . . ." and the adjective definition will be the part outside the parentheses: "of or from . . . ."

run *v.* (cause) to move at a pace faster than walking.

The above should be read as two definitions: "cause to move at a pace faster than walking" and "move at a pace faster than walking." The two definitions have been telescoped into one for saving space.

3. To show alternative structures, as in the following:

de·sir·ous (di·ZYE·rus) *adj.* desiring or wishing: *A mother is desirous of her children's good; She is desirous that they (should) do well in life.*

In the last sentence, *should* is placed in parentheses to show that both "She is desirous that they do well in life" and "She is desirous that they should do well in life" are correct.

Other examples:

Boys ganged (up) together at the corner.

in (or **out of**) **gear** connected (or not connected) to the motor; hence, working (or not working) properly.

gift of (the) gab

lead someone (on) a merry chase.

4. To enclose short grammar and usage notes and other explanations. Square brackets are used for this purpose, as in the following entries:

a·bed (uh·BED) *adj. & adv.* [literary use] in bed: *to lie abed of a Sunday morning.*

a·ghast (uh·GAST) *adj.* [used after its noun] horrified: *She was aghast; Everyone stood aghast at the sight.*

Dominion Day *n.* [former name] Canada Day.

(b) PREPOSITIONS IN ITALICS

Giving prepositions in italics, as in the following examples, is another space-saving device. The definition itself shows how to use the headword, so no illustrative sentence is given. Thus, **evict,** as shown below, should be used in a sentence like "to evict someone from his house," not "out of his house," etc.

evict *v.* oust or discharge a tenant *from* a house or land by legal process.

moon *v.* spend time or wander *about* or *around* idly.

mull *v.* ponder *over* a problem, proposal, etc.

sally *v.* go *forth* or set *out* suddenly, as if in attack.

scuffle *v.* to struggle *with* someone at close quarters.

(c) SMALL CAPITALS

Small capitals indicate cross-references which should be looked up for a formal definition or for more information. Thus:

apices See APEX.

holloware . . . cf. FLATWARE.

—— kind of *Informal.* same as SORT OF.

should *pt.* of SHALL.

(d) QUOTED WORDS AND PHRASES

Occasionally, you may find a word or phrase given in quotes instead of boldface as you might expect. Such quotes are used to show that the quoted word or phrase is outside the scope of this dictionary to be entered and defined fully. However, the word or phrase is being used to explain a meaning because of its relevance in the particular context in which it appears. Thus:

leech *n.* **1** a small worm, also called "bloodsucker," once used in medicine to remove blood from patients.

milk *n.* **1** . . . **2** a similar liquid, as found in a coconut, the latex of trees and plants, or "milk of magnesia."

In the above definitions, "bloodsucker" and "milk of magnesia" are not entered in the dictionary. But they should help to clarify the meanings of **leech** and **milk** respectively.

VII. LETTERS TO THE EDITOR

Users of *The Penguin Canadian Dictionary* are invited to write to the lexicographer at the address given below on anything connected with the dictionary: comments, criticisms, suggestions, requests for more information, etc. are welcome. Please enclose a stamped, self-addressed envelope to facilitate a reply.

Thomas M. Paikeday
c/o Penguin Books Canada Limited
2801 John Street
Markham, Ontario, L3R 1B4

Aa

A or **a** (AY) *n.* **A's** or **a's 1** the first letter of the English alphabet. **2** [used to indicate the first, highest, or best of a group]: *He got an A on the test; grade A eggs; an A1 student; We enjoy a triple-A credit rating.*
— **combining form.** shaped like an A: *an A-frame house; an A-line skirt; an A-tent.*

a (AY, uh) *indef. art.* **1** a single thing but not a particular one: *a bird, book, boy.* **2** a single group: *a lot of books; a few boys.* **3** [used with "many" before singular nouns for plural meaning]: *many a book* (= many books). **4** [used with "of"]: *birds of a feather* (= of the same kind). — *prep.* each: *twice a week.*

a- *prefix.* **1** on: *afire, ashore; The house is a-building* (= being built). **2** not: *amoral, asexual, asocial.*

aard·vark (ARD·vark) *n.* a South African anteater.

ab- *prefix.* away; from: *abduct, aberrant, abnormal.*

a·back (uh·BAC) *adv.*: *He was taken aback* (= startled) *by the announcement.*

a·ban·don (uh·BAN·dun) *v.* give up or desert: *the order to abandon ship; He abandoned his car in the snow; He abandoned it to its fate.*
— *n.* carefree manner: *She sang with wild abandon; He drove with reckless abandon.* — **a·ban·don·ment** *n.*

abandoned (uh·BAN·dund) *adj.* **1** deserted: *an abandoned house.* **2** shameless: *an abandoned sinner.*

a·base (uh·BACE) *v.* **a·bas·es, a·based, a·bas·ing** lower or humble *oneself.* — **a·base·ment** *n.*

a·bate (uh·BATE) *v.* **a·bates, a·bat·ed, a·bat·ing** make or become less: *The storm has abated; drugs to abate pain.* — **a·bate·ment** *n.: a tax abatement.*

ab·bre·vi·ate (uh·BREE·vee·ate) *v.* **-ates, -at·ed, -at·ing** shorten: *to abbreviate a word, phrase, story, visit; "Professor" can be abbreviated to "Prof."*
— **ab·bre·vi·a·tion** (-AY·shun) *n.*

ABC *n.* **ABC's 1** the alphabet: *as easy or simple as ABC.* **2** basics or fundamentals: *the ABC's of driving a car.*

ab·di·cate (AB·duh·cate) *v.* **-cates, -cat·ed, -cat·ing** give up a position, power, right, etc.: *King Edward VIII abdicated in 1936; He abdicated the throne; She abdicated her responsibilities.*
— **ab·di·ca·tion** (-CAY·shun) *n.*

ab·do·men (AB·duh·mun, ab·DOH·mun) *n.* **1** the human belly. **2** the last segment of an insect's body.

ab·dom·i·nal (ab·DOM·uh·nul) *adj.* having to do with the human belly: *to suffer from abdominal pain.*

ab·duct (ab·DUCT) *v.* take away someone by force; kidnap: *The infant was abducted from its home.*
— **ab·duc·tion** *n.* — **ab·duc·tor** *n.*

a·bed (uh·BED) *adj. & adv.* [literary use] in bed: *to lie abed of a Sunday morning.*

ab·er·rant (ab·ER·unt) *adj.* not normal in behaviour; deviant.

ab·er·ra·tion (ab·uh·RAY·shun) *n.* **1** deviation: *a mental aberration.* **2** distortion: *Optical aberrations cause bad focussing.*

a·bet (uh·BET) *v.* **a·bets, a·bet·ted, a·bet·ting** encourage in doing wrong: *to aid and abet a thief; The rumours were aided and abetted by leaks from confidential sources.* — **a·bet·tor** or **a·bet·ter** *n.*

a·bey·ance (uh·BAY·unce) *n.* suspension: *a law held in abeyance; a rule that has fallen into abeyance* (= disuse).

ab·hor (ub·HOR) *v.* **ab·hors, ab·horred, ab·hor·ring** to hate with disgust: *He abhors getting drunk; He abhors drunkenness.*
— **ab·hor·rence** *n.: He holds drug dealers in abhorrence.*
— **ab·hor·rent** *adj.: Child abuse is abhorrent to human nature.*

a·bide (uh·BIDE) *v.* **a·bides,** *pt. & pp.* **a·bode** or **a·bid·ed, a·bid·ing 1** put up with a person or thing: *He's so nasty no one can abide him; People like Mother*

Teresa can't abide human misery. **2** stay: *"Abide with me"; You can rely on him to **abide by** (=keep) his promises; **abiding** (=lasting) happiness.*

a·bil·i·ty (uh·BIL·uh·tee) *n.* **-ties** power or skill: *the human being's ability to think; a woman of great ability; He did the job to the best of his ability* (= as well as he could); *to appreciate, demonstrate, display, recognize, show ability; creative, exceptional, innate, natural, outstanding, remarkable ability.*

ab·ject (AB·ject) *adj.* low or degrading: *He had to make an abject apology; to live in abject poverty; abject submission.* — **ab·ject·ly** *adv.*

a·blaze (uh·BLAZE) *adj.* on fire: *a house set ablaze; He was ablaze* (=filled) *with fury.*

a·ble (AY·bul) *adj.* having the means or power: *The child is able to walk by itself; an able* (=skilful or talented) *lawyer, ruler.* — **a·bly** (-blee) *adv.*

-able *adj. suffix.* that can be done, as specified: *applicable, avoidable, bearable, bendable, readable.*

able-bodied (AY·bul·bod·eed) *adj.* having a healthy body: *an able-bodied citizen, man, woman, worker; An **able-bodied** or **able seaman** ranks above an ordinary seaman.*

a·bloom (uh·BLOOM, long "OO") *adj.* in flower: *Trees are abloom in early spring.*

ab·nor·mal (ab·NOR·mul) *adj.* not normal: *abnormal behaviour, weather.* — **ab·nor·mal·ly** *adv.*
— **ab·nor·mal·i·ty** (ab·nor·MAL·uh·tee) *n.*: *a congenital abnormality.*

a·board (uh·BORD) *adv. & prep.* on, onto, or in a ship, train, plane, etc.: *All aboard! Come aboard! Let's go aboard; Welcome aboard!*

a·bode (uh·BODE) *pt. & pp.* of ABIDE.
— *n.* a place where one lives; dwelling: *Al took up his abode here in the 1920s; a man of no fixed abode* (=address).

a·boi·deau (AB·uh·doh) *n.* **-deaus** or **-deaux** (-doze) *Cdn.* **1** in the Maritimes, a sluice gate in a dam for letting out flood water while preventing the inflow of sea water at high tide. **2** the dam or dike itself. Also **a·boi·teau** (-toh), *pl.* **-teaus** or **-teaux** (-toze).

a·bol·ish (uh·BOL·ish) *v.* do away with a custom, practice, or institution: *Lincoln abolished slavery in the U.S.*

ab·o·li·tion (ab·uh·LISH·un) *n.* an abolishing, esp. of capital punishment, slavery, etc.
— **ab·o·li·tion·ist** *n. & adj.*

A-bomb (AY·bom) *n.* an atomic bomb.

a·bom·i·na·ble (uh·BOM·uh·nuh·bul) *adj.* loathsome or disgusting: *an abominable crime; The **Abominable Snowman** is said to be a humanoid, hairy beast that lives in the Himalayas.* — **a·bom·i·na·bly** *adv.*
— **a·bom·i·na·tion** (-NAY·shun) *n.*: *He thinks TV dinners that pack little meat and sell for high prices are an abomination.*

a·bo·rig·i·nal (ab·uh·RIJ·uh·nul) *adj.* having existed first in a place: *aboriginal languages, people, plants, rights, rocks.*

— *n.* a member of an aboriginal people; also **ab·o·rig·i·ne** (-RIJ·uh·nee).

a·born·ing (uh·BORN·ing) *adv.* [literary use] while being born or produced: *an independence movement that died aborning.*

a·bort (uh·BORT) *v.* end a plan or process before completion: *to abort a flight on takeoff; to abort a fetus, pregnancy.*

a·bor·tion (uh·BOR·shun) *n.* termination of a pregnancy: *to get, have, induce an abortion; to do* or *perform an abortion on a woman; a therapeutic abortion; legalized abortion; women wanting abortion on demand; spontaneous abortion* (=miscarriage).

a·bor·tion·ist *n.* [unfavourable use] one who favours or effects the abortion of unwanted fetuses.

a·bor·tive (uh·BOR·tiv) *adj.* that fails to succeed: *an abortive attempt, coup, effort.*

a·bound (uh·BOWND) *v.* have or exist in large numbers: *Fish abound in this lake; The lake abounds in* or *with fish.*

a·bout (uh·BOWT) *prep. & adv.* **1** in, on, or near; around: *I saw him about here; We are about 2 km from the river; It is about time; The guests were seated about* (on the lawn); *It was late when she set about* (=started) *getting dinner ready.* **2** concerning: *Tell me about her; How about that? What's it all about? Let's be quick about it* (= Let's do it quickly).
— *adj.* **1** active: *He is up and about at 6 a.m. every day.* **2** ready: *She was about to leave; He's **not about to** * (=is very unwilling to) *resign.*

about-face (uh·BOWT·face) *n.* a reversing, esp. of attitude: *The politician did an about-face after the election.*
— *v.* **-fac·es, -faced, -fac·ing** turn to face the opposite way.

a·bove (uh·BUV) *prep.* higher, earlier, or more than: *We are flying above the clouds; We value honour above wealth; **Above all**, we try to be honest.*
— *adv.*: *See page 10 above; a kite flying above.*
— *adj.*: *the above words; The words above are to be deleted; It's 40 degrees above* (= above zero).
— *n.*: *The orders came from above* (= from the superiors); *none of the above* (= above-mentioned words, items, etc.).

a·bove·board (uh·buv·BORD) *adj. & adv.* without dishonesty: *She's always quite open and aboveboard in her dealings.*

ab·ra·ca·dab·ra (AB·ruh·cuh·DAB·ruh) *n.* **1** word or speech supposed to have magical effect. **2** jargon; gibberish.

a·bra·sion (uh·BRAY·zhun) *n.* **1** a rubbing away. **2** a scraped part or area, as on the skin.

a·bra·sive (uh·BRAY·siv) *adj.* **1** that grinds and polishes: *an abrasive material like sand; n.: Diamonds are used as abrasives.* **2** rough or irritating: *a fellow with an abrasive manner; He's an abrasive personality.*

a·breast (uh·BREST) *adj. & adv.* side by side: *They marched two abreast; TV helps him **keep abreast of*** (= stay informed about) *current events.*

a·bridge (uh·BRIJ) v. **a·bridg·es, a·bridged, a·bridg·ing** shorten or condense a book: *an abridged edition.* — **a·bridg·ment** or **a·bridge·ment** n.

a·broad (uh·BRAWD) adv. **1** out of one's country: *He has been abroad 10 years; went abroad as a reporter; He's now returning **from abroad**.* **2** widespread: *A rumour is abroad that he is dead.*

a·brupt (uh·BRUPT) adj. sharp, not slow or smooth: *an abrupt turn in the road; an abrupt descent; his abrupt manner of taking leave.* — **a·brupt·ly** adv.; **a·brupt·ness** n.

ab·scess (AB·ses) n. a collection of pus in a body tissue: *an abscess of the gums;* **adj.:** *an **abscessed** tooth.*

ab·scond (ab·SCOND) v. sneak off and hide: *He absconded with the money; absconded from the country; the **absconding** thief.* — **ab·scond·er** n.

ab·sence (AB·sunce) n. a being absent: *It happened during his absence; an unexplained absence; He's noted for his frequent absences from work.*

ab·sent (AB·sunt) adj. not present: *He was absent without leave from his duties; was absent (from school) on Monday; the absent student.* — **prep.** [legal use] without: *Absent proof of purchase, a refund is impossible.* — **v.** (ab·SENT) be absent: *He absented himself from duty for many days.* — **ab·sent·ly** (AB·sunt·lee) adv.

ab·sen·tee (ab·sun·TEE) n. & adj. (one) who is absent: *No absentees today; an absentee landlord; An absentee rate of 4.6% is considered unacceptable.*

ab·sen·tee·ism (ab·sun·TEE·iz·um) n. habitual or customary absence: *school absenteeism; Three percent is considered normal absenteeism in business.*

absentee voting n. Cdn. voting by people who are temporarily away from their ridings.

absent-minded (ab·sunt·MINE·did) adj. inattentive or forgetful. — **ab·sent·mind·ed·ly** adv. — **ab·sent·mind·ed·ness** n.

ab·so·lute (AB·suh·loot, long "oo") adj. complete or perfect: *the absolute truth; absolute proof, trust; The accused was given an **absolute discharge** (with no criminal record) because of new evidence; An absolute (= despotic) ruler has absolute or unlimited power.*

ab·so·lute·ly (AB·suh·loot·lee) adv. completely or entirely: *He's absolutely mistaken.* — **interj.** (-LOOT.lee) certainly!

absolute zero n. the lowest temperature possible, −273.15° C.

ab·so·lu·tion (ab·suh·LOO·shun) n. remission of sin through a church sacrament: *A priest pronounces absolution at the end of a confession.*

ab·solve (ab·ZOLV) v. **ab·solves, ab·solved, ab·solv·ing** to free: *to absolve someone from blame, guilt, obligations, promises, sins.*

ab·sorb (ab·ZORB) v. **1** take in, as a sponge does a liquid: *Paper absorbs moisture; Rugs absorb sound; The small companies were absorbed into a large conglomerate.* **2 absorbed** adj. with attention completely taken up: *a philosopher found absorbed in thought; completely, deeply, thoroughly, totally absorbed; She's quite absorbed in her homework; especially absorbed with or by math problems; He finds chess quite **absorbing** (= taking up all his attention).* — **ab·sorb·en·cy** n. — **ab·sorb·ent** adj. — **ab·sorp·tion** n.

ab·stain (ab·STAIN) v. keep away on principle or in self-denial: *to abstain from alcohol, meat, smoking, voting.* — **ab·stain·er** n.

ab·sten·tion (ab·STEN·shun) n. an act of abstaining, as from voting: *10 in favour, 7 against, and 3 abstentions.*

ab·sti·nence (AB·stuh·nunce) n. the act of abstaining in self-denial: *He practises complete or total abstinence from liquor, meat, tobacco, etc.* — **ab·sti·nent** (-nunt) adj.

ab·stract (ab·STRACT) v. take out or remove something from a mass or body: *to abstract iron from ore; A pickpocket abstracts (= steals) money from a purse; The idea of greenness is abstracted (= taken by the mind) from green objects; to abstract (= summarize) an essay in 100 words; The philosopher wore an **abstracted** (= lost in thought) look;* **ab·stract·ed·ly** adv. — **n.** (AB·stract) summary: *a 100-word abstract of a thesis.* — **in the abstract** in theoretical terms: *He talks in the abstract without giving concrete examples.* — **adj.** (AB·stract) existing only in the mind, removed from reality: *Greenness is an abstract idea; Abstract art does not represent real objects.* — **ab·strac·tion** (ab·STRAC·shun) n.

ab·struse (ab·STROOSE) adj. difficult for the lay person to understand: *Higher mathematics is an abstruse discipline.*

ab·surd (ab·ZURD) adj. not sensible; ridiculous: *It's absurd to ask for such a big raise; It's patently, totally absurd.* — **ab·surd·ly** adv. — **ab·sur·di·ty** (-duh·tee) n.: *the height of absurdity.*

a·bun·dance (uh·BUN·dunce) n. plenty: *a life of abundance; There's food in abundance after a harvest; There's an abundance of food.*

a·bun·dant (uh·BUN·dunt) adj. plentiful: *Food is abundant after a harvest; a country abundant in raw materials; There's abundant evidence for pressing charges.* — **a·bun·dant·ly** adv.

a·buse (uh·BYOOZ) v. **a·bus·es, a·bused, a·bus·ing 1** use or treat badly: *No tool lasts long if abused; to abuse an animal by beating it; Employees abuse a trust by stealing.* **2** insult: *He got drunk and abused his boss.* — **n.** (uh·BYOOSE) **1** wrong or improper use: *drug abuse; abuse of language, power, privileges, trust; a used car that has taken a lot of abuse.* **2** bad treatment: *child abuse; physical abuse.* **3** insult: *a term of abuse; verbal abuse; words of abuse; She heaped, hurled, showered abuse (= insults) on him.* — **a·bu·sive** (-siv) adj.; **a·bu·sive·ly** adv.

a·but (uh·BUT) v. **a·buts, a·but·ted, a·but·ting** have a common border or end with something: *His garage abuts on or upon my lot.*

a·bys·mal (uh·BIZ·mul) adj. extremely bad: *His record is abysmal; an abysmal failure; his abysmal ignorance.*

a·byss (uh·BIS) *n.* a hole that is too deep to measure: *a gaping, yawning abyss; the abyss* (= depth) *of ignorance, shame, sin.*

ac·a·deme or **Ac·a·deme** (AC·uh·deem) *n.* the world of scholars, esp. at the university level: *the groves* or *halls of academe* (= the world of universities). Also **ac·a·de·mi·a** (-DEE·mee·uh) *n.*

ac·a·dem·ic (ac·uh·DEM·ic) *adj.* **1** having only theoretical value: *How he managed to pass is now academic.* **2** having to do with teaching and studying: *the **academic freedom** of a professor who can say what he thinks without fear; The **academic year** usually starts in September.* — *n.* a professor. — **ac·a·dem·i·cal·ly** *adv.*

a·cad·e·my (uh·CAD·uh·mee) *n.* **-mies 1** a society of learned people: *an academy of science; the French Academy.* **2** a school for special studies: *a military, naval, riding academy; We studied together at the academy; an academy for girls.*

Academy Award *n.* an annual award of the Academy of Motion Picture Arts and Sciences of Hollywood for outstanding achievements in film making; an Oscar.

A·ca·di·an (uh·CAY·dee·un) *n. & adj. Cdn.* (person) of or from **Acadia,** the French-speaking region of New Brunswick and Nova Scotia or a parish of Louisiana settled by people deported from there: *the picturesque **Acadian Trail** (= motor route) through the region of New Brunswick where descendants of the Acadians deported in 1755 and 1758 live; Acadian French.* See also CAJUN.

ac·cede (ak·SEED) *v.* **-cedes, -ced·ed, -ced·ing 1** agree, esp. after being persuaded: *She acceded to the blackmailer's demands; to accede to a treaty.* **2** assume: *to accede to an office, to a position, to the throne.* — **ac·ces·sion** (ac·SESH·un) *n.*

ac·cel·er·ate (ac·SEL·uh·rate) *v.* **-ates, -at·ed, -at·ing** speed up: *to accelerate an engine; The car can accelerate to 60 km/h in 10 seconds.* — **ac·cel·er·a·tion** (-RAY·shun) *n.*

ac·cel·er·a·tor (ac·SEL·uh·ray·tur) *n.* the gas pedal of an automobile: *to step on* or *depress the accelerator; to ease up on* or *let up on the accelerator; the accelerator pedal.*

ac·cent (AC·sent) *n.* **1** a foreign style of speaking, esp. from one's own point of view: *When the Texan Lyndon Johnson became U.S. president, Texans said at last they had a president who could speak English without an accent; She speaks with a heavy, middling, neutral, slight, strong, thick accent; He affects, assumes, cultivates, imitates, puts on a British accent when travelling in the U.K.; She can speak French with no accent at all; His Canadian accent was evident from the way he pronounced words like "about" and "mouse"; But he got rid of his accent after a few years abroad.* **2** emphasis placed on a syllable in speaking or a mark placed on a written word: *Most English words have their accent on the first syllable; French words have acute, grave, and circumflex accents* (= accent marks); *"Rôle" is often written with a circumflex accent.* **3** emphasis: *The accent was on the layered look in women's fashions; an overcoat with a London accent* (= character). — *v.* (also ac·SENT) emphasize: *The accented syllable of "accord" is the second; Makeup accents her good*

looks; *a product that accents the flavour of good food; He speaks a heavily accented English* (= with a heavy foreign accent).

ac·cen·tu·ate (ac·SEN·choo·ate) *v.* **-ates, -at·ed, -at·ing** to accent or emphasize: *to accentuate the positive.* — **ac·cen·tu·a·tion** (-choo·AY·shun) *n.*

ac·cept (ac·SEPT) *v.* receive and approve: *to accept a gift, proposal; to accept something blindly, fully, readily; to be accepted* (as a member) *in high society; an **accepted*** (= generally approved) *fact, opinion.*

ac·cep·ta·ble (ac·SEP·tuh·bul) *adj.* **1** that can be accepted; agreeable: *Is this acceptable to you? The terms of a contract have to be mutually acceptable to the parties concerned; completely, fully acceptable.* **2** endurable: *pollen count that is considered acceptable; an acceptable level of emission from a factory.* — **ac·cep·ta·bly** (-blee) *adv.* — **ac·cep·ta·bil·i·ty** (-BIL·uh·tee) *n.*

ac·cep·tance (ac·SEP·tunce) *n.* an act of accepting or being accepted: *three refusals and no acceptances; a belief that has gained wide acceptance; a theory that has found universal acceptance; the blind acceptance of a dogma.*

ac·cep·ta·tion (ac·sep·TAY·shun) *n.* accepted meaning: *the usual acceptation of a word.*

ac·cess (AC·ses) *n.* a going to or reaching a place: *a password for gaining* or *getting access to computer data; He was denied access; Can we grant her access to our records? direct, easy, free, limited, random, unlimited access; The stairs are the only access to* (= means of reaching) *those rooms; The rooms are not easy of access* (= not easy to reach); *the **access time** between requesting and receiving data from a computer storage medium such as a disk.* — *v.* gain access to something: *to access computer data.*

ac·ces·si·ble (ac·SES·uh·bul) *adj.* within reach: *A hospital should be easily accessible to all; an accessible* (= approachable) *leader.* — **ac·ces·si·bly** (-blee) *adv.* — **ac·ces·si·bil·i·ty** (-BIL·uh·tee) *n.*

ac·ces·sion (ac·SESH·un) *n.* **1** an acceding, assuming, or attaining: *an heir's accession to the throne; accession to an office, to a position of power, to leadership; a nation's accession to independence.* **2** something added: *a library's new accessions* (= additions, esp. books).

ac·ces·so·ry (ac·SES·uh·ree) *n.* **-ries 1** a nonessential item added as an extra: *Tires are not auto accessories, but tape decks are; The shop sells pins, rings, bracelets, and other accessories; matching accessories; adj.: an accessory designer, feature, store.* **2** helper: *an accessory to a crime; An **accessory before** or **after the fact** is not involved in the actual committing of the crime.*

access road *n. Cdn.* road providing access to a region or expressway.

ac·ci·dent (AC·suh·dunt) *n.* **1** a mishap, esp. one causing hurt or damage: *He met with* or *had an accident; The accident occurred* or *happened* or *took place on the highway; He was (involved) in a hit-and-run accident; how to prevent automobile accidents; a bad, dreadful, fatal, frightful, horrible, nasty, serious, unfortunate accident.* **2** chance: *It was (by) pure accident that I found the loot; I met her **by accident.***

— **ac·ci·den·tal** (-DEN·tul) *adj.*
— **ac·ci·den·tal·ly** *adv.*

ac·claim (uh·CLAIM) *v.* **1** applaud or hail: *They acclaimed him leader; He was acclaimed (as) a hero for saving the child's life.* **2** *Cdn.* elect without opposition: *The mayor was acclaimed.*
— *n.* praise: *The book received wide acclaim from critics.*

ac·cla·ma·tion (ac·luh·MAY·shun) *n.* **1** an act of acclaiming. **2** *Cdn.* an unopposed election: *She won by acclamation; There were no acclamations in last year's election.*

ac·cli·mate (AC·luh·mate) *v.* **-mates, -mat·ed, -mat·ing** same as ACCLIMATIZE.
— **ac·cli·ma·tion** (ac·luh·MAY·shun) *n.*

ac·cli·ma·tize (uh·CLYE·muh·tize) *v.* **-tiz·es, -tized, -tiz·ing** to accustom: *We become acclimatized to a new climate, environment, situation; to acclimatize ourselves to new surroundings.*
— **ac·cli·ma·ti·za·tion** (-tuh·ZAY·shun) *n.*

ac·co·lade (AC·uh·lade) *n.* great appreciation or praise: *to bestow an accolade on someone; The play received accolades in the media.*

ac·com·mo·date (uh·COM·uh·date) *v.* **-dates, -dat·ed, -dat·ing 1** lodge: *This room can accommodate four people.* **2** adjust or adapt: *to accommodate to new surroundings.* **3** do a favour for someone: *He accommodated her with a loan; a very accommodating* (= obliging) *neighbour.*

ac·com·mo·da·tion (ac·COM·uh·DAY·shun) *n.* **1** lodging and related services: *Hotel accommodation was scarce during the Olympics; first-class, overnight, tourist, travel accommodations; a hotel with accommodations for 300 people.* **2** favour: *He did it as an accommodation for a friend.* **3** settlement: *to come to, make, reach, seek, work out an accommodation with the opposite party.* **4** an adaptation or adjustment: *an accommodation to wartime conditions.*

ac·com·pa·ni·ment (uh·CUM·pun·i·munt) *n.* something that accompanies: *a piano accompaniment to a song; They danced to the accompaniment of drums.*

ac·com·pa·ny (uh·CUM·puh·nee) *v.* **-nies, -nied, -ny·ing 1** go along with someone: *The child's mother accompanied her.* **2** to play or sing supporting a solo part: *to accompany a singer on the piano.*

ac·com·plice (uh·COM·plis) *n.* a companion in wrongdoing: *She was an unwilling accomplice; an accomplice in or to a crime.*

ac·com·plish (uh·COM·plish) **1** *v.* succeed in doing; achieve: *to accomplish an objective; What can we accomplish in half an hour? Landing on the moon is now an accomplished fact.* **2 accomplished** *adj.* talented: *She's an accomplished actor; accomplished at acting and singing.*

ac·com·plish·ment (uh·COM·plish·munt) *n.* **1** skill acquired by great effort: *It's no mean accomplishment to be able to play the piano; sewing, cooking, and such accomplishments.* **2** achievement: *a woman of many accomplishments.*

ac·cord (uh·CORD) *v.* **1** give or grant: *We accorded him a hero's welcome.* **2** agree: *His actions do not accord with his words.*
— *n.* agreement: *to reach an accord with Russia about arms control; a peace accord between the U.S. and Russia; to live in perfect accord* (= harmony); *He signed the agreement of his own accord* (= willingly); *The motion was passed with one accord* (= unanimously).

ac·cord·ance (uh·COR·dunce) *n.* agreement or harmony: *The goods were shipped in accordance with your wishes.*

according (uh·COR·ding) *adj.* in harmony or agreement: *You'll be punished according as* (= depending on how or whether) *you sin.*
— **according to 1** as stated by an authority: *the creation according to the Bible; It's 8:25 according to this watch.* **2** on the basis of something: *shoes classified according to size.*
— **according to Hoyle** according to the rules; the way it is usually done.
— **ac·cord·ing·ly** *adv.* in agreement: *These are the rules, act accordingly.*

ac·cor·di·on (uh·COR·dee·un) *n.* a musical instrument worked with a boxlike bellows and a keyboard at each end: *a skirt with accordion pleats (like an accordion's bellows).* — **ac·cor·di·on·ist** *n.*

ac·cost (uh·COST) *v.* approach uninvited: *to be accosted by beggars; A police officer accosted the demonstrators and told them to move on.*

ac·count (uh·COWNT) *v.* consider or reckon: *An accused is accounted innocent until proven guilty; Account yourself lucky you were not killed in the accident; Someone has to account for* (= explain) *the missing money.*
— *n.* **1** a report: *a press account; to give or render an account to one's superiors; an accurate, biassed, detailed, eyewitness, running, true, vivid account of what happened; a newspaper account of the incident; a great man by all accounts.* **2** a transaction: *to settle an account by paying up; I have an account in* (= dispute) *to settle with him.* **3** consideration: *When you take account of everything or when you take everything into account, there's nothing to be sorry about; He was late on account of* (= because of) *rain; No one will be excused on any account* (= for any reason); *The bank president was held to account* (= was accountable) *for an embezzlement by a loan officer; a journey undertaken on the company's account* (= behalf); *Don't be late on my account* (= for my sake). **4** business arrangement: *to keep, open a savings account at a bank;*

a chequing account; All receipts are paid into our current account; active, dormant, inactive accounts. 5 client: *an advertising account; an **account executive** (in charge of a client's business).*
— **accounts** 1 record of money transactions; books: *to keep accounts; He's good at accounts* (= keeping accounting records). 2 differences: *the settling of accounts and vendettas; to square accounts.*

ac·count·a·ble (uh·COWN·tuh·bul) *adj.* responsible or answerable: *I am accountable to my superiors for my actions; My superiors will be held accountable for my actions.* — **ac·count·a·bil·i·ty** (-BIL·uh·tee) *n.*

ac·count·an·cy (uh·COWN·tun·see) *n.* the systematic keeping of business records.

ac·count·ant (uh·COWN·tunt) *n.* one trained in keeping business records or money accounts; bookkeeper: *A **chartered accountant** is called a **certified public accountant** in the U.S.*

account executive See ACCOUNT, *n.* 5.

accounting (uh·COWN·ting) *n.* the system of bookkeeping used by accountants or their work: *cost accounting.*

ac·cred·it (uh·CRED·it) *v.* 1 send out officially: *an envoy accredited to the Vatican.* 2 recognize: *an accredited authority on the subject; an (officially) accredited university.* 3 attribute or credit: *a discovery accredited to Newton.* — **ac·cred·i·ta·tion** (-uh·TAY·shun) *n.*

ac·crue (uh·CROO) *v.* **ac·crues, ac·crued, ac·cru·ing** add on gradually: *Interest accrues to an account from savings deposits; the interest accrued on the remaining balance of a loan.* — **ac·cru·al** (uh·CROO·ul) *n.*

ac·cu·mu·late (uh·CUE·myuh·late) *v.* **-lates, -lat·ed, -lat·ing** pile or heap up: *Snow accumulates in the winter; to accumulate knowledge, riches, a fortune.* — **ac·cu·mu·la·tion** (-LAY·shun) *n.*

ac·cu·ra·cy (AC·yuh·ruh·see) *n.* the quality of being accurate: *scientific accuracy; the accuracy of your figures.*

ac·cu·rate (AC·yuh·rit) *adj.* having no errors: *an accurate aim, clock, figure, report; The report is accurate in every detail; Is it accurate to say that 365 days make a year? an accurate* (= careful and exact) *typist.* — **ac·cu·rate·ly** *adv.*

ac·cursed (uh·CURST) *adj.* hated or hateful: *the accursed custom of slavery.* Also **ac·curst.**

ac·cu·sa·tion (ac·yoo·ZAY·shun) *n.* a charge of wrongdoing: *to bring* or *make an accusation of murder against someone; a damaging, false, grave, groundless, sweeping accusation.*

ac·cu·sa·tive (uh·CUE·zuh·tiv) *n. & adj.* (a grammatical case) indicating object: *"Me" is the accusative (case) of "I."*

ac·cu·sa·to·ry (uh·CUE·zuh·tor·ee) *adj.* accusing: *his accusatory looks; She spoke in an accusatory tone; to point an accusatory finger at someone.*

ac·cuse (uh·KYOOZ) *v.* **-cus·es, -cused, -cus·ing** charge with an offence: *He is accused of murder; He stands accused (= accused person) in the murder case; She is another of **the accused** (= accused*

people). — **ac·cus·er** *n.*

ac·cus·tom (uh·CUS·tum) *v.* make used to something: *He accustomed himself to the cold; got accustomed* (= used) *to the cold; He's out for his **accustomed** (= usual) walk; She is **accustomed to** (= used to) working late.*

ace *n.* 1 the highest of a set of playing cards: *the ace of spades; an ace card.* 2 in tennis or handball, a serve that is not touched by the receiver: *He dealt his opponent 19 aces during the game; He fired and scored many aces.* 3 an expert: *He's an ace at flying; a bullpen ace; a relief ace; adj.: an ace pilot, pitcher; our ace reliever.*
— **ace in the hole** *Informal.* a hidden advantage: *When oil became scarce, some nations turned to coal as their ace in the hole.*
— **ace up one's sleeve** *Slang.* a hidden and tricky advantage.
— *v.* **ac·es, aced, ac·ing** 1 in tennis, etc., win a point against one's opponent. 2 *Slang.* win, as with an A grade: *The new car aced the test drive; She **aced it** (= did it very well).*

a·cer·bic (uh·SUR·bic) *adj.* acidic or sharp-tasting: *an acerbic critic, style, writer; acerbic comments, humour, wit.*
— **a·cer·bi·ty** (uh·SUR·buh·tee) *n.* **-ties:** *No one can stand the acerbity of his wit; We are tired of his acerbities.*

ache (AKE) *n.* a dull continuous pain: *a backache, headache, stomachache; He suffers from **aches and pains.***
— *v.* **aches, ached ach·ing** have an ache: *My back aches; She is aching (Informal for wanting very much) to go home; aching for her loved ones.*
— **ach·y** (AY·kee) *adj.*

a·chieve (uh·CHEEV) *v.* **a·chieves, a·chieved, a·chiev·ing** gain by overcoming difficulties: *to achieve an aim, a goal, an objective, success in life.*
— **a·chieve·ment** *n.: a brilliant, crowning, dazzling, great, major, outstanding, signal, superb achievement in science.* — **a·chiev·a·ble** *adj.*
— **a·chiev·er** *n.: a high achiever.*

A·chil·les' heel (uh·KIL·eez·) *n.* mortal weakness or weak point, like the heel of **Achilles,** the legendary Greek hero of the "Iliad."

achy See ACHE.

ac·id (AS·id) *n.* 1 a sour substance with a biting quality: *Corrosive acids eat into metal.* 2 *Slang.* LSD; *adj.: an acid freak, pad, trip; acid rock (music).*
— *adj.* 1 bitingly sour: *The lime is an acid fruit.* 2 sharp: *She has an acid tongue; an acid wit.*
— **a·cid·ic** (uh·SID·ic) *adj.;* **a·cid·i·ty** (-uh·tee) *n.*
— **ac·id·ly** (AS·id·lee) *adv.*

ac·id·head (AS·id·hed) *n. Slang.* an LSD user.

a·cid·i·fy (uh·SID·uh·fye) *v.* **-fies, -fied, -fy·ing** make or become sour or acid.

acid rain or **acid precipitation** *n.* rain or snow containing acids formed in the atmosphere by industrial pollutants such as sulphur dioxide.

acid rock *n.* rock music with drugs as theme.

acid test *n.* a decisive test, as for gold which acids do not attack.

ac·know·ledge (ak·NOL·ij) *v.* -ledg·es, -ledged, -ledg·ing **1** admit: *He acknowledged defeat; acknowledged that he had been beaten; acknowledged me to be the winner; She gratefully acknowledged receipt of the letter; She acknowledged* (= admitted receiving) *the letter.* **2** give a sign of recognition: *He acknowledged me in the crowd; She acknowledged me as the winner.*
— **ac·know·ledg·ment** or **ac·know·ledge·ment** *n.*: *He made a public acknowledgment of his mistake; a receipt issued in acknowledgment of a payment.*

ac·me (AC·mee) *n.* the highest point: *to attain* or *reach the acme of her career as a dancer.*

ac·ne (AC·nee) *n.* a skin disease that causes pimples.

a·corn (AY·corn) *n.* the nut of an oak tree.

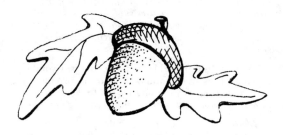

a·cous·tic (uh·COO·stic) or **a·cous·ti·cal** (-stuh·cul) *adj.* **1** relating to sound or hearing: *an acoustic* or *acoustical coupler for a phone; the acoustic nerve; Acoustic tiles absorb sound; the acoustical difference between an empty theatre and a full one; acoustical properties, qualities, shortcomings.* **2** not electrically amplified: *an acoustic guitar; acoustic and electric pianos; acoustic jazz.*
— **a·cous·tics** *n.pl.* **1** [takes sing. v.] the science of sound: *Acoustics is taught here.* **2** [takes pl. v.] sound qualities of enclosed spaces: *The acoustics of this auditorium are good.*

ac·quaint (uh·QUAINT) *v.* make oneself familiar: *She's new here and has to acquaint herself thoroughly with her job, then get acquainted with* (= meet and know) *her fellow workers; to be casually, closely, intimately acquainted with someone.*

ac·quaint·ance (uh·QUAIN·tunce) *n.* **1** personal knowledge or familiarity: *a lawyer's close acquaintance with law; I'd like to make his acquaintance* (= meet him); *to keep up, renew, strike up an acquaintance with someone; to have a nodding, passing, slight acquaintance with someone.* **2** a person one has met but does not know well: *She's only a casual acquaintance of mine, not a close friend.*

ac·qui·esce (ak·wee·ES) *v.* -esc·es, -esced, -esc·ing agree passively: *He found it hard to acquiesce in the umpire's ruling.* — **ac·qui·es·cence** (-unce) *n.*

ac·quire (uh·QUIRE) *v.* -quires, -quired, -quir·ing get

by effort: *to acquire wealth, a taste for music; Speech is an acquired, not inborn skill; an acquired, not inherited character* or *characteristic.* — **ac·quire·ment** *n.*

ac·qui·si·tion (ac·wuh·ZISH·un) *n.* the act of acquiring or something acquired: *the acquisition of knowledge; Our museum's latest acquisition is a Picasso.*

ac·quis·i·tive (uh·QUIZ·uh·tiv) *adj.* eager to get and keep things: *A chipmunk is acquisitive by nature; The lady is acquisitive of lands and wealth.*
— **ac·quis·i·tive·ness** *n.*

ac·quit (uh·QUIT) *v.* -quits, -quit·ted, -quit·ting **1** to free someone of a charge: *The accused was acquitted; He was acquitted of murder.* **2** to conduct: *He acquitted himself well at the interview; She acquitted herself like a pro.*

ac·quit·tal (uh·QUIT·ul) *n.* an act or instance of being acquitted of a charge instead of being convicted: *A jury brings in an acquittal; He was convicted on one charge but won acquittals on the others.*

a·cre (AY·cur) *n.* **1** a unit of land area equal to 4 840 sq. yds. (4.047 m²). **2 acres** *pl.* lands; estate: *to clear a forest for cultivable acres; green acres.*

a·cre·age (AY·cur·ij) *n.* amount of land; area in acres.

ac·rid (AC·rid) *adj.* **1** sharp and biting to the taste or smell: *acrid fumes, smoke.* **2** sharp and bitter in tone: *acrid words.* — **ac·rid·ly** *adv.*
— **ac·rid·ness** or **ac·rid·i·ty** (ac·RID·uh·tee) *n.*

ac·ri·mo·ni·ous (ac·ruh·MOH·nee·us) *adj.* characterized by acrimony: *an acrimonious debate.*
— **ac·ri·mo·ni·ous·ly** *adv.*

ac·ri·mo·ny (AC·ruh·moh·nee) *n.* bitterness of language or tone.

ac·ro·bat (AC·ruh·bat) *n.* one who performs on a tightrope, trapeze, etc., as at a circus.
— **ac·ro·bat·ic** (-BAT·ic) *adj.*: *a trapeze artist's acrobatic skills.*

acrobatics *n.pl.* **1** [takes sing. v.] the skill of an acrobat: *Her acrobatics is of Olympic standard.* **2** [takes pl. v.] the feats of an acrobat: *Some of her acrobatics are scary.*

ac·ro·nym (AC·ruh·nim) *n.* a pronounceable word formed by joining the first letters of a phrase, as Alcan ("Aluminum Canada") and NATO ("North Atlantic Treaty Organization").

a·cross (uh·CROS) *prep.* & *adv.* from one side to the other: *Let's walk across (the street); He lives across* (= on the opposite side of) *the street; The street is 50 m across; She lives across from* (= opposite) *us; He went across the border from Windsor; He works across the border in Detroit; Detroit is across the border* (= in the U.S.); *our neighbours **across the border** (Cdn. for in the U.S.); The news was flashed across the nation; People from across* (= from all over) *the country flocked to the capital; Honesty is the best policy, but it is difficult to get it across to people* (= make them appreciate it); *I ran* or *came across* (= met) *an old friend yesterday.*
— **across the board** equally for all categories: *Pay scales were raised across the board; **adj.**: an across-the-board pay raise, price increase, tax, tax hike.*

a·cros·tic (uh·CROS·tic) *n.* a geometric arrangement of words from which a new word can be read, as NEWS from North, East, West, and South arranged in a column.

a·cryl·ic (uh·CRIL·ic) *n.* **1** a synthetic substance in the form of paints, textile fibres such as Acrilan and Orlon, and transparent resins such as Lucite and Plexiglas; *adj.*: *acrylic acid; an acrylic fibre, plastic, paint, painting, resin, substance.* **2** a picture painted in acrylic: *an exhibition of watercolours, oils, and acrylics.*

act *n.* **1** something done: *an act of faith, folly, heroism, love, mercy, war; a kind act; a class act* (Informal for a person or thing that is admirable); *an act* (= law) *of Parliament; caught in the act* (= action) *of stealing; to get into the act* (= participate). **2** performance: *a circus act; a drama in five acts* (= parts); *a nightclub act; The child is **putting on an act*** (Informal for putting on a show) *to get sympathy; He was told to **clean up his act*** (Informal for act properly) *or resign; Let's **get our act together*** (= get organized).
— *v.* do something: *We acted quickly to put out the fire; He's acting* (= performing as) *the clown; Act your age* (= Behave more maturely)!; *Lawyers **act for*** (= represent) *their clients; She acts* (= does what is needed) *on their advice; She acts* (= behaves) *politely toward her competitors; Some people act* (= take action) *out of fear; Lou is acting as* (= temporarily filling the position of) *principal; Lou is the **acting*** (= temporary) *principal.*
— **act up** *Informal.* behave badly: *The child acts up when his parents are away; My arthritis acts up* (= gives trouble) *in cold weather; It acts up on me now and then.*

ac·tion (AC·shun) *n.* **1** the act or process of doing; also, what is done: *the corrosive action of acid on metal; Watch the action on the stage; The action has been dragging so far, but it is beginning to pick up; legal action; to institute or take action in a court of law; Firefighters go into action* (= start work) *at a moment's notice; They put a plan into action; They take action to stop fires; Good examples spur us into action; "Actions speak louder than words"; soldiers killed or missing **in action*** (= in battle); *enemy action; He saw action* (= took part in the fighting) *during World War II; A car is out of action* (= useless) *without fuel; affirmative action; a concerted, decisive, delaying, direct, disciplinary, drastic, emergency, hasty, immediate, job, police, prompt, rearguard, remedial, reflex, vigorous action; Go where the action* (Informal for activity) *is.* **2** a lawsuit: *to bring an action against the defaulter; A judge may dismiss an action; a civil action; class action.*

ac·tion·a·ble (AC·shuh·nuh·bul) *adj.* giving cause for a legal action: *actionable behaviour; an actionable offence, procedure.*

ac·ti·vate (AC·tuh·vate) *v.* -vates, -vat·ed, -vat·ing make active, as by an outside agent: *Smoke activates the alarm; Heat activates chemical processes; **Activated charcoal** (treated with steam and air) is used in filters as a purifying agent.* — **ac·ti·va·tion** (-VAY·shun) *n.*

ac·tive (AC·tiv) *adj.* having life and motion: *He continues to lead an active life at 75; An active volcano erupts from time to time; Tennis is an active sport; an active* (= not dormant) *business account; an active* (= not silent) *partner; a soldier on **active duty*** (= not retired or on reserve status).* — **ac·tive·ly** *adv.*

active voice *n.* a form of sentence in which the doer is the subject of the verb, as "Students write exams" as opposed to "Exams are written by students" (PASSIVE VOICE).

ac·tiv·ist (AC·tuh·vist) *n.* one who resorts to direct action to achieve something for the common good: *animal rights activists; farm activists; peace activists.*

ac·tiv·i·ty (ac·TIV·uh·tee) *n.* -ties the state of doing or something done: *There was a burst of activity just before the Christmas festival; Our school was buzzing or humming with activity; to break off or terminate a prohibited activity; Terrorist activity has been curbed; Business activity is paralysed by the strike; There's political and subversive activity still going on behind the scenes; intellectual, physical, scientific activity; We engage in, participate in, take part in cultural activities at school; Running is an activity that requires effort; recreational and social activities such as chess and folk-dancing; Holidays are a good time for outside activities; He's too busy studying to engage in extracurricular activities.*

act of God *n.* an unforeseeable accident that is beyond human control, as an earthquake, flood, or tornado: *The insurance company considered the broken water main an act of God and refused to pay for the damage.*

ac·tor (AC·tur) *n.* one who plays a role, as in a play or movie: *a famous actor of Hamlet; a character actor; to cast an actor in the role of Hamlet; Trudeau was a key actor in the patriation of our Constitution.*
— **ac·tress** (-tris) *fem.*

ac·tu·al (AC·choo·ul) *adj.* real and existing, not imagined, estimated, etc.: *The actual cost was less than the estimate; an actual happening.*
— **ac·tu·al·ly** (-uh·lee) *adv.*
— **ac·tu·al·i·ty** (-AL·uh·tee) *n.* -ties.

ac·tu·al·ize (AC·choo·uh·lize) *v.* -iz·es, -ized, -iz·ing make actual; bring into being: *to actualize one's plans; People actualize* (= fulfill) *themselves through their work.*

ac·tu·ar·y (AC·choo·air·ee) *n.* -ar·ies a statistician who calculates insurance risks, premiums, annuities, etc.
— **ac·tu·ar·i·al** (-AIR·ee·ul) *adj.*

ac·tu·ate (AC·choo·ate) *v.* -ates, -at·ed, -at·ing **1** motivate for action: *to be actuated by compassion, greed, malice, self-interest.* **2** put in operation: *the pressure that actuates a brake system; an actuating device.* — **ac·tu·a·tion** (-AY·shun) *n.*

ac·tu·a·tor (AC·choo·ay·tur) *n.* one that puts something in operation: *Control actuators keep an aircraft level; a brake actuator; valve actuators.*

a·cu·i·ty (uh·CUE·uh·tee) *n.* sharpness or keenness, esp. of perception: *mental acuity; visual acuity; acuity of hearing.*

a·cu·men (uh·CUE·mun) *n.* keenness of insight and judgment: *to demonstrate, display, show good business* *acumen; a lawyer's legal acumen.*

ac·u·punc·ture (AC·yoo·punk·chur) *n.* a method of treating disease and pain by inserting needles at specific points on the body, traditionally used by the Chinese. — **ac·u·punc·tur·ist** *n.*

a·cute (uh·CUTE) *adj.* 1 critical or severe: *an acute shortage of water; He's in acute pain.* 2 of diseases, likely to come to a crisis, but of short duration; not chronic: *acute gastritis, indigestion; an acute-care hospital.* 3 keen or sharp: *a dog's acute sense of hearing; an acute thinker; an **acute angle** (of less than 90°).*

ad *n. Informal.* an advertisement: *"Teachers Wanted" is a want ad for teachers; a help-wanted ad; a classified, not display ad.*

ad- *prefix.* to; toward: *adjoin, administer, advert.*

ad·age (AD·ij) *n.* a popular saying in long use; proverb; maxim: *"Look before you leap" is an old adage.*

Ad·am (AD·um) *n.* in the Bible, the name of the first man: *I would **not know him from Adam** (= could not recognize him).*

ad·a·mant (AD·uh·munt) *adj.* unchanging in behaviour; unyielding: *He won't change his mind – he's quite adamant about it; He's adamant that the proposal be dropped.* — **ad·a·mant·ly** *adv.*

a·dapt (uh·DAPT) *v.* modify something or oneself to suit a different situation: *a story adapted for TV; a screenplay adapted from a novel; He found it hard to adapt (himself) to the new climate; Cactuses are adapted to life in the desert.*
— **a·dap·ta·ble** (-tuh·bul) *adj.*
— **a·dapt·a·bil·i·ty** (-tuh·BIL·uh·tee) *n.*
— **ad·ap·ta·tion** (ad·up·TAY·shun) *n.*: *an adaptation of a novel for TV.*
— **a·dapt·er** or **a·dap·tor** (uh·DAP·tur) *n.*

add *v.* join something to another: *He added sugar to my coffee; It added to (= increased) the taste; He added (= also said) that no cream was available; You get 6 if you add 1, 2, and 3; He can add (= do sums) and subtract; We **add on** new wings to our main building as business expands; We **add to** (= increase) our staff; His stories don't **add up** (= make sense); Those smiles **add up to** (= amount to) mischief.*
— **add fuel to the fire** or **flame** *Informal.* make a problem, situation, etc. worse.
— **add insult to injury** make matters even worse, as by taunting after hurting.

ad·dict (AD·ict) *n.* one who does something habitually and compulsively, esp. one who uses narcotics: *a confirmed addict; a drug addict.*
— *v.* (uh·DICT) devote oneself to such use: *a patient who is chronically, hopelessly addicted to drugs.*
— **ad·dic·tion** (uh·DIC·shun) *n.*: *addiction to drugs; Physical dependence produces addiction.*
— **ad·dic·tive** (-tiv) *adj.*: *Cocaine, heroine, tobacco, etc. are addictive; They are addictive substances.*

ad·di·tion (uh·DISH·un) *n.* 1 the process or an act of adding: *to do an addition.* 2 a person or thing added: *The new addition to our family is a girl; He gets a salary and a bonus **in addition**; gets a bonus **in addition to** (= as well as) his salary.*
— **ad·di·tion·al** *adj.*; **ad·di·tion·al·ly** *adv.*

ad·di·tive (AD·uh·tiv) *n.* an added substance: *Colour is often an additive in foods; an additive ingredient.*

ad·dle (AD·ul) *v.* **ad·dles, ad·dled, ad·dling** 1 of eggs, make or become rotten: *an addled egg.* 2 make or become confused: *Alcohol addles rather than clarifies the mind.*

addle-brained (AD·ul·braind) *adj.* confused or muddled: *an addle-brained agitator.*
Also **ad·dle·head·ed** or **ad·dle·pat·ed.**

ad·dress (uh·DRES) *v.* 1 speak to someone: *to address an audience; People address important officials respectfully; We address the French teacher as "Madam."* 2 write the destination on something being sent: *to address envelopes, mail.* 3 apply oneself to a question, problem, etc.: *The speaker addressed himself to the problem of unemployment; to address (= deal with) a problem.*
— *n.* 1 an elaborate speech: *to deliver* or *give a presidential address; an eloquent, keynote, inaugural, moving, stirring address; an address about social reform.* 2 (also AD.res) the location of a person or business: *Our address is "1776 Chalkdene Grove, Mississauga, Ont."; Did you leave a forwarding address when you changed your address? I couldn't find you at the old address; Write your return address on the top left corner of the envelope; a business address; home address; permanent address; temporary addresses.*
4 the location of information in computer memory.

ad·dress·ee (ad·res·EE) *n.* one to whom something such as a letter is addressed.

ad·duce (uh·DUCE, *rhyme:* produce) *v.* **ad·duc·es, ad·duced, ad·duc·ing** give as an example or as evidence.

a·dept (uh·DEPT) *adj.* skilled or expert: *Yun is adept in playing the violin; Guy is adept at billiards; the adept touch of the artist.*
— *n.* (AD·ept) one who is adept.
— **a·dept·ly** (uh·DEPT·lee) *adv.*; **a·dept·ness** *n.*

ad·e·quate (AD·uh·quit) *adj.* sufficient to satisfy a need; enough: *remuneration adequate for the work done; supplies that are barely adequate to the need.*
— **ad·e·quate·ly** *adv.*
— **ad·e·quate·ness** or **ad·e·qua·cy** (-kwuh·see) *n.*

ad·here (ad·HERE) *v.* **-heres, -hered, -her·ing** stick firmly: *Glue helps things to adhere to each other; to adhere (= be devoted) to a plan, policy; to adhere closely, strictly, stubbornly.*
— **ad·he·sion** (ad·HEE·zhun) *n.*

ad·her·ent (ad·HEER·unt) *n.* close follower and supporter: *an adherent of the civil rights movement.*
— **ad·her·ence** (-unce) *n.*

ad·he·sive (ad·HEE·siv) *n.* a sticky substance: *Gum is an adhesive; Patriotism serves as an adhesive (= something that sticks parts together) for national unity.*
— *adj.* sticking, sticky, or stuck: *adhesive paper used for labels or stickers; adhesive paste used in bookbinding; Paperbacks come with adhesive (= not stitched but "perfect") binding; a bandage kept in place with adhesive tape.* — **ad·he·sive·ness** *n.*

ad hoc *adj.* for a particular purpose: *an ad hoc committee to study street lighting.*

ad ho·mi·nem (ad·HOM·uh·num) *adj. & adv.* attacking the person rather than addressing the issue: *You're arguing ad hominem; to use an ad hominem approach, argument; an ad hominem style; to resort to ad hominem measures.*

a·dieu (uh·DEW) *n. & interj.* **a·dieus** or **a·dieux** (-DEWZ) farewell: *We bade him adieu; We said adieu.*

ad in·fi·ni·tum (AD·in·fuh·NYE·tum) *adv. Latin.* without limit; endlessly: *You can count 1, 2, 3, 4, and so on ad infinitum.*

ad·ja·cent (uh·JAY·sunt) *adj.* near or next: *the house adjacent to ours.* — **ad·ja·cent·ly** *adv.* — **ad·ja·cen·cy** *n.*

ad·jec·tive (AJ·ic·tiv) *n.* a word that qualifies a noun, as "good" in "the good book" or "The book is good."

ad·join (uh·JOIN) *v.* be next to and touching something: *My property adjoins his; Adjoining the kitchen is our dining room.*

ad·journ (uh·JURN) *v.* **1** suspend a meeting or session: *We adjourned for lunch; adjourned for a week.* **2** *Informal.* move to another place: *Shall we adjourn to the living room?* — **ad·journ·ment** *n.*

ad·judge (uh·JUJ) *v.* **ad·judg·es, ad·judged, ad·judg·ing** **1** award by law, as by a judge: *The house was adjudged to his ex-wife.* **2** judge: *Jim was adjudged (to be) the winner of the debate.*

ad·ju·di·cate (uh·JOO·duh·cate) *v.* **-cates, -cat·ed, -cat·ing** **1** settle a claim judicially: *to adjudicate a dispute.* **2** serve as a judge or referee: *to adjudicate on a case; to adjudicate a debate, a music festival.* — **ad·ju·di·ca·tor** *n.* — **ad·ju·di·ca·tion** (-CAY·shun) *n.*

ad·junct (AJ·unct) *adj.* attached to something without forming a part of it: *an adjunct professor (not a faculty member).* — *n.* an addition: *an adjunct to or of something.*

ad·jure (uh·JOOR) *v.* **-jures, -jured, -jur·ing** urge earnestly or solemnly: *The minister adjured the young offender to think of his future.* — **ad·ju·ra·tion** (aj·uh·RAY·shun) *n.*

ad·just (uh·JUST) *v.* **1** change slightly so as to suit a new condition: *The eyes adjust (themselves) to light; Sound volume should be adjusted to the size of the audience; Do not adjust your (TV) set; Please adjust the dial to "Low"; to adjust (= adapt oneself) to a new climate; He is well adjusted to his new environment.* **2** settle: *An insurance adjuster adjusts claims after adjusting (= determining the amount of) the losses.* — **ad·just·a·ble** *adj.* — **ad·just·er** or **ad·jus·tor** *n.; **ad·just·ment** *n.*

ad lib *adv. Informal.* in a free style, without using a script or musical score.

ad-lib (ad·LIB) *adj.* free-style: *an ad-lib comment, joke, performance.* — *v.* **-libs, -libbed, -lib·bing** deliver lines or a speech spontaneously. — *n.* a free-style comment or remark. — **ad-lib·ber** *n.*

ad·mail *n.* the direct-mail component of the postal service; junk mail.

ad·man *n.* **-men** a man in the advertising business.

ad·mass (AD·mas) *n.* **1** the section of a population that is easily influenced by mass advertising. **2** a mass-marketing system.

ad·min·is·ter (ad·MIN·is·tur) *v.* **1** manage: *to administer a department; to administer to (= help with) the needs of a community.* **2** direct the taking of something: *to administer a medicine, an oath of allegiance.*

ad·min·is·tra·tion (ad·MIN·is·TRAY·shun) *n.* **1** an administering: *the administration of justice by the courts; a course in business administration; public administration of resources.* **2** government: *a civilian administration; military administration; the Diefenbaker administration.*

ad·min·is·tra·tive (ad·MIN·is·truh·tiv) *adj.* having to do with administration: *administrative duties, reform, red tape, responsibility.* — **ad·min·is·tra·tor** (-stray·tur) *n.* one who administers or manages: *the administrator of an estate; a civil administrator; school administrators.*

ad·mi·ra·ble (AD·muh·ruh·bul) *adj.* that deserves to be admired: *an admirable performance;* **ad·mi·ra·bly** *adv.*

ad·mi·ral (AD·muh·rul) *n.* **1** in Canada, a naval rank equal to that of an army general. **2** a naval officer ranking above a captain or commodore.

ad·mi·ra·tion (ad·muh·RAY·shun) *n.* **1** an act of admiring or being admired; a feeling of wonder, esteem, or approval: *to arouse, command, express, win admiration; to feel admiration for someone; He looks at her with admiration; He looks up to her in admiration; He's filled with admiration for her; Admiration can be blind, deep, grudging, mutual, sincere, strong, undying.* **2** one who is admired: *She is the admiration of her friends.*

ad·mire (ad·MIRE) *v.* **-mires, -mired, -mir·ing** regard with wonder, esteem, or approval: *She admires him greatly; admires his family; admires him for his many achievements; admires his being so successful in his profession.*

ad·mis·si·ble (ad·MIS·uh·bul) *adj.* worthy of being allowed, esp. in court: *admissible evidence.* — **ad·mis·si·bil·i·ty** (-BIL·uh·tee) *n.*

ad·mis·sion (ad·MISH·un) *n.* **1** entrance with rights, privileges, etc.: *to apply for or seek admission to a school; to be denied, granted, refused admission; Admission to the army is restricted and selective, not open or free; He gained admission by fair means.* **2** entrance fee: *The admission to the show is $65; The general admission (for unreserved seats) is $45.* **3** acknowledgment or confession: *to make an admission of guilt; a damaging admission; an admission that he had helped in the crime; He was guilty by or on his own admission.*

ad·mit (ad·MIT) *v.* **-mits, -mit·ted, -mit·ting** **1** allow: *Latecomers will not be admitted to the show; This rule does not admit of (Formal for allow or tolerate) exceptions.* **2** acknowledge: *The accused readily admitted to the police that he had taken part in the burglary; He admitted to (Formal for confessed) his complicity in the crime; admitted to his stealing the money; admitted (to) stealing the money.*

ad·mit·tance (ad·MIT·unce) *n. Formal.* physical entrance to a place: *He tried to gain admittance to the show; was denied admittance.*

ad·mit·ted·ly (ad·MIT·id·lee) *adv.* as admitted: *Boys and girls, admittedly, are different from each other.*

ad·mix (ad·MIX) *v.* mix together; mix in.
— **ad·mix·ture** (ad·MIX·chur) *n.*

ad·mon·ish (ad·MON·ish) *v. Formal.* warn someone mildly but seriously: *The principal admonished the students for being lazy; admonished them to be more diligent.* — **ad·mon·i·tor·y** (-uh·tor·ee) *adj.*
— **ad·mon·i·tion** (ad·muh·NISH·un) *n.*

ad nau·se·am (ad·NAW·zee·um) *adv.* to a sickening degree: *He keeps repeating his jokes ad nauseam.*

a·do (uh·DOO) *n.* fuss or bother: *The child made much ado about* or *over being ignored; Without further* or *more ado, he left the scene.*

a·do·be (uh·DOH·bee) *n.* a structure of sun-dried bricks; *adj.: an adobe house, wall.*

ad·o·les·cence (ad·uh·LES·unce) *n.* the period between childhood and maturity.
— **ad·o·les·cent** *n. & adj.: Teenagers are adolescents; her adolescent shyness.*

a·dopt (uh·DOPT) *v.* **1** take as one's own child: *The childless couple adopted an orphan girl; adopted her as their own.* **2** take up and use as one's own: *to adopt a foreign costume, custom, language.* **3** agree to; accept: *A meeting adopts a resolution.*
— **a·dop·tion** *n.: Disowned children are put up for adoption; an adoption agency.*
— **a·dop·tive** (uh·DOP·tiv) *adj.: Guy's adoptive* (= not natural) *parents; their adoptive* (= adopted) *child Guy.*

a·dore (uh·DOR) *v.* **-dores, -dored, -dor·ing** **1** worship: *"We adore thee, O Lord!"* **2** *Informal.* be extremely fond of a person or thing: *A mother adores her baby; She adores singing in public; He adores the couple for their devotion to the cause.*
— **a·dor·a·ble** *adj.;* **a·dor·a·bly** (-blee) *adv.*
— **ad·o·ra·tion** (ad·uh·RAY·shun) *n.*

a·dorn (uh·DORN) *v.* decorate: *She adorns herself with jewels.* — **a·dorn·ment** *n.*

ad·re·nal (uh·DREE·nul) *adj.* relating to two glands, one above each kidney: *an adrenal secretion.*

ad·ren·al·in or **ad·ren·al·ine** (uh·DREN·uh·lin) *n.* a hormone made by the **adrenal glands** and secreted into the blood during anger, fear, etc., preparing the body for quick action: *a shot of adrenalin; Watching hockey gets his adrenalin flowing* or *going* or *pumping.*

a·drift (uh·DRIFT) *adj. & adv.* drifting without aim or guidance: *a boat found adrift on the lake; It was cast adrift by someone; Crowds of demonstrators were turned adrift on the streets.*

a·droit (uh·DROIT) *adj.* skilful: *an adroit politician; an admirer adroit at* or *in flattery.*

ad·u·la·tion (aj·uh·LAY·shun) *n.* servile praise; flattery: *the adulation of followers.*

a·dult (uh·DULT, AD·ult) *n.* a mature living being, esp. a person of legal age: *Consenting adults may enter into*

an agreement to do anything that is not illegal.
— **adj.:** *an adult butterfly (past the pupa stage); adult* or *continuing education (offered to adults who want to improve their knowledge or skills); an adult movie (to which children are not admitted).*
— **a·dult·hood** (short "oo") *n.*

a·dul·ter·ant (uh·DUL·tuh·runt) *n.* something that adulterates: *Water may be an adulterant in wine.*

a·dul·ter·ate (uh·DUL·tuh·rate) *v.* **-ates, -at·ed, -at·ing** make impure by adding something inferior or foreign: *The wine was adulterated with water;* **a·dul·ter·a·tor** *n.*
— **a·dul·ter·a·tion** (-tuh·RAY·shun) *n.*

a·dul·ter·ous *adj.* having to do with adultery: *an adulterous husband, relationship, wife.*
— **a·dul·ter·ous·ly** *adv.*

a·dul·ter·y (uh·DUL·tuh·ree) *n.* **-ter·ies** a married person's sexual relationship with someone other than the legal spouse: *to commit adultery with someone.*
— **a·dul·ter·er** *n.;* **a·dul·ter·ess** *fem.*

ad va·lor·em (ad·vuh·LOR·um) *adj.* according to the value: *an ad valorem (customs) duty; an ad valorem levy, tax.*

ad·vance (ad·VANCE) *v.* **-vanc·es, -vanced, -vanc·ing** **1** come or go forward: *an advancing army; It advances against the enemy; advances to* or *toward the country's borders; advances into enemy territory; Prices advance* (= increase) *with inflation.* **2** put forward: *to advance an opinion unasked; She was advanced* (= promoted) *to a higher pay bracket; We advanced* (= lent) *him $100 till payday; The date of publication has been advanced (to an earlier date).*
— **n.** **1** an advancing or something advanced: *an advance of $100; an advance paid to an author against royalties; Our army made an advance* (= forward movement) *against the enemy; It pressed the advance to* or *toward the country's borders and into enemy territory.* **2** progress: *the advance of high technology; the* **advances** (= developments) *made in microcomputers.* **3** **advances** *pl.* overtures: *The management made advances to the union; The union rebuffed* or *rejected the advances; She resisted his advances* (= acts of wooing).
— **in advance** before due time: *A month's rent was paid in advance; royalties paid in advance* (= ahead of sales or publication).
— **adj.** ahead of time; prior: *The police had advance information of the plot; an advance copy, notice, party, payment; advance publicity.*

advanced (ad·VANST) *adj.* being ahead: *an advanced level of achievement; advanced English; an advanced student; advanced studies; the industrially advanced countries of Europe; A man of 90 is rather advanced in years* (= old).

advance man *n.* one who prepares a tour ahead of a political candidate.

ad·vance·ment (ad·VANCE·munt) *n.* a moving forward: *the advancement of peace; rapid, slow advancement; to block, further, speed one's professional advancement.*

advance poll *n. Cdn.* a poll held for the convenience of those who expect to be absent from their ridings on election day; also, the number of votes (advance votes) cast.

ad·van·tage (ad·VAN·tij) *n*. superiority or what results from it: *Education is an advantage when one is applying for a job; The educated have an advantage over the uneducated; the advantages of education; a clear, decided, mutual, obvious, unfair advantage; He used his public office to personal advantage* (= gain); *He wouldn't* **take advantage of** (= exploit) *her youth; Disadvantages outweigh advantages; His education worked to his advantage in getting promoted; He was at an advantage because of his education; He used his education to good advantage; In tennis, a server says, "Advantage in!"* (= a chance to score the next point and the game). — **ad·van·ta·geous** (ad·vun·TAY·jus) *adj.: A change of wind will be advantageous to us; It would be advantageous to wait a little.* — **ad·van·ta·geous·ly** *adv.*

ad·vent (AD·vent) *n*. a coming or arrival of something awaited: *the advent of spring; the advent of space travel; The season of* **Advent**, *a period before Christmas, commemorates the coming of Christ.*

ad·ven·ture (ad·VEN·chur) *n*. a risky, exciting, or challenging experience: *the adventures of Ulysses; an explorer's spirit of adventure; People have* or *meet with adventures; bold, breathtaking, exciting, thrilling adventures; a sailor in search of high adventure; It's an adventure to sail* or *sailing the high seas.* — *v*. **-tures, -tured, -tur·ing** dare to go *into* a place, *on* an undertaking.

ad·ven·tur·er (ad·VEN·chur·ur) *n*. **1** one who undertakes adventures: *a dauntless, intrepid adventurer.* **2** one who seeks his fortune by soldiering or unscrupulous means.

ad·ven·tur·ess (ad·VEN·chur·us) *n*. **1** a woman who schemes to obtain wealth and rank: *a bold adventuress.* **2** a woman who undertakes adventures.

ad·ven·tur·ous (ad·VEN·chur·us) *adj*. **1** full of adventure: *an adventurous expedition, life.* **2** daring: *an adventurous explorer;* also **ad·ven·ture·some.**

ad·verb (AD·vurb) *n*. a word modifying a verb, adjective, or another adverb, as "very" and "slowly" in "She's very good" and "He speaks very slowly." — **ad·ver·bi·al** (ad·VUR·bee·ul) *adj.*

ad·ver·sa·ri·al (ad·vur·SAIR·ee·ul) *adj*. adversary or opposing: *an adversarial relationship.*

ad·ver·sa·ry (AD·vur·sair·ee) *n*. **-ries** an opponent: *a bold, formidable, worthy adversary.* — *adj*. opposing or antagonistic: *the adversary climate in labour relations; divorce and such adversary proceedings; in an adversary role; the adversary system of union-management relations.*

ad·verse (AD·vurce, ad·VURCE) *adj*. opposing or unfavourable: *an adverse decision; adverse winds, working conditions; conditions that are adverse to our interests.* — **ad·verse·ly** *adv.*

ad·ver·si·ty (ad·VUR·suh·tee) *n*. **-ties** misfortune: *patience in adversity; to face, overcome adversity; the* **adversities** (= hardships) *of life, of old age.*

ad·ver·tise (AD·vur·tize) *v*. **-tis·es, -tised, -tis·ing**

announce something by a paid notice in a journal, on TV, radio, etc.: *to advertise a job vacancy; to advertise that a vacancy exists; advertise for an editor.* — **ad·ver·tis·er** *n.*

ad·ver·tise·ment (ad·vur·TIZE·munt) *n*. a notice advertising something; ad: *to place, publish, run, take out an advertisement for an editor.*

advertising (AD·vur·tye·zing) *n*. **1** advertisements: *a paper that carries no advertising; outdoor advertising using billboards; word-of-mouth advertising.* **2** the preparation and publishing of advertisements; *adj.: the advertising manager of a newspaper; an advertising agency, brochure, campaign, department, firm, slogan; advertising material, revenue, standards.*

ad·vice (ad·VICE) *n*. **1** opinion given by a person on what to do in a given situation: *Seek advice when you need help; A father gives* or *offers advice to his son; a bit* or *piece* or *word of advice; professional advice on a legal matter; She acted on* or *upon, not against her lawyer's advice; She refused to deal with him* **on advice of** *counsel; to disregard, follow, refuse, take, turn a deaf ear to advice; friendly, good, misleading, parting, sage, sensible, sound, unasked-for, unsolicited advice; Our advice to you is to see another lawyer.* **2** a notice or information, as about a delivery to be expected: *a remittance advice; shipping advices from our exporters.*

ad·vis·a·ble (ad·VYE·zuh·bul) *adj*. recommended: *Rest is advisable when you are tired; It is advisable to rest when you're tired.* — **ad·vis·a·bil·i·ty** (-BIL·uh·tee) *n.*

ad·vise (ad·VIZE) *v*. **-vis·es, -vised, -vis·ing** **1** give advice: *The doctor advised her to take rest; The doctor advised* (= recommended) *rest; a well* **advised** *rest.* **2** give notice: *We will advise you when it arrives; will keep you* **advised** (= informed) *till then.* — **ad·vis·er** or **ad·vi·sor** *n.: an adviser to the government on security matters.*

ad·vis·ed·ly (ad·VYE·zid·lee) *adv*. after consideration: *a word used advisedly.*

ad·vise·ment (ud·VIZE·munt) *n*. [legal use] careful consideration: *The court agreed to take the matter under advisement.*

ad·vi·so·ry (ud·VYE·zuh·ree) *adj*. giving advice: *an advisory body, committee, council, opinion; to act in an advisory capacity, role.* — *n*. a warning report: *A weather advisory has been issued.*

ad·vo·ca·cy (AD·vuh·cuh·see) *n*. the advocating of something: *the advocacy of better day care; adj.: a citizen advocacy group for lowering taxes; advocacy advertising, as about butter being better than margarine; advocacy journalism (with much personal involvement by the reporter).*

ad·vo·cate (AD·vuh·kit) *n*. one who defends or supports a person or cause, as a lawyer: *Gandhi was a strong advocate of nonviolence.* — *v*. (AD·vuh·cate) **-cates, -cat·ed, -cat·ing** defend or support: *Gandhi advocated nonviolence; He advocated disobeying unjust laws.*

ae·gis (EE·jis) *n*. auspices or protection: *The nations of the world meet under the aegis of the U.N.*

ae·on (EE·on) *n.* same as EON.

aer·ate (AIR·ate) *v.* -ates, -at·ed, -at·ing infuse with a gas, as soda water with carbon dioxide: *Blood is aerated with oxygen in the lungs; aerated water.*
— aer·a·tion (air·AY·shun) *n.*

aer·i·al (AIR·ee·ul) *adj.* of, in, or by air: *an aerial attack, battle, survey; a firefighter's aerial ladder; aerial photography.* — *n.* a TV or radio antenna.
— aer·i·al·ly *adv.*

aer·i·al·ist *n.* one who performs on a trapeze, tightrope, etc. in a circus.

aer·ie (AIR·ee) *n.* same as EYRIE.

aero- *combining form.* of the air, gases, or aircraft: *aerobic, aerodrome, aeronaut.*

aer·o·bat·ic (air·oh·BAT·ic) **1** *adj.* having to do with feats performed with an airplane: *an aerobatic display.* **2 aerobatics** *n.pl.* [takes sing. v.] aerobatic feats.

aer·o·bic (air·OH·bic) **1** *adj.* having to do with improving the body's use of oxygen: *her aerobic capacity; aerobic exercises.* **2 aerobics** *n.pl.* [takes sing. v.] aerobic exercises or their performance: *Aerobics is good for you.*

aer·o·dy·nam·ic (AIR·oh·dye·NAM·ic) *adj.* having to do with the forces exerted by gases in motion: *aerodynamic design, drag, efficiency, forces, looks, styling of sports cars.*

aer·o·gram (AIR·oh·gram) *n.* an air letter.

aer·o·naut (AIR·uh·nawt) *n.* one who operates an airship, balloon, etc. — aer·o·nau·tic (-NAW·tic) *adj.*

aer·o·nau·tics (air·uh·NAW·tics) *n.pl.* [takes sing. v.] the science of the design, manufacture, and operation of aircraft.

aer·o·pause (AIR·uh·pawz) *n.* the altitude above the earth at which the air is too thin for airplanes to fly.

aer·o·plane (AIR·uh·plane) *n. Brit.* airplane.

aer·o·quay (AIR·uh·kee) *n.* an airport terminal building with facilities for passengers and docklike bays for airplanes, as Terminal One in Toronto.

aer·o·sol (AIR·oh·sol) *n.* a container for spraying a liquid under pressure; *adj.: an aerosol bomb* (=can), *deodorant; a product sold in aerosol form; an aerosol insecticide, spray.*

aer·o·space (AIR·oh·space) *n.* the part of space in which airplanes, rockets, etc. travel; *adj.: aerospace industries, medicine, research.*

aer·y (AIR·ee) *adj.* ethereal.
— *n.* same as EYRIE.

aes·thete (ES·theet, "th" as in "thin") *n.* one who appreciates artistic beauty.
— aes·thet·ic (es·THET·ic) or aes·thet·i·cal *adj.*
— aes·thet·i·cal·ly *adv.*

aes·thet·ics (es·THET·ics) *n.pl.* [takes sing. v.] the philosophy of artistic beauty.

aether same as ETHER.

a·far (uh·FAR) *adv.* far away: *Explorers went afar in search of new lands; They came from afar to meet the*
Pope.

af·fa·ble (AF·uh·bul) *adj.* pleasant to talk to: *an affable person; an affable* (=friendly) *smile.*
— af·fa·bly (-blee) *adv.*
— af·fa·bil·i·ty (-BIL·uh·tee) *n.*

af·fair (uh·FAIR) *n.* **1** a temporary love relationship: *He is having* or *carrying on an affair with his colleague; a casual, clandestine, illicit, love, romantic, secret, tempestuous affair.* **2** a business or event: *A wedding is a social affair; Our wedding was a private affair; a delicate, dull, formal, gala, informal, shabby, sinister, sordid, ugly affair; to cover up, hush up, investigate an affair; an **affair of honour*** (=duel); *That's his affair* (=concern), *not yours.* **3 affairs** *pl.* matters of general interest: *current affairs; to conduct affairs of state; to arrange, manage, settle, straighten out one's affairs; cultural affairs; the Minister of External* or *Foreign Affairs; an expert in international affairs; national affairs; the Minister of Veterans Affairs.*

af·fect (uh·FECT) *v.* **1** have an influence on a person or thing: *Smoking affects your health; Metals are affected by heat and cold; Everyone was much **affected*** (=moved) *by the tragedy; It affected everyone deeply, profoundly, strongly; The tragedy was a very **affecting*** (=moving) *experience; She spoke to us **affectingly*** (=feelingly) *about it.* **2** pretend: *He affects ignorance of what happened; She affected an air of innocence; She affected not to hear; an **affected*** (=artificial) *Oxford accent.* — af·fec·ted·ly *adv.*

af·fec·ta·tion (af·ek·TAY·shun) *n.* behaviour or attitude that is assumed or put on for show: *His Oxford accent is a mere affectation.*

af·fec·tion (uh·FEK·shun) *n.* **1** feeling of love for someone: *to demonstrate, display, return, show affection; to feel affection for someone; to gain* or *win someone's affection; a deep, strong, warm affection; to alienate a spouse's affections and cause a separation.* **2** disease: *TB is an affection of the lungs.*
— af·fec·tion·ate (-shun·it) *adj.: She is very affectionate to* or *toward her friends.* — af·fec·tion·ate·ly *adv.*

af·fi·da·vit (af·uh·DAY·vit) *n.* a written statement made on oath: *Lawyers file affidavits on behalf of clients.*

af·fil·i·ate (uh·FIL·ee·ate) *v.* -ates, -at·ed, -at·ing connect as a member or branch: *The parent company affiliated a new store; Now the two are affiliated; They are affiliated to* or *with a national chain; A left-wing organization would be unlikely to affiliate itself with a right-wing movement.*
— *n.* (-ee·it) a member or branch: *The new store is an affiliate of the national chain; the broadcasting affiliate of a media giant.*
— af·fil·i·a·tion (-AY·shun) *n.: schools in affiliation with a university; party, political, religious affiliations.*

af·fin·i·ty (uh·FIN·uh·tee) *n.* -ties **1** connection based on kinship or common interests: *There are relatives by birth and by affinity* (=marriage); *In-laws are tied by bonds of affinity, not by blood; the close affinity of Canadian English with American; the many affinities between Canadian and American English in pronunciation, vocabulary, etc.; An **affinity card** is a credit card issued to an **affinity group** such as a trade or professional organization, school alumni, or* *customers of an airline.* **2** attraction based on kinship: *to feel, have, show an affinity to one's relatives; the strong affinity of Canadian English for American words.*

af·firm (uh·FURM) *v.* say firmly: *She affirmed her innocence; affirmed that she was innocent.*
— **af·fir·ma·tion** (af·ur·MAY·shun) *n.*

af·fir·ma·tive (uh·FIR·muh·tiv) *adj.* saying "yes"; positive: *an affirmative response; a program of* **affirmative action** *to give women and minorities equal opportunity with the majority in employment, school admissions, etc.*
— *n.* the "yes" form of answer: *He replied* **in the affirmative;** *The* **affirmative** (= the ayes or "yes" side) *won the debate.* — **af·fir·ma·tive·ly** *adv.*

af·fix (uh·FIX) *v.* attach or add: *to affix a signature to a document.* — *n.* (AF.ix) a prefix or suffix.

af·flict (uh·FLICT) *v.* cause suffering to someone: *He is afflicted with gout.*
— **af·flic·tion** (-FLIC·shun) *n.: Gout is an affliction of the joints; We sympathize with him in his affliction.*

af·flu·ent (AF·loo·unt) *adj.* increasingly prosperous; well-to-do: *our affluent relatives; an affluent family, society, suburb; We live in affluent times; He is affluent in worldly goods.* — **af·flu·ence** *n.*

af·ford (uh·FORD) *v.* **1** be able to spare the time, money, etc. for something: *Can we afford two cars? I can't afford* (= am unable) *to miss work; I could ill afford to go on leave without pay.* **2** give or furnish: *Music affords us pleasure.*
— **af·for·da·ble** *adj.: The homeless are looking for affordable housing at affordable prices.*

af·front (uh·FRUNT) *v.* offend openly or knowingly.
— *n.* an open or intentional expression of disrespect: *She took it as an affront; an affront to her dignity; Her dignity suffered an affront; a shocking affront; It was indeed an affront to common decency.*

a·fi·cio·na·do (uh·fish·uh·NAH·doh) *n., pl.* **-dos** a devotee, enthusiast, or fan: *an aficionado of the theatre.*

a·field (uh·FEELD) *adj. & adv.* [used after its noun or verb] away from home: *He wandered* **far afield** *and got lost.*

a·fire (uh·FIRE) *adj. & adv.* [used after its noun or verb] on fire: *The house was set afire; politicians afire with* (= consumed by) *patriotic love.*
Also **a·flame** (uh·FLAME).

a·float (uh·FLOTE) *adj. & adv.* [used after its noun or verb] floating: *to set a leaking boat afloat again; to keep a company afloat* (= save it from bankruptcy); *There are rumours afloat* (= going around) *that the company is about to go under.*

a·flut·ter (uh·FLUT·ur) *adj.* [used after its noun or verb] excited: *John was all aflutter over the approaching examinations; aflutter with nervousness.*

a·foot (uh·FOOT) *adj.* [used after its noun] under way: *A scheme is afoot to raise funds for a new university.*

a·fore·men·tioned (uh·FOR·men·shund) *adj.* mentioned before.

a·fore·said (uh·FOR·sed) *adj.* referred to above.

a·foul (uh·FOWL) *adj. & adv.* [used after its noun or verb] entangled.
— **run** or **fall afoul of** be in conflict or collision with something: *It ran afoul of the other ship in the dark; to run afoul of the law.*

a·fraid (uh·FRAID) *adj.* [used after its noun] **1** fearful: *He's deathly, terribly afraid of water; afraid to swim; afraid that he might drown; Are you afraid of being late?* **2** sorry that something is, was, or will be as specified: *I'm afraid we are late; I'm afraid so; Will he survive? I'm afraid not.*

A-frame *adj.* of a building, having steep roofs overhanging the sides and meeting in a steep A-like point: *an A-frame cottage, house.*
— *n.* an A-shaped structure.

a·fresh (uh·FRESH) *adv.* [used after its verb] anew or again: *He starts afresh after each failure.*

Af·ri·can (AF·ruh·cun) *n.* a person of or from Africa.
— *adj.: He's African by birth; Swahili is an African language.*

Af·ro (AF·roh) *n.* a style of doing the hair in a dense bushy mass.
— *adj.* of Africa, Afros, etc.: *He came to work sporting an Afro haircut.*

Afro-American *n. & adj.* Black American: *a school of Afro-American studies.*

aft *adj. & adv.* to, at, or near the rear of a craft: *an aft sail; Let's go aft; the lavatories aft (of the airplane).*

af·ter (AF·tur) *prep.* following: *Jill comes after Jack; Jack is named after* (= same as) *his father, but he takes after* (= is like) *his mother; a woman after* (= according to) *my own heart; The police are after* (= pursuing) *him; This happens day after day* (= daily) *in city after city* (= in every city); *You were expected here at 10 and now it is 20 after* (= 10:20); *We're human* **after all** (= in spite of everything).
— **after hours** past the regular closing time, as after school or work: *a convenience store that is open after hours; adj.: an after-hours bar, club, job.*
— *adj.* later or following: *In after years, he regretted his actions;* **adv.***: Jack fell ill first, Jill came after; Both died shortly after; conj.: He stayed long after the others had left.*

af·ter·care (AF·tur·care) *n.* treatment following discharge from hospital or prison.

af·ter·ef·fect (Af·tur·i·fect) *n.* a secondary or later effect: *a drug with no aftereffects or side effects.*

af·ter·glow (AF·tur·gloh) *n.* **1** the glow seen in the sky after a sunset. **2** a pleasant feeling remaining after an experience: *in the afterglow of victory.*

af·ter·life (AF·tur·life) *n.* life after death.

af·ter·math (AF·tur·math) *n.* **1** a second crop, esp. of hay. **2** an outcome or result: *famine and disease as the aftermath of war; In the aftermath of the famine, people began to emigrate.*

af·ter·noon (af·tur·NOON) *n.* the time between noon and evening: *We started work at one o'clock in the afternoon; on Saturday afternoon; We worked all afternoon; We are not used to working afternoons on Saturdays.*
— *adj.* (AF·tur·noon): *an afternoon conference, nap.*

after-shave (AF·tur·shave) *n.* a scented lotion to dab on the face after shaving.

af·ter·taste (AF·tur·taist) *n.* **1** a taste remaining in the mouth, as after eating or drinking something: *Mouthwashes leave an aftertaste; a nice, pleasant, unpleasant aftertaste.* **2** a lingering feeling of a previous experience: *a bitter aftertaste; an aftertaste of last night's outburst.*

af·ter·tax (AF·tur·tax) *adj.* after taxes are deducted: *aftertax profits.*

af·ter·thought (AF·tur·thought) *n.* something that comes to mind after the occasion has passed.

af·ter·ward or **af·ter·wards** *adv.* after that; later: *He fell ill and died shortly afterward.*

a·gain (uh·GAIN) *adv.* more times: *You can say that again; Not again, dear; I've told you **again and again** or **time and time again** (= repeatedly) not to do it; She might say yes, **and again** or **and then again** (= on the other hand) she might not; I got $200 – first $100, and then **as much again** (= an equal amount) as bonus; **Now and again** (= sometimes) our neighbours offer to cut our grass.*

a·gainst (uh·GENST, "G" as in "go") *prep.* opposing: *to swim against the current; I'm against a picnic today; Don't lean against the wall; Two against one is unfair; Take an umbrella against (= in preparation for) the chance of rain; two houses **over against** (= facing) each other.*

a·gape (uh·GAPE) *adj.* [used after its noun] with mouth wide open: *The children were agape with astonishment.*

ag·ate (AG·it, "G" as in "go") *n.* a semiprecious stone coloured in patches or bands.

a·ga·ve (uh·GAH·vee) *n.* a tropical plant with thick fleshy leaves and a long flower stalk.

age *n.* **1** a period or length of life: *He's 15 years of age; At age 15, he hopes to live to a ripe old age; an advanced, early, tender, young age; in middle age when you are 40 to 65 years old; You don't look your age (= You seem younger than you are); children of school age; retirement age; to reach the venerable age of 90; an old woman bent with age; people of all ages; to **act** or **be one's age** (= to behave reasonably); It seems **ages** (Informal for a long time) since we met; 15 is below the*

age of consent *for marriage; She has reached the **age of discretion** (= of legal responsibility); At 18 one is **of age** (= legally an adult) in many countries; You're supposed to have **come of age** at 18; There are attempts to reduce the **age of majority** (= of legal independence) from 18; He has to produce an age-of-majority card before buying liquor; An old man is **over age** for military service; At 15, you are **under age** (= too young) to drive.* **2** a historical or cultural stage: *the Stone Age of civilization; the Victorian Age; the Age of Mammals; World War II ushered in the nuclear age; the age of automation; the progress of civilization through **the ages** (= the centuries; history).*
— *v.* **ag·es, aged, ag·ing** or **age·ing** grow or make old: *Some age faster than others; Wine is aged in storage casks after fermentation to develop its flavour.*

aged *adj.* **1** (AIJD) having age as specified: *a pensioner aged 90.* **2** (AY·jid) advanced in age: *an aged pensioner; a home for the aged; the sick and **the aged** (= old people).* **3** (AIJD) matured: *aged cheese, wine.*

age·less *adj.* **1** always young: *an ageless beauty.* **2** eternal: *the ageless genius of Shakespeare.*

age·ism (AY·jiz·um) *n.* discrimination based on age: *Racism, sexism, and ageism have not yet been eliminated.* Also **ag·ism** *n.*

age·long *adj.* lasting a very long time: *the end of an age-long tyranny.*

a·gen·cy (AY·jun·see) *n.* **-cies 1** an office or service: *advertising, law-enforcement, news, regulatory, ticket, travel agencies; He works at an employment agency; an intelligence agency for gathering information secretly.* **2** means of doing something: *Miracles are beyond human agency.*

a·gen·da (uh·JEN·duh) *n.* **-das** list of things to be done, as on a program: *to draw up or make up an agenda; a hidden agenda; What's the next item on the agenda?*

a·gent (AY·junt) *n.* one who acts for another: *an enemy agent; He was not a free agent in the negotiatons; A literary agent helps authors deal with publishers; a real-estate agent; a press agent; shipping agent; A secret agent spies for his government; The spy was a double agent; Catalysts are chemical agents; a cleaning agent (= substance) such as soap.*

agent general *n.* *Cdn.* a Canadian province's commercial representative abroad.

age of consent, age of discretion, age of majority See AGE.

age-old *adj.* existing for a very long time: *an age-old custom, institution; age-old problems, questions, rivalries.*

ag·gran·dize (uh·GRAN·dize) *v.* **-diz·es, -dized, -diz·ing** make *oneself* greater in power, wealth, or position.
— **ag·gran·dize·ment** (uh·GRAN·diz·munt) *n.*: *personal aggrandizement at public expense; territorial aggrandizement of the superpowers.*

ag·gra·vate (AG·ruh·vate) *v.* **-vates, -vat·ed, -vat·ing** make worse or more serious: *His excuses only aggravated the quarrel; **aggravated assault** using a deadly weapon;*

his **aggravating** (= annoying) *behaviour.*
— **ag·gra·va·tion** (-VAY·shun) *n.*

ag·gre·gate (AG·ruh·gate) *v.* -gates, -gat·ed, -gat·ing collect together in a mass or cluster.
— **adj.** (-git) forming a collection or cluster: *The blackberry and the raspberry are aggregate fruits; aggregate marks, sales.*
— in the aggregate collectively; as a whole.
— **ag·gre·ga·tion** (-GAY·shun) *n.* collection: *an aggregation of museum exhibits.*

ag·gres·sion (uh·GRESH·un) *n.* **1** an act of attacking first: *They vowed never to commmit (an act of) aggression against a neutral nation; armed, naked, outright, unprovoked aggression.* **2** aggressiveness: *Aggression is manifested in overt and covert ways by destruction, greed, ambition, etc.*

ag·gres·sive (uh·GRES·iv) *adj.* **1** tending to attack: *the aggressive instinct; an aggressive nation; an aggressive weapon (made for use in attack).* **2** forceful or energetic: *an aggressive approach, campaign, sales rep, style; aggressive leadership.*
— **ag·gres·sive·ly** *adv.*; **ag·gres·sive·ness** *n.*

ag·gres·sor (uh·GRES·ur) *n.* one who commits aggression: *The Nazis were branded the aggressors in World War II.*

ag·grieved (uh·GREEVD) *adj.* having suffered grief or hurt: *Jane felt aggrieved she didn't get a raise; felt aggrieved about not getting a raise; She's the aggrieved party.*

a·ghast (uh·GAST) *adj.* [used after its noun] horrified: *She was aghast; Everyone stood aghast at the sight.*

ag·ile (AJ·ile, AJ·ul) *adj.* quick and nimble: *a leopard's agile movements; her agile wit.*
— **ag·ile·ly** *adv.* — **a·gil·i·ty** (uh·JIL·uh·tee) *n.*

ag·ism (AY·jiz·um) *n.* same as AGEISM.

ag·i·tate (AJ·uh·tate) *v.* -tates, -tat·ed, -tat·ing disturb or stir up: *the sea agitated by a storm; She seemed agitated by the delay; to agitate* (= arouse public opinion) *strongly for or against a piece of legislation.*
— **ag·i·ta·tion** (-TAY·shun) *n.*
— **ag·i·ta·tor** *n.* one that stirs: *Our washer needs a new agitator; a political agitator (who stirs up people).*

a·gleam (uh·GLEEM) *adj.* [used after its noun] gleaming.

a·glit·ter (uh·GLIT·ur) *adj.* [used after its noun] glittering.

a·glow (uh·GLOH) *adj.* [used after its noun] glowing: *Her face was aglow with joy.*

ag·lu or **ag·loo** (AG·loo) *n. Cdn.* a breathing hole made in ice by seals.

ag·nos·tic (ag·NOS·tic) *n.* one who asserts that the existence of God and the supernatural are unknowable: *He's not an atheist but an agnostic; his agnostic position, views.* — **ag·nos·ti·cism** (-tuh·siz·um) *n.*

a·go (uh·GO) *adv.* [used after a verb in the past tense] back in time: *I saw him 50 years ago; That was long ago; It was long ago that I saw him last.*

a·gog (uh·GOG) *adj.* excited: *The town was all agog (with excitement); The announcement left the town agog; The town was agog over the victory.*

ag·o·nize (AG·uh·nize) *v.* -niz·es, -nized, -niz·ing be in agony: *Tim is agonizing over his homework; He has an agonized* (= distressed) *look; They had an agonizing* (= distressing) *time in a hijacked plane; adv.: Service is agonizingly* (= distressingly) *slow here.*

ag·o·ny (AG·uh·nee) *n.* -nies intense pain or suffering in body or mind: *the agony of suspense; The accident victim spent hours in mortal agony before dying; We are in great agony to learn the worst; Why prolong the agony when we can open the envelope and get it over with?*

a·grar·i·an (uh·GRAIR·ee·un) *adj.* having to do with land ownership, farms, etc.: *an agrarian party serving agrarian interests.*

a·gree (uh·GREE) *v.* a·grees, a·greed, a·gree·ing **1** say yes; concur: *I agree with you completely, entirely, fully, readily, wholeheartedly about reaching a settlement; I couldn't agree (with you) more; I agree on or to a compromise; I agree that it is a good deal; We agreed on the terms of the deal; We agreed to sign the deal; We are agreed* (= satisfied) *it is a good deal.* **2** be in harmony: *John's account agrees with Jane's; In "He go," the verb doesn't agree with the subject; Seafood and this climate don't agree with me* (= suit my well-being).

a·gree·a·ble (uh·GREE·uh·bul) *adj.* **1** ready to agree: *an agreeable negotiator, I'm agreeable to the idea.* **2** pleasing: *an agreeable smile, voice; The idea is agreeable to me* (= I like the idea).
— **a·gree·a·ble·ness** *n.* — **a·gree·a·bly** *adv.*

a·gree·ment (uh·GREE·munt) *n.* **1** the act of agreeing: *We are in full agreement on the question; to settle all disputes by mutual agreement.* **2** accord, treaty, or contract: *to carry out, come to, conclude, enter into, reach, sign, work out an agreement; to break, denounce, violate an agreement; a binding, contractual, gentleman's, iron-clad, tacit, tentative agreement; an agreement between two parties; an agreement on or about a disputed matter; an agreement to pay a monthly rent; an agreement that the rent would be paid on the first of each month.* **3** grammatical concord: *"She do his own hair" lacks agreement in number and gender; It should read "She does her own hair."*

ag·ri·busi·ness (AG·ruh·biz·nis) *n.* the farming industry, including equipment, fertilizers, and related services.

ag·ri·cul·ture (AG·ruh·cul·chur) *n.* **1** farming or husbandry. **2** the science of farming.
— **ag·ri·cul·tur·al** (-CUL·chur·ul) *adj.*
— **ag·ri·cul·tur·al·ly** *adv.*
— **ag·ri·cul·tur·ist** or **ag·ri·cul·tur·al·ist** *n.*

a·grol·o·gy (uh·GROL·uh·jee) *n.* a branch of agriculture dealing with soils. — **a·grol·o·gist** *n.*

a·gron·o·my (uh·GRON·uh·mee) *n.* the science of land management and production of crops.
Also **ag·ro·nom·ics** (ag·ruh·NOM·ics) *n.pl.* [used with sing. v.]. — **a·gron·o·mist** (uh·GRON·uh·mist) *n.*

a·ground (uh·GROUND) *adj. & adv.* [used after its noun or verb] of a craft, touching the bottom in shallow water: *The ship ran aground; It was fast aground.*

a·gue (AIG·yoo) *n.* a usually malarial fever with periodic chills and sweating.

ah or **a·ha** (ah·HAH) *interj.* indicating surprise, triumph, pain, etc.: *Ah, yes, I remember; Aha! I've caught you red-handed.*

a·head (uh·HED) *adj. & adv.* [used after its noun or verb] forward: *Look straight ahead when driving; We are far ahead of everyone else; Watch the road ahead of you; Go ahead and tell us; We're trying to get ahead (=succeed) in life; My watch is ahead by a couple of minutes; We'll be ahead of time when we get there; You're **ahead of the times** (= very modern); to **get ahead of** (= outdo) the competition and stay ahead; She always seems to get **ahead of the game** (Slang for to have an advantage); The captain ordered **full speed ahead** (= to go at full speed).*

a·hem (uh·HEM) *interj.* [like a clearing of the throat] used to attract attention.

-aholic *suffix* [forming n. or adj. like "alcoholic"] addicted to what is specified: *sleepaholic, spendaholic, workaholic.*

a·hoy (uh·HOY) *interj.* used by sailors to warn or hail: *Ship ahoy!*

aid *n.* help: *He went to her aid; He was charged with giving aid and comfort to the enemy; to cut off, extend, give, offer, provide, render aid to poor nations; economic, financial, and foreign aid; to withdraw aid; TV is an audio-visual aid; a hearing aid; rhymes, mnemonics, and such memory aids; teaching aids such as chalkboards and wallmaps; a benefit performance in aid of the Red Cross.*
— *v.* help: *They aided her with money; aided him in his work; a publication that was **aided and abetted** by her friends.*

aide (AID) *n.* helper or assistant: *a nurse's aide; teacher's aide; He works as an aide to the president.*

aide-de-camp (AID·duh·camp) *n., pl.* **aides-de-camp** (AID·duh-) a military officer who is an assistant to a senior officer.

aid·man *n.* **-men** a medical aide in a field unit.

AIDS (AIDZ) *n.* "acquired immune deficiency syndrome," an often fatal disorder causing severe damage to the body's defences against disease.

ail *v.* be ill: *an ailing child; an ailing economy; What ails her (= is making her ill)?*

ai·le·ron (AY·luh·ron) *n.* a movable section of the rear edge of an airplane's wing that helps it to turn left or right.

ail·ment (AIL·munt) *n.* illness: *a common ailment; minor ailments.*

aim *v.* direct an object, remark, or action: *Aim your gun at the target; Aim for the bull's-eye; The remark was aimed at the whole group; She is aiming to be a lawyer; aiming for success.*
— *n.* **1** an aiming: *Take aim carefully before shooting; Keep a steady aim at the target.* **2** purpose: *people with no aim in life; His long-range aim was to become a teacher, the immediate aim to get a degree; Our final aim should be to be happy; Idealistic and lofty aims are hard to achieve.*
— **aim·less** *adj.*: *an aimless existence, life.*
— **aim·less·ly** *adv.*; **aim·less·ness** *n.*

ain't [nonstandard or informal] am not; are not; is not; has not; have not: *I ain't gonna do it; Egalitarian it ain't; You ain't seen nothin' yet.*
— **Ain't I?** *Informal.* Am I not?

air *n.* **1** atmosphere, esp. the mixture of gases surrounding the earth: *We need air to breathe; We inhale air and exhale carbon dioxide; Open the windows for a breath of fresh air; balmy, bracing, brisk, crisp, dry, foul, humid, polluted, refreshing, stale air; A blast of hot air hit me as I opened the furnace door; Birds fly in the air; to travel by air (= in an airplane); There is a rumour in the air (= going around); Our plans disappeared into thin air (= completely) when our money was stolen; A program is either on or off the air (= being or not being broadcast); She likes to **take the air** (= go out for fresh air) after dinner; The result of the election is **up in the air** (= uncertain); She will be **walking on air** (= elated) if she wins.* **2** a manner: *There's an air of dignity about her; a detached, nonchalant, superior, triumphant air; He puts on **airs** (= unnatural ways of behaviour) to impress people.* **3** a tune or melody: *The band played a martial air.*
— *v.* expose to the air: *A stuffy room needs to be aired; to air (= go public with) a grievance; The grievances got a good **airing** (= discussion) at the meeting.*

air·bag *n.* a protective bag designed to inflate in front of an automobile passenger in a crash.

air base *n.* an operating headquarters for military aircraft.

air·borne (AIR·born) *adj.* carried by air; flying: *airborne invasion, pollen, seeds; an airborne warning and control system; Drinks are served only after the airplane becomes airborne (= when it is up in the air).*

air·brain *n.* same as AIRHEAD.

air brake *n.* a brake worked by compressed air.

air·brush (AIR·brush) *n.* a compressed-air device for touching up artwork.
— *v.* apply the airbrush to artwork: *Blemishes on a photo can be airbrushed away.*

air·bus *n.* a wide-bodied passenger jet aircraft.

air·condition (air·cun·DISH·un) *v.* control humidity, temperature, etc. using a refrigerating device called an air-conditioner: *an air-conditioned car, room; He works in air-conditioned comfort; central **air-conditioning** for the whole building.* — **air-conditioner** *n.*

air·craft (AIR·craft) *n. sing. & pl.* an airplane or other air vehicle including helicopters and balloons: *enemy aircraft; an unidentified aircraft; Many aircraft were shot down in the battle.*

aircraft carrier *n.* a warship with a deck for aircraft to land and take off.

air cushion vehicle *n.* a vehicle that travels on a cushion of air by means of jets or fans blowing downward and raising it a few metres above ground or water.

air·drop (AIR·drop) *v.* **-drops, -dropped, -drop·ping** deliver cargo or personnel by parachute. — *n.* such a delivery.

air express *n.* the shipping of parcels by air; **Air Express** *Service mark.*

air·fare *n.* fare for an airplane trip.

air·field *n.* a field where airplanes land and take off.

air filter *n.* a device for filtering out dust, pollen, etc. from an engine, air-conditioner, etc.

air·foil *n.* a controlling part of an airplane such as a wing, rudder, or aileron.

air force *n.* the air arm of a nation's armed forces.

air gun *n.* a gun that is worked by compressed air or a gas and uses BB shot or pellets.

air·head *n. Informal.* one who is silly or stupid.

air hole *n.* a hole for passing or getting air, esp. a breathing hole for water animals, as in the ice covering a pond or river.

air lane *n.* a path regularly used by airplanes.

air·less *adj.* without movement of air: *an airless room.*

air letter *n.* a letter mailed by air that consists of a sheet of paper folded, sealed, and addressed without an envelope.

air·lift *n.* the transporting of people and supplies by air. — *v.:* *Supplies were airlifted to the disaster area.*

air·line *n.* a regular passenger service by air: *a commuter, domestic, feeder, international, national airline.*

air·lin·er (AIR·lye·nur) *n.* an airline's passenger plane.

air·lock *n.* **1** a blockage caused by air, as in a water pipe. **2** an airtight chamber, as in a caisson.

air·mail *n.* the transporting of mail by air: *a letter sent via* or *by airmail to Japan.* — *v.:* to airmail a letter.

air·man *n.* **-men 1** a member of an air force, esp. one in the lower ranks. **2** an aviator.

air mattress *n.* a pad that is inflated for use as a mattress.

air mile *n.* same as NAUTICAL MILE.

air·mo·bile (AIR·moh·bil) *adj.* of ground troops, that are moved to combat areas by air, usually by helicopter.

air piracy *n.* aircraft hijacking. — **air pirate** *n.*

air pistol *n.* a handgun that is worked by compressed air or a gas and uses BB shot or pellets.

air·plane *n.* a heavier-than-air machine with fixed wings that is powered by a propeller or jet: *to board, bring down* or *shoot down, land, ditch, fly, hijack, navigate an airplane; An airplane crashes, cruises at a certain altitude, gains altitude as it goes up, lands* or *touches down at airports, loses altitude when there is flight trouble, levels off after reaching an altitude, taxis along the runway before taking off.*

air plant *n.* a plant that grows on another plant, drawing nourishment from air and rain, as mosses.

air·play *n.* the playing of a song or musical composition by a radio station.

air pocket *n.* a partial vacuum or other atmospheric condition that makes an aircraft lose altitude while in flight.

air pollution *n.* contamination of the air by industrial gases, automobile exhausts, etc.

air·port *n.* a place with established facilities for planes, passengers, and cargo: *to land at an airport.*

air pump *n.* a piece of equipment for compressing or removing air.

air raid *n.* an attack by armed aircraft on a ground target: *to carry out* or *conduct an air raid; an air raid alert.*

air rifle *n.* a rifle that is worked by compressed air or a gas and uses BB shot or pellets.

air·ship *n.* a lighter-than-air craft equipped with power for propulsion and steering; dirigible.

air show *n.* **1** a display of aircraft and their manoeuvres: *to put on* or *stage an air show.* **2** an exhibition of the aircraft and aerospace industry.

air·sick *adj.* nauseated from the movements of an aircraft. — **air·sick·ness** *n.*

air·space *n.* the space above a country over which it has jurisdiction.

air·speed *n.* the speed of an aircraft relative to the air through which it flies.

air strike *n.* an attack from the air.

air strip *n.* a strip of ground used as an airfield; landing strip.

air·tight *adj.* **1** too tight for air to get in or out. **2** flawless: *an airtight alibi, argument.*

air time *n.* flight time: *The airtime between Toronto and Montreal is about an hour.*

air-to-air (AIR·too·AIR) *adj.* directed from an aircraft to a target in the air: *air-to-air combat, missiles.*

air-to-ground (AIR·tuh·GROUND) *adj.* directed from an aircraft to a ground target.

air waves *n. pl.* the medium of transmission of radio and TV: *the newest star of the national air waves.*

air·way *n.* **1** a route used by airplanes. **2** air passageway to the lungs, to a mine, etc.

air·wom·an (AIR·woom·un) *n.* **-wom·en** a woman aviator or member of an air force.

air·wor·thy (AIR·wur·thee) *adj.* of airplanes, fit to be flown. — **air·wor·thi·ness** *n.*

air·y (AIR·ee) *adj.* **air·i·er, -i·est 1** having plenty of air circulating in it: *an airy room.* **2** light-hearted or breezy: *an airy greeting.* — **air·i·ly** *adv.;* **air·i·ness** *n.*

aisle (ILE) *n.* a passageway between two rows of seats, shelves, etc. as in an auditorium or supermarket: *to clear the aisles; to walk up the aisle to the altar; Nuts and candy are in Aisle* (= row) *7B.* — **aisled** *adj.*

a·jar (uh·JAR) *adj.* [used after its noun] of a door, hinged window, etc., partly open: *The door is ajar.*

a·kim·bo (uh·KIM·boh) *adj. & adv.* with the hands on the hips and the elbows pointing outward: *He stood with arms akimbo barring her way.*

a·kin (uh·KIN) *adj.* related; of the same stock: *"Three" is akin to the German "drei."*

à la or **a la** (AH·lah) *prep.* in the style or after the manner of a person or thing: *tragedy à la Shakespeare.*

al·a·bas·ter (AL·uh·bas·tur) *n.* a soft, white stone that resembles marble.
— *adj.* made of or like alabaster: *an alabaster vase; her alabaster skin.*

à la carte (ah·luh·CART) *adj. & adv.* ordered from a menu item by item, not as a complete meal: *an à la carte dinner.*

a·lac·ri·ty (uh·LAC·ruh·tee) *n.* eager readiness: *The MPs acted with alacrity to vote themselves a raise.*

à la mode (al·uh·MODE) *adj.* in the fashion: *"Apple pie à la mode" is served with ice cream.*

a·larm (uh·LARM) *n.* **1** sudden fear: *The news caused alarm; People expressed, felt great alarm at what was happening.* **2** warning: *Sound the fire alarm; The alarm was set to go off at 6 a.m.; to activate, deactivate, give, raise, set off, sound, turn off an alarm; a burglar alarm; false alarm; smoke alarm; Leave the building when the alarm goes off, rings, sounds; the alarm (signal) of an* **alarm clock.**
— *combining form:* *A three-alarm fire has three companies of firefighters and vehicles responding; a four-alarm* (*Informal for* very hot) *Indian curry.*
— *v.* frighten: *We didn't mean to alarm you; Don't be alarmed; an* **alarming** *state of affairs.*

a·larm·ist (uh·LARM·ist) *n.* one who raises alarms needlessly. — *adj.:* *alarmist views on the Soviet threat.*

a·las (uh·LAS) *interj.* indicating regret, anxiety, sorrow, etc.

al·ba·tross (AL·buh·tros) *n.* **-tross·es** a large-winged seabird related to the petrel: *The charge of accepting a bribe proved an albatross around his neck* (= something that impaired his effectiveness).

al·be·it (awl·BEE·it) *conj. Formal.* although; admittedly: *There's still a chance, albeit slim.*

al·bi·nism (AL·buh·niz·um) *n.* lack of skin coloration that results in very pale skin, white hair, and pink eyes from birth.

al·bi·no (al·BYE·noh) *n.* a human or animal born with albinism.

al·bum (AL·bum) *n.* **1** a book in which stamps, photographs, or other objects are kept as a collection. **2** a record of several pieces of music or a set of such records.

al·bu·men (al·BYOO·mun) *n.* **1** the white of an egg. **2** the protein substance which forms egg white, found also in many plant and animal tissues and juices, better known as **al·bu·min.**

al·che·my (AL·cuh·mee) *n.* miraculous change of the ordinary into something precious, like the turning of base metals into gold, as attempted by medieval chemists. — **al·chem·ist** *n.*

al·co·hol (AL·cuh·hol) *n.* **1** a liquid forming the intoxicating element of drinks such as beer, wine, and whisky, also called "ethyl alcohol": *grain alcohol; to distill, make alcohol; pure, unadulterated alcohol.* **2** such a drink: *to abstain from alcohol; The tavern reeked of alcohol.* **3** any chemical compound similar to alcohol: *methyl* or *wood alcohol; rubbing alcohol.*

al·co·hol·ic (al·cuh·HOL·ic) *adj.* containing alcohol: *an alcoholic drink.*
— *n.* one who suffers from excessive use of alcohol: *a chronic alcoholic;* **al·co·hol·ism** (AL·cuh·hol·iz·um) *n.*

al·cove (AL·cohv) *n.* **1** a nook or recessed room, as in a library. **2** a sheltered area in a garden.

al den·te (ahl·DEN·tay) *adj. Italian.* firm to the teeth when cooked; not soft: *Cook the spaghetti until tender but al dente.*

al·der·man (ALL·dur·mun) *n.* **-men** a member of a municipal council.

ale *n.* a beerlike liquor brewed from malt and hops.

a·lert (uh·LURT) *adj.* watchful and ready to act, as a sentinel on duty: *an alert security guard; alert in answering the door; Be always alert to danger.*
— *v.* warn: *The siren alerted us to the danger of an air raid.*
— *n.* **1** a warning signal: *to call, call off, cancel an alert; to place* or *put the army on alert; a full alert; red alert; in a state of alert; during an air raid alert* (= during the period of the warning); *Be* **on the alert** (= on the lookout) *for pickpockets.*
— **a·lert·ly** *adv.;* **a·lert·ness** *n.*

ale·wife *n.* **-wives** a herringlike fish used for food, fertilizer, etc.

a·lex·i·a (uh·LEX·ee·uh) *n.* reading inability caused by brain damage.

al·fal·fa (al·FAL·fuh) *n.* a cloverlike plant used as fodder.

al·fres·co (al·FRES·coh) *adj. & adv.* in the open air: *to dine alfresco; an alfresco breakfast on the patio.*

al·ga (AL·guh) *n., pl.* **-gae** (-jee) seaweed, pond scum, or such primitive form of plant life.
— **al·gal** (-gul) *adj.*

al·ge·bra (AL·juh·bruh) *n.* a branch of mathematics that uses symbols in place of quantities.
— **al·ge·bra·ic** (-BRAY·ic) or **al·ge·bra·i·cal** *adj.*

al·go·rithm (AL·guh·rith·um, "th" as in "the") *n.* a set of rules in a mathematical operation for solving a problem.

a·li·as (AY·lee·us) *adv.* also known as: *Jones, alias Johnson.*
— *n.* an assumed name: *a criminal with many aliases, checking in at hotels under a new alias each time.*

al·i·bi (AL·uh·bye) *n.* an accused person's plea that he was elsewhere when the crime was committed: *His alibi wouldn't hold up; to break* or *disprove an alibi; to establish an alibi; to confirm someone's alibi; an airtight, foolproof, unassailable alibi; He provided no alibis* (*Informal for* excuses) *for his absence.*

al·ien (AY·lee·un) *n.* foreigner: *an enemy alien; illegal aliens coming in across the border; registration of aliens; a visit by aliens* (= extraterrestial beings) *from Mars.*
— *adj.* foreign: *a naturalized citizen of alien origin; a way of life that is alien to our culture.*

al·ien·ate (AY·lee·uh·nate) *v.* **-ates, -at·ed, -at·ing** cause to be withdrawn, estranged, or separated: *youth feeling alienated from society.*

al·ien·a·tion (AY·lee·uh·NAY·shun) *n.* a transferring; withdrawal: *He suffered alienation from his associates; A third party is sued for **alienation of affection** between* (= transference of love away from) *spouses.*

a·light (uh·LITE) *v.* **a·lights,** *pt. & pp.* **a·light·ed** or **a·lit** (uh·LIT), **a·light·ing** descend: *to alight from a cab; The bird alighted on a branch.*
— *adj.* [used after its noun] **1** on fire: *to set a house alight.* **2** lit or bright: *a cloudless night alight with stars; faces alight with joy.*

a·lign (uh·LINE) *v.* arrange properly, as in a line: *The front wheels need aligning; He aligned himself* (= formed an alliance) *with the leftists.*
Also **a·line, a·lines, a·lined, a·lin·ing.**
— **a·lign·ment** or **a·line·ment** *n.: The wheels are either in or out of alignment.*

a·like (uh·LIKE) *adj.* [used after its noun] similar: *Identical twins always look alike.*
— *adv.* similarly: *The law treats everyone alike.*
— **a·like·ness** *n.*

al·i·ment (AL·uh·munt) *n.* food to keep the body functioning.

al·i·men·ta·ry (al·uh·MEN·tuh·ree) *adj.* having to do with nourishment: *The alimentary canal* or *tract extends from the mouth to the anus; The alimentary system consists of the intestines, digestive glands, etc.*

al·i·mo·ny (AL·uh·moh·nee) *n.* **-nies** an allowance paid by one spouse to the other on separation or divorce: *The courts usually award alimony to an unemployed spouse.*

aline, alinement See ALIGN.

A-line *adj.* of garments, in the shape of an "A," esp. with a flared bottom: *an A-line skirt.*

alit a *pt.* or *pp.* of ALIGHT.

a·live (uh·LIVE) *adj.* living: *Is the snake dead or alive? The abortion issue is very much alive* (= not dead); *A claim must be kept alive* (= active) *in order to be valid; He's not only breathing but quite **alive to** (= conscious of) what is happening around him; The sleepy town is **alive with** (= full of) tourists in the summer.*
— **alive and kicking** or **alive and well** *Informal.* quite well and healthy.

al·ka·li (AL·kuh·lye) *n.* **-lis** or **-lies** a substance such as caustic soda that combines with acids to form salts.
— **al·ka·line** *adj.*

all (AWL) *adj.* the whole number, amount, extent, etc.

of a group or class: *It rained all day; We are all mortal; The ambulance came with all speed; Ito, of all people, would never do such a thing; It's sunny all year round in the tropics.*
— *pron.* [takes pl. v. when used as pl. subject] the whole number, amount, etc.: *All are mortal; All is not lost;* [used with "of" before a personal pron. or to express limited meaning] *All of them work hard; I mean all the women; all of the women who are employed here; He's a child **after all** (= in spite of everything); Anyone **at all** (= in any way) for tennis? There are 200 **in all** (= altogether).*
— *n.* everything: *You must give your all for this cause; In his will, Joe left his all to his wife.*
— *adv.* wholly: *a child left all by himself; I'm all in favour of the idea; He came with all possible speed; I told you **all along** (= all the time) to be careful; The job is **all but** (= almost) done; I'm **all in** (Informal for tired); **All in all** (= as a whole), it was a fair deal; a small country whose army numbers **all of** (= at least) 500; They went **all out** (= with full effort) to help the refugees; She has travelled **all over** (= everywhere in) the world; That's Dad **all over** (= behaviour typical of Dad); Are you **all right** (= safe, well, etc.)? He didn't do much work, **all the same** (= anyhow; nevertheless) he got paid; I feel **all the worse** (= so much the worse) for the medication; The trip cost me $300 **all told** (= altogether).*
— **all quiet on the Western front** *Informal.* It's calm and peaceful (at the place mentioned).
— **all the time:** *Some people complain all the time* (= habitually); *Lou was driving around without a licence and I knew it all the time* (= throughout that period).

Al·lah (AL·uh, AH·luh) *n.* in Islam, the supreme being; God.

all-American (all·uh·MER·uh·cun) *adj.* **1** wholly American: *an All-American team.* **2** the best American: *an All-American quarterback.*

all-around (ALL·uh·round) same as ALL-ROUND.

al·lay (uh·LAY) *v.* make less: *to allay one's anger, apprehensions, doubts, fears, pain, trouble.*

all-Canada (all·CAN·uh·duh) *adj.* confined to Canada: *an all-Canada pipeline, route, service.*

all-Canadian (all·cuh·NAY·dee·un) *adj.* consisting entirely of Canadian people or resources: *an all-Canadian achievement, company, conference, hockey team, show.*

all-clear *n.* a signal indicating the end of an air raid or other threat.

al·le·ga·tion (al·luh·GAY·shun) *n.* an alleging or what is alleged: *a false, serious, unsubstantiated, vague allegation about someone; an allegation of theft against Jon; an allegation that Jon has stolen $200; to deny, drop, make, refute, retract, withdraw an allegation.*

al·lege (uh·LEJ) *v.* **al·leg·es, al·leged, al·leg·ing** put forward a claim, accusation, excuse, etc. without proof: *He alleged that she stole the money; She is the alleged thief; $200 is alleged to have been stolen; Poverty has been alleged* (as reason) *for the theft.*
— **al·leg·ed·ly** (-id·lee) *adv.*

al·le·giance (uh·LEE·junce) *n.* loyalty owed to one's country, a government, cause, leader, etc.: *an oath of allegiance; They pledged* or *swore allegiance to the flag; true, unfailing, unswerving allegiance; to disavow* or *forsake one's allegiance to a cause.*

al·le·go·ry (AL·uh·gor·ee) *n.* **-ries** a story with characters, places, and events representing abstractions such as patience, purity, truth, and justice: *George Orwell's "Animal Farm" is an allegory.*
— **al·le·gor·ic** (al·uh·GOR·ic) or **al·le·gor·i·cal** *adj.*

al·le·lu·ia (al·uh·LOO·yuh) *interj.* same as HALLELUJAH.

al·ler·gen (AL·ur·jun) *n.* something that causes an allergy. — **al·ler·gen·ic** (al·ur·JEN·ic) *adj.*

al·ler·gic (uh·LUR·jic) *adj.* sensitive to particular things: *He's allergic to milk; an allergic reaction; She's quite allergic* (*Informal* for disinclined) *to math.*

al·ler·gist (AL·ur·jist) *n.* an allergy specialist.

al·ler·gy (AL·ur·jee) *n.* **-gies** an abnormal sensitivity to particular things such as foods, smoke, dust, pollen, or insect venom: *An allergy is acquired, developed.*

al·le·vi·ate (uh·LEE·vee·ate) *v.* **-ates, -at·ed, -at·ing** make more bearable; lessen: *to alleviate misery, pain, suffering.* — **al·le·vi·a·tion** (-AY·shun) *n.*

al·ley (AL·ee) *n.* **al·leys** a narrow passageway, as between rows of buildings: *the stray cat in our back alley; a blind alley* (= road closed at one end); *The ball rolled down the alley* (= bowling lane) *and knocked down the pins; Stamp-collecting is not* **up** or **down my alley** (*Informal* for not my area of interest).

alley cat *n.* a stray cat.

all-fired *adj. & adv.* extreme or extremely: *His all-fired nerve! He's so all-fired arrogant.*

All Fools' Day *n.* April 1; April Fools' Day.

all fours *n. pl.* **1** all four legs. **2** a person's arms and legs or hands and knees: *to scrounge around* **on all fours.**

All·hal·lows (all·HAL·oze) *n.* same as ALL SAINTS' DAY.

al·li·ance (uh·LYE·unce) *n.* a union, association, or relationship: *We entered into* or *formed an alliance with our neighbours against a common threat; an alliance to watch for prowlers; a military alliance; an unholy political alliance between opposition parties; to dissolve an alliance.*

allied, allies See ALLY.

al·li·ga·tor (AL·uh·gay·tur) *n.* a reptile similar to the crocodile but with a broader snout.

all-important *adj.* of the greatest importance.

all-inclusive *adj.* inclusive of everything: *an all-inclusive charge.*

al·lit·er·ate (uh·LIT·uh·rate) *v.* **-ates, -at·ed, -at·ing** have or use the same initial sound in successive words, as "Cossack commanders cannonading came."
— **al·lit·er·a·tion** (AL·uh·tuh·RAY·shun) *n.*

all-night·er (ALL·nye·tur) *n.* a party, session, etc. lasting all night: *He studied in all-nighters and cram sessions.*

al·lo·cate (AL·uh·cate) *v.* **-cates, -cat·ed, -cat·ing** give funds, space, duties, etc. to someone or for a specific purpose: *to allocate funds for education; money allocated to charities.*
— **al·lo·ca·tion** (al·uh·CAY·shun) *n.*: *to make an allocation; allocations to charities; the allocation of funds for health care.*

al·lo·cu·tion (al·uh·CUE·shun) *n.* a formal authoritative address, as of the Pope.

al·lo·phone (AL·uh·fone) *n. Cdn.* in French Canada, one who speaks a language other than French or English: *Francophones, Anglophones, and allophones.*

al·lot (uh·LOT) *v.* **al·lots, al·lot·ted, al·lot·ting** assign or distribute: *the time allotted to each speaker; A fixed time is allotted for each question.* — **al·lot·ment** *n.*

all-out *adj.* using all resources: *Al made an all-out effort to win; the threat of all-out war.*

all·o·ver (ALL·oh·vur) *adj.* covering the whole surface: *an allover pattern.*

al·low (uh·LOW, *rhyme:* HOW) *v.* let have, be, or do: *He allows his son $10 a week; allows him to play on the street; He allows himself no luxuries; No smoking is allowed; An hour is allowed for lunch; The judge allowed* (= agreed to) *the claim; He allowed that it was reasonable; Considering all those fringe benefits, she* **allows as how** (*Informal* for concedes) *she has no complaints; The judge did not* **allow for** (= take into consideration) *his age in sentencing him; This rule* **allows of** (= admits of) *no exception.*
— **al·low·a·ble** *adj.*; **al·low·ed·ly** (-id·lee) *adv.*

al·low·ance (uh·LOW·unce) *n.* **1** a granting or conceding: *the allowance of a claim; to make allowances for human error; the road allowances* (= property) *appropriated by the Government of Canada.* **2** a sum granted: *His son gets a weekly allowance of $10; He gets a cost-of-living allowance in addition to wages; the Family Allowance for children under 18; a trade-in allowance deducted from the price of a new car; a sales rep's travel allowance.* **3** a difference allowed in the size of mating machinery parts for various kinds of fit.

al·loy (AL·oy, uh·LOY) *n.* a combination of one metal with another of lower quality, as brass (copper with zinc or tin) and steel (iron with carbon).
— *v.* mix, as a metal, with something of lower quality; hence, debase.

all-points bulletin *n.* a police advisory issued in all directions, as when a fugitive is being sought.

all right *adj. & adv.* **1** in good order; satisfactory: *I was feeling sick, but I'm all right now; She's doing all right in school.* **2** yes; certainly: *All right, you may go to the movie.*

all-right *adj. Slang.* passably good: *an all-right fellow.*

all-round *adj.* accomplished in every way: *an all-round candidate, student.*

All Saints' Day *n.* November 1, a day to commemorate Christian saints; Allhallows.

All Souls' Day *n.* November 2, a day of prayer for the dead.

all·spice *n.* the spice obtained from the berry of a West Indian shrub.

all-terrain vehicle (ALL·tuh·rain-) *n.* a motor vehicle that has large, balloonlike tires, designed for use on rough, marshy, or sandy ground, as on farms.

all-time *adj. Informal.* **1** of record level: *an all-time high, low, record.* **2** that takes up all one's time: *an all-time job.*

al·lude (uh·LOOD, long "OO") *v.* **al·ludes, al·lud·ed, al·lud·ing** refer, usually indirectly: *The speaker alluded to them in passing (without mentioning names).*

al·lure (uh·LOOR) *v.* **al·lures, al·lured, al·lur·ing** attract by something that offers pleasure, reward, etc.: *Beauty allures men and women; an **alluring** (=tempting) sight.*
— *n.* attraction: *the allure of riches;* also **al·lure·ment.**

al·lu·sion (uh·LOO·zhun) *n.* an alluding: *to make an allusion to the past.* — **al·lu·sive** (uh·LOO·siv) *adj.*
— **al·lu·sive·ly** *adv.;* **al·lu·sive·ness** *n.*

al·ly (uh·LYE, AL·eye) *v.* **al·lies, al·lied, al·ly·ing** unite by some relationship or bond: *I am allied to them by marriage; Canada allied (itself) with the British in World War II against the Axis powers; Dutch and English are **allied** (=related) languages; to lobby for allied interests.*
— *n., pl.* **al·lies** one united to another: *a faithful, staunch friend and ally; The U.S. and Britain were the chief **Allies** in World War II.*

al·ma ma·ter (AL·muh·MAY·tur) *n.* the institution in which one was educated.

al·ma·nac (ALL·muh·nac) *n.* a calendar-based annual publication giving information about the sun, moon, and tides and miscellaneous other useful data.

al·might·y (all·MYE·tee) *adj.* all-powerful: *the almighty dollar; fear of **the Almighty** (=God); the Cree hero and martyr called "Almighty Voice" (1874 – 97).*

al·mond (AH·mund, AL-) *n.* an edible nut that is oval-shaped with pointed ends or the tree bearing it; *combining form: an **almond-eyed** (=Oriental) beauty.*

al·most (ALL·mohst) *adv.* very nearly: *I am almost finished; She said almost nothing of importance in her lecture.*

alms (AHMZ) *n.pl.* money, clothes, food, etc. given to the poor as charity: *to dispense alms for the needy.*

alms·house *n.* a home for poor people.

al·oe (AL·oh) *n.* **al·oes 1** a fleshy African plant of the lily family with sharp-pointed spiny leaves: *The century plant, called also the "American aloe," is an agave.* **2 aloes** [with sing. v.] a purgative prepared from aloe juice.

a·loft (uh·LOFT) *adv.* high up in the air: *flags flying aloft; to soar aloft like a kite.*

a·lo·ha (uh·LOH·huh) *interj.* Hawaiian greeting or farewell.

a·lone (uh·LONE) *adv. & adj.* [used after its noun] **1** by oneself: *He likes to eat alone; She was left alone with no one to talk to; You can find her alone reading in a corner of the library.* **2** only: *He lives for money alone; God alone knows what happened.*
— **let alone** not to mention: *He can't even afford a car, let alone a house.*
— **let** or **leave alone** not interfere with a person or thing: *Let her alone.*
— **let well enough alone** leave things as they are.

a·long (uh·LONG) *adv. & prep.* **1** from one end to the other: *cars parked along the street.* **2** onward: *We were driving along (the highway); Bring your friends along with you; Bring them along; I knew about her **all along** (= all the time); It happened **along about** (Informal for near) noon; Tell them I'll **be along** (Informal for be there).*

a·long·shore *adv.* by the shore.

a·long·side *adv. & prep.* side by side: *a bike driven alongside (of) a car; The bike was driving alongside when hit.*

a·loof (uh·LOOF, long "OO") *adj. & adv.* **1** at a distance: *He holds or keeps (himself) aloof in company; He remains or stands aloof from others.* **2** reserved or withdrawn: *his aloof expression, manner; He's an aloof character.* — **a·loof·ly** *adv.;* **a·loof·ness** *n.*

a·loud (uh·LOWD) *adv.* so as to be heard: *Please read aloud; He called aloud (=loudly) for help.*

alp *n.* a high mountain.

al·pac·a (al·PAC·uh) *n.* **1** a South American animal of the camel family that yields wool. **2** its wool or the soft and resilient cloth made from it.

al·pha (AL·fuh) *n.* the first letter of the Greek alphabet.
— **alpha and omega** the beginning and the end.

al·pha·bet (AL·fuh·bet) *n.* the letters used to write a language; the ABC: *The English alphabet is phonetic and symbolic; the Arabic, Greek, Hebrew, Roman alphabets.*

al·pha·bet·ic (al·fuh·BET·ic) or **al·pha·bet·i·cal** (·BET·uh·cul) *adj.* 1 using an alphabet: *Most languages have alphabetic systems of writing; Chinese characters are not alphabetic but pictographic.* 2 in the order of the letters of the alphabet: *words in alphabetical order.* — **al·pha·bet·i·cal·ly** *adv.*

al·pha·bet·ize (AL·fuh·buh·tize) *v.* -iz·es, -ized, -iz·ing put in alphabetical order.

al·pha·nu·mer·ic (AL·fuh·new·MER·ic) *adj.* with letters and numbers combined: *Canada's alphanumeric postal code.*

alpha rhythm *n.* the relaxed rhythmic activity of the brain as observable on a machine called "electroencephalograph," normally between 8 and 13 cycles per second; slow brain wave: *Biofeedback teaches you to generate alpha rhythms.* Also **alpha wave.**

Al·pine or **al·pine** (AL·pine) *adj.* 1 having to do with high mountains: *an alpine glacier, hut, plant, pond, rose, tent, wilderness; Alpine skiing includes downhill and slalom events; the Teutonic, Mediterranean, and the shorter, darker, and broad-headed alpine racial types.* 2 **alpine** very high: *the alpine increase in fat consumption.*

al·pin·ism (AL·puh·niz·um) *n.* mountain-climbing, esp. in the **Alps,** a European mountain system; **al·pin·ist** *n.*

al·read·y (all·RED·ee) *adv.* 1 by the time specified: *The train had already left when I reached the station.* 2 even before the specified time: *Have you finished already?*

al·right (all·RITE) *adj. & adv. Nonstandard.* all right.

al·so (ALL·soh) *adv.* as well: *She also was there; Not only Jim but also his wife saw her.*

also-ran *n. Informal.* a defeated candidate, contestant, etc.

al·tar (ALL·tur) *n.* a raised structure or table used in divine worship: *to kneel at an altar; to lead her to the altar* (= marry her, esp. in a church).

altar boy or **altar girl** *n.* a boy or girl who assists a priest at religious ceremonies.

al·tar·piece (ALL·tur·peece) *n.* a painting or other work of art at the back of an altar.

al·ter (ALL·tur) *v.* change partially: *to alter clothes to suit a fashion; A ship alters course, direction; He has altered; His whole outlook has altered since returning from abroad; altered states of consciousness attained by clairvoyance, telepathy, whirling, etc.; Circumstances alter cases* (= change the situation). — **al·ter·a·ble** *adj.* — **al·ter·a·tion** (all·tuh·RAY·shun) *n.: to make major, minor, slight alterations in a story.*

al·ter·ca·tion (all·tur·CAY·shun) *n.* a noisy argument; quarrel: *He had an altercation with his neighbour about or over the location of a fence; altercations between spouses.*

alter ego *n.* a second self; also, an intimate friend.

al·ter·nate (ALL·tur·nate) *v.* -nates, -nat·ed, -nat·ing occur, arrange, or do by turns: *Jack and I alternate in doing the dishes; We alternate between cooking and washing; We alternate one job with another; Farmers alternate* (= rotate) *crops to save the soil.*

— *adj.* 1 following each other by turns: *Jack and I do the dishes on alternate days.* 2 substitute; alternative: *We went by an alternate route; alternate sources of energy such as the sun, wind, and water.* — *n.* (-nit) a substitute: *convention delegates and their alternates; Have meat or some meat alternate in your diet.*

al·ter·nate·ly (ALL·tur·nate·lee) *adv.* one after the other; by turns: *She laughed and cried alternately as she told the story of the ups and downs of her life.*

al·ter·na·tive (all·TUR·nuh·tiv) *n.* a choice between two or more possibilities: *Facing dismissal, he has no alternative but to resign; Resignation is the only alternative to being fired; Can you propose or suggest another alternative? At this time, changing jobs is not a viable alternative; His boss has various alternatives* (= choices). — *adj.* 1 substitute: *an alternative plan of escape.* 2 offering something different from the established, conventional, traditional, etc.: *an alternative life style; an alternative school offering alternative education using a nontraditional curriculum; the anti-apartheid alternative press of South Africa.* — **al·ter·na·tive·ly** *adv.*

al·though (all·THOH, "TH" as in "the") *conj.* in spite of the fact that: *Al's able to walk although he's very ill.*

al·ti·tude (AL·tuh·tude) *n.* height above sea level: *to reach an altitude of 9 000 km; a high altitude; Airplanes cruise at that altitude; They lose altitude in bad weather; Nothing grows at those altitudes.*

al·to (AL·toh) *n.* -tos 1 the lowest female voice. 2 a singer or instrument in this range of voice.

al·to·geth·er (all·tuh·GETH·ur, "TH" as in "the") *adv.* on the whole: *The expenses came to $500 altogether; Things are not altogether bad.* — **in the altogether** *Informal.* in the nude.

al·tru·ism (AL·troo·iz·um) *n.* selfless concern for the welfare of others; opposed to EGOISM. — **al·tru·ist** *n.* — **al·tru·is·tic** (·IS·tic) *adj.*

¹**al·um** (AL·um) *n.* a colourless crystalline compound of aluminum used medically and in manufacturing.

²**a·lum** (uh·LUM) *n. Informal.* alumnus or alumna.

a·lu·mi·num (uh·LOO·muh·num) *n.* a light white metal; *Brit.* **al·u·min·i·um** (al·yoo·MIN·yum).

a·lum·na (uh·LUM·nuh) *n., pl.* **-nae** (-nee) a former female student of a particular school: *the Nurses Alumnae Association.*

a·lum·nus (uh·LUM·nus) *n., pl.* **-ni** (-nye) a former male student of a particular school.

al·ways (ALL·waze, -wiz) *adv.* at all times: *He is always punctual; She is always* (= repeatedly) *asking to go to the movies.*

Alz·hei·mer's disease (ALTS·hye·murz-) *n.* a degenerative disease of the brain cells.

am *first person sing. pres. indicative* of BE.

a·main (uh·MAIN) *adv.* [old use] at full speed; hastily; with full strength.

a·mal·gam (uh·MAL·gum) *n.* **1** a mercury alloy, as used in teeth fillings. **2** a blending or union, esp. of organizations.

a·mal·ga·mate (uh·MAL·guh·mate) *v.* -mates, -mat·ed, -mat·ing unite or combine without loss of identity, as labour unions: *Municipalities often amalgamate with others into regional governments; Our town is amalgamated with Metro; The Amalgamated Mine Workers of Nova Scotia.*
— **a·mal·ga·ma·tion** (-MAY·shun) *n.*

a·mass (uh·MAS) *v.* heap up or accumulate: *He quickly amassed a fortune by trading in stocks;* **a·mass·ment** *n.*

am·a·teur (AM·uh·tur, -choor) *n.* **1** one who engages in a hobby, sport, or other activity without accepting payment; nonprofessional: *Some amateurs turn professional after acquiring some skill and experience.* **2** an inexperienced practitioner of an art or skill: *a rank amateur.*
— *adj.* nonprofessional: *an amateur athletic association; The Canadian Amateur Sports and Physical Fitness Development Services; an amateur competition; amateur hockey; an amateur painter; amateur radio.*
— **am·a·teur·ism** *n.*

am·a·teur·ish (am·uh·TUR·ish, -CHOOR·ish) *adj.* unskilled or inexperienced.

a·maze (uh·MAZE) *v.* a·maz·es, a·mazed, a·maz·ing bewilder or be bewildered or confused: *I'm amazed to hear you didn't get the job; I'm amazed that you have been bypassed; quite amazed at their decision; The decision amazes me; It's **amazing** that she can refuse such a good job.* — **a·maz·ing·ly** *adv.*
— **a·maze·ment** *n.: To my complete, total, utter amazement, she refused the job; We stared in amazement at each other; I expressed my amazement at or with her refusal.*

am·a·zon (AM·uh·zon) *n.* a strong aggressive woman, like the **Amazons,** a warriorlike race of women of Greek myth. — **am·a·zo·ni·an** (-ZOH·nee·un) *adj.*

am·bas·sa·dor (am·BAS·uh·dur) *n.* the official representative of a foreign government: *the U.S. ambassador to Canada; An ambassador is sometimes recalled for consultations at home; an ambassador-at-large; a goodwill ambassador; a roving ambassador.*
— **am·bas·sa·dor·ship** *n.*
— **am·bas·sa·dor·i·al** (-DOR·ee·ul) *adj.*

am·ber (AM·bur) *n.* a yellowish-brown fossil resin used in jewellery.
— *adj.* of the colour of amber: *The traffic light goes amber for a few seconds before turning red.*

am·bi·dex·trous (am·bi·DEX·trus) *adj.* **1** able to use both hands equally well. **2** skilful or versatile. **3** deceitful or double-dealing.

am·bi·ence or **am·bi·ance** (AM·bee·unce) *n.* surrounding atmosphere or environment: *a restaurant famous for its ambience and good food.*

am·bi·ent (AM·bee·unt) *adj.* surrounding: *a mountain peak concealed by ambient clouds; Ambient tobacco smoke in the workplace is hurtful to nonsmokers; The blind can locate themselves by an ambient vision that works subconsciously.*

am·bi·gu·i·ty (am·big·YOO·uh·tee) *n.* -ties the state of being ambiguous or something ambiguous: *to avoid ambiguity; an ambiguity about or concerning his position; to clear up or remove an ambiguity.*

am·big·u·ous (am·BIG·yoo·us) *adj.* having more than one meaning: *an ambiguous position, response, term, wording.* — **am·big·u·ous·ly** *adv.*

am·bit *n.* a sphere of influence or authority; bounds or scope: *within the ambit of his power.*

am·bi·tion (am·BISH·un) *n.* a strong desire to achieve a goal: *men and women of ambition; the many ambitions of our younger days; to achieve, attain, fulfill, realize, restrain one's ambition; The Nobel prize spurred or stirred his ambition to become a scientist; It was his greatest ambition (=goal); an aggressor's territorial ambitions; his boundless, overweening, unbridled ambition and greed.*

am·bi·tious (am·BISH·us) *adj.* having ambition: *an ambitious youth; She is ambitious to win an Olympic gold; an ambitious attempt, plan, undertaking; a program that is too ambitious for our budget; Hamilton, the "Ambitious City."*

am·biv·a·lent (am·BIV·uh·lunt) *adj.* having conflicting feelings about the same object or person: *ambivalent attitudes, feelings, reactions; The government seems ambivalent about its policy toward refugees.*
— **am·biv·a·lence** *n.*

am·ble (AM·bul) *n.* an easy, leisurely gait, as of a horse.
— *v.* -bles, -bled, -bling move at an amble: *He ambled along while we stopped for a chat.* — **am·bler** *n.*

am·bro·sia (am·BROH·zhuh) *n.* **1** in classical myths, the food of the gods. **2** anything considered very delicious.
— **am·bro·sial** *adj.*

am·bu·lance (AMB·yuh·lunce) *n.* a vehicle for taking the sick and wounded to hospital.

ambulance chaser *n. Informal.* a lawyer who goes after accident victims urging them to sue for damages, etc.

am·bu·lant (AMB·yuh·lunt) *adj.* walking about.

am·bu·la·to·ry (AMB·yuh·luh·tor·ee) *adj.* having to do with walking: *Ambulatory medical care is given in emergency and outpatient departments; ambulatory patients.*

am·bus·cade (AM·bus·cade) *n.* same as AMBUSH.

am·bush (AM·bush) *n.* **1** a lying in wait to attack by surprise; also, such a trap or the attackers: *to attack an enemy from ambush; to lie in ambush for them; to lay or set an ambush (=trap) for the enemy; to draw them into the ambush; The enemy ran into the ambush; They had been trapped by ambush.* **2** such an attack: *The enemy was greeted with an ambush of automatic weapons fire.*
— *v.* -bush·es, -bushed, -bush·ing attack from ambush: *The enemy was ambushed and defeated.*

a·me·ba, a·me·bic (uh·MEE-) same as AMOEBA, AMOEBIC.

a·mel·io·rate (uh·MEEL·yuh·rate) *v.* -rates, -rat·ed, -rat·ing to make a condition, plight, situation, etc. better or more tolerable: *to ameliorate the condition of the poor; The situation did not ameliorate (=improve).*
— **a·mel·io·ra·tion** (-RAY·shun) *n.*

a·men (ay·MEN, ah·MEN) *interj.* expressing agreement, as to a prayer: *Everyone said amen.*

a·me·na·ble (uh·MEE·nuh·bul, uh·MEN·uh·bul) *adj.* responsive: *a child who is amenable to reason; We are amenable to compromise.* — **a·me·na·bly** *adv.*
— **a·me·na·ble·ness** or **a·me·na·bil·i·ty** (-BIL·uh·tee) *n.*

a·mend (uh·MEND) *v.* change in order to improve: *to amend one's life; to amend a constitution, a resolution, the wording of a law.* — **a·mend·ment** *n.*

a·mends *n.pl.* [takes sing. or pl. v.] reparation for a harm or hurt: *Al made amends for his past misdeeds.*

a·men·i·ty (uh·MEN·uh·tee, uh·MEE·nuh·tee) *n.* **-ties** **1** a feature that makes a place or facility more comfortable: *a hotel with amenities such as sauna and colour TV; They offer amenities for relaxation and enjoyment.* **2 amenities** *pl.*: *to exchange amenities* (=greetings); *to observe the amenities* (=courtesies) *of diplomacy.*

A·mer·i·can (uh·MER·uh·cun) *n.* **1** a person of or from North or South America, esp. a U.S. national: *a Middle American* (=Midwesterner; also, middle-class American); *a Native American* (=Indian). **2** English as used in the U.S.: *General American;* also **American English.**
— *adj.* having to do with North and/or South America or their peoples or cultures, esp. the U.S.: *as American as apple pie; the American dream of prosperity and happiness.*

A·mer·i·can·ism (uh·MER·uh·cuh·niz·um) *n.* a word, usage, cultural trait, etc. that is typical of the United States: *In spite of their Americanisms, they escaped from the country passing as Canadians.*

A·mer·i·can·ize (uh·MER·uh·cuh·nize) *v.* **-iz·es, -ized, -iz·ing** make American.
— **A·mer·i·can·i·za·tion** (-nuh·ZAY·shun) *n.*

American plan *n.* a hotel charging rate that includes room and meals; cf. EUROPEAN PLAN.

American Sign Language *n.* a system of manual signs used by the deaf in North America. Also **ASL.**

Am·er·ind (AM·uh·rind) or **Am·er·ind·i·an** (-RIN·dee·un) *n. & adj.* American Indian; Native American.

Am·es·lan (AM·us·lan) *n.* same as AMERICAN SIGN LANGUAGE.

am·e·thyst (AM·uh·thist, "th" as in "thin") *n.* **1** a gem of a purple or violet colour. **2** its colour.

a·mi·a·ble (AY·mee·uh·bul) *adj.* friendly and good-natured: *an amiable leader, personality, tone of voice; He lectured us in a relaxed and amiable fashion; a bunch of amiable eccentrics.* — **a·mi·a·bly** *adv.*
— **a·mi·a·ble·ness** or **a·mi·a·bil·i·ty** (-BIL·uh·tee) *n.*

am·i·ca·ble (AM·uh·cuh·bul) *adj.* showing goodwill and love of peace: *amicable coexistence, negotiations; an amicable agreement, departure, parting of the ways; an amicable meeting between labour and management; the amicable settlement of a dispute; an amicable separation; She spoke to the rioters in an amicable tone.* — **am·i·ca·bly** *adv.*

a·mid (uh·MID) or **a·midst** (uh·MIDST) *prep.* in the midst of something: *The child got lost amid the confusion of the fair.*

a·mid·ships (uh·MID·ships) *adv.* toward the middle of a craft, as between a ship's bow and stern: *The aircraft was broken amidships, with the cockpit landing in one place and the tail section in another.*

a·midst same as AMID.

a·mi·go (uh·MEE·goh) *n.* **-gos** (-goze) *Spanish.* a friend.

a·miss (uh·MIS) *adj. & adv.* [used after its noun or verb] wrong or wrongly: *Something went amiss with the arrangements; Is something amiss? Don't* **take** *my words* **amiss.**

am·i·ty (AM·uh·tee) *n.* **-ties** friendly relations: *to live in amity like good neighbours.*

am·mo·ni·a (uh·MONE·yuh) *n.* a strong-smelling gas used in refrigeration, fertilizers, and as a liquid cleaning agent.

am·mu·ni·tion (am·yuh·NISH·un) *n.* objects for firing, as bullets, shells, grenades, and rockets, with their fuzes, charges, etc.: *live ammunition; The scandal provided ammunition* (=firing materials) *for press attacks against the government.*

am·ne·sia (am·NEE·zhuh) *n.* loss of memory, often temporary.

am·nes·ty (AM·nus·tee) *n.* **-ties** a general pardon granted by a government, esp. to political offenders: *to declare an amnesty for political prisoners; The U.S. granted amnesty posthumously to General Lee in 1975.*
— *v.* **-ties, -tied** (-teed), **-ty·ing** pardon, esp. a group.
— *adj.*: *The Amnesty Act of 1849 offered a pardon for those who took part in the 1837 rebellions; an* **amnesty day** *for returning overdue books without paying fines; the 1972* **amnesty program** *for illegal immigrants to legalize their status.*

a·moe·ba (uh·MEE·buh) *n.* **-bas** or **-bae** (-bee) a microscopic one-celled organism found in soil and water that multiplies by splitting into two independent cells.

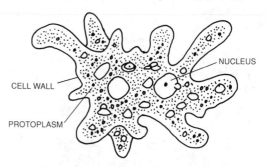

NUCLEUS

CELL WALL

PROTOPLASM

a·moe·bic (uh·MEE·bic) *adj.* having to do with amoebas: *amoebic dysentery.*

a·mok (uh·MUK, -MOK) *adv.* **run amok** rush about wildly in a murderous frenzy.

a·mong (uh·MUNG) *prep.* **1** in the middle of a group: *a town nestled among the hills; Einstein is among* (=one of) *the greatest men of science.* **2** to, with, by, etc. a group: *how to share $100 among seven people; Discuss it among yourselves.* Also **amongst.**

a·mor·al (ay·MOR·ul) *adj.* neither moral nor immoral: *an infant's amoral* (=innocent) *behaviour.*
— **a·mor·al·ly** *adv.*

am·o·rous (AM·uh·rus) *adj.* related to love, esp. sexual: *amorous advances, glances, inclinations, love, novels, verse, women.*

a·mor·phous (uh·MOR·fus) *adj.* 1 having no definite shape or form: *an amorphous mass of clay; a writer's amorphous style.* 2 not crystalline: *amorphous glass, minerals.*

a·mor·tize (AM·ur·tize, uh·MOR·tize) *n.* -tiz·es, -tized, -tiz·ing pay off a mortgage, debt, etc. by instalment payments. — **am·or·ti·za·tion** (-tuh·ZAY·shun) *n.*

a·mount (uh·MOWNT) *n.* a quantity, esp. as a mass: *a large amount of money; the full amount asked for; a considerable, enormous, huge, moderate, negligible, small, substantial amount; No amount of discussion will help.*
— *v.* add up: *His debts amount to $10 000; disloyalty amounting to treason; He never amounted to anything as a mayor.*

a·mour (uh·MOOR) *n.* a love affair, esp. one that is illicit.

am·per·sand (AM·pur·sand) *n.* the symbol "&" meaning "and."

am·phet·a·mine (am·FET·uh·meen, -min) *n.* a compound drug used as a nasal decongestant or as a stimulant.

am·phib·i·an (am·FIB·ee·un) *n.* 1 an animal such as a frog or seal that can live in water and on land. 2 a vehicle such as an aircraft, tank, or truck that can operate on land and water.

am·phib·i·ous (am·FIB·ee·us) *adj.* 1 adapted for land and water: *amphibious troops.* 2 carried out on land and water: *an amphibious attack.*
— **am·phib·i·ous·ly** *adv.;* **am·phib·i·ous·ness** *n.*

am·phi·the·a·tre (AM·fuh·thee·uh·tur, "th" as in "thin") *n.* a building with an arena or stage in the middle and rows of seats rising around it. Also **am·phi·the·a·ter.**

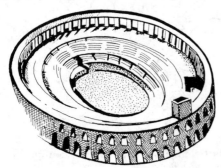

am·ple (AM·pul) *adj.* -pler, -plest more than adequate in size, capacity, or amount: *a car with ample room for four passengers; an income that is ample for all his needs; a man of ample means.* — **am·ple·ness** *n.*

am·pli·fi·er (AM·pluh·fye·ur) *n.* an amplifying device: *an electronic amplifier for strengthening sound and picture signals.*

am·pli·fy (AM·pluh·fye) *v.* -flies, -flied, -fly·ing make larger or fuller: *to amplify a narrative with details; a device to amplify* (=strengthen) *a voice or electric current.* — **am·pli·fi·ca·tion** (-fuh·CAY·shun) *n.*

am·pli·tude (AM·pluh·tude) *n.* fullness or largeness, as the extent to which a pendulum or wave oscillates.

am·ply (AM·plee) *adv.* in an ample manner.

am·pu·tate (AM·pyuh·tate) *v.* -tates, -tat·ed, -tat·ing cut off a limb by surgery.
— **am·pu·ta·tion** (-TAY·shun) *n.*

am·pu·tee (AM·pyuh·tee) *n.* one who has had a limb cut off by surgery.

a·muck (uh·MUK) *adv.* same as AMOK.

am·u·let (AM·yuh·lit) *n.* something worn on one's person as protection against evil; charm; talisman.

a·muse (uh·MUZE) *v.* a·mus·es, a·mused, a·mus·ing to interest lightly; engage the attention humorously: *He kept the children amused by telling them stories; Your jokes don't amuse me very much; It amuses me that he would use such a ploy; to amuse oneself by playing solitaire; She amused the audience with little tricks; We were* **amused** *at* or *by her tricks; We were greatly, highly, thoroughly, very much amused by what we saw; We found it very* **amusing;** *It was amusing to all of us.*
— **a·muse·ment** *n.: a party to provide amusement for the company; Much to our amusement, no one appeared at the party; People found amusement in all sorts of diversions.*

amusement park *n.* a place of outdoor entertainment equipped with rides, booths for games, snack bars, etc. Also **amusement centre** or **center.**

an (AN, 'n) *indef.art.* the form of "a" used when a vowel sound follows: *an event; an honour; an M.A.*

a·nach·ro·nism (uh·NAC·ruh·niz·um) *n.* 1 an error of putting persons, things, or events together that are too far removed in time, as "Alexander the Great attacked Washington." 2 a person or thing that is out of its proper time: *Horse-drawn vehicles seem anachronisms to most people.* — **a·nach·ro·nis·tic** (-NIS·tic) *adj.*

an·a·con·da (an·uh·CON·duh) *n.* a large South American tropical snake that crushes its prey in its coils.

a·nae·mi·a (uh·NEE·mee·uh) same as ANEMIA.

an·aes·the·sia, etc. same as ANESTHESIA, etc.

an·a·gram (AN·uh·gram) *n.* a word or group of words formed by rearranging the letters of another word: *"Agitator" is an anagram for "I got a rat."*

a·nal (AY·nul) *adj.* having to do with the anus.

an·al·ge·si·a (an·ul·JEE·zhuh) *n.* absence of the sense of pain.

an·al·ge·sic (an·ul·JEE·zic) *n.* a pain-killing drug or ointment.
— *adj.* pain-killing: *Heating pads, warm baths, etc. have an analgesic effect.*

a·nal·o·gous (uh·NAL·uh·gus) *adj.* similar or comparable: *The fin of a fish is analogous to a wing in its function; The two processes are not analogous (with each other).*

an·a·logue or **an·a·log** (AN·uh·log) *n.* something similar or parallel to something else in properties or functions: *The gill of a fish is the analogue of a lung; a meat analogue made from soya beans.*

analogue or **analog computer** *n.* a calculating device in which numbers correspond directly to quantities such as weights or lengths, as on a ruler.

a·nal·o·gy (uh·NAL·uh·jee) *n.* **-gies 1** likeness or similarity between things that are unlike each other; extended comparison: *He drew* or *made an analogy between a watch and the universe; an analogy based on their orderly movement; a close, not superficial analogy; the analogy of the universe to* or *with a watch.* **2** a process of reasoning or comparison based on similarity: *He argued* or *reasoned by false analogy that since one of the twins likes popcorn the other must too.* **3** word formation based on similarity: *It was by analogy that "cows" came to replace "kine"; "Cows" was formed on the analogy of other plurals.*
— **an·a·log·i·cal** (an·uh·LOJ·uh·cul) *adj.*
— **an·a·log·i·cal·ly** *adv.*

an·a·lyse or **an·a·lyze** (AN·uh·lize) *v.* **-lys·es** or **-lyz·es, -lysed** or **-lyzed, -lys·ing** or **-lyz·ing** make an analysis of something: *to analyse a substance for carbon; to analyse a sentence into its parts; to analyse causes, motives, people.* — **an·a·lys·er** or **an·a·lyz·er** *n.*

a·nal·y·sis (uh·NAL·uh·sis) *n., pl.* **-ses** (-seez) **1** the separation of something into its parts: *to make chemical analyses of substances into their constituent elements.* **2** an examination of the parts of anything or a statement of the result of such a study: *Your analysis of the poem is very penetrating; a careful, in-depth, painstaking, thorough analysis; On further analysis, the scheme was found to be a fraud; In the last, final, ultimate analysis, most of life's joys are transitory.* **3** psychoanalysis: *to undergo analysis on a therapist's couch.*

an·a·lyst (AN·uh·list) *n.* one who makes an analysis, as a psychoanalyst or chemist: *a financial analyst; systems analyst.*

an·a·lyt·i·cal (an·uh·LIT·uh·cul) *adj.* of or using analysis: *an analytical mind; analytical chemistry, psychology, skills.* Also **an·a·lyt·ic** *adj.*
— **an·a·lyt·i·cal·ly** *adv.*

analyze *v.* See ANALYSE.

an·ar·chy (AN·ur·kee) *n.* **-chies** lawlessness or disorder caused by absence of government or control: *complete, total, utter anarchy; Anarchy reigned during the riot.*
— **an·ar·chism** (-kiz·um) *n.;* **an·ar·chist** (-kist) *n.*
— **a·nar·chic** (uh·NAR·kic) or **a·nar·chi·cal** *adj.*

a·nath·e·ma (uh·NATH·uh·muh, "TH" as in "thin") *n.* **1** a curse invoking damnation: *The church used to declare* or *pronounce anathemas on nonconformists such as heretics and schismatics; An anathema could be lifted from a sinner after he had done penance.* **2** a hated person or thing: *Liquor is anathema to her.*

a·nath·e·ma·tize (uh·NATH·uh·muh·tize) *v.* **-tiz·es, -tized, -tiz·ing** curse or excommunicate.

an·a·tom·i·cal (an·uh·TOM·uh·cul) *adj.* having to do with anatomy. — **an·a·tom·i·cal·ly** *adv.*

a·nat·o·mist (uh·NAT·uh·mist) *n.* an expert in anatomy.

a·nat·o·mize (uh·NAT·uh·mize) *v.* **-miz·es, -mized, -miz·ing** examine the structure of something, as by dissecting it.

a·nat·o·my (uh·NAT·uh·mee) *n.* **-mies 1** the science of the structure of bodies and their parts: *comparative anatomy of different animals.* **2** a structure or analysis: *the anatomy of a frog, murder, poem.*

-ance or **-ence** *n.* suffix indicating action, state, quality, or amount: *abundance, dependence, resistance.* Also **-ancy** or **-ency**: *consistency, truancy.*

an·ces·tor (AN·ses·tur) *n.* a person from whom one is descended; forebear: *our remote ancestors; Worship of ancestors is common in many cultures.*
— **an·ces·tral** (an·SES·trul) *adj.*

an·ces·try (AN·ses·tree) *n.* **-tries** a line of ancestors; lineage: *Most white people are of European ancestry; Public schools admit children of all ancestries and religions; North American blacks trace their ancestry to Africa.*

an·chor (ANK·ur) *n.* **1** a heavy object lowered by cable from a ship to hold it in place: *A ship casts* or *drops anchor in a harbour; It **rides at anchor** while anchored; It **weighs anchor** (= takes up the anchor) and sails away.* **2** a team leader, as the coordinator of a telecast; also **an·chor·man, anchor person, an·chor·wom·an. 3** a person in a responsible or sensitive position, as the one finishing a relay race or at the end of a tug-of-war team.
— *v.* secure or moor, as a ship or balloon: *The posts are firmly anchored in the ground.*

an·chor·age (ANG·cur·ij) *n.* a place to anchor, as a bay or harbour.

an·cho·vy (AN·choh·vee) *n.* **-vies** a small herringlike fish.

an·cien re·gime (ahn·SYAHN·ray·ZHEEM) *French.* the old order, as in France before the Revolution.

an·cient (AYN·shunt) *adj.* belonging to olden days: *an ancient monument; tales of ancient Rome; That's ancient history!*
— *n.* an aged person: *according to **the ancients** (= people of olden days).*
— **an·cient·ly** *adv.;* **an·cient·ness** *n.*

an·cil·lar·y (AN·suh·lair·ee) *adj.* in a helping role: *Logic is ancillary to philosophy; an ancillary subject.*

-ancy See -ANCE.

and *conj.* **1** used to join words, phrases, sentences, etc. **2** referring to the second of a pair: *ham and* (= and eggs).
— **and how!** *interj.* expressing emphatic agreement: *Did she win? And how!*

and·i·ron (AN·dye·urn) *n.* one of a pair of metal holders for keeping logs in a fireplace.

and/or *conj.* [used when "and" or "or" may be read as the connective]: *We serve coffee with cream and/or sugar* (= with cream and sugar, with cream, or with sugar).

an·droid (AN·droid) *n.* a creature such as an automaton or a robot having human form; also *adj.*

an·drol·o·gy (an·DROL·uh·jee) *n.* the medical specialty concerned with the male reproductive tract and its diseases.

an·ec·dote (AN·ic·dote) *n.* a short, often humorous or instructive account of an incident in a person's life: *to narrate, relate, tell an anecdote of one's childhood; a funny, witty anecdote.* — **an·ec·dot·al** (-DOH·tul) *adj.*

a·ne·mi·a (uh·NEE·mee·uh) *n.* weakness or paleness from lack of red cells in the blood: *pernicious anemia; sickle-cell anemia.* — **a·ne·mic** *adj.*

an·e·mom·e·ter (an·uh·MOM·uh·tur) *n.* an instrument for measuring the force and speed of winds.

an·er·oid (AN·uh·roid) *adj.* not using fluid: *An **aneroid barometer** indicates air pressure by means of an elastic metal disk connected to a needle.*

an·es·the·sia (an·is·THEE·zhuh, "TH" as in "thin") *n.* loss of the sense of pain, cold, touch, etc., as by use of an anesthetic: *Local anesthesia in a part of the body, as when extracting teeth, wears off after a time; General anesthesia puts a person to sleep during surgery; Deep hypnosis can produce or induce anesthesia in a subject.*

an·es·thet·ic (an·is·THET·ic) *adj.* causing anesthesia. — *n.* an anesthetic agent such as ether: *to administer or give an anesthetic to a patient; to have or take an anesthetic; He was operated on while under (an) anesthetic.* — **an·es·thet·i·cal·ly** *adv.*

an·es·thet·ist (uh·NES·thuh·tist) *n.* a physician who administers anesthetics.

a·new (uh·NEW) *adv.* [used following its verb] again or afresh: *After a short ceasefire, fighting broke out anew.*

an·gel (AIN·jul) *n.* **1** a spiritual being, usually in the role of a heavenly messenger: *a guardian angel; The nurse was like a ministering angel to him.* **2** one regarded as good and lovely: *You're an angel!* — **an·gel·ic** (an·JEL·ic) or **an·gel·i·cal** (-uh·cul) *adj.* — **an·gel·i·cal·ly** *adv.*

angel cake or **angel food cake** *n.* a white fluffy cake made with egg whites.

angel dust *n. Slang.* **1** the tranquilizer "PCP" sniffed or smoked as a narcotic. **2** a synthetic heroin.

an·ger (ANG·gur) *n.* strong feeling of hurt or displeasure; ire: *to arouse, express, show, stir up anger; to allay, appease, calm, swallow one's anger; He used to vent his anger on his family; He felt a blind, burning, deep-seated, seething, unbridled anger at being fired from his job; anger toward society; burning with anger; In a blaze or fit of anger, he yelled at his boss; He struck*

in anger; an outburst of repressed anger.
— *v.* **an·gers, an·gered, an·ger·ing** make or be angry: *Foul play angers him; It angers him to think that people can get away with murder.*

an·gi·na (an·JYE·nuh) *n.* any illness characterized by spasmodic pain, esp. **angina pec·to·ris** (-PEC·tuh·ris), a heart ailment accompanied by sudden bursts of chest pain. — **an·gi·nal** *adj.*

An·glais (ang·GLAY) *n. French.* an English-speaking Canadian, as referred to by French Canadians.

an·gle (ANG·gul) *n.* **1** the space between two lines or surfaces that meet: *an obtuse angle that is complementary to an acute angle; the angle of a roof; a right angle (of 90 degrees).* **2** a deviation from a straight line: *The leaning tower of Pisa stands at a slight angle; a hat set at a rakish angle.* **3** a point of view; aspect: *two accounts from different angles; Look at it from various angles; When something is offered free, you suspect an angle (Informal for motive) or a gimmick somewhere.* — *v.* **-gles, -gled, -gling 1** to fish with a hook or try to get as with a fishhook: *to angle for trout, for an invitation, for compliments.* **2** to slant or bias: *an angled account of the incident.* — **an·gler** *n.*

an·gle·worm (ANG·gul·wurm) *n.* an earthworm used as a bait; dew worm.

An·gli·can (ANG·gluh·cun) *n. & adj.* a member of the Church of England or a related church: *The Anglican Church of Canada and the U.S. Episcopal Church are in the Anglican Communion.*
— **An·gli·can·ism** (-cuh·niz·um) *n.*

an·gli·cize (ANG·gluh·size) *v.* **-ciz·es, -cized, -ciz·ing** make something English.
— **an·gli·ci·za·tion** (-suh·ZAY·shun) *n.*
Also **an·gli·fy, -fies, -fied, -fy·ing.**

An·glo (ANG·gloh) *n.* **-glos** a white English-speaking North American.

Anglo- *combining form.* English: *Anglo-Canadian, Anglo-Catholic, Anglo-French, Anglo-Saxon.*

An·glo·phile (ANG·gluh·file) *n.* an admirer of English and things English.

An·glo·phobe (ANG·gluh·fobe) *n.* one who hates or fears England and things English.

An·glo·phone or **an·glo·phone** (ANG·gluh·fone) *n.* in a multilingual nation, one whose first language is English.
— *adj.* English-speaking: *Canada's Anglophone population.*

Anglo-Saxon (ANG·gloh·SAX·un) *n.* **1** a member or descendant of the Angles, Saxons, and Jutes who settled in Britain in the 5th and 6th centuries: *people of Anglo-Saxon descent; the Anglo-Saxon establishment; a white Anglo-Saxon Protestant.* **2** the Old English language. **3** of English speech and writing, consisting of plain and simple, sometimes unrefined, words: *four-letter Anglo-Saxon words.*

an·gry (ANG·gree) *adj.* **-gri·er, -gri·est 1** full of anger: *The boss got or became angry at or with us for being late; He's always angry about something or other; She's never angry at being pestered by kids; She was angry to find out what happened; angry that her child had stolen something; an angry look; the angry (= stormy) sea.*

2 inflamed; red: *an angry wound.* — **an·gri·ly** *adv.*

an·guish (ANG·gwish) *n.* intense pain, esp. of the mind: *The child's disappearance caused much anguish in the community; The parents were in deep mental anguish at or over what might have happened.*
— *v.* be in pain: *He anguishes over trifles; wears an* **anguished** (= pained) *expression.*

an·gu·lar (ANG·yuh·lur) *adj.* 1 having an angle or angles; sharp-cornered: *an angular structure.* 2 bony or stiff-looking: *an angular face; angular features.* 3 measured by an angle: *the angular distance; an angular measure; angular velocity.*
— **an·gu·lar·ly** (-lur·lee) *adv.*
— **an·gu·lar·i·ty** (-LAIR·uh·tee) *n.*

an·i·mal (AN·uh·mul) *n.* a living being that has sensation and can move about: *Both beasts and human beings are animals; We are rational animals; Some wild animals can be domesticated; to train an animal to do tricks; draft animals such as the horse and camel; Wolves are pack animals; People butcher, hunt, neuter, slaughter, skin, stuff, trap animals; caged, carnivorous, flesh-eating, predatory animals; Ants are social animals; He's a mere animal* (= brute) *in his eating habits; Some of us are party animals, others are political animals; There's something of the animal* (= animal nature) *in all of us; There is **no such animal*** (= no person or thing) *as the average Canadian.*
— *adj.* having to do with animals: *Lard and butter are animal fats;* **animal husbandry** (= care of domestic animals for milk and meat); *the animal kingdom as opposed to the vegetable; Food is one of our animal* (= physical) *needs; an animal* (= sensual) *appetite; our animal* (= brutish) *desires, instincts; an **animal rights activist*** (= one who campaigns for humane treatment of animals); *animal spirits* (= overflow of liveliness).

an·i·mal·ism (AN·uh·muh·liz·um) *n.* the belief in and practice of sensuality as a way of life.
— **an·i·mal·ist** *n.* — **an·i·mal·is·tic** (-LIS·tic) *adj.*
— **an·i·mal·i·ty** (-MAL·uh·tee) *n.*

an·i·mal·ize (AN·uh·muh·lize) *v.* -iz·es, -ized, -iz·ing cause to become like an animal.
— **an·i·mal·i·za·tion** (-luh·ZAY·shun) *n.*

an·i·mate (AN·uh·mit) *adj.* living; active: *Plants are part of animate nature.*
— *v.* (AN·uh·mate) -mates, -mat·ed, -mat·ing 1 give life, vigour, or interest to something: *a debate animated by lively wit; an animated discussion, expression, face;* **an·i·mat·ed·ly** *adv.* 2 make a moving picture using drawings: *to animate a story; An **animated cartoon** is a series of drawings photographed like a moving picture.*
— **an·i·ma·tion** (an·uh·MAY·shun) *n.: a dead body in suspended animation; the animation of a story by a cartoonist.*

an·i·ma·tor (AN·uh·may·tur) *n.* one who makes an animated cartoon.

an·i·mism (AN·uh·miz·um) *n.* the belief that inanimate things such as rocks, winds, and rivers have souls.
— **an·i·mist** *n.* — **an·i·mis·tic** (-MIS·tic) *adj.*

an·i·mos·i·ty (an·uh·MOS·uh·tee) *n.* -ties intense dislike bordering on hostility: *to arouse* or *stir up animosity in the community; racial and religious animosities; It's natural to feel animosity against* or *to* or *toward the*

favoured few; the animosity between religious sects; a burning, deep-seated, seething, violent animosity.

an·i·mus (AN·uh·mus) *n.* dislike based on ill will or prejudice.

an·kle (ANK·ul) *n.* the part of a leg that links the foot to the calf: *to sprain* or *twist one's ankle; the ballerina's well-turned* (= shapely) *ankles; The child stood* **ankle-deep** *in mud.*

an·klet (ANK·lit) *n.* 1 an ankle ornament, as a band or chain. 2 a short sock.

an·nals (AN·ulz) *n. pl.* historical records: *The trade pact opened a new chapter in the annals of Canadian-American relations.* — **an·nal·ist** (AN·uh·list) *n.*

an·neal (uh·NEEL) *v.* toughen and temper glass, metal, etc. by slow cooling and heating.

an·nex (uh·NEX) *v.* take and attach, usually a territory, to itself: *A city sometimes annexes a suburb.*
— *n.* (AN·ex) something attached, as an addition to a building: *a hospital annex for outpatients; a clause added as an annex to the treaty.*
— **an·nex·a·tion** (-AY·shun) *n.*

an·ni·hi·late (uh·NYE·uh·late) *v.* -lates, -lat·ed, -lat·ing destroy completely: *to annihilate an army, city, plan.*
— **an·ni·hi·la·tion** (-LAY·shun) *n.*

an·ni·ver·sa·ry (an·uh·VUR·suh·ree) *n.* -ries the yearly recurring date of an event: *1987 marked the 20th anniversary of her arrival in Canada; to celebrate, commemorate an anniversary; a golden, silver, wedding anniversary; It takes 65 years to reach one's diamond anniversary; what to do on the next anniversary; adj.: an anniversary celebration, dinner.*

an·no Dom·i·ni (an·oh·DOM·uh·nee, -nye) *adv. Latin.* [usually abbreviated as A.D.] in the year of the Lord (following Christ's birth): *in A.D. 1867.*

an·no·tate (AN·uh·tate) *v.* -tates, -tat·ed, -tat·ing provide a text with notes: *an annotated edition of Shakespeare.* — **an·no·ta·tor** *n.*
— **an·no·ta·tion** (-TAY·shun) *n.: to make marginal annotations on a manuscript; a text edited with copious annotations.*

an·nounce (uh·NOWNCE) *v.* **an·nounc·es, an·nounced, an·nounc·ing** 1 make known publicly: *to announce a wedding date; They announced that they would wed on January 4; It was announced to the press; He announces news and weather on radio.* 2 state the name of a person, flight, etc. on arrival: *The butler announced the guests.* — **an·nounce·ment** *n.*

an·nounc·er (uh·NOWN·sur) *n.* one who announces programs, reads news, etc. on radio or TV.

an·noy (uh·NOY) *v.* irritate or disturb: *Phone calls annoy her; She is annoyed by too many phone calls; She is annoyed at* or *with him for making too many calls; She is annoyed that he often calls in the middle of the night.*
— **annoying** *adj.: Phone calls can be very annoying; Callers are annoying to people who wish to be left alone; It's annoying that people try to sell things by phone.*
— **an·noy·ing·ly** *adv.*

an·noy·ance (uh·NOY·unce) *n.* **1** the feeling of being annoyed: *To her great annoyance, he arrived very late; Much to his own annoyance, she had left the scene; She felt and showed annoyance at or over or with his behaviour; She expressed her annoyance that he always kept her waiting.* **2** one that annoys; nuisance: *Boarders proved to be an annoyance to the family.*

an·nu·al (AN·yoo·ul) *adj.* **1** yearly; of a year: *your annual income; Marigolds and zinnias are annual plants (that complete the life cycle in one year).* **2** every year: *Birthdays are annual events; an annual meeting; Cross-sections of tree trunks show **annual rings** indicating each year's growth.*
— *n.* **1** annual plant. **2** yearbook. — **an·nu·al·ly** *adv.*

an·nu·i·tant (uh·NEW·uh·tunt) *n.* one who receives an annuity.

an·nu·i·ty (uh·NEW·uh·tee) *n.* **-ties** a fixed sum of money paid yearly on an investment.

an·nul (uh·NUL) *v.* **an·nuls, an·nulled, an·nul·ling** cancel or make a marriage, law, etc. void.
— **an·nul·ment** *n.: The Pope grants annulments.*

an·nu·lar (AN·yoo·lur) *adj.* ringlike: *an annular eclipse showing the rim of the heavenly body like a ring.*

an·nu·lus (AN·yuh·lus) *n.* **-lus·us** or **-li** (·lye) a ringlike part, marking, or formation.

an·o·dyne (AN·uh·dine) *n.* a drug that relieves pain, as codeine: *Time is the anodyne of sorrow.*

a·noint (uh·NOINT) *v.* **1** apply oil or ointment to someone, esp. as a religious rite: *The sacrament **Anointing of the sick** was formerly called "extreme unction."* **2** consecrate: *to anoint a queen; Elizabeth II was anointed queen in 1953.*

a·nom·a·ly (uh·NOM·uh·lee) *n.* **-lies** (·leez) something irregular or abnormal, as stairs that lead nowhere: *the anomaly of time in the movie "Back to the Future"; the anomaly of large houses lying vacant while more and more people live on the streets.*
— **a·nom·a·lous** (·lus) *adj.: the anomalous situation of an unknown French play becoming a huge hit in its English version.*

an·o·mie (AN·uh·mee) *n.* loss of faith in human nature and social values. Also **an·o·my.**

a·non (uh·NON) *adv.* soon: *But more of that anon.*
— **ever and anon** now and then.

a·non·y·mous (uh·NON·uh·mus) *adj.* with no name given: *an anonymous author, call, caller, letter.*
— **a·non·y·mous·ly** *adv.*
— **a·no·nym·i·ty** (an·uh·NIM·uh·tee) *n.*

an·o·rex·i·a (an·uh·REX·ee·uh) *n.* an eating disorder, esp. of young women, characterized by loss of appetite and resulting starvation from anxiety to control weight; in full "anorexia nervosa."
— **an·o·rex·ic** (·REX·ic) *n. & adj.* (patient) having anorexia.

an·oth·er (uh·NUTH·ur, "TH" as in "the") *pron. & adj.* an additional, different, or similar one: *This cup is broken, get me another; Have another drink; She's a brilliant physicist, another Einstein.*

an·swer (AN·sur) *n.* a reply to a question: *to give, offer,* provide an answer to a question; *The answer is No; I have nothing more to say in answer to your question; an appropriate, blunt, curt, civil, evasive, glib, negative, positive, ready, straight, vague, witty answer; the right answer; the wrong answer; Even doctors don't have or know all the answers to your health problems; Dieting may be the answer* (= solution) *to his weight problem; The CN Tower is Canada's answer* (= matching response) *to the world's tallest structures.*
— *v.* say or act in answer: *to answer a question; Please answer the phone; A stick will answer* (= suit) *my purpose very well; Don't **answer back** (= reply rudely) to your mother; You will have to **answer for** (= be responsible for) the broken china; An **answering service** handles phone calls for clients.*
— **answer to 1** explain to: *You'll have to answer to the manager.* **2** correspond: *This one answers to the description of the missing dog.* **3** respond: *He answers to the name "Tiger."*

an·swer·a·ble (AN·sur·uh·bul) *adj.* responsible: *We are answerable to our superiors for carrying out our duties.*

ant *n.* any of a family of small social insects related to bees: *a colony of ants; army ants; He's got **ants in his pants** (Slang for He's very restless or anxious).*

ant- same as ANTI-.

ant·ac·id (an·TAS·id) *n.* a chemical that neutralizes acidity, as baking soda.

an·tag·o·nism (an·TAG·uh·niz·um) *n.* opposition or hostility between persons: *to arouse, stir up antagonism between friends; People feel a strong antagonism to or towards anyone seen as a threat to their livelihood.*

an·tag·o·nist (an·TAG·uh·nist) *n.* adversary or opponent: *a formidable antagonist.*
— **an·tag·o·nis·tic** (·NIS·tic) *adj.*

an·tag·o·nize (an·TAG·uh·nize) *v.* **-iz·es, -ized, -iz·ing** make someone hostile: *He antagonized the rest of the class by giving special consideration to a few.*

Ant·arc·tic (ant·ARC·tic, ·AR·tic) *adj.* of the south polar region of the Earth: *The **Antarctic Circle,** the parallel at 66° 33' S, encloses the South Frigid Zone; the Antarctic Ocean.*

an·te (AN·tee) *n.* a stake put up by a poker player.
— **raise the ante** raise the price.
— *v.* **-tes,** *pt. & pp.* **-ted** or **-teed, -te·ing** put up an ante.
— **ante up** *Informal.* pay one's due share in a joint venture.

ante- *n. & v. prefix.* before; prior: *antechamber, antedate.*

an·te·ce·dent (an·tuh·SEE·dunt) *n.* a person or thing going before, as a word or phrase to which a pronoun refers: *In the sentence, "When I borrow a book I return it," "book" is the antecedent of "it"; a nonentity with no **antecedents** (= known ancestors).*
— *adj.* preceding: *antecedent circumstances.*
— **an·te·ce·dent·ly** *adv.*
— **an·te·ce·dence** (·dunce) *n.*

an·te·cham·ber (AN·tee·chame·bur) *n.* a side room leading into a larger room.

an·te·date (AN·tee·date) *v.* **-dates, -dat·ed, -dat·ing**

1 date a document, cheque, etc. earlier than the actual date. **2** happen earlier than another event.

an·te·di·lu·vi·an (AN·tee·duh·LOO·vee·un) *adj.* very ancient, antiquated, or obsolete: *an antediluvian custom.*
— *n.* one who is antediluvian: *He's an antediluvian in his attitude to TV.*

an·te·lope (AN·tuh·lope) *n.* a deerlike animal such as the chamois, gazelle, and pronghorn.

an·te·na·tal (an·tee·NAY·tul) *adj.* before-birth; prenatal.

an·ten·na (an·TEN·uh) *n.* **1** a wire, rod, or dish used in sending or receiving TV and radio signals; aerial: *a loop antenna; a TV antenna.* **2** *pl.* also **an·ten·nae** (·TEN·ee) a hornlike feeler on the head of an insect.

an·te·ri·or (an·TEER·ee·ur) *adj.* coming before in position or time.

an·te·room (AN·tee·room) *n.* a small room opening into one larger; waiting room.

an·them (ANTH·um) *n.* a hymn of praise, devotion, or triumph: *our national anthem; the college anthem; A band plays* or *strikes up an anthem.*

ant·hill *n.* a pile of earth thrown up by ants at the entrance to their nest.

an·thol·o·gy (an·THOL·uh·jee) *n.* **-gies** (·jeez) collection of writings, usually on one theme by many authors.
— **an·thol·o·gist** *n.*

an·thro·poid (AN·thruh·poid) *adj.* humanlike: *the anthropoid apes.*
— *n.* an ape such as the chimpanzee, gibbon, or gorilla.

an·thro·pol·o·gy (an·thruh·POL·uh·jee) *n.* the study of human origins, characteristics, and cultural development.
— **an·thro·pol·o·gist** *n.*
— **an·thro·po·log·i·cal** (·puh·LOJ·uh·cul) *adj.*

anti- *prefix* [indicating opposition]: *antacid, anti-American, anticapitalist.*

an·ti (AN·tee) *n.* **-tis** *Informal.* one who opposes something: *The vote was three pros and two antis;* **prep.**: *She is anti everything foreign.*

an·ti·air·craft (an·tee·AIR·craft) *adj.* for use against aircraft: *an antiaircraft gun.*

an·ti·bac·te·ri·al (AN·tee·bac·TEER·ee·ul) *adj.* that checks or protects from bacteria: *an antibacterial agent.*

an·ti·bi·ot·ic (AN·tee·bye·OT·ic) *n.* a substance such as penicillin that can destroy or prevent the growth of harmful microorganisms: *A broad-spectrum antibiotic is effective against a wide variety of diseases.*

an·ti·bod·y (AN·tee·bod·ee) *n.* **-bod·ies** a substance produced in the blood to fight disease germs, poisons, etc.

an·tic (AN·tic) *n.* a clownish act; caper.
— *adj.* ludicrous; odd.
— *v.* **-tics, -ticked, -tick·ing** cut capers: *A buffoon antics on the stage.*

an·tic·i·pate (an·TIS·uh·pate) *v.* **-pates, -pat·ed, -pat·ing** foresee something and act accordingly: *We anticipated trouble during the strike; anticipated*

missing our mail; Anticipating rain, we took an umbrella.
— **an·tic·i·pa·tion** (·PAY·shun) *n.*: *We look forward to your visit with eager* or *keen anticipation; We took an umbrella in anticipation of rain.*

an·ti·cli·max (an·tee·CLY·max) *n.* a sudden descent from the serious to the trivial in a series of events or in what is said or done: *The rain was an anticlimax to the victory parade.* — **an·ti·cli·mac·tic** (·clye·MAC·tic) *adj.*

an·ti·clock·wise (an·tee·CLOCK·wize) *adj. & adv.* in the direction opposite to the movement of a clock's hands.

an·ti·cy·clone (an·tee·SYE·clone) *n.* a rotating system of winds originating from a centre of high pressure.
— **an·ti·cy·clon·ic** (AN·tee·sye·CLON·ic) *adj.*

an·ti·de·pres·sant (AN·tee·duh·PRES·unt) *adj.* tending to prevent emotional depression.
— *n.* an antidepressant drug; also called "energizer."

an·ti·dote (AN·tuh·dote) *n.* a remedy against poison, evil, or other harm: *There are specific antidotes for* or *against* or *to various poisons.*
— **an·ti·do·tal** (·DOH·tul) *adj.*

an·ti·freeze (AN·tee·freez) *n.* a substance added to gasoline, radiator coolant, etc. to prevent freezing.

an·ti·gen (AN·tuh·jun) *n.* a foreign substance such as a virus or pollen that produces antibodies when it enters the body. — **an·ti·gen·ic** (an·tuh·JEN·ic) *adj.*

an·ti·his·ta·mine (an·tee·HIS·tuh·meen) *n.* a medicine for colds and allergies.

an·ti·knock (an·tee·NOCK) *n.* a fuel additive that reduces the noise of too rapid combustion in an engine.

an·ti·mag·net·ic (AN·tee·mag·NET·ic) *adj.* esp. of a watch, made with nonmagnetic metals to ensure constant movement of parts.

an·ti·nu·cle·ar (an·tee·NEW·clee·ur) *adj.* opposed to the use of nuclear energy for any purpose.

anti-nuke (an·tee·NUKE) *n. & adj. Slang.* (one) opposed to nuclear arms, nuclear energy, etc.

an·tip·a·thy (an·TIP·uh·thee, "th" as in "thin") *n.* **-thies** deep dislike or an object of it: *the antipathy of cats to water; Lotteries were a lifelong antipathy of his.*

an·ti·per·son·nel (AN·tee·pur·suh·NEL) *adj.* in war, designed for use against humans rather than materials: *an antipersonnel bomb.*

an·ti·per·spi·rant (an·tee·PUR·spuh·runt) *n.* a cosmetic preparation for checking perspiration.

an·tip·o·de (an·TIP·uh·dee) *n.* **1** Antipodes *pl.* a diametrically opposite place or region of the earth, esp. Australia and New Zealand: *Canberra is in the Antipodes.* **2** something that is contrary to another: *Thrift and prodigality are antipodes; Violence is the antipode of peace.* — **an·tip·o·de·an** (·DEE·un) *adj.*

an·ti·pol·lu·tion (AN·tee·puh·LOO·shun) *adj.* designed to counteract or prevent pollution: *antipollution devices, measures.*

an·ti·quar·i·an (an·tuh·QUAIR·ee·un) **1** *adj.* antique in interest: *a vast antiquarian collection.* **2** *n.* same as ANTIQUARY.

an·ti·quar·y (AN·tuh·quair·ee) *n.* **-quar·ies** one who collects or studies antiquities.

an·ti·quat·ed (AN·tuh·quay·tid) *adj.* out of date or old-fashioned: *a man of antiquated ideas.*

an·tique (an·TEEK) *n.* a once useful object that is now of mostly cultural value, as a century-old piece of furniture, pottery, or costume.
— *adj.* **1** having to do with antiques: *an antique dealer; antique furniture; an antique shop.* **2** ancient: *an antique city; antique heroes.*

an·tiq·ui·ty (an·TIK·wuh·tee) *n.* **-ties 1** great age: *discarded because of its antiquity.* **2** former times: *great men of antiquity.* **3** *pl.* ancient remains: *Greek and Roman antiquities.*

anti-Semite (an·tee·SEM·ite) *n.* one who hates Jews.
— **anti-Semitic** (AN·tee·suh·MIT·ic) *adj.*

an·ti·sep·tic (an·tuh·SEP·tic) *adj.* **1** destroying disease germs: *Carbolic acid and alcohol are antiseptic agents.* **2** lifeless or sterile because extremely clean.
— *n.* an antiseptic agent.

an·ti·so·cial (an·tee·SOH·shul) *adj.* **1** not sociable: *an antisocial fellow, life.* **2** against the good of society: *Stealing is antisocial.*

an·tith·e·sis (an·TITH·uh·sis, "TH" as in "thin") *n., pl.* **-ses** (-seez) **1** a contrasting idea or expression, as "Give me liberty or give me death!" **2** something that is contrasting: *Private ownership is the very antithesis of Communism; the antithesis between good and evil.*

an·ti·tox·in (an·tee·TOX·in) *n.* an antibody or serum injected against a disease.

an·ti·trades (AN·tee·trades) *n.pl.* winds blowing in an opposite direction to the trade winds.

an·ti·trust (AN·tee·trust) *adj.* having to do with laws against business monopolies: *antitrust legislation; an antitrust suit.*

ant·ler (ANT·lur) *n.* a branched horn of an animal of the deer family: *Deer lock antlers in a fight; They shed their antlers each winter and grow new ones in the spring.*

ant·lered (ANT·lurd) *adj.* having antlers.

an·to·nym (AN·tuh·nim) *n.* a word that means the opposite of another: *"Black" is the antonym of "white."*

a·nus (AY·nus) *n.* the opening at the end of the alimentary canal.

an·vil (AN·vil) *n.* a heavy block on which to hammer metals into shape.

anx·i·e·ty (ang·ZYE·uh·tee) *n.* **1** fear in thinking of what may happen: *a mother's anxiety for her child's safety; to relieve her anxiety; deep, grave, great, high anxiety; In his anxiety about the trip, he forgot to pay his rent.* **2** *pl.* **-ties** an instance of such fear: *the anxieties of unemployment.* **3** eagerness: *a pupil's anxiety to please his teacher.*

anx·ious (ANK·shus) *adj.* **1** worried or troubled: *She spent many anxious hours waiting for her child; She was anxious for the child's safety; anxious about what might happen.* **2** very eager: *Neighbours were anxious to help; They were anxious that she shouldn't worry.*

— **anx·ious·ly** *adv.*

an·y (EN·ee) *adj.* one out of many or some out of much of something [in positive statements and in questions when an affirmative answer is expected]: *Do we have any oranges? Any old hat will do; Just any of them will suffice; as any child could tell you;* [with implied negative] *There's hardly any time left; He spoke without any hesitation.*
— *pron.* some: *I have no money – have you any?*
— *adv.* to some degree: *Has her luck improved any? Is she any better today? Is the book any good at all?*
— **at any rate** in whatever case; at least.
— **in any case** or **event** whatever happens.

an·y·bod·y (EN·ee·bod·ee) *pron.* **1** any person; anyone: *Anybody home? Do you have anybody to mind the baby? It's anybody's guess* (= a question no one can answer). **2** any person of importance: *Is she anybody here?*

an·y·how (EN·ee·how) *adv.* anyway; nevertheless.

an·y·more (EN·ee·more) *adv.* any longer.

an·y·one (EN·ee·wun) *pron.* any person; anybody.

an·y·place (EN·ee·place) *adv.* anywhere.

an·y·thing (EN·ee·thing) *n., pron. & adv.* any one thing or something: *You don't see anything in the dark; He will do anything for money; She is anything but* (= not at all) *fat; He cried like anything* (*Informal* for a great deal).

an·y·time (EN·ee·time) *adv.* at any time: *He may call anytime now.*

an·y·way (EN·ee·way) *adv.* in any way.

an·y·where (EN·ee·where) *adv. & pron.* in or to any place.

an·y·wise (EN·ee·wise) *adv.* in any manner.

A-OK *adj. & adv. Informal.* quite all right.

A1 or **A one** *adj. Informal.* excellent.

a·pace (uh·PACE) *adv.* [used after its verb] quickly.

a·part (uh·PART) *adj. & adv.* [used after its noun or verb] away from each other: *two houses three miles apart; they are far apart; I took him apart* (= aside) *for a private chat; Don't tear the thing apart* (= into parts); *Handle it carefully or it will fall apart* (= go to pieces); *Twins are difficult to tell apart* (= distinguish); *Joking apart* (= excepted), *I want to go to the moon; The apes are a class apart* (= separate) *from other animals; They are worlds apart* (= very different) *from humans; Apart from* (= besides) *errors, the book is also out of date.*

a·part·heid (uh·PAR·tate, -tide) *n.* the political policy of racial segregation in South Africa.

a·part·ment (uh·PART·munt) *n.* a suite of rooms for living in; flat: *a bachelor, duplex, efficiency, high-rise, penthouse, studio apartment.*

apartment block or **building** or **house** *n.* a building containing many apartments.

apartment hotel *n.* a hotel containing apartments with housekeeping facilities for guests on a temporary or permanent basis.

ap·a·thet·ic (ap·uh·THET·ic, "TH" as in "thin") *adj.* showing apathy: *He is apathetic to* or *toward the poor; quite apathetic about their condition.*

ap·a·thy (AP·uh·thee, "th" as in "thin") *n.* lack of feeling or interest; indifference: *He feels apathy toward the poor; to show apathy; to cast off* or *shed* or *throw off one's apathy and do something.*

ape *n.* 1 a large tailless monkey such as a chimpanzee, gibbon, or gorilla; one of the "great apes" or "higher apes." 2 any monkey. 3 one who mimics another's behaviour like an ape. 4 a clumsy person.
— **go ape** *Slang.* 1 go crazy. 2 go crazy *over* an object of admiration.
— *v.* **apes, aped, ap·ing** imitate someone or someone's behaviour in a silly way.

ap·er·ture (AP·ur·chur) *n.* an opening or hole, as of a camera.

a·pex (AY·pex) *n.* **a·pex·es** or **ap·i·ces** (AP·uh·seez) the highest point or climax: *at the apex of her fortunes.*

a·pha·sia (uh·FAY·zhuh) *n.* loss of the ability to use or understand language, resulting from brain damage.
— **a·pha·si·ac** (-zee·ac) or **a·pha·sic** (-zic) *n. & adj.*

a·phid (AY·fid) or **a·phis** (AY·fis) *n.* **a·phids** or **a·phi·des** (-fuh·deez) a small insect that lives on the juice of plants.

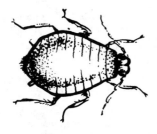

aph·o·rism (AF·uh·riz·um) *n.* a pithy expression of a general truth, as the saying "The dog is man's best friend." — **aph·o·ris·tic** (af·uh·RIS·tic) *adj.*

a·pi·ar·i·an (ay·pee·AIR·ee·un) *adj.* having to do with beekeeping.
— *n.* beekeeper; also **a·pi·a·rist** (AY·pee·uh·rist).

a·pi·ar·y (AY·pee·air·ee) *n.* **-ar·ies** a box for keeping bees in hives.

apices See APEX.

a·pi·cul·ture (AY·puh·cul·chur) *n.* beekeeping.

a·piece (uh·PEECE) *adv.* [used after its verb] to or for each: *They cost $5 apiece.*

a·plomb (uh·PLOM) *n.* poise or self-confidence in bearing or behaviour: *She spoke with the aplomb typical of a professional who knows her job.*

ap·ne·a (AP·nee·uh) *n.* stoppage of breathing for a minute or two: *Sleep apnea has been blamed in infant crib deaths.*

a·poc·a·lypse (uh·POC·uh·lips) *n.* a revelation or prophecy of something final and conclusive, as in the **Apocalypse,** or the "Book of Revelation," the last book of the Bible: *Are we facing a nuclear apocalypse* (= end)?
— **a·poc·a·lyp·tic** (-LIP·tic) or **a·poc·a·lyp·ti·cal** (-LIP·tuh·cul) *adj.*

a·poc·ry·pha (uh·POC·ruh·fuh) *n. pl.* writings from a dubious source connected with something authentic, like the **Apocrypha** attached to the Bible.
— **a·poc·ry·phal** (-ful) *adj.* unauthentic: *an apocryphal account, anecdote, book, story.*

ap·o·gee (AP·uh·jee) *n.* 1 the point in an orbit (as of a satellite) or trajectory (as of a rocket) that is farthest from the earth: *There is a difference of over 50 000 km between the moon's apogee and "perigee."* 2 the highest point; apex: *to reach the apogee of one's career.*

a·po·lit·i·cal (ay·puh·LIT·uh·cul) *adj.* not related to politics.

ap·o·lo·get·ic (uh·pol·uh·JET·ic) *adj.* making an apology: *an apologetic smile; He was apologetic about his absence.* — **a·pol·o·get·i·cal·ly** *adv.*

ap·o·lo·gi·a (ap·uh·LOH·jee·uh) *n.* a formal defence of one's position.

a·pol·o·gist (uh·POL·uh·jist) *n.* one who speaks or writes in defence of a cause: *an apologist for the cause.*

a·pol·o·gize (uh·POL·uh·jize) *v.* **-giz·es, -gized, -giz·ing** make an apology: *He apologized to them for his rudeness.*

a·pol·o·gy (uh·POL·uh·jee) *n.* **-gies** 1 an expression of regret for an offence: *He made* or *offered no apology for his rude remarks; They demanded an apology; an abject, humble, public, sincere apology.* 2 a poor specimen or substitute: *a mere apology for the real thing.*

ap·o·plec·tic (ap·uh·PLEC·tic) *adj.* showing symptoms of apoplexy: *an apoplectic attack, stroke; an apoplectic* (= paralyzing) *fit, fury, rage.*

ap·o·plex·y (AP·uh·plex·ee) *n.* stroke resulting in partial paralysis.

a·pos·ta·sy (uh·POS·tuh·see) *n.* **-sies** an abandoning of one's religious faith, political party, or other allegiance: *his apostasy from the priesthood.*

a·pos·tate (uh·POS·tate, -tit) *n.* one guilty of apostasy: *an apostate from the Catholic faith; an apostate priest.*

a pos·te·ri·o·ri (AY·poh·steer·ee·OH·rye, -ree) *adj. & adv.* of reasoning, proceeding from effect to cause, not a priori.

a·pos·tle (uh·POS·ul) *n.* 1 one of Christ's twelve disciples. 2 a first missionary: *the apostle to the Indies.* 3 leader of a movement: *an apostle of women's rights.*

a·pos·to·late (uh·POS·tuh·lit, -late) *n.* the work of an apostle: *Mother Teresa's apostolate of mercy; lay apostolates such as the Christian Family Movement.*

a·pos·tol·ic (ap·uh·STOL·ic) *adj.* 1 having to do with Christ's disciples: *the apostolic church established by Peter; in apostolic times.* 2 papal: *the apostolic blessing; an apostolic delegate.*

a·pos·tro·phe (uh·POS·truh·fee) *n.* 1 a punctuation mark indicating possession *(John's),* plural *(3 A's),* or contraction *(isn't).* 2 a rhetorical passage addressed to an imaginary or absent person or a personified object, as "Milton! thou shouldst be living at this hour."

a·poth·e·car·y (uh·POTH·uh·cair·ee, "TH" as in "thin") *n.* -car·ies a pharmacist; druggist.

ap·o·thegm (AP·uh·them, "th" as in "thin") *n.* a short, pithy saying or maxim such as "Honesty is the best policy."

a·poth·e·o·sis (uh·poth·ee·OH·sis, "th" as in "thin") *n.*, *pl.* -ses (-seez) glorification or idealization: *He was the apotheosis of chivalry.*

ap·pall or **ap·pal** (uh·POL) *v.* **ap·palls** or **ap·pals,** **ap·palled, ap·pal·ling** fill with shock and dismay: *We are appalled at or by the misery of the poor; We are appalled to see the misery around us; We are appalled that such conditions could exist among us; the **appalling** condition of the slums.*

ap·pa·rat·chik (ah·puh·RAH·chik) *n.* [contemptuous use] a functionary or bureaucrat working for a Communist party; flunky.

ap·pa·ra·tus (ap·uh·RAT·us, -RAY·tus) *n.* -tus or -tus·es equipment for a specific task: *a gym apparatus; laboratory apparatus; a party's election apparatus* (= organization).

ap·pa·rel (uh·PAIR·ul) *n.* clothing, esp. outer; attire: *wearing apparel.*
— *v.* -els, -elled or -eled, -el·ling or -el·ing clothe: *children brightly apparelled for a festival; Nature seemed apparelled* (= adorned) *in celestial light.*

ap·par·ent (uh·PAIR·unt) *adj.* 1 visible; evident: *His limp is quite apparent; It soon became clearly, increasingly apparent who was lying; It was apparent to all that Jon was telling the truth.* 2 seeming: *an apparent advantage, contradiction.*
— **ap·par·ent·ly** *adv.*

ap·pa·ri·tion (ap·uh·RISH·un) *n.* a supernatural vision; ghost; spectre: *a strange apparition in the middle of the night.*

ap·peal (uh·PEEL) *n.* 1 an earnest call for help: *an appeal to the public; He made an appeal for funds, mercy; a desperate, final, last, ringing, stirring appeal; an eloquent, emotional, irresistible appeal.* 2 a sending of a case to a higher court for a new hearing or an application for it: *to deny, dismiss, file, lodge, lose, reject, throw out, win an appeal; an appeal against a decision; an appeal from a lower court; He took the appeal to the Supreme Court; There was no appeal from their decision.* 3 interest or attraction: *a show that has lost its appeal; box-office appeal; sales, sex, snob appeal.*
— *v.* 1 request earnestly: *The convict appealed to the King for clemency; appealed to him to be merciful.* 2 refer to a higher authority: *They appealed against the lower court's decision; The decision was appealed to the Supreme Court.* 3 interest or attract: *a movie appealing to the young; A picture is more **appealing** than words.*
— **ap·peal·ing·ly** *adv.*

ap·pear (uh·PEER) *v.* 1 become visible: *The sun appears on a clear day.* 2 arrive: *The boss hadn't appeared by 11 a.m.; Police appeared on the scene (of the crime); They appeared at the door; They appeared unannounced; The president appeared in person.*

3 seem: *She appeared dejected; She appeared to have suffered much; It appeared (to us) that the case was lost.* 4 to be published: *A book appears on the market; An essay appears in print; Stories appear in the papers.* 5 present oneself: *He was ordered to appear in court on a charge of speeding; to appear before a committee; Actors appear on stage.* 6 act as a lawyer: *She appeared for the prosecution; appeared against the accused.*

ap·pear·ance (uh·PEER·unce) *n.* 1 an appearing: *the timely appearance of the police; The lawyer was making her first appearance in court; At first appearance, she makes a good impression; a guest appearance on a TV show; a cameo appearance; personal appearance; He **puts in an appearance** (= appears for a short while) at work every day.* 2 outward impression: *He gives an appearance of honesty; From or To all appearances, he is honest; One cannot judge by appearances alone; A candidate has to be neat in appearance; the immaculate appearance of her home; a dishevelled, shabby, unkempt, untidy appearance; Although broke, he tries to **keep up appearances** (= appear to be all right).*

ap·pease (uh·PEEZ) *v.* **ap·peas·es, ap·peased, ap·peas·ing** pacify by satisfying: *to appease his hunger; It's useless to try to appease an aggressor.*
— **ap·pease·ment** *n.*

ap·pel·lant (uh·PEL·unt) *n.* one who appeals to a higher court.

ap·pel·late (uh·PEL·ut) *adj.* having power to hear appeals: *an appellate court, judge, jurisdiction.*

ap·pel·la·tion (ap·uh·LAY·shun) *n.* the act of naming; also, a designation, as "Her Majesty, the Queen."

ap·pend (uh·PEND) *v.* add at the end of a document; affix: *a chart appended to a statement.*

ap·pend·age (uh·PEN·dij) *n.* 1 an added part: *Frills are decorative appendages to costumes.* 2 a body part such as an arm, tail, or fin: *The appendix is an appendage of the large intestine.*

ap·pen·dec·to·my (ap·un·DEC·tuh·mee) *n.* -mies surgical removal of the appendix.

ap·pen·di·ci·tis (uh·pen·duh·SYE·tis) *n.* inflammation of the appendix.

ap·pen·dix (uh·PEN·dix) *n.* -dix·es or -di·ces (-duh·seez) 1 section added at the end of a book or document: *There are two appendixes to the book.* 2 short tubelike appendage of the large intestine: *The appendix may burst or rupture when it is inflamed.*

ap·per·tain (AP·ur·tain) *v.* belong rightfully: *duties that appertain to his office.*

ap·pe·tite (AP·uh·tite) *n.* a natural desire of the body, esp. for food: *to curb, satisfy, spoil, take away, whet one's appetite; to work up an appetite for dinner; sexual appetite; a healthy, hearty, insatiable, ravenous, voracious appetite; Good appetite!*

ap·pe·tiz·er (AP·uh·tye·zur) *n.* a food or drink meant to stimulate the appetite.

ap·pe·tiz·ing (AP·uh·tye·zing) *adj.* stimulating the appetite: *an appetizing smell from the kitchen.*
— **ap·pe·tiz·ing·ly** *adv.*

ap·plaud (uh·PLAWD) *v.* express approval, as by clapping hands: *The audience applauded heartily, loudly; His election was applauded* (= praised) *by everyone.*

ap·plause (uh·PLAWZ) *n.* an applauding: *Loud applause greeted the winner; She spoke to the prolonged, thunderous applause of her admirers; a burst, ripple, round of applause; Her speech drew, got, won applause* (= praise) *for her party.*

ap·ple (AP·ul) *n.* a round fleshy fruit with a core of seeds or the tree bearing it: *cooking apples such as Rome Beauty; eating apples such as Delicious and McIntosh; baked apples; candied apples; a real slick apple* (*Slang* for guy); *There's a **rotten apple*** (= undesirable character) *in every group; an **apple of discord** like the golden apple inscribed "For the most beautiful" which caused rivalry among Aphrodite, Athena, and Hera of Greek myth.*
— **the apple of one's eye** a very dear one.

ap·ple·cart (AP·ul·cart) *n.* esp. **upset one's** or **the applecart,** upset a system, undertaking, plan, or situation; disprove a theory, etc.

ap·ple·jack (AP·ul·jack) *n.* a liquor distilled from cider.

apple pie *n.* the commonest of fruit pies which is made with apples.
— **apple-pie** *adj.: a motherhood-and-apple-pie issue* (= one that deals with traditional North American values); *I found everything **in apple-pie order*** (= neat and orderly arrangement).

apple-polish *v. Informal.* curry favour with someone.

ap·ple·sauce (AP·ul·sawce) *n.* **1** stewed apples in pulp form. **2** *Slang.* nonsense.

ap·pli·ance (uh·PLY·unce) *n.* a piece of equipment: *electric kettles, irons, and such small appliances; a major appliance such as a dishwasher or refrigerator; kitchen appliances.*

ap·pli·ca·ble (AP·luh·cuh·bul, uh·PLIC·uh·bul) *adj.* that applies: *a law applicable to the situation.*
— **ap·pli·ca·bly** *adv.*
— **ap·pli·ca·bil·i·ty** (-BIL·uh·tee) *n.*

ap·pli·cant (AP·luh·kunt) *n.* one who applies for a job, loan, etc.

ap·pli·ca·tion (ap·luh·CAY·shun) *n.* **1** a request: *His job application is on file; a formal, written application; to file, make, put in, reject, send in, screen, submit, turn down, withdraw an application; Forms are available to the public on* or *by application; to file, fill in, fill out, submit an application form.* **2** a putting on: *two applications of the ointment.* **3** a putting into practice: *the application of a new method; the application of theory to practice.* **4** bearing or reference: *a discovery with many applications in daily life.* **5** attention: *with close application to detail, to one's studies.*

applied (uh·PLIDE) *adj.* put to practical use: *applied arts, chemistry, mathematics, research, sciences.*

ap·pli·qué (ap·luh·KAY) *n.* a decorative design or ornament cut out for attaching to something.
— *v.* **-qués, -quéd, -qué·ing:** *an appliquéd floral design.*

ap·ply (uh·PLY) *v.* **ap·plies, ap·plied, ap·ply·ing**

1 make a request: *to apply for a job; He applied to the bank for a loan; Students apply* (= seek admission) *to universities; They apply to be admitted.* **2** put on: *to apply two coats of paint to a wall; Apply the brakes to stop the car.* **3** put in practice: *to apply a rule.* **4** have a bearing on a person or thing: *This rule applies in all cases; It applies to you.* **5** devote to some end: *to apply oneself to studies.* — **ap·pli·er** (uh·PLY·ur) *n.*

ap·point (uh·POINT) *v.* **1** set or fix a time or place: *We met at the appointed time and place.* **2** assign to a position: *Jim was appointed to the vacancy; was appointed to serve as manager; was appointed (as) manager.* **3 appointed** *adj.* furnished or equipped: *a well-appointed office.*

ap·poin·tee (uh·poin·TEE) *n.* one who is appointed.

ap·point·ment (uh·POINT·munt) *n.* **1** an agreement to meet: *to break, cancel, fix, keep, make an appointment with a doctor; an appointment to see the doctor; visits by appointment only.* **2** an assignment to a position: *a letter of appointment following a job offer; She received an appointment as manager of the company and held it for three years; a temporary appointment, not a permanent one.* **3 appointments** *pl.* furnishings: *a car's interior appointments and exterior design.* **4** [used on product labels] **by appointment** to approved by Her Majesty the Queen, etc.

ap·por·tion (uh·POR·shun) *v.* allot as a share or portion: *The judge apportioned blame for the accident equally between the parties; liability apportioned among those responsible.* — **ap·por·tion·ment** *n.*

ap·po·site (AP·uh·zit) *adj.* relevant and suitable: *an apposite answer, comparison, quotation, remark, suggestion; a proposal apposite to the occasion.*

ap·po·si·tion (ap·uh·ZISH·un) *n.* the placing of a noun next to another noun as an explanation: *In "Jack the giant-killer," "the giant-killer" is in apposition to* or *with "Jack."*

ap·prais·al (uh·PRAY·zul) *n.* an appraising; estimate of worth: *to give* or *make an appraisal; an objective appraisal of the facts.* — **ap·prais·er** *n.*

ap·praise (uh·PRAIZ) *v.* **ap·prais·es, ap·praised, ap·prais·ing** estimate the worth or value of a gem, house, situation, etc. as an expert: *a painting appraised at $1 million.*

ap·pre·ci·a·ble (uh·PREE·shuh·bul) *adj.* capable of being measured or perceived: *an appreciable rise in temperature; an appreciable improvement.*
— **ap·pre·ci·a·bly** *adv.*

ap·pre·ci·ate (uh·PREE·shee·ate) *v.* **-ates, -at·ed, -at·ing 1** understand the meaning or value of something: *I fully appreciate the risks involved; Not everyone appreciates poetry; Everyone likes to be appreciated; We deeply, greatly, highly, sincerely appreciate your help; We appreciate your helping us; We appreciate the fact that you went out of your way to help us; I would appreciate* (= like to have) *your help.* **2** rise in value: *House prices appreciate in the spring.*
— **ap·pre·ci·a·tion** (-AY·shun) *n.: to demonstrate, display, express, show our appreciation for your services; The honorary degree was given in appreciation of her services to the country.*

— **ap·pre·ci·a·tive** (-shee·uh·tiv) *adj.: an appreciative gesture, glance, letter; We are deeply appreciative of your help.*

ap·pre·hend (ap·ruh·HEND) *v.* **1** arrest: *to apprehend a burglar.* **2** anticipate with fear: *to apprehend danger in the dark.*

ap·pre·hen·sion (ap·ruh·HEN·shun) *n.* **1** fear or foreboding: *The mother felt grave apprehension for her child's safety; Everyone tried to allay her apprehensions and to reassure her.* **2** conception: *He was under a wrong apprehension; He had no clear apprehension of the situation.* **3** a seizing or arrest: *the apprehension of stolen goods; the apprehension of the thief.*

ap·pre·hen·sive (ap·ruh·HEN·siv) *adj.* fearful: *He was apprehensive about or for or of what might happen; He was apprehensive that the child might get lost.*
— **ap·pre·hen·sive·ly** *adv.*

ap·pren·tice (uh·PREN·tis) *n.* a learner in a trade or profession: *law apprentices; an apprentice to an electrician; An apprentice graduates as a journeyman.*
— *v.* **-tic·es, -ticed, -tic·ing** place someone as an apprentice: *He apprenticed his son to a tailor.*
— **ap·pren·tice·ship** *n.: an apprenticeship in carpentry; to fill an apprenticeship (position); to serve an apprenticeship (term).*

ap·prise (uh·PRIZE) *v.* **ap·pris·es, ap·prised, ap·pris·ing** *Formal.* advise or inform: *Apprised of danger, he fled the country.*

ap·proach (uh·PROHCH) *v.* **1** move near or nearer to a person or thing: *Night was fast approaching; as we approached Toronto; The pilot was directed to approach the airport from the east.* **2** go to someone with a specific aim: *to approach the bank for a loan; to approach the boss about a raise; to approach the manager with a suggestion.*
— *n.* an approaching: *to find a means of approach to the snowbound airport; to make an approach for a bank loan; A pilot makes his approach with the landing gear down and the flaps lowered; He took the unusual approach of calling on the manager at his home; It was not a judicious approach to the problem; a forthright, pragmatic, rational, scholarly, scientific approach; They fled at our approach; With the approach of Christmas, business booms; an approach from a sales rep; She spurned his approaches* (= advances); *The police sealed all approaches* (= means of approach) *to the city.*

ap·proach·a·ble (uh·PROH·chuh·bul) *adj.* that can be approached: *a quite approachable* (= friendly) *boss.*
— **ap·proach·a·bil·i·ty** (-BIL·uh·tee) *n.*

ap·pro·ba·tion (ap·ruh·BAY·shun) *n.* approval with pleasure.

ap·pro·pri·ate (uh·PROH·pree·ate) *v.* **-ates, -at·ed, -at·ing** **1** make one's own: *He tends to appropriate what he borrows.* **2** assign to a specific purpose: *the funds appropriated by government for education.*
— *adj.* (-pree·it) proper or suitable: *It's not appropriate to wear casual clothes to a formal banquet; Wear something appropriate to the occasion; What is appropriate for me may not be appropriate for you; It is appropriate that everyone be suitably attired; appropriate technology that is appropriate to the economic conditions of the country or area where it is to be used.* — **ap·pro·pri·ate·ly** *adv.*

ap·pro·pri·a·tion (uh·PROH·pree·AY·shun) *n.* money allotted for a purpose in a budget: *The government makes appropriations for various departments; an appropriation bill.*

ap·prov·al (uh·PROO·vul) *n.* act of approving: *Her project met with or received or won his approval; received his stamp of approval; a seal of approval; He gave his approval for the project; approval to carry on with it; his complete, tacit, unqualified approval; The goods were shipped on approval* (= to be returned if not acceptable).

ap·prove (uh·PROOV) *v.* **ap·proves, ap·proved, ap·prov·ing** **1** accept as satisfactory: *She examined his plan and approved it wholeheartedly.* **2** view favourably: *She approved of his plan.*

ap·prox·i·mate (uh·PROX·uh·mit) *adj.* nearly accurate or exact: *her approximate age; our approximate time of arrival.*
— *v.* (-mate) **-mates, -mat·ed, -mat·ing** come near to something; approach: *John's record approximates the champion's; a figure approximated* (= brought near) *to the nearest million.* — **ap·prox·i·mate·ly** (-mit·lee) *adv.*
— **ap·prox·i·ma·tion** (-MAY·shun) *n.*

ap·pur·te·nance (uh·PUR·tuh·nunce) *n.* an appendage, accessory, or adjunct: *a company car, expense account, and such appurtenances of his office.*

a·pres-ski (ah·pray·SKEE) *n.* the relaxation period after skiing; *adj.: apres-ski clothes, parties.*

ap·ri·cot (AP·ruh·cot, AY·pruh-) *n.* an orange-coloured oval fruit similar to the peach.

A·pril fool (AY·prul-) *n.* a victim of a practical joke on April 1, **April Fool's Day.**

a pri·o·ri (ah·pree·OR·ee, ay·pry·OR·eye) *adj. & adv.* of reasoning, proceeding from cause to effect, not a posteriori.

a·pron (AY·prun) *n.* **1** a garment worn in front and tied behind to protect clothes while working: *a man tied to his wife's apron strings* (= overly dependent on his wife). **2** a front part, as of a stage.

ap·ro·pos (ap·ruh·POH) *adj. & adv.* relevant and timely: *Your remark is quite apropos; apropos of* (= with reference to) *what you said yesterday.*

apt *adj.* **1** appropriate: *an apt observation.* **2** likely or inclined: *Students are apt to work too hard on the eve of examinations.* **3** naturally suited: *She's apt at solving problems.* — **apt·ly** *adv.*

ap·ti·tude (AP·tuh·tude) *n.* natural ability or capacity: *a leader with a special aptitude for solving problems; to demonstrate or show a natural aptitude for music; a mechanical aptitude; a scholastic aptitude test for determining a candidate's areas of special fitness.*

aq·ua (AK·wuh) *n., pl.* **-uae** (-wee) or **-uas** water.
— *adj.* aquamarine.

aq·ua·cul·ture (AK·wuh·cul·chur) *n.* **1** the cultivation of fish and water plants, usually in an artificial stream, pond, etc. **2** same as HYDROPONICS.
— **aq·ua·cul·tur·al** (-CUL·chur·ul) *adj.*

— aq·ua·cul·tur·ist *n.*

aq·ua·farm (AK·wuh·farm) *n.* an artifical pond or other body of water used in aquaculture.

aqua-lung (AK·wuh·lung) *n.* an underwater breathing apparatus; scuba; **Aqua-Lung** *Trademark.*

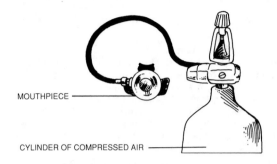

MOUTHPIECE

CYLINDER OF COMPRESSED AIR

aq·ua·ma·rine (ak·wuh·muh·REEN) *n.* a bluish-green beryl. — *adj.* bluish-green.

aq·ua·plane (AK·wuh·plane) *n.* a board pulled by a motorboat, which one rides on water standing up.

a·quar·i·um (uh·KWAIR·ee·um) *n.* **-i·ums** or **-i·a** 1 container for displaying water animals and plants. 2 an establishment housing many such displays.

a·quat·ic (uh·KWOT·ic, -KWAT·ic) 1 *adj.* having to do with water: *The water lily is an aquatic plant; aquatic animals; aquatic sports such as swimming and sailing.* 2 aquatics *n. pl.* water sports.

aq·ue·duct (AK·wuh·duct) *n.* 1 an elevated channel for bringing water from a distance. 2 a structure supporting such a channel.

a·que·ous (AY·kwee·us, AK·wee·us) *adj.* dissolved in water; watery: *an aqueous solution of a medication.*

aq·ui·cul·ture (AK·wuh·cul·chur) *n.* same as AQUACULTURE.

aq·ui·line (AK·wuh·line) *adj.* like an eagle: *An aquiline nose is shaped like an eagle's beak.*

Ar·ab (AIR·ub) *n.* a person of or from an Arabic-speaking country.
— *adj.* having to do with the Arabs: *the Arab bloc; the Arab Common Market; Arab countries, culture, customs; the United Arab Emirates; the Arab-Israeli Wars; the Arab League; Arab University.*

ar·a·besque (air·uh·BESK) *n.* 1 an architectural design with intertwining flowers, foliage, and geometric figures: *an arabesque design, style.* 2 a ballet pose in which one leg is extended horizontally behind the dancer with the foot pointed and the knee straight. 3 in music, a florid melodic figure or a composition based on one.

A·ra·bi·an (uh·RAY·bee·un) *n.* a person of or from Arabia, the peninsula between the Red Sea and the Persian Gulf.
— *adj.* having to do with Arabia or the Arabs: *the Arabian camel, Desert, horse, Peninsula, Sea.*

Ar·a·bic (AIR·uh·bic) *n.* a Semitic language spoken in Arabia, Jordan, Syria, Iraq, and Northern Africa.

— *adj.* having to do with the language and culture of the Arabs: *the Arabic alphabet, language, numerals; Arabic poetry.*

Arabic numeral *n.* any of the symbols 1, 2, 3, 4, 5, 6, 7, 8, 9, and 0.

ar·a·ble (AIR·uh·bul) *adj.* suitable for cultivation: *arable land.*

ar·bi·ter (AR·buh·tur) *n.* one recognized as the authority on a disputed matter: *The dictionary is the arbiter of correct usage for most people.*

ar·bi·tra·ble (AR·buh·truh·bul) *adj.* capable of being arbitrated.

ar·bi·trage (AR·buh·trij) *n.* the buying and selling of currency, stocks, commodities, etc. in different markets at the same time to profit from price differences.
— **ar·bi·trag·er** *n.*

ar·bi·trar·y (AR·buh·trair·ee) *adj.* 1 not based on reason: *an arbitrary decision.* 2 despotic: *a dictator's arbitrary powers, rule.* — **ar·bi·trar·i·ly** *adv.*

ar·bi·trate (AR·buh·trate) *v.* **-trates, -trat·ed, -trat·ing** 1 judge between disputing parties: *someone to arbitrate between the parties.* 2 settle by arbitration: *When talks failed, they arbitrated the dispute.*
— **ar·bi·tra·tion** (-TRAY·shun) *n.* the settlement of a dispute by judge or arbiter: *to go to, resort to arbitration; compulsory arbitration; The parties had to agree to binding arbitration because the dispute affected the public interest.* — **ar·bi·tra·tor** (-tray·tur) *n.*

ar·bo·re·tum (ar·buh·REE·tum) *n.* **-tums** or **-ta** a place where trees and shrubs are grown and displayed.

ar·bour or **ar·bor** (AR·bur) *n.* a shady corner formed by overhanging vegetation.

ar·bu·tus (ar·BYOO·tus) *n.* 1 a plant of the heath family with fragrant pink or white flowers and red berries. 2 the "trailing arbutus," also called "Mayflower," Nova Scotia's floral emblem.

arc *n.* anything curved like a bow, as a segment of a circle.
— *v.* **arcs, arced** or **arcked, arc·ing** or **arck·ing** form or move in an arc, as an electrical discharge across two points.

ar·cade (ar·CADE) *n.* 1 a covered passageway lined with shops. 2 an amusement centre: *a penny arcade; pinball arcade; video-game arcades; coin-operated arcade games.* 3 a series of arches with columns supporting them.

Ar·ca·di·a (ar·CAY·dee·uh) *n.* a region of quiet contentment, like a district of ancient Greece of the same name.
— **Ar·ca·di·an** *n. & adj.: Arcadian beauty, innocence, simplicity.*

ar·cane (ar·CANE) *adj.* hidden or mysterious: *arcane issues, knowledge, language, matters, references, subjects.*

arch *n.* a curved structure built over a passage, as in gateways and bridges; also, anything similar: *a triumphal arch; the twin golden arches of a fast-food chain; the superior arch of his eyebrows; the arch of the* *foot.*

— *v.* curve like an arch: *A rainbow arched over the field; with eyebrows arched in amazement.*
— *adj.* **1** saucy or roguish in a playful manner: *"Rhymes with rich," said the arch heading of the story about the rich but unpopular lady.* **2** chief: *the arch enemy, rival, villain.* — **arch·ly** *adv.*; **arch·ness** *n.*

ar·chae·ol·o·gy (ar·kee·OL·uh·jee) *n.* the study of human history as seen in fossils, tombs, artifacts, etc.
— **ar·chae·o·log·i·cal** (-uh·LOJ·uh·cul) *adj.: to dig at an archaeological site.*

ar·cha·ic (ar·CAY·ic) *adj.* of an earlier period: *the archaic language of the Bible; archaic laws, vocabulary.*

ar·cha·ism (AR·kee·iz·um) *n.* an archaic word: *"Forsooth" is an archaism for "truly."*

arch·an·gel (ARK·ain·jul) *n.* an angel of the highest order.

arch·bish·op (ARCH·bish·up) *n.* a bishop of the highest rank.

arch·bish·op·ric (arch·BISH·up·ric) *n.* an archbishop's jurisdiction or position.

arch·di·o·cese (arch·DYE·uh·sis) *n.* the diocese of an archbishop.

arch·duch·y (arch·DUCH·ee) *n.* **-duch·ies** the territory of an archduke.

arch·duke (ARCH·duke) *n.* a prince of the former royal family of Austria; *fem.* **arch·duch·ess** (arch·DUCH·is).
— **arch·du·cal** (arch·DEW·cul) *adj.*

arch·en·e·my (arch·EN·uh·mee) *n.* **-mies** chief enemy, esp. Satan.

ar·che·ol·o·gy (ar·kee·OL·uh·jee) same as ARCHAEOLOGY.

arch·er (ARCH·ur) *n.* one who uses a bow and arrows.

arch·er·y (ARCH·uh·ree) *n.* the art of shooting with a bow and arrows.

arch·fiend (arch·FEEND) *n.* chief fiend, esp. Satan.

Arch·ie Bunk·er (AR·chee·BUNK·ur) *n.* a bigot or redneck, like the character of that name in the TV sitcom "All in the Family": *the Archie Bunker mentality.*

ar·chi·e·pis·co·pal (AR·kee·i·PIS·cuh·pul) *adj.* having to do with an archbishop.

ar·chi·pel·a·go (ar·cuh·PEL·uh·go) *n.* **-gos** or **-goes** a group of islands: *the Philippine archipelago; the Canadian archipelago of the Far North.*

ar·chi·tect (AR·cuh·tect) *n.* one who designs buildings and supervises their construction.

ar·chi·tec·ton·ic (AR·cuh·tec·TON·ic) **1** *adj.* having to do with architectural principles. **2 architectonics** *n. pl.* [with sing. or pl. v.] the science of architecture; also, the design of a building.

ar·chi·tec·ture (AR·cuh·tec·chur) *n.* **1** the art or science of building: *Byzantine, Colonial, Gothic, Greek, Modern, Roman architecture.* **2** building design: *the architecture of a church.* **3** the manner in which the components of a computer system are put together.
— **ar·chi·tec·tur·al** (ar·cuh·TEC·chur·ul) *adj.: an architectural beauty, disaster, marvel.*

ar·chive (AR·kive) *n.*, usually **archives**, *pl.* **1** a historical document or public record: *The archives of the Hudson's Bay Company were moved from London to Winnipeg in 1974.* **2** a place where such materials are kept: *the Provincial Archives of Manitoba.*
— **ar·chi·val** (-kye·vul) *adj.*
— **ar·chi·vist** (AR·cuh·vist) *n.*

arch·way (ARCH·way) *n.* a passageway with an arch over it.

arc·tic or **Arc·tic** (ARC·tic, AR·tic) *adj.* **1** usually **Arctic**, having to do with **the Arctic**, the north polar region: *The **Arctic Circle**, the parallel at 66° 33' N, encloses the North Frigid Zone; the **Arctic char** (= variety of salmon); the **Arctic fox, owl**; an Arctic plant; Canada's Arctic sovereignty over the mainland and the islands of the Arctic archipelago; the Arctic winter.* **2** usually **arctic**, bitterly cold: *arctic air, weather; an arctic (= frigid) disposition.*

ar·dent (AR·dunt) *adj.* intensely devoted, enthusiastic, or zealous: *an ardent lover; his ardent desire for freedom; an ardent champion of the feminists.*
— **ar·dent·ly** *adv.*

ar·dour or **ar·dor** (AR·dur) *n.* intensity of feeling: *to cool or dampen one's ardour; his patriotic ardour; the public's ardour for the new government; the **ardours** (= passions) of youth.*

ar·du·ous (AR·joo·us) *adj.* requiring much energy and effort: *an arduous climb uphill.*

are (AR) the form of BE used with *you, we, they.*

ar·e·a (AIR·ee·uh) *n.* **1** the extent of a surface: *a vast area of desert; an area of three hectares.* **2** a specific kind of area: *a built-up area; the catchment area of a river; an economically depressed area; a desert, disaster, drainage, high-pressure, low-pressure, metropolitan area; a penalty area in soccer; a play, residential, rural, service area; the slum area of a city; a staging area for the military; a rural area; urban area.* **3** a specific portion of an area: *to close off, rope off an area; an **area rug** (covering part of a floor).* **4** a sphere of knowledge or activity: *an area of knowledge; his area of specialty.* — **ar·e·al** *adj.*

area code *n.* a usually three-digit number designating a telephone area.

ar·e·a·way (AIR·ee·uh·way) *n.* a small sunken area for light and air or for access to a basement.

a·re·na (uh·REE·nuh) *n.* **1** an enclosed area used for a show or sports activity; also, a building housing one: *a sports arena; the Winnipeg Arena* (= stadium). **2** a sphere of activity, esp. one involving struggle or competition: *in the political arena.*

arena rat *Cdn. Slang.* same as RINK RAT.

arena theatre or **theater** *n.* a theatre with the stage in the centre; "theatre-in-the-round."

aren't (ARNT) are not: *They aren't here yet; I'm a bit late, aren't I?* (Informal for *am I not?*).

ar·gent (AR·junt) *n. & adj.* [old or rare] silver.

ar·go·sy (AR·guh·see) *n.* **-sies 1** a fleet of merchant ships. **2** rich cargo.

ar·got (AR·gut, AR·goh) *n.* the private language of a particular group, esp. that of the underworld.

ar·gu·a·ble (AR·gyoo·uh·bul) *adj.* 1 questionable or doubtful: *That there is life on other planets is arguable; an arguable issue.* 2 that can be supported by reasoning: *It is arguable that life could exist on other planets.* — **ar·gu·a·bly** (-blee) *adv.*: *Einstein is arguably the greatest scientist of the twentieth century.*

ar·gue (ARG·yoo) *v.* -**gues**, -**gued**, -**gu·ing** 1 give reasons in order to persuade, attack, or defend: *People argued for and against capital punishment; We argue with our children; We argue about or over their grades; Lawyers argue cases; Some argue ably; to argue that all are equal; to argue calmly, logically, heatedly, vehemently; She argued me into buying a new house; I argued her out of selling our old car; The children have stopped arguing* (= quarrelling). 2 indicate or show: *a tough decision that argues a lot of maturity.*

ar·gu·ment (ARG·yoo·munt) *n.* 1 a giving of reasons for or against something: *a cogent, compelling, convincing, persuasive, telling, valid, weak argument; to drive home, present, press, put forward, refute an argument; his argument that the death penalty should be restored; The judge heard the closing arguments of plaintiff and defendant.* 2 dispute or quarrel: *An argument breaks out between neighbours; an argument about or over repairing a fence; to get into or have an argument with the neighbours; a bitter, heated, loud, violent argument; The police settled the argument; The rain clinched the argument about where to hold the picnic.*

ar·gu·men·ta·tion (ARG·yuh·men·TAY·shun) *n.* the process of reasoning.

ar·gu·men·ta·tive (arg·yuh·MEN·tuh·tiv) *adj.* fond of arguing or disputing.

a·ri·a (AR·ee·uh) *n.* a vocal solo with accompaniment during an opera or oratorio.

ar·id (AIR·id) *adj.* 1 dry or parched: *an arid desert.* 2 dull: *an arid discourse.* — **a·rid·i·ty** (uh·RID·uh·tee) *n.*

a·right (uh·RITE) *adv.* rightly; all right.

a·rise (uh·RIZE) *v.* **a·ris·es, a·rose, a·ris·en** (uh·RIZ·un), **a·ris·ing** 1 come to be: *If the need arises, phone for help; Superstitions arise* (= result) *from ignorance.* 2 [old use] rise: *Arise and go home.*

ar·is·toc·ra·cy (air·is·TOC·ruh·see) *n.* -**cies** 1 the nobility: *British aristocracy.* 2 an elite group or a government by the elite.

ar·is·to·crat (uh·RIS·tuh·crat) *n.* a member of an elite group. — **a·ris·to·crat·ic** (-CRAT·ic) *adj.*

a·rith·met·ic (uh·RITH·met·ic) *n.* computation with numbers, using addition, subtraction, multiplication, and division. — **ar·ith·met·ic** (air·ith·MET·ic) or **ar·ith·met·i·cal** (-tuh·cul) *adj.* — **a·rith·me·ti·cian** (uh·rith·muh·TISH·un) *n.*

-arium *n. suffix.* denoting place or relationship: *aquarium, herbarium, honorarium, sanitarium.*

ark *n.* 1 a chest or box: *The Israelites kept the two tablets containing the Ten Commandments in the **Ark of the Covenant**; The scrolls of the Torah are kept in an ark in synagogues.* 2 a huge boat like the one in which Noah and his family were preserved during the Flood.

arm *n.* 1 either of one's two upper limbs: *to cross, fold, raise, swing, wave one's arms; to twist someone's arms* (= use pressure); *She threw her arms around the child and hugged her; to stand with arms akimbo; We saw Dick walking **arm in arm*** (= with arms linked) *with Jane; She was received **with open arms*** (= warmly); *It won't cost you **an arm and a leg*** (= a lot of money) *to eat at that restaurant; to be kept at **arm's length*** (= at a distance). 2 something resembling an arm: *the arms of a chair, shirt; the tone arm or pickup of a record player; The Gulf of California is an arm of the North Pacific; The army and navy are arms* (= branches) *of the military; One should be afraid of **the long arm of the law*** (that has power to seize, control, etc.). 3 **arms** *pl.* weapons: *the right to bear arms; the call to arms when a war breaks out; to **lay down one's arms*** (= surrender); *to **present arms** in salute; **royal arms*** (= coat of arms); ***small arms*** (= guns); *soldiers kept under arms* (= armed) *at all times; They decided to **take up arms*** (= fight) *against drunken drivers; The people were **up in arms*** (= ready to fight) *over the new taxes; to accelerate, curb, step up the **arms race** between the superpowers.* — *v.* 1 equip with weapons: *an ordinance to arm the citizenry against the enemy; They armed themselves to meet the attack; Take care, he's armed and dangerous; an armed camp; an armed robbery of a bank; The terrorists were **armed to the teeth*** (= heavily armed). 2 get ready for action: *He came armed with a letter from the president; to arm a missile before firing; The alarm will go off only if armed; **armed neutrality*** (= state of readiness to fight while remaining neutral); *the **armed services** or **forces*** (= army, navy, air force, etc.).

ar·ma·da (ar·MAH·duh) *n.* 1 a fleet of warships. 2 a flotilla.

ar·ma·dil·lo (ar·muh·DIL·oh) *n.* -**los** a small burrowing animal with a protective shell of bony plates.

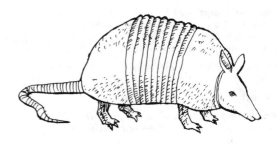

Ar·ma·ged·don (ar·muh·GED·un, "G" as in "go") *n.* the final conflict between good and evil, as foretold in the Bible.

ar·ma·ment (AR·muh·munt) *n.* 1 weapons and supplies: *armaments of war; the armaments industry.* 2 the process of arming for war.

ar·ma·ture (AR·muh·chur) *n.* **1** the rotating part of a dynamo or motor, in which current is produced. **2** a protective covering.

arm·chair (ARM·chair) *n.* a chair with armrests.
— *adj.* [used before its noun] theoretical or unrealistic: *armchair critics, generals, philosophers, strategy, theorizing, travellers.*

armed forces *n. pl.* the military, naval, and air forces of a country.

arm·ful *n.* -fuls as much as can be held in one arm or in both together.

arm·hole *n.* an opening in a garment for the wearer's arm.

ar·mi·stice (AR·muh·stis) *n.* an agreement to stop fighting, as after a war: *to agree on, declare, make, sign, suspend, violate, work out an armistice.*

arm·let (ARM·lit) *n.* a band worn on an arm around the sleeve.

arm·lock *n.* same as HAMMERLOCK.

armor same as ARMOUR.

ar·mor·i·al (ar·MOR·ee·ul) *adj.* pertaining to heraldry: *The armorial bearings* (= coat of arms) *of Canada have a sprig of maple on a silver shield and the royal arms of England, Scotland, Ireland, and France.*

armory same as ARMOURY.

ar·mour or **ar·mor** (AR·mur) *n.* **1** a usually metal protective covering, as the steel platings of ships and tanks: *a medieval soldier's suit of armour; heavy and light armour; a police officer wearing soft body armour; Bullets couldn't pierce the armour; You think a knight in shining armour will protect you; I see a **chink in his armour*** (= a weak point in an apparently strong position); *an armour-plated vehicle.* **2** armoured cars, tanks, etc.: *The city was ringed by troops, armour, and artillery.*

ar·moured or **ar·mored** (AR·murd) *adj.* **1** covered with armour: *an armoured car.* **2** equipped with armour-covered vehicles, guns, etc.: *an armoured column, corps, division.*

ar·mour·y or **ar·mor·y** (AR·muh·ree) *n.* **ar·mour·ies** or **ar·mor·ies 1** a place for making or storing arms; arsenal. **2** armouries *pl. Cdn.* a headquarters building of reserve units of the armed forces.

arm·pit *n.* the hollow under the arm where it joins the body.

arm·rest *n.* support for the arm or elbow.

arm-twisting (ARM·twist·ing) *n.* pressure to force someone to do something. — **arm-twister** *n.*

arm wrestling *n.* a trial of strength between two who sit across a table, rest their elbows on it, grip each other's hand, and try to force each other's arm down.

ar·my (AR·mee) *n.* **-mies 1** a trained and organized group, esp. military: *to command, deploy, drill, equip, field, mobilize, overrun, raise, rout an army; to join the army; to put an army to flight; a rebel, regular, standing, volunteer army; the Salvation Army; an army of workers.* **3** any similar group: *an army of ants.*

a·ro·ma (uh·ROH·muh) *n.* the penetrating and usually pleasant odour of foods, wines, spices, etc.: *aromas wafting from the kitchen; coffee with a fine aroma; a delicate, fragrant, pleasant aroma; a perfume with a woodsy aroma; the dungy aromas* (= smells) *around a zoo.*

ar·o·mat·ic (air·uh·MAT·ic) *adj.* fragrant: *an aromatic bark, tobacco.*

arose *pt.* of ARISE.

a·round (uh·ROUND) *adv. & prep.* **1** in a circle: *to drive around (the block); He measures 70 cm around (the waist); a patient who needs watching **around the clock*** (= 24 hours). **2** here and there in a place: *to browse around (in a library); Stick around (here).* **3** *Informal.* near or nearly: *a car costing around $20 000.* **4** on the other side: *He went around the corner.* **5** in the opposite way: *Turn around!*
— **be around** *Informal.* be active, seen, well-known, etc.: *She has been around for some time and is listed in the Who's Who; Is that famous singer still around?*
— **first** (or **second** etc.) **time around** on the first (or second, etc.) occasion.
— **get around** *Informal.* find time to do something: *I never got around to answering that letter.*

a·rouse (uh·ROWZE) *v.* **a·rous·es, a·roused, a·rous·ing 1** awaken: *He was aroused from sleep.* **2** evoke: *to arouse pity; behaviour that arouses suspicion.*
— **a·rous·al** *n.*

aroused *adj.* excited: *The patient gets violent when aroused; to be sexually aroused; Interest in a subject is aroused more easily by pictures than by words.*

ar·raign (uh·RAIN) *v.* call before a court to be charged: *He was arraigned on a charge of spreading malicious reports.* — **ar·raign·ment** *n.*

ar·range (uh·RAINJ) *v.* **-rang·es, -ranged, -rang·ing** set up in a certain way: *books neatly arranged on shelves; She arranged the flowers tastefully in vases; to arrange for a loan; Ask the bank manager to arrange a loan for a client; to arrange a meeting for 8 p.m.; to arrange that we should meet at 8 p.m.; He has arranged to meet with us at 8 p.m.; a composition arranged* (= adapted) *for the piano.*

ar·range·ment (uh·RANGE·munt) *n.* **1** an arranging: *to make* or *work out an arrangement for our next meeting; a meeting by special arrangement; under an arrangement with the Minister concerned; to complete the **arrangements*** (= preparations) *for us to meet in Ottawa.* **2** something arranged: *a floral, flower, seating, working arrangement.*

ar·rant (AIR·unt) *adj.* downright; utter: *What arrant nonsense!*

ar·ray (uh·RAY) *n.* **1** a splendid or imposing arrangement or display: *an army in battle array; an array of jewellery; beautiful in her bridal array; an array of facts and figures.* **2** an arrangement of elements forming a unit: *a radio antenna array; an array of solar cells.*
— *v.:* *She was arrayed* (= dressed) *like a queen; Troops array* (= position) *themselves for battle; They are arrayed against the enemy.*

ar·rears (uh·REERZ) *n. pl.* overdue debts or other

unfulfilled obligations: *arrears of rent, work; He is in arrears with* (= owing) *his rent; His rent is in arrears* (= being owed).

ar·rest (uh·REST) *v.* **1** capture and hold legally: *Police arrested the suspect; a ship arrested after an oil spill; an arresting* (= attention-capturing) *view of the lake.* **2** stop growth, development, etc.: *a drug to arrest the growth of the AIDS virus.*
— *n.* **1** legal detention: *The police make arrests saying "You are under arrest"; He was placed* or *put under arrest; He tried to resist arrest; charged the police with wrongful arrest; The arrest was made for murder; an arrest made on a murder charge; a house arrest* (= being kept under guard at home); *She made a citizen's arrest and handed over the thief to the police; to issue an arrest warrant.* **2** stoppage: *cardiac arrest; a case of respiratory arrest after receiving muscle-relaxing drugs.*

ar·ri·val (uh·RYE·vul) *n.* an arriving: *The crowd awaited the hero's arrival; arrival at the airport, in town, from abroad; the baby's arrival* (= birth); *early and late arrivals* (= people who come early and late); *adj.: the arrival lounge on the arrival level of an airport; arrival time.*

ar·rive (uh·RIVE) *v.* **ar·rives, ar·rived, ar·riv·ing** reach, esp. a place: *We arrived in London safe and sound; To arrive on time is better than arriving early or late; A baby arrives* (= is born); *We arrived at an agreement, a decision; The wedding day arrived* (= came) *at last; Votes showed that the young politician had arrived* (= attained recognition).

ar·ro·gance (AIR·uh·gunce) *n.* a haughty manner or attitude: *the arrogance of power; his insufferable arrogance; the arrogance of the newly rich; He had the arrogance to ask for a 50% raise.*

ar·ro·gant (AIR·uh·gunt) *adj.* excessively or unpleasantly sure of oneself: *He's arrogant towards the poor; an arrogant demand.* — **ar·ro·gant·ly** *adv.*

ar·ro·gate (AIR·uh·gate) *v.* **-gates, -gat·ed, -gat·ing** take or claim without right: *He arrogated too much authority to himself.* — **ar·ro·ga·tion** (-GAY·shun) *n.*

ar·row (AIR·oh) *n.* **1** slender, pointed shaft used as a missile shot from a bow: *straight as an arrow; a poisoned arrow; a spent arrow.* **2** an arrowlike figure [♦] used to point, as on a sign or a map.

ar·row·head (AIR·oh·hed) *n.* the pointed tip of an arrow.

arse (ARS) same as ASS (buttocks).

ar·se·nal (AR·suh·nul) *n.* a place where arms and ammunition are made or stored: *The dictionary is an arsenal* (= storehouse) *of words.*

ar·sen·ic (AR·suh·nic) *n.* a poisonous chemical element used in insecticides, weed-killers, etc.

ar·son (AR·sun) *n.* the wrongful burning of property: *to commit arson; Arson is suspected in the fire.*

ar·son·ist (AR·suh·nist) *n.* one who commits arson.

art *n.* **1** the creation or expression of beauty: *works of art such as paintings and sculptures; the fine arts of painting and sculpture; abstract, commercial, folk, modern, pop, primitive art.* **2** skilled activity: *to practise*

the art of writing; the occult art; the applied, graphic, industrial, language, liberal, martial, performing, plastic arts; There's an art to it (= a knack of doing it). **3** usually **arts** *pl.* the humanities, as distinguished from science: *a Bachelor of Arts.* **4** artfulness or cunning; also, tricks: *His wily arts didn't fool her.*
— *v.* [old use] the form of BE used with "thou."

art bank *n.* a collection of paintings, hangings, sculptures, etc., as the one maintained by the Canada Council.

ar·te·fact same as ARTIFACT.

ar·te·ri·al (ar·TEER·ee·ul) *adj.* of or like an artery: *arterial blood, railways, roads.*
— *n.* a through street or expressway.

ar·ter·y (AR·tuh·ree) *n.* **-ter·ies 1** any of the tubular vessels that carry blood from the heart to every part of the body: *a blocked* or *occluded coronary artery; ruptured artery; hardening of the arteries due to cholesterol buildup.* **2** a main route of transportation or communication: *a major artery; traffic artery.*

art·ful *adj.* **1** showing art or skill. **2** crafty; cunning: *an artful guy; an artful blend of truth and falsehood.*
— **art·ful·ly** *adv.;* **art·ful·ness** *n.*

art gallery *n.* **1** a permanent exhibition of paintings and other works of art, less comprehensive than an **art museum** which may also contain displays of science, history, etc. **2** a private establishment for the marketing of art.

ar·thrit·ic (ar·THRIT·ic, "TH" as in "thin") *adj.* having to do with arthritis.— *n.* an arthritic patient.

ar·thri·tis (ar·THRYE·tis) *n.* inflammation of the body joints.

ar·ti·cle (AR·tuh·cul) *n.* **1** a particular thing, item, or object: *an article of clothing, food, furniture; secondhand articles; toilet articles like soap and cologne; the genuine article* (= real thing); *Little Lee is quite an article (Informal for quite cute or clever).* **2** a section or clause of a document: *the articles of a constitution; an article of faith* (= a basic belief); *They filed "articles of association"* (= bylaws) *governing the day-to-day running of the company.* **3** a nonfiction essay or story: *a magazine article.* **4** same as DEFINITE ARTICLE or INDEFINITE ARTICLE.
— *v.* **-cles, -cled, -cling** *Cdn.* bind by a contract or serve as a law apprentice, accounting student, etc.: *She was articled to the firm of Smith & Smith; She articled with Smith & Smith; She articled in Regina; an articled clerk; an articling law student.*

ar·tic·u·lar (ar·TIK·yuh·lur) *adj.* having to do with body joints: *articular cartilages, membranes.*

ar·tic·u·late (ar·TIK·yuh·lit) *adj.* **1** of speech, clear and distinct. **2** of a person, able to express thoughts clearly: *So excited, he was barely articulate.*
— *v.* (ar·TIK·yuh·late) **-lates, -lat·ed, -lat·ing** express or speak distinctly.
— **articulated** joined together: *An articulated bus is preferred to a double-decker; articulated railway cars.*
— **ar·tic·u·late·ly** (-lit·lee) *adv.*
— **ar·tic·u·la·tion** (-LAY·shun) *n.*

ar·ti·fact (AR·tuh·fact) *n.* a product of human hands, esp. an item of archaeological interest: *Bits of charcoal, stone tools, and other artifacts 16 000 years old were found at the dig; the artifacts recovered from the Titanic; The book is a mere literary artifact with no artistic value.*

ar·ti·fice (AR·tuh·fis) *n.* 1 skill used to trick or deceive: *Some sales people are masters of artifice.* 2 an inventive trick or expedient: *the various artifices used in displaying merchandise.*

ar·ti·fic·er (ar·TIF·uh·sur) *n.* a skilled worker.

ar·ti·fi·cial (ar·tuh·FISH·ul) *adj.* 1 made by human skill, not natural: *an artificial gene, limb, lung, sweetener; artificial blood, light, silk; an artificial (earth) satellite; artificial insemination (of a female); artificial intelligence (programmed into a computer); artificial respiration (by mechanical or manual methods).* 2 affected, not natural: *an artificial smile.* — **ar·ti·fi·cial·ly** (-uh·lee) *adv.* — **ar·ti·fi·ci·al·i·ty** (AR·tuh·fish·ee·AL·uh·tee) *n.*

ar·til·ler·y (ar·TIL·uh·ree) *n.* 1 mounted guns of large calibre: *field artillery; heavy artillery.* 2 a branch of an army equipped with such guns.

artily, artiness See ARTY.

ar·ti·san (AR·tuh·zun, -zan) *n.* a manually skilled worker, as a tailor or carpenter.

ar·tist *n.* 1 one who practises a fine art, as a painter or sculptor: *a gifted, struggling, talented artist; a sidewalk artist.* 2 one who practises a skilled activity, sometimes of a shady nature: *a con artist; escape artist; makeup artist; ripoff artist; software artist (= hacker); trapeze artist.* — **ar·tis·tic** (ar·TIS·tic) *adj.* — **ar·tis·ti·cal·ly** *adv.*

ar·tiste (ar·TEEST) *n.* a professional entertainer, esp. a singer, actor, or dancer.

art·ist·ry (AR·tis·tree) *n.* artistic skill or quality: *the brilliant artistry of a fireworks display.*

art·less *adj.* 1 free from cunning: *a child's artless questions.* 2 natural, not artificial: *the artless grace of the gazelle.* 3 lacking artistry: *an artless contraption.* — **art·less·ly** *adv.;* **art·less·ness** *n.*

art museum See ART GALLERY.

art·work *n.* 1 the work of a painter, sculptor, etc.: *Inuit artwork on display.* 2 the graphic portions of a printed text. 3 typeset and graphic matter assembled for printing.

art·y (AR·tee) *adj.* **art·i·er, -i·est** *Informal.* artistic in a showy or pretentious way. — **art·i·ly** *adv.;* **art·i·ness** *n.*

Ar·y·an (AIR·ee·un) *n.* 1 a member of a prehistoric people from whom most of the peoples of Europe, India, and Iran are descended; also, their family of languages. 2 [in racist use] white Caucasian, often non-Jewish.

as (AZ) *adv.* 1 in or to the same degree: *See that oak – our flagpole has to be as tall.* 2 for instance: *felines, as lions and leopards.* — **conj.** 1 in the same way as: *tall as an oak; He did as promised; The papers report everything as it happens.* 2 while: *He wept as he told the story.* 3 because: *He stopped work as he was tired.* 4 though: *Tall as John is,*

he's shorter than Jim. 5 with the result that: *I wasn't so worried as to lose sleep over it.*
— **prep.** 1 in the character or position of someone: *Speaking as a lawyer, I am against it.* 2 like: *cool as a cucumber.*
— **as ... as** [indicating sameness]: *He's as busy as a bee; as far as the North Pole; She's as good as gold; I'll be as happy as a lark.*
— **as far as** *Informal.* as for: *As far as getting a gold medal, I believe she will.*
— **as for** [used in the beginning of a sentence or clause] as regards: *As for me, I don't like going to work on Sunday.*
— **as from** as of: *You are hired as from Monday.*
— **as if** or **as though**: *It looks as though it might rain* (= as it usually looks if it is going to rain).
— **as is** unchanged: *a scratched chair sold as is at a reduced price.*
— **as of** [indicating starting time]: *As of now, there are 30 of us; As of last week he was all right.*
— **as to** as regards: *As to me, I don't like going to work on Sunday; My pal is indifferent as to* (= about) *when he is asked to work.*

as·cend (uh·SEND) *v.* go higher up: *to ascend a mountain, river; mist ascending from a valley; the ascending part of the aorta, colon, etc.; ascending tones in music.* — **ascend the throne** become king or queen.

as·cend·an·cy (uh·SEN·dun·see) *n.* dominance: *to attain* or *gain ascendancy over a rival.* Also **as·cend·en·cy.**

as·cen·dant (uh·SEN·dunt) *adj.* rising in influence or power: *His star is in the ascendant.* Also **as·cen·dent.**

as·cend·er (uh·SEN·dur) *n.* one that ascends, as the part of an "l" or "f" that is above the body of the letter.

as·cen·sion (uh·SEN·shun) *n.* the act of ascending: *Christ's Ascension* (= the Christian belief of Christ's going bodily into Heaven); *one's ascension to power, the presidency, stardom, the throne.*

as·cent (uh·SENT) *n.* a climbing upward: *their victorious ascent of Everest; They made the ascent in many stages; The first part was a gradual, not a steep ascent* (= way going up); *their slow ascent* (= climb) *uphill; an ascent* (= slope) *of 15 degrees; the theory of the ascent* (= rise) *of man from the apes.*

as·cer·tain (as·ur·TAIN) *v.* find out with certainty: *to ascertain the truth, the facts of a story; to ascertain that he is still alive.* — **as·cer·tain·a·ble** (-TAY·nuh·bul) *adj.*

as·cet·ic (uh·SET·ic) *adj.* self-denying in regard to life's comforts, esp. with a religous motive. Also **as·cet·i·cal** (-uh·cul).
— **n.** one who leads an ascetic life: *an ascetic's regimen of life; an ascetic who fasts on Fridays.*
— **as·cet·i·cism** *n.*

as·cribe (uh·SCRIBE) *v.* **-cribes, -cribed, -crib·ing** attribute a cause or quality to something as typical of it: *an artifact ascribed to the Stone Age; Many errors can be ascribed to ignorance; He ascribes his successes to luck.* — **as·crip·tion** *n.*

a·sex·u·al (ay·SEK·shoo·ul) *adj.* without sexual activity; sexless: *Budding and cell division are forms of asexual reproduction.*

ash *n.* **1** a tree with compound leaves and tough wood; also, the wood. **2** the soft, grey, powdery substance left after burning: *The place was covered with volcanic ash; dust, ash, and cinders; soda ash* (= sodium carbonate). **3 ashes** *pl.: The wood was burned to ashes; to rake the ashes after a fire; a town reduced to ashes; the ashes of a cremated person; to spread the ashes to the winds; A phoenix is believed to rise from its ashes.*

a·shamed (uh·SHAMED) *adj.* [used after its noun] feeling shame: *He's ashamed to go on welfare; ashamed that he can't find a job; thoroughly ashamed of himself.*

ash can *n.* a can for trash; also, a garbage can.

ash·en (ASH.un) *adj.* **1** pale like the colour of ashes: *Her face was ashen with fear.* **2** made of ash wood.

a·shore (uh·SHORE) *adv. & adj.* [used after its noun or verb] to or on the shore: *The refugees were put* or set *ashore by an unknown ship; They went ashore without being caught; came ashore yesterday; They are now ashore in RCMP custody.*

ash·tray *n.* a small dish for tobacco ash, cigar butts, etc.

ash·y *adj.* **ash·i·er, -i·est** like ashes: *an ashy deposit.*

A·sian (AY.zhun, -shun) *adj.* having to do with Asia: *Asian affairs; the Asian flu; the Asian Games; an Asian-American immigrant.*
— *n.* a person of or from Asia: *the **Central Asians** of Tibet, Mongolia, and Sinkiang (China); **North Asians** of the U.S.S.R., from the Urals to the Pacific; **Southwest Asians** of Afghanistan, the Arabian Peninsula, Cyprus, Iran, Iraq, Jordan, Lebanon, Sinai, Syria, and Turkey.* See also EAST ASIAN, SOUTH ASIAN, SOUTHEAST ASIAN.

A·si·at·ic (ay·shee·AT·ic) *n. & adj.* [old use, now derogatory in reference to persons] same as ASIAN: *the asiatic elephant.*

a·side (uh·SIDE) *adv.* [used after its verb] to one side: *to push, put, shove, take a person or thing aside; to stand aside; The high court set aside* (= rejected) *the lower court's decision; Joking aside* (= apart), *I remain firm in my view; Only adults were present, **aside from** (= except for) a few infants.*
— *n.* **1** an actor's words that other actors are not supposed to hear. **2** digression: *He told the story as an aside to the class.*

as·i·nine (AS·uh·nine) *adj.* utterly stupid: *a silly and asinine excuse; an asinine joke, policy; asinine behaviour.* **— as·i·nin·i·ty** (-NIN·uh·tee) *n.*

ask *v.* **1** call for an answer: *to ask a question; She asked him point-blank how old he was; Ask me another!* (*Informal for* I don't know the answer). **2** request: *She asked him his name; He asked her to wait; He asked his friend for a loan; asked a favour of his friend; She asked to be excused; He asked that the matter be kept secret; Guests normally ask leave of their hosts; We ask advice of friends; He asked help from his buddy; He asked for help; She asked for* or *asked to see the boss; He was asking too much* or *asking for the moon; Please ask* (= invite) *him in; He was hoping she would ask him out* (= ask for a date); *She never asked him back* (= invited him in return); *You asked for it* (*Informal for* provoked it); *He was asking for* (= inviting) *trouble; A free sample is yours **for the asking*** (*Informal for* You can get it merely by asking); *the **asking price** (= maximum price desired by a seller).* **3** inquire: *Jim asks after you; He asks about your health; We had to ask our way around the town.*

a·skance (uh·SKANCE) *adv.: He looked askance* (= with disapproval or suspicion) *at my suggestion.*

a·skew (uh·SKEW) *adj. & adv.* [used after its noun or verb] **1** leaning to one side: *Your hat is a bit askew; a picture hung askew on the wall.* **2** amiss: *when things go askew.*

a·sleep (uh·SLEEP) *adj. & adv.* [used after its noun or verb] in or into a state of sleep: *He fell asleep at his desk; He's fast asleep; sound asleep; My foot is asleep* (= numb).
— asleep at the switch *Informal.* negligent in one's duty; not vigilant.

asp *n.* a small venomous snake.

as·par·tame (AS·pur·tame) *n.* a low-calorie sugar substitute.

as·pect (AS·pect) *n.* appearance, as from one point of view: *to study a question in all its aspects; a house with a southern aspect* (= exposure); *a man of solemn aspect* (= look or mien); *a frightening, grim, humorous aspect.*
— as·pec·tu·al (as·PECK·choo·ul) *adj.*

as·pen (AS·pun) *n.* a poplar with leaves that flutter in the slightest wind: *the quaking aspen.*

as·per·i·ty (as·PER·uh·tee) *n.* **-ties** harshness or roughness of a tone, temper, weather, surface; also, an instance of it: *the asperities of life in the Arctic.*

as·perse (uh·SPURCE) *v.* **-pers·es, -persed, -pers·ing** slander: *He was aspersed with damaging allegations.*

as·per·sions (as·PUR·shun) *n.* slanderous remark: *The story cast aspersions on his good name.*

as·phalt (AS·fault) *n.* a mixture of sand or gravel with a brownish black bituminous substance that is used in paving streets.
— *v.* pave with asphalt: *to asphalt a street.*

asphalt jungle *n.* a crowded city viewed as a place hard to survive in.

as·phyx·i·ate (as·FIX·ee·ate) *v.* **-ates, -at·ed, -at·ing** suffocate or be suffocated by carbon monoxide poisoning, electric shock, strangulation, etc.
— as·phyx·i·a·tion (-ee·AY·shun) *n.*

as·pic (AS·pic) *n.* **1** a jelly made with fish or meat stock. **2** [old use] asp.

as·pi·rant (AS·puh·runt) *n.* one who aspires: *an aspirant to the ministry; aspirants for a position.*

as·pi·rate (AS·puh·rate) *v.* **-rates, -rat·ed, -rat·ing 1** utter with an "h" sound: *He has a tendency to aspirate his "it" into "hit."* **2** draw in, as by suction: *Liquid aspirated down the windpipe could cause suffocation.* — *adj.* (-rit) aspirated: *The "h" is not aspirate in "honour" and "hour."*

as·pi·ra·tion (as·puh·RAY·shun) *n.* **1** desire to attain a goal or an instance of it: *lofty, noble aspirations; a subject people's aspirations to independence; Priesthood was one of his early aspirations.* **2** the pronouncing of an "h" sound as in "hit." **3** a drawing in, out, up, etc. by suction, as into the lungs or windpipe: *The mucus was removed from the patient's windpipe by aspiration.*

as·pire (uh·SPIRE) *v.* **-pires, -pired, -pir·ing** have a desire to attain a goal: *to aspire after fame, knowledge; He aspires to become a doctor; She aspires to the highest office of the land.*

as·pir·in (AS·pur·in) *n.* a white crystalline drug for relieving pain and fever; also, a tablet of it: *The doctor told me to take two aspirin(s) and call him in the morning; Use buffered aspirin to protect your stomach; an aspirin tablet.* — **Aspirin** *Trademark.*

ass *n.* **1** a braying animal related to the horse but smaller; donkey. **2** stupid person: *Don't make an ass of yourself; a pompous ass; "The law is an ass"* (= The law needs to be changed). **3** [slang use, sometimes vulgar] the buttocks: *Get off your ass; He's a pain in the ass; She's up to her ass in work.*

as·sail (uh·SAIL) *v.* attack violently, as with repeated blows: *Relentless winds assailed the coast; He was assailed bitterly by his foes; assailed with doubts, insults, questions.* — **as·sail·ant** (-unt) *n.*

as·sas·sin (uh·SAS·in) *n.* a murderer of a prominent person, esp. a hired killer.

as·sas·si·nate (uh·SAS·uh·nate) *v.* **-nates, -nat·ed, -nat·ing** kill as an assassin. — **as·sas·si·na·tion** (-NAY·shun) *n.*: *political assassinations; an assassination carried out by a hired killer; character assassination (by slander).*

as·sault (uh·SAULT) *n.* **1** an attack, esp. a violent and sudden one: *They carried out, led, made an assault against the fortress; an assault on enemy positions; The fortress was taken by assault; an all-out, armed, military assault; the final assault on Mount Everest; She considers rock music an assault on her ears.* **2** [legal use] a physical threat: *If you strike at someone and miss, that constitutes only assault; If you hit, you commit* **assault and battery** (= threat with actual use of force). **3** [legal use] an attack: *aggravated assault such as assault with a deadly weapon; He was charged with attempted rape and indecent assault; sexual assault* (= rape). — *adj.*: *assault troops; an assault weapon.* — *v.* attack: *He was assaulted in the street.* — **as·sault·er** *n.*

as·say (AS·ay, as·AY) *n.* a test or analysis of a precious metal, ore, drug, etc. to determine quality or composition: *a biological assay or bio-assay.* — *v.* **1** analyse or test: *a theme that she assays in her novels.* **2** attempt or try: *Many have assayed to conquer Everest.*

as·sem·ble (uh·SEM·bul) *v.* **-bles, -bled, -bling 1** gather together: *The principal addressed the assembled staff.* **2** put together: *to assemble automobiles.*

as·sem·bler (uh·SEM·blur) *n.* **1** one that assembles. **2** a computer program for automatically converting assembly-language instructions into machine language. **3** an assembly language.

as·sem·bly (uh·SEM·blee) *n.* **-blies 1** an assembling: *the daily assembly before school begins; Our Charter of Rights guarantees freedom of peaceful assembly; an unlawful assembly of picketers; the Assembly of First Nations* (= national organization of Native Canadians); *a gear assembly (of transmission parts).* **2** a legislative body: *to convene an assembly; a legislative assembly; Quebec's National Assembly; the U.N. General Assembly.*

assembly language *n.* a programming language in which several elementary operations are grouped together in each command, the commands being directly convertible to machine language.

assembly line *n.* a factory system in which each worker does a specific operation in assembling a product: *He spends all day on an assembly line.*

as·sem·bly·man (uh·SEM·blee·mun) *n.* **-men** a member of a legislative body: *In Prince Edward Island, a councillor and an assemblyman are elected from each of 16 electoral districts.*

as·sent (uh·SENT) *v.* express acceptance or adherence: *to assent to an opinion, proposal.* — *n.* agreement: *a nod of assent; They withheld their assent to the proposal; A bill is given royal assent* (= acceptance) *after passage through both houses.*

as·sert (uh·SURT) *v.* claim or say forcefully: *He asserted his innocence; asserted that he was innocent.* — **assert oneself** insist on one's rights.

as·ser·tion (uh·SUR·shun) *n.* an asserting: *to make a bold, sweeping, unfounded assertion against someone; to deny, refute an assertion; her assertion of innocence; her assertion that she is innocent.*

as·ser·tive (uh·SUR·tiv) *adj.* that asserts oneself or itself: *an assertive young woman; an assertive check design.* — **as·ser·tive·ly** *adv.*; **as·ser·tive·ness** *n.*

assertiveness training *n.* training to help one act with self-confidence and get positive results.

as·sess (uh·SES) *v.* **1** determine a payment as damages, a fine, levy, or tax or impose it: *Each member was assessed $300 as fee.* **2** estimate property, income, etc. for taxation: *properties assessed at $50 000 and up.* **3** evaluate: *to assess the merit of a thesis; to assess a situation.* — **as·sess·ment** *n.* — **as·ses·sor** (-ur) *n.*

as·set (AS·et) *n.* **1** a person or thing that is considered valuable or useful: *Experience is a valuable asset in a job applicant; She is an asset to the firm; a valuable asset.* **2 assets** *pl.* property that may be used to pay one's debts, as cash, merchandise, accounts receivable, real estate, securities, trademarks, and good will: *to realize, unfreeze assets; current, family, financial, frozen,* *hidden, intangible, liquid, personal assets.*

as·sid·u·ous (uh·SIJ·oo·us) *adj.* diligent and unremitting in one's effort: *She was assiduous in her efforts to get top marks; studied with assiduous application; a most assiduous critic.* — **as·sid·u·ous·ly** *adv.* — **as·si·du·i·ty** (as·uh·DEW·uh·tee) *n.*

as·sign (uh·SINE) *v.* **1** give out as someone's share: *A teacher assigns work; He assigned us an easy task.* **2** appoint to a post or duty: *A reporter is assigned to a story.* **3** name or specify: *to assign an hour for a ceremony; to assign a motive for a murder; to assign* (= ascribe) *an artifact to a certain culture.* **4** [legal use] transfer ownership: *to assign a book's copyright.* — *n.* same as ASSIGNEE. — **as·sign·a·ble** *adj.* — **as·sign·er** or **as·sign·or** *n.*

as·sign·ee (uh·sye·NEE) *n.* one to whom an ownership or right is legally assigned.

as·sign·ment (uh·SINE·munt) *n.* **1** task or duty assigned: *The teacher gave us a math assignment* (= homework); *That was one tough assignment she handed out; Most of us did the assignment; Some were late to hand in the assignment.* **2** task or mission: *a reporter sent on a special assignment; He was on **assignment** in Mexico for a month; an assignment to report on the earthquake; He carried out his assignment brilliantly; a dangerous, difficult, easy, overseas, rough, tough assignment; an assignment* (= appointment) *to a foreign embassy.* **3** an act of assigning, esp. a transfer of ownership.

as·sim·i·late (uh·SIM·uh·late) *v.* **-lates, -lat·ed, -lat·ing** **1** take something in and make it similar to itself: *The body assimilates food by digestion; The mind assimilates* (= absorbs) *knowledge.* **2** make or become similar to something: *The "p" sound in "cupboard"* (CUB·urd) *is assimilated to "b"; Canada has assimilated millions of people from all over the world; New Canadians try to assimilate into* or *to a community; They assimilate with the rest of the population.* — **as·sim·i·la·tion** (-LAY·shun) *n.*

as·sist (uh·SIST) *v. Formal.* to help; aid: *to assist at an operation, in taking pictures, with the staging of a play.* — *n.* in a game, an instance of helping a teammate, as to make a putout or score a goal: *She made three baskets and two assists during the game; He could get out the car only with an assist* (*Informal* for a helping hand) *from his wife.* — **as·sis·tance** (-tunce) *n.: to give, offer, provide, render assistance to someone; clerical assistance; Phone 411 for directory assistance; She was of great assistance to us during the emergency; considerable, economic, financial, legal, material, technical assistance.*

as·sis·tant (uh·SIS·tunt) *n.* one who helps: *a marketing assistant; office assistants; research assistants; teaching assistants; an assistant to the president; adj.: an assistant manager, professor.*

as·size (uh·SIZE) *n.* **1** an inquest by judge and jury. **2** assizes *pl.* periodic sessions of a law court: *at the current assizes of the Ontario Supreme Court in Guelph; the Summer Assizes of the Manitoba Court of Queen's Bench.*

as·so·ci·ate (uh·SOH·shee·ate, -see·ate) *v.* **-ates, -at·ed, -at·ing** **1** join or be connected: *Jones and Smith are associated in a law firm; to associate with bad characters; The Associated Press is an association of newspapers.* **2** to link in the mind: *Children associate birthdays with gifts.* — *n.* (also -shee·it, -see·it) companion or colleague. — *adj.* associated in function, but not fully in regard to privileges and responsibilites: *an associate editor, judge, member; An **associate professor** ranks below a full professor but above an assistant professor; Some colleges award an **associate degree** after two years of study.*

as·so·ci·a·tion (uh·SOH·see·AY·shun) *n.* **1** the act of associating: *articles of association* (= incorporation); *the association* (= linking) *of ideas in the mind.* **2** connection: *He has ended his association with that company; He has started a new business in close association with his brothers.* **3** a group or union: *to form an association; The Commonwealth of Nations is a free association of countries with British connections; a bar association* (= lawyers' association); *an association of Ontario farmers.*

as·so·ci·a·tive (uh·SOH·see·ay·tiv, -see·uh·tiv) *adj.* **1** depending on association: *an associative idea, image; associative learning by the linking of ideas.* **2** in mathematics, not dependent on order of grouping: *Addition and multiplication are associative operations.*

as·sort·ed (uh·SOR·tid) *adj.* of various kinds; miscellaneous: *a box of assorted candies, greeting cards; cats, dogs, and assorted other pets; an **ill-assorted*** (= badly matched) *pair.* — **as·sort·ment** *n.: We carry a wide assortment of greeting cards.*

as·suage (uh·SWAGE) *v.* **as·suag·es, as·suaged, as·suag·ing** lessen or pacify feelings, desires, etc. that need satisfaction: *to assuage one's fears.*

as·sume (uh·SUME – "YOO" or "OO") *v.* **as·sumes, as·sumed, as·sum·ing** **1** suppose: *Let's assume there's life on Mars; Never assume too much when dealing with a stranger; Everyone is **assumed** to be innocent until proven guilty.* **2** take a responsibility, right, etc. as one's own: *to assume the role of a mediator; The junta assumed dictatorial powers; a very **assuming*** (= presumptuous) *young man.* **3** take on: *She assumes her new duties on Monday; The problem assumed awesome proportions; to assume* (= put on) *an air of indifference.*

as·sump·tion (uh·SUM·shun) *n.* **1** an assuming or something assumed: *He made an assumption that proved to be erroneous; a false assumption; not a reasonable, safe, or valid assumption; an assumption about something he had no proof of; an assumption of guilt; He proceeded on the assumption that the money had been stolen.* **2** a taking up: *No date has been set for the assumption of office by the new mayor; the **Assumption*** (= taking up into Heaven of the Virgin Mary).

as·sur·ance (uh·SHOOR·unce) *n.* an assuring or being assured: *He spoke with assurance* (= confidence); *He had given us every assurance that we would get the contract; He gave us assurances* (= promises) *of a quick decision; assurances that the decision would be made before the end of the week.*

as·sure (uh·SHOOR) *v.* **as·sures, as·sured, as·sur·ing**
make someone certain of something; guarantee: *The car is quite safe, I can assure you; I can assure you of its roadworthiness.*

assured (uh·SHOORD) *adj.* sure or secure: *Her future is assured, thanks to the inheritance; There is an assured demand for newer and better computers; The "mutual assured destruction" (MAD) of the superpowers in case of a nuclear war acts as a deterrent; Rest assured* (= confident) *your child will recover.*
— *n.* a person in whose favour an insurance policy is issued; an insured.
— **as·sur·ed·ly** (uh·SHOOR·id·lee) *adv.*
— **as·sur·ed·ness** *n.*

as·ter·isk (AS·tuh·risk) *n.* a star-shaped figure (*) used as a reference mark; *adj.: an asterisked* (= indicated by asterisk) *footnote.*

a·stern (uh·STURN) *adj. & adv.* [used after its noun or verb] at or toward the rear of a ship; behind: *The boat came up astern of the ship.*

as·ter·oid (AS·tuh·roid) *n.* any of the many small planets orbiting around the sun between Mars and Jupiter.

asth·ma (AZ·muh) *n.* a chest disease marked by coughing, wheezing, and other breathing difficulties.

asth·mat·ic (az·MAT·ic) *n.* an asthma patient; *adj.: an asthmatic attack.*

a·stig·ma·tism (uh·STIG·muh·tiz·um) *n.* a focussing defect in a lens, esp. of the eye, which results in blurred vision. — **as·tig·mat·ic** (as·tig·MAT·ic) *n. & adj.*

a·stir (uh·STUR) *adj. & adv.* [used after its noun or verb] 1 in an excited state: *a town astir with the news of victory.* 2 out of bed; awake.

as·ton·ish (uh·STON·ish) *v.* surprise so greatly as to seem unbelievable: *I was astonished to hear of your successes; I am astonished at your behaviour; I am astonished that you can do such things; Your acrobatic feats astonish me; an astonished spectator.*
— **astonishing** *adj.: The acrobat can perform some really astonishing feats; They are astonishing to watch.*
— **as·ton·ish·ing·ly** *adv.*
— **as·ton·ish·ment** *n.: To our astonishment, she succeeded in every one of them; Everyone stared in astonishment at her performance; They expressed astonishment at her skills.*

as·tound (uh·STOWND) *v.* strike with sudden surprise: *We were astounded at or by the news; astounded that such a thing could happen.*
— **astounding** *adj.: It was astounding to hear that she had broken the previous record; an astounding feat.*
— **as·tound·ing·ly** *adv.*

a·strad·dle (uh·STRAD·ul) *adv.* [used after its verb] astride: *She rides astraddle.*
— *prep.: seated astraddle her horse.*

as·tral (AS·trul) *adj.* pertaining to the stars; stellar: *astral influences.*

a·stray (uh·STRAY) *adj. & adv.* [used after its noun or verb] away from the right course: *How did he go astray? He was led astray by bad companions.*

a·stride (uh·STRIDE) *adj. & adv.* with legs on either side: *She likes to ride her horse astride; Astride riding seems safer.*
— *prep.: He came sliding down astride a banister; The city grew astride* (= on both sides of) *the river.*

as·trin·gent (uh·STRIN·junt) *adj.* tending to contract blood vessels, tissues, etc.
— *n.* an astringent substance: *Shaving lotions contain astringents.*

as·trol·o·gy (uh·STROL·uh·jee) *n.* the study of the influence of stars on human affairs. — **as·trol·o·ger** *n.* — **as·tro·log·i·cal** (as·truh·LOJ·uh·cul) *adj.*

as·tro·naut (AS·truh·nawt) *n.* a person trained for space flights. — **as·tro·naut·ic** (-NAW·tic) or **as·tro·naut·i·cal** (-tuh·cul) *adj.*

astronautics *n. pl.* [takes sing. v.] the science of making and operating spacecraft.

as·tro·nom·i·cal (as·truh·NOM·uh·cul) *adj.* 1 having to do with astronomy. 2 extraordinarily large: *an astronomical price, sum.*

as·tron·o·my (uh·STRON·uh·mee) *n.* -mies the science of heavenly bodies. — **as·tron·o·mer** *n.*

as·tute (uh·STUTE, "YOO" or "OO") *adj.* shrewd and sagacious, esp. in aiming for advantage: *an astute lawyer, politician, remark; She is very astute at persuading people.* — **as·tute·ly** *adv.;* **as·tute·ness** *n.*

a·sun·der (uh·SUN·dur) *adv.* [used after its verb] separated into parts: *families torn asunder by war; driven, forced, rent asunder.*

a·sy·lum (uh·SYE·lum) *n.* 1 protection or sanctuary: *Refugees seek political asylum; Asylum is not denied in genuine cases; Most receive* or *are granted asylum.* 2 [former use] refuge or hospital: *lunatic asylum; mental asylum.*

at *prep.* [indicating] 1 position in time, place, etc.: *I met her at noon; I'll see you at school.* 2 direction, movement, rate, degree, etc.: *Aim at the target; to drive at top speed; men at work; nations at war; He's at it* (Informal for busy with it) *again.* 3 manner, condition, state, etc.: *a body at rest; goods sold at auction; We're happy at his victory.*

ate *pt.* of EAT.

A-tent *n.* an A-shaped tent with no vertical wall.

a·the·ism (AY·thee·iz·um, "th" as in "thin") *n.* the denial of God's existence. — **a·the·ist** *n.*
— **a·the·is·tic** (-IS·tic) or **a·the·is·ti·cal** (-IS·tuh·cul) *adj.*

ath·e·ne·um or **ath·e·nae·um** (ath·uh·NEE·um, "th" as in "thin") *n.* 1 an institution of learning. 2 a literary or scientific club.

a·thirst (uh·THIRST) *adj.* [used after its noun] longing: *athirst for adventure, freedom, glory, news.*

ath·lete (ATH·leet, "TH" as in "thin") *n.* one trained to compete in athletics: *an all-round, amateur, world-class athlete; professional athletes.*

ath·let·ic (ath·LET·ic) 1 athletics *n. pl.* [takes sing. v.] physical exercises, sports, and games: *intercollegiate athletics.* 2 *adj.* having to do with athletics: *an athletic event; a man of athletic build; his athletic prowess; An athletic support* (= elastic belt and pouch for the genitals) *is worn by men during athletics.*

at home (at·HOME) *n.* a reception held at one's home.
— **at-home** *adj.*: *at-home entertaining, parties; an at-home dress (suitable for home wear).*

-athon *combining form.* an activity that is like a marathon in duration: *bikeathon, skiathon, telethon, walkathon, workathon.*

at·i·gi (AT·uh·ghee) *n. Cdn.* a hooded fur jacket or parka used in the North.

At·lan·tic (at·LAN·tic) *adj.* having to do with the **Atlantic Ocean** lying between the Americas in the west and Europe and Africa in the east: *the **Atlantic Provinces** of Newfoundland, Prince Edward Island, Nova Scotia, and New Brunswick.*

at·las (AT·lus) *n.* a book of maps.

at·mos·phere (AT·mus·feer) *n.* **1** the air surrounding the Earth or a similar gaseous envelope around any heavenly body: *a polluted atmosphere; rarified atmosphere; the upper atmosphere.* **2** the environment of any place: *We met in a friendly atmosphere; a formal, informal, relaxed, stifling, tense atmosphere; This restaurant is crowded, but it has real atmosphere* (= a distinctive ambience).

at·mos·pher·ic (at·mus·FEER·ic, -FER·ic) **1** *adj.* of the atmosphere: *an atmospheric disturbance; atmospheric pressure.* **2 atmospherics** *n.pl.* disturbances caused in radio reception by natural phenomena, as during a storm.

at·oll (AT·ol) *n.* a ring of coral reefs and islands enclosing a lagoon.

at·om (AT·um) *n.* **1** the smallest particle of an element that may be involved in chemical reactions: *the splitting of the atom; to harness **the atom*** (= atomic energy). **2** a tiny bit; jot: *There's not an atom of truth in what he says.*

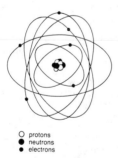

○ protons
● neutrons
• electrons

atom bomb *n.* a very destructive weapon that uses the energy, or **atomic energy**, released by the splitting of atomic nuclei. Also **atomic bomb.**

a·tom·ic (uh·TOM·ic) *adj.* having to do with atomic energy; nuclear: *the atomic age; the **atomic club*** (= nations possessing nuclear weapons); *atomic physics, warfare; a very precise **atomic clock;** an **atomic pile** or reactor; an atomic warhead.*

at·o·mize (AT·uh·mize) *v.* **-iz·es, -ized, -iz·ing** reduce a liquid, esp. a medicine or perfume into a fine spray using a device called an "atomizer"; **at·o·miz·er** *n.*

— **at·om·i·za·tion** (-muh·ZAY·shun) *n.*

a·ton·al (ay·TOH·nul) *adj.* of music, not based on a key.
— **a·ton·al·ly** *adv.*
— **a·to·nal·i·ty** (ay·toh·NAL·uh·tee) *n.*

a·tone (uh·TONE) *v.* **a·tones, a·toned, a·ton·ing** make up for a wrong: *He atoned for past misdeeds by philanthropy.*

a·tone·ment (uh·TONE·munt) *n.* satisfaction for wrongdoing; amends: *in atonement for his sins; to make atonement for his misdeeds.*

a·top (uh·TOP) *prep. & adv.* on top: *The balloon landed atop a building; a bird perched atop of a tower.*

a·tro·cious (uh·TROH·shus) *adj.* **1** wicked or horrifying. **2** *Informal.* very bad: *Her manners are atrocious; an atrocious necktie.*

a·troc·i·ty (uh·TROS·uh·tee) *n.* **-ties** something atrocious: *death-camp atrocities; the horrible atrocities committed by the Nazis;* [Informal] *the atrocities of bad spellers.*

at·ro·phy (AT·ruh·fee) *n.* the wasting away or stop in growth of a body part or tissue, as in polio.
— *v.* **-phies, -phied, -phy·ing** affect with atrophy: *Skills atrophy from lack of practice; an atrophied limb.*

atta- *combining form.* that's the; that's a: *attaboy, attagirl; Attaway, baby!*

at·ta·boy (AT·uh·boy) or **at·ta·girl** (AT·uh·girl) *interj.* expressing encouragement; way to go!: *Attaboy, Ashley!*

at·tach (uh·TACH) *v.* **1** unite one to another by a bond or tie so as to keep them together: *to attach a label to a parcel; a garage attached to a house; a school attached to a university; I attach my signature to a petition; two friends deeply attached to each other; He's strongly attached to his family.* **2** attribute or be attributed: *Do you attach any political significance to the mayor's speech? No blame attaches to his spouse for John's conduct; What's the use of attaching blame without suggesting a cure?* **3** take away by legal writ: *A debtor's property may be attached.*
— **at·tach·ment** *n.*: *to feel a close, strong attachment to one's family; It was no mere sentimental attachment; He formed some lasting attachments* (= friendships) *while at college; A vacuum cleaner comes with several attachments* (= devices).

at·ta·ché (at·uh·SHAY, uh·TASH·ay) *n.* **1** a diplomatic official: *a cultural, military, naval, press attaché.* **2** also **attaché case,** a thin suitcase for carrying papers.

at·tack (uh·TAK) *n.* **1** an offensive action against a person or thing: *The French launched or mounted an attack on England; England came or **was under attack;** They launched an attack against enemy forces; Attack is the best form of defence; to blunt, carry out, press, lead, make, provoke, repel, repulse, spearhead an attack; an air, all-out, enemy attack; a concerted, frontal, mock, pre-emptive, sneak, surprise attack; An attack may fail, fizzle out, succeed.* **2** an aggressive speech or writing: *a newspaper attack on Government policies; a bitter, blistering, scurrilous, vicious, wanton attack.* **3** an affliction: *to have an attack of measles; He died of a heart attack; a fatal, recurrent, slight, sudden attack.* **4** start of an activity: *to make a fresh attack on a*

problem.
— v. make an attack: *to attack the enemy; A disease attacks the body; Who attacked first? She was attacked viciously in the media.* — **at·tack·er** *n.*

attagirl See ATTABOY.

at·tain (uh·TAIN) *v.* **1** reach a state, position, goal, etc.: *to attain the age of 21; to attain success by hard work.* **2 attain to** succeed in reaching: *to attain to great power and glory; to attain to man's estate.* — **at·tain·a·ble** *adj.*

at·tain·ment *n.* the act of attaining or something attained, esp. something distinguished; accomplishment: *a position difficult of attainment; a woman of great cultural attainments.*

at·tempt (uh·TEMT) **1** *v.* make an effort to do something; try: *Many failed in attempting (to climb) Everest; He attempted the same exam three times; She was charged with attempted murder.* **2** *n.* an effort or try: *an attempt at the Olympic gold; an attempt at being funny; an attempt to be funny; to make an attempt* (= attack) *on the premier's life; The attempt was foiled* or *thwarted; an abortive, all-out, bold, concerted, deliberate, feeble, first, fruitless, futile, half-hearted, last-ditch, premature, successful attempt; He gave up after repeated attempts.*

at·tend (uh·TEND) *v.* **1** be present at a place or function: *to attend church, meetings, school; The meeting was well attended; a speech attended* (= accompanied) *by shouts from the audience.* **2** pay attention to a person or thing: *Let's attend to our duties; Sales clerks attend to* (= help) *customers; Nurses attend* (= care for) *the sick; Waiters* **attend on** (= serve) *customers; Students attend* (= listen to what is being taught) *in class.*

at·ten·dance (uh·TEN·dunce) *n.* a being present: *No doctor is in attendance on Sundays; Attendance is compulsory at school; average, low, poor attendance; attendance falls* or *goes down, goes up; Attendance is checked daily; Attendance* (= count of people attending) *is taken in the morning; He expects his employees to* **dance attendance on** (= be servile to) *him.*

at·ten·dant (uh·TEN·dunt) **1** *adj.* attending: *the attendant* (= on duty) *nurse; evils* **attendant on** (= connected with) *a war.* **2** *n.* a person in a specified service: *a flight attendant; parking-lot attendant; wedding attendant; She worked as an attendant to the princess.*

at·ten·tion (uh·TEN·shun) *n.* the act of listening or caring: *a note for the boss's attention; The wound requires immediate attention; Please bring it to the nurse's attention; to attract, capture, catch, command, distract, divert, draw, hold, retain, rivet someone's attention; to devote, escape, focus one's attention; one's undivided attention; close, meticulous, personal, rapt attention; with great attention to detail; The soldiers are standing* **at attention** (= in an erect posture), *not at ease; They have been called to attention; They come to* or *snap to attention; Students should* **pay attention** (= listen carefully) *to what is taught; The youngster liked the* **attentions** (= courtesies) *he received; Young children have a very short* **attention span** (= period during which they can concentrate on one thing).*

at·ten·tive (uh·TEN·tiv) *adj.* paying attention: *Teachers like attentive pupils; Be attentive* (= considerate) *to her needs.* — **at·ten·tive·ly** *adv.*

at·ten·u·ate (un·TEN·yoo·ate) *v.* **-ates, -at·ed, -at·ing** make or become thin or weak, less dense, harmful, etc.: *Wire is attenuated by being drawn out; a body attenuated by lack of nourishment; to attenuate the amplitude of a signal; a drug prepared in an attenuated form for medicinal use.*
— **at·ten·u·a·tion** (-AY·shun) *n.* lessening: *The high green walls along the highway are for the attenuation of noise.*

at·test (uh·TEST) *v.* bear witness to the truth or genuineness of something: *a signature attested by two witnesses; They attest (to) its genuineness.* — **at·tes·ta·tion** (at·uh·STAY·shun) *n.*

at·tic (AT·ic) *n.* a room or space just under a roof.

at·tire (uh·TIRE) *n.* dress or clothes: *casual attire; civilian attire; dressed in formal attire.*
— *v.* **at·tires, at·tired, at·tir·ing** array: *attired in regal splendour.*

at·ti·tude (AT·uh·tude) *n.* **1** the way one feels or thinks about something: *a cooperative attitude; to assume* or *take an attitude of defiance; his attitude towards his superiors; a belligerent, cavalier, condescending, defiant, firm, hands-off, holier-than-thou, liberal, negative, positive, reverent, scornful, selfish attitude; the attitude that his needs always come first.* **2** a pose, position, or posture: *She stood in the doorway in a threatening attitude* (= posture); *A signal was sent to shift the attitude* (= position in the sky) *of a space station veering out of control; arabesques and attitudes* (= ballet poses).* — **strike an attitude** assume a posture.

at·tor·ney (uh·TUR.nee) *n.* **-neys 1** person with legal authority to act for another; lawyer: *to hire, retain an attorney; a defence, district, prosecuting attorney.* **2** legal authority: *a power of attorney appointing someone to act for the signer.*

attorney general *n.* **attorneys general** or **attorney generals** the chief law officer of a country, province, or state; minister of justice.

at·tract (uh·TRACT) *v.* draw toward one: *Honey attracts bees; The goings-on attracted everyone's attention; Joe felt attracted to Jane.*

at·trac·tant (uh·TRAC·tunt) *n. & adj.* (something) that attracts: *an attractant scent; a sex attractant; attractants and repellents.*

at·trac·tion (uh·TRAC·shun) *n.* **1** an attracting: *magnetic attraction and repulsion.* **2** charm: *Joe feels a strong attraction to Jane; an irresistible attraction; sexual attraction.* **3** something that attracts: *a country's scenic, tourist attractions; The movie was a box-office attraction.*

at·trac·tive (uh·TRAC·tiv) *adj.* that attracts: *a beautiful and attractive child; a sexually attractive figure; an attractive bargain; an offer that sounds very attractive to everyone.* — **at·trac·tor** or **at·tract·er** *n.*

at·trib·ute (uh·TRIB·yoot) *v.* **-utes, -ut·ed, -ut·ing** consider as belonging to a person or thing: *He attributes*

his successes to luck; a play attributed to Bacon; Revenue Canada says income from money loaned to your wife will be attributed to you.
— n. (AT·ruh·bute) an inherent characteristic: *Being all-powerful is one attribute of God.*
— at·tri·bu·tion (at·ruh·BYOO·shun) *n.: The politician wouldn't say it for attribution* (= wouldn't be quoted).

at·tri·tion (uh·TRISH·un) *n.* **1** a wearing away; gradual weakening: *A war of attrition could destroy both sides.* **2** reduction in personnel through resignations, retirements, and deaths: *the high rate of attrition in our senior staff; $300 000 was saved by attrition and $1 million by cutbacks.*

at·tune (uh·TUNE) *v.* **at·tunes, at·tuned, at·tun·ing** tune: *A mother's ears are attuned to her children's voices.*

a·twit·ter (uh·TWIT·ur) *adj. & adv.* [used after its noun or verb] *Informal.* twittering; excited.

a·typ·i·cal (ay·TIP·uh·cul) *adj.* not typical; unusual: *behaviour that is atypical of children.*

au·burn (AW·burn) *n. & adj.* reddish brown: *His hair is a shiny auburn; her auburn hair.*

au cou·rant (oh·coo·RAHN) *adj. French.* modern or up to date: *Everyone likes to be au courant; to be au courant with fashion changes; an au courant fashion, style.*

auc·tion (AWK·shun) *n.* sale by bidding: *The house was put up for auction; sold by auction; I bought it at an auction; The auction was held in London; The auction took place last year.*
— v. auction off sell at auction.
— auc·tion·eer (awk·shuh·NEER) *n.*

au·da·cious (aw·DAY·shus) *adj.* bold in an impudent or daring manner: *It was audacious of him to ask his teacher for a date; an audacious act.*
— au·dac·i·ty (aw·DAS·uh·tee) *n.: sheer audacity; He had the audacity to reject the hand held out by her.*

au·di·ble (AW·duh·bul) *adj.* loud enough to be heard: *in an audible voice.* **— au·di·bly** (·blee) *adv.*
— au·di·bil·i·ty (·BIL·uh·tee) *n.*

au·di·ence (AW·dee·unce) *n.* **1** a group of listeners or spectators, as in an auditorium or theatre: *The meeting attracted* or *drew a large audience; an appreciative, enthusiastic audience; a capacity, captive, live, passive, responsive, select, standing-room-only, sympathetic audience.* **2** those reached by books and media: *a TV audience; a novelist with a large audience* (= readership); *high audience ratings.* **3** a formal interview: *to seek an audience with the Pope; I was at a papal audience; The Queen received us in audience; to give* or *grant an audience to someone.* **4** an opportunity to be heard: *If once given audience, some complaints only get worse.*

au·di·o (AW·dee·oh) **1** *n.* the sound portion of a telecast or film, distinguished from the video; *adj.: an audio component, frequency, tape; audio equipment.* **2** *combining form.* having to do with hearing: *audiology, audiophile, audiovisual.*

au·di·ol·o·gy (aw·dee·OL·uh·jee) *n.* the science of hearing; **au·di·ol·o·gist** (·OL·uh·jist) *n.*

au·di·o·phile (AW·dee·uh·file) *n.* one who is fond of hi-fi equipment and sound reproduction as a hobby: *High-quality audiophile records sell at premium prices.*

au·di·o·vis·u·al (AW·dee·oh·VIZH·oo·ul) **1** *adj.* having to do with both audio and visual communication: *audiovisual aids; Audiovisual education uses films, record players, and slides; audiovisual teaching materials.* **2 audiovisuals** *n. pl.* audiovisual aids used in education.

au·dit (AW·dit) *n.* **1** an official checking and verification of business accounts: *to carry out* or *conduct an annual audit; He lives in fear of a tax audit.* **2** a report of such a checking.
— v. 1 officially examine a business account. **2** attend a course of study, but not for credit.

au·di·tion (aw·DISH·un) *n.* a trial given to an actor, singer, etc. before hiring: *The recruiter holds auditions at his hotel.*
— v. 1 give an audition to someone: *The director was auditioning actors yesterday.* **2** perform for trial: *Three girls auditioned for the leading role; They auditioned to play the leading role.*

au·di·tor (AW·duh·tur) *n.* **1** one who audits. **2** listener.

Auditor General *n. Cdn.* an officer who audits the accounts of the Federal Government and crown corporations and reports to Parliament.

au·di·to·ri·um (aw·duh·TOR·ee·um) *n.* **-ri·ums** or **-ri·a** (·ree·uh) **1** a hall or theatre for seating audiences. **2** a building containing one.

au·di·to·ry (AW·duh·tor·ee) *adj.* having to do with hearing: *Auditory nerves connect the ear to the brain.*

audit trail *n.* a record of transactions that can be traced from a computer output back to the original document.

auf Wie·der·se·hen (owf·VEE·dur·zay·un) *German.* farewell!

au·ger (AW·gur) *n.* any of various tools for boring holes in wood, in the earth, etc.

aug·ment (awg·MENT) *v.* make or become larger: *to augment one's income with a sideline; a stream augmented by rains.* **— aug·men·ta·tion** (·TAY·shun) *n.*

au gra·tin (oh·GRAH·tin) *adj. French.* of dishes, with a light crust of bread crumbs or grated cheese: *egg and spinach au gratin.*

au·gur (AW·gur) *n.* one who foretells the future; soothsayer.
— v. 1 foretell, esp. from signs and omens. **2** be a sign of; bode: *A long drought does not augur well for a good harvest; It augurs ill for everyone.*

au·gu·ry (AUG·yuh·ree) *n.* **-ries 1** divination. **2** a sign or omen.

au·gust (aw·GUST) *adj.* majestic: *an august personage.*
— au·gust·ly *adv.;* **au·gust·ness** *n.*

Au·gust (AW·gust) *n.* the 8th month of the year, having 31 days.

au jus (oh·ZHOO) *adj. French.* of cooked meat, served with its own juices.

auld *adj. Scottish.* old, as in **auld lang syne** (awld·lang·zyne), the good old days.

au na·tu·rel (oh·nah·too·REL) *adj. French.* 1 in the natural state; nude. 2 of food, plainly cooked.

aunt (ANT, AHNT) *n.* one's father's or mother's sister; also **aun·tie, aun·ty,** *Informal.*

au pair (oh·PAIR) 1 *adj.* having to do with a domestic arrangement for exchange of services, as a foreign student living in a French home doing light housework while going to school: *an au pair girl, program, placement agency, student.* 2 *n.* a young person in such an arrangement: *Most au pairs find the experience rewarding.*

au·ra (AW·ruh) *n.* -ras or -rae (-ree) 1 a distinctive atmosphere or quality, esp. about a person: *an aura of holiness, mystery.* 2 a ring or circle of light or other emission: *a glittering aura; the electrical aura around a hydro station.*

au·ral (AW·rul) *adj.* of the ear: *aural comprehension, memory; an aural surgeon.* — **au·ral·ly** *adv.*

au re·voir (oh·ruv·WAR) *n. & interj. French.* good-bye.

au·ri·cle (AW·ruh·cul) *n.* 1 the external ear. 2 the earlike part of any other organ, as the upper chambers of the heart.

au·ro·ra (uh·ROR·uh) *n.* -ras or -rae (-ree) flashes of light seen in the night sky, esp. near the poles. — **au·ro·ral** (-rul) *adj.*

aurora aus·tra·lis (-aw·STRAY·lis) *n.* the aurora seen in southern regions.

aurora bo·re·al·is (-bor·ee·AL·is) *n.* the aurora of northern skies.

aus·pice (AWS·pis) *n.* usually **auspices** *pl.* patronage: *a meeting held **under the auspices** of the Y.M.C.A.*

aus·pi·cious (aw·SPISH·us) *adj.* having good omens; propitious: *an auspicious day for starting on a journey.* — **aus·pi·cious·ly** *adv.*

Aus·sie (AW·see) *n. & adj. Informal.* Australian.

aus·tere (aw·STEER) *adj.* strict and self-disciplined in manner or style: *an austere monk; an austere, unadorned style.* — **aus·tere·ly** *adv.* — **aus·ter·i·ty** (aw·STER·uh·tee) *n.: to practise austerity.*

au·teur (oh·TUR) *n.* the creative force behind an artistic production: *The film director, not the author of the screenplay, is seen as the real auteur of a film.*

au·then·tic (aw·THEN·tic, "TH" as in "thin") *adj.* reliable, as true to the original; genuine: *an authentic signature.* — **au·then·ti·cal·ly** *adv.*

au·then·ti·cate (au·THEN·tuh·cate) *v.* -cates, -cat·ed, -cat·ing prove or determine to be authentic: *an authenticated Picasso; a painting authenticated as genuine.* — **au·then·ti·ca·tion** (-CAY·shun) *n.*

au·then·tic·i·ty (au·then·TIS·uh·tee) *n.* the state of being authentic: *to doubt, establish, prove, question, vouch for the authenticity of a signature.*

au·thor (AW·thur, "th" as in "thin") *n.* one who makes or originates something, esp. something written: *an anonymous, classical, contemporary, noted author; a prolific author of romances; a Latin author; to translate a Latin author* (= author's book); *the author of a plot.* — *v.* be the author of something: *Shakespeare authored many plays.* — **au·thor·ship** *n.*

au·thor·i·tar·i·an (aw·THOR·uh·TAIR·ee·un) *adj.* demanding submission to authority without regard to individual freedom: *an authoritarian government.* — **au·thor·i·tar·i·an·ism** *n.*

au·thor·i·ta·tive (aw·THOR·uh·tay·tiv) *adj.* having authority: *an authoritative source of information; an authoritative text.* — **au·thor·i·ta·tive·ly** *adv.*

au·thor·i·ty (aw·THOR·uh·tee) *n.* -ties 1 the power or right to do something: *an order issued under the authority of a judge; the authority to arrest a suspect; A president speaks with authority; She is a woman of authority; Luc never abuses or oversteps his authority; to assume, defy, deny, invoke, reject, undermine, wield authority; absolute, full, legal, ministerial, parental, royal, supreme authority; to delegate authority for day-to-day government; to exercise authority over a department; The department is under her authority; Orders are issued on or by her authority; She is **in authority*** (= charge) *there.* 2 the authorities *pl.* government officials: *Crimes have to be reported to the authorities; the civil, government, local authorities.* 3 a person, institution, etc. having expert knowledge: *He is the greatest living authority on the subject; He cited or invoked the dictionary as authority for his usage of the term; He invoked the authority of his dictionary; a competent, irrefutable, leading, outstanding, reliable, respected, unimpeachable authority; I can tell you on good authority that he is still alive; I can assure you on the highest authority that it is so.*

au·thor·i·za·tion (aw·thuh·ruh·ZAY·shun) *n.* official permission: *to give, grant, receive, revoke authorization to begin work on the project; authorization for the work to begin.*

au·thor·ize (AW·thuh·rize) *v.* -iz·es, -ized, -iz·ing permit or allow officially: *The minister has authorized the expenditure; He has authorized us to spend the money; We are authorized to do it; King James I's **Authorized Version** of the Bible.*

au·tism (AW·tiz·um) *n.* a mental disorder of children that is characterized by daydreaming and other signs of withdrawal from reality. — **au·tis·tic** (aw·TIS·tic) *adj.: Autistic children are often mute.*

auto- *combining form.* 1 of or by oneself: *autocrat, autograph.* 2 automatic: **autopilot** (= machinelike piloting device). 3 having to do with automobiles: *automaker,* **automan** (= automaker); *automotive.*

au·to (AW·toh) *n.* -tos an automobile: *the auto industry; an auto part.*

au·to·bahn (AW·toh·bahn) *n.* a German superhighway.

au·to·bi·og·ra·phy (AW·toh·bye·OG·ruh·fee) *n.* -phies an author's own life history. — **au·to·bi·og·ra·pher** (-ruh·fur) *n.* — **au·to·bi·o·graph·i·cal** (-bye·uh·GRAF·uh·cul) *adj.*

au·toc·ra·cy (aw·TOC·ruh·see) *n.* -cies government by

an autocrat.

au·to·crat (AW·tuh·crat) *n.* one who has absolute power. — **au·to·crat·ic** (-CRAT·ic) *adj.*

au·to·graph (AW·tuh·graf) *n.* a person's signature given for its sentimental value. — *v.* put an autograph on something: *Authors autograph their books for buyers; a movie star's autographed portrait.*

au·to·mak·er (AW·toh·may·kur) *n.* an automobile manufacturer.

au·to·mate (AW·tuh·mate) *v.* -mates, -mat·ed, -mat·ing operate or control a process, equipment, or system automatically, esp. by use of computers and robots.

au·to·mat·ic (aw·tuh·MAT·ic) *adj.* **1** self-acting, as machines under set conditions: *a fully automatic camera; a radio receiver with automatic frequency control; a car's automatic gearshift, transmission; the **automatic pilot** (= device for automatically piloting an airplane; "autopilot"); an automatic rifle (= machine gun); an **automatic teller machine** for making cash withdrawals, deposits, etc.* **2** machinelike in action: *an automatic (= routine) annual pay raise; an automatic (= unconscious) response.* — **au·to·mat·i·cal·ly** (-uh·cuh·lee) *adv.*

au·to·ma·tion (aw·tuh·MAY·shun) *n.* the automatic control and operation of a process, as by use of computers or robots: *Automation replaces much unskilled labour.*

au·tom·a·ton (aw·TOM·uh·tun) *n.* -tons or -ta (-tuh) a robot or similar self-acting mechanism.

au·to·mo·bile (AW·tuh·moh·BEEL) *n.* a self-propelled, usually four-wheeled passenger vehicle: *to drive, operate, ride in, park an automobile.* — *adj.:* *automobile industry, insurance, production, repairs, safety, sales; an automobile association, dealer, engine, policy.*

au·to·mo·tive (aw·tuh·MOH·tiv) *adj.* having to do with automobiles: *an automotive engine, part, worker; the automotive industry.*

au·to·nom·ic (aw·tuh·NOM·ic) *adj.* governing involuntary actions: *the autonomic nervous sytem.*

au·ton·o·my (aw·TON·uh·mee) *n.* -mies self-government: *to grant, seek autonomy.* — **au·ton·o·mous** (-mus) *adj.*

au·top·sy (AW·top·see) *n.* -sies the examination of a corpse to determine cause of death; post-mortem: *to do an autopsy on an accident victim.* — *v.* -sies, -sied, -sy·ing perform an autopsy on a body: *Those dead of unknown causes are usually autopsied.*

au·to·route (AW·toh·root) *n.* in Quebec, France, etc., an expressway.

au·to·stra·da (aw·toh·STRAH·duh) *n.* an Italian expressway.

au·to·sug·ges·tion (AW·toh·suh·JES·chun) *n.* mental suggestion to oneself; self-hypnosis.

au·tumn (AW·tum) *n.* the season between summer and winter; fall. — **au·tum·nal** (aw·TUM·nul) *adj.*

aux·il·ia·ry (awg·ZIL·yuh·ree) *adj.* having a helping, subordinate, or supplementary function: *an auxiliary organization, police force, power plant; An auxiliary verb such as "is" or "can" is used with another verb, as in "is gone" or "can go."* — *n., pl.* -ries an auxiliary person, institution, etc.: *an auxiliary (= bishop) assisting a diocesan bishop; a nursing auxiliary (= member of a nursing group); a women's auxiliary (= organization of women helpers).*

a·vail (uh·VAIL) *v.* be of use or advantage; profit: *A last-minute effort will avail us nothing; It won't avail against the heavy odds we face; He bought a house to **avail himself of** (= make use of) a tax deduction.* — *n.* avails *pl.* profits. — **to no avail, of no avail, to little avail**, or **of little avail** of no help: *The strike was of no avail in forcing a settlement.*

a·vail·a·ble (uh·VAY·luh·bul) *adj.* obtainable: *Front row seats are not easily available to the general public; Balcony seats are readily available; He was too busy to be available (= free) for an interview; He couldn't make himself available (to be interviewed).* — **a·vail·a·bil·i·ty** (-BIL·uh·tee) *n.*

av·a·lanche (AV·uh·lanch) *n.* a massive descent of loose earth, snow, or rock from a mountain: *The skiers were buried under an avalanche; an avalanche of mail from an enthusiastic public.* — *v.* overwhelm or bombard: *The Minister was avalanched with questions from reporters.*

a·vant-garde (ah·vahnt·GARD) *n.* the front line or vanguard of a movement, esp. in the arts: *an avant-garde art form.*

av·a·rice (AV·uh·ris) *n.* greed for money combined with miserliness: *the avarice of a usurer.* — **av·a·ri·cious** (av·uh·RISH·us) *adj.:* *the avaricious usurer.*

a·vast (uh·VAST) *interj.* [nautical use] away!

a·venge (uh·VENJ) *v.* a·veng·es, a·venged, a·veng·ing take revenge for a wrong or on behalf of the wronged one: *Hamlet wanted to avenge his father's murder; to avenge his father; to avenge himself on or upon Claudius.* — **a·ven·ger** *n.*

av·e·nue (AV·uh·new) *n.* **1** a street, usually a wide one: *a tree-lined avenue; He lives on Bernard Avenue.* **2** an approach: *to explore every avenue or all avenues to a peaceful settlement.*

a·ver (uh·VUR) *v.* a·vers, a·verred, a·verr·ing *Formal.* assert confidently.

av·er·age (AV·uh·rij) *n.* the arithmetic mean: *To calculate or work out the average of three numbers, you add them up and divide the sum by 3; 4 is the average of 1, 3, and 8; She is well **above average** (= the ordinary level of achievement) in her class; She has an A average in all subjects; Our car uses 7 L of gas per 100 km **on the** or **on an average** (= normally).* — *adj.* common or ordinary: *The average student gets a pass mark; She has an above average I.Q.* — *v.* -ag·es, -aged, -ag·ing do, get, or come to an average: *Her pay averages $800 a week; She averages 30 hours on the job each week; Losses and gains **average out** (= even out) to a small profit each year.*

a·verse (uh·VURCE) *adj.* disinclined or opposed to something because of distaste or repugnance: *an austere man averse to any kind of self-indulgence.*

a·ver·sion (uh·VUR·zhun) *n.* the state of being averse; dislike: *Some people have a built-in aversion to smoking; Some take an aversion to smoking; a deep, distinct, marked aversion to certain things; TV is one of his pet aversions* (= objects of aversion).

aversion therapy *n.* a method of treatment that makes a bad habit or behaviour repugnant to the patient.

a·vert (uh·VURT) *v.* **1** turn away: *The child averted her eyes from the scary picture.* **2** prevent a danger or misfortune: *A strike was averted at the last moment.*

a·vi·an (AY·vee·un) *adj.* of birds: *an avian enthusiast.*

a·vi·ar·y (AY·vee·air·ee) *n.* **-ries 1** a bird cage. **2** a house for birds, as in a zoo.

a·vi·a·tion (ay·vee·AY·shun) *n.* flying as an art, science, or industry: *civil, military aviation; **Aviation medicine** deals with illnesses peculiar to flyers and astronauts.*

a·vi·a·tor (AY·vee·ay·tur) *n.* an airplane pilot.

av·id (AV·id) *adj.* eager to have and enjoy more and more of something: *an avid golfer; an avid reader of romances; Midas was avid* (= greedy) *for gold.* — **av·id·ly** *adv.* — **a·vid·i·ty** (uh·VID·uh·tee) *n.*

a·vi·on·ics (ay·vee·ON·ics) *n.pl.* [takes sing. v.] electronics applied to aviation and astronautics. — **a·vi·on·ic** *adj.*

av·o·ca·do (av·uh·CAD·oh) *n.* **-dos** or **does** a greenish, pear-shaped tropical fruit, its colour, or the tree bearing it.

av·o·ca·tion (av·uh·CAY·shun) *n.* a side occupation or hobby pursued with dedication. — **av·o·ca·tion·al** *adj.*

a·void (uh·VOID) *v.* keep away from something harmful or undesirable: *Drive on the right to avoid collisions; to avoid colliding with oncoming traffic; There are loopholes for avoiding taxes without having to evade them; He studiously tries to avoid taxes; She avoids fatty foods **like the plague** (Informal for* totally). — **a·void·a·ble** *adj.;* **a·void·a·bly** *adv.* — **a·void·ance** (-unce) *n.*

av·oir·du·pois (av·ur·duh·POIZ) *n.* **1** the weight system based on pounds and ounces. **2** *Informal.* one's weight: *a man of great moral avoirdupois.*

a·vow (uh·VOW) *v.* acknowledge openly; admit with assurance in the face of hostility: *He avows himself (to be) an animal rights activist; He's an **avowed** animal rights activist.* — **a·vow·al** *n.* — **a·vow·ed·ly** (-id·lee) *adv.*

a·vun·cu·lar (uh·VUNK·yuh·lur) *adj.* characteristic of an uncle: *She doesn't like his avuncular manner.*

aw *interj.* expressing disappointment, regret, and such feelings: *Aw, come on! Aw shucks!*

a·wait (uh·WAIT) *v.* wait for a person or thing: *I await your reply.*

a·wake (uh·WAKE) *adj.* **1** roused from sleep: *He's fully awake; wide awake.* **2** alert or aware: *a new recruit who is awake to his duties; the alpha rhythm of the awake brain.*

— *v.* **a·wakes,** *pt.* **a·woke** or **a·waked,** *pp.* **a·waked, a·woke,** or **a·wok·en,** *pres. part.* **a·wak·ing** to wake up; be roused: *I awoke at 6 yesterday; awoke from a sound sleep; awoke to the sound of the radio; I awoke to find everyone gone.*

a·wak·en (uh·WAY·kun) *v. pt. & pp.* **a·wak·ened** awake; wake up: *a bugle's awakening call; I was awakened by the alarm; My fears were awakened.*

awakening *n.* a waking up: *a rude, sudden awakening; the new awakening* (= awareness) *about animal rights.*

a·ward (uh·WORED) *v.* give officially on the basis of merit, as a decoration, prize, or ruling: *They award scholarships to needy students; The Glenn Gould Prize is awarded for distinction in music; The judge awarded custody of the children to their father.* — *n.* something awarded: *She received an award made annually by the Canada Council; a money award; Some awards are granted on the basis of need; The fastest horse was given the highest award; a Genie Award for the best actor; Who presented the awards? an arbitration award* (= ruling).

a·ware (uh·WARE) *adj.* **1** conscious or having knowledge of something: *I am aware of my rights; Are you aware that you were late for work all last week? I have recently become aware of a new trend; I'm keenly, painfully, very much aware of my shortcomings.* **2** informed: *a politically aware student; These youths are aware, well-adjusted people.* — **a·ware·ness** *n.*

a·wash (uh·WOSH) *adj. & adv.* [used after its noun or verb] being washed; flooded: *The dish was just bits of meat and vegetables awash in murky gravy; a speech awash* (= flowing) *with self-pity.*

a·way (uh·WAY) *adv.* [used after its verb] **1** at a distance from the speaker or from a place, person, etc. referred to: *Get away from the fire! Please go away!* [in exclamations] *Away with the nuisance!* **2** far: *She's away down on the list; away back in 1926.* Also **way,** *Informal.* **3** on: *Time is ticking away; He's grinding away at his task.* — *adj.* **1** distant: *Our school is only 2 km away; Lee is far away in Taiwan; The boss is away* (= gone) *on business.* **2** [used before its noun] away from home: *There are special football trains to away games (played at the opponent's place, not a "home game"); the away team.* — **do away with** get rid of; kill. — **far and away** or **out and away** very much. — **right away** or **straight away** at once: *Go home right away!*

awe (AW) *n.* a mixed emotion of fear, respect, wonder, reverence, etc., esp. as felt toward something supernatural: *The heavens inspire awe in us; Our boss is held **in awe** by everyone at work; The subjects stand **in awe** of Her Majesty.* — *v.* **awes, awed, aw·ing** fill with awe: *a poet awed by nature's wonders; The tourists seemed **awed into** silence.*

a·weigh (uh·WAY) *adj.* suspended: *With anchors aweigh, the boat put out to sea.*

awe·some (AW·sum) *adj.* **1** *Informal.* quite impressive: *His achievements are awesome.* **2** causing awe: *an awesome sight.*

awe·strick·en (AW·strick·un) or **awe·struck** *adj.* filled with awe.

aw·ful (AW·ful) *adj. Informal.* **1** terrible: *an awful crime.* **2** very bad: *his awful manners; It was an awful mistake; We feel awful about it; It's awful that we had to go through with it.* **3** very great: *an awful lot of waiting; I don't know an awful lot about computers.* — *adv. Slang.* very: *It's awful hot in here!*

aw·ful·ly (AW·fuh·lee) *adv. Informal.* very: *35° Celsius is awfully hot; You're awfully nice.*

a·while (uh·WHILE) *adv.* for some time: *Stay awhile and have a coffee.*

awk·ward (AWK·wurd) *adj.* **1** clumsy; graceless: *awkward movements; He is awkward with mechanical tools.* **2** uncomfortable: *an awkward posture.* **3** difficult to handle; embarrassing: *a lawyer dealing with awkward facts; found herself in an awkward position; She felt awkward dealing with that client.* — **awk·ward·ly** *adv.;* **awk·ward·ness** *n.*

awn *n.* bristle or bristles on the head of a grass or cereal grain; beard: *Barley, oats, etc. have awns; adj.: Some fruits and leaf-tips are also awned* (= having bristles).

awn·ing *n.* an overhanging shelter, often of canvas, above a door or window.

awoke, awoken a *pt. & pp.* of AWAKE.

A·WOL (AY·wall) **1** *adj.* absent without official leave, esp. from the military: *to go AWOL.* **2** *awol n.* one who goes AWOL.

a·wry (uh·RYE) *adj. & adv.* [used after its noun or verb] askew; amiss: *a scheme that went awry.*

axe or **ax** (AX) *n., pl.* **ax·es** (AK·siz) a tool with a heavy cutting blade fitted parallel to the handle: *He came out swinging an axe; A lumberjack wields an axe.* — **get the axe** *Informal.* be terminated: *The employees and the project got the axe.* — **have an axe to grind** *Informal.* have a private, selfish motive.

— *v.* **ax·es, axed, ax·ing** cut, get rid of, etc. with an axe: *The lumberjack axed down the tree; Many TV shows have been axed* (= cancelled) *because of poor ratings.*

axes *pl.* of AX, AXE or AXIS.

ax·i·om (AK·see·um) *n.* a self-evident truth or principle: *Everyone accepts the axiom that the whole equals the sum of its parts; Change is an axiom of the fashion world.* — **ax·i·o·mat·ic** (-uh·MAT·ic) *adj.*

ax·is (AK·sis) *n., pl.* **ax·es** (AK·seez) **1** a straight line around which an object rotates or is symmetrical: *The earth rotates on its axis.* **2** a reference line: *the x and y axes of a graph.*

THE EARTH'S AXIS

ax·le (AK·sul) *n.* **1** a shaft that turns with a wheel or wheels attached to it. **2** a fixed shaft with bearings at either end for wheels: *an automobile's axis; the **axle tree** of a wagon or carriage.*

a·ya·tol·lah (ah·yuh·TOL·luh) *n.* **1** a title for a distinguished Muslim clergyman. **2** a powerful leader.

aye *adv.* **1** (AY) *Poetic.* forever. **2** (EYE) yes: *Aye, aye, sir!* — *n.* (EYE) a yes vote or voter: *The ayes have it.*

az·ure (AZH·ur) *n.* sky-blue: *the azure sky.*

Bb

B or **b** (BEE) *n.* **B's** or **b's** **1** the second letter of the English Alphabet. **2** second in a series, esp. second highest or best: *He received a B (grade) in math.*

B.A. *n.* **B.A.'s** the degree of Bachelor of Arts or one holding it: *He took a history B.A.; He's a B.A. in history.*

baa (BAH) *v.* **baas, baaed** (BAHD), **baa·ing** bleat, as a sheep does. — *n.* the bleating of a sheep.

bab·ble (BAB·ul) *v.* **bab·bles, bab·bled, bab·bling** **1** talk very freely, foolishly, or indistinctly, as a baby does: *to babble a secret; He babbled something in her ear.* **2** murmur: *a babbling brook.*
— *n.* such talk or murmur: *a baby's babble; a confused babble; the incessant babble heard at a bazaar.*
— **bab·bler** *n.*

babe *n.* **1** a baby: *a babe in arms.* **2** *Slang.* [intimate male use] a girl or woman as a sex object.
— **babe in the woods** an innocent or helpless person.

ba·bel (BAY·bul, BAB·ul) *n.* a noisy confusion: *He tried to make himself heard above the babel of voices; a babel of dialects.*

ba·biche (bah·BEESH, BAB·ish) *n.* *Cdn.* thongs or lacings of rawhide, as used in making snowshoes.

ba·boon (ba·BOON) *n.* a big monkey with a muzzle like a dog's.

ba·by (BAY·bee) *n.* **-bies** **1** an infant: *Only women can have babies; A pregnant woman normally carries a baby to term* or *carries a baby for nine months; A premature baby is not a full-term baby; A doctor or midwife delivers babies; a new-born baby; Mothers nurse babies, but anyone may change them* (= change their diapers); *Babies are weaned from breast to bottle in the first few months; She sang "Rock a bye baby!" and lulled him to sleep in the cradle; Babies babble, burp, coo, crawl, creep, drool, teethe; Some babies are stillborn; test-tube babies.* **2** the youngest of a group: *the baby of the family.* **3** a childish person: *You're some baby!* **4** [used in a familiar way to address or to refer to someone] *Slang.* a person: *You've come a long way, baby!* **5** *Slang.* [often offensive] sex object; babe. **6** an object of special care or concern: *The dictionary project is my baby.*
— *adj.* **1** of or for a baby: *baby clothes, shoes; a baby face* (= face like a baby's); *a **baby walker*** (= device to help a baby to walk). **2** very young or small: *a baby bird, monkey, seal.*
— *v.* treat with excessive care: *to baby a new car.*

— **ba·by·hood** (BAY·bee·hood, short "oo") *n.*
— **ba·by·ish** *adj.*

baby beef *n.* ·beef from a one- or two-year-old calf.

baby bonus *n.* *Cdn. Informal.* Family Allowance.

baby boom *n.* the sudden increase in the birth rate experienced in the late 1940s as a result of veterans rejoining their families after World War II.

baby boomer *n.* a member of a social and economic group composed of those born during the baby boom and noted for their materialistic lifestyles and habits in the 1980s, with yuppies forming the upper crust.

baby buggy or **baby carriage** *n.* a buggy for pushing infants in.

baby bust *n.* the decline in the birth rate experienced in the 1970s because of changing social attitudes and economic conditions.

baby-sit (BAY·bee·sit) *v.* **-sits, -sat, -sit·ting** look after a child while its parents are away: *Eve baby-sits for Mrs. Smith; baby-sits her two children;* **baby-sitter** *n.* Also **babysit, babysitter.**

bach *n.* *Slang.* a bachelor.
— *v.* **bach it** *Informal.* live a single life during one's spouse's absence.

bach·e·lor (BACH·uh·lur) *n.* **1** an unmarried man: *a confirmed bachelor; eligible bachelors.* **2** one who has received an undergraduate degree: *Bachelor of Arts; Bachelor of Engineering; She's working on her **bachelor's** (degree).* **3** an apartment in which the living room doubles as the bedroom; also **bachelor apartment.** — **bach·e·lor·hood** (short "oo") *n.*

bach·e·lor·ette (bach·uh·luh·RET) *n.* **1** *Cdn.* a smaller-size bachelor apartment. **2** an unmarried young woman living by herself.

bachelor girl *n.* *Informal.* an independent single young woman; career woman.

bachelor pad *n.* *Informal.* a bachelor's living quarters.

bachelor party *n.* a party for a bridegroom to mark the end of his bachelorhood.

back *n.* **1** the rear part of the human body or the corresponding part in animals: *my aching back; seated*

on a horse's back; a stab in the back; She was lying on
her back; At the end of February we say we have broken
the back of (= been through most of) the winter; He
broke his back (= worked very hard) to finish writing the
book on time. **2** anything that supports or covers the
back: the back of a chair, dress, etc. **3** a part that is
behind the front: the back of the head; the back of a
book; a room at the back of the house; He was seated in
the back (= back seat) of the car; I know it like the back
of my hand (= thoroughly). **4** a player stationed in the
backfield.
— **(in the) back of** Informal. behind: Stand back of the
line; a tennis court in the back of the house; The
experience remained in the back of my mind (= in the
subconscious).
— **behind one's back** in one's absence or without one's
knowledge.
— **be on one's back** harass one: He complains that the
boss is on his back all day.
— **get off one's back** stop harassing one: Get off my
back, will you?
— **get (or put) one's back up** make (or become)
uncooperative or angry.
— **have one's back to the wall** be in a desperate
situation.
— **on one's back** sick in bed.
— **adj. 1** in, at, or toward the rear: a back alley, fence,
flip, room, shed; back concessions, country. **2** of the
past: I was born way back in 1926; a periodical's back
issues (that are no longer on sale); back pay, rent (that is
owing); Things are back to normal after the strike (= as
they were before the strike).
— **adv. 1** at or toward the rear: Stand back! **2** in reserve
or restraint: Hold back your best card. **3** in, at, or
toward an earlier time, state, or position: Bring the
book back; It happened back in 1910. **4** in return: to
pay back a loan.
— **go back on one's promise** or **word** fail to keep one's
promise.
— **v. 1** move backward or to the rear: to back (a car)
into a parking space; to back a car out of a garage.
2 bet on; support: to back a candidate; to back the right
horse. **3** form the back of or provide backing for
something: High cliffs backed the beach. **4** have the
back in a certain place: Our house backs on a park.
— **back and fill 1** of automobiles, go back and forth in
an effort to get out when bogged down in snow or mud.
2 Informal. be changing one's mind; be undecided.
— **back away** withdraw: They backed away without
starting a fight.
— **back down** withdraw from a stand one has taken.
— **back east** in or into the eastern part of the country, in
Canada, esp. the Atlantic Provinces, Quebec, or
Ontario, as viewed from the West.
— **back off** or **out** withdraw: He decided to back off
from his initial demands; to back out of a commitment.
— **back up 1** support: Jim backed up her story; He
backed her up. **2** accumulate and clog: The drain is
backed up. **3** move in reverse: He backed up to the
loading dock; The teacher backed up and repeated the
earlier part of the lesson.

back·ache n. a dull pain in the lower back: a nagging,
persistent backache.

back bacon n. Cdn. bacon made from loin cuts with less
fat than bacon from the sides; Canadian bacon.

back bench n. one of the seats in a legislature for
members who are not in the front benches occupied by
the cabinet or shadow cabinet: a career on the back
benches; applause from the back benches.
— **back-bench** adj.: a back-bench M.P.
— **back-bench·er** n.

back·bite v. -bites, -bit, -bit·ten, -bit·ing speak ill of
someone who is absent. — **back·bit·er** n.

back·board n. in basketball, the upright rebound board
behind the basket.

back·bone n. **1** the spinal column. **2** courage or
resolution: to have the backbone to stand up to a bully.
3 main support: Customers are the backbone of a
business.

back·breaking (BACK·bray·king) adj. of work, very
tiring.

back burner n. usually on the back burner, in a
position of low priority.

back·check·ing n. in hockey and lacrosse, the harrying
of an advancing opposing player by a forward while
backing away to defend the goal.

back concessions n.pl. Cdn. esp. in eastern Canada,
rural regions.

back country n. unsettled area behind a settled one.

back·date v. -dates, -dat·ed, -dat·ing put a date on a
document that is earlier than the actual date: The
contract was backdated to January 1; a backdated
cheque.

back door n. a rear entrance: to get in by or through the
back door (using unfair influence).
— **back-door** adj. indirect, devious, or dishonest: back-
door businesses, influence.

back·drop n. **1** a usually painted cloth hung at the back
of a stage. **2** background: Recent events provide a
backdrop for the present situation; the present situation
seen against the backdrop of recent events.

back·er n. a supporter of a candidate, horse in a race,
project, etc.: the financial backer of a project.

back·field n. the football players or their positions
behind the line of scrimmage.

back·fire n. **1** a fire set to check a forest or prairie fire
by burning off its fuel. **2** an improperly timed fuel
explosion, as in an automobile engine.
— **v.** -fires, -fired, -fir·ing happen in a way opposite to
what is intended: a plan that backfired.

back flip n. a backward somersault or dive.

back·ground n. **1** ground or setting behind something,
as distant scenery in a painting or music for a movie:
music to serve as an appropriate background for the
performance; a leader who likes to stay in the
background (= in a less visible or important place);
adj.: background knowledge, information, music, noise.
2 conditions that influence something: She has a good
family background; an academic, educational
background; a broad, cultural, historical, political,
religious background; He has no background

(= experience) *for the job; the background of* (= conditions existing before) *the war; The politician was speaking to reporters on background* (= for information only, not to be quoted).

back·hand *adj. & adv.* with the hand in the position opposite to the usual one: *a backhand stroke in tennis (with the back of the hand forward); backhand writing (slanting to the left).*
— *n.* a backhand stroke or writing.

back·hand·ed (BACK·han·did) *adj. & adv.* 1 backhand. 2 having an opposite intent; sarcastic: *a backhanded apology, compliment.*

backing *n.* 1 support or strengthening. 2 material used for this.

back·lash *n.* hostile reaction: *the backlash against the new taxes.*

back·log *n.* a piling up of something that should have been attended to, as work: *to accumulate, build up, reduce a backlog; a growing backlog of orders waiting to be filled.*

back number *n. Informal.* a person or thing that is out of date, as an old issue of a magazine.

back order *n.* a purchase order waiting to be filled.

back·pack *n.* a knapsack, esp. on a metal frame.
— *v.* hike with or carry in a backpack; **back·pack·er** *n.*

back·ped·al (BACK·ped·ul) *v.* 1 pedal backward. 2 retreat: *to backpedal on a promise.*

back·seat *n.* a secondary position, as a seat in the back of a vehicle: *a distinguished Canadian who won't take a backseat to anyone else in the world.*

backseat driver *n.* a passenger who offers unwanted advice to the driver.

back·side *n.* the buttocks.

back·slap·per (BACK·slap·ur) *n.* an effusively friendly person.

back·slide *v.* -slides, *pp.* -slid or -slid·den, -slid·ing fall back into lax ways, esp. morally. — **back·slid·er** *n.*

back·spin *n.* a spin that makes a ball slow down or bounce backward.

back·stage *adv.* 1 in or to the area behind the stage, not seen by the audience: *He went backstage to congratulate the actors.* 2 in private; behind the scenes: *What goes on backstage is anybody's guess.*

back·stretch *n.* the racetrack straightaway opposite the homestretch.

back·stroke *n.* a style of swimming on one's back: *to do or swim the backstroke.*

back talk *n.* an impudent retort.

back-to-back *adj. & adv.* 1 with the backs against each other: *Before a duel, the opponents stand back-to-back; to photocopy back-to-back* (= on both sides of the paper). 2 *Informal.* one after another: *We had ten wins back-to-back; exhausted from back-to-back interviews with job applicants.*

back·track *v.* 1 go back the way one came. 2 retreat; back down.

back·up *n.* 1 a backing up of a flow: *a backup of sewage, traffic.* 2 support or substitute: *extra equipment as backup in case of a breakdown;* **adj.**: *a backup airplane, computer, disk, plan, power supply.*

back·ward (BACK·wurd) *adv.* 1 to the back or past; with the rear leading. 2 in the wrong way; to a worse condition: *He bends* or *leans over backward* (= tries extraordinarily hard) *to please his customers.* Also **back·wards.**
— *adj.* 1 turned toward the back in time or space: *a backward flow, glance, journey, look, step.* 2 slow in development: *a backward region, student; He is backward in his studies but not backward* (= shy or diffident) *in speaking his mind.*
— **backwards and forwards** to and fro.
— **back·ward·ness** *n.*

back·wash *n.* 1 air or water thrown back, as by a propeller or oars. 2 a resulting situation; aftermath.

back·wa·ter (BACK·wot·ur) *n.* 1 a body of water without a current or flow, as a lagoon or inlet. 2 an unprogressive area: *a cultural backwater of civilization.*

back·woods *n. pl.* 1 thinly populated forest land. 2 a remote and backward area.
— **back·woods·man** *n.* **-men.**

back·yard *n.* an area at the back of one's house.

ba·con (BAY·cun) *n.* cured and smoked hog flesh: *crisp, lean, smoked bacon; a rasher of bacon; Canadian bacon; bacon and eggs for breakfast.*
— **bring home the bacon** *Informal.* 1 provide for one's family. 2 win the prize; succeed.
— **save one's bacon** *Informal.* escape danger or trouble.

bac·te·ri·a (bac·TEER·ee·uh) *n. pl.* microscopic organisms that cause disease, fermentation, etc.
— **bac·te·ri·al** (-ee·ul) *adj.*: *a bacterial canker.*
— **bac·te·ri·um** *sing.*

bad *adj. comp.* **worse** (WURSE), *superl.* **worst** (WURST) not good; having undesirable qualities: *bad language, news; a bad boy* (= boy who misbehaves); *bad plumbing (that leaks); Smoking is bad* (= unhealthy); *an egg gone bad* (= rotten); *He looks bad* (= sick); *I feel bad* (= sorry) *about it; Too bad* (= unfortunate) *you lost; a bad cheque (that bounces); a bad* (= severe) *cold; a bad*

debt (that cannot be collected); bad ice (that is thin or melting).
— **not bad** *Informal.* not unsatisfactory; fairly good; also **not half bad** or **not so bad.**
— *adv.* [nonstandard] badly: *He wasn't hurt that bad in the accident.*
— *n.* **the bad** what is bad: *to take the bad with the good.*
— **go from bad to worse** get worse from day to day.
— **in bad** *Informal.* in disfavour *with* someone.
— **to the bad** *Informal.* to or in a bad condition: *a good man who went to the bad; He was put to the bad (= put in debt) by his generosity towards friends; He was about $1 million to the bad (= in debt).* — **bad·ness** *n.*

bad blood *n.* ill will.

bad·die or **bad·dy** (BAD·ee) *n.* **bad·dies** *Slang.* one that is really bad; bad guy or villain.

bade (BAD) a *pt.* of BID.

badge (BAJ) *n.* an emblem or device worn to show one's membership or rank: *a police officer's badge; a badge of slavery such as the language of the conqueror.*

badg·er (BAJ·ur) *n.* a digging animal of the weasel family with white markings on its head.
— *v.* pester or torment without ceasing: *She was badgered with questions by reporters; He was badgered into joining the party.*

bad·lands *n. pl.* dry barren land eroded into strange shapes: *the badlands of Alberta.*

bad·ly (BAD·lee) *adv.* **1** in an undesirable manner: *He behaved badly.* **2** very much: *a badly needed book.* **3** [nonstandard] bad: *I feel badly about it.*

bad·min·ton (BAD·min·tun) *n.* a racket game in which a shuttlecock is hit back and forth over a net.

bad-mouth *v. Slang.* speak badly of a person or thing.

bad news *n. Informal.* a person, situation, event, etc. that is unpleasant or unwelcome.

baf·fle (BAF·ul) *v.* **baf·fles, baf·fled, baf·fling** frustrate by confusing or puzzling: *a baffling mystery; a mystery that completely baffles me.*
— *n.* a device for slowing or redirecting the flow of air, water, etc. — **baf·fle·ment** *n.*

baf·fle·gab (BAF·ul·gab) *n. Informal.* jargon used by bureaucrats, academics, etc., as when a nanny paid by the government was described as "a member of the staff who interfaces with the children in a habitual way."

bag *n.* **1** a container of paper, cloth, etc., usually one that can be opened and closed: *a bag of sugar; a brown-bag* or *brown-paper bag; a duffel, kit, flight, garment, grab, grocery bag; a padded jiffy bag; an overnight, paper, plastic, shopping, sleeping, tea, tote bag; She uses a punching bag for working out her frustrations; He packed his bags (= suitcases, etc.) and left; He was told to clear out **bag and baggage** (= with all his possesions); Check your bags (= luggage) at the check-in counter.* **2** the amount of game shot or caught.
— **in the bag** *Informal.* assured of success; sewed up.
— *v.* **bags, bagged, bag·ging 1** put into a bag or bags. **2** shoot or catch game.

ba·gel (BAY·gul) *n.* a hard, leavened, ring-shaped roll.

bag·gage (BAG·ij) *n.* **1** suitcases, personal effects, etc. that one travels with; luggage: *to check baggage before boarding; carry-on baggage; excess baggage.* **2** burden or impediment: *a speech loaded with patronizing baggage; the psychological baggage of preconceived ideas.*

bag·gat·a·way (buh·GAT·uh·way) *n. Cdn.* formerly, a native Indian game from which lacrosse developed.

bag·gy (BAG·ee) *adj.* **bag·gi·er, bag·gi·est** sagging or bulging like a bag: *baggy trousers.*

bag lady *n.* a homeless, usually elderly woman who carries her possessions in a shopping bag.

bag·man (BAG·mun) *n.* **-men 1** *Cdn.* the fund-raiser of a political party. **2** *Slang.* a racketeer who collects money, pays out bribes, etc.

bag·pipe *n.* usually **bag·pipes,** *pl.* a wind instrument consisting of a bag with pipes attached to it: *to play the bagpipes.*

bah *interj.* expressing contempt, disgust, etc.

bail *n.* **1** a scoop, bucket, etc. for bailing water out of a boat. **2** the semicircular handle of a kettle or pail. **3** a security of money posted to free someone from jail until the trial: *Carl was granted bail; The bail was set at $50 000; He was set free on a $50 000 bail; was freed or released on bail; Friends had put up or posted or provided or stood bail for him; Others were denied bail; They had trouble making or raising bail; No one would go bail for them; However, Carl jumped or skipped bail and failed to appear in court; He forfeited bail; The bail was forfeited to the Crown.*
— *v.* **1** grant bail to someone. **2** release on bail.
— **bail out 1** get someone released on bail. **2** clear a boat of water by dipping: *They bailed the water out of the boat.* **3** parachute from an airplane: *The pilot bailed out of the plane before it crashed.*
— **bail·a·ble** (-luh·bul) *adj.*: *a bailable offence, person.*

bail·ee (bay·LEE) *n.* a person to whom property is entrusted as bail.

bail·iff (BAY·lif) *n.* **1** an official who assists in a courtroom. **2** a sheriff's assistant.

bail·i·wick (BAY·lee·wick) *n.* **1** a bailiff's jurisdiction. **2** one's area of expertise or activity: *She doesn't accept work that is outside her bailiwick.*

bail·or *n.* a person who puts up property or money as bail.

bails·man *n.* **-men** a bondsman.

bait *n.* a lure or enticement, as food placed in a trap or on a hook to catch animals or fish: *a tempting bait; to hold out, nibble at, offer, put out, set out bait; to rise to the bait; to swallow or take the bait.*
— *v.* **1** put bait in or on something: *to bait a hook, trap.* **2** torment mercilessly for fun, as in bear-baiting.
— **bait·er** *n.*

bait and switch *n.* a sales tactic of attracting customers with a low-priced item in the hope of selling higher-priced goods.

bake *v.* **bakes, baked, bak·ing** cook, dry, or harden by dry heat, as in an oven or kiln: *to bake a cake for the party; bricks baked in the sun; a can of (Boston)* **baked beans** (= baked white dry beans with salt pork in tomato sauce). — *n.* a social event at which baked food is usually served, as a clambake.

bake·ap·ple (BAKE·ap·ul) *n.* *Cdn.* in the Atlantic Provinces, a "cloudberry" which resembles a small raspberry: *A bakeapple festival is held annually at L'Anse Amour, Newfoundland.*

bak·er (BAY·kur) *n.* one who bakes and sells bread, rolls, cakes, etc.

baker's dozen *n.* a dozen plus one.

bak·er·y (BAY·kuh·ree) *n.* **-ries** where baked goods are made or sold.

bake·shop *n.* a bakery.

baking powder *n.* a leavening agent containing baking soda, starch, and acid.

baking soda *n.* a sodium compound used as a leavening agent.

bal·ance (BAL·unce) *n.* **1** a weighing instrument, usually one supported in the centre with pans hanging on either side: *His future hangs* **in the balance** (= is uncertain). **2** a state in which both sides are equal: *The rider tried to keep his balance; He lost his balance and fell; He was thrown off balance; He couldn't recover his balance before falling; to strike a balance between being harsh and lenient; Why disturb* or *upset the delicate balance that exists in the community? The books are in* **balance** (= Debit equals credit); *In a minority government, a third party may hold the* **balance of power** *by aligning itself with one or the other of the two leading parties; the strategic balance of power in the Middle East; a system of checks and balances* (= controls) *for the even distribution of power.* **3** harmony or proportion: *a picture with a good balance of weights and colours.* **4** remainder or difference: *I paid $55 of the $100 due and she paid the balance* (= $45); *The last line of the statement shows your bank balance; a country's foreign-trade balance* or **balance of trade** (= difference of value between imports and exports); *The trade balance is favourable if exports exceed imports.* — **off balance** unsteady: *The boat got off balance and turned over; He was caught off balance* (= unprepared) *and failed the test.* — **on balance** all in all: *On balance, it was a fair deal.* — *v.* **-anc·es, -anced, -anc·ing** make, come, or be in a state of equilibrium: *He balanced the cup on his knee; to balance a budget so that there is neither surplus nor deficit; to balance the pros and cons* (= weigh the relative merits) *of an issue; The gains balance* (= equal) *the losses; A* **balanced diet** *has the right kinds and quantities of foods; the* **balancing act** *of finding more money without raising taxes.*

balance sheet *n.* a financial statement showing assets, liabilities, and net worth.

bal·co·ny (BAL·cuh·nee) *n.* **-nies** **1** an overhanging gallery in a theatre, auditorium, etc. **2** an outside projecting platform with a railing around it.

bald (BAWLD) *adj.* **1** without the usual covering, esp. of hair on the head or something resembling it: *I'm bald under my hat; A bald tire has no tread left; A* **bald cypress** *tree is a conifer that loses its leaves unlike other conifers that are evergreens; The* **bald eagle** *has a white head; the treeless* **bald prairie.** **2** plain or blunt: *a bald statement, style of writing.* — **bald·ly** *adv.;* **bald·ness** *n.*

bal·der·dash (BAWL·dur·dash) *n.* nonsense.

balding *adj.* becoming bald: *the balding head of a balding man.*

bale *n.* a large package of goods or material, compressed and bound: *a bale of cotton, hay.* — *v.* **bales, baled, bal·ing** make cotton, hay, newspaper, etc. into bales. — **bal·er** *n.*

bale·ful *adj.* threatening evil; ominous: *a baleful glance, influence, look, stare.* — **bale·ful·ly** *adv.*

balk (BAWK) *v.* **1** refuse to proceed: *Some horses balk at the slightest obstacle; When it was time to do as promised, she balked; He balked at the idea of a pay cut.* **2** frustrate by putting obstacles in the way: *The police balked the efforts of the gang.* — *n.* in baseball, an illegal hesitation by the pitcher. — **balk·y** *adj.:* *a balky horse, mule.*

ball (BAWL) *n.* **1** a usually round object, esp. one used in sports: *a golf ball; tennis ball; a cue ball used in billiards; When in danger, the hedgehog curls up in a ball; a sterile absorbent cotton ball; a fortune-teller's crystal ball; a medicine ball used for exercise; to bat, bounce, catch, drop, fumble a ball; A ball is dead when it has ceased to bounce; a ball of string; the ball* (= sole) *of the foot.* **2** a game played with a ball, esp. baseball; *adj.:* *a ball boy (fielding tennis balls); ball games such as football and tennis; a ball park, player.* **3** in baseball, a batted or pitched ball: *foul ball; fast ball; low ball.* **4.** a formal dancing party: *a costume, fancy-dress, inaugural, masked ball; I met her at a ball.* **5** *Slang.* a good time: *We had a ball.* — **be** or **get** or **have on the ball** *Informal.* efficient or alert: *She's really on the ball in her job; Her boss doesn't have to tell her to get on the ball; It didn't take the boss long to find out what she had on the ball* (= how good she was). — **play ball** cooperate *with* someone. — **start the ball rolling** begin an activity. — *v.* form into a ball. — **ball up** *Slang.* **1** ruin or spoil something organized, as a plan, project, etc. **2** confuse: *Your explanation has me all balled up.*

bal·lad (BAL·ud) *n.* **1** a narrative song in stanzas, esp. a folk song. **2** a popular love song. — **bal·lad·eer** (bal·uh·DEER) *n.*

bal·last (BAL·ust) *n.* **1** heavy material carried to stabilize a ship, aircraft, etc.: *to drop, take on ballast.* **2** crushed stone used in making concrete or to hold railway ties in place. — *v.* load with ballast.

ball bearing *n.* **1** a bearing with small steel balls turning to reduce friction. **2** such a ball.

bal·le·ri·na (bal·uh·REE·nuh) *n.* a female ballet dancer.

bal·let (BAL·ay) *n.* an elaborate, graceful, stylized form of dance: *to dance, perform, stage a ballet; classical, folk, water ballet.* — **bal·let·ic** (ba·LET·ic) *adj.*

bal·let·o·mane (ba·LET·uh·mane) *n.* a ballet enthusiast. — **bal·let·o·ma·ni·a** (-MAY·nee·uh) *n.*

bal·lis·tic (buh·LIS·tic) **1** *adj.* having to do with the flight of a projectile: *A **ballistic missile** is powered only while ascending, reaching its target in free flight.* **2 ballistics** *n.pl.* [takes sing. v.] the study of the motion and behaviour of bullets, rockets, bombs, etc.; *adj.: a ballistics expert, laboratory, test.*

bal·loon (buh·LOON) *n.* an airtight bag filled with helium, hot air, etc. and often used to lift loads into the atmosphere: *to blow up, deflate, fly, inflate a balloon; a trial balloon; weather balloon.* — **bal·loon·ist** *n.*

bal·lot (BAL·ut) *n.* **1** a piece of paper used in secret voting containing a list of candidates: *Cast your ballot; an absentee ballot; Spoiled ballots are invalidated; void ballots.* **2** the act, method, or right of voting: *They voted by secret ballot, not open ballot; a straw ballot* (= straw poll). **3** the votes cast or the result: *ballots for and against a proposal; The ballot was against the death penalty.*
— *v.* vote or decide by ballot: *The balloting went on till 6 a.m.; They were balloting for a new leader.*

ballot box *n.* a box into which ballots are put by voters: *to stuff the ballot boxes* (= put fraudulent votes in a ballot box). — **ballot stuffing** *n.*

ball·park *n.* a baseball field: *A **ballpark figure** (= a figure that is a reasonable estimate) for that project is $500 000; It may cost around $500 000, in that ballpark* (= range).

ball·point pen *n.* a pen with a ball bearing for a point, which rolls ink from a cartridge onto the paper.

ball·room *n.* a large hall for social dancing.

ball·sy (BALL·zee) *adj. Slang.* cocky and aggressive: *a ballsy fellow.*

bal·ly·hoo (BAL·ee·hoo) *n.* extravagant and noisy advertising.
— *v.* **-hooes, -hooed, -hoo·ing** praise or publicize with ballyhoo.

balm (BAHM, BOM) *n.* **1** an aromatic medicinal ointment or lotion: *a healing balm.* **2** something soothing: *the balm of friendship and understanding.*

balm·y (BAH·mee, BOM·ee) *adj.* **balm·i·er, -i·est** mild and soothing, not hot or cold: *the balmy beaches of Bermuda; a balmy breeze, climate; a balmy region of steady sunshine; a balmy temperature of 5°C; balmy weather.*

ba·lo·ney (buh·LOH·nee) *n.* **1** bologna sausage. **2** *Slang.* false and worthless talk; bunk.

bal·sam (BAWL·sum) *n.* the fragrant resin of several trees, used esp. in medicines.

bal·us·trade (BAL·us·trade) *n.* a row of posts with a rail on top of them.

bam·boo (bam·BOO) *n.* a tall, woody, often hollow-stemmed grass used for fishing poles, making huts, etc.; *adj.: a bamboo hut; bamboo shoots.*

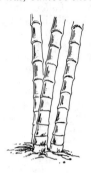

bam·boo·zle (bam·BOO·zul) *v.* **-zles, -zled, -zling** *Informal.* cheat or deceive: *He bamboozled her into buying an old encyclopedia, saying it would help to improve her child's grades; The old man was bamboozled out of his savings.*
— *n.: a monumental bamboozle* (= deception).
— **bam·boo·zler** *n.*

ban *v.* **bans, banned, ban·ning** officially disapprove of and prohibit a show, book, organization, person, or activity: *The troublemakers were banned from entering the school; a book banned in Boston; Ban the bomb!*
— *n.* an official prohibition: *the nuclear test ban; They put or placed a ban on smoking in the office; a movie under a ban imposed by the government; The ban was lifted later.*

ba·nal (buh·NAL, BAY·nul) *adj.* commonplace or dull: *banal compliments, humour, remarks.*

ba·na·na (buh·NAN·uh) *n.* **1** a long, curved tropical fruit with a yellowish peel. **2** *Slang.* a person playing a role: *the top banana* (= leading comic); *second banana; They are two tough bananas.* **3 bananas** *pl. Slang.* crazy: *She'll go bananas with boredom; Your music is driving me bananas.* **4 bananas** *interj.* nonsense.

banana belt *n. Cdn.* a region of relatively mild weather, esp. a southerly region of Canada: *in the banana belt* (= Okanagan Valley) *of British Columbia.*

banana republic *n.* any small Latin American country whose economy depends mostly on fruits, esp. one ruled by a despot.

banana seat *n.* an elongated bicycle seat.

banana split *n.* a dessert of ice cream with split banana.

band *n.* **1** a thin strip of flexible material used around something: *a hat band; a rubber band; the gold band around the rim of a cup; a wedding band* (= metal ring). **2** a range of radio frequencies: *a citizens' band; a short wave band; a broad-band radio antenna.* **3** a group of musicians playing on brass, woodwind, and percussion instruments: *a band playing in the park; a five-piece, jazz, marching, military, school, steel, string band; Strike up the band! The band struck up and played "O*

Canada"; *Everyone got up and started shouting to* **beat the band** (*Informal for* with much noise). **4** a united group of people or animals: *a band of deer, Indians; a roving band* (= gang) *of marauders, outlaws, robbers, thieves.* **5** *Cdn.* a Canadian Indian group, as on a reserve, recognized by the government as an administrative unit. **6 bands** *pl.* a pair of strips hung from the front of the collar in academic, clerical, and legal costumes. **7 bands** *pl.* braces for the teeth.
— *v.* **1** put an identifying band around: *Birds are banded, released, and captured again for studying their travel routes; the naturally* **banded** (= striped) *rattlesnake.* **2** get together for a common purpose: *They banded together for protection; The students banded together to vote against a fee increase.*

band·age (BAN·dij) *n.* a strip of gauze or cloth used to bind or cover an injured part of the body: *to apply, put on, remove a bandage.*
— *v.* **-ag·es, -aged, -ag·ing** put a bandage on a body part, wound, etc.

band-aid *n.* a small adhesive gauze bandage used to cover cuts.
— *adj.* temporary or stop-gap: *a band-aid approach, measure; a mere band-aid solution to a perennial problem; to give band-aid treatment when major surgery is called for.* — **Band-Aid** *Trademark.*

ban·dan·a or **ban·dan·na** (ban·DAN·uh) *n.* a large brightly coloured handkerchief or scarf.

ban·dit (BAN·dit) *n.* **-dits** or **-dit·ti** (ban·DIT·ee) an outlaw, esp. one of a band of robbers: *a masked bandit; one-arm bandit* (*Informal for* slot machine).
— **ban·dit·ry** (BAN·dit·ree) *n.*

ban·do·leer or **ban·do·lier** (ban·duh·LEER) *n.* a cartridge belt worn across the chest and over one shoulder.

band·wag·on (BAND·wag·un) *n.* a large, decorated wagon used to carry a band in a parade.
— **climb** or **hop** or **jump on the bandwagon** support a cause when it is winning, esp. in a political campaign.

ban·dy (BAN·dee) *v.* **-dies, -died, -dy·ing** knock back and forth; exchange gossip, insults, etc., esp. frivolously or in anger: *All they did was bandy words about; They bandied words with their opponents instead of debating the issues.* — *adj.* curved outwards: *bandy legs.*

bandy-legged (BAN·dee·leg·id) *adj.* bowlegged.

bane *n.* **1** a cause of death or woe: *the bane of one's existence; Alcohol proved to be the bane of his life.* **2** *combining form.* poison: *fleabane, flybane, ratsbane, wolfsbane.*

bane·ful (BANE·ful) *adj.* evil: *the baneful influence of drugs on society.*

bang *v.* **1** strike hard or with a loud noise: *She banged on the door; She accidentally banged her head against the door; Don't let the door bang behind you; She banged into him* (= met him by accident) *on her way back; He was banging away* (= working hard) *at his old typewriter.* **2** handle roughly or noisily: *He was pretty banged up at the initiation ceremony.* **3** cut hair in bangs.
— *n.* **1** a sudden loud noise: *He slammed the door with*

a bang; the "big bang" theory of the origin of the universe. **2** noisy blow. **3** *Slang.* a thrill: *You'll get a bang out of this.* **4** usually **bangs** *pl.* fringe of hair cut squarely across the forehead.
— *adv. Informal.* directly or exactly: *He ran bang into the wall; to stay bang up to date; Prices go up and bang go savings; He arrived bang on the hour; That's bang on* (= exactly right); *a* **bang-up** (= first-rate) *finish, job.*

ban·gle (BANG·gul) *n.* **1** a rigid bracelet worn on the wrist or ankle. **2** an ornament hanging from this.

ban·ish *v.* **1** expel from a country: *Convicts used to be banished instead of being hanged; He was banished from England; banished to Australia.* **2** send away, esp. from the mind: *how to banish care and woe.*
— **ban·ish·ment** (BAN·ish·munt) *n.*

ban·is·ter or **ban·nis·ter** (BAN·is·tur) *n.* the railing along a set of stairs: *to slide down the banister.*

bank *n.* **1** a pile or heap: *a bank of snow; a bank of clouds.* **2** usually **banks** *pl.* a shallow area under water; shoal: *the Grand Banks* (= fishing banks) *of Newfoundland.* **3** the edge of a body of water: *the two banks of a river; standing on the opposite bank; a rugged bank.* **4** the inward tilt of a vehicle, esp. an aircraft, as it turns: *The pilot put the plane into a steep bank.* **5** the slant in a road or course at a curve. **6** a row or tier, as of oars, organ keys, etc.: *film crews with their banks of floodlights; a bank* (= set) *of elevators.* **7** a business establishment that deals in money deposits, loans, etc.: *a central, chartered, national, savings bank; Banks may close, collapse, fail.* **8** a reserve or supply for drawing from: *a blood bank; data banks full of information; eye banks; food banks for the hungry.*
— *v.* **1** pile up; also, heap fuel, ashes, etc. on a fire to slow its burning: *The camper banked the fire and went to sleep.* **2** tilt: *This turn is too steeply banked for the average driver.* **3** put money in a bank: *She banks her savings.* **4** do business at a bank: *Where do you bank?*
— **bank on** rely on: *We banked on her support; She was banking on having more money to spend.*
— **bank·a·ble** *adj.*

bank barn *n. Cdn.* a barn built into a hillside so that the upper storey may be entered from one side and the lower from the other.

bank·book *n.* a bank customer's record of deposits and withdrawals.

bank card *n.* a card issued by a bank for electronic banking or as a credit card.

bank·er *n.* **1** one who owns or manages a bank: *Banker's hours used to be from 10 to 3.* **2** *Cdn.* a boat or person engaged in fishing off the Grand Banks of Newfoundland.

bank note *n.* a note issued by a bank guaranteeing payment of a stated sum to bearer.

bank rate *n.* the interest rate set by a country's national bank, as what the Bank of Canada charges on loans to the chartered banks.

bank·roll (BANK·role) *n. Informal.* a supply of ready money.

— *v.* finance: *a new project bankrolled by some bold investors.*

bank·rupt *n.* 1 a person or business legally declared unable to pay creditors fully. 2 one totally lacking in a specified quality: *a moral bankrupt.*
— *v.* make bankrupt: *Farmers complain of being bankrupted by quotas, levies, etc.*
— *adj.* unable to pay debts or meet obligations: *Companies go bankrupt; a bankrupt corporation; a government bankrupt* (= devoid) *of leadership.*

bank·rupt·cy (BANK·rup·see) *n.* **-cies** bankrupt condition: *The struggling businessman declared* or *filed for* or *petitioned for* or *went into personal bankruptcy to get rid of his debts; companies driven to bankruptcy by the recession.*

ban·ner (BAN·ur) *n.* 1 a flag or standard, esp. a large strip of cloth bearing a slogan: *to unfurl a banner; banners waving* or *fluttering in the wind; America's star-spangled banner; Campaign banners were stretched across the streets of Rome.* 2 rallying point: *People gathered under the banner of socialism.* 3 an across-the-page newspaper headline.
— *adj.* outstanding: *a banner year for the school's swimming team.*

bannister same as BANISTER.

banns *n.pl.* the announcement in church of an intended marriage: *Banns are usually published* or *announced on three successive Sundays.*

ban·quet (BANK·wit) *n.* an elaborate feast, usually in honour of a person or event: *to arrange, cater, give, hold a banquet; a farewell, formal, lavish, state, sumptuous, wedding banquet; I met him at the banquet for the new mayor.*

ban·shee *n.* in Irish and Scottish folklore, a female spirit whose wail foretells a death in the house: *screaming like a banshee; a raving banshee.*

ban·tam (BAN·tum) *n.* 1 a dwarfish but aggressive breed of domestic fowls. 2 a small aggressive person.
— *adj.* aggressive though small: *a bantam battalion, league; her bantam spirit; a bantam hockey team.*

ban·ter (BAN·tur) *n.* playful teasing: *good-natured, light, witty banter; to exchange banter with friends.*
— *v.* 1 tease good-humouredly. 2 joke playfully *with* someone.

ban·zai (bahn·ZYE) *interj.* a Japanese cheer or battle cry.

banzai attack *n.* a usually suicidal mass attack.

bap·tism (BAP·tiz·um) *n.* 1 a baptizing: *to administer, receive, undergo baptism.* 2 an initiation: *a soldier's baptism of fire* (= first experience of combat).
— **bap·tis·mal** (bap·TIZ·mul) *adj.: a baptismal font, name, rite; baptismal vows, water.*

Bap·tist (BAP·tist) *n.* a member of a Protestant church that baptizes mature believers by immersion.

bap·tize (bap·TIZE, BAP·tize) *v.* **-tiz·es, -tized, -tiz·ing** 1 admit a person to a church by a rite using water. 2 give a first name to; christen: *He was baptized John; They baptized him John.* 3 initiate or inaugurate: *a party thrown to baptize a new barbecue.*

bar *n.* 1 a regular oblong piece, as of wood or metal: *an iron bar; a bar of soap; a candy bar.* 2 a bar used to block a passage or fasten a door: *a window bar; a bar to progress; a colour bar between whites and blacks.* 3 something made of a bar: *a wrecking bar; the horizontal and parallel bars for gymnasts; the torsion bar of an automobile's suspension; ballerinas warming up at the bar* (= barre); *a typewriter's space bar* (= lever). 4 a band, as of colour or sunlight; *adj.: a bar chart* or *graph; a bar code.* 5 a sales counter, as one serving drinks: *Joe's bar and grill; Tim drinks at the bar every evening; He drops into the bar on his way home; He met his wife at the bar; a cash bar at a convention; a singles bar; cosmetics bar; salad bar; snack bar.* 6 a law court: *the prisoner at the bar; before the bar of conscience; the bar of public opinion.* 7 **the bar** the legal profession: *Law students read for the bar; They are called* or *admitted to the bar; Judges are normally chosen from the bar.* 8 a vertical line dividing a staff of music into measures; also, a portion so divided: *He played a few bars of "O Canada."*
— **behind bars** in prison.
— *v.* **bars, barred, bar·ring** 1 fasten with a bar: *Bar the door.* 2 exclude: *The heckler was barred from future meetings; They barred* (= forbade) *his attending the meetings.*
— *prep.* excepting: *bar none; bar one; also* **barring:** *Everyone, barring Tim, was present; Barring* (= except in case of) *a miracle, the sun should rise tomorrow.*

barb *n.* 1 a backward-turned point, as on a fishhook or arrow. 2 something sharp or cutting, as criticism or sarcasm: *to sling barbs of ridicule at a poet; her barbs of wit.*

bar·bar·i·an (bar·BAIR·ee·un) *n.* 1 a member of a primitive or relatively less developed culture. 2 an uncultured person or brute.
— *adj.* uncivilized: *barbarian customs, hordes, peoples.*

bar·bar·ic (bar·BAIR·ic) *adj.* wild, uncivilized, or exotic: *barbaric customs, ornaments, people; the barbaric splendour of a temple's interior.*

bar·bar·ism (BAR·buh·riz·um) *n.* 1 a primitive level of civilization: *to live in barbarism.* 2 a cruel or savage act or trait. 3 a nonstandard usage such as "irregardless."

bar·bar·i·ty (bar·BAIR·uh·tee) *n.* **-ties** 1 a cruel or savage act or custom: *the barbarities of warfare.* 2 a primitive or uncultured condition: *living in barbarity; Nazism was a regression to barbarity.*

bar·ba·rous (BAR·buh·rus) *adj.* 1 savage; brutal; uncivilized. 2 of words and expressions, nonstandard.
— **bar·ba·rous·ly** *adv.*

bar·be·cue (BAR·buh·cue) *n.* 1 an outdoor pit, fireplace, or portable grill for roasting meats. 2 a party at which such food is served: *Canadians have barbecues in the summer.*
— *v.* **-cues, -cued, -cu·ing** 1 cook on a barbecue. 2 cook with a seasoned sauce, or **barbecue sauce,** made with tomatoes and vinegar.

barbed *adj.* having barbs: *a barbed* (= sarcastic) *comment.*

barbed wire *n.* wire with sharp points along it, used for fences or barricades: *Barbed wire was strung around the compound.*

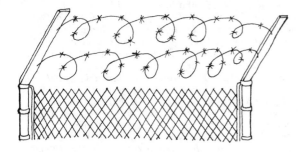

bar·ber (BAR·bur) *n.* one who cuts hair, shaves beards, etc. as a trade.

bar·ber·shop (BAR·bur·shop) *n.* a barber's place of business.

barbershop quartet *n.* a group of four male harmonized voices singing popular songs.

Bar·bie doll (BAR·bee-) *n.* **1** a popular brand of miniature adult blond blue-eyed doll; **Barbie Doll**, *Trademark.* **2** *Slang.* a mindless person.

bar·bi·tu·rate (bar·BICH·ur·it) *n.* a sedative or sleep-inducing drug that is potentially addictive.

barb·wire *n.* same as BARBED WIRE.

bar code *n.* a code of bars and numbers printed on products for use in computerized checkout and inventory systems, esp. the "universal product code."

bard *n.* a tribal poet or minstrel: *"the Bard of Avon"* (= Shakespeare).

bare *adj.* **bar·er, bar·est 1** without its natural or usual covering, as shoes for the feet: *bare feet; a bare head; He uprooted the tree with his bare hands; the bare* (= unadorned) *facts; bare walls; a bare* (= empty) *cupboard; a hillside **bare of** vegetation; to **lay bare*** (= expose) *the facts, secrets, the truth of a story.* **2** mere: *the bare necessities of life; a budget cut to the bare bones* (= essentials); *They won with a bare* (= scanty) *majority; the bare* (= stark) *truth.*
— *v.* **bares, bared, bar·ing** lay bare or reveal: *The dog growled and bared its teeth.*

bare-bones *adj.* having only the bare essentials: *a bare-bones budget, operation, style of writing.*

bare·faced *adj.* shameless: *a barefaced liar, lie.*

bare·foot *adj. & adv.* without shoes: *to run barefoot in the park; the **barefoot doctors*** (= medical auxiliaries) *of China's rural areas.* Also **bare·foot·ed.**

bare·hand·ed (BARE·han·did) *adj.* with empty hands, as without a tool or weapon.

bare·head·ed (BARE·hed·id) *adj. & adv.* with head exposed; hatless.

bare·leg·ged (BARE·leg·id) *adj. & adv.* with no leg-covering: *barelegged children shivering on street corners.*

bare·ly *adv.* **1** scantily: *a barely furnished room.* **2** scarcely: *She had barely met him when he proposed; He barely survived the fire.* — **bare·ness** *n.*

bar·fly *n.* **-flies** *Slang.* one who regularly drinks in bars.

bar·gain (BARG·in) *n.* **1** an agreement or deal to buy, sell, etc.: *to make or seal or strike a bargain with someone; a sales rep who drives a hard bargain; But he always meets his end of the bargain or keeps his side of the bargain* (= carries out what he has agreed to do); *She tried to make the best of a **bad bargain*** (= do her best in the difficult situation). **2** something bought at a low price: *People shop for bargains; trying to find or get good bargains; It's a real bargain at that price.*
— **in** or **into the bargain** in addition.
— *v.* negotiate terms, as of a deal or contract: *to bargain with a sales rep for a used car; to bargain over the terms of a lease; collective bargaining; plea bargaining.*
— **bargain on** or **for** expect or anticipate: *He met with trouble he hadn't bargained for.*

bargain-basement *adj.* [used before its noun] cheap or inexpensive: *The new airline started bargain-basement flights across the Atlantic; a bargain-basement deal, fare, figure, price.*

bargaining chip *n.* something used in negotiations to gain an advantage or concession from the opposite party: *The question of overtime pay was used as a bargaining chip during the final negotiations.*

barge (BARJ) *n.* **1** a big flat-bottomed freight boat used on canals, rivers, etc. **2** a finely decorated ceremonial boat: *Cleopatra's barge on the Nile.*
— *v.* **barg·es, barged, barg·ing 1** transport by barge. **2** move or intrude clumsily or rudely: *He has a way of barging into a room; He barges in without knocking; He barges in on people's conversations.*

bar·i·tone (BAIR·uh·tone) *n.* a male singing voice lower than tenor and higher than bass: *He sings baritone; He's a baritone (singer).*

bark *n.* **1** a short gruff sound typically made by a dog; "bow-wow": *a loud bark; an angry bark; "His bark is worse than his bite"* (= He is frightening but harmless). **2** the tough outer covering of woody stems and roots: *to peel the bark off trees.*
— *v.* **1** utter a bark: *Dogs bark at strangers.* **2** speak sharply or hoarsely: *an officer who barks orders.* **3** take the bark off a tree. **4** *Informal.* scrape the skin of a body part: *He fell and barked his shin.*
— **bark up the wrong tree** have one's efforts, criticisms, etc. misdirected; be on the wrong track.

bar·keep·er *n.* **1** a bartender. **2** owner of a bar serving liquor. Also **bar·keep.**

bark·er *n.* one who loudly calls out to attract people, esp. to a sideshow or sale.

bar·ley (BAR·lee) *n.* a grain used for food and in making beer and whisky.

bar·maid *n.* a woman who serves drinks in a bar.

bar·man *n.* **-men** a bartender.

bar mitz·vah (bar·MITS·vuh) *n.* **1** a Jewish ceremony for a 13-year-old boy to mark his taking on of religious responsibility. **2** such a boy.

barm·y *adj.* **barm·i·er, -i·est** crazy or foolish: *They have gone totally barmy to join in the gold rush.*

barn *n.* **1** a large building for sheltering farm equipment, animals, crops and feed, etc.; *adj.*: *It's no use locking the barn door after the horse has escaped; Her speech was a **barn burner*** (*Slang* for something sensational or exciting). **2** a similar building for buses, trucks, etc.

bar·na·cle (BAR·nuh·cul) *n.* a marine shellfish that fastens itself firmly to rocks, timbers, ship hulls, etc.: *clinging barnacles.*

barn·storm *v.* tour the countryside giving plays, speeches, or exhibitions of stunt flying.

barn·yard *n.* a yard near a barn.
— *adj.* earthy: *low barnyard humour.*

ba·rom·e·ter (buh·ROM·uh·tur) *n.* **1** an instrument for measuring atmospheric pressure: *A barometer falls, rises, is steady.* **2** an indicator of change: *Polls are a barometer of public opinion.*
— **bar·o·met·ric** (bair·uh·MET·ric) *adj.*

bar·on (BAIR·un) *n.* **1** a peer of the lowest inherited rank; *fem.* **bar·on·ess. 2** a magnate: *a beef, cattle, coal, mining, oil baron; the barons of the board room.*
— **baron of beef** two sirloins joined at the backbone.
— **bar·on·age** (BAIR·uh·nij) *n.*

ba·ro·ni·al (buh·ROH·nee·ul) *adj.* **1** of a baron: *baronial privileges.* **2** large or ample: *baronial rooms; a house of baronial dimensions.*

ba·roque (buh·ROKE) *adj.* in a 17th century style noted for florid ornamentation, bordering on the grotesque: *baroque architecture, furniture, music, opera, poetry, sculpture; a **baroque garden** with canals, cascades, and fountains; a **baroque pearl** (of irregular shape).*

bar·racks (BAIR·uks) *n.pl.* [takes sing. or pl. v.] a building housing soldiers: *The RCMP barracks house local detachments and serve as training centres; a school built like a barracks; refugee barracks.*

bar·rage (buh·RAHZH) *n.* **1** a heavy, sustained burst of artillery fire. **2** a continuous stream: *a barrage of abuse, complaints, goals, questions; a barrage of balloons sent up by protestors.*
— *v.* **bar·rag·es, bar·raged, bar·rag·ing** hit with a barrage: *The speaker was barraged with questions.*

barrage balloon *n.* a balloon flown anchored to the ground with a cable to obstruct enemy aircraft.

barre (BAR) *n.* a horizontal rod attached to a wall that ballet dancers use for balance when practising: *Ballet training begins at the barre.*

barred See BAR.
— **barred** *adj.* having bars: *a barred window.*

bar·rel (BAIR·ul) *n.* **1** a round cask with bulging sides; drum: *Petroleum products are measured in barrels of 159 L.* **2** a cylindrical part of an apparatus or machine, esp. the firing tube of a gun. **3** *Informal.* a great amount: *a barrel of fun, laughs.*
— **over a barrel** *Informal.* at someone's mercy.
— *v.* **bar·rels, bar·relled** or **bar·reled, bar·rel·ling** or **bar·rel·ing 1** pack in a barrel. **2** *Slang.* travel at high speed: *stopped by police while barrelling along the highway.*

barrel-chested *adj.* having a broad chest.

bar·ren (BAIR·un) *adj.* **1** not bearing fruit; unproductive: *a barren desert, region; a barren* (= sterile) *woman.* **2** devoid: *Animals are not barren of intelligence; an attempt that was barren of results.*
— *n.***1** usually **barrens** *pl.* a barren region. **2** *Cdn.* the **Barrens** or **Barren Ground** or **Barren Grounds** or **Barren Lands** the thinly populated sub-Arctic tundra area of Northern Canada, from Hudson Bay west to the Great Slave and Great Bear lakes, in which only grasses, mosses, etc. grow. — **bar·ren·ness** *n.*

bar·ri·cade (BAIR·uh·cade) *n.* a hastily built rampart or barrier, esp. one blocking a street: *to place* or *set up a barricade; to remove* or *take down a barricade; a barbed-wire barricade; Man the barricades, citizens!*
— *v.* **-cades, -cad·ed, -cad·ing** block, obstruct, or protect, esp. with a barricade.

bar·ri·er (BAIR·ee·ur) *n.* something that blocks, hinders, or separates, esp. a fence or wall: *to erect, overcome, place, remove, set up barriers; Do not cross a police barrier; Watch how easily the horse takes the barrier; cultural, language, social barriers; to break down the barriers between the races; barriers to progress; the boom of a supersonic plane breaking the sound* or *sonic barrier as it approaches the speed of sound.*

barring (BAR·ing) *prep.* See BAR.

bar·ri·o (BAH·ree·oh) *n.* **-os** a Spanish-speaking part of an American city.

bar·ris·ter (BAIR·is·tur) *n.* a lawyer, esp. one who argues cases: *A Canadian lawyer is both barrister and solicitor.*

bar·room *n.* a room with a bar for selling liquor.

bar·row (BAIR·oh) *n.* **1** a mound over an ancient grave site. **2** a wheelbarrow or handcart.

bar·stool *n.* a high stool used at a bar.

bar·ten·der (BAR·ten·dur) *n.* one who serves liquor at a bar.

bar·ter *v.* to trade without using money: *The trapper bartered his furs for a rifle.*
— *n.* the practice of bartering goods and services: *The pioneers engaged in barter with the natives; Barter precedes a money economy; People form barter clubs for making cashless trades and evading taxes.*

bas·al (BAY·sul) *adj.* having to do with the base or basis: *a basal reader (textbook); basal* (= very light) *anesthesia.*

basal metabolism *n.* the minimal amount of energy used by an organism for cell activity, respiration, and circulation, as when at rest.

base *adj.* **1** greedy and selfish; ignoble: *base cowardice.* **2** of metals, not precious: *a base coin made with an alloy; brass, lead, zinc, and such base* (= not "noble") *metals.* — **base·ly** *adv.;* **base·ness** *n.*
— *n.* **1** the lower or supporting part of a statue, figure, etc.: *the base of a triangle.* **2** the number on which a numbering system is built: *10 is the base of the decimal system.* **3** a camp or town supplying food, equipment, etc. for a military or other undertaking: *to set up a base of operations; a forward base; an army, military, missile, naval base; The power base of the party is among the peasantry; the base camp of the mountain climbers.*

4 the main ingredient: *a paint with an oil base.* 5 a substance that reacts with an acid to form a salt: *Strong bases are called alkalis.* 6 the part of a word to which affixes are added; stem: *The base of "mistakenly" is "take."* 7 in baseball, one of the four points to be touched for a run to count: *to **touch base*** (= be in contact) *with someone; The speaker **touched all bases*** (= points to be considered) *in his keynote address.*
— **base on balls** a baseball batter's advance to first base after being pitched four balls.
— **get to first base with** *Informal.* begin to have any success with someone.
— **off base** *Informal.* mistaken or unprepared.
— *v.* **bas·es, based, bas·ing** 1 place at a base: *a journalist based in New Delhi.* 2 have or provide a foundation for something: *a story based upon facts; a movie based on a novel.*

base·ball *n.* a game played by two teams of nine players each on a diamond-shaped field with a bat and ball; also, the ball.

base·less (BAIS·lis) *adj.* without foundation: *a baseless allegation.*

base·line *n.* 1 in baseball, one of the four lanes connecting the bases. 2 a line serving as a base, esp. in surveying.

base·ment (BAIS·munt) *n.* 1 the foundation of a building. 2 the lowest storey, at least partly underground: *a finished basement with a kitchen and recreation room; the bargain basement of a department store.*
— *adj:* *a basement apartment, kitchen, office; a basement bargain* (= cheap bargain).

base pay *n.* pay exclusive of overtime and other additions.

bases *pl.* of BASE or BASIS.

bash *v. Informal.* hit very hard; smash: *He bashed his head against the wall; union-bashing by management.*
— *n. Slang.* a party: *a birthday bash; the bash for her 21st birthday.*

bash·ful *adj.* shy, as a child or youth; sensitive and timid. — **bash·ful·ly** *adv.;* **bash·ful·ness** *n.*

bas·ic (BAY·sic) *adj.* 1 fundamental: *a basic outline of the course; life's basic necessities; students who commit errors in basic English; The three R's are basic to education; to take basic training in life-saving.* 2 in chemistry, having to do with a base.
— *n.* 1 something basic; usually **basics** *pl.: The negotiators got down to basics; the basics of algebra.* 2 **Basic** or **BASIC** a computer language using common English terms. — **bas·i·cal·ly** (-sic·lee) *adv.*

ba·sin (BAY·sin) *n.* 1 an open, shallow, rounded vessel for water; also, a sink. 2 a usually enclosed body of water, as a harbour or pond: *a tidal basin.* 3 the area passed through by a river. 4 a broad, rounded depression in a land mass.

ba·sis (BAY·sis) *n., pl.* **ba·ses** (BAY·seez) foundation: *a case with a firm* or *solid basis on evidence; the scientific basis of a theory; a complaint without any basis; It rests on a shaky basis; The new president put the company on*

a sound economic basis; Common interests are or form or provide a good basis* (= common ground) *for friendship; friends on a first-name basis* (= footing); *He is paid on a monthly basis* (= arrangement); *He was hired on the basis of* (= relying on) *recommendations.*

bask *v.* enjoy being exposed to warmth, love, admiration, etc.: *See the people basking on the beach; They like to bask in the sunshine; to bask in glory.*

bas·ket (BAS·kit) *n.* 1 a container usually made of interwoven strips of wood, cane, fibre, etc.: *to weave a basket; a laundry basket made of plastic; picnic basket; wastepaper basket; a basket of apples* (= apples in a basket). 2 a round hoop fitted with an open, hanging net that forms the goal in basketball. 3 a throw of the ball through the hoop that counts as a score: *to make, miss, score, shoot, sink a basket.*

bas·ket·ball (BAS·kit·ball) *n.* a game played with an inflated round ball by two teams of five players each; also, the ball.

basket case *n.* a totally incapacitated person or entity: *Some poor countries are true basket cases; to bring corporate basket cases* (= bankrupt companies) *back to health.*

bas·ket·ful (BAS·kit·ful) *n.* the contents of a basket.

bas mitz·vah (bahs·MITS·vuh) same as BATH MITZVAH.

Basque (BASK) *n.* a member of an ethnically unique people of the Pyrenees; also, their language.
— *adj.:* *the Basque country; the Basque provinces of northern Spain; Basque separatists.*

bass (BAYCE) *adj.* of the lowest pitch of male voice: *a bass drum, singer, voice.*
— *n.* 1 a male singer or an instrument with a bass range. 2 the lowest part in harmonic arrangements: *He sings a deep bass.* 3 (BASS) any of a group of spiny-finned game fishes of lakes and seas.

bas·tard (BAS·turd) *n.* 1 *Slang.* [abusive use] an offensive person. 2 an illegitimate child.
— *adj.* 1 illegitimate. 2 inferior: *bastard mahogany.*
— **bas·tard·ly** *adj.* base or vicious: *a bastardly trick.*

bas·tard·ize (BAS·tur·dize) *v.* **-iz·es, -ized, -iz·ing** 1 make or declare bastard. 2 corrupt or debase: *He speaks a bastardized French.*

baste *v.* **bastes, bast·ed, bast·ing** 1 fasten with large stitches: *The tailor basted the hem of the skirt before stitching it.* 2 beat or scold soundly: *a good, sound, thorough basting for using foul language.* 3 pour drippings, sauce, etc. over meat or fish while it is cooking: *basted turkey.*

bas·tion (BAS·chun) *n.* 1 a fortified projection of a wall or rampart. 2 a strong position: *a club that was the last bastion of male chauvinists.*

bat *n.* 1 a stick or paddle for hitting the ball in baseball, cricket, etc.: *He swung his bat to hit the ball.* 2 a type of nocturnal animal, including the vampire and the "flying fox," that has wings of membrane: *blind as a bat.* 3 a blow.
— **at bat** taking one's turn as a hitter in baseball.
— **off the bat** *Informal.* without any delay; right away: *right off the bat.*

— *v.* **bats, bat·ted, bat·ting 1** hit with a bat. **2** flutter eyelids: *She didn't **bat an eye*** (= showed no surprise) *at the news.*
— **go to bat for** (or **against**) defend (or oppose) someone.

batch *n.* a group of things or people processed at one time: *a fresh batch of bread, dough, loaves; a batch of pea soup; a new batch of problems, trainees; **batch processing** of many transactions together on a computer.*

ba·teau (ba·TOH) *n. Cdn., pl.* **ba·teaux** (-TOZE) a flat-bottomed light boat, usually with narrow bow and stern.

bated (BAY·tid) *adj.* usually **with bated breath,** holding the breath in excitement, expectation, fear, etc.

bath *n.* **1** a washing of the body in water: *to take a bath in the morning; Stockholders **took a bath** (Informal for* suffered a financial loss) *when the market crashed.* **2** the water, tub, or room used for bathing: *to draw a bath; Run the bath till the tub is half full; A sauna is a steam bath; whirlpool bath; an apartment with a bedroom, kitchen, and bath; one and a half baths* (= one four-piece bathroom and a two-piece washroom). **3 baths** *pl.* a building with bathing pools and rooms: *Roman baths; Turkish baths.*

bathe ("th" as in "the") *v.* **bathes, bathed, bath·ing 1** take or subject to a bath: *to bathe a child; We bathe in warm water.* **2** go swimming: *to bathe in the sea; a **bathing** beach, beauty, cap, costume; bathing trunks.* **3** soak: *Bathe your foot in warm water; We bathe in the sun; The meadows were **bathed** in* (= covered with) *sunlight; He was all **bathed*** (= wet) *with sweat.*
— **bath·er** *n.*

bathing suit *n.* a swimsuit.

bath mitz·vah (baht·MITS·vuh) *n.* a ceremony for a girl similar to the bar mitzvah.

ba·thos (BAY·thos, "th" as in "thin") *n.* **1** a sudden transition from the sublime to the trivial. **2** overdone or insincere pathos.

bath·robe *n.* a loose robe worn when going to and from a bath, for lounging, etc.

bath·room *n.* **1** a room for taking baths, usually one with a toilet, washbasin, and bathtub or shower. **2** a washroom or lavatory.

bath·tub *n.* a tub for bathing.

bat·mitz·vah (baht·MITS·vuh) *n.* same as BATH MITZVAH.

ba·ton (buh·TON, *rhyme:* ON) *n.* **1** a light stick used by the conductor to direct an orchestra: *a great performance under the baton of Seiji Ozawa.* **2** any similar rod or staff, as one carried as a symbol of authority: *A drum majorette leads a parade twirling a baton in display; In a relay race, each runner of a team carries a baton and hands* or *passes it to the next runner; a field marshal's baton; The police made a baton* (= truncheon) *charge to disperse the mob.*

bats·man (BATS·mun) *n.* **-men** a batter in baseball or cricket: *the lead-off batsman.*

batt (BAT) *n.* a batting of cotton, wool, or other material: *friction-fit batts of fibreglass for insulation.*

bat·tal·ion (buh·TAL·yun) *n.* **1** a military unit made up of two or more companies, batteries, etc.: *Hitler's big battalions.* **2** a large organized group: *battalions of census takers.*

bat·ten (BAT·un) *n.* a long thin board used for flooring or to fasten other boards in place.
— *v.* **1 batten down the hatches** secure a ship's hatch covers, esp. before a storm. **2** thrive or grow fat: *He leads a life of ease battening on the generosity of relatives.*

bat·ter *n.* **1** in baseball, one whose turn it is to bat. **2** a beaten mixture of flour, milk, eggs, etc. that can be poured for cooking or used as a coating: *pancake batter.*
— *v.* strike or pound heavily or repeatedly: *to batter away at a door; The police had to batter down the door; The dollar took a battering in foreign exchange markets yesterday; The storm battered the coast for several days.*

battered *adj.* beaten up or worn, as from hard use: *a battered old car, house, sailboat; a battered competition, economy, foreign currency, plan; a home for battered* (= physically abused) *women.*

bat·ter·y (BAT·uh·ree) *n.* **bat·ter·ies 1** a device for storing or generating electricity: *to charge the storage battery of an automobile; Most flashlight batteries cannot be recharged; A car battery charges itself as the engine runs; When a battery discharges* or *runs down, it is a dead battery.* **2** a set of similar things used together, as an array of guns: *An artillery battery is commanded by a captain; A battalion is composed of two or more batteries; a missile battery; He had to face a battery of press cameras; a battery of questions, searchlights, tests and X rays.* **3** the unlawful use of force by one person against another, esp. an attack: *He was charged with assault and battery; Even touching a person in a hostile way could constitute battery; Surgery without informed consent was ruled battery upon the patient.* **4** in baseball, the pitcher and catcher.

batting *n.* flat wads of the fibres of cotton, wool, etc. as used in furniture stuffing: *Cotton batting is used in bandages.*

batting average *n.* a person's level of success or achievement, as of a baseball player at bat: *an M.P. with a low batting average with his constituents.*

bat·tle (BAT·ul) *n.* a conflict or struggle, esp. a large armed combat: *the Battle of Queenston Heights; wounds received in battle; soldiers killed in battle; a battle for supremacy; a battle of wits, words; "The first blow is half the battle"; We lost a few battles but won*

the war; to do or *give* or *join battle with the enemy; to fight, terminate, wage a battle; a bloody, decisive, fierce, losing, naval, pitched, raging, royal, running battle; The will led to a long battle among* or *between the family members for* or *over possession of the house; the continuing battle against inflation; to take up one's battle station; the **battle of the bulge** (Informal for struggle to get rid of body fat).*
— *v.* **bat·tles, bat·tled, bat·tling** to fight: *to battle against* or *with someone for* or *over something.*

battle-axe or **battle-ax** (BAT·ul·ax) *n.* -ax·es **1** a heavy axe used as a weapon. **2** *Informal.* an aggressive domineering woman.

battle cry *n.* a slogan or cry used as encouragement in a conflict.

battle fatigue *n.* same as SHELL SHOCK.

bat·tle·field (BAT·ul·feeld) *n.* the site of a battle: *on the battlefields of Normandy; a bloody battlefield;* **adj.**: *battlefield areas, casualties, dress, trails.*

bat·tle·front (BAT·ul·frunt) *n.* where a battle is being fought: *the greenline battlefront dividing the eastern and western parts of the city; along, at, from, on the battlefront.*

bat·tle·ground (BAT·ul·ground) *n.* a battlefield, esp. an area of conflict: *The island became a major battleground for logging companies, environmentalists, and Native Canadians.*

bat·tle·ship *n.* a warship of the most heavily armed class.

bat·ty (BAT·ee) *adj.* **bat·ti·er, bat·ti·est** *Informal.* crazy or eccentric: *He's gone batty from the strain; the bored and batty who watch TV all day.*

bau·ble (BAW·bul) *n.* a worthless, showy trinket.

baud *n.* a data transmission speed of one bit per second: *a 1 200-baud modem.*

baulk, baulky same as BALK, BALKY.

bawd·y *adj.* **bawd·i·er, -i·est** obscene or indecent in a humorous way: *bawdy jokes, songs; charged with keeping a common **bawdy house** (= brothel).*
— *n.*: *Chaucer's bawdy* (= coarse language and humour). — **baw·di·ly** *adv.*; **baw·di·ness** *n.*

bawl *v.* shout, cry, or weep loudly: *to bawl like a baby; The boss **bawled him out** (Informal for scolded him vigorously) for sleeping on the job.*

bay *n.* **1** a deep, continuous barking, esp. of hunting dogs. **2** the position of someone who is cornered or checked: *The sniper kept* or *held the police **at bay**; a wild boar **brought to bay** by hounds.* **3** a separate compartment: *a bomb bay in an aircraft; the sick bay* (= infirmary) *of a ship.* **4** a recess in an outer wall, esp. one with a window, or **bay window. 5** a body of water extending into the land, usually smaller than a gulf, sometimes an estuary: *the Bay of Fundy.* **6** a kind of laurel whose leaves, or **bay leaves**, are used dried in cooking and to weave garlands. **7 bays** *pl.* fame and honour.
— *adj.* reddish-brown: *a bay horse.*
— *v.* give repeated prolonged barks: *a dog baying at the moon.*

bay·o·net (BAY·uh·net) *n.* a heavy knife made to be attached to a rifle barrel for hand-to-hand combat: *The soldiers advanced with bayonets fixed; a bayonet thrust.*
— *v.* **-nets, -net·ted** or **-net·ed, -net·ting** or **-net·ing** stab with a bayonet.

ba·zaar (buh·ZAR) *n.* **1** a marketplace, as in Middle Eastern countries: *It happened in a bazaar in Cairo; In some villages, public life centres around the bazaar; I purchased some curios at the village bazaar.* **2** a sale of assorted goods, usually for a charity: *I met her at the bazaar; The Hadassah Bazaar is an annual event in Toronto; a church bazaar.* Also **ba·zar.**

BB *n.* shot of 0.4572 cm (0.18 in) diameter, as used in air guns.

be (BEE) *auxiliary v.* (I) **am**; (you, we, they) **are**; (he, she, it) **is**; *pt.* (I, he, she, it) **was,** (you, we, they) **were**; *pp.* **been** (BIN); **be·ing 1** [used to show existence]: *Is there life on Mars? Old Pete is no more; Dick and Jane were here; That was a week ago; They will be here tomorrow; Let "l" be the speed of light; **Be that as it may** (= in spite of that), everyone is expected to attend the wedding; If I am to be punished for telling the truth, **so be it** (= let it be so).* **2** [used to join subject and predicate]: *To work is to pray; This is my hat; The sky is blue; The dog is a mammal.* **3** [used with a present participle to show continued action]: *He is sitting on the fence.* **4** [used with a past participle to form the passive voice]: *They were hit by a car.* **5** [used with "to" to show futurity, expectation, duty, etc.]: *She hopes to be a lawyer some day; The missing man was to have come to last night's party.*

beach (BEECH) *n.* a shallowly sloping shore usually covered with sand or small stones: *a private beach belonging to a cottage; a cottage situated on* or *at the beach; the sandy beaches of Georgian Bay; the tidal beaches of the Bay of Fundy; the **Beaches** (= lakeshore) district of the city;* **adj.**: *a beach house, umbrella.*
— *v.* bring or force onto a beach: *to beach a boat, whale; a **beached** (Informal for unemployed) fisherman.*

beach ball *n.* an inflated ball for playing on the beach.

beach bum *n. Informal.* one who spends a lot of time on beaches, esp. a surfer.

beach·comb·er (BEECH·coh·mur) *n.* a person who lives on what may be picked up along the beach.

beach·head (BEECH·hed) *n.* a fortified advance position on a beach held by invading forces: *to establish and secure a beachhead.*

beach·wear *n.* clothes to wear on the beach.

bea·con (BEE·cun) *n.* a fire, lighthouse, buoy, radio signal, or other device used to guide or warn ships, aircraft, etc.: *Aeronautical beacons mark the route to an airport; Radio beacons are of great help to ships in foggy weather; Laura Secord's shining example should serve as a beacon* (= guiding light) *to all of us.*

bead (BEED) *n.* a small globular object of glass, wood, etc. pierced for stringing together: *prayer beads; beads* (= droplets) *of dew, perspiration, sweat.*
— **draw a bead on** take aim at.
— **say** or **count** or **tell one's beads** say prayers, as with a rosary.
— *v.* ornament with beads: *a beaded dress, vest; Drops of sweat beaded* (= formed into beads) *on his brow.*

bead·y (BEE·dee) *adj.* **bead·i·er, -i·est** small, round, and shiny: *beady eyes.*

bea·gle (BEE·gul) *n.* a small hound with a smooth coat and drooping ears.

beak (BEEK) *n.* 1 a hard, sharp, often hooked mouth structure, esp. a bird's bill. 2 *Informal.* the human nose. — **beaked** *adj.*

be-all and end-all *n.* the whole: *Her kids are the be-all and end-all of her existence.*

beam (BEEM) *n.* 1 a long, heavy piece of wood, steel, etc. used in building: *The beams and girders supporting a building are laid horizontally, with the columns carrying their load.* 2 the crosspiece of a ship, balance, etc.: *A gymnast's performance on the **balance beam** includes jumping, lying, running, standing, and turning in a two-minute routine.* 3 a stream of rays, waves, particles, etc.: *the high beam and low beam of an automobile's headlight; a radio beam guiding aircraft; A **beam weapon** can fire laser beams against enemy missiles; a beam of hope.*
— **on** or **off the beam** *Informal.* on or off the right track.
— *v.* 1 send in a beam: *The TV program was beamed to North America via satellite from Europe; propaganda beamed at countries behind the Iron Curtain.* 2 smile radiantly: *She was beaming with joy.*

bean (BEEN) *n.* 1 an edible, usually kidney-shaped seed of a pod-bearing plant or the seed of the coffee shrub: *broad, kidney, lima, navy, pinto, string beans; snap or wax beans; Green beans are used without shelling; canned beans; Baked beans, a favourite Boston dish, is made with dried beans.* 2 *Informal.* the head; *v.* to hit on the head.
— **full of beans** *Informal.* 1 very lively. 2 quite mistaken.
— **spill the beans** *Informal.* reveal a secret.

bean·bag *n.* a cushionlike seat used on the floor, consisting of a cloth bag filled with beans or polystyrene beads. Also **beanbag chair.**

bean·ie (BEE·nee) *n.* a small skullcap.

bear (BAIR) *n.* 1 a large, thick-furred, short-tailed mammal: *There are black, brown, grizzly, kodiak, polar, and wild bears; a stuffed teddy bear.* 2 a gruff or clumsy person.
— *v.* **bears,** *pt.* **bore,** *pp.* **borne** or **born, bear·ing** 1 carry: *Mules bear loads; The right to bear arms was*
crucial in pioneer days; She can bear herself with dignity under the most malicious attacks; "Beware of people who come bearing gifts"; Do not bear* (= give) *false witness; He has to bear* (= take) *the blame for this; Let's bear that in mind* (= remember it); *She bears them no grudge* (= feels no grudge toward them) *for the defeat she suffered.* 2 suffer or endure without being broken: *He can't bear the pain; She can't bear to look at him suffering; He just can't bear the sight of blood; She can't bear being alone at night; People used to be branded and made to bear the mark of slavery all their lives; Can this theory bear* (= stand) *examination? a case that bears* (= is worth) *looking into; a strong witness who can **bear up*** (= remain strong) *under any cross-examination; Please **bear with*** (= be patient with) *me for another minute while I finish the story.* 3 give birth to offspring: *Women bear children; She has borne two sons; The baby was born in 1987; a child born of a poor woman; a child borne by a poor woman; Trees bear* (= yield) *fruit.* 4 lean or press: *Guilt bears heavily on a killer's mind; Here are some facts bearing on* (= relating to) *the case; Remember to bear* (= go toward) *right or to the right at the next lights; Watch that truck **bearing down*** (= coming threateningly) *on you from behind; Facts will **bear out*** (= confirm) *the truth; The rich sometimes **bring their influence to bear*** (= exert influence) *on people in power.* — **bear·er** *n.*

bear·a·ble (BAIR·uh·bul) *adj.* that can be endured: *The pain is bearable.*

beard (BEERD) *n.* 1 the hair on a man's face: *to grow a beard; to shave off, stroke, trim one's beard; a bushy, light, neat, thick, trim beard.* 2 a similar bristly growth on a plant or animal, as in the **bearded seal** of the Arctic.
— *v.* **beard the lion in his den** face a person boldly on his own ground.

bearing (BAIR·ing) *n.* 1 how one comports oneself: *a man of noble bearing; a dignified, military, regal, royal bearing.* 2 a part supporting a machine's moving part: *a ball bearing; roller bearing; The bearing has burned out.* 3 relation: *This story has no direct bearing on the case.* 4 direction: *to take a bearing on the tower with a compass; The fog was so thick we lost our **bearings*** (= sense of direction or position).

bear·ish (BAIR·ish) *adj.* negative in direction or attitude: *The stock market is bearish on corn prices and friendly to bullish for soybeans; He's somewhat bearish on our hopes of winning.*

beast (BEEST) *n.* 1 an animal, esp. a four-legged one: *a wild beast; The camel is a **beast of burden*** (= animal used for carrying loads). 2 a cruel or coarse person: *He behaves like a beast; The beast* (= beastlike nature) *in him acts up now and then.*
— **beast·ly** *adj.* **-li·er, -li·est** very bad: *I'm suffering from a beastly cold; beastly manners, savagery; adv.: It's beastly* (= extremely) *cold outside.* — **beast·li·ness** *n.*

beat (BEET) *v.* **beats,** *pt.* **beat,** *pp.* **beat** or **beat·en, beat·ing** 1 strike repeatedly: *He was robbed and beaten by thugs; was beaten brutally, mercilessly, severely, viciously; to beat the drum; to beat eggs in a cup; gold beaten into leaves; the beating of wings; Watch the rain*

beating against the window; An adult's heart beats about 72 times a minute; to beat (=mark) time with the foot; to **beat swords into ploughshares** (=go from war to peace); to beat a person into submission; He was beaten unconscious; was found beaten to death; People will **beat a path to your door** (=come and see you) if you do something remarkable. **2** defeat or outdo: I can beat him at chess; He beat me out in the math test; She beat him to the corner (by getting there first); He was beaten (Informal for tricked) for $5; Bicycling beats (=is preferable to) walking. **3** pulsate regularly, as the heart, a flying bird's wings, etc. **4** travel with difficulty, repeatedly, or to find something: hunters beating the woods for game.
— **beat a retreat** withdraw or retreat quickly.
— **beat about** or **around the bush** avoid coming to the point.
— **beat down 1** descend mercilessly: The sun beat down on the parched earth all summer. **2** reduce or make someone reduce a price: to beat the price down to $100; He haggled and beat me down to $100.
— **beat it** Slang. leave quickly.
— **beats me** Informal. puzzles me: It beats me how she does it; How she does it beats me; How does she do it? Beats me.
— **beat the rap** Slang. escape being punished.
— **beat the pants** or **socks off someone** Slang. clobber or trounce someone.
— **beat up** Informal. thrash soundly: to beat someone up or beat up on someone.
— **off the beaten track** or **path** out of the accustomed route: We ate at a restaurant off the beaten track.
— **n. 1** a time unit or accent in music. **2** regular or rhythmic striking: People danced to the beat of the drum; a steady, rhythmic beat; the beat of the heart; an irregular beat. **3** a path travelled or job done regularly: a police officer walking her beat.
— **adj.** Informal. tired; exhausted: I'm dead beat.

be·a·tif·ic (bee·uh·TIF·ic) adj. blissful: a beatific expression, smile; the beatific vision (of God).

be·at·i·fy (bee·AT·uh·fye) v. -fies, -fied, -fy·ing **1** make blissful. **2** in the Roman Catholic church, officially declare a dead person to be in heaven.
— **be·at·i·fi·ca·tion** (-fuh·CAY·shun) n.

beating n. an act of striking repeatedly or its effect: a brutal, severe, vicious beating at the hands of thugs; Our team got or took a merciless beating (=lost badly) in the finals.

beat-up adj. Slang. battered or damaged: a beat-up old car.

beau (BOH) n. beaus or beaux (BOZE) **1** a fine-looking dandy. **2** a woman's escort or suitor: a steady beau of hers.

beaut (BYOOT, long "YOO") n. Slang. [often ironic] something of superlative quality: Your hat's a real beaut!

beau·te·ous (BYOO·tee·us) adj. [poetic use] beautiful.

beau·ti·cian (byoo·TISH·un) n. one who cuts or styles hair and provides other beauty treatments such as manicures and facials.

beau·ti·ful (BYOO·tuh·ful) adj. having beauty; pleasing to the mind or senses: a beautiful child, day, girl, scene,

song; The ballet was beautiful to watch; the **beautiful people** (=people of wealth and fashion).
— **beau·ti·ful·ly** adv.

beau·ti·fy (BYOO·tuh·fye) v. -fies, -fied, -fy·ing make or become beautiful.
— **beau·ti·fi·ca·tion** (-fuh·CAY·shun) n.

beau·ty (BYOO·tee) n. -ties **1** a combination of pleasing qualities: Does makeup really enhance your beauty? **2** a person or thing having attractive qualities, esp. a woman: a dazzling, raving, striking, wholesome beauty; bathing beauties on the beach; Feminists frown upon **beauty contests** as exploitation of women; a beauty queen; The car is a beauty (Cdn. for great)!

beauty shop or **beauty parlour** or **beauty salon** n. a business establishment giving cosmetic care to women's hair, hands, and face.

beaux arts (boh·ZAR) n. pl. the fine arts.

bea·ver (BEE·vur) n. a large rodent with flat tail and strong incisors noted for its activity: a large colony of beavers; He's busy as a beaver; a **beaver dam** (built by beavers); He works like a beaver (=is very industrious); the **beaver pelt** tag of authenticity of a piece of native art or craft; an eager beaver (=very zealous) reporter.

be·calmed (bi·CAHMD) adj. made motionless by lack of wind: a ship becalmed in the South Seas.

became pt. of BECOME.

be·cause (bi·CAWZ, -CUZ) conj. for the reason that: I like the hat because it fits me; I like it **because of** (=on account of) its fit.

beck n. a summoning gesture: A slave had to be at his master's **beck and call** (=ready to obey on command) all day.

beck·on (BECK·un) v. summon, esp. with a gesture of the hand or head: He beckoned to her; beckoned her to follow him to the office.

be·come (bi·CUM) v. -comes, -came, -come, -com·ing **1** come or grow to be: Children become adults; She wants to become a doctor; He wants to become rich and famous; What **became of** (=happened to) your old car? **2** suit: It ill becomes one to swear in public.

becoming adj. suitable and attractive: She came dressed in a very becoming fashion for the interview; The hat is very becoming to you; **be·com·ing·ly** adv.

bed n. **1** a piece of furniture for sleeping: a bunk, double, king-size, queen-size, rollaway, single, sofa, twin

bed; a trundle bed; water beds; a feather bed (= mattress); *We* **go to bed** (= retire to sleep) *at 11; The kids are put to bed at 9; We try to get out of bed at 6; She likes to lie or stay late in bed on holidays; Maids make or make up beds* (= arrange beds) *in hotel rooms; I had to take to my bed* (= remain in bed) *with a fever all last week; She pays for her* **bed and board** (= food and lodging); *a* **bed-and-breakfast** *establishment* (= inn or guesthouse offering lodging and breakfast). **2** a place where something lies: *miners working on a bed of coal; the bed of a river; the bed of the ocean; a house built on a bed* (= foundation) *of concrete.* **3** a piece of ground for planting: *a flower bed.*
— **get up on the wrong side of the bed** *Informal.* wake up in a bad mood.
— **go to bed with** *Informal.* have sex with someone.
— **make the bed** arrange a bed for use.
— *v.* **beds, bed·ded, bed·ding 1** put or go to bed: *We had to* **bed** *down on the floor.* **2** plant, as in a bed: *plants ready for bedding; posts bedded* (= embedded) *in concrete.* **3** lay out in a bed: *to bed out the plants.*

be·daub (bi·DAWB) *v.* smear or smudge: *a wall bedaubed with mud.*

be·daz·zle (bi·DAZ·ul) *v.* **-daz·zles, -daz·zled, -daz·zling 1** blind with brightness. **2** dazzle or confuse.

bed chesterfield *n.* a sofa bed.

bed·clothes *n. pl.* sheets and blankets for a bed.

bedding (BED·ing) *n.* **1** bedclothes or material to sleep on. **2** a building foundation.

be·deck (bi·DEK) *v.* ornament or adorn.

be·dev·il (bi·DEV·ul) *v.* **-ils, -illed** or **-iled, -il·ling** or **-il·ing** plague or confuse: *The use of nuclear power is an issue that bedevils humanity.* — **be·dev·il·ment** *n.*

be·dew (bi·DEW) *v.* wet or sprinkle, as with dew: *a face bedewed with tears.*

bed·fel·low (BED·fel·oh) *n.* one sharing a bed: *Politics makes strange bedfellows* (= makes very different people come together).

be·dim (bi·DIM) *v.* **-dims, -dimmed, -dim·ming** make dim.

bed·lam (BED·lum) *n.* uproar and confusion.

Bed·ou·in (BED·oo·in) *n.* an Arab who leads a nomadic life.

bed·pan *n.* a pan used in bed or at bedside as a toilet.

bed·post *n.* one of the corner supports on an old-fashioned bed such as a four-poster: *This is* **between you and me and the bedpost** (*Informal for* confidential).

be·drag·gled (bi·DRAG·uld) *adj.* wet, limp, and dirty: *bedraggled clothes.*

bed·rid·den (BED·rid·un) *adj.* confined to bed by age or illness.

bed·rock *n.* solid rock under soil, loose rock, etc.: *Philosophers consider morality the bedrock* (= basis or foundation) *of civilization.*
— *adj.* fundamental or crucial: *a bedrock decision, quality, question.*

bed·room *n.* a room for sleeping: *Mom and Dad use the*

master bedroom; We've a spare bedroom for guests; **adj.:** *a bedroom city or suburb from which people commute to work in a crowded metropolis; Our town is a bedroom community of Montreal.*

bed·side *n.* the area close to a bed, as of a sick person: *We were at her bedside during her last moments.*
— *adj.:* *a bedside lamp; a doctor's fine bedside manner; a book for bedside reading.*

bed·sore *n.* a sore caused by being bedridden.

bed·spread *n.* a decorative cover for the bedclothes.

bed·stead (BED·sted) *n.* a frame for the springs and mattress of a bed.

bed·time *n.* the time one usually goes to bed: *It's past your bedtime.*

bee *n.* **1** a small four-winged stinging insect that gathers nectar from flowers: *a colony of queen bees, worker bees, and drones; a swarm of bees flying away to form a new colony; An African breed of aggressive killer bees has been spreading northward from Brazil since 1957; She's as busy as a bee; He keeps bees as a hobby.* **2** a busy gathering or activity: *a knitting, quilting, sewing, spelling, spinning bee.*
— **bee in one's bonnet** *Informal.* a notion or idea that is a preoccupation or obsession: *She's got a bee in her bonnet about eating only vegetables.*

beech *n.* a hardwood tree with silvery grey bark and edible nuts.

beef *n.* **1** *pl.* **beeves** (BEEVZ) the meat of full-grown cattle: *Prime beef is the meat of steers and young cows; Bull and cow are other classes of beef; Choice, good, and utility are various grades of beef; cuts of beef such as brisket, chuck, and round; Beef may be braised, broiled, roasted, stewed; corned beef* (= beef cured by salting); *ground beef* (= minced by grinding); *a herd of good beef* (= beef cattle); *Texas beeves.* **2** brawn or strength: *The singer needs to put more beef in her voice.* **3** *pl.* **beefs** *Informal.* a complaint: *to have a beef.*
— *v.* **1** *Informal.* complain: *What's he beefing about?* **2 beef up** strengthen: *to beef up a police force; to beef up security for the royal visit.*

beef·cake *n. Informal.* a pictorial display of muscles on the male body.

beef·steak (BEEF·stake) *n.* a thick slice of beef for broiling, frying, etc.

beef·y *adj.* strong-looking: *a beefy bodyguard, bouncer.*

bee·hive *n.* **1** a hive of bees or one made for them. **2** a busy place: *a beehive of activity.*

bee·keep·er (BEE·kee·pur) *n.* one who tends domesticated bees for their honey. — **bee·keep·ing** *n.*

bee·line *n.* shortest route: *They made a beeline for the cafeteria when the bell rang.*

been *pt.* of BE: *I've* **been to** (= visited) *Europe.*

beep *n.* a short high-pitched tone given as a signal.
— *v.* give or make a beep: *She beeped* (= sounded) *her horn to warn the bicyclist.*

beep·er *n.* a beeping device, esp. a radio receiver carried on one's person for receiving signals to phone customers, patients, etc.

beer *n.* 1 an alcoholic drink made from malted barley and hops: *a bottle, can, glass, mug, stein of beer; light beer with less alcohol;* **Near beer** has low alcohol content. 2 a soft drink made from extracts of roots, bark, etc.: *ginger beer; root beer.*
— *adj.: a* **beer belly** (*Slang* for potbelly or a man with one); *a zoo with a* **beer garden** (*where beer is sold); a* **beer joint** (*Slang* for beer tavern).

beer parlour *n. Cdn.* a room set apart for serving beer to the public; beverage room.

beer slinger *n. Cdn. Informal.* one who serves beer in a beer parlour.

beer·y *adj.* beer·i·er, -i·est having to do with beer: *a beery flavour, lunch, tavern.*

beet *n.* a plant with edible red or white roots: *as red as a beet.*

bee·tle *n.* an insect with hard forewings covering the flying wings when at rest: *Some well-known beetles are the June bug, the ladybug, and the firefly.*
— *v.* bee·tles, bee·tled, bee·tling 1 overhang: *beetling cliffs.* 2 to scurry.
— *adj. & combining form.* overhanging or projecting: *a hairy man with beetle brows.*
— beetle-browed or beetling *adj.*

beeves a *pl.* of BEEF.

be·fall (bi·FAWL) *v.* be·falls, be·fell, be·fall·en, be·fall·ing happen to someone: *No one knows what strange fate befell him.*

be·fit (bi·FIT) *v.* -fits, -fit·ted, -fit·ting be appropriate to a person or thing: *He came dressed as befits someone of his rank; in clothes befitting a prince; dressed in* **befitting** (= appropriate) *style.*

be·fore (bi·FOR) *adv.* earlier or formerly: *This has happened before; same as before.*
— before long soon.
— *prep.* 1 earlier than: *the day before yesterday; on or before October 11.* 2 ahead of: *She puts honour before everything else.* 3 in front of: *He knelt before the queen; a case before* (= being considered by) *the court.*
— *conj.* sooner than: *He would beg or borrow before he would steal.*

be·fore·hand (bi·FOR·hand) *adj. & adv.* in advance; ahead of time: *Let me know beforehand; It's wise to be ready beforehand in case of trouble.*

be·foul (bi·FOWL) *v.* make dirty; foul: *a stream befouled by city wastes.*

be·friend (bi·FREND) *v.* 1 act as a friend to someone: *to befriend the needy.* 2 make a friend of someone: *She befriended the new girl in class.*

be·fud·dle (bi·FUD·ul) *v.* -fud·dles, -fud·dled, -fud·dling confuse, as with drink. — be·fud·dle·ment *n.*

beg *v.* begs, begged, beg·ging 1 ask for handouts: *He begs for a living* or *He lives by begging; He is so desperate he would beg, borrow, or steal; He begs his bread (as charity).* 2 ask formally: *I beg to differ.* 3 ask earnestly: *I humbly beg your forgiveness; I must beg a favour of you; I beg (of) you to forgive me; I beg for mercy; I beg your pardon; I beg pardon of you.*
— beg off ask to be released from an obligation.

— **beg the question** assume the truth of what is to be proved.
— **go begging** have few buyers: *Houses go begging during a depression.*

be·gan *pt.* of BEGIN.

be·get (bi·GET) *v.* -gets, *pt.* -got, *pp.* -got·ten or -got, -get·ting 1 be the father of someone: *Abraham begot Isaac.* 2 cause: *Poverty begets crime.*

beg·gar (BEG·ur) *n.* one who begs for a living: *"Beggars can't be choosers"* (= One shouldn't criticize what is received free).
— *v. Formal.* make poor: *He was beggared by the loss of his job; The sight of Everest* **beggared description** (= was too great for words to describe).

beg·gar·ly (BEG·ur·lee) *adj.* very poor: *long hours and beggarly wages.*

beg·gar·y (BEG·uh·ree) *n.* great poverty.

be·gin (bi·GIN, "G" in "go") *v.* -gins, -gan, -gun, -gin·ning start to do or exist: *Let's begin the lesson; Please begin at* (= start from) *the beginning; We begin* (= start work) *on a new lesson today; We are beginning to see the light* (= understand it); *When did life begin* (= come into being) *on Earth? The alphabet begins with ABC; ABC begins the alphabet; Let's begin to read* or *begin reading; The pileup on the highway was so bad the police* **couldn't begin to** (= come near to) *sort it out; Let's begin by singing the national anthem* or *Let's begin with the national anthem; You have to be interested in the book* **to begin with** (= as the first step).
— be·gin·ner (bi·GIN·ur) *n.: We are all beginners when we learn something new; He's a mere beginner* (= one lacking in skill and experience).

beginning (bi·GIN·ing) *n.* a start or starting: *In or At the beginning we had no idea of what to do; We made a good beginning; Today marks the beginning of a new era; a new beginning after many failures; the beginning of the end of the war; Start at the beginning; from the beginning of the poem; the very beginning; Can you recite the poem from* **beginning to end?** *a millionaire who rose from humble* **beginnings** (= origins); *the* **beginnings** (= early stages) *of a settlement.*
— *adj.* basic or elementary: *a beginning course, dictionary, student.*

be·gone (bi·GON) *interj. Poetic.* Go away: *"Begone, dull care!"*

begot, begotten See BEGET.

be·grime (bi·GRIME) *v.* -grimes, -grimed, -grim·ing to make dirty: *a mechanic with hands begrimed with grease and dirt.*

be·grudge (bi·GRUJ) *v.* -grudg·es, -grudged, -grudg·ing envy or resent: *Let's not begrudge him his good fortune.* — be·grudg·ing·ly *adv.*

be·guile (bi·GUILE) *v.* -guiles, -guiled, -guil·ing 1 deceive by charm and persuasion: *He was beguiled into betraying his plans; He was beguiled out of all his savings; a pretty tale to beguile* (= entertain) *fools (with).* 2 pass time pleasantly: *She reads to beguile her leisure hours.* — be·guile·ment *n.* — be·guil·er *n.*

begun *pp.* of BEGIN.

be·half (bi·HAF) *n.* interest or benefit: *a lawyer acting in her client's behalf.*
— **on** or **in behalf of** in the interest of someone: *A lawyer acts on* or *in behalf of his client; She spoke on behalf of* (= representing) *all of us.*

be·have (bi·HAIV) *v.* -haves, -haved, -hav·ing
1 conduct oneself according to a standard: *Children are taught to behave (well); to behave respectfully toward teachers; Billy, behave yourself* (= behave properly)*! how to behave in public; to behave like civilized people.*
2 perform or act: *The machine behaved well during the tests; How do acids behave in the presence of alkalis?*

be·hav·iour or **be·hav·ior** (bi·HAIV·yur) *n.* a way of behaving or acting: *Be on your best behaviour* (= Behave properly)*; The drugged man showed strange behaviour; animal behaviour; social behaviour; to study the behaviour of animals under varying conditions; abnormal, criminal, disciplined, disruptive, infantile, irrational, modest, normal, obsequious, scandalous, sullen, ungentlemanly, unorthodox, unruly behaviour; His sentence was reduced for good behaviour (in prison); adj.: a behaviour pattern; behaviour modification, therapy.*
— **be·hav·iour·al** or **be·hav·ior·al** *adj.: a behavioural problem; Psychology and sociology are **behavioural sciences.***

be·head (bi·HED) *v.* cut off the head of someone: *Traitors used to be beheaded.*

beheld *pt. & pp.* of BEHOLD.

be·hest (bi·HEST) *n.* a command or urgent request: *We act at your behest; at the behest of friends and relatives.*

be·hind (bi·HINED) *adv.* in, to, or at the rear, a previous place or time, etc.: *We were seated behind, not in front of her; the child he left behind in Vietnam; to remain* or *stay behind when everyone is gone; a pupil falling* or *lagging behind in school* (= slow at learning)*; He's behind* (= in arrears) *in* or *with his rent; He's behind by $900.*
— **prep.** 1 later than: *He finished behind the others.* 2 in or to the rear of a person or thing: *He is behind you; What is behind* (= hidden by) *this clever scheme? Jimmy does naughty things **behind his mother's back*** (= unknown to her)*; activity going on **behind the scenes*** (= in secret)*; adj.: a behind-the-scenes activity.*
3 supporting: *We are solidly behind you all the way.*
— **n.** Informal. buttocks: *He fell on his behind.*

be·hind·hand (bi·HINED·hand) *adv.* in arrears or backward: *Your dues are behindhand this month; You're behindhand with the rent; You're also behindhand with* or *in your homework; You're never behindhand in offering to help when we have a party.*

be·hold (bi·HOLED) *v.* -holds, -held, -hold·ing gaze upon something: *Lo and behold, the rabbit is gone! Open your eyes and behold the wonders of nature!*
— **be·hold·er** *n.: "Beauty is in the eye of the beholder."*

be·hold·en *adj.* [sometimes ironical] obliged: *I'm not beholden to anyone for the wealth I have accumulated; She's truly beholden to you for your kindness.*

beige (BAIZH) *n. & adj.* yellowish brown.

being (BEE·ing) *v.* See BE.
— **n.** 1 existence; life: *the question of being as opposed to becoming; brought into being by peculiar circumstances; How did the universe come into being?* 2 one that exists or is thought to exist: *an extraterrestrial being; human beings; a mortal being; We are rational beings; Ghosts are supernatural beings.* 3 one's nature: *He loved her with his whole being.*
— **for the time being** for the present; for now.

be·la·bour or **be·la·bor** (bi·LAY·bur) *v.* 1 attack with blows or words. 2 dwell too long on a subject; labour: *The lecturer belaboured the point for a whole hour.*

be·lat·ed (bi·LAY·tid) *adj.* delayed: *Happy New Year and a belated Merry Christmas!* — **be·lat·ed·ly** *adv.*

be·lay (bi·LAY) *v.* -lays, -layed, -lay·ing 1 secure a rope around a cleat or pin, called **belaying pin** on a ship. 2 secure a mountain climber by a rope. 3 [nautical use] stop: *Belay there!*

belch *v.* let out something noisily or violently, esp. stomach gas: *Babies are said to "burp," not belch; The chimneys belched smoke.*
— **n.** an act of belching or what is belched: *Someone let out a belch which disturbed the speaker; The volcano released* or *emitted a great belch of fire.*

be·lea·guer (bi·LEE·gur) *v.* -guers, -guered, -guer·ing besiege or harass: *a beleaguered town; the beleaguered diplomats in a troubled country.*

bel·fry (BEL·free) *n.* -fries 1 a chamber in a bell tower in which bells are hung; also, the bell tower.
— **have bats in one's belfry** Informal. be eccentric or crazy.

be·lie (bi·LYE) *v.* -lies, -lied, -ly·ing prove false: *Facts belied her story; His face belied* (= gave a false idea of) *his true feelings; Fate belied* (= disappointed) *our hopes.*

be·lief (bi·LEEF) *n.* the act of believing or something believed: *Nothing could shake her belief in God; They tried their best to make her give up* or *relinquish her beliefs; the religious beliefs expressed in her writings; superstitious beliefs held by the people; He did it in the belief that he was right; erroneous, false, mistaken beliefs; It is my firm belief* (= opinion) *that he was telling the truth; Some of the reports about him are **beyond belief*** (= impossible to believe).

be·lieve (bi·LEEV) *v.* -lieves, -lieved, -liev·ing 1 accept as true: *I believe his story; to believe firmly, mistakenly, sincerely, strongly; a story about him that is hard to believe; I cannot believe it of him; We all know and believe that we will die some day; That's the truth, believe me.* 2 have faith: *Do you believe in exercise* (= consider it as worth anything)*?* 3 suppose: *I believe you trust him; I believe so; Do you think he did it? I believe not.*
— **be·liev·a·ble** *adj.: a believable story.*
— **be·liev·er** *n.: the fellowship of true believers; a firm, sincere, strong believer in life after death.*

be·lit·tle (bi·LIT·ul) *v.* -lit·tles, -lit·tled, -lit·tling make seem small: *Don't belittle her merits; a belittling* (= disparaging) *remark.*

bell *n.* 1 a hollow, usually metallic object that makes a ringing sound when struck: *church bells; I didn't hear the door bell* (= the striking of the bell)*; I hear wedding bells* (= I think they are going to get married)*; Bells chime, peal, ring, sound, toll; to ring* or *sound a bell;*

The boxer was saved by the bell (because the round ended before he was counted out by the referee).
2 something with the typical bell's flared shape: *the bell of a flower; a diving bell.* **3** a measure of time (half an hour) at sea: *Call the watch at six bells.*
— *v.* flare like a bell: *a belled skirt.*

bell-bottom (BELL·bot·um) *adj.* flaring at the bottom of the leg: *bell-bottom trousers,* or **bell-bottoms** *n. pl.*

bell-boy or **bell-hop** *n.* a club or hotel employee who carries luggage, runs errands, etc.

bell captain *n.* one who is in charge of bellhops.

belle (BEL) *n.* a popular and handsome woman: *a Southern belle.*
— **the belle of the ball** the favourite woman of the party.

belles-let·tres (bel·LET·ruh) *n. pl.* [takes sing. v.] literature as one of the fine arts.
— **bel·let·rist** (bel·LET·rist) *n.*
— **bel·le·tris·tic** (bel·let·RIS·tic) *adj.*

bellhop same as BELLBOY.

bel·li·cose (BEL·uh·cose) *adj.* disposed to start a fight: *a bellicose mood, nation, people; to live in bellicose estrangement.* — **bel·li·cos·i·ty** (-COS·uh·tee) *n.*

bel·lig·er·ent (buh·LIJ·uh·runt) *adj.* **1** engaged in war or hostile activities: *the belligerent powers of the Middle East; a country that is belligerent toward its neighbour.* **2** aggressive by nature: *a belligerent, swaggering bully.*
— *n.* a belligerent person or state: *The U.N. condemned the belligerents.* — **bel·lig·er·ent·ly** *adv.*
— **bel·lig·er·ence** (-runce) *n.*

bell·man *n.* -men a bellhop.

bel·low (BEL·oh) *v.* make a deep roar, as a bull, or shout in this way: *He bellowed with pain; He bellows out orders to his men.* — *n.* a bellowing roar or shout.

bel·lows (BEL·oze) *n. sing. & pl.* **1** a usually hand-operated device for blowing air, as to fan a fire: *Let me show you how to use* or *operate a bellows; See how the bellows works.* **2** something resembling a bellows, as the pleated part of an accordion.

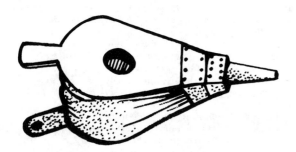

bells *n. pl. Informal.* bell-bottoms.

bells and whistles *n. pl. Informal.* accessories or frills, as of a computer system.

bell·weth·er (BELL·weth·ur, "th" as in "the") *n.* a person or thing considered as the indicator of a trend: *The weekly interest rates set by the Bank of Canada are*

the bellwether for the chartered banks to raise or lower their lending rates.

bel·ly (BEL·ee) *n.* **bel·lies** **1** the cavity of the body that includes the stomach and bowels, esp. when bulging: *He has pain in his belly; a beer belly (= potbelly); Les Halles, which housed the world's biggest food market, was called "the belly of Paris"; He has always been a slave to his belly (= a glutton);* ***adj.:*** *He did a **belly flop** (hitting the water stomach first); a belly (= deep, hearty) laugh; Many companies **went belly up** (Slang for collapsed or failed) during the last recession.* **2** the inside of an animal, aircraft, etc.: *in the belly of a whale; the belly of a ship; the price of live hogs and frozen **pork bellies** (= sides of pork for making bacon) on the Chicago Mercantile Exchange.*
— *v.* **bel·lies, bel·lied, bel·ly·ing** swell out: *a sail bellying in the wind.*

bel·ly·ache (BEL·ee·ake) *n.* an abdominal pain.
— *v.* **-aches, -ached, -ach·ing** *Slang.* complain in a grumbling manner: *What are you bellyaching about? Quit your bellyaching.*

bel·ly·but·ton (BEL·ee·but·un) *n. Informal.* the navel.

belly dance *n.* an erotic Middle Eastern dance performed by a woman. — **belly dancer** *n.*

bel·ly·ful (BEL·ee·ful) *n. Informal.* all that one wants or can take: *That country has had its bellyful of war and famine.*

be·long (bi·LONG) *v.* **1** be related to another as owned: *The dog belongs to Jim; Jim **belongs to** (= is a member of) the Rotary Club; a community in which you feel a sense of **belonging** (= closeness).* **2** have one's proper place: *Home is where you belong; The chair belongs in the corner; All these words belong under "B".*
— **be·long·ing** *n.;* **be·long·ing·ness** *n.*

belongings *n. pl.* movable possessions: *our earthly belongings; your personal belongings.*

be·lov·ed (bi·LUV·id) *adj.* very much loved: *She was beloved by* or *of all who came to know her; her beloved husband.* — *n.* a beloved one: *Dearly beloved!*

be·low (bi·LOH) *prep.* lower than: *It's 10 below zero (Celsius); She went below deck; The Dead Sea is below sea level; He is below (= under) 21; A major is below a colonel in rank.*
— *adv.* in, to, or at a lower position: *It is 10 below (= 10° below zero) right now; See page 85 below (= further on).*
— **down below** in the lower part of a house, ship, etc.
— **here below** on earth.

belt *n.* **1** a band of material worn around the waist: *the belt of her dress; to buckle, loosen, undo one's belt; Fasten your seat belts; a cartridge belt; life belt; money belt; safety belt; shoulder belt; She is a black belt in judo; Jim holds a brown belt in karate; It's not fair to hit one **below the belt**; We **tighten our belts** (= consume less) in hard times; We stop eating out as a **belt-tightening** measure; She has years of experience **under her belt** (= to her credit).* **2** an endless strap used to move or drive something: *a conveyor belt; the fan belt of an engine.* **3** an area distinct in some way: *a belt of* trees; a **Bible Belt** (= region of fundamentalist believers in the Bible); *a corn, cotton, farm, fruit belt; the prairie grain belt; a green belt (of parkland); the nickel belt around Sudbury; a parkway belt.* 4 *Slang.* a whack. 5 *Slang.* a swallow of drink: *No belt for the road, please!* — *adj.* encircling or ringing: *a **belt highway** bypassing an urban area; a **belt line** service of ferries touching the islands.* — *v.* 1 encircle with a belt. 2 *Slang.* beat, as with a belt: *She belted him one.* 3 *Slang.* gulp or guzzle: *to belt down one cola after another.* — **belt out** sing something forcefully.

bel·ve·dere (BEL·vuh·deer) *n.* a structure providing a fine view, as an open gallery or a summerhouse.

be·moan (be·MOHN) *v.* mourn over: *to bemoan a loss.*

be·muse (bi·MYOOZ) *v.* -mus·es, -mused, -mus·ing have one confused or lost in thought: *The retired politician was bemused by the fact that he received no job offers; a bemused smile.*

bench *n.* 1 a long seat for two or more people: *a park bench; a **bench seat** (that extends the full width of an automobile).* 2 a long, sturdy work table: *a work bench.* 3 the office of a judge: *a lawyer appointed to the bench; a ruling from the bench; the bar and **the bench*** (= judges collectively). 4 **benches** *pl.* places in a legislature: *There was much shouting from the opposition benches; He spent two terms on the back benches before joining the cabinet.* — **on the bench** 1 sitting as a judge. 2 not playing in the game: *He got two minutes on the bench (as penalty).* — *v.* put or keep someone on a bench, as unable to play: *He was benched for two minutes for using a profanity; benched by the umpire.*

bench·er *n.* 1 a judge or magistrate. 2 a member of a governing body of the legal profession such as the Law Society of Upper Canada.

bench·mark or **bench mark** *n.* 1 a reference point in surveying. 2 a measuring standard: *a court decision that will serve as a benchmark in future cases; a benchmark decision.*

bench warrant *n.* a court order to have someone arrested: *to issue a bench warrant.*

bend *v.* bends, bent, bend·ing 1 make, be, or become crooked or curved: *Bend down and touch your toes; Try to bend this bar; a wire bent into a coat hanger; Trees bend in the wind; The highway bends to the right after the bridge.* 2 submit or cause to submit: *She refused to bend to his will.* 3 direct or turn: *to bend one's efforts to a task; a lobby group that is **bending the MPs' ears*** (*Informal* for pressuring them) *about auto insurance rates; a session that really bent (Informal for made a powerful impact on) her mind; They **bend over backward** (= try very hard) to please customers.* — *n.* a crooked or curved form or part: *a sharp bend in the road.*

bend·er *n.* *Slang.* a drinking spree.

be·neath (bi·NEETH, "TH" as in "thin") *prep.* 1 below: *the valley beneath the mountain; She looked down at the valley beneath.* 2 unworthy of someone: *Is manual work beneath you? behaviour that is **beneath*** (= unworthy of even) **contempt.**

ben·e·dic·tion (ben·uh·DIC·shun) *n.* a blessing, esp. one at the end of a church service.

ben·e·fac·tion (ben·uh·FAC·shun) *n.* a charitable gift, as given by a benefactor.

ben·e·fac·tor (ben·uh·FAC·tur) *n.* one who helps another, esp. by donations.

ben·e·fice (BEN·uh·fis) *n.* a church position, as of a vicar, or the income that goes with it.

be·nef·i·cent (buh·NEF·uh·sunt) *adj.* doing good, esp. charitable works. — **be·nef·i·cence** *n.*

ben·e·fi·cial (ben·uh·FISH·ul) *adj.* helpful or favourable: *Fresh air is beneficial to health; It's especially beneficial for office workers; He finds it beneficial to exercise regularly.* — **ben·e·fi·cial·ly** *adv.*

ben·e·fi·ci·ar·y (ben·uh·FISH·ee·air·ee) *n.* -aries one who receives a benefit, as from an insurance policy, trust, or will: *His wife was named as the beneficiary of his insurance policy.*

ben·e·fit (BEN·uh·fit) *n.* 1 something that does good; advantage: *Is nuclear power a benefit to humanity? It has to be properly used to be of benefit to anyone; Use it to humanity's benefit rather than for destruction; the benefits of dieting; We derive, get, reap many benefits from good habits; Because of insufficient evidence, the accused was given **the benefit of the doubt** and acquitted.* 2 financial help or payment: *a death benefit; Most companies provide fringe benefits such as sick leave and a dental plan; a tax benefit; retirement benefits; She collected disability, maternity, sickness, strike, unemployment, and other benefits during her long career.* 3 a performance, sale, etc. to help a person or cause: *to have or hold a benefit; The play was staged as a benefit; a benefit performance.* — *v.* 1 do good to someone: *Wars benefit no one.* 2 derive good: *Everyone benefits by experience; Only the lucky few benefit from* (= get) *windfalls.*

be·nev·o·lence (buh·NEV·uh·lunce) *n.* desire to do charitable deeds: *acts of benevolence.* — **be·nev·o·lent** *adj.*: *She was benevolent to or toward the poor.* — **be·nev·o·lent·ly** *adv.*

be·night·ed (bi·NYE·tid) *adj.* unenlightened: *his benighted ideas on immigration.* — **be·night·ed·ly** *adv.*

be·nign (bi·NINE) *adj.* 1 kind and gracious: *a benign old man; a benign smile; a benign* (= mild) *climate; The armed forces complain of **benign neglect*** (= indifference) *on the part of the government in regard to manpower and resources.* 2 not harmful or malignant: *a benign tumour;* also **be·nig·nant** (bi·NIG·nunt): *a benignant, not cancerous growth.* — **be·nig·ni·ty** (bi·NIG·nuh·tee) *n.* -ties.

ben·i·son (BEN·uh·sun) *n.* [old use] a blessing.

bent *adj.* 1 curved or crooked. 2 determined: *She's bent on becoming a lawyer; He seems bent on mischief.* — *n.* a natural inclination: *her artistic bent; his bent for mischief; She followed her bent and became a lawyer.*

bent *pt.* of BEND.
— **bent on** or **upon** determined on something: *youths bent on winning.*
— **bent out of shape** *Slang.* 1 drunk. 2 extremely upset.

be·numb (bi·NUM) *v.* deaden the feelings: *hands benumbed by cold; the benumbing effect of sorrow.*

be·queath (bi·KWEETH, "TH" as in "thin") *v.* hand down or leave money, possessions, etc., esp. in a will, *to someone after one's death.*

be·quest (bi·KWEST) *n.* 1 an act of bequeathing: *to make a bequest to one's favourite charity.* 2 something bequeathed.

be·rate (bi·RATE) *v.* -rates, -rat·ed, -rat·ing scold severely: *The security guard was berated for sleeping on the job.*

be·reave (bi·REEV) *v.* -reaves, *pt. & pp.* -reaved or -reft, -reav·ing deprive by death: *a dead man's bereaved family; The bereaved husband wept by his wife's coffin; The **bereaved** (relatives) stood around the grave.* — **be·reave·ment** *n.*

be·reft (bi·REFT) *adj.* deprived: *a refugee bereft of kin; a life bereft of joy; a future bereft of all hope.*

berm *n.* 1 a ridge or other barrierlike formation: *The building is surrounded by a berm* (= high mound of earth) *which protects it from street noise.* 2 a shoulder, as of a road, or shoulderlike formation or ledge.

Ber·mu·da shorts (bur·MYOO·duh-) or **Ber·mu·das** *n. pl.* knee-length shorts.

ber·ry (BER·ee) *n.* **ber·ries** 1 a usually small, fleshy fruit with many seeds, as a blueberry or strawberry: *to pick berries; Botanically, a tomato is a berry although it looks like a fruit and is used as a vegetable.* 2 a dried seed: *coffee berries.*

ber·serk (bur·SURK) *adj. & adv.* in or into a destructive frenzy: *The soccer fans went berserk and caused some destruction.*

berth *n.* 1 a sleeping place in a ship, railway car, etc. 2 an anchoring place for a ship.
— **give a wide berth to** keep a safe distance from a person.
— *v.* put into or occupy a berth.

be·seech (bi·SEECH) *v.* -seech·es, *pt. & pp.* -seeched or -sought (-SAWT) , -seech·ing *Formal.* beg earnestly: *Mercy, I beseech you! I beseech you to show mercy.*

be·set (bi·SET) *v.* -sets, -set, -set·ting attack on all sides: *a traveller beset by robbers; a mind beset with fears; Pride was the king's **besetting** (= predominant) sin.*

be·side (bi·SIDE) *prep.* at or near the side of a person or thing: *The garage is beside the house, not attached to it.*
— **beside oneself** distraught or agitated *with* despair, fear, grief, joy, rage, etc.: *She was beside herself* (= very angry) *when she found out the truth.*
— **beside the point** irrelevant.

besides (bi·SIDES) *prep. & adv.* in addition to: *Besides being smart, he's hardworking; He owns a cottage besides his house; He owns a house and a cottage besides.*

be·siege (bi·SEEJ) *v.* -sieg·es, -sieged, -sieg·ing lay siege to a person or thing; surround: *a city besieged by enemy troops; Employment agencies were besieged* (= crowded around) *by the jobless; Employers were besieged* (= pressed) *with applications.*

be·smear (bi·SMEER) *v.* smear or sully: *a wall besmeared with paint; a besmeared reputation.*

be·smirch (bi·SMURCH) *v.* harm a reputation: *His writings besmirched her good name.*

be·som (BEE·zum) *n.* a broom, as used in the game of curling.

be·sot·ted (be·SOT·id) *adj.* intoxicated: *He was besotted with her charms.*

besought a *pt. & pp.* of BESEECH.

be·span·gle (bi·SPANG·gul) *v.* -gles, -gled, -gling decorate with spangles: *a star-bespangled sky.*

be·spat·ter (bi·SPAT·ur) *v.* spatter or soil with dirt, calumny, etc.

be·speak (bi·SPEEK) *v.* -speaks, -spoke, -spok·en, -speak·ing be a sign of something: *an omen that bespeaks good fortune.*

bespoke (bi·SPOKE) *adj.* custom-made: *a bespoke jacket, suit; a bespoke* (= custom) *tailor.*

be·sprin·kle (bi·SPRING·kul) *v.* -kles, -kled, -kling sprinkle: *a lawn besprinkled with dew.*

best *adj.* superl. of GOOD: *May the best man win; It's best that we remain silent on the subject; The dog is man's best friend; She thought it best to ignore the man.*
— *n.* something that is best: *For the idealist, the best is not good enough; The best is yet to come; He tried his very or level best to do a good job; He did his best on the job; gave his best to the company; He came dressed in his **Sunday best*** (= best clothes) *so as to look his best; He was not in the best of health; It was too much to hope for at the best of times; The weather is at its best in the spring; Jan is the best in her class; Jon is the next or second best; To the best of my knowledge* (= as far as I know), *he has never been married; Please give my best* (*Informal for* best wishes) *to the family; All the best!*
— *adv.* superl. of WELL: *Luc came out best; He did the best in the exams; The Bible is the best-selling book of all time.*
— **as best one can** as well as possible.
— **at best** under the most favourable conditions.
— **for the best** good or well: *It's all for the best, don't worry.*
— **get the best of** defeat; outwit.
— **had best** ought to: *I'd best stay in school.*
— **make the best of** do as well as possible despite something unfavourable: *to make the best of a bad bargain.*
— **the best of both worlds** the good aspects of two different situations without any of their disadvantages.
— **the best part of** almost all of something: *He was absent for the best part of the day.*
— **with the best (of them)** as well as any.
— *v.* outdo: *The boxer was bested in a fair fight.*

bes·tial (BES·tee·ul, BES·chul) *adj.* of or like beasts; savage: *bestial cruelty.* — **bes·tial·ly** *adv.* — **bes·ti·al·i·ty** (-AL·uh·tee) *n.*

be·stir (bi·STUR) *v.* -stirs, -stirred, -stir·ring *Formal.* make active: *It's morning, let's bestir ourselves!*

best man *n.* a bridegroom's male attendant.

be·stow (bi·STOH) *v.* give as an honour or gift: *They bestowed a doctorate on or upon him.* — **be·stow·al** (-ul) *n.*

be·stride (bi·STRIDE) *v.* -strides, -strode, -strid·den, -strid·ing sit, stand, or get astride: *The knight bestrode his horse.*

best·sell·er (best·SEL·ur) *n.* a book, record, etc. that sells better than others of its kind: *Dictionaries are perennial bestsellers.*

bet *n.* 1 an agreement that the one who is wrong about an outcome will give something, usually a sum of money, to the one who is right; wager: *We made a $100 bet that we would win the election; They accepted the bet; A bookmaker is taking bets on who will form the next government; She wouldn't have done it except on a bet; He hedges his bets* (= protects himself) *by placing bets on more than one horse.* 2 that on which a bet is made: *His team is a safe bet (to win); In this weather, your best bet* (= safest alternative) *is to take the train.* — *v.* bets, *pt. & pp.* bet or bet·ted, bet·ting 1 make a bet; wager (usually money): *We bet (him) $50 that he would lose the vote; He bets only on horses; off-track betting.* 2 claim as though betting: *I bet she'll win.* — **you bet!** *Informal.* certainly!

be·ta (BAY·tuh) *n.* the second letter of the Greek alphabet.

be·take (bi·TAKE) *v.* -takes, -took, -tak·en, -tak·ing cause *oneself* to go: *They betook themselves to the air waves in a propaganda blitz.*

be·think (bi·THINK) *v.* -thinks, -thought, -think·ing make oneself recall or reconsider: *Bethink yourself of your patriotic duty.*

be·tide (bi·TIDE) *v.* befall: *Woe betide you if you fail this test!*

be·times (bi·TIMES) *adv.* in good time; early in the day, year, etc.

be·to·ken (bi·TOH·kun) *v.* be a sign of: *preparations betokening war.*

betook *pt.* of BETAKE.

be·tray (bi·TRAY) *v.* 1 be disloyal by breach of faith: *He betrayed his best friend to his enemies; to betray one's country, a trust; He felt betrayed* (= forsaken) *when his family ignored him in his time of need.* 2 reveal on purpose: *to betray a confidence, secret.* 3 show, esp. unwittingly: *His shaking hands betrayed his nervousness.* — **be·tray·al** (bi·TRAY·ul) *n.*

be·troth·al (bi·TROH·thul, bi·TROTH·ul, "TH" as in "thin") *n.* engagement to be married.

be·trothed (bi·TROTHED, bi·TROTHT) *adj.* engaged to be married. — *n.* an engaged person.

bet·ter (BET·ur) *adj., comp.* of GOOD: *Is he any better today? He's much better than he was last week; Mom kissed the sore spot and made it **all better;** It's better to give than to receive; It's better that we give rather than take from others; He's better at chess than at tennis.* — *adv. comp.* of WELL: *You better believe it* (Informal for *You're absolutely right*).
— **better half** *Informal.* one's spouse.
— **better off** in a better condition.
— **for better or (for) worse** whatever happens: *He is your spouse for better or for worse.*
— **get the better of** outdo or overcome.
— **had better** ought to.
— **the better part of** more than half of something: *He was absent for the better part of the day.*
— **think better of** reconsider.
— *n.* one that is better: *the better of the two; a change for the better* (= an improvement); *Events took a turn for the better; $5 000 or better* (= more); *Listen to your elders and **betters*** (= superiors).
— *v.* improve: *He bettered himself by training; was able to better* (= outdo) *his previous record.*

bet·ter·ment (BET·ur·munt) *n.* improvement, esp. of society: *She devoted her life to the betterment of humanity.*

bet·tor (BET·ur) *n.* one who bets. Also **bet·ter.**

be·tween (bi·TWEEN) *prep.* indicating 1 [a midway position, place, time, degree, etc.]: *the road between here and Ottawa; some time between 7 and 8 p.m.; a position between two extremes.* 2 [joint or related ownership, action, connection, etc.]: *We own 100 hectares between the two of us; **Between them,** the three women have over 100 years of experience on this job; just **between you and me*** (= confidentially). 3 [choice involving two or more]: *I can't choose between the two ties; a race between chuckwagons; the main differences between the three of us.*
— **between you and I** [overcorrect form of "between you and me"]
— *adv.:* *He eats only breakfast and supper, with snacks in between; Her visits have become **few and far between*** (= very rare).

be·twixt (bi·TWIXT) *prep. & adv.* between: *The peacemaker was caught betwixt and between (the two parties).*

bev·er·age (BEV·rij) *n.* a drink other than water: *to order a beverage with one's meal; alcoholic beverages; carbonated beverages.*

beverage room *n. Cdn.* same as BEER PARLOUR.

bev·y (BEV·ee) *n.* **bev·ies** group: *a bevy of girls, deer, larks, phone calls, projects, quails, roes.*

be·wail (bi·WAIL) *v.* lament: *to bewail one's fate, misfortune.*

be·ware (bi·WARE) *v.* be careful or cautious: *Let the buyer beware; Beware of the dog.*

be·wil·der (bi·WIL·dur) *v.* puzzle and confuse: *He was bewildered by everything that had happened that night; a bewildered look; a **bewildering** array of artifacts for sale.* — **be·wil·der·ment** *n.*

be·witch (bi·WICH) *v.* **1** cast a magic spell on, esp. with evil intent: *He's easily bewitched by flattery.* **2** charm: *a bewitching beauty, smile; Macbeth was bewitched into contemplating murder.*

be·yond (bi·YOND) *prep.* **1** on the other side: *You can't see beyond the horizon; She was told not to stay beyond midnight; How time never ends is beyond me* (= more than I can understand). **2** outside the limits: *She was grateful beyond measure for the kindness shown to her husband; to live beyond one's means and go broke; a subject that is really beyond my depth* (= beyond my understanding); *behaviour that is beyond the pale* (= unacceptable); *He was found guilty of murder beyond a reasonable doubt; It has been proven beyond the shadow of a doubt; a beautiful scene that is beyond words to describe.*
— *adv.* farther on: *The view stretches to the horizon and beyond.*
— **the (great) beyond** the afterlife.

bi·an·nu·al (bye·AN·yoo·ul) *adj.* occurring twice a year; semiannual. — **bi·an·nu·al·ly** *adv.*

bi·as (BYE·us) *n.* **bi·as·es 1** an inclination for or against something; prejudice: *a hiring policy that shows strong bias against women and minorities; a deep-rooted bias; Some companies have a bias toward or for or in favour of younger personnel.* **2** a slanting line across the weave of a fabric: *a bias seam; cloth that is cut on the bias* (= diagonally); *a radial, not bias (ply) tire.*
— *v.* **bi·as·es, bi·assed** or **bi·ased, bi·as·sing** or **bi·as·ing** prejudice: *His experience biassed him against bureaucrats.*

bi·assed or **bi·ased** (BYE·ust) *adj.* prejudiced: *The juror was rejected because he seemed very biassed; The report was biassed against the elderly; It seemed biassed toward younger people.*

bi·ath·lon (bye·ATH·lun) *n.* a sport or skill combining skiing and rifle-shooting.

bib *n.* **1** a cloth tied under a child's chin at meals: *He appeared in his best bib and tucker* (*Informal* for best clothes) *for her graduation.* **2** the top part of an apron or overalls.
— *v.* [as combining form] drink excessively: *a wine-bibber; a brawling, beer-bibbing heavyweight.*

Bi·ble (BYE·bul) *n.* **1** the sacred scriptures, esp. of the Christians: *The Koran is the Bible of the Muslims.* **2 bible** an authoritative book of reference: *the bible of the trade.* — **Bib·li·cal** or **bib·li·cal** (BIB·luh·cul) *adj.*

bib·li·og·ra·phy (bib·lee·OG·ruh·fee) *n.* **-phies 1** a list of books and articles on a topic or by one author: *an annotated bibliography.* **2** the study of editions, history, etc. of published works. — **bib·li·o·graph·ic** (-uh·GRAF·ic) or **bib·li·o·graph·i·cal** (-uh·cul) *adj.*

bi·cam·er·al (bye·CAM·uh·rul) *adj.* having two houses of legislature: *the bicameral system.*

bi·cen·ten·ni·al (bye·sen·TEN·ee·ul) *n. & adj.* a 200th anniversary or its celebration: *to celebrate, mark, observe a bicentennial; a bicentennial celebration, project, year.* Also **bi·cen·te·nar·y** (bye·sen·TEN·uh·ree, -TEE·nuh·ree).

bi·ceps (BYE·seps) *n. sing. & pl.* the muscle at the front of the upper arm: *A wrestler likes to flex his biceps.*

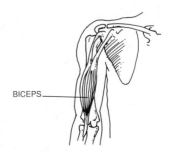

BICEPS

bick·er (BICK·ur) *v.* quarrel pettily: *to bicker with a salesclerk about* or *over the price of a small article; the constant bickering going on between the children.*

bi·cus·pid (bye·CUS·pid) *n. & adj.* (a tooth) having two points: *We have eight bicuspids, or pre-molars; bicuspid teeth.*

bi·cy·cle (BYE·suh·cul) *n.* a two-wheeled vehicle, usually driven by pedals, with a seat and handlebars: *to get on* or *mount a bicycle; An exercise bicycle is a stationary bicycle.*
— *v.* **-cles, -cled, -cling** ride a bicycle: *He was bicycling along the highway; bicycling home at night.*
— **bi·cy·clist** *n.*

bid *v.* **bids,** *pt.* **bid,** *pp.* **bid** or **bid·den, bid·ding 1** *pt.* **bade** (BAD), tell: *They bade him be silent; She bids us farewell today.* **2** offer a price at an auction: *She bid $50 for the chair.* **3** in bridge, declare the trump suit and how many points or tricks one will make: *His partner had bid three hearts.* **4** try to get, win, etc.: *Six firms bid on the work contract; Everyone wanted to bid for the painting; The new stadium bids fair to* (= seems likely to) *become a world attraction.*
— *n.* **1** an act of bidding or offering: *to call for, enter, file, invite, make, submit bids; to raise one's bids; an opening bid; sealed bids; Three hearts could be a bad bid; The work contract was up for bids; Six firms put in bids* (= offers) *for the contract.* **2** an attempt to get, win, etc.: *a bid for popular support; He made a desperate bid to regain his lost influence.* — **bid·der** *n.*

bid·da·ble (BID·uh·bul) *adj.* **1** *Informal.* ready to obey. **2** worth bidding on: *a biddable hand in bridge.*

bidding *n.* **1** offering of bids: *The bidding opened at $100 000.* **2** command: *His secretary is not supposed to make coffee at his bidding; He would like someone to do his bidding* (= do what he commands) *at all times.*

bide *v.* **bides,** *pt.* **bode** or **bid·ed,** *pp.* **bid·ed, bid·ing** [old use] wait or remain.
— **bide one's time** await one's opportunity.

bi·en·ni·al (bye·EN·ee·ul) *adj.* **1** occurring every two years: *a biennial convention.* **2** lasting two years: *a biennial plant; n.: The beet and carrot are biennials.*
— **bi·en·ni·al·ly** *adv.*

bier (BEER) *n.* a movable stand for a coffin or corpse.

bi·fo·cal (bye·FOH·cul) **1** *adj.* having two focal lengths: *a bifocal lens.* **2 bifocals** *n. pl.* spectacles with divided lenses for distant and close vision.

big *adj.* **big·ger, big·gest 1** large in regard to size, weight, or bulk; not small: *a big box; a store that carries special sizes of clothes for big* (= large) *and tall men; a woman big* (= pregnant) *with child; the Big Apple* (= New York). **2** important or powerful: *He's a big man on campus; a big fish* or *gun* or *shot; big business, government.* **3** full-grown; older: *You're a big boy now; your big brother, sister.* **4** generous: *a big benefactor with a big heart; It's big of him to apologize.* **5** boastful: *big talk; What's the big idea* (= Why are you so boastful or aggressive)?
— **big on** *Informal.* enthusiastic about something: *He's big on parties for all occasions.*
— **big with** *Informal.* popular with someone: *Miniskirts are big with the younger set.*
— **too big for one's boots** or **breeches** too cocky or self-important.
— *adv. Informal.* **1** on a grand scale: *Think big.* **2** boastfully: *He talks big but achieves little.*
— **big·ness** *n.*

big·a·my (BIG·uh·mee) *n.* the crime of being married to two people where the law allows marriage to only one person at a time: *to commit, practise bigamy.*
— **big·a·mist** *n.* — **big·a·mous** *adj.*

Big Brother *n.* **1** a layman who volunteers to befriend a fatherless boy. **2** the all-powerful leader of an authoritarian state: *Big Brother is watching you.*
— **Big Broth·er·ism** *n.*

big deal *n. Informal* [usually ironical] something of importance: *So you got a Cadillac – big deal! Don't make such a big deal out of your Cadillac; Getting a Cadillac is no big deal these days.*

Big·foot *n.* See SASQUATCH.

big·horn *n.* a large-horned wild sheep of the Rocky Mountains.

bight *n.* **1** a gently curving bay. **2** the slack or looped part of a rope.

big leagues *n. pl. Informal.* the major leagues in baseball.

big name *n. Informal.* a well-known, popular person, esp. an entertainer.
— **big-name** *adj.: a big-name actor.*

big·ot (BIG·ut) *n.* an intolerant, blindly prejudiced person: *a fanatical, narrow-minded bigot.*
— **big·ot·ed** *adj.: a bigoted attitude; He's bigoted against minorities.*

big·ot·ry (BIG·uh·tree) *n.* **-tries** bigoted attitude or behaviour: *to stir up* or *arouse bigotry.*

big-ticket *adj. Slang.* high-priced: *a big-ticket item.*

big time *n. Slang.* the top level of a field such as entertainment: *The singer hit the big time.*
— **big-time** *adj.: big-time crime; a big-time operator* (= wheeler-dealer); *a big-time outfit, spender.*

big top *n. Informal.* the main tent of a circus: *life under the big top* (= life in the circus).

big·wig *n. Informal.* an important person.

bike *n. Informal.* a bicycle or motorcycle: *to ride a bike.*

— *v.* **bikes, biked, bik·ing.** — **bik·er** *n.*

bi·ki·ni (bi·KEE·nee) *n.* a woman's scanty two-piece bathing suit.

bi·lat·er·al (bye·LAT·uh·rul) *adj.* made by or affecting both sides equally: *a bilateral agreement, policy, treaty; An animal's body has bilateral symmetry, but a potato doesn't.* — **bi·lat·er·al·ly** *adv.*

bile *n.* **1** a greenish-yellow fluid produced in the liver. **2** bad temper.

bilge (BILJ) *n.* **1** water that collects in the bottom of a ship. **2** *Slang.* nonsense.

bi·lin·gual (bye·LING·gwul) *adj.* having to do with two languages: *a bilingual country, document, person, school, service; U.S. schools provide bilingual education in native languages other than English.*

bi·lin·gual·ism (bye·LING·gwuh·liz·um) *n.* the use of two languages, esp. the Canadian government policy of using French and English on an equal footing.

bil·ious (BIL·yus) *adj.* **1** having to do with the bile: *a bilious attack; The colour is a bilious yellow.* **2** ill-tempered: *a bilious old man.* — **bil·i·ous·ness** *n.*

bilk *v.* cheat, esp. by taking money: *He bilked the poor widow out of her savings.* — **bilk·er** *n.*

bilk joint *n. Slang.* a shop that cheats its customers; gyp joint.

bill *n.* **1** a list of payments due: *Guests settle their hotel bills before checking out; We ran up a huge bill for phone calls last month.* **2** a list of items, as on a menu, theatre program, etc.: *a bill of fare* (= menu). **3** a poster: *Post no bills (on this wall)!* **4** a piece of paper money: *to change* or *break a $100 bill; He tried to pass a counterfeit $20 bill; Marked bills are used by police to catch thieves.* **5** a proposed law: *to draft, introduce, oppose, pass, propose, reject, shelve, support, veto, vote down a bill; In 1982 Bill C-127 was before Parliament; The bill was railroaded through the House.* **6** a certificate or similar document: *a bill of health, rights, sale; a bill of exchange* (= draft). **7** the hard mouth parts of a bird; beak.
— **fill** or **fit the bill** *Informal.* meet the requirements.
— **foot the bill** *Informal.* settle the bill; make the payment: *He footed the bill for the whole party.*
— *v.* **1** present with a bill: *Please bill us at the end of the month; to bill for services rendered.* **2** advertise with bills: *Ali was billed as the world's greatest; Jim was billed to appear as Macbeth.*
— **bill and coo** kiss and caress.

bill·board *n.* a signboard for posters, notices, etc.: *billboard advertising.*

bil·let (BIL·it) *n.* **1** a soldier's lodging in a civilian's house: *an officer's billet.* **2** a lodging assigned to someone as a guest in a private home.
— *v.* to quarter troops by billet: *The platoon was billeted in our village.*

bill·fold *n.* a wallet.

bil·liards (BIL·yurdz) *n.* a game played by striking hard balls with a cue on a rectangular, cloth-covered table.
— **billiard** *adj.: a billiard ball, player, table.*

billing *n.* a display of performers' names according to their importance: *a Canadian actor who gets top billing in New York.*

bil·lings·gate (BIL·ingz·gate) *n.* vulgar abuse.

bil·lion (BIL·yun) *n.* **1** a thousand million; 1 000 000 000: *Ten billion dollars; billions of dollars.* **2** [British use] a million million; 1 000 000 000 000. — **bil·lionth** (BIL·yunth) *n. & adj.*

bil·lion·aire (bil·yuh·NAIR) *n.* one whose wealth amounts to at least a billion dollars, francs, etc.

bill of goods *n.* a shipment of merchandise to sell: *We have been sold a bill of goods (Informal for cheated).*

bill of health *n.* a certificate of good health: *to get, give (someone), receive a clean bill of health.*

bill of rights *n.* a declaration of the basic rights of a people: *The Canadian Charter of Rights and Freedoms (Part I of the 1982 Constitution Act) replaced the 1960 Bill of Rights.*

bil·low (BIL·oh) *n.* a swelling or surging mass, as a large wave of water. — *v.* rise, swell, or roll in billows: *Smoke billowed from the burning oil well.* — **bil·low·y** *adj.*: *the billowy ocean; an airy billowy dress for summer wear.*

bil·ly (BIL·ee) *n.* **bil·lies** *Informal.* a small club carried by a police officer; nightstick; truncheon; also called "billy club."

billy goat *n.* a male goat.

bim·bo (BIM·boh) *n. Slang.* **-bos** *Informal.* a dumb or insignificant person.

bi·month·ly (bye·MUNTH·lee) *adj.* **1** occurring once in two months. **2** [loosely] occurring twice a month; semimonthly. — *n., pl.* **-lies** a bimonthly publication.

bin *n.* a large box or container for storage: *a coal bin; a grain bin.*

bi·na·ry (BYE·nuh·ree) *adj.* having two parts, elements, etc.: *Orange and green are binary colours composed of two primary colours; a binary star (= two stars revolving around each other); The binary digits are 0 and 1; In the binary system or code or notation, 5 is written as 0101.*

bind (BINED) *v.* **binds, bound** (BOWND), **bind·ing** **1** to tie: *She binds her hair with ribbons; Reapers bind sheaves of wheat; The suspect was bound to a post until the police arrived.* **2** bandage: *A nurse bound up his wounds.* **3** obligate or constrain: *an apprentice bound to serve for three years; The contract binds you to deliver on time; He was bound over (= made to promise in court) to keep the peace.* **4** stick together or cause to cohere: *Cement binds gravel well.* **5** strengthen or decorate an edge with braid, tape, etc. **6** fasten a book's pages together or inside a cover, as done in a bindery: *a book bound in leather.* — *n. Informal.* a difficult situation: *The loss of his job put him in a financial bind; She was in the double bind of being sick and jobless.*

bind·er (BINE·dur) *n.* **1** a folder that holds paper together: *a loose-leaf binder; ring binder.* **2** one that binds: *a book binder; Cut grain has been tied with*

binder twine instead of binder wire since the 1880s. **3** a binding clause of a contract specifying a condition, as in an insurance agreement.

bind·er·y (BINE·duh·ree) *n.* **-ries** a place where books are bound.

binding (BINE·ding) **1** *n.* something that binds, as a book's cover, the boot fastenings on skis, etc.: *cloth, leather binding; to sew on a binding* (= strip of fabric). **2** *adj.* obligatory: *A contract is binding on or upon the parties concerned.*

binge (BINJ) *n. Informal.* a spree: *to go on a shopping binge; a scoring binge in hockey; a binge of borrowing and spending.*

bin·go (BING·go) *n.* **-gos** a gambling game played on cards with numbered squares. — *interj.* expressing suddenness: *Bingo! said the winner of the game; When the lunch bell goes, bingo! They drop everything and leave.*

bin·oc·u·lar (buh·NOK·yuh·lur, bye-) **1** *adj.* using or for use by both eyes at once: *a binocular microscope; binocular vision.* **2 binoculars** *n.pl.* an optical instrument like a telescope with lens tubes for both eyes, as opera glasses or field glasses: *a pair of binoculars; She trained her binoculars on her favourite horse.*

bi·no·mi·al (bye·NOH·mee·ul) *n.* **1** a mathematical expression consisting of two terms linked by a + or −sign, as "3x − 4xy." **2** a two-word scientific name indicating genus and species, as "Equus caballus" (horse) and "Equus asinus" (ass). — *adj.*: *a binomial equation, expression, series, system; binomial nomenclature; the binomial theorem.*

bio (BYE·oh) **1** *n.* [short form] biography, esp. a short one. **2** *combining form.* having to do with life or living things: *bioassay, biochemistry, bioethics, biohazard.*

bi·o·cide (BYE·uh·cide) *n.* **1** a substance that can destroy life, as DDT. **2** the destruction of life.

bi·o·clean (BYE·uh·cleen) *adj.* free from microorganisms, esp. harmful ones.

bi·o·de·grad·a·ble (BYE·oh·di·GRAY·duh·bul) *adj.* able to be broken down by biological agents, esp. bacteria: *Plastics are not biodegradable; biodegradable paper.*

bi·o·eth·ics (bye·oh·ETH·ics) *n.pl.* [takes sing. v.] the ethics of biological research and its application to medicine, as in artificial insemination, genetic engineering, and organ transplants.

bi·o·feed·back (bye·oh·FEED·back) *n.* the technique of mental control of the body's unconscious processes, as by using a machine that monitors brain waves.

bi·o·flick (BYE·oh·flick) *n. Slang.* a TV show or movie based on a person's life story.

bi·og·ra·phy (bye·OG·ruh·fee) *n.* **-phies** the story of a person's life as written by another. — **bi·og·ra·pher** *n.* — **bi·o·graph·ic** (bye·uh·GRAF·ic) or **bi·o·graph·i·cal** (-uh·cul) *adj.*

bi·o·haz·ard (bye·oh·HAZ·urd) *n.* a hazard resulting from a biological agent such as a virus or a dangerous environmental condition.

bi·o·log·i·cal (bye·uh·LOJ·uh·cul) *adj.* having to do with living organisms: *a biological agent, pesticide, science, system; biological wastes; a biological parent* (= birth parent).

biological clock *n.* a built-in timing system controlling cyclical behaviour in organisms, as sleeping patterns, bird migrations, and the blossoming of flowers.

biological warfare *n.* warfare using poisonous germs, insects, etc. to destroy plant, animal, and human life.

bi·ol·o·gy (bye·OL·uh·jee) *n.* the science of living organisms and life processes. — **bi·ol·o·gist** *n.*

bi·o·mass (BYE·oh·mas) *n.* vegetable and animal waste materials used as a source of energy; *adj.: Wood, garbage, and other biological wastes form biomass fuels that produce renewable energy; biomass energy; a biomass reactor.*

bi·ome (BYE·ohm) *n.* a typical community of plants and animals based on a particular climate: *a grassland, a tropical forest, or a tundra biome.*

bi·on·ics (bye·ON·ics) *n. pl.* the study and design of electronic devices modelled on living things. — **bi·on·ic** *adj.: a child with a bionic arm.*

bi·op·sy (bye·OP·see) *n.* -**sies** the removal and diagnostic examination of fluid or tissue from a living body.

bi·o·rhythm (BYE·oh·rith·um, "th" as in "the") *n.* the rhythm of cyclical behaviour in organisms, as in sleeping and waking.

bi·o·sphere (BYE·us·feer) *n.* that part of the earth and the atmosphere in which life is found.

bi·ot·ic (bye·OT·ic) *adj.* caused by or having to do with living things: *the biotic environment.*

bi·par·ti·san (bye·PAR·tuh·zun) *adj.* having to do with two sides or parties: *a bipartisan committee.* — **bi·par·ti·san·ship** *n.*

bi·par·tite (bye·PAR·tite) *adj.* divided into two parts: *a bipartite agreement; bipartite leaves.*

bi·ped (BYE·ped) *adj. & n.* two-footed (animal): *Humans are biped animals; We are bipeds.*

bi·plane (BYE·plane) *n.* an airplane with two main wings one above the other.

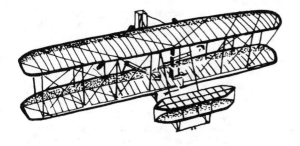

bi·ra·cial (bye·RAY·shul) *adj.* having to do with two races: *a biracial society.* — **bi·ra·cial·ism** *n.*

birch *n.* **1** a hardwood tree whose smooth bark peels off in layers. **2** a bunch of birch twigs used to give a

whipping.
— *v.* whip: *Criminals used to be birched as punishment.*

bird *n.* **1** a two-legged, feathered, winged animal: *as free as a bird; Birds build nests, sing, soar, twitter, warble; game, migratory, wading, water birds; "A bird in the hand* (= something already possessed) *is worth two in the bush"; "Birds of a feather* (= people of the same kind) *flock together."* **2** *Informal.* a person: *He's a rare bird at these meetings; a clever, literary, strange bird; a funny* (= eccentric) *bird; a wise old bird.* **3** *Informal.* a shuttlecock, clay pigeon, missile, satellite, etc. that flies or seems to: *The first commercial communications satellite called "Early Bird" was launched in 1965.* **4** *Slang.* [derogatory] a young woman; chick.
— **for the birds** *Slang.* worthless: *Al says economics is strictly for the birds.*
— **the birds and the bees** *Informal.* the basic facts about sex: *Raj learned about the birds and the bees in Family Studies class.*

bird·brain *n.* a stupid person. — **bird·brained** *adj.*

bird call *n.* the cry of a bird: *to imitate birdcalls.*

bird dog *n.* **1** a sporting dog such as a pointer or retriever that smells the air and locates game birds shot down by the hunter. **2** *Slang.* a talent scout, detective, chaperone, or other person or instrument that works like a bird dog.
— **bird-dog** *v.* -**dogs,** -**dogged,** -**dog·ging:** *He was assigned to bird-dog* (= tail) *the suspect around town.*

bird·er *n. Informal.* a birdwatcher.

bird·ie (BUR·dee) *n.* **1** in golf, a one-under-par score on a hole. **2** a little bird.

bird of passage *n.* **1** a migratory bird. **2** *Informal.* one who moves or travels about constantly.

bird of prey *n.* a bird such as the eagle or hawk that kills other animals for food.

bird·seed *n.* an assorted mixture of seeds for feeding birds.

bird's-eye *adj.* **1** quick or general: *a bird's-eye view.* **2** with markings like a bird's eye: *the bird's-eye maple used esp. for veneers; a bird's-eye pattern.*

bird·watch·ing (BURD·woch·ing) *n.* the study of birds in their natural surroundings. — **bird·watch·er** *n.*

birth *n.* a being born or coming into existence: *Many Canadians are British by birth; He weighed only six pounds (2.72 kg) at birth; You have one **birth date,** or date of birth, but many birthdays; She gave **birth to** (= brought forth) triplets; It was a difficult birth (= act of giving birth); a breech, multiple, premature birth; a man of noble birth (= parentage); Today marks the birth (= beginning) of a new era; adj.: birth defects such as birthmarks, cleft palate, and colour blindness; The project was aborted after enduring or suffering many birth pangs.*

birth control *n.* the use of a device or method to prevent pregnancy: *People like to practise birth control under the name "family planning."*

birth·day *n.* the anniversary of a birth: *to celebrate, mark, reach a birthday; on her 90th birthday; Happy* *birthday (to you)! **adj.:** a birthday boy, card, girl, party, present.*

birthday suit *n. Informal.* the state of nudity, as when an infant is born.

birth·ing *n.* the act of giving birth: *a birthing centre, room.*

birth·mark *n.* a mark on the skin that is present from birth.

birth mother *n.* the woman who gives birth to a child.

birth parent *n.* the birth mother or the man who fathers a child; a natural or biological, not adoptive parent of a child.

birth·place *n.* one's place of birth.

birth·rate *n.* the ratio of births to total population in an area: *the falling birthrate; a rising birthrate.*

birth·right *n.* a right to an inheritance, citizenship, etc. based on when or where one is born.

birth·stone *n.* a gemstone symbolizing the month of one's birth, as garnet (January), amethyst (February), etc.

bis·cuit (BIS·kit) *n.* **1** a small bread or roll leavened without yeast: *soda biscuits; tea biscuits.* **2** *Brit.* a cracker or cookie: *a cream biscuit; sweet biscuits.*

bi·sex·u·al (bye-SEK·shoo·ul) *adj.* having to do with both sexes: *Bisexual people are sexually attracted to members of both sexes; Earthworms are bisexual* (= have both male and female organs).
— *n.* a bisexual person, animal, or plant.
— **bi·sex·u·al·i·ty** (-AL·uh·tee) *n.*

bish·op (BISH·up) *n.* **1** a clergyman who usually heads a diocese and has authority over other clergy. **2** a chess piece that moves diagonally.

bish·op·ric (BISH·up·ric) *n.* a bishop's rank, office, or jurisdiction.

bi·son (BYE·sun) *n. sing. & pl.* a wild, oxlike bovine with large shaggy head and a hump at the shoulders: *a herd of bison; The bison is the emblem of Manitoba; The European bison and the North American buffalo are related species.*

bit *n.* **1** a small portion, amount, interval, etc.: *a bit of paper; a tiny bit; bits and pieces of information gathered from hearsay; Wait a bit* (=little while); *He tried to do his bit* (=fair share); *She's **every bit*** (=quite) *like her father and **every bit*** (=just) **as** *talented as her brother; He's **a bit of a*** (=somewhat of a) *comic; You can do the whole thing **bit by bit*** (=little by little); *The shelf is **a bit*** (=slightly) *too high; She's not **the least bit*** (=not at all) *worried; He admits to cheating **a little bit**; That's **quite a bit*** (=more than a little) *to admit.* **2** the cutting edge of a tool, esp. one for boring and drilling: *a brace and bit; a drill bit.* **3** the part of a bridle held in a horse's mouth: *He has a tendency to **take the bit in his mouth*** (=take charge) *and do things his own way.* **4** in entertainment, a short act or routine; *adj.:* *a bit part in a play; a bit player.* **5** *Informal.* a stereotyped act, behaviour, speech, etc.: *Her husband did the jealousy bit.* **6** in computers, a binary digit representing the smallest unit of information, as a 0 or 1: *A byte is eight bits long in the oldest microprocessors; The first modems used to receive and transmit data at 300 bits per second; a third-generation 32-bit microprocessor; In **bit-mapped** graphics, a bit in the computer memory controls each pixel of the display.*

bitch *n.* **1** *Slang.* a woman looked on with scorn. **2** *Slang.* anything that causes one to complain: *Money is such a bitch; this bitch of a toothache!* [used as intensifier] *a or one bitch of a* (*Slang* for a very bad) *job.* **3** *Slang.* something admirable; lulu: *a or one bitch of an album; It's a bitch; a **bitching*** (=very) *good single.* **4** [formal use] the adult female of a dog or other canine.
— *v. Slang.* **1** complain: *He's always bitching about something or other.* **2** botch or bungle: *The project was bitched up by incompetent workers.*

bitch·y (BICH·ee) *adj.* **bitch·i·er, -i·est** *Slang.* spiteful or ill-tempered.

bite *v.* **bites,** *pt.* **bit,** *pp.* **bit·ten** or **bit, bit·ing** seize, pierce, or cut with or as if with the teeth, as a dog, snake, or mosquito: *Dogs bite letter carriers; Fish bite at baits, but they aren't biting today; She likes to bite into or on an apple; She bit off a large piece; Snow tires bite into snow; fingers bitten by frost; He would never **bite the hand that fed him*** (=be ungrateful).
— **bite one's tongue** restrain oneself from saying something.
— **bite the bullet** suffer something painful without complaining.
— **bite the dust** be utterly defeated.
— *n.* **1** an act of biting: *dog, insect, mosquito, snake bites; a dog with a powerful bite* (=biting ability). **2** what is bitten off: *He took a big bite out of my apple; There's just enough time to grab* or *have a quick bite* (*Informal* for light meal); *The new taxes take a big bite* (=deduction) *from* or *out of our earnings.*
— **put the bite on** *Slang.* press someone for money or favours.

bite-size or **bite-sized** *adj.* small and easy to use: *Dice the sausage into bite-size pieces; a newspaper featuring bite-size stories.*

biting (BYE·ting) *adj.* sharp or stinging: *a biting odour, wind; biting criticism, sarcasm.* — **bit·ing·ly** *adv.*

bit·ter *adj.* **1** having a sharp, unpleasant taste: *bitter*

medicine; *a **bitter pill to swallow*** (= an unpleasant fact). **2** harsh or unpleasant: *That was bitter news to hear; bitter winter weather; to fight to the **bitter end*** (= the very end, even if unpleasant). **3** expressing sorrow or resentment: *She is bitter about the defeat; a bitter disappointment; He shed bitter tears.* **4** full of hatred: *a bitter dispute, enemy.*
— *n.* **1** something bitter: *He soon learned to **take the bitter with the sweet**.* **2** **bitters** *n.pl.* a usually alcoholic bitter liquid used as a tonic or cocktail flavouring.
— **bit·ter·ly** *adv.*
— **bit·ter·ness** *n.*: *There's a touch of bitterness in her poetry; He feels bitterness toward his former employers; He gave vent to his bitterness about or over their exploiting him.*

bit·ter·sweet (BIT·ur·sweet) *adj.* painful though pleasant: *a bittersweet memory; those bittersweet jokes about the loss of his job.*
— *n.* **1** a climbing vine with orange seed pods. **2** a climbing vine with poisonous berries.

bi·tu·men (bi·TUE·mun) *n.* asphalt, tar, or other viscous substance used to surface roads.
— **bi·tu·mi·nous** (-muh·nus) *adj.* soft: *bituminous coal, crude oil, molasses.*

bi·valve (BYE·valv) *n.* any mollusc with two hinged shells, as a clam.
— *adj.* having two movable parts, like a clamshell: *The pea has a bivalve pod.*

biv·ou·ac (BIV·uh·wac) *n.* a temporary camp in the open, esp. for soldiers: *They are on bivouac; gone on bivouac; They set up a bivouac in the mountains.*
— *v.* **-acs, -acked, -ack·ing**: *The platoon bivouacked in the woods; They bivouacked at a former army barracks.*

bi·week·ly (bye·WEEK·lee) *adj. & adv.* **1** once every two weeks. **2** [loosely] twice a week; semiweekly.
— *n., pl.* **-lies** a biweekly publication.

bi·year·ly (bye·YEER·lee) *adj. & adv.* **1** once every two years. **2** loosely, twice a year; semiyearly.

biz *n.* [short form] business: *show biz; the biz world; Banking biz is big biz.*

bi·zarre (buh·ZAR) *adj.* strikingly odd, eccentric, or fantastic: *bizarre appearance, behaviour; a bizarre series of events; He led a bizarre life.*

blab *v.* **blabs, blabbed, blab·bing** *Informal.* talk foolishly, as by revealing a secret or something confidential.
— *n.* **1** one who blabs. **2** a blab's chatter.

blab·ber (BLAB·ur) **1** *v.* **blab·bers, blab·bered, blab·ber·ing** to talk or communicate foolishly or indiscreetly. **2** *n.* one who blabs.

blab·ber·mouth (BLAB·ur·mouth) *n. Informal.* one who blabbers: *the blabbermouths who give away secrets.*

black *n.* **1** the colour that is opposed to white: *basic black; jet black; Put it down **in black and white*** (= in writing); *a company operating **in the black*** (= making a profit, not in the red). **2** a pigment, clothing, etc. of black: *The widow wore black (in mourning); Black is beautiful; black tie.* **3** also **Black**, a person of African origin: *Canadian blacks and other minorities; Congress of Black Women of Canada.*
— *v.* make or become black; blacken: *A shoeshine boy*

blacks shoes.
— **black out 1** to faint. **2** cover or darken: *All lights had to be blacked out during the war; A power failure blacked out much of Ontario and New York in 1965; The censor blacked out certain parts of the story.*
— *adj.* **1** very dark; of the colour black: *a black flag; **black gold*** (= petroleum). **2** dirty: *hands black with grease.* **3** bad in some way: *a black* (= gloomy) *future, night; a black* (= morbid) *depression; a black* (= angry) *look; the **Black Death** (from bubonic plague) of the 1300s; Two disastrous **Black Fridays** left many U.S. investors bankrupt in 1869 and 1873; The same thing happened on **Black Monday**, 19 October 1987.* **4** also **Black** having to do with the black people: *a black family, ghetto, leader, neighbourhood; black culture, history, politics, power, studies; a black Hebrew sect; the black Jews of Ethiopia; a **Black English** dialect; "I am a Canadian, a man, and a black man in that order," said Lincoln Alexander; the **Black Panthers** (= militant group of American blacks).*

black-and-blue (BLACK·un·BLOO) *adj.* darkly bruised, as from a beating.

black-and-white (BLACK·un·WHITE) *adj.* **1** not in colour: *a black-and-white drawing, movie.* **2** clearcut; not grey: *It's not a black-and-white issue; He thinks of morals in black-and-white terms.*

black art *n.* witchcraft.

black·ball *n.* a negative vote, esp. against a prospective member or employee.
— *v.* keep out or exclude: *After much blackballing by France, Britain was allowed to join the Common Market in 1973.*

black belt *n.* **1** the highest rating in judo or karate. **2** a person thus rated.

black·ber·ry (BLAK·ber·ee) *n.* **-ber·ries** the fleshy but seedy fruit of a bramble bush.

black·board *n.* a dark, smooth board for writing on with chalk: *to erase a blackboard; to write on the blackboard.*

black box *n.* **1** the flight recorder of an aircraft. **2** any complex electronic device whose mode of operation is unknown to the user.

black·en (BLACK·un) *v.* to darken or sully: *He came out of the scandal with his name blackened.*

black eye *n. Informal.* **1** a dark bruise around the eye: *to get a black eye.* **2** a bad reputation: *The rumours gave him a black eye.*

black·guard (BLAG·urd) *n.* a villainous or foul-mouthed person.

black hole *n.* **1** a region in outer space of such great density and gravity that even light cannot escape from it. **2** a dungeon.

black humour or **black humor** *n.* comedy stressing the morbid and the absurd.

blacking *n.* a substance for blackening something, esp. shoes.

black·jack *n.* **1** a short leather-covered club with a flexible handle. **2** a card game, also called "twenty-one."

— *v.* **1** hit with a blackjack. **2** force someone by threatening, as if with a blackjack.

black light *n.* ultraviolet or infrared light that is invisible.

black·list *n.* a list of people who are disapproved of. — *v.* to put someone on such a list.

black lung *n.* a lung disease caused by breathing coal dust.

black magic *n.* witchcraft.

black·mail *n.* **1** payment extorted, esp. by a threat of discreditable exposure: *to pay blackmail.* **2** such extortion: *to commit blackmail.*
— *v.* subject someone to blackmail: *She was blackmailed into submission.* — **black·mail·er** *n.*

black market *n.* the buying and selling of goods and exchanging money in violation of government regulations: *It's available on the black market; Tourists are warned against black market dealings in foreign countries.* — **black marketer** or **marketeer** *n.*
— **black-marketing** or **black-marketeering** *n.*

black·out *n.* a blacking out, as in the absence of light, consciousness, etc.: *Blackouts are imposed* or *ordered in wartime; The news blackout was lifted when the emergency was over.*

black sheep *n.* a person considered disgraceful by the rest of a group: *the black sheep of the family.*

black·smith *n.* one who works with iron, esp. one who shoes horses.

black tie *n.* a tuxedo or the black bow tie that is worn with it.

black-tie *adj.* requiring semiformal costume: *The banquet was a black-tie affair.*

black.top *n.* asphalt or similar material for surfacing roads.
— *v.* -tops, -topped, -top·ping: *a freshly blacktopped driveway.*

blad·der (BLAD·ur) *n.* **1** a bag of membrane that collects urine from the kidneys: *a full bladder; to empty one's bladder* (= urinate). **2** any similar object, as the air bag inside a football.

blade *n.* **1** the thin, flat cutting part of a sword, knife, axe, skate runner, etc.: *a blunt, dull, sharp blade; a razor blade; the rotary blade of a mower.* **2** a similar part on a propeller, oar, paddle, etc. **3** the long flat leaf of a grass or cereal. **4** a spirited young man.

blah *n. Informal.* **1** baloney or bunk: *all the blah you hear about freedom and democracy.* **2** boredom: *a case of the February blahs at the end of winter; adj.: a blah* (= bored) *attitude; a blah* (= boring) *performance.*

blame *v.* blames, blamed, blam·ing consider someone responsible for something bad: *They blamed the pitcher for the loss; Don't blame it on me; I'm not to blame* (= responsible) *for it.*
— *n.* responsibility for something bad: *It was hard to fix the blame for the broken window; The blame seemed to fall on Guy; Everyone put the blame on him; They laid the blame at his door; Guy tried to shift the blame to someone else; Matt took the blame in the end.*
— **blam·a·ble** (BLAY·muh·bul) *adj.*

blame·wor·thy (BLAME·wur·thee) *adj.* deserving blame.

blanch *v.* make or become pale or white: *His face blanched with fear; He blanched at the gruesome sight; blanched almonds (with skin removed); Fruit, vegetables, etc. are blanched* (= boiled briefly) *before being frozen.*

bland *adj.* **1** pleasing or soothing, not irritating: *a bland diet, smile.* **2** dull: *a bland character, leader, personality, report.*

blan·dish (BLAN·dish) *v.* persuade using flattery; cajole. — **blan·dish·er** *n.;* **blan·dish·ment** *n.*

blank *adj.* having nothing on or in it; empty: *a blank expression, look, page, sheet of paper, space, stare; a blank cartridge (with no bullet); The police have run into a blank wall* (= have no leads) *in their investigation; a blank window (with no decoration); Suddenly my mind went blank* (= I couldn't recall anything); *It was blank* (= absolute) *terror.*
— *n.* something blank or empty: *Fill in the blanks; Keys are cut from blanks; A starter pistol fires only blanks; Our investigations drew a blank (Informal for* were unsuccessful).
— *v.* reduce to nothing: *They blanked the Bruins 2-0* (= the Bruins scored nothing); *He blanked out* (= deleted) *the offending words; Suddenly my mind blanked out* (= I couldn't remember anything).

blank cheque or **blank check** *n.* **1** a signed cheque with the amount to be filled in by the recipient. **2** freedom of action: *He was given a blank cheque to negotiate a contract.*

blan·ket (BLANK·it) *n.* **1** a large cloth covering used for warmth, esp. on a bed: *a woollen blanket.* **2** a covering: *a blanket of snow.*
— *v.* cover like a blanket: *A fog blanketed the coast.*
— *adj.* covering all cases: *a blanket amnesty, authorization, condemnation, pardon, refusal, rule, veto.*

blare *v.* blares, blared, blar·ing sound or call out loudly and brashly: *The radio blared out the news.*

blar·ney (BLAR·nee) *n.* flattery or coaxing: *That's sheer blarney!*
— **kiss the Blarney Stone** get skill in coaxing and flattering.

bla·sè (blah·ZAY) *adj.* bored by too much of something: *TV viewers are blasè about all the sex and violence they watch.*

blas·pheme (blas·FEEM) *v.* -phemes, -phemed, -phem·ing speak impiously about God or something sacred: *to blaspheme (against) God; He is prone to blaspheme when tipsy.* — **blas·phem·er** *n.*
— **blas·phe·mous** (BLAS·fuh·mus) *adj.*
— **blas·phe·mous·ly** *adv.*

blas·phe·my (BLAS·fuh·mee) *n.* -mies contemptuous treatment, esp. in words, of anything considered divine; also, an instance of it: *to commit blasphemy; to utter blasphemies against Allah.*

blast *n.* **1** a powerful gust of air, gases, etc.: *The spark set off a blast; a blast of hot air; the trumpet's blast* (= loud sound); *They worked away at full blast (Informal for* at maximum capacity). **2** an explosion or

the shock wave from it: *a bomb blast.* **3** a critical or abusive attack: *an icy blast; a vicious blast; a withering blast against the Opposition.* **4** a blight that withers plants. **5** *Slang.* a wild good time; ball. **6** *Slang.* a miserable failure; bomb or flop.
— *v.* **1** explode: *Danger, blasting! Rockets blast off* (= take off with an explosion) *from the launch pad.* **2** criticize violently: *editorials blasting the government.* **3** wither: *blasted flowers; the blasted* (= blighted or darned) *idiot!*

blast·off *n.* the takeoff of a rocket, missile, etc.

blat *v. Informal.* bleat; also, speak loudly.

bla·tant (BLAY·tunt) *adj.* openly offensive; flagrant: *a blatant falsehood; He acted in blatant disregard of the rules of decency.* — **bla·tant·ly** *adv.*

blath·er (BLATH·ur, "TH" as in "the") *v.* talk foolishly and without making sense: *to blather about truth and justice.* — *n.* such talk: *sheer blather.*

blaze *n.* **1** the sudden shooting up of a flame: *The fire burst into a blaze; They tried to extinguish* or *put out the blaze.* **2** something similar to a blaze: *the blaze of the tropical sun; in the full blaze of publicity; a blaze* (= outburst) *of fury; the blaze* (= brilliant display) *of fall colours; Go to blazes!* (= hell).
— *v.* **blaz·es, blazed, blaz·ing** burn furiously: *a blazing inferno; blazing with anger.*
— **blaze a trail** mark out a path, as through the woods: *Amelia Earhart blazed a trail for women pilots.*
— **blaze away** keep shooting *at* someone.

blaz·er (BLAY·zur) *n.* a light sports jacket, often blue with metal buttons.

bla·zon (BLAY·zun) *n.* **1** a coat of arms. **2** a showy display.
— *v.* **1** publicize widely: *a billboard blazoning forth the virtues of the new soft drink.* **2** display or adorn.

bleach (BLEECH) *v.* make or become pale or white: *She bleached her hair blond; sun-bleached bones.*
— *n.* a bleaching agent: *laundry bleach; liquid bleach.*

bleach·ers (BLEE·churz) *n. pl.* tiers of usually roofless seats for spectators.

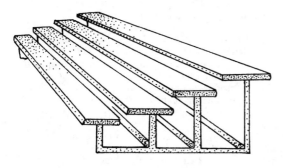

bleak (BLEEK) *adj.* **1** barren and windswept: *bleak cliffs.* **2** cold and raw: *a bleak wind.* **3** gloomy: *The company faces a bleak future.*

blear·y (BLEER·ee) *adj.* esp. of eyes, blurred or unclear from fatigue, tears, etc. — **bleary-eyed** *adj.*

bleat (BLEET) *v. & n.* (make) the cry of a calf, goat, or sheep.

bleed *v.* **bleeds, bled, bleed·ing** **1** shed blood: *He lay there bleeding profusely from his wounds; He bled to death; My heart bleeds* (= feels sympathy) *for him; The injured tree is bleeding* (= losing its sap); *internal bleeding from the stomach.* **2** draw blood, etc. from: *The thugs bled him white* (= took all his money). **3** extend or run from its regular position: *Some colours bleed* (= run) *when wet; a bleeding check pattern; the bleeding "madras" fabric; a bleeding illustration (that goes to the edge of the page); Allow tire pressure to bleed off* (= be released) *by slightly opening the valve.*

bleeding heart *n.* **1** a person overly sympathetic to the disadvantaged. **2** a perennial plant with heart-shaped pink, white, or rosy-red flowers.

bleep *adj. Slang.* taboo or vulgar: *A bleep* (= beep) *sound replaces coarse language on TV meant for family viewing; a bleep job.*
— *n.* a beep or what it stands for: *the bleeps of a Geiger counter; He's been called a meddler, fascist, and a bleep* ("four-letter word").

blem·ish *n.* a surface imperfection or flaw, as a stain or spot: *a beautiful skin marred by blemishes; She was acquitted without the least blemish on her character.*
— *v.* to spoil or taint, as by a blemish.

blench *v.* flinch or draw back: *He blenched as the light suddenly shone on him; He blenched at the dazzling light.*

blend *v.* mix or combine into one: *The ingredients should be blended rather than beaten; architecture that blends with the environment; She blended in with the crowd; A chameleon blends into its surroundings; voices blending (together) in harmony; Blended whisky is composed of several whiskies or other spirits.*
— *n.* something blended: *a blend of teas; "Smog" is a blend of "smoke" and "fog."* — **blend·er** *n.*

bless *v.* **bless·es,** *pt. & pp.* **blessed** or **blest, bless·ing** **1** make holy, happy, good, etc.: *God bless you! She is blessed* (= favoured) *with good health.* **2** ask divine favour for a person or thing: *The minister blessed his congregation.*

bless·ed (BLES·id) *adj.* **1** holy: *the blessed martyrs; the Blessed Virgin.* **2** fortunate: *Blessed are the merciful.*
— **bless·ed·ly** *adv.;* **bless·ed·ness** *n.*

blessing *n.* **1** a prayer for divine favour, as grace said at a meal: *to bestow a blessing on someone; a priestly blessing; Who will ask the blessing* (= say grace)? **2** a grant of divine favour; happy event: *It was a blessing that I missed the ill-fated flight; When you feel like complaining, count* (= remember) *your blessings; My missing the flight turned out to be a blessing in disguise because the plane was forced to land; Nuclear power may be considered as a mixed blessing (that has good and bad aspects).* **3** approval: *He did it with his wife's blessing; She gave her blessing to the project.*

blew *pt.* of BLOW.

blight *n.* **1** a disease that causes plants to wither or die: *a potato blight.* **2** decay or the resulting ugliness: *urban blight; Slums are a blight on the landscape; Childhood misery cast a blight on* or *upon her future.*

—*v.* affect with blight: *a blighted apple tree; her blighted hopes; blighted neighbourhoods.*

blimp *n.* **1** a nonrigid airship: *the Good Year blimp.* **2** *Slang.* a fat person.

blind (BLINED) *adj.* **1** unable to see: *He's blind as a bat; He turned a blind eye to* (= pretended not to notice) *what was going on.* **2** not using vision: *We made a blind landing because of fog;* **adv.***: a pilot flying blind in a storm.* **3** wanting in perception, reason, judgment, forethought, etc.: *blind to his fate; blind with fury; blind chance, faith, love.* **4** hidden: *a blind intersection; a blind alley* (= road closed at one end); *the blind* (= windowless) *side of a house; a blind spot (that a driver cannot see except by checking over the shoulder).* **5** involving the unknown: *a blind purchase.*
—*v.* make blind: *Paul was blinded by the light; rushed with blinding speed; blinded by fury; Love blinded her to his faults.*
—*n.* something to shut out light: *Venetian blinds; to adjust, draw, lower, raise the blinds.*
—**blind·ly** *adv.;* **blind·ness** *n.*

blind date *n.* **1** a date between people who have never met. **2** either partner.

blind·er *n.* one of a pair of flaps blocking a horse's sideways vision.

blind·fold *v.* tie a cloth over the eyes of someone.
—*n.* a cloth so used.

blind·side *v.* hit unexpectedly, as a car from a side that the driver cannot see.

blind spot *n.* **1** a place one cannot see. **2** a weakness or failing, esp. one the subject is unaware of: *an all-round scholar with but one blind spot.*

blind trust *n.* an arrangement for one's financial affairs to be handled by another person without one's own involvement so as to avoid conflict of interest when holding public office.

blink *v.* **1** shut and open the eyes quickly, as when dazzled by light: *He listened to the charge without once blinking* (= showing any surprise); *Teachers sometimes blink at* (= ignore) *mischievous behaviour; The child tried to blink away or blink back* (= repress) *her tears.* **2** to flicker or flash lights on and off: *the blinking cursor on a computer screen.*
—*n.* an act of blinking; glimmer.
—**on the blink** *Slang.* out of order.

blink·er *n.* **1** a flashing light. **2** a blinder.

blip *n.* a dot of light on a radar screen.
—*v.* **blips, blipped, blip·ping** to erase electronically and substitute a bleep: *A censor may blip words or lines from a sequence.*

bliss *n.* complete, serene happiness: *heavenly, marital, pure, wedded bliss; "Ignorance is bliss" (when you don't know the worst); It was bliss to be without TV for a few days.*
—*v.* **bliss out** *Slang.* go into a state of ecstacy, as under the influence of a guru.
—**bliss·ful** *adj.;* **bliss·ful·ly** *adv.*

blis·ter (BLIS·tur) *n.* **1** a patch of skin raised and filled with fluid, as from a rubbing or burn: *Blisters burst, form.* **2** a similar bulging, as on paint or metal: *Some tablets come in a blister pack of clear plastic bubbles on*

a cardboard strip.
—*v.* form blisters: *Her new shoes blistered her heel; His hands blister easily; The paint is blistering off.*

blistering *adj. & adv.* very hot or angry: *the blistering heat of the midday sun; in the blistering sun; a blistering attack, look, tongue; blistering words; It's blistering hot in here.*

blithe ("th" as in "the") *adj.* cheerful and carefree: *blithe spirits.* —**blithe·ly** *adv.*

blith·er·ing (BLITH·uh·ring, "TH" as in "the") *adj. Informal.* foolish: *the blithering idiot! his blithering innocence.*

blitz *n.* **1** a lightning-fast military attack. **2** an intensive campaign: *a public relations blitz.*
—*v.* overwhelm: *Video games have blitzed the science toys market; The Canadiens blitzed* (= beat) *the Nordiques 7-1.*

bliz·zard (BLIZ·urd) *n.* a severe snowstorm driven by high winds: *A blizzard struck in March and raged through the weekend; a blizzard* (= enormous amount) *of bills, greeting cards, paperwork, streamers and confetti.*

bloat *v.* swell, as with fat, gas, vanity, etc.: *a bloated belly, carcass; He suffers from a bloated ego; bloated figures on a financial statement; He has a bloated head* (= high opinion of himself).

blob *n.* a shapeless mass; also, a spot of colour: *a blob of grease, paint.*

bloc *n.* a usually political grouping of nations, parties, etc. for a common purpose: *a Communist bloc; the NATO bloc; a voting bloc; Soviet bloc nations.*

block *n.* **1** a solid mass of wood, stone, metal, etc., usually with at least one flat side: *a concrete block for building; a chopping block; an engine block containing the cylinders; Children play with building blocks of wood, plastic, etc.; a runner's starting block* (= brace). **2** a hindrance: *He has a mental block about anything alcoholic; He proved a stumbling block in our efforts to raise money.* **3** a building with many units: *an apartment block; office block; the Centre Block on Parliament Hill.* **4** an urban area with streets on all four sides: *a building that occupies an entire city block; neighbours who live in the same block; I went around the block in search of the child, then walked ten blocks* (= block lengths) *to the school; the new kid on the block* (*Slang* for newcomer). **5** a number of company shares, seats close together, lines of type, etc.: *to delete, exchange, move blocks* (= sections) *of text on the video display.* **6** an auction platform: *The painting goes on the block* (= up for sale by bidding) *tomorrow.* **7** *Slang.* the head.
—*v.* **1** hinder or obstruct: *A fallen tree blocked the road; a blocked-up nose; players trying to block one another's moves.* **2** support with a block: *It's safer to block up the other wheels before changing a tire.*
—**block off** close or seal off: *The firefighters had to block off the street for safety's sake.*
—**block out 1** make a sketch or plan in outline: *The artist blocked out a sketch of his painting;* also **block in.** **2** cover part of a picture or view. — **block·age** (-ij) *n.*

block·ade (block·ADE) *n.* a blocking off of the access to a city, harbour, etc.: *the blockade of Cuba during the 1962 missile crisis; to break, impose, lift, maintain a blockade; Ships trying to run the blockade* (= to slip through) *were fired at.* — *v.* to impose a blockade.

block·bust·er (BLOCK·bus·tur) *n. Informal.* **1** a very powerful bomb. **2** something with a very powerful impact: *The show was a blockbuster.*

block·head (BLOCK·hed) *n.* a stupid person.

block letter *n.* a capital letter: *a headline in big block letters.*

block parent *n.* a volunteer parent to whose home children can go for protection in case of trouble from molesters, bullies, etc. on the street: *the block parent sign displayed on a window.*

bloke *n. Brit. Informal.* a fellow or guy.

blond *adj.* **1** yellowish or light-coloured: *blond complexion; blond hair and blue eyes; blond furniture, lace, silk, skin, wood.* **2** having blond hair: *a blond child with blond parents.*
— *n.* a blond person, esp. male: *Though her parents are blonds, she is a brunette.*

blonde (BLOND) *n.* a blond woman or girl: *There are not many natural platinum blondes (with very light hair); She resents being typecast as a dumb blonde.*
— *adj.* esp. of women, having blond hair: *the blonde lady over there.*

blood (BLUD) *n.* **1** the red fluid in veins and arteries: *Blood coagulates, clots, congeals, curdles, flows; Blood spurts from a wound; to donate blood to a blood bank; to draw, let, lose blood; to shed or spill blood by killing; Blood is typed or grouped as A, AB, B, and O; pure blood; whole blood;* **blood sports** *(that involve bloodshed) such as fox-hunting.* **2** life or vigour: *The younger employees inject fresh or new blood into a company; old blood* (= personnel); *The book was written at the cost of a lot of blood, sweat, and tears; tired blood* (*Informal* for rundown condition of body). **3** passion or feeling: *There's bad blood* (= ill feeling) *between the two brothers; murdered* **in cold blood** (= cruelly and without feeling); *She's careful never to respond* **in hot blood** (= a temper). **4** family or descent: *The two are related by blood; "Blood is thicker than water"; a horse of good blood; a woman of royal blood; Poetry* **runs in their blood** (= They have been poets for generations); *They are your own flesh and blood* (= relatives); *We're all* **blood** (= blood brothers); *It's* **too rich for our blood** (= It's too expensive).
— **make someone's blood boil** (or **run cold** or **freeze**) make someone angry (or frightened).

blood and thunder *n.* violent melodrama.

blood bank *n.* a place where blood is stored for use in transfusions.

blood·bath *n.* a massacre.

blood brother *n.* **1** one's brother by birth. **2** one's brother or kin by a ceremony of mixing blood from one's body with that of another. **3** *Slang.* a fellow black.

blood cell *n.* a red or white corpuscle of the blood.

blood·count *n.* the number of red and white cells in an amount of blood.

blood·cur·dling (BLUD·curd·ling) *adj.* terrifying.

blood doping *n.* injection of an athlete with his own blood ("hemoglobin") to improve performance.

blood·ed 1 *adj.* of fine pedigree: *blooded horses.* **2** *combining form.* having a certain kind of blood: *cold-blooded, full-blooded, hot-blooded, red-blooded, warm-blooded.*

blood·hound *n.* a large, long-eared, keen-scented tracking dog.

blood·less *adj.* **1** without violence or bloodshed: *a bloodless coup, revolution.* **2** lacking vigour or feeling: *a cerebral, bloodless style of verse.*

blood·let·ting (BLUD·let·ing) *n.* **1** therapeutic bleeding. **2** bloodshed.

blood·line *n.* a line of direct descent.

blood·mo·bile (BLUD·moh·beel) *n.* a truck, van, etc. outfitted for collecting blood donations.

blood pressure *n.* the pressure of the blood on the blood-vessel walls: *High or elevated blood pressure and low blood pressure are bad symptoms.*

blood relative *n.* a relative related by birth, not marriage.

blood·shed *n.* the violent shedding of blood; killing.

blood·shot *adj.* of the eyes, red from inflammation.

blood·stain *n.* a dark stain made by blood.
— **blood·stained** *adj.*

blood stream *n.* the flow of blood in the arteries, veins, capillaries, etc.

blood test *n.* the clinical testing of a blood sample.

blood·thirst·y (BLUD·thurs·tee) *adj.* eager to kill.

blood·y (BLUD·ee) *adj.* **blood·i·er, -i·est 1** of, containing, or stained with blood; bleeding: *a bloody nose, sword.* **2** having to do with bloodshed: *a bloody persecution, tyrant.* **3** *Slang.* damned: *a bloody miracle, nuisance, shame;* **adv.:** *We may bloody well get out of here; Writing a book is bloody hard work.*
— **scream** or **cry** or **yell bloody murder** or **blue murder** *Informal.* make an outcry; complain loudly.

bloody-minded *adj.* **1** bloodthirsty. **2** tiresome or cantankerous. — **bloody-mindedness** *n.*

bloom (long "oo") *n.* **1** a flower or flowering state: *Lay out your garden carefully to ensure bloom from spring to fall; The trees are* **in bloom** or **in full bloom** (= full

of flowers) *in May.* **2** a flourishing condition: *He died in the (full) bloom of youth; The bloom may fade, as the company is heading for bankruptcy; Soon, the bloom was off their romance.*
— *v.* **1** of plants and trees, have flowers. **2** flourish; glow with health.

bloom·er *n.* **1** one that flowers. **2** *Informal.* blooper.

bloomers *n.pl.* **1** baggy women's trousers gathered at the knee. **2** women's underpants of this style.

blooming *adj. Informal.* darned: *a blooming idiot.*

bloop·er (BLOO·pur) *n. Informal.* a stupid mistake.

blos·som (BLOS·um) *n.* a flower, esp. of a fruit tree: *cherry blossoms; when apples are **in blossom*** (= flowering).
— *v.* to flower or develop: *Youth blossom into the leaders of tomorrow; a chance meeting that blossomed into a romance.* — **blos·som·y** *adj.*

blot *n.* a stain, as of spilled ink: *The incident left a blot on his good name.*
— *v.* **blots, blot·ted, blot·ting 1** put a blot on something; stain. **2** absorb, esp. spilled ink, with absorbent paper.
— **blot out 1** cover over: *The smoke and dust blotted out the sun.* **2** destroy: *to blot the memories of the war; to blot it out of one's memory, mind.*

blotch *n.* an irregular discoloration or stain, esp. a skin blemish.
— **blotch·y** *adj.* **blotch·i·er, -i·est:** *a blotchy complexion.*

blot·ter *n.* **1** a sheet of blotting paper. **2** a daily record sheet: *the police blotter of arrests, charges, etc.*

blotting paper *n.* a soft paper used to dry ink after writing.

blot·to (BLOT·oh) *adj. Slang.* in a drunk state: *He was blotto and couldn't remember a thing afterward.*

blouse (rhyme: "house") *n.* **1** a loose shirtlike garment, esp. for women: *a full blouse; a peasant blouse.* **2** a kind of smock or shirt, as worn by artists, peasants, sailors, etc.
— *v.* **blous·es, bloused, blous·ing** fall in a fold *above* or *over* a hip, boot, etc.: *a dress bloused below a collar of antique lace; bloused at the waist.*

blou·son (BLOW·son, BLOO·son – "OW" as in "HOW," *rhyme:* on) *n.* a blouse or dress with material blousing over the waistband: *a blouson of soft fabric with striped borders; a blouson top.*

blow (BLOH) *v.* **blows, blew** (BLOO), **blown, blow·ing 1** of air, be in motion: *The wind is blowing hard.* **2** make a stream of air with the mouth or nose: *He blew her a kiss; When the tea is hot, he blows on it; to blow out* (= extinguish) *a candle; to blow one's nose (to clear it); She came in puffing and blowing* (= panting) *after jogging; **There she blows*** (= There is the whale spouting air and water)! **3** move or be moved by wind: *A leaf blew down from the tree.* **4** make or do by blowing: *a child blowing bubbles; to blow* (= sound) *a bugle, horn, trumpet, whistle.* **5** burst, as a fuse, tire, etc.; explode: *She will **blow her top*** (*Informal* for lose her temper or explode) *when she finds out.* **6** *Informal.* spend extravagantly: *Charlie blew $1 000 at the races.* **7** *Slang.*

bungle: *The actor blew his lines.*
— **blow in** or **into** *Informal.* arrive unexpectedly: *He blew into town with a new show.*
— **blow it** *Informal.* ruin one's chances.
— **blow one's horn** or **trumpet** brag or boast.
— **blow someone's mind** *Slang.* evoke feelings of admiration, awe, etc. or overwhelm: *Your new car will blow his mind.*
— **blow one's top** or **lid** or **stack** *Slang.* lose one's temper. Also **blow a gasket** or **fuse.**
— **blow over** pass over or be finished: *Wait till the storm blows over; Let the controversy blow over.*
— **blow the lid off** *Slang.* uncover: *He threatened to blow the lid off the whole scandal.*
— **blow the whistle** *Informal.* report *on* someone or something to the authorities.
— **blow up 1** explode: *a bridge blown up by terrorists.* **2** *Informal.* get very angry. **3** make larger; enlarge or inflate.
— *n.* **1** a hard stroke: *He dealt* or *delivered* or *struck him a crushing blow; a knockout blow; The crowd heaped* or *rained blows on him; She's still reeling under the blows received; He took a blow to* or *on his chin; It was a low blow* (= was unfair) *to question his motives; a blow to his hopes; Her speech struck a blow for reform; a blow against tyranny; to cushion, deflect, dodge, parry, ward off a blow; a decisive, glancing, hard, heavy, mortal, resounding, severe, staggering, telling blow; Tell me what happened **blow by blow*** (= in detail); *a **blow-by-blow*** (= detailed) *account of what happened; They **come to blows** or start **exchanging blows*** (= begin fighting) *as soon as they start arguing.* **2** a blowing, as of the nose. **3** a heavy storm.

blow-dry *v.* to dry hair using a blow dryer.

blow dryer *n.* an electric blower for drying the hair.

blow·gun *n.* a tube for shooting a dart by blowing.

blow·out *n.* **1** a bursting of a tire; flat tire: *to have a blowout; fix a blowout.* **2** an uncontrollable flow of oil or gas from a well. **3** *Slang.* something overwhelming or out of the ordinary: *The 38-16 score was the second blowout in a row in the Superbowl; The record sale was clearly a blowout; the annual Mardi Gras blowout* (= noisy celebration); *adj.:* *a great blowout party, weekend.*

blow·pipe *n.* a tube for forcing in air, as to fan a fire, blow glass, launch a missile, etc.

blow·sy (BLOW·zee, "OW" as in "how") *adj.* **-si·er, -si·est** untidy and coarse: *She played the blowsy and boozy Lady Hamilton.* Also **blow·zy.**

blow·torch *n.* a portable torch for shooting a gasoline flame under pressure.

blow-up *n.* **1** an explosion. **2** an enlarged photograph. **3** a fit of anger.

blow·y *adj.* **blow·i·er, -i·est** windy.

blowzy See BLOWSY.

BLT *n.* **BLTs** *Slang.* a sandwich of bacon, lettuce, and tomato.

blub·ber *n.* fat, esp. of whales, seals, etc.
— *v.* weep noisily; **blub·ber·er** *n.* — **blub·ber·y** *adj.*

blub·ber·head (BLUB·ur·hed) *n. Slang.* stupid person;

fathead.

blu·cher (BLOO·cur, -chur) *n.* a style of shoe in which the vamp is one piece with the tongue.

bludg·eon (BLUJ·un) *n.* a short heavy club.
— *v.* beat with a bludgeon: *The baby seals were bludgeoned to death; She was bludgeoned* (= coerced) *into joining them.*

blue (BLOO) *n.* 1 the colour of a cloudless daytime sky; also, something in this colour, as clothing or a dye: *a patch of blue; The colour is a light blue; She was decked in blue; clothes washed in blue.* 2 the blue: *into the blue* (= sky); *out in the blue* (= ocean); *the big blue* (= blue-chip corporation or conservative party); *The news came as a bolt from the blue* (= as a shock); *The principal appeared out of the blue* (= unexpectedly).
— **blues** *pl.* 1 a melancholy mood: *to sing the blues* (*Informal for* to complain); *the blue-collar blues* (= boredom and depression) *of assembly-line workers; the Monday morning blues.* 2 a slow, sad style of jazz, characterized by so-called "blue" notes sung or played a half-tone flat.
— *adj.* blu·er, blu·est 1 of the colour blue: *a face blue with cold; blue eyes and blond hair; Blue ice is safer to skate on than brownish or dark ice.* 2 gloomy: *He's feeling somewhat blue today; He's developed blue flu* (*Slang for* He's calling in sick). 3 puritannical: *Sunday blue laws.* 4 noble or aristocratic: *born of blue blood.* 5 conservative: *a true-blue Canadian; He's more of a red Tory than a blue or even pink one.* 6 *Informal.* off-colour; risqué: *blue jokes, language, movies.*
— **blue around the gills** *Informal.* looking or feeling sick.
— **once in a blue moon** very rarely. — **blu·ish** *adj.*

blue baby *n.* a baby born with a bluish skin from a heart defect.

blue·ber·ry (BLOO·ber·ee) *n.* -ber·ries the small, edible, dark-blue fruit of a wild or cultivated shrub.

blue·blood *n.* aristocrat: *The zoo board was a group of bluebloods.*

blue-blooded (BLOO·blud·id) *adj.* of aristocratic birth.

blue book *n.* an official publication: *a blue book* (= listing) *of socially prominent people; a 2 000-page Blue Book of the Government's spending estimates.*

blue box *n.* 1 an electronic device for bypassing telephone circuits and making illegal toll-free calls. 2 a box for putting out recyclable waste such as cans and bottles.

blue cheese *n.* a creamy white cheese with veins of bluish mould.

blue chip *n.* an expensive, secure investment stock: *The original $50 investment is a blue chip today; The rally on the stock exchange was led by established blue chips.*
— **blue-chip** *adj.* highly valued: *a "Blue Chip" savings account; a blue-chip client, corporation, investment, visitors' list.*

blue-collar (BLOO·coll·ur) *adj.* having to do with manual or industrial workers: *a blue-collar job, neighbourhood, stronghold; the blue-collar trades; tensions between white-collar and unionized blue-collar workers.*

blue·grass *n.* 1 a grass with bluish stems, common in Kentucky. 2 Southern country music played on string instruments; *adj.: the Saskatoon bluegrass band; a bluegrass musical festival; the bluegrass style of music; Bluegrass Canada '74 was a weekend affair.*

blue·ing same as BLUING.

blue jay *n.* a bold and loud bird of Eastern Canada and the U.S. with a crested head and blue and white feathers.

blue jeans *n.* jeans of heavy blue denim.

blue·nose *n.* 1 a puritan. 2 **Bluenose** a Nova Scotian; rarely, a New Brunswicker: *The most famous Bluenose of all is the schooner launched at Lunenburg in 1921 and shown on the back of the Canadian dime since 1936.*

blue·nosed *adj.* puritannical: *those blue-nosed censors.*

blue pages *n.pl.* a section of the telephone directory printed on blue paper, in which government agencies are listed.

blue-pencil (BLOO·PEN·sul) *v.* -cils, -cilled or -ciled, -cil·ling or -cil·ing delete or edit out.

blue·print *n.* 1 a kind of photographic reproduction of building plans, maps, etc.: *to draw up* or *make up a blueprint.* 2 a detailed plan: *a blueprint for peace, progress, reform; adj.: the blueprint stage of a plan; v.: to blueprint a plan, program.*

blue ribbon *n.* an award of excellence.
— **blue-ribbon** *adj.* composed of specially qualified or distinguished members: *a blue-ribbon audience, committee, jury, panel.*

blue-sky *adj.* having no practical value or application: *a blue-sky estimate, figure; blue-sky thinking; blue-sky* (= worthless) *stock; a blue-sky law designed to protect investors from fraudulent stockbrokers.*

blue streak *n.* a rapid stream of words: *The child was chattering* or *talking a blue streak about learning to write his name at school that day.*

bluff *v.* mislead or intimidate by a false show of confidence or strength: *He was only bluffing, didn't really mean it; tried to bluff me into lending him money.*
— *n.* 1 an attempt to threaten or mislead: *I didn't fall for* (= was not deceived by) *his bluff; He backed down when she called his bluff* (= challenged him). 2 a steep, flat-fronted cliff or bank: *on a high bluff overlooking the South Saskatchewan River; the Scarborough Bluffs overlooking Lake Ontario.* 3 *Cdn.* a grove of trees, as in "Oak Bluff" (Manitoba) and "Poplar Bluff" (Saskatchewan): *the lines of cool bluffs in the Minesing Swamp near Lake Simcoe.*
— *adj.* 1 steep and flat-fronted: *a bluff shoreline.* 2 blunt and good-natured: *his bluff refusal.*

blu·ing or **blue·ing** (BLOO·ing) *n.* a blue laundering additive.

blun·der *n.* a mistake made from ignorance or stupidity: *He committed a costly blunder; a grave, stupid, terrible blunder; It was a tactical blunder not to consult her.*
— *v.* 1 move clumsily: *He blundered through the*

jungle. **2** make a foolish mistake: *He blundered; She* **blundered upon** *the solution to the puzzle* (= found it by mistake).

blun·der·buss (BLUN·dur·bus) *n.* **1** a wide-muzzled old-fashioned gun. **2** one who blunders.

blunt *adj.* **1** without a sharp edge; dull: *a blunt knife, object, pencil.* **2** plainspoken: *Forgive my being blunt; I'm a blunt person.*
— *v.* make or become blunt: *He blunted his axe on the rock; Alcohol blunts your senses.*
— **blunt·ly** *adv.;* **blunt·ness** *n.*

blur *v.* **blurs, blurred, blur·ring** make or become indistinct or dim: *blurred vision.*
— *n.* something indistinct: *The cars raced past in a blur; You can see it only as a blur in the picture.*
— **blur·ry** *adj.: a blurry photograph.*

blurb *n.* a publisher's write-up of a book, printed on its dust jacket.

blurt *v.* say without thinking: *The child blurted out the secret.*

blush *v.* turn red in the face from shame, modesty, etc.: *She blushes readily; He blushed for* or *with shame; He blushes at the mere mention of the subject.*
— *n.* **1** a reddening of the face: *The story brought a deep blush to his cheeks.* **2** appearance: *the blush of dawn in the morning sky; the first blush of youth; The plan may seem harmless* **at first blush** (= at first sight).
— **blush·ful** *adj.*

blush·er *n.* face rouge that is pink; also **blush** or **blush-on.**

blus·ter (BLUS·tur) *v.* **1** blow in heavy gusts. **2** speak or act in noisy threats or boasts.
— *n.* such behaviour: *a bully's empty bluster.*
— **blus·ter·er** *n.*

blus·ter·y (BLUS·tuh·ree) *adj.* blowing or windy: *a blustery day; blustery weather.*

B.O. or **BO** (BEE.oh) *n. Informal.* body odour.

bo·a (BOH.uh) *n.* **1** a tropical snake, esp. the **boa constrictor,** which crushes and swallows its prey. **2** a long scarf of feathers or fluffy fur.

boar (BOR) *n.* **1** a male pig. **2** a fierce Old World wild pig.

board (BORD) *n.* **1** a long, thin, rectangular piece of wood: *boards for a boardwalk.* **2** a flat piece of material for a special use: *Bristol boards for artwork; a bulletin board; chess board; cutting board; dart board; diving board; drawing board; ironing board; sounding board; a computer's circuit board; a book's* **board covers** *(made of stiff material).* **3** a table for serving food: *room and board* (= meals). **4** an official council: *the editorial board; to serve on a board of directors; the chairman of the board; a liquor control board; parole board; school board; a board of education, health, studies, trade.*
— **above board** open and honest.
— **across the board** affecting every member of the group: *a pay raise of 5% across the board;* **adj.:** *an across-the-board pay raise.*
— **go by the board** become forgotten, abandoned, lost, etc.; fail completely.
— **on board 1** aboard a ship, train, etc.: *the people on*

board a bus. **2** into a working relationship: *Come on board* (= Join us)! Also **aboard.**
— **the boards** *n. pl.* **1** in hockey and lacrosse, the board fence enclosing the rink or field. **2** the stage: *An actor is said to tread the boards; She was off the boards for a year because of illness.*
— *v.* **1** cover or shut with boards: *The windows were boarded up before the storm.* **2** get on a ship, bus, train, etc.: *a boarding pass; Flight 181 is now boarding* (= being boarded). **3** provide with meals and usually lodging for regular payment: *Our landlady boards 10 students; I boarded my horse* (= arranged with a stable for its lodging and feed) *when I went on holidays.* **4** *Cdn.* in hockey and box lacrosse, to bodycheck an opponent into the boards.

board·er *n.* one who pays for meals and often a room: *She takes in boarders.*

boarding *n. Cdn.* in hockey and box lacrosse, an illegal bodychecking of an opponent; also **board-checking.**

board of control *n. Cdn.* the executive group of certain large cities composed of the mayor and several controllers.

board·room *n.* the conference room in which a governing body such as a school board or board of directors meets.

board·sail·ing (BORD·say·ling) *n.* same as SAILBOARDING.

board·walk *n.* a sidewalk or beach promenade built of boards.

boast (BOHST) *v.* **1** speak of one's abilities, deeds, etc. with too much pride: *He likes to boast about* or *of his wealth; to boast that he is wealthy.* **2** be proud to have: *The town boasts a new concert hall.*
— *n.* a boasting or the subject of it: *to make an idle, vain, proud boast; Some of his claims are just empty boasts.*
— **boast·ful** *adj.;* **boast·ful·ly** *adv.;* **boast·ful·ness** *n.*

boat (BOHT) *n.* **1** a vessel for water travel, esp. a small open one: *to launch, row, sail, swamp, upset a boat; a patrol boat; We crossed the Channel by boat; A boat heaves, pitches, rolls, sails.* **2** a dish for serving sauces: *a gravy boat.*
— **in the same boat** in the same circumstances.
— **miss the boat** miss one's opportunity.
— **rock the boat** *Informal.* cause problems by disturbing the way things are.
— *v.* **1** travel in a boat: *to go boating; Anne boated down the river.* **2** take in a boat: *He boated the 1 000-pounder (fish) in 30 minutes.*

boat·er *n.* **1** one who boats. **2** a flat-topped hard straw hat.

boat·man (BOHT·mun) *n.* **-men** a man who operates, works with, or deals in boats.

boat people *n. pl.* refugees fleeing or arriving by boat.

boat·swain (BOH·sun) *n.* a ship's petty officer in charge of the deck, hull, anchor, etc.

bob *v.* **bobs, bobbed, bob·bing 1** move up and down, as a cork on water. **2** come up or in suddenly: *He bobbed into the room.* **3** cut short: *a horse with a bobbed tail.*

— *n.* **1** a rapid up-and-down movement: *a bob of the head.* **2** a float for a fishing line. **3** a woman's short hair style. **4** a small weight, as on a plumb line.

bob·by *n.* **bob·bies** *Brit. Informal.* a policeman.

bobby pin *n.* a small ridged hair clip.

bobby-soxer (BOB·ee·sox·ur) *n. Informal.* a teen-age girl of the 1940s, esp. one who wore ankle-high **bobby socks** or **sox** folded over the shoes.

bob·cat *n.* a spotted, tan or reddish brown North American wildcat.

bob·skate *n. Cdn.* a child's skate consisting of runners that are strapped on to boots.

bob·sled *n.* **1** a joined pair of short sleds. **2** a heavy racing sled with two sets of runners, a steering wheel, and brakes. — *v.* **-sleds, -sled·ded, -sled·ding.**

bock or **bock beer** *n.* a dark, sweetish beer.

bod *n. Slang.* **1** body: *Most people have neither the bods nor the boodle to dress in fashion.* **2** person: *Thousands of sweaty bods packed the stadium.*

bode **1** *pt.* of BIDE. **2** *v.* **bodes, bod·ed, bod·ing** be a sign of something to happen: *A long drought does not bode well for a good harvest; It bodes ill for a good harvest; It bodes us no good.*

bod·ice (BOD·is) *n.* the fitted upper portion of a woman's dress.

bod·ied (BOD·eed) *combining form.* having a body, as specified: *an able-bodied sailor; a full-bodied wine; wide-bodied aircraft.*

bod·i·ly (BOD·uh·lee) *adj.* of the body, not of the mind: *charged with assault causing bodily harm; a bodily illness, organ.*
— *adv.* **1** in person, not in spirit: *A spirit cannot be bodily present.* **2** as a whole: *The group walked out bodily; He was lifted bodily and thrown out of the bar.*

bod·kin *n.* **1** a pointed instrument such as a kind of awl or an ornamental hairpin. **2** a needle for pulling tape or ribbon through something.

bod·y *n.* **bod·ies** **1** the physical structure of an organism, esp. of a human: *a sound mind in a healthy body; the body beautiful;* **Over my dead body** (= It can't be done while I'm alive)! *We need two warm bodies* (*Informal* for persons) *for the moving job; The body* (= corpse) *of the President will lie in state; She loved him* **body and soul** (= totally). **2** a physical object: *a solid body; to remove dust particles and such foreign bodies*

from the eye; The moon is a celestial or *heavenly body.* **3** the trunk or main part: *the body of the essay; an automobile body (exclusive of chassis and engine).* **4** a large mass: *A lake is a body of water; a body of evidence, information, knowledge.* **5** a group or unit: *an advisory, deliberative, governing body; the body politic; the student body; The workers walked out* **in a body** (= all together). **6** a bodylike quality, esp. thickness: *Her hair has body; This paint has body; a wine with body* (= richness).

body bag *n.* a plastic or rubber bag used for removing corpses.

body blow *n.* a severe setback or defeat, as a hard blow between neck and waistline in boxing: *The new legislation administered* or *dealt a body blow to the insurance industry.*

body·check *n.* in hockey and lacrosse, a checking of an opposing player by hitting from the front or side and above the knees with one's hip or shoulder. Also *v.*

body English *n.* body movements reflecting a player's desire to control a ball after throwing it.

bod·y·guard (BOD·ee·gard) *n.* one or more guards protecting a person.

body language *n.* postures, gestures, etc. as expressing feelings, thoughts, or attitudes: *Leo can read both Italian and Italian body language.*

body pack *n.* a wireless device secretly worn on the person, as of an undercover police officer, for transmitting and recording conversations.

body politic *n.* the people as a political unit under a government.

body rub *n.* a nonmedical massage, as given in a massage parlour; *adj.:* *a body-rub parlour, studio.*

body shirt *n.* a close-fitting shirt-and-pantie combination that is sewn or snapped at the crotch.

body snatcher *n.* one who illegally digs up corpses, esp. for dissection.

body stocking *n.* a close-fitting light garment covering the trunk and often the legs and arms.

bof·fin (BOF·un) *n. Informal.* a technical expert: *a computer boffin.*

bof·fo (BOF·oh) *adj. Informal.* successful, as a box-office hit: *a boffo Kung Fu movie.*
— *adv.* well: *It did boffo at the box office.*

bog *n.* an area of wet marshy ground: *a peat bog.*
— *v.* **bogs, bogged, bog·ging** get stuck in or as if in a bog; mire: *The talks (got) bogged down on the question of overtime; a student* **bogged down** *in* or *with homework.*

bo·gan (BOH·gun) *n. Cdn.* in the Maritimes, a slow or sluggish stream that flows into a river.

bo·gey (BOH·ghee) *n.* **-geys** **1** a frightening spirit or something feared: *The final examinations were his bogey;* also **bo·gy** or **bo·gie,** *pl.* **-gies.** **2** in golf, one stroke over par on a hole. — *v.* make this score.

bog·gle (BOG·ul) v. **bog·gles, bog·gled, bog·gling** be bewildered: *The mind boggles at the idea of limitless space and time; Space and time boggle* (= bewilder) *the mind.*

bo·gus (BOH·gus) adj. fake: *a bogus 20-dollar bill.*

bogy See BOGEY.

Bo·he·mi·an or **bo·he·mi·an** (boh·HEE·mee·un) n. one, esp. an artist, who lives in an unconventional manner; **adj.:** *a Bohemian life style.*

boil v. **1** cause a liquid to bubble and vaporize by heating to the temperature at which it changes to gas: *Let's boil some water in the kettle; We have a boiling kettle (of water); Water boils,* or *reaches the **boiling point,** at 100°C.* **2** cook or sterilize in boiling water: *to boil an egg.* **3** seethe: *He's boiling with rage; He's boiling (mad)! the boiling rapids of the Niagara River.*
— **boil down** condense by boiling: *Your essay is too long – boil it down to 500 words; It all boils down* (= amounts) *to greed.*
— **n. 1** the state of boiling: *to bring the water to a boil; Water comes to a boil at 100°C; Keep it at a gentle boil for 10 minutes.* **2** a swollen and pus-filled skin infection: *A boil comes to a head and bursts when ripe.*

boil·er n. a tank, pot, etc. in which water is boiled, as for steam power or cooking.

boil·er·plate (BOY·lur·plate) n. **1** steel plate for making boilers. **2** *Informal.* standardized material, as syndicated news and features supplied to small newspapers by metropolitan dailies in stereotyped form on plates.

boiler room n. **1** a room in which boilers are located. **2** *Informal.* a high-pressure sales operation conducted from a back room full of solicitors using telephones and prepared sales pitches. Also **boiler shop, bucket shop.**

bo·ing (BOH·ing) [like the sound of a plucked string] *interj.* expressing ecstasy or vibrations: *When the baton landed on the twirler's head, the boys went boing.*

bois·ter·ous (BOIS·tur·us) adj. noisily exuberant: *his boisterous good humour; a boisterous* (= rowdy) *party.*

bold adj. **1** courageous; daring: *a bold adventurer; He felt a bit nervous, but put on a bold front; He **made bold** to ask her age; If I may be so bold as to ask your age, madam?* **2** impudent: *a bold youth.* **3** distinctly visible: *The hills stood out against the sky in bold outline; He painted it with a few bold strokes of the brush.* **4** steep: *a bold cliff.* — **bold·ly** adv.; **bold·ness** n.

bold·face n. a heavy, dark style of type, as **this.**

bold·faced adj. **1** in boldface. **2** impudent: *the boldfaced youth.*

boll (BOLE) n. a round seed pod, as of cotton, flax, etc.

bo·lo·gna (buh·LOH·nee) n. a large sausage of smoked mixed meats; also **bolony** or **bologna sausage.**

Bol·she·vik (BOLE·shuh·vik) adj. Communist; also, extremely radical. — **Bol·she·vism** n.
— **Bol·she·vist** n. & adj.

bol·ster (BOLE·stur) n. **1** a long, thin, firm pillow, cushion, etc. used as a support. **2** a support.
— v. prop up: *a pep talk to bolster their sagging spirits.*

bolt n. **1** a rod or bar used to fasten a door, window, etc.

2 a metal fastener made of a rod or pin with threads on one end and a head at the other: *nuts and bolts.* **3** a roll of cloth. **4** a blast of lightning: *Her resignation came as a **bolt from the blue** (= shock). **5** a dash, as if to escape: *The dog made a bolt for the door.*
— **have shot one's bolt** exhausted oneself, as in old age: *It's tragic that some young people have shot their bolt by age 20.*
— **sit bolt upright** sit stiffly erect.
— v. **1** fasten the bolt on something: *Shut the door and bolt it; It bolts* (= is bolted) *at the bottom.* **2** run away, as if scared: *The horse bolted from the barn; His supporters suddenly bolted; They bolted the Liberals and joined the Tories.* **3** swallow food rapidly: *Don't bolt (down) your lunch.* **4** sift using a sieve, etc.: *to bolt flour, grain.*

bomb (BOM) n. **1** a projectile filled with explosives, gas, incendiary material, etc.: *to deactivate, defuse, detonate, drop, explode, set off a bomb; A bomb explodes* or *goes off; an atom, atomic, clean, hydrogen, incendiary, letter, stink, time bomb; a smart* (= guided) *bomb; Ban the Bomb* (= the atomic bomb)! **2** an aerosol spray can. **3** *Slang.* a total failure: *The book was a bomb.*
— v. **1** destroy or attack with bombs: *to bomb a city;* **adj.:** *a **bombing** attack, raid, run.* **2** *Slang.* be a total failure: *The show bombed.*

bom·bard (bom·BARD) v. attack with or as if with heavy guns: *Warships bombarded the coast; The prime minister was bombarded with letters and telegrams.*
— **bom·bard·ment** n.

bom·bar·dier (bom·buh·DEER) n. **1** a crew member of a bomber who aims and releases the bombs. **2** *Cdn.* a snow vehicle with a set of skis in front and wheels on endless tracks at the rear; **Bombardier** *Trademark.*

bom·bast (BOM·bast) n. pretentious and lofty writing or speech. — **bom·bas·tic** (bom·BAS·tic) adj.

bomb bay n. a compartment on the underside of a bomber from which bombs are released.

bombed (BOMD) adj. *Slang.* intoxicated: *Some of those drivers are anywhere from tipsy to flat-out bombed; He's bombed* or **bombed out** *on drugs.*

bomb·er (BOM·ur) n. an airplane designed to drop bombs: *a fighter bomber; long-range bomber.*

bomber jacket n. a short jacket, usually leather, of the kind worn by air crew.

bomb·proof adj. able to resist a bomb explosion: *a bombproof basement.*

bomb·shell n. **1** a bomb. **2** someone or something that creates a sensation: *He dropped a bombshell when he announced the winner; an actress described as a **blond bombshell*** (= strikingly attractive blonde).

bomb·sight n. a bomb-aiming device used in aircraft.

bo·na fi·de (BOH·nuh·fide, BOH·nuh·FYE·dee) adj. without intent to deceive; genuine: *a bonafide offer to purchase; bonafide hotel guests; bonafide reasons for delay.*

bo·nan·za (buh·NAN·zuh) n. something very profitable or rewarding: *The movie proved a box-office bonanza.*

bond *n.* **1** something that unites, ties, obliges, etc.: *a man and woman united in the bond of matrimony; They strengthened their bond by signing a contract; a bond of friendship with someone; to break the bonds* (=fetters) *of slavery; The slaves cast off their bonds and became free; Mortar makes a good bond* (=cement or adhesive) *between bricks.* **2** a pledge or guarantee, as an insurance agreement to pay an employer for loss caused by an employee: *a fidelity bond or surety bond; a bail bond; He furnished or posted a bond for $10 000; He forfeited the bond by not delivering as promised; fiduciary bonds.* **3** a pledge by a government or corporation to repay a loan with interest on a specified date: *Canada Savings Bonds; I cashed in or redeemed my bonds before they matured.* **4** a strong, superior kind of paper; also called "bond paper."
— **in bond** of imported goods, in storage in a bonded warehouse awaiting payment of taxes: *whisky bottled in bond.*
— *v.* **1** join or unite: *two boards bonded (together) by glue; a fire-hose covering of bonded fabric; A newborn is ready to bond to anyone, but an older child takes longer; This **baby bonding*** (=emotional union betweeen mother and baby) *is believed to begin soon after birth.* **2** guarantee a worker with a bond: *a bonded housemaid.* **3** place goods in a bonded warehouse till tariffs are paid: *bonded goods, whisky.*

bond·age (BOND·ij) *n.* slavery or serfdom: *He lived all his life in bondage to his creditors.*

bonded warehouse *n.* a warehouse for the storage of dutiable goods, the operator of it having bonded himself to secure the payment before goods are released.

bonds·man (BONDS·mun) *n.* **-men** one who provides bail; surety.

bone *n.* the hard substance of vertebrate skeletons or a piece of it: *He fell and broke a bone; A doctor set the fractured bone; Broken bones knit; Language is often a **bone of contention*** (=subject of dispute) *in bilingual societies; I have **a bone to pick with*** (*Informal for* a complaint against) *you; Services have been **cut to the bone*** (=drastically reduced) *because of budget cuts; I knew or could feel **in my bones*** (=had a deep-seated feeling) *this was going to happen; He **makes no bones about*** (=does not feel bothered by) *telling everyone he dropped out of school; She stood there in fright chilled or frozen to the bone.*
— *v.* **bones, boned, bon·ing** take the bones out of something: *to bone a fish.*
— **bone up** study hard: *He's boning up on his math; boning up for his finals.*

bone china *n.* a fine china made of white clay mixed with bone ash.

bone-dry *adj.* very dry.

bone·head *n. Slang.* a stupid person.
— *adj.: a bonehead* (=stupid) *statement; bonehead English* (=basic composition) *for people who can't write.*

bon·er (BOH·nur) *n. Slang.* blunder or blooper.

bon·fire (BON·fire) *n.* a large fire built outdoors, as for a celebration: *They built a bonfire and sat around it.*

bon·go (BONG·go) *n.* **-gos 1** either of a pair of small drums, called **bongo drums**, joined together for playing with the hands. **2** an African antelope with narrow white stripes.

bon·ho·mie (bon·uh·MEE) *n.* good-natured amiability; also **bon·hom·mie.**

bon·kers (BONK·urz) *adj. Slang.* nuts or crazy: *offbeat, bizarre, a little bonkers; He went bonkers in that movie; He seems even more bonkers in this movie than in previous ones.*

bon mot (bohn·MOH) *n., pl.* **bons mots** (-MOZE), a witty remark, as "Students of the world arise; you've nothing to lose but your marks!"

bon·net (BON·it) *n.* a head covering for women and children that is tied under the chin; also, any hood or covering.

bon·ny or **bon·nie** *adj.* **bon·ni·er, bon·ni·est** *Scot. & Brit.* healthy and good-looking: *a bonny lass.*

bon·sai (bon·SYE) *n. sing. & pl.* **1** an ornamental dwarf tree: *the bonsai gardens of Japan.* **2** the art of growing bonsai.

bo·nus (BOH·nus) *n.* **-nus·es** something paid or given as an extra: *Everyone received a Christmas bonus of $500; a **bonus shot*** (=extra free throw) *in basketball.*

bon vi·vant (bon·vi·VAHNT) *n.* one who likes good food and drink and other pleasures of life.

bon voy·age (bon·voy·AZH) *n.* farewell; (Have a) pleasant trip!

bon·y (BOH·nee) *adj.* **bon·i·er, -i·est 1** having to do with bones: *a bony fish* (full of bones); *a bony growth* (like a bone). **2** having prominent bones: *bony faces, features, hands, knees.*

bon·zo (BON·zoh) *adj. Slang.* nuts or crazy.

boo *interj. & n., pl.* **boos** a sustained sound made to show disapproval or to startle when made abruptly: *He sneaked up behind her and said "Boo!"*
— *v.* **boos, booed, boo·ing** make a "boo" at someone: *They booed him; He was booed off the stage.*

boob (long "oo") *n. Slang.* **1** a dolt. **2** booboo: *a report that is replete with financial boobs.* **3** a woman's breast.

boo·boo *n.* **-boos** *Slang.* a blunder: *to make a booboo.*

boob tube *n. Slang.* TV or a TV set.

boo·by (BOO·bee) *n.* **-bies 1** a doltish person. **2** a swimming sea bird that lights on ships and easily allows itself to be caught.

booby prize *n.* a prize given to a loser in fun.

booby trap *n.* a deceptive object that explodes or injures when touched: *to set a booby trap.*
— *v.*: *Terrorists booby-trapped the car and it exploded.*

boo·dle (BOO·dul) *n. Slang.* 1 a large amount; caboodle. 2 money, esp. as a bribe or loot from corrupt practices.

boo·gie or **boo·gy** (BOOG·ee, short or long "OO") *n.* rock music for dancing.
— *v.* **boo·gies, boo·gied, boo·gy·ing** to dance to rock music. Also **boo·gey.**

boogieman See BOGEYMAN.

book *n.* 1 a set of paper or similar sheets bound along one edge: *to bind a book; a book bound in leather.* 2 a literary, historical, etc. composition of some length: *to ban a book; to charge* or *check a book out of a library; to bring out, copyright, dedicate, edit, pirate, publish, put out, review, revise a book; to typeset a book* or *set a book in type; to write a book; Books appear* or *come out* or *are published; A book goes out of print when it is sold out and is not reprinted; a* **closed book** (= a person or thing that is not well-known; also, an investigation that is finished); an **open book** (= a person or thing that is accessible); *a coffee-table book; library book; picture book; rare book; a book translated from Arabic; The Bible is often called* **the (Good) Book;** *A phone book is a reference book; a book on carpentry.* 3 a main division of such a work: *Genesis is the first book of the Bible.* 4 **books** *pl.* financial and such records: *Accountants keep books; Auditors audit* or *go over* or *inspect the books; New members are entered on the books; Is he in the good or bad books of* (= in or out of favour with) *the president?* 5 something packaged in booklike form: *a book of coupons, matches, tickets; a cheque, phone, phrase book.*
— **by the book** correctly or properly, according to the rules: *Let's go* or *play by the book.*
— **make book** make or take bets.
— **throw the book at someone** punish someone severely by making all possible charges and giving the maximum penalties.
— *v.* 1 engage in advance: *to book a room in a hotel; to book seats on a flight; a night club tour booked by a travel agent; Area hotels are booked up solid* (= no more rooms available); *A* **booking** (= engagement or reservation) *was made, then cancelled.* 2 make a charge against someone: *He was booked for theft.* 3 declare: *Employees sometimes book off sick as a job action; Hospitals book off* or *out of service due to shortage of beds.*

book·case *n.* a piece of furniture having bookshelves.

book club *n.* a company that sells books at a discount to members.

book·end *n.* something used to keep a row of books upright: *a pair of bookends; people from the bookends of Canada* (= from coast to coast).

book·ie (BOOK·ee) *n. Slang.* bookmaker.

book·ish *adj.* based on books, not practical: *the bookish views of a bookish scholar; a bookish* (= pedantic or affected) *style of writing.*

book·keep·er (BOOK·kee·pur) *n.* one who keeps business records and accounts.

book·keep·ing *n.* accountancy; also, the work: *Who does the bookkeeping for your company?*

book·let *n.* a thin, usually paperbound book.

book·mak·er (BOOK·may·kur) *n.* one who accepts bets, usually on races.

book·mak·ing (BOOK·may·king) *n.* the business of taking bets, as on horses.

book·man (BOOK·mun) *n.* **-men** 1 one who loves books. 2 a bookseller or book publisher.

book·mark *n.* something put in a book to mark a place.

book·mo·bile (BOOK·moh·beel) *n.* a truck equipped as a mobile library or book store.

book·sell·er (BOOK·sel·ur) *n.* one who runs a bookstore.

book·shelf *n.* **-shelves** a shelf to keep books on.

book·shop or **book·store** *n.* a place where books are sold.

book value *n.* in accounting, a firm's assets minus its liabilities or an asset's depreciated value.

book·worm *n.* 1 an insect that eats into books. 2 an avid reader or student.

boom *n.* 1 a long horizontal pole, as one used to hold out the bottom edge of a sail, support a load on a derrick, hold a microphone, etc. 2 a barrier: *a boom of connected logs used to contain floating timber; An ice boom builds up in the Niagara River at Lake Erie during the winter; Sandbags filled with absorbent material were placed as booms along the channel to prevent the oil spill from entering the river.* 3 a deep, loud sound: *a sonic boom.* 4 a sudden increase: *the postwar baby boom; The boom has passed its peak; the* **boom-and-bust** *cycle (of prosperity and depression).*
— **lower the boom** *Informal.* crack down *on* someone.
— *v.* 1 make or utter with a deep resonant sound: *Guns boomed in the distance; Tchaikovsky's 1812 Overture, complete with cannons booming on cue.* 2 become suddenly prosperous, famous, active, etc.: *Business is booming; Industry boomed after World War II; Compact disk sales boomed in the late 1980s.*

boom·er·ang (BOO·muh·rang) *n.* 1 a curved stick thrown as a weapon that returns to the thrower. 2 something that rebounds to its author's disadvantage: *The politician had thrown a boomerang by his dirty tricks.* — *v.*: *His dirty tricks boomeranged on him.*

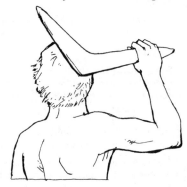

boom town *n.* a suddenly prosperous town.

boon *n.* a great blessing or benefit: *Insulin has been a boon to diabetics; Grant me one boon* (=favour).

boon companion *n.* close friend.

boon·docks *n.pl. Informal.* a rural or backwoods area.

boon·dog·gle (BOON·dog·ul, long "OO") *n. Informal.* waste of public funds: *The Commission was a massive financial boondoggle with $15 million gone down the drain.*

boor (rhyme: "poor") *n.* a rude or coarse person, esp. a rustic: *He's just a boor, not a gentleman.*
— **boor·ish** *adj.*: *boorish manners.*

boost (long "oo") *v.* raise: *a pep talk to boost his morale; to boost prices, production, sales; Ads are used to boost* (=promote) *a product.*
— *n.* a raising or increase: *Give me a boost up the tree; a boost in salary; The promotion was a big boost to his ego.*

boost·er *n.* one that boosts: *Civic boosters try to attract conventions to their cities; a morale booster.*
— *adj.*: *Jumper cables or booster cables are used for jump-starting a car by connecting its dead battery to the live battery of another; a booster rocket for launching a spacecraft.*

booster shot *n.* a supplementary dose of vaccine or antigen.

boot (long "oo") *n.* **1** heavy footwear covering part of the leg: *rubber boots; work boots.* **2** a kick: *He got the boot* (=got fired) *after only a week on the job.*
— **lick someone's boots** behave like a slave toward someone.
— **to boot** as well: *a good student and a soccer player to boot.*
— *v.* **1** kick. **2 boot out** *Informal.* dismiss, esp. from a job. **3** start a computer: *I boot up my computer by turning on the power, popping the DOS disk in Drive 0, and pressing the "on" button.*

boot·black *n.* one who cleans and shines shoes and boots.

boot camp *n.* in the U.S., a basic training centre for new recruits to the coast guard, navy, etc.

boot·ee or **boot·ie** *n.* a baby's shoe made of soft cloth.

booth *n.* a small enclosed area, esp. a private stall or compartment: *a phone booth; the projection booth in a movie theatre; voting booth; A restaurant booth has a table and two bench seats.*

boot·leg *v.* **-legs, -legged, -leg·ging** make, buy, or sell liquor illegally: *Saccharin-sweetened soft drinks were being bootlegged* (=sold) *in some stores even after the ban; a bootlegging operation.*
— *n. & adj.*: *He bought some bootleg; some bootleg gin.* — **boot·leg·ger** *n.*

bootleg turn *n.* an abrupt turning around of an automobile using the emergency brake.

boot·strap *n.* **1** a strap at the top of a boot for pulling it on: *She has pulled herself up by her own bootstraps* (=risen from depression or depression by her own efforts without outside help). **2** a short routine of instructions for loading a program into a computer.

boot·y *n.* **boot·ies** goods seized jointly by pirates, soldiers in a war, etc.

booze *n. Informal.* alcoholic drink.
— *v.* **booz·es, boozed, booz·ing** drink to excess.
— **booz·er** *n.* — **booz·y** *adj.*

bop *n. & v.* **bops, bopped, bop·ping** *Slang.* hit: *a bop on the head.*

bor·der (BOR·dur) *n.* **1** an edge or boundary, esp. between two states, countries, etc.: *The goods were smuggled across* or *over the border from the U.S.; Detroit is close to the Canadian border; Niagara Falls is at* or *on the border; It is warmer south of the border; Anyone may go as far as* or *up to the U.S. border; to cross, draw, establish, fix, patrol a border; to slip across a border; a closed, common, disputed, recognized, unguarded border.* **2** a strip outlining an edge: *a lace border on a cuff.*
— *v.* provide with a border: *Trees bordered the grounds; His actions border on* (=are close to) *the insane.*

bor·der·land (BOR·dur·land) *n.* land near a border; fringe area: *the borderland* (=intermediate condition) *between waking and sleeping.*

bor·der·line (BOR·dur·line) *n.* a line marking a border: *on the borderline between passing and failing.*
— *adj.* marginal: *He's not quite insane, but a borderline case; a borderline pass in a test.*

bore *pt.* of BEAR.
— *v.* **bores, bored, bor·ing 1** make a usually long, narrow hole, esp. by drilling or digging: *to bore a tunnel; to bore a hole through concrete.* **2** make tired by repeating, being dull, etc.: *I won't bore you with the details; We were bored to death; We were bored having nothing to do; bored stiff* (=very bored); *It was boring to be in that city.*
— *n.* **1** a bored hole: *the bore* (=hollow) *of a pipe, gun, etc.* **2** a boring person or thing: *a frightful, insufferable, utter bore.* **3** a tidal wave with a steep front.

bo·re·al (BOR·ee·ul) *adj.* having to do with the North: *a boreal bog, chickadee, owl; boreal forests full of needleleaf trees.*

bore·dom (BOR·dum) *n.* the condition of being bored: *He fell asleep out of utter boredom; It was sheer boredom watching that movie.*

born *a pp.* of BEAR.
— *adj.* **1** brought forth by birth: *A child is born (to its parents); a child born of poor parents; a woman born to lead; We are born free.* **2** natural: *a born genius, leader, loser; Poets are born* (=They are so by nature), *not made.*

born-again (BOR·nuh·gain) *adj.* reborn spiritually: *a born-again Baptist, Tory.*

borne *a pp.* of BEAR.

bor·ough (BUR·oh) *n.* **1** a municipality within a metropolitan area: *North York used to be a borough of*

Metro Toronto; New York City has five boroughs. 2 in various countries, an incorporated town, village, or county.

bor·row (BOR·oh) *v.* 1 get from another to use for a time: *Can I borrow $50 (from you) till payday? books borrowed from the library.* 2 take and use: *Did you borrow $5 from my wallet? "Pizza" was borrowed from Italian into English; it's an Italian* **borrowing** (= word adopted from Italian); *a patient living on* **borrowed time** (= living beyond the expected period).
— **bor·row·er** *n.*

bosh *n. Informal.* nonsense!

bosk or **bos·ket** (BOS·kit) *n.* a thicket or small grove.

bos·om (BOOZ·um, long or short "OO") *n.* 1 the chest or breasts: *She held the baby to her bosom; a matronly woman with an ample bosom; Under the jacket, he wore a shirt with a bosom* (= front) *and no back.* 2 close relationship: *He was received into the bosom of the church; in the bosom of one's family;* **adj.:** *his bosom* (= very close) *buddy, friend.*

boss *n.* one who gives orders, as an employer or foreman: *She is the absolute* or *undisputed boss around here; He's only a straw boss* (= with very little power); *party bosses of politics.*
— *v.* act like a boss towards: *His older brother likes to boss him around.* — **boss·y** *adj.*

bo·sun (BOH·sun) *n.* boatswain. Also **bos'n, bo's'n,** or **bo'sun.**

bot·a·ny (BOT·uh·nee) *n.* the science of plants.
— **bot·a·nist** *n.*
— **bo·tan·i·cal** (buh·TAN·uh·cul) *adj.: botanical gardens, specimens.*

botch *v.* bungle a job: *Joe was told to fix the car, but he botched it (up); a botched job.*

both (BOHTH, "th" as in "thin") *adj.* the one as well as the other: *I met both boys; I spoke to both the boys.*
— **pron.:** *I met both* (= the two) *of the boys.*
— **both ... and:** *I met both Jon and Tim; Jon is both older and wiser; Tim can both sing and dance.*

both·er (BOTH·ur, "TH" as in "the") *v.* disturb or trouble: *He bothers me when I am busy; bothers me about a loan; bothers everyone with his problems; It bothers me (to hear) that he is dishonest; He never bothers* (= takes the trouble) *to ask for what he wants; Please don't* **bother yourself** (= trouble yourself) *about fixing me lunch; Don't* **bother with** *it.*
— *n.* trouble or concern: *It is a bother to have to hire relatives; Relatives are sometimes a bother* (= source of concern) *to employers.* Also **both·er·a·tion** (-uh·RAY·shun) *n.*

bot·tle (BOT·ul) *n.* 1 a usually narrow-necked container for liquids: *a wine bottle; a bottle of wine* (= traditionally 25 oz / 710 ml); *a bottle of pop; Give the baby her bottle* (= nursing bottle); *a baby bottle* or *nursing bottle; a hot-water bottle; a disposable, no-deposit, no-return bottle; returnable bottles.* 2 **the bottle** *Informal.* use of alcohol, esp. in excess: *The poor fellow took to the bottle to drown his grief; He would hit the bottle every night.*

— *v.* **bot·tles, bot·tled, bot·tling** put in a bottle: *bottled beer; It's not healthy to* **bottle up** (= repress) *your anger.*

bot·tle·neck (BOT·ul·nek) *n.* anything hindering progress or causing a slowdown, as a narrow spot in a busy road: *We were caught* or *trapped in a bottleneck; to eliminate a bottleneck; a bottleneck in the production line.*

bot·tom (BOT·um) *n.* 1 the part that is underneath or lowest: *the bottom of the ocean, ship, stairs, well; It sank to the bottom; a suitcase with a false bottom (for hiding things); New recruits start at the bottom and work their way up; Let's get to the bottom* (= clear up the mystery) *of this affair; The bottom fell out of the coffee market* (= Coffee prices collapsed); *At bottom* (= Basically) *he's a good fellow; She loved him* **from the bottom of her heart** (= most sincerely). 2 *Informal.* buttocks: *The baby fell on her bottom.*
— **bottoms up** [a drinking toast]: *Bottoms up, for Team Canada!*
— *adj.* lowest or last: *That's my bottom offer; You can* **bet your bottom dollar** (*Informal* for everything you have) *I won't lose.*
— *v.* of prices, etc. that vary over time, reach the lowest level before going up again: *The recession seems to be bottoming out.*

bot·tom·less (BOT·um·lus) *adj.* (as if) having no bottom: *It seemed a bottomless pit; the bottomless depths of the ocean; a bottomless mystery.*

bottom line *n. Informal.* the result that counts, as the final figure in a financial statement, showing a profit or loss.
— **bottom-line** *adj.* 1 concerned with profits: *a bottom-line executive; The president has to be a bottom-line person; bottom-line publishing.* 2 realistic: *a bottom-line approach.*

bou·doir (BOO·dwar) *n.* a woman's private bedroom or sitting room.

bouf·fant (boo·FAHNT) *adj.* puffed out or full: *a bouffant coiffure, hairdo, skirt, sleeve.*

bough (rhyme: "how") *n.* a main branch of a tree.

bought *pt. & pp.* of BUY.

bouil·la·baisse (bool·yuh·BACE) *n.* a chowder containing many kinds of fish and shellfish: *a bouillabaise* (= stew) *of taxes.*

bouil·lon (BOOL·yon) *n.* a clear broth.

boul·der (BOLE·dur) *n.* a large, usually rounded stone.

boul·e·vard (BOOL·uh·vard) *n.* 1 a broad, often tree-lined street: *the boulevards of Winnipeg;* [as a name] Lake Shore Boulevard. 2 the grassy strip between a sidewalk and the street. 3 a median dividing a highway.

bounce *v.* **bounc·es, bounced, bounc·ing** 1 move up and down elastically: *a child bouncing a ball; The ball bounced off the wall; it bounced down the road; He bounced* (= jumped) *to his feet; He bounced out into the street; a* **bouncing** (= strong and healthy) *baby boy.*

2 *Informal.* of a cheque, be returned because of insufficient funds: *Cheques that bounce are known as "rubber cheques."* **3** *Slang.* eject for rowdy behaviour, as a bouncer.
— **bounce back** *Informal.* start again with new vigour, as after a defeat.
— *n.* **1** a bouncing: *I missed the ball on the first bounce.* **2** vigour or enthusiasm: *There's a bounce to his stride.* **3 the bounce** *Slang.* a dismissal; the bum's rush.
— **bounc·er** *n.*

bound (BOWND) *pt. & pp.* of BIND: *The body was found bound and gagged.*
— *adj.* **1** tied or obligated: *He's morally bound to inform the police; Spouses are bound by marriage vows.* **2** certain: *It is bound to rain today.* **3** going to a place: *homeward bound; They're bound for home; east-bound traffic.* **4** *combining form.* confined: *He felt duty-bound to support his boss; house-bound because of illness; an ice-bound expressway; No takeoffs from a snow-bound airport.*
— **bound up with** or **in** closely connected with something: *a question bound up with what is right and wrong; a devoted husband whose interests are bound up in family matters.*
— *v.* **1** leap, spring, jump, etc.: *kangaroos bounding across the plain.* **2** form the boundary of a place: *The U.S. bounds Canada in the south.*
— *n.* **1** a bounding: *He cleared the fence in a single bound.* **2** usually, **bounds,** a limit, border, or boundary: *Who sets the bounds for outside activities? He acted beyond the bounds of reason; Her joy knew no bounds; She kicked the ball out of bounds; Bars and nightclubs are **out of bounds** (= forbidden) to children.*
— **by leaps and bounds** very rapidly.

bound·a·ry (BOWN·duh·ree) *n.* **-ries** a line, plane, point, etc. that forms a limit or border: *Canada has a common boundary with the U.S.; The 60th parallel forms the boundary between the Yukon and B.C.*

bound·en *adj.* obligatory: *It's our bounden duty to help the poor.*

bound·less *adj.* having no limits: *boundless enthusiasm.*

boun·ti·ful (BOWN·tuh·ful) *adj.* plentiful: *blessed with a bountiful harvest; Nature's bountiful gifts.*
Also **boun·te·ous** (BOWN·tee·us).
— **boun·ti·ful·ly** or **boun·te·ous·ly** *adv.*

boun·ty (BOWN·tee) *n.* **-ties 1** generous giving; liberality: *The farmer's market looked like a display of the earth's bounty; silos full of the field's bounty; the endless bounty of TV.* **2** a reward or grant offered by a government: *a cash bounty offered for wolf pelts; The government used to pay a bounty on wolves; Two bounty hunters kidnapped him and took him back to the U.S.*

bou·quet *n.* **1** (boh·KAY, boo·KAY) a bunch of cut flowers: *brickbats and bouquets* (= compliments). **2** (boo·KAY) an aroma, as of wine, brandy, etc.: *a wine with an elegant bouquet.*

bour·geois (boorzh·WAH) **1** *n. sing. & pl.* a member of the middle class, esp. a property owner, shopkeeper, etc.; capitalist. **2** *adj.* capitalistic in outlook: *Bourgeois attitudes undermine the arts.*

bout (BOWT) *n.* **1** a spell of an activity: *a boxing bout; drinking bout.* **2** an attack or outbreak: *a bout of (the) flu; a severe bout of diarrhea.*

bou·tique (boo·TEEK) *n.* a small fashionable shop.

bo·vine (BOH·vine) *adj.* **1** of or like an ox or cow: *The antelope is a bovine animal; bovine malaria.* **2** slow and dull: *his bovine laziness.*

¹**bow** (rhyme: "how") *v.* bend the head or body, esp. as a sign of respect, submission, etc.: *They bow before the altar; We bow to* (= accept) *the inevitable; to **bow down to*** (= submit to) *a dictatorship; He's too self-respecting to **bow and scrape*** (= behave slavishly); *an old man bowed* (= bent) *with age; a widow **bowed down*** (= weighed down) *with grief; She decided to **bow out*** (= get out) *of her job; to **bow to*** (= agree to) *his mother's wishes.*
— *n.* **1** a bending of the head or body: *made a low bow; The ballerina **took a bow*** (= came back on stage to receive applause) *at the end of the recital.* **2** the front part of a ship; opposed to STERN.

²**bow** (BOH) *n.* **1** a weapon for shooting arrows: *He drew his bow and shot an arrow.* **2** a light stick strung with horsehair for playing a violin, viola, etc. **3** a knot with loops: *Tie a bow in her hair.* **4** something curved, esp. a rainbow.
— *v.* **1** bend or curve. **2** play with a bow: *to bow a fiddle.*

bowd·ler·ize (BOWD·luh·rize, BOWD *rhymes with* LOUD) *v.* **-iz·es, -ized, -iz·ing** revise a book, play, etc. so as to remove portions considered improper in a family setting; expurgate: *Shakespeare was bowdlerized by Thomas Bowdler; a bowdlerized edition of the Bible.*

bow·el (BOW·ul, *rhyme:* vowel) *n.* **1** an intestine: *He has pain in his bowels; loose **bowels*** (= feces); *a bowel movement* (= emptying of the bowels). **2 bowels** *pl.* deep interior: *down in the bowels of the coal mine.*

bow·er (BOW·ur, *rhyme:* OUR) *n.* a recess shaded by trees or vines.

bow·er·y (BOW·uh·ree, BOW *rhymes with* HOW) *n.* the part of a city inhabited by the poor and homeless.

bowl (BOLE) *n.* **1** a deep, rounded dish: *a finger, punch, salad, sugar bowl; a bowl of rice or soup* (= rice or soup in a bowl); *the bowl* (= bowl-shaped part) *of a smoking pipe.* **2** a heavy ball used in games such as bowling; also, a throw of such a ball.
— *v.* **1** play at bowling: *He goes bowling on weekends.* **2** roll a ball or hoop.
— **bowl along** move quickly along.
— **bowl over** fall or roll over: *The car bowled over and caught fire; She came round the corner and nearly bowled me over; I was **bowled over*** (= stunned or overwhelmed) *by the announcement.*

bowl·der (BOLE·dur) *n.* same as BOULDER.

bow·legs (BOH·legs) *n.pl.* legs curved outward.
— **bow·leg·ged** (-leg·id) *adj.*

bow·ler (BOH·lur) *n.* a stiff round hat with a narrow brim; derby.

bowling (BOH·ling) *n.* a game in which a ball is rolled down a wooden lane to knock over wooden pins; *adj.: a bowling ball, lane, pin; a bowling green* (= grass plot) *for "lawn bowling."*

bowling alley *n.* a building with many bowling lanes.

bow·man (BOH·mun) *n.* -men an archer.

bow·string (BOH·string) *n.* a cord for an archer's bow.

bow tie (BOH·tie) *n.* a necktie that is worn knotted into a bow.

box *n.* 1 a usually rectangular receptacle or container, often with a lid: *a box of candy; You can rent a post office box for receiving your mail; a safety deposit box (in a bank); a suggestion box; What's on the box* (Slang for TV) *tonight? a box lunch (packed in a box).* 2 a marked-off or enclosed area: *a jury box; a lacrosse box; witness box; Nobles used to have special boxes at the opera; a penalty box (in hockey); a press box (for journalists); a news item printed in a box* (= rectangular area marked like a box). 3 a booth or small shelter: *a sentry box.* 4 a blow with the open hand: *a box on the ear.*
— *v.* 1 put into a box: *The apartment is so small she feels boxed in; boxed candy.* 2 strike with the open hand: *to box someone's ears.* 3 engage in boxing.

box·car *n.* an enclosed freight car.

box·er *n.* 1 one who boxes; pugilist. 2 a sturdy, deep-chested dog with a short coat.

boxer shorts *n.pl.* undershorts like a prizefighter's shorts.

box·ing *n.* the sport of fighting with one's fists.

Boxing Day *n. Cdn.* a holiday following Christmas Day, marked by special sales of Christmas merchandise.

box·la (BOX·luh) *n. Cdn.* [short form] box lacrosse.

box lacrosse *n. Cdn.* lacrosse as played indoors in a hockey rink but on a wooden floor.

box office *n.* 1 the ticket office at a theatre. 2 money taken at a box office: *Studios use the weekend box office to calculate how well a movie is doing; Many movies helped the 1989 box office.* 3 a financial success or successful show: "Star Wars" *was good box office.*
— **box-office** *adj.* 1 having to do with the box office: *a box-office record; box-office sales; That movie was the biggest box-office draw of the season; The box-office*

gross or *take is determined by the number of tickets a movie sells over the weekend.* 2 successful: *The movie was a box-office hit, thanks to the star's box-office performance.*

box score *n.* a tabulated summary of the plays of a baseball game, as usually given in a box in a newspaper.

box spring *n.* a mattress base made of coil springs in a box.

boy *n.* 1 a male child: *delivery boys; newspaper boys; shoeshine boys; That's a good boy! a fair-haired boy* (= favourite); *a whipping boy (who takes all the blame); a **boy wonder** (who arouses admiration); **That's my boy** (= well done)!* 2 *Informal.* a member of a team: *She's trying to be one of the boys; He's out drinking with the boys; an old boys' association; the old boy network.* 3 [offensive] a male servant.
— *interj.* expressing admiration: *Boy, is she hitting it! Oh boy!* — **boy·hood** *n.*
— **boy·ish** *adj.*; **boy·ish·ly** *adv.*

boy·cott (BOY·cot) *v.* refuse to have anything to do with a person, product, place, function, etc.
— *n.* such a measure: *They imposed a boycott of* or *on nonunion products.*

boy·friend *n. Informal.* a male friend, esp. a girl's steady escort.

Boy Scout *n.* a member of the **Boy Scouts,** an international club for boys aged 11 to 17 that stresses outdoor life and helpfulness to others.

bo·zo (BOH·zoh) *n. Slang.* one with little brains, like "Bozo the Clown."

bra (BRAH) *n.* [short form] a brassiere.

brace *n.* 1 something used to support, clamp, hold things in place, etc.: *He wears a brace to support his weak leg; a back, knee, leg, neck, rib brace; a brace supporting the east wall.* 2 either of the signs { } used to enclose linked words, numbers, etc. 3 a crank-shaped handle for holding and turning a drilling bit: *brace and bit.* 4 *sing. & pl.* a pair of a kind taken together: *several brace of partridges, quail; a brace of columns, M.P.s, pistols.*
— **braces** 1 a wire device worn on the teeth for straightening them. 2 suspenders for holding up trousers.
— *v.* **brac·es, braced, brac·ing** 1 strengthen or support, esp. with a brace. 2 prepare: *Brace yourself for some bad news; to brace up to the inevitable.* 3 invigorate: *A cold shower will brace you up in the morning; the bracing mountain air.*

brace·let (BRACE·lit) *n.* an ornament worn around the arm or wrist: *a charm bracelet.*

brack·en (BRAK·un) *n.* a large common fern with a tough stem.

brack·et (BRACK·it) *n.* 1 a usually L-shaped device to support a shelf or balcony, wall lamp, etc. 2 a shelf so supported. 3 either of the signs ( ) used to enclose words, numbers, etc.: *a list of names with ages shown in brackets.* 4 one of a pair of parentheses [ ] or braces { }: *angle, round, square brackets.* 5 a range or group: *Teenagers are in the 13-19 age bracket; A higher income bracket means a higher tax bracket.*

— *v.* **1** support with a bracket. **2** enclose, link, or set aside with or as if with brackets: *a bracketed phrase.*

brack·ish *adj.* slightly salty: *brackish water from a lake.*

brag *v.* **brags, bragged, brag·ging** speak of one's abilities, deeds, etc. with too much pride; boast: *He brags about his clothes; That is nothing to brag about; He brags that he is the world's greatest boxer.*
— **brag·ger** or **brag·gart** (BRAG·urt) *n.*

brag·ga·do·ci·o (brag-uh-DOH-shee-oh) *n.* **-os 1** a braggart. **2** boasting or cockiness: *the political braggadocio of the ruling party.*

Brah·ma (BRAH·muh) or **Brah·man** (-mun) *n.* **1** in Hinduism, the creator. **2** a hump-backed breed of cattle related to the Indian zebu: *The white Brahma bull is also known as "Brahmany bull."*

Brah·min (BRAH·mun) *n.* **1** an upper-class member of the Establishment, esp. in New England: *the Boston Brahmins.* **2** Also **Brah·man,** a Hindu of the highest caste.

braid *n.* an interwoven or plaited cord of three or more strands: *her braids of hair; gold or silver braid* (= ornamental trim).
— *v.* do into braids: *She wears her hair braided into pigtails.*

braille or **Braille** (BRAIL) *n.* a writing system for the blind that uses raised dots for characters which are read by touching.

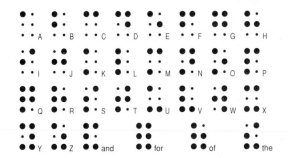

brain *n.* **1** the centre of a vertebrate's nervous system and thought processes, located in the head: *The brain consists of two hemispheres that control opposite sides of the body; a boy who has computers **on the brain*** (*Informal for* constantly on his mind); *He blew his **brains** out* (= shot himself through the head); *adj.: brain damage, death; a brain scan, surgeon, tumour, wave.* **2** mind or intelligence: *She has a good brain for math; a student with **brains.*** **3** an intelligent person: *some of the best brains in physics.*
— **pick someone's brain** or **brains** get and use someone's ideas.
— **rack** or **beat** or **cudgel one's brains** think hard *over* a problem.

brain·child *n. Informal.* someone's new idea or invention.

brain death *n.* death as determined by the permanent cessation of brain activity and shown by a flat EEG ("electroencephalograph" output).

brain drain *n.* the emigration of scientists, professionals, etc. from a country: *to plug the brain drain to the U.S.; the brain drain from Third World countries to Europe and North America.*

brain·storm *n.* a sudden inspired idea: *to have a brainstorm; adj.: A brainstorming session is held by a problem-solving group to pool their ideas.*

brains trust or **brain trust** *n.* a group of unofficial advisers.

brain·wash *v.* force a person *into* accepting a radically new set of beliefs.

brain wave *n.* **1** a rhythmic electric impulse in the brain. **2** a brainstorm.

brain·y *adj.* **brain·i·er, -i·est** having a good intellect.

braise (BRAIZ) *v.* **brais·es, braised, brais·ing** to brown and simmer slowly: *braised beef.*

brake *n.* **1** a device for stopping a vehicle: *to apply* or *put on* or *step on the brakes; The car may skid if you jam on* or *slam on the brakes; an emergency brake; a car with power steering and power brakes; Brakes jam, lock, fail, hold, screech; He decided to put a brake on too rapid expansion of the business.* **2** bracken. **3** a thicket, as of cane plants.
— *v.* use a brake: *The car may skid if you brake suddenly; The bus braked* (= stopped) *abruptly before a red light; the **braking** capability, equipment, system of a vehicle.*

brake·man (BRAKE·mun) *n.* **-men** an assistant to a train conductor or engineer.

bram·ble *n.* a prickly shrub or vine such as the blackberry or loganberry.

bran *n.* the coarse seed covering of cereals that is separated by sifting: *oat bran; wheat bran.*

branch *n.* a part, division, or extension that is separate from the main body: *to trim the branches of a tree; the branch of a river; the various branches of medicine; a chartered bank with a network of branches; a branch office.*
— *v.* put out or separate into branches: *Latin, Greek, etc. **branched off** in prehistoric times; A newspaper **branches out** into book publishing.*

branch plant *n.* a business that is the subsidiary of a foreign company.

brand *n.* **1** a label or mark identifying a particular product: *Colas are sold under many brands; two popular brands* (= varieties) *of cola; He drinks only name brand colas* (= well-known brands); *"Cola" itself was originally a **brand name*** (= registered trademark). **2** a piece of burned or burning wood; hence, an iron **(branding iron)** used red-hot to mark cattle, criminals, etc. **3** a mark made by a branding iron. **4** a stigma: *the brand of Cain,* i.e. of *"murderer."*
— *v.* **1** to mark, as with a brand: *an experience forever branded on his memory.* **2** stigmatize: *The spy was branded (as) a traitor.*

bran·dish *v.* wave around or display, as if to threaten: *to brandish a sword.*

brand-new *adj.* absolutely new and unused.

bran·dy *n.* **-dies** a liquor distilled from wine, as cognac, or from fermented fruit juices: *peach brandy.*
— *v.* **-dies, -died, -dy·ing** treat or preserve with brandy: *brandied cherries.*

brash *adj.* impudently self-assertive: *a brash young man.*
— **brash·ly** *adv.;* **brash·ness** *n.*

brass *n.* **1** an alloy of copper and either zinc or tin. **2** an object or things made of brass: *a shop specializing in brass; brasses such as fittings and ornaments; the strings and brass* or *brasses* (= brass instruments) *of an orchestra.* **3** *Informal.* brazen impudence: *He had the brass to ask me again for a loan.* **4** high-ranking officers, executives, etc. as a group: *army brass; the top brass of the industry.*
— **get down to brass tacks** get down to specific details.
— *adj.* made of brass: *a brass doorknob; a hoodlum wearing brass knuckles.*

brass hat *n. Slang.* a high-ranking officer.

bras·siere (bruh·ZEER) *n.* a woman's undergarment to support the breasts.

brass tacks *n.pl.* basic facts; essentials.

brass·ware *n.* things made of brass.

brass·y *adj.* **brass·i·er, -i·est 1** of or like brass. **2** harsh and blaring: *a brassy hairdo, voice.*

brat *n.* a bad-mannered child: *a spoiled brat.*
— **brat·ty** *adj.*

bra·va·do (bruh·VAH·doh) *n.* a false and swaggering courage.

brave *adj.* courageous: *It was brave of him to attempt the rescue.*
— *n.* an American Indian warrior: *a brave from the Kahnawake Reserve.*
— *v.* **braves, braved, brav·ing** challenge or endure with courage: *It was going to be rough, but he decided to brave it out.* — **brave·ly** *adv.*

brav·er·y (BRAY·vuh·ree) *n.* the quality of being brave: *to demonstrate, display, show bravery.*

bra·vo (BRAH·voh) *interj. & n.* **-vos** a shout of approval.

brawl *n.* a noisy, disorderly fight or quarrel: *a barroom brawl; a drunken brawl.*
— *v.:* *to brawl in barrooms.* — **brawl·er** *n.*

brawn *n.* **1** big powerful muscles: *The bully was all brawn and no brains.* **2** pickled pork. — **brawn·y** *adj.*

bray *n.* the noisy, harsh call of a donkey; *v.: Stop braying like an ass.*

bra·zen (BRAY·zun) *adj.* **1** of or like brass: *brazen candlesticks.* **2** of sounds, blaring; brassy. **3** shameless or impudent: *brazen lies; a brazen-faced liar.*
— **bra·zen·ly** *adv.;* **bra·zen·ness** *n.*

bra·zier (BRAY·zhur) *n.* **1** a brass-worker. **2** a metal container holding live coals, as for grilling meat.

breach (BREECH) *n.* **1** a violation: *He committed a breach of etiquette; charged with breach of contract; a breach of the peace* (= public disturbance); *She charged him with breach of promise (to marry) and sued for damages.* **2** a cessation of friendship: *to cause a breach;*

Other friends tried to heal the breach but to no avail. **3** a break, gap, or rift: *to close a breach; a breach in the castle wall.* — *v.* make a breach in something; break.

bread (BRED) *n.* **1** a basic item of food made of baked flour: *a loaf of bread; sliced bread; unleavened bread; white bread; whole wheat bread; bread and butter; to put bread* (= food) *on the table; She will **break bread*** (= share a meal) *with people of any race or creed.* **2** livelihood: *to beg, earn one's bread; He works hard for his daily bread; A dishonourable discharge would have **taken the bread out of his mouth*** (= made it impossible for him to earn a living); *Writing stories is her **bread and butter*** (= chief source of income), *not a hobby; a bread-and-butter letter (expressing thanks for hospitality).* **3** *Slang.* money; dough.
— *v.* coat with breadcrumbs: *breaded veal cutlets.*

bread-and-butter *adj.* of basic importance: *a bread-and-butter course, issue; a bread-and-butter customer (on whom a business depends for its main income).*

bread·bas·ket (BRED·bas·kit) *n.* **1** a basket for bread or rolls. **2** a grain-growing area: *The Prairies are the breadbasket of Canada.*

bread·board *n.* **1** a board to knead or cut bread on. **2** a board for laying out experimental electric circuits.

bread·crumb (BRED·crum) *n.* a tiny piece of bread broken off from a loaf or slice.

bread line *n.* a line of people waiting for food given as charity.

bread·stuff *n.* grain, flour, etc. for making bread.

breadth (BREDTH) *n.* **1** width: *It is 10 cm in breadth; has a breadth of 10 cm; He escaped by a hair's breadth* (= very small distance). **2** scope or range: *breadth of culture, interests, learning; He shows great breadth of mind about religion; He claims to have travelled (through) **the length and breadth** of Canada* (= from coast to coast).

bread·win·ner (BRED·win·ur) *n.* one whose earnings support a family.

break (BRAKE) *v.* **breaks, broke, bro·ken, break·ing 1** separate into two or more pieces, esp. by force: *The baseball broke the window; to break off* (= detach) *a small piece of dough.* **2** burst: *A blister breaks; Waves break on the beach.* **3** make or become inoperative: *The toilet is broken; it won't flush.* **4** disturb the order, continuity, etc. of something: *Soldiers break step while marching on a bridge; a scrape that breaks the skin.* **5** pause; interrupt: *We break for lunch at noon.* **6** reduce the force of something: *The shrubs broke his fall from the window.* **7** make submissive: *to break a wild horse; Suffering broke his spirit; was tortured until he broke* (= became submissive). **8** violate: *People break the law, their promises, speed limits; Supersonic planes break the sound barrier; the crime of **breaking and entering** a place* (= burglary); *She broke* (= exceeded) *all records.* **9** make a sudden move or change: *They broke for cover when the rain came.* **10** come out suddenly: *Dawn breaks; A boy's voice breaks* (= changes suddenly) *during puberty; Prisoners broke loose during the riot; a reporter sent to cover a breaking* (= developing) *news story; Who will break* (= disclose) *the news to the poor widow?*

— **break away** get away: *The hostages broke away from their captors.*

— **break down 1** become inoperative or fail: *The car broke down; Marriages break down; Our negotiations broke down; He broke down* (= lost control) *and wept.* **2** separate into parts: *to break down a compound into its parts.* **3** overcome: *to break down social barriers.*

— **break even** of a business, have income equalling expenses.

— **break in 1** enter by force: *How did the burglars break in? Carla broke in on our conversation.* **2** prepare a person or thing for new duties, use, etc.: *to break in a new recruit; A new car has to be broken in gradually.* **3** interrupt: *At the height of the drama, the announcer broke in with a bulletin.*

— **break into 1** enter by force: *Burglars broke into our house.* **2** get into or begin a new activity, state, etc.: *to break into journalism; to break into print* (= have something published); *to break into song* (= begin singing), *to break into* (= begin to use) *one's savings; to break into* (= have) *a cold sweat because of fear.*

— **break off 1** stop abruptly: *She broke off her engagement; The lecturer broke off in mid-sentence; to break off diplomatic relations.* **2** separate: *a splinter group that broke off from the party.*

— **break out 1** begin suddenly: *A war breaks out; He broke out in* (= developed) *a rash; She broke (out) into tears.* **2** get out: *Convicts break out of prison during a riot; Canada breaks out of a recession.* **3** take out for distribution or consumption: *Let's break out the champagne and celebrate.*

— **break up 1** disperse: *Break it up* (= Stop fighting)!; *The radicals broke up* (= separated) *into splinter groups.* **2** end, esp. a relationship: *Children suffer most when a family breaks up; Pat broke up with Sue.* **3** *Informal.* erupt or make erupt into laughter: *The joke broke up the audience.* **4** *Cdn.* of ice on lakes, rivers, roads, etc., thaw in the spring: *the breaking up of winter roads.* — **n. 1** a breaking or something broken: *I see a break in the glass.* **2** a pause or change from what is going on: *Let's take a break; waiting for a break in the (bad) weather; Give me a break! a lucky break* (= piece of good luck). **3** a dash: *The hostages made a break for it when the lights went out.* — **break·a·ble** *adj.*

break·age (BRAY·kij) *n.* a breaking, the extent of it, or the loss caused.

break·a·way (BRAY·kuh·way) *n.* **1** a breaking away, as from a group. **2** in hockey, lacrosse, etc., an offensive move or run by a player that leaves defenders far behind. — **adj. 1** that has broken away: *a breakaway group, sect.* **2** made to break easily, as for stage use: *a breakaway chair.*

break·danc·ing (BRAKE·dan·sing) *n.* an acrobatic dance of teenage youths characterized by writhings, tumblings, and shows of balance; also **break·ing.** — **break·dance** *v.*

break·down *n.* **1** failure: *a breakdown of machinery.* **2** collapse: *a nervous breakdown.* **3** analysis: *a breakdown of population figures by area.*

break·er *n.* **1** one that breaks: *a circuit breaker.* **2** a wave that breaks into foam on a beach, reef, etc.

break·fast (BREK·fust) *n.* the morning meal: *He has breakfast in bed; a continental, hurried, not substantial breakfast; Cereals are used as breakfast foods;* **v.:** *He breakfasts on ham and eggs.*

break-in *n.* an act of entering by force: *a break-in by burglars.*

break·neck *adj.* dangerous: *to drive at breakneck speed.*

break·out *n.* an escape, as out of prison.

break·through *n.* a sudden advance, as through obstacles: *medical, scientific breakthroughs.*

break·up *n.* **1** a breaking up: *the breakup of a marriage.* **2** *Cdn.* the breaking up of ice on water in the spring: *spring breakup.*

breast (BREST) *n.* **1** a mammary gland, esp. in a human: *an infant at its mother's breast.* **2** the front of an upper human torso or the similar part in animals: *He beat his breast* (= chest) *in sorrow; A child with a pigeon or chicken breast* (= protruding chest) *could use vitamin D; a breast of chicken, fowl, lamb* (= specified meat with bone and muscle). **3** the seat of emotions: *Anger rose in his breast; You will feel better if you* **make a clean breast of** (= confess) *the affair.*

breast-feed *v.* **-feeds, -fed, -feed·ing** feed a baby at the breast, not from a bottle.

breast-stroke *n.* a swimming stroke done with the arms sweeping to the sides and back to the breast.

breath (BRETH, "TH" as in "thin") *n.* **1** the act or power of breathing: *Keep quiet and don't waste your breath; Save your breath* (= Don't waste your time talking); *He stuck to the story to his* **last breath** (= till death); *He was so evasive he seemed to say yes and no in* **the same breath** (= at the same time); *to draw or take a deep breath;* **Don't hold your breath** (= Don't wait too eagerly); *She awaited his arrival with bated breath* (= in suspense); *The scene is so beautiful it* **takes your breath away** (= it is thrilling); *stopped to regain his breath when he was* **out of breath** (= breathing very hard from exertion); *He spoke* **under** or **below his breath** (= in a whisper). **2** a slight breeze: *a breath of fresh air; There's a breath* (= hint) *of spring in the air.* — **breath·less** *adj.: The finalists stood breathless with expectation.* — **breath·less·ly** *adv.*

breath·a·lyz·er (BRETH·uh·lye·zur) *n.* a device for measuring the alcohol in a person's blood by analysing a breath sample. — **Breath·a·lyz·er** *Trademark.*

breathe (BREETH, "TH" as in "the") *v.* **breathes, breathed, breath·ing 1** take in and expel air: *a jogger breathing heavily; We breathe in* (= take in air) *and breathe out* (= expel air) *all the time; a wine left to breathe* (= develop flavour by exposure to air); *Ask me while I yet breathe* (= while I am alive). **2** utter: *Don't breathe a word of this to anyone.* **3** blow or exhale: *Dragons breathe fire and smoke; He breathed his last* (= died). **4** inspire: *The money breathed new life into the project.* **5** say softly or in a whisper: *"I love you," she breathed.*

— **breathe down someone's neck** *Informal.* be annoyingly close behind someone.

— **breathe easy** *Slang.* relax.

breath·er (BREE·thur, "th" as in "the") *n.* **1** *Slang.* one who breathes heavily, esp. one making an obscene phone call. 2 *Informal.* a short rest: *Take a breather.*

breath·tak·ing (BRETH·tay·king) *adj.* thrilling: *a breathtaking view.*

bred *pt. & pp.* of BREED.

breech *n.* 1 buttocks. 2 the part of a gun behind the bore or barrel. 3 **breeches** (BRICH·iz) *pl.* trousers, esp. knee-length ones: *riding breeches.*

breed *v.* **breeds, bred, breed·ing** 1 produce offspring: *Rabbits breed fast.* 2 cause or originate: *Poverty breeds crime; Disease breeds in unsanitary conditions; Unsanitary conditions are the **breeding ground** of disease.* 3 raise; rear: *He was born and bred in this country; the well-bred manners of a person of (good) **breeding*** (= upbringing); *"What is bred in the bone will not go out of the flesh"* (= Hereditary characteristics are hard to get rid of). 4 produce animals by controlled mating: *Williams breeds fine hunting dogs.* — *n.* a kind, sort, etc. produced by breeding: *a new breed of horse.*

breed·er *n.* one that breeds: *a horse breeder; a breeder* (= causer) *of trouble.*

breeze *n.* a light wind: *A cool breeze blows; a gentle breeze; That job is a breeze* (*Slang for* easy task); *to **shoot the breeze*** (*Slang for* chat). — *v.* **breez·es, breezed, breez·ing** go quickly and easily: *She breezed into the room.*

breez·y *adj.* with breezes blowing: *a breezy day; a gossip columnist's breezy* (= light and easy) *style.*

breth·ren [old & formal use] *pl.* of BROTHER.

Bret·on (BRET·un) *n.* a person of or from Brittany, France; also, the Celtic language of Brittany; *adj.: fine Breton cuisine.*

brev·i·ty (BREV·uh·tee) *n.* the quality of being brief or short: *"Brevity is the soul of wit."*

brew *v.* prepare tea, beer, etc. by steeping, boiling, etc.: *Trouble is brewing* (= forming). — *n.* something brewed, esp. beer. — **brew·er** *n.*

brew·er·y (BROO·uh·ree) *n.* **-er·ies** a place where beer or ale is brewed.

brewis (BROOZE) *n.* in Newfoundland, a stew prepared with hard tack (biscuit) and salt cod or pork.

bri·ar (BRY·ur) *n.* same as BRIER.

bribe *n.* a gift, esp. of money, given to influence someone's conduct improperly. — *v.* **bribes, bribed, brib·ing** corrupt or influence someone with a bribe: *The babysitter bribed the children with promises of candy.* — **brib·er·y** (BRY·buh·ree) *n.*

bric-a-brac (BRIC·uh·brac) *n.* small ornamental knickknacks.

brick *n.* 1 a rectangular building block of baked clay: *Bricks are laid in rows to cover a wall; bricks and mortar; arrested for throwing bricks* (= brickbats) *at the police.* 2 something like a brick: *a brick of ice cream; a brick* (*Slang for* kilogram pack) *of marijuana; to hit the bricks* (*Slang for* be out on the streets); *You dropped a brick* (*Slang for* committed a gaffe); *The criticism hit him **like a ton of bricks.***

— *v.* pave or construct with bricks: *It's better to brick up the old doorway.*

brick·bat *n.* a piece of brick used as a missile: *The speech received both bouquets and brickbats* (= insults).

brick·lay·er (BRICK·lay·ur) *n.* one who builds with bricks. — **brick·lay·ing** *n.*

brid·al (BRY·dul) *adj.* having to do with a wedding: *a bridal bouquet, shower; a hotel's bridal suite.*

bride *n.* a woman about to be or recently married. — **bride·groom,** *masc.*

brides·maid *n.* a bride's female attendant.

bridge *n.* 1 a structure providing passage across a depression, esp. a waterway: *a bridge built across a river; The bridge collapsed; "We will **cross that bridge*** (= deal with it) *when we come to it."* 2 something similar to a bridge: *The bridge connecting a pair of glasses rests on the bridge of the nose; a removable dental bridge (of artificial teeth attached to one's natural teeth); Faith is the bridge from despair to salvation.* 3 a raised platform on a ship, from which commands are given. 4 a four-handed card game, esp. "contract bridge" or "auction bridge."
— **burn one's bridges (behind one)** leave oneself no way back.
— *v.* **bridg·es, bridged, bridg·ing** be a bridge, join with a bridge, or build a bridge over: *to bridge the gap.*

bridge·head *n.* a fortified advance position established to protect troops as they cross, land, or invade enemy territory.

bri·dle (BRY·dul) *n.* 1 on a horse's head, the harness to which the reins are attached; hence, a control or curb: *the bridle* (= loop) *of a snowshoe.* 2 a holding or controlling device: *the bridle of a kite, waterskiing towline.*
— *v.* **-dles, -dled, -dling** 1 put a bridle on an animal: *to bridle a pony; Bridle* (= control) *your temper.* 2 raise the head with the chin tucked in, as a sign of scorn, anger, etc.: *She bridles at the suggestion that she cheated.*

brief (BREEF) *adj.* 1 short in length or duration: *a brief visit.* 2 short and concise: *a brief letter, memorandum, reply.*
— *n.* 1 a condensed summary, esp. of a legal case: *to file, present, submit a brief; He **holds no brief for*** (= does not argue for) *feminists but believes in the equality of the sexes; **In brief*** (= in a few words), *we won the case.* 2 **briefs** *pl.* men's short, close-fitting

underpants.
— *v.* give essential information or instructions to: *to brief a lawyer on a case;* **brief·ing** *n.* — **brief·ly** *adv.*

brier (BRY·ur) *n.* a plant such as the blackberry and the wild rose having a thorny, woody stem: *Brer Rabbit hid in the brier patch.* Also **briar.**

bri·gade (brig·ADE) *n.* **1** a military unit of two or more battalions or regiments. **2** a group with special tasks or duties: *the fire brigade.* **3** *Cdn.* same as FUR BRIGADE.

brig·a·dier (brig·uh·DEER) *n.* an army officer ranking just above a colonel.

bright *adj.* shining with much light: *a bright light, star; a bright* (= brightly coloured) *green hat; a bright* (= cheerful) *prospect; a bright* (= intelligent) *young girl.*
— *adv.:* *The stars shone bright* (= brightly).
— **bright and early** quite early.
— **bright·ly** *adv.;* **bright·ness** *n.*

bright·en (BRY·tun) *v.* make or become bright: *The sun brightens the landscape; Her face brightened at the prospect of going to Paris.* — **bright·en·er** *n.*

bril·liant (BRIL·yunt) *adj.* exceptionally bright: *brilliant fall colours; brilliant sunshine; a brilliant red; a brilliant star; a brilliant* (= clever) *manoeuvre; a brilliant* (= splendid) *prospect; a brilliant* (= intelligent) *young composer, student.* — **bril·liant·ly** *adv.*
— **bril·liance** (-yunce) or **bril·lian·cy** *n.*

brim *n.* the edge or rim of a cup, bowl, etc.: *Fill it to the brim; a hat with a wide brim* (= projecting rim).
— *v.* **brims, brimmed, brim·ming** be full to the brim: *a glass so full it's brimming over; She was brimming (over) with joy.* — **brim·ful** *adj.*

brim·stone *n.* sulphur: *The preacher called down fire and brimstone on sinners* (= threatened them with punishment).

brine *n.* **1** salt-saturated water. **2** the ocean.

bring *v.* **brings, brought** (BRAWT), **bring·ing 1** cause to come along with: *She brought a friend to the party; I'll take the books to the library if you will bring them to me.* **2** cause a person or thing to come to a certain place, be in a certain condition, etc.: *Parents bring children into the world; The sun brings warmth; He was brought to grief by fate; The plaintiff brings a charge (before a court); He couldn't bring himself to do it.* **3** sell for: *What will it bring on the open market?*
— **bring about** cause: *Moral decay can bring about the fall of a civilization.*
— **bring someone around** persuade: *It's difficult to bring her around to our point of view.*
— **bring down 1** present officially: *to bring down a budget.* **2 bring down the house** score a great success, as when the whole audience applauds.
— **bring forth** give birth to young, not hatch: *Mammals bring forth their young.*
— **bring home the bacon** *Informal.* **1** earn enough to support the family. **2** be successful.
— **bring off** do successfully: *He can bring off the most difficult feats when you least expect it.*
— **bring out** reveal: *Nothing like a couple of drinks to bring out the beast in him; The publishers will bring out* (= publish) *her new book in the fall.*
— **bring to** or **around** revive from unconsciousness.

— **bring up** raise: *Jim brought up the subject of money; Parents try to bring up their children as good citizens; He gulped it down but brought it up* (= vomited it) *in no time.*

brink *n.* the edge of a steep drop: *You may look down but be careful not to go over the brink; a company on the brink* (= verge) *of bankruptcy.*

brink·man·ship (BRINK·mun·ship) *n.* the strategy of pushing a risky situation to the crisis point.

brisk *adj.* quick-moving: *proceeded at a brisk pace; a brisk sale, walk; The air was brisk; Trading was brisk on the stock exchange.* — **brisk·ly** *adv.;* **brisk·ness** *n.*

bris·tle (BRIS·ul) *n.* a short, stiff hair, as on an animal, a brush, etc.
— *v.* **-tles, -tled, -tling** raise the bristles: *Fido's hair bristles when he is angry; The dog bristles at the sight of cats; She bristled with* (= showed) *indignation; The plan bristles* (= is thick) *with objections.*

Brit *n.* & *adj. Slang.* Briton; British; Britisher.

Bri·tan·nic (bri·TAN·ic) *adj.* British: *Her Britannic Majesty.*

Brit·i·cism (BRIT·uh·siz·um) *n.* a characteristically British word or idiom, as "lorry" for "truck."

Brit·ish *adj.* having to do with **Britain** (= England, Scotland, and Wales) or its people: *British English, immigrants, imports, subjects; the **British Isles** (= Britain, Ireland, and nearby islands).*
— *n.* **1 the British** the people of Britain. **2** also **British English,** the English language as spoken in Britain.

Brit·on (BRIT·un) *n.* **1** a native of Britain. **2** one of the pre-Anglo-Saxon people of Great Britain.

brit·tle (BRIT·ul) *adj.* hard but very easily broken: *brittle bones, glass; a tense and brittle* (= fragile) *manner.*
— *n.* a brittle candy with nuts: *peanut brittle.*

broach (BROHCH) *v.* bring up: *Now is the time to broach the subject of a raise with the boss.*

broad (BRAWD) *adj.* **1** wide from side to side: *a broad avenue; 100 m broad.* **2** wide in scope; general: *a broad rule; in the broadest sense of the word; the broad outlines of a subject.* **3** clear or expansive: *the broad ocean; in broad daylight.* **4** obvious: *a broad accent, hint.* **5** ribald: *noted for his broad humour; broad comedy.* **6** liberal and tolerant: *He has broad views on religion.* — *n. Slang.* [offensive] a woman.
— **broad·ly** *adv.*

broad axe *n. Cdn.* an axe with a broad blade used for shaping logs into timber; also **broad ax.**

broad·band *adj.* having a wide range of frequencies; hence, general: *broadband objectives, radio systems.*

broad·brush *adj.* rough or general: *broadbrush estimates; a broadbrush indictment.*

broad·cast *v.* **-casts,** *pt.* & *pp.* **-cast** or **-cast·ed, -cast·ing 1** transmit widely, esp. by radio or television: *The program was broadcast live from the studio; They broadcast it live.* **2** scatter seed widely.
— *n.* a broadcasting or something broadcast: *a live broadcast; We interrupt this broadcast for a special*

announcement; *a broadcast beamed to the Soviet Union;* **adj.:** *broadcast journalism* (= radio and TV); *a broadcast satellite (that transmits TV signals); broadcast* (= wide) *sowing;* **adv.:** *seed sown broadcast* (= widely).

broad·en (BRAW·dun) *v.* make or become broad or broader: *The river broadens here; Reading broadens the mind.*

broad jump same as LONG JUMP.

broad·leaf *adj.* having broad, flat leaves and hard wood: *The beech, maple, oak, etc. are broadleaf, not needleleaf trees, which lose their leaves in the fall.*

broad·loom *n.* wide carpeting: *wall-to-wall broadloom; a piece of broadloom (carpeting).*

broad-minded (BROAD·mine·did) *adj.* tolerant or liberal; not narrow-minded.

broad·side *n.* 1 the side of a ship or similar vehicle; **adv.:** *The car was hit broadside by the truck;* **adj.:** *a broadside* (= sideways) *hit.* 2 a firing of all the guns on one side of a ship: *They fired a broadside at the enemy; He delivered a broadside* (= barrage of criticism or abuse) *against the opposition.* 3 a large sheet of paper printed usually across its central fold, as for advertising, political tracts, etc.; also **broad·sheet.**

broad-spectrum (BROAD·spec·trum) *adj.* effective against a wide variety of something: *a broad-spectrum antibiotic for treating many diseases.*

bro·cade (broh·CADE) *n.* a rich fabric with a raised design, as of gold or silver.

bro·chure (broh·SURE) *n.* a pamphlet: *an advertising brochure.*

brogue (BROHG) *n.* 1 an Irish accent: *She speaks with a soft Irish brogue; He asked me in a heavy brogue where I was from; a faint, rich, thick, Scottish brogue.* 2 a stout oxford shoe with a perforated pattern; wingtip.

broil *v.* cook by direct exposure to flame or great heat: *Meat may be broiled in a range or on a grill.*
— **broiled** *adj.:* *broiled fish; char-broiled chicken.*

broil·er *n.* 1 a pan or grill for broiling. 2 a young chicken suitable for broiling.

broke *pt.* of BREAK.
— **adj.** *Informal.* having no money: *The business went broke last year; He was flat broke at the end of the month.*
— **go for broke** make a big try, staking everything.

bro·ken (BROH·kun) *pp.* of BREAK.
— **adj.** 1 uneven: *broken ground.* 2 crushed or beaten: *His pride was broken by the defeat; a broken heart.* 3 disunited, esp. by divorce: *children from broken homes; a broken family, marriage.* 4 incorrectly spoken: *He answered in broken French.*
— **bro·ken·ly** *adv.;* **bro·ken·ness** *n.*

broken-down *adj.* worn out; useless: *a broken-down car in a junkyard.*

broken-hearted *adj.* overcome by grief: *a sad and broken-hearted lover.*

bro·ker (BROH·kur) *n.* an agent for buying, selling, making contracts, etc.: *a customs broker; marriage*

broker; *a power broker of the underworld; We need an honest broker* (= mediator) *to mediate the dispute.*

bro·ker·age (BROH·kuh·rij) *n.* 1 a broker's fee. 2 the business of a broker.

bro·mide (BROH·mide) *n.* 1 a potassium compound used as a drug to calm the nerves. 2 a dull, obvious remark or idea; also, its author.

bron·chi·al (BRONK·ee·ul) *adj.* having to do with bronchitis: *bronchial pneumonia.* — **bron·chi·al·ly** *adv.*

bron·chi·tis (brong·KYE·tis) *n.* inflammation of the air passages from the lungs and those of the nose, throat, etc.

bron·co (BRONG·coh) *n.* **-cos** in the West, a wild or half-tamed horse: *the bucking bronco; bronco busting* (= taming).

Bronx cheer *n.* *Slang.* a noise of disapproval; raspberry.

bronze (BRONZ) *n.* 1 an alloy of copper and tin. 2 a work of art made of bronze. 3 the yellowish or reddish brown colour of bronze.
— *v.* **bron·zes, bronzed, bronz·ing** 1 give a bronze colour to: *a beachcomber bronzed by the sun; Some people bronze* (= cast in bronze) *baby shoes and other keepsakes and souvenir items.*
— *adj.* having to do with bronze: *Bronze tools and weapons mark the **Bronze Age** of civilization.*

brood (long "oo") *n.* the offspring in one family, as baby birds hatched at one time: *the Smiths and their noisy brood* (= children).
— *v.* 1 hatch eggs by sitting on them. 2 ponder or worry: *He tends to brood about his losses; It's no use brooding over your past.* 3 look over from a close or commanding position: *From the CN Tower, I could brood over all of Toronto.*
— *adj.* meant for breeding or hatching: *a brood mare; a brood range for waterfowl breeding; a brood stock of salmon.*

brood·er (BROO·dur) *n.* 1 one that broods or worries. 2 a bird that hatches eggs. 3 a heated enclosure for raising chicks without a hen.

brooding *adj.* 1 threatening: *a sheer brooding cliff; the brooding eyes of a bull.* 2 intense or keen: *a brooding drama, painting, woodcut; the brooding emotional intensity of the music.*

brood·y *adj.* ready or inclined to brood: *a broody hen; a broody poetic soul.*

brook (short "oo") *n.* a small stream: *babbling brooks.*
— *v.* put up with: *a dictator who would brook no differences of opinion.*

broom (short or long "oo") *n.* a brushlike tool with a long handle, used for sweeping: *"A new broom sweeps clean"* (= A new administration will make drastic changes).

broth (rhyme: "cloth") *n.* a clear stock left after boiling meat or vegetables in water: *beef broth; clear broth.*

broth·el (BROTH·ul, "TH" as in "thin") *n.* a prostitute's place of business; whorehouse.

broth·er (BRUTH·ur, "TH" as in "the") *n.* 1 a son of the same parents: *Cain and Abel were brothers.* 2 a fellow member of a particular group: *They became blood brothers by mixing each other's blood in a ceremony; A black man refers to his fellows as soul brothers; Brother John is a lay brother* (= not priest) *of a religious order.*

broth·er·hood (BRUTH·ur·hood, short "oo") *n.*
1 brotherly bond or feeling: *the brotherhood of nations; the brotherhood of man; universal brotherhood; to live in peace and brotherhood.* **2** an organization of people who share a belief, occupation, etc.: *the Brotherhood of Indian Nations; the Brotherhood of Railway and Airline Clerks.*

brother-in-law (BRUTH·ur·in·law) *n.* **brothers-in-law**
1 a spouse's brother. **2** the husband of a spouse's sister. **3** a sister's husband.

broth·er·ly (BRUTH·ur·lee) *adj.* of or like a brother: *a brotherly feeling; brotherly love.*

brougham (BROME, BROOM, BROO.um, long "OO") *n.* an early type of limousine with an open driver's seat.

brought *pt. & pp.* of BRING.

brou·ha·ha (broo·HAH·hah) *n.* an uproar or fuss: *a brouhaha over a silly question of protocol.*

brow (rhyme: "how") *n.* **1** the ridge over the eyes; eyebrow: *He knit his brows in a frown.* **2** the forehead: *a wrinkled brow.*

brow·beat *v.* -beats, -beat, -beat·en, -beat·ing intimidate, esp. by stern looks or speech: *a browbeaten clerk; He was browbeaten into withdrawing his remark.*

brown *n. & adj.* (of) the colour of chocolate: *her dark brown hair; the dark brown of her hair; a brown bear such as the grizzly; brown coal* (= "lignite"); *brown* (= unpolished) *rice.*
— *v.* make or become brown, esp. by cooking.
— **browned off** *Slang.* bored; also, angry.
— **brown·ish** *adj.*

brown-bag *v. Informal.* -bags, -bagged, -bag·ging *Informal.* carry one's own food or liquor to a restaurant, club, etc. or carry a lunch to work or school, esp. in a brown paper bag. — **brown-bagger** *n.*
— **brown-bagging** *n.*

brown belt *n.* **1** a rank in karate or judo below the black belt. **2** a person holding this rank.

brown·ie (BROW·nee) *n.* **1** a helpful little elf.
2 **Brownie** a junior member of the Girl Guides, usually aged seven to nine. **3** a flat, rich, usually chocolate cake with nuts.

Brownie points *n. pl. Informal.* credit or approval, like a Brownie earning her badges.

brown·out *n.* a partial reduction of lighting during a power shortage: *There are brownouts and occasional blackouts in our town.*

browse (BROWZ) *v.* brows·es, browsed, brows·ing
1 go through or examine books, merchandise, etc. in a casual way: *"Come in and browse," the sign said; Feel free to browse through the store.* **2** nibble on grass, young shoots, etc.: *Cows browse in the field; They browse on grass, shrubs, twigs; to browse off young trees.*
— *n.* a browsing or what is browsed: *Tender shoots,*

shrubs, and twigs are good browse for cattle; a book good only for a browse; The Art Gallery is holding a browse this evening.

bru·in (BROO·in) *n.* a bear.

bruise (BROOZE) *n.* an injury that discolours the skin without breaking it: *cuts and bruises.*
— *v.* bruis·es, bruised, bruis·ing **1** inflict or suffer a bruise: *He fell off the bike and bruised his knee; a bruised apple* (with its skin broken). **2** hurt the feelings of: *his bruised ego.*

bruis·er (BROO·zur) *n. Informal.* a big, strong, pugnacious man.

bruit (BROOT, long "OO") *v.* spread or circulate a rumour, story, etc.: *the names being bruited about on campus for the post of president.*

bru·lé or **bru·le** (broo·LAY) *n. Cdn.* **1** a burned area of forest. **2** **Brulé** a Métis.

brunch *n.* a late-morning meal combining breakfast and lunch: *a Sunday brunch.*

bru·net (broo·NET) *n.* a man or boy with dark hair; *fem.* **bru.nette** (broo·NET).
— **brunet** *adj.* brown in colour; having dark hair and complexion: *Both her parents happen to be brunet.*

brunt *n.* the hardest or greatest part: *They bore the brunt of the attack.*

brush *n.* **1** an area covered with low, rough shrubs and small trees: *He walked through thick brush.* **2** broken or cut branches; brushwood: *a brush fence, fire.* **3** a utensil made of bristles fastened in a handle, for applying paint, shaving cream, etc. or for cleaning teeth, clothing, hair, floors, etc. **4** a light touch, encounter, or skirmish: *Her last illness was a close brush with death; He had a brush with the police.*
— *v.* **1** clean, arrange, or spread with a brush: *to brush the hair, teeth; to brush a coat clean; He brushed the dust off the book; She knows how to **brush off** (= get rid of) unwelcome offers; You had better **brush up** or **brush up on** your* (= refresh your knowledge of) *math.* **2** touch lightly; graze: *The bullet only brushed his head; She brushed past me in the crowd without noticing.*

brush·off *n. Informal.* an abrupt cold rejection: *He got a swift brushoff when he tried his sales pitch on her.*

brush wolf *n. Cdn.* coyote.

brush·wood *n.* **1** a thicket. **2** cut or broken branches of trees.

brusque (BRUSK) *adj.* impolitely abrupt; curt: *his brusque manner.* — **brusqe·ly** *adv.;* **brusque·ness** *n.*

bru·tal (BROO·tul) *adj.* **1** cruel or savage: *a brutal attack, lie, manner, murder, slaying; brutal violence; this brutal winter weather; It was brutal of her to refuse his apology.* **2** harsh but true: *the brutal facts, truth.*
— **bru·tal·ly** *adv.*

bru·tal·i·ty (broo·TAL·uh·tee) *n.* -ties a brutal act or condition: *They suffered many brutalities such as being beaten and kicked; the brutality of war.*

bru·tal·ize (BROO·tul·ize) *v.* **1** make brutal: *He was brutalized by hard work and poverty.* **2** treat brutally: *The kidnappers brutalized their victim.*

brute (BROOT, long "OO") *n.* **1** an irrational animal. **2** a coarse, cruel, or unthinking person: *Alcohol brings out the brute in him; They arrested the drunken brute.* — *adj.* **1** unthinking, not rational: *a brute animal, beast; He won by sheer brute strength; the brute* (= harsh but true) *facts of the case.* **2** savage or stupid: *his brute manners, mentality; Some kill out of brute spite.*

bru·tish (BROO·tish) *adj.* savage: *the primitive's brutish condition.*

bub *n. Slang.* [unfriendly use] fellow: *When Big Brother asks questions, bub, you answer.*

bub·ble (BUB·ul) *n.* **1** a roundish, enclosed, usually hollow object: *She blows bubbles for fun; soap bubbles; A bubble bursts when pricked; He's so allergic to the air he lives in a plastic bubble; a mere **bubble brain** or **bubblehead** (Slang for stupid person).* **2** an unrealistic or delusive idea or scheme: *The real estate bubble burst after a few months of high profits.* **3** something bubble-shaped, as a kind of woman's hairdo or a car (**bubble car**) with a transparent dome top, or **bub·ble·top**. — *v.* **bub·bles, bub·bled, bub·bling** make or sound like bubbles: *She was bubbling with enthusiasm; a child bubbling over with excitement.*

bubble gum *n.* chewing gum that can be blown into bubbles. — *adj.:* the *bubble-gum set* (*Informal* for preteens).

bub·ble·head·ed (BUB·ul·hed·id) *adj. Slang.* silly or light-headed.

bubble memory *n.* data storage by means of bubbles formed on magnetic silica film, each bubble or its absence representing a binary digit.

bub·bly (BUB·lee) *adj.* **1** having or like bubbles: *the bubbly champagne.* **2** spirited or enthusiastic: *in a bubbly mood; a bubbly personality; in bubbly spirits.* — *n., pl.* **bub·blies** *Informal.* champagne: *Let's break out the bubbly!*

buc·ca·neer (buck-uh·NEER) *n.* a pirate or freebooter.

buck *n.* **1** *Slang.* dollar or money: *how to make a fast buck; You're talking **big bucks** (= a great deal of money); She looks like **a million bucks** (= She's gorgeous).* **2** a full-grown male animal, esp. a deer: *There are bucks, bulls, stags, and harts of the antlered kind; a buck rabbit.* **3** a vigorous young man: *the young buck you see on a motorbike.* **4** a bucking. — *v.* **1** leap and plunge, as a horse trying to throw the rider off: *a bucking bronco; The raft bucked and heaved in the stormy sea.* **2** resist: *to buck a trend; You can't buck the system.* — **buck for** *Informal.* strive hard for something: *to buck for a promotion.* — **buck up** cheer up. — **pass the buck** *Informal.* pass on blame or responsibility to someone: *Let's pass the buck to the other department; **The buck stops here** (= No appeal to anyone higher)!*

buck·a·roo (BUCK·uh·roo) *n., pl.* **-roos** *Informal.* cowboy.

buck·et (BUCK.it) *n.* **1** a pail or the amount it holds, or **buck·et·ful. 2** the scoop of a dredge, steam shovel, etc. **3 the bucket** *Slang.* jail; cooler.

— **kick the bucket** *Slang.* die.

bucket seat *n.* a car seat with a rounded back, for one passenger.

bucket shop *n.* same as BOILER ROOM.

buck·le (BUCK·ul) *n.* **1** a device for fastening a strap or belt: *to undo a buckle.* **2** a fold, wrinkle, bend, etc. — *v.* **-les, -led, -ling 1** secure with a buckle: *to buckle a belt; The knight buckled on his sword; Please buckle up your seat belt.* **2** collapse or give way, esp. under heat or pressure: *The pavement buckled in the hot sun; The landing gear buckled as the plane landed; The boxer buckled the champ's knees* (= made them bend) *with a straight right.* — **buckle down** start working very hard: *It's time to buckle down and get the job done.* — **buckle under** yield: *She won't buckle under to pressure from anyone.*

buck-passer (BUCK·pass·ur) *n.* one who passes the buck. — **buck-passing** *n.*

buck·shot *n.* a large size of lead shot: *Some people file lawsuits like scattering buckshot; The madman peppered the crowd with buckshot.*

buck·skin *n.* a soft, strong, yellowish-grey leather: *buckskin leggings.*

bu·col·ic (bew·COL·ic) *adj.* having to do with shepherds or pastoral life: *bucolic pleasures, poetry.*

bud *n.* **1** a partly opened flower: *rose buds.* **2** a sprouting plant part containing immature leaves, flowers, etc. **3** something at its beginning stage. — *v.* **buds, bud·ded, bud·ding 1** put out buds. **2** begin to develop: *a budding poet.* — **nip in the bud** stop something at an early stage.

Bud·dhist (BOOD·ist, short or long "OO") *n.* a follower of **Buddhism,** a religion founded in India by the **Buddha** in the fifth century B.C. — *adj.:* a *Buddhist monastery, monk.*

bud·dy (BUD.ee) *n.* **bud·dies** *Informal.* a companion or pal: *his bosom buddy; an army buddy; an old buddy of mine; the **buddy system** of pairing together for protection, appointing friends to jobs, not charging fellow police officers, etc.* — **buddy up** to get very close to or get chummy with someone.

buddy-buddy *adj. Slang.* very friendly or familiar: *It doesn't look good for teachers to act too buddy-buddy with their students.*

budge *v.* **budg·es, budged, budg·ing** move the slightest bit: *Stay here and don't budge! The stubborn mule couldn't be budged.*

budg·et (BUJ.it) *n.* **1** a statement of expected expenditure and income: *our annual budget; a balanced, federal, household, itemized budget; A budget has to be drawn up; adj.:* a *budget cut, item; the Finance Minister's **budget speech** in the House of Commons.* **2** an allocated sum: *We have a budget of only $1 000 for new books.* **3** a limited amount of money to spend: *I can't afford luxuries, I'm on a budget.* — *adj.* inexpensive: *budget meals at budget prices; a budget store.*

— *v.* make a budget: *We've budgeted $1 000 for new books; A busy man must budget his time, budget every minute of his day* (= plan in detail how his time is spent).

budg·ie (BUJ·ee) *n. Informal.* a parakeet with green, yellow, and blue feathers.

buff *n.* 1 a block or wheel covered with soft leather, velvet, etc. that is used for polishing. 2 a brownish yellow. 3 *Informal.* bare skin: *a beach for sunning yourself in the buff.* 4 *Informal.* a devotee or enthusiast: *a jazz buff.*
— *adj.* of the colour buff.
— *v.* polish, esp. with a buff: *He waxed and buffed the wooden floor.*

buf·fa·lo (BUFF·uh·loh) *n.* -lo or -los a kind of wild ox such as the North American bison, the **Cape buffalo** of Africa, and the domesticated **water buffalo** of India: *a place where a dwindling herd of wild buffalo still roam.*
— *adj.:* Indians used to eat **buffalo berry** with **buffalo meat;** to light a fire with **buffalo chips** (made of dried dung); A **buffalo jump** is where buffalo used to be stampeded over a cliff for killing.
— *v.* -loes, -loed, -lo·ing *Slang.* confuse: *We're totally buffaloed by the statement from Ottawa.*

buff·er *n.* 1 one that buffs. 2 something that lessens the effect of an impact, shock, etc.: *He acted as a buffer between the warring parties; an alkaline buffer to neutralize the acid reaction of aspirin in the stomach;* hence **buffered aspirin.** 3 a temporary storage device in a computer; memory: *Clear the buffer.*

buffer state *n.* a neutral country between two rival powers.

buffer zone *n.* an area separating two armies.

¹**buf·fet** (BUF·it) *v.* blow or toss about: *an airplane buffeted by heavy winds; a tragic character buffeted by fate.* — *n.* a blow, esp. with the hand.

²**buf·fet** (buh·FAY) *n.* 1 a sideboard: *a hutch and buffet for the dining room.* 2 a meal with food set out on a table or sideboard for guests to serve themselves: *an all-you-can-eat buffet.*

buf·foon (buh·FOON, long "OO") *n.* a clown or habitual joker: *He likes to play the buffoon at parties.* — **buf·foon·er·y** *n.*

bug *n.* 1 any insect or insectlike animal, esp. a pest: *bed bugs; June bugs.* 2 *Informal.* a disease-causing germ or virus: *There's a flu bug going around; Mom was bitten by the hula-hoop bug* (= craze) *in her teens.* 3 *Informal.* an enthusiast: *a ham radio bug.* 4 *Informal.* a fault or problem in a machine or process: *He's working the bugs out of his robot; to get the bugs out of a computer program.* 5 a hidden listening device: *a bug installed in a telephone; Bugs had been planted even in flowerpots.*
— *v.* bugs, bugged, bug·ging 1 *Slang.* pester or annoy: *Something seems to be bugging him.* 2 hide a microphone in something: *They bugged the spy's telephone line.* 3 tap a conversation, speaker, etc. unknown to the speaker: *an illegally bugged conversation (monitored by an unauthorized party).*
— **bug off** *Slang.* get lost.
— **bug out** *Slang.* evade: *to bug out of a responsibility.*

bug·a·boo (BUG·uh·boo) *n. Informal.* a bogey or frightening spirit.

bug·bear *n.* 1 a source of persistent annoyance: *Little brothers can be the bugbear of a teenager's life.* 2 a bogey or bugaboo.

bug-eyed *adj.* with eyes sticking out: *He was bug-eyed with astonishment.*

bug·ger (BUG·ur) *n. Slang.* 1 one who bugs; also, one who plants bugs. 2 [familiar use] bastard: *You little bugger!*

bug·gy (BUG·ee) *n.* **bug·gies** a light, usually four-wheeled carriage: *a baby buggy; dune buggy; luggage buggies at an airport; shopping buggy; the horse and buggy* (= carriage).

bu·gle (BEW·gul) *n.* a small, trumpetlike brass instrument: *Boy Scouts play the bugle at ceremonies; Military life is marked by bugle calls.* — **bu·gler** *n.*

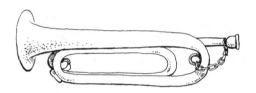

build (BILD) *v.* **builds, built, build·ing** 1 construct barns, bridges, dwellings, houses, etc.: *Birds build nests; a novel built around one central character; shelves built into a wall; a statue built out of clay; a relationship built* (= based) *on trust.* 2 develop: *There's a crowd building outside; We're building* (= expanding) *for the future.*
— **build up** 1 increase or accumulate: *to build up a supply of cash; to build up hope, muscles, strength.* 2 develop with buildings. 3 promote: *ads to build up a new product.*
— *n.* figure or physique: *a man of heavy build; husky build.* — **build·er** *n.*

build-down *n.* a slowing down of the arms race between the superpowers by eliminating nuclear weaponry instead of building them up.

building *n.* 1 a structure with walls and a roof, as a house, barn, factory, etc.: *to build, demolish, erect, put up, renovate a building; The building was gutted by fire; an apartment building; a dilapidated, ramshackle, tumbledown, tall building.* 2 the act or trade of building: *prefabricated building; road building;* **adj.:** *Children play with* **building blocks;** *the building industry; a building machine such as a crane, bulldozer, or concrete mixer; building codes, construction, materials, permits, stones, trades.*

build-up *n.* an increase: *a military build-up on a country's border; She received a big build-up* (= boost) *in the media; traffic build-up* (= congestion) *during rush hour.*

built-in *adj.* forming an integral part: *walls with built-in bookshelves; a built-in closet; a built-in, not detached garage; a plan with a built-in drive for profits.*

built-up *adj.* developed with buildings: *the heavily built-up downtown area.*

bulb *n.* 1 something with a rounded, bulging end: *an electric light bulb; the rubber bulb of a syringe.* 2 a roundish underground bud from which a plant such as a tulip or onion grows; also, such a plant.
— **bul·bous** (BUL·bus) *adj.* having bulbs or shaped like a bulb: *a bulbous nose.*

bulge (BULJ) *n.* an outward swelling: *bulges of fat on the body; the battle of the bulge (Informal for the struggle to keep slim); The post-war baby boom showed a bulge (= temporary rise) in the population curve.*
— *v.* **bulg·es, bulged, bulg·ing** swell: *Santa carries a sack bulging with toys.*

bu·lim·i·a (byoo·LIM·ee·uh) *n.* an eating disorder arising from anxiety to control one's weight in which the patient goes on an eating binge followed by fasting, using laxatives, vomiting, etc.

bulk *n.* 1 volume, quantity, mass, etc., esp. if great: *The elephant raised its bulk and stood up; a lumbering bulk of a beast; The bulk (= greater part) of an iceberg is under water; groceries sold in bulk (= in quantity) rather than in packages; Material of the same kind is sent through the mails as bulk mail at special bulk rates.* 2 food material that is not digested: *Fibre adds bulk to diet to stimulate bowel movement;* also **bulk·age** (-ij) . — *v.* appear large or important.

bulk·head *n.* a vertical partition in a ship, airplane, etc.: *a fireproof bulkhead; the bulkhead separating an automobile engine from the body.*

bulk·y *adj.* **bulk·i·er, -i·est** having bulk: *a bulky package; a bulky (= large and clumsy) person; a bulky (= relatively heavy) sweater; a bulky food such as bran; A bulky vegetable adds fibre to the diet.*

bull (short "oo") *n.* 1 an adult male of the ox family or of large animals such as the elephant, moose, seal, walrus, and whale. 2 an investor who buys stocks expecting prices to rise. 3 *Slang.* nonsense.
— **bull in a china shop** one who is clumsy or tactless.
— **shoot the bull** *Slang.* talk idly.
— **take the bull by the horns** deal boldly with a difficult situation.
— *adj.* 1 male: *a bull calf, moose.* 2 characterized by rising prices: *a bull market.*

bull·dog *n.* a short-haired dog with a pug nose and strong jaws.
— *v.* attack like a bulldog, as in bulldogging.

bull·dog·ging (BULL·dog·ing) *n.* in rodeos, the stunt of plunging from horseback to the neck of a steer to wrestle it to the ground; steer wrestling.

bull·doze *v.* **-doz·es, -dozed, -doz·ing** 1 push, clear, gouge, etc. using a bulldozer: *They bulldozed a path through the jungle.* 2 force: *He bulldozed his way through the crowd; People were bulldozed (= intimidated or forced) into signing the petition.*

bull·doz·er (BOOL·doh·zur) *n.* a heavy tractor with a wide frontal blade for digging, pushing earth, grading, etc.

bul·let (BOOL·it, short "OO") *n.* a small metal projectile shot from a gun: *He died in a hail of bullets; The bullet trains of Japan reach speeds of up to 200 km/h.*

bul·le·tin (BOOL·uh·tin, short "OO") *n.* 1 an announcement, esp. of news: *a late news bulletin about the earthquake.* 2 a periodical report, esp. for a society, group, etc.

bulletin board *n.* 1 a board to post notices on. 2 a privately operated network for exchange of information among computerists which they may access via the telephone lines; also **bulletin-board system** or **BBS.**

bullet-proof *adj.* safe from bullets: *a bullet-proof vest.*

bull·fight *n.* a spectacle in which a **bull·fight·er** provokes and then kills a fierce bull in a sport called **bull·fight·ing.**

bull·frog *n.* a large frog whose male has a deep croak.

bull·head·ed (BULL·hed·id) *adj.* unthinkingly stubborn.

bull·horn *n.* a small battery-powered megaphone, as used by police when dealing with a crowd; loud-hailer.

bul·lion (BOOL·yun, short "OO") *n.* gold or silver, esp. in bars.

bull·ish *adj.* 1 bull-like. 2 expecting, having, or causing a price rise: *the bullish growth of a computer giant; a bullish market; bullish speculators.* 3 *Informal.* enthusiastic or hopeful: *I'm bullish on or about Team Canada; a bullish outlook.* — **bull·ish·ness** *n.*

bull·pen *n.* 1 a pen for bulls; also, a special enclosure in a jail. 2 in baseball, a warming-up area for relief pitchers.

bull session *n.* an informal, unstructured discussion.

bull's-eye *n.* a circle marking the centre of a target: *He hit the bull's-eye; She scored a bull's-eye (hit).*

bul·ly (BOOL·ee, short "OO") *n.* **bul·lies** one who threatens or is cruel to a weaker person.
— *v.* **bul·lies, bul·lied, bul·ly·ing** be a bully to someone: *He bullies the younger children during recess; She was bullied (= threatened) into agreeing.*
— *adj. & interj.* splendid!

bul·wark (BOOL·wurk, short "OO") *n.* 1 a defensive wall or rampart. 2 usually **bulwarks** *pl.* an extension of the ship's side above the deck to provide protection for people and objects on deck. 3 a protection or defence: *Freedom of expression is a bulwark of democracy; a bulwark against tyranny.*

bum *n.* 1 a loafer, vagrant, or hobo: *a beach bum; ski bum; welfare bum.* 2 *Informal.* a buttock.
— **on the bum** *Informal.* 1 living as a bum. 2 malfunctioning.
— **the bum's rush** *Slang.* ejection by force; instant dismissal: *He was given the bum's rush when he became abusive.*
— *v.* **bums, bummed, bum·ming** *Slang.* 1 live by begging; loaf: *to bum around.* 2 beg; cadge: *He bummed a cigarette off her.*
— *adj. Slang.* bad: *bum advice; an athlete with a bum knee; the victim of a bum rap (= false charge); a bum steer (= bad direction or tip).*

bum·ber·shoot (BUM·bur·shoot) *n. Informal.* umbrella: *It's always bumbershoot weather in certain parts of B.C.*

bum·ble·bee (BUM·bul·bee) *n.* a large, hairy, black-and-yellow bee.

bum·mer (BUM·ur) *n. Slang.* a bad experience: *The trip was really a bummer.*

bump *v.* **1** collide with or knock forcibly: *She bumped against a chair; I bumped into her in the dark; bumped into (Informal for chanced to meet) an old friend at the convention.* **2** *Informal.* displace: *He was bumped from the overbooked flight; The gangsters decided to bump off (Slang for kill) the informer.*
— *n.* **1** a blow or collision. **2** a bulge or hump: *a bump on his head.*

bump·er (BUM·ur) *n.* **1** a metal bar protecting either end of an automobile: *a bumper sticker with a slogan on it; The bumper-to-bumper traffic crawled to a halt.* **2** a brimful cup of drink; hence, something exceptionally large; *adj.: a bumper crop, harvest; a bumper issue (of a journal).*

bump·kin *n.* an awkward or naive person: *city slickers and country bumpkins.*

bump·tious (BUMP·shus) *adj.* arrogantly self-assertive.
— **bump·tious·ly** *adv.*

bump·y *adj.* **bump·i·er, -i·est** having or marked by bumps: *a bumpy ride, road.*

bun *n.* **1** a roll: *a cheese bun; cinnamon bun; onion bun.* **2** a coil of hair at the back of the head: *A ballerina wears her hair in a bun.*

bunch *n.* **1** a number of similar things growing or fastened together: *a bunch of bananas, flowers, keys; Some grasses grow in bunches (= tufts).* **2** *Informal.* group: *a bunch of fellow workers, girls; She is the best of the bunch.*
— *v.* gather together: *Let's bunch up before the fire; a dress bunched up at the back.* — **bunch·y** *adj.*

bun·dle (BUN·dul) *n.* **1** a number of things tied together or wrapped up; package: *a bundle of sticks; a bundle of clothes for the cleaners; She's a bundle of nerves (= very nervous) at exam time.* **2** *Informal.* a great amount of money: *He made a bundle on the stock market.*
— *v.* **bun·dles, bun·dled, bun·dling 1** tie or pack into a bundle: *We'll bundle up the newspapers for pickup; Let's bundle up (= dress warmly) and go for a walk; She bundled up her child against the cold.* **2** dispatch quickly: *She bundled the children off to school.*

bun·ga·low (BUNG·guh·loh) *n.* a house of one or one-and-one-half stories: *a back-split bungalow.*

bun·gle (BUNG·gul) *v.* **-gles, -gled, -gling** do or work clumsily or improperly; botch: *He bungled the job; bureaucratic bungling; n.: It was a technological bungle.* — **bun·gler** *n.*

bun·ion (BUN·yun) *n.* a swollen, painful deformity of the first joint of the big toe.

bunk *n.* **1** a sleeping place, esp. a narrow bed or berth. **2** *Slang.* meaningless talk.
— *v.* sleep in or provide with a bed, often a makeshift one: *We bunked in the old cabin.*

bunk bed *n.* one of a pair of beds set one above the other.

bunk·er *n.* **1** a storage area for fuel oil, coal, etc. on a ship. **2** a fortified, often underground shelter. **3** in golf, a hazard, as a sandy hollow or mound of earth.

bunk·house *n.* a house equipped with sleeping bunks, as for cowhands on a ranch.

bun·kum (BUNK·um) *n. Slang.* nonsense; bunk.

bun·ny *n.* **bun·nies** *Informal.* a rabbit.

bunt *v.* hit a baseball a short distance with a half swing; *n.: The batter reached first base on a bunt.*

bunt·ing *n.* a light cloth for flags, streamers, etc.

buoy (BOO·ee, BOY) *n.* **1** a floating marker anchored to indicate a channel, hidden hazard, etc.: *A bell buoy rings when tossed by the waves.* **2** a ring-shaped device for keeping a person afloat; life buoy.
— *v.* (BOY) **1** mark with buoys. **2** keep afloat: *a barrel buoyed up by water; a balloon buoyed up by air; The good news buoyed up (= cheered) her spirits.*

buoy·an·cy (BOY·un·see) *n.* the ability to float: *A bladder provides buoyancy for fish; The buoyancy of water (to keep objects floating on it) increases with density.*

buoy·ant (BOY·unt) *adj.* **1** able to float or keep something afloat: *Cork is naturally buoyant.* **2** cheerful: *He seemed in buoyant good spirits; Real estate enjoys a buoyant (= resilient) market in the spring.*
— **buoy·ant·ly** *adv.*

bur or **burr** *n.* **1** the prickly seedcase or fruit of some plants; also, such a plant. **2** a person or thing that sticks to one like a bur. — **bur·ry** *adj.*

bur·ble (BUR·bul) *v.* make a bubbling noise: *The percolator started burbling; She burbled (= said or spoke) excitedly.*

bur·bot (BUR·but) *n.* a freshwater fish of the cod family.

bur·den (BUR·dun) *n.* **1** something carried, as a ship's cargo; load: *The camel is a beast of burden; Distribute the burden by shifting weights.* **2** a responsibility, task, or worry: *He was a heavy burden to everyone in his final days; His age placed a big burden on his relatives; Jane bore the burden of caring for him all by herself; But he was not a financial burden; The burden was relieved only by his death; The burden of proof (= obligation to prove one's point) rests with the accuser.* **3** the central idea or theme: *the burden of the argument; the burden of her song.*
— *v.* load: *a heavily burdened horse; Let's not burden him with our problems.* — **bur·den·some** *adj.*

bu·reau (BYOOR·oh) *n.* **-reaus** or **-reaux** (-oze) **1** a chest of drawers; dresser. **2** an office: *a better business bureau; credit bureau; news bureau; tourist bureau; weather bureau; the (U.S.) Federal Bureau of Investigation.*

bu·reau·cra·cy (byoo·ROC·ruh·see) *n.* **-cies 1** a graded organization of nonelected public officials. **2** an administrative system bound by fixed rules and red tape: *an aging, faceless, incompetent, overgrown, swollen bureaucracy.*

bu·reau·crat (BYOOR·uh·crat) *n.* an official working in a bureaucracy.
— **bu·reau·crat·ic** (byoor·uh·CRAT·ic) *adj.: a tale of bureaucratic bungling.*

burg *n. Informal.* a city or town.

bur·geon (BUR·jun) *v.* **1** to sprout leaves or buds. **2** expand or develop rapidly: *the burgeoning electronics industry.*

bur·ger (BUR·gur) *n. Informal.* a hamburger.
— *combining form.* **1** a patty in a bun: *eggburger; fishburger.* **2** a hamburger: *a cheeseburger* (= hamburger with cheese); *soyaburger* (= hamburger with soya protein).

bur·gess (BUR·jis) *n.* **1** a citizen of a borough. **2** *Cdn.* in Saskatchewan, a property owner or ratepayer.

burgh (BURG) *n.* an incorporated Scottish town; borough.

burgh·er (BUR·gur) *n.* a solid citizen, as of a burgh or town.

bur·glar (BURG·lur) *n.* one who commits burglary: *A cat burglar goes in and out like a cat; A **burglar alarm** warns about burglars.*

bur·glar·ize (BUR·gluh·rize) *v.* **-iz·es, -ized, -iz·ing** *Informal.* break into a house as a thief: *They found their home burglarized and vandalized when they returned from Florida.*

bur·gla·ry (BUR·gluh·ree) *n.* **-ries** the breaking and entering of a building to commit a crime, esp. robbery.

bur·gle (BUR·gul) *v.* **-gles, -gled, -gling** same as BURGLARIZE.

Bur·gun·dy (BUR·gun·dee) *n.* **-dies 1** a usually red table wine, esp. one made in Burgundy, France. **2** a dark reddish brown colour.

bur·i·al (BER·ee·ul) *n.* the act of burying a body: *The burial took place at sea; a burial ground.*

bur·lesque (bur·LESK) *n.* **1** an entertainment featuring striptease acts, coarse humour, etc. **2** a travesty or parody.
— *v.* **-lesques, -lesqued, -lesqu·ing** imitate satirically or humorously.

bur·ly (BUR·lee) *adj.* **-li·er, -li·est** big and strong; husky: *a big burly fellow.*

burn *v.* **burns,** *pt. & pp.* **burned** or **burnt, burn·ing**
1 be or set on fire and suffer its effects: *a burning house; It'll burn to the ground, burn to ashes; He burned his hand in the oven; The meat was burned to a crisp; Joan of Arc was burned at the stake; She was burned to death; was burned alive; Fire burns* (= gives off great heat). **2** suffer the burning effects of acid, radiation, or electricity. **3** consume as fuel: *Our furnace burns gas; The first stage of the rocket burns for two minutes.*
4 feel or make feel hot: *the burning sands of the desert; I held on to the rope although it burned* (= the skin came off) *my hands as I slid down; She had burning ears from the cold; her cheeks burning with shame; ears burning* (= very eager) *to hear about the scandal; He was burning with desire; It **burns me up** (Informal for makes me angry) that I wasn't given a chance.* **5** spend freely: *I don't have money to burn.* **6** *Slang.* cause

damage to someone: *He decided to quit the business after getting burned the first time.*
— **burn one's boats** or **bridges** *Informal.* leave oneself no means of escape or return.
— **burn out** to become exhausted after a time and unable to carry on, as in some lines of work: *a burned-out teacher.*
— *n.* **1** a burning or an injury or mark made by burning: *A first-degree burn only reddens the skin; a slow burn* (= rising fury) *leading to a blowup.* **2** a firing of a rocket engine.

burn·er *n.* something that burns, heats, or emits flame, esp. a heating element or a stove: *a gas burner; The less urgent business is put on the back burner* (= position of low priority), *others on the front burner* (= position of high priority).

bur·nish *v.* polish: *a burnished mahogany table; burnished steel;* **bur·nish·er** *n.* — *n.* lustre or gloss.

burn·out *n.* **1** the cessation of firing of a rocket or jet engine. **2** exhaustion: *Some people suffer burnout after a time in a strenuous job; teacher burnout.*

burnt a *pt. & pp.* of BURN.

burp *n.* a soft belch: *The baby let out a burp.*
— *v.* belch or cause to belch: *A baby is burped after feeding.*

burp gun *n.* an automatic pistol or light machine gun.

burr *n.* **1** a rough edge left by cutting, drilling, etc. **2** a roughly trilled "r" sound: *the Scottish burr.* **3** a whirring sound. **4** same as BUR.

bur·ro (BUR·oh) *n.* a small donkey.

bur·row (BUR·oh) *n.* a tunnel or hole dug by a rabbit, mole, etc.
— *v.* **1** dig a burrow: *Muskrats burrow into the banks of streams.* **2** search, move, or progress as if by digging a burrow: *He's burrowing through books and papers in search of evidence.*

bur·sar (BUR·sur) *n.* the treasurer of a college or university.

bur·sa·ry (BUR·suh·ree) *n.* **-ries 1** the treasury of a college or university. **2** a small scholarship: *The student received a bursary.*

burst *v.* **bursts, burst, burst·ing 1** explode; break, esp. from internal pressure: *A bomb bursts; The creek burst its banks; He burst out laughing; The police burst into the house; She burst into tears; She burst out of the house crying; Don't **burst in on** or **upon** (= interrupt) us when we are busy.* **2** be very full: *Granaries are bursting with grain; The child was bursting to tell us the news; The room is so crowded it seems to **burst at the seams**.*
— *n.* **1** a bursting: *a burst* (= series of shots) *of machine-gun fire; The sentry fired a burst at the escaping convicts.* **2** an outbreak, spurt, or effort: *a burst of applause, energy, speed.*

bur·y (BER·ee) *v.* **bur·ies, bur·ied, bur·y·ing 1** hide in the ground: *buried treasure.* **2** put a corpse in the ground, underwater, etc., esp. with funeral rites: *to bury a body; He was buried alive in the landslide.*
3 hide: *The child buried her face in the pillow; He tried to forget his sorrow by burying* (= occupying) *himself in work; decided to **bury the hatchet** (= make peace) and*

be friends.

bus *n.* **bus·es** or **bus·ses** a large public conveyance usually having a fixed route and stopping points: *They caught a bus; boarded the bus; The children came by bus; Those who **miss the bus** (Informal for* lose the opportunity) *this time may not get another chance.*
— *v.* **bus·es** or **bus·ses, bused** or **bussed, bus·ing** or **bus·sing** **1** travel by bus: *We bus to school; We are bused* (= transported) *back at 3:30 p.m.* **2** act as a busboy or busgirl.

bus·boy *n.* a waiter's helper who sets and clears tables; *fem.* **bus·girl.**

bush (short "oo") *n.* **1** a small woody plant with many branches but no central stem, as the lilac or the rose; shrub. **2** wild, uninhabited land, esp. if forested: *to stay in the bush.* **3** *Cdn.* a wooded area near a cleared one. **4** *Cdn.* in the Prairies, wooded land near the plains. **5** grove: *a maple bush; sugar bush.*
— **beat around** or **about the bush** approach or discuss a topic without coming to the point.
— *v.* be thick like a bush.
— *adj.* **1** *Slang.* amateur; hence, second-rate: *a bush league, performance.* **2** *Cdn.* of the bush: *a bush line* (= airline serving the bush country); *a bush fire; bush lot* (= wooded part of a farm); *the bush pilots who fly into the bush country; an impassable bush* (= rural) *road; bush telegraph.*
— **bush·y** *adj.* **bush·i·er, -i·est:** *a bushy beard; a fox's bushy tail.*

bushed *adj.* **1** *Informal.* exhausted. **2** *Cdn. Informal.* lonely and depressed.

bush·el (BOOSH·ul, short "OO") *n.* a measure for bulky articles: *We sell apples by the bushel; A bushel of corn weighs 25.4 kg.*

bush league *n. Slang.* a minor league, considered second-rate.
— **bush-league** *adj.* second-rate: *to improve the bush-league status of their hockey team; a bush-league speech.*

Bush·man (BOOSH·mun, short "OO") *n.* **-men** a member of a nomadic people of southwestern Africa, properly called "the San"; formerly **bushman, -men.**

bush·whack (BOOSH·whack) *v.* **1** live in the bush, esp. in hiding. **2** make one's way through the bush. **3** ambush or raid. — **bush·whack·er** *n.*

busi·ness (BIZ·nis) *n.* **1** work or occupation: *Sales people travel on business; to mix business with pleasure; Each one minds his own business; That's none of your business* (= rightful concern); *Waiting in line is tiresome business* (= activity); *I **mean business** (= I am in earnest); **adj.:** a **business card** bearing a company's name; The **business end** of a tool, weapon, etc. is the end with which the action is performed, as the muzzle of a gun.* **2** a commercial undertaking such as a store or factory: *He gave up his job and went into business (for himself); Many businesses closed down or went out of business during the recession.* **3** commerce or trade: *She is in show business; Business is picking up after the recession; Business is booming; They are trying to drum up business for the new agency; We want your business; We'd like to do business with you.*

busi·ness·like *adj.* efficient or purposeful: *Let's be businesslike and not waste any time.*

busi·ness·man (BIZ·nis·mun) *n.* **-men** one engaged in business, esp. as an owner or boss.
— **busi·ness·wom·an** *n.* **-wom·en.**

busk·er (BUS·kur) *n.* a street musician or entertainer.

bus·kin *n.* a thick-soled, high-laced boot, as worn formerly by actors.

busman's holiday *n.* a vacation spent in activity similar to one's usual work.

buss *n. & v. Informal.* kiss.

bus stop *n.* a stopping point on a bus route.

bust *n.* **1** a sculpture of a person's head and upper chest. **2** a woman's bosom. **3** *Slang.* a police arrest or raid. **4** a failure or collapse: *the cycle of boom and bust; California or bust!* **5** punch.
— *v. Slang.* **1** burst, break, punch, tame, etc.: *He busted my toy! She busted his nose; The trees are busting into bloom; a bronco-busting cowboy.* **2** of police, arrest: *He was busted for peddling drugs; They busted* (= raided) *the joint.* **3** demote: *He was busted to private.* **4** make or become penniless: *busted until payday.*

bust·er *n. Slang.* **1** one that busts or breaks: *a bronco buster; fuzz buster* (= speedtrap beater); *fuzz-buster buster; ghost busters.* **2** [hostile use] fellow: *Relax, buster!*

bus·tle (BUS·ul) *n.* **1** busy activity: *the hustle and bustle of trading on the stock exchange; The bustle subsides when the bell rings.* **2** formerly, a cushion that makes a woman's skirt stick out at the back: *a maid in a bustle, apron, and lace cap.*
— *v.* **-tles, -tled, -tling** move or work busily and fussily: *She bustles the children off to school at 8 everyday; the bustling stock exchange; It bustles with activity.*

bust·y *adj. Informal.* big-breasted.

bus·y (BIZ·ee) *adj.* **bus·i·er, -i·est** **1** active: *as busy as a bee; a busy marketplace, typist; She had a busy day at work; He's busy with his homework; Homework keeps him busy; Dad is busy cooking; The phone is busy* (= in use), *as you can tell by the **busy signal**.* **2** of a design, having too many distracting details.
— *v.* **bus·ies, bus·ied, bus·y·ing** make busy or active: *He busies himself with hobbies at weekends.*
— **bus·i·ly** *adv.*

bus·y·bod·y (BIZ·ee·bod·ee) *n.* **-bod·ies** a nosey or meddlesome person.

bus·y·work (BIZ·ee·wurk) *n.* useless work to keep one occupied.

but *conj.* **1** yet; however; on the contrary: *She is short but thin; He visited, but could not stay long.* **2** if not; other than: *He would have come but that he was too busy.*
— *prep.* except: *Everyone but Mei-Li had left the scene; Everyone but he or him had left the scene; He wouldn't be alive today **but for** the operation; It happened on the **last day but one** (= second day) before the wedding.*
— *adv.* [formal use] only: *There was but one survivor.*

— **n.** an exception, condition, etc.: *no buts about it; no ands ifs or buts.*

butch (short "oo") *n. Slang.* an aggressively masculine person.

butch·er (BOOCH·ur, short "OO") *n.* **1** one who kills or dresses meat for sale or consumption. **2** a brutal mass killer. **3** one who botches a job; bungler.
— **v.** slaughter: *They butcher cattle, hogs, and sheep; Thousands were butchered in the war; He butchered* (= bungled) *the job.*
— **butch·er·y** (BOOCH·uh·ree) *n.* **-er·ies.**

but·ler *n.* a chief male house-servant.

butt *n.* **1** a large cask. **2** the larger or handle end: *the butt of a pistol, rifle.* **3** a remaining or broken end: *a cigarette butt.* **4** an object of ridicule: *Bob is the butt of many jokes.* **5** a butting. **6** *Slang.* buttocks: *Will you please get off your butt and do something?*
— **v.** strike or push with the head or horns, as a goat does: *to butt against a wall.*
— **butt in** *Informal.* interfere: *She doesn't like to butt in when they're talking privately; never butts in on their conversation.*
— **butt out** *Slang.* stop interfering.

butte (BYOOT, long "OO") *n.* an isolated, flat-topped hill with steep sides, as in southern Alberta and Montana.

butt-end *v. Cdn.* in hockey and lacrosse, to jab or thrust an opponent with the handle of the stick. Also *n.*

but·ter (BUT·ur) *n.* **1** a thick, rich food product made by churning cream: *a pat of butter; a whole stick of butter; fresh butter; rancid butter; sweet* (= unsalted) *butter; Fry it in butter.* **2** a similar product: *apple butter; peanut butter.*
— **v.** spread butter on something: *to butter a toast; He knows how to **butter up** or **up to** (= flatter) his boss to get a raise.* — **but·ter·y** *adj.*

but·ter·cup (BUT·ur·cup) *n.* a shiny yellow wildflower.

but·ter·fat (BUT·ur·fat) *n.* the fatty part of milk that is churned into butter.

but·ter·fin·gers (BUT·ur·fing·gurz) *n. Slang.* one who is clumsy and drops things: *a regular butterfingers.*

but·ter·fly (BUT·ur·fly) *n.* **-flies** a slender, often colourful, four-winged insect that flies by day, flitting from flower to flower: *the monarch butterfly; a social butterfly who has time only for parties; He has **butterflies** or **butterflies in his stomach** (= a nervous feeling) just before an exam.*

but·ter·milk (BUT·ur·milk) *n.* the milky liquid left after cream is churned for butter, made commercially by fermenting skim milk.

but·ter·scotch (BUT·ur·scotch) *n.* a syrup, candy, or flavouring made with butter and brown sugar.

but·tock (BUT·uck) *n.* **1** either of the two fleshy rounded parts at the back of the hips. **2 buttocks** *pl.* the seat or rump.

but·ton (BUT·un) *n.* **1** a disk or knob used to fasten or ornament clothing. **2** a similar object: *Push* or *press the button for help; He **pushed the panic button** (= panicked); He's wearing a campaign button (= badge)*

*on his lapel; He always arrives at 9 **on the button** (= exactly).*
— **v.** fasten with a button: *Button (up) your shirt.*
— **button up** or **button one's lip** *Slang.* be quiet.

buttoned-down or **button-down** *adj. Informal.* conventional or conservative.

buttoned-up *adj. Informal.* prim and serious-minded.

but·ton·hole (BUT·un·hole) *n.* a slit or loop through which a button is passed.
— **v. -holes, -holed, -hol·ing** stop and force someone to listen.

but·tress (BUT·ris) *n.* an external support built against a wall; hence, any support.
— **v.** support: *to buttress a wall; a poor thesis buttressed with a long bibliography.*

bux·om (BUX·um) *adj.* plump and attractive: *a buxom young matron.*

buy *v.* **buys, bought** (BAWT), **buy·ing** acquire by payment in cash or kind: *He will buy me a car from a dealer; Dealers buy wholesale and sell retail; a temptation for impulse buying; panic buying of stocks; Our freedom was bought with their lives; He tried to buy his way into the club; The lawyer was accused of trying to buy* (= bribe) *the jury; No one will buy* (*Slang* for believe) *that story.*
— **buy into** purchase shares in a company.
— **buy out** buy someone's shares or controlling interest in a business.
— **buy time** *Informal.* to stall so as to gain time.
— **buy up** buy as much as one can of something.
— **n.** *Informal.* purchase: *a good buy; a great buy* (= bargain) *at such a low price.*
— **buy·er** *n.: It's a **buyer's market** when prices are low.*

buzz *v.* **1** make a vibrating, prolonged, z-like sound: *bees buzzing in the field; a market buzzing with activity; Buzz* (= telephone) *for room service; When he became a nuisance, she told him to **buzz off** or **along** (Slang for go away).* **2** fly an airplane low over: *They buzzed the enemy ship.*
— **n.** a buzzing sound: *the buzz of bees, rumour; the buzz of a saw; He appeared promptly at my buzz* (= when I pressed the buzzer); *Give me a buzz* (*Informal* for phone call) *when you are free.*

buz·zard (BUZ·urd) *n.* a bird of the vulture family: *The "turkey buzzard" is a New World vulture.*

buz·zer (BUZ·ur) *n.* a signalling device that makes a buzzing sound.

buzz word *n.* a high-sounding bit of jargon: *a computer buff who uses buzz words like "telecommute" and "wetware."*

by *prep.* **1** beside; near; at: *It's over by the door; I stopped by her house* (= visited her) *on my way back.* **2** through the agency of: *a book by Margaret Atwood; to Ottawa by way of Montreal; trapped by a snowstorm.* **3** during: *He works by night; The payment is due by* (= on or before) *May 31.* **4** according or in relation to: *Play by the rules; a lawyer by profession; He swears by the Bible.* **5** past: *She went by us at full speed.* **6** to the extent of: *He missed the bus by 15 minutes.* **7** in the amount, lot, or unit of something: *apples by the bushel; You pay by the hour.* **8** [used to indicate multiplication, division, linking of dimensions, etc.]: *Multiply 2 by 7 to get 14; Divide 14 by 2 to get 7.*
— *adv.: Keep close by* (= near) *in case of trouble; Don't lay it by* (= aside) *just yet; Stop by* (= visit) *on your way home; She drove by* (= past) *just now.*
— **by and by** eventually.
— **by and large** on the whole.
— **by oneself** without others.
— **by the by** or **by the way** incidentally.

bye *n.* an advance to the next round of a tournament because there is no other contestant with whom one can be paired: *Smith drew a bye; a bye to the semi-finals.*
— *interj. Informal.* good-bye: *Bye now!*

by-election (BY·i·lec·shun) *n.* a special election to fill a vacant seat between regular elections.

by·gone (BY·gon) *adj.* past: *in bygone days.*
— *n.: "Let bygones be bygones"* (= Forgive and forget).

by·law *n.* a rule or regulation passed by a company, city, etc. to regulate its own affairs.

by·line *n.* the writer's name printed at the head of a newspaper story.

by·pass *n.* a road or passage around something: *Take the bypass to avoid city traffic; a coronary bypass (around the blocked portion of an artery).*
— *v.* go around: *The canal bypasses the rapids.*

by·path *n.* a secondary or rarely used path or road.

by·product (BY·prod·uct) *n.* something produced incidentally to the chief product: *Molasses and syrup are by-products of sugar manufacture.*

by·stand·er (BY·stan·dur) *n.* a nonparticipating onlooker: *An innocent bystander was hit by the runaway car.*

byte *n.* a unit of computer data usually consisting of 8 bits.

by·way *n.* **1** a bypath: *highways and byways.* **2** a less known topic or area: *in the byways of history.*

by·word *n.* **1** a proverbial saying. **2** a person or thing that is typical of a quality: *The newspapers are not all bywords for accuracy.* **3** watchword or guiding principle: *Efficiency is the byword for kitchen designers.*

By·zan·tine (BIZ·un·teen) *adj.* **1** having to do with the Byzantine Empire (A.D. 395 – 1453) and its culture, esp. its architecture. **2** characterized by intrigue: *a Byzantine struggle for power; the Byzantine world of big corporations linked to political parties.*

C or **c** (SEE) *n.* **C's** or **c's 1** the third letter of the English alphabet. **2** the third in a series; third highest: *a grade of C.*

cab *n.* **1** a taxicab: *to call for a cab; hail, hire, take a cab; to go in a cab; to go by cab.* **2** the driver's compartment of a truck, crane, locomotive, etc.

ca·ba·na (cuh·BAN·uh) *n.* a shelter used as a bathhouse near a beach or swimming pool.

cab·a·ret (cab·uh·RAY) *n.* **1** a restaurant providing liquor and light entertainment. **2** the entertainment itself.

cab·bage (CAB·ij) *n.* a vegetable with a dense round head of thick leaves: *heads of cabbage; He ordered a dish of corned beef and cabbage.*

cab·bage·town (CAB·ij·town) *n. Cdn.* a run-down city area; *adj.: Toronto's Cabbagetown district; a Cabbagetown merchant.*

cab·by or **cab·bie** (CAB·ee) *n. pl.* **cab·bies** *Informal.* one who drives a taxicab; also **cab·driv·er.**

cab·in (CAB·in) *n.* **1** a small, rough dwelling of one storey: *Pioneers lived in log cabins.* **2** a room on a ship or boat: *a first-class cabin; a cabin boy* (= servant boy on a ship). **3** an enclosed space in an airplane for crew, cargo, or passengers.

cabin cruiser *n.* a small powered craft with built-in living facilities.

cab·i·net (CAB·uh·nut) *n.* **1** a cupboardlike structure for housing or displaying objects or equipment: *a china cabinet; the cabinet of a console TV; a filing cabinet for the office; a kitchen cabinet.* **2** the advisory council of a head of state or chief executive of a government: *a decision taken in cabinet; a coalition cabinet; a mere kitchen cabinet (Informal for unofficial advisory group); the shadow cabinet (of the opposition party); adj.: She's at a cabinet meeting; a cabinet minister, reshuffle.*

cabin fever *n. Cdn.* surliness and depression resulting from prolonged confinement indoors, esp. during the Northern winter.

ca·ble (CAY·bul) *n.* **1** a rope of large diameter, usually of steel or fibre. **2** the anchor cable of a ship: *The cable broke and our ship began to drift.* **3** a unit of length equal to 100 or 120 fathoms; also **cable length.** **4** a bundle of insulated electrical conductors. **5** a cablegram: *He sent us a cable from Europe.*
— *v.* **ca·bles, ca·bled, ca·bling** send a cablegram to

someone: *He cabled us from Europe; cabled for money; cabled that he was broke.*

cable car *n.* a car drawn by a moving cable, as on a hill or across a canyon.

cable TV *n.* TV using a central antenna to serve a whole community.

cab·man (CAB·mun) *n.* **-men** a male cabby.

ca·boo·dle (cuh·BOO·dul) *n. Slang.* **the whole (kit and) caboodle** the whole lot.

ca·boose (cuh·BOOSE) *n.* **1** the car at the end of a freight train with sleeping and kitchen facilities for the train crew. **2** *Cdn.* a mobile bunkhouse used by lumberjacks. **3** *Cdn.* a horse-drawn vehicle made of a small cabin on runners and equipped with a stove for use in the winter.

cab·stand *n.* a parking place for taxicabs waiting for passengers.

cac·ci·a·to·re (cah·chuh·TOR·ee) *adj.* cooked with tomatoes, onions, and herbs: *veal cacciatore; chicken cacciatore.*

cache (CASH) *n.* **1** a hiding place, originally for food and supplies for future use. **2** goods hidden in a cache.
— *v.* **cach·es, cached, cach·ing** hide: *The explorers cached their provisions in a cave.*

cache memory *n.* in a computer system, a high-speed buffer-type memory into which instructions and programs are loaded from the main memory.

ca·chet (cash·AY) *n.* **1** a mark or seal as an indication of official approval on a letter or document. **2** a mark of excellence or authenticity. **3** a design or advertisement stamped or printed on mail.

cack·le (CACK·ul) *v.* **1** make the shrill cry of a hen or goose. **2** laugh in such a way: *to cackle with glee.*
— *n.* a hen's cry or laughter like it: *Cut the cackle* (*Informal* for Stop the pointless chatter).

cac·tus (CAC·tus) *n., pl.* **-tus·es** or **-ti** (-tye) a leafless, spiny desert plant with fleshy stems.

cad *n.* an ungentlemanly ill-mannered person.
— **cad·dish** *adj.*

ca·dav·er (cuh·DAV·ur) *n.* a dead body, esp. a corpse for dissection.

ca·dav·er·ous (cuh·DAV·uh·rus) *adj.* corpselike; pale and gaunt.

cad·dy (CAD·ee) *n.* **cad·dies 1** also **cad·die,** one hired to assist a golfer to carry clubs. **2** a small container or chest, esp. one for tea.
— *v.* **cad·dies, cad·died, cad·dy·ing** act as a caddie.

ca·dence (CAY·dunce) *n.* **1** a rhythm or flow of sound. **2** a timed measure, as for a march or dance. **3** modulation of pitch and volume of the voice; hence, the general character of the voice: *the pleasant cadence of her speech.* **4** a musical progression toward an harmonic conclusion. — **ca·denced** *adj.*

ca·den·za (cuh·DEN·zuh) *n.* a parenthetic ornamental flourish, either vocal or instrumental, just before the end of a work of music.

ca·det (cuh·DET) *n.* **1** a student in a military academy or one receiving military training, as a member of a "cadet corps": *an army cadet; military cadet; naval cadet; police cadet; a space cadet* (= a spaced-out person). **2** a 16- to 21-year-old Girl Guide: *In the U.S.,* **Cadette** *Girl Scouts are 12 to 14 years old.*

cadge *v.* **cadg·es, cadged, cadg·ing** *Slang.* get by begging: *trying to cadge cigarettes from passers-by.*
— **cadg·er** *n.*

Cad·il·lac (CAD·uh·lac) *n.* something considered as the most outstanding of its kind: *the Cadillac of copying machines; adj.: a Cadillac plan, service;* **Cadillac** *Trademark.*

cad·re (CAD·ree) *n.* **1** a trained group, esp. military or political, forming the core of a larger organization: *A cadre of revolutionaries operated in each village.* **2** a revolutionary group or a member of one: *A high-ranking cadre arrived at the local meeting in a chauffeured car.*

Cae·sar or **cae·sar** (SEE·zur) *n.* an absolute ruler, like the emperors of ancient Rome; **Cae·sar·ism** (-riz·um) *n.*

cae·sar·e·an or **Cae·sar·e·an** (si·ZAIR·ee·un) *n.* the delivery of a fetus by surgical incision into the uterus: *The baby was delivered by caesarean; A caesarean had to be performed;* also **caesarean** or **Caesarean section.** Also **cae·sar·i·an, Cae·sar·i·an.**

Caesar salad *n.* a tossed salad of greens, eggs, and anchovies with olive oil, lemon juice, and seasonings.

ca·fé (ca·FAY, cuh·FAY) *n.* a small restaurant or bar. Also **ca·fe.**

caf·e·te·ri·a (caf·uh·TEER·ee·uh) *n.* a restaurant where customers serve themselves at a counter and carry food to the tables: *a school cafeteria; adj.: The cafeteria plan, approach, or concept of compensation allows employees to pick and choose their benefits; a cafeteria selection of courses.*

caf·feine or **caf·fein** (ca·FEEN) *n.* a stimulant drug found in tea, coffee, chocolate, and colas.

caf·tan (CAF·tan, -tun) *n.* **1** a long-sleeved Middle Eastern men's tunic reaching to the ankles and worn with a sash. **2** a caftanlike shirt or dress worn in Western countries as casual wear.

cage *n.* **1** an enclosure for animals, consisting of an open structure of metal or wooden bars or wire. **2** a similar structure or enclosure: *the batting cage of baseball players in training; an elevator cage; a bank teller's cage; the rib cage of the chest.* **3** [in news headings] basketball; *adj.: a cage coach, title.*
— *v.* **cag·es, caged, cag·ing** put or keep in a cage.

cag·er (CAY·jur) *n.* [in news headings] a basketball player.

cag·ey (CAY·jee) *adj.* **cag·i·er, -i·est** *Informal.* **1** cunning: *the cagey fox.* **2** cautious: *The politician was cagey about committing himself.*
— **cag·i·ly** *adv.;* **cag·i·ness** *n.*

ca·hoots (cuh·HOOTS, long "OO") *n. Slang.* **in cahoots (with)** in partnership, usually of an improper nature.

Cain *n.* a murderer, like the son of Adam and Eve in the Bible who killed his brother Abel: *the mark* or *brand of Cain.* — **raise Cain** *Slang.* make a big commotion.

caisse pop·u·laire (KES·pop·yuh·LAIR) *n. Cdn.* in Quebec, a credit union.

cais·son (CAY·son, *rhyme:* on) *n.* **1** formerly, a horse-drawn, usually two-wheeled ammunition wagon. **2** a watertight chamber filled with air under high pressure, used for underwater construction.

ca·jole (cuh·JOLE) *v.* **-joles, -joled, -jol·ing** persuade or coax, esp. with flattery; wheedle: *The child was cajoled into the dentist's chair.* — **ca·jol·er·y** *n.*

Ca·jun (CAY·jun) *n.* a Louisianian descended from French immigrants exiled from Acadia in the 18th century.

cake *n.* **1** a sweet loaf, baked and often iced, usually in a thick disk shape: *a piece* or *slice of cake; a birthday cake; layer cake; wedding cake.* **2** something made into a round flat shape: *fish cake; barley cakes; a cake of soap.*
— **a piece of cake** *Informal.* something very easy to accomplish.
— **have one's cake and eat it too** want to enjoy the advantages without accepting the disadvantages of a deal.
— **take the cake** *Informal.* deserve a prize: *This takes the cake for the dullest novel of the year.*

cake·walk *n.* **1** a show dance characterized by an elaborate walk with a high prance. **2** *Slang.* a piece of cake; breeze.

cal·a·bash (CAL·uh·bash) *n.* **1** a tropical American tree bearing a fruit gourd; also, the gourd. **2** a bottle, bowl, pipe, etc. made from this gourd.

ca·lam·i·ty (cuh·LAM·uh·tee) *n.* **-ties** a grave misfortune that befalls a person or people: *The marriage proved to be the greatest calamity of his life; A collision with a kangaroo was the only calamity of our Australian tour.* — **ca·lam·i·tous** (-uh·tus) *adj.*

ca·lash (cuh·LASH) *n.* **1** a four-passenger carriage with a folding top. **2** the folding top of a carriage. **3** formerly, a woman's folding hood or bonnet. **4** a calèche.

cal·ci·fi·ca·tion (CAL·suh·fuh·CAY·shun) *n.* hardening by calcium formation: *Bones are formed by calcification; In old age, calcification of joints may set in.*

cal·ci·fy (CAL·suh·fye) *v.* **-fies, -fied, -fy·ing** harden by accumulation of calcium.

cal·cine (CAL·sine) *v.* **-cines, -cined, -cin·ing** reduce to quicklime or similar dry powder by heating but not melting. — **cal·ci·na·tion** (-suh·NAY·shun) *n.*

cal·ci·um (CAL·see·um) *n.* a soft, whitish, metallic element found in combination in limestone, chalk, marble, bone, etc.

cal·cu·late (CAL·kyuh·late) *v.* **-lates, -lat·ed, -lat·ing** **1** compute mathematically or scientifically: *Actuaries calculate insurance premiums.* **2** evaluate or predict by common sense: *to calculate the consequences of an action.* — **cal·cu·la·ble** (-luh·bul) *adj.;* **cal·cu·la·bly** *adv.*

calculated *adj.* deliberate: *a calculated attempt, insult; a plan **calculated** (= designed) to cause delay; We're taking a **calculated risk** (with chances of failure already estimated).*

calculating *adj.* shrewd or clever in a selfish way: *a cold and calculating villain.*

cal·cu·la·tion (cal·kyuh·LAY·shun) *n.* **1** the process or result of calculating. **2** shrewd deliberation.

cal·cu·la·tor (CAL·kyuh·lay·tur) *n.* one that calculates, esp. an electronic machine that does arithmetic computations: *a pocket calculator.*

cal·cu·lus (CAL·kyuh·lus) *n.* **1** *pl.* **-lus·es** a system of computing using algebraic symbols: *differential and integral calculus.* **2** *pl.* **-li** (-lye) an abnormal stonelike growth in the body: *urinary calculi* (= kidney stones).

cal·dron (CAWL·drun) same as CAULDRON.

ca·lè·che or **ca·leche** (cuh·LESH) *n. Cdn.* a two-wheeled, one-horse carriage with a folding top, used as a sightseeing vehicle in Quebec and other cities.

cal·en·dar (CAL·un·dur) *n.* **1** a system for determining the days, weeks, and months of a year; also, a table or chart showing this: *the Chinese, Gregorian, Julian calendar; a perpetual calendar (useful for many years); Our **calendar year** runs from January to December.* **2** an ordered list; schedule: *a school calendar; a calendar of events; That's not on my calendar this week.* — *v.* record on a calendar or schedule.

cal·en·der (CAL·un·dur) *n.* a finishing machine used to give a gloss to cloth, paper, etc.

calf (CAF) *n.* **calves** (CAVZ) **1** the thick, fleshy back part of the lower leg. **2** the young of cattle and other large mammals such as the elephant, moose, porpoise, and whale: *A cow is said to be **in calf** (= pregnant); Veal is calf meat.* **3** calfskin.

calf love *n.* same as PUPPY LOVE.

calf·skin or **calf** *n.* leather made from calf hides.

Calgary red·eye *n. Cdn.* a popular Western drink of tomato juice mixed with an equal amount of beer.

caliber same as CALIBRE.

cal·i·brate (CAL·uh·brate) *v.* **-brates, -brat·ed, -brat·ing** **1** fix or adjust the graduations of a measuring instrument: *a well calibrated thermometer.* **2** find the calibre of a tube. — **cal·i·bra·tion** (-BRAY·shun) *n.*

cal·i·bre or **cal·i·ber** (CAL·i·bur) *n.* **1** the diameter of a bullet or other projectile: *A .20 [pronounced "twenty"] calibre bullet is 20/200 in. (5.08 mm) in diameter.* **2** the inside diameter of a tube or the barrel of a gun: *Smooth-bore guns use bullets of the same calibre as the bore.* **3** quality or excellence: *work of high calibre; A woman of her calibre is hard to find.*

cal·i·co (CAL·i·coh) *n.* **-cos** or **-coes** a rough cotton cloth with a printed pattern: *a **calico cat** (= spotted cat).*

cal·i·per (CAL·uh·pur) *n.* same as CALLIPER.

cal·is·then·ics (cal·us·THEN·ics, "TH" as in "thin") *n.* same as CALLISTHENICS.

calk (CAWK) *v.* same as CAULK.

call *v.* **1** summon; ask to come: *Did you call me? She felt called to the service of the poor.* **2** visit in person: *The plumber will be calling soon; Please call again; to call at a place.* **3** to telephone: *Tell her to call home; Our doctor will be calling soon; Many employees have called in sick today.* **4** deem or consider: *We'll call it even and go home.* **5** name: *Let's call the baby Jacques; The media called her a hero.* **6** to shout or cry: *Please call for help; a bird calling for its mate.* **7** require or demand, as a loan to be paid, cards to be shown in a game, etc.: *The bank has called the loan; This calls for an explanation.* **8** end: *The game was called because of rain.* **9** say or read out aloud: *to call the roll.*
— **call in 1** summon as help: *to call in a consultant.* **2** withdraw from circulation, as old currency.
— **call off 1** cancel: *to call off an investigation.* **2** read out aloud; also **call out.**
— **call on** pay a short visit to someone.
— **call someone's bluff** *Informal.* challenge a pretentious claim.
— **call someone on the carpet** *Informal.* summon for or give a rebuke.
— **call the shots** *Informal.* be in charge.
— **call up 1** (cause to) recollect. **2** to telephone. **3** bring or summon to an active state: *Young people are called up for military service; to call up images, text, etc. on a computer screen.*
— *n.* **1** a summoning: *a strike call; a call to battle; above and beyond the **call of duty** (= more than what one's job requires); a divine call to the ministry; a bugle call* (= signal); *Doctors are **on call** (= available) in an emergency; a close call* (= narrow escape). **2** a visit: *Few doctors make house calls any more.* **3** an act of telephoning: *collect calls; A local call is not a long-distance call; station-to-station calls; We placed or made an operator-assisted person-to-person call to Jim; The*

operator put my call through to Baffin Island; a toll call; Will someone take that call, please? **4** decision or ruling: *a bad call by an umpire in baseball.* **5** a cry or shout: *a call for help; a bird's mating call; a roll call* (= reading aloud of the roll); *Please stay **within call*** (= close enough to hear being called). **6** a demand: *There are too many calls on my time; a loan to be repaid on call.* **7** in card games, a bid. — **call·er** *n.*

call·back *n.* a manufacturer's notice to consumers to return a defective product; recall.

call·board *n.* a bulletin board for notices or schedules, as for theatre rehearsals or train times.

call girl *n.* a prostitute available by telephone.

cal·lig·ra·phy (cuh·LIG·ruh·fee) *n.* penmanship; fine handwriting. — **cal·lig·ra·pher** *n.* — **cal·lig·ra·phic** (cal·uh·GRAF·ic) *adj.*

call-in *n.* same as PHONE-IN.

calling *n.* a profession, occupation, or religious vocation.

calling card *n.* a card bearing a person's name and address. Also **visiting card.**

cal·li·per (CAL·uh·pur) *n.* **1** usually **callipers** *pl.* an instrument with two curved legs, for measuring thicknesses or the diameters of tubes. **2** either of two plates that press against a rotating part, as the wheel of a bicycle or the disc of a car's wheel, to act as a brake: *calliper brakes.*

cal·lis·then·ics (cal·us·THEN·ics, "TH" as in "thin") *n.pl.* simple physical exercises designed to develop grace and strength. — **cal·lis·then·ic** *adj.*

call number *n.* a set of letters and numbers by which a library book and its place on the shelves is identified.

cal·los·i·ty (cal·OS·uh·tee) *n.* **-ties 1** callousness. **2** a callus.

cal·lous (CAL·us) *adj.* **1** toughened: *A callus is skin become callous by constant pressure or friction.* **2** insensitive: *He showed callous disregard for her condition; He seems callous to suffering; It was callous of him to ignore her.* — **cal·lous·ly** *adv.;* **cal·lous·ness** *n.*

cal·low (CAL·oh) *adj.* youthful and inexperienced: *a callow lad, youth.* — **cal·low·ness** *n.*

call-up *n.* a summons to military service.

cal·lus (CAL·us) *n.* **cal·lus·es** a tough, thickened area of skin or bark: *If you wear tight shoes, calluses may appear on the soles of your feet.* — *v.* form a callus on the skin: *Hard physical labour callused his hands; Soak the callused area in warm water.*

calm (COM, CAHM) *n.* **1** a state of peacefulness; serenity: *Nothing could disturb the calm of her repose.* **2** at sea, a time or condition of no wind; doldrums: *the calm before the storm.* — *adj.* peaceful: *a calm and cool reaction.* — *v.* make or become quiet: *We tried to calm her; to calm her fears; Will you **calm down** and stop screaming?* — **calm·ly** *adv.;* **calm·ness** *n.*

cal·o·rie (CAL·uh·ree) *n.* **ries 1** a unit for measuring heat energy. **2** the amount of energy produced by a food

when used up by the body: *food calories; A workman needs up to 6 000 calories a day; A boiled egg supplies about 80 calories; She **counts calories** (of everything she eats); Junk food is high in calories but they are empty calories with little nutritive value.* — **ca·lor·ic** (cuh·LOR·ic) *adj.* energy-producing: *the caloric value of foods.*

cal·u·met (CAL·yuh·met) *n. Cdn.* the Indian peace pipe as known in French Canada.

cal·um·ny (CAL·um·nee) *n.* **-nies** a malicious falsehood or accusation: *They heaped calumny on him.* — **ca·lum·ni·ous** (cuh·LUM·nee·us) *adj.* — **ca·lum·ni·ous·ly** *adv.*

calve (CAV) *v.* **calves, calved, calv·ing** bear a calf. — **calves** *pl.* of CALF.

Cal·vin·ism (CAL·vuh·niz·um) *n.* the doctrines of **John Calvin,** a French theologian, esp. predestination and salvation by grace. — **Cal·vin·ist** *n. & adj.* — **Cal·vin·is·tic** (-NIS·tic) *adj.*

calyces a *pl.* of CALYX.

ca·lyp·so (cuh·LIP·soh) *n.* **-sos** a type of West Indian folk song: *They danced to calypso rhythms.*

ca·lyx (CAY·lix, CAL·ix) *n.* **-lyx·es** or **-ly·ces** (-luh·seez) the outer ring of usually green, leaflike sepals covering a flower bud.

ca·ma·ra·de·rie (cam·uh·RAD·uh·ree) *n.* fellowship and loyalty among friends or comrades.

cam·ber (CAM·bur) *n.* **1** a slight upward arching, as of a road surface in the middle. **2** the adjustment of automobile wheels to make them closer together at the bottom. — *v.* to arch upward slightly.

Cam·bo·di·an (cam·BOH·dee·un) *n. & adj.* (a person) of or from the Southeast Asian country of **Cambodia.**

cam·boose (cam·BOOSE) *n. Cdn.* **1** formerly, the central open fireplace in log shanties used by lumbermen and voyageurs. **2** such a log shanty itself.

cam·cord·er (CAM·cor·dur) *n.* a camera-equipped videotape recorder for taking pictures and viewing them immediately afterwards.

came *pt.* of COME.

cam·el (CAM·ul) *n.* a domestic, cud-chewing beast of burden with a humped back and long neck: *the two-humped Bactrian camel; The Arabian camel has one hump.*

cam·el·back (CAM·ul·back) *n.* **1** the back of a camel: *We crossed the desert on camelback.* **2** a rubber compound used in retreading tires.

camel's hair *n.* a fabric made with camel's hair or a substitute: *The artist's **camel's-hair brush** is made of squirrel's-tail hair.*

Cam·em·bert (CAM·um·bare) *n.* a creamy, rich cheese of French origin.

cam·e·o (CAM·ee·oh) *n.* **-os 1** a small carving raised above its background, as on a layered gem, shell, medallion, etc. **2** in drama, television, or films, a brief appearance by a famous person: *a cameo role.* — *v.* **-os, -oed, -o·ing** portray or present in cameo.

cam·er·a (CAM·uh·ruh) *n.* an apparatus for taking photographs or motion pictures: *a TV camera; video camera; The **candid camera** shows people as they really are; She refused to be interviewed **on camera** (= live); an off-camera interview.*
— **in camera** in privacy.

cam·er·a·man (CAM·uh·ruh·man, ·mun) *n.* -men a TV or movie camera operator.

cam·i·sole (CAM·uh·sole) *n.* a woman's sleeveless undergarment covering the torso.

cam·ou·flage (CAM·uh·flahzh) *n.* **1** an appearance or disguise that imitates the surroundings. **2** materials for such a disguise. **3** any deceptive concealment.
— *v.* -flag·es, -flaged, -flag·ing to conceal by camouflage: *They camouflaged the tanks with saplings.*

camp *n.* **1** a group of rough and temporary shelters, esp. military or recreational, usually in the country; also, the members or location of such a group: *to pitch a camp; an army camp; an armed camp (of rioters); fishing camp; mining camp; a summer camp for children; trailer camp; We'll **break camp** (= pack up) and leave at dawn; adj.: a camp bed, chair.* **2** a side in a debate or fight: *He belongs to the opposite camp.* **3** *Slang.* something so exaggerated, unnatural, or outlandish as to be considered amusing: *high camp; low camp.*
— *adj. Slang.* outlandish or oversentimental in appeal: *camp art, clothes, fashions; dresses and oversized camp shirts.*
— *v.* make, shelter in, or live in a camp; also **camp out.**

cam·paign (cam·PAIN) *n.* an organized activity aimed at a specific goal: *an election campaign; fund-raising campaign; whispering campaign (of spreading slander); to organize, mount or launch, wage a campaign.*
— *v.* to conduct a campaign: *The candidate campaigned from door to door, for freedom, and against censorship.* — **cam·paign·er** *n.*

cam·per (CAM·pur) *n.* **1** one who lives in a camp, esp. a recreational camp. **2** a vehicle adapted for camping: *a camper truck.*

camp·fire *n.* **1** an open fire at a camp. **2** the gathering or meeting held around it.

camp follower *n.* an unofficial member of a party; hanger-on.

camp·ground *n.* a camping area, often public, with facilities provided.

cam·phor (CAM·fur) *n.* an aromatic, medicinal gum obtained from an evergreen tree of the laurel family.

cam·phor·at·ed (CAM·fuh·ray·tid) *adj.* treated with camphor: *camphorated oil.*

camp meeting *n.* an evangelistic meeting held outdoors and lasting several days.

camp·o·ree (cam·puh·REE) *n.* a regional assembly or outing of Scouts or Guides; cf. JAMBOREE.

camp robber *n. Cdn.* same as CANADA JAY.

camp·site *n.* a place fit or prepared for a camp.

camp·stool *n.* a portable, folding stool.

cam·pus (CAM·pus) *n.* -pus·es the land and buildings of an educational institution: *the university campus; Some students live on campus; off-campus activities.*

camp·y *adj.* **camp·i·er, -i·est** *Slang.* interesting because exaggerated or unusual: *campy acting, fun; campy pink flamingo statues.*

can *auxiliary v., pt.* **could** (COOD, short "OO") [indicating] **1** ability: *He can swim; He can be nasty at times.* **2** likelihood: *What could have happened to him?* **3** capacity or permission; may: *I can not accept that cheque; You can go now.*
— *v.* **cans, canned, can·ning 1** preserve in cans or jars: *We can tomatoes; a jar of canned preserves.* **2** *Slang.* fire from a job. **3** *Slang.* stop: *Can that chatter!*
— *n.* **1** a metal container or what it contains: *garbage can; milk can; tin can; a can of peas.* **2** *Slang.* jail. **3** *Slang.* toilet.

Can·a·da (CAN·uh·duh) *n.* **1** a Canada Savings Bond. **2** formerly, Upper or Lower Canada. **3** a Canada goose: *There's a flock of Canadas going south.*

Canada Day *n.* a national holiday on July 1 to mark the anniversary of the establishment of the Dominion of Canada in 1867; formerly **Dominion Day.**

Canada goose *n.* a wild goose with a black head and neck, seen migrating south from Canada for the winter.

Canada jay *n.* a grey-feathered jay with a crestless head noted for stealing food and camp refuse; also known as "camp robber," "lumberjack," "moose bird," etc.

Ca·na·di·an (cuh·NAY·dee·un) *n. & adj.* (a person) of or from Canada: *He's Canadian by birth, not a naturalized Canadian; Both are Canadian citizens; a **New Canadian** who has recently come to Canada as a landed immigrant.*

Ca·na·di·a·na (cuh·NAY·dee·AN·uh) *n.pl.* things of Canadian cultural interest, as art, books, furniture, etc.: *a Canadiana collection, museum.*

Canadian bacon same as BACK BACON.

Canadian English *n.* the English language as used in Canada, esp. as distinguished from British and American English.

Canadian football *n.* the Canadian version of North American football with 12 players on each side instead of 11 and played on a field of different size from American football.

Canadian French *n.* the French language as used in Quebec and elsewhere in Canada and distinguished from the French spoken in Europe.

Ca·na·di·an·ism (cuh·NAY·dee·uh·niz·um) *n.* **1** a word, pronunciation, usage, or custom distinctive of Canada. **2** devotion to Canada and its customs, traditions, etc.: *His Canadianism cannot be questioned.* **3** the state of being distinctively Canadian: *Canadianism is tied to national unity.*

Ca·na·di·an·ist (cuh·NAY·dee·uh·nist) *n.* a specialist in Canadian studies or Canadiana.

Ca·na·di·an·ize (cuh·NAY·dee·uh·nize) *v.* **-iz·es, -ized, -iz·ing** make Canadian in character, customs, ownership, etc.: *Immigrants become Canadianized over the years; to Canadianize industries, textbooks.*

Ca·na·di·en (cuh·nay·dee·EN) *n.* a French Canadian;

fem. **Ca·na·di·enne** (cuh·nay·dee·EN).

ca·nal (cuh·NAL) *n.* 1 an artificial waterway: *a shipping canal; an irrigation canal.* 2 a duct or passage in the body: *the alimentary canal.*

ca·nal·boat (cuh·NAL·boat) *n.* a barge for use on canals.

ca·nal·ize (cuh·NAL·ize, CAN·uh·lize) *v.* **-iz·es, -ized, -iz·ing** 1 build a canal or canals through an area. 2 direct something into or provide with a channel or outlet: *to canalize activities, energies, feelings.* — **ca·nal·i·za·tion** (-luh·ZAY·shun) *n.*

ca·na·pé (CAN·uh·pee) *n.* a cracker or piece of toast, with a tasty topping, forming an appetizer: *anchovy canapés.*

ca·nard (cuh·NARD) *n.* a false rumour spread purposely; hoax.

ca·nar·y (cuh·NAIR·ee) *n.* **-nar·ies** 1 a small, bright yellow songbird of the finch family. 2 a bright yellow; *adj.: a canary dress.*

can·cel (CAN·sul) *v.* **-cels, -celled** or **-celed, -cel·ling** or **-cel·ing** 1 cross out or delete: *to cancel a word; to cancel a postage stamp (to prevent re-use); to cancel a cheque (to make it invalid).* 2 annul or withdraw: *to cancel an appointment, a game, meeting, order, reservation, show, subscription, trip.* 3 in arithmetic, to remove a common element from both parts of an equation or fraction. 4 neutralize or counterbalance: *The two arguments* **cancel each other out.**
— *n.* a crossing out, annulment, or something cancelled.
— **can·cel·la·tion** (-LAY·shun) *n.: The cancellation made the cheque nonnegotiable.*

can·cer (CAN·sur) *n.* a malignant growth in a body part or the disease that causes it: *Smoking may lead to cancer of the lungs; One may develop lung cancer; She has breast cancer; inoperable cancer; terminal cancer; Electoral corruption is a cancer* (= growing evil) *in the body politic.* — **can·cer·ous** *adj.: a cancerous growth.*

can·de·la·brum (can·duh·LAH·brum) *n.* a usually ornamental candlestick with several branches; also **can·de·la·bra** (-bruh), **-bras.**

can·did *adj.* 1 truthful and sincere: *He was candid with me; candid about what he knew of the case; People don't always appreciate candid criticism.* 2 informal; unposed: *a few candid shots; The* **candid camera** *(used for quick informal pictures) never lies.*
— **can·did·ly** *adv.*

can·di·da·cy (CAN·duh·duh·see) *n.* the act or condition of being a candidate: *He announced his candidacy; She withdrew her candidacy; His candidacy was unopposed.*

can·di·date (CAN·duh·date, -dit) *n.* 1 one who competes for a position: *an electoral candidate; a candidate for mayor.* 2 one who is eligible: *a Ph.D. candidate; a candidate for admission to the school.*

can·died (CAN·deed) *adj.* 1 encrusted or cooked with sugar: *candied apples, dates, fruit.* 2 sweet or flattering: *candied words.*

can·dle (CAN·dul) *n.* a usually cylindrical mass of tallow, wax, etc. with a wick of fibre through it, which is burned for the light of its flame: *A candle is lit.*
— **burn the candle at both ends** work too hard without getting enough rest.

can·dle·light (CAN·dul·lite) *n.* light shed by a candle: *to dine by candlelight.*

can·dle·pow·er (CAN·dul·pow·ur) *n.* light intensity, as measured by a standard unit called a "candle."

can·dle·stick (CAN·dul·stick) *n.* a holder for a single candle.

can-do (CAN·doo) *adj. Informal.* willing and able to carry out a task: *a can-do attitude, image, person, spirit, style.*

can·dour or **can·dor** (CAN·dur) *n.* the quality of being candid: *the candour of a child's expression; She spoke with complete candour; Her candour was disarming.*

Can-du or **CANDU** (CAN·doo) *n. Cdn.* the Canadian heavy-water system for generating nuclear energy; *adj.: the Candu design, reactor, system.*

can·dy (CAN·dee) *n.* **-dies** (-deez) a sweet food made in various shapes with fruit, nuts, flavouring, etc.: **Cotton candy** or **candy floss** is made of spun sugar.
— *v.* **-dies, -died, -dy·ing** encrust with sugar: *a recipe for candying apples.*

candy cane *n.* a red-striped Christmastime peppermint candy in the shape of a walking stick with a curved handle.

candy-striped *adj.* with thin, bright-coloured stripes on a plain, usually white background.

candy striper *n.* a young volunteer nursing assistant.

cane *n.* 1 a thin, woody, usually flexible stem of a grass like sugar cane and bamboo, of a palm like rattan, or of other plants like the raspberry. 2 such a plant itself. 3 material, esp. rattan, woven into chairs, baskets, etc. 4 a walking stick. 5 a rod for flogging.
— *v.* **canes, caned, can·ing** 1 make or repair with cane. 2 flog.

cane sugar *n.* sugar made from sugar cane.

can·ine (CAY·nine) *adj.* having to do with the group of animals that includes dogs, jackals, wolves, and foxes: *the canine devotion of a pet dog.*
— *n.* 1 a dog. 2 one of the four sharp teeth between the incisors and pre-molars; also **canine tooth.**

can·is·ter (CAN·is·tur) *n.* 1 light container of metal, plastic, etc. with a lid, used for storing tea, flour, crackers, etc. 2 a cylindrical projectile containing shot, tear gas, etc. 3 the tank or container of a vacuum cleaner. 4 the boxlike filtering part of a gas mask.

can·ker (CANK·ur) *n.* 1 a disease that eats away tissue, as a rot or rust in plants. 2 a small sore in the mouth, or **canker sore.** 3 a plant-eating insect larva, or **can·ker·worm.** — **can·ker·ous** *adj.*

Can-Lit (CAN·lit) *n. Informal.* Canadian literature: *a CanLit course, program.*

can·na·bis (CAN·uh·bis) *n.* 1 the dried flowering tops of the female hemp plant, the source of marijuana and hashish. 2 marijuana. 3 the plant itself.

canned *pt. & pp.* of CAN: *canned beef, food, fruit, goods.*
— *adj.* recorded for reproduction: *canned applause, laughter, music; a newspaper with many cartoons, crossword puzzles, and such canned features.*

can·ner (CAN·ur) *n.* one that cans: *home canners; a pressure canner.*

can·ner·y (CAN·uh·ree) *n.* **can·ner·ies** a canning factory.

can·ni·bal (CAN·uh·bul) *n.* **1** one who eats human flesh: *a cannibal tribe.* **2** an animal, as a spider, that feeds on its own kind. **3** a brutal savage. — **can·ni·bal·ism** *n.*
— **can·ni·bal·is·tic** (-buh·LIS·tic) *adj.*

can·ni·bal·ize (CAN·uh·buh·lize) *v.* **-iz·es, -ized, -iz·ing** tear up old equipment, machines, etc. for parts to repair other equipment with: *He cannibalized a lawn mower and a motorbike to build his go-cart.*

can·nis·ter (CAN·is·tur) *n.* same as CANISTER.

can·non (CAN·un) *n.* **-nons** or **-non** a large, heavy gun mounted on a platform or carriage which fires a heavy metal shot: *to load and fire a cannon.*

can·non·ade (can·uh·NADE) *n.* a prolonged volley of cannon fire. Also *v.* **-ades, -ad·ed, -ad·ing.**

can·non·ball (CAN·un·ball) *n.* a heavy metal ball used as a cannon shot.
— *v. Informal.* move quickly and with great force.

can·non·eer (can·uh·NEER) *n.* one who tends and fires cannon.

cannon fodder *n.* soldiers considered merely as expendable war materiel.

can·not (CAN·ot, cuh·NOT) [the commoner and less emphatic form of "can not"] can not: *I cannot sing; I cannot but* (= must) *admire his singing.*

can·ny (CAN·ee) *adj.* **can·ni·er, can·ni·est 1** shrewd or cunning: *a canny businessman, politician, trader.* **2** thrifty: *a canny landlord.* — **can·ni·ly** *adv.*

ca·noe (cuh·NOO) *n.* **-noes** a slender boat with pointed ends, usually moved by paddles: *a birchbark canoe.*
— *v.* **-noes, -noed, -noe·ing** travel or transport in a canoe: *He canoed the load across the bay.*

ca·noe·ist (cuh·NOO·ist) *n.* one who paddles a canoe.

ca·noe·man (cuh·NOO·mun) *n. Cdn.* a canoeist or voyageur.

can of worms *n. Informal.* a source of trouble; Pandora's box.

ca·no·la (cuh·NOH·luh) *n. Cdn.* **1** a variety of the rape plant, used as fodder and for its oil; formerly, rape, rapeseed. **2** the oil or meal prepared from it.

can·on (CAN·un) *n.* **1** a principle or rule of behaviour: *This goes against the canons of good taste, decency.* **2** a law or rule of the church: *Nearly 1 800 canons comprise the Code of Canon Law.* **3** a list of items accepted as genuine and essential to a body of works: *to establish the canon of Shakespeare's works; books that are outside the canon of the Bible; the Confucian canon.* **4** a cleric serving in a cathedral. **5** a form of music, as a round, involving two or more parts or voices.

ca·ñon (CAN·yun) *n.* same as CANYON.

ca·non·i·cal (cuh·NON·uh·cul) *adj.* **1** accepted or authoritative: *the canonical books of the Bible.* **2** according to canon law. — **ca·non·i·cal·ly** *adv.*

can·on·ize (CAN·uh·nize) *v.* **-iz·es, -ized, -iz·ing** in the Catholic Church, declare officially as a saint in heaven. — **can·on·iz·a·tion** (-nuh·ZAY·shun) *n.*

canon law *n.* a body of laws and regulations of the Catholic Church.

can·o·py (CAN·uh·pee) *n.* **-pies** (-peez) an overhanging cover, esp. for ornamentation or protection: *A canopy is used over a four-poster bed; a canopy of trees; the canopy* (= cockpit cover) *of an airplane.*
— *v.* **-pies, -pied, -py·ing** cover with a canopy: *a canopied entrance.*

canst [old use] the form of CAN used with "thou."

cant *n.* **1** language that is peculiar or secretive: *thieves' cant* (= argot); *lawyer's cant* (= jargon). **2** empty, hypocritical, conventional speech: *all this cant about virtue; v.: They will cant about charity but won't give a penny.* **3** a sloping or angled surface, edge, or position; slant.

can't (CANT) cannot.

can·ta·loupe or **can·ta·loup** (CAN·tuh·lope) *n.* a small, orange-fleshed muskmelon with a hard, ribbed rind.

can·tan·ker·ous (can·TANK·uh·rus) *adj.* quarrelsome or bad-tempered: *a cantankerous old man.*

can·ta·ta (cun·TAH·tah) *n.* a piece of choral music with solos and accompaniment, usually dramatic, though not acted.

can·teen (can·TEEN) *n.* **1** a place that sells refreshments and small provisions: *a factory canteen.* **2** a recreation centre, esp. at a military base. **3** a small metal flask for liquids, usually canvas-covered.

can·ter (CAN·tur) *n.* a gentle gallop: *He rode at a canter; v.: The horse cantered along.*

cant-hook *n. Cdn.* a pole with a jawlike hook attached to its side, used to move floating logs.

can·ti·cle (CAN·tuh·cul) *n.* a song or chant, usually from the Bible, used in a church service.

can·ti·le·ver (CAN·tuh·lee·vur) *n.* a projecting structure or support fastened only at one end, as under a balcony or at either end of a bridge.

cantilever bridge *n.* a bridge built of cantilevers at either end.

can·to (CAN·toh) *n.* **-tos** a major division of a long poem.

can·ton (CAN·tun) *n.* **1** an administrative division, as in France, Quebec, etc. **2** a territorial division, esp. a state in Switzerland.
— *v.* **1** divide or apportion. **2** quarter troops in lodgings.

Can·ton·ese (can-tuh·NEEZ) *n.* **1** *sing. & pl.* a person of or from Canton, China. **2** the regional language of Canton.
— *adj.: the Cantonese dialect; a Cantonese restaurant.*

can·ton·ment (can-TONE·munt, can-TON·munt – "TON" *rhymes with* "ON") *n.* **1** the billeting of troops. **2** a temporary housing for troops.

can·tor (CAN·tur) *n.* a solo or lead singer in a church or synagogue.

Ca·nuck (cuh·NUCK) *n. & adj. Cdn. Slang.* [sometimes offensive or patronizing in non-Canadian use] Canadian: *my Canuck friend; a cute young Canuck; "Johnny Canuck" is supposed to personify Canada.*

can·vas (CAN·vus) *n.* **1** a strong, coarsely woven cloth used for sails, tents, etc. **2** something made using canvas, as an oil painting on canvas.
— **under canvas 1** with sails spread. **2** in tents.
— *adj.* made of canvas: *canvas deck shoes.*
— *v.* **-vas·es, -vased, -vas·ing** cover with canvas.

can·vass (CAN·vus) *v.* **1** go about asking for something; solicit: *to canvass donations, opinions, orders, votes; She's canvassing for the Heart Fund; He has canvassed everyone in sight and every house on this street.*
2 examine thoroughly or consider in detail: *to canvass ballots after votes are cast.*
— *n.* a canvassing: *a door-to-door canvass for the election candidate; a complete canvass* (= examination) *of the proposal.* — **can·vass·er** *n.*

can·yon (CAN·yun) *n.* a deep narrow valley with high, sheer walls; gorge.

cap *n.* **1** a soft, light head-covering: *a baseball cap; bathing cap; nurse's cap; skull cap; The graduates came to the ceremonies in cap* (= mortarboard) *and gown; She put on her thinking cap* (= started thinking); *He came to me cap in hand* (= humbly). **2** any covering, lid, or topmost part: *bottle caps; mushroom caps; The budget places a cap* (= upper limit) *on expenditures.*
3 percussion cap, esp. a small explosive charge in a paper capsule for use in a toy gun called a **cap pistol** or **cap gun.**
— *v.* **caps, capped, cap·ping 1** place a cap on something; cover. **2** improve on something; outdo: *He can cap that trick.*

ca·pa·bil·i·ty (cay-puh·BIL·uh·tee) *n.* **-ties** ability or potential: *She demonstrated her capabilities on the very first day; the capability to do a good job; a job that is within and not beyond her capabilities; the nuclear capability of the superpowers.*

ca·pa·ble (CAY·puh·bul) *adj.* competent: *a capable manager; He did a capable job.*
— **capable of** with the potential for something: *He is quite capable of winning the scholarship; a problem that is capable of solution.* — **ca·pa·bly** *adv.*

ca·pa·cious (cuh·PAY·shus) *adj.* able to hold a great deal: *a capacious dining room.*
— **ca·pa·cious·ly** *adv.;* **ca·pa·cious·ness** *n.*

ca·pac·i·ty (cuh·PAS·uh·tee) *n.* **-ties 1** the ability to receive, hold, absorb, produce, etc.: *your earning capacity; a woman of great mental capacity; her capacity for learning; a theatre with a large seating capacity; a storage capacity of 30 tons; The theatre was filled **to capacity*** (= to the limit); *A capacity crowd filled the theatre; a factory operating at peak capacity; He's working at his full capacity.* **2** position or role: *in an advisory capacity; He was acting in his official capacity; in his capacity as president.*

ca·par·i·son (cuh·PAIR·uh·sun) *n.* a decorative covering for a horse and its harness; rich finery.
— *v.* cover with rich finery: *The trees were caparisoned in autumn gold.*

cape *n.* **1** a full, sleeveless outer garment hanging from the shoulders. **2** a point of land projecting into a sea, lake, etc., as the Cape of Good Hope.

cape·lin (CAPE·lin) *n.* a small fish of the smelt family.

ca·per (CAY·pur) *n.* **1** a light playful jump. **2** a prank or trick: *a childish caper; the 1980 Canadian caper of rescuing Americans from Iran.* **3** *Slang.* a crime.
— **cut a caper** or **capers** to frolic about; also, play a prank: *Clowns like to cut capers before a crowd.*
— *v.* leap about or frolic: *a lamb capering across the meadow.*

cap·ful *n.* the amount that a bottle cap can hold.

cap gun See CAP, *n. 3.*

cap·il·lar·y (CAP·uh·lair·ee, cuh·PIL·uh·ree) *adj.* having a small bore; hairlike: *a capillary tube.*
— *n., pl.* **-il·lar·ies** a capillary tube, esp. any of the tiny blood vessels linking the arteries to the veins.

cap·i·tal (CAP·uh·tul) *adj.* **1** most important or serious: *an act of capital folly; a capital offence* (= murder); *to impose capital punishment* (= death penalty). **2** excellent: *a capital meal.*
— *n.* **1** capital city: *municipal, national, provincial capitals; a world capital such as Tokyo or New York; the crime capital* (= main centre of crime) *of North America.* **2** capital letter. **3** the often ornate top of a pilaster or column. **4** material or financial assets engaged in or available for business expenditure: *to invest, raise, tie up, withdraw capital; The Government made political capital* (= gain) *out of the scandal involving the Opposition; the working capital* (for running a business). **5** capitalists or investors collectively: *Much capital left Quebec during the 1970s.*
— **cap·i·tal·ly** *adv.*

capital city *n.* chief city, esp. a governmental centre.

capital goods *n. pl.* goods such as machinery and equipment used in the production of other goods.

capital-intensive *adj.* requiring the investment of capital more than of labour: *Atomic power plants are capital-intensive whereas coal-burning plants are labour-intensive.*

cap·i·tal·ism (CAP·uh·tuh·liz·um) *n.* an economic system with free markets and private ownership of capital.

cap·i·tal·ist (CAP·uh·tuh·list) *n.* **1** a person who owns invested capital. **2** one who supports capitalism. — **cap·i·tal·is·tic** (-tuh·LIS·tic) *adj.*

cap·i·tal·ize (CAP·uh·tuh·lize) *v.* **-iz·es, -ized, -iz·ing 1** write with or as a capital letter: *Names are capitalized.* **2** take advantage of or profit from something: *to capitalize on someone else's bad luck.* **3** supply capital for something: *to capitalize a business venture.*

capital letter *n.* a large letter, as A, B, or C.

capital ship *n.* a warship of the highest rank.

capital stock *n.* the total amount of capital invested in a corporation issued as shares.

cap·i·ta·tion (cap·uh·TAY·shun) *n.* a per-capita tax or levy.

cap·i·tol (CAP·uh·tul) *n.* a legislature building in the U.S.

ca·pit·u·late (cuh·PICH·uh·late) *v.* **-lates, -lat·ed, -lat·ing** surrender or yield: *He finally capitulated to their demands.* — **cap·i·tu·la·tion** (-LAY·shun) *n.*

cap·let (CAP·lit) *n.* a coated medicine tablet that is oval-shaped like a capsule.

cap·lin (CAP·lin) *n.* same as CAPELIN.

ca·pon (CAY·pon, *rhyme:* on) *n.* a rooster, castrated and fattened for eating.

ca·pote (cuh·POTE) *n.* a hooded cloak or cape.

cap pistol See CAP, *n. 3.*

ca·price (cuh·PREECE) *n.* a change of mind without any apparent reason; whim; fickleness: *He did it merely out of caprice; It was pure caprice on his part.* — **ca·pri·ci·ous** (cuh·PRISH·us) *adj.: a capricious lover; capricious weather.* — **ca·pri·ci·ous·ly** *adv.;* **ca·pri·ci·ous·ness** *n.*

cap·si·cum (CAP·suh·cum) *n.* a shrubby plant that bears hot or sweet peppers.

cap·size (CAP·size) *v.* **-siz·es, -sized, -siz·ing** overturn or upset: *The canoe capsized in the storm.*

cap·stan (CAP·stun) *n.* **1** an upright rotating cylinder on which a cable, as in lifting weights, is wound. **2** a similar spindle that moves the tape in a tape recorder at a constant speed.

cap·su·lar (CAP·suh·lur) *adj.* in, of, or like a capsule.

cap·sul·ate (CAP·suh·late) or **cap·sul·at·ed** (-lay·tid) *adj.* enclosed in a capsule.

cap·sule (CAP·sul, -sule) *n.* **1** an enclosed protective covering, as for seeds, spores, oral doses of medicine, etc. **2** a separable enclosure for people, instruments, etc. in an airplane or rocket: *The space capsule almost burned on re-entry; A time capsule contains items typical of the time when it is deposited for future discovery.* — *v.* **-sules, -suled, -sul·ing** capsulize. — *adj.* brief and concise: *a capsule account, biography, course, history, news report.*

cap·sul·ize (CAP·suh·lize) *v.* **-iz·es, -ized, -iz·ing 1** put into a capsule. **2** express concisely: *capsulized news.*

cap·tain (CAP·tin) *n.* **1** a leader: *the captain of the baseball team; a bell captain; captains* (= outstanding people) *of industry.* **2** a military officer ranking just below major. **3** a naval officer ranking just below commodore or rear admiral. **4** the commander of a ship, fortress, garrison, etc. **5** the chief pilot of an airliner. — *v.* lead: *He captained the squad all season.* — **cap·tain·cy** (-see) *n.* **-cies.** — **cap·tain·ship** *n.*

cap·tion (CAP·shun) *n.* **1** a brief legend under a picture or cartoon. **2** a subtitle in a movie. **3** a heading or title. — *v.* put a caption on something: *The artist captions his own cartoons.*

cap·tious (CAP·shus) *adj.* **1** overly critical; carping. **2** designed to confuse and trap; sophistical: *captious questions.* — **cap·tious·ly** *adv.;* **cap·tious·ness** *n.*

cap·ti·vate (CAP·tuh·vate) *v.* **-vates, -vat·ed, -vat·ing** enthrall or charm: *He was captivated by her beauty.* — **cap·ti·va·tion** (-VAY·shun) *n.*

cap·tive (CAP·tiv) *n.* **1** one who is confined against his will, esp. a prisoner of war. **2** one who is captivated. — *adj.* **1** captured and confined: *a captive bird; The prisoner hated his captive condition; He was taken and held captive for many years.* **2** forced, as by circumstances: *a captive audience, market.* — **cap·tiv·i·ty** (cap·TIV·uh·tee) *n.*

cap·tor (CAP·tur) *n.* one who captures: *the captor and his captives.*

cap·ture (CAP·chur) *v.* **-tures, -tured, -tur·ing 1** seize by force or other means: *Spiders trap and then capture insects; a captured city; Her performance captured our attention; The 1980 Winter Olympics captured Canada's imagination.* **2** record permanently: *his face as captured on film; the capturing of computer data by keyboarding, scanning, etc.* — *n.* the act of capturing or one that has been captured.

Cap·u·chin (CAP·yoo·chin) *n.* **1** a Franciscan friar distinguished by a special hood. **2 capuchin** a type of South American monkey with hair on its crown resembling a monk's hood.

car *n.* **1** an automobile: *a getaway car; police car; sports car;* **armoured car** (= closed truck carrying money); *to break in a new car; to jack up, road-test, tune up a car; adj.: a car bed for infants; a car bomb (planted by terrorists); a car coat (3·4 of full length).* **2** a wheeled vehicle on rails: *a cattle car; dining car; railway car.* **3** a compartment for passengers, freight, etc. in an elevator, cable car, dirigible, etc.

ca·rafe (cuh·RAF) *n.* a bottle for serving wine, water, coffee, etc.

car·a·mel (CAIR·uh·mul) *n.* **1** burnt sugar that is dark and bitter, used for colouring and flavouring. **2** a rich, chewy candy.

car·a·pace (CAIR·uh·pace) *n.* a bony protective shell, as of a turtle, lobster, etc.

car·at (CAIR·ut) *n.* **1** same as KARAT. **2** a unit of weight of gems, equal to 200 mg.

car·a·van (CAIR·uh·van) *n.* **1** a party of traders, pilgrims, etc. travelling together for safety; hence, a line of vehicles: *a circus caravan.* **2** a van.

car·a·van·sa·ry (cair·uh·VAN·suh·ree) *n.* **-ries** an inn for caravans; also **car·a·van·se·rai** (-rye, -ray), **-rais.**

car·a·vel (CAIR·uh·vel) *n.* a small sailing ship of the 15th and 16th centuries with a high stern and broad bow.

car·a·way (CAIR·uh·way) *n.* the aromatic seeds of a parsleylike herb used for seasoning; also, the herb.

car·bine (CAR·been, -bine) *n.* a light rifle with a short barrel.

car·bo·hy·drate (car·boh·HYE·drate) *n.* a compound of carbon, oxygen, and hydrogen, as cellulose, starch, and sugar.

car·bon (CAR·bun) *n.* **1** the common element of all organic compounds, esp. coal, petroleum, and other fuels: *Diamond is pure carbon.* **2** a carbon paper or a carbon copy.

car·bon·ate (CAR·buh·nate) *v.* **-ates, -at·ed, -at·ing** mix with carbon dioxide: *Soda water is carbonated; a carbonated drink.* — **car·bon·a·tion** (-NAY·shun) *n.*

carbon black *n.* a fine powdered carbon used as a pigment in ink.

carbon copy *n.* **1** a copy of a document made using carbon paper. **2** something very similar to its original: *a mere carbon copy of the foreign edition;* **carbon-copy** *v.*

carbon dioxide *n.* a heavy, odourless, colourless, incombustible gas produced by fermentation, combustion, and respiration.

carbon monoxide *n.* a light, odourless, colourless, combustible, very poisonous gas, as produced by automobile engines.

carbon paper *n.* a thin sheet coated on one side with a carbon-based pigment and inserted between sheets of paper for copying what is being written or typed.

car·bun·cle (CAR·bung·cul) *n.* **1** a painful inflammation under the skin which produces pus. **2** a red garnet.

car·bu·ret·or (CAR·buh·ray·tur) *n.* in internal combustion engines, a device which combines air and fuel for proper burning.

car·ca·jou (CAR·cuh·zhoo) *n. Cdn.* a wolverine.

car·cass (CAR·cus) *n.* **1** an animal corpse, esp. one dressed for use as meat. **2** *Informal.* the human body. **3** useless remains: *the carcass of a wrecked car.*

car·cin·o·gen (car·SIN·uh·jun) *n.* a cancer-causing substance. — **car·ci·no·gen·ic** (CAR·sin·oh·JEN·ic) *adj.*

card *n.* **1** a small, usually stiff, rectangular piece of paper used for many purposes: *a business card; a calling card, or visiting card; a plastic credit card for charging purchases to an account; a get-well card; a greeting card for a birthday or Christmas; an identity card; index cards for a card file; a membership card; playing card; a report card showing a pupil's progress at school; score card.* **2 cards** *pl.* any game using playing cards. **3** a program at an event, esp. sports. **4** *Informal.* a witty or eccentric person. **5** a computer's internal plug-in circuit board. **6** a wire brush for combing and cleaning unspun

cotton or wool; *v.: to card wool;* **card·er** *n.* — **in the cards** likely to happen; probable.

card·board *n. & adj.* a thick board made of several layers of paper pulp; *adj.: a cardboard box; a cardboard* (= stereotyped) *character.*

card-carrying *adj.* **1** officially registered: *a card-carrying Communist.* **2** *Informal.* identifiable as such: *a card-carrying Nazi, neurotic, pacifist.*

card catalogue or **card catalog** *n.* a file usually made on index cards and arranged in alphabetical order, esp. one for books; also **card file.**

car·di·ac (CAR·dee·ac) *adj.* having to do with the heart or heart disease: *a cardiac arrest, condition, disease, shock, surgeon, unit.*

car·di·gan (CAR·duh·gun) *n.* a sweater or knitted jacket that opens down the front.

car·di·nal (CAR·duh·nul) *n.* **1** a dignitary of the Roman Catholic Church ranking next below the pope. **2** a crested red finch of North America. **3** a bright red. — *adj.* principal: *a cardinal goal, principle;* the **cardinal numbers** (= 1, 2, 3, etc. as opposed to the ordinals, 1st, 2nd, 3rd, etc.); *North, South, East, and West are the four* **cardinal points** *of the compass; The four* **cardinal virtues** *are fortitude, justice, prudence, and temperance.*

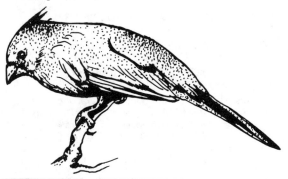

card index *n.* same as CARD CATALOGUE.

car·di·o·gram (CAR·dee·uh·gram) *n.* same as ELECTROCARDIOGRAM.

car·di·o·lo·gy (car·dee·OL·uh·jee) *n.* the study of the heart, its diseases, and their treatment. — **car·di·ol·o·gist** *n.*

car·di·o·pul·mo·nar·y (CAR·dee·oh·PUL·muh·nair·ee) *adj.* having to do with the heart and lungs: *A heart-attack victim is given* **cardiopulmonary resuscitation** *(CPR) to restore breathing and circulation.*

card·sharp, card·sharp·er or **card shark** *n. Informal.* one skilled in winning card games by cheating.

care *n.* **1** worry or anxiety: *to be free from care.* **2** supervision: *patients under a doctor's care; the tender loving care of parents; children left in our care; entrusted to the care of foster parents; child care; children in need of day care; a day care centre; extended care for the elderly; a hospital's intensive care unit.* **3** attention or caution: *to exercise care; Handle with care; with the utmost care;* **Take care** *to fasten your seat belt.* **4** a cause of anxiety; responsibility: *a life*

that is free from cares and worries.
— *v.* **cares, cared, car·ing 1** feel anxiety, interest, or liking: *Who cares? I care about the future; a warm and* **caring** *person.* **2** be concerned: *I could or couldn't care less* (= I don't care); *You can do what you like,* **for all I care** (= I don't care).
— **care for 1** take care of someone: *Nurses care for the sick.* **2** desire: *Do you care for some coffee?* **3** like or want: *I don't care for it at all.*
— **(in) care of** at the address of someone.
— **take care of** look after someone: *Parents take care of children.*

ca·reen (cuh·REEN) *v.* **1** tip a ship to one side, esp. for cleaning; tilt or lean. **2** rush headlong unsteadily: *The car careened downhill and hit a curb.*

ca·reer (cuh·REER) *n.* **1** a progression through life or a special period or aspect of it: *your business career; school career; He made or carved out a career for himself in the army; He retired at 65 after a distinguished or brilliant career in the army; She had a chequered career; a successful career as a diplomat;* **adj.**: *a* **career decision** *(that may affect one's career); a* **career diplomat** (= a diplomat all through his career); *a* **career girl** *or* **woman** *(who continues in her profession after marriage).* **2** speed: *The racing car broke down* **in full career** (= at full speed).
— *v.* move swiftly; hurtle.

care·free *adj.* without care or worry: *She leads a carefree life.*

care·ful *adj.* using care: *Be careful near the fire; Be careful not to touch it; He did a careful job; She's very careful about details; Be extremely careful with explosives.* — **care·ful·ly** *adv.;* **care·ful·ness** *n.*

care·less (CARE·lus) *adj.* **1** showing lack of care: *a careless error, observation, worker; He was quite rash and careless about consequences; It was careless of him to drive without buckling up.* **2** carefree or effortless: *an easy, careless grace.*
— **care·less·ly** *adv.;* **care·less·ness** *n.*

ca·ress (cuh·RES) *n.* **1** a loving touch, stroke, kiss, or hug. **2** a light touch: *the caress of a gentle breeze.*
— *v.* touch lovingly or lightly: *They caressed each other; A warm breeze caressed her cheek.* — **ca·ress·ing·ly** *adv.*

car·et (CAIR·ut) *n.* the mark [ ] used to show where something is to be inserted in written or printed matter.

care·tak·er (CAIR·tay·kur) *n.* one hired to oversee and maintain property, buildings, etc., often in the owner's absence.
— *adj.* temporary: *a caretaker government.*

care·worn *adj.* marked by grief or anxiety: *a haggard, careworn face.*

car·fare *n.* the price of a bus or streetcar ride.

car·go *n.* **-gos** or **-goes** the goods loaded in a ship, airplane, truck, etc.: *to carry, haul, load, take on cargo;* **adj.**: *a cargo liner, plane, ship.*

car·goed (CAR·gode) *adj.* loaded: *ships cargoed with gold.*

car·hop *n.* one who waits on cars at a drive-in restaurant.

Car·ib·be·an (cair·uh·BEE·un) *adj.* having to do with the region between the West Indies and Central and South America: *the Caribbean Sea; a Caribbean vacation (on one of the Caribbean islands).*
— *n.* the Caribbean Sea.

car·i·bou (CAIR·uh·boo) *n.* a large North American deer similar to the reindeer.

car·i·ca·ture (CAIR·uh·cuh·choor, -chur) *n.* an exaggerated or distorted picture or writing that makes fun of one's peculiarities: *"Don Quixote" is a caricature of the romantic hero.*
— *v.* **-tures, -tured, -tur·ing** represent in caricature: *The politician was caricatured in the paper as a clown.*
— **car·i·ca·tur·ist** (CAIR·uh·cuh·CHOOR·ist, -cuh·chuh·rist) *n.*

car·ies (CAIR·eez) *n.* decay affecting bones or teeth.

car·il·lon (CAIR·uh·lon, *rhyme:* on) *n.* a set of tuned bells played by means of a keyboard; also, the music played. — **car·il·lon·er** (-luh·nur) or **car·il·lon·neur** (-luh·NUR) *n.*

car·i·ole or **car·ri·ole** (CAIR·ee·ole) *n.* **1** a small horse-drawn carriage. **2** a covered cart. **3** *Cdn.* a light open horse- or dog-drawn sleigh; also called "carryall." **4** *Cdn.* a dogsled that can carry a single passenger lying down.

car·load *n.* in shipping by rail, the amount that a freight car can hold.

car·nage (CAR·nij) *n.* massive killing.

car·nal (CAR·nul) *adj.* **1** sensual or fleshly: *Lust is carnal; He was charged with having* **carnal knowledge** *of* (= sex with) *a minor.* **2** worldly: *the pursuit of carnal pleasure; carnal pursuits.* — **car·nal·ly** *adv.*
— **car·nal·i·ty** (car·NAL·uh·tee) *n.*

car·na·tion (car·NAY·shun) *n.* **1** a cultivated herb with many-petalled red, purple, pink, yellow, or white flowers: *red carnations.* **2** the flower or its medium-red colour.

carney or **carnie** same as CARNY.

car·ni·val (CAR·nuh·vul) *n.* **1** the pre-Lent season of merrymaking or revelry; **adj.**: *a carnival atmosphere, dance; the carnival season, spirit; a charity ball with a carnival theme; Mardi Gras is carnival time in New Orleans; a carnival-style winter festival.* **2** a festival: *a carnival weekend get-together at a ski resort; a winter carnival complete with a carnival queen; The show is a carnival on ice; The Food Fair is a culinary carnival.* **3** a travelling outfit providing rides, games, etc. in public places.

car·ni·vore (CAR·nuh·vore) *n.* **1** a flesh-eating mammal, as a cat, dog, bear, or seal. **2** a plant that feeds on insects.

car·niv·or·ous (car·NIV·uh·rus) *adj.* flesh- or insect-eating: *a carnivorous animal, plant.*

car·ny, car·nie or **car·ney** (CAR·nee) *n.* **-nies** or **-neys** *Informal.* **1** a carnival or fair; **adj.**: *a carny midway, salesman, ride.* **2** a carnival worker; also, his argot or jargon: *The barker is talking carny.* — **adj.**: *popcorn, candied apples, and such carny food.*

car·ol (CAIR·ul) *n.* a joyous song, often devotional or

laudatory: *Christmas carols.*
— *v.* **car·ols, car·olled** or **car·oled, car·ol·ling** or **car·ol·ing 1** sing carols: *We used to go carolling on Christmas eve.* **2** sing joyously: *We could hear robins carolling to the spring.*

car·om (CAIR·um) *n.* **1** a hit and rebound. **2** in billiards, a shot where the cue ball rebounds from one ball to strike another.
— *v.* hit and rebound: *The truck caromed off the wall.*

ca·rot·id (cuh·ROT·id) *adj.* having to do with the two large arteries that carry blood via the neck to the head.
— *n.* either of these arteries, one on each side of the neck.

ca·rous·al (cuh·ROW·zul, "OW" as in "HOW") *n.* a noisy drinking party or spree; carouse.

ca·rouse (cuh·ROWZE) *v.* **-rous·es, -roused, -rous·ing** revel and drink heavily.
— *n.* a rowdy drinking party.

car·ou·sel or **car·rou·sel** (cair·uh·SEL) *n.* a merry-go-round.

carp *n.* an edible, large-scaled fish found in quiet, fresh waters.
— *v.* find fault pettily or captiously: *He's always carping at something or other; a carping critic with a carping tongue.*

car·pen·ter (CAR·pun·tur) *n.* a workman who builds and repairs wooden objects, as houses, ships, etc.; *v.: a well-carpentered house.* — **car·pen·try** (-tree) *n.*

car·pet (CAR·pit) *n.* a thick, heavy covering for floors and stairs: *The boss called her **on the carpet** (=reprimanded her) for her negligence; They rolled out the red carpet for (=gave a warm reception to) the visiting dignitary; a carpet of grass, leaves, snow.*
— *v.* cover with carpet: *a room carpeted with broadloom; wall-to-wall **carpeting** (=floor covering).*

car·pet·ing (CAR·pit·ing) *n.* carpet material; also, carpets collectively.

car pool *n.* a cooperative of automobile commuters who take turns driving the others in his or her own car.

car·port *n.* an automobile shelter, usually under an extension of a house's roof.

car·riage (CAIR·ij) *n.* **1** a wheeled passenger vehicle: *a baby carriage; horse-drawn carriages.* **2** the transport of goods. **3** posture or bearing: *an erect, proud carriage.* **4** a movable support: *a gun carriage; typewriter carriage.*

carriage trade *n.* the wealthy, esp. their patronage.

car·ri·er (CAIR·ee·ur) *n.* **1** one that carries: *an aircraft carrier; letter carrier; a paper carrier doing a carrier route; A mosquito is the carrier of malaria; A carrier remains unaffected while infecting others.* **2** a commercial transporter: *a common carrier; public carrier.* **3** a box or basket on a vehicle, esp. a bicycle.

carrier pigeon *n.* a message-carrying pigeon.

car·rion (CAIR·ee·un) *n.* dead, rotting flesh.
— *adj.* carrion-eating: *the carrion beetle, crow.*

car·rot (CAIR·ut) *n.* **1** the edible, orange root of a vegetable. **2** an inducement: *the carrot and the stick; a*

bunch of financial carrots to attract buyers.

carrot-and-stick *adj.* alternately rewarding and punishing: *the carrot-and-stick approach, policy, technique.*

carrousel same as CAROUSEL.

car·ry (CAIR·ee) *v.* **car·ries, car·ried, car·ry·ing 1** hold and convey; bear: *a donkey carrying a load; She carries herself with dignity; She is carrying (= is pregnant with) her second child; Her views carry a lot of weight (Informal for are highly valued) around here.*
2 transport: *a pipe carrying water.* **3** travel: *Voices carry over the water.* **4** hold: *Carry your head high.* **5** take: *They carried the joke a bit too far.* **6** win: *The motion carried; The ayes carried the day.* **7** entail: *Any job carries some responsibility.* **8** support a debtor, an enterprise, etc.: *He carried the firm through hard times.* **9** have for sale: *We don't carry that line of goods.* **10** publish or broadcast: *Stories carried by the morning papers are also carried on the evening news.*
— **carry away** be unduly influenced: *He tends to get a little carried away sometimes; He was carried away by anger.*
— **carry on 1** continue: *to carry on a conversation; He was carrying on with it past midnight; Let's carry on in spite of the weather.* **2** have an affair with someone: *He was carrying on with his neighbour's wife.*
— **carry out** fulfil or perform: *to carry out a duty, plan, promise, threat.*
— **carry over** move forward, as in bookkeeping.
— *n., pl.* **car·ries 1** the act or manner of carrying: *the **fireman's carry** (= two people taking a person's arm and leg on either side).* **2** the range of a projectile. **3** a portage.

car·ry·all (CAIR·ee·all) *n.* any very spacious carriage, automobile, shopping bag, etc.

carrying charge *n.* the interest charged for paying in instalments.

carrying-on (CAIR·ee·ing·on) *n.* **carryings-on** improper behaviour between two persons.

carry-on (CAIR·ee·on) *n.* a piece of luggage small enough to fit under an airplane seat, which a passenger is allowed to carry on board: *carry-on and checked bags; carry-on baggage, items; carry-on and cargo-hold luggage.*

car·ry·out (CAIR·ee·out) *n. & adj.* same as TAKE-OUT.

car·ry·o·ver (CAIR·ee·oh·vur) *n.* what is left over or carried over, as in bookkeeping: *a carryover of three days' unfinished business.*

car·sick *adj.* nauseated, esp. while travelling in a car, train, etc. — **car·sick·ness** *n.*

cart *n.* **1** a sturdy, two-wheeled utility vehicle usually drawn by horses, oxen, etc. **2** any light, wheeled vehicle: *a golf cart; grocery cart; shopping cart.*
— **put the cart before the horse** reverse the right order of things.
— *v.* transport or convey: *to cart produce to market; Despite their protests, the children were carted off to bed.*

carte blanche (CART·blahnsh) *n., pl.* **cartes blanches** (CART·blahnsh) a free hand; full discretionary power:

It was as if industries had been given carte blanche to pollute the air and water.

car·tel (car·TEL) *n.* a monopolistic group of commercial interests: *a closed cartel of medical specialists; to break up a cartel; The OPEC oil cartel forced prices up in the 1970s.*

Car·te·sian (car·TEE·zhun) *adj.* having to do with the French philosopher and mathematician René Descartes: *a Cartesian cordinate, plane, product.*

car·ti·lage (CAR·tuh·lij) *n.* a flexible, tough tissue related to the bone; gristle: *a torn cartilage;* **car·ti·lag·i·nous** (-LAJ·uh·nus) *adj.*

car·tog·ra·phy (car·TOG·ruh·fee) *n.* the science of making maps and charts; **car·tog·ra·pher** *n.*

car·ton (CAR·tun) *n.* a cardboard box; container in which milk, cigarettes, or other articles are sold; also, its contents.

car·toon (car·TOON) *n.* 1 a humorous or satirical drawing. 2 a comic strip. 3 an animated cartoon. — **car·toon·ist** *n.*

car·tridge (CAR·trij) *n.* 1 a case or capsule of material, as film, ink, and tape, for use in an apparatus: *a video-game cartridge.* 2 a usually cylindrical case containing the explosive charge and primer for a gun: *a blank cartridge; spent cartridges.*

cart·wheel *n.* a sideways handspring: *to turn cartwheels for fun.*

carve (CARV) *v.* **carves, carved, carv·ing** 1 cut out or form artistically; sculpture: *carved woodwork; figurines carved in wood; a figure carved out of stone.* 2 divide: *to carve up the meat into pieces; to carve* (= slice and serve) *a turkey; a carving knife.* — **carv·er** *n.*

carving *n.* a carved object or the act or occupation of making such objects: *an ivory carving; wood carvings; Wood carving is her hobby.*

car·wash *n.* a place equipped for washing automobiles.

Cas·a·no·va (cas·uh·NOH·vuh) *n.* a man who has many love affairs with women.

cas·cade (cas·CADE) *n.* a steep waterfall or series of waterfalls or something resembling it: *a window adorned with cascades of lace.* — *v.* **-cades, -cad·ed, -cad·ing** fall like or in a cascade: *The stream cascades over a cliff.*

case *n.* 1 a situation or an instance of it: *a clear case of fraud; a case in point* (= relevant instance); *The doctor saw three cases of measles today; Luc is not an isolated case; a terminal case of cancer; If that's the case, you're in trouble! a basket case (that is quite helpless); Please get off my case (Slang for stop bothering me); a case study* (= analysis of a case history). 2 a situation as a matter of litigation: *Lawyers argue cases; A case goes to trial; Courts hear or try cases; The defence rests its case* (= has finished its presentation); *"Case dismissed," said the judge; You don't have a case (that is strong); He lost the case; The case was settled out of court; the detective who finally cracked the case* (= solved the crime); **Case law** *is established by decisions in court cases.* 3 a container or its contents: *an attaché case; a glass display case; packing case; A case of pop contains 24 cans.* 4 a

cover: *a pillow case; watch case.* 5 the frame for a door or window. 6 a grammatical variation of a noun, pronoun, or adjective: *"They," "them," and "their" are in the nominative, objective, and possessive cases respectively.*
— **in any case** anyhow.
— **in case** in the event: *In case of emergency dial zero; Take your umbrella in case it rains; Take your umbrella just in case.*
— *v.* **cas·es, cased, cas·ing** 1 *Informal.* inspect in preparation for theft: *Burglars case a bank first; He had cased the joint before breaking in.* 2 put in a case: *to case a window.*

case history *n.* the facts about a subject's past and present that are useful for a medical or social study.

case·load *n.* the number of cases handled by a court, social worker, etc.

case·work *n.* social work involving individual cases; **case·work·er** *n.*

cash *n.* ready money or its equivalent as payment: *We always pay (in) cash for groceries; Pay cash either in currency or by cheque; Cold cash and no cheques, please; I ran out of cash and charged my purchases to a credit card; We carry only petty cash for daily expenses; The terms were strictly cash on delivery; adj.: a cash advance* (= loan charged to a bank card); *a cash bar (at a reception where guests may buy drinks); a cash discount (allowed to customers who pay in cash or within a certain period); the cash flow* (= after-tax net income) *of a business.*
— *v.* exchange for cash: *to cash a cheque, money order.*
— **cash in** 1 turn into cash, as bonds or gambling chips, and withdraw. 2 *Informal.* die: *It was time for him to cash in (his chips).*
— **cash in on** exploit fully; profit from something: *He cashed in on his sudden fame; to cash in on a favourable market.*

cash crop *n.* a crop that is grown for sale, not for consumption on the farm.

cash·ier (ca·SHEER) *n.* 1 one who receives the payments from customers: *a cashier at a supermarket checkout.* 2 a financial officer of a bank or company.
— *v.* dismiss, esp. in disgrace: *a clerk cashiered for embezzlement.*

cashier's cheque *n.* a cheque issued by a bank, drawn on its own funds, as given to borrowers.

cash·less *adj.* without cash: *a cashless society in which all transactions would be carried out by electronic funds transfer.*

cash·mere (CAZH·meer) *n.* 1 a soft fabric originally made from the wool of goats from Tibet and northern India. 2 such wool or a garment made with it.

cash register *n.* a machine, with a drawer for cash, that records sales, totals bills, etc.

casing (CAY·sing) *n.* what encloses something, as the airtight inner liner of a car tire, the skin of a sausage, the covering of a rifle cartridge, the interior frame of a door or window opening, or the steel lining of an oil well.

ca·si·no (cuh·SEE·noh) *n.* **-nos** a public establishment for amusements, esp. gambling: *a gambling casino.*

cask *n.* a barrel for liquids or the amount it holds.

cas·ket (CAS·kit) *n.* 1 a coffin. 2 a small box for valuables.

cas·se·role (CAS·uh·role) *n.* 1 a deep, usually covered dish for baking and serving food. 2 food cooked in a casserole: *to bake a casserole; a meat casserole; lima bean casserole.*

cas·sette (cuh·SET) *n.* a cartridge for photographic film or magnetic tape for use in a camera, tape player, etc.

cas·si·no (cuh·SEE·noh) *n.* a card game.

cast *v.* **casts, cast, cast·ing** 1 throw: *An angler casts a line; Fishermen cast nets; A snake casts* (= discards) *its skin; Voters cast* (= deposit) *ballots; actions that cast doubts on his competence; His remarks* **cast aspersions on** (= slandered) *her good name; He left the Liberals and* **cast in his lot** (= joined with) *the Tories.* 2 form in a mould: *to cast a bronze statue.* 3 assign an actor to a role: *Burton was cast as Caesar; He was cast in the hero's role.* 4 calculate: *to cast a horoscope.*
— **cast about** search: *Hounds cast about for a scent; a prisoner casting about for* (= seeking) *a means of escape.*
— **cast off** free a ship from a dock.
— *n.* 1 a throw: *a cast of the dice.* 2 something thrown or discarded: *a worm cast* (= excrement). 3 something moulded, esp. a rigid plaster-of-Paris dressing for a broken limb: *Her leg is in a (plaster) cast.* 4 the actors in a play: *a cast of characters; a star-studded cast; supporting cast.* 5 colour or quality: *a ruddy cast; a noble cast of mind.*

cas·ta·nets (cas·tuh·NETS) *n. pl.* a pair of small, hollowed-out pieces of wood, ivory, etc. held in the hand and clicked together for rhythm, used esp. in Spanish dancing.

cast·a·way (CAST·uh·way) *adj.* thrown away; set adrift: *a castaway sailor;* ***n.:*** *The castaways landed on the beach.*

caste (CAST) *n.* 1 a usually hereditary social class defined by rigid barriers, as in traditional Hinduism. 2 status or prestige: *He was afraid of losing caste.*

cast·er or **cas·tor** (CAS·tur) *n.* 1 a ball or swivelling wheel fitted to the legs of furniture, machines, etc. to make moving easier. 2 a small container for salt, relish, vinegar, etc. for use at the table.

cas·ti·gate (CAS·tuh·gate) *v.* **-gates, -gat·ed, -gat·ing** reprove strongly; punish; **cas·ti·ga·tor** (-gay·tur) *n.*

— **cas·ti·ga·tion** (-GAY·shun) *n.*

casting *n.* 1 something moulded or cast: *a brass casting.* 2 the excrement of earthworms. 3 a snake's discarded skin.

casting vote *n.* a chairperson's vote used to break a tie.

cast iron *n.* a hard, nonmalleable iron-carbon alloy made by casting.
— **cast-iron** *adj.* made or as if made of cast iron: *a cast-iron rod; a cast-iron* (= hardy) *constitution; a cast-iron* (= rigid) *policy, rule; a cast-iron* (= strong) *stomach, will.*

cas·tle (CAS·ul) *n.* 1 a large fortified dwelling or group of buildings, esp. one built in the Middle Ages; stronghold: *"A man's home is his castle"; a visionary who spends a lot of time* **building castles in the air** or **in Spain** (= daydreaming). 2 in chess, a rook.

cast-off *adj.* discarded: *cast-off clothes, skin.*

cast·off *n.* someone or something discarded: *dressed in his brother's castoffs.*

cas·tor (CAS·tur) *n.* 1 same as CASTER. 2 a beaver hat.

castor oil *n.* a thick yellow oil obtained from the beans of a tropical plant and used as a purgative, lubricant, etc.

cas·trate (CAS·trate) *v.* **-trates, -trat·ed, -trat·ing** remove the testicles of a human or animal: *Farmers castrate hogs to fatten them for market.*
— **cas·tra·tion** (cas·TRAY·shun) *n.*

cas·u·al (CAZH·oo·ul) *adj.* 1 accidental; chance: *a casual meeting.* 2 informal: *He comes to work in casual clothes; He adopts a casual attitude to work; He sounded quite casual* (= indifferent) *about losing his job.* 3 occasional: *We hire casual labour for seasonal work.*
— **cas·u·al·ly** *adv.;* **cas·u·al·ness** *n.*

cas·u·al·ty (CAZH·ul·tee) *n.* **-ties** 1 a victim (wounded, missing, or killed) of an accident or military action: *a traffic casualty; heavy casualties inflicted on the enemy; They suffered many casualties.* 2 a victim: *Automation claims many casualties among manual labour; He was a casualty of the electronic revolution.*

cas·u·ist·ry (CAZH·oo·is·tree) *n.* **-tries** 1 subtle reasoning about right and wrong. 2 a clever but false rationalization; sophistry. — **cas·u·ist** *n.*
— **cas·u·is·tic** (cazh·oo·IS·tic) *adj.*

cat *n.* 1 a mammal of the same family as the lion, lynx, leopard, and panther, esp. a small domesticated species kept as a pet or to catch mice: *A cat meows; Cats purr when at ease; an alley cat; stray cats.* 2 *Informal.* a malicious gossipy woman. 3 *Slang.* a caterpillar tractor.
— **let the cat out of the bag** reveal a secret.

cat·a·clysm (CAT·uh·cliz·um) *n.* a sudden, destructive change, as a great flood or war.
— **cat·a·clys·mic** (-CLIZ·mic) *adj.*

cat·a·combs (CAT·uh·cohmz) *n. pl.* underground burial places connected by tunnels and chambers.

cat·a·logue or **cat·a·log** (CAT·uh·log) *n.* a complete, organized, often descriptive list, as of merchandise, library books, art exhibits, etc.: *a college catalogue listing course offerings.*

— *v.* **-logues** or **-logs**, **-logued** or **-loged**, **-logu·ing** or **-log·ing** make a catalogue of something: *He has his stamp collection all neatly catalogued.*
— **cat·a·logu·er** or **cat·a·log·er** *n.*

ca·tal·y·sis (cuh·TAL·uh·sis) *n.*, *pl.* **-ses** (-seez) the process of change induced in a chemical reaction by a catalyst.

cat·a·lyst (CAT·uh·list) *n.* **1** an agent that induces or speeds up a change without itself undergoing change: *Enzymes act as catalysts in digestion.* **2** one who unintentionally causes a change: *She was a catalyst of the feminist movement; a catalyst for reform.*
— **cat·a·lyt·ic** (-LIT·ic) *adj.*

catalytic converter *n.* an antipollution device used in automobiles to render exhaust gases harmless.

cat·a·lyze (CAT·uh·lize) *v.* **-lyz·es**, **-lyzed**, **-lyz·ing** act on or change, as a catalyst does: *The discovery of the New World catalyzed world exploration.*

cat·a·mar·an (cat·uh·muh·RAN) *n.* **1** a slender raft of logs, usually propelled by a paddle. **2** a twin-hulled sailboat. **3** *Cdn.* in Newfoundland, a sled or sleigh used for winter transportation.

cat·a·pult (CAT·uh·pult) *n.* **1** a device for launching or hurling objects, as airplanes from a ship, pilots from an airplane, or missiles and stones in ancient warfare. **2** slingshot.
— *v.* throw by or as if by a catapult: *He was catapulted to fame by his marriage to the princess; He catapults out of bed at five each morning.*

cat·a·ract (CAT·uh·ract) *n.* **1** a great rush or flood of water, esp. a steep waterfall. **2** blurred vision resulting from a clouding of the eye's lens: *Elderly people develop cataracts; to remove a cataract by an operation.*

ca·tas·tro·phe (cuh·TAS·truh·fee) *n.* something that ends as a great disaster: *A bank failure is a catastrophe affecting millions of people.*
— **cat·a·stroph·ic** (cat·uh·STROF·ic) *adj.*: *a disaster of catastrophic proportions;* **cat·a·stroph·i·cal·ly** *adv.*

cat·bird *n.* a grey North American songbird with a mewing call.
— **in the catbird seat** *Informal.* in an advantageous position.

cat·call *n.* a loud, rude noise expressing disapproval of a speaker, performer, etc.; *v.*: *The singer was booed and catcalled off the stage.*

catch *v.* **catch·es**, **caught** (CAWT), **catch·ing** **1** take and hold: *to catch a ball; a barrel to catch rain in.* **2** get or grasp: *to catch sight of him; trying to catch her meaning.* **3** overtake or intercept: *Catch him before he leaves; He was at the station to catch the last train; There isn't enough time to catch a movie.* **4** apprehend: *You never catch him sleeping on the job; to catch a culprit red-handed.* **5** get or be tangled, stuck, etc.: *a finger caught in the door.* **6** be affected by something: *to catch (a) cold; A house catches fire.* **7** take hold: *flames catching on wood.* **8** act as a catcher.
— **catch at** reach out to grasp; seize on: *"A drowning man will catch at a straw."*
— **catch it** *Informal.* be scolded.
— **catch on** become well-known or popular: *Slogans tend to catch on.*

— **catch on to** come to understand: *The child soon caught on to what the adults were saying.*
— **catch one's breath** to rest: *After running for a while, I stopped to catch my breath.*
— **catch up** come up from behind and reach a person or thing: *A police cruiser catches up with a speeding car; He takes catnaps to catch up on lost sleep; He has a lot of catching up to do in math.*
— **caught up in** involved in something: *a premier caught up in a scandal; teens caught up in* (= carried away by) *the latest fads.*
— *n.* **1** the act of catching; also, a simple ball game. **2** what is caught: *a small catch of fish; a good catch; the day's catch; His wife is a real catch* (= good find). **3** a latch; fastener: *a safety catch.* **4** a small fragment or piece; snatch: *Catches of songs could be heard.* **5** a break in the voice, as caused by fear or anxiety. **6** an unforeseen or hidden complication or problem: *What's the catch? It sounds so good there must be a catch to it.*

catch·all *n.* one that applies to many different things: *"Flu" is a catchall term for many illnesses.*

catch-as-catch-can (CACH·uz·cach·CAN) *adj.* haphazard or random: *catch-as-catch-can wrestling; a hurried catch-as-catch-can news report.*

catch·er *n.* in baseball, one who receives the pitcher's throw behind home plate.

catching *adj.* **1** contagious. **2** catchy or easily remembered.

Catch-22 *n.* a situation in which one is victimized either way, as when an applicant is refused jobs because he lacks job experience and lacks experience because he is refused jobs.

catch·up *n.* same as KETCHUP.

catch-up *n.* a coming up from being behind; recovery: *Their wages had slipped so far behind the rest of the industry, the union demanded a 35% raise for catch-up; Playing catch-up is sometimes a losing game.*

catch·word *n.* **1** a word or phrase that is merely catchy: *His speech was full of catchwords like "challenge" and "commitment."* **2** a guide word, as at the top of this page.

catch·y *adj.* **catch·i·er**, **-i·est** **1** that catches one's attention and stays in the mind: *a catchy song, title, tune.* **2** tricky: *a catchy question.*

cat·e·chism (CAT·uh·kiz·um) *n.* **1** a set of questions and answers used for instruction, esp. in religion. **2** oral instruction or examination by question and answer.
— **cat·e·chist** *n.*

cat·e·chize (CAT·uh·kize) *v.* **-chiz·es**, **-chized**, **-chiz·ing** question closely or instruct by questioning: *The teacher catechized him in geography.*

cat·e·gor·i·cal (cat·uh·GOR·uh·cul) *adj.* unqualified or unconditional: *a categorical denial, rejection, statement.*

cat·e·go·rize (CAT·uh·guh·rize) *v.* **-riz·es**, **-rized**, **-riz·ing** **1** classify: *She categorized the group as tall, medium, and short.* **2** label: *a phenomenon categorized as supernatural.*
— **cat·e·go·ri·za·tion** (-ruh·ZAY·shun) *n.*

cat·e·go·ry (CAT·uh·gor·ee) *n.* -go·ries a basic division or class, esp. in logic or philosophy: *The parts of speech are categories of words; He's too great a guy to fit into any category of genius.*

ca·ter (CAY·tur) *v.* 1 furnish a reception, party, etc. with food, entertainment, or other service: *We cater for all occasions; We will cater the banquet.* 2 gratify: *He caters to her every whim.* — **ca·ter·er** *n.*

cater-corner or **cater-cornered** *adj.* diagonal; kitty-corner: *two gas stations cater-corner to each other at a junction;* **adv.:** *a sofa set cater-corner across the room.*

cat·er·pil·lar (CAT·ur·pil·ur) *n.* 1 a usually hairy, wormlike larva of a butterfly, moth, etc. 2 a vehicle moved by two endless metal tracks instead of wheels: *a caterpillar tractor;* **Caterpillar** *Trademark.*

cat·er·waul (CAT·ur·wall) *v.* howl or screech like a cat; also *n.*

cat·fish *n.* a scaleless fish with a big head and whiskers like a cat's.

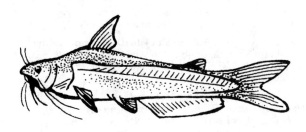

cat·gut *n.* a tough string made of the intestines of sheep, horses, etc. and used for sutures, stringing rackets, etc.

ca·thar·sis (cuh·THAR·sis, "TH" as in "thin") *n., pl.* -ses (-seez) a purification or release, esp. of the emotions, by witnessing tragic drama or by some other outlet or expression.

ca·thar·tic (cuh·THAR·tic) *adj.* purifying or purging. — *n.* a strong laxative.

ca·the·dral (cuh·THEE·drul, "TH" as in "thin") *n.* the principal church of a diocese: *A cathedral ceiling has exposed beams and often a skylight.*

cath·e·ter (CATH·uh·tur, "TH" as in "thin") *n.* a long, flexible tube inserted into a canal or cavity in the body, usually to remove fluid, as urine from the bladder.

cath·ode-ray tube (CATH·ode·ray·tube) *n.* a vacuum tube in which a beam of electrons throws images on to a screen, as in radar and TV.

cath·o·lic (CATH·uh·lic) *adj.* 1 wide or general in appeal, interest, etc.: *a person of very catholic tastes; a movie of catholic appeal;* **cath·o·lic·i·ty** (-LIS·uh·tee) *n.* 2 **Catholic** having to do with the Roman Catholic Church: *a Catholic priest.* — *n.* a member of the Roman Catholic Church: *Protestants and Catholics.* — **Ca·thol·i·cism** (cuh·THOL·uh·siz·um) *n.*

cat·kin *n.* a long, drooping cluster of flowers, as on the birch or willow.

cat·like *adj.* like a cat; silent: *catlike footsteps.*

cat·nap *n.* a brief, light sleep. Also *v.* -naps, -napped, -nap·ping.

cat·nip *n.* a fragrant mint much liked by cats.

CAT scan *n.* a picture produced by a **CAT scanner,** a computerized X-ray machine that produces three-dimensional pictures by scanning the images of a series of cross-sections.

cat's cradle *n.* a game in which a string, looped through the fingers in intricate but symmetrical designs, is transferred from player to player.

cat's-eye *n.* -eyes a gem, marble, etc. that reflects light with a distinctive gleam.

cat's-paw *n.* one used by another to do something risky or disreputable.

cat·sup *n.* same as KETCHUP.

cat·swing *n.* same as CAT-TRAIN.

cat·tle (CAT·ul) *n.pl.* 1 cows, bulls, and other domestic bovines collectively: *a herd of cattle; to brand cattle; drive cattle; Cowboys round up cattle.* 2 humans considered with contempt or pity: *The refugees were herded like cattle into the camp.*

cat·tle·man (CAT·ul·mun) *n.* -men a rancher or cowboy.

cat·train *n. Cdn.* a train of large sleds carrying goods pulled by a caterpillar tractor.

cat·ty *adj.* **cat·ti·er, cat·ti·est** *Informal.* slyly spiteful: *a catty child; She was somewhat catty about giving her rival due credit.* — **cat·ti·ly** *adv.;* **cat·ti·ness** *n.*

catty-corner or **catty-cornered** *adj. & adv.* same as KITTY-CORNER(ED).

cat·walk *n.* a narrow, usually elevated walkway, as along a bridge.

Cau·ca·sian (caw·CAY·zhun) *n.* a person of the racial group to which most Europeans belong.

Cau·ca·soid (CAW·cuh·soid) *adj.* [former use] having to do with the races that are mostly white, including the light-skinned peoples of north Africa, southwest Asia, and the Indian subcontinent; also *n.*

cau·cus (CAW·cus) *n.* a political party's meeting to debate policy, select candidates, etc. — *v.* hold a caucus: *They caucused all night.*

caught *pt. & pp.* of CATCH.

caul·dron or **cal·dron** (CAWL·drun) *n.* a large vat or pot for boiling: *a witch's cauldron.*

cau·li·flow·er (CAW·lee·flow·er) *n.* 1 the large white flower head of a kind of cabbage. 2 the plant itself.

cauliflower ear *n.* an ear misshapen and scarred by blows received in boxing.

caulk (CAWK) *v.* seal or make tight usually with a filler, seams in a boat, pipe joints, cracks, etc.; **caulk·er** *n.*

caus·al (CAW·zul) *adj.* having to do with a cause: *There seems no causal connection between her death and his disappearance;* **cau·sal·ly** *adv.* — **cau·sal·i·ty** (caw·ZAL·uh·tee) *n.*

cau·sa·tion (caw·ZAY·shun) *n.* **1** the act of causing. **2** cause-and-effect relation. **3** cause.

'cause *Informal.* because.

cause (CAWZ) *n.* **1** one that produces or is responsible for an effect, change, etc.: *The cause of the fire is unknown; She died of natural causes.* **2** grounds; reason: *He was fired from his job for cause; a court order to show cause why a judgment should not be executed; There's no cause for alarm; There's good cause to celebrate.* **3** a goal actively pursued or strongly supported: *to advance the cause of justice; The money is for a worthy cause; You are fighting for a lost cause; He made common cause with the enemy.* **4** a legal case. — *v.* **caus·es, caused, caus·ing** bring about; make happen: *What caused the accident? He caused us a lot of trouble.*

cause cé·lè·bre (CAWZ·suh·LEB·ruh) *n., pl.* **causes cé·lè·bres** (CAWZ·suh·LEB·ruh) a famous case or controversy: *The abdication of King Edward VIII became a cause célèbre.*

cause·way *n.* a raised road or path across water or marshy ground.

caus·tic (CAW·stic) *adj.* **1** able to destroy or eat into (esp. flesh) chemically; corrosive: *the caustic action of soda and potash.* **2** sharp or biting: *a caustic remark; his caustic wit.* — *n.* a caustic agent. — **caus·tic·i·ty** (caw·STIS·uh·tee) *n.*

caustic soda *n.* a corrosive alkali used in bleaching, making soap, etc.

cau·ter·ize (CAW·tuh·rize) *v.* **-iz·es, -ized, -iz·ing** burn abnormal or injured tissue with a hot iron, caustic, or laser beam to kill infection, remove diseased tissue, etc. — **cau·ter·i·za·tion** (-ruh·ZAY·shun) *n.*

cau·tion (CAW·shun) *n.* **1** regard for safety; wariness: *Drive with caution on icy roads; Exercise caution when walking on wet floors; Use extreme caution while handling explosives; He threw caution to the winds and jumped into the current.* **2** a warning: *the judge's caution against repeating the offence; Caution! Wet Floor.* — *v.* warn or admonish: *He cautioned her against driving too fast; cautioned her not to drive so fast; cautioned her about the dangers.*

cau·tion·ar·y (CAW·shuh·nair·ee) *adj.* warning of danger: *cautionary advice; a cautionary sign, tale.*

cau·tious (CAW·shus) *adj.* careful or wary: *She is cautious of strangers; cautious about travelling at night; cautious in the use of drugs; cautious with firearms.* — **cau·tious·ly** *adv.;* **cau·tious·ness** *n.*

cav·al·cade (CAV·ul·cade) *n.* **1** a parade or procession, as of horses. **2** a progression: *a cavalcade of historical events.*

cav·a·lier (cav·uh·LEER) *n.* **1** an armed rider. **2** a gallant; lady's escort. — *adj.* casual or off-hand: *a cavalier attitude; He acts with cavalier indifference to the rights of others.* — **cav·a·lier·ly** *adv.*

cav·al·ry (CAV·ul·ree) *n.* **-ries 1** mobile troops on horseback or in armoured vehicles: *a cavalry unit of tanks and armoured personnel carriers.* **2** horses and riders collectively. — **cav·al·ry·man** *n.* **-men.**

cave *n.* an underground cavity with an opening, usually on a cliff or hillside: *to explore a cave.* — *v.* **caves, caved, cav·ing** esp. **cave in 1** collapse inward: *The old tunnel caved in.* **2** give in or yield: *Don't cave in to pressure.*

ca·ve·at (CAY·vee·ut) *n. Formal.* a caution.

caveat emp·tor (-EMP·tor) *Latin.* "Let the buyer beware," i.e. Make sure of a product's quality before buying it.

cave-in *n.* the occurrence or site of a collapse in a mine, tunnel, etc.

cave·man *n.* **1** a cave dweller of prehistoric times. **2** *Informal.* a strong but crude man.

cav·ern (CAV·urn) *n.* a huge or vast cave.

cav·ern·ous (CAV·ur·nus) *adj.* **1** full of caverns: *a cavernous mountain.* **2** of or like a cavern: *a cavernous* (= large and hollow) *structure; cavernous* (= deep-set) *eyes; a cavernous* (= resonant) *voice; the cavernous* (= large and spacious) *Grand Hotel.*

cav·i·ar or **cav·i·are** (CAV·ee·ar) *n.* the salted eggs of salmon and other fishes eaten as an appetizer.

cav·il (CAV·ul) *v.* **-ils, -iled** or **-illed, -il·ing** or **-il·ling** needlessly criticize or object to something; carp: *to cavil at little delays; This is no time to cavil about trivialities.* — **cav·il·er** or **cav·il·ler** *n.*

cav·i·ty (CAV·uh·tee) *n.* **-ties** a hollow place in a solid body: *the abdominal cavity; Dentists fill cavities (in teeth); the oral cavity (of the mouth).*

ca·vort (cuh·VORT) *v.* prance; caper: *See the horse cavorting in the field; young bucks cavorting on the dance floor.*

caw *n.* the harsh call of a crow, raven, etc. — *v.*: *Rooks cawed from the treetops.*

cay·enne or **cayenne pepper** (kye·EN-) *n.* a spicy, red pepper made from capsicum fruits.

CB *n.* a range of radio frequencies meant for two-way communication between private parties; citizens band: *In CB slang, "chicken coop" means "weigh scales for trucks."*

CB·er (SEE·bee·ur) *n. Informal.* one who uses a CB radio.

cease (SEECE) *v.* **ceas·es, ceased, ceas·ing** come to an end or discontinue: *The music faded and then ceased; Extinct animals are those that have ceased to exist; The rebels were ordered to cease fire; an order to **cease and desist** (from something illegal); It snowed without ceasing all January.* — *n.*: *It snowed **without cease** (= without end or pause) all January.*

cease-fire *n.* a pause in open warfare: *to declare, work out, sign, observe a cease-fire; The cease-fire was broken soon after it went into effect; adj.: a cease-fire order from the U.N.*

cease·less *adj.* endless; continual: *ceaseless activity, enmity, noise, rivalry, tumult.* — **cease·less·ly** *adv.*

ce·dar (SEE·dur) *n.* **1** an evergreen coniferous tree with reddish, hardy, fragrant wood. **2** the wood: *a cedar* *chest, fence; a cedar-lined closet.*

cede (SEED) *v.* **cedes, ced·ed, ced·ing** surrender a property, claim, right, etc. esp. by treaty: *Some land was ceded to the Crown by the Indians.*

CEGEP (SAY·jep) *n.* **CEGEPs** *Cdn.* in Quebec, a community college of general and professional training: *Candidates should have three years of CEGEP or equivalent technical college.*

ceil·ing (SEE·ling) *n.* **1** the interior, overhead covering of a room. **2** an upper limit, as on prices and wages, visibility, operable altitude for an airplane, etc.: *to put or set a ceiling on rents; They lifted the ceiling after a year.*
— **hit the ceiling** or **roof** *Slang.* lose one's temper.

ce·leb (suh·LEB) *n. Informal.* a celebrity or famous person.

cel·e·brant (SEL·uh·brunt) *n.* **1** a priest officiating at a ceremony. **2** a celebrator: *New Year's Eve celebrants.*

cel·e·brate (SEL·uh·brate) *v.* **-brates, -brat·ed, -brat·ing 1** hold festivities, rites, etc. in honour of an event: *He celebrated the victory with champagne; Most Christians celebrate Christmas on December 25.* **2** praise publicly; make known: *to celebrate the memory of the war heroes.* **3** perform solemnly: *to celebrate a marriage, Mass.* — **cel·e·bra·tor** (-bray·tur) *n.*
— **cel·e·bra·tion** (-BRAY·shun) *n.*

celebrated (SEL·uh·bray·tid) *adj.* famous: *France is celebrated for its wines; celebrated as a producer of fine wines.*

ce·leb·ri·ty (suh·LEB·ruh·tee) *n.* **-ties 1** renown or fame. **2** a famous person: *a Hollywood celebrity; local celebrities.*

cel·e·ry (SEL·uh·ree) *n.* a plant of the parsley family, grown for its crisp, edible stem: *a bunch of celery; a stick of celery.*

ce·les·tial (suh·LES·chul) *adj.* **1** having to do with the sky or the heavens: *The sun, moon, and stars are celestial bodies; The* **celestial equator** *runs through the sky directly above the earth's equator.* **2** heavenly or divine: *a goddess's celestial beauty.* — **ce·les·tial·ly** *adv.*

cel·i·bate (SEL·uh·bit) *n.* one who stays unmarried, esp. by religious vow. — *adj.: a celibate life, nun, priest.*
— **cel·i·ba·cy** (-buh·see) *n.*

cell *n.* **1** a small, separate space, as in a honeycomb. **2** a similar room to accommodate a monk, prisoner, etc. **3** a basic unit of a larger structure: *a blood cell* (= the smallest independent unit of living tissue); *a dry cell* (= the basic component of an electric battery); *a binary cell* (= the basic storage unit of a computer memory); *a Communist cell* (= the smallest unit of the party).

cel·lar (SEL·ur) *n.* **1** a usually underground storage room; also, its contents, esp. a store of wine. **2** basement.
— **in the cellar** *Informal.* in last place in a sports league.

cel·lo (CHEL·oh) *n.* **cel·los** a large bass instrument of the violin family. — **cel·list** *n.*

cel·lo·phane (SEL·uh·fane) *n.* a thin, transparent moisture-proof wrapping material used to keep foods,

cigarettes, etc. fresh.

cel·lu·lar (SEL·yuh·lur) *adj.* **1** cell-like; porous: *cellular rubber.* **2** consisting of cells: *cellular communications, radio, service.*

cellular telephone *n.* a radiotelephone system for vehicles, in which a chain of transmitting stations, or cells, each serving a small area, relays the messages.

cel·lu·lite (SEL·yuh·lite, -leet) *n.* fat or a fatty substance that accumulates under the skin, said to be the cause of bulges on thighs, hips, and buttocks.

cel·lu·loid (SEL·yuh·loid) *n.* a flammable, colourless material used for toys, combs, photographic film, etc.
— *adj.* having to do with films; hence, artificial or unreal: *celluloid characters; the celluloid world of the movies;* **Celluloid** *Trademark.*

Cel·si·us (SEL·see·us) *adj.* having to do with the temperature scale having 0 and 100 degrees as the freezing and boiling points of water respectively.

Cel·tic (KEL·tic, SEL·tic) *adj.* of a group of languages that include Gaelic, Welsh, Breton, and Cornish.

ce·ment (suh·MENT) *n.* **1** a substance, esp. a powder of clay and lime, pastelike when mixed with water but hardening to a stony mass and used to bind building materials, make concrete, etc.: *Cement is poured into forms; The cement sets as concrete;* **Paper cement** *and* **rubber cement** *are adhesives.* **2** a hard crust covering the roots of a tooth.
— *adj.* concrete: *a cement floor, sidewalk.*
— *v.* bind or cover with cement: *He cemented over the crack in the wall; Shared experiences help to cement* (= join firmly) *a friendship.*

cem·e·ter·y (SEM·uh·tair·ee) *n.* **-ter·ies** a burial ground.

cen·o·taph (SEN·uh·taf) *n.* a monument to a person buried elsewhere: *a cenotaph of the Unknown Soldier.*

cen·ser (SEN·sur) *n.* a vessel for burning incense during religious ceremonies.

cen·sor (SEN·sur) *n.* **1** one authorized to prohibit or edit movies, news, books, etc. to make them conform to standards of morality, security requirements, etc.: *The censor cut 10 minutes from the film.* **2** one of two officials of ancient Rome who conducted the census and supervised public morals.
— *v.* subject to censorship: *Mail from the troops was censored; Ten minutes were censored* (= cut) *from the film.* — **cen·sor·ship** *n.*

cen·so·ri·al (sen·SOR·ee·ul) *adj.* having to do with a censor: *censorial powers.*

cen·so·ri·ous (sen·SOR·ee·us) *adj.* fault-finding.
— **cen·so·ri·ous·ly** *adv.*

cen·sure (SEN·shur) *n.* **1** harsh criticism or disapproval, esp. of an authoritative or official nature: *the censure of the church; a censure motion against the government.* **2** censorship.
— *v.* **-sures, -sured, -sur·ing** subject to censure: *The professor and his teachings were censured by the authorities.*

cen·sus (SEN·sus) *n.* an official count of the population, usually including a record of age, sex, occupation, etc.: *Statistics Canada makes partial surveys in the years* *ending with 6 and complete censuses in the years ending with 1.*

cent *n.* a unit or piece of money equal to 1/100 of the dollar; penny: *He didn't have a **red cent*** (*Slang for* any money at all) *left in his account; If I may put* or *add* or *throw my **two cents** in* (*Slang for* If I may offer a little advice).

cen·taur (SEN·tor) *n.* a monster of Greek myths that is half man and half horse.

cen·te·nar·i·an (sen·tuh·NAIR·ee·un) *n.* one who is at least 100 years old.

cen·te·nar·y (sen·TEN·uh·ree) *n. & adj.* -nar·ies (of) a 100th anniversary or its celebration.
Also **cen·ten·ni·al** (sen·TEN·ee·ul).

center See CENTRE.

cen·ti·grade (SEN·tuh·grade) *n.* former term for CELSIUS.

cen·ti·gram (SEN·tuh·gram) *n.* 1/100 of a gram; **cen·ti·gramme** *Brit.*

cen·ti·me·tre (SEN·tuh·mee·tur) *n.* 1/100th of a metre; also **cen·ti·me·ter.**

cen·tral (SEN·trul) *adj.* **1** at or near the centre: *a central area, place, position; the **central city** (= core of a metropolitan area); A hospital has to have a central* (= easy-to-reach) *location; The countries south of Mexico and north of South America make up **Central America;** the annual Central Canada Exhibition in Ottawa; the **Central Provinces** of Ontario and Quebec lying between the Atlantic Provinces and the Western Provinces.* **2** main or dominant: *a central authority; a central library and its branches; the central government in a country's capital; a computer's **central processing unit;** Freedom is **central to** (= essential to) our way of life.* **3** operated from one main location: *a house with central air-conditioning, heating, and vacuum.*
— *n.* a main telephone exchange or one of its operators.
— **cen·tral·ly** *adv.*

cen·tral·ize (SEN·truh·lize) *v.* -iz·es, -ized, -iz·ing **1** bring to a centre: *Business is centralized in the downtown area.* **2** put government, offices, etc. under one main control: *Certain functions are centralized in the Federal Government.*

cen·tre or **cen·ter** (SEN·tur) *n.* **1** the point equally distant from a figure's outermost edges: *the centre of a circle; She hit the target right in the centre* or *hit the target dead centre; adj.: the Centre Block of the*

Parliament Buildings; the centre spot, zone. **2** a focus of activity: *an amusement, civic, community, crisis, cultural, day-care, health, immigration, nerve, shopping centre; Paris is a centre for fashion; An active person is said to be at the centre of things; The astronaut was the centre of attention all evening.* **3** a player stationed in the middle: *The centre passes the ball to the quarterback.* **4 Centre** political moderates or their position.
— *v.* **1** put or be at the centre: *to centre a heading on the page; The children centred around the storyteller.* **2** concentrate or focus: *The story centres on a kidnap attempt; The student's efforts were centred on winning a scholarship.*

cen·tre·fold or **cen·ter·fold** (SEN·tur·fold) *n.* a picture spread across the stapled or stitched centre of a magazine, often on a foldout.

centre of gravity or **center of gravity** *n.* the point at or on which a body will balance.

cen·tre·piece or **cen·ter·piece** (SEN·tur·piece) *n.* a decorative object that is placed in a central position.

cen·trif·u·gal (sen·TRIF·yoo·gul) *adj.* tending to move away from the centre: *The centrifugal force tends to pull a rider away from the centre of a merry-go-round.*

cen·trip·e·tal (sen·TRIP·uh·tul) *adj.* tending to move toward the centre: *The centripetal force keeps you moving in a circular path on a merry-go-round.*

cen·trist (SEN·trist) *n.* a member of a moderate political party: *a centrist position between Right and Left.*
— **cen·trism** *n.*

cen·tu·ry (SEN·chuh·ree) *n.* -ries **1** a period of 100 years: *The 20th century A.D. runs from 1901 through 2000; People have become more and more civilized over* or *through the centuries.* **2** any group or series of 100 similar things: *A cricket batsman scores a century* (= 100 runs).

ce·ram·ic (suh·RAM·ic) *n.* **1 ceramics** *pl.* [takes sing. v.] the art of making earthenware, porcelain, etc. by firing clay or a similar material. **2** a product of ceramics: *Ceramics include bricks, cement, pottery, and sewer products; adj.: ceramic industries, tiles.*
— **ce·ram·ist** or **ce·ram·i·cist** *n.*

ce·re·al (SEER·ee·ul) *n.* **1** a grass producing an edible grain, as wheat, oats, and rice; also, such a grain; *adj: cereal crops, grasses, grains, products.* **2** food made from a cereal grain: *ready-to-eat breakfast cereals such as cornflakes (cold cereal); a hot cereal such as oatmeal.*

ce·re·bral (suh·REE·brul, SER·uh·brul) *adj.* **1** having to do with the brain: *cerebral cortex, palsy.* **2** intellectual: *a hard cerebral style of verse.* — **ce·re·bral·ly** *adv.*

cer·e·brate (SER·uh·brate) *v.* -brates, -brat·ed, -brat·ing use the brain; cogitate; think.
— **cer·e·bra·tion** (-BRAY·shun) *n.*

cer·e·mo·ni·al (ser·uh·MOH·nee·ul) *adj.* accompanied by or associated with ceremony: *The priest made a ceremonial offering; He donned ceremonial robes for the occasion.*
— *n.* a ceremony or ritual; **cer·e·mo·ni·al·ly** *adv.*

cer·e·mo·ni·ous (ser·uh·MOH·nee·us) *adj.* full of or fond of ceremony: *A coronation is not a simple but a*

ceremonious affair; ceremonious courtesy, devotion, greetings; a ceremonious bow, occasion, procession, religion, welcome.
— **cer·e·mo·ni·ous·ly** *adv.*; **cer·e·mo·ni·ous·ness** *n.*

cer·e·mo·ny (SER·uh·moh·nee) *n.* **-nies 1** a set of prescribed formal acts appropriate to a function such as a wedding or religious rite; also, the function itself: *to perform a religious ceremony; a flag-raising ceremony; funeral ceremony; marriage ceremony.* **2** formality: *The burial was conducted with appropriate ceremony; Everyone joined in the celebrations* **without ceremony**; *There's no need to* **stand on ceremony** (= be formal) *among friends.*

ce·rise (suh·REECE) *n. & adj.* clear, bright red or cherrylike colour.

cer·tain (SUR·tun) *adj.* **1** limited: *He received a certain portion of the profits; I trust him to a certain extent.* **2** particular but not specified: *I met a certain Mr. Smith; The play has a certain appeal;* **pron.**: *Certain of his friends deserted him.* **3** completely sure: *sure and certain; We are certain to win; We are certain about winning; quite certain of the outcome; It is quite certain* (= sure as proven) *that the earth is round; I know* **for certain** (= without doubt) *it rained yesterday.*
— **cer·tain·ly** *adv.*

cer·tain·ty (SUR·tun·tee) *n.* **-ties 1** sureness of mind: *We can state with certainty that it will not rain today; Our certainty has been shaken by the darkening skies; There is no certainty of our winning in a lottery.* **2** a definite or proven fact or belief: *It's a physical certainty that the sun will rise tomorrow; That 2 + 2 is 4 is a mathematical certainty; It is a moral certainty* (= generally true) *that mothers love their offspring; We know this* **for a certainty** (= without a doubt).

cer·ti·fi·a·ble (sur·tuh·FYE·uh·bul) *adj.* **1** that can be certified: *a certifiable candidate, result.* **2** so ill mentally that the authorities have to be notified: *a certifiable lunatic.*
— **cer·ti·fi·a·bly** *adv.*: *The patient seems certifiably dead; Hughes was certifiably insane.*

cer·tif·i·cate (sur·TIF·uh·kit) *n.* a usually official document testifying to a qualification, fact, etc.: *a birth, death, gift, marriage, teaching certificate; He cashed (in) his savings certificate; to issue a certificate of deposit, ownership, vaccination.*
— **cer·ti·fi·ca·tion** (SUR·tuh·fuh·CAY·shun) *n.*

cer·ti·fy (SUR·tuh·fye) *v.* **-fies, -fied, -fy·ing 1** declare, endorse, guarantee, etc., usually by a certificate: *The mechanic has certified the car is roadworthy; a car certified to be roadworthy; certified (as) roadworthy; A* **certified cheque** *cannot be refused or returned because the money is being held by the bank; Users of* **certified mail** *will get a receipt signed by the addressee;* **Certified milk** *has to meet official standards; a* **certified public accountant** *from the U.S.* (= chartered accountant). **2** declare to be insane: *A certified (mental) case is normally hospitalized.* — **cer·ti·fi·er** *n.*

cer·ti·tude (SUR·tuh·tude) *n. Formal.* sureness; certainty: *There's no absolute certitude about life after death; We cannot assert this with the certitude of mathematical truths.*

cer·vix (SUR·vix) *n., pl.* **-vic·es** (-vi·seez) or **-vix·es** the

neck-shaped lower end of the uterus.
— **cer·vi·cal** *adj.*: *cervical cancer; a cervical* (= neck) *collar.*

ce·sar·e·an or **ce·sar·i·an** (si·ZAIR·ee·un) *n. & adj.* same as CAESAREAN.

ces·sa·tion (ses·AY·shun) *n.* a ceasing: *a brief cessation of pain.*

ces·sion (SESH·un) *n.* a ceding or something ceded, as territory.

cess·pool (SES·pool) *n.* a covered pit or buried tank for sewage.

Cha·blis (SHAB·lee) *n.* a dry, white wine.

cha-cha (CHAH·chah) *n.* **1** a ballroom dance of Latin American origin. **2** the music for it. Also **cha-cha-cha**.
— *v.* **-chas, -chaed, -cha·ing** dance the cha-cha.

cha·dor (CHUD·or) *n.* a long, usually black garment traditionally worn by Muslim women draped around the body from head to foot.

chafe *v.* **chafes, chafed, chaf·ing 1** be irritated or impatient: *students chafing at restrictions; workers chafing under heavy loads.* **2** rub so as to warm hands, skin, etc. **3** wear away by rubbing action: *Friction from clothing can cause chafing of the skin; a sore caused by a chafing harness.*

chaff *n.* **1** the husks of grain and other matter discarded in threshing: *to separate the wheat from the chaff* (= trivial or worthless material). **2** light teasing; banter.
— *v.* tease jovially: *to chaff a guy about his girl friends.*
— **chaff·er** *n.*

chaff·y (CHAF·ee) *adj.* **chaff·i·er, -i·est 1** like chaff; worthless. **2** full of chaff.

cha·grin (shuh·GRIN) *n.* distress or irritation at failure, embarrassment, etc.: *To his great chagrin, his younger brother got the job.*
— *v.* **-grins, -grined, -grin·ing** cause chagrin to someone: *He was chagrined to learn that a rival got the job; felt chagrined at being rejected for the job; was chagrined that he didn't get the job.*

chain *n.* **1** a flexible series of connected metal links used for binding, transmitting power, etc. **2 chains** *pl.* fetters or bonds: *the chains of love.* **3** a unit of linear measure: *The "surveyor's chain" is 66 ft. (20.12 m); The "engineer's chain" is 100 ft. (30.48 m).* **4** a series of usually similar, connected things: *a coast-to-coast supermarket chain; a chain of events; a chain of atoms.* **5** same as CHAIN STORE.
— **in chains** in an enslaved condition.
— *v.* bind, connect, or confine by or as if by chains: *a dog chained to a post.*

chain gang *n.* a group of prisoners chained together for outdoor labour.

chain letter *n.* a letter asking the recipient to send copies of it to others who are to do the same.

chain mail *n.* flexible body armour made of meshed metal links.

chain reaction *n.* a usually self-sustaining series of events, esp. chemical or nuclear reactions, each of which causes the next one in the series.

chain saw *n.* a portable power saw with the teeth driven on an endless chain.

chain-smoke *v.* -smokes, -smoked, -smok·ing smoke a continuous series of cigarettes. — **chain smoker** *n.*

chain store *n.* one of a chain of retail stores owned by one company; also **chain.**

chair *n.* 1 a seat with a back support: *a deck chair; easy chair; rocking chair; swivel chair; a dentist's chair; a dentist with a great* **chairside** *manner.* 2 a position of dignity, authority, etc., as a professorship: *to endow, establish a chair in linguistics; Mrs. Chen was appointed to the chair; We need someone to* **take the chair** (= to preside) *in the absence of the president.* 3 a chairman; chairperson: *Address all questions to the chair, please; Wait for the chair to recognize you; A new chair is to be elected.* 4 the electric chair for executing criminals: *He was sent to the chair.*
— *v.* preside: *to chair a meeting.*

chair car *n.* a railway car with reclining seats; parlour car.

chair lift *n.* a ski lift with chairs to ride in.

chair·man (CHAIR·mun) *n.* -men 1 the person presiding at a meeting; president. 2 the head of a board, committee, etc.: *the department chairman; the chairman of the board.* — **chair·man·ship** *n.*

chair·per·son (CHAIR·pur·sun) *n.* one who presides over a meeting or heads a group such as a committee.

chaise (SHAYZ) *n.* a light, two- or four-wheeled pleasure carriage.

chaise longue (SHAYZ·long) *n., pl.* **chaise longues** (-longz) or **chaises longues** (SHAYZ·longz) a chair with the seat extended to support the legs. Also **chaise lounge** (-lownj).

cha·let (sha·LAY) *n.* 1 a Swiss dwelling with balconies and large projecting eaves. 2 a house, cottage, etc. in similar style. 3 an Alpine herdsman's hut.

chal·ice (CHAL·is) *n.* 1 a goblet, esp. a cup for Eucharistic wine. 2 the cup-shaped part of a flower.

chalk (CHAWK) *n.* 1 a soft, white limestone. 2 prepared chalk or a substitute used to write on chalkboards: *to write with chalk; a piece of chalk.*
— *v.* rub, treat, write, etc. with chalk.
— **chalk up** 1 record or score: *He chalked up three wins against one defeat.* 2 attribute: *He chalked up his mistakes to youth and inexperience.*
— **chalk·y** *adj.* **chalk·i·er, -i·est.**

chalk·board (CHAWK·board) *n.* a usually black or green board prepared for writing on with chalk and used as a visual aid.

chal·lenge (CHAL·unj) *v.* **chal·leng·es, chal·lenged, chal·leng·ing** 1 demand identification: *He gave the password when challenged by the sentry.* 2 invite to take part in a duel, game, etc.; dare: *She challenged him to a game of tennis; challenged him to fight.* 3 excite to effort, courage, etc. 4 question the truth of something; dispute: *to challenge a will; to challenge* (= object to) *a prospective juror.*
— *n.* 1 demand: *The sentry gave the challenge, "Who goes there?"* 2 a dare: *The boxer issued a challenge to*
all comers; *There was no one to take up or accept or respond to the challenge; a formidable challenge; a challenge to human dignity.* 3 a situation calling for one's best efforts: *Journalism offers many challenges to a resourceful writer; It was a challenge just to keep breathing while waiting for help.* 4 objection: *The challenge was upheld and the juror was dropped.*
— **chal·leng·er** *n.*

cham·ber (CHAIM·bur) *n.* 1 a hall for assemblies, receptions, etc.: *an audience chamber; reception chamber.* 2 a council, board, legislative body, etc.: *The Senate and the House of Commons are the two chambers, or houses, of a bicameral legislature.* 3 any enclosed space: *a combustion chamber; gas chamber; torture chamber; the upper and lower chambers of the heart; A charge or cartridge is held in the chamber of a firearm.* 4 a room, esp. a bedroom: *a lady's chamber.* 5 **chambers** *pl.* a judge's office.

cham·ber·lain (CHAIM·bur·lin) *n.* a high official at court, as a treasurer or the steward of a lord or monarch.

cham·ber·maid (CHAIM·bur·maid) *n.* a maid who makes beds and cleans rooms.

chamber music *n.* music written for small groups to perform, as in a string quartet.

chamber of commerce *n.* an association of local businesses promoting a community's commercial interests.

chamber pot *n.* a vessel used as a toilet in a bedroom.

cha·me·le·on (cuh·MEEL·yun) *n.* 1 a lizard that changes colour to match its surroundings. 2 a changeable person.

cham·ois (SHAM·ee) *n. sing. & pl.* 1 a soft leather used esp. as a polishing cloth. 2 (*also* sham·WAH) a goatlike mountain antelope of Europe and western Asia.

champ *v.* chew or bite vigorously; gnash the teeth.
— **champ (at) the bit** show impatience or restlessness to begin something.
— *n. Informal.* a champion.

cham·pagne (sham·PAIN) *n.* a sparkling wine, usually white, originally from France: *pink champagne; She broke out the champagne to celebrate her victory.*

cham·pi·on (CHAM·pee·un) *v.* fight for a cause, person, etc.; defend.
— *n.* 1 a valiant defender: *a champion of freedom.* 2 one holding first place or winning first prize, esp. in sports: *the defending champion of the world*

heavyweight title; **adj.:** *a champion boxer, poodle.*
— **cham·pion·ship** *n.*

chance *n.* **1** an apparently uncaused event; luck: *It was by pure* or *sheer chance that we met in Moscow; I am not taking any chances* (= risks); **adj.:** *a chance discovery, meeting.* **2** opportunity: *a chance for success; a chance to compete in the Olympics; He hasn't got a chance; doesn't have a ghost of a chance; He let his chance slip by; missed his chance.* **3** possibility: *There's only a slight* or *slim chance he'll win now; There's little* or *small chance of his winning; the chances of being a winner; (The) chances are he may lose; She stands a good chance of winning; He doesn't* **stand a chance** *against such heavy odds; He has entered anyhow* **on the off chance** (= on the remote possibility) *of his rival dropping out.*
— *v.* **chanc·es, chanced, chanc·ing 1** meet, come, happen, etc. accidentally: *He chanced on the discovery; He chanced to be there when it happened.* **2** hazard or risk: *It's too dangerous; don't chance it!*

chan·cel·lor (CHAN·suh·lur) *n.* a high official, as the heads of some European governments, the titular heads of some universities, church officials in charge of diocesan business, and judges in courts of equity.
— **chan·cel·lor·ship** *n.*

chan·cer·y (CHAN·suh·ree) *n.* **-cer·ies 1** the office or rank of a chancellor. **2** an office of public archives; record office. **3** a court of equity.

chanc·y (CHAN·see) *adj.* **chanc·i·er, -i·est** *Informal.* risky: *accidents caused by chancy driving; Fortune-telling is a chancy occupation.*

chan·de·lier (shan·duh·LEER) *n.* a many-branched hanging light fixture: *crystal chandeliers.*

change *v.* **chang·es, changed, chang·ing 1** make or become different: *Jack changed his name; changed it from Smith to Jones; His beliefs have changed radically; One experience changed his life; He changes colour when you mention it; Can you change a dollar (for quarters, dimes, etc.)?* **2** exchange: *I changed seats with her; We changed seats; to change dollars for francs.* **3** enter, put, take, etc. something in place of something else: *We change trains at the next stop; Let's change into beachwear; Later we'll change for dinner; Don't forget to change the baby* (= baby's diaper).
— **change the channel** *Slang.* change the topic of conversation.
— **change hands** pass from one owner to another.
— **change one's tune** alter one's story or attitude.
— *n.* **1** an alteration or difference: *the change of seasons from summer to fall; a refreshing, welcome change in the weather; There's a marked, striking change in his appearance with the hairpiece on; The new posting brought about* or *effected a drastic change in our life style; Let's eat out for a change* (= for variety); *People go away on weekends for a change of pace from the hectic life of the city; Sweeping changes in government are taking place; The new government is a change for the better; He had a change of heart* (= change in thinking or attitude). **2** something to be substituted: *Bring just one change of clothes; The doctor ordered a change of diet; a change of address.* **3** money returned from an overpayment: *The waiter brought back change.* **4** money in smaller units, esp.

coins: *$10.15 is $10* **and change;** *Listen to the loose change jingling in his pocket; small change; Let the waiter keep the change; Do you have change for a dollar? a* **change purse** *for keeping change.* **4** a pattern or sequence for ringing bells.
— **ring the changes** ring bells through all possible variations: *In his book, he rings all the changes on East versus West.*
— **chang·er** *n.;* **change·ful** *adj.;* **change·less** *adj.*

change·a·ble *adj.* capable of change: *a changeable temperament; changeable as the weather.*

change·house *n.* a building for bathers to change clothes in.

change·ling *n.* a child substituted for one that is stolen.

change of life *n.* menopause.

change·o·ver (CHANGE·oh·vur) *n.* a complete conversion from one system, activity, etc. to another: *the changeover from the imperial to the metric system.*

chan·nel (CHAN·ul) *n.* **1** a long, narrow, usually deep way for something to pass in, as a groove, duct, stream bed, the navigable part of a waterway (*a shipping channel*), or a large strait (*the English Channel*). **2** any path of transmission, communication, or activity, as a frequency range for one radio or TV signal: *Let's change the channel for a better program.* **3 channels** *pl.* official lines of communication: *diplomatic, military channels; a petition sent through the proper channels.*
— *v.* **-nels, -nelled** or **-neled, -nel·ling** or **-nel·ing** make a channel for or in something: *He channels his money into profitable ventures; channels his profits to worthy causes.* Also **chan·nel·ize** (CHAN·uh·lize) *v.* **-iz·es, -ized, -iz·ing.**

chan·son (SHAN·song, -sun) *n.* a song.

chant *n.* **1** a melody in which many words are sung to one note, esp. a religious song: *Gregorian chant.* **2** a rhythmic and repetitive utterance: *the chant of the mob outside the embassy.*
— *v.* **1** sing or speak in a chant: *The demonstrators chanted slogans outside the embassy.* **2** sing about a subject: *a poet chanting his love's virtues.* — **chant·er** *n.*

cha·os (KAY·os) *n.* total disorganization: *to bring order out of chaos.* — **cha·ot·ic** (kay·OT·ic) *adj.*

chap *v.* **chaps, chapped, chap·ping** to dry, roughen, or crack because of cold, wind, etc.: *Too much dishwashing had chapped his hands; Apply petroleum jelly to chapped lips.*
— *n.* **1** *Informal.* a fellow; guy. **2 chaps** (also SHAPS) *pl.* protective leggings worn by cowboys over their trousers.

chap·el (CHAP·ul) *n.* **1** a small church. **2** a small room for worship in a large church or cathedral. **3** a place of worship in a home, school, prison, etc. **4** a religious service held in a school: *to go to chapel; She's never late for chapel.*

chap·er·on or **chap·er·one** (SHAP·uh·rone) *n.* a mature person who escorts a single young woman or supervises a social gathering of young people: *Teachers help out as chaperons at school dances.*
— *v.* **-ons** or **-ones, -oned, -on·ing:** *Teachers and parents chaperon school dances.*
— **chap·er·on·age** (-roh·nij) *n.*

chap·lain (CHAP·lin) *n.* a clergyman serving in a public institution such as a club, hospital, prison, school, etc. or with the military. — **chap·lain·cy** *n.* **-cies.**

chap·ter (CHAP·tur) *n.* **1** a major division of a book: *an introductory chapter; Chapter 3, verse 42 of the Koran says, "Oh Mary, Lo Allah has chosen thee and made thee pure and hath preferred thee above [all] the women of creation"; The novel closes with a chapter on the wedding; School was an exciting chapter* (= period) *of her youth; Her previous marriage is a closed chapter of her life* (= something to be forgotten). **2** a local branch of a society: *Our I.O.D.E. chapter meets monthly.* **3** a meeting of canons, monks, etc.
— **chapter and verse** exact authority: *Can you cite or give or put down or quote chapter and verse for what you say? I know the whole story chapter and verse* (= thoroughly).

Chapter 11 *n.* a provision in U.S. law for a business to reorganize itself while facing bankruptcy: *The firm has filed for protection from creditors under Chapter 11 of the U.S. Bankruptcy Code.*

char·ac·ter (CAIR·uc·tur) *n.* **1** the distinctive personality of a person, group, etc.: *a man of fine character; Suffering builds character* (= moral strength); *adj.: character assassination* (= slandering); *character formation, traits; A* **character witness** *gives evidence in a legal action about the character of a person.* **2** a person in a story, drama, etc.: *"Hamlet," unlike "Julius Caesar," is a fictitious character; the leading character in a novel; adj.: a character actor, part, sketch.* **3** a distinguishing property; nature: *Each one has a character of his own; a directive of an official character.* **4** [usually derogatory] a person: *He's quite a character* (= an eccentric); *a dangerous, shady, suspicious character; an obnoxious, unpleasant character; a most unforgettable character.* **5** a symbol, as a letter or ideogram: *Roman characters; special characters such as mathematical symbols; italic characters* (= characters in italic style).
— **in** (or **out of**) **character** true (or false) to one's nature or role: *An actor should always be in character.*

char·ac·ter·is·tic (CAIR·uc·tuh·RIS·tic) *n.* an identifying or distinctive property: *Stripes are a distinguishing characteristic of the zebra.*
— *adj.* identifying or distinctive: *the characteristic odour of chlorine gas; Hospitality is characteristic of most cultures.* — **char·ac·ter·is·ti·cal·ly** *adv.*

char·ac·ter·ize (CAIR·uc·tuh·rize) *v.* **-iz·es, -ized, -iz·ing 1** portray or describe as being of a certain kind: *Iago is characterized as a villain.* **2** be characteristic of or give a characteristic to something: *The zebra is characterized by its stripes; Thoroughness characterizes her work.* — **char·ac·ter·i·za·tion** (-ruh·ZAY·shun) *n.*

cha·rade (shuh·RAID) *n.* **1** a pretence or false show: *The discussion proved to be a mere charade.* **2 charades** *pl.* [takes sing. *v.*] a game in which each participant acts out words and phrases that have to be guessed.

char·coal *n.* **1** a dark grey, light, porous material made by partially burning wood, bone, etc. and used as fuel, in filters, etc. **2** a crayon or pencil made of this substance. **3** a sketch done with it.

charge *v.* **charg·es, charged, charg·ing 1** fill, load, or saturate: *The air was charged with excitement; We have to charge our battery; The mechanic charges it up.* **2** impose on, as a task, responsibility, instruction, etc.: *He charged her with the task of reorganizing the office.* **3** ask (so much) in payment: *We will have to charge (you) for it; We can't charge less than $500; We charge by the minute* (= for each minute). **4** accuse, esp. officially: *The police charged her with speeding; They charged that she was driving 25 km over the limit.* **5** rush forward: *She charged into the store when the doors opened, but charged out again to get her purse from the car; The bull charged at us.* **6** record an item as an obligation or debt: *He went shopping and charged a lot of clothes; Books are charged out of a library by patrons.*
— *n.* **1** a load, as a quantity of explosive, electricity, etc.: *a positive or negative charge of electricity; a depth charge used against submarines; A charge explodes when set off.* **2** duty, custody, command, responsibility, etc.; also, a subject of such responsibility: *the judge's charge* (= instruction) *to the jury; a babysitter's little charges, or babies placed in the sitter's charge* (= custody); *A sitter is put* **in charge of** (= responsible for) *a baby; Is she still in charge? Will someone please* **take charge?** **3** a price or cost: *an admission charge; There's a basic cover charge (for your place at the table) besides the charge for food and drink; The operator announcing the collect call asked, "Will you accept charges?" Will that be cash or charge* (= charge to your account)? **4** an accusation: *to bring, drop, face, level, press, withdraw a charge; a baseless, false, frivolous, trumped-up charge; The police laid a charge of reckless driving against her; She denied the charge; The judge threw out the charge; She was arrested on another charge.* **5** an attack: *a fierce cavalry charge; to fight off a charge; the charge of the Light Brigade.* **6** *Informal.* a thrill: *an emotional charge; He got a real charge out of it.* — **charge·a·ble** (CHAR·juh·bul) *adj.*

charge account *n.* an arrangement for buying on credit.

charge card *n.* a card issued by a firm to customers for charging purchases to an account, usually up to a maximum limit; credit card.

charg·er *n.* **1** person or thing that charges: *a battery charger.* **2** a war horse.

charge sheet *n.* an indictment.

char·i·ot (CHAIR·ee·ut) *n.* a light, horse-drawn, two-wheeled cart, used formerly in racing, war, parades, etc. — **char·i·o·teer** (-uh·TEER) *n.*

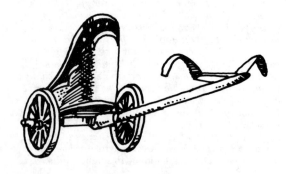

cha·ris·ma (cuh·RIZ·muh) *n.* 1 divine grace or healing power. 2 a magical quality of arousing the devotion of one's followers: *a leader with charisma.*

char·is·mat·ic (cair·iz·MAT·ic) *adj.* 1 having to do with divine healing power: *a charismatic church, movement.* 2 arousing devotion: *a charismaic leader, personality.*

char·i·ty (CHAIR·uh·tee) *n.* 1 love of fellow humans: *St. Paul urged faith, hope, and charity; "Charity begins at home".* 2 a forgiving attitude: *He treated his enemies with charity; They pleaded for charity.* 3 *pl.* **-ties** aid to the poor and needy; almsgiving: *to dispense, distribute, give charity; charity for widows and orphans.* 4 a charitable institution: *Give to your favourite charity; charities such as the Salvation Army.*
— **char·i·ta·ble** (-tuh·bul) *adj.*

char·la·tan (SHAR·luh·tun) *n.* one claiming skills or knowledge that he does not have; phony; quack.
— **char·la·tan·ism** *n.*

charm *n.* 1 an attractive or pleasing personal quality: *the charm of youth; She turns on her charm when she wants something from her dad; a woman of irresistible charm; She exudes charm; Her presence lends charm to any gathering.* 2 a magic formula, ritual, object, etc.: *He wears a charm to ward off the evil eye.*
— **work like a charm** function exactly as desired; succeed completely.
— *v.* attract, please, win over, etc. by charm: *We would be charmed to accept your invitation; We are charmed by the prospect of meeting her; She seems to lead a charmed life (safe from dangers and difficulties); No one likes to break into his charmed (= exclusive) circle of friends.* — **charm·er** *n.*

charming *adj.* attractive or pleasing: *It's charming to watch children perform; a charming personality; She is charming to everyone;* **charm·ing·ly** *adv.*

chart *n.* 1 a sheet or display showing special information with graphics, tables, etc.: *a weather chart; a patient's clinical chart; a flow chart (= diagram) showing the systems or operations of a computer.* 2 a map, esp. one for sea navigation. 3 **charts** *pl.* the listings of sales by rank, esp. of songs: *Her album was number one on the charts; It topped the charts.*
— *v.* map out using a chart; plan in detail: *to chart the position of a ship; to chart out a sales campaign.*

chart·er *n.* 1 a written authorization founding or giving rights to a corporation, university, etc.: *to apply for a charter; to grant a charter to trade in a territory; a charter (= original) member of a society.* 2 a constitution or manifesto of political principles: *the Canadian Charter of Rights and Freedoms.* 3 a travel arrangement in which a group hires a bus, ship, airplane, etc.: *a charter flight.*
— *v.* 1 give a charter to an institution: *The Federal Government charters banks to do business in Canada.* 2 hire or lease: *to charter a bus for a trip to the zoo; to charter a flight to Canada.*
— **chartered** *adj.* given rights by government charter: *a chartered accountant, chartered life underwriter.*

chartered bank *n.* *Cdn.* a privately owned bank chartered by Parliament to operate nationally.

char·y (CHAIR·ee) *adj.* **char·i·er, -i·est** 1 cautious: *She is chary about throwing away money; chary of being too*

generous. 2 sparing: *a curmudgeon who is chary of kind words.* — **char·i·ly** *adv.*; **char·i·ness** *n.*

chase (CHACE) *v.* **chas·es, chased, chas·ing** 1 pursue; hunt; fetch quickly: *to chase after name and fame.* 2 drive away: *Chase that dog off the lawn.* 3 *Informal.* rush: *The boys went chasing down the street.* 4 engrave or emboss metal: *a chased silver teapot.*
— *n.* 1 pursuit: *The police caught the robbers after a short chase; the thrill of **the chase** (= hunting).* 2 that which is hunted. 3 a groove, slot, etc.
— **give chase** pursue.
— **lead someone (on) a merry chase** make someone work hard toward a goal but in vain.

chas·er (CHAY·sur) *n.* 1 *Informal.* a light drink following hard liquor: *whisky with a beer chaser.* 2 a person or thing that chases: *an ambulance chaser; a skirt* or *woman chaser.*

chasm (CAZ·um) *n.* 1 a deep gap: *a yawning chasm.* 2 a rift, as between former friends.

chas·sis (SHAS·ee, CHAS·ee) *n., pl.* **chas·sis** (-eez) 1 a supporting framework, as of a car, truck, radio, or TV set. 2 the landing-gear assembly of an airplane.

chaste *adj.* 1 free from improper sexual relations: *a chaste life, woman; a chaste (= celibate) priest.* 2 simple in style, plain, unadorned, etc.: *chaste diction, prose, wit.* — **chaste·ly** *adv.*; **chaste·ness** *n.*

chas·ten (CHAY·sun) *v.* correct by punishing; purify: *The defeat had a chastening influence on his behaviour.*
— **chas·ten·er** *n.*

chas·tise (chas·TIZE) *v.* **-tis·es, -tised, -tis·ing** punish by a beating or severe remprimand.
— **chas·tise·ment** (CHAS·tiz·munt, chas·TIZE-) *n.*

chas·ti·ty (CHAS·tuh·tee) *n.* the state of abstaining from sexual relations: *the religious vows of poverty, chastity, and obedience.*

chat *v.* **chats, chat·ted, chat·ting** talk in a light, easy manner: *In Ottawa he goes to parties to meet and **chat up** (= try to make friends with) bureaucrats.*
— *n.* a chatting: *a chat about old times; a chat between friends; Franklin Roosevelt's famous fireside chats on radio.*

cha·teau (sha·TOH) *n.* **-teaus** or **-teaux** (-TOZE) a French castle; manor-house.

chat·e·laine (SHAT·uh·lain) *n.* the mistress of a chateau, castle, or large household.

chat·tel (CHAT·ul) *n.* an article of personal property that can be moved from place to place, unlike real estate such as land and houses: *a chattel mortgage.*

chat·ter (CHAT·ur) *n.* 1 a rapid series of brief, meaningless or mechanical sounds, as of a squirrel, birds, monkeys, the sound of typewriter keys, teeth clicking from cold, etc. 2 fast, idle conversation: *endless, idle, incessant chatter.*
— *v.* 1 rattle: *teeth chattering from the cold.* 2 indulge in chatter: *No chattering in class, please!* **chat·ter·er** *n.*

chat·ter·box (CHAT·ur·box) *n.* *Informal.* one who talks idly and without stopping.

chat·ty (CHAT·ee) *adj.* **chat·ti·er, chat·ti·est 1** inclined to chat. **2** informal: *a chatty letter, news report.*
— **chat·ti·ly** *adv.;* **chat·ti·ness** *n.*

chauf·feur (SHOH·fur) *n.* one employed as the driver of a car.
— *v.* drive as a chauffeur: *He chauffeured his boss around town.*

chau·vin·ism (SHOH·vuh·niz·um) *n.* a blind, unreasonable, often aggressive loyalty to one's nation, race, sex, etc.: *male chauvinism.*
— **chau·vin·ist** *n.* — **chau·vin·is·tic** (-NIS·tic) *adj.*

cheap (CHEEP) *adj.* **1** costing comparatively little money, effort, etc.: *The car is cheap at that price; It's cheaper to live in the suburbs than in the city.* **2** selling goods at a low price: *a cheap store.* **3** low in value; of low quality: *a cheap hotel; cheap shoes; a cheap shot* (= an unfair statement or attack); *a cheap threat, trick.* **4** *Informal.* ashamed: *He felt cheap after cheating his friend.* **5** *Informal.* stingy.
— *adv. Informal.* at a cheap price: *to buy cheap and sell dear.* — **cheap·ly** *adv.;* **cheap·ness** *n.*

cheap·en (CHEE·pun) *v.* make or become cheap: *goods cheapened by a shrinking market.*

cheap·ie (CHEE·pee) or **cheap·o** (CHEE·poh) *n. Slang.* a cheap article.

cheap·skate *n. Slang.* a stingy person.

cheat (CHEET) *v.* **1** take from someone by dishonesty or deceit: *An impostor cheated her out* (= deprived her) *of her money; Jim doesn't like to **cheat on** (= be unfaithful to) his wife.* **2** act or play dishonestly: *Jim cheats at cards.* **3** deprive of something: *An illness cheated him of his hopes.* **4** elude or escape from something: *He cheated death while the other passengers were killed in the crash.*
— *n.* **1** an act of cheating; also, a trick or deception. **2** one who cheats.

check *n.* **1** a control: *Keep your horse in check; a body check in hockey; the **checks and balances** (= controls for the even distribution of power) built into an administration; Your (chess) king is in check (= in a threatened position).* **2** an examination or verification; hence, a check or tick (✓) showing that a check has been made: *The police made a spot check of all cars that came by; They ran a check for prior convictions; A background check is made of all applicants.* **3** a token for reclaiming one's hat, baggage, etc.: *a hat check; a rain check for making a later claim or purchase.* **4** a small square or a regular pattern of squares: *red and white checks on the tablecloth.* **5** a bill in a restaurant, bar, etc. **6** same as CHEQUE.
— *v.* **1** stop: *He checked his urge to talk back.* **2** in chess, to threaten the king. **3** examine, inspect for accuracy, proper condition, etc.: *Please check my figures; If you're in doubt, check it out! The police checked into his story and checked through his files.* **4** tick with a check mark: *Please check in this box.* **5** correspond or refer to a list, original copy, authority, etc.: *His version checks with mine; It checks out* (= It's accurate); *I'll have to check with* (= speak to) *the boss on this.* **6** process something for another to have, use, store,

etc.: *Cashiers check out groceries; The airline checked our baggage through* (= accepted it for shipment) *to London; Patrons check* (= borrow) *books out of libraries; Library clerks check* (= give) *them out.*
— **check in (at)** or **check into** formally enter a hotel, factory, etc.; sign in: *We'll check into some hotel; Let's check in at the Laurier.*
— **check up on** or **check on** find out more about a person or thing: *The police checked up on his background.*
— **check out (of)** formally leave an establishment after paying dues, etc.: *Let us check out of this hotel; Now is the time to check out.*

checkbook same as CHEQUEBOOK.

checked *adj.* having a pattern of squares: *a checked shirt, table cloth.*

check·er *n.* **1** a piece used in the game of checkers. **2** one who checks: *a checker at the supermarket counter.*

check·ered (CHECK·urd) *adj.* having a pattern of varying colours or shapes: *a checkered tablecloth; the checkered beetle, lily; a **checkered career** (with many ups and downs).*

checking account *n.* see CHEQUING ACCOUNT.

check·list *n.* a list of items to be referred to and verified.

check·mate *n.* in chess, a position of check which cannot be escaped; hence, total defeat. Also *v.* **-mates, -mat·ed, -mat·ing.**

check·off *n.* the automatic deduction of union dues from a pay cheque.

check·out *n.* a checking out or where it is done: *a supermarket checkout; an express checkout; a checkout counter.*

check·up *n.* **1** an inspection. **2** a medical examination.

cheek *n.* **1** the part on either side of the face below the eyes: *dimpled, rosy, ruddy cheeks; a starving man with hollow, sunken cheeks; couples dancing cheek to cheek; to turn the other cheek* (= patiently suffer injury instead of retaliating). **2** something like a cheek, esp. a buttock. **3** *Informal.* impudence: *He owes me money and had the cheek to phone me collect.*
— **cheek by jowl** close together.

cheek·y *adj.* **cheek·i·er, -i·est** impudent: *a cheeky student;* **cheek·i·ness** *n.*

cheep *n.* a weak, high-pitched cry, as of a young bird.

cheer *n.* **1** a shout of enthusiasm or encouragement: *loud and prolonged cheers; Three cheers for democracy!* **2** joyous mood; hopeful state of mind: *Be of good cheer.* **3** hospitality; hence, food and drink: *Christmas cheer.*
— **cheers** *interj.* used as a drinking toast.
— *v.* **1** make or become glad; hearten: *Let's cheer up; things will improve.* **2** shout a cheer; support: *Let's all cheer for the home team; cheer them on to victory.*

cheer·ful (CHEER·ful) *adj.* **1** having or causing cheer: *a bright and cheerful day.* **2** willing: *a cheerful helper.*
— **cheer·ful·ly** *adv.;* **cheer·ful·ness** *n.*

cheer·i·o (CHEER·ee·oh) *interj. & n.* **-os** *Informal.*

good-bye; also, cheers!

cheer·y *adj.* **cheer·i·er, -i·est** marked by or causing cheerfulness: *a cheery greeting, welcome.*
— **cheer·i·ly** *adv.;* **cheer·i·ness** *n.*

cheese (CHEEZ) *n.* a protein-rich food made from pressed milk curd.
— *v.* **cheese it!** *Slang.* scram! depart!
— **cheesed off** *Slang.* disgusted.

cheese·cake *n.* **1** a cake made of cottage or cream cheese in a crust of sweet crumbs. **2** *Informal.* pictorial display of attractive, scantily clad women; also, such attractiveness; *adj.: cheesecake pictures, magazines.*

cheese·cloth *n.* a light, porous cotton gauze.

cheese·par·ing (CHEEZ·pair·ing) *n.* **1** stinginess. **2** a trifle saved by a miser; *adj.: petty, cheesepairing economics.*

chees·y *adj.* **chees·i·er, -i·est** **1** like cheese. **2** *Slang.* inferior; tawdry: *a dingy room with cheesy furnishings.*
— **chees·i·ness** *n.*

chef *n.* a cook, esp. a head cook.

chem·i·cal (KEM·uh·cul) *adj.* having to do with chemistry: *a chemical bomb, burn, change, compound, experiment, formula, process, reaction; chemical apparatus, engineering, warfare.*
— *n.* a chemical substance. — **chem·i·cal·ly** *adv.*

chem·ist (KEM·ist) *n.* **1** a chemistry specialist. **2** *Brit.* a pharmacist or druggist.

chem·is·try (KEM·is·tree) *n.* **-tries** **1** the science of the composition, combination, and reactions of substances and their elements: *analytical, inorganic, physical chemistry; the chemistry of copper.* **2** how various elements work in combination: *your body chemistry; the odd chemistry* (= workings) *of mob hysteria; There's a special chemistry* (= bond of sympathy) *at work between Mario and Marcie.*

chem·o·ther·a·py (kee·moh·THER·uh·pee, kem·oh-) *n.* treatment of disease using chemicals.

cheque or **check** (CHEK) *n.* a signed authorization for a bank to pay money from one's account: *We always pay by cheque; We issue, make out, write out cheques in favour of people; Cheques are drawn on the bank against our account; People present cheques to a bank; They cash or deposit cheques; Bad or N.S.F. cheques bounce; Our cheques are covered (with sufficient money in the account) so they will clear instead of bouncing; Most people will honour a travel* or *traveller's cheque purchased from a bank, exactly like a cashier's cheque or certified cheque; A blank cheque (that may be used to withdraw an indefinite amount of money) should be given only to the most trustworthy.*

cheque·book or **check·book** *n.* a book of blank cheques.

chequebook journalism *n.* the practice of paying news sources for exclusive rights to a story.

chequ·ing account or **checking account** *n.* a bank account against which cheques may be drawn.

cher·ish (CHER·ish) *v.* **1** hold dear: *a noble cause embraced and cherished by the masses.* **2** keep in mind with attachment or affection: *a cherished memory; We*

had cherished hopes of his return.

cher·ry (CHER·ee) *n.* **cher·ries** **1** a firm, small, fleshy red fruit of a tree of the rose family; also, the tree itself or its wood. **2** bright red colour.

cher·ub (CHER·ub) *n.* **1** a chubby, rosy-faced child. **2** *pl.* **-ub·im** an angel.

che·rub·ic (chuh·ROO·bic) *adj.* angelic: *a cherubic face.*

chess *n.* a game played on a checkerboard, or **chess·board,** by two people, each using 16 pieces called **chess·men,** *sing.* **chess·man.**
— *adj.: a chess game, master, match, piece.*

chest *n.* **1** the front of the body, from the bottom of the ribs to the neck: *a man's hairy chest; the barrel chest (of a lung patient); You'll feel much better if you get it **off your chest** (by telling someone).* **2** a storage or shipping box with a lid: *a tool chest; a young woman's **hope chest** (of clothes and furnishings kept in anticipation of marriage); medicine chest* (=cabinet). **3** a treasury or fund: *the community chest; a war chest for use in a strike or other aggressive action.* **4** a piece of furniture with drawers for clothes; also **chest of drawers.**

ches·ter·bed (CHES·tur·bed) *n.* a chesterfield or sofa that can be opened out into a bed.

ches·ter·field (CHES·tur·field) *n.* a sofa with a well-padded back and upright arm-rests.

chest·nut *n.* **1** the edible nut, enclosed in a prickly case, of a tree of the beech family; also, the tree itself or its wood: *We roast chestnuts for eating.* **2** a reddish brown: *a chestnut horse.* **3** a stale joke, story, theme, etc.: *The new movie gives another roasting to the old chestnut about identical twins getting mixed up.*

chev·a·lier (shev·uh·LEER) *n.* a member of an order of merit such as the French Legion of Honour.

chew (CHOO) *v.* grind or mash with the teeth; masticate: *It's good to chew our food well; He likes to chew on mints after dinner.*
— **chew out** *Slang.* scold severely.
— **chew over** *Slang.* ponder or discuss thoroughly.
— **chew the rag** or **fat** *Slang.* talk casually; chat: *The two old friends chewed the rag for over an hour.*
— *n.* **1** an act of chewing: *Give it a good chew.* **2** something chewed, esp. a quid of tobacco.

chewing gum *n.* a sticky substance such as the solidified latex of certain trees sweetened and flavoured for chewing: *a piece* or *stick of chewing gum.*

chew·y *adj.* **chew·i·er, -i·est** thick and requiring some chewing: *She likes cookies that are chewy rather than crisp.*

chic (SHEEK) *adj.* elegant and fashionable: *a chic dress, hat, lady; It's chic to be thin.*
— *n.* sophistication; stylishness: *feminine chic; radical chic* (= left-wing politics considered fashionable); *Texas chic* (= style featuring Western boots, hats, etc.)

chi·can·er·y (shi·CAY·nuh·ree) *n.* **-er·ies** artful or sophistic trickery; also, a deception or trick.

Chi·ca·no (chi·CAH·noh) *n.* **-nos** an American of Mexican origin; *adj.*: *Chicano Americans; the Chicano community.*

chi·chi (SHEE·shee) *adj.* very refined or elegant, often to excess. — *n.* a person, thing, or quality that is chichi.

chick *n.* 1 a young domestic fowl: *a hen and its chicks.* 2 [slang term of familiarity] a young woman.

chick·a·dee (CHICK·uh·dee) *n.* 1 a small, grey, black-capped North American bird. 2 *Slang.* darling: *My little chickadee!*

chick·en (CHICK·un) *n.* 1 the common barnyard fowl, raised for its flesh and eggs: *the clucking chicken; a brood of chickens; It's not wise to **count one's chickens before they are hatched*** (= act on the basis of premature hopes); *fried chicken* (= fried chicken flesh). 2 *Slang.* a coward: *When it comes to fighting, he's a chicken; to **play chicken*** (= exchange challenges in hopes that the other will back down before the actual showdown).
— *adj. Slang.* 1 cowardly: *He's chicken;* also **chicken-hearted** and **chicken-livered.** 2 adhering to petty details or rules.
— **chicken out** withdraw because of fear.

chick·let or **chic·let** (CHICK·lit) *n.* a small piece of candied chewing gum.

chide *v.* **chides,** *pt.* **chid** or **chid·ed,** *pp.* **chid, chid·ed** or **chid·den, chi·ding** scold mildly: *She chided her daughter for being late.*

chief *n.* the leader of a group, organization, etc.: *an Indian chief; our fire chief; the police chief; Hey Chief!*
— *adj.* 1 highest ranking: *the chief executive officer of a company; the Chief Justice of the Supreme Court; the Chief Executive* (= President) *of the U.S.* 2 most important: *my chief worry.*

chief·ly *adv.* 1 first of all; especially: *His diet is meant chiefly to reduce weight; Chiefly, he has to avoid fat.* 2 mainly or mostly: *His diet consists chiefly of nonfat foods.*

chief of staff *n.* a senior military officer or a head physician.

chief of state *n.* a constitutional head, as the British sovereign in Canada.

chief·tain (CHEEF·tun) *n.* a chief, esp. of a tribe, clan, band, etc.: *a Scottish chieftain.*
— **chief·tain·cy** *n.* **-cies.**

chif·fon (shi·FON) *n.* a light, diaphanous fabric of silk, nylon, etc., as used for wedding dresses.
— *adj.* light and fluffy: *pineapple chiffon pie.*
— **chif·fon·y** (SHIF·uh·nee) *adj.*: *a chiffony silk scarf.*

chil·blain (CHIL·blain) *n.* an itchy, red swelling of the fingers, toes, ears, or nose caused by exposure to cold: *to catch chilblains.*

child (CHILED) *n., pl.* **chil·dren** (CHIL·drun) 1 baby; infant: *A mother conceives a child; She carries a child for nine months, when she is **with child*** (= pregnant); *She has* or *gives birth to a child; She nurses her child till she goes back to work; a child at a day-care centre.* 2 one who is growing up: *to adopt, feed, indulge, pamper, spoil a child; a bright, gifted, happy, intelligent, loving, mischievous, obedient, precocious, sensitive, young child; delinquent children; a neglected, problem, stubborn, unruly, wayward child; an underprivileged child; Legally, you are still a child at 16; adj.: child care, guidance, labour, psychology, welfare.* 3 offspring: *the only child of her parents; Our children have married and left; the children* (= descendants) *of Adam; the children of Israel* (= Jews). 4 a product of a particular period or influence: *a child of his times; a child of the 1960s.*

child·hood *n.* the state or period of being a child: *He had a happy childhood; an oldster in his **second childhood*** (= being senile).

child·bear·ing (CHILD·bair·ing) *n. & adj.* childbirth: *pregnancy and childbearing; a woman of childbearing age; Most women's childbearing years are between the ages of 25 and 44.*

child·birth *n.* the act of giving birth.

child·ish *adj.* foolish and immature: *It's childish of him to act like that; a childish prank.*
— **child·ish·ly** *adv.;* **child·ish·ness** *n.*
— **child·less** *adj.*: *a childless couple.*

child·like *adj.* like a child, esp. innocent, naive, etc.: *She spoke with childlike candour.*

child·proof *adj.* that children cannot open, damage, etc.: *a child-proof bottle, cap, lock.*

children's aid society *n. Cdn.* a private social service agency funded by government to look after the needs of children lacking parental care.

child's play *n.* an easy or trivial job: *Assembling computers is child's play to him.*

chil·i (CHIL·ee) *n.* **chil·ies** 1 the pod of a tropical American capsicum, dried to make a pungent pepper, often ground to make **chili powder** seasoning; also, the plant. 2 a hot dish with chili, meat, beans, etc.; also **chili con car·ne** (CHIL·ee·cun·CAR·nee),

chill *n.* 1 a feeling of coldness: *The ghost story sent chills up her spine; The death cast a chill over the proceedings; She put the glass near the fire to take the chill off the drink; It's easy to catch a chill* (= cold) *in that draft.* 2 cool weather: *the chill of a fall day; He walked out into the chill of the night.*
— *adj.* uncomfortably cool: *a chill December wind; She silenced him with a chill* (= cold) *stare.*
— *v.* 1 make or get cold: *The skiers were chilled to the bone; Chill the wine before serving; a chilling wind.* 2 discourage; dampen: *to chill friendliness, spirits; His negative attitude chilled our plans; a chilling effect; a **chilling*** (= frightening) *drama, observation, reminder,*

tale, truth.

chill·er *n.* one that chills: *Meat is transported in special chillers; a chiller (=scary book or movie) called "Thirteen Ghosts."*

chill factor *n.* same as WINDCHILL.

chil·li same as CHILI (pepper).

chill·y (CHILL·ee) *adj.* **chill·i·er, -i·est** cold: *a chilly wind; chilly temperatures, weather; a chilly greeting, reception; chilly conditions, news, relations.*
— **chill·i·ly** *adv.*; **chill·i·ness** *n.*

chimaera same as CHIMERA.

chime *n.* 1 a bell, as in a clock. 2 usually **chimes** *pl.* a set of bells rung in melody: *We have chimes instead of a doorbell; Chimes sounded in the distance.*
— *v.* **chimes, chimed, chim·ing** 1 ring or sound, esp. in harmony: *The clock chimed three.* 2 agree: *Your idea chimes with my own.*
— **chime in** join in a conversation, song, etc. with agreement or harmony: *"So do I," she chimed in.*

chi·me·ra or **chi·mae·ra** (kye·MEER·uh) *n.* 1 a monster of Greek myth with a lion's head, goat's body, and serpent's tail. 2 a terrible or bizarre fantasy; something unrealistic or illusory.

chi·mer·i·cal (kye·MER·uh·cul) *adj.* illusory or impractical: *a chimerical plan for reform; a vision of prosperity built on chimerical foundations.*

chim·ney (CHIM·nee) *n.* **-neys** 1 a vertical vent for the smoke and gases from a factory, fireplace, furnace, stove, etc.: *He smokes like a chimney.* 2 a glass tube shielding a lamp flame: *a chimney that is black with soot.*

chi·mo (CHEE·moh, CHY-) *interj. Cdn.* in the North, greetings! [as a toast] cheers!

chimp *n. Informal.* chimpanzee.

chim·pan·zee (chim·pan·ZEE, -PAN·zee) *n.* an intelligent, middle-sized African ape.

chin *n.* the part of the lower jaw below the lower lip: *a portly gentleman with a double chin.*
— *v.* **chins, chinned, chin·ning** pull *oneself* up, as from a bar while hanging by the hands until the chin is level with or above the hands.
— **keep one's chin up** not to get discouraged.
— **take it on the chin** suffer courageously.

chi·na (CHYE·nuh) *n.* porcelain, esp. tableware of porcelain: *fine china; a set of china; Set the best china for our company; a china doll.*

Chi·na·town (CHYE·nuh·town) *n.* the Chinese quarter of a large city outside China.

Chin·ese (chye·NEEZ) *n. sing. & pl.* 1 a native of China or a descendant of one. 2 one of a group of related languages of China, esp. Mandarin.
— *adj.* pertaining to the nation, people, culture, or language of China: *a set of Chinese boxes (in a nested arrangement); Chinese cabbage, checkers, cookies, food, lantern, laundry, puzzle, restaurant; the Chinese Empire (from about 2200 B.C. to the Chinese Revolution of A.D. 1911); the Chinese Wall (=the Great Wall of China).*

chink *n.* 1 a small crack: *a chink in his armour (=weak point).* 2 a sharp, metallic click.
— *v.* 1 fill in cracks: *The pioneers chinked their log cabins with clay and straw, moss, etc. before winter.* 2 make a clicking sound: *You could hear coins chinking in his pocket.*

chin·less *adj.* lacking strength of character: *Our chinless wonders haven't won a game all season.*

Chi·nook (shuh·NOOK, long or short "OO") *n.* 1 (a member of) any of a group of American Indian tribes of northwestern U.S. 2 the language of a Chinook tribe, as **Chi·nook·an.** 3 chinook *Cdn.* a warm Pacific wind that blows across the Rockies in the winter down into Alberta and Saskatchewan.

Chinook Jargon *n.* a trade language of western North America based on Chinook.

chintz (CHINTS) *n.* a brightly patterned cotton cloth, usually with a glossy finish.

chintz·y (CHINT·see) *adj.* **chintz·i·er, -i·est** 1 of or decorated with chintz. 2 cheap and tacky: *a chintzy approach, bargain, job, publicity stunt.* 3 stingy.

chin-up *n.* the exercise of chinning oneself.

chip *n.* 1 a small cut or broken piece: *Wood chips littered the carpenter's shop; chocolate chips.* 2 a flaw showing where a chip has been made: *a chip in the glass.* 3 a gambling token: *He **cashed in his chips** (Slang for died); Let **the chips fall where they may** (=Let actions take their natural course); when **the chips are down** (=in a critical situation).* 4 a thin, crispy snack: *corn chips; potato chips.* 5 a small strip of something edible: *fish and chips (=french fries).* 6 an integrated circuit: *computer chips; logic chips; silicon chips.*
— **chip off the old block** one just like his father.
— **chip on one's shoulder** a grievance: *He has a chip on his shoulder about being passed up for promotion.*
— **in the chips** *Slang.* having much money.
— *v.* **chips, chipped, chip·ping** 1 cut or shape by chipping. 2 knock a chip from something: *Some cups and plates chip; He fell and chipped a tooth.*
— **chip in** contribute.

chip·munk *n.* a small striped ground-dwelling North American squirrel.

chip·per *n.* a person or machine that chips.
— *adj. Informal.* cheerful; vigorous; lively: *chipper as a sparrow.* — *v.* **chipper up** cheer up.

chip·py *adj. Cdn. Slang.* rough or aggressive: *a chippy game, player.*

chip shot *n.* in golf, a short lobbed shot onto the green.

chi·ro·prac·tic (kye·ruh·PRAC·tic) *n.* the treatment of disease by the manipulation of the spine or other parts of the body: *Doctor of Chiropractic.*

chi·ro·prac·tor (KYE·ruh·prac·tur) *n.* a chiropractic doctor.

chirp *v.* utter a high, short sound, as small birds and insects such as crickets and grasshoppers do.
— *n.* a tweet; peep.

139

chir·rup (CHUR·up) *v.* **1** chirp repeatedly. **2** make a similar noise, esp. by sucking, as in urging a horse forward; *n.: the chirrup of bullets whizzing by.*

chis·el (CHIZ·ul) *n.* a metal tool with a sloped cutting edge used to shape or cut wood, stone, or metal.
— *v.* **-els, -elled** or **-eled, -el·ling** or **-el·ing 1** shape or work with a chisel: *to chisel a groove in a plank; a finely chiselled figure.* **2** *Informal.* cheat or get by cheating: *The crook chiselled us out of $100.*

chis·el·ler or **chis·el·er** (CHIZ·uh·lur) *n. Slang.* a cheat or swindler.

chit *n.* **1** a short note. **2** a voucher for food, drink, merchandise, etc.: *meal chits.* **3** *Informal.* a child.

chit·chat *n.* small talk; chat.

chiv·al·ry (SHIV·ul·ree) *n.* **1** the qualities of a perfect knight, such as courage, courtesy, and honour: *Is chivalry dead?* **2** the system of medieval knighthood: *the age of chivalry* (= Middle Ages).
— **chi·val·ric** (shi·VAL·ric) *adj.* having to do with chivalry: *the chivalric code; chivalric rites.*
— **chiv·al·rous** (SHIV·ul·rus) *adj.* having or showing chivalry: *his chivalrous manner; a chivalrous gentleman of the old school with chivalrous notions.*
— **chiv·al·rous·ly** *adv.;* **chiv·al·rous·ness** *n.*

chlo·ri·nate (CLOR·uh·nate) *v.* **-nates, -nat·ed, -nat·ing** treat with chlorine or a compound of it, usually to purify, esp. water. — **chlo·ri·na·tor** (-nay·tur) *n.*
— **chlo·ri·na·tion** (-NAY·shun) *n.*

chlo·rine (CLOR·een) *n.* a greenish-yellow, poisonous, foul-smelling gas used to disinfect, bleach, etc.

chlo·ro·form (CLOR·uh·form) *n.* a volatile, pleasant-smelling liquid, used as an anesthetic, in refrigerants, etc. — *v.* anesthetize with chloroform; also, kill.

chlo·ro·phyll or **chlo·ro·phyl** (CLOR·uh·fil) *n.* the green colouring in plant cells which is necessary for photosynthesis.

chock *n.* a block or wedge used to support or keep a barrel, wheel, boat hull, etc. from moving.
— *v.* block with a chock or chocks: *We chocked the rear wheels before jacking up the car.*
— *adv.* as close, tight, etc. as possible.

chock-a-block (CHOCK·uh·bloc) *adj. & adv.* close(ly): *families crammed chock-a-block into tenements; The tenements are chock-a-block with people.*

chockbore same as CHOKEBORE.

chock-full *adj.* as full as possible: *a room chock-full of books and papers.*

choc·o·late (CHOCK·lit) *n.* **1** a powder, syrup, solid, etc. made from roasted and processed seeds of the "cacao" tree. **2** a food made with chocolate: *a cup of hot chocolate (drink); a bar of milk chocolate.* **3** a deep reddish brown colour.
— *adj.: a chocolate bar, cake, candy, drink, flavour; a chocolate chip cookie; chocolate colour, ice cream.*

choc·o·lat·y or **choc·o·lat·ey** (CHOCK·luh·tee) *adj.* like chocolate: *She likes everything sweet and chocolaty; It's a chocolaty brown.*

choice *n.* **1** the act or power of choosing: *a matter of choice; The choice is difficult; She did it of her own choice; He remains a bachelor by choice.* **2** something chosen; selection: *the people's choice; a poor choice of words; a bad, first, good, happy, intelligent, judicious, random, wise choice; Aluminum is the material of choice* (= the preferred one) *for a lightweight plane; Take your choice (from the lot).* **3** an alternative: *the choice between marriage and the single life; the choice among many possibilities; Your reasons are so compelling, I have no choice but to agree.* **4** the best: *the choice of the lot.* **5** a variety to choose from; selection: *We offer a wide choice of colours.*
— *adj.* **choic·er, choic·est** very good in quality or kind: *a choice portion of the turkey; the choicest cuts of meat.*

choir (QUIRE) *n.* **1** a group of singers, esp. in a church: *to sing in a choir.* **2** a section of an orchestra with instruments of the same type: *the brass choir.* **3** the part of a church used by the choir.
— **choir·boy** *n.;* **choir·girl** *n.*

choke *v.* **chokes, choked, chok·ing 1** have or cause difficulty in breathing: *The heavy smoke choked us up; Pollution is choking our lakes and rivers; He choked on a piece of meat; It was death by choking; a baseball team that is choking* (*Slang* for collapsing). **2** limit the flow of air, water, etc.; clog: *a pipe choked with mud; a flower bed choked with weeds; He choked back his tears; was too choked up* (= overcome with emotion) *to go on with his speech; Parliament decided to choke off* (= end) *the debate.* **3** grip a bat, golf club, etc. closer to the hitting end: *The burly six-footer choked up on the bat two inches.*
— *n.* **1** the action or sound of choking. **2** the air valve in a carburetor. **3** a narrowing of the bore of a gun near the muzzle; also **choke·bore.**

chok·er (CHOH·kur) *n. Informal.* something worn around the neck, as a short, close-fitting necklace.

chol·er·a (COLL·uh·ruh) *n.* a severe contagious disease of the digestive system which often results in death.

chol·er·ic (COLL·uh·ric, cuh·LER·ic) *adj.* hot-tempered: *He is choleric by temperament; He's of a choleric disposition.*

cho·les·ter·ol (cuh·LES·tuh·rol) *n.* a fatty substance in body tissues: *Fatty meats, butter, and eggs are high in cholesterol; Cutting down on cholesterol helps prevent hardening of the arteries.*

chomp *v.* chew hard; champ: *He chomps on his cigar.*

choose (CHOOZ) *v.* **choos·es, chose** (CHOZE), **cho·sen**
(CHOH·zun), **choos·ing 1** pick according to one's
judgment; select: *He chooses his partners carefully; We
choose at random when all are equally good; We can
also choose by lot or by tossing a coin; to choose from
many applicants for a job; The judges found it difficult
to choose between the two finalists; One was chosen as
the winner; He was chosen to fill the vacancy; a
candidate of her own choosing.* **2** decide by oneself: *I
chose to live in Canada; I will do as I choose.*

choos·y or **choos·ey** (CHOO·zee) *adj.* **choos·i·er, -i·est**
Informal. fussy in choosing; picky: *She's very choosy
about what she wears.* — **choos·i·ness** *n.*

chop *v.* **chops, chopped, chop·ping 1** cut with a heavy
blade, as an axe, cleaver, etc.: *He chopped down the
tree; chopped up the logs into firewood; finely chopped
onions* (= cut into small pieces). **2** hit with a short, sharp
stroke: *He chopped the ball.*
— *n.* **1** a chopping blow: *He cut the cable with one
chop; a karate chop that splits wood.* **2** a piece chopped
off, esp. a small cut of meat and bone: *lamb, mutton,
pork, veal chops.* **3** an official permit or stamp of
quality: *first-chop goods* (= goods of top quality). **4** a
short, jerky motion, as of waves. **5 chops** *pl.* the jaws
and surrounding flesh: *Fido licks his chops after a meal.*

chop·per *n.* **1** a person or thing that chops: *a food
chopper; meat chopper.* **2** *Informal.* a helicopter.
3 *Slang.* a motorcycle with its front modified, as one
without fenders; customized motorcycle.

chop·py (CHOP·ee) *adj.* **chop·pi·er, chop·pi·est**
irregular or changeable: *a choppy sea, wind.*
— **chop·pi·ly** *adv.*; **chop·pi·ness** *n.*

chop·sticks *n. pl.* one of a pair of slender sticks held in
one hand and used by the Chinese, Japanese, Koreans,
etc. as an eating utensil.

cho·ral (COR·ul) *adj.* having to do with a choir or
chorus: *a choral arrangement, group, society; the three-
part choral odes between the episodes of a Greek
tragedy; choral music sung by a chorus as part of an
opera; choral reading by many in unison.*
— **chor·al·ly** *adv.*

cho·rale or **cho·ral** (cuh·RAL) *n.* **1** a simple choral
hymn, esp. in a Lutheran church service. **2** its melody as
set in harmony for voices or instruments: *a Bach
chorale.* **3** a choir.

chord (CORD) *n.* **1** a set of three or more musical notes
sounded together in harmony. **2** a line linking two
points on a curve or circle. **3** an emotional response or
reaction: *Her sad story struck a sympathetic chord in the
audience.* — *v.* harmonize: *to chord a guitar.*

chore *n.* a tiresome job, esp. a routine task: *The job was
quite a chore; John does his chores before breakfast; the
daily chore of taking out the garbage.*

chor·e·o·graph (COR·ee·uh·graf) *v.* create the
choreography for a dance: *a well choreographed show.*
— **chor·e·o·graph·er** (-ee·OG·ruh·fur) *n.*

chor·e·og·ra·phy (cor·ee·OG·ruh·fee) *n.* the art of
designing dances or ballets; also, the dancing.
— **chor·e·o·graph·ic** (-GRAF·ic) *adj.*

cho·rine (COR·een) *n.* *Informal.* a chorus girl.

chor·is·ter (COR·is·tur) *n.* **1** a member of a choir, esp. a
choirboy. **2** a choir leader.

chor·tle (CHOR·tul) *v.* **-tles, -tled, -tling** give a gleeful,
throaty chuckle: *She chortled in triumph.*
— *n.*: *a chortle of delight.*

cho·rus (COR·us) *n.* **1** a choir. **2** any group of people
who sing, dance, recite, etc. together, esp. the
supporting players in a musical drama: *a mixed chorus.*
3 the part performed by a chorus; also, a piece of
harmonic music written for a chorus. **4** something said
or sung in unison: *a chorus of praise; "Absolutely," they
said in chorus;* (= all together). **5** a repeated part of a
song or tune; refrain.
— *v.* **-rus·es, -russed** or **-rused, -rus·sing** or **-rus·ing**
utter in unison.

chorus boy or **chorus girl** *n.* a young man or young
woman who sings and dances in the chorus of a musical
show or revue.

chose, chosen See CHOOSE.
— **cho·sen** (CHOH·zun) *adj.* selected or preferred: *the
chosen few; the chosen people.*

chow (rhyme: "how") *n.* *Informal.* food.
— *v.* **chow down** eat.

chow·chow *n.* a relish made of pickled chopped
vegetables.

chow·der (CHOW·dur) *n.* **1** a thick stewlike soup
usually of seafood with a milk base. **2** a similar dish:
clam chowder; corn chowder.

chrism (CRIZ·um) *n.* consecrated oil used in church
sacraments.

chris·ten (CRIS·un) *v.* **1** baptize: *I christen* (= name)
thee Margaret. **2** name and dedicate formally, as a ship.

Chris·ten·dom (CRIS·un·dum) *n.* Christians collectively;
also, the Christian world.

Chris·tian (CRIS·chun) *adj.* having to do with Christ, his
teachings, the religion based on them, or its followers:
*Christian charity, churches, concern for others;
Christian countries, ethics, piety; the Christian era
(starting with the birth of Christ); the Christian or
church year (according to the church calendar).*
— *n.* a believer in Christ or Christianity.

Chris·ti·an·i·ty (cris·chee·AN·uh·tee) *n.* **1** a religion
based on Christ's teachings. **2** the state of being
Christian: *No one doubts his Christianity; but his
Christianity doesn't go so far as turning the other cheek.*

Chris·tian·ize (CRIS·chuh·nize) *v.* **-iz·es, -ized, -iz·ing**
make Christian in belief or character.

Christian name *n.* name given at baptism; a Christian's
first name.

Christ·like (CRY·) *adj.* like Christ; exhibiting patience,
purity, and other virtues.

Christ·mas (CRIS·mus) *n.* a Christian festival
celebrating the birth of Christ observed on December 25
(or January 7 in Eastern churches): *We wish you a Merry*

Christmas; I'm hoping for a white Christmas (with snowfall).
— *adj.: a Christmas card, carol, Day, Eve, gift, greeting, seal; Christmas cheer.*
— **Christ·mas·sy** or **Christ·mas·y** (-muh·see) *adj.*

Christ·mas·tide (CRIS·mus·tide) *n.* the Christmas festival season, esp. December 24 to January 6.

Christ·mas·time (CRIS·mus·time) *n.* the time of the year around Christmas.

Christmas tree *n.* a usually evergreen tree decorated and set up at Christmas: *to trim a Christmas tree* (= decorate it).

chro·mat·ic (croh·MAT·ic) *adj.* 1 having to do with colour. 2 in music, having to do with the **chromatic scale** which proceeds by half-tones: *a chromatic harmonica.*

chrome (CROME) *n.* 1 chromium-plated trim, as of an automobile. 2 chromium; also, an alloy or pigment made with it; *adj.: chrome green* (= permanent green colour used in printing textiles); *Chrome leather (tanned using a chromium solution) is used for shoe uppers, handbags, etc.; chrome steel, yellow.*
— **chro·mic** (CROH·mic) *adj.*

chro·mi·um (CROH·mee·um) *n.* a hard grey metal used in alloys, pigments, corrosion-resistant plating, etc.

chro·mo·some (CROH·muh·sohm) *n.* any of the gene-bearing bodies in a cell's nucleus.
— **chro·mo·so·mal** (-SOH·mul) *adj.*

chron·ic (CRON·ic) *adj.* constant and long-lasting: *a chronic complainer, complaint, condition, disease, head cold, indigestion, patient, rebellion, sufferer, worry; a chronic-care facility, patient.* — **chron·i·cal·ly** *adv.*

chron·i·cle (CRON·uh·cul) *n.* a bare historical record of events; account: *He kept a daily chronicle of events while in captivity.*
— *v.* -cles, -cled, -cling narrate or record as in a chronicle: *He chronicled his days in captivity; He has chronicled the history of the Roman Empire.*
— **chron·i·cler** *n.*

chron·o·graph (CRON·uh·graf) *n.* any device for precisely measuring time, as a stopwatch.
— **chron·o·graph·ic** (-GRAF·ic) *adj.*

chron·o·log·i·cal (cron·uh·LOJ·uh·cul) *adj.* 1 according to chronology: *Tell us what happened in chronological order* (= order of earliest happenings first). 2 measured by time: *He has a low mental age compared with his chronological* (= actual) *age.* — **chron·o·log·i·cal·ly** *adv.*

chro·nol·o·gy (cruh·NOL·uh·jee) *n.* -gies 1 the determination or arrangement of the dates and sequence of events: *The chronology of prehistory is still uncertain.* 2 a list or table showing this: *the chronology of the war.*
— **chro·nol·o·gist** *n.*

chro·nom·e·ter (cruh·NOM·uh·tur) *n.* a precise watch or clock.

chrys·a·lis (CRIS·uh·lis) *n.* -lis·es 1 the pupa of an insect; also, its firm cocoon. 2 something immature but developing; also, a cocoonlike protection: *youth emerging from the chrysalis of naivety.*

chub·by (CHUB·ee) *adj.* chub·bi·er, chub·bi·est plump or fleshy: *the chubby faces of children.*

chuck *v.* 1 tap or pinch lightly, esp. under the chin. 2 *Informal.* toss easily; throw: *She chucked the ball to him.* 3 *Informal.* throw away; dismiss: *to chuck out old shoes; Chuck it, it's hopeless now.*
— *n.* 1 a tap or pinch: *a loving chuck.* 2 a throwing: *a quick chuck to the outfield.* 3 a device for holding a tool, bit, or piece of work in a drill, lathe, etc. 4 a cut of beef from the neck to the shoulder blade: *ground chuck; adj.: a chuck steak.* 5 *Cdn.* a large body of water, esp. the ocean.

chuck·le (CHUCK·ul) *v.* -les, -led, -ling laugh gently or to oneself: *She chuckled quietly and left the room; What was she chuckling about? was chuckling with glee at his blooper.*
— *n.* a chuckling: *They had a good chuckle over what happened; She let out a hearty chuckle; a satisfied chuckle; a chuckle of mirth.*

chuck·wag·on (CHUCK·wag·un) *n.* a wagon carrying food and kitchen equipment for feeding loggers, cowboys, etc.

chuckwagon race *n. Cdn.* in Western Canada, a race between chuckwagons as part of a rodeo or stampede.

chug *n.* a short, heavy, dull sound, as of a labouring engine.
— *v.* chugs, chugged, chug·ging make this sound or move while doing so: *an old car chugging up the hill; The train chugged along.*

chum *n.* 1 *Informal.* a close friend; buddy: *We were chums at school; We're old chums.* 2 *Cdn.* a variety of Pacific salmon found along the coast of British Columbia.
— *v.* chums, chummed, chum·ming make friends: *The two seem to be chumming up well; my son chumming up with yours.*

chum·my *adj.* chum·mi·er, chum·mi·est *Informal.* friendly: *He was very chummy with her; was acting too chummy for a total stranger.*
— **chum·mi·ly** *adv.;* **chum·mi·ness** *n.*

chump *n. Informal.* a dupe; fool.

chunk *n.* a thick, heavy piece; hence, a large amount: *a chunk of wood; You're asking for a big chunk of my time.*

chunk·y *adj.* chunk·i·er, -i·est 1 stocky or thickset: *a man of chunky build; The dictionary is a chunky volume; The puffin is a chunky bird.* 2 having chunks in it: *a thick, chunky soup.*
— **chunk·i·ly** *adv.;* **chunk·i·ness** *n.*

church *n.* 1 a building for public, usually Christian worship: *to consecrate* or *dedicate a church.* 2 a religious service: *They attend* or *go to church on Sundays; We were late for church; We met at church; I saw her in church; We went home after church.* 3 [descriptive or generic use] Christians as a body: *the Catholic church; a Christian church; an evangelical church; a fundamentalist church; the universal church.* 4 **Church** an organized group or a denomination within this body: *the Anglican, Baptist, Catholic, Episcopal, Established, Lutheran, Mennonite, Methodist, Mormon,*

Orthodox, Presbyterian, Protestant, United Church; the Church of England; as the Church teaches. **5** religious as opposed to secular power: *separation of church and state.* **6** the clergy or clerical profession: *She entered the church at 25.* — **adj.:** *a church assembly, burial, school, service, wedding.*

church·go·er (CHURCH·go·ur) *n.* a regular attender of church. — **church·go·ing** *n. & adj.*

church·man (CHURCH·mun) *n.* **-men** a clergyman: *a leading Anglican churchman.*

church·war·den (CHURCH·wor·dun) *n.* an elected lay official of an Anglican or Episcopal church.

church·wom·an (CHURCH·wom·an) *n.* **-wom·en** an active woman member of a church.

church·yard *n.* the grounds of a church, esp. as a burial place.

churl *n.* an ill-bred, bad-tempered person; boor. — **churl·ish** *adj.: churlish manners.* — **churl·ish·ly** *adv.;* **churl·ish·ness** *n.*

churn *n.* a container for agitating milk or cream to make butter. — *v.* **1** make butter in a churn. **2** produce or suffer violent agitation: *A motor boat churns the water; the churning waters of the rapids; The car churned (=moved with churning effect) through the snowbank.* — **churn out** produce rapidly and mechanically: *He churns out one trashy novel after another.*

chute (SHOOT, long "OO") *n.* **1** a waterfall or rapids. **2** a passage or channel for shooting or sliding things down: *a mail chute; the emergency escape chute of an airliner; the discharge chute of a lawn mower.* **3** *Informal.* a parachute.

chutz·pa or **chutz·pah** (HOOT·spuh, short "OO") *n. Informal.* **1** boldness or aggressiveness: *a woman of hope and chutzpa.* **2** gall or nerve.

ciao (CHOW) *interj. Informal.* greetings; goodbye.

ci·der (SYE·dur) *n.* the pressed juice of apples, used as a beverage, either unfermented (**sweet cider**) or fermented (**hard cider**), and to make vinegar, applejack, etc.

ci·gar (suh·GAR) *n.* a cylindrical roll of tobacco for smoking: *He kept puffing on his cigar as he talked.*

cig·a·rette (sig·uh·RET) *n.* a roll of finely cut tobacco covered with thin paper; also **cig·a·ret.**

cinch *n.* **1** the belt used to fasten a saddle or pack on a horse. **2** *Slang.* a firm grip; hence, a certainty; something easy to do or guaranteed: *The job is a cinch; It's a cinch that he'll win; He'll win – that's a cinch; He's a cinch to win.* — *v.* **1** tighten a belt or cinch. **2** *Slang.* make sure of something: *They cinched the game in the last quarter; They had it cinched.*

cin·der (SIN·dur) *n.* **1** a piece of hard, solid residue of burning coal or wood; *adj.: a cinder-block building, bunker.* **2** glowing coals; embers. **3 cinders** *pl.* ashes: *It was reduced to cinders.* — **cin·der·y** *adj.*

Cin·der·el·la (sin·duh·REL·uh) *n.* a person or thing that is neglected or unrecognized like the fairy-tale character

of that name: *Libraries sometimes become the Cinderellas of educational budgeting: a Cinderella (=neglected) resource.*

cin·e·ma (SIN·uh·muh) *n.* **1** the art, industry, or medium of motion-picture films; also, films collectively: *the influence of American cinema on Canadian culture.* **2** *Brit.* a movie or movie theatre; **cin·e·mat·ic** (sin·uh·MAT·ic) *adj.*

cin·e·ma·theque (sin·uh·muh·TEK) *n.* a small theatre for innovative and experimental films.

cin·e·ma·tog·ra·phy (sin·uh·muh·TOG·ruh·fee) *n.* the art of making movies, esp. the photographic aspects.

cinema ve·ri·té (-ver·uh·TAY) *n.* film-making in a style suggesting documentary realism; also, such a film.

ci·pher (SYE·fur) *n.* **1** zero (0) as indicating no quantity; hence, a nonentity. **2** a coding system for concealing the meaning of a text; also, a coded message: *messages in cipher; spies trying to break a cipher without its key.* **3** any Arabic numeral. — *v.* **1** solve or calculate arithmetically. **2** express information in a code.

cir·ca (SUR·cuh) *prep.* about: *born circa 1900.*

cir·ca·di·an (sur·CAY·dee·un) *adj.* in biology, acting or occurring in roughly 24-hour cycles: *the circadian rhythm of our eating and sleeping patterns.*

cir·cle (SUR·cul) *n.* **1** a closed round plane curve or the area bounded by it: *A compass is used to draw circles; Satellites describe circles around their planets; They joined hands and formed a circle around the pole; The Arctic and Antarctic Circles are polar circles; a traffic circle.* **2** something resembling a circle: *a circle of admirers; jobseekers caught in a vicious circle of lack of experience and consequent unemployment; People move in academic, business, close, diplomatic, exclusive, family, financial, inner, intimate, political, professional circles; the circle (= cycle) of the seasons; to go around or talk **in circles** without getting anywhere.* — **come full circle** return to the starting point after a sojourn. — *v.* **-cles, -cled, -cling** enclose or move in a circle: *The teacher circled six errors; The jet circled (above) the airport.*

cir·clet (SUR·clit) *n.* a small circle, esp. as an ornament: *She had a gold circlet around her neck.*

cir·cuit (SUR·kit) *n.* **1** the path, distance, or journey around something: *A fence marks the circuit of the estate; the circuit of the moon around the earth.* **2** a regular course travelled by a sales rep, preacher (**circuit rider**), judge (**circuit judge**), entertainer, athletic competitor, etc.: *the professional golf circuit; the lecture circuit; a band playing the nightclub circuit; the cocktail party circuit.* **3** the path of an electric current, with its wiring and other equipment: *Current flows when the circuit is closed; If the current stops, there's a break in the circuit somewhere; A dangerous short circuit results when the main circuit is bypassed; a computer's **circuit board** on which chips are mounted.*

circuit breaker *n.* a device for stopping the flow of electricity under special conditions such as overload:

The current stops when a circuit breaker is tripped.

cir·cu·i·tous (sur·CUE·uh·tus) *adj.* lengthy and indirect; roundabout: *They took a circuitous route to avoid reporters.* — **cir·cu·i·tous·ly** *adv.*

cir·cuit·ry (SUR·cuh·tree) *n.* -ries 1 the design or components of an electrical circuit. 2 such circuits collectively.

cir·cu·lar (SURK·yuh·lur) *adj.* having to do with the circle: *A quadrant is a unit of circular measure; a circular* (= circuitous) *explanation; circular reasoning; a **circular file** (Informal for wastebasket); a circular letter, notice (distributed to many); a circular* (= round) *saw.* — *n.* an advertisement, leaflet, etc. for mass distribution: *We send out circulars to the public; to distribute circulars from door to door.* — **cir·cu·lar·i·ty** (-LAIR·uh·tee) *n.*

cir·cu·late (SURK·yuh·late) *v.* -lates, -lat·ed, -lat·ing move, often in a circuit, from place to place, person to person, etc.: *A fan circulates air in a room; Please circulate this memo; Blood circulates in the body; The host circulates among the guests; A popular paper circulates widely.*

cir·cu·la·tion (surk·yuh·LAY·shun) *n.* 1 the act of circulating, esp. of blood in the body: *Exercise helps improve circulation if you suffer from poor circulation; The government puts money into circulation; Bills are withdrawn from circulation as they get old; They cease to be in circulation.* 2 the distribution or total sales of a periodical: *a paper with a limited or small circulation; The Times enjoys a wide, national circulation; an enormous circulation of two million.*

cir·cu·la·to·ry (SUR·kyuh·luh·tor·ee) *adj.* having to do with the circulation of the blood: *He died of circulatory failure.*

cir·cum·cise (SUR·cum·size) *v.* -cis·es, -cised, -cis·ing cut off the foreskin of a male or "clitoris" of a female. — **cir·cum·ci·sion** (-SIZH·un) *n.*

cir·cum·fer·ence (sur·CUM·fuh·runce) *n.* 1 the perimeter of a circle or other figure: *three kilometres in circumference.* 2 outer boundary; periphery.

cir·cum·flex (SUR·cum·flex) *n.* a mark written above a vowel (as in â) to show its quality, pitch, etc.

cir·cum·lo·cu·tion (SUR·cum·loh·CUE·shun) *n. Formal.* an indirect, evasive expression using too many words.

cir·cum·nav·i·gate (sur·cum·NAV·uh·gate) *v.* sail all the way around, esp. the world: *Magellan was the first to circumnavigate the world.* — **cir·cum·nav·i·ga·tion** (-GAY·shun) *n.*

cir·cum·scribe (SUR·cum·scribe) *v.* -scribes, -scribed, -scrib·ing 1 draw a line around something. 2 restrict, limit in scope, etc.: *a narrowly circumscribed field of specialization.*

cir·cum·spect (SUR·cum·spect) *adj.* aware of possible consequences; cautious and prudent: *She is very circumspect when dealing with strangers.* — **cir·cum·spec·tion** (-SPEC·shun) *n.*

cir·cum·stance (SUR·cum·stance, -stunce) *n.* 1 a fact or occurrence associated with a person or event: *It was*

snowing heavily, the roads were slippery, the driver was exhausted, and such circumstances of the accident; a combination of circumstances pointing to the accused's guilt; He was absent without warning because of unforeseen circumstances; Acts of God are circumstances beyond our control. 2 chance: *She was a victim of circumstance.* 3 condition or situation: *Use of force is justified in certain circumstances such as to defend oneself; She pleaded extenuating circumstances; He lived in straitened circumstances* (= financial hardship); **Under** or **In no circumstances** would he tell a lie; **Under** or **In the circumstances,** the judge had to show mercy. 4 ceremony: *an emperor's life of pomp and circumstance.*

cir·cum·stan·tial (sur·cum·STAN·shul) *adj.* 1 having to do with or determined by circumstances; incidental: *circumstantial evidence with no direct proof.* 2 with full details of the circumstances of time and place: *a circumstantial account, report.* — **cir·cum·stan·tial·ly** *adv.*

cir·cum·vent (sur·cum·VENT) *v.* 1 overcome by craft: *a plan circumvented by the enemy.* 2 get around; avoid: *a plan to circumvent the rules.* 3 encircle: *circumvented by perils.*

cir·cus (SUR·cus) *n.* -cus·es 1 a usually travelling entertainment consisting of trained animals, acrobats, clowns, etc. performing in a tent: *a three-ring circus.* 2 *Slang.* an uproarious display or entertainment: *The show was too much of a circus for one man to handle.*

cis·tern (SIS·turn) *n.* a storage tank for water, esp. rainwater.

cit·a·del (SIT·uh·dul) *n.* 1 a fortress: *the citadel overlooking Quebec City; the Halifax Citadel.* 2 a stronghold or refuge: *a citadel of democracy, freedom.*

ci·ta·tion (sye·TAY·shun) *n.* 1 quotation: *He has citations to prove his point; a citation* (= passage) *from the Bible.* 2 summons: *He was issued a citation for contempt of court; a citation to appear in court.* 3 commendation: *She received a citation for bravery.*

cite *v.* cites, cit·ed, cit·ing 1 quote; also, list, refer to, or bring forward as proof, example, etc.: *He likes to cite passages from the Koran; Job is often cited as a model of patience.* 2 call to appear in court. 3 commend for bravery, dedication, etc.

cit·i·fy (SIT·uh·fye) *v.* -fies, -fied, -fy·ing make refined; urbanize: *There's a citified air about him.*

cit·i·zen (SIT·uh·zun) *n.* 1 a member of a state, owing allegiance to it and having full rights in it: *A natural-born citizen is a citizen by birth; One can become a naturalized Canadian citizen if one is a landed immigrant; She is considered a **citizen of the world** with a cosmopolitan outlook.* 2 one who lives in or was born in a specified city: *the citizens of Toronto.* 3 a civilian: *a law-abiding, leading, prominent, solid citizen; our senior citizens; They complained of being treated as second-class citizens; He made a **citizen's arrest** and held the burglar till the police arrived.* — **cit·i·zen·ly** *adj.*: *citizenly virtues.*

cit·i·zen·ry (SIT·uh·zun·ree) *n.* citizens collectively: *an informed citizenry; the citizenry of Rome.*

cit·i·zen·ship (SIT·uh·zun·ship) *n.* the status of being a citizen: *to acquire, give up, grant, receive, renounce, revoke a citizenship; a certificate of citizenship; dual citizenship* (= citizenship of two countries).

cit·rus (SIT·rus) *n.* **1** a thorny, evergreen tree bearing acid fruit, as the orange, grapefruit, lemon, and lime. **2** such a fruit. — **cit·rous** (-rus) *adj.*

cit·y (SIT·ee) *n.* **cit·ies** a large or important town, esp. one that is incorporated: *Victoria is a capital city; a densely populated city; People working in the city tend to live in the suburbs; satellite cities around a metropolitan area; Kitchener and Waterloo are twin cities in southwestern Ontario; Overcrowding, poverty, and crime are some of the problems of the inner* (= central) *city.*
— *adj.: A city council has legislative and administrative powers over a city; a city editor* (= local news editor); *the city fathers* (= city administrators); *city limits* (= city boundaries).

city hall or **City Hall** *n.* **1** a municipal government building. **2** a bureaucratic administration: *"You can't fight city hall" (because it is futile).*

city slicker *n.* a sophisticated and wily person with city manners.

civ·ic (SIV·ic) **1** *adj.* having to do with a city, citizenship, etc.: *your civic duties; our civic pride; Our civic centre contains the municipal headquarters and facilities for games and other community activities.* **2** civics *n.pl.* [takes sing. v.] the study of the rights and duties of citizenship in relation to government.

Civic Holiday *n. Cdn.* the first Monday in August observed as a public holiday, known also as Simcoe Day in Ontario, Heritage Day in Alberta, British Columbia Day, and Saskatchewan Day.

civ·ies same as CIVVIES.

civ·il (SIV·ul) *adj.* **1** pertaining to the citizens in their relationship to the state: *our civil liberties and rights as guaranteed in the Charter of Rights; the civil and criminal codes of law; to bring a civil action against someone in a civil court; to resort to civil disobedience* (= disobedience against the government to agitate for reform); *a civil war (between factions within a nation).* **2** pertaining to the people as distinguished from the military or religious: *civil aviation; civil defence in wartime; Civil engineering deals with roads, tunnels, and other public works; The civil name of Pope John Paul II was Karol Wojtyla; the civil* (= government) *service; a civil* (= not religious) *marriage.* **3** civilized: *We live in a civil society; Keep a civil tongue in your head; At least be civil if you can't be polite or courteous; It was civil of her to invite him.* — **civ·il·ly** *adv.*

ci·vil·i·an (suh·VIL·yun) *n.* a member of the general public, not a member of the military, police, etc.
— *adj.: a civilian award; a soldier's return to civilian life; a return to civilian rule after military rule.*

ci·vil·i·ty (suh·VIL·uh·tee) *n.* **-ties** politeness; also, a polite act.

civ·i·li·za·tion (SIV·uh·luh·ZAY·shun) *n.* **1** a high degree of cultural, social, and technological development: *to introduce, spread civilization.* **2** the culture of a time, place, people, etc.: *the rise and fall of civilizations since* prehistoric times; *Many ancient civilizations have been stamped out* or *destroyed* or *wiped out by invaders; the decay and collapse of the Aztec civilization; Western civilization has its roots in Greek and Roman culture.* **3** the act of civilizing: *the civilization of conquered nations.* **4** the comforts of modern society: *It took us many days to get back to civilization after getting lost in the jungle.*

civ·i·lize (SIV·uh·lize) *v.* **-liz·es, -lized, -liz·ing** bring to a higher degree of civilization: *The conquerors tried to civilize the conquered.*

civilized *adj.* refined or cultured: *civilized behaviour, manners; a civilized country, dialogue, home, society; the civilized world that we live in; a civilized afternoon of ballet and some TV.*

civ·vies (SIV·eez) *n.pl. Informal.* civilian or regular attire as distinguished from a uniform.

clack *v.* **1** make a short, hard sound: *She clacked down the stairs in her clogs.* **2** chatter: *clacking tongues.* Also *n.* — **clack·er** *n.*

clad *adj.* [old pp. of CLOTHE] clothed or covered: *a warmly clad hunter; a scantily clad bather; a partially, lightly, fully clad body; an emperor clad in rags; the ivy-clad towers of the university; an iron-clad guarantee; a clad coin containing two outer layers of a copper-nickel alloy bonded to a core of pure copper; stone cladding* (= facing or covering) *for your home.*

claim *v.* **1** assert as a fact or right: *He claimed the crown (as his); claimed that the crown was his; claims to get more mileage with his new car.* **2** take: *The fire claimed three lives; Let's claim* (= ask for and get) *our bags.*
— *n.* **1** a demand, request, or assertion of something, esp. as a right: *to enter, file, put forward, put in, submit a claim; A claim for compensation or damages against the offending party was settled out of court; The prospector staked (out) his claim to the territory (by marking it off with stakes); There are too many claims on my time by family, colleagues, and friends for me to do any community work; His claim to fame is based on his scientific discoveries; to lay claim to an inheritance.* **2** something claimed, esp. land: *A rival prospector jumped his claim* (= took it illegally).

claim·ant (CLAY·munt) *n.* one who claims: *a claimant to the throne.*

clair·voy·ance (clair·VOY·unce) *n.* the ability to perceive what is beyond the senses; also, sharp intuition.
— **clair·voy·ant** *n. & adj.;* **clair·voy·ant·ly** *adv.*

clam *n.* **1** a bivalve mollusc often used for food. **2** *Informal.* one who doesn't talk much.
— *v.* **clams, clammed, clam·ming 1** dig for clams. **2 clam up** stop talking.

clam·bake *n.* **1** an outdoor party at which clams are steamed or baked. **2** any large, lively social gathering.

clam·ber (CLAM·bur) *v.* climb awkwardly, usually with both hands and feet: *He clambered up the hill; clambered over the fence; clambered into a bus.*

clam·my (CLAM·ee) *adj.* **clam·mi·er, clam·mi·est** unpleasantly moist, cool, and sticky: *clammy hands,* *skin.* — **clam·mi·ly** *adv.;* **clam·mi·ness** *n.*

clam·our or **clam·or** (CLAM·ur) *n.* a loud noise or shouting; a violent protest, demand, etc.: *a public clamour for reform; a clamour against the new bill.* — *v.* make a clamour: *children clamouring for attention; a crowd of demonstrators clamouring to see the minister.* — **clam·or·ous** *adj.;* **clam·or·ous·ly** *adv.*

clamp *n.* 1 a band, vise, etc. for holding objects together. 2 a firm grip. — *v.* 1 fasten or hold firmly, as in a clamp. 2 impose: *to clamp controls on rising prices; to clamp on a curfew.* — **clamp down** *Informal.* impose restrictions: *The authorities are finally clamping down; They're clamping down on tax evaders.* — **clamp·down** *n.*

clam·shell *n.* 1 the shell of a clam. 2 a dredging bucket hinged like such a shell.

clan *n.* 1 a group of families, as among Indian tribes or Scottish highlanders, based on descent from a common ancestor: *a gathering of the clans.* 2 a group of associates or relatives; clique: *a Mafia clan; a clan of poets, power brokers, writers.*

clan·des·tine (clan·DES·tin) *adj.* secret or underhand: *a clandestine love affair, meeting.*

clang *n.* a loud, ringing, metallic sound: *the clang of steel.* — *v.: The dinner bell clanged at 6:00.*

clan·gour or **clan·gor** (CLANG·ur, -gur) *n.* a prolonged clang; clanging din.

clank *n.* an abrupt, loud, metallic sound; *v.: chains clanking in the dungeon; The door clanked shut.*

clan·nish *adj.* forming a group that excludes outsiders: *People become less clannish as they get more educated; their clannish loyalties.* — **clan·nish·ly** *adv.;* **clan·nish·ness** *n.*

clans·man (CLANZ·mun) *n.* -men a member of a clan. — **clans·wom·an** *n.* -wom·en.

clap *n.* 1 a loud, flat noise, as of the palms of two hands struck sharply together. 2 applause. 3 a loud explosive noise: *a clap of thunder.* 4 a blow or slap. — *v.* **claps, clapped, clap·ping** 1 strike the palms together; make a clapping noise; applaud: *to clap hands with joy; The clapping went on for five minutes after the speech.* 2 slap: *to clap someone on the back.* 3 move, put, do, etc. suddenly and roughly: *They clapped him in irons; He was clapped in jail; A 10% duty was clapped on imports.*

clap·trap *n.* cheap rhetoric used in a speech, writing, etc. merely to win applause: *mere claptrap; cant and claptrap sentiment.*

clar·et (CLAIR·ut) *n.* 1 a dry red table wine. 2 its purplish red colour.

clar·i·fy (CLAIR·uh·fye) *v.* -fies, -fied, -fy·ing make or become clear: *The situation will clarify as events develop; Clarify your meaning, position, views; clarified* (= purified) *butter.* — **clar·i·fi·ca·tion** (-fuh·CAY·shun) *n.*

clar·i·net (clair·uh·NET) *n.* a single-reed woodwind instrument with finger holes and keys. — **clar·i·net·tist** or **clar·i·net·ist** *n.*

clar·i·on (CLAIR·ee·un) *n.* a medieval type of trumpet. — *adj.* clear and ringing: *the bugle's clarion call.*

clar·i·ty (CLAIR·uh·tee) *n.* clearness: *clarity of the atmosphere; the clarity of a diamond; His arguments came through with forceful clarity; clarity of expression, thinking, speech, vision.*

clash *n.* 1 a conflict or disagreement: *a bloody, violent clash; the clash of* or *between opposing armies, interests, personalities; a clash with the neighbours.* 2 a loud, confused, usually metallic sound of colliding: *the clash of cymbals, weapons.* — *v.* 1 to conflict: *Red and green clash in the picture; Our troops clashed with the enemy; The two factions clashed* (= argued) *over the seating arrangements.* 2 collide: *oildrums clashing together.*

clasp *n.* 1 a fastener, as a pin, hook, buckle, etc.: *a tie clasp.* 2 a firm grip or embrace. — *v.* 1 fasten with or as with a clasp: *a sweater clasped at the neck.* 2 grip with the hand; embrace: *He clasped the picture to his breast.*

class *n.* 1 a distinctive group with a common characteristic and name: *Apes, bears, mice, etc. form the class of mammals.* 2 a social division based on status, economic function, etc.: *an educated, leisure, middle, privileged, ruling, underprivileged, upper, working class; social classes; adj.: a class conflict, distinction, struggle; class bias, consciousness, differences, hatred, superiority, warfare.* 3 a group defined by quality, level, condition, etc.: *cabin, economy, tourist class; She usually travels first-class; He passed with first-class honours; a second-class citizen; She is in a class of her own* (= has no equal). 4 a group of students, or **class·mates,** instructed together, usually in the same room, or **class·room:** *to attend classes; to call off, cancel, conduct, dismiss, hold, give a class; to cut, go to, miss, schedule classes; to sit in on a Hebrew class; the freshman, sophomore class; The class of 98 graduates in the year 1998.* 5 *Informal.* style, high quality, etc.: *a woman with class; Kay doesn't have much class.* — *v.* put in a class; classify: *She is classed as a genius.*

class act *n. Informal.* a person or thing of outstanding quality.

class action *n.* a law suit brought on behalf of all parties affected by an alleged injustice.

clas·sic (CLASS·ic) *adj.* **1** of the highest quality; of traditionally recognized importance, value, excellence, etc.: *the classic style of Milton.* **2** standard or typical: *a classic example of mismanagement; the classic symptoms of smallpox.*
— *n.* **1** a person, thing, or event considered as classic in quality: *Homer is a Greek classic; This salad is a culinary classic.* **2 classics** *pl.* Greek and Roman literature.

clas·si·cal (CLASS·uh·cul) *adj.* **1** having to do with ancient Greek or Roman culture or its qualities of simplicity, form, purity, etc.: *classical literature; a classical scholar; the classical music of Beethoven and Mozart.* **2** classic: *written in classical style.*
— **clas·si·cal·ly** *adv.*

clas·si·cism (CLASS·uh·siz·um) *n.* adherence to the stylistic standards of ancient Greece and Rome, as clarity, form, restraint, and grace. — **clas·si·cist** *n.*

classified (CLASS·uh·fied) *adj.* **1** designated as secret: *classified information; a classified report on nuclear weapons.* **2** arranged by topic: *classified advertising.*

clas·si·fy (CLASS·uh·fy) *v.* **-fies, -fied, -fy·ing** put in groups according to type, topic, etc.
— **clas·si·fi·a·ble** (-fye·uh·bul) *adj.*
— **clas·si·fi·ca·tion** (-fuh·CAY·shun) *n.*

classmate, classroom See CLASS.

class·y *adj.* **class·i·er, -i·est** *Slang.* having class: *a very classy car, dress, hotel, style.*

clas·tic (CLAS·tic) *adj.* **1** formed from pieces of older rock: *a clastic sandstone.* **2** that can be taken apart: *a clastic anatomical model.*

clat·ter (CLAT·ur) *v.* move with or make a loud rattling sound: *Pots and pans clattered out of the cabinet.*
— *n.* rattling noise: *the clatter of pots and pans.*

clause (CLAWZ) *n.* **1** a part of a sentence having its own subject and verb: *main and subordinate* or *dependent clauses.* **2** a section of a document: *an escalator clause; grandfather clause; penalty clause.*

claus·tro·pho·bi·a (claw·struh·FOH·bee·uh) *n.* an abnormal fear of closed spaces such as elevators.
— **claus·tro·pho·bic** *adj.*

claw *n.* **1** a usually sharp, curving nail on the foot of a bird, lizard, cat, etc.; also, the pincer of a lobster, some insects, etc.: *Cats can retract their claws.* **2** anything shaped like a claw, as the curved, split head of a hammer (**claw·ham·mer**) used for pulling nails.
— *v.* grasp, scratch, dig, or move using or as if using claws: *a dog clawing at a locked door.*

clay *n.* **1** a fine-grained kind of earth, soft when wet, used for moulding, brick-making, and ceramics: *potter's clay; modelling clay.* **2** wet ground or mud. **3** the human body: *this mortal clay.*

clay·ey (CLAY·ee) *adj.* **clay·i·er, -i·est** containing clay: *clayey soil.*

clean (CLEEN) *adj.* **1** free from dirt: *a clean shirt; an immaculately clean home; a spotlessly clean house; a **clean room** (free of dust, germs, etc.).* **2** free from anything undesirable, as obscenity (*a clean joke; good clean fun*), pollution (*a clean blast, bomb; the Clean Air Act*), dishonesty (*a clean game*), complications (*the*

clean lines of a work of art), illegal drugs, sin, etc. **3** complete or thorough: *a clean sweep of the polls; a clean profit of $100 000.*
— **come clean** *Slang.* confess: *They were forced to come clean under interrogation.*
— *adv.* **1** in a clean manner: *Let's play it clean.* **2** completely: *We're clean out of provisions; Stay clean out of sight.*
— *v.* make or become clean: *to clean the kitchen; He doesn't mind cleaning up after his sister; A cleaner in baseball is supposed to clean* or *clear the bases* (= hit a home run with players on bases).
— **clean out** empty: *Please clean out your desk before leaving; The burglars cleaned out the shop; The shop was cleaned out of its inventory.*
— **clean up** *Informal.* make a large profit; make a killing: *They cleaned up on the business deal; The book is just out and cleaning up.*
— **clean up one's act** *Informal.* behave properly.
— **cleaning** *n.* act of cleaning: *Give it a thorough cleaning; Only dry cleaning will remove those spots; our annual spring cleaning of the house.* — **clean·ness** *n.*

clean-cut *adj.* **1** having distinct outlines: *a clean-cut analysis of the problem; a clean-cut unambiguous statement; It's pretty clean-cut that he is not telling the whole truth.* **2** neat and wholesome: *a clean-cut young man; our clean-cut image as a party.*

clean·er *n.* a person or thing that cleans: *a pipe cleaner; drain cleaner; vacuum cleaner; street cleaners; She was taken **to the cleaners*** (= defrauded of all her money).

clean·ly (CLEN·lee) *adj.* **-li·er, -li·est** habitually clean and tidy: *the cat's reputation as a cleanly animal.*
— *adv.* (CLEEN·lee) without making a mess: *The knife goes cleanly into the cheese.*
— **clean·li·ness** (CLEN-) *n.:* personal cleanliness; "*Cleanliness is next to godliness.*"

cleanse (CLENZ) *v.* **cleans·es, cleansed, cleans·ing** clean and purify: *to cleanse a wound; to cleanse the air; to cleanse your heart of sin; a **cleansing** cream for your skin.*

cleans·er (CLEN·zur) *n.* a solvent or detergent for cleaning: *a kitchen cleanser.*

clean·up *n.* **1** a thorough cleaning. **2** a large profit.

clear (CLEER) *adj.* **1** free from dimness or darkness, as a cloudless sky: *on a clear day; clear glass.* **2** free from anything unwanted or obscuring, as blurring (*a clear outline, tone, vision*), debt or deduction (*a clear profit, title*), obstruction (*clear sailing ahead*), contents (*a ship clear of cargo*), flaws or blemishes (*a clear complexion*), guilt (*a clear conscience*), or contact (*stand clear*). **2** free from doubt; obvious to the mind: *Is that clear to you? Are you clear about it? I'd like to make this crystal clear; It is clear that we have lost; It's as clear as day.* **3** keen or perceptive: *She has a clear head for math.*
— *n.* **in the clear** *Informal.* free of suspicion, danger, or obstructions: *The dropping of all charges left the suspect in the clear.*
— *adv.* **1** in a clear manner: *I read you loud and clear* (= understand you perfectly). **2** completely: *It flew clear across the lake.*
— *v.* **1** make or become clear: *The sky is clearing; to clear up a difficulty, misunderstanding; They cleared the snow from the driveway; cleared the land of trees;*

He was cleared of the murder charge; *The rash will take time to* **clear up** (= heal). **2** make money as net profit: *We cleared $1 million last year.* **3** pass through checking procedures; get or give approval: *an article cleared for publication; It has been cleared with the censors; A flight is cleared for takeoff; We were cleared to land; The motion cleared the committee.* **4** go over, under, past, etc. without touching: *The horse cleared the fence.* — **clear out** *Informal.* **1** go away; leave: *He cleared out before he was thrown out.* **2** clean out: *He's clearing out his desk before leaving.* — **clear the air** resolve differences or tensions. — **clear·ly** *adv.*; **clear·ness** *n.*

clear·ance (CLEER·unce) *n.* **1** the distance at which something is removed from another; clearing space: *a bridge with enough clearance for trucks to pass under.* **2** a permission or authorization: *customs clearance; A pilot receives clearance to land; a security clearance; clearance papers.* **3** a clearing: *slum clearance; a warehouse clearance; a* **clearance sale** *(at reduced prices).*

clear-cut 1 *adj.* distinctly outlined; hence, plain: *a clear-cut case of fraud; a clear-cut answer, definition, guarantee, issue, rule, victory.* **2** *n.* an area completely cleared of trees.

clear-eyed *adj.* clearly thought-out; discerning: *a good, well-acted, clear-eyed production.*

clear-headed (CLEER·hed·id) *adj.* sensible; mentally clear.

clearing (CLEER·ing) *n.* an area in the woods that is free of trees.

clear·ing·house (CLEER·ing·house) *n.* a central office, as for clearing cheques between banks: *a clearinghouse for information; a publishers' clearinghouse (for selling publications at a discount).*

clear-sighted *adj.* clear-eyed.

cleat (CLEET) *n.* **1** a projection, as on the sole of a shoe to get a grip. **2** on boats, a two-horned projection around which a rope may be wound.

cleav·age (CLEE·vij) *n.* a splitting or division: *the direction of cleavage in a gem; the sharp cleavages existing in society; a neckline cut low on a dress to show cleavage* (= the division between a woman's breasts).

cleave (CLEEV) *v.* **1** cleaves, cleaved, cleav·ing cling: *Traditional societies tend to cleave to age-old customs.* **2** cleaves, *pt.* cleft, cleaved or clove (CLOHV), *pp.* cleft, cleaved or clo·ven (CLOH·vun), cleav·ing split or divide: *to cleave a piece of wood, a stick; The devil is often pictured with cloven feet; Cattle, deer, pigs and such animals have cloven hoofs.*

cleav·er (CLEE·vur) *n.* a butcher's heavy, broad-bladed chopping tool: *a meat cleaver.*

clef *n.* a symbol on a musical staff indicating the pitch of the notes.

cleft a *pt. & pp.* of CLEAVE. — *adj.* split: *a cleft lip, palate.* — *n.* a fissure or split: *a cleft in the rock.*

clem·en·cy (CLEM·un·see) *n.* mercy, as of a judge toward an offender: *a plea for clemency; to beg for,*

deny, seek, show clemency.

clem·ent (CLEM·unt) *adj.* **1** mild, not harsh: *clement weather.* **2** lenient or forgiving: *a clement judge.*

clench *v.* close, grip, or fasten tightly: *to clench one's teeth; a clenched fist.* — *n.* a tight grip.

cler·gy (CLUR·jee) *n.* [usually takes pl. v.] a body of people in religious service, as monks, priests, rabbis, or nuns: *The clergy are distinguished from the laity.* — **cler·gy·man** *n.* -men. — **cler·gy·wom·an** *n.* -wom·en.

cler·ic *n.* a member of the clergy.

cler·i·cal (CLER·uh·cul) *adj.* **1** having to do with clerks, office work, etc.: *typing and such clerical skills; a clerical error.* **2** having to do with the clergy: *a clerical collar;* **cler·i·cal·ism** *n.*

clerk (CLURK) *n.* **1** an office worker, as one who types, files, etc. **2** an official in charge of records and regular business: *a city, county, court clerk; the clerk* (= chief administrative officer) *of the legislature.* **3** a person in a sales or service function: *a desk clerk; room clerk in a hotel; sales clerk.* **4** a cleric: *a clerk in holy orders.* — *v.* work as a clerk: *Karen clerks in her father's store; She started her law career clerking for a judge.* — **clerk·ship** *n.*

clev·er (CLEV·ur) *adj.* **1** showing quickness of mind, even if not deep or thorough: *a clever child, reply, student.* **2** showing cleverness: *a clever answer, book, idea, trick.* **3** deft: *She is clever with her hands; clever at arranging flowers.* — **clev·er·ly** *adv.*; **clev·er·ness** *n.*

cli·ché (clee·SHAY) *n.* an expression, image, sentiment, situation, or theme considered hackneyed or overused among a group or at a particular time: *"Winds of change" was popular in the 1960s but has now become a cliché; A feminist who has toppled quite a few clichés; They think of Canada in clichés of Mounties, polar bears, and snow.*

cli·chéd (clee·SHADE) *adj.* that has become a cliché: *"Last but not least" is a clichéd expression; a clichéd phrase, sentiment.*

click *n.* **1** a short, sharp metallic sound, as of cocking a gun. **2** a sucking sound. — *v.* **1** make a click: *A soldier clicks his heels when he comes to attention; She clicked her tongue in delight; He clicks his teeth impatiently; Before he could finish the sentence, the receiver was clicked off* (= the connection was cut off with a click); *The camera clicked when we were not looking; Something clicked* (= flashed in the mind) *and I knew we had the right answer.* **2** *Informal.* to be a success: *The two seem to have clicked with each other; The new show clicked instantly with the prime-time audience.*

cli·ent (CLYE·unt) *n.* one who receives the services of a professional in a dependent relationship: *an accountant's, agent's, lawyer's clients; a welfare client* (= recipient); *a client* (= dependent) *state.*

cli·en·tele (clye·un·TEL) *n.* clients collectively.

cliff *n.* a high, steep-faced rocky prominence: *a rugged, sheer, steep cliff; to scale a cliff using ropes.*

cliff·hang·er (CLIFF·hang·ur) *n.* **1** a serialized

adventure story or movie whose episodes end in suspense. **2** a suspenseful situation: *The game was a cliffhanger till the last play.*

cli·mac·ter·ic (clye·MAC·tuh·ric) *n.* a period of major change, esp. the menopause.

cli·mac·tic (clye·MAC·tic) *adj.* forming a climax: *the climactic final assault on Berlin.*

cli·mate (CLYE·mit) *n.* **1** the average weather of a region: *the cold climate of Canada; a damp, dry, hot, humid, invigorating, mild, temperate, tropical, warm, wet climate.* **2** a region considered in regard to its weather: *We live in a cold climate; Many birds move to a warmer climate in the winter.* **3** the temper or condition of a place or time: *the political climate of Portugal.*
— **cli·mat·ic** (clye·MAT·ic) *adj.*: *climatic changes; the climatic variations of the seasons.*

cli·max (CLYE·max) *n.* **1** the most important or significant, often final part or event; culmination: *a dramatic climax; The revelations bring the story to a thrilling climax; to mark, reach, work up to a climax.* **2** orgasm.
— *v.* **-max·es, -maxed, -max·ing** attain or bring to a climax: *The Olympic win climaxed her efforts.*

climb (CLIME) *v.* **1** ascend; go up: *The moon climbed the night sky; Our stock is climbing; to climb a hill, mountain; to climb to the top.* **2** move along, up, down, etc. by using the hands and feet: *Any baby can climb out of that crib; Jack fell while climbing a tree; The infant climbed onto her mother's knees; It was easier to climb down the mountain; to climb aboard a wagon.*
— *n.* a climbing: *The pilot put the plane into a steep climb; It was a hard, rough, tortuous climb up the mountain; It is a gradual climb to the top.*
— **climb·er** *n.*: *a mountain climber; social climber.*

clime *n. Poetic.* region; also, climate.

clinch *v.* **1** fasten firmly; hence, make certain or final: *The salesman clinched the deal; Our team clinched the victory in the final moments of the game; We also clinched the championship.* **2** in boxing, hold tight; *n.*: *The boxers went into a clinch.*

clinch·er *n.* a deciding or conclusive argument, element, event, etc.

cling *v.* **clings, clung, cling·ing** hang on, as if attached, to something: *Children cling to their mothers; children clinging together in the cold; A cooking odour may cling to the kitchen; to cling to a hope; a **clinging vine** (Informal for* a person too dependent on another).

cling·stone *n.* a kind of peach whose flesh adheres to the pit.

clin·ic *n.* **1** a medical treatment facility for outpatients: *a health clinic.* **2** such a facility run cooperatively by many specialists: *an abortion, dental, family-planning clinic.* **3** any centre for instruction, counselling, or a similar service: *a legal-aid clinic; a storefront clinic to give financial advice; shoe clinic* (= repair shop); *a writers' clinic* (= short course of instruction).

clin·i·cal (CLIN·uh·cul) *adj.* **1** having to do with treatment of illness: *a clinical examination, thermometer; a doctor's clinical training, experience;*

the tests used in clinical psychology. **2** coldly analytical: *a clinical evaluation, interest, tone; a psychologist's clinical attitude to a marriage breakup.*

clink *v.* make a short, sharp, ringing sound: *They clinked glasses in a toast.* Also *n.*

clink·er *n.* **1** a piece of fused, incombustible residue left when coal is burned; slag. **2** *Slang.* anything bad, as a flaw or failure, a blooper, lemon, or turkey: *a clinker of a play.* **3** *Slang.* jail: *He was tossed into the clinker.*

clip *v.* **clips, clipped, clip·ping 1** cut off, cut out, or cut short, esp. with shears, scissors, etc.: *to clip pictures from magazines; a terse, clipped style of speech; hair clipped short; The plane clipped a sea wall and disintegrated on impact.* **2** hold tightly, esp. fasten with a clip: *He clipped his card to the memo.* **3** *Informal.* hit with a short, quick blow. **5** *Slang.* cheat, esp. by overcharging.
— *n.* **1** a device for fastening or holding things together: *a paper clip; tie clip; a cartridge clip* (= feeding mechanism); *There were four bullets in the clip but none in the chamber.* **2** speed: *We were moving along at a fast clip.* **3** a piece or clipping: *a clip from a movie; film clip; clips from her speeches;* also **clipping**: *nail clippings; press clippings.*

clip·board *n.* a small writing board having a clip to hold paper with.

clip joint *n.* an establishment, esp. a night club, that cheats customers.

clip·per (CLIP·ur) *n.* **1** often **clippers** *pl.* a tool for clipping, esp. shears for hair, wool, etc. **2** a long, narrow sailing ship; hence, any fast means of travel.

clique (CLEEK) *n.* a small exclusive group, usually social or political.
— **cli·quish** (CLEE·kish) *adj.*: *serving narrow, cliquish interests.*

cloak (CLOKE) *n.* **1** a loose, usually sleeveless outer garment. **2** a concealment or disguise intended to deceive: *under the cloak of darkness; the cloak of friendship; attacking under the cloak of anonymity.*
— *v.* cover with a cloak for the purpose of deceiving: *plans cloaked in secrecy; hospitality that cloaks treachery.*

cloak-and-dagger (CLOKE·un·dag·ur) *adj.* having to do with spies: *James Bond's cloak-and-dagger adventures.*

cloak·room *n.* a room where coats, hats, etc. may be left for a time.

clob·ber (CLOB·ur) *v. Informal.* strike hard and repeatedly; defeat soundly; trounce: *They got clobbered in the finals.*

clock *n.* a device for measuring or indicating time: *the hands of a clock; to stop the clock; cuckoo clock; Workers check in and out of the factory by punching the time clock; a time bomb with a clock ticking inside; an alarm clock set to go off at 6 a.m.; when the clock strikes six; A watch is a clock made to be worn; to set the clock forward for daylight saving time; to **turn the clock back** on progress; It was a race **against the clock** to reach there before closing time; He watched at his sick child's bedside **around the clock** (= day and night); adj.: a clock mechanism, pendulum, radio, tower; a*

clock watcher (who is more interested in leaving work than in doing a good job).
— *v.* check with a clock or other device: *The police clocked the speeder at 120 km/h.*

clock·wise *adj. & adv.* in the same direction a clock's hands move in.

clock·work *n.* the mechanism of a clock; also, any similar machinery: *Everything went* **like clockwork** (= smoothly and precisely) *at the reception.*

clod *n.* 1 a lump of earth, mud, etc. 2 a dolt, lout, or boor. — **clod·dish** *adj.: his cloddish manners.*

clod·hop·per (CLOD·hop·ur) *n.* 1 a rustic, clumsy, or stupid person. 2 a heavy thick-soled shoe or boot.

clog *n.* 1 a heavy, wooden or wooden-soled shoe or boot. 2 a block of wood, as tied to the leg of an animal to prevent it from wandering; hence, an encumbrance.
— *v.* **clogs, clogged, clog·ging** fill up and block or slow down: *a drain clogged with grease; Rush-hour traffic clogs the highways.* — **clog·gy** (CLOG·ee) *adj.*

clois·ter (CLOY·stur) *n.* 1 a covered walk with an open colonnade facing usually on a quadrangle. 2 a place secluded for religious life; monastery or convent; *v.: to be secluded from the world.*

clone *n.* 1 an exact copy of its parent, as a plant variety multiplied from rooted cuttings. 2 an imitation of a commercial product, as of a computer.
— *v.* **clones, cloned, clon·ing** produce as a clone.

clonk *v. & n.* (make) a dull, hollow thump.

clop *v.* **clops, clopped, clop·ping** make the sharp, hollow sound of a horse's hoof on pavement; *n.* this sound.

close (CLOZE) *v.* **clos·es, closed, clos·ing** 1 stop up an opening or passage; shut: *The border has been closed off; Please close the door; close it tight; They have closed the carwash for repairs; It's closed to the public; You can't close your eyes to the truth.* 2 to conclude or end: *Let us close our meeting; We'll close with the national anthem; The matter is closed; Our stocks closed strong (on the exchange); to close* (= finalize) *a deal with someone; to close a sale* (= finish the transactions on it). 3 make or become close with no space between parts: *Close your hand into a fist; The order was given to close* (= join) *ranks; The troops closed with* (= engaged) *the enemy; as night closed around us; Police closed on the escaped convict.*
— **close down** stop entirely: *a factory closed down by a strike.*
— **close in** encircle and advance upon: *The hunters closed in on the fox; closed in for a kill.*
— **close out** sell all of a store's goods; sell a business; *adj.: a close-out sale.*
— *n.* a conclusion: *The sunset marks the close of day; to bring our talks to a close; as the meeting draws to a close; "Yours truly" is a complimentary close to a letter.*
— *adj. & adv.* (rhyme: "dose") **clos·er, clos·est** 1 with little space between parts or elements; densely packed: *a close weave; soldiers in close ranks; precise, close reasoning.* 2 very near: *She lives close to work; Don't get too close to the cage; Ray's relationship with the neighbours is getting* **too close for comfort;** *a close copy of the original; That's close but not quite correct; a*

patient under *close observation; He was close to tears; two close* (= intimate) *friends who are close to each other; an attack at close range; Has anyone seen Bigfoot* **at close quarters?** *Stay close by; The bullet hit close to the mark.* 3 nearly equal: *a close contest, decision, election, finish, match; The race is too close to call; a close score of 6-5; The vote was close.* 4 closed in; cramped: *a prisoner in close confinement; a period of close* (= restricted) *credit; Open a window, it's close* (= hot and humid) *in here.* 5 concealed; secretive: *as close as an oyster; He's close* (= stingy) *with his money.*
— **play close to the chest** or **vest** be secretive.
— **close·ly** *adv.;* **close·ness** *n.*

close call or **close shave** *n. Informal.* a narrow escape.

closed caption *n.* a TV subtitle that is invisible except on receivers equipped with a decoder, as used by the hearing-impaired.
— **closed-captioned** *adj.;* **closed-captioning** *n.*

closed circuit *n.* 1 an unbroken circuit. 2 radio or TV transmission by wire, not broadcasting: *He watched the show from his hospital bed by closed circuit.*

closed shop *n.* an establishment in which only members of a labour union are hired.

close·fist·ed (CLOSE·fis·tid) *adj.* stingy; miserly.

close·knit *adj.* strongly united: *a close-knit group.*

close·mouthed *adj.* cautious in speaking; secretive: *She's closemouthed about his past.*

clos·et (CLOZ·it) *n.* 1 a small room or cabinet for storage of clothes, household goods, etc.: *a broom, china, linen closet; a bedroom with a walk-in closet; to come out of* **the closet** (= condition of concealment). 2 a room for private meetings, study, prayer, etc.
— *adj.* secret or covert: *a closet addict, racist; closet loyalties.*
— *v.* be alone with another in private conference: *He was closeted with his advisors for an hour.*

close-up (CLOSE·up) *n.* a picture taken at close range: *a close-up look at moon craters; a revealing close-up* (= detailed study).

clo·sure (CLOH·zhur) *n.* 1 an act of closing or a device for closing: *plant closures; a Velcro closure.* 2 the closing off of a legislative debate by taking a vote: *to apply, invoke closure.*

clot *n.* a mass of thickened liquid, esp. blood: *A clot forms to prevent loss of blood from a cut or wound.*
— *v.* **clots, clot·ted, clot·ting** thicken or coagulate.

cloth ("TH" as in "thin") *n.* 1 a woven, knitted, or felted fabric of natural or synthetic fibres. 2 a piece of this for a specific purpose, as a tablecloth: *a loin cloth; strips of cloth.* 2 **the cloth** the clergy.

clothe ("TH" as in "the") *v.* **clothes,** *pt. & pp.* **clothed** or **clad, cloth·ing** put clothes on; dress: *clothed in silk; a partially clothed body; villainies clothed* (= covered) *in fine words.*

clothes (CLOTHES, CLOZE) *n. pl.* garments; coverings: *to change, put on, strip off, take off, wash, wear clothes; civilian, night, old, plain, shabby,* summer, Sunday, swaddling, tailor-made, trendy, winter clothes; **"The emperor has no clothes"** (= What has long been accepted as true turns out to be false, as in the story of "The Emperor's New Clothes").

clothes·horse n. 1 a frame to hang clothes on; also clothes hanger. 2 an affectedly fine dresser.

clothes·pin n. a clip for holding clothes on a line, or clothes·line.

clothes·press n. a clothes closet, wardrobe, or chest for clothes.

cloth·ier (CLOH·thee·ur, "th" as in "the") n. 1 one who makes or sells clothing. 2 a cloth dealer.

cloth·ing (CLOH·thing, "th" as in "the") n. clothes: an article of clothing; to model, put on, wear clothing; custom-made, heavy, light, outer, protective, summer, used, warm, winter clothing.

cloud n. 1 a distinct, visible mass of water vapour hanging high in the air: Rain clouds form in the sky; Threatening clouds gather on the horizon; storm clouds; Clouds scud across the sky; Clouds are dispersed by the wind; dark, heavy, mushroom, scattered, storm, thick clouds; Clouds are seeded to produce rain. 2 any light or puffy visible mass in the air: a cloud of dust. 3 swarm: a cloud of locusts, horsemen. 4 something that causes gloom, threatens, or bodes ill: a cloud on the horizon; the gathering clouds of war; "Every cloud has a silver lining" (= There is always a brighter side to a gloomy situation).
— in the clouds in a fanciful dream; also, impractical.
— on cloud nine Slang. joyfully elated.
— under a cloud 1 depressed. 2 in disgrace: He left under a cloud when he quit his job.
— v. cover or become covered with or as if with clouds: The sky is clouding over; Anger clouded his face; He suffers from clouded vision; a clouded reputation.
— cloud·less adj.

cloud·ber·ry (CLOUD·ber·ee) n. -ber·ries Cdn. a wild raspberry of northern regions; bakeapple.

cloud·burst n. a sudden downpour.

cloud-cuckoo-land (CLOUD·cook·oo·land) n. the world of fantasy.

cloud seeding n. the scattering of chemicals in clouds to cause rainfall.

cloud·y (CLOW·dee) adj. cloud·i·er, -i·est 1 covered with clouds: Partly cloudy skies are forecast. 2 not clear: a cloudy day; cloudy notions.
— cloud·i·ly adv.; cloud·i·ness n.

clout (rhyme: "out") v. Informal. 1 hit hard with the hand. 2 in baseball, hit a ball far.
— n. Informal. 1 a heavy blow: a clout on the snoot. 2 influence, esp. political: an M.P. who has or wields clout in Ottawa; Lou has a lot of clout with the prime minister.

clove (CLOHV) n. 1 the dried flower bud of an Asiatic evergreen tree used as a spice called cloves. 2 one of the segments of a compound bulb: a clove of garlic.
— v. a pt. of CLEAVE.

clo·ven (CLOH·vun) a pp. of CLEAVE.

— **adj.** split: Cattle and sheep have cloven hoofs; the **cloven foot** (= Satan).

clo·ver (CLOH·vur) n. a plant with thick purple, pink, or white flower heads, used for pasturage: A four-leaf clover is a sign of good luck; Since winning the lottery, he has been living **in (the) clover** (= in luxury).

clo·ver·leaf (CLOH·vur·leef) n. -leafs or -leaves (-leevz) a highway interchange having ramps forming the shape of a four-leaf clover.

clown (rhyme: "down") n. 1 a professional jester or buffoon, esp. in a circus or parade. 2 an awkward, ill-mannered person. 3 one who constantly jokes or acts silly: He likes to act or play the clown when others are talking seriously.
— v. act as or like a clown; play jokes or act silly: He likes to clown around when others are talking seriously.
— clown·ish adj.; clown·ish·ly adv.; clown·ish·ness n.

cloy v. satiate, esp. with something sweet or rich; sate; surfeit: Too much candy can be cloying; cloy·ing·ly adv.

club n. 1 a thick, heavy, usually tapered piece of wood used as a weapon. 2 a stick for striking the ball in various sports: a golf club. 3 a playing card marked with a stylized black clover leaf; also, the marking: **Clubs** (= the suit so marked) is or are trumps. 4 a group of people united for a social, sporting, charitable, or similar purpose; also, their meeting place: a book, country, fan, glee, tennis, yachting club; to break up, disband, form, organize a club; China joined the nuclear club in 1964; Welcome to the club (= You are in similar company)!
— v. clubs, clubbed, club·bing 1 beat with or as with a club: Hunters club baby seals to death. 2 join: The children clubbed together to buy their teacher a present.

club·by (CLUB·ee) adj. club·bi·er, club·bi·est sociable in an exclusive or clannish way.

club·foot n. a usually congenital malformation of the foot; also, a foot so malformed.

cluck v. 1 make the sound of a hen calling her chicks. 2 make a similar sound with the tongue, as to coax a horse, express interest or concern, etc.
— n. 1 a clucking sound: a cluck of approval. 2 Slang. a dull or incompetent person.

clue (CLOO) n. a word, thing, or idea that suggests the solution to a puzzle, mystery, crime, etc.: The police have uncovered some vital clues to the murderer's identity; to discover, find, furnish, supply a clue; Crossword puzzles provide you with clues across and

*clues down; He does **not have a clue** (Informal for* does not know) *what we are talking about.*
— *v.* **clues, clued, clu·ing** or **clue·ing** give a clue to someone: *Please clue me in on what happened.*

clump *n.* 1 a mass or lump. 2 a group of trees, plants, etc. standing or growing together. 3 the sound of tramping feet. — *v.* walk heavily.

clum·sy (CLUM·zee) *adj.* -si·er, -si·est 1 awkward; unwieldy; uncoordinated: *a clumsy amateur, weapon; It's so clumsy of him to drop it; He's a bit clumsy with his hands; She's rather clumsy at knitting.* 2 inept: *a clumsy apology.* — **clum·si·ly** *adv.;* **clum·si·ness** *n.*

clung *pt. & pp.* of CLING.

clunk *n.* the heavy, flat sound of metal being struck.

clunk·er *n. Slang.* 1 a noisy old machine in poor repair, esp. a car. 2 a clumsy person; duffer. 3 *Slang.* a flop or failure.

clunk·y *adj.* clumsy or ungraceful: *clumsy shoes.*

clus·ter *n.* a group of similar objects situated together: *a cluster of grapes; adj.: A **cluster bomb** contains smaller bombs that scatter hundreds of steel shards over a wide area; A **cluster headache** attacks in a series over several hours.*
— *v.* be, gather, or place in a cluster: *We saw people clustered on street corners; They clustered in small groups; Some clustered around the speaker.*

clutch *v.* 1 grasp or hold suddenly or tightly, esp. with hands or claws; make a grab: *"A drowning man will clutch at a straw"; She clutched her child to her breast.* 2 operate a clutch mechanism.
— *n.* 1 the act of clutching; also, a tight hold: *in the **clutches** (=* power) *of the devil, of the enemy.* 2 a device for engaging and disengaging a drive mechanism from the motor, as in a standard-shift automobile: *Depress the clutch to the floor when changing gears; Release the clutch after use; Riding the clutch (with the left foot on it) causes needless wear on the clutch.* 3 *Informal.* a critical or dangerous situation: *a friend you can count on **in the clutch.*** 4 a nest of eggs or the chicks hatched from them; also, a group of similar individuals: *A clutch of graduates formed the end of the procession.*

clut·ter (CLUT·ur) *n.* a disordered state; jumble; also, things in a disorganized state: *the clutter on his desk; Advertising clutter in magazines is more bearable than on TV because TV commercials intrude on the program.*
— *v.* litter with a disorganized mass of objects: *His desk is always cluttered up.*

c'mon (cuh·MON) *Informal.* come on: *C'mon in, Jane; Aw, C'mon off it! C'mon Canada!*

co- *prefix.* together; jointly: *coauthor, coheir, cooperate.*

coach *n.* 1 an enclosed passenger vehicle, as a bus, railway car, or four-wheeled carriage (*a stage coach*). 2 a class of airline or train travel lower than first-class. 3 one who trains or instructs others, esp. athletes, students, and singers: *a baseball, drama, voice coach.*
— *v.* train or tutor: *Bill had to be coached for his finals; was coached in French and math.*

coach·man *n.* -men the driver of a carriage or coach.

co·ag·u·late (coh·AG·yuh·late) *v.* -lates, -lat·ed, -lat·ing change a liquid or become changed to a solid or thick semisolid state; clot; set: *The white of the egg coagulates when boiled.* — **co·ag·u·la·tion** (-LAY·shun) *n.*

coal (COLE) *n.* 1 an organic, black or brown, combustible rock used as a fuel; also, a piece of this for burning: *He shovels coal into the furnace.* 2 a piece of glowing wood, coal, etc.; ember: *The yogi can walk a bed of (live) coals; We cooked it over hot coals.*
— **rake** or **haul over the coals** reprimand severely.
— *v.* provide with or take on a supply of coal.

co·a·lesce (coh·uh·LES) *v.* -les·ces, -lesced, -les·cing grow together or unite, as the edges of a wound when healing: *The parties coalesced into one.*
— **co·a·les·cence** *n.;* **co·a·les·cent** *adj.*

coal field *n.* a region rich in coal.

coal gas *n.* a gas made from coal, used for heating, lighting, etc.

co·a·li·tion (coh·uh·LISH·un) *n.* a usually temporary union of people, political parties, states, etc. for a common purpose: *They formed a coalition; a coalition of or between the Liberals and the N.D.P.; The coalition was about to fall apart; The coalition dissolved or broke up for the election; a rainbow coalition (of members of various ethnic groups).*

coal tar *n.* a thick, black liquid by-product obtained from soft coal.

coarse (CORSE) *adj.* **coars·er, coars·est** 1 ordinary; inferior; hence, vulgar; unrefined; offensive: *coarse food, language, manners.* 2 consisting of large, rough particles; having a rough texture or appearance: *coarse sand; coarse-grained wood.*
— **coarse·ly** *adv.;* **coarse·ness** *n.*

coast (COHST) *n.* 1 the land along the sea: *The boat sank off the coast of Newfoundland; People live along the coast; a town located on the coast; She campaigned **(from) coast to coast** (=* across the nation); *He thought the **coast was clear** (=* it was safe) *when everyone had left.* 2 a slope for sledding or tobogganing. 3 the act of coasting.
— *v.* 1 sail along a seacoast. 2 move without acceleration or effort, as sledding down a hill, gliding on a bicycle without pedalling, etc.
— **coast·al** *adj.: coastal shipping, waters.*

coast·er *n.* a pad or disk placed under a glass to protect the surface it rests on.

coast guard or **Coast Guard** *n.* the military and police force which patrols a nation's seacoast and territorial waters. — **coast·guards·man** *n.* -men.

coat *n.* 1 a sleeved outer garment reaching at least to the waist: *She had a coat on; She took off her coat; an all-weather coat; a mink, fur, winter coat.* 2 a natural outer covering, as an animal's fur or feathers: *the silky coat of a cocker spaniel.* 3 a thin layer covering something, as paint on a wall: *We put on or applied a second coat; an outer, protective coat or coating of wax.*
— *v.* apply or be a coat on something: *a floor coated with wax; Frost coated the window.*
— **coat·ed** *adj.: coated aspirin; a camera with a coated lens to eliminate reflections; smooth, coated paper used for artwork.*

coat hanger *n.* a hanger for a coat, dress, etc. that is made of wire, wood, or plastic in the shape of a person's shoulders with a hook at the top for hanging in a closet.

coat of arms *n.* the heraldic insignia of a person, family, institution, etc.

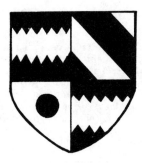

coat·tail *adj.* dependent or derivative: *a protective coattail provision in the law; coattail power, prestige.* — **coattails** *n.pl.* 1 the back flaps of a coat. 2 a politician's popularity that is strong enough to carry a follower to victory: *He rode to victory* **on the coattails** *of the prime minister.*

co·au·thor (coh·AW·thur) *n.* a collaborating author; *v.:* *The husband-and-wife team coauthored the report.*

coax (COHX) *v.* use persistent kindness, flattery, or effort to persuade or to produce a desired effect: *He coaxed his mother into agreeing; He had to coax the old car up the hill.* — **coax·ing·ly** *adv.*

cob *n.* 1 the woody core of an ear of corn: *corn on the cob.* 2 a male swan. 3 a thickset horse with short legs.

co·balt blue (COH·bault·) *n.* a deep-to-greenish blue.

cob·ble (COB·ul) *v.* **cob·bles, cob·bled, cob·bling** 1 pave with cobblestones: *the cobbled streets of Spain.* 2 make or repair, esp. footwear. 3 make roughly and quickly: *It was cobbled up* or *together in a hurry.* — *n.* same as COBBLESTONE.

cob·bler *n.* 1 one who repairs shoes. 2 a deep fruit pie with a thick crust only on top: *cherry cobbler; peach cobbler.*

cob·ble·stone (COB·ul·stone) *n.* a rounded stone of medium size, as used for paving.

co·bra (COH·bruh) *n.* a poisonous snake of Asia and Africa that can spread its neck skin into a hood.

cob·web *n.* 1 a web or a fine thread spun by a spider. 2 something flimsy but ensnaring: *cobwebs of suspicion.*

co·ca (COH·cuh) *n.* a South American shrub whose dried leaves are the source of cocaine.

co·caine (coh·CAIN) *n.* a drug made from the dried leaves of the coca, and used as a local anesthetic, stimulant, or addictive narcotic. Also **co·cain.**

cock *n.* 1 the adult male of common barnyard fowl; also, any male bird: *cock robin.* 2 a valve for controlling liquid or gas flow; faucet: *the drain cock of a boiler; the fuel cock of an engine.* 3 the hammer of a gun; also, its raised position, when ready for firing. 4 a small, cone-shaped pile, usually of hay.

— **the cock of the walk** a domineering or overbearing person.

— *v.* 1 turn up or to one side: *The horse cocked its ear; He cocked a quizzical eye; He wears his hat cocked.* 2 put in a position of readiness to fire or hit: *to cock a gun; to cock a fist or arm.*

cock·a·doo·dle·doo (COCK·uh·doo·dul·DOO) *n.* the crowing of a cock.

cock·a·ma·mie or **cock·a·ma·my** (cock·uh·MAY·mee) *adj. Slang.* nonsensical; silly.

cock-and-bull story *n.* an improbable story or excuse.

cock·a·too (COCK·uh·too) *n.* **-toos** a large crested parrot with feathers of white, red, orange, etc.

cock·crow *n.* sunrise; dawn.

cocked hat *n.* a hat with its brim turned up so as to form three corners.

— **knock into a cocked hat** *Informal.* beat competition, plans, etc. thoroughly.

cock·er *n.* same as **cocker spaniel,** a small breed of spaniel with long ears, silky coat, and a square muzzle.

cock·eye *n.* a squinting eye.

cock·eyed *adj.* 1 cross-eyed; askew. 2 *Slang.* absurd or foolish: *a cockeyed idea, notion, scheme.*

cock·fight *n.* a fight between gamecocks.

cock·le (COCK·ul) *n.* 1 a weed that grows in grainfields. 2 an edible shellfish; **cock·le·shell** *n.*
— **warm the cockles of one's heart** make one feel pleased and happy.

Cock·ney or **cock·ney** (COCK·nee) *n.* **-neys** 1 a native of London, esp. its East End. 2 the distinctive dialect of London's East End: *the Cockney accent.*

cock·pit *n.* 1 an enclosed area for cockfights: *So many battles were fought in New Jersey, the state has earned the nickname "Cockpit of the Revolution."* 2 the room in an airplane for the pilot and, in the larger planes, for the pilot and crew: *In the smallest planes, the pilot shares the cockpit with a passenger.* 3 a similar place for the pilot of a boat or driver of a racing car.

cock·roach (COCK·rohch) *n.* a nocturnal insect pest found esp. in houses.

cocks·comb *n.* 1 the red, fleshy, comblike crest on a rooster's head. 2 coxcomb.

cock·sure *adj.* arrogantly self-confident.

cock·tail *n.* 1 a mixed, usually iced alcoholic drink such as a martini. 2 an appetizer: *fruit cocktail; shrimp cocktail.*

cock·y *adj.* **cock·i·er, -i·est** jauntily conceited; cocksure. — **cock·i·ly** *adv.;* **cock·i·ness** *n.*

co·coa (COH·coh) *n.* 1 chocolate in powder form; also, a beverage made with this. 2 a light reddish brown.

co·co·nut (COH·cuh·nut) *n.* the large fruit of a tropical palm (**coconut palm**), which is a husk-covered, hard-shelled seed containing a milky fluid (**coconut milk**), and lined with an edible white meat that yields an oil (**coconut oil**) used in soaps, foods, etc. Also **co·coa·nut.**

co·coon (cuh·COON, long "OO") *n.* **1** the fibrous covering spun by some insect larvae as a case for the pupa. **2** the egg case spun by spiders and other insects: *A nation emerges from its political cocoon when it gains independence.*

co·coon·ing (cuh·COO·ning) *n.* living isolated from society: *the new cocooning trend.*

cod *n.* a fish of northern waters valuable for food.

cod·der (COD·ur) *n. Cdn.* a cod fisherman or cod fishing boat used in the Maritimes.

cod·dle (COD·ul) *v.* **cod·dles, cod·dled, cod·dling** **1** pamper. **2** cook in water just below the boiling point: *coddled eggs.*

code *n.* **1** a systematic collection of laws or regulations: *The Napoleonic Code is the basis of Quebec's civil law; a building, civil, criminal, moral, penal, unwritten code; motor vehicle code; the Revenue Canada tax code; a human rights code; a code of ethics, honour; a dress code for students.* **2** a set of usually arbitrary symbols that carry meaning; language: *the Morse code of dots and dashes; They established a telephone code for identification of callers – one ring, then hang up and dial again; the computer's binary machine code of zeros and ones; a spy trying to break or crack or decipher the enemy's code; a message sent in code; the three-digit telephone area code; the Canadian postal code; the American zip code; DNA contains the genetic code that determines our inherited characteristics.*
— *v.* **codes, cod·ed, cod·ing** put into a code: *a coded message.*

co·deine or **co·dein** (COH·deen) *n.* a mild narcotic derived from opium, used esp. as a sedative and a cough suppressant.

code name *n.* a name used to disguise the identity of a secret agent or operation.

code word *n.* a word with a disguised or hidden meaning, as given by parents to children for use as a password for identifying an authorized stranger.

cod·fish *n.* same as COD.

codg·er (COJ·ur) *n. Informal.* an aging and somewhat odd fellow: *a shrewd old codger like my grandfather.*

cod·i·fy (COD·uh·fye, COH·duh-) *v.* **-fies, -fied, -fy·ing** collect and systematize laws, regulations, etc. into a code.
— **cod·i·fi·ca·tion** (-fuh·CAY·shun) *n.* the codification of unwritten laws into statutes.

co·ed (COH·ed) *n. Informal.* a female student at a coeducational school.
— *adj. Informal.* coeducational; also, having to do with coeds: *a coed school, fashion.*

co·ed·u·ca·tion (COH·ej·uh·CAY·shun) *n.* the education of males and females together in the same school or class. — **co·ed·u·ca·tion·al** *adj.*

co·ef·fi·cient (coh·uh·FISH·unt) *n.* a number that is the measure of a property or characteristic: *Each material has a different coefficient of expansion; The treatment of women and minorities is a coefficient* (= measure or yardstick) *of our culture.*

co·erce (coh·URSE) *v.* **-erc·es, -erced, -erc·ing** **1** compel or restrain by fear, violence, etc.: *a pacifist coerced into joining the army.* **2** gain or effect by force: *a coerced signature.* — **co·er·cion** (coh·UR·shun) *n.* — **co·er·cive** (-siv) *adj.*

co·ex·ist (coh·ig·ZIST) *v.* exist at the same place and time: *Nations have to coexist (with one another) in peace and amity.*
— **co·ex·is·tence** (-tunce) *n.: the peaceful coexistence of the superpowers.*

cof·fee (COF·ee) *n.* a caffeine-containing beverage made from the roasted and ground seeds **(coffee beans)** of a small tropical tree; also, the tree or its seeds: *to brew, grind, grow, make, percolate, stir, strain coffee; black, decaffeinated, fresh, instant, strong, weak coffee; a cup of coffee; to take a* **coffee break** *(at work); a* **coffee shop** *(=café) in a hotel; a* **coffee table** *(used in front of a sofa); a* **coffee table book** *(=large illustrated book for display on a coffee table).*

cof·fee·house (COF·ee·house) *n.* a restaurant serving coffee and light refreshments, often acting as a social gathering place.

cof·fer (COF·ur) *n.* **1** a strongbox or vault for storing valuables. **2** **coffers** *pl.* fund or treasury: *the municipal coffers.*

cof·fin (COF·in) *n.* a usually oblong box used to bury the dead in: *The coffin was lowered into the grave.*

cog *n.* **1** a tooth or projection, usually on a gear or wheel used to transmit motion, as in a bicycle; also, a cogwheel. **2** a person or thing seen as an unimportant though a necessary part of a large, impersonal operation.

co·gent (COH·junt) *adj.* powerfully convincing, as by its logic and rigour: *cogent arguments, reasons.*
— **co·gent·ly** *adv.* — **co·gen·cy** (COH·jun·see) *n.*

cogged (COGD) *adj.* fitted with cogs: *the cogged rails of a cog railway.*

cog·i·tate (COJ·uh·tate) *v.* **-tates, -tat·ed, -tat·ing** think intently about something; ponder: *She cogitated over or on or about her next move.*
— **cog·i·ta·tion** (-TAY·shun) *n.*

cog·nac (CONE·yak) *n.* a fine brandy.

cog·nate (COG·nate) *adj.* related by common origin: *English and Hindi are cognate languages.*

cog·ni·tion (cog·NISH·un) *n.* **1** the process of knowing, including perceiving and thinking. **2** the result of this; perception or thought.
— **cog·ni·tive** (COG·nuh·tiv) *adj.*

cog·ni·zance (COG·nuh·zunce) *n.* conscious knowledge of something; awareness: *The accused had no cognizance of the events that followed; The court took* **cognizance of** *(= recognized) extenuating circumstances in sentencing the accused.*
— **cog·ni·zant** (-zunt) *adj.: He was fully cognizant of the serious nature of the charge.*

cog·wheel *n.* a wheel with cogs around the edge.

co·hab·it (COH·hab·it) *v.* live together like husband and wife without being married: *Dick cohabited with Jane before marrying; They were cohabiting.*
— **co·hab·i·ta·tion** (coh·HAB·uh·TAY·shun) *n.*

co·heir (coh·AIR) *n.* a joint heir: *The brothers were coheirs to the estate.*

co·here (coh·HEER) *v.* -heres, -hered, -her·ing stick together as one mass; hence, connect logically: *Your arguments don't cohere; The first part of the essay doesn't cohere with the last.*
— **co·her·ence** (coh·HEER·unce) *n.*

co·her·ent (coh·HEER·unt) *adj.* holding together or connected: *coherent ideas, reasoning, thought; coherent* (= intelligible) *speech.* — **co·her·ent·ly** *adv.*

co·he·sion (coh·HEE·zhun) *n.* physical sticking together of parts: *Unity within a party depends on cohesion among the membership; Solids are more difficult to separate than liquids or gases because of the greater cohesion between molecules.* — **co·he·sive** (-siv, -ziv) *adj.* — **co·he·sive·ly** *adv.;* **co·he·sive·ness** *n.*

co·hort (COE·hort) *n.* 1 originally, a division of soldiers in a Roman legion; hence, a group. 2 associate or companion: *The burglar and his cohorts were caught red-handed.*

coif *n.* 1 a tight-fitting cap. 2 a hair style.

coif·feur (cwah·FUR) *n.* a male hairdresser; *fem.* **coif·feuse** (cwah·FURZ).

coif·fure (cwah·FYOOR) *n.* a hair style; coif.

coil *v.* to wind or move in a spiral or round shape; loop: *A snake coils around its prey; Coil the rope and hang it up; String is coiled into balls.*
— *n.* 1 a series of connected loops or circles: *a radiator coil.* 2 one loop of this: *a coil of hair.* 3 a length of conducting wire wound spirally around a nonconducting core; also, a device using this: *an induction coil; the ignition coil of an automobile engine.*

coin *n.* 1 a piece of metal money: *He collects coins as a hobby; Drop a coin into the slot; We flip* or *throw* or *toss a coin to decide between alternatives; counterfeit, gold, rare, valuable coins; words that are common coin* (= widely used) *in the language; She returned the insult in his own* or *in the same coin* (= insulted him back); *the other side of the coin* (= the opposite side of the issue). 2 coins collectively: *He insisted on payment with* or *in coin* (= in cash). 3 *Slang.* money.
— *v.* 1 to mint coins from metal. 2 create a new word, phrase, etc.: *Did Churchill coin "iron curtain"?*
— **coin money** make a big profit. — **coin·er** *n.*

coin·age (COIN·ij) *n.* 1 the act of minting coins. 2 the coins minted. 3 an invented word or phrase: *"Canola" is a Canadian coinage for use instead of "rapeseed."*

co·in·cide (coh·in·SIDE) *v.* -cides, -cid·ed, -cid·ing 1 occupy or occur at the same point in space or time: *Her graduation coincided with her birthday.* 2 be identical; agree: *Our tastes in music coincide.*

co·in·ci·dence (coh·IN·suh·dunce) *n.* 1 a coinciding. 2 a remarkable and seemingly accidental instance of events happening together: *What a coincidence that both of you came today! It happened by a happy, odd, remarkable, strange coincidence; by mere, pure, sheer coincidence.* — **co·in·ci·den·tal** (-suh·DEN·tul) *adj.*

coin machine *n.* a coin-operated vending machine; slot machine.

co·i·tus (COE·it·us) *n.* sexual intercourse. — **co·i·tal** *adj.*

coke *n.* 1 a clean, hot-burning fuel used esp. in metal industries, made by removing gases from a bituminous coal, or coking coal. 2 *Slang.* cocaine: *a coke peddler, sniffer.* 3 **Coke** *Trademark.* the soft drink "Coca-Cola."

co·la (COH·luh) *n.* 1 any of several African trees that bear caffeine-containing nuts, or **cola nuts,** used as a flavouring and in medicines. 2 the extract of this nut. 3 a carbonated drink flavoured with cola extract. 4 a *pl.* of COLON. 5 **COLA** cost-of-living adjustment to wages, benefits, etc.

cold *adj.* 1 of a low temperature as compared to a norm, esp. body temperature: *a cold day; I feel cold; cold hands; cold to the touch.* 2 lacking in sympathy, encouragement, feeling, etc.: *a cold personality; She's cold towards her in-laws; His words were cold comfort; His appeals left him cold* (= did not impress or excite him); *cold* (= depressing) *facts; They asked for payment in cold* or *hard cash* (= money that you can feel). 3 clear or objective: *in the cold light of reality; the cold logic of her argument.* 4 *Informal.* unconscious: *The accident knocked him cold; He was out cold on the floor.*
— **in cold blood** without emotion: *murdered in cold blood.*
— **throw** or **pour cold water on something** discourage a plan, hopes, etc.
— *adv.* 1 *Informal.* absolutely; perfectly: *He turned me down cold when I asked for a raise; She knew the family law cold and could cite chapter and verse from memory.* 2 *Informal.* without preparation, warning, warm-up, etc.: *He went into the examination cold; She came to the job cold with no previous experience; You should be able to pick up a dictionary cold and use it right away.*
— *n.* 1 a condition of cold, esp. cold weather: *He went out into the cold without a coat; come in from the cold* (= come back into favour); *No one should be left out in the cold; biting, bitter, extreme, intense, severe cold.* 2 a viral infection that causes a stuffed or runny nose: *You'll catch (a) cold if you sit in that draft; the common cold; to come down with, contract, fight off, have, nurse, shake off, throw off a cold; a bad, chest, head, lingering, severe, slight cold.*
— **cold·ly** *adv.;* **cold·ness** *n.*

cold-blooded (COLD·blud·id) *adj.* 1 without feeling; ruthless: *a cold-blooded approach, killer, murder.* 2 having a body temperature that varies with the environment: *Birds and mammals are not cold-blooded animals, but fishes and reptiles are.*

cold call *n.* a call made without prior warning or introduction to a prospective customer, employer, etc.

cold cream *n.* a cleansing and softening cream for the skin.

cold cut *n.* a slice of cold meat.

cold-eyed *adj.* unemotional; dispassionate.

cold feet *n.* a lack of courage or self-confidence: *He got cold feet and withdrew his application.*

cold shoulder *n. Informal.* deliberate indifference; a snub: *He was given the cold shoulder when he applied to join the club.*
— **cold-shoulder** *v.: Let's not cold-shoulder an old friend.*

cold snap *n.* a sudden period of cold weather.

cold sore *n.* a blister on the lips, usually accompanying a cold or fever.

cold storage *n.* 1 refrigerated storage for preserving food, fur coats, etc. 2 putting away of an idea, plan, etc. until needed: *It's in* or *gone* or *put into cold storage.*

cold turkey *Slang.* 1 *n.* behaviour or procedure that is abrupt, as sudden withdrawal from an addictive drug. 2 *adv.* abruptly: *to take kids off heroin cold turkey; He quit smoking cold turkey; Do it cold turkey; He went cold turkey and quit smoking.*
— **cold-turkey** *adj.*: *a cold-turkey approach; a week of cold-turkey withdrawal from TV.*

cold war *n.* a state of suppressed, nonmilitary hostility between nations.

cole·slaw (COLE·slaw) *n.* finely shredded raw cabbage as a salad; also **cole slaw.**

col·ic (COLL·ic) *n.* severe abdominal pain.
— **col·ick·y** *adj.*: *a colicky infant.*

col·i·se·um (col·uh·SEE·um) *n.* a large multipurpose stadium for sports or other public entertainment.

col·lab·o·rate (cuh·LAB·uh·rate) *v.* **-rates, -rat·ed, -rat·ing** 1 work together: *He collaborated with her on the project; They collaborated.* 2 cooperate with an invading or occupying force: *He was accused of collaborateing with the Nazis.*
— **col·lab·o·ra·tion** (-RAY·shun) *n.*
— **col·lab·o·ra·tor** (-LAB·uh·ray·tur) *n.*: *a wartime collaborator; The collaborator was convicted of treason.*

col·lage (cuh·LAHZH) *n.* an artistic composition using diverse items; bits of paper, wood, cloth, etc. glued onto a board: *That essay is a mere collage of quotations.*

col·lapse (cuh·LAPS) *v.* **-laps·es, -lapsed, -laps·ing** 1 fall down or break down: *The bridge collapsed during the flood; collapsed from the force of the water; collapsed under its weight; The plot collapsed* (= failed completely). 2 fall helpless or become unable to function: *He collapsed under the strain; collapsed from mental fatigue.*
— **n.** a breakdown or failure: *the collapse of a roof during a storm; the collapse of a business venture; an economic, emotional, mental, total collapse.*
— **col·lap·si·ble** *adj.* that can be folded for storage: *a collapsible bed, chair.*

col·lar (COLL·ur) *n.* 1 something that encircles the neck, esp. the part of a garment that does so, the leather band around a dog's neck, or the similar part of a harness: *a button-down, Roman, stiff, turndown collar; People get **hot under the collar*** (= angry). 2 something resembling a collar, as on a pipe.
— **v.** 1 put a collar on something. 2 seize; detain; arrest. — **col·lar·less** *adj.*

col·late (col·LATE) *v.* **-lates, -lat·ed, -lat·ing** 1 compare closely and note variants: *a scholar collating ancient texts; to collate one text with another.* 2 assemble pages in proper order, as after photocopying.
— **col·la·tor** (-LAY·tur) *n.*

col·lat·er·al (cuh·LAT·uh·rul) *adj.* 1 from the same ancestors by a different line of descent; not lineal:

Brothers, uncles, etc. are collateral relations, not like parents and children; a collateral branch of the family. 2 parallel; also, supporting: *collateral evidence.* 3 secured by a guarantee of repayment: *The bank manager offered us a **collateral loan;** She asked for collateral* (= guaranteeing) *funds, security.*
— **n.** property pledged as security for a loan or obligation: *to put up collateral for a loan.*

col·league (COLL·eeg) *n.* an associate, esp. a fellow member of a profession.

col·lect (cuh·LECT) *v.* 1 bring or come together into a group or mass: *People collected on street corners; They collected around the speaker; He collects coins as a hobby.* 2 get control of oneself, one's thoughts, etc.: *a calm and **collected*** (= not distracted) *manner.* 3 ask for and receive payment, taxes, and such dues: *The paper boy comes collecting on Fridays; to collect benefits, bills, debts, pensions; He collected on his insurance.* 4 pick up: *to collect a parcel at the post office; to collect one's date.*
— **adj. & adv.** paid for by the receiver: *Children phone home collect; They make collect calls.*

col·lect·i·ble or **col·lect·a·ble** (cuh·LEC·tuh·bul) *n.* an object fancied by someone, as for its aesthetic appeal or nostalgic value: *Licence plates, fountain pens, and such collectibles are not fancied by collectors of art, coins, stamps, etc.*

col·lec·tion (cuh·LEC·shun) *n.* the act of collecting or what is collected: *an art, butterfly, coin, private, stamp collection; to take up a collection for the homeless;* **adj.**: *a collection agency, letter.*

col·lec·tive (cuh·LEC·tiv) *adj.* having to do with a group or unit: *collective action; a collective agreement between labour and management; a collective bargaining unit; a **collective farm** worked and managed by a group; a **collective noun** such as "class" or "flock"; the collective ownership of property* (= ownership in common); *NATO is an agency of collective security.*
— **n.** a collective organization: *an editorial collective (of journalists); a worker's collective.* — **col·lec·tive·ly** *adv.*

col·lec·tor *n.* one who collects: *an art, garbage, stamp, tax, trash collector; an avid collector of rare books; a book that has become a collector's item.*

col·lege (COLL·ij) *n.* 1 an institution of higher education: *to go to college after high school; graduate from college; She tried to put him through college* (= pay for it); *He dropped out, failed out* or *flunked out of college; a business, community, junior, military college; a college of dentistry, education, pharmacy; She's away at college; made friends in college; back from college after graduation; out of college looking for work.* 2 a group of people with common duties: *an electoral college; the College of Cardinals.*

col·le·giate (cuh·LEE·jut) *adj.* 1 having to do with a college or colleges: *a collegiate church, dictionary, education, library, institution, student, textbook; collegiate level, life, standards, types.* 2 *Cdn.* having to do with a collegiate institute.
— **n.** *Cdn.* in some provinces, a high school with special facilities and staff; also **collegiate institute.**

col·lide (cuh·LIDE) *v.* **col·lides, col·lid·ed, col·lid·ing** 1 come into violent contact: *The car collided head-on* with a truck; *They collided on the highway.* **2** come directly in conflict; clash: *The Government and the Opposition collide constantly during question period.*

col·lie (COLL·ee) *n.* a large long-haired dog originally bred in Scotland to herd sheep.

col·lier·y (COLL·yuh·ree) *n.* **col·lier·ies** a coal mine with its equipment and buildings.

col·li·sion (cuh·LIZH·un) *n.* a colliding: *a head-on, midair, near collision; a collision between two planes; one plane in collision with another; The government is on a **collison course** with the labour unions unless they drop the bill.*

col·lo·cate (COLL·uh·cate) *v.* -cates, -cat·ed, -cat·ing exist side by side or close together: *"Door" collocates with "ajar," "back," "front," "close," "lock," "open," "shut," etc. in numerous idioms and structures.*

col·lo·cation (col·uh·CAY·shun) *n.* a collocating: *the collocation of "open" and "door" in a phrase like "open-door policy."*

col·lo·qui·al (cuh·LOH·kwee·ul) *adj.* characteristic of informal conversation: *a colloquial expression, as "forty winks" for "a short nap."*— **col·lo·qui·al·ly** *adv.*

col·lo·qui·al·ism (cuh·LOH·kwee·uh·liz·um) *n.* a colloquial word or phrase; an informal expression: *"Fly off the handle" is a colloquialism for "lose one's temper."*

col·lo·quy (COLL·uk·wee) *n.* -quies **1** a usually formal dialogue or conversation. **2** a work written in this form.

col·lu·sion (cuh·LOO·zhun) *n.* secret agreement for an improper or fraudulent purpose: *a spy working in collusion with the enemy; There was collusion between them.*

co·logne (cuh·LONE) *n.* a perfumed liquid made of fragrant oils in an alcohol base.

co·lon (COH·lun) *n.* **1** a punctuation mark [:] used before a list, example, quotation, etc. **2** *pl.* -lons or -la (-luh), the lower part of the large intestine leading to the rectum.

colo·nel (CUR·nul) *n.* a military officer ranking above a lieutenant colonel and below a brigadier general, usually in command of a regiment.

co·lo·ni·al (cuh·LOH·nee·ul) *adj.* **1** [often derogatory] having to do with a colony or colonies: *colonial oppression, possessions, power; Canada's colonial status ended with Confederation in 1867.* **2** **Colonial** having to do with the period of U.S. history before independence: *colonial architecture, furniture.*

— **co·lo·ni·al·ism** (-uh·liz·um) *n.*; **co·lo·ni·al·ly** *adv.*

col·o·nist (COLL·uh·nist) *n.* one who lives in a colony, esp. a first settler.

col·o·nize (COLL·uh·nize) *v.* -niz·es, -nized, -niz·ing settle in a place or establish a colony: *North America was colonized by the Dutch, French, and British.* — **col·o·ni·za·tion** (-nuh·ZAY·shun) *n.*

col·on·nade (coll·uh·NADE) *n.* a row of evenly spaced columns usually supporting one side of the roof of a large building.

col·o·ny (COLL·uh·nee) *n.* -nies **1** a dependency in a distant land controlled and settled from the mother country: *Thirteen former British colonies first made up the U.S.; Hong Kong ceases to be a crown colony in 1998.* **2** a group of individuals of the same kind or calling living in one area: *an artists' colony; a leper colony; penal colony; a colony of ants.*

color, colorant *n. & v.* See COLOUR, COLOURANT.

col·or·a·tion (cull·uh·RAY·shun) *n.* the state or manner of being coloured.

col·or·a·tu·ra (cull·uh·ruh·TOOR·uh) *n.* **1** elaborate or ornamental passages in music. **2** a soprano specializing in such music.

colorblind, colorcast, colored, colorfast, etc. See COLOURBLIND, etc.

co·los·sal (cuh·LOSS·ul) *adj.* of human creations, huge or of vast proportions; like a colossus: *a colossal dam on the Nile; a colossal structure; his colossal pride, stupidity; What a colossal waste!*— **co·los·sal·ly** *adv.*

co·los·sus (cuh·LOSS·us) *n., pl.* -los·si (-los·eye) or -los·sus·es something of huge size, like a statue of Apollo in ancient Rhodes: *Bell Canada is a colossus of Canadian industry.*

col·our or **col·or** (CULL·ur) *n.* **1** the quality of things as they appear in light: *the bright colours of the rainbow; Red, blue, and yellow are the primary colours; attractive, brilliant, dark, dull, gaudy, rich, strong colours; the soft or subdued, not loud or harsh, colours of an evening scene; the vivid, warm colours of a painting; painted in natural colour; Colours should match or blend, not clash; a movie in living colour! Our garden is a riot of colour; He described her performance in glowing colours;* **adj.:** *a colour film, painting, photography, printing; colour harmony, television.* **2** skin colour, esp. as indicating health or embarrassment: *She lost colour while in hospital; Rest and recuperation brought colour back to her cheeks; He changes colour whenever the subject is mentioned; a person **of colour** (=nonwhite).* **3** **the colours** a flag, emblem, etc. of a nation, military unit, etc.: *the ceremony of trooping the colours; to serve with the colours (=military); You see him in his true colour or colours (=nature); She passed the test **with flying colours** (=victoriously).* **4** a lively or interesting quality: *Writers use dialect to add or lend local colour to a story.* **5** appearance: *greed under the colour of frugality; a new twist that gives a false colour to what happened; false evidence that gives or lends colour (=the appearance of truth) to the charges.* **6** painting: *oil, water colours.*

— *v.* **1** change the colour of something: *She coloured*

her hair brown. **2** alter or misrepresent: *a story coloured by the reporter's prejudices.* **3** change colour; blush: *He colours at the very mention of the subject.*

col·our·ant or **col·or·ant** (CULL·ur·unt) *n.* a colouring agent like dye, ink, or paint.

col·our·blind or **col·or·blind** (CULL·ur·blined) *adj.* unable to perceive or distinguish certain colours. — **col·our·blind·ness** or **col·or·blind·ness** *n.*

col·our·cast or **col·or·cast** (CULL·ur·cast) *v.* telecast in colour; *n.: a colourcast of the Santa Claus parade.*

col·oured or **col·ored** (CULL·urd) *adj.* **1** having colour. **2** distorted; biassed: *a highly coloured account of what happened.* **3** non-Caucasian, esp. Black: *Is he coloured or white?* — *n., pl.* **coloured** or **colored, coloureds** or **coloreds** a racially mixed person: *the coloureds of South Africa.*

col·our·fast or **col·or·fast** (CULL·ur·fast) *adj.* having colours that will not fade or run: *colourfast cotton.*

col·our·ful or **col·or·ful** (CULL·ur·full) *adj.* **1** having strong or attractive colours: *a colourful costume, scene.* **2** lively or interesting: *a colourful character.* — **col·our·ful·ly** or **col·or·ful·ly** *adv.*

colt *n.* **1** a young horse, donkey, etc., esp. a male. **2** an inexperienced youth.

colt·ish *adj.* frisky; lively: *coltish escapades.* — **colt·ish·ly** *adv.*

col·umn (COLL·um) *n.* **1** a pillar, with its base and capital, usually supporting a roof or upper storey. **2** something resembling this: *the spinal column; vertebral column; the steering column of an automobile; a column of figures to be added; a column of smoke rising from a chimney; This page has two columns (of print).* **3** a file or row: *a tank column; a column of soldiers.* **4** a regular feature in a newspaper or magazine: *correspondence columns; a gossip, obituary, sports column; a syndicated column.* — **col·umned** *adj.* — **col·um·nar** (cuh·LUM·nur) *adj.*

col·um·nist (COLL·um·ist, -um·nist) *n.* one who writes a newspaper column: *a gossip columnist; political columnist.*

com- *prefix.* together: *compact, compatriot, compress.*

co·ma (COH·muh) *n.* a prolonged period of deep unconsciousness, esp. as caused by injury, poison, or disease: *to slip into a coma; to come out of a coma.*

co·ma·tose (COH·uh·tose, *rhyme:* dose) *adj.* of, like, or affected with coma: *a comatose patient, state.*

comb (COHM) *n.* **1** a toothed instrument for arranging and sometimes holding the hair in place: *a tortoise-shell comb; We examined the records with a fine-tooth comb* (= very carefully). **2** the fleshy, usually red crest on a rooster's head. **3** the crest of a wave. — *v.* **1** arrange, clean, etc. with a comb. **2** search thoroughly: *The police combed the house for clues.*

com·bat (cum·BAT) *v.* **-bats, -bat·ted** or **-bat·ed, -bat·ting** or **-bat·ing** fight or oppose: *Help combat heart disease; how to combat terrorism.* — *n.* (COM·bat) a fight, esp. active warfare as opposed to military support: *to engage in* or *to go into combat; a close, deadly, hand-to-hand, military, mortal combat;*

adj.: a combat mission, team; a combat unit wearing combat boots.

com·bat·ant (cum·BAT·unt) *n.* a person engaged in combat.

combat fatigue same as SHELL SHOCK.

com·bat·ive (cum·BAT·iv) *adj.* ready or eager to fight: *He's in a combative mood; She did it in a combative spirit.*

combat zone *n.* an area in which fighting is going on.

com·bi·na·tion (com·buh·NAY·shun) *n.* **1** the act or state of combining or being combined. **2** a united entity or group: *a free, rare, strange combination; a number-password combination for accessing a database.* **3** the series of letters and numbers that, when turned on a dial, will open a lock, or **combination lock,** as on a bank vault.

com·bine (cum·BINE) *v.* **-bines, -bined, -bin·ing** come or bring together; unite: *Let's combine our efforts; We'll combine business with pleasure; Husbands and wives often combine as partners in business.* — *n.* (COM·bine) **1** a mobile machine that both cuts and threshes grain. **2** a combination, esp. of business interests, sometimes unethical: *a business combine; dairy combine; The powers of The Restrictive Trade Practices Commission are derived from the Federal Combines Investigation Act.*

combining form *n.* a form in which a word combines with other words or word elements to make new compounds and derivatives, as "auto-," "counter-," "-crat," "demo-," "multi-," and "-pede."

comb·ings (COH·mingz) *n.pl.* loose hair, wool, etc. removed by combing.

com·bo (COM·boh) *n. Informal.* a small group of musicians: *a jazz combo.*

com·bus·ti·ble (cum·BUS·tuh·bul) *n. & adj.* (something) that is capable of burning: *combustible liquids such as gasoline and cooking oil; Paper, cloth, and wood are combustible materials; All these are combustibles.* — **com·bus·ti·bil·i·ty** (-BIL·uh·tee) *n.*

com·bus·tion (cum·BUS·chun) *n.* a chemical reaction in a gaseous medium with release of heat; burning: *spontaneous combustion of rags soaked with oil; the internal combustion engine of an automobile.*

come (CUM) *v.* **comes, came, come, com·ing 1** move toward a position, condition, or state thought of as near the speaker: *Please come to our house; He's coming down the street; He came at me with a big smile; Water comes to a boil at 100°C.* **2** occur; happen: *Christmas comes once a year; F comes before G in the alphabet; Z comes last; She will be a year older,* **come** *February* (= when February arrives). **3** originate: *He comes of good stock; She comes from Alberta; Chicks come from eggs; I know where you're* **coming from** (*Informal* for I know what you mean). — **come across 1** appear: *He comes across as a radical in his books.* **2** also **come upon,** find or meet unexpectedly: *I came across* or *upon an old friend at the party.* — **come along** make an appearance: *We wanted to hail the first cab that came along; Then along comes this*

nearly empty bus.
— **come around 1** recover: *She has come around quickly after her recent illness.* **2** change *to* a different opinion or stand.
— **come away** leave: *Each came away with a different impression of the show.*
— **come back** return, esp. to fame, power, status, etc.
— **come between** cause trouble between or separate two people.
— **come by** acquire or get: *Good editors are hard to come by these days.*
— **come clean** *Slang.* tell the whole truth; confess.
— **come down:** *an heirloom that has come down* (= that originated) *from our ancestors; The teacher came down hard on the students* (= punished them severely); *This talk about more money – it all comes down* (= amounts) *to greed; He came down* (= became afflicted) *with measles.*
— **come in for** be subjected to something: *The new play came in for some harsh comment.*
— **come into** receive, esp. by inheritance: *She will come into $500 000 on her aunt's death.*
— **come off 1** become detached. **2** happen; succeed; fare.
— **come off it!** or **come on!** *Informal.* stop behaving like that!
— **come on** present oneself aggressively: *She's coming on a bit too strong for me; He comes on* (= comes across or appears) *rather dumb.*
— **come out:** *Young women used to come out* (= debut) *at 18; She came out* (= turned out) *in her best outfit; They come out with* (= publish) *a dozen books each month.*
— **come through** give or do what is required: *It takes time for them to come through with a contract offer.*
— **come to 1** amount to: *That comes to $50.95.*
2 (-TOO) regain consciousness: *The boxer came to within moments of the knockout.*
— **come up roses** happen as desired.
— **come up with** *Informal.* produce: *Try to come up with a better idea.*
— **come what may** no matter what happens.
— **how come?** *Informal.* why?

come·back *n.* **1** a return to power or status; recovery. **2** a retort.

come·down *n.* a coming down in power or position.

co·me·di·an (cuh·MEE·dee·un) *n.* **1** one who acts in a comedy. **2** an amusing person, esp. a professional entertainer: *a nightclub, stand-up, TV comedian.* — **co·me·di·enne** (-dee·EN) *fem.*

com·e·dy (COM·uh·dee) *n.* -**dies 1** a play with a light, amusing tone: *a musical comedy; situation comedy.* **2** a dramatic piece with a happy ending; hence, this type, as opposed to tragedy. **3** an amusing aspect, event, etc. — **co·me·dic** (cuh·MEE·dic) *adj.: He had a long comedic career; her comedic talents.*

come·ly (CUM·lee) *adj.* -**li·er**, -**li·est** attractive; good-looking. — **come·li·ness** *n.*

come-on *n. Slang.* an allurement; inducement: *Pens are being handed out as come-ons to attract customers.*

com·er (CUM·ur) *n. Informal.* a promising or rapidly advancing person: *He is ready to take on all comers.*

com·et (COM·it) *n.* a celestial body, esp. one orbiting the sun, with a small, bright centre, a glowing "head" around it, and often a long glowing "tail."

come·up·pance (cum·UP·unce) *n. Informal.* just retribution; deserts: *You'll get your comeuppance.*

com·fort (CUM·furt) *v.* soothe or console: *to comfort them in their hour of sorrow.*
— *n.* **1** consolation; also, a person or thing that gives consolation: *a source of joy and comfort; Your letter was a great comfort; The low marks were cold comfort; to* **take comfort** *in* or *from recent improvements in our performance.* **2** ease or well-being; also, something that causes this: *Three in the front seat is too close for comfort; to live in comfort; a resort with all the comforts of home.*

com·fort·a·ble (CUM·fur·tuh·bul) *adj.* being in a state of or giving comfort: *He's quite comfortable in bed; a comfortable chair, pew; She enjoys a comfortable income.* — **com·fort·a·ble·ness** *n.*; **com·fort·a·bly** *adv.*

com·fort·er (CUM·fur·tur) *n.* **1** a warm quilt. **2** a soft, woollen scarf.

com·fy (CUM·fee) *adj.* -**fi·er**, -**fi·est** *Informal.* comfortable: *a nice comfy pillow for my baby.*

com·ic (COM·ic) *adj.* **1** having to do with comedy or cartoons: *a comic actor, character, section of a newspaper.* **2** humorous or amusing in a thoughtful way: *a comic effect, sense; comic spirit.*
— *n.* **1** a humorous person, esp. a professional comedian. **2** *Informal.* a comic book. **3 comics** *pl.* a section of comic strips, as in a newspaper; funnies: *full-colour comics.*

com·i·cal (COM·uh·cul) *adj.* provoking laughter; hilariously funny: *a comical air, outfit, performance, scene.* — **com·i·cal·ly** *adv.*

comic book *n.* a booklet of comic strips telling adventurous or humorous stories.

comic strip *n.* a series of drawings telling a humorous or adventurous story.

coming *adj.* **1** approaching: *the coming attractions at our theatre.* **2** *Informal.* showing promise of success: *the coming thing in neckwear.*
— *n.* advent: *the coming of winter; The* **comings and goings** (= movements or activities) *of the new neighbours amused everyone; Christians await the* **Second Coming** *of the Messiah.*

com·ma (COM·uh) *n.* a punctuation mark (,) showing a slight separation or pause within a sentence or clause.

com·mand (cuh·MAND) *v.* **1** order with authority: *He commanded them to cease fire; He commanded that they cease fire; the **commanding officer*** (= the one in authority). **2** receive as one's due: *Knowledge commands respect; She commands a six-figure salary.* **3** have in one's control; also, overlook in a controlling manner: *The fort commands the valley; a fort built on **commanding** heights.*
— *n.* **1** an order or the giving of it: *to carry out, execute, give, issue, obey commands; At whose command did you open fire?* **2** authority or ability to give commands: *Who is in command? the chain of command from the Chief of Staff down; to assume, exercise, place in, put in, relinquish, take over command; He was in firm command of or over the regiment till the end.* **3** a military force or similar organization: *the armed forces under a unified command; the Maritime Command of the Canadian Armed Forces for air-and-sea naval support of operations; the Strategic Air Command; a decision made by the military high command* (= top commanders). **4** control: *She has a good, fluent command of Spanish.*

com·man·dant (COM·un·dant) *n.* a commanding officer.

com·man·deer (com·un·DEER) *v.* seize by force, esp. by military order.

com·mand·er (cuh·MAN·dur) *n.* **1** one who commands, esp. a commanding officer: *the commander of a unit.* **2** a naval officer ranking just below a captain, as in the Maritime Command of the Canadian Armed Forces.

com·mand·ment (cuh·MAND·munt) *n.* a command or precept, esp. **Commandment,** one of the ten laws given by God to Moses: *to keep the commandments; the Ten Commandments.*

command module *n.* the section of a spacecraft containing astronauts and main controls and designed for reentry.

com·man·do (cuh·MAN·doh) *n.* **-dos** or **-does** (-doze) **1** a member of a small military force trained for quick raids into enemy territory. **2** the force itself.

command performance *n.* an entertainment given at the request of a ruler or head of state; hence, an inspired or engineered action or show.

command post *n.* the field headquarters of a fighting unit.

com·mem·o·rate (cuh·MEM·uh·rate) *v.* **-rates, -rat·ed, -rat·ing** **1** honour or keep the memory of a person or event. **2** be a memorial to a person or event: *a plaque commemorating war dead.*
— **com·mem·o·ra·tion** (-RAY·shun) *n.*
— **com·mem·o·ra·tive** (-ruh·tiv) *adj.: a commemorative stamp.*

com·mence (cuh·MENCE) *v.* **com·men·ces, com·menced, com·menc·ing** *Formal.* begin or start: *Let the games commence; The ceremonies commenced at noon.*

com·mence·ment (cuh·MENCE·munt) *n.* **1** a beginning: *the commencement of the ceremony.* **2** a ceremony for the granting of degrees or diplomas: *at the commencement on May 23; adj.: commencement ceremony, exercises.*

com·mend (cuh·MEND) *v.* **1** praise; recommend: *She was highly commended for her work.* **2** entrust to another's care: *In his will, he commended his children to his sister's care.*
— **com·men·da·tion** (com·un·DAY·shun) *n.*

com·men·da·ble (cuh·MEN·duh·bul) *adj.* praiseworthy: *a commendable action; his highly commendable bravery.* — **com·men·da·bly** *adv.*

com·men·su·ra·ble (cuh·MEN·shuh·ruh·bul) *adj.* measurable by the same standard, as numbers evenly divisible by the same whole number: *21 and 28 are commensurable* (= divisible by 7).

com·men·su·rate (cuh·MEN·shuh·rit) *adj.* proportionate: *He was paid a salary commensurate to his worth; Pay has to be commensurate with work performed.*

com·ment (COM·ent) *n.* an explanatory or critical note, remark, or reaction: *a critical, cryptic, fitting, nasty, off-the-record, passing comment; The incident aroused or caused or evoked or provoked considerable comment in the press; "No comment," the politician replied; Comments made about or on the incident are off the record.*
— *v.* make a comment: *He commented that everyone seemed happy; refused to comment on or about the incident.*

com·men·tar·y (COM·un·tair·ee) *n.* **-tar·ies** **1** usually **commentaries,** memoirs or a simple narrative. **2** a systematic series of comments, as on a text or a sports event: *He wrote a commentary on the Koran; He gave a running commentary* (= oral play-by-play comments) *on the game.* **3** something that illustrates or reflects on a subject: *Pollution is a sad commentary on civilization.*

com·men·ta·tor (COM·un·tay·tur) *n.* one who reports and comments on news and politics on radio or TV.

com·merce (COM·urse) *n.* **1** the buying and selling of commodities; trade: *to carry on, develop, engage in, expand commerce with other countries; overseas commerce; the commerce between Canada and the U.S.; a Chamber of Commerce.* **2** dealings; social relations: *no commerce with the enemy; Latin used to be the language of commerce in Vatican circles.*

com·mer·cial (cuh·MUR·shul) *adj.* **1** having to do with commerce: *a commercial agent, attaché, bank, bureau, centre, development, undertaking; commercial art, courses, education, grade, law, photography, programs, transport, treaties.* **2** oriented to profit-making: *Commercial television relies on advertising; academic and commercial publishers.*
— *n.* a radio or TV advertisement: *a commercial sponsored by a bank.* — **com·mer·cial·ly** *adv.*

com·mer·cial·ism (cuh·MUR·shuh·liz·um) *n.* excessive emphasis on the making of a profit.

com·mer·cial·ize (cuh·MUR·shuh·lize) *v.* **-iz·es, -ized, -iz·ing** make commercial; put something on a commercial basis: *the highly commercialized North American Christmas (with a lot of buying and selling).*

Com·mie (COM·ee) *n. & adj. Informal.* communist; also **Com·my, com·mie,** *pl.* **Com·mies, com·mies.**

com·mis·sar (COM·uh·sar) *n.* a communist party official who watches over army officers and others to ensure their conformity to the wishes of the party: *a political commissar.*

com·mis·sar·y (COM·uh·sair·ee) *n.* **-sar·ies 1** a store selling food and other provisions at a temporary site or work camp. **2** a lunchroom, esp. in a movie studio.

com·mis·sion (cuh·MISH·un) *n.* **1** an act of committing: *the commission of a crime; sins of omission and commission.* **2** the granting of certain military ranks or the rank itself: *to award, confer, earn, grant, win a commission.* **3** a task entrusted to someone: *She received a commission from City Hall to paint a mural; to execute a commission.* **4** a group entrusted with a task, often as a government agency: *to appoint* or *establish a fact-finding, investigating, planning commission; a Royal Commission on the status of women; The commission was disbanded after it reported; the Canadian High Commission* (= embassy) *in Jamaica.* **5** a sales rep's fee, usually a percentage of the sale price: *a 10% commission on all sales.*
— in (or **out of**) **commission** in (or out of) working order or active service: *The plant has been in commission since 1980; It was put out of commission by a fire for a few days.*
— v. give a commission: *A lieutenant is a commissioned officer; He was commissioned an officer cadet; The king commissioned him to explore the West; a painting commissioned by the city.*

com·mis·sion·aire (cuh·mish·uh·NAIR) *n.* a uniformed attendant or guard on duty at the entrance to a hotel, club, large shop, office, etc.: *The Canadian Corps of Commissionaires is composed of former members of the armed forces.*

com·mis·sion·er (cuh·MISH·un·ur) *n.* **1** a member of a commission. **2** the head of a usually governmental agency: *the commissioner of education; the Canadian High Commissioner* (= ambassador) *in a Commonwealth country.* **3** an administrative head: *a Salvation Army commissioner; a commissioner of the Girl Guides.*

com·mit (cuh·MIT) *v.* **-mits, -mit·ted, -mit·ting 1** do something wrong or bad: *to commit aggression, atrocities, blackmail, blunders, crimes, mistakes, suicide.* **2** put in a special place: *to commit a person to prison, to a mental hospital; to commit a poem to memory; He never committed his thoughts to paper.* **3** pledge or promise oneself or resources to an action or use: *to commit funds to a project; He won't commit himself* (= say anything definite or binding) *on that issue; He is* **committed** (= devoted) *to helping the poor, to his principles.*

com·mit·ment (cuh·MIT·munt) *n.* **1** a pledge or promise: *He gave* or *made a firm commitment to invest in our firm; a commitment that he would invest in our firm; He was unable to meet such heavy financial commitments.* **2** devotion: *a deep, total commitment to helping the poor.*

com·mit·tal (cuh·MIT·ul) *n.* a committing to a special place, as a body to a grave: *a committal* (= burial) *service.*

com·mit·tee (cuh·MIT·ee) *n.* an appointed or elected group that considers, acts on, promotes, or reports on particular matters: *to appoint, establish, form, organize, set up a committee; an ad-hoc, advisory, finance, select, standing, steering committee; a* **committee of the whole** (= of all members of a legislative body); *a committee for economic development; to sit on a committee (as a member); a committee on inner-city schools.*

com·mode (cuh·MODE) *n.* **1** a chest of drawers. **2** a portable washstand in a cupboard. **3** a low chair enclosing a chamber pot.

com·mod·i·ty (cuh·MOD·uh·tee) *n.* **-ties** an article of use, esp. one transported and traded, as farm and mining products, textiles, and lumber: *a marketable commodity; to trade in commodities on the* **commodity exchange** or **commodity market.**

com·mo·dore (COM·uh·dor) *n.* **1** a wartime navy officer ranking just below a rear admiral. **2** the head of a yacht club, fleet, etc.

com·mon (COM·un) *adj.* **1** having to do with more than one: *Laws serve the common good; common interests; two apartments separated by a common* (= shared) *wall; A public park is common* (= public) *property; English is the common language of the Commonwealth of Nations; to meet on common ground (acceptable to the parties concerned); Falling asleep is a weakness* **common to** *all of us.* **2** frequent; usual; general: *Cows are a common sight on the rural landscape; They are quite common; a matter of common knowledge; a common experience, occurrence; in common parlance; words in common use.* **3** ordinary; without distinction of quality or rank: *a common criminal, flower, lawyer, sailor, soldier; the common cat, people; common courtesy, decency; common salt; a* **common or garden variety** *of an article; an old senator who has lost the* **common touch** (= gift of communicating with the common people). **4** having no quality; inferior: *the common speech of the uneducated; common manners; She looks rather common in that hairdo.*
— n. 1 a piece of land owned by and open to the public: *cows grazing on the village common; property held* **in common with** (= shared by) *the rest of the family.* **2 commons** *pl.* the common people. **3 the Commons** the House of Commons, the lower house of Parliament. **— com·mon·ly** *adv.;* **com·mon·ness** *n.*

common carrier *n.* a commercial concern for carrying goods, people, or messages nationwide, as Bell Canada.

com·mon·er (COM·un·ur) *n.* one without noble rank.

common factor or **common divisor** *n.* a number that divides evenly into two or more numbers: *8 is a common factor of 16 and 24.*

common ground *n.* shared opinions or interests.

common law *n.* the uncodified body of law based on custom and court decisions.
— common-law *adj. & adv.: a common-law marriage* (= one based on cohabitation and valid by common law); *a common-law husband, wife; They lived common-law for many years.*

com·mon·place (COM·un·place) *n.* **1** a frequent thing. **2** a trite or obvious remark or topic; platitude: *You've*

just stated a commonplace; It's a commonplace to say families are breaking up.
— *adj.* ordinary or usual: *a movie with a commonplace theme; It's becoming commonplace for families to break up.*

common sense *n.* ordinary practical judgment that is not based on sophistication: *He had the common sense not to contradict the boss; to show* or *use good, plain common sense.*
— **common-sense** or **com·mon·sen·si·cal** (com·un·SEN·suh·cul) *adj.*

com·mon·weal (COM·un·weel) *n.* the public good.

com·mon·wealth (COM·un·welth) *n.* **1** the body of citizens in a state. **2** a nation or state: *the Commonwealth of Australia; the Commonwealth of Massachusetts.* **3** an association of sovereign states, esp. the **Commonwealth of Nations** made up of Britain and former British colonies.

com·mo·tion (cuh·MOH·shun) *n.* noisy confusion; tumult: *The announcement caused, created, raised a commotion in the audience; The commotion soon subsided.*

com·mu·nal (cuh·MEW·nul, COM·yoo·nul) *adj.* **1** having to do with a commune or a system of common property; shared: *a communal farm; communal living.* **2** having to do with a community or ethnic group: *communal strife.*

com·mune (cum·YOON) *v.* -munes, -muned, -mun·ing converse, esp. mentally: *Poets commune with Nature.*
— *n.* (COM·yoon) **1** a group of people living and working together; community: *a hippie commune.* **2** the smallest division of government in some European countries, esp. France, resembling a township. **3** in a Communist country, a communal unit or settlement: *Chinese communes.*

com·mu·ni·ca·ble (cuh·MEW·nuh·cuh·bul) *adj.* that can be easily communicated; contagious or infectious: *Mumps is a communicable disease.*

com·mu·ni·cate (cuh·MEW·nuh·cate) *v.* -cates, -cat·ed, -cat·ing **1** pass on to or share with another: *to communicate a disease, information, feelings, thoughts; We were not allowed to communicate by letter or telephone with the outside world.* **2** allow passage between: *two communicating rooms.* **3** administer or receive Holy Communion. — **com·mu·ni·ca·tor** *n.*

com·mu·ni·ca·tion (cuh·mew·nuh·CAY·shun) *n.* **1** the act or means of communicating: *to cut off communications; to establish communication with the trapped miners; stay in communication with the outside world; The Federal Department of Communications is in charge of radio, TV, satellites, telephone, films, etc.; adj.: the communications guru Marshall McLuhan; Keep communication lines open; the communications media, technology; a communications satellite; Computers need communications software to send and receive data.* **2** a message: *The outpost received a communication from headquarters; to address, direct, send communications to headquarters; a direct, official, personal, private communication; a privileged* (=confidential) *communication between priest and penitent.*

com·mu·ni·ca·tive (cuh·MEW·nuh·cuh·tiv) *adj.* willing to talk; not secretive: *a child who is not very communicative; a communicative disposition.*

com·mu·nion (cum·YOON·yun) *n.* **1** a sharing: *a communion of interests.* **2** fellowship; a group of people connected by religion: *the communion of saints; the Anglican Communion.* **3** intimate communication: *to hold communion with oneself.* **4 Communion** Holy Communion or the Lord's Supper: *to administer, receive, take Communion.*

com·mu·ni·qué (cuh·MEW·nuh·cay) *n.* an official announcement, esp. to the press; bulletin: *They issued a joint communiqué after the summit meeting; a communiqué on* or *about what they had discussed.*

com·mu·nism (COM·yuh·niz·um) *n.* **1** a social system based on the collective ownership of wealth and the absence of social class. **2 Communism** the revolutionary communist system, as practised esp. in the U.S.S.R., based on the theories of Marx and Lenin and controlled by the **Communist Party.**
— **com·mu·nist** or **Com·mu·nist** *n. & adj.*
— **com·mu·nis·tic** (com·yuh·NIS·tic) *adj.*

com·mu·ni·ty (cuh·MEW·nuh·tee) *n.* -ties **1** a group of people living in one place, esp. the population of a town, region, etc.: *a leader who has the support of the whole community; a close-knit community; a protected community; adj.: community antenna television* (=cable TV); *a community chest* (=fund for charitable purposes); *a community* (=not teaching) *hospital; community property (jointly held by husband and wife).* **2** a group of people with similar interests: *an academic, business, ethnic, Jewish, religious, scientific community; Ottawa's diplomatic community.* **3** identity: *a community of interests and views.*

community college *n.* **1** *Cdn.* a post-secondary educational institution for training in occupations and skills. **2** a junior college serving and supported by a regional community.

com·mu·ta·tion (com·yuh·TAY·shun) *n.* a commuting: *a commutation ticket (usually at a reduced rate for commuters).*

com·mute (cuh·MYOOT, long "YOO") *v.* -mutes, -mut·ed, -mut·ing **1** change or substitute, esp. reduce the severity of a penalty: *The death sentence was commuted to life imprisonment.* **2** travel regularly between home and place of work: *People commute to work by car, rail, and bus; They commute between city and suburb; People commute daily from the suburbs to the city.*
— *n.* trip: *It's a two-hour commute to work.*
— **com·mu·ter** *n.*

Commy same as COMMIE.

com·pact (com·PACT) *adj.* **1** densely packed; solid: *a compact mass.* **2** condensed: *a compact style of writing.* **3** occupying a small space: *a compact volume.*
— *n.* (COM·pact) **1** a small car. **2** an agreement: *to make a trade compact with the U.S.; a compact between labour and management.* **3** a small case for face powder.
— *v.* (cum·PACT) pack tightly together.
— **com·pact·ly** *adv.*; **com·pact·ness** *n.*

compact disc (COM·pact·) *n.* a diskette containing music or data recorded in digital form and read by an optical laser.

com·pac·tor (cum·PAC·tur) *n.* a machine for compacting earth to a firm density or trash into small bundles.

com·pan·ion (cum·PAN·yun) *n.* one that accompanies another; close associate: *a boon, close, faithful, inseparable, life, travelling companion; hired as a companion for an elderly lady; A companion volume contains the index to the encyclopedia.*

com·pan·ion·a·ble (cum·PAN·yun·uh·bul) *adj.* easy to associate with; sociable: *a leader who has made politics and humanity companionable; a companionable smile.* — **com·pan·ion·a·bly** (-blee) *adv.*

com·pan·ion·ship (cum·PAN·yun·ship) *n.* association or fellowship: *She used to enjoy his companionship; They lived in close companionship for many years.*

com·pa·ny (CUM·puh·nee) *n.* **-nies 1** a group of people who work or play together, as a musical or theatrical troupe, the officers and men of a ship, or a military unit smaller than a battalion. **2** a business organization: *to establish, form a company; a finance, holding, insurance, investment, joint-stock, limited, shipping company; The company failed, went bankrupt; a* **company doctor** *(retained by a company to care for its employees).* **3** guest(s): *We're having company for supper.* **4** one's associates or companions: *"A man is known by the company he keeps"; mixed company (including men and women); present company (= those present); He had to* **part company** *with (= leave) them on Monday morning.* **5** companionship; fellowship: *the pleasure of your company at supper; He sought the company of the learned; They proved good company; He drinks only* **in company** *(= socially); He drinks* **in company with** *(= together with) friends.* — **keep company 1** associate: *a man and a woman keeping company; He is known to keep company with shady characters.* **2** accompany: *Keep her company.*

com·pa·ra·ble (COM·puh·ruh·bul) *adj.* able or worthy to be compared: *Apples and pears are not comparable in many respects; goods of comparable value.* — **com·pa·ra·bly** *adv.*

com·par·a·tive (cum·PAIR·uh·tiv) *adj.* **1** compared to something else; relative: *a comparative stranger.* **2** having to do with or using comparison: *comparative advertising, anatomy; a comparative adjective such as "more" and "greater" in "much-more-most" and "great-greater-greatest"; n.: "Better" is the comparative of "good."* — **com·par·a·tive·ly** *adv.*

com·pare (cum·PARE) *v.* **1** examine to note differences and similarities: *to compare apples and or with oranges; Compared to or with oranges, apples are generally sweeter; They compare (= may be compared) advantageously, favourably.* **2** liked to a person or thing: *Apples cannot be compared to oranges in all respects.* **3** be equally good when compared: *Fast food can't compare with home-cooked meals.*

com·par·i·son (cum·PAIR·uh·sun) *n.* a comparing: *to draw, make a comparison between two things; Some things are beyond comparison; the many points of comparison (= similarity) between the two.*

— **comparison with** when or if compared with: *One suffers by comparison with the other; One seems a bargain in comparison with the other.*

comparison-shop *v.* to shop for the best value by comparing prices and brands of competing items at various stores.

com·part·ment (cum·PART·munt) *n.* a division of a space, structure, etc.; separate room or area: *a first-class compartment; watertight compartment; the glove compartment of a car.*

com·pass (CUM·pus) *n.* **1** a device for indicating direction, esp. one with a magnetic needle that points north: *the 32 points (= directions) of the compass; a mariner's compass.* **2** usually **compasses** *pl.* a V-shaped device with two hinged legs for drawing circles, measuring distances, etc. **3** extent; boundary: *Some things are beyond the compass of our imagination.* — *v.* same as ENCOMPASS.

com·pas·sion (cum·PASH·un) *n.* sorrow or sympathy for another's sufferings, with desire to help: *to arouse, display, show, feel compassion for the poor; to act out of compassion; a deep, profound, strong sense of compassion.*

com·pas·sion·ate (cum·PASH·uh·nit) *adj.* having compassion: *a tender, compassionate heart.* — **com·pas·sion·ate·ly** *adv.*

com·pat·i·ble (cum·PAT·uh·bul) *adj.* able to live, function, or get along together: *a compatible companion, pair; One is compatible with the other.* — **com·pat·i·bil·i·ty** (-BIL·uh·tee) *n.*

com·pa·tri·ot (cum·PAY·tree·ut) *n.* **1** a fellow citizen. **2** a colleague.

com·peer (cum·PEER, COM·peer) *n.* a person of equal rank; peer; also, a comrade: *They were compeers at a military training camp.*

com·pel (cum·PEL) *v.* **-pels, -pelled, -pel·ling 1** force: *Famine compelled him to steal.* **2** get by force, pressure, etc.: *The troops compelled submission from the people.*

compelling (cum·PEL·ing) *adj.* causing respect, interest, belief, etc.; forceful: *a compelling line of argument; a compelling tale.*

com·pen·di·um (cum·PEN·dee·um) *n., pl.* **-di·a** (-dee·uh) or **-di·ums** a short but comprehensive summary.

com·pen·sate (COM·pun·sate) *v.* **-sates, -sat·ed, -sat·ing 1** pay someone to make up for something: *to* compensate a worker for injury suffered at work. **2** to make up for a defect or variation: *He drove faster to compensate for the time lost; His boldness only compensates for an inner timidity.*

com·pen·sa·tion (com·pun·SAY·shun) *n.* equivalent payment: *to make, offer, pay adequate, appropriate compensation; compensation for injury suffered.*

com·pen·sa·to·ry (cum·PEN·suh·tor·ee) *adv.* that compensates or makes up: *She was awarded compensatory damages of $6 000 for the damaged car; compensatory education for disadvantaged children.*

com·pete (cum·PEET) *v.* -petes, -pet·ed, -pet·ing **1** vie for or as if for a prize; strive: *to compete in sports; to compete with his rivals; They are competing for the gold medal.* **2** be as good as: *The corner store cannot compete with the supermarket.*

com·pe·tence (COM·puh·tunce) *n.* ability or fitness: *The court questioned the competence of the witness; his competence to give evidence; his competence in the language; to acquire, gain the necessary competence for a teaching position; It was beyond, not within the competence of the court to try the case.*

com·pe·tent (COM·puh·tunt) *adj.* sufficiently able, qualified, etc.: *a highly competent judge of character; a competent scholar; She is competent in her subject; competent as a classicist; competent to teach the subject; She could do a competent (=satisfactory) job.* — **com·pe·tent·ly** *adv.*

com·pe·ti·tion (com·puh·TISH·un) *n.* **1** opposition or rivalry: *He faces bitter, cutthroat, healthy, keen, stiff, strong competition; There's free competition among or between rivals; competition for control of the market; One is in competition with the others.* **2** a contest or match: *a literary, music, sports competition; an open competition for a prize.* **3** one's rivals: *Try to undercut or undersell the competition; The competition is hard to beat.*

com·pet·i·tive (cum·PET·uh·tiv) *adj.* liking or ready to compete: *a fiercely, keenly competitive spirit; competitive sports; We are competitive with (= as good as) our rivals.*

com·pet·i·tor (cum·PET·uh·tur) *n.* one who competes: *a formidable, strong, unscrupulous competitor.*

com·pile (cum·PILE) *v.* -piles, -piled, -pil·ing collect information from different sources and prepare a volume: *to compile a dictionary, encyclopedia, list, volume of ballads.* — **com·pil·er** *n.* — **com·pi·la·tion** (com·puh·LAY·shun) *n.*

com·pla·cen·cy (cum·PLAY·sun·see) *n.* the state of being complacent: *a smug complacency about the future.* Also **com·pla·cence** (-sunce).

com·pla·cent (cum·PLAY·sunt) *adj.* self-satisfied; unconcerned: *He's quite complacent about the future; an air of complacent superiority.* — **com·pla·cent·ly** *adv.*

com·plain (cum·PLAIN) *v.* express or describe one's dissatisfaction, discomfort, annoyance, etc.: *He complains of an aching back; complains about the neighbour's dog; complains to his wife; complains bitterly, constantly, loudly.*

com·plain·ant (cum·PLAIN·unt) *n.* [legal use] one who makes a complaint.

com·plaint (cum·PLAINT) *n.* **1** an act of complaining; also, an accusation or grievance: *He brought, filed, lodged, made, registered a complaint with the police against his neighbour; It was a bitter, legitimate, loud complaint; He had grounds or cause for complaint; They did not disregard, ignore, reject his complaint; They acted on, responded to his complaint.* **2** a cause for complaining, esp. an illness: *a stomach complaint.*

com·plai·sant (cum·PLAY·zunt, -sunt) *adj.* eager to please; obliging: *a complaisant attitude.* — **com·plai·sant·ly** *adv.* — **com·plai·sance** (-sunce) *n.*

com·pleat (cum·PLEET) *adj.* [old spelling of "complete"] proficient or expert: *"The Compleat Angler"; the compleat family man, politician, showman, swimmer.*

com·ple·ment (COM·pluh·munt) *n.* **1** something that completes: *Fine wine is a complement to good food.* **2** a word or words completing a predicate, as "fine" in "I feel fine." **3** a complete set or number: *a full complement of 32 teeth; a ship with its complement (= crew) of men.* — *v.* (cum·pluh·MENT) complete: *The couple complement each other; The hairdo complements her good looks.*

com·ple·men·ta·ry (com·pluh·MEN·tuh·ree) *adj.* that completes: ***Complementary colours,** as red and green, combine in light to form white; Green is complementary to red;* ***Complementary angles** add up to a right angle.*

com·plete (cum·PLEET) *adj.* **1** having all of its parts; entire: *a complete deck of cards; a dinner complete with cake and coffee.* **2** perfect; thorough: *complete happiness; a complete fool, stranger, waste.* **3** concluded; finished: *The job is complete.* — *v.* -pletes, -plet·ed, -plet·ing **1** make complete or entire: *to complete a circle, collection, set.* **2** finish doing: *to complete a contract, job, mission, task; the completed exercise, lesson.* — **com·plete·ly** *adv.;* **com·plete·ness** *n.* — **com·ple·tion** (-PLEE·shun) *n.:* *Our work is nearing completion; We get paid on completion of work.*

com·plex (cum·PLEX, COM·plex) *adj.* **1** composed of distinct but connected parts; not simple: *a complex sentence with main clause and subordinate clauses; complex fractions, numbers.* **2** complicated: *a problem too complex for a ten-year-old.* — *n.* (COM·plex) **1** a combination of related things, as buildings: *an apartment complex; an industrial complex; vitamin B complex.* **2** any obsessive fear, belief, etc.: *People suffer from complexes; the Electra, inferiority, Oedipus, superiority complex.* — **com·plex·i·ty** (cum·PLEX·uh·tee) *n.* **-ties.**

com·plex·ion (cum·PLEK·shun) *n.* **1** the natural colour and texture of the skin, esp. of the face: *a clear, dark, fair, pale, ruddy, sallow complexion.* **2** character or aspect: *Nuclear bombs have altered the complexion of modern warfare.* — **com·plex·ioned** (-shund) *combining form:* *dark-, fair-, light-complexioned.*

com·pli·ance (cum·PLY·unce) *n.* the act of complying or obeying: *a delivery made **in compliance with** a customer's wishes; compliance with rules and*

regulations.
— adj.: *a compliance department, officer.*

com·pli·ant (cum·PLY·unt) *adj.* tending to comply, give in, or yield; **com·pli·ant·ly** *adv.*

com·pli·cate (COM·pluh·cate) *v.* **-cates, -cat·ed, -cat·ing** make complex, involved, or difficult: *Why complicate matters? a* **complicated** (= hard to analyse, solve, or understand) *problem.*

com·pli·ca·tion (com·pluh·CAY·shun) *n.* a complicated condition: *to avoid complications; Complications may arise or set in during an illness.*

com·plic·i·ty (cum·PLIS·uh·tee) *n.* association in guilt: *He is suspected of complicity in the plot; complicity between law enforcement officials and drug pushers.*

com·pli·ment (COM·pluh·munt) *n.* **1** an expression of praise, admiration, or politeness: *She paid her secretary a compliment; a compliment on his good work; Children fish for compliments; He lavished or showered compliments on his wife; Please give or convey our sincere compliments to the chef; a back-handed compliment.* **2 compliments** *pl.* usually formal greetings: *a book presented with the author's compliments; We received it (with the) compliments of the author; The author conveys, presents, sends his compliments.*
— v. (-ment) pay a compliment to someone: *We complimented the cook on her fine cooking.*

com·pli·men·ta·ry (com·pluh·MEN·tuh·ree) *adj.* **1** expressing a compliment: *the complimentary close of a letter, as "Yours truly"; a complimentary remark.* **2** gratis or free: *Coffee is complimentary; a complimentary copy of our book.*

com·ply (cum·PLY) *v.* **-plies, -plied, -ply·ing** act in accordance with something: *They swore never to comply with terrorists' demands.*

com·po·nent (cum·POH·nunt) *n.* one of the parts of a complex object or group: *Copper and tin are the main components of bronze; Speakers are essential components of a stereo system.*
— adj. constituent: *a component element, part.*

com·port (cum·PORT) *v.* **1** behave: *He comported himself well, with dignity.* **2** be in agreement with or suitable to something: *Poor manners do not comport with high ideals.*
— n. (COM·port) a shallow stemmed serving dish.

com·pose (cum·POZE) *v.* **-pos·es, -posed, -pos·ing** **1** make up or constitute, as out of parts or elements: *Air is mainly composed of oxygen and nitrogen.* **2** create, esp. a work of music or literature: *to compose an ode, opera, poem, song, speech; He sings as well as composes* (= writes music). **3** set type, as a compositor. **4** settle: *Let's compose our differences.* **5** gain control of oneself: *to compose oneself, one's feelings, thoughts; She remained* **composed** (= in control of herself) *throughout the cross-examination.*
— com·pos·ed·ly (cum·POH·zid·lee) *adv.*

com·pos·er (cum·POH·zur) *n.* one who writes music or songs: *a popular composer; a major composer such as Mozart.*

com·pos·ite (COM·puh·zit, cum·POZ·it) *adj.* **1** made

up of distinct separate parts: *a composite photograph, portrait, print; a composite sketch of a suspect prepared by a police artist.* **2** belonging to a large family of plants having compound flower heads: *The daisy and the dandelion are composite flowers.*
— n. something that is composite: *His character was a composite of instinct and education.*

composite school (COM·puh·zit-) *n. Cdn.* a secondary school providing instruction in academic, commercial, and technical subjects.

com·po·si·tion (com·puh·ZISH·un) *n.* **1** the act, art, or result of composing: *to perform, play a (musical) composition; to write an English composition* (= essay); *All our composition* (= typesetting) *is done by computer.* **2** the arrangement of parts or elements: *a photographer with a good sense of composition; the ethnic composition* (= makeup) *of a population.*

com·pos·i·tor (cum·POZ·uh·tur) *n.* a typesetter.

com·post (COM·post, *rhyme:* most) *n.* a combination of decayed plant matter, garbage, and manure, used as a fertilizer; **adj.:** *a compost heap.*

com·po·sure (cum·POH·zhur) *n.* calmness: *She kept her composure in spite of provocations; to lose, regain, retain one's composure.*

com·pote (COM·pote) *n.* **1** fruit stewed or preserved in a syrup. **2** a shallow, stemmed dish for serving fruit, nuts, etc.

com·pound (COM·pownd) *n.* **1** the area enclosing a group of buildings, as of a factory, prison, or residences. **2** something made by the union of two or more parts or elements, as a word such as "spaceship" or a substance such as common salt (sodium and chlorine) or water (hydrogen and oxygen).
— adj. having many parts: *the compound eye of insects; a compound leaf, number, sentence.*
— v. (cum·POWND) **1** mix together or produce by combining: *A pharmacist sometimes compounds drugs as prescribed; Water is compounded of hydrogen and oxygen.* **2** calculate compound interest: *Interest on your savings is compounded quarterly.* **3** make greater: *to compound an error; The huge waves compounded the problem for the survivors in the lifeboat.*

compound fracture *n.* a broken bone causing an open wound in the skin.

compound interest *n.* interest charged on the principal of the debt and the accumulated interest.

com·pre·hend (com·pri·HEND) *v.* **1** grasp mentally; understand: *Do you comprehend the endlessness of time?* **2** include in its scope: *The humanities comprehend a whole range of subjects.*

com·pre·hen·si·ble (com·pri·HEN·suh·bul) *adj.* understandable: *The theory of relativity is not comprehensible to the lay person.*
— com·pre·hen·si·bly (-suh·blee) *adv.*
— com·pre·hen·si·bil·i·ty (-suh·BIL·uh·tee) *n.*

com·pre·hen·sion (com·pri·HEN·shun) *n.* understanding: *A theory that is beyond the lay person's comprehension; It defies, eludes comprehension.*

com·pre·hen·sive (com·pri·HEN·siv) *adj.* inclusive of everything: *a comprehensive examination, insurance* coverage.

comprehensive school *n. Cdn.* same as COMPOSITE SCHOOL.

com·press (cum·PRES) *v.* -press·es, -pressed, -press·ing pack or squeeze into a smaller space; condense: *We could compress this essay into a paragraph; Tires contain compressed air (under more than atmospheric pressure); a compressed style of writing; a compressed three-day work week.*
— *n.* (COM·press) a pad of gauze or cloth used to apply moisture, heat, cold, or pressure to the body, as to stop bleeding or relieve pain.
— **com·pres·sion** (cum·PRESH·un) *n.:* *the extreme compression of his style; the compression chamber of an auto engine.* — **com·pres·sor** *n.*

com·prise (cum·PRIZE) *v.* -pris·es, -prised, -pris·ing 1 be made up of; contain: *Our team comprises 18 players.* 2 *Informal.* make up; compose: *18 players comprise our team; Our team is comprised of 18 players.*

com·pro·mise (COM·pruh·mize) *n.* 1 the settlement of a difference or disagreement by concessions on both sides: *to work out an acceptable, fair, reasonable compromise with the opposite party; They agreed on, came to, reached a compromise after much negotiation; a compromise between labour and management; The domed stadium is a compromise between* (=a combination of) *a football field and a baseball park.* 2 a concession of something bad or wrong: *We can't agree to a compromise of principles.*
— *v.* -mis·es, -mised, -mis·ing 1 settle by or make a compromise: *Labour compromised with the management; They compromised on several key issues.* 2 to damage something: *We cannot compromise principles; Dick compromised his reputation by accepting a bribe; He has been in many* **compromising** *positions, situations.*

comp·trol·ler (cun·TROH·lur) *n.* same as CONTROLLER.

com·pul·sion (cum·PUL·shun) *n.* 1 an act of compelling or the state of being compelled: *He lied under compulsion; She felt a moral compulsion to tell the truth.* 2 an obsessive urge: *a neurotic compulsion; the truthful man who feels a compulsion to tell a lie.*
— **com·pul·sive** (-siv) *adj.: a compulsive liar, neurosis, smoker.*

com·pul·so·ry (cum·PUL·suh·ree) *adj.* required by law or regulation: *Primary school attendance is compulsory for children; compulsory arbitration, auto insurance, military service; the* **compulsory figures** *of skating and gymnastic competitions.*

com·punc·tion (cum·PUNK·shun) *n.* a feeling of guilt, regret, or remorse: *He cheats without the slightest compunction; He feels no compunction about cheating.*

com·pute (cum·PYOOT) *v.* -putes, -put·ed, -put·ing calculate mathematically or with a computer.
— **com·pu·ta·tion** (comp·yoo·TAY·shun) *n.*

com·put·er (cum·PEW·tur) *n.* an electronic machine that stores, manipulates, and analyses information, and performs mathematical calculations: *analogue, desktop, digital, general-purpose, home, mainframe, personal*

computers; *to program a computer; The bank's computer is often down* (= not functioning).
— **com·put·er·ist** *n.*

com·put·er·ize (cum·PEW·tuh·rize) *v.* -iz·es, -ized, -iz·ing prepare, make more efficient, or produce by means of a computer: *to computerize an accounting system, business; computerized bookkeeping, data, factories, jobs, typesetting, traffic signals.*
— **com·put·er·i·za·tion** (-ruh·ZAY·shun) *n.*

com·rade (COM·rad) *n.* 1 an associate or pal: *a comrade in arms* (= fellow fighter). 2 **Comrade** a member of a left-wing group, esp. a communist.
— **com·rade·ly** *adj.* — **com·rade·ship** *n.*

con *adv., prep. & n.* See PRO AND CON.
— *n. Slang.* a convict.
— *v.* cons, conned, con·ning 1 *Slang.* swindle; cheat: *She was conned into signing the contract; a scheme for conning people out of their savings;* **adj.:** *a con artist, game, man.* 2 [old use] study something carefully in order to learn it: *to con one's lessons.*

con·cave (con·CAVE) *adj.* curved inward like the inside surface of a ball. — **con·cav·i·ty** (-CAV·uh·tee) *n.* -ties.

con·ceal (cun·SEEL) *v.* keep secret or out of sight; hide: *The guerrilla leader always carried a concealed weapon.*
— **con·ceal·ment** *n.*

con·cede (cun·SEED) *v.* -cedes, -ced·ed, -ced·ing 1 admit as true or valid; acknowledge: *He conceded our point; conceded that he had lost the election.* 2 yield; give up: *They conceded the game after five innings; In the final stages of a vote count, the runner-up often concedes the election to the leading candidate.*

con·ceit (cun·SEET) *n.* a too high estimation of one's own worth: *a pompous chap, full of conceit.*
— **con·ceit·ed** *adj.*

con·ceive (cun·SEEV) *v.* -ceives, -ceived, -ceiv·ing 1 become pregnant with a child: *A woman conceives a child; Sterile women can't conceive.* 2 form an idea or notion; imagine: *the "average Canadian" as conceived by statisticians; Can you conceive of a unicorn in our zoo? They have conceived a great dislike for him.*
— **con·ceiv·a·ble** (-vuh·bul) *adj.*
— **con·ceiv·a·bly** (-vuh·blee) *adv.*

con·cen·trate (CON·sun·trate) *v.* -trates, -trat·ed, -trat·ing 1 focus or fix one's attentions, efforts, etc.: *to concentrate our energies on the task in hand.* 2 make a solution stronger: *frozen concentrated orange juice.*
— *n.* a concentrated food product: *Vitamin C concentrate; Dilute the concentrate to make soup.*

con·cen·tra·tion (con·sun·TRAY·shun) *n.* 1 the act or state of concentrating: *Noises tend to disturb our concentration; She is lost in deep concentration.* 2 something concentrated: *troop concentrations along the border; a concentration* (= broad study) *in physical sciences.* 3 strength: *the concentration of a solution.*

concentration camp *n.* a prison camp for prisoners of war, political prisoners, and other internees.

con·cen·tric (con·SEN·tric) *adj.* having a common centre or axis: *Tree trunks show concentric annual rings; the concentric circles of a target.*

con·cept (CON·sept) *n.* a usually general idea or notion of a class or thing: *The concept of tallness is formed from tall objects; to formulate, frame a concept; clear, vague, valid concepts; the old concept of the earth as being flat; the concept that the earth is round.*

con·cep·tion (cun·SEP·shun) *n.* **1** the act or process of conceiving: *the conception of a child in the womb; Does life begin at conception? the conception of new ideas in the mind.* **2** concept or idea: *He has no conception of what she's talking about; the popular conception of the sun as going around the earth.*

con·cep·tu·al·ize (cun·SEP·choo·uh·lize) *v.* **-liz·es, -lized, -liz·ing** form a concept of an object: *It's hard to conceptualize the infinity of space.*

con·cern (cun·SURN) *v.* **1** be the business of someone: *Does that concern you? a letter addressed "To Whom It May Concern"; a memo* **concerning** (= regarding) *absentees.* **2** interest or involve oneself: *Courts are concerned with justice; As far as I am concerned, all days are equally good; People should concern themselves with the running of their country; a* **concerned** *citizen.* **3** cause worry or anxiety to someone: *She has reason to be concerned when her child is late from school; She is concerned about* or *over* or *for her child's safety; concerned that her child may get lost; a* **concerned** *parent.*
— *n.* **1** something that involves or concerns someone: *This is no concern of mine.* **2** regard or anxiety: *a question that arouses, causes, gives us concern; We expressed, felt, showed, voiced our concern about* or *over the matter; our concern that she might die of the illness; We did it out of concern for her health; Crime is an object of considerable, grave, growing, particular, public, serious concern; Her illness is a cause of deep concern to us.* **3** a business: *a mining concern; a going* (= successful) *concern; a paying* (= profitable) *concern.*

con·cert (CON·surt) *n.* **1** a program of public musical entertainment: *A concert is cancelled, given, held, staged; people at a concert; a band concert; pop concert; rock concert.* **2** unity in action, opinion, etc.: *the concert of Europe against Napoleonic France.*
— in concert in harmony: *acting, working in concert with others; voices raised in concert against the new bill.*

con·cert·ed (cun·SUR·tid) *adj.* mutually planned or accomplished; combined: *The Opposition made concerted efforts to topple the Government.*

con·cer·ti·na (con·sur·TEE·nuh) *n.* a small, accordionlike musical instrument: *high prison fences topped with concertinas* (= coils) *of barbed wire.*

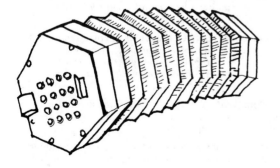

con·cer·to (cun·CHAIR·toh) *n.* **-tos** a piece of music for one or more solo instruments and orchestra: *to perform, play a concerto; a piano concerto; a violin concerto.*

con·ces·sion (cun·SESH·un) *n.* **1** the act of conceding or something conceded: *a concession to public demand.* **2** a piece of land or a privilege granted by a government or business, esp. to operate an industry or other business: *a mining concession; a parking concession; a food concession at a fair.* **3** *Cdn.* a subdivision in township surveys of Ontario and Quebec: *front concessions along the baseline; back concessions* (= rural regions); *a concession line* (= survey line).

concession road *n. Cdn.* esp. in Ontario, one of a series of roads running east and west between concessions, or subdivisions, and connected by side roads running north and south.

con·ci·erge (con·see·AIRZH) *n.* **1** the doorkeeper and usually custodian of a building, esp. an apartment building. **2** a hotel official who caters to the special needs of guests.

con·cil·i·ate (cun·SIL·ee·ate) *v.* **-ates, -at·ed, -at·ing** win the goodwill of someone; placate.

con·cil·i·a·tion (cun·SIL·ee·AY·shun) *n.* the act or state of conciliating, esp. the settlement of a dispute by compromise with the help of a third party.
— con·cil·i·a·tor (-ay·tur) *n.*
— con·cil·i·a·to·ry (-ee·uh·tor·ee) *adj.*

con·cise (cun·SICE) *adj.* brief but expressing much; terse: *a concise expression, report, style.*
— con·cise·ly *adv.*; **con·cise·ness** *n.*
— con·ci·sion (cuh·SIZH·un) *n.*: *the concision of her style.*

con·clave (CON·clave) *n.* a private or secret assembly, esp. of cardinals to elect a new pope: *a party conclave.*

con·clude (cun·CLOOD, long "OO") *v.* **-cludes, -clud·ed, -clud·ing** **1** end or finish: *The fair concluded on Friday; We concluded the meeting at 9 p.m.* **2** decide on the basis of evidence: *The court concluded that he was guilty.* **3** agree on or settle something: *to conclude a business deal with Japan.*

con·clu·sion (cun·CLOO·zhun) *n.* **1** end: *at the conclusion of the meeting;* **In conclusion** (= In ending), *I would like to thank everyone concerned.* **2** inference or judgment: *to arrive at, bring to, come to, draw, jump to a conclusion; an erroneous, inevitable, reasonable, valid conclusion; The jury reached the conclusion that the accused was guilty; It was not a foregone* (= predetermined) *conclusion.*

con·clu·sive (cun·CLOO·siv) *adj.* decisive or final for ending doubt: *conclusive evidence, proof.*
— con·clu·sive·ly *adv.*

con·coct (cun·COCT) *v.* **1** prepare (usually a food or drink) by mixing together. **2** invent: *a concocted excuse, plot, story.*
— con·coc·tion (cun·COC·shun) *n.*: *a new concoction whipped up for the occasion.*

con·com·i·tant (cun·COM·uh·tunt) *adj.* happening along with something else; accompanying: *circumstances concomitant with an event;* ***n.***: *Disease is a concomitant of poverty.*

con·cord (CON·cord) *n.* harmony or agreement, as in music, grammar (i.e. case, number, gender, or person), or between people: *an era of peace and concord between England and France; when France lived in concord with England.*

con·cor·dance (cun·COR·dunce) *n.* a listing of each word of a text in its context: *to compile a Shakespeare concordance.*

con·cor·dant (cun·COR·dunt) *adj.* agreeing; harmonious: *actions that are concordant with our principles; concordant musical notes.*

con·course (CON·corse) *n.* 1 a large space milling with people, as the main hall of a railway terminal or a broad thoroughfare: *the vast concourse of Union Station; the main concourse of an airport; an underground shopping concourse.* 2 a coming together; hence, a great crowd: *a concourse of circumstances, events, people.*

con·crete (CON·creet) *adj.* 1 existing in real experience of the senses, not abstract: *We need concrete evidence, examples, facts, figures, proof; a concrete noun such as "book," "flower," "girl"; A beautiful flower is beauty **in the concrete.*** 2 specific or definite, not vague or general: *We need concrete ideas, plans, proposals, terms; concrete thoughts that we can act upon.* 3 made of concrete: *concrete masonry; a concrete building block, mix, road surface, shelter, slab, walkway, wall; a concrete mixer (that mixes concrete); a **concrete jungle** full of skyscrapers.*
— *n.* a hard building material made of sand, small stones, and cement: *to pour concrete into forms for hardening; pre-stressed, ready-mix, reinforced concrete; precast concrete used for pipes, beams, and girders.*
— *v.* (con·CREET) -cretes, -cret·ed, -cret·ing pave or coat with concrete: *a concreted sidewalk.*

con·cu·bine (CONK·yuh·bine) *n.* a woman kept by a man as his mistress or secondary wife.

con·cur (cun·CUR) *v.* -curs, -curred, -cur·ring *Formal.* agree: *I concur fully, completely with you; I concur with your opinion; We concur that the building should be torn down; They concur in supporting abolition.*

con·cur·rence (cun·CUR·unce) *n.* agreement: *The Grits were in full concurrence with the Tories; The bill was passed with the concurrence of all parties.*

con·cur·rent (cun·CUR·unt) *adj.* 1 taking place at the same time: *two concurrent three-year sentences; a concurrent resolution (passed by both houses of a legislature).* 2 meeting or tending to meet at a point: *concurrent forces, lines.* — **con·cur·rent·ly** *adv.*

con·cus·sion (cun·CUSH·un, "USH" as in "rush") *n.* a severe shock or injury to the brain, as by a fall or blow on the head: *to receive, suffer a concussion; a severe, simple, slight concussion.*

con·demn (cun·DEM) *v.* 1 utter strong criticism of a person or thing: *atrocities condemned by humanity.* 2 declare guilty: *He was condemned as a traitor; condemned for selling secrets to the enemy.* 3 to sentence or doom: *A murderer is condemned to death; He was condemned to 10 years in jail; condemned to live the rest of his life in disgrace.* 4 declare unfit for use: *a condemned bridge, building.*
— **con·dem·na·tion** (con·dum·NAY·shun) *n.*

con·dense (cun·DENSE) *v.* -dens·es, -densed, -dens·ing 1 make or become more dense or concentrated: *Water vapour condenses as dew; to condense light rays with a lens;* **condensed** (= evaporated and sweetened) *milk.* 2 express in fewer words: *to condense an essay into a paragraph; to condense it to half its length; a story in condensed form; a condensed version of the novel.*
— **con·den·sa·tion** (con·den·SAY·shun) *n.*

con·de·scend (con·di·SEND) *v.* be gracious enough to do something that is beneath one's dignity: *He condescended to meet with the servants; His manner was somewhat **condescending** (= patronizing).*
— **con·de·scend·ing·ly** *adv.*
— **con·de·scen·sion** (-SEN·shun) *n.*

con·dign (cun·DINE) *adj.* deserved, though harsh: *condign punishment.*

con·di·ment (CON·duh·munt) *n.* a food seasoning, as relish, mustard, or spices.

con·di·tion (cun·DISH·un) *n.* 1 **conditions** *pl.* circumstances: *Under normal conditions it doesn't snow in July; weather conditions; unsanitary working conditions; abnormal, difficult, ideal, squalid conditions; economic conditions; market conditions.* 2 a state of being, fitness, or health, seen as changeable: *a motor in good running condition; in bad, excellent, operating, poor, terrible condition; a patient in critical, fair, good, satisfactory, serious, stable condition; He's either **in** or **out of condition** (= physically fit or unfit) for a marathon.* 3 what something depends on for its being or happening; requirement: *the terms and conditions of an offer; a condition of the offer; the essential conditions for survival; to fulfil, impose, meet, satisfy, set, stipulate a condition; a bail condition; He spoke **on condition that** he not be identified.* 4 a disease: *to have a heart condition; a skin condition such as acne.*
— *v.* 1 make conditional: *She led a life conditioned by her mother's whims.* 2 put into good condition: *Exercise conditions your body; an aerobic conditioning program.* 3 accustom or train: *Pavlov conditioned dogs to expect food every time a bell rang; a conditioned reflex, response.* — **con·di·tion·al** *adj.*

con·di·tion·er (cun·DISH·nur) *n.* a cosmetic or other substance added to something to improve its quality: *a hair, skin, water conditioner.*

con·do (CON·doh) *n.* -dos *Informal.* a condominium building.

con·dole (cun·DOLE) *v.* -doles, -doled, -dol·ing feel or express sympathy: *They condoled with her on her husband's death.*

con·do·lence (cun·DOH·lunce) *n.* (expression of) sympathy: *We conveyed, expressed, offered our heartfelt, sincere condolences to the widow; a letter of condolence; Our condolences on the death of your husband.*

con·dom (CON·dum) *n.* a thin rubber sheath for the penis, for use in sexual intercourse to prevent infection and as a contraceptive.

con·do·min·i·um (con·duh·MIN·ee·um) *n.* a residential building or complex in which single units are owned individually and the common property is owned and maintained jointly; also, a unit in this.

con·done (cun·DOHN) *v.* **-dones, -doned, -don·ing** overlook or implicitly forgive (misbehaviour): *She would condone sloppiness, but not skipping school.*

con·dor (CON·dur) *n.* a large vulture.

con·duce (cun·DUCE, *rhyme:* produce) *v.* **-duc·es, -duced, -duc·ing** tend to lead: *an atmosphere that conduces to study.*
— **con·du·cive** (-DEW·siv) *adj.:* *an atmosphere that is conducive to study.*

con·duct (CON·duct) *n.* **1** behaviour: *He was charged with disorderly conduct; conduct unbecoming an officer; early parole for good conduct.* **2** management: *the conduct of foreign affairs.*
— *v.* (cun·DUCT) **1** lead or guide: *A guide conducts a tour; She conducts tourists through the museum; He conducts them into and out of the building.* **2** manage: *the officer conducting the company's financial affairs.* **3** behave: *She conducts herself like a professional; He conducts himself with dignity.* **4** transmit: *The ability to conduct heat or electricity is one of the physical properties of matter.*

con·duc·tion (cun·DUC·shun) *n.* transmission of heat or electricity by contact.

con·duc·tor (cun·DUC·tur) *n.* **1** the leader or director of an orchestra or choir. **2** the person in charge of a bus, passenger train, etc. **3** something that enables heat, electricity, or sound to pass through: *a lightning conductor.*

con·duit (CON·dit, -doo·it) *n.* a pipe, channel, or tubing for carrying liquids, enclosing electric wires, etc.: *The secretary acted as a conduit (of information) to the minister.*

cone *n.* **1** a three-dimensional surface or solid with a usually circular base, tapering to a point. **2** anything in this shape: *an ice-cream cone; the cone of a volcano; a pine cone* (= the dry, scaly fruit of a pine).

con·es·to·ga (con·is·TOH·guh) *n.* a sturdy covered wagon used esp. by prairie pioneers. Also **Conestoga wagon.**

con·fec·tion (cun·FEC·shun) *n.* a sweet treat, as candy, pastry, or ice cream; delicacy. — **con·fec·tion·er** *n.*

con·fec·tion·er·y (cun·FEC·shuh·nair·ee) *n.* **-er·ies 1** confections collectively. **2** a confectioner's shop.

con·fed·er·a·cy (cun·FED·uh·ruh·see) *n.* **-cies** an alliance of countries or states: *They formed a confederacy among the states; A Confederacy of 11 southern U.S. states broke away from the Union in 1860 – 61.*

con·fed·er·ate (cun·FED·uh·rate) *v.* **-ates, -at·ed, -at·ing** join or form into an alliance of people, organizations, states, etc.
— *n.* (-uh·rit) **1** an ally or accomplice. **2** a supporter of the Confederacy; *adj.: a confederate army, dollar, government; the 11 Confederate States of America.*

con·fed·er·a·tion (cun·FED·uh·RAY·shun) *n.* **1** the act of confederating. **2** an alliance or union, esp. of states or countries: *The 13 colonies called their confederation the United States of America; the Articles of Confederation; the Confederation of National Trade Unions.* **3 Confederation** *Cdn.* the federal union of the Canadian provinces, starting with Ontario, Quebec, New Brunswick, and Nova Scotia in 1867: *Newfoundland joined Confederation in 1949, as the tenth province.*

con·fer (cun·FUR) *v.* **-fers, -ferred, -fer·ring 1** consult; exchange views: *Let's confer with the president on* or *about the new budget.* **2** grant or bestow: *to confer an honorary degree on the ambassador.* — **con·fer·ment** *n.*

con·fer·ee (con·fuh·REE) *n.* **1** one on whom something is conferred. **2** one taking part in a conference.

con·fer·ence (CON·fuh·runce) *n.* **1** a conferring or consulting: *I had a conference with my son's teacher; a news, press, staff conference; a conference between the two parties; a conference of teachers; a conference on teaching methods; The boss is in conference.* **2** a league of sports teams, schools, etc.
— *v.* confer: *Teachers conference with parents.*

conference call *n.* a telephone call for talking with different people in different places at the same time.

con·fess (cun·FES) *v.* **1** acknowledge or admit, usually a crime or fault: *I confess that I was mistaken; I confess my mistake; I confess to being mistaken; He confessed to everything he was charged with; He confessed to the police.* **2** tell one's sins to a priest to seek God's forgiveness: *I confess my sins; I confess to having sinned.* **3** of a priest, absolve someone from sins.
— **con·fes·sed·ly** (cun·FES·id·lee) *adv.*

con·fes·sion (cun·FESH·un) *n.* **1** the act or result of confessing, esp. a written statement or the telling of one's sins: *I have a confession to make; The "people's court" forced him to sign a confession; The confession was extorted from him; a forced, full, public confession; The accused repudiated, took back, withdrew her confession when she was set free; He made a voluntary deathbed confession that he was the real murderer; Priests hear confessions and forgive sins; to go to confession during Lent.* **2** a declaration of religious beliefs: *a confession of faith.* **3** a Christian denomination; communion: *the various confessions within Christianity.*

con·fes·sion·al (cun·FESH·uh·nul) *n.* an enclosure for private confession.

con·fes·sor (cun·FES·ur) *n.* **1** one who confesses. **2** a priest who hears confessions.

con·fet·ti (cun·FET·ee) *n. pl.* [takes sing. v.] little pieces of coloured paper for throwing about in celebrations, esp. at weddings.

con·fi·dant (CON·fuh·dant) *n.* a person trusted with personal secrets; *fem.* **con·fi·dante** (con·fuh·DANT, CON·fuh·dant).

con·fide (cun·FIDE) *v.* -fides, -fid·ed, -fid·ing **1** tell or give to another in secrecy or trust; entrust: *the folly of confiding secrets to strangers; The child was confided to a neighbour's care.* **2** trust: *She confides in her parents.*

con·fi·dence (CON·fuh·dunce) *n.* **1** trust; reliance: *I place* or *put no confidence in his promises; He enjoyed, gained, had, won our confidence; She inspires, instills confidence in her followers; I have absolute, every, perfect confidence in your ability; Our confidence was shaken by his behaviour.* **2** a feeling of assurance in oneself: *to face the future with confidence; He lacked the confidence to invest in the project.* **3** a trusting secrecy: *The news was told in strictest confidence; She took her brother into her confidence.* **4** a secret: *They used to exchange confidences; would never betray a confidence; He was accused of violating a confidence.* — *adj.* swindling; con: *a confidence game, man, trick.*

con·fi·dent (CON·fuh·dunt) *adj.* sure of oneself; certain: *a confident and aggressive sales rep; She is confident of the outcome of the trial; confident that she will win.* — **con·fi·dent·ly** *adv.*

con·fi·den·tial (con·fuh·DEN·shul) *adj.* **1** secret: *a strictly personal and confidential letter; confidential information, papers.* **2** trusted with private affairs: *a confidential assistant, secretary, servant.* — **con·fi·den·tial·ly** *adv.* — **con·fi·den·ti·al·i·ty** (CON·fuh·den·shee·AL·uh·tee) *n.*

con·fig·u·ra·tion (cun·FIG·yuh·RAY·shun) *n.* a particular arrangement of parts or components; outline or shape: *the configuration of atoms in a molecule; a planetary configuration; the configuration of the ocean floor.*

con·fine (cun·FINE) *v.* -fines, -fined, -fin·ing keep within limits or barriers; restrict: *His social life was confined to weekends; a soldier confined to quarters; Avoid arguments and confine yourself to the facts.*

con·fine·ment (cun·FINE·munt) *n.* a being confined: *He was put in solitary confinement; It happened during her confinement in hospital.*

con·fines (CON·fines) *n. pl.* limits: *Stay within the confines of your home.*

con·firm (cun·FURM) *v.* **1** strengthen: *Adversity only confirmed him in his resolve.* **2** verify: *The rumour was confirmed by later developments.* **3** make firm or definite: *to confirm an airline reservation; The decision has to be confirmed by the president; The children were confirmed (as members by a religious rite) at 13.* — **con·fir·ma·tion** (con·fur·MAY·shun) *n.*

con·firmed (cun·FURMD) *adj.* settled or unchanging: *a confirmed alcoholic, bachelor, invalid.*

con·fis·cate (CON·fis·cate) *v.* -cates, -cat·ed, -cat·ing seize property by public authority: *The heroin was confiscated by the police.* — **con·fis·ca·tor** *n.* — **con·fis·ca·tion** (con·fis·CAY·shun) *n.*

con·fla·gra·tion (con·fluh·GRAY·shun) *n.* a big fire, esp. one that is very destructive.

con·flict (CON·flict) *n.* **1** a fight; struggle: *an armed, direct conflict between two nations; a conflict about* or *over territorial rights; a conflict among the neighbours; Neighbours come into conflict with each other; to provoke, resolve a conflict.* **2** a clash of opposing interests or viewpoints: *the unending conflict between religion and politics; a conflict of interest (between an official's public duty and private interest); His version of the accident is in conflict* (= disagreement) *with yours.* — *v.* (cun·FLICT) be in opposition; clash: *My interests conflict with yours; People are torn by* **conflicting** *desires.*

con·form (cun·FORM) *v.* **1** correspond to or be like a pattern: *a building that conforms to specifications.* **2** comply with a law, rules, or customs: *In many schools, students have to conform to a dress code.*

con·for·ma·tion (con·fur·MAY·shun) *n.* **1** a formation or structure. **2** the build of a racehorse.

con·form·i·ty (cun·FOR·muh·tee) *n.* **1** agreement: *His actions were in conformity with his beliefs; We acted in conformity with his wishes; conformity with the law.* **2** obedience: *in conformity to the rules, to local customs.*

con·found (cun·FOUND) *v.* **1** confuse by surprising: *The weather confounded the forecasters; to confound one's critics, foes, opponents.* **2** mix up: *They had confounded fact with fancy.*

con·found·ed *adj.* [euphemism] damned: *You confounded idiot!*

con·frere (CON·frair) *n.* **1** a fellow member of a religious community. **2** *Informal.* colleague.

con·front (cun·FRUNT) *v.* come or bring face to face with; meet and challenge: *The two armies confronted each other along the border; He had nothing to say when confronted with the facts.*

con·fron·ta·tion (con·frun·TAY·shun) *n.* active face-to-face opposition: *an atmosphere of confrontation; Question period in the House of Commons is a time of confrontation between Government and Opposition; It provoked a direct confrontation with the police; the civil rights confrontations of the 1960s.*

con·fuse (cun·FUZE) *v.* -fus·es, -fused, -fus·ing **1** bewilder or perplex: *I'm quite confused by the conflicting versions of the incident; I find it quite* **confusing.** **2** fail to distinguish: *Let's not confuse the issues; People always confuse Tim and* or *with his twin brother.* — **con·fus·ed·ly** *adv.;* **con·fus·ing·ly** *adv.*

con·fu·sion (cun·FEW·zhun) *n.* **1** a mixing up: *the confusion of tongues at the Tower of Babel; It caused, created, was a scene of utter confusion; Complete confusion reigned.* **2** disorder: *Arrangements were thrown into confusion by a last-minute change of plans.*

con·geal (cun·JEEL) *v.* thicken or solidify, as by freezing; coagulate or clot: *congealed blood.* — **con·geal·ment** *n.* — **con·ge·la·tion** (con·juh·LAY·shun) *n.*

con·gen·ial (cun·JEEN·yul) *adj.* **1** of similar tastes and character: *congenial companions.* **2** agreeable or

pleasing: *work that is congenial to his temperament; a congenial atmosphere, climate, weather.*
— con·gen·ial·ly *adv.*
— con·ge·ni·al·i·ty (-nee·AL·uh·tee) *n.*

con·gen·i·tal (cun·JEN·uh·tul) *adj.* **1** present from birth: *a congenital abnormality, defect; congenital blindness, brain damage, heart disease; He has a congenital aversion to math.* **2** born: *a congenital latecomer, shoplifter; her congenital altruism.*
— con·gen·i·tal·ly *adv.*

con·gest·ed (cun·JES·tid) *adj.* too full or clogged: *downtown streets congested with traffic; a congested airport, area, schedule, slum; congested lungs* (= clogged by blood).
— con·ges·tion (-chun) *n.: to relieve traffic congestion during the rush hour; nasal congestion; congestion of the lungs.*

con·glom·er·ate (cun·GLOM·uh·rit) *n.* **1** a composite mixture: *Toronto is a conglomerate of world cultures.* **2** a corporation with widely diversified enterprises and interests.

con·grat·u·late (cun·GRACH·uh·late) *v.* -lates, -lat·ed, -lat·ing express pleasure at another's success or good luck: *a message congratulating her on her graduation.*
— con·grat·u·la·tion (-LAY·shun) *n.: We extend, offer our deep, hearty, sincere, warmest congratulations on or upon your graduation.*
— con·grat·u·la·to·ry (-luh·tor·ee) *adj.: a congratulatory message.*

con·gre·gate (CONG·gruh·gate) *v.* -gates, -gat·ed, -gat·ing gather together.

con·gre·ga·tion (cong·gruh·GAY·shun) *n.* **1** a gathering. **2** people attending a place of worship, esp. those present at a service. — con·gre·ga·tion·al *adj.*

con·gress (CONG·grus) *n.* **1** a meeting or convention: *to convene, hold a congress; a party congress.* **2** a national legislature: *the U.S. Congress.*

con·gress·man (CONG·grus·mun) *n.* -men a member of the U.S. House of Representatives.
— con·gress·wom·an *n.* -wom·en.

con·gru·ous (CONG·groo·us) *adj.* in agreement or harmony; congruent: *actions that are not congruous with stated principles.* — con·gru·ous·ly *adv.*

con·ic (CON·ic) or con·i·cal (CON·uh·cul) *adj.* shaped like or pertaining to a cone: *a conical cap; The parabola and ellipse are conic sections; a conic or conical projection* (= map with radiating meridians and concentric parallels).

con·i·fer (CON·uh·fur) *n.* a cone-bearing, usually evergreen tree or bush, as pine, spruce, and fir.
— co·nif·er·ous (coh·NIF·uh·rus) *adj.: coniferous forests, trees.*

con·jec·ture (cun·JEK·chur) *v.* -tures, -tured, -tur·ing to guess because of insufficient evidence: *We can only conjecture that no lives have been lost in the accident; a conjectured estimate, figure.*
— *n.* a report based on mere conjecture.
— con·jec·tur·al (cun·JEK·chuh·rul) *adj.*

con·ju·gal (CON·juh·gul) *adj.* having to do with marriage: *the conjugal bliss of a couple; a spouse's conjugal rights.* — con·ju·gal·ly *adv.*

con·ju·gate (CON·juh·gate) *v.* -gates, -gat·ed, -gat·ing give the inflected forms of a verb.
— con·ju·ga·tion (con·juh·GAY·shun) *n.: "Take-took-taken" is a strong conjugation; "Call," "move," and "add" belong to weak conjugations using "-ed" for the past tense and past participle.* — con·ju·ga·tion·al *adj.*

con·junc·tion (cun·JUNK·shun) *n.* **1** union or alignment: *The storm was caused by a rare conjunction of the Earth, Sun, and Moon; a note to be read in conjunction with the report.* **2** a connecting word: *"But," "and," "or," etc. are conjunctions used to link words, phrases, and clauses.*

con·junc·ture (cun·JUNK·chur) *n.* a combination of circumstances, esp. a critical situation.

con·jure *v.* -jures, -jured, -jur·ing **1** (cun·JOOR) *Formal.* appeal to, esp. by an oath: *I conjure you by all that's holy to hear my plea.* **2** (CUN·jur, CON·jur) summon spirits, the devil, etc. by a spell or magic; also, produce by magic: *Magicians conjure rabbits out of their hats.*
— **a name to conjure with** a person or thing that is very important.
— **conjure up** call or bring to mind: *The music conjured up visions of the Orient.*
— con·jur·er or con·jur·or (CUN·jur·ur, CON-) *n.*

conk *v. Informal.* hit over the head.
— **conk out** *Informal.* **1** stop functioning suddenly: *Our motor conked out.* **2** collapse with fatigue; lose consciousness: *Father just conked out after a hard day.* **3** *Slang.* die: *Quit smoking before you conk out.*

con·nect (cuh·NECT) *v.* **1** link, join, or be joined: *My telephone line is connected to the rest of the system; The operator can connect me with anyone who has a telephone; Our telephone was connected up only yesterday; I am connected to my in-laws by marriage; I have been connected with them since my marriage; closely, intimately, loosely connected; We catch a connecting flight out of Montreal; I didn't connect you* (= link you mentally) *with the person who called yesterday.* **2** in sports, hit, shoot, throw, etc. successfully: *connected for a line drive.*
— con·nect·ed·ly *adv.*
— con·nect·er or con·nec·tor *n.*

con·nec·tion (cuh·NEC·shun) *n.* **1** a link or linkage: *There must be a loose connection in the wiring somewhere; Please speak up, we seem to have a bad connection; to establish a connection between smoking and cancer; to break or sever our connection with that party; a close, intimate connection; a tenuous connection; a company with many foreign, international connections* (= ties); *an executive with many business, professional, and social connections* (= acquaintances); *to make a connection; I missed my connection* (= connecting flight) *in Montreal; the French Connection (Slang for drug dealer).* **2** an influential person: *He got the job through connections on his wife's side.*
— **in connection with** in relation to: *They mentioned his previous job in connection with the present one.*
— **in this** or **that** or **what connection** in relation to this or that or what: *In what connection did he mention my name?*

conning tower *n.* the observation tower on top of a submarine.

con·nip·tion (cuh·NIP·shun) *n. Informal.* a fit of violent rage, alarm, excitement, etc.: *Grandma will have a conniption* or *conniptions if she finds out.* Also **conniption fit.**

con·nive (cuh·NIVE) *v.* **con·nives, con·nived, con·niv·ing 1** intentionally ignore wrongdoing: *Some officials connived at the use of drugs by athletes.* **2** secretly cooperate or conspire to do something wrong or unlawful: *He is known to be conniving with underworld figures to traffic in heroin.*

con·nois·seur (con·uh·SUR) *n.* an expert in an area of artistic taste: *a connoisseur of art, furniture, wines.*

con·no·ta·tion (con·uh·TAY·shun) *n.* what a word means besides its strict or denotative meaning: *the unpleasant connotations of "capitalist."*
— **con·no·ta·tive** (CON·uh·tay·tiv) *adj.*

con·note (cuh·NOTE) *v.* **con·notes, con·not·ed, con·not·ing** of words, convey as a meaning secondary to the strict meaning or denotation: *"Foreign" may connote hostility, but "imported" connotes distinctiveness.*

con·quer (CONK·ur) *v.* gain mastery of a person or thing: *to conquer a country, one's fears, bad habits; to conquer a people (by defeating them); a member of a conquered race; to conquer a mountain (by climbing it).*
— **con·quer·or** *n.*

con·quest (CONG·kwest) *n.* the act of conquering or something conquered: *the Norman Conquest (of England); Alexander consolidated his conquests as he extended them eastward; the conquest of Mt. Everest; a final conquest; world conquests; Don Juan made the conquest of his lady's heart; Mexico was a Spanish conquest (= conquered territory).*

con·quis·ta·dor (con·QUIS·tuh·dor, cong·KEE·stuh·dor) *n.* **-dors** a 16th-century Spanish conqueror in Central or South America.

con·san·guin·i·ty (con·sang·GWIN·uh·tee) *n.* relationship by blood: *Marriage is prohibited within certain degrees of consanguinity.*

con·science (CON·shunce) *n.* the awareness of right and wrong that prompts one to do good and avoid evil: *a cold-blooded murderer whose conscience never bothers him; He stole something and had it on his conscience all week; He had a guilty conscience; He had to return it to its owner in all conscience (= in truth or fairness); returned it as a matter of conscience; He could say with a clear conscience that he hadn't stolen anything; She appealed to their conscience to release the innocent prisoner; a prisoner of conscience (in jail because of political or religious beliefs); conscience money (paid to ease one's conscience).*

con·sci·en·tious (con·shee·EN·shus) *adj.* **1** ruled by or according to one's moral convictions: *A conscientious objector refuses to go to war.* **2** scrupulous and painstaking: *She's very conscientious about her duties.*
— **con·sci·en·tious·ly** *adv.*

con·scious (CON·shus) *adj.* **1** aware of or alert to: *He is fully conscious of the risks involved; quite conscious that there are risks involved.* **2** awake or mentally active: *The patient became conscious and started moving.* **3** aware of oneself, one's thoughts, and one's actions: *Breathing is not a conscious activity; a conscious artist, choice; He made a conscious (= deliberate) effort to improve.*
— **con·scious·ly** *adv.*

con·scious·ness (CON·shus·nis) *n.* **1** the state of being conscious: *He was struck on the head and lost consciousness; It was hours before he recovered or regained consciousness.* **2** awareness: *He tried to raise the consciousness of the community to the danger of an epidemic; class, political, social consciousness.*

con·script (cun·SCRIPT) *v.* to compel by law into military service: *Canadians were conscripted into the army in 1917.*
— *n.* (CON·script) one conscripted or drafted; draftee.
— **con·scrip·tion** (con·SCRIP·shun) *n.*

con·se·crate (CON·suh·crate) *v.* **-crates, -crat·ed, -crat·ing** make sacred or set aside as sacred, hallowed, or for religious use: *Bread and wine are consecrated during Mass; She consecrated (= dedicated) her life to painting.*
— **con·se·cra·tion** (con·suh·CRAY·shun) *n.: the consecration of a new chapel.*

con·sec·u·tive (con·SEK·yuh·tiv) *adj.* following one after the other; successive: *He missed three consecutive days of school.* — **con·sec·u·tive·ly** *adv.*

con·sen·sus (cun·SEN·sus) *n.* general agreement: *They could not reach a consensus on capital punishment or its abolition; There was a consensus that a vote on the question be postponed; consensus politics (based on agreement).*

con·sent (cun·SENT) *v.* give approval; agree: *He consented to be operated on; consented to the operation; He did it as a consenting adult.*
— *n.* agreement: *He gave, refused, withheld his consent; a plan adopted by common consent; general, mutual, parental, tacit consent; A patient's informed consent is required for an operation.*

con·se·quence (CON·suh·quence) *n.* **1** a result or effect: *We have to take the consequences of our actions; far-reaching, grave, inevitable, unforeseen consequences; Her hard work was recognized and in consequence she was promoted.* **2** importance: *a matter of little or no consequence; a woman of some consequence in our society.*

con·se·quent (CON·suh·quent) *adj.* following logically or resulting as a consequence: *a major fire with a consequent loss of lives; The position was declared vacant consequent on or upon his resignation.*
— **con·se·quent·ly** *adv.*

con·se·quen·tial (con·suh·QUEN·shul) *adj.* **1** following as a result: *consequential damages.* **2** of importance: *consequential changes in taxation; a consequential appointment, decision.* **3** self-important: *His consequential manner doesn't impress anyone.*

con·ser·va·tion (con·sur·VAY·shun) *n.* the preservation or careful and controlled use, esp. of natural resources: *energy, forest, fuel, soil, water, wildlife conservation;* *adj.: a conservation officer; a conservation road (giving access to a conservation area).* — **con·ser·va·tion·ist** *n.*

con·ser·va·tism (cun·SUR·vuh·tiz·um) *n.* a tendency to keep things as they are and resist social or political change.

con·ser·va·tive (cun·SUR·vuh·tiv) *adj.* 1 conforming to moderate or traditional tastes, views, etc.: *He wears conservative clothes; a conservative* (= rather low) *estimate; a conservative* (= solid or safe) *investment portfolio.* 2 given to conservatism: *conservative politics, politicians; a conservative government.*
— *n.* 1 a conservative person: *a dyed-in-the-wool conservative; a political conservative; a small "c" conservative.* 2 **Conservative** a member or supporter of a conservative party such as the Progressive-Conservative Party of Canada; Tory. — **con·ser·va·tive·ly** *adv.*

con·ser·va·to·ry (cun·SUR·vuh·tor·ee) *n.* -ries 1 a school of music, drama, etc. 2 a glass-covered building or room for growing plants and flowers.

con·serve (cun·SURV) *v.* -serves, -served, -serv·ing 1 keep in unchanged condition for later use, esp. from waste or destruction: *to conserve one's energy, resources.* 2 preserve fruit by stewing with sugar.
— *n.* (*also* CON·surv): *a strawberry conserve.*

con·serv·er (cun·SUR·vur) *n.* one that conserves: *Our survival depends on changing from a consumer society to a **conserver society.***

con·sid·er (cun·SID·ur) *v.* think about with a purpose: *They considered her application; took time to consider; They considered it carefully, favourably; considered* (= believed or judged) *her qualified, intelligent, a genius; They had considered him (to be) not promotable; They considered her (as a candidate) for his job; considered her as his replacement; He considered* (= contemplated) *resigning, his alternatives, where to go; They said he had done a good job, **all things considered*** (= everything being taken into account); *He had done a good job, **considering;** an especially good job **considering*** (= taking into account) *his inexperience, considering that he was inexperienced; That was their **considered*** (= studied) *opinion.*

con·sid·er·a·ble (cun·SID·uh·ruh·bul) *adj.* important enough to be considered; great or large: *a person of considerable influence; a considerable amount, sum, weight; a man of considerable means* (= wealthy man); *She went to considerable trouble to help us.*
— **con·sid·er·a·bly** *adv.*

con·sid·er·ate (cun·SID·uh·rit) *adj.* thoughtful of others: *a polite, considerate young man.*

con·sid·er·a·tion (cun·SID·uh·RAY·shun) *n.* 1 careful thought: *His considerations on mortality give one food for thought; But have some consideration for her feelings; The award was made in consideration of her services to the community; The application is submitted for your consideration; We will take everything into consideration; Nothing will be left out of consideration; It is under consideration; They voted after lengthy consideration; On careful consideration, we have decided to reject it; On no consideration* (= in no case) *can we make an exception to the rules.* 2 something to consider: *Location is an important consideration in buying a house; an overriding consideration; Money is of no consideration* (= importance) *when we are looking for*

the best; *He sold everything for $1 plus other considerations* (= benefits); *He will assign you a better seat, for a consideration* (= payment).

con·sign (cun·SIGN) *v.* 1 give over: *an orphan consigned to the state's custody; to consign papers to the fire.* 2 send goods, esp. to an agent for sale.
— **con·sign·or** or **con·sign·er** *n.*

con·sign·ment (cun·SIGN·munt) *n.* a shipment of goods to a dealer: *It was shipped **on consignment*** (= to be paid for if and when sold).

con·sist (cun·SIST) *v.* 1 be made up or composed: *The team consists of six players.* 2 have as basis: *Loyalty consists in devotion to a person or cause.*

con·sis·ten·cy (cun·SIS·tun·see) *n.* -cies 1 degree of thickness or solidity of a thick liquid: *soil of gummy consistency; the consistency of molasses, syrup.* 2 conformity to previous actions, principles, etc.

con·sis·tent (cun·SIS·tunt) *adj.* conforming, not contradictory: *He followed a consistent policy throughout his career; a report that is not consistent with the facts; He has been a consistent* (= regular) *loser.*
— **con·sis·tent·ly** *adv.*

con·so·la·tion (con·suh·LAY·shun) *n.* comfort in sorrow or disappointment: *Her children were a consolation to the widow in her sorrow; They afforded consolation; Friends offered consolation; She received many letters of consolation; It was a consolation to know or consolation knowing that the children were safe; a consolation that no one else was hurt; a $100 000 grand prize and a $2 000 **consolation prize.***

con·sole (CON·sole) *n.* 1 a cabinet for a TV, radio, etc. that sits on the floor. 2 that part of an organ having the stops, keys, pedals, etc.; also, an electrical control panel, as of a washing machine or stove: *A computer operator sits at a console* (= desklike control unit).
— *v.* (cun·SOLE) -soles, -soled, -sol·ing lessen the unhappiness of someone; comfort: *to console a widower on his wife's death; They consoled themselves with thoughts of a better future.*

con·sol·i·date (cun·SOL·uh·date) *v.* -dates, -dat·ed, -dat·ing 1 form or combine into one mass or organization: *a consolidated* (= central) *school in a rural area; a consolidated* (= unified) *school district.* 2 make secure or firm; strengthen: *to consolidate the company's position; Studying for an exam consolidates what you have learned.* — **con·sol·i·da·tion** (-DAY·shun) *n.*

con·som·mé (CON·suh·may, con·suh·MAY) *n.* a clear soup made from meat or vegetables.

con·so·nant (CON·suh·nunt) *adj.* in harmony or agreement: *a statement not consonant with his previous policies.*
— *n.* a sound or letter other than the vowels "a," "e," "i," "o," and "u."

con·sort (CON·sort) *n.* a ruling monarch's spouse: *Prince Philip is the Queen's consort; the queen consort* (= king's wife).
— *v.* (cun·SORT) 1 associate: *He consorts with drug pushers.* 2 agree: *Their actions do not consort with their principles.*

con·sor·ti·um (cun·SOR·shee·um, -SOR·tee·um) *n.*, *pl.* -ti·a (-shee·uh) a combination of banks, large companies, etc. for a large-scale investment or other activity: *an oil-pipeline consortium; The Canadian Consortium for Computing in the Humanities.*

con·spec·tus (cun·SPEC·tus) *n.* an overall view; a summary of something under consideration.

con·spic·u·ous (cun·SPIC·yoo·us) *adj.* noticeable; remarkable: *He has been conspicuous for his charitable works; The president was* **conspicuous by her absence** *(because she should have been present); the* **conspicuous consumption** *of luxuries by the newly rich.*
— **con·spic·u·ous·ly** *adv.*

con·spir·a·cy (cun·SPEER·ruh·see) *n.* -cies a secret planning, esp. by a group to act jointly to do something wrong; also, the plan or plot: *The Riel Rebellion began as a conspiracy; a criminal conspiracy to commit arson, murder; a conspiracy with the army to take over a government; to crush, foil a conspiracy; to hatch, organize a conspiracy against the leadership; a conspiracy of silence by witnesses unwilling to testify.*
— **con·spir·a·tor** (-tur) *n.*
— **con·spir·a·tor·i·al** (-TOR·ee·ul) *adj.*

con·spire (cun·SPIRE) *v.* -spires, -spired, -spir·ing 1 plot together secretly: *They were accused of conspiring to overthrow the government.* 2 work together: *Many events conspired to spoil their plans.*

con·sta·ble (CON·stuh·bul) *n.* 1 a police officer of the lowest rank. 2 formerly, the chief officer in a royal household.

con·stab·u·lar·y (cun·STAB·yoo·lair·ee) *n.* -ries 1 a police force. 2 an armed paramilitary force: *the Irish constabulary.*

con·stant (CON·stunt) *adj.* 1 continual or unchanging: *There's a constant flow of water from the spring; the constant round of parties; constant current, velocity, voltage.* 2 faithful: *a constant companion, spouse.*
— *n.* in mathematics and physics, an unchanging factor or quantity, not a variable.
— **con·stant·ly** *adv.* — **con·stan·cy** *n.*

con·stel·la·tion (con·stuh·LAY·shun) *n.* 1 a group of stars, as the Great Bear, Gemini, etc. 2 a group of celebrities: *a constellation of movie stars.*

con·ster·na·tion (con·stur·NAY·shun) *n.* shock or dismay that bewilders or confuses: *The announcement caused consternation in the audience; People looked for the exit in consternation; To their consternation, the doors were found locked.*

con·sti·pate (CON·stuh·pate) *v.* -pates, -pat·ed, -pat·ing cause constipation.

con·sti·pa·tion (con·stuh·PAY·shun) *n.* difficulty in emptying the bowels.

con·stit·u·en·cy (cun·STICH·oo·un·see) *n.* -cies 1 an electoral district or riding represented by a member of a legislature. 2 a body of voters, supporters, or clients.

con·stit·u·ent (cun·STICH·oo·unt) *n.* 1 a member of a constituency: *The M.P. writes to her constituents regularly.* 2 a part or component: *Fat is one of the constituents of milk.*
— *adj.* 1 electoral: *a constituent body.* 2 component: *Fat is a constituent part of milk.* 3 empowered to write

or change a constitution: *a constituent assembly.*

con·sti·tute (CON·stuh·tute) *v.* -tutes, -tut·ed, -tut·ing 1 be the parts of something; form; make up: *Twelve people normally constitute a jury; an action that constitutes fraud.* 2 set up; appoint: *to constitute an assembly; a duly constituted representative.*

con·sti·tu·tion (con·stuh·TUE·shun) *n.* 1 the makeup of anything, esp. a person's physical condition: *a weak constitution; Exercise is good for your constitution.* 2 the basic rules or laws of a state, nation, corporation, club, etc.: *Canada's new* **Constitution** *was proclaimed on April 17, 1982.*

con·sti·tu·tion·al (con·stuh·TUE·shuh·nul) *adj.* 1 physical: *a constitutional tendency to gain weight; a constitutional inability to tell a lie.* 2 according to a constitution: *Is this law constitutional? a constitutional amendment, convention; The United Kingdom is a* **constitutional monarchy,** *the monarch having only limited power.*
— *n. Informal.* a walk taken for one's health: *She's out for her constitutional.*

con·strain (cun·STRAIN) *v.* restrain or confine: *He was constrained in iron chains; Clothes that constrain you may affect the safety of your driving.*

con·strained (cun·STRAIND) *adj.* 1 forced or obliged: *The judge said he felt constrained to impose a long jail sentence.* 2 strained or artificial: *a constrained laugh, smile.*

con·straint (cun·STRAINT) *n.* 1 compulsion: *The prisoner obeyed only* **under constraint.** 2 restriction: *the constraints of military discipline; legal constraints; to impose, place, put constraints on or upon trade between countries.*

con·strict (cun·STRICT) *v.* make smaller or tighter, as by tension: *to constrict arteries, blood vessels, tissues.*
— **con·stric·tion** *n.;* **con·stric·tive** (-tiv) *adj.*

con·stric·tor (cun·STRIC·tur) *n.* 1 a muscle that compresses, as those of the throat used in swallowing. 2 a snake that kills its prey by squeezing, as a boa or python.

con·struct (cun·STRUCT) *v.* build skilfully by putting parts together: *to construct an argument, bridge, model airplane; Students of geometry construct triangles.*
— **con·struc·tor** *n.*

con·struc·tion (cun·STRUCK·shun) *n.* 1 the act of building, a building, or the way something is built: *Our new house is under construction* (= being built); *commercial, modular, residential construction; a shoddy construction* (= building); *Everyone wears a helmet on a construction site.* 2 the building industry: *He is in construction; adj.: the construction business, boom; a construction engineer, firm.* 3 interpretation: *She put the wrong construction on something I said.* 4 arrangement of words: *the construction of a sentence; an idiomatic construction* (= phrase or sentence).

con·struc·tive (cun·STRUC·tiv) *adj.* useful: *constructive criticism.* — **con·struc·tive·ly** *adv.*

con·strue (cun·STROO) *v.* -strues, -strued, -stru·ing 1 interpret: *The meaning of a sentence sometimes depends on how you construe it; He construed her words* *as an insult rather than as a compliment.* **2** analyse grammatically: *Long and involved sentences are hard to construe.*

con·sul (CON·sul) *n.* an official appointed to protect a country's citizens and business interests in a foreign city. — **con·su·lar** (-lur) *adj.*

con·sul·ate (CON·suh·lit) *n.* the position, residence, or offices of a consul.

con·sult (cun·SULT) *v.* ask or refer to for advice or information: *He's gone to consult his lawyer about the case; She frequently consults her dictionary while studying; We have to consult* (= have regard for) *our own best interests; He consults* (= confers) *with his wife before making any decision; Our company consulted for* (= gave advice to) *the Royal Commission.*

con·sult·ant (cun·SUL·tunt) *n.* one who can give expert advice on a specific subject: *a business, educational, legal, medical, tax consultant; He works as a consultant for an engineering firm; a consultant to the minister on tax reform; a consultant in linguistics, a consultant* (= medical specialist) *in children's diseases.* — **con·sul·tan·cy** *n.* **-cies.**

con·sul·ta·tion (con·sul·TAY·shun) *n.* the act of consulting: *She holds consultations with her staff about or on all important matters; It's better not to disturb her when she is in consultation.*

con·sul·ta·tive (cun·SUL·tuh·tiv) *adj.* advisory: *a consultative assembly, committee, council; The lawyer advised her in his consultative capacity.*

con·sum·a·ble (cun·SOO·muh·bul, -SYOO·muh·bul) *n.* something that can be consumed or used up: *food, fuel, and other consumables; office consumables such as pads and pencils.* — **adj.**: *a consumable book* (= a workbook that is used and then discarded); *consumable goods, items, supplies.*

con·sume (cun·SOOM, -SYOOM, long "OO") *v.* **-sumes, -sumed, -sum·ing 1** use up; eat or drink; purchase and use for oneself: *They consumed a lot of popcorn.* **2** destroy: *The house was consumed by fire.* **3** take up completely; engross: *Physics consumes all her time and energy; It's her consuming interest.*

con·sum·er (cun·SOO·mur, -SYOO·mur) *n.* a user of goods and services, as opposed to producer: *the Consumers' Association.* — **adj.**: *a consumer cooperative; consumer appeal, awareness, credit, demand, education, protection, research, resistance; the consumer price index* (= cost-of-living index); *a consumer society (that consumes products and services unnecessarily).*

consumer goods *n. pl.* goods such as food, appliances, and automobiles that are produced for the use of the general public.

con·sum·er·ism (cun·SOO·mur·iz·um, con·SYOO-) *n.* a movement for protecting consumers from false advertising, unsafe products, etc. — **con·sum·er·ist** *n.*

con·sum·mate (CON·sum·it, cun·SUM·it) *adj.* complete or perfect, esp. skilled: *a consummate artist, liar, politician, virtuoso.* — *v.* (CON·suh·mate) **-sum·mates, -sum·mat·ed, -sum·mat·ing** to complete or fulfill: *to consummate a*

marriage (with an act of sexual intercourse); to consummate a deal, merger. — **con·sum·ma·tion** (-MAY·shun) *n.*

con·sump·tion (cun·SUMP·shun) *n.* **1** a consuming or being consumed: *the consumption of food; consumption by fire; an engine's fuel consumption* (= amount used up). **2** tuberculosis of the lungs.

con·sump·tive (cun·SUMP·tiv) *adj.* **1** having to do with consuming: *the consumptive needs of society.* **2** having to do with tuberculosis: *a consumptive cough.* — *n.* a tuberculosis patient.

con·tact (CON·tact) *n.* **1** the touching of two objects; also, the state of being in touch or having a communications link: *to come in(to), establish, make, maintain, stay in, bring into, break off, lose contact with someone; She has not been in contact* (= in touch) *for some time; to have body, close, cultural, intimate, direct, eye, face-to-face, personal, physical, radio contact; at the point of contact; The bomb exploded on contact with the ground.* **2** an electrical connection: *a device for breaking contact.* **3** an acquaintance: *business, international, professional, social contacts.* — *v.* to place, come, or get in contact with someone: *Let me contact headquarters first.* — *adj.*: *contact cement, dermatitis, man, period, person, printing; contact flying by observing landmarks; contact transmission of diseases.*

contact lens *n.* a light corrective lens placed over the pupil of the eye.

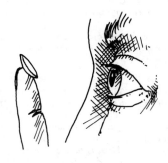

contact sport *n.* a sport such as football or hockey that involves body contact and blocking.

con·ta·gion (cun·TAY·jun) *n.* **1** the passing of a disease from one person to another by contact. **2** a disease so passed on or its cause. **3** the general spread of an idea, emotion, bad influence, etc.: *Steps have to be taken before the contagion spreads among the student population.*

con·ta·gious (cun·TAY·jus) *adj.* **1** spreading by contact: *Plague is extremely, highly contagious; Strictly speaking, malaria is not contagious but infectious.* **2** loosely, infectious: *a contagious viral disease.* **3** catching: *Her enthusiasm is contagious; contagious laughter.*

con·tain (cun·TAIN) *v.* **1** hold within oneself or itself: *Her coin purse contains 75 cents; This bottle contains* (= has a capacity of) *two litres; 6 contains* (= is divisible exactly by) *2 and 3.* **2** hold in check; hold back: *They tried to contain the enemy on the left flank; to contain a fire; to contain an oil spill using booms; Green belts of* *parkland are used to contain urban sprawl; She can't contain herself for joy; He can't contain his enthusiasm.* — **con·tain·er** *n.*

con·tain·ment (cun·TAIN·munt) *n.* a containing or checking: *the containment of rising insurance rates.*

con·tam·i·nant (cun·TAM·uh·nunt) *n.* something that contaminates: *radioactive contaminants in the water.*

con·tam·i·nate (cun·TAM·uh·nate) *v.* -nates, -nat·ed, -nat·ing to dirty, infect, or taint by contact: *Pesticides can contaminate the water supply.* — **con·tam·i·na·tion** (-NAY·shun) *n.*

con·tem·plate (CON·tum·plate) *v.* -plates, -plat·ed, -plat·ing think about or look at thoughtfully: *to contemplate the view from the hilltop; He says he never contemplated quitting the team.* — **con·tem·pla·tor** (-play·tur) *n.*

con·tem·pla·tion (con·tum·PLAY·shun) *n.* thoughtful consideration: *the contemplation of beauty.*

con·tem·pla·tive (cun·TEM·pluh·tiv) *adj.* given to contemplation: *a contemplative life, monk, religious order.* — *n.* one who lives a life of contemplation.

con·tem·po·ra·ne·ous (cun·TEM·puh·RAY·nee·us) *adj.* occurring at the same period as another: *a contemporaneous event; The Suez crisis of 1956 was contemporaneous with the Hungarian uprising.*

con·tem·po·rar·y (cun·TEM·puh·rair·ee) *adj.* 1 existing at the same period as another: *Laurier's life was contemporary with Queen Victoria's reign.* 2 modern; present-day: *contemporary English, events, furniture, styles, trends.* — *n., pl.* -ries a person of the same period as another: *Laurier was a contemporary of Queen Victoria; Joe and I were contemporaries in school.*

con·tempt (cun·TEMPT) *n.* 1 a regarding or being regarded as base, negligible, worthless, etc.; scorn: *Cowards deserve contempt; They should be treated with contempt; deep, profound, total, utter contempt; The bikers demonstrated, displayed, showed contempt for the law.* 2 a challenging of the authority or dignity of a judge or legislature: *He was held in contempt of court for disobeying a court order;* **civil contempt** (= disobedience of a decree issued by a court); **criminal contempt** (= flouting of a judge's authority in court). — **con·tempt·i·ble** *adj.*: *contemptible behaviour; It was contemptible* (= deserving contempt) *of him to spit in front of her.* — **con·temp·ti·bly** *adv.*

con·temp·tu·ous (cun·TEM·choo·us) *adj.* full of or showing contempt; scornful: *a contemptuous look, sneer; a biker who is contemptuous of all authority; It was contemptuous of him* (= showing contempt) *to spit in front of her.*

con·tend (cun·TEND) *v.* 1 compete, as in combat or debate, *for* a prize, position, etc. *with* someone: *The pioneers had to contend with the elements.* 2 claim or maintain: *He contends that you misled him.* — **con·tend·er** *n.*: *the leading contender; a likely contender for the leadership of the party.*

con·tent (CON·tent) *n.* 1 **contents** *pl.* what is contained: *the contents of a box; a book's table of contents; the contents of a confidential letter; a content*

sale (of everything in a house). 2 substance: *All objects have form and content; a book with no intellectual content; the content analysis of a book, film, etc.* 3 amount contained: *The salt content of butter is about 3%.* 4 (cun·TENT) satisfaction: *He ate to his heart's content.* — *v.* (cun·TENT) satisfy or please: *a modest man who contents himself with what he has achieved; a* **contented** *life, look, smile.* — *adj.* (cun·TENT) satisfied: *He is content with his lot in life; content to remain as a clerk.*

con·ten·tion (cun·TEN·shun) *n.* 1 disagreement or rivalry that shows itself in fighting and controversy: *a bone of contention between the two parties; two advertisers appearing in contention* (= competition) *with each other.* 2 a disputed statement: *to rebut, refute a contention; It is his contention that you misled him.*

con·ten·tious (cun·TEN·shus) *adj.* 1 causing rivalry or dissent: *a contentious argument that never ends; a contentious claim that is hard to settle.* 2 having a fighting attitude: *a contentious and argumentative fellow; his contentious nature.*

con·tent·ment (cun·TENT·munt) *n.* a satisfied state: *a life of peace and contentment.*

con·test (CON·test) *n.* 1 competition: *a baby, beauty, oratorical contest; to enter, hold, judge, stage a contest; a contest among friends; a contest between teams; a contest for a prize.* 2 a fight or dispute: *a bitter, hard-fought, close, one-sided contest.* — *v.* (cun·TEST) 1 compete for something: *to contest a seat in an election.* 2 fight or argue over something: *He always contests his parking tickets in court.* — **con·test·a·ble** *adj.* — **con·test·ant** *n.*

con·text (CON·text) *n.* the surrounding words that determine a word's meaning: *a display showing key words in their contexts; I was unfairly quoted out of context; a dangerous admission to make in the context* (= circumstances) *of the trial.*

con·tig·u·ous (cun·TIG·yoo·us) *adj.* touching along all or most of one side; next in space or time: *Canada is contiguous with* or *to the U.S.; A movie is made up of contiguous still pictures.* — **con·ti·gu·i·ty** (con·tig·YOO·uh·tee) *n.*

con·ti·nence (CON·tuh·nunce) *n.* self-restraint, esp. the ability to control a bodily need or function such as sex, urination, or evacuation.

con·ti·nent (CON·tuh·nunt) *adj.* having to do with or showing continence. — *n.* 1 one of the seven large continuous land masses, i.e., Africa, Antarctica, Asia, Australia, Europe, and North and South America: *Britain is in the continent of Europe.* 2 **the Continent** mainland Europe in relation to Britain: *Britons like to holiday on the Continent.*

con·ti·nen·tal (con·tuh·NEN·tul) *adj.* 1 pertaining to a continent: *The Antarctic is one continental glacier; the* **continental drift** *theory of the movement of continents; A* **continental shelf** (= sloping sea bed) *contains continental deposits washed down by rivers.* 2 **Continental** or **continental** European: *a Continental army; a* **continental breakfast** *of coffee and rolls.* — *n.* a person from mainland Europe.

Continental Divide *n.* the high ground formed by the Rocky Mountains separating rivers flowing to the Atlantic from those flowing to the Pacific.

con·tin·gen·cy (cun·TIN·jun·see) *n.* -**cies** a possibility that depends on chance or uncertain conditions: *An unforeseen contingency may arise; Be prepared for all contingencies; To provide for every contingency is impossible.*
— *adj.*: *a contingency plan; a* **contingency fee** *(chargeable only if specified conditions are met); a* **contingency fund** *(to cover unexpected losses); a* **contingency table** *(for studying the likelihood of certain events occurring).*

con·tin·gent (cun·TIN·junt) *adj.* possible but uncertain; dependent: *His arrival is contingent on* or *upon the weather.*
— *n.* a number of things or a group of people forming part of a larger group: *a contingent of cavalry, ships, troops; A French contingent joined the British.*

con·tin·u·al (cun·TIN·yoo·ul) *adj.* repeated frequently; periodic but unceasing: *a beach eroded by the continual action of the waves; Her sleep was disturbed by the continual barking of a dog.* — **con·tin·u·al·ly** *adv.*

con·tin·u·ance (cun·TIN·yoo·unce) *n.* a continuation or its duration: *his continuance in office; the continuance of a crisis.*

con·tin·u·a·tion (cun·TIN·yoo·AY·shun) *n. a continuing or resumption of an action: His next book will be a continuation of the story.*

con·tin·ue (cun·TIN·yoo) *v.* -**ues**, -**ued**, -**u·ing** 1 go on being or doing something; carry on: *The strike continues; He wants to continue in his job; to continue as a clerk; to continue on his career, journey; to continue at the factory; to continue with his work; to continue for another year; She continues to make* or *making mistakes; The trains continue to be late; The nuisance continues unabated; It may continue all summer; The lecture continued after lunch; He takes night courses at a school of* **continuing education** (= adult education). 2 resume: *He continued the lecture after lunch.* 3 extend: *The mandate was continued for another year.* 4 adjourn: *The hearing was continued for a week.*

con·tin·u·i·ty (con·tuh·NEW·uh·tee) *n.* 1 a continuous quality: *Chapter 3 breaks the continuity of the story.* 2 the working script showing the scenario for a movie, TV, or radio production, not the shooting script. 3 linking material for a TV or radio program.

con·tin·u·ous (cun·TIN·yoo·us) *adj.* without a break in space or time: *a continuous line of cars; the continuous passage of time.* — **con·tin·u·ous·ly** *adv.*

con·tin·u·um (cun·TIN·yoo·um) *n.* a continuous extent or series: *Time and space are continuums; Einstein's space-time continuum; Car prices vary along a continuum.*

con·tort (cun·TORT) *v.* twist out of shape; deform: *a face contorted by rage.* — **con·tor·tion** *n.*

con·tour (CON·toor) *n.* the outline of a surface of varying dimensions: *We flew low hugging the contours of the ground to elude enemy radar; the smooth, sweeping contours of a car's aerodynamic design; clothes that outline the contours of the body.*
— *adj.* following the contours: *a contour chair;* **Contour lines** connect points of equal elevation, as shown on a **contour map.**

con·tra (CON·trah) *n.* a member of a right-wing guerrilla group in Nicaragua.

con·tra·band (CON·truh·band) *n. & adj.* illegal or smuggled goods: *contraband liquor.*

con·tra·cep·tion (con·truh·SEP·shun) *n.* the prevention of conception: *to practise, use contraception.*

con·tra·cep·tive (-tiv) *n.* an agent used to prevent conception: *a chemical, herbal, oral, vaginal contraceptive; adj.*: *a contraceptive measure; a variety of contraceptive devices, methods, techniques.*

con·tract (CON·tract) *n.* an agreement, esp. if legally binding: *a legal, marriage, valid, void contract; a secretly arranged sweetheart contract* or *deal* (= secret deal); *to assign, award, breach, break, cancel, carry out, conclude, draw up, enter into, execute, negotiate, ratify, repudiate, violate a contract; There's a contract out for Caputo* (Informal for Someone has been hired to kill Caputo); *the contract on Caputo.*
— *v.* 1 agree in a contract: *They contracted to supply steel for the railway; The railway contracted with the company for steel supplies; Railways usually* **contract out** *the job of supplying steel.* 2 (cun·TRACT) acquire something unwanted: *to contract debts, bad habits, diseases, obligations; a marriage contracted* (= entered into) *for unworthy reasons.* 3 (cun·TRACT) make or become smaller, as by drawing in: *Cold contracts metals; The triceps muscle contracts as the arm is straightened; "I'm" is the* **contracted** (= shortened) *form of "I am"; to contract* (= wrinkle) *one's brow in a frown.*
— **con·trac·tion** (cun·TRAC·shun) *n.*: *"It's" is the contraction for "It is"; Call the doctor when the contractions (of the uterus) are less than ten minutes apart and last for half a minute.*
— **con·trac·tor** *n.*: *a building, electrical, plumbing contractor.* — **con·trac·tu·al** (cun·TRAC·choo·ul) *adj.* — **con·trac·tu·al·ly** *adv.*

con·tra·dict (con·truh·DICT) *v.* state the opposite or deny the truth or correctness of something: *One can't contradict facts; Facts may contradict your claims; The two stories contradict each other; He's always contradicting his superiors; Stop contradicting!*

con·tra·dic·tion (con·truh·DIC·shun) *n.* a contradicting: *an apparent, basic, clear, glaring, inherent, internal contradiction; a story full of discrepancies and contradictions; His practice is in sharp contradiction with* or *to his principles; "Square circle" is a contradiction in terms.*
— **con·tra·dic·to·ry** (-tuh·ree) *adj.*: *two contradictory versions of the same incident, one contradictory to the other.*

con·trap·tion (cun·TRAP·shun) *n. Informal.* a gadget: *to build, put together, slap together a contraption; a new-fangled contraption for polishing shoes.*

con·tra·ri·wise (con·TRAIR·ee·wize) *adv.* in a contrary manner.

con·tra·ry (CON·trair·ee) *adj.* **1** opposed: *His actions were contrary to company policies; two contrary* (= contrasting) *examples; two contrary* (= incompatible) *statements; a ship tossed by contrary* (= adverse) *winds.* **2** (*also* cun·TRAIR·ee) temperamentally opposed to obedience: *Mary is quite contrary; a contrary child.*
— *n., pl.* **-ries** something opposite: *He was reported to be cruel;* **On the contrary,** *he was very kind; He seemed very kind despite all reports* **to the contrary.**

con·trast (con·TRAST) *v.* **1** set in opposition to show differences: *Compare and contrast their behaviour.* **2** exhibit differences when placed, seen, etc. together: *Her behaviour contrasts sharply with his.*
— *n.* (CON·trast) **1** comparison: *In contrast to or By contrast with Ottawa, Toronto is mild in winter.* **2** difference in comparison: *Vancouver is or presents a harsh, sharp, startling contrast to Ottawa; The contrast between the two cities is striking; The picture lacks contrast (between light and dark tones).*

con·tra·vene (CON·truh·veen) *v.* **-venes, -vened, -ven·ing** go against or conflict with something: *a structure that contravenes the building code.*
— **con·tra·ven·tion** (-VEN·shun) *n.:* *It's been built in contravention of the building code.*

con·trib·ute (cun·TRIB·yoot) *v.* **-utes, -ut·ed, -ut·ing** give jointly with others: *We contributed clothing, money, time, etc. for the refugees; We regularly contribute to the United Way, to charity; to contribute ideas, knowledge, etc. to a project; to contribute an article, poem, story, etc. to a magazine; Many things* **contributed to** (= jointly brought about) *his downfall.*
— **con·tri·bu·tion** (con·truh·BYOO·shun) *n.:* *She made or sent in a (charitable) contribution; a generous, monetary, token, voluntary contribution to charity; He made many brilliant, key, major, notable, original, outstanding, remarkable, valuable contributions to knowledge; His contribution* (= article) *was accepted by the editor.*
— **con·trib·u·tor** (cun·TRIB·yoo·tur) *n.:* *a generous, regular contributor to charity; a prolific contributor to scholarly journals.*

con·trib·u·to·ry (cun·TRIB·yoo·tor·ee) *adj.* contributing: *a contributory cause of the accident; the accident victim's* **contributory negligence** *in not watching the traffic.*

con·trite (CON·trite) *adj.* sorrowful about having done wrong, with a firm purpose of amendment: *He prayed for forgiveness with a humble and contrite heart; a contrite sinner; He shed contrite tears.*

con·tri·tion (cun·TRISH·un) *n.* sorrow for having done wrong: *an act of contrition; He expressed, felt, showed contrition for his sins.*

con·triv·ance (cun·TRY·vunce) *n.* something contrived: *a new contrivance for peeling potatoes.*

con·trive (cun·TRIVE) *v.* **-trives, -trived, -triv·ing** plan and accomplish something cleverly or ingeniously: *The burglar contrived a way to break into the house; contrived to break in by an air vent; She escaped from the fire by a rope ladder contrived out of bedsheets; a* **contrived** (= laboured or artificial) *alibi, excuse, gaiety.*

con·trol (cun·TROLE) *v.* **-trols, -trolled, -trol·ling** direct or restrain in order to keep within limits or on a course: *He can control his horse, but not his temper; a car controlled by radio.*
— *n.* **1** power of directing or restraining; also, an act of controlling: *to assume or take control of a situation; to establish, exercise, exert control over the people working for you; They finally brought the fire* **under control;** *The car went out of control; He lost control of the car and landed in a ditch; absolute, close, full, government, lax, loose, parental, remote, strict control; birth, cost, damage, emission, fire, flight, flood, gun, mission, pest, quality, rent, stress, thought control; She wrested control of the plane from the hijacker; Her husband took over the* **controls** (= controlling mechanism) *after freeing himself; He remained at the controls for the rest of the flight.* **2 controls** *pl.* restrictions: *to impose wage and price controls; to introduce rent controls; The government tightened controls on liquor sales; The controls were lifted or removed after a time.* **3** a standard used for comparison: *The first group got much better than the controls* (= members of the "control group") *who were not given the drug.*
— *adj.:* *a control centre, panel; a* **control rod** *of a nuclear reactor; the* **control stick** *of an airplane; a control tower, unit.*
— **con·trol·la·ble** (-luh·bul) *adj.*
— **con·trolled** (cun·TROLED) *adj.:* *a freeway with* **controlled access** *(having interchanges for exits and entrances); a magazine with* **controlled circulation** *(distributed free in select areas); a controlled celebration, economy, manner, voice; A* **controlled experiment** *(using a standard for comparison) has to be carried out under controlled conditions;* **controlled substances** (= drugs).

con·trol·ler (cun·TROH·lur) *n.* **1** one who directs: *an air-traffic controller; flight controller.* **2** one who supervises finances and spending; comptroller. **3** *Cdn.* an elected member of the board of control and city council of certain large cities.

con·tro·ver·sial (con·truh·VUR·shul) *adj.* **1** arousing controversy: *Abortion is a bitterly, highly controversial issue, question, subject; a controversial author, figure.* **2** fond of controversy: *a controversial philosopher.*
— **con·tro·ver·sial·ly** *adv.*

con·tro·ver·sy (CON·truh·vur·see) *n.* **-sies** a conflict of opinion; dispute: *the bitter, furious, heated, lively, public, spirited controversy over or about abortion; the controversy between pro-life and pro-choice groups; Abortion arouses, causes, fuels, stirs up much controversy; a controversy that is hard to settle; He got into a controversy with the administration.*

con·tro·vert (CON·truh·vurt) *v.* argue against or about: *a much controverted issue.* — **con·tro·ver·ti·ble** *adj.*

co·nun·drum (cuh·NUN·drum) *n. Formal.* **1** a riddle involving a pun; e.g. "When is a dress like a chair? When it is sat·in." **2** a hard-to-solve, confusing problem: *the conundrum of balancing the budget without raising taxes.*

con·va·lesce (con·vuh·LES) *v.* **-lesc·es, -lesced, -lesc·ing** recover after an illness or injury; get better: *She is convalescing from her recent illness.*
— **con·va·les·cence** (-unce) *n.:* *It happened during her convalescence.*
— **con·va·les·cent** (-unt) *n. & adj.:* *A* **convalescent home** *is a home for convalescents.*

178

con·vec·tion (cun·VEC·shun) *n.* internal movement in a liquid or gas, caused esp. by variation in heating: *Heating takes place by conduction, convection, and radiation;* **adj.:** *A space heater sets up convection currents; A* **convection oven** *blows and circulates hot air uniformly around the food; the sun's* **convection zone** *just below its surface.*
— **con·vec·tion·al** *adj.: Equatorial forests thrive on convectional rains.*

con·vene (cun·VEEN) *v.* **-venes, -vened, -ven·ing** come or bring together in a body: *The mayor convened the town council; The meeting convenes at 3 p.m.*
— **con·ve·nor** or **con·ven·er** *n.*

con·ven·ience (cun·VEEN·yunce) *n.* **1** the quality of being convenient: *the convenience of shopping by telephone; a* **marriage of convenience** *(entered into for gaining some advantage, not out of love).* **2** ease or personal comfort: *We will see you* **at your convenience;** *words arranged in alphabetical order* **for your convenience. 3** something that helps ease or comfort: *It's a great convenience to live* or *living near the rapid transit; the microwave oven, electric kettle, and such modern conveniences; Is there a powder room, washroom, or convenience* (= toilet) *here?*

convenience food *n.* prepackaged, easy-to-prepare food, as a TV dinner.

convenience store *n.* a small store carrying basic food items and other necessities that is open long hours.

con·ven·ient (cun·VEEN·yunt) *adj.* adapted for one's ease or comfort: *five convenient locations to shop; a convenient illness during exam week; Is next week convenient for you? It's very convenient living* or *to live near the rapid transit; It's very convenient that you can take the subway to work.* — **con·ven·ient·ly** *adv.*

convenor See CONVENE.

con·vent (CON·vunt) *n.* a community of nuns or where they live.

con·ven·tion (cun·VEN·shun) *n.* **1** a meeting, esp. of delegates: *to hold a convention; an annual, constitutional, national, party, political, sales convention; a convention centre.* **2** an international agreement: *a copyright convention; the Geneva conventions providing for the humane treatment of war prisoners and wounded.* **3** accepted custom or usage; also, a practice so sanctioned: *Whether you kiss or rub noses is a matter of convention; a mere convention; a social convention; not a rigid convention; the conventions of art, communication, games, language, parliamentary practice, religion, warfare.*

con·ven·tion·al (cun·VEN·shuh·nul) *adj.* **1** customary: *It is conventional to shake hands over a deal; a conventional greeting; The fleur-de-lis is a conventional representation of the lily;* **conventional wisdom** (= a belief or set of commonly held beliefs); *conventional as opposed to nuclear warfare.* **2** ordinary: *a conventional dictionary, lifestyle, product, view; clothes that are too conventional for special occasions.*
— **con·ven·tion·al·ly** *adv.*

con·verge (cun·VURGE) *v.* **-verg·es, -verged, -verg·ing** move toward a common point or goal: *The demonstrators converged on Parliament Hill;*

Converging lines meet.
— **con·ver·gence** *n.;* **con·ver·gent** *adj.*

con·ver·sant (cun·VUR·sunt, CON·vur·sunt) *adj.* having knowledge or familiarity: *a lawyer thoroughly conversant with contract law.*

con·ver·sa·tion (con·vur·SAY·shun) *n.* a talk between two or more people: *the fine art of conversation; to begin, break off, bug, carry on, have, hold, interrupt, monitor, monopolize, stimulate, strike up, tap, tape, terminate a conversation; She tried hard to make conversation but the other party was not interested; an animated, intimate, light, lively, private, serious, telephone conversation; I couldn't help overhearing fragments* or *scraps of their conversation; He had a conversation about cats with Joan; He was in conversation with Joan for two hours; Collectibles make great* **conversation pieces** (= items having curiosity or novelty value).
— **con·ver·sa·tion·al** *adj.;* **con·ver·sa·tion·al·ly** *adv.*
— **con·ver·sa·tion·al·ist** *n.: a skilled and witty conversationalist.*

con·verse 1 (cun·VERSE) *v.* **-vers·es, -versed, -vers·ing** talk informally: *He can converse fluently about Germany in German with fellow students.*
2 (CON·verse) *n. & adj.* opposite: *Her generosity is the converse of his stinginess; a converse proposition, theorem.*

con·verse·ly (cun·VERSE·lee) *adv.* in the opposite way: *Our summer is New Zealand's winter, and conversely* (= Our winter is New Zealand's summer).

con·ver·sion (cun·VUR·zhun, -shun) *n.* **1** a converting or being converted; change: *the conversion of rooming houses to apartments; conversion of data to machine-readable form; a table for metric conversion; methods of conversion* (= refining) *of crude oil to make gasoline; He underwent a sudden conversion* (= religious change) *from Christianity to Islam; He also made some conversions* (= converts) *among his friends.* **2** illegal use of another's property: *The bailiff was charged with theft by conversion of $500* (= illegal use of property worth $500).

con·vert (cun·VURT) *v.* **1** change or adapt to a different form, use, etc.: *Alchemists wanted to convert base metals like lead to gold; We had to convert a lot of dollars to rupees for a vacation in India; to convert a barn into a restaurant; They will convert to production of the new model in July; She converted to Islam; Canada converted to the metric system long ago;* **Converted rice** *has been processed to preserve its mineral and vitamin content.* **2** persuade someone or be persuaded to adopt new principles, esp. as a religion: *He was converted from Baptist to Buddhism; He converted voluntarily; He's a* **converted** *Buddhist.* **3** illegally use another's property as one's own.
— *n.* (CON·vurt) one who has been converted: *a convert to Hinduism.*

con·vert·er (cun·VUR·tur) *n.* a converting device: *a pocket metric converter; an electrical converter for changing AC to DC; a catalytic converter; a hand-held cable-TV converter for viewing many channels.*

con·vert·i·ble (cun·VUR·tuh·bul) *adj.* that can be converted: *a bond that is convertible to stock; Dollars*

are freely convertible into other currencies; a convertible sofa that opens out into a bed.
— *n.* a car with a folding roof.

con·ver·tor (cun·VUR·tur) *n.* same as CONVERTER.

con·vex (CON·vex) *adj.* rounded outward, as the outer surface of a ball: *a convex lens.*
— **con·vex·i·ty** (cun·VEX·uh·tee) *n.* -ties.

con·vey (cun·VAY) *v.* 1 carry from place to place; conduct: *a pipe to convey water.* 2 pass on; communicate: *I conveyed my sympathies to the bereaved.* 3 transfer ownership of a property: *The title to the land was conveyed from the school to the church; The land was conveyed to the church.*

con·vey·ance (cun·VAY·unce) *n.* 1 a conveying; moving or transferring: *the conveyance of freight; the conveyance of an estate; a deed of conveyance.* 2 a means of conveying; vehicle: *a public conveyance.*

conveyor or **conveyor belt** *n.* an endless belt, chain, etc. for moving objects, as on an assembly line or at a supermarket checkout.

con·vict (cun·VICT) *v.* declare or prove guilty: *He was convicted of theft; a convicted thief.*
— *n.* (CON·vict) one serving a prison term.

con·vic·tion (cun·VIC·shun) *n.* 1 a convicting: *Jon received a conviction for petty theft; That is just one of the many convictions the prosecutor got last year; The conviction was overturned on appeal.* 2 firm belief: *a burning, deep, firm, life-long, strong conviction that truth will win; He's a pacifist by conviction; He has the courage of his convictions to refuse to go to war; a story that carries conviction* (= that is convincing).

con·vince (cun·VINCE) *v.* -vinc·es, -vinced, -vinc·ing persuade; bring to a firm belief: *I am convinced of his innocence; He convinced me that he is innocent; He convinced (Informal for persuaded) me to tell it to the judge; I am absolutely, completely, firmly, thoroughly convinced (= persuaded) that he is innocent; His arguments are very convincing (= persuasive).*
— **con·vinc·ing·ly** *adv.: He argues convincingly.*

con·viv·i·al (cun·VIV·ee·ul) *adj.* fond of, suited to, or having good company, good food, and good drink: *a convivial host; We had a convivial time at the party.*
— **con·viv·i·al·ly** *adv.*
— **con·viv·i·al·i·ty** (-ee·AL·uh·tee) *n.*

con·vo·ca·tion (con·vuh·CAY·shun) *n.* an assembly of churchmen, members of a university, etc.: *A convocation is held when degrees are to be conferred.*

con·voke (cun·VOKE) *v.* -vokes, -voked, -vok·ing *Formal.* summon for a deliberative or legislative purpose: *to convoke an assembly, congress, parliament.*

con·voy (CON·voy) *v.* accompany as protection on a journey: *Aircraft convoyed the tankers.*
— *n.* 1 an armed escort, as for ships: *They sailed under convoy of aircraft.* 2 a group travelling together for safe or orderly transport: *a convoy of merchant ships; All shipping moved in convoys during World War II.*

con·vulse (cun·VULSE) *v.* -vuls·es, -vulsed, -vuls·ing throw into a convulsion or spasm; shake violently: *She was convulsed with laughter.*

con·vul·sion (cun·VUL·shun) *n.* 1 an involuntary, powerful muscular contraction; fit or seizure: *Epileptics go into convulsions.* 2 a powerful sudden or spasmodic action, as a revolution, earthquake, etc.: *The audience was thrown into convulsions of laughter; There were convulsions of panic during the stock market crash.*

coo *n.* 1 the low, gentle murmuring of doves. 2 any similar sound.
— *v.* coos, cooed, coo·ing: *the billing and cooing going on park benches.*

cook (short "oo") *v.* 1 prepare for eating by boiling, baking, frying, etc.: *We need someone to cook a meal for us; to cook us a meal; Who will cook supper? The eggs are cooking (= being cooked) now; He does all our cooking; good home cooking.* 2 treat with heat. 3 *Informal.* happen: *What's cooking?* 4 *Slang.* falsify; also, botch: *The embezzler cooked the (account) books.* 5 *Slang.* do or feel the right thing: *Now you're cooking!*
— **cook one's goose** *Informal.* ruin oneself completely.
— **cook up** *Informal.* concoct or invent: *to cook up an excuse, plan, plot, pretext, story, tale.*
— *n.* one who cooks: *the head cook; a short-order cook.*

cook·book *n.* a book of recipes.

cook·ie or **cook·y** (COOK·ee, short "OO") *n.* 1 a small, usually flat cake made from a stiff, sweet dough: *a fortune cookie (containing a flattering or humorous message folded inside); caught with his hand in the cookie jar (= caught accepting bribes); That's how or the way the cookie crumbles (= how the matter resolves itself)!* 2 *Slang.* person; guy: *a tough cookie.*

cook·out *n.* a meal prepared and eaten outdoors, as on an outing: *to have a cookout.*

cool (long "oo") *adj.* 1 somewhat cold; also, protecting or relieving from heat: *a cool summer; a cool summer jacket.* 2 unemotional: *Keep, remain, stay cool (= calm); Keep a cool head; She is cool as a cucumber (= unexcited); cool (= restrained) jazz; He was cool (= unfriendly) toward us; was cool to (= unreceptive of) the new idea; According to McLuhan, radio is a hot medium, involving more listener participation to complete its communication than such cool media as films and T.V.* 3 *Slang.* excellent; admirable: *It isn't cool to be jealous; It's cool not to take drugs; The Calgary Winter Games cost a cool $1 billion.*
— **play it cool** *Slang.* be casual and impassive.
— *n.* 1 something cool: *the cool of a summer night.* 2 *Slang.* composure: *He blew his cool; He lost his cool and yelled at her; She kept her cool and just walked away.*
— *v.* make or become cool: *Leave him to cool off or cool down, he'll come back; Tell him to cool it (Slang for relax); an air-cooled engine; the cooling-off period during which you may cancel a sales contract.*
— **cool one's heels** *Informal.* be forced to wait.
— **cool·ly** *adv.;* **cool·ness** *n.*

cool·ant (COO·lunt) *n.* a fluid used, as in an engine, to remove excess heat: *to add coolant to the radiator.*

cool·er (COO·lur) *n.* 1 one that cools or a cooling container or room. 2 a cool drink, esp. one that is slightly alcoholic. 3 **the cooler** *Slang.* jail; slammer.

cool·ie (COO·lee) *n.* an unskilled, often exploited Oriental labourer.

coon (long "oo") *n. Informal.* raccoon: *I haven't seen him in a **coon's age*** (= for a long time).

coop (long "oo") *n.* **1** a cage, pen, etc., esp. for poultry: *a chicken coop.* **2** *Slang.* a jail: *The convict **flew the coop*** (= escaped).
— *v.* confine: *The jury was cooped up in a hotel during the trial.*

co-op (COH·op) *n.* cooperative: *We do all our shopping at the co-op (store); **adj.**: a co-op housing project; a co-op student in a co-op system; see* COOPERATIVE EDUCATION.

co·op·er·ate (coh·OP·uh·rate) *v.* -ates, -at·ed, -at·ing work with others, esp. for a common goal: *to cooperate on a project with neighbours; They cooperated in building a fence.*
— **co·op·er·a·tion** (-RAY·shun) *n.*: *We had the close, complete, whole-hearted cooperation of the teaching community; We appreciate your cooperation with us in this enterprise; This dictionary was prepared in cooperation with teachers.* — **co·op·er·a·tor** *n.*
Also **co-operate, co-operation, co-operator.**

co·op·er·a·tive (coh·OP·ur·uh·tiv) *adj.* **1** having to do with cooperation: *in a cooperative mood.* **2** having to do with an enterprise owned and usually operated by members for their own benefit: *a cooperative apartment house, film club, health facility, savings-and-loan institution.*
— *n.* a cooperative enterprise, esp. a store: *consumers', farmers', producers', workers' cooperatives; handicraft cooperatives in Atlantic Canada; fishing cooperatives; recreation cooperatives.* — **co·op·er·a·tive·ly** *adv.*
Also **co-operative, co-operatively.**

cooperative education *n.* an educational program in which students spend alternating periods in school and at study-related work in industry on a year-round basis.

co-opt (coh·OPT) *v.* **1** choose as a partner or colleague: *A committee can co-opt more members.* **2** absorb into a culture, organization, etc.; also, take over: *a revolutionary co-opted by the system.*

co·or·di·nate (coh·OR·duh·nit) *adj.* of equal importance or rank; parallel: *the coordinate clauses of a compound sentence.*
— *n.* **1** something coordinate: *shirt-pant-sweater coordinates* (= matching clothes) *in navy blue.* **2** a letter or number used as a reference in precisely locating something: *the X and Y coordinates of a graph; "L-7" gives the coordinates of Chalkdene Grove on the map.*
— *v.* (-nate) -ates, -at·ed, -at·ing **1** make or become coordinate: *"And," "but," "hence," etc. are coordinating conjunctions.* **2** work or cause to work harmoniously together: *a coordinated assault on the fortress; a coordinating editor; a colour-coordinated outfit.*
— **co·or·di·nate·ly** (-nit·lee) *adv.*; **co·or·di·na·tor** (-nay·tur) *n.*
Also **co-ordinate, co-ordinately, co-ordinator.**

co·or·di·na·tion (coh·OR·duh·NAY·shun) *n.* **1** a coordinating. **2** the harmonious functioning of various muscles in a complex action: *Brain injury may cause poor coordination, as in cerebral palsy.*
Also **co-or·di·na·tion.**

coot (long "oo") *n.* **1** any of several ducklike water birds: *bald as a coot; silly* or *stupid as a coot.*

2 *Informal.* a silly, usually old man or woman: *crazy as a coot.*

cop *v.* cops, copped, cop·ping *Slang.* capture, seize, or steal: *The bird had been copped from his coop.*
— **cop a plea** plead guilty to a lesser charge in order to avoid being tried on a more serious one.
— **cop out** *Slang.* withdraw from or avoid commitment; back out: *He copped out of or on his obligation to pay back the loan.*
— *n. Slang.* a police officer.

cope *n.* **1** an outer, enveloping cloak worn by clergy during ceremonies. **2** anything that covers like a cope; canopy. **3** a top part: *the cope* (= top half) *of a mould enclosing a pattern to be cast.*
— *v.* copes, coped, cop·ing contend, usually successfully; come to grips: *troubled teenagers trying to cope with life; Some just can't cope.*

cop·i·er (COP·ee·ur) *n.* one that copies, esp. a duplicating machine.

co·pi·lot (COH·pye·lut) *n.* an assistant pilot.

cop·ing (COH·ping) *n.* the rooflike topping of a stone or brick wall.

co·pi·ous (COH·pee·us) *adj.* plentiful in quantity or in words, speech, etc.: *a copious discharge of steam; a text provided with copious notes.*
— **co·pi·ous·ly** *adv.*; **co·pi·ous·ness** *n.*

cop-out or **cop·out** *n. Slang.* a copping or backing out: *Resignation is an easy cop-out; He thought his easy life was a real cop-out and no challenge; Your answer is a cop-out.*

cop·per (COP·ur) *n.* **1** a reddish-brown metal or its colour. **2** *Brit.* a penny. **3** *Slang.* a police officer; cop.
— *adj.*: *copper bracelets, mining, ore, tan, wire.*
— **cop·per·y** *adj.*

copse (COPS) *n.* a thicket of shrubs or small trees.

cop·ter (COP·tur) *n. Informal.* helicopter.

cop·u·late (COP·yuh·late) *v.* -lates, -lat·ed, -lat·ing engage in coitus *with* someone.
— **cop·u·la·tion** (-LAY·shun) *n.*

cop·y (COP·ee) *n.* cop·ies **1** a close imitation or duplication of an original: *a copy of the Mona Lisa; fair and rough copies of a manuscript; a certified true copy of the document; a carbon copy of a letter; Make me a clean Xerox copy; Save the master copy; Run off 500 copies for me; Keep an extra copy as backup copy.* **2** a single specimen of a printed text, photograph, etc.: *a first printing of 100 000 copies; Authors autograph copies of their books for friends; leather-bound presentation copies; advance copies sent to reviewers; the hard copy printout from a computer; back copies* (= issues) *of a periodical.* **3** draft material to be typeset; manuscript; hence, the words of an advertisement: *the layout of copy and illustrations; Editors check copy produced by writers; newspaper copy; the copy desk of a newspaper.* **4** subject matter for a story: *Scandals make good copy for the papers.*
— *v.* cop·ies, cop·ied, cop·y·ing reproduce closely or imitate: *He likes to copy from friends; He slavishly copies what the others do; Children tend to copy their*

parents; Text copies better (= gives better photocopies) *than pictures; a **copying machine*** (= photocopier).

cop·y·book (COP·ee·book) *n.* a book containing samples of proper handwriting.

copy boy *n.* a boy who helps in a newspaper office doing errands, delivering copy, etc.

cop·y·cat (COP·ee·cat) *n. Informal.* a slavish imitator of others.

copy desk *n.* a desk where newspaper copy is edited before typesetting.

copy-edit (COP·ee·ed·it) *v.* edit a manuscript for publication.

copy-editor (COP·ee·ed·uh·tur) *n.* one who edits copy and, often, writes headings, as for a newspaper.

cop·y·ist (COP·ee·ist) *n.* one who makes written copies.

cop·y·right (COP·ee·rite) *n.* an author's legal right to reproduce, sell, publish, etc. a work of art, literature, music, etc.: *Authors and publishers apply for, claim, hold, secure copyrights in* or *on their works; The Department of Consumer and Corporate Affairs registers* or *grants copyrights in Canada; You will infringe (a) copyright if you copy a book that is under copyright.*
— *v.: to copyright a play, story, work; a copyrighted poem.*

cop·y·writ·er (COP·ee·rye·tur) *n.* one who writes advertising copy.

co·quet·ry (COH·kuh·tree) *n.* **-tries** a flirting act or attitude.

co·quette (coh·KET) *n.* a woman who frivolously seeks men's attentions. — **co·quet·tish** (coh·KET·ish) *adj.*

cor·al (COR·ul) *n.* 1 a stonelike substance formed from the skeletons of marine polyps; also, such a polyp. 2 a deep or yellowish pink or red.
— *adj.: a coral atoll, island, reef.*

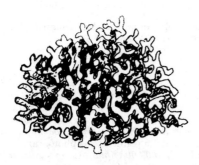

cord *n.* 1 a thin rope of several strands or fibres; hence, something similar: *an extension cord for a lamp; our vocal cords; the umbilical cord of a fetus; the spinal cord of nerve tissue; the cords* (= ribs) *on corduroy cloth; **Cords*** (= corduroy pants) *are not allowed by our dress code.* 2 a measure of cut wood piled 4 ft. × 4 ft. × 8 ft. (approximately 1.2 m × 1.2 m × 2.4 m).
— *v.* 1 tie or provide with a cord or cords. 2 pile wood in a cord.

cord·age (COR·dij) *n.* 1 cords and ropes collectively,

esp. the ropes of a ship's rigging. 2 the number of cords of wood in a given area.

cor·dial (COR·jul) *adj.* warm and hearty: *She was cordial to* or *toward us; He sent us cordial greetings; a cordial letter, welcome.*
— *n.* a liqueur; also, a stimulant. — **cor·dial·ly** *adv.*
— **cor·di·al·i·ty** (cor-dee-AL·uh·tee) *n.* **-ties.**

cord·less (CORD·lus) *adj.* operating without cord, i.e. by battery power: *a cordless electric shaver, telephone.*

cor·don (COR·dun) *n.* 1 a line of police, soldiers, or forts guarding or isolating an area: *They formed a cordon to keep back the crowds; The police threw a cordon around the area.* 2 a decorative cord worn as a sign of honour.
— *v.* put a protective cordon around something: *The police cordoned off the area.*

cor·du·roy (COR·duh·roy) *n.* 1 a stout-ribbed fabric. 2 corduroys *pl.* trousers made of this. 3 *Cdn.* same as **corduroy road,** a road built of logs laid across it in parallel rows, usually in a swampy area.

core *n.* 1 the centre of something, as the hard, seed-containing part in fruits: *an apple core; the core of the earth, sun; the core of a nuclear reactor; the centre core of a multi-lane highway; the downtown core; a 3% hard core of unemployable people; Explicit sex distinguishes hard-core from soft-core pornography.* 2 essence: *the core of the argument; the common core of meaning in the usages of a word; Prejudice is at the core of the problem.*
— **to the core** completely: *He is good, honest, conservative, rotten to the core.*
— *adj.* central: *a core factor to be borne in mind; a program of interdisciplinary **core courses;** a **core curriculum** of basic subjects; the random-access **core memory** of a computer using magnetic storage techniques; the 9:30-to-3:30 **core period** of a flexible-hours system when all personnel must be on the job; the **core vocabulary** of a reading program.*
— *v.* remove the core of a fruit. — **cor·er** *n.*

core city *n.* the centre of a large urban area; inner city; central city.

cork *n.* 1 the thick outer bark of a Mediterranean oak (**cork oak**) used for bottle stoppers, insulation, floats, etc. 2 a stopper for a bottle, esp. one made of cork: *to pop* or *remove a cork.*

corked (CORKT) *adj.* fouled by a bad cork: *corked wine.*

cork·screw *n.* a pointed metal spiral with a handle, used for pulling corks from bottles.

corn *n.* 1 a cultivated cereal grass bearing kernels on large ears; maize; also, the kernels or ears of this: *an ear of corn; corn on the cob; to grow, raise, husk corn; hybrid, Indian, sweet, young corn.* 2 any cereal grass or its seeds, esp. the dominant grain of an area. 3 *Slang.* something outdated or oversentimental. 4 a thickening of the skin at a point of friction or pressure, esp. on the feet.

cor·ne·a (COR·nee·uh) *n.* the transparent covering over the pupil and iris of the eye.
— **cor·ne·al** *adj.: a corneal transplant.*

corned beef *n.* beef cured by salting: *corned beef on rye.*

cor·ner (COR·nur) *n.* **1** the intersection of two lines, planes, or streets: *It's in the corner of the room; a figure with four square corners; meet me at* or *on the corner of King and Yonge streets; the upper right corner of a page; He hit his head on the corner of the cupboard; The phone booth is around the corner; You'll see it when you turn* or *round the corner.* **2** an area or region, esp. a quiet or remote place: *a quiet corner of the library; thoughts passing through the dark corners of the mind; a blind corner (that you cannot see); I could see what was going on out of the corner of my eye; People came from the (four) corners of the earth* or *globe; from all corners of the world; The news was flashed to every corner of the earth; I'm in your corner (Informal for* I'm your supporter). **3** a difficult position to escape from: *He found himself backed into a corner; He had painted himself into a corner; a tight corner; The patient has turned the corner (=*improved) *after being on the critical list.* **4** sufficient control of a commodity to force a price rise: *We have a corner on wheat (=* on the wheat market).
— **around the corner** very near: *They live around the corner; Christmas is just around the corner.*
— **cut corners** economize.
— *v.* **1** turn a corner: *Slow down for cornering.* **2** drive into a corner: *a fugitive cornered by the police.* **3** gain control of something: *to corner the market on wheat.*

cor·ner·stone (COR·nur·stone) *n.* **1** a stone joining walls at a corner, often one ceremonially laid in a building's foundation: *The mayor will lay the cornerstone of the new city hall.* **2** basic foundation: *Free elections are the cornerstone of democracy.*

corn·meal *n.* meal coarsely ground from corn.

corn·row (CORN·roh) *n.* a style of arranging hair in braided rows placed flat on the scalp.

corn snow *n.* coarse-grained snow resulting from melting and refreezing.

corn·starch *n.* a refined corn flour used to thicken sauces and in making **corn sugar,** dextrose, and **corn syrup** which contains glucose.

cor·nu·co·pi·a (cor·nuh·COH·pee·uh) *n.* **1** a horn of plenty, shown overflowing with fruits. **2** an abundance: *a cornucopia of fringe benefits.*

corn·y (COR·nee) *adj.* **corn·i·er, -i·est** *Informal.* rustic; old-fashioned; hackneyed; oversentimental: *a corny joke; corny old love songs; Just because I look corny, it doesn't mean I am, says Dolly.*

co·rol·la (cuh·ROL·uh, -ROH·luh) *n.* the petals around a flower.

cor·ol·lar·y (cuh·ROL·uh·ree, COR·uh·lair·ee) *n.* **-ol·lar·ies** a logical consequence; result; accompanying fact: *Good health comes as a corollary to good eating habits; good eating habits and the corollary good health.*

cor·o·nar·y (COR·uh·nair·ee) *adj.* **1** of or like a crown; encircling. **2** having to do with the arteries that conduct blood to the heart muscle: *coronary artery; a coronary care unit for heart patients; coronary heart disease.*
— *n., pl.* **-nar·ies** a blockage in a coronary artery in the heart caused by a blood clot.

cor·o·na·tion (cor·uh·NAY·shun) *n.* the crowning of a king, queen, pope, etc.: *to hold a coronation.*

cor·o·ner (COR·uh·nur) *n.* a public official who investigates deaths that may not be from natural causes.

cor·o·net (cor·uh·NET) *n.* **1** a jewelled headband; ornamental garland. **2** a smaller crown worn by nonsovereign nobility or royalty.

corpora *pl.* of CORPUS.

cor·po·ral (COR·puh·rul) *n.* **1** in the Canadian Armed Forces, a noncommissioned officer below sergeant. **2** a similar rank in the Ontario Provincial Police. **3** a similar rank in the army or marines of the U.S. and other countries. — *adj.* physical: *corporal punishment.*

cor·po·rate (COR·puh·rit) *adj.* **1** of, like, or shared by a united group: *corporate action, effort, endeavour, responsibility.* **2** having to do with a corporation: *a corporate body, bond, chain, crime, elite, headquarters, image, sponsor; A company's distinctive policies and behaviour styles constitute its **corporate culture**; corporate greed, income tax, law, property, structure.*

cor·po·ra·tion (cor·puh·RAY·shun) *n.* a group such as a business firm or municipality that is authorized to act as one legal entity: *The Borough of North York became a corporation in 1979; the Canadian Broadcasting Corporation; to dissolve, establish* or *set up* or *form, manage, run a corporation; a charitable* or *nonprofit corporation such as the Red Cross; commercial, foreign-owned, multinational, municipal corporations.*

corps (COR) *n. sing. & pl.* **1** an organized group of people following the same occupation: *the diplomatic corps in Ottawa; the press corps; a volunteer corps; the **Corps of Commissionaires** (=* former members of the armed forces who work as private guards, watchmen, etc.). **2** a branch of the armed forces providing a special service: *a medical corps; the Signal Corps; the U.S. Marine Corps; the Corps of Engineers.* **3** an army unit made up of more than one division: *an air, army corps; a corps of marines.*

corpse (CORPS) *n.* a dead, usually human body: *to lay out a corpse for burial; to bury, dig up a corpse; to exhume a corpse for an autopsy.*

corps·man (COR·mun) *n.* **-men** same as AIDMAN.

cor·pus (COR·pus) *n., pl.* **-por·a** (-puh·ruh) **1** a body of writings or texts: *the corpus of Shakespeare's works; to collect* or *gather a corpus of materials for a dictionary.* **2** the main part of a bodily organ or structure.

cor·pus·cle (COR·puh·sul) *n.* **1** a small, free-floating blood or lymph cell: *red and white corpuscles.* **2** a tiny particle, as in early theories of electricity and light propagation.

cor·ral (cuh·RAL) *n.* **1** a pen for horses or cattle. **2** a defensive circle of vehicles, as wagons.
— *v.* **cor·rals, cor·ralled, cor·ral·ling** *Informal.* surround and catch: *Cowboys corral wild horses; Police corral drug dealers; A party whip corrals (=*gathers) *votes.*

cor·rect (cuh·RECT) *v.* **1** set right what is wrong: *to correct abuses, errors, excesses, mistakes; Eyeglasses correct vision.* **2** point out errors in a person or thing: *to correct exam papers, Parents have to correct* (= discipline) *their children.*
— *adj.* **1** free from fault or error, often according to a standard: *the correct information; a correct answer, translation; Is it correct that he was fired? She's correct in thinking he was fired, but he claims it is more correct to say he resigned.* **2** proper: *correct behaviour, manners; a correct young man.*

cor·rec·tion (cuh·REC·shun) *n.* **1** a correcting: *if I may make a correction; to mark corrections in a text.* **2** that which makes or marks a correction: *The clock needed a correction of two minutes.* **3** the treatment of offenders: *The correction of criminals outside the prison is usually by putting them on probation.*
— **cor·rec·tion·al** *adj.* having to do with correction: *a correctional centre* or *facility* (= jail); *correctional institutions; a correctional officer* (= prison guard); *correctional standards.*
— **cor·rec·tive** *adj.* meant to correct; remedial: *corrective justice, lenses, surgery, training; a corrective measure; n.: Glasses are a corrective for faulty vision.*
— **cor·rect·ly** *adv.;* **cor·rect·ness** *n.*

cor·re·late (COR·uh·late) *v.* **-lates, -lat·ed, -lat·ing** stand in or bring into a mutual or systematic relationship: *We correlate lower speed limits with greater safety.*
— *n.* a correlated factor: *The diameter of a circle is a correlate of its circumference.*
— **cor·re·la·tion** (cor·uh·LAY·shun) *n.: There's a correlation between lower speed limits and greater safety.*

cor·rel·a·tive (cuh·REL·uh·tiv) *adj.* corresponding: *strikes and the correlative loss of productivity.*

cor·res·pond (cor·uh·SPOND) *v.* **1** agree: *Actual costs do not correspond with budget estimates.* **2** be parallel or similar: *The Latin "pater" corresponds to the English "father"; Our Senate corresponds to the British House of Lords; the* **corresponding** *period of the last financial year.* **3** communicate by mail: *They corresponded (with each other) for many years before meeting; a* **corresponding member** *of a society (who lives far away and keeps in touch by mail).*

cor·re·spond·ence (cor·uh·SPOND·unce) *n.* **1** conformity or agreement: *His actions have no close correspondence with his promises; There is no one-to-one correspondence between sounds and letters, as "c" may sound as (s) in "nice" and (k) in "cat"; the correspondence between theory and practice; the correspondences* (= similarities) *between the two jobs.* **2** communication by letter: *to break off, carry on* or *conduct a correspondence; business, commercial, personal correspondence; She was in correspondence with her parents about marrying Jim; The correspondence between them has not been published; A* **correspondence course** *is conducted by mail.*

cor·re·spond·ent (cor·uh·SPOND·unt) *adj.* corresponding: *inflation and correspondent wage increases.*
— *n.* one who communicates by mail, esp. a newspaper reporter: *our London correspondent; a foreign, special,* war correspondent.

cor·ri·dor (COR·uh·dor) *n.* **1** a long passageway or hall: *Room 233 is down the corridor; Room 204 is across the corridor from 201; You walk through a long, narrow, winding corridor to reach her office; the* **corridors of power** (= places of influence) *reserved to the elite.* **2** a narrow path for access or transportation: *a high-speed rail corridor to downtown; Highway 401 is in the crowded commuter corridor north of Metro Toronto; land acquired for a transportation corridor.*

cor·rob·o·rate (cuh·ROB·uh·rate) *v.* **-rates, -rat·ed, -rat·ing** support someone's evidence, a theory, etc.: *An independent witness corroborated her story.*
— **cor·rob·o·ra·tion** (-RAY·shun) *n.*

cor·rode (cuh·RODE) *v.* **cor·rodes, cor·rod·ed, cor·rod·ing** eat away, destroy, or deteriorate slowly, as by chemical action: *a badly corroded battery terminal.*
— **cor·ro·sion** (cuh·ROH·zhun) *n.*

cor·ro·sive (cuh·ROH·siv) *adj.* that corrodes: *the corrosive action of salt water; a corrosive agent, effect; corrosive substances such as acid, cleaning fluid, and drain cleaner.* — *n.* a corrosive substance.

cor·ru·gate (COR·uh·gate) *v.* **-gates, -gat·ed, -gat·ing** form into parallel ridges and furrows: *corrugated iron roofing; corrugated paper; a corrugated* (= furrowed) *brow.* — **cor·ru·ga·tion** (-GAY·shun) *n.*

cor·rupt (cuh·RUPT) *adj.* **1** no longer pure; made evil, tainted, or immoral: *children made corrupt by the bad example of their elders; corrupt desires; a corrupt life; the corrupt* (= changed by usage) *form of a word.* **2** dishonest: *a corrupt customs official, judge, politician; corrupt practices such as bribery and ballot-box stuffing.*
— *v.* make corrupt: *The old man was charged with corrupting youth; Power corrupts; Bodies corrupt* (= decay); *Malayalam "kattil" was corrupted* (= changed by usage) *to English "cot."*
— **cor·rupt·er** or **cor·rup·tor** *n.*
— **cor·rup·tion** *n.: political corruption; bribery and corruption; "Cot" is actually a corruption* (= changed form) *of Malayalam "kattil."* — **cor·rupt·ly** *adv.*

cor·sage (cor·SAHZH) *n.* a small bouquet worn by a woman on the shoulder, waist, or wrist.

cor·set (COR·sut) *n.* a tight, often laced, woman's undergarment for shaping the figure.

cor·tege or **cor·tège** (cor·TEZH) *n.* a following of attendants; also, a procession: *a funeral cortege.*

cor·tex (COR·tex) *n., pl.* **-ti·ces** (-tuh·seez) or **-tex·es** an outer layer of covering tissue on an organ or plant part: *adrenal, cerebral cortex; The cortex, or middle layer of bark, contains chlorophyll.*

cor·ti·cal (COR·tuh·cul) *adj.* of a cortex, esp. of the brain cortex.

co·sign (COH·sine) *v.* sign a document along with another signer.

cosily, cosiness See COSY.

cos·met·ic (coz·MET·ic) *n.* **1** a substance, as lipstick, face powder, eye shadow, etc. for beautifying the skin,

hair, nails, etc.: *to apply, put on, use cosmetics.*
2 anything that superficially covers up defects.
— *adj.* serving to improve appearance: *a cosmetic cream, preparation; a name that has only cosmetic appeal; a merely cosmetic antipoverty program; cosmetic surgery.* — **cos·met·i·cal·ly** *adv.*

cos·mic (COZ·mic) *adj.* 1 having to do with the cosmos: *cosmic forces, harmony;* **Cosmic rays** *enter our atmosphere from outer space.* 2 huge; endless: *the cosmic proportions of our universe; its cosmic vastness.* — **cos·mi·cal·ly** *adv.*

cos·mo·naut (COZ·muh·nawt) *n.* a Soviet astronaut.

cos·mo·pol·i·tan (coz·muh·POL·uh·tun) *adj.*
1 representing the whole world: *Recent immigration has made Toronto one of the most cosmopolitan cities of Canada; The "peregrine falcon" is a cosmopolitan bird (that once lived throughout the world); a cosmopolitan background, centre, clientele, community, metropolis, population, society.* 2 not narrow or regional in outlook: *the cosmopolitan world of art; The cosmopolitan person is at home in any part of the world; a cosmopolitan atmosphere, charm, lifestyle, taste, vision.*
— *n.* one who is cosmopolitan: *a cosmopolitan and a famous world traveller.*

cos·mos (COZ·mus, COZ·mos) *n.* the universe as an ordered whole; hence, any complex, harmonious system.

cost *n.* 1 the price of something: *the high cost of housing; The average cost of a home goes up each spring; a cost that is hard to bear; We estimated the unit cost* (= what each copy would cost) *of the publication; We put* or *set the cost at $25; She decided to fight the election* **at all costs** or **at any cost** *without stopping to* **count the cost;** *He won the election at the cost of his health, home, and family; It was a terrible cost to pay; a service provided at no cost to the taxpayer.* 2 expenses: *We are trying to cut* or *reduce heating costs; His parents spared no cost to put him through college; He was fined $500 and* **costs** (= expenses of the lawsuit); *They paid his court costs; There are direct, fixed, indirect, overhead costs to be considered.*
— *v.* 1 **costs, cost, cost·ing** require or entail as a payment or loss: *Houses cost too much; How much did it cost? It cost (us) $200 000; His mistake cost him dearly; It cost him his job.* 2 **costs, cost·ed, cost·ing** determine the cost of something: *We costed out the book to determine if it was publishable.*

co-star (COH·star) *n.* a star of equal rank.
— *v.* **-stars, -starred, -star·ring:** *Vivien Leigh co-starred with Clark Gable in "Gone With the Wind"; Vivien Leigh co-starred in the movie.*

cost-effective (cos·tuh·FEC·tiv) *adj.* beneficial in proportion to the cost: *Computerization is cost-effective; cost-effective measures; a cost-effective system.*

cost·ly *adj.* **-li·er, -li·est** that costs a great deal: *costly furs and jewels; a costly production delay; a costly victory; It's costly to replace the stolen furs.*
— **cost·li·ness** *n.*

cost of living *n.* the average cost of food, shelter, clothing, and other necessities: *The cost of living has gone up twofold during the last 10 years; The strikers' demands included a better* **cost-of-living allowance** or **COLA;** *The* **cost-of-living index** *is a measure of how*

the cost of living changes periodically.

cos·tume (COS·tyoom, -toom – long "oo") *n.* a set of clothes: *an academic, ballet, bathing, ethnic, folk, Halloween, Indian, national, native, peasant, stage costume.*
— *v.* **-tumes, -tumed, -tum·ing** dress: *an actress costumed in Elizabethan style.*
— **cos·tum·er** (cos·TUE·mur) or **cos·tum·i·er** (cos·TUE·mee·ur) *n.*

costume jewellery or **costume jewelry** *n.* inexpensive artificial ornaments made of glass, plastics, wood, leather, etc.

co·sy (COH·zee) *adj.* **co·si·er, co·si·est** 1 snug and comfortable: *the cat sleeping in a cosy corner of the sofa.* 2 *Informal.* beneficial as the result of a secret arrangement: *a cosy little deal.*
— *v.* **-sies, -sied, -sy·ing** become friendly with someone: *The Tory government was accused of* **cosying up to** *America.*
— *n., pl.* **-sies** a covering for a teapot to keep it warm: *a tea cosy.* — **co·si·ly** *adv.;* **co·si·ness** *n.* Also **co·zy.**

cot *n.* 1 a narrow bed of canvas over a usually collapsible frame. 2 also **cote** (COHT), a shelter or shed, esp. for animals: *a dove cot.*

cot death *n.* same as CRIB DEATH.

co·te·rie (COH·tuh·ree) *n.* a usually exclusive circle of people with a shared interest: *a literary coterie.*

cot·tage (COT·ij) *n.* a small, usually rural house; also, a summer house: *We drive to the cottage on weekends.*
— **cot·tag·er** *n.*

cottage cheese *n.* a soft, mild cheese made from soured skim milk.

cottage industry *n.* a small-scale manufacturing activity carried on as from home.

cot·ter or **cotter pin** *n.* a split pin used to hold parts in place, inserted through a hole and fastened by spreading the tips.

cot·ton (COT·un) *n.* 1 thread or cloth made from the white, fluffy seed hairs of a bushy plant. 2 the seed hairs or the plant itself: *absorbent cotton; a bale of cotton; to pick cotton.*
— **cotton on to** *Informal.* understand.
— **cotton to** take a liking to someone.
— **cot·ton·y** *adj.: The wind carries the feathered, cottony dandelion seeds far and wide.*

cotton candy *n.* a fluffy candy spun from melted sugar.

cotton-picking *adj. Informal.* damned: *Politicians should keep their cotton-picking hands out of the private lives of people.*

couch (COWCH) *n.* a piece of furniture for sitting or lying down; sofa: *the psychoanalyst's couch; a studio couch.*
— *v.* 1 lay or lie on or as on a couch: *Ambushers couched in the bushes.* 2 to phrase: *a request couched in diplomatic language.*

couch potato *n.* one who spends too much time watching TV.

cou·gar (COO·gur) *n.* a large, light-brown wildcat.

cough (CAWF) *v.* 1 emit air forcefully and noisily from the lungs: *a fit of coughing.* 2 utter or expel by coughing: *He coughed up the fishbone that was choking him; She had no problem **coughing up** (Slang for producing) the cash they demanded.*
— *n.:* *a cold with a bad cough; a hacking, heavy, persistent cough.*

could (COOD, short "OO") *pt.* of CAN [also used to express possibility, condition, permission, etc.]: *Could I see you for a minute? It could happen here; It could be serious if help doesn't arrive fast.*

could·n't (COOD·unt, short "OO") could not.

cou·lee (COO·lee) *n. Cdn.* in the Prairies, a stream bed or gully that is usually dry in summer.

coun·cil (COWN·sil) *n.* a body or assembly chosen to discuss, advise, administer, or legislate: *the executive council; student council; The Privy Council; The Security Council; The mayor convened the town council.*

coun·cil·lor (COWN·suh·lur) *n.* 1 a member of a council; also **coun·cil·or.** 2 in Prince Edward Island, one of the legislators elected by the property owners.

coun·sel (COWN·sul) *v.* **-sels, -selled** or **-seled, -sel·ling** or **-sel·ing** give advice to someone: *The lawyer counselled his client about her problem; He counselled her against acting rashly; counselled her to be patient; He counselled (=urged) patience; She felt good about having counselled with (=consulted) him.*
— *n.* 1 advice: *to give, offer counsel; sage, wise counsel; Let us **take counsel together** (=discuss this together), then **take counsel with** (=get advice from) our lawyer; I don't like to **keep my own counsel** (=keep my plans secret).* 2 *sing. & pl.* legal adviser(s); lawyer(s): *legal counsel; Queen's Counsel; counsel (=a lawyer) for the defence; counsel for the prosecution.*

counselling or **counseling** (COWN·suh·ling) *n.* the giving of advice: *career, family, guidance, marriage, vocational counselling.*

coun·sel·lor or **coun·se·lor** (COWN·suh·lur) *n.* 1 adviser: *a career counsellor at our high school; a guidance counsellor; He's a counsellor at the High Commission; a counsellor to the ambassador; a counsellor in the State Department.* 2 a lawyer.

count *v.* 1 recite numbers in order: *Children learn to count (in ascending order); Can you count (from one) to ten in French? Before a rocket lifts off, they say, "T*

minus *30 seconds and counting" (down to zero); They* **count down** *(in reverse order) to zero.* 2 match a series of objects to such a series of numbers; total up: *Count your change; Let's **count heads** or **noses** to see how many are here.* 3 consider: *Count yourself lucky to be alive; They'll count an 80% mark as an A; It counts (=is considered) as an A; If you count Jim (=take him into consideration), there are six of us; Please **count me in** (=include me) as a member; If it's something illegal, you can **count me out** (=leave me out); A boxer is **counted out** (=loses) if he doesn't get up in ten seconds after being knocked down.* 4 depend or rely: *Never **count on** the weather; You can **count (up)on** us for help, to support you; You can **count on** winning (=expect to win).* 5 be of significant value: *Nowadays connections in high places don't **count for** much; Your marks count; They **count toward** qualifying for admission to college; One low mark won't **count against** you.*
— *n.* 1 a counting or the resulting number: *Someone please **keep count** of the guests; Let's make or take an accurate, correct, exact body count; He got it right on the third count; What's the count (=total) now? The count stands at 237; It's 239 by my count; We've now **lost count** of them because of newcomers.* 2 a charge in an indictment: *five counts of robbery; He was found guilty on all counts.* 3 a European noble whose rank is analogous to that of an earl. — **count·a·ble** *adj.*

count·down *n.* a counting backward to the zero hour: *The countdown began at 16:00 hours; the final countdown for the moon flight; The countdown continues, ". . . 3, 2, 1, lift off!"*

coun·te·nance (COWN·tuh·nunce) *n.* 1 a person's face, esp. as expressing feelings: *an angry, happy, hideous, pleasant countenance.* 2 approval: *As vegetarians, we cannot give or lend countenance to killing in any form.* 3 composure; self-control: *Her icy stare put him **out of countenance**; The joke was so funny she could not **keep her countenance** (=could not help laughing).*
— *v.* **-nan·ces, -nanced, -nanc·ing** approve or tolerate: *We cannot countenance killing in any form.*

count·er *n.* 1 one that counts: *a calorie counter's guide to dieting.* 2 a token, chip, etc. used for counting or in games. 3 a long table, board, or other flat surface for displaying wares, conducting business, serving or preparing food, etc.: *a bargain, jewellery, kitchen, lunch counter; Drugs sold **over the counter** don't need a prescription; over-the-counter trading of securities (through a broker); Sometimes payments, sales, etc. are made **under the counter** (=illicitly).* 4 the opposite; a checking action: *an effective counter to the attack.*
— *adj. & adv.* contrary: *Sorry, but your ideas go or run counter to accepted theories.*
— *v.* act or speak in opposition to a person or thing; strike or answer back; offset: *efforts to counter inflationary losses; Her opponent countered that the question was irrelevant; The boxer countered (the blow) with a left hook.*

coun·ter·act (cown·tur·ACT) *v.* oppose or offset: *a drug to counteract the poison.*

coun·ter·at·tack (COWN·tur·uh·TACK) *n. & v.* attack in response: *They lost the battle, but counterattacked the next day; to launch, make a counterattack against the enemy.*

coun·ter·bal·ance (cown·tur·BAL·unce) *v.* **-anc·es,**
-anced, -anc·ing oppose with equal weight; offset.
— *n.* (COWN·tur·bal·unce) a weight or force that
balances or offsets another: *He boasts many strengths as
a counterbalance to his one weakness.*

coun·ter·claim (COWN·tur·claim) *n.* an opposing claim,
as in law against a plaintiff: *to bring, enter, make, plead
a counterclaim against the plaintiff.*
— *v.: The defendant counterclaimed $2 million.*

coun·ter·clock·wise (cown·tur·CLOCK·wize) *adj. & adv.*
opposite in direction to the turning of a clock's hands.

coun·ter·cul·ture (COWN·tur·cul·chur) *n.* a culture
with values opposed to the rest of society, as among
youth: *The new counterculture is more into vegetables
than drugs.* — **coun·ter·cul·tur·al** (-CUL·chuh·rul) *adj.*

coun·ter·feit (COWN·tur·fit) *v.* make an imitation or
replica, as of currency, so as to deceive or cheat: *They
went to jail for counterfeiting (bills); He only
counterfeited grief when she died.*
— *n. & adj.: This $20 bill seems a counterfeit; It's a
counterfeit twenty.*

coun·ter·in·tel·li·gence (COWN·tur·in·TEL·uh·junce)
n. action to thwart or mislead enemy spies or saboteurs:
to conduct counterintelligence.

coun·ter·mand (COWN·tur·mand) *v.* revoke or call back
an order with an opposite order.

coun·ter·mea·sure (COWN·tur·mezh·ur) *n.* opposing
measure: *Canada sometimes takes countermeasures
against foreign tariffs.*

coun·ter·of·fen·sive (COWN·tur·uh·fen·siv) *n.* an
offensive in anticipation of an attack: *to launch or
undertake a counteroffensive against the invaders.*

coun·ter·part (COWN·tur·part) *n.* one that is similar or
analogous: *The Secretary of State met her Russian
counterpart; Our prime minister has a counterpart in
the Russian premier; He is the counterpart of or to our
prime minister.*

coun·ter·point (COWN·tur·point) *n.* **1** a melody in
contrasting harmony to the main melody; also, music
having this. **2** a foil or contrast for something: *The
funeral was a sad counterpoint to springtime.*

coun·ter·poise (COWN·tur·poiz) *n.* counterbalance;
equilibrium. Also *v.* **-pois·es, -poised, -pois·ing.**

coun·ter·pro·duc·tive (COWN·tur·pruh·DUC·tiv) *adj.*
having results opposite to those desired: *The punishment
was so severe it proved to be counterproductive.*

coun·ter·sign (COWN·tur·sign) *v.* sign an already signed
document to authenticate it.
— *n.* such a signature; also **coun·ter·sig·na·ture.**

coun·ter·vail (COWN·tur·vail) *v.* **1** act against
successfully; counteract: *a countervailing pressure to
take action; countervailing advice; countervailing
military strength.* **2** compensate: *a countervailing
tendency, tariff.*

count·ess (COWN·tis) *n.* an earl's or count's wife or
widow.

count·less (COUNT·lis) *adj.* too numerous to be
counted: *countless hordes of insects; countless numbers
of people.*

coun·tri·fied (CUN·truh·fide) *adj.* rustic; also, rural: *a
countrified design, setting, version.*

coun·try (CUN·tree) *n.* **-tries 1** a nation; also, its
territory: *to govern or rule or run a country; a civilized,
developing, host, neighbouring, Third-World country.*
2 a district or region: *mountainous country.* **3** a rural
area: *living out in the country; the back, open, rough,
rugged country.*
— *adj.* **1** rural: *country roads.* **2** rustic: *country
bumpkins, manners.* **3** having to do with country music:
a country singer.

country club *n.* a suburban social club, usually having a
golf course and other sports facilities.

country cousin *n.* a relative from the country who is new
to city ways.

country-dance (CUN·tree·dance) *n.* a native English
folk dance in which dancers are arranged in two facing
lines, a square, or a circle.

coun·try·man (CUN·tree·mun) *n.* **-men 1** a man from
one's own country; compatriot. **2** (*also* **-man**) a rustic.

country mile *n. Informal.* long distance: *to walk a
country mile; the best politician within a country mile of
Parliament Hill.*

country music *n.* a modernization of the rural folk
music of southern and western United States.

coun·try·side (CUN·tree·side) *n.* a rural area: *Let's visit
the countryside; The whole countryside* (= rural
population) *is behind the farmers.*

coun·try·wom·an (CUN·tree·wom·an) *n.* **-wom·en 1** a
woman from one's own country; compatriot: *She led her
countrywomen in a 15-year campaign for equal rights.*
2 a rustic woman.

coun·ty (COWN·tee) *n.* **-ties** the major administrative
division of a state, province, or of a country, as in
Britain: *Since 1969, counties have been grouped under
regions in Ontario.*

coup (COO) *n.* **coups** (COOZ) **1** a sudden, strikingly
successful action: *Smith scored a big coup over his rivals
by being first.* **2** a sudden, usually violent change in
government: *to carry out, stage a coup; a bloodless
coup; a bloody coup by the army; a military coup;* also
coup d'é·tat (-day·TAH).

coupe (COOP) *n.* a closed, two-door car smaller than a
sedan: *a hatchback coupe.*

cou·pé (coo·PAY) *n.* **1** a closed carriage that seats two
people inside and the driver outside. **2** a coupe.

cou·ple (CUP·ul) *v.* **-ples, -pled, -pling** join or link
together; unite: *A locomotive is coupled to a train.*
— *n.* **1** two similar things: *a couple of old boots that
don't match as a pair.* **2** *Informal.* a few: *a couple of
days back.* **3** two people, esp. a man and a woman
considered as partners or mates: *a married couple;
unmarried couples; couples swirling on the dance floor.*
4 a link or fastener.

cou·pler (CUP·lur) *n.* one that couples: *A railway car
has a coupler at each end.*

cou·plet (CUP·lit) *n.* two consecutive, usually rhyming
lines of verse in the same metre, as: *"Those who in*

quarrels interpose / Must often wipe a bloody nose."

cou·pon (COO·pon, CUE-) *n.* **1** a ticket, part of a package or advertisement, etc. entitling the bearer to a discount, refund, etc. or for use in ordering by mail: *to detach, redeem a coupon.* **2** a detachable interest certificate on a bond: *to clip coupons.*

cour·age (CUR·ij) *n.* the ability to persevere in the face of danger or hardship; bravery: *to demonstrate* or *display* or *show courage; to get up* or *muster* or *summon up courage; a woman of great courage; He lacks the courage to stand up for his rights; It takes courage to do it; the dauntless* or *indomitable courage of our pioneers; grim, moral, physical courage; He has the **courage of his convictions** to do what he thinks is right.*
— **cou·ra·geous** (cuh·RAY·jus) *adj.*
— **cou·ra·geous·ly** *adv.*

cou·reur de bois (coo·RUR·duh·bwah) *n.* **cou·reurs de bois** (coo·RUR·duh-) *Cdn.* formerly, a French or Métis woodsman and fur trader: *a latter-day coureur de bois on a weekend of orienteering.*

cou·ri·er (COOR·ee·ur, CUR·ee·ur) *n.* one who carries messages, official papers, goods, etc.: *to dispatch a courier to the head office; We'll send it to you by courier; a diplomatic courier;* ***adj.:*** *courier delivery, services, traffic.*

course (CORSE) *n.* **1** a progression in space or time: *the course of events; the winding course of a river.* **2** the normal order, development, or duration: *the course of true love; The disease has run its course* (= is over); *He does favours for friends **as a matter of course*** (= as something normal or natural); *You will receive a reply **in due course*** (= when it is time); *They lost $5 million **in the course of*** (= during) *a month.* **3** route; direction: *What course are we sailing? to chalk out a course of action; Your only course may be to flee; to stay* (= persevere in) *the course; to steer* (= pursue) *the course; The plane went **off course** and was shot down by the enemy; Our plane is **on course** for Vancouver.* **4** a study program: *They conduct* or *give* or *offer* or *teach courses in many areas; a course in calculus; a course on family planning; They cancel, introduce, organize, plan courses; Students may audit* or *sit in on courses; They complete, drop, drop out of, enrol for, fail, pass, register for, sign up for, take, withdraw from courses; There are advanced, beginning, correspondence, demanding, difficult, easy, elective, elementary, extension, graduate, gut, intensive, intermediate, introductory, laboratory, lecture, makeup, noncredit, refresher, required, rigorous, survey, undergraduate courses; Courses cover, deal with, treat subjects.* **5** an ordered series: *a course of lectures, studies; to undergo a course of treatment; a six-course dinner; a course* (= layer) *of bricks.*
— **of course 1** certainly: *Of course, she's right.* **2** as one would expect: *Everyone, of course, has to pay a fee.*
— *v.* **cours·es, coursed, cours·ing 1** move, run, or flow swiftly: *Blood courses through the veins.* **2** hunt, esp. deer or rabbits, with hounds.

course·ware (CORS·ware) *n.* software for teaching purposes.

court (CORT) *n.* **1** a judge or judges who try legal cases; also, the place where this is done: *to take a person to court; to testify in court; in open court; A court*

*adjourns; to hold court; Too many cases clog the courts; an appellate, circuit, county, criminal, district, family, federal, high, juvenile, moot, municipal, night, probate, small claims, superior, supreme, traffic, trial court; Order in the court! a court of appeals, chancery, common pleas, equity, law; The **Court of Queen's Bench*** (= superior court) *of Manitoba.* **2** an open area with one or more buildings around it; courtyard. **3** an open area for playing a game such as tennis or basketball. **4** a king, queen, etc. with his or her family, retinue, advisers, and ministers; an assembly of this; also, a royal palace: *The royal family holds court; Visitors are presented at court; at the Court of St. James* or *at St. James's* (= at the British royal court); *a court jester.*
— *v.* try to gain the favour or love of someone; woo; also, tempt: *Those who drink and drive are courting disaster.*
— **out of court 1** without a trial: *a case settled out of court.* **2** unworthy of being given a hearing: *His wild schemes are quite out of court; They will be **laughed out of court*** (= dismissed as ridiculous).
— **pay court to someone** *Formal.* try to please or woo someone.

cour·te·ous (CUR·tee·us) *adj.* gracious and considerate in manner. — **cour·te·ous·ly** *adv.*

cour·te·san (COR·tuh·zun) *n.* a prostitute with a wealthy or high-ranking clientele; also **cour·te·zan.**

cour·te·sy (CUR·tuh·see) *n.* **-sies** (an instance of) polite, considerate, well-mannered behaviour: *He showed us every courtesy; her professional, unfailing courtesy; as a courtesy to* or *toward new customers; He didn't have the courtesy to answer our letters; He did us the courtesy of not interrupting our conversation; as common courtesy dictates; Coffee and donuts are **courtesy of*** (= offered with the compliments of) *the management.*

court·house *n.* a building housing law courts.

cour·ti·er (COR·tee·ur) *n.* a member of a royal court.

court·ly (CORT·lee) *adj.* **-li·er, -li·est** polite and dignified; refined: *courtly love, manners; the courtly Mr. Smith.* — **court·li·ness** *n.*

court-martial (CORT·marsh·ul) *n.* **courts-martial** or **court-martials 1** a military court that tries offenders against military law. **2** such a trial: *to hold a court-martial; a general, special, summary court-martial.*
— *v.* **-tials, -tialled** or **-tialed, -tial·ling** or **-tial·ing:** *He was court-martialled for disobeying orders.*

court·ship *n.* a wooing.

court·yard *n.* an open area surrounded by buildings or such an area inside a large building.

cous·in (CUZ·in) *n.* **1** a child of one's aunt or uncle; also called "first cousin": *a first cousin once removed* (= first cousin's child). **2** relative: *a distant cousin; kissing cousins* (= close relatives); *Words are **cousin*** (= related) *to the deed.*

couth (COOTH, long "OO") *n.* refinement or polish: *Our cook has more couth than your maitre d'.*

cou·ture (coo·TOOR) *n.* the work of a couturier.

cou·tu·ri·er (coo·TOOR·ee·ur) *n.* one who designs and makes high-fashion clothes for women.

— **cou·tu·ri·ère** or **cou·tu·ri·ere** (-ee·ur), *fem.*

cove (COHV) *n.* a small usually sheltered bay.

cov·e·nant (CUV·uh·nunt) *n.* 1 a formal and serious agreement: *God's covenant with Noah; the UN Covenant on Economic, Social, and Cultural Rights; a death covenant signed by lovers.* 2 a provision, as in a deed: *a covenant between real estate developers and home buyers restricting rooftop TV antennas; to ease restrictive covenants on homes.*
— *v.: They covenanted to deliver the steel on August 18 for a sum of $750.*

cov·er (CUV·ur) *v.* 1 to be or place something in front of, on top of, etc., esp. so as to conceal or protect; hence, lie or extend over something: *Snow covered the mountain; He covered his tracks to avoid detection; Will you **cover for** me* (= take my place) *while I'm away? a war hero covered with glory; Nixon was accused of **covering up*** (= concealing the truth) *in the Watergate affair.* 2 deal with something: *This book covers the whole subject; a reporter covering* (= reporting on) *the coronation live; I can't cover* (= travel over) *more than 900 km a day; money to cover* (= pay for) *all expenses.* 3 protect: *The house and contents are covered by this insurance policy; It covers you against all perils; The shortstop shifted to cover third base; Cover me (by shooting at the enemy) while I run for help; Keep him covered (by pointing your gun) so he won't escape; Bill covered* (= accepted) *my bet.*
— *n.* 1 something that covers, hides, or protects: *Put the cover on the box; a book mailed under separate cover* (= in another envelope); *a cloud, dust, mattress, pillow cover; a book with a torn cover; He read the book from **cover to cover;** They sought cover (during the attack); to provide air cover* (= protection) *for an advancing army; a sniper firing from cover; His business is just a cover for his spying; When the shooting starts, **take cover.*** 2 a place setting for one person at a table: *Covers were laid for 10.*
— **under cover** in concealment: *to work under cover as a spy; He came here under cover of darkness; State budgets are kept under cover till the last minute.*

cov·er·age (CUV·ur·ij) *n.* 1 a covering by insurance: *to provide coverage; comprehensive* or *full coverage.* 2 a reporting: *the coverage of an election; live TV coverage; The election received complete, extensive, full, wide coverage in the media.*

cover charge *n.* a fixed additional charge in a restaurant, night club, etc.

covered wagon *n.* a pioneer wagon with an arched roof of canvas.

cover girl *n.* a glamorous young woman, as one who appears on a magazine cover.

cov·er·let (CUV·ur·lit) *n.* a bedspread.

cover letter *n.* a letter that explains or supports something enclosed; also **covering letter.**

cover story *n.* 1 the leading story in a magazine as pictured on its cover. 2 a story made up to hide something.

cov·ert (COH·vurt, CUV·urt) 1 *adj.* hidden or disguised, esp. illegal and protected: *the Intelligence Agency's covert actions, operations.* 2 *n.* a hiding place,

esp. for game. — **cov·ert·ly** *adv.*

cover-up (CUV·ur·up) *n.* a device or attempt to hide something: *the Watergate cover-up.*

cov·et (CUV·it) *v.* strongly desire what is another's: *She coveted Jane's car and constantly borrowed it.*
— **cov·et·ous** (-us) *adj.: She is envious of Jane's good looks and covetous of her car.*

cow *n.* 1 an adult female bovine; also, an adult female walrus, elephant, dolphin, moose, etc.: *Holy cow! You can argue, complain, sit there, wait **till the cows come home*** (= forever), *but nothing will happen.* 2 **cows** [in cowboy use] cattle.
— *v.* intimidate: *They were cowed into submission.*

cow·ard (COW·urd) *n.* one shamefully lacking in courage: *an abject, dastardly, dirty coward.*
— *adj.: his coward* (= cowardly) *cries, deceit; a coward deed.* See also COWARDLY.

cow·ard·ice (COW·ur·dis) *n.* lack of courage: *to show cowardice; abject, moral, rank cowardice; the streak of cowardice in his makeup.*

cow·ard·ly (COW·urd·lee) *adj. & adv.* lacking courage: *a cowardly deed, excuse, lion.* — **cow·ard·li·ness** *n.*

cow·boy *n.* one who tends cattle on a ranch; also **cow·hand.**

cow chip *n.* a dried piece of cattle dung used as a fuel.

cow·er (COW·ur) *v.* huddle or cringe in fear.

cow·girl *n.* a woman who tends cattle on a ranch.

cow·hand *n.* a cowboy.

cowl (rhyme: "howl") *n.* a hood on a monk's habit.

cow·lick *n.* a tuft of hair that stubbornly sticks up.

cow·man *n.* -men a cattle rancher.

co-worker (COH·wur·kur) *n.* a fellow worker.

cow·poke or **cow·punch·er** (COW·punch·ur) *n.* Informal. a cowboy.

cox *n.* Informal. coxswain.

cox·comb *n.* a foolish, conceited fop.

cox·swain *n.* one who commands a ship's boat or a racing shell.

coy *adj.* 1 bashful: *a coy manner, smile, suggestion.* 2 pretending to be shy; also, teasing: *a coy reply; He was coy about his plans to run for mayor.*
— **coy·ly** *adv.;* **coy·ness** *n.*

coy·o·te (kye·OH·tee, KYE·ote) *n.* a small western North American wolf.

co·zy (COH·zee) *adj.* -zi·er, -zi·est same as COSY.

crab *n.* 1 a ten-legged, broad-shelled aquatic animal. 2 a "crab louse": *Crab lice infest the armpits, chest, etc. of a patient; The patient has **crabs.*** 3 a crab apple. 4 an ill-tempered grumbler.
— *v.* **crabs, crabbed, crab·bing** Informal. 1 complain ill-temperedly: *He keeps on crabbing that the winter is too long.* 2 ruin by meddling: *Don't crab my act.*

crab·bed (CRAB·id) *adj.* 1 crabby. 2 barely legible because cramped: *crabbed handwriting.*

crab·by (CRAB·ee) *adj.* **crab·bi·er, crab·bi·est** ill-tempered or complaining.
— **crab·bi·ly** *adv.;* **crab·bi·ness** *n.*

crack *v.* **1** make or cause to make a short, sharp noise: *to crack a whip; thunder cracking in the distance; He's good at cracking* (= telling) *jokes.* **2** break without separating into pieces: *The glass cracked in the heat; a cracked egg.* **3** change suddenly to a higher or a hoarse sound: *His voice cracked with emotion.* **4** distil petroleum into its component chemicals. **5** *Informal.* solve: *Detective Brown cracked the case.* **6** hit sharply. **7** *Informal.* open: *a student who didn't crack one book all year; She tried to make him crack a smile; They were nabbed by police before they could crack the brew; to crack* (= open by force) *a safe, vault.*
— **crack down** become more strict: *Police crack down on drunk drivers at Christmas.*
— **crack up 1** especially of a car or plane, crash: *The airliner cracked up because of metal fatigue.* **2** break down laughing. **3** *Informal.* break down mentally. **4 cracked up** reputed: *not quite what it is cracked up to be.*
— **get cracking** *Informal.* get moving or working fast: *Better get cracking if you want to finish on time.*
— *n.* **1** a sudden sharp sound, as of a whip, rifle fire, or thunder. **2** a narrow split or gap: *He looked through a crack in the wall.* **3** a cracking: *a crack in his voice.* **4** break: *We set out at the crack of dawn.* **5** a sharp blow: *a crack of the whip; I'll have a crack* (*Informal* for make an attempt) *at it; She likes to make cracks* (= quips or wisecracks) *about his bald head.* **6** a very pure form of cocaine for smoking.

crack·down *n.* imposition of strict measures: *The police launch a crackdown on drunken driving at Christmas.*

crack·er *n.* **1** a thin, dry biscuit: *graham, soda, salted crackers.* **2** a firecracker. **3** a party favour that opens with a snapping noise.

cracker-barrel *adj. Informal.* plain and down-to-earth: *a cracker-barrel discussion; her cracker-barrel humour, philosophy.*

crack·er·jack (CRACK·ur·jack) *adj. & n. Slang.* first-rate (person or thing).

crack·le (CRACK·ul) *v.* **-les, -led, -ling** make small cracking noises: *the crackling fire; a crackling* (= bubbly) *wine.*
— *n.* **1** a crackling noise: *the crackle of small-arms fire.* **2** many small cracks on china or porcelain; hence **crack·le·ware** *n.*

crack·pot *n. & adj. Informal.* eccentric: *There are some crackpots among the experts; some crackpot idea, notion, scheme, theory.*

cra·dle (CRAY·dul) *n.* **1** a baby's bed on rockers: *to rock a cradle.* **2** a frame to support something, esp. a telephone handset: *She tapped the cradle buttons to alert the operator but got disconnected.* **3** birthplace: *Charlottetown is the "Cradle of Confederation" because an 1864 conference held there led to Confederation; The Mediterranean region is believed to be the cradle of Western civilization.*
— **from the cradle to the grave** all one's life.
— **rob the cradle** have a much younger spouse or sweetheart.

— *v.* **-dles, -dled, -dling** place in or rock as if in a cradle: *She cradled his head in her lap.*

cradle-board (CRAY·dul·bord) *n. Cdn.* a device consisting of a board to which a bag is attached for carrying an infant on the back, as used by native Indian mothers.

craft *n.* **1** *sing. & pl.* a vessel or aircraft: *a landing craft; Small craft were swamped in the storm.* **2** *pl.* **crafts** a skill or skilled trade: *to learn, master, ply* or *practise a craft; arts and crafts; the people in a craft* (= occupation); *a craft union.* **3** sly cunning; skill in deceiving.

crafts·man (CRAFTS·mun) *n.* **-men** a skilled worker; artisan: *a master craftsman.* — **crafts·man·ship** *n.*

craft·y (CRAF·tee) *adj.* **craft·i·er, -i·est** showing craft; sly: *a crafty fox.* — **craft·i·ly** *adv.;* **craft·i·ness** *n.*

crag *n.* a rugged, steeply projecting mass of rock.
— **crag·gy** *adj.* **crag·gi·er, crag·gi·est:** *a craggy mountain.* — **crag·gi·ness** *n.*

cram *v.* **crams, crammed, cram·ming 1** fill too full or too fast; jam: *He crammed his books into the locker; a suitcase crammed full of* or *with clothes.* **2** feed or eat too much or too fast. **3** study hard at the last minute: *He's cramming for the test;* **n.:** *a desperate cram on the eve of the exam.* — **cram·mer** *n.*

cramp *n.* a sharp and painful muscle contraction: *He got a cramp in his leg while swimming; Bad eating habits may cause* **cramps** (= abdominal pain); *writer's cramp* (= stiffness of hand muscle).
— *v.* **1** suffer a cramp: *My leg cramped while I was asleep.* **2** restrict or place in a small space: *We are somewhat cramped for space; cramped accommodation; A heavy meal could* **cramp your style** (= spoil ease of performance). **3** turn a vehicle's wheels sharply.

cran·ber·ry (CRAN·ber·ee) *n.* **-ber·ries** a small red berry, used esp. for jelly and juice.

crane *n.* **1** a long-legged, long-necked wading bird similar to a heron or stork. **2** a hoisting machine having a projecting arm or a horizontal track: *He operates cranes.*
— *v.* **cranes, craned, cran·ing** stretch one's neck for a better view.

crank *n.* **1** a handle or rod bent at right angles to a rotating shaft: *Turn the crank to work the grinder.* **2** *Informal.* an eccentric and mischievous person; **adj.:** *a crank letter, phone call.*
— *v.* start or operate with a crank.

— **crank out** churn out: *a novelist who cranks out three romances a year.*

— **crank up** *Informal.* start up, as early auto engines.

crank·y *adj.* **crank·i·er, -i·est 1** irritable; eccentric. **2** working badly or fitfully.

cran·ny (CRAN·ee) *adj.* **cran·nies** a small corner or crevice: *He looked in every nook and cranny of the house for the lost diamond.*

crap 1 *n.* [vulgar] excrement; something worthless: *That's a pile of crap! He never expected to get or to have to take that kind of crap* (= nonsense). **2 craps** *pl.* [takes sing. v.] a gambling game played with two dice; *adj.: a crap game, table.*

crash *v.* **1** collide, break, fall, land, etc. with a great noise or damage: *The car crashed through a store window; It crashed into a wall; China crashed to the floor; The plane crashed in flames; The stock market crashed* (= collapsed) *on October 19, 1987.* **2** *Informal.* enter without permission or invitation: *to crash a party.* **3** *Slang.* sleep in a place without having to pay: *The poor guy used to crash with friends when he was broke.* — *n.* **1** a crashing sound: *a loud or resounding crash; the crash of sheet metal, of waves on the shore.* **2** a crashing, esp. a collision or collapse: *a plane crash; the stock market crash of 1987.* — *adj.* **1** done in the least possible time: *a crash course, diet, program, project; a submarine's crash* (= fast) *dive.* **2** having to do with crashing: *a **crash helmet** worn by motorcyclists for protection; A **crash landing** is a forced landing of an aircraft that damages it; a foam **crash mat** for gym use; the specially equipped **crash truck** used for aid at the scene of a plane crash.*

crash pad *n.* *Slang.* a place for nonpaying, temporary guests.

crass *adj.* grossly stupid: *crass avarice, behaviour, commercialism, ignorance, incompetence, stupidity; It was crass of him to offer her money for a labour of love.*

crate *n.* a storage or shipping case, esp. one made of wooden slats. — *v.* **crates, crat·ed, crat·ing** put in a crate: *The movers crated our piano.*

cra·ter (CRAY·tur) *n.* a funnel- or bowl-shaped hollow, as the mouth of a volcano: *a bomb crater; the craters on the moon.*

crave *v.* **craves, craved, crav·ing 1** ask for; beg: *to crave for forgiveness, mercy.* **2** desire strongly to satisfy a physical or emotional need: *to crave (for) admiration; to crave (after) affection; to crave (for) a drink; He feels or has a powerful or strong **craving** for a smoke even after quitting.*

cra·ven (CRAY·vun) *adj.* absolutely lacking in courage; cowardly: *a craven fear.* — *n.* coward: *a base craven.* — **cra·ven·ly** *adv.*

craw *n.* a bird's crop or animal's stomach. — **stick in the** or **one's craw** be unacceptable to one: *The appointments were so partisan that it stuck in our craw.*

crawl *v.* **1** move by pulling the body along the ground like a snake or worm; hence, move slowly; creep: *a crawling insect; A baby crawls on the floor till it can walk; Traffic crawled along at 15 km/h; to crawl out from under the table; to crawl into somebody's favour* (by being overly nice); *She's too self-respecting to crawl* (= degrade herself) *for a favour.* **2** swim a crawl stroke. **3** be covered with crawling things: *The kitchen floor was crawling with ants; a scary movie that makes your flesh crawl* (= feel as if covered with crawling things). — *n.* **1** a crawling movement; slow pace: *Rush-hour traffic slowed to a crawl; a backsplit house with **crawl space** beneath the first floor.* **2** a fast swimming stroke with alternate overarm movements, done lying prone with face in the water. — **crawl·er** *n.*

craw·ly *adj.* creepy.

cray·on (CRAY·on, -un) *n.* **1** a drawing stick of charcoal, coloured wax, or chalk: *coloured crayons.* **2** a drawing made with this. — **crayoned** *adj.* done with a crayon: *a crayoned drawing, message, sketch.*

craze *v.* **craz·es, crazed, craz·ing** make or become crazy: *He was crazed with fear.* — *n.* a short-lived fad or mania: *the current, latest, newest craze that is sweeping North America.*

cra·zy (CRAY·zee) *adj.* **-zi·er, -zi·est** *Informal.* **1** insane: *He's crazy as a loon; She's dieting **like crazy*** (= wildly). **2** extremely fond: *She's crazy about or for or over him.* **3** foolish or eccentric: *a crazy idea, scheme; He drives me crazy; It was crazy of him to do that.* — *n., pl.* **-zies** a crazy person. — **craz·i·ly** *adv.;* **craz·i·ness** *n.*

crazy quilt *n.* a quilt of multi-coloured, irregular pieces.

creak (CREEK) *v.* make a harsh, squeaking sound like that of unoiled door hinges; *n.: a terrible creak in the bedroom floor.* — **creak·i·ly** *adv.;* **creak·i·ness** *n.* — **creak·y** *adj.* **creak·i·er, -i·est 1** full of creaks: *creaky old stairs.* **2** rundown: *a creaky old building; a creaky old man.*

cream (CREEM) *n.* **1** the yellowish, fatty content of milk from which butter is made: ***Coffee cream*** or ***cereal cream*** *has 18-20% butterfat; "Half-and-half" is 12% cream; Whipped cream has 32-40% butterfat and is made by whipping cream.* **2** a food made with cream: *cream of tomato soup.* **3** something with a thick, smooth consistency, as a cosmetic or liqueur: *to apply cleansing, cold, facial, hand, shaving, skin, vanishing cream; "Irish Cream" (liqueur); cream sherry.* **4** a light, yellowish white colour. **5** the best part: *These kids are **the cream of the crop.*** — *v.* **1** work to a creamy consistency; also, add cream to something. **2** remove the best of something: *Recruiters creamed off the best of us.* **3** *Slang.* hit hard and decisively: *They got creamed; He'll cream the ball on one shot.* — **cream·y** *adj.* **cream·i·er, -i·est:** *whipped to a creamy consistency.*

cream cheese *n.* a soft, smooth cheese made with cream.

cream·er *n.* **1** a pitcher for cream. **2** an artificial coffee whitener for use instead of cream.

cream puff *n.* **1** a pastry made with cream. **2** *Slang.* one who is out of condition; sissy: *He's bright and athletic* *and no cream puff.*

crease (CREECE) *n.* a line or wrinkle made usually by folding or pressing: *to iron out* or *remove the creases from a dress.*
— *v.* **creas·es, creased, creas·ing 1** make creases in something: *Permanent press clothes don't crease easily.* **2** graze with a bullet.

cre·ate (CREE·ate) *v.* **-ates, -at·ed, -at·ing 1** cause to exist: *The Bible says God created heaven and earth; Laurence Olivier **created the part** (= was first to act the role).* **2** cause: *The news created a lot of confusion, enthusiasm, excitement; The judgment created a disturbance, precedent, sensation.* **3** raise to a rank or title: *The pope creates cardinals.*

cre·a·tion (cree·AY·shun) *n.* **1** a creating; something created: *Do you believe in creation, evolution, or both? That piece of marble is one of Henry Moore's best creations.* **2** the world: *He looked all over creation for the fountain of youth.*

cre·a·tive (cree·AY·tiv) *adj.* that creates: *the creative arts, imagination, impulse; his creative powers; her creative talents as an artist; his creative efforts, genius; Novels, plays, and poems are creative (= imaginative) writing.* — **cre·a·tiv·i·ty** (-ay·TIV·uh·tee) *n.*

cre·a·tor (cree·AY·tur) *n.* one who creates: *Henry Moore is the creator (= sculptor) of "The Archer"; God **the Creator.***

crea·ture (CREE·chur) *n.* one that has been created, esp. an animal or other being considered as dependent on a creator: *a poor creature; "all creatures great and small"; Martian creatures; Are human beings creatures of circumstances or circumstances the creatures of humans? The UFO is a creature of his imagination.*

creature comforts *n.pl.* physical comforts, as good food and shelter.

crèche (CRESH, CRAISH) *n.* **1** a scene representing Christ born in a stable. **2** a day-care centre.

cre·dence (CREED·unce) *n.* belief: *The rumours did not gain much credence; Few attach* or *give* or *lend credence to rumours.*

cre·den·tials (cri·DEN·shulz) *n.pl.* documents stating one's right or ability to fill an office, do a job, etc.: *Ambassadors present their credentials at a ceremony; The school board examined his credentials as a teacher.*

cre·den·za (cri·DEN·zuh) *n.* a usually legless sideboard or bookcase.

cred·i·bil·i·ty (cred·uh·BIL·uh·tee) *n.* the quality of being credible: *The MPs who performed as they promised established their credibility; others lost their credibility; Their words lack,* or *strain credibility;* **adj.:** *Those who don't tell the truth will face a credibility crisis* or *develop a **credibility gap** (= lack of trust).*

cred·i·ble (CRED·uh·bul) *adj.* believable: *a credible story.* — **cred·i·bly** *adv.*

cred·it (CRED·it) *v.* **1** believe: *a story that is hard to credit.* **2** attribute: *a fable credited to Aesop; We credit him with inventiveness.* **3** enter as a payment into an account: *$5 000 has been credited to your account.*
— *n.* **1** belief: *a theory that has gained credit in recent*

times; *New data have lent credit to the theory.*
2 recognition or honour: *Give credit where credit is due; She deserves credit; Her work does credit to her intelligence, reflects credit on her school; Her teachers can take credit for her work; They get some credit for being learned; It is to their credit that she graduated; With all due credit to those who helped her, she is a credit (= source of recognition) to her family; the **credits** (= acknowledgments) at the beginning or end of a show.* **3** financial reliability; also, the amount of money that may be borrowed or the time allowed for repayment: *Stores allow* or *extend* or *give* or *offer credit to customers; Some are denied* or *refused credit; consumer credit; to buy goods **on credit** (= to be paid for later).*
— *adj.:* *a **credit addict** who can't control his buying on credit; A **credit bureau** keeps people's credit records; A **credit card** is issued to people for buying on credit up to a maximum line of credit* or **credit line**; *a **credit report** following a credit check.*

cred·it·a·ble (CRED·i·tuh·bul) *adj.* worthy of praise: *a creditable performance.*

Cred·i·tiste (cred·i·TEEST) *n. & adj.* (a member) of the Social Credit Rally of Quebec.

cred·i·tor (CRED·uh·tur) *n.* a person to whom one owes money: *How will you pay off your creditors?*

credit union *n.* a cooperative savings-and-loan institution.

cre·do (CREE·doh, CRAY·) *n.* **-dos** a belief, esp. religious, or its statement; creed: *Equal pay for work of equal value is part of our credo.*

cre·du·li·ty (cruh·DEW·luh·tee) *n.* readiness to believe easily: *a story that strains our credulity.*

cred·u·lous (CREJ·uh·lus) *adj.* too willing to believe: *He is credulous, but her story is not credible.*
— **cred·u·lous·ly** *adv.;* **cred·u·lous·ness** *n.*

creed *n.* same as CREDO: *the Apostles' Creed; to adhere to a political, religious creed; people of all creeds (= religions) and colours.*

creek (CREEK, CRIK) *n.* a small stream.
— **up the creek (without a paddle)** *Informal.* in trouble.

creep *v.* **creeps, crept, creep·ing 1** move gradually or stealthily, close to the ground: *A cat creeps slowly toward a mouse; Vines creep along the ground and up trees and walls.* **2** appear unnoticed: *Errors creep into our work; Old age creeps up on us; the **creeping** (= slowly advancing) materialism of our times.* **3** feel as if something is creeping over one: *The noise made my flesh creep.*
— *n.* **1** *Informal.* creepy feeling: *a spooky old house that gives me **the creeps**.* **2** *Slang.* a petty or very unpleasant person. — **creep·er** *n.*

creep·y *adj.* **creep·i·er, -i·est** feeling or causing fear or disgust.
— **creep·i·ly** *adv.;* **creep·i·ness** *n.* Also **creepy-crawly.**

cre·mate (CREE·mate) *v.* **-mates, -mat·ed, -mat·ing** burn up a dead body. — **cre·ma·tion** (cri·MAY·shun) *n.*

cre·ma·to·ry (CREE·muh·tor·ee) *n.* **-ries** a furnace or building for cremating.
Also **cre·ma·to·ri·um** (-TOR·ee·um) *n.*

crème (CREM, CREEM) *n.* a sweet, creamy liqueur, as chocolate-flavoured **crème de ca·ca·o** (CREEM·duh·COH·coh, CREEM·duh·cuh·CAH·oh) or mint-flavoured **crème de menthe** (CREEM·duh·MAHNT, -MENTH).

crepe or **crêpe** (CRAPE) *n.* 1 a thin fabric with a crinkled surface. 2 a thin, crepelike paper; also **crepe paper.**

crept *pt. & pp.* of CREEP.

cre·scen·do (cri·SHEN·doh) *adj. & adv.* gradually growing in volume.
— *n.*: *The symphony ended with a deafening crescendo; The complaints rose to* or *reached a crescendo; a crescendo of complaints.*

cres·cent (CRES·unt) *n.* the shape of the moon when less than half of it is visible, having one convex and one concave edge: *the Cross and the* **Crescent** (= Islamic symbol); *He lives on Chalkdene Crescent* (= curved side street whose ends open on to a busier street); *the* **crescent moon; a crescent roll** *(pastry).*

crest *n.* 1 a tuft, comb, etc. on top of an animal's head. 2 top: *the crest of a hill, wave.* 3 a coat of arms or other heraldic device. — *v.* come to or form a crest.

crest·fal·len (CREST·faw·lun) *adj.* dejected or disappointed.

cre·tin (CRET·in, CREE·tin) *n.* 1 one afflicted with cretinism. 2 an idiot. — **cre·ti·nous** *adj.*

cre·vasse (cri·VAS) *n.* a deep crack in a glacier or an embankment.

crev·ice (CREV·is) *n.* a narrow opening; fissure.

crew *n.* a group that works together: *the crew of an airplane; The ground crew services the airplanes; the crew of a ship, racing shell; a camera crew; repair crew; stage crew; The whole crew* (*Informal* for group or crowd) *was present.* — *v. pt.* of CROW.

crib *n.* 1 a high-sided baby's bed. 2 a manger. 3 a bin or small building for grain storage. 4 *Informal.* a translation or other aid used dishonestly by a student; pony. 5 an extra hand for the dealer in cribbage.
— *v.* **cribs, cribbed, crib·bing** 1 shut up or confine. 2 *Informal.* cheat on an exam; use a crib. — **crib·ber** *n.*

crib·bage (CRIB·ij) *n.* a card game in which scores are kept using pegs on a board (**cribbage board**).

crib death *n.* the sudden death of infants in their sleep because of breathing disturbances. Also **cot death, SIDS, sudden infant death syndrome.**

crick·et (CRICK·it) *n.* 1 a grasshopperlike insect whose male chirps by rubbing his wings together. 2 a British game played between teams of 11 using a ball, bat, and two wickets: *Cheating is not cricket* (= sportsmanlike behaviour). — **crick·et·er** *n.*

cried *pt. & pp.* of CRY.

cri·er (CRY·ur) *n.* one who cries out, shouting announcements, sales pitches, etc.: *the town crier shouting "Oyez, Oyez!"*

crime *n.* 1 a major illegal act; felony or misdemeanour: *to commit* or *perpetrate a crime; to investigate, prevent, report a crime; an atrocious, brutal, daring, heinous,* *horrible, infamous, major* or *serious crime; a minor* or *petty crime; an outrageous, vicious, violent crime; a crime of passion; a crime against humanity, society; war crimes; a victimless crime such as gambling; a white-collar crime such as fraud or embezzlement.* 2 criminal behaviour; law-breaking: *to deter, eradicate* or *stamp out* or *wipe out crime; organized crime;* **adj.**: *crime detection, prevention, rates, syndicates.* 3 a disgraceful or regrettable condition or act: *It's a crime that there are homeless people dying in the winter.*

crim·i·nal (CRIM·uh·nul) *adj.* 1 having to do with crime: *a criminal investigation, record; A* **criminal lawyer** *specializes in* **criminal law**; *judged guilty of* **criminal negligence** (= reckless disregard of others' safety). 2 guilty of a crime: *a criminal gang, offender.*
— *n.* one guilty of a crime: *to apprehend* or *arrest a criminal; to pardon, parole, release, rehabilitate a criminal; a common, habitual, hardened, infamous, notorious, war criminal; a band* or *gang of criminals.*
— **crim·i·nal·ly** *adv.* — **crim·i·nal·i·ty** (-NAL·uh·tee) *n.*

crimp *v.* 1 make wavy, corrugated, bent, etc. 2 pinch, as the edges of a pie crust, to seal together. 3 inhibit or restrict: *Changes in taste have crimped demand for certain goods.*
— *n.* a crimping or restraint: *Police raids have* **put a crimp in** (= hindered) *the gambling business.*

crim·son (CRIM·zun) 1 *n.* a purplish red; *adj.*: *a crimson rose; the crimson snows of the Arctic reddened by an alga.* 2 *v.* make crimson.

cringe *v.* **cring·es, cringed, cring·ing** 1 crouch, draw back, or cower in fear. 2 fawn servilely: *a cringing coward.*

crin·kle (CRINK·ul) *v.* **-kles, -kled, -kling** 1 (cause to) wrinkle or crease, esp. a surface: *How did this note get crinkled up? He crinkled his nose in disapproval.* 2 rustle.
— *n.* wrinkle: *Crinkles form around his eyes when he smiles.*

crin·kly (CRINK·lee) *adj.* **-kli·er, -kli·est** 1 wrinkled: *crinkly hair.* 2 rustling: *crinkly silk.*

cripe *interj.* [used as an expletive]: *Cripes! The cops are here; Holy cripe!*

crip·ple (CRIP·ul) *n.* [uncomplimentary use] a physically disabled person or animal.
— *v.* **crip·ples, crip·pled, crip·pling** make a cripple; hence, weaken or damage: *Storms crippled rescue efforts; Arthritis is a crippling disease.* — **crip·pler** *n.*

cri·sis (CRY·sis) *n., pl.* **-ses** (-seez) a critical or crucial situation, as when a patient may either live or die: *to aggravate, avert, cause, defuse, forestall, overcome, precipitate, provoke, ride out, settle, stir up a crisis; a grave, serious, impending, mounting crisis; a cabinet crisis, an economic* or *financial crisis; an energy, environmental, food, housing, identity, mid-life, monetary, political, population crisis; The government faced a crisis over the scandal; the crisis in housing; a* **crisis centre** (where people can phone for advice in a personal crisis).

crisp *adj.* 1 firm and easy to break: *crisp bacon, carrots, crackers, lettuce; a crisp new dollar bill.* 2 well-defined; clear and precise: *a crisp architectural design,*

illustration, reply, speech. **3** bracing: *the crisp morning air.*
— *v.* make crisp: *well-crisped bacon.*
— *n.* something crisp: *The toast was burned* **to a crisp.**
— **crisp·ly** *adv.;* **crisp·ness** *n.*
— **crisp·y** *adj.* **crisp·i·er, -i·est** of food, crisp: *the crispy noodles served with Chinese food; crispy French fries.*

criss·cross *v.* **1** make crossing lines on. **2** move back and forth over: *Searchlights crisscrossed the night sky.*
— *n.* a set of crossing lines; hence, tick-tack-toe; *adj.:* a *crisscross design; crisscross sandals.*
— *adv.* **1** in a crisscross manner: *sticks lying crisscross on the floor.* **2** awry: *plans that went crisscross.*

cri·te·ri·on (cry·TEER·ee·un) *n.,* pl. **-i·a** or **-i·ons** a standard of judgment: *Wealth is no criterion of worth; to meet* or *satisfy the criteria for party leader.*

cri·te·ri·um (cry·TEER·ee·um) *n.* a bicycle race of many laps over a short course as opposed to a city-to-city road race.

crit·ic (CRIT·ic) *n.* **1** one who criticizes: *The senator answered his critics.* **2** one who discusses and judges esp. works of art: *a newspaper's art, drama, literary, music critic; a social critic; a harsh, severe, unkind critic; an impartial critic.*

crit·i·cal (CRIT·uh·cul) *adj.* **1** of or being a crisis; crucial: *a patient in serious but not critical condition; Oxygen is critical to our survival; It is critical that we have enough air to breathe.* **2** faultfinding: *a highly critical account; He was somewhat critical of my scholarship.* **3** of critics or criticism; evaluative: *a critical review of the book.* — **crit·i·cal·ly** *adv.*

critical mass *n.* a condition that is necessary for maintaining a state or producing a result, as the minimum mass of fissionable material required to maintain a nuclear reaction.

criticise same as CRITICIZE.

crit·i·cism (CRIT·uh·siz·um) *n.* **1** the judgment of art, literature, etc. by a critic: *constructive, fair, sober, valid criticism; literary criticism;* **textual criticism** *of the Bible (for reconstructing its original words).*
2 disapproval; faultfinding; also, an expression of this: *barbs of criticism; to arouse, express, offer, provoke, stir up, take criticism; to level criticism at someone; to subject someone to criticism; He tempers his criticism with wit; adverse, biting, damaging, devastating, mild, nitpicking, petty, scathing, severe, sharp, sweeping, unsparing, withering criticism.*

crit·i·cize (CRIT·uh·cize) *v.* **-ciz·es, -cized, -ciz·ing**
1 find fault with a person or thing: *He always criticizes her; criticizes her for being lazy; to criticize harshly, severely, sharply.* **2** evaluate critically: *to criticize a painting, performance, recital; to criticize fairly; to criticize her style, works.* Also **criticise.**

cri·tique (cri·TEEK) *n.* a critical review, discussion, or analysis: *to give* or *present a critique.*

crit·ter (CRIT·ur) *n. Informal.* creature: *Inflation is a hungry critter that has eaten away 45 cents of every dollar in just 25 years.*

croak (CROKE) *n.* the low, rough sound made by a frog.
— *v.* **1** make a croak; utter with such a sound: *a crabby*

old fellow croaking his orders. **2** *Slang.* kill or die.
— **croak·er** *n.*

cro·chet (croh·SHAY) *n.* a heavy lace made with one hooked needle.
— *v.* **-chets, -cheted, -chet·ing:** *a crocheted sweater.*
— **cro·chet·er** (-SHAY·ur) *n.*

crock *n.* **1** a pot, jar, etc. of earthenware: *They struck a crock of gold with the bestseller; That's baloney, a real* **crock of it** *(Slang for* potful of something disgusting). **2** *Slang.* one that is disliked, esp. one who is old, drunk, etc.

crock·er·y (CROCK·uh·ree) *n.* earthenware or crocks collectively.

croc·o·dile (CROC·uh·dile) *n.* a large, swimming reptile with a long tail and strong jaws coming to a sharper point than an alligator's: *to shed* **crocodile tears** *(= to pretend sorrow).*

cro·cus (CROH·cus) *n.* **-cus·es** or **-ci** (-sye) a flower related to the iris, with yellow, purple, or white blooms: *The "prairie crocus" is Manitoba's floral emblem.*

crois·sant (cruh·SAHNT) *n.* a crescent-shaped roll of rich pastry.

cro·ny (CROH·nee) *n.* **-nies** a partisan friend: *a government crony; political crony; cronies of the ruling party.*

crook (short "oo") *n.* **1** *Informal.* a thief or swindler: *"I'm not a crook," he said when arrested.* **2** a hooked stick, tool, or part, esp. a shepherd's staff.
— *v.* bend: *He goes whenever she crooks her little finger (to summon him).*
— **crook·ed** (-id) *adj.* **1** bent or curving. **2** dishonest.
— **crook·ed·ly** *adv.;* **crook·ed·ness** *n.*

croon (long "oo") *v.* sing or hum softly; also, sing a song in a soft voice: *to croon a lullaby.*

croon·er (CROO·nur) *n.* a professional singer of popular songs who uses a soft, smooth voice.

crop *n.* **1** an agricultural product: *a good crop of corn; Ontario's maple syrup crop; a crop of wool; to gather* or *harvest* or *reap a crop; Trees bear* or *yield crops; Farmers dust* or *spray crops; to rotate crops; a bountiful* or *bumper* or *record crop; a cash, staple crop; a poor crop; adj.: crop insurance; crop rotation, surpluses.* **2** a group or batch: *a new crop of trainees.* **3** a pouchlike part in a bird's gullet. **4** a whip handle; also, a short riding whip. **5** a close haircut; *adj.: crop marks (for indicating where a picture is to be cropped).*

— *v.* **crops, cropped, crop·ping 1** cut off short; cut the ends off something: *closely cropped hair; to crop a hedge, a horse's tail or ear, edges of a book or photograph: She cropped the grass short.* **2** plant a crop on land: *to crop a few hectares with corn.*
— **crop up** arise, turn up, or occur without warning: *the problems that crop up at work.*

crop-dusting (CROP·dus·ting) *n.* the spraying of pesticides on crops from an aircraft.

crop·per (CROP·ur) *n.* one that crops; sharecropper.
— **come a cropper** fail; come to grief: *The prosecutor came a cropper himself for padding his payroll.*

cross *n.* **1** a vertical post or beam with a horizontal piece near the top, like the **Cross** on which Christ was crucified: *Christians make the sign of the cross.* **2** a burden or affliction: *We all have our crosses to bear.* **3** an X-like mark: *As he couldn't write, he made or marked his cross on the deed.* **4** a hybrid: *The mule is a cross between a horse and a donkey.*
— *v.* **1** go or reach from one side to the other: *to cross the street; to cross from one side to the other; to cross over to the other side; She never omits to **cross her t's and dot her i's** (= is very careful about detail).* **2** draw a line or cross through to cancel: *to cross out an error.* **3** meet and pass by something: *Other unionized workers refused to cross their picket line; King Street doesn't cross* (= intersect) *Queen; She used to **cross my path** in the office; It never did **cross my mind** (= occur to me) to ask her out; I must have got my **wires crossed** (= made some mistake).* **4** place across one another: *People cross their fingers for good luck.* **5** make the sign of the cross on or over oneself: *Christians cross themselves in prayer.* **6** oppose or thwart: *He never crossed a guy for doing what he thought was right.* **7** cause to breed with a different species of animal or variety of plant: *You get a mule if you cross a donkey with a horse.*
— **cross my heart** *Informal.* I swear I am telling the truth.
— *adj.* **1** crosswise or intersecting: *the cross street at the next traffic lights; cross traffic, ventilation; the **cross·bar** of a cross, goalpost, bicycle frame; the **cross·beam** of a cross.* **2** contrary; opposing: *cross talk between two groups.* **3** angry: *She's cross at or with me for being late.*
— **cross·ly** *adv.;* **cross·ness** *n.*

cross·bones *n.pl.* two thighbones laid across one another: *A "skull and crossbones" is a symbol of death.*

cross·breed *v.* **-breeds, -bred, -breed·ing** breed or cause to breed with a different species, variety, etc.: *sheep that have been crossbred.*
— *n.* a crossbred plant or animal: *The mule is a crossbreed.*

cross-country (CROSS·cun·tree) *adj. & adv.* **1** across open country: *a cross-country event, marathon, resort; cross-country skiing, trails; to run cross-country.* **2** across a nation: *a cross-country manhunt, poll, tour; cross-country hearings.*

cross·cut *v.* **-cuts, -cut, -cut·ting** cut across a wood grain, course, etc.
— *adj.* **1** for crosscutting: *a crosscut saw.* **2** sawed or cut across the grain.
— *n.* a shortcut: *a crosscut through the schoolyard.*

cross-examine (cross·ig·ZAM·in) *v.* **-ines, -ined, -in·ing**

question closely to check someone's previous answers.
— **cross-examination** (-uh·NAY·shun) *n.*

cross-eye *n.* an eye turned inward toward the nose.
— **cross-eyed** *adj.: We're all going cross-eyed reading reports that don't tell us anything.*

cross-fertilize (CROSS·FUR·tuh·lize) *v.* **-liz·es, -lized, -liz·ing 1** of a plant or flower, cause or undergo pollination by another plant or flower. **2** interact, influence, or enrich *by* or *with* ideas, cultures, etc. from different sources.
— **cross-fertilization** (-luh·ZAY·shun) *n.*

cross·fire *n.* intersecting lines of gunfire: *bystanders caught in a crossfire.*

crossing *n.* **1** an intersection: *a grade or level crossing; railway or railroad crossing.* **2** an act of crossing: *We had a rough, not smooth, Atlantic crossing; We made the border crossing at Niagara Falls.* **3** a place for crossing a street, river, etc.: *a deer crossing; pedestrian crossing; school crossing; There is a border crossing in Niagara Falls; A **crossing guard** helps children cross a street.*

cross-purpose (CROSS·pur·pus) *n.* an opposed though unintended purpose: *Tom and Jerry work at cross-purposes with no benefit to the company.*

cross-reference (CROSS·REF·ur·unce) *n.* a reference to another part of the same book, list, etc.

cross·road *n.* an intersecting or connecting road.
— **crossroads** *pl.* [takes sing. or pl. v.] **1** a meeting point for roads, travellers, cultures, etc.: *Look for signs at the next crossroads.* **2** a point where one must choose or decide: *We are at the crossroads of our career.*

cross section *n.* **1** a place or piece cut at right angles to the axis of something. **2** a sample representation of the whole: *a poll based on a cross section of the population.*

cross talk *n.* garbled sounds intruding from another telephone, radio, or tape channel.

cross·walk *n.* a pedestrian crossing marked on a street.

cross·ways *adj. & adv.* across; diagonally: *The child lay crossways on the bed.* Also **cross·wise.**

crotch *n.* the point where two tree branches fork or where the legs diverge at the human pelvis: *the crotch of a pair of pants.*

crotch·et·y (CROCH·uh·tee) *adj.* eccentric and ill-tempered: *a crotchety old fellow.*

crouch (CROWCH) **1** *v.* lower the body with legs bent and limbs tucked in, as in cringing or preparing to run or leap. **2** *n.* such a position.

crow (CROH) *n.* **1** a common black bird with a harsh call. **2** a crowing: *We'll start at cock's crow.*
— *v.* **1** *pt.* also **crew,** utter a rooster's shrill cry. **2** feel or express triumph; exult: *The track star says his new record is nothing to crow about.* **3** make happy sounds as a baby does.
— **as the crow flies** in a straight line: *Ottawa to Montreal is 200 km but much shorter as the crow flies.*
— **eat crow** be humiliated: *The minister had to eat crow and apologize in Parliament.*

crow·bar *n.* a steel or iron bar used for prying or as a lever.

crowd *n.* **1** a large group of people forming a mass; also, the masses: *He likes to be one of the crowd, to go along with the crowd, not stand out from the crowd.* **2** a group with a shared interest: *Last night we joined the theatre crowd.*
— *v.* **1** gather in a crowd: *People crowded into the room; then crowded around the speaker.* **2** fill or cram to excess: *They crowded the hallways.* **3** press, shove, stand close to, etc.: *They crowded the shoppers out of their way; Don't crowd the driver; Don't crowd* (= pressure) *me! He is crowding* (= close to) *50 and still a bachelor.*
— **crowd (on) sail** spread more sail to increase speed.

crown *n.* **1** a garland or wreath for the head; also, a jewelled headdress, diadem, etc.: *a crown of thorns; the martyr's crown* (= honour); *the world heavyweight crown* (= title). **2** **the Crown** a monarch or government: *territories ceded to* **the Crown** (= the monarch); *adj.: a* Crown (= government) *attorney; a* **crown colony** (= British overseas possession); *Crown* (= government) *lands or reserves in various provinces; a* **crown prince** or **princess** (= heir apparent). **3** the top or a crownlike part of something, esp. of a tree, tooth, or head.
— *v.* **1** put a crown on someone; also, honour as someone: *Elizabeth II was crowned Queen.* **2** be at the top or best point: *Her career was crowned with a Nobel prize; Winning the Nobel was her* **crowning** *glory.* **3** cap a tooth with an artificial crown. **4** *Informal.* hit over the head.

Crown corporation *n.* *Cdn.* a government-owned but independently run company or agency such as Canada Post and Ontario Hydro.

cru·ces (CROO·seez) a *pl.* of CRUX.

cru·cial (CROO·shul) *adj.* decisive for the future: *a crucial decision; a decision that is crucial to or for our future; a crucial moment, operation, point, question, test; It's crucial that you take this test.*
— **cru·cial·ly** *adv.*

cru·ci·ble (CROO·suh·bul) *n.* a heat-resistant pot or container for heating esp. metals to a very high temperature.

cru·ci·fy (CROO·suh·fye) *v.* **-fies, -fied, -fy·ing** execute by nailing or tying to a cross; hence, persecute or torment in punishment.

crud *n.* *Slang.* a deposit of dirt or filth; hence, one that is worthless or disgusting.

crude *adj.* **1** raw or unprocessed: *crude oil, ore, rubber.* **2** unrefined or insensitive: *his crude behaviour, life; crude habits, people, remarks.* **3** rough or unfinished: *crude ideas, log cabins, methods, paintings, schemes, shelters, workmanship.*
— *n.* crude petroleum: *the price of domestic crude.*
— **crude·ly** *adv.*

cru·el (CROO·ul) *adj.* causing grief or pain; inhumane; harsh: *a cruel and unusual punishment; a cruel blow, disease, predicament, remark, wind, taskmaster, treatment, tyrant; He can be cruel to animals; It was cruel of him to let the cat out in the cold.*
— **cru·el·ly** *adv.*

cru·el·ty (CROO·ul·tee) *n.* **-ties** the quality of being cruel or a cruel action: *His actions demonstrate or*

display or exhibit cruelty; deliberate, wanton cruelty to animals; Mental cruelty is sometimes charged in divorce cases; the cruelty of neglecting children, of trapping wild animals; the cruelties of war.

cruise (CROOZ) *v.* **cruis·es, cruised, cruis·ing 1** sail, drive, or fly in an unhurried way or with no particular goal, as for pleasure, to patrol an area, etc.: *He cruised around the world in pursuit of pleasure; a taxi cruising for a fare; to cruise a street looking for pickups; John is cruising for a bruising* (*Informal* for looking for trouble). **2** operate at optimum speed and efficiency: *The high gear is for cruising; Our plane cruises at an altitude of 30 000 ft. (9 144 km); The* **cruising speed** *is not the maximum speed.*
— *n.* voyage: *to go on or take a cruise in the Mediterranean; a Caribbean cruise; a shakedown cruise; world cruise; a car with* **cruise control** (*to automatically maintain a constant speed*).

cruise missile *n.* a small, pilotless, long-range jet-powered missile that flies low to elude enemy radar.

crumb (CRUM) *n.* **1** a scrap or small fragment, as of bread. **2** *Slang.* a contemptible person.
— *v.* break something into crumbs or cover with crumbs.

crum·ble (CRUM·bul) *v.* **-bles, -bled, -bling 1** break into small pieces: *He crumbled the cookie; It crumbled easily.* **2** collapse or disintegrate: *The building crumbled into ruins; Their marriage crumbled.*

crum·my (CRUM·ee) *adj.* **crum·mi·er, crum·mi·est** *Slang.* worthless; cheap; wretched: *He felt crummy in the morning; had the crummy idea of calling in sick; read a crummy book; had a crummy lunch; got a crummy deal.*

crum·ple (CRUM·pul) *v.* **-ples, -pled, -pling 1** crush or become crushed into wrinkles: *She crumpled the letter and threw it away; a crumpled fender.* **2** collapse or break down: *The accused crumpled to the floor under questioning and admitted her guilt; She crumpled in a faint.*

crunch *v.* **1** chew, grind, crush, etc. with a loud noise; hence, make such a noise: *to crunch potato chips; Snow crunches underfoot in subzero weather.* **2** to process: *Computers crunch numbers besides performing logical operations.*
— *n.* **1** a crunching. **2** a difficult situation; pinch: *True friends don't desert us in a crunch; when it comes to the crunch; an energy crunch* (= shortage); *crunch* (= critical) *negotiations.*
— **crunch·y** *adj.: crunchy corn chips, snow.*

cru·sade (croo·SADE) *n.* a zealous battle for a cause: *to conduct, embark on, engage in, go on, join, launch a crusade; the crusade against abortion; the crusade for women's rights.*
— *v.* **-sades, -sad·ed, -sad·ing:** *Some crusade against, others for, abortion on demand; a crusading knight.*
— **cru·sad·er** *n.: an equal rights crusader.*

crush *n.* **1** press or squeeze so as to break or damage; crumple so as to wrinkle: *She was crushed into the corner by the mob; You crushed my new suit.* **2** grind or break into small pieces: *crushed ice.* **3** overcome or destroy: *She felt crushed; a crushing defeat.*
— *n.* **1** a crushing; also, a dense crowd of people:

Children were trampled in the crush. **2** *Informal.* a strong temporary attraction; infatuation: *He had a youthful crush on his arts teacher.* **3** a fruit-juice drink: *lemon crush.*

crust *n.* **1** the hard surface of a loaf of bread; also, an end piece made mostly of this. **2** a pastry shell: *pie crust.* **3** any hard outer layer, as of the earth: *A crust forms on snow when it freezes again after beginning to melt: The snow crusted over during the night.* **4** *Informal.* impudence: *He had the crust to ask me for another loan.*
— **crust·y** *adj.*: *crusty French bread; a crusty snow cover; a crusty (= bad-tempered) old major.*

crutch *n.* a prop or aid, esp. a stick with a padded crosspiece that rests in the armpit, used as a support for walking: *to walk on* or *with crutches; The injured skier was on crutches for many weeks.*

crux *n.* **crux·es** or **cru·ces** (CROO·seez) the essential or crucial point: *the crux of the matter, negotiations; the crux of the argument, problem.*

cry *v.* **cries, cried, cry·ing** **1** sob and weep; shed tears: *He cried with genuine sorrow; No use crying over spilled milk; She cried for joy on hearing the good news; She never goes crying (= complaining) to the media; But she cried her heart out when Jim lost; then cried herself to sleep; He spent all day crying in his beer (Informal for feeling sorry for himself).* **2** shout; call out: *the boy who cried "wolf" (= raised a false alarm); They're ready to cry havoc (= warn of disaster) at the least suspicion of wrongdoing.* **3** announce or proclaim: *a peddler crying his wares.* **4** utter a characteristic call, as birds, hounds, etc.
— **cry out** appeal: *The plight of the homeless cries out for attention; a heinous crime that cries out to heaven for vengeance; People always cry out (= protest) against injustices.*
— **for crying out loud** *Slang.* for heaven's sake; for Pete's sake.
— *n., pl.* **cries** **1** a bout of weeping: *Flo felt better after a good cry.* **2** a shout: *a cry for help; to give, raise, utter a cry; an anguished, heart-rending, loud, lusty, piercing, plaintive cry; a battle cry or war cry; a rallying cry.* **3** a characteristic call: *the cries of infants; the cry of the wolf.*
— **a far cry** something quite different: *Fast food is a far cry from home-cooked meals.*

cry·ba·by (CRY·bay·bee) *n.* **-bies** one who cries or complains too much; *adj.*: *a crybaby act, attitude, plea.*

crying *adj.* **1** demanding attention: *a crying need; a crying (= scandalous) shame.* **2** having to do with crying: *a crying jag, room, towel.*

cry·on·ic (cry·ON·ic) **1** *adj.* having to do with the freezing of bodies for later revival: *Cryonic societies keep freshly-dead bodies in cryonic suspension to prevent deterioration, hoping to revive them.* **2** **cryonics** *n. pl.* [takes sing. v.] the preservation of bodies by freezing.

cryp·tic (CRIP·tic) *adj.* secret or mystifying: *a cryptic comment, message, note, remark; the Mona Lisa's cryptic smile.*

crys·tal (CRIS·tul) *n.* **1** colourless transparent quartz;

adj.: *She tells fortunes by gazing into a crystal ball; People engage in crystal-gazing (= speculation) when they don't have evidence on which to base a judgment.* **2** a high-quality glass used for tableware: *fine crystal goblets; Why, it's clear as crystal! Let me make our views crystal clear.* **3** a clear cover over a watch face. **4** a naturally formed three-dimensional structure of the molecules of a substance as it passes to the solid state: *ice, salt, sugar crystals.*

crys·tal·line (CRIS·tuh·line, -lin) *adj.* having to do with crystals: *the crystalline structure of some gems; crystalline clarity, salt.*

crys·tal·lize (CRIS·tuh·lize) *v.* **-tal·liz·es, -tal·lized, -tal·liz·ing** **1** form into crystals; take on crystalline structure. **2** take on a fixed, definite form: *vague ideas that crystallized into a theory.*

cub *n.* **1** a young bear, lion, fox, etc. **2** a novice: *a cub (reporter).* **3** a Boy Scout aged 8 to 10.

cube *n.* **1** a solid shape bounded by six equal squares: *bread, ice, sugar cubes.* **2** the product of a number multiplied by itself twice: *The cube of 2 (= 2 x 2 x 2) is 8; The **cube root** of 8 is 2; to find* or *extract the cube root of 8.*
— *v.* **cubes, cubed, cub·ing** **1** multiply by itself twice: *8 is 2 cubed.* **2** shape or cut into cubes.

cu·bic (CUE·bic) *adj.* **1** cube-shaped; also **cu·bi·cal.** **2** extended in three dimensions: *One cubic metre is the volume of a cube one metre long, one metre wide, and one metre deep.* **3** raised to or relating to the third degree: *a cubic equation, measure.*

cu·bi·cle (CUE·buh·cul) *n.* a small room or compartment: *a dormitory cubicle; a separate cubicle for each typist.*

cuck·oo (COO·coo) *n.* **1** a bird with a distinctive call that lays its eggs in other birds' nests. **2** *Informal.* a foolish or silly person.
— *adj.* crazy or silly: *He was nearly cuckoo with fear; a head full of cuckoo notions.*

cu·cum·ber (CUE·cum·bur) *n.* a long, thin, green vegetable with a white flesh; also, the vine it grows on: *She stays **cool as a cucumber** under provocation.*

cud *n.* a mouthful of food that animals such as cattle, deer, and camels bring up from their stomachs for rechewing. — **chew the cud** ponder or ruminate.

cud·dle (CUD·ul) *v.* **cud·dles, cud·dled, cud·dling** hold or nestle close; hug: *People cuddle up for greater* *warmth; They cuddle up with their children; Children cuddle up to their parents for the warmth of affection.*

cud·dle·some (CUD·ul·sum) or **cud·dly** (CUD·lee) *adj.* good for cuddling: *It looks so cute and cuddlesome; a cuddlesome baby, kitten.*

cudg·el (CUJ·ul) *n.* a stout club: *Lou's the only one around to* **take up the cudgels for** (= go to the defence of) *the underdog.*
— *v.* -els, -elled or -eled, -el·ling or -el·ing beat wih a cudgel: *The victim was cudgelled to death; Hard as I* **cudgelled my brains** (= Though I thought hard), *I couldn't solve the problem.*

cue *n.* 1 a signal indicating when the next speech, action, etc. should occur in a play; hence, a hint or indication: *to give the cue; They* **take their cue** *from their bosses; The postal workers walked out* **on cue** *from headquarters.* 2 a long tapered stick used to strike the ball (**cue ball**) in billiards and similar games.
— *v.* cues, cued, cu·ing 1 hit a billiard ball, etc. with a cue stick. 2 give a cue or indication to help a person or thing into a specific place: *to cue an actor on his lines* (= prompt him); *Let's cue her in to* (= explain to her) *what happened; to cue* (= insert) *a few songs into the script.*

cue card *n.* 1 a large piece of cardboard with writing on it, held by a stagehand to prompt a television performer. 2 a small card held in the hand as a memory aid.

cuff *n.* a band or folded piece of cloth on the end of a shirt sleeve or pant leg: *pleated and* **cuffed** *pants.*
— *v.* strike, usually lightly with an open hand: *a bear cub cuffed into line by its mother.*
— **off the cuff** impromptu: *Raj spoke off the cuff; an off-the-cuff remark.*
— **on the cuff** on credit: *Ed buys his groceries on the cuff.*

cui·sine (kwi·ZEEN) *n.* a style of cooking; also, food so cooked: *the best Breton cuisine.*

cu·li·nar·y (CUE·luh·nair·ee, CULL·uh·) *adj.* of kitchens or cookery: *his culinary expertise, skills.*

cull *v.* select or gather: *to cull flowers from the garden; quotations culled from Keats; the annual culling of seals; the culling* (= reducing) *of fleets for consolidating the navy; to cull* (= go over) *a field for grain.*
— *n.* 1 a culling: *the cull of grey seals.* 2 something discarded: *As the culls are thrown out, 50 kg of carrots shrinks to 30.*

cul·mi·nate (CULL·muh·nate) *v.* -nates, -nat·ed, -nat·ing reach its climax or best point: *The growing discontent culminated in a full-scale riot.*
— **cul·mi·na·tion** (cull·muh·NAY·shun) *n.*: *Her Nobel prize was the culmination of years of hard work.*

cul·pa·ble (CUL·puh·bul) *adj.* deserving blame because of something done or omitted: *His attitude was blameworthy and his actions culpable; culpable homicide, negligence, stupidity; culpable but not guilty.*
— **cul·pa·bly** *adv.* — **cul·pa·bil·i·ty** (-BIL·uh·tee) *n.*

cul·prit *n.* an accused or guilty person.

cult *n.* 1 a system of religious worship: *the cult of saints, of the Virgin Mary, of Zeus.* 2 a faddish or abnormal devotion to a person, thing, or idea: *the cult of old*

movies; a fertility, personality, religious, satanic cult; **adj.**: *a cult festival, figure, following, image, member, object; cult indoctrination.* — **cult·ism** *n.*

cult·ist *n.* one who practises a cult: *a field dominated by kooks, cultists, and quasi-religious fanatics.*

cul·ti·vate (CULL·tuh·vate) *v.* -vates, -vat·ed, -vat·ing 1 prepare soil and grow plants, trees, etc.: *to cultivate crops, gardens, the land, plantations, the soil, trees.* 2 grow or foster: *to cultivate an atmosphere of goodwill, a good image, an interest in music, friendships, opportunities, relationships, tastes, values.* 3 to seek the goodwill of someone: *Political aspirants cultivate politicians; Politicians cultivate the electorate.*
— **cultivated** *adj.* refined or improved: *wild and cultivated roses; We like to appear cultivated; a cultivated accent, air of sophistication, style, taste.*
— **cul·ti·va·ble** (-vuh·bul) *adj.*
— **cul·ti·va·tion** (-VAY·shun) *n.*
— **cul·ti·va·tor** (-vay·tur) *n.*

cul·tur·al (CULL·chuh·rul) *adj.* having to do with culture: *a cultural attaché; cultural deprivation, exchange, history, inheritance, interests, mosaics, nationalism, revolution, societies; In a changing world, societies and institutions that are slow to adapt to change are said to suffer from* **cultural** *or* **culture lag.**
— **cul·tur·al·ly** *adv.*

cul·ture (CULL·chur) *n.* 1 intellectual and emotional refinement; enlightenment: *a man of little culture; a woman of great culture; centres of culture and civilization; to bring culture to the people; to develop, disseminate, foster, spread culture.* 2 the result of such refinement; the arts, beliefs, customs, etc. of a group as a whole: *Aztec, Chinese, Greek culture; ancient, corporate, ethnic, human, mass, material, modern, tribal culture; Canada is a mosaic of cultures.* 3 growth or development: *the culture of the mind; beauty culture; physical culture.* 4 something grown, as in a laboratory: *to grow bacterial cultures; the culture for making Oka cheese; clones produced by tissue culture; a yogurt culture grown in Bulgaria.*
— *adj.*: *the* **culture shock** *of being thrust suddenly into a different society; a* **culture vulture** (= somewhat pretentious devotee of the arts) *who has no time for movies.*

cultured (CULL·churd) *adj.* 1 refined: *a cultured gentleman.* 2 artificially cultivated: *a cultured pearl, variety of rose.*

cum·ber·some (CUM·bur·sum) *adj.* awkward or unwieldy: *a cumbersome device, operation, process; a cumbersome bureaucracy.*

cu·mu·la·tive (CUE·myuh·luh·tiv) *adj.* increasing by accumulation or continued addition: *the cumulative effect of long hardship; cumulative interest (added to the principal sum and earning more interest).*
— **cu·mu·la·tive·ly** *adv.*

cun·ning (CUN·ing) *adj.* 1 cleverly deceptive: *a cunning fox, scheme, trick.* 2 skilfully made or done: *a cunning piece of workmanship.* 3 cute: *a cunning little girl; a cunning red dress.*
— *n.* 1 skill in deception; craftiness. 2 skill or dexterity: *The wood carving shows cunning.* — **cun·ning·ly** *adv.*

cup *n*. 1 a small, bowllike container, usually with a handle: *a cup and saucer; a coffee, drinking, loving, paper, plastic cup; He drained the cup to the dregs; a bra with cups in sizes A, B, C, D, and DD (for 31 to 54 bust sizes).* 2 a cupful; an 8 oz. (236.59 ml) measure of capacity: *a cup of tea.* 3 prize or trophy, usually a loving cup: *a challenge cup; the Grey Cup; Stanley Cup; We lost, they won the cup.*
— **in one's cups** drunk; intoxicated.
— *v.* **cups, cupped, cup·ping** shape or put into a cup: *He cupped his hand under his chin; Jo sat with her chin cupped in her hand.* — **cup·ful** *n.*

cup·board (CUB·urd) *n.* a small cabinet or closet: *a kitchen with built-in cupboards; The cupboard is bare* (= Nothing is available) *at our local employment office.*

cu·pid (CUE·pid) *n.* a small, winged boy representing the Roman god of love: *She likes to play cupid making matches.*

cup of tea *n.* what interests one; one's own thing: *Skiing is not my cup of tea; Skiing's a different cup of tea* (= different thing) *from skating.*

cur·a·ble (KYOOR·uh·bul) *adj.* that can be cured.

cu·rate (KYOOR·it) *n.* a clergyman who is assistant a parish priest.

curate's egg *n.* something with both good and bad qualities.

cur·a·tive (KYOOR·uh·tiv) *adj.* able to cure: *curative power, value; **n.**: a curative for fever.*

cu·ra·tor (cue·RAY·tur, CURE·uh·tur) *n.* one who administers a museum, art gallery, etc.

curb *n.* 1 a check or restraint: *a curb on drunk driving.* 2 a strap or chain used with a bit to check a horse. 3 a raised border for a street or driveway; *adj.: curb crawling* (= going around in one's car looking for pickups); *curb service* (= service at the curb).
— *v.* control abruptly: *to curb one's curiosity, dog, enthusiasm, temper.*

cur·dle (CUR·dul) *v.* **-dles, -dled, -dling** 1 thicken milk into curd. 2 seem to thicken: *The scream in the middle of the night curdled their blood with fear.*

cure (KYOOR) *n.* 1 a healing: *to effect, provide, work a cure; a complete, sure, miraculous cure.* 2 a drug or therapy that heals: *a cure for the common cold; a rest cure; water cure.*
— *v.* **cures, cured, cur·ing** 1 heal; make better: *to cure people of their ills; a plan to cure the world's problems.* 2 preserve bacon, fish, etc. by salting, smoking, etc.: *Tobacco is cured by drying.*

cure-all *n.* a supposedly universal cure; panacea.

cur·few *n.* an evening hour at which one must be off the streets: *to impose a midnight curfew; disciplined for violating the curfew; a curfew of 8 p.m. for children under 15; The curfew has been lifted.*

cu·ri·o (CUE·ree·oh) *n.* **-os** a novel or unusual object; curiosity.

cu·ri·os·i·ty (cue·ree·OS·uh·tee) *n.* **-ties** 1 a being curious: *to arouse, excite, pique, satisfy, whet one's curiosity; a healthy, idle, intellectual, natural, unquenchable curiosity; She did it out of curiosity; her curiosity about the goings-on.* 2 a novel or unusual object: *the curiosities sold at a souvenir shop.*

cu·ri·ous (KYOOR.ee.us) *adj.* 1 eager to know: *She is curious to know what happened; I'm curious about her background; He's just curious.* 2 too eager to know; inquisitive: *He's so curious; curious eyes, neighbours, questions.* 3 peculiar: *a curious state of affairs; Isn't it curious that he left without a word? What a curious thing to say!*— **cu·ri·ous·ly** *adv.*

curl *n.* something with a curved shape, esp. a ringlet of hair: *Her hair falls in curls; a curl of the lips; a curl of smoke; the curl of a wave about to break.*
— *v.* 1 give a curl to something: *She helped Mary curl her hair; Her fees will curl your hair (Informal for will shock you).* 2 form in a curl or curls: *Smoke curls from the pipe; He's curled up in front of the TV; The cat curls up into a ball.*

curl·ing *n.* a game in which round stones are slid toward a target across ice by two teams of four each.

curl·y *adj.* **curl·i·er, -i·est** having or being in curls: *naturally curly hair; his curly head.*

cur·mudg·eon (cur·MUJ·un) *n.* a cantankerous old person. — **cur·mudg·eon·ly** *adv.*

cur·rant (CUR·unt) *n.* 1 a sour berry related to the gooseberry: *red currants; black currant jelly.* 2 a small seedless dried grape used esp. in baking: *currant wine.*

cur·ren·cy (CUR·un·see) *n.* **-cies** 1 the state or duration of being current; general use: *a coin that is no more in currency; It went out of currency; The rumour gained, had, enjoyed currency; wide currency.* 2 money circulating as legal tender: *to call in, issue, print, withdraw currency; hard, foreign, paper, soft, stable, weak currencies; currency exchange rates.*

cur·rent (CUR·unt) *adj.* 1 circulating: *a current coin.* 2 now occurring; of the present: *Read the papers for current events; a current affairs TV program dealing with current issues; Money kept in a **current account** may be withdrawn on demand; **Current assets** are readily convertible to cash.* 3 generally accepted; prevalent: *current theories of the universe; the current usage of a word.*
— *n.* 1 something flowing in a path, as air, water, or electricity: *The Gulf Stream is a warm current; air currents; an underwater current; the flow of electric current; alternating and direct currents.* 2 a course or tendency: *It's easier to swim with, not against the current; the current of 20-century liberalism; the current of unrest that swept campuses in the 1960s.*

cur·rent·ly (CUR·unt·lee) *adv.* at present: *legislation currently under review.*

cur·ric·u·lum (cuh·RICK·yuh·lum) *n., pl.* **-la** or **-lums** a school's program of studies: *Music is on the school curriculum; a basic or core curriculum; to draw up or design a curriculum; a curriculum* (= set of courses) *in math.*

curriculum vi·tae (-VYE·tee) *n.* a résumé; vita.

cur·ry (CUR·ee) *n.* **cur·ries** a sauce or dish seasoned with **curry powder**, a spicy mixture of turmeric and

other spices: *a hot curry; mild curry; chicken, fish, vegetable curry.*
— *v.* **cur·ries, cur·ried, cur·ry·ing 1** prepare with curry: *curried chicken.* **2** brush or rub down a horse using a brush with metal teeth, or **cur·ry·comb** (-cohm).
— **curry favour** gain favour: *He's trying to curry favour by flattery and with gifts; She tried to curry favour with the principal.*

curse *n.* **1** a calling down of evil on someone or something: *to pronounce* or *put a curse (up)on someone; to lift a curse; under the curse of their ancestors.* **2** an oath, esp. one using a sacred name: *to utter a curse against someone.* **3** a bane or scourge: *Scurvy was the curse of old-time sailors.*
— *v.* **curs·es,** *pt. & pp.* **cursed** or **curst, curs·ing 1** swear at someone: *She cursed her attacker for what he did to her.* **2** afflict: *He was cursed with poverty in old age.*

cur·sed (CUR·sid, CURST) *adj.* hateful.

cur·sor (CUR·sur) *n.* on a video display unit, a manually controllable pointer of flashing light used as a position indicator.

cur·so·ry (CUR·suh·ree) *adj.* quick or hurried: *a cursory inspection, reading of a book.*
— **cur·so·ri·ly** (-ruh·lee) *adv.*

curt *adj.* short or brusque; nearly rude: *a curt response to a complaint;* **curt·ly** *adv.*

cur·tail (cur·TAIL) *v.* cut short; reduce: *to curtail expenditure.* — **cur·tail·ment** *n.*

cur·tain (CUR·tun) *n.* a piece of fabric hung before a stage, window, etc. to veil or shut off view: *to close, draw, hang, lower, open, put up, raise a curtain; to pull the curtains (shut); shower, stage, theatre curtains; to raise, ring up, ring down the curtain on a performance; The curtain goes up* or *rises on a scene; The curtain comes down* or *drops* or *falls on a scene; His first show proved to be* **curtains** (*Informal* for the end) *for him.*
— *v.* furnish or conceal with a curtain: *One end of the cabin was* **curtained off** *for the ladies.*

curtain call *n.* a performer's return to the stage in answer to prolonged applause: *to take curtain calls.*

curt·sy (CURT·see) *n.* **-sies** a bow of respect by women made by bending the knees: *Mia made* or *bobbed* or *dropped a graceful curtsy to the audience.*
— *v.* **-sies, -sied, -sy·ing:** *She curtsied to the Queen.*

cur·va·ceous (cur·VAY·shus) *adj.* having a full and rounded figure: *a curvaceous young woman.*

cur·va·ture (CUR·vuh·chur) *n.* a curving or curved part: *the curvature of space, of the earth; a deformity called "curvature of the spine."*

curve *n.* **1** a line, shape, or outline that bends with no straight portion: *a hairpin* or *horseshoe curve; the alluring curves of her figure; a sharp curve in the road; The road describes* or *makes a curve to the east; to plot a curve* (= graph) *using coordinates; your learning curve.* **2** a baseball pitched so as to swerve near the batter: *He threw me a curve* (= tried to trick me) *but to no avail; a* **curve·ball** (= tricky move) *that came close to cheating.*

— *v.* **curves, curved, curv·ing** bend: *The road curves quite sharply to the east.*

cush·ion (COOSH·un, short "OO") *n.* **1** a pillow or pad for sitting, lying, or kneeling on. **2** something that absorbs shock or protects from a blow or shock: *An air cushion vehicle such as a Hovercraft rides on a cushion of air; A savings account will prove to be a cushion when you lose your job.*
— *v.* protect from or absorb the shock of something: *a youth cushioned from the realities of life by his protective parents.*

cush·y (COOSH·ee, short "OO") *adj.* **cush·i·er, -i·est** easy or comfortable: *a cushy job, life, post.*

cusp *n.* a pointed end or peak, as of a leaf or tooth.

cus·pid (CUS·pid) *n.* a single-pointed or canine tooth.

cuss *n. & v. Informal.* same as CURSE but milder in tone: *The punks started hollering and cussing at us; a* **cuss word** (= swear word).

cus·tard (CUS·turd) *n.* a dessert made with a milk-and-egg mixture.

cus·to·di·an (cus·TOH·dee·un) *n.* one who has custody, esp. of a property; caretaker or janitor.

cus·to·dy (CUS·tuh·dee) *n.* **-dies 1** safekeeping; guardianship: *The divorced couple fought for custody of the child; The mother was awarded* or *granted custody; She received, took custody of her child; joint custody (shared by both parents); a custody dispute.* **2** legal detention: *He was held overnight in protective custody; police custody; Suspects are* **taken into** or **put in** *custody.*

cus·tom (CUS·tum) *n.* **1** a conventional usage: *to cherish, establish, observe* or *practise customs; an ancient, local, old, pagan, quaint, tribal custom; It's our custom to bury the dead rather than cremate them; It is my custom* (= habit) *to go for a walk after supper.* **2** customs *pl.* duty on imported goods: *We paid $100 in customs on the camera imported from Europe.* **3** customs *pl.* [takes sing. v.] the department that levies this or a post manned by it: *Customs never closes; We had nothing to declare at customs; had no problem getting our baggage through customs; We cleared* or *got through* or *passed through* or *went through customs quickly.*
— *adj.* making or made to order: *Custom tailors make custom clothes.*
— *combining form.* to order: *a custom-built house; custom-fitted covers; custom-made suits; custom-tailored clothes; to live in custom-tailored comfort.*

cus·tom·ar·y (CUS·tuh·mair·ee) *adj.* conventional: *It's customary among us to bury the dead; It's customary* (= usual) *for me to go for a walk daily; my customary* (= regular or habitual) *walk.*

cus·tom·er (CUS·tuh·mur) *n.* **1** one who purchases something, esp. regularly: *They offer gifts to attract customers; a cash customer who has no use for credit; a prospective, satisfied, steady customer.* **2** a person; fellow: *a shrewd, tough customer; an ugly customer* (= violent person).

cus·tom·ize (CUS·tuh·mize) v. -miz·es, -mized,
-miz·ing build or alter something to specifications.

cut v. cuts, cut, cut·ting 1 separate or pierce something
with a sharp edge or object: *She cut the apple in two; to
cut a loaf into slices; He cut* (= pierced) *his leg on the
barbed wire.* 2 make or do something by or as if by
cutting: *to cut diamonds, glass; to cut a road through
the mountains; to cut a slice from a loaf; to cut*
(= record and produce) *a phonograph record; He cuts
his hair* (= gets a haircut) *every month; a farmer cutting*
(= harvesting) *wheat; She cut* (= struck) *the horse with
her whip; a cold wind that cuts you to the bone; The
baby has cut her first tooth* (= Her first tooth has pierced
the gum); *She cut her teeth* (= had her early training) *as
a journalist on "The Times"; to cut* (= make) *a deal.*
3 reduce or shorten: *We cut the work week to 30 hours;
She has cut her hair; Censors cut movies; His sarcastic
wit really cut* (= hurt) *her; She was cut to the quick*
(= deeply hurt); *He was cut short* (= reduced to silence)
in the middle of a call. 4 absent oneself from somewhere
without leave: *He cut class to go to the movie.*
5 intersect: *where Sixth Avenue cuts Second Street; to
cut* (= go directly) *across a field; Another driver cut me
off* (= got in my way without warning), *then suddenly
cut* (= changed direction) *to the right lane.* 6 divide a
deck of cards. 7 yield to cutting: *This cheese is so soft it
cuts easily.* 8 dilute: *to cut a drink with water.*
9 remove: *Ammonia cuts grease and dirt; She was cut
out of* (= excluded from) *his will.*
— **cut a figure** make an impression: *He cut a sorry
figure with his humour.*
— **cut and run** run away quickly.
— **cut back** prune: *to cut back the shrubbery; She has
cut back on* (= reduced) *her smoking.*
— **cut both ways** have good and bad effects.
— **cut down** reduce: *She has cut down on smoking; She
cut him down to size* (= made him feel less important;
deflated him).
— **cut ice with someone** have influence; make an
impression: *His wild claims cut no ice with me.*
— **cut in** intrude, as move in front of another car;
interrupt: *He cut in on our conversation; Ed cut in when
Joe and Kay had just started dancing.*
— **cut it** Slang. succeed; hack it.
— **cut off** separate; interrupt; discontinue; deprive of
something: *They cut off our heat; We got lost and were
cut off from civilization for a while.*
— **cut out** 1 Informal. stop: *Cut out that noise; Time to
cut out* (= leave quickly). 2 suited: *He's not cut out to be
a lawyer; not cut out for a legal career.* 3 planned and
ready: *The astronauts have their work cut out for them.*
— **cut up** Informal. 1 criticize harshly. 2 play pranks,
clown around, etc. 3 upset: *He's really cut up about the
loss.*
— *n.* a cutting or its result: *a cut on the chin from
shaving; a superficial, not deep cut; cuts made in a story
by the censors; a choice cut of beef; The road ran
through a cut in the mountain; a crew cut; a stylish cut
of hair, clothes; Everyone took a 20% cut* (= reduction)
*in pay last year; a budget cut; tax cut; a cut in
expenditure; staff cuts; Each got a 20% cut* (Slang for
share) *of the profits; Cadillacs are **a cut above***
(= superior to) *other cars; a write-up illustrated with cuts*
(= pictures).

cut-and-dried or **cut-and-dry** adj. already prepared, as
by formula; routine: *a cut-and-dried answer, plan,
solution.*

cut-back n. a reduction: *a budgetary cutback; a cutback
in expenditure.*

cute adj. cut·er, cut·est 1 pretty; dainty: *Babies are
cute; a cute little hat.* 2 affectedly pleasing; artificial: *a
cute act.* 3 Informal. frivolous or disrespectful: *He tried
to be cute with her.* 4 Informal. sly or tricky.
— **cute·ly** adv.; **cute·ness** n.

cute·sy or **cute·sie** (CUTE·see) adj. cute in a mannered
or deliberate way.

cu·tie or **cu·tey** (CUE·tee) n. Informal. a charming and
inoffensive young person.

cut-off n. a cutting off or what results from it: *She wears
cutoffs* (= jeans cut short) *in the summer; cutoffs*
(= shortcuts) *built to eliminate winding roads.*
— **adj.:** *a cutoff period, point, valve; the cutoff date
(when an agreement ends).*

cut-out n. a pattern, picture, part (as the back of a
dress), etc. designed to be or that has been cut out.

cut-rate adj. having to do with reduced prices: *cut-rate
airlines, fares, fees, financing, gasoline, methods, offers,
prices, stores.*

cut-throat n. a murderer.
— **adj.** merciless; bloodthirsty: *cutthroat competition.*

cutting n. a short slip for propagation of a plant.
— **adj.** hurting the feelings: *cutting remarks.*

cutting edge n. the forefront of something developing: *a
company that is at or on the cutting edge of computer
technology.*

cy·an (SYE·un) n. a greenish blue.

cy·ber·net·ics (sye·bur·NET·ics) n.pl. [takes sing. v.] the
comparative study of information flow and control
processes in humans and machines.
— **cy·ber·net·ic** adj.

cy·borg (SYE·borg) n. a human being who depends on
mechanical parts for the carrying out of bodily
functions.

cy·cla·mate (SYE·cluh·mate) n. an artificial salt of
sodium or calcium used as a sugar substitute.

cy·cle (SYE·cul) n. 1 a periodic action or event or the
time taken for it: *the cycle of the seasons; Alternating
current reverses direction at 60 cycles per second; the
four stages in the life cycle of the butterfly; a business,
economic, menstrual cycle.* 2 circle: *The earth
completes its cycle around the sun in one year; to **come
full cycle*** (= come back to the starting point). 3 a
bicycle, tricycle, or motorcycle.
— v. -cles, -cled, -cling ride a cycle. — **cy·clist** n.

cy·cli·cal (SYE·clic·ul) adj. occurring in a cycle;
regularly repeating: *the cyclical swings of the real-estate
market; the cyclical nature of the hotel industry; a
cyclical pattern.* Also **cy·clic.**

cy·clone (SYE·clone) *n.* a spiralling wind formation that includes hurricanes and tornados.
— **cy·clon·ic** (sye·CLON·ic) *adj.*

cy·clo·ram·a (sye·cluh·RAM·uh) *n.* a large picture painted on a circular wall.

cyl·in·der (SIL·un·dur) *n.* the round solid or hollow shape of a pencil, tin can, water pipe, etc.
— **cy·lin·dri·cal** (suh·LIN·druh·cul) *adj.*

cyn·ic (SIN·ic) *n.* one who sneers at the goodness of human nature and actions, attributing everything to self-interest.
— **cyn·i·cal** (-uh·cul) *adj.: She is cynical about his idealism.* — **cyn·i·cism** (-uh·siz·um) *n.*

cy·press (SYE·press) *n.* an evergreen tree of the pine family with scalelike leaves.

cyst (SIST) *n.* an abnormal sac in the body containing fluid. — **cys·tic** *adj.*

czar or **tsar** (ZAR) *n.* **1** a baron; also, an autocrat: *an energy czar; oil czar; a financial, gambling czar.* **2** a Russian emperor (until 1917); *fem.* **cza·ri·na** or **tsa·ri·na** (zah·REE·nuh). — **czar·ist** or **tsar·ist** *n. & adj.*

Dd

D or **d** (DEE) *n.* **D's** or **d's** the fourth letter of the English alphabet.

dab *v.* **dabs, dabbed, dab·bing** put on, touch, or strike with a light, quick, usually soft stroke: *a child dabbing paste on paper; He dabbed at his eyes with a handkerchief; He dabbed his eyes.*
— *n.*: *A quick dab removed the smudge; Put a little dab of butter on the toast.*

dab·ble (DAB·ul) *v.* **dab·bles, dab·bled, dab·bling**
1 spatter with water; splash. **2** play splashing in the water: *Ducks dabbled in the pond.* **3** work or do something amateurishly: *an amateur who dabbles in science; a banker who likes to dabble at gardening; One of the kids was caught dabbling with drugs.*
— **dab·bler** *n.*

dad *n. Informal.* father.

dad·dy (DAD·ee) *n.* **dad·dies 1** [child's word] father.
2 *Informal.* most respected member of a group; dean: *the daddy of all living mayors; the grand daddy of them all.*

daf·fo·dil (DAF·uh·dil) *n.* a yellow flower with long stems and narrow leaves that blooms in early spring.

daf·fy (DAF·ee) *adj.* **daf·fi·er, daf·fi·est** *Informal.* crazy or daft: *a daffy idea; Lu shows a talent for daffy comedy.* — **daf·fi·ness** *n.*

daft *adj.* **1** insane. **2** foolish: *The speech was a bit daft.*

dag·ger (DAG·ur) *n.* **1** a pointed, two-edged knife used for stabbing. **2** a mark (†) used for reference.
— **at daggers drawn** in open hostility *with* some.
— **look daggers** at stare at someone with hate or fury.

dai·ly (DAY·lee) *adj.* of, for, done, or occurring every day: *our daily newspaper; He was paid a daily rate of $500.*
— *adv.*: *Take two pills thrice daily.*
— *n., pl.* **-lies** a newspaper put out every weekday.

dain·ty (DAIN·tee) *adj.* **-ti·er, -ti·est 1** delicate and pleasing: *a dainty centrepiece for the table; a dainty dance step.* **2** fussy; fastidious: *a dainty eater.*
— *n., pl.* **-ties** a delicacy.
— **dain·ti·ly** *adv.*; **dain·ti·ness** *n.*

dair·y (DAIR·ee) *n.* **dair·ies 1** also **dairy farm,** a farm specializing in milk production; *adj.*: *dairy breeds of cattle; dairy cattle, products.* **2** a place where milk and milk products are kept, processed, or sold.
— **dair·y·maid** *n.*
— **dair·y·man** *n.* **-men.; dair·y·wom·an** *n.* **-wo·men.**

dai·sy (DAY·zee) *n.* **-sies** a composite flower with white rays and a yellow centre; also, any similar flower: *as fresh as a daisy; to pick off the daisy petals one by one to determine whether or not something is going to happen; The dead are supposed to* **push up daisies** *from their graves; adj.: The apartment flip was a* **daisy chain** (= linked series) *of deals that drove up the price at each sale; Letter-quality printers use an interchangeable* **daisy-wheel** *with letters around its rim.*

dale *n.* a valley: *through hill and dale.*

dalles (DAL·us, DALZ) *n.pl. Cdn.* the rapids of a river flowing in a narrow channel between high rock walls: *the dalles of the Winnipeg River.*

dal·li·ance (DAL·ee·unce) *n.* a dallying or flirtation: *a brief dalliance with a young actress.*

dal·ly (DAL·ee) *v.* **dal·lies, dal·lied, dal·ly.ing 1** waste time; dawdle: *a child dallying over a meal.* **2** trifle or play: *He dallied with the idea till it was too late; She was merely dallying with his affections* (= flirting).

dam *n.* **1** an obstacle built across a watercourse to hold back the flow: *to build, construct, erect a dam; a storage dam; A dam bursts and floods a valley.* **2** a mother, esp. of a four-legged animal: *a thoroughbred horse with registered sire and dam.*
— *v.* **dams, dammed, dam·ming:** *They dammed the creek to make a duck pond; It is unhealthy to* **dam up** (= bottle up) *your anger.*

dam·age (DAM·ij) *n.* **1** injury or hurt, esp. one resulting in loss: *to cause* or *do damage to something; inflict damage on someone; to repair* or *undo a damage; His car suffered* or *sustained a $2 000 damage in the* accident; *The damage from the fire was extensive; a damage set at $50 000; a grave damage to her reputation; a great, irreparable, serious, severe damage; Lasting* or *permanent damage was done; light* or *slight damage; irreversible damage to the brain from interruption of oxygen supply; fire, flood, material, property, structural, widespread damage.* **2 damages** *pl.* money as a recompense for loss or impairment: *to award, claim, pay, receive, recover damages for defamation of character; Compensatory, exemplary, nominal, punitive damages are awarded by courts.* — *v.* **-ag·es, -aged, -ag·ing** cause or suffer damage: *She damaged her toy; Smaller cars damage more easily; an easily damaged* (= easy to damage) *car; a badly damaged building.*

dame *n.* **1** lady: *Dame Fortune.* **2 Dame** a British title for women corresponding to knight. **3** *Slang.* [used by men] a woman; broad.

damn (DAM) *v.* **1** condemn: *the damned and the saved; a play damned by the critics.* **2** *Slang.* curse or swear saying "damn": *I'll be damned if I know; Damn it all!* — **damn with faint praise** praise so slightly as to imply fault. — *n. Slang.* a damning: *He doesn't* **give** or **care a damn** (= doesn't care at all); *It's* **not worth a damn** (= is worthless); *People want answers and* **by damn** (= damn it!) *they're going to get them.* — **damn** or **damned** *adj. & adv. Slang.* **1** absolute; utter: *a damn fool.* **2** very: *You damn well know it; A damn fine mess we're in now.* — **damnedest** (DAM·dist) *Slang.* **1** worst: *the damnedest mess under the sun.* **2** utmost: *We'll do* or *try our damnedest to get out of it.* — **dam·na·ble** (DAM·nuh·bul) *adj.*

dam·na·tion (dam·NAY·shun) *n.* a damning or being damned: *souls sent to eternal damnation.*

damp *adj.* moderately wet; having absorbed moisture: *My shoes were damp from the rain; An automatic washer fills itself, washes, rinses, and* **damp-dries** *clothes* (= dries them partially) *before shutting off.* — *n.* **1** a moderate wetness. **2** a harmful gas, as in coal mines. — *v.* **1** make damp. **2** reduce enthusiasm, force, or power: *The defeat didn't damp his spirit.* Also **damp·en.** — **damp·ness** *n.*

damp·er *n.* something that reduces or damps, as a plate for checking the draft in a flue, or a felt pad for stopping a piano string's vibration: *The news of the tragedy put a damper on the party.*

dam·sel (DAM·zul) *n.* [old use] a maiden: *Knights used to rescue damsels in distress.*

dance *v.* **danc·es, danced, danc·ing** **1** move the body and feet rhythmically, usually to music; also, perform a particular dance step: *He's dancing in the rain; to dance the cha-cha; She's not the girl to* **dance to someone's tune** (= to be in someone else's power). **2** move lightly, esp. up and down: *a boxer dancing around the ring.* — *n.* **1** a set of dancing movements, as the tango or waltz; also, music for it: *to do* or *perform a dance; a dance with the bride; a circle* or *round dance; a barn, belly, classical, folk, formal, modern, square, sword, tap, war dance.* **2** a party given for dancing: *She went to the school dance; made new friends at the dance; He sat*

out the whole dance because of a sprained ankle. **3** dancing: *a school of dance.* — **danc·er** *n.* — **dancing** *n.:* *aerobic, ballroom, social, belly, break, folk, tap dancing.*

dan·de·lion (DAN·duh·lye·un) *n.* a bright-yellow composite flower having edible, jagged leaves. — *adj.:* *dandelion blossoms, greens, salad, wine.*

dan·der (DAN·dur) *n. Informal.* **get one's dander up** make or become angry.

dan·dle (DAN·dul) *v.* **-dles, -dled, -dling** bounce a child up and down, as on one's knee or in one's arms.

dan·druff (DAN·druf) *n.* whitish flakes of dead skin from the scalp.

dan·dy (DAN·dee) *n.* **-dies** **1** a man who is overly stylish and careful in dress; fop. **2** *Informal.* something excellent of its type: *That's a dandy.* — *adj.* **-di·er, -di·est** excellent: *That is fine and dandy by me!*

dan·ger (DAIN·jur) *n.* exposure to or risk of harm; also, a source of this: *An open manhole constitutes, creates, represents a danger to people; a clear and present danger; People are exposed to, face, run the danger of falling in; There's a danger that they may fall in; a deadly* or *grave* or *mortal danger of breaking one's neck; an imminent* or *impending danger; She sensed the danger; The danger was averted; He fell into the lake and was in danger of his life; was out of danger after a few days; adj.: danger money, pay.*

dan·ger·ous (DAIN·juh·rus) *adj.* liable to cause harm or loss unless dealt with carefully: *It's dangerous to play with fire; Firefighting is a dangerous occupation; The escaped convict is armed and dangerous; a dangerous person, place, thing.* — **dan·ger·ous·ly** *adv.*

dan·gle (DANG·gul) *v.* **-gles, -gled, -gling** hang loosely and swing; also, make to do so: *Fish dangled from a hook; He dangled it before* or *in front of his cat.*

Dan·ish (DAY·nish) *adj.* having to do with Denmark or its people: *Danish cheese.* — *n.* **1** the Danish language. **2** a rich pastry, usually with filling and icing; also **Danish pastry.**

dank *adj.* injuriously or unpleasantly damp: *a dank dungeon.* — **dank·ly** *adv.;* **dank·ness** *n.*

dap·per (DAP·ur) *adj.* (of men of small build) trim or smartly dressed: *a dapper fellow, youth; He looks quite dapper in his new suit; looks a bit too dapper for manual work.*

darb *n. Cdn. Slang.* a remarkable person or thing; lulu.

dare *v.* **dares** [or **dare** if followed by verb without "to"], **dared, dar·ing** **1** challenge: *She dared him to dive after her.* **2** have the boldness to do something: *if he dares to dive after her; if he dare dive after her; He dared not dive after her; didn't dare to dive after her; How dare he defy her?* **3** face boldly: *Brave men dare great dangers.* — *n.* a challenge: *He did it on a dare; He took the dare.* — **dar·er** *n.*

dare·dev·il (DARE·dev·il) *n.* one who acts with reckless courage: *a daredevil stunt.*

dare·say *v.* [used in pres. tense, first person sing.]

venture to say: *I daresay it is cold outside; You're right, I daresay.*

daring (DAIR·ing) *n.* bravery or boldness: *an act, man, woman, work of great daring.*
— *adj.* brave or bold: *a daring action, crime, dress, effort, hero, idea, movie, plan, robbery, thing.*
— dar·ing·ly *adv.*

dark *adj.* 1 lacking in light; not bright or light: *a dark and stormy night; It was pitch dark; a dark (= overcast) day; dark blue; dark hair; a deep dark (= mysterious) secret; **dark glasses** (= sunglasses).* 2 unenlightened: *the **Dark Ages** of early medieval Europe; Africa was once known as the **Dark Continent** (= unexplored continent).* 3 gloomy; also, evil or angry: *a dark look.*
— *n.* darkness: *Ed visited us in the dark of night; Some birds come out after dark (= nightfall); She kept him **in the dark** (= in ignorance) about her plans.*
— dark·ly *adv.*
— dark·ness *n.*: *complete or pitch or total darkness; when darkness falls.*

dark·en (DARK·un) *v.* dim or obscure: *Clouds darkened the sky; Her face darkened with rage; She told him never to **darken her door** (= visit her) again.*

dark horse *n.* a contestant whose strength is still unknown.
— dark-horse *adj.*: *a dark-horse candidate, contender; dark-horse odds.*

dar·ling *n.* a dearly loved person or thing: *Is that you, darling? grandma's little darling; the darling of the film industry.*
— *adj.*: *a darling child, dog; my darling Mimi; What a darling (Informal for charming) purse!*

darn 1 *v.* repair a hole, garment, etc. by interlacing yarn or thread: *to darn old socks.* 2 *n.* a hole thus repaired. 3 *n., v., adj. & adv. Informal.* damn: *Darn it! I don't give a darn; I heard no such darn thing; a darn good excuse.*

darned *adj. & adv. Informal.* same as DARN, 3.
— darned·est utmost: *He did or tried his darnedest to find the lost key.*

dart *n.* 1 a pointed missile that is thrown, blown by a blowgun, etc.: *The game of **darts** is played by aiming darts at a target on a board.* 2 a sudden, fast movement.
— *v.* throw or move with sudden speed: *The frog darts out his tongue to catch a fly; She darted a glance at him; See the rabbits darting across the road.*

dash *v.* 1 move, throw, or strike with violent speed: *The winner dashed (= ran) across the finish line; As the bombs fell, people dashed for cover; In his fury, he dashed (= threw) the cup to the floor; Her hopes were dashed (= destroyed); She revived when he dashed (= splashed) water on her face; Five minutes is all it takes to **dash off** (= write hastily) a letter.* 2 mix with a bit of another substance: *water dashed with vinegar.*
— **dash it (all)!** *Informal.* damn it (all)!
— *n.* 1 a fast move, throw, or strike: *People made a quick dash for cover; a 100-m dash (= race or sprint); A dash (= splashing) of water on the face revived her.* 2 a small amount added or mixed in: *Add a dash of vanilla extract; a dash of colour, salt, whisky.* 3 vigorous,

spirited action: *She plays with dash and vigour.* 4 a punctuation mark (-). 5 dashboard: *I always keep a flashlight and road maps under the dash.*

dash·board *n.* an instrument panel below a vehicle's windshield.

dash·er *n.* the ledge along the top of the boards of a hockey rink; hence, *Cdn.* the boards.

dashing *adj.* spirited; also, stylish: *a dashing young lieutenant.*

da·ta (DAY·tuh, DAT·uh) *n. pl.* [used with sing. or pl. v. depending on sentence structure] basic information; facts as a basis for analysis: *biographical, scientific, statistical data; to cite, evaluate, gather, keyboard, punch in, retrieve, store, transmit data; Raw data is* [not *are*] *fed into the computer for processing; Great masses of data are* [not *is*] *confusing even to a computer; Census figures, school records, and such kind of data is or are called "derived data."*

data bank *n.* a large collection of computerized information; also, the place housing it: *Are data banks a threat to privacy?*

da·ta·base (DAY·tuh·base) *n.* an organized collection or file of information stored in a computer; also, the software for this.

dat·a·ble or **date·a·ble** (DAY·tuh·bul) *adj.* that can be dated: *a datable piece of pottery.*

data processing *n.* operations to convert, store, analyse, and retrieve data in usable form. — **data processor** *n.*

date *n.* 1 the time at which something exists, happens, is made, etc., esp. the day, month, and year: *to fix or set a date for our meeting; 1867 is a significant date in Canadian history; a **cut-off date** (= deadline) for applications; A library book should be returned on the **due date** stamped on it; a target date for completion; at a certain date; at a later date; on a future date; one's **date of birth**; Today's date is August 26.* 2 *Informal.* a social meeting, esp. between a male and female; also, a person with whom one has a date: *to have, make a date for lunch; Dick is Jane's date; They are out on a date; He broke (= did not keep) his date with Jan; a blind date; double date; a date (= appointment) with destiny.* 3 the sweet oblong fruit of a palm tree.
— **out of date** old-fashioned; obsolete: *Daily papers go or get or become out of date every day.*
— **to date** until now: *We have 125 replies to date since the ad appeared.*
— **up to date** using or knowing current information or methods: *We have to bring the boss up to date on what happened while he was away; to bring or make a publication up to date for a new edition; adj.: an up-to-date edition.*
— *v.* dates, dat·ed, dat·ing 1 record or mark the date on something: *a postcard dated 31 March.* 2 determine or show the date or age of a person or thing: *Carbon 14 is used to date artifacts; That expression dates you, Grandpa (= shows you to be of an earlier generation).* 3 have or make a date (with) someone: *Is your sister old enough to date (boys)? She's into computer **dating**.*
— **date back to** or **date from** be in existence since: *Thanksgiving dates back to pioneer days; The October observance dates from 1957.*

dated (DAY·tid) *adj.* old-fashioned.

dateable See DATABLE.

date·less *adj.* 1 undated. 2 timeless; also, too old to date. 3 undying: *dateless fame.*

date·line *n.* the place and date of origin of a document or story, as "Moose Jaw, July 8."

date rape *n.* rape committed on one's partner during a date.

dating bar *n.* a bar for single people to find dates in.

da·tum (DAY·tum, DAT·um) *n., pl.* -ta or -tums [used technically; see DATA for pl. use] an item of information; a given fact: *a sense datum; a datum of consciousness, experience.*

daub *v.* 1 smear or coat, as with grease, clay, plaster, etc.: *to daub plaster on a wall; His hands were daubed* (=soiled) *with ink.* 2 paint crudely or rapidly. — *n.* 1 material for daubing: *a hut made of wattle and daub* (=mud or clay). 2 a daubing; smear or stain; also, a crude painting. — **daub·er** *n.*

daugh·ter (DAW·tur) *n.* 1 a female offspring: *an adopted daughter; foster daughter; She is like a daughter to me, says her neighbour.* 2 a descendant or product thought of as female: *Italian, French, Spanish, etc. are daughters of Latin; Radon daughters are the harmful radioactive decay products of radon gas; adj.: the daughter languages of Latin; a daughter cell, product.* — **daugh·ter·ly** *adj.*: *She cared for the elderly with daughterly devotion.*

daunt *v.* frighten or discourage: *The prospect was rather daunting; She went ahead,* **nothing daunted** (=frightened by nothing). — **daunt·less** *adj.*: *her dauntless courage; a dauntless hero.*

dau·phin (DAW·fin) *n.* till 1830, the title of the eldest son of a king of France.

dav·en·port (DAV·un·port) *n.* a large couch, often a day bed.

daw·dle (DAW·dul) *v.* -dles, -dled, -dling waste time; idle: *to dawdle over breakfast; Stop dawdling, says Mom; Don't dawdle your summer away.* — **daw·dler** *n.*

dawn *n.* 1 the first light of day; daybreak: *We'll start at dawn; at the crack or break of dawn; Dawn breaks in the east; Wake up at dawn.* 2 beginning: *at the dawn of civilization, of history; the dawn of hope, of a new era.* — *v.* become light at sunrise; hence, begin to develop, be clear, etc.: *Day dawns (when the sun rises); The day dawns bright on a clear day; An idea* **dawns on** or **upon** *you (gradually); It dawned on her that she was free at last.*

day *n.* 1 the period from sunrise to sunset: *a cool, cold, hot, sultry, sunny, warm day; an eventful, memorable, opening, red-letter, wedding day;* **The day** (= The important day) *finally arrived; Montreal by day* (= daytime sightseeing in Montreal) *is less exciting than Montreal by night; Most people work* **days** *and sleep nights.* 2 the 24-hour period from midnight to midnight: *the seven days of the week; What time of day is it?* 3 the part of a day one works: *Our day starts at 9;*

We work an 8-hour day; Some are paid by the day or on a **day-to-day** *basis; She did the job in a day; She took the day off on Friday; She is off for the day* (= the rest of the day). 4 a period or stage of existence; age or era: *in days of yore; in days to come; in Columbus's day; back in the old days; during the good old days in Europe; the halcyon days of our youth; It happened just the other day; one of these days* (= in the near future); *the dog days of summer; You'll rue the day you do such a thing;* **In this day and age** *no one should have to sleep in parks; His days are numbered* (= has only a limited time left). 5 a period of success, opportunity, power, etc.: *"Every dog has his day"; a retired politician who has had his day.* 6 success in a contest: *We've carried or won the day; The day is ours; They lost the day.*
— **all in a day's work** the normal thing to happen.
— **call it a day** consider it the end of the day; stop working.
— **day after day** or **day in, day out** or **day in and day out** every day; always.
— **day and night** continually.
— **day in court** a chance to be heard before being judged.
— **make one's day** make one quite happy: *"You made my day," said the woman when told she had won the contract.*

day bed *n.* a couch that may be converted to a bed.

day care *n.* care of children outside of home and school, usually while the parents are at work, as provided at a **day-care centre** or **day nursery**.

day·dream *n.* a reverie; an unrealistic, pleasant thought; *v.: She daydreams about lottery wins.*

day·light *n.* 1 sunlight; daytime: *Rani likes to read by daylight; The bank was robbed in broad daylight.* 2 understanding, like reaching the end of a long journey in the dark: *We're longing to* **see daylight** *on this issue.* 3 daylights Slang. insides or wits: *The boxer had the daylights whipped or beaten or walloped out of him; He scared the (living) daylights out of her with his scream.*

day nursery See DAY CARE.

Day One or **day one** *n.* the beginning of an enterprise or activity: *The business has been a success from Day One.*

daze *v.* **daz·es, dazed, daz·ing** bewilder or confuse by something sudden and excessive: *The tragedy left him dazed; He was dazed by the tragedy; n.: He was in a daze for hours after being hit on the head.*

daz·zle (DAZ·ul) *v.* **daz·zles, daz·zled, daz·zling** dim the vision of someone or overpower, as by bright light or brilliance: *Highbeams dazzle drivers in the opposing lane; a dazzling beauty, display; She dazzles me by her wit.* Also *n.*

D-day *n.* the starting date for a military or other operation, as 6 June 1944, when the Allies invaded Europe: *D-day minus two* (= two days before D-day).

dea·con (DEE·cun) *n.* an assistant to a minister or a clergyman ranking next to a priest; *fem.* **dea·con·ess**.

de·ac·ti·vate (dee·AC·tuh·vate) *v.* -vates, -vat·ed, -vat·ing make inactive or nonfunctional: *He deactivated the time bomb before it could go off.*
— **de·ac·ti·va·tion** (DEE·ac·tuh·VAY·shun) *n.*

dead (DED) *adj.* **1** no longer alive: *Jon was left there for dead; He wasn't playing dead; was dead as a dodo* or *doornail; He had been shot dead; He is now dead and buried; He's dead and gone; She would **not be caught dead** dealing* (*Informal for* would never deal) *with a thug again.* **2** like death or being dead: *dead with fatigue; He collapsed in a dead faint; a criminal who is **dead to*** (=insensible of) *all shame; ears dead* (=numb) *with the cold; a dead* (=lifeless) *party; a dead* (=out of play) *ball; a dead* (=chargeless) *battery; The telephone line is dead; It has gone dead* (=There's no dial tone); *dead* (=infertile) *soil; The ship fell into a dead* (=complete) *calm.* **3** exact or unerring: *I hit it dead centre; with dead accuracy; He's a dead shot with a rifle; It's a dead certainty; Your smile is a dead giveaway* (=sure sign); *a dead ringer* (=lookalike).
— **dead to the world** *Slang.* drunk, fast asleep, or unconscious.
— *adv.* quite: *Are you dead certain? Medicine is dead last in his career choices; We are dead set against dealing with terrorists; It's dead perfect; He's dead tired; It's dead* (=directly) *ahead; He stopped dead* (=as if dead) *in his tracks; He's dead beat* (*Slang for* quite exhausted) *and dead broke* (*Slang for* penniless).
— *n.* **1** dead people: *the quick* or *living and the dead; Lazarus rose from the dead.* **2** a state resembling death: *the dead* (=quietest part) *of the night; in the dead* (=coldest part) *of winter.*

dead·beat *n. Slang.* one who does not pay his debts or fair share.

dead duck *n. Slang.* one sure to be finished with or killed: *One wrong move and you are a dead duck.*

dead·en (DED·un) *v.* **1** deprive of sensation: *a soul deadened by the blows of fate.* **2** dull or weaken: *pain deadened by drugs.* **3** to sound-proof.

dead end *n.* **1** a street, hall, alley, etc. closed at the other end. **2** something with no chance for progress.

dead-end *adj.* closed at the other end: *a dead-end street; a dead-end job with no possibility of advancement; dead-end kids* (of the slums) *fighting for survival.*

dead·head *v. Informal.* of pilots, fly between assignments: *He's deadheading home to Toronto after the London-Montreal flight.*
— *n.* **1** *Cdn.* a log sticking out of the surface of water as a snag to navigation. **2** *Slang.* a freeloader, klutz, bore, etc. **3** a commercial vehicle without its usual payload. **4** a faded flower head.

dead heat *n.* a race or contest between two, as in an election, that ends in a tie.

dead letter *n.* **1** a letter that cannot be delivered or returned, as because of an illegible address. **2** a rule or law no longer enforced though not yet repealed.

dead·line *n.* the time by which something must be done: *to establish, extend, meet, miss, set a deadline; to work against a deadline* (=work to meet the deadline).

dead·lock *n.* a standstill resulting from two unrelenting forces: *to break a deadlock; reach a deadlock; v.: Union and management deadlocked over wage increases.*

dead·ly (DED·lee) *adj.* **-li·er, -li·est 1** likely to cause

death: *assault with a deadly weapon; to use deadly force in self-defence; deadly machine-gun fire; a deadly disease, duel, poison; the seven **deadly sins** that cause spiritual death.* **2** deathlike: *a deadly silence.* **3** extreme; absolute: *in deadly earnest.* **4** unerring: *a deadly aim; with deadly accuracy.* — *adv.* very: *a deadly dull speech.*

dead-on *adj.* precisely on time or target: *You're dead-on; his dead-on aim, timing.*

dead·pan 1 *adj.* without expression or emotion: *a deadpan comedian, face; his deadpan humour.* **2** *n.* a deadpan expression; poker face: *A shy smile split her deadpan.* **3** *v.* **-pans, -panned, -pan·ning** say in a deadpan style: *"All men are created equal," she deadpanned.*

dead reckoning *n.* the determination of a ship's location by using a compass and logbook but not astronomical observations.

dead ringer *n. Slang.* one who looks exactly like another; lookalike: *He's a dead ringer for Elvis Presley.*

dead weight *n.* the weight of anything that is heavy and motionless; hence, a heavy burden.

dead·wood *n.* **1** wood that is dead on a tree. **2** a useless burden, as redundant personnel.

deaf (DEF) *adj.* unable to hear: *He's deaf as a post; stone deaf; She was deaf* (=unwilling to pay heed) *to his pleas; She turned a deaf ear; the blind and **the deaf*** (=deaf people). — **deaf·ness** *n.*

deaf·en (DEF·un) *v.* make deaf: *a deafening crash, noise; the deafening roar of machinery.*

deaf-mute *n. & adj.* (one) who is deaf and dumb.

deal (DEEL) *v.* **deals, dealt** (DELT), **deal·ing 1** give out; distribute, esp. cards to players: *to deal someone four aces; The dictator dealt a blow to free speech.* **2** do business: *Realtors deal in real estate.*
— **deal with** treat: *how to deal with the public; The book deals with* (=is about) *slavery.*
— *n.* **1** a quantity or degree: *a good deal of money; The twins look a good deal alike; Lu spent a great deal of time on the job.* **2** a turn to deal: *Is it my deal now?* **3** a business arrangement: *Let's do* or *make a deal; to strike a deal, to cut* (*Slang for* make) *a deal with someone; a package deal; Our sales reps close* or *wrap up deals; It turned out to be a bad deal.* **4** treatment: *He wanted a fair deal; He got a rough* or *rotten* or *raw deal.* **5** bargain: *We have a great deal on carpets; He got a square deal* (=fair bargain); *The reforms promised a new deal* (=greater social justice) *for the poor; Big deal* (=something impressive)! **6** fir or pine wood cut into planks; also, a plank of this.

deal·er *n.* **1** one who deals: *The dealer also shuffles the cards.* **2** one who deals in goods or wares: *an art, book, car, junk dealer; a dealer in used cars.* **3** *Cdn.* in Newfoundland, a middleman between fishermen and merchants.

deal·er·ship (DEE·lur·ship) *n.* a franchised sales agency: *a hardware dealership; a dealership covering Quebec.*

dealing *n.* business: *I have no dealings with liars; He's capable of crooked dealing* (=behaviour).

dean (DEEN) *n.* **1** the head of a faculty or other division in a university: *Dean of Humanities; Dean of Men; The* ***dean's list*** *recognizes students with very high marks.* **2** a senior or most respected member: *the dean of Canadian historians.* **3** the head of a body of canons, as in a cathedral. — **dean·ship** *n.*

dear (DEER) *adj.* **1** beloved: *a child who is dear to her heart; She holds her dear; her dearest child;* ***n.:*** *Come, my dear; You're a real dear!* **2** warmly regarded: *a dear old buddy; Dear Mr. Smith.* **3** expensive: *It's dear at the price.* **4** sincere: *His dearest hope was for peace.* — ***interj.:*** *O dear! Dear, dear, what's wrong? Dear me!* — **dear·ly** *adv.;* **dear·ness** *n.*

Dear John or **Dear John letter** *n.* a letter from a wife or girlfriend, esp. to a soldier away from home, breaking off a relationship.

dearth (DURTH) *n.* a scarcity, as of food: *in time of dearth and famine; a crippling dearth of raw materials.*

death (DETH) *n.* the act of dying or the state of being dead; also, a cause of this: *He loved her till death; "Till death do us part," as they vowed at marriage; Riel was dignified in death as in life; to cause, face, feign death; the painful, lingering death of the terminally ill; a slow death; It was living death; He died a natural death; a sudden, untimely death in a crash; the crib death of infants; death by drowning, fire, hanging, lethal injection; He was beaten, burnt, shot, starved to death; He met a violent death at the hands of terrorists; She's mourning her brother's death; He was sent to death without a trial; sentenced to death; was put to death by firing squad; Arms dealers are called "merchants of death"; Death to fascism!* — **at the point of death** or **at death's door** near death, as from illness. — **be the death of** cause the death of someone: *That job will be the death of her.* — **catch** or **take one's death of something** suddenly become seriously ill with something. — **death on** devastation to: *a collection agency that is death on defaulters.* — **to death** too much: *bored to death; I've studied the problem to death; Let's not work ourselves to death.*

death·bed *n.* **1** the bed one is dying on. **2** one's last hours of life; ***adj.:*** *a deathbed confession, repentance, scene.*

death·blow *n.* a blow that kills; anything destructive: *The sudden withdrawal of grant money dealt a deathblow to the project.*

death·less *adj.* immortal: *deathless prose.*

death·like *adj.* resembling death: *a deathlike pallor.*

death·ly *adj.* resembling or causing death: *a deathly silence, wound;* ***adv.:*** *It was deathly quiet outside.*

death row *n.* a section of prison housing those awaiting execution: *to be on death row.*

death warrant *n.* **1** an order authorizing an execution. **2** *Informal.* doom: *You'll be signing your own death warrant if you do that.*

death wish *n.* a wish for oneself or another to be dead.

deb *n.* a debutante.

de·ba·cle (di·BAH·cul) *n.* a sudden rout, disaster, or collapse.

de·bar (di·BAR) *v.* **-bars, -barred, -bar·ring** shut out, as from a right or privilege; prevent: *He was debarred from the meetings.* — **de·bar·ment** *n.*

de·base (di·BACE) *v.* **-bas·es, -based, -bas·ing** lower in position, character, or value: *debased coinage, morals.* — **de·base·ment** *n.*

de·bate (di·BATE) *v.* **-bates, -bat·ed, -bat·ing 1** discuss or consider an issue from both sides: *I debated for a long time whether to join or not.* **2** participate in a formal contest of argument: *to debate heatedly* or *hotly with the opposition; the debating club; a good debating style.* — *n.* a debating: *to conduct, hold, moderate a debate; an acrimonious, bitter, heated, lively, spirited debate; a parliamentary debate; a debate in parliament; the ongoing debate about capital punishment.* — **de·bat·a·ble** *adj.* — **de·bat·er** *n.*

de·bil·i·tate (di·BIL·uh·tate) *v.* **-tates, -tat·ed, -tat·ing** make weak or feeble: *a debilitating disease, effect, foreign debt, illness, injury.* — **de·bil·i·ty** *n.*

deb·it (DEB·it) *n.* **1** a sum owed, as recorded in an account. **2** a drawback or disadvantage. — *v.* charge: *Please debit the purchase to* or *against my account; Debit my account with the entire amount.*

debit card *n.* a card for effecting electronic funds transfer from buyer's bank account to seller's.

deb·o·nair or **deb·o·naire** (deb·uh·NAIR) *adj.* jaunty or dashing. — **deb·o·nair·ly** *adv.*

de·brief (di·BREEF) *v.* question a diplomat, astronaut, etc. at the end of a mission to obtain information. — **de·brief·ing** *n.*

de·bris or **débris** (duh·BREE, DAY·bree) *n.* broken remains; rubble: *to clear the debris of an earthquake.*

debt (DET) *n.* **1** what one owes to another, esp. in money: *I had a $5 000 debt; I owe her a debt of gratitude; to cancel, contract, discharge, get into, go into, incur, pay, pay off, recover, run up, settle, wipe out a debt; The creditor wrote off the unpaid debt; the national debt; a* ***debt of honour*** *(= debt based on one's sense of honour for its repayment, as in betting).* **2** the condition of owing: *Everyone tries to stay out of debt; He was deeply in debt from borrowing money to start a business.*

debt·or (DET·ur) *n.* one who owes a debt, as opposed to creditor; ***adj.:*** *a debtor country, nation.*

de·bug (dee·BUG) *v.* **-bugs, -bugged, -bug·ging** remove the bugs from a machine, process, or environment: *to debug a computer program; The room was searched for hidden microphones and thoroughly debugged.*

de·bunk (dee·BUNK) *v. Informal.* show the falsity of something: *The survey debunked the myths about everyone being able to read and write; to debunk a claim, notion, theory, view.*

de·but (di·BYOO, DAY·byoo) *n.* a first performance or appearance: *She didn't wait till 21 to make her debut (= formal appearance in society); She made her debut as a child actor at age five.*

dec·ade (DEC·ade) *n.* a ten-year period or set: *The decade of the 1980s runs from 1980 to 1989.*

dec·a·dence (DEC·uh·dunce) *n.* a decline or decay in standards, esp. in art or morals: *the current educational decadence that contributes to the high level of illiteracy; the decadence of Byzantine art.*
— **dec·a·dent** *n. & adj.: decadent art, civilization, culture, movements.*

de·camp (di·CAMP) *v.* 1 break camp and leave. 2 run away, usually secretly: *The club's treasurer decamped with $10 000.*

de·cant (di·CANT) *v.* pour a liquid gently, so as not to stir up the sediment: *The wine was decanted into smaller bottles.*

de·cap·i·tate (di·CAP·uh·tate) *v.* -tates, -tat·ed, -tat·ing cut off the head of someone; behead.
— **de·cap·i·ta·tion** (-uh·TAY·shun) *n.: decapitation by guillotine.*

de·cath·lon (di·CATH·lon, *rhyme:* on) *n.* a contest consisting of ten track-and-field events, as in the Olympics.

de·cay (di·CAY) *v.* 1 lose power, health, beauty, etc.: *Everything on earth decays; The magnetism of even permanent magnets decays in time; When the orbit of a satellite decays, it loses speed and altitude and falls to earth.* 2 decompose or disintegrate: *Meat decays if left outside the refrigerator; Some radioactive substances decay* (= lose atomic particles) *faster than others.*
— *n.* 1 loss of health, beauty, power, etc.: *the decay of the patient's mental faculties; a once-booming town now fallen into decay.* 2 decomposition or disintegration: *how to prevent tooth decay; the moral decay of our time; the slow decay of radium.*

de·cease (di·SEECE) *n.* [formal use with reference to people recently dead] death or demise.
— **de·ceased** *n. & adj.* dead: *to pay our respects to the deceased; her deceased husband; He is now deceased.*

de·ceit (di·SEET) *n.* 1 dishonesty: *behaviour full of deceit; practised deceit.* 2 a trick: *the con man's various deceits.*
— **de·ceit·ful** *adj.: a deceitful ad campaign; deceitful statistics.*

de·ceive (di·SEEV) *v.* -ceives, -ceived, -ceiv·ing mislead deliberately, as by lying, trickery, or cheating: *The company was deceived into hiring the illegal immigrant.*

de·cel·er·ate (dee·SEL·uh·rate) *v.* -ates, -at·ed, -at·ing go or cause to go more slowly: *A driver decelerates the engine by taking the foot off the gas pedal or by applying the brakes; A spacecraft decelerates by reversing the thrust of the engines; Business activity decelerates as the economy slows down.*
— **de·cel·er·a·tion** (-RAY·shun) *n.*

de·cen·cy (DEE·sun·see) *n.* 1 the quality of being decent; also, a propriety: *Observe the decencies when in good company.* 2 kindness, courtesy, or sense of obligation: *He doesn't have a spark of decency; We should have the decency to call and cancel a date we cannot keep; Common decency demands it.*

de·cen·ni·al (di·SEN·ee·ul) *adj.* 1 of or lasting 10 years. 2 occurring every 10 years: *the decennial census.*
— *n.* a tenth anniversary.

de·cent (DEE·sunt) *adj.* 1 conforming to social conventions in regard to behaviour: *decent and respectable people; a decent chap, man, student, woman; It was decent of her to pay for our meal; Don't come in yet, I'm not decent* (= dressed)! 2 *Informal.* quite good: *a decent job, salary.* — **de·cent·ly** *adv.*

de·cen·tral·ize (dee·SEN·truh·lize) *v.* -iz·es, -ized, -iz·ing distribute something concentrated, as power, population, or industry, over a wider area: *to decentralize the federal bureaucracy.*
— **de·cen·tral·i·za·tion** (-luh·ZAY·shun) *n.*

de·cep·tion (di·SEP·shun) *n.* 1 a deceiving or being deceived; deceit: *to practise deception.* 2 a trick, lie, etc.: *a magician's deceptions; a deliberate deception.*
— **de·cep·tive** (-tiv) *adj.*
— **de·cep·tive·ly** *adv.: a deceptively simple question.*

dec·i·bel (DES·uh·bel) *n.* the unit of intensity of sound: *A whisper measures 20 decibels, an automobile horn up to 90; Teachers try to keep the* **decibel level** (= noise level) *down in their classrooms.*

de·cide (di·SIDE) *v.* -cides, -cid·ed, -cid·ing 1 settle or resolve: *The issue was decided by flipping a coin; The court case was decided in favour of Mr. Smith; The jury decided for* (= in favour of) *the defendant.* 2 make up one's mind: *I couldn't decide what to do with the money; to decide whether I wanted a cat or a dog; I found it difficult to decide between them; Finally I decided against having a pet; I decided to buy a new TV; We also decided on a vacation; We decided that we would go to the Bahamas.* 3 cause to decide: *A sense of fair play decided me on the question.*

decided *adj.* definite: *a decided advantage; a very decided* (= determined) *young man.*

deciding *adj.* that settles a controversy or contest: *the deciding game, run, vote.*

de·cid·u·ous (di·SIJ·oo·us) *adj.* of leaves, antlers, etc., falling off or out at a certain time: *Baby teeth are deciduous; Fame and glory are often deciduous* (= passing quickly); *Deciduous trees* (= with deciduous leaves) *make a deciduous forest.*

dec·i·mal (DES·uh·mul) *adj.* of or based on units of ten or tenths: *decimal currency; the decimal system of weights and measures.*
— *n.* a fraction (**decimal fraction**) such as 0.05.

dec·i·mate (DES·uh·mate) *v.* -mates, -mat·ed, -mat·ing destroy a large portion of a group: *cities decimated by plague; to decimate the enemy forces, buffalo herds.*

de·ci·pher (di·SYE·fur) *v.* interpret something written despite illegibility or a code; decode: *Even pharmacists have problems deciphering doctors' prescriptions.*

de·ci·sion (di·SIZH·un) *n.* 1 a deciding or resolution; also, a statement of this: *The judge's decision was appealed to a higher court; to arrive at, hand down, make, overrule, reach, render, reverse a decision; an arbitrary, just, final, landmark, momentous, rash decision; a split* (= not unanimous) *decision; a decision to go ahead with the plan.* 2 the ability to decide; also, determined firmness: *Lu lacks decision; His wife is a woman of decision.*

de·ci·sive (di·SYE·siv) *adj.* **1** determining or deciding; crucial: *the decisive moment of the war; a decisive victory.* **2** definite: *a decisive advantage.* **3** determined or firm: *a leader of decisive judgment.*
— de·ci·sive·ly *adv.*; de·ci·sive·ness *n.*

deck *n.* **1** a floor of a ship, esp. the main one: *to swab the deck; the main deck; promenade deck; the flight deck of an aircraft where the pilot sits; The flight deck of an aircraft carrier is used for landings and takeoffs; the upper or top deck of a double-decker; Hit the deck* (*Slang* for lie low) *when shooting starts; A deck chair is a folding chair used on a ship's deck.* **2** a platform or other surface similar to a ship's deck: *a sun deck.* **3** a pack of cards: *to cut, shuffle, stack a deck.* **4** a tape deck.
— clear the decks make ready.
— on deck present and ready: *The next batter is on deck; If I were on deck, this wouldn't have happened.*
— *v.* **1** provide or cover with a deck. **2** adorn or decorate: *Deck the halls; a bride decked out in all her finery.* **3** *Slang.* knock down to the floor, esp. with the fist: *The Twins decked* (= beat) *the Cardinals in the World Series.*

de·claim (di·CLAIM) *v.* **1** recite or speak dramatically. **2** attack verbally: *to declaim against inflation and unemployment without doing anything about it.*
— dec·la·ma·tion (dec·luh·MAY·shun) *n.*
— de·clam·a·to·ry (di·CLAM·uh·tor·ee) *adj.*

dec·la·ra·tion (dec·luh·RAY·shun) *n.* an announcement or statement: *Jack made a false declaration to customs; The accused issued a solemn declaration of innocence; the American Declaration of Independence in 1776; In 1959, the United Nations adopted the Declaration of the Rights of the Child.*

declaration day *n. Cdn.* a day on which candidates are declared duly elected after the official vote count.

de·clar·a·to·ry (di·CLAIR·uh·tor·ee) or **de·clar·a·tive** (di·CLAIR·uh·tiv) *adj.* making a statement: *a declaratory sentence such as "I love you."*

de·clare (di·CLAIR) *v.* **-clares, -clared, -clar·ing** **1** state or make known formally; announce: *The judges declared Jim the winner; declared Jim elected; declared Jim to have won the election; Iraq declared war on Iran; Iran declared that it would fight to the finish; Do you have anything to declare* (*that is dutiable*)? **2** state definitely: *Ed declared his love for Jane; declared that he loved her; They declared themselves* (*to be*) *for marriage,* (*to be*) *against or opposed to divorce; Well, I declare!* (= I am surprised). **3** in bridge, name a trump suit or "no-trump." — dec·lar·er *n.*

de·clas·si·fy (dee·CLAS·uh·fye) *v.* **-fies, -fied, -fy·ing** make secret papers public or no longer classified.

de·cline (di·CLINE) *v.* **-clines, -clined, -clin·ing** **1** slope or move downwards: *At the village, the land declines rapidly to the valley below; Her health, influence, power is declining* (= going from a better to a worse condition); *She is in her declining years* (= last part of life). **2** say no or refuse politely: *She declined his kind offer of a ride.*
— *n.* a going down or moving from a better to a worse position: *the decline and fall of the Roman Empire; a sharp decline in prices caused by an oversupply; The*
patient suffered or went into a gradual, steady decline; Interest in large cars was on the decline (= going down) *when gas prices were going up.*

de·code (dee·CODE) *v.* **-codes, -cod·ed, -cod·ing** translate out of code: *to decode a message in cipher; to decode a TV signal.*
— de·cod·er *n.* an electronic decoding device: *Decoders are used to unscramble TV transmissions.*

de·com·pose (dee·cum·POZE) *v.* **-pos·es, -posed, -pos·ing** break down into component parts; rot.
— de·com·po·si·tion (DEE·com·puh·ZISH·un) *n.*

de·com·pres·sion (dee·cum·PRESH·un) *n.* the releasing of pressure: *The hostages were taken to a hospital for decompression after their release by the terrorists; The quickest way to put out a fire on an aircraft is decompression* (= getting rid of the oxygen); *Decompression sickness is caused by a too rapid release from pressure, as when deep-sea divers or caisson workers surface too quickly.*

de·con·ges·tant (dee·cun·JES·tunt) *n.* something that relieves congestion: *nasal decongestants; a decongestant spray.*

de·con·trol (dee·cun·TROLE) *v.* **-trols, -trolled, -trol·ling** remove government controls from commodities, prices, gold coins, etc.: *to decontrol the economy.*

dé·cor or **de·cor** (day·COR) *n.* the style of decoration of a room or the layout of what is displayed in it: *a Scandinavian décor.*

dec·or·ate (DEC·uh·rate) *v.* **-ates, -at·ed, -at·ing** **1** beautify what is plain by adding colour or ornament: *We have to decorate the basement for the party.* **2** make a place suitable for living in: *The landlord is supposed to decorate the apartment by painting, wallpapering, etc. before we move in.* **3** honour with an award, medal, etc.: *a soldier decorated for heroism.*
— dec·or·a·tion (-RAY·shun) *n.*: *A decoration for bravery was awarded to the police officer; Remembrance Day has replaced Decoration Day which the Royal Canadian Legion and IODE used to observe; In December, it's time to put up Christmas decorations.*
— dec·o·ra·tor (DEC·uh·ray·tur) *n.*: *an interior decorator.*

de·co·rum (di·COR·um) *n.* seemliness or propriety in speech, action, appearance, etc.: *Strict decorum is observed during a royal visit.*
— dec·o·rous (DEC·uh·rus, di·COR·us) *adj.*

de·coy (di·COY) *n.* something used to draw others into danger, as a wooden bird to lure real birds within range of a hunter. — *v.* trick or lure into a trap.

de·crease (di·CREECE) *v.* **-creas·es, -creased, -creas·ing** grow or cause to grow smaller, less, etc.: *to decrease defence capability; Will you please decrease the volume* (*Informal* for lower the volume or speak softer)?
— *n.* (DEE·creece): *A 75% decrease in car insurance rates is unlikely; There has been a gradual, steady decrease in industrial accidents; Traffic deaths seem to be on the decrease.* — de·creas·ing·ly *adv.*

de·cree (di·CREE) *n.* an official order or judgment, as of a court of law or a ruler: *to enact, issue, rescind, revoke a decree; a divorce decree.*

— *v.* **-crees, -creed, -cree·ing 1** to issue a decree: *Parliament decreed that the death penalty be abolished.* **2** bring into being by decree: *The government decreed a day of public mourning in honour of the dead hero.*

de·crep·it (di·CREP·it) *adj.* worn-out or broken-down, esp. by long use.

de·cry (di·CRY) *v.* **-cries, -cried, -cry·ing** criticize openly and strongly: *The Opposition decried the Government's feeble efforts at reform.*

ded·i·cate (DED·uh·cate) *v.* **-cates, -cat·ed, -cat·ing 1** devote or commit, as to a sacred use, to a cause, etc.: *institutions dedicated to the preservation of freedom; to dedicate a chapel; A humanitarian is one who is dedicated to helping others.* **2** address a book, song, etc. to someone as a mark of honour: *He dedicated the book to his wife.* — **ded·i·ca·tion** (-CAY·shun) *n.*

dedicated *adj.* **1** devoted to a cause: *a dedicated person, worker.* **2** set apart for a special use: *a dedicated machine, network channel, procedure, program, system.*

de·duce (di·DUCE, *rhyme:* produce) *v.* **-duc·es, -duced, -duc·ing** infer by reasoning: *If A equals B and B equals C, then we deduce that A equals C.* — **de·duc·i·ble** (-suh·bul) *adj.*

de·duct (di·DUCT) *v.* take away or subtract: *Tuition fees may be deducted from income on tax returns.*

de·duc·tion (di·DUC·shun) *n.* **1** a deducing or conclusion: *a logical deduction by Sherlock Holmes; a deduction that the death was a suicide.* **2** a deducting: *Allowable deductions from income include charitable donations; We try to claim as many deductions as possible to reduce the amount of tax to be paid.*

de·duc·tive (di·DUC·tiv) *adj.* of or characterized by inference from premises to conclusions: *deductive and inductive logic.* — **de·duc·tive·ly** *adv.*

deed *n.* **1** something done; action: *the brave deeds done or performed by heroes; chivalrous, daring, heroic, noble, wicked deeds; a friend who is faithful in word and deed.* **2** a signed legal document, esp. one conferring ownership of property: *Who holds the deed (= title) to this land?* — *v.* convey by deed: *The property had been deeded to him by his late wife.*

dee·jay (DEE·jay) *n. Informal.* a disk jockey.

deem *v. Formal.* believe or consider: *The scout deemed it unwise to light a fire in that area; She threatens to do as she deems fit.*

deep *adj.* **1** being or extending far down or in something: *the deep blue sea; The rocket was lost deep in space; He seems deep (= immersed) in thought; Sam is very deep (= involved) in debt; a deep (= large) discount, price cut; the deep (= underlying meaning, not surface) structure of a sentence.* **2** from front to back: *The sofa is 224 cm wide and 91 cm deep; The crowd that lined the street was ten deep in places along the route.* **3** from a depth: *Take a deep breath.* **4** of sound, low in pitch: *a deep voice.* **5** of colour, rich or dark: *a deep red.* **6** profound or thorough: *deep emotions; a deep sleep; a deep silence; a deep, scholarly study; He found himself in **deep water** (= in trouble) in calculus.*

7 mysterious: *a deep secret.* **8** very serious or grave: *He was in deep trouble for skipping school.* — **go off the deep end** *Informal.* yield to anger or excitement. — *adv.* in a deep manner: *We dug deep in the earth; The children were lost deep in the woods; He works deep into the night; "Still waters run deep."* — *n.* depth: *in the deep of the night; denizens of the deep* (= ocean) . — **deep·ly** *adv.*

deep·en (DEE·pun) *v.* become or make deeper: *the deepening gloom.*

deep-freeze *n.* **1** a freezer for quickly freezing food. **2** a suspension of action; cold storage: *We had to put the plan in (the) deepfreeze because of lack of funds.* Also *v.* **deep·freez·es,** *pt.* **-froze** or **-freezed,** *pp.* **-froz·en** or **-freezed, -freez·ing.**

deep-fry *v.* **-fries, -fried, -fry·ing** fry potatoes, onions, etc. immersed in oil or fat: *French fries are deep-fried; deep-fried potatoes.*

deep pocket *n. Informal.* wealth: *Lawyers think accountants are the ones with the deep pocket.*

deep-rooted (DEEP·ROO·tid) *adj.* firmly implanted, as a plant with deep roots: *a deep-rooted dislike, dissatisfaction; deep-rooted anxieties, fears, frustrations, prejudices, problems, traditions.*

deep-sea *adj.* having to do with the deep parts of the sea: *deep-sea diver, diving, exploration.*

deep-seated (DEEP·see·tid) *adj.* **1** well below the surface: *a deep-seated illness.* **2** same as DEEP-ROOTED.

deep-set (DEEP·set) *adj.* deeply set: *deep-set eyes.*

deep space *n.* space beyond the moon or solar system.

deer *n. sing. & pl.* any of a group of ruminant animals having cloven hooves, including moose, elk, white-tailed deer, and caribou: *a herd of deer; the fawn (= young one) of a deer; a female deer (= doe); a male deer (= buck or stag); deer meat (= venison).*

de·face (di·FACE) *v.* **-fac·es, -faced, -fac·ing** disfigure the surface or lettering of something: *He was arrested for defacing the War Memorial.* — **de·face·ment** *n.*

de fac·to (di·FAC·toh) *adj. & adv.* in actual fact; actual or actually: *De facto slavery still exists although de jure it has been abolished in most countries.*

de·fame (di·FAME) *v.* **-fames, -famed, -fam·ing** injure someone or someone's reputation by libel or slander. — **de·fam·er** *n.*

— **def·a·ma·tion** (def·uh·MAY·shun) *n.*
— **de·fam·a·to·ry** (di·FAM·uh·tor·ee) *adj.*

de·fault (di·FAULT) *v.* 1 fail to do something, as appear in court, repay a loan, or enter a contest: *He defaulted on his debt and lost his credit rating.* 2 of a variable in a computer system, return to its preset value: *If a margin width is not specified by the user, the computer defaults to the 12-space setting.*
— *n.* 1 a failure to do what is expected of one: *The plaintiff lost his case by default; She went ahead as planned in default of* (= lacking) *instructions to the contrary.* 2 a particular value to which a variable is set in a computer system: *By default* (= Unless instructed otherwise), *all text is printed out with a 12-space left margin; Twelve spaces is the default margin.*

def·con (DEF·con) *n.* defence condition, a state of military alert: *Defcon ranges from Defcon I* (= state of war) *to Defcon V* (= combat readiness).

de·feat (di·FEET) *v.* 1 frustrate or thwart: *to defeat a bill in parliament; To talk too much about the security system is to defeat its very purpose.* 2 beat: *to defeat the enemy in battle; The Yankees were defeated 2 to 1.*
— *n.* a defeating: *the defeat of the Yankees: They met, suffered defeat at the hands of the Blue Jays; to admit, invite defeat; a crushing, shameful, total defeat.*

de·feat·ism (di·FEE·tiz·um) *n.* a too ready acceptance or expectation of defeat.
— **de·feat·ist** *adj.*: *a defeatist attitude.*

def·e·cate (DEF·uh·cate) *v.* -cates, -cat·ed, -cat·ing empty the bowels. — **def·e·ca·tion** (-CAY·shun) *n.*

de·fect (di·FECT) *n.* a lack, fault, or imperfection: *to correct speech defects such as lisping and stuttering; a glaring defect; a birth defect; a congenital, hearing, mental, physical, structural defect.*
— *v.* to desert to another cause, party, country, etc.: *The Soviet athletes defected to the U.S.; They defected from Russia.* — **de·fec·tion** *n.* — **de·fec·tor** *n.*

de·fec·tive (di·FEC·tiv) *adj.* having a defect: *She returned the defective appliance to the store; A defective verb such as "ought" lacks some of the usual forms as in "take-took-taken-taking."*
— *n.* a subnormal person: *Mental defectives are not accepted for military training.*

de·fence or **de·fense** (di·FENCE) *n.* 1 an act or means of defending: *"Offence is the best form of defence;" civil defence; a defence of his position on disarmament; to conduct, organize, put up a defence; a heroic, military, national, strong defence; She spoke in defence of freedom and democracy; a mutual defence pact.*

defence mechanism *n.* an unconscious mental process or reaction of protection against unpleasant truths or feelings.

de·fend (di·FEND) *v.* 1 fight for a person or cause; also, argue in defence of something: *to defend yourself against an attacker; I defend your right to speak; to defend a proposal under attack.* 2 speak in a law court for someone accused or sued, the **de·fen·dant.** 3 to contest a claim or action.

de·fend·er (di·FEN·dur) *n.* one who defends: *a staunch defender of the underprivileged; the challenger and the defender* (= holder) *of a title; a public defender* (= lawyer assigned to defend the poor).

de·fen·si·ble (di·FEN·suh·bul) *adj.* that can be defended: *a defensible claim.*

de·fen·sive (di·FEN·siv) *adj.* 1 defending: *a defensive play, position, weapon.* 2 acting as though under attack: *He is rather defensive about his views; a defensive battery of tests ordered out of fear of being sued for malpractice; a defensive, negative, and poorly motivated group of employees.*
— **on the defensive** 1 defending oneself: *Their aggressiveness kept us on the defensive.* 2 acting as though under attack: *Mention of the subject puts him on the defensive; He goes on the defensive when the subject is mentioned.*

de·fer (di·FUR) *v.* -fers, -ferred, -fer·ring 1 put off until later; postpone: *The judge deferred sentencing the convicted man; People buy on credit with a down payment followed by equal amounts of deferred payments.* 2 yield to another's opinion or judgment, esp. as a courtesy: *I defer to your greater knowledge and experience in the matter.*

def·er·ence (DEF·uh·runce) *n.* courteous respect: *in deference to the feelings of others.*
— **def·er·en·tial** (-REN·shul) *adj.*

de·fer·ment (di·FUR·munt) *n.* a delaying of induction into the military: *draft deferment for a student who is at college.* Also **de·fer·ral** (di·FUR·ul).

de·fi·ance (di·FYE·unce) *n.* 1 a challenge: *explorers bidding defiance to nature.* 2 bold refusal to obey: *"Over my dead body," he said in defiance; He acted in defiance of* (= defying) *public opinion.*
— **de·fi·ant** (di·FYE·unt) *adj.*: *a defiant young hoodlum.* — **de·fi·ant·ly** *adv.*

de·fi·cien·cy (di·FISH·un·see) *n.* the lack of something necessary or its amount: *a severe mental deficiency; to suffer from iron deficiency; a deficiency of $200 in the account; mineral deficiencies in the diet; nutritional deficiencies; vitamin deficiencies; Scurvy is a deficiency disease.*

de·fi·cient (di·FISH·unt) *adj.* lacking something necessary: *a diet that is deficient in vitamin C; a deficient* (= insufficient) *supply of nutrients.*

def·i·cit (DEF·uh·sit) *n.* the amount by which a sum is too small: *huge budgetary deficits; an operating deficit; trade deficits; The Montreal Olympics chalked up a $1 billion deficit; deficit spending (using borrowed money).*

de·file (di·FILE) 1 *v.* -files, -filed, -fil·ing make dirty or impure; desecrate or dishonour: *a murderer's hands defiled with blood.* 2 *n.* (*also* DEE·file) a narrow pass or valley.

de·fine (di·FINE) *v.* -fines, -fined, -fin·ing 1 state the meaning of a word: *Please define your terms; "Square" may be defined as "a plane figure with four equal sides and angles."* 2 state or show the limits of something; specify: *a law defining the powers of the police; A position paper defines or outlines one's position or views on a subject; The height of the first hill defines the roller coaster and its momentum to do the whole track*

without mechanical help. **3** show the edge or shape of something: *a clearly defined shape; a sharply defined TV picture.*
— **de·fin·a·ble** (-nuh·bul) *adj.* — **de·fin·er** *n.*

def·i·nite (DEF·uh·nit) *adj.* **1** well defined; clear and distinct: *A plan should have a definite goal in view; Tall players have a definite advantage over others in basketball.* **2** certain: *It's not definite yet that anyone will be here on Monday morning; I want a definite answer from you before Friday evening; Let us be definite about it.*
— **def·i·nite·ly** *adv.: That is definitely* (= clearly) *untrue; My answer is, most definitely (yes)! No, definitely not!*— **def·i·nite·ness** *n.*

def·i·ni·tion (def·uh·NISH·un) *n.* **1** a defining or determining, esp. a statement of a word's meaning: *the dictionary definition of a word; to formulate, provide, write a definition; By definition* (= As the very term suggests), *a delta is a triangular piece of land.* **2** distinctness or clarity: *a picture with good definition; High-definition TV gives clearer and brighter pictures; Eyebrow pencils give definition to brows, mustaches, and beards.*

de·fin·i·tive (di·FIN·uh·tiv) *adj.* **1** conclusive: *a definitive yes-or-no reply; a definitive decision, order of the highest court.* **2** the most complete and reliable to date: *a definitive study; the definitive text of Shakespeare.* **3** explicitly defining: *a definitive statement of the party's position on disarmament.*

de·flate (di·FLATE) *v.* -flates, -flat·ed, -flat·ing **1** let the air or gas out of something inflated: *to deflate a tire.* **2** reduce the self-esteem of someone conceited: *to deflate his ego.* **3** reduce prices or the money supply in the economy: *deflated prices; a deflated economy.*
— **de·fla·tion** (-FLAY·shun) *n.*

de·flect (di·FLECT) *v.* turn aside or from a straight course: *light rays deflected by a prism; to deflect from the straight and narrow path.*

de·fog (di·FOG) *v.* -fogs, -fogged, -fog·ging remove fog or condensation. — **de·fog·ger** (di·FOG·ur) *n.*

de·form (di·FORM) *v.* destroy the natural form of something; disfigure; also, become deformed: *Thalidomide deformed fetuses in the wombs of mothers who took the drug; Anger and hate deform faces; the deformed* (= misshapen) *limbs of Thalidomide children.*
— **de·for·ma·tion** (dee·for·MAY·shun) *n.*

de·form·i·ty (di·FOR·muh·tee) *n.* -ties a physical or moral flaw; disfigurement: *Clubfoot is a congenital deformity of the foot.*

de·fraud (di·FRAUD) *v.* deprive someone of something by fraud; swindle: *The bank was defrauded of $1 million.*

de·fray (di·FRAY) *v.* pay for costs or expenses: *a collection to defray the costs of the convention.*

de·frost (di·FROST) *v.* **1** thaw: *to defrost frozen meat.* **2** free or make free of ice or frost: *Some refrigerators have to be defrosted when ice builds up in the freezer section; Automobiles have a windshield defrosting system.*

deft *adj.* skilful, quick, and facile: *the deft fingers of a*

surgeon or pianist; a deft performance; the deft touches of an artist's brush.*

de·funct (di·FUNCT) *adj.* no longer existing; dead: *a defunct committee, idea, species; the now defunct Montreal Star newspaper.*

de·fuse (dee·FUZE) *v.* -fus·es, -fused, -fus·ing **1** remove the fuse of an explosive: *to defuse a bomb.* **2** make less dangerous or tense: *to defuse a dangerous crisis; to defuse an explosive situation.*

de·fy (di·FYE) *v.* -fies, -fied, -fy·ing **1** dare or challenge, esp. with mocking contempt: *I defy you, punk! She defied him to take the lie detector test; His feats seemed to defy even death; Those who defy the law get arrested.* **2** to exceed the power of something; resist: *beauty that defies description; a problem that defies solution.*

de·gen·er·ate (di·JEN·uh·rate) *v.* -ates, -at·ed, -at·ing decline to a worse condition: *The debate degenerated into a brawl.*
— **adj. & n.** (-uh·rit) (one) that is degraded, as from normality: *a degenerate people; a drunken degenerate (person); degenerate art forms.*
— **de·gen·er·a·tion** (-uh·RAY·shun) *n.: Accumulation of fat around the heart, liver, etc. causes fatty degeneration interfering with their proper functioning.*
— **de·gen·er·a·tive** (-uh·tiv) *adj.: Arthritis is a degenerative disease; the degenerative nature of drug addiction.*

de·grad·a·ble (di·GRAY·duh·bul) *adj.* that can break down chemically: *Biologically degradable materials do not pollute the environment; degradable detergents, plastics.* — **de·grad·a·bil·i·ty** (-BIL·uh·tee) *n.*

deg·ra·da·tion (deg·ruh·DAY·shun) *n.* a degrading: *moral degradation; public degradation; a life of misery and hopeless degradation.*

de·grade (di·GRADE) *v.* -grades, -grad·ed, -grad·ing **1** decrease in rank, quality, or moral character; corrupt or disgrace: *Abuse of children degrades society; A man degrades himself by abusing children; It is degrading to human nature.* **2** break down chemically.

de·gree (di·GREE) *n.* **1** a level or stage in a progression or series: *We have students at every degree of proficiency; people of all degrees and conditions in life; It's true to a great or large degree; a man who was wealthy to the highest or last degree; "Less" and "greater" are in the comparative degree of "little" and "great"; First-degree murder is the most serious murder, but a third-degree burn is the worst kind of burn; They really gave him the third degree (Informal for mental or bodily torture).* **2** a relative amount or manner: *Everyone can tolerate pain to a or to a certain or to some degree; I don't mind the cold in the slightest degree; The patient's health is improving by degrees* (= step by step). **3** a unit of measurement, as for temperature or angles: *32 degrees Fahrenheit or 0 degree Celsius is the freezing point of water; a 90-degree* (= right) *angle.* **4** a rank or title awarded by a college or university: *She's working for a degree in economics; She will receive or take her degree after four years of study; a bachelor's, master's, doctoral or doctor's degree; An honorary degree* (= not an earned one) *was bestowed or conferred on our mayor.*

degree day *n.* the number of degrees by which the daily average temperatures of a region fall below 18 degrees Celsius during a year, used as an index of coldness during the heating season: *The average number of degree days in the Toronto area is 4 214; A colder climate means more degree days.*

de·hu·man·ize (dee·HEW·muh·nize) *v.* -iz·es, -ized, -iz·ing make machinelike or inhuman: *a dehumanized assembly-line job; movies that degrade and dehumanize women; the dehumanizing aspects of solitary confinement.*
— **de·hu·man·i·za·tion** (-nuh·ZAY·shun) *n.*

de·hu·mid·i·fy (dee·hew·MID·uh·fye) *v.* -fies, -fied, -fy·ing reduce the moisture content of something, esp. air. — **de·hu·mid·i·fi·er** *n.*
— **de·hu·mid·i·fi·ca·tion** (-fuh·CAY·shun) *n.*

de·hy·drate (dee·HYE·drate) *v.* -drates, -drat·ed, -drat·ing dry, esp. foods to preserve them: *dehydrated coffee* (=instant coffee).
— **de·hy·dra·tion** (dee·hye·DRAY·shun) *n.* drying of the body: *High fever, heavy perspiration, etc. may cause dehydration.*

de·ice (DEE·ice) *v.* -ic·es, -iced, -ic·ing make or keep free of ice: *In freezing weather, airplanes have to be deiced before takeoff.*
— **de·ic·er** *n.*: *an electric windshield deicer.*

deign (DAIN) *v.* of God and people in high station, be gracious and kind enough to do something: *The king deigned to visit us.*

de·i·ty (DEE·uh·tee) *n.* -ties **1** a divine being or divinity. **2** the **Deity** God.

de·ja vu or **dé·jà vu** (day·zhah·VEW) *n.* a feeling of having previously experienced a novel situation: *a profound sense of deja vu; an impression of deja vu; a story with an element of deja vu.*

de·ject·ed (di·JEC·tid) *adj.* sad and downcast.
— **de·jec·tion** *n.*: *the gloomy dejection of a disappointed man.*

de ju·re (dee·JOOR·ee) *adj. & adv.* by right; legal: *A de jure government in exile does not have de facto power.*

deke (DEEK) *Cdn. Slang. v.* in hockey and box lacrosse, draw a defending player out of position by faking a shot or movement. — *n.* such a shot or movement.

de·lay (di·LAY) *v.* **1** put off until a later time; make late: *A snowstorm delayed our train; It delayed our arrival; A delayed-action bomb was defused by the army; a delayed penalty in hockey.* **2** linger; be late: *Don't delay!*
— *n.* a delaying or being delayed: *Please reply without delay; This is a matter that brooks no delay; There was a two-hour delay before the flight took off.*

de·lec·ta·ble (di·LEC·tuh·bul) *adj.* pleasing and delicious: *a delectable fruit; a delectable combination of flavours; n.: the many delectables at a food fair.*

de·lec·ta·tion (di·lec·TAY·shun) *n.* delight and entertainment: *a juggling act presented for your delectation.*

del·e·gate (DEL·uh·gate) *v.* -gates, -gat·ed, -gat·ing **1** select as a representative: *He was delegated to represent his nation at the conference.* **2** entrust to someone as an agent: *A leader must know how to delegate authority.*
— *n.* (-git) one selected as a representative: *convention delegates.*

del·e·ga·tion (del·uh·GAY·shun) *n.* **1** a delegating. **2** a group of delegates: *to head a delegation; a delegation from the Vatican; to send a delegation to a foreign country.*

de·lete (di·LEET) *v.* -letes, -let·ed, -let·ing strike out or omit: *to delete a word, a name from a list.*
— **de·le·tion** (-LEE·shun) *n.*

del·e·te·ri·ous (del·uh·TEER·ee·us) *adj.* harmful: *the deleterious effects of smoking; Smoking is deleterious to health.*

del·i (DEL·ee) *n.* -is *Informal.* a delicatessen.
— *adj.: a deli counter; deli food.*

de·lib·er·ate (di·LIB·uh·rate) *v.* -ates, -at·ed, -at·ing consider carefully; take counsel: *to deliberate about a move, on a subject, over a decision.*
— *adj.* (-rit) **1** intentional; well thought out: *a deliberate act, attempt to injure someone; deliberate cruelty; a deliberate decision, effort, misuse of words; a deliberate overdose.* **2** slow and careful: *He's precise and deliberate in his enunciation; She took a deliberate step forward.* — **de·lib·er·ate·ly** *adv.*; **de·lib·er·ate·ness** *n.*

de·lib·er·a·tion (di·LIB·uh·RAY·shun) *n.* **1** careful pondering: *the judge's lengthy deliberations.* **2** deliberateness: *the deliberation with which the murder was committed.*
— **de·lib·er·a·tive** (-tiv) *adj.: A legislature is a deliberative body.*

del·i·ca·cy (DEL·uh·cuh·see) *n.* -cies **1** delicateness: *Proposing marriage is a matter of extreme, great delicacy; the delicacy of her health.* **2** a dainty or choice food: *We specialize in delicacies such as snails; We also have other delicacies of the palate.*

del·i·cate (DEL·uh·kit) *adj.* **1** pleasing; fine, as because of lightness, softness, intricacy, subtlety, etc.: *a delicate fabric; a delicate shade of pink; a delicate weave.* **2** needing care and tact or great skill and sensitivity: *the delicate question of her divorce; a delicate surgical operation; a delicate* (=easily damaged) *lace dress; a delicate* (=frail) *child.* **3** having refined sensitivity, skill, tact, sensory discrimination, etc.: *She has a delicate ear for music.* — **del·i·cate·ly** *adv.*; **del·i·cate·ness** *n.*

del·i·ca·tes·sen (del·uh·cuh·TES·un) *n.* **1** a shop selling ready-to-eat food such as smoked meats, cheeses, salads, etc. **2** [takes pl. v.] such food.

de·li·cious (di·LISH·us) *adj.* very pleasing, esp. to the taste or smell: *What is that delicious smell from the kitchen? Your cooking is delicious; the delicious* (=delightful) *irony of it all; Red Delicious and Golden Delicious apples* (=sweet apple varieties).
— **de·li·cious·ly** *adv.*; **de·li·cious·ness** *n.*

de·light (di·LITE) *v.* to take great pleasure or cause someone great pleasure: *a hunter who delights in the chase; The new toy delighted Billy; Billy was delighted with the new toy; We're delighted to meet you; We're delighted that you are in town.*
— *n.* great pleasure: *Watching her dance was sheer*

delight; She plays pranks on boys with intense delight; She takes great delight in tormenting her kid brother; We enjoyed the delights of his well-furnished table.
— **de·light·ful** *adj.: an absolutely delightful book.*
— **de·light·ful·ly** *adv.*

de·lin·e·ate (di·LIN·ee·ate) *v.* -ates, -at·ed, -at·ing sketch or portray; hence, outline in words: *to delineate a character, plan.* — **de·lin·e·a·tion** (-AY·shun) *n.*

de·lin·quen·cy (di·LINK·wun·see) *n.* behaviour that is contrary to accepted social norms: *acts of juvenile delinquency.*

de·lin·quent (di·LINK·wunt) *adj.* 1 overdue or unpaid: *a delinquent account; delinquent debts, taxes.* 2 guilty by acting against or by neglect of duty or rules: *He has been delinquent in paying his dues,*
— *n.* a deliquent person: *a juvenile delinquent; tax delinquents.*

de·lir·i·ous (di·LEER·ee·us) *adj.* excited, as with an attack of delirium: *a child delirious with high fever; She was delirious with joy.*
— **de·lir·i·ous·ly** *adv.: She was deliriously happy.*

de·lir·i·um (di·LEER·ee·um) *n.* -i·ums or -i·a 1 a short mental disturbance characterized by excited activity, disordered speech, confusion, etc.: *The child was in a delirium with high fever.* 2 a frenzied excitement: *She went into a delirium of joy on learning the good news.*

de·liv·er (di·LIV·ur) *v.* 1 set free; rescue: *to deliver the hostages from the terrorists.* 2 send to a target, terminal, audience, or other receiving end: *Letter carriers deliver* (= hand over or convey) *mail to people's homes; They used to deliver six days a week; The boxer can deliver* (= send) *a hard punch; to deliver a lecture, sermon; She delivered* (= read or said) *her speech well; She is so popular she could also deliver votes to anyone who can gain her support; She always delivers on* (= performs) *her promises.* 3 help to give birth: *Midwives and obstetricians deliver babies; Who delivered your wife* (= assisted at her delivery)? *She felt relieved when she had delivered herself of* (= produced or expressed) *her views on the subject.*
— **deliver (the goods)** perform as expected or required: *Can he deliver?*
— **de·liv·er·ance** (di·LIV·uh·runce) *n.*

de·liv·er·y (di·LIV·uh·ree) *n.* -er·ies 1 a delivering or the manner of delivering: *You accept* or *take delivery of the parcel sent "cash on delivery" after paying for it; Payment is collected on delivery of the parcel; general, rural, special delivery (of mail); an emergency, overnight, prompt delivery; a weapons delivery system for quick retaliation in case of a surprise attack.* 2 manner of speaking: *an orator with effective delivery; fast or slow delivery.* 3 childbirth: *She had an easy, normal delivery, not a breech delivery; the **delivery room** of a hospital.*

dell *n.* a small, usually wooded glen: *the cottage in the dell.*

del·ta (DEL·tuh) *n.* 1 the fourth letter of the Greek alphabet (Δ, δ). 2 a usually triangular area of silt or sand formed at a river mouth: *the delta of the Nile.*
— *adj.* delta-shaped: *the triangular swept-back delta wing of an airplane.*

de·lude (di·LOOD, long "OO") *v.* -ludes, -lud·ed, -lud·ing mislead into believing what is false.

del·uge (DEL·yooj, long "oo") *n.* a flood, downpour, etc.
— *v.* -ug·es, -uged, -ug·ing flood: *a movie star deluged with fan mail.*

de·lu·sion (di·LOO·zhun) *n.* a deluding, esp. a persistent false belief in something unreal: *His offer is a snare and a delusion; He suffers from delusions of grandeur such as thinking he is the Saviour; He cherishes, clings to, is under, or labours under the delusion that he is the Saviour.* — **de·lu·sive** (-siv) *adj.*

de·luxe (di·LUX, di·LOOKS, long or short "OO") *adj.* of outstanding luxury or comfort: *a deluxe sedan; a hotel rated "triple A, deluxe, superior accommodation."*

delve *v.* delves, delved, delv·ing dig deeply, as in study: *to delve into old land deeds.*

dem·a·gogue or **dem·a·gog** (DEM·uh·gog) *n.* a leader who manipulates the people's passions.
— **dem·a·gog·ic** (-GOJ·ic) *adj.* — **dem·a·gog·uer·y** (-gog·uh·ree) or **dem·a·go·gy** (-goh·jee) *n.*

de·mand (di·MAND) *v.* 1 ask for vehemently or as a right: *We demand justice; She demands an apology from you; He demands to be satisfied; He demands that she resign her job; Her job is more **demanding** than her husband's; it is very **demanding** of her energies.* 2 require: *a situation that demands tactful handling.*
— *n.* 1 a demanding or being demanded: *The lady refused to yield to his demands; to drop, give in to, make, meet, reject, satisfy a demand; a demand for compensation; He makes too many demands on her time and patience; A "demand loan" is repayable **on demand** (= when asked for); a demand bill, deposit, note; Dictionaries are always very much **in demand** (= needed).* 2 the readiness and ability to buy a product: *the law of supply and demand; As the demand increases, the supply decreases and scarcity results; Can advertising create a demand? There's a brisk, great, strong demand for certain goods.*

de·mar·cate (dee·MAR·cate) *v.* -cates, -cat·ed, -cat·ing mark the boundaries of; separate: *Pope Alexander VI tried to demarcate the New World between Spain and Portugal along the 48-degree-west line of longitude.*
— **de·mar·ca·tion** (DEE·mar·CAY·shun) *n.: The line of demarcation was ignored by the French, English, and the Dutch.*

de·mean (di·MEEN) *v.* degrade or debase: *People demean themselves by dishonesty; Manual work ennobles rather than demeans us; Some people consider manual work very **demeaning**.*

de·mean·our or **de·mean·or** (di·MEE·nur) *n.* outward behaviour as expressing attitude towards others: *She spends hours practising the demeanour of a lawyer in court.*

de·ment·ed (di·MEN·tid) *adj.* insane.

de·mer·it (dee·MER·it) *n.* 1 a fault or offence. 2 a score against one for this: *a student with three demerits for being late; The driver received three demerit points for disobeying a traffic signal.*

de·mil·i·ta·rize (dee·MIL·uh·tuh·rize) *v.* **-riz·es, -rized, -riz·ing** keep free of military equipment and troops: *the demilitarized neutral zone between North and South Korea.*

de·mise (di·MIZE) *n. Formal.* decease; death: *Upon her uncle's demise, she gained title to the property.*

dem·i·tasse (DEM·i·tas) *n.* a small cup for serving strong black coffee.

dem·o (DEM·oh) *n. Informal.* **1** a demonstration, esp. a record or tape as a sample of someone's talent. **2** an automobile, program diskette, tape, etc. used as a demonstrator. **3** *Slang.* a political demonstration.

de·mo·bi·lize (di·MOH·buh·lize) *v.* **-iz·es, -ized, -iz·ing** free from military service: *to demobilize an army after a war.* — **de·mo·bi·li·za·tion** (-luh·ZAY·shun) *n.*

de·moc·ra·cy (di·MOC·ruh·see) *n.* **-cies 1** government by the people. **2** a political system so governed, either directly or through representatives: *the foundations of our democracy; constitutional, parliamentary, representative democracy.*

dem·o·crat (DEM·uh·crat) *n.* **1** one who believes in government by the people. **2 Democrat** a member of the U.S. Democratic Party. — **dem·o·crat·ic** (-CRAT·ic) *adj.*

de·moc·ra·tize (di·MOC·ruh·tize) *v.* **-tiz·es, -tized, -tiz·ing** make or become democratic: *to democratize a nation, organization, political system.*

de·mol·ish (di·MOL·ish) *v.* wreck totally; tear down: *The old hotel has been demolished; His arguments were demolished by the evidence produced in court.* — **dem·o·li·tion** (dem·uh·LISH·un) *n.: a **demolition bomb** for wrecking buildings; the **demolition derby** of ramming cars together till only one is running; He was hit by a brick at a **demolition site** (of a building).*

de·mon (DEE·mun) *n.* **1** a devil or evil spirit. **2** an evil person or thing: *a spelling demon* (= hard-to-spell word); *He avoids the demon rum like the plague.* **3** one who acts with great zeal or skill: *He's a demon for homework; His teacher is a demon for punctuality.* — **de·mon·ic** (di·MON·ic) *adj.*

de·mo·ni·ac (di·MOH·nee·ac) or **de·mo·ni·a·cal** (dee·muh·NYE·uh·cul) *adj.* **1** of or like a demon. **2** possessed by the devil.

de·mon·stra·ble (di·MON·struh·bul) *adj.* that can be demonstrated or proved: *That the earth is round is a demonstrable fact.* — **de·mon·stra·bly** *adv.: The flat earth theory is demonstrably absurd.*

dem·on·strate (DEM·un·strate) *v.* **-strates, -strat·ed, -strat·ing 1** show or prove, as by examples or reasoning: *to demonstrate the fallacy of an argument; Please demonstrate that this machine works; demonstrate also how it works; Now please demonstrate the machine to my wife* (= show her how it works). **2** display one's views, feelings, etc. by parading, shouting, etc.: *Children demonstrate their affection by hugging and kissing; Pacifists demonstrate against the war; They demonstrate for peace.* — **dem·on·stra·tor** (-stray·tur) *n.* — **dem·on·stra·tion** (-STRAY·shun) *n.*

de·mon·stra·tive (di·MON·struh·tiv) *adj.* **1** displaying one's feelings openly: *demonstrative actions, affection, behaviour, persons.* **2** that demonstrates; giving proof: *evidence that is demonstrative of the truth.* — **de·mon·stra·tive·ly** *adv.*

de·mor·al·ize (di·MOR·uh·lize) *v.* **-iz·es, -ized, -iz·ing** weaken the morals, morale, or discipline of someone: *a young girl demoralized by a bad home environment; The army was quite demoralized by the defeat.* — **de·mor·al·i·za·tion** (-luh·ZAY·shun) *n.*

de·mote (di·MOTE) *v.* **-motes, -mot·ed, -mot·ing** lower in rank or station: *He was demoted because he was lazy; He was demoted to work on the assembly line.* — **de·mo·tion** (di·MOH·shun) *n.*

de·mur (di·MUR) *v.* **-murs, -murred, -mur·ring** *Formal.* object or take exception: *He demurred at my offer; n.: She accepted it without demur.* — **de·mur·rer** *n.*

de·mure (di·MURE) *adj.* **-mur·er, -mur·est** reserved and modest: *Raquel appeared demure in a high-necked blouse tied with a bow at the throat; She struck a demure pose for the photographer.* — **de·mure·ly** *adv.*

de·mur·rage (di·MUR·ij) *n.* **1** the delay of a cargo conveyance beyond the time for loading or unloading. **2** a compensation for this delay: *to pay demurrage to ship companies and railways.*

den *n.* **1** a quiet, cozy room, as a study. **2** a wild animal's lair: *Daniel in the lion's den.* **3** a squalid or hidden dwelling: *a gambling den; opium den; a den of iniquity; a den of thieves.*

de·ni·al (di·NYE·ul) *n.* a denying or a statement of it: *the denial of a charge, of justice, of a child* (as one's own); *the denial that the child is one's own; a flat, outright, strong denial.*

den·i·grate (DEN·uh·grate) *v.* **-grates, -grat·ed, -grat·ing** blacken, esp. someone's name; also, belittle: *He was accused of denigrating her character and motives.* — **den·i·gra·tion** (-GRAY·shun) *n.*

den·im (DEN·um) *n.* a heavy, twilled cotton cloth: *jeans of blue denim; Usually **denims*** (= denim-made clothes) *are for casual wear.*

den·i·zen (DEN·uh·zun) *n.* a plant or animal that has made a certain place its home: *the denizens of the forest; the finny denizens* (= fishes, etc.) *of the deep.*

de·nom·i·na·tion (duh·NOM·uh·NAY·shun) *n.* **1** a naming or designating. **2** a name, esp. of a class, group, etc.: *coins of small denominations* (= dimes, nickels, etc.). **3** a particular sect or group: *religious denominations; Protestants of various denominations.* — **de·nom·i·na·tion·al** (-shuh·nul) *adj.: a denominational school run by the Seventh Day Adventists.*

de·nom·i·na·tor (duh·NOM·uh·nay·tur) *n.* the number below the line in a fraction; divisor: *¼ and ¾ have the same denominator; They have a common denominator; The **lowest** or **least common denominator** of ½, ⅔, and ¾ is 12.*

de·no·ta·tion (dee·noh·TAY·shun) *n.* the strict meaning of a word or what is referred to by it: *A logician considers a word's denotation, but a writer has to weigh also its connotations.*

de·note (di·NOTE) *v.* **-notes, -not·ed, -not·ing** mean or indicate; be the symbol for something: *A skull and crossbones denotes death or danger.*

de·nounce (di·NOUNCE) *v.* -nounc·es, -nounced, -nounc·ing **1** repudiate or reject: *The new government denounced the old treaty as a mere scrap of paper; Smith denounces* (= condemns publicly) *drug abuse and drug pushers roundly in his speeches.* See DENUNCIATION. **2** accuse or inform against someone: *Smith denounced his neighbour to the police as a drug pusher;* **de·nounce·ment** (-munt) *n.*

dense (DENCE) *adj.* dens·er, dens·est **1** having a great deal in a small space; compact; thick: *a dense cloud of smoke; through dense jungles.* **2** *Informal.* not bright; thick-headed. — **dense·ly** *adv.;* **dense·ness** *n.*

den·si·ty (DEN·suh·tee) *n.* -ties **1** concentration: *the high density of population in urban areas; Traffic density reaches its peak during the rush hour.* **2** compactness of substance; relative weight: *Because of its lower density, ice floats in water.*

dent *n.* an impression made by hitting or pressing in: *a dent in the fender; to hammer out a dent; After two days he had hardly made a dent in the work* (= any appreciable start on the work) *that had accumulated.* — *v.* make a dent in something: *A tin can is easily dented.*

den·tal (DEN·tul) *adj.* having to do with teeth or dentistry: *dental decay, hygiene; a dental surgeon, technician; dental consonants such as "t" and "d."*

dental floss *n.* a strong, flat thread for cleaning between teeth.

dental hygienist *n.* one who assists a dentist, esp. by cleaning teeth.

dental plate *n.* a denture.

den·ti·care (DEN·tuh·care) *n.* a dental insurance program sponsored by government.

den·ti·frice (DEN·tuh·fris) *n.* a powder, paste, etc. for cleaning teeth; toothpaste.

den·tin (DEN·tin) or **den·tine** (DEN·teen) *n.* the hard, dense body of a tooth under the enamel.

den·tist (DEN·tist) *n.* one professionally trained to care for teeth.

den·tis·try (DEN·tis·tree) *n.* a dentist's art or profession.

den·ture (DEN·chur) *n.* a set of false teeth: *full and partial dentures; A denture therapist makes dentures.*

den·tur·ist (DEN·chur·ist) *n.* one who makes and fits dentures; denture therapist.

de·nude (di·NUDE) *v.* -nudes, -nud·ed, -nud·ing make bare: *hillsides denuded of trees by excessive logging.* — **de·nu·da·tion** (DEE·new·DAY·shun) *n.*

de·nun·ci·a·tion (di·NUN·see·AY·shun) *n.* a denouncing or condemnation: *to issue, make a denunciation; a bitter, scathing, sweeping, vehement denunciation of government policy.*

de·ny (di·NYE) *v.* -nies, -nied, -ny·ing **1** refuse to accept, recognize, etc.: *He denied the charge; denied that he was guilty; He denied knowing anything about*

it; *to deny categorically, flatly, strongly, vehemently; Normally, a mother will not deny* (= disown) *her own children.* **2** refuse to give; say no to something: *All appeals were denied; She was denied admittance, bail, her civil rights; It takes an ascetic to deny oneself* (= manage without the things one needs).

de·o·dor·ant (dee·OH·duh·runt) *n.* a deodorizer for the body: *to apply* or *put on a deodorant; a roll-on, spray, stick, under-arm deodorant; a deodorant spray.*

de·o·dor·ize (dee·OH·duh·rize) *v.* -iz·es, -ized, -iz·ing remove or mask the unpleasant odour of something: *to deodorize a room.* — **de·o·dor·iz·er** *n.*

de·part (di·PART) *v. Formal.* leave: *Trains depart for various destinations from Union Station; Bogus refugees may be told to depart Canada; Queen Victoria departed this life* (= died) *in 1901.*
— **depart from** deviate or stray: *to depart from the path of virtue; to depart from the subject; to depart from the truth and tell a falsehood; to depart from the usual custom.*
— **departed** *n. & adj.* dead: *the dear departed; our departed brethren.*

de·part·ment (di·PART·munt) *n.* **1** a division of a larger organization: *the editorial department of a newspaper; the linguistics department of the School of Arts and Science; the Department* (= Ministry) *of Labour; France is divided into departments instead of provinces or states; The various departments of a department store sell different kinds of goods.* **2** an area of interest or knowledge: *Sorry, not my department! In the weather department, the forecast calls for a snowy day.*
— **de·part·men·tal** (dee·part·MEN·tul) *adj.*

de·par·ture (di·PAR·chur) *n.* a departing: *This procedure marks a departure from established routine; a departure from routine; His departure for Europe was sudden and unannounced; adj.: the departure date, gate; The departure level of the airport has a departure lounge.*

de·pend (di·PEND) *v.* **1** rely on or trust: *You can depend on* or *upon her to get things done.* **2** be contingent on or determined by something: *Whether we'll have a picnic or not depends on the weather.*

de·pend·a·ble (di·PEN·duh·bul) *adj.* trustworthy: *a dependable worker.*
— **de·pend·a·bil·i·ty** (-duh·BIL·uh·tee) *n.*

de·pend·ence (di·PEN·dunce) *n.* a depending: *drug dependence; a youth suffering from a dependence on* or *upon drugs.* Also **de·pend·ance.**

de·pend·en·cy (di·PEN·dun·see) *n.* -cies dependence; also, something dependent, as a region ruled by but not forming part of another country: *The Falkland Islands are a British dependency; a colonial dependency.*

de·pend·ent (di·PEN·dunt) *adj.* **1** relying on another, esp. for food, shelter, etc.: *Children are dependent on their parents; There's a tax deduction for each dependent child.* **2** subordinate: *a dependent clause, nation, territory.*
— *n.: the parents and six dependents* (= children, seniors, etc.). Also **de·pend·ant.**

de·pict (di·PICT) *v.* portray in a picture or in words: *a rural landscape depicted in watercolours; It is depicted* in great detail; *It depicts sheep grazing in a meadow; It depicts sheep as grass-eating animals.* — **de·pic·tion** *n.*

de·plane (di·PLANE) *v.* -planes, -planed, -plan·ing get off an airplane: *to deplane at an airport.*

de·ple·ta·ble (di·PLEE·tuh·bul) *adj.* that can be used up: *Coal is a depletable, not renewable resource.*

de·plete (di·PLEET) *v.* -pletes, -plet·ed, -plet·ing empty out or exhaust: *Overspending has depleted our resources; We have been depleted of our funds, riches, stores, wealth; Now we have to deplete* (= lessen) *a massive debt.* — **de·ple·tion** (di·PLEE·shun) *n.: the rapid depletion of our natural resources.*

de·plor·a·ble (di·PLOR·uh·bul) *adj.* regrettable or lamentable: *a deplorable incident; a deplorable lack of cleanliness.* — **de·plor·a·bly** *adv.*

de·plore (di·PLORE) *v.* -plores, -plored, -plor·ing feel deep regret about something: *We deplore the condition of the poor; Everyone deplores corruption.*

de·ploy (di·PLOY) *v.* arrange strategically: *The government deployed troops at the site of the demonstration.* — **de·ploy·ment** *n.*

de·po·lit·i·cize (dee·puh·LIT·uh·size) *v.* -ciz·es, -cized, -ciz·ing remove from the realm of politics: *efforts to depoliticize the Olympics.*

de·pop·u·late (dee·POP·yuh·late) *v.* -lates, -lat·ed, -lat·ing reduce the population of a place greatly or totally: *The Black Death once depopulated Europe.* — **de·pop·u·la·tion** (-LAY·shun) *n.*

de·port (di·PORT) *v.* 1 conduct oneself: *She deports herself with dignity; deports herself well at interviews.* 2 expel an alien or criminal from a country: *Convicts used to be deported from England to Australia.* — **de·por·ta·tion** (dee·por·TAY·shun) *n.*

de·por·tee (di·por·TEE) *n.* a deported person.

de·port·ment (di·PORT·munt) *n.* one's cultivated behaviour or conduct: *a woman of fine bearing and deportment.*

de·pose (di·POZE) *v.* -pos·es, -posed, -pos·ing 1 remove from power or office: *an emperor deposed by the army.* 2 testify under oath, usually in writing.

de·pos·it (di·POZ·it) *v.* 1 put money or valuables for safekeeping, as a security, etc.: *She deposits $100 each week in a savings account; adj.: deposit insurance, slips.* 2 leave or lay down: *gravel deposited by receding glaciers.* — *n.* what is deposited: *She tries to keep money on deposit to cover her cheques; She makes a deposit at the beginning of each month; You leave a small deposit on returnable pop bottles; You forfeit your deposit if you don't return the bottles; newly discovered* **deposits** (= masses or accumulations) *of coal, gas, iron, minerals, oil.* — **de·pos·i·tor** (di·POZ·uh·tur) *n.*

dep·o·si·tion (dep·uh·ZISH·un) *n.* written testimony taken under oath: *He made a sworn deposition before a judge that he had witnessed what had happened that night.*

de·pos·i·to·ry (di·POZ·uh·tor·ee) *n.* -ries a place for depositing things: *a depository for secret government documents; a school board's textbook depository; a* **depository library** *(officially designated to receive publications).*

de·pot (DEE·poh) *n.* 1 a place for storing and distributing things, esp. military supplies: *an ammunition depot.* 2 a bus or railway station.

de·prave (di·PRAVE) *v.* -praves, -praved, -prav·ing make wicked or perverted; corrupt: *youth depraved by bad influences; a* **depraved** *criminal, mind, youth.* — **de·prav·i·ty** (di·PRAV·uh·tee) *n.* -ties.

dep·re·cate (DEP·ruh·cate) *v.* -cates, -cat·ed, -cat·ing 1 disapprove of or plead against something: *a banker deprecating plans for monetary reform.* 2 [loosely] belittle: *a quiet, shy* **self-deprecating** *man.* — **dep·re·ca·tion** (-CAY·shun) *n.*

de·pre·ci·ate (di·PREE·shee·ate) *v.* -ates, -at·ed, -at·ing 1 lessen the value of; fall in value: *Once it is out of the showroom, a car begins to depreciate; It depreciates in value.* 2 disparage. — **de·pre·ci·a·tion** (-shee·AY·shun) *n.*

dep·re·da·tion (DEP·ruh·DAY·shun) *n.* a plundering or laying waste: *the harsh depredations of estate taxes.*

de·press (di·PRESS) *v.* 1 press or push down: *to depress a lever, pedal.* 2 make sad: *The bad news depressed his spirits; It depressed him that his wife was ill; He was* **depressed** *to learn of his wife's illness; He found the news from the hospital* **depressing.** 3 make poor economically: *Unemployment, business failures, etc. tend to depress the economy; a* **depressed** *area with poverty and high unemployment.*

de·pres·sant (di·PRES·unt) *n. & adj.* one that depresses: *a depressant drug for a heart condition; a depressant to calm the nerves.*

de·pres·sion (di·PRESH·un) *n.* 1 a period of severe reduction in economic activity: *What causes a depression? an economic, major, minor depression; the Great Depression of the 1930s.* 2 a state of extreme sadness; dejection: *chronic, deep, severe depression.* 3 an area lower than its surroundings: *A meteorite that fell near Hudson Bay caused a depression that is 640 km wide.* — **de·pres·sive** (di·PRES·iv) *adj.*

de·pres·sor (di·PRES·ur) *n.* one that depresses: *a tongue depressor used by a physician; adj.: a depressor muscle; a depressor nerve (that lowers arterial blood pressure).*

dep·ri·va·tion (DEP·ruh·VAY·shun) *n.* the state of being deprived: *a child raised in hunger and deprivation (of the necessities of life); the many deprivations* (= lacks or wants) *suffered by poor children.*

de·prive (di·PRIVE) *v.* -prives, -prived, -priv·ing take or keep something away from someone: *a prisoner deprived of his civil rights; A* **deprived child** *grows up without parental affection, a normal home life, etc.*

depth *n.* 1 the quality or degree of deepness: *The lake is 200 m in depth; a submarine cruising at a depth of 100 m; She shows great depth of learning; The study lacks depth* (= is superficial). 2 a deep thing or place: *in the depths of outer space; the depths of the Great Depression; the depths of despair; fish that live in the ocean depths; at depths of up to 200 m; I'm grateful from the depths of my heart; adj.: to drop a* **depth**

bomb or **depth charge** *to destroy a submarine; a depth finder;* **depth psychology** *dealing with unconscious mental processes.*
— **in depth** thoroughly and with penetration: *She studied it in depth;* **adj.***: an in-depth* (= thorough) *news report.*
— **out of** or **beyond one's depth** more than one is competent to do: *You may get lost if you venture too far beyond your depth in mathematics.*

dep·u·ta·tion (dep·yuh·TAY·shun) *n.* a person or group appointed to represent and act on behalf of others; delegation.

de·pute (di·PYOOT, long "OO") *v.* -putes, -put·ed, -put·ing 1 appoint someone to act for one: *The Prime Minister deputes a senior minister to act as his deputy.* 2 assign a job, one's authority or power, etc. to someone; delegate: *He deputes his authority to a senior minister.*

dep·u·ty (DEP·yuh·tee) *n.* -ties 1 one appointed to act officially for another: *My deputy* (= assistant) *will run things while I'm away;* **adj.***: a deputy minister, sheriff.* 2 a people's representative: *a deputy of the Quebec National Assembly; a deputy of the French legislature; A Chamber of Deputies and a Senate form the Italian parliament.*

de·rail (di·RAIL) *v.* run or cause to run off the rails: *The train derailed; Who derailed it?* — **de·rail·ment** *n.*

de·range (di·RAINJ) *v.* -rang·es, -rang·ed, -rang·ing make disturbed, disordered, or insane: *a deranged killer; a mentally deranged patient.* — **de·range·ment** *n.*

der·by (DUR·bee, *Brit.* DAR·bee) *n.* -bies 1 a hat with a rounded crown and a thin, rolled brim. 2 **Derby** any of several annual horse races: *the Kentucky Derby; Epsom's Derby at Surrey, England.* 3 an open race or contest: *a dog derby* (= dog-team race); *a soapbox derby* (= coasting race for small engineless cars made of wooden boxes); *demolition derby.*

de·reg·u·la·tion (DEE·reg·yuh·LAY·shun) *n.* the removal of unnecessary government regulations and restrictions in trade and industry.

der·e·lict (DER·uh·lict) *adj.* 1 neglectful: *He was found derelict in his duty.* 2 abandoned: *a derelict car rusting in a field; his derelict condition.*
— *n.* one that is abandoned, as a ship at sea or a vagrant cast out by society.

der·e·lic·tion (der·uh·LIC·shun) *n.* an abandoning or a neglecting, as of duty.

de·ride (di·RIDE) *v.* -rides, -rid·ed, -rid·ing laugh at with contempt; ridicule.

de ri·geur (duh·ree·GUR) *adj.* required by fashion or social convention: *Black tie is de rigeur for men at a formal dinner dance.*

de·ri·sion (di·RIZH·un) *n.* a deriding or ridiculing: *an object of derision; He aroused* or *provoked derision wherever he went selling snake oil.*
— **de·ri·sive** (di·RYE·siv) *adj.: derisive jeers, laughter, nicknames, publicity, references; a derisive* (= trifling) *sum.* Also **de·ri·so·ry** (-suh·ree) *adj.*
— **de·ri·sive·ly** *adv.*

de·riv·a·tive (di·RIV·uh·tiv) *adj.* derived from another source: *His poetry is very derivative* (= based on or borrowed from other sources).
— *n.* something derived: *"Classify" is a derivative of "class"; Polystyrene and such plastics are made from petroleum derivatives such as ethylene.*

de·rive (di·RIVE) *v.* -rives, -rived, -riv·ing 1 receive from a source: *He derives great satisfaction from his work; "Word" is derived from Old English; a conclusion derived* (= inferred or deduced) *from wrong premises.* 2 come from a source: *Much of our vocabulary derives from Anglo-Saxon; problems deriving from social changes.* 3 trace the origin of something, esp. a word: *Etymologists derive words.*
— **der·i·va·tion** (der·uh·VAY·shun) *n.*

de·rog·a·to·ry (di·ROG·uh·tor·ee) *adj.* disparaging or insulting: *a derogatory remark; The remark was deleted as derogatory of* or *to* or *toward a section of the community.* — **de·rog·a·to·ri·ly** *adv.*

der·rick (DER·ic) *n.* a hoisting apparatus that can be assembled or disassembled on a work site.

der·ri·ère (der·ee·AIR) *n.* the buttocks.

der·ring-do (der·ing·DOO) *n.* bold deeds; reckless bravery: *a desperate deed of derring-do.*

des·cant (DES·cant) *n.* a sung or played harmony to a simple melody; any song: *the nightingale's amorous descant.*
— *v.* (des·CANT) sing; also, comment at length: *a physicist descanting on the theme of solar energy.*

de·scend (di·SEND) *v.* 1 move or extend downward; go down on or along something: *a hillside descending to the sea; We descend a staircase to reach the basement.* 2 sink in character or stoop: *She would never descend to name-calling and such tactics.* 3 come from ancestors: *He is descended from a royal family; Are the higher animals descended from lower forms of life? an heirloom that has descended* (= been passed by inheritance) *in the Ito family.* 4 attack suddenly; swoop or pounce: *The police descended on the convict's hideout.*

de·scend·ant (di·SEN·dunt) *n.* one in relation to one's grandparents or ancestors: *children, grandchildren, and later descendants; direct* (= lineal) *and collateral descendants; Queen Elizabeth II is a descendant of the family of Windsor.*

de·scent (di·SENT) *n.* 1 a descending: *the plane's rapid descent from 5 000 m; the descent of pirates on the coast.* 2 a downward slope: *a gradual descent; steep descent.* 3 ancestry or lineage: *Pedro is of Mexican descent; to trace one's descent.*

de·scribe (di·SCRIBE) *v.* -scribes, -scribed, -scrib·ing 1 write or tell about a person or thing, esp. with graphic detail: *Describe the house you live in; Please describe it to us; describe it in detail, minutely, vividly; Describe how it is kept; Would you describe it as palatial?* 2 outline: *a set of compasses used to describe an arc.*
— **de·scri·ba·ble** (-buh·bul) *adj.*

de·scrip·tion (di·SCRIP·shun) *n.* 1 a describing, esp. a picture of a person or thing in words: *to give, provide a detailed description of the scene; an accurate, blow-by-blow, exact, lively, matter-of-fact, objective, picturesque, vivid description; a suspect who fits the*

description; who answers to the description given by the police; a job description; It's so good that it beggars, defies description (= so good it cannot be described in words). 2 kind or type: They carry merchandise of every description; a swindler of the worst description; Someone of that description cannot be trusted.
— de·scrip·tive (-tiv) adj.: a descriptive account; descriptive writing. — de·scrip·tive·ly adv.

de·scrip·tor (di·SCRIP·tur) n. an index term in an information retrieval system.

de·scry (di·SCRY) v. -scries, -scried, -scry·ing catch sight of: The lookout descried a ship on the horizon.

des·e·crate (DES·uh·crate) v. -crates, -crat·ed, -crat·ing violate a holy place; treat sacrilegiously.
— des·e·cra·tion (-uh·CRAY·shun) n.

de·seg·re·gate (dee·SEG·ruh·gate) v. -gates, -gat·ed, -gat·ing eliminate racial segregation in a place: to desegregate beaches, churches, schools.
— de·seg·re·ga·tion (-GAY·shun) n.

de·sen·si·tize (dee·SEN·suh·tize) v. -tiz·es, -tized, -tiz·ing make insensitive or less sensitive to irritants such as allergens, suffering, etc.

¹des·ert (DEZ·urt) n. a region barren of plant life because of limited rainfall: an arid, trackless desert; the Sahara Desert; a desert (= uninhabited) island.

²de·sert (di·ZURT) v. leave from a place of duty without permission: He deserted his wife and children; He deserted them to join the army; When his courage deserted him (= failed), he deserted his regiment and deserted (= went over) to the enemy.
— n. something deserved; reward or punishment: a villain who got his just deserts.
— de·ser·tion (di·ZUR·shun) n.

de·serve (di·ZURV) v. -serves, -served, -serv·ing be worthy of something: She deserved better (treatment) than that; She deserved well of them for her services; She deserved to be rewarded; The punishment was richly, well deserved; an allowance given to **deserving** candidates; to those who are **deserving of** help.
— de·ser·ved·ly (-vid·lee) adv.

de·sign (di·ZINE) n. 1 the combination of colour, shape, parts, etc. in something; also, a decorative pattern: We need a mural with good design for the reception area; a dress with a paisley design; a school of fashion design. 2 a plan, blueprint, outline, etc.: designs for a new school; a design engineer. 3 an intention, esp. evil: He had sinister **designs** against or on or upon his nephew's inheritance; His answers were vague **by design** (= deliberately).
— v. 1 intend or plan: a job designed to lead to promotion; designed as a stepping stone to a career; designed for ambitious youth. 2 make a design for something: They design airplanes for the military.

des·ig·nate (DEZ·ig·nate) v. -nates, -nat·ed, -nat·ing 1 specify or indicate: The region was designated (as) a disaster area to qualify for aid; Striking is not allowed in services designated as essential; powers designated as being under state jurisdiction. 2 select for an office, task, etc.: They designated her to lead the delegation; The **designated hitter** bats for the pitcher during a baseball game.

— adj. picked out but not yet holding office: The president designate takes office on January 1.
— des·ig·na·tion (-NAY·shun) n.

de·sign·er (di·ZYE·nur) n. one who designs: a fashion designer; an interior designer.
— adj. made by a noted designer; hence, high-quality: designer clothes with designer labels; designer fashions, jeans, wallpaper; a genius with designer brains.

designer drug n. a synthesized narcotic such as crack that is more potent than the natural variety.

designing (di·ZYE·ning) 1 n. the art or work of creating designs. 2 adj. cunningly scheming: a designing fellow, woman.

de·sire (di·ZIRE) v. -sires, -sired, -sir·ing 1 wish or long for something: to desire to be happy; to desire someone to make her happy. 2 request: The Queen desired an audience with the Pope.
— n. a desiring or something desired: He looked at the car with great desire; to arouse, create, express, feel, satisfy, stifle, suppress, whet a desire; an ardent, blind, burning, fervent, intense, keen, passionate, strong, unfulfilled desire; the desire for fame and glory; a desire to excel in everything.
— de·sir·a·ble adj.; de·sir·a·bly adv.
— de·sir·a·bil·i·ty (-ruh·BIL·uh·tee) n.

de·sir·ous (di·ZYE·rus) adj. desiring or wishing: A mother is desirous of her children's good; She is desirous that they (should) do well in life.

de·sist (di·ZIST) v. Formal. stop: a court order to cease and desist (from an illegal action).

desk n. 1 a flat-topped piece of furniture for writing: He cleared his desk and quit his job; adj.: a desk calendar, diary, job. 2 a counter, stand, etc. for doing business: The receptionist sits at the reception desk; Hotel guests register at the front desk; The desk clerk will help you. 3 a department: a newspaper's city desk.

desk-top adj. suitable for use on a desk: a desk-top calculator, computer, copier; **Desk-top publishing** uses a microcomputer and laser printer.

des·o·late (DES·uh·lit) adj. 1 not fit for habitation, esp. barren, deserted, ravaged, etc.: a desolate Arctic plain. 2 cheerless; lonely; abandoned: a desolate old dwelling.
— v. (-late) -lates, -lat·ed, -lat·ing make desolate: farmlands desolated by a tornado.
— des·o·la·tion (des·uh·LAY·shun) n.: The fire left desolation in its wake; the complete, utter desolation of the landscape; The loner lived in desolation and misery.

de·spair (di·SPAIR) v. lose all hope: Don't despair; Columbus never despaired of reaching India.
— n. loss of hope: He struggled hard to overcome despair; He gave up his efforts in despair; He ended his life out of sheer, total, utter despair; The earthquake was the despair (= cause of the feeling of loss) of all his hopes.

des·patch (dis·PATCH) n. & v. same as DISPATCH.

des·per·a·do (des·puh·RAH·doh) n., pl. -dos or -does a reckless criminal or outlaw.

des·per·ate (DES·puh·rit) adj. ready to do anything because of despair: a desperate criminal; a last

desperate effort, move; a desperate crime (committed in despair); The refugees are desperate (= in great need) *for help; They are in desperate* (= grave) *need.*
— **des·per·ate·ly** *adv.;* **des·per·ate·ness** *n.*

des·per·a·tion (des·puh·RAY·shun) *n.* the state of being desperate: *He acted out of desperation; He jumped into the sea in desperation; She led a life of quiet desperation unable to achieve her ambition; a national policy directed against hunger, poverty, desperation, and chaos.*

des·pi·ca·ble (di·SPIC·uh·bul, DES·pic·uh·bul) *adj.* that deserves to be despised; utterly worthless and contemptible: *a despicable act; despicable behaviour, morality.* — **des·pi·ca·bly** *adv.*

de·spise (di·SPIZE) *v.* **-spis·es, -spised, -spis·ing** have utter contempt or disdain for a person or thing: *People are despised for their cowardice; Lepers used to be the most despised and rejected of people.*

de·spite (di·SPITE) *prep.* in spite of: *The child got hurt despite attempts to protect him;* [old use] *She stayed out late* **in despite of** *her parents' warning.*

de·spoil (di·SPOIL) *v.* rob or plunder: *She fell into evil company and was soon despoiled of her innocence.*

de·spo·li·a·tion (di·SPOH·lee·AY·shun) *n.* robbery or pillaging: *Bandits were responsible for the despoliation of the village.*

de·spond (di·SPOND) *v.* lose hope and lose heart. — *n.: the slough of despond.*

de·spond·en·cy (di·SPON·dun·see) *n.* a feeling of utter hopelessness and discouragement: *sheer despondency.*

de·spond·ent (di·SPON·dunt) *adj.* sad and hopeless: *a despondent lover; quite despondent about* or *over his rejection.*

des·pot (DES·pot, DESP·ut) *n.* a ruler with unlimited power, often cruel and unjust; tyrant: *He owned the company and ruled over it like a despot.*
— **des·pot·ic** (des·POT·ic) *adj.;* **des·pot·i·cal·ly** *adv.*
— **des·pot·ism** (DES·puh·tiz·um) *n.*

des·sert (di·ZURT) *n.* a course of fruit, pie, sweet foods, etc. at the end of a meal.

des·ti·na·tion (des·tuh·NAY·shun) *n.* the place something or someone is going to: *your place of departure and destination; a traveller's (city or country of) destination; to arrive at a destination; to reach one's final, ultimate destination; the destination of a letter, parcel, ship.*

des·tine (DES·tin) *v.* **-tines, -tined, -tin·ing** have as destination, goal, or purpose: *Our mortality destines us for death; Some of us are destined to be great; travellers* **destined** *for the Bahamas; students* **destined** *to enter college* or **destined for** *college; Princess Elizabeth was* **destined to** (= later did) *become queen, as we now know.*

des·ti·ny (DES·tuh·nee) *n.* **-tin·ies** a course or end that seems determined in advance, esp. something great or noble: *to achieve, decide, fulfil, shape one's destiny; It was her destiny to win a Nobel prize.*

des·ti·tute (rhyme: "substitute") *adj.* **1** needy or penniless: *He died leaving his family destitute.* **2** devoid: *a boulevard destitute of trees.*

des·ti·tu·tion (des·tuh·TUE·shun) *n.* extreme poverty: *He lived in destitution all his life.*

de·stroy (di·STROY) *v.* demolish or undo: *a hotel destroyed by fire; a king destroyed by pride; His efforts at reform were destroyed by the Depression; Rabid dogs are routinely destroyed* (= killed).

de·stroy·er (di·STROY·ur) *n.* **1** one that destroys. **2** a small, fast warship.

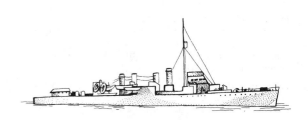

de·struct (di·STRUCT) *n.* the deliberate destroying of a missile in flight; *adj.: a destruct sequence, signal;* also *v.*
— **de·struct·i·bil·i·ty** (-tuh·BIL·uh·tee) *n.*
— **de·struct·i·ble** (-tuh·bul) *adj.*
— **de·struc·tor** *n.*

de·struct·ion (di·STRUC·shun) *n.* a destroying: *the complete, total destruction caused by a tornado; the willful and wanton destruction of property carried out by vandals; The preacher called down death and destruction on sinners; Drugs proved to be his destruction* (= cause or means of destruction).

de·struct·ive (di·STRUC·tiv) *adj.* that destroys: *destructive criticism; Criticism can be destructive of creativity; his destructive tendencies; a very destructive storm.*

des·ul·to·ry (DES·ul·tor·ee) *adj.* not thorough or well organized; fitful or disconnected: *He carries out his duties in a desultory fashion, manner, way; desultory efforts, research.*

de·tach (di·TACH) *v.* separate or disengage: *to detach a coupon from the book; A number of men were detached and sent to scout ahead.*

detached (di·TACHT) *adj.* **1** not connected: *A detached house stands by itself; A semi-detached house shares a wall with another house.* **2** with detachment; impartial: *a detached view.*

de·tach·ment (di·TACH·munt) *n.* **1** lack of prejudice; impartiality. **2** a body of people, ships, etc. detached for special service: *an RCMP detachment.*

de·tail (di·TAIL, DEE·tail) *n.* **1** a particular or small item or part; also, details in general or their treatment: *I won't bore you with the details of my plan; I will fill in, furnish the details later; graphic, gruesome, lurid, sordid, microscopic, minor, minute, technical details; to treat a subject in great detail; a painter devoting great attention to detail; an account of the incident given* **in detail.** **2** a group assigned to a specific task: *a fatigue detail; to form a work detail; a platoon on guard detail* (= duty or task).

— *v.* **1** list or tell in detail: *to detail the new taxes.*
2 detach for a specific task; assign: *two corporals detailed to guard the prisoner; a unit detailed for a duty.*
— **de·tailed** *adj.*: *a detailed account, analysis, plan, proposal, report, study.*

de·tain (di·TAIN) *v.* **1** hold back; delay: *We were detained at customs for two hours.* **2** keep in custody.

de·tain·ee (dee·TAY·nee) *n.* a person in detention; prisoner: *political detainees.*

de·tect (di·TECT) *v.* find out or discover: *a machine to detect the presence of radioactive matter; She detected three adding errors in the bill.*
— **de·tec·ta·ble** or **de·tec·ti·ble** (di·TEC·tuh·bul) *adj.*
— **de·tec·tion** (-shun) *n.*

de·tec·tive (di·TEC·tiv) *n.* one who investigates crimes, finds criminals, etc.: *private detectives; a police detective;* **adj.**: *a detective agency, novel, story; detective fiction.*

de·tec·tor (di·TEC·tur) *n.* one that detects: *traffic signals triggered by detectors placed on the roadway; a metal detector; mine detector; smoke detectors; to take a lie-detector test.*

dé·tente or **de·tente** (day·TAHNT) *n.* a lessening of strain or hostility, as between nations: *the policy of détente with the Soviets.*

de·ten·tion (di·TEN·shun) *n.* a detaining: *He was held in detention as a preventive measure; a house of detention* (= jail); *a* **detention centre** or **detention home** *(for young offenders).*

de·ter (di·TUR) *v.* **-ters, -terred, -ter·ring** hinder or discourage: *Does the threat of counter-attack deter nations from building nuclear bombs?* — **de·ter·ment** *n.*

de·ter·gent (di·TUR·junt) *n.* a cleaning agent, esp. a synthetic soap substitute: *a laundry detergent; liquid detergents; the detergent action of gasoline additives in cleaning off engine deposits caused by the burning of fuel.*

de·te·ri·o·rate (di·TEER·ee·uh·rate) *v.* **-rates, -rat·ed, -rat·ing** make or become weaker, worse, etc.: *Polio causes muscles to deteriorate; The strike situation is deteriorating.* — **de·te·ri·o·ra·tion** (-RAY·shun) *n.*

de·ter·mi·na·tion (di·TUR·muh·NAY·shun) *n.* a determining or being determined: *the determination of the speed of light; She showed dogged, firm, iron, unyielding determination in prosecuting the case; his determination* (= firm intention) *to succeed; The court took several days to come to a final determination of* (= decision on) *the case.*

de·ter·mine (di·TUR·min) *v.* **-mines, -mined, -min·ing**
1 resolve or decide; also, cause to decide: *He determined to change his life; He was determined to change his life; a* **determined** (= firm or resolute) *young man.* **2** fix beforehand; cause: *Is intelligence determined solely by heredity?* **3** settle or resolve: *The courts determine questions of guilt and innocence; They determine who is guilty and who is innocent.* **4** ascertain or find out: *to determine the position of a ship by radar; a committee to determine next year's budget needs; to determine where the next Olympics will be held; to*

determine that a child is in need of protection; an investigation to determine whether a charge should be laid.

de·ter·rence (di·TUR·unce) *n.* the act or a means of deterring.
— **de·ter·rent** *n. & adj.*: *a nuclear deterrent; the ultimate deterrent; The H-Bomb is a great deterrent to another world war.*

de·test (di·TEST) *v.* hate intensely; abhor: *She detests any kind of dishonesty.* — **de·test·a·ble** (-uh·bul) *adj.*

de·throne (di·THRONE) *v.* **-thrones, -throned, -thron·ing** remove from a throne or other position of power: *a dethroned emperor.* — **de·throne·ment** *n.*

det·o·nate (DET·uh·nate) *v.* **-nates, -nat·ed, -nat·ing** explode or cause to explode: *to detonate a bomb; A bomb detonates; to detonate dynamite;* **det·o·na·tion** (-NAY·shun) *n.*
— **det·o·na·tor** (-nay·tur) *n.*: *A detonator is used to set off a charge.*

de·tour (DEE·toor) *n.* **1** a roundabout or secondary route used when the main road is closed: *The police set up a detour around the troubled area.* **2** any roundabout way.
— *v.* make a detour: *to detour around bureaucratic obstacles.*

de·tox (DEE·tox) *n. & v. Informal.* [short form] detoxify or detoxification: *to detox an addict; a detox centre for sobering up; a detox program.*

de·tox·i·fy (dee·TOX·uh·fye) *v.* **-fies, -fied, -fy·ing** remove a poison or its effect from a body, system, etc.
— **de·tox·i·fi·ca·tion** (-uh·fuh·CAY·shun) *n.*

de·tract (di·TRACT) *v.* take away; diminish: *a scar that detracts from his good looks.*
— **de·trac·tion** *n.*; **de·trac·tor** (-tur) *n.*

det·ri·ment (DET·ruh·munt) *n.* harm or damage: *He stayed in his high-pressure job to the detriment of his health.*
— **det·ri·men·tal** (-MEN·tul) *adj.*: *the detrimental effects of smoking; Smoking is detrimental to health.*

de·tri·tus (di·TRY·tus) *n.* material remaining after disintegration or breakdown: *a room littered with pop bottles, plastic cups, and such detritus of a late-night party.*

deuce (DEWCE) *n.* **1** a two in the game of cards or dice. **2** a tie score in tennis. **3** *Informal.* [used as intensifier] devil: *What* **the deuce** *are you doing here?*

de·val·ue (dee·VAL·yoo) *v.* **-values, -valued, -valu·ing** reduce the value of currency in international trade: *to devalue the dollar.* — **de·val·u·a·tion** (-yoo·AY·shun) *n.*

dev·as·tate (DEV·uh·state) *v.* **-tates, -tat·ed, -tat·ing**
1 destroy totally; lay waste: *The invading army devastated the town.* **2** overwhelm: *We were devastated by the news of the tragedy.*
— **devastating** *adj.* very destructive, effective, stunning, etc.: *a devastating analysis, argument, beauty, bore, dinner, fire, flood, tornado, war; her devastating humour, wit.*
— **dev·as·ta·tion** (-uh·STAY·shun) *n.*: *Flood and*

earthquakes caused complete, total devastation (= destruction).

de·vel·op (di·VEL·up) *v.* **1** grow or cause to grow larger, better, more mature, more complex, etc.: *Caterpillars develop from eggs; They develop into adult butterflies; a child's developing body; Reading develops the mind; a fully developed plan; prosperous and (industrially) developed nations like Canada and Britain; aid to* **developing** (= less-developed) *countries.* **2** make or become visible, active, usable, clear, etc.: *Film is developed by treating it with chemicals (so that the picture can be seen); Farmland is being developed* (= built on) *for new housing and industry.* **3** acquire gradually: *She developed an interest in politics.* — **de·vel·op·er** *n.*: *Real-estate developers buy land to build on and to sell.*

de·vel·op·ment (di·VEL·up·munt) *n.* a developing or something developed, esp. an occurrence or new state of affairs: *the development of the butterfly through its various stages; A dwarf is a case of arrested development; recent developments in international trade; a new housing development* (= group of buildings). — **de·vel·op·men·tal** (-up·MEN·tul) *adj.*

development road *n. Cdn.* an access road leading to a region where natural resources are being developed.

de·vi·ant (DEE·vee·unt) *n. & adj.* (one) that deviates: *Only a minority of physicians are deviant in regard to medical ethics; deviant behaviour such as vandalism; to be intolerant of the deviant* (= deviant people). — **de·vi·ance** (-unce) *n.*

de·vi·ate (DEE·vee·ate) *v.* **-ates, -at·ed, -at·ing** turn away, esp. from a standard or norm: *to deviate from what is customary, from a plan, from the truth; His later beliefs deviate sharply from his earlier views.* — **de·vi·a·tion** (-AY·shun) *n.*

de·vice (di·VICE) *n.* **1** something devised, as a scheme or plan: *a clever device for fooling the competition; a mnemonic device for remembering a list of names.* **2** a usually mechanical invention: *a labour-saving device like the electric toothbrush; A bug is a listening device; a new device for catching mice; an intra-uterine device (for birth control).* **3** a design or emblem, as on a coat of arms: *a heraldic device.* — **leave to one's own devices** allow to do what one will or can.

dev·il (DEV·ul) *n.* **1** a demon; [as a mild oath]: *It's* **a devil of a** (= extremely bad instance of a) *job to fix that car; What* **the devil** *did he mean?* **2** a wicked or reckless person. **3** *Informal.* a person in regard to luck: *a lucky devil; the poor devil.* **4** a printer's helper: *pranks of the printer's devil* (= printing errors). — **the Devil** the supreme evil spirit. — **between the devil and the deep (blue) sea** in an unpleasant dilemma. — **the devil to pay** much trouble. — **give the devil his due** be fair or honest about a bad or disliked person. — **go to the devil 1** [a milder form of] go to hell! **2** be ruined, esp. morally. — **play the devil with** upset or ruin. — **speak of the devil (and he appears)** [said when one who is being referred to comes along]. — *v.* **-ils, -illed** or **-iled, -il·ling** or **-il·ing 1** badger or

torment. **2** prepare, esp. ham or eggs, with hot seasonings.

dev·il·ish (DEV·uh·lish) **1** *adj.* like the devil, esp. mischievous. **2** *adv. Informal.* extremely: *He was devilish lucky.* — **dev·il·ment** or **dev·il·ry, -ries** or **dev·il·try** (-tree), **-tries** *n.* mischief: *street kids who are always up to some deviltry or other.*

devil-may-care *adj.* not caring; reckless: *a devil-may-care attitude, flying ace, person.*

devil's advocate *n.* one who presents the opposite side of an argument.

de·vi·ous (DEE·vee·us) *adj.* **1** not straight: *The stream followed a devious path through the wood.* **2** underhand; not straightforward: *He made his fortune by devious means.*

de·vise (di·VIZE) *v.* **-vis·es, -vised, -vis·ing 1** contrive or invent: *to devise a siphon to bring water into the house.* **2** plot: *They devised the murder of the king.*

de·void (di·VOID) *adj.* having none of or totally without something: *a tyrant devoid of any human feelings.*

de·volve (di·VOLV) *v.* **-volves, -volved, -volv·ing** pass on authority, power, etc. to someone else: *The new responsibilities devolved on* or *upon the oldest son.*

de·vote (di·VOTE) *v.* **-votes, -vot·ed, -vot·ing** set apart or dedicate for a special purpose: *to devote one's life to politics; He devotes a lot of his spare time to his hobby; She has devoted herself entirely to the service of her community.*

devoted (di·VOH·tid) *adj.* very dedicated, faithful, or loving: *a devoted companion, helper, husband, mother, wife; a devoted student of music; Two parents who are completely, entirely devoted to their family.*

dev·o·tee (dev·uh·TEE) *n.* a devoted worshipper, follower, supporter, etc.: *the devotees of Zeus; a devotee of baseball.*

de·vo·tion (di·VOH·shun) *n.* **1** a devoting or being devoted, esp. great love or loyalty: *a soldier's unswerving devotion to duty; a child's blind devotion to its parents; a dog's slavish devotion to its master; her absolute, complete, deep, thorough, undying devotion to the cause of freedom.* **2** religious or spiritual dedication: *She practises yoga with great devotion; It's better not to disturb her when she is at her* **devotions** (= prayers or worship). — **de·vo·tion·al** *adj.*: *devotional music (used in a religious service).*

de·vour (di·VOUR, *rhyme:* OUR) *v.* **1** eat greedily: *The monster ravenously devoured everything in sight.* **2** consume: *He was devoured with curiosity; a house devoured by flames.* **3** read, look at, listen to, etc. greedily: *He devours whodunits at the rate of two a week.*

de·vout (di·VOWT) *adj.* **1** very pious: *a devout follower of the Buddha; a devout attitude, supporter, worshipper; The devout (people) were assembled in the temple.* **2** earnest or heartfelt: *She spent her last moments in devout prayer; It's my devout wish that you will succeed.* — **de·vout·ly** *adv.;* **de·vout·ness** *n.*

dew *n.* moisture that condenses on cool bodies at night.

dew point *n.* the air temperature at which dew forms.

dew worm *n. Cdn.* an earthworm used as fishing bait.

dew·y (DEW·ee) *adj.* **dew·i·er, -i·est** wet (as) with dew: *Dora's dewy eyes; her dewy-eyed innocence.*

dex·ter·i·ty (dex·TER·uh·tee) *n.* **1** skill in using the hands: *Some manual dexterity is required to thread a needle.* **2** clever skill: *Lawyers have the dexterity to get a witness to say what they want to hear.*

dex·ter·ous (DEX·tuh·rus) *adj.* **1** skilful with one's hands: *You need dexterous fingers to untie a knot.* **2** mentally quick or clever: *a dexterous lawyer, manager; her dexterous handling of people.* **3** done with dexterity: *a dexterous highwire act.* Also **dex·trous** (DEX·trus).

dex·trose (DEX·trose, *rhyme:* dose) *n.* a pure form of sugar found in grapes, honey, and animal body fluids and used in jams, canning fruits, and in candy.

di·a·be·tes (dye·uh·BEE·teez, -tus) *n.* a disease in which a deficiency of natural insulin causes excess sugar in the blood and urine. — **di·a·bet·ic** (dye·uh·BET·ic) *n. & adj.: He's a diabetic; a diabetic patient.*

di·a·bol·ic (dye·uh·BOL·ic) or **di·a·bol·i·cal** (-uh·cul) *adj.* devilish; evil or cruel: *a diabolical plan to kidnap a child.*

di·a·dem (DYE·uh·dem) *n.* a crown, wreath, etc. worn by a sovereign.

di·ag·nose (dye·ug·NOSE, *rhyme:* DOSE) *v.* **-nos.es, -nosed, -nos·ing** identify, esp. a disease, from symptoms: *The doctor diagnosed measles; The mechanic diagnosed the problem as a clogged carburetor.*

di·ag·no·sis (dye·ug·NOH·sis) *n., pl.* **-ses** (-seez) the identification of a disease, problem, the nature of something, etc.: *The doctor's diagnosis was measles; A second opinion confirmed the diagnosis that it was a case of measles; The diagnosis of measles proved to be correct; a diagnosis of current economic problems.* — **di·a·gnos·tic** (-NOS·tic) *adj.* having to do with diagnosis: *a diagnostic test; diagnostic equipment.* — **di·a·gnos·ti·cian** (-nos·TISH·un) *n.*

di·ag·o·nal (dye·AG·uh·nul) *adj.* **1** running from one corner to the opposite in a figure of at least four sides. **2** on a slant; oblique. — *n.* **1** a diagonal line, as a virgule. **2** a cloth with a slanting weave; twill. — **di·ag·o·nal·ly** *adv.*

di·a·gram (DYE·uh·gram) *n.* a sketch or line drawing used to show the structure, functioning, etc. of something. — *v.* **-grams, -grammed** or **-gramed, -gram·ming** or **-gram·ing** make a diagram of something: *The statistician diagrammed the results of his survey.*

di·al (DYE·ul) *n.* **1** a circular surface used to indicate measures of time, temperature, etc.: *the dial of a wrist watch; a barometer dial.* **2** a disk that can be turned to select, adjust, etc. an apparatus: *Tune in to a radio station or TV channel by using a knoblike dial; Modern telephones have push-buttons instead of a dial for making calls.*

— *v.* **-als, -alled** or **-aled, -al·ling** or **-al·ing** use a dial; also, operate, select, etc. by using a dial: *We dial 411 for information; We can dial many places around the globe direct* (= without operator assistance); *She dialled the correct code to open the safe.*

dial-a- *combining form* [used to indicate a service available by telephone]: *dial-a-bus, -date, -doctor, -joke, -pizza, -prayer, -thought.*

di·a·lect (DYE·uh·lect) *n.* a regionally or socially distinct form of a language, esp. if nonstandard: *the Ottawa Valley dialect of Canadian English; In Southern Georgian dialect, "I wouldn't" becomes "Ah woon."* — **di·a·lec·tal** (-LEC·tul) *adj.*

di·a·lec·tic (dye·uh·LEC·tic) *n.* reasoned discussion; logic. — *adj.* also **dialectical:** *dialectical materialism.*

di·a·logue or **di·a·log** (DYE·uh·log) *n.* **1** a conversation; hence, a literary work representing a conversation or the conversational element in a literary work: *the Socratic dialogues of Plato; a play with a fast-paced dialogue.* **2** constructive discussion: *the ongoing dialogue between Protestants and Catholics; efforts to have a meaningful dialogue with the militants.* — *v.* discuss in order to exchange opinions and reach a consensus: *World leaders dialogue at a summit meeting.*

dial tone *n.* the buzzing sound indicating that a telephone line is open for use.

di·am·e·ter (dye·AM·uh·tur) *n.* the greatest width of a figure, esp. a line through the centre of a circle, sphere, cylinder, etc.: *The ball is 38 cm in diameter.*

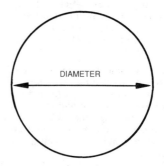

DIAMETER

di·a·met·ri·cal (dye·uh·MET·ruh·cul) *adj.* **1** of or on a diameter. **2** totally opposite: *diametrical viewpoints.* Also **di·a·met·ric.** — **di·a·met·ri·cal·ly** (-cuh lee) *adv.: two ideologies diametrically opposed to each other.*

di·a·mond (DYE·uh·mund) *n.* **1** a crystalline form of nearly pure carbon and the hardest naturally occurring mineral, used as a gem and as an industrial abrasive: *a cut, flawless, perfect, sparkling diamond; A diamond is cut, ground, polished, and set in a ring or crown.* **2** a figure having four equal sides and two pairs of equal angles, one of which is acute. **3** something so shaped, as a playing card marked with this shape in red or a baseball field, esp. the infield. — **diamond in the rough** a good person with unpolished manners.

diamond anniversary or **diamond jubilee** *n.* a 60th or 75th year.

di·a·per (DYE·pur, DYE·uh·pur) *n.* an absorbent cloth folded around a baby like underpants: *to change diapers; disposable diapers; a toddler clad only in his diaper; a new government still in diapers* (= in its infancy); *diaper rash.*
— *v.* put a diaper on someone: *how to diaper a baby; The driver of the horse carriage was charged with failing to diaper his animals.*

di·aph·a·nous (dye·AF·uh·nus) *adj.* of fabrics, fine and able to be seen through: *diaphanous material; a diaphanous blouse.*

di·ar·rhe·a or **di·ar·rhoe·a** (dye·uh·REE·uh) *n.* too frequent and watery bowel movements: *an attack of diarrhea; No one can stand his verbal diarrhea* (*Informal* for talkativeness); *a propensity for backseat driving and diarrhea of the mouth.*

di·ar·y (DYE·uh·ree) *n.* **-ar·ies** a day-by-day record of one's thoughts, experiences, etc.: *Lu keeps a diary; He writes in his diary every night at bedtime.* — **di·a·rist** *n.*

Di·as·po·ra (dye·AS·puh·ruh) *n.* **1** the Jews living outside Israel. **2** also **diaspora** a scattering of a people: *Palestinians living in the diaspora in Lebanon, Kuwait, Jordan, etc.; the Irish diaspora in North America.*

di·a·ton·ic scale (dye·uh·TON·ic-) *n.* the standard eight-tone musical scale.

di·a·tribe (DYE·uh·tribe) *n.* a violent criticism: *a bitter diatribe against union leaders; a diatribe on gasoline prices.*

dib *n.* a small marble.
— **dibs** *pl.* **1** a game played with marbles. **2** *Informal.* money or dollars.

dib·ble (DIB·ul) *n.* a pointed gardener's tool for making holes, as for bulbs, seeds, and slips.

dice *n.pl., sing.* **dice** or **die 1** small cube(s) having one to six spots on its respective sides, used in games and gambling: *to roll, throw the dice; a roll of the dice; Beware of loaded dice!* **2** [takes sing. v.] a game played with dice.
— **no dice** *Slang.* no luck; nothing doing.
— *v.* **dic·es, diced, dic·ing 1** play with dice. **2** chop into small cubes: *to dice carrots.*

dic·ey (DYE·see) *adj.* **dic·i·er, -i·est** *Informal.* risky or uncertain: *His chances of getting a summer job are a bit dicey.*

di·chot·o·my (dye·COT·uh·mee) *n.* **-mies** division into two, usually opposed parts: *the dichotomy between black and white, of theory and practice, of East versus West.*

dick·ens (DICK·unz) *n.* [used as an intensifier] deuce; devil: *People are mad as the dickens; How the dickens did this happen? What the dickens are you doing? Where the dickens is your dad?*

dick·er *v.* bargain or haggle: *to dicker with a car dealer; to dicker for bargains; to dicker over the exchange value of the Canadian dollar.*

dick·ey (DICK·ee) *n.* **-eys 1** a detachable false shirt or blouse front worn under a jacket or sweater. **2** a little bird. **3** *Cdn.* a hooded pullover.

dic·ta (DIC·tuh) *n.* a *pl.* of DICTUM.

dic·tate (DIC·tate) *v.* **-tates, -tat·ed, -tat·ing 1** read or say something for someone else to write down: *an executive dictating a letter to his secretary.* **2** command with authority; give orders: *Don't let your kid brother dictate to you; Victors dictate the terms of surrender.*
— *n.* order or command: *the dictates of conscience.*
— **dic·ta·tion** (dic·TAY·shun) *n.*: *Some give dictation and others take* or *take down dictation.*

dic·ta·tor (DIC·tay·tur, dic·TAY·tur) *n.* one who dictates, esp. an absolute, usually unconstitutional ruler; tyrant: *a benevolent dictator; a military dictator.*
— **dic·ta·tor·ship** *n.*
— **dic·ta·tor·i·al** (dic·tuh·TOR·ee·ul) *adj.*

dic·tion (DIC·shun) *n.* **1** choice of words for expressing ideas: *poor diction.* **2** the way one pronounces words: *a singer with clear diction.*

dic·tion·ar·y (DIC·shuh·nair·ee) *n.* **-ar·ies 1** a book listing words in alphabetical order, with pronunciation, meaning, and other information on them: *to compile, consult, refer to a dictionary; a desk, collegiate, etymological, pocket, pronouncing, unabridged dictionary.* **2** a book that translates words of one language into another: *a Russian-English dictionary.* **3** a reference list, as of words for checking spelling stored in a word-processing system.

dic·tum (DIC·tum) *n.* **-tums** or **-ta** a formal pronouncement of one's opinion.

did *pt.* of DO.

di·dac·tic (dye·DAC·tic) *adj.* intended to teach; moralizing: *didactic poetry, writers; a didactic manner, style.* — **di·dac·ti·cism** *n.*

did·dle (DID·ul) *v.* **did·dles, did·dled, did·dling** *Informal.* **1** cheat: *People get tired of being diddled; He got diddled out of his reserved seat.* **2** waste time with trivialities: *He diddled away a month on useless research.* **3** juggle or handle carelessly: *Stop diddling with the china.*

did·dler *n.* *Slang.* a sex offender.

did·n't (DID·unt) did not.

di·do (DYE·doh) *n.* **-dos** or **-does** *Informal.* mischievous trick; caper.

die (DYE) *n.* **1** sing. of DICE. **2** *pl.* **dies** a hard metal device used to shape material, as by stamping coins or medals, by cutting threads on a screw, or by extrusion, as wire.
— **the die is cast** the step is taken and there is no going back.
— *v.* **dies, died, dy·ing 1** stop living, existing, or functioning: *People die by the sword, die by their own hands* (= kill themselves), *die for their beliefs, die in action* (= in battle); *The engine just died on us; The "right to bear arms" is a tradition that dies hard; People were dying off one by one with the plague; The passenger pigeon died out* (= became extinct) *years ago; Pete didn't like to retire because he wanted to die in harness* (= die while still actively working); *a gunfighter who died with his boots on* (= while still active). **2** lose power, vigour, or force: *We waited for the wind to die down* or *die away before sailing.* **3** *Informal.* desire very much: *Lou is dying to go to the dance; Jo still dies for a cigarette now and then.*

die·hard *n.* one who stubbornly refuses to give in or change; *adj.:* *diehard conservatives, hockey fans, leftists, traditionalists.*

die·sel (DEE·zul) *n.* **1** also **diesel engine** an internal-combustion engine without spark plugs that burns oil by the heat of air compression; *adj.:* *diesel fuel, motor, oil.* **2** a truck, locomotive, etc. driven by such an engine.

di·et (DYE·ut) *n.* **1** one's regular food and drink; also, a special regimen: *He lives on a diet of French fries and cola; Everyone needs a balanced, nutritious diet; poor people on a starvation diet; He went on a low-fat diet to lose weight; a crash, high-calorie, high-fibre, high-protein, low-cholesterol diet; She's on a salt-free diet; Al's reading is a steady diet of cheap westerns; adj.:* *a diet cola, pop.* **2** an assembly or parliament: *The Japanese Diet consists of two houses; The Diet of Worms, Germany, declared Martin Luther a heretic in 1521.* — *v.* eat or drink according to rules: *He lost 10 kg by dieting for a few months.*

di·e·ta·ry (DYE·uh·tair·ee) *adj.* having to do with diet: *Jewish dietary laws; dietary fibre* (= roughage).

di·e·tet·ic (dye·uh·TET·ic) **1** *adj.* of or for a diet, esp. a restricted one: *high-priced dietetic foods; low-sodium foods from the dietetic section of the supermarket; dietetic soft drinks.* **2** **dietetics** *n.pl.* the study of healthy diets.

di·e·ti·tian or **di·e·ti·cian** (dye·uh·TISH·un) *n.* one trained to plan meals for a hospital, restaurant, school cafeteria, etc.

dif·fer (DIF·ur) *v.* **1** be different: *Tom and I differ widely; We differ in many respects; I differ from him in my attitude to food.* **2** disagree: *We differ about* or *on* or *over almost everything; He differs with me on what to eat; "I beg to differ"* (= I disagree with you), *he says; After much arguing, we are hungry and **agree to differ** or **disagree.***

dif·fer·ence (DIF·ur·unce) *n.* **1** the fact or a way of being different; what distinguishes: *There's no difference between our viewpoints; Whether we stay or go makes no difference to me; a slight difference of opinion; The only difference between the cars is their colour; Can you tell the difference? There's a world of* (= a considerable) *difference between them; marked, striking, irreconcilable, minor, subtle, superficial differences.* **2** the amount by which things differ: *The difference between 18 and 6 is 12.* **3** a disagreement: *to compose, reconcile, set aside, settle, thrash out differences between parties; differences among friends.* — **make a difference** be important; matter. — **split the difference** divide the difference equally; hence, compromise: *The negotiators split the difference for a 7% raise (halfway between 5% and 9%).*

dif·fer·ent (DIF·uh·runt) *adj.* not the same; dissimilar: *Her opinions are very different from his; much more different than he imagined; quite different to what her mother-in-law thought; as different as night and day; How do you like my new tie? Well, it's different* (= unusual); *I called seven different* (= separate or distinct) *times; Order a different* (= another) *meal if they're out of fish.* — **different strokes for different folks** People and their

ways differ. — **dif·fer·ent·ly** *adv.*

dif·fer·en·tial (dif·uh·REN·shul) *adj.* of or expressing a difference or distinction: *a differential fee for foreign students; a differential price for foreign and domestic buyers of petroleum; She complained of getting differential* (= discriminatory) *treatment at work.* — *n.* an absolute or percentage difference: *There's a 15% wage differential between the two job classifications.*

dif·fer·en·ti·ate (dif·uh·REN·shee·ate) *v.* **-ates, -at·ed, -at·ing** be, make, have, or recognize a difference: *He is colour-blind and can't differentiate between colours; He can't differentiate red from green; The two varieties are differentiated by colour.* — **dif·fer·en·ti·a·tion** (DIF·uh·ren·shee·AY·shun) *n.*

dif·fi·cult (DIF·uh·cult) *adj.* **1** requiring effort, strength, skill, patience, etc.; not easy: *It is difficult to get through medical school; I have a difficult problem for homework.* **2** hard to please, manage, get along with, etc.: *a difficult child who has been spoiled by his parents.*

dif·fi·cul·ty (DIF·uh·cul·tee) *n.* **-ties 1** the fact or quality of being hard or troublesome: *a task of extraordinary difficulty; He reads German with some difficulty; She's in serious difficulty; She has difficulty paying for her groceries.* **2** something that is difficult; trouble or problem: *to be faced with, to come across, encounter, experience, face, meet difficulties; to run into difficulties; when difficulties arise; The businessman found himself in financial difficulties; One has to clear up, overcome, resolve, surmount difficulties to achieve anything.*

dif·fi·dent (DIF·uh·dunt) *adj.* not self-confident; timid: *He declined the offer with a diffident smile.* — **dif·fi·dent·ly** *adv.* — **dif·fi·dence** *n.*

dif·fract (di·FRACT) *v.* break up light rays into bands of light and dark or of different colours, as when passing around the edge of an object or through a small slit, hole, or grating. — **dif·frac·tion** *n.*

dif·fuse (di·FYOOZE) *v.* **dif·fus·es, dif·fused, dif·fus·ing** spread out widely: *The smell of perfume diffused through the room.* — *adj.* (di·FYOOSE) **1** diffused: *Diffuse light produces no glare.* **2** verbose: *a diffuse, rambling report.* — **dif·fuse·ly** *adv.;* **dif·fuse·ness** *n.*

dif·fu·sion (di·FEW·zhun) *n.* a diffusing or spreading: *the diffusion of gases in the air; the diffusion of knowledge through books and schools.* — **dif·fu·sive** (-siv) *adj.:* *the diffusive power of gases.*

dig *v.* **digs, dug, dig·ging 1** break up or scoop out earth, esp. for making or getting things: *Gardeners dig in the garden (to prepare it for planting); to dig a grave, a hole; to dig potatoes (out of the ground).* **2** poke: *She dug me in the ribs with her umbrella; Her umbrella was digging into my ribs; She never stopped digging at* (= harassing and teasing) *me the whole afternoon.* **3** *Slang.* notice; like; understand: *Dig that car! He doesn't dig abstract art.* **4** search and explore: *to dig into the literature on UFOs; You have to dig long and hard to get anything out of him; That's easy digging* (= an easy thing to do); *She digs deep into her pockets to give* (= She gives generously) *to charity.*

— **dig in 1** *Informal.* begin to eat or work: *She brought out the sandwiches and told us to dig in.* **2** take a firm position; dig oneself a trench: *He dug in his heels for both principle and politics.*

— **dig out** or **dig up** find (out) by much looking or research: *a reporter trying to dig up some information.* — *n.* **1** a poke; hence, a pointed remark: *She likes to take a dig at me now and then.* **2** an archaeological excavation or its site: *The class has gone on a dig to look for Indian artifacts.* **3 digs** *pl. Informal.* diggings; lodgings; quarters.

di·gest (DYE·jest) *n.* a short compilation or summary, esp. from diverse sources: *a legal digest; a weekly news digest.*
— *v.* (di·JEST) **1** summarize and arrange. **2** break down food for absorption into the blood stream, as in the digestive system. **3** assimilate mentally: *I have read the report but have not digested everything.*
— **di·gest·i·ble** (di·JES·tuh·bul) *adj.*

di·ges·tion (di·JES·chun) *n.* the system for digesting or the ability to digest food: *a man with a delicate digestion.*
— **di·ges·tive** (-tiv) *adj.* having to do with digestion: *Saliva and bile are digestive juices; The food canal and the accessory glands make up the digestive system.*

dig·ger (DIG·ur) *n.* a person who digs or a tool for digging.

diggings (DIG·ingz) *n. pl.* **1** what is dug out. **2** a place where digging is being done. **3** *Informal.* a place to live. Also **digs.**

dig·it (DIJ·it) *n.* **1** a finger, thumb, or toe. **2** an Arabic numeral: *five-digit figures (from 10 000 to 99 999).*

dig·i·tal (DIJ·uh·tul) *adj.* **1** having to do with numbers: *A digital (as opposed to an analogue) computer calculates using binary numbers; a digital clock radio; A digital watch does not have hands.* **2** binary-coded: *Digital recording of sound eliminates wow and flutter; digital audio tape, discs.* — **dig·i·tal·ly** *adv.*

dig·i·tize (DIJ·uh·tize) or **dig·i·tal·ize** (DIJ·uh·tul·ize) *v.* **-iz·es, -ized, -iz·ing** convert data, images, or sounds to digital or computer-readable form. — **dig·i·tiz·er** *n.*
— **dig·i·ti·za·tion** (-tuh·ZAY·shun) *n.*

dig·ni·fied (DIG·nuh·fide) *adj.* having dignity: *an aloof, dignified demeanour.*

dig·ni·fy (DIG·nuh·fye) *v.* **-fies, -fied, -fy·ing** give dignity to: *The mayor dignified the school fair with her presence.*

dig·ni·tar·y (DIG·nuh·tair·ee) *n.* **-tar·ies** a person in a high rank or office: *a foreign dignitary; visiting dignitaries.*

dig·ni·ty (DIG·nuh·tee) *n.* **-ties 1** intrinsic worth or value: *the dignity of human suffering.* **2** respect owed to one: *They were treated with great dignity.* **3** a calm, stately manner: *She lived and died in dignity; She never lost her dignity; She maintained her dignity under provocation.* **4** a high rank or office: *the dignity of her office.*

di·gress (dye·GRES) *v.* stray from the main subject.
— **di·gres·sion** (dye·GRESH·un) *n.: The historian included a digression on tribal customs; It was a digression from the main theme.*

— **di·gres·sive** (-siv) *adj.: a loose, digressive style of storytelling.*

dike *n.* a bank or levee to prevent flooding of low ground.

di·lap·i·dat·ed (duh·LAP·uh·day·tid) *adj.* falling to pieces; broken-down: *a dilapidated condition, house, truck.* — **di·lap·i·da·tion** (-uh·DAY·shun) *n.*

di·late (dye·LATE) *v.* **-lates, -lat·ed, -lat·ing 1** make wider or bigger: *eye drops to dilate the pupils for a checkup.* **2** write or speak at length: *The lecturer dilated on* or *upon his favourite subject.*
— **di·la·tion** (-LAY·shun) *n.*

dil·a·tor·y (DIL·uh·tor·ee) *adj.* causing or inclined to delay or slow down: *a dilatory approach to homework; Filibuster is a dilatory tactic; dilatory proceedings in committee.* — **dil·a·tor·i·ly** *adv.;* **dil·a·tor·i·ness** *n.*

di·lem·ma (duh·LEM·uh) *n.* **1** a situation in which one is faced with competing alternatives: *Tim was in a dilemma when by mistake he arranged two dates for the same evening; He was* **on the horns of a dilemma.** **2** any difficult or problematic situation.

dil·i·gent (DIL·uh·junt) *adj.* hard-working or painstaking: *a diligent pupil; He's always diligent in his work.* — **dil·i·gent·ly** *adv.* — **dil·i·gence** *n.*

dill *n.* an herb used in pickling.

dill pickle *n.* a cucumber pickled with dill.

dil·ly (DIL·ee) *n.* **dil·lies** *Slang.* something remarkable: *The snowfall in June was a dilly.*

dil·ly·dal·ly (DIL·ee·DAL·ee) *v.* **-dal·lies, -dal·lied, -dal·ly·ing** waste time, esp. by hesitating or loitering.

di·lute (dye·LOOT, di·LOOT – long "OO") *v.* **-lutes, -lut·ed, -lut·ing** weaken by adding something else: *to dilute wine with water;* **adj.:** *dilute acid.*
— **di·lu·tion** (-LOO·shun) *n.*

dim *adj.* **dim·mer, dim·mest 1** not bright or clear: *dim lighting; a dim chance, future, hope, image, memory, outlook, prospect, recollection.* **2** not seeing clearly: *Her eyes were dim and she couldn't see.*
— **take a dim view** of regard something with disapproval or scepticism.
— *v.* **dims, dimmed, dim·ming** make or become dim.
— **dim·ly** *adv.;* **dim·ness** *n.*
— **dims** *n. pl.* an automobile's parking lights.

dime *n.* a ten-cent coin: *Computers are* **a dime a dozen** (= cheap or easy to get) *these days.*

di·men·sion (di·MEN·shun) *n.* **1** a measurable magnitude, as length, width, and depth: *Time is often thought of as a fourth dimension.* **2** size; also, importance or range: *a disaster of great dimensions; The tragedy assumed serious dimensions as the bodies were uncovered.*
— **di·men·sion·al** *adj.: We live in a three-dimensional world.* — **di·men·sion·al·ly** *adv.*

di·min·ish (di·MIN·ish) *v.* make or become smaller, less strong, etc.: *The force of the wind gradually diminished; She felt diminished by their cruel remarks; an enterprise affected by the law of* **diminishing returns** (= profit becoming proportionately less as effort

is increased beyond a certain point).
— **di·mi·nu·tion** (dim·uh·NEW·shun) *n.*

di·min·u·tive (di·MIN·yuh·tiv) *adj.* very small.
— *n.* a suffix denoting smallness, as "-ie," "-let," or
"-kin" or a word formed with one, as *birdie, bracelet, or
catkin.*

dim·mer (DIM·ur) *n.* **1** a switch for dimming an electric
light. **2** dimmers *pl.* the low-beam headlights of an
automobile; also, parking lights.

dim·ple (DIM·pul) *n.* a small depression, esp. in a body
part, as on the cheeks or chin: *the dimples on a golf
ball.*
— *v.* -ples, -pled, -pling make or form dimples in: *Her
cheeks dimple when she laughs.* — **dim·ply** *adj.*

dim·wit *n. Informal.* a simpleton.
— **dim·wit·ted** (DIM·wit·id) *adj.*

din *n.* a continuous, confused loud noise: *Her voice
could be heard above the din; The crowd made such a
din she had to shout at the top of her voice.*
— *v.* dins, dinned, din·ning force with a din; tell
repeatedly: *Industriousness was dinned into him as a
child.*

dine *v.* dines, dined, din·ing eat dinner; also, provide
with dinner: *We dine at home most of the time; We dine
on whatever is in the fridge; We usually dine out* (= eat
at a restaurant) *once a week; They like to wine and dine*
(= treat with food and drink) *their clients.*

din·er (DYE·nur) *n.* **1** one who is dining: *Busboys are
not supposed to speak to the diners.* **2** a restaurant car
on a train; also, a restaurant built like one: *We had ham
and eggs at Pete's diner.*

di·nette (dye.NET) *n.* a nook or alcove for eating in: *a
dinette set* (= table and chairs) *for your apartment.*

ding *n.* **1** also ding·dong the sound of a bell.
2 *Informal.* a tiny dent; *v.: Some clumsy driver dinged
our car.*

ding-a-ling (DING·uh·ling) *n. Slang.* a crazy person.

ding·bat *n. Informal.* a stupid person.

ding·dong *n.* **1** a bell or its sound. **2** *Slang.* an eccentric
person; nut.

din·ghy (DING·ee, -ghee) *n.* -ghies **1** a small rowboat.
2 an inflatable raft for emergency use.

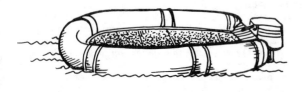

ding·us (DING·us) *n. Slang.* a gadget; something whose
name does not come to mind.

din·gy (DIN·jee) *adj.* ding·i·er, -i·est dark and dirty;
shabby: *a dingy coal-mining town; a dingy room in a
cheap hotel.* — **din·gi·ly** *adv.;* **ding·i·ness** *n.*

dining lounge *n.* a dining room licensed to serve liquor
with meals.

din·ky (DINK·ee) *adj. Slang.* -ki·er, -ki·est small and
insignificant: *dinky toys; a dinky restaurant.*

din·ner (DIN·ur) *n.* **1** the main meal of the day, at noon
or in the evening: *to eat, have, make, prepare dinner;
What are we having for dinner? a TV dinner; We were
at dinner when he called; It happened during dinner.*
2 a formal meal; banquet.

din·ner·ware (DIN·ur·ware) *n.* plates, bowls, cups, etc.
for serving dinner.

di·no·saur (DYE·nuh·sor) *n.* **1** any of the often large,
now extinct reptiles of the Mesozoic era, found in fossils.
2 something out-of-date or obsolete.

dint *n.* a dent.
— **by dint of** by the effort or force of something: *He got
rich by dint of hard work.*

di·ox·in (dye·OX·un) *n.* a most poisonous chemical
which occurs as a by-product in manufacturing
pesticides and is believed to cause cancer and genetic
defects in people exposed to it.

dip *v.* dips, dipped, dip·ping **1** immerse briefly in a
liquid: *A fabric is dipped into a vat of dye; to dip pen in
ink.* **2** ladle or scoop out; hence, reach down into to take
out: *Dip water from the bucket with a cup; Hard times
forced them to dip into their life savings to pay the rent.*
3 go down: *The moon dipped behind the trees; Prices
dipped at the end of the year.* **4** go down and up again;
make to do so: *to dip a flag in salute.* **5** read or study
superficially: *We dipped into Russian history.*
— *n.* **1** a dipping, esp. a brief swim: *I'm going to take a
quick dip in the pool.* **2** something to dip finger food in:
a cheese dip; an onion-and-garlic dip for potato chips.
3 a downward slope, depression, or course: *a dip in the
road.*

di·plo·ma (di·PLOH·muh) *n.* a certificate of educational
accomplishment: *Your degree is awarded on a diploma;
The diplomas are awarded or conferred or given out or
presented at convocations and graduation ceremonies; a
high-school diploma; A teacher has a degree, a
diploma, or a certificate in education.*

di·plo·ma·cy (di·PLOH·muh·see) *n.* the art of a
diplomat; skill in conducting relations between countries
or people; tact: *the elaborate etiquette of international
diplomacy; dollar diplomacy; gunboat diplomacy; quiet
diplomacy; shuttle diplomacy; street diplomacy; Our
manager relies on or uses or resorts to diplomacy rather
than force to solve inter-personal problems.*

dip·lo·mat (DIP·luh·mat) *n.* **1** one empowered to
represent a government in dealing with another
government: *a career diplomat who has been long in the
Federal Service.* **2** one who is tactful and skilful in
dealing with people.

dip·lo·mat·ic (dip·luh·MAT·ic) *adj.* **1** tactful in dealing
with delicate situations: *a diplomatic supervisor skilled
at settling disputes.* **2** having to do with ambassadors:
*diplomatic duties, representatives, service; A nation's
diplomatic corps or **mission** working in the capital of a*

foreign country includes the ambassador or high commissioner, ministers, counsellors, consuls, attachés, clerks, etc.; to enjoy, grant, have, withdraw **diplomatic immunity** (= freedom from arrest, search, seizure, taxes, etc.).

di·plo·ma·tist (di·PLOH·muh·tist) *n.* a person with the qualities of a diplomat.

dip·stick *n.* a stick dipped in a liquid, as engine oil, to measure its depth.

dip·sy-do (dip·see·DOO) *n. Slang.* a complicated or tricky act, as a hard-to-hit curveball.

dipsy-doo·dle (dip·see·DOO·dul) *n. Slang.* 1 dipsy-do: *She did a dipsy-doodle with her hand to show how she felt about him.* 2 a deception or deceiver.
— *v.* **-dles, -dled, -dling** move around in a deceptive manner.

dire *adj.* **dir·er, dir·est** 1 terrible; disastrous: *dire threats.* 2 extreme; very difficult: *in dire need, poverty, straits.*

di·rect (di·RECT, dye-) *v.* 1 send or address: *Please direct your reply to him, c/o Mrs. Smith; remarks directed to* or *at his employees; The criticism was directed* (= pointed) *at* or *against the media; Better direct* (= aim) *your efforts to* or *toward something constructive; Can you direct* (= guide) *me to the library?* 2 give orders or guidance to someone; control or regulate: *She directs the children's department in the library; He's on the set directing a movie; The manager directed her staff to remain calm; She directed that the police be called; Police direct traffic.*
— *adj.* 1 straight; unswerving; not stopping, interrupted, etc.: *in a direct line from A to B; a direct hit on target.* 2 with nothing intervening or mediating: *in direct sunlight; a direct* (= unbroken) *line of descent; Dialogue reported in* **direct discourse,** or **direct speech,** *quotes the words as spoken; a* **direct tax** *(such as income tax) paid by the person on whom it is levied.* 3 blunt; straightforward; candid: *direct answers.* 4 diametrical: *Hate is the direct antithesis of love; a direct opposite.*
— *adv.* in a straight manner: *We flew from Toronto to Vancouver direct; They appealed direct to the voters.*

di·rec·tion (di·REC·shun) *n.* 1 management: *He works under the direction of experts; A program is required to give direction to our work.* 2 often **directions** *pl.* instructions on how to use or do something, get somewhere, etc.: *to follow, give, issue detailed directions for using the lawn mower; She had left directions with her husband in case the parcel arrived.* 3 where something is facing or going, as North, South, left, up, etc.; way: *Which direction did he go? in the opposite, right, wrong direction; The wind blew the papers in all directions; new directions in literary criticism; Al has a poor sense of direction* (= is always getting lost).

di·rec·tion·al (di·REC·shuh·nul) *adj.* having to do with direction: *a directional radio antenna (for signals from a particular direction); the right and left directional* (= turn) *signals.*

di·rec·tive (di·REC·tiv) *n.* an order or rule: *The Minister has issued directives on hiring minority citizens; a directive that men and women (must) be given equal opportunity.*

di·rect·ly *adv.* 1 in a direct or straightforward manner: *smiling directly at us.* 2 immediately: *We'll leave directly after work.* — **di·rect·ness** *n.*

direct mail *n.* advertising matter mailed to people on a list, as by a mail-order house.

di·rec·tor (di·REC·tur) *n.* one who directs: *an editorial director; a funeral, managing, movie, program director; a director of the company* (= member of the Board of Directors).

di·rec·to·ry (di·REC·tor·ee) *n.* **-ries** an alphabetical list of names along with addresses, phone numbers, etc.: *a city directory; telephone directory; a Canadian directory that gives many facts and figures about people and institutions.*

dirge (DIRJ) *n.* a song or poem lamenting someone's death: *a funeral dirge.*

dir·i·gi·ble (DEER·uh·juh·bul, duh·RIJ·uh·bul) *n.* an airship. — *adj.* steerable.

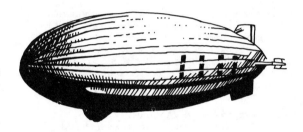

dirt *n.* 1 soil or earth: *Children like to play in the dirt; Everyone hit the dirt* (Slang for fell to the ground) *when the firing started; adj.: a dirt bike* (= trail bike); *a dirt farmer (who farms by himself); a dirt road* (= unpaved road); *a dirt track for bikes.* 2 grime or filth: *Detergents help wash dirt off clothes; He treats his men like dirt* (Slang for with utter contempt). 3 corruption or obscenity; pornography: *There's little dirt on TV during prime time; a campaign to get dirt off the newsstands; I just heard some dirt* (= slanderous gossip) *about the Joneses.*
— **dirt cheap** *Informal.* very cheap: *You can buy it dirt cheap; at dirt-cheap prices.*
— **dirt poor** so poor as to be without most of the essentials of life.
— **eat dirt** *Informal.* accept humiliating treatment; retract a statement.

dirt·y (DUR·tee) *adj.* **dirt·i·er, -i·est** 1 soiled; unclean: *dirty clothes, dishes, hands.* 2 unfair; low; base: *a dirty job, trick; political dirty tricks; dirty work;* **dirty pool** (Slang for trickery). 3 immoral; taboo; smutty: *a dirty book, movie, word; dirty language; the stereotype of "the dirty* (= lecherous) *old man."* 4 stormy or hostile: *dirty weather; He gave us a dirty look.*
— *adv.* in a dirty way: *to fight dirty; talk dirty.*
— *v.* **dirt·ies, dirt·ied, dirt·y·ing** make dirty: *The children were told not to* **dirty their hands** (= shame themselves) *by stealing and lying.* — **dirt·i·ness** *n.*

dirty linen *n.* private affairs of an embarrassing nature: *The Smiths never air* or *wash* or *hang out their dirty* *linen in public.* Also **dirty laundry.**

dis·a·bil·i·ty (dis·uh·BIL·uh·tee) *n.* **-ties** the state of being disabled: *Blindness is a physical disability; Dyslexia is a learning or reading disability* (= disorder); *Some disabilities are caused by illness, others by injury; the disabilities of illiterate adults; adj.: disability benefits, insurance; a disability pension for a wounded veteran.*

dis·a·ble (dis·AY·bul) *v.* **-bles, -bled, -bling** make unable, unfit, unqualified, etc., as by wounding: *a disabled car left on the road shoulder; a tank disabled by a land mine; Marriage disabled* (= disqualified) *her from inheriting.*

disabled *adj.* handicapped: *a disabled veteran; the dead and the disabled; Children who are learning disabled and physically disabled are given special help; the mentally disabled* (= mentally ill or retarded).

dis·a·buse (dis·uh·BYOOZE) *v.* **-bus·es, -bused, -bus·ing** free of mistaken ideas: *to disabuse a person of his errors.*

dis·ad·van·tage (dis·ud·VAN·tij) *n.* something that harms, works against, hinders, etc.; drawback: *Those who hadn't helped out in the kitchen were clearly at a disadvantage in the cooking contest; Everything seemed to work to our disadvantage; We all have certain aptitudes that outweigh or offset our disadvantages; Not knowing how to read is a decided disadvantage when applying for a job.*

disadvantaged (dis·ud·VAN·tijd) *adj.* lacking an acceptable basic standard of living, educational opportunities, civil rights, etc.: *an economically disadvantaged neighbourhood; a disadvantaged sector of our society; a disadvantaged youngster.*
— **dis·ad·van·ta·geous** (dis·AD·vun·TAY·jus) *adj.*

dis·a·gree (dis·uh·GREE) *v.* **-grees, -greed, -gree·ing** **1** fail to agree; differ: *People disagree on or about or over many things; Often we disagree sharply with our best friends; Sometimes we* **agree to disagree** *(on matters of opinion), but not when the bank balance disagrees with the cheque book register.* **2** cause distress or upset: *Sea food disagrees with some.* — **dis·a·gree·ment** *n.*

dis·a·gree·a·ble (dis·uh·GREE·uh·bul) *adj.* **1** ill-tempered: *a disagreeable old grouch.* **2** unpleasant: *a disagreeable day at work; Sea food is disagreeable to some.* — **dis·a·gree·a·ble·ness** *n.;* **dis·a·gree·a·bly** *adv.*

dis·al·low (dis·uh·LOW, *rhyme:* HOW) *v.* refuse to allow or accept officially: *The review board disallowed his claim; to disallow an appeal.*

dis·ap·pear (dis·uh·PEER) *v.* cease to be seen: *The magician made the rabbit disappear; Then he disappeared from view himself; Whales are disappearing* (= dying out) *because of excessive hunting.*
— **dis·ap·pear·ance** (-unce) *n.*

dis·ap·point (dis·uh·POINT) *v.* let someone down: *It disappointed us that we lost the Canada Cup; The team disappointed us.*
— **disappointed** *adj.: We are deeply disappointed by his poor performance; We were disappointed at or with his grades; not really disappointed in him; He too was disappointed to learn that he had failed.*
— **disappointing** *adj.: the disappointing turnout at our*

annual picnic; It's disappointing that so few turned up.
— **dis·ap·point·ment** (-munt) *n.: The picnic was a bit of a disappointment; We felt and expressed our disappointment at or about or over the poor turnout; a bitter, deep, keen, profound disappointment; To our great disappointment, the picnic had to be cancelled.*

dis·ap·prove (dis·uh·PROOV) *v.* **-ap·proves, -ap·proved, -ap·prov·ing** not accept or approve; have or express a bad opinion: *Father disapproves of long hair.* — **dis·ap·prov·al** (-PROO·vul) *n.*

dis·arm (dis·ARM) *v.* **1** take weapons away from someone; also, reduce or do away with military strength: *The police disarmed the robber; Germany and Japan were disarmed after World War II.* **2** make less hostile; make favourably inclined: *to disarm opposition; Her confession disarmed their suspicions; He won over the audience with a* **disarming** *smile.*
— **dis·ar·ma·ment** (-muh·munt) *n.: nuclear disarmament.*

dis·ar·ray (dis·uh·RAY) *n.* disorganized condition; disorder: *Her clothes were in disarray; As the rain fell, the procession broke up in total disarray; v: papers disarrayed by the wind.*

dis·as·sem·ble (dis·uh·SEM·bul) *v.* **-bles, -bled, -bling** take or come apart: *to disassemble a bicycle for shipping.*

dis·as·so·ci·ate (dis·uh·SOH·shee·ate) *v.* **-ates, -at·ed, -at·ing** end or break off an association with a person or thing: *She disassociated* (= dissociated) *herself from their activities.*

dis·as·ter (diz·AS·tur) *n.* **1** a great misfortune causing much death or damage: *It was a major disaster for the nation and a personal calamity for the minister responsible; He was courting disaster when he made that decision; The disaster could have been averted; Another disaster or near disaster is impending.* **2** a total failure: *The Edsel and the Bricklin were disasters of the car industry.*
— **adj.: The hurricane-stricken town was declared a** **disaster area** *by the government; A* **disaster film** *or* **movie** *capitalizes on fires, crashes, etc.*
— **dis·as·trous** (diz·AS·trus) *adj.: There was a disastrous drought last year; It would be disastrous to wait and see what happens instead of doing something about it.*
— **dis·as·trous·ly** *adv.*

dis·a·vow (dis·uh·VOW) *v. Formal.* to claim that one does not know about, does not approve of, or is not associated with something: *She disavowed the incriminating evidence; to disavow an intention, responsibility.* — **dis·a·vow·al** (-ul) *n.*

dis·band (dis·BAND) *v.* break up an organization: *to disband a committee, company, organization, regiment; The group disbanded after a few months.*

dis·bar (dis·BAR) *v.* **-bars, -barred, -bar·ring** expel as a lawyer: *to be disbarred from practice.*
— **dis·bar·ment** *n.*

dis·be·lief (dis·bi·LEEF) *n.* refusal to believe: *They stood aghast in utter disbelief; The story aroused widespread disbelief and suspicion.*

dis·burse (dis·BURCE) *v.* **-burs·es, -bursed, -burs·ing** pay out or distribute: *The government disbursed the*

authorized funds to the school boards.
— dis·burse·ment *n.*: *a treasurer in charge of disbursements of research grants; a lawyer's bill of fees, charges, and disbursements.*

disc *n.* **1** a phonograph record: *to cut* (=make) *a disc.* **2** a cartilage pad between vertebrae: *Al slipped* (=dislocated or ruptured) *a disc while playing football.* **3** a round, flat part or plate: *a kit including a buffer, adapter, and six sanding discs; the sun's disc* (=disclike figure); *the **disc pad** of an automobile's **disc brake**.* Also **disk.**

dis·card (dis·CARD) *v.* get rid of something; throw away, as a used carton.
— n. (DIS·card) something discarded, as a card or cards, an old library book, etc.: *Many old values have been thrown **into the discard** since World War II.*

disc drive *n.* a computer device for reading or writing data using discs.

dis·cern (di·SURN, -ZURN) *v.* perceive or distinguish: *We were able to discern mountains in the distance.*
— discerning *adj.*: *an astute and discerning judge of character; the discerning eye; a discerning audience.*
— dis·cern·i·ble *adj.*; **dis·cern·ment** *n.*

dis·charge (dis·CHARGE) *v.* **-charg·es, -charged, -charg·ing 1** send forth or unload the contents of something: *The bus discharged its passengers; to discharge waste into rivers and lakes; to discharge a ship of its cargo; to discharge the cargo; The Niagara River discharges into Lake Ontario; Batteries discharge electricity; The battery is discharged* (=dead); *Discharge* (=fire) *your rifle in the air; The pistol discharged accidentally.* **2** be free of an obligation: *Jim has discharged his debts* (=paid them); *We discharge our duties (by doing them).* **3** let go of someone or something: *A prisoner is discharged early on parole; a clerk discharged* (=dismissed) *for theft; He had been discharged dishonourably from the Navy.*
— n. (also DIS·charge) **1** a sending forth or emptying: *the discharge of the cargo from the ship's hold; a discharge of pus and blood from a wound; The patient continued to improve after his discharge from the hospital; an electrical discharge such as a spark across a gap.* **2** the fulfilling of an obligation: *the discharge of his legal responsibilities as a husband.* **3** dismissal: *He received an honourable discharge; The discharge (papers) came in the mail.*

dis·ci·ple (di·SYE·pul) *n.* a student or follower, esp. one of Christ's 12 apostles.

dis·ci·pli·nar·i·an (DIS·uh·pluh·NAY·ree·un) *n.* one who believes in and enforces strict discipline: *a strict disciplinarian and a good principal.*
— dis·ci·pli·nar·y (-nair·ee) *adj.*: *disciplinary action; a disciplinary body, committee, measure, problem.*

dis·ci·pline (DIS·uh·plin) *n.* **1** an area of learning: *medicine and affiliated disciplines such as nursing and pharmacy; Nadia won all four disciplines* (=balance beam, uneven bars, vault, and floor exercises) *for the gymnastic title.* **2** training to produce self-control, obedience, proper conduct, etc.; also, the results of this: *Principals try to establish and maintain discipline in their schools; They crack down on violations of discipline; Conduct that undermines discipline is not*

tolerated; Discipline can be firm, harsh, lax, loose, slack, stern, strict; iron discipline; Military discipline means automatic unquestioning obedience; He lives in monastic discipline under the vows of poverty, chastity, and obedience; Where's your party discipline? **3** corrective punishment: *the discipline committee of the Teachers' Federation.*
— v. -plines, -plined, -plin·ing 1 subject to corrective punishment: *Children used to be disciplined by being spanked.* **2** correct and train: *Children are best disciplined while young.*

disciplined *adj.* marked by discipline: *a disciplined writer; well disciplined kids; highly disciplined troops; It takes a disciplined* (=organized and trained) *mind to compile a dictionary.*

disc jockey *n.* a host of a program featuring recorded music.

dis·claim (dis·CLAIM) *v.* claim that one has no knowledge of or connection with something: *He disclaimed complicity in the plot.*

dis·claim·er (dis·CLAY·mur) *n.* a statement that disclaims something.

dis·close (dis·CLOZE) *v.* **-clos·es, -closed, -clos·ing** make visible or known; reveal: *The convict disclosed the names of his accomplices; He disclosed that he had been in jail before; A **disclosing agent** shows where brushing is required by staining the plaque around teeth.*

dis·clo·sure (dis·CLOH·zhur) *n.* a disclosing or something disclosed: *The public, sensational, startling disclosures made in the media shocked the nation.*

dis·co (DIS·coh) *n.* **-cos** *Informal.* a discotheque or discotheque music; *adj.*: *disco dancing, music, sounds; the disco craze, scene; a disco bar, hit, star, tape.*
— v. -coes, -coed, -co·ing dance to disco music: *They discoed all night.*

dis·col·our or **dis·col·or** (dis·CULL·ur) *v.* change or spoil in colour, as by fading, stains, or running of the dye.
— dis·col·or·a·tion (DIS·cull·uh·RAY·shun) *n.*

dis·com·bob·u·late (dis·cum·BOB·yuh·late) *v.* **-lates, -lat·ed, -lat·ing** *Informal.* upset or confuse: *He discombobulates his older colleagues by appearing at work casually dressed.*

dis·com·fit (dis·CUM·fit) *v.* defeat and confuse or disconcert: *She felt utterly discomfited by his disappearance just when he was most wanted.*
— dis·com·fi·ture (-fuh·chur) *n.*

dis·com·fort (dis·CUM·furt) *n.* lack of comfort, bodily or mental; unease; also, an instance or cause of this: *to put up with the discomforts of travel; to bear small physical discomforts without complaining.*
— v.: *He is discomforted by his tight shoes.*

dis·com·pose (dis·cum·POZE) *v.* **-pos·es, -posed, -pos·ing** upset the composure, poise, or order of: *He seemed a bit discomposed by the sudden bad news.*
— dis·com·po·sure (-POH·zhur) *n.*

dis·con·cert (dis·cun·SURT) *v.* ruin the calm self-control of someone; perturb: *He was disconcerted to find his hairpiece missing; That was quite **disconcerting**.*

dis·con·nect (dis·cuh·NECT) v. break the connection of something: *to disconnect one freight car from another; to disconnect* (= unplug) *a toaster.*

disconnected (dis·cuh·NEC·tid) adj. 1 not well linked; not coherent: *a disconnected narrative; disconnected thoughts.* 2 not connected: *disconnected hydro, telephone, TV.*

dis·con·tent (dis·cun·TENT) n. a lack of contentment or satisfaction: *They tried to stir up discontent among the employees; Soon there was widespread discontent about vacations, discontent at low wage scales, discontent with the whole working environment.* — **dis·con·tent·ed** adj.: *It is unfortunate that she is discontented with her job.*

dis·con·tin·ue (dis·cun·TIN·yoo) v. **-ues, -ued, -u·ing** cease or cause to cease; break off: *She discontinued paying rent until the leak was fixed.* — **dis·con·tin·u·ance** (-yoo·unce) or **dis·con·tin·u·a·tion** (DIS·con·tin·yoo·AY·shun) n.

dis·con·ti·nu·i·ty (DIS·con·tuh·NEW·uh·tee) n. **-ties** a gap or break.

dis·cord (DIS·cord) n. 1 disagreement or dispute: *to stir up discord in a community; discord between parents; discord among family members; Domestic or family discord sometimes leads to broken homes; the apple of discord* (= cause of rivalry and contention). 2 disharmony in music; a harsh dissonance; din. — **dis·cor·dant** (-dunt) adj.

dis·co·theque (DIS·cuh·tek) n. a club for dancing to recorded music.

dis·count (DIS·count) n. an amount deducted for early payment, buying in bulk, etc.: *A 5% discount is given on cash purchases; a cash discount; Slightly soiled goods are sold at a discount; A discount store sells goods at reduced prices.* — v. 1 reduce the price of something; deduct an amount from the price: *We discount all goods in the warehouse; We discount 5% from the regular price.* 2 allow for or anticipate bias, exaggeration, etc.; also, disregard as unreliable: *We tend to discount the rumours heard through the grapevine and the sensational stories in the press.* — **dis·count·a·ble** adj.: *discountable merchandise.* — **dis·count·er** n.

dis·coun·te·nance (dis·COW·tuh·nunce) v. **-nanc·es, -nanced, -nanc·ing** Formal. 1 disconcert: *She seemed a little discountenanced at being kept waiting.* 2 disapprove: *a disciplinarian who discountenances habitual tardiness.*

dis·cour·age (dis·CUR·ij) v. **-ag·es, -aged, -ag·ing** 1 make less confident, hopeful, or courageous; dishearten: *The troops were discouraged by the early defeats; They sat there discouraged at or about or over what had happened; It was discouraging to see their efforts wasted.* 2 deter: *Heavy seas discouraged the rescuers from jumping into the water; It discouraged rescue efforts.* — **dis·cour·age·ment** n.

dis·course (DIS·corse) n. 1 a formal speech; treatise: *a philosophical discourse.* 2 verbal communication: *terms used in ordinary discourse;* "He said 'I will come' " is **direct discourse** (= quotation of speaker's own words),

but "He said that he would come" is **indirect discourse** (= speaker's words as reported by someone else). — v. **-cours·es, -coursed, -cours·ing** 1 speak or write at length: *He discourses on* or *upon many matters in his book.* 2 converse: *Teachers don't like students discoursing too much about unrelated topics in class.*

dis·cour·te·ous (dis·CUR·tee·us) adj. rude and ill-mannered: *He was fired for being discourteous to customers.* — **dis·cour·te·ous·ly** adv.

dis·cour·te·sy (dis·CUR·tuh·see) n. **-sies** rudeness: *He apologized for his discourtesies; a grave discourtesy; She can't stand the discourtesy of being kept waiting.*

dis·cov·er (dis·CUV·ur) v. 1 get knowledge of something: *Police discovered several clues to the mystery; The body was finally discovered in the bushes; Children go to museums to discover how things work.* 2 be first to learn of, see, etc. a person or thing: *Did the Vikings discover Newfoundland?*

dis·cov·er·y (dis·CUV·uh·ree) n. **-er·ies** a discovering or what has been discovered: *the revolutionary discovery that the Earth goes around the Sun; the dramatic, exciting, startling, world-shaking discovery of the New World; Banting and Best made the discovery of insulin; a medical, scientific discovery; the discovery of new talent for the stage; the recent discoveries in space.*

Discovery Day n. a public holiday in Newfoundland and Labrador and in the Yukon Territory observed on the third Monday in August.

dis·cred·it (dis·CRED·it) v. 1 damage the believability of a person or thing: *The revelations were meant to discredit the opposition; The flat-earth theory has long been discredited.* 2 disbelieve: *One tends to discredit many of the rumours dished up in the papers.* — n. loss of good name or its cause: *The fact that he lied will be remembered by his discredit by future generations; He is a discredit to his school; Lying brings discredit to* or *on any self-respecting person; It throws discredit* (= disbelief) *on everything he has ever said.* — **dis·cred·i·ta·ble** (dis·CRED·uh·tuh·bul) adj.: *discreditable conduct, behaviour.*

dis·creet (dis·CREET) adj. 1 having or showing discretion and good judgment, esp. in speech: *She is very discreet in talking to the media; She keeps a discreet distance from them; Often she keeps a discreet silence or says, "Sorry, no comment!"* 2 tastefully modest: *She is known for her discreet charm; Her office is the picture of discreet elegance.* — **dis·creet·ly** adv.

dis·crep·an·cy (dis·CREP·un·see) n. **-cies** a disagreement; conflict: *a glaring discrepancy; There are numerous, serious, wide discrepancies between the two versions of the incident.* — **dis·crep·ant** (-unt) adj.: *two widely discrepant versions of the same incident.*

dis·crete (dis·CREET) adj. distinct and individual; separate: *a stereo set made up of four discrete component units.*

dis·cre·tion (dis·CRESH·un) n. 1 discernment; judgment: *He backed out saying, "Discretion is the better part of valour"* (= Why take an unnecessary risk). 2 freedom to choose or act as one wishes: *I leave this to*

your discretion; One may not marry before the **age of discretion** (= age of legal responsibility); *He has been authorized to incur expenses* **at his discretion.**
— **dis·cre·tion·ar·y** (dis·CRESH·uh·nair·ee) *adj.: the discretionary powers of a judge.*

discretionary income *n.* money left after paying for life's necessities, taxes, etc.

dis·crim·i·nate (dis·CRIM·uh·nate) *v.* **-nates, -nat·ed, -nat·ing 1** make or see a distinction, esp. in an intelligent way: *to discriminate between good and bad poetry; to discriminate good poetry from bad; to discriminate among many equally good options; a man of* **discriminating** *taste in clothes.* **2** act differently towards someone as a result of prejudice: *a club that discriminates against women (by excluding them).*

dis·crim·i·na·tion (dis·CRIM·uh·NAY·shun) *n.* **1** the ability to discriminate: *He doesn't show much discrimination in his choice of clothes.* **2** prejudice: *to practise discrimination; discrimination against minorities in housing; Minority groups are subjected to discrimination in various ways; age, racial, religious, sex discrimination; reverse discrimination (against members of the majority group).*

dis·crim·i·na·to·ry (dis·CRIM·uh·nuh·tor·ee) *adj.* that discriminates: *Discriminatory tariffs promote trade with some nations and discourage it with others; discriminatory* (= biassed) *hiring, laws, policies, practices.*

dis·cur·sive (dis·CUR·siv) *adj.* **1** moving from topic to topic freely: *a discursive letter.* **2** logical, not intuitive: *discursive reasoning.*

dis·cus *n.* **-cus·es 1** a heavy, round, flattish disc thrown for distance as a contest. **2** this contest; also **discus throw.**

dis·cuss (dis·CUS) *v.* talk about or consider a topic in all its aspects in speech or writing: *Let's discuss it with our friends; We discussed how we might put the money to good use.*

dis·cus·sion (dis·CUSH·un, "USH" as in "rush") *n.* a discussing or its presentation; discourse: *to have, lead, provoke a discussion; to bring up a subject for discussion; A subject comes up for discussion; It is presently under discussion; an animated, frank, heated, lively, open, quiet, spirited discussion; a panel discussion.*

dis·dain (dis·DAIN) *v.* consider or reject as unworthy: *He disdained to accept the award because he thought he*

deserved something better.
— *n.* haughty contempt: *the look of proud disdain on his face.*
— **dis·dain·ful** *adj.: He's disdainful of peers who have come up from the ranks; a disdainful silence.*
— **dis·dain·ful·ly** *adv.*

dis·ease (di·ZEEZ) *n.* a deviation of a plant or animal body from its healthy state; illness: *how the body fights disease; heart disease; the causes and symptoms of diseases; the breakout of a disease; the cure for a disease; the spread of a disease; to contract or come down with a disease; an acute, chronic, communicable, congenital, contagious, deadly, fatal, infectious, incurable, occupational, rare, social, tropical, venereal disease; Air pollution is a disease of industrial societies.*
— **dis·eased** (-ZEEZD) *adj.: diseased crops; a diseased liver.*

dis·em·bark (dis·em·BARK) *v.* go or put ashore from a ship.

dis·em·bow·el (dis·em·BOW·ul, *rhyme:* VOWEL) *v.* **-els, -elled** or **-eled, -el·ling** or **-el·ing** remove the bowels from a body: *To clean a chicken for cooking means to disembowel it.* — **dis·em·bow·el·ment** *n.*

dis·en·chant (dis·en·CHANT) *v.* set free from mistaken belief or enchantment: *He became disenchanted with the life of an actor;* **dis·en·chant·ment** *n.*

dis·en·gage (dis·en·GAGE) *v.* **-gag·es, -gaged, -gag·ing** free from being engaged, involved, or committed: *Depressing the clutch pedal disengages the clutch and disconnects the engine from the transmission; Troops were disengaged from the border confrontation.*
— **dis·en·gage·ment** *n.*

dis·en·tan·gle (dis·en·TANG·gul) *v.* **-gles, -gled, -gling 1** free from something that tangles or ties up: *He's trying to disentangle his hair from the comb.* **2** untangle: *to disentangle a snarled ball of wool.*

dis·fa·vour or **dis·fa·vor** (dis·FAY·vur) *n.* the state of being disapproved of or being out of favour: *He looks upon* or *regards* or *views foreigners with disfavour; He fell into disfavour with his boss.*
— *v. Formal.* not favour: *a plan disfavoured by the board of directors.*

dis·fig·ure (dis·FIG·yur) *v.* **-ures, -ured, -ur·ing** mar the appearance of: *a child disfigured by a burn; The scar disfigures her face; a badly disfigured body.*
— **dis·fig·ure·ment** *n.*

dis·fran·chise (dis·FRAN·chize) *v.* **-chis·es, -chised, -chis·ing** deprive someone of a right, esp. citizenship rights or the right to vote.

dis·gorge (dis·GORJ) *v.* **-gorg·es, -gorged, -gorg·ing** spew forth, esp. something swallowed; hence, give up or discharge: *a dragon disgorging smoke and flame; a river disgorging into the ocean.*

dis·grace (dis·GRACE) *n.* a loss of favour, good name, or honour; also, a cause of this: *Being poor is no disgrace but the condition of the poor is a disgrace to our civilization; Soldier, you've brought disgrace on your regiment; He had to leave his position* **in disgrace;** *He had* **fallen into disgrace** *with his superiors.*
— *v.* **-grac·es, -graced, -grac·ing** bring disgrace on someone: *He disgraced himself by his behaviour; He was*

publicly disgraced by being removed from office.
— **dis·grace·ful** *adj.* shameful: *disgraceful behaviour.*

dis·grun·tle (dis-GRUN·tul) *v.* -tles, -tled, -tling make ill-humoured by displeasing: *a fisherman disgruntled at* or *over* or *with the rainy weather.*

dis·guise (dis-GUYZ) *v.* -guis·es, -guised, -guis·ing change the appearance of a person or thing so as to conceal identity; also, cover up; hide: *The warship was disguised to look like a merchant vessel; a robber disguised as a police officer; We can't disguise the fact that many people who have been through high school are still illiterate; to disguise one's feelings.*
— *n.* a disguising or disguised condition; also, a means of disguise such as a wig, mask, or clothes: *a clever disguise; He put on a disguise and went to the Halloween party; He shed* or *threw off that disguise and assumed the disguise of a policeman; He made no disguise of* (= did not hide) *his intentions; He went to the party **in disguise**; Losing that job proved a **blessing in disguise** for he immediately got a much better one.*

dis·gust (dis-GUST) *n.* a feeling of sickened distaste, repugnance, or offence: *He discovered to his utter disgust that the vegetable dish contained meat; He felt, expressed disgust at what had happened.*
— *v.* cause disgust to someone: *His drunken behaviour thoroughly disgusted her; When he sobered up, he said he was **disgusted** with it himself; Everyone thought it was quite **disgusting** to watch.* — **dis·gust·ing·ly** *adv.*

dish *n.* 1 a shallow, concave container for food. 2 a serving of food; also, food prepared in some way. 3 *Slang.* a good-looking person. 4 *Slang.* what meets one's taste; one's cup of tea. 5 same as EARTH STATION. 6 **dishes** *pl.* plates, cups, bowls, etc. collectively, as left after meals: *Who'll do the dishes? We used to wash dishes to earn pocket money; The dishes are soaking now; You have to wash, rinse, and stack the dishes; She got a set of dishes* (= food containers) *for her bridal shower.*
— *v.* put in a dish: *It's Dad's turn to dish the dinner; Dish it up, Dad!*
— **dish out** or **up 1** put food into a dish. **2** *Informal.* give out, esp. freely: *Teachers dish out homework to students; It's easier to **dish it out** (= give blame or punishment) than to take it.*

dis·ha·bille (dis-uh-BEEL) *n.* the state of being partly or carelessly dressed, as in a robe or negligee: *Mom keeps telling Dad never to answer the door in dishabille.*

dis·heart·en (dis-HAR·tun) *v.* discourage; dismay: *The defeat disheartened us all; We all felt **disheartened**; It was quite **disheartening** to lose the very first game.*

dished (DISHT) *adj.* concave like a dish.

di·shev·el (duh-SHEV·ul) *v.* -els, -elled or -eled, -el·ling or -el·ing disorder, muss, or rumple hair or clothing; also, do so to a person: *Children return from play all dishevelled; his dishevelled appearance; The wind dishevelled his hair.*

dis·hon·est (dis-ON·ist) *adj.* not truthful or honest: *It's dishonest to lie, cheat, steal, and break promises; dishonest profits (as from smuggled goods).*

dis·hon·es·ty (dis-ON·is·tee) *n.* -ties 1 lack of honesty. 2 a dishonest act: *petty dishonesties.*

dis·hon·our or **dis·hon·or** (dis-ON·ur) *n.* a lack or loss of respect, honour, etc.; shame; also, a cause of this: *"Death before dishonour" went the battle cry as they refused to yield to the enemy.*
— *v.* 1 disgrace. 2 show disrespect to a person or thing: *Let's not dishonour our noble traditions.* 3 refuse to pay or cash a bill, cheque, etc.
— **dis·hon·our·a·ble** (-ur·uh·bul) *adj.*: *a dishonourable discharge from the military;* **dis·hon·our·a·bly** *adv.*

dish·wash·er (DISH·wosh·ur) *n.* a person or machine that washes dishes: *to load* or *stack a dishwasher.*

dish·y (DISH·ee) *adj. Slang.* attractive: *a dishy singer.*

dis·il·lu·sion (dis·i·LOO·zhun) *v.* to free one of illusions or misconceptions: *He was living in a world of fantasy, but no one tried to disillusion him; He ended up a very **disillusioned**(= disappointed and embittered) man.*
— **dis·il·lu·sion·ment** *n.*

dis·in·cline (dis·in·CLINE) *v.* -clines, -clined, -clin·ing be or make unwilling: *People seem **disinclined** to work on Monday mornings.*

dis·in·fect (dis·in·FECT) *v.* make free of disease germs: *Drinking water is disinfected with chlorine; to disinfect a room.*

dis·in·fect·ant (dis·in·FEC·tunt) *n. & adj.* (something) that disinfects.

dis·in·gen·u·ous (dis·in·JEN·yoo·us) *adj.* not honest, open, or sincere: *a disingenuous reply to the lawyer's question; It's disingenuous to say there is nothing to the rumour in order to divert attention.*

dis·in·te·grate (dis·IN·tuh·grate) *v.* -grates, -grat·ed, -grat·ing break up into smaller or component parts: *Most meteoroids disintegrate and burn up in the atmosphere.* — **dis·in·te·gra·tion** (-tuh·GRAY·shun) *n.*

dis·in·ter (dis·in·TUR) *v.* -ters, -terred, -ter·ring dig up from the earth or a grave; exhume; **dis·in·ter·ment** *n.*

dis·in·ter·est·ed (dis·IN·tris·tid, -tuh·res·tid) *adj.* 1 unbiassed or impartial: *a disinterested observer, offer, generosity, service.* 2 uninterested or indifferent: *He looked bored and disinterested; disinterested and uninformed clerks.*

dis·joint·ed (dis·JOIN·tid) *adj.* 1 broken at the joints: *a disjointed turkey.* 2 badly connected; lacking unity: *a rambling and disjointed* (= incoherent or badly connected) *account, narrative; disjointed images, sentence structure, thoughts; What a disjointed society we live in!*

disk *n.* a storage device in the shape of a thin, flat phonograph record for recording and reading back data using a drive mechanism: *floppy disk; hard* or *rigid disk; optical disks read by laser beams; to format a disk; copy on to a disk; make a backup disk; a **disk pack** (= stack of disks). Also **disc.**

disk·ette (dis·KET) *n.* a floppy disk.

dis·like (dis·LIKE) *v.* -likes, -liked, -lik·ing not like: *Joe dislikes spinach; Jane dislikes playing with dolls.*
— *n.* a not liking: *a feeling of dislike; a cordial, deep, hearty, violent dislike; a dislike for* or *of dogs; Our dog has taken a strong dislike to the neighbour's cat; But the cat shows no dislike for Fido; The roommates don't*

know each other's likes and dislikes yet.

dis·lo·cate (DIS·loh·cate, dis·LOH·cate) *v.* **-cates, -cat·ed, -cat·ing** move, esp. a bone of the body, from its proper position: *a dislocated shoulder; store sales dislocated* (=changed) *by a recession.* — **dis·lo·ca·tion** (-loh·CAY·shun) *n.*

dis·lodge (dis·LOJ) *v.* **-lodg·es, -lodged, -lodg·ing** move forcibly from a position: *Artillery fire dislodged the enemy's infantry; The blow dislodged the filling from the tooth.*

dis·loy·al (dis·LOY·ul) *adj.* not loyal; unfaithful: *Troops disloyal to the government attacked the president's palace.* — **dis·loy·al·ly** *adv.* — **dis·loy·al·ty** (-tee) *n.* **-ties.**

dis·mal (DIZ·mul) *adj.* gloomy or depressing: *orphans facing a dismal future; dismal weather; their dismal failure, outlook, performance, record, showing.*

dis·man·tle (dis·MAN·tul) *v.* **-tles, -tled, -tling** to strip something of covering, equipment, weapons, etc.: *the dismantled hulk of an abandoned bus; a large desk* **dismantled** (=taken apart) *for shipping.*

dis·may (dis·MAY) *v.* dishearten, make afraid, or daunt, esp. about a problem to be resolved: *The students were dismayed at the teachers' strike; dismayed to think they might fail the exam.* — **n.:** *The results of the exam filled us with dismay; We felt and expressed dismay at the number of failures; To our dismay, even the best student had failed.* — **dis·may·ing·ly** *adv.*

dis·mem·ber (dis·MEM·bur) *v.* **1** cut or tear the limbs from a body: *a dismembered corpse.* **2** divide or tear into pieces: *The Church was dismembered by the Reformation.* — **dis·mem·ber·ment** *n.*

dis·miss (dis·MIS) *v.* **1** allow or cause to leave; send away: *Class dismissed!* **2** release from a job, service, etc.: *He dismissed his chauffeur for reckless driving; was dismissed from his job.* **3** put out of one's mind; also, reject in court: *He dismissed the rumours as nonsense; "Case dismissed," said the judge.*

dis·miss·al (dis·MIS·ul) *n.* a being dismissed or sent away: *a curt dismissal; early dismissal because of snow.*

dis·mount (dis·MOUNT) *v.* **1** get down or cause to get off from a horse, vehicle, etc.: *Bicyclists are supposed to dismount and walk at a pedestrian crossing; The knight was dismounted by his opponent in a joust.* **2** remove something from its mounting: *to dismount a cannon from its carriage.* — **n.** an act of dismounting: *The gymnast dislocated an ankle on his dismount from the high bar.*

dis·o·be·di·ence (dis·uh·BEE·dee·unce) *n.* refusal to obey: *a soldier court-martialled for disobedience; civil disobedience; willful disobedience.* — **dis·o·be·di·ent** (dis·uh·BEE·dee·unt) *adj.:* *a disobedient child; disobedient to his parents.*

dis·o·bey (dis·uh·BAY) *v.* refuse or fail to obey: *dismissed for disobeying orders.*

dis·or·der (dis·OR·dur) *n.* **1** a lack of orderly arrangement; disarray: *He leaves his room in disorder; The army retreated in disorder.* **2** a disturbance in functioning; mild disease: *a bowel, brain, intestinal,*

mental, personality, respiratory, stomach disorder. **3** an upset to the public peace: *to restore order where there is disorder; social disorders; Violent disorders* (= riots) *broke out in the country.*

dis·or·dered (dis·OR·durd) *adj.* marked by disorder: *He left the office in a disordered condition; a badly disordered desk; a disordered* (= sick) *mind.*

dis·or·der·ly (dis·OR·dur·lee) *adj.* **1** disorganized or disarrayed: *a disorderly pile of junk.* **2** unruly or riotous: *arrested for being drunk and disorderly; disorderly conduct* (such as fighting in public). — **dis·or·der·li·ness** *n.*

dis·or·gan·ize (dis·OR·guh·nize) *v.* **-iz·es, -ized, -iz·ing** break up the orderly or systematic organization of a schedule, service, system, timetable, etc.: *Firing the department head disorganized operations; The department is now a* **disorganized** *mess.* — **dis·or·gan·i·za·tion** (-nuh·ZAY·shun) *n.*

dis·o·ri·ent (dis·OR·ee·unt) *v.* cause to be lost or confused by taking one out of one's familiar surroundings: *People become disoriented if shut up in a dungeon for some time; the* **disoriented** (= aimless) *youth of today.* — **dis·o·ri·en·ta·tion** (-TAY·shun) *n.*

dis·own (dis·OWN) *v.* deny that one owns, knows, or is connected with a person or thing; reject: *children disowned by their parents.*

dis·par·age (dis·PAIR·ij) *v.* **-ag·es, -aged, -ag·ing** *Formal.* cause to be less well thought of; also, treat or talk about a person or thing slightingly: *a* **disparaging** *remark; adv.: He talked* **disparagingly** *about his rivals.*

dis·pa·rate (DIS·puh·rit, dis·PAIR·it) *adj.* fundamentally unlike: *Apples and oranges are not so disparate as chalk and cheese.* — **dis·par·i·ty** (dis·PAIR·uh·tee) *n.* **-ties:** *the wide disparity in incomes; the great disparity between pay scales for men and women.*

dis·pas·sion·ate (dis·PASH·uh·nit) *adj.* calmly impartial; unemotional: *a cool dispassionate examination of the problem.* — **dis·pas·sion·ate·ly** *adv.*

dis·patch (dis·PATCH) *v.* **1** send with directness or great speed: *Ambulances were dispatched to the scene of the accident; radio-dispatched delivery.* **2** deal with or finish quickly; also, kill quickly: *He dispatches the morning's business before lunch; The bull was dispatched at the end of the bullfight.* — **n. 1** a dispatching. **2** fast efficiency: *She worked with great dispatch to stop the trouble before it spread.* **3** a message, report, etc., as for a government, a news service, or the military: *to file, send a dispatch; He was* **mentioned in dispatches** (for bravery in battle).

dis·patch·er (dis·PATCH·ur) *n.* one who sends out trains, buses, taxis, etc. on schedule or as needed.

dis·pel (dis·PEL) *v.* **-pels, -pelled, -pel·ling** get rid of something by scattering or driving off: *The sun dispelled the early morning fog; The new evidence dispelled all doubts; to dispel fears, gloom, hopes, illusions, myths, notions, rumours, suggestions; The light that the book shed on the subject dispelled the mists of ignorance.*

dis·pen·sa·ry (dis·PEN·suh·ree) *n.* **-ries** a place where medicines are prepared and given out in a school, factory, hospital, etc.

dis·pen·sa·tion (dis-pen-SAY-shun) *n.* **1** a dispensing: *the dispensation of the laws.* **2** an exemption from a rule of law: *a papal dispensation allowing remarriage; No dispensation can be granted from divine law.* **3** an ordering of events; also, a resulting system or rule: *to live under the Christian dispensation; Capitalists fled from the new dispensation in Russia after the Revolution.*

dis·pense (dis-PENCE) *v.* **-pens·es, -pensed, -pens·ing** distribute or give out: *to dispense alms to the poor, food to the hungry; Courts dispense justice; Pharmacists dispense* (= prepare and give out) *medicines.*
— **dispense with** do without a person or thing: *Shall we dispense with the formalities?* — **dis·pen·sa·ble** *adj.*

dis·pen·ser (dis-PEN-sur) *n.* one that dispenses, esp. a device for the convenient dispensing of something: *a cash dispenser; the ice dispenser of a fridge; a soap dispenser; tape dispenser; towel dispenser.*

dis·per·sal (dis-PUR-sul) *n.* a dispersing or scattering: *the natural dispersal of seeds; the dispersal of a crowd.*

dis·perse (dis-PURCE) *v.* **-pers·es, -persed, -pers·ing** **1** break up and distribute: *The crowd dispersed when the riot police appeared; new chemicals to disperse oil slicks in the harbour; In an emulsion, one liquid is dispersed or suspended in another, as oil in water.* **2** spread widely: *Seeds are dispersed in various ways by the wind, water, people, and animals; Maples are found widely dispersed in Canada.*
— **dis·per·sion** (-PUR-shun) *n.*

dis·pi·rit (di-SPEER-it) *v.* make sad, downcast, or discouraged: *The players were dispirited by repeated failures.*

dis·place (dis-PLACE) *v.* **-plac·es, -placed, -plac·ing** move from its proper place: *a ship that displaces 12 000 tons (of water); After World War II many **displaced persons** (= those uprooted by war and political unrest) came to Canada.*

dis·place·ment (dis-PLACE-munt) *n.* a displacing or what is displaced: *the displacement of Jon as the club's treasurer; Naval ships are rated according to their displacement (of water equal to their weight in long tons).*

dis·play (dis-PLAY) *v.* expose clearly to the view; show or exhibit: *A store window is used to display merchandise; He thought to display his learning at the convention, but only succeeded in displaying his ignorance.*
— *n.* a displaying: *a dazzling, impressive, lavish, ostentatious, spectacular display of new fashions; Select the one you like from the display; a display of courage; Private matters are not for public display; to make, put on a vulgar display of one's wealth; a modest display of one's talents; a graphic display presented on the VDT; a video display; window display;* **adj.**: *a display cabinet, case, window.*

dis·please (dis-PLEEZ) *v.* **-pleas·es, -pleased, -pleas·ing** be unpleasing to someone; annoy.

dis·pleas·ure (dis-PLEZH-ur) *n.* the feeling one has when displeased: *to incur the displeasure of the queen; He showed his displeasure with the day's happenings.*

dis·pos·a·ble (dis-POH-zuh-bul) *adj.* **1** available to be used: *your disposable income* (= take-home pay). **2** to be used and then thrown away: *a disposable diaper, pop bottle;* **n.**: *Disposables add to the garbage.*

dis·pos·al (dis-POH-zul) *n.* **1** a disposition or arrangement: *the disposal of chessmen on a board.* **2** a getting rid of something: *sewage disposal; waste disposal; the disposal* (= sale) *of the family farm; the disposal* (= giving away) *of grandpa's property according to his will.* **3** a device, usually fitted in the kitchen sink, for shredding garbage which is then flushed down the drain; disposer.
— **at one's disposal** to be used as one desires: *I'm at your disposal but she is not; She has placed her chauffeur at your disposal.*

dis·pose (dis-POZE) *v.* **-pos·es, -posed, -pos·ing** **1** make willing or likely: *She is not disposed* (= not in the mood) *to receive visitors today; The government is either well or ill **disposed** to your request* (= favours or disfavours it). **2** set in order; arrange: *troops disposed in battle array; "Man proposes, God disposes."*
— **dispose of** get rid of a person or thing: *the dangers of disposing of nuclear wastes.*

dis·pos·er (dis-POH-zur) *n.* same as DISPOSAL, 3.

dis·po·si·tion (dis-puh-ZISH-un) *n.* **1** a disposing of something; also, the power to dispose or use: *The heirs have disposition of the land; disposition of property by sale or gift.* **2** the way something is disposed; arrangement: *an elegant disposition of furniture.* **3** one's general tendency; temperament: *a woman of a pleasant disposition; a buoyant, genial, sunny, mild disposition.*

dis·pos·sess (dis-puh-ZES) *v.* deprive someone of possession, esp. of land; evict: *They were dispossessed of their land; dispossessed dirt farmers.*
— **dis·pos·ses·sion** *n.*

dis·pro·por·tion·ate (dis-pruh-POR-shuh-nit) *adj.* out of proportion to something: *Your pay is disproportionate* (= low compared) *to the work involved; A disproportionate* (= too large) *amount of time is spent on coffee breaks.*

dis·prove (dis-PROOVE) *v.* **-proves, -proved, -prov·ing** prove wrong or false: *Creationists and evolutionists try to disprove each other's theories.*

dis·pu·ta·tious (dis-pew-TAY-shus) *adj.* given to arguing: *a disputatious committee; He is of a disputatious turn of mind.*

dis·pute (dis-PYOOT, long "OO") *v.* **-putes, -put·ed,**

-put·ing 1 argue or debate about something: *The speaker offered to dispute (the issue) with all comers; I do not dispute that the earth is round; The brothers are always disputing* (= quarrelling). **2** argue against the rightness or truth of something: *to dispute a claim, decision, election, statement, will.* **3** oppose or fight for in defence of something: *We'll dispute every inch of ground before yielding.*
— *n.* an argument or quarrel, esp. one that is heated: *The argument led to a dispute; an acrimonious, bitter, sharp dispute; Religious disputes have ended in bloodshed; to arbitrate, resolve, settle a dispute; Her claim to first prize is **beyond dispute*** (= cannot be disputed); *The contract settlement is still **in dispute*** (= being disputed). — **dis·pu·ta·ble** (-tuh·bul) *adj.*
— **dis·put·er** or **dis·pu·tant** (DIS·pyoo·tunt, dis·PEW·tunt) *n.*

dis·qual·i·fy (dis·QUAL·uh·fye) *v.* **-fies, -fied, -fy·ing** make or declare unfit, ineligible, or unentitled: *The racehorse was disqualified because it was drugged.*
— **dis·qual·i·fi·ca·tion** (-fuh·CAY·shun) *n.*

dis·quiet (dis·KWY·ut) *v.* upset the peace of mind or disturb the security of someone: *People are disquieted by news of friction between the superpowers; a very **disquieting** report.*
— *n.* worry or anxiety: *a feeling of disquiet; We endured months of disquiet during the trial.*

dis·re·gard (dis·ruh·GARD) *v.* pay no attention or respect to something: *Please disregard this notice if you have already paid; Let's not disregard the advice of older and wiser people.*
— *n.* lack of attention or respect: *Willful disregard of rules could land you in trouble; his disregard for his elders.* — **dis·re·gard·ful** (dis·ri·GARD·ful) *adj.*

dis·re·pair (dis·ri·PAIR) *n.* the state of being neglected and needing repairs: *a bridge that is in disrepair.*

dis·rep·u·ta·ble (dis·REP·yuh·tuh·bul) *adj.* having a bad reputation: *a disreputable businessman; a disreputable part of town.*

dis·re·pute (dis·ri·PYOOT, long "YOO") *n.* a state of ill repute; disgrace: *The theatre fell into disrepute when it was taken over by the new management; It has been held in disrepute ever since.*

dis·res·pect (dis·ris·PECT) *n.* absence of respect: *without disrespect to our seniors; with no disrespect to our traditions; No disrespect was intended or meant.*
— **dis·res·pect·ful** *adj.*: *a disrespectful remark.*

dis·robe (DIS·robe) *v.* **-robes, -robed, -rob·ing** take off clothing, esp. outer robes: *She disrobed and dived into the pool.*

dis·rupt (dis·RUPT) *v.* break apart; hence, disturb or disorder: *attempts to disrupt debate in the Commons.*
— **dis·rup·tion** *n.*: *the total disruption of service caused by a strike; temporary disruptions in TV transmission.*
— **dis·rup·tive** (-tiv) *adj.*: *the disruptive behaviour of disruptive strikers.*

dis·sat·is·fac·tion (DIS·sat·is·FAC·shun) *n.* the state of being dissatisfied: *The strikers expressed deep, keen, widespread dissatisfaction about or with working conditions.*

dis·sat·is·fied (dis·SAT·is·fide) *adj.* not satisfied;

discontented: *He's dissatisfied at not getting a raise; a dissatisfied worker who is dissatisfied with his pay.*

dis·sect (dis·SECT) *v.* **1** cut into pieces for anatomical study: *to dissect a frog in biology class.* **2** analyse very finely.
— **dis·sec·tion** *n.*: *a dissection* (= analysis) *of the causes of the revolution.*

dis·sem·ble (di·SEM·bul) *v.* **-bles, -bled, -bling 1** hide under a false guise: *He dissembled his emotions.* **2** feign or pretend: *He was merely dissembling sympathy.*
— **dis·sem·bler** *n.* — **dis·sem·blance** (-blunce) *n.*

dis·sem·i·nate (di·SEM·uh·nate) *v.* **-ates, -at·ed, -at·ing** spread widely or to many people.
— **dis·sem·i·na·tion** (-NAY·shun) *n.*: *the wide dissemination of knowledge through radio and TV.*

dis·sen·sion (di·SEN·shun) *n.* disagreement, esp. one causing hostility; quarrel: *They tried to sow dissension among the workers; to stir up dissension between rival groups.*

dis·sent (di·SENT) *v.* not agree; hold a different opinion: *One of the justices dissented from the views of the others; He gave a **dissenting** opinion.*
— *n.* disagreement, as nonacceptance of the teachings of a church: *a matter that brooks no dissent; Some churches tolerate no dissent from traditional doctrines.*
— **dis·sent·er** (di·SEN·tur) *n.*

dis·ser·ta·tion (dis·ur·TAY·shun) *n.* a long essay, esp. a doctoral thesis: *a dissertation on or about the novels of Margaret Atwood.*

dis·ser·vice (dis·SUR·vis) *n.* a harmful or injurious action: *Doing the children's homework is not only doing them a disservice but also a disservice to the cause of education.*

dis·si·dence (DIS·uh·dunce) *n.* disagreement or dissent.
— **dis·si·dent** *adj.*: *the expulsion of dissident trade unionists;* **n.**: *political dissidents of the Soviet system.*

dis·sim·i·lar (dis·SIM·uh·lur) *adj.* not similar; unlike: *Cats are not dissimilar to lions and leopards; comparison of dissimilar jobs for giving equal pay.*
— **dis·sim·i·lar·i·ty** (DIS·suh·muh·LAIR·uh·tee) *n.* **-ties.**

dis·sim·u·late (dis·SIM·yuh·late) *v.* **-lates, -lat·ed, -lat·ing** hide the truth; dissemble: *The job applicant dissimulated about his university degrees.*
— **dis·sim·u·la·tor** (-lay·tur) *n.*
— **dis·sim·u·la·tion** (-LAY·shun) *n.*

dis·si·pate (DIS·uh·pate) *v.* **-pates, -pat·ed, -pat·ing 1** disperse: *morning fog dissipated by the sun.* **2** vanish or fade away, or cause to do so; hence, waste foolishly; engage in wasteful, excessive pleasures: *a fortune dissipated by bad investments; a rich young man who dissipates his wealth by gambling in casinos.*
— **dis·si·pa·tion** (dis·uh·PAY·shun) *n.*: *a life of drunken dissipation.*

dis·so·ci·ate (di·SOH·shee·ate) *v.* **-ates, -at·ed, -at·ing** separate from association; cut off: *The Minister dissociated herself from the views expressed by her colleagues.* — **dis·so·ci·a·tion** (-AY·shun) *n.*

dis·so·lute (DIS·uh·loot) *adj.* profligate, immoral, and dissipated. — **dis·so·lute·ly** *adv.;* **dis·so·lute·ness** *n.*

dis·solve (di·ZOLV) *v.* **-solves, -solved, -solv·ing** 1 (make) go into solution; also, disappear as into a liquid: *Sugar dissolves in coffee; You dissolve it by stirring; Coffee dissolves sugar* (= takes it in solution); *On the screen, one scene dissolves* (= fades out and blends) *into the next; **n.**: The scenes changed in a series of dissolves.* 2 bring to an end: *to dissolve a marriage, parliament, partnership; Parliament dissolves at the end of a session; The child dissolved in tears* (= broke down and wept) *when his toy was crushed.*

dis·suade (di·SWADE) *v.* **dis·suades, dis·suad·ed, dis·suad·ing** advise or persuade not to do something: *We dissuaded her from quitting her job.* — **dis·sua·sion** (-SWAY·zhun) *n.*

dis·taff (DIS·taff) *n.* 1 a stick for holding wool or flax for use in spinning. 2 women collectively; also, womanly occupations. — *adj.* female: *He's related to the Silvas on the distaff side.*

dis·tance (DIS·tunce) *n.* a measure of separation in space or time or of remoteness in similarity or relation: *the distance between Halifax and Vancouver; the distance from Halifax to Vancouver; We have travelled quite a distance* (= a long way) *to come here; We can see the sea in the distance* (= far away); *at a distance of a few kilometres; to cover, run, walk a distance; Let's keep a safe distance behind the car in front; Don't close the distance between our car and theirs; a braking, short, shouting, stopping, striking, walking distance; in the remote distances of history when the English language didn't exist.* — **go** or **last the distance** stay in or last till the end of something that requires sustained effort. — **keep one's distance** remain aloof or detached. — **keep someone at a distance** prevent someone from becoming friendly. — *v.* **-tanc·es, -tanced, -tanc·ing** place or keep at a distance: *We distanced ourselves from the policies of the new leaders.*

dis·tant (DIS·tunt) *adj.* not close; far; away: *on the distant horizon; in the not too distant future; a distant relative; The school is two kilometres distant from our house; He acknowledged us with a rather distant* (= cold and aloof) *smile.* — **dis·tant·ly** *adv.*

dis·taste (dis·TAIST) *n.* dislike or aversion: *She shows a strong distaste for romantic novels.* — **dis·taste·ful** *adj.*

dis·tend (dis·TEND) *v.* swell, as from internal pressure: *the distended tummies and skeletal frames of starving children.*

dis·til or **dis·till** (dis·TIL) *v.* **-tils** or **-tills, -tilled, -til·ling** 1 fall or cause to fall in drops, as by the condensation of vapour: *If you distil salt water you get pure distilled water; Salt is distilled from* or *out of sea water; Sometimes water distils through rocks and wets their surface; Flowers distil nectar.* 2 extract or emerge as the essential element: *a book that is the distilled wisdom of the ancients.* 3 produce or purify by distillation: *Malted barley is distilled to make whisky; A licence is required for distilling liquors; Whisky, gin, rum, etc. are **distilled** liquors* or *spirits; The world's two*

largest **distilling** *companies are Canadian; the* **distilling** *industry.* — **dis·til·la·tion** (dis·tuh·LAY·shun) *n.*

dis·till·er (dis·TIL·ur) *n.* one who distils, esp. a producer of distilled alcoholic beverages.

dis·tinct (dis·TINCT) *adj.* 1 different; individual; clearly specified: *The Maltese, Manx, Persian, and Siamese are four distinct breeds of cat; They are distinct from one another; The Inuit are a distinct group within Canadian society; Quebec has been declared a distinct society in the Canadian Constitution.* 2 clearly perceived or perceivable; well-defined: *Tall players have a distinct advantage in basketball; the distinct profile of a woman; There's a distinct hint of fall in the air.* — **dis·tinct·ly** *adv.;* **dis·tinct·ness** *n.*

dis·tinc·tion (dis·TINK·shun) *n.* 1 a distinguishing or making a difference, as in treatment: *We pay our employees without distinction of sex.* 2 a difference; also, a trait, characteristic, etc. that makes a difference: *a philosopher who can draw* or *make a subtle distinction between being and becoming; to blur a distinction; a clear-cut, dubious, fine, nice distinction.* 3 excellence; special honour; superiority; also, something in recognition of this: *She passed the examination with distinction; She won many academic distinctions; a statesman of distinction; He enjoys* or *has* or *holds the dubious distinction of being the world's fattest man.*

dis·tinc·tive (dis·TINK·tiv) *adj.* marking the distinctness of something; characteristic: *the distinctive aroma of coffee; The aroma is distinctive of that type of coffee.* — **dis·tinc·tive·ly** *adv.;* **dis·tinc·tive·ness** *n.*

dis·tin·guish (dis·TING·gwish) *v.* 1 mark as different: *Speech distinguishes people from animals.* 2 perceive a difference; discriminate: *to distinguish between good and bad art.* 3 perceive or make out: *We were barely able to distinguish the hills in the distance.* 4 make famous, respected, etc.: *to distinguish oneself by gallantry in battle.* — **dis·tin·guish·a·ble** (-gwish·uh·bul) *adj.*

distinguished *adj.* 1 famous or eminent: *a distinguished author; the Distinguished Service Medal.* 2 having a dignified and superior manner: *a distinguished accent, gentleman, lady.*

dis·tort (dis·TORT) *v.* 1 twist out of its normal shape or condition. 2 alter or twist the truth, a story, etc. — **dis·tor·tion** (-TOR·shun) *n.: The government claimed that the newspaper story was a gross distortion of the truth.*

dis·tract (dis·TRACT) *v.* draw one's attention away from something: *Don't distract me when I am trying to concentrate; A phone call distracted her from her homework.* — **distracted** *adj.* upset emotionally; bewildered by conflicting thoughts: *She wore a distracted look; to be distracted by* or *with anxiety, fear, grief.*

dis·trac·tion (dis·TRAC·shun) *n.* the state of being distracted or something that draws away one's attention: *She doesn't like distractions when trying to concentrate on her work; On weekends she looks for any distractions* (= amusements) *available in town; She was once driven to distraction* (= mental confusion) *by loneliness.*

dis·traught (dis·TRAWT) *adj.* mentally agitated or upset: *She was distraught with fear and pain; Hamlet was distraught* (= mad).

dis·tress (dis·TRESS) *n.* great danger or suffering of a temporary nature that calls for relief: *Wars bring distress and misery; to alleviate the distress of famine in Africa; economic, financial, distress; He suffered great distress of body and mind; She felt deep distress at or over being unable to help; gastric distress* (= trouble); *Knights were supposed to rescue* **damsels in distress.** — *adj.: distress merchandise sold at a loss; Their houses were seized and sold at distress prices; a distress sale; the distress slaughter of cattle for lack of fodder; "Mayday" and "SOS" are* **distress signals** *used by airplanes and ships.* — *v.* cause distress to someone: *We're distressed to hear you are ill; a* **distressed area** *with high unemployment, poverty, etc.; a* **distressing** *report about the famine in Africa; It's* **distressing** *to think of so many children starving to death.* — **dis·tress·ful** *adj.*

dis·trib·ute (dis·TRIB·yoot, long "oo") *v.* -utes, -ut·ed, -ut·ing 1 divide or pass out among many, esp. in shares: *a magazine distributed nationwide to homeowners in selected areas; Tips received are distributed equally among the staff.* 2 put into classes or kinds. 3 spread: *Distribute the manure evenly on the lawn.* — **dis·trib·u·tion** (dis·truh·BYOO·shun) *n.: the distribution of food among the hungry; the distribution network of a marketing firm.* — **dis·trib·u·tor** (dis·TRIB·yuh·tur) *n.*

dis·trict (DIS·trict) *n.* an area or region, esp. one with a specific character or marked out for a judicial or administrative purpose: *a business, electoral, farming, financial, residential, school, theatre district.*

dis·trust (dis·TRUST) *n.* an absence of faith, confidence, trust, etc.: *the deep distrust between labour and management; the popular distrust of computers.* — *v.* not trust: *Everyone distrusts flatterers.* — **dis·trust·ful** *adj.;* **dis·trust·ful·ly** *adv.*

dis·turb (dis·TURB) *v.* 1 upset the peace, quiet, etc. of a place or person: *Don't disturb people who are asleep; The shots disturbed the quiet of the night; She was disturbed to hear someone had broken into her home; The picketer was charged with* **disturbing the peace** (= causing public disorder); *She found the news quite* **disturbing.** 2 upset mentally: *a ward for* **disturbed** *patients.* 3 trouble: *Don't disturb yourself for me.* — **dis·turb·er** *n.: arrested as a disturber of the peace.*

dis·turb·ance (dis·TUR·bunce) *n.* a disturbing; disorder or trouble: *to cause, create, make, put down, quell a disturbance; widespread political disturbances and riots.*

dis·u·nite (dis·yoo·NITE) *v.* -nites, -nit·ed, -nit·ing cause something or someone to become separate: *a family disunited by quarrels over an inheritance.* — **dis·u·ni·ty** (dis·YOO·nuh·tee) *n.*

dis·use (dis·YOOSE) *n.* the state of not being used: *a railway line that has fallen into disuse.* — **dis·used** *adj.: a disused mine shaft.*

ditch *n.* a trench dug in the earth, often containing water: *There are deep drainage ditches on the roadside; an irrigation ditch; to fight* **to the last ditch** (= to the end). — *v.* 1 dig a ditch around or in a place. 2 drive a car into a ditch; also, land a plane on water. 3 *Slang.* get rid of a person or thing; dump: *The project was ditched when funds ran out.*

dith·er (DITH·ur, "TH" as in "the") *n.* a state of nervous excitement or confusion: *He was all in a dither over his wedding.* — *v.* act indecisively: *He dithers instead of taking action.*

dit·to (DIT·oh) *n.* **dit·tos** 1 the same as above. 2 a mark (") placed beneath something to be repeated; also **ditto mark.** 3 duplicate.

dit·ty (DIT·ee) *n.* **dit·ties** a simple little song: *a popular ditty.*

di·ur·nal (dye·UR·nul) *adj.* 1 daily: *the diurnal motion of the heavens due to the diurnal rotation of the earth.* 2 having to do with the daytime: *a diurnal, not nocturnal animal; Diurnal flowers close up at night.* — **di·ur·nal·ly** *adv.*

dive *v.* **dives,** *pt.* **dived** or **dove** (DOHV), *pp.* **dived, div·ing** 1 plunge head-first into water, as a swimmer; hence, submerge, as a submarine, descend deeply, as an aircraft, or leap from an aircraft, as a parachutist. 2 enter vigorously into an activity: *He dives into homework as soon as he gets home.* 3 rush, dart, or plunge: *The rabbit dived into its hole as we approached; Stock prices dived* (= fell sharply) *during the Depression.* — *n.* a diving: *The submarine made a crash dive* (= sudden diving) *into the depths; a high dive from the diving board; a head-first dive; The pilot put his plane into a steep dive; The boxer took a dive* (= faked a knockout). — **div·er** *n.: a deep-sea diver; scuba diver.*

di·verge (duh·VURJ, dye·VURJ) *v.* -verg·es, -verged, -verg·ing draw apart; move away from something: *rays that diverge from a central point; This is the point where our views diverge.* — **di·ver·gence** (-junce) *n.: a divergence of viewpoints.* — **di·ver·gent** (-junt) *adj.: widely divergent interests.*

di·vers (DYE·vurz) *adj. Formal.* several and various: *divers beliefs; the divers origins of words.*

di·verse (dye·VURSE) *adj.* different in kind; of various kinds: *people of diverse backgrounds.* — **di·verse·ly** *adv.*

di·ver·si·fy (dye·VUR·suh·fye) *v.* -fies, -fied, -fy·ing make various or diverse, esp. to extend business activities into different fields: *A company diversifies to protect itself from market changes; a well-diversified investment portfolio.* — **di·ver·si·fi·ca·tion** (-fuh·CAY·shun) *n.*

di·ver·sion (di·VUR·zhun, dye-) *n.* 1 a pastime or entertainment: *golf, bridge, and such diversions.* 2 an action or manoeuvre that draws attention, activity, etc. aside: *a diversion of trade from one market to another; a diversion of funds from education to road maintenance.* 3 an alternative route for traffic bypassing a regular road that is closed for the time being; detour. — **di·ver·sion·ar·y** (-zhuh·nair·ee) *adj.: a diversionary attack, manoeuvre, raid, tactic.*

di·ver·si·ty (dye·VUR·suh·tee) *n.* variety of things not related to one another: *a population with a diversity of backgrounds; a woman with a diversity of interests.*

di·vert (di·VURT, dye-) *v.* 1 turn aside: *to divert a stream from its natural course to a farm for irrigation.* 2 turn away; distract: *a false attack to divert the enemy fire.* 3 amuse: *video games to divert children.*

di·vest (dye·VEST, di-) *v.* deprive of clothes, property, rights, etc.; strip: *a boxer divested of his title; a company forced to **divest itself of** (= get rid of) some of its holdings.*
— **di·vest·i·ture** (-VEST·i·chur) or **di·vest·ment** *n.*

di·vide (di·VIDE) *v.* **-vides, -vid·ed, -vid·ing** 1 separate, esp. into parts or groups; distribute: *Divide the books into fiction and nonfiction; The kids divided up the pie among themselves; We divide the expenses and each pays a share; The path divides here into two branches; A **divided highway** has a centre strip separating traffic in opposite directions; She's wearing a **divided skirt** (that looks like a skirt but is made like trousers); We have to draw a **dividing line** (= line of separation) between what is and what is not allowed.* 2 cause disagreement: *The caucus was sharply divided on or over the issue; the policy of **divide and rule** (by setting parties against one another in order to have your own way).* 3 determine how many times one number is contained in another: *You get 3 when you divide 7 into 21; 36 divided by 9 is 4; 4 divides into 36 nine times.*
— *n.* a dividing, esp. a watershed: *the Rockies are called the "Great Divide"; the great divide (= death) that everyone has to cross.* — **di·vid·er** (di·VYE·dur) *n.*

div·i·dend (DIV·uh·dend) *n.* 1 a number to be divided, as 10 in "10 divided by 2." 2 a stockholder's share of profits; also, the total of all of these; hence, a bonus: *to declare a dividend; a stock dividend.*

di·vine (di·VINE) *adj.* **-vin·er, -vin·est** 1 of or like a god; having to do with God; theological: *Plato thought the planets were divine beings; King James I of England believed in the **divine right** of kings (= God-given right to rule); divine law, manifestation; the divine Saviour; divine service, wisdom, worship.* 2 extremely good; superb; delightful: *a positively divine dress; His cooking is simply divine; a divine car, play; divine weather.*
— *n.* a scholar or student of theology.
— *v.* **-vines, -vined, -vin·ing** 1 foretell or predict by magic or special insight: *a **divining** rod for finding water.* 2 conjecture or guess: *to divine her intentions; to divine what she means.* — **di·vine·ly** *adv.*
— **di·vi·ner** *n.* — **div·i·na·tion** (div·uh·NAY·shun) *n.*

di·vin·i·ty (di·VIN·uh·tee) *n.* **-ties** 1 the state of being divine; also, deity. 2 theology: *students of divinity; a Doctor of Divinity.*
— the **Divinity** God.

di·vis·i·ble (di·VIZ·uh·bul) *adj.* able to be divided, esp. evenly: *7 is not evenly divisible by 3.*
— **di·vis·i·bil·i·ty** (-BIL·uh·tee) *n.*

di·vi·sion (di·VIZH·un) *n.* 1 the act of dividing: *cell division; to do long division (e.g. Divide 37 428 by 59); the **division sign** (÷); Adam Smith advocated **division of labour** (= each employee doing a part of the complete process).* 2 the state of being divided: *There are sharp divisions in the party between Right and Left; The*

division bells *of a legislature summon members to gather for voting.* 3 a line, boundary, etc. that divides: *an arbitrary division between young and old.* 4 the result of dividing; a part, portion, section, class, etc., esp. a large unit in the armed forces or a part of a league in sports: *an airborne, armoured, motorized division; the CFL's Western Division.*
— **di·vi·sion·al** *adj.*

di·vi·sive (di·VYE·siv) *adj.* tending to divide: *Abortion is a divisive issue.* — **di·vi·sive·ly** *adv.*; **di·vi·sive·ness** *n.*

di·vorce (di·VORCE) *n.* 1 the complete legal termination of a marriage: *Dick and Jane got a divorce; She filed or sued for divorce; an uncontested divorce; The divorce was granted; It was divorce by mutual consent; divorce and reconciliation.* 2 a deep separation: *the divorce of church and state.*
— *v.* **-vorc·es, -vorced, -vorc·ing** split up, as when a marriage is legally ended: *a divorced couple; They got divorced; Dick divorced (= split up with) his wife; He's now divorced from his wife; He is a dreamer divorced from the realities of daily life.*

di·vor·cé (di·vor·SAY) *n.* a divorced man.
— **di·vor·cée** or **di·vor·cee** (di·vor·SEE, -SAY), *fem.*

di·vulge (di·VULJ) *v.* **-vulg·es, -vulged, -vulg·ing** make known something secret: *He refused to divulge details of campaign expenses to the press.*

div·vy (DIV·ee) *v.* **div·vies, div·vied, div·vy·ing** *Slang.* divide: *robbers divvying up the loot.*

diz·zy (DIZ·ee) *adj.* **diz·zi·er, diz·zi·est** 1 having a whirling unsteady feeling in the head; giddy and prone to fall; also, causing this feeling: *Looking down from the tower made him dizzy; He was dizzy from the height; Dizzy with success, he lost his head.* 2 *Informal.* silly or lightheaded: *a dizzy teenager.*
— *v.* **diz·zies, diz·zied, diz·zy·ing** make dizzy: *She was dizzied by the height; the dizzying heights of fame.*
— **diz·zi·ly** *adv.*; **diz·zi·ness** *n.*

do (DOO) *v.* **does** (DUZ), *pt.* **did**, *pp.* **done** (DUN), **do·ing** 1 perform: *to do a good job; We'll do our best to help; to do (= fulfill) one's duty; He did (= completed) five years in the military; What's done is done (= it cannot be changed); What do you do (= work at) for a living? Our class is doing (= presenting) "Hamlet."* 2 make: *to do a painting; Do (= grant) us a favour.* 3 cause or effect: *Kindness does wonders; Foul play does no good.* 4 deal with, work on, etc. to achieve an aim: *to do the dishes; Who does your hair? I can't do (= deal successfully with) this sum! He does (Slang for uses or takes) drugs.* 5 fasten; also **do up**: *Do your shirt (up).* 6 behave: *Do to others as you would like them to do to you; Do as I say, not as I do! Taking the knife to your mouth – it's just not **done** (= not considered proper behaviour).* 7 suffice or serve: *This hat will do nicely, although I could have done with a better one; My knapsack will **do duty for** a pillow; We had to **make** the old carpet **do** for another year; When times are hard, you **make do with** what you have or simply **do without**; We have to **do without** a lot of luxuries.* 8 get on; fare: *How do you do? How are you doing in your new job?* 9 move at a specified speed; travel: *Your car was doing 120 km/h; The book tells you how to do (= tour) Europe on $50 a day.* 10 cook: *How do you like your steak done?*

11 cheat: *Many people were done out of their savings by the scam.* **12** [as an auxiliary verb in questions, negations, inversions; for emphasis; to refer to an earlier verb]: *Do you know what I know? I do not; Never did I see such a thing! I do declare! Run as fast as I do.*
— **do a job** or **number on** *Slang.* treat roughly; confound, esp. by deception.
— **do away with** get rid of something; also, kill someone.
— **do by** deal with or treat: *"Do as you would be done by,"* says the Golden Rule.
— **do for** attend to or care for someone: *They do for you in the rest home.*
— **do in** *Slang.* **1** kill: *He was done in by gangsters.* **2** tire out: *I'm all done in after a hard day at work.*
— **do justice to** handle or treat as one deserves or requires.
— **do the trick** produce the desired result.
— **have to do with:** *She won't have anything to do* (= have any business) *with door-to-door sellers; This has to do with* (= is about) *selling her house.*
— *n., pl.* **dos** or **do's 1** something to be done: *Too many **do's and don'ts*** (= rules and customs) *cramp your style.* **2** *Informal.* a party or social event: *They had a big do at the country club.*

doc *n. Slang.* **1** doctor. **2** guy or fellow: *What's up, doc?*

doc·ile (DOS·ile, DOS·ul, DOH·sile) *adj.* easy to teach, control, etc.; submissive: *a docile child, horse, patient, pupil.* — **doc·ile·ly** *adv.*
— **do·cil·i·ty** (doh·SIL·uh·tee) *n.*

dock *n.* **1** the place for the accused in a courtroom. **2** an area of water beside a pier or between piers: *Ships are brought into dock for repairs; "Graving" docks (for cleaning and tarring a ship's bottom) and floating docks are dry docks (in which a ship can lie out of the water); a wet dock (with water at a constant level, free from tides).* **3** a pier or wharf; hence, a loading platform: *labour trouble at or in or on the docks.*
— *v.* **1** cut off the end of something; hence, make a deduction from something due: *to dock a horse's tail; Wages were docked for being late.* **2** move or come into a dock; hence, link two spacecraft together in space; also, become so linked: *A ship docks at a port; A spacecraft docks with another; a docking manoeuvre.*

dock·et (DOCK·it) *n.* a list, as of court cases tried or to be tried, things to be done, contents of a package, etc.: *What's on the docket today?*
— *v.* put a summary of a case on a docket; list a case for action before a court.

doc·tor (DOC·tur) *n.* **1** a physician; an M.D.: *Patients see doctors; Doctors see and treat their patients; the barefoot doctors of China (who cover rural areas on foot); This is not exactly **what the doctor ordered*** (= what is beneficial or desirable). **2** one who holds a doctorate degree, as a Ph.D.: *He got his **doctor's*** (degree) *last year; Who shall decide when **doctors disagree*** (= when the experts can't agree on it)?
— *v.* **1** treat medically: *She was doctored back to health by our family doctor.* **2** repair or mend: *My programmer has doctored the software so now it runs without a hitch.* **3** alter so as to deceive: *an accountant accused of doctoring the books* or *accounts;* **doctored** (= loaded) *dice; He didn't know the cat had been doctored* (= castrated) *when he paid for it; A doctored* (= drugged or strengthened) *wine has a different aroma.*

doc·tor·al (DOC·tuh·rul) *adj.* having to do with the academic doctorate: *a doctoral candidate, degree, hood; a post-doctoral research fellow.*

doc·tor·ate (DOC·tuh·rit) *n.* a university degree of the highest level: *She was awarded a doctorate in economics; D.Phil., Ed.D., Ph.D., etc. are usually earned doctorates (based on attending a university); D.D., D.Litt., LL.D., etc. may be honorary doctorates.*

doc·tri·naire (doc·truh·NAIR) *adj.* applying a preconceived doctrine without regard to reality or practical problems.

doc·trine (DOC·trin) *n.* something taught, as a set of theories, dogmas, basic beliefs, etc.: *the doctrines of the Church of England; to apply, disprove, establish, preach a doctrine; a sound doctrine.*
— **doc·tri·nal** (DOC·truh·nul, doc·TRY·nul) *adj.*

doc·u·dra·ma (DOC·yuh·dram·uh) *n.* a dramatic piece based on historical facts produced for TV or as a movie: *The CBC did a docudrama on the life and work of Emily Carr.*

doc·u·ment (DOC·yuh·munt) *n.* an official paper, as a deed or birth certificate, forming the proof or basis of something: *to submit a document as evidence in court; an authentic document; Copiers are great at document processing.*
— *v.* (-ment) support with documents or references: *to document a claim, report, thesis; The historian documented her study by citing references.*

doc·u·men·ta·ry (doc·yuh·MEN·tuh·ree) *adj.*
1 concerning or being documents: *Citizenship certificates of two countries are documentary proof of dual citizenship; documentary evidence.* **2** wholly factual and unbiassed: *a documentary film, report.*
— *n., pl.* **-ries** a film or TV show of this nature: *a documentary on the harmful effects of pesticides.*

doc·u·men·ta·tion (DOC·yuh·men·TAY·shun) *n.* (the providing of) documents or references: *The software comes with good documentation* (= operating instructions).

dod·der (DOD·ur) *n.* a parasitic vine of the morning-glory family that grows on other plants by means of suckers.
— *v.* tremble or move shakily because of old age.
— **dod·der·er** *n.*

dodge (DOJ) *v.* **dodg·es, dodged, dodg·ing** avoid by a trick or sudden movement; move trickily or quickly: *He went to Mexico to dodge the draft; to dodge a blow by ducking; He dodged behind a rock; He dodges in and out of traffic.*
— *n.* **1** a dodging; means of evasion: *to use investments as a tax dodge.* **2** a clever scheme, expedient, or plan.
— **dodg·er** *n.: a draft dodger; tax dodger.*

do·do (DOH·doh)) *n.* **1** a long-extinct, flightless bird: *The plan is dead as the* or *a dodo.* **2** a stupid or old-fashioned person.

doe (DOH) *n.* a full-grown female of an animal such as the deer, antelope, rabbit, goat, etc. whose male is a buck.

do·er (DOO·ur) *n.* one who does, esp. a person of vigorous action.

does See DO.

doe·skin (DOH·skin) *n.* a soft leather of the skin of a doe or lamb.

does·n't (DUZ·unt) does not.

doff *v.* take off: *He doffed his coat and boots at the door; The President doffed (=lifted) his hat to the crowd.*

dog *n.* **1** a domesticated canine such as a poodle or beagle: *There are attack dogs like the pit-bull terrier, police dogs like German shepherds, sheep dogs, sled dogs, sporting dogs, toy dogs (=very small breeds), working dogs, etc.; Wild (=not domesticated) dogs include coyotes, foxes, jackals, and wolves; to curb one's dog; a guard, guide, mad, seeing-eye, stray dog; to work* **like a dog** *(=very hard).* **2** *Informal.* a fellow; also, a low worthless person: *a dirty dog; lucky dog; a running dog (=lackey); It shouldn't happen to a dog (=What I have experienced is too bad); He led* **a dog's life** *(=wretched existence).* **3** *Slang.* something considered a total failure: *The book was a dog; it never sold.* **4** an andiron; also, any of several devices for holding and gripping.
— **a dog's age** *Informal.* a very long time.
— **dog in the manger** one who selfishly guards something so that others may not use it; *adj.: a dog-in-the-manger policy.*
— **go to the dogs** *Informal.* be ruined, morally, physically, etc.
— **let sleeping dogs lie** do not disturb a situation and cause unnecessary trouble.
— **put on the dog** show off as though wealthy and refined.
— *v.* **dogs, dogged, dog·ging** track, pursue, etc. like a dog; hence, beset: *an expedition dogged by mishaps and problems.*

dog days *n.pl.* the hottest days of the summer.

dog-ear *n.* a turned-down corner of a page.
— **dog-eared** *adj.*

dog-eat-dog (DOG·eet·DOG) *adj.* marked by ruthless competition: *this dog-eat-dog world; It's so dog-eat-dog in some courses that students turn to cheating.*

dog·fight *n.* **1** a rough fight, as between dogs. **2** an aerial combat between two or more fighter planes: *They engaged in a dogfight.*

dog·ged (DOG·id) *adj.* persistent or stubborn: *her dogged determination; his dogged loyalty, persistence.*
— **dog·ged·ly** *adv.;* **dog·ged·ness** *n.*

dog·gie bag *n.* same as DOGGY BAG.

dog·gone *adj. Informal.* damn: *Doggone it, how did it happen? That doggone pooch has eaten the cat food.*

dog·gy *n.* **dog·gies** [child's word] dog.

doggy bag *n.* a bag for taking leftovers from a restaurant, as if for one's dog.

dog·house *n.* a shelter for a dog.
— **in the doghouse** *Informal.* in a state of disfavour.

dog·ma (DOG·muh) *n.* a belief or set of beliefs held strongly and often on the basis of authority, esp. that of a church.

dog·mat·ic (dog·MAT·ic) *adj.* **1** of dogma: *dogmatic theology (concerned with the content of the Christian faith).* **2** asserted by authority alone: *a dogmatic statement; A scientist cannot be dogmatic (=too assertive) about questions that cannot be verified.* Also **dog·mat·i·cal.** — **dog·mat·i·cal·ly** *adv.*
— **dog·ma·tism** (DOG·muh·tiz·um) *n.*

do-good·er (DOO·good·ur) *n. Informal.* a well-meaning but impractical and naive social reformer.

dog·wood *n.* a small tree or shrub with four-leaved greenish-white flowers and bright-red fruits: *The "flowering dogwood" is the floral emblem of British Columbia.*

doings *n.pl.* things that are done or that occur.

do-it-yourself (DOO·it·yur·SELF) *adj.* of or meant for use by the consumer rather than by a paid supplier: *a book on do-it-yourself plumbing repairs; a do-it-yourself backyard barbecue.* — **do-it-your·self·er** *n.*

dol·drums (DOLE·drumz, DOLL-) *n.pl.* **1** a region near the equator where there are light, changeable winds and many calms: *a sailing ship in the doldrums (=becalmed).* **2** a period or mood of depression, listlessness, inactivity, etc.: *He has been* **in the doldrums** *since losing his job.*

dole *n. Informal.* a grant of assistance, as food, clothes, or money, to the needy, esp. a payment by government to the unemployed: *He was on the dole for many months before he found a new job.*
— *v.* **doles, doled, dol·ing** give out as charity, or sparingly, bit by bit: *a social worker who doled out sympathy to all and sundry.*

dole·ful *adj.* causing, having, or expressing sorrow.
— **dole·ful·ly** *adv.*

doll *n.* **1** a small figure in the form of a human, esp. used as a child's toy: *a paper doll; rag doll.* **2** *Informal.* an attractive or lovable person.
— *v.* **doll up** *Informal.* dress finely, as for a special occasion: *She dolled herself up for the school prom.*

dol·lar (DOLL·ur) *n.* the basic money unit in Canada, the U.S., Australia, and other countries: **Dollar for dollar** *(=considering prices), this car is second to none; Everyone likes* **dollars** *(Informal for money).*

dollar diplomacy *n.* **1** the use of a government's power to further its overseas economic or financial interests. **2** diplomacy helped by financial resources.

dollies See DOLLY.

dol·lop (DOLL·up) *n.* an amount or serving: *a dollop of whipped cream; We need large dollops of cash; You need an extra dollop of skill to do a good job.*

dol·ly (DOLL·ee) *n.* **dol·lies 1** [child's word] a doll. **2** a low, wheeled platform, as used for moving heavy objects, for getting under an automobile, for moving a TV or movie camera around on, etc.

dol·phin (DOLL·fin) *n.* a small, whalelike sea mammal: *a school of dolphins; a bull* (= male) *dolphin; the calf* (= young) *and cow* (= female) *of a dolphin.*

dolt *n.* a stupid person. — **dolt·ish** *adj.*

do·main (doh·MAIN) *n.* **1** an area under one's rule or control: *the Queen's domain; Our riding has always been the domain of the Tories.* **2** a range or field of activity or concern: *Medicine is in the general domain of science; What is not copyrighted, patented, or trademarked is in the public domain; public domain software.*

dome *n.* **1** a hemispherical roof, vault, etc. **2** *Slang.* head: *Get that into your thick dome!*

do·mes·tic (duh·MES·tic) *adj.* **1** of or concerning the household, home life, etc.: *a domestic quarrel between the maid and the homemaker; a domestic scene of love and peace; Butlers are in domestic service; **domestic science*** (= home economics); *She's not your domestic type of woman (who enjoys home life and working at home).* **2** having to do with one's own country; not foreign: *domestic crude oil, industries, markets, politics, prices, wines.* **3** tame, not wild: *cats, dogs, cows, ducks, pigs, and such domestic animals.*
— *n.* a servant in someone's home, esp. a female.
— **do·mes·ti·cal·ly** *adv.*

do·mes·ti·cate (duh·MES·tuh·cate) *v.* **-cates, -cat·ed, -cat·ing** make accustomed to living in human environments, out of the wild: *domesticated varieties of wheat; domesticated cattle; You can train an animal to work only after domesticating it.*
— **do·mes·ti·ca·tion** (-CAY·shun) *n.*
— **do·mes·tic·i·ty** (duh·mes·TIS·uh·tee) *n.*

dom·i·cile (DOM·uh·sile, -sul) *n.* the place of one's habitual residence: *Your will is settled according to the law of the place where you had your official domicile when you made the will even if you changed your domicile afterward.*
— *v.* **-ciles, -ciled, -cil·ing** have or provide with a domicile: *a Quebecker domiciled in Manitoba.*

dom·i·nant (DOM·uh·nunt) *adj.* **1** dominating or prevailing: *the dominant idea or theme in her books; Russians are the dominant group in the U.S.S.R.; a dominant influence in his life; a dominant passion; a dominant* (= overlooking) *cliff.* **2** in genetics, overpowering another gene or trait parallel to it; not recessive or latent: *Brown eyes are dominant over blue when genes for both are present.*
— **dom·i·nance** (-nunce) *n.*

dom·i·nate (DOM·uh·nate) *v.* **-nates, -nat·ed, -nat·ing 1** have control, authority, or influence: *Seniors try to dominate over the juniors; Our team dominated the league this year.* **2** overlook: *the cliffs dominating the city.* — **dom·i·na·tion** (-NAY·shun) *n.*

dom·i·neer (DOM·uh·neer) *v.* rule over, esp. tyrannically: *The stronger ones tend to domineer over the weaker; He's a big **domineering** bully.*

do·min·ion (duh·MIN·yun) *n.* **1** sovereign power or its exercise: *in the days of the Empire, when Britain had dominion over land and sea; Many nations have been freed from the dominion of the colonial powers since World War II.* **2** the field or territory over which dominion is exercised; domain: *the king's dominions; British settler colonies were raised to the status of dominion (having self-rule but owing allegiance to the Crown); In 1867, Canada was the first country to become a **Dominion**.*

Dominion Day *n.* [former name] Canada Day.

dom·i·no (DOM·uh·noh) *n.* **-nos** or **-noes** [takes sing. v.] a game in which oblong pieces with one to six spots on either half are placed end to end so that the halves match each other; also, such a piece.

domino effect *n.* the fall of one item of an arranged series causing the collapse of the next on or toward which it is leaning and so on down the line; chain reaction.

domino theory *n.* the belief that a Communist takeover in one nation will lead to its neighbours also falling to the Communists.

don *n.* **1 Don** a respectful term of address for men in Spanish: *Don Carlos.* **2** an official in charge of a student dormitory in some Canadian colleges. **3** a Mafia leader.
— *v.* **dons, donned, don·ning** put on clothing, hats, etc.

do·nate (DOH·nate, doh·NATE) *v.* **-nates, -nat·ed, -nat·ing** give, esp. to a worthy cause: *We donate used clothes to the Salvation Army.*
— **do·na·tion** (doh·NAY·shun) *n.*: *to make a donation; a donation to charity; political donations from corporations.*

done *pp.* of DO.
— *adj.* **1** cooked: *How do you like your steak done – rare, medium-rare, medium, or well? I like it **done to a turn** or **done to a T*** (= just right). **2** considered proper: *Eating peas with your knife – it's not the done thing.* **3** finished: *We're done with the dishes; a done deal; "You're done," he threatened; I'm **done for** or **done in** or **done up*** (= quite exhausted).
— **done·ness** *n.*: *Degrees of doneness may be dialled on certain microwave ovens.*

don·key (DONK·ee) *n.* **-keys 1** an ass: *A donkey brays; Donkeys go heehaw.* **2** a headstrong or stupid person.
— **a donkey's years** *Slang.* a long time.

donkey work *n.* the work of a drudge: *Computers take much of the donkey work out of our lives.*

do·nor (DOH·nur) *n.* one who donates: *a blood donor; organ donor.*

Don Qui·xo·te (don·kee·HOH·tee) *n.* an idealistic, impractical fighter of evil, as the hero of a satiric novel of the same name by Cervantes.

don't do not.
— *n.* a prohibition or order not to do something: *do's and don'ts.*

do·nut (DOH·nut) *n.* a ring of leavened dough fried in fat: *It's customary to dunk donuts in coffee; the 24-hour donut shops where he used to hang out.*

doo·dad (DOO·dad) *n.* a small object or ornament, esp. one whose name has been temporarily forgotten: *See the clutter of doodads on the coffee table.*

doo·dle (DOO·dul) *v.* **-dles, -dled, -dling** draw idly and aimlessly, esp. while preoccupied.
— *n.* a drawing so made. — **doo·dler** *n.*

doom (long "oo") *n.* a judgment, esp. an adverse one; also, a grim fate: *The judge pronounced his doom and condemned him to death; He was sent to his doom in the electric chair; He awaited his doom on death row; The day of doom drew near; The soldier went to his doom bravely; Many things have been foretold about the* **crack of doom** (= end of the world); *messengers of* **doom and gloom.**
— *v.* consign to a bad fate; condemn: *They were doomed to die young; a plan doomed to failure from the beginning.*

dooms·day (DOOMZ·day) *n.* the end of the world; the day of God's final judgment on the world: *He's going to do nothing* **till doomsday.**

door (DORE) *n.* **1** a hinged, swinging, or sliding panel that covers an entrance, esp. to a house, room, etc.: *A door is hung on its hinges; to break down, close, force, lock, open, shut, slam a door; Visitors arrive at the door; They knock on the door; The door was ajar; a back, double, front, revolving, side, sliding, storm door; a meeting held* **behind closed doors** (= in secret); *The Smiths live next door.* **2** a doorway; hence, a means or path of access: *the door to the next room; Education opens the door to many careers; to* **show someone the door** (= ask politely to leave); *The boss* **laid the blame at the secretary's door;** *She told him never to* **darken her door** (= visit her) *again; He earns his living by selling encyclopedias from* **door to door** (= house to house); *a* **door-to-door** *salesman; The car accident* **closed** *or* **shut** *or* **slammed the door** *on* (= made impossible) *his hopes of a medical career.*

door·mat *n.* **1** a mat for wiping the feet at a door. **2** *Informal.* one who passively suffers insults, etc. from others.

door·step *n.* a step or steps in front of an outside door.

door·way *n.* an opening or entrance fitted with a door: *to stand in the doorway; the doorway to freedom, health, a new career.*

dope *n.* **1** a liquid, esp. a viscous one, used to give desired properties to a surface. **2** any adulterant or additive such as antiknock in gasoline, preservatives in foods, or stimulants for race horses. **3** *Informal.* a narcotic or other intoxicating drug: *They don't take dope.* **4** *Slang.* a dull or half-witted person. **5** *Slang.* special information: *What's the latest dope about the project?*
— *v.* **dopes, doped, dop·ing** apply or give dope to a person or thing: *to dope an athlete, a horse; the doping of blood to improve athletic performance; Silicon is doped with impurities in making transistors and chips.*

dope·ster (DOPE·stur) *n. Slang.* one who claims to know and be able to tell what will happen in the world of sports, politics, etc.

dop·ey or **dop·y** (DOH·pee) *adj.* **dop·i·er, -i·est** *Slang.* dazed, as if drugged: *He was feeling dopey after the drink.*

dorm *n. Informal.* [short form] dormitory.

dor·mant (DOR·munt) *adj.* asleep or inactive: *Some plants and animals are dormant in winter; a dormant volcano; passions that lie dormant; ways of arousing our dormant interest in art.* — **dor·man·cy** (-mun·see) *n.*

dor·mer or **dormer window** *n.* a window set upright in and projecting from a sloping roof.

dor·mi·to·ry (DOR·muh·tor·ee) *n.* **-ries** a room or building with sleeping accommodations for a large group.

dor·sal (DOR·sul) *adj.* of or on the back: *a dorsal fin.*
— **dor·sal·ly** *adv.*

dos·age (DOH·sij) *n.* the amount of a dose.

dose *n.* **1** an amount of medicine or treatment given at one time: *to administer, give, measure out, take a dose of medicine; to give someone* or *get a* **dose of one's own medicine** (= give or get the same kind of treatment as one gives to others); *a lethal* or *fatal dose.* **2** *Slang.* an infection of a venereal disease.
— *v.* **dos·es, dosed, dos·ing** treat: *Mother used to dose us with vitamin pills in the winter.*

dost (DUST) [old word] the form of DO used with "thou."

dot *n.* a small point, speck, etc., as over an "i" or "j": *the dots and dashes of the Morse Code; She always arrives* **on the dot** (= on time).
— *v.* **dots, dot·ted, dot·ting** **1** mark or make with a dot: *a dotted line; Editors take care to* **dot their i's and cross their t's** (= to be precise, minutely correct, etc.). **2** form a dot or dots: *Fishing boats dot the lake.*
— **sign on the dotted line** agree fully to what is asked.

dot·age (DOH·tij) *n.* advanced old age with deteriorating mental faculties: *An old man in his dotage is said to be in his second childhood.*

dote *v.* **dotes, dot·ed, dot·ing** **1** be feeble-minded with old age. **2** be excessively fond of someone: *She just dotes on her son; Kumar is a* **doting** *father and a loving husband.*

doth (DUTH) [old word] does.

dot matrix *n.* a pattern of dots, as an oblong with five dots across and seven down, from which letters, numbers, etc. are formed for computer output: *a dot-matrix printer, not a daisywheeler.*

dot·ty (DOT·ee) *adj.* **dot·ti·er, dot·ti·est** **1** full of dots. **2** *Informal.* feeble-minded; eccentric: *a dotty friend, idea, notion.*

dou·ble (DUB·ul) *adj.* **1** twice as much, many, strong, etc.; two instead of one: *a double thickness of paper; an egg with a double yolk.* **2** twofold; in a pair: *double doors; a double boiler.* **3** for two: *a double harness; a double bed.* **4** having two senses, characters, etc.; hence, deceitful: *Jones led a double life as a* **double**

agent (=spy working from within a government); *a word with a double meaning; The company kept double books, one with correct records and the other with false records to cheat on taxes.* **5** having more petals than normal: *a double rose.* **6** an octave below normal: *a double bass.*
— *adv.* two together; two instead of one; twofold: *Fold it double; They ride double on his bike; You may see double when hit on the head.*
— *n.* **1** a double quantity, strength, etc.: *12 is the double of 6; Make it a double* (=twice the usual serving). **2** one that is just like another; hence, a substitute, as for an actor. **3** in baseball, a hit that allows the batter to get to second base. **4** a sharp turn or evasion while running. **5 doubles** *pl.* a game with two players on each side: *men's doubles; mixed doubles; women's doubles.*
— **on the double** *Informal.* at an extra pace; very fast.
— *v.* **-bles, -bled, -bling 1** make or become double: *Double your money; House prices have doubled in ten years.* **2** fold in two; also, close up: *He doubled his fists in anger.* **3** go around a cape, headland, etc. **4** serve or stand in for another: *The stuntman doubled for the star in the fire scene.* **5** serve two purposes; play two roles: *The cook doubles as our dishwasher* (*Informal* for plays a second role as dishwasher). **6** turn sharply or back on one's path: *The dogs doubled back to find the scent again.*
— **double up 1** bend, esp. one's body, or fold double: *Hit in the stomach, he doubled up in pain.* **2** share, esp. accommodations, in pairs: *They doubled up to make room for everybody; Pat doubled up with Lou.*

double check *n.* a careful rechecking of something for accuracy or a similar purpose; **double-check** *v.*

double-cross *v. Informal.* betray by doing the opposite of what was agreed to.
— *n.* such an action; **double-crosser** *n.*

double date *n.* a date involving two couples.
— **double-date** *v.* **-dates, -dat·ed, -dat·ing.**

double-deal *v.* act with duplicity; deceive or cheat.
— **double-dealing** *n. & adj.;* **double-dealer** *n.*

double-header (DUB·ul·HED·ur) *n.* two baseball games between the same teams on the same day.

double jeopardy *n.* the position of an accused person being tried a second time for the same crime.

double take *n.* delayed reaction to something unusual, as by a second glance, often used as a comic device: *He did a double take.*

double talk *n.* ambiguous or nonsensical talk that appears to make sense.

dou·bly (DUB·lee) *adv.* to twice the degree or amount; also, in a double manner: *He's doubly indebted to her as his wife and breadwinner; to be doubly sure.*

doubt (DOWT) *n.* **1** the state of being uncertain: *I'm in doubt* (=in uncertainty) *about the outcome of the race; He will beyond doubt or without doubt* (=certainly) *win the race; He'll no doubt* (=certainly) *win the race.* **2** a lack of certainty, conviction, or trust; disbelief: *Is there any doubt (as to) whether it will rain or snow? I have my doubts about his innocence; Many have expressed doubt that he is innocent; But I don't want to raise doubts in your mind; Let's give him the benefit of*

the doubt; *To cast doubt on his intentions is not fair; to entertain, feel, harbour doubts about something; to dispel, express, resolve, voice a doubt about the matter; beyond the shadow of a doubt; a deep, gnawing, lingering, reasonable, serious, slight, strong doubt.*
— *v.* be uncertain or distrustful about something; also, think unlikely: *It's not that I doubt your words; I don't doubt that you are telling the truth; We doubt very much that he will come; We strongly doubt whether or if he is alive at all.* — **doubt·er** *n.*

doubt·ful *adj.* unsure or uncertain: *We feel doubtful about tomorrow's weather; It's doubtful that it will rain; The outcome is still doubtful; a man of doubtful* (=questionable) *character.* — **doubt·ful·ly** *adv.*

doubting Thomas *n.* a persistent or habitual doubter.

doubt·less *adj. & adv.* without doubt; no doubt: *He will doubtless be here by supper time.* — **doubt·less·ly** *adv.*

douche (DOOSH, long "OO") *n.* a stream of water sent against a part or into a cavity of the body, esp. for washing: *a vaginal douche.*
— *v.* **douch·es, douched, douch·ing** apply or use a douche.

dough (DOH) *n.* **1** a soft, elastic mixture of flour, liquid, etc. prepared for baking: *to knead, mix, roll, work dough; firm, flaky, stiff dough; The dough has to rise before bread can be baked.* **2** *Slang.* money.

dough·nut (DOH·nut) *n.* [older spelling] DONUT.

dough·ty (DOW·tee) *adj.* **-ti·er, -ti·est** brave; valiant.

dough·y (DOH·ee) *adj.* like dough: *doughy bread* (=bread not baked long enough); *a doughy* (=soft and pale) *complexion.*

dour (DOO·ur, DOW·ur, *rhyme:* OUR) *adj.* **1** [in Scots use] stern or obstinate: *a dour Scot; dour and taciturn.* **2** gloomy; silent and ill-tempered: *a man who is dour in disposition; his dour determination, looks, silence.*

douse *v.* **dous·es, doused, dous·ing 1** plunge into a liquid; drench: *The arsonist doused the house with gasoline and set it on fire; We had pancakes doused in maple syrup.* **2** *Informal.* put out: *to douse the lights, enthusiasm, hopes, rumours.*

dove (DOHV) a *pt.* of DIVE.
— *n.* (DUV) **1** a pigeon, esp. a small, wild one: *Doves coo.* **2** a gentle or peaceful person, esp. one opposed to war or military threats; one who is not a hawk.
— **dov·ish** *adj.*

dove·tail *n.* a wedge-shaped projection fitted into a groove in another piece to make a joint firm and solid. — *v.* fit together thus: *a cabinet with dovetailed corners; One corner dovetails into the other; Your interests dovetail (with) ours; Our plans dovetailed perfectly.*

dow·a·ger (DOW·uh·jur, DOW *rhymes with* HOW) *n.* a widow having title or property from her dead husband; hence, an older woman of social standing: *the dowager duchess.*

dow·dy (DOW·dee, DOW *rhymes with* HOW) *adj.* -di·er, -di·est shabby or plain in clothes or appearance. — **dow·di·ly** *adv.;* **dow·di·ness** *n.*

dow·er (DOW·ur, DOW *rhymes with* HOW) *n.* 1 a dowry. 2 a widow's share of her husband's property for her lifetime. — *v.* provide with a dowry or dower.

down *adv.* 1 at or toward a lower position, quieter or worse state, smaller volume, etc.: *The stars will come out when the sun goes down; Sit down! He came down with the flu; She's trying to quiet down the children; Cut down the essay to 2 000 words.* 2 southwards; also, away from the speaker: *He's gone down to Florida; Let's walk down to the plaza; He's gone down South (= to the southern states of the U.S.).* 3 as partial payment, usually in cash: *He paid $10 000 down on the house.* 4 in writing: *Put it down in your diary.* 5 in subjection: *They had been held down as slaves for centuries.* 6 toward a later time: *down through the ages.*
— **down and out** *Informal.* destitute, friendless, etc.
— **down at the heels** *Informal.* in a shabby or run-down condition.
— **down east** in or to eastern North America, esp. the Atlantic Provinces and New England, as viewed from the West: *CBC's "Don Messer's Jubilee" was down east music.*
— **down home 1** *Cdn.* down east: *down home in Cape Breton.* 2 in the southern U.S.: *down home in Louisiana.*
— **down in the dumps** or **down in the mouth** *Informal.* depressed or sad.
— **down on** *Informal.* hostile to someone: *People are down on him for always being late to work.*
— **down on one's luck** *Informal.* unfortunate.
— **down the drain** *Informal.* lost or gone.
— **down to the ground** completely: *The promotion suits him down to the ground.*
— *adj.* 1 in or at a low position: *The hydro lines were down after the storm; You don't hit or kick a man when he is down; the down elevator; The down pipe carries rain water from the roof; He's down on all fours under the table searching for the missing ring; The computer is down (= not working).* 2 out of play: *The ball is down on the 10-yard line.* 3 behind; trailing: *They're down 6-0 in the sixth inning.* 4 completed: *one down, two to go.* 5 less active, ill, or despondent: *She's down with a cold; He's feeling a bit down these days; Don't let these misunderstandings get you down (= bother you too much).*
— *prep.* 1 down along, through, etc.: *He ran down the hill; down the ages.* 2 to or at a lower or later point: *to sail down the river; That's two kilometres down the road; Ten years down the road anything could happen.* 3 along: *I was walking down the road.*
— *n.* 1 **downs** *pl.* grassy uplands. 2 a decline: *ups and*

downs; This is a real boost after the downs we've been having. 3 in Canadian football, any of three attempts to advance the ball 10 yards: *Second down and three yards to go.* 4 very fine fluffy feathers or hair: *the down on a teenager's chin.* 5 same as DOWNER.
— *v.* cause to go or be down: *He downed the ball on the 25-yard line; They downed (= defeated) the Dodgers 5-2.*

down-at-the-heels *adj.* shabby or run-down.

down·beat *n.* a descending stroke of a conductor's baton showing the principal accent in a measure. — *adj.* 1 gloomy; realistic and grim. 2 casual and relaxed.

down·burst *n.* a powerful downdraft or downward surge of air.

down·cast *adj.* pointed down; dejected: *with downcast eyes.*

down·draft *n.* a draft with a downward tendency: *a downdraft in the chimney caused by tall trees near it; A powerful downdraft was responsible for the airplane crash.*

down·er *n. Slang.* 1 a depressant drug, as a barbiturate or tranquillizer. 2 a depressing experience; bad trip.

down·fall *n.* 1 a heavy fall of snow or rain. 2 a sudden fall from power, wealth, etc. or the cause of this: *Drink was his downfall; Addictions bring about people's downfall; We knew he was heading for a downfall.*
— **down·fall·en** (DOWN·fall·un) *adj.*

down·grade *n.* 1 a downward slope. 2 any path of decline: *an aging leader on the downgrade.*
— *v.* -grades, -grad·ed, -grad·ing lower the status, pay, importance, etc. of a person or thing: *His condition has been downgraded from "serious" to "critical"; a hurricane downgraded to storm status.*

down·heart·ed (DOWN·har·tid) *adj.* depressed.

down·hill *adj. & adv.* downward along a hill or to a lower status, condition, etc.: *It's downhill from here on (Informal for The hard part is over).*
— *n.* a downhill skiing race.
— **down·hill·er** (DOWN·hill·ur) *n.*

down·link *n.* communication from a satellite or spacecraft to the ground.

down·load *v.* transfer data, programs, etc. from one computer's storage to another's.

down payment *n.* a first payment made at the time of purchase: *to make a down payment on a home.*

down·play *v.* play down; de-emphasize: *The company downplayed the seriousness of the oil spill.*

down·pour *n.* a very heavy rain: *a sudden torrential downpour.*

down·right *adj.* 1 plainspoken or candid. 2 thoroughgoing or absolute: *a downright falsehood; adv.: He got downright hostile.*

down·scale *adj.* socially or economically inferior; not upscale.

down·side *n. Informal.* a downward trend or aspect: *The downside of that proposal is that it would cost a lot* to implement; *Better not say anything downside* (= negative) *on this issue.*

down·stairs *adv.* down a set of stairs; on or to a lower floor: *Who lives downstairs? Let's go downstairs.* — *adj.*: *She is downstairs; in the downstairs apartment.* — *n.*: *The downstairs has been painted.*

down·stream *adj. & adv.* in the direction of flow: *The boat floated downstream; The lamb was drinking downstream from the wolf; pollutants found downstream of or from the chemical company; Refining and marketing are the downstream end of the petroleum business; downstream assets, operations, products, profit; A downstream holding company owns the insurance company's miscellaneous interests.*

down·swing *n.* 1 a downward swing, as of a golf club. 2 a decline, as in business: *TV ratings were on the downswing when the program was cancelled.*

down·time *n.* time of inactivity, as of a machine or factory, or of leisure, as of a worker.

down-to-earth *adj.* practical: *a down-to-earth approach, attitude, manner, nature, theory; down-to-earth advice, prices.*

down·town *n.* the lower, central, or business district of a city or town. — *adj. & adv.* in or to downtown: *He has gone downtown; to downtown Montreal; downtown businesses, offices, stores.*

down·trod·den (DOWN·trod·un) *adj.* trampled, as by tyranny; oppressed.

down·turn *n.* same as DOWNSWING.

down under or **Down Under** *n. & adv. Informal.* Australia or New Zealand: *The boomerang comes from down under; She's vacationing down under.*

down·ward *adj. & adv.* toward a lower, inferior, or later place, condition, etc.; also **down·wards** *adv.*

down·wind *adj. & adv.* in the direction the wind is blowing: *the downwind side of the mountains.*

down·y *adj.* **down·i·er, -i·est** of, like, or covered with down.

dow·ry (DOW·ree) *n.* **-ries** the property that a woman brings to her husband at marriage; hence, a natural talent or gift: *Brains were the best dowry her family could provide for her.*

dowse (DOWZE) *v.* **dows·es, dowsed, dows·ing** use a divining rod. — **dows·er** *n.*

doy·en (DOY·un) *n.* the senior member of a group; dean: *the doyen of Canadian historians; fem.* **doy·enne** (DOY·en).

doze *n.* a short nap; light sleep. — *v.* **doz·es, dozed, doz·ing**: *He is dozing in the sun; I tend to **doze off** while watching TV.*

doz·en (DUZ·un) *n.* a group of 12: *three dozen eggs; A baker's dozen is one more than a round dozen; Eggs are sold in dozens; We sell **dozens of** (= lots of) eggs every day.* — **doz·enth** *adj.*

doz·y (DOH·zee) *adj.* **doz·i·er, -i·est** drowsy or sleepy.

drab *adj.* **drab·ber, drab·best** 1 greyish- or yellowish-brown. 2 dull; faded; monotonous: *It's a drab brown; the drab grey walls; the drab routine of an assembly-line job.* — *n.* drab colour or a drab cloth. — **drab·ly** *adv.*; **drab·ness** *n.*

Dra·co·ni·an or **dra·co·ni·an** (dray·COH·nee·un) *adj.* very harsh or strict like Draco, a lawgiver of ancient Greece: *a Draconian law, measure, rule; the Draconian approach; its Draconian cruelty; a budget that is more Draconian than austere; a Draconian but pragmatic policy.*

draft *n.* 1 an act of drawing or pulling or what is drawn: *a draft* (= drink) *of water; We've beer on draft* (= to be drawn from a cask or keg); *You're sitting in a draft* (= current of air) *by the window; a draft of fish* (= amount caught in a net at one time). 2 a device for controlling air flow in a fireplace or wood stove. 3 the depth of water drawn by a ship: *a ship's draft* (= distance between water line and bottom of the keel); *vessels of shallow draft.* 4 a paper directing a bank to pay a specified amount to the person in whose favour it is drawn: *a bank draft for $1 000; a draft on a Winnipeg branch of the bank.* 5 a sketch or plan of work to be done, made usually by a draftsman. 6 a preliminary version of something written: *to make, prepare a preliminary, rough draft of the speech; the final, polished draft.* 7 a selection, as of new players by sports teams; also, of people for military service by a **draft board**: *During the Vietnam war, Americans used to dodge the draft by immigrating to Canada.* 8 the state of being forced, as by popular pressure: *He was unwilling to be a candidate but wouldn't refuse a draft.* — *adj.* 1 on draft: *draft beer.* 2 preliminary or rough: *a draft contract, manuscript; a draft version of the bill.* 3 used for pulling loads: *In the Third World,* **draft animals** *such as horses, oxen, mules, donkeys, and water buffalo still do much of the work of trucks and tractors.* — *v.* 1 select by a draft: *to be drafted into the army.* 2 compose, sketch, or draw up, esp. in rough form: *to draft a letter, memo, proposal.*

draft·ee (draf·TEE) *n.* a person selected by a draft board for military service.

drafts·man (DRAFTS·mun) *n.* **-men** 1 one who prepares mechanical drawings, designs, plans, sketches, etc., as for making buildings and machines. 2 one who draws up official documents. 3 one who is skilled in drawing: *a gifted draftsman; An artist is more than a draftsman.* — **drafts·man·ship** *n.*

draft·y *adj.* **draft·i·er, -i·est** exposed to currents of air: *a drafty hallway, room.* — **draft·i·ness** *n.*

drag *n.* 1 something dragged, as a net, harrow, sledge, etc. 2 a dragging or something that slows or hinders, esp. the resistance of air or fluid to a moving body: *An airplane uses thrust to overcome aerodynamic) drag; Drag increases with speed; a drag on the economy.* 3 *Slang.* a female attire worn by a man: *Tim appeared at the party in drag;* **adv.**: *Are you going to the party drag* (= with a partner) *or stag?* 4 *Informal.* one that is boring: *Life can become a drag during summer; Dan is such a drag* (= bore) *when he starts talking about computers.* 5 *Slang.* a puff on a cigar, cigarette, etc.: *She took a drag on his cigar.* 6 *Slang.* a street: *the main*

drag. **7** a drag race.
— v. drags, dragged, drag·ging 1 pull or draw with difficulty, esp. along the ground; trail; hence, move or cause to move slowly, tediously, against one's will, etc.: *He had to drag the tree behind the cart; Don't drag me into your problems; He dragged his son off to see the ball game; Time drags near lunch hour; The meeting* **dragged on** *for hours; Don't* **drag out** *the meeting with useless questions.* **2** search or fish with a net, hook, etc.: *The police had the river dragged for the missing body.* **3** *Slang.* puff: *to drag on a cigar, cigarette, etc.*
— drag one's feet or **heels** move or act slowly and without making the required effort: *He was dragging his feet on the job.* **— drag·ger** *n.*

drag·net *n.* **1** a fishing net pulled across the bottom of a body of water. **2** a set of coordinated procedures for finding people wanted by police.

drag·on (DRAG·un) *n.* in myths, a large lizard or snake, winged and usually fire-breathing: *Has modern science slain the dragon of superstition?*

drag·on·fly (DRAG·un·fly) *n.* **-flies** a flying insect with four large, gauzy wings, which feeds on insects caught in flight.

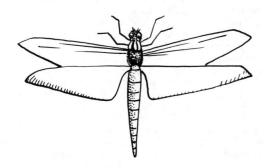

Dragon Lady *n.* a powerful or intimidating woman.

dra·goon (druh·GOON) *n.* a heavily armed cavalryman.
— v. harass or coerce: *He was dragooned into (joining) the organization.*

drag race *n.* an acceleration race over a short, straight course (**drag strip**), often between specially built cars (**drag·sters**).

drain *v.* **1** draw or flow out of a place; hence, exhaust or make empty: *to drain gasoline from the tank; Lou felt drained at the end of the exams.* **2** dry by drawing liquid from a place: *to drain land for farming; a creek that drains the region; The region drains* (= empties its water) *into the creek.* **3** become emptied or exhausted: *Her enthusiasm drained away.*
— n. 1 a means of draining, as a drainpipe: *to block, clean out, clear, clog, unclog a drain; Morality seems to be going down the drain and little is being done about it.* **2** a draining, depletion, etc.: *a drain on his financial resources; a brain drain to the U.S.*

drain·age (DRAY·nij) *n.* **1** a draining; also, a system of ditches, pipes, etc. for draining. **2** that which is drained off. **3** an area drained; also **drainage basin.**

drain·pipe *n.* a pipe for carrying off water or other unwanted liquid.

drake *n.* a male duck.

dra·ma (DRAH·muh, DRAM·uh) *n.* **1** a play for the stage, TV, or radio. **2** the art or institution of the theatre or plays: *a student of Japanese drama.* **3** a unified series of exciting events: *a hostage drama at the embassy; The drama unfolded right in front of them.*

dra·mat·ic (druh·MAT·ic) *adj.* **1** of or for drama: *dramatic irony, unity.* **2** vivid, striking, exciting, etc.: *a rather dramatic entrance; Events took a dramatic turn.* **3 dramatics** *n.pl.* [usually takes pl. v.] dramatic behaviour; also, theatrical performance or production.
— dra·mat·i·cal·ly *adv.*

dram·a·tist (DRAM·uh·tist) *n.* a playwright.

dram·a·tize (DRAM·uh·tize) *v.* **-tiz·es, -tized, -tiz·ing 1** adapt for dramatic presentation. **2** present or regard dramatically: *He always dramatizes his problems.*
— dram·a·ti·za·tion (-tuh·ZAY·shun) *n.*

drank *pt.* of DRINK.

drape *v.* **drapes, draped, drap·ing 1** cover or hang with cloth in loose folds; hang cloth thus: *a coffin draped with black cloth; He came out with a towel draped over his head.* **2** hang or rest casually or loosely: *His arm was draped over her shoulders.*
— n. 1 draped cloth. **2 drapes** *pl.* curtains: *window drapes; to draw, hang, open the drapes.*

dra·per·y (DRAY·puh·ree) *n.* **-per·ies 1** draped cloth; also, the draping or arranging of material. **2 draperies** *pl.* curtains.

dras·tic (DRAS·tic) *adj.* harsh or extreme: *The revolt was put down with drastic measures; The punishment was rather drastic; They took drastic steps.*
— dras·ti·cal·ly *adv.*

draught (DRAFT) *n., adj. & v.* same as DRAFT.

draughts·man, draught·y same as DRAFTSMAN, DRAFTY.

draw *v.* **draws,** *pt.* **drew,** *pp.* **drawn, draw·ing 1** pull with effort; hence, move gradually or slowly: *an engine drawing a long train; a carriage drawn by horses; to draw* (= close) *the drapes; The racer drew ahead; A small boat draws alongside (of) a ship; I had to* **draw him aside** *for a private word.* **2** attract: *Sugar draws ants; a threat that draws no reply; a speech that drew cheers; May I draw your attention to the smoke rising from your roof?* **3** pull in; inhale: *He likes to draw at or on his pipe while thinking what to say; He says he will defend his country while he draws breath* (= as long as he lives); *He draws courage from her example; The cat drew in its claws; a chimney that draws* (= lets or causes air to flow) *well.* **4** pull out; extract: *She drew the sword from the scabbard; The gunfighter drew and fired; to draw lots; to draw water from a well; to draw money from the bank; a bank account drawing* (= earning) *good interest; to draw a chicken* (= have its entrails taken out). **5** shape, make larger or longer, as by stretching or pulling: *Please draw the strings tight.* **6** move gradually and steadily: *The meeting is drawing to a close; Night draws on; Death draws nearer every moment.* **7** portray with lines or words; sketch; write out: *to draw a picture; She drew him in a thoughtful mood.* **8** infer or make: *to draw a conclusion; to draw an analogy between two things.* **9** of ships, etc., need a depth of water to float in: *Loaded boats draw more*

water than empty ones. **10** bend a bow for shooting an arrow. **11** tie a contest: *Canada drew against the Soviet Union; We drew in the hockey game.* **12** steep: *The tea has to draw before being served.*
— **draw a blank** be unsuccessful.
— **draw down** consume or deplete: *A war draws down military supplies.*
— **draw on 1** approach or come near: *When winter drew on we were short of supplies; The brown horse is beginning to draw in the black one.* **2** take from somewhere: *He can draw on his great fund of knowledge; a cheque drawn on a trust company; a cheque drawn on or against an account.*
— **draw out 1** prolong. **2** induce to talk: *He drew out the old-timer on the hardships of the Depression years.*
— **draw the line** set a limit not to be gone past: *We have to draw the line at $10 000 for expenses.*
— **draw up 1** set in order; also, straighten stiffly: *She drew herself up in her chair and listened intently.*
2 draft: *to draw up a treaty, will.* **3** come to a stop: *The car drew up in front of us.*
— **n. 1** a drawing: *a fast-draw gunfighter; Lou is quick on the draw* (*Informal* for quick to react); *Pat is slow on the draw* (*Informal* for sluggish); *They held a lucky draw* (= raffle or lottery). **2** something drawn, esp. a tied contest: *The game ended in a draw.* **3** an attraction: *Niagara Falls is a powerful draw for tourists.* **4** a gully or valley.

draw·back *n.* a disadvantage or hindrance.

draw·down *n.* a reduction or depletion.

draw·er *n.* **1** one that draws. **2** a container in a desk, bureau, etc. that slides in and out: *to close, open, pull out, push in a drawer.* **3 drawers** *pl.* underpants.

drawing *n.* the act or skill of portraying by drawn lines; also, a representation so made; an act or instance of drawing: *She's good at drawing; Her pencil drawings are on display at the gallery; a draftsman's mechanical drawing; a freehand drawing; A line drawing has no shaded areas.*

drawing board *n.* a board used for drawing up plans: *The project is on the drawing board; Back to the **old drawing board*** (= We start again at the planning stage)!

drawing card *n.* attraction: *The hotel's drawing card is a good sandy beach.*

drawl *n.* a way of speaking that lengthens the vowel sounds: *a Texas drawl.*
— *v.:* *"Naw," he drawled, "no problem."*

drawn *adj.* strained and haggard.

dread (DRED) *v.* fear greatly: *He dreads horror movies; She dreads being called up in the middle of the night.*
— *n.* great fear: *The fugitive lived in dread of being caught.*

dread·ful *adj.* causing dread; also, very unpleasant or severe: *dreadful news; a dreadful storm; It's dreadful to sit there and listen to speeches all day.*
— **dread·ful·ly** *adv.*

dread·locks *n.pl.* an Afro-style hairdo of tightly curled and matted strands of hair.

dream (DREEM) *n.* **1** a group of subjective images, thoughts, etc. in a sleeper's mind; also, a reverie or daydream: *Everyone has dreams; Some interpret dreams; a bad, recurring, visionary, wild dream; a childhood dream about a pot of gold.* **2** a vision or ideal, esp. if considered as unreal: *Her dream was to win an Olympic gold; The wedding was like a dream come true; I have a dream of people living in harmony; What we achieved was beyond our wildest dreams.*
3 something very desirable or excellent: *Our vacation was a dream; The new car runs like a dream* (= without problems); *a **dream factory*** (= movie studio); *the **dream machine*** (= the TV industry).
— *v.* **dreams,** *pt. & pp.* **dreamed** or **dreamt** (DREMT), **dream·ing 1** have a dream: *Joe dreamed about waking up rich.* **2** be in a reverie; daydream. **3** suppose or imagine: *He never dreamed that one day he would win a Nobel prize; I wouldn't **dream of** having you pay the bill; They tried hard to **dream up** (= invent) some excuse for being so late.* — **dream·er** *n.*

dream·y (DREE·mee) *adj.* **dream·i·er, -i·est 1** given to daydreaming: *a dreamy child, disposition; He's too dreamy to be a responsible babysitter.* **2** like a dream: *dreamy music; the dreamy quality of the scene; a dreamy recollection, smile, vision.* **3** *Informal.* perfect or lovely: *a dreamy car, companion, dress; It sounds dreamy; dreamy eyes.*
— **dream·i·ly** *adv.;* **dream·i·ness** *n.*

drear·y (DREER·ee) *adj.* **drear·i·er, -i·est** causing boredom, low spirits, etc.; gloomy: *a dreary chore; It's very dreary working on the same book day after day.* Also **drear** *Poetic.* — **drear·i·ly** *adv.;* **drear·i·ness** *n.*

dreck *n.* *Slang.* something cheap and useless; rubbish or trash: *the dreck of downtown streets.*

dredge *n.* a scoop, bucket, net, etc. for dragging along the bottom of a body of water; also, a ship fitted with this.
— *v.* **dredg·es, dredged, dredg·ing 1** clean or deepen a channel or harbour with a dredge. **2** gather or search for with a dredge: *to dredge oysters in the shallows; trying to **dredge up** news about the scandal.* **3** sprinkle or coat: *to dredge meat cubes with flour; to dredge spices over something.*

dregs *n.pl.* **1** the sediment from a liquid, esp. a drink. **2** the most worthless part: *the dregs of society.*

drench *v.* wet thoroughly or soak: *We were thoroughly drenched by a sudden downpour; drenched to the skin; a fugitive drenched in despair.*

dress *v.* **1** put clothes on a person: *A mother dresses her child; Don't come in, I'm dressing; to dress* (= put on formal clothes) *for dinner; Mourners dress in black; to dress elegantly, lightly, smartly, warmly; She went out to the costume party dressed as a fairy, dressed like a butterfly.* **2** decorate: *to dress a display window.* **3** comb and arrange hair; groom an animal. **4** put or get troops in straight lines. **5** prepare for cooking or use; finish: *a pre-dressed chicken; dressed leather; dressed lumber.* **6** apply a dressing to a wound.
— **dress down** scold vigorously.
— **dressed to the teeth** or **dressed to kill** dressed very finely or fancily.
— **dress up** dress specially or formally: *She went out dressed up as a spacewoman; She dressed up her children as little goblins; Everyone came to the party nicely dressed up.*

— **n. 1** clothing, esp. outer: *casual, formal, informal dress; He appeared in his native dress; neglect of one's dress; a full-dress affair.* **2** a woman's or girl's one-piece outer garment: *The ladies were in long cocktail dresses; a low-cut, maternity, short, summer, tight dress.*
— **adj.** of clothes, formal: *a dress shirt; dress shoes; a dress affair (requiring formal clothes).*

dress circle *n.* the first tier of seats in a theatre, where formal dress was once required.

dress·er *n.* **1** one who dresses: *a careful dresser; a fine dresser.* **2** a bureau or chest of drawers, usually with a mirror.

dressing *n.* **1** a bandage, medication, etc. applied to a wound: *to apply a dressing to a wound; put on a dressing; to remove, replace a dressing.* **2** a sauce for salads, etc.: *a creamy French dressing.* **3** a bread-and-seasoning stuffing, as for poultry.

dressing gown *n.* an informal robe worn while lounging, preparing to dress, etc.

dress rehearsal *n.* a rehearsal in full costume.

dress·y *adj.* **dress·i·er, -i·est 1** given to fancy dressing: *dressy women; the dressy crowd.* **2** stylish or formal: *dressy clothes for a dressy cocktail party; a dressy black suit good for dressy occasions.*

drew *pt.* of DRAW.

drib·ble (DRIB·ul) *v.* **drib·bles, drib·bled, drib·bling 1** flow or fall in a small, unsteady stream; allow or cause to do so; also, slobber. **2** in sports, move the ball or puck by a series of bounces, taps, or kicks.
— **n. 1** what dribbles down: *A dribble of saliva fell from the baby's mouth; The donations came in dribbles.* **2** an act of dribbling: *a rapid dribble at centre court.*

dribs and drabs *n. pl. Informal.* tiny amounts: *They could save only in dribs and drabs.*

dried, drier, dries, driest See DRY, DRYER.

drift *n.* **1** aimless movement; also, one's course while drifting. **2** a movement; tendency; also, tenor, gist, etc.: *the drift of the political situation; the drift of their conversation; if you get the drift* (=meaning). **3** a bank of sand or snow piled up by wind. **4** a glacial deposit of rock debris.
— **v. 1** move aimlessly, esp. with a current, breeze, etc.; stray idly; cause to drift: *a boat drifting south along the coast; It was drifting with the current; Some of the debris drifted back to the beach; They started to drift apart* (=lose interest in each other) *over the years; Customers were still drifting in at closing time; We drifted off to sleep during the show; people drifting through life without even having learned to read.* **2** pile or be piled up in a drift: *drifting sand, snow.*

drift·er *n.* one that drifts, esp. a homeless wanderer; bum.

drill *n.* **1** a tool for making a hole in something hard: *a dentist's drill; a hand drill such as a brace and bit; to operate a power drill.* **2** a repeated series of physical or mental exercises used in teaching, esp. a military procedure for training in marching and use of weapons: *a fire drill; pronunciation drill; spelling drill; A military drill is conducted by a* **drill·mas·ter. 3** a furrow to plant seeds in; also, a machine that plants seeds in rows of holes and furrows: *a seed drill.*
— **v. 1** make a hole with a drill: *We are drilling for oil.* **2** *Informal.* throw a ball hard and fast or shoot a puck so as to penetrate the defence: *He drilled it through.* **3** train with or undergo a drill: *The teacher drilled his class in the multiplication tables; He had German* **drilled** (=instilled) **into** *him at school.* — **drill·er** *n.*

dri·ly (DRY·lee) *adv.* same as DRYLY.

drink *v.* **drinks, drank, drunk, drink·ing 1** swallow a liquid: *to drink water.* **2** take in mentally or with the senses: *tourists drinking in the sights of Paris.* **3** consume alcoholic beverages: *He drinks like a fish; He drinks to excess; He sometimes goes missing after a bout of* **drinking. 4** make or take part in a toast: *Let's* **drink to** *the bride and groom; Let's drink a toast to them; I'll* **drink to that** (=I agree).
— **drink someone under the table** get one's drinking partner drunk while remaining sober oneself.
— **drink up** finish one's drink.
— **n. 1** a beverage; also, an amount drunk: *Have a drink; Let me fix you a drink; to make, mix, nurse, pour, take, toss off a drink; a mixed, soft, stiff, strong drink.* **2** alcoholic beverages; also, their excessive use: *He was driven to drink by loneliness.*
— **drink·a·ble** *n. & adj.*
— **drink·er** *n.: a hard* or *heavy drinker (of liquor).*

drip *v.* **drips, dripped, drip·ping 1** fall or let fall in drops: *Water is dripping from the tap; water dripping off the roof; a dripping faucet.* **2** be overflowing or soaked: *a voice dripping with irony; He came in* **dripping** (=quite) *wet.*
— **n.** a dripping or the noise of it: *the steady drip of a leaking faucet.*

drip-dry *adj.* of clothes, made to dry while hung dripping wet.

drippings *n. pl.* juices that drip from cooking fat meat: *to make gravy from the drippings; Drippings help reinforce the flavour of the meat.*

drive *v.* **drives, drove** (DROHV), **driv·en, driv·ing** (DRY·ving) **1** make to move in some direction or to a target or goal: *to drive cattle to market; The golfer drove the ball from the tee; to drive a nail* (=hit it with a hammer) *into a wall; What are you* **driving at** (=suggesting)? *The lecturer tried to make a point and* **drive it home** *with a story.* **2** force to move fast or violently; force to work: *A south wind drove us on; The boss drives his workers very hard.* **3** bore; drill; dig: *to drive a tunnel under the canal; to drive a well.* **4** compel; impel; put into a state: *He was driven to despair by the tragedy; The pain drove her mad; His behaviour drives me crazy* or *mad (Informal for irritates me).* **5** give power or motion: *an engine driven by steam.* **6** operate, ride in, or convey in a vehicle: *to drive a car; She drives her children to school, then drives to work; Please drive me home; I saw him* **drive down** *the street; Let's* **drive up** *to the house over there and ask our way.* **7** carry on; conduct: *I got the car at a low price by* **driving a hard bargain** (= by negotiating skilfully).
— **n. 1** a driving, esp. a trip in a car: *Let's go for, go on, take a drive in the new car; a test drive; It's an easy 10-minute drive to work.* **2** a herding together or movement of animals: *a cattle drive.* **3** a driving of a ball: *a line drive to centre field.* **4** a road; also,

driveway: *the Lakeshore Drive*. **5** a campaign: *a charity drive; to initiate, launch a drive for funds; a fundraising drive*. **6** energy or dynamism: *a sales rep with plenty of drive; She has the drive to see the project through*. **7** a strong urge or impulse: *The sex drive is an elemental drive*. **8** a mechanism that transmits motion: *a belt drive; a motorcycle with a chain drive; the disk drive or tape drive in which a computer's magnetic storage media are rotated; a fluid, four-wheel, frontwheel (automobile) drive*.

drive-in *adj.* providing service to patrons who remain in cars: *a drive-in bank, movie, takeout window;* also *n.*

driv·el (DRIV·ul) *n.* meaningless or silly talk.

drive·line *n.* same as DRIVETRAIN.

driv·er (DRY·vur) *n.* one who drives: *a truck driver; Your **driver's licence** is issued by the government; Who is in the **driver's seat*** (= controlling position)?

drive shaft *n.* a shaft that transmits motion, as to the rear axle of an automobile.

drive-through *n.* a drive through a place in one's automobile; also, such a place.
— *adj.* that one may drive through: *a drive-through carwash, game park, pickup window, zoo*.

drive·train *n.* the parts that carry power from an automobile's engine to the driving wheels, comprising the transmission, the drive shaft, universal joints, and the differential gears.

drive-up *adj.* same as DRIVE-IN: *the drive-up window of a bank*.

drive·way *n.* **1** a usually short private road to one's garage, parking lot, house, etc.: *to pave* or *surface a driveway*. **2** a semi-private road, as through a housing complex or shopping centre: *Vehicles may not be parked on driveways*. **3** *Cdn.* a scenic drive: *the driveway along the Niagara River*.

driving *adj.* **1** having great force or producing a strong effect: *a driving ambition, concern, energy, force, influence, power, rain*. **2** having to do with the operation of a motor vehicle: *driving gloves; a driving lesson, school, test; safe driving practices; n.: careless, defensive, drunk, reckless driving*.

driz·zle (DRIZ·ul) *v.* **driz·zles, driz·zled, driz·zling** rain or sprinkle in fine droplets: *a misty drizzling rain*. Also *n.* — **driz·zly** *adj.: a cold drizzly day*.

droll (DROLE) *adj.* quaintly amusing: *a droll sense of humour*.

drone *n.* **1** a nonworking male honeybee serving only for reproductive purposes; hence, a parasitic idler. **2** a pilotless aircraft guided by remote control: *to send up drones for target practice*. **3** a low humming or monotonous sound or voice; also, a pipe of a bagpipe that makes such a sound steadily.
— *v.* **drones, droned, dron·ing** utter such a sound: *The speaker droned on with the financial report*.

drool *v.* **1** run or let saliva run from the mouth: *a drooling infant*. **2** *Informal.* show excessive pleasure at or in anticipation of something: *She's drooling over the chance to go to Europe*.

droop *v.* sag or hang down: *pants that droop down your rear end; a man with drooping shoulders; She drooped her head in shame; My spirits drooped* (= I was dispirited) *at the bad news*.
— *n.:* *There's a slight droop to one eye; the vast droop of his belly*.

droop·y *adj.* sagging or floppy: *The flowers are droopy from the drought; a droopy-eared rabbit; droopy eyelids; droopy-eyed workers; modishly droopy* (= oversized) *knits such as cardigans and polo shirts*.

drop *n.* **1** a tiny, usually globular mass of liquid: *a drop of water; The coffee is good to the last drop; cough, ear, eye, nose **drops*** (= medication); *knockout **drops*** (= drugs). **2** a tiny amount: *He's had a drop too much to drink* (= is drunk); *When we are trying to collect $40 million, $9.95 is a mere **drop in the bucket**, but every drop counts*. **3** a drop-shaped pendant, candy, etc.: *gum drops*. **4** a falling, descent, or decrease: *the sheer drop of the mountain face; a sharp drop in the price of gas; a sudden drop in temperature; a drop in height from 20 000 to 10 000 m; You're looking down a drop* (= cliff or slope) *of 5 000 m*. **5** a dropping or deposit or a place for it: *a parachute drop of supplies; a mail drop for letters; The spy made the drop; He deposited the papers at the drop*. **6** something to be lowered, as a stage curtain (**drop curtain**) or a trapdoor.
— **at the drop of a hat** promptly; without hesitation.
— **get the drop on someone** *Slang.* have an advantage over someone.
— *v.* **drops, dropped, drop·ping 1** fall or let fall, as in drops; lower; decrease; descend: *to drop a bomb; drop a coin into the slot; Prices drop when demand is low; The troops were dropped by parachute*. **2** fall or cause to fall as from weakness, a blow, wounds, etc.: *to drop from exhaustion; The hunter dropped the moose with one shot; The wounded were dropping to the ground like flies*. **3** move to a position that is inferior, less active, or further back: *Our horse is beginning to **drop back** in the race; We never expected him to **drop behind** in class; to drop behind the others*. **4** say or write casually: *to drop a hint, a name; Do drop us a card when you get there*. **5** cease connection with a person or thing: *Pat dropped his old friends and **dropped out of sight*** (= disappeared); *He drops* (= omits) *his g's and says readin', writin', etc*. **6** put down; deposit: *Please drop this letter in the mailbox; Can you drop me at Fifth Street?* **7** visit informally: *Please **drop in** on us sometime; I may **drop around** on Monday*. **8** *Slang.* take a narcotic in pill or capsule form: *He started smoking pot and dropping* (= swallowing) *acid*.
— **drop dead** *interj. Slang.* get lost; go to hell.
— **drop off 1** decrease: *Attendance drops off toward the end of the month*. **2** leave: *She dropped off a package for you; to drop* (= fall) *off to sleep watching TV; Please drop* (= let) *me off at the next stop*.
— **drop out** withdraw from a contest, school (before graduating), from conventional society, etc.

drop·in *n.* **1** a casual visitor. **2** a place for informal visits: *a dropin centre for teens*.

drop-off *n.* **1** a dropping off; decline. **2** *Informal.* delivery.

drop·out *n.* one who drops out: *a high-school dropout*.

droppings *n. pl.* animal excrement: *animal, bird droppings*.

dross *n.* 1 a scum of waste formed on molten metals. 2 worthless impurities; rubbish. — **dross·y** *adj.*

drought (DROWT) *n.* an extended period of unusually dry weather.

drove *pt.* of DRIVE.
— *n.* a herd or large group, as of animals, moving or driven: *droves of cattle on the road to market; droves of flies; People left the area in droves because of the chemical spill, others stayed home in droves.*

dro·ver (DROH·vur) *n.* one who herds animals, esp. to market.

drown *v.* 1 kill or die by submersion in liquid, esp. water: *He didn't kill himself, he drowned; Did someone drown him? He tried to drown* (=get rid of) *his sorrows at the local lounge.* 2 flood or overwhelm: *The speaker was drowned out by the noise of the traffic.*

drown·proof·ing (DROWN·proo·fing) *n.* a technique for avoiding drowning by relaxing and using one's natural buoyancy.

drowse (DROWZ) *v.* **drows·es, drowsed, drows·ing** sleep lightly; doze: *to drowse away the time.*
— *n.:* *He was in a drowse when the book dropped to the floor.*

drow·sy (DROW·zee, DROW *rhymes with* HOW) *adj.* 1 feeling or making one feel heavy and dull: *I feel drowsy after sitting in the sun; a drowsy day.* 2 quiet or inactive: *a drowsy village.*
— **drow·si·ly** *adv.;* **drow·si·ness** *n.*

drub *v.* **drubs, drubbed, drub·bing** thrash or defeat soundly.

drudge *n.* one who does menial, boring, or plodding work: *Samuel Johnson described the dictionary maker as a harmless drudge.* Also *v.* **drudg·es, drudged, drudg·ing.**

drudg·er·y (DRUJ·uh·ree) *n.* **-ries** the work of a drudge: *He writes poetry to escape the drudgery of a dishwashing job; the sheer drudgery of housework.*

drug *n.* 1 a substance administered in medicines to affect the body: *an over-the-counter drug; prescription drug; a proprietary, not generic drug; a habit-forming, miracle, powerful, toxic, wonder drug.* 2 a narcotic, hallucinogen, barbiturate, etc., esp. if addictive or abused: *hard and soft drugs; to peddle, push, sell, take, traffic in illicit drugs; He had been on drugs for some time when he was found dead; adj.:* *drug abuse, addict, addiction, dealer, pusher.*
— *v.* **drugs, drugged, drug·ging** 1 give a drug to someone, esp. affect with a narcotic: *The spy was drugged and carted away in a crate.* 2 mix a drug with something: *The drink was drugged.*

drug·gist *n.* one who sells drugs, esp. a retail pharmacist.

drug·o·la (druh·GOH·luh) *n.* Slang. a bribe in the form of illicit drugs.

drug·store *n.* a retail pharmacy that sells prescription drugs and other articles.

drum *n.* 1 a hollow cylinder or other shape with a membrane stretched over an open end, beaten as a percussion instrument: *to beat, play, roll a drum; a bass drum; the roll of the drums.* 2 eardrum. 3 a drumlike cylinder, as a barrel or a cartridge holder for a machine gun: *the brake drum of an automobile.* 4 the sound of a beaten drum; also **drum·beat.**
— *v.* **drums, drummed, drum·ming** 1 play a drum; make a similar noise, as by tapping one's fingers or by beating the wings, as a bird does. 2 force by repetition: *It had been drummed into his head from early childhood that lying is bad.*
— **drum out** expel from a group in disgrace.
— **drum up** get by persistent canvassing or effort: *to drum up business, customers, interest, support.*

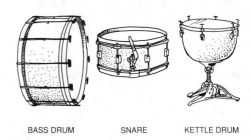

BASS DRUM   SNARE   KETTLE DRUM

drum ma·jor·ette (-may·juh·RET) *n.* a female baton twirler of a band.

drum·mer *n.* one who plays a drum: *Individualists* **hear** or **march to a different drummer** (=are unconventional, doing their own thing).

drunk *pp.* of DRINK.
— *adj.* intoxicated: *a drunk driver; He seemed drunk; drunk as a skunk; charged with drunk and disorderly conduct.*
— *n.* 1 a bout of drunkenness. 2 drunkard: *to roll* (=rob) *a drunk.*

drunk·ard (DRUNK·urd) *n.* one who is drunk, esp. habitually.

drunk·en (DRUNK·un) *adj.* 1 drunk: *drunken drivers; drunken driving; a drunken-driving charge; They are not a drunken lot.* 2 having to do with being drunk: *a drunken argument, incident, party, shouting match; He was staggering about in a drunken stupor.*
— **drunk·en·ly** *adv.;* **drunk·en·ness** *n.*

drunk tank *n.* a cell for people arrested for drunkenness.

dry *adj.* **dri·er, dri·est** 1 not wet or moist: *the dry sand; dry as a bone; dry as dust* (=uninteresting); *There was not a dry* (=not crying) *eye at the funeral; a dry well (that has no water); The well has gone or run dry; dry land (that is not under water); a dry* (=not yielding milk) *cow.* 2 having or providing little rain: *a dry area, region, season; in dry weather; the* **Dry belt** *between Moose Jaw, Sask., and Medicine Hat, Alta.* 3 having to do with solids, not liquids: **dry goods** *such as cloth, clothing, etc.;* **Dry measure** *uses pints, quarts, pecks, and bushels to measure grain, vegetables, etc.* 4 served without butter or jam: *dry toast.* 5 without moisture or lubrication: *a dry cough.* 6 prohibiting alcoholic drink;

also, supporting prohibition: *a dry county, district.*
7 not sweet: *a dry wine.* **8** plain or unadorned: *a dry* (= dull) *recitation of facts; his dry* (= subtly witty or ironic) *humour.*
— **not dry behind the ears** *Informal.* immature or naive; wet behind the ears.
— *v.* **dries, dried, dry·ing** make or become dry: *clothes drying in the sun; We dry them in a dryer;* **Dried** *fish, food, fruit, meat, milk, etc. keep longer.*
— **dry out** detoxify from the effects of alcohol.
— **dry up** *Slang.* stop talking.
— **dry·ly** *adv.;* **dry·ness** *n.*

dry-clean *v.* clean clothes, etc. with a solvent other than water. — **dry-cleaner** *n.;* **dry-cleaning** *n.*

dry dock *n.* a watertight dock that may be emptied of water to hold a ship under repair or one being built. — **dry-dock** *v.* put a ship in a dry dock.

dry·er *n.* a machine, appliance, or person that dries: *a clothes dryer.*

dry ice *n.* solid carbon dioxide used as a cooling agent and for stage effects: *Dry ice passes from solid to vapour at -78.5 degrees Celsius;* **Dry Ice** *Trademark.*

dry rot *n.* **1** decay of seasoned wood from within by the action of fungi. **2** inner decay.

dry run *n.* a rehearsal or trial: *to do* or *make a dry run.*

du·al (DEW·ul) *adj.* having to do with two; twofold; double: *a dual alliance, personality; dual citizenship, nationality; Training vehicles have dual controls; a truck trailer with dual tires; dual-purpose cattle (raised for milk and beef).* — **du·al·i·ty** (dew·AL·uh·tee) *n.*

du·al·ism (DEW·uh·liz·um) *n.* the belief that the world is composed of two basic principles or forces, as good and evil, matter and form, yin and yang, etc. — **du·al·ist** *n. & adj.*

dub *v.* **dubs, dubbed, dub·bing** **1** add new voices or sounds to a movie or sound track: *to dub in English dialogue for a French film; to dub a French film into English.* **2** dress leather by rubbing a greasy paste (**dub·bin**) into it. **3** tap with a sword to make a knight: *The queen dubbed him a knight.* **4** give a new name, title, or nickname to: *They dubbed him "The King of Hearts."*
— *n.* **1** *Slang.* a bungler. **2** what is dubbed in a sound track.

du·bi·ous (DEW·bee·us) *adj.* **1** doubting or mistrustful: *She's dubious about* or *of your claims.* **2** causing doubt; questionable: *a dubious claim, behaviour; rather dubious business practices; a man of dubious character.* — **du·bi·ous·ly** *adv.*

duch·ess (DUCH·is) *n.* **1** a duke's wife. **2** a woman who rules a duchy.

duch·y (DUCH·ee) *n.* **duch·ies** dukedom; land ruled by a duke or duchess, as Luxembourg.

duck *n.* **1** a web-footed water bird smaller than a goose: *Ducks and ducklings quack and waddle about; Jane has taken to computers like a duck to water* (= readily). **2** a strong, tightly woven, usually cotton cloth for lightweight apparel. **3** **ducks** *pl.* clothes, esp. pants, made of duck.
— **like water off a duck's back** producing no effect.

— *v.* **1** lower oneself, one's head, body, etc. to avoid being seen or hurt: *He didn't duck fast enough to avoid the bullet; He should have ducked behind a car; boxers dodging and ducking in the ring; She came in late and ducked* (= moved quickly) *into her office.* **2** evade or dodge: *to duck issues, questions, reporters; She is ducking all phone calls this morning, but she won't* **duck out of** *her real obligations.* **3** submerge in water for a short time: *They ducked him in the pond.*

duck·ling *n.* a young duck.

duck·y *adj.* **duck·i·er, -i·est** *Informal.* **1** pleasing or excellent: *just ducky.* **2** corny.

duct *n.* a tube, pipe, channel, etc. for the flow of air, liquids, etc. or for electrical wires and cables: *hot air ducts for heating the home; the tear ducts; The salivary and oil-producing glands also have ducts.* — **duct·less** *adj.*

duc·tile (DUCK·tile, -tul) *adj.* **1** of solids, able to be stretched or drawn into shape without breaking: *Copper, aluminum, silver, etc. are ductile.* **2** docile or easily led.

dud *n.* **1** *Informal.* a bomb or shell that fails to explode; hence, a failure, a worthless person, or something that is without effect: *a dud cheque.* **2** **duds** *pl. Informal.* clothes; also, one's belongings: *a young guy dressed in Mountie duds.*

dude (DEWD) *n.* **1** *Informal.* a dandy or fop; hence, a city dweller or Easterner in the West. **2** *Slang.* a guy or fellow.

dude ranch *n.* a ranch run as a vacation spot for guests, sometimes called "guest ranch" or "resort ranch."

dudg·eon (DUJ·un) *n.* an angry fit of indignation: *He stalked out of the room in high dudgeon.*

due *adj.* **1** to be paid or submitted, esp. payable immediately; owed: *Your rent is due on the first of each month; The homework is due on Monday; a loan that falls* or *comes due at the end of June.* **2** proper or suitable: *with all due respect; It will be done in due time; You will hear from us in due course; The right to* **due process** (= fair treatment according to the laws) *is guaranteed by the Constitution.* **3** expected or scheduled: *The baby is due any day now; Our bus was due (to arrive) at 4:30; He is due for a pay raise* (= He can expect a pay raise).
— **due to** **1** attributable to something: *game cancellations due to rain.* **2** *Informal.* because of something: *game cancelled due to rain.*
— *adv.* directly: *Miami is due south of Toronto on the same longitude; due east, north, west.*
— *n.* **1** something owed to or deserved by someone: *Let's* **give the devil his due** (= give deserved credit even to one's enemy). **2** **dues** *pl.* a fee, as for membership: *We pay annual membership dues of $50; He has* **paid his dues** (*Informal for* earned what he is enjoying through hard work, suffering, etc.).

du·el (DEW·ul) *n.* **1** a formal combat between two people, as to settle a point of honour: *Ho challenged Lou to a duel; But Lou doesn't fight duels.* **2** a contest between two: *a duel to the death; a duel of wits.*
— *v.* **du·els, du·elled** or **du·eled, du·el·ling** or **du·el·ing.** — **du·el·list** or **du·el·ist** *n.*

du·et (dew·ET) *n.* **1** a piece of music for two singers or players: *to play, sing a duet.* **2** the performing pair: *a male duet.*

duff *n.* **1** a flour pudding made in a cloth bag. **2** decaying matter covering the ground in forests. **3** *Slang.* buttocks: *to get off one's duff.*

duffel same as DUFFLE.

duf·fer (DUF·ur) *n. Informal.* one who is bumbling and incompetent, esp. such a golfer.

duf·fle or **duf·fel** (DUF·ul) *n.* **1** coarse, thick-napped woollen cloth. **2** [short form] duffle bag; duffel coat; duffel sock.

dug *pt. & pp.* of DIG.

dug·out *n.* **1** a canoe made of a hollowed-out tree trunk. **2** a rough shelter dug at least partly into the ground. **3** a roofed and sunken shelter for baseball players. **4** *Cdn.* in the Prairies, a reservoir dug on a farm, in which water from rain and snow is collected for use in irrigation, watering livestock, etc.

duke *n.* **1** a nobleman of rank next below prince. **2** a ruler of a duchy or **duke·dom** (often a small state in Europe). **3** **dukes** *pl. Informal.* fists: *to put up one's dukes.*

dul·cet (DUL·sit) *adj.* sweet or soothing, esp. to the ear.

dul·ci·mer (DUL·suh·mur) *n.* either of two musical instruments with steel strings; also **dul·ci·more.**

dull *adj.* **1** not perceiving sharply: *dull hearing; He's just a little dull, not stupid or dense; a dull-witted* (= slow in understanding) *fellow.* **2** sluggish; not active: *a week of dull trading on the stock exchange.* **3** not sharp, bright, or clear: *a dull knife, light, sword; dull grey walls; dull sounds; a dull thud.* **4** boring or tedious: *a dull speech; The book is dull reading.* **5** overcast: *a dull day.* — *v.* make dull: *a mind dulled by drugs; Candy dulls the appetite; The knife has been dulled by rough use.* — **dul·ly** *adv.;* **dull·ness** *n.*

dull·ard (DULL·urd) *n.* a stupid person.

du·ly (DEW·lee) *adv.* in a due and proper way, time, etc.: *a duly elected official.*

dumb *adj.* **1** unable to speak, either by birth or temporarily: *She was struck dumb with shock; a dumb animal, creature; the deaf and* **the dumb** (= deaf-mutes). **2** silent: *a dumb show.* **3** *Informal.* stupid: *He played dumb and didn't say a word.* — **dumb·ly** *adv.;* **dumb·ness** *n.*

dumb·bell *n.* **1** a short bar with often rounded weights on either end, lifted for exercise. **2** *Slang.* a stupid person.

dumb·found *v.* strike speechless for a moment, as with amazement: *He was dumbfounded to hear that he had been fired from his job; utterly dumbfounded at or by the news.* Also **dum·found.**

dumb terminal *n.* a terminal without independent processing capability that operates only when connected to a computer; not a smart or intelligent terminal.

dum·my *n.* **dum·mies 1** a model human figure: *a dummy used by a ventriloquist; a tackling dummy (used for boxing practice).* **2** an imitation or substitute for something, as one acting secretly for another person; *adj.:* *a dummy corporation; a dummy gun (that only looks like a real one).* **3** *Slang.* a mute person; also, a stupid person. **4** the exposed hand of the declarer's partner in bridge. — *v.* **dum·mies, dum·mied, dum·my·ing** usually **dummy up,** refuse to answer questions.

dump *v.* **1** unload, empty, or drop in a large mass: *They dump the garbage behind the building; Did she dump* (= drop) *him or was it the other way around? Data is dumped* (= transferred) *from computer memory to storage or to an output terminal.* **2** sell in large quantities abroad at a low price: *Surplus goods are sometimes dumped abroad to keep domestic prices up.* — **dump on** *Slang.* unload bad feelings on someone, as by complaining or criticizing. — *n.* **1** a place for dumping something: *a garbage dump; a trash dump; a municipal dump; an ammunition dump* (= storage depot). **2** *Slang.* a run-down, dirty place: *This apartment is a real dump!* — **the dumps** *Informal.* a depressed state of mind: *to feel down in the dumps over a defeat.*

dump·ling *n.* a ball of dough boiled or steamed, unstuffed for serving with meats, or stuffed with fruit as a dessert.

dump·ster (DUMP·stur) *n.* a large bin for dumping trash; **Dumpster,** *Trademark.*

dump truck *n.* a truck with a body that can be tilted up to unload through a tailgate.

dump·y *adj.* **dump·i·er, -i·est 1** short, squat, and plump: *a dumpy bird.* **2** shabby or grungy: *a dumpy dress, restaurant, room.*

dun *adj.* dull greyish-brown. — *n.* **1** this colour; also, a dun horse. **2** a dunning. **3** one who duns. — *v.* **duns, dunned, dun·ning** ask a debtor repeatedly for payment.

dunce *n.* a slow-witted person: *He had to wear a dunce cap as punishment.*

dun·der·head (DUN·dur·hed) *n.* a stupid person: *a blundering dunderhead.*

dune *n.* a hill of sand made by the wind.

dune buggy *n.* a light automobile adapted, as by fitting with wide tires, for driving on soft sand.

dung *n.* excrement, esp. from animals, used as fertilizer. — **dung·y** *adj.*

dun·geon (DUN·jun) *n.* a dark, usually underground jail or cell.

dunk *v.* **1** submerge or dip into a liquid: *He likes to dunk his donut (in coffee).* **2** throw a basketball into the hoop with the hand reaching over the rim. — *n.* **1** a dunking; dip: *He had a good dunk in the lake.* **2** *Slang.* a basketball shot made by dunking; also **dunk shot.** — **dunk·er** *n.*

du·o (DEW·oh) *n.* **-os** a duet; hence, any pair.

dupe *v.* **dupes, duped, dup·ing** cheat by catching off guard or while suspecting nothing; make a fool of someone; trick: *He was duped into believing the car was new.*

— *n.* one who is easily duped.

du·ple (DEW·pul) *adj.* double: *duple metre; duple time (with two beats to the bar).*

du·plex (DEW·plex) *adj.* double: *a duplex apartment, house; duplex* (= two-ply) *paperboard.*
— *n.* **1** a house having two separate dwelling units; also **duplex house. 2** an apartment having rooms on two floors; also **duplex apartment.**

du·pli·cate (DEW·pluh·cate) *v.* -cates, -cat·ed, -cat·ing **1** make or become double; also, do or occur again: *to duplicate one's earlier performance.* **2** copy exactly, as with a **duplicating machine** or **du·pli·ca·tor** (-cay·tur).
— *adj.* (-kit) double; being an exact copy: *duplicate keys; In* **duplicate bridge,** *each hand is replayed by different players.*
— *n.* (-kit) an exact copy; a double of something: *to make a duplicate of the application; an application prepared* **in duplicate** (= with an exact copy of the original). — **du·pli·ca·tion** (-CAY·shun) *n.*

du·plic·i·ty (dew·PLIS·uh·tee) *n.* -ties deception by acting so as to conceal one's real intent or feelings.
— **du·plic·i·tous** (-uh·tus) *adj.*

du·ra·ble (DURE·uh·bul) *adj.* long-lasting, esp. despite use and wear: *cars, appliances, furniture, and such* **durable goods;** *durable construction, equipment, fashions, friendships, leaders, products, relations; a durable peace.* — **du·ra·bil·i·ty** (-BIL·uh·tee) *n.*

durable press *n.* a chemical process for fixing the shape, creases, etc. of a garment and making it wrinkle-resistant. — **durable-press** *adj.*

du·ra·tion (dure·AY·shun) *n.* the time during which something lasts or continues to exist: *an illness of short duration; The facilities were closed* **for the duration** *(of the strike).*

du·ress (dew·RES) *n.* illegal use of threats or force such as imprisonment to make someone do something: *One is not obliged to keep a promise made* **under duress.**

dur·ing (DURE·ing) *prep.* **1** throughout the course of time of something: *It's hot during the summer.* **2** at one point in the course of something: *He was wounded during the battle.*

durst [old form] *pt.* of DARE.

dusk *n.* the partial darkness of twilight: *Some flowers close at dusk; Dawn and dusk last very long at the poles during winter.*

dusk·y *adj.* dusk·i·er, -i·est **1** dim; darkish; gloomy. **2** dark-skinned; swarthy.
— **dusk·i·ly** *adv.*; **dusk·i·ness** *n.*

dust *n.* **1** fine particles of solid matter; fine powdery earth: *A layer of dust covered the furniture lying in storage; Books were gathering dust in the library; Dust was collecting* or *settling everywhere; Children playing in the dirt kick up* or *raise quite a dust; Water is sprinkled on dirt roads to lay the dust; a cloud, layer, particle of dust; The debate will resume when the dust settles* (= when the confusion is over); *We return to dust when we die.* **2** something resembling dust: *The sun was formed from a swirling mass of gases and cosmic dust; gold dust; radioactive dust; volcanic dust.*
— **bite the dust** die in battle; be defeated.

— **dust and ashes 1** [indicating worthlessness]: *The king did penance for his misdeeds in dust and ashes (put on the head as a sign of repentance).* **2** [indicating disillusion or disappointment]: *His hopes turned into dust and ashes.*
— **shake the dust from one's feet** leave in anger or contempt.
— **throw dust in someone's eyes** mislead or confuse.
— *v.* **1** remove the dust from something: *Those books need dusting; Make sure you dust them off as you take them down.* **2** sprinkle with dust or any powder: *The detective dusted the fingerprints with white powder; She dusted sugar over the cakes; There is a light* **dusting** *of snow on the ground.*

dust·bin *n.* garbage can.

dust·er *n.* **1** a person or implement that dusts: *a crop duster; feather duster.* **2** a light housecoat.

dust jacket *n.* the printed protective wrapper of a hardcover book.

dust·up *n.* a quarrel or fight: *a dustup between two neighbours.*

dust·y *adj.* dust·i·er, -i·est filled with or like dust: *a dusty old insurance policy; a dusty brown; a dusty village.*

Dutch *adj.* of the Netherlands, its people, or their language.
— **the Dutch** *n.pl.* the people of the Netherlands.
— **go Dutch** *Informal.* have each pay his or her own share, as on a date.
— **in Dutch** *Informal.* [derogatory] in trouble.

Dutch courage *n.* *Informal.* [derogatory] bravery inspired by alcohol.

Dutch treat *n.* *Informal.* an entertainment for which each person pays for his or her own share.

Dutch uncle *n.* *Informal.* [derogatory] one given to making harsh and forthright criticisms: *He talked to her like a Dutch uncle.*

du·ti·a·ble (DEW·tee·uh·bul) *adj.* subject to duty: *goods dutiable at 25%.*

du·ti·ful (DEW·tuh·ful) *adj.* doing one's duty; obedient: *a dutiful child, servant.* — **du·ti·ful·ly** *adv.*

du·ty (DEW·tee) *n.* -ties **1** something that one ought to do: *Do your duty; Duty (comes) before pleasure; Her devotion to duty is well-known; He's always ready to answer* or *obey the call of duty; It's our democratic duty to vote; our patriotic duty to defend our country; our bounden duty to our country; He did it out of a sense of duty; an official charged with dereliction of duty; to take on a duty; to carry out, discharge, do, perform, shirk one's duty; a civic, moral, official, pleasant duty; When duty calls, she cannot wait; A doctor is* **duty bound** (= obliged by duty) *to save a life if possible.* **2** active service, esp. military: *He saw active duty during World War II; fatigue duty; guard duty; overseas duty; Marcie is* **on duty** *from 9 a.m.; She'll be* **off duty** *at 5 p.m.; My typewriter will* **do duty for** (= serve as) *my writing equipment while my word processor is being serviced; the duty nurse (who is on duty).* **3** a tax, esp. one on imported or exported goods: *import and export* duties; *Customs duties are levied before sales taxes; Excise duties are paid on goods and services produced within a country; A duty was imposed on imported books and later lifted.*

duty-free *adj.* free of customs duties: *duty-free goods from a duty-free shop.*

du·vet (DEW·vay) *n.* a down-filled quilt used as bed covering; also called "continental quilt."

dwarf (DWORF) *n.* **dwarfs** or **dwarves** (DWORVZ) 1 an abnormally small adult person, plant, or animal. 2 in folk tales, a deformed or ugly dwarf with magic powers.
— *v.* cause to be or remain too small: *the Japanese art of dwarfing trees; The aircraft carrier dwarfed the boats near it.*
— *adj.*: *dwarf* (= undersized) *cattle that are born stunted; a dwarf tree (such as a bonsai).*
— **dwarf·ish** *adj.*

dwell *v.*, *pt. & pp.* **dwelled** or **dwelt** stay or remain for a long time; live in a place: *to dwell among the mountains, in a cottage, on an island.*
— **dwell on** or **upon** think, speak, write, etc. about something at some length: *The speaker dwelt at length on choosing a career; Let's dwell a little* (= spend some time) *on this topic.*
— **dwell·er** *n.*: *cave dwellers; city dwellers.*

dwelling *n.* a building in which one lives; residence: *the humble dwelling of a poor peasant.*

dwin·dle (DWIN·dul) *v.* **-dles, -dled, -dling** make or become less by steady degrees: *our dwindling oil resources; By 1830, the Beothuk population had dwindled to zero.*

dye *n.* 1 a substance used to colour or stain something, esp. fabrics, leather, hair, etc. 2 the resultant colour: *a villain of the deepest dye* (= of the worst kind).
— *v.* **dyes, dyed, dye·ing** to colour or be coloured in this way: *She dyed her hair brown.* — **dy·er** *n.*

dyed-in-the-wool (dyed·in·thuh·WOOL) *adj.* firm or devoted: *a dyed-in-the-wool conservative, socialist; a dyed-in-the-wool establishment attitude.*

dying See DIE.

dy·nam·ic (dye·NAM·ic) *adj.* having to do with motion; not static: *the dynamic balancing of a wheel while it is rotating; potential and dynamic energy; a dynamic* (= functional), *not organic disease; "Crescendo," "forte," "piano," etc. are dynamic terms used in dynamic marking of sheet music for loudness and* softness; **Dynamic RAM** *(computer memory) keeps data one bit at a time at an address and for only a fraction of a second unlike static RAM; a dynamic period of history; a dynamic* (= energetic) *personality; a dynamic* (= active) *sales campaign.*
— *n.* 1 a force that produces change or action in society: *the inner dynamic that drives the young social reformer.* 2 **dynamics** *n. pl.* [with sing. v.] the physical study of motion and the forces producing it: *Dynamics is a branch of mechanics; the dynamics of social reform; population dynamics; The group dynamics of people working together is studied in sociology.*
— *combining form:* aerodynamics, hydrodynamics, thermodynamics.

dy·na·mism (DYE·nuh·miz·um) *n.* 1 action or power arising from energy: *the dynamism of her personality.* 2 the theory that whatever happens is the result of forces acting on mind and matter.

dy·na·mite (DYE·nuh·mite) *n.* 1 an industrial blasting explosive: *a stick of dynamite.* 2 *Informal.* a person or thing having great energy and appeal: *The singer was hailed by her fans as dynamite; Our new sports car is 1 000 kg of pure dynamite; a vacuum-cleaner that is just dynamite for homes and offices.*
— *v.* **-mites, -mited, -mit·ing** blow up with dynamite: *The terrorists dynamited the bridge.* — **dy·na·mit·er** *n.*

dy·na·mo (DYE·nuh·moh) *n.* **-mos** 1 an electrical generator. 2 a forceful and energetic person: *a dancing dynamo; stage dynamos; a heart-throbbing dynamo of a singer.*

dy·nas·ty (DYE·nuh·stee, DIN·uh-) *n.* **-ties** a series of rulers or powerful leaders of one family; also, their rule: *The Great Wall was built during the Ch'in dynasty which collapsed in 206 B.C.; A dynasty is established, founded, overthrown.* — **dy·nas·tic** (dye·NAS·tic) *adj.*

dys·en·ter·y (DIS·un·tair·ee) *n.* **-ter·ies** an infection of the large intestine marked by painful, often bloody diarrhea.

dys·func·tion (DIS·funk·shun) *n.* an impairment of normal functioning.

dys·lex·i·a (dis·LEX·ee·uh) *n.* abnormal difficulty in reading, often caused by brain damage.
— **dys·lex·ic** *n. & adj.*

dys·pep·si·a (dis·PEP·see·uh) *n.* disturbed or difficult digestion; indigestion. — **dys·pep·tic** *n. & adj.*

dys·tro·phy (DIS·truh·fee) *n.* **-phies** 1 a disorder characterized by neural or muscular degeneration: *muscular dystrophy.* 2 faulty nutrition.

E or **e** (EE) *n.* **E's** or **e's** the fifth letter of the English alphabet; hence, the fifth in a series.

each (EECH) *pron.* every one of two or more taken separately: *He spoke to each of them; to each of the children; to each and every one of them;* [with pl. v.] *Lou and Pat each have a house; They each have their* (*Informal for* his or her) *house; Each of the houses is* or *are for sale; They looked at each other* and their broker; *They all looked at each other* or *one another.* — *adj.*: *a gift for each child.* — *adv.* to or for each: *The tickets cost $50 each.*

ea·ger (EE·gur) *adj.* full of desire; keenly wanting: *a sales clerk eager to please customers; He is eager for appreciation; Rani is an eager beaver* (= diligent person) *who never rests.* — **ea·ger·ly** *adv.;* **ea·ger·ness** *n.*

ea·gle (EE·gul) *n.* **1** a large, powerful bird of prey having keen vision: *the bald eagle of the North; golden eagle; An eagle soars; the scream of an eagle; The eagle-eyed* (= sharp-eyed) *forest ranger spotted smoke in the distance.* **2** in golf, a score of two under par on a hole.

ea·glet (EEG·lit) *n.* a young eagle.

ear (EER) *n.* **1** the organ of hearing, esp. its visible, outer part; hence, the sense of hearing: *The hearing organ consists of the inner ear, middle ear, and outer ear (including the "ear canal"); He has a good ear for music; Dissonant voices grate on our ears; She had her ears pierced for earrings; He can wiggle his ears; Some animals perk or prick up their ears when listening; Our ears perked up* or *pricked up* (= We became attentive) *as Joe went up to the mike to announce the winner; You have my ear* (= attention); *Tell me, I'm all ears* (= listening); *Friends and comrades, lend me your ears* (= pay attention)! *The boy genius set the computer world on its ear* (*Informal for* caused a revolution in the computer world); *I can play that song by ear* (= without written music); *I forgot my lines, so I played it by ear* (= improvised); *Dad turned a deaf ear* (= refused to listen) *to his pleas for more money; His pleas fell on deaf ears; He's up to his ears* (= deeply) *in debt.* **2** the grain-bearing spike of a cereal such as corn or wheat.

ear·drop *n.* a hanging ornament for the ear; also, an earring.

ear·drum *n.* a vibrating membrane between the outer ear and middle ear.

eared *adj. & combining form.* having an ear or specified kind of ear: *The sea lion is an eared seal; a dog-eared book; golden-eared wheat; a sharp-eared listener.*

ear·ful (EER·ful) *n.* something startling or unpleasant: *She got an earful from her parents for being late.*

earl (URL) *n.* a British peer ranking below a marquis but above a viscount. — **earl·dom** *n.*

ear·ly (UR·lee) **-li·er, -li·est 1** *adj. & adv.* near the beginning of a period; before (in time); not late; soon: *I go to bed early and rise early; Trees are in bud in early spring; "The early bird catches the worm"* (= gets the prize); *Please reply at your earliest convenience.* **2** *adj.* of a historical period or epoch: *Early* (= prehistoric) *man chipped tools from stone; Early American* (= Colonial) *furniture; Early English (1200 – 1300); Early Victorian* (= of the earlier part of Queen Victoria's reign). — **early on** at or during an early stage *in* a period or activity.

ear·mark *n.* a mark to identify, designate, etc.: *a book that has all the earmarks* (= characteristics) *of sound scholarship.* — *v.*: *funds earmarked* (= set aside) *for charity, emergencies.*

ear·muffs *n. pl.* coverings for the ears against cold, noise, etc.

earn (URN) *v.* deserve or gain as reward, wages, profit, etc.: *to earn a living; Savings deposits earn interest; You get two or more weeks of earned vacation in a year; His community work earned him gratitude; It earned respect and admiration for him.* — **earn·er** *n.*

ear·nest (UR·nist) *adj.* serious and eager: *an earnest attempt to succeed; an earnest appeal, effort, worker.* — **in earnest** serious: *Surely, you can't be in earnest! I am in earnest about getting a degree; But he began studying in earnest* (= seriously) *only on the eve of the exam.* — *n.* a pledge or surety: *His first poem was an earnest of greater works to come; earnest money (paid as surety).* — **ear·nest·ly** *adv.;* **ear·nest·ness** *n.*

earnings *n. pl.* money that one earns: *his annual earnings; the average earnings of a postal worker; your net earnings after deducting expenses from gross earnings.*

ear·ring *n.* a ring, stud, etc. worn as an ear ornament.

ear·shot *n.* hearing range: *She was out of earshot when he called for help; Try to stay within earshot in case I need you.*

ear·split·ting (EER·split·ing) *adj.* painfully loud or high-pitched.

earth (URTH, "TH" as in "thin") *n.* **1** often **Earth,** the planet we live on: *The Earth rotates on its axis and revolves around the Sun; The Moon circles* or *orbits the Earth once in about 30 days.* **2** the world and its inhabitants: *All earth rejoiced at the news.* **3** dry land; ground; also, soil or dirt: *She is interested in everything that moves between the earth and the sky; the cultivation of the earth; a pot filled with earth.*
— **down to earth** sensible and realistic.
— **on earth** [as an intensive] **1** of all things: *How* (or *Where, When, Why,* etc.) *on earth did this happen?* **2** on this planet: *our life on earth; as if he were the last man on earth.*
— **run to earth** search and find someone or something.

earth·born *adj.* mortal.

earth·bound *adj.* **1** tied to earthly things. **2** worldly; unimaginative.

earth·en (URTH·un) *adj.* of earth or baked clay: *an earthen dam, floor, jar, jug, pot, tile.*

earth·en·ware (UR·thun·ware) *n.* pottery made of coarse porous clay.

earth·ly *adj.* **-li·er, -li·est 1** of the earth; also, worldly or temporal: *our earthly existence.* **2** [used negatively] possible: *no earthly chance; no earthly hope; Any earthly need for an umbrella today? What earthly use is that piece of junk?* — **earth·li·ness** *n.*

earth·mov·er (URTH·moo·vur) *n.* a bulldozer.

earth·quake *n.* a shaking of the earth: *a devastating earthquake; A major earthquake measuring 8.1 on the Richter scale struck Mexico in 1985.*

earth·shak·ing (URTH·shay·king) *adj.* of profound significance: *an earthshaking discovery, event; a matter of earthshaking importance.*

earth station *n.* a dish-shaped antenna for receiving TV signals directly from orbiting satellites; dish.

earth·work *n.* piled up earth used for defence; embankment.

earth·worm *n.* a smooth, reddish-brown, segmented worm that burrows in moist soil.

earth·y *adj.* **earth·i·er, -i·est** of or like earth; hence, crude or vulgar: *earthy humour, wit.* — **earth·i·ness** *n.*

ease (EEZ) *n.* **1** comfort; relaxation: *a millionaire's life of ease; Stand at ease* (= with feet apart)! **2** naturalness; poise: *the reassuring ease of her manner.* **3** facility: *She passed the exam with ease.*
— **at ease** or **at one's ease** not feeling nervous or troubled.
— **ill at ease** nervous or troubled.
— **put someone at his** or **her ease** make someone feel at ease.
— **take one's ease** relax.
— *v.* **eas·es, eased, eas·ing 1** make less painful or difficult: *The windfall cheque eased his money troubles; He was given an injection to ease the pain.* **2** move effortlessly or slowly: *She eased the car into the parking space; He eased himself into the corner of the sofa; Unwanted employees are* **eased out** (= relieved) *of their jobs.*
— **ease up** or **off** relax: *Ease off a little on a holiday;* **Ease up on** (= Don't be so hard on) *the poor fellow.*
— **ease·ful** *adj.;* **ease·ful·ly** *adv.*

ea·sel (EE·zul) *n.* a frame or tripod to support an artist's canvas, a blackboard, etc.

ease·ment (EEZ·munt) *n.* in law, a limited right, as of passage, on land owned by another: *Your property deed may include an easement for a hydro right of way.*

eas·i·ly (EE·zul·ee) *adv.* in an easy way; without doubt: *She won easily; She is easily the winner.* — **eas·i·ness** *n.*

east (EEST) *n.* where the sun rises; the direction opposite west: *Montreal is east of Toronto.*
— **the East 1** the eastern part of the world, of a country, region, town, etc., esp. the countries in Asia: *the three wise men from the East; the Far East; the Middle East; the Near East; the East trying to meet the West.* **2** the Soviet Union and allied nations of Eastern Europe: *the thawing of relations between the East and the West.*
— **back east** or **down east** in or to the eastern part of the country, esp. the Atlantic Provinces, Quebec, or Ontario, as viewed from the West.
— *adj.* & *adv.*: *the East Indies* (= Southeast Asia); *an east wind* (from the east); *A ship sailing east* (= to the east) *is* **east·bound**.

East Asian *n.* & *adj.* (a person) of or from the region comprising eastern China, Japan, North and South Korea, Taiwan, and nearby islands.

East·er (EES·tur) *n.* a Christian spring festival commemorating Christ's resurrection.

east·er·ly (EES·tur·lee) *adj.* & *adv.* **1** toward the east: *Cape Spear, Newfoundland, is Canada's most easterly point.* **2** from the east: *an easterly wind.*
— *n., pl.* **-lies** an easterly wind.

east·ern or **East·ern** (EES·turn) *adj.* of, to, or from the east: *the Eastern Hemisphere; the Eastern Orthodox churches; the eastern red cedar; the Eastern Shore of Nova Scotia; Eastern Standard Time used in Eastern Canada and U.S.; the Eastern Townships of Quebec.*
— **east·ern·er** or **East·ern·er** *n.*

East Indian *n.* & *adj.* (a person) of or from the Indian subcontinent.

east·ward (EEST·wurd) *n., adj.* & *adv.* (to) the east: *an eastward journey, movement, tendency; to fly, sail, spread eastward; The ship sailed eastward across the Atlantic.* Also **east·wards** *adv.*

eas·y (EE·zee) *adj.* **eas·i·er, -i·est** involving little effort; without constraints; not hard; smooth: *as easy as ABC; as easy as (apple) pie; an easy book (that is easy to read); It's not easy getting a book published; It's easy for you to say that; an easy lesson, life, mind, pace, victory; to get a loan on easy terms; to repay a loan in easy instalments; easy money (obtained improperly); to complete a journey by easy stages* (= a short distance at a time); *Pat's affable, easy manners; He's an easy touch* (= easy to get money out of); *a woman of easy virtue* (= of poor morals); *adv.*: *It's easier said than done.*
— **easy come, easy go** easy to get and to spend: *With*

money, it was always easy come, easy go for him.
— **easy does it** do it in a relaxed manner.
— **go easy** use moderation: *Go easy on that cake, Billy.*
— **on easy street** *Informal.* without financial worries.
— **take it easy** or **take things easy** relax.

eas·y·go·ing (ee·zee·GO·ing) *adj.* having a relaxed attitude.

easy mark *n. Informal.* one easy to impose upon.

eat (EET) *v.* **eats, ate, eat·en, eat·ing** take in with the mouth and swallow: *something to eat; We eat to live; to eat a meal; to eat out (at a restaurant); to eat greedily, heartily, voraciously; Rust eats away* (= corrodes) *metal; The sea eats away at* (= takes away bit by bit; erodes) *our shores; Acids eat into* (= damage) *metal; Moths eat* (= make) *holes in cloth; What's eating (Informal for bothering) you? Inflation eats up* (= consumes) *whatever profit we make; He had to eat* (= take back) **his words** *when she proved him wrong.*
— **eat one's heart out** be jealous; also, be bitterly sorry.
— **eat out of one's hand** be submissive to another; obey eagerly.
— *n.* esp. **eats** *pl. Slang.* food. — **eat·er** *n.*

eat·a·ble (EE·tuh·bul) *n. & adj.* (something) that is fit to eat: *These bananas are a bit too ripe to be eatable; Any eatables in that basket?*

eat·er·y (EE·tur·ee) *n.* **-ries** *Informal.* restaurant.

eaves (EEVZ) *n. pl.* the lower edges of a roof projecting beyond the walls of the house.

eaves·drop *v.* **-drops, -dropped, -drop·ping** listen secretly: *Lou was caught eavesdropping on their conversation; electronic eavesdropping by the secret police.* — **eaves·drop·per** *n.*

ebb *n.* the flowing back of the tide; hence, a decline: *the ebb and flow of fortune; The fortunes of the party are at a low ebb these days.*
— *v.: Life seemed to ebb away fast as he neared his end.*

eb·on·y (EB·uh·nee) *n.* **-on·ies** the hard, dark wood of a tropical tree. — *adj.: an ebony statue; a child with lovely ebony* (= black) *hair.*

e·bul·lience (i·BUL·yunce) *n.* a being ebullient; exuberance.

e·bul·lient (i·BUL·yunt) *adj.* bubbling, as with excitement or enthusiasm: *an ebullient optimism, personality, spirit, style; in an ebullient mood; She was her usual ebullient self.*

e·bul·li·tion (eb·uh·LISH·un) *n.* outburst: *an ebullition of joy.*

ec·cen·tric (ek·SEN·tric) *adj.* **1** odd or peculiar: *his eccentric behaviour; He's eccentric in his habits; It's eccentric to wear a mismatched pair of socks; n.* an eccentric person. **2** not concentric; off centre: *Pluto moves in an eccentric orbit around the sun; an eccentric wheel for up-and-down movement.*
— **ec·cen·tric·i·ty** (ek·sen·TRIS·uh·tee) *n.* **-ties.**

ec·cle·si·as·tic (i·KLEE·zee·AS·tic) *n.* a clergyman.
— **ec·cle·si·as·ti·cal** (-tuh·cul) *adj.* having to do with the church as an institution: *ecclesiastical affairs, authority, calendar, controversy, history, power, provinces,*

superiors.

ech·e·lon (ESH·uh·lon) *n.* a level of authority or responsibility: *Vice-presidents are in the higher echelons of a company; the upper echelons of society.*

ech·o (EK·oh) *n.* **-oes** a reflected or repeated sound, as heard around caves, in the mountains, etc.: *Some churches produce echoes; a radar echo.*
— *v.* **-oes, -oed, -o·ing 1** make an echo or reverberate: *His voice echoed across the valley.* **2** repeat: *a child echoing her mother's words.*

e·cho·ic (ek·OH·ic) *adj.* imitative in sound: *"Ding-dong" is echoic of a bell.*

é·clat (ay·CLAH) *n.* a splendid success that draws praise from everyone: *She performed the number with great éclat.*

ec·lec·tic (i·CLEC·tic) *adj.* drawing or drawn from various sources: *her eclectic taste in furniture.*
— *n.* a philosopher, artist, etc. who uses eclectic methods. — **ec·lec·ti·cism** *n.*

e·clipse (i·CLIPS) *n.* the darkening of the sun (solar eclipse) by the moon's shadow or of the moon (lunar eclipse) by the earth's shadow: *a total eclipse; a partial eclipse; He has been in eclipse* (= in darkness or hiding) *since his recent defeat at the polls.*
— *v.* **e·clips·es, e·clipsed, e·clips·ing** overshadow: *a movie star eclipsed by her more famous daughter.*

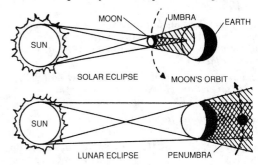

e·clip·tic (i·CLIP·tic) *n.* the sun's apparent annual path through the celestial sphere.

ec·logue (EC·log) *n.* a short pastoral poem.

e·co·cide (EE·cuh·cide, EC·uh-) *n.* environmental destruction, esp. by pollutants.

e·col·o·gy (ee·COL·uh·jee) *n.* **1** the study of the relationship between organisms and their environment; also, this relationship. **2** an environmental system: *the ecology of a lake; This dictionary describes the linguistic ecology of words in their grammatical and meaning relationships.* — **e·col·o·gist** (-jist) *n.*
— **e·co·log·i·cal** (ee·cuh·LOJ·uh·cul) *adj.*
— **e·co·log·i·cal·ly** *adv.*

e·co·nom·ic (ee·cuh·NOM·ic, ec·uh-) *adj.* **1** having to do with economics or economy: *the economic growth of a nation; the Canadian movement for economic nationalism; Some nations claim an economic zone beyond their coastal waters for fishing and other purposes.* **2** economical: *an economic measure to save money.*

e·co·nom·i·cal (ee·cuh·NOM·uh·cul, ec·uh-) *adj.* not wasteful of resources: *Spending money on a freezer is economical in the long run; It is economical to buy a freezer if you use food in large quantities.* — **e·co·nom·i·cal·ly** *adv.*

economics (ee·cuh·NOM·ics, ec·uh-) *n. pl.* [takes sing. v.] the science of the production, distribution, and consumption of goods and services.

e·con·o·mist (i·CON·uh·mist) *n.* a specialist in economics.

e·con·o·mize (i·CON·uh·mize) *v.* **-iz·es, -ized, -iz·ing** be economical. — **e·con·o·miz·er** *n.*

e·con·o·my (i·CON·uh·mee) *n.* **-mies 1** management and use of resources, esp. how a country's money supply, industry, and trade work: *the state of our economy; how the economy is run; political economy* (= economics); *to achieve* ***economies of scale*** (= benefits of large-scale production that lowers unit cost). **2** thrift or an instance of it: *We try to practise economy; They did it with great economy of effort and expense; the little economies that help us save money.* **3** a system of managing resources: *We live in a free-enterprise economy; a planned economy; A major strike could cripple a capitalist economy; a rural economy; the socialist economies of Eastern Europe.* — *adj.* designed to save money: *an economy car such as a subcompact; an economy-class airline ticket; an economy drive or measure to cut costs; a package in economy size.*

e·co·sys·tem (EE·coh·sis·tum, EC·uh-) *n.* the system of harmonious relationships between living and nonliving things of nature and their environment: *the ecosystem of a forest or lake.*

ec·sta·sy (EC·stuh·see) *n.* **-sies** rapture, esp. of delight: *pure, sheer ecstasy; He was in ecstasy over his wedding.* — **ec·stat·ic** (ic·STAT·ic) *adj.*

-ectomy *combining form.* surgical removal: *appendectomy, hysterectomy, vasectomy.*

ec·u·men·i·cal (ek·yoo·MEN·uh·cul) *adj.* having to do with the Christian church as a whole; promoting church unity. — **ec·u·men·i·cal·ly** *adv.*

ec·u·men·ism (EK·yuh·muh·niz·um) *n.* the movement for church unity.

ec·ze·ma (eg·ZEE·muh, EC·suh·muh) *n.* a skin inflammation with redness, itching, and lesions.

ed·dy (ED·ee) *n.* **ed·dies** a circular current of water, wind, fog, dust, etc. — *v.* **ed·dies, ed·died, ed·dy·ing** to whirl: *Convention crowds eddied about in the hotel lobby.*

E·den (EE·dun) *n.* in the Bible, the garden where Adam and Eve first lived; hence, a paradise.

edge (EJ) *n.* **1** the cutting side of a blade: *the cutting edge; the leading* (= front) *edge and trailing* (= back) *edge of an airplane's wing; Our company is* ***on the cutting*** *or* ***leading edge*** *of* (= is a leader in) *computer technology; Oil producing nations* ***have an edge on*** (= advantage over) *the world market; That cookie* ***took the edge off*** (= dulled) *my appetite.* **2** a border or brink; boundary: *to trim the edges of a lawn; at the water's edge; to stand at the edge of a precipice and look down.* — **on edge** edgy or nervous.

— *v.* **edg·es, edged, edg·ing 1** form a border or trimming on. **2** move gradually, as to get in or put someone out of a place: *The Grits edged out the Tories with just a handful of votes.* — **edg·er** *n.*

edge·ways or **edge·wise** *adv.* with the edge forward; sideways.

edg·y (EJ·ee) *adj.* **edg·i·er, -i·est** tense or anxious: *He's a bit edgy about what might happen.* — **edg·i·ness** *n.*

ed·i·ble (ED·uh·bul) *adj.* fit to eat; eatable: *an edible variety of mushroom.* — *n.* usually **edibles** *pl.* food. — **ed·i·bil·i·ty** (-BIL·uh·tee) *n.*

e·dict (EE·dict) *n.* an order of the highest authority; decree.

ed·i·fice (ED·uh·fis) *n.* an imposing building.

ed·i·fy (ED·uh·fye) *v.* **-fies, -fied, -fy·ing** improve morally; uplift: *A teacher's conduct is supposed to edify the students; an edifying example.* — **ed·i·fi·ca·tion** (-fuh·CAY·shun) *n.;* **ed·i·fi·er** (-fye·ur) *n.*

ed·it (ED·it) *v.* prepare a manuscript, newspaper, film, tape, etc. for publication or presentation.

e·di·tion (i·DISH·un) *n.* **1** the form in which a book, newspaper, or radio or TV program is presented to the public: *to bring out a new edition of Shakespeare; an abridged, annotated, critical, paperback, revised edition; the evening edition of the news; the city edition of a daily; a morning edition.* **2** the copies of a publication printed at one time: *The first edition of her book was sold out in a few weeks.* **3** a form in which something is presented or appears: *a specially equipped limited edition of 200 cars of a particular model; She is a younger edition of her mother; One edition in gold and 10 in silver of the Canadian Olympic coins were issued in 1988.*

ed·i·tor (ED·uh·tur) *n.* **1** one who edits: *a newspaper's city editor; a copy editor; a technical editor.* **2** a viewing device for editing film or videotape. — **ed·i·tor·ship** *n.*

ed·i·to·ri·al (ed·uh·TOR·ee·ul) *adj.* having to do with an editor, editors, or opinions: *an editorial article, opinion, page; our editorial director.* — *n.* an article containing an editor's opinion.

ed·i·to·ri·al·ize (ed·uh·TOR·ee·uh·lize) *v.* **-iz·es, -ized, -iz·ing** express opinions, esp. inappropriately: *It's not considered professional to editorialize in the news columns; Just give us the facts without editorializing.*

Ed·sel (ED·sul) *n.* a flop or failure, like an automobile of that name produced by Ford from 1958 to 1960.

ed·u·ca·ble (EJ·oo·cuh·bul) *adj.* capable of being educated or trained: *special classes for educable mentally handicapped children.* — **ed·u·ca·bil·i·ty** (-BIL·uh·tee) *n.*

ed·u·cate (EJ·oo·cate) *v.* **-cates, -cat·ed, -cat·ing** instruct in order to develop knowledge or skills; send to school or pay for someone's schooling: *Parents educate their children; to educate the public not to waste food; She was educated* (= went to school) *in Europe; educated at Cambridge; a highly* ***educated*** *writer; An* ***educated guess*** (based on some knowledge of the facts) *is likely to be right.* — **ed·u·ca·tor** (-cay·tur) *n.*

ed·u·ca·tion (ej·uh·CAY·shun) *n.* 1 schooling; also, mental development: *The state provides free and compulsory education up to age 16; adult, college, continuing, high school, in-service, liberal, physical, remedial, sex, university, vocational education; a good general education; higher educations and incomes.* 2 teaching; also, the study of teaching methods, principles, etc.: *boards of education; A faculty of education trains teachers.*

ed·u·ca·tion·al (ej·uh·CAY·shuh·nul) *adj.* 1 having to do with education: *an educational association, book, degree, film, foundation, influence; educational materials, psychology, resources, standards, systems, television, theories.* 2 helping to improve the mind; instructive: *an educational experience.*
— **ed·u·ca·tion·al·ly** *adv.*

ed·u·ca·tive (EJ·uh·cay·tiv) *adj.* helping to improve the mind; instructive: *an educative experience, force; the educative value of field trips.*

eel *n.* a snakelike fish: *slippery as an eel; Anglers bob for eels* (= fish for eels using a bundle of worms).

e'er (AIR) *adv.* Poetical. ever.

ee·rie or **ee·ry** (EER·ee) *adj.* -ri·er, -ri·est weird or mysterious in a frightening manner: *eerie shadows dancing on a wall; an eerie cry from the swamp; an eerie atmosphere.* — **ee·ri·ly** *adv.*

ef·face (i·FACE) *v.* ef·fac·es, ef·faced, ef·fac·ing remove or blot out something as if by rubbing away.

ef·fect (i·FECT) *n.* 1 what is produced by a cause: *The drug had some effect on him; It took effect immediately; He felt the effects of the drug; an adverse, beneficial, dramatic, exhilarating, far-reaching, harmful, hypnotic, marginal, profound, salutary, side effect; An effect wears off; Sometimes you sleep off the ill effects of a drug; All his counselling was to no effect.* 2 power to produce a result: *Advice has no effect on him; a former custom that is no more in effect* (= operation); *It has in effect* (= in practice) *fallen into disuse; a proclamation to give effect to a new law.* 3 a resulting impression: *He raises his voice merely for effect; Special sound effects are used in movies; a science-fiction movie with fancy special effects.* 4 meaning or intent: *You can start on Monday and I'll give you a letter to that effect.* 5 effects *pl.* goods: *personal effects such as clothing and jewellery; household effects.*
— *v.* bring about; realize: *The treaty effected a settlement; The medicine will effect a cure;* **ef·fect·er** *n.*

ef·fec·tive (i·FEC·tiv) *adj.* 1 producing the desired effect: *Antibiotics are effective against bacteria; The steps we are taking will be effective; effective measures; They will be effective in controlling crime; a forceful and effective speaker; The new timetable will be effective* (= in effect or operative) *as of Monday.* 2 actual: *the effective strength of an army after allowing for the sick and wounded; the effective membership of our organization after all the resignations.*
— **ef·fec·tive·ly** *adv.;* **ef·fec·tive·ness** *n.*

ef·fec·tor (i·FEC·tur) *n.* a muscle, gland, etc. that can respond to a nerve impulse.

ef·fec·tu·al (i·FEC·choo·ul) *adj.* adequate to achieve a desired effect: *an effectual demand that brought a prompt response; The steps we took proved to be effectual; an effectual measure, punishment, remedy.*
— **ef·fec·tu·al·ly** *adv.*

ef·fec·tu·ate (i·FEC·choo·ate) *v.* -ates, -at·ed, -at·ing make effectual; put into effect: *to effectuate a settlement.*

ef·fem·i·nate (i·FEM·uh·nit) *adj.* womanish; soft or delicate. — **ef·fem·i·na·cy** (-uh·see) *n.*

ef·fer·vesce (ef·ur·VES) *v.* -vesc·es, -vesced, -vesc·ing 1 of liquids, bubble and hiss as gas is let off. 2 be ebullient or excited.
— **ef·fer·ves·cence** *n.;* **ef·fer·ves·cent** *adj.*

ef·fete (i·FEET) *adj.* worn out or decadent: *the effete aristocracy, Athenians; an effete civilization.*

ef·fi·ca·cious (ef·uh·CAY·shus) *adj.* esp. of medicines, sure to have the desired effect: *an efficacious remedy.*

ef·fi·ca·cy (EF·uh·cuh·see) *n.* the quality of being efficacious: *a drug of proven efficacy; the efficacy of a cure.*

ef·fi·cien·cy (i·FISH·un·see) *n.* the quality of being efficient: *A machine operates at peak or maximum efficiency when the energy put into it is the same as the work produced; degrees of efficiency; The less the friction, the higher the efficiency of a machine; conditions that impair, lower, reduce efficiency; adj.:* An **efficiency apartment** *usually consists of a room and kitchenette;* An **efficiency expert** *aims to make a business or system more efficient.*

ef·fi·cient (i·FISH·unt) *adj.* producing the desired result with the least waste of resources; capable: *an efficient executive, method, worker; a manager who is efficient in the use of resources; the efficient action of heat in raising temperature; Heat is the efficient cause of many chemical changes; Gas is more efficient than oil for home heating.* — **ef·fi·cient·ly** *adv.*

ef·fi·gy (EF·uh·jee) *n.* -gies a portrait or other representation of a notable person: *the effigy of the Queen on Canadian coins; a sculptured effigy on a tomb, coin, etc.; the effigies* (= statues) *in Madam Tussaud's Wax Museum; The dictator was burned in effigy* (= in a crude representation).

ef·flu·ence (EF·loo·unce) *n.* an outflow; emanation.

ef·flu·ent (EF·loo·unt) *adj.* flowing out, as a stream from a lake or reservoir.
— *n.* chemically treated sewage or factory waste.

ef·fort (EF·urt) *n.* energy required to do something; hence, a strong attempt or its result: *Power steering takes little effort; His efforts were greatly appreciated; He spared no effort to make a success of the project; He made an all-out, conscious, desperate, frantic, gallant, heroic effort to succeed; He put forth a valiant effort to achieve his goal; He redoubled his efforts toward the end.*

ef·fron·ter·y (i·FRUN·tuh·ree) *n.* -ter·ies boldness in defying norms of courtesy or propriety; impudence: *the effrontery to ask for a 25% raise when others are getting only 5%.*

ef·ful·gence (i·FUL·junce) *n.* splendour or brilliance.
— **ef·ful·gent** (-junt) *adj.*

ef·fu·sive (i·FEW·siv) *adj.* marked by a pouring out, esp. of feelings: *an effusive* (= *gushing*) *speech, welcome; an effusive volcanic eruption; Effusive rocks are formed of solidified lava.* — **ef·fu·sive·ly** *adv.;* **ef·fu·sive·ness** *n.*

e·gad (i·GAD) *interj.* a mild oath: *Egad! He actually gave to charity.*

e·gal·i·tar·i·an (i·GAL·uh·TAIR·ee·un) *n. & adj.* (one) supporting equality for all. — **e·gal·i·tar·i·an·ism** *n.*

egg *n.* **1** the oval or round body laid by birds, reptiles, fishes, etc. that hatches into a living young: *Hens lay and hatch eggs; We beat, boil, fry, poach eggs; devilled, fried, hard-boiled, scrambled, soft-boiled eggs.* **2** an egg cell. **3** *Slang.* a person: *She's a good egg; bad egg; rotten egg.*
— **egg on one's face** *Informal.* embarrassment from having blundered.
— *v.* **egg someone on** incite or urge: *His companions egged him on to enter the race.*

egg·beat·er (EG·bee·tur) *n.* **1** a rotary device for beating eggs. **2** *Slang.* helicopter.

egg·head *n. Slang.* [derogatory] an intellectual.

e·gis (EE·jis) *n.* same as AEGIS.

e·go (EE·goh, EG·oh) *n.* **e·gos** **1** the thinking, feeling, and acting being as perceived by oneself: *one's alter ego* (= another self). **2** self-esteem: *Everyone tries to feed or flatter his ego; Being ignored hurt his ego; He had an inflated ego.*

e·go·cen·tric (ee·goh·SEN·tric, eg·oh-) *n. & adj.* (one) who is self-centred.

e·go·ism (EE·goh·iz·um, EG·oh-) *n.* self-centredness or conceit; opposed to ALTRUISM. — **e·go·ist** (-ist) *n.*
— **e·go·is·tic** (-IS·tic) or **e·go·is·ti·cal** (-tuh·cul) *adj.*

e·go·tism (EE·guh·tiz·um, EG·uh-) *n.* a more overt and annoying kind of egoism, expressed in speech and behaviour. — **e·go·tist** *n.*
— **e·go·tis·tic** (ee·guh·TIS·tic, eg·uh-) or **e·go·tis·ti·cal** (-tuh·cul) *adj.*

ego trip *n.* a self-centred or self-realizing activity.
— **ego-trip** *v.* **-trips, -tripped, -trip·ping.**
— **e·go·trip·per** (EE·goh·trip·ur, EG·oh-) *n.*

e·gre·gious (i·GREE·jus) *adj.* outstandingly bad: *an egregious blunder, error, waste; an egregious example of wasteful spending.*
— **e·gre·gious·ly** *adv.;* **e·gre·gious·ness** *n.*

eh (AY) *interj.* [used at the end of an utterance in a doubtful or questioning way]: *from Canada, eh?*

eight (ATE) *n., adj. & pron.* one more than seven; the number 8 or VIII: *There are eight of them; eight girls; That's an eight (card).*

eight ball *n.* in pool, a black ball numbered 8.
— **behind the eight ball** *Slang.* in a hazardous position.

eighth (AITTH) *n.* **1** the next after the seventh. **2** one of eight equal parts, as of an octave.
— *adj.:* *the eighth part of the series; an eighth part.*

eight·y (AY·tee) *n., adj. & pron.* **1** ten times eight; 80 or LXXX. **2** **the eighties** the numbers, years, etc. from 80 through 89. — **eight·i·eth** (-ith) *n. & adj.*

ei·ther (EE·thur, EYE-, "th" as in "the") *pron.* (the) one or the other: *Either of the twins can wear this; adj.: Sit on either stool; He can write with either hand* (= both hands); *conj.: Say either yes or no; Have either a candy bar, a yogurt, or an ice cream.*
— *adv.* also: *If you don't go, I won't either.*

e·jac·u·late (i·JAK·yuh·late) *v.* **-lates, -lat·ed, -lat·ing** discharge, esp. semen.
— **e·jac·u·la·tion** (-yuh·LAY·shun) *n.*

e·ject (i·JECT) *v.* throw out: *The rowdies were ejected from the room.*
— **e·jec·tion** (i·JEC·shun) *n: The pilot bailed out of the disabled aircraft in his **ejection seat.***

eke (EEK) *v.* **ekes, eked, ek·ing** add to something; supplement: *He had to take two jobs to **eke out** a living.*

e·lab·o·rate (i·LAB·uh·rit) *adj.* **1** worked out in great detail: *an elaborate plan, plot; elaborate excuses, precautions, preparations.* **2** ornate: *elaborate decorations; an elaborate design, pattern.*
— *v.* (-rate) **-ates, -at·ed, -at·ing** add more detail to something: *He hinted at the rumour but would not elaborate (on it).*
— **e·lab·o·rate·ly** *adv.;* **e·lab·o·rate·ness** *n.*
— **e·lab·o·ra·tion** (-RAY·shun) *n.*

e·lan (ay·LAHN) *n.* spirit or enthusiasm; dash or verve: *She joined the activities with great elan.*

e·lapse (i·LAPS) *v.* **e·laps·es, e·lapsed, e·laps·ing** of time, to pass; go by: *Many years elapsed before their first child was born.*

e·las·tic (i·LAS·tic) *adj.* **1** rubberlike or stretchable: *an elastic band, belt, tape; Knead the dough until it is smooth and elastic; the clown's elastic face.* **2** capable of returning to its original shape or form: *A steel spring is elastic; the elastic temperament of one who is never let down; her elastic optimism.*
— *n.* a fabric interwoven with rubber strands; also, a garter or band made of this.

e·las·tic·i·ty (ee·las·TIS·uh·tee) *n.* the quality of being elastic: *All substances have some elasticity; Rubber has great elasticity; Words in common use have much elasticity of meaning.*

e·las·ti·cize (i·LAS·tuh·size) *v.* **-ciz·es, -cized, -ciz·ing** make elastic: *an elasticized waistband.*

e·late (i·LATE) *v.* **e·lates, e·lat·ed, e·lat·ing** fill with high spirits, as by joy, pride, etc.: *Everyone was elated at or over the victory.* — **e·la·tion** (i·LAY·shun) *n.*

el·bow (EL·boh) *n.* the outer part of the joint between the upper and lower arm, esp. bent, as when jostling, working, etc.; also, this shape; *adj.: an elbow pipe joint; elbow macaroni.*
— **at one's elbow** close by.
— **out at (the) elbows** in worn-out clothes; hence, poverty-stricken.
— *v.* use the elbow to do something: *He elbowed everyone out of his way; He elbowed (his way) through the crowd; In hockey and box lacrosse, **elbowing** an opponent* (= hitting an opponent with the elbow) *results in a penalty.*

elbow grease *n. Informal.* hard work.

elbow room *n*. space to move in comfortably: *There was no elbow room in the packed train; The new recruit was given plenty of elbow room* (= freedom) *for trying out new ideas.*

El Chea·po or **el chea·po** (el·CHEE·poh) *n. Slang.* a person or thing that is cheap or shoddy: *He's an El Cheapo; an el cheapo vacation.*

eld·er (EL·dur) *adj.* older or senior: *your elder brother; an elder statesman.*
— *n.* a respected older member of a tribe, community, church, family, etc.: *Listen to your elders.*

el·der·ly (EL·dur·lee) *adj.* [respectful use] old: *homes for the elderly.*

el·dest (EL·dist) *adj.* oldest, esp. of surviving family members.

El Do·ra·do or **El·do·ra·do** (el·duh·RAH·doh) *n.* -dos a legendary place that is rich in gold.

e·lect (i·LECT) *v.* choose, esp. in a formal way, as by voting: *Eloi was unanimously elected mayor as Eve's successor; They elected him to succeed Eve; Yves elected* (= chose) *law rather than politics for a career.*
— *adj.* chosen: *the president elect (who has not yet assumed charge); the elect few.*
— **the elect** *n. pl.* a specially chosen group: *the elect of God (chosen for salvation).*

e·lec·tion (i·LEC·shun) *n.* the act or process of electing: *to carry, concede, decide, fix, hold, lose, swing, win an election; a close, free, rigged, runoff election.*

e·lec·tion·eer (i·LEC·shuh·NEER) *v.* work for the success of a candidate or party in an election.

e·lec·tive (i·LEC·tiv) *adj.* based on or having to do with an election: *the elective office of president; an elective government, official; elective* (= nonessential) *surgery.*
— *n.* an optional subject in a program of studies.

e·lec·tor (i·LEC·tur) *n.* one having the right to elect; voter. — **e·lec·tor·al** (-tuh·rul) *adj.*

electoral district *n. Cdn.* a constituency represented by a member of the House of Commons or of a provincial legislature.

e·lec·tor·ate (i·LEC·tuh·rit) *n.* people qualified to vote, collectively.

e·lec·tric (i·LEC·tric) *adj.* 1 also **e·lec·tri·cal**, having to do with electricity: *an electric battery; an electric guitar, light, organ; electric heating; an **electric broom*** (= vacuum cleaner); *the **electric eel*** (= an eel capable of giving electric shocks); *electrical activity, equipment, industries; an electrical circuit, discharge, engineer, storm, worker.* 2 exciting or thrilling: *The reaction of the audience was electric; The air was electric with excitement; an electric performance, personality; electric* (= very bright) *blue.* — **e·lec·tri·cal·ly** *adv.*

electric chair *n.* 1 (sentence of) death by electrocution: *a murderer sent to the electric chair.* 2 the chair used in this.

electric eye *n.* same as PHOTOELECTRIC CELL.

e·lec·tri·cian (i·lec·TRISH·un) *n.* one who installs, operates, or repairs electrical equipment.

e·lec·tric·i·ty (i·lec·TRIS·uh·tee) *n.* a form of energy generated by friction, induction, or chemical changes, and capable of producing heat, light, etc., as observed in natural phenomena such as lightning and in certain fishes and eels; also, electric current, esp. as a public utility.

e·lec·tri·fy (i·LEC·truh·fye) *v.* -fies, -fied, -fy·ing 1 charge with electricity; hence, excite or thrill: *The whole town was electrified by the news.* 2 provide or equip with electricity: *to electrify a rural area.*
— **e·lec·tri·fi·er** (-truh·fye·ur) *n.*
— **e·lec·tri·fi·ca·tion** (-truh·fuh·CAY·shun) *n.*

e·lec·tro·car·di·o·gram (i·LEC·truh·CAR·dee·uh·gram) *n.* a tracing made by an electrocardiograph.

e·lec·tro·car·di·o·graph (i·LEC·truh·CAR·dee·uh·graf) *n.* an instrument that detects and records the electrical impulses produced by heartbeats.

e·lec·tro·cute (i·LEC·truh·cute) *v.* -cutes, -cut·ed, -cut·ing kill by the action of electricity.
— **e·lec·tro·cu·tion** (-truh·CUE·shun) *n.*

e·lec·trode (i·LEC·trode) *n.* a conductor of outgoing or incoming current in an electrical circuit.

e·lec·tro·mag·net (i·LEC·truh·MAG·nit) *n.* a magnet that has a coil of wire around it through which a current is passed to magnetize it.
— **e·lec·tro·mag·net·ic** (-truh·mag·NET·ic) *adj.*: *Radio waves, light, X rays, gamma rays, etc. are forms of electromagnetic radiation produced when electric and magnetic fields act together.*
— **e·lec·tro·mag·net·ism** (-truh·MAG·nuh·tiz·um) *n.*

e·lec·tron (i·LEC·tron) *n.* any of the negatively charged particles in an atom.

e·lec·tron·ic (i·lec·TRON·ic) *adj.* having to do with electronics: *an electronic flash camera; TV and such electronic journalism; the **electronic cottage*** (= home as computer-linked workplace); ***electronic data processing*** *using computers; **electronic surveillance*** *by bugging, wiretaps, etc.* — **e·lec·tron·i·cal·ly** *adv.*

electronic funds transfer *n.* transfer of money from one account to another via computer communications, as by automatic teller machines and debit cards.

electronic mail *n.* transmission and distribution of messages by electronic means such as the telephone, facsimile, telex, videotext, and communicating word processors.

electronic music *n.* music composed of sounds produced with electronic devices, assembled on magnetic tape, and played through loudspeakers.

electronics *n. pl.* the science of the behaviour and control of electrons through vacuums, semiconductors, and gases for use in devices such as the electron tube, photoelectric cell, and transistor.

e·lec·tro·stat·ic (i·LEC·truh·STAT·ic) *adj.* having to do with static electricity: *Electrostatic printing, as xerography, reproduces originals without ink or pressure, using an electrically charged black powder.*

el·e·gance (EL·uh·gunce) *n.* the quality of being elegant; refinement or polish: *the elegance of the furnishings; sartorial elegance; sheer elegance; a taste for elegance; She writes with grace and elegance; the elegance of a mathematical equation.*

el·e·gant (EL·uh·gunt) *adj.* rich and luxurious but restrained in style; graceful, tasteful, or polished: *an elegant diction, dresser, restaurant, writer; an elegant young man with elegant manners; a charming and elegant lady; She leads a life of elegant ease.*
— **el·e·gant·ly** *adv.*

el·e·gi·ac (el·uh·JYE·ac, i·LEE·jee·ac) *adj.* in the form of an elegy; hence, sad or mournful.
— **el·e·gi·a·cal** (-JYE·uh·cul) *adj.*

el·e·gy (EL·uh·jee) *n.* **-gies** a melancholy poem, usually one mourning the dead, as Gray's "Elegy."

el·e·ment (EL·uh·munt) *n.* **1** something basic, esp. a basic or constituent part: *Fire, air, earth, and water were once considered the four basic elements of nature; All matter is composed of 100-odd (chemical) elements; an essential, vital element of the story; the human element* (=factor) *in the story; There is an element* (=particle) *of truth in what he says; the* **elements** (=rudiments) *of algebra; the French element* (=component) *in the English vocabulary; the Sea, Land, and Air elements* (=branches) *of the Canadian armed forces; criminal, extremist, subversive, undesirable elements* (=members) *of society; the heating element* (=unit) *of an electric kettle.* **2** the environment, esp. as made up of the forces of nature; hence, rough weather: *A storm-tossed vessel is at the mercy of the* **elements;** *Out of water, a fish is* **out of its element;** *She's* **in her element** (=doing what she likes best) *as a social worker.*

el·e·men·tal (el·uh·MEN·tul) *adj.* having to do with natural forces: *elemental gods representing the forces of nature; the elemental fury of a volcano in action; the elemental problem of survival; sex, hunger, and such elemental urges; an artist's elemental characters, music, themes.*

el·e·men·ta·ry (el·uh·MEN·tuh·ree) *adj.* basic or fundamental: *elementary arithmetic; That's elementary, my dear Watson; the electron, proton, and such supposedly indivisible* **elementary particles** *of matter; The first six (or sometimes eight) grades constitute* **elementary school.**

el·e·phant (EL·uh·funt) *n.* a huge mammal of Africa or Asia with a long snout, or trunk, and ivory tusks growing from either side of its upper jaw: *An elephant trumpets; a herd of elephants; a rogue elephant that has gone wild; the calf* (=young) *of an elephant; a cow* (=female) *elephant; a bull* (=male) *elephant.*

el·e·phan·tine (el·uh·FAN·tine, -teen) *adj.* of or like elephants; huge, clumsy, etc.

el·e·vate (EL·uh·vate) *v.* **-vates, -vat·ed, -vat·ing** **1** lift or raise, esp. to a higher rank, plane, or quality: *a commoner elevated to the peerage; An* **elevated railway** *is elevated on tracks above street level allowing other traffic to pass underneath.* **2** make better in mind or soul; elate or exhilarate: *an elevating religious experience; sagging spirits elevated by success.*

el·e·va·tion (el·uh·VAY·shun) *n.* **1** a raising: *the elevation of bishops to the cardinalate.* **2** height: *We were flying at an elevation of 20 000 m; You get a good view of the countryside from this elevation* (=hill); *at an elevation* (=angular distance) *of 30 degrees above the horizon.* **3** the exterior design of a building: *the front, rear, side elevation; a house model with a choice of three elevations.*

el·e·va·tor (EL·uh·vay·tur) *n.* **1** a cage or platform for travelling up and down in a building or mine: *There's a bank of elevators on the main floor; Take the up elevator to the top floor; adj.: an elevator lobby, operator, shaft.* **2** a tall structure in which grain is stored: *a prairie elevator.* **3** a movable horizontal flap on the tail section of an aircraft for making it go up and down.

e·lev·en (i·LEV·un) *n., adj. & pron.* one more than 10; the number 11 or XI: *There are eleven of them; eleven boys; a football eleven* (=team) . — **e·lev·enth** *n. & adj.*

eleventh hour *n.* just before it is too late: *The program was cancelled at the eleventh hour because of bad weather.*
— **eleventh-hour** *adj.: the eleventh-hour cramming for an exam; an eleventh-hour decision.*

elf *n.* **elves** (ELVZ) a mischievous little fairy.
— **elf·in** or **elf·ish** *adj.*

e·lic·it (i·LIS·it) *v.* draw out: *a question that didn't elicit a response from anyone.*
— **e·lic·i·ta·tion** (-uh·TAY·shun) *n.*

el·i·gi·ble (EL·uh·juh·bul) *adj.* qualified or fit to be chosen: *Citizens are eligible to vote; Eve is eligible for admission to a university; an eligible bachelor or woman (who will make a suitable spouse); an eligible voter; eligible income for refundable tax credit.*
— **n.** an eligible person: *a list of eligibles.*
— **el·i·gi·bil·i·ty** (-juh·BIL·uh·tee) *n.*

e·lim·i·nate (i·LIM·uh·nate) *v.* **-nates, -nat·ed, -nat·ing** get rid of from within: *Body wastes are eliminated; In a tournament, losers in the first rounds are eliminated until a single champion remains; to tighten a budget by eliminating unnecessary expenses.*
— **e·lim·i·na·tion** (-uh·NAY·shun) *n.: the elimination of poverty and hunger from the earth.*

e·li·sion (i·LIZH·un) *n.* an eliding: *Contractions result from elisions as in "didn't" and "they've."*

e·lite (i·LEET, ay·LEET) *n.* **1** [takes pl. v.] a group considered to be superior: *a private school for the elite; the elite of society; adj.: the creation of an elite force; a small elite group.* **2** a size of typewriter type that gives 12 characters to the linear inch.

e·lit·ism (i·LEE·tiz·um, ay·LEE-) *n.* rule by an elite.
— **e·lit·ist** *adj.* having to do with the elite: *Is racing an elitist sport? an elitist approach, attitude, image.*

e·lix·ir (i·LIK·sur) *n.* a fragrant alcoholic syrup containing medicine: *The alchemists sought the elixir of life, a mythical substance that would prolong life indefinitely.*

ell *n.* 1 something L-shaped, as a joint of tubing or an annex to a building. 2 a former measure of cloth length, equal to 45 in. (112 cm): *"Give him an inch he'll take an ell"* (= take too much).

el·lipse (i·LIPS) *n.* **el·lip·ses** (-siz) an oval-shaped symmetrical closed curve.

el·lip·tic or **el·lip·ti·cal** (i·LIP·tuh·cul) *adj.* 1 of or like an ellipse: *an elliptic arch; elliptical geometry.* 2 marked by ellipsis: *elliptical language.*
— **el·lip·ti·cal·ly** *adv.: The earth moves elliptically around the sun.*

el·o·cu·tion (el·uh·CUE·shun) *n.* the art of public speaking. — **el·o·cu·tion·ist** *n.*

e·lon·gate (i·LONG·gate) *v.* **-gates, -gat·ed, -gat·ing** make or become longer, esp. out of proportion: *Stretching upwards elongates your spine; an elongated figure.*
— *adj.* elongated: *an elongate leaf.*
— **e·lon·ga·tion** (ee·long·GAY·shun) *n.*

e·lope (i·LOPE) *v.* **e·lopes, e·loped, e·lop·ing** run away together to get married: *Jane eloped with Dick; They eloped.* — **e·lope·ment** *n.* — **e·lop·er** *n.*

el·o·quent (EL·uh·quent) *adj.* forceful or fluent in expression: *an eloquent speech; eloquent gestures.*
— **el·o·quent·ly** *adv.* — **el·o·quence** *n.*

else *adj.* [following modified pronoun] other: *Anyone else? someone else's book.*
— *adv.* 1 in a different manner; at a different place or time: *How else? Where else shall we go?* 2 otherwise: *Finish the job, (or) else you won't be paid; Finish it in time **or else,** he was warned.*

else·where *adv.* somewhere else.

e·lu·ci·date (i·LOO·suh·date) *v.* **-dates, -dat·ed, -dat·ing** make something clear by illustrating or explaining: *to elucidate a meaning, problem, text.*
— **e·lu·ci·da·tion** (-suh·DAY·shun) *n.*

e·lude (i·LOOD, long "OO") *v.* **e·ludes, e·lud·ed, e·lud·ing** escape mental or physical grasp by some cunning quality: *The answer to this riddle eludes me; He was arrested after eluding the police for two years.*
— **e·lud·er** *n.* — **e·lu·sion** (-zhun) *n.*

e·lu·sive (i·LOO·siv) *adj.* hard to get, catch, or grasp: *an elusive concept; She's elusive like a will-o'-the-wisp.*
— **e·lu·sive·ly** *adv.*; **e·lu·sive·ness** *n.*

elves *pl.* of ELF.

E·ly·si·an (i·LIZH·un) *adj.* having to do with Elysium, or **Elysian Fields,** the paradise of Greek myth.

'em [short form] them: *Let 'em go.*

e·ma·ci·ate (i·MAY·shee·ate, -see·ate) *v.* **-ates, -at·ed, -at·ing** make very thin or waste away, as by hunger or illness. — **e·ma·ci·a·tion** (-AY·shun) *n.*

em·a·nate (EM·uh·nate) *v.* **-nates, -nat·ed, -nat·ing** 1 originate, as from a source: *From where do these rumours emanate?* 2 emit: *the authority she emanates!*

— **em·a·na·tion** (-NAY·shun) *n.*

e·man·ci·pate (i·MAN·suh·pate) *v.* **-pates, -pat·ed, -pat·ing** to free from slavery or restraint.
— **e·man·ci·pa·tor** (-pay·tur) *n.*

e·man·ci·pa·tion (i·MAN·suh·PAY·shun) *n.* a freeing, as from slavery: *the emancipation of slaves from bondage; the emancipation of women; the emancipation of Irish Catholics in 1829.*

e·mas·cu·late (i·MAS·kyuh·late) *v.* **-lates, -lat·ed, -lat·ing** castrate; hence, weaken: *freedom of speech emasculated by censorship.*
— **e·mas·cu·la·tion** (-LAY·shun) *n.*

em·balm (im·BAHM, -BOM) *v.* 1 preserve a dead body from decay using spices, chemicals, etc.; hence, preserve. 2 perfume.

em·bank (im·BANK) *v.* protect or support with an embankment.

em·bank·ment (im·BANK·munt) *n.* a bank of earth, stone, etc. raised to hold back water or support a roadway: *the embankment along the river Thames in London.*

em·bar·go (im·BAR·go) *n.* **-goes** a temporary government order prohibiting commerce with a foreign country, esp. the movement of ships or goods: *to impose, place, put an embargo on arms shipments to South Africa; charged with shipping high tech items to Russia while under embargo; to lift or remove the economic embargo against trade with Cuba.*
— *v.* **-goes, -goed, -go·ing** prohibit or hold up: *Mail to Canada is embargoed in the U.S. during a postal strike; A press release embargoed till 6 p.m. may not be published before 6 p.m.*

em·bark (im·BARK) *v.* 1 put passengers or cargo on board ship, airplane, etc. 2 get on board: *She embarked for Europe from Halifax; He is embarking* (= setting out) *on a new career as an engineer.*
— **em·bar·ka·tion** (em·bar·KAY·shun) *n.*

em·bar·rass (im·BAIR·us) *v.* 1 make or become uneasy or nervous: *parents embarrassed by a child's behaviour; a sensitive child who embarrasses easily; She was embarrassed to find her name in the papers; embarrassed about or at or over the publicity she was subjected to; It is **embarrassing** that so many people arrived after the guest of honour.* 2 hinder ease of movement; burden: *students embarrassed by heavy workloads; pensioners much embarrassed for life's necessities in inflationary times.*
— **em·bar·rass·ment** *n.: His shoplifting became an embarrassment to his family; social embarrassments of the underprivileged (who cannot afford good clothes, cars, etc.); a wealthy man's embarrassment of riches* (= riches so excessive he doesn't know how to use them).

em·bas·sy (EM·buh·see) *n.* **-bas·sies** 1 a mission from one head of state to another. 2 an ambassador and his or her staff, the position of an ambassador, an ambassador's residence, or an ambassador's offices abroad: *You can find him at or in the embassy.*

em·bat·tled (em·BAT·uld) *adj.* engaged in battle: *an embattled city, presidency.*

em·bed (im·BED) *v.* -beds, -bed·ded, -bed·ding fix firmly; also, plant: *bricks embedded in mortar; The human embryo begins to develop embedded in the uterus wall.*

em·bel·lish (im·BEL·ish) *v.* decorate with added ornamentation; enhance: *a somewhat embellished truth, though not a falsehood.* — **em·bel·lish·ment** *n.*

em·ber (EM·bur) *n.* a glowing piece of wood or coal in the remains of a fire: *a dying, glowing ember; the last ember of hope; the glow of burning embers; live embers; to fan the embers into a fire; an ember pit.*

em·bez·zle (im·BEZ·ul) *v.* -bez·zles, -bez·zled, -bez·zling steal money, securities, etc. entrusted to one's care: *An assistant manager was charged with embezzling $2 million from the bank; He had embezzled this money over several years.* — **em·bez·zle·ment** *n.* — **em·bez·zler** *n.*

em·bla·zon (im·BLAY·zun) *v.* 1 decorate with a coat of arms or other insignia. 2 extol. — **em·bla·zon·ment** *n.*

em·blem (EM·blum) *n.* an object or design used to represent something characteristic of it: *The beaver and the maple leaf are both emblems of Canada; Each province has a floral emblem; the hammer-and-sickle emblem of Soviet communism.* — **em·blem·at·ic** (em·bluh·MAT·ic) *adj.*: *The cross is emblematic of Christianity and symbolic of suffering.*

em·bod·y (im·BOD·ee) *v.* -bod·ies, -bod·ied, -bod·y·ing 1 give form to an ideal, thought, feelings, etc.; personify: *Democratic ideals are embodied in our Constitution.* 2 incorporate: *The newer cars embody many gas-saving features.* — **em·bod·i·ment** *n.*: *Solomon was the embodiment of wisdom.*

em·bold·en (im·BOLE·dun) *v.* give someone the courage *to do something.*

em·boss (im·BOSS) *v.* 1 make a design, lettering, etc. stand out on a surface; 2 decorate in relief: *an embossed business card; embossed stationery.*

em·brace (im·BRACE) *v.* -brac·es, -braced, -brac·ing 1 clasp with the arms to show love or friendship; hug: *He embraced her; Father and son embraced.* 2 contain or include: *a program of education embracing the arts and sciences.* 3 accept or take up: *He left home to embrace the monastic life.* — *n.* hug: *a loving, tight, warm embrace; the passionate embraces of Romeo and Juliet.*

em·broi·der (im·BROY·dur) *v.* 1 embellish, esp. with embroidery. 2 exaggerate: *He embroidered the original story beyond recognition.*

em·broi·der·y (im·BROY·duh·ree) *n.* -der·ies 1 the ornamenting of fabrics with needlework; also, embroidered work. 2 an embellishment or exaggeration.

em·broil (im·BROIL) *v.* involve a person or country in trouble, esp. in a quarrel: *He found himself embroiled in controversy.* — **em·broil·ment** *n.*

em·bry·o (EM·bree·oh) *n.* -os a developing plant in its seed or such an animal in its egg or mother's womb, esp. during the first two months of pregnancy in humans: *The researchers inserted rat genes into mouse embryos; the marketing of frozen Holstein embryos; adj.: an embryo implant, transference, transplant; embryo*

research.
— **in embryo** in an undeveloped stage.
— **em·bry·on·ic** (-ON·ic) *adj.* developing.

em·cee (EM·see) *n. Informal.* [short form] master of ceremonies.
— *v.* -cees, -ceed, -cee·ing act as emcee: *Who is emceeing? a beauty pageant emceed by a TV star.*

em·er·ald (EM·ur·uld) *n.* a bright green precious stone or its colour; *adj.: emerald green; "The Emerald Isle"* (= Ireland).

e·merge (i·MURJ) *v.* e·merg·es, e·merged, e·merg·ing come forth, as if from hiding; come out into view: *Venus emerged from the sea; to emerge from the shadows into light; After the first round, she emerged as the leading contender for the championship; New viruses have emerged* (= evolved as new forms) *recently.*

e·mer·gen·cy (i·MUR·jun·see) *n.* -cies a situation arising suddenly that needs quick action, as a flood or heart attack: *In case of (an) emergency* or *In an emergency, don't panic; An emergency was declared in the area; a life-threatening, national, serious emergency; a state of emergency.*
— *adj.: Cars are equipped with an **emergency brake** or parking brake for use if the foot brakes fail; She pulled the **emergency cord** and stopped the train; **emergency equipment** such as a first-aid kit, flares, and tow line; an emergency exit, landing; a car's emergency lights; Ambulances, fire trucks, etc. are emergency vehicles; an emergency situation; an emergency warning given on radio about a tornado.*

e·mer·gent (i·MUR·junt) *adj.* emerging or coming forth: *the newly emergent nations of Africa.*
— **e·mer·gence** (-junce) *n.*

e·mer·i·tus (i·MER·uh·tus) *adj.* of a professional, retired from active service: *a professor emeritus of McGill University; the emeritus organist of our cathedral.*
— *n., pl.* -ti (-tye); *fem.* -ta, *pl.* -tae (-tee).

em·i·grate (EM·uh·grate) *v.* -grates, -grat·ed, -grat·ing go *from* one country or region to settle in another: *They emigrated from Taiwan and immigrated to Canada; Canadians emigrate to the U.S. to live in the Sunbelt.*
— **em·i·grant** (-grunt) *n. & adj.*
— **em·i·gra·tion** (-GRAY·shun) *n.*

é·mi·gré (EM·uh·gray) *n.* a political fugitive, as the Hungarians and Czechs who fled the communist revolutions in their countries.

em·i·nence (EM·uh·nunce) *n.* prominent or distinguished position: *a woman of great eminence as a physicist; We looked at the horizon from an eminence* (= elevated spot) *overlooking the sea; Your Eminence* [form of addressing a cardinal]; *His Eminence said so.*
— **em·i·nent** *adj.: an eminent physician; He is eminent as a diplomat; She is eminent in her field.*
— **em·i·nent·ly** *adv.*

em·is·sar·y (EM·uh·sair·ee) *n.* -is·sar·ies 1 one sent on an official mission; messenger: *an emissary from the Kremlin.* 2 a secret agent or spy.

e·mis·sion (i·MISH·un) *n.* an emitting or something discharged: *Automobile emissions cause pollution; the emission* (= streaming out) *of electrons from an electrode.*

e·mit (i·MIT) *v.* **e·mits, e·mit·ted, e·mit·ting** send out or discharge heat, fumes, odours, sounds, etc. — **e·mit·ter** *n.*

Em·my (EM·ee) *n.* **Em·mys** an annual award for outstanding TV producers, performers, etc.

e·mol·u·ment (i·MOL·yuh·munt) *n.* usually **emoluments** *pl. Formal.* reward for work, usually other than wages: *health insurance, pension scheme, and such emoluments besides a salary; the emoluments* (= perks) *of an office; the emoluments* (= trappings) *of power.*

e·mote (i·MOTE) *v. Informal.* **e·motes, e·mot·ed, e·mot·ing** act emotionally.

e·mo·tion (i·MOH·shun) *n.* an intense feeling, as joy, anger, love, or fear: *The speech stirred up* or *whipped up the emotions of the mob; their pent-up emotions; the conflicting emotions of love of one's religion and loyalty to the nation; He left the scene with mixed emotions.* — **e·mo·tion·al** *adj.: an emotional appeal, character, disorder, outburst, plea.* — **e·mo·tion·al·ism** *n.* — **e·mo·tion·al·ly** *adv.: People sometimes act emotionally rather than rationally; an emotionally handicapped child with behaviour problems.*

e·mo·tive (i·MOH·tiv) *adj.* causing strong feeling: *words with emotive associations; an emotive concept, expression; emotive language, words, utterances.*

em·pan·el (im·PAN·ul) *v.* **-els, -elled** or **-eled, -el·ling** or **-el·ing** same as IMPANEL.

em·path·ic (em·PATH.ic) *adj.* of or showing empathy.

em·pa·thize (EM·puh·thize, "th" as in "thin") *v.* **-iz·es, -ized, -iz·ing** have empathy: *to empathize with someone.*

em·pa·thy (EM·puh·thee, "th" as in "thin") *n.* identification with another's feelings or ideas: *He has plenty of sympathy but little empathy with the poetry of suffering.*

em·per·or (EM·pur·ur) *n.* the male ruler of an empire.

em·pha·sis (EM·fuh·sis) *n., pl.* **-ses** (-seez) special stress put on syllables, words, thoughts, actions, etc. because of their relative importance.

em·pha·size (EM·fuh·size) *v.* **-siz·es, -sized, -siz·ing** stress: *The speaker emphasized each point by pounding the table with his fist.*

em·phat·ic (em·FAT·ic) *adj.* **1** expressed with force or spoken with emphasis: *an emphatic denial, gesture, opinion, statement; an emphatic "No"; "She does swim" is an emphatic form of utterance; "Herself," "himself," "itself," etc. are emphatic pronouns.* **2** sure or certain: *He's quite emphatic in his views; He's emphatic about having seen Bigfoot; an emphatic* (= striking) *success, victory.* — **em·phat·i·cal·ly** *adv.*

em·pire (EM·pire) *n.* **1** a group of territories under a sovereign ruler, usually an emperor: *to break up, consolidate, rule an empire.* **2** sovereign rule. **3** an extensive business or other organization with unified control: *to build up a financial empire; publishing empire; adj.: an empire builder; empire building.*

em·pir·ic (em·PEER·ic) *n.* one who relies on practical experience rather than on theory.

em·pir·i·cal (em·PEER·uh·cul) *adj.* **1** based on experiment and observation: *Your existence is an empirical fact, but that of ghosts is not; the empirical method of scientific procedure.* **2** based merely on practical experience: *an amateur doctor's empirical remedies.*

em·place·ment (em·PLACE·munt) *n.* **1** positioning: *the emplacement of American missiles in Europe.* **2** a platform on which heavy guns are placed for firing.

em·plane (em·PLANE) *v.* board a plane: *We emplaned at 3 p.m. but were cleared for takeoff only at 4.*

em·ploy (em·PLOY) *v.* make use of or put to work on a regular basis: *I would like to hire you for occasional jobs but couldn't afford to employ you as a staffer; A housewife not gainfully employed doesn't pay income tax; methods employed to get votes; Skills not employed may go to waste; how to employ your spare time.* — *n.* service: *They have 200 people in their employ.*

em·ploy·a·ble (em·PLOY·uh·bul) *adj.* that can be employed: *an employable immigrant with employable skills.*

em·ploy·ee (em·PLOY·ee, em·ploy·EE) *n.* one who is employed: *We're not taking on any more employees; to fire, hire, sack employees.* — **em·ploy·er** (-PLOY·ur) *n.: an equal-opportunity employer.*

em·ploy·ment (em·PLOY·munt) *n.* an employing or being employed, esp. a job: *a housewife who has no problem finding (outside) employment; to give, seek employment; New industries provide employment to the unemployed; part-time, seasonal, steady employment; Employment peaks, rises, is up in the summer, down in the winter; An* **employment agency** *places workers and bills employers for the service.*

em·po·ri·um (em·POR·ee·um) *n.* **-ri·ums** or **-ri·a** (-ee·uh) a large retail store with a variety of goods.

em·pow·er (em·POW·ur) *v.* give someone power, authority, or ability *to* do something.

em·press (EM·pris) *n.* an emperor's wife or the woman ruler of an empire.

emp·ty (EMP·tee) *adj.* **-ti·er, -ti·est** lacking the usual content: *"Empty vessels make the most sound"; The house is empty* (= the people who live in it are out) *but not vacant; an empty chair, lot, room; weasel words that are empty of meaning;* **empty calories** *(of foods with no nutritive value); an empty* (= valueless) *display; an empty* (= unreal) *dream; empty* (= idle) *hours; empty* (= hollow) *pleasures; an empty* (= meaningless) *promise; an empty* (= ineffective) *threat; an empty word* (= not a content word) *like "from" or "but" which has grammatical function rather than meaning.* — *n., pl.* **-ties:** *Return the empties* (= containers) *for refund or refill.* — *v.* **-ties, -tied, -ty·ing** make or become empty, as by pouring out the contents: *to empty a cup; The St. Lawrence empties* (= discharges) *into the Atlantic; The hall emptied* (= became empty) *at the sound of the siren; The streets seemed to have been emptied of traffic.* — **emp·ti·ly** (-tuh·lee) *adv.;* **emp·ti·ness** *n.*

empty nester *n.* one whose home is empty since the children have grown up and left.

empty set *n.* in mathematics, a set without members; null set.

em·py·re·an (em·pye·REE·un, em·PEER·ee·un) *n.* the highest heaven; also, the sky.
— *adj.* heavenly or sublime. Also **em·py·re·al** *adj.*

e·mu (EE·mew) *n.* a large flightless bird of Australia, related to but smaller than an ostrich.

em·u·late (EM·yuh·late) *v.* -lates, -lat·ed, -lat·ing try to equal or excel an admired person or the person's qualities: *He tried to emulate his father's courage.*
— **em·u·la·tor** (-lay·tur) *n.*
— **em·u·la·tion** (-LAY·shun) *n.*

en·a·ble (en·AY·bul) *v.* -bles, -bled, -bling give ability or capacity to someone, esp. legally: *Education enables one to qualify for better jobs; The U.S. Congress has to pass enabling legislation to enable a territory to become a state.*

en·act (in·ACT) *v.* 1 make a bill into law; **en·act·ment** *n.* 2 act out a role on stage.

en·am·el (i·NAM·ul) *n.* 1 a hard, glasslike substance used to decorate and protect the surface of metal, glass, or pottery: *Kitchen appliances and bathroom fixtures are often finished in enamel; en·am·el·ware metal products.* 2 a kind of glossy paint, as used on walls, bicycles, and automobiles. 3 the hard outer covering of a tooth.
— *v.* -els, -elled or -eled, -el·ling or -el·ing decorate with or as with enamel: *an enamelled brick, earring, plate.* — **en·am·el·ler** or **en·am·el·er** *n.*

en·am·oured or **en·am·ored** (i·NAM·urd) *adj.* captivated or charmed: *He's quite enamoured of her.*

en bloc *adv.* as a whole; all together: *They walked out en bloc; They voted en bloc to kill the legislation.*

en·camp (en·CAMP) *v.* camp or put soldiers, etc. in a camp; **en·camp·ment** *n.*

en·case (in·CASE) *v.* -cas·es, -cased, -cas·ing put in or as if in a case: *a bronze plaque encased in concrete.*

-ence See ·ANCE.

en·ce·phal·ic (en·suh·FAL·ic) *adj.* of or near the brain.

en·ceph·a·li·tis (en·SEF·uh·LYE·tis) *n.* inflammation of the brain. — **en·ceph·a·lit·ic** (-uh·LIT·ic) *adj.*

en·chain (in·CHAIN) *v.* 1 to chain. 2 captivate; hold fast.

en·chant (in·CHANT) *v.* charm, as if with magic; bewitch: *an enchanted forest.*

— **en·chant·er** *n.; fem.* **en·chant·ress** (-tris)
— **en·chant·ing** *adj.* — **en·chant·ment** *n.*

en·chi·la·da (en·chuh·LAH·duh) *n.* a rolled tortilla with a filling of meat or cheese, peppers, etc.
— **the big enchilada** *Slang.* the boss.
— **the whole enchilada** *Slang.* the whole thing.

en·cir·cle (en·SUR·cul) *v.* circle. — **en·cir·cle·ment** *n.*

en·clave (EN·clave, AHN-) *n.* a territory of one country lying inside the boundaries of another: *Goa was a Portuguese enclave in India.*

en·close (in·CLOZE) *v.* -clos·es, -closed, -clos·ing 1 include, as in an envelope or parcel: *A $100 cheque is enclosed herewith; Please find enclosed a cheque for $100.* 2 shut up as with a fence: *a garden enclosed with a wall; an enclosed convent (of cloistered nuns).*

en·clo·sure (in·CLOH·zhur) *n.* 1 something that shuts up, as surrounding walls. 2 an enclosed space, as a corral. 3 something enclosed, as a cheque with a covering letter.

en·code (in·CODE) *v.* -codes, -cod·ed, -cod·ing put a message into code or add codes to data or text: *A text is encoded by replacing its words with arbitrary symbols; to encode data for computer processing.*

en·cod·er (in·COH·dur) *n.* an encoding device: *In a colour telecast, the three primary colour signals are combined in an encoder for transmission.*

en·co·mi·um (en·COH·mee·um) *n.* -mi·ums or -mi·a (-mee·uh) *Formal.* an expression of high praise; eulogy.

en·com·pass (en·CUM·pus) *v.* 1 contain, as if encircled: *a mind that could encompass vast knowledge.* 2 accomplish: *a plot that encompassed his ruin.*

en·core (AHNG·core) *interj.* once more! repeat!: *The audience shouted, "Encore!"*
— *n.* 1 a popular call to repeat a stage performance or act: *The audience insisted on an encore; v.: The audience encored the violinist three times.* 2 a repetition made in response to such a call: *to do, play, sing an encore.*

en·coun·ter (in·COWN·tur) *v.* come up against; confront: *to encounter difficulties.*
— *n.* 1 an unexpected meeting: *a brief, casual, chance, close, fleeting encounter.* 2 a confrontation: *an encounter with a burglar; a bloody, sudden, ugly encounter; Members of an encounter group meet in sensitivity-training sessions to talk about and act out hostile feelings and reactions to help them get along with others more effectively.*

en·cour·age (in·CUR·ij) *v.* -ag·es, -aged, -ag·ing 1 give courage, hope, confidence, support, etc. to someone, esp. to do something: *A teacher encourages students to work harder; She doesn't encourage their disturbing others.* 2 stimulate or hearten: *We were encouraged to hear we had won; The news encouraged us; The news was quite encouraging.* — **en·cour·age·ment** *n.*

en·croach (in·CROHCH) *v.* trespass or intrude gradually *on* or *upon* someone's land, time, or other property: *The sea encroaches on land by erosion.*
— **en·croach·ment** *n.*

en·crust (in·CRUST) *v.* cover with, form, or form into a crust: *The shoes were encrusted with mud; Ice encrusted*

the water in the tank.
— **en·crus·ta·tion** (en·crus·TAY·shun) *n.*

en·cum·ber (in·CUM·bur) *v.* burden, obstruct, or crowd so as to hinder freedom of movement or action: *He doesn't like to be transferred, as he is encumbered with a large family of dependents; an estate encumbered with debts; a backyard encumbered with junk; a page encumbered with footnotes.*
— **en·cum·brance** (-brunce) *n.*

en·cy·clo·pe·di·a (en·SYE·cluh·PEE·dee·uh) *n.* a book or set of books providing wide information on every field of knowledge or on a specific area if a specialized work: *an encyclopedia of science and technology; She's a **walking encyclopedia*** (= well-informed in all subjects).
— **en·cy·clo·pe·dic** (-PEE·dic) *adj.* wide-ranging: *a scholar of encyclopedic knowledge.*
Also **en·cy·clo·pae·di·a; en·cy·clo·pae·dic.**

end *n.* **1** an extremity or limit, as of a line or of anything extended in space or time: *Tie a knot at each end of the rope; The rope measures 10 m **from end to end**; the front end and rear end of a car; I watched the game **from beginning to end**; Ends play at each end of the line of scrimmage in football; We can't lend you any more money because you have reached **the end of the line** – you already owe too much; The news was broadcast to **the ends of the earth** (= to the remotest places on earth); The Minister was at or on the receiving end of the public outcry; Let's hear your end (= side) of the story; The unemployed find it hard to **make (both) ends meet** (= make income equal expenditures); It rained for days **on end** (= continuously); The gruesome sight made his hair **stand on end** (= horrified him and made him feel as if the hair on his head was rising stiffly).* **2** a finish: *to **put an end to** the nuisance; at the end of the day; He fought for his rights to the bitter end; The meeting came to an end at midnight; The old man was nearing his end (= death); **In the end** (= At last), everyone parted as friends; He gave us **no end** (= a great deal) of trouble.* **3** a piece of anything having extension: *Take all the candle ends off the cake; the **odds and ends** (= miscellaneous things) left over after a party.* **4** goal or purpose: *to accomplish, achieve one's ends; Have your end clearly in view; Does the **end justify the means** (= Does the result justify the means used to achieve it)?*
— *v.* come or bring to a close: *High school ends with graduation; They end all meetings by singing the national anthem; We ended the dinner with a dessert; The game ended in a draw.*
— **end up** finish: *The bellhop ended up owning the hotel; He ended up (as) the company president; The gunman ended up in jail.*

en·dan·ger (en·DAIN·jur) *v.* put in danger, as of death: *Drunk drivers endanger lives; With so few left, whooping cranes are an **endangered species** (threatened with extinction).*

en·dear (en·DEER) *v.* make dear or lovable: *Children have a way of endearing themselves to everyone; the **endearing** ways of children.* — **en·dear·ing·ly** *adv.*

en·dear·ment (en·DEER·munt) *n.* expression of affection, as a word or touch: *a term of endearment such as "honey."*

en·deav·our or **en·deav·or** (en·DEV·ur) *v. Formal.* make an attempt, esp. in an earnest and sustained manner: *Most parents endeavour to provide their children with a good education;* **n.:** *a lifetime of honest endeavour to reform the legal system.*

ending *n.* the last part: *a story with a happy ending; "Hamlet" has a tragic ending; "-es" is a plural ending* (= suffix).

end·less (END·lis) *adj.* **1** without end, eternal or boundless, or seeming so: *an endless nuisance; the endless stretch of the heavens.* **2** with the ends joined together, thereby making continuous: *the endless track of a snowmobile or bulldozer.*

end·most *adj.* farthest.

end of steel *n. Cdn.* the end of a railway line or a town located there.

en·dor·phin (en·DOR·fun) *n.* a hormone compound produced in the nerve cells of the body to relieve pain and tension: *Exercise stimulates the release of endorphins in the body.*

en·dor·sa·tion (EN·dor·SAY·shun) *n. Cdn.* approval or support.

en·dorse (en·DORCE) *v.* **-dors·es, -dorsed, -dors·ing** **1** sign a cheque, money order, or a document, usually on the back, to indicate approval. **2** approve of or support a candidate, product, service, etc.
— **en·dorse·ment** *n.*

en·dow (en·DOW, *rhyme:* HOW) *v.* provide someone with money, property, talents, or other assets: *Nature endowed her with beauty and wit.*
— **en·dow·ment** *n.: The new school was provided with a million-dollar endowment* (= fund); *An endowment insurance policy matures at a specified date and is paid as a lump sum.*

end product *n.* the final result of a process or of a series of activities; finished product.

end run *n.* a football play in which the ball carrier tries to run around one end of the opponent's line; hence, a tactic for getting around opposition: *to make or try an end run around a person or situation.*

end table *n.* a small low table used beside a sofa or other piece of furniture.

en·due (en·DUE) *v.* **-dues, -dued, -du·ing** usually **endued with,** provided with a quality.

en·dur·ance (en·DURE·unce) *n.* the state or power of enduring or bearing: *You need great endurance to run a marathon; an athlete's powers of endurance; The agony was beyond her endurance (= impossible to bear); When the pain became past endurance she just fainted; a 19-day **endurance race** of automobiles; a gruelling **endurance test** of one's patience.*

en·dure (en·DURE) *v.* **-dures, -dured, -dur·ing** **1** bear something or someone, esp. for a long time; tolerate: *to endure noise, pain, suffering.* **2** continue in existence, esp. in spite of opposite influences; last: *Even great works of art do not endure forever; an **enduring** peace.*
— **en·dur·a·ble** (-uh·bul) *adj.*

end use *n.* the final use to which a product is put.
— **end-user** or **end-consumer** *n.*

end·ways or **end·wise** *adj. & adv.* with the end forward; lengthwise.

en·e·my (EN·uh·mee) *n.* **-mies 1** one who hates or wishes to harm another: *to conquer, overcome, rout an enemy; The escaped killer was considered public enemy number one; an arch, bitter, common, mortal, political, powerful, sworn enemy.* **2** anything harmful or injurious: *A bad habit could be one's own worst enemy; Lethargy is the enemy of progress.*

en·er·get·ic (en·ur·JET·ic) *adj.* vigorous or forceful. — **en·er·get·i·cal·ly** *adv.*

en·er·gize (EN·ur·jize) *v.* **-giz·es, -gized, -giz·ing** rouse into action or give energy to. — **en·er·giz·er** (-JYE·zur) *n.*

en·er·gy (EN·ur·jee) *n.* **-gies 1** capacity for action; ability to do work: *a youngster full of energy; He starts each day in a burst of energy; Without proper guidance, he would dissipate his energy in useless pursuits; Hot weather saps his energy; He should concentrate his energy on doing one thing at a time; His energies have to be redirected in useful ways; Pat's energies are now being applied or devoted to winning a gold medal; Lou expended her energies in the cause of consumer rights; She's a person of boundless, limitless, unflagging energy.* **2** usable power: *Chemical, electrical, mechanical, and solar energy are different kinds of energy, while kinetic and potential energy are different forms of mechanical energy; Atomic energy was first harnessed in the 1940s; renewable sources of energy such as the sun, wind, and tides; We may be facing an **energy crisis** (= acute energy shortage) unless we conserve our nonrenewable oil and natural gas resources.*

en·er·vate (EN·ur·vate) *v.* **-vates, -vat·ed, -vat·ing** lessen the physical, mental, or moral vigour of someone, as by a hot, damp climate or overindulgence in luxury, alcohol, drugs, etc. — **en·er·va·tion** (-VAY·shun) *n.*

en·force (en·FORCE) *v.* **-forc·es, -forced, -forc·ing** compel or force, esp. obedience, understanding, etc.: *Police enforce the law; Some laws are strictly enforced; a period of enforced idleness due to hospitalization; to enforce an argument using facts and figures.* — **en·force·able** *adj.;* **en·force·ment** *n.*

en·forc·er (en·FOR·sur) *n.* **1** one who enforces. **2** one whose job is to enforce the will of a gang leader by threats and punishment: *Professional hockey teams have enforcers who use intimidating tactics against opposing players.*

en·fran·chise (en·FRAN·chize) *v.* **-chis·es, -chised, -chis·ing 1** give voting rights to a group: *to become enfranchised as Canadian citizens.* **2** set slaves free. — **en·fran·chise·ment** (-chiz·munt, -chize·munt) *n.*

en·gage (en·GAGE) *v.* **-gag·es, -gaged, -gag·ing 1** be busy; occupy or involve: *Scientists are engaged in research; He engaged the hostess in conversation; Japan is engaged in trade with many countries; matters that engage our attention all day.* **2** make involved, as machine parts meshing or people fighting: *As you release the clutch, it engages a "flywheel" connected to the engine; If the gears don't engage, you have a problem; He engaged the enemy in hand-to-hand combat.* **3** promise or bind oneself: *Marc is engaged to (marry) Mia; Mia and Marc are engaged (to be married); They got engaged last week; an **engaged** couple.* **4** hire: *to engage a lawyer; We engaged a student as our tour guide; We engaged her to show us around her hometown.*

en·gage·ment (en·GAGE·munt) *n.* **1** an agreement or promise: *to announce an engagement* (= betrothal); *She broke off her engagement (to marry) and returned the **engagement ring.*** **2** an arrangement to meet someone: *The boss has cancelled all outside engagements because of a cold; He has many luncheon, social, and speaking engagements; Previous or prior engagements prevent him from seeing surprise visitors.* **3** an action involving combat: *The territory was recaptured after a brief naval engagement with the enemy.*

engaging (en·GAY·jing) *adj.* pleasing or charming: *her engaging manner, smile.*

en·gen·der (en·JEN·dur) *v.* give rise to or produce something: *Fear often engenders violence.*

en·gine (EN·jun) *n.* **1** a mechanism, esp. one that uses fuel energy to produce work: *an air-cooled, diesel, gasoline, internal-combustion, jet, radial, reciprocating, rotary, steam, V-8 engine; to rev up, tune up, turn off, warm up an engine; Engines break down, idle, sputter, stall, work; Some engines burn too much gasoline; an engine that runs on alcohol; a fire engine* (= fire truck). **2** a machine used for military purposes: *medieval engines of warfare such as battering rams.*

en·gi·neer (en·juh·NEER) *n.* one who designs, manages, or operates machinery and systems to utilize power and materials: *a professional engineer such as a chemical, civil, electrical, electronic, or mechanical engineer; A sanitary engineer deals with aspects of public health such as water supply, sewage disposal, etc.; a locomotive engineer* (= driver); *technicians such as operating engineers in charge of machines and plants, radio engineers, sound engineers, and stationary engineers in charge of generators, compressors, etc.*
— *v.* plan and make, as an engineer does: *a well engineered car; Some foods are scientifically engineered* (= fabricated) *for higher nutritional value and longer shelf life; a demonstration engineered* (= caused and managed) *by students.*

engineering *n.* the profession of an engineer; the scientific use of energy and materials for practical purposes.

Eng·lish (ING·glish) *n.* **1** the Germanic language of England, used also in the British Commonwealth, the U.S., and other countries: *Old English* or *Anglo-Saxon* *(to about A.D. 1100), Middle English (1100 – 1500), and Modern English; British English is sometimes called "English English"; Correct English is called the King's or Queen's English; Current English is contemporary English; good English; in plain English* (= plainly speaking). **2 the English** *pl.* the people of England. **— adj.** having to do with England, its people, or its language: *the English Channel, foxhound, language, setter; English grammar, history, literature; English Canada* or *English-speaking Canada (where English speakers predominate).*

Eng·lish·man (ING·glish·mun) *n.* **-men** a man of or from England; **Eng·lish·wom·an** *n.* **-wom·en.**

en·gorge (en·GORJ) *v.* **-gorg·es, -gorged, -gorg·ing** **1** swallow greedily: *Leeches engorge on their victims' blood.* **2** distend with fluid or blood: *an engorged river ready to burst its banks.*

en·grave (en·GRAVE) *v.* **-graves, -graved, -grav·ing** **1** cut, carve, or etch letters, designs, etc. in wood, stone, metal, etc., esp. for printing from. **2** impress: *childhood experiences engraved in our memory.* **— en·grav·er** *n.;* **en·grav·ing** *n.*

en·gross (en·GROSE, *rhyme:* DOSE) *v.* absorb the entire attention of someone: *a child deeply engrossed in her homework; an engrossing thriller.*

en·gulf (en·GULF) *v.* swallow up, as by waves: *The flames soon engulfed the building; He was engulfed by fear; Poverty and misery engulfed the family as a result of the disaster.*

en·hance (en·HANCE) *v.* **-hanc·es, -hanced, -hanc·ing** raise or increase value, beauty, or other desirable quality: *Home improvements enhance the value of property; Prestige is enhanced by victories; Beauty may be enhanced by makeup; A computer can enhance the quality of photographs transmitted from space by filling in missing bits of data, etc.* **— en·hance·ment** *n.*

e·nig·ma (uh·NIG·muh) *n.* **1** a person who is perplexing because of a mixture of conflicting qualities: *Nick is an enigma because he is kind to strangers and harsh to his neighbours.* **2** something that is ambiguous or cryptic in nature: *The riddle of the Sphinx about the human being ("Who goes on four legs in the morning, on two at noon, and on three at night?") was an enigma to everyone except Oedipus who solved it.* **— en·ig·mat·ic** (en·ig·MAT·ic) or **en·ig·mat·i·cal** *adj.* difficult to interpret: *the Mona Lisa's enigmatic smile; an enigmatic figure, personality, style.*

en·join (en·JOIN) *v. Formal.* command: *They were enjoined to keep the matter secret; They were enjoined not to speak to the press; Secrecy was enjoined* (= imposed) *on them.*

en·joy (en·JOY) *v.* take pleasure in something: *He likes school, enjoys games, enjoys doing homework; He is enjoying himself* (= having fun). **— en·joy·a·ble** (·JOY·uh·bul) *adj.:* *We had a highly enjoyable time at the party.* **— en·joy·ment** *n.:* *Hobbies provide enjoyment during leisure hours; She derives great enjoyment from watching hockey.*

en·large (en·LARGE) *v.* **-larg·es, -larged, -larg·ing** make or become larger: *a copier that enlarges and reduces originals.* **— enlarge on** or **upon** discuss at length. **— en·large·ment** *n.*

en·light·en (en·LITE·un) *v.* inform, esp. so as to remove misunderstanding, error, etc.: *Can you enlighten me on the nature of your research project? Her speech was instructive and enlightening; an enlightened* (= well-informed) *public; Enlightened self-interest guided Canada and the U.S. in their trade negotiations.* **— en·light·en·ment** *n.*

en·list (en·LIST) *v.* join or get someone to join the military or a cause or undertaking: *to enlist in the armed forces for three years; She enlisted her young son in the navy; We enlisted the help of our neighbours in controlling street crime; an enlisted man in the armed forces (not a commissioned officer).* **— en·list·ment** *n.*

en·liv·en (en·LYE·vun) *v.* put life into a party, dull surroundings, etc.

en masse (en·MAS) *adv.* all together; in one body: *The staff resigned en masse.*

en·mesh (en·MESH) *v.* take in or as if in a net; entangle: *He found himself enmeshed in his own web of lies.*

en·mi·ty (EN·muh·tee) *n.* **-ties** hostility or hatred, as between enemies: *to stir up enmity against, among, between, toward people.*

en·no·ble (en·NOH·bul) *v.* **-bles, -bled, -bling** raise to noble rank or add dignity; also, make noble: *Suffering purifies and ennobles character.*

e·nor·mi·ty (i·NOR·muh·tee) *n.* **-ties 1** outrageous or monstrous quality: *the enormity of a crime, offence, of his wickedness.* **2** *Informal.* vastness or immensity: *the enormity of a problem, task.*

e·nor·mous (i·NOR·mus) *adj.* very much exceeding the normal size, amount, or degree: *an enormous appetite; at enormous expense; an enormous waste.* **— e·nor·mous·ly** *adv.*

e·nough (i·NUF) *adj.* [with reference to number or quantity, not degree, as "sufficient" in "necessary and sufficient condition"; used after, not before, a countable noun in sing., as in "man enough to apologize"] sufficient: *There are blankets enough* (= sufficient number) *for everyone; There is enough food* (= a sufficient quantity of it) *for everyone; food enough for everyone; money enough to buy food; enough people to help us; people enough to help us.* **— n. & pron.** a sufficient number or amount: *That will be enough; I've had enough of this; We have enough and to spare* (= more than sufficient); *"Enough is enough"* (= That's the limit); *He was enough of a fool* (= foolish enough) *to cheat in the exam.* **— adv.** sufficiently: *Sure enough, he was late (as usual); She's well enough to sit up in bed; glad enough* (= quite glad) *to get out of the hospital.*

enquire, enquiry same as INQUIRE, INQUIRY.

en·rage (en·RAGE) *v.* **-rag·es, -raged, -rag·ing** put in a rage or anger; infuriate: *He was enraged to hear that he had been fired for no reason; quite enraged at* or *by* or *with the treatment he was receiving.*

en·rap·ture (en·RAP·chur) *v.* -tures, -tured, -tur·ing transport with joy.

en·rich (en·RICH) *v.* make rich; improve in quality: *White enriched bread (has added food value); Flour and rice are enriched by replacing the vitamins lost in milling the grain; vitamin-enriched cereal; a new laser process to enrich uranium* (= increase its fissionable U-235 content) *for use in nuclear reactors.* — **en·rich·ment** *n.*

en·rol or **en·roll** (en·ROLE) *v.* -rols or -rolls, -roled or -rolled, -rol·ing or -roll·ing enter on a roll or list, as a member of a body of students, electors, or of a club: *Students enrol in* or *for a course; A school enrols students in courses.* — **en·rol·ment** or **en·roll·ment** *n.*

en route (ahn·ROOT) *adv.* on the way *to* or *from* a place.

en·sconce (en·SCONCE) *v.* -sconc·es, -sconced, -sconc·ing establish oneself securely or snugly: *There she is, enjoying my book ensconced in her favourite chair.*

en·sem·ble (ahn·SAHM·bul) *n.* 1 an integrated set or whole whose parts together produce a single effect, as a matching costume and accessories. 2 music of several parts, a group of singers or actors performing cooperatively, etc.: *an ensemble called the New Chamber Orchestra.*

en·shrine (en·SHRINE) *v.* -shrines, -shrined, -shrin·ing enclose in or as in a shrine; hence, keep or cherish as sacred: *civil rights enshrined in the Constitution.*

en·shroud (en·SHROWD) *v.* to shroud or veil.

en·sign (EN·sun) *n.* 1 (*also* EN·sine) a flag or emblem: *The Red Ensign was Canada's flag until 1965.* 2 the lowest rank of commissioned officer in the U.S. Navy.

en·si·lage (EN·suh·lij) *n.* ensiled green fodder.

en·sile (en·SILE) *v.* -siles, -siled, -sil·ing preserve fodder in a silo.

en·slave (en·SLAVE) *v.* -slaves, -slaved, -slav·ing make a slave of someone. — **en·slave·ment** *n.*

en·snare (en·SNARE) *v.* -snares, -snared, -snar·ing 1 to snare or trap: *to ensnare a rabbit.* 2 catch, as in a net.

en·sue (en·SUE) *v.* -sues, -sued, -su·ing follow, esp. as a consequence; result: *After the heavy rains a flood ensued; There was a drought and then a famine in the ensuing year.*

en·sure (en·SURE) *v.* -sures, -sured, -sur·ing make certain or secure; guarantee: *Registration ensures delivery of mail; It ensures mail against loss, theft, etc. but does not ensure its being delivered on time; The weatherman cannot ensure that it will or will not rain tomorrow.*

en·tail (en·TAIL) *v.* make something a necessary requirement: *Success entails hard work.*

en·tan·gle (en·TANG·gul) *v.* -gles, -gled, -gling 1 of hair, string, etc., make tangled or twisted together: *He got entangled in the net he was laying to catch birds.* 2 make or be tangled in a difficult or perplexing situation: *He became entangled in a dispute with neighbours; She doesn't like to become entangled with other people's problems.*
— **en·tan·gle·ment** *n.*: *He doesn't like entanglements* (= involvements) *in* or *with his in-laws' affairs; Barbed-wire entanglements* (= fences) *are used as barriers in ground warfare.*

en·ter (EN·tur) *v.* 1 go or come in: *Knock before entering; to enter by a side door; The burglar entered the house through the window;* [as a stage direction] *Enter Romeo* (= Romeo enters). 2 get into or join a group, list, record, etc.: *to enter the army, a profession, the practice of law; It's time to enter* (= enrol) *your child in school; Words are entered in a dictionary; The accused entered a plea of guilty; Don't* **enter into** (= start) *arguments with customers; to* **enter on** or **upon** (= begin) *a new career.*

en·ter·prise (EN·tur·prize) *n.* 1 a project or undertaking that requires initiative and risk-taking: *a business enterprise; commercial enterprises; a joint enterprise; The company started as a private enterprise.* 2 initiative and risk-taking: *a woman of great enterprise; Ours is a* **free enterprise** *society; She's quite* **enterprising** (= marked by enterprise).

en·ter·tain (en·tur·TAIN) *v.* 1 receive as a guest: *The Siegels were entertaining the Khans last night; They entertain a lot on weekends.* 2 please or amuse with something planned or prepared: *Clowns know how to entertain children with funny acts; The talk was instructive and* **entertaining.** 3 be ready and willing to consider: *to entertain doubts, ideas, opinions, pleas, proposals, suggestions.* — **en·ter·tain·er** *n.*
— **en·ter·tain·ment** *n.*: *Stage shows provide live entertainment; TV affords entertainment for the bed-ridden; It is pure entertainment to watch babies playing.*
— *adj.*: *the entertainment industry* (= TV, radio, movies, music records, etc.); *an entertainment tax (on stage and screen performances); an instructive book with some entertainment value.*

en·thral or **en·thrall** (en·THRAWL) *v.* -thrals or -thralls, -thralled, -thrall·ing captivate by fascinating.

en·throne (en·THRONE) *v.* -thrones, -throned, -thron·ing put on a throne; hence, exalt: *Mercy is "enthroned in the hearts of kings."* — **en·throne·ment** *n.*

en·thuse (en·THEWZ) *v.* -thus·es, -thused, -thus·ing *Informal.* show, feel, or express with enthusiasm: *"A marvellous movie," she enthused; We're all enthused, but let us not get too enthused about it.*

en·thu·si·asm (en·THEW·zee·az·um) *n.* intense interest or admiration approaching zeal for a person, pursuit, cause, etc.: *to arouse, demonstrate, display, kindle, radiate, show, stir up enthusiasm for a cause; He expressed great enthusiasm about* or *over the new leader; her boundless, unbridled, wild enthusiasm; Let's not dampen her enthusiasm by telling her the party may be cancelled.*

en·thu·si·ast (en·THEW·zee·ast) *n.* one who is keenly interested in an activity or cause: *a sports enthusiast; an enthusiast for women's rights.*
— **en·thu·si·as·tic** (-zee·AS·tic) *adj.*: *He is an enthusiastic admirer of hers; She seems enthusiastic about* or *over her new responsibilities.*

— en·thu·si·as·ti·cal·ly *adv.*

en·tice (en·TICE) *v.* **-tic·es, -ticed, -tic·ing** lure or tempt by skilful or crafty means: *The youth was enticed into running away from home; He was enticed with promises of becoming rich.* — **en·tice·ment** *n.*

en·tire (en·TIRE) *adj.* unbroken as a unit; with no parts left out; complete in extent or degree: *Her entire savings amount to $1.98; The entire day was spent in conferences; an entire set of the encyclopedia; The skeleton was whole and entire; You have my entire support; I'm in entire agreement with you; He was in entire ignorance of what happened; an entire* (= not gelded or castrated) *horse.*
— **en·tire·ly** *adv.* completely: *I agree with you entirely; time spent entirely on useless pursuits; That's entirely different, unnecessary.*
— **en·tire·ty** *n.*: *The proposal was rejected **in its entirety.***

en·ti·tle (en·TYE·tul) *v.* **-tles, -tled, -tling 1** give a claim or right to something: *Your age entitles you to retirement benefits; You are entitled to your opinions.* **2** title: *a book entitled "Roots."*
— **en·ti·tle·ment** *n.*: *entitlements such as welfare and unemployment benefits.*

en·ti·ty (EN·tuh·tee) *n.* **-ties** a person or thing that has independent existence: *Many believe that body and soul are separate entities; Canada is one entity formed out of two founding nations; Ethnic groups are cultural entities; They try to preserve their entity* (= existence) *and individuality.*

en·tomb (en·TOOM, long "OO") *v.* to place in a tomb or mausoleum; bury. — **en·tomb·ment** *n.*

en·tou·rage (ahn·too·RAHZH) *n.* a group of attendants; retinue: *the Queen's entourage.*

en·trails (EN·trailz) *n.pl.* the inner parts, esp. intestines, from a body; guts.

en·train (en·TRAIN) *v.* put or go on board a train.

¹**en·trance** (EN·trunce) *n.* **1** the act of entering; entry: *His entrance was very dramatic, thanks to the marching band he had hired; He made a grand, triumphal entrance into the stadium; Actors have to know their exits and entrances; A woman's formal entrance into society used to be at a debut; September 10, 1939, marks Canada's entrance into World War II.* **2** a door or other passageway: *There is an entrance to the house from the garage; The service entrance is for deliveries; A guard is posted at the entrance; Do not block the entrance, or **en·trance·way.*** **3** permission or right to enter; admission: *No one with a valid ticket is refused entrance; High school graduates are qualified for entrance to a university; There is no **entrance fee** for club members.*

²**en·trance** (en·TRANCE) *v.* **-tranc·es, -tranced, -tranc·ing** transport with joy, as in a trance or dream: *The crowd stood entranced by the beauty of the pageant; They were entranced with the music, entranced at the pageantry, quite entranced over the whole show; It held them entranced for over an hour; an **entrancing** sight.* — **en·tranc·ing·ly** *adv.*

en·trant (EN·trunt) *n.* one who enters, esp. in a race or contest: *He was one of many entrants in the marathon.*

en·trap (en·TRAP) *v.* **-traps, -trapped, -trap·ping** catch in or as in a trap: *The police were accused of entrapping them into selling the drug.* — **en·trap·ment** *n.*

en·treat (en·TREET) *v.* ask earnestly and persuasively: *The child entreated her mother to let her watch a late movie.*

en·treat·y (en·TREE·tee) *n.* **-treat·ies** an earnest request: *Their entreaties for mercy fell on deaf ears.*

en·trée or **en·tree** (AHN·tray) *n.* **1** means of entering or the right to enter: *Eminent position or outstanding achievements are the usual entrées to the Who's Who; You pay heavily to gain entrée into certain clubs.* **2** the main dish of a meal.

en·trench (en·TRENCH) *v.* put trenches around something; hence, fortify or make secure: *His success in the war further entrenched his position.*
— **en·trench·ment** *n.*

en·tre·pre·neur (ahn·truh·pruh·NOOR) *n.* one who organizes and manages a business, assuming risks and seeking profits.
— **en·tre·pre·neur·i·al** (-NOOR·ee·ul) *adj.*

en·trust (en·TRUST) *v.* **1** trust someone with a responsibility: *I entrust you with my dog.* **2** trust a responsibility to someone: *I entrust Fido to your care.*

en·try (EN·tree) *n.* **-tries 1** the act, right, or a place of entering: *Canada's entry into World War II; Each entry starts with "Dear Diary"; The hero made a triumphal entry into the city; a burglar's forced entry into a house; He gained entry by breaking a window.* **2** the act of placing in a record or listing, as of words entered alphabetically in a dictionary; also, a thing or person so entered, as in a competition: *All entries have to be postmarked no later than December 31; A dictionary entry starts with the word's spelling; Bookkeepers make entries for each item of income and expense.*
— *adj.: An entry blank or form is filled out and submitted for entering a contest; entry criteria, fees, rules, visas, an **entry word** (= headword) in a dictionary; an **entry-level** (= lowest level) job such as dishwasher or stockroom clerk.*

en·twine (en·TWINE) *v.* **-twines, -twined, -twin·ing** twist or weave together or around.

e·nu·mer·ate (i·NEW·muh·rate) *v.* **-ates, -at·ed, -at·ing 1** list or name one by one: *My reasons are too many to enumerate; to enumerate the advantages, circumstances, facts, qualities, various items.* **2** count: *to enumerate the population of an area; to enumerate* (= make a census of) *a province.* **3** *Cdn.* to enter in or make a list of voters prior to an election: *Voters have to be enumerated before they can vote.* — **e·nu·mer·a·tor** (-ray·tur) *n.* — **e·nu·mer·a·tion** (-RAY·shun) *n.*

e·nun·ci·ate (i·NUN·see·ate) *v.* **-ates, -at·ed, -at·ing 1** pronounce distinctly: *Actors have to enunciate clearly for the audience to hear what they are saying.* **2** set forth systematically: *to enunciate a doctrine, principle, theory.*
— **e·nun·ci·a·tion** (-AY·shun) *n.*: *an announcer with good enunciation* (= manner of pronunciation).

en·vel·op (en·VEL·up) *v.* **-ops, -oped, -op·ing** cover completely: *mountain tops enveloped in mist.*
— **en·vel·op·ment** *n.*

en·ve·lope (EN·vuh·lope, AHN-) *n.* a cover, esp. a flat paper container for mailing letters in: *We address, stamp, and seal envelopes before mailing; Please enclose a stamped, self-addressed envelope for a quick reply; a pay envelope (containing wages or pay cheque); a window envelope (with the mailing address showing through an opening covered by transparent paper).*

en·ven·om (en·VEN·um) *v.* taint with venom or poison; also, embitter.

en·vi·a·ble (EN·vee·uh·bul) *adj.* worthy of being envied: *My former helper is now in an enviable position as company president.* — **en·vi·a·bly** *adv.*

en·vi·ous (EN·vee·us) *adj.* feeling or showing envy: *Cinderella's sisters were envious of her beauty and jealous of her success with the prince.* — **en·vi·ous·ly** *adv.*

en·vi·ron·ment (en·VYE·run·munt) *n.* surroundings or habitat, esp. as affecting the development of an individual or community: *A child's own family should be the most healthy environment for its upbringing; to clean up, preserve, protect, pollute the environment* (= the air, water, soil, scenery, etc. around us). — **en·vi·ron·men·tal** (-MEN·tul) *adj.*: *Pesticides, exhaust fumes, and industrial wastes cause environmental pollution; Environmental art, sculpture, and theatre involve or engage the viewer as well as artist; An environmental protection agency deals with environmental problems.* — **en·vi·ron·men·tal·ist** *n.*

en·vi·rons (en·VYE·runz) *n.pl.* surroundings; also, suburbs: *a city and its environs; commuters from outside the environs of the city.*

en·vis·age (en·VIZ·ij) *v.* **-ag·es, -aged, -ag·ing** form a mental picture of something, esp. under a particular aspect such as the future; visualize: *The lobbyist envisaged many problems in the proposed legislation; We envisage that the proposal will be accepted without delay.*

en·vi·sion (en·VIZH·un) *v.* form a mental picture of something, as if in a vision: *to envision a world full of peace and happiness.*

en·voy (EN·voy, AHN·voy) *n.* **1** a messenger, esp. a government official sent on a mission: *The president despatched his personal envoy to Rome to negotiate the treaty; An envoy extraordinary is a diplomatic official ranking next below an ambassador.* **2** a short farewell message in the form of a literary postscript or concluding stanza; also **en·voi.**

en·vy (EN·vee) *n.* **-vies** a feeling of wishing that one had what another enjoys; also, the object of such feeling: *Kay was consumed or green with envy; Lee's red convertible was the envy of the neighbourhood; an object of envy; In a community racked by petty jealousies and envies many things are done out of mere envy; People feel, show envy when others arouse or stir up envy by their behaviour.* — *v.* **-vies, -vied, -vy·ing** feel envy toward someone: *Eve envies Flo; Many girls envy her curly hair; I envy your good fortune, but I don't envy you your job.*

en·zyme (EN·zime) *n.* a catalytic substance found in yeast and digestive juices: *Body irritants may be released by enzyme detergents used in dissolving stains.*

e·on (EE·un, EE·on) *n.* a long and indefinite period of time; an age: *Eons have passed since the universe came into being.*

e·phem·er·al (i·FEM·uh·rul) *adj.* **1** short-lived or passing, as glory or pleasures: *art that has only ephemeral value; writings of ephemeral interest; He only had a temporary, if not ephemeral, influence on poetry.* **2** originally, lasting no more than a few days, as certain plants, insects, etc.

ep·ic (EP·ic) *n.* **1** a long poem in a majestic style and with a heroic theme: *Greek and Roman epics by Homer and Virgil; The Ramayana is a Sanskrit epic; A folk epic is one that has been handed down orally from prehistoric times.* **2** a long story that is full of adventure and heroism: *action-packed western movie epics.* — *adj.* heroic and adventurous: *the epic deeds of Ulysses; an epic battle, drama, struggle; a tragedy of epic* (= vast) *proportions.*

ep·i·cure (EP·uh·cure) *n.* a person with a highly refined taste for food and wine.

ep·i·cu·re·an (EP·uh·kew·REE·un) *adj.* given to sensuous pleasure, esp. of eating and drinking. — *n.* same as EPICURE.

ep·i·dem·ic (ep·uh·DEM·ic) *adj.* spreading rapidly, as contagious diseases: *Measles could become epidemic if not controlled; an epidemic attack, fever; Dieting has reached epidemic proportions.* — *n.* **1** an epidemic disease: *a cholera, flu, typhoid epidemic; Epidemics break out, spread, if they are not contained or controlled; An epidemic touched off or triggered by a flu bug in 1918 became a pandemic.* **2** any rapid development, as of a fad: *The hula hoop started an epidemic in the 1950s.*

ep·i·gram (EP·uh·gram) *n.* a terse witty saying, esp. one with a paradox in it, e.g. "Revenge is a kind of wild justice."

ep·i·graph (EP·uh·graf) *n.* a motto or quotation written at the front of a building, statue, tomb, etc. or at the beginning of a book or chapter.

ep·i·lep·sy (ep·uh·LEP·see) *n.* **-sies** a chronic nervous disorder marked by convulsions and unconsciousness. — **ep·i·lep·tic** (-tic) *n.* one who has epilepsy. — *adj.*: *an epileptic fit.*

ep·i·logue or **ep·i·log** (EP·uh·log) *n.* a concluding act or piece, as at the end of a play, poem, etc.

e·pis·co·pal (i·PIS·cuh·pul) *adj.* having to do with bishops: *episcopal government, jurisdiction; The (Protestant) Episcopal Church in the U.S. belongs to the Anglican communion.*

e·pis·co·pate (i·PIS·cuh·pit) *n.* **1** a bishop's rank, term of office, or see. **2** bishops collectively.

ep·i·sode (EP·uh·sode) *n.* **1** an incident in a continuous course of events that is complete in itself, as in a literary or artistic work. **2** such a musical passage. **3** any occurrence or event: *a coronary episode; an episode of his childhood.* — **ep·i·sod·ic** (-SOD·ic) *adj.*; **ep·i·sod·i·cal·ly** *adv.*

e·pis·tle (i·PIS·ul) *n.* **1** *Formal.* a letter. **2** **Epistle** one of the apostolic letters of the New Testament.

ep·i·taph (EP·uh·taf) *n.* a short inscription, as on a tombstone or tablet, in memory of a dead person.

ep·i·thet (EP·uh·thet) *n.* a word or phrase to characterize someone, usually descriptive, as "doubting Thomas," often disparaging, as "bloody fool": *a colourful epithet; a racist who often hurls, shouts harsh, offensive, vile epithets at people; His speeches are marked by epithet* (= name-calling) *and abuse.*

e·pit·o·me (i·PIT·uh·mee) *n.* 1 a summary or abstract giving essential features. 2 a person or thing that typifies a specified quality: *Satan is the epitome of evil.*

e·pit·o·mize (i·PIT·uh·mize) *v.* **-miz·es, -mized, -miz·ing** 1 make a summary of something. 2 typify: *Satan epitomizes evil.*

ep·och (EP·uc, EE·poc) *n.* a period of time, esp. with reference to some memorable event; era: *The earth was covered by glaciers during the glacial epoch; Space exploration has ushered in a new epoch in human history; Our landing on the moon marks a new epoch; It was an **epoch-making** event.* — **ep·och·al** (EP·uh·cul) *adj.*

ep·o·nym (EP·uh·nim) *n.* a person from whom an institution, place, theory, movement, etc. is said to get its name: *A. G. Eiffel is the eponym of the Eiffel Tower.*

ep·on·y·mous (ep·ON·uh·mus) *adj.* giving one's name: *the eponymous edifice of A. G. Eiffel; the eponymous hero* (= Anne) *of "Anne of Green Gables."*

eq·ua·ble (EK·wuh·bul) *adj.* not liable to change suddenly; steady: *an equable temper.* — **eq·ua·bly** (-blee) *adv.* — **eq·ua·bil·i·ty** (-BIL·uh·tee) *n.*

e·qual (EE·kwul) *adj.* of the same amount, number, size, value, degree, spread, advantage, etc.: *We are all created equal; A dollar divides into four equal parts of 25 cents each; It's equal in value to four quarters; A quarter is equal to 25 cents; Minorities deserve equal employment opportunities* (with the majority groups); *Women fought for equal rights with men; We want equal pay for work of equal value; an **equal-opportunity** employer* (who gives an equal chance to everyone regardless of sex, race, religion, age, etc.); *the **equal sign*** (=); *the right to **equal time** on radio or TV to air an opposing view; I don't feel **equal to*** (= fit enough for) *my usual walk today.* — *n.* one that is equal: *David and Goliath were not equals; Goliath had no equal in physical strength.* — *v.* **e·quals, e·qualled** or **e·qualed, e·qual·ling** or **e·qual·ing** be or make equal to a person or thing: *Two plus two equals four; Her record has not been equalled, let alone broken; There was no one to equal Goliath in strength.* — **e·qual·ly** *adv.*

e·qual·i·ty (ee·KWOL·uh·tee) *n.* **-ties** the state or an instance of being equal: *to achieve* or *attain equality of opportunity; equality between the sexes; equality among the various sections of the population.*

e·qual·i·za·tion (EEK·wuh·luh·ZAY·shun) *n. Cdn.* the practice of the federal government making grants to the poorer provinces to supplement their tax revenues: *equalization grants, payments.*

e·qual·ize (EEK·wuh·lize) *v.* **-iz·es, -ized, -iz·ing** make equal, even, or uniform. — **e·qual·i·zer** *n.*

e·qua·nim·i·ty (eek·wuh·NIM·uh·tee) *n.* evenness of mind or temper: *She listened to the bad news with equanimity; It didn't upset her equanimity.*

e·quate (ee·QUATE) *v.* **e·quates, e·quat·ed, e·quat·ing** treat one thing as equal to another: *We don't equate happiness with wealth.* — **e·quat·a·ble** *adj.*

e·qua·tion (ee·QUAY·shun) *n.* 1 a sentence using symbols that says two expressions containing at least one variable element in them are equal: *a chemistry equation showing a reaction; a mathematical equation such as "a + b = 0"; to formulate, solve, state an equation.* 2 a variable element in a complex whole: *the human equation; personal equation.* 3 a condition involving an equivalent relationship: *the supply and demand equation; The movement of people between suburbs and cities is one of the prime equations of our social history.*

e·qua·tor (ee·QUAY·tur) *n.* an imaginary circle around a sphere, esp. the earth or a heavenly body, that divides it equally into two hemispheres; also, the corresponding circle in the celestial sphere: *Canada is north of the equator.* — **e·qua·tor·i·al** (eek·wuh·TOR·ee·ul) *adj.: an equatorial current.*

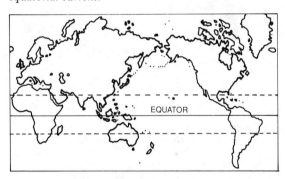

e·ques·tri·an (i·QUES·tree·un) *adj.* on horseback: *Cross-country riding, and show jumping are equestrian events; a circus performer's equestrian skills; an equestrian statue* (showing someone on horseback). — *n.* a horseback rider; *fem.* **e·ques·tri·enne** (i·ques·tree·EN).

e·qui·dis·tant (eek·wuh·DIS·tunt) *adj.* equally distant: *Montreal and New York are equidistant from Vancouver.*

e·qui·lat·er·al (eek·wuh·LAT·uh·rul) *adj.* having all sides equal: *an equilateral triangle.*

e·qui·lib·ri·um (eek·wuh·LIB·ree·um) *n.* state of balance: *He lost his equilibrium and fell into the river; The canals of the inner ear are what help us maintain our equilibrium; Adding weights to one pan of a balance will upset the equilibrium.*

e·quine (EE·quine, EK·wine) *adj.* having to do with horses: *equine encephalitis, events, flu, research, stars, vets.* — *n.* a horse.

e·qui·nox (EEK·wuh·nox) *n.* either of two times of the year when the sun crosses the equator and day and night are of equal length all over the globe: *autumnal equinox; spring* or *vernal equinox.* — **e·qui·noc·tial** (-NOK·shul) *adj.*

e·quip (i·QUIP) v. **e·quips, e·quipped, e·quip·ping**
supply or provide with what is needed to make an
occupation or function more efficient: *a car equipped
with power steering; a party well equipped for camping
out; First aid equips you to deal with life-and-death
emergencies.*
— **e·quip·ment** n.: *military equipment; office
equipment; sports equipment such as bats, gloves,
masks, and helmets.*

e·quip·age (EK·wuh·pij) n. a carriage with horses,
driver, and attendants.

e·qui·poise (EK·wuh·poiz) n. 1 even balance;
equilibrium. 2 a force or weight that restores balance;
counterbalance.

eq·ui·ta·ble (EK·wuh·tuh·bul) adj. characterized by
equity: *Preferential hiring of minority candidates is
considered equitable by some and unjust by others.*
— **eq·ui·ta·bly** adv.

eq·ui·ty (EK·wuh·tee) n. **-ties** 1 fairness or justice;
hence, a law that goes beyond common law and statutes,
based on reason and the spirit of the law: *a court of
equity.* 2 what a property is worth beyond what is owed
on it: *The equity on your home increases as you pay off
the mortgage.* 3 **equities** pl. the ordinary shares of a
corporation.

e·quiv·a·lent (i·KWIV·uh·lunt) adj. having equal force,
value, effect, significance, etc.: *Send us $20 or an
equivalent amount in pounds; A mile is equivalent to
1.609 km.*
— n.: *Today's dollar is the equivalent of a quarter some
years back; Few words have exact equivalents in
different languages.* — **e·quiv·a·lence** n.

e·quiv·o·cal (i·KWIV·uh·cul) adj. 1 capable of more
than one interpretation; hence, ambivalent or deceptive:
*an equivocal answer, attitude, reply, statement; He
sounded equivocal about joining the party.* 2 of
language or behaviour, doubtful or questionable: *Does
dual citizenship mean equivocal loyalties?*

e·quiv·o·cate (i·KWIV·uh·cate) v. **-cates, -cat·ed,
-cat·ing** use words of double meaning in order to
deceive. — **e·quiv·o·ca·tor** (-cay·tur) n.
— **e·quiv·o·ca·tion** (-CAY·shun) n.

-er 1 n. suffix. agent or other person or thing related to
something specified: *gardener, singer, six-footer.*
2 comparative suffix: *harder, taller, wiser.*

e·ra (EER·uh, AIR·uh) n. a period of time, esp. one
starting from a particular event or one with distinctive
characteristics: *the Christian era; in the Victorian era;
The automobile ushered in a new era in transportation.*

e·rad·i·cate (i·RAD·uh·cate) v. **-cates, -cat·ed, -cat·ing**
completely get rid of something that has established
itself; uproot or eliminate: *reforms to eradicate social
injustices; a program to eradicate poverty; to eradicate
bad habits, crime, diseases, ignorance, illiteracy, vice.*
— **e·rad·i·ca·tion** (-CAY·shun) n.

e·rase (i·RACE) v. **e·ras·es, e·rased, e·ras·ing** wipe out,
esp. by rubbing or scraping, as a by a rubber **e·ras·er,**
or magnetically, as by a tape recorder's **erase head.**
— **e·ras·a·ble** (-suh·bul) adj.; **e·ras·ure** (i·RAY·zhur) n.

ere (AIR) prep. & conj. [old use] before.

e·rect (i·RECT) adj. upright, esp. straight, not bent or
lying down: *Soldiers stand erect; an erect post; Apes
don't have the erect posture of human beings.*
— v. 1 make erect: *to erect (= put up) a building,
flagpole, statue, tent.* 2 establish: *a monument erected
in memory of war heroes.* — **e·rec·tion** n.
— **e·rect·ly** adv.; **e·rect·ness** n.; **e·rec·tor** n.

e·rec·tile (i·REC·tul) adj. capable of erection: *an erectile
organ; erectile tissue.*

er·go (UR·goh) adv. therefore; hence.

er·go·nom·ics (ur·guh·NOM·ics) n. pl. the science of
human work and efficient working conditions.

er·mine (UR·min) n. 1 the white winter fur of a weasel,
that is valuable as trimming and is traditionally used on
the robes of judges and European peers as a symbol of
rank; adj.: *ermine caps, coats, jackets; ermine-lined
boots; an ermined judge in her ermine-trimmed robe.*
2 the animal itself.

e·rode (i·RODE) v. **e·rodes, e·rod·ed, e·rod·ing** wear
away by gradual action, esp. of water, wind, acid, etc.:
*Canyons are spectacular examples of the eroding power
of water; Running water erodes soil and rocks; It erodes
(= forms by wearing away) channels on the face of the
earth.* — **e·ro·sion** (i·ROH·zhun) n.

e·rog·e·nous (i·ROJ·uh·nus) adj. sexually sensitive or
arousing: *the erogenous parts of the body; erogenous
zones.*

e·rot·ic (i·ROT·ic) adj. having to do with sexual love.
— **e·rot·i·cal·ly** adv.

e·rot·i·ca (i·ROT·uh·cuh) n. pl. erotic literature, art,
etc.

err (UR, AIR) v. do or be wrong: *"To err is human, to
forgive divine"; You can never err on the side of honesty
(= You can never be too honest).*

er·rand (ER·und) n. a trip to do something for someone
else, as to deliver a message; also, the object of the trip:
*His job is to run errands for everyone in the office;
Florence Nightingale's errands of mercy as a nurse.*

er·rant (ER·unt) adj. 1 roving: *an errant knight.*
2 straying: *errant sheep.*

er·rat·a (uh·RAT·uh, uh·RAH-) n. pl. errors made in a
book or other publication.

er·rat·ic (uh·RAT·ic) adj. irregular or eccentric: *erratic
behaviour; an erratic clock.*

er·ro·ne·ous (uh·ROH·nee·us) adj. mistaken or
incorrect: *the erroneous assumption that the earth is
flat; erroneous ideas, notions.* — **er·ro·ne·ous·ly** adv.

er·ror (ER·ur) n. something mistaken, a wrong or
incorrect action, a misplay or failure in a game, etc.:
*She's in error about my birth date; an error in
judgment; an error compounded by mismanagement;
The accident was caused by human error; to commit,
correct, make, rectify an error; a clerical, costly,
egregious, flagrant, glaring, grievous, serious, tactical
error; Lou opened Lee's letter by or in error (= by
mistake); He repented of his errors (= moral wrongs) in
his old age.*

er·satz (UR·zahts, ER-) adj. a substitute or imitation

product, considered inferior: *Margarine is ersatz butter; the ersatz culture of the newly rich.*

erst·while (URST·while) *adj.* of a little while ago; former: *Her erstwhile admirer is marrying someone else tomorrow.*

er·u·dite (ER·yuh·dite, ER·uh-) *adj.* learned or scholarly: *an erudite man, scholar, woman; an erudite work in literary criticism.*

er·u·di·tion (er·yuh·DISH·un) *n.* learning and scholarship, esp. of the specialized kind: *a man of great erudition whose works are not for the masses; His books show amazing erudition without being pedantic.*

e·rupt (i·RUPT) *v.* break out or burst forth: *Volcanoes erupt (lava); Hot water and steam erupt from geysers; A riot erupted; Milk teeth erupt during a baby's first year.*
— **e·rup·tion** *n.*: *rashes and other skin eruptions; a volcanic eruption.*

es·ca·late (ES·cuh·late) *v.* **-lates, -lat·ed, -lat·ing** rise as on an escalator; hence, increase, expand, intensify, develop, etc.: *A small incident escalates into a major confrontation.* — **es·ca·la·tion** (-LAY·shun) *n.*

es·ca·la·tor (ES·cuh·lay·tur) *n.* **1** a moving staircase on an endless belt: *the up escalator and the down escalator.* **2** same as **escalator clause,** a provision for adjusting wages, prices, etc. upward under specified conditions.

es·cal·lop (es·CAL·up, es·COLL·up) *n.* same as SCALLOP.

es·ca·pade (ES·cuh·pade) *n.* an adventurous act, esp. one involving freedom from restraint: *a childish Halloween escapade that turned into a tragedy.*

es·cape (es·CAPE) *v.* **-capes, -caped, -cap·ing 1** get away or get away from somewhere: *Convicts try to escape from prison; Air has escaped from the tire; A cry of pain escaped her lips; Her name escapes (= eludes) me.* **2** stay free of something: *Many criminals escape being caught; He escaped death by sheer luck.*
— *n.* an escaping or a means of escaping: *a narrow, hairbreadth escape from death; The burglar made good (= effected) his escape before the police arrived; to foil or thwart an escape; an escape from captivity; the escape of air from a tire; Romances are her favourite escape (from reality); He clambered down the fire escape (= emergency staircase).*
— *adj.*: *an escape hatch; Escape literature frees us from the pressures of reality; escape mechanism, valve, velocity.*

es·cap·ee (es·CAY·pee, es·cay·PEE) *n.* one who has escaped, esp. from confinement. Also **es·cap·er** (es·CAY·pur).

es·cap·ism (es·CAY·piz·um) *n.* flight from unpleasant realities, responsibilities, etc. by means of diversions.
— **es·cap·ist** *n. & adj.*: *an escapist attitude, fantasy, myth, show; escapist literature.*

es·car·got (es·car·GOH) *n.* **-gots** a garden snail that is eaten as a delicacy.

es·carp·ment (es·CARP·munt) *n.* a steep slope or embankment of considerable length: *The Niagara Escarpment runs from the Niagara River to Tobermory at the north end of the Bruce Peninsula.*

es·chew (es·CHOO) *v.* shun or avoid with special care: *to eschew vice and practise virtue.*

es·cort (ES·cort) *n.* a person or group accompanying another to give protection or as courtesy: *The police provided an escort for the procession; They proceeded under police escort; She came to the dance without an escort* (= male companion).
— *v.* (es·CORT) go with someone as an escort: *The receptionist escorted the visitor to the door; Fifty aircraft escorted the royal yacht.*

-ese *suffix.* **1** *n. & adj.* (a person) of or from a country: *Assamese, Chinese, Portuguese.* **2** *n.* a jargon or occupational dialect: *bureaucratese, computerese, legalese.*

Es·ki·mo (ES·kuh·moh) *n.* **-mos 1** one of a native people of the Arctic, properly called "the Inuit." **2** their language. — **Es·ki·mo** or **Es·ki·mo·an** (-MOH·un) *adj.*

Eskimo dog *n. Cdn.* a breed of powerful dog used to pull sleds in the Arctic: *The Siberian husky is an Eskimo dog.*

es·o·ter·ic (es·uh·TER·ic) *adj.* unintelligible except to those initiated: *an esoteric doctrine, system; esoteric ideas, literature.*

es·pe·cial (es·PESH·ul) *adj.* special in a pre-eminent manner; exceptional: *A special consideration was given in her especial case because of the disability.*
— **es·pe·cial·ly** *adv.*

es·pi·o·nage (ES·pee·uh·nahzh, -uh·nij) *n.* spying for political, military, or industrial purposes: *to conduct or engage in espionage.*

es·pla·nade (es·pluh·NAHD, -NADE) *n.* a place designated as a public walk or drive, usually along a shore.

es·pous·al (i·SPOW·zul) *n.* **1** an espousing of a cause or idea. **2 espousals** *pl.* formerly, betrothal or wedding ceremonies.

es·pouse (es·POWZE) *v.* **-pous·es, -poused, -pous·ing** advocate or take up: *to espouse a cause; the values that we espouse in our society.*

es·prit de corps (es·PREE·duh·COR) *n.* group spirit; comradeship.

es·py (es·PYE) *v.* **-pies, -pied, -py·ing** catch sight of, esp. something small or partly hidden.

-esque *adj. suffix.* like: *arabesque, Disneyesque, picturesque, statuesque.*

es·quire (ES·quire) *n.* an Anglo-Saxon title of courtesy used formally after a man's surname, esp. by lawyers, men and sometimes women, instead of "Mr." or other prefixed title: *Chris Capone, Esq., Barrister & Solicitor.*

-ess *n. suffix.* female: *empress, lioness, mistress;* [derogatory] *Jewess, negress, poetess.*

es·say (ES·ay) *n.* **1** a literary composition, usually short and in prose, less formal than a treatise; **es·say·ist** *n.* **2** (*also* es·AY) a trial or attempt.
— *v.* (*usually* es·AY) attempt: *Before leaping in, she essayed to find out how deep the water was;* **es·say·er** *n.*

es·sence (ES·unce) *n.* **1** the basic or most important nature or quality, as the "greenness" of grass: *She is the* very essence of good manners; The essence of good manners is thoughtfulness; That is what it means *in essence* (= essentially); Time is *of the essence* (= a most important consideration) in an emergency. **2** something abstracted, extracted, or distilled, as the gist of a speech, a meat extract, a perfume, etc.

es·sen·tial (i·SEN·shul) adj. having to do with essence: Food is necessary for survival, but life jackets are essential for safety in water; It's essential that everyone wear a life jacket; Breathing is essential to life; "Attar of roses" is an **essential oil** extracted from rose petals. — n.: The three R's are the essentials of a good education; the bare or basic essentials for survival in the jungle. — **es·sen·tial·ly** adv.

est or **EST** n. a psychological training program for developing one's personality and potential.

es·tab·lish (uh·STAB·lish) v. set up on a firm foundation: a company established in 1827; A dentist establishes himself in a neighbourhood; Much evidence is needed to establish a motive; It was finally established that he was innocent; the state-established Church of England; It takes time for a practice to get established (= accepted) as a custom; Words get established by usage.

es·tab·lish·ment (uh·STAB·lish·munt) n. **1** an establishing or thing established, as a household or business with all its members or employees. **2** a controlling group: the literary establishment; the medical establishment. **3** the **Establishment**, the dominant social group; the elite: the Toronto Establishment; The Establishment prefers pinstripes to jeans.

es·tate (is·TATE) n. **1** a large property, including a house: He owns a large tea estate; a coffee estate; rubber estate; an industrial estate (= an area of factories). **2** what one owns, esp. as left by a deceased person: to come into an estate (= inherit property); real estate (= immovable property); adj.: an **estate tax** (= succession duty); an **estate wagon** (Brit. for station wagon). **3** condition or stage in life: A boy reaches man's estate (= adulthood as a man); The nobles, clergy, and common people were the **three estates**; the **fourth estate** (= journalists).

es·teem (is·TEEM) n. great regard: She is held in high esteem as a surgeon; She rose in the esteem of her staff as the years went by, while others fell in their esteem. — v. regard highly: your esteemed journal; a highly esteemed lawyer; I esteem (= consider) it an honour to write for your paper.

esthete, esthetic, etc. same as AESTHETE, AESTHETIC, etc.

es·ti·ma·ble (ES·tuh·muh·bul) adj. worthy of esteem.

es·ti·mate (ES·tuh·mate) v. **-mates, -mat·ed, -mat·ing** judge or give an approximate calculation of the worth, size, etc. of something: We estimate that the project will cost $100 000; We estimate the cost to be $100 000; The cost is estimated at $100 000; to estimate the damage done to a car; to estimate a job in regard to cost or fee; to estimate a population. — n. (-mit) an opinion, esp. an approximate calculation: to give, make, submit an estimate; What's your estimate for producing this book? a ballpark,

conservative, preliminary, rough estimate; By my estimate, it will cost around $750 000. — **es·ti·ma·tor** (-may·tur) n.

es·ti·ma·tion (es·tuh·MAY·shun) n. **1** an opinion or judgment: In our estimation, the project is not workable. **2** esteem: She was held in high estimation by all.

es·tranged (es·TRAINJD) adj. alienated from friend or relative: He lived alone, estranged from family and friends. — **es·trange·ment** n.

es·tu·ar·y (ES·choo·air·ee) n. **-ar·ies** the mouth of a large river into which the tide flows from the sea.

et al. (et·AL) n. pl. and the other people: Luc, Guy, Mimi, et al.

et cet·er·a (et·SET·uh·ruh, -SET·ruh) n. pl. [usually shortened to "etc."] and the rest; and the like: cats, dogs, hamsters, etc.; lawyers, doctors, engineers, etc. (= and such people); books, papers, pencils, **and the et ceteras** (Informal for other such).

etch (ECH) v. **1** produce a drawing or other design on a metal or glass plate by the action of acid: an etched design, figure. **2** engrave deeply: a tragic event etched forever in her memory; a sharply etched character, feature. — **etch·er** n.

e·ter·nal (i·TUR·nul) adj. **1** having no beginning or end in time; timeless: the eternal life of heavenly beings; Because of its long history, Rome has been called the "Eternal city"; The "eternal triangle" of a third party involved with a couple is a favourite theme in romances; the eternal (= unchanging) verities of truth and justice; God **the Eternal;** the eternal (= perpetual) flame burning at a memorial. **2** Informal. seeming never to stop; ceaseless: the eternal chatter of gossips; eternal complaining; an eternal nuisance; Hope springs eternal for the optimist in us. — **e·ter·nal·ly** adv.

e·ter·ni·ty (i·TUR·nuh·tee) n. **-ties 1** endlessness of time. **2** an infinite or seemingly endless period: an eternity of anxious waiting; It seemed like an eternity; an **eternity ring** set with a continuous row of stones.

eth·a·nol (ETH·uh·nol) n. ethyl alcohol.

e·ther (EE·thur, "th" as in "thin") n. **1** a colourless, volatile, sweet-smelling liquid used as an anesthetic. **2** the invisible substance once thought to fill all space.

e·the·re·al (i·THEER·ee·ul, "TH" as in "thin") adj. heavenly; also, airy; light: her ethereal beauty; ethereal music. — **e·the·re·al·ly** adv.

eth·ic (ETH·ic, "TH" as in "thin") n. **1** a rule of conduct; also, a system of such rules: The Protestant work ethic says work is ennobling. **2 ethics** pl. [takes sing. v.] moral philosophy; also, the moral quality of an action: Ethics is taught in schools; Infants don't understand the ethics of taking things without asking. **3 ethics** pl. [takes pl. v.] rules of conduct: His professional ethics are faultless.

eth·i·cal (ETH·uh·cul) adj. agreeing with a professional standard: The firing was quite legal though not ethical; Whatever be his morals, he's very ethical as a lawyer; the ethical, moral, and social questions raised by surrogate parenthood; ethical issues, standards, systems; **ethical drugs** (= prescription drugs). — **eth·i·cal·ly** adv.

Eth·i·o·pi·an (ee·thee·OH·pee·un, "th" as in "thin") **1** *n.* & *adj.* (a person) of or from **Ethiopia**, an East African country. **2** [rarely] black in complexion.

eth·nic (ETH·nic, "TH" as in "thin") *adj.* [sometimes hostile in the sense of "foreign"] having to do with people, esp. minorities, grouped according to language, nationality, race, or religion; ethno·cultural: *The French are an ethnic group in the U.S. but one of the two founding nations of Canada; an ethnic background, community, custom, food, newspaper, restaurant, riding; ethnic culture, origins, sensibilities, theatre; the ethnic vote; the ethnic Chinese of the U.S.S.R.; Think ethnic* (= Be proud of your heritage)!; *"Heritage languages" is more polite than ethnic languages; an ethnic* (=racial) *joke, slur.*
— *n.* [usually derogatory] a member of an ethnic group: *Multiculturalism is not just for ethnics; Jews, blacks, and other ethnics.*
— **eth·ni·cal·ly** *adv.: The Scots and the Irish are ethnically quite close.*

eth·nic·i·ty (eth·NIS·uh·tee) *n.* the fact or quality of being ethnic: *immigration quotas based on ethnicity.*

eth·no·cul·tur·al (eth·noh·CUL·chuh·rul) *adj.* ethnic.

eth·nog·ra·phy (eth·NOG·ruh·fee) *n.* the study of racial and cultural groups.

eth·nol·o·gy (eth·NOL·uh·jee) *n.* the anthropology of racial and cultural groups, their origins, distribution, and characteristics. — **eth·nol·o·gist** *n.*
— **eth·no·log·ic** (eth·nuh·LOJ·ic) or **eth·no·log·i·cal** (-uh·cul) *adj.*

e·thos (EE·thos) *n.* the underlying moral and ethnic character of a person or group; code of values.

eth·yl (ETH·ul, "TH" as in "thin") *n.* the hydrocarbon base of common alcohol, ether, etc.

eth·yl·ene (eth·uh·LEEN) *n.* a gaseous hydrocarbon with an unpleasant odour, used as an anesthetic, to make polyethylene, and in **ethylene glycol**, automobile antifreeze.

et·i·quette (ET·uh·kut, -ket) *n.* conventional rules of behaviour, as in polite society, a particular profession, etc.: *the etiquette prescribed for weddings; courtroom etiquette; military etiquette; Social etiquette includes table manners.*

et seq. *n. pl.* and the following ones, as pages of a book.

-ette *n. suffix.* **1** female: *majorette, suffragette, usherette.* **2** small; also, imitation or substitute: *cigarette, leatherette, flannelette.*

et·y·mol·o·gy (et·uh·MOL·uh·jee) *n.* **-gies 1** the history of a particular word: *to determine* or *trace the etymology of "OK."* **2** the study of the origin and development of words. — **et·y·mol·o·gist** (-jist) *n.*
— **et·y·mo·log·i·cal** (et·uh·muh·LOJ·uh·cul) *adj.*

eu- *n.* & *adj. prefix.* good; well; true: *euphemism, euphonious, euphoria.*

Eu·cha·rist (YOO·cuh·rist) *n.* Communion or the consecrated bread and wine used in it: *Christians celebrate the Eucharist on Sundays; Catholics receive the Eucharist during Mass.*
— **Eu·cha·ris·tic** (-RIS·tic) or **Eu·cha·ris·ti·cal** (-tuh·cul) *adj.*

eu·gen·ics (yoo·JEN·ics) *n. pl.* [takes sing. v.] the science of improving the human race by selective control of reproduction and thereby heredity.
— **eu·gen·ic** *adj.;* **eu·gen·i·cal·ly** *adv.;* **eu·gen·i·cist** *n.*

eu·lo·gy (YOO·luh·jee) *n.* **-gies** a formal speech or a piece of writing in high praise of a person, as at a funeral: *The minister delivered a touching eulogy for the war dead; The letter was an eloquent eulogy to the leader of the expedition.* — **eu·lo·gist** *n.*
— **eu·lo·gis·tic** (-JIS·tic) *adj.*

eu·lo·gize (YOO·luh·jize) *v.* **-giz·es, -gized, -giz·ing** praise highly, as in a eulogy. — **eu·lo·giz·er** *n.*

eu·nuch (YOO·nuk) *n.* a castrated boy or man.

eu·phe·mism (YOO·fuh·miz·um) *n.* an inoffensive term used in place of another considered overused or offensive, e.g. "funeral director" for "undertaker."
— **eu·phe·mis·tic** (yoo·fuh·MIS·tic) *adj.*

eu·pho·ni·ous (yoo·FOH·nee·us) *adj.* having euphony: *euphonious music; "Syllabication" is more euphonious than "syllabification."*

eu·pho·ny (YOO·fuh·nee) *n.* **-nies** pleasantness or smoothness of sounds, esp. spoken.

eu·pho·ri·a (yoo·FOR·ee·uh) *n.* a feeling of well-being or high spirits, esp. as produced by drugs such as amphetamines or cocaine: *in a state of euphoria; A feeling of euphoria came over her when she heard the great news.* — **eu·phor·ic** *adj.*

Eur·a·sian (yoo·RAY·zhun) **1** *adj.* having to do with Europe and Asia considered as one land mass. **2** *n.* a person of mixed European and Asian descent.

eu·re·ka (yoo·REE·kuh) *interj.* indicating triumph at a discovery, as Archimedes exclaimed ("I've found it" in Greek) on solving a problem.

Eu·ro·dol·lars (YOOR·uh·doll·urz) *n. pl.* U.S. dollars deposited in foreign banks for use as currency in Europe.

Eu·ro·pe·an (yoor·uh·PEE·un) *n.* & *adj.* (a person) of or from Europe: *Asians and Europeans; The European Common Market* or *Economic Community of 12 nations as trading partners; European immigrants, population.*

eu·tha·na·si·a (yoo·thuh·NAY·zhuh) *n.* the causing of death in order to end prolonged suffering in terminal cases; mercy killing.

eu·troph·ic (yoo·TROF·ic) *adj.* polluted by excess of nutrients such as phosphates from human wastes.

e·vac·u·ate (i·VAC·yoo·ate) *v.* **-ates, -at·ed, -at·ing 1** to empty: *to evacuate the bowels, stomach; to evacuate* (=discharge) *bodily wastes.* **2** withdraw from a place: *They were told to evacuate the area before the hurricane struck; to evacuate a city; to evacuate* (=remove) *people from a disaster area; The order to evacuate came in the middle of the night.*
— **e·vac·u·a·tion** (-AY·shun) *n.: to carry out a mass evacuation from a disaster area.*

e·vac·u·ee (i·VAC·yoo·ee) *n.* an evacuated person.

e·vade (i·VADE) *v.* **e·vades, e·vad·ed, e·vad·ing** use trickery or skill to escape or dodge enemies, responsibilities, and other unwelcome things: *She successfully evaded the reporter's questions; Taxes may be legally avoided but not evaded; During the 1960s, many Americans moved to Canada to evade the draft.* — **e·vad·er** *n.*

e·val·u·ate (i·VAL·yoo·ate) *v.* **-ates, -at·ed, -at·ing** determine the amount, quality, or value of nonmaterial things such as evidence, someone's performance, career, etc.: *to evaluate a plan, play.* — **e·val·u·a·tion** (-AY·shun) *n.* appraisal: *to make a critical, fair, objective evaluation of a poem.*

ev·a·nes·cent (ev·uh·NES·unt) *adj.* tending to fade away from sight; vanishing: *an evanescent dream.* — **ev·a·nes·cence** *n.*

e·van·gel·i·cal (i·van·JEL·uh·cul) *adj.* **1** relating to the four Gospels. **2** of Protestant churches such as the Methodist and Baptist, stressing faith and the preaching of the Gospels rather than ritual and good works for salvation. — *n.* a member of such a church.

e·van·gel·ist (i·VAN·juh·list) *n.* **1 Evangelist** one of the four who wrote the Gospels: Matthew, Mark, Luke, and John. **2** a preacher, esp. a Gospel revivalist.

e·van·gel·ize (i·VAN·juh·lize) *v.* **-iz·es, -ized, -iz·ing** preach the Gospel to a people: *St. Columba evangelized the Scots; St. Thomas evangelized India.*

e·vap·o·rate (i·VAP·uh·rate) *v.* **-rates, -rat·ed, -rat·ing** **1** change a liquid or solid into a gas: *Heat evaporates water;* **Evaporated milk** *is milk thickened by evaporating for canning.* **2** become gaseous: *Water evaporates into vapour or steam; Hopes may evaporate* (= disappear) . — **e·vap·o·ra·tion** (-RAY·shun) *n.*

e·va·sion (i·VAY·zhun) *n.* an act of evading: *a charge of tax evasion.*

e·va·sive (i·VAY·siv) *adj.* evading: *an evasive answer; The pilot took evasive action to avoid a midair collision.*

Eve (EEV) *n.* **1** in the Bible, the first woman and the wife of Adam. **2** also **eve,** the evening or day before: *Christmas Eve; on the eve of* (= the time just before) *our wedding.*

e·ven (EE·vun) *adj.* **1** of equal level: *The water level rose and was even with the pavement; an even* (= smooth) *surface.* **2** having equal intervals; uniform or regular: *the even hum of an engine.* **3** that divides equally, leaving no remainder: *The property was divided in even shares among the three sons; 2, 4, 6, 8, etc. are even numbers; Give me an even* (= exact) *dozen.*
4 equal: *Give the girls an even break with the boys; an even* (= fifty-fifty) *chance; to bet even money* (= have odds of winning what one has risked); *He vowed to* **get even** with (= get revenge on) *her for tricking him; The business is beginning to* **break even** (= have gains equalling losses) *after ten years; After a long fight, Lee called it* **even steven** or **stephen** *with Lou and continued to be friends.*
— *adv.* [to emphasize a comparison]: *He can't even walk, let alone run; John is tall, but his sister is even taller; The patient died* **even as** (= just as) *the doctor arrived; She won't go* **even if** *she is invited; He is still sore,* **even so** (= still) *he should forgive her; Lou refuses to eat* **even though** (= although) *he is hungry.*
— *v.* make or become even or equal: *Use the trimmer to*

even the edges; *Losses and gains* **even out** *over the years; Our team* **evened up** *the score in the second period.* — **e·ven·ly** *adv.;* **e·ven·ness** *n.*

even-handed (EE·vun·HAN·did) *adj.* impartial: *A judge metes out even-handed justice.*

eve·ning (EEV·ning) *n.* the final part of day and the early part of night: *Good evening (to you)! (Good) evening! I'll see you at seven (o'clock) in the evening* (= 7 p.m.); *a gala evening; We stay home* **evenings** (*Informal* for in the evenings).

e·vent (i·VENT) *n.* **1** a happening, esp. one of relative importance: *The first day of school is an event in a child's life; A birth is a blessed event; Read the papers for current events; A disastrous event took place* or *occurred last year on this day; the dramatic events of the hijacking and rescue of the passengers; a historical event such as the signing of a treaty; The publication of a book is a literary event; the main events of last year; a major event of her childhood; a media event; sporting event; tragic event; Everyone can be* **wise after the event** (= can give advice about something after it has happened). **2** an item in a program of sports: *track and field events; swimming events.* **3** result or consequence that is unforeseen or beyond human control: *In that event we shall have to sell our house and move into an apartment.*
— **at all events** or **in any event** whatever happens.
— **in the event of** or **that** in case of.

even-tempered (EE·vun·TEM·purd) *adj.* calm: *an even-tempered woman.*

e·vent·ful (i·VENT·ful) *adj.* full of noteworthy events: *an eventful day at work.* — **e·vent·ful·ly** *adv.*

e·ven·tide (EE·vun·tide) *n.* [old use] evening.

e·ven·tu·al (i·VEN·choo·ul) *adj.* of an event, happening as a final effect: *the eventual defeat of the enemy; the eventual outcome of the war; our eventual victory.* — **e·ven·tu·al·ly** *adv.*

e·ven·tu·al·i·ty (i·VEN·choo·AL·uh·tee) *n.* **-ties** a possible outcome: *In the eventuality of a hailstorm, an umbrella may not help much.*

ev·er (EV·ur) *adv.* **1** at any time; by any chance: *Have you ever been to P.E.I.? Does Sue ever complain? Does she ever* (= She does)! *She is a complainer, if ever there was one* (= She is a perfect example of a complainer); [used after *how, what, when, where,* and *who* for added force] *How ever did this happen? Who ever told you that?* **2** at all times; forever: *Yours ever* or *Ever yours* or *Yours as ever* [used at the close of an informal letter]; *faithful as ever; lived happily ever after.* **3** [following a superlative]: *the greatest boxer ever* (= that ever lived)!
— **ever and anon** *Poetic.* every now and then.
— **ever so** *Informal.* very: *This has happened ever so often; in ever so many cases; Thank you ever so much.*
— **for ever and a day** always.

ev·er·green (EV·ur·green) *n.* a plant or tree that has green leaves all year round, as pine, spruce, etc.: *Most tropical plants are evergreens.* Also *adj.*

ev·er·last·ing (ev·ur·LAST·ing) *adj.* lasting an eternity. — **ev·er·last·ing·ly** *adv.*

ev·er·more (ev·ur·MORE) *adv.* forever.

ev·er·y (EV·ree) *adj.* **1** each of a group [including all, or one after another if indefinite]: *Trains leave here every hour; It happens every day; Not every Tom, Dick, and Harry (Informal for the ordinary person) goes to college.* **2** all possible [with abstract noun]: *You have every reason to be proud of your children.*
— **every last one** *Informal.* every one.
— **every now and then** or **every now and again** occasionally; also **every once in a while** and **every so often.**
— **every which way** *Informal.* in all directions.

ev·er·y·bod·y (EV·ree·bod·ee, -bud·ee) *pron.* everyone: *Everybody loves somebody;* **Everybody and his brother** *walks over Jim's lawn.*

ev·er·y·day (EV·ree·day) *adj.* daily; hence, common or ordinary: *words that are in everyday use; An everyday occurrence is one that happens very commonly; everyday English, expenses, happenings, incidents, language, life, objects, shoes; clothes for everyday wear at home, work, or school.*

ev·er·y·one (EV·ree·wun) *pron.* every person.

ev·er·y·thing *n. & pron.* every thing; all: *a gift for the woman who has everything; Children are everything* (= very important) *to her.*

ev·er·y·where (EV·ree·where) *adv.* in or to every place: *Look everywhere.* Also **ev·er·y·place.**

e·vict (i·VICT) *v.* oust or discharge a tenant *from* a house or land by legal process.
— **e·vic·tion** (i·VIC·shun) *n.;* **e·vic·tor** *n.*

ev·i·dence (EV·uh·dunce) *n.* something that supports an assertion: *Possession of stolen property is evidence of theft; The testimony of witnesses proved strong evidence that he had committed the crime; not mere hearsay evidence; a signed receipt produced in evidence against a defaulter; to dig up, find, furnish, gather, piece together, suppress, turn up, unearth, withhold evidence; The incriminating evidence had been planted on the accused; ample, circumstantial, compelling, conclusive, damaging, documentary, substantial, telltale evidence; a body of evidence; not a piece, scrap, shred of evidence against the accused; The bulk of the evidence is undeniable; The hit-and-run car was nowhere* **in evidence** (= to be seen); *One of the accused* **turned Queen's** or **King's** or **state's evidence** (= joined the prosecution) *and testified against the others.*
— *v.* **-denc·es, -denced, -denc·ing** be a sign of something: *Spontaneous tears evidenced his sorrow.*

ev·i·dent (EV·uh·dunt) *adj.* clear and plain to the understanding: *Her language showed her evident displeasure; It was evident that she was displeased.*
— **ev·i·dent·ly** *adv.*

e·vil (EE·vul) *n.* something very bad, harmful, or unlucky: *to root out the evils of drug abuse; Is idleness or money the root of all evil? When both candidates are unsuitable, one has to choose* **the lesser of two evils;** *Politics is a* **necessary evil** (that cannot be avoided).
— *adj.* to ward off the **evil eye** (= the look bringing bad luck); *an* **evil-minded** (= malicious) *gossip; the* **Evil One** (= the Devil).

e·voc·a·tive (i·VOC·uh·tiv) *adj.* evoking: *an incident evocative of old memories.*

— **ev·o·ca·tion** (ev·uh·CAY·shun) *n.*

e·voke (i·VOKE) *v.* **e·vokes, e·voked, e·vok·ing** call forth; elicit, esp. a response from the mind or emotions.

ev·o·lu·tion (ev·uh·LOO·shun) *n.* an evolving or development; also, a result of this: *The evolution of the horseless carriage into the automobile; the organic evolution of higher forms of life from the lower; Darwin's theory of evolution by natural selection; evolution as opposed to creation by God.*
— **ev·o·lu·tion·ar·y** (-shuh·nair·ee) *adj.*
— **ev·o·lu·tion·ism** *n.;* **ev·o·lu·tion·ist** *n.*

e·volve (i·VOLV) *v.* **e·volves, e·volved, e·volv·ing** develop gradually: *Did the modern horse evolve from the "Eohippus" of 65 million years ago?*

ewe (YOO) *n.* a female sheep.

ex 1 *prep.* from; out of: *Goods are shipped ex warehouse; She is here ex officio.* **2** *prefix.* out of: *excommunicate, export, expurgate.* **3** *prefix.* former: *ex-convict, ex-president, ex-wife.* **4** *n., pl.* **ex·es** *Informal.* one's divorced spouse. **5 the Ex** *n. Cdn. Informal.* an exhibition such as the Canadian National Exhibition and the Central Canada Exhibition.

ex·ac·er·bate (eg·ZAS·ur·bate) *v.* **-bates, -bat·ed, -bat·ing** aggravate or make worse: *to exacerbate anxieties, concerns, fears, problems, situations.*
— **ex·ac·er·ba·tion** (-BAY·shun) *n.*

ex·act (eg·ZACT) *adj.* **1** agreeing in every detail; correct: *an exact copy; the exact size of a room; Passengers should pay exact fares in tickets, tokens, or cash since the driver carries no change; the* **exact same** (Nonstandard for very same) *man I met yesterday.* **2** characterized by or capable of precision: *The calculations are exact in every detail; an exact aim, calculation; Psychology is not an* **exact science** *like physics or chemistry.* — **ex·act·ly** *adv.;* **ex·act·ness** *n.*
— *v.* obtain forcefully what is demanded: *a disciplinarian who exacts obedience from everyone; Tributes were exacted from conquered nations.*
— **ex·ac·tion** *n.*
— **exacting** *adj.: an exacting work schedule; a child who is very exacting in his demands.*

ex·ac·ti·tude (eg·ZAC·tuh·tude) *n.* the quality or an instance of exactness: *a woman of great exactitude.*

ex·ag·ger·ate (eg·ZAJ·uh·rate) *v.* **-ates, -at·ed, -at·ing** magnify or overstate something: *Cartoonists exaggerate facial features out of proportion; She always exaggerates; a greatly or grossly* **exaggerated** *account of what happened.* — **ex·ag·ger·a·tion** (-RAY·shun) *n.*

ex·alt (eg·ZAWLT) v. raise in rank, power, dignity, glory, etc.; elevate or glorify: *the tendency to exalt commonplace things to the skies; He has an **exalted** opinion of himself.*
— **ex·al·ta·tion** (eg·zawl·TAY·shun) n.: *great joy and exaltation.*

ex·am (eg·ZAM) n. *Informal.* an examination or a set of examination questions; *adj.: exam fever; exam results.*

ex·am·i·na·tion (eg·ZAM·uh·NAY·shun) n. 1 a close inspection or study: *the examination of a new theory; A physician does or makes a physical examination of* or *on a patient; a careful, cursory, in-depth, superficial, thorough examination; On close examination, the painting was found to be a fake.* 2 a test or set of questions: *a competitive, comprehensive, difficult, easy, entrance, final, makeup, oral, placement, qualifying, written examination in a subject, on a topic; to administer, conduct, draw up, fail, give, make up, monitor, supervise, take an examination.*

ex·am·ine (eg·ZAM·in) v. -ines, -ined, -in·ing 1 closely inspect a patient, situation, etc.: *The insurance adjuster examined the car for damages; to examine carefully, closely, thoroughly.* 2 interview, question, or test an applicant, student, witness, etc.: *She was examined in all subjects.* — **ex·am·in·er** n.

ex·am·i·nee (eg·ZAM·uh·NEE) n. a person being tested at an examination.

ex·am·ple (eg·ZAM·pul) n. 1 a person or thing that is typical of the rest of a group: *Canines – **for example,** dogs and wolves; the worst example of a polluted stream; to cite, give, provide an example; a classic, concrete, glaring, illustrative, prime, typical example.* 2 one likely to be followed or copied: *He was punished as an example to* or *for the whole class; The teacher made an example of him; The religious leader taught by precept and personal example; to follow an example; a shining, striking example of a model student; Parents should **set a good example** for their children.*

ex·as·per·ate (eg·ZAS·puh·rate) v. -ates, -at·ed, -at·ing irritate or annoy intensely: *Unnecessary delays exasperate everyone; We are **exasperated** at* or *by unnecessary delays in mail delivery; Delays can be very **exasperating**.* — **ex·as·per·a·tion** (-RAY·shun) n.

ex·ca·vate (EX·cuh·vate) v. -vates, -vat·ed, -vat·ing make a hollow in; hence, dig or dig out: *an excavating machine to dig a building foundation; Archaeologists excavate ancient ruins; Pompeii was excavated* (= uncovered by digging). — **ex·ca·va·tor** (-vay·tur) n. — **ex·ca·va·tion** (-VAY·shun) n.

ex·ceed (ek·SEED) v. go beyond: *to exceed the speed limit; She exceeds* (= surpasses) *everyone in creativity.* — **ex·ceed·ing·ly** adv. extremely: *exceedingly difficult, simple, well.*

ex·cel (ek·SEL) v. -cels, -celled, -cel·ling surpass others: *He excels at tennis; She excels in math.*

ex·cel·lence (EK·sul·unce) n. excellent quality: *a student noted for excellence at piano-playing; her excellence in singing; Music is just one of her many excellences.*

Ex·cel·len·cy (EK·sul·un·see) n. -cies [a title of honour used in addressing the Governor General of Canada, a foreign head of state or ambassador, an archbishop, etc.]: *Her, His, Your Excellency; their Excellencies the American ambassador and his wife.*

ex·cel·lent (EK·sul·unt) adj. outstanding or very good: *an excellent job, player, record, student; I'm in excellent physical condition; Excellent* (= Superb)! — **ex·cel·lent·ly** adv.

ex·cept (ek·SEPT) v. leave out; exclude.
— **prep. & conj.** but: *Everyone except him was there; I'm OK except (that) I have a slight headache; I'm OK **except for** a slight headache.*

ex·cep·tion (ek·SEP·shun) n. 1 an excepting or excluding; also, a person or thing excepted: *Everyone makes mistakes and I'm no exception; "The exception proves the rule"* (= Without a rule, there could be no exception). 2 an objection: *She **takes exception*** (= objects) *to his language.*

ex·cep·tion·al (ek·SEP·shuh·nul) adj. unusual: *weather that is exceptional for this time of year; an exceptional case; exceptional* (= gifted or handicapped) *children.* — **ex·cep·tion·al·ly** adv.

ex·cerpt (ek·SURPT) v. take out passages *from* a source. — **n.** (EK·surpt) an extract; passage taken *from* a source.

ex·cess (ek·SES) n. what is greater than or exceeds a limit: *An excess of expenditure over income means you are in debt; He was given to gambling, drinking, and such excesses; The company has assets **in excess of*** (= more than) *$3 billion; He was left broken-hearted, having loved her **to excess*** (= too much). — **adj.** (EK·ses): *A higher rate is charged for excess baggage; an excess profits tax.* — **ex·ces·sive** (ek·SES·iv) adj.

ex·change (ex·CHANGE) v. -chang·es, -changed, -chang·ing give a thing in return for something else; give and receive: *a customer exchanging his gift for something better; We exchange greetings at Christmas; to exchange* (= change or swap) *seats with someone.* — **n.** 1 a trade or swapping: *an exchange of prisoners after a war; a watch given in exchange for coupons; cultural exchanges between nations; an overseas **exchange student** under a scholarship program.* 2 a place for exchanging things or services: *a commodity exchange; stock exchange; telephone exchange (where lines are connected).* 3 money or a document for setting or adjusting payments, currency differences, etc.: *Exports earn foreign exchange; a bill of exchange* (= draft); *the **exchange rate** on the American dollar.* — **ex·change·a·ble** adj.

ex·cheq·uer (ex·CHEK·ur, EX·chek·ur) n. 1 the national treasury: *Britain's Chancellor of the Exchequer is the finance minister.* 2 *Informal.* finances.

ex·cise 1 (EK·size, -sice) n. a tax or duty charged within a country on the manufacture and sale of goods such as liquor and tobacco, on purchases in the form of sales tax, and on services in the form of business licenses, entertainment tax, etc. 2 (ek·SIZE) v. -cis·es, -cised, -cis·ing remove by cutting out: *to excise an objectionable part from a book.* — **ex·ci·sion** (-SIZH·un) n.: *the surgical excision of diseased tissue.*

282

ex·cite (ek·SITE) *v.* -cites, -cit·ed, -cit·ing 1 arouse the thoughts or feelings of someone; also, thrill: *The discovery excited the kids.* 2 stir up or make active: *Rumours excite curiosity; a hive of excited bees in hot pursuit.*
— **ex·cit·a·ble** (-tuh·bul) *adj.*
— **ex·cit·a·bil·i·ty** (-tuh·BIL·uh·tee) *n.*

excited *adj.* stirred up: *She was excited* (= thrilled) *to learn she had won; He got quite excited* (= angry) *about or at or over the treatment he received.*
— **ex·cit·ed·ly** *adv.*

exciting *adj.* thrilling: *an exciting adventure; an exciting bit of news; It's exciting to watch thrillers.*

ex·claim (ex·CLAIM) *v.* utter suddenly and vehemently: *"Ouch," she exclaimed in pain; He exclaimed: "I didn't do it!"*
— **ex·cla·ma·tion** (ex·cluh·MAY·shun) *n.*: *an exclamation of joy; This* [!] *is an **exclamation mark** or **point**.*
— **ex·clam·a·to·ry** (ex·CLAM·uh·tor·ee) *adj.*: *An exclamatory word or sentence is ended with an exclamation mark, as "Alas!"*

ex·clude (ex·CLOOD, long "OO") *v.* -cludes, -clud·ed, -clud·ing 1 keep out or prohibit from somewhere: *No one is excluded on the basis of age, sex, or colour.* 2 leave out of consideration: *We cannot exclude the possibility of theft of the missing money; The bill comes to $400 **excluding** minor expenses.*

ex·clu·sion (ex·CLOO·zhun) *n.* what is excluded: *gifts, benefits, and other nontaxable exclusions (on a tax return); He studies algebra **to the exclusion of** (= so as to exclude) other branches of mathematics.*

ex·clu·sive (ex·CLOO·siv) *adj.* that excludes: *an exclusive news story (that no other media may carry); A patent gives exclusive rights to an inventor* (= rights that no one else can have); *Ours used to be an exclusive neighbourhood (with only people of one social group or income bracket); an exclusive attitude; an exclusive feature (that no other product has); exclusive attention, jurisdiction, possession, privileges, use; an exclusive (not multiple) listing by a realtor for a certain period; Truth and untruth are mutually exclusive* (= It's either the one or the other); *an **exclusive economic zone** claimed by countries beyond their coastal waters to protect fishing and mineral rights; a car that costs $20 000 **exclusive of** (= not including) optional items.*
— *n.* an exclusive story or article.
— **ex·clu·sive·ly** *adv.*; **ex·clu·sive·ness** *n.*

ex·com·mu·ni·cate (ex·cuh·MEW·nuh·cate) *v.* -cates, -cat·ed, -cat·ing cut off from membership, esp. of a church, by a formal act of **ex·com·mu·ni·ca·tion** (-CAY·shun) *n.*

ex·co·ri·ate (ex·COR·ee·ate) *v.* -ates, -at·ed, -at·ing 1 strip off the skin from a surface. 2 criticize a book, performance, person, etc. severely: *a play excoriated by the critics.* — **ex·co·ri·a·tion** (-ee·AY·shun) *n.*

ex·cre·ment (EX·cruh·munt) *n.* waste from the bowels: *human excrement.*

ex·crete (ex·CREET) *v.* -cretes, -cret·ed, -cret·ing eliminate from the body.
— **ex·cre·tion** (ex·CREE·shun) *n.*: *Sweat, carbon*

dioxide, urine, etc. are bodily excretions.
— **ex·cre·to·ry** (EX·cruh·tor·ee) *adj.*: *the body's excretory functions.*

ex·cru·ci·at·ing (ex·CROO·shee·ay·ting) *adj.* 1 of mental or bodily pain, acute: *an excruciating agony, fear, pain.* 2 extreme or intense: *with excruciating care; excruciating delight; in excruciating detail; an excruciating regard for correctness.*

ex·cur·sion (ex·CUR·zhun) *n.* a journey made with the intention of returning to the starting-point; hence, a pleasure trip by air, train, ship, etc.; also, the people in it: *We went on an excursion to collect specimens; a botany excursion from school; The excursion was due back at 5 p.m.; a round-trip economy **excursion ticket**.*

ex·cuse (ex·KYOOZE) *v.* -cus·es, -cused, -cus·ing overlook an offence or offending person: *Excuse me, ma'am; If you will excuse our interrupting; Please excuse us for interrupting; Excuse my (poor) French; We excuse you this time; We won't excuse your rudeness another time; You're excused from classes till you are better; You are excused* (= You may leave); *I will **excuse myself*** (= be absent) *for the rest of this session; Please **excuse me*** (= allow me to get out).
— *n.* (ex·KYOOSE) an act or instance of excusing: *to accept, find, make, reject an excuse; He tried to make up an excuse for being late; an excellent, good, plausible, valid excuse; There's no excuse* (= justification) *for always being late; the flimsy excuse that the watch is faulty; It sounds like a feeble excuse to get a new watch; A faulty watch is a lame excuse; That gadget is a poor excuse for* (= example of) *a watch.*
— **ex·cus·a·ble** (-suh·bul) *adj.*: *an excusable offence.*

ex·e·cra·ble (EX·uh·cruh·bul) *adj.* detestable: *an execrable crime; his execrable manners; her execrable tastes.* — **ex·e·cra·bly** *adv.*

ex·e·cute (EX·uh·cute) *v.* -cutes, -cut·ed, -cut·ing 1 carry out to completion; put into effect: *to execute an agreement, plan, portrait, search warrant, transaction; The government executes what parliament legislates; Nurses execute doctors' orders; A deed is executed when it is signed, sealed, and delivered; Each step has to be executed gracefully in performing a dance; He died without naming anyone to execute his will.* 2 put a condemned person to death: *He was executed by hanging; was executed as a traitor.*

ex·e·cu·tion (ex·uh·CUE·shun) *n.* 1 an executing or the manner of it: *the execution of justice; the execution of a dance, plan, will.* 2 the putting to death of a condemned person: *The sentence was passed, but the execution was delayed by appeals; execution by electrocution, hanging; to carry out an execution; a public execution by firing squad.* — **ex·e·cu·tion·er** *n.*

ex·ec·u·tive (ig·ZEK·yuh·tiv) *adj.* having to do with the carrying out of a function; hence, managerial: *an executive committee, director, officer, secretary; The RCMP is an executive arm of government; secrecy in the guise of **executive privilege** of confidentiality; An executive chauffeur drives executives around; an executive* (= managerial) *chef.*
— *n.* 1 the executive branch of government: *the judiciary and the executive.* 2 a business manager: *the chief executive; the top executives of a corporation.*

ex·ec·u·tor (ig·ZEK·yuh·tur) *n.* one who is to carry out the provisions of a will. — **ex·ec·u·trix** *fem.*

ex·em·plar (ig·ZEM·plar, -plur) *n.* an ideal pattern or a model worthy of imitation.

ex·em·pla·ry (ig·ZEM·pluh·ree) *adj.* being an example to others: *She was praised for exemplary behaviour; He was awarded **exemplary damages** (as a warning to others) besides compensation for the loss.*

ex·em·pli·fy (ig·ZEM·pluh·fye) *v.* -flies, -flied, -fly·ing serve as a typical example of something: *Mother Teresa exemplifies service.*
— **ex·em·pli·fi·ca·tion** (-fuh·CAY·shun) *n.*

ex·empt (ig·ZEMPT) *v.* to free from a general obligation or requirement: *No one is exempted from paying taxes;* ***adj.**: Certain goods are exempt from duty.*
— **ex·emp·tion** (-ZEMP·shun) *n.: She was granted an exemption from jury duty; tax exemptions; Dependents may be claimed as exemptions (to reduce taxable income).*

ex·er·cise (EX·ur·cize) *v.* -cis·es, -cised, -cis·ing **1** put to active use or work: *He walks the dog to exercise him; It's good to exercise (the body) for 30 minutes daily; to exercise hard, regularly, strenuously, vigorously; **adj.**: an exercise break (from work); an exercise program.* **2** exert: *to exercise restraint in the use of energy; In sending them to jail, the judge was only exercising his powers; They were quite **exercised** (= troubled) about or over his remarks.*
— *n.* **1** the use or exertion of an organ, faculty, etc.: *Take a little exercise every day, says the doctor; Swimming is an excellent form of vigorous exercise; physical exercises; warming-up exercises; Teaching requires the exercise of care and patience; The object of the exercise has to be kept in mind, or it may become an exercise in futility; a lesson followed by exercises* (= tasks); *an exercise book.* **2** **exercises** *pl.* a program or operation in many parts: *military exercises near the war zone; naval exercises in the Persian Gulf; to hold graduation or commencement exercises* (= ceremonies).

ex·ert (ig·ZURT) *v.* put or bring into action; exercise or wield: *to exert authority; You must **exert yourself** (= try hard) to achieve anything.*
— **ex·er·tion** (ig·ZUR·shun) *n.: the exertion of undue influence; the diplomat's exertions in the cause of peace.*

ex·hale (ex·HALE) *v.* -hales, -haled, -hal·ing breathe out or give out vapour, smoke, odours, etc.: *We inhale oxygen and exhale carbon dioxide; Please exhale slowly; the odours exhaling* (= rising) *from the sewage plant.*
— **ex·ha·la·tion** (ex·huh·LAY·shun) *n.*

ex·haust (ig·ZAWST) *v.* to empty out, drain off, or use up strength, supplies, or other contents: *an exhausted oil well; Overspending exhausts our resources; He exhausted the subject* (= discussed it thoroughly) *within the hour; You must feel quite **exhausted** (= too tired to go on) after the climb; It was an **exhausting** (= very tiring) climb.*
— *n.* what exhausts or is exhausted: *Use the fan as an air exhaust; Mufflers reduce the noise of car exhausts; Exhaust fumes are mostly carbon monoxide.*
— **ex·haus·ti·ble** *adj.*

ex·haus·tion (ig·ZAWS·chun) *n.* **1** great fatigue or tiredness: *He collapsed on the floor out of sheer exhaustion; in a state of exhaustion; heat exhaustion* (= a milder form of heatstroke). **2** a using up: *the exhaustion of our resources, supplies.*

ex·haus·tive (ig·ZAWS·tiv) *adj.* dealing completely with a subject; thorough: *an exhaustive inquiry, search, study.*

ex·hib·it (ig·ZIB·it) *v.* to display for public notice: *Artists exhibit their work; evidence exhibited in court; He listened to the verdict without exhibiting* (= showing) *the least emotion.*
— *n.* something exhibited, as an art object or collection or a piece of legal evidence: *to mount* or *organize an art exhibit; A work of art by Picasso was on exhibit; The murder weapon was entered as Exhibit A* (= the first piece of evidence). — **ex·hib·i·tor** or **ex·hib·it·er** *n.*

ex·hib·i·tion (ex·uh·BISH·un) *n.* a public showing, esp. an organized display: *an art exhibition; An exhibition is put on* or *staged; trade exhibitions* (= fairs); *He made an exhibition of himself* (= made himself ridiculous) *by crying like a baby.*

ex·hil·a·rate (ig·ZIL·uh·rate) *v.* -rates, -rat·ed, -rat·ing fill with high spirits: *Some are scared rather than exhilarated by a roller-coaster ride; Young people find the ride an **exhilarating** experience.*
— **ex·hil·a·ra·tion** (-RAY·shun) *n.*

ex·hort (ig·ZORT) *v.* urge earnestly, as a preacher does: *She exhorted them to study hard for the examinations.*
— **ex·hor·ta·tion** (eg·zor·TAY·shun) *n.*

ex·hume (ex·HUME, igz·HUME – *rhyme:* assume) *v.* -humes, -humed, -hum·ing dig a corpse out of its grave; hence, bring to light from a buried state.
— **ex·hu·ma·tion** (ex·hyuh·MAY·shun) *n.*

ex·i·gen·cy (EX·uh·jun·see) *n.* -cies a situation of need requiring urgent action: *An unexpected exigency arose; the **exigencies** (= demanding conditions) of life in a war zone.*

ex·ile (EG·zile, EK·sile) *v.* -iles, -iled, -il·ing force someone or oneself to leave home or country for a period: *Napoleon was exiled from France; He was exiled to Elba.*
— *n.* an exiled person, the person's banishment, or its period: *Napoleon was sent into exile twice; He died in exile on Saint Helena; Ugandan exiles in Canada.*

ex·ist (ig·ZIST) *v.* to be; have being or life: *Do ghosts exist? We can't exist without food; You can't exist long on bread and water.*

ex·ist·ence (ig·ZIS·tunce) *n.* the state of existing: *the existence of ghosts; Will the universe go out of existence? the miserable existence of the poor; the precarious existence* (= life) *of a wanted man; to eke out an existence* (= a living) *by taking in laundry.*
— **ex·ist·ent** (-tunt) *adj.*

ex·it (EG·zit, EK·sit) *n.* **1** a way out, as from a stage, building, or highway: *a plane's emergency exits; a window exit; There's no exit from the rear; The exit to the balcony was closed.* **2** a going out, departure, or death: *He felt sick and made a hasty exit from the meeting; **exits and entrances** (= when to come on stage and leave); an **exit poll** of voters as they come out after voting to find out who might be winning.*
— *v.* **1** go out: *We exited from the highway to Main*

Street; Some exited by the fire escape, others through windows. **2** [as a stage direction] (He, she, or it) goes out: "(Antigonus) exit, pursued by a bear."

ex·o·dus (EX·uh·dus) *n.* a departure in large numbers, like that of the Israelites from ancient Egypt: *There's a mass exodus from the city to the country on summer weekends.*

ex of·fi·ci·o (ex·uh·FISH·ee·oh) *adj. & adv.* by virtue of one's official position: *She is a member of the board ex officio; an ex officio member of the board.*

ex·on·er·ate (ig·ZON·uh·rate) *v.* -ates, -at·ed, -at·ing clear or free someone of guilt or responsibility for an action: *The verdict completely exonerated him from the charge.* — **ex·on·er·a·tion** (-uh·RAY·shun) *n.*

ex·or·bi·tant (ig·ZOR·buh·tunt) *adj.* excessive or unreasonable: *exorbitant demands, prices, profits.* — **ex·or·bi·tant·ly** *adv.*

ex·or·cise (EX·or·size) *v.* -cis·es, -cised, -cis·ing **1** expel an evil spirit from a possessed person by solemn commands: *He exorcised the devil from Lu.* **2** free such a person or haunted place of an evil spirit: *He exorcised Lu of the devil.* Also **ex·or·cize.** — **ex·or·cism** *n.; ex·or·cist* *n.*

ex·ot·ic (ig·ZOT·ic) *adj.* **1** of plants, fishes, foods, fashions, words, etc., introduced from abroad; not indigenous or native: *The African violet is an exotic plant that is native to Kenya and Tanzania.* **2** strangely fascinating or attractive: *exotic colours; an exotic nightclub dancer.*

ex·pand (ex·PAND) *v.* make or become larger, esp. in extent, by unfolding, opening, spreading, etc.: *Heat expands metals; A flooded river may expand into a lake; to expand a short story into a novel; A professor* **expands on** or **upon** (= explains at length) *a theme during a lecture.* — **ex·pand·a·ble** or **ex·pan·si·ble** *adj.* — **ex·pan·sion** *n.*

ex·panse (ex·PANCE) *n.* a large surface or stretch: *the broad expanse of his chest; the wide expanse of the grassy plain; the vast expanses of outer space.*

ex·pan·sive (ex·PAN·siv) *adj.* **1** capable of or causing expansion: *the expansive force of heat on metals.* **2** of people, friendly and willing to talk: *She was in an expansive mood; A small compliment will make him expansive; an expansive personality.*

ex par·te (ex·PAR·tee) *adj. & adv.* [legal use] without benefit to the other party: *an ex parte judgment, order; The case was heard ex parte* (= in the absence of the other party).

ex·pa·tri·ate (ex·PAY·tree·ate) *v.* -ates, -at·ed, -at·ing **1** withdraw oneself from one's native country and settle abroad: *He expatriated himself to England on retirement.* **2** exile; also, deprive of acquired citizenship: *a Russian dissident expatriated from the U.S.S.R.* — *n.* a person settled abroad in relation to his or her native country: *Ukrainian expatriates in North America.* — **ex·pa·tri·a·tion** (-AY·shun) *n.*

ex·pect (ex·PECT) *v.* look forward to, usually with certainty, often with hope or confidence: *Much is expected of* or *from a nation's leaders; People expect them to deliver on their election promises; I'm expecting*

company; *I expect they'll be here by noon; They'll be here by noon,* **I expect** (= I suppose); *His wife is* **expecting** (= pregnant); *She's expecting a boy.* — **ex·pect·a·ble** *adj.*

ex·pect·an·cy (ex·PEC·tun·see) *n.* -cies the state of expecting or something expected: *There was an air of expectancy in the room when the hero was announced; Paintings have a greater life expectancy than film.* — **ex·pect·ant** (-tunt) *adj.: an expectant father, mother* (expecting a baby to be born). — **ex·pect·ant·ly** *adv.*

ex·pec·ta·tion (EX·pec·TAY·shun) *n.* **1** the act of expecting: *She had every expectation of winning the gold medal; He stayed home that day in expectation of* (= expecting) *a visit.* **2** **expectations** *pl.* what is hoped for or the basis of hoping: *to have great* or *high expectations of winning; Contrary to expectations, everyone did well at school; He didn't fall short of expectations; He came up to, exceeded, met, surpassed expectations; He succeeded beyond all expectations.*

ex·pec·to·rant (ex·PEC·tuh·runt) *n.* a medicine that helps to expectorate.

ex·pec·to·rate (ex·PEC·tuh·rate) *v.* -rates, -rat·ed, -rat·ing cough up phlegm; discharge sputum; also, spit. — **ex·pec·to·ra·tion** (-RAY·shun) *n.*

ex·pe·di·en·cy (ex·PEE·dee·un·see) *n.* -cies suitability for a specific, usually selfish purpose, without regard for principles: *political expediency.* Also **ex·pe·di·ence** (-unce).

ex·pe·di·ent (ex·PEE·dee·unt) *n.* a device of convenience: *a phone call as an expedient for leaving a meeting.* — *adj.* politically wise: *The legislators thought it expedient to vote themselves a raise now rather than after the election.*

ex·pe·dite (EX·puh·dite) *v.* -dites, -dit·ed, -dit·ing help speed up a plan, service, etc.: *Enclose a self-addressed stamped envelope to expedite a reply; Postal codes are used to expedite the processing of mail.* — **ex·pe·dit·er** or **ex·pe·di·tor** *n.*

ex·pe·di·tion (ex·puh·DISH·un) *n.* **1** a journey of people, ships, etc. organized for a specific purpose: *to go on, launch, lead, mount, organize an expedition; an archaeological, military, scientific, whaling expedition; an expedition to the Arctic; an expedition across the Sahara Desert; a cod-fishing expedition; to go on a* **fishing expedition** (to look for information). **2** the quality of being expeditious: *Food was dispatched with expedition to the famine-stricken area.*

ex·pe·di·tion·ar·y (ex·puh·DISH·uh·nair·ee) *adj.* having to do with a military expedition: *Cuban expeditionary forces in Angola.*

ex·pe·di·tious (ex·puh·DISH·us) *adj.* with easy and efficient speed; without delay: *fast and expeditious service; an expeditious answer, journey, method, move, plan.* — **ex·pe·di·tious·ly** *adv.*

ex·pel (ex·PEL) *v.* -pels, -pelled, -pel·ling force out: *Air is expelled from the lungs in breathing; Students may be expelled* (= dismissed) *from school for serious misbehaviour.*

ex·pend (ex·PEND) v. use up large sums, resources, etc.: *the energies expended on* or *in tracking down Bigfoot.*
— **ex·pend·a·ble 1** *adj.* that may be disposed of: *expendable supplies; an expendable regiment.*
2 expendables *n. pl.* supplies such as paper, pencil, and ink.

ex·pend·i·ture (ex·PEN·duh·chur) n. a spending or what is spent: *Every project requires the expenditure of time, money, energy, and other resources; capital expenditures on building, equipment, and such assets; We are trying to curb, curtail, cut down (on), reduce unnecessary expenditure; expenditures for luxuries.*

ex·pense (ex·PENCE) n. **1** cost considered usually as large: *She was put through college at her parents' expense; They were put to great expense; They went to great expense; They spared no expense to educate their children; Buying a car is a considerable expense for most families; A gas guzzler is a great expense* (= cause of expenditure); *to incur* or *run up an expense; to curb, curtail, cut down (on), defray, reduce, reimburse, share expenses; The school was built at government expense, not at our expense; They tried to increase volume* **at the expense of** *quality.* **2 expenses** *pl.* money for incidental expenditure: *a sales representative who gets a salary, car, and expenses.*

expense account n. a record of business expenses that are repaid to the employee.

ex·pen·sive (ek·SPEN·siv) *adj.* high-priced.
— **ex·pen·sive·ly** *adv.*

ex·pe·ri·ence (ex·PEER·ee·unce) n. what one lives through, i.e. sees, feels, does, etc.; what happens to one; also, the knowledge gained: *Everyone learns by* or *from experience; We acquire, gain, get experience from doing things; broad, direct, firsthand, hands-on, practical, previous, wide experience; childhood experiences; to have an enlightening, harrowing, memorable, painful, pleasant, rewarding, unforgettable experience.*
— v. **-enc·es, -enced, -enc·ing 1** have experience of something: *He had never experienced starvation.*
2 experienced *adj.* having experience: *a qualified and experienced teacher; She's experienced at* or *in teaching the handicapped.*

ex·per·i·ment (ex·PER·uh·munt) n. a controlled action or process to discover something unknown or to test or demonstrate a known fact: *to carry out, conduct, perform an experiment; a chemistry experiment; an experiment in international cooperation.*
— v. carry out experiments: *The Wright brothers experimented with different types of airplanes; Scientists experiment on mice and guinea pigs.*
— **ex·per·i·men·ta·tion** (-men·TAY·shun) n.
— **ex·per·i·men·tal** (ex·PER·uh·MEN·tul) *adj.* having to do with experiments: *an experimental farm operated by the federal government to do agricultural research; an experimental variety of wheat; in the experimental stage of development; experimental* (= practical), *not theoretical knowledge, sciences;* **ex·per·i·men·tal·ly** *adv.*

ex·pert (EX·purt) n. one who is highly skilled and knowledgeable: *a handwriting expert; an expert in arranging flowers; an expert on warranties; an expert at detecting flaws.*
— *adj.* (*also* ex·PURT) having special skill and knowledge: *an expert typist, witness; She's expert at calligraphy; your expert advice, opinion.*
— **ex·pert·ly** *adv.;* **ex·pert·ness** n.

ex·per·tise (ex·pur·TEEZ) n. an expert's skill or knowledge: *technical expertise; expertise in labour relations; the expertise to mediate a dispute.*

ex·pi·ate (EX·pee·ate) v. **-ates, -at·ed, -at·ing** atone for something: *to expiate a crime.*
— **ex·pi·a·tion** (-AY·shun) n.

ex·pi·ra·tion (ex·puh·RAY·shun) n. a breathing out or expiring: *expiration and inspiration; The mayor decided to run again at the expiration* (= end) *of his first term in office.*

ex·pire (ex·PIRE) v. **-pires, -pired, -pir·ing** breathe out; hence, breathe one's last: *He expired before next of kin could be called; Your licence has expired* (= come to an end).

ex·pi·ry (ex·PYE·uh·ree, EX·puh·ree) n. **-ries** an expiring: *A driving licence may be renewed on expiry; the expiry date.*

ex·plain (ex·PLAIN) v. make something clear and understandable: *You were absent yesterday – please explain; I can explain my absence; Al explained why he was absent; He explained that he was ill; He didn't try to* **explain it away** (= avoid an explanation by giving excuses).
— **explain oneself 1** make one's meaning clear. **2** justify one's conduct. — **ex·plain·a·ble** *adj.*
— **ex·pla·na·tion** (ex·pluh·NAY·shun) n.: *A full explanation is called for; the reasons given in explanation of his absence.*
— **ex·plan·a·to·ry** (ex·PLAN·uh·tor·ee) *adj.*

ex·ple·tive (EX·pluh·tiv) n. an obscenity: *a mild expletive; an edited story with expletives deleted.*

ex·pli·ca·ble (EX·pluh·cuh·bul) *adj.* explainable: *puzzling but explicable behaviour.*

ex·pli·cate (EX·pluh·cate) v. **-ates, -at·ed, -at·ing** analyse or interpret a passage, theory, etc.
— **ex·pli·ca·tion** (-CAY·shun) n.

ex·plic·it (ex·PLIS·it) *adj.* clearly stated, explained, or pictured; not implicit or vague: *The rules are explicit on that point; explicit language, sex, violence in movies.*
— **ex·plic·it·ly** *adv.*

ex·plode (ex·PLODE) **1** v. **-plodes, -plod·ed, -plod·ing** burst with a loud noise: *A boiler may explode under pressure; A bomb explodes or has to be exploded* (= blown up); *Pent-up discontent explodes* (= erupts) *into a riot; She exploded with fury* (= suddenly became furious) *when she realized she had been cheated; Science has exploded* (= disproved) *many myths and superstitions; an exploding* (= suddenly expanding) *population.* **2 exploded** *adj.* of a drawing, model, or view of a mechanism, showing components separated but in their relative positions: *an exploded view of a carburetor.*

ex·ploit (EX·ploit) n. a daring deed; feat: *the heroic exploits performed by Hercules.*
— v. (*usually* ex·PLOIT) make use of, often in an unfair or selfish manner: *They exploited her generosity.*
— **ex·ploit·a·tive** (-uh·tiv) or **ex·ploit·ive** *adj.*: *exploitative actions, treatment; an exploitative wage*

offer. — **ex·ploi·ta·tion** (ex·ploy·TAY·shun) *n.*

ex·plo·ra·tion (ex·pluh·RAY·shun) *n.* an exploring: *space exploration; Champlain's explorations led to the founding of New France.*

ex·plore (ex·PLORE) *v.* -plores, -plored, -plor·ing search a new region so as to learn about it: *a lunar rover to explore the moon's surface; A surgeon explores a wound.* — **ex·plor·er** *n.*
— **ex·plor·a·to·ry** (-uh·tor·ee) *adj.*: *an exploratory voyage; exploratory surgery.*

ex·plo·sion (ex·PLOH·zhun) *n.* 1 an exploding or its noise: *What caused the explosion? an explosion set off or touched off by a lighted cigarette.* 2 sudden expansion or increase: *knowledge explosion; population explosion.*

ex·plo·sive (ex·PLOH·siv) *n.* a substance that can cause an explosion: *TNT is a high explosive that detonates relatively fast; Gunpowder is a low explosive; plastic explosives* (= bombs); *to set off an explosive; The explosive had been planted in the baggage.*
— **adj.** capable of exploding: *an explosive situation created by a public injustice; Lee has an explosive temper.* — **ex·plo·sive·ly** *adv.*; **ex·plo·sive·ness** *n.*

ex·po (EX·poh) *n.* -pos *Informal.* an international exhibition or world's fair: *Expo 67 was held in Montreal; Expo 86 in Vancouver.*

ex·po·nent (ex·POH·nunt) *n.* one that expounds; hence, one that favours or promotes a policy, method, theory, etc.: *a leading exponent of free trade.*

ex·po·nen·tial (ex·puh·NEN·shul) *adj.* very rapid: *A population that multiplies itself in a short period is increasing* or *growing at an exponential rate.*
— **ex·po·nen·tial·ly** *adv.*

ex·port (ex·PORT) *v.* send or carry away to a foreign country, esp. goods for sale: *Cars are exported from Japan to North America.*
— **n.** (EX·port) an exporting or thing exported: *our exports and imports.*

ex·pose (ex·POZE) *v.* -pos·es, -posed, -pos·ing 1 lay open; hence, display or reveal: *A bikini exposes much of the body; He was charged with exposing himself* (= displaying his body indecently) *on the beach.* 2 leave unprotected: *Children are exposed to much violence on TV; Ancient Spartans used to expose unwanted infants* (= kill by leaving them outside); *exposed to the elements.* 3 uncover sensitized film or plate for taking picture.

ex·po·sé (ex·poh·ZAY) *n.* an exposition, esp. an exposure of a crime or scandal.

ex·po·si·tion (ex·puh·ZISH·un) *n.* 1 an explanation in spoken or written form. 2 a large exhibition: *fairs and expositions.*

ex·pos·i·tor (ex·POZ·uh·tur) *n.* one who explains or interprets.
— **ex·pos·i·tor·y** (-tor·ee) *adj.*: *expository writing.*

ex·po·sure (ex·POH·zhur) *n.* 1 an exposing or being exposed: *a corrupt politician afraid of public exposure in the media; wide exposure* (= publicity); *The abandoned infant died of exposure (to the elements); charged with indecent exposure (of the body); a film with 24 exposures* (= pictures) *per roll; An exposure meter measures light intensity to determine the correct*

exposure time for a picture. 2 aspect or facing: *Houses with a southern exposure get more sun in the winter.*

ex·pound (ex·POWND) *v.* set forth or explain a doctrine, theory, writings, etc. systematically, as by an authority on the subject: *to expound the theory of relativity; He expounded for hours on the need for pay equity.*

ex·press (ex·PRESS) *v.* 1 put thoughts or feelings into words, music, signs, or symbols: *Parents express their concerns to teachers; He's learning to express himself in correct English; A nod expresses assent; a sign* (÷) *that expresses division.* 2 squeeze out juice, oil, milk, etc. from its source. 3 send by express: *We'll express the parcel to Vancouver.*
— **adj.** 1 clearly and directly stated: *express permission; He's here with the express purpose of talking to you; This was her express wish; She's the express* (= exact) *image of her mother.* 2 fast and direct: *an express elevator, highway, mail service, messenger, train.*
— **adv.** by express: *Send it express to Vancouver.*
— **n.** a bus, train, or other service for transporting people or things quickly and directly; also, the things thus transported.

ex·pres·sion (ex·PRESH·un) *n.* 1 something that expresses thoughts and feelings, as a word, phrase, gesture, look, sigh, or tone: *a colloquial, common, idiomatic, slang, technical expression* (= word or phrase); *an angry, grave, serious, happy, pained, puzzled, vacuous expression* (= look); *the expression of sadness on his face.* 2 the expressing of meaning, beauty, feelings, etc.: *She sings with expression; Her feelings sometimes find expression in poetic language; a statue that is beautiful beyond expression* (= beyond words).

ex·pres·sive (ex·PRES·iv) *adj.* serving to express: *words that are expressive of emotions; a very expressive* (= meaningful) *gesture, look, word.*
— **ex·pres·sive·ly** *adv.*

ex·press·ly (ex·PRES·lee) *adv.* clearly or explicitly: *The rules expressly forbid it.*

ex·press·way (ex·PRES·way) *n.* a limited-access divided highway for high-speed traffic.

ex·pro·pri·ate (ex·PROH·pree·ate) *v.* -ates, -at·ed, -at·ing take land from the owner for public use, as for schools, parks, airports, etc.
— **ex·pro·pri·a·tion** (-AY·shun) *n.*

ex·pul·sion (ex·PUL·shun) *n.* an expelling or being expelled or forced out: *a student facing expulsion from school for cheating on exams.*

ex·punge (ex·PUNJ) *v.* -pung·es, -punged, -pung·ing remove completely: *The judge ordered certain remarks expunged from the records.*

ex·pur·gate (EX·pur·gate) *v.* -gates, -gat·ed, -gat·ing purify a book or other writing of morally objectionable matter: *an expurgated edition of Shakespeare.*
— **ex·pur·ga·tion** (-GAY·shun) *n.*

ex·qui·site (EX·kwuh·zit, ex·QUIZ·it) *adj.* 1 of great excellence because of elaborate workmanship, delicate texture, keenness of taste, etc.: *exquisite beauty, grace, joy, taste; an exquisite* (= finely made) *design, lace.*

2 keenly felt: *exquisite agony, pain.*
— **ex·qui·site·ly** *adv.*

ex·tant (EX·tunt, ex·TANT) *adj.* of documents, paintings, life forms, etc., still existing: *Only one copy of the book is extant; one of the few extant varieties of the dying species.*

ex·tem·po·rize (ex·TEM·puh·rize) *v.* **-riz·es, -rized, -riz·ing** devise as something temporary; improvise: *An actor extemporizes when he forgets his lines; an extemporized shelter.*

ex·tend (ex·TEND) *v.* **1** stretch out in length, area, scope, time, etc.: *hands extended in welcome; Birds extend their wings when they fly; The drought-stricken area extends as far as the coast; Canadian sovereignty extends* (= reaches) *from the Atlantic to the Pacific; Our sovereignty extends* (= spreads) *over the Arctic; to extend* (= prolong) *a vacation by another week; The deadline has been extended to December 31; He* **extended himself** (= tried very hard) *and suffered a nervous breakdown; Nursing homes provide* **extended care** *(beyond what a hospital can) to the sick and disabled; an* **extended family** *of relatives under the same roof with the nuclear family.* **2** offer or convey: *to extend someone aid, credit, greetings, hospitality, an invitation, a loan, a welcome; She extended her sympathy to the bereaved family.*

ex·ten·sion (ex·TEN·shun) *n.* an extending or something extended as a continuation or addition: *He has been granted an extension of leave; Lou happened to listen in on the extension (telephone) when Pat called Lee; the extension of our knowledge; an extension to a house; an* **extension cord** *for an electrical appliance.*

ex·ten·sive (ex·TEN·siv) *adj.* having great extent of area, scope, influence, etc.: *She has extensive knowledge of her subject; Plentiful land is put to* **extensive farming** *though without intensive cultivation.*
— **ex·ten·sive·ly** *adv.*

ex·tent (ex·TENT) *n.* the degree, scope, or area of extension: *the extent of one's hopes, influence, knowledge; We trust him to a certain extent and no further; to the extent of $500.*

ex·ten·u·at·ing (ex·TEN·yoo·ay·ting) *adj.* making an offence or guilt seem less serious: *His licence was not suspended because of extenuating circumstances.*
— **ex·ten·u·a·tion** (-AY·shun) *n.: the reasons given in extenuation of his conduct.*

ex·te·ri·or (ex·TEER·ee·ur) *n.* the immediate outside: *the brick exterior of a house; Her stern exterior hides a soft heart; shooting the exteriors* (= outdoor scenes) *for a movie.*
— *adj.: a house with a handsome exterior design; exterior architectural features; an auto's exterior finish, styling, trim; Our car has two exterior mirrors; an oil-based exterior paint; an exterior staircase that serves as a fire escape; a building's exterior walls.*
— **ex·te·ri·or·ly** *adv.*

ex·ter·mi·nate (ex·TUR·muh·nate) *v.* **-nates, -nat·ed, -nat·ing** **1** destroy by killing: *a poison to exterminate rats.* **2** eliminate or wipe out: *Has smallpox been completely exterminated?*
— **ex·ter·mi·na·tor** (-nay·tur) *n.*
— **ex·ter·mi·na·tion** (-NAY·shun) *n.: the extermination of mice.*

ex·ter·nal (ex·TUR·nul) **1** *adj.* on or from the outside, esp. as not related; not internal: *Rubbing alcohol is for external use; external evidence from outside the work under study; an external influence; the minister for* **external** (= foreign) **affairs. 2 externals** *n.pl.* outward aspects or features such as one's clothing, manners, etc.: *the externals of religious practice.* — **ex·ter·nal·ly** *adv.*

ex·tinct (ex·TINCT) *adj.* no longer existing or active: *an extinct volcano; an extinct animal such as the dodo or dinosaur.*
— **ex·tinc·tion** (-shun) *n.: the extinction of one's hopes; the extinction of the passenger pigeon.*

ex·tin·guish (ex·TING·wish) *v.* put out or put an end to something: *to extinguish a fire; to extinguish hopes, passions, rights.* — **ex·tin·guish·er** *n.*

ex·tir·pate (EX·tur·pate) *v.* **-pates, -pat·ed, -pat·ing** root out a race, family, species, evil, etc.
— **ex·tir·pa·tion** (-PAY·shun) *n.*

ex·tol or **ex·toll** (ex·TOLE) *v.* **-tols** or **-tolls, -tolled, -toll·ing** praise highly; exalt: *The poem extols the virtue and courage of the heroine.*

ex·tort (ex·TORT) *v.* get confessions, money, promises, etc. *from someone by force or intimidation.*
— **ex·tor·tion** (-shun) *n.*
— **ex·tor·tion·ate** (-shuh·nit) *adj.: extortionate demands, fees, interest rates, prices, taxes.*
— **ex·tor·tion·er** or **ex·tor·tion·ist** *n.*

ex·tra (EX·truh) *adj. & adv.* more or larger than normal: *available at no extra cost; more work for extra pay; an extra added attraction; an extra dry champagne; extra large eggs; an extra special quality.*
— *n.* something or someone extra, as an additional favour, a special edition of a newspaper, or an actor for a minor role: *Extra! Extra! Read all about it! The epic film used 2 500 extras.*

ex·tract (ex·TRACT) *v.* draw out by physical or mental effort: *to extract* (= pull) *a tooth; to extract metal from ore (by mechanical separation); to extract* (= press) *juice from fruit; to extract* (= take out) *a passage from a book; to extract a confession (from an unwilling person).*
— **ex·trac·tor** *n.*
— *n.* (EX·tract) something extracted: *an extract from Shakespeare; a cosmetic extract like musk; a lemon, meat, vanilla extract.*

ex·trac·tion (ex·TRAC·shun) *n.* **1** an act of extracting: *the extraction of teeth.* **2** a person's ancestry: *a woman of noble extraction; people of British extraction.*

ex·trac·tive (ex·TRAC·tiv) *adj.* that extracts: *Lumbering, fishing, and mining are extractive industries; extractive agriculture, processes.*

ex·tra·cur·ric·u·lar (EX·truh·cuh·RIC·yuh·lur) *adj.* outside the regular curriculum: *sports, dramatics, hobbies, and such noncredit extracurricular activities of students.*

ex·tra·dite (EX·truh·dite) *v.* **-dites, -dit·ed, -dit·ing** deliver a prisoner *from* one country *to* another to be tried for a crime committed there.
— **ex·tra·di·tion** (-DISH·un) *n.*

ex·tra·mar·i·tal (ex·truh·MAIR·uh·tul) *adj.* outside marriage; adulterous: *extramarital affairs, relationships.*

ex·tra·mu·ral (ex·truh·MYOOR·ul) *adj.* outside the school or between schools: *an extramural event; extramural sports.*

ex·tra·ne·ous (ex·TRAY·nee·us) *adj.* **1** from outside: *pollution from extraneous substances.* **2** not relevant or germane: *an extraneous remark; an incident extraneous to the theme of the story.* — **ex·tra·ne·ous·ly** *adv.*

ex·traor·di·nar·y (ex·TROR·duh·nair·ee) *adj.* not ordinary; unusual. — **ex·traor·di·nar·i·ly** *adv.*

ex·trap·o·late (ex·TRAP·uh·late) *v.* **-lates, -lat·ed, -lat·ing** to follow a trend beyond the established range, as by extending a graph or curve: *We extrapolate costs, figures, findings, results, samples, surveys; a population estimate extrapolated* (= obtained by extrapolating) *from current census figures; In the late 1960s, demographers extrapolated* (= estimated) *that the world population would reach 10 billion by A.D. 2000; Scientists often extrapolate* (= extend their judgments) *from tests on animals to human risks in using a drug.* — **ex·trap·o·la·tion** (-LAY·shun) *n.*

ex·tra·sen·so·ry (ex·truh·SEN·suh·ree) *adj.* outside normal sense perception.

ex·tra·ter·res·tri·al (ex·truh·tuh·RES·tree·ul) *adj.* beyond the earth's atmosphere: *extraterrestrial beings, exploration, life, navigation.*

ex·tra·ter·ri·to·ri·al (EX·truh·ter·uh·TOR·ee·ul) *adj.* extending beyond one's territory: *extraterritorial ambitions, jurisdiction, privileges, rights.*

ex·trav·a·gance (ex·TRAV·uh·gunce) *n.* the quality or an instance of being extravagant: *the extravagance of her spending habits; He considers it an extravagance to eat out frequently.*

ex·trav·a·gant (ex·TRAV·uh·gunt) *adj.* **1** excessive: *extravagant claims, demands, praise, prices, spending.* **2** wasteful: *an extravagant life style, spender; He's rather extravagant in his spending, in his tastes.* — **ex·trav·a·gant·ly** *adv.*

ex·trav·a·gan·za (ex·TRAV·uh·GAN·zuh) *n.* a spectacular stage or screen production; also, such an event: *a week-long extravaganza with stage shows, fiddler contests, livestock shows, beauty pageants, and fireworks.*

ex·treme (ex·TREEM) *adj.* **1** farthest away, esp. from a middle: *the extreme edge of a cliff.* **2** of the highest degree: *the extreme heat of summer; in extreme cold, danger, old age, pain, poverty; with extreme joy, kindness, patience; an extreme case of insanity.* **3** of people and ideas, not moderate: *extreme opinions, views; the extreme left wing of a political party; the extreme right.* **4** excessive or drastic: *to use extreme measures; to take extreme action.* — *n.* something that is extreme or situated at either end: *to go from one extreme to the other; the extremes of joy and despair; It was disappointing* **in the extreme** (= extremely); *She went to* **extremes** (= the utmost limits) *to save a few dollars.* — **ex·treme·ly** *adv.* — **ex·tre·mism** (-miz·um) *n.;* **ex·tre·mist** *n. & adj.*

ex·trem·i·ty (ex·TREM·uh·tee) *n.* **-ties** an extreme condition, degree, or part: *in the extremity of despair;*

Friends were a great help in her extremity; people driven **to the last extremity** (= to death) *by famine; The* **extremities** (= hands and feet) *are the first to feel the cold.*

ex·tri·cate (EX·truh·cate) *v.* **-cates, -cat·ed, -cat·ing** free someone or oneself from a difficult situation: *to extricate oneself from a financial mess, a sticky situation, a web of lies.* — **ex·tri·ca·ble** (-cuh·bul) *adj.* — **ex·tri·ca·tion** (-CAY·shun) *n.*

ex·trin·sic (ex·TRIN·sic) *adj.* [formal use] outside the essential nature of something; not inherent or intrinsic: *facts that are extrinsic to the subject under discussion.*

ex·tro·vert (EX·truh·vurt) *n.* one whose interests are in other people and in the world outside rather than in oneself: *There is more of the extrovert than introvert in the more outgoing among us;* also **ex·tra·vert.** — **ex·tro·ver·sion** or **ex·tra·ver·sion** *n.* — *adj.: an extrovert personality.* Also **ex·tro·vert·ed** or **ex·tra·vert·ed.**

ex·trude (ex·TROOD, long "OO") *v.* **-trudes, -trud·ed, -trud·ing** **1** stick out or force out. **2** shape by forcing out a ductile material such as metals, plastics, and rubber through a die: *a pasta machine that extrudes everything from noodles to macaroni.* — **ex·tru·sion** (-TROO·zhun) *n.* — **ex·tru·sive** (-TROO·siv) *adj.*

ex·u·ber·ant (ig·ZOO·buh·runt) *adj.* **1** overflowing with cheer: *an exuberant youth; in an exuberant mood.* **2** profuse in growth: *the exuberant vegetation of a tropical jungle.* — **ex·u·ber·ance** (-runce) *n.*

ex·ude (ig·ZOOD, ex·YOOD, long "OO") *v.* **-udes, -ud·ed, -ud·ing** come out or send out, as sweat through pores: *a hostess exuding charm.* — **ex·u·da·tion** (ex·yuh·DAY·shun) *n.*

ex·ult (ig·ZULT) *v.* rejoice in triumph; be jubilant: *to exult at her success; to exult in the victory; to exult over (winning) the gold medal; to exult* (= crow) *over someone's defeat.* — **ex·ult·ant** (-tunt) *adj.;* **ex·ult·ant·ly** *adv.* — **ex·ul·ta·tion** (EG·zul·TAY·shun, EX·ul-) *n.*

eye *n.* **1** the organ of sight: *He wears a patch over his left eye (which is blind); blond hair and blue eyes* (= irises); *to give someone a black eye* (= bruised eye); *the green eye of jealousy; to blink, drop, lift, raise, rest, roll, squint, strain one's eyes; She is so calm she can be charged with theft and not bat an eye* (= show any emotion); *an eagle eye* (= keen sight). **2** a look or glance: *to cast an eye on something; Feast your eyes on* (= Enjoy the sight of) *our manicured lawn; to fix one's eye on something; She was so attractive he couldn't take his eyes off her; He ran his eyes over the front page looking for his name; to give someone the glad eye* (= a seductive glance); *He's a flirt with a roving or wandering eye; an anxious, critical eye; to ward off the evil eye* (= a look that is supposed to bring harm); *a jaundiced* (= jealous) *eye; a sharp, suspicious eye; a watchful or weather eye; prying, piercing eyes; There's more to it than* **meets the eye** (= more than is seen); *a confidential document* **for your eyes only** (= not to be copied or shared with anyone). **3** the power of seeing; hence, observation or judgment: *good, strong, weak eyes; As an M.P., she is always in the public eye* (= being seen by the public); *He was guilty in the eyes* (= judgment) *of the law.* **4** one that detects: *an electric eye* (= photoelectric cell); *a private eye* (= detective). **5** something resembling an eye, as a needle's hole, buds on a potato, the calm centre of a developing hurricane, a bull's-eye, etc.

— **close** or **shut one's eyes to** ignore a situation that calls for action.

— **eye for an eye** retaliation in kind.

— **have an eye for** have the ability to see clearly: *She has an eye for detail; He has a good eye for bargains.*

— **lay** or **set eyes on** look at or see the first time: *He loved her from the moment he set eyes on her.*

— **make eyes at** look amorously at someone; ogle.

— **see eye to eye with** agree with someone.

— **throw dust in someone's eyes** deceive someone intentionally.

— **with an eye to** having as one's purpose: *He requested an appointment with an eye to asking for a loan.*

— **with one's eyes open** fully aware of what may happen.

— **with the naked eye** without the aid of an optical instrument such as a microscope or telescope.

— *v.* **eyes, eyed, ey·ing** or **eye·ing** look at, observe, or watch: *The policeman eyed him critically; The professor eyed her quizzically.*

eye appeal *n.* visual attractiveness: *Colour is added to foods for eye appeal.*

eye·ball *n.* the ball-shaped part of an eye: *I'm up to my eyeballs in work.*

— **eyeball to eyeball** *Informal.* face to face: *an eyeball-to-eyeball confrontation that makes one person blink.*

— *v. Informal.* look closely at someone: *The guard was supposed to eyeball the prisoner at all times.*

eye·brow *n.* the arch of bone and growth of hair over

each eye: *a man with bushy eyebrows; The court ruling raised eyebrows* (= caused a sensation) *around the country.*

eye contact *n.* the meeting of two people's eyes: *She avoids eye contact with strangers in the big city.*

eyed (IDE) *adj. & combining form.* having eyes or eyelike markings: *an eyed design; eyed like a peacock; almond-eyed, cockeyed, one-eyed, sharp-eyed.*

eye·ful *n.* a sight, view, or person likely to please one: *Eve's quite an eyeful; He got an eyeful* (= more than he expected to see) *when he looked into the room.*

eye·lash *n.* a hair or fringe of hairs on the edge of the upper or lower eyelid.

eye·let (EYE·lit) *n.* a small hole, usually rimmed with metal, as for a shoelace to pass through, or edged with stitches, as in embroidered designs.

eye·lid *n.* the upper or lower fold of skin over an eye: *drooping, swollen eyelids.*

eye·lin·er (EYE·lye·nur) *n.* a cosmetic preparation applied to the base of the eyelashes.

eye-opener (EYE·oh·puh·nur) *n.* **1** something that surprises and enlightens: *The results of the literacy survey came as an eye-opener to educators.* **2** *Informal.* an early-morning drink.

eye·piece *n.* the viewing lens of a microscope, telescope, etc.

eye shadow *n.* a cosmetic preparation applied on the upper eyelids.

eyes-only *adj.* to be read only by the addressee: *an eyes-only document, message; information shared on an eyes-only basis.*

eye·sore *n.* an unpleasant sight.

eye·tooth *n., pl.* **-teeth** an upper canine tooth: *It is a privilege anyone would **give his eyeteeth** for* (= It is a great privilege).

eye·wash *n.* **1** an eye lotion. **2** *Informal.* something said or done to impress or flatter.

eye·wit·ness (EYE·WIT·nis) *n.* one who can testify about a happening, having seen it in person: *an eyewitness to the accident; an eyewitness account.*

eying See EYE.

ey·rie (AIR·ee, EYE·ree) *n.* **-ries** a nest, as an eagle's, placed high: *The hawk swooped down from its eyrie; There's an eyrie of a restaurant atop the CN Tower.* Also **aerie, aery, eyry.**

Ff ▾ ▾ ▾ ▾

F or **f** (EF) *n.* **F's** or **f's** the sixth letter of the English alphabet; hence, the sixth in a series.

fa (FAH) *n.* in music, the fourth tone of the diatonic scale.

fa·ble (FAY·bul) *n.* 1 a story with a moral and animals as characters. 2 a myth or invention.

fa·bled (FAY·buld) *adj.* famous in legends or stories: *the fabled monster of Loch Ness; the fabled golden waves of prairie wheat.*

fab·ric (FAB·ric) *n.* 1 a material, as flannel or other cloth, that is put together by weaving, knitting, or felting: *a fine fabric of linen fibres; synthetic, textile, and other fabrics.* 2 any structure of different elements: *None of the original fabric of the old cathedral remains today; the fabric of society weakened by civil wars.*

fab·ri·cate (FAB·ruh·cate) *v.* -cates, -cat·ed, -cat·ing 1 create by putting parts together: *the separately fabricated parts of a house; a pre-fabricated building; Margarine, bacon bits, coffee creamers, etc. are **fabricated foods**.* 2 make up in order to deceive: *to fabricate an excuse, explanation, falsehood, story.* — **fab·ri·ca·tion** (-ruh·CAY·shun) *n.: That report was pure fabrication; an outright fabrication.* — **fab·ri·ca·tor** (-cay·tur) *n.*

fab·u·lous (FAB·yuh·lus) *adj.* like a fable; hence, incredible or wonderful: *the fabulous treasures of sunken ships; I'm in fabulous health.* — **fab·u·lous·ly** *adv.: a fabulously wealthy man.*

fa·cade or **fa·çade** (fuh·SAHD, -SADE) *n.* 1 the front of a building: *the facade of a church.* 2 a false or put-on appearance: *His humility is a mere facade.*

face *n.* 1 the front of the human head; hence, an expression or look: *a beautiful, familiar, moon, oval, round, ruddy, strange, ugly face; Al made a face at Lu; Children make faces in the mirror; an angry, funny, poker, straight, serious face* (= expression); *She looked him **in the face*** (= directly); *They finally met **face to face*** (= in person); *He married her **in the face of*** (= facing) *opposition from her family; The new evidence **flies in the face of*** (= contradicts) *previous testimony; It seems a good plan **on the face of it*** (= judging by appearances); *She called him a liar **to his face**; A **face guard** or **face mask** is worn by players to protect the face from injury.* 2 the front, main, or outer surface: *the face of a clock; the faces of a crystal; Industry has changed the face* (= appearance) *of the land.* 3 dignity or prestige: *He **lost face** by refusing the challenge; She **saved face** by rewording her statement.* — *v.* **fac·es, faced, fac·ing** 1 look or be turned toward something: *Our house faces south.* 2 meet a person in a brave or daring manner; confront: *He couldn't face his mother after telling a lie; He backed down when faced with the facts; Ming knew she was innocent and she calmly **faced down*** (= defeated) *the crowd without saying a word; They had to **face up** to the truth* (= accept it courageously). 3 provide a surface or trimming to something: *Our house is faced with brownstone; a walnut veneer **facing*** (= front); *a military coat's **facings*** (= cuffs, collar, and trimmings).

face·down *n.* a confrontation or showdown. — *adv.* with the face down: *The body was lying facedown; Cards are dealt facedown on the table.*

face·less *adj.* having no distinctive character: *the faceless crowds of large cities.*

face·lift *n.* 1 cosmetic surgery for getting rid of facial wrinkles and such signs of age. 2 treatment to improve appearance: *The city hall got a facelift for the centennial.*

face-off *n.* 1 the opening play in hockey in which two opposing players face each other: *Our team won the face-off.* 2 a confrontation: *The Cuban missile crisis was a superpower face-off that brought the world to the brink of war.*

face-saving *adj.* that saves face or avoids embarrassment: *a face-saving compromise, measure.*

fac·et (FAS·it) *n.* one of many sides, aspects, or phases, as a surface of a cut gem: *An insect's compound eye has six lensed facets; to study a problem in all its facets.*

fac·et·ed (FAS·it·id) *adj.* having a facet or facets: *a faceted rock crystal; a multi-faceted personality.*

fa·ce·tious (fuh·SEE·shus) *adj.* aiming to be humorous, esp. by witty remarks in a serious or inappropriate situation: *facetious humour; a facetious remark, reply.*

face-to-face (FACE·tuh·face) *adj.* direct: *a face-to-face confrontation, meeting, talk.*

face value *n.* 1 the stated value, as on a bond or bill. 2 apparent value or meaning: *I took his word at face value.*

fa·cial (FAY·shul) *adj.* of the face: *a facial expression, massage, treatment; facial features; **facial tissue** (paper)*

for use as a handkerchief.
— *n.* a treatment for the face, as given in a beauty parlour: *to get a facial.* — **fa·cial·ly** *adv.*

fac·ile (FAS·ul, -ile) *adj.* [sometimes derogatory, depending on context] quick and easy: *a facile answer, disposition, liar, method, mind, narrator, nature, pen, remark, solution, task, tongue, victory, wit, writer; a sales rep's facile pitch.* — **fac·ile·ly** *adv.*

fa·cil·i·tate (fuh·SIL·uh·tate) *v.* -tates, -tat·ed, -tat·ing make a process, result, etc. easier: *to facilitate a reply, task; Labour-saving devices facilitate work.*
— **fa·cil·i·ta·tor** (-tay·tur) *n.*
— **fa·cil·i·ta·tion** (-TAY·shun) *n.*

fa·cil·i·ty (fuh·SIL·uh·tee) *n.* -ties 1 the quality that makes a particular action easy or simple: *the dog's natural facility in swimming; Mia plays the piano with great facility; Yves has no facility with languages.* 2 something that helps an activity: *a correctional facility* (=prison); *recreational facilities; a university with excellent research facilities; Schools provide facilities for study such as books and libraries; swimming pools, tennis courts, and such sports facilities; an indoor swimming facility; airports, bus services, and other travel facilities; He operates a computer facility* (=installation); *Would you like to use the facilities* (=washroom)?

fac·sim·i·le (fac·SIM·uh·lee) *n.* 1 an exact copy, esp. of something graphic. 2 same as FAX.

fact *n.* something that is real, actual, or true: *Is the UFO story fact or fiction? Give me some **facts and figures*** (=precise information); *an accepted, established, hard, historic, incontestable, irrefutable, proven, well-known fact; the bare facts; to ascertain, check, confirm, establish, ignore, verify a fact; to cite, distort, embellish, embroider, evaluate, face, interpret, marshall, present, twist (the) facts; Pollution is a fact of life; the **facts of life*** (=basics of sex and reproduction); *A helper in a crime could be an accessory **before** or **after the fact*** (=before or after the committing of the crime); ***As a matter of fact*** (=actually or really), *UFOs are fiction; No one, **in fact**, has touched a UFO; **In point of fact**,* (=actually) *they don't exist.*

fact finder *n.* an investigator, esp. as a member of a committee, as in labour disputes: *a **fact-finding** committee, mission, tour.*

fac·tion (FAC·shun) *n.* 1 a minority group within an organization, working against its larger interests; clique: *a party torn by warring factions; an extremist faction.* 2 party strife.
— **fac·tion·al** *adj.*: *factional conflicts, disputes, feuds, fighting, strife, warfare.*

fac·tor (FAC·tur) *n.* 1 a circumstance or element contributing to a result: *Strength of materials is a safety factor in construction; a common factor; deciding factor; major factor; the wind-chill factor.* 2 a number which multiplied by another equals a given number: *3 and 6 are factors of 18.* 3 a trading agent: *a fur company factor.*

fac·to·ry (FAC·tuh·ree) *n.* -ries a building in which products are manufactured; industrial plant: *He works at or in an automobile factory; a factory hand* (=factory worker).

fac·to·tum (fac·TOH·tum) *n. Formal.* one who does all kinds of work around a house or office.

fac·tu·al (FAC·choo·ul) *adj.* agreeing with facts: *a factual account, report.* — **fac·tu·al·ly** *adv.*

fac·ul·ty (FAC·ul·tee) *n.* -ties 1 an ability or power: *the faculty of speech; a faculty for remembering names; a will made while in full possession of one's faculties.* 2 an academic division: *the faculty of arts.* 3 a teaching staff, esp. of a college or university: *She is on the medical faculty; The faculty is on strike; **adj.**: a faculty club, common room, lounge, member.*

fad *n.* a temporary fashion or craze: *The hula hoop was a great fad of the 1950s; a food fad; the latest or newest fad; a passing fad; Is the denim fad about to fade?*
— **fad·dish** *adj.*; **fad·dist** *n.*

fade *v.* fades, fad·ed, fad·ing become faint: *The music faded in the distance; well-worn faded jeans; Childhood memories fade with age; worn brakes that fade* (=lose stopping power).
— **fade in** (or **out**) 1 of motion pictures, appear or make appear (or disappear) gradually. 2 of sounds, make or become more (or less) distinct.

fag *v.* fags, fagged, fag·ging work hard until tired: *He's fagging away at his tasks; He's too fagged out to stay awake.*
— *n. Slang.* 1 a cigarette. 2 [short form] faggot.
— **fag end** *n. Informal.* the extreme end: *Everyone is tired at the fag end of the day.*

fag·got or **fag·ot** (FAG·ut) *n.* 1 a bundle of sticks or of iron rods. 2 *Slang.* [derogatory] a male homosexual.

Fahr·en·heit (FAIR·un·hite) *adj.* having to do with a thermometer scale with 32° as the freezing point and 212° as the boiling point of water: *the Fahrenheit scale; a Fahrenheit thermometer.*

fail *v.* 1 be wanting, lacking, or negligent: *He has brains but fails in diligence; Those failing to do their homework are given detentions; Words fail us when our hearts are full; an old woman in failing* (=weakening) *health.* 2 be unsuccessful: *He failed the test; failed dismally, miserably; failed in math; Crops may fail during a drought; Trees fail to bear fruit; Businesses fail; Her confidence failed her when she got up to speak; Don't fail* (=disappoint) *me when I need you most; The teacher failed* (=did not pass) *those who scored below 50%.* — **without fail** surely: *I'll be there without fail.*

failing *n.* weakness: *Laziness is one of his failings.*
— ***prep.*** in the absence of something: *You have to produce your birth certificate, failing which you may not be registered.*

fail-safe *adj.* providing safety against failure: *a fail-safe device to open doors in an emergency.*

fail·ure (FAIL·yur) *n.* lack of success or an instance of it: *The party was a failure; business failures; Many businesses end in failure; They prove to be failures; their failure to make a profit; a crop, engine, heart, power failure; He was an abject, complete, dismal, hopeless, miserable, total failure in algebra, but not a failure in life.*

faint *adj.* weak or feeble: *She felt faint and was about to*

collapse; *He spoke in a faint voice, whisper; faint praise; I don't have the faintest idea where she is.*
— *v.* become unconscious: *He fainted on hearing the bad news.*
— *n.* state of unconsciousness: *He fell into a faint; She came out of the faint in no time.*
— faint·ly *adv.*; faint·ness *n.*

faint-hearted (FAINT·har·tid) *adj.* lacking courage; timid.

fair 1 *adj. & adv.* treating both sides alike without selfish considerations: *a fair and impartial judge; a fair businessman, decision, judgment; Turn about is* **fair play;** *Let's play fair; to be fair to customers; He always gets what he wants by* **fair means or foul** (= with or without fraud); *It's not fair* (= according to the rules of boxing) *to hit anyone below the belt.* **2** *adj.* [in the general sense of "good" or "pleasing"]: *a patient in fair condition; a fair* (= moderately good) *guess; fair* (= light in colour) *hair, skin; a fair* (= attractive) *maiden; fair* (= clear) *weather; a fair* (= favourable) *wind; the* **fair sex** (= women). **3** *n.* an exhibition of agricultural or industrial goods: *a county, state, trade, world's fair.*
— **fair and square** honestly: *She is fair and square in her dealings; She deals fair and square with everyone; Lin hit Luc fair and square* (= straight) *on the nose.*
— fair·ly *adv.* in a fair manner: *We treat our employees fairly* (= justly); *He looks fairly* (= reasonably) *happy.*
— fair·ness *n.*

fair·ground or **fair·grounds** *n.* a place to hold fairs, carnivals, and other outdoor events.

fair shake *n. Informal.* an even chance: *to get a fair shake.*

fair·way *n.* the mowed area of a golf course between tee and green.

fair-weather (FAIR·weath·ur) *adj.* changeable; hence, untrustworthy: *a fair-weather friend.*

fair·y (FAIR·ee) *n.* **fair·ies 1** a supernatural being resembling humans but usually much smaller, sometimes winged, often mischievous and endowed with magical powers: *Cinderella's* **fairy godmother. 2** *Slang.* [derogatory] a male homosexual.

fairy tale *n.* a story for children about fairies, fantasies, and magical happenings: *Grimm's Fairy Tales.*
— **fairy-tale** *adj.* having the qualities of fairy tales: *a fairy-tale house, princess, romance, valley; Your story is pure fairy-tale* (= all made up).

fait ac·com·pli (FATE·ah·cohm·PLEE), *pl.* **faits ac·com·plis** (FATE·ah·cohm·PLEE) an accomplished fact; hence, something that cannot be helped or changed.

faith *n.* **1** trust or belief: *She had faith in the justice system; Her faith was shaken by the jury's verdict; He didn't lose faith; a deep, enduring, strong faith; Labour and management bargained* **in good faith** (= with sincerity); *They showed* **good faith** (= good will) *by signing a contract; She* **kept faith** *with* (= was loyal to) *him in good times and bad; a Hindu by faith and by conviction; We take many things* **on faith** *in the absence of proof.* **2** a particular belief or religion: *to keep the faith; renounce one's faith; He considers his religion the true faith; non-Christian faiths.*

faith·ful *adj.* loyal or dedicated: *a faithful employee, husband, wife; a faithful servant who was faithful to his master; faithful in everything.*
— *n.* [takes pl. v.] practising believers: *The faithful attend services regularly; the party faithful* (of a political party). — faith·ful·ly *adv.*; faith·ful·ness *n.*

faith·less *adj.* without faith; also, disloyal.

fake *v.* **fakes, faked, fak·ing** pretend or counterfeit: *a painting style that is hard to fake; to fake an accident and collect insurance; to fake the goalie* (= draw the goalie out of position) *and shoot a goal.*
— *adj.* false or sham: *a fake masterpiece;* *n.*: *Her French accent is only a fake.*

fal·con (FAL·cun) *n.* a hawk used in the sport of hunting birds.

fall (FAWL) *v.* **falls, fell, fall·en, fall·ing 1** drop or move down: *Leaves fall from trees in autumn; Soldiers fall in battle, dead or wounded; He slipped and fell on the floor; to fall headlong into a well; Children fall down on the ice; to fall down the stairs; to fall off a horse; to fall out of bed; During a storm, trees fall over, fall across power lines; The roof fell in* (= collapsed) *under the weight of the snow; Temperatures fall in the winter.* **2** occur, happen, or move into a new state or condition: *Night falls early in December; December 25 fell on a Sunday in 1988; People fall asleep, fall ill, fall in love with each other, fall into error, fall into evil ways, fall on hard times* (= become poor). **3** decline in power, position, value, etc.: *The ocean bed falls sharply a few kilometres from the shore; Stocks fell to their lowest value ever on Black Monday; A government falls* (= suffers defeat) *when it loses support; A country falls to* (= is conquered by) *the enemy; His face fell* (= suddenly took on a look of disappointment) *because it was bad news.*
— **fall back** give way or retreat: *Troops were falling back all along the front.*
— **fall back on** turn to for help: *a friend to fall back on in time of need.*
— **fall behind** fail to keep up with something: *Some runners soon fell behind; to fall behind in one's payments.*
— **fall down on the job** fail to do the job.
— **fall flat** fail completely: *His plans and her jokes always fall flat.*
— **fall for** *Informal.* **1** fall in love with someone: *He fell for her right away.* **2** be deceived by something: *We won't fall for that trick.*
— **fall foul of** quarrel, clash, or lose favour with

someone: *He fell foul of his boss; to fall foul of the law.*
— **fall in** get in formation: *The troops were ordered to fall in.*
— **fall into 1** begin: *to fall into conversation with someone.* **2** be classified: *People fall into different groups.*
— **fall into line** comply or obey: *The dissidents won't fall into line.*
— **fall in with** meet or join: *How did he fall in with criminal elements?*
— **fall off** become less: *The membership of the party began to fall off after they lost the election.*
— **fall on** or **upon 1** attack eagerly: *Hungry children fall on the food as soon as served; Troops fall upon an enemy.* **2** be the duty of someone: *It falls on her as the chair to preside over the meeting.*
— **fall out (with)** quarrel (with): *Al and Lu fell out with each other over buying a new car; They had a **falling out**.*
— **fall over backward(s)** or **fall (all) over oneself** try very hard; be very eager: *These waiters fall over backward to give good service; He fell (all) over himself trying to help me.*
— **fall short** fail to reach a goal: *The results fell short of expectations.*
— **fall through** fail: *Wild schemes often fall through.*
— **fall to 1** belong, as right or duty: *It falls to her as the chair to preside over the meeting.* **2** begin doing something: *The children fell to doing their chores.*
— **n. 1** the act or result of falling; drop or collapse: *a fall on the ice; a fall from power; a sharp fall in demand, prices, temperature; the fall of a government; a free fall (under the pull of gravity alone); The tree branches helped break his fall; Niagara Falls is not a high fall or falls; his fall from grace; After **the Fall** of Adam and Eve (= expulsion from paradise), to err is human.* **2** autumn: *Schools open in the fall.*

fal·la·cy (FAL·uh·see) *n.* **-cies** false or erroneous reasoning; an incorrect or deceptive idea: *Prejudices are based on old fallacies.*
— **fal·la·cious** (fuh·LAY·shus) *adj.*

fall fair *n.* *Cdn.* a fair held in the fall with exhibits of farm products and entertainment.

fall guy *n.* *Informal.* scapegoat.

fal·li·ble (FAL·uh·bul) *adj.* subject to error: *We are fallible creatures.* — **fal·li·bly** *adv.*
— **fal·li·bil·i·ty** (·uh·BIL·uh·tee) *n.*

fall·out *n.* **1** radioactive particles from a nuclear explosion in the air: *a fallout shelter.* **2** an unforeseen result; side effect.

fal·low (FAL·oh) *adj.* **1** unseeded or unused: *fields that lie fallow.* **2** light brownish yellow.

false (FAWLSE) *adj.* **fals·er, fals·est** not true or correct: *What you heard was a false alarm set off by mistake; False arguments don't convince anyone; false (= illegal) arrest and imprisonment; Drugs were found in the **false bottom** (= secret compartment) of his suitcase; a false ceiling (hung below the ceiling joists); a ship flying false colours (to deceive the authorities); false (= fake) diamonds; a false (= unfaithful or disloyal) friend; to put up a false front (= deceptive appearance); He gained admission by false pretences; false (= ill-founded) pride, sense of security; a false start before the pistol is fired; A*

false step made her stumble and fall; a set of false (= artificial) teeth; a false (= incorrect) verdict; false weights (for cheating customers).*
— **play false** cheat or trick someone.
— **false·ly** *adv.;* **false·ness** *n.*

false·hood (FAWLSE·hood, short "oo") *n.* an untruth or lie: *an absolute, obvious, outright, utter falsehood.*

fal·set·to (fawl·SET·oh) *n.* **-set·tos** an artificially high singing voice, esp. of a tenor: *to sing falsetto.*

fal·si·fy (FAWL·suh·fye) *v.* **-fies, -fied, -fy·ing** make or prove false: *a clerk fired for falsifying the records; The evidence falsifies your conclusion.*
— **fal·si·fi·ca·tion** (·fuh·CAY·shun) *n.*

fal·si·ty (FAWL·suh·tee) *n.* **-ties** falseness: *the truth or falsity of a claim.*

fal·ter (FAWL·tur) *v.* **-ters, -tered, -ter·ing** waver or hesitate in gait, resolve, speech, etc.: *He faltered and fell down the stairs; Our courage began to falter; She faltered out a few words before passing out; The engine faltered and stopped dead; He falters in his resolve to see the project through; a faltering enterprise; a few faltering steps.* — **fal·ter·ing·ly** *adv.*

fame *n.* great reputation or renown: *an ambitious man eager for fame and fortune; to achieve, attain, seek, win fame; At the height of his fame, he was still poverty-stricken.*

famed *adj.* famous: *a region famed for its lakes.*

fa·mil·ial (fuh·MIL·yul) *adj.* having to do with a family: *Most familial diseases are inherited; familial relationships.*

fa·mil·i·ar (fuh·MIL·yur) *adj.* having to do with close association: *a familiar (= well-known) voice; familiar to everyone; an all too familiar slogan; good friends on familiar (= intimate or informal) terms; Children should not get familiar with strangers; experts who are thoroughly familiar (= acquainted) with the problem.*
— **n.** a companion or friend: *A black cat was believed to be a witch's familiar (= spirit in animal form).*
— **fa·mil·i·ar·ly** *adv.*

fa·mil·i·ar·i·ty (fuh·MIL·ee·AIR·uh·tee) *n.* **-ties** closeness: *The lawyer showed lack of familiarity with (= knowledge of) the case; She resents such familiarities (= liberties) as necking and petting; She moves about with easy familiarity (= informality) among her guests.*

fa·mil·i·ar·ize (fuh·MIL·yur·ize) *v.* **-iz·es, -ized, -iz·ing** make familiar: *He familiarized himself with the facts of the case.*

fam·i·ly (FAM·uh·lee) *n.* **-lies 1** the social unit of parents and children: *a broken family; a close family; an extended family of relatives living under the same roof; Al comes from a good family; The nuclear family is your immediate family; Love of music runs in the family (= is hereditary); **adj:** a family doctor, movie, practitioner, restaurant; a **family room** (for recreation); family medicine, planning, ties.* **2** one's children: *a couple without a family; to raise a family; to start a family; to clothe, feed, and support a family.* **3** any group or set with a common origin or with similar characteristics: *Cougars belong to the cat family; English and Hindi are in the Indo-Aryan family of languages; a plant family; a* *notorious Mafia family.*

Family Allowance *n. Cdn.* an allowance paid by the Federal Government for the parents, usually to the mother, of each dependent child under age 18.

family tree *n.* a chart showing the ancestors and descendants of a family.

fam·ine (FAM·un) *n.* a widespread and serious shortage, esp. of food: *a country struck by famine.*

fam·ish (FAM·ish) *v.* -ish·es, -ished, -ish·ing suffer or make suffer from extreme hunger: *the famished look of war orphans; I missed lunch, I'm famished (Informal for very hungry).*

fa·mous (FAY·mus) *adj.* very well-known and esteemed: *a famous professor; France is famous for its wines; famous as a wine-producing country.*
— **fa·mous·ly** *adv. Informal.* very well: *They got along famously for 20 years.*

fan *n.* **1** a semicircular, often folding device for blowing air for ventilation or cooling: *a fan of feathers.* **2** something fan-shaped: *the fan hitch method of harnessing a team of sled dogs.* **3** a rotary device equipped with blades or vanes for blowing air: *a ceiling fan; electric fan; exhaust fan; table fan; to turn off, turn on a fan; the fan of a radiator.* **4** an enthusiastic follower or admirer; buff: *a football fan; an ardent fan of Anne Murray;* **adj.:** *fan clubs, letters, magazines, mail.*
— *v.* **fans, fanned, fan·ning:** *A room packed with people fanning themselves (= using fans); The speech helped fan (= fire up) the flames of rebellion; Their anger was fanned (= raised) into fury by the mob orator; Police and neighbours fanned out (= spread out) over the neighbourhood in search of the missing child; a (baseball) batter who fans (= strikes out); to fan (= miss the hockey puck) on a shot or pass.*

fa·nat·ic (fuh·NAT·ic) *n. & adj.* (one who is) uncritically enthusiastic about something religious, political, etc.: *a religious fanatic; a fanatic cult; Mario is fanatic about fresh air; Pin is a fanatic for vegetarianism.*
— **fa·nat·i·cal** (-uh·cul) *adj.: fanatical ideas; a fanatical sect.* — **fa·nat·i·cal·ly** *adv.;* **fa·nat·i·cism** *n.*

fan belt *n.* the belt that drives the fan of a radiator.

fan·ci·er (FAN·see·ur) *n.* one with a special interest in particular types of birds, animals, plants, or articles.: *a dog fancier; an orchid fancier; a fancier of fine wines.*

fan·ci·ful (FAN·suh·ful) *adj.* overimaginative: *a fanciful poet; fanciful tales.*

fan·cy (FAN·see) *n.* an idea or imagination of a passing or trifling nature: *She can afford to do whatever strikes her fancy; Jo felt a sudden fancy for heart-shaped cookies; Advertisers use words and pictures to tickle your fancy; Aunt Ada took quite a fancy to her young niece; Science fiction is not mere fancy but the product of fertile imaginations; creatures of fancy such as fairies and dragons; a poet's flights of fancy.*
— *adj.* unusual or out-of-the-way: *a fancy costume; fancy goods; $50 000 seems a fancy price for a used car; Sensible children don't wear fancy shoes to school.*
— *v.* -cies, -cied, -cy·ing **1** imagine: *She fancies she'll be a doctor in five years; He fancies setting up a thriving business.* **2** like: *Pat doesn't fancy him as a doctor; Lu*

doesn't fancy working late.

fancy dress *n.* imaginative costume, as for a masquerade.

fancy-free *adj.* free from serious romantic attachments.

fan·fare *n.* **1** a sounding of trumpets; hence, a flourish. **2** publicity: *a narrow win announced with great fanfare.*

fang *n.* **1** one of the sharp and pointed teeth of carnivorous mammals; canine tooth: *The tiger bared its fangs menacingly.* **2** a venomous tooth of a reptile.

fan·ny (FAN·ee) *n.* fan·nies *Slang.* the buttocks.

fan·ta·size (FAN·tuh·size) *v.* -siz·es, -sized, -siz·ing daydream: *Everyone fantasizes now and then; The orphan child fantasizes that she is with her family; She is fantasizing about being reunited with her family; Pat fantasizes (= daydreams about) Ray and vice versa.*

fan·tas·tic (fan·TAS·tic) *adj.* **1** strange and unreal: *a fantastic story that no one will believe.* **2** *Informal.* incredible or wonderful: *a fantastic movie; a fantastic idea, price.* Also **fan·tas·ti·cal.** — **fan·tas·ti·cal·ly** *adv.*

fan·ta·sy (FAN·tuh·see) *n.* -sies something imagined or invented in a literary or artistic way that has little correspondence with reality: *Tolkien's "Lord of the Rings" is high fantasy; Space travel is no longer a fantasy; He lives in a world of fantasy full of heroic deeds; He indulges in fantasies but doesn't act them out.*
— **fan·ta·sist** *n.*

fan·zine (FAN·zeen) *n.* a magazine for fans, esp. of science fiction.

far *adj.* **far·ther** (FAR·thur, "th" as in "the") or **fur·ther** (FUR-), **far·thest** (-thist) or **fur·thest** distant or remote: *a far country; in the far future; the far ends of the earth; Calgary is farther from Toronto than from Winnipeg; the farthest of the three cities; The winter is far from over in March; Despotism is a far cry (= a long way) from democracy.*
— *adv.* at, to, or from a distance in time or position: *We like to travel far; He lives farther down the road; a job far (= much) easier than the old one; As or So far as I can tell, it won't rain today; This is the best deal by far (= without doubt); Lee is far and away (= beyond doubt) the best baker around here; She carried her message far and wide (= everywhere); Far be it from me to (= I would never) question his sincerity; Do I doubt his sincerity? Far from it! She will go far (= succeed) in her career; So far (= till now), she has done well.*

far·a·way (FAR·uh·way) *adj.* **1** distant: *faraway voices.* **2** dreamy: *a faraway look in his eyes.*

farce *n.* a humorous play full of funny situations and ridiculous happenings; hence, a mockery: *The new censorship laws make a farce of freedom of speech.*
— **far·ci·cal** (FAR·suh·cul) *adj.*

fare *v.* fares, fared, far·ing **1** get on; do: *How did he fare in his new job? She fared well at the exam; She couldn't have fared any better.* **2** [old use] go or travel.
— *n.* **1** a fee paid for transportation: *The fare to the airport is $20; People pay the fare that is charged; a cheap, economy, excursion, full, half, reduced fare; air, airplane, bus, plane, taxi, train fares.* **2** a paying

passenger: *The cabbie took his fare to the airport.*
3 food or diet: *plain, simple, wholesome fare.*

Far East *n.* eastern Asia, esp. China, Japan, Korea, and nearby islands; rarely, Southeast Asia.

fare·well (fare·WEL) *interj.* good-bye.
— *n.* an expression of good wishes at parting: *She made her farewell; He bade her farewell; a fond farewell; sad farewell; farewell to family and friends; adj.: a farewell party, speech.*

far·fetched *adj.* contrived and unlikely: *a story too far-fetched to be true.*

far-flung *adj.* **1** widely scattered: *the far-flung oases of the Sahara.* **2** distant: *the far-flung corners of the earth.*

farm *n.* **1** a tract of land on which crops are grown and livestock raised: *to manage, run a farm; to work on a farm; chicken, dairy, fruit, poultry, sheep, truck farms; adj.: a farm corporation; farm credit, exports, income, law, life, machinery, organizations, property, sales, supports.* **2** a minor-league baseball or hockey team associated with or owned by a major league club; also **farm club.**
— *v.* cultivate crops and raise livestock on a farm: *Over half the world's people farm for a living.*
— **farm out** send work out to be done by others: *Many publishers farm out editorial jobs; The children were farmed out (=sent) to relatives when their mother was ill.*

farm·er *n.* one who farms: *a dirt farmer; Gentlemen farmers farm for pleasure; grain farmers from the Prairies; a sheep farmer from Australia; a farmer cooperative; a farmers' alliance, market, union.*
— **farming** *n. & adj.: collective farming; subsistence farming; wheat farming; the farming business; farming operations.*

farm·hand *n.* one who works on a farm for wages.

farm·house *n.* the dwelling house on a farm.

farm·land *n.* land that is or can be used for agriculture.

farm·stead *n.* the land and buildings of a farm.

farm·yard *n.* the area next to or surrounded by buildings of a farm.

Far North *n.* Canada's Arctic and sub-Arctic regions lying north of the provinces.

far-off *adj.* remote: *the far-off times and places of one's childhood.*

far-out *adj.* **1** very distant: *the far-out stars of our galaxy.* **2** *Informal.* far from the ordinary; unconventional: *a far-out design, sect; far-out music.*

far-reaching *adj.* having wide-ranging effects or importance: *Far-reaching tax reforms have been proposed.*

far·row (FAIR·oh) *n. & v.* (give birth to) a litter of pigs.

far·see·ing (FAR·see·ing) *adj.* able to see far, esp. showing foresight; farsighted.

far·sight·ed (FAR·sye·tid) *adj.* **1** able to see ahead, esp. the future effects of one's actions; not shortsighted: *a farsighted leader.* **2** not able to see near objects as clearly as distant ones.
— **far·sight·ed·ness** *n.: Convex glasses are worn to correct farsightedness.*

farther *a comp.* of FAR.

far·ther·most (FAR·thur·most, "th" as in "the") *adj.* remotest.

farthest *a superl.* of FAR.

far·thing (FAR·thing, "th" as in "the") *n.* **1** an old British coin worth one fourth of a penny. **2** something small or of little value; a small sum.

fas·ci·nate (FAS·uh·nate) *v.* **-nates, -nat·ed, -nat·ing** captivate, esp. in an irresistible or compelling way: *Poetry fascinates him; a **fascinating** personality, speech.*
— **fas·ci·na·tion** (-NAY·shun) *n.*

fas·cism (FASH·iz·um) *n.* a political system or philosophy based on absolute loyalty to a one-party dictatorship, militarism, and usually racism and nationalism. — **fas·cist** *n. & adj.*

fash·ion (FASH·un) *n.* **1** the manner or way of doing something: *He walks in a peculiar fashion; people of all fashions (= types); women of fashion (= of social prominence); He can speak Chinese **after a fashion** (= moderately well).* **2** what is current in styles of dress, speech, conduct, etc. at a particular time or place: *Designers set fashions; the latest fashions; Miniskirts come into fashion now and then; What is **in fashion** today may go **out of fashion** tomorrow; a fashion show.*
— *v.* make in a creative way: *a figure fashioned out of clay.*

fash·ion·a·ble (FASH·uh·nuh·bul) *adj.* stylish.
— **fash·ion·a·bly** *adv.*

fast *adj.* **1** swift or rapid: *a fast runner; a fast highway (on which you can drive fast); the **fast lane** (= passing lane) of a highway; life in the **fast lane** (= a pleasure-oriented life); a fast watch (that runs ahead of the actual time).* **2** firm or secure: *a fast hold on a rope; Make the rope fast to the post.* **3** steadfast: *They've been fast friends since childhood.* **4** nonfading: *cloth dyed in fast colours.* **5** dishonest or deceptive: *He's out to make a fast buck; They pulled **a fast one** (Slang for clever trick) on me.*
— *adv.: Pat is driving too fast; The child is fast (= deeply) asleep; to hold fast to one's faith; He **plays fast and loose** (= acts in an undependable way) with his friends, with her affections.*
— *v.* abstain from food for losing weight, as penance, in protest, etc.: *She fasts during Lent.*
— *n.* **1** avoidance of food: *to observe a (religious) fast; He will break his fast only if his demands are met.* **2** one that fastens: *a door fast; A stern fast is a rope or cable.*

fas·ten (FAS·un) *v.* make fast, as by tying or gluing: *a door fastened with a bolt and chain; He drives with his eyes fastened (= fixed) on the road in front.*

fas·ten·er or **fas·ten·ing** *n.* a device that fastens, as a zipper, hook, clip, etc.

fast food *n.* food such as hamburgers and hot dogs that may be prepared and served quickly.
— **fast-food** *adj.: the fast-food industry; a fast-food chain, franchise, outlet, restaurant.*

fas·tid·i·ous (fas-TID·ee·us) *adj.* hard to please, being too critical of the quality of food, clothes, etc.; fussy: *She's a fastidious dresser; a man of fastidious tastes; She*

is fastidious about her china.
— fas·tid·i·ous·ly *adv.;* fas·tid·i·ous·ness *n.*

fast·ness *n.* **1** a secure place or stronghold: *robbers hiding in the fastnesses of the jungle; the mountain fastnesses of the Rockies.* **2** the quality of being fast or firm.

fast-talk *v. Informal.* persuade by fast and often deceitful talking.

fast-track *v.* go or send faster through a program or operation than planned: *to fast-track a student through high school; adj.: a fast-track deal, method, procedure, student.*

fat *n.* **1** an oily substance of animal tissue; also, vegetable oil used as a cooking medium: *potatoes fried in deep fat; Some are more inclined to fat* (= to become fleshy) *than others; excess body fat; The body makes cholesterol from saturated fats* (= fatty acids). **2** anything rich or superfluous: *to trim the fat off a heavy budget; He lives off the fat of the land* (= in luxury).
— **chew the fat** *Informal.* chat.
— **the fat is in the fire** the damage is done; there will be trouble.
— *adj.* fat·ter, fat·test filled out with fat: *fat cattle; a fat man; a fat bank account (with plenty of money in it); a fat farm (Informal for spa that helps people lose weight); He charges fat* (= heavy) *fees; fat* (= fertile) *lands; He won't listen to anyone because of his fat head* (= stupidity); *a fat pocketbook (full of money); Fat chance* (= No chance at all)! *It'll do a fat lot of good (Informal for no good at all).*
— fat·ly *adv.;* fat·ness *n.*

fa·tal (FAY·tul) *adj.* causing death: *a fatal accident; fatal injuries; the fatal hour (that cannot be avoided).*
— fa·tal·ly *adv.*

fa·tal·ism (FAY·tuh·liz·um) *n.* the belief or attitude that events, esp. unlucky ones, are predetermined and inevitable. — fa·tal·ist *n.* — fa·tal·is·tic (-LIS·tic) *adj.*

fa·tal·i·ty (fuh·TAL·uh·tee) *n.* -ties **1** deadliness: *the fatality of a disease like AIDS or cancer.* **2** a death as the result of a disaster: *highway fatalities; traffic fatalities during a snowstorm; The highway fatality rate is much worse than in the air.*

fat·back *n.* dried and salted fat from a hog's back.

fat cat *n. Informal.* a wealthy person: *the bankers and other fat cats of the financial world.*

fate *n.* **1** the inevitable outcome of events, often unfavourable: *blind, cruel fate; He met with a terrible fate being mauled to death by a bear; As sure as fate, the police were waiting around the corner; By a strange stroke of fate, the same thing happened the next day; the fate* (= death) *that awaits all of us; He was going out to meet his fate* (= destiny) *when he got on the highway; as fate decreed; The judgment sealed or decided his fate.* **2** Fates three goddesses of Greek and Roman myths who ruled people's lives.

fat·ed (FAY·tid) *adj.* marked by fate: *Prisoners fated to die are said to be on "death row"; the ill-fated voyage of the Titanic.*

fate·ful (FATE·ful) *adj.* decisive for the future: *The fateful hour of the jury's fateful verdict.*
— fate·ful·ly *adv.*

fat·head *n. Slang.* a stupid person. — fat·head·ed *adj.*

fa·ther (FAH·thur, FAW-, "th" as in "the") *n.* **1** a male parent; hence, originator: *the father of the child; the Fathers of Confederation who met in Charlottetown in 1867; Canada's founding fathers; Edward Teller, the father of the hydrogen bomb; Satan, the father of lies; our fathers* (= ancestors); *Our Father* (= God); *the city fathers* (= administrators). **2** Father [used also as a prefixed title] a Christian priest; Dear Father Smith.
— *v.* be the father or begetter of someone: *Jim fathered the orphan child; The child was wrongly fathered* (= imposed on as father) *on Joe.*
— fa·ther·hood *n.* — fa·ther·less *adj.*
— fa·ther·ly (FAH·thur·lee, FAW-); fa·ther·li·ness *n.*

father-in-law *n.* fathers-in-law the father of one's spouse.

fa·ther·land (FAH·thur·land, FAW-) *n.* one's native or ancestral country.

fath·om (FATH·um, "TH" as in "the") *n.* a measure of depth equal to 6 ft. (1.8 m).
— *v.* to sound a depth; hence, get to the bottom of something; figure out: *He speaks so little, it's difficult to fathom his intentions; to fathom what he means.*
— fath·om·a·ble *adj.*

fath·om·less (FATH·um·lis) *adj.* not fathomable or understandable: *a fathomless mystery; the fathomless depths of outer space.*

fa·tigue (fuh·TEEG) *n.* **1** weariness from exertion resulting in reduced capacity for work: *battle* or *combat fatigue; mental fatigue; metal fatigue (resulting from long use under stress); physical fatigue.* **2** fatigues *pl.* work clothing: *army fatigues.*
— *v.* fa·tigues, fa·tigued, fa·tigu·ing become weary or worn: *The raids confused and fatigued the army; A fatigued axle (with fatigued metal parts) may crack or break under continued strain.*

fatigue duty *n.* military duty of a menial nature, carried out in work clothes.

fat·ten (FAT·un) *v.* make or become fat.

fat·ty (FAT·ee) *adj.* fat·ti·er, fat·ti·est **1** containing fat: *Fatty acids contain many carbon atoms; a fatty* (= greasy) *food.* **2** *Informal.* overweight or too plump: *the fatty one over there.*
— *n., pl.* fat·ties *Informal.* a fat person.

fat·u·ous (FACH·oo·us) *adj.* stupid and self-satisfied.

fau·cet (FAW·sit) *n.* a fixture with a valve-device for drawing liquid from a pipe or cask; tap or spigot.

fault *n.* an imperfection, flaw, or error: *Everyone has faults; a service fault in tennis; The San Andreas Fault is a visible break in the rock stratum; to correct, overlook his faults; Who was at fault* (= to blame) *in the accident? She's generous to a fault* (= excessively); *He is always tring to find fault with* (= blame) *someone.*
— *v.* blame: *You can't fault her driving for the flat tire; You can't fault it on her driving.*
— fault·find·er (FAULT·fine·dur) *n.;* fault·find·ing *n.*

& adj.
— fault·less *adj.*; fault·less·ly *adv.*; fault·less·ness *n.*

fault·y (FAWL·tee) *adj.* fault·i·er, -i·est defective: *a faulty electrical connection; a fire resulting from faulty wiring.* — fault·i·ly *adv.*; fault·i·ness *n.*

fau·na (FAW·nuh) *n.* the animal life or animals of a particular period or region: *the flora and fauna of the Queen Charlotte Islands.*

faux pas (FOH·PAH) *n., pl.* faux pas (FOH·PAH) a social blunder; also, an embarrassing mistake.

fave *n. & adj. Informal.* favourite: *a cult fave like "Star Trek"; What's your fave sport?*

fa·vour or **fa·vor** (FAY·vur) *n.* 1 friendly regard or approval: *to look on someone with favour; justice without fear or favour; to curry, find, gain favour with someone; She fell out of favour with her boss; We are all in favour of a holiday; Luck is in our favour; a cheque made out in favour of John Doe (who is to get the money).* 2 a token of this, as a gift or an act of kindness: *Do me a small favour; noisemakers and such party favours.*
— *v.* 1 have or show favour for a person or thing: *Which candidate do you favour for the post? He favours his nephew Al; She favoured her cousin with (= gave her cousin) the job; He was heavily favoured to get it.* 2 resemble: *She favours her father.*
— fa·vour·a·ble or fa·vor·a·ble (FAY·vur·uh·bul) *adj.: weather that is favourable for a picnic.*
— fa·vour·a·bly or fa·vor·a·bly *adv.*

fa·vour·ite or **fa·vor·ite** (FAY·vur·it) *n.* a favoured person or thing: *Al is her favourite; a heavy, strong favourite for the presidency; adj.: a child's favourite toy; a teacher's favourite pupil; one of Canada's favourite sons* (= popular and famous people).

fa·vour·it·ism or **fa·vor·it·ism** (FAY·vur·it·iz·um) *n.* partiality toward particular people: *to show favouritism.*

fawn *n.* a young deer less than a year old or its pale yellowish brown colour.
— *v.* show friendliness by cringing or flattery: *Some dogs fawn on people* (= show love by climbing on them, etc.); *He fawns on his bosses.*

fax *n.* 1 an electronic machine for transmitting documents and pictures via the telephone lines; also **fax** or **facsimile machine.** 2 a document or picture received by fax.
— *v.* communicate with or transmit by fax: *I faxed London; I'll fax the contract to you and put the cheque in the mail.*

fay *n.* an elf or fairy.

faze *v.* faz·es, fazed, faz·ing *Informal.* upset: *Nothing could ever faze him.*

fear (FEER) *n.* an emotion felt in the presence of danger or some threat to one's well-being: *the fear of darkness; a fear of heights; to allay, arouse, express, feel, instill, kindle, overcome, show fear; The warning struck fear into our hearts; a grave, groundless, idle, lingering, mortal, sudden fear; the salutary fear* (= reverence) *of God; She tiptoed for fear of waking the baby.*
— *v.* feel fear or be afraid: *She fears to fly; We fear for his life; He fears that his life may be in danger.*
— fear·ful *adj.*; fear·ful·ly *adv.*; fear·ful·ness *n.*

fear·some *adj.* frightful: *the fearsome subject of AIDS, a fearsome disease; It has fearsome implications, prospects; It has already taken a fearsome toll; a tennis champion with a fearsome* (= intimidating) *forehand.*

fea·si·ble (FEE·zuh·bul) *adj.* 1 possible to carry out or do, esp. conveniently: *It's possible to drive 1 000 km nonstop, but hardly feasible; It's not a feasible plan.* 2 plausible: *a feasible story considering the circumstances.* — fea·si·bil·i·ty (-BIL·uh·tee) *n.*

feast (FEEST) *n.* 1 an elaborate or sumptuous meal: *a wedding feast; The smorgasbord was a feast for the eyes and the palate.* 2 a religious festival: *Hanukkah, the Feast of Lights.*
— *v.* entertain with a feast: *He feasts his friends on his birthday; Feast your eyes on* (= Enjoy the sight of) *my manicured lawn.*

feat (FEET) *n.* a remarkable deed or exploit: *to perform herculean feats of strength; a brave, brilliant, outstanding, remarkable feat; It's no mean feat to climb Everest.*

feath·er (FETH·ur, "TH" as in "the") *n.* one of the light, soft, thin outgrowths covering a bird's body: *as light as a feather; to smooth her ruffled feathers* (= calm her down); *"Birds of a feather* (= of the same kind) *flock together."*
— **feather in one's cap** an accomplishment.
— *v.* supply or furnish with feathers: *a feathered arrow, dart; our feathered friends, the birds; He was fired for trying to feather his nest* (= enrich himself by using his position). — feath·er·y (FETH·uh·ree) *adj.*

fea·ture (FEE·chur) *n.* 1 an outstanding detail or quality: *the physical features of a region; a characteristic, distinctive, distinguishing, noteworthy, redeeming feature; a child with delicate, handsome, soft, striking features (of face).* 2 an outstanding item offered in a newspaper, store, etc.: *a double feature* (= two films shown one after another); *standard and optional features for a new car; a special feature; adj.: a feature article, presentation, story, writer; a feature-length* (= full-length) *movie.*
— *v.* -tures, -tured, -tur·ing be or make a feature of something: *a store that features discounts; Who was featured in that movie? featured as the hero.*
— fea·ture·less *adj.: a featureless landscape; the featureless wastes of the Sahara.*

fe·ces (FEE·seez) *n. pl.* waste from the intestines.
— fe·cal (FEE·cul) *adj.*

feck·less (FEK·lis) *adj.* ineffective, futile, or

irresponsible: *a young woman abandoned by her feckless lover; He thinks those who pay taxes are foolish and feckless and those who don't are smart; He plays the part of a virtuous, feckless, and wimpy youth.*
— **feck·less·ly** *adv.*; **feck·less·ness** *n.*

fe·cund (FEC·und, FEE-) *adj.* fruitful or fertile: *the fecund earth; da Vinci's fecund genius.*
— **fe·cun·di·ty** (fi·CUN·duh·tee) *n.*

fed *pt. & pp.* of FEED.
— **fed up** *Informal.* tired and disgusted: *He's fed up with TV.*
— **fed** or **Fed** *n. Informal.* 1 a federal government agent or official. 2 **the feds** or **the Feds** *pl.* the federal government or its officials. 3 **the Fed** a federal government agency.

fed·er·al (FED·ur·ul) *adj.* 1 having to do with a federation: *a federal organization, party, union.* 2 having to do with a central government: *a federal affair, body, commission, district, policy, system; federal funding; a Federal Building (housing federal government offices); The U.S. Federal Bureau of Investigation corresponds to the Canadian RCMP; The Federal Court of Canada deals with Crown revenues, maritime law, and other specialized matters; the Federal Government in Ottawa; the Federal Parliament.*
— **fed·er·al·ly** *adv.*

fed·er·al·ize (FED·ur·uh·lize) *v.* **-iz·es, -ized, -iz·ing** unite into a federal union or put under federal control.

fed·er·ate (FED·uh·rate) *v.* **-ates, -at·ed, -at·ing** unite into a federation.

fed·er·a·tion (fed·uh·RAY·shun) *n.* a union of many member nations, states, or organizations.

fee *n.* a charge or payment for a privilege or service: *to charge a fee for admission; fees for services; a contingency, entrance, lawyer's, membership, registration, tuition fee; For a (nominal) fee, the shop will hold an item for you; They waived his fee; She split her fees with him.*

fee·ble (FEE·bul) *adj.* **-bler, -blest** 1 weak from sickness or age: *a feeble old man; a feeble voice.* 2 ineffective: *a feeble attempt, cry; feeble efforts.* — **fee·bly** *adv.*

fee·ble·mind·ed (FEE·bul·mine·did) *adj.* mentally retarded. — **fee·ble·mind·ed·ly** *adv.*
— **fee·ble·mind·ed·ness** *n.*

feed *v.* **feeds, fed, feed·ing** 1 give food or as food to someone: *Mother feeds the baby; Feed this to the cat; Caterpillars **feed on** (= eat) leaves; breast, forced, intravenous **feeding.*** 2 supply or provide: *to feed data into a computer; A TV reporter feeds her stories to the network; news to feed (= satisfy) your curiosity.*
— *n.* 1 food for animals: *cattle feed.* 2 material to feed into a machine or furnace. 3 a feeding mechanism.

feed·back *n.* in automatic systems, the return of part of the output as input, as in the on-and-off switching in a home heating system; hence, any similar process: *positive and negative feedbacks; This dictionary was compiled with the help of feedback from teachers and students.*

feel *v.* **feels, felt, feel·ing** 1 be aware of or experience something or one's own state of being: *A nail or hair cannot feel; How do you feel? I feel bad, cold, fine, good, hot, proud, sorry, warm; He feels such an idiot to have done that; You will feel better after resting; She feels cheated; He feels for her in her misery; He feels pity for her; She feels like a fool; Do you **feel like** taking a walk? No, I don't **feel up to** it today.* 2 perceive by touching: *The doctor felt her pulse; She could feel it beat(ing); She felt about in her bag for the key; A blind man **feels his way** about in the dark; The room feels warm (= One feels warm in it).* 3 believe or think: *He feels strongly about cruelty to animals; He feels that animals should not be killed for food; Let's **feel out** (= find out the thinking of) the membership on this question.*
— *n.* 1 the sense of touch: *She has a good feel (= intuition) for poetry that sells; He took a feel of (= did an act of feeling) her pulse.* 2 how something feels when touched: *the soft feel of silk.*

feel·er *n.* 1 one that feels, as an insect's antenna. 2 an observation or suggestion to find out what a person thinks: *to put out* or *throw out a feeler.*

feeling *n.* 1 the sense of touch. 2 an experience of sensation or emotion, esp. as influencing one's thought: *a feeling of joy; a gut feeling; a numb feeling; What are your feelings on capital punishment? to arouse or stir up popular feeling on an issue; to lose feeling in one's foot; a deep, eerie, friendly, gloomy, hostile, intense, queasy, sinking, uneasy feeling; to harbour feelings of hatred; no hard feelings; one's innermost, intimate, pent-up feelings; He sounds as if his **feelings** (= sensitivities) have been hurt; a man of delicate, sensitive feelings.*
— *adj.* sensitive or sympathetic: *a feeling remark.*
— **feel·ing·ly** *adv.*

feet *pl.* of FOOT.

feign (FAIN) *v.* pretend: *to feign illness; He's only feigning he's ill; She wants to feign (= make up) an excuse for her absence; a feigned (= pretended) attack.*

feint (FAINT) *n.* pretence: *a surprise attack after (making) a feint of retreating.*
— *v.* pretend: *He dribbled the ball after feinting a pass.*

feist·y (FYE·stee) *adj.* **feist·i·er, -i·est** spirited or fighting: *a feisty politician.*

fe·lic·i·tate (fuh·LIS·uh·tate) *v.* **-tates, -tat·ed, -tat·ing** *Formal.* congratulate someone *on* an occasion of joy, as a wedding or graduation.
— **fe·lic·i·ta·tion** (-TAY·shun).

fe·lic·i·tous (fuh·LIS·uh·tus) *adj.* delightful or delightfully expressed: *a felicitous occasion; a most felicitous way of expressing herself; a felicitous expression.*

fe·lic·i·ty (fuh·LIS·uh·tee) *n.* **-ties** 1 happiness or good fortune. 2 gracefulness of expression; also, a graceful expression: *the felicity of her style, wit.*

fe·line (FEE·line) *n.* an animal of the cat family: *Lions and tigers are felines;* **adj.**: *He crept forward with feline (= catlike) stealth.*

fell 1 *pt.* of FALL. 2 *v.* strike down or cut down: *The giant felled the tree with one blow of the axe.* 3 *adj.* fierce or deadly: *He took care of everything **at one fell swoop** (= suddenly and all at once).* 4 *n.* an animal's hide; pelt.

fel·lah (FEL·uh) *n. Informal.* fellow; also **fel·ler.**

fel·low (FEL·oh) *n.* 1 *Informal.* a male person. 2 a companion: *They were fellows at school; The fellow* (=mate) *to this glove is missing; The world has not produced a fellow* (= peer) *to Shakespeare's genius; adj.: our fellow citizens; fellow humans; fellow feeling* (=sympathy); *fellow traveller* (= communist sympathizer). 3 a member of a learned society; also, a student on a fellowship: *research, senior, teaching fellows.*

fel·low·man (FEL·oh·man) *n.* **-men** a fellow human being.

fel·low·ship (FEL·oh·ship) *n.* 1 companionship or community: *to foster, promote good fellowship in the neighbourhood; the fellowship of humanity; united in fellowship with our brothers and sisters.* 2 at a university, a position or award given to a graduate student as a help.

fel·on (FEL·un) *n.* one who has committed a felony.

fel·o·ny (FEL·uh·nee) *n.* **-nies** a crime such as arson, rape, or robbery that is more serious than a misdemeanour.

felt 1 *pt. & pp.* of FEEL. 2 *n.* a fabric made of wool mixed with fur, hair, etc., matted together by steam and pressure instead of being woven or knitted: *a pool table covered with felt; a felt hat.* — *v.* make into felt.

felting *n.* felt cloth.

fe·male (FEE·male) *adj.* 1 of the sex that produces eggs or bears young: *a female animal.* 2 forming a receptacle for a corresponding male part: *the female organ of pollination; The vagina is a female structure; a female electric socket; A bolt turns in the female groove inside a nut.* — *n.* a female person, animal, flower, etc.

fem·i·nine (FEM·uh·nin) *adj.* having to do with women or their characteristics: *a feminine fashion; the feminine gender; feminine graces, hygiene; the feminine suffix "-ess."* — *n.* a feminine word: *"She" and "actress" are feminines.* — **fem·i·nin·i·ty** (-NIN·uh·tee) *n.*

fem·i·nism (FEM·uh·niz·um) *n.* the women's rights movement or its principles. — **fem·i·nist** *n. & adj.*

fem lib *n. Informal.* women's liberation.

femme fa·tale (fem·fuh·TAL) *n., pl.* **femmes fatales** (fem-fuh·TALZ) a very seductive woman.

fen *n.* esp. in England, a marsh or swamp.

fence *n.* 1 a barrier of stakes, stones, or wire put around property for protection and privacy: *to build, erect, put up a fence; a barbed-wire, chain-link, chicken-wire, picket, snow fence.* 2 a receiver of stolen goods. 3 a place where such goods are bought and sold. — **on the fence** hesitating about which side of a dispute to join: *to sit on the fence.* — **to mend fences** *Informal.* to improve relations with people. — *v.* **fenc·es, fenced, fenc·ing** 1 enclose or keep out with a fence. 2 practise the sport of fencing. 3 parry questions. 4 buy and sell stolen goods. — **fenc·er** *n.*

fence-mending *n.* the improving of a neglected relationship.

fencing *n.* 1 swordplay using a foil or sabre. 2 material for putting up a fence.

fend *v.* defend: *She used judo to fend off her attacker; He had to fend* (= provide) *for himself after his parents died.*

fend·er *n.* a protective or shielding device, as the metal covers over an automobile's tires, the screen in front of a fireplace, or a buffer for protecting a ship's side when docking: *the fender benders* (= minor automobile collisions) *during a storm.*

fe·ral (FEER·ul) *adj.* untamed or wild: *He fell into a feral rage.*

fer·ment (FUR·ment) *n.* 1 yeast, bacteria, or a similar thing that causes fermentation. 2 a state of agitation or unrest: *when the nation was in ferment; the ferment that swept communist nations in 1989.* — *v.* (fur·MENT) cause fermentation: *Yeast ferments the starch in bread dough; Cheese is a fermented food* (made by fermentation).

fer·men·ta·tion (fur·men·TAY·shun) *n.* a change such as the souring of milk or ripening of cheese brought about by the action of enzymes, bacteria, etc.

fern *n.* one of a large group of flowerless plants with stems and fronds which reproduce by means of spores: *the fiddlehead fern of New Brunswick.*

fe·ro·cious (fuh·ROH·shus) *adj.* 1 fierce or bloodthirsty: *a ferocious animal, beast.* 2 extreme: *pangs of ferocious hunger.*

fe·roc·i·ty (fuh·ROS·uh·tee) *n.* **-ties** fierce cruelty or a ferocious act.

fer·ret (FER·it) *n.* a weasellike animal trained for use by hunters and rat-catchers. — *v.* **ferret out** search out facts, secrets, the truth, etc.

fer·ry (FER·ee) *n.* **fer·ries** a conveyance, as a boat, hydrofoil, or aircraft, esp. across water. — *v.* **fer·ries, fer·ried, fer·ry·ing** cross or convey, as by ferry: *People and cars are ferried to and from Prince Edward Island; Airplanes are ferried* (= flown) *from the factory to delivery points.* — **fer·ry·boat** *n.* — **fer·ry·man** *n.* **-men.**

fer·tile (FUR·tul) *adj.* productive of young, crops, seeds, ideas, etc.: *fertile eggs, land, soil, women; a storyteller's fertile imagination.* — **fer·til·i·ty** (fur·TIL·uh·tee) *n.: multiple births caused by fertility drugs.*

fer·til·ize (FUR·tul·ize) *v.* **-iz·es, -ized, -iz·ing** make fertile, as by use of manure on land or by impregnating an egg cell. — **fer·til·iz·er** (-lye·zur) *n.* — **fer·til·i·za·tion** (-uh·ZAY·shun) *n.*

fer·vent (FUR·vunt) *adj.* showing earnestness or devotion; impassioned: *a fervent plea for mercy; a fervent prayer;* **fer·vent·ly** *adj.*

fer·vour or **fer·vor** (FUR·vur) *n.* earnestness or enthusiasm; zeal: *religious fervour.*

-fest *combining form.* festival: *filmfest, funfest, Octoberfest, songfest, talkfest.*

fes·tal (FES·tul) *adj.* having to do with a religious feast; also, festive: *a festal celebration, day, occasion.*

fes·ter (FES·tur) *n.* a small ulcer or sore filled with pus. — *v.* **1** form pus: *A wound festers.* **2** rankle or cause to rankle: *Hatred festered in his mind.*

fes·ti·val (FES·tuh·vul) *n.* a special period of celebration: *to hold a Christmas, dance, drama, folk, music festival; "Hanukkah," the festival of lights; the Stratford Festival (of staged plays); the Tulip Festival; Festival Canada (of the performing arts) held in Ottawa.*

fes·tive (FES·tiv) *adj.* having to do with a feast or festival; joyous or gay: *New Year's is a festive occasion; Everyone is in a festive mood; a festive air, atmosphere, celebration, crowd, event, feeling, season, spirit; festive garments.*

fes·tiv·i·ty (fes·TIV·uh·tee) *n.* **-ties** merrymaking; also, a festive activity: *The festivities ended with fireworks.*

fes·toon (fes·TOON, long "OO") *n.* a garland of flowers or other decorative material for hanging in a loop. — *v.:* *a room festooned with garlands and streamers for a party.*

fe·tal (FEE·tul) *adj.* of a fetus: *the curled-up fetal position characteristic of a fetus in the womb.*

fetch *v.* **1** bring or get: *Go and fetch some water from the well; Please fetch me some water; The car will fetch $5 000 if you sell it now.* **2** draw forth: *to fetch a sigh, groan, tears.* **3** *Informal.* deal: *She fetched him one on the jaw.* — **fetch up** stop: *The car skidded off the highway and fetched up against a tree.*

fetching *adj. Informal.* attractive or admirable: *a fetching appearance, hat, personality, smile; in a fetching pose.* — **fetch·ing·ly** *adv.*

fete or **fête** (FAIT) *n.* a lavish entertainment or party, often one held outdoors. — *v.* **fetes** or **fêtes, fet·ed** or **fêt·ed, fet·ing** or **fêt·ing** honour with a feast: *The Olympic hero was feted everywhere he went.*

fet·id (FET·id, FEE·tid) *adj. Formal.* stinking: *The air was fetid with the smell of rotting garbage.*

fet·ish (FET·ish, FEE·tish) *n.* **1** an idol, image, or other object carried around for its supposed magical powers. **2** a blind devotion: *He makes a fetish of washing his hands before and after meals.* — **fe·tish·ism** *n.*

fet·ter (FET·ur) *n.* **1** a shackle for the feet. **2** a restraint: *the fetters of superstition.* — *v.* hamper or restrain.

fet·tle (FET·ul) *n.* **in fine fettle** in good physical condition.

fe·tus (FEE·tus) *n.* a developing animal embryo, esp. an unborn infant after the first two months of conception.

feud (FEWD) *n.* a long-lasting quarrel, esp. between families or clans, often vengeful and bitter: *to stir up a feud; a blood feud* (= arising from a violent crime); *a family feud over an inheritance.* — *v.* carry on a feud: *The Smiths have been feuding with the Joneses over an inheritance.*

feu·dal (FEW·dul) *adj.* having to do with feudalism: *a feudal fief, lord, society, vassal; feudal laws, tenure; the feudal system.*

feu·dal·ism (FEW·dul·iz·um) *n.* the economic, social, and political system of medieval Europe binding vassals to the military service of their lords from whom they received fiefs of land and buildings and serfs or peasants to work the land. — **feu·dal·is·tic** (-duh·LIS·tic) *adj.*

fe·ver (FEE·vur) *n.* **1** abnormally high body temperature: *to come down with a fever; a high, intermittent, recurrent, slight fever.* **2** a disease: *glandular, hay, rheumatic, scarlet, typhoid, yellow fever.* — **fe·ver·ish** *adj.*

fever pitch *n.* a restless or excited state: *Emotions had reached* or *were at a fever pitch before the riot.*

few *n., adj. & pron.:* Few (= not many) *books are missing; 100 or fewer* (= a smaller number); *Only* **a few** (= some) *have been destroyed; Such cases are* **few and far between** (= rare); **Quite a few** (= A good many) *are lost;* **The few** (= The minority) *that are missing should be found.*

fey *adj.* fairylike, whimsical, or strange: *a fey character; a fey and chance event.*

fi·an·cé (fee·ahn·SAY) *n.* a man engaged to be married; *fem.* **fi·an·cée** (-SAY).

fi·as·co (fee·AS·coh) *n.* **-cos** or **-coes** an utter failure: *The conference ended in a complete, total, utter fiasco.*

fi·at (FEE·at, -ut) *n.* an executive, usually arbitrary, order; decree.

fib *n.* a trivial little lie. — *v.* **fibs, fibbed, fib·bing.** — **fib·ber** *n.*

fi·bre or **fi·ber** (FYE·bur) *n.* **1** a threadlike strand of an animal, vegetable, or mineral substance such as muscle tissue, wool, cotton, or asbestos: *Rayon, fibreglass, and nylon are synthetic fibres; Beans, bran, bread, and cereals are high in dietary fibre.* **2** this spun or woven into materials with strength and toughness. **3** strength or character: *a man of strong moral fibre.*

fi·bre·glass or **fi·ber·glass** (FYE·bur·glas) *n.* finespun glass woven into cloth, made into plastic material for boards, or in woolly form as insulation; **Fiberglas** *Trademark.*

fibre optics or **fiber optics** *n. pl.* [takes sing. v.] transmission of light around bends and in curves through a bundle of flexible filaments of glass or plastic. — **fibre-optic** or **fiber-optic** *adj.*

fi·brous (FYE·brus) *adj.* having fibres or like fibre.

-fic *suffix.* making: *acidific, deific, honorific, horrific, pacific.*

fiche (FEESH, FISH) *n.* [short form] microfiche.

fick·le (FICK·ul) *adj.* changeable like the weather; inconstant: *a fickle mind; fickle weather.*

fic·tion (FIC·shun) *n.* **1** something made up in the mind: *pure fiction.* **2** literature of imagination including novels, short stories, and plays: *romance fiction; science fiction.*
— **fic·tion·al** *adj.* of fiction: *fictional characters, literature.*

fic·ti·tious (fic·TISH·us) *adj.* imaginary or invented: *a fictitious account; a fictitious character like Oliver Twist; fictitious heroes; "John Doe" is a fictitious name; He checked in under a fictitious* (=false) *name.*

fic·tive (FIC·tiv) *adj.* not genuine; also, fictional: *the fictive world of TV.*

fid·dle (FID·ul) *Informal. n.* **1** a violin: *to play the fiddle; (as) fit as a fiddle* (=quite healthy). **2** a falsification of accounts: *a tax fiddle.*
— *v.* **fid·dles, fid·dled, fid·dling 1** play on a violin. **2** tamper with, esp. accounts: *an accountant caught fiddling tax returns.* — **fid·dler** *n.*

fid·dle·head (FID·ul·hed) *n. Cdn.* the tightly curled frond of the ostrich fern of New Brunswick eaten as a delicacy.

fid·dle·sticks (FID·ul·sticks) *interj.* nonsense!

fi·del·i·ty (fuh·DEL·uh·tee, fye-) *n.* **-ties** loyalty, esp. continuing faithfulness to a duty or trust: *to swear lifelong fidelity to one's marriage vows; a **fidelity bond** insuring against dishonesty or negligence.*

fidg·et (FIJ·it) *v.* move or act nervously or restlessly: *to fidget with one's hands.*
— *n.* this condition or a person who fidgets.
— **the fidgets** *n. pl.* a fit of nervousness. — **fidg·et·y** *adj.*

fi·du·ci·ar·y (fi·DEW·shee·air·ee) *adj.* held or holding in trust; of a trustee: *Executors act in a fiduciary capacity.*
— *n., pl.* **-ar·ies** a trustee.

fie (FYE) *interj.* shame: *Fie on you!*

fief (FEEF) *n.* an estate granted by a feudal lord to a vassal; hence, one's sphere of operation; also **fief·dom.**

field (FEELD) *n.* **1** a piece of open land, esp. one put to a specific use, as for a crop, pasture, etc.: *a corn field; Farmers work in the fields; They plough, till, work the fields; a landing field (for aircraft); coal, gold, oil fields; a baseball, football, playing field; on the soccer field; a field of ice; a field of fire (where shooting goes on).* **2** an area of interest, influence, or activity: *Surgery is outside my field; in the field of medicine; The Moon is within the Earth's gravitational field; the Earth's magnetic field; Lou doesn't go steady, but **plays the field*** (=dates various people).
— *adj.* having to do with a battlefield: *field artillery, batteries, hospitals, officers.*
— *v.* **1** in baseball, cricket, etc., catch or stop a batted ball; hence, defend or tackle: *a skilled diplomat who fields reporters' questions with ease.* **2** put people on a field: *Our party fielded 200 candidates in the last election.*

field day *n.* **1** a day for outdoor sports or activities. **2** an occasion of unrestricted freedom or enjoyment: *The Blue Jays had a field day against the Tigers.*

field glasses *n. pl.* binoculars for outdoor use; also **field glass.**

field hockey *n.* hockey played on a field of grass.

field marshal *n.* in some countries, an army officer ranking next below a commander in chief.

field-test *v.* test a product or method under actual conditions of use.

field trip *n.* a trip for students to gain knowledge outside of the classroom.

field·work *n.* work done in a field of activity, as by a sociologist or surveyor.

fiend (FEEND) *n.* **1** the devil; hence, an evil spirit or a wicked person. **2** *Informal.* one devoted or addicted to something: *a bridge fiend; fresh-air fiend; hockey fiend.*
— **fiend·ish** *adj.*

fierce (FEERCE) *adj.* **fierc·er, fierc·est** extremely violent in temper or manner: *a fierce battle, dog; fierce loyalty; the fierce heat of summer; It was fierce (Informal for very bad) of me to lose my temper.*
— **fierce·ly** *adv.;* **fierce·ness** *n.*

fi·er·y (FYE·uh·ree) *adj.* **fi·er·i·er, -i·est** like fire; burning: *a fiery sunset; a fiery* (=full of fire) *speech; a fiery* (=inflamed) *sore.*

fi·es·ta (fee·ES·tuh) *n.* esp. in Spanish-speaking countries, a religious or secular festival.

fife *n.* a flutelike musical instrument, used with drums.

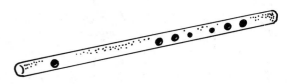

fif·teen (fif·TEEN) *n., adj. & pron.* five more than 10; 15 or XV. — **fif·teenth** *n. & adj.*

fifth *n., pron. & adj.* (the one) following the fourth; 1/5: *Who's the fifth? the fifth in line; the fifth boy; a fifth (of a U.S. gallon of liquor); to take or invoke the Fifth or Fifth Amendment (of the U.S. Constitution against a person being forced to testify against himself or herself).*

fifth column *n.* a subversive group working secretly for a foreign country.

fif·ty (FIF·tee) *n. & adj.* **-ties 1** one more than 49; 50 or L. **2** **the fifties** *n. pl.* numbers, years, etc. ending in 50 through 59: *She's in her fifties; The fifties were a time of reconstruction in Europe.* — **fif·ti·eth** (-tee·ith) *n. & adj.*

fifty-fifty *adj. & adv. Informal.* equal or equally: *a fifty-fifty chance of winning; Divide it fifty-fifty between us; Let's go fifty-fifty on it.*

fig *n.* **1** a small tree bearing many-seeded pear-shaped fruit. **2** something contemptible: *She doesn't give or* *care a fig for* or *about his opinion; It's not worth a fig.*

fight (FITE) *v.* **fights, fought** (FAWT), **fight·ing 1** to struggle or contend against a person or thing: *to fight bravely, clean, desperately, dirty; to fight about* or *over a fence; to fight with* (= against) *one's neighbours; to fight with* (= using) *guns; to fight her fear of the dark; to fight like dogs; Team Canada fights against Russia; Children fight among themselves; We have to fight for survival; He couldn't* **fight back** *his tears; She* **fought off** *sleep by pinching herself; Pat is determined to* **fight it out** or **fight to the finish;** *Lee would never* **fight shy of** (= avoid facing) *the truth.* **2** achieve by fighting: *Fight your way through life; The battle was well fought.* — *n.* a struggle or conflict: *to get into, pick, provoke a fight with someone; to put up a last-ditch fight against the new bill; a bitter, desperate, fierce fight to the death; a fight to reduce taxes; a fight for justice; A fight breaks out, starts, a fist fight; Who won the fight? He's still full of fight* (= fighting spirit) *though thrice beaten.* — **fight·er** *n.*

fighting chance *n.* a chance to win after a hard struggle.

fig leaf *n.* a leaf used traditionally in sculpture to hide nudity.

fig·ment (FIG·munt) *n.* something made up: *a mere figment of the imagination.*

fig·u·ra·tive (FIG·yuh·ruh·tiv) *adj.* using figures of speech; not literal. — **fig·u·ra·tive·ly** *adv.*

fig·ure (FIG·yur) *n.* **1** number or amount; also, a numeral: *Her salary runs to six figures; Did the sales rep mention a figure? a ballpark, exact, round figure; Accountants should be good at* **figures** (= math). **2** a shape or pattern: *A parabola is a geometric figure; the 69 "school figures" of figure skating; The airplane did a* **figure eight. 3** the shape of one's body: *She diets to keep her figure; He's a handsome figure; an imposing, impressive, striking, trim figure; an artist good at figure drawing.* **4** personage: *a familiar, national, political, prominent, public, underworld figure; Napoleon is a historical figure.* **5** an appearance or likeness; image: *Clowns cut funny figures; a ridiculous, sorry figure; She was the figure of misery; similes, metaphors, and such* **figures of speech.** — *v.* **-ures, -ured, -ur·ing 1** do sums: *That's too much to figure up without a calculator.* **2** imagine, picture, or estimate: *I figured we would be late; But I didn't* **figure on** *being* (= expect to be) *that late; I had figured* (= relied) *on* or *upon your helping us; It's difficult to* **figure out** (= understand) *what this poem means.* **3** appear prominently: *Galahad figures in Arthurian legends; plain, not* **figured** (= patterned) *wallpaper.*

fig·ure·head (FIG·ur·hed) *n.* **1** an ornamental carved figure on the bow of a ship. **2** a person in a high position but without real power.

fig·u·rine (fig·uh·REEN) *n.* a statuette.

fil·a·ment (FIL·uh·munt) *n.* a thread or a threadlike part, as the wire that glows in an electric bulb.

filch *v.* steal something of small value casually: *to filch candy from a counter.* — **filch·er** *n.*

file *n.* **1** a container such as a folder, drawer, or cabinet for keeping papers in order, usually threaded with a wire, rod, or other device. **2** such a system or the set of

papers: *to close, keep, make up, open a file on someone; Your application is* **on file,** *says the* **file clerk. 3** a row of persons, animals, or things, one behind the other: *At the sound of the alarm, the pupils marched out* **in file;** *Indians walking their trail* **in single file. 4** a smoothing or grinding metal tool with a ridged surface: *a nail file.* — *v.* **files, filed, fil·ing 1** enter into an official record: *to file an application, a lawsuit; She filed* (= applied) *for divorce; Correspondents file* (= send) *stories for publication; Please file away these papers* (= enter them in the office records). **2** move one behind the other: *Shoppers kept filing in all day; The Opposition M.P.s filed out of the Commons in protest; Thousands filed past the coffin of the dead leader.* **3** smooth or grind away: *The rough edge will hurt unless filed away; a carpentry floor sprinkled with iron* **filings** (= particles).

fi·let (fi·LAY, FIL·ay) *n.* same as FILLET.

fil·i·al (FEL·ee·ul, FIL·yul) *adj.* of a son or daughter: *filial love, respect.*

fil·i·bus·ter (FIL·uh·bus·tur) *n.* the use of delaying tactics to obstruct passage of a bill in a legislature, esp. by prolonged speech-making: *The Tories carried on* or *conducted* or *engaged in a filibuster against the Maple Leaf flag from June 15 to December 14, 1964.* — *v.* use filibustering: *to filibuster a bill; U.S. Senator Huey Long filibustered 15 hours in 1935.*

fil·i·gree (FIL·uh·gree) *n.* ornamental, lacelike openwork of gold or silver wire. — *v.* **-grees, -greed, -gree·ing** adorn with or as if with filigree: *Our picture window was filigreed with frost.*

fill *v.* **1** put something into a space so as to occupy it fully: *to fill a glass with water; It's filled to overflowing; a room filled to capacity; filled with people; Dentists fill cavities with porcelain; Please fill out this form; sails* **filled out** *by the wind; Please* **fill up** *my gas tank; It was a* **filling** *meal.* **2** supply what is called for; fulfill: *to fill an order, doctor's prescription, requirement.* **3** put someone or oneself into a position or office: *An employment agency helps fill vacancies; Ms. Smith has filled the principalship; She was qualified enough to* **fill the bill** (= meet the job requirements); *The vice-principal* **fills in** (= substitutes) *for the principal when the latter is away; He later* **fills her in** (= brings her up to date) *on what happened during her absence.* — *n.* a filling or its amount: *Earth, gravel, and garbage are used as fills; They drank their fill; She had her fill (of food); He ate his fill from the buffet.*

fil·let (FIL·it) *n.* **1** a ribbonlike strip or band. **2** (*also* fi·LAY, FIL·ay) a slice of boneless, lean meat or fish; filet: *fillet of fish, sole; trout fillets.* — *v.* to bone and slice fish or meat into fillets: *to clean and fillet a catch of fish.*

fill-in *n.* a substitute person or thing.

filling *n.* something used to fill something else: *a cheese filling for a sandwich; The dentist put in a temporary filling; a plastic filling.*

filling station *n.* same as GAS STATION.

fil·lip (FIL·up) *n.* **1** an outward flip of a finger from the thumb, as in flicking a crumb off a sleeve. **2** something that goads or stimulates: *The tax was abolished as a fillip to industry.*

fil·ly (FIL·ee) *n.* **fil·lies** a young female horse.

film *n.* **1** a membrane or similar layer, as of oil in water. **2** a thin flexible material coated with a light-sensitive substance and made into sheets or rolls for taking photographs: *to develop, load, rewind, splice, wind film.* **3** a motion picture: *to ban, censor, direct, edit, make, produce, rate, release, review, shoot, show a film; an action, adult, adventure, disaster, documentary, feature, gangster, propaganda, silent film.* — *v.* **1** photograph: *a movie filmed on location in Spain.* **2** coat: *tabletops filmed with dust.*

film·y *adj.* **film·i·er, -i·est 1** thin: *a filmy curtain.* **2** hazy: *a filmy windowpane.*

fil·ter (FIL·tur) *n.* **1** a porous device for straining out dust, smoke, germs, or impurities from a liquid or gas medium in which they are suspended. **2** the porous material used, such as felt, paper, sand, or charcoal. **3** a device or substance for absorbing certain light rays and frequencies: *the colour filter of a camera lens.* — *v.* **1** remove using a filter: *Air conditioners filter out the dust and pollen from the air.* **2** subject to the action of a filter: *Use filtered water.* **3** pass or move slowly, as through a filter: *Refugees filter into the country; They filter through the border.*

filth *n.* **1** foul dirt. **2** moral corruption or obscenity.

filth·y *adj.* **filth·i·er, -i·est** disgustingly dirty: *a filthy room, window; to work in filthy conditions; filthy lucre* (*Informal for* money); *adv.: a TV series featuring filthy* (=extremely) *rich characters.*

fil·tra·tion (fil·TRAY·shun) *n.* the process of filtering: *a city's water filtration plant.*

fin *n.* **1** a winglike or fanlike organ of a fish used for swimming, turning, and balancing its body in water. **2** any similar structure: *the tail fin of an aircraft; the cooling fins of a radiator.*

fi·nal (FYE·nul) *adj.* last and decisive: *a final decision; the final hour; our final offer.* — *n.* something final, as a deciding game, the last examination in a course, etc.: *to take one's finals in Grade 12.* — **fi·nal·ly** (-lee) *adv.*

fi·na·le (fuh·NAH·lee, -NAL·ee) *n.* the conclusion or last part, as of a play or piece of music: *the grand finale of her career.*

fi·nal·ist (FYE·nuh·list) *n.* one who takes part in the finals of a competition.

fi·nal·i·ty (fye·NAL·uh·tee) *n.* **-ties** conclusiveness: *When Mom says something with finality, that's it.*

fi·nal·ize (FYE·nul·ize) *v.* **-iz·es, -ized, -iz·ing** make final: *Our plans have yet to be finalized.* — **fi·nal·i·za·tion** (-luh·ZAY·shun) *n.*

fi·nance (fuh·NANCE, FYE·nance) *n.* **1** (the science of) the management of money, esp. public revenue: *an expert in finance; high finance; the Minister of Finance.* **2 finances** *pl.* money resources; funds. — *v.* **-nanc·es, -nanced, -nanc·ing** provide or get money for something: *The bank financed his new car; A finance company would have demanded a lien on his salary and charged a higher interest.* — **fi·nan·cial** (-NAN·shul) *adj.: a family's financial affairs, difficulties, matters; insurance companies,* banks, and such financial institutions; Bankers move in financial circles; the financial records; a financial (=fiscal) year. — **fi·nan·cial·ly** *adv.*

fin·an·cier (fuh·nan·SEER) *n.* **1** an investor. **2** an expert in finance.

finch *n.* a small bird that has a sharp, cone-shaped bill for crushing seeds.

find (FINED) *v.* **finds, found, find·ing 1** come upon by accident or by searching: *The child found a dime and shouted, "Finders keepers, losers weepers"; Please find me a cab; Water finds* (=naturally reaches) *its own level; A river finds its way* (=moves along) *to the sea; Please find out* (=learn or ascertain) *when the flight arrives.* **2** decide: *The jury found against the accused and for the defendant.* **3** experience or perceive: *He finds moths interesting; She finds people forgetting her in her old age; He was found wanting in diligence; He found himself in trouble.* **4** provide or supply: *to find funds for a project; A broker charges a finder's fee to arrange a mortgage on a house.* — **find fault** complain about: *He finds fault with everything and everybody.* — **find oneself** discover one's own abilities: *After trying several jobs, he finally found himself as a social worker.* — *n.* a finding or something found: *The new recruit is a real find; Al held up a dime as the day's find; an archaeological find; a lucky find; rare find.*

fin-de-siè·cle (fan·duh·see·EK·luh) *adj.* having to do with the close of the 19th century: *the fin-de-siècle* (=decadent) *Versailles of Louis XIV.*

finding *n.* **1** discovery: *the findings of modern science.* **2** a decision, as of a jury. **3 findings** *pl.* things other than basic materials: *A notions department supplies a dressmaker's findings such as buttons, threads, and zippers.*

fine *adj.* **fin·er, fin·est:** *I feel fine* (=very good); *a fine* (=excellent) *young woman; fine* (=bright or clear) *weather; Gold alloy that is 18 carats fine is 75% pure gold; the fine* (=sharp) *edge of a knife; the fine point of a pen (that writes thin); fine* (=very small or thin) *wire; a fine* (=subtle or nice) *distinction; fine* (=delicate) *lace; Sand is finer* (=has smaller particles) *than gravel; their finest hour* (=moment of glory); *The fine arts are painting, sculpture, and architecture, sometimes also poetry, music, drama, and dancing; one of the city's finest* (=a police officer). — *adv.: Friday will suit me fine* (=quite well); *fine-drawn* (=thinly or delicately drawn) *wire, arguments, distinctions; Fibreglass is made of fine-spun glass.* — *n.* a sum of money paid as a penalty or punishment: *to impose, levy, slap a fine on someone; a heavy, mandatory, stiff fine.* — *v.* impose a fine on someone: *The judge fined him $50 for speeding.*

fine print *n.* the less favourable parts of a contract or agreement, which are usually printed in small type.

fin·er·y (FYE·nuh·ree) *n.* **-er·ies** showy clothes, jewellery, etc.: *a bride in all her finery.*

fi·nesse (fuh·NES) *n.* **1** skilfulness: *a diplomat who can manage people with great finesse.* **2** cunning, as used in card games.

— *v.* **-ness·es, -nessed, -ness·ing** use finesse; also, accomplish by finesse: *to finesse an appointment to the position; He finessed my queen* (= took the card trick) *with his jack.*

fine-tune (fine·TUNE) *v.* **-tunes, -tuned, -tun·ing** regulate by making small adjustments: *to fine-tune an engine; A government tries to fine-tune the economy* (= make it stable) *with tax cuts, spending increases, etc.*

fin·fish *n.* a true fish, not a shellfish such as an oyster or other mollusc.

fin·ger (FING·gur) *n.* **1** one of the five divisions of the hand, esp. any of the four exclusive of the thumb: *index* or *trigger finger; middle finger; ring* (= third) *finger; little finger; Everyone jumps when she snaps her fingers; to* **point the finger** or **an accusing finger** *at someone; a warning finger; No one could* **lay** or **put their finger on** (= find out) *what had gone wrong; The finger of suspicion seemed to point to her* (= She was the suspect); *But no one dared* **lay a finger on** (= harm) *her or* **lift a finger against** (= oppose) *her.* **2** anything corresponding to or resembling a finger: *the finger of a glove; a finger of light coming through a hole in the roof.*
— **keep** or **have one's fingers crossed** be hopeful.
— *v.* **-gers, -gered, -ger·ing 1** touch with or use the fingers on something, as a musical instrument in playing it. **2** *Informal.* point out a victim, potential loot, etc.

finger bowl *n.* a small bowl for rinsing the fingers at a meal.

fin·gered (FING·gurd) *adj. & combining form.* having or involving fingers: *giant trees with fingered roots; the keyboarder's fleet-fingered accuracy; a fumble-fingered fielder; a light-fingered pickpocket.*

finger food *n.* snacks that may be picked up and eaten with the fingers.

fin·ger·print (FING·gur·print) *n.* an impression of the lines that form arches, loops, and whorls on the fingertips, used as a positive means of identification: *a set of fingerprints; v.:* *The suspect was arrested, photographed, and fingerprinted.*

fin·ger·tip (FING·gur·tip) *n.* the tip of a finger: *He has several languages* **at his fingertips** (= at his command).

fin·i·cky (FIN·uh·kee) *adj.* fussy in taste or standards: *a finicky dresser, eater; finicky about the least things.*

fi·nis (FIN·is, FYE·nis) *n.* **-nis·es** a formal conclusion or end, as written at the end of a book, movie, etc.

fin·ish (FIN·ish) *v.* **1** bring to completion: *Of the 12 who*

started the race, *only four finished; Let me finish* (= reach the end of) *this chapter; We finished the meeting by singing* or *with "O Canada"; I'm not finished with you yet* (= Don't leave yet); *She hopes to* **finish up** *at the top of her class.* **2** make complete: *a roughed-in fireplace that needs finishing; Give the tabletop a finishing touch with this paint; A* **finishing school** *prepares young women for social life.*
— *n.* **1** the final part of something: *"The Charge of the Light Brigade" was a fight to the finish; the close, hair-breadth, photo finish of a horse race.* **2** something used in finishing or a finished quality: *paints, varnishes, waxes, and such finishes; the glossy finish of art paper; His manner lacks finish* (= polish).

finished *adj.* polished: *a finished performance; finished furniture.*

fi·nite (FYE·nite) *adj.* having limits; neither infinite nor infinitesimal: *our finite existence.*

fink *n. Slang.* an undesirable person such as a strikebreaker or informer.
— **fink out** *Slang.* back out like a fink.

fin·ny (FIN·ee) *adj.* **fin·ni·er, fin·ni·est** having to do with fins or fish: *the finny deep* (= ocean filled with fish); *the finny whale; the finny population (of fishes).*

fir *n.* a pyramid-shaped coniferous evergreen tree of the pine family.

fire *n.* **1** a burning or its flame, fuel for burning, the destruction caused by a blaze, etc.: *to sit around a picnic fire; Your house may* **catch fire** *(and burn) if you smoke in bed; a house* **on fire** (= burning); *You're playing with fire* (= something dangerous); *to bank, build, contain, douse, extinguish, kindle, light, make, put out, set, stamp out, start, stir, stoke a fire; to bring a fire under control; to strike fire using a flint; A fire breaks out, goes out, rages, roars, smoulders, spreads.* **2** something resembling a fire, as strong feeling, zeal, or enthusiasm: *eyes full of fire; He didn't have to* **set the world on fire** (= do anything spectacular). **3** a discharge of firearms or an action resembling it: *Hold your fire! to cease, draw, exchange fire; cross fire; rapid fire; rifle fire; baptism of fire; a decision still* **hanging fire** (= being considered); *We will* **open fire** (= start shooting) *when we sight the enemy; The politician was* **under fire** (= under attack) *from the media.*
— *v.* **fires, fired, fir·ing 1** (cause to) burn, bake, get hot, etc.: *Pottery is fired* (= baked) *in a kiln; adventure stories that fire* (= excite) *the imagination; Sam left the meeting all* **fired up** (= excited) *at the imagined insult.* **2** shoot: *First he fired in the air, then into the crowd; fired point-blank at her; The press* **fired away** *with questions throughout the interview; He prefers to* **fire off** (= write and send) *memos rather than talk.* **3** dismiss from a job: *He was told to resign or be fired.*

fire·arm *n.* a hand weapon such as a rifle or pistol that fires a bullet or shell using gunpowder.

fire·bomb *n.* a bomb designed to start a fire; *v.:* *Terrorists firebombed the embassy.*

fire·box *n.* **1** the fire-containing chamber of a furnace or boiler, as in a steam engine. **2** a box with a signalling device for alerting a fire station.

fire·brand *n*. **1** a piece of burning wood. **2** an agitator.

fire·break *n*. *Cdn*. a strip of land that has been cleared of everything flammable to prevent the advance of a spreading fire.

fire·bug *n*. *Informal*. a maniac who sets fire to things.

fire chief *n*. the head of a firefighting department.

fire·clay *n*. a clay that can withstand high temperatures and is used to line furnaces and kilns.

fire·crack·er *n*. (FIRE·crack·ur) *n*. a firework consisting of a paper roll of explosive and a fuse.

fire drill *n*. an exercise to teach the proper evacuation procedure in case of a fire.

fire engine *n*. an automotive truck for transporting firefighters and their equipment.

fire escape *n*. **1** a fireproof stairway outside a building. **2** a ladder or other means of escaping a fire.

fire·fight·er (FIRE·fye·tur) *n*. one trained to fight fires. — **fire·fight·ing** *n*.

fire·fly *n*. -**flies** a night beetle that gives off flashes of light; also called "lightning bug."

fire·hall *n*. *Cdn*. a building in which fire engines and firefighters are housed. Also **firehouse, fire station.**

fire hydrant *n*. a street outlet to draw water from in case of a fire.

fire·man (FIRE·mun) *n*. -**men 1** a firefighter. **2** one who attends to a furnace.

fire·place *n*. a place for an open fire, esp. a framed one built in a room at the base of a chimney.

fire·plug *n*. same as FIRE HYDRANT.

fire·pow·er (FIRE·pow·ur) *n*. the firing capacity and effectiveness of a military unit or weapon.

fire·proof *adj*. that resists burning: *a fireproof building; fireproof clothing.*
— *v*. **1** cover with fire resistants such as stone, brick, etc.: *to fireproof a building.* **2** treat with fire retardants such as ammonium phosphate, borax, and zinc chloride: *to fireproof clothing.*

fire·reels *n.pl*. *Cdn*. [old use] fire engine.

fire sale *n*. *Informal*. a sale at a very low price, as of something damaged by fire.

fire·screen *n*. a screen placed in front of a fireplace as protection against flying sparks.

fire·side *n*. a hearth: *to sit by the fireside; The president went on TV with an informal **fireside chat** instead of giving a formal press conference.*

fire station *n*. a firehall.

fire·storm *n*. **1** a huge fire, as from a nuclear explosion or bombing raid, which generates inrushing winds fanning it. **2** a similar phenomenon: *A firestorm of telegrams and phone calls hit Parliament Hill.*

fire·trap *n*. a place from which escape in case of fire would be practically impossible.

fire truck *n*. a fire engine.

fire·wa·ter (FIRE·wot·ur) *n*. *Informal*. alcoholic liquor.

fire·wood *n*. wood for fuel.

fire·work *n*. **1** a device that produces noise and light, as a firecracker or rocket. **2 fireworks** *sing. & pl.* a spectacular display using firecrackers, rockets, etc.

firing line *n*. the front line of an activity, controversy, campaign, etc.

firing squad *n*. a group of soldiers that carries out a death sentence by firing or fires a volley of shots in salute.

firm *adj*. **1** not affected by pressure, movement, or change: *healthy, firm muscles; as firm as a rock; an infant that is firm on its feet; a firm offer, price; The dollar remained firm against the yen on the money market.* **2** fixed or resolute: *a firm voice; a teacher who is firm* (= strict) *with pranksters; She's firm in her religious beliefs;* ***adv.:*** *Stand firm and do not yield; the basic beliefs that we all hold firm.*
— *v*. make or become firm: *Prices are firming up after going down; Let's firm up the contract and close the deal.*
— *n*. a business enterprise or partnership: *He manages an advertising firm.* — **firm·ly** *adv.;* **firm·ness** *n*.

fir·ma·ment (FUR·muh·munt) *n*. the sky considered as a dome with stars fixed in it.

firm·ware *n*. software that comes with a computer, written into its random access memory from which it cannot be accidentally erased.

first *adj*. coming before all others in time, position, rank, etc.: *I was the first to arrive; Who is first (in rank) in the class?*
— *adv.* **1** for the first time; before all others: *Who came in first? when I first met you.* **2** in the first place: *First, I have to finish my homework; I have to finish my homework first.*
— *n*. a person, thing, place, etc. that is first: *She is a strong first; He is among the first; the first and the best of my pupils; **At first** (= In the beginning) I didn't recognize her.*

first aid *n*. emergency care given to a sick or injured person: *to administer* or *give first aid.*
— **first-aid** *adj.: a first-aid kit; first-aid training, treatment, workers.*

first base *n*. in baseball, the base that a runner has to touch first.
— **get to first base** *Informal*. take the first step towards a goal.

first-born *n*. the oldest child.

first class *n*. the first group in a classification system.
— **first-class** *adj. & adv.: sealed letters and such first-class mail; She always flies first-class; a first-class passenger.*

first floor *n*. **1** the ground floor. **2** [in U.K. & Europe] the floor above the ground floor.

first-hand *adj. & adv.* obtained from the original source; not secondhand: *I learned it (at) first-hand; It's first-hand information.*

first lady *n*. **1** also **First Lady**, the wife of a chief of state, as the wife of the U.S. president: *Canada's first lady is the Governor General (if a woman) or the Governor General's wife.* **2** the leading woman of an art or profession: *the first lady of ballet.*

first·ly *adv.* [used in listing items] in the first place; first: *Firstly, you are too young, secondly, you are still in school.*

first name *n.* given name, as opposed to the family name or middle names.
— **first-name** *adj.* familiar or friendly: *We are on a first-name basis.*

first person *n.* a pronoun or verb such as "I," "he," "you," or "we" and "am," "is," or "are" that refers to the speaker or writer: *An autobiography is written in the first person; adj.: a first-person account, narrative.*

first-rate *adj. & adv.* excellent: *a first-rate hotel with first-rate accommodation, a first-rate performance, player, scholar.*

first strike *n.* a nuclear attack in anticipation of one by the enemy.
— **first-strike** *adj.: the enemy's first-strike capability.*

first string *n.* the best group of players, not alternates or substitutes. — **first-string** *adj.* first-rate.

fis·cal (FIS·cul) *adj.* having to do with public revenue or corporate finance: *Canada's fiscal history; fiscal policies; the fiscal year* (= accounting period) *ending March 31; the budget for fiscal 1991.*

fish *n., pl.* fish or **fish·es** (fish species) **1** a water animal with fins, gills, and scales: *to catch fish; Fish bite at bait; a school* or *shoal of fish; Fish may be baked, broiled, filleted, fried, frozen, smoked; the birds of the air and the fishes of the sea; the miracle of the multiplication of the loaves and fishes performed by Jesus; a queer fish* (*Informal for* strange person); *to feel like a fish out of water* (= out of one's natural environment). **2** the flesh of fishes used as food: *tuna fish balls; fish and brewis.*
— *v.* **1** try to catch fish: *He's fishing by the pond; She rarely goes fishing.* **2** search for, catch, or pull out: *Children fish for compliments; He fished out his will from a cabinet; to fish in troubled waters* (= take advantage of a troubled situation); *a fishing expedition* (to find evidence of the required kind).

fish-and-chips *n. pl.* a dish of fried fish and French fries.

fish·bowl *n.* a glass bowl for keeping live fish, open to view from all sides.

fish·er *n.* **1** a marten. **2** one who catches fish; also **fish·er·man, -men.**

fish·er·y (FISH·uh·ree) *n.* **-er·ies 1** fishing as a business. **2** an establishment for processing fish.

fish flake *n. Cdn.* in Newfoundland, a platform for drying cod.

fish·wife *n.* **-wives** a foul-mouthed woman.

fish·y *adj.* **fish·i·er, -i·est 1** dull-looking like a fish's eye. **2** slippery; hence, of doubtful value: *a fishy story; something fishy about the plan.*

fis·sile (FIS·ul) *adj.* that can be split; fissionable.

fis·sion (FISH·un) *n.* a splitting apart: *Nuclear fission releases energy, as in atomic bombs; Algae, amoebas, and such simple organisms multiply by cellular fission.*
— **fis·sion·a·ble** (-nuh·bul) *adj.*

fis·sure (FISH·ur) *n.* a crack or break, as in rocks, or in the skin or a membrane.

fist *n.* a tightly closed or clenched hand, as in hitting: *to clench the fist; to shake one's fist at someone; the iron fist of the oppressor.*

fis·ti·cuffs (FIS·ti·cuffs) *n. pl.* a fight using fists: *to engage in fisticuffs.*

fit *adj.* **fit·ter, fit·test** suited to a certain purpose, occasion, or use: *food that is fit for a king; news that is fit to be printed; The struggle for existence results in the survival of the fittest; She keeps fit as a fiddle by regular exercise; adv.: He thought* or *saw fit to invite some and leave out others.*
— *v.* **fits, fit·ted, fit·ting** to be right or the right size: *"If the cap fits, wear it"; a punishment that fits the crime; His education and experience fit* (= qualify) *him for the job; But will he fit into* (= be suitable for) *our group? The new building fits in* (= blends) *with the surroundings; all fitted out* (= equipped or dressed) *for a costume party; a room fitted up as a studio.*
— *n.* **1** how something fits: *The cut of his coat is good but the fit is poor; a loose, snug, tight fit.* **2** a sudden attack or convulsion; seizure: *an epileptic fit; He fired her in a fit* (= outburst) *of fury; He throws a fit* (= tantrum) *now and then; She studies by fits and starts* (= not regularly). — **fit·ness** *n.* — **fit·ter** *n.*

fit·ful *adj.* irregular or restless: *She spent a fitful night with high fever; fitful sleep.* — **fit·ful·ly** *adv.*

fitting *adj.* suitable or appropriate: *a fitting answer to a rude question; a fitting occasion for a speech; It is fitting and proper that we honour her with a reception.*
— *n.* **1** an adjustment of clothes to make them fit properly: *a customer who insists on several fittings before her suit is finished; a fitting room.* **2** a small, detachable machine part: *elbows, clamps, and such pipe fittings.*

five 1 *n. & adj.* the number of the fingers of one hand; 5 or V. **2** *n.* a group of five or something numbered 5 or having five units, as a basketball team, playing card, domino, or five-dollar bill.

fix *v.* **fix·es, fixed, fix·ing 1** make firm or steady: *to fix the door with a doorstop.* **2** fasten: *to fix a shelf to a wall; On whom shall we fix the blame? Carl fixed his gaze on Chris.* **3** repair: *to fix a leaking faucet; We need someone to fix up the house before we move in.* **4** arrange or set up: *to fix an appointment for 2 p.m.; The hairdresser will fix your hair; I could fix dinner for you; She fixed me up in a good hotel, then fixed me up with a new job.* **5** *Informal.* influence dishonestly: *The race was fixed; He tried to fix the jury; a company charged with price fixing.* **6** *Informal.* punish: *He threatened to fix me.*
— *n.* **1** position: *Navigators used to get the fix of their ships from the stars; The executive with two luncheon appointments was in a fix* (= awkward situation). **2** *Slang.* a dishonest influencing or a contest or situation so influenced. **3** *Slang.* a shot of a narcotic: *a fix of heroin.* **4** something to which one is addicted: *He can't do without his weekly fix of golf.*

fix·ate *v.* **-ates, -at·ed, -at·ing** have a fixation on a person or thing: *The man was fixated on the idea that the young actress was in love with him.*

fix·a·tion (fik·SAY·shun) *n.* a fixing of one's interest on a person or thing as an obsession: *The man had a fixation on* or *for* or *over* or *with the young actress.*

fixed (FIXT) *adj.* fastened or firm: *the fixed* (= unmoving) *gaze of a dead person; a pensioner on a fixed* (= unchanging) *income; a race suspected of being fixed* (= dishonestly arranged); *A fixed star is so far away, its position never seems to change.* — **fix·ed·ly** (FIX·id·lee) *adv.;* **fix·ed·ness** *n.*

fixings *n. pl. Informal.* accessories: *a turkey served with all the fixings.*

fix·ture (FIX·chur) *n.* a person or thing that is part of a situation or place: *A chandelier is a lighting fixture; plumbing fixtures; He's been so long with the company, he seems a fixture in the office.*

fizz *n.* a drink that gives out bubbles with a hissing sound; hence, liveliness: *how to put more fizz into your business.* — *v.* make a fizz: *You can drink it while it fizzes.*

fiz·zle (FIZ·ul) *v.* **fiz·zles, fiz·zled, fiz·zling** end feebly after a lively start; fail: *The party fizzled out when most of the guests didn't arrive.* — *n.* a fiasco.

flab *n. Informal.* excess of flabby flesh.

flab·ber·gast (FLAB·ur·gast) *v.* dumbfound: *They were flabbergasted to hear the best student had failed.*

flab·by (FLAB·ee) *adj.* **flab·bi·er, flab·bi·est** lacking firmness or strength: *flabby flesh, muscles, will; the flabby generation of TV watchers.*

flac·cid (FLAC·sid, FLAS·id) *adj.* **1** flabby: *flaccid muscles.* **2** limp or feeble: *droopy and flaccid from the heat.*

flack *n.* **1** *Slang.* a press agent. **2** [nonstandard] flak or criticism. — *v.* act as a flack: *to flack for a movie star; a heavily flacked* (= publicized) *production.*

flag *n.* **1** a piece of fabric, usually with a distinctive coloured design, used as an emblem or banner, often hoisted on a **flagpole** or **flagstaff**: *to dip, fly, lower, raise, run up, wave a flag; the white flag (of surrender); a ship sailing under the Liberian flag; a flag flying at half-mast.* **2** a slab of paving stone, or **flag·stone.** — *v.* **flags, flagged, flag·ging** **1** to signal: *We flagged down the first cab that came along.* **2** droop or slacken: *As time wore on, interest seemed to flag; a pep talk to revive their flagging spirits.*

flag·on (FLAG·un) *n.* a vessel with a spout, handle, and lid for holding wine or other liquor at the table.

fla·grant (FLAY·grunt) *adj.* of errors, offences, etc., openly and notoriously bad: *flagrant cheating, crime, error, injustice, mutiny, violations.* — **fla·grant·ly** *adv.*

flag·ship *n.* **1** a ship carrying the officer in command of a fleet or squadron. **2** the most important of its group: *the flagship store of the company in the Eaton Centre.*

flag·waving (FLAG·way·ving) *n.* a patriotic but boastful appeal to the emotions.

flail *n.* a farm tool for threshing grain. — *v.* strike with or wave arms about as with a flail.

flair *n.* a keen sense or taste: *She shows a distinctive flair for clothes.*

flak *n.* **1** antiaircraft gunfire: *A flak jacket protects the wearer from flying shell fragments.* **2** *Informal.* criticism: *to take the flak when something goes wrong.*

flake *n.* **1** a small, thin piece or mass: *a flake of snow; flakes of rust; soap flakes; flakes of chocolate.* **2** *Slang.* an eccentric; nut. — *v.* **flakes, flaked, flak·ing** fall off in flakes: *Old paint tends to flake off.* — **flake off** *Slang.* beat it. — **flake out** *Slang.* **1** collapse or lie down exhausted. **2** fail or flop.

flak·y (FLAY·kee) *adj.* **flak·i·er, -i·est** **1** having to do with flakes: *a crisp and flaky pie crust.* **2** *Slang.* eccentric: *the oddball's flaky behaviour.* — **flak·i·ly** *adv.;* **flak·i·ness** *n.*

flam·bé (flahm·BAY) *n.* a dessert or other dish served flaming.

flam·boy·ant (flam·BOY·unt) *adj.* flamelike in form or character; hence, ornate or showy. — **flam·boy·ance** (-unce) *n.*

flame *n.* **1** a brightly burning fire: *to kindle a flame; The car burst into flame on impact; It was in flames.* **2** *Informal.* a sweetheart: *my old flame; your first flame.* — *v.* **flames, flamed, flam·ing** blaze, grow hot, glow, or burst out like a flame: *the flaming fall colours; cheeks flaming with emotion; Her eyes flamed with fury.*

flame·out *n.* a jet-engine failure due to faulty fuel combustion.

fla·min·go (fluh·MING·go) *n.* **-gos** or **-goes** a water bird with long legs and neck, curved bill, and pink feathers.

flam·ma·ble (FLAM·uh·bul) *adj.* that easily catches fire, as gasoline. — **flam·ma·bil·i·ty** (-BIL·uh·tee) *n.*

flange (FLANJ) *n.* a projecting rim of a wheel, rail, girder, etc. — *v.* **flang·es, flanged, flang·ing:** *pipe ends flanged and bolted together.*

flank *n.* **1** the fleshy side above the hips; also, a cut of beef corresponding to this part. **2** a side, as of a mountain, a military or football formation, etc. — *v.* **1** be placed beside: *She appeared in public flanked by bodyguards.* **2** attack from the side: *The troops were flanked and overpowered in a surprise attack.*

flan·nel (FLAN·ul) *n.* **1** a soft, warm woollen cloth with a napped surface. **2** **flannels** *pl.* flannel trousers or woollen underwear.

flap *n.* 1 a broad, flat piece of material attached on one side, as the cover of a pocket, the gummed end of an envelope, or the hinged back sections of a plane's wings. 2 the sound of wings beating the air or of oars on water. 3 *Informal.* a stir or commotion: *The students were in a flap about or over the exam results.*
— *v.* flaps, flapped, flap·ping make flaps or move by making flaps: *Sails flapped in the wind; A young bird flaps it wings.*

flap·jack *n.* a pancake.

flap·pa·ble (FLAP·uh·bul) *adj.* easily upset.

flap·per (FLAP·ur) *n.* 1 one that flaps, as a broad fin or a bird learning to fly. 2 a woman of the 1920s who was aggressively unconventional in dress and manners.

flare *n.* 1 an outburst of flame or a short-lived, unsteady blaze of light, as a rocket signal shot into the air or a solar eruption. 2 a candlelike light used as a marker on the ground: *They set up or set out flares at the crash site to warn approaching motorists.* 3 **flares** *pl.* a pair of bell-bottomed trousers.
— *v.* flares, flared, flar·ing 1 burst into flame: *The candle sputtered, flared, and went out; when trouble flares* (= erupts); *He tends to flare up* (= get excited) *at the least provocation.* 2 widen towards the bottom: *He flared his nostrils in a grimace; a flared cuff.*

flare-up *n.* an outburst, sudden increase, or intensification: *a flare-up of hostilities.*

flash *n.* 1 a sudden, brief brilliance, as of lightning or of a camera flashbulb; hence, any similar feeling or display: *a flash of inspiration, wit; the hot flashes or flushes* (= feeling of warmth) *experienced during menopause.* 2 a brief period or something lasting only an instant: *I remembered the whole episode in a flash; First came a telex flash, then the full obituary; the flash of her smile.*
— **a flash in the pan** a brilliant but short-lived effort or attempt.
— *v.* 1 give out a sudden light: *a signal flashing every few seconds; a cursor that flashes* (= blinks) *off and on; His eyes were flashing* (= glowing) *with fury.* 2 happen or do something in a sudden or passing manner: *Headlights flashed* (= quickly passed) *by on the highway; A train flashed* (= suddenly came) *into view; Canadian Press flashed* (= sent out with speed) *the news across the nation; The policeman flashed* (= quickly showed) *his badge and walked in.*
— *adj.* sudden or instantaneous: *a flash burn caused by exposure to radiation; She drills her class in spelling, math, etc. using flash cards (bearing words, figures, etc. to be shown briefly); a flash flood following a heavy rainfall.*

flash·back *n.* a narration or portrayal, esp. in a play or movie, of an episode from the past, as in suddenly recalling a past event.

flash·er *n. Informal.* one who exposes himself indecently.

flash-forward (FLASH·for·wurd) *n.* the showing of a future occurrence as a dramatic device in movies and TV.

flash·light *n.* a hand-held electric lamp.

flash point *n.* 1 the lowest temperature at which a flammable substance will catch fire in the presence of a flame. 2 a place where hostilities may flare up: *a flash point of racial unrest.*

flash·y *adj.* flash·i·er, -i·est gaudy or showy in a cheap way: *a flashy dress.*

flask *n.* a container for carrying liquids.

flat *adj.* flat·ter, flat·test 1 horizontal and plane, not round, high, or thick: *the flat top of a table; a flat* (= deflated) *tire.* 2 not changeable; absolute: *a flat denial, refusal; a flat rate of interest.* 3 of colours, tastes, sounds, and other perceptions, not distinctive: *a flat, not glossy paint; a flat musical note (that is below the normal pitch); soda pop that has gone flat* (= stale).
— *adv.* absolutely: *He placed flat last in the competition; The bridge will help islanders get to the mainland in nothing flat* (= in no time at all); *He fell flat on the floor; All his plans have fallen flat* (= failed).
— **flat out** 1 outright: *She flat out denied the charges; It was flat out incompetent of him to say such things; a flat-out assertion without any proof.* 2 at full speed: *He drove flat out to the hospital.*
— *n.* 1 something flat, as a deflated tire, swampland, or the palm of the hand: *to change, fix, have a flat (tire).* 2 an apartment. 3 in music, a half pitch below the note, as indicated by the symbol [♭].
— *v.* flats, flat·ted, flat·ting make or become flat.
— flat·ly *adv.;* flat·ness *n.*

flat·bed *n.* a truck or trailer whose body is a platform without sides.

flat·car *n.* a railway freight car without sides or roof.

flat·foot *n., pl.* -feet a condition in which the arch of the instep has flattened.

flat·foot·ed (FLAT·foot·id) *adj. & adv. Informal.* in an unready condition: *to be caught flatfooted.*

flat·ten (FLAT·un) *v.* make or become flat: *The toy was flattened when a truck ran over it; A tapeworm has a flattened* (= flat) *body.*

flat·ter (FLAT·ur) *v.* please a person by something that makes him or her feel good, as praising: *He tried to flatter her about or on her good looks; I feel flattered; The portrait flatters her* (= represents her favourably); *He flatters himself on* (= is pleased with) *his musical talent; I find the award quite flattering to my ego.*
— **flattered** *adj.* pleased: *I'm flattered to receive the award; flattered that I've been chosen for the award; She feels flattered by or at all the attention she's getting.*
— flat·ter·er *n.;* flat·ter·ing·ly *adv.*
— flat·ter·y *n.* flat·ter·ies.

flat·u·lence (FLACH·uh·lunce) *n.* accumulation of gas in the stomach or intestines.

flat·u·lent (FLACH·uh·lunt) *adj.* 1 having or causing flatulence. 2 windy or pompous.

flat·ware *n.* flat tableware such as plates, knives, and spoons.

flaunt *v.* 1 display or parade oneself, one's wealth, or one's possessions. 2 flutter or wave proudly: *to flaunt a banner, flag.*

flau·tist ("au" as in "cause" or as in "how") *n.* same as FLUTIST.

fla·vour or **fla·vor** (FLAY·vur) *n.* **1** the taste and smell that are characteristic of a substance: *Spices, fruit, etc. have natural flavours; the strong flavour of certain cheeses; They sell ice cream in 101 flavours.* **2** a pleasing quality: *romances with an exotic flavour; Spices impart flavour to bland foods.*
— *v.* give a flavour to something: *Vanilla extract is used to flavour ice cream; "Vanillin" is an artificial* **flavouring.**

flaw *n.* an imperfection such as a crack or blemish that mars something structurally: *the flaw in a gem; the flaws and fallacies of your reasoning; a character flaw* (= weakness); *the fatal flaw that destroyed Hamlet.*

flawed (FLAUD) *adj.* having a flaw: *a flawed diamond; a character flawed by a lack of will power.*

flax *n.* an herb or shrub that is raised for its fibre used to make linen and coarse yarns.

flax·en (FLAX·un) *adj.* **1** made of flax. **2** pale-yellow: *flaxen hair.*

flay *v.* **1** strip off the skin of a person or animal: *He was almost flayed alive for not doing his chores.* **2** criticize or scold harshly: *M.P.s flaying at each other in parliament.*

flea (FLEE) *n.* a tiny, wingless jumping insect that sucks the blood of animals.

flea collar *n.* an animal collar containing insecticide that repels fleas.

flea market *n.* an open-air bazaar that sells cheap, often used, goods.

fleck *n.* a spot or patch: *floating flecks* (= flakes) *of snow.* — *v.* mark with flecks: *skin flecked with freckles.*

fled *pt. & pp.* of FLEE.

fledge *v.* **fledg·es, fledged, fledg·ing** grow or equip with or as if with feathers: *to fledge an arrow; a full-fledged acrobat; a mere* **fledg·ling** or **fledge·ling** (= beginner) *of a poet.*

flee *v.* **flees, fled, flee·ing** run away, as from danger or evil: *to flee from a fire; to flee a scene; to flee the country; to flee west* (= to the west).

fleece *n.* a sheep's or similar animal's coat of wool.
— *v.* **fleec·es, fleeced, fleec·ing** **1** shear sheep. **2** strip someone of belongings: *Con men fleeced him of his savings.*

fleec·y *adj.* **1** like, covered with, or made of fleece: *fleecy clouds.* **2** woollen: *warm fleecy underwear.*

fleet *n.* a unified group: *a fleet of aircraft, automobiles, bicycles, ships.*
— *adj.* swift: *Antelopes are fleet of foot.*
— **fleet·ing** *adj.* passing swiftly: *Worldly joys are fleeting; a fleeting glimpse.*
— **fleet·ing·ly** *adv.: He thought she spoke to him fleetingly in a dream.*

flesh *n.* **1** the soft tissue beneath the skin, esp. the muscle and fat of animals: *Animal flesh is used as meat; Some stories make your flesh creep* (= horrify); *flesh-coloured* (= yellowish pink) *tights.* **2** the body or bodily nature: *She dreamed she saw her dead child* **in the flesh** (= alive); *"The spirit is willing but the flesh is weak"; to*

mortify the flesh by penance; Your own **flesh and blood** (= blood relatives) *are closer to you than in-laws.*
— **press the flesh** shake hands with people, as when campaigning for election.
— *v.* feed, grow, or fill out with flesh: *a well-fleshed steer; An artist fleshes out a sketch with live figures.*

flesh·pot *n.* place of luxurious living: *to long for the fleshpots of one's native land; Saint-Tropez is one of the fleshpots of France.*

flesh·y *adj.* **flesh·i·er, -i·est** **1** fat: *a soft and fleshy Cupid; Do I look a bit too fleshy?* **2** having to do with flesh: *the fleshy side of your fingertips; a fleshy intestinal growth; Apples are fleshy fruits.*

fleur-de-lis (flur·duh·LEE) *n.* **fleurs-de-lis** (flur·duh·LEEZ) a lilylike design used on early French flags and in the four corners of the Quebec flag.

flew *pt.* of FLY.

flex *v.* **1** bend a limb. **2** contract a muscle.

flex·i·ble (FLEX·uh·bul) *adj.* **1** that can be bent without breaking: *Wire, leather, etc. are flexible.* **2** adaptable: *a flexible mind, schedule; He's quite flexible in his decisions; flexible working hours.*
— **flex·i·bly** (-blee) *adv.*
— **flex·i·bil·i·ty** (-BIL·uh·tee) *n.*

flick *n.* **1** a light, quick stroke or movement, as of a whip; also, the snapping sound made by it. **2** *Slang.* a movie.
— *v.* **1** make a flick or strike with a flick: *a pocket knife that can be flicked open or shut; He flicked a crumb off his sleeve; She flicked* (= switched) *on a light.* **2** flip: *to flick through a volume.*

flick·er *v.* waver or flutter: *a flickering fire that is about to die.*
— *n.* a spark: *Is there a flicker of hope left? a pure liquid without a flicker of colour or scent.*

flied *a pt.* of FLY (baseball sense).

fli·er (FLY·ur) *n.* **1** one that flies, as an aviator. **2** handbill; flyer. **3** *Informal.* a reckless enterprise.

flight (FLITE) *n.* **1** the act of flying: *a long flight over the Atlantic; the seasonal flights of birds to warmer climes; a flight* (= group) *of geese; I put her on a flight to Paris; the touchdown of Flight 202 (airliner) from London; a bumpy, chartered, connecting, domestic, scheduled, shakedown, solo, space, test flight; the flight of time; flights* (= soaring heights) *of ambition, fancy, wit; a* **flight attendant** *such as a steward or air hostess;*

A **flight bag** has to fit under the seat in front of the passenger; Planes land on an aircraft carrier's **flight deck;** the ostrich, emu, penguin, and such **flightless** birds; the **flight path** of an airplane, missile, or spacecraft; The **flight recorder,** or black box, of an aircraft records the voices in the cockpit and technical data; An astronaut has to be in top **flight-worth-y** condition. **2** the act of fleeing: *the flight of slaves by the underground railroad to Canada; the flight* (= transfer) *of capital to foreign enterprises; The defeated armies were* **put to flight** (= made to flee); *They* **took flight** or **took to flight** (= fled). **3** a set or series: *We went up two flights of stairs.*

flight-y *adj.* **flight-i-er, -i-est** light-headed or frivolous. — **flight-i-ly** *adv.*

flim-sy (FLIM-zee) *adj.* **-si-er, -si-est** thin or frail: *a flimsy defence; flimsy evidence, excuses.* — *n.* a sheet of thin paper. — **flim-si-ly** *adv.;* **flim-si-ness** *n.*

flinch *v.* draw back from something painful or requiring courage: *She never flinches from doing what has to be done; He can take the worst news without flinching.*

fling *v.* **flings, flung, fling-ing 1** throw sharply and with force: *She flung her books on the table and strode out; He was flung into jail without being charged; Lou spoke out against the regime, flinging all caution to the winds.* **2** dash or rush: *He flung out of the room in a huff.* — *n.* **1** a casual attempt: *She had a fling at journalism before becoming a teacher; a last fling* (= spree of self-indulgence). **2** a Scottish dance: *the Highland fling.*

flint *n.* a hard quartz that gives off sparks when struck with steel.

flint-y *adj.* **flint-i-er, -i-est 1** having flint: *a flinty rock.* **2** hard and unyielding: *a flinty disposition, heart, look; the flinty general.*

flip *v.* **flips, flipped, flip-ping 1** toss or move something jerkily so that it turns on its side: *Let's flip a coin to settle the matter; She flipped through the book looking for pictures.* **2** flick or strike: *to flip at a fly; to flip marbles out of a ring; He flipped* (*Slang* for lost self-control) *when he was fired from his job.* — *n.* a flipping: *a flip of the coin; a* **flip chart** (of sheets hinged at the top for flipping over); the **flip-down** seats in a theatre; a **flip-top** can of pop. — *adj.* **flip-per, flip-pest** *Informal.* flippant: *She sounded flip but really meant it.*

flip-flop *n.* **1** a backward somersault. **2** a change, as of opinion, resembling a somersault: *Politicians do or make flip-flops on issues after hearing from the people.* **3** a flat, open-toed, backless shoe or slipper. — *v.* **-flops, -flopped, -flop-ping** do a flip-flop.

flip-pant (FLIP-unt) *adj.* of attitudes and expressions, not respectful: *a flippant answer to a serious question.* — **flip-pan-cy** *n.*

flip-per (FLIP-ur) *n.* a broad, flat fin or blade: *Seals, sea lions, and whales have paddlelike flippers; a diver's rubber flippers.*

flip side *n. Informal.* the back of a phonograph record.

flirt *v.* **1** play at love: *to flirt with people; to flirt* (= trifle or toy) *with danger.* **2** flutter or flick: *the flirting of a*

bird's tail. — *n.* one who flirts. — **flir-ta-tion** (-TAY-shun) *n.;* **flir-ta-tious** (-shus) *adj.*

flit *v.* **flits, flit-ted, flit-ting** flutter or fly about like a bee or butterfly: *thoughts flitting across a troubled mind; Time flits by.*

float (FLOTE) *v.* stay on the surface of a fluid or move along lightly: *Cork floats on water; He doesn't swim, can't even float; to float* (= raise) *a sunken ship; A bond issue is floated* (= placed for sale) *on the market; to float* (= launch) *a company, idea, loan, proposal, scheme.* — *n.* something that floats: *Cork is used as a float on a fishing line; the floats* (= exhibits on wheels) *in a parade; Planes that land on water have floats* (= airtight structures) *instead of wheels; an orange float* (= orange pop with a lump of ice cream floating on top); *a credit card company with a float* (= money in transit) *totalling billions of dollars because of uncashed traveller's cheques; the yen's upward float* (= rise) *in value against the U.S. dollar.* — **float-er** *n.* — **float-a-tion** (floh-TAY-shun) *n.*

floating *adj.* that moves or changes: *The* **floating decimal** *moves to the left of a display as a number like 1772.2532 is changed to* 1.7722532×10^3; *the floating exchange value of a currency; a resort town with a floating population; the two bottom* **floating ribs** (not attached in front).

flock *n.* **1** a group of animals of the same kind: *a flock of birds, sheep.* **2** a group of worshippers: *A pastor tends his flock.* — *v.* group: *Children flocked around the ice-cream vendor; "Birds of a feather flock together."*

floe *n.* a sheet or broken-off piece of floating ice.

flog *v.* **flogs, flogged, flog-ging 1** whip or beat with a stick: *to flog a mule; You're flogging a dead horse* (= fighting a dead issue). **2** *Informal.* sell or publicize: *a vendor flogging his wares.* — **flog-ger** *n.*

flood (FLUD) *n.* **1** a great flow or overflow of water, as of rivers after heavy rains, when the tide rises in a **flood-tide,** or when a sluice, or **flood-gate,** is opened in a dam: *a raging flood; The flood inundated the valley before beginning to subside.* **2** anything similar: *a flood of light, tears, words;* **the Flood** (= deluge) *of Noah's time.* — *v.* flow or cause to flow like a flood: *The spring thaw flooded basements; The river flooded* (= overflowed).

flood-light *n.* a large light used for lighting the outdoors: *Niagara Falls is lit by floodlights.* — *v.* **-lights,** *pt. & pp.* **-light-ed** or **-lit, -light-ing** light by using floodlights.

floor (FLOR) *n.* **1** the inside bottom surface, as of a room: *a marble floor; a floor of hardwood; the ocean floor; on the first floor of the house; ground, main, top, upper floor.* **2** where a legislature or similar body meets: *on the floor of the Senate; a motion from the floor* (= where members sit, not from the platform); *to cross the floor* (and join another party). **3** the right to speak in a legislature: *Mr. Speaker, may I have the floor? to get, take the floor; to yield the floor to another member; to give someone the floor.* **4** a lower limit: *a floor (price) of $12 and a ceiling of $15.* — *v.* **1** provide with a floor, as of tiles or wood: *We* *floored the ground with tiles; marble, parquet, and other types of **flooring**.* **2** knock down or defeat someone: *to floor a boxer; He seemed utterly **floored** (= confounded) by the question.*

floor·board *n.* a board or one of the strips forming a floor.

floor exercise *n.* a gymnastic exercise performed without an apparatus.

floor leader *n.* the leader of a party in a legislature.

floor manager *n.* a manager who supervises store clerks and looks after customers.

floor show *n.* an entertainment presented at a nightclub or restaurant.

flop *v.* **flops, flopped, flop·ping** move about or drop down in a loose or clumsy way: *You could hear the fish flopping on the deck; She flopped into bed in exhaustion; The office is no place for flopping (= lounging); The play flopped (= failed).*
— *n. Informal.* failure: *The play was a total flop.*

flop·house *n.* a cheap hotel.

flop·py (FLOP·ee) **1** *adj.* **flop·pi·er, flop·pi·est** soft and flexible, like a hound's ear. **2** *n., pl.* **flop·pies** a flexible diskette for storing computer data; also **floppy disk.**

flo·ra (FLOR·uh) *n.* the plant life or plants of a specified region or period: *the **flora and fauna** of Newfoundland.*
— **flo·ral** (-ul) *adj.* having to do with flowers: *a floral arrangement, bouquet, emblem, wreath.*

flor·id (FLOR·id) *adj.* **1** of a complexion, flushed, as with emotion. **2** ornate or showy: *a florid prose style.*

flor·ist (FLOR·ist) *n.* one who grows or deals in flowers.

floss *n.* **1** soft, silky fluff or fibre, as spun by silkworms, or candy spun from sugar. **2** silk yarn or thread, as used in embroidery or as "dental floss" to clean between teeth; *v.: Brush and floss your teeth daily, says the dentist.*

floss·y *adj.* **floss·i·er, -i·est** like floss, esp. showy or stylish.

flo·ta·tion (floh·TAY·shun) *n.* same as FLOATATION.

flo·til·la (floh·TIL·uh) *n.* a small fleet or a fleet of small ships.

flot·sam (FLOT·sum) *n.* floating debris, as from a shipwreck: *the **flotsam and jetsam** (= discards and derelicts) of a nation destroyed by war.*

flounce *v.* **flounc·es, flounced, flounc·ing** move *off* or *out* of a place with an abrupt or jerky motion, as if in impatience or disdain.
— *n.* **1** such a movement. **2** a wide, rufflelike strip of cloth gathered and sewed on by its upper edge around a skirt. — **flounc·y** *adj.*

floun·der ("ou" as in "out") *v.* struggle or stumble about as in deep snow: *to flounder through a memorized speech.*
— *n.* **1** a floundering: *The team's flounder at the start of the season cost them the title.* **2** a saltwater fish with a flattened body and both eyes on the same side of the head.

flour (rhyme: "our") *n.* the powdered and sifted meal of a cereal such as wheat for baking bread, biscuits, etc.
— *v.* coat or cover with flour or a similar product.

flour·ish (FLUR·ish) *v.* **1** prosper or thrive: *The Aztec civilization flourished in Mexico before the Spanish conquest; She's flourishing as a lawyer.* **2** wave about or brandish: *to flourish a sword.*
— *n.* a waving or showy movement, writing, or musical passage: *a flourish (= fanfare) of trumpets.*

flout *v.* treat advice, laws, orders, etc. with scorn.
— *n.* a scornful act or speech. — **flout·er** *n.*

flow (FLOH) *v.* move or seem to move smoothly and steadily, as a stream of water: *Rivers flow into the ocean; eyes flowing with tears; hair that flows in the wind; wealth flowing out of an exploited nation; The flowing (= rising) tide swells a river.*
— *n.* a smooth and steady pouring: *the flow of words from a fluent speaker; the ebb and flow of tides; the flow of electricity from the negative to the positive pole of a battery; to staunch the flow of blood; cash flow; the flow of traffic.*

flow chart *n.* a diagram showing the movement of materials and personnel in operating a plant or the steps in a complex process.

flow·er (rhyme: "our") *n.* **1** the seed-producing part of a plant, usually having colourful petals, scent, and honey: *a bouquet of fragrant flowers; to pick or pluck flowers; cut flowers for sale; Flowers bloom, fade, wilt, wither.* **2** a plant cultivated for its flowers: *to plant and grow flowers.* **3** a blossoming or flourishing part or period: *Bamboos are rarely seen **in flower**; Lou was plucked from life in the flower (= best part) of youth.*
— *v.* bloom or develop: *Some plants flower once and wither away; the early flowering of her poetical genius; The "rose window" has a **flowered** design.*

flower child *n.* a hippie.

flower girl *n.* a young girl attending a bride with flowers.

flow·er·y *adj.* **-er·i·er, -er·i·est** **1** full of flowers: *a flowery dress, pattern.* **2** ornate: *flowery speech, writing.*

flown (FLONE) *pp.* of FLY.

flu (FLOO) *n.* influenza: *Asian flu; swine flu; a new strain of flu (virus); a touch of (the) flu; a flu shot.*

flub *n. & v.* **flubs, flubbed, flub·bing** *Informal.* bungle.

fluc·tu·ate (FLUK·choo·ate) *v.* **-ates, -at·ed, -at·ing** vary irregularly: *fluctuating temperatures; fluctuating between highs and lows.* — **fluc·tu·a·tion** (-AY·shun) *n.*

flue (FLOO) *n.* a passage such as a pipe or tube for conveying smoke, air, etc., as in a chimney or pipe organ.

flu·ent (FLOO·unt) *adj.* esp. of writing or speech, flowing smoothly: *a fluent speaker; her fluent command of the language; She speaks fluent English.*
— **flu·ent·ly** *adv.* — **flu·en·cy** *n.*

fluff *n.* **1** soft fur or feathers, as inside a pillow. **2** nap, as on a woollen blanket. **3** something woolly or light. **4** a blunder, esp. in saying one's lines on the stage.
— *v.* **1** make even or larger by shaking: *Pillows are fluffed up.* **2** *Informal.* slip up on something: *I hope no*

one fluffs a line when we go on stage.

fluff·y *adj.* **fluff·i·er, -i·est** appearing fluffed or made larger: *a fluffy angel cake; a fluffy chick.*

flu·id (FLOO·id) *n.* a liquid or gaseous substance such as water, mercury, or air: *Drink plenty of fluids; AIDS is transmitted through body fluids such as blood and semen.*
— *adj.* of or like fluids: *a fluid diet (of nonsolid foods); cash, savings, and such fluid assets; a fluid (= unstable) situation.* — **flu·id·i·ty** (floo·ID·uh·tee) *n.*

fluke *n. Informal.* a stroke of luck: *She won by a fluke; It was a pure fluke.* — **fluk·y** (FLOO·kee) *adj.*

flume *n.* **1** a narrow, deep valley or channel. **2** a flowing channel or chute used in irrigation, logging, mining, etc.

flum·moxed (FLUM·uxt) *adj. Slang.* confused or confounded.

flung *pt.* of FLING.

flunk *v. Informal.* fail in school work: *Some students flunked the math test; They flunked in math, but they didn't* **flunk out of** (= get dismissed from) *school.*

flun·ky (FLUNK·ee) *n.* **-kies** [contemptuous term] a menial servant or lackey; also **flun·key, -keys.**

flu·o·res·cence (floo·uh·RES·unce) *n.* the property of transforming radiations such as ultraviolet rays and X rays into a different wavelength or colour; also, light thus emitted.
— **flu·o·res·cent** (-unt) *adj.: a fluorescent lamp* or *tube; fluorescent light; a fluorescent screen (coated with fluorescent material).*

fluo·ri·date (FLOR·uh·date) *v.* **-dates, -dat·ed, -dat·ing** add fluorides to drinking water.
— **fluor·i·da·tion** (-DAY·shun) *n.*

fluo·ride (FLOR·ide, FLOO·uh·ride) *n.* a fluorine compound, as used in water and toothpastes to prevent tooth decay.

fluo·rine (FLOR·een, FLOO·uh·reen) *n.* a gaseous chemical element.

fluor·o·car·bon (floo·ur·uh·CAR·bun) *n.* a fluorine-carbon compound used as lubricant, refrigerant, or aerosol propellant.

flur·ry (FLUR·ee) *n.* **flur·ries 1** a sudden gust of wind, fall of snow, or shower of rain: *the first flurry of rain; High winds, wet flurries (of wet snow), and snow squalls are forecast.* **2** a brief commotion: *a flurry of activity, announcements, calls, goals, letters, punches, trading on the stock exchange.*
— *v.* **flur·ries, flur·ried, flur·ry·ing** agitate or disturb: *He got all flurried when the boss asked to see him.*

flush *v.* **1** make or become red or glowing: *cheeks flushed with joy.* **2** make flow: *to flush a toilet; They flushed the guerrillas out* (= made them come out) *with tear gas.*
— *n.* **1** an excited condition; glow: *in the first flush of victory.* **2** a rapid flow or outgrowth: *the first flush of spring grass.* **3** a hand of the same suit of cards.
— *adj.* **1** glowing with vigour: *the flush faces of healthy youth.* **2** abundant or prosperous: *Oil-rich nations were flush with money in the 1970s.* **3** even or level: *a flush*

door without panels; lines printed flush on the left; **adv.:** *a flush left margin; The puck hit him flush* (= directly) *on the chin.*

flus·ter (FLUS·tur) *v.* upset or make nervous: *Let's not get flustered.*
— *n.* a state of nervousness or confusion: *The school was thrown into a fluster by the mayor's visit.*

flute (long "oo") *n.* **1** a high-pitched wind instrument consisting of a slender tube with finger holes along its stem and a hole at one end for blowing. **2** one of the ornamental grooves or furrows running parallel along a column; also, a similar groove in a garment, furniture leg, or armour. — **flut·ed** (FLOO·tid) *adj.*
— **flut·ing** (FLOO·ting) *n.*

flut·ist (FLOO·tist) *n.* one who plays a flute.

flut·ter (FLUT·ur) *v.* beat or flap rapidly and irregularly: *to flutter one's eyelids; The chick fluttered its wings as if to fly; Flags flutter in the wind; The patient's pulse fluttered awhile before regaining its rhythm; Waiters flutter about* (= move about quickly) *taking orders during the lunch hour.*
— *n.* rapid flapping or agitation: *the flutter of wings; She put us in a flutter (Informal for excited state) by appearing unannounced; Bad acoustics could cause wow and flutter* (= rise and fall in pitch more rapid than wow) *in sound reproduction.*

flux *n.* a flow or flowing: *the flux of the tides; the flux of electricity, particles, radiation, time; Languages are in a continual state of flux* (= change).

fly *v.* **flies, flew** or **flied** (baseball sense), **flown** (FLONE), **fly·ing** move swiftly and lightly, as a bird through the air: *He would like to fly or at least learn to fly a plane; Lou has never flown in a plane; They fly (by) Air Canada; We fly (= arrive by plane) into New York; They flew (across) the Atlantic in a balloon; a pilot who flew refugees out of Ethiopia; He has flown many bombing missions; a ship flying before the wind; Windows flew open during the storm; The batter flied (the ball) to centre field; a brilliant idea that would not fly (Informal for succeed); a testimony that* **flies in the face of** (= contradicts) *the facts as we know them; a man who* **flies into a rage** (= gets enraged) *when something goes wrong; He* **flies off the handle** (= gets angry) *at the least provocation; A Brownie qualifies to* **fly up** (= be promoted) *to Girl Guide; In her fury she* **let fly** (= burst out) *with four-letter words; But she came out of the grilling* **with flying colours** (= victorious).
— *n., pl.* **flies 1** a winged insect such as the housefly or

dragonfly: *We swat flies.* **2** a flying part, as the flapping edge of a flag. **3** a flap, as in a garment to hide buttons, zipper, etc. or one serving as the door of a tent. **4** a baseball batted high in the air; also **fly ball.**
— **fly in the ointment** something that lessens the value or usefulness of what it affects, as an unwelcome guest at a party.
— **on the fly** while flying: *Lou caught the ball on the fly; She's so busy she always eats on the fly* (= hurriedly).

fly·blown *adj.* contaminated or spoiled, as covered with larvae of flies.

fly·by *n.* **-bys** a craft's flight close to or past an object under observation, esp. an object in space such as Mars or the moon.

fly-by-night *adj.* that quits without paying debts or meeting contractual obligations: *a fly-by-night operator.*

fly·er *n.* same as FLIER.

flying saucer *n.* a mysterious flying object, esp. one disk-shaped, reportedly seen in the skies.

flying squad *n.* a rapidly mobile unit, esp. of police, for special tasks.

flying wing *n. Cdn.* the twelfth player of a football team with a variable position behind the scrimmage line.

fly·leaf *n.* **-leaves** a blank page at the beginning or end of a book.

fly·pa·per (FLY·pay·pur) *n.* a strip of sticky paper for catching flies.

foal *n.* the young of an animal of the horse family; colt or filly. — *v.* give birth to a colt or filly.

foam *n.* **1** a mass of fine bubbles, as formed in or on a liquid by agitation, fermentation, etc. **2** a rigid or spongy material made by the dispersal of bubbles in liquid rubber, plastic, etc.
— *v.* make foam: *boiling, foaming water; a rabid dog foaming at the mouth.* — **foam·y** *adj.*

fob *n.* a short ribbon, chain, etc., often with an ornament, attached to a pocket watch or key ring: *his and hers key fobs.*
— *v.* **fobs, fobbed, fob·bing** trick someone or impose something on someone by trickery: *They **fobbed her off** with a lemon of a car; They **fobbed off** a lemon on her.*

fo·cal (FOH·cul) *adj.* of or at a focus: *The Olympic Games become the focal point of world attention every four years.*

fo·cus (FOH·cus) *n.* **-cus·es** or **-ci** (FOH·sye) **1** the meeting point of rays of light, heat, or sound. **2** focal length or distance. **3** an adjustment of this to get a sharp image: *A photograph is **in focus** (= clear) or **out of focus** (= blurred); Bring the image **into focus.*** **4** centre of attention.
— *v.* **-cus·ses** or **-cus·es, -cussed** or **-cused, -cus·sing** or **-cus·ing** adjust a lens, the eyes, etc. so as to get a sharp image: *to focus the camera on a scene; Let's focus* (= concentrate) *our attention on the environment.*

fod·der (FOD·ur) *n.* coarse or dried food for farm animals, as alfalfa, corn, hay, etc.

foe *n.* an enemy, esp. an actively hostile one: *a bitter, formidable, implacable foe.*

foe·tal, foe·tus same as FETAL, FETUS.

fog *n.* thick mist or cloud that is close to the ground and cuts visibility: *in dense, heavy, light fog; a patch of fog; Wait till the fog clears, lets up, lifts.*
— *v.* **fogs, fogged, fog·ging 1** cover with fog: *a fogged car window.* **2** be or become obscured or bewildered: *Liquor tends to fog the mind.*

fog·bound *adj.* hampered or prevented by fog: *a rash of accidents on a fogbound expressway; We were fogbound for many days; fogbound travellers.*

fog·gy (FOG·ee) *adj.* **fog·gi·er, fog·gi·est** full of fog; cloudy: *in foggy conditions, weather; I don't have the foggiest notion of what she means.*
— **fog·gi·ly** *adv.;* **fog·gi·ness** *n.*

fo·gy (FOH·gee, "g" as in "go") *n.* **-gies** one who is old-fashioned in thinking and behaviour: *an old fogy.* Also **fo·gey, -geys.**

foil *n.* **1** a thin-rolled sheet of a metal such as tin, aluminum, lead, or gold, as used for wrapping. **2** a person or thing that acts as a sharp contrast setting another off, as a "straight man" for a comedian. **3** a blunted sword used in fencing. **4** a hydrofoil: *a boat with submerged foils; a foil-borne craft.*
— *v.* thwart or frustrate, as by throwing pursuers off a scent: *The guards foiled the prisoner's attempt to escape.*

foist *v.* palm off: *useless stuff foisted on unwary customers.*

fold *v.* **1** bend or double over, as to wrap or enclose: *A letter is folded to put in an envelope; candy folded* (= wrapped) *in foil; He stood there with folded arms (crossed over his chest) refusing to lend a hand; She knelt with hands folded* (= pressed together) *in prayer; the picture of a child folded in her mother's embrace* (= held to her breast); *A **folding** door made of hinged panels or accordion pleats is used for closets and as a room divider.* **2** *Informal.* fail: *A business folds (up) when broke.*
— *n.* **1** a folding or bend: *hidden in the folds of a drape.* **2** a sheep pen; also, a flock, esp. a church congregation: *the prodigal's return to the fold.*

-fold *combining form.* number of parts or times as specified: *manifold, myriadfold, threefold, triplefold, twofold.*

fold·er *n.* something folded, as a file for papers or an advertising leaflet.

fo·li·age (FOH·lee.ij) *n.* leaves of a plant or tree.

fo·li·o (FOH·lee·oh) *n.* **-os 1** a leaf of a book. **2** a page number. **3** formerly, the largest book size resulting from sheets of paper folded only once.

folk (FOKE) **1** *n. & combining form.* the common people, esp. as a social or cultural group: *city folk, country folk, fisher folk, kinsfolk, gentlefolk, menfolk, womenfolk.* **2 folks** *n.pl. Informal.* people: *old folks; How are your folks* (= family, esp. parents)?
— *adj.* that is traditional with the common people: *folk art, ethics, literature, medicine, psychology, speech, theatre; a folk ballad, belief, custom, dance, singer, song, tale, tune; a folk Mass with folk music; **folk rock*** (= folk songs sung to a rock rhythm).

folk·lore *n.* the traditional customs, beliefs, sayings, etc. of a people, handed down from generation to generation.

folk·sy (FOKE·see) *adj.* **-si·er, -si·est** *Informal.* friendly or sociable in style.

folk·way *n.* a habit or custom common within a social group.

fol·low (FOLL·oh) *v.* **1** go or come after: *Christmas follows Thanksgiving; Your shadow follows you closely; The reasons are as follows; a sales representative who follows up letters with phone calls; a follow-up visit; The man emigrated and his family followed suit* (= did the same); *to follow through* (= go ahead) *with a plan; service offered as a follow-through after sales.* **2** to result or ensue: *Wars follow from enmities.* **3** obey: *Communists follow Lenin's doctrines; to follow blindly, faithfully.* **4** understand: *a lecturer difficult to follow.* — **fol·low·er** *n.*

following (FOLL·oh·ing) **1** *adj.* that follows: *for the following reasons; My reasons are the following.* **2** *n.* group of followers: *a political party with a large following.* **3** *prep.* after: *a dance following dinner.*

fol·ly (FOLL·ee) *n.* **fol·lies** (-eez) **1** lack of good sense or an instance of it: *the folly of accepting rides from strangers; It was folly not to listen to advice; the follies and excesses of youth.* **2** **follies** *pl.* a revue: *ice follies.*

fo·ment (foh·MENT) *v.* **1** stir up something that is below the surface: *to foment discontent, hatred, rebellion, trouble.* **2** apply something hot and moist such as a compress or poultice to a painful body part. — **fo·men·ta·tion** (-men·TAY·shun) *n.*

fond *adj.* loving, often excessively: *a fond belief, husband, kiss, look, wife; a fond parent; fond and foolish hopes; with fondest love; He's fond of her.* — **fond·ly** *adv.;* **fond·ness** *n.*

fon·dle (FON·dul) *v.* **-dles, -dled, -dling** pet or caress lovingly.

font *n.* **1** a bowl or basin for holy water, esp. one used at baptism: *a baptismal font.* **2** a style of printing type, as Helvetica and Baskerville. **3** a complete set of type of the same size and style.

food (long "oo") *n.* something to be consumed, esp. to sustain life or nourish growth: *People die for lack of food and water; food and drink; Fertilizers are plant foods; the Scriptures as food for the soul.*

food bank *n.* an agency that collects food donations and distributes them to the needy.

food chain *n.* a series of organisms that depend on one another for food, as mice on grass, owls on mice, bacteria on dead bodies which then become nutrients for the grass.

food cycle *n.* the cycle formed by the various food chains in an ecological system such as a forest or lake.

food processor *n.* an electrical kitchen appliance that chops, slices, mixes, shreds, etc.

food·stuff *n.* anything such as grain, meat, vegetables, etc. that has food value.

food web *n.* same as FOOD CYCLE.

fool *n.* **1** a silly or idiotic person. **2** a jester, as in the

Middle Ages.
— *v.* **1** trick or deceive: *People get fooled on April 1.* **2** *Informal.* act like a fool: *Stop fooling around and start studying; She fooled away her time till the eve of exams; It's dangerous to fool with explosives.*

fool·er·y (FOO·luh·ree) *n.* **-er·ies** a foolish action or foolish behaviour.

fool·har·dy (FOOL·har·dee) *adj.* **-di·er, -di·est** foolishly daring. — **fool·har·di·ness** *n.*

fool hen *n. Cdn.* a species of grouse, as Canada spruce goose, that is easy to catch.

fool·ish (FOO·lish) *adj.* showing lack of good sense and judgment: *a foolish action, young man.* — **fool·ish·ly** *adv.;* **fool·ish·ness** *n.*

fool·proof *adj.* so safe or simple as not to be mishandled, misunderstood, etc. even by a fool.

fool's paradise *n.* a state of happiness based on false hopes or illusions.

foot (short "oo") *n., pl.* **feet 1** the part of the leg that touches the ground when one is standing or walking: *to gain, get to, shuffle, stamp one's feet; children in their stocking feet (without footwear); The whole city is at your feet from this hilltop; Children living nearby go to school on foot* (= walking); *She put her foot down* (= was firm) *and refused to admit latecomers; Let's put our best foot forward* (= appear at our best) *for the interview; Small children tend to get under foot* (= in the way). **2** something corresponding to a foot: *the foot of a chair, stocking.* **3** a part opposed to the head or top part: *at the foot of the bed, hill, page, sail.* **4** a measure of length based on the human foot, equal to 12 in. (0.3048 m). **5** a unit of verse based on the syllable: *"Five and twenty sailors" has three feet.*
— **set foot** enter: *Troublemakers are not allowed to set foot in Canada; Al was told never to set foot on Canadian soil.*
— *v.* **1** find the sum of a column of figures. **2** pay costs, a bill, etc.: *to foot the bill.*
— **foot it** walk: *They had to foot it home after missing the bus.*

foot·age (FOOT·ij) *n.* **1** length measured in feet. **2** a length of motion-picture film: *library footage; newsreel footage.*

foot·ball *n.* **1** a game played between two teams defending a goal at either end of a field and using an inflated ball; also, rugby or soccer. **2** the ball used in any of these games.

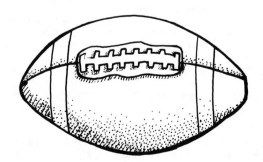

foot-dragging (FOOT·drag·ing) *n.* failure to act with the required promptness.

foot·ed *adj. & combining form.* having feet as specified: *a child's footed pajamas; barefooted; clubfooted; pussyfooted; splayfooted; We are two-footed animals; web-footed.*

-foot·er *combining form.* a person or thing in regard to height or length: *a strapping, big-boned six-footer; The superstore is a 100 000-square-footer; a formidable eight-footer of an alligator; a small 12-footer boat; Greg fired a 10-footer* (= hockey shot) *into the open net; She putted a 25-footer on the twelfth hole.*

foot·fall *n.* the sound of a footstep.

foot·hill *n.* a hill at the foot of higher mountains: *The foothills of Alberta are the "high country" between the prairies and the Rockies.*

foot·hold *n.* **1** a place to hold on to with a foot. **2** a secure or advantageous position: *a firm foothold; to establish, gain, secure a foothold.*

foot·ing *n.* **1** a placing of the feet: *to keep, lose one's footing.* **2** a foothold or something forming a foot, as the lowest part of a building foundation. **3** basis: *on an equal, friendly, sure, war footing.*

foot·less *adj.* **1** having no feet or foundation. **2** clumsy or inept.

foot·lights *n. pl.* a row of stage lights at foot level.

foot·lock·er (FOOT·lock·ur) *n.* a chest kept at the foot of one's bed, esp. in barracks.

foot·loose *adj.* free to move about or do as one pleases: *footloose and fancy free.*

foot·man (-mun) *n.* **-men** a male servant doing odd jobs; doorman.

foot·note *n.* a note placed at the foot of a page or end of a chapter or book explaining or amplifying a text: *the footnotes to the volume.*

foot·pad *n.* a padded foot of a soft-landing spacecraft.

foot·race *n.* a running race.

foot·rest *n.* a support on which to rest the feet.

foot·sie (FOOT·see) *n.* [child's word] foot.
— **to play footsie with** *Informal.* to flirt with an idea, group, plan, etc., like playing by touching feet under the table.

foot soldier *n.* an infantryman.

foot·step *n.* the sound or impression made by feet: *There were footsteps leading to the spot where the body was found; to dog someone's footsteps; a disciple who follows **in the footsteps of** (= follows the example of) his master.*

foot·stool *n.* a low stool to rest the feet on.

foot·wear *n.* things to wear on the feet, as shoes, boots, and slippers.

fop *n.* a vain person. — **fop·pish** *adj.*

for (FOR, fur) *prep.* [indicating purpose, goal, object, fitness, exchange, duration, etc.]: *to go for a walk; to catch a plane for Ottawa; a gift for you; She has a good ear for music; We slept for 10 hours; The eggs are for hatching, not for eating; a restaurant famous for fine cooking; A lawyer acts for her clients; a child named for* (= same as) *her mother; I stayed home for* (= because of) *many reasons; a good guy **for all I care** (Informal for but I'm indifferent); a good guy **for all I know** (Informal for probably).*
— *conj.* [not used to begin a sentence] because: *I'm not going, for I am ill.*

for·age (FOR·ij) *n.* a search or what is searched out for food, esp. grass and winter fodder for farm animals.
— *v.* **-ag·es, -aged, -ag·ing** wander in search, esp. of food: *Hunting and gathering tribes live by foraging; to forage for firewood.*

for·ay (FOR·ay) *n.* a raid, as into enemy territory: *a scoring foray in football; to make forays* (= advances or incursions) *into the U.S. market.* — *v.* make a raid.

forbad or **forbade** *pt.* of FORBID.

for·bear (for·BARE) *v.* **-bears, -bore, -borne** (-BORN) , **-bear·ing 1** keep from doing or saying; also, be patient and control oneself. **2** same as FOREBEAR.
— **for·bear·ance** (-unce) *n.*

for·bid (for·BID) *v.* **-bids,** *pt.* **-bad** or **-bade** (-BAD), *pp.* **-bid·den, -bid·ding** order not to do something: *She had expressly forbidden her children to smoke; Strangers are forbidden use of the cottage; God forbid (such a calamity)! God forbid that I should ever say such a thing!*

forbidden fruit *n.* something wished for but not permitted.

forbidding *adj.* that causes fear or dislike: *The pool looks cold and forbidding; a man of forbidding appearance.* — **for·bid·ding·ly** *adv.*

forbore, forborne See FORBEAR.

force *n.* **1** physical, mental, or moral power or strength, esp. its active use: *to apply, resort to, use force to open a door; We renounce the use of force; armed, brute, deadly, moral, physical force; a show of force; She can move objects by sheer force of will; We go on making the same mistakes by force of habit; "Absolutely" has greater force than "Yes"; the force of inertia as used in the wheels of toys; a centrifugal, centripetal, irresistible, magnetic force* (= energy). **2** a body of people: *an air, occupation, peace-keeping, police, sales force; a task force to study speed limits; the work force* (= workers); *to **join forces with** the opposition; the armed **forces*** (= army, navy, etc.); ***forces of nature** such as storms and earthquakes.*
— **in force:** *Lower speed limits are now in force* (= in effect); *Volunteers came out in force* (= great numbers) *to help disaster victims.*
— *v.* **forc·es, forced, forc·ing** get something done by overcoming resistance: *He forced the door (open); a confession forced from the prisoner; promises forced out of someone; a bribe forced on or upon an official; She had to force her way through the crowd.*

forced (FORST) *adj.* done with the use of force: *a forced confession, entry; forced feeding; a plane's forced landing; smiles that look forced* (= artificial); *a forced-air heating system.*

force·ful *adj.* that has force: *a forceful personality,*

presentation, speaker, style.
— **force·ful·ly** *adv.;* **force·ful·ness** *n.*

for·ci·ble (FOR·suh·bul) *adj.* **1** obtained or done by the use of force: *forcible confinement; a burglar's forcible entry; Rowdies are liable to forcible ejection from the nightclub.* **2** showing force: *a rather forcible argument.*
— **for·ci·bly** *adv.*

ford *n.* a place in a stream that is shallow enough to cross by wading or driving through.
— *v.* cross: *to ford a river.*

fore *adj.* in the front or forward, not back or aft: *the fore end of a firearm; a page's fore edge (opposite the back or stitched edge); the fore hatch of a ship.*
— *adv.* toward the bow of a ship.
— **fore and aft** at, to, or from bow and stern.
— **fore-and-aft** *adj.* lengthwise: *a fore-and-aft rigged ship; a fore-and-aft cap in British army style.*
— *n.* front: *a candidate who has* **come to the fore** *only recently.*
— *interj.* used as a warning: *The golfer shouted "Fore" and swung her club.*
— *combining form.* before or front: *forefather, fore-loader, forerunner.*

fore·arm *n.* the part of the arm between elbow and wrist.
— *v.* (for·ARM) arm beforehand: *"Forewarned is forearmed."*

fore·bear or **for·bear** *n.* ancestor.

fore·bode (for·BODE) *v.* -bodes, -bod·ed, -bod·ing esp. of things, predict or warn about something unfavourable: *a dream foreboding a fatal crash.*

foreboding *n.* a feeling of something about to happen: *dark forebodings of disaster, of the end of the world.*

fore·cast *v.* tell beforehand: *Snow is forecast for Christmas; economic indicators forecasting a recession.*
— *n.* a foretelling or prediction.

fore·cas·tle (FOKE·sul) *n.* the raised deck near a ship's bow.

fore·close (for·CLOSE) *v.* -clos·es, -closed, -clos·ing close in advance: *A mortgage is foreclosed and the property sold if payments are not kept up; an embargo to foreclose trade with a nation.*
— **fore·clo·sure** (-CLOH·zhur) *n.*

fore·doom (for·DOOM) *v.* doom beforehand: *a plot foredoomed to failure because it was not kept secret.*

fore·fa·ther (FOR·fah·thur) *n.* an ancestor.

fore·fin·ger (FOR·fing·gur) *n.* the finger next to the thumb.

fore·foot *n.* -feet one of the front feet of an animal or insect with four feet or more.

fore·front *n.* the extreme front; position of the greatest importance: *in the forefront of the struggle.*

fore·gath·er *v.* same as FORGATHER.

fore·go (for·GO) *v.* -goes, -went, -gone, -go·ing **1** go before or precede: *From the* **foregoing** *facts, we deduce that the earth is round; The case was so strong the verdict was a* **foregone conclusion** *(known in advance).* **2** same as FORGO.

fore·ground *n.* the part of a picture that appears closest to the viewer: *The children were in the foreground of the picture with a chalkboard in the background.*

fore·hand *n.* **1** in tennis and such racket games, a stroke with the palm of the hand turned forward. **2** a similar shot or pass in hockey.
— *adj.:* *a forehand drive, grip, stroke.*

fore·head (FOR·id, FOR·hed) *n.* the part of the face above the eyebrows.

for·eign (FOR·in) *adj.* having to do with an outside country or place: *a foreign accent; English is a foreign language in Ethiopia; The* **foreign minister** *is in charge of a government's foreign affairs; our foreign policy; Laziness is foreign to her nature; Dust, grit, and such foreign bodies may get into our eyes; native-born children of foreign-born parents.* — **for·eign·er** *n.*

fore·know (for·NOH) *v.* -knows, -knew, -known, -know·ing have prior knowledge, esp. by use of divine or psychic power. — **fore·know·ledge** (-NOL·ij) *n.*

fore·limb *n.* a foreleg or a corresponding arm, fin, or wing.

fore·lock *n.* a lock of hair, as of a horse, growing just above the forehead.

fore·man (FOR·mun) *n.pl.* -men **1** the leader of a jury. **2** one in charge of workers or a section of a plant; *fem.* **fore·wom·an, -wom·en.**

fore·mast *n.* the mast near a ship's bow.

fore·most *adj. & adv.* first in position or importance: *I am first and foremost a Canadian; the foremost champion of women's rights.*

fore·named *adj.* before-mentioned; aforesaid.

fo·ren·sic (fuh·REN·sic) *adj.* having to do with courts of law or argumentation: *a lawyer's forensic abilities; A body is sent to a* **forensic laboratory** *for a post-mortem;* **forensic medicine** *(= medical science applied to legal questions).*

fore·run·ner (FOR·run·ur) *n.* **1** one who goes before another preparing the way; precursor. **2** a warning sign or symptom: *A sore throat is sometimes a forerunner of the flu, measles, etc.*

fore·see (for·SEE) *v.* -sees, -saw, -seen, -see·ing see or realize in advance what is going to happen.
— **fore·see·a·ble** (-SEE·uh·bul) *adj.:* *in the forseeable future.*

fore·shad·ow (for·SHAD·oh) *v.* indicate something to follow; give advance warning of something: *events foreshadowing war.*

fore·shore *n.* the part of a shore covered during high tide.

fore·sight *n.* the act or power of foreseeing: *The principal acted with foresight in sending the children home before the storm.*

fore·sight·ed (FOR·sye·tid) *adj.* having or using foresight: *Their foresighted planning averted a famine.*

for·est (FOR·ist) *n.* a large wooded area; also, the trees and underbrush in it: *to clear a forest; a dense, evergreen, hardwood, impenetrable, primeval, virgin*

forest; a (tropical) rain forest; a town hidden under a forest of TV antennas.
— **adj.**: forest conservation; a forest fire, product, ranger, region, reserve; a **forested** (= wooded) area.

fore·stall v. take advance action to prevent or get ahead of: early negotiations to forestall a strike.

for·est·er (FOR·is·tur) n. **1** one trained in forestry. **2** one in charge of a park or forest; also **forest ranger**.

for·est·ry (FOR·is·tree) n. the science of forest cultivation and management of timber resources.

fore·taste n. a first experience of something to happen: The balmy weather was a foretaste of spring; a foretaste of victory. — **v.** (fore·TAIST) -tastes, -tast·ed, -tast·ing.

fore·tell (for·TELL) v. -tells, -told, -tell·ing indicate beforehand; predict.

fore·thought n. **1** previous consideration. **2** foresight.

for·ev·er (fur·EV·ur) n. **1** an endlessly long time: He was taking forever to finish his speech. **2** adv. endlessly; always: Nothing lasts forever; They lived happily forever; also **for·ev·er·more** (-ur·MORE).

fore·warn v. warn in advance of something.

forewoman See FOREMAN.

fore·word n. a short preface to a book.

for·feit (FOR·fit) v. lose or be deprived of something as a punishment: Drunk drivers forfeit their licence; The bail was forfeited to the Crown when Joe failed to appear in court; **adj.**: The bail was forfeit to the Crown.
— **n.** a forfeiting: Murderers used to be punished by forfeit of their lives; also **for·fei·ture** (-fi·chur) n.

for·fend (for·FEND) v. [old use] forbid: Heaven forfend!

for·gath·er (for·GATH·ur, "TH" as in "the") v. assemble or come together.

forgave pt. of FORGIVE.

forge (FORJ) n. **1** a furnace in which metal is heated or wrought. **2** a smithy.
— **v.** forg·es, forged, forg·ing **1** form or shape, as metal in a forge: Blacksmiths forge metals by beating them into shape while red-hot on an anvil; to forge a horseshoe, tool, utensil; bonds of friendship forged at school. **2** make or imitate falsely: to forge a cheque, passport, signature; **for·ger** n. **3** move suddenly with speed and power: The horse that was last began forging into the lead toward the end; It **forged ahead** and won the race.

for·ger·y (FOR·juh·ree) n. -ger·ies **1** a counterfeiting of cheques and documents, paintings, signatures, etc. **2** something forged: The Hitler diaries were found to be forgeries.

for·get (fur·GET) v. -gets, -got, -got·ten, -get·ting **1** fail to remember: I forgot to bring my homework to school; I forgot about bringing it (= I didn't bring it); I clean forgot; I completely forgot about it in the morning rush. **2** neglect or disregard: Let's forget about your unfinished work; Just forget it.
— **forget oneself 1** say or do something improper. **2** be unselfish: She forgets herself in the service of others.
— **for·get·ta·ble** (fur·GET·uh·bul) adj.

for·get·ful (fur·GET·ful) adj. apt to forget; also, negligent: to be forgetful of the needs of others.
— **for·get·ful·ly** adv.; **for·get·ful·ness** n.

for·give (fur·GIV) v. -gives, -gave, -giv·en, -giv·ing pardon, esp. give up the wish to punish: I forgive and forget hurts, forgive enemies, but never forgive (= cancel) debts. — **for·giv·a·ble** adj.

for·go (fur·GOH) v. -goes, -went, -gone, -go·ing do without something in a self-denying way, usually because of practical considerations: She worked nights, often forgoing sleep.

forgot, forgotten See FORGET.

fork n. **1** a tool with a handle and two or more prongs or tines for eating, pitching hay, etc.; also, something resembling it, as a tuning fork. **2** where branches of a tree, stream, or road meet; also, one of the branches: Winnipeg is at the fork of the Red and Assiniboine rivers. **3** forks pl. area around a river fork.
— **v. 1** use a fork to lift, throw, dig, etc. **2** divide into forks or branches, as a river or road does.
— **fork over** or **out** or **up** Informal. hand over money.
— **forked** adj.: a forked stick; forked (= zigzag) lightning; the forked tongue of a serpent; to speak with a **forked tongue** (= to be untruthful).
— **fork·ful** n. -fuls.

for·lorn (for·LORN) adj. wretched and forsaken: the deserted and forlorn look of hungry children.
— **for·lorn·ly** adv.

forlorn hope n. a nearly hopeless enterprise.

form n. **1** shape or structure: water in the form of ice and snow; The Greek god Proteus could assume or take or take on any form; the form and content of a poem; in an abridged, condensed, convenient, handy, revised form; She is in excellent, good, superb form (= condition) today; He was not **in form** (= in good condition) yesterday; light, heat, and other forms (= kinds) of energy. **2** a way, method, or manner of doing something: "Good morning" is the accepted form of greeting before noon; It's considered bad form (= behaviour) to smoke at an interview; They don't like it in **any manner, shape, or form**; I'm not talking about mere forms and ceremonies. **3** a frame or mould: Concrete is poured into forms for setting. **4** a document to be filled out: an application form; tax forms.
— **v.** to shape, take shape, put into shape, etc.: Frost is forming on the window; a party formed of friends and relatives; a figure formed out of clay; habits formed in childhood; Please form yourselves into circles.

-form combining form. having form, as specified: cruciform, uniform, vermiform.

form·al (FOR·mul) adj. in accordance with a form, rule, custom, or convention: A tuxedo is a formal costume; A contract is a formal agreement; a formal garden laid out in geometrical designs; a formal invitation.
— **form·al·ly** adv. — **for·mal·ism** n.

for·mal·i·ty (for·MAL·uh·tee) n. -ties **1** attention to forms and ceremonies; hence, stiffness. **2** a rule, custom, or convention: to complete, cut out, go through the formalities.

for·mal·ize (FOR·muh·lize) v. -iz·es, -ized, -iz·ing make formal or give a form to: The fleur-de-lis is a formalized

iris flower; language formalized as grammar rules.
— **for·mal·i·za·tion** (-luh·ZAY·shun) *n.*

for·mat (FOR·mat) *n.* shape, design, or arrangement: *Books are published in many formats, as hardcover, leatherbound, paperback, etc.; a meeting in the format of a panel discussion.*
— *v.* **-mats, -mat·ted, -mat·ting** put in a format: *to format a diskette (in tracks and sectors) for recording data; to format text for printing out with appropriate margin widths, line spacing, etc.; book formatting by computer.*

for·ma·tion (for·MAY·shun) *n.* **1** a forming or manner of forming: *the formation of ice on a lake; a battle, close, cloud, football, tight formation.* **2** something formed: *planes flying in formation; Gibraltar is a huge rock formation.*

for·ma·tive (FOR·muh·tiv) *adj.* having to do with growth and formation: *the formative influences of home, school, and society; the formative years of childhood.*

for·mer (FOR·mur) *adj.* **1** previous: *stories of former times.* **2** the first-mentioned of two: *Of Lou and Lee, the former is a girl.* — **for·mer·ly** *adv.* in the past.

for·mi·da·ble (FOR·muh·duh·bul, for·MID·uh·bul) *adj.* causing awe, admiration, and alarm: *a formidable list of qualifications; a formidable opponent, task, threat.*

form·less *adj.* shapeless: *Fluids are formless; the voices of formless (=immaterial) beings.*

form letter *n.* a letter so written that copies of it may be dated and addressed to many people.

for·mu·la (FORM·yuh·luh) *n.* **-las** or **-lae** (-lee) **1** a set expression, esp. one for a specific use: *"You're welcome" is a polite formula for acknowledging thanks; "I baptize thee..." is a baptismal formula.* **2** a set of symbols expressing a scientific truth: *the chemical formula for water; a mathematical formula for the area of a circle.* **3** a set of specifications or a plan, preparation, recipe, etc. in which one is used: *to make up, prepare, warm up the baby's formula (=milk mixture); a soap-making formula; to devise a formula; a formula for success; a proven formula; a Formula One racing car (built to specifications).*

for·mu·late (FORM·yuh·late) *v.* **-lates, -lat·ed, -lat·ing** **1** express in a formula or systematically: *Einstein formulated relativity.* **2** prepare using a formula: *Pharmacists formulate prescriptions.*
— **for·mu·la·tion** (-LAY·shun) *n.*

for·sake (fur·SAKE) *v.* **-sakes, -sook, -sak·ing** give up a person or thing to which one is attached: *Friends forsook him when he was in jail; bad habits that he forsook on marrying.*

for·swear (for·SWARE) *v.* **-swears, -swore, -sworn, -swear·ing** swear solemnly to avoid something considered bad, as a habit.
— **forswear oneself** perjure oneself.

fort *n.* a fortified place; also, a permanent army post: *Fort York in Toronto; The fort fell to the Americans in 1813; They went out shopping, leaving the children to hold the fort (=look after the house).*

forte (FORT) *n.* one's strong point: *I'm a plumber,*

carpentry is not my forte.

for·te (FOR·tay, -tee) *adj. & adv.* in music, loud(ly) and strong(ly).

forth *adv.* forward or onward: *He went forth to meet her; From that day forth (=on), they have been friends.*
— **and so forth** et cetera.
— **back and forth** to and fro.

forth·com·ing (FORTH·cum·ing) *adj.* coming forward or approaching: *No help seemed forthcoming; our forthcoming movie attractions.*

forth·right *adj. & adv.* straightforward or frank: *He was very forthright in his answers; He told them forthright that the pay was too low.*

forth·with *adv.* at once: *He made his speech and forthwith left the meeting to catch his flight.*

for·ti·fy (FOR·tuh·fy) *v.* **-fies, -fied, -fy·ing** strengthen: *to fortify a town with a fortress; a soul fortified by suffering; Milk is fortified with vitamins and minerals; Fortified wines have up to 21% alcohol.*
— **for·ti·fi·ca·tion** (-fuh·CAY·shun) *n.*

for·ti·tude (FOR·tuh·tude) *n.* strength of mind that enables one to endure pain, misfortune, etc. patiently: *intestinal fortitude (=guts).*

fort·night *n.* a period of two weeks.

fort·night·ly (FORT·nite·lee) *n. & adj.* (a periodical) appearing every two weeks: *a fortnightly journal;* **adv.:** *We publish fortnightly.*

for·tress (FOR·tris) *n.* a fortified place: *to besiege, storm, take a fortress; A fortress falls to the enemy.*

for·tu·i·tous (for·TUE·uh·tus) *adj.* of a fortunate event, happening by chance: *a fortuitous event, meeting.*
— **for·tu·i·tous·ly** *adv.*

for·tu·nate (FOR·chuh·nit) *adj.* of people and circumstances, lucky: *We were saved from fire by a fortunate change of wind; It's fortunate the wind changed; We were fortunate to be saved from the fire.*
— **for·tu·nate·ly** *adv.*

for·tune (FOR·chun) *n.* **1** one's lot or luck: *It was her good fortune to be born in that family; the bad fortune to be hit by a truck; "Fortune (=good fortune) favours the brave"; He left home to try his fortune as a sailor; our changing fortunes; the fortunes of war; when fortune smiles on us; the goddess of fortune with her wheel of fortune (=chance); A stroke of good fortune made her a millionaire; She tells fortunes (=predicts good and bad things to come) for a living; a fortune cookie (containing a prediction or maxim).* **2** wealth: *He's after fame and fortune; to accumulate, amass, come into, inherit, run through, squander a fortune; an enormous, vast, family fortune; That sofa will cost you a fortune (=a large sum of money); a Fortune 500 (=one of the top 500 in income) company; a fortune hunter (who seeks wealth, esp. by marriage).*

for·ty (FOR·tee) *adj., pron. & n.* **1** four times 10; 40 or XL: *forty acres; some forty of them; She scored a forty; Give me an even forty.* **2** the forties *n.pl.* numbers, years, etc. ending in 40 through 49: *The early forties were war years.* — **for·ti·eth** (-tee·ith) *n. & adj.*

forty winks *n.pl. Informal.* a short nap.

fo·rum (FOR·um) *n.* **-rums 1** a place for public discussion: *TV as a forum of public affairs; They held an open forum on or about traffic safety.* **2** a tribunal.

for·ward (FOR·wurd) *adj.* toward the front, not backward: *a forward leap, march, movement; a forward* (=pushy) *young man with very forward* (=bold) *views; forward planning (for the future); forward buying of grain (for later delivery).*
— *adv.* to a front position: *to bring* or *put forward a proposal for reform; to come, rush, step forward; I look forward to our meeting (with pleasure); From that time forward* (=onward), *he was very careful; Put the clock forward* (=advance it) *by one hour in the spring.* Also **for·wards.**
— *n.* a front-line player in team games such as hockey and basketball.
— *v.* **1** send: *We will forward your mail to the new address.* **2** promote: *to forward a plan, scheme.*

forwent *pt.* of FORGO.

fos·sil (FOS·ul) *n.* **1** a hardened remnant of an animal or plant dating from a previous geological period, preserved in rock or in coal deposits: *a fossil fern; the fast depletion of the earth's fossil fuels such as coal, oil, and natural gas.* **2** an antiquated person: *an old fossil of a philosopher.*

fos·sil·ize (FOS·uh·lize) *v.* **-iz·es, -ized, -iz·ing 1** change into a fossil: *the fossilized remains of prehistoric humans.* **2** become set or rigid in one's ways.
— **fos·sil·i·za·tion** (-luh·ZAY·shun) *n.*

fos·ter *v.* **1** help to grow or develop: *to foster good habits in children.* **2** encourage or cultivate: *hopes fostered by promises.*

foster brother or **foster sister** *n.* a child raised by foster parents.

foster home *n.* a private home in which children needing special care are placed by agencies such as children's aid societies.

foster parent *n.* one acting in the place of a natural parent in taking care of children.

fought *pt. & pp.* of FIGHT.

foul (rhyme: "howl") *adj.* **1** rotten or filthy; hence, disagreeable: *the foul air around a garbage dump; medicine with a foul taste; We were warned of foul* (=stormy) *weather; foul language* (=swearing); *a foul* (=violent) *crime; Chimney sweeps clean out the soot from foul* (=dirty) *chimneys.* **2** not fair; against rules: *a foul ball that lands outside the foul lines in foul territory; by fair means or foul* (=by honest or dishonest means). **3** tangled: *foul ropes.*
— *adv.* in a foul manner: *to play foul; Those who go* or *fall* or *run foul of* (=get in trouble with) *the law may go to jail.*
— *v.* make foul: *Auto exhausts foul the air; Their last-minute change of mind fouled up* (=spoiled or ruined) *our plans.*
— *n.* anything foul, as an infraction of a rule, a collision or entangling, or a foul ball.
— **foul·ly** *adv.;* **foul·ness** *n.*

fouling *n.* a messy deposit, as in a sewage pipe or in the barrel of a gun after firing.

foul-mouthed *adj.* using foul language; abusive.

foul play *n.* **1** unfair play. **2** treacherous violence, esp. murder: *He met with foul play; The police suspected foul play when the missing person's clothes were found in the bush.*

foul-up *n.* *Informal.* a mixup or mess.

found *v.* **1** *pt. & pp.* of FIND: *the lost-and-found columns of a newspaper.* **2** establish: *a company founded in 1847; an argument founded* (=based) *on facts, not hearsay evidence.* **3** cast metal, as in a foundry.
— *adj.* discovered, not made as such: **Found art** *uses found objects such as driftwood, shells, and junk;* **found poems** *composed by rearranging found fragments of writing from newsprint, laundry lists, etc.; You can't have a steady income from **found money**.*

foun·da·tion (fown·DAY·shun) *n.* **1** base: *Our house rests on a concrete foundation; a firm, solid, strong foundation; a cosmetic foundation for applying makeup; to undermine a foundation; a story without foundation* (=basis); *adj.:* a foundation garment such as a corset or girdle with bra; to lay the foundation stone of a building.* **2** an endowed institution: *a charitable foundation; a science foundation; a foundation for humanitarian work.*

found·er (FOWN·dur) *n.* **1** one who founds an institution. **2** one who casts metals.
— *v.* collapse or fail: *A horse founders from overwork and limps; a business that foundered during the recession; A ship foundered in the storm* (=filled with water and sank).

found-in *n.* *Cdn.* a person arrested for being in an illegal establishment such as a gambling place or brothel.

found·ling *n.* an abandoned infant of unknown parents.

found·ry (FOUND·ree) *n.* **-ries** a shop where metal is moulded into products such as engine blocks, dies, and printing type.

fount *n.* **1** a source or font. **2** a fountain.

foun·tain (FOWN·tun) *n.* **1** a spring of water, esp. an artificial jet or flow supplied by pipes and having a basinlike receptacle: *We first met at the office (water) fountain; A soda fountain* (=counter) *sells sodas, milkshakes, etc.* **2** source: *a fountain of knowledge, wisdom; He went in quest of the fountain of youth.*

foun·tain·head (FOWN·tun·hed) *n.* the original source, as of a stream: *God as the fountainhead of all wisdom.*

four (FOR) *n., pron. & adj.* one more than three; the number 4 or IV: *four limbs; four of them; Infants crawl around on all fours* (=hands and feet).

four·fold *adj. & adv.* four times: *a fourfold* (=400%) *increase; It increased fourfold.*

four-letter word *n.* **1** any of the most vulgar words of English that refer to sex, excretion, and related bodily parts. **2** any disgusting word or name.

four-poster *n.* a bed with four posts to support a canopy.

four·some *n.* a group of four persons, as for a game of golf.

four·square *adj. & adv.* square-shaped; hence, solidly

based, unyielding, or forthright.

four·teen (for·TEEN) *n., adj. & pron.* four more than 10; the number 14 or XIV. — **four·teenth** *n. & adj.*

fourth (FORTH) *n., adj. & adv.* **1** next after third: *the fourth gear of a car; He placed fourth in the exam.* **2** one of four equal parts.

fourth estate *n.* the public press or journalism.

Fourth World *n.* the poorest nations of the world.

fowl *n.* a bird, esp. a large domestic bird such as a chicken, duck, goose, or turkey or their flesh used as food. — *v.* hunt or catch wild fowl. — **fowl·er** *n.*

fowling piece or **fowling gun** *n.* a lightweight shotgun.

fox *n.* **1** a small, wild, flesh-eating, bushy-tailed canine animal, usually considered crafty and sly: *A fox yelps; a fox's cub* or *pup; a female fox* (= vixen). **2** a crafty or sly person: *a wise old fox.* — *v.* to trick by craftiness.

fox·hole *n.* a hole dug as a shelter against gunfire for one or two soldiers.

fox·y *adj.* **fox·i·er, -i·est** like a fox: *a foxy* (= wily) *old trader; the foxy* (= soured or grapey) *flavour of certain wines; foxy* (= rotting) *ice; a foxy* (*Slang* for sexually attractive) *woman.*

foy·er (FOY·ur, FOY·ay) *n.* an entrance hall or lobby, esp. one used as a lounge: *in the foyer of an apartment building, hotel, theatre.*

fra·cas (FRAY·cus) *n.* a noisy fight or brawl.

frac·tion (FRAK·shun) *n.* **1** a broken part of a whole, esp. a fragment or insignificant portion: *Our candidate got only a fraction of the vote.* **2** in math, a quantity expressed with a numerator and denominator: *A common fraction such as 2/5 can be changed to the decimal fraction 0.4.* — **frac·tion·al** (-nul) *adj.: fractional currency such as dimes, nickels, and quarters.*

frac·tious (FRAK·shus) *adj.* rebellious; also, irritable or peevish.

frac·ture (FRAK·chur) *n.* a breaking, esp. a break or crack in a bone, rock, gem, etc.: *Physicians set fractures* (= broken bones); *Fractures heal, knit; a compound, greenstick, hairline, simple fracture.* — *v.* **frac·tures, frac·tured, frac·tur·ing** break: *Bones fracture in various ways.*

frag·ile (FRAJ·ile, -ul) *adj.* easy to break or destroy: *a fragile toy, truce; in a fragile condition; a fragile environment; fragile happiness, health.* — **fra·gil·i·ty** (fruh·JIL·uh·tee) *n.*

frag·ment (FRAG·munt) *n.* a broken-off part; also, an incomplete part, as of a conversation, or an unfinished work, as Coleridge's poem "Kubla Khan." — *v.* break up or split up: *Is our society fragmenting as it gets more and more diversified? We face the prospect of fragmented families; a fragmented narrative (that lacks unity); a decentralized, fragmented organization, fragmented into small groups; a fragmented industry, market, society.* — **frag·men·tar·y** (-mun·tair·ee) *adj.* — **frag·men·ta·tion** (-TAY·shun) *n.*

fra·grant (FRAY·grunt) *adj.* pleasant-smelling: *a fragrant air, flower, garden.* — **fra·grance** *n.*

frail *adj.* weak or delicate: *a man in frail health; a frail beauty, constitution, flower, smile, voice; frail excuses, hands, happiness, hopes, humanity.*

frail·ty *n.* weakness or fault, esp. moral: *human frailty.*

frame *n.* **1** a structure, esp. a basic or skeletal system that gives something its shape or form: *a man of slender frame; the wooden frame of a frame house.* **2** the borders of a picture or of a pair of glasses: *Bright weather puts her in a cheerful frame of mind* (= mood). **3** something having a frame, as an individual picture on a strip of motion-picture film, one of the series of question-and-answer steps into which a topic is divided in programmed instruction, one of the 10 sequences in which scores are recorded at bowling, etc.: *a time frame* (= period) *of six months.* — *v.* **frames, framed, fram·ing 1** put a border round: *He stood there framed in the doorway; the constitution as originally framed* (= put in shape) *by the Fathers of Confederation.* **2** *Informal.* implicate falsely: *She was framed by agents who had planted the drugs in her room; It was a frame-up.* — **fram·er** *n.*

frame of reference *n.* a set of axes or coordinates: *a graph drawn with a time-temperature frame of reference; a judgment made without a clear frame of reference* (= set of standards).

frame·work *n.* **1** structure: *an ancient ship with a wooden framework.* **2** set of standards: *free elections within the framework of a democratic society.*

fran·chise (FRAN·chize) *n.* **1** the right granted by a government to vote: *to exercise one's franchise; Federal franchise was made universal in Canada in 1920.* **2** the right granted by a government or company to market a product or operate a service: *We have* or *hold a fried-chicken franchise.*

Franco- *combining form.* French: *Franco-American, Franco-Canadian, Franco-Ontarian.*

Fran·co·phone or **fran·co·phone** (FRANK·uh·fone) *n. Cdn.* a French-speaking person in a multilingual society: *Canadian Francophones, Anglophones, and allophones.* — *adj.* French-speaking: *the Francophone nations of Africa.*

Frang·lais or **frang·lais** (frang·GLAY) *n. & adj.* French mixed with English, as "le cash, les girls."

frank *adj.* freely expressing what one feels or thinks: *a frank confession, exchange of views; I'll be frank with you; brutally frank; She's frank but fair.*
— *n. Informal.* a frankfurter.
— *v.* send or mark mail for postage-free transmission, as by using an authorized sign instead of stamps: *a franked self-addressed envelope; franked or metered mail; a franking machine.*

Frank·en·stein (FRANK·un·stine) *n.* a monster that endangers its own creator.

frank·fur·ter (FRANK·fur·tur) *n.* a smoked sausage of beef or pork.

fran·tic *adj.* wildly excited; frenzied: *a frantic rush to catch the bus; a frantic search for the wallet; It would drive anyone frantic (= crazy).* — **fran·ti·cal·ly** *adv.*

frat *n. Informal.* a fraternity.

fra·ter·nal (fruh·TUR·nul) *adj.* 1 brotherly: *fraternal love; fraternal societies (of Elks, Foresters, Knights of Columbus, etc.).* 2 developed from different egg cells, whether male or female: *fraternal quadruplets, twins;* cf. IDENTICAL. — **fra·ter·nal·ly** *adv.*

fra·ter·ni·ty (fruh·TUR·nuh·tee) *n.* -ties 1 brotherliness: *a feeling of fraternity; equality and fraternity; a fraternity (= brotherly commonness) of interests.* 2 a group of people of the same profession or interests: *the medical fraternity (= physicians); Greek-letter fraternities (of male students) such as Phi Delta Theta have chapters in Canadian universities; a fraternity pin or badge.*

frat·er·nize (FRAT·ur·nize) *v.* -niz·es, -nized, -niz·ing associate in a friendly manner: *Neighbours fraternize with one another.*
— **fra·ter·ni·za·tion** (-nuh·ZAY·shun) *n.*

frat·ri·cide (FRAT·ruh·cide) *n.* 1 one who kills a brother or sister. 2 such an act. — **frat·ri·ci·dal** (-SYE·dul) *adj.*

Frau (rhyme: "how") *n., pl.* **Frau·en** (FROW·un) German for "Mrs."; also, a wife.

fraud *n.* a trick, trickster, or trickery: *The charity was a fraud (= trick for exploiting people); found guilty of fraud (= trickery); consumer fraud (for tricking consumers); mail fraud (= use of the mails for cheating purposes); vote fraud; welfare fraud (for tricking the government of welfare money); to commit, expose, perpetrate a fraud; a pious fraud (= deception for religious purposes); Is Flo a fraud (= trickster) or a genuine scholar?*

fraud·u·lent (FRAW·juh·lunt) *adj.* dishonest or deceptive: *a fraudulent claim.*
— **fraud·u·lent·ly** *adv.* — **fraud·u·lence** (-lunce) *n.*

fraught (FRAUT) *adj.* loaded with something bad: *a scheme fraught with peril; an undertaking fraught with danger.*

Fräu·lein (FROY·line) *n.* the German for "Miss"; hence, an unmarried young woman.

fray *n.* a noisy quarrel or dispute: *to enter, get into, join the fray.*
— *v.* wear through or become worn by rubbing: *a frayed cuff; Deer fray their antlers against trees to rub off dry skin; frayed (= worn out or strained) nerves, tempers.*

fraz·zle (FRAZ·ul) *v.* **fraz·zles, fraz·zled, fraz·zling** make or become exhausted or frayed: *frazzled nerves after a frazzling birthday bash; frazzled businessmen, executives, motorists, parents, teachers.*
— *n.* an exhausted condition: *worn to a frazzle.*

freak (FREEK) *n.* 1 a person or thing that is unusual, unexpected, odd, or queer: *a double-headed freak of nature; saved from ruin by a freak of fortune;* **adj.:** *a freak accident; A freak snowstorm hit us in July.* 2 *Slang.* a user of an illicit drug; hence, an addict or devotee, as of a cult: *an acid freak; baseball freaks; film freaks.*
— *v.* **freak out** *Slang.* have an extreme mental reaction: *to freak out on drugs; to freak out of (= withdraw from) society.*

freak-out *n. Slang.* the act of freaking out or one who has freaked out.

freck·le (FRECK·ul) *n.* a small, brownish spot on the skin.
— *v.* **-les, -led, -ling** mark or become marked with freckles: *The sun freckkles the skin; The tendency to freckle diminishes as you grow older.*
— **freck·led** *adj.: a freckled face, forehead, nose.* Also **freck·ly** *adv.*

free *adj.* **free·er, free·est** not bound or hampered: *All are born free and equal, but not free from care; free of debt; a prisoner free on parole; We enjoy free speech in a democracy; Feel free to browse around; He was fired for being too free with (= for freely using) company funds; to be free with advice (= to give unasked-for advice); I've two free (= gratis) tickets to the show; the **free fall** of an apple from a tree; There's no such thing as a **free lunch** (= Everything has some hidden obligation or liability attached); an employee given a **free hand** (= freedom of action); to give **free rein** to your thoughts; a **free zone** (where goods may be received without paying duties); You can have it **for free** (= without charge); her engaging **free and easy** (= relaxed and uninhibited) manner.*
— **free on board** or **f.o.b.** placed without charge on board customer's vehicle: *goods free on board (at) our warehouse.*
— *combining form:* *lead-free gas; salt-free diet; sugar-free gum.*
— *adv.* without restraints: *Dogs should not run free in a people's park; Who sets or turns them free? Children are admitted free (= without charge).* See also FREELY.
— *v.* **frees, freed, free·ing** make free: *people freed from slavery; to free a room of dust; to free up teachers for more teaching duties.*

free·bie or **free·bee** *n. Informal.* something given free, as complimentary tickets.

free·boot·er (FREE·boo·tur) *n.* a plunderer.

free·born *adj.* not born in slavery.

free·dom (FREE·dum) *n.* the state, right, or privilege of being free: *Do we enjoy the freedom to do what we like? to abridge, curtail, gain, secure, win freedom; academic, personal, political, religious freedom; The Canadian Charter of Rights and Freedoms guarantees freedom of conscience and religion, freedom of thought and expression, freedom of assembly, and freedom of association; He was granted the freedom of (= privilege* of travelling freely in) *the city; Children have the freedom of the house.*

free enterprise *n.* the capitalist economic system with a minimum of government control.

free flight *n.* the flight of a rocket after its fuel is burned up.

free-for-all (FREE·fur·all) *n.* a contest in which anyone may take part, usually with no rules; hence, a brawl.

free·hand *adj.* done without mechanical aids: *a freehand drawing.*

free lance *n.* one who is not committed to any one employer; also **free-lanc·er.**
— **free-lance** *adj.: a free-lance artist, editor, journalist.*
— *v.* **-lanc·es, -lanced, -lanc·ing** work as a free lance: *Since resigning, she has been free-lancing as a consultant.*

free·load *v. Informal.* get things or make a living at another's expense; sponge.

free love *n.* sexual love without marriage or other social restrictions.

free·ly *adv.* in a free manner: *People can roam freely through our malls; They can mingle freely with the crowds and spend freely in the shops; They speak freely and openly about restrictions; They pay freely agreed prices; He freely* (= without being forced) *admitted his guilt.*

free port *n.* a port without import and export duties, as Singapore or Hong Kong.

free-standing *adj.* without external supports: *The CN Tower is our tallest free-standing structure; a free-standing clinic (not attached to a hospital).*

free·style *n.* swimming or figure skating with no specified style.

free trade *n.* trade between nations without the restrictions of customs, duties, protective tariffs, etc.

free university *n.* a student-run university devoted to subjects of the students' own choice and without grades, credits, and such restrictions.

free verse *n.* verse without the structure imposed by a metre or rhyme.

free·way *n.* **1** a main highway allowing free flow of traffic with fully controlled accesses and grade-separated interchanges. **2** a toll-free highway.

free·wheel·ing (free·WHEEL·ing) *adj.* moving along unrestrained or uninhibited: *a freewheeling discussion.*

free will *n.* the power of free choice, esp. in regard to one's salvation.
— **free-will** *adj.* voluntary: *a free-will offering.*

free world *n.* the countries outside Communist rule.

freeze *v.* **freez·es, froze, froz·en, freez·ing** harden or solidify with cold: *Water freezes at 0°C or 32°F, the* **freezing point** *of water; It's freezing (weather) outside; It froze last night; The homeless may freeze to death; A bridge freezes* (= ices) *fast because of its exposure; As the ghost appeared, the audience sat frozen to their seats; The runner froze* (= stopped) *in his tracks when the police shouted "Freeze!" Dentists freeze the jaw (using an*

anesthetic) *before pulling a tooth; Lakes* **freeze over** *during a wintry night; You can argue* **until hell freezes over** (*Informal for* forever); *We'll believe you* **when hell freezes over** (*Informal for* We'll never believe you).
— *n.* a freezing or frozen condition: *The last ships to leave the canal were caught in the freeze; We were in a deep freeze all January; to impose a freeze on prices and wages to halt inflation.*

freeze-dry *v.* **-dries, -dried, -dry·ing** dehydrate by freezing and evaporating: *freeze-dried coffee, foods, medicines.*

freez·er *n.* a chest or room in which perishable foods are preserved frozen.

freeze-frame *n.* a still frame of a motion picture when stopped: *the freeze-frame button of a VCR.*

freeze-up *n. Cdn.* the freezing up of water and soil in early winter or its duration.

freight (FRATE) *n.* **1** goods carried by water, land, or air transportation or the charge for it: *a freight car, train; Most students pay the full freight* (= fees, etc.) *without any financial aid.* **2** a freight train made up of freight cars: *He jumped a freight for Vancouver.*
— *v.* send by or load with freight.

freight·er *n.* a ship or plane carrying freight.

French *n.* **1** the language of France, Quebec, etc.: *Acadian French; Canadian French; Louisiana French; Parisian French.* **2** **the French** the people who speak French, as people of or from France, French Canada, etc.
— *adj.* having to do with France and other French-speaking countries and regions: *The French Academy; French colonial (architecture); the French community; French cuisine, culture, dialects, history; The French and Indian War (1754 – 1763); French literature, the French population; the French Quarter (of New Orleans); the French Revolution; the* **French shore** *(of Newfoundland from Cape St. John to Cape Ray, of Nova Scotia between Yarmouth and Digby); French wines.*
— **French·man** (-mun) *n.* **-men; French·wom·an** *n.* **-wom·en.**

French Canada *n.* **1** Quebec and other parts of Canada where French is spoken. **2** French Canadians as a group.

French Canadian *n.* **1** a Canadian of French origin; Franco-Canadian. **2** the Canadian French language. Also *adj.*

French dressing *n.* a salad dressing of oil, vinegar, and seasonings.

French fact *n. Cdn.* the distinct cultural entity of French Canada.

French fries *n.pl.* deep-fried strips of potato.
— **French-fry** *v.* **-fries, -fried, -fry·ing** fry potatoes, shrimps, onion rings, etc. in deep fat. Also **french-fry.**

French toast *n.* a slice of bread dipped in an egg-and-milk mixture and sautéed.

fre·net·ic (fri·NET·ic) *adj.* frenzied or fanatic.
— **fre·net·i·cal·ly** *adv.*

fren·zied (FREN·zeed) *adj.* full of frenzy: *He shook his fists in a frenzied rage.*

fren·zy (FREN·zee) *n.* **-zies** emotional agitation tending to violent activity: *in a wild frenzy; a frenzy of despair.*

fre·on (FREE·on) *n.* a commercially produced fluorocarbon fluid, used as a refrigerant, solvent, etc.; **Freon** *Trademark.*

fre·quen·cy (FREEK·wun·see) *n.* **-cies** the number of times that cycles, oscillations, or other repeated things or events are found in a given period or sample: *Our electric current has a frequency of 60 cycles per second; "The" has the highest frequency among English words; Accidents happen with alarming frequency during holiday weekends; Each radio station is on a different frequency (of radio waves); radio transmission by **frequency modulation** instead of amplitude modulation.*

fre·quent (FREE·kwunt) *adj.* occurring often: *a frequent visitor to the zoo.* — *v.* (free·KWENT) go to habitually: *a restaurant frequented by students.* — **fre·quent·ly** *adv.*

fresh *adj.* **1** new or pure, not stale, used, preserved, etc.: *fresh as a daisy; the fresh morning air; Fresh meat is not salted, canned, or frozen; to make a fresh start in life after failures; a tragedy still fresh in our memories; She was fresh (= recently) out of school when she married; a **fresh breeze** blowing 29 – 38 km/h.* **2** inexperienced: *He's rather fresh on the job.* **3** *Informal.* bold or impudent: *Don't get fresh with me!*

fresh·en (FRESH·un) *v.* make fresh: *a cream to freshen your complexion; Use the powder room to **freshen up** before dinner.* — **fresh·en·er** *n.:* *an air freshener; skin freshener.*

fresh·et (FRESH·it) *n.* a rush of fresh water, as from a thaw or heavy rain.

fresh·man (FRESH·mun) *n.* **-men** a beginner, esp. a first-year student; *adj.:* *freshman composition, English; a freshman congressman, senator (in his or her first year).*

fresh·wa·ter (FRESH·wau·tur) *adj.* **1** of or living in lakes and streams, not in salt water: *a freshwater fish.* **2** inexperienced: *a freshwater sailor.* **3** out-of-the-way or obscure: *a freshwater college.*

fret *v.* **frets, fret·ted, fret·ting** **1** worry or be vexed: *He tends to fret and fume about or over trifles; a child fretting against parental control.* **2** eat away or corrode: *river banks fretted by the force of water.* — *n.* **1** *Informal.* state of agitation or irritation: *to get in a fret when something goes wrong.* **2** erosion. **3** one of the ridges as guides for fingering across the fingerboard of a guitar, banjo, etc.

Freud·i·an (FROY·dee·un) *adj.* having to do with Sigmund Freud, the founder of psychoanalysis: *A "Freudian slip" is supposed to reveal something in the unconscious mind.*

fri·a·ble (FRY·uh·bul) *adj.* crumbly, as dry soil.

fri·ar (FRY·ur) *n.* a member of a mendicant Roman Catholic order of monks, as a Carmelite or Franciscan.

fric·tion (FRIK·shun) *n.* **1** resistance from rubbing of one thing against another: *Oil is used to reduce friction between moving metal parts.* **2** disagreement or unpleasantness: *to create friction between employees and management; office frictions due to personality differences; family frictions.*

Fri·day (FRY·dee, -day) *n.* **1** the sixth day of the week. **2** a faithful helper: *my man Friday; girl Fridays; A clerk Friday wanted.*

fridge short form of REFRIGERATOR.

fried *pt. & pp.* of FRY.

friend (FREND) *n.* **1** one who likes, has common interests with, and desires another's good without being related: *my good friend Flo; a close personal friend, but not a boy friend or girl friend; a bosom, fair-weather, faithful, false, fast, intimate, life-long, loyal, mutual, special, staunch friend; a friend in need; the art of making and keeping friends; a friend of the poor; a **friend of the court** (= advisor); Who goes there, friend or foe? our friend (= the person or stranger) over there; **man's best friend** (= dog).* **2** friends: *I'm friends (= on friendly terms) with Ray; He's trying to make friends with (= be a friend of) everyone; Al and Lu just made friends (= made up) after a good fight.* **3** **Friend** a Quaker: *the Society of Friends.*

friend·ly (FREND·lee) *adj.* **-li·er, -li·est** of or like a friend: *friendly advice, arguments, disputes, dogs, games, greetings, manner, smiles, spirit, welcome; to be friendly to or toward or with someone.* — **friend·li·ness** *n.*

friend·ship *n.* the condition of being friends or an instance of it: *to break up, cement, cherish, cultivate, destroy, develop, promote, strike up a friendship; a firm, lifelong, strong, warm friendship between two people; the bonds of friendship among school chums; a long friendship; friendships that last.*

frier same as FRYER.

fright (FRITE) *n.* fear, esp. when sudden and passing: *Your Halloween costume gave me quite a fright; Her hat was a real fright (Informal for fearsome thing).*

fright·en (FRY·tun) *v.* cause to feel sudden fear or become afraid: *a child frightened into submission; Her screams frightened off the attacker; adj.:* *the **frightening** experience of being kidnapped; adv.:* *the **frighteningly** high numbers of highway deaths.*

fright·ful *adj.* **1** terrible: *a frightful tragedy.* **2** *Informal.* [intensifier]: *What a frightful snob! He left in a frightful hurry.*

fright·ful·ly (FRITE·fuh·lee) *adv.* **1** alarmingly. **2** *Informal.* very: *I'm frightfully sorry.*

frig·id (FRIJ·id) *adj.* **1** extremely cold, as in the **Frigid Zone,** either of the two regions within the Arctic and Antarctic circles: *frigid air, temperatures, water, weather, winds.* **2** cold or aloof in manner: *He received a frigid reception; frigid relations between spouses.* — **frig·id·ly** *adv.* — **fri·gid·i·ty** (fri·JID·uh·tee) *n.*

frill *n.* **1** a ruffle or similar edging or trimming: *frills and furbelows.* **2** something serving as an ornament: *rebates, gifts, and other frills to attract shoppers: Some consider out-of-school trips educational frills.* — **frill·y** *adj.*

fringe (FRINJ) *n.* **1** a border ornament or trimming of loose threads or cords, as on a shawl or rug, often tied in

bunches: *a clipped fringe of hair over the forehead.*
2 the outer edge or limit: *criminals, drug pushers,
thieves, and others on the fringes of society; the lunatic
fringe (of people with extremist views); the poor TV
reception experienced in* **fringe areas** (= outer areas);
We provide pension, health insurance, and such **fringe
benefits** *to employees.*
— *v.* **fring·es, fringed, fring·ing** border: *trees fringing
a lawn; a fringing coral reef growing outward from the
shoreline; Some flowers have fringed petals (with
borders).*

frip·per·y (FRIP·uh·ree) *n.* **frip·per·ies 1** cheap finery.
2 affected elegance: *the fripperies of speech and
behaviour.*

fris·bee *n.* a saucer-shaped plastic disk for tossing back
and forth in games; **Fris·bee** *Trademark.*

frisk *v.* **1** move in a lively, playful manner: *lambs
frisking about in the sun.* **2** search a person for
concealed weapons or goods, as police do after an arrest.

frisk·y *adj.* **frisk·i·er, -i·est** lively or playful: *a frisky
little pup.* — **frisk·i·ly** *adv.;* **frisk·i·ness** *n.*

frit·ter (FRIT·ur) *n.* a small cake of fried batter
containing corn, sliced fruit, fish, or other filling.
— *v.* waste little by little: *to fritter away one's time and
energies on* or *in useless pursuits.*

fritz *n.* **on the fritz** *Slang.* out of order; on the blink:
Our TV goes on the fritz now and then.

friv·o·lous (FRIV·uh·lus) *adj.* **1** trivial: *to waste money
on frivolous baubles.* **2** light-minded or giddy: *frivolous
behaviour; a frivolous remark.* — **friv·o·lous·ly** *adv.*
— **fri·vol·i·ty** (fri·VOL·uh·tee) *n.*

friz or **frizz** *v.* form hair into tight little curls.
— *n.* such hair.

friz·zle (FRIZ·ul) *v.* **friz·zles, friz·zled, friz·zling 1** frizz
or curl. **2** sizzle, fry, or broil.

friz·zly (FRIZ·lee) or **friz·zy** (FRIZ·ee) *adj.* curly: *frizzly
hair.*

fro (FROH) *adv.* **to and fro** to somewhere and back;
back and forth.

frock *n.* **1** formerly, an outer garment or robe worn by
friars and monks; also, a man's double-breasted **frock-
coat. 2** a woman's or child's dress.

frog *n.* **1** a small, tailless, amphibious jumping animal
with long hind legs and webbed feet: *the croaking of
frogs.* **2** *Informal.* hoarseness; also **frog in the throat.**

frol·ic (FROL·ic) *n.* play or fun, esp. of a light-hearted,
carefree nature.
— *v.* **-ics, -icked, -ick·ing** make merry; gambol about.
— **frol·ick·er** *n.* — **frol·ic·some** (-sum) *adj.*

from (FRUM, FROM) *prep.* **1** [indicating a starting
point or source]: *It's 10 km from home to school; I know
him from way back in the old country; It's a great idea
from my point of view; cars priced from $20 000 to $30
000; Tell her from me she's wrong; A picture painted
from life has to look lifelike; She knows about rockets
from the ground up; Mistakes happen from time to
time.* **2** [indicating a cause or motive]: *shivering from
the cold; It sounds fine from what I was told; speaking
from envy.* **3** [indicating a difference or distinction]:
*Humans are different from animals; Can you tell a frog
from a toad?*

frond *n.* **1** a large leaf: *banana fronds; fern fronds;
palm fronds.* **2** a tender coiled shoot: *the fronds of the
fiddlehead fern.*

front (FRUNT) *n.* **1** the forward or most important part
or side: *The driver is seated in front; a shirt front
covered by a tie; Top marks place you in front; a cold
front* (= air mass) *moving in from the Arctic; a
stationary front; a warm front; to park* **in front of** *a
house; They pay you* **up front** (= in advance). **2** a scene
of activity: *No news from the western front (of battle);
the fighting going on at the front; trouble brewing on
the labour front.* **3** land or a road facing a body of
water: *a villa on the lake front; river front; sea front.*
4 a face or cover: *His geniality is a mere front; He put
on a bold, brazen front; a travel business used as a front*
(= façade) *for a spy operation.*
— *adj.* forward: *the* **front end** *and rear end of a car;
fighting in* or *on the front lines; The most important
news makes* **the front page;** *a front seat;* **front money**
(*Informal* for advance payment).
— *v.* face: *The cottage fronts on a lake; windows
fronting the street.*

front·age (FRUNT·ij) *n.* **1** (extent of) land between a
building and a street, river, or lake that it faces. **2** a
building's exposure: *a church with a southern frontage;
the frontage* (= width) *and depth of a building lot.*

front·al (FRUN·tul) *adj.* having to do with the front: *a
direct, frontal assault, attack; the frontal lobe of the
brain.*

front burner *n.* usually **on the front burner,** in a
position of priority; cf. BACK BURNER.

front-end *n.* having to do with the front: *the front-end
costs of buying a home; a* **front-end loader** (= tracked
construction vehicle with a scoop in front for picking up
earth, fodder, etc.).

fron·tier (frun·TEER) *n.* **1** the border between two
countries: *a shooting incident on the Sino-Soviet
frontier.* **2** a region whose borders are being extended
into newly explored territory: *the new frontiers opened
up by space exploration; to advance, cross, extend a
frontier; the frontiers of medicine; in the frontier days
when the pioneers were moving West; a frontier town.*

fron·tiers·man (frun·TEERZ·mun) *n.* **-men** a man living
on the frontier.

front office *n.* headquarters; hence, administrative authority.

front-runner (FRUNT·run·ur) *n.* the leading contender.

frost *n.* a freezing, the state of being frozen, or frozen dew, vapour, or hoarfrost: *There's a touch of frost in the air; the severe frost of January.*
— *v.* cover with or like frost: *to frost a cake.*
— **frosted** *adj.*: *a frosted car window (covered with frost); frosted* (=nontransparent) *glass for bathroom windows, electric bulbs, etc.); crunchy frosted flakes (covered with sugar); a frosted cake (covered with icing).*

frost·bite *n.* injury to skin and body tissue from exposure to cold.
— *v.* -bites, -bit, -bit·ten, -bit·ing: *a frostbitten foot.*

frost heave *n.* a heaving of the ground caused by moisture freezing underneath.

frosting *n.* 1 icing. 2 *Informal.* an extra bonus: *The bonus payment was the frosting on the cake.*

frost·y *adj.* frost·i·er, -i·est 1 freezing or covered with frost. 2 cold or unfriendly: *a frosty welcome.*

froth *n.* foam, esp. as scum; hence, something worthless: *a discussion that was all froth and no substance; v.: an overworked horse frothing at the mouth.*
— **froth·y** *adj.*: *a frothy discussion.*

fro·ward (FROH·urd) *adj.* of people, difficult to manage; willful. — **fro·ward·ness** *n.*

frown (rhyme: "down") *v.* 1 wrinkle the forehead, as in disapproval: *It's no use frowning at your poor grades.* 2 show displeasure: *Teachers frown on* or *upon latecomers.* — *n.* a frowning expression or face.

frow·zy (FROW·zee, "OW" as in "how") *adj.* -zi·er, -zi·est untidy or unkempt; also **frow·sy.**

froze See FREEZE.

fro·zen (FROH·zun) *adj.* 1 hardened by cold: *frozen food (kept in a freezer); frozen hard in the cold; Ice is water frozen solid; a frozen lake, water main; the Frozen North* (=the Arctic). 2 made motionless, stiff, or fixed: *He stood there frozen with fear; Rents have been frozen* (=fixed) *for two years; All foreign assets were frozen* (=prohibited from being removed) *while the war was on.*

fruc·ti·fy (FRUC·tuh·fye) *v.* -fies, -fied, -fy·ing bear fruit; make productive: *plans that didn't fructify.*

fru·gal (FROO·gul) *adj.* sparing, not wasteful; simple in regard to food, clothing, etc.: *a frugal meal, people; frugal habits.* — **fru·gal·ly** *adv.*
— **fru·gal·i·ty** (froo·GAL·uh·tee) *n.*

fruit (FROOT) *n.* 1 the edible, often sweet, fleshy, and juicy part of a plant or tree, as apples, bananas, or grapes: *We grow fruits and vegetables in our backyard; Trees bear fruit; canned, dried, fresh, frozen, luscious fruit; forbidden fruit.* 2 any seed-bearing or useful plant product, as pea pods, cereal grains, green peppers, and such vegetables: *thanksgiving for the fruits of the earth.* 3 product or result: *the fruits of our labour; work that did not bear fruit.*

fruit·cake *n.* 1 a rich cake containing raisins, nuts, spices, etc. 2 *Informal.* an eccentric or insane person: *He's nutty as a fruitcake.*

fru·i·tion (froo·ISH·un) *n.* fulfilment or realization: *the fruition of our hopes; when our plans finally came to fruition; to bring them to fruition.*

fruit·y (FROO·tee) *adj.* fruit·i·er, -i·est rich or mellow in flavour, tone of voice, interest, etc.

frump *n.* one who is shabby or dowdy, esp. a woman; also, this quality: *Frump is out, glamour is in.*
— **frump·ish** or **frump·y** *adj.*

frus·trate (FRUS·trate) *v.* -trates, -trat·ed, -trat·ing prevent someone from accomplishing something or getting something done; make someone ineffective: *She felt frustrated in her attempts to educate her child; It was frustrating for her to try to do it all by herself.*
— **frus·tra·tion** (frus·TRAY·shun) *n.*: *a life of loneliness and frustration; It was no use venting his frustrations on his family; Some take to drinking to forget their frustrations.*

fry *v.* fries, fried, fry·ing cook in a pan or on a griddle, esp. using fat: *Please fry me two eggs; "Out of the frying pan into the fire"* (=From something bad into something worse).
— *n.* 1 *pl.* fries, something fried, as FRENCH FRIES. 2 an outdoor social gathering at which fried food is served: *a fish fry.* 3 *sing.* & *pl.* small, esp. young fish: *The small fry* (=children) *are also invited.*

fry·er *n.* 1 a utensil for deep-frying. 2 a chicken suitable for frying, usually larger than a BROILER.

fud·dle *v.* fud·dles, fud·dled, fud·dling confuse or stupefy, as with drink.

fud·dy-dud·dy *n.* -dud·dies *Informal.* a fussy or old-fashioned, usually elderly person.

fudge (FUJ) *n.* 1 a rich, soft, often chocolate-flavoured candy. 2 nonsense.
— *v.* fudg·es, fudged, fudg·ing falsify or cheat: *to fudge on one's income tax return; to fudge* (=hedge) *on a promise; to fudge* (=dodge) *an issue.*

fu·el (FEW·ul) *n.* a substance such as coal, gasoline, ethane, or oil which, when burned, produces heat or power: *We ran out of fuel and were stranded on the highway; Uranium and hydrogen are atomic fuels liberating energy by fusion or fission; Fossil fuels will one day be exhausted; He managed only to add fuel to the fire* (=make the situation worse).
— *v.* fu·els, fu·elled or fu·eled, fu·el·ling or fu·el·ing supply with or get fuel: *a plane fuelling up before a flight.*

fu·gi·tive (FEW·juh·tiv) *n.* one who flees: *a fugitive from justice; Dogs were used to track down the fugitives; adj.: the fugitive slaves; He tried to finish the job during the fugitive* (=fleeting) *hours of daylight.*

-ful *suffix.* 1 *n.* [pl. sometimes as "cupsful"] amount for filling: *cupful, handful, spoonful.* 2 *adj.* full of, as specified: *sorrowful, soulful, tuneful.*

ful·crum ("ful" as in "dull" or "full") *n.* -crums or -cra (-cruh) 1 the point of leverage or support, as of a crowbar. 2 the means of exerting pressure or influence.

ful·fil or **ful·fill** (full·FIL) *v.* -fils or -fills, -filled, -fil·ling perform, carry out, realize, complete, etc. something that is expected or required: *to fulfil a duty, promise, prophecy; customers' orders to be fulfilled* (= filled); *in search of a fulfilling* (= satisfying) *job; She fulfilled herself as a physician after trying nursing and teaching.* — **ful·fil·ment** or **ful·fill·ment** *n.*

full (short "oo") *adj.* complete in number, amount, extent, etc.; having everything needed to fill or satisfy: *The glass is full to the brim; It is full of water; "Full speed ahead!" shouted the captain; I'll cooperate to the fullest extent; a full skirt that is generous with material; a garden in full bloom; a popular movie playing to full houses; an associate professor promoted to full professor; a full-service gas station.* — *adv.: The ball hit her full* (= squarely) *in the face; Al knows full* (= quite) *well he is wrong.* — *n.: I was paid in full* (= all that had to be paid). — *v.* **fulls, fulled, full·ing 1** make full: *a dress fulled with wide folds.* **2** shrink and thicken wool and other cloths, as a **full·er** does. — **ful·ly** *adv.*

full-blooded *adj.* purebred; hence, vigorous or genuine: *full-blooded capitalism, patriotism, a full-blooded judicial inquiry.*

full-blown *adj.* fully grown or mature: *full-blown flowers; The roadside check could lead to a full-blown breath test at the police station; It was not a conference, but a full-blown convention; The nomination race was the start of a full-blown election campaign; The slowdown developed into a full-blown strike; a full-blown inquiry, personality, success.*

full-bodied *adj.* having much flavour or strength: *a rich, full-bodied, fruity wine; the brew's full-bodied taste; a glossy full-bodied production.*

full-course *adj.* **1** consisting of an appetizer or salad, main dish, dessert, and beverage: *a full-course dinner, lunch, meal.* **2** involving one complete lap of a racecourse: *a full-course caution flag, caution period.*

full-dress *adj.* observing all formalities: *a full-dress parliamentary debate.*

full-fledged *adj.* fully developed; of full rank.

full-length *adj.* having regular length: *standing before a full-length mirror in a full-length dress; a full-length movie, portrait.*

full moon *n.* the moon in its fully illuminated phase.

full-scale *adj.* not reduced in size; complete: *a full-scale attack, investigation, operation, production, riot, war.*

full time *n.* the full working day, as from 9 to 5; *adv.: She works here full time; adj.: a full-time, not part-time employee doing full-time work.*

ful·mi·nate (FUL·muh·nate, "FUL" as in "DULL") *v.* **-nates, -nat·ed, -nat·ing** thunder forth threats, denunciations, etc.: *the media fulminating against restrictions on freedom of the press.* — **ful·mi·na·tion** (-NAY·shun) *n.*

ful·some (FULL·sum, short "oo") *adj.* excessive or insincere: *fulsome flattery, praise.*

fum·ble *v.* **-bles, -bled, -bling 1** fail to catch a ball; hence, bungle: *a fumbled job.* **2** grope clumsily: *He fumbled about in the dark for the key he dropped; Then fumbled with the lock* (= handled it clumsily in the dark).

fume *n.* a choking or offensive gas, smoke, or vapour, as from an exhaust: *It's dangerous to inhale the fumes.* — *v.* **fumes, fumed, fum·ing 1** treat: *Oak wood is fumed with ammonia gas for a darker colour.* **2** be angry: *The boss is fuming about* or *at* or *over the slow mail delivery.*

fun *n.* amusement or what provides amusement; sport: *Skating is fun; We had a lot of fun skating; Children throw snowballs for fun* or *in fun; Guy likes to poke fun at* or *make fun of Cora's walk; The rain spoiled the fun; Life is not all fun and games.* — *adj.* providing enjoyment: *We had a fun time at the party; It's not fun or funny to tease dumb animals.*

func·tion (FUNK·shun) *n.* **1** the kind of work that a person or thing is supposed to do: *The heart's function is to pump blood; a bodily function; the functions of a bank; the mathematical functions of a calculator; Each part has its own function to perform* or *fulfill.* **2** a formal occasion such as a wedding or an opening ceremony: *to attend a function; a social function.* **3** a variable quantity that is related to another: *A circle's radius is a function of its area.* — *v.* operate or perform: *The new computer is functioning well; We need someone to function as chairperson of the meeting.*

func·tion·al (FUNK·shuh·nul) *adj.* having to do with operation rather than structure or decoration: *functional architecture; a functional disorder with no organic causes for the organ's not working properly; A functional illiterate, in spite of some schooling, is unable to perform minimally as a literate (e.g. fill out an application for a driver's licence).* — **func·tion·al·ly** *adv.*

func·tion·ar·y (FUNK·shuh·nair·ee) *n.* **-ar·ies** an official with routine duties.

fund *n.* **1** a stock or supply, as of money: *Give to the heart fund; to establish* or *set up a fund; an entertaining speaker with a fund of anecdotes.* **2 funds** *pl.* money, esp. ready money: *We pay in Canadian funds; The cheque was returned because of insufficient funds (in the account); Welfare payments come out of public funds; to disburse, pay out, raise funds for a project; the funds required to get it going; Our funds dried up* or *ran out toward the end of the year; a hospital built out of private funds; (equal) matching funds offered by the government.* — *v.* **1** provide funds for something: *a federally funded program.* **2** convert: *A short-term debt is funded into a long-term one at a fixed interest rate.*

fun·da·men·tal (fun·duh·MEN·tul) *adj.* essential or basic: *a citizen's fundamental rights and freedoms as in the Canadian Charter.* — *n.* a fundamental principle or fact: *the fundamentals of algebra.* — **fun·da·men·tal·ly** *adv.*

fun·da·men·tal·ism (fun·duh·MEN·tul·iz·um) *n.* belief in or the following of a literal interpretation of the rules of a religion. — **fun·da·men·tal·ist** *n. & adj.*

fu·ner·al (FEW·nur·ul) *n.* a ceremony honouring a dead person before cremation or burial: *to conduct, hold a funeral; a military, state funeral; a funeral director*

(= undertaker or mortician).
— **fu·ner·ar·y** *adj.*: *a funerary urn.*

funeral home or **funeral parlour** *n.* an establishment where the dead are embalmed and prepared for burial or cremation, often with a chapel for visiting mourners.

fu·ne·re·al (few·NEER·ee·ul) *adj.* gloomy or dismal: *a funereal expression.*

fun·gi·cide (FUN·juh·cide) *n.* a fungus-destroying chemical.

fun·gus (FUNG·gus) *n., pl.* **-gi** (-jye) or **-gus·es** any of the lowest members of the plant kingdom having no stems, leaves, flowers, or chlorophyll, including mushrooms, moulds, and mildews.
— **fun·gal** (-gul) or **fun·gous** (-gus) *adj.*

funk *n. Informal.* 1 panic; lack of courage; also, a state of depression: *blue funk; in a deep funk.* 2 an art form using strange or bizarre objects. 3 funky music.

funk·y *adj.* **funk·i·er, -i·est** *Slang.* 1 smelly or earthy; hence, down-to-earth. 2 fashionable or trendy: *funky rock music; the funky platform shoes of the 1970s.*
— **funk·i·ness** *n.*

fun·nel (FUN·ul) *n.* 1 a wide-mouthed, tapering utensil for pouring liquids, grain, etc. into a narrow-mouthed container; hence, anything of similar shape: *the funnel of a tornado.* 2 a smokestack or flue.
— *v.* **fun·nels, fun·nelled** or **fun·neled, fun·nel·ling** or **fun·nel·ing** send through a funnel: *the funnelling of aid to poor countries; state secrets funnelled out through the embassies.*

fun·nies *n. pl.* comic strips or a section of a newspaper containing these.

fun·ny (FUN·ee) *adj.* **fun·ni·er, fun·ni·est** 1 amusing: *very funny; That's not funny!* 2 *Informal.* tricky or strange: *a funny feeling; There's something funny about his absence; Isn't it funny that there's no one home? funny* (= counterfeit) *money.*
— **fun·ni·ly** *adv.;* **fun·ni·ness** *n.*

funny bone *n.* 1 a sensitive spot at the back of the elbow that produces a painful tingling sensation when struck. 2 one's sense of humour.

fur *n.* 1 the soft, thick hair of mink, ermine, fox, etc. 2 this processed and made into a garment. 3 a furlike coating, as on a sick person's tongue or the lime deposit on a surface, as of a kettle.
— *adj.* having to do with fur: *a fur coat, company, post, trail; fur farming, trade.*
— **make the fur fly** *Informal.* create an uproar.
— *v.* **furs, furred, fur·ring** cover or become covered with fur: *a furred kettle.*

fur·be·low (FUR·buh·loh) *n.* a flounce, ruffle, or something showy or superfluous: *frills and furbelows.*

fur·bish *v.* burnish; also, renovate.

fur brigade *n. Cdn.* formerly, a fleet of canoes, dog sleds, carts, etc. carrying goods from inland trading posts.

Fu·ries (FYOOR·eez) *n. pl.* three snake-haired female avengers of Greek and Roman myths.

fu·ri·ous (FYOOR·ee·us) *adj.* filled with fury; hence, wild or violent: *a furious attack, storm; working at a*

furious pace; Flo is furious about or *at* or *over being bumped from the flight; furious that she missed her appointment.* — **fu·ri·ous·ly** *adv.*

furl *v.* roll up a flag, umbrella, sail, etc.

fur·lough (FUR·loh) *n.* leave of absence from duty, esp. in the military: *He's home on furlough.*
— *v.* give furlough to someone.

fur·nace (-nis) *n.* a chamber in which fuel is burned to heat buildings, melt metals, etc.: *a blast furnace; coal furnace; to stoke a furnace; Our home furnace is a gas furnace; oil furnace.*

fur·nish *v.* supply, provide, or equip with what is useful or needed: *a library well furnished with books; a loan to furnish an apartment (with furniture, drapes, etc.); a tastefully furnished living room; music furnished* (= provided) *by a band; Can you furnish* (= give) *one good reason why you're late?*

furnishings *n. pl.* 1 furniture, carpets, cushions, etc. 2 dress accessories, esp. men's.

fur·ni·ture (FUR·nuh·chur) *n.* the usually movable equipment such as chairs, tables, and beds for living or working, as for a home, office, or ship: *garden furniture; lawn furniture; unfinished furniture (ready for painting, etc.); upholstered furniture.*

fu·ror (FYOOR·or) *n.* a noisy outburst from a crowd; uproar: *The announcement created a furor in the audience.*

fur·ri·er (FUR·ee·ur) *n.* one who processes or deals in furs.

fur·row (FUR·oh) *n.* a track cut in the ground by a plough; also, anything similar, as a rut made by a wheel or a deep wrinkle on one's brow.
— *v.* make a furrow: *a face furrowed with age.*

fur·ry *adj.* made of, covered with, or soft like fur.
— **fur·ri·ness** *n.*

fur·ther ("th" as in "the") *adj. & adv.* 1 [a comp. of FAR] farther; more distant: *Go no further.* 2 additional: *No further action is necessary; The show is over until further notice; adj.: He refused to discuss it any further* (= more).
— *v.* advance or promote: *to further the aims of justice.*
— **fur·ther·ance** (FUR·thur·unce) *n.: steps taken in furtherance of his aims.*

fur·ther·more (FUR·thur·more) *adv.* moreover.

fur·thest *adj. & adv.* a superl. of FAR.

fur·tive (-tiv) *adj.* stealthy or sneaky: *The child took a few furtive steps and stole a glance into the room.*
— **fur·tive·ly** *adv.;* **fur·tive·ness** *n.*

fu·ry (FYOOR·ee) *n.* **-ries** 1 rage or frenzy tending to violence: *the proverbial fury of a scorned woman; He flew into a fury when told he had lost the bid; He vented his fury on* or *upon everyone around; pent-up, savage, unbridled fury; the fury of the elements* (= stormy weather). 2 **Fury** any of the FURIES or one like them.

fuse (FEWZ) *n.* 1 a slow-burning wick ("safety fuse") as used in blasting: *Don't light the fuse yet; Ho has a short fuse (Informal for* is short-tempered). 2 a mechanical or electrical device, usually **fuze,** for setting off an

explosive charge, as in guns and shells: *to arm* or *set a fuse; a percussion fuse; a time fuse.* **3** a cartridge or plug containing a wire or metal strip that melts and breaks an electrical circuit as a safety device: *to blow (out) a fuse; What made the fuse blow (out)? to change a fuse.*
— **blow a fuse** *Informal.* lose one's temper.
— *v.* **fus·es, fused, fus·ing 1** melt, esp. unite or blend by melting together: *furnaces to fuse zinc and copper into brass; One party fused with the other; a new party fused* (= formed) *out of many factions.* **2** equip a bomb, mine, etc. with a fuse; also **fuze.**

fu·see (few·ZEE) *n.* **1** a large-headed friction match. **2** a signal flare used on railroads and highways.

fu·se·lage (FEW·suh·lahzh) *n.* the body of an airplane housing the controls, crew, passengers, and cargo.

fu·si·ble (FEW·zuh-) *adj.* that can be fused: *Alloys are more fusible than pure metals.*
— **fu·si·bil·i·ty** (-BIL·uh·tee) *n.*

fu·sil·lade (FEW·suh·lade, -lahd) *n.* rapid gunfire: *a fusillade of questions from the press.*

fu·sion (FEW·zhun) *n.* **1** a fusing or melting: *the fusion of metals in making alloys.* **2** union: *the fusion of many cultures in a nation; the nuclear fusion of atoms in the hydrogen bomb; a fusion bomb.*

fuss *n.* unnecessary bother, esp. about trivial things: *He kicked up a fuss* (= row) *because I spilled some soup; What a fuss she makes about* or *over her picture in the paper!*
— *v.* make a fuss: *He fusses a lot about* or *over his wife and kids; Don't fuss with that dress, it looks all right; Flo fussed about* (= behaved anxiously) *all morning but achieved little.*

fuss·budg·et (FUSS·buj·it) or **fuss·pot** *n. Informal.* one who fusses over trifles.

fuss·y *adj.* **fuss·i·er, -i·est:** *He's very fussy* (= particular) *about his steaks; a dress too fussy* (= full of details requiring much attention) *to make in one day.*
— **fuss·i·ly** *adv.;* **fuss·i·ness** *n.*

fus·tian (FUS·chun) *n.* **1** a coarse twilled cloth with a velvety pile. **2** inflated talk or writing; bombast;

claptrap.

fus·ty *adj.* **-ti·er, -ti·est 1** stale-smelling or musty. **2** old-fashioned; out-of-date.
— **fus·ti·ly** *adv.;* **fus·ti·ness** *n.*

fu·tile (FEW·tul, -tile) *adj.* of no use; ineffectual: *All his attempts proved futile; It's futile to argue with him; a futile question; a futile* (= frivolous) *young man.*
— **fu·tile·ly** *adv.* — **fu·til·i·ty** (few·TIL·uh·tee) *n.*

fu·ton (FEW·ton, FOO-, *rhyme:* "on") *n.* a thin mattress used for sleeping on the floor.

fu·ture (FEW·chur) *n.* **1** time to come after the present; also, events to come: *We face an uncertain future; a bleak, bright, promising, unforeseeable future; to look into, plan, predict the future; in the distant, immediate, near future; Who knows what the future may bring; a career with a future* (= bright prospects); *He'll be more careful* **in future;** *savings to provide* **for the future.** **2** an English verb form constructed with "shall" and "will," as "We will go." **3 futures** *pl.* commodities and stocks bought for future acceptance or delivery.
— *adj.:* *the future tense of a verb; our future life (after death); the* **future shock** *or distress of coping with the rapid changes in modern society.*
— **fu·tu·ri·ty** (few·TURE·uh·tee, few·CHOOR·uh·tee) *n.* **-ties.**

futz (FUTZ) *v. Slang.* **futz around** loaf or fool around.

fuze See FUSE.

fuzee same as FUSEE.

fuzz (FUZ) *n. sing. & pl.* **1** loose, fluffy fibres, particles, or hairs, as of down or wool, or as on a peach or a caterpillar's back. **2 the fuzz** *Slang.* the police; a police officer. — *v.* make or become fuzzy.

fuz·zy (FUZ·ee) *adj.* **fuz·zi·er, fuz·zi·est** of or like fuzz; hence, blurred or indistinct: *a fuzzy photograph; fuzzy thinking; a politician whose speeches are fuzzy on the issues; the fuzzy set of "average Canadians"* (= a grouping with no sharply defined boundaries).
— **fuz·zi·ly** *adv.;* **fuz·zi·ness** *n.*

-fy *v. suffix.* make or become: *glorify, liquefy, magnify, simplify.*

G or **g** (JEE) *n.* **G's** or **g's** the seventh letter of the English alphabet; hence, the seventh in a series.

gab *v.* **gabs, gabbed, gab·bing** *Informal.* talk rapidly, excessively, or thoughtlessly; chatter.
— *n.* esp. **the gift of (the) gab,** fluency of speech.
— **gab·ber** *n.*

gab·ble (GAB·ul) *v.* **gab·bles, gab·bled, gab·bling**
1 talk quickly or incoherently; jabber or babble.
2 cackle.
— *n.* confused and voluble talk: *the gabble at a bazaar.*

gab·by (GAB·ee) *adj.* **gab·bi·er, gab·bi·est** *Informal.* talkative. — **gab·bi·ness** *n.*

gab·fest *n. Informal.* a gathering; also, a prolonged chat or gossiping.

ga·ble (GAY·bul) *n.* the triangular part of a wall at the end of a ridged roof: *a farmhouse called "Green Gables"; a gable window* (= a window in a gable or with a gable design). — **ga·bled** *adj.*

GABLE

gad *v.* **gads, gad·ded, gad·ding** roam or wander about: *The government ministers were accused of gadding about at public expense.*

gad·a·bout (GAD·uh·bowt) *n. Informal.* a rambler looking for fun.

gad·fly *n.* **-flies 1** a horsefly. **2** a persistently annoying person.

gadg·et (GAJ·it) *n.* **1** a small mechanical device. **2** a trivial object. — **gadg·et·ry** (-ree) *n.*

gaff *n.* **1** a pole with an iron hook used to land fish. **2** *Slang.* abuse.
— **stand the gaff** endure harsh treatment.
— *v.* land a fish with a gaff.

gaffe (GAF) *n.* a clumsy social blunder: *to make a gaffe.*

gaf·fer (GAF·ur) *n.* an old man.

gag *v.* **gags, gagged, gag·ging 1** prevent speech by stopping up the mouth; hence, restrain free speech. **2** block off or obstruct; hence, choke or retch: *to gag a valve; He gagged on his first puff of tobacco.* **3** make or tell jokes.
— *n.* **1** anything that stops the mouth or prevents speech: *A gag kept the kidnapped man from crying for help; the dictator's gag on the press; Courts sometimes issue **gag orders** on the media.* **2** *Informal.* an amusing joke or trick: *The flying saucer turned out to be a gag; Someone did it for a gag.*

ga·ga (GAH·gah) *adj. Slang.* wildly enthusiastic: *The kids went gaga for* or *over Superman.*

gage (GAIJ) *n.* **1** a pledge or challenge to fight. **2** formerly, a glove, hat, or similar object thrown down as a gesture of defiance. **3** same as GAUGE.
— *v.* **gag·es, gaged, gag·ing.**

gag·gle (GAG·ul) *n.* a flock, group, or cluster: *a gaggle of geese, people; a gaggle of streamers flying from the car window.*

gag·man *n.* **-men** a writer of jokes or comic routines.

gai·e·ty (GAY·uh·tee) *n.* **-ties 1** the state of being gay or cheerful. **2** gay or festive entertainment: *to join in the gaieties of the season.* **3** bright, showy appearance: *gaiety of dress.*

gai·ly *adj.* in a gay manner: *a gaily caparisoned horse; gaily coloured packages; gaily decorated lunchboxes; a house gaily painted in pink; a gaily wrapped gift.*

gain *v.* obtain or acquire, esp. as an achievement, addition, advantage, or profit: *He gained recognition by his memoirs; Our firm gained $10 000 in the deal; You gain weight by overeating; The climbers soon gained* (= reached) *the summit; This clock gains* (= is faster by) *a few seconds each day; He's slowly gaining strength after his recent illness; A faster runner was **gaining on*** (= drawing nearer to) *the champion; We tried to **gain*** (= win) ***him over** to our side.*
— *n.* something obtained or increased; profit: *the gains made last year in sales volume; a considerable, enormous, notable, tangible, tremendous gain; a gain in efficiency; losses and gains; a tax on capital gains; ill-gotten gains.*

gain·ful *adj.* profitable.
— **gain·ful·ly** *adv.*: *gainfully employed* (= working for a living).

gain·say *v.* **-says, -said, -say·ing** deny or contradict: *It cannot be gainsaid that he is popular; There is no gainsaying his popularity.* — **gain·say·er** *n.*

gait *n.* 1 manner or style of moving on foot: *a heavy, shambling, steady, unsteady gait; the comic Charlie Chaplin gait; the loping gait of Steve Fonyo walking across Canada.* 2 a horse's trot, pace, canter, or gallop: *After breaking stride at the half-mile mark, our horse got back on gait to finish second.*
— **-gait·ed** *combining form.* having a gait as specified: *heavy-gaited; slow-gaited; a smooth-gaited animal.*

gai·ter (GAY·tur) *n.* an outer covering for the leg reaching from the instep to ankle, mid-calf, or knee; legging or spat.

ga·la (GAY·luh, GAL·uh) *n.* a celebration or festival.
— *adj.* festive: *a gala evening; The party was a gala affair, event; a gala occasion.*

ga·lac·tic (guh·LAC·tic) *adj.* 1 having to do with a galaxy: *galactic cluster, nebulae; galactic noise from the Milky Way.* 2 huge or large: *a galactic amount, sum; of galactic proportions.*

gal·ax·y (GAL·uk·see) *n.* **-ax·ies** 1 one of the many systems of stars, gas, and cosmic dust that form the universe, esp. the **Galaxy**, or the Milky Way. 2 a collection of illustrious people or things: *a galaxy of movie stars.*

gale *n.* 1 a strong wind: *a sudden gale; gale-force winds (32 to 63 mph or 50 to 102 km/h).* 2 an outburst: *gales of laughter.*

gall (GAWL) *n.* 1 a bitter secretion of the liver; bile. 2 anything bitter to endure; rancour or resentment. 3 *Informal.* impudence: *After cheating on the exam, the student had the unmitigated gall to accuse others of cheating.* 4 a sore caused by chafing.
— *v.* rub a sore spot on the skin; hence, annoy: *It galls me to have to wait for latecomers.*

gal·lant (GAL·unt) *adj.* 1 brave or dashing: *a gallant knight, soldier.* 2 [not used of people] stately or noble: *as gallant a ship as ever sailed; a gallant attempt, deed, display, effort, fight; a gallant (= high-spirited) horse.* 3 (guh·LANT) courteous, esp. polite to women: *the gallant attentiveness of a gallant escort; a gallant knight.*
— *n.* (guh·LANT) a stylish young man, esp. a lady's man.

gal·lant·ry (GAL·un·tree) *n.* **-ries** brave, spirited, or courteous behaviour or action: *a soldier's gallantry in battle; He displayed gallantry; courted her with little gallantries.*

gall·blad·der (GAWL·blad·ur) *n.* a sac situated under the liver in which excess bile is stored.

gal·ler·y (GAL·uh·ree) *n.* **gal·ler·ies** 1 a long, narrow outdoor balcony; porch. 2 a balcony in a theatre or public place, esp. the topmost balcony; also, the people seated in this area. 3 any group of spectators: *a performance applauded by the gallery; the*

parliamentary press gallery; the peanut gallery; They would much rather play to the gallery (= cater to the tastes of the masses) *than try to impress the elite.* 4 a long, narrow room or passageway; underground tunnel or passage: *a shooting gallery* (= indoor range). 5 an institution for displaying or selling works of art: *a picture gallery; the National Art Gallery.*

gal·ley (GAL·ee) *n.* 1 a ship of former times propelled by oars and sails. 2 the kitchen of an airplane or ship. 3 in printing, a tray holding type that has been set. 4 proof of typeset matter in single columns; also **galley proof.**

Gal·lic (GAL·ic) *adj.* having to do with Gaul or France: *Caesar's Gallic wars; a Gallic accent.*

Gal·li·cism (GAL·uh·siz·um) *n.* a French custom or characteristic.

gal·li·vant (GAL·uh·vant) *v.* roam about seeking fun.

gal·lon (GAL·un) *n.* a liquid measure equal to 4 quarts or 8 pints: *A U.S. gallon is 3.78 litres; The imperial gallon is 4.55 litres.*

gal·lop (GAL·up) *n.* the fastest pace of a horse or other four-legged animal: *She rode away at full gallop.*
— *v.* to move at this pace: *a horse galloping across a field; galloping inflation.*

gal·lows (GAL·oze) *n.* **-lows** or **-lows·es** a structure of usually two upright posts and a crossbeam used for hanging condemned criminals: *to be sent to the gallows.*

gallows humour *n.* humour based on a terrifying situation.

Gal·lup poll (GAL·up-) *n.* a survey of public opinion on a certain issue.

gal·lus·es (GAL·us·iz) *n.pl. Regional.* suspenders.

ga·lore (guh·LORE) *adj.* [used after its noun] in great numbers: *a big sale with bargains galore.*

ga·losh (guh·LOSH) *n.* a high rainproof overshoe: *a pair of galoshes.*

gal·van·ic (gal·VAN·ic) *adj.* producing electric current; also, electrical in effect: *a galvanic battery; The announcement produced a galvanic* (= nervous) *reaction.*

gal·va·nize (GAL·vuh·nize) *v.* **-niz·es, -nized, -niz·ing** 1 stimulate with electric current; hence, excite or startle: *The stock market was galvanized into activity by the encouraging news.* 2 to coat metal with rustproof zinc. — **gal·va·niz·er** *n.*
— **gal·va·ni·za·tion** (-nuh·ZAY·shun) *n.*

gam *n. Slang.* a leg, esp. of a woman.

gam·bit *n.* 1 a way of beginning a chess game by sacrificing a minor piece to gain an advantage. 2 an opening move, esp. a strategic one.

gam·ble (GAM·bul) *v.* **-bles, -bled, -bling** 1 bet or play games of chance; risk or lose something by gambling: *He gambled away the money he had won.* 2 take a risk or speculate: *to gamble on the stock market; We gambled on having good weather for the picnic.*
— *n.* a risky act: *to take a gamble on a new product.*
— **gam·bler** *n.*

gam·bol (GAM·bul) v. -bols, -bolled or -boled, -bol·ling or -bol·ing run friskily: *The lambs gambolled on the hillside.*

gam·brel (GAM·brul) or **gambrel roof** n. a roof, as of barns, that has two slopes on each side.

game n. 1 a form of playing; diversion or pastime; also, a competitive activity: *a game of chance; games of skill; a board game such as chess or checkers; parlour games; video games; word games and puzzles; numbers game* (=lottery); *war games* (=manoeuvres); *the Commonwealth, Olympic, summer, winter games* (=competitions). 2 a single contest in a competition: *to play a game; He won three out of four games; He threw the last game; The game was called because of rain; a championship, close, fair game; a home game (played at one's own place), not an away game.* 3 the number of points needed to win it: *21 points is a game in casino.* 4 any activity similar to sports in risk-taking, planning, competitiveness, etc.: *the game of diplomacy; the advertising game; a cat-and-mouse game (of constant escapes and captures); a con or confidence game; the mating game; a waiting game* (=strategy); *We saw through his game* (=deception). 5 animals hunted for food or sport; also, their flesh: *to eat deer and other game; to hunt for game; to stalk game; big game such as lions and elephants; small game such as rabbits and squirrels; Anyone is fair game for the April Fool;* adj: *a game park, preserve, or reserve (for the preservation of wild life).*
— **the game is up** the plan has failed.
— **to play the game** behave honourably according to rules.
— v. games, gamed, gam·ing to gamble.
— adj. 1 plucky or brave; also, ready: *a game youth; I'm game for a ride.* 2 lame: *a game leg.*

game fish n. a fish that is sought for sport with a hook and line.

game·keep·er (GAME·kee·pur) n. a person taking care of wildlife on a private reserve.

game plan n. planned strategy: *a politician's game plan.*

game point n. the point before the end of a game; also, the winning point.

games·man·ship (GAMES·mun·ship) n. skill in winning games, esp. by stratagems.

game·ster (GAIM·stur) n. a gambler.

game theory n. a mathematical method of determining the best strategy in games, business, war, etc.

game warden n. an official who enforces hunting and fishing regulations.

gamey same as GAMY.

gam·in (GAM·un) n. a street urchin; waif.

ga·mine (guh·MEEN) n. a roguish but charming girl.

gam·mon (GAM·un) n. 1 a smoked ham or side of bacon. 2 nonsensical or deceptive talk.

gam·ut (GAM·ut) n. a complete musical scale; hence, the full range of anything variable: *the whole gamut of emotions from joy to despair; At this resort, accommodation runs the gamut from small guest houses to large luxury hotels.*

gam·y (GAY·mee) adj. gam·i·er, -i·est 1 having the flavour of game, esp. when spoiled; hence, racy. 2 plucky. — gam·i·ness n.

gan·der (GAN·dur) n. 1 a male goose. 2 *Slang.* a look, esp. a close one, as if craning one's neck: *to take a gander at the goings-on.*

gang n. 1 a group of people associating or working together: *a road gang repairing streets; a work gang.* 2 a band of criminals or delinquents: *a gang of thieves; a juvenile gang; street gangs; to break up, form, join a gang.* 3 *combining form.* a set of similar items or units arranged to work together: gang drill, gang hook, gangplough, gangsaw, gangswitch.
— v. form into groups: *Boys ganged (up) together at the corner; The children decided to **gang up on** or **against** (Informal for* join and attack) *the bully.*

gang·land n. the gangster world.

gan·gling (GANG·gling) adj. -gli·er, -gli·est tall, thin, and awkward; loosely built. Also **gan·gly.**

gang·plank n. a removable ramp for boarding or leaving a ship.

gang·plough or **gang·plow** n. a plough equipped with several ploughshares.

gan·grene (GANG·green, gang·GREEN) n. the dying of body tissue due to interruption of the blood supply: *Gangrene may set in after a severe burn.*
— v. -grenes, -grened, -gren·ing: *A foot gangrened by frostbite may have to be amputated.*
— gan·gre·nous (-gruh·nus) adj.

gang·saw n. a set of several saws working together.

gang·ster (GANG·stur) n. a criminal or racketeer.

gang·way n. 1 a passageway. 2 a gangplank.
— interj. make way!

gaol (JAIL) n. *Brit.* jail. — **gaol·er** n.

gap n. 1 an opening or break: *A missing tooth leaves a gap; to bridge, close, fill a gap; a mountain gap in the Rockies; a wide gap.* 2 an obvious difference or disparity: *There's a gap of many years in your narrative; Lying builds up a credibility gap; the gender gap (between the sexes); the generation gap between parents and children; America's missile gap with the Soviets; our trade gap (between imports and exports) with Japan.*

gape v. gapes, gaped, gap·ing 1 open widely, esp. open the mouth to yawn: *The abandoned quarry gaped before us; a gaping wound.* 2 stare with the mouth open: *tourists gaping at the wonders of the Grand Canyon.*
— n. a gaping: *to stifle a bored gape; with the mouth open in a gape of surprise.*

ga·rage (guh·RAHZH, -RAHJ) n. 1 a shelter for cars: *a house with an attached garage; a built-in garage; a (public) parking garage.* 2 a car repair shop.
— v. -rag·es, -raged, -rag·ing put or keep in a garage.

garage sale n. a sale of used household articles held at the seller's home.

garb n. 1 clothing or style of dress: *a nun's garb; Everyone came in formal garb.* 2 outward appearance: *to give confusion the garb of order.*
— v. wear as garb: *She was garbed in her graduation*

cap and gown.

gar·bage (GAR·bij) *n.* **1** discarded food: *We dispose of garbage separately from trash.* **2** anything discarded as worthless: *They pick up garbage twice a week; No dumping of garbage on this lot; That's a lot of garbage* (= nonsense); *adj.: The plastic garbage bag is a Canadian innovation; a garbage can.*

gar·ble (GAR·bul) *v.* -bles, -bled, -bling distort, misrepresent, or intentionally scramble: *a garbled message.*

gar·den (GAR·dun) *n.* **1** a plot of land for growing flowers, fruit, or vegetables: *to maintain, plant, water, weed a garden; flower garden; kitchen garden; vegetable garden; adj.: a garden hose for watering the lawn; tomatoes and other garden vegetables.* **2** any fertile area: *a lush resort in the garden spot of our province.* **3** an area for public recreation: *a botanical, formal, rock, zoological garden.*
— *v.* work in a garden: *Few Canadians garden in the winter; landscape gardening* (= designing).
— **gar·den·er** *n.*

garden variety *n.* a common or ordinary kind: *a garden variety restaurant.*

gar·gan·tu·an or **Gar·gan·tu·an** (gar·GAN·choo·un) *adj.* enormous or huge: *a gargantuan appetite.*

gar·gle (GAR·gul) *v.* -gles, -gled, -gling rinse the throat with liquid kept in motion by exhaled breath.
— *n.* liquid for gargling: *a salt-water gargle for a sore throat.*

gar·goyle (GAR·goil) *n.* a grotesquely shaped waterspout projecting from the gutter of a building.

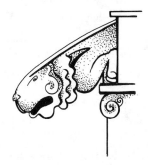

gar·ish (GAIR·ish) *adj.* gaudy or showy; glaring.
gar·land (GAR·lund) *n.* a wreath of leaves or flowers.
— *v.* decorate with a garland: *a bride garlanded with roses.*

gar·lic *n.* **1** a plant related to the onion. **2** its strong-smelling bulb used in cooking: *a clove of garlic; There's a whiff of garlic in his office.* — **gar·lick·y** *adj.*

gar·ment (GAR·munt) *n.* an article of clothing: *a foundation garment; adj.: the garment district of the city; the garment industry; garment workers; a garment bag* (= travel bag that folds in two).

gar·ner (GAR·nur) *v.* gather and store away: *to garner support, votes.*

gar·net (GAR·nit) *n.* a glossy mineral whose deep-red variety is used as a gem.

gar·nish *v.* decorate or adorn, esp. food: *to garnish a platter with parsley.*
— *n.: a garnish of parsley.*

gar·nish·ee (gar·nuh·SHEE) *v.* -ees, -eed, -ee·ing legally withhold a debtor's money to pay the debts: *wages garnisheed by the loan company.*

gar·nish·ment (GAR·nish·munt) *n.* a notice to garnishee.

ga·rotte *n.* See GARROTE.

gar·ret (GAIR·it) *n.* an attic.

gar·ri·son (GAIR·uh·sun) *n.* **1** the troops stationed in a fortified place. **2** the fort itself.
— *v.* to station troops, etc.: *Our troops were garrisoned in Europe during the war.*

garrison state *n.* a country dominated by military personnel.

gar·rote or **ga·rotte** (guh·ROT, -ROTE) *n.* **1** strangulation by an iron collar, cord, wire, etc. **2** the device used.
— *v.* gar·rotes or ga·rottes, gar·rot·ed or ga·rot·ted, gar·rot·ing or ga·rot·ting kill by garrote: *The robber garroted his victim with a wire.*

gar·ru·lous (GAIR·uh·lus) *adj.* talkative or wordy.
— **gar·ru·lous·ly** *adv.*
— **gar·ru·lous·ness** or **gar·ru·li·ty** (guh·ROO·luh·tee) *n.*

gar·ter *n.* a band or strap to hold up a stocking.
— *v.* to support with a garter.

gas *n.* gas·es **1** a shapeless fluid like air which can expand indefinitely. **2** any gas or volatile liquid that is used as a fuel, anesthetic, poison, irritant, or illuminant, esp. gasoline: *The stalled car was out of gas; Step on the gas* (= accelerator pedal) *to go faster; coal gas; laughing gas* (= nitrous oxide); *natural gas for home heating; Turn on the gas before lighting it; mustard gas; nerve gas; tear gas; toxic gas; stomach gas* (= flatulence); *adj.: a gas range; a criminal executed in a gas chamber* (with poison gas). **3** *Slang.* a source of great pleasure or excitement: *The roller coaster is a real gas.*
— *v.* gas·es, gassed, gas·sing **1** supply with gas: *to gas up a car before a trip.* **2** *Slang.* talk idly and boastfully: *He often gases about his fishing trips.*

gas-guzzler (GAS·guz·lur) *n.* a large automobile with a low gas mileage.

gash *n.* a long, deep wound.
— *v.* make a gash in something: *legs gashed by barbed wire.*

gas·o·line or **gas·o·lene** (GAS·uh·leen, gas·uh·LEEN) *n.* a flammable liquid distilled from petroleum and used as a motor fuel; gas: *high-octane, leaded, lead-free, unleaded, premium, regular gasoline.*

gasp *v.* **1** breathe in sharply, as from shock. **2** pant: *an asthmatic gasping for breath; The winded messenger gasped his story* (= told it while gasping for breath).
— *n.* a gasping: *an audible gasp; to give, let out a gasp; a gasp for air.*
— **at the last gasp** on the point of death.

gas·pe·reau (gas·puh·ROH) *n. Cdn.* a type of Atlantic coast herring; alewife.

Gas·pe·sian (gas·PAY·zhun, -PEE·zhun) *n. Cdn.* a person of or from the Gaspé Peninsula.

gas station *n.* where gasoline, oil, etc. for motor vehicles are sold.

gas·sy (GAS·ee) *adj.* **gas·si·er, gas·si·est** full of or producing stomach gas; flatulent.

gas·tric *adj.* having to do with the stomach.

gate *n.* 1 a movable barrier hung on a post which controls passage through an entrance in a fence, wall, castle, etc.: *the starting gate of a racetrack; to wait at the gate.* 2 a door or valve controlling water flow in a canal, dam, lock, etc.; also, a gateway. 3 the total amount of money taken or the number of spectators at an event. 4 a computer circuit having one output activated by a combination of signals to the inputs.
— **give someone the gate** *Slang.* dismiss or reject someone.

gate-crash *v. Informal.* enter without an invitation or without paying: *to gate-crash a party.*
— **gate-crash·er** *n.*

gate·way *n.* 1 an opening for a gate. 2 a means of entrance: *the gateway of heaven; Vancouver, the gateway to the Orient.*

gath·er (GATH·ur, "TH" as in "the") *v.* 1 bring together: *He gathered his friends for the reunion.* 2 collect or assemble: *A farmer gathers his crop; A detective gathers evidence; Children gather around their teacher.* 3 accumulate or increase: *Old books gather dust in the library; A car gathers speed as it rolls downhill.* 4 draw: *She gathered a shawl around herself; to gather one's brows in a frown; a skirt gathered at the waist (into pleats or folds).* 5 infer or conclude: *I gather you're not interested.*
— *n.* a very small pleat: *She removed the gathers to remodel the dress.* — **gath·er·er** *n.*

gathering (GATH·ur·ing) *n.* a coming together: *a gathering of clouds before a storm; Thanksgiving and other family gatherings; a public gathering; a social gathering.*

gating (GAY·ting) *n.* the rearresting of potentially dangerous prisoners as soon as they are released after a jail term.

gauche (GOHSH) *adj.* awkward, esp. socially.

gau·che·rie (goh·shuh·REE) *n.* a clumsy or tactless action; awkwardness.

gau·cho (GOW·choh, "OW" as in "HOW") *n.* -chos a cowboy of the South American plains.

gaud (GAWD) *n.* a cheap ornament or trinket.

gaud·y (GAW·dee) *adj.* **gaud·i·er, -i·est** tastelessly colourful; flashily ornamented.
— **gaud·i·ly** *adv.;* **gaud·i·ness** *n.*

gauge (GAIJ) *n.* 1 a standard measurement, as for the thickness of wire, widths of railway tracks, sizes of bores, etc.: *Trains run on broad, narrow, and standard gauges; a 12-gauge shotgun; Wire gauges vary from No. 000000 (15 mm) to No. 51 (0.022301 mm).* 2 a measuring instrument: *a fuel, oil, pressure, rain gauge; a water-level gauge; wind gauge.* 3 a means of estimating or judging: *Looks are no sure gauge of character.*

— *v.* **gaug·es, gauged, gaug·ing** to measure or judge: *a director gauging an actor's performance.*

gaunt *adj.* 1 thin-looking: *He was gaunt and weak; a gaunt* (= elegant-looking) *fashion model.* 2 desolate or grim-looking: *the gaunt brow of a cliff.*
— **gaunt·ness** *n.*

gaunt·let (GAWNT·lit, GONT·lit) *n.* 1 a protective glove, esp. from a suit of armour. 2 two rows of armed people who strike a person forced to run between them; hence, any ordeal: *His work had to* **run the gauntlet** *of critics worldwide before being accepted.*
— **pick up** or **take up the gauntlet** accept a challenge.
— **throw down the gauntlet** challenge someone to fight.

gauze (GAUZ) *n.* a thin, transparent, loosely-woven fabric.

gave *pt.* of GIVE.

gav·el (GAV·ul) *n.* a small mallet used by a judge, auctioneer, or the chairperson of a meeting: *a rap of the gavel.*
— **gavel-to-gavel** from beginning to end of a meeting.

gawk *v.* to stare stupidly: *to gawk at people.*
— *n.* an awkward or clumsy person.

gawk·y (GAW·kee) *adj.* **gawk·i·er, -i·est** awkward or clumsy: *a growing boy's gawky limbs.*
— **gawk·i·ness** *n.* — **gawk·ish** *adj.*

gay *adj.* **gay·er, gay·est** 1 *Informal.* homosexual: *a gay bar;* also *n.* 2 joyous; lively; merry; given to (social) pleasure. 3 brightly coloured: *a gay Caribana costume.* 4 licentious or immoral: *a gay dog.*
— **gai·ly** or **gay·ly** *adv.* — **gay·e·ty** same as GAIETY.

gaze *v.* **gaz·es, gazed, gaz·ing** to look steadily and with fascination.
— *n.* a gazing: *an admiring, intense, steady, wistful gaze; Their eyes met in a bewildered gaze.*

ga·ze·bo (guh·ZEE·boh, -ZAY·boh) *n.* -bos or -boes a belvedere.

ga·zelle (guh·ZEL) *n.* -zelles a small, swift, graceful antelope of Asia and Africa.

ga·zette (guh·ZET) *n.* 1 an official government journal. 2 [used in titles of newspapers]: *The Montreal Gazette.*
— *v.* -zettes, -zet·ted, -zet·ting publish or list in a gazette.

gaz·et·teer (gaz·uh·TEER) *n.* a dictionary of names of places, seas, rivers, mountains, etc.

gear (GEER, "G" as in "go") *n.* 1 a toothed wheel that meshes with another toothed element to transmit motion, often in a system of such gears: *Drivers change, reverse, shift gears; to put a car in low, high, reverse, top gear; Gears jam, lock, mesh, stick; a worm gear; a gear shift.* 2 equipment, esp. tools or clothing for a special purpose: *The soldier left his gear in the barracks; to pack camping gear for a trip; fishing, hunting, skiing gear.* 3 fashion: *dressed in the latest gear; trendy gear.*
— **in** (or **out of**) **gear** connected (or not connected) to the motor; hence, working (or not working) properly.
— **in high gear** 1 in the highest speed range. 2 at high efficiency.
— *v.* 1 connect, as by gears: *A car's rear wheels are*

geared to the motor; A factory's production is geared (= adjusted) *to demand.* **2** equip or get ready: *hikers geared for an outing; a team gearing up for a game.*

gear·box *n.* an automobile transmission.

gear·shift *n.* a device for changing from one gear to another.

gear·wheel *n.* cogwheel.

gee (JEE) *interj.* expressing surprise: *Gee, aren't we lucky!*

geek ("g" as in "go") *n. Slang.* a weirdo or freak.

geese *pl.* of GOOSE.

gee whiz *interj.* same as GEE.
— **gee-whiz** *adj. Informal.* surprisingly good: *a gee-whiz kid.*

geez (JEEZ) *interj.* same as GEE.

gee·zer (GEE·zur, "g" as in "go") *n. Slang.* an eccentric old man.

gel (JEL) *n.* a jellylike substance formed by the thickening of a colloidal solution.
— *v.* **gels, gelled, gel·ling 1** form a gel: *Egg white gels when heated.* **2** take shape; jell: *Somehow our plans failed to gel.*

gel·a·tin or **gel·a·tine** (JEL·uh·tin) *n.* a gluelike substance used in drugs and cooking.
— **ge·lat·i·nous** (juh·LAT·uh·nus) *adj.*

geld (JELD) *v.* to neuter a male animal; castrate: *a gelded horse.*

geld·ing *n.* a castrated animal, esp. a horse.

gem (JEM) *n.* a precious or semiprecious stone cut and polished as a jewel; hence, anything highly valued: *A Picasso was the gem of his art collection.*

gem·i·nate (JEM·uh·nate) *v.* **-ates, -at·ed, -at·ing** make or become double or paired.

Gem·i·ni (JEM·uh·nye, -nee) *n. Cdn.* any of the annual awards made by the Academy of Canadian Cinema and Television for excellence in television production.

gem·mol·o·gy or **gem·ol·o·gy** (jem·OL·uh·jee) *n.* the study of gems. — **gem·mol·o·gist** or **gem·ol·o·gist** *n.*

gem·stone *n.* a stone that may be cut and polished as a gem.

gen·darme (ZHAHN·darm) *n.* a soldier serving as a policeman, esp. in France.

gen·dar·mer·ie or **gen·dar·mer·y** (zhahn·DAR·muh·ree) *n.* a body of gendarmes.

gen·der (JEN·dur) *n.* **1** sex: *the female gender; male gender;* **adj.:** *gender differences, equality; the gender factor; gender politics, stereotyping; gender-neutral legislation; In 1985, there was a gender gap* (= differences in attitudes, values, etc. because of sex) *in federal politics, with six percent more women favouring the Liberals than the Conservatives.* **2** one of the grammatical categories into which words are grouped: *the feminine, masculine, neuter gender; common gender.*

gene (JEEN) *n.* a unit of chromosome that determines the inheritance of a certain characteristic.

ge·ne·al·o·gy (jee·nee·AL·uh·jee) *n.* **-gies** a record or study of family history; lineage or pedigree.
— **ge·ne·al·o·gist** (-jist) *n.*
— **ge·ne·a·log·i·cal** (JEE·nee·uh·LOJ·uh·cul) *adj.*

gene pool *n.* all the genes in a breeding population.

genera a *pl.* of GENUS.

gen·er·al (JEN·ur·ul) *adj.* **1** applicable to or true of the whole; common, prevalent, or widespread; not limited, specialized, precise, or detailed: *a general feeling of unrest in society; All bears have the same general features, but they differ in colour and size; She quickly sketched the general outline of the scheme; reforms for the general welfare of the public; The Jeep is a **general-purpose*** (= good for a variety of uses and users) *vehicle; a general* (= national or provincial) *election.* **2** having the highest rank: *a store's general manager; a general secretary; the U.N. General Assembly.*
— *n.* **1** what is general: *His report concentrates on the general and ignores specifics; The weather, **in general*** (= usually), *is rainy throughout April.* **2** an officer of the highest rank, as in the military: *the general of the army; postmaster general; the superior general of a religious order.* **3** an officer ranking above a colonel: *a brigadier general; lieutenant general; major general.*
— **gen·er·al·ship** *n.*

gen·er·al·i·ty (jen·uh·RAL·uh·tee) *n.* **-ties 1** something general: *The lecturer spoke in generalities; sweeping generalities.* **2** the greater part: *The generality of people pay their taxes.*

gen·er·al·ize (JEN·ur·uh·lize) *v.* **-iz·es, -ized, -iz·ing** speak in general terms: *He frequently generalizes without revealing specific plans; to generalize about a whole group based on experience with a few members; The scientist generalized a law from several experiments.* — **gen·er·al·i·za·tion** (-luh·ZAY·shun) *n.*

gen·er·al·ly (JEN·ur·uh·lee) *adv.* in general: *Generally speaking, it's a friendly town; an obscure fact that is not generally known.*

general practitioner *n.* a physician who is not a specialist.

general store *n.* a store selling a wide variety of merchandise but not in separate departments.

gen·er·ate (JEN·uh·rate) *v.* **-ates, -at·ed, -at·ing** bring into being, as by a process: *heat generated by burning coal; a diplomat generating good will; Insects generate countless offspring.*
— **gen·er·a·tive** (-ur·uh·tiv, -uh·ray·tiv) *adj.*

gen·er·a·tion (jen·uh·RAY·shun) *n.* **1** the act of generating: *the generation of electricity at Niagara Falls.* **2** all people of about the same age range considered as one step in the line of descent: *Children are the younger generation; the coming, next, older, post-war, present generation; a future, lost, past generation; Four generations* (= children, parents, grandparents, and great-grandparents) *of Smiths were at the family reunion; Parents talking to their teenagers help bridge the **generation gap.***
— **gen·er·a·tor** (JEN·uh·ray·tur) *n.*

ge·ner·ic (juh·NER·ic) *adj.* having to do with an entire group, class, or genus; hence, general, not specific: *Thorns are a generic feature in roses; generic software that is compatible with many computers; The generic (= not trademarked) name for Coke, Pepsi, etc. is cola; a generic (= not brand-name) drug.* — **ge·ner·i·cal·ly** *adv.*

gen·er·ous (JEN·ur·us) *adj.* giving freely; noble or magnanimous; ample or abundant: *He gave up his seat in a generous act; She gave us a generous share of the profits; Gigi is generous in giving to the poor; Jean is quite generous with his time and money;* **gen·er·ous·ly** *adv.* — **gen·er·os·i·ty** (-ROS·uh·tee) *n.* **-ties.**

gen·e·sis (JEN·uh·sis) *n., pl.* **-ses** (-seez) the coming into being of something; origin: *The Book of Genesis starts with the creation of the universe.*

gene-splicing *n. Informal.* same as GENETIC ENGINEERING.

ge·net·ic (juh·NET·ic) **1** *adj.* having to do with origin and heredity. **2 genetics** *n.pl.* [takes sing. v.] the study of heredity and variations in related plants and animals. — **ge·net·i·cal·ly** *adv.* — **ge·net·i·cist** *n.*

genetic code *n.* the organization of chemical elements in the chromosome determining the characteristics passed on from generation to generation.

genetic engineering *n.* scientific manipulation of genes or gene processes to create or eliminate traits.

ge·nial (JEEN·yul) *adj.* **1** favourable to life or growth: *Oranges thrive in Spain's genial climate.* **2** cheerful and amiable: *The genial host made us feel welcome.* — **ge·nial·ly** *adv.* — **ge·ni·al·i·ty** (jee·nee·AL·uh·tee) *n.*

-genic *adj. suffix.* producing: *carcinogenic, eugenic, photogenic.*

ge·nie (JEE·nee) *n.* **1 -nies** or **-ni·i** (-nee·eye) a supernatural being, often serving humans, like those in the Arabian Nights stories: *The threat of a holocaust is so great, people feel we should stuff the nuclear genie back in the bottle.* See also GENIUS. **2 Genie** *Cdn.* any of the annual awards made by the Academy of Canadian Cinema and Television for artistic excellence in theatrical shorts and documentaries.

gen·i·tal (JEN·uh·tul) *adj.* having to do with reproduction: *the genital organs.* — **gen·i·tal·ly** *adv.*

gen·i·tal·i·a (jen·uh·TAIL·yuh) or **gen·i·tals** (JEN·uh·tulz) *n.pl.* the external sex organs: *female, male genitalia.*

gen·i·us (JEEN·yus) *n.* **-us·es 1** exceptional natural ability or inclination, esp. great intellectual capacity or creativity: *Gigi has a genius for learning languages; There's a spark of genius in everything she does.* **2** a person with such ability: *a budding genius; mathematical, mechanical, musical geniuses; Einstein was a rare genius; An I.Q. of 150 or more makes you a "genius" according to the Terman index.* **3** *pl.* **ge·ni·i** (JEE·nee·eye) the distinctive spirit of an age, nation, place, or group: *F. Scott Fitzgerald captured the genius of the "Lost Generation."* **4** one who strongly influences another: *his evil genius.*

gen·o·cide (JEN·uh·cide) *n.* the systematic destruction

of a racial, political, or cultural group. — **gen·o·ci·dal** (-SYE·dul) *adj.*

gen·re (ZHON·ruh) *n.* a type or kind, esp. of literary or artistic composition: *Science fiction is a 20th-century genre.*

gent (JENT) *n. Informal.* a man.

gen·teel (jen·TEEL) *adj.* polite and stylish, esp. affectedly or prudishly elegant: *She learned the genteel arts in finishing school; an old lady living in genteel poverty; the genteel quarters of Vancouver.*

gen·tile or **Gen·tile** (JEN·tile) *n.* **1** an outsider, as among Jews and Mormons: *a Jew married to a gentile woman.* **2** formerly, a heathen or pagan.

gen·til·i·ty (jen·TIL·uh·tee) *n.* **-ties 1** the condition of being of gentle birth; refinement: *an air of old-fashioned gentility.* **2** people of gentle birth; aristocracy.

gen·tle (JEN·tul) *adj.* **-tler, -tlest 1** kind and considerate; of things, not harsh, rough, violent, etc.: *He was soothed by her gentle voice; a mother's gentle (= soft) touch; a gentle (= mild) detergent for dry skin; Apply gentle (= moderate) heat; I barely heard the gentle (= soft) knock; a wild horse now gentle (= tame) as a lamb; nearly flat terrain with only a gentle (= slow) incline.* **2** of the upper classes, refined or well-bred: *Do good manners go with gentle birth?* — *v.* **-tles, -tled, -tling** make gentle or tame: *Soft music gentles his nerves.* — **gen·tly** *adv.*; **gen·tle·ness** *n.*

gen·tle·folk or **gen·tle·folks** *n.pl.* people of good upbringing.

gen·tle·man (JEN·tul·mun) *n.* **-men** a polite or well-bred man: *Hello, ladies and gentlemen; an unwritten gentleman's agreement (based on trust); A valet used to be referred to as a "gentleman's gentleman."* — **gen·tle·man·ly** *adv.*

gen·tle·wom·an (JEN·tul·wom·an) *n.* **-wom·en** a lady; also, a female attendant of a woman of rank.

gen·try (JEN·tree) *n.* **-tries 1** people of gentle birth: *The new governor entertained the local gentry; the landed gentry.* **2** people of a specified class: *the teaching gentry.*

gen·u·ine (JEN·yoo·in, *rarely* JEN·yoo·ine) *adj.* **1** real and not fake: *a genuine antique, coin, Picasso.* **2** true or sincere: *genuine sorrow.* — **gen·u·ine·ly** *adv.*; **gen·u·ine·ness** *n.*

ge·nus (JEE·nus) *n., pl.* **gen·er·a** (JEN·uh·ruh) or **ge·nus·es** a kind, sort, or class, esp. a plant or animal classification under "family," comprising many "species": *Genus "Rosa" has hundreds of rose species.*

ge·o·cen·tric (jee·uh·SEN·tric) or **ge·o·cen·tri·cal** (-truh·cul) *adj.* with the earth as centre: *the old geocentric theory of the universe.*

ge·og·ra·phy (jee·OG·ruh·fee) *n.* **-phies** the science of the earth's natural features, climate, inhabitants, resources, etc.— **ge·og·ra·pher** *n.* — **ge·o·graph·ic** (jee·uh·GRAF·ic) or **ge·o·graph·i·cal** (-uh·cul) *adj.*

ge·ol·o·gy (jee·OL·uh·jee) *n.* **-gies** the science of the structure and history of the earth's crust. — **ge·ol·o·gist** (-jist) *n.* — **ge·o·log·ic** (jee·uh·LOJ·ic) or **ge·o·log·i·cal** *adj.*

— ge·o·log·i·cal·ly *adv.*

ge·om·e·try (jee·OM·uh·tree) *n.* the mathematics of points, lines, angles, surfaces, and solid figures. — ge·o·met·ric (jee·uh·MET·ric) or ge·o·met·ri·cal (-ruh·cul) *adj.* — ge·o·met·ri·cal·ly (-cuh·lee) *adv.*

ge·o·sta·tion·ar·y (jee·uh·STAY·shuh·nair·ee) or **ge·o·syn·chro·nous** (jee·uh·SINK·ruh·nus) *adj.* of an artificial communications satellite, orbiting at the same speed and in the same direction as the earth so that it can act as a fixed relay station.

ge·ot·ro·pism (jee·OT·ruh·piz·um) *n.* the tendency, as of a plant's roots, to grow downward because of the earth's gravity.

ger·i·at·rics (jer·ee·AT·rics) *n.* [with sing. v.] a branch of medicine dealing with aging and the diseases of the aged. — ger·i·at·ric *adj.*

germ (JURM) *n.* 1 the seed, bud, or earliest form of a living thing: *the oil-rich wheat germ.* 2 source or origin: *Inspiration is the germ of poetry.* 3 a microscopic creature, as a bacterium; microbe.

Ger·man (JUR·mun) *adj.* having to do with Germany, its language, or its people. — *n.* 1 a person of or from Germany. 2 the German language.

-german *combining form.* 1 having the same parents: *a brother-german; sisters-german.* 2 closely related: *a cousin-german* (= first cousin).

ger·mane (jur·MAIN) *adj.* closely related: *Your sex is germane to the question of parenthood, but not even relevant to your becoming a lawyer.*

Ger·man·ic (jur·MAN·ic) *adj.* German in origin: *Germans, Dutch, English, etc. are Germanic peoples speaking Germanic languages.*

ger·mi·nate (JUR·muh·nate) *v.* -nates, -nat·ed, -nat·ing begin to grow; sprout; also, cause to sprout. — ger·mi·na·tion (-NAY·shun) *n.*

Ge·sta·po (guh·STAH·poh) *n.* -pos the Nazi German secret police.

ges·tate (JES·tate) *v.* -tates, -tat·ed, -tat·ing carry in the womb; hence, develop slowly.

ges·ta·tion (jes·TAY·shun) *n.* pregnancy or its period: *a ten-month period of gestation; a project that has been 10 years in gestation* (= development).

ges·tic·u·late (jes·TIK·yuh·late) *v.* -lates, -lat·ed, -lat·ing make vigorous gestures, esp. instead of words: *Too shocked to speak, he gesticulated helplessly.* — ges·tic·u·la·tion (-yuh·LAY·shun) *n.*

ges·ture (JES·chur) *n.* 1 a motion of the body expressing or emphasizing an idea or feeling: *Nodding is a common gesture for "Yes"; In East Indian dancing, every gesture and movement has a meaning; an angry gesture; a gesture of appreciation.* 2 any act or remark indicating attitude: *The offer was a conciliatory gesture; a bold, friendly, grand, noble gesture; She gave up her seat as a kind gesture to the man on crutches.* — *v.* -tures, -tured, -tur·ing communicate by gesture: *She gestured to the waiter to bring the tab.*

Ge·sund·heit (guh·ZOONT·hite) *interj.* [said when someone sneezes] Bless you!

get *v.* gets, *pt.* got, *pp.* got or got·ten 1 obtain or acquire, as by earning, buying, catching a disease, etc.: *I must get a better job; You must get some rest; How did he get such a good deal? She got herself new shoes; Go and get me a drink; Add 5 and 8 to get 13; The children got colds.* 2 reach or cause to reach a place, condition, state, etc.: *We have to get home early; He's planning to get married; Let's not get* (= enter) *into an argument; Can you get* (= make) *him to listen? He didn't get the message; He got himself in trouble with the police; You have to get after* (= put pressure on) *him; Wayne doesn't want to get between* (= try to separate) *a man and his wife; to get* (= become) *angry, drunk, excited; to get even with someone; We're getting nowhere waiting for the bus; Let's get rid of the trash.* 3 *Informal.* overcome physically or emotionally, as by capturing, killing, irritating, puzzling, etc.: *The Mounties got* (= captured) *their man; Her pleas finally got* (= overcame) *him; Nothing gets* (= annoys) *me more than loud chewing.* 4 *Informal.* understand or hear: *I didn't get you.* 5 have, esp. as an obligation: *Our team has got to win!* 6 manage or contrive: *When will I get to see the dentist? We finally got the car going.* 7 communicate with someone: *Please get her on the phone.* 8 beget: *Abraham got Isaac.*

— **get across** make or become clear: *to get a message across to the class.*

— **get along** manage fairly well: *We used to get along on $100 a week; They find it hard to **get along with*** (= stay on good terms with) *each other.*

— **get around** 1 circulate: *Word got around that the boss had resigned.* 2 evade: *He tried to get around the rules.* 3 trick, esp. by flattery. 4 find the time for doing something: *I never got around to answering that letter.*

— **get at** 1 to reach: *Keep drugs where the kids can't get at them; to get at the truth by study and prayer.* 2 to reach indirectly: *He was accused of trying to get at* (= bribe) *the jury; What are you getting at* (= implying)?

— **get away** leave or escape: *The burglars got away.*

— **get away with** succeed in something: *People shouldn't be getting away with cheating; He practically got away with murder.*

— **get back at** take revenge: *Jean is trying to get back at Marie for the snub.*

— **get by** manage: *Can you get by without a loan?*

— **get down** take up: *When you get down to it, it's no problem; Let's get down to business.*

— **get it** *Informal.* be punished: *He got it for being late.*

— **get it (all) together** or **get one's act together** *Informal.* to get organized or function in an organized way.

— **get off** leave or escape: *Let's get off the bus; A smart lawyer got him off* (= helped him escape punishment).

— **get off on** *Slang.* get pleasure or excitement from something: *to get off on drugs; She gets off on horror movies.*

— **get on** go up on or into something: *to get on a train; Noisy children get on his nerves* (= make him nervous); *They are quite active though getting on* (= advancing) *in years; She gets on* (= is friendly) *with everyone.*

— **get out** go out: *He quickly got out of town; if word of our plans gets out* (= escapes).

— **get over** forget: *He'll soon get over the shock of her death.*

— **get through 1** finish: *I get through my homework before bedtime.* **2** survive: *The homeless try to get through the winter.* **3** establish communication: *He couldn't get through to the operator.*
— **get together** assemble: *Teachers get together with the principal now and then.*
— **get to one** *Informal.* disturb: *His nagging is beginning to get to me.*
— **get up** arise, as from bed or the table..
— *n.* **1** an animal offspring; also, the offspring of a male animal collectively. **2** in Jewish law, a religious divorce: *A husband has the authority to give a get but the wife may refuse to accept it.*

get·a·way (GET·uh·way) *n. Informal.* escape: *The robbers made a quick getaway in their getaway car.*

get-together (GET·tuh·geth·ur) *n.* an informal social gathering.

get-up *n.* costume: *He came to the party in a bizarre get-up; an elaborate get-up.*

get-up-and-go (GET·up·un·GO) *n. Informal.* initiative or energy: *Vito has get-up-and-go; Leo lacks get-up-and-go.*

gey·ser (GUY·zur) *n.* a spring that periodically ejects columns of hot water and steam.

G-force *n.* the force of gravity: *Astronauts encounter high G-forces during blastoff and re-entry.*

ghast·ly (GAST·lee) *adj.* **-li·er, -li·est 1** terrifying or horrible; also, very unpleasant. **2** ghostlike or deathly; pale. — **ghast·li·ness** *n.*

ghet·to (GET·oh) *n.* **-tos** or **-toes** a section of a city inhabited by a minority group obliged to live there for economic, legal, or social reasons: *the former Jewish ghettos of anti-Semitic countries; an inner-city ghetto; urban ghettos.*

ghost (rhyme: "post") *n.* **1** the spirit of a dead person, supposed to appear to the living as a pale, shadowy form: *to see a ghost at night; a ghost story.* **2** a faint trace, suggestion, or shadow, as a secondary television or photographic image: *Ghosts result when the TV set receives direct as well as reflected images; a candidate without a ghost of a* (= the least) *chance.* **3** one who ghosts a book or speech.
— **give up the ghost** *Informal.* die.
— *v. Informal.* write another person's autobiography, speech, etc. for payment. — **ghost·ly** *adj.*

ghost town *n.* a deserted town which was once flourishing, as one abandoned after a gold rush.

ghost·write *v.* **-writes, -wrote, -writ·ten, -writ·ing** same as GHOST: *a ghostwritten autobiography.*

ghoul (GOOL) *n.* a legendary evil spirit that robs graves and feeds on the dead. — **ghoul·ish** *adj.*

GI (JEE·eye) *n., pl.* **GI's** or **GIs** a U.S. serviceman, esp. an enlisted soldier: *GI Joe.*
— *adj.* issued by the military or conforming to military regulations: *a GI haircut.*

gi·ant (JYE·unt) *n.* a huge, imaginary humanlike being of enormous strength; hence, a person or thing of great size or powers: *Bell Canada is a corporate giant; the "San Francisco Giants" (baseball team).*

— *adj.* huge or great in size: *a giant redwood tree; the long, zigzag* **giant slalom** *in skiing.*

giantism same as GIGANTISM.

gib·ber (JIB·ur, GIB·ur) *v.* speak rapidly and unintelligibly; chatter.

gib·ber·ish (JIB·ur·ish, GIB-) *n.* meaningless talk or chatter; nonsense.

gib·bet (JIB·it) *n.* a gallows.
— *v.* **1** hang on a gibbet. **2** hold up to public ridicule.

gib·bon (GIB·un) *n.* a small, long-armed ape of Southeast Asia and the East Indies.

gibe (JIBE)) *v.* **gibes, gibed, gib·ing** make jeering remarks; taunt or sneer: *Siblings gibe at each other.*
— *n.* a taunt or sneer: *Siblings trade gibes at each other.* Also **jibe.**

gid·dy (GID·ee) *adj.* **gid·di·er, gid·di·est** having or causing dizziness; hence, frivolous or fickle: *to climb to giddy heights; a giddy young flirt.* — **gid·di·ness** *n.*

gift *n.* **1** something given; a present: *to give a birthday gift; wedding gifts; He lavished gifts on his spouse; a million-dollar gift to charity; an outright gift with no conditions attached.* **2** a natural ability or talent: *She has a gift for drawing; Some are more* **gifted** (= talented) *than others.* **3** the act or power of giving: *a job within the mayor's gift.*

gig ("g's" as in "go") *n.* **1** an open, two-wheeled, horse-drawn carriage. **2** a long, light ship's boat. **3** a fishing spear. **4** *Slang.* a job, esp. a one-time engagement for a jazz or rock musician. Also *v.* **gigs, gigged, gig·ging.**

gi·ga- (JIG·uh-) *combining form.* one billion: *gigabit, gigabyte, gigacycle, gigaton, gigawatt.*

gi·gan·tic (jye·GAN·tic) *adj.* giantlike; huge or immense in size.

gi·gan·tism (jye·GAN·tiz·um) *n.* excessive growth of the body or of plants.

gig·gle ("g's" as in "go") *v.* **gig·gles, gig·gled, gig·gling** laugh in a silly or nervous way: *He kept giggling all through the speech.*
— *n.* such a laugh: *She gave a shrill giggle at the remark.*

gild ("g" as in "go") *v.* **gilds,** *pt. & pp.* **gild·ed** or **gilt, gild·ing** cover with gold leaf or gold-coloured material; hence, make deceptively attractive in appearance: *It makes no sense to* **gild the lily** (= unnecessarily adorn something beautiful). — *n.* same as GUILD.

gilding n. an outer layer of gold: *the gilding on a bracelet; a mere gilding* (= surface coating) *of politeness.*

gilt a *pt.* and *pp.* of GILD; also *adj.*
— *n.* same as GILDING.

gilt-edge or **gilt-edged** *adj.* of the highest quality: *Gilt-edge securities are safe investments.*

gim·let (GIM·lit, "G" as in "go") n. **1** a small hole-boring hand tool with a screw point. **2** a cocktail made with gin or vodka.

gim·me (GIM·ee, "G" as in "go") *Slang.* v. "give me": *Gimme a break.*
— *n.* **1** something easily obtained: *A gimme goal has nothing to do with good hockey.* **2** the tendency of children to be constantly asking for things advertised on TV: *It's always gimme, gimme with kids who watch too much TV; Commercials promote* **the gimmes.**

gim·mick (GIM·ik, "G" as in "go") n. an ingenious device, scheme, deception, or concealed condition: *a sports car equipped with the latest gimmicks; pens given out as an advertising gimmick; promotional gimmicks.*
— **gim·mick·ry** (-ree) n. **-ries.** — **gim·mick·y** *adj.*

gimp ("g" as in "go") n. a lame person or walk.
— **gimp·y** *adj.*

gin (JIN) n. **1** an alcoholic liquor distilled from grain. **2** a trap or snare. **3** a machine for removing cotton seeds from the fibres.
— *v.* **gins, ginned, gin·ning** remove seeds from cotton.

gin·ger (JIN·jur) n. **1** a tropical plant with a pungent underground stem used as a spice. **2** the spice itself. **3** *Informal.* liveliness or spirit. — **gin·ger·y** *adj.*

ginger ale n. a ginger-flavoured carbonated soft drink.

gin·ger·bread (JIN·jur·bred) n. **1** a ginger-flavoured molasses cake. **2** gaudy or elaborate ornamentation, as on houses.
— *adj.* elaborately ornamented: *gingerbread architecture; a gingerbread clock; gingerbread design, men, trim.*

gin·ger·ly (JIN·jur·lee) *adj.* very careful or cautious: *He picked up the worm in a gingerly manner.*

gip, Gipsy same as GYP, GYPSY.

gi·raffe (juh·RAF) n. a cud-chewing African animal with a very long neck and legs and a tawny, spotted coat.

gird v. **girds,** *pt. & pp.* **gird·ed** or **girt, gird·ing**
1 encircle with a belt; hence, surround: *a city girded by ramparts; "Thou hast girded* (= invested) *me with gladness."* **2** fasten or tie: *His sword was girded on; trousers girded up with rope; He girded himself* (= prepared) *for the blow.*
— **gird (up) one's loins** prepare for action.

gird·er n. a main horizontal supporting beam.

gir·dle (GUR·dul) n. an encircling or confining band, esp. a woman's elasticized undergarment worn about the hips and waist.
— *v.* **-dles, -dled, -dling** encircle: *a park girdled by trees.*

girl n. **1** a female child or a young unmarried woman: *a chorus, college, dancing, flower, pinup girl.* **2** [offensive when used instead of "woman"]: *a career girl; working girls.* **3** [offensive to women] a female servant. **4** a sweetheart or female companion; also, a girlfriend: *the girl of his dreams.* — **girl·hood** n.; **girl·ish** *adj.*

girl Friday n. See FRIDAY.

girl·friend n. *Informal.* a girl who is one's friend or sweetheart.

Girl Guide n. a member of the Girl Guides, a character-building organization for girls aged 7 to 17 years.

gir·lie (GUR·lee) *adj. Informal.* having to do with the physical aspect of women: *I want a design that is feminine without being girlie; a girlie calendar with girlie pictures; a girlie magazine.*

Girl Scout n. a member of the Girl Scouts of America, a youth organization corresponding to the Girl Guides.

girt 1 a *pt. & pp.* of GIRD. **2** *v.* put a girdle around; gird.

girth n. **1** the measurement around something; circumference. **2** a band around an animal's body to hold a saddle or pack on its back.

gis·mo (GIZ·moh) n. same as GIZMO.

gist (JIST) n. the essential or main point: *to get the gist of an argument.*

give (GIV) v. **gives, gave, giv·en, giv·ing 1** hand over: *I gave her a book; to give to charity; How much will he give (as a price) for the car? Let's give the devil* (= let him have) *his due.* **2** provide or present: *to give a concert, party, reading, speech.* **3** devote: *He has given his life to the cause.* **4** produce: *Cows give milk.* **5** yield: *Any lock will give if forced.* **6** afford a view; open: *The windows give onto the yard.*
— **give away 1** give as a gift. **2** present a bride to the groom. **3** reveal: *Don't give away the secret.*
— **give in** yield: *He had to give in to her demands.*
— **give it to someone** *Informal.* scold or beat.
— **give or take** add or subtract a small number: *200 people, give or take a few.*
— **give out 1** distribute or make known. **2** wear out; break down; become exhausted.
— **give to understand** cause to understand; assure.
— **give up 1** surrender or devote oneself, one's energies, life, time, etc. entirely to something: *Mother Teresa has given up her life to helping the poor.* **2** stop doing, trying, or hoping: *to give up smoking; I give up* (guessing the answer); *They gave up* (= stopped trying to find) *the cat for lost.*
— **give way** yield: *to give way to pressure; The bridge gave way* (= collapsed).
— **what gives?** *Informal.* what is the matter?: *What gives with him? Is he mad or something?*
— *n.* a yielding under pressure; elasticity: *A concrete walk has no give; I see some give in their attitude.*

give-and-take (GIV·un·TAKE) n. a fair exchange, esp. of ideas or remarks; banter.

give·a·way (GIV·uh·way) n. **1** an unintentional revelation: *a dead giveaway.* **2** something given away without charge.

giv·en *adj.* **1** specified: *on a given date; within a given time.* **2** assumed: *Given that all are mortal, how can he*

hope to live forever? **n.**: *Mortality is a given.*
3 habitually disposed: *a boy given to bullying.*

given name *n.* first name; a name given to a person, as at baptism, not surname or family name.

giz·mo (GIZ·moh) *n.* **-mos** *Slang.* a device or gadget.

gla·cial (GLAY·shul) *adj.* 1 relating to glaciers or to a glacial epoch, a period, as the Ice Age, when much of the earth was covered by glaciers. 2 very cold: *a glacial disposition.* 3 very slow: *The negotiations are moving at a glacial pace.* — **gla·cial·ly** *adv.*

gla·cier (GLAY·shur) *n.* a huge body of ice slowly moving downhill or spreading across land.

glad *adj.* **glad·der, glad·dest** 1 causing or feeling joy or pleasure: *a glad occasion; glad tidings.* 2 pleased: *I'm glad to hear the good news; I'm glad to help; to give someone the* **glad eye** (= a seductive glance).

glad·den (GLAD·un) *v.* make or become glad.

glade *n.* an open space in a forest.

glad hand *n.* a jovial, often insincere greeting.
— **glad-hand** *v.*: *a candidate glad-handing the voters.*

glad·i·a·tor (GLAD·ee·ay·tur) *n.* a man trained to fight for public entertainment in ancient Rome.

glad·some *adj.* joyful; cheerful; delightful: *the gladsome news.*

glam·or·ize (GLAM·uh·rize) *v.* **-iz·es, -ized, -iz·ing** make glamorous; idealize.
— **glam·or·i·za·tion** (-uh·ruh·ZAY·shun) *n.*

glam·our or **glam·or** (GLAM·ur) *n.* alluring charm, romance, or excitement: *the glamour of Hollywood; a woman with an aura of glamour; The glamour soon wore off;* *adj.*: *a glamour boy, girl.* — **glam·or·ous** *adj.*

glance *v.* **glanc·es, glanced, glanc·ing** 1 strike and be deflected obliquely: *a glancing blow; She threw the stone so that it glanced off the water.* 2 look quickly: *She glanced at us as she passed by.* 3 to flash or gleam with light: *Swords glanced in the sun.*
— **n.** 1 a quick look: *to steal a glance at someone; to exchange glances; a fleeting, furtive, knowing, shy, sidelong, wistful, withering glance; She saw what was going on with a glance through the window.* 2 gleam: *the glance of swords in the sun.*

gland *n.* an organ such as the liver or kidneys that produces a fluid like bile for body use or urine for excretion: *The adrenal gland is a ductless gland, sweat glands have ducts.*

glan·du·lar (GLAN·juh·lur) *adj.* having to do with glands: *Mononucleosis is called "glandular fever."*

glare *v.* **glares, glared, glar·ing** 1 shine with a harsh, painfully bright light: *glaring neon lights.* 2 stare angrily or fiercely: *They glared at each other.*
— **n.** 1 the effect of a harsh light: *to perform under the glare of television lights; in the full glare of publicity.* 2 an angry look: *Sam shot a glare of hatred at Lou.*

glaring *adj.* conspicuous: *a glaring case of misconduct; a glaring deficiency, discrepancy, error, example, inconsistency, injustice, lapse, omission, weakness.*

glas·nost (GLAS·nost) *n.* campaign of openness in

dealing with the people, as started by the Soviet leader Mikhail Gorbachev.

glass *n.* 1 a hard, brittle, usually transparent substance made by melting sand with lime, potash, etc. 2 an object made of glass: *milk served in a glass; They clinked glasses and drank to each other's health; a wine glass; The glass* (= mirror) *reflected his face; He saw the moon through a glass* (= telescope). 3 **glasses** *pl.* eyeglasses or binoculars: *dark, field, opera, reading, sun glasses.* 4 the amount contained in a drinking glass: *a glass of milk;* also **glass·ful.**
— *adj.* made of glass: *a glass eye; "Those who live in glass houses should not throw stones"* (= Do not blame others when you are as bad as they).

glass·y *adj.* **glass·i·er, -i·est** 1 smooth like glass: *a glassy sheet of ice.* 2 lifeless or expressionless: *a glassy stare.*
— **glass·i·ly** *adv.*

glaze *v.* **glaz·es, glazed, glaz·ing** 1 provide a window frame, etc. with glass. 2 cover pottery or food with a smooth, glossy surface: *glazed chicken breast.*
— **n.**: *Hot water dulled the china's glaze; a glaze of ice on the pond.*

gla·zier (GLAY·zhur) *n.* one who fits windows, etc. with glass.

gleam (GLEEM) *n.* 1 a brief flash or dim glow of light: *the gleam in her eyes; a gleam of sunshine.* 2 a brief or faint show: *a gleam of hope, interest.*
— *v.*: *A fire gleamed in the dark; eyes momentarily gleaming with humour.* — **gleam·y** *adj.*

glean (GLEEN) *v.* 1 pick up the grain left by reapers. 2 gather facts, news, etc. bit by bit: *facts gleaned from old magazines.* — **glean·er** *n.*

glee *n.* 1 lively delight: *to dance with glee.* 2 an unaccompanied song for three or more different singing voices. — **glee·ful** *adj.*; **glee·ful·ly** *adv.*

glee club *n.* a group organized for singing choral songs.

glen *n.* a narrow valley.

glib *adj.* **glib·ber, glib·best** smooth and fluent, often in an insincere way: *a glib excuse.*

glide *v.* **glides, glid·ed, glid·ing** 1 move along smoothly and with ease. 2 descend in a plane without using the engine.
— **n.**: *the prone glide and back glide in swimming; the plane's long glide to the ground.*

glid·er (GLY·dur) *n.* one that glides, esp. an engineless aircraft kept aloft by air currents: *A glider soars upward or across the sky.*

glim·mer (GLIM·ur) *v.* give a weak, flickering light; appear dimly: *stars glimmering in the distant sky.*
— **n.** a faint light: *the faint glimmer of distant candlelight; a glimmer of hope; a story without even a glimmer of truth.*

glimpse (GLIMPS) *v.* **glimps·es, glimpsed, glimps·ing** see or look at briefly and hastily.
— **n.** a brief sight: *I caught a glimpse of the speeding car.*

glint *n.* 1 a flash or gleam of light. 2 a brief appearance.
— *v.* flash briefly: *Light glinted from the crystal glasses;*

With each turning, the story glints with a different light.

glis·ten (GLIS·un) *v.* shine brightly by reflecting light; sparkle: *Dew glistens on the grass;* also *n.*

glis·ter (GLIS·tur) *v.* [old use] glisten.

glitch *n.* 1 an unwanted surge of electricity or a false electronic signal. 2 *Informal.* a minor mishap or malfunction: *an unexpected glitch; the glitches and gremlins that bug computers.*

glit·ter (GLIT·ur) *v.* 1 shine brightly with a flashing light; sparkle: *a glittering diamond.* 2 be showy or attractive: *the glittering costumes worn by rock singers.* — *n.* 1 sparkle: *the glitter of diamonds; a circus parade's glitter; to decorate costumes with glitter* (= small, shiny objects). 2 *Cdn.* same as **glitter ice,** ice left on trees and other exposed objects by freezing rain.

glitz·y (GLIT·see) *adj.* **glitz·i·er, -i·est** showy or gaudy: *a glitzy restaurant.*

gloat (GLOTE) *v.* take pleasure in a greedy, selfish, or sadistic manner: *to gloat over a rival's misfortune.*

glob *n.* a drop or globule; also, a rounded lump.

glob·al (GLOH·bul) *adj.* 1 of the whole earth; worldwide: *global changes, implications; a global war.* 2 all-inclusive: *a global command, search, view.* — **glob·al·ism** (-liz·um) *n.* — **glob·al·ly** *adv.*

global village *n.* the concept of the world reduced to a small community by high-speed transportation and communications.

globe *n.* 1 anything spherical, esp. the earth or a model of it: *The equator girdles the globe.* 2 a nearly round glass object, as a fishbowl.

globe·trot *v.* **-trots, -trot·ted, -trot·ting** travel all over the world. — **globe·trot·ter** *n.*

glob·u·lar (GLOB·yuh·lur) *adj.* 1 spherical. 2 composed of globules.

glob·ule (GLOB·yool) *n.* a tiny ball or drop.

gloom (long "oo") *n.* darkness or dimness: *an all-pervading gloom; the gloom of winter; The bad news cast gloom* or *a gloom over the audience; a cloud, pall of gloom; tales of doom and gloom; There is gloom about* or *over the future of the environment.* — **gloom·y** *adj.*

glo·ri·fy (GLOR·uh·fye) *v.* **-fies, -fied, -fy·ing** 1 give praise, honour, worship, or glory to a person or thing; also, exalt to heaven: *a martyr glorified after death.* 2 make something seem more splendid than it actually is: *TV seems to glorify violence.* — **glo·ri·fi·er** (-fye·ur) *n.* — **glo·ri·fi·ca·tion** (-fuh·CAY·shun) *n.*

glo·ri·ous (GLOR·ee·us) *adj.* 1 having, giving, or deserving glory: *a glorious deed, past, reign, victory.* 2 magnificent or delightful: *the glorious fall weather; We had a glorious time at the party.* — **glo·ri·ous·ly** *adv.*

glo·ry (GLOR·ee) *n.* **-ries** 1 great honour, fame, or praise, esp. of God: *Glory to God in the Highest; Olympic gold brings glory to a nation; to bask in the glory of victory.* 2 the source of renown; splendour or magnificence: *Long hair was her glory; the glory that was Rome.* 3 heavenly bliss: *a painting of saints in heavenly glory.* — **in one's glory** in a state of great joy, gratification, etc. — *v.* **-ries, -ried, -ry·ing** rejoice proudly: *to glory in one's exploits.*

gloss *n.* 1 a shiny surface; lustre: *a high gloss finish.* 2 a deceptive appearance. 3 a commentary on, a brief note within, or a translation of a text. — *v.* explain or annotate. — **gloss over** try to ignore or hide: *The report glosses over the details of the scandal.*

glos·sa·ry (GLOS·uh·ree) *n.* **-ries** a short dictionary of difficult or technical words: *a glossary at the end of a textbook.*

glos·sy (GLOS·ee) *adj.* **gloss·i·er, -i·est** having a lustrous surface: *a glossy finish, paint.* — *n., pl.* **glos·sies** a magazine or photograph printed on smooth, shiny paper. — **gloss·i·ly** *adv.;* **gloss·i·ness** *n.*

glove (GLUV) *n.* 1 a fitted hand covering with separated fingers: *kid, leather, rubber gloves; The nickname fits him like a glove; The gloves were coming off (in preparation for a fight) and charges were laid.* 2 a large padded leather covering used on the hand in baseball, boxing, etc.

gloved (GLUVD) *adj.* wearing gloves: *He was warmly gloved against the cold.*

glow (GLOH) *v.* 1 shine brightly and steadily because or as though intensely heated: *glowing embers; a glowing* (= highly favourable) *account, description.* 2 have a bright, reddish colour; flush or blush: *His cheeks glowed with embarrassment.* 3 show warm emotion: *glowing with pride in his son.* — *n.* 1 brightness: *the glow of burning coal; the soft glow of a lamp.* 2 warmth or warm colour: *the ruddy glow of health on her cheeks; to feel a glow of affection.*

glow·er (GLOW·ur, "OW" as in "HOW") *v.* stare angrily or sullenly. — *n.* a scowl.

gloze *v.* **gloz·es, glozed, gloz·ing** gloss over.

glue (GLOO) *n.* a sticky substance used to join things, esp. one made from animal gelatin. — *v.* **glues, glued, glu·ing** stick: *a broken cup glued together.* — **glue·y** (GLOO·ee) *adj.*

glum *adj.* **glum·mer, glum·mest** gloomy, sullen, or morose. — **glum·ly** *adv.;* **glum·ness** *n.*

glut *v.* **gluts, glut·ted, glut·ting** 1 fill or feed to excess: *to glut one's appetite.* 2 oversupply a market: *The price of gas went down when the world markets were glutted with oil.* — *n.* an oversupply: *There's a glut of cookbooks on the market.*

glut·ton (GLUT·un) *n.* one who overeats or has a too large capacity for something: *He's a glutton for work.* — **glut·ton·ous** *adj.* — **glut·ton·y** *n.* **glut·ton·ies.**

gnarl (NARL) *n.* a twisted, protruding knot on a tree.

gnarled or **gnarl·y** *adj.* knotty or misshapen.

gnash (NASH) *v.* grind together: *He gnashed his teeth in rage.*

gnat (NAT) *n.* any tiny, winged, usually biting insect.

gnaw (NAW) *v.* **1** consume, corrode, or produce by biting: *a dog gnawing (at) a bone; Mice gnaw holes.* **2** torment: *Remorse gnawed at his heart; gnawing anxiety, hunger, pain.*

gnome (NOME) *n.* a dwarf of folklore who lives underground and guards treasures of precious ores: *the fabled gnomes* (= powerful bankers) *of Swiss banks.*

gno·mic (NOH·mic) *adj.* having to do with maxims and aphorisms: *gnomic poetry, verse.*

gnom·ish (NOH·mish) *adj.* dwarfish, like a gnome.

go *v.* **goes** (GOZE), **went, gone** (GON, GAWN), **go·ing** **1** move away to or from a place: *You can go now; I'll be gone by 5 p.m.* **2** move or pass on: *There's a rumour going through school; another year to go before I graduate; My eyesight is going* (= weakening); *Fifty dollars will not go far* (= purchase much) *at today's prices.* **3** be active: *The machine goes when you switch it on.* **4** move or tend *to* someone or something: *You shouldn't have gone to such trouble for me; This fact goes to prove he was wrong; She had to go to court to establish her claim.* **5** be, become, or be put in a certain way or condition: *Where will this sofa go? She will go mad when she hears this; Many go hungry all over the world; Some go broke; How did the interview go? The cork went pop.*
— **go along** go forward in agreement: *They tried to go along with his wishes; To get along with Joe you have to go along with him.*
— **go ape** *Slang.* go crazy: *Fans are going ape over that star.*
— **go at** devote oneself to something: *She goes at everything she takes up with energy.*
— **go back on** break: *to go back on a promise.*
— **go by the board** be abandoned: *The project went by the board when the director died.*
— **go down** be entered in the records: *He'll go down in history as a great general.*
— **go for 1** apply to a person or thing: *What I said about Al – the same goes for you too.* **2** attack: *The animal went for his face.* **3** *Informal.* approve of: *The government knew that the people wouldn't go for the increased taxes.* See also GOING.
— **go in for** take an interest in something: *I don't go in for the latest fashions.*
— **go it alone** act alone: *She decided to go it alone when her partner backed out.*
— **go off 1** take place: *How did the meeting go off?* **2** explode: *The bomb didn't go off.*
— **go on 1** happen: *What's going on in town?* **2** judge by: *We need some facts and figures to go on.* **3** continue: *Don't go on being late.*
— **go one better** do better: *The competition tried to go one better by cutting prices.*
— **go out 1** go steady: *Jack is going out with Jill.* **2 go out** to feel for someone: *Our hearts go out to the children of broken homes.*
— **go over 1** examine: *An accountant went over the company's books.* **2** desert to another group: *a spy who went over to the enemy.*
— **go through 1** pass: *He went through a red light and got hit.* **2** endure: *the hard times she went through.*
— **go through with** carry out: *to go through with a marriage, performance, plan.*
— **go under** fail: *Many businesses go under during a recession.*
— **go up to** approach: *She went up to the officer and asked the way.*
— **go with** go steady: *Jack is going with Jill.*
— **go without** carry on wanting something: *When food is scarce, some have to go without.*
— **let go** release or relax: *The child wouldn't let go of her mother's hand; A very reserved man at work, he lets himself go during office parties.*
— *n.* *Informal.* attempt: *He will have another go at the top prize next year; to make a go* (= success) *of the new enterprise.*
— **from the word go** from the very start.
— **no go** failure: *It was no go each time he applied for membership.*
— **on the go** active: *vitamins for people on the go from 9 to 5.*
— *adj.* *Informal.* in perfect order: *All systems are go for the blastoff.*

goad (GODE) *n.* **1** a pointed rod used to urge animals forward. **2** a driving impulse.
— *v.* drive: *Examinations goad students into activity; Students are goaded to study hard.*

go-ahead (GOH·uh·hed) *n.* *Informal.* permission or signal to proceed: *Wait for the leader to give the go-ahead; We got the go-ahead for the project.*

goal (GOLE) *n.* **1** a desired aim, attained after some effort: *to achieve, reach, realize, set a goal; an immediate goal; the ultimate goal of one's ambition.* **2** in a race or in games such as hockey and football, the place to be reached for winning or scoring; also, such a score: *to kick* or *make a goal; She scored two goals in one minute.*

goal·ie (GOH·lee), **goal·keep·er** (GOLE·kee·pur) or **goal·tend·er** (GOLE·ten·dur) *n.* a player who defends a goal against the opposing team.

goat (GOTE) *n.* **1** a cud-chewing, horned, and usually bearded animal related to the sheep: *A goat baas* or *bleats; a young goat* (= kid); *a female goat* (= doe, nanny); *a male goat* (= buck or billy goat). **2** *Informal.* a scapegoat: *Education sometimes becomes the goat of government spending.*
— **get one's goat** *Informal.* annoy or irritate someone.

goat·ee (goh·TEE) *n.* a small, pointed beard on the chin.

goat·herd *n.* one who tends goats.

goat·skin *n.* a container of leather made from a goat's skin.

gob *n.* 1 *Slang.* a sailor in the U.S. Navy. 2 *Informal.* a lump or mass; also **gob·bet** (GOB·it).

gob·ble (GOB·ul) *v.* **gob·bles, gob·bled, gob·bling** 1 swallow greedily: *He gobbled up the food in a hurry.* 2 make the throaty sound of a male turkey, or **gob·bler.**

gob·ble·dy·gook or **gob·ble·de·gook** (GOB·ul·dee·gook, long or short "oo") *n. Informal.* speech or writing that is incomprehensible or meaningless because of its pompous or involved style.

go-between (GOH·bit·ween) *n.* an intermediary or messenger between two parties.

gob·let (GOB·lit) *n.* a bowl-shaped drinking cup with a stem and foot but no handles.

gob·lin (GOB·lin) *n.* a mischievous elf or sprite of folklore.

go-cart *n.* 1 a small, low-slung toy wagon. 2 a kart.

god *n.* 1 a supreme being considered as supernatural and immortal; also, a male deity or idol: *heathen gods; the god of love.* 2 **God** the creator and ruler of the universe for those who believe in one supreme being: *Thank God he's alive; God willing, I hope to pass my final exam; Compulsory arbitration means someone must play God* (= make a binding decision). 3 a deified person or thing.
— **a sight** or **feast for the gods** something wonderful.

god·child *n.* **-chil·dren** one sponsored by a godparent, as at baptism; a **god·daugh·ter** or **god·son.**

god·dess (GOD·is) *n.* a female god.

god·fa·ther (GOD·fah·thur) *n.* 1 a man who sponsors a person at baptism. 2 *Informal.* don or boss: *an underworld godfather; adj.: a godfather figure; the godfather image.*

god·for·sak·en (god·fur·SAY·kun) *adj.* desolate or dismal: *a godforsaken place.*

god·head *n.* 1 a divinity. 2 **Godhead** God.

god·less (GOD·lis) *adj.* not religious; also, wicked.
— **god·less·ness** *n.*

god·ly (GOD·lee) *adj.* **-li·er, -li·est** having reverence for God: *a godly life, person.* — **god·li·ness** *n.*

god·moth·er (GOD·muth·ur) *n.* a woman sponsoring a person at baptism.

god·par·ent (GOD·pair·unt) *n.* a godfather or godmother.

god·send *n.* something much-needed or desired that one gets as if sent by God: *A maid can be a real godsend to the busy homemaker.*

god·son See GODCHILD.

God·speed (god·SPEED) *n.* success: *to bid* or *wish one Godspeed.*

go·fer (GOH·fur) *n. Slang.* one who fetches things for another: *file clerks, receptionists, and assorted gofers.*

go-get·ter (GOH·get·ur) *n. Informal.* one who is aggressively ambitious.

gog·gle (GOG·ul) 1 *v.* **gog·gles, gog·gled, gog·gling** stare with bulging or suprised eyes *at* something.

2 **goggles** *n.pl.* large protective eyeglasses as worn by welders, motorcyclists, and divers.

goggle-eyed (GOG·ul·ide) *adj.* having staring eyes: *The goggle-eyed audience never took their eyes off her; a goggle-eyed fish (with bulging eyes).*

go-go *n.* 1 a discotheque. 2 discotheque dancing.
— *adj.: a go-go dancer cavorting on the stage; the go-go* (= unrestrained) *pace of twentieth-century life; a go-go* (= speculative) *investment fund; a very go-go* (= stylish) *jacket and slacks.*

going *n.* moving: *the coming and going* (= departure) *of winter; We find the going* (= progress) *tougher than expected; Let's leave the place **while the going is good*** (= while it is easy to leave).
— *adj.: a going concern* (= smoothly running business); *the best candidate going* (= available); *The going* (= prevailing) *rate for this job is $50 an hour; a lucky young woman who has many things **going for*** (= in favour of) *her; She's 12, **going on*** (= approaching) *13; It's **going to*** (= about to) *rain.*

going-over (go·ing·OH·vur) *n.* 1 a thorough examination. 2 a scolding or beating.

goings-on (go·ing·ZON) *n.pl. Informal.* happenings looked upon with disapproval: *The goings-on in that house were the talk of the town.*

gold *n.* 1 a bright-yellow precious metal used for jewellery and as international currency; hence, money: *to prospect for gold; We struck gold; Liz is as good as gold* (= very good). 2 a bright yellow. 3 *Cdn.* a record or album that has sold between 50 000 and 100 000 copies in Canada. 4 in the U.S., a record that has sold one million copies or 500 000 copies as an album.

gold·en (GOLD·un) *adj.* 1 made of gold: *the golden calf; a golden ring.* 2 bright yellow: *golden hair.* 3 flourishing or prosperous: *the golden age of poetry; the golden years of retirement; the **Golden Horseshoe** of Ontario* (= heavily urbanized, crescent-shaped area along Lake Ontario, from Oshawa to St. Catherines); *the **golden boy** or **golden-haired boy*** (= favourite) *of our corporation; The Golden Boy of Winnipeg represents eternal youth; a **golden handshake*** (= huge severance pay); *a golden* (= 50th year) *anniversary, jubilee; a **golden oldie** (Informal for* something old but still popular, as a song); *a golden* (= valuable) *opportunity.*

golden ager *n. Informal.* a person over 65 years old.

golden calf *n.* 1 in the Bible, an idol worshipped by the Israelites. 2 wealth as an object of worship.

golden parachute *n.* guarantee of a large severance payment to a top executive in the event of a company takeover.

golden rule *n.* a basic rule of conduct, esp. "Treat others as you would like them to treat you."

gold·eye *n. Cdn.* a freshwater fish that is used smoked as a table delicacy.

gold·fish *n.* a fancy variety of carp with bright colours ranging from gold to red, kept in glass bowls as ornamental fish.

gold·smith *n.* a worker skilled in making articles of gold; also, a dealer in them.

golf (GOLF, GAWLF) *n.* a game played with a small, hard ball and long-handled **golf clubs** on an outdoor **golf course** or **golf links** having a series of 9 or 18 holes: *to play a round of golf* (= complete circuit of all the holes). — *v.* play golf. — **golf·er** *n.*

Go·li·ath (guh·LYE·uth) *n.* in the Bible, a giant killed by David.

gol·ly (GOL·ee) *interj.* expressing surprise, pleasure, etc.: *By golly, he did it; Oh, golly gee!*

-gon *combining form.* a figure with angles as specified: *octagon, pentagon, polygon.*

gon·do·la (GON·duh·luh) *n.* **1** a long, narrow boat with peaked prow and stern, as used on the canals of Venice. **2** something resembling a gondola such as an enclosed suspended car used as a ski lift, a car suspended from under an airship, a low-sided open-topped railway car, or **gondola car,** or bulk freight such as coal, etc.

gon·do·lier (gon·duh·LEER) *n.* one who rows or poles a gondola.

gone *pp.* of GO. **1** away: *I'll be gone for two days; He's gone to* (= away in) *Europe; I've gone* (= been) *to Europe; The disease is too far gone* (= too advanced) *for us to do anything.* **2** *Informal.* removed from reality: *He wore a gone expression; He's quite gone on* (= in love with) *her.*

gon·er (GON·ur) *n. Informal.* a person or thing beyond help: *One glance from her and you're a goner!*

gon·zo (GON·zoh) *adj. Slang.* weird or bizarre.

goo *n. Slang.* **1** anything thick and sticky, as glue. **2** sentimentality: *nostalgia without the goo.* — **goo·ey** (GOO·ee) *adj.*

good (short "oo") *adj., comp.* **bet·ter** (BET·ur), *superl.* **best** having a desirable quality: *Rain is good for crops, but bad for a picnic; She's good at or in manual work; good with her hands; good to her in-laws; Isn't it good to be home at last!* 2 + 2 = 4 **holds good** (= is true) *under all conditions; She's been away a good* (= considerable) *while; so tired I'm as good as* (= almost) *dead; a round-trip ticket that is good for* (= valid for) *a year; This pen is no good* (= useless). — *n.* **1** what is good: *Do good and avoid evil; The laws work for the common good; Happiness is the highest good; What good is food you can't eat? I'm telling you for your own good; A teacher tries to bring out the good in every student; Some come to no good* (= yield no good result); *Sound advice, well taken, works to our good.* **2** **goods** *pl.* movable personal property; also, merchandise; things for sale: *capital, consumer, durable, manufactured goods.* — **for good (and all)** forever. — **have the goods on** *Slang.* know something bad about a person that others don't. — *adv. Informal.* well: *I can't see good through the fog; It's raining good and* (= really) *heavy.* — **make good 1** succeed: *Unsuccessful throughout life, he made good by marrying a wealthy widow.* **2** put into effect: *to make good one's escape; make good (on) a promise, a threat.* **3** pay for something: *to make good a*

good-bye or **good·bye** *interj. & n., pl.* **-byes** farewell.

good-for-nothing (GOOD·fur·nuth·ing) *n.* one who is worthless or disreputable.

good·ly (GOOD·lee) *adj.* **-li·er, -li·est** considerable: *a goodly sum of money.*

good·ness (GOOD·nis) *n.* the condition or quality of being good, esp. morally: *Goodness knows I tried; For goodness' sake, stop arguing.*

Good Sa·mar·i·tan (-suh·MAIR·uh·tun) *n.* one who takes pity on another in misery and offers help unselfishly.

good will *n.* **1** friendly feeling. **2** the reputation enjoyed by a business that is valued as one of its assests. — **good·will** *adj.* promoting good will: *a goodwill gesture, mission, tour; The Goodwill Industries work for the handicapped.*

good·y (GOOD·ee) *n.* **good·ies** *Informal.* something good, esp. to eat. — *adj.* affectedly pious or moral. — *interj.* a child's exclamation indicating delight.

goody-goody *n.* one who is affectedly or abjectly good.

goof *n. Slang.* **1** blunder. **2** a stupid person. — *v.* make a blunder: *Somebody goofed and the wedding cake never arrived; Those who goof around* (= waste time) *all day never get anything done; He was fired for goofing off* (= loafing) *on the job.*

goof-off *n. Slang.* a shirker.

goof·y (GOO·fee) *adj.* **goof·i·er, -i·est** silly or crazy.

gook (long or short "oo") *n. Slang.* something sticky or slimy.

goon (long "oo") *n. Slang.* **1** a ruffian, as one hired to break up strikes or help prison guards: *a goon squad.* **2** a stupid person.

goop (long "oo") *n. Slang.* something semiliquid and sticky: *goops of ink from a ball-point pen.*

goose (rhyme: "loose") *n., pl.* **geese** a web-footed bird that is smaller than a swan, to which it is related, and considered stupid: *A goose cackles or honks; a flock or gaggle of geese; a young goose* (= gosling); *a male goose* (= gander); *You silly goose! to kill the goose that lays golden eggs* (= to destroy a source of wealth out of greed). — **cook one's goose** See COOK. — *v. Slang.* to prod a person in the buttocks: *to goose up* (= raise) *sales, wages.*

goose bumps *n.pl.* a skin condition resembling a plucked goose's skin caused by cold, fear, etc.; also **goose flesh, goose pimples.**

go·pher (GOH·fur) *n.* **1** a burrowing rodent with large cheek pouches; also called "pocket gopher." **2** a ground squirrel of the prairies related to the chipmunk. **3** same as GOFER.

Gor·dian knot (GOR·dee·un-) *n.* something intricate like the knot that could not be untied and was cut by Alexander the Great with a quick, bold stroke.

gore *n.* **1** clotted blood. **2** a long, triangular or wedge-shaped piece of cloth inserted in a garment, sail, etc. to

adjust width or shape.
— *v.* gores, gored, gor·ing pierce or wound with a horn or tusk.

gorge (GORJ) *n.* 1 a narrow canyon with steep walls. 2 a mass, as of ice, choking a passage. 3 a seam on a coat where the collar meets the lapel.
— make one's gorge rise of something gruesome, to disgust or make one want to vomit.
— *v.* gorg·es, gorged, gorg·ing stuff with food: *children at a party gorging themselves with* or *on cake.*

gor·geous (GOR·jus) *adj.* splendid, esp. in a colourful way: *trees in gorgeous fall colours; gorgeous weather; a gorgeous day, sunset; Isn't she gorgeous! fifty gorgeous dancers kicking on the stage.*

go·ril·la (guh·RIL·uh) *n.* an African ape, the largest of the anthropoids.

gorm·less (GORM·lis) *adj. Informal.* senseless.

gorp *n. Informal.* a snack of high-energy food, as dried fruits, nuts, and seeds.

gor·y (GOR·ee) *adj.* gor·i·er, gor·i·est bloody; hence, horrible: *Spare us the gory details.*

gosh *interj.* an exclamation of surprise: *By gosh!*

gos·pel (GOS·pul) *n.* 1 truth accepted without question, esp. gospel truth, as from the Christian Gospels, the first four books of the New Testament. 2 Christianity: *to spread the gospel; St. Thomas preached the gospel in India; a gospel singer of devotional folk songs, spirituals, etc.*

gos·pel·ler or gos·pel·er (GOS·pul·ur) *n.* a gospel preacher.

gos·sip (GOS·ip) *n.* 1 idle talk about other people and their private affairs: *Where did he pick up that piece of gossip? Who's spreading the gossip? the gossip about Dick and Jane.* 2 a person who indulges in gossip: *an idle, malicious, vicious gossip.*
— *v.: People gossip about unwed mothers and fathers.*
— gos·sip·y *adj.*

got *pt. & pp.* of GET.
— have got *Informal: Have you got* (= do you have) *a match? I have got to* (= must) *go home now.*

gotch·a (GOCH·uh) *Informal.* "I got you!"

Goth·ic (GOTH·ic) *n. & adj.* 1 (the language) of a Germanic people of the 3rd to 5th centuries A.D.: *a Gothic tribe.* 2 a style of architecture developed in Europe in the Middle Ages: *the pointed Gothic arch; Gothic cathedrals.* 3 fiction dealing with the supernatural and the grotesque: *Gothic books, fiction; 19th century Gothic novels.*

got·ta (GOT·uh) *Informal.* "have got to." See GOT.

got·ten (GOT·un) a *pp.* of GET.

gouge (GOWJ, "OW" as in "HOW") *n.* 1 a chisel with a concave blade for cutting grooves and holes. 2 a channel or hole made with a gouge.
— *v.* goug·es, gouge, goug·ing 1 dig or scoop out, as with a gouge: *Torturers gouged out his eyes.* 2 *Informal.* extort money from someone: *The shopkeeper used to gouge his customers; He was charged with (price) gouging.* — goug·er *n.*

gourd (GORD, GOORD) *n.* 1 the fruit of a vine such as the cucumber, pumpkin, or squash. 2 a hard-shelled fruit such as the calabash that is dried for use as a container.

gour·mand (GOOR·mund, -mahnd) *n.* a lover of good food and wine.

gour·met (GOOR·may) *n.* a discriminating expert of food and drink: *an expensive gourmet restaurant.*

gout (GOWT) *n.* a disease characterized by swelling of the joints, esp. that of the big toe.
— gout·y *adj.* gout·i·er, -i·est: *gouty arthritis (caused by gout); a gouty joint; a gouty toe (suffering from gout).*

gov·ern (GUV·urn) *v.* control or regulate: *Children must learn to govern their temper; conduct governed by moral principles; The British Sovereign merely reigns and does not govern; Supply and demand govern prices; "to" governs "him," not "he" as in "Give it to him"; a college's governing body.*
— gov·ern·a·ble (-nuh·bul) *adj.*
— gov·ern·ance (-nunce) *n.*

gov·ern·ess (GUV·urn·is) *n.* a woman who teaches and supervises children in their home.

gov·ern·ment (GUV·urn·munt) *n.* 1 rule or governing: *Democracy is government by the people.* 2 a system of governing: *a central, communist, democratic, federal, local, municipal, national, parliamentary, provincial government.* 3 a governing body of people such as the prime minister and cabinet: *the fault of the last government; a Conservative government; Liberal government; a caretaker, coalition, good, minority, parliamentary, provisional, strong, totalitarian, weak government; to head, live under, overthrow, run, seize a government; shouting from the government benches of the legislature; government and opposition; Who will form the next government* (= Who will be the next prime minister or premier)? *The government was about to fall; The government* (= ministers) *are pleased to announce a cut in spending; the governments* (= nations) *represented at the U.N.; the government leaders* (= party spokesmen) *of the Commons and the Senate.*
— gov·ern·men·tal (-MEN·tul) *adj.*

gov·er·nor (GUV·ur·nur) *n.* 1 the appointed head of a state or colony. 2 a member of a governing body or "board of governors."

governor general *n.* a chief governor: *the Governor General of Canada.*

gown (rhyme: "down") *n.* 1 a long, loose outer garment or robe, as worn by judges and academics, or a woman's formal dress, as worn at a wedding. 2 a similar garment: *dressing gowns; a hospital gown.*
— *v.* dress in a gown: *Candidates come capped and gowned for a graduation ceremony.*

grab *v.* grabs, grabbed, grab·bing 1 grasp suddenly, esp. in an eager or greedy manner: *A dog grabs at a bone.* 2 *Informal.* take or get: *Grab a pencil and write this down; Something that grabs your attention; The Soviets grabbed the lead in the third period; He grabbed her by the arms; She grabbed hold of the grab bar*

when she slipped in the bath. **3** *Informal.* make an impression on someone: *Five dollars for a cup of coffee – how does that grab you?*
— **n.** a snatch or grasp: *an elected office **up for grabs** every four years.* — **grab·ber** *n.*

grab bag *n.* **1** a bag of assorted items sold at a fixed price. **2** miscellaneous assortment: *The politician offered a grab bag of promises.*

grab·by (GRAB·ee) adj. **grab·bi·er, grab·bi·est** avaricious.

grace *n.* **1** a pleasing quality such as charm, beauty, or elegance: *Gazelles run fast with effortless grace; He's full of faults but for one saving grace* (= quality); *A defeated candidate concedes an election with **good** or **bad grace**; Jane puts on little **airs and graces** to impress people.*
2 Your or **Her** or **His Grace** [title used in addressing or referring to an archbishop, duke, or duchess]. **3** favour or good will: *Adam's disobedience and fall from grace; divine grace; a state of grace; three days of grace to return a book without penalty after it is due.* **4** a short prayer, as before or after a meal.
— **in one's good** (or **bad**) **graces** favoured (or disliked) by one.
— **v. grac·es, graced, grac·ing 1** bring charm or elegance to something: *The Queen graced the occasion by* or *with her presence.* **2** honour someone, as with a title.

grace·ful *adj.* attractive in form, movement, or behaviour: *a graceful animal, dance, gesture.*
— **grace·ful·ly** *adv.;* **grace·ful·ness** *n.*

gra·cious (GRAY·shus) *adj.* having or showing qualities befitting a high station in life, as courtesy, indulgence, and elegance: *the Queen's gracious smile; She's gracious towards everyone; a gracious gesture, speech; a suburban mansion fit for gracious living.*
— **interj.** indicating surprise: *Good gracious!*

grad *n. Informal.* a graduate.

gra·da·tion (gruh·DAY·shun, gray-) *n.* a step or degree in something showing progressive change: *the gradations from violet to red in the rainbow.*

grade *n.* **1** one of a series of steps or degrees: *school grades from 1 to 12; He rose from the grades of warrant officer to the rank of captain.* **2** a classification according to quality: *Canada Fancy, Light, Medium, and Dark grades of maple syrup; prime, choice, and other grades of American beef; There are several sizes of grade A eggs; grades of coal, lumber.* **3** an achievement rating as A, B, C, D, E, F (fail), or S (satisfactory): *to get, give, receive a grade; Everyone except those receiving F **make the grade*** (= pass). **4** a road level or ground level: *A basement is below grade; There is no grade separation between road and railway at a **grade crossing*** (= level crossing). **5** a grade crossing. **6** the slope of a road or railway.
— **v. grades, grad·ed, grad·ing 1** classify: *Only steer and heifer can be graded prime beef; a term paper graded "A".* **2** level or slope: *to clear a right of way and grade it for a highway.*

grad·er (GRAY·dur) *n.* **1** one that grades, esp. an earth-levelling machine: *a road grader.* **2** a school pupil in a specific grade: *first grader; second grader.*

grade school *n.* [U.S. use] elementary school; also **the grades.**

grade separation *n.* a crossing that uses an overpass or underpass.

grad·u·al (GRAJ·oo·ul) *adj.* by steps or degrees; little by little. — **grad·u·al·ism** (-liz·um) *n.*
— **grad·u·al·ly** *adv.*

grad·u·ate (GRAJ·oo·ate) *v.* **-ates, -at·ed, -at·ing**
1 finish a course of study: *Al graduated from McGill with honours.* **2** give a diploma to someone: *Al was graduated with honours.* **3** mark or divide into gradations: *a thermometer graduated in degrees Celsius; a tax rate so graduated that higher incomes are taxed more than lower incomes.*
— **n.** (-oo·it) one who has graduated: *a Queens graduate; an honours graduate; adj.: a graduate degree, engineer, nurse; a graduate student working on her M.A.* — **grad·u·a·tion** (-AY·shun) *n.*

graf·fi·to (gruh·FEE·toh) *n., pl.* **-ti** (-tee) a crude drawing or writing done on a public wall, rock, etc.

graft *v.* **1** join a shoot or bud, called "scion," from one plant or tree to another, called "stock," and make it grow: *Several varieties of a plant may be grafted on to the same stock.* **2** produce a new or improved fruit, flower, etc. **3** transplant skin or bone in this manner. **4** of politicians, public officials, etc., make money by illegal means.
— **n. 1** something grafted: *different types of graft such as cleft, splice, and saddle; A skin graft was done, but it didn't take.* **2** illegally made money: *graft in the form of protection money.*

gra·ham (GRAY·um) *adj.* made of fine, unsifted whole-wheat: *graham crackers, flour.*

grain *n.* **1** a small, hard seed, esp. a cereal or its plant; also, cereal seeds collectively: *to grind, grow, mill, store grain; Our chief food grain is wheat; the world's grain consumption.* **2** a tiny, hard bit or particle: *grains of pollen, sugar; coarse, not fine grains of salt, sand, stone, etc.; Take tall tales **with a grain of salt*** (= with skepticism). **3** a unit of weight equal to ¼ carat. **4** the fibre pattern of wood, layer arrangement of coal, stone, etc.: *Punctuality goes **against the grain*** (= natural inclination) *of some people.*

grained *adj.* marked like wood, marble, etc.

grain·y *adj.* **grain·i·er, -i·est** having a grain or texture; consisting of particles: *the speckled, grainy appearance of a photographic enlargement.* — **grain·i·ness** *n.*

-gram *combining form.* **1** something recorded or drawn: *cablegram, diagram, monogram.* **2** number of grams: *kilogram, milligram.*

gram·mar (GRAM·ur) *n.* **1** the rules governing the formation of words and the structure of sentences. **2** correctness of spoken or written expression.
— **gram·mar·i·an** (gruh·MAIR·ee·un) *n.*

gram·mat·i·cal (gruh·MAT·uh·cul) *adj.* having to do with grammar or correct grammar: *a grammatical error; good grammatical English.*
— **gram·mat·i·cal·ly** *adv.*

Gram·my (GRAM·ee) *n*. **Gram·mys** or **Gram·mies** any of the annual awards for achievements in the recording industry.

gramps *n*. *Informal*. grandfather.

gran·a·ry (GRAN·uh·ree, GRAY·nuh·ree) *n*. **-ries** a storehouse for threshed grain: *The Prairies are the granary* (= area of grain production) *of Canada*.

grand *adj*. **1** large in size or importance: *a grand finale, jury, piano, staircase, total; the Grand Trunk Railway*. **2** high in rank or dignity: *a grand old man, rabbi*. **3** *Informal*. very satisfying: *We had a grand time at the party*.
— *n*. *sing*. & *pl*. *Slang*. $1 000: *fifty grand* (= $50 000).

gran·dam or **gran·dame** *n*. [old use] an old woman, esp. a grandmother.

grand·child *n*. **-chil·dren** a child of one's son or daughter; a **grand·son** or **grand·daugh·ter**.

grande dame (grahn·DAHM) *n*., *pl*. **grandes dames** (grahn·DAHM) *French*. an elderly woman of prestige: *the grande dame of classical ballet*.

grand·daugh·ter (GRAN·daw·tur) *n*. See GRANDCHILD.

gran·dee (gran·DEE) *n*. **1** a Spanish or Portuguese nobleman of the highest rank. **2** an all-important personage.

gran·deur (GRAN·jur) *n*. greatness or magnificence of appearance, style, quality, nobility, etc.: *The dictator suffered from delusions of grandeur*.

grand·fa·ther (GRAN·fah·thur, -faw·thur) *n*. See GRANDPARENT.

grandfather clause *n*. a legal provision for favouring a special group: *In 1975, the Canadian Parliament repealed a grandfather clause favouring foreign publications*.

grandfather clock *n*. a large clock that stands on the floor in a tall, upright case.

gran·dil·o·quent (gran·DIL·uh·kwunt) *adj*. pompous in diction and tone.

gran·di·ose (GRAN·dee·ose) *adj*. **1** imposing or magnificent. **2** showy or pompous.

grand jury *n*. in the U.S., a jury of usually more than 12 persons that hears evidence and decides whether to indict an accused person for trial by a petit jury.

grand·ma (GRAN·mah, -muh) *n*. *Informal*. grandmother.

grand·mas·ter (GRAN·mas·tur) *n*. an unusually skilled player, esp. an international winner in chess.

grand·moth·er (GRAN·muth·ur) *n*. See GRANDPARENT.

grand·pa (GRAN·pah) *n*. *Informal*. grandfather.

grand·par·ent (GRAN·pair·unt) *n*. a parent of one's father or mother; a grandfather or grandmother.

grand slam *n*. **1** a winning of all the four major golf or tennis championships in one year. **2** in baseball, a home run hit with a runner on each base: *a grand slam homer*.

grandson See GRANDCHILD.

grand·stand *n*. the main seating place for the spectators at a sporting event.
— *v*. *Informal*. make an attention-getting display, or **grandstand play**, as in baseball.

grange (GRAINJ) *n*. a farm or farmhouse with its barn and other buildings.

gran·ite (GRAN·it) *n*. a hard rock with grains of minerals in it.
— **gra·nit·ic** (gruh·NIT·ic) *adj*. like granite in firmness and endurance.

gran·ny or **gran·nie** (GRAN·ee) *n*. **gran·nies** *Informal*. **1** a grandmother or elderly woman. **2** a fussy person.

gra·no·la (gruh·NOH·luh) *n*. a prepared breakfast cereal of rolled oats and other ingredients that is used as a health food.

grant *v*. **1** allow a request, permission, claim, etc.: *to grant leave of absence to an employee; I grant that my statement was a bit misleading*. **2** confer property or other right or benefit: *Governments grant pensions to widows of veterans*.
— **take for granted** assume: *Don't take it for granted that you will get a raise every year; You can't take anyone for granted (as dependable) these days*.
— *n*. something granted, as money, lands, etc.: *to award, give, receive a grant for a project; a Canada Council grant; a grant to attend a convention; block grants of fixed amounts made by the federal government*. — **gran·tor** or **grant·er** *n*.

grant-in-aid (gran·tun·AID) *n*. **-aids** a money grant or subsidy given to a person or institution for an educational or public-service project.

grants·man·ship (GRANTS·mun·ship) *n*. the art of obtaining grants.

gran·u·lar (GRAN·yuh·lur) *adj*. grainy: *"Corn snow" is granular; the granular white cells in the bloodstream*.
— **gran·u·lar·i·ty** (-LAIR·uh·tee) *n*.

gran·u·late (GRAN·yuh·late) *v*. **-lates, -lat·ed, -lat·ing** **1** form granules: *granulated honey, sugar*. **2** become granular or roughen: *A wound surface granulates in healing; granulated leather*.
— **gran·u·la·tion** (-LAY·shun) *n*.

gran·ule (GRAN·yool) *n*. **1** a grain or small crystal, as of sugar or snow pellets. **2** one of the small, short-lived patches of gas in the sun's photosphere.

grape *n.* **1** the small, round, juicy berry that grows in clusters on various woody vines: *to pick grapes; press grapes for wine; a bunch of grapes; a case of sour grapes (as when the fox said the grapes he couldn't reach must be sour).* **2** such a vine or the usually dark, purplish-red colour of the fruit.

grape·fruit *n.* a large, round, yellowish citrus fruit.

grape·shot *n.* small iron balls formerly used as cannon shot.

grape·vine *n.* **1** a grape-bearing vine. **2** *Informal.* word-of-mouth spreading of news, gossip, etc.: *We heard it by* or *on* or *through the office grapevine.*

graph (GRAF) *n.* a chart or drawing using lines, curves, bars, or circles ("pie chart") to present in picture form relationships between quantities: *a graph showing the changes of temperature during the day.*
— *v.* show in graph form: *Student attendance may be graphed against school days along a pair of axes.*

-graph *combining form.* a recording instrument or something recorded: *autograph, monograph, telegraph.*

graph·ic *adj.* **1** vivid or realistic: *a graphic description of the massacre; too graphic for children to watch on TV.* **2** having to do with graphs; also **graph·i·cal.** **3** having to do with drawing, painting, printing, engraving, etc., or the **graphic arts.**
— *n.* **1** a work of graphic art. **2** a graphic display by computer on a video screen.
— **graphics** *n.pl.* [with sing. v.] **1** design, including type, using graphic arts; also, graphic arts itself. **2** production of graphic displays, as on a video screen: *computer graphics.* — **graph·i·cal·ly** *adv.*

-graphy *combining form.* writing or something written, as a treatise or science: *biography, calligraphy, cryptography, geography.*

grap·ple (GRAP·ul) *v.* **grap·ples, grap·pled, grap·pling** **1** grip and hold. **2** struggle or wrestle: *There were more problems than she could* **grapple with** *in one day.*
— *n.* **1** a struggle. **2** a grasping or holding device; also **grappling hook** or **iron.**

grasp *v.* seize and hold firmly, as with the hand: *The swimmer grasped at* or *for the rope thrown to her; She grasped it firmly; They grasped her by the arm and pulled her in; He's eager to grasp at any available opportunity; an idea that is not difficult to grasp* (= understand).
— *n.* hold: *a firm grasp; He has a good grasp of Russian grammar; a thorough grasp of her subject; Success seems within her grasp* (= reach).

grasping *adj.* greedy or avaricious.

grass *n.* **1** any of various plants with jointed stems and long, narrow leaves eaten by grazing animals and cultivated on lawns: *blades of grass; a tuft of grass; to cut* or *mow the grass; Please don't walk on the grass* (= lawn). **2** any cereal grass such as wheat, barley, or corn. **3** *Slang.* marijuana.
— **grass·y** *adj.* **grass·i·er, -i·est.**

grass hockey *n.* *Cdn. Informal.* field hockey.

grass·hop·per (GRAS·hop·ur) *n.* a leaping insect that feeds on leaves and destroys crops.

grass·land *n.* pasture land: *the southern grasslands region of the Prairie Provinces.*

grass roots *n.pl. Informal.* the common people who form the basic strength of any popular movement: *Prosperity should trickle down to the grass roots; The defeated party had to be rebuilt from the grass roots up.*
— **grass·root** or **grass·roots** *adj.: a grassroot issue; at the grassroot level; a grassroot movement for reform; a candidate with grassroot support.*

grate *v.* **grates, grat·ed, grat·ing** **1** grind by scraping or rubbing: *to grate cabbage, cheese.* **2** scrape or scratch or make a rasping sound, as an iron gate on its hinges: *Harsh voices grate on* (= irritate) *our ears.*
— *n.* **1** a framework of bars forming a protective screen, as in a window; grill. **2** a horizontal framework of bars for holding burning fuel, as in a fireplace.
— **grat·er** *n.* — **grat·ing** *n.*

grate·ful *adj.* **1** thankful: *We're grateful to you for helping us; grateful for your help; grateful that you could help.* **2** pleasing: *a grateful task.*
— **grate·ful·ly** *adv.*

grat·i·fy (GRAT·uh·fye) *v.* **-fies, -fied, -fy·ing** give pleasure to; satisfy: *fancies that gratify one's desires; We are gratified at* or *by* or *over* or *with the results; gratified to learn of your success; The results are really gratifying.* — **grat·i·fi·ca·tion** (-fuh·CAY·shun) *n.*

grat·is (GRAT·is, GRAY·tis) *adj. & adv.* free of charge: *tickets mailed gratis; gratis copies of a new book.*

grat·i·tude (GRAT·uh·tude) *n.* thankfulness: *our deep, profound, undying gratitude; to express, feel, show (one's) gratitude for favours received.*

gra·tu·i·tous (gruh·TUE·uh·tus) *adj.* unjustified; uncalled-for: *gratuitous advice; a gratuitous insult, remark.*

gra·tu·i·ty (gruh·TUE·uh·tee) *n.* **-ties** a small money gift; tip.

grave *adj.* **grav·er, grav·est** weighty; hence, serious or solemn: *a grave doubt; grave consequences; a mourner's grave expression.*
— *n.* **1** a hole dug in the ground to bury a corpse: *A coffin is lowered into a grave; to lay flowers on a grave; People pray at his grave; a grave desecrated by body snatchers; bodies buried in mass graves; an unmarked grave; the watery grave of those who die at sea; from* **the cradle to the grave** (= all through life); *He has* **one foot in the grave** (= is near death); *It's enough to make him* **turn over in his grave** (= It's so shocking). **2** a mound of earth or tomb. **3** a mark originally indicating a vowel of low pitch, as in French words like "blasè," used also to mark prominence of syllable, as in "an agèd genius"; also **grave accent.**
— *v.* **graves,** *pt.* **graved,** *pp.* **grav·en** or **graved, grav·ing** **1** carve; hence, impress deeply: *idols and such* **graven images** *of stone and wood.* **2** clean and tar a ship's bottom: *the graving docks of shipyards.*
— **grave·ly** *adv.;* **grave·ness** *n.*

grav·el (GRAV·ul) *n.* rock fragments, pebbles, etc. that are coarser than sand: *Streams and melting glaciers formed gravel pits; gravel in the urine* (= particles of kidney stones).

— **grav·el·ly** *adj.* like gravel; harsh-sounding: *a gravelly voice.*

grave·stone *n.* an inscribed stone or monument marking a grave.

grave·yard *n.* a cemetery: *an auto graveyard; A graveyard shift (of workers) starts near midnight.*

grav·i·tate (GRAV·uh·tate) *v.* -tates, -tat·ed, -tat·ing move or tend to or toward a place by or as if by gravity: *Heavier substances gravitate to the bottom of a liquid faster than lighter ones; two kindred spirits gravitating* (=attracted) *toward each other.*
— **grav·i·ta·tion** (-TAY·shun) *n.*
— **grav·i·ta·tion·al** *adj.*: *There's no gravitational force at the centre of the earth.*

grav·i·ty (GRAV·uh·tee) *n.* -ties 1 the force of gravitation, esp. the earth's pull on objects: *the law of gravity; Gravity causes weight; The lower an object's centre of gravity* (=weight), *the more stable it is.* 2 weightiness or seriousness: *Do you realize the gravity of the situation?*

gra·vy (GRAY·vee) *n.* -vies 1 sauce made by thickening with flour, seasoning, etc. the juice given off by meat in cooking. 2 *Slang.* a surplus beyond what is expected or needed.

gray, graybeard, gray matter See GREY, etc.

gray·mail *n.* a kind of blackmail by threat of public exposure.

graze *v.* graz·es, grazed, graz·ing 1 feed on grass: *sheep grazing in the meadow; The shepherds graze them.* 2 touch, scrape, or scratch in passing: *The bullet grazed his head.* — *n.* a grazing or abrasion.

grease (GREECE) *n.* a thick oily substance such as melted animal fat; lubricant: *a detergent that cuts* (=dissolves) *grease; The wheel needs a spot of grease; nothing like elbow grease* (=hard work) *to get things done; Clowns, actors, etc. use grease paint.*
— *v.* (GREECE, GREEZ) greas·es, greased, greas·ing 1 smear with grease; lubricate: *Will higher pay grease the wheels of bureaucracy* (=make it more efficient)? 2 *Slang.* to bribe, esp. **grease the hand** or **palm** of someone.

greas·y (GREE·see) *adj.* greas·i·er, -i·est 1 containing grease: *greasy food.* 2 soiled with grease: *greasy hands.*

greasy spoon *n. Slang.* a cheap, unsanitary restaurant.

great (GRATE) *adj.* 1 imposing in size or degree: *a great artist, friend, idea, judge, king, loss, man, occasion, ruler, writer; the great toe* (=big toe); *the great train robbery; the Great Confederacy* (=league of the Iroquois); *Alexander the Great; a great deal of fun; the great majority of people; A great many of us don't smoke; the Great Wall of China; the Great War of 1914 – 1918; once in a great while; He's a great one for* (*Informal* for good at) *throwing parties; the four great powers* (=nations). 2 remarkable or surprising: *He shows great ignorance.* 3 *Informal.* very good: *You're great! It was great of you to come to our rescue; The party was great fun; Pat's the greatest!* (=a remarkably good person). — **great·ly** *adv.*; **great·ness** *n.*

great·coat *n.* a heavy overcoat.

Great Dane *n.* a large, graceful, strong, short-coated mastiff.

great-grandchild (great·GRAN·child) *n.* -chil·dren a child of one's grandchild.

great·heart·ed (great·HAR·tid) *adj.* 1 noble or generous. 2 fearless.

Great Lakes *n. pl.* the lakes Ontario, Erie, Huron, Michigan, and Superior.

greed *n.* excessive desire for money, food, power, etc.: *Midas showed insatiable greed for gold; a man consumed with greed.*

greed·y *adj.* -i·er, -i·est having great desire for food, money, etc.: *a child who is greedy for candy; to get greedy; a greedy moneylender.*
— **greed·i·ly** *adv.*; **greed·i·ness** *n.*

Greek *n.* a person of or from Greece; also, the language of Greece: *Your poetry is all Greek to* (=unintelligible to) *me; ancient warfare using Greek fire* (=chemical mixture that burns on contact with water).

green *n. & adj.* 1 the colour of greenery: *Fertilizers helped the green revolution in developing countries; the Green Chamber* (=House of Commons) *has green carpeting; to be green with envy; the green-eyed monster* (=jealousy). 2 a grassy plot: *the village green; a (golf) putting green.* 3 the colour of unripe fruit; hence, immature or inexperienced: *a green team of reporters.* 4 the colour symbolizing hope, promise, safety, etc.: *You can turn left only on a green (light); We've got the green light from the boss (to go ahead).*
— **greens** *n. pl.* 1 green leaves and branches. 2 a golf course or its putting green.
— *v.* make or become green or younger; revitalize: *the greening of the nation, thanks to young immigrants.*
— **green·ness** *n.*

green belt *n.* a belt of trees and parks around a heavily built-up area.

green·er·y (GREE·nuh·ree) *n.* -er·ies grass and other growing vegetation.

green·horn *n. Informal.* a new arrival or recruit, esp. one who is easily duped.

green hornet *n. Cdn.* a civilian employee of a police force who issues parking tickets.

green·house *n.* a glass- or plastic-covered building for climate-controlled cultivation of plants.

greenhouse effect *n.* the warming of the earth's lower atmosphere resulting from pollutants such as carbon dioxide blocking the escape of solar heat back into space.

green·mail *n.* the forcing of a company to buy back its shares at a premium price from a speculator threatening a takeover.

green manure *n.* fertilizer made up of growing plants such as alfalfa, grasses, peas, beans, etc. ploughed into the soil.

green paper *n.* a government document containing proposals on a subject of reform for public discussion.

green power *n.* power based on money.

green revolution *n.* increased production of food grains in developing countries, aided by fertilizers, pesticides, and new high-yield varieties.

green·room *n.* offstage waiting room for performers.

green thumb *n.* skill in gardening.

greet *v.* meet someone, esp. to welcome: *Guests are greeted at the door; The announcement was greeted with laughter.*

greeting *n.* **1** the act of one who greets or its expression: *a cordial, formal, friendly, warm greeting; The mayor extended an official greeting* (= welcome) *to the visitors; He began the letter with the greeting* (= salutation) *"Sir."* **2 greetings** *pl.* wishes: *to exchange greetings at Christmas; to extend* or *send greetings to friends; our cordial, friendly, warm, warmest greetings; birthday, holiday, season's greetings; a greeting card.*

gre·gar·i·ous (gruh·GAIR·ee·us) *adj.* **1** tending to herd or flock together: *the gregarious instinct in animals such as sheep; Some solitary bees and wasps are gregarious* (= They build their nests close together). **2** sociable, not solitary: *a witty and gregarious fellow.*

grem·lin *n.* a goblin usually blamed for mechanical mishaps: *The gremlins changed a letter and the forecast said "wild weather."*

gre·nade (gruh·NADE) *n.* a small bomb thrown by hand or fired from a rifle.

grew *pt.* of GROW.

grey or **gray** (GRAY) *adj.* **1** of the dull colour that is a blend of black and white or the colour of aging hair. **2** dismal or dreary. **3** vague or indeterminate: *a grey area of morality.*
— *n.* a grey colour, animal such as a grey horse, or grey cloth.
— *v.* make or become grey: *hair greyed by age.*

grey·beard *n.* an old man.

Grey Cup *n.* *Cdn.* **1** a football trophy awarded each fall to the best professional team in Canada. **2** the deciding game: *a ticket for the Grey Cup.*

grey eminence *n.* one who secretly exercises power.

grey market *n.* a method of dealing based on the ability to pay without doing anything illegal as in black market.

grey matter *n.* the greyish tissue of the brain and spinal cord; hence, intelligence.

grid *n.* **1** a framework resembling a grate or grill;

gridiron. **2** something resembling a grid, as the lead plate in a storage battery, a football field, an interconnecting network of radio or television stations, a system of horizontal and vertical lines for locating points on a map, etc.: *the rectangular grid road system in Alberta.*

grid·dle (GRID·ul) *n.* a heavy, flat metal plate for cooking bacon, pancakes (**griddle cake**), etc.

grid·i·ron (GRID·eye·urn) *n.* **1** a grill for broiling. **2** anything resembling this, as a football field, the structure above a stage for manipulating scenery, or a clock pendulum with rods of different metals.

grid·lock *n.* a traffic jam so tight that no movement is possible.

grief (GREEF) *n.* acute sorrow, esp. one of short duration caused by some misfortune: *He almost went mad with grief when his wife died; Some have died of grief; Hopes of a lifetime **came to grief** (= failed) when the bank crashed;* [exclamation of dismay] *Good grief!*

griev·ance (GREE·vunce) *n.* a complaint or its real or imagined cause: *The fired worker nursed a grievance against his boss; to air* or *vent a grievance publicly; He filed* or *launched* or *submitted a grievance to the higher authorities; They heard and redressed the grievance; the grievance procedure to settle a dispute.*

grieve (GREEV) *v.* **grieves, grieved, griev·ing 1** cause or feel grief: *It grieves us to hear Al is no more; Everyone grieves over his death; The whole nation grieves for him.* **2** appeal as a grievance: *She grieved her dismissal to the labour union.*

griev·ous (GREE·vus) *adj.* causing suffering; hence, severe or grave: *a grievous crime, loss, wound, wrong; grievous pain.* — **griev·ous·ly** *adv.*; **griev·ous·ness** *n.*

grill *n.* **1** a gridiron. **2** a dish of broiled meat, fish, etc.: *a mixed grill of meats and vegetables.* **3** a small restaurant, or **grill-room.** **4** usually **grille**, a protective metal screen or grating, as in front of an automobile radiator. **5** a vent or window covered with a grating.
— *v.* **1** broil: *to grill a hamburger; a grilled cheese sandwich.* **2** torture with questions: *Lawyers grill witnesses.*

grill·work *n.* a pattern of grilles.

grim *adj.* **grim·mer, grim·mest 1** fierce, not relenting: *a battle fought with grim resolve.* **2** horrible or ghastly: *the grim prospect of unemployment; a joke too grim to laugh at.*

grim·ace (GRIM·is, gruh·MACE) *n.* a twisted or distorted face, as of one in pain or trying to amuse.
— *v.* **-ac·es, -aced, -ac·ing** make a grimace: *She grimaced in disgust at the toad on the table.*

grime *n.* dirt, esp. soot, rubbed into a surface such as the skin.

grim·y (GRY·mee) *adj.* **grim·i·er, -i·est** covered with grime: *the grimy faces of miners.*

grin *n.* **1** a broad smile showing the teeth. **2** a baring of teeth in anger, pain, or scorn.
— *v.* **grins, grinned, grin·ning** make a grin or express by a grin: *She nodded and grinned her approval; The pain was bad but he had to **grin and bear it.***

grinch *n.* a person or thing that spoils a celebration, as in the story of the Grinch who stole Christmas gifts.

grind (GRINED) *v.* **grinds, ground, grind·ing 1** reduce to powder by friction, as grain in a mill: *to grind wheat into flour.* **2** rub or press together, as teeth by an angry person or when a crank turns: *to grind out music on a hand organ; The train ground to a halt just short of the landslide.* **3** work hard or long: *a diligent worker grinding away at her tasks.*
— *n.* **1** hard work or study: *the dull grind of compiling a seed catalogue.* **2** a grinding or its result: *coffee of a coarse grind* (= particle size). **3** *Informal.* a hard-working student: *He became a grind so as to get the best exam results.*

grind·stone *n.* **1** a millstone. **2** a sharpening and polishing instrument with a revolving stone.

grip *n.* **1** a firm hold or tight grasp: *to lose, relax, release, tighten one's grip; a firm, tight, vise-like grip; a country in the grip of a famine; to get a good grip on oneself* (= have self-control); *a youngster who* **comes to grips with** (= tries to deal with) *reality.* **2** a way of holding a racket or golf club. **3** something to hold with, as a handle. **4** a handbag or small suitcase. **5** a stagehand in a film production crew.
— *v.* **grips, gripped, grip·ping** have a firm hold: *The scared child gripped its mother's hand; a novel that grips your interest.* — **grip·ping·ly** *adv.*

gripe *v.* **gripes, griped, grip·ing** *Informal.* complain.
— *n.* **1** *Informal.* complaint. **2 gripes** *pl.* pain in the intestines.

grippe (GRIP) *n.* influenza.

gris·ly (GRIS·lee) *adj.* **gris·li·er, -li·est** horrible or ghastly: *a grisly murder.*

grist *n.* **1** ground grain such as meal or flour. **2** grain to be ground, as in a **grist·mill.**
— **grist to** or **for one's mill** matter for profit or advantage to oneself.

gris·tle (GRIS·ul) *n.* cartilage, esp. in table meats.
— **gris·tly** (GRIS·lee) *adj.*

grit *n.* **1** fine gravel, sand, or coarse-grained sandstone: *"All sand and no dirt, clear grit all the way through,"* said the leader about the kind of people he wanted. **2 Grit** *Cdn.* a member of the Liberal Party of Canada, formerly "Clear Grit Party." **3 grits** *n. pl.* coarsely ground corn, oats, wheat, etc.; esp. in southern U.S., ground corn eaten boiled or fried. **4** obstinate courage or pluck: *true grit.*
— *v.* **grits, grit·ted, grit·ting** clench or grind the teeth in determination: *She gritted her teeth and bore the pain.*

grit·ty (GRIT·ee) *adj.* **grit·ti·er, grit·ti·est 1** like grit; sandy: *medication with a gritty texture; the electric guitar's gritty wail; She complained of a gritty feeling in the eyes.* **2** plucky or brave: *a gritty effort; a gritty little girl.*

griz·zled (GRIZ·uld) *adj.* grey-haired; streaked with grey: *a grizzled beard.*

griz·zly (GRIZ·lee) **1** *n., pl.* **griz·zlies** a massive, greyish, ferocious bear of North America; also **grizzly bear. 2** *adj.* greyish like a grizzly.

groan (GRONE) *n.* a deep sound made from the throat to express pain, disapproval, grief, etc.: *the groans of the wounded on a battlefield.*
— *v.* make a groan: *She groaned with dismay on seeing her son's report card; a banquet table groaning under a load of food.*

groat (GROTE) *n.* a former British coin worth four pennies; hence, a trifling sum.

gro·cer (GROH·sur) *n.* a retailer of food and other household supplies.

gro·cer·y (GROH·suh·ree) *n.* **-cer·ies** a grocer's store or the food products sold in one: *Supermarkets sell* **groceries** *and nonfood items.*

gro·dy (GROH·dee) same as GROTTY.

grog·gy (GROG·ee) *adj.* **grog·gi·er, grog·gi·est** *Informal.* drunk or feeling like it, as from sleep; shaky or dazed. — **grog·gi·ly** *adv.;* **grog·gi·ness** *n.*

groin *n.* **1** the fold or depression between belly and thigh. **2** in architecture, the curved edge formed by two intersecting vaults. **3** a jettylike structure to protect a coast from wave erosion.

grom·met (GROM·it) *n.* a ring or loop used as a fastening or reinforcement or to protect an opening or the thing passing through it.

groom (long "oo") *n.* **1** a bridegroom. **2** a man or boy who takes care of horses.
— *v.* **1** take care of a horse, dog, etc. by cleaning and currying. **2** make neat and tidy in appearance: *a well-groomed man; Good* **grooming** *is a must for success.* **3** prepare someone for an office: *She is being groomed for the presidency.*

grooms·man (GROOMZ·mun) *n.* **-men** a bridegroom's attendant.

groove *n.* **1** a channel, furrow, or rut; hence, a routine. **2** *Slang.* something enjoyable.
— **in the groove** *Slang.* in top form; working smoothly, like a needle playing in the groove of a phonograph record; groovy.
— *v.* **grooves, grooved, groov·ing** *Slang.* react with empathy: *to groove to swing music; to groove with someone; everyone grooving* (= enjoying) *in his or her own way.*

groov·y (GROO·vee) *adj. Slang.* **groov·i·er, -i·est** swinging; excellent: *a groovy hairstyle.*

grope *v.* **gropes, grop·ed, grop·ing** feel one's way about as if blind or uncertain: *We groped around in the dark; always groping for a better word.*
— *n.* an act of groping.

gross (rhyme: "dose") *adj.* **1** extremely bad or objectionable, as being coarse, vulgar, or indecent: *a gross error, injustice; gross misconduct, negligence; his gross table manners.* **2** whole or entire, with nothing deducted: *a physician's gross income before overhead, salaries, etc. are paid out; a company's gross sales.*
— *n.* **1** *pl.* **gross·es** the total amount. **2** *sing. & pl.* 12 dozen; 144: *six gross of eggs.*
— *v.* earn before deductions: *How much did you gross last year?*
— **gross out** *Slang.* taunt so as to disgust.

gro·tesque (groh·TESK) *adj.* unnatural or fantastic in appearance, shape, or manner; bizarre and ludicrous: *A gargoyle is a grotesque form of caricature.*
— *n.* a painting or sculpture containing medallions, sphinxes, foliage, etc.

grot·to (GROT·oh) *n.* **-tos** or **-toes** a cave or a cavelike place, garden shelter, or shrine.

grot·ty (GROT·ee) *adj. Slang.* grotesque or miserably bad; also, disgusting: *feeling dead grotty!*

grouch *n. Informal.* **1** a grumbler. **2** a grumbling or sulky mood. **3** a complaint.
— *v.* complain in a surly, ill-tempered manner.
— **grouch·y** *adj.* — **grouch·i·ly** *adv.*

ground *pt. of* GRIND.
— *n.* **1** the earth's surface, as distinguished from the air: *Leaves fall to the ground; Plants grow in fertile ground; to* **break ground** *for a new building; Keep your* **feet on the ground** (= Be practical in your thinking); *He built the company* **from the ground up;** *The ground (connection) of an appliance conducts leaking electricity to earth; an airline's ground* (= land) *crew; Airline mechanics are ground-based; fighter planes directed by ground-controlled radar; a ground-to-air missile; The new business has still to* **get off the ground** (= make a start). **2** soil or land: *dry, firm, frozen, hallowed, wet ground.* **3** a part of the earth's surface: *We own a piece of ground in Florida; a breeding, burial, camping, dumping, forbidden, hunting, parade, picnic, proving ground; You're on shaky ground if you say the earth is flat; Research theses are supposed to* **break new ground,** *not rehash old discoveries; a flag with a gold crescent on a green ground* (= background). **4** the bottom: *the ground of the ocean where "groundfish" live.* **5** a fighting position: *We are on common ground on this issue; You are on safe ground; Don't* **shift your ground** *in the middle of an argument; Continue fighting and don't* **give ground; Hold** *or* **stand your ground;** *Is mercy killing* **gaining** *or* **losing ground?**
— **grounds 1** dregs: *coffee grounds left in a cup.* **2** a specific area: *the grounds of an estate, hospital, mansion, school; hunting and fishing grounds.* **3** basis or reasons: *On what grounds did she resign? Does she have any grounds to sue us? You've no grounds for complaint; no ample, solid, sufficient grounds.*
— **cut the ground from under someone's feet** destroy someone's plans or arguments, as by anticipating them.
— *v.* put or base on the ground: *a pilot grounded by illness; aircraft grounded by fog; You're grounded* (= punished by having privileges withdrawn) *for a week; arguments grounded on facts (as basis); a graduate student well* **grounded** (= trained), *or with a good* **grounding** (= training), *in the basic arts and sciences; an appliance grounded (electrically) by its own metal frame.*

ground floor *n.* **1** the floor nearest to the ground. **2** *Informal.* a position of advantage, as at the outset of a venture: *The man who owns the business* **got in on the ground floor.**

ground glass *n.* **1** nontransparent glass with a roughened surface. **2** glass in powder form.

ground·hog *n.* woodchuck: *the Groundhog Day tradition of determining the length of the winter by the shadow cast by the animal on February 2.*

ground·less *adj.* baseless.

ground·ling *n.* **1** a plant or animal whose habitat is close to the ground. **2** a person of inferior artistic taste.

ground rule *n.* a basic rule, as of a game.

ground squirrel *n.* any burrowing animal of the squirrel family, as the groundhog, prairie dog, or woodchuck.

ground·swell *n.* **1** stormy water in the ocean, caused by a distant storm or earthquake. **2** a growing wave of popular concern, support, etc.: *There was a groundswell of public support for the nurses' demands.*

ground·work *n.* basis or foundation: *To lay the groundwork for a good education, start with the three R's; Have you done the groundwork* (= spadework) *for your project?*

ground zero *n.* a point on the ground directly above or beneath an exploding atomic bomb.

group (GROOP) *n.* a number of persons, animals, or things belonging, classed, or associated together: *a group of students; an affinity, age, blood, encounter, ethnic, peer, pressure, special-interest, splinter group; English and Dutch belong to the Germanic group of languages; Battalions and squadrons form military groups or units; a low* **group insurance** *rate for club employees and members; physicians in* **group practice** *practising* **group medicine.**
— *v.* form or arrange into a group: *They group around the leader; Girl Guides are grouped* (= divided) *into Brownies, Guides, and Rangers; All races are grouped* (= classed) *under the human species.*

group home *n. Cdn.* a publicly funded home for deprived children or for the handicapped in need of care.

group·ie (GROO·pee) *n. Informal.* **1** a camp follower or fan. **2** a young, usually female fan of a pop group, esp. one who follows them for sexual relations.

grouse *n. sing. & pl.* a game bird resembling domestic fowl: *the ruffed grouse; the Canada spruce grouse* (= fool hen).
— *v.* **grous·es, groused, grous·ing** *Informal.* grumble.
— *n. Informal.* a complaint. — **grous·er** *n.*

grout (GROWT) *n.* a thin mortar or plaster.
— *v.* fill up a space, as between tiles, finish a wall, ceiling, etc., or fix with grout.

grove (GROHV) *n.* a small wood without underbrush; group of trees: *an orange grove; the groves of academe* (= the academic world).

grov·el (GRUV·ul, GROV·ul) *v.* **-els, -elled** or **-eled, -el·ling** or **-el·ing** crawl or cringe at the feet of or before someone feared: *to grovel in the dust; to grovel to the boss.*

grow (GROH) *v.* **grows, grew** (GROO), **grown** (GRONE), **grow·ing** develop, as animals and plants from seed, gradually getting bigger: *Trees and plants grow from seeds; Children grow up to be leaders of society; They grow out of their clothes (which become too small for them); A small business grows into a corporate giant; People grow their hair* (= let it get longer); *Days grow* (= gradually become) *shorter in the* *fall; Habits seem to* **grow on** *us like vines on walls; the* **growing pains** (= stresses and strains) *of childhood and youth.* — **grow·er** *n.*

growl *v. & n.* **1** (make) a low, throaty sound, as a dog warning an approaching stranger, thunder in the distance, or the stomach of a hungry person; rumble: *Fido always growls at strangers; Al growled his thanks and left.* **2** grumble roughly.

grown *pp.* of GROW.
— *adj.* mature: *a grown man.*

grown-up *n. & adj.* adult.

growth (GROHTH) *n.* a growing, what has grown, or amount grown: *the rapid growth of grass in the spring; tumours and such cancerous growths; his growth in maturity; to foster, promote, retard, stunt growth; population growth; a* **growth company** *or* **growth industry** *with greater than average growth; A* **growth ring**, *or annual ring, shows a year's growth of wood.*

groyne (GROIN) *n.* a jettylike groin built to reduce sea erosion.

grub *v.* **grubs, grubbed, grub·bing** dig (up); also, rummage about: *A farmer grubs up tree roots and stumps to clear new land; to grub for potatoes; to grub around in the garbage for a missing ring; He grubs away at his menial tasks.*
— *n.* **1** an insect larva, as of a beetle; also, a toiler; drudge. **2** *Slang.* food.

grub·by (GRUB·ee) *adj.* **grub·bi·er, grub·bi·est**
1 grimy: *grubby hands.* **2** infested, as cattle or sheep, with fly maggots.

grub·stake *n.* food and equipment supplied in return for a share of the proceeds, as merchants used to supply gold prospectors in return for a share of their gold.

grudge (GRUJ) *n.* ill will against another: *to bear or owe someone a grudge; It's not healthy to harbour or nurse grudges; He acts as though he has or bears or carries or holds a grudge* (= reason for ill will) *against her; What's the use of carrying on a grudge? a* **grudge fight** *to avenge a defeat.*
— *v.* **grudg·es, grudged, grudg·ing** resent or envy: *I don't grudge doing him a favour although he charges for everything he does; I don't grudge him all the money he makes.*
— **grudging** *adj.* reluctant or unwilling: *He's very grudging in his generosity; a grudging admiration, apology, approval, gesture, respect, support.*

gru·el (GROO·ul) *n.* liquid food, as for invalids, made by boiling meal in water or milk; a thin porridge.

gru·el·ling or **gru·el·ing** (GROO·uh·ling) *adj.* exhausting or tiring; demanding: *a gruelling contest, experience, race, training session.*
— *n.* something that is gruelling.

grue·some (GROO·sum) *adj.* causing fear and loathing because of something frightful or hideous: *gruesome details; a gruesome scene of bloodshed.*

gruff *adj.* **1** rough, not polite: *gruff manners.* **2** having a deep and harsh voice: *a gruff reply, sergeant, voice.*

grum·ble *v.* **grum·bles, grum·bled, grum·bling** growl, mutter, or rumble in a surly or peevish manner: *It's no*

use grumbling about or at or over the weather; He grumbled his thanks.
— *n.* a rumble or complaint. — **grum·bler** *n.*

grump·y *adj.* **grump·i·er, -i·est** *Informal.* grouchy or ill-humoured: *He's always grumpy about poor heating.*
— **grump·i·ly** *adv.;* **grump·i·ness** *n.*

grunge *n. Slang.* the condition of being grungy; squalor or shabbiness.

grun·gy (GRUN·jee) *adj.* **-gi·er, -gi·est** *Slang.* shabby or squalid: *a grungy movie house.*

grunt *n.* **1** the short, deep guttural sound made by a hog. **2** an expression of boredom, disapproval, effort, etc. **3** an ocean fish of the Atlantic coast, such as the "pigfish" and "sailor's choice" that grunts when taken out of water.
— *v.* make or express with a grunt: *She was grunting and groaning with pain; He merely grunted his approval.*

guar·an·tee (gair·un·TEE) *n.* a promise or pledge to carry out a service or to replace, repair, or refund the price of a product if it proves unsatisfactory: *a TV set with a year's guarantee; a five-year guarantee against manufacturing defects; He has given a firm guarantee that the car won't break down; We insist on written guarantees; Health and wealth are no guarantees of happiness.*
— *v.* **-tees, -teed, -tee·ing** **1** stand behind: *We guarantee everything we sell.* **2** promise or pledge: *We guarantee satisfaction; We guarantee the car to be roadworthy; We guarantee that it will not break down; We guarantee it against all defects.*
— **guar·an·tor** (GAIR·un·tor) *n.*

guar·an·ty (GAIR·un·tee) *n.* **-ties** **1** a usually written agreement to pay another's debt if the latter fails to pay. **2** something given or taken as security for this promise.
— *v.* **-ties, -tied, -ty·ing** same as GUARANTEE: *to put up collateral to guaranty a loan.*

guard (GARD) *v.* protect or defend, esp. by watching over someone or something against possible harm or danger or to prevent escape, as the Coast Guard or a sentry does: *to guard the borders from smugglers; a vaccination to guard against a disease; "We will see" was his* **guarded** (= cautious) *reply.*
— *n.* a person, group, or thing that guards: *an armed guard; crossing guard; honour guard; prison guard; security guard; The house is under guard; A watchdog keeps guard over a house; A sentry stands guard at a gate; He was hit when he let his guard* (= defensive stance as in boxing) *down; He was caught* **off guard** (= unprepared); *Citizens* **stand on guard** *over* (= ready to defend) *their country.*
— **on** (or **off**) **one's guard** prepared (or unprepared).

guard·i·an (GAR·dee·un) *n.* a custodian, esp. one in charge of a minor, a mentally incompetent person, or of his or her property: *Parents are their children's "guardians by nature";* **adj.:** *a guardian angel, spirit.*

guard·rail *n.* a protective railing, as at the side of a staircase or highway.

guard·room *n.* **1** a room for the use of guards. **2** a room for keeping prisoners.

gu·ber·na·to·ri·al (GOO·bur·nuh·TOR·ee·ul) *adj.* of a governor or his or her office.

guck *n. Slang.* a gooey or mucky substance.
— **guck·y** *adj.*

guer·ril·la (guh·RIL·uh) *n.* a member of a volunteer force of irregulars fighting in small bands, usually behind enemy lines, using hit-and-run tactics, sabotage, kidnappings, and such terrorist actions; *adj.: a guerrilla attack, band; the guerrilla warfare of the Irish Republican Army; an urban guerrilla group.* Also **gue·ril·la.**

guess (GESS, "G" as in "go") *n.* a usually correct estimate or judgment made without sufficient evidence: *Your guess is as good as mine; It's anybody's guess; I will hazard* or *make a guess.*
— *v.* **1** make a guess: *Can you guess her height? Guess who's coming to dinner.* **2** *Informal.* suppose: *I guess I was wrong.*

guess·ti·mate (GES·tuh·mut) *n. Informal.* an estimate based on guessing.

guest (GEST, "G" as in "go") *n.* **1** a person receiving hospitality or being entertained at a home, club, etc.: *We have guests tonight (for supper); an honoured, unexpected, unwelcome guest; wedding guests; Be my guest (Informal for* Help yourself)! **2** a patron of a hotel or restaurant: *a regular guest.* **3** a performer invited to take part in a show or program.
— *adj.* having to do with being a guest: *a guest appearance, column, editor, worker.*

guff *n. Informal.* empty talk: *No one will fall for that guff; I don't have to take any guff from you.*

guf·faw (guh·FAW) *n.* a coarse or loud laugh.
— *v.* give a guffaw: *to guffaw at an off-colour joke.*

guid·ance (GUY·dunce) *n.* direction such as given to students on what courses to take ("educational guidance"), in choosing a career ("vocational guidance"), or to a missile in flight by means of radar, computers, etc.: *parental guidance; under the guidance of a counsellor.*

guide (GIDE, "G" as in "go") *n.* **1** a person or thing that shows the way, as on a tour. **2** a guidebook: *a guide to Paris.*
— *v.* **guides, guid·ed, guid·ing** act as a guide: *Let your conscience guide your decision; He guided us around Paris.*

guide·line *n.* usually **guidelines** *pl.* advice on policy by a controlling authority: *to establish new guidelines for energy conservation; to adhere to* or *follow guidelines.*

guide word *n.* a word placed at the top of a page showing the first or last entry on it, as in this dictionary.

guild (GILD, "G" as in "go") *n.* **1** an association of people with a common interest, as of merchants or craftsmen of the same trade. **2** a labour union.

guile (GILE, "G" as in "go") *n.* slyness and cunning; deceit: *a man full of guile; She spoke without guile.*
— **guile·ful** *adj.;* **guile·less** *adj.*

guil·lo·tine (GIL·uh·teen, "G" as in "go") *n.* a heavy blade slid down grooves in an upright frame, used to execute people by beheading.
— *v.* (gil·uh·TEEN) **-tines, -tined, -tin·ing** kill using a guillotine: *People were guillotined during the French Revolution.*

guilt (GILT, "G" as in "go") *n.* the fact or feeling of having done wrong: *a lawyer trying to establish guilt; to admit guilt in the accident; guilt by association; a guilt-ridden conscience.*

guilt·y *adj.* **guilt·i·er, -i·est** having done wrong: *The jury found Jim guilty of theft; They pronounced him guilty; guilty as charged; a verdict of guilty; a guilty verdict; He had pleaded not guilty; a not guilty plea; a* **guilty conscience** (= feeling of guilt). — **guilt·i·ly** *adv.*

guin·ea pig (GIN·ee, "G" as in "go") *n.* a furry rodent much used as a subject for scientific testing.

guise (GUYZ) *n.* a garb or outward aspect, esp. a deceptive one: *treachery in* or *under the guise of friendship.*

gui·tar (guh·TAR) *n.* a musical instrument with six strings that are plucked or strummed. — **gui·tar·ist** *n.*

gu·lag (GOO·lahg) *n.* a forced-labour camp for prisoners, as in the Soviet Union.

gulch *n.* a deep, narrow ravine.

gulf *n.* **1** a large arm of an ocean extending into the land, as the Gulf of St. Lawrence: *the* **Gulf Shore** *of Nova Scotia and New Brunswick; the* **Gulf States** *of Texas, Louisiana, Mississippi, Alabama, and Florida (near the Gulf of Mexico).* **2** a chasm or wide gap: *a yawning gulf; the widening gulf between rich and poor nations.*

gull *n.* **1** a long-winged, grey-and-white ocean bird useful as a scavenger around shore waters. **2** an easy victim of cheating; dupe.
— *v.* to dupe: *Con men gulled her out of her savings; She was gulled into thinking she would get rich quickly.*

gull·i·ble (GUL·uh·bul) *adj.* easily fooled, being too trusting: *a gullible youth.*
— **gul·li·bil·i·ty** (-BIL·uh·tee) *n.*

gul·ly (GULL·ee) *n.* **gul·lies** a small ravine, esp. one worn by running water.

gulp *v.* swallow hastily or nervously: *He gulped it down and hurried to the door; She bravely gulped back* (= suppressed) *her tears.*

— *n.*: *He drank the medicine in* or *at one gulp.*
— **gulp·er** *n.*

gum *n.* 1 usually **gums** *n.pl.* the firm, pink supporting tissue around the base of the teeth. 2 a sticky, water-soluble sap of trees such as the plum and peach, used for drugs, candy, etc., esp. **gum arabic** obtained from an African tree: *to chew gum; a stick of gum; a wad of gum.*
— *v.* **gums, gummed, gum·ming** 1 smear or treat with something gummy. 2 *Slang.* clog or mess up: *Keep the plans secret and don't let anyone* **gum up** (= spoil) *the works.*

gum·my (GUM·ee) *adj.* **gum·mi·er, gum·mi·est** covered with or giving off gum; sticky.

gump·tion *n. Informal.* readiness to act according to common sense; guts: *the gumption to say no without fear of offending.*

gum·shoe *n.* 1 a rubber overshoe. 2 **gumshoes** *pl.* sneakers. 3 *Slang.* detective.
— *v.* **-shoes, -shoed, -shoe·ing** go about quietly as if wearing sneakers.

gun *n.* 1 a weapon using an explosive, usually **gun·pow·der**, to shoot a bullet, shell, or other missile through a metal tube, esp. a cannon or machine gun; also, a rifle, pistol, or revolver: *to aim, carry, draw, fire, load, pack a gun; to hold a gun to someone's head; to turn a gun on someone; A gun fires, goes off, jams; a big gun* (*Informal* for big shot); *the smoking gun* (= conclusive evidence). 2 something resembling a gun, as an "air gun" or an engine's throttle. 3 a gunman: *to hire a gun.* 4 *Slang.* [jocular use] *"You son of a gun"* (= bastard)!
— **great guns** *Informal.* fast and furiously toward success: *She's going* or *blowing great guns as a cabinet minister.*
— **jump the gun** start too soon or get a head start: *The competition jumped the gun on our announcement.*
— **spike one's guns** frustrate one's efforts.
— **stick to one's guns** refuse to retreat.
— **under the gun** under pressure *to* do something.
— *v.* **guns, gunned, gun·ning** 1 shoot (at) with a gun: *President Sadat was gunned down by assassins.* 2 rev: *bikers gunning their motors.*
— **gunning for** trying to get something desired or to capture and punish someone: *The Oilers will be gunning for the Hawks in tomorrow's game; a Crown attorney gunning for a conviction.*

gunboat diplomacy *n.* diplomacy by means of military threats.

gun·fire *n.* the firing of guns: *to come under heavy gunfire; a barrage, burst, hail of gunfire; an exchange of gunfire between police and snipers.*

gung-ho *adj. Informal.* eager and enthusiastic: *The union members were all gung-ho for* or *about the strike; A gung-ho atmosphere reigned at the meeting; They were so gung-ho they had no doubt they would win.*

gunk *n. Slang.* something thick and messy: *where to dump the gunk dredged from the lake.*

gunk hole *n. Cdn.* a small cove or fishing harbour.

gun·man (GUN·mun) *n.* **-men** an armed gangster.

gun·met·al (GUN·met·ul) *n.* 1 a dark, bluish grey bronze used for gears, bearings, valves, and steam fittings. 2 a dark bluish grey.

gun·point *n.* the point of a gun: *He was taken and held* **at gunpoint** (= under threat of being shot).

gun·shot *n.* a shot, shooting, or range of a gun: *They were fired on when they came within gunshot of the enemy.*

gun·sling·er (GUN·sling·ur) *n.* a gunman or gunfighter.

gur·gle (GUR·gul) *n.* the bubbling sound of water poured from a narrow-neck bottle: *the happy gurgle of a baby.*
— *v.* **-gles, -gled, -gling** make a gurgle: *a gurgling baby, brook.*

gu·ru (GOOR·oo) *n.* 1 a Hindu religious teacher or guide. 2 a guide or leader in a specific field: *our communications guru Marshall McLuhan; Yogi Berra, the guru of baseball.*

gush *v.* 1 pour out copiously, as water from a spring: *Blood gushed forth from the wound.* 2 express oneself effusively. — *n.* a copious flow.

gush·er *n.* 1 one who gushes. 2 an oil well that flows without pumping: *They hit the first gusher in North America at Oil Springs, Ont., in 1857.*

gush·y *adj.* **gush·i·er, -i·est** *Informal.* effusive or sentimental.

gus·sie or **gus·sy** (GUS·ee) *v.* **gus·sies, gus·sied, gus·sy·ing** *Slang.* smarten or dress up: *to get gussied up for a party.*

gust *n.* a sudden burst or rush of wind: *a gust of emotion, fire, rain, smoke; fitful gusts of wind.*
— *v.* blow in gusts: *strong winds gusting to 60 km/h.*

gus·to (GUS·toh) *n.* zest or relish: *She devours westerns with great gusto.*

gust·y *adj.* **gust·i·er, -i·est** marked by gusts: *a gusty day.*

gut *n.* the alimentary canal or a part of it, esp. intestines.
— **guts** *n.pl.* 1 bowels or entrails. 2 *Informal.* the essential or working parts. 3 *Informal.* pluck or courage: *He doesn't have the guts to stand up to the bully, but has the guts* (= impudence) *to talk back to his mother.*
— **hate someone's guts** dislike someone intensely.
— *v.* **guts, gut·ted, gut·ting** disembowel; hence, destroy the inside of something: *a building gutted by fire.*
— *adj. Informal.* 1 vital or basic: *the gut issues of the campaign; a gut* (= easy-to-pass) *course.* 2 from one's inner self: *to make a gut call on whether someone is lying; a gut feeling of what is right; his gut reaction.*
— **gut·less** *adj. Informal.* cowardly.

guts·y *adj.* **guts·i·er, -i·est** *Slang.* bold or lusty.

gut·ter (GUT·ur) *n.* 1 a channel such as the ditch along the side of a street or the trough at the edge of a roof for carrying away rainwater or the groove on either side of a bowling alley. 2 a low or wretched place: *the language of the gutter; He was dragged down into the gutter by bad companions.*
— *v.* to stream: *rainwater guttering downhill; wax running down the sides of a guttering candle.*

gut·ty (GUT·ee) *adj.* **gut·ti·er, gut·ti·est** *Slang.* **1** gutsy. **2** basic or strongly evocative; having gut quality.

guy ("g" as in "go"; rhyme: "my") *n. Informal.* **1** a fellow: *guys and girls; She was trying to be one of the guys; a great guy; a nice guy; a regular guy* (= a good sport); *a wise guy* (= a conceited fellow); *You* **guys** (= boys and/or girls; fellows). **2** a steadying or guiding rope, chain, or wire attached to a tent or tower. — *v.* **1** secure with a guy or guys: *The CN Tower is a free-standing, not guyed structure.* **2** *Informal.* tease or ridicule.

guz·zle (GUZ·ul) *v.* **guz·zles, guz·zled, guz·zling** eat or drink something greedily. — **guz·zler** *n.*

gym (JIM) *n.* [short form] gymnasium; also, physical education.

gym·kha·na (jim·KAH·nuh) *n.* **1** a place for athletic contests. **2** a contest or meet for horseriders or automobile drivers: *the Antique Car Club's gymkhana at Fort York.*

gym·nas·tic (jim·NAS·tic) **1** *adj.* having to do with gymnastics: *world gymnastic championships; gymnastic exercises, manoeuvres, tumbles.* **2 gymnastics** *n.pl.* exercises for physical fitness: *She does gymnastics daily after school; There's more gymnastics* (= the art) *than choreography in jazz dancing; adj.: gymnastics championships, contests, teams.*

gyp (JIP) *v.* **gyps, gypped, gyp·ping** *Slang.* cheat or swindle: *They gypped him out of his share of the booty.* — *n.* cheater or swindler; also, a cheating: *a gyp artist, joint.*

Gyp·sy (JIP·see) *n.* **-sies 1** a member of a wandering people, properly called "Romany," originally from India, with a language of their own; also **gyp·sy.** **2 gypsy** one who leads a wandering life; *adj.: a gypsy cab (cruising for fares without a licence); gypsy music; a gypsy trucker* (= independent operator).

gy·rate (JYE·rate) *v.* **-rates, -rat·ed, -rat·ing** turn with a swinging motion in a circular or spiral course, as a tornado, a figure skater, or a spinning top: *the gyrating hips of a rock singer.* — **gy·ra·tion** (jye·RAY·shun) *n.*

Hh

H or **h** (AICH) *n.* **H's** or **h's 1** the eighth letter of the English alphabet; hence, the eighth in a series. **2** anything H-shaped.

hab·er·dash·er·y (HAB·ur·dash·uh·ree) *n.* **-er·ies 1** hats, ties, shirts, socks, etc. for men. **2** a store that sells such items.

hab·it (HAB·it) *n.* **1** a settled tendency or disposition, acquired by practice, to perform an action almost automatically: *He was in the habit of taking drugs; It is hard to **kick a habit*** (*Slang for* to break a bad habit); *to acquire, develop, form good habits; an incurable, repulsive habit; It's dangerous to make a habit of smoking in bed; a disciplined woman with regular habits; She gets up at the stroke of five by force of habit; She does it out of habit.* **2** a costume, as of nuns and priests: *a Carmelite habit.* **3** a characteristic mode or appearance: *the prismatic or pyramidal habit of a crystal; the twining habit of a vine.*

hab·it·a·ble (HAB·uh·tuh·bul) *adj.* able to be inhabited: *this habitable globe.*

hab·it·ant (HAB·uh·tunt) *n. Cdn.* a settler, esp. a farmer, of French Canada or Louisiana.

hab·i·tat (HAB·uh·tat) *n.* **1** natural habitation, esp. of a plant or animal. **2** an underwater laboratory.

hab·i·ta·tion (hab·uh·TAY·shun) *n.* **1** occupancy. **2** a home or settlement.

habit-forming *adj.* addictive: *Habit-forming drugs include narcotics, barbiturates, and tranquillizers.*

ha·bit·u·al (huh·BICH·oo·ul) *adj.* done by habit: *his habitual courtesy; Dad is a habitual snorer; his habitual* (= customary) *place at the head of the table.*
— **ha·bit·u·al·ly** *adv.*

ha·bit·u·ate (huh·BICH·oo·ate) *v.* **-ates, -at·ed, -at·ing** make used to something: *a dog habituated to being let out at night; She habituated herself to the harsh climate.* — **ha·bit·u·a·tion** (-AY·shun) *n.*

ha·bit·u·é (huh·BICH·oo·ay) *n.* a frequenter or regular attender: *a habitué of Maple Leaf Gardens.*

Habs *n.pl. Cdn.* the Montreal Canadiens hockey team.

hack *v.* **1** cut or chop crudely: *They hacked their way through the dense jungle; He hacked at the weeds with a hoe; to hack something to pieces; a wild beast found hacked to death.* **2** *Slang.* manage successfully: *He just couldn't hack it as a journalist.* **3** *Informal.* work as a

hack driver: *a student who works part-time at hacking.*
— *n.* **1** a common horse that may be hired for riding. **2** an old or worn-out horse: *a jaded old hack.* **3** a drudge or hireling: *a literary hack; a party hack; a hack job* (= drudgery). **4** *Informal.* a taxicab.

hack·er *n.* **1** an amateur computer whiz, esp. one who uses his expertise to break into computer systems. **2** *Informal.* an amateur: *a miserable hacker of a golf player.*

hacking cough *n.* a dry cough without discharge of phlegm.

hack·le (HACK·ul) *n.* **1** a neck feather of a fowl. **2 hackles** *pl.* hairs on a dog's neck that bristle when it is angry.
— **raise the hackles of** or **get one's hackles up** *Informal.* become or make someone angry or ready to fight.

hack·man (HACK·mun) *n.* **-men** a cabdriver.

hack·ney (HACK·nee) *n.* **-neys** a common horse or a carriage or coach for hire.
— **hack·neyed** (-need) *adj.* clichéd: *a hackneyed expression.*

had *pt. & pp.* of HAVE.

Ha·des (HAY·deez) *n.* **1** in Greek myth, the underworld. **2 hades** *pl. Informal.* hell.

had·n't (HAD·unt) had not.

hadst *Archaic.* the form of "had" used with THOU.

hag *n.* an ugly old woman, esp. a witch.

hag·gard (HAG·urd) *adj.* careworn or emaciated.
— **hag·gard·ly** *adv.*

hag·gle (HAG·ul) *v.* **hag·gles, hag·gled, hag·gling** argue *about* or *over* a price or bargain.
— *n.* such a bargaining.

hail *n.* **1** a shout or cheer. **2** frozen raindrops falling during a thunderstorm; also, a shower of such frozen raindrops. **3** a shower of bullets, blows, or anything similar.
— *v.* **1** greet or call to someone: *They hailed us as we drove by; We were **within hail*** (= within hailing distance); *Stand at the curb and hail a cab; He was hailed as the new leader; They hailed the decision a great victory.* **2** shower hail or like hail: *It was hailing on and off all afternoon; The mob hailed insults at him.*
— **hail from** come from: *Our Chinese neighbours hail*

from Taiwan.
— *interj.* expressing greeting: *All hail! Hail to the chief!*

hail·er (HAY·lur) *n.* a bullhorn.

hair *n.* **1** any of the fine, threadlike outgrowths from the skin of mammals, esp. from the human head: *not a single hair.* **2** such hairs collectively: *a fine head of hair; a shock of hair; curly, kinky, straight, thick, thinning, unruly, wavy hair; a curl* or *lock of hair; auburn, black, blond, brown, dark, grey, light, red, white hair; He brushes, combs, loses, parts, strokes his hair; Our dog sheds his hair everywhere; She braids, colours, cuts, does, dyes, shampoos, trims, washes her hair.*
— **by a hair** by a small margin: *He lost the election by a hair.*
— **by a hair's breadth** by a very short distance; narrowly: *We missed* or *escaped being hit by a hair's breadth.*
— **get in one's hair** *Slang.* annoy one.
— **let one's hair down** act in an uninhibited manner; be unrestrained.
— **not turn a hair** show no reaction.
— **split hairs** make too fine distinctions.
— **to a hair** exactly.
— **hair·less** *adj.;* **hair·like** *adj.*

hair-breadth *n. & adj.* (by) a very small distance: *We had a hair-breadth escape in the accident.*

hair·line *n.* **1** the outline of the hair above the forehead: *the receding hairline of a balding man.* **2** a very thin line: *a hairline crack or fracture; a questionable hairline decision; a hairline space.*

hair·pin *n.* a U-shaped metal or plastic pin used by women to keep their hair in place: *a **hairpin bend** in the road.*

hair-raiser (HAIR·ray·zur) *n.* something terrifying, esp. a story. — **hair-raising** *adj.*

hairs·breadth or **hair's-breadth** *n. & adj.* same as HAIR-BREADTH.

hair·split·ting (HAIR·split·ing) *n.* the making of too fine distinctions.

hair trigger *n.* a delicately adjusted trigger that operates by the slightest pressure.
— **hair-trigger** *adj.: hair-trigger laughter, nerves; a hair-trigger temper.*

hair·y *adj.* **hair·i·er, -i·est 1** covered with hair: *a hairy chest; the hairy woodpecker.* **2** of or like hair: *the hairy vetch.* **3** *Informal.* difficult or dangerous: *a hairy situation, time.*

hairy-chested (HAIR·ee·ches·tid) *adj.* virile or robust.

hal·cy·on (HAL·see·un) *adj.* peaceful and prosperous: *in the halcyon days of one's youth.*

hale *adj.* **hal·er, hal·est** healthy: *a hale and hearty golden ager.*
— *v.* **hales, haled, hal·ing** haul: *He was haled into court to answer a charge.*

half (HAF) *n. & pron., pl.* **halves** (HAVZ) one of two equal parts making up something: *Seven is just half of 14; "Half a loaf is better than no bread"* (= Something is better than nothing); *I want my half of it; Divide the cake **in half** or **into halves;** one's **better half** (Informal*

for spouse); *A year and a half has passed; One and a half* or *One and one half years have passed.*
— **by half** by far.
— *adj. & pron.* being a half: *He'll be here in a half hour* or *in half an hour; sold at half price.*
— *adv.* to half: *A half empty glass is half full; a potato that is only half cooked; We start work at half past eight* (= 8:30).
— **not half bad** *Informal.* not at all bad; fairly good.

half-and-half *n., adj. & adv.* (a mixture, as of milk and cream) consisting of two equal parts.

half-baked *adj. Informal.* poor in planning or judgment: *a half-baked idea, scheme, visionary, youth.*

half-cocked *adj.* without full thought or consideration, like a firearm whose hammer is pulled back only halfway before firing.

half-heart·ed (HAF·har·tid) *adj.* unwilling or uninterested. — **half-heart·ed·ly** *adv.*

half-mast *n.* the position of flying a flag halfway from the top of its mast as a sign of respect to a dead person or as a distress signal. Also **half-staff.**

half-truth *n.* a deceptive statement giving only some of the facts.

half·way *adj. & adv.* **1** midway: *We live halfway between the two bus stops; He's halfway through the book; He had walked halfway across the street when he was hit.* **2** incomplete or incompletely: *a halfway measure, point; You can't leave halfway through a haircut.*
— **go halfway** or **meet someone halfway** do one's share toward accomplishing something: *I'll take up the project only if you will go halfway with me; Joe agreed to meet Jim halfway.*

halfway house *n.* a centre for housing former drug addicts, convicts, mental patients, etc. while they are being prepared to return to society.

hall *n.* **1** a common passageway such as a corridor; hallway. **2** a foyer or lobby. **3** a large room for meetings, parties, etc.: *a concert, convention, lecture, mess, study, town hall; Massey Hall.* **4** an educational or residential building containing offices, housing a dormitory, etc.: *Athabasca Hall; the **halls of ivy*** (= academic life).

hal·le·lu·jah or **hal·le·lu·iah** (hal·uh·LOO·yuh) *interj.* "Praise the Lord." — *n.* a hymn with this theme.

hall·mark 1 *n. & v.* (put) an official mark guaranteeing quality, as Goldsmith's Hall in London used to stamp on gold and silver objects. **2** *n.* a distinguishing characteristic: *the hallmarks of a gentleman, of a good education.*

hal·lo (huh·LOH) *n., v. & interj.* **hal·los, hal·loed, hal·lo·ing** call or shout to greet or attract attention. Also **hal·loa** (huh·LOH).

hall of fame *n.* a memorial building in honour of celebrated people: *the Hockey Hall of Fame.*

hal·loo (huh·LOO) *n., v. & interj.* **-loos, -looed, -loo·ing** hallo, esp. as used to urge hounds on in hunting.

hal·lowed (HAL·ode, *also* HAL·oh·wid *in* "Hallowed be thy name") *adj.* blessed: *We are on hallowed ground.*

Hal·low·een or **Hal·low·e'en** (hal·oh·WEEN) *n.*
Allhallows Eve; October 31, esp. the evening: *Children go seeking treats on Halloween; to scare away the goblins at Halloween; Happy Halloween!* **adj.:** *a Halloween costume, mask, night, parade, party, prank, robbery, tradition.*

hal·lu·ci·nate (huh·LOO·suh·nate) *v.* **-nates, -nat·ed, -nat·ing** (cause) to see or experience things that are unreal or dreamlike, as when delirious or under the influence of a drug.
— **hal·lu·ci·na·tion** (·NAY·shun) *n.*
— **hal·lu·ci·na·to·ry** (-nuh·tor·ee) *adj.*

hal·lu·ci·no·gen (huh·LOO·suh·nuh·jun) *n.* a drug such as LSD that makes one hallucinate.
— **hal·lu·ci·no·gen·ic** (-nuh·JEN·ic) *adj.*

hall·way *n.* a passageway or corridor.

ha·lo (HAL·oh, HAY·loh) *n.* **-los** or **-loes** a circle of light, as sometimes seen around the sun, moon, or other heavenly body and symbolically pictured around the heads of saints and similar personages as a mark of glory.

halt (HAWLT) *n.* a usually brief stop: *The traffic came to a halt at the crash site; a grinding* or *screeching halt; The strike brought operations* **to a halt;** *effective steps to* **call a halt** *to wasteful spending.*
— *v.* **1** (cause) to stop: *Halt! Who goes there? measures to halt inflation; The marchers halted for refreshments.* **2** hesitate or waver.
— *adj.* [old use] lame: *to cure the halt and the sick.*

hal·ter (HAWL·tur) *n.* **1** a rope or strap around the neck, as for leading a horse, esp. one connected to a headstall, a noose for hanging, etc. **2** death by hanging. **3** a woman's backless bodice, often **halter top**, held by a strap around the back of the neck; *adj.:* *a halter dress, gown, neckline.*
— *v.* tie with or put a halter on a person or animal; hence, restrain.

halt·ing *adj.* **1** faltering or wavering: *He testified in a halting voice.* **2** lame or limping: *his halting gait.*
— **halt·ing·ly** *adv.*

halve (HAV) *v.* **halves, halved, halv·ing 1** divide or share equally. **2** reduce to half: *The strength of the enemy was halved after the battle.*

halves (HAVZ) *n.pl.* of HALF.
— **by halves** incompletely: *to do a job by halves.*
— **go halves** share equally.

ham *n.* **1** the back of a thigh and buttock, as of a pig, esp. as salted and dried or smoked meat: *a breakfast of ham and eggs; He squatted on his* **hams.** **2** *Informal.* a showy performer: *a ham actor; a radio ham* (= amateur radio operator). **3** *Informal.* a theatrical demonstration: *a 90-minute TV special full of tears and ham; It was pure ham.*
— *v.* **hams, hammed, ham·ming** overact: *He had to* **ham it up** *to make an impression.*

ham·burg·er (HAM·bur·gur) *n.* ground beef, a patty of such meat, or a patty grilled and sandwiched in a split bun.

ham·mer (HAM·ur) *n.* **1** a pounding tool, usually with a metal head set crosswise at the end of a wooden handle. **2** anything similar, as one of the wooden mallets inside a piano, an auctioneer's gavel, the striking mechanism of a firing pin, or a bone of the middle ear: *Unclaimed articles go* or *come* **under the hammer** (= the auctioneer's gavel, for auction sale); *a* **hammer-and-tongs** (= vigorous) *approach to a problem.*
— *v.* work with or as if with a hammer; strike with repeated blows; hence, work hard: *Lou hammers at her typewriter six hours a day; She's* **hammering away** *at her Ph.D. thesis; to* **hammer out** *a solution to a vexing problem.*

hammer and sickle *n.* a Communist emblem symbolizing the labourer and the farmer, as on the flag of the Soviet Union.

ham·mer·lock (HAM·ur·lock) *n.* a wrestling hold in which the opponent's arm is held twisted behind his back.

ham·mock (HAM·uck) *n.* a cradlelike swinging couch, as one of netted cord slung by its ends between supports.

ham·per (HAM·pur) *v.* impede the movement or hinder the freedom of someone: *A heavy snowfall hampered our progress.*
— *n.* a large covered basket or container, as for food, wine, laundry, or mail.

ham·string *n.* **1** either of the two tendons at the back of the knee connecting the thigh muscles. **2** in four-footed animals such as the horse, a large tendon at the back of the hock.
— *v.* **-strings**, *pt. & pp.* **-strung** or **-stringed, -string·ing** cripple or disable, (as if) by cutting the hamstring: *press freedom hamstrung by restrictions.*

hand *n.* **1** the end part of the forearm that is below the wrist, used for grasping and holding: *We shook hands over the deal; to clasp, hold, take someone's hand; to clap, cup, lower, raise, wring one's hands; to* **lay one's hands on** (= seize; also, touch, as in blessings or religious ceremonies) *someone; to lead, take somebody by the hand; He picked it up with his bare hands.* **2** a limb or other part similar to the human hand in appearance or use: *a monkey's hands* (= forelimbs) *and feet; a hand* (= bunch) *of bananas; The hands of a clock tell the time.* **3** a person or a person's action, skill, or power: *"All hands on deck"; hired hands; ranch hands; Please give* or *lend me a hand with this job; He would have no hand in wrongdoing; He's an old hand at basket-weaving; She writes a legible hand; He rules with a firm hand; an iron hand in a velvet glove; He fell* **into the**

hands of the enemy. **4** what is given with the hand: *The audience gave her a big hand* (= round of applause); *He decided to ask her hand* (= promise) *in marriage; the warm hand* (= offer) *of friendship.* **5** the cards dealt to or held by a player in a game; also, a round of play: *to have, hold, show, tip one's hand; a good, strong, weak hand.*
— **at hand** close by: *The nurse is at hand if you need help; Peace was at hand after many years of war.*
— **at first hand** directly: *I heard it at first hand, not at second hand* (= indirectly).
— **from hand to mouth** on a day-to-day basis: *With no money in the bank, we are practically living from hand to mouth.*
— **in hand** under control or in one's possession: *The situation is well in hand; The money we have in hand is not sufficient.*
— **hand in glove** or **hand and glove** in close cooperation *with* someone.
— **hand in hand** together: *Lee and Lou walking hand in hand.*
— **hands down** easily: *She won the game hands down.*
— **hands off** take your hands off: *Hands off my bike!*
— **on hand** within reach: *Please make sure coffee and donuts are on hand; I'll be on hand* (= present) *to help out.*
— **on one's hands** at one's disposal: *When I have time on my hands no one needs me!*
— **on the one** (or **other**) **hand** from one (or another) point of view: *On the one hand, we have a job opening; on the other hand, we can't afford to hire one more.*
— **out of hand 1** out of control: *Don't let the situation get out of hand.* **2** forthwith: *The petition was rejected out of hand.*
— *v.* give or do with the hand or as if with the hand: *She handed him his drink; He courteously handed her into the car; Did you* **hand in** *your work? She's so successful everyone* **hands it** (= gives credit) *to her.*
— **hand down** give: *an opinion handed down by a court; a legend handed down* (= passed along) *from generation to generation.*
— **hand out** distribute: *to hand out flyers, food.*
— **hand over** transfer to someone: *The robber asked the teller to hand over the cash (to him); Mr. Lyon will hand over charge to the new teacher tomorrow.*

hand·ball *n.* a game played by striking a rubber ball with the hand against a wall or board.

hand·book *n.* a manual or guidebook.

hand·cart *n.* a cart that is pulled or pushed by hand.

hand·cuff *n.* one of a pair of metal rings joined by a short chain, used in restraining prisoners.
— *v.* **1** put handcuffs on someone; manacle. **2** check or hinder: *The goalkeeper was handcuffed by the deflected shot.*

-handed *combining form.* having or using hands as specified: *a left-handed writer; a two-handed stroke; heavyhanded; right-handed; single-handed.*

hand·ed·ness *n.* one's natural preference for either the left or the right hand.

hand·ful *n.* **-fuls 1** what the hand can hold; hence, a small number or amount. **2** *Informal.* a person or thing that is hard to manage.

hand·gun *n.* a firearm such as a pistol that is held and fired with one hand.

hand·i·cap (HAN·di·cap) *n.* **1** a disadvantage or hindrance: *Poverty is a handicap to progress; The poor are under a handicap; We try to overcome our handicaps.* **2** an adjustment of time, distance, or weight made for individual competitors in a contest or game to give the weaker ones an advantage or the stronger ones a disadvantage. **3** a game or race in which such handicaps are given, as in golf or horse racing.
— *v.* **-caps, -capped, -cap·ping 1** be at a disadvantage: *He is handicapped by a speech defect; the* **handicapped** *such as the deaf, blind, crippled, retarded, and mentally ill.* **2** give a handicap to someone: *In trapshooting, competitors may be handicapped up to nine metres.* — **han·di·cap·per** *n.*

hand·i·craft *n.* **1** the skilful making of articles by hand. **2** a trade or art using such skill, as ceramics or basket-weaving. **3** a handicraft product or artifact.
— **hand·i·craft·er** or **hand·i·crafts·man** *n.* **-men.**

hand·i·work (HAN·di·wurk) *n.* handwork; also, work done personally; an individual achievement: *Some see the universe as the handiwork of God.*

hand·ker·chief (HANK·ur·chif) *n.* **-chiefs** or **-chieves** (-cheevz) **1** a usually square piece of cloth carried on one's person for blowing one's nose, wiping the face, etc. **2** a kerchief.

han·dle (HAN·dul) *n.* the part of a tool, door, cup, etc. for holding, grasping, or manipulating it.
— **fly off the handle** *Informal.* lose one's temper.
— **get a handle on** grasp mentally: *It took time for them to get a handle on the situation.*
— *v.* **han·dles, han·dled, han·dling 1** take, operate, manage, or control (as if) with one's hand or hands: *A crowd has to be tactfully handled; The Oilers handled* (*Slang for* defeated) *the Leafs with ease; a case that requires delicate, gentle, tactful* **handling.** **2** respond to control: *a car that handles well.*

hand·maid or **hand·maid·en** (HAND·may·dun) *n.* **1** formerly, a female personal attendant. **2** helper: *Logic is the handmaid of philosophy.*

hand-me-down *n.* something, as a garment, handed down from an older person.
— *adj.* secondhand or cheap: *an ill-fitting hand-me-down suit.*

hand·out *n. Informal.* something handed out as charity, as a free gift, as promotional literature, or as an official version of a news event.

hand·pick *v.* **1** pick fruits or vegetables. **2** choose: *to handpick one's supporters or aides.*

hand·picked *adj.* **1** personally selected, often unfairly: *a handpicked group of supporters.* **2** carefully selected: *The winning candidate had a group of handpicked advisors.*

hand·shake *n.* **1** a friendly clasping and shaking of each other's hands: *a warm handshake.* **2** a money gift made on parting: *a golden handshake.*

hands-off *adj.* noninterfering: *a hands-off approach, attitude, policy, stand.*

hand·some *adj.* **hand·som·er, hand·som·est 1** [esp. of males] good-looking: *a handsome design, face, fellow, horse, suitor, volume, woman, young man; a tall handsome stranger; handsome stationery; Our handsome hulk likes to flaunt himself in front of the mirror.* **2** generous: *a handsome amount, gift, payment, profit, settlement; handsome treatment.* — **hand·some·ly** *adv.*

hands-on *adj.* involving active participation: *a hands-on course, demonstration, experience.*

hand-to-hand *adj. & adv.* close together; involving physical contact: *They fought hand-to-hand; a hand-to-hand combat.*

hand-to-mouth *adj.* spending or consuming with no provision for the future; precarious: *a hand-to-mouth existence.*

hand·writ·ing (hand·RYE·ting) *n.* writing by hand or its style. — **hand·writ·ten** (hand·RIT·un) *adj.*

hand·y *adj.* **hand·i·er, -i·est 1** readily available: *Keep your pencils handy.* **2** skilled, usually without training, in odd jobs: *Jean is handy at plumbing, Jan is handy with a lawnmower; Joe is handy around the house.* **3** convenient: *A food processor is very handy for kitchen chores; It's handy to have labour-saving gadgets; An eraser will* **come in handy** (= be convenient) *for corrections.* — **hand·i·ly** *adv.;* **hand·i·ness** *n.*

hand·y·man (HAN·dee·man) *n.* **-men** one who does odd jobs.

hang *v.* **hangs,** *pt. & pp.* **hanged** (in "kill" senses) or **hung, hang·ing 1** attach, fasten, or suspend so as to swing or turn freely: *A coat is hung on a hook; Pictures hang on the wall; We hang out the laundry to dry; He hangs his head in shame; was condemned to be hanged (by the neck); He was hanged for murder; He didn't have to hang himself;* **Hang it** (= Damn it)! **2** cover or furnish with something suspended, as a wall with tapestry or a window with drapes. **3** be or seem suspended, as when undecided, idle, etc.: *Time is hanging on his hands* (= He has free time) *since he quit his job; His career hangs* (= depends) *on your recommendation.*
— **hang around** or **about** *Informal.* loiter or stand by idly.
— **hang back** be reluctant: *Billy is so shy he hangs back from group activities.*
— **hang in there** *Informal.* don't give up; stay put.
— **hang loose** *Informal.* be relaxed.
— **hang on** keep one's hold or grip: *to hang on to a lifebuoy, to an heirloom, to old customs, to a piece of property.*
— **hang out** *Informal.* live or stay: *Where do you hang out? The donut shop is where he hangs out* (= is often found); *Be careful who you hang out* (= keep company) *with.*
— **hang up** put back on a hanger or hook, as the receiver at the end of a phone call: *She hung up on* (= cut off) *the harassing caller.*
— **let it all hang out** *Informal.* let one's hair down; be uninhibited.
— *n.* **1** the way something hangs: *I don't like the hang of that curtain.* **2** *Informal.* how something is done or what something means: *I'm trying to get the hang of this poem.* **3** *Informal.* a trifle: *I don't care a hang or give a*

hang about root beer.

hang·ar (HANG·ur) *n.* a shed or shelter, as for aircraft.

hang·dog *adj.* sneaking or shamefaced: *a hangdog look.*

hanger-on *n.* **hangers-on** [contemptuous use] a follower or dependent.

hang gliding *n.* the sport of gliding or soaring using a kitelike device, that carries the glider harnessed underneath it.

hanging *adj.* **1** that hangs: *a hanging basket, bookcase, plant; a* **hanging judge** (*known for death sentences*); *The Hanging Gardens of Babylon are said to have been laid out on a terrace.* **2** deserving death by hanging: *Murder used to be a hanging crime.* **3** **hangings** *n. pl.* things hung, as draperies or curtains: *silk hangings.*

hang-loose *adj.* relaxed; uninhibited.

hang·out *n. Slang.* a place where one hangs out; a frequented resort.

hang·o·ver (HANG·oh·vur) *n. Informal.* aftereffects of a drinking bout, such as headache, dizziness, and depression.

hang-up *n. Slang.* a mental or emotional problem.

hank *n.* a coil or loop: *a hank of hair, thread.*

han·ker (HANK·ur) *v.* long or crave for something that makes one restless in its pursuit: *Some hanker after riches, others hanker for thrills; He has been hankering (= wanting) to go back to Europe ever since he landed here; In his old age he began to long for peace and happiness after a lifetime of* **hankering** *for or after wealth.*

Han·sard (HAN·surd) *n.* the published record of the proceedings of a parliament or legislature.

Ha·nuk·kah (HAH·nuh·kuh) *n.* a Jewish festival in December; also called "Feast of Lights."

hap *n.* [old use] happening; also, a chance or lot.
— *v.* **haps, happed, hap·ping** occur by chance; happen.

hap·haz·ard (hap·HAZ·urd) *adj.* careless or chancy: *a haphazard filing of papers;* **adv.:** *books left haphazard over the desks.*
— *n.:* *gifts selected* **at haphazard.**
— **hap·haz·ard·ly** *adv.*

hap·less (HAP·lis) *adj.* unlucky. — **hap·less·ly** *adv.*

hap·ly *adv.* by chance.

hap·pen (HAP·un) *v.* take place or be, esp. by chance: *The accident happened on the highway; I just happened to be at the scene; You're late, what happened?* **As it happens,** (= It turns out) *our new car had a flat tire; Accidents* **happen to** (= are experienced by) *lots of people.*
— **happen on** or **upon** meet or find something by chance.

happening (HAP·un·ing) *n.* **1** what happens or takes place. **2** an event, activity, or performance of a spontaneous or vital nature with many participants, as "action painting" or "living theatre."

hap·pen·stance (HAP·un·stance) *n.* a chance circumstance or happening: *"Once may be happenstance, but twice is coincidence."*

hap·py (HAP·ee) *adj.* **hap·pi·er, hap·pi·est 1** having peace and contentment: *a happy childhood, family, home, marriage.* **2** pleased: *We are happy to accept your invitation; happy that you are getting married; very happy about the marriage; Everyone is happy for* (*Informal for* pleased with) *you; a "happy face" sweater* (*with such a design*). **3** fortunate or lucky: *a happy chance, coincidence.* **4** apt or felicitous: *a happy choice of words; a happy idea, remark, thought.*
— **hap·pi·ly** *adv.;* **hap·pi·ness** *n.*

-happy *combining form.* happy with or dazed by something, as specified: *bomb-happy, gold-happy, slap-happy, trigger-happy.*

happy-go-lucky (HAP·ee·goh·LUCK·ee) *adj.* easygoing or light-hearted.

happy hour *n.* an early evening hour when a bar sells liquor at a discount.

ha·ra·ki·ri (HAH·ruh·KEER·ee) *n.* suicide by disembowelment, as once practised by the samurai.

ha·rangue (huh·RANG) *n.* a long and loud, esp. scolding speech; tirade.
— *v.* **-rangues, -rangued, -rangu·ing** address in or deliver a harangue.

har·ass (HAIR·us, huh·RAS) *v.* bother or torment unceasingly, as by repeated calls, raids, demands, cares, worries, etc. — **har·ass·ment** *n.*

har·bin·ger (HAR·bin·jur) *n.* one that goes before another to announce what is to come: *The early-blooming primrose has been called the harbinger of spring.*

har·bour or **har·bor** (HAR·bur) *n.* **1** a protected area of deep water on the coast of a sea or lake where ships may dock. **2** a place of safety or refuge; shelter.
— *v.* **1** come to anchor. **2** be or give a hiding place to an undesirable person, thing, or feeling: *hair that harbours fleas; to harbour feelings of revenge.*

hard *adj.* **1** too firm to penetrate, cut, or crush: *a hard nut, rock, muscle.* **2** of liquor, high in alcohol content, as rye or gin. **3** difficult to form lather with soap: *hard water.* **4** backed by gold or readily convertible to other currencies: *hard currency such as dollars, pounds, etc.* **5** not soft, weak, tentative, or visionary: *a hard and unyielding character; The police need hard evidence to get a murder conviction; It was a hard decision to let* him go; the hard facts of reality; Let's take a good hard look before deciding. **6** tough to endure: *No work is too hard for Lu; a* **hard luck story** (*meant to get sympathy and help*); *the hard* (= distressing) *times of unemployment; The fired employee left with no hard* (= harsh) *feelings; The baby gave us a hard* (= rough) *time when we ran out of milk; He said hard* (= unkind) *things to his wife; hard* (= severe) *winter weather; Everyone hates* **hard and fast** (= very rigid) *rules; We were* **hard put to** *find* (= had great difficulty in finding) *a night's lodging in that strange city; a big spender who is* **hard up** *for* (*Informal for* in great need of) *money at the end of each month.* **7** demanding great physical or mental effort; not easy: *a hill that is hard to climb; the long, hard march to freedom; Some habits are hard to break; a list of hard words; an earphone for the* **hard of hearing** (= those who don't hear well); *Lee's just playing* **hard-to-get** (*Informal for* pretending to be not easily won over).
— *adv.* in a hard manner: *The lake is frozen hard enough to skate on; Students work hard before a test; Try hard to succeed; Running makes you breathe hard; We are* **hard hit** (= We suffer) *by misfortunes; It will* **go hard with you** (= You will have a difficult time) *if you don't pay up; He took the defeat very hard* (= found it difficult to endure); *Superstitions* **die hard** (= remain in existence); *The church is* **hard by** (= close to) *the school.*

hard·ball *n. Slang.* tough or aggressive action: *to play hardball* (= be callous or ruthless); *hardball politics.*

hard-boiled *adj.* **1** boiled with its shell until firm inside: *a hard-boiled egg.* **2** *Informal.* tough or callous: *a hard-boiled businesswoman.*

hard copy *n.* a printout as distinguished from a video display.

hard-core *adj.* chronic or extreme: *the hard-core unemployed and unemployables of a community; explicit hard-core pornography.*

hard-cover (HARD·cuv·ur) *adj.* bound in cloth, board, or other stiff cover, not paperback: *a hardcover book, edition.*

hard drug *n.* an addictive drug such as cocaine or heroine.

hard·en *v.* **1** make hard or become solidified. **2** make or become unfeeling or pitiless: *hardened by training; a hardened criminal; Do not harden your hearts.*

hard hat *n.* **1** a protective helmet worn by miners, construction workers, etc.; hence, *Informal.* a construction worker. **2** an outspoken reactionary.

hard·head·ed (HARD·hed·id) *adj.* **1** stubborn. **2** practical or realistic: *a hardheaded businesswoman.*

hard·heart·ed (HARD·har·tid) *adj.* cruel or unfeeling.

har·di·hood (HAR·di·hood, short "oo") *n.* **1** daring or sturdiness. **2** audacity or boldness.

hard line *n.* an unyielding position: *The boss is taking a hard line against absenteeism.*
— **hard-line** *adj.* unyielding in policy, esp. political: *a hard-line nationalist, position, stand.* — **hard-liner** *n.*

hard·ly *adv.* **1** barely; almost not: *I can hardly walk; Hardly anyone turned up at the meeting; You can* *hardly expect to be paid for such poor work.* **2** [old use] in a hard manner: *He was dealt with hardly and severely.*

hard-nosed *adj. Informal.* shrewd and tough: *a hard-nosed politician.*

hard·scrab·ble (HARD·scrab·ul) *adj.* **1** earning a bare subsistence. **2** of land, barren: *hardscrabble coal country.*

hard sell *n. Informal.* high-pressure salesmanship: *the hard sell used to make kids eat wholesome foods.* — *adj.*: *a hard-sell campaign, commercial, hustler, promotion, tactic.*

hard·ship *n.* a hard-to-bear condition such as hunger, sickness, poverty, and pain.

hard·ware *n.* **1** metal articles, tools, utensils, etc.: *a hardware store.* **2** weaponry, equipment, etc.: *military hardware.* **3** apparatuses such as the physical units of a computer system, not programs or software.

hard-wired *adj.* directly connected to a computer, not via telephone lines.

hard·wood *n.* tough, compact wood, as of broad-leaved trees such as the oak, ebony, and mahogany: *a hardwood floor.*

har·dy (HAR·dee) *adj.* **hard·i·er, -i·est** strong and robust: *our hardy pioneers; hardy annuals that can endure the frost.* — **hard·i·ly** *adv.;* **hard·i·ness** *n.*

hare *n.* a rabbitlike furry animal but larger and with longer ears, a split upper lip, and powerful hind legs; jack rabbit: *Hares do not burrow but are very active in the spring; "to run with the hare and hunt with the hounds"* (= to play a double game, supporting both sides); *"mad as a March hare"* (when it is rutting).

har·em (HAIR·um) *n.* **1** a group of women kept by one man, as in a Moslem household. **2** an animal's mates collectively.

hark *v.* [literary use] listen! — **hark back** recall or refer back *to* an earlier subject or time.

harm *n.* hurt with pain or distress: *Some drugs do more harm than good; to undo the harm caused by pollutants; grave, grievous, irreparable, severe harm to the environment; There's no harm in watching a little TV.* — *v.* cause harm. — **harm·ful** *adj.;* **harm·ful·ly** *adv.*

har·mon·ic (har·MON·ic) *adj.* having to do with musical harmony: *a harmonic balance, concept, design, element.* — *n.* **1** a musical overtone. **2 harmonics** *pl.* [takes sing. v.] the science of musical sounds.

har·mo·ni·ous (har·MOH·nee·us) *adj.* **1** arranged so that the parts agree: *The structure is a harmonious mass of shapes and colours; nature and art forming a harmonious whole.* **2** agreeing in feelings, actions, etc.: *the harmonious relationships among our neighbours.* **3** concordant or well-sounding: *a harmonious melody.*

har·mo·nize (HAR·muh·nize) *v.* **-niz·es, -nized, -niz·ing** be in or make harmony: *Complementary colours harmonize well; music harmonized in chords.* — **har·mo·ni·za·tion** (-nuh·ZAY·shun) *n.*

har·mo·ny (HAR·muh·nee) *n.* **-nies 1** musical agreement of sounds, esp. of various tones and chords. **2** agreement in thoughts, feelings, words, actions, etc.; accord: *to act in harmony with the others; to achieve social harmony.* **3** any orderly arrangement: *the harmony of colour and form in a painting; the peace and harmony in a happy family; racial harmony; people living in harmony with the environment.*

har·ness (HAR·nis) *n.* **1** a combination of straps, bands, etc. for hitching an animal to what it pulls, as a horse to a carriage or plough. **2** similar trappings to tie a person to a parachute, restrain an automobile driver for safety, or have a child or dog in one's control. — **in harness** at one's regular occupation: *He never took a vacation and died in harness.* — *v.* **1** put a harness on an animal: *to harness dogs to a sled.* **2** utilize the power of water, wind, atomic energy, etc.

harp *n.* an ancient stringed musical instrument, played by plucking its strings with the fingers. — *v.* play on a harp. — **harp on** or **upon** refer continually to a tiresome subject. — **harp·ist** *n.*

har·py (HAR·pee) *n.* **-pies** a cruel and greedy person like the **Harpies** of Greek myth, winged monsters with a woman's head and bird's body.

har·ri·er (HAIR·ee·ur) *n.* **1** a breed of dog smaller than the English foxhound, used to hunt hares. **2** a cross-country runner. **3** one who harries. **4** a kind of hawk that preys on rodents, reptiles, and poultry.

har·row (HAIR·oh) *v.* **1** break up and level ploughed ground, as with a harrow. **2** lacerate, wound, or distress: *The hijacking was a harrowing* (= painful and distressing) *experience.* — *n.* an implement with a set of revolving disks (**disk harrow**) or one with spikes or teeth for breaking and smoothing the soil.

har·ry (HAIR·ee) *v.* **har·ries, har·ried, har·ry·ing 1** harass or torment. **2** raid or pillage.

harsh *adj.* **1** disagreeably rough to the senses: *a harsh climate, colour, flavour, portrait, sound.* **2** cruel or unfeeling: *a harsh parent; He is too harsh with his children.*

har·vest (HAR·vist) *n.* **1** the season for gathering in grain, fruit, vegetables, etc.: *We bring in* or *reap the harvest in the fall; an abundant, bountiful, poor, rich harvest.* **2** the gathering in or what is gathered: *a bountiful harvest of wheat; The seal harvest has suffered at the hands of animal rights activists.* **3** the fruit or reward of one's labours. — *v.* reap: *to harvest grain; Quebec producers harvest several million gallons of maple syrup each year; A donated organ has to be used soon after it is harvested* (= removed from the body); *to harvest a new crop of cultures grown in the lab.* — **har·vest·er** (HAR·vis·tur) *n.*

has third person sing. of HAVE.

has-been (HAZ·bin) *n. Informal.* a person or thing whose heyday is past: *The singer was superrich and a has-been by age 20.*

hash *v.* **1** chop into small pieces for cooking. **2** make a mess of something. **3** *Informal.* discuss: *We hashed over it* or *hashed it over before making a decision.*
— **hash out** settle a question by discussing.
— *n.* **1** cooked food hashed and fried or baked. **2** a mixture or hodgepodge. **3** *Slang.* [short form] hashish.
— **make a hash of** make a mess of something.
— **settle one's hash** *Informal.* subdue, silence, or put down someone.

hash browns *n.pl.* diced, boiled, and browned potatoes; also **hash brown potatoes.**

hash·ish (hash·EESH) *n.* an intoxicating drug prepared from an Asiatic plant; also **hash·eesh.**

has·n't (HAZ·unt) has not.

has·sle (HAS·ul) *n.* *Informal.* a wrangle, argument, or tussle.
— *v.* **has·sles, has·sled, has·sling 1** have a hassle: *to hassle with the referee over* or *about a foul call.* **2** harass or pester: *Will you stop hassling me?*

hast [old use] the form of "have" used with THOU.

haste *n.* hurry, esp. in a careless manner: *"Haste makes waste"; "The more haste, the less speed"* (= The more you rush the less you achieve); *He made haste* (= hurried up) *and cooked up a tasteless meal; In his haste, he even forgot to add salt.*

has·ten (HAY·sun) *v.* **1** hurry or speed up: *He was told to hasten and fix us something to eat.* **2** be quick: *Let me hasten to add that I didn't cook this dinner.*

has·ty (HAY·stee) *adj.* **hast·i·er, -i·est 1** quick: *He made a hasty exit after dinner.* **2** too quick or quick-tempered; rash: *a hasty decision.* — **has·ti·ly** *adv.*

hat *n.* a head covering with a brim and crown for formal or outdoor wear: *to don and doff hats; a straw hat; top hat; Names were picked out of a hat* (= by lot); *Hats off* (= Congratulations) *to Jim for coming out first in his class; Three-D movies are old hat* (= nothing new); *You pass the hat around to take up a collection; She threw her hat into the ring* (= entered the contest) *as a candidate for election; You don't have to keep it under your hat* (*Informal* for keep it private or confidential).
— **hat in hand** humbly.

hatch *n.* **1** an opening, as in a ship's deck for loading cargo: *Down the hatch it went.* **2** a trapdoor covering it: *to batten down the hatches before a storm.* **3** an opening or door in a spacecraft or aircraft: *an escape hatch.* **4** a set of hatched lines; also **hatch·ing.**
— *v.* **1** draw or engrave fine parallel lines for a shading effect. **2** keep eggs warm so as to bring out the young. **3** bring forth young or come out from eggs. **4** plot or scheme: *prisoners hatching an escape plot.*
— **hatch·er** *n.*

hat·check *adj.* having to do with the checking of coats and hats: *a hatcheck girl, stand.*

hatch·et (HACH·it) *n.* a small, short-handled axe, as used to kill; tomahawk.
— **bury the hatchet** make peace after a fight.

hatchet job *n.* *Informal.* an unfair attack in a publication: *The TV program did a hatchet job on the Prime Minister.*

hatchet man *n.* *Informal.* one hired to deal viciously with opponents.

hate *v.* **hates, hat·ed, hat·ing 1** dislike intensely, usually with malice and a tendency to hurt. **2** do not like: *Cats hate water; He hates ice cream; She hates to disturb you.*
— *n.* hostility or an object of it.
— *adj.:* *a hate campaign; flooded by hate mail; hate propaganda.* — **hate·ful** *adj.;* **hate·ful·ly** *adv.*

hath [old use] has.

ha·tred (HAY·trud) *n.* ill will or strong dislike: *Joe's hatred of* or *for skunks; to arouse, express, feel, show, stir up hatred toward people of other races and colours; Racists are consumed* or *filled with hatred.*

haugh·ty (HAW·tee) *adj.* **-ti·er, -ti·est** proud in bearing or manner, esp. scornful of others.
— **haugh·ti·ly** *adv.;* **haugh·ti·ness** *n.*

haul *v.* **1** pull or tug with sustained force; hence, transport: *the hauling of freight by truck and train.* **2** shift or change, as a wind or a sailing ship's course.
— **haul up** order to appear on trial: *He was hauled up before a judge.*
— *n.* a load, amount, or distance hauled: *They fled with a million-dollar haul; a short-haul* (= short-distance) *flight.*
— **in** or **over the long haul** *Informal.* over a long period.

haunch *n.* hindquarter, including hip, buttock, and top of thigh: *A dog sits on its haunches; a haunch* (= loin and leg) *of venison.*

haunt *v.* visit continually or seem to stay in a place, as a spirit inhabiting a house; hence, plague or obsess: *Memories from the past haunted her in her dreams; That house is haunted* (by a ghost); *a haunting melody* (that stays in one's mind).
— *n.* a frequently visited place: *to revisit the haunts of one's youth; a favourite haunt of criminals.*

have (HAV, huv, uv) *v.* **has** (HAZ, huz, uz), **had** (HAD, hud, ud), **hav·ing 1** hold or possess: *We have a home; What are we having for dinner? Please have a chair* (= Please sit down); *She's having* (= bearing or begetting) *a baby; She had two children by her first husband; Always have* (= keep) *my advice in mind; I won't have* (= tolerate) *any pranksters in my class; The police have nothing on* (= no evidence against) *us; We have nothing against* (= don't dislike) *the police.* **2** cause: *He's having his tonsils removed; We'll have someone (to) fix the faucets; Let's have a pizza delivered.* **3** [indicating necessity or obligation]: *It's midnight, I have (got) to go.* **4** [indicating completed action]: *Everyone has arrived; She'll have left by now.*
— **have coming** deserve: *She had the raise coming to her after winning the contract.*
— **have done with** cease or stop: *One last time and we shall have done with gambling.*
— **have had it** *Informal.* reach an end with something: *I have had it – no more loans for you.*
— **have it out** settle *with* someone by fighting or arguing.
— **have on** be wearing: *I had nothing on when I came into the world.*
— **have to do with 1** be related to something: *Geology has to do with the earth.* **2** associate with something:

She won't have anything to do with him.
— **the haves and the have-nots** the rich and the not so rich.

ha·ven (HAY·vun) *n.* a harbour or refuge.

have-not *n.* one that does not have something, esp. one with little material resources: *the haves and the have-nots of society; the nuclear powers and the have-nots.*

have·n't (HAV·unt) have not.

hav·oc (HAV·uc) *n.* widespread harm or destruction, as caused by an earthquake or tornado: *The storm wreaked havoc on the town; a scandal that **played havoc with** (= greatly damaged) many reputations.*

haw *n.* See HEM AND HAW.

hawk *n.* **1** a bird of prey with sharp eyesight, similar to eagles but smaller. **2** one who favours war, not a dove. — *v.* **1** hunt with or like hawks. **2** peddle wares by shouting, as a hawker does. **3** clear the throat noisily. — **hawk·ish** *adj.*

hawk·er *n.* a huckster: *the hawkers and vendors of downtown streets.*

hawk-eyed *adj.* sharp-eyed.

hay *n.* cut and dried grass, alfalfa, clover, etc. for use as fodder.
— **hit the hay** *Slang.* go to bed.
— **make hay while the sun shines** make the most of an opportunity.
— *v.* mow grass, etc. and prepare hay.

hay·mak·er (HAY·may·kur) *n. Slang.* a knockout blow.

hay·ride *n.* a pleasure ride taken by a group in an open vehicle, esp. at night.

hay·seed *n.* **1** grass, seed, chaff, etc. from hay. **2** *Slang.* a rustic or bumpkin.

hay·wire *n.* wire for tying up bales of hay.
— **go haywire** *Slang.* of a person or operation, go crazy or get upset.

haz·ard (HAZ·urd) *n.* **1** a risk or chance: *A stunt man's life is full of hazards; Careless smoking is a fire hazard and secondhand smoke is a health hazard; a hazard to health; occupational hazards.* **2** an obstacle in golf.
— *v.* venture or expose to risk: *to hazard* (= make) *a guess.*

haz·ard·ous (HAZ·ur·dus) *adj.* risky or dangerous: *Smoking is hazardous to health; a hazardous journey, undertaking; hazardous materials, occupations; hazardous foods (that may get spoiled if not refrigerated); the disposal of hazardous industrial wastes that may contaminate the environment.*

haze *n.* **1** a mist, smoke, dust, etc. thinly spread in the air, reducing visibility: *A haze hung over the morning countryside.* **2** vagueness.
— *v.* **haz·es, hazed, haz·ing** force newcomers to a group, as among students, to do humiliating things.

haz·el (HAY·zul) *n.* a kind of shrub or tree bearing small, edible, light-brown nuts.
— *adj.* light or yellowish brown.

ha·zy (HAY·zee) *adj.* **-zi·er, -zi·est** misty, smoky, or vague: *hot, humid, and hazy summer weather; hazy notions.* — **ha·zi·ly** *adv.;* **ha·zi·ness** *n.*

he (HEE) *n. & pron., objective* HIM, *possessive* HIS; *pl.* THEY, *objective* THEM, *possessive* THEIR(S). the male animal or human being referred to: *Is the calf a he or a she? "He* (= he or she) *who hesitates is lost."*

head (HED) *n.* **1** the part of the body containing the brain, eyes, ears, nose, and mouth; the top part in humans and front part in quadrupeds: *to bare, bow, drop, hang, lift, nod, raise, scratch, shake, toss, turn one's head; hold one's head high (in self-respect); to hang one's head in shame.* **2** the chief, top, upper, or leading part of anything: *the head of a bed, column, corporation, department, family, household, pin, procession; Racism rears its ugly head in our cities; the head* (= source) *of a river; the head of a ship* (= the bow, etc.); *a movement **gathering head*** (= strength); *The Prime Minister is the head of the Canadian government, but the sovereign or the Governor General is the **head of state**.* **3** *sing. & pl.* individual(s): *500 head of cattle; The party costs $25 a head to cater.* **4** the cutting or hitting part of a hammer, golf club, ends of a drum, etc. **5** mind or brains: *He has a good head for figures; She keeps a clear head in difficult situations; She uses her head to solve problems; a level head; older and wiser heads than mine.* **6** [short form] headland; heading; headword.
— **cannot make head or tail of something** cannot understand it.
— **give someone his** or **her head** let one do as he or she likes.
— **go to someone's head** affect one's mind, as to intoxicate or make conceited: *Success went to his head.*
— **head over heels** completely or recklessly.
— **keep** (or **lose**) **one's head** keep (or lose) one's self-control.
— **out of one's head** *Informal.* crazy; also **off one's head.**
— **over one's head 1** beyond one's grasp. **2** without regard to one's claims or authority: *to complain to the boss over the supervisor's head.*
— **to a head:** *A boil comes to a head before bursting; bring matters to a head* (= crisis point).
— **turn someone's head** make one giddy or conceited: *Success in the stock market turned his head.*
— *adj.* having to do with the head or being a head: *a head cold; a head clerk, gate, table.*
— *v.* **1** be the head of something: *A president heads a corporation; a letter headed with a place and date; The committee is headed by a woman.* **2** go in a certain direction: *We head home after school; to head east; to head* (= turn) *a boat toward shore; They took steps to **head off*** (= prevent) *trouble.*

-head *combining form. Slang.* addict: *acidhead, pothead, teahead.*

head·ache (HED·ake) *n.* **1** pain in the head: *a severe, sick, splitting headache.* **2** *Informal.* a source of annoyance. — **head·ach·y** (-ay·kee) *adj.*

head·board *n.* a board or frame at the head of something, as of a bed.

head cold *n.* a common cold affecting the nasal passages.

head·dress *n.* a usually elaborate covering for the head.

-headed *combining form.* having a head as specified: *double-headed, light-headed, muddle-headed.*

head-first *adj. & adv.* (done or going) with the head first: *to dive head-first into a pool.*

head·gear *n.* 1 headdress. 2 the harness for an animal's head.

head·hunt·er (HED·hun·tur) *n.* 1 formerly, a member of a tribe that killed their enemies and kept their heads as trophies. 2 an aggressive personnel recruiter.

heading *n.* 1 a topic or title placed at the beginning or top of a piece of writing. 2 the travelling direction of a ship or plane.

head·land *n.* a point of land projecting into water; cape.

head·light *n.* a bright light of a locomotive or automobile.

head·line *n.* a printed line at the top of a page or at the head of a news story: *a banner headline; a robbery that made headlines* (= important news) *all over the country.* — *v.* -lines, -lined, -lin·ing make or be the main attraction or news event.

head·lock *n.* a wrestling hold in which the opponent's head is held under one's arm.

head·long *adj. & adv.* 1 with the head first: *a headlong plunge.* 2 with uncontrolled speed or force; reckless(ly): *He ran headlong into oncoming traffic.*

head·mas·ter (HED·mas·tur) *n.* in some schools, the principal. — **head·mis·tress** *fem.*

head of steel *n. Cdn.* same as END OF STEEL.

head-on *adj. & adv.* frontal(ly); direct(ly): *The car ran head-on into a bus; The government decided to tackle the deficit head-on by cutting its wasteful spending; two companies competing head-on against each other; head-on competition; a head-on collision, confrontation.*

head·quar·ters (HED·kwor·turz) *n. pl.* [takes sing. or pl. v.] 1 administrative centre. 2 a place from where orders are issued for a police force, army, etc.

head·rest *n.* 1 a support for the head, as in a barber's chair. 2 same as **head restraint,** a support at the top of an automobile seat's back to protect the occupant, esp. in a rear-end collision.

head·set *n.* a pair of headphones or earphones, often with an attached transmitter.

head·ship *n.* the office or position of a head.

head shop *n.* a shop selling accessories for the users of illicit drugs.

head start *n.* the advantage of a start ahead of one's peers or competitors: *to get a headstart on the work lying ahead.*

head·strong *adj.* rash or foolish in having one's own way: *a headstrong child.*

head·way *n.* 1 progress or advance: *to gain* or *make headway against something.* 2 headroom. 3 the interval between two successive buses, trains, etc. on the same route.

head·word *n.* a word that forms the heading of a paragraph, dictionary entry, etc.

head·y *adj.* **head·i·er, -i·est** 1 apt to affect the head, as an intoxicant: *Being mayor for a day was a heady experience.* 2 rash or impetuous.

heal (HEEL) *v.* 1 make or get well, as a wound, sore, burn, etc.; cure a disease or sick person. 2 end breached relations. 3 free from or get rid of something bad: *Time heals all sorrows.*

health (HELTH, "TH" as in "thin") *n.* 1 sound condition of body or mind: *to enjoy, promote good health; to recover* or *regain one's health; bad, broken, delicate, failing, fragile, robust health; occupational health; public health.* 2 a toast drunk to wish someone well: *We drank her health; To your health!*

health food *n.* food that is naturally health-giving, as grown without the use of chemicals and not subjected to processing.

health·ful *adj.* good for the health; health-giving: *a healthful climate; healthful eating; the healthful properties and value of spinach; healthful foods, music, snacks.*

health resort *n.* a place having a spa; also **health spa.**

health·y *adj.* **health·i·er, -i·est** 1 having good health: *a sound mind in a healthy body.* 2 showing or giving health: *a healthy appearance, appetite, climate, habit.* — **health·i·ly** *adv.;* **health·i·ness** *n.*

heap (HEEP) *n.* 1 a mass or pile of things: *a heap of rubbish; a scrap heap.* 2 *Informal.* a large amount: *a heap of sand; a heap of trouble.* — *v.* 1 form into a heap: *to heap* (= amass) *riches, wealth; to heap* (= load) *a plate with food.* 2 give a heap of something to someone: *to heap gifts, insults, praises on someone; to heap someone with gifts.*

hear (HEER) *v.* **hears, heard** (HURD), **hear·ing** 1 perceive by the ear: *I hear the birds sing(ing); I hear you loud and clear; You heard what I said.* 2 listen to something: *to hear a lecture, recitation; You better hear what I have to say; Courts hear* (= listen to and try) *cases.* 3 receive information: *to hear about an accident; I never heard of such a thing; We heard from him yesterday.*

hearing *n.* 1 the sense by which sounds are perceived: *acute, keen, impaired hearing; Some are hard of hearing; the hearing impaired (people).* 2 a range of this perception; earshot: *Parents are careful about what they say in the hearing of children.* 3 a listening or receiving of information: *He was given a patient hearing by the committee; to conduct* or *hold a hearing; to testify at a hearing; a fair, impartial, open hearing.*

heark·en (HAR·kun) *v.* [old use] listen *to* prayer, etc.; heed.

hear·say (HEER·say) *n.* something one has heard but not verified, as a rumour or gossip: *mere hearsay; hearsay evidence.*

hearse (HURSE) *n.* a vehicle for taking the dead to the grave.

heart (HART) *n.* **1** the hollow, muscular organ that pumps blood throughout the body, traditionally considered as the seat of one's feelings, esp. love, sympathy, courage, etc., and the centre or most vital part of one's being: *a hard* (= cruel) *heart; a heavy, light heart (in regard to feeling); a kind heart; a brave, faint, stout, strong, weak heart (in regard to courage); Let's not lose heart but take heart* (= courage); *a **heart of gold*** (= generous nature); *Hearts ache, beat, bleed, fail, palpitate, throb; He broke her heart* (= made her very sad); *to gladden, harden, steal, win someone's heart; to speak from the heart* (= speak sincerely); *She is in the very heart* (= centre) *of things; Pat has no heart for* (= does not like) *housework; She had a change of heart* (= of feeling). **2** a heart-shaped figure, as on a playing card; also, a card so marked: *the queen of hearts.*
— **after one's own heart** as one likes or desires it.
— **at heart** in one's innermost nature.
— **by heart** by or from memory: *to get, know, learn, recite a poem by heart.*
— **from the bottom of one's heart** sincerely.
— **have a heart** be kind; don't ask for so much.
— **set one's heart:** *His heart is set against* (= He is opposed to) *marrying her; The announcement set our hearts at rest* (= made us feel at ease); *Her heart is set on winning* (= She is determined to win) *a gold medal.*
— **take to heart:** *He took the warning to heart* (= was much moved by it).
— **with all one's heart** with all sincerity and good will.

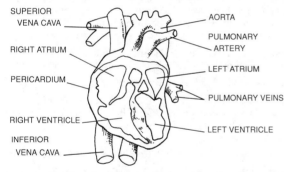

SUPERIOR VENA CAVA
AORTA
PULMONARY ARTERY
RIGHT ATRIUM
LEFT ATRIUM
PERICARDIUM
PULMONARY VEINS
RIGHT VENTRICLE
LEFT VENTRICLE
INFERIOR VENA CAVA

heart·burn *n.* a burning feeling as if from near the heart, caused by the rising up of stomach acid.

heart·burn·ing (HART·burn·ing) *n.* intense jealousy or resentment.

-hearted *combining form.* having a heart as specified: *hard-hearted, stout-hearted, weak-hearted.*

heart·en (HAR·tun) *v.* cheer up.

heart·felt *adj.* sincere or genuine: *our heartfelt apology, sympathy, thanks.*

hearth (HARTH) *n.* **1** the floor near a fireplace; fireside. **2** home or family life.

hearth·stone *n.* **1** the stone forming a hearth. **2** home.

heart·land *n.* the central or vital region of a country, institution, movement, etc.

heart·sick or **heart·sore** *adj.* sick at heart.

heart·strings *n. pl.* one's deepest feelings: *to tug at someone's heartstrings.*

heart·throb *n.* **1** a heartbeat. **2** *Informal.* a person one is infatuated with.

heart-to-heart (HART·tuh·HART) *adj.* frank and sincere: *They made up after a heart-to-heart talk.*

heart·warm·ing (HART·war·ming) *adj.* kindling feelings of warmth and geniality.

heart·y *adj.* **heart·i·er, -i·est 1** full of vigour and enthusiasm: *a hearty welcome.* **2** showing or promoting good health: *a hearty appetite, eater, meal.*
— **heart·i·ly** *adv.;* **heart·i·ness** *n.*

heat (HEET) *n.* **1** the quality of being hot to the touch; high temperature; the form of energy that causes expansion, melting, etc.: *to generate, produce, radiate heat; to alleviate the heat of the summer; blistering, dry, extreme, intense, low, oppressive, radiant, red, stifling, white heat.* **2** great feeling or excitement: *He said it in the heat of the argument; a female mammal **in heat*** (= recurring period or condition of sexual excitement). **3** a single effort; hence, a preliminary round, as in a race, that qualifies candidates for the finals: *She won the first heat; a dead heat* (= a tie). **4** *Informal.* pressure: *to put the heat on someone; to apply the heat to force a confession.*
— *v.* **1** make or become hot or warm: *to heat water for coffee.* **2** excite or become excited.
— **heat·ed** *adj.: a heated wire, argument, discussion.*

heat exchanger *n.* a device of the type of an automobile radiator for changing heat from one medium to another for elimination or for use, as in a nuclear reactor.

heath (HEETH, "TH" as in "thin") *n.* **1** open wasteland covered by shrubs such as heather. **2** any of a family of shrubs and plants including the blueberry, cranberry, and arbutus.

heath·en (HEE·thun, "th" as in "thin") *n.* **-then** or **-thens 1** a person of no religion or culture. **2** formerly, one who is not a Christian, Jew, or Moslem: *heathen customs.*

heat pump *n.* a refrigerating apparatus for extracting heat from the air, ground, water, etc. so as to cool the place that heat is taken from or to heat what it is delivered to.

heat·stroke or **heat stroke** *n.* illness from exposure to excessive heat.

heave (HEEV) *v.* **heaves,** *pt. & pp.* **heaved** or **hove** (HOHV), **heav·ing 1** lift and move something heavy: *A ship heaves anchor and sails away; They heaved the stone through the window.* **2** move in a rising and falling manner: *the heaving waves; Her stomach heaves at the sight of blood; He heaved a sigh of relief; A ship **heaves in** or **into sight** on the horizon; The ground heaves* (= bulges) *from an earthquake; Sailors heave at* or *on* (= pull) *a rope.*
— **heave to** stop, as a sailing ship.
— *n.* **1** rise and fall: *the heave of the sea; with a mighty heave* (= pull or throw). **2 heaves** *pl.* a lung disease of horses, marked by difficult breathing and heaving sides.
— **heave ho!** the cry of sailors pulling in the anchor.

heave-ho *n. Informal.* dismissal.

heav·en (HEV·un) *n.* **1** a place of great happiness. **2 Heaven** God's supposed dwelling place; where the

blessed go after death.
— **move heaven and earth** do one's utmost.
— **the heavens** *pl.* the firmament.
— **heavens!** or **for heaven's sake!** exclamation of surprise, protest, etc.
— **heav·en·ly** *adj.*
— **heav·en·ward** (HEV·un·wurd) *adj. & adv.;* also **heav·en·wards** *adv.*

heav·y (HEV·ee) *adj.* **heav·i·er, -i·est** having great weight; hence, hard: *a heavy load, rain; a heavy blow; heavy features, fighting, news, reading, traffic; They made it heavy going for him at work; a heavy* (= hard to digest) *meal; a heavy* (= sorrowful) *heart; a heavy* (= hard to endure) *odour; a heavy* (= sound) *sleeper; a heavy drinker and smoker (who drinks and smokes a lot); a heavy* (= abundant) *vote.*
— *adv.: a deed that lies heavy on his conscience; Time hangs heavy on her hands* (= drags).
— *n., pl.* **heav·ies 1** something heavy, as a large wave. **2** a strong person hired for protection, as a bouncer, or one of consequence. **3** an actor in a nonheroic or villainous role. — **heav·i·ly** *adv.;* **heav·i·ness** *n.*

heavy-duty (HEV·ee·DEW·tee) *adj.* designed for hard use; durable: *a heavy-duty shock absorber; heavy-duty machinery, shoes.*

heavy-handed (HEV·ee·HAN·did) *adj.* **1** awkward. **2** cruel or oppressive.

heavy-hearted (HEV·ee·HAR·tid) *adj.* sad or gloomy.

heavy metal *n.* amplified electronic rock music with a heavy beat.

heav·y·weight (HEV·ee·wait) *n.* **1** a boxer weighing over 175 lb. (81 kg for Olympics). **2** *Informal.* a person of much intelligence or consequence.

heck *n. & interj. Informal.* hell: *What the heck! a heck of a job.*

hec·tare *n.* a metric unit of area equal to 10 000 square metres.

hec·tic (HEC·tic) *adj.* busy or exciting: *a hectic day, life, pace, period, time.*

hec·tor (HEC·tur) *n.* a bully or blusterer, like **Hector,** Trojan hero.
— *v.: The Opposition tries to hector the Government whenever they get a chance.*

he'd (HEED) he had; he would.

hedge (HEJ) *n.* **1** a row of bushes planted as a fence. **2** a boundary, barrier, or means of protection, as against financial loss: *an investment as a hedge against inflation; a hedge fund.*
— *v.* **hedg·es, hedged, hedg·ing** enclose or protect: *hedged in* or *about by restrictions; to hedge a bet by making one also on the opposite side; to hedge against commodity price changes by selling futures; a politician accused of hedging on the issues* (= of being evasive).
— **hedg·er** *n.*

heed *v.* pay attention to: *to heed a warning.*
— *n.* attention or notice: *to pay* or *give heed to advice; He took no heed of warnings.*

hee·haw *n. & v.* bray; also, guffaw.

heel *n.* **1** the hindmost part of a foot, below the ankle.

2 anything resembling a human heel in shape, function, or position, as the hock of an animal or hind toe of a bird, the hind part of a shoe or sock, an end crust of bread, or any bottom part or portion. **3** *Informal.* a despicable person.
— **be at someone's heel, on someone's heel, on the heels of someone** or **upon someone's heels** be close behind someone.
— **cool one's heels** *Informal.* be kept waiting.
— **down at the heel** or **heels** in a shabby condition.
— **hard on someone's heels** close to someone.
— **take to one's heels** flee.
— *v.* **1** furnish with a heel; also, follow closely behind, as a dog in pursuit. **2** lean to one side. **3** make a ship list.

heft *n. Informal.* weight or bulk.
— *v.* lift or heave.

heft·y *adj.* **hef·ti·er, hef·ti·est 1** heavy or bulky; well-built: *a hefty man.* **2** considerable or large: *a hefty pay hike.* — **heft·i·ly** *adv.;* **heft·i·ness** *n.*

heif·er (HEF·ur) *n.* a young cow that has not yet had a calf.

heigh-ho (HYE·hoh, HAY·hoh) *interj.* expressing joy, surprise, boredom, etc.

height (HITE) *n.* **1** how high or tall a person or thing is: *The CN Tower is 553 m in height.* **2** elevation or altitude: *flying at a height of 3 000 m above sea-level; the precipitous height of a cliff.* **3** the topmost point: *at the height of his career; It is the height of folly to say such a thing.* **4 heights** *pl.* an eminence or hill: *Battle of Queenston Heights; the dizzying heights of fame.*

height·en (HIGH·tun) *v.* **1** bring to a height or become high or higher. **2** make or become greater; increase.

height of land *n. Cdn.* a watershed or divide.

Heim·lich manoeuvre (HIME·lik-) *n.* a method of forcing out what is lodged in a choking person's windpipe by hugging from behind and applying pressure to the abdomen.

hei·nous (HAY·nus) *adj.* hatefully bad: *a heinous crime.*

heir (AIR) *n.* one who is in line to inherit another's property, as **heir apparent** if no stronger claimant is possible, and **heir presumptive** till a nearer relative is born; *pl.* **heirs apparent, heirs presumptive.**

heir·ess (AIR·is) *n.* a female heir, esp. one inheriting great wealth.

held *pt. & pp.* of HOLD.

hel·i·cal (HEL·uh·cul) *adj.* like a screw; spiral: *helical gears.*

hel·i·cop·ter (HEL·uh·cop·tur) *n.* an aircraft that lifts off vertically, flies, and hovers with the aid of large rotor blades mounted horizontally on its top.

hel·i·pad (HEL·uh·pad) *n.* a helicopter-landing surface.

hel·i·port (HEL·uh·port) *n.* a helicopter airport; also, a helipad.

hel·i·ski (HEL·i·skee) *v.* **-skis, -skied, -ski·ing** to ski using a helicopter to reach the top of the slopes.
— *adj.: a heli-ski operator, program.* — **hel·i·ski·ing** *n.*

he·li·um (HEE·lee·um) *n.* a lightweight gas used in

industry, as a filler for balloons, and in medicine.

he'll (HEEL) he will; he shall.

hell *n.* 1 in Christianity and other religions, a place of eternal torment as punishment for damned souls. 2 *Slang.* [used to emphasize anything good or bad]: *Who the hell is he?*
— **all hell broke loose** conditions became very chaotic.
— **hell of a** *Slang.* very bad, good, etc. as implied: *a hell of a nuisance; one hell of a nice girl.*
— **just for the hell of it** *Informal.* for kicks.

hell-bent *adj. & adv. Informal.* fully intent *on* achieving something; recklessly aiming *for* a goal or *to* achieve something.

hell-for-leather (HELL·fur·LETH·ur) *adj. & adv. Informal.* hell-bent.

hell·hole *n. Informal.* a detestable place.

hel·lo (huh·LOH) *n. & interj.* an exclamation of greeting or response.

hel·lu·va (HEL·uh·vuh) [a respelling of the slang phrase "hell of a"] very good, bad, etc., as implied or expressed: *a helluva* (= very bad) *job; You're one helluva* (= very good) *guy.*

helm *n.* 1 a ship's steering wheel or gear. 2 a position of control: *to take over the helm of government; at the helm of the nation.*

hel·met (HEL·mut) *n.* a protective covering for the head: *crash, safety, steel helmet.* — **hel·met·ed** *adj.*

helms·man (HELMZ·mun) *n.* **-men** one who steers a ship.

help *v.* 1 provide someone with a useful thing or needed service: *Please help me set the table; to help with the dishes; to help us in our preparations; to help a patient (get) into a wheelchair; someone to help out in the kitchen; Do help yourself to the drinks; Who'd like another helping* (= portion) *of cake?* 2 improve or make better: *a medicine to help your cough.* 3 avoid: *I couldn't help falling asleep during the show; He cannot help but* (= is obliged to) *admire her patience.*
— *n.* 1 aid or assistance. 2 a person or other source of aid: *Help wanted; kitchen help at $25 an hour.*

help·mate *n.* a helpful partner, as one's spouse; also **help·meet** [old use].

hel·ter-skel·ter (HEL·tur·skel·tur) *adv.* in confusion or disorderly haste.
— *adj.: a helter-skelter condition, militia, retreat.*

hem *n.* 1 the usually folded and sewn-down border or edge of a garment: *to let out, lower, raise, straighten, take up a hem.* 2 the sound of clearing the throat.
— *v.* **hems, hemmed, hem·ming** 1 put a hem on a garment. 2 enclose or confine: *a lake hemmed in or about or around by hills; He felt hemmed in on all sides by his enemies.* 3 make the sound of clearing the throat.
— **hem and haw** 1 hesitate in speech. 2 stall or put off doing something.

he-man *n.* **-men** *Informal.* an obviously virile man.

hemi- *prefix.* half: *hemiplegia, hemisphere.*

hem·i·sphere (HEM·us·feer) *n.* half of a sphere, esp. the northern, southern, western, or eastern half of the

earth. — **hem·i·spher·i·cal** (-FER·uh·cul) *adj.*

hem·line *n.* a hem, esp. the bottom edge of a skirt as determining its length.

hen *n.* a female bird, esp. of the domestic fowl: *a cackling* or *clucking hen; Hens lay eggs.*

hence *adv.* from this place, time, source, or origin: *Many years hence we shall all be gone; "Grapes are sour," hence* (= consequently) *the sour-grapes philosophy.*

hench·man (HENCH·mun) *n.* **-men** a right-hand man, often a self-serving political follower.

hep *adj. Slang.* hip or aware.

hep·cat *n. Slang.* one who is hip or aware.

hepta- *combining form.* seven: *heptagon* (= seven-sided figure), *heptameter* (= seven-footed verse), *heptarchy* (= rule by seven).

her (HUR, ur) *pron.* objective or possessive case of SHE: *I saw her; her face; I'm older than her* (*Informal for* she); *That's her* (*Informal for* she).
— **hers** (HURZ) *pron.: The purse is hers; his books and hers; Hers are cleaner.*

her·ald (HER·uld) *n.* 1 formerly, a public official in charge of announcements, ceremonies, coats-of-arms, etc. 2 an announcer or harbinger. Also *v.: Birds herald the dawn.* — **he·ral·dic** (huh·RAL·dic) *adj.*

her·ald·ry (HER·ul·dree) *n.* **-ries** 1 coats of arms or their science and art. 2 heraldic pomp: *with great pomp and heraldry.*

herb (URB, HURB) *n.* any seed plant with fleshy stems that is used for food and in medicines and perfumes.

her·bal (UR·bul, HUR-) *adj.* 1 having to do with herbs: *an herbal remedy.* 2 medicinal: *the herbal qualities of poison ivy.*

her·cu·le·an or **Her·cu·le·an** (hurk·yuh·LEE·un, hur·KEW·lee·un) *adj.* having or requiring great strength like that of Hercules, a hero of Greek and Roman myths, famous for 12 feats of strength: *a herculean effort, feat, labour, task, workload; herculean dimensions, measures, proportions, strength.*

herd *n.* 1 a group of large animals such as cattle, horses, and elephants that are kept or that live together: *to round up, tend a herd.* 2 a crowd of common people or children: *the common herd; the herd instinct (to stay and act in a group).*
— **ride herd on** supervise people closely like cowboys herding cattle.
— *v.* form into or take care of as a herd or flock, as a herdsman does. — **herds·man** *n.* **-men.**

here (HEER) *n. & adv.* 1 at, in, to, or into this place: *Come here, Joe; Here I come.* 2 at this point or time: *Let's pause here for a moment.*
— **here below** on earth.
— **here goes!** *Informal.* [announcing something about to be done].
— **here you are!** *Informal.* [said when handing over something asked for].
— **neither here nor there** not relevant.
— **up to here** *Informal.* to the utmost: *People have had it up to here with all sorts of taxes.*

here·af·ter (heer·AF·tur) *n. & adv.* (in) the future or the life after the present: *Hereafter we are going to be on time; Who knows what may happen in the hereafter?*

here·by (heer·BY) *adv. Formal.* by this means, as by a document; in this way.

he·red·i·tar·y (huh·RED·uh·tair·ee) *adj.* 1 by inheritance: *a hereditary ruler, title.* 2 by heredity: *a hereditary characteristic.* 3 traditional: *hereditary beliefs, customs, enemies, loyalties.*

he·red·i·ty (huh·RED·uh·tee) *n.* -ties 1 the passing on of parental characteristics to offspring through genes. 2 such qualities, traits, etc. or the tendency to inherit them.

here·in (here·IN) *adv. Formal.* in this document, matter, etc.

here·of (heer·OV) *adv. Formal.* of or about this.

here·on (heer·ON) *adv. Formal.* on this.

here's (HEERZ) here is.

her·e·sy (HER·uh·see) *n.* -sies an opinion or belief, esp. religious, that is opposed to the orthodox or established position: *He was accused of preaching heresy.*
— **her·e·tic** (-uh·tic) *n. & adj.*
— **he·ret·i·cal** (huh·RET·uh·cul) *adj.*

here·with (heer·WITH, "TH" as in "the") *adv.* with this: *A cheque is enclosed herewith.*

her·it·age (HER·uh·tij) *n.* what is inherited, as a title, property, languages, traditions, etc.: *a cultural, family, priceless, proud, rich heritage; the teaching of heritage* (= ethnic) *languages in schools.*

her·mit (HUR·mit) *n.* a recluse, esp. religious.

her·mit·age (HUR·muh·tij) *n.* a hermit's secluded dwelling place.

her·ni·a (HUR·nee·uh) *n.* a bulging of an organ through weakened tissue surrounding it; rupture.

he·ro (HEER·oh) *n.* -roes one admired for noble qualities or exploits, as the central characters in novels, plays, etc.: *a folk, military, popular, war hero.*

he·ro·ic (hi·ROH·ic) *adj.* 1 of, about, or like heroes: *Courage and nobility are heroic qualities; The "Odyssey" is a heroic poem.* 2 daring and bold: *to take heroic measures.* 3 **heroics** *n.pl.* extravagant or showy behaviour. Also **he·ro·i·cal** *adj.;* **he·ro·i·cal·ly** *adv.*

her·o·in (HER·oh·in) *n.* a pain-relieving, habit-forming narcotic.

her·o·ine (HER·oh·in) *n.* a female hero.

her·o·ism (HER·oh·iz·um) *n.* 1 great courage or bravery. 2 the qualities and actions of a hero or heroine.

Herr (HAIR) *n., pl.* **Her·ren** *German.* 1 a man. 2 [as title] Mr. or Sir.

her·ring (HER·ing) *n.* a small, widely used food fish of the North Atlantic.

her·ring·bone (HER·ing·bone) *n.* a pattern of rows of slanted lines arranged like the ribs on a herring's spine, as in twilled fabrics, bricklaying, or a climbing step in skiing.

herring choker *n. Cdn. Slang.* a New Brunswicker or Maritimer.

hers See HER.

her·self (hur·SELF) *pron.* reflexive or emphatic of SHE: *Kay is proud of herself; sitting all by herself; She's not quite herself* (= as she normally is) *when unwell; She herself said it.*

he's (HEEZ) he is; he has.

hes·i·tant (HEZ·uh·tunt) *adj.* doubtful or undecided: *He was hesitant about jumping down from the flaming building.* — **hes·i·tant·ly** *adv.* — **hes·i·tan·cy** *n.* -cies.

hes·i·tate (HEZ·uh·tate) *v.* -tates, -tat·ed, -tat·ing 1 be doubtful or undecided: *She hesitated before saying "yes"; He hesitated about jumping* or *hesitated to jump into the water.* 2 talk or act doubtfully or undecidedly: *"He who hesitates is lost."*— **hes·i·tat·ing·ly** *adv.*
— **hes·i·ta·tion** (-TAY·shun) *n.*

hetero- *combining form.* other or different: *heterodox, heterogeneous, heterosexual.*

het·er·o·dox (HET·ur·uh·dox) *adj.* not orthodox.

het·er·o·ge·ne·ous (het·ur·uh·JEE·nee·us) *adj.* composed of different kinds of things; not homogeneous: *a heterogeneous group, population.*

het·er·o·sex·u·al (het·ur·uh·SEK·shoo·ul) *adj.* 1 attracted to the opposite sex, not homosexual; also *n.* 2 of different sexes: *heterosexual twins.*

heu·ris·tic (hew·RIS·tic) *adj.* based on or involving trial and error: *a heuristic approach, computer program, teaching method.*

hew *v.* hews, *pt.* hewed, *pp.* hewed or hewn, hew·ing 1 cut or form by cutting or chopping, as with an axe or chisel: *hewn timber; The enemy was hewn down in battle; to hew one's way through a jungle.* 2 hold fast or adhere: *to hew to rules and regulations.* — **hew·er** *n.*

hex *n.* a magic spell.
— *v.* put a hex on a person or thing; jinx.
— *adj.* 1 hexagonal: *a bolt with a hex head.* 2 hexadecimal: *a hex pad (or keyboard) with 16 keys.*

hexa- *combining form.* six: *hexagon, hexameter, hexapod.*

hex·a·dec·i·mal (hex·uh·DES·uh·mul) *adj.* having to do with 16: *The hexadecimal code uses the base 16 instead of the 10 of the decimal code.*

hex·a·gon (HEX·uh·gon) *n.* a polygon of six angles and sides. — **hex·ag·o·nal** (hek·SAG·uh·nul) *adj.*

hex·am·e·ter (hek·SAM·uh·tur) *n.* six-footed verse.

hex·a·pod (HEX·uh·pod) *n. & adj.* (an insect) having six legs.

hey (HAY) *interj.* used to ask a question, attract attention, or express surprise.

hey·day *n.* the time of greatest strength, prosperity, etc.: *in the heyday of colonialism.*

hi (HYE) *interj.* hello: *Hi there! Hi Joe! Hi neighbour!*

hi·ba·chi (hi·BAH·chee) *n.* -chis a charcoal-burning brazier and grill, as used for preparing food at the dining table: *a Japanese restaurant with hibachi cuisine.*

hi·ber·nate (HYE·bur·nate) *v.* -nates, -nat·ed, -nat·ing
pass the winter in an inactive condition: *bats, bears,
chipmunks, and such hibernating animals.*
— **hi·ber·na·tion** (-NAY·shun) *n.*

hic·cup (HIC·up) *n.* the sharp, clicking noise of a
breathing spasm, or hiccups *pl.*
— *v.* **hic·cups, hic·cupped** or **hic·cuped, hic·cup·ping**
or **hic·cup·ing** make hiccups: *how to stop hiccupping.*
Also **hic·cough** (HIC·up).

hick *n. & adj.* [often contemptuous] rustic: *Is he a hick
or a city slicker? a mere hick town.*

hidden tax *n.* an indirect tax such as an excise or
customs duty.

hide *v.* **hides, hid, hid·den** (HID·un), **hid·ing**
(HYE·ding) 1 keep or remain secret or out of sight: *The
sun is hidden by the clouds; a code word with a hidden
meaning; Children play **hide-and-seek;** He has gone
into hiding to escape the publicity.* 2 *pt.* **hid·ed**
Informal. flog or thrash: *to give a good hiding to
someone.* — *n.* a raw or tanned skin of a large animal.

hide·a·way (HYE·duh·way) *n.* a place of seclusion,
refuge, or retreat, as a quiet restaurant; *adj.: The sofa
opens out to show a hideaway bed.*

hide·bound *adj.* 1 of cattle, with the skin sticking close
to the body. 2 narrow-minded and obstinate.

hid·e·ous (HID·ee·us) *adj.* extremely ugly or revolting.

hide·out *n.* a place of hiding, as of guerrillas.

hie (HYE) *v.* **hies, hied, hy·ing** or **hie·ing** [old or poetic
use] hasten: *Hie hither; He hied him* or *himself to the
chase.*

hi·er·ar·chy (HYE·ur·ar·kee) *n.* -chies 1 a graded or
ranked organization, as of authority in the church, in a
civil service, etc.: *the military hierarchy; He rose in the
hierarchy from lieutenant to general.* 2 the body of
people in higher authority: *They appealed to the
hierarchy to bend a little.* 3 a graded series: *a hierarchy
of values governing conduct.*
— **hi·er·ar·chic** (-AR·kic) or **hi·er·ar·chi·cal** *adj.*

hi·er·o·glyph (HYE·ur·uh·glif) *n.* same as
hi·er·o·glyph·ic (hye·ur·uh·GLIF·ic) *n.* a picture or
symbol expressing an idea, as in ancient Egyptian and
Aztec writing.
— *adj.* 1 of or like hieroglyphics. 2 hard to read.

hi·fa·lu·tin (hye·fuh·LOO·tun) *adj.* same as
HIGHFALUTIN.

hi-fi (HYE·fye) *n. & adj.* high fidelity (equipment).

hig·gle·dy-pig·gle·dy ((HIG·ul·dee·PIG·ul·dee) *adj. &
adv.* in disorder; jumbled.

high *adj.* 1 being above the ground, esp. to a
considerable distance: *a high mountain; How high is it?
1 000 m high; The cupboard is too high for me (to
reach); the high (= top) shelf; a high dive (from a great
height).* 2 great or advanced in quality or extent,
importance, seriousness, etc.: *a high priest; high school;
to drive at high speed; high crimes, principles,
standards, treason; the **higher apes** (= anthropoids);
higher education (= college); a high manner (= conceit);
high noon (at its peak); Pat's in high spirits after
exercising; high voice (in pitch).* 3 *Informal.*
intoxicated, esp. under the influence of a drug: *to get
high on hashish.*
— *adv.* at or to a height: *Birds fly high in the air; Stars
shine high up in the sky; Tempers ran high during the
debate.*
— *n.* something that is high: *a record that hits a new
high; an all-time high; the highs and lows of
atmospheric pressure; highs induced by narcotics, yoga,
jogging, etc.; commands issued **from on high** (= as if
from heaven).*
— **high and dry** stranded; all alone: *They were left
high and dry on a treetop.*
— **high and low** everywhere: *to search high and low.*
— **high and mighty** important people: *the follies of the
high and mighty.*

high beam *n.* a beam of headlight switched to illuminate
the way far ahead.

high·born *adj.* of noble birth.

high·boy *n.* a high chest of drawers mounted on
relatively tall legs.

high·brow *n. & adj. Informal.* (one) of supposedly great
knowledge or culture.

high command *n.* the top leadership of an organization:
the Tory high command.

High Commission *n.* the embassy of one Commonwealth
country in another. — **High Commissioner** *n.*

high-end *adj.* top-range in price and sophistication: *A
high-end computer costs millions of dollars.*

high-energy *adj.* 1 having to do with particle
accelerators: *High-energy astronomy studies high-energy
phenomena such as X rays and cosmic rays; high-energy
physics.* 2 dynamic: *high-energy foods, music.*

higher-up *n. Informal.* one in a higher rank or position.

high-fa·lu·tin or **high-fa·lu·ting** (hye·fuh·LOO·tun) *adj.
Informal.* high-sounding or bombastic.

high fidelity *n.* sound reproduction with high accuracy
and low distortion.
— **high-fidelity** *adj.: a high-fidelity amplifier; high-
fidelity reception.*

high-five *n.* a slapping together of the raised palms of two people as a greeting or farewell.

high-fly·er (HIGH·fly·ur) *adj.* 1 one that flies high, esp. a stock that rises in value more quickly than other stocks. 2 an extravagant or high-spending person. — **high-flying** *adj.: a high-flying financial company, real-estate dealer, specialty store.*

high-flown (HYE·flone) *adj.* excessively high or bombastic.

high frequency *n.* a radio frequency of 3 to 30 megahertz.

high-grade *adj.* of high quality or value: *high-grade bonds, ore, performance.*

high-handed (HYE·HAN·did) *adj.* 1 overbearing in manner. 2 without consideration for others' feelings: *the new manager's high-handed way of running things.*

high-hat *adj. Slang.* snobbish. — *v.* -hats, -hat·ted, -hat·ting treat snobbishly.

high jinks *n.pl.* boisterous fun; horseplay.

high·land (HYE·lund) *adj. & n.* (having to do with) a region that is higher than its surroundings, as the Highlands of northern and western Scotland: *highland cattle, meadows; a **Highland fling** (= dance of the Scottish Highlands). — **high·land·er** or **High·land·er** *n.*

high-level (HYE·LEV·ul) *adj.* 1 involving persons of high rank: *a high-level meeting of cabinet ministers.* 2 of a computer programming language, using almost the same language as the user, as Basic.

high·light *n.* a very prominent aspect or feature, as a light-reflecting spot on a shiny object: *the highlight of her career, of the evening, of a celebration.* — *v.* -lights, -light·ed, -light·ing 1 be a highlight of something: *a year highlighted by achievements in science.* 2 give prominence to something: *Word-processing programs highlight misspelled words for correction; to highlight one's features using makeup; She prefers highlighting or streaking to colouring her hair.*

high·lin·er (HYE·lye·nur) *n.* in the Maritimes, the member of a fishing fleet that brings in the largest catch; also, its captain.

high·ly *adv.* 1 at a high level or standard: *a highly classified document; a highly placed official.* 2 very (much): *a highly entertaining act; He speaks highly (= well) of her.*

high-minded (HYE·MINE·did) *adj.* marked by high principles or feelings.

high·ness (HYE·nis) *n.* high state. — **Her** or **His** or **Your Highness** [style of addressing or referring to royalty].

high-octane *adj.* of gasoline, having a high octane content; hence, high-powered or dynamic.

high-pressure (HYE·PRESH·ur) *adj.* 1 using aggressive methods, esp. in selling. 2 involving much worry and tension: *a high-pressure job.*

high-rise *adj.* having many stories: *a high-rise apartment block.* — *n.* such a building: *There are high-rises, mid-rises,* and walkups.

high-riser (HYE·rye·zur) *n.* 1 a high-rise. 2 a bicycle with high handlebars.

high·road *n.* 1 a main road. 2 a direct or easy route: *the highroad to fame.*

high roller *n.* one who spends freely or gambles recklessly.

high school *n.* secondary school consisting of grades 9 through 12, if four-year, or 10 through 12 if "senior high school."

high seas *n.pl.* the open ocean outside of national jurisdictions.

high-spirited *adj.* brave or proud: *a high-spirited youth; a high-spirited* (=frisky) *horse.*

high-sticking (HYE·STICK·ing) *n.* in hockey and lacrosse, a foul resulting from a player using the stick above shoulder level, esp. to hurt an opponent.

high-strung *adj.* easily excited.

high tech (HYE·tek) *n. Informal.* high technology. — **high-tech** *adj.*

high technology *n.* technology used in highly sophisticated computers and other electronic devices.

high-tension (hye·TEN·shun) *adj.* high voltage: *a high-tension wire.*

high-test *adj.* 1 same as HIGH-OCTANE. 2 of high standard.

high-ticket *adj.* of merchandise, expensive: *a high-ticket item.*

high tide *n.* 1 (the time of) the highest level of the tide. 2 climax.

high time *n.* a time allowing no more delay: *It is high time we did something about this problem.*

high·way *n.* 1 a public road: *a divided highway; limited-access highway; the Queen's Highway; the Trans-Canada Highway.* 2 highroad: *the highway to success.*

high·way·man (HYE·way·mun) *n.* -men a highway robber.

high wire *n.* rope or cable stretched high for aerialists to perform on; tightrope.

hi·jack (HYE·jack) *v.* seize control of an airplane, bus, truck, etc. for extortion purposes. — *n.* a hijacking. — **hi·jack·er** *n.*

hike *v.* hikes, hiked, hik·ing 1 go on a long walk; tramp or march. 2 *Informal.* pull up and hitch: *She hiked up her skirt and waded across the stream.* 3 raise or increase: *Prices are hiked to keep up with inflation.* — *n.* 1 a long walk or march: *to go on a hike.* 2 a raising or increase: *the new hike in taxes.* — **take a hike** *Slang.* Go away! — **hik·er** *n.*

hi·lar·i·ous (huh·LAIR·ee·us) *adj.* causing great merriment: *a hilarious account, joke, party, tale; her hilarious humour.* — **hi·lar·i·ty** (-uh·tee) *n.*

hill *n.* 1 an elevation on the earth's surface, smaller than a mountain: *the rolling hills of the prairies; a steep hill; to head for the hills* (*Informal for* run away and hide); *to live in the hills; an office located on Parliament Hill* (or *the Hill) in Ottawa.* 2 a pile, heap, or mound, as an anthill or molehill.
— **over the hill** past one's prime, as a retired person.

hill·bil·ly (HIL·bil·ee) *n.* **-bil·lies** a person from a backwoods region, esp. of southeastern U.S.

hill·ock (HILL·uck) *n.* a small hill.

hill·y *adj.* **hill·i·er, -i·est** 1 full of hills: *a hilly region; hilly country.* 2 steep: *a hilly slope.*

hilt *n.* the handle of a sword, dagger, or similar weapon or tool.
— **to the hilt** or **up to the hilt** to the very limit: *dressed to the hilt; in debt up to the hilt; She lived to the hilt.*

him *pron.* objective case of HE: *She knows him; She's older than him* (*Informal for* he); *It's him* (*Informal for* he) *all right.*

Hi·ma·la·yan (him·uh·LAY·un, huh·MAHL·yun) *adj.* having to do with the **Himalayas,** the world's highest mountain system.

him·self (him·SELF) *pron.* reflexive or emphatic form of HE: *He's not quite himself* (= as he normally is) *today; He likes to work by himself* (= alone); *He himself did it.*

hind (HINED) *n.* 1 the adult female of the red deer. 2 a British farm hand.
— *adj.* **hind·er, hind·most** or **hind·er·most** (HINE·dur·most) rear or back.

hin·der (HIN·dur) *v.* 1 keep back or restrain: *Thick underbrush hindered our moving forward; hindered us from moving forward.* 2 prevent the progress of a person or thing: *We were hindered in our rescue efforts by a snowstorm.*

hindmost See HIND.

hind·quar·ter (HINED·kwor·tur) *n.* 1 the back half of a side of beef, lamb, etc. 2 **hindquarters** *pl.* a quadruped's hind pair of legs; haunches.

hin·drance (HIN·drunce) *n.* 1 an obstacle: *a hindrance rather than a help; a hindrance to progress.* 2 [legal use] the act of hindering: *We have to be free to work without let or hindrance.*

hind·sight (HINED·site) *n.* a looking back after the event; understanding of what should have been done: *In hindsight* or *With (the benefit of) hindsight, he would have sent the letter by courier instead of mailing it.*

Hin·du (HIN·doo) *n.* a follower of Hinduism.

Hin·du·ism (HIN·doo·iz·um) *n.* the main religion of India, with worship of many gods, the caste system, and belief in reincarnation.

hinge (HINJ) *n.* 1 a natural or artificial joint on which a door, gate, lid, knees, clamshells, etc. move, turn, or depend. 2 a pivotal or determining factor.
— *v.* **hing·es, hinged, hing·ing** 1 join: *a cover hinged to move up and down.* 2 depend: *Everything hinges on* or *upon her decision.*

hint *n.* an indirect or slight indication: *to drop a hint;*

Can you give me a hint? a hint about what you're up to; He left the place at the first hint of trouble; a broad or *obvious hint; a gentle* or *subtle hint; the merest hint of suspicion; He can* ***take a hint*** (= understand what is meant); *There's a hint* (= trace) *of frost in the air.*
— *v.* make a hint: *She didn't suggest leaving, but hinted at the lateness of the hour; She hinted to us that it was getting late.*

hin·ter·land (HIN·tur·land) *n.* 1 the inland region behind a coast, as one served by a port. 2 a region far from any urban centre.

hip *n.* 1 the joint of the thighbone with the ear-shaped **hip·bone** of the pelvis; also **hip·joint.** 2 the fleshy side below the waist covering a hipjoint: *to wiggle one's hips; close-fitting* ***hip-huggers*** (= pants).
— **shoot from the hip** *Slang.* act impulsively or recklessly.
— *adj.* **hip·per, hip·pest** *Slang.* alert to or informed about what is new and modish; not square: *He is hip to what's going on; hip designer clothes; one of the city's hippest nightspots.*
— *v. Slang.* 1 keep someone up to date; wise up. 2 make a person hip.

hipped *adj.* 1 *Slang.* obsessed: *hipped on golf.* 2 *adj. & combining form.* having a hip or the specified type of hip: *a hipped roof with sloped instead of vertical ends; broad-hipped; narrow-hipped suits.*

hip·pie or **hip·py** (HIP·ee) *n.* **hip·pies** *Slang.* a dropout from conventional society who lives a carefree life in communes, with long hair, practising free love, mysticism, doing drugs, etc. — **hip·pie·dom** *n.*

hip·po (HIP·oh) *n.* **hip·pos** *Informal* for **hip·po·pot·a·mus** (hip·uh·POT·uh·mus) *n.* **-mus·es** or **-mi (-mye),** a large-headed, short-legged, thick-skinned African animal that lives in rivers and marshy ponds.

hire *v.* **hires, hired, hir·ing** 1 engage for pay, esp. on a temporary basis: *to hire help, workers; Casual workers try to hire on* (= get hired) *during a strike; a hired gun.* 2 get or give the use of a thing or the work or services of a person in return for payment: *to hire out a labourer or tool.*
— *n.* a hiring, hired person, or payment for one: *to make a hire; a good worker worth every penny of his hire; cabs for hire; workmen on hire.*

hire·ling *n. & adj.* (one) who will do anything for pay; mercenary.

his (HIZ) *adj. & pron.* of or to him: *Those are his; his neckties; a friend of his.*

hiss *v.* 1 make a sharp sound, as of air escaping from a tire or of geese and snakes when excited. 2 show disapproval by hissing: *The speaker was so unpopular the audience hissed at his jokes; He was hissed off the stage.*
— *n.* a hissing: *He had to leave amid hisses and hoots from spectators.*

hist (PSST) *interj.* used to attract attention.

his·tor·ic (his·TOR·ic) *adj.* 1 famous or important in history: *the historic event of the patriation of Canada's* *constitution; the historic interest of a "national historic park" such as Signal Hill; the historic moment of the signing of a treaty; preserving a historic site such as the "Plains of Abraham"; We have written records of events that have happened within historic times* (= from about 5 000 years ago); *things of historic value.* **2** historical: *certain historic practices in regard to hiring women and minorities; historic* or *historical relationships between England and France.*

his·tor·i·cal (his·TOR·uh·cul) *adj.* **1** having to do with history or having reference to the past: *a historical event, novel, play, society, study; the historical method of working from the past to the present; certain historical* or *historic relationships.* **2** factual, not fictitious: *historical characters and events.* — **his·tor·i·cal·ly** *adv.*

his·to·ry (HIS·tuh·ree) *n.* **-ries 1** a branch of knowledge dealing with the recording and study of past events: *ancient, cultural, medieval, military, modern history; the natural history* (= study of the nature and development) *of butterflies.* **2** historical records: *ruins of an era before the dawn of history; The Calgary Olympics was news in 1988, but now it is history* (= a past event); *It will go down in history as a great success; to trace the history* (= events) *of a nation through the centuries.* **3** a historical account: *a short history of Canada; the case history of a patient; an oral history based on interviews; a patient with a history* (= past) *of heart trouble; Does history* (= the past) *repeat itself? The landing on the moon made history* (= It was so important).

his·tri·on·ics (his·tree·ON·ics) *n.pl.* [takes sing. or pl. v.] **1** dramatic representation; dramatics. **2** affected display of emotion; artificial manner. — **his·tri·on·ic** *adj.*

hit *v.* **hits, hit, hit·ting 1** come against with force; strike, not miss: *The car hit (against) a tree; The driver hit his head on the roof; The dart hit the bull's-eye; a good fielder who couldn't hit* (= bat); *a nation hard hit* (= severely affected) *by famine; The media hit hard at* (= attacked) *the government; The minister hit back at the media; He hit out against his attackers.* **2** reach or find: *Drive on till you hit the highway; an event that hit the headlines; She hit on* or *upon* (= found by chance) *a clever plan; The two hit it off* (= got along well) *from the beginning.*
— *n.* **1** a blow or stroke, esp. one getting to what is aimed at: *The player chalked up* or *scored more misses than hits; a direct hit; an unfair hit below the belt.* **2** success: *Our play was a box-office hit; a smash hit.* **3** *Slang.* dose or portion: *a hit of cocaine.*
— *adj. Slang.* having to do with murder: *a hit squad, team.*
— **hit-and-run** *adj.: a hit-and-run military tactic; a hit-and-run baseball play; a hit-and-run driver wanted by police.*
— **hit-or-miss** *adj.: a hit-or-miss* (= aimless) *effort.*
— **hit·ter** *n.*

hitch (HICH) *v.* **1** pull or move jerkily; yank: *He hitches up his trousers before sitting down.* **2** fasten or attach: *a sleeve that hitches on to a doorknob; a horse hitched* (= harnessed) *to a wagon; a trailer hitched behind a car; an author hitching up* (= joining) *with an agent.* **3** *Informal.* hitchhike: *He hitched a ride home instead of walking.*
— *n.* **1** pull: *to give a hitch to a sock that won't stay up.* **2** knot: *He tied his donkey to a tree with a hitch of the rope.* **3** obstacle: *Everything went off without a hitch.* **4** service: *He did a two-year hitch in the navy.*

hitch·hike *v.* **-hikes, -hiked, -hik·ing** travel by getting rides along the way. — **hitch·hik·er** *n.*

hith·er (HITH·ur, "TH" as in "the") *adj. & adv.* to or on this side: *Come hither, darling!* [old use]; *Kay's come-hither* (= attractive) *appeal, charm, looks.*
— **hither and thither** here and there; also **hither and yon.**

hith·er·to (hith·ur·TOO) *adv.* until now.

hit list *n.* a list or people, projects, etc. to be eliminated.

hit man *n.* a hired murderer.

hit parade *n.* a listing of popular hit songs.

hive *n.* **1** a beehive; hence, a place of busy activity. **2 hives** *pl.* [takes sing. or pl.v.] an itching and burning skin rash caused by allergies.
— *v.* **hives, hived, hiv·ing 1** put bees or settle in a hive: *Beekeepers hive bees; to hive off* (= separate) *one unit from a group.* **2** lay up for future use: *Bees hive honey.*

hoa·gy or **hoa·gie** (HOH·gee, "g" as in "go") *n.* **-gies** a hero sandwich.

hoard *v.* get and store away money, goods, etc. for future use or sale.
— *n.* what is hoarded: *a squirrel's hoard of nuts for the winter; a miser's hoard of wealth; the profiteer's hoard of scarce commodities.* — **hoard·er** *n.*

hoarding *n.* **1** a temporary fence of boards put up around a work site. **2** *Brit.* a billboard.

hoar·frost *n.* white frost; frozen dew; ice crystals.

hoarse *adj.* **hoars·er, hoars·est** of sounds or voice, rough and husky. — **hoarse·ness** *n.*

hoar·y *adj.* **hoar·i·er, -i·est 1** white or grey. **2** white-haired with age: *He shook his hoary head; a hoary* (= ancient) *legend, past.* — **hoar·i·ness** *n.*

hoax (HOKES) *n.* a fraud or practical joke: *a literary hoax.*
— *v.* trick: *The publisher was hoaxed into buying fake diaries of Hitler.*

hob *n.* **1** an elf or hobgoblin. **2** a shelf or ledge at the back or side of a fireplace. **3** the target peg in quoits. **4** a gear-cutting metal device.
— **play hob** *Informal.* make mischief with something.

hob·ble (HOB·ul) *v.* **hob·bles, hob·bled, hob·bling** move in an awkward walk, as of a horse whose front legs are tied: *an injured skier hobbling around on crutches.* Also *n.*

hob·ble·de·hoy (HOB·ul·dee·hoy) *n.* a clumsy or gawky, esp. adolescent youth.

hob·by (HOB·ee) *n.* **hob·bies** a leisure-time activity or pursuit outside of one's main occupation, indulged in for fun and profit: *to pursue a hobby.* — **hob·by·ist** *n.*

hob·by·horse (HOB·ee·horse) *n.* **1** a child's rocking horse or a stick with a horse's head. **2** one's favourite topic or pet theory.

hob·nob *v.* -nobs, -nobbed, -nob·bing associate familiarly with important or influential people.

ho·bo (HOH·boh) *n.* -bos or -boes a tramp.

Hob·son's choice (HOB·sunz-) *n.* a choice with no alternative.

hock *n.* **1** the backward-bending hind-leg joint of a horse, cat, etc. or the corresponding joint of a fowl's leg. **2** *Slang.* pawn; also *v.*
— **in hock** indebted: *He was in hock to loan sharks.*

hock·ey (HOK·ee) *n.* **1** a game played on ice by opposing teams of six each, wearing skates and equipped with sticks having curved ends to drive a disk, or puck, into the opposite side's goal: *The first hockey game is said to have been held in Victoria Park, Montreal, in 1875.* **2** same as FIELD HOCKEY.

hock·shop *n.* pawnshop.

ho·cus-po·cus (HOH·cus·POH·cus) *n.* **1** a meaningless formula; deceptive talk. **2** trickery; sleight of hand.

hod *n.* **1** an open trough or box fixed to the top of a staff, used for carrying bricks or mortar up ladders, etc. **2** a coal scuttle.

hodge·podge *n.* a jumble or mixture.

hoe *n.* a farm tool consisting of a thin blade set across the end of a long handle.
— *v.* hoes, hoed, hoe·ing cut, weed, or loosen soil with a hoe.

hog *n.* **1** a pig, esp. one raised for meat. **2** a coarse, filthy, or selfish person. **3** one who is selfish: *a road hog.*
— **eat** or **live off the hog, eat** or **live on the hog, eat** or **live high on the hog** *Slang.* live a luxurious life.
— **go the whole hog** *Informal.* go all the way.
— *v.* hogs, hogged, hog·ging grab or use selfishly: *Al likes to hog both lanes of the freeway.*

hog·gish *adj.* filthy, greedy, or selfish.

hog-tie *v.* -ties, -tied, -ty·ing or -tie·ing make helpless, as by tying the feet.

Hog·town *n.* [nickname] Toronto.

hog·wash *n.* **1** swill. **2** baloney or nonsense.

hog-wild *adj. Informal.* wild with excitement: *to go hog-wild.*

ho-hum *interj.* expressing boredom.

— *adj.* dull or boring: *a ho-hum routine.*

hoi pol·loi (HOY·puh·LOY) *n. pl.* the common people.

hoist *v.* raise or lift, as a flag or sail, usually with some mechanical means.
— *n.* a hoisting or a hoisting machine, as derricks and cranes.

hoke *v.* hokes, hoked, hok·ing *Slang.* esp. **hoke up,** overplay a stage or screen part in a cheap or sensational manner.
— **hok·ey** (HOH·kee) *adj.*: *hokey humour; a hokey production number; Sounds a bit hokey to me.*

ho·kum (HOH·kum) *n. Slang.* bunk; humbug.

hold *v.* holds, held, hold·ing have or take in one's possession, as by the hand or in one's physical or mental power: *a mother holding a child; Hold yourself erect;* ***Don't hold your breath*** (= Don't be expecting it to happen); *a package being held for you at the post office; to hold* (= defend) *a fort against invaders; beliefs held* (= kept) *by people; Past mistakes will not be held* (= taken into account) *against you; She's held in great esteem by all; to hold* (= adhere) **to** *a promise; to hold someone* (= make him adhere) *to his word; to hold* (= consider) *life cheap; Borrowers are held* (= considered legally) *responsible for what they borrow; a staff meeting to be held* (= made to happen) *at 4 p.m.; The cease-fire seems to be holding* (= continuing); *a rule that* ***holds good*** *or* ***true*** (= applies) *in all cases; He's trying to* ***hold down*** (= stay in) *a job long enough to pay his debts; The preacher* ***held forth*** (= talked) *for over an hour.*
— **hold it!** stop what you are doing!
— **hold on** *Informal.* **1** keep on holding: *Hold on to your hat.* **2** wait: *Hold on, there!*
— **hold one's own** keep one's position in the face of opposition.
— **hold out 1** continue resisting: *to hold out against the enemy; a labour union holding out for* (= refusing to settle and demanding) *more concessions.* **2** offer: *to hold out hopes of a settlement.*
— **hold over 1** postpone or retain. **2** keep or stay for a longer period: *The movie was held over for 10 weeks.*
— **hold up 1** maintain or continue: *to hold up under the strains of a job.* **2** stop, esp. by force: *to hold up a train.*
— **left holding the bag** left responsible for someone else's unfinished work.
— *n.* **1** a holding, manner of holding, thing to hold by or with, a holding influence, or an order to hold: *to relax, relinquish one's hold on something; a wrestler's hold; Put a hold* (= holding order or stop) *on that.* **2** a cargo compartment in a ship or airplane.
— **catch, get, grab, lay, seize** or **take hold of** seize or get possession of something.
— **on hold** in waiting condition: *to put a telephone caller on hold; Our plans are on hold.*
— **take hold** have an effect.

holding *n.* **1** land or other property. **2 holdings** *pl.* stocks and bonds.
— *adj.*: *a holding* (= delaying) *action; a holding* (= waiting) *area; a holding* (= temporary) *home for youths in trouble with the law; a holding tank (for temporary storage).*

holding pattern *n.* an oval flight course at a specified height for an aircraft awaiting clearance to land; hence, a stationary condition: *The candidates had to go into* or *were put in a holding pattern for half an hour.*

hold·out *n.* 1 refusal to agree or submit. 2 a person or group resisting thus.

hold·o·ver (HOLE·doh·vur) *n.* a person or thing remaining from a previous time: *Hippies are holdovers from the 1960s.*

hold·up *n.* a stoppage, esp. a forcible one for robbery.

hole *n.* 1 an opening in or through something; hence, a pit, cave, burrow, etc.: *to bore* or *dig a hole; fill in a hole; a gaping, yawning hole in the floor.* 2 a dingy or dirty place; an awkward position. 3 in golf, one of the usually 18 hollows on the green; also, a single play from tee to hole: *to shoot a **hole in one**.*
— **in the hole** in difficulties, esp. in debt.
— **pick holes in** pick out errors or flaws in, as in an argument.
— *v.* **holes, holed, hol·ing** 1 make a hole in something. 2 drive into a hole.
— **hole up** hide oneself: *Ann Frank was holed up in an attic for two years.*

hole-in-the-wall *adj. Informal.* modest or unpretentious: *a hole-in-the-wall restaurant.*

-holic *combining form.* addicted to something specified: *alcoholic, chocoholic, crediholic, workaholic.*

hol·i·day (HOL·uh·day) *n.* 1 a day of freedom from work, usually for a religious or other celebration: *We observe a holiday in honour of Queen Victoria; a legal, paid, public holiday; Sundays and other statutory holidays; The Civic Holiday is a summer holiday.* 2 a period of rest: *to take a holiday (from work).* 3 vacation: *He is on holiday; I go on holiday* or *holidays next month; Schools are closed during the summer holidays.*
— *adj.*: *a holiday mood; holiday pay; **holiday weekend** (= "long weekend" of three days).*
— *v.* spend a holiday or vacation. — **hol·i·day·er** *n.*

holier-than-thou, holiness See HOLY.

ho·lis·tic (hoh·LIS·tic) *adj.* having to do with the whole system rather than a part of it: *Holistic medicine treats the whole body rather than affected parts; the holistic approach; holistic ecology, psychology.*

hol·ler (HOL·ur) *n. & v. Informal.* shout or yell.

hol·low (HOL·oh) *adj.* 1 empty, not solid inside: *a hollow ball.* 2 concave: *a hollow dish, lens.* 3 looking sunken or sounding empty: *hollow cheeks, eyes, laughter; a hollow tube, voice.* 4 not real or genuine; false: *hollow hopes, promises, settlements.*
— *n.* a cavity; depression; valley.
— *v.* make hollow: *river banks hollowed by erosion; a container hollowed out of a gourd.*
— *adv. Informal.* thoroughly: *The boxer beat him hollow in no time.* — **hol·low·ness** *n.*

hol·low·ware (HOL·oh·ware) *n.* tableware such as bowls, cups, etc.; cf. FLATWARE. Also **hol·lo·ware.**

Hol·ly·wood (HOL·ee·wood) *n.* the home of the American motion-picture industry.
— *adj.* expensive, lavish, or extravagant: *a movie made with Hollywood effects.*

hol·o·caust (HOL·uh·caust) *n.* a large-scale destruction, esp. of lives, as by fire: *a nuclear holocaust;* **the Holocaust** *of Jews under the Nazis.*

hol·o·gram (HOLL·uh·gram, HOH·luh-) *n.* a three-dimensional image produced by laser: *Holograms are used on credit cards, etc. as a security device.*

ho·lus-bo·lus (HOH·lus-BOH·lus) *adj. & adv. Informal.* all at once: *They had to learn it holus-bolus; their heavy-handed holus-bolus approach.*

ho·ly (HOH·lee) *adj.* **-li·er, -li·est** 1 worthy of worship or reverence, esp. because of spiritual perfection: *a holy man; the Holy Ghost* or *Holy Spirit.* 2 belonging to or devoted to God: *a holy day such as the Passover or Good Friday;* **Holy Communion** (= Eucharist); **the Holy Land** (= Palestine); *to take* **holy orders** (= ordination as a Christian priest or minister); **holy water** *(blessed for religious use); 1975 was observed as a Holy Year in Rome.* — **ho·li·ness** *n.*
— **holier-than-thou** (HOH·lee·ur·than·THOU) *adj.* implying superior goodness: *a holier-than-thou attitude, manner, politician, smugness.*
— **Your** or **His Holiness** [title used in addressing or referring to the Pope].

hom·age (HOM·ij) *n.* an act or show of reverence: *An eternal flame burns in homage to the war dead; People come to pay homage to them at the cenotaph.*

home *n.* 1 one's dwelling place, where one belongs, often including family and surroundings: *"Home sweet home"; Some prefer to make their homes in the suburbs; University students often live away from home; to build, establish a home in Canada; provide a good home for the children; an ancestral, country, foster, mobile, summer, winter home; Some children come from broken homes* (= families); *He feels quite* **at home** (= ease) *in this country; This country has been home to him for 50 years; She is* **not (at) home** *after 8* (= She is out or not receiving calls). 2 an establishment: *to manage, operate, run a home for the aged; a convalescent, detention, funeral, nursing, rest, retirement home.* 3 a native place or habitat: *Alaska is the home of the "kodiak bear."* 4 in games, a goal or home plate.
— *adj.* having to do with home: *home computer, front, office; a* **home game** *(played at home, not away);* **home ice** (= hockey rink where a home game is played); *Natives fight for* **home rule** (= self-rule); *seen on* **home screens** (= on TV).
— *adv.* 1 at or to one's home: *He's gone home; The B.N.A. Act was brought home* (= patriated to Canada) *in 1982.* 2 to the point aimed at: *Drive the nail home; The point was* **brought home to** (= impressed on) *him.*
— *v.* **homes, homed, hom·ing** go, return, or send home: *The* **homing pigeon** *is trained to carry written messages home over long distances; The infrared* **homing system** *of a missile to make it* **home in on** *its target; An aircraft landing in fog will* **home onto** *a radar signal for guidance.*

home·base same as HOME PLATE.

home·bod·y (HOME·bod·ee) *n.* **-bod·ies** a person who prefers home and family to outside attractions: *a homebody who enjoys spending time with his wife and children.*

home·bound *adj.* forced to stay home all the time, as

when disabled.

home·brew n. 1 home-made alcoholic beverage, esp. beer. 2 *Cdn. Informal.* a football or hockey player trained in Canada, not an import.

home·com·ing (HOME·cum·ing) n. an arrival at or return to one's home or school, esp. an annual campus celebration.

home economics n. pl. [takes sing. v.] the management of a household as a course of study, including housekeeping, cooking, child care, etc.; domestic science.

home fries n. pl. potatoes served boiled, sliced, and fried.

home-grown adj. grown or produced at home: *home-grown fruit, politicians, vegetables.*

home·land n. 1 one's native land: *the question of a homeland for Palestinian Arabs.* 2 a semi-independent region established for a black tribe within South Africa.

home·ly adj. -li·er, -li·est suited to home life; hence, plain or plain-looking: *homely pleasures, virtues; Eleanor Roosevelt was a homely woman; a homely metaphor; to give the story a homely touch.* — **home·li·ness** n.

home·made adj. made at home, not commercially: *a homemade cake; furniture that looks homemade* (= lacking finish).

home·mak·er (HOME·may·kur) n. a manager of a household, esp. a housewife.

home plate n. the slab beside which a baseball batter stands while batting.

hom·er (HOH·mur) n. *Informal.* a home run in baseball. — v. hit a homer.

home·room n. a room where all members of a class report.

home run n. a baseball hit that enables the batter to touch all bases and return to home plate.

home·sick adj. sad because away from home. — **home·sick·ness** n.

home·spun 1 n. cloth spun or made at home. 2 adj. plain: *homespun manners, wit.*

home·stead (HOME·sted) n. a place, including land and buildings, where a family settled and made its home: *the homestead rights of a farmer's wife.*

home·stretch n. the last stretch of a race track before the finish line: *In June, we are on the homestretch* (= in the concluding part) *of the school year.*

home·town n. a city or town where one lived while growing up.

home·ward (HOME·wurd) adj. & adv. toward home: *a homeward trek; travelling homeward.* Also **home·wards** adv.

home·work n. work done at home, esp. schoolwork outside the classroom: *Both debaters had apparently done their homework* (= prepared themselves).

home·y (HOH·mee) adj. hom·i·er, -i·est having the atmosphere of a home.

hom·i·cide (HOM·uh·side) n. 1 one who kills another. 2 the crime itself: *justifiable homicide committed in self-defence; an allegation of negligent homicide against the driver; the homicide squad (of a police force).* — **hom·i·ci·dal** (-SYE·dul) adj.

hom·i·ly (HOM·uh·lee) n. -lies (-leez) 1 a sermon. 2 a moralizing speech.

homo- *combining form.* same: *homogeneous, homograph, homosexual.*

ho·mo (HOH·moh) n. 1 [short form] homogenized milk. 2 pl. -mos [short form] homosexual.

ho·mo·ge·ne·ous (HOH·muh·JEE·nee·us) adj. of the same kind or of uniform composition, not heterogeneous. — **ho·mo·ge·ne·i·ty** (-juh·NEE·uh·tee) n.

ho·mog·e·nize (huh·MOJ·uh·nize) v. -niz·es, -nized, -niz·ing make homogeneous: *Homogenized milk has its fat particles evenly distributed so that cream does not separate and come to the top.*

hom·o·graph (HOM·uh·graf) n. a word that is the same as another in spelling, but different in pronunciation and meaning, as "lead" (n.) and "lead" (v.)

ho·mol·o·gous (huh·MOL·uh·gus) adj. corresponding in origin, structure, etc.: *The flipper of a seal and the foreleg of a horse are homologous.*

hom·o·logue or **hom·o·log** (HOM·uh·log) n. a homologous thing or part: *The flipper of a seal is the homologue of a horse's foreleg.*

hom·o·nym (HOM·uh·nim) n. 1 same as HOMOPHONE. 2 a word that is the same as another in pronunciation and spelling, but different in meaning, as "bear" (v.) and "bear" (n.)

hom·o·phile (HOM·uh·file) n. & adj. same as HOMOSEXUAL.

hom·o·pho·bi·a (hom·uh·FOH·bee·uh) n. fear of homosexuality.

hom·o·phone (HOM·uh·fone) n. a word that is pronounced like another, as "bear" and "bare," or "shoe" and "shoo."

Ho·mo sa·pi·ens (HOH·moh·SAY·pee·unz, -SAP·ee·unz) n. the "intelligent human being" as a species, from about 300 000 B.C.

ho·mo·sex·u·al (hoh·muh·SEK·shoo·ul) n. a person who is sexually attracted to those of the same sex. — adj. having to do with sexual attraction between members of the same sex: *a homosexual act, group, relationship; the homosexual community, condition, orientation.* — **ho·mo·sex·u·al·i·ty** (-shoo·AL·uh·tee) n.

hon·cho (HON·choh) n. -chos *Informal.* boss or chief: *the top news honcho of the local TV station.*

hone v. hones, honed, hon·ing sharpen a razor, knife, or other cutting tool using a hone: *to hone one's skills; a well muscled, fine-honed acrobat.* — n. a fine-grained stone.

hon·est (ON·ist) adj. 1 of people, honourable and truthful; not lying, cheating, or stealing: *an honest politician; an honest broker* (= neutral mediator); *I do feel sorry, honest* (= I'm sincere). 2 having to do with an honest person: *an honest effort, face, living, mistake,*

opinion, piece of work; honest goods, profits.
— hon·est·ly *adv.* — hon·es·ty *n.*

hon·ey (HUN·ee) *n.* -eys 1 the sweet, thick, golden
liquid made by hon·ey·bees from the nectar of flowers
and stored in honeycombs. 2 anything sweet like honey.
3 *Informal.* darling: *I'm waiting, honey; My new
computer is a real honey.*
— *v.* hon·eys or hon·ies, hon·eyed or hon·ied,
hon·ey·ing sweeten: *honeyed words (that are sweet as
honey); He staved off eviction by honeying up (= talking
sweetly to) the landlady.*

hon·ey·comb (HUN·ee·come, *rhyme:* "home") *n.* 1 a
wax structure of six-sided cells, made by bees.
2 anything resembling this.
— *v.: a landscape honeycombed with apartments.*

hon·ey·dew (HUN·ee·dew) *n.* 1 a sweet and sticky
substance found on leaves and stems of plants, secreted
by aphids and such insects. 2 a **honeydew melon** which
has a whitish rind and sweet, green flesh.

honey locust *n.* a tree of the pea family with a slender
trunk and featherlike foliage, whose pods contain a
sweetish pulp.

hon·ey·moon (HUN·ee·moon) *n.* 1 the vacation taken
by a newly married couple: *to go on a honeymoon.* 2 an
initial period of harmonious relations, as between
newlyweds: *The honeymoon has ended.*
— *v.: They honeymooned in Las Vegas.*
— hon·ey·moon·er *n.*

hon·ey·suck·le (HUN·ee·suck·ul) *n.* a shrub or vine with
trumpet-shaped, nectar-filled flowers.

honk *n.* a wild goose's cry or a similar sound, as of an
automobile horn.
— *v.* make a honk: *He parked outside and honked for
his friend to come out; The cyclist doesn't like to be
honked at.*

hon·ky-tonk (HONG·kee·tonk) *n. Slang.* a cheap
nightclub or dancehall.
— *adj.: honky-tonk music; a honky-tonk cafe, singer.*

honor See HONOUR.

hon·o·rar·i·um (on·uh·RAIR·ee·um) *n.* -i·ums or -i·a
(-ee·uh) a voluntary fee offered for a professional service.

hon·o·rar·y (ON·ur·air·ee) *adj.* given or done as an
honour: *an honorary consultant, degree, position.*

hon·or·if·ic (on·uh·RIF·ic) *adj.* conferring or showing
respect.
— *n.* an honorific word or title, as "Excellency" or "Sir."

hon·our or **hon·or** (ON·ur) *n.* 1 keen personal sense of
right and wrong: *a man of honour; I give you my word
of honour; a duel fought as an affair of honour; to take
a pledge on one's honour; a code of honour; an honour
box* (= newspaper vending box) *based on the honour
system* (of trusting people to observe the rules). 2 respect
felt or shown to a person: *Dr. Bethune is held in high
honour in China; He's an honour* (= source of respect) *to
Canada; in honour of our war heroes; a guard of
honour; Olympic winners bring or do honour to their
countries; Your* or *Her* or *His Honour* [title of respect
for judges and certain officials]; *to do the honours*
(= observe the formalities of being a host or hostess); *the
Queen's honours list; buried with full military honours.*
3 credit or distinction: *to confer an honour on someone;
a dubious honour; the great, high honour of being
chosen "woman of the year"; She's an honour student on
the honour roll* (= list of outstanding students); *He
passed with honours.*
— *v.* to respect: *He felt honoured by the invitation; All
credit cards are honoured* (= accepted) *here.*

hon·our·a·ble or **hon·or·a·ble** (ON·ur·uh·bul) *adj.*
having, showing, causing, or worthy of honour: *an
honourable deed; an honourable discharge from the
army after years of faithful service; the honourable
member* (= M.P.) *for York Centre.*
— **the Honourable** [title prefixed to the names of
various justices, cabinet ministers, speakers of
legislatures, etc.]: *the Honourable (John Doe,) Minister
of Finance.*
— hon·our·a·bly or hon·or·a·bly (-uh·blee) *adv.*

-hood (short "oo") *n. suffix.* 1 state or quality:
childhood, falsehood. 2 group: *brotherhood,
neighbourhood.*

hood (short "oo") *n.* 1 a covering for the head and neck
or something looking like one, as the fold of cloth over
the back of a parka, an automobile engine's metal cover,
a canopy over a cooking range or window, the expanded
neck of a cobra, the crests of certain birds, etc.: *to check
under the hood (of a car for mechanical problems);
adj.: a hooded* (= having a hood) *crow, pitcher plant,
seal.* 2 [short form] hoodlum.

hood·lum (long "oo") *n.* a young ruffian, esp. a member
of a street gang.

hoo·doo *n.* -doos 1 a strange rock formation in the
shape of columns formed by wind and water erosion, as
in the badlands in Alberta. 2 *Informal.* bad luck or a
person or thing bringing it. 3 same as VOODOO.

hood·wink (short "oo") *v.* mislead or dupe, as if by
blindfolding.

hoo·ey (HOO·ee) *n. & interj. Slang.* nonsense; bunk.

hoof (short or long "oo") *n.* hoofs or hooves the hard,
horny covering on the feet of animals such as horses,
pigs, and cattle: *the cloven hoof* (= sign of Satan); *Retail
meat costs several times what it is worth on the hoof*
(= as live animals).
— *v. Informal.* walk: *Let's hoof it to the store.*
— hoofed *adj.* having hoofs.

hook (short "oo") *n.* 1 a curved or bent piece of stiff
material, as metal or wood, for catching, as a *fish hook,*

to hang things on, as a *coat hook,* or as in a **hook and eye** (= fastening device with a hook and a loop). **2** a strike or blow, as in boxing, given with a curving motion.
— **by hook or by crook** by any means, fair or foul.
— **off the hook** *Informal.* out of trouble; free of responsibility.
— *v.* catch fish, etc. with a hook or get by a trick: *She hooked herself a customer.*
— **hook up** connect or set up a radio, telephone, etc.

hooked *adj.* **1** bent like a hook, having hooks, or made by hooking: *a hooked rug.* **2** *Informal.* addicted: *Don't get hooked on drugs.*

hook·er *n. Slang.* a prostitute.

hook·up *n.* a radio or telephone setup, esp. a network of radio and television stations.

hook·y *n.* **play hooky** *Informal.* stay out of school without permission.

hoo·li·gan (HOO·luh·gun) *n.* a hoodlum.

hoop (long "oo") *n.* a large ring, as one of the flat bands holding the staves of a barrel together, any of the flexible rings forming a frame to hold out a **hoop skirt,** or a ring used as a **hula hoop** for twirling around the hips.

hoop·la (short "oo") *n. Informal.* ballyhoo; hullabaloo: *What's all the hoopla about?*

hooray same as HURRAH.

hoot (long "oo") *n.* **1** the cry of an owl: *She doesn't give a hoot* (*Informal for* doesn't care the least bit). **2** *Slang.* something laughably funny: *It was a real hoot to see the teachers in their Halloween costumes.*
— *v.* shout in disapproval or scorn: *The audience hooted at the speaker; He was hooted off the stage.*

hootch (long "oo") *n. Slang.* inferior or illicitly made alcoholic liquor.

hoot·en·an·ny (HOO·tun·an·ee) *n.* **-an·nies** an informal folk-singing party.

hooves a *pl.* of HOOF.

hop *n.* **1** a short leap on one foot, as in hopscotch, or on both feet, as birds do, or on all fours, as frogs. **2** *Informal.* a short trip or plane flight: *It's a short hop from Vancouver to Victoria.* **3** *Slang.* dope, esp. opium. **4** a vine whose dried flower clusters, or **hops,** are used to flavour beer, ale, etc.
— *v.* **hops, hopped, hop·ping** make a hop: *to hop out of bed when the alarm goes; rabbits hopping across a field; He had to hop about with one foot in a cast; to hop* (= board) *a train; a fence low enough to hop* (= leap over).
— **hop up** *Informal.* supercharge: *to hop up an engine.*
— **hopped up** *Slang.* under the influence of narcotics.
— **hopping mad** *Informal.* very angry.

hope *n.* **1** a confident belief that something will be realized as desired: *Any hope of success? to dash, dispel, raise, thwart someone's hopes; high hopes; I'm writing you in hopes of or in the hope of finding my lost luggage; to abandon, give up, stir up hope; to cherish, entertain, express, nurse, voice a hope; a faint, false, fervent, fond, idle, illusory, realistic, slight, vain hope;*

in high hopes; hopes come true, fade; Not a flicker, glimmer, ray, spark of hope was left; The thing seemed beyond, past hope. **2** the thing hoped for, reason for hoping, or a person one has hopes in: *She's the hope of the family.*
— *v.* **hopes, hoped, hop·ing** wish and expect: *Let's hope for the best; I hope so; I hope not; She didn't hope to recover, but kept hoping against hope.*

hope·ful *n. & adj.* (a person) feeling or giving hope: *We are hopeful of victory; a hopeful sign; young medical-school hopefuls.*
— **hope·ful·ly** *adv.: She waited hopefully for the results; Hopefully* (*Informal for* It is hoped), *everyone will pass.*
— **hope·ful·ness** *n.*

hop·head *n. Slang.* a drug addict.

hop·per *n.* **1** one that hops, esp. an insect such as the locust. **2** a container that is emptied from the bottom, as a railway car for bulk freight such as coal, a seeding machine or drill, etc.: *Your application is in the hopper* (= to be considered in its turn).

-hopping *combining form.* sampling or checking one after another: *(TV) channel-hopping, job-hopping, restaurant-hopping, table-hopping (at a restaurant).*

horde (HORD) *n.* a crowd or throng, esp. one considered as invading or rapacious: *the Tartar hordes; hordes of children, locusts, shoppers, tourists.*

ho·ri·zon (huh·RYE·zun) *n.* **1** where earth and sky seem to meet: *Ships appear on the horizon.* **2** the limit of one's experience or perception: *travel for broadening one's horizons.*

hor·i·zon·tal (hor·uh·ZON·tul) *n. & adj.* (a line, surface, direction, etc.) that is level, not vertical; flat or even: *a gymnast performing on the horizontal bars.*
— **hor·i·zon·tal·ly** *adv.*

horn *n.* **1** either of a pair of hard, bony projections on the head of a hoofed animal. **2** a similar protrusion, as on the head of a snail or insect. **3** the substance that horns, birds' beaks, hoofs, fingernails, etc. are made of. **4** a container hollowed out of horn. **5** a brass-wind instrument or other sounding device: *a hunting horn, French horn, automobile horn; to blow or sound the horn; to blow or toot one's own horn* (= to boast).
— **on the horns of a dilemma** perplexed.
— **take the bull by the horns** be bold.
— *v.* **horn in** *Informal.* intrude or butt in *on* a conversation, etc.

horned *adj.* having horns or something hornlike: *the horned owl, toad.*

hor·net (HOR·nit) *n.* any of several large social wasps that give painful stings.

hornet's nest *n.* a source of unexpected trouble: *to stir up a hornet's nest* (= provoke an angry reaction all around).

horn of plenty same as CORNUCOPIA.

horn·y *adj.* **horn·i·er, -i·est 1** *Slang.* lustful or excited. **2** made of horn; also, hard or calloused.

hor·o·scope (HOR·uh·scope) *n.* an astrological forecast based on the signs of the zodiac.

hor·ren·dous (hor·EN·dus) *adj.* liable to instil horror: *horrendous cruelties and atrocities; horrendous red tape.*

hor·ri·ble (HOR·uh·bul) *adj.* **1** dreadful: *a horrible torture chamber.* **2** *Informal.* extremely unpleasant: *a horrible odour.* — **hor·rib·ly** *adv.*

hor·rid (HOR·id) *adj.* frightful: *such horrid manners!* — **hor·rid·ly** *adv.*

hor·ri·fy (HOR·uh·fye) *v.* **-fies, -fied, -fy·ing** cause to feel horror; shock: *He was horrified by the atrocities; horrified at the prospect of death; a horrifying scene.*

hor·ror (HOR·ur) *n.* **1** fear mixed with revulsion: *the horror of a child witnessing a crime; They looked on in horror.* **2** something that causes such feeling: *the horrors of wasteful government spending; adj.: a horror film, movie, story; a story full of horror and suspense.*

horse *n.* **1** a strong, four-legged, solid-hoofed animal with a mane and a long tail of hair, used for riding and for pulling or carrying loads: *to break in, harness, mount, ride, saddle, shoe a horse; Horses buck, canter, gallop, neigh, trot, whinny; a young horse* (=foal); *a female horse* (=mare); *a young female horse* (=filly); *a male horse* (=stallion); *a young male horse* (=colt); *a castrated male horse* (=gelding); *to **back the wrong horse*** (=be on the losing side); *to **flog a dead horse*** (=continue discussing a dead issue). **2** a piece of gymnasium equipment used for vaulting. **3** a supporting frame, as a clotheshorse or sawhorse.
— **from the horse's mouth** *Informal.* authoritatively: *I got my facts straight from the horse's mouth.*
— **horse of another** or **of a different colour** a different matter.
— **look a gift horse in the mouth** criticize something received as a gift.
— *v.* **horse around** *Informal.* fool around.

horse·back *adv. & adj.* on a horse's back: *to ride horseback; horseback riding.*

horse·play *n.* boisterous play.

horse·pow·er (HORS·pow·ur) *n.* a unit of engine power: *a 2 000-horsepower automobile engine; The runner suddenly lost horsepower and started trailing.*

horse race *n.* **1** a race between horses. **2** a closely fought race.

horse sense *n. Informal.* common sense.

horse·shoe (HORS·shoo) *n.* **1** a U-shaped metal plate nailed to a horse's hoof for protection. **2 horseshoes** *pl.* a game of pitching horseshoes so as to get them around a stake 40 feet (12.20 m) away.
— *adj.* horseshoe-shaped: *a horseshoe magnet, table.*

horse trading *n.* buying and selling with much bargaining, many concessions, etc.

horse·whip *n.* a whip for driving horses.
— *v.* **-whips, -whipped, -whip·ping** beat with a horsewhip.

hors·ey or **hors·y** (HOR·see) *adj.* **hors·i·er, -i·est** fond of or having to do with horses or horse racing: *the horsey set frequenting the racetracks.* — **hors·i·ness** *n.*

hose (HOZE) *n.* **1** *pl.* **hos·es** a tube of flexible material for watering, putting out fires, etc.: *a garden hose; to train a hose on a mob.* **2** *sing. & pl.* same as HOSIERY.

3 *sing. & pl.* tight breeches formerly worn by men.
— *v.* **hos·es, hosed, hos·ing** put water on with a hose: *to hose a lawn; to hose down a stone-throwing mob.*

ho·sier·y (HOH·zhuh·ree) *n.* socks and stockings.

hos·pice (HOS·pis) *n.* **1** a lodging for travellers. **2** a home for the sick or poor.

hos·pi·ta·ble (HOS·pit·uh·bul, hos·PIT·uh·bul) *adj.* **1** kind and courteous to guests and others seeking hospitality. **2** receptive: *The boss is hospitable to new ideas.*

hos·pi·tal (HOS·pit·ul) *n.* an institution where sick and injured are treated.

hos·pi·tal·i·ty (hos·puh·TAL·uh·tee) *n.* **-ties** friendly and generous treatment of guests and strangers: *warm hospitality; to extend, offer, show hospitality; to abuse someone's hospitality; the **hospitality suite** of a hotel for guests to socialize in at a convention.*

hos·pi·tal·ize (HOS·pit·ul·ize) *v.* **-iz·es, -ized, -iz·ing** put a patient into a hospital for medical, surgical, or related care. — **hos·pi·tal·i·za·tion** (-ul·uh·ZAY·shun) *n.*

host (rhyme: "most") *n.* **1** one who receives and accommodates or entertains a guest: *Calgary **played host to** (=hosted) the Winter Olympics in 1988.* **2** an organism such as a plant or animal on which a parasite feeds, or an embryo into which a graft is transplanted. **3** in a computer system, a central database or the controlling computer of a network of terminals. **4** a large number, originally an army: *hosts of relatives; a host of objections.* **5** a wafer used in Holy Communion. **6** **Host** such a consecrated wafer.
— *v.* act as a host or emcee for a TV show or other event.

hos·tage (HOS·tij) *n.* a person handed over or seized and held as a pledge or guarantee: *Twenty passengers were taken hostage during the hijacking.*

hos·tel (HOS·tul) *n.* an inexpensive lodging: *a hostel for the homeless; a youth hostel (for travelling youth).*

hos·tel·er (HOS·tul·ur) *n.* a hostel guest.

hos·tel·ry (HOS·tul·ree) *n.* **-ries** an inn or hotel.

host·ess (HOH·stis) *n.* **1** a woman who entertains invited guests. **2** a woman who works in an entertaining or service role, as in managing a hotel, in a restaurant or dance hall, as an airline stewardess, etc.: *an air hostess* (=flight attendant).

hos·tile (HOS·tul, -tile) *adj.* **1** of an enemy: *a hostile army, force, ruler.* **2** unfriendly or unsuitable: *a hostile book reviewer; His attitude was openly hostile; He was received with hostile looks; a hostile mood; A hot climate is hostile to polar bears.* — **hos·tile·ly** *adv.*

hos·til·i·ty (hos·TIL·uh·tee) *n.* **-ties 1** a hostile act or condition: *to arouse, display, express, feel, show hostility; to stir up hostility between people; the strikers' hostility to or toward management.* **2 hostilities** *pl.* war: *the outbreak of hostilities between Arabs and Israel; the suspension of hostilities after the Six-Day War.*

hot *adj.* **hot·ter, hot·test 1** having a high temperature: *Fire is hot; a hot day; hot weather; boiling, piping,*

scalding hot water. **2** sharp or pungent to the taste: *a hot curry, pepper.* **3** similar in effect to high heat or something that is hot: *Running makes you hot; a hot* (=fiery) *temper; a hot* (=fresh) *scent; police in hot* (=very close) *pursuit of a getaway car; a place getting too hot* (=dangerous) *for lawbreakers; a hot* (=live) *wire.* **4** *Slang.* causing heat; excited or passionate: *a hot* (=wanted) *criminal; hot* (=stolen) *merchandise; hot* (=fashionable) *jazz; Radio is a hot medium unlike movies and TV because of more listener participation; a hot* (=very interesting) *tip about some hot news; He's a good student but* **not so hot** (*Slang* for rather mediocre) *in athletics.*
— **make it hot for someone** *Informal.* make things uncomfortable for someone.
— **hot·ly** *adv.;* **hot·ness** *n.*

hot air *n. Slang.* empty talk or writing.

hot·bed *n.* a place of rapid growth, as a glass-covered bed of earth heated by fermenting manure: *Slums are the hotbeds of vice and crime.*

hot-blooded (HOT·BLUD·id) *adj.* easily excited; reckless.

hot·cake *n.* pancake.
— **sell like hotcakes** *Informal.* sell rapidly.

hot dog *n.* **1** a sandwich made with a hot frankfurter in a split roll. **2** *Slang.* a skier or skateboarder who performs stunts, esp. one who shows off.
— *interj. Slang.* an exclamation of approval or enthusiasm.
— **hot·dog** *v.* **-dogs, -dogged, -dog·ging** *Slang.* to show off, as skiers and skateborders. — **hot·dog·ger** *n.*

ho·tel (hoh·TEL) *n.* a commercial establishment providing food and lodging, esp. for travellers; *adj.:* *Hotel clerks register guests; Hotel guests check in and out all day.*

hot·foot *n.* **-foots** the prank of lighting a match in the welt of a shoe of an unsuspecting person.
— *adv. Informal.* in haste.
— *v.* **hotfoot it** *Informal.* go hastily.

hot·head *n.* a rash or fiery-tempered person.
— **hot·head·ed** *adj.*

hot·house *n.* a heated greenhouse.

hot line *n.* **1** a direct telephone or other communication line for use in a crisis: *A hotline was set up between Moscow and Washington.* **2** a phone-in radio or TV show.

hot potato *n. Informal.* a troublesome question or subject that no one wants to handle.

hot rod *n. Slang.* an automobile modified for fast acceleration and speeds.
— **hot rod·der** (HOT·ROD·ur) *n.*

hot seat *n. Slang.* a situation or position in which one is subject to harassment or criticism.

hot·shot *n. & adj. Slang.* (one) who is flashily skilful: *a hotshot of an amateur; a hotshot amateur.*

hot spot *n.* **1** a popular resort or meeting place. **2** a scene of social unrest, trouble, or hostilities. **3** a polluted or contaminated area. **4** a region of great heat, as inside the earth or near a spreading fire.

hot tub *n.* a large wooden tub of hot water to sit and socialize in.

hot water *n. Informal.* trouble: *He found himself in hot water.*

hound *n.* **1** a short-haired, long-eared hunting dog that tracks its prey by scent: *a pack of hounds.* **2** *Informal.* an enthusiastic pursuer: *an autograph hound; party hound; publicity hounds.*
— *v.* keep chasing: *a debtor hounded by creditors; The creditors hounded him to pay up; He was hounded out of office by the media when they learned about his past.*

hour (OUR) *n.* **1** one of the 24 periods of 60 minutes each into which a day is divided: *a clock that shows* or *tells the hour, minute, and second; It strikes every hour on the hour; the wee* **hours** *of the morning (from 1 a.m. on); Casual workers are paid by the hour; The next train leaves within an hour.* **2** a moment in time: *She thinks 4 a.m. is an ungodly hour for waking up; Friends helped him in his hour of need; Everyone gathered at the appointed hour; The hour of decision had arrived; her* **finest hour** (=moment or period of greatest glory). **3** any fixed period: *Our lunch hour is from 12:30 to 1:15 p.m.; Our office* **hours** *are from 9 to 5; the morning and afternoon rush hour; Buses are more frequent during peak hours; the zero hour (when an event is to begin).*
— **after hours** after the regular school or business hours.
— **keep late, odd, regular, strange, etc. hours** go to bed late, work during odd, regular, strange, etc. hours.

hour·glass *n.* a time-measuring device consisting of two glass bulbs containing enough sand or liquid to run for an hour through the narrow neck connecting the top bulb to the bottom one: *her shapely* **hourglass figure** *(that is narrow at the waist).*

hour·ly *adv. & adj.* by the hour: *Some are paid hourly; an hourly rate of pay.*

house *n.* **hous·es** (HOW·ziz) **1** a living place, esp. as an establishment, often including a family and servants, headed by a parent and managed by a "lady of the house" or a "man of the house": *Father* **keeps house** (=does the housework) *nowadays; to build, demolish, put up, renovate, tear down a house; a brick, country, detached, dilapidated, frame, haunted, prefabricated, ramshackle, rooming, row, summer, town house; a swallow's hanging house; a snail with its house on its back; Elizabeth II is from the royal House* (=family including ancestors and descendants) *of Windsor; the*

*house of David; a fraternity house ; the **houses of heaven*** (= 12 portions of the zodiac, each with its own sign and name). **2** an organization or institution: *a boarding, disorderly, gambling, halfway, mail-order, publishing, safe house; a house of correction, detention; The drinks are **on the house*** (= free); *the **House of Commons*** (= the lower house of a parliament); *a **house of ill fame*** (= brothel). **3** an assembly or audience: *They played to a full* or *packed house, not to an empty house; Is there a doctor in the house? We are holding an open house (when everyone is welcome to drop in); Her singing never fails to **bring the house down*** (Informal for be loudly applauded).
— *v.* (HOWZ) **hous·es, housed, hous·ing** put into a house: *The refugees were housed in tents; old furniture housed in the attic.*

house·break·ing (HOUSE·bray·king) *n.* the act of breaking into a house to commit a crime.

house·bro·ken (HOUSE·broh·kun) *adj.* of a domestic pet, trained to live in a house, esp. knowing where to defecate and urinate.

house·call *n.* a visit by a professional to the home of a customer: *Few doctors make housecalls any more.*

house·clean·ing (HOUSE·clee·ning) *n.* getting rid of bad conditions, as in cleaning a house and its furnishings.

house·hold *n.* a group of people such as a family living in a house: *to run a household.*
— *adj.* domestic: *household articles, effects, expenses; a **household word*** (= a familiar name or saying).

house·hold·er (HOUSE·hole·dur) *n.* the head of a house of family and servants.

house·hus·band (HOUSE·huz·bund) *n.* a man who manages a household while his wife has an outside job.

house·keep·er (HOUSE·kee·pur) *n.* one who manages a household.

house·keep·ing (HOUSE·kee·ping) *n.* **1** washing, cooking, and such work; housework: *a light housekeeping cabin, suite.* **2** bookkeeping, paperwork, and such domestic details of business management.
— *adj.* having kitchen facilities: *a large housekeeping suite at $300 a day; a housekeeping cabin, unit.*

house·lights *n. pl.* lights in a theatre auditorium, as opposed to stage lights.

house·maid *n.* a female servant doing housework.

house·moth·er (HOUSE·muth·ur) *n.* a woman in charge of young people living together, as in a dormitory.

house sitter *n.* a person who looks after a house during the absence of its regular occupant.

house·top *n.* roof: *This is private, don't shout it **from the housetops.***

house·wares *n. pl.* dishes, small appliances, and such kitchen equipment and household articles.

house·warm·ing (HOUSE·warm·ing) *n.* a party to celebrate one's moving into a new home.

house·wife *n.* -wives the woman head of a household.
— **house·wife·ly** *adj.*

house·wif·er·y (HOUSE·wye·fuh·ree) *n.* housekeeping.

house·work *n.* washing, cooking, and other housekeeping work.

housing *n.* **1** the providing of shelter: *low-income, public, student, subsidized, substandard housing.* **2** houses collectively; lodging: *open housing without racial discrimination; overpopulation and housing problems.* **3** a frame, box, plate, etc. for holding a mechanical part in place. **4** an ornamental saddle cover.

hove (rhyme: "drove") a *pt. & pp.* of HEAVE.

hov·el (HOV·ul, HUV·ul) *n.* a miserable dwelling; hut.

hov·er (HOV·ur, HUV·ur) *v.* be in a fluttering, suspended, or lingering state: *a bird hovering over its nest; The patient hovered between life and death; The temperature outside hovered around zero.*

how *adj. & adv.* **1** in what way, state, condition, etc.: *Hello, how are you? She will show you how to do it; No one knows how this happened.* **2** to what degree, extent, effect, etc.: *How old are you? How do you mean? Tell us how much you're asking; How* (= at what price) *do you sell these goods?* **3** *Informal.* why: *How is that?* **4** by what name: *How are you known around here?*
— **and how!** *Informal.* very much so!
— **how about** what do you say to (something): *How about buying me a drink?*
— **how come?** *Informal.* Why: *How come* (= Why is it that) *you're late?*
— **how do you do?** [used formally on being introduced] hello!
— *n.:* *the hows and whys of a situation.*

how·dy (HOW·dee) *interj. Informal.* hello.

how·e'er (how·AIR) [poetical form] however.

how·ev·er (how·EV·ur) *conj. & adv.* **1** in whatever way or to whatever extent: *I couldn't persuade her however hard I tried; However did you manage that?* **2** nevertheless; but: *I'm busy; however, I will come.*

howl *v. & n.* **1** (give) a long, loud, and mournful cry, as dogs and wolves: *It howled with pain; It let out a howl of pain.* **2** yell or shout from amusement or scorn: *The speaker was mercilessly howled down; They howled at him; He was howled off the stage.*

howl·er *n.* **1** one that howls. **2** *Informal.* a ridiculous blunder.

howling *adj.: a howling* (= desolate) *wilderness; a howling* (Informal for great) *success.*

how·so·ev·er (how·soh·EV·ur) *adv.* in whatever way or to whatever extent; however.

how-to *adj.* giving practical instructions on how to do something: *a how-to book on carpentry.*

Hoyle (HOIL) in **according to Hoyle,** according to the rules; exactly.

hub *n.* **1** the central part around which a wheel turns. **2** a centre of activity: *In Ontario, Sudbury is sometimes called "the hub of the North."*

hub·bub (HUB·ub) *n.* **1** confused noise, as of a milling crowd. **2** uproar.

hub·by (HUB·ee) *n.* **hub·bies** *Informal.* husband.

hub·cap *n.* a metal cap covering the end of an axle.

hu·bris (HEW·bris) *n.* extreme arrogance.

huck·ster (HUCK·stur) *n.* **1** a peddler of small articles. **2** a loud or petty sale rep. **3** *Slang.* an adman, esp. a producer of commercials.
— *v.* peddle or promote: *a commercial huckstering holiday homes in Florida.*

hud·dle (HUD·ul) *n.* a closely packed group, as of football players between plays.
— *v.* crowd together or confer in a huddle.
— **hud·dler** *n.*

hue (HEW) *n.* colour, esp. as the modification of a basic colour; tint: *Vermilion is a darker hue of red.*

hue and cry *n.* a shouting of alarm; outcry: *They raised a hue and cry over the referee's decision.*

-hued *combining form.* coloured: *many-hued, multi-hued, reddish-hued.*

huff *n.* a fit of peevish anger: *He protested and walked out of the room in a huff.* — **huff·y** *adj.*

hug *v.* **hugs, hugged, hug·ging 1** clasp closely in an embrace. **2** cling or stay close to something: *a low-slung car that hugs the road; The bus moved forward, hugging the right side of the highway.*
— *n.* a close embrace. — **hug·ger** *n.*

huge (HYOOJ) *adj.* **hug·er, hug·est** very large in mass or bulk: *a huge belly, deficit; a huge (= great in scope) undertaking.*

hug·ger-mug·ger (HUG·ur·mug·ur) *n.* a confused condition; disorder.

huh *interj.* expressing contempt, surprise, question, etc.

hulk *n.* a heavy, unwieldy, or clumsy person or thing, as an old ship or automobile that is out of service: *a rusted old hulk of a vehicle; the hulk of the Titanic; the concrete-and-glass hulks dominating our city skyline; a hulk of a beast; a lumbering hulk; a big **hulking** heavyweight of a man.*

hull *n.* **1** the outer covering of a fruit or seed. **2** the calyx of some fruits such as the strawberry. **3** the outer frame on which a ship or similar vessel floats: *the double hull of a submarine.*

hul·la·ba·loo (HUL·uh·buh·loo) *n.* **-loos** clamour or disturbance.

hum *v.* **hums, hummed, hum·ming** make a low, continuous sound with lips closed, as in sounding out a melody without words: *to hum a tune; an office humming with activity.*
— *n.* a humming: *the hum of bees, machines, a busy concourse.* — **hum·mer** *n.*

hu·man (HEW·mun, YOO·mun) *adj.* having to do with the form and characteristics of people: *To err is human; a human error; the human body; a human-interest story; human consumption, existence, resources, rights, weaknesses.*
— *n.* a person, or human being.
— **hu·man·ly** *adv.;* **hu·man·ness** *n.*

hu·mane (hew·MANE) *adj.* **1** kind and sympathetic: *humane treatment of prisoners; a humane society for the protection of children and animals.* **2** humanistic:

humane studies; Doctor of Humane Letters.

hu·man·ism (HEW·muh·niz·um, YOO·muh-) *n.* a movement or philosophy emphasizing human worth and values, as opposed to a supernatural or ascetic view of life: *secular humanism.* — **hu·man·ist** *n. & adj.*
— **hu·man·is·tic** (-NIS·tic) *adj.*

hu·man·i·tar·i·an (hew·MAN·uh·TAIR·ee·un) *n.* a person such as a philanthropist who promotes human welfare: *a humanitarian concern.*
— **hu·man·i·tar·i·an·ism** (-uh·niz·um) *n.*

hu·man·i·ty (hew·MAN·uh·tee) *n.* **-ties 1** mankind: *the good of humanity; Since World War II, deportation of civilians has been considered a crime against humanity.* **2** a human or humane quality. **3 the humanities** *pl.* branches of learning concerned with culture, not science, as religion, philosophy, languages, literature, history, and the fine arts: *The Canadian Federation for the Humanities promotes scholarship and research in the humanities.*

hu·man·ize (HEW·muh·nize, YOO·muh-) *v.* **-iz·es, -ized, -iz·ing** make or become human or humane.
— **hu·man·iz·er** *n.*
— **hu·man·i·za·tion** (-muh·nuh·ZAY·shun) *n.*

hu·man·kind (HEW·mun·kined) *n.* same as MANKIND.

hu·man·oid (HEW·muh·noid) *n.* a nearly human creature, as prehistoric types such as the Neanderthal man and the androids of science fiction.

human rights *n. pl.* fundamental civil, economic, political, and social rights, as of a free human being.

hum·ble (HUM·bul) *adj.* **-bler, -blest 1** modest and unpretentious. **2** lacking in self-respect: *a man of humble birth; forced to eat **humble pie** (= to make a humble apology).*
— *v.* **-bles, -bled, -bling** make humble: *a proud man humbled in defeat; The king humbled himself in penance.* — **hum·ble·ness** *n.* — **hum·bly** (-blee) *adv.*

hum·bug *n.* a person or thing that is a fraud.
— *v.* **-bugs, -bugged, -bug·ging** deceive or trick.
— *interj.* nonsense!

hum·ding·er (HUM·DING·ur) *n. Slang.* someone or something that is extraordinary or striking; a beaut.

hum·drum *adj.* commonplace or boring: *a humdrum routine.*

hu·mid (HEW·mid) *adj.* of the air, moist or damp.
— **hu·mid·ly** *adv.*

Hu·mi·dex (HEW·mi·dex) *n. Cdn.* a measure of discomfort based on the combined effect of heat and humidity.

hu·mid·i·fy (hew·MID·uh·fye) *n.* **-fies, -fied, -fy·ing** make the air humid, as with a **hu·mid·i·fi·er.**

hu·mid·i·ty (hew·MID·uh·tee) *n.* dampness, esp. the amount of it in the air.

hu·mil·i·ate (hew·MIL·ee·ate) *v.* **-ates, -at·ed, -at·ing** to humble or disgrace someone; hurt someone's self-esteem: *a **humiliating** defeat.*
— **hu·mil·i·a·tion** (-AY·shun) *n.*

hu·mil·i·ty (hew·MIL·uh·tee) *n.* **-ties** the quality of being genuinely humble; lack of false pride.

hu·mon·gous or **hu·mun·gous** (hew·MUNG·gus) *adj.* *Slang.* large in size or extent: *a humongous birthday cake.*

hu·mor·ous (HEW·mur·us) *adj.* amusing or funny. — **hu·mor·ous·ly** *adv.*

hu·mour or **hu·mor** (HEW·mur) *n.* **1** an amusing quality, as of a funny or ludicrous situation. **2** the capacity to appreciate this: *a good sense of humour.* **3** an expression of it in speech or writing: *black, deadpan, earthy, gallows, infectious, irrepressible, slapstick, subtle, wry humour; a humour magazine.* **4** a state of mind; also, a fancy or whim: *to be in bad humour; in good humour; She's in no humour to be the butt of practical jokes.* — **out of humour** in a bad mood. — *v.* indulge: *Children, the sick, and the cranky have to be humoured now and then.* — **hu·mor·ist** *n.*

hump *n.* a lumpy formation, as on the back of a camel or as a deformity, as of a hunchback, or **hump·back.** — **over the hump** *Informal.* past a difficult period or phase. — *v.* arch: *A cat humps its back when excited.*

humph *n. & interj.* a snorting sound expressing doubt, dissatisfaction, etc.

humungous same as HUMONGOUS.

Hun *n.* **1** one of a warlike Asiatic people who invaded Europe in the 4th and 5th centuries A.D. **2 hun** a vandal.

hunch *n.* **1** *Informal.* a feeling of what is going to happen; premonition or foreboding: *I took the umbrella on a hunch; I had a hunch it was going to rain.* **2** a hump; *v.*: *pupils hunched in concentration over their books; He sat hunched up in a sulky mood.*

hunch·back *n.* a person with a curvature of the spine; humpback.

hun·dred (HUN·drud) *n. & adj.* ten times ten; 100 or C: *three hundred boys; hundreds* (= a large number) *of boys.*

hun·dred·fold (HUN·drud·fold) *n., adj. & adv.* (being) a hundred times as much or as many.

hun·dredth (HUN·drudth, "th" as in "thin") *n. & adj.* (being) a 100th part.

hung *pt. & pp.* of HANG. — **hung up** *Slang.* having a hang-up or mental fixation: *a kid who is really hung up on sports; Sam is so hung up about age; Al is hung up on* (= infatuated by) *every girl he meets.*

hun·ger (HUNG·gur) *n.* **1** pain or discomfort of the stomach because of the body's need for food: *to alleviate, appease, gratify, satisfy one's hunger.* **2** starvation: *People die of hunger during a famine; Prisoners go on a **hunger strike** to enforce demands or in protest.* **3** any strong desire or craving: *the hunger for knowledge.* — *v.* have such a desire: *A child hungers for affection; to hunger after justice.*

hung jury *n.* a jury that cannot agree on a verdict.

hun·gry (HUNG·gree) *adj.* **-gri·er, -gri·est** feeling hunger or a similar strong desire: *a hungry stomach; the hungry eyes of starving people; People go hungry in poor countries; the Hungry Thirties of the Depression years; souls hungry for salvation.* — **hun·gri·ly** *adv.*

hunk (HUNK) *n.* *Informal.* **1** a well-built man: *quite a hunk of a fellow.* **2** a large chunk or slice: *a hunk of bread, cheese, meat; She popped a hunk of jello into his gaping mouth.*

hun·ker (HUNK·ur) **1** *v.* squat down on one's haunches. **2 hun·kers** *n. pl.* haunches.

hun·ky-do·ry (hunk·ee·DOR·ee) *adj.* *Slang.* quite satisfactory; fine.

hunt *v.* **1** chase, harry, kill, or catch game for food or sport. **2** search: *to hunt down an escaped convict; Researchers hunt for information in the library; Police hunt up evidence; the **hunt-and-peck** method of typing.* — *n.* a hunting, search, or a group hunting party: *to organize a hunt for big game.* — **hunt·er** *n.* — **hunts·man** (-mun) *n.* **-men; hunt·ress** (-tris) *n.*

hur·dle (HUR·dul) *n.* **1** an obstacle or barrier to jump over: *to clear or take a hurdle.* **2 hurdles** *pl.* a race in which the competitors have to clear many hurdles. — *v.* **-dles, -dled, -dling** jump over or overcome an obstacle. — **hur·dler** *n.*

hurl *v.* throw with force or violence, as a javelin or spear: *The two boxers hurled themselves at each other; The mob started hurling insults at the speaker.* — *n.* a forcible throw: *a hurl of the discus.*

hurl·y-burl·y (HUR·lee·bur·lee) *n.* **-burl·ies** turmoil or uproar.

hur·rah (huh·RAH) *n., v. & interj.* shout of joy or approval; cheer: *the last hurrah* (= final moment of glory). Also **hur·ray** (-RAY).

hur·ri·cane (HUR·uh·cane) *n.* a whirling tropical storm with winds of 73 mi. (117 km) per hour or more: *the eye of a hurricane; A hurricane hits or strikes, then blows itself out; adj.: A **hurricane lamp** or **lantern** has a chimney to protect its flame from winds; a hurricane warning, watch.*

hur·ry (HUR·ee) *v.* **hur·ries, hur·ried, hur·ry·ing** make haste, often with some excitement and confusion: *Hurry up if you want to be on time.* — *n.*: *We were in a hurry to catch the train; In the hurry, she forgot her purse.* — *adj.*: *a hurried departure;* **hur·ried·ly** *adv.*

hurt *v.* **hurts, hurt, hurt·ing** feel or cause pain physically or mentally: *She hit a stone and hurt her foot; The injured foot hurts; She hurt herself; She was badly hurt; He hurt her feelings by saying "no"; She was deeply hurt; It hurts to see her suffer.* — *n.* a feeling of pain: *The hurt was forgotten but the scars remained.*

hurt·ful *adj.* harmful.

hur·tle (HUR·tul) *v.* **-tles, -tled, -tling** rush or move with a clattering or rattling sound: *A train hurtles past at a crossing; The truck skidded and hurtled across the street into a shop window; Rocks came hurtling down the mountainside.*

hus·band (HUZ·bund) *n.* a male spouse: *a devoted, doting, jealous, unfaithful husband; common-law*

husbands.
— **v.** manage economically: *to husband one's resources, strength.*

hus·band·man (HUZ·bund·mun) *n.* **-men** [old use] farmer.

hus·band·ry (HUZ·bund·ree) *n.* farming: *animal husbandry* (= care of farm animals).

hush *n., v. & interj.* quiet or silence: *A hush fell over the audience as a ghost appeared on the stage; to **hush up** a secret by paying **hush money** to the person likely to tell.*

hush-hush *adj.* secret or confidential: *a hush-hush manner, subject.*

husk *n.* the outer covering of cereals, esp. corn.
— **v.** remove the husk of a cereal. — **husk·er** *n.*

husk·y *adj.* **husk·i·er, -i·est** **1** hoarse: *a husky voice.* **2** big and strong.
— **n.** **-kies** **1** a husky person. **2** *Cdn. Informal.* an Inuit; also **Husky.** **3** a hardy sled dog of the Arctic; also called "Siberian husky."
— **husk·i·ly** *adv.;* **husk·i·ness** *n.*

hus·tle (HUS·ul) *v.* **-tles, -tled, -tling** **1** act aggressively to get something done: *You have to hustle in times of unemployment; to hustle to find work.* **2** rush or push someone to get something done: *a child hustled off to bed after watching TV late; The gate-crasher was hustled out the door; Cabbies were hustling people for rides.* **3** sell aggressively or deceitfully: *a boy caught hustling stolen goods; Tickets to the game were being hustled for $500 each.*
— **n.** **1** a hustling quality: *a used-car sales rep who lacks hustle* (= drive); *the hustle and bustle of a big city; He makes a living by some hustle (Informal for* racket) *or other.* **2** a ballroom dance using disco music.
— **hus·tler** *n.*

hut *n.* a small, plain or crudely built dwelling or cabin.

hutch *n.* **1** a cupboard with shelves for dishes, etc.: *a combined buffet and hutch for the dining room.* **2** a pen or coop, as a rabbit cage; also, a shack: *a hatchback model of an automobile equipped with a hutch* (= foldable tent).

hutz·pa or **hutz·pah** (HOOT·spuh) same as CHUTZPAH.

huz·za or **huz·zah** (huh·ZAH) same as HURRAH.

hy·brid (HYE·brid) *n. & adj.* (anything) of mixed origin or structure, as the mule (from a jackass and a mare) or "oramon" (from "orange" and "lemon"): *"Talkative" is a hybrid word that is half English and half Latin in origin.* — **hy·brid·ism** *n.*

hy·drant (HYE·drunt) *n.* a discharge pipe with a nozzle, connected to a water main and serving as a street outlet for water to put out fires: *to turn on a fire hydrant.*

hy·draul·ic (hye·DRAW·lic) **1** *adj.* working with water or liquid pressure: *a hydraulic brake; Hydraulic cement hardens under water; hydraulic engineering.* **2** **hydraulics** *n. pl.* [takes sing. v.] physics dealing with the behaviour of liquids at rest and in motion.
— **hy·draul·i·cal·ly** *adv.*

hy·dro (HYE·droh) *n. Cdn.* hydroelectric power, electricity as a utility, or an agency that distributes it: *Our hydro was cut off by a storm; your monthly bill for hydro; a cheque made out to Ontario Hydro.*
— **adj.** hydroelectric: *hydro companies, dams, equipment, lines, poles, power, stations, utilities.*

hydro- *combining form.* water or hydrogen-containing: *hydrocarbon, hydroelectric, hydroplane.*

hy·dro·e·lec·tric (hye·droh·i·LEC·tric) *adj.* having to do with the generation of electricity by water power.

hy·dro·foil (HYE·droh·foil) *n.* **1** a vessel that skims over water at high speeds using winglike structures attached to its hull. **2** such a structure.

hy·dro·gen (HYE·druh·jun) *n.* a gaseous element that combines with oxygen to form water.

hydrogen bomb *n.* an extremely powerful nuclear weapon whose energy is derived from the fusion of hydrogen atoms.

hy·dro·plane (HYE·druh·plane) *n.* a motorboat whose hull is so shaped as to enable it to skim over water at high speeds.

hy·dro·plan·ing (HYE·druh·play·ning) *n.* the dangerous gliding of a rubber-tired vehicle on a wet pavement when the vehicle reaches a critical high speed.

hy·dro·pon·ics (hye·druh·PON·ics) *n. pl.* [takes sing. v.] the growing of plants in water, with nutrients added, instead of in soil.
— **hy·dro·pon·ic** *adj.;* **hy·dro·pon·i·cal·ly** *adv.*

hy·e·na (hye·EE·nuh) *n.* a wolflike animal of Africa and Asia, considered cowardly, with a weird cry like a hysterical laugh: *a pack of hyenas.*

hy·giene (HYE·jeen) *n.* the observance and practice of health standards: *dental, feminine, mental, personal, public hygiene.*
— **hy·gi·en·ist** (HYE·jee·nist, hye·JEE·nist) *n.*

hy·gi·en·ic (hye·JEE·nic, hye·jee·EN·nic) *adj.* sanitary or healthful.

hying a *pres. part.* of HIE.

hype *n. Slang.* **1** exaggerated promotion; hence, deception: *The book needs a little luck and a lot of hype to sell well; hard-sell hype; the poetic hype of copywriters; the hype about the redeeming social value of cheap movies.* **2** same as HYPODERMIC. **3** a drug addict.
— **v.** **hypes, hyped, hyp·ing** **1** promote in a sensational manner: *the business of hyping sex and violence on TV; a movie hyped as a hot romance.* **2** falsify or fake: *to hype production costs; a hyped package.* **3** stimulate or excite, as by a drug injection: *People get hyped for*

hockey games; They are hyped up by all the hoopla; a **hyped-up** (= phony) *sales campaign.*

hy·per (HYE·pur) *adj. Slang.* **1** overactive: *a hyper child.* **2** overexcited: *Let's not get hyper about it.*

hyper- *prefix.* more than normal: *hyperactive, hyperinflation, hypersensitive.*

hy·per·ac·tive (hye·pur·AC·tiv) *adj.* more active than normal; overactive: *a hyperactive child.* — **hy·per·ac·tiv·i·ty** (HYE·pur·ac·TIV·uh·tee) *n.*

hy·per·bo·le (hye·PUR·buh·lee) *n.* a figure of speech using exaggeration for effect, as in "She looked daggers." — **hy·per·bol·ic** (hye·pur·BOL·ic) *adj.*

hy·per·mar·ket (HYE·pur·MAR·kit) *n.* a supermarket combined with a department store.

hy·per·text (HYE·pur·text) *n.* a computer system for accessing large interconnected bodies of textual and graphic information on specific topics as desired by the user.

hy·phen (HYE·fun) *n.* a punctuation mark used to show word division, as in compound words like "high-level," or in syllable division, as at the end of a line.

hy·phen·ate (HYE·fuh·nate) *v.* **-ates, -at·ed, -at·ing** use a hyphen in a word: *"High-level" is a hyphenated compound word; a hyphenated surname.* — **hy·phen·a·tion** (-NAY·shun) *n.*

hyphenated *adj.* of supposedly divided allegiance, as an "Irish-Canadian" or "Franco-German": *a hyphenated Canadian.*

hyp·no·sis (hip·NOH·sis) *n., pl.* **-ses** (-seez) a trancelike condition in which a subject will act according to the suggestions of the person who induces the condition, or **hyp·no·tist** (HIP·nuh·tist) *n.* — **hyp·not·ic** (-NOT·ic) *adj.*

hyp·no·tize (HIP·nuh·tize) *v.* **-tiz·es, -tized, -tiz·ing** induce hypnosis in a subject.

hy·po (HYE·poh) *n.* **1** same as HYPE. **2** *Informal.*

hypodermic.

hypo- *prefix.* beneath or less than: *hypocentre, hypodermic, hypothyroid.*

hy·po·cen·tre (hye·poh·CEN·tur) *n.* same as GROUND ZERO.

hy·poc·ri·sy (hi·POC·ruh·see) *n.* **-sies** a pretending to be what one is not, esp. very good or religious.

hy·po·crite (HIP·uh·crit) *n.* one who pretends to be good or religious. — **hyp·o·crit·i·cal** (-CRIT·uh·cul) *adj.* — **hyp·o·crit·i·cal·ly** *adv.*

hy·po·der·mic (hye·puh·DUR·mic) *adj.* beneath the skin: *a hypodermic syringe with a hypodermic needle for giving a hypodermic injection.*

hy·poth·e·sis (hye·POTH·uh·sis) *n.* **-ses** (-seez) an assumed or likely explanation of a set of facts for further study or verification: *a working hypothesis; to advance* or *propose a hypothesis; Later discoveries confirmed our hypothesis.*

hy·poth·e·size (hye·POTH·uh·size) *v.* **-siz·es, -sized, -siz·ing** make a hypothesis; assume on the basis of a set of facts: *to hypothesize about what might happen; Columbus hypothesized that he could reach India if he sailed west.*

hy·po·thet·i·cal (hye·puh·THET·uh·cul) *adj.* conjectural: *Who will start a nuclear war is a hypothetical question.*

hys·te·ri·a (his·TEER·ee·uh, -TER·ee·uh) *n.* uncontrollable excitement, as in a neurotic condition brought on by an unbearable situation: *In a fit of hysteria, she smashed all her china; Mass hysteria resulted in a stampede; War hysteria led to the jailing of innocent civilians.* — **hys·ter·ic** (-TER·ic) *n. & adj.*

hys·ter·i·cal (his·TER·uh·cul) *adj.* **1** wildly excited: *Let's not get hysterical about it; hysterical behaviour, laughter.* **2** *Informal.* wildly funny: *a hysterical joke.*

hysterics *n. pl.* a fit of uncontrollable laughter or crying.

Ii

I or **i** (EYE) *n.* **I's** or **i's** **1** the ninth letter of the English alphabet. **2** the Roman numeral for "1."

-ible same as -ABLE: *admissible, audible, expansible, forcible, intelligible.*

-ic *suffix.* **1** *adj.* having to do with: *hysteric, poetic, scenic;* also **-ical.** **2** *n.* a person or thing: *arithmetic, emetic, lunatic.*

ice *n.* **1** water frozen solid or as a layer: *to form, make, melt, produce ice; crushed, dry, pack ice.* **2** a frozen dessert of sweetened fruit juice without milk or cream; *water ice.* **3** *Slang.* diamonds. **4** *Slang.* a crystalline form of the drug "speed."
— *adj.: the* **Ice Age** *when much of the earth was under ice; an* **ice bag** *of crushed ice for relieving body pain; an* **ice pick** *for picking or breaking ice.*
— *v.* **-ic·es, iced, ic·ing** cover with, become covered with, turn to, or make cool with ice: *The bridge ices in cold weather and gets slippery.*
— **iced** *adj.* containing ice: *iced coffee, tea.*
— **break the ice** make a start, esp. by overcoming some initial difficulty.
— **cut no ice with someone** *Informal.* have no effect on someone.
— **on ice** *Informal.* **1** in reserve: *The remaining applications were put on ice.* **2** safely assured: *The bargain is on ice.*
— **on thin ice** in a dangerous position.

ice·berg *n.* a huge piece of ice broken off from a glacier floating in the sea with only its tip showing above water: *The Titanic hit* or *struck an iceberg and sank; That's only* **the tip of the iceberg** (= the visible part of something larger and deeper).

ice cream *n.* a frozen dessert of sweetened and flavoured cream.

ice floe *n.* a sheet of floating sea ice.

ice hockey *n.* same as HOCKEY.

ice milk *n.* a dessert similar to ice cream but made with skim milk.

ice storm *n.* a storm in which rain freezes as it falls, coating everything with a glaze of ice.

ice water *n.* **1** water from melting ice. **2** water chilled for drinking.

ic·ing (EYE·sing) *n.* a sweet, creamy mixture for coating cakes and such baked goods; frosting.
— **icing on the cake** pleasure or benefit beyond what is expected.

i·con (EYE·con) *n.* **1** an image or figure, as a picture symbol shown on a video display representing a task to be performed by the computer. **2** in the Orthodox Eastern Church, a sacred painting or mosaic.

i·cy (EYE·see) *adj.* **i·ci·er, -i·est** **1** of, covered with, or like ice: *an icy road.* **2** cold: *an icy reception, stare, wind.* — **i·ci·ly** *adv.;* **i·ci·ness** *n.*

I'd (IDE) I had; I should; I would.

i·de·a (eye·DEE·uh) *n.* **1** a mental image, thought, or meaning; concept: *Words express ideas; This was not my idea of a picnic; She has hit upon a new idea; to communicate, disseminate ideas; to dismiss, endorse, entertain, favour, implement, reject an idea; to toy with an idea; a brilliant, clear, clever, crazy, daring, fixed, fantastic, far-fetched, fresh, ingenious, novel, rough, silly, vague idea; not the faintest* or *slightest idea what he means; Do you get the idea* (= understand)? **2** plan or scheme: *What's the big idea? a man of* **ideas** (= resourcefulness).

i·de·al (eye·DEE·ul, eye·DEEL) *n.* **1** a perfect type: *the ideal school.* **2** a goal to achieve: *a woman of high, lofty, noble ideals; to attain* or *realize an ideal.*
— *adj.* **1** perfect: *This is ideal weather for a picnic.* **2** abstract or imaginary: *A geometrical point is a purely ideal concept.* — **i·de·al·ly** *adv.*

i·de·al·ism (eye·DEE·ul·iz·um, eye·DEE·liz·um) *n.* **1** thought or behaviour based on how things ought to be rather than how they are in reality; hence, the neglecting of practical matters. **2** in art, literature, etc., representation of imagined types rather than of exact likenesses. — **i·de·al·ist** *n.*
— **i·de·al·is·tic** (-uh·LIS·tic) *adj.*
— **i·de·al·is·ti·cal·ly** *adv.*

i·de·al·ize (eye·DEE·uh·lize, eye·DEEL·ize) *v.* **-iz·es, -ized, -iz·ing** form an ideal; think of as ideal: *an idealized vision of reality.*
— **i·de·al·i·za·tion** (-luh·ZAY·shun) *n.*

i·den·ti·cal (eye·DEN·tuh·cul) *adj.* exactly alike: *the identical voice I heard yesterday; two men wearing identical ties; One tie is identical to* or *with the other; Unlike fraternal twins,* **identical twins** *develop from the same egg cell.*

i·den·ti·fy (eye·DEN·tuh·fye) *v.* **-fies, -fied, -fy·ing** **1** know or establish the identity of a person or thing; recognize: *Can you identify that voice? A voice can be*

identified by the speaker's accent; We can identify two main issues in this campaign. **2** associate: *He's reluctant to identify (himself) with the radicals.* **3** sympathize: *a dramatic character with whom the audience identifies.*
— **i·den·ti·fi·a·ble** (-FYE·uh·bul) *adj.*
— **i·den·ti·fi·ca·tion** (-fuh·CAY·shun) *n.*

i·den·ti·ty (eye·DEN·tuh·tee) *n.* **-ties 1** sameness: *We work together because of identity of interests.* **2** who somebody or what something is: *to establish the identity of an anonymous caller; a case of mistaken identity; A mask hides your identity; Come out and reveal your identity; Show your **identity card** as proof of your name and age; an adolescent suffering an **identity crisis** because of internal changes and social pressures.* **3** individuality: *Multiculturalism gives people of various origins a sense of identity; cultural identity.*

id·i·om (ID·ee·um) *n.* **1** a particular language or dialect with its distinctive characteristics: *Shakespeare wrote in the idiom of the Elizabethans.* **2** an expression that is peculiar to a particular language: *"Get one's goat" is an idiom that is hard to translate into another language.* **3** an individualistic style: *the Shakespearean idiom.*
— **id·i·o·mat·ic** (-uh·MAT·ic) *adj.*

id·i·o·syn·cra·sy (ID·ee·uh·SINK·ruh·see) *n.* **-sies** a peculiarity of style or behaviour, as a mannerism, a writer's style, or one's reaction to a drug.
— **id·i·o·syn·crat·ic** (-sing·CRAT·ic) *adj.*

id·i·ot (ID·ee·ut) *n.* a very stupid person: *a blithering, blooming, perfect idiot; the village idiot; You stupid idiot!*— **id·i·ot·ic** (-ee·OT·ic) *adj.;* **id·i·ot·i·cal·ly** *adv.*

idiot box *n. Slang.* a television set.

idiot card *n. Slang.* a cue card for prompting a performer.

i·dle (EYE·dul) *adj.* **i·dler, i·dlest 1** not active: *Money lies idle if not invested; Machinery stands idle during a strike; an idle but not lazy worker who happens to be on strike; an idle mind.* **2** lazy: *the idle rich; "Idle folks have the most labour."* **3** useless or worthless: *idle conversations, curiosity, gossip, pleasures, rumours, threats; It's idle to deny that the earth is round.*
— *v.* **i·dles, i·dled, i·dling:** *to idle away* (= waste) *a summer; workers idled by layoffs; An automobile left idling* (= with the engine running but not engaged) *wastes gas.* — **i·dler** *n.* — **i·dle·ness** *n.* — **i·dly** *adv.*

i·dol (EYE·dul) *n.* **1** an object of worship, esp. a statue; hence, a false god: *the worship of idols.* **2** an object of ardent admiration: *a fallen idol; matinee idol; movie idols.*

i·dol·ize (EYE·duh·lize) *v.* **-iz·es, -ized, -iz·ing** regard or treat as an idol: *She was idolized as the incarnation of beauty; Mammon is wealth idolized.*

i·dyll or **i·dyl** (EYE·dul) *n.* a simple, charming, and picturesque, hence, usually rural scene or description: *the idylls of Theocritus; Tennyson's "Idylls of the King" are stories about King Arthur.*

i·dyl·lic (eye·DIL·ic) *adj.* full of beauty and peace: *an idyllic existence without cares and worries; in the idyllic surroundings of a country home.*

if *conj.* **1** in case: *You'll get wet if it rains; I wouldn't do it if I were you; Please attend, if at all possible.*

2 whether: *Ask if she will come.* **3** granting or allowing; even: *It will cost only $10, if that; Few, if any, lives were lost; I don't believe in UFOs because they are, if **anything**, illusions.* **4** though: *a welcome if unexpected change; **as if** I didn't know.*
— *n.* condition: *It's a big if whether nuclear arms will be eliminated; Your money will be refunded with no **ifs, ands, or buts.***

if·fy (IF·ee) *adj.* **if·fi·er, if·fi·est** *Informal.* uncertain or chancy: *The outcome is iffy.*

ig·loo (IG·loo) *n.* **-loos** a dome-shaped Inuit dwelling made of blocks of compact snow: *An authentic piece of Inuit art or craft carries the "igloo tag."* Also **ig·lu.**

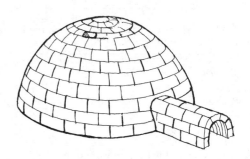

ig·nite (ig·NITE) *v.* **-nites, -nit·ed, -nit·ing** catch or set on fire. — **ig·nit·a·ble** (-tuh·bul) *adj.*

ig·ni·tion (ig·NISH·un) *n.* **1** an igniting. **2** an apparatus or device for igniting the fuel in an engine: *The car keys are in the ignition; to turn off, turn on the ignition; a rocket's ignition system.*

ig·no·ble (ig·NO·bul) *adj.* not noble; shameful: *an ignoble end.* — **ig·no·bly** *adv.*

ig·no·min·y (IG·nuh·min·ee) *n.* **-min·ies 1** disgrace or humiliation: *the ignominy of defeat.* **2** a disgraceful action, quality, or outcome: *He was subjected to many ignominies as a war prisoner.*
— **ig·no·min·i·ous** (-MIN·ee·us) *adj.*
— **ig·no·min·i·ous·ly** *adv.*

ig·no·ra·mus (ig·nuh·RAY·mus) *n.* **-mus·es** an ignorant person.

ig·no·rance (IG·nuh·runce) *n.* the state of being ignorant: *abysmal, blissful, profound, total ignorance of or about the facts; to act in ignorance of the facts; to betray, display, show ignorance.*

ig·no·rant (IG·nuh·runt) *adj.* **1** lacking knowledge or education: *an ignorant answer, rustic.* **2** unaware: *He was ignorant of what went on behind his back.*
— **ig·no·rant·ly** *adv.*

ig·nore (ig·NOR) *v.* **-nores, -nored, -nor·ing** pay no attention to a person or thing: *to ignore an insult; Facts cannot be ignored; He felt ignored by the others.*

i·kon (EYE·con) *n.* a sacred painting or mosaic; icon.

ilk *n.* kind or class: *people **of that** or **her** or **his** or **their** ilk.*

I'll (ILE) I will; I shall.

ill *adj. & adv. comp.* **worse** (WURSE), *superl.* **worst**

(WURST).
— **adj. 1** bad: *to stir up ill feeling among friends; He bore no one ill will; The place has fallen into ill repute.* **2** sick: *He's ill with the flu; She's fallen ill too; Everyone is taken ill and has gone home; Some are desperately, gravely, seriously, terminally ill; All are physically ill; No one is emotionally or mentally ill; Lu is a little nervous and* **ill at ease** (= uncomfortable) *in company.*
— **adv.** badly: *He never speaks ill of his neighbours; She fared ill at the examination; He was generous when he could ill* (= scarcely) *afford to be.*
— **n.** something bad, esp. sickness or evil: *the ills of our mortal existence, of our society.*
— **combining form. 1** badly: *ill-conceived, ill-considered, ill-defined, ill-equipped, ill-fitting, ill-founded, ill-informed, ill-prepared, ill-suited, ill-timed, ill-trained, ill-treat.* **2** bad: *ill-health, ill-treatment, ill-wisher.*

ill-advised (ILL·ud·VIZED) *adj.* acting or done without good advice or proper consideration: *You would be ill-advised to call in sick when you want to go out shopping.* — **ill-advisedly** *adv.*

ill-bred *adj.* badly brought up; rude: *an ill-bred cad.*

ill-disposed (ILL·dis·POZED) *adj.* unsympathetic: *We are ill-disposed to listen to complaints on a Monday morning; People are ill-disposed toward chronic complainers.*

il·le·gal (i·LEE·gul) *adj.* against the law, esp. not permitted by the rules: *It is illegal to go through a red light; If you specify Drive 3 with only two online, that's illegal; an illegal move in chess; illegal possession of firearms; an illegal alien, immigrant.*
— **n.** one who enters a country illegally.
— **il·le·gal·ly** *adv.*

il·le·gal·i·ty (il·ee·GAL·uh·tee) *n.* **-ties 1** unlawfulness. **2** an illegal act.

il·le·git·i·mate (il·uh·JIT·uh·mit) *adj.* **1** born of parents not married to each other: *an illegitimate child, son.* **2** contrary to law, custom, or logic: *an illegitimate claim to property; an illegitimate conclusion, expression, use of funds.* — **il·le·git·i·mate·ly** *adv.*
— **il·le·git·i·ma·cy** (-uh·muh·see) *n.*

ill-fated (IL·FAY·tid) *adj.* with an evil fate; unlucky: *the ill-fated voyage of the Titanic.*

ill-gotten (IL·GOT·un) *adj.* obtained by evil means: *ill-gotten gains, goods, wealth.*

il·lic·it (i·LIS·it) *adj.* not allowed by law or by the rules: *an illicit act, love affair, relationship; illicit sale of drugs; illicit trade.*

il·lit·er·ate (i·LIT·ur·it) *adj.* **1** uneducated, esp. not knowing how to read or write. **2** lacking basic knowledge in one's field of study.
— **n.** an illiterate person: *a functional illiterate who can't fill out an application for a job.*
— **il·lit·er·a·cy** (-ur·uh·see) *n.* **-cies.**

ill-mannered (IL·MAN·urd) *adj.* having bad manners; rude.

ill-natured (IL·NAY·churd) *adj.* of a mean disposition; disagreeable. — **ill-naturedly** *adv.*

ill·ness *n.* sickness: *to get over a slight illness; a grave,*

mental, serious, sudden, terminal illness.

il·log·i·cal (i·LOJ·uh·cul) *adj.* not logical or sensible.
— **il·log·i·cal·ly** *adv.*
— **il·log·i·cal·i·ty** (-uh·CAL·uh·tee) *n.* **-ties.**

ill-tempered (IL·TEM·purd) *adj.* having a bad temper; irritable.

il·lu·mi·nate (i·LOO·muh·nate) *v.* **-nates, -nat·ed, -nat·ing 1** supply with light: *Gas lamps used to illuminate our streets; a neighbourhood illuminated* (= decorated) *by Christmas lights.* **2** make clear or explain: *to illuminate an obscure passage; a very* **illuminating** *discussion.* **3** decorate initial letters, borders, etc. of a manuscript with colours and designs, as in the Middle Ages. Also **il·lu·mine** (i·LOO·min), **-mines, -mined, -min·ing.**
— **il·lu·mi·na·tion** (-NAY·shun) *n.*

il·lu·sion (i·LOO·zhun) *n.* a misleading effect produced on the eye or mind: *the illusion of movement produced by a series of still pictures; an optical illusion; He was under the illusion* (= false belief) *that wealth would make him happy; to cherish, create, dispel, harbour an illusion.*

il·lu·so·ry (i·LOO·suh·ree) *adj.* based on or due to an illusion; deceptive: *illusory hopes; an illusory peace.*

il·lus·trate (IL·us·trate) *v.* **-trates, -trat·ed, -trat·ing 1** provide with pictures, diagrams, etc.: *to illustrate a book, lecture; We illustrate word meanings with examples of usage.* **2** make clear or lucid: *Falling objects illustrate gravity.* — **il·lus·tra·tor** (-tray·tur) *n.*

il·lus·tra·tion (il·us·TRAY·shun) *n.* an example or picture that illustrates: *Meanings are explained in this dictionary by illustration in context more than by definitions; verbal, not pictorial illustrations; to give, offer, provide an illustration; to draw an illustration* (= analogy).

il·lus·tra·tive (i·LUS·truh·tiv, IL·us·tray·tiv) *adj.* serving to illustrate: *an illustrative example; sentences that are illustrative of word meanings.*

il·lus·tri·ous (i·LUS·tree·us) *adj.* brilliantly eminent or distinguished: *our illustrious predecessors; an illustrious career, family, name.*

I'm (IME) I am.

im·age (IM·ij) *n.* **1** a graphic, optical, or electronic representation of a scene or object, as in a mirror, photograph, on TV, etc.: *a mirror image; a visual image; an image reflected in water.* **2** likeness: *the very image of her father; a spitting image of her mother; "God created man in his own image."* **3** a physical representation, as a statue or idol: *the worship of images.* **4** a mental picture or concept: *the ivory-tower image of bankers; the corporate image of our company projected through the media; They hired a public-relations firm to improve their public image; an image they didn't want to promote.* **5** the expression of a mental concept, esp. a simile or metaphor: *drama as the image of life; the images of death in Shakespeare's plays.*
— **v. -ages, -aged, -ag·ing 1** form an image of an object: *a bust of the premier imaged in bronze; a slide that images sharply on the screen.* **2** imagine: *a scene hard to image, given so few details.*

im·age·ry (IM·ij·ree) *n.* mental images or their figurative expression, as in poetry: *poetry full of vivid imagery.*

i·mag·i·na·ble (i·MAJ·uh·nuh·bul) *adj.* capable of being visualized: *the worst imaginable scenario of a tragedy; the most beautiful sight imaginable.*
— **i·mag·i·na·bly** *adv.*

i·mag·i·nar·y (i·MAJ·uh·nair·ee) *adj.* not real but imagined: *UFOs may not be entirely imaginary; Many of our fears are imaginary; the imaginary square root of a negative quantity.*

i·mag·i·na·tion (i·maj·uh·NAY·shun) *n.* the power to imagine: *the fertile imagination of storytellers; to defy, excite, fire, stagger, stir someone's imagination; to use one's imagination; Try to see it in your imagination; an active, creative, feeble, lively, wild imagination; By no stretch of the imagination could such a thing happen; A resourceful executive has imagination and judgment; Your ghost story sounds like mere imagination* (= use of imagining power or an imagined object) *to me.*

i·mag·i·na·tive (i·MAJ·uh·nuh·tiv) *adj.* **1** able to picture things or form new ideas: *an imaginative child; Ida is imaginative but Peg is more practical.* **2** having to do with the imagination: *an imaginative answer; imaginative literature.*

i·mag·ine (i·MAJ·in) *v.* **-ines, -ined, -in·ing 1** form an image of something: *Imagine yourself flying like a bird.* **2** think or conceive of something: *Can you imagine someone living without TV for a whole year? I can imagine her becoming* or *as our next prime minister; I imagine* (= suppose) *that's what she wants to be.*

im·bal·ance (im·BAL·unce) *n.* lack of balance or proportion, as between two aspects of the same thing: *to correct the imbalance between our earning power and our spending habits; affirmative action to redress the imbalance in our hiring policies.*

im·be·cile (IM·buh·sul) *n.* one who is very foolish or stupid. — **im·be·cil·ic** (-SIL·ic) *adj.*
— **im·be·cil·i·ty** (-SIL·uh·tee) *n.*

im·bibe (im·BIBE) *v.* **-bibes, -bibed, -bib·ing 1** to drink, esp. alcoholic liquor. **2** absorb an atmosphere, ideas, principles, etc.: *You go to Paris to imbibe the true French spirit.*

im·bue (im·BEW) *v.* **-bues, -bued, -bu·ing** soak or permeate; hence, inspire: *to be imbued with an idea, principle, spirit.*

im·i·tate (IM·uh·tate) *v.* **-tates, -tat·ed, -tat·ing** be, look, or act like another person or thing: *a successful novelist as a model for aspiring writers to imitate* (= emulate); *Do not imitate* (= mimic) *people as an ape or parrot does; She can imitate* (= reproduce) *any bird call; wallpaper imitating* (= resembling) *wood panelling.*
— **im·i·ta·tor** *n.*

im·i·ta·tion (im·uh·TAY·shun) *n.* an act of imitating or something that is a copy: *art as the imitation of life; "Imitation is the sincerest form of flattery"; Beware of cheap imitations; This is a pale imitation* (= poor copy) *of the original painting; He can do imitations* (= impressions) *of just about anyone; verses composed* **in imitation of** *a poet's style.*
— *adj.* fake: *an imitation diamond; imitation leather.*
— **im·i·ta·tive** (-tay·tiv) *adj.;* **im·i·ta·tive·ly** *adv.*

im·mac·u·late (i·MAC·yuh·lit) *adj.* perfect or flawless: *a house in immaculate condition; an immaculate copy of the original painting; She left everything in immaculate order; the Immaculate Virgin Mary (conceived without original sin).* — **im·mac·u·late·ly** *adv.*

im·ma·te·ri·al (im·uh·TEER·ee·ul) *adj.* **1** unimportant: *It's wholly immaterial how you get here provided you're on time.* **2** not material but spiritual.

im·me·di·a·cy (i·MEE·dee·uh·see) *n.* **-cies** direct relevance to the present time, place, etc.: *a question that lacks immediacy and urgency; a sense of immediacy and excitement; the immediacies* (= urgent needs) *of life.*

im·me·di·ate (i·MEE·dee·ut) *adj.* with nothing coming between: *an immediate reply (without any delay); our immediate* (= next-door) *neighbour on the right; the immediate* (= near), *not remote cause of the death; one's immediate family* (= parents, children, and siblings).
— **im·me·di·ate·ly** *adv.*

im·me·mo·ri·al (i·muh·MOR·ee·ul) *adj.* going back beyond memory: *an immemorial* (= ancient) *custom; a custom that has come down to us* **from time immemorial.**

im·mense (i·MENCE) *adj.* **1** so large as to seem difficult to measure: *an immense amount of wealth; an immense difference; immense rocks of immense size; immense gains, importance, waste.* **2** *Informal.* splendid; very good: *an immense poem.*
— **im·mense·ly** *adv.* — **im·men·si·ty** (-suh·tee) *n.*

im·merse (i·MURSE) *v.* **im·mers·es, im·mersed, im·mers·ing 1** lower into a liquid so as to be covered by it: *To learn to swim, you've to be able to immerse yourself in water; Keep your head immersed.* **2** involve deeply: *He's deeply immersed in his homework; She sat immersed in thought.*

im·mer·sion (i·MUR·zhun) *n.* a dipping in: *baptism by immersion; total immersion in a language;* **adj.:** *an* **immersion program** *of language teaching (with the students using the language all the time and for all subjects); an immersion school; the electric coil of an* **immersion heater** *for liquids.*

im·mi·grant (IM·uh·grunt) *n.* **1** a nonnative admitted to a country to settle in it: *an immigrant from Ethiopia; an immigrant to this country; an illegal immigrant without a work permit; a landed immigrant (accepted as a permanent resident of Canada); hardworking immigrants;* **adj.:** *immigrant labour; a native-born Canadian of immigrant parents; an immigrant visa.* **2** a new plant or animal observed in a region: *an immigrant bird.*

im·mi·grate (IM·uh·grate) *v.* **-grates, -grat·ed, -grat·ing** come into a country to live in it: *Recent settlers have immigrated to Canada from various parts of the world, but the native peoples migrated here from Asia in prehistoric times.* — **im·mi·gra·tion** (-GRAY·shun) *n.*

im·mi·nent (IM·uh·nunt) *adj.* likely or about to happen soon without further warning: *A storm is imminent when black clouds gather; the imminent danger of an explosion.* — **im·mi·nence** *n.*

im·mod·est (i·MOD·ist) *adj.* **1** bold, not modest: *an immodest costume.* **2** indecent: *immodest behaviour.*

— **im·mod·es·ty** (-is·tee) n.

im·mo·late (IM·uh·late) v. -lates, -lat·ed, -lat·ing kill as a sacrifice: *The Buddhist monk immolated himself in a fire.* — **im·mo·la·tion** (-LAY·shun) n.

im·mo·ral (i·MOR·ul) adj. morally wrong, esp. in sexual matters. — **im·mor·al·ly** adv.

im·mo·ral·i·ty (im·uh·RAL·uh·tee) n. -ties 1 vice. 2 an immoral act or practice.

im·mor·tal (i·MOR·tul) adj. everlasting, not subject to death: *our immortal soul; Madame Curie's immortal fame as a physicist.*
— **n.** a very famous person: *the immortals of the Greek and Roman pantheon; the 40 immortals* (= members) *of the French Academy.*
— **im·mor·tal·i·ty** (im·or·TAL·uh·tee) n.

im·mor·tal·ize (i·MOR·tul·ize) v. -iz·es, -ized, -iz·ing make immortal: *Shakespeare has been immortalized by his plays.*

im·mov·a·ble (i·MOO·vuh·bul) adj. that cannot be moved; hence, unyielding: *steadfast and immovable in purpose; land, trees, buildings and such* **immovables.**
— **im·mov·a·bly** adv.
— **im·mov·a·bil·i·ty** (-BIL·uh·tee) n.

im·mune (IM·yoon) adj. free or protected from something disagreeable to which one is normally liable: *To be immune from error is humanly impossible; a world made immune from smallpox; immune against attacks; immune to measles, polio, etc.; the body's immune defence system; TV viewers made immune* (= insensitive) *to violence; The* **immune response** *or* **reaction** *causes rejection of foreign tissue.*

im·mu·ni·ty (i·MEW·nuh·tee) n. the state or condition of being immune: *An infant is born with passive immunity against* or *to certain diseases; an acquired, active, developed, natural immunity; Diplomats are protected by diplomatic immunity from being charged for offences.*

im·mu·nize (IM·yuh·nize) v. -niz·es, -nized, -niz·ing make immune, as by giving injections: *to immunize a traveller against typhoid.*
— **im·mu·ni·za·tion** (-nuh·ZAY·shun) n.

imp n. 1 a young demon. 2 a mischievous child.

im·pact n. 1 a striking together; collision: *a steering column designed to collapse on impact (during a collision); an impact crater made by a meteorite hitting the earth.* 2 an influence for change; effect: *TV has considerable impact on* or *upon our culture; The family breakup had a strong emotional impact on the children.*
— **v.** 1 pack in: *refugees impacted into slums; An* **impacted** *wisdom tooth (pressed against another tooth) is taken out because it cannot break through the gum.* 2 have an effect on something: *Laser printers have impacted (on) the publishing business considerably.*

im·pair (im·PAIR) v. harm or lessen the quality, value, strength, etc. of something: *Drugs could impair your health.*
— **impaired** adj. 1 Cdn. with one's faculties weakened by alcohol: *an impaired driver; a charge of impaired driving.* 2 handicapped: *hearing impaired (people); the visually impaired.* — **im·pair·ment** n.

im·pan·el (im·PAN·ul) v. -els, -elled or -eled, -el·ling or -el·ing 1 put a person on a list for jury duty. 2 select a jury.

im·part (im·PART) v. give, esp. by sharing: *the imparting of knowledge to pupils; stage lighting designed to impart an air of mystery to the scene; Spices impart flavours to foods.*

im·par·tial (im·PAR·shul) adj. not partial to any side; fair or unbiassed: *an impartial judge.*
— **im·par·tial·ly** adv.
— **im·par·ti·al·i·ty** (-shee·AL·uh·tee) n. -ties.

im·pass·a·ble (im·PASS·uh·bul) adj. that cannot be travelled over or through: *an impassable road; a mountain pass made impassable by snow and ice.*

im·passe (IM·pass) n. -pass·es a deadlock, like a passage closed at one end: *The talks are at* or *have reached an impasse; To break the impasse, one party has to yield a little.*

im·pas·sioned (im·PASH·und) adj. full of feeling: *an impassioned appeal, plea, speech.*

im·pas·sive (im·PASS·iv) adj. not showing emotion: *a face impassive in suffering.*

im·pa·tience (im·PAY·shunce) n. 1 lack of patience: *His impatience with the screaming child didn't help much.* 2 eager restlessness: *In his impatience to drive away, he forgot to release the brake.*

im·pa·tient (im·PAY·shunt) adj. lacking patience: *a sales clerk who is impatient with customers; Pupils grow impatient for the class to be dismissed; a man in a hurry, always impatient of the least delay.*
— **im·pa·tient·ly** adv.

im·peach (im·PEECH) v. 1 charge a public official such as a judge, senator, or president with misbehaviour: *President Nixon was about to be impeached for the Watergate coverup.* 2 question or discredit: *to impeach a person's honour or motives.*
— **im·peach·a·ble** (-uh·bul) adj.; **im·peach·ment** n.

im·pec·ca·ble (im·PECK·uh·bul) adj. without error or flaw: *her impeccable taste.* — **im·pec·ca·bly** adv.

im·pede (im·PEED) v. -pedes, -ped·ed, -ped·ing slow up the movement or progress of someone or something by getting in the way.

im·ped·i·ment (im·PED·uh·munt) n. a hindrance or obstruction: *an impediment to growth, marriage, progress; a speech impediment* (= defect) *such as stuttering or stammering.*

im·ped·i·men·ta (im·PED·uh·MEN·tuh) n.pl. baggage, supplies, and such encumbrances, as of an army on the march: *Cameras, binoculars, maps, and other impedimenta of espionage.*

im·pel (im·PEL) v. -pels, -pelled, -pel·ling urge or drive forward, as by a strong desire: *Duty to society impelled Al to help the police; It impelled him into reporting the hit-and-run driver.*

im·pend (im·PEND) v. be about to happen, as if dropping from a suspended state: *the* **impending** *crisis, examinations, trial.*

im·pen·e·tra·ble (im·PEN·uh·truh·bul) *adj.* **1** that cannot be penetrated or understood: *an impenetrable jungle, metal, mystery.* **2** not receptive to influences: *an impenetrable mind.* — **im·pen·e·tra·bly** *adv.* — **im·pen·e·tra·bil·i·ty** (-BIL·uh·tee) *n.*

im·per·a·tive (im·PER·uh·tiv) *adj.* **1** having the nature of a command: *"Stop!" is in the **imperative mood**.* **2** that must be done: *It is imperative that we set out at once.* — *n.* something commanded: *Food and fresh air are physiological imperatives* (= necessities); *English imperatives* (= sentences in the imperative mood) *usually have no expressed subject, as in "Go home!"*

im·per·cep·ti·ble (im·pur·SEP·tuh·bul) *adj.* not easily perceived: *The difference in texture is imperceptible to the touch; Growth occurs by imperceptible* (= slow) *degrees.* — **im·per·cep·ti·bly** *adv.*

im·per·fect (im·PUR·fict) *adj.* not perfect; defective: *imperfect knowledge, understanding.*

im·per·fec·tion (im·pur·FEC·shun) *n.* lack of perfection; deficiency or fault: *Gems with slight imperfections are sold at reduced prices.*

im·pe·ri·al (im·PEER·ee·ul) *adj.* **1** of an empire, emperor, or empress: *Her Imperial Majesty; an imperial guard, power; the imperial gallon; the imperial system of measurement.* **2** having or showing authority, majesty, or superior quality: *to live in imperial grandeur; the imperial presidency.*

im·per·il (im·PER·ul) *v.* **-ils, -illed** or **-iled, -il·ling** or **-il·ing** endanger or jeopardize.

im·pe·ri·ous (im·PEER·ee·us) *adj.* **1** overbearing or domineering: *an imperious aristocrat, face, gesture, look, manner, person, voice.* **2** imperative or urgent: *an imperious command, demand, need.*

im·per·ish·a·ble (im·PER·ish·uh·bul) *adj.* enduring or indestructible: *a statue cast in imperishable bronze.* — **im·per·ish·a·bly** *adv.*

im·per·son·al (im·PUR·suh·nul) *adj.* **1** without reference to any person: *an impersonal directive, suggestion.* **2** having no personal feeling: *an impersonal force (as of the elements).*

im·per·son·ate (im·PUR·suh·nate) *v.* **-ates, -at·ed, -at·ing** play the part of or pretend to be someone: *an actor impersonating a lunatic; charged with impersonating a police officer.* — **im·per·son·a·tor** (-nay·tur) *n.* — **im·per·son·a·tion** (-NAY·shun) *n.*

im·per·ti·nent (im·PUR·tuh·nunt) *adj.* **1** not showing due respect, esp. by interfering in another's business: *an impertinent child, intrusion.* **2** not relevant. — **im·per·ti·nence** *n.*

im·per·vi·ous (im·PUR·vee·us) *adj.* **1** not capable of being passed through: *cloth that is impervious to moisture.* **2** not affected by something: *one who is impervious to criticism, pity, reason.*

im·pet·u·ous (im·PECH·oo·us) *adj.* **1** marked by impulsive force: *impetuous speed, torrents.* **2** rash, not thoughtful: *an impetuous nature, outburst.* — **im·pet·u·ous·ly** *adv.* — **im·pet·u·os·i·ty** (-oo·OS·uh·tee) *n.*

im·pe·tus (IM·puh·tus) *n.* a driving force or impulse: *A rock rolls downhill under the impetus acquired from gravity; a new agreement to give a fresh impetus to trade.*

im·pi·e·ty (im·PYE·uh·tee) *n.* **-ties 1** lack of reverence. **2** an impious act.

im·pinge (im·PINJ) *v.* **-ping·es, -pinged, -ping·ing 1** make an impact: *Billiard balls impinge on one another; where a ray of light impinges on a surface.* **2** encroach: *measures that impinge on* or *upon individual rights.* — **im·pinge·ment** *n.*

im·pi·ous (IM·pee·us, im·PYE·us) *adj.* irreverent or profane.

imp·ish *adj.* of an imp; mischievous: *an impish grin; the impish suggestion to echo Kennedy's famous Berlin speech and declare in Frankfurt, "I am a Frankfurter."*

im·plac·a·ble (im·PLAC·uh·bul, -PLAY·cuh·bul) *adj.* that cannot be appeased: *an implacable enemy, foe, hatred.* — **im·plac·a·bly** *adv.* — **im·plac·a·bil·i·ty** (-BIL·uh·tee) *n.*

im·plant (im·PLANT) *v.* plant or fix firmly, as in the mind: *high ideals implanted in children.* — *n.* (IM·plant) something implanted in living tissue: *When a transplant is not possible, an artificial heart implant may be the answer; a breast implant following surgical removal of the breast; dental implants (of false teeth).*

im·ple·ment (IM·pluh·munt) *n.* a tool or device used in some activity: *The plough and shovel are farm implements; A sword, gun, etc. are implements of war.* — *v.* (-ment) to effect or carry out: *to implement a decision, order, plan, reform.* — **im·ple·men·ta·tion** (-mun·TAY·shun) *n.*

im·pli·cate (IM·pluh·cate) *v.* **-cates, -cat·ed, -cat·ing** show someone to have a role, usually in something bad: *a confession implicating others in the robbery; He was implicated but not directly involved in the fraud.*

im·pli·ca·tion (im·pluh·CAY·shun) *n.* an implicating or something inferred: *the implications of being fired rather than resigning.*

im·plic·it (im·PLIS·it) *adj.* **1** implied or suggested, not expressed: *an implicit permission; obligations implicit in the contract.* **2** unhesitating; absolute: *implicit faith; Some parents expect implicit obedience from their children.*

im·plode (im·PLODE) *v.* **-plodes, -plod·ed, -plod·ing** burst inward, as when a vacuum tube breaks: *stars that implode; McLuhan wrote about the imploding* (= contracting) *energies of the modern world.* — **im·plo·sion** (im·PLOH·zhun) *n.*

im·plore (im·PLORE) *v.* **-plores, -plored, -plor·ing** beg someone earnestly, as if in distress, *to* do or avoid something. — **im·plor·ing·ly** *adv.*

im·ply (im·PLY) *v.* **-plies, -plied, -ply·ing 1** hint at or suggest without saying: *His smile seemed to imply agreement; to imply that he had no objection.* **2** signify or suggest as a logical consequence without being expressed in words: *Rights imply duties; an **implied***

warranty such as that a seller has the right to sell the goods, that what is sold is basically suitable for the intended purpose, etc.

im·port (im·PORT) *v.* 1 bring in, as merchandise, from a foreign country: *goods imported from abroad; goods imported into Canada.* 2 mean or signify: *What does that remark import?*
— *n.* (IM·port) 1 something brought in from an external source: *Balance of trade depends on imports and exports.* 2 *Cdn.* an imported professional hockey or football player. 3 signification; also, significance or importance: *the full import of his words; matters of great import; international, sociological import.*

im·por·tance (im·POR·tunce) *n.* the quality of being important; significance: *Conservation is a subject of vital importance to* or *for the human race; great, historic, paramount, some, utmost importance; to acquire, assume importance; to attach* or *attribute importance to something.*

im·por·tant (im·POR·tunt) *adj.* 1 meaning much; of significant quality or value: *an important announcement; VIPs are very important people; Is a fancy car important to one's social status? not important for me; What's important is to do good and avoid evil; It's most important that everyone be happy.*
2 pretentious: *The mayor looks very important in her robe.*
— **im·por·tant·ly** *adv.:* *"More importantly" is not as elegant a phrase as "What is more important."*

im·por·tu·nate (im·POR·chuh·nit) *adj.* persistent in asking: *an importunate beggar, petitioner; an importunate* (= pressing) *demand.*

im·por·tune (im·por·TUNE) *v.* **-tunes, -tuned, -tun·ing** ask someone repeatedly and annoyingly *to* do something. — **im·por·tu·ni·ty** (-TUE·nuh·tee) *n.* **-ties.**

im·pose (im·POZE) *v.* **-pos·es, -posed, -pos·ing** 1 to place as a burden *on* or *upon* someone: *A fine is imposed on delinquents.* 2 take advantage of someone: *Uninvited guests impose themselves on their hosts; Sorry to impose on your generosity.*
— **im·po·si·tion** (im·puh·ZISH·un) *n.*

imposing (im·POH·zing) *adj.* impressive because of size, excellence, or appearance: *an imposing building, display, personality.*

im·pos·si·ble (im·POS·uh·bul) *adj.* that cannot be; not possible to be done, to be true, to tolerate, etc.: *It's impossible to please everyone; It's physically impossible for me to be in two places at once; That's impossible* (= cannot be true)! *The ancients thought it practically impossible to fly; almost, virtually, well-nigh impossible; an impossible* (= difficult) *situation, student, task.*
— *n.:* *to attempt the impossible; The astronauts did the impossible by landing on the moon.*
— **im·pos·si·bly** *adv.*
— **im·pos·si·bil·i·ty** (-BIL·uh·tee) *n.* **-ties.**

im·pos·tor (im·POS·tur) *n.* one who deceives or cheats others by pretending to be someone else; also **im·pos·ter.**

im·pos·ture (im·POS·chur) *n.* a fraud or deception.

im·po·tent (IM·puh·tunt) *adj.* 1 lacking power or strength: *a new defence system that would make* or *render nuclear weapons impotent and obsolete; The UN has proved impotent in preventing hundreds of regional wars since it was established; Humans are impotent against the forces of nature; grinding his teeth in impotent fury.* 2 esp. of males, unable to complete the sexual act. — **im·po·tence** or **im·po·ten·cy** *n.*

im·pound (im·POUND) *v.* 1 put in a pound, as a stray animal or towed vehicle. 2 seize and hold evidence in legal custody. 3 collect and confine in a reservoir: *water impounded behind dams.*

im·pov·er·ish (im·POV·ur·ish) *v.* deprive of the essentials of a healthy existence: *the impoverished nations of the Fourth World; an **impoverished** land (without much plant or animal life or with its resources exhausted).*
— **im·pov·er·ish·ment** *n.*

im·prac·ti·ca·ble (im·PRAC·tuh·cuh·bul) *adj.* 1 not practicable or feasible; unrealistic: *an impracticable plan, policy, scheme, suggestion; It's impracticable to follow his advice.* 2 impossible to put to use: *an impracticable course, invention, path, road.*

im·prac·ti·cal (im·PRAC·tuh·cul) *adj.* not sensible or realistic: *an impractical planner; It's impractical to keep a limousine to go to the corner store.*
— **im·prac·ti·cal·i·ty** (-CAL·uh·tee) *n.*

im·preg·na·ble (im·PREG·nuh·bul) *adj.* 1 that cannot be overcome by force: *an impregnable fortress; an impregnable argument, belief.* 2 that can be impregnated. — **im·preg·na·bly** *adv.*

im·preg·nate (im·PREG·nate) *v.* **-nates, -nat·ed, -nat·ing** 1 make pregnant; fertilize ovum. 2 charge or fill: *The sea air is impregnated with salt; to impregnate wood with a preservative.*
— **im·preg·na·tion** (im·preg·NAY·shun) *n.*

im·press (im·PRES) *v.* 1 stamp or imprint: *a fossil impressed in rock.* 2 fix strongly on the mind or feelings: *He impressed us with his learning; He impresses us as a learned man; She impresses on everyone the urgency of her mission; Some children are not easily impressed; Everyone is deeply, favourably, greatly, highly, strongly **impressed.*** 3 force someone to serve in the armed forces: *people impressed into the military.* — **im·press·ment** *n.*
— **im·press·i·ble** (-uh·bul) *adj.*

im·pres·sion (im·PRESH·un) *n.* an act of impressing or a result of it: *a thumb impression; to create an impression; to make a favourable impression on* or *upon the judges; a deep, erroneous, false, lasting, pleasant, profound, strong, vivid impression; I was under the impression that I had lost the bid; a 20 000-copy impression* (= printing) *of a book; a comedian good at doing impressions* (= imitations) *of celebrities.*

im·pres·sion·a·ble (im·PRESH·un·uh·bul) *adj.* sensitive to influences: *the impressionable minds of children; Childhood is an impressionable period.*

im·pres·sive (im·PRES·iv) *adj.* making a strong, esp. favourable impression on the mind or feelings: *an impressive ceremony, sight, speaker.*
— **im·pres·sive·ly** *adv.;* **im·pres·sive·ness** *n.*

im·print (im·PRINT) *v.* mark by pressure; impress: *an unforgettable experience forever imprinted on our*

minds; *A newborn animal may become permanently imprinted* (= attached) *to* or *on* or *by the parent, handler, etc. whom it first recognizes.*
— **n.** (IM·print) 1 something imprinted: *the imprint left by feet on wet cement; a great teacher who left her imprint* (= distinctive mark) *on a whole generation of students; Her writings bear the imprint of genius; the imprint* (= lasting effect) *of years of suffering on his face.* 2 the publisher's name and the place and date of publication printed in a book, usually at the foot of the title page.

im·pris·on (im·PRIZ·un) *v.* put in prison; hence, confine.

im·prob·a·ble (im·PROB·uh·bul) *adj.* not probable; unlikely: *a highly improbable story;* **im·prob·a·bly** *adv.* — **im·prob·a·bil·i·ty** (-BIL·uh·tee) *n.*

im·promp·tu (im·PROMP·tyoo, -choo) *adj. & adv.* done on the spur of the moment: *an impromptu concert, guided tour, press conference.*

im·prop·er (im·PROP·ur) *adj.* not suitable, correct, in good taste, etc.: *Is it improper to cast your ballot in your own favour?* — **im·prop·er·ly** *adv.*

im·pro·pri·e·ty (im·prop·RYE·uh·tee) *n.* -ties 1 lack of propriety: *the crass impropriety of chewing gum in church.* 2 an improper act, remark, language use, etc.

im·prove (im·PROOV) *v.* -proves, -proved, -prov·ing make or become better: *The patient is improving; how to improve your chances; land improved* (= made more valuable) *by cultivation; It's not easy to* **improve on** or **upon** (= do better than) *nature.*
— **im·prov·a·ble** *adj.*

im·prove·ment (im·PROOV·munt) *n.* an improving or getting better; also, its result: *Your grades show an improvement; A "B" grade is an improvement on* or *over* (= is better than) *a "C"; You have brought about a marked improvement in your work; a decided, distinct, great, major, minor, substantial improvement; There is room for more improvement; home improvement (to make the house more useful or valuable).*

im·prov·i·dent (im·PROV·uh·dunt) *adj.* not providing for the future; thriftless: *his improvident habits, nature.*
— **im·prov·i·dent·ly** *adv.*
— **im·prov·i·dence** *n.*

im·pro·vise (IM·pruh·vize) *v.* -vis·es, -vised, -vis·ing make or do something without preparation or prepared material: *We had to spend the night in an improvised shelter; a pop singer who improvises as he sings; The actor improvised her lines.*
— **im·prov·vis·er** or **im·pro·vi·sor** *n.*
— **im·pro·vi·sa·tion** (IM·prov·uh·ZAY·shun) *n.*

im·pru·dent (im·PROO·dunt) *adj.* not prudent; rash or indiscreet. — **im·pru·dence** *n.*

im·pu·dent (IMP·yuh·dunt) *adj.* shamelessly rude or impertinent. — **im·pu·dent·ly** *adv.* — **im·pu·dence** *n.*

im·pugn (im·PYOON) *v.* attack a person's motives, character, action, or statement as false or worthless.

im·pulse (IM·pulse) *n.* 1 a sudden driving force or impetus; also, its effect: *He was acting on* or *under a mere impulse without any reflection; She felt an irresistible impulse to fly home; the impulse of curiosity,*

hunger; **impulse buying** *by shoppers (who decide to buy on the spur of the moment).* 2 stimulus: *an electrical impulse; nerve impulses.*

im·pul·sion (im·PUL·shun) *n.* an impelling or impelling force; impetus.

im·pul·sive (im·PUL·siv) *adj.* 1 impelling: *an impulsive force.* 2 done or acting on impulse: *an impulsive child, demand, retort.*

im·pu·ni·ty (im·PYOO·nuh·tee) *n.* freedom from punishment, injury, or other consequence: *One seldom breaks the law with impunity.*

im·pure (im·PYOOR) *adj.* not pure, clean, or chaste.

im·pur·i·ty (im·PYOOR·uh·tee) *n.* -ties
1 contamination. 2 foreign matter, as in food, water, air, etc.

im·pute (im·PYOOT) *v.* -putes, -put·ed, -put·ing charge or attribute: *She is not guilty of the crimes imputed to her; to examine actions without imputing motives.* — **im·pu·ta·tion** (imp·yuh·TAY·shun) *n.*

in *prep.* 1 enclosed by limits of space, time, etc.: *She's in the house; It happened in a minute; He's rolling in the snow; Go in* (= into) *the house.* 2 [indicating various relationships]: *green in colour; girl in a million; a degree in science; a party in his honour; to go in search of help; It's not in him* (= characteristic of him) *to say "No" to a request for help; He's a generous man* **in that** (= because) *he gives to charities.*
— **adv.**: *Come in, please; She isn't in; All latecomers are* **in for** (= going to have) *trouble today; Don't let everyone* **in on** (= make them acquainted with) *the secret; Tell only those who are* **in with** (= friends with) *us.*
— **adj.**: *The votes are in* (= have been received) *and counted; a train on the in* (= inside) *track; It is in* (*Informal for* fashionable) *to eat out; an in* (= private) *group, joke, word.*
— **n.**: *She has been here so long she knows all the* **ins and outs** *of the place; the ins* (= power group) *of a society; She could get you an in with* (*Informal for* introduction to) *her boss.*
— **combining form**: *in-depth study, in-service training; an in-crowd* (= clique); *drive-in, sit-in, stand-in, teach-in, wader-in.*
— **prefix.** 1 to or on the inside: *inbound, incoming, indoors, insight.* 2 lack of: *inability, inaccessible.* [Such compounds may be formed by prefixing "in" to many nouns, adjectives, and verbs. The spelling, meanings, pronunciation, and usages of such compounds remain the same as "in" plus the base word in each case. The entries that follow are the most frequently used or the ones that are distinctive in one respect or another.]

in ab·sen·ti·a (in·ub·SEN·shuh) *Latin.* in his, her, or their absence: *He was tried in absentia; a degree conferred in absentia* (= without the candidate being present).

in·ac·cu·ra·cy (in·AC·yuh·ruh·see) *n.* -cies lack of accuracy or an instance of it: *a glaring inaccuracy; the many inaccuracies in the report.*

in·ac·tion (in·AC·shun) *n.* absence of action: *government inaction on the issue.*

in·ad·e·quate (in·AD·uh·kwit) *adj.* not adequate; unable to cope with a situation: *supplies that are inadequate to meet the demand; He feels very inadequate in his job.*
— **in·ad·e·quate·ly** *adv.*
— **in·ad·e·qua·cy** (-kwuh·see) *n.* -cies.

in·ad·vert·ent (in·ud·VUR·tunt) *adj.* **1** inattentive. **2** unintentional.
— **in·ad·vert·ent·ly** *adv.: She inadvertently left the door unlocked.* — **in·ad·vert·ence** *n.*

in·al·ien·a·ble (in·AIL·yuh·nuh·bul) *adj.* that cannot be taken away, as basic or fundamental rights.
— **in·al·ien·a·bly** (-blee) *adv.*
— **in·al·ien·a·bil·i·ty** (-BIL·uh·tee) *n.*

in·ane (in·ANE) *adj.* -an·er, -an·est empty of meaning; also, silly: *an inane expression, remark, smile.*
— **in·an·i·ty** (in·AN·uh·tee) *n.* -ties.

in·ap·ti·tude (in·AP·tuh·tude) *n.* lack of aptitude or skill.

in·ap·pro·pri·ate (in·uh·PROH·pree·ate) *adj.* not appropriate: *a costume that is inappropriate to the occasion; inappropriate behaviour, remarks.*

in·apt (in·APT) *adj.* not apt or suitable: *an inapt companion, remark, term.*

in·ar·tic·u·late (in·ar·TIK·yuh·lit) *adj.* **1** unable to speak fluently and readily: *an inarticulate child.* **2** incoherent or irrational: *He burst into an inarticulate rage.*

in·as·much as (in·uz·MUCH·as) *conj.* to the extent that; since.

in·au·gu·ral (in·AUG·yuh·rul) *n.* a ceremony or speech that inaugurates a function.
— *adj.: the U.S. president's inaugural address, ball, parade; inaugural celebrations, festivities.*

in·au·gu·rate (in·AWG·yuh·rate) *v.* -rates, -rat·ed, -rat·ing **1** make a formal beginning of a new era, policy, institution, etc. **2** install a new president in office.
— **in·au·gu·ra·tion** (-RAY·shun) *n.*

in·board *adj. & adv.* in the hull or toward the middle of a ship, boat, or other craft.
— *n.* an inboard engine of a motorboat.

in·born *adj.* of qualities, existing at birth; innate: *an inborn talent.*

in·bound *adj.* inward bound: *an inbound flight; inbound traffic.*

in·breed *v.* -breeds, -bred, -breed·ing breed from closely related plants, animals, or persons, esp. in order to preserve purity of stock or strain: *Inbred corn has been fertilized with its own pollen; hereditary illnesses due to inbreeding within a group, as by marriage between first cousins; Travel broadens the mind, inbreeding* (= narrow social or cultural life) *does not.*

in·cal·cu·la·ble (in·CALK·yuh·luh·bul) *adj.* **1** too great or too many to be counted: *incalculable harm.* **2** unpredictable: *an incalculable mood, temper.*
— **in·cal·cu·la·bly** *adv.*

in·can·des·cent (in·can·DES·unt) *adj.* glowing red-hot or white-hot, as the filament of an electric lamp, or **incandescent lamp.** — **in·can·des·cence** (-unce) *n.*

in·can·ta·tion (in·can·TAY·shun) *n.* the use of words chanted as a magical formula or spell; also, such words.

in·ca·pac·i·tate (in·cuh·PAS·uh·tate) *v.* -tates, -tat·ed, -tat·ing disqualify; disable; make incapable.
— **in·ca·pac·i·ta·tion** (-TAY·shun) *n.*

in·car·cer·ate (in·CAR·suh·rate) *v.* -ates, -at·ed, -at·ing imprison. — **in·car·cer·a·tion** (-RAY·shun) *n.*

in·car·nate (in·CAR·nit) *adj.* **1** having bodily form: *the devil incarnate.* **2** personified: *a moneylender who is greed incarnate.*
— *v.* (-nate) -nates, -nat·ed, -nat·ing **1** make or be incarnate. **2** be the embodiment of: *She incarnates all wifely virtues.* — **in·car·na·tion** (-NAY·shun) *n.*

in·cen·di·ar·y (in·SEN·dee·air·ee) *n. & adj.* -ar·ies a person or thing that sets fire: *He was arrested as an incendiary; an incendiary bomb, crime; an incendiary speech* (= one that stirs up violence).

in·cense (IN·sense) *n.* the perfume or smoke from a gum or spice burned for fragrance, usually as part of a ritual.
— *v.* (in·SENSE) in·cens·es, in·censed, in·cens·ing make someone very angry *at, by, with,* or *against* someone or something.

in·cen·tive (in·SEN·tiv) *n. & adj.* something such as an award, bonus, loan, pay, etc. tending or designed to stimulate or encourage someone to greater effort or output: *a powerful, strong incentive to work harder; adj.: an incentive bonus, pay.*

in·cep·tion (in·SEP·shun) *n.* beginning or commencement of a plan, undertaking, organization, business, program, etc.: *It has been a failure from its very inception.*

in·ces·sant (in·SES·unt) *adj.* ceaseless or uninterrupted: *incessant complaining, noises, phone calls, rain.*
— **in·ces·sant·ly** *adv.*

in·cest (IN·sest) *n.* sexual relations between those closely related by blood, as father and daughter or uncle and niece. — **in·ces·tu·ous** (in·SES·choo·us) *adj.*

inch *n.* **1** a unit of length that is one-twelfth of a foot (2.54 cm). **2** a unit of rainfall, snow, or pressure, based on the height in inches of a liquid in a specified container, as of mercury in a barometer: *Three inches of rain fell during April.* **3** the smallest amount or least bit: *She wouldn't yield an inch.*
— **by inches 1** gradually; also **inch by inch. 2** only just: *He missed the target by inches.*
— **every inch** completely: *She's every inch a lady.*
— **within an inch of:** *She came within an inch of* (= very close to) *losing the election.*
— *v.* move little by little, or inch by inch, *along, back, forward,* etc.: *The shy child inched away and hid behind her mother.*

in·ci·dence (IN·suh·dunce) *n.* **1** the falling or striking of a projectile, ray, or beam on a surface: *the angle of incidence of light rays.* **2** the rate or frequency with which something occurs: *the incidence of an indirect tax on the manufacturer or consumer; the growing incidence of crime; There were 16 incidences of vandalism during the first month of school.*

in·ci·dent (IN·suh·dunt) *n.* an occurrence, esp. one of minor significance, usually related to something major:

a border incident leading to war; An incident happens, occurs, takes place; to cover up, provoke, suppress an incident; an amusing, curious, funny, humorous, strange, touching, ugly incident.
— **adj. 1** falling or striking: *light incident on or upon a photographic subject.* **2** incidental: *duties incident to the office of principal.*

in·ci·den·tal (in·suh·DEN·tul) *adj.* that happens or is likely to happen along with something else that is more important: *problems incidental to setting up in business; incidental* (= casual) *expenses, or* **incidentals** *n. pl.*

in·ci·den·tal·ly (in·suh·DEN·tul·ee) *adv.* by the way.

in·cin·er·ate (in·SIN·uh·rate) *v.* -ates, -at·ed, -at·ing burn to ashes, as in an incinerator.
— **in·cin·er·a·tion** (-RAY·shun) *n.*
— **in·cin·er·a·tor** (-ray·tur) *n.*

in·cip·i·ent (in·SIP·ee·unt) *adj.* just beginning to be or become apparent: *a boy with an incipient growth of facial hair; the incipient life of a fetus; my incipient old age.* — **in·cip·i·ence** *n.*

in·ci·sion (in·SIZH·un) *n.* a gash or cut, as in a surgical operation.

in·ci·sive (in·SYE·siv) *adj.* keen or cutting: *an incisive approach to problem-solving; an incisive mind.*
— **in·ci·sive·ly** *adv.;* **in·ci·sive·ness** *n.*

in·ci·sor (in·SYE·zur) *n.* any of the sharp-edged cutting teeth in front of a mammal's upper and lower jaws.

in·cite (in·CITE) *v.* -cites, -cit·ed, -cit·ing **1** stir up: *to incite hatred; to incite a riot.* **2** urge: *to incite a person to action, violence; His speech incited the crew to mutiny.* — **in·cite·ment** *n.*

in·clem·en·cy *n.* -cies severity or harshness: *the inclemencies of the weather.*

in·clem·ent (in·CLEM·unt) *adj.* **1** severe or harsh: *an inclement judge, ruler.* **2** rough or stormy: *the inclement elements, weather.*

in·cli·na·tion (in·cluh·NAY·shun) *n.* an inclining: *the inclination* (= angle) *of an orbit from the equator; He led a life of ease following every inclination* (= liking) *of body and mind; an unwelcome visitor with no inclination* (= disposition) *to leave.*

in·cline (in·CLINE) *v.* -clines, -clined, -clin·ing **1** cause to slope, lean, or bend: *with head inclined in prayer; Use an* **inclined plane** *such as a plank or ramp at an angle for raising loads.* **2** be or make favourable, willing, or disposed: *She's inclined to think her son is innocent.* — **n.** (IN·cline) a slope.

inclose, inclosure same as ENCLOSE, ENCLOSURE.

in·clude (in·CLOOD, long "OO") *v.* -cludes, -clud·ed, -clud·ing take in as part of something: *Batteries are not included in the price; All are included among "human beings."*

in·clu·sion (in·CLOO·zhun) *n.* an including or something included: *the inclusion of a book in the approved list.*

in·clu·sive (in·CLOO·siv) *adj.* including: *February 1st to 10th inclusive* (= including both days); *an inclusive* (= including much or all) *charge, list, rate; It costs only $350* **inclusive of** (= counting) *taxes.*

in·cog·ni·to (in·COG·nuh·toh, in·cog·NEE·toh) *adj., adv. & n.* -tos with a concealed or disguised identity: *a king travelling incognito; an incognito that is hard to penetrate.*

in·come (IN·cum) *n.* money that comes in, or other benefit or gain received, on account of services or capital, esp. in a given period: *to earn an income; to live within, not beyond one's income; an annual, fixed, net income; the per capita income of a country; the* **income tax** *collected by governments.*

in·com·ing (IN·cum·ing) *n. & adj.* coming in: *the incoming of the tide; the incoming* (= new) *chairman, mail, traffic, year.*

in·com·pa·ra·ble (in·COM·pur·uh·bul) *adj.* that cannot be compared, esp. being unequalled: *Jan's incomparable beauty, skill, wit.*

in·com·pat·i·ble (in·cum·PAT·uh·bul) *adj.* not compatible *with* one another, as different drugs, blood types, temperaments, etc.
— **in·com·pat·i·bil·i·ty** (-BIL·uh·tee) *n.*

in·con·nu (IN·cuh·new) *n. Cdn.* a whitefish of Northern waters.

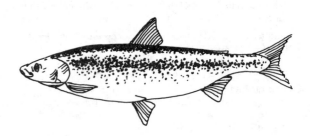

in·con·sol·a·ble (in·cun·SOH·luh·bul) *adj.* that cannot be consoled: *an inconsolable child, grief, widow.*
— **in·con·sol·a·bly** *adv.*

in·con·ti·nent (in·CON·tuh·nunt) *adj.* **1** not continent or having self-control, esp. in regard to sex. **2** unable to control one's bladder or bowels: *The paralysis made her incontinent.* — **in·con·ti·nent·ly** *adv.*
— **in·con·ti·nence** *n.*

in·con·ven·ience (in·cun·VEEN·yunce) *n.* **1** lack of comfort or ease: *Dogs barking at night are a cause of much inconvenience to neighbours.* **2** something that is inconvenient: *a considerable, great, slight inconvenience; to put up with the inconveniences of travel.*
— **v.** -ienc·es, -ienced, -ienc·ing cause trouble or bother to: *I hope that my stay will not inconvenience you.* — **in·con·ven·ient** (-yunt) *adj.*

in·cor·po·rate (in·COR·puh·rate) *v.* -rates, -rat·ed, -rat·ing **1** unite into or combine with so as to form one body: *a plan incorporating many suggestions.* **2** make into a legal body or corporation: *A business is* *incorporated for limiting the liability of investors; an* **incorporated** *town.* — in·cor·po·ra·tion (-RAY·shun) *n.*

in·cor·po·re·al (in·cor·POR·ee·ul) *adj.* not having material form, as angels and spirits; spiritual.

in·cor·ri·gi·ble (in·COR·uh·juh·bul) *adj.* that cannot be changed or reformed: *an incorrigible habit, youth.* — in·cor·ri·gi·bly *adv.* — in·cor·ri·gi·bil·i·ty (-BIL·uh·tee) *n.*

in·crease (in·CREECE) *v.* -creas·es, -creased, -creas·ing make or become greater in size, degree, number, etc.: *World population is increasing every minute; Prices increase with demand.* — *n.* (IN·creece) growth or its result: *an increase of 10° from the normal; a slight increase in productivity; Prices seem always* **on the increase** *in our economy.*

in·creas·ing·ly (in·CREE·sing·lee) *adv.* more and more.

in·cred·i·ble (in·CRED·uh·bul) *adj.* too unusual or improbable to believe: *an incredible feat of endurance.* — in·cred·i·bly *adv.*

in·cre·du·li·ty (in·cruh·DEW·luh·tee) *n.* disbelief: *Incredulity was written all over his face.*

in·cred·u·lous (in·CREJ·uh·lus) *adj.* showing disbelief: *an incredulous expression, look, shaking of the head.* — in·cred·u·lous·ly *adv.*

in·cre·ment (IN·cruh·munt) *n.* amount or quantity of increase: *the annual increments in a wage scale.* — in·cre·men·tal (-MEN·tul) *adj.*

in·crim·i·nate (in·CRIM·uh·nate) *v.* -nates, -nat·ed, -nat·ing accuse of or involve in wrongdoing: *He was suspected of the crime because of incriminating circumstances.* — in·crim·i·na·tion (-NAY·shun) *n.* — in·crim·i·na·to·ry (-nuh·tor·ee) *adj.*

incrust, incrustation same as ENCRUST, ENCRUSTATION.

in·cu·bate (INK·yuh·bate) *v.* -bates, -bat·ed, -bat·ing 1 sit on eggs or brood as a female bird does. 2 artificially develop eggs, cultures of microorganisms, premature infants, etc. 3 of germs, develop in a body before symptoms of the infection appear. — in·cu·ba·tion (-BAY·shun) *n.: Measles has an incubation period of 10 to 14 days.*

in·cu·ba·tor (INK·yuh·bay·tur) *n.* 1 an apparatus for keeping premature babies under controlled conditions till they are ready to live in a normal atmosphere. 2 an apparatus for keeping eggs warm while being hatched.

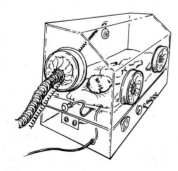

in·cul·cate (in·CUL·cate, IN·cul·cate) *v.* -cates, -cat·ed, -cat·ing impress ideas, habits, facts, etc. into the minds

of others, esp. by frequent repetition: *Prejudice is often inculcated in children by parents.* — in·cul·ca·tion (in·cul·CAY·shun) *n.*

in·cum·ben·cy (in·CUM·bun·see) *n.* -cies 1 the term of office of an incumbent. 2 a duty or obligation.

in·cum·bent (in·CUM·bunt) *n. & adj.* a person holding an office or position: *Mr. Jones, the present incumbent; candidates challenging the incumbent mayor; The judge felt it* **incumbent on** *or* **upon** *him* (= felt it to be an obligation) *to impose a jail term.*

incumber, incumbrance same as ENCUMBER, ENCUMBRANCE.

in·cur (in·CUR) *v.* -curs, -curred, -cur·ring meet with or bring down on oneself an inconvenience or something unpleasant: *to incur debts, dislike, displeasure, expenses, hatred.*

in·cur·sion (in·CUR·zhun) *n.* an invasion or raid: *armed incursions by guerrillas into British territory.*

in·debt·ed (in·DET·id) *adj.* owing money, gratitude, etc.: *We are deeply indebted to you for taking care of our child.* — in·debt·ed·ness *n.*

in·de·cen·cy (in·DEE·sun·see) *n.* -cies 1 lack of decency. 2 an obscene act or expression: *a charge of gross indecency in a public place.*

in·de·cent (in·DEE·sunt) *adj.* 1 not decent or becoming: *It's indecent of you to come out of the bathroom with nothing on; He married his brother's widow in indecent haste.* 2 morally bad or obscene: *Rape is a more serious crime than* **indecent assault;** *charged with* **indecent exposure** (of genitals). — in·de·cent·ly *adv.*

in·de·ci·sive (in·duh·SYE·siv) *adj.* 1 not decisive or conclusive: *The battle was indecisive.* 2 vacillating: *Hamlet was indecisive about avenging his father's death.*

in·deed (in·DEED) *adv.* certainly; really. — *interj.* expressing surprise, doubt, irony, etc.

in·de·fat·i·ga·ble (in·duh·FAT·uh·guh·bul) *adj.* untiring or tireless: *She was indefatigable in the service of the company.* — in·de·fat·i·ga·bly *adv.*

in·def·i·nite (in·DEF·uh·nit) *adj.* not definite; not defining, precise, or certain: *an indefinite answer such as "Maybe"; an indefinite period of time; indefinite pronouns such as "some," "few," and "many"; an indefinite article* (= "a" or "an"). — in·def·i·nite·ly *adv.;* in·def·i·nite·ness *n.*

in·del·i·ble (in·DEL·uh·bul) *adj.* that cannot be erased or blotted out: *an indelible ink, impression, memory;* in·del·i·bly *adv.*

in·del·i·cate (in·DEL·uh·kit) *adj.* lacking delicacy or propriety; coarse or tactless: *It was indelicate of him to point out her error in public.* — in·del·i·ca·cy (-cuh·see) *n.* -cies.

in·dem·ni·fy (in·DEM·nuh·fye) *v.* -fies, -fied, -fy·ing insure: *money set aside to indemnify workers against loss of job; to indemnify them against or for losses, damages, legal actions; to indemnify depositors in case of bank failure.* — in·dem·ni·fi·ca·tion (-fuh·CAY·shun) *n.*

in·dem·ni·ty (in·DEM·nuh·tee) *n.* **-ties 1** in Canada, the annual salary received by a member of Parliament or of a legislature: *the sessional* (= annual) *indemnity.* **2** security or insurance: *life insurance with double indemnity in case of accidental death.* **3** compensation such as war reparations exacted from a defeated nation.

in·dent (in·DENT) *v.* **1** make a dent, notch, or recess on an edge or border: *The first line of a paragraph is indented a few spaces from the left margin; coves and capes that indent a coastline.* **2** make a dent or depression, as of a pattern on metal; hence, stamp: *an asphalt that indents easily.*
— *n.* a notch or indention.
— **in·den·ta·tion** (in·den·TAY·shun) *n.*
— **in·dent·er** or **in·den·tor** *n.*

in·den·tion (in·DEN·shun) *n.* an indenting or the blank space left by indenting a line or paragraph: *Make a paragraph indention of five spaces.*

in·den·ture (in·DEN·chur) *n.* a written contract, usually **indentures**, esp. a contract binding one to someone else's service: *He was apprenticed to a carpenter by indentures.*
— *v.* **-tures, -tured, -tur·ing** bind by indentures: *Plantation workers used to be slaves, indentured servants, or immigrants.*

in·de·pend·ence (in·duh·PEN·dunce) *n.* the quality of being independent; freedom: *The United States gained or won its independence from Britain; They declared independence on July 4, 1776; Many nations have achieved independence since World War II; Satellite countries don't enjoy political independence; Some have lost their independence to the superpowers.*

in·de·pend·ent (in·duh·PEN·dunt) *adj.* free from the rule, control, or influence of others: *Everyone would like to become independent (of others); an independent businessman, country, income, inquiry, operator, opinion, thinker; She is a woman of **independent means** (having private resources); a fiercely independent nationalist; He has nothing **independent of** (= apart from) his pension.*
— *n.: He sits in the Commons as an independent (not belonging to any party).* — **in·de·pend·ent·ly** *adv.*

in-depth *adj.* profound or thorough: *an in-depth interview, report, study.*

in·de·scrib·a·ble (in·duh·SCRYE·buh·bul) *adj.* that cannot be described or is beyond description: *He was in indescribable pain.*

in·dex (IN·dex) *n.* **-dex.es** or **-di.ces** (-duh·seez)
1 something that points or indicates: *Growth rings are an index of a tree's growth; "The face is the index of the mind."* **2** the forefinger, or **index finger**. **3** a fist sign beside a note or paragraph. **4** same as THUMB INDEX. **5** a listing of authors or subjects, as at the end of a book or in a library catalogue: *an author index; a card index* (= catalogue); *subject index; to compile, do, make an index to a book; the former Roman Catholic Index of books prohibited as harmful to faith or morals.* **6** the percentage variation from a normal, as in prices, wages, cost of living, etc.: *the cost-of-living index.* **7** a figure (as 3 in ab³) showing the power to which a mathematical quantity is raised. **8** the amount that a light ray bends, or **index of refraction,** in passing into a different

medium: *The lower a gem's refractive index the less its lustre.*
— *v.* **1** provide with an index: *The book is well indexed.* **2** adjust to the cost-of-living index: *an indexed pension; the indexing of wages, interest, etc.*
— **in·dex·a·tion** (-AY·shun) *n.*

In·di·an (IN·dee·un) *n.* **1** a member of one of the many groups of people considered natives of North America: *The Indians and the Inuit are Native Canadians; Status Indians include treaty Indians and others; Joe's just **one of the Indians*** (= not a chief). **2** a person of or from India; East Indian.
— *adj.* having to do with North American Indians or their languages: *the Department of Indian Affairs; an **Indian club*** (= wooden club for exercise); *an Indian reserve; an **Indian superintendent*** (formerly "Indian agent" or representative of the Federal Government).

Indian file *n.* single file.

Indian summer *n.* a brief period of unusually mild weather sometimes occurring late in the fall.

in·di·cate (IN·duh·cate) *v.* **-cates, -cat·ed, -cat·ing** point to, point out, signify, or state briefly: *A clock's hands indicate time; A nod indicates assent; She indicated that it was their last meeting; Lee's language is so poor that remedial English seems indicated.*
— **in·di·ca·tion** (-CAY·shun) *n.*

in·dic·a·tive (in·DIC·uh·tiv) *adj.* indicating or pointing out something: *symptoms indicative of a disease; In "She is gone" and "Are you coming?" the verbs are in the **indicative mood,** not imperative or subjunctive.*
— **in·di·ca·tor** (IN·duh·cay·tur) *n.*

indices a *pl.* of INDEX.

in·dict (in·DITE) *v.* charge with a crime.
— **in·dict·a·ble** (in·DYE·tuh·bul) *adj.*

in·dict·ment (in·DITE·munt) *n.* **1** an indicting: *Criminal cases are tried on indictment; A grand jury hands up an indictment to a judge; to issue, return, quash an indictment; to bring an indictment against someone for a crime.* **2** condemnation or accusation: *The accountant's report was a stinging indictment of wasteful spending; a sweeping indictment against the government.*

in·dif·fer·ence (in·DIF·ur·unce) *n.* **1** lack of interest: *to affect, display, feign indifference towards someone; a cool, studied indifference to flattery.* **2** lack of concern, esp. as to the importance of something: *Careless work shows his indifference; his indifference about good work habits; Her opinions are a matter of indifference to me; a marked indifference to the demands of justice.*

in·dif·fer·ent (in·DIF·ur·unt) *adj.* **1** showing no interest; apathetic: *She couldn't remain indifferent in a family dispute; He's not indifferent to the sufferings of the poor.* **2** mediocre: *a novel of indifferent quality.*

in·di·gence (IN·duh·junce) *n.* privation or need.

in·dig·e·nous (in·DIJ·uh·nus) *adj.* belonging or proper to a particular region, country, soil, or climate as native to it, not exotic or imported: *an indigenous people, species; The Australian aborigines are the indigenous inhabitants of the country; Koalas are indigenous to Australia.*

in·di·gent (IN·duh·junt) *n. & adj.* (one) who is needy.

in·di·gest·i·ble (in·duh·JES·tuh·bul) *adj.* of foods, difficult to digest.

in·di·ges·tion (in·duh·JES·chun) *n.* poor digestion: *Some foods cause indigestion; an attack of indigestion; Arguing at meals gives me indigestion.*

in·dig·nant (in·DIG·nunt) *adj.* righteously angry or scornful: *She is indignant with her boss about* or *at* or *over not being given a raise.* — **in·dig·nant·ly** *adv.*

in·dig·na·tion (in·dig·NAY·shun) *n.* anger caused by an injustice: *public indignation; righteous indignation; to arouse, feel, show indignation; to express indignation about* or *at* or *over being kept waiting unnecessarily.*

in·dig·ni·ty (in·DIG·nuh·tee) *n.* -ties something done or said that hurts one's dignity or self-respect: *indignities inflicted on the poor; to suffer indignities.*

in·di·rect (in·duh·RECT) *adj.* 1 not straight or straightforward; devious: *an indirect answer, dealing, method, route; Unlike sales tax, an indirect tax is included in the price of a product.* 2 secondary: *an indirect cause; indirect discourse* (= reported speech); *In "Give me the pen," "me" is the indirect object.* — **in·di·rect·ly** *adv.*; **in·di·rect·ness** *n.*

in·dis·cre·tion (in·dis·CRESH·un) *n.* 1 lack of discretion; imprudence. 2 an indiscreet act or remark: *youthful indiscretions.*

in·dis·crim·i·nate (in·dis·CRIM·uh·nit) *adj.* 1 without care in making choices or decisions: *an indiscriminate reader; indiscriminate in her attacks, compliments, friendships.* 2 haphazard: *an indiscriminate pile.* — **in·dis·crim·i·nate·ly** *adv.*

in·dis·pen·sa·ble (in·dis·PEN·suh·bul) *adj.* absolutely essential: *Food is indispensable for* or *to living beings.* — **in·dis·pen·sa·bly** *adv.* — **in·dis·pen·sa·bil·i·ty** (-BIL·uh·tee) *n.*

in·dis·posed (in·dis·POZED) *adj.* 1 not well disposed: *He's indisposed to help you.* 2 slightly ill: *The boss is indisposed.* — **in·dis·po·si·tion** (IN·dis·puh·ZISH·un) *n.*

in·dis·sol·u·ble (in·di·SOL·yuh·bul) *adj.* that cannot be undone; lasting.

in·dite (in·DITE) *v.* -dites, -dit·ed, -dit·ing compose a poem, speech, letter, etc.

in·di·vid·u·al (in·duh·VIJ·oo·ul) *n.* a separate person, animal, or thing: *the rights of the individual as opposed to those of society as a whole; treat children as individuals; each individual of a species; an obnoxious individual* (= person). — *adj.* having to do with an individual: *There is standing room besides individual seating for 200; lectures followed by individual coaching; an individual* (= distinctive) *style.* — **in·di·vid·u·al·ly** (-uh·lee) *adv.*

in·di·vid·u·al·i·ty (IN·duh·vij·oo·AL·uh·tee) *n.* -ties 1 the sum of a person's distinctive characteristics. 2 one's individual condition or existence. 3 an individual characteristic or trait.

in·di·vid·u·al·ize (in·duh·VIJ·oo·uh·lize) *v.* -iz·es, -ized, -iz·ing make individual: *individualized instruction of students; a style that individualizes* (= distinguishes) *her performance.* — **in·di·vid·u·al·i·za·tion** (-luh·ZAY·shun) *n.*

in·doc·tri·nate (in·DOC·truh·nate) *v.* -nates, -nat·ed, -nat·ing teach a specific doctrine, esp. fill a subject's mind *with* or *in* the beliefs of a particular party or sect. — **in·doc·tri·na·tion** (-NAY·shun) *n.*

in·do·lent (IN·duh·lunt) *adj.* idle or lazy: *an indolent worker; an indolent* (= inactive) *ulcer; an indolent* (= painless) *cyst or tumour.* — **in·do·lence** (-lunce) *n.*

in·dom·i·ta·ble (in·DOM·uh·tuh·bul) *adj.* unconquerable or unyielding: *indomitable courage, spirit, will.* — **in·dom·i·ta·bly** *adv.*

in·door (IN·dore) *adj.* done, used, situated, etc. within a building: *an indoor facility, game, pool; indoor photography.* — **in·doors** (IN·DORZ) *adv.*: *to go, keep, stay indoors.*

indorse same as ENDORSE.

in·du·bi·ta·ble (in·DEW·buh·tuh·bul) *adj.* that cannot be doubted; certain. — **in·du·bi·ta·bly** *adv.*

in·duce (in·DUCE) *v.* -duc·es, -duced, -duc·ing 1 bring about: *drugs to induce sleep; induced abortion, labour; induced current (induced by electrical conduction).* 2 influence or persuade: *a carrot to induce a donkey to proceed.*

in·duce·ment (in·DUCE·munt) *n.* external influence or attempt to entice or tempt one to action: *to offer* or *provide inducements; a strong inducement; scholarships as inducements to study.*

in·duct (in·DUCT) *v.* install, enrol, or introduce someone *into* an office or position, the military, *to* a benefice, etc. — **in·duct·ee** (in·duc·TEE) *n.* — **in·duc·tor** *n.*

in·duc·tion (in·DUC·shun) *n.* 1 the process of inducing electrical or magnetic properties: *induction coils, heating.* 2 an inducting, as into military service or an office; *adj.*: *induction ceremonies, papers.* 3 process of reasoning from particular facts to general principles; opposite of DEDUCTION; also, a conclusion so reached. — **in·duc·tive** (in·DUC·tiv) *adj.*: *inductive logic.*

indue same as ENDUE.

in·dulge (in·DULJ) *v.* -dulg·es, -dulged, -dulg·ing yield or give in to one's pleasures, wants, wishes, or whims: *to indulge a fondness for or craving for candy; a sick child who needs some indulging; She rarely indulges in abusive language.*

in·dul·gence (in·DUL·junce) *n.* 1 an indulging or something one indulges in. 2 in the Roman Catholic Church, remission of punishment due for sins. 3 tolerance or forbearance: *The lecturer craved the indulgence of a tired audience.* — **in·dul·gent** *adj.*; **in·dul·gent·ly** *adv.*

in·dus·tri·al (in·DUS·tree·ul) *adj.* having to do with industries: *modern industrial nations of the West; an industrial* (= synthetic) *diamond; a suburban area zoned as an industrial park for businesses and industries; Factory production was speeded up by machines during England's Industrial Revolution from about 1750.* — **in·dus·tri·al·ist** (-uh·list) *n.* — **in·dus·tri·al·ly** *adv.*

in·dus·tri·al·ize (in·DUS·tree·uh·lize) *v.* -iz·es, -ized, -iz·ing make or become industrial: *Material progress lies*

*in industrializing; Japan is highly **industrialized;** the industrialized nations of the West.*
— **in·dus·tri·al·i·za·tion** (-luh·ZAY·shun) *n.*

in·dus·tri·ous (in·DUS·tree·us) *adj.* naturally hard-working: *an industrious clerk, housewife; industrious like ants and bees.*
— **in·dus·tri·ous·ly** *adv.;* **in·dus·tri·ous·ness** *n.*

in·dus·try (IN·dus·tree) *n.* -tries 1 a business activity or enterprise: *Primary or extractive industries such as fishing and mining, secondary or manufacturing industries, and distributive industries that serve the consumer; a basic, cottage, key industry; heavy, light, steel, textile, tourist, travel industry; Industries spring up; to build up or develop industries; Canadian industry (collectively).* 2 habitually hard-working quality; systematic effort: *Diligence and industry got her to the top.*

in·dwell·ing (IN·dwel·ing) *adj.* dwelling within: *an indwelling force, principle, spirit.*

in·e·bri·ate (in·EE·bree·ate) *v.* -ates, -at·ed, -at·ing *Formal.* intoxicate.
— *n.* (-it) a drunkard. — *adj.* drunk.
— **in·e·bri·a·tion** (-AY·shun) *n.*

in·ef·fa·ble (in·EF·uh·bul) *adj.* not capable of being expressed in words: *that old ineffable charm; an ineffable mystery, sadness; the ineffable happiness of Heaven; ineffable beauty; the ineffable name of Jehovah (too sacred to be uttered).* — **in·ef·fa·bly** *adv.*

in·ef·fi·cient (in·uh·FISH·unt) *adj.* not working well enough to produce results quickly: *an inefficient administration, government, machine, manager, measure, method.* — **in·ef·fi·cient·ly** *adv.*
— **in·ef·fi·cien·cy** *n.*

in·el·i·gi·ble (in·EL·uh·juh·bul) *n. & adj.* (one who is) not eligible or suitable.
— **in·el·i·gi·bil·i·ty** (-BIL·uh·tee) *n.*

in·e·luc·ta·ble (in·i·LUC·tuh·bul) *adj.* not to be struggled with or avoided: *ineluctable fate.*

in·ept (in·EPT) *adj.* utterly lacking in skill or dexterity; incompetent: *an inept comparison, question, remark; He's quite inept at or in handling people; a brave but inept* (= bungling) *military officer.* — **in·ept·ly** *adv.*
— **in·ept·i·tude** or **in·ept·ness** *n.*

in·e·qual·i·ty (in·ee·KWOL·uh·tee) *n.* -ties difference in status, opportunities, etc. between two or more social groups: *the inequalities between the rich and the poor.*

in·ert (in·URT) *adj.* lacking inherent power or quality, as to act or move: *The accident victim lay inert; an inert electorate; Neon is an inert gas that does not combine with other elements.* — **in·ert·ly** *adv.;* **in·ert·ness** *n.*

in·er·tia (in·UR·shuh) *n.* 1 the tendency of matter to remain in its state of rest or motion unless acted on by an outside force: *the self-adjusting **inertia reel** of a safety belt; an aircraft engine with an **inertia starter** that has a wheel spun by hand.* 2 inertness or sluggishness: *Sheer inertia makes him stay in bed all morning.*
— **in·er·tial** (-shul) *adj.: an inertial force; inertial resistance; a missile kept on course by means of an inertial guidance or navigation system.*

in·es·cap·a·ble (in·uh·SCAY·puh·bul) *adj.* that cannot be escaped; inevitable, as a logical conclusion, moral necessity, etc. — **in·es·cap·a·bly** *adv.*

in·ev·i·ta·ble (in·EV·uh·tuh·bul) *adj.* unavoidable, as a natural occurrence or phenomenon: *Death is inevitable; an inevitable delay, result, war; a tourist with his inevitable camera.* — **in·ev·i·ta·bly** *adv.*
— **in·ev·i·ta·bil·i·ty** (-BIL·uh·tee) *n.*

in·ex·haust·i·ble (in·ig·ZAWS·tuh·bul) *adj.* 1 that cannot be exhausted: *the ocean's inexhaustible riches.* 2 tireless: *a man of inexhaustible energy.*
— **in·ex·haust·i·bly** *adv.*

in·ex·o·ra·ble (in·EX·uh·ruh·bul) *adj.* that cannot be altered by begging or entreaty; relentless: *a dictator's inexorable demands; the condemned man awaiting his inexorable doom; the inexorable logic of her reasoning.*
— **in·ex·o·ra·bly** *adv.*

in·ex·pe·ri·ence (in·ek·SPEER·ee·unce) *n.* lack of experience or consequent lack of skill, wisdom, etc.
— **in·ex·pe·ri·enced** *adj.*

in·ex·tri·ca·ble (in·EX·tri·cuh·bul, in·ik·STRIC·uh·bul) *adj.* 1 impossible to extricate oneself from: *inextricable difficulties.* 2 impossible to disentangle: *an inextricable problem.* — **in·ex·tri·ca·bly** *adv.*

in·fal·li·ble (in·FAL·uh·bul) *adj.* not capable of failing or being wrong: *an infallible authority, method, remedy, test.* — **in·fal·li·bly** *adv.*
— **in·fal·li·bil·i·ty** (-BIL·uh·tee) *n.*

in·fa·mous (IN·fuh·mus) *adj.* having or giving a scandalous reputation: *infamous and unprofessional conduct; an infamous crime, plot, traitor.*

in·fa·my (IN·fuh·mee) *n.* -mies 1 a disgraceful or wicked act. 2 disgrace or wickedness: *the infamy of Pearl Harbour.*

in·fan·cy (IN·fun·see) *n.* -cies 1 the state or period of being an infant. 2 any initial period: *in Caxton's days when printing was in its infancy.*

in·fant (IN·funt) *n.* a baby: *no extra charge for infants; to nurse, suckle, wean an infant; a new-born infant; premature infants.*
— *adj.: **infant mortality** (= death before age one); an infant* (= young) *nation; Mozart was an infant prodigy.*

in·fan·ti·cide (in·FAN·tuh·side) *n.* the killing of an infant; also, the killer.

in·fan·tile (IN·fun·tile, -til) *adj.* having to do with infancy: *infantile behaviour; **infantile paralysis** (= polio).*

in·fan·try (IN·fun·tree) *n.* -tries 1 the branch of an army consisting of troops. 2 troops trained and equipped to fight on foot.

in·fat·u·ate (in·FACH·oo·ate) *v.* -ates, -at·ed, -at·ing affect a person with a foolish, usually short-lived passion. — **in·fat·u·a·tion** (-AY·shun) *n.*

in·fect (in·FECT) *v.* 1 cause an unhealthy condition in a body part; become diseased, as with a germ or virus: *An open wound may become infected.* 2 to influence or affect: *The teacher infected the whole class with her enthusiasm.*

in·fec·tion (in·FEC·shun) *n.* **1** disease caused by a spreading virus or bacterium: *a secondary infection such as sinusitis resulting from a virus cold; airborne infections.* **2** the act or process of infecting: *Infection sets in if a wound is not attended to; the rate, risk, route, source of infection; the infection* (= affecting) *of young minds with dangerous ideas.*
— **in·fec·tious** (in·FEC·shus) *adj.*: *infectious mononucleosis; infectious* (= spreading) *laughter.*
— **in·fec·tor** *n.*

in·fer (in·FUR) *v.* -**fers**, -**ferred**, -**fer·ring 1** conclude from facts or evidence. **2** loosely, to imply.
— **in·fer·ence** (IN·fur·unce) *n.*
— **in·fer·en·tial** (in·fuh·REN·shul) *adj.* based on facts or evidence: *an inferential judgment.*

in·fe·ri·or (in·FEER·ee·ur) *n. & adj.* (one) that is lower in position, merit, or quality.
— **in·fe·ri·or·i·ty** (-OR·uh·tee) *n.*

in·fer·nal (in·FUR·nul) *adj.* hellish or damned: *an infernal region, scheme.* — **in·fer·nal·ly** *adv.*

in·fer·no (in·FUR·noh) *n.* -**nos** a hell-like place or condition: *a blazing, raging, roaring, towering inferno.*

in·fest (in·FEST) *v.* overrun in large numbers, as with pests or parasites: *Slugs infest a green garden; hair infested with lice.* — **in·fes·ta·tion** (in·fes·TAY·shun) *n.*

in·fi·del (IN·fuh·dul) *n.* a religious unbeliever.

in·fi·del·i·ty (in·fuh·DEL·uh·tee) *n.* -**ties 1** (act of) disloyalty between spouses; unfaithfulness: *conjugal infidelity; marital infidelities.* **2** lack of religious faith.

in·fight·ing (IN·fight·ing) *n.* **1** fighting within a group, as between associates. **2** fighting at close quarters, as in boxing or fencing. — **in·fight·er** *n.*

in·fill *n.* the filling in of empty spaces, as with new housing in a densely built-up area: *New housing is created by infill, renovation, and conversion.*
— *adj.*: *infill housing; an infill development, house, project, site; infill drilling of oil wells.*

in·fil·trate (IN·fil·trate, in·FIL·trate) *v.* -**trates**, -**trat·ed**, -**trat·ing** pass gradually through or into something; penetrate a region or organization secretly with hostile intent. — **in·fil·tra·tor** (-tray·tur) *n.*
— **in·fil·tra·tion** (-TRAY·shun) *n.*

in·fi·nite (IN·fuh·nit) *adj.* endlessly great or vast: *God's infinite goodness; her infinite patience; God* **the Infinite** *(being).* — **in·fi·nite·ly** *adv.*

in·fin·i·tes·i·mal (IN·fin·uh·TES·uh·mul) *adj.* that is extremely minute: *The chances of your contracting the disease are infinitesimal; The odds are infinitesimal.*
— *adv.*: *They are* **in·fin·i·tes·i·mal·ly** *small.*

in·fin·i·tive (in·FIN·uh·tiv) *n.* a verb form that is not limited to any person, number, or tense, as "to go" in "I (or We, They, etc.) want (or wanted) to go."

in·fin·i·ty (in·FIN·uh·tee) *n.* -**ties** something infinite such as an indefinite number: *10/3 equals 3.333* **to infinity.**

in·firm (in·FURM) *adj.* not firm or strong; esp., weak because of age.

in·fir·ma·ry (in·FUR·muh·ree) *n.* -**ries 1** a small hospital. **2** a dispensary.

in·fir·mi·ty (in·FUR·muh·tee) *n.* -**ties 1** weakness or illness. **2** a flaw of character.

in·flame (in·FLAME) *v.* -**flames**, -**flamed**, -**flam·ing 1** make or become excited: *words apt to inflame a mob to fury.* **2** make or become sore or swollen: *an inflamed wound.* — **in·flam·ma·tion** (in·fluh·MAY·shun) *n.*

in·flam·ma·ble (in·FLAM·uh·bul) *adj.* that catches fire easily: *Gasoline is highly inflammable; He has an inflammable* (= easily excitable) *temper.*
— **in·flam·ma·bil·i·ty** (-BIL·uh·tee) *n.*

in·flam·ma·to·ry (in·FLAM·uh·tor·ee) *adj.* apt to inflame: *an inflammatory speech; an inflammatory lung condition.*

in·flate (in·FLATE) *v.* -**flates**, -**flat·ed**, -**flat·ing** expand, as with air, or increase abnormally: *to inflate a tire; an ego inflated with pride; prices inflating at an annual rate of 30%.*
— **in·flat·a·ble** (in·FLAY·tuh·bul) *adj.*: *an inflatable mattress, toy, vest.*

in·fla·tion (in·FLAY·shun) *n.* rise of prices and fall in the buying power of money: *creeping, double-digit, galloping, rampant, runaway inflation.*

in·fla·tion·ar·y (in·FLAY·shuh·nair·ee) *adj.* causing inflation: *Credit buying is inflationary; an inflationary wage settlement; unemployment during an inflationary recession; Wages and prices rise in an inflationary spiral.*

in·flect (in·FLECT) *v.* change or vary: *to inflect the tone or pitch of voice; to inflect the form of a word to show number, gender, tense, etc.*
— **in·flec·tion** *n.* **1** tone: *"No!" has a falling inflection, but "No?" has a rising inflection.* **2** suffix showing a grammatical change; also, a form so changed: *"-ed," "-ing," "-est," and other inflections; inflections of "go" such as "goes" and "gone."*

in·flex·i·ble (in·FLEX·uh·bul) *adj.* rigid or unyielding in thought or will: *He's inflexible in his demands.*
— **in·flex·i·bly** *adv.*
— **in·flex·i·bil·i·ty** (-BIL·uh·tee) *n.*

in·flex·ion (in·FLEC·shun) *n.* same as INFLECTION.

in·flict (in·FLICT) *v.* give or impose suffering, punishment, or anything painful *on* or *upon* someone: *The speech was so boring, the audience felt it was being inflicted on them.* — **in·flic·tion** *n.*

in·flight (IN·flite) *adj.* during flight: *an inflight movie; inflight refuelling.*

in·flu·ence (IN·floo·unce) *n.* indirect power or its effect: *the moon's influence on tides; a man of much influence but no real authority; accused of influence peddling; He was caught driving* **under the influence** *(of liquor); to bring influence to bear on an issue; to exert influence on a person; to flaunt, strengthen, use one's influence; to wield influence; a bad, cultural, moderating, moral, outside, positive, powerful, salutary influence; She's a good influence* (= person exerting influence) *on him; an influence for good.*
— *v.* -**enc·es**, -**enced**, -**enc·ing** have or use influence: *Do stars influence our fate? a jury influenced by news stories.*

in·flu·en·tial (in·floo·EN·shul) *adj.* having or using much influence: *Many factors were influential in arriving at*

this decision; an influential lobbyist, senator.
— in·flu·en·tial·ly *adv.*

in·flux *n.* a flowing in; inflow: *the influx of refugees into a country.*

in·fo·bit (IN·foh·bit) *n.* a bit of information as stored in a database.

in·fo·mer·cial (in·fuh·MUR·shul) *n.* a short TV feature advertising a product or service.

in·form (in·FORM) *v.* give facts or news to; tell someone: *a letter to inform you of or about our decision; Neighbours sometimes inform on or against each other to the police.* — in·form·er *n.*

in·for·mal (in·FOR·mul) *adj.* not formal in style, esp. of speech or writing; colloquial; **in·for·mal·ly** *adv.* — in·for·mal·i·ty (in·for·MAL·uh·tee) *n.* **-ties.**

in·for·mant (in·FOR·munt) *n.* one who supplies information, usually for professional use, as to the police.

in·for·ma·tion (in·fur·MAY·shun) *n.* **1** facts, data, news, etc.: *He is full of information but lacks judgment; to classify, collect, dig up, divulge, find, furnish, leak, provide information; to feed information into a computer; to retrieve information from a database; to withhold information from the authorities; computerized information storage and retrieval; classified, confidential, detailed, first-hand, inside, reliable, secondhand, secret information; For your information, we are closed on Sundays.* **2** the communication of facts, news, etc.: *director of information;* **adj.:** *an information bureau, officer.* — in·for·ma·tion·al (-shun·ul) *adj.*

in·for·ma·tive (in·FOR·muh·tiv) *adj.* instructive: *an informative leaflet, lecture, talk.* — in·for·ma·tive·ly *adv.*

informed *adj.* knowing the facts: *Sterilization requires informed consent; Do keep us informed of your progress; a well-informed journalist.*

in·for·mer·cial (in·fur·MUR·shul) *n.* same as INFOMERCIAL.

in·frac·tion (in·FRAC·shun) *n.* infringement or violation: *a minor infraction of a rule.*

in·fra·red (in·fruh·RED) *n. & adj.* (beyond) the red end of the visible spectrum: *Infrared rays are used to detect heat from weather satellites and to photograph without light.*

in·fra·struc·ture (in·fruh·STRUK·chur) *n.* installations, facilities, roads, and such basic services and equipment to back up an undertaking.

in·fre·quent (in·FREE·kwunt) *adj.* not frequent; rare: *an infrequent visitor.* — in·fre·quent·ly *adv.*

in·fringe (in·FRINJ) *v.* -fring·es, -fringed, -fring·ing break or violate: *a publication infringing a copyright; something that* **infringes on** or **upon** *a private right or territory.* — in·fringe·ment *n.*

in·fu·ri·ate (in·FYOOR·ee·ate) *v.* -ates, -at·ed, -at·ing make furious; enrage.

in·fuse (in·FYOOZE) *v.* -fus·es, -fused, -fus·ing **1** pour liquid over something; hence, steep or let soak tea,

herbs, etc. **2** instil a quality *into* people or minds; inspire people or minds *with* a quality: *flagging spirits infused with fresh courage.* — in·fu·sion (in·FEW·zhun) *n.*

in·gen·ious (in·JEEN·yus) *adj.* inventive and skilful in thought or action: *an ingenious device, explanation, theory; He's ingenious at finding excuses.* — in·gen·i·ous·ly *adv.;* in·gen·i·ous·ness *n.*

in·ge·nu·i·ty (in·juh·NEW·uh·tee) *n.* skill and cleverness in designing: *human ingenuity.*

in·gen·u·ous (in·JEN·yoo·us) *adj.* not trying to hide one's feelings or intentions; simple and artless: *a child's ingenuous answer, explanation, smile.*

in·gest (in·JEST) *v.* take into the body like food; absorb. — in·ges·tion (-chun) *n.*

in·glor·i·ous (in·GLOR·ee·us) *adj.* **1** disgraceful: *an inglorious end.* **2** obscure or little-known: *"Some mute inglorious Milton here may rest."*

in·grain (in·GRAIN) *v.* work into the grain or fibre: *habits ingrained in us from childhood; deeply ingrained prejudices; an* **ingrained** (= out-and-out) *liar.* — *n.* (IN·grain) yarn, carpeting, etc. dyed before manufacture.

in·gra·ti·ate (in·GRAY·shee·ate) *v.* -ates, -at·ed, -at·ing try to bring oneself into favour with someone: *The killer would first try to ingratiate himself into the confidence of his victims; Canada doesn't need to ingratiate itself with* or *to the U.S.* — **ingratiating** *adj.: his ingratiating behaviour, cuteness, an ingratiating melody, voice, smile.*

in·grat·i·tude (in·GRAT·uh·tude) *n.* ungratefulness: *base, rank ingratitude.*

in·gre·di·ent (in·GREE·dee·unt) *n.* something that goes into the making of a mixture, esp. of a food or medicinal preparation: *the ingredients of a cocktail; basic ingredients; the essential ingredients of chivalry.*

in·hab·it (in·HAB·it) *v.* live or dwell in a place. — in·hab·i·ta·ble (-tuh·bul) *adj.*

in·hab·it·ant (in·HAB·uh·tunt) *n.* one inhabiting a place: *America's original inhabitants; a city of two million inhabitants.*

in·hale (in·HALE) *v.* -hales, -haled, -hal·ing breathe in air, vapour, smoke, etc. — in·ha·la·tion (in·huh·LAY·shun) *n.*

in·here (in·HEER) *v.* -heres, -hered, -her·ing *Formal.* belong or be inherent *in* something.

in·her·ent (in·HEER·unt, in·HAIR·unt) *adj.* existing as an inborn or inseparable quality: *the inherent goodness of human nature; basic rights inherent in citizenship.* — in·her·ent·ly *adv.*

in·her·it (in·HER·it) *v.* receive as a bequest in a will, as a hereditary trait, or as something passed along: *a chair he inherited from his grandfather; She inherited a financial mess from her predecessor.* — in·her·it·ance (-unce) *n.*

in·hib·it (in·HIB·it) *v.* **1** forbid a person from doing something: *Clean-air signs inhibit most smokers from* *lighting up in public.* **2** hinder an action or process. — **in·hib·i·tor** *n.*

in·hi·bi·tion (in·huh·BISH·un) *n.* a check, esp. a mental blocking of one's own thinking or behaviour.

in-house *adj. & adv.* inside a group or institution: *artwork for a book done in-house rather than by an agency; an in-house line, publication, system; in-house staff, training.*

in·hu·man (in·HEW·mun) *adj.* not human: *Cannibalism is cruel and inhuman; inhuman poverty and misery; His stamina seems inhuman.* — **in·hu·man·ly** *adv.*

in·hu·mane (in·hew·MAIN) *adj.* not showing humanity or kindness: *inhumane treatment of animals.*

in·hu·man·i·ty (in·hew·MAN·uh·tee) *n.* **-ties** cruelty or barbarity: *man's inhumanity to man.*

in·hume (in·HUME) *v.* **-humes, -humed, -hum·ing** bury or inter. — **in·hu·ma·tion** (in·hew·MAY·shun) *n.*

in·im·i·cal (in·IM·uh·cul) *adj.* **1** *Formal.* hostile: *an inimical attitude, force, glance.* **2** harmful: *drugs inimical to good health.* — **in·im·i·cal·ly** *adv.*

in·iq·ui·ty (in·IK·wuh·tee) *n.* **-ties** wickedness or a wicked act: *a den of iniquity.* — **in·iq·ui·tous** (-tus) *adj.*

in·i·tial (i·NISH·ul) *adj.* being the beginning of a series; first: *the initial letter of a word; in the initial stages of our negotiations; initial claims, impressions, plans, steps; My initial reaction was to refuse.* — *n.* the first letter, esp. of a name: *John Smith's* **initials** (=J.S.). — *v.* **-tials, -tialled** or **-tialed, -tial·ling** or **-tial·ing** mark with initials: *to initial a correction.*

in·i·tial·ize (i·NISH·ul·ize) *v.* **-iz·es, -ized, -iz·ing** of a computer process or device, to set to a starting position or value.

in·i·tial·ly (i·NISH·uh·lee) *adv.* at first.

in·i·ti·ate (i·NISH·ee·ate) *v.* **-ates, -at·ed, -at·ing** **1** begin; get going: *to initiate a plan, project; to initiate talks.* **2** admit a person into a special group or to a field of knowledge or activity: *a day for initiating new members; He was initiated into the Knights of Columbus.* — **in·i·ti·a·tion** (-AY·shun) *n.*

in·i·ti·a·tive (i·NISH·ee·uh·tiv) *n.* **1** the action of taking a first step: *She does things on her own initiative; a peace initiative; The stronger nation should take the initiative for peace talks.* **2** the ability required for this; hence, enterprise: *a woman who shows great initiative.*

in·ject (in·JECT) *v.* introduce or force into, as serum into the bloodstream or fuel into the cylinders of an internal-combustion engine: *funds to inject new life into an ailing business.* — **in·jec·tion** *n.* — **in·jec·tor** *n.*

in·junc·tion (in·JUNK·shun) *n.* an order, esp. one issued by a court, to do or not do something, as during a labour strike: *A court delivers, grants, hands down, issues an injunction against picketing; an injunction to prevent picketing.*

in·jure (IN·jur) *v.* **-jures, -jured, -jur·ing** hurt or do harm or damage: *people injured in an accident; to be badly, fatally, seriously, severely, slightly injured; to put on a look of* **injured** *innocence.*

in·ju·ri·ous (in·JOOR·ee·us) *adj.* harmful: *Bad publicity is injurious to a business; Some habits are injurious to health.*

in·jur·y (IN·juh·ree) *n.* **-ries 1** bodily hurt: *injuries suffered in an accident; to inflict, receive, suffer, sustain an injury; a bodily, fatal, great, internal, minor, physical, serious, severe, slight injury; head injuries; injuries to the head.* **2** wrong or injustice: *an injury to one's pride, to one's reputation; the forgiveness of injuries; to* **add insult to injury** (= annoy besides hurting).

in·jus·tice (in·JUS·tis) *n.* **1** lack of justice: *a sense of injustice; social injustice.* **2** an unjust act: *to commit an injustice; to do someone an injustice* (= judge him or her unfairly); *to redress an injustice; a blatant, flagrant, gross injustice; rank injustice; the injustices of life.*

ink *n.* a coloured liquid for writing, printing, or drawing: *a blob of ink; indelible, invisible, marking ink.* — *v.* cover, mark, or stain with ink.

ink-jet printer *n.* a quiet, high-speed computer printer that works by spraying ink.

ink·ling *n.* a hint or vague notion: *to get, have an inkling of the meaning; I didn't have the faintest* or *slightest inkling of it; to give someone an inkling of the problem.*

in·laid (IN·laid, in·LAID) *adj.* decorated with a design, material, etc. set in the surface as an inlay: *an inlaid table top.*

in·land (IN·lund) *adj.* **1** situated in or toward the interior of a country: *an inland town; inland waterways such as canals, rivers, and lakes;* ***adv.:*** *to go inland; travel inland by boat.* **2** domestic or internal: *sources of inland revenue such as income tax and excise, estate, and gift taxes.*

in-law *n. Informal.* a relative by marriage. — *combining form:* *brother-in-law, father-in-law, mother-in-law, sister-in-law.*

in·lay *v.* **-lays, -laid, -lay·ing 1** set in or insert a piece of wood or metal, pattern, or illustration into a surface. **2** decorate thus. — *n.* something inlaid, as a mosaic, bone graft, or dental filling.

in·mate *n.* a person living with others, esp. one confined in a prison or institution.

in·most *adj.* most inward; secret: *one's inmost thoughts.*

inn *n.* **1** a hotel. **2** in names, a restaurant or tavern.

in·nards (IN·urdz) *n.pl. Informal.* internal organs, parts, or workings.

in·nate (IN·ate, i·NATE) *adj.* existing from birth or by nature in a person or thing; inborn: *an innate defect, instinct, strength, vigour.*

in·ner (IN·ur) *adj.* situated farther in, esp. deep inside: *an inner organ of the body; the earth's inner core; inner* (= mental or spiritual) *peace; an influential* **inner circle** *of friends; the overcrowded, poverty-stricken, and crime-ridden* **inner city** *being abandoned in favour of* *the suburbs; a nonconformist* **inner-directed** *personality; the inflatable* **inner tube** *of a bicycle tire; one's* **in·ner·most** *thoughts and desires.*

in·ning (IN·ing) *n.* **1** in baseball, a play period in which both teams have a turn at bat. **2** such a turn. **3** innings *pl.* opportunity for action.

inn·keep·er (IN·kee·pur) *n.* the owner or manager of a hotel.

in·no·cence (IN·uh·sunce) *n.* the quality or state of being innocent: *to maintain, prove, show one's innocence; an air of injured innocence* (= undeserved hurt); *people living in a state of primitive innocence* (= unspoiled by civilization).

in·no·cent (IN·uh·sunt) *adj.* **1** doing or having done no harm or wrong; not deserving punishment for an offence: *He was declared innocent of the charge of theft; Many innocent people were killed in the bombing.* **2** harmless: *innocent enjoyment; We're having some innocent fun; innocent amusements, pastimes, pleasures.* **3** without guile; hence, naive or simple: *an innocent infant, question; too innocent to be suspicious of anyone.* — *n.* a child or simple-minded adult. — **in·no·cent·ly** *adv.*

in·noc·u·ous (i·NOK·yoo·us) *adj.* **1** harmless or inoffensive: *an innocuous drug.* **2** unexciting: *an innocuous speech.*

in·no·vate (IN·uh·vate) *v.* -vates, -vat·ed, -vat·ing **1** make changes: *You can't innovate without the principal's approval.* **2** bring in something new as a change: *Who innovated this procedure?* — **in·no·va·tive** (-vay·tiv) *adj.*

in·no·va·tion (in·uh·VAY·shun) *n.* **1** introduction of a change: *The 1980s were a period of innovation in computer technology.* **2** the making of changes: *Progress comes about through innovation.* **3** a new method, device, or other change: *microwaves and such recent innovations in kitchen equipment.*

in·nu·en·do (i·new·EN·doh) *n.* -does an indirect derogatory remark or hint: *His jokes are full of sexual innuendo; to make innuendoes about someone's private life.*

in·nu·mer·a·ble (i·NEW·muh·ruh·bul) *adj.* too numerous to be counted.

in·oc·u·late (i·NOC·yuh·late) *v.* -lates, -lat·ed, -lat·ing introduce a serum or vaccine into the body, usually by injection, to give immunity *against* infectious diseases such as smallpox and measles. — **in·oc·u·la·tion** (-LAY·shun) *n.*

in·of·fen·sive (in·uh·FEN·siv) *adj.* unoffending: *an inoffensive remark.*

in·op·er·a·ble (i·NOP·uh·ruh·bul) *adj.* that cannot be surgically operated upon: *an inoperable tumour.*

in·op·er·a·tive (i·NOP·uh·ruh·tiv) *adj.* not working; without effect: *The previous boss's directives are inoperative today.*

in·or·di·nate (i·NOR·dun·it) *adj.* disorderly or immoderate: *an inordinate affection, demand, passion, period of time.* — **in·or·di·nate·ly** *adv.*

in·put *v.* -puts, *pt. & pp.* -put·ted or -put, -put·ting put into a machine or system as raw materials for manufacturing, data for processing, etc. — *n.* what is input, as a contribution or reaction: *A government tries to get input from the public on a proposed piece of legislation; capital, labour, and other inputs required for a new product.*

in·quest *n.* **1** a coroner's inquiry to find out the cause of a suspicious death. **2** the jury holding it or their finding.

in·quire (in·QUIRE) *v.* -quires, -quired, -quir·ing *Formal.* ask: *to inquire about what happened last night; Mother inquires after you* (= asks about your health); *The police inquire into suspicious deaths; a child with an inquiring* (= curious and alert) *mind.* — **in·quir·er** *n.*

in·quir·y (in·QUIRE·ee, INK·wuh·ree) *n.* -quir·ies **1** a request for information: *We made many discreet inquiries about her condition; Thanks for your kind inquiries.* **2** a formal investigation: *to conduct, hold, launch, make an official inquiry into a scandal.*

in·qui·si·tion (ink·wuh·ZISH·un) *n.* an intensive or ruthless questioning: *to conduct an inquisition into his teachings on religion and morals.* — **in·quis·i·tor** (in·KWIZ·uh·tur) *n.* — **in·quis·i·to·ri·al** (-TOR·ee·ul) *adj.*

in·quis·i·tive (in·KWIZ·uh·tiv) *adj.* questioning or curious in a prying manner.

in-residence (in·REZ·uh·dunce) *combining form.* of an artist or professional, having duties as a teacher, consultant, etc.: *a poet-in-residence at a university; a writer-in-residence.*

in·roads *n. pl.* an invasion or encroachment: *Automation has made deep inroads into our work habits; to make inroads on* or *upon one's health, savings, time.*

in·sane *adj.* **1** formerly, having to do with the mentally ill: *an insane asylum.* **2** *Informal.* very foolish: *What an insane idea!*

in·san·i·ty (in·SAN·uh·tee) *n.* **1** severe mental illness: *He was judged not guilty of murder by reason of insanity; He pleaded temporary insanity due to a nervous condition.* **2** extreme foolishness: *outright, pure, sheer insanity.*

in·sa·ti·a·ble (in·SAY·shuh·bul) *adj.* that cannot be satisfied: *an insatiable appetite; his insatiable greed.*

in·scribe (in·SCRIBE) *v.* -scribes, -scribed, -scrib·ing write in or engrave in a lasting manner: *a tombstone inscribed with one's name; words indelibly inscribed in her memory; to inscribe a book* (= autograph or dedicate it). — **in·scrip·tion** (in·SCRIP·shun) *n.*

in·sect *n.* **1** a small, six-legged creature such as a fly, mosquito, or beetle. **2** a wingless or crawling creature such as a spider or tick.

in·se·cure (in·si·CURE) *adj.* not secure or feeling safe: *an insecure child; He seems very insecure in his job; an insecure job that may end any time; He feels insecure about going out at night; an insecure hold, lock.*

— in·se·cure·ly *adv.*
— in·se·cu·ri·ty (-CURE·uh·tee) *n.* -ties.

in·sem·i·nate (in·SEM·uh·nate) *v.* -nates, -nat·ed,
-nat·ing **1** put semen into a female animal or egg: *She
was artificially inseminated with the sperm of her
husband.* **2** inject a new element into something old: *to
inseminate an old show with new characters.*
— in·sem·i·na·tion (-NAY·shun) *n.*

in·sen·si·ble (in·SEN·suh·bul) *adj.* **1** not sensitive: *to be
insensible to the feelings of others.* **2** unconscious or
numb: *He lay there insensible and bleeding; quite
insensible of what was going on around him.* **3** not easy
to sense or perceive: *It grew cold by insensible degrees.*

in·sep·a·ra·ble (in·SEP·uh·ruh·bul) **1** *adj.* that cannot
be parted or separated: *inseparable companions; twins
who are inseparable from each other.* **2** **inseparables**
n. pl. inseparable persons or things.

in·sert (in·SURT) *v.* put something into a place where it
belongs: *to insert a key into a lock; to insert new names
in a list.*
— *n.* (IN·surt) something inserted: *an 8-page
advertising insert* (= supplement) *of a newspaper; See
enclosed package insert for dosage information.*
— in·ser·tion (in·SUR·shun) *n.: ornamental lace
insertions in cloth.*

in-service *adj.* received in the course of one's
employment: *in-service training.*

in·set *v.* -sets, -set, -set·ting set in something: *a picture
inset with the text.*
— *n.* something inset or inserted.

in·shore *adj. & adv.* close to the shore, not offshore: *an
inshore boat race; the grey whale of inshore waters; the
annual whale migration of codfish; Fish that don't
swim inshore get caught offshore; the inshore catch of
fish; inshore fishing, fishing grounds, fisheries, fleets,
plants, winds.*

in·side *n.* an inner side, position, part, etc.: *the inside of
a room; one horse overtaking another* **on the inside**
(= in the inside lane); *the insides* (= internal organs) *of
the body.*
— *adj.: inside information; an* **inside job** (= a crime
committed with the help of someone inside the
organization that is the victim); *an inside page;* **the
inside track** (= advantageous position).
— *prep.: Fido is inside the house.*
— *adv.: We stay inside when it rains; We'll be back*
inside of (= within) *an hour; an umbrella turned* **inside
out** *by the wind; She knows the place inside out*
(= thoroughly).

in·sid·er (in·SYE·dur) *n.* one who belongs to a group or
place, and is often specially privileged: *Stock market
insiders have confidential information from company
managers, directors, etc.; an* **insider trading** *scandal
(resulting from exploiting confidential information).*

in·sid·i·ous (in·SID·ee·us) *adj.* treacherous; working
secretly: *an insidious disease, influence, plot.*

in·sight *n.* power to see into and understand a situation:
*to gain, have an insight into their mode of life; The
book provides deep insights about their life.*
— in·sight·ful *adj.*

in·sig·ni·a (in·SIG·nee·uh) *n.* -ni·a or -ni·as a
distinguishing mark of position or rank, as on a military
uniform; emblem.

in·sin·cere (in·sin·SEER) *adj.* not sincere.
— in·sin·cer·i·ty (-SER·uh·tee) *n.* -ties.

in·sin·u·ate (in·SIN·yoo·ate) *v.* -ates, -at·ed, -at·ing
1 hint or imply something dishonourable about a
person: *to insinuate that Joe is a thief.* **2** introduce
oneself into a place artfully or slyly: *He insinuated
himself into her affections.*
— in·sin·u·a·tion (-AY·shun) *n.*

in·sip·id (in·SIP·id) *adj.* without flavour; dull or
tasteless.— in·sip·id·ly *adv.*
— in·si·pid·i·ty (in·suh·PID·uh·tee) *n.* -ties.

in·sist (in·SIST) *v.* be firm about a request, statement,
or demand: *He insisted on accompanying her; He
insisted that she shouldn't go out alone; He insisted on it
and she agreed.*
— in·sist·ence (-unce) *n.;* in·sist·ent (-unt) *adj.*

in·so·far (in·soh·FAR) *adv.* to such a degree or extent:
insofar as I'm concerned.

in·so·lent (IN·suh·lunt) *adj.* openly defiant or insulting,
esp. to a superior. — in·so·lence *n.*

in·sol·u·ble (in·SOL·yuh·bul) *adj.* **1** that cannot be
dissolved. **2** not solvable.

in·sol·va·ble (in·SOL·vuh·bul) *adj.* not solvable.

in·sol·vent (in·SOL·vunt) *adj.* unable to pay debts;
bankrupt: *an insolvent debtor, estate.*
— in·sol·ven·cy *n.*

in·sou·ci·ant (in·SOO·see·unt) *adj. Formal.* pert and
unconcerned: *an insoiciant joy, manner, person.*
— in·sou·ci·ance *n.*

in·spect (in·SPECT) *v.* examine carefully and critically,
as for errors or defects: *to inspect a factory for safety; to
inspect a school; to inspect troops (officially); to inspect
someone's work (for accuracy).* — in·spec·tor *n.*

in·spec·tion (in·SPEC·shun) *n.* an inspecting: *to carry
out, conduct, make an inspection; a cursory, visual
inspection; On closer inspection, the signature was
found to be forged.*

in·spi·ra·tion (in·spuh·RAY·shun) *n.* **1** an influence of
the mind or feelings that prompts one to be creative:
*artistic inspiration; poetic inspiration; She started
writing on a sudden inspiration; The classics often give
or provide inspiration to a writer; Shakespeare has been
the inspiration for many playwrights; lifelong*

companions who were a source of mutual inspiration; divine inspiration (= inspiration from God); to derive or draw inspiration from Scripture; a lengthy essay without a flash or spark of inspiration. **2** a breathing in: The chest expands during inspiration.
— in·spi·ra·tion·al (-RAY·shuh·nul) adj.: inspirational literature, music, performance; an inspirational leader, manager, message, player, speaker.

in·spire (in·SPIRE) v. -spires, -spired, -spir·ing breathe in; hence, be the cause of life, vigour, new thought or feeling, etc.: The talk inspired his men with confidence; it inspired them to carry on with the struggle; a very **inspiring** talk; Her warning inspired fear and respect in their hearts; rumours inspired by malice.
— in·spir·er n.

inspired adj. **1** clever and accurate: an inspired guess. **2** creative of thoughts and feelings: a prophet's inspired words.

in·sta·bil·i·ty (in·stuh·BIL·uh·tee) n. lack of stability, firmness, or determination.

in·stall (in·STAWL) v. -stalls, -stalled, -stall·ing put or establish a person, thing, or oneself in a place or position: The faucet was installed by the plumber; a ceremony to install a new president; to install Jones as president; She installs herself in front of the TV after supper every day.
— in·stal·la·tion (in·stuh·LAY·shun) n.

in·stal·ment or in·stall·ment (in·STAWL·munt) n. any of several parts, as of a large amount, long story or article, etc. due at regular intervals: an encyclopedia published in instalments; We paid for the freezer in instalments; We purchased it on the **instalment plan.**

in·stance (IN·stunce) n. **1** a person, thing, or event considered as a case or example: We could cite or give many instances of her generosity; an isolated, rare instance; **In the first instance,** he wasn't invited, and then he stayed too long; Students need good reference books – dictionaries **for instance. 2** request or urging: She was invited at my instance.
— v. -stanc·es, -stanced, -stanc·ing illustrate or cite: an attitude of disrespect instanced by his recent conduct.

in·stant (IN·stunt) n., adj. & combining form. a moment, esp. the present: Come here this instant!
— adj.: Instant coffee is quickly prepared; instant gratification, success; TVs with an **instant-on** button need no warm-up time; an **instant replay** of the videotape of a striking segment of a live telecast; an instant-start fluorescent tube. — in·stant·ly adv.

in·stan·ta·ne·ous (in·stun·TAY·nee·us) adj. coming or happening in an instant: instantaneous death by electrocution; instantaneous reaction.
— in·stan·ta·ne·ous·ly adv.

in·stead (in·STED) adv. in place: I'll have tea **instead of** coffee; She would like an ice cream instead.

in·sti·gate (IN·stuh·gate) v. -gates, -gat·ed, -gat·ing incite or provoke a person, usually to something considered bad: to instigate an assassination, quarrel, rebellion; to instigate workers to strike.
— in·sti·ga·tion (-GAY·shun) n.
— in·sti·ga·tor (-gay·tur) n.

in·stil or in·still (in·STIL) v. -stils or -stills, -stilled,

-still·ing **1** put in drop by drop: nose drops to be instilled in each nostril thrice daily. **2** impart gradually: Parents and teachers instil good habits in or into children; to instil knowledge, love of work, principles.
— in·stil·ment or in·still·ment n.

in·stinct n. an unlearned, inborn tendency to behave in a certain way: the basic instincts; the herd, hunting, mating, and survival instincts; the instinct for self-preservation; the maternal instinct to protect the young; a human, natural instinct; animal, predatory instincts; an unerring instinct (= knack or gift) for the right expression.
— adj. instinct with filled or charged with: a poem instinct with beauty.

in·stinc·tive (in·STINK·tiv) adj. not thought out but spontaneous: an instinctive awareness, dislike, fear, reaction, understanding. — in·stinc·tive·ly adv.

in·sti·tute (IN·stuh·tute) v. -tutes, -tut·ed, -tut·ing initiate or establish: to institute a legal action, award, inquiry; to institute changes, charges, policies, criminal proceedings, programs, rules; to institute a halt to trading.
— n. **1** an organization for art, science, or education, esp. an advanced or specialized school, as one in technical subjects: a technical institute; a collegiate institute; an institute for advanced study. **2** a short teaching program: a summer institute.

in·sti·tu·tion (in·stuh·TYOO·shun) n. **1** an organization for educational, religious, or social work: a charitable, educational, financial institution; an institution endowed by the state. **2** an establishing or thing established, as a law or custom: the institution of marriage; slavery abolished as an institution; She is quite an institution around here (= has been here for a long time).

in·sti·tu·tion·al (in·stuh·TYOO·shuh·nul) adj. having to do with institutions: Apartheid is institutional racism; institutional care for the infirm; institutional advertising (as opposed to product advertising) for generating good will. — in·sti·tu·tion·al·ly adv.

in·struct (in·STRUCT) v. give information to someone clearly and directly: Teachers instruct pupils in a subject; A client instructs his lawyer; A judge instructs a jury; He was instructed (= ordered) to exercise daily.
— in·struc·tor (-tur) n.: a language instructor; an instructor in music. — in·struc·tor·ship n.

in·struc·tion (in·STRUC·shun) n. a direct command or set of directions: to await, carry out, follow, give, issue, receive instructions; Pupils take instruction from teachers; English is our medium of instruction; She had left written instructions for us; Lawyers act on their client's instructions; a judge's instruction to the jury; A computer executes millions of instructions per second; Read the instructions before starting the engine; an instruction manual. — in·struc·tion·al adj.

in·struc·tive (in·STRUC·tiv) adj. serving to teach: an instructive and entertaining talk.

in·stru·ment (IN·struh·munt) n. a person or thing used as a means, esp. an implement for delicate scientific or artistic use: A stringed musical instrument; a string instrument; to play an instrument; a blunt, sharp,

surgical instrument; a navigational instrument such as a compass; A deed of conveyance is a legal instrument (= document); *He refused to be used as an instrument of subversion; Only instruments are used in* **instrument flying** *and landing, as in fog.*
— **v.** (-ment) equip with instruments: *a system fully instrumented for safety; an instrumented landing on Mars.*

in·stru·men·tal (in·struh·MEN·tul) *adj.* 1 serving as a means: *an editor instrumental in the publication of many books.* 2 having to do with instruments: *instrumental music.* — **in·stru·men·tal·ist** *n.*
— **in·stru·men·tal·i·ty** (-TAL·uh·tee) *n.* -ties a serving as a means; agency.

in·suf·fer·a·ble (in·SUF·ur·uh·bul) *adj.* unbearable: *an insufferable bore; insufferable insolence.*
— **in·suf·fer·a·bly** *adv.*

in·su·lar (IN·suh·lur) *adj.* 1 of or like an island in being isolated from the surroundings. 2 narrow-minded, as an islander is assumed to be.
— **in·su·lar·i·ty** (-LAIR·uh·tee) *n.*

in·su·late (IN·suh·late) *v.* -lates, -lat·ed, -lat·ing isolate or separate a conductor or source of energy such as heat, sound, or electricity with a nonconducting material so as to keep from losing or transferring energy: *a well-insulated house; Parents try to insulate their children from the cruelty of the real world.*
— **in·su·la·tion** (-LAY·shun) *n.*

in·su·lin (IN·suh·lin) *n.* a sugar-reducing hormone.

in·sult (IN·sult) *n.* something insolent, rude, or contemptuous that humiliates another: *to avenge, take, swallow an insult; to fling* or *hurl insults at the speaker; The speech was an insult to their intelligence; to add insult to injury.*
— **v.** (in·SULT) do or say something that is an insult: *She felt deeply insulted; a very* **insulting** *remark.*

in·su·per·a·ble (in·SOO·pur·uh·bul) *adj.* that cannot be overcome or passed over: *an insuperable barrier, difficulty, obstacle, problem; insuperable odds.*

in·sur·ance (in·SHOOR·unce) *n.* an undertaking to compensate or protect against specified losses in return for a fee: *to carry, take out, underwrite insurance; accident, automobile, collision, disability, fire, group, health, homeowner's, life, no-fault, term insurance; insurance on property; insurance against loss, fire, etc.; She's in insurance* (= the insurance business); *He collected $3 000 insurance (money) on his car; She pays $400 insurance (as premium) annually; Your insurance (policy) doesn't cover acts of God; Take your umbrella as insurance* (= protection) *(against getting wet).*

in·sure (in·SHOOR) *v.* -sures, -sured, -sur·ing 1 give, take, or get insurance on a property, person, life, etc.: *You can insure your life for a huge sum of money; No one can be insured against dying.* 2 same as ENSURE.

insured *n.* a person whose property or life is insured.

in·sur·gen·cy (in·SUR·jun·see) *n.* -cies a minor revolt.

in·sur·gent (in·SUR·junt) *n.* a person rising up or acting against an established government; rebel.
— **in·sur·gence** *n.*

in·sur·rec·tion (in·suh·REC·shun) *n.* an armed uprising

or outbreak, usually short-lived, against established authority: *to crush, foment, put down, quell, stir up an insurrection; The military was called out to suppress the insurrection; an armed insurrection.*
— **in·sur·rec·tion·ist** *n.*

in·tact (in·TACT) *adj.* untouched or whole in spite of something that might have impaired or damaged it: *The parcel was delivered intact; Nothing was left intact after the storm.*

in·take *n.* 1 an opening where a fluid enters a container: *The* **intake manifold** *of a carburetor connects it with the engine cylinders.* 2 a taking in, esp. of a fluid through a narrow opening. 3 the amount of liquid or gas taken in.

in·tan·gi·ble (in·TAN·juh·bul) 1 *adj.* that cannot be touched, felt, or grasped by the mind: *Goodwill is an intangible business asset; the intangible charisma of leadership.* 2 *n.pl.* stocks, bonds, patents, and such intangibles (that are not material assets).
— **in·tan·gi·bly** *adv.*

in·te·gral (IN·tuh·grul, in·TEG·rul) *adj.* 1 essential as part of a whole: *Limbs are integral parts of our bodies.* 2 formed of such parts: *an integral design.* 3 whole or unbroken: *an integral personality, structure.*
— **n.** a whole number or a whole.

in·te·grate (IN·tuh·grate) *v.* -grates, -grat·ed, -grat·ing make into or become a whole; bring parts together into one, as different racial groups in society: *Immigrants try to integrate into Canadian society; to integrate with the rest of the population; an* **integrated school** *(for members of various races, religions, etc.);* **integrated software** *combining a spreadsheet with word processing; transistors, resistors, and capacitors in one* **integrated circuit** *instead of being wired together.*
— **in·te·gra·tion** (-GRAY·shun) *n.*

in·teg·ri·ty (in·TEG·ruh·tee) *n.* 1 trustworthy moral character: *a man of integrity.* 2 soundness or completeness of anything: *a treaty guaranteeing territorial integrity; a dramatization that lacks artistic integrity.*

in·tel·lect (IN·tuh·lect) *n.* mind or intelligence: *a woman of keen intellect; one of the greatest intellects of our time.*

in·tel·lec·tu·al (in·tuh·LEC·choo·ul) *adj.* having to do with or interested in things of the mind rather than of the body or emotions: *Chess is an intellectual game; reasoning, judgment, and such intellectual processes; a woman of intellectual tastes.*
— **n.** an intellectual person: *Academics are intellectuals.* — **in·tel·lec·tu·al·ly** *adv.*

in·tel·lec·tu·al·ize (in·tuh·LEC·choo·uh·lize) *v.* -iz·es, -ized, -iz·ing make intellectual or treat intellectually, esp. without considering emotional aspects; philosophize.

in·tel·li·gence (in·TEL·uh·junce) *n.* 1 ability to learn, understand, remember, and respond to situations requiring use of the mind: *high, keen, limited, low, native, remarkable, sharp, superior intelligence; an intelligence test.* 2 news or information of a vital nature: *Spies collect* or *gather intelligence; foreign, industrial,* *military intelligence; The Canadian Security Intelligence Service; The U.S. Central Intelligence Agency.*

in·tel·li·gent (in·TEL·uh·junt) *adj.* having intelligence: *an intelligent child, dog, woman; an intelligent observation (showing intelligence); An intelligent or smart terminal can process data besides receiving and transmitting it like a dumb terminal.*
— in·tel·li·gent·ly *adv.*

in·tel·li·gent·si·a (in·TEL·uh·JENT·see·uh) *n. sing.* or *pl.* the intellectual class of a society.

in·tel·li·gi·ble (in·TEL·uh·juh·bul) *adj.* that can be understood by the mind: *an unreasonable but intelligible explanation.* — in·tel·li·gi·bly *adv.*
— in·tel·li·gi·bil·i·ty (-BIL·uh·tee) *n.*

in·tem·per·ate (in·TEM·puh·rit) *adj.* not moderate or showing self-control: *an intemperate outburst; a man of intemperate habits (esp. in regard to drinking).*
— in·tem·per·ate·ness *n.* — in·tem·per·ance *n.*

in·tend (in·TEND) *v.* **1** have as an aim or purpose: *I intend to go home after school; What do you intend doing after school?* **2** mean: *an offence that was not intended; a book intended as a gift.*

in·tend·ant (in·TEN·dunt) *n.* the head of a French colonial government, as Jean Baptiste Talon in 17th century Quebec.

in·tend·ed (in·TEN·did) *n.* husband or wife to be: *a note from your intended.*
— *adj.* meant or planned: *a gift intended for the bride; the parents of the intended* (= prospective) *bride.*

in·tense (in·TENCE) *adj.* of a high degree; sharply focussed; very keen: *intense happiness, heat, light, pain; an intense personality (strong in head and heart); an intense woman.* — in·tense·ly *adv.*
— in·ten·si·ty (in·TEN·suh·tee) *n.* -ties.

in·ten·si·fy (in·TEN·suh·fye) *v.* -fies, -fied, -fy·ing make or become more intense; strengthen: *to intensify activities, the competition, concerns, cooperation, demands, efforts, a search; Attacks, charges, negotiations, pressure, problems, speculation, trends intensify.* — in·ten·si·fi·er (-fye·ur) *n.*
— in·ten·si·fi·ca·tion (-fuh·CAY·shun) *n.*

in·ten·sive (in·TEN·siv) *adj.* thorough or concentrated, not extensive: *an intensive* (= in-depth) *study; a hospital's intensive care unit for critically ill patients; intensive farming to produce several crops each year with heavy use of labour, fertilizers, etc.*
— *combining form:* capital-intensive, labour-intensive.

in·tent (in·TENT) *n.* what is intended or meant; intention: *malicious intent; assault with intent to kill; the intent* (= meaning) *of a message.*
— to all intents and purposes in every way; practically.
— *adj.* attentive or earnest: *an intent look; a student intent on passing her exams.* — in·tent·ly *adv.*

in·ten·tion (in·TEN·shun) *n.* **1** what is intended: *He had no intention of seeing her; She had every intention of seeing him; She stuck to her intention to see him.* **2** intentions plans, as in regard to a person one is interested in: *What are his intentions in regard to her?*

honorable intentions; "The road to hell is paved with good intentions" (= Good intentions are useless without good performance).

in·ten·tion·al (in·TEN·shuh·nul) *adj.* with an intended aim or purpose; deliberate: *an intentional snub.*
— in·ten·tion·al·ly *adv.*

in·ter (in·TUR) *v.* -ters, -terred, -ter·ring *Formal.* bury a corpse.

inter- *combining form.* between or among; each other: *interact, interchange, interface.*

in·ter·act (in·tur·ACT) *v.* act on or influence each other: *Students and teachers interact with each other.*
— in·ter·ac·tion (-AC·shun) *n.*

in·ter·ac·tive (in·tur·AC·tiv) *adj.* acting on each other; two-way: *an interactive communication system; interactive cable TV.*

in·ter·cede (in·tur·SEED) *v.* -cedes, -ced·ed, -ced·ing plead with someone in authority for a favour: *The suspended student asked me to intercede with the principal for his reinstatement; I interceded on his behalf.*

in·ter·cept (in·tur·SEPT) *v.* cut off, stop, or seize a moving person or thing before reaching the destination: *to intercept a letter in the mail; to intercept a fleeing convict; to intercept a forward pass in football; to intercept the flow of oil.* — in·ter·cep·tion (-shun) *n.*
— in·ter·cep·tor (-tur) *n.*

in·ter·ces·sion (in·tur·SESH·un) *n.* an interceding, as by prayer or mediation. — in·ter·ces·sor (-SES·ur) *n.*
— in·ter·ces·so·ry (-SES·uh·ree) *adj.*

in·ter·change (in·tur·CHANGE) *v.* **1** exchange. **2** cause two things to change places or to happen by turns.
— *n.* (IN·tur·change) an interchanging, esp. a junction in the shape of a cloverleaf, diamond, etc. designed for unchecked flow of traffic between a highway or freeway crossing a secondary road or another freeway.
— in·ter·change·a·ble (-CHAIN·juh·bul) *adj.*

in·ter·con·ti·nen·tal (IN·tur·con·tuh·NEN·tul) *adj.* between or across continents: *an intercontinental ballistic missile, railway; intercontinental migration.*

in·ter·course (IN·tur·corse) *n.* dealings, as between people: *social intercourse; sexual intercourse* (= sexual act); *intercourse* (= communing) *with the Deity.*

in·ter·dict (in·tur·DICT) *v.* prohibit or forbid by decree: *People interdicted under the Liquor Licence Act may not enter a liquor store or licenced premises.*
— *n.* (IN·tur·dict) a prohibition.

in·ter·est (IN·trist, -tuh·rist) *n.* **1** condition or feeling of wanting to know or learn about and share or take part in something: *She takes interest in education; That's not her only interest* (= subject of interest) *in life; a dull story without much interest* (= interesting quality); *to arouse, generate, lose, show, stir up, revive interest in the arts; a deep, intense, keen, lively interest; a story with much human interest; a conflict of interest between private and public interest; a story of some interest to the general public; The government has the national interest in view; Teachers work in the interest or in the interests* (= for the good) *of students.* **2** a group of

people with a common concern: *an undertaking supported by the business interests of the town; banking interests; oil interests; shipping interests; steel interests; A ban on smoking is opposed by certain vested interests; a (special) interest group of tobacco growers.* **3** benefit or advantage: *People tend to look after their own interests; to guard, promote, protect their interests; Whose interests does this project serve? a clash of interests; He sold his interest (= share) in the farm.* **4** money charged or paid for the use of money: *The bank lends money at a certain interest; Savings deposits bear* or *pay* or *yield interest; Banks pay interest on deposits; Interest accrues to deposits; Interest is added to the principal; Interest is charged on loans.*
— *v.* cause interest in someone: *Nothing interests him more than video games; Could I interest you in a new car?*
— **interested** *adj.* **1** having or showing interest: *I'm interested in a new car at this time; You'll be interested to hear about our bargain prices; My wife is an interested party to a car deal; an interested look.* **2** having a personal interest: *a sales rep with an interested motive.*

in·ter·face (IN·tur·face) *n.* a common surface or boundary through which two bodies, regions, or systems interact or communicate: *A union station is the transportation interface of a large city; Publishing is the interface between authors and the reading public; v.: Authors interface with the public through publishers.*

in·ter·fere (in·tur·FEER) *v.* -feres, -fered, -fer·ing get in the way of people or affairs: *to interfere in a family dispute; They hesitated to interfere between the spouses; Nothing unforeseen should interfere with our plans; The catcher interfered by hampering the batter's swing; a very interfering (= meddlesome) neighbour.*
— **in·ter·fer·ence** (-unce) *n.*: *unwarranted foreign interference in a country's internal affairs; They will brook no interference from the superpowers; We won't tolerate any interference with our plans; His secretary was supposed to run interference (Informal for handle the problems) between him and his creditors.*

in·ter·fer·on (in·tur·FEER·on) *n.* a protein molecule produced by cells to fight a viral infection.

in·ter·im (IN·tur·im) *n.* the time that comes between: *She was without a job in the interim while management changed hands; adj.: an interim arrangement, loan, payment, report.*

in·te·ri·or (in·TEER·ee·ur) *adj.* inside or inner, not exterior: *a house's interior walls; Style, colour, pattern, etc. are elements of interior design used in interior decoration of houses, offices, automobiles, etc. to make them pleasant and comfortable.*
— *n.* the inner or inside part: *the interior of a building; the interior of British Columbia (away from the Pacific coast); The U.S. Department of the Interior looks after the nation's natural resources.*

in·ter·ject (in·tur·JECT) *v.* throw in a remark, question, etc. abruptly between other things: *"Hold it!" he interjected as I was about to continue.*

in·ter·jec·tion (in·tur·JEC·shun) *n.* something interjected, esp. an exclamatory word considered as a part of speech, as "alas," "ouch," etc.

in·ter·lace (in·tur·LACE) *v.* -lac·es, -laced, -lac·ing **1** pass over and under each other. **2** arrange this way, as reeds or fibres in basket-weaving: *an interlacing pattern; roads interlacing with rivers on a map.*

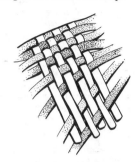

in·ter·lard (IN·tur·lard) *v.* mix or intersperse: *a speech interlarded with anecdotes.*

in·ter·leaf (IN·tur·leef) *n.* -leaves a usually blank leaf inserted between the leaves of a book.
— **in·ter·leave** (-leev) *v.* -leaves, -leaved, -leav·ing: *illustrated pages interleaved with print.*

in·ter·lock (in·tur·LOCK) *v.* **1** lock or fit tightly together, as the pieces of a jigsaw puzzle. **2** operate together, as railway signals.
— *n.* an interlocking condition, device, or arrangement: *an automobile with an interlock that prevents the driver from starting the engine without first buckling up; A microwave has two interlock systems to prevent it from operating if the door is even slightly open.*

in·ter·mar·ry (in·tur·MAIR·ee) *v.* -mar·ries, -mar·ried, -mar·ry·ing marry or become connected by marriage across racial, religious, or familial boundaries: *Jews intermarrying with gentiles.*
— **in·ter·mar·riage** (-ij) *n.*: *intermarriage between Catholics and Protestants.*

in·ter·me·di·ar·y (in·tur·MEE·dee·air·ee) *n.* -ar·ies a go-between or mediator; *adj.: an intermediary role; an intermediary stage of development.*

in·ter·me·di·ate (in·tur·MEE·dee·it) *adj.* being in between two things: *an intermediate shade of green; an automobile of intermediate size (= midsize, between standard and compact); The intermediate grades (= usually 7 through 10) of school link junior and senior grades; an intermediate range ballistic missile (that travels up to 1 500 mi. / 2 414 km).*

in·ter·min·gle (in·tur·MING·gul) *v.* -gles, -gled, -gling mingle or mix together: *The plainclothes police intermingled with the crowd.*

in·ter·mit·tent (in·tur·MIT·unt) *adj.* stopping and starting again: *an intermittent fever; an intermittent volcano erupting in cycles.* — **in·ter·mit·tent·ly** *adv.*

in·ter·mo·dal (in·tur·MOH·dul) *adj.* of several modes: *an intermodal container that can be shipped by plane, rail, truck, or ship.*

in·tern or **in·terne** (IN·turn) *n.* a medical or other professional receiving in-service training.
— *v.* (in·TURN) **1** be an intern: *She interned in St.*

John's. **2** confine, esp. suspected aliens, in a certain place, as during wartime. — **in·tern·ship** *n.*

in·ter·nal (in·TUR·nul) *adj.* inside or inner, not external: *Hormones are internal secretions; a computer's* **internal memory** *(to hold data being processed) as opposed to its external storage; the internal combustion within an engine's cylinders; an* **internal-combustion engine;** *A historical reference in a book is* **internal evidence** *of its date of publication;* **Internal medicine** *deals with the nonsurgical treatment of diseases of the heart, lungs, stomach, and such internal organs; a government's* **internal revenue** *derived from taxing domestic goods and services, not from export and import duties.* — **in·ter·nal·ly** *adv.*

in·ter·na·tion·al (in·tur·NASH·uh·nul) *adj.* having to do with relationships between nations: *an international airport where planes land from foreign countries; the Canada-U.S. international border; International law deals with war, peace, and neutrality; the high seas, or* **international waters,** *200 miles (= 321.9 km) from a country's shore.* — **in·ter·na·tion·al·ly** *adv.*

interne same as INTERN.

in·ter·nee (in·tur·NEE) *n.* a person confined as an alien during wartime, as North Americans of Japanese ancestry during World War II. — **in·tern·ment** *n.*

in·ter·per·son·al (in·tur·PUR·suh·nul) *adj.* (having to do with relations) between persons: *interpersonal communications, conflicts, relationships; a leader with good interpersonal skills (for managing people).*

in·ter·plan·e·tar·y (in·tur·PLAN·uh·tair·ee) *adj.* between planets or in their region: *interplanetary travel; an interplanetary probe into interplanetary space.*

in·ter·play (IN·tur·play) *n.* interaction: *the interplay of coloured lights at Niagara Falls.*

in·ter·po·late (in·TUR·puh·late) *v.* -lates, -lat·ed, -lat·ing **1** insert new or spurious matter *into* a passage or text. **2** alter it thus: *interpolated passages in Shakespeare.* — **in·ter·po·la·tion** (-LAY·shun) *n.*

in·ter·pose (in·tur·POZE) *v.* -pos·es, -posed, -pos·ing put forward or place *between* or *among* others: *a remark interposed at the wrong moment; Al got hurt when he interposed himself between the fighters.*

in·ter·pret (in·TUR·prit) *v.* explain or bring out a meaning that is not apparent: *to interpret a dream; to interpret an author; to interpret a dramatic role (by one's acting); to interpret (= translate) for foreign tourists.*
— **in·ter·pre·ta·tion** (-pruh·TAY·shun) *n.*
— **in·ter·pret·er** (-prit·ur) *n.*

in·ter·ra·cial (in·tur·RAY·shul) *adj.* having to do with different races: *an interracial incident, marriage.*

in·ter·re·late (IN·tur·ruh·LATE) *v.* -lates, -lat·ed, -lat·ing have or bring into a mutual relationship.
— **in·ter·re·la·tion·ship** *n.*

in·ter·ro·gate (in·TER·uh·gate) *v.* -gates, -gat·ed, -gat·ing question a prisoner, witness, etc. formally and systematically in a search for facts; **in·ter·ro·ga·tion** (-GAY·shun) *n.* — **in·ter·ro·ga·tor** (-gay·tur) *n.*

in·ter·rog·a·tive (in·tuh·ROG·uh·tiv) *n.* used in asking a question: *an interrogative adverb such as "when,"*

"where," or "why"; *interrogative pronouns such as* "who" *and* "what."

in·ter·rupt (in·tuh·RUPT) *v.* **1** make a break in the continuity of something: *to interrupt a flow; An accident interrupts traffic; to interrupt study, work; Highrises interrupt (= obstruct) our view.* **2** break in upon a person, his speech, etc.: *Sorry to interrupt you; Am I interrupting anything?*
— *n.* a computer's ability to interrupt the execution of one routine and take up another without waiting for the first to finish. — **in·ter·rup·tion** (-RUP·shun) *n.*

in·ter·sec·tion (in·tur·SEC·shun) *n.* a crossing or the place of crossing, as of lines, streets, etc.: *traffic accidents at a busy intersection; a railway crossing that is considered a dangerous intersection.*

in·ter·sperse (in·tur·SPURCE) *v.* -spers·es, -spersed, -spers·ing put here and there between or among other things: *to intersperse statuary among the flowers in a garden; greenery interspersed with flowers.*

in·ter·stel·lar (in·tur·STEL·ur) *adj.* between stars or in their region: *interstellar cloud, space, travel.*

in·ter·stice (in·TUR·stis) *n.* -stic·es a narrow opening, crack, or similar intervening space, as in network.

in·ter·twine (in·tur·TWINE) *v.* -twines, -twined, -twin·ing twine together; interlace: *Four strands of wool are intertwined to make four-ply yarn.*

in·ter·val (IN·tur·vul) *n.* a break or gap of space, time, pitch, or other factor: *trees planted at intervals of 10 m; a medication to be taken at regular intervals; Buses leave here at short intervals; labour pains at 10-minute intervals; a brief, lucid interval (= limited period) during an illness; A* **major interval** *(= pitch difference between two tones) chromatically reduced by a semitone becomes a minor interval.*
— **at intervals** here and there; also, now and then.

in·ter·vene (in·tur·VEEN) *v.* -venes, -vened, -ven·ing **1** be, come, or go between events, persons, etc.: *to intervene in a family dispute; the intervening period between their separation and reunion; The government can intervene to end a strike; Before he could graduate, war intervened.* **2** [legal use] to act as an intervenor.

in·ter·ve·nor or **in·ter·ven·er** (in·tur·VEE·nur) *n.* an interested party given standing at a judicial hearing.

in·ter·ven·tion (-VEN·shun) *n.* an act of intervening: *an armed, divine, military intervention.*

in·ter·view (IN·tur·vyoo) *n.* **1** a personal conversation, as between an employer and job applicant or a journalist and a subject: *to conduct, do, give, grant an interview; a live, telephone, taped, TV interview.* **2** a news story or article setting forth a conversation: *The interview appeared yesterday.*
— *v.: The personnel manager interviews candidates for jobs; The politician refused to be interviewed on camera; She was interviewed via satellite.*

in·tes·tin·al (in·TES·tuh·nul) *adj.* of the intestines: *an intestinal bypass operation;* **intestinal fortitude** *(= pluck or guts).*

in·tes·tine (in·TES·tin) *n.* the alimentary tube from the end of the stomach to the anus, divided into the narrow "small intestine" and the wider "large intestine"; bowel. — *adj.* within a country: *intestine strife.*

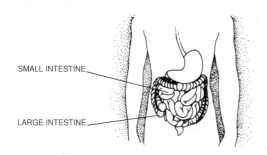

SMALL INTESTINE

LARGE INTESTINE

in·ti·ma·cy (IN·tuh·muh·see) *n.* -cies **1** personal closeness: *the intimacy between spouses.* **2** an intimate act, esp. sexual.

in·ti·mate (IN·tuh·mit) *adj.* personally close or familiar: *two friends on intimate terms; They are intimate with each other; the intimate atmosphere of a nightclub; an intimate nightclub; an intimate relationship; an intimate knowledge of the subject.* — *n.* one who is intimate: *an intimate of Leslie's.* — *v.* (-mate) -mates, -mat·ed, -mat·ing *Formal.* suggest delicately or indirectly: *to intimate one's wishes; He has intimated to the family that he would like to visit them.* — **in·ti·mate·ly** *adv.* — **in·ti·ma·tion** (-MAY·shun) *n.*

in·tim·i·date (in·TIM·uh·date) *v.* -dates, -dat·ed, -dat·ing frighten by display of superior strength, power, learning, etc.: *a witness intimidated into silence.* — **in·tim·i·da·tion** (-DAY·shun) *n.*

in·to (IN·too) *prep.* [indicating movement toward or to the inside of]: *She went into the room; bumped into him by accident; to translate from French into English; She fell ill in October when she was a month into Grade 7; She is now into* (Informal for involved in) *cooking; She's so into cooking, she has no time to watch TV; 4 into 20* (= 20 divided by 4) *is 5.*

in·tol·er·a·ble (in·TOL·ur·uh·bul) *adj.* too much to endure; unbearable: *He screamed in intolerable pain; The "Intolerable Acts" of the British Parliament drove the American colonies to war.* — **in·tol·er·a·bly** *adv.*

in·tol·er·ance (in·TOL·ur·unce) *n.* **1** the quality of being intolerant: *racial intolerance; religious intolerance.* **2** allergy or sensitivity to something: *intolerance to specific drugs; A person with alcoholic intolerance should not touch liquor.*

in·tol·er·ant (in·TOL·ur·unt) *adj.* not tolerant, esp. of other's opinions or beliefs; bigoted: *He's too **intolerant of** opposition to be a democrat.*

in·to·na·tion (in·tuh·NAY·shun) *n.* **1** the act or style of intoning or chanting: *intonation of the Psalms.* **2** the rise and fall of the voice in speech: *Questions have a rising intonation.*

in·tone (in·TONE) *v.* -tones, -toned, -ton·ing recite a prayer, psalm, etc. in a singing voice or in a monotone.

in·tox·i·cate (in·TOX·uh·cate) *v.* -cates, -cat·ed, -cat·ing make drunk or as if drunk: *Power intoxicates; He was intoxicated by the idea of getting rich by gambling.* — **in·tox·i·ca·tion** (-CAY·shun) *n.*

intra- *combining form.* within; inside of: *intracity, intramolecular, intramural, intrastate.*

in·tran·si·tive (in·TRAN·suh·tiv) *adj.* of a verb, that does not need a direct object. — *n.* an intransitive verb such as "arrive," "seem," or "lie." — **in·tran·si·tive·ly** *adv.*

in·tra·ve·nous (in·truh·VEE·nus) *adj.* within or into a vein or veins: *intravenous feeding; an intravenous anesthetic, injection.* — **in·tra·ve·nous·ly** *adv.*

intrench same as ENTRENCH.

in·trep·id (in·TREP·id) *adj.* brave and fearless, esp. against new or unknown dangers: *an intrepid explorer, fireman; Canadian Sir William Stephenson was called Intrepid as a master spy for British Security in World War II.* — **in·tre·pid·i·ty** (in·truh·PID·uh·tee) *n.*

in·tri·ca·cy (IN·truh·cuh·see) *n.* -cies the quality of being intricate or something that is intricate: *the intricacies of diplomacy, of a plot.*

in·tri·cate (IN·truh·kit) *adj.* hard to follow or understand, being complicated like a maze or elaborate like filigree work: *an intricate pattern, plot, problem.* — **in·tri·cate·ly** *adv.*

in·trigue (IN·treeg) *n.* a secret, often underhanded plot or scheme, as for the overthrow of someone or an illicit love affair: *to engage in domestic intrigue; The palace was a hotbed of intrigue; a web of intrigue.* — *v.* -trigues, -trigued, -trig·uing **1** make or carry out a secret plan or plot: *He gets ahead by intriguing against his rivals.* **2** interest greatly: *a story opening that is likely to intrigue the reader; I'm intrigued by or with the story opening; She found the revelation very **intriguing*** (= strangely fascinating).

in·trin·sic (in·TRIN·sic) *adj.* existing within, as something essential or inherent, not extrinsic: *Beauty is intrinsic to beautiful objects; the intrinsic merit or worth of a painting besides its snob value; the intrinsic value of an object apart from its usefulness; The intrinsic value of a coin is what its metal is worth.* — **in·trin·si·cal·ly** *adv.*

in·tro·duce (in·truh·DUCE) *v.* -duc·es, -duced, -duc·ing **1** bring in or put in: *It's not advisable to introduce a knife into the mouth like a spoon; to introduce a new subject for discussion.* **2** bring forward for getting acquainted: *A chairman introduces a speaker (to the audience); I introduced myself to him; a party to introduce* (= begin or open) *the New Year.*

in·tro·duc·tion (in·truh·DUC·shun) *n.* an introducing: *the debut as a formal introduction to society; She replied to the introduction by saying "How do you do"; the introduction of printing in or into Europe; a letter of introduction; to write an introduction to a book.* — **in·tro·duc·to·ry** (-DUC·tuh·ree) *adj.*

in·tro·spec·tion (in·truh·SPEC·shun) *n.* an examining of one's own thoughts and feelings. — **in·tro·spec·tive** (-tiv) *adj.;* **in·tro·spec·tive·ly** *adv.*

in·tro·vert (IN·truh·vurt) *n.* one who is more concerned with his or her own thoughts and feelings than with the world outside, not an extrovert. — **in·tro·vert·ed** *adj.* — **in·tro·ver·sion** (-VUR·zhun, -VUR·shun) *n.*

in·trude (in·TROOD) *v.* **-trudes, -trud·ed, -trud·ing** thrust or push in where not invited or expected: *to intrude on a person's privacy; May I intrude? The enemy forces intruded into our territory; a bore who intrudes his views on everyone.* — **in·trud·er** *n.*: *He locks the gate to his backyard to keep out intruders.* — **in·tru·sion** (-TROO·zhun) *n.*

in·tru·sive (in·TROO·siv) *adj.* forcing in: *intrusive behaviour, person; Molten magma forms intrusive rocks by pushing up from below the surface.* — **in·tru·sive·ly** *adv.*; **in·tru·sive·ness** *n.*

intrust same as ENTRUST.

in·tu·i·tion (in·tyoo·ISH·un) *n.* **1** direct insight without conscious reasoning: *Experienced people sense things by intuition.* **2** something known or learned by such insight: *Our intuitions may fail in moments of panic.* — **in·tu·i·tive** *adj.*; **in·tu·i·tive·ly** *adv.*

In·u·it (IN·oo·it) *n. sing. & pl.* Eskimo (people or language): *the Inuit Tapirisat* (= Eskimo Brotherhood) *of Canada.*

in·un·date (IN·un·date) *v.* **-dates, -dat·ed, -dat·ing** overflow, as in a flood; deluge: *employers inundated with job applications.* — **in·un·da·tion** (-DAY·shun) *n.*

in·ure (in·YOOR) *v.* **-ures, -ured, -ur·ing** *Formal.* accustom oneself to something hard to bear: *to become inured to cold, danger, hardship, hunger.*

in·vade (in·VADE) *v.* **-vades, -vad·ed, -vad·ing** enter another's territory to conquer or as if to take possession: *a household invaded by unexpected guests; Army worms invade fields.* — **in·vad·er** *n.*

in·va·lid (IN·vuh·lid) *n.* a person who is weak or sickly: *He remained an invalid all his life; a home for invalids.* — *v.* disable or render weak: *He was invalided by a bomb blast and invalided* (= released) *out of the military.* — *adj.* (in·VAL·id) not valid: *an invalid claim, cheque, marriage.* — **in·val·id·ly** *adv.*

in·val·i·date (in·VAL·uh·date) *v.* **-dates, -dat·ed, -dat·ing** deprive of legal force or effect: *The most recent will invalidates any previous wills.* — **in·val·i·da·tion** (-DAY·shun) *n.*

in·val·u·a·ble (in·VAL·yoo·uh·bul) *adj.* of value that cannot be estimated; priceless. — **in·val·u·a·bly** (-blee) *adv.*

in·var·i·a·ble (in·VAIR·ee·uh·bul) *adj.* habitual and unchanging. — **in·var·i·a·bly** (-uh·blee) *adv.*: *He is invariably late on Monday mornings.*

in·va·sion (in·VAY·zhun) *n.* an invading, as by an attacking force, disease germs, etc.: *to carry out, launch, repel, repulse an invasion; the annual invasion of tourists in the summer; the invasion of privacy by electronic snooping.* — **in·va·sive** (-siv) *adj.* that invades the body: *an invasive cancer; A biopsy is an invasive diagnostic examination.*

in·vec·tive (in·VEC·tiv) *n.* a violent attack in words, spoken or written: *The media hurled a torrent of invective or invectives against the censorship laws.*

in·vei·gle (in·VAY·gul, -VEE·gul) *v.* **-gles, -gled, -gling** mislead someone or obtain something by trickery: *He was inveigled into buying worthless stock.*

in·vent (in·VENT) *v.* make up or think up something new: *Who invented the ballpoint pen? The child is good at inventing excuses.* — **in·ven·tor** *n.*

in·ven·tion (in·VEN·shun) *n.* an inventing or something invented: *Modern inventions make living comfortable; an ingenious invention; a report that is pure invention; "Necessity is the mother of invention"* (= is what makes people invent things).

in·ven·tive (in·VEN·tiv) *adj.* having the ability to invent: *an inventive mind; our inventive capacity, powers.* — **in·ven·tive·ly** *adv.*; **in·ven·tive·ness** *n.*

in·ven·to·ry (IN·vun·tor·ee) *n.* **-ries 1** an itemized list of goods in stock, property, etc., as for valuation: *to make or take an inventory of stock.* **2** the things so listed: *a sale to reduce inventory; the annual marking down of inventory; The shop will be closed next week for inventory; We like fast inventory turnover.* — *v.* **-ries, -ried, -ry·ing**: *We inventory stock monthly.*

in·verse (IN·vurse) *adj.* inverted or reversed, esp. mathematically: *an inverse function; Addition and subtraction are inverse operations.* — *n.*: *a/b is the inverse of b/a.* — **in·verse·ly** *adv.*: *Light intensity is inversely related to distance* (= The larger the distance the less intense the light).

in·vert (in·VURT) *v.* turn in an opposite direction, esp. upside down: *A mirror reverses its image, a lens inverts it; Quotation marks are **inverted commas.*** — **in·ver·sion** (in·VUR·zhun, -shun) *n.*: *the inversion of subject and verb in "Did I?"; **Temperature inversion** traps smoke and noxious gases in the air.*

in·vest (in·VEST) *v.* **1** spend or put out money, time, energy, and such resources with the expectation of later benefit: *People invest heavily in Canada Savings Bonds;* **in·ves·tor** *n.* **2** *Formal.* clothe or endow a person *with* an office, dignity, authority, right, etc.; **in·ves·ti·ture** (in·VES·tuh·chur) *n.*

in·ves·ti·gate (in·VES·tuh·gate) *v.* **-gates, -gat·ed, -gat·ing** search into a situation or incident systematically so as to learn the facts. — **in·ves·ti·ga·tion** (-GAY·shun) *n.*: *to carry out, conduct, make an investigation; a criminal, cursory, impartial, perfunctory, thorough investigation; a case that is under police investigation.* — **in·ves·ti·ga·tive** (-gay·tiv) *adj.* — **in·ves·ti·ga·tor** (-gay·tur) *n.*

in·vest·ment (in·VEST·munt) *n.* an investing of money and such resources: *an investment of $5 million; a long-term investment; investments in blue chip stocks; Education is a good investment for life.* — *adj.*: *an investment banker, company, counsellor.*

in·vet·er·ate (in·VET·ur·it) *adj.* of a habit, custom, practice, feeling, etc., long-established: *an inveterate prejudice, smoker; an inveterate* (= habitual) *liar.*

in·vid·i·ous (in·VID·ee·us) *adj.* tending to cause envy or animosity: *an invidious comparison, discrimination, rule.* — **in·vid·i·ous·ly** *adv.;* **in·vid·i·ous·ness** *n.*

in·vig·o·rate (in·VIG·uh·rate) *v.* **-rates, -rat·ed, -rat·ing** fill with vigour.
— **invigorating** *adj.*: *The swim was very invigorating; an invigorating climate, tonic.*
— **in·vig·o·ra·tion** (-RAY·shun) *n.*

in·vin·ci·ble (in·VIN·suh·bul) *adj.* that cannot be overcome or subdued: *invincible courage, ignorance.*
— **in·vin·ci·bly** *adv.*
— **in·vin·ci·bil·i·ty** (-BIL·uh·tee) *n.*

in·vi·o·late (in·VYE·uh·lit) *adj.* not violated; sacred or pure: *to keep an oath inviolate; the shrine's inviolate sanctity.*

in·vis·i·ble (in·VIZ·uh·bul) *adj.* not visible; out of sight or hidden: *the invisible side of the moon; Germs are invisible to the naked eye.*
— **in·vis·i·bly** *adv.;* **in·vis·i·bil·i·ty** (-BIL·uh·tee) *n.*

in·vi·ta·tion (in·vuh·TAY·shun) *n.* an inviting: *to decline, extend, issue, send, spurn an invitation; to send out invitations to a wedding; printed invitations; an invitation to attend a wedding; a cordial, formal, informal invitation; Admission is by invitation only.*
— **in·vi·ta·tion·al** *adj.*: *an invitational lecture not open to the public; an invitational tennis tournament.*

in·vite (in·VITE) *v.* **-vites, -vit·ed, -vit·ing** ask politely to be present somewhere or to do something: *to invite a guest; He was invited to the wedding; Your costume may invite* (= provoke) *comment; an inviting* (= attractive or alluring) *sight.* — **in·vit·ing·ly** *adv.*

in vi·tro (in·VEE·troh) *adv.* in an artificially maintained condition, as an embryo in a test tube, not **in vi·vo** (in·VEE·voh), or in the living body.
— **in-vitro** *adj.*: *an in-vitro fertilization.*

in·vo·ca·tion (in·vuh·CAY·shun) *n.* **1** an invoking or appeal to God or similar higher power. **2** the words or formula used.

in·voice (IN·voice) *n.* a list of goods or services provided showing payment due for them: *an invoice for books shipped.*
— *v.* **-voic·es, -voiced, -voic·ing 1** enter on an invoice: *to invoice an order.* **2** bill: *to invoice a customer.*

in·voke (in·VOKE) *v.* **-vokes, -voked, -vok·ing** appeal to a higher power such as God or spirits or to an authority, as of a law, ruling, etc. for help or protection: *a prayer invoking God's blessing; penalties invoked only in times of national crises; to invoke aid, mercy, special privileges.*

in·vol·un·tar·y (in·VOL·un·tair·ee) *adj.* not willed or controlled by the will, as reflex actions: *an involuntary action, movement; the involuntary muscles of the intestines.* — **in·vol·un·tar·i·ly** (-TAIR·uh·lee) *adv.*

in·vo·lute (IN·vuh·loot) *adj.* **1** rolled inward, as the scrolls of an "Ionic" column. **2** curled in a spiral, as some shells. **3** intricate or involved.

in·volve (in·VOLV) *v.* **-volves, -volved, -volv·ing 1** enfold or include: *a job that involves manual work; Rights involve duties.* **2** concern or entangle: *I would like to help you without involving myself in* or *with your*

private life; And let's not involve the children in this.
— **involved** *adj.* **1** closely connected or concerned: *Leo is emotionally involved with Lee; At first they didn't want to get involved* (= have a close relationship). **2** complicated: *an involved explanation, question, sentence, style.* — **in·volve·ment** *n.*

in·vul·ner·a·ble (in·VUL·nur·uh·bul) *adj.* that cannot be attacked or hurt: *an invulnerable argument, fortress, position; a fortress that is invulnerable to attack.*
— **in·vul·ner·a·bly** *adv.*

in·ward (IN·wurd) *adj.* directed toward the inside; inner: *an inward curve, slant; one's inward nature.*
— *adv.*: *inward bound;* also **in·wards.**
— **in·ward·ly** (IN·wurd·lee) *adv.*: *He was inwardly happy at her discomfort.*

in·wrought (in·RAWT) *adj.* of a pattern or decoration, woven or worked in.

i·o·dine (EYE·uh·din) *n.* a chemical element found in sea water and sea weed, used as an antiseptic.

i·o·ta (eye·OH·tuh) *n.* **1** the ninth letter of the Greek alphabet, corresponding to "i." **2** the least bit or amount; jot: *I didn't get one iota of help from him.*

IOU (EYE·oh·YOO) *n.* **IOUs** a written promise ("I owe you") to repay money or debts owed.

IQ (EYE·cue) *n.* **IQs** a measure of intelligence: *a high, low IQ; an IQ test.*

i·rate (eye·RATE) *adj. Formal.* angry: *an irate customer, driver.* — **i·rate·ly** *adv.*

ire *n.* wrath, as shown in looks, words, actions, etc.: *to arouse someone's ire.* — **ire·ful** *adj.*

ir·i·des·cent (eer·uh·DES·unt) *adj.* displaying rainbowlike colours when seen from different angles, as mother-of-pearl. — **ir·i·des·cence** *n.*

i·ris (EYE·ris) *n.* **1** a plant with sword-shaped leaves bearing three-petalled flowers of varying colour, stylized as the fleur-de-lis. **2** the coloured part around the pupil of the eye.

I·rish (EYE·rish) *n.* a person of or from Ireland.
— **get one's Irish up** *Informal.* arouse one's temper.
— *adj.* having to do with the people of Ireland or their language: *Irish fairy tales, literature, moss, potato famine, setter, stew, Sweepstakes, terrier, whiskey, wolfhound.*
— **I·rish·man** (EYE·rish·mun) *n.* **-men; I·rish·wom·an** (EYE·rish·woom·un) *n.* **-wom·en.**

irk *v.* cause a feeling of weariness or annoyance in someone: *It irks us to have to pay so much tax.* — **irk·some** *adj.*: *an irksome delay, task; irksome restrictions.*

i·ron (EYE·urn) *n.* **1** a hard, strongly magnetic, heavy metallic element used for tools and machinery, esp. as steel: *cast, crude, pig, scrap, wrought iron.* **2** any tool or weapon of iron, a golf club, etc.: *branding iron* (= a branding device); *climbing or grappling iron* (= a hook); *a clothes iron; curling iron* (= instrument for curling hair; rarely, a curling stone); *soldering iron* (= tool for applying solder); *waffle iron* (= utensil); *to **pump iron*** (= be a weight-lifter). **3 irons** *pl.* handcuffs or shackles: *They put him in irons.* — *v.* press and smooth cloth with a heated iron. — **iron out** smooth out confusion, differences, difficulties, etc. — *adj.* made of or like iron in hardness: *an iron constitution, hand, lady, ore; The dictator ruled with an **iron fist** for 25 years; an **iron hand in a velvet glove*** (= ruthlessness masked by softness). — **ironing** *n.* clothes ironed or for ironing: *to do the ironing.*

i·ron·clad (EYE·urn·clad) *adj.* difficult to get out of, as if armoured with iron plates: *an ironclad guarantee.*

ironic, ironical See IRONY.

iron lung *n.* an artificial respiratory chamber in which a paralysed person can be kept alive for treatment.

i·ron·stone (EYE·urn·stone) *n.* **1** iron ore. **2** a type of hard white English pottery.

i·ron·ware (EYE·urn·ware) *n.* pots, tools, etc. of iron; hardware.

i·ron·work·er (EYE·urn·wur·kur) *n.* a person whose work is the erecting and connecting of the structural steel framework of buildings.

i·ron·works (EYE·urn·wurks) *n. sing. & pl.* a place where iron and steel products are made.

i·ro·ny (EYE·ruh·nee) *n.* **-nies** a saying, happening, or situation that is apparently contrary to what is intended or desirable, as when one says "Wonderful!" about something infuriating: *bitter irony; dramatic irony; a touch of irony; tragic irony; By an **irony of fate**, he received his inheritance the day he died.* — **i·ron·ic** or **i·ron·i·cal** (eye·RON·uh·cul) *adj.* — **i·ron·i·cal·ly** *adv.*

ir·ra·di·ate (i·RAY·dee·ate) *v.* **-ates, -at·ed, -at·ing** expose to rays of light or other radiation: *a countenance irradiated with joy; food preserved by being irradiated with gamma rays or electrons.* — **ir·ra·di·a·tion** (-AY·shun) *n.*

ir·ra·tion·al (i·RASH·uh·nul) *adj.* **1** not endowed with reason: *Animals are irrational creatures; He became irrational with rage.* **2** contrary to reason: *Superstitions are irrational.* — **ir·ra·tion·al·ly** (-nuh·lee) *adv.* — **ir·ra·tion·al·i·ty** (-NAL·uh·tee) *n.* **-ties.**

ir·rec·on·cil·a·ble (i·REC·un·SYE·luh·bul) *adj.* that cannot be reconciled or brought into harmony: *an irreconcilable enemy; irreconcilable differences of attitude.* — **ir·rec·on·cil·a·bly** (-luh·blee) *adv.*

ir·re·gard·less (eer·uh·GARD·lis) *adj.* [nonstandard use] See REGARDLESS.

ir·reg·u·lar (i·REG·yuh·lur) *adj.* not obeying the usual rules, as in conduct, organization, or features: *an irregular coastline; irregular behaviour, breathing; an irregular marriage (that is contrary to rules); irregular troops; "go-went-gone" are parts of an **irregular verb**.* — **ir·reg·u·lar·ly** *adv.* — *n.* a soldier not of a regular army. — **ir·reg·u·lar·i·ty** (-LAIR·uh·tee) *n.* **-ties.**

ir·rel·e·vant (i·REL·uh·vunt) *adj.* not pertinent or to the point. — **ir·rel·e·vant·ly** *adv.* — **ir·rel·e·vance** *n.*

ir·rep·a·ra·ble (i·REP·ur·uh·bul) *adj.* that cannot be repaired or put right: *to do irreparable harm.*

ir·re·spec·tive (eer·uh·SPEC·tiv) *adj.* regardless of something: *irrespective of colour, creed, or sex.*

ir·rev·o·ca·ble (i·REV·uh·cuh·bul) *adj.* that cannot be revoked or altered. — **ir·rev·o·ca·bly** (-blee) *adv.*

ir·ri·gate (EER·uh·gate) *v.* **-gates, -gat·ed, -gat·ing** supply with flowing water or other liquid, as land for cultivation or a body part to cleanse it. — **ir·ri·ga·tor** (-gay·tur) *n.* — **ir·ri·ga·tion** (-GAY·shun) *n.*

ir·ri·ta·ble (EER·uh·tuh·bul) *adj.* **1** easily irritated. **2** highly sensitive to irritants, as skin or other plant or animal tissue.

ir·ri·tant (EER·uh·tunt) *n.* something causing irritation: *The barking at night proved an irritant to neighbourly relations; an irritant poison.*

ir·ri·tate (EER·uh·tate) *v.* **-tates, -tat·ed, -tat·ing** **1** annoy in such a way that nothing can be done about it: *His comments irritated the speaker.* **2** stimulate biologically, as by light, heat, pressure, or touch. **3** make sore or sensitive, as mucous membranes by irritant poisons such as arsenic and lead: *Too much chlorine in the swimming pool irritates the eyes.* — **ir·ri·ta·tion** (eer·uh·TAY·shun) *n.*

ir·rupt (i·RUPT) *v. Formal.* **1** rush in or burst in: *The drug squad irrupted into the apartment.* **2** of a species, to increase suddenly in numbers. — **ir·rup·tion** (-shun) *n.* — **ir·rup·tive** (-tiv) *adj.*

is (IZ) See BE.

-ish *adj. suffix.* of or like, esp. somewhat inclined to be: *girlish, reddish, sixish (Informal for about 6), uppish.*

Is·lam·ic (is·LAH·mic) *adj.* having to do with the religion founded by Mohammed: *Islamic ceremonies, unity; the Islamic code, law, people, religion, republic, revolution, world.*

is·land (EYE·lund) *n.* **1** a usually small land mass surrounded by water: *Green Gables is in Prince Edward Island; They live on Vancouver Island; We live in Bowen Island; on an island in the Caribbean; Robinson Crusoe's deserted island; a tropical island.* **2** any isolated place such as a "traffic island" for the safety of pedestrians. — **is·land·er** *n.*

isle (ILE) *n.* a small island.

is·let (EYE·lit) *n.* a tiny island.

ism (IZ·um) **1** *n. Informal.* a doctrine or cause, as communism, fascism, jingoism, etc. **2** *suffix.* conduct, condition, or quality: *archaism, fascism, heroism, liberalism.*

is·n't (IZ·unt) is not.

i·so·late (EYE·suh·late) *v.* -lates, -lat·ed, -lat·ing **1** separate from others: *to isolate one animal from the rest of the herd; a few **isolated** instances (that are not part of a general pattern).* **2** obtain a substance in a free or uncombined state.

i·so·la·tion (eye·suh·LAY·shun) *n.* physical separation imposed by circumstances: *Robinson Crusoe's life of isolation; A hospital's **isolation ward** is for patients with contagious diseases.*

i·so·met·ric (eye·suh·MET·ric) *adj.* **1** having equality of measure: *An isometric crystal, as a cube-shaped one, has three equal axes; isometric drawing, line, projection.* **2** involving contraction of muscles without shortening; not isotonic: *Isometric exercises, or **isometrics,** involve tensing (with little movement) of muscles against each other or against a fixed object.*

i·so·ton·ic (eye·suh·TON·ic) *adj.* **1** of solutions, having the same osmotic pressure. **2** involving shortening of a muscle, not isometric: *an isotonic contraction, exercise.*

is·sue (ISH·oo) *v.* **is·sues, is·sued, is·su·ing 1** put forth or put out: *to issue a proclamation, stamps and coins, a publication; clothing issued to G.I.s* **2** come out: *smoke issuing from a chimney.*
— *n.* **1** what is issued or comes out: *to bring out or publish a new **issue** of an old book; an issue consisting of 2 000 copies; back issues and current issues of a journal; a pair of government-issue boots; He died without issue* (= offspring). **2** result or outcome: *to await the issue of an election.* **3** subject of a dispute or controversy: *to address, bring up, face, raise, straddle an issue; Let's not make such an issue of it; to cloud, confuse, duck, evade, settle the issue; a burning, dead, divisive, sensitive, side, substantive issue; Let's not **force the issue*** (= force a decision); *The point **at issue*** (= in dispute) *is not how it happened but why; He hesitated to **take issue*** (= disagree) *with his boss.* — **is·su·er** *n.*

-ist *n. suffix.* person of specified occupation or persuasion: *atheist, botanist, communist, humorist, specialist.*

it *pron., possessive* ITS, *pl.* THEY, *objective* THEM, *possessive* THEIR *or* THEIRS **1** the understood subject to which an action refers: *We all heard it; Tell her about it; Don't make such a big deal of it.* **2** an indefinite or impersonal subject or object: *Who is it? "It never rains but it pours"; It's nice to see you; She's quite **with it*** (*Slang for* up to date).
— *n.* in children's games such as tag, the player who initiates the action, as catching, finding, etc.

I·tal·ian (i·TAL·yun) *n.* a person of or from Italy or the Romance language spoken there.
— *adj.* having to do with Italy: *Italian immigrants; the Italian language.*

i·tal·ic (i·TAL·ic, eye-) *n.* a type or letter that slants to the right: *This is italic; printed in italics.*
— *adj.* **1** Italic having to do with ancient Italy, its people, or their dialects. **2** having to do with italics: *an italic letter, passage, sentence, type.*

i·tal·i·cize (i·TAL·uh·size) *v.* -ciz·es, -cized, -ciz·ing print in italics or underline to indicate italics.

itch *n.* **1** skin irritation that makes one want to scratch: *an ointment to relieve your itch.* **2** a restless, uneasy longing or desire: *the **seven-year itch** (to have an affair after seven years of marriage); Mites cause **the itch,** or scabies; an itch for gold.*
— *v.* have an itch: *I'm itching to get at him; I have itching ears (eager to hear what comes next); the itching palm of an avaricious man.*
— **itch·y** *adj.* **itch·i·er, -i·est.** — **itch·i·ness** *n.*

i·tem (EYE·tum) *n.* a separate unit or article in an enumeration, list, or group: *a budget item; collector's item; luxury item; news items.*

i·tem·ize (EYE·tuh·mize) *v.* -iz·es, -ized, -iz·ing list in detail: *an itemized bill instead of a general statement.*
— **i·tem·i·za·tion** (-muh·ZAY·shun) *n.*

i·tin·er·ant (eye·TIN·ur·unt) *n.* one travelling from one place to another: *an itinerant judge, musician, preacher, seller.*

i·tin·er·ar·y (eye·TIN·uh·rair·ee) *n.* -ar·ies **1** a plan, route, or record of a journey. **2** a traveller's guidebook.

-itis *n. suffix.* a disease or diseaselike condition: *appendicitis, bronchitis, electionitis* (= election fever).

it'll it will, it shall.

it's it is; it has.

its *adj. & pron.* possessive of IT: *Two of its legs are missing; They are its (legs).*

it·self (it·SELF) *pron.* emphatic or reflexive form of IT: *the very thing itself; A catalyst works without itself being affected; a machine able to run **by itself;** The book speaks **for itself;** TV watching is not bad **in itself.***

I've I have.

i·vo·ry (EYE·vuh·ree) *n.* **1** the hard, creamy-white substance of the tusks of elephants, walruses, etc. **2 ivories** *pl. Slang.* things made of ivory, as piano keys, teeth, billiard balls, or dice.
— *adj.* of or like ivory; creamy white.

ivory tower *n.* a place or condition of existence away from the harsh realities of life: *Some see universities as ivory towers.*

i·vy (EYE·vee) *n.* **i·vies** a creeping and climbing evergreen vine with smooth and shiny leaves, five-pointed in the common "English ivy."

-ize *v. suffix.* cause to be, become, or treat (like): *alphabetize, finalize, legalize.*

J or **j** (JAY) *n.* **J's** or **j's** the 10th letter of the English alphabet.

jab *n.* a quick poke with something pointed or a blow as in boxing: *to throw a jab; a left jab; right jab.*
—*v.* **jabs, jabbed, jab·bing** give a jab: *Jan's umbrella jabbed me in the ribs.*

jab·ber (JAB·ur) *n. & v.* chatter *about* something.

jab·ber·wock·y (JAB·ur·wock·ee) *n.* gibberish; meaningless syllables.

jack *n.* **1** a male, esp. a young fellow or helper: *They fired every man Jack (of them); "A jack of all trades and master of none."* **2** a playing card with a picture of a knave: *A jack ranks below king and queen.* **3** a simple mechanism or device, as a machine to lift the wheel of an automobile, or an outlet or receptacle for plugging in a telephone, etc. **4** something handy, as a pebble or piece used in the children's game of **jacks,** a small ball or flag, etc.
—*v.* **jack up 1** raise: *to jack up a car to change a tire.* **2** raise prices, wages, etc.

jack·al (JACK·awl, -ul) *n.* a foxlike wild dog that hunts in packs by night and feeds on carrion: *a pack of jackals.*

jack·ass *n.* **1** a male donkey. **2** a stupid person.

jack·boot *n.* a heavy military boot; hence, oppression or bullying behaviour: *jackboot tactics.*

jack·boot·ed (JACK·boo·tid) *adj.* ruthless: *jackbooted force, militarism.*

jack·et (JACK·it) *n.* **1** a short coat: *a bomber, dinner, flak, life, sports, suit jacket.* **2** an outer covering: *a book's dust jacket; the jacket (=skin) of a potato; the jacket (=sleeve) of a record.*

jack·knife *n.* **-knives 1** a large pocketknife. **2** a dive in which the body is doubled up in midair before straightening up to hit the water.
—*v.* **-knifes, -knifed, -knif·ing** double up like a jackknife, as two railway cars in an accident: *A tractor-trailer jackknifed on the main highway.*

jack-of-all-trades (jack·uv·ALL·trades) *n., pl.* **jacks-of-all-trades** one who can do different kinds of work though not as an expert in any of them.

jack·pot *n.* the accumulated stakes of a poker game or a similar big prize or windfall: *He hit the jackpot (=won the biggest prize).*

jack rabbit *n.* a long-eared North American hare with strong hind legs: *the jack-rabbit (=sudden) starts of a hot rodder.*

jack-up *n.* an increase.

jade *n.* **1** a hard, tough, green or white gemstone used for carvings and jewellery; *adj.* light-green. **2** a worn-out horse. **3** a disreputable woman.
—*v.* **jades, jad·ed, jad·ing** to dull or wear out, as with hard work or overindulgence in something: *a jaded appetite, look.*

jag *v.* **jags, jagged, jag·ging** cut or tear unevenly: *a jagged edge.*
—*n.* **1** a pointed projection, as of rock. **2** *Slang.* a drinking bout or spree. **3** *Informal.* a fit: *a crying jag.*

jail *n.* a prison, esp. one for temporary confinement or for minor offences: *to go to jail, be sent to jail, serve time in jail; He broke out of jail and is now missing.*
—*v.* confine in or as if in jail.

jail·bird *n.* **1** *Informal.* a prisoner. **2** a habitual lawbreaker.

jail·break *n.* an escape from prison: *to attempt, make a jailbreak.*

jail·er or **jail·or** (JAY·lur) *n.* a person in charge of a jail or prisoners.

jam *v.* **jams, jammed, jam·ming 1** press, squeeze, or wedge in between two surfaces: *a finger jammed in a car door.* **2** block or get blocked, get caught in, etc.: *logs jamming a river; clothes jammed into a suitcase; a bus jammed (full) with passengers; The car skidded when the driver jammed on the brakes; A jammed lock or window is hard to open; enemies jamming (=interfering with) each other's radio messages.*

—*n.* **1** a place with so many people or things that movement is impossible: *a log jam in a river; a traffic jam at a busy intersection; If you're in a jam (Informal for tight spot) give me a call.* **2** a fruit preserve: *to spread jam on toast; It's* **jam tomorrow, jam yesterday, but never jam today** (= Your present performance is never as good as your boasts about the past and the future)!

jamb or **jambe** (JAM) *n.* a leglike upright piece forming part of a frame, as of a door.

jam·bo·ree (jam·buh·REE) *n.* **1** a large gathering for revelry or festivities. **2** a Boy Scout rally.

jam·packed *adj.* tightly packed, as a stadium with spectators.

jam session *n. Informal.* a lively gathering of musicians playing improvisations.

jan·gle (JANG·gul) *n.* a harsh, usually metallic clashing noise, as of pots and pans: *Screaming children jangle on* (= upset) *his nerves.*
—*v.* **-gles, -gled, -gling** make a jangle.

jan·i·tor (JAN·uh·tur) *n.* a person in charge of the cleaning, heating, and maintenance of a building; custodian. — **jan·i·tor·i·al** (-TOR·ee·ul) *adj.*

ja·pan (juh·PAN) *n.* a hard varnish as on Japanese lacquerware.
—*v.* **-pans, -panned, -pan·ning** give a glossy finish with japan.

Jap·a·nese (jap·uh·NEEZ) *n. sing. & pl.* **1** a person of or from Japan. **2** *pl.* the people of Japan.
—*adj.: Japanese Canadians; the Japanese cherry tree, language, maple, mink, porcelain, spaniel, yew.*

jape *n. & v.* **japes, japed, jap·ing** jest or gibe.
— jap·er *n.* — jap·er·y *n.*

jar *n.* **1** a wide-mouthed container, usually round, for holding liquids, cosmetics, canned fruit, etc.: *a cookie jar; a "Mason jar" for home canning.* **2** a harsh, esp. grating shock or sound.
—*v.* **jars, jarred, jar·ring** cause a jar: *nerves jarred by the shaking and rattling of the long ride; jarring* (= discordant) *colours, opinions, sounds.*

jar·gon (JAR·gun, -gon) *n.* **1** language that is unintelligible because it is meaningless or obscure. **2** the language of a particular occupational group or profession: *legal jargon; trade jargon.*

jas·per (JAS·pur) *n.* **1** an opaque, usually red, yellow, or brown granular quartz. **2** *Slang.* guy.

jaun·dice (JAWN·dis) *n.* a liver ailment resulting in a yellow discoloration of the skin and eyes: *a jaundiced* (= jealous or prejudiced) *eye, view.*
—*v.* **-dic·es, -diced, -dic·ing** be afflicted with jaundice.

jaunt *n.* a short pleasure trip or excursion: *to go on a jaunt through the hills.* — *v.* take a jaunt.

jaun·ty (JAWN·tee) *adj.* **-ti·er, -ti·est** stylish: *a hat set at a jaunty angle; jaunty* (= lively and carefree) *steps.*
— jaun·ti·ly *adv.;* jaun·ti·ness *n.*

ja·va (JAH·vuh) *n. Slang.* coffee.

jav·e·lin (JAV·lin, JAV·uh·lin) *n.* a light wooden or metal spear, esp. one over 8.5 ft. (260 cm) long, thrown for distance as a field sport.

jaw *n.* **1** either of the two sets of bones containing teeth and forming the mouth: *the lower jaw; upper jaw; He dislocated his jaw; with her jaws set in determination.* **2 jaws** *pl.* a mouth or narrow entrance to a valley, channel, etc.: *the jaws of death.* **3** a gripping or holding part, as of a vise. **4** *Slang.* a talk or chat: *a good jaw with an old friend.* **5** *Slang.* a lengthy, boring, or scolding talk.
—*v.* to talk or talk to someone in a lengthy or boring manner: *He got jawed at; to jaw a situation out with someone.*

jaw·bone *n.* **1** a bone of a jaw, esp. a lower jaw. **2** *Cdn.* in the West, credit: *Oaltal wanted a little jawbone until they brought in the winter's catch of furs; "No jawbone," the sign said.*
—*v.* **-bones, -boned, -bon·ing** *Informal.* pressure or persuade using speech power, esp. to comply with government controls.

jaw·break·er (JAW·bray·kur) *n. Informal.* something that is hard on the jaws, as a kind of candy or a hard-to-pronounce word.

Jaws of Life *Trademark.* a cutting device used in rescuing people trapped in wreckage.

Jay·cee *n.* a member of a junior chamber of commerce, a worldwide organization for leadership training and community work.

jay·walk *v.* of pedestrians, cross a street without regard to traffic regulations. — jay·walk·er *n.*

jazz *n.* **1** music developed by American blacks, characterized by emotional appeal, fast rhythms, and improvisation. **2** *Slang.* empty talk; nonsense: *... and all that jazz* (= and the rest of the stuff). **3** a style of gymnastic dancing based on rock music.
—*adj.: a jazz band; jazz fans, music.*
—*v.* play music as jazz.
— **jazz up** *Slang.* add life, colour, or appeal to something: *a news report that is too jazzed up to be true.*

jazz·y *adj.* **jazz·i·er, -i·est** **1** like jazz. **2** *Slang.* lively or showy: *a jazzy new suit.*
— jazz·i·ly *adv.;* jazz·i·ness *n.*

jeal·ous (JEL·us) *adj.* **1** fearful or suspicious about losing what is one's own to a rival, as a loved one or one's rights: *a jealous husband; a jealous* (= watchful) *guardian of religious freedom; Lee walked out in a jealous rage.* **2** envious: *rivals jealous of each other.*
— jeal·ous·ly *adv.*

jeal·ous·y (JEL·uh·see) *n.* **-ous·ies** resentfulness against rivals; also, envy: *to arouse, feel jealousy; fierce, petty, professional jealousy.*

jeans (JEENZ) *n. pl.* pants made of denim or similar cloth: *blue jeans.*

jeer *n.* a scoffing cry or remark; ridicule.
—*v.* scoff or ridicule: *to jeer at someone or something.*
— jeer·ing·ly *adv.*

jeez *interj.* expressing surprise; gee.

Je·ho·vah (ji·HOH·vuh) *n.* God, as in the Old Testament.

jell *v.* 1 become like jelly; set. 2 *Informal.* of ideas, plans, etc., take definite form: *He's been in a dozen careers that have not jelled.* — *n.* jelly.

jel·li·fy (JEL·uh·fye) *v.* -fies, -fied, -fy·ing change into jelly.

jel·ly (JEL·ee) *n.* jel·lies 1 a semisolid, partly transparent food made from fruit juices, starch, etc. by the thickening action of gelatin. 2 any jellylike substance such as the tissue of jellyfish. — *v.* jel·lies, jel·lied, jel·ly·ing congeal as jelly: *a jellied salad.*

jel·ly·fish (JEL·ee·fish) *n.* 1 an umbrella-shaped sea animal trailing stinging tentacles. 2 a spineless person.

jeop·ard·ize (JEP·ur·dize) *v.* -iz·es, -ized, -iz·ing put in jeopardy; endanger or imperil.

jeop·ard·y (JEP·ur·dee) *n.* -ard·ies danger or peril: *The refugee claimed his life would be in jeopardy if he returned home.*

jerk *n.* 1 a quick, sharp pull, push, or twist. 2 a muscular contraction or twitch, as when the knee is tapped by a physician. 3 *Slang.* one considered as stupid, foolish, or irritating. — *v.* 1 pull quickly and sharply: *She jerked her arm away from her captor; a train jerking its way uphill.* 2 cut beef, etc. into strips for drying and preserving: *Reindeer meat may be jerked, smoked, or canned.* — jerk·y *adj.* jerk·i·er, -i·est. — jerk·i·ly *adv.*

jer·ry-built (JER·ee·bilt) *adj.* shoddily or cheaply constructed.

jer·sey (JUR·see) *n.* -seys a close-fitting pullover made of a plain-stitch knitted fabric.

jest *n.* something said for fun, often to tease or mock: *She said it only in jest* (= not seriously). — *v.* laugh at or joke: *She doesn't jest about her work.*

jest·er *n.* a clown or fool, as in a medieval court.

jet *n.* 1 a stream of water, steam, flame, etc. sent out under pressure, as through a narrow nozzle or spout. 2 such an opening or vent. 3 a jet-propelled aircraft: *to fly, pilot a jet.* — *adj.* deep glossy black. — *v.* jets, jet·ted, jet·ting 1 spout or gush: *water jetting from a fountain.* 2 travel by jet: *to jet over to London.*

jet-black *adj.* very black.

jet lag *n.* exhaustion felt after jetting through several time zones because of the disruption of the body's 24-hour biological rhythms. Also **jet fatigue, jet syndrome.**

jet·lin·er (JET·lye·nur) *n.* a commercial jet airliner.

jet·port *n.* an airport for jet airplanes.

jet·pro·pelled (JET·pruh·PELD) *adj.* driven by jet propulsion.

jet propulsion *n.* the forward reaction of burned gases shooting backward from an engine through exhausts.

jet·sam (JET·sum) *n.* 1 jettisoned cargo washed ashore: *flotsam and jetsam.* 2 social derelicts and such rejected elements of society.

jet set *n.* fashionable people who make frequent air journeys, esp. in the pursuit of pleasure.

jet stream *n.* 1 any of several wide bands of strong winds blowing at high altitudes from west to east. 2 a jet engine exhaust.

jet·ti·son (JET·uh·sun) *v.* throw goods overboard in an emergency so as to lighten a ship or aircraft. — *n.* such goods.

jet·ty (JET·ee) *v.* jet·ties, jet·tied, jet·ty·ing jut out into the water, as a landing pier or breakwater. — *n.* a jettying wall or other structure.

Jew *n.* a follower of Judaism; Hebrew: *the Ashkenazic, Sephardic, and Oriental Jews; The child is a Jew if the mother is Jewish.*

jew·el (JOO·ul) *n.* 1 a precious stone or gem: *priceless jewels; to mount a jewel;* **crown jewels** (= crown, sceptre, etc. used by royalty on official occasions). 2 a jewelled ornament; hence, something or someone very precious: *India was the jewel in the British Crown; Jo is a jewel of a wife.* — *v.* -els, -elled or -eled, -el·ling or -el·ing adorn or set with a jewel: *a jewelled crown.* — jew·el·ler or jew·el·er (JOO·ul·ur) *n.*

jew·el·le·ry or **jew·el·ry** (JOO·ul·ree) *n.* jewels collectively: *costume jewellery.*

Jew·ish *adj.* having to do with Jews: *David is Jewish; He was born on 20 June 1945, or 9 Tammuz 5705 according to the* **Jewish** or **Hebrew calendar** *dating from creation at 3760 B.C.; a Jewish community.* — **Jew·ish·ness** *n.*

Jew·ry (JOO·ree) *n.* 1 Jewish people. 2 formerly, a Jewish ghetto.

jib *n.* 1 a triangular sail set ahead of the foremast. 2 a shying horse. — *v.* jibs, jibbed, jib·bing refuse to move forward, as a shying horse.

jibe 1 *v.* jibes, jibed, jib·ing agree: *Your story doesn't jibe with his.* 2 same as GIBE.

jif·fy (JIF·ee) *n.* jif·fies *Informal.* moment: *I'll be back in a jiffy.*

Jiffy bag *Trademark.* a padded bag for mailing books, pictures, etc.

jig *n.* 1 a lively folk dance, often in triple time, or the music for it. 2 a device that works with an up-and-down motion, as a spoon-shaped fishing lure or a mechanical coal cleaner. 3 a device for holding machine work in position and guiding a tool that works on it, as in machine embroidery.

RINK IT AIN'T A REEM

— **the jig is up** it's hopeless; it's over.
— *v.* **jigs, jigged, jig·ging 1** dance a jig. **2** jerk or move up and down.

jig·ger (JIG·ur) *n.* a measure for serving liquor, usually 1.5 ounces.

jig·gle (JIG·ul) *n.* a slight shake or jerk.
— *v.* **jig·gles, jig·gled, jig·gling** give a jiggle.
— **jig·gly** *adj.*

jigsaw puzzle *n.* a picture sawed into small irregular pieces for fitting back together: *to put together a jigsaw puzzle.*

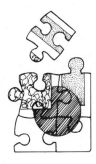

jilt *v.* cast off a lover faithlessly or unfeelingly.
— *n.* one who jilts. — **jilt·er** *n.*

jim·my (JIM·ee) *n.* **jim·mies 1** a short crowbar used especially by burglars. **2 jimmies** *pl.* bits of candy sprinkled on pastry and ice cream for decoration.
— *v.* **jim·mies, jim·mied, jim·my·ing** pry open with a jimmy.

jin·gle (JING·gul) *n.* **1** a clinking sound like that of little bells, coins, or keys striking together. **2** a verse or music that is catchy because of the sound repetitions in it: *an advertising jingle.*
— *v.* **-gles, -gled, -gling** make a clinking sound: *keys jingling in his pocket.* — **jin·gly** (-glee) *adj.*

jin·go (JING·go) *n.* **-goes** one who is jingoistic.

jin·go·ism (JING·go·iz·um) *n.* the attitude or policy of chauvinistic aggressiveness toward other countries.
— **jin·go·ist** *n.* — **jin·go·is·tic** (-IS·tic) *adj.*

jinx *v.* to bring bad luck to someone.
— *n.* a person or thing that jinxes: *to put a jinx on someone.*

jit·ters (JIT·urz) *n. pl. Informal.* the fidgets; a fit of nervousness: *a bad case of the jitters; She had the jitters just before she went on stage.*

jit·ter·y (JIT·uh·ree) *adj.* nervous.

jive *n. Slang.* **1** swing music or dancing; jazz. **2** talk that is insincere or tiring.
— *v.* **jives, jived, jiv·ing 1** tease or kid. **2** dance to or play jive music.
— *adj.* pretentious; insincere; phoney.

job *n.* **1** a piece of work, esp. one done for pay: *He does a good job in his present position; a backbreaking, difficult job; a hatchet job; a snow job; a put-up job; a handyman hired to do **odd jobs** around the house.* **2** employment: *to get, give up, hold, hold down, hunt for, land, look for, lose, quit, take a job; a part-time or full-time job; a cushy, demanding, desk, menial, soft, steady job; summer jobs for students; a job application; He was fired for drinking **on the job** (= while on duty).* **3** *Informal.* a criminal act: *to do a job; He pulled a job at* (= robbed) *the corner store; an inside job.*
— *v.* **jobs, jobbed, job·bing** sell goods purchased wholesale or in large quantities, piece by piece or in small quantities to retailers.

job action *n.* a tactic such as a slowdown, sick-out, or demonstration used by employees instead of striking.

job bank *n.* a computerized system that matches job vacancies with unemployed workers.

job·ber (JOB·ur) *n.* **1** one who does piecework or one who jobs as a middleman. **2** one who uses a position of trust for private ends.

job-hop·ping (JOB·hop·ing) *n.* frequent changing of jobs for financial gain.

job sharing *n.* the sharing of a full-time position by two people working in shifts.

jock *n. Informal* [short form] **1** disc jockey; jockey. **2** jockstrap. **3** *Slang.* a male athlete.

jock·ey (JOCK·ee) *n.* **1** one who rides horses in races. **2** one who guides the movement of something, as specified: *a car jockey; disc jockey.*
— *v.* **-eys, -eyed, -ey·ing 1** ride a horse in a race. **2** try to gain an advantage by skilful manoeuvring: *to jockey for position; to jockey someone or something into position.* **3** trick or cheat someone *into* doing something.

joc·u·lar (JOCK·yuh·lur) *adj.* **1** fond of joking: *a jocular fellow.* **2** meant to be funny: *She said it in a jocular vein.* — **joc·u·lar·i·ty** (-LAIR·uh·tee) *n.*

Joe or **joe** *n. Slang.* fellow or guy: *She's such a good Joe I don't feel threatened by her; not a dumb Joe but a real smartie.*
— *adj.* ordinary: *She started at the bottom doing the Joe jobs.*

jog *n.* **1** a little shove or nudge. **2** a notch or a projecting part; also, unevenness. **3** a sharp and brief change of direction, as in a road.
— *v.* **jogs, jogged, jog·ging 1** give a jog: *She has to jog her husband's memory sometimes.* **2** move along with a shaking motion: *a horse jogging along. People jog for exercise.* — **jog·ger** *n.*

John or **john** (JON) *n. Slang.* **1** a toilet. **2** a prostitute's client.

John Doe *n.* a person whose true name is unknown.

john·ny (JON·ee) *n.* **john·nies** a short gown worn by hospital patients.

Johnny Canuck *n.* See CANUCK.

Johnny-come-lately *n.* **-lies 1** a newcomer. **2** an upstart.

join *v.* **1** bring or come together with another person or thing: *broken pieces joined together; One piece is joined to another; a junction where one street joins another; to join two people in matrimony.* **2** associate with or come into the company of another or others: *to join the armed forces; She will join us in a minute; She'll join in with us; Let's join in the chorus; Let's join hands and say a prayer in silence; Later we will join forces with our allies* *and fight our common enemy; We'll join with them in the fight.* — **join battle** start fighting.

join·er *n.* **1** a person or thing that joins, esp. a carpenter or woodworker specializing in intricate joining work. **2** *Informal.* one who likes to join groups.

joint *n.* **1** a joining or place of joining: *a pipe joint; the ball-and-socket joint of the shoulder; a dovetail joint; mitre joint; mortise and tenon joint; rivetted joint; a kneelike toggle joint; universal joint; welded joint.* **2** a jointed part or division: *the middle joint of a finger; a butcher's joint* (= section) *of meat for roasting.* **3** *Slang.* a cheap establishment such as a hotel, restaurant, or other place where people meet: *two would-be burglars casing a joint; a booze joint; clip joint.* **4** *Slang.* a marijuana cigarette.
— *v.* **1** fit together for joining: *Insects have jointed legs; a perfectly jointed space suit.* **2** divide or cut up at the joints, as a butcher does.
— *adj.* shared or sharing: *a joint bank account; the Joint Chiefs of Staff (forming a military advisory board); divorced parents given* **joint custody** *of a child; a joint editor, secretary.* — **joint·ly** *adv.*

joist *n.* one of the parallel beams supporting a floor or ceiling from wall to wall.

joke *n.* **1** something that arouses laughter, as a funny story, remark, or prank: *to crack, take, tell a joke; a clean, coarse, crude, dirty, funny, off-colour, practical, sick, stale joke; It's no joke to lose your job; Children play jokes on each other on April Fool's Day; Sometimes you can carry a joke too far; Better not make a joke of personal handicaps; the butt or object of a joke; The joke was on me.* **2** a person or thing to laugh at: *He's the joke of the village; The math test was a joke* (= was very easy).
— *v.* **jokes, joked, jok·ing** jest or tease: *to joke with someone about something;* **Joking** *aside, how serious is the loss?* — **jok·ing·ly** *adv.*

jok·er (JOH·kur) *n.* **1** one who jokes; also **joke·ster.** **2** in some games, an extra card useful as a wild card or highest trump. **3** a tricky clause, phrase, or word inserted in a document to nullify its effect.

jol·lies (JOL·eez) *n.pl. Slang.* fun or pleasure: *They get their jollies by partying.*

jol·ly (JOL·ee) *adj.* **jol·li·er, jol·li·est** full of fun; merry.
— *v.* **jol·lies, jol·lied, jol·ly·ing** **1** to humour someone. **2** make fun of someone good-naturedly.
— **jol·li·ly** *adv.*

jolt *n.* a sudden jerk, knock, or surprise: *The news of death came as a jolt to his loved ones; a severe jolt.*
— *v.* give or experience a jolt: *It jolted everyone; It jolted us out of our smugness.* — **jolt·y** *adj.*

Jones·es (JONE·siz) *n.pl.* **keep up with the Joneses** slavishly follow what everyone else is doing, esp. in acquiring material things.

josh *v. Informal.* tease playfully. — **josh·er** *n.*

jos·tle (JOS·ul) *v.* **-tles, -tled, -tling** push or shove, as in a crowd: *Children jostle with each other; They are jostling for position.* — *n.* a jostling.

jot *n.* a very small amount; iota: *I don't care one jot; There's not a jot of truth in the story.*

— *v.* **jots, jot·ted, jot·ting** write down hastily and briefly. — **jot·ter** *n.*

joual (ZHWAHL) *n. Cdn.* dialectal Canadian French as used by the less literate.

jounce (JOWNCE) *n. & v.* **jounc·es, jounced, jounc·ing** jolt or bounce. — **jounc·y** *adj.: a jouncy ride in a jeep.*

jour·nal (JUR·nul) *n.* **1** a daily account or record such as a diary or log, a daily publication such as a newspaper, or a daily bookkeeping record: *I keep a journal during the school term.* **2** a magazine or periodical: *a learned journal; professional journals; scholarly journals; to edit, publish, put out, subscribe to a journal.*

jour·nal·ese (jur·nuh·LEEZ) *n.* language and style that is typical of newspapers and magazines.

jour·nal·ism (JUR·nuh·liz·um) *n.* **1** the gathering and publishing of news through the mass media: *I tried journalism for a career.* **2** journalistic writing: *Journalism is not always literature.* **3** newspapers and magazines collectively: *advocacy journalism; yellow journalism.* — **jour·nal·ist** *n.*
— **jour·nal·is·tic** (-LIS·tic) *adj.*

jour·ney (JUR·nee) *n.* a trip, usually of some duration, to a definite place: *to go on, make, set out on, undertake a journey; a journey across the Sahara; a journey into or through the jungle; a long day's journey; a round-the-world journey; a pleasant, safe, sentimental, tiring journey; It's a journey* (= distance) *of 3 000 km.*
— *v.* **-neys, -neyed, -ney·ing** go on a journey: *to journey from Montreal to Vancouver.*

jour·ney·man (JUR·nee·mun) *n.* **-men** a qualified and experienced though not a master workman; *adj.: a journeyman carpenter, mechanic, plumber, writer.*

joust (JOWST, JUST, JOOST) *n.* combat using lances between two knights on horseback, esp. as part of a medieval tournament, or **jousts** *pl.*
— *v.* engage in a joust.

jo·vi·al (JOH·vee·ul) *adj.* full of good humour and fun: *in a jovial mood.* — **jo·vi·al·ly** *adv.*
— **jo·vi·al·i·ty** (-AL·uh·tee) *n.*

jowl (rhyme: "howl") *n.* **1** the jaw: *a man with heavy jowls.* **2** the lower, hanging part of a face or head, as of cattle, fowl, the head and shoulders of salmon, etc.: *a messy desk with diskettes lying* **cheek by jowl** (= side by side) *with papers.* — **jow·ly** *adj.*

joy *n.* great delight or happiness: *Words cannot express our joy; We feel joy; Her face radiates joy; It's a joy to behold; He couldn't hide his joy that everyone was at the party; He finds, takes joy in teasing people; She leaped for or with joy on hearing the news; the joys and sorrows of life.*

joy·ful *adj.* full of or causing joy: *That was joyful news; Everyone is joyful about or over the victory.*
— **joy·ful·ly** *adv.*

joy·ous (JOY·us) *adj.* full of or endowed with joy: *a joyous family, heart, mood, occasion.*

joy ride *n.* a ride taken for the fun of it, often using unlawful means, as in a stolen automobile: *The boys were on a joy ride when they crashed; They had gone on*

a joy ride in the neighbour's van.
— **joy rider** *n.* — **joy riding** *n.*

joy·stick *n.* a lever that moves in many directions to control an airplane or a computer display.

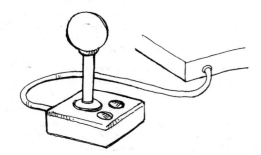

ju·bi·lant (JOO·buh·lunt) *adj.* showing great joy; exultant: *to be jubilant about* or *at* or *over something.* — **ju·bi·lant·ly** *adv.*

ju·bi·la·tion (joo·buh·LAY·shun) *n.* rejoicing; glee: *a poem expressing jubilation at the Olympic gold; Great jubilation was felt all over the country.*

ju·bi·lee (JOO·buh·lee) *n.* a time of rejoicing or celebration, esp. an anniversary: *a diamond jubilee* (= 60th year); *golden jubilee* (= 50th year); *silver jubilee* (= 25th year).

Ju·da·ic (joo·DAY·ic) *adj.* of the Jews or Judaism: *Judaic beliefs; the Judaic religion.*

Ju·da·ism (JOO·duh·iz·um) *n.* the Jewish religion or way of life: *Conservative Judaism; Orthodox Judaism; Reform Judaism; a policy of toleration of Judaism and opposition to Zionism.*

ju·das (JOO·dus) *n.* a traitor, like the disciple Judas who betrayed Jesus.

judge (JUJ) *n.* **1** one who decides, esp. a public official in a court of law who hears and decides cases; a justice: *a fair, impartial, harsh judge; a hanging* (= severe) *judge; a circuit, district, provincial, trial judge; a Supreme Court judge.* **2** one who decides questions of merit, taste, etc.; referee: *a fair judge; I'm a poor judge of wines.*
— *v.* **judg·es, judged, judg·ing** decide or settle: *the court's power to judge cases; It's not safe to judge by* or *from appearances; Better to judge from the facts; to judge a person guilty; to judge how old Jan is; motives that are hard to judge* (= criticize); *I judged it better to remain silent; Who's judging* (at) *the beauty contest?*
— **judge·ship** *n.*

judg·ment or **judge·ment** (JUJ·munt) *n.* a judging, its result such as an opinion or a sentence, or the ability to judge: *to form* or *make a judgment; to hand down, pass, pronounce, render judgment; to sit in judgment on a case; to display, exercise, reserve judgment; to show good judgment; a subjective value judgment; In my judgment, he's at fault; an error of judgment; to pass judgment without hearing both sides; The judgment went against him; an accident that seemed a judgment on* (= punishment for) *his driving habits.*
— **judg·men·tal** or **judge·men·tal** (-MEN·tul) *adj.*

ju·di·cial (joo·DISH·ul) *adj.* of a judge: *a judicial decision, district, mind, process, review.*
— **ju·di·cial·ly** *adv.*

ju·di·ci·ar·y (joo·DISH·ee·air·ee) *adj.* of the administration of justice: *judiciary proceedings.*
— *n., pl.* **-ar·ies** the court system as a branch of government: *The legislature, executive, and the judiciary are the three branches of government; the independence of the judiciary; The judiciary* (= judges collectively) *helps mould our lives as social beings.*

ju·di·cious (joo·DISH·us) *adj.* wise in deciding, sound in judgment: *a judicious decision, parent, selection; judicious use.* — **ju·di·cious·ly** *adv.*

ju·do (JOO·doh) *n.* a Japanese sport or weaponless method of self-defence in which balance, timing, leverage, etc. are used to throw an opponent.

ju·do·ka (joo·DOH·kuh) *n. sing. & pl.* a judo player.

jug 1 *n.* a large, narrow-mouthed container, usually with a handle, for liquids: *a milk jug.* **2** *n. Slang.* jail. **3** *v.* **jugs, jugged, jug·ging** *Slang.* put in jail.

jug·ger·naut (JUG·ur·nawt) *n.* something massive and overpowering that crushes everything in its path.

jug·gle (JUG·ul) *v.* **jug·gles, jug·gled, jug·gling** manipulate or play tricks with figures, facts, or words, as one may do with balls, plates, etc. by tossing them up and catching them as a feat of dexterity. — **jug·gler** *n.*

jug·gler·y (JUG·luh·ree) *n.* **jug·gler·ies** sleight of hand; trickery; fraud.

jug·u·lar (JUG·yoo·lur) *adj.* of the neck or throat, esp. of the two large **jugular veins** that take blood down from the head and neck to the heart.
— *n.* a jugular vein: *They **went for the jugular*** (= attacked the weakest point).

juice (JOOSE) *n.* **1** the liquid part or essence of plant or animal tissue: *orange juice; the natural juices or gravy of meat; digestive juices; the gastric juice of the stomach; the creative juices* (= creative inspiration). **2** *Slang.* a fuel such as electricity or gasoline that supplies power; also, alcoholic liquor.
— *v.* **juic·es, juiced, juic·ing:** *music to **juice up*** (= enliven) *a party.*

juice·head *n. Slang.* an alcoholic.

juic·er (JOO·sur) *n.* a kitchen appliance for extracting juice from fruit.

juic·y (JOO·see) *adj.* **juic·i·er, -i·est 1** full of juice. **2** *Informal.* exciting because of its being scandalous or racy. — **juic·i·ly** *adv.;* **juic·i·ness** *n.*

ju·ju (JOO·joo) *n.* a form of popular Nigerian music.

ju·jube (JOO·joob, -joo·bee) *n.* a lozenge of gummy, fruit-flavoured candy.

ju·lep (JOO·lup) *n.* an iced and sweetened drink of whisky or brandy flavoured with mint; also **mint julep.**

ju·li·enne (joo·lee·EN) *adj.* cut into long thin strips: *julienne potatoes.*

jum·ble (JUM·bul) *n.* a disorderly mass or confusion.
— *v.* **-bles, -bled, -bling** mix up in a jumble.

jum·bo (JUM·boh) *adj. & n.* **-bos** something very large of its kind: *a jumbo jet (airliner); a jumbo size bottle; a jumbo burger.*

jump *v.* move with sudden muscular effort using the feet and legs: *She jumps into bed at 10 p.m. and jumps out of bed at 5 a.m.; He jumped in and drove off; She escaped by jumping (into) a passing train; This is where the train jumped the tracks* (= got derailed); *He jumped clear of the building; Everyone jumped for or with joy; Grandpa dropped his book and jumped to his feet; He jumped to* (= came quickly to) *our defence; Cats jump from roof to roof; Horses jump over fences; Let us not jump to conclusions before all the facts are in; Prices jump as supplies dwindle; She jumped at* (= eagerly seized) *the long-awaited opportunity; He jumped* (= started ahead of) *the green light; He jumps on* (= scolds) *his students at the slightest disturbance; The bondsman lost his money when the prisoner jumped bail* (= disappeared).
— **jump the gun** See GUN.
— *n.* a jumping: *He made a parachute jump; The high jump is a track-and-field event; a quantum* (= sudden and dramatic) *jump; Oil prices took a jump yesterday; to keep one jump ahead* (= one step ahead) *of the competition.*
— **have** or **get the jump on someone** anticipate or get an advantage over someone.

jump·er *n.* **1** a person or thing that jumps: *Jump* or *Jumper cables close an electrical circuit by jumping or bypassing a break in it.* **2** a loose jacket or sleeveless dress worn to protect one's clothes. **3 jumpers** *pl.* same as ROMPERS.

jumping-off point or **place** *n.* point of departure.

jump-start *n.* the starting of a car using booster cables to recharge the battery; *v.: A "defibrillator" is used to jump-start failed hearts in emergency rooms.*

jump suit *n.* a parachutist's one-piece suit or a similar woman's suit of top and trousers belted in the middle.

jump·y *adj.* **jump·i·er, -i·est** jittery or nervous: *What are you so jumpy about?*
— **jump·i·ly** *adv.;* **jump·i·ness** *n.*

junc·tion (JUNK·shun) *n.* **1** a joining. **2** a place of joining, as of roads.

junc·ture (JUNK·chur) *n.* a joining, esp. a critical moment in the coming together of events: *At that juncture he was lost for words.*

jun·gle (JUNG·gul) *n.* **1** a wildly overgrown tropical forest: *the dense jungles of central Africa, Brazil, etc.* **2** a place hard to survive in: *the jungle of city slums; the asphalt jungle; the blackboard jungle of teaching; the concrete jungle of our great cities; It's a jungle out there!*

jun·ior (JOON·yur) *n.* a person younger or lower in rank than another who is senior: *John Smith, Jr.* (= Junior, son of John Smith); *a college or high school junior (in his or her next-to-last year).*
— *adj: my junior brother; a junior member of the staff; a junior minister, partner; She's junior in rank; She's junior to me by two years* or *She's my junior by two years.*

junior college *n.* a college offering two-year programs, either as the first two years for a bachelor's degree or as technical training for semiprofessional jobs.

junior high school *n.* usually, grades 7, 8, and 9 of school.

junior varsity *n.* a school or college team composed of those less qualified and experienced than the varsity.

junk *n.* **1** worthless stuff: *Children who eat junk, listen to junk, talk junk, and watch junk may grow up to be dopes.* **2** *Slang.* a narcotic, esp. heroin. **3** a Chinese flat-bottomed ship with four-cornered sails and a high poop.
— *v.* discard as junk: *She junked her old car.*

junk bond *n.* a high-yield but speculative bond issued by a company for buying back its stocks or for financing a takeover.

junk·et (JUNK·it) *n.* an excursion or trip, esp. one taken by someone at public or company expense: *a Las Vegas gambling junket; She went on a free junket to hunt geese at James Bay.* — *v.* go on a junket.

junk food *n.* a food such as candy, potato chips, cake, or soda that has little nutritive value.

junk·ie or **junk·y** (JUNK·ee) *n.* **-kies** *Informal.* a drug addict.

junk mail *n.* unsolicited third-class mail such as advertising circulars; also called "direct mail."

junk·yard *n.* an area in which junk is kept, as for resale: *mean as a junkyard dog.*

Juno Award *n. Cdn.* the top annual award of the Canadian recording industry, made in various categories.

jun·ta (HOON·tuh, JUN-) *n.* a group of military men ruling a country after a coup d'état: *a revolutionary junta; government by junta.*

ju·rid·i·cal (joo·RID·uh·cul) *adj.* having to do with the administration of justice. — **ju·rid·i·cal·ly** *adv.*

ju·ris·dic·tion (joor·is·DIC·shun) *n.* legal authority in regard to its extent or territory: *matters outside, under, within a court's jurisdiction; a court that has jurisdiction over a case.*

ju·ris·pru·dence (joor·is·PROO·dunce) *n.* **1** the science or philosophy of law. **2** legal knowledge or skill.

ju·rist (JOOR·ist) *n.* a legal scholar such as a judge or lawyer. — **ju·ris·tic** (joor·IS·tic) *adj.*

ju·ror (JOOR·ur) *n.* one who takes an oath as a member of a jury: *A juror may be challenged before being selected.*

ju·ry (JOOR·ee) **1** *n., pl.* **-ries** a select group of people who hear evidence and give a verdict, as in a court trial, who determine the cause of a death in an inquest, or who decide the winner in a contest: *judge and jury; trial by jury; the jury system; to charge, impanel, instruct, sequester, swear in a jury; to fix* (= dishonestly influence) *a jury; Citizens are called on to serve on a jury; a coroner's jury; grand jury; petit jury; A jury reaches a verdict after deliberating; The jury is out on the issue* (= The issue is still undecided). **2** *adj.* for temporary use: *a jury mast; a jury-rigged* (= makeshift) *camera mount for shooting the action from various angles.*

ju·ry·man (JOOR·ee·mun) *n.* **-men** a juror.
— **ju·ry·wom·an** *n.* **-wom·en.**

just *adj.* due or appropriate according to a moral, social, esthetic, or other standard: *a just and upright man; He got his just reward; just deserts; a just and impartial decision; a just measure, praise, price; Trudeau's concept of "the just society."*
— *adv.* **1** exactly or nearly as stated or at a certain time or place: *I saw her just now; I'm not sleepy just now; I'll do just as you say; That's just what I need; You just missed the bus; it just left.* **2** *Informal.* simply; truly; really: *I'm just fine; That looks just perfect.*
— **just the same** even so; nevertheless.
— **just·ly** *adv.*

jus·tice (JUS·tis) *n.* **1** a being just; fairness: *peace on earth and justice to all.* **2** just treatment, esp. by process of law: *to dispense, mete out, obstruct, pervert, render justice; the frontier justice of pioneer days; the poetic justice of falling into one's own trap; a miscarriage of justice; travesty of justice; to bring someone to justice; justice tempered with mercy; Justice should prevail; "Justice delayed is justice denied"; The picture did not* **do justice** *to her* (= did not treat her fairly); *Another portrait was ordered* **in justice to** (= in fairness to) *her demands; The Department of Justice under the Minister of Justice looks after the administration of justice in Canada.* **3** a judge: *the Chief Justice of Canada; a Supreme Court justice; a* **justice of the peace** (= local magistrate).

jus·ti·fy (JUS·tuh·fye) *v.* **-fies, -fied, -fy·ing** make or show to be just or right: *conduct that is difficult to justify; Does a good end justify evil means? A printed line is justified* (= made the same length) *by spacing out the words; This dictionary is printed with a ragged right margin instead of a justified* (= even) *one.*
— **jus·ti·fi·a·ble** (-FYE·uh·bul) *adj.;* **jus·ti·fi·a·bly** (-blee) *adv.* — **jus·ti·fi·ca·tion** (-fuh·CAY·shun) *n.*

jut *n.* a projection, part, etc. made or formed so as to stick out or stand out, as a balcony or jetty.
— *v.* **juts, jut·ted, jut·ting** stick out: *Piers* **jut out** *into the water.*

ju·ve·nile (JOO·vuh·nul, -nile) *n.* **1** a young and immature person. **2** a young plant or animal such as a two-year-old race horse.
— *adj.:* *a juvenile acting role; a juvenile phase of development; A* **juvenile court** *deals with* **juvenile delinquents** (= young offenders below the legal age, usually 18); **juvenile diabetes** *(that develops before age 20).*

jux·ta·pose (JUX·tuh·poze) *v.* **-pos·es, -posed, -pos·ing** put close together or side by side *with* something, as for comparison or contrast.
— **jux·ta·po·si·tion** (-puh·ZISH·un) *n.*

K or **k** (KAY) *n.* **K's** or **k's** the 11th letter of the English alphabet.

Kab·loo·na or **Kab·loo·nah** (kab·LOO·nuh) *n. Cdn. sing. & pl.* a white person among the Inuit: *an Arctic community of 400 Inuit and 15 Kabloona* (= whites).

kaf·fee·klatsch (COF·ee·clach) *n.* an informal social gathering at which coffee is served.

kaf·fi·yeh (kah·FEE·yuh) *n.* an Arab headdress of cloth held in place by a cord wound round the head: *Yasser Arafat with his customary checkered kaffiyeh and dark glasses.*

ka·lei·do·scope (kuh·LYE·duh·scope) *n.* a tube fitted with mirrors that reflect coloured beads and pieces of glass at one end in an endless variety of patterns as the tube is rotated and viewed.
— **ka·lei·do·scop·ic** (-SCOP·ic) *adj.*

ka·mi·ka·ze (kah·muh·KAH·zee) *n.* a Japanese suicide attack or a plane or pilot making one.
— *adj.* suicidal, reckless, or self-destructive: *a kamikaze driver.*

Kam·loops trout *n. Cdn.* a variety of rainbow trout found in the lakes of British Columbia.

kan·ga·roo (kang·guh·ROO) *n.* **-roos** an Australian mammal that carries its young in a pouch outside the mother's body and with powerful hind legs on which it hops about: *a mob of kangaroos.*

kangaroo court *n.* an unauthorized court, often a mock one, as set up by prison inmates.

ka·put (kuh·POOT, long "OO") *adj. Informal.* **be** or **go kaput** fail; be finished: *All our money is gone, vanished, kaput!*

kar·at (CAIR·ut) *n.* a 1/24 part used as the unit for specifying the proportion of gold in an alloy: *In 10-karat gold, 10/24 of it is pure gold.*

ka·ra·te (kuh·RAH·tee) *n.* an Oriental form of unarmed combat using kicks, punches, and "chops" aimed at the most vulnerable parts of the opponent's body.

kar·ma (KAR·muh) *n.* in Buddhism and Hinduism, life and actions as determining one's fate; hence, fate or destiny.

kart *n.* a small, low, four-wheeled, one-seater vehicle used for racing, or **kart·ing.**

kay·ak (KYE·ak) *n.* a light Inuit canoe having a deck top covered with seal skin and a cockpit in the middle for the paddler.

kay·o (KAY·oh) *n. Slang.* a knockout in boxing.
— *v.* **-os, -oed, -o·ing** knock out or beat out.

keel *n.* **1** the main timber or steel piece laid lengthwise along the hull of a boat to support its framework. **2** a ridgelike part.
— **on an even keel 1** in a level position. **2** stable or steady.
— *v.* **keel over 1** turn over, as a boat. **2** *Informal.* collapse or faint.

keen *adj.* **1** having a fine edge: *a keen blade.* **2** sharp or biting: *keen eyesight, pain.* **3** very eager; full of enthusiasm: *keen competition; She's keen on winning; keen about learning to fly.* **4** *Slang.* wonderful.
— *n.* a wailing or lamentation; *v.* make a sound suggesting it. — **keen·ly** *adv.; ***keen·ness** *n.*

keep *v.* **keeps, kept, keep·ing 1** continue to have and hold in one's possession, control, or care: *You may not keep library books beyond the due date; Parents don't keep their children from school without good reason; Pets should be kept off the streets; Please ***keep off*** (= stay away from) the grass; Please keep out of the way of the ambulance; Drivers must keep to the right of the road; The family wanted to keep the wedding a secret; They wanted to keep it to themselves; What keeps* (= prevents) *you from going? They keep* (= raise) *hogs on the farm; We don't keep people waiting; a well-kept lawn; Teachers have to ***keep after*** (= urge) *students to make them do their best; Everyone, please ***keep to*** (= remain in) *your rooms; He ***keeps very much to himself*** (= avoids meeting people) *since his wife died.*

2 maintain or preserve without change of condition: *Salt keeps meat from spoiling; It helps to keep the roads clear of snow; A coat keeps you warm; We keep children amused; Please keep quiet in the library; Teachers keep students at their work; Students keep on* (=continue) *attending school till graduation; We have to keep up payments on a loan.* **3** be faithful to something: *to keep an appointment, the law, a promise, a treaty.*
— **keep abreast of** stay informed of something: *to keep abreast of the latest advances in computers.*
— **keep up with** go as fast as a person or thing and not fall behind: *a fast runner who is difficult to keep up with; Supply has to keep up with demand; to keep up with the neighbours* (=do as well as one's neighbours); *to keep up* (=stay up to date) *with what's going on around us.*
— *n.* **1** support or livelihood: *Maria earns her keep by taking care of the kids.* **2** the strongest part of a fort or castle.
— **for keeps 1** for the winner to keep. **2** *Informal.* on a continuing basis: *The winter has set in for keeps by January.* — **keep·er** *n.*

keeping *n.* **1** care: *something entrusted to your keeping.* **2** accordance: *a practice that is in keeping with custom.*

keep·sake *n.* something to keep in memory of someone; memento.

keg *n.* a small cask or barrel: *a powder keg.*

ken *v.* **kens, kenned, ken·ning** *Scottish.* know or have knowledge of something.
— *n.* range of knowledge: *Some things are beyond our ken; matters within our ken.*

ken·nel (KEN·ul) *n.* **1** a doghouse. **2** often **kennels** *pl.* a place that breeds or boards dogs.
— *v.* **ken·nels, ken·nelled** or **ken·neled, ken·nel·ling** or **ken·nel·ing** keep in a doghouse.

kept 1 *pt. & pp.* of KEEP. **2** *adj.* maintained for sexual relations: *a kept boy, woman.*

ker- *prefix.* forming interjections: *kerplunk, kerpow, kerthump!*

ker·chief (KUR·chif) *n.* **-chiefs** or **-chieves** (-cheevz) **1** a usually square piece of cloth used by women as a head covering or scarf. **2** a handkerchief.

ker·fuf·fle (kur·FUF·ul) *n. Informal.* commotion or fuss.

ker·nel (KUR·nul) *n.* **1** a seed of the corn plant or a grain of wheat or other cereal. **2** the inner, edible part of a nut, fruit pit, etc. **3** the core or essence: *the kernel of an argument; a kernel of truth.*

ker·o·sene (KAIR·uh·seen) *n. Cdn.* a thin fuel oil distilled from petroleum.

kes·trel (KES·trul) *n.* a small falcon or hawk.

ketch·up *n.* a seasoned sauce, esp. a thick one made of tomatoes.

ket·tle (KET·ul) *n.* a metal container for boiling liquids: *A kettle boils.*
— **kettle of fish** a matter or affair: *a different kettle of fish; a fine* or *pretty kettle of fish* (=a mess).
— **pot calling the kettle black** blaming someone when

suffering from the same fault.

key (KEE) *n.* **keys 1** a small metal device with one end cut in a particular design for fitting into the keyhole of a door, padlock, etc. to lock or unlock it: *to cut, fit, insert, match, turn a key; the key to a room; a master key; skeleton key; a bunch of keys; car keys; ignition keys.* **2** something shaped or used like a key: *the key of a tin can; an old clock that is wound with a key.* **3** something that provides access or entry, as the solution to a problem or the explanation of a set of symbols: *a dictionary's pronunciation key; the key* (=answer) *to the exercises; the key to a mystery.* **4** one of a set of disks or buttons forming a keyboard operated with the fingers, as in playing certain musical instruments, operating a typewriter, or a key punch machine: *Strike* or *Press the "shift" key to type a capital letter.* **5** a musical scale or system based on a basic tone or keynote, as "C major"; hence, a tone or style of expression: *He spoke in a low key; the key signature* (=sharps or flats placed after the clef) *of a staff of music.*
— *adj.* important or controlling: *a key advisor, area, factor, figure, issue, player, role; key personnel; Doing your homework is absolutely key to being promoted.*
— *v.* **keys, keyed, key·ing 1** tune: *a properly keyed violin; The speech was keyed to the mood of the audience; deluxe colour-keyed seat belts* (harmonized according to colour); *crazy fans keyed up* (=excited) *to a fever pitch.* **2** type: *to key in data for computer processing.*

key·board *n.* a set of disks or buttons on a musical instrument, typewriter, etc. for its manual operation.
— *v.* enter text, data, etc. into a processing system using a keyboard: *Matter had to be keyboarded for typesetting.*

key club *n.* a private club whose members usually have keys to the premises.

key grip *n.* the head of a stage crew.

key·hole *n.* a hole in a door, padlock, etc. for inserting its key: *a child peeping through a keyhole.*

key·note *n.* **1** the basic note of a musical scale. **2** the basic idea or policy theme, as set forth in a **keynote speech** or **address** given at a convention.
— *v.* **-notes, -not·ed, -not·ing** give the keynote or keynote address of a meeting. — **key·not·er** *n.*

key·pad *n.* a small keyboard, often handheld, having buttons for input of data: *a numeric keypad integrated with the computer keyboard.*

key punch *n.* a machine for punching cards or tapes for data processing.
— **key·punch** or **key·stroke** *v.* same as KEYBOARD.

key·stone *n.* **1** the central, topmost stone of an arch. **2** central principle: *Freedom is the keystone of democracy.*

key·stroke *n.* a tap of a key, as in keyboarding.

key·word *n.* a word that forms the key or guide to other words, as a guide word at the top of a dictionary page: *a computer program for showing the keywords of a document in their contexts; a keyword-in-context program.* Also **key word.**

kha·ki (KAK·ee, KAH·kee) *n.* **1** a strong, twilled, yellowish-brown cloth for uniforms, esp. military. **2** the colour or a uniform made of khaki. **3 khakis** *pl.* such a uniform.
— *adj.* **1** dull yellowish-brown. **2** made of khaki cloth.

khan (KAHN, KAN) *n.* a Turkish title, now used for "Mister" in some Central Asian countries.

kib·ble (KIB·ul) *v.* **kib·bles, kib·bled, kib·bling** grind coarsely. — *n.* coarsely ground meal.

kib·butz (ki·BOOTS) *n., pl.* **kib·but·zim** (ki·boot·SEEM) an Israeli collective farm: *They live on the Kibbutz Eindor; were married at the same kibbutz.*

kib·itz (KIB·its) *v. Informal.* look on at a card game and offer unwanted advice: *to kibitz* (= chat) *with the crowd standing around.*

kib·itz·er (KIB·it·sur) *n.* one who kibitzes; hence, a meddler.

ki·bosh (KYE·bosh) *n. Slang.* **put the kibosh on** put an end to something; squelch.

kick *v.* **1** strike out with a foot, esp. forward: *Keep kicking to stay afloat; a horse that kicks; The cow kicked the pail.* **2** force or move by a kick: *A soccer ball is kicked; Slip-on shoes are easy to kick off.* **3** *Informal.* complain or grumble. **4** *Slang.* get rid of a habit.
— **kick around 1** discuss ideas, suggestions, etc. informally. **2** treat with no consideration: *When Dick retires, you won't have anyone to kick around any more.*
— **kick in** *Informal.* **1** contribute one's share. **2** become active or operational.
— **kick off** *Informal.* begin a campaign, proceedings, a project, etc. as by putting a ball in play with a kickoff.
— **kick over** start operating, as an automobile engine beginning to fire.
— **kick up** *Informal.* start: *to kick up trouble.*
— *n.* **1** a kicking: *a football kick; a free kick in soccer; a penalty kick; a kick in the groin, behind; a kick in the teeth* (= an embarrassing rejection); *the kick* (= recoil) *of a gun when fired.* **2** *Informal.* thrill: *I get a kick out of studying words; Flat pop has no kick* (= life or strength) *to it; People start using drugs for kicks.*

kick·back *n. Informal.* money illegally paid back to a patron in return for a benefit such as a job, business, contract, etc.: *to take kickbacks for arranging mortgages.*

kick·er *n.* **1** one that kicks. **2** *Slang.* something that gives a kick or jolt, as a punch line or a catch.

kick·off *n.* **1** in football and soccer, a place kick. **2** *Informal.* the start of an activity: *the kickoff of a campaign.*

kick·stand *n.* on a bicycle or motorcycle, a short metal bar that is kicked into position to stand the vehicle up when not in use.

kick·y *adj.* **kick·i·er, -i·est** *Slang.* exciting; providing kicks.

kid *n.* **1** *Informal.* a child; also, a young man or woman; *adj.: my kid* (= younger) *brother; mere kid stuff (suitable for kids).* **2** a young goat, its flesh for food, or its skin or leather, or **kid·skin,** used for shoes and gloves.
— *v.* **kids, kid·ded, kid·ding 1** tease: *to kid a guy about his girl friends.* **2** fool: *You're kidding!* [exclamation of unbelief].
— **kid·der** *n.* — **kid·ding·ly** *adv.*

kid·dy or **kid·die** *n.* **kid·dies** a small child.

kid glove *n.* a glove made of the skin of a young goat: *A temperamental person has to be handled with kid gloves* (= carefully).

kid·nap *v.* **-naps, -napped** or **-naped, -nap·ping** or **-nap·ing** abduct someone, usually for ransom or as a hostage. — **kid·nap·per** or **kid·nap·er** *n.*

kid·ney (KID·nee) *n.* **-neys 1** either of a pair of bean-shaped organs situated at the back above the waist that separates waste matter from the blood and passes it as urine into the bladder: *A calculus or kidney stone is a hard mineral deposit in a kidney.* **2** nature or sort: *a man of a different kidney.*

kidskin See KID.

kid·vid *n. Slang.* children's TV.

kill *v.* **1** cause death or cause the death of someone: *"Thou shalt not kill"; Cain killed Abel; a soldier killed in action; a killing* (= exhausting) *job.* **2** do away with something: *They played cards to kill time till dinner; Journalists kill stories they cannot use.* **3** *Slang.* make one laugh to exhaustion: *We killed ourselves laughing; You're absolutely killing* (= very funny).
— **kill two birds with one stone** do two things by one effort.
— *n.* a killing or something killed, as by a hunter or beast, an aircraft or missile shot down, etc.: *Hounds move in for the kill when the exhausted prey is run to the ground.*

kil·ler (KIL·ur) *n.* one that kills: *a serial killer (who commits a series of murders); when the killer strikes again; adj.: the African killer bees advancing from the south; a killer satellite; a killer whale* (= large voracious porpoise capable of killing a whale).

killing *n.* **1** slaughter: *the killing of whales.* **2** *Informal.* a profit or windfall, as from a sale: *He made a killing in stocks by selling them when the market peaked.*

kill·joy *n.* one who spoils others' fun.

kiln (KIL, KILN) *n.* a high-temperature furnace or oven for making lime, bricks, ceramics, pottery, etc.
— *v.* burn, bake, or dry in a kiln.

ki·lo (KEE·loh, KILL·oh) *n.* **-los** [short form] kilogram or kilometre.

kilo- *prefix.* one thousand: *kilobaud, kilobit, kilobyte, kilocycle, kilohertz, kilometre, kilopascal, kilorad.*

kil·o·gram or **kil·o·gramme** (KIL·uh·gram) *n.* a unit of weight equal to 1 000 grams.

ki·lo·me·tre or **ki·lo·me·ter** (kuh·LOM·uh·tur, KIL·uh·mee·tur) *n.* unit of length equal to 1 000 metres.

kilt *n.* a knee-length pleated skirt, usually of tartan, worn by men in the Scottish Highlands; *adj.: a kilted* (= kilt-wearing) *regiment.*

kilt·er *n.* in **out of kilter** *Informal.* not in proper working order.

ki·mo·no (kuh·MOH·noh) *n.* **-nos** the traditional Japanese outer garment of men and women, a long, loose robe with a wide sash around the waist.

kin *n.* a relative or kinsman; also, relatives or kindred: *He's no kin of mine; An accident victim's identity is not disclosed before **next of kin** (= nearest relatives) are informed; adj.: He's kin to me.*

-kin *suffix.* little: *catkin, elfkin, lambkin, napkin.*

kind (KINED) *adj.* sincerely sympathetic and considerate: *Be kind to animals; He had a kind word for everyone; It was kind of her to baby-sit for us.* — *n.* **1** a natural group of people, animals, plants, etc.: *He's one of our own kind; our kind of people; birds of all kinds.* **2** nature or characteristic: *Being short or tall is a difference of degree, not of kind; He said nothing of the kind* (= of that nature). — **in kind**: *The insult was paid back in kind* (= in the same manner); *Payment used to be accepted in cash or in kind* (= in goods or produce). — **kind of** *Informal.* same as SORT OF. — **of a kind 1** of the same kind: *two of a kind.* **2** of a poor quality.

kind·a (KINE·duh) *Slang.* kind of; sort of.

kin·der·gar·ten (KIN·dur·gar·tun) *n.* a class or school preparing four- and five-year-olds for first grade by games and other activities.

kind·heart·ed (KINED·HAR·tid) *adj.* kind by nature; kind and gentle.

kin·dle (KIN·dul) *v.* **-dles, -dled, -dling 1** set on fire: *to kindle firewood; to kindle a fire; Each substance has its own **kindling** temperature.* **2** light up or arouse like fire: *to kindle anger, interest, passion; a face kindled with joy.*

kindling *n.* material such as dry wood that easily catches fire: *tinder, kindling, and firewood to build a campfire.*

kind·ly (KINED·lee) *adj.* **kind·li·er, -li·est 1** disposed to be kind; friendly: *a kindly old gentleman; kindly attentions.* **2** agreeable: *a kindly climate.*

— *adv.* in a kind manner: *His words were kindly meant; Thank you kindly; Few dogs **take kindly to** (= accept or like) cats.* — **kind·li·ness** *n.*

kind·ness (KINED·nis) *n.* kind nature, treatment, or a kind act: *to show kindness to or toward animals; the milk of human kindness; the many kindnesses done to me; to repay or return kindnesses.*

kin·dred (KIN·drid) *adj.* naturally related or similar: *kindred facts, languages, natures, souls, spirits, tribes.*

ki·ne·sics (kye·NEE·six) *n. pl.* the study of bodily movements and gestures as part of language.

ki·net·ic (kye·NET·ic) *adj.* of or by motion: *A falling object has **kinetic energy**.*

kinette *fem.* of KINSMAN.

kin·folk or **kin·folks** *n. pl.* family or relatives. Also **kins·folk.**

king *n.* **1** a male sovereign: *the King of Denmark; A king ascends* or *mounts his throne.* **2** a male person or animal supreme in a certain sphere or class: *The lion is the king of the beasts; a king among men; the king of the mountain; when comedy was king; an oil king* (= tycoon). **3** a chess piece or playing card designated as king. — **king·ly** *adj.* — **king·ship** *n.*

king·dom (KING·dum) *n.* **1** a king's domain or territory: *the kingdom of Alfred the Great; the United Kingdom.* **2** a division: *the animal, vegetable or plant, and mineral kingdoms of the natural world.* — **kingdom come** life after death. — **till kingdom come** forever.

King James Bible or **King James Version** *n.* a version of the Bible published in 1611 under King James I; Authorized Version.

king·mak·er (KING·may·kur) *n.* a person with power and influence to make someone ruler or leader.

king·pin *n.* **1** in bowling games, the chief or front pin. **2** *Informal.* the most important person or thing: *the kingpin of the underworld.*

king's evidence See EVIDENCE.

king·size or **king·sized** *adj. Informal.* large: *a kingsize cigarette, meal; kingsize sheets for a **kingsize bed** (approximately 78 × 80 in. / 1.98 × 2.03 m).*

King's post *n. Cdn.* formerly, a fishing or fur-trading post in Quebec.

kink *n.* **1** a twist or tight curl, as in hair, wire, or rope. **2** something that obstructs or prevents smooth operation: *a few kinks to be ironed out in our plan; the only kink* (= quirk) *in his personality.* **3** a muscle spasm. — *v.* bend or curve: *Railway tracks may expand and kink upward under intense heat.*

kink·y (KINK·ee) *adj.* having kinks: *kinky hair; kinky goods* (Slang for goods obtained by crooked means); *kinky* (= far-out or off-beat) *clothes.*

kins·folk (KINZ·folk) *n. pl.* same as KINFOLK.

kin·ship *n.* family relationship: *Animal lovers feel a kinship with the animal world.*

kins·man (KINZ·mun) *n.* -men 1 relative, esp. a male; **kins·wom·an, -wom·en,** *fem.* 2 **Kinsman** a member of a **Kinsmen Club,** a service club for men between the ages of 21 and 45 and women and other auxiliaries, founded in Hamilton, Ontario, in 1920; **ki·nette** (kuh·NET) *fem.*

ki·osk (KEE·osk) *n.* a lightly built, open-sided structure, as a bandstand, newsstand, or booth: *a newspaper kiosk.*

Kir·li·an (KUR·lee·un) *adj.* having to do with a characteristic aura observed around an object when an electric charge is passed through it: *Kirlian photography.*

kiss *n.* 1 a caress with the lips: *to blow someone a kiss; to steal a kiss; a loving, passionate, tender kiss.* 2 a gentle touch. 3 a small cake or candy: *chocolate kisses.* — *v.* caress or express with a kiss: *the moonlight kissing the treetops; She kissed them "good night"; He had to* **kiss good-bye to** (= give up) *his hopes of becoming a lawyer.* — **kiss·a·ble** *adj.*

kiss-and-tell (KIS·un·tel) *adj.* talking about one's confidential relationships: *the kiss-and-tell stories of a kiss-and-tell aide.*

kiss·er *n.* 1 one who kisses. 2 *Slang.* mouth.

kissing cousin *n.* a close relative: *This sauce seems a kissing cousin to the commercial product.*

kissing disease same as MONONUCLEOSIS.

kiss of death *n.* a well-intentioned action that actually proves harmful or ruinous.

kit *n.* a set of tools, supplies, parts, etc. for a specific use: *a first-aid kit; model airplane kit; shaving kit; survival kit; travelling kit; a military kit bag.* — **the whole kit and caboodle** *Informal.* the whole lot.

kitch·en (KICH·un) *n.* a room or place for cooking food: *"Get out of the kitchen if you can't stand the heat."*

kitch·en·ette or **kitch·en·et** (kich·uh·NET) *n.* a small kitchen or cooking facility.

kite *n.* 1 a device for flying in the air at the end of a long string, made of a light, usually geometrical framework covered with paper or plastic. 2 bird of prey of the hawk family noted for its long, narrow wings and graceful gliding. — **go fly a kite!** *Informal.* get lost! — *v.* to fly or soar: *to kite cheques* (= issue bad cheques in an attempt to make or get money); *Prices go on kiting as inflation soars.*

kith and kin *n. pl.* friends and relatives.

kitsch (KICH) *n.* trashy art or its pretentious quality. — **kitsch·y** *adj.*

kit·ten (KIT·un) *n.* a young cat.

kit·ten·ish (KIT·un·ish) *adj.* playful like a cat; coquettish.

kit·ty (KIT·ee) *n.* **kit·ties** 1 [pet name] cat or kitten. 2 a fund of money, esp. one pooled for a common purpose: *no money in the kitty.*

kitty-corner or **kitty-cornered** *adj.* same as CATER-CORNER(ED).

ki·wi (KEE·wee) *n.* 1 a flightless, shaggy, long-billed bird of New Zealand. 2 *Informal.* a New Zealander. 3 an egg-sized fruit with fuzzy brown skin; also **kiwi fruit.**

Klan *n.* the Ku Klux Klan or one of its chapters. — **Klans·man** *n.* -men.

klatsch (CLACH) *n.* an informal social gathering.

klax·on (CLAX·un) *n.* a warning signal or horn, as used by ambulances and such emergency vehicles; **Klaxon** *Trademark.*

klee·nex *n.* a handkerchief made of tissue paper; **Kleenex** *Trademark.*

kleig light *n.* same as KLIEG LIGHT.

klep·to·ma·ni·a (klep·tuh·MAY·nee·uh) *n.* an obsessive impulse to steal, esp. things that the thief, or **kleptomaniac,** has no use for.

klieg light (KLEEG-) *n.* a high-intensity carbon-arc light used on motion picture sets.

klutz *n.* *Slang.* a clumsy person. — **klutz·y** *adj.*

knack (NAK) *n.* ability to do something with cleverness and skill: *It's easy to do once you get the knack of it; He has a knack for getting into trouble.*

knap·sack (NAP·sack) *n.* a soldier's or hiker's bag for supplies, carried strapped to the back.

knave (NAVE) *n.* 1 a rogue or dishonest person. 2 a jack (playing card). — **knav·ish** *adj.*

knav·er·y (NAY·vuh·ree) *n.* -eri·es rascality or roguery.

knead (NEED) *v.* work by pressing and squeezing dough, clay, muscles, etc. — **knead·er** *n.*

knee (NEE) *n.* the leg joint between thigh and lower leg, protected in front by the kneecap: *He dandled the child on his knee; Your first language is usually learned* **at your mother's knee** (= as a child); *to bring someone* **to his** or **her knees** (= force someone to obey or submit); *to ask for forgiveness* **on bended knee(s).** — *v.* **knees, kneed, knee·ing** touch or hit with the knee.

knee·cap *n.* the bone covering the knee.

knee-deep *adj.* sunk to the knees: *knee-deep in mud; found himself knee-deep in trouble.*

knee-high *adj.* reaching the knees: *She waded through knee-high water.*

knee·hole *n.* a space, as in a desk, for the user's knees.

knee-jerk *adj.* of behaviour, predictable as being automatic like a reflex action: *a knee-jerk reaction, response.*

kneel (NEEL) *v.* **kneels,** *pt. & pp.* **knelt** or **kneeled, kneel·ing** go down on one's knee or knees, as in prayer: *to kneel before the altar.*

knell (NELL) *v.* ring a bell solemnly, as at someone's death.
— *n.* such a ringing or its sound; hence, the indication of an end: *"The curfew tolls the knell of parting day"; Black Monday sounded the death knell of the enterprise.*

knelt a *pt. & pp.* of KNEEL.

knew *pt.* of KNOW.

knick·ers (NIK·urz) *n.pl.* loose breeches gathered at the knee; also **knick·er·bock·ers** (NIK·ur·bok·urz).

knick·knack (NIK·nak) *n.* a small trivial or dainty article or trinket.

knife (NIFE) *n.* **knives** (NIVES) **1** a cutting tool with a blade and handle, as used with a fork for eating: *a bread, butcher, carving, kitchen, paring, pocket, steak knife.* **2** a cutting blade, as of a lawnmower.
— **under the knife** *Informal.* undergoing surgery.
— *v.* **knifes, knifed, knif·ing** stab or cut through with or as if with a knife.

knight (NITE) *n.* **1** in the Middle Ages, a military man honoured as a loyal servant of the king: *Francis was dubbed knight by the Queen.* **2** a British rank just below baronet with the title "Sir." **3** a man of chivalry. **4** a member of an order or society of "Knights" such as the **Knights of Columbus,** a Roman Catholic fraternal society. **5** a chess piece shaped like a horse's head.
— *v.* make a knight: *Charlie Chaplin was knighted by the Queen in 1975.*

knight·hood *n.* **1** the rank of a knight; also, knights collectively. **2** chivalry.

knight·ly *adj.* chivalrous or brave.

knit (NIT) *v.* **knits,** *pt. & pp.* **knit** or **knit·ted, knit·ting 1** make a fabric or article of clothing by looping, instead of weaving, thread or yarn closely together with long needles: *to knit a sweater; A fractured bone knits* (= joins together) *in course of time; a close-knit group of researchers; a closely knit family; Her brow was knit* (= drawn together) *in a frown; an individualist who sticks to his own **knitting*** (= minds his own business). — **knit·ter** *n.*

knit·wear *n.* knitted clothing.

knives *pl.* of KNIFE.

knob (NOB) *n.* **1** a rounded bulge made for ornament or as a handle fixed to a door, drawer, etc.: *Turn the knob to tune the radio; control knobs.* **2** a small rounded hill.
— **knobbed** (NOBD) *adj.*
— **knob·bly** (-lee) or **knob·by** *adj.*

knock (NOK) *n.* a sharp blow with something hard or solid, as a fist, knuckles, gavel, etc.: *a loud knock on the door; the hard knocks one has to take in the struggle to make a living; It's a hard-knock world.*
— *v.* strike, pound, or collide: *to knock at or on a neighbour's door; The boxer was knocked down in the* first round; *The ball knocked the vase off the table; No one likes to knock* (*Informal* for attack or criticize) *a colleague; An engine that knocks* (= makes a rattling noise) *needs antiknock in the fuel or no-knock gasoline.*
— **knock about** or **around 1** roam around. **2** treat someone roughly.
— **knock back** drink a quantity of liquor.
— **knock down 1** to fell. **2** indicate an auctioned item as sold, with a knock of the gavel. **3** disassemble: *furniture that comes knocked down in a carton.*
— **knock off** *Informal.* **1** deduct: *We'll knock 10% off the price.* **2** stop work or other activity: *We knock off* (*work*) *at 5 p.m.; Will you please **knock it off*** (= stop behaving like that)? **3** finish routinely: *a prolific writer who knocks off one book after another.* **4** overcome or kill.
— **knock out 1** defeat, as in boxing, or put a pitcher out of a game of baseball. **2** make inoperative: *power lines knocked out by a storm; Two drinks are enough to **knock him out*** (= make him unconscious).
— **knock together** put together or compose hastily.
— **knock·er** *n.*

knock-kneed *adj.* with the legs bent inward at the knees so that they touch in walking.

knock·off *adj.* routinely finished or cheaply copied: *The ad said, "Ours is a brand-name computer, not some shoddy knockoff clone."*

knock·out *n.* **1** a defeat: *He won it on a technical knockout; It was a knockout blow; He was stupefied by knockout drops* (*that make one unconscious*) *in his drink.* **2** *Informal.* something outstanding: *You're a knockout! a knockout performance.*

knoll (NOLE) *n.* a small rounded hill; mound.

knot (NOT) *n.* **1** a tie or fastening made with one or more cords, ropes, etc.: *to loosen, tie, undo, untie a knot; a square knot* (= symmetrical double knot). **2** something that resembles a knot in closeness, intricacy, or lumpiness of form: *a figure-eight knot; knots of people standing around chatting; Why tie yourself in knots* (= get nervous) *over nothing?* **3** a hard, cross-grained mass formed in wood, as in knotty pine. **4** one nautical mile per hour.
— **tie the knot** *Informal.* get married.
— *v.* **knots, knot·ted, knot·ting 1** tie in a knot; tangle in knots. **2** unite closely or form into a hard lump.

knot·hole *n.* a hole left by a knot that has fallen out of a board or tree trunk.

knot·ty (NOT·ee) *adj.* **knot·ti·er, knot·ti·est** having knots: *knotty pine wood; a knotty* (= complex) *problem.*

knout (NOWT) *n.* a whip of a kind formerly used in Russia. — *v.* flog with a knout.

know (NO) *v.* **knows, knew** (NEW), **known** (NOHN), **know·ing** be well acquainted with a person or thing, having the subject firmly in the mind or memory: *Do I know you? You know me from school days; He knows her by name; She knows him to be a great spender; She knows it for a fact* (= knows it to be true); *He knows how to type; She knows the song by heart; Infants don't know* (= distinguish) *right from wrong; He should know better*

than to make promises he can't keep; I will let you know (= inform you) *when the parcel arrives; Mother knows best* (= is the best guide).
— *n.: people who are **in the know*** (*Informal for* having inside information).
— **know·a·ble** (NOH·uh·bul) *adj.*

know-all or **know-it-all** *n. Informal.* a person pretending to know everything.

know-how *n. Informal.* expertise or practical knowledge: *the know-how to operate a business.*

knowing *adj.* having knowledge in a special way: *a knowing glance, look, smile, wink.*
— **know·ing·ly** *adv.: She wouldn't knowingly hurt a fly.*

knowl·edge (NOL·ij) *n.* a knowing or understanding; also, what is known: *the knowledge of good and evil; knowledge of oneself; She denied all knowledge of the missing money; His resignation is a matter of common knowledge; It's common knowledge that he has resigned; a good working knowledge of Italian; extensive, intimate, intuitive, profound, rudimentary, superficial knowledge of something; Some things are beyond our knowledge; It has come to our knowledge that you are operating without a licence; a book of knowledge; "Knowledge is power"; her great fund of knowledge; to absorb, accumulate, acquire, assimilate, communicate, gain, impart, soak up knowledge; to brush up, parade one's knowledge of a subject.*
— **to (the best of) one's knowledge** as far as one knows.

knowl·edge·a·ble (NOL·ij·uh·bul) *adj.* well-informed; intelligent. — **knowl·edge·a·bly** *adv.*

knuck·le (NUCK·ul) *n.* **1** a finger joint, esp. one joining a finger to the rest of the hand: *She cracked her knuckles in agony; to rap someone on* or *over the knuckles* (= punish or chastise). **2** the knee or hock joint of an animal such as a pig used as food.
— *v.* **-les, -led, -ling; knuckle down** apply oneself earnestly *to* a job, task, work, etc.
— **knuckle under** submit or yield *to* a person or similar thing.

knuck·le·head (NUCK·ul·hed) *n. Informal.* a stupid person.

knurl (NURL) *n.* **1** a small projection or knob. **2** a ridge formed of such, as the milling on the edge of a coin.

knurled (NURLD) *adj.* **1** milled, as the edge of a coin. **2** gnarled.

KO (KAY·oh) *v.* **KO's, KO'd, KO'ing** *Slang.* in boxing, to knock out; hence, defeat: *Leafs KO'd the Flyers.*
— *n.* a knockout in boxing. Also **K.O., k.o.**

ko·a·la (koh·AH·luh) *n.* a small tree-dwelling Australian marsupial.

kook (long "oo") *n. Slang.* one considered crazy or eccentric. — **kook·y** *adj.;* **kook·i·ness** *n.*

ko·sher (KOH·shur) *adj.* **1** of a food or establishment, meeting the requirements of Jewish dietary law: *kosher chicken.* **2** legitimate or proper: *a deal that's not quite kosher.*

kow·tow ("ow" as in "how") *v.* show slavish respect *to* someone. — *n.* an act of kowtowing.

kraft *n.* tough paper made from wood pulp for use in wrappers, etc.

Krem·lin *n.* the Soviet government, formerly housed in the citadel of Moscow called "the Kremlin."

ku·dos (CUE·dos) *n.* [usually takes sing. *v.*, rarely pl.; rarely "kudo" sing.] *Informal.* credit for an achievement; glory or fame: *to deserve, get, receive, win kudos; Kudos to the winners!*

kung fu (kung·FOO) *n.* the Chinese form of karate.

kvetch *v. Slang.* complain in a nagging or whining manner; gripe. — *n.* one who complains thus.

Kwa·ki·u·tl (kwah·kee·YOO·tul) *n.* a member of a group of native Indians of Vancouver Island.

KWIC (KWIC) *n.* "keyword-in-context," a computer-generated index for retrieving keywords of a document together with portions of the surrounding text.

L l▾▾▾

L or **l** *n.* **L**'s or **l**'s **1** the 12th letter of the English alphabet. **2** also **l**, the Roman numeral for 50. **3 L,** *pl.* **L**'s something L-shaped, as an extension forming a right angle with the main building or a pipe-joint.

lab *n.* [short form] laboratory.

la·bel (LAY·bul) *n.* **1** a slip attached to something to identify or describe it, its ownership, or its destination: *clothes carrying a union label.* **2** designation: *the part-of-speech label of a dictionary entry.*
— *v.* **-bels, -belled** or **-beled, -bel·ling** or **-bel·ing** assign a person or thing to a particular class: *All luggage should be labelled with your name and address; He was labelled (as) a communist because of his leftist leanings.*
— **la·bel·ler** or **la·bel·er** *n.*

labor See LABOUR.

lab·or·a·to·ry (LAB·ruh·tor·ee, luh·BOR·uh·tor·ee) *n.* **-ries** a place for scientific research or manufacture, esp. of drugs and chemicals.

la·bo·ri·ous (luh·BOR·ee·us) *adj.* **1** requiring much labour or hard work: *a laborious business, style of writing; laborious research, tasks; a slow and laborious climb; a laborious (=laboured) excuse.* **2** industrious or hard-working: *a laborious craftsman, researcher, worker.*

la·bour or **la·bor** (LAY·bur) *n.* **1** hard work or exertion, esp. physical: *He was sentenced to five years' hard labour; child, forced, manual, menial, slave labour; An electric dishwasher is a labour-saving device.* **2** the pains of childbirth: *A pregnant woman goes into labour; She was in labour for two hours; false labour; induced labour.* **3** a piece of work; task: *the labours of Hercules; Volunteers offer to help others as a labour of love (not for money).* **4** workers as distinguished from management; also, labour unions collectively: *migrant labour; organized labour; seasonal labour; skilled labour; Service industries tend to be labour-intensive (=investing much on labour) rather than capital-intensive.*
— *v.* work, esp. with much effort: *a truck labouring uphill with a heavy load; a practical-minded woman who labours under no delusions; She labours all day as a maid; Why labour a point that is so obvious? the laboured (=heavy) breathing of an asthmatic.*
— **la·bour·er** or **la·bor·er** *n.*

Labour Day or **Labor Day** *n.* the first Monday of September, a legal holiday in Canada and the U.S. in honour of workers.

labour union or **labor union** *n.* a workers' organization for the protection of their rights as wage-earners, esp. by collective bargaining.

Lab·ra·dor (LAB·ruh·dor) *n. Cdn.* a powerful breed of hunting dog, originally from Labrador; also **Labrador retriever.**

Labrador tea *n. Cdn.* a tea made from an evergreen bog plant common in the North.

lab·y·rinth (LAB·uh·rinth) *n.* a confusing network of passageways; maze: *a hedge labyrinth; We got lost in a labyrinth of back alleys.*

lab·y·rin·thine (lab·uh·RIN·thin) *adj.* like a labyrinth; complicated.

lac *n.* a resinous substance deposited by insects on the "acacia" trees of Asia.

lace *n.* **1** open fabric woven in patterns with threads of linen or similar soft material: *delicate, exquisite, fine lace;* **adj.:** *a lace border, edging;* **lace fern** (with lacelike fronds); *a lacewing butterfly.* **2** an ornamental braid used for trimming uniforms. **3** a string or cord pulled through eyelets to tie a shoe, tighten a corset, etc.
— *v.* **lac·es, laced, lac·ing 1** tie with a lace: *to lace up a shoe.* **2** trim: *a uniform laced with gold (lace); a statement laced with accusations of wrongdoing; coffee laced with rum (=with rum added).*
— **lace into 1** attack physically. **2** criticize severely.

lac·er·ate (LAS·uh·rate) *v.* **-ates, -at·ed, -at·ing** tear flesh or tissues irregularly.
— **lac·er·a·tion** (-RAY·shun) *n.: a laceration caused by a fishhook.*

lace·work *n.* lace; also, any lacelike decoration.

lack *v.* be without or not have enough of something needed: *A novice lacks experience; She's not lacking in enthusiasm; The well-to-do seem to* **lack for nothing.**
— *n.* absence or shortage of something needed: *For lack of fresh air we had to move to another place; The plants died through lack of rain.*

lack·a·dai·si·cal (lack·uh·DAY·zuh·cul) *adj.* lacking enthusiasm or interest.

lack·ey (LAK·ee) *n.* -eys 1 a footman. 2 a servile follower; toady.

lack·lus·tre (LACK·lus·tur) *adj.* dull or drab: *his lacklustre performance on the job.* Also **lack·lus·ter.**

la·con·ic (luh·CON·ic) *adj.* brief to the point of seeming curt: *a laconic announcement, answer, reply; laconic in expression; a laconic person; his laconic wit, writing style.*

lac·quer (LAK·ur) *n.* a resinous varnish made from the sap of certain Asiatic trees and from compounds of lac.
— *v.* to coat metal, wood, etc. with lacquer: *a lacquered vase.* — **lac·quer·er** *n.*
— **lac·quer·work** or **lac·quer·ware** *n.*

la·crosse (luh·CROS) *n. Cdn.* a field game played between teams using sticks with a webbed pouch at one end to carry and throw a small rubber ball into the opposing team's goal.

lact- *combining form.* derived from milk: *lactase, lactic, lactose.*

lac·tase (LAC·tace) *n.* an enzyme that helps in the digestion of milk sugar.

lac·tate *v.* -ates, -at·ed, -at·ing produce milk through a mammary gland: *A mother begins to lactate soon after the baby's birth.*
— **lac·ta·tion** (lac·TAY·shun) *n.: Cows have a lactation period of about 10 months.*

lac·tic acid *n.* acid of sour milk.

lac·tose *n.* the sugar of milk.

la·cu·na (luh·CUE·nuh) *n.* -nas or -nae (·nee) 1 a gap, esp. a missing part of a text or manuscript. 2 a cavity in a bone or cartilage.

lac·y (LAY·see) *adj.* lac·i·er, -i·est of or like lace.
— **lac·i·ness** *n.*

lad *n.* a youth; also, a fellow: *a young lad and his lass.*

lad·der (LAD·ur) *n.* a climbing device, usually a framework of two long sidepieces connected by rungs: *to climb, go up, mount a ladder; a rope ladder; up the social ladder (to membership in exclusive clubs).*

lad·die (LAD·ee) *n. Scottish.* lad.

lade *v.* lades, *pt. & pp.* lad·ed or lad·en, lad·ing load, as cargo on a ship: *a bill of lading.*

lad·en (LAY·dun) *adj.* burdened: *a tree laden with fruit; a ship fully laden with merchandise.*

la-di-da or **la-de-da** (lah·dee·DAH) *adj. Informal.* affectedly polished or refined; excessively genteel: *There's nothing fancy or la-di-da about the boutique.*

la·dle (LAY·dul) *n.* a long-handled spoon with a cup-shaped bowl.
— *v.* la·dles, la·dled, la·dling dip out with a ladle: *to ladle the gravy, soup.* — **la·dler** *n.*

la·dy (LAY·dee) *n.* -dies 1 a woman of refinement or high social position: *lords and ladies; quite a lady; a lady by birth.* 2 [as a title]: *Lady Chatterly; Lady Diana; Lady Luck* (= "luck" personified). 3 [as a polite term or euphemism] woman: *Ladies and gentlemen; the first lady of Canadian ballet; the leading lady of the play; the young lady who baby-sits for us; the lady* (= mistress) *of the house; the (homeless) bag ladies of our streets;* **ladies of the evening** (= prostitutes).

lady beetle or **la·dy·bug** (LAY·dee·bug) *n.* a small round beetle with a bright red or yellow spotted back, useful against plant lice. Also **la·dy·bird.**

la·dy·fin·ger (LAY·dee·fing·gur) *n.* a finger-shaped spongecake.

lady-in-waiting *n.* ladies-in-waiting a queen's or princess's attendant.

la·dy·like (LAY·dee·like) *adj.* like a lady; also, suitable for a lady: *Linda is quite ladylike; her ladylike manners.*

la·dy·love (LAY·dee·luv) *n.* a sweetheart.

la·dy·ship (LAY·dee·ship) *n.* 1 a lady's rank or position. 2 **Ladyship** [preceded by "Her" or "Your" used in referring to or addressing a woman with the title "Lady"].

lady's man *n.* a man who is very attentive to women or fond of their company.

lady's-slipper (LAY·deez·slip·ur) *n.* a wild orchid with flowers shaped like a slipper: *The pink lady's-slipper is the floral emblem of Prince Edward Island.*

lag *v.* lags, lagged, lag·ging fall behind instead of keeping up: *Those who lag behind in class need special help; As the speaker droned on, interest lagged; The order of play is decided by lagging* (= tossing balls toward a "lag line," as in marbles, or a boundary in billiards).
— *n.* interval or amount by which a person or thing lags: *the time lag between the flash and the sound of the firing; the* **cultural** or **culture lag** *between social institutions and the advancement of science; jet lag.*

la·ger or **lager beer** (LAH·gur·) *n.* a light, mellow beer that has been stored up to six months.

lag·gard (LAG·urd) *n. & adj.* one who falls behind: *a laggard at homework; walking at a laggard* (= slow) *pace.*

la·goon (luh·GOON) *n.* a shallow body of water near or

connected with a larger one: *the lagoons of Venice.*

laid *pt. & pp.* of LAY.

laid-back *adj. Slang.* relaxed in style; easy-going: *the look of a laid-back dude; the laid-back life of Californians; Vancouver is more laid-back than Toronto.*

lain *pp.* of LIE.

lair *n.* the den of a wild animal.

laird *n.* in Scotland, a landowner.

lais·sez faire (les·ay·FAIR) *n.* the principle of noninterference by government in private enterprise. — **laissez-faire** *adj.*

la·i·ty (LAY·uh·tee) *n.* **-ties** lay people, as distinguished from clergy.

lake *n.* **1** a body of water surrounded by land: *a cottage on* or *at the lake.* **2** a pool of oil, tar, lava, etc.

lake trout *n.* a char of the region of the Great Lakes.

lal·ly·gag (LAH·lee·lag) *n.* same as LOLLYGAG.

lam *v.* **lams, lammed, lam·ming** *Slang.* flee. — *n.* **on the lam** in flight or in hiding: *He spent three years on the lam from the police.*

la·ma (LAH·muh) *n.* a Buddhist monk of Tibet or Mongolia.

lamb (LAM) *n.* **1** the young of sheep: *the bleating of lambs; a sacrificial lamb; He was led like a lamb to the slaughter.* **2** a person thought of as young and innocent. **3** lamb's meat or skin: *New Zealand spring lamb.* — *v.* bring forth a lamb.

lam·bast or **lam·baste** (lam·BAIST, -BAST) *v.* **-bastes, -bast·ed, -bast·ing** *Informal.* thrash or scold severely.

lam·bent (LAM·bunt) *adj.* of a flame, playing lightly or gently over a surface: *lambent light; her lambent* (=gently brilliant) *wit.* — **lam·bent·ly** *adv.* — **lam·ben·cy** *n.*

lamb·kin *n.* a little lamb.

lamb·skin *n.* (leather from) a lamb's skin.

lame *adj.* **lam·er, lam·est 1** crippled or limping: *a lame man; lame in one leg; a lame* (=painful) *back; a lame* (=weak) *excuse.* **2** *Slang.* square; not up to date. — *v.* **lames, lamed, lam·ing** make lame. — **lame·ly** *adv.;* **lame·ness** *n.*

lame·brain *n. Informal.* a slow-witted person.

lame duck *n.* **1** one who is disabled or helpless. **2** a public official serving the last part of his or her term after being defeated in a reelection. — **lame-duck** *adj.: a lame-duck president waiting out his lame-duck term.*

la·ment (luh·MENT) *n.* **1** an expression of grief, as by wailing or in a poem or song. **2** an elegy or dirge. — *v.* grieve or mourn: *a widow lamenting the death of her husband; Mothers lament for* or *over their missing children; our late lamented* (=mourned for) *friend.* — **lam·en·ta·ble** (LAM·un·tuh·bul, luh·MEN-) *adj.: a lamentable tragedy; the lamentable* (=regrettable) *condition of our roads.* — **lam·en·ta·bly** *adv.* — **lam·en·ta·tion** (lam·un·TAY·shun) *n.*

lam·i·nate (LAM·uh·nate) *v.* **-nates, -nat·ed, -nat·ing 1** cover with a layer of clear plastic: *to laminate a diploma or picture.* **2** split, beat, or roll, as metal, into layers. **3** make in layers bonded together as plywood, safety glass, and plastics: *a laminated board.* — *adj.* (-nit) laminated: *a laminate beam, tabletop.* — **lam·i·na·tion** (-NAY·shun) *n.*

lamp *n.* a device that gives light or heat using electricity, gas, oil, kerosene, etc.: *a floor, incandescent, reading, safety, table lamp; to light, turn down, turn off, turn on a lamp.*

lam·poon (lam·POON) *n.* a satirical piece of writing ridiculing a person or organization. — *v.* attack someone using a lampoon. — **lam·poon·er·y** *n.*

lance *v.* **lanc·es, lanced, lanc·ing** pierce or cut open with a lance or lancet: *to lance a boil.* — *n.* **1** a sharp-pointed instrument such as the large, steel-tipped wooden spear used by medieval knights. **2** same as LANCET. **3** a cavalryman armed with a lance; also **lan·cer.**

lan·cet (LAN·sit) *n.* a small two-edged surgical knife.

land *n.* **1** the solid surface of the earth: *Columbus sighted land; He reached land; dry land; to clear land* (=the ground) *for cultivation; to travel by, on, over land; arable, barren, cultivable, fertile land* (=soil); *a small parcel of land; The house price is inclusive of land* (=plot); *a plot of land; a publicly owned* **land bank** (=parcels of land appropriated by government) *for a housing project.* **2** country: *this land of ours; the Holy Land of Palestine; your native land; the Promised Land of Israel; in no man's land* (=neutral territory); *back in the land* (=realm) *of the living.* — *v.* **1** come or bring to land: *Passengers land at an airport; where to land a plane; how to land a fish.* **2** *Informal.* get: *She could easily land a job or contract; Theft could land you in jail; Pat landed him one* (*Informal* for punched him) *on the nose.*

landed *adj.: the* **landed gentry** *(who own land); a* **landed immigrant** *(who has legally taken up residence in Canada);* **landed property** *(=real estate).*

land·fall *n.* **1** land sighted after a voyage by sea, balloon, etc.: *The Shetland Islands were important landfalls for the Vikings on their way to Britain.* **2** a landing: *The hurricane is on its way to landfall in Florida; It's expected to make landfall by dawn.*

land·fill *n.* disposal of garbage or rubbish by burying it layer by layer under earth: *a sanitary landfill site.*

land·form *n.* a physical feature of the earth's surface, as a hill or plateau.

land grant *n.* gift of land by a government for agricultural colleges, railways, etc.

land·hold·er (LAND·hole·dur) *n.* an owner or occupant of land.

landing *n.* **1** a coming or bringing to land: *We made a safe, smooth, soft landing in heavy fog; a bumpy, crash, easy, emergency, forced, hard landing; a landing by parachute.* **2** the level part at either end of a flight of stairs: *I came to rest on the landing, with no broken bones at all.*

—*adj.*: a **landing craft** *for bringing people and equipment close to shore from a ship; The undercarriage or* **landing gear** *of an aircraft consists of wheels or floats; a* **landing strip** (= airstrip).

land·la·dy (LAND·lay·dee) *n.* **-dies** *fem.* of LANDLORD.

land·locked *adj.* **1** surrounded by land, as a bay, harbour, or inland country. **2** confined to fresh water, as fish: *landlocked salmon.*

land·lord *n.* **1** one who rents property to others: *an absentee landlord; slum landlords.* **2** the keeper of an inn or rooming house.

land·lub·ber (LAND·lub·ur) *n.* [sailor's term] one who is not used to the sea.

land·mark *n.* **1** something that stands out on a landscape, serving to identify a locality. **2** a memorable event: *The moon-landing was a landmark in the history of space travel;* **adj.**: *a landmark decision of the Supreme Court; President Sadat's landmark visit to Israel.*

land·mass *n.* a continent or similar large unbroken area of land.

land office *n.* a government office recording sales and transfers of public lands.
— **land-office** *adj. Informal.* busy and rapid: *doing a land-office business; the land-office demand for a new product.*

land·scape *n.* land scenery or a picture of it: *a beautiful, bleak, gloomy, stark landscape; the lunar landscape; landscape painting.*
— *v.* **-scapes, -scaped, -scap·ing** redesign land and what is on it so as to please the eye, as a **landscape architect** or **landscape gardener** does.

land·slide *n.* **1** the sliding of a mass of earth or rocks down a slope; also, such a displaced mass. **2** in an election, a large majority of votes: *She won by a landslide;* **adj.**: *a landslide defeat, re-election, victory.*

lane *n.* a narrow way, path, or strip, esp. one marked out or designated for runners, aircraft, ships, automobiles, etc. going in the same direction: *to change, shift lanes; the fast lane (on the extreme left of a highway); an inside lane; the passing lane; The shoulder lane is the slow lane.*

lan·guage (LANG·gwij) *n.* **1** a system of communication, esp. human speech or the speech of one group of people: *your native language; her first language; national and official languages; English is a world language; an ancient, classical, dead, foreign, modern, second, universal language; colloquial, formal, idiomatic, informal, literary, nonstandard, spoken, standard, substandard, written language; African and Asian languages; Esperanto is an artificial, not a natural language; the sign language of the deaf; to acquire, butcher, enrich, learn, massacre, master a language; the language of the blind; high-level and low-level computer languages; machine language; programming languages; a* **language laboratory** *for learning to speak languages.* **2** style of verbal expression: *abusive, bad, coarse, diplomatic, dirty, flowery, foul, obscene, offensive, plain, polite, rough, simple, strong language; Pardon my language! the* **language arts** *of reading, speaking, listening, and writing.*

lan·guid (LANG·gwid) *adj.* tired or bored, as on a hot and humid day; not disposed to exert oneself.
— **lan·guid·ly** *adv.;* **lan·guid·ness** *n.*

lan·guish (LANG·gwish) *v.* **1** suffer from languor; pine or droop: *a promising genius now languishing in prison.* **2** lose energy or vigour: *the languishing looks of a forlorn lover.*

lan·guor (LANG·gur) *n.* **1** weakness, sluggishness, or indifference caused by enervating conditions. **2** effeteness or softness: *the languor of a tropical existence.*
— **lan·guor·ous** *adj.*: *a life of languorous ease.*
— **lan·guor·ous·ly** *adv.*

lank *adj.* **1** straight, with a tendency to bend, as tall grass or to lie limp, as hair; **lank·ly** *adv.;* **lank·ness** *n.* **2** awkwardly lean and tall; also **lank·y** *adj.* **lank·i·er, -i·est**: *a lanky-legged colt;* **lank·i·ly** *adv.;* **lank·i·ness** *n.*

lan·tern *n.* **1** a portable lamp with a light inside a frame: *a Chinese lantern; hurricane lantern; kerosene lantern.* **2** a chamber or case to hold or regulate a light, as the top part of a lighthouse or a small windowed turret crowning a dome. **3** an early projector called "magic lantern."

lantern-jawed (LAN·turn·jawd) *adj.* with the lower jaw projecting beyond the upper one.

lap *n.* **1** the knees and thighs of a sitting person forming a place where something may be held: *a child in her mother's lap; brought up in the lap of luxury; His fate is* **in the lap of the gods** (= beyond human help). **2** the loose front part of a garment when held up to hold or catch something. **3** an overlapping part. **4** one circuit of a racecourse: *on the last lap of the journey.* **5** a splashing sound.
— *v.* **laps, lapped, lap·ping 1** lay partly over another, as shingles on a roof: *a lapped seam.* **2** wrap or enfold, as with a canvas or in a blanket. **3** drink, as cats and dogs do; hence, beat gently with a splashing sound: *waves lapping a shore; Be wary of lapping up* (= eagerly consuming) *advice from strangers.*

lap belt *n.* a safety belt across the lap, as in an automobile.

lap·board *n.* a board placed over the lap for use as a table or desk.

lap·dog *n.* a small pet dog.

la·pel (luh·PEL) *n.* the folded-back part of a coat coming down from the collar.

lapse (LAPS) *n.* **1** a slip of the tongue, memory, or pen: *a lapse in judgment; literary lapses.* **2** a slipping back into depression, sin, savagery, etc. **3** a passage into a coma or into silence. **4** the ending of a privilege through neglect or of a custom through disuse.
— *v.* **laps·es, lapsed, laps·ing**: *Your lease lapses* (= ends) *unless renewed in three days; a once splendid palace now lapsed* (= fallen) *into ruin; a lapsed* (= nonpractising) *Catholic.*

lap·top *n.* a portable computer that is smaller than a briefcase.

lar·ce·ny (LAR·suh·nee) *n.* **-nies** [legal use] theft: *Grand larceny is theft of goods of greater value than in petty larceny.* — **lar·ce·nist** *n.*

— lar·ce·nous (-suh·nus) *adj.*

lard *n.* the melted and clarified fat of hogs.
— *v.* put bacon on or into slits in meat to improve its flavour: *a poor speech though larded with biblical quotations.*

lard·er *n.* **1** pantry: *a well-stocked larder.* **2** food supply.

large (LARJ) *adj.* **larg·er, larg·est** big in dimensions or quantity: *the large calorie, intestine; a large fortune, household; large powers; on a large scale; pictures (as) large as (in) life; a **larger-than-life** (=* great) *personality.*
— *adv.: a threat looming large on the horizon; Disappointment was writ large on his face.*
— **at large:** *The rapist is at large* (= free); *The police are appealing to the public at large* (= as a whole); *A congressman-at-large represents an entire state; an editor-at-large in charge of a variety of publications.*
— **by and large** in general.

large-hearted *adj.* generous.

large·ly *adv.* **1** for the most part: *Joe is largely to blame for what happened.* **2** generously: *They contributed largely of their wealth to the campaign.* — **large·ness** *n.*

large-scale *adj.* large in scale or dimensions: *a large-scale map; large-scale abuses, computers, cultivation, distribution, industries, operations, projects, waste.*

lar·gess or **lar·gesse** (LAR·jis) *n.* a generous or showily large bestowal or gift.

larg·ish (LAR·jish) *adj.* somewhat large.

lark *n.* **1** any of a family of small songbirds, esp. the skylark. **2** *Informal.* a frolic or prank: *For a lark, the wanted man dialed the police but got caught instead.*
— *v.: They were larking all night in the park.*

lar·ri·gan (LAIR·uh·gun) *n. Cdn.* a knee-high, oil-tanned boot with a moccasin foot.

lar·va (LAR·vuh) *n., pl.* **-vae** (-vee) or **-vas** the immature, usually wormlike stage of an insect, as a caterpillar, grub, or maggot. — **lar·val** (-vul) *adj.*

lar·yn·gi·tis (lair·un·JYE·tis) *n.* hoarseness from inflammation of the throat.

la·sa·gna (luh·ZAHN·yuh) *n.* a dish of noodles in ribbon form baked with layers of chopped meat, cheese, and tomato sauce; also **la·sa·gne.**

las·civ·i·ous (luh·SIV·ee·us) *adj.* lewd or lustful.
— **las·civ·i·ous·ness** *n.*

lase (LAZE) *v.* **las·es, lased, las·ing** emit or subject to

laser light.

la·ser (LAY·zur) *n.* a device producing an intense, penetrating beam of light which is used in scanning images, printing, playing records, surgery, cutting metal, etc.
— *adj.: a laser printer; laser technology; a laser* (= optical) *disc.*

lash *n.* **1** the flexible striking part of a whip. **2** eyelash. **3** a stroke or blow, as with a whip. **4** something that hurts like a lash.
— *v.* **1** beat or whip: *a tiger lashing its tail; sails lashed by a wind; We could hear the rain lashing against the window; Editorials lashed out at* or *against the tax increases; The government lashed back at the media; The mob was lashed into a fury by one speaker after another; a tongue-lashing he'll never forget.* **2** tie or bind with a rope, cord, chain, etc.

lashing *n.* material with which to tie or bind.

lass *n.* **1** a young girl. **2** a sweetheart, esp. **las·sie** (LAS·ee) *Scottish.*

las·si·tude (LAS·uh·tude) *n.* weariness resulting from dejection, overexertion, etc.

las·so (LAS·oh, la·SOO) *n.* **-sos** or **-soes** a cowboy's rope with a noose at one end for catching or roping livestock.
— *v.* **las·soes, las·soed, las·so·ing** rope or catch with a lasso. — **las·so·er** *n.*

last *adj.* a *superl.* of LATE. **1** coming at the end of a series; hence, lowest in importance: *the last boy in his class; the last man I want to see; a drug of last resort; He is **on his last legs** (=* at the end of his resources). **2** coming after all others in time; hence, latest or most recent: *your last letter; on the **last day but one** (=* two days before the end) *of the school term; the **Last Judgment** (=* God's judgment when the world ends); *She changed her mind at the **last minute** (when it was almost too late); the last rites for the dying; her last will and testament; to have the **last laugh** (=* be successful over the others in the end).
— *adv.: Z comes last in the alphabet; She was fine when I last saw her.*
— *v.* continue to exist and be useful: *Well-made goods last a long time; provisions to last a winter; The funds lasted us* (= were enough for) *a year.*
— *n.* **1** a last person or thing: *Yesterday's game was the last of the series.* **2** a foot-shaped block on which to form or repair a shoe, used by cobblers.
— **at last** or **at long last** after a long time.
— **breathe one's last** die.
— **stick to one's last** mind one's own business.
— **to the last** to the very end.
— **last·ly** *adv.*

last-ditch *adj.* having to do with a final effort: *a last-ditch attempt, effort, measure; our last-ditch supporters.*

last hurrah *n.* a final attempt before quitting, as in politics.

lasting *adj.* continuing indefinitely: *a lasting effect, friendship, impression, solution; a just and lasting peace.*

last name *n.* a family name or surname.

last post *n.* a bugle call sounded at lights-out time, military funerals, and memorial services; taps.

last straw *n.* the last of many intolerable things, like the straw that broke the camel's back in the fable.

last word *n.* **1** the final say or authority: *Mom always has to have the last word in family disputes; Dad's book is the last word on how to conduct an argument.* **2** *Informal.* the latest or most fashionable thing: *the last word in beachwear.*

latch *n.* a fastening device inside a door, window, etc. consisting of a small lever falling into a notch, which may be opened from the outside by a latchkey or a **latch·string** passed outside through a hole in the door. — *v.* fasten: *a cabin door latched shut; a lonesome child looking for someone to* **latch on to** (*Informal for* attach oneself to).

latch·key *n.* **1** a key to the front door of a house that is accessible from the outside. **2** a child left alone at home after school because the parents are at work; also **latchkey child.**

late *adj.* **lat·er** or **lat·ter**, **lat·est** or **last** **1** coming or happening after an expected time: *She's never late for work; was late in going to bed; a bit too late with his application; The supper was late.* **2** at an advanced time: *a late-night party; a late supper near midnight; the late city edition of a newspaper; the late 1980s* (= 1989, 1988, etc.). **3** recent in regard to death, retirement, or other event: *her late husband; a late model car; our late mayor; the late floods.* — *adv.* **lat·er**, **lat·est** or **last** **1** after the usual or expected time: *We arrived late; We had lunch later on in the afternoon; We returned late at night.* **2** recently: *our late lamented friend; as late as last week.* — **of late** lately or recently. — **sooner or later** at some time in the future.

late·ly *adv.* recently.

la·tent (LAY·tunt) *adj.* lying hidden though in existence: *one's latent abilities, qualities; the latent undeveloped image captured on film.* — **la·tent·ly** *adv.* — **la·ten·cy** *n.*

lat·er·al (LAT·ur·ul) *adj.* sideways: *a lateral, not terminal bud; a lateral movement; a **lateral pass** (thrown toward the sidelines or away from the opposing team's goal) in football.* — **lat·er·al·ly** *adv.*

la·tex (LAY·tex) *n.* **1** the milky juice from the bark of plants and trees such as rubber. **2** a rubber or plastic emulsion, as used in paints and adhesives.

lath ("th" as in "the" or as in "thin") *n.* one of the thin, narrow strips of wood or metal forming a lattice or a framework for plastering, as for the walls of a frame house. — *v.* cover or line with laths.

lathe (LAITH, "TH" as in "the") *n.* a machine for shaping pieces of wood, metal, etc. by turning them against a cutting tool. — *v.* **lathes, lathed, lath·ing** shape on a lathe.

lath·er (LATH·ur, "TH" as in "the") *n.* froth or foam, as produced by soap and water or by a sweating horse: *Why work yourself into a lather* (*Slang for* state of excitement) *over nothing?*

— *v.* cover with or form lather: *Men lather the face before shaving with a blade; Soap does not lather in hard water.* — **lath·er·y** *adj.*

lath·ing ("th" as in "the" or as in "thin") or **lath·work** *n.* laths or their installation.

Lat·in *n.* **1** the language of ancient Rome. **2** one who speaks a language such as French, Italian, Portuguese, or Spanish that is descended from the ancient Latin language; one who is from the Mediterranean region; *adj.: a Latin nation; the Latin temperament; the **Latin Church*** (= Roman Catholic Church); *a **Latin American** country (of the Western Hemisphere south of the U.S.).*

lat·ish (LAY·tish) *adj. & adv.* somewhat late.

lat·i·tude (LAT·uh·tude) *n.* **1** the distance north or south of a point on the globe from the equator, measured in degrees: *Medicine Hat is at a latitude of 50 degrees North.* **2** a place or region with reference to its latitude: *cold, high, low latitudes.* **3** degree of freedom of thought or action: *Older children are allowed greater latitude than younger ones in regard to watching TV.* — **lat·i·tu·di·nal** (-TUE·dun·ul) *adj.*

la·trine (luh·TREEN) *n.* a toilet for the use of many, as in a barracks, camp, or factory.

lat·ter (LAT·ur) *adj.* a comp. of LATE. **1** later or more recent: *the latter half of May* (= May 16 to May 31). **2** the last-mentioned, usually the second of two: *Of Jack and Jill, the latter is the younger; Of Tom, Dick, and Harry, the latter* (= Harry) *is the baby.*

latter-day (LAT·ur·day) *adj.* of recent times: *a latter-day problem; a latter-day Shakespeare; a **Latter-day Saint*** (= Mormon).

lat·ter·ly (LAT·ur·lee) *adv.* recently.

lat·tice (LAT·is) *n.* **1** a framework of crossed wooden or metal strips. **2** a window, door, or gate with such a framework. — **lat·ticed** (LAT·ist) *adj.*

laud *n. & v.* praise or acclaim. — **laud·a·ble** (LAW·duh·bul) *adj.* — **laud·a·bly** (-blee) *adv.*

laud·a·to·ry (LAW·duh·tor·ee) *adj.* expressing praise: *a laudatory speech; laudatory verses.*

laugh (LAF) *v.* make the sounds, facial expressions, and bodily movements of one who is amused, joyous, scornful, etc.: *People laugh at his jokes; They laugh with him; Some burst out laughing; "He who laughs last laughs longest"* (= The one who succeeds in the end is the best). — **laugh at** ridicule: *People used to be laughed at for wanting to go to the moon.* — **laugh off** dismiss with a laugh, as something of no consequence. — **laugh out of court** ridicule and get rid of someone. — **laugh up one's sleeve** laugh or ridicule secretly. — *n.* **1** an act of laughing: *anything to get a laugh; He did it for laughs.* **2** *Informal.* something that causes laughter. — **laugh·a·ble** (LAF·uh·bul) *adj.* — **laugh·a·bly** (-blee) *adv.*

laugh·er *n. Slang.* a game that is an easy win.

laugh·ing·stock (LAF·ing·stok) *n.* an object of ridicule: *He made a laughingstock of himself with his claims of UFO sightings.*

laugh·ter (LAF·tur) *n.* the sound or action of laughing: *His wild claims provoked laughter; contagious, convulsive, derisive, hearty, hysterical, infectious, raucous, uproarious, subdued laughter; The audience broke up in gales of laughter.*

launch 1 *n.* an open motorboat used for short trips; also, a large boat carried by a warship. **2** *v.* set in motion, as a ship slid into water or a missile shot into the air: *money to launch her in business; to launch an attack against the enemy; to launch threats; to launch into a tirade against gambling.* **3** *n.* a launching.

launch pad or **launching pad** *n.* a platform from which a missile or spacecraft is launched, usually at a **launching site** such as Cape Canaveral, Florida, by means of a **launch vehicle** (= a rocket system to boost a spacecraft into orbit).

launch window *n.* a limited period suitable for launching a spacecraft depending on the position of the planets.

laun·der (LAWN·dur) *v.* **1** wash and iron clothes, linens, etc. **2** improve or make acceptable: *a laundered version of the real story; a public-relations firm hired to launder the image of the corporation.* **3** make illegal funds clean by channeling through a third party such as a foreign bank to hide their source.
— **laun·der·er** *n.; fem.* **laun·dress** (-dris).

laun·dro·mat (LAWN·druh·mat) *n.* a self-service laundry; **Laundromat** *Trademark.*

laun·dry (LAWN·dree) *n.* **-dries 1** a place for laundering clothes, etc. **2** a batch of such items before or after laundering: *clean, dirty laundry; to do, dry, fold, iron the laundry.*

laundry list *n.* a long and routine list of items.

lau·re·ate (LOR·ee·it) *n.* one honoured with a special prize or title: *a poet laureate; Nobel laureates.*

lau·rel (LOR·ul) *n.* **1** a tropical tree or shrub with aromatic leaves used by the ancient Greeks to crown victorious athletes. **2 laurels** *pl.* fame or victory: *He was never content to **rest on his laurels** (= be satisfied with his accomplishments).*

Lau·ren·tian (law·REN·shun) *adj.* having to do with the St. Lawrence River: *the Laurentian Mountains* or *the Laurentians of Eastern Canada; the Laurentian Shield.*

Lau·ren·tide (LAW·ren·tide) *adj. Cdn.* having to do with the Laurentian region or Quebec.

la·va (LAH·vuh, LAV·uh) *n.* melted rock from a volcano; also, this solidified.

lav·a·lier or **lav·a·liere** (lav·uh·LEER) *n.* **1** an ornament worn on a necklace. **2** a microphone used that way.

lav·a·to·ry (LAV·uh·tor·ee) *n.* **-ries** a toilet, a washbowl with running water, or a washroom equipped with either or both.

lave *v.* **laves, laved, lav·ing** [poetical use] wash or bathe.

lav·en·der (LAV·un·dur) *n.* **1** the pale-purple flowers and leaves of a fragrant European mint: *He's all **lavender and old lace** (= very gentle-mannered).* **2** a pale-purple; also *adj.*

lav·ish (LAV·ish) *adj.* spending or spent very generously and freely: *lavish expenditure, gifts, praise; He's lavish in his praise and lavish with her money.*
— *v.* bestow or spend liberally: *the love and care lavished on children.*
— **lav·ish·ly** *adv.;* **lav·ish·ness** *n.*

law *n.* **1** a written or unwritten rule or regulation governing conduct, recognized by a society: *the laws of hospitality, morality; the law of the land; A bill becomes law when passed by parliament; According to the law, you have to drive on the right; It is against the law to drink and drive; Governments maintain law (= control imposed by laws) and order in society; He went to law (= a court of law) to establish his claim; You read or study law for several years before entering the law (= legal profession) to practise law; Try not to get into trouble with the law (= police); No one is above the law (= free from it); Better leave it to the police and not **take the law into your own hands** (= try to enforce the law yourself); Observe **the Law** (= God's commands in the Old Testament) and the prophets; to administer, adopt, annul, break, challenge, cite, enact, flout, interpret, promulgate, repeal, strike down, violate a law; a blue, dietary, just, lemon, licensing, stringent, unwritten, zoning law.* **2** a type of law: *canon, civil, common, constitutional, criminal, family, international, Islamic, labour, maritime, martial, military, municipal, statutory law; the Mosaic law (of Moses); She's a Doctor of Laws.* **3** any rule or principle: *Newton's laws of motion; a law of nature such as gravitation; the **law of the jungle** (based on who is stronger or more powerful); the laws of hockey; the law of supply and demand.*

law-abiding *adj.* obedient to the law: *a law-abiding citizen.*

law·ful *adj.* according to the law: *a lawful arrest, claim, heir; by all lawful means.*
— **law·ful·ly** *adv.;* **law·ful·ness** *n.*

law·giv·er (LAW·giv·ur) *n.* one who makes laws; lawmaker. — **law·giv·ing** *n. & adj.*

law·less (LAW·lis) *adj.* **1** without laws: *a lawless life, tribe.* **2** breaking the law; disorderly: *lawless behaviour, violence; a lawless gang.*

law·mak·er (LAW·may·kur) *n.* one who helps make laws, as a legislator.

law·man (LAW·mun) *n.* **-men** a law officer such as a sheriff or marshal.

lawn *n.* a plot of close-cropped, grass-covered land for recreation or as part of landscaping: *to mow a lawn.*

law·suit *n.* a case in a law court: *to bring, file, lose, settle, win a lawsuit against a party.*

law·yer (LAW·yur) *n.* one qualified to practise law, advising and representing clients in legal matters: *to hire, retain a lawyer.*

lax *adj.* loose or relaxed, not tight or strict: *lax habits, morals; a school that is somewhat lax in discipline; lax fibre, tissue; lax soil (in texture).*
— **lax·i·ty** or **lax·ness** *n.* — **lax·ly** *adv.*

lax·a·tive (LAX·uh·tiv) *n.* a medicine that helps to make the bowels loose.

lay *v.* **1** *pt.* of LIE: *He lay down to sleep.* **2** **lays, laid, lay·ing** cause to lie; hence, set or put down, esp. in a particular way: *A bricklayer lays bricks; to lay chairs around a room; He laid* (Nonstandard *for* lay) *down to sleep; It's time to lay the book aside and* **lay** (= arrange) **the table** *for dinner; I'll lay* (= make) *a bet the baby will be a boy; I'll lay* (= bet) *you $50 it will be a girl; Our teacher lays* (= puts) *much emphasis on neatness; a well-laid* (= well-made) *plan; Birds lay* (= produce) *eggs; A good rain will lay* (= settle) *the dust; The exorcist tried to lay* (= get rid of) *the ghost; She* **lays claim to** (= claims) *her uncle's estate; He lost his cool and started to* **lay about him** (= hit out) *with his hockey stick; a committee to* **lay down** (= declare authoritatively) *rules and regulations; They managed to* **lay hold of** (= grab) *the burglar; It's wise to* **lay in** (= store up) *provisions for winter; The paint has been* **laid on** (= applied) *rather thick; Please* **lay out** (= arrange) *these pages in proper order; You* **lay over** (= stop and wait) *in Rome and catch a flight the next day for Bombay; the cemetery where grandpa was* **laid to rest** (= buried); *She is* **laid up** (= sick in bed) *with the flu.*
— **lay off 1** make workers idle: *Thousands were laid off when the factory closed.* **2** stop doing something bad: *The superpowers should lay off* (= stop interfering with) *Third World countries; Better lay off* (= stop using) *drugs; Lay off* (= Stop annoying), *will you?*
— *n.* **1** the way something is laid or lies: *the lay of the land as seen from the air.* **2** *Slang.* partner for sexual intercourse. **3** a narrative poem for singing; also, a song or tune: *"The Lay of the Last Minstrel."*
— *adj.* nonprofessional, esp. not of the clergy: *lay people; a book that is too technical for lay readers.*

lay·a·bout (LAY·uh·bowt) *n.* an idle and lazy person.

lay·a·way (LAY·uh·way) *n.* an article reserved for a customer on payment of a deposit to be claimed later after the full price is paid: *We buy Christmas gifts in October on the layaway plan.*

lay·er (LAY·ur) *n.* **1** one that lays: *All our hens are good layers.* **2** one thickness or stratum, esp. one of several: *an even, outer, protective, uneven layer; the bottom, top layer; adj.: a layer cake with a filling between the layers; the layered look of clothes worn one over the other.*

lay·er·ing (LAY·ur·ing) *n.* **1** the wearing of clothes in layers. **2** a method of growing roots for a new plant from a twig or shoot still attached to its parent.

lay·ette (lay·ET) *n.* an outfit of clothes, blankets, etc. for a newborn infant.

lay·man (LAY·mun) *n.* **-men** one who is an outsider in relation to a particular profession, as one who is not a clergyman.

lay·off *n.* **1** a temporary dismissal of an employee. **2** the duration of such unemployment.

lay·out *n.* the arrangement of parts of something organized: *the layout of an advertisement, camp, newspaper page.*

lay·o·ver (LAY·oh·vur) *n.* a break or stop in the course of a journey.

lay·per·son (LAY·pur·sun) *n.* same as LAYMAN.

laze *v.* **laz·es, lazed, laz·ing** be lazy or idle.

la·zy (LAY·zee) *adj.* **-zi·er, -zi·est 1** not willing to work or exert oneself: *a lazy fellow, youth.* **2** having to do with a lazy person: *a lazy excuse, habit.* **3** slow-moving or sluggish: *a lazy current, stream; a lazy eye* (= poor vision resulting from weak eye nerves).
— **la·zi·ly** *adv.*; **la·zi·ness** *n.*

la·zy·bones (LAY·zee·bones) *n. Informal.* a lazy person.

lea (LEE) *n.* a meadow or pasture.

leach (LEECH) *v.* **1** be subject to washing action: *Silver-plated cups that leech too much lead are a health hazard; the leaching field of a sewage system.* **2** remove by washing action: *Heavy rainfall can leach out minerals from fertile soil; the leaching method of separating metal from ore.*

¹lead (LEED) *v.* **leads, led, lead·ing 1** show the way by going in front, directing, or guiding: *You lead, we follow; Please lead the way; a mob led by a troublemaker; He leads them by promises; What led* (= induced or made) *them to follow him? He will* **lead them down the garden path** (= deceive them); *He'll* **lead them (on) a merry chase** (= send them on a useless pursuit); *the events* **leading up to** (= preparing the way for) *the war.* **2** be first in something: *She leads (the class) in all subjects; the float that leads the parade; the batter who leads off in an inning.* **3** pass life, time, etc. in a particular way: *She leads a happy life.*
— *n.* **1** one that leads, as the principal part in a play: *to play the lead; the lead* (= leading) *role of Macbeth; the lead car, dog, hand; The story has a good lead* (= opening paragraph); *The police are tracking down some leads* (= clues) *on the murder; Dogs should be on a lead* (= leash). **2** a leading: *someone to take the lead in organizing the show; We'll follow his lead.* **3** a being first, as in a race: *We are in the lead; We've to hold, maintain the lead; We have a commanding lead over* (= wide margin by which we lead) *the competition.*
— **lead·er** *n.*; **lead·er·ship** *n.*

²lead (LED) *n.* **1** a soft, heavy, bluish-grey metallic element that is poisonous in compounds such as "lead acetate" and "lead arsenate." **2** something made of lead, as bullets, a plumb bob, or a strip of metal to space out lines of type. **3** the material ("graphite") used in pencils.

— **get the lead out** *Slang.* hurry up; hustle.

— *v.* to cover, mix, treat, weight, or fix glass in position with lead.

— *adj.* made of or with lead: *a lead pipe; a lead* (= graphite) *pencil.*

lead·ed (LED·id) *adj.* containing lead: *leaded gasoline.*

lead·en (LED·un) *adj.* made of or like lead in weight, colour, dullness, etc.: *leaden limbs, skies, spirits, thoughts.*

lead·ing 1 (LED·ing) *n.* metal strips for spacing out lines of type. **2** (LEE·ding) *adj.* that leads: *the leading character in a play; one of our leading* (= influential) *citizens; the* **leading** (= front) *edge of an airfoil, of a warm front; at the leading edge of technology; a* **leading question** (*so worded as to suggest the desired answer).*

lead time *n.* the time required for a plan or project to be carried out, as in manufacturing a new product.

leaf (LEEF) *n.* **leaves** (LEEVZ) **1** one of the thin, flat, green parts of a tree or plant: *a fig leaf; tea leaves; Leaves rustle in the wind.* **2** something similar to a leaf such as a flower petal, a sheet of paper or metal, a movable part of a table's top, a door, or a gate: *The dome was covered with gold leaf.*

— *v.* **1** to bear leaves: *Many trees and plants leaf in the spring.* **2** look through casually: *to leaf through a book, magazine.*

leaf·age (LEE·fij) *n.* leaves or foliage.

leaf·let (LEEF·lit) *n.* **1** a printed, often folded sheet, as for direct-mail advertising: *a propaganda leaflet.* **2** a small leaf or a part of a compound leaf.

leaf·y (LEE·fee) *adj.* **leaf·i·er, -i·est** having many leaves: *Lettuce is a leafy vegetable.*

league (LEEG) *n.* **1** an alliance of organizations with common interests, as in politics or sports: *the League of Nations (1920 – 1946); the League of Canadian Poets; major league* (= class or category) *baseball; big, bush, minor league.* **2** formerly, a measure of distance, usually equal to three nautical miles (5.556 km).

— **in league** allied with someone.

— **out of one's league** *Informal.* out of one's own class.

leak (LEEK) *v.* allow something to go in or out, as through a hole or crack: *a leaking boat; Water leaks into a boat; They are accused of leaking state secrets to the press; Air is leaking out* (= escaping) *from the tire; Truth will leak out.*

— *n.* a leaking or something that leaks: *The pipe sprang a leak; to stop the leak; to plug a security leak; a politically inspired news leak.*

leak·age (LEE·kij) *n.* a leak, what has leaked out, or its amount.

leak·y (LEE·kee) *adj.* **leak·i·er, -i·est** that leaks: *a leaky boat, roof.*

lean (LEEN) *v.* **leans,** *pt. & pp.* **leaned** or **leant, lean·ing 1** bend or incline from a normal position *toward, against, on,* or *upon* something, as for support: *to lean a ladder against a wall; the Leaning Tower of Pisa; a doctrine leaning toward heresy.* **2** rely: *Friends lean on each other in times of crisis.*

— **lean on** *Informal.* force or urge someone to do something.

— **lean over backward(s)** try very hard to please someone; bend over backward.

— *n.* inclination; also, leaning.

— *adj.* **1** without much fat: *lean meat; He's of a lean and wiry build.* **2** meagre or scanty: *a fuel mixture that is too lean* (= not rich enough) *for proper burning.*

— **lean·ness** *n.*

leap (LEEP) *n.* a jump or spring, esp. one suggesting lightness: *a great leap forward.*

— **by leaps and bounds** swiftly.

— *v.* **leaps,** *pt. & pp.* **leaped** or **leapt** (LEEPT, LEPT), **leap·ing** jump or cause to jump over something: *horses leaping a fence; "Look before you leap"; An idea leaped to her mind; to leap at* (= grasp eagerly) *an opportunity.*

leap·frog *v. & n.* **-frogs, -frogged, -frog·ging** (leap over as in) a game in which players jump, with legs spread wide, over the bent back of each of the other players: *to play leapfrog; One labour union tries to leapfrog* (= get more than) *the wages gained by another.*

leap year *n.* a year of 366 days, with February 29 as the extra day, occurring every fourth year.

learn (LURN) *v.* **learns,** *pt. & pp.* **learned** (LURND) or **learnt, learn·ing 1** acquire a skill or knowledge, as by study or experience: *to learn a poem by heart; Children learn to walk; They learn by* or *from experience; to learn dancing* or *to dance* or *how to dance; adj.:* a **learned** *habit, lesson, response, skill.* **2** come to know: *I learned about the lottery; learned that he is now a millionaire; I learned the news from TV.*

learn·ed (LUR·nid) *adj.* having to do with learning; scholarly: *a learned book, profession, scholar, society.*

learning *n.* **1** knowledge, esp. of the formal or advanced kind: *a man of great learning; higher learning; not mere book learning.* **2** the act of learning: *programmed learning; adj.: A child with a* **learning disability** *may need special help with reading and math; A* **learning curve** *or* **graph** *shows progress in learning.*

lease (LEECE) *n.* **1** a contract by which one person (**lessor**) lets another (**lessee**) have the use of property such as land, buildings, automobiles, etc. for a certain period on payment of a rent: *A lease may expire* or *run out if not renewed.* **2** the right thus acquired, its period, or the property itself: *Surgery could give you a* **new lease on life** (= chance to continue living).

— *v.* **leas·es, leased, leas·ing** give or take a lease on something: *to lease a car from a dealer.* — **leas·er** *n.*

lease·hold *n.* property held by a lease.

— **lease·hold·er** *n.*

leash (LEESH) *v.* check or hold an animal on a leash.

— *n.* a line, chain, or strap: *a child* **straining at the leash** (= trying hard) *to be free of parental control.*

least (LEEST) *adj.* a *superl.* of LITTLE; smallest, slightest, or lowest: *I'm not the least bit worried.*

— *n.* what is smallest, slightest, or lowest: *The least I ask is 25 cents; If you can't pay it,* **at least** *say "Thank you."*

— **not in the least** not at all.

— *adv.* a *superl.* of LITTLE: *He likes Mondays least.*

least·wise *adv. Informal.* at any rate. Also **least·ways** [regional].

439

leath·er (LETH·ur, "TH" as in "the") *n.* 1 animal skin prepared for making shoes, coats, gloves, etc. 2 such an article. — *adj.* made of leather; also **leath·ern.**

leath·er·y (LETH·uh·ree) *adj.* tough and pliable like leather.

leave (LEEV) *v.* **leaves, left** or **leaved** (def. 4), **leav·ing** 1 go or depart from a place: *a flight leaving (Montreal) for London; She just left (here).* 2 let a person or thing be; let remain: *Don't leave the baby alone; She left the door open; There was no one left in the house; The injured dog was left for* (= abandoned as) *dead; I left* (= forgot) *my wallet at school; I leave it to your good judgment; The decision is left up to you; His arguments* **leave me cold** (= unimpressed). 3 let a person have: *His rich uncle left him a fortune.* 4 **leaves, leaved, leav·ing** put forth leaves.
— **leave off** stop or cease.
— **leave out** omit or ignore.
— **leave something, somewhat** or **a great deal** or **a lot** or **much to be desired** be not as good as it should be: *Your homework leaves somewhat to be desired.*
— *n.* 1 permission: *He asked leave to speak; She has a year's leave* (= free time away from duty); *maternity, sick leave; terminal leave* (before retirement); *a sailor on shore leave; He was granted* **leave of absence** (= permission to be absent) *from duty; She's back home* **on leave;** *It was time to* **take leave of** (= to leave) *his family; He seems to have* **taken leave of his senses** (= He's acting strangely). 2 **leaves** See LEAF.
— **leaved** *adj. & combining form.* having leaves as specified: *a lovely tree when fully leaved; a four-leaved clover.*

leav·en (LEV·un) *n.* 1 a substance such as yeast or baking powder, also called **leav·en·ing,** that causes fermentation in batter or dough by releasing carbon dioxide which lightens and raises it. 2 a spreading influence bringing about change.
— *v.* 1 make batter or dough rise. 2 lighten, temper, or enliven: *poetry leavened with wit.*

leaves *pl.* of LEAF.

leave-taking (LEEV·tay·king) *n.* parting or farewell.

leavings *n.pl.* what is left; leftovers or remnants.

lech·er *n.* a man who indulges in lechery or lust.

lech·er·y (LECH·uh·ree) *n.* lust; lewdness; debauchery.
— **lech·er·ous** (-uh·rus) *adj.*

lec·tern (LEC·turn) *n.* a tall reading stand, usually with a slanted top, as used by a lector.

lec·tor (LEC·tur) *n.* a person who reads to the congregation at a church service.

lec·ture (LEC·chur) *n.* 1 an instructive talk, as given to a class of students: *Professors deliver, students attend lectures.* 2 a scolding.
— *v.* **-tures, -tured, -tur·ing** give a lecture to someone; also, scold: *The teacher lectured him on his poor marks.*
— **lec·tur·er** *n.: a lecturer in or on Canadian literature.*
— **lec·ture·ship** *n.*

led *pt. & pp.* of LEAD.

ledge (LEJ) *n.* a narrow shelf or ridge standing out from an upright surface: *a window ledge; a ledge of rock near*

a shore.

ledg·er (LEJ·ur) *n.* a book in which money transactions are recorded.

lee *n.* 1 a side, as of a ship or island, that is sheltered from the wind. 2 shelter: *in the lee of a wall.*
— *adj.* sheltered or away from the wind; leeward, not windward: *a lee shore, tide; the lee side of a ship.*

leech *n.* 1 a small worm, also called "bloodsucker," once used in medicine to remove blood from patients. 2 a hanger-on.
— *v.* drain or exhaust: *work that leeches one's energy.*

leer *n.* a sly, suggestive, or evil glance.
— *v.* look with a leer at someone.

leer·y *adj.* **leer·i·er, -i·est** *Informal.* suspicious or wary *of* someone or something.

lees (LEEZ) *n.pl.* dregs or sediment, as of wine during fermentation.

lee·ward (LEE·wurd, LOO·wurd) *adj. & adv.* away from the wind; toward the lee. — *n.* the lee side.

lee·way *n.* 1 leeward drift of a ship or aircraft from its true course; also, the degree of such deviation. 2 a margin of safety or tolerance; freedom or elbow room: *Allow some leeway for human error; Don't give too much leeway to laziness.*

left *n.* 1 the side of the body or the hand to the north when one is facing east: *Your heart is on your left.* 2 a left turn: *Take a left at the lights.* 3 **the left** or **the Left** in politics, a liberal or radical position, party, or person, esp. one advocating social and economic reform: *the extreme, far Left.* 4 a punch with the left hand: *to deliver* or *throw a left.*
— *adv. & adj.* on or toward the left: *Turn left at the lights; No left turn is allowed on a red light.*
— **left·ist** *adj.: a leftist position, view.*
— *pt. & pp.* of LEAVE.

left-handed *adj. & adv.* using or done with the left hand: *He is left-handed; a left-handed pitch; He pitches left-handed; a left-handed* (= insincere) *compliment.*

left·o·ver (LEFT·oh·vur) *n.* something that is left or unused, as scraps of food: *We don't serve leftovers to our guests; It looks like a leftover from the previous government.*

left wing *n.* 1 a front-line player or position to the left of centre, as in hockey. 2 the more radical section of a political party. — **left-wing** *adj.* — **left-wing·er** *n.*

left·y *n.* **left·ies** *Informal.* a left-handed person.

leg *n.* 1 one of the limbs in humans and animals used for support and for moving about: *to cross one's legs in sitting; Walk around the room to stretch your legs a little; a cat's hind legs; He does* **not have a leg to stand on** (= has no valid defence). 2 any part suggesting a leg, as of trousers, of a table, chair, etc. 3 one of the stages of a course, as in a relay race or journey: *She is on the last leg of her journey.*
— **on one's last legs** near collapse.
— **pull one's leg** *Informal.* tease; also, trick in fun, not maliciously.
— *v.* **legs, legged, leg·ging** *Informal.* go on foot: *The*

car broke down and we had to leg it the rest of the way.

leg·a·cy (LEG·uh·see) *n.* **-cies 1** an inheritance or bequest. **2** anything handed down from the past or by predecessors: *a lasting legacy of the war.*

le·gal (LEE·gul) *adj.* involving the law or its knowledge or use: *to take legal action; legal advice; the **legal age*** (= age of majority); *in her legal capacity as the child's guardian; in legal control, ownership; a **legal holiday*** (set by law) *such as Thanksgiving; the legal profession; your legal rights and responsibilities; a **legal pad** or **tablet** of legal-size paper (measuring 8.5 x 14 in. / about 20 x 36 cm); a legal system; One thousand pennies may not be **legal tender*** (= money acceptable in payment of a debt). — **le·gal·ly** *adv.* — **le·gal·i·ty** (lee·GAL·uh·tee) *n.*

le·gal·ism (LEE·guh·liz·um) *n.* **1** strict adherence to the letter of the law. **2** a legal expression or rule. — **le·gal·is·tic** (-LIS·tic) *adj.*

le·gal·ize (LEE·guh·lize) *v.* **-iz·es, -ized, -iz·ing** make legal: *Gambling was legalized in the form of government-run lotteries.* — **le·gal·i·za·tion** (-luh·ZAY·shun) *n.*

leg·end (LEJ·und) *n.* **1** a story or tradition connected with the history of a people, as the story of St. George and the Dragon: *Mother Teresa's work with the poor made her a living legend; She became a legend in her own lifetime.* **2** an inscription, as on a medal. **3** an explanation, as of an illustration or of symbols used on a chart or map.

leg·end·ar·y (LEJ·un·dair·ee) *adj.* having to do with legend: *the legendary tales about Charlemagne; He became a legendary figure even during his life.*

leg·ged (LEG·id, LEGD) *adj. & combining form.* with legs as specified: *to sit cross-legged; a long-legged colt, the one-legged marathoner Steve Fonyo; spindly legged jeans; a three-legged race.*

leg·ging *n.* a leg-covering: *woollen leggings for children.*

leg·gy (LEG·ee) *adj.* **leg·gi·er, leg·gi·est** having long legs: *a leggy sprinter; Leggy colts look awkward.*

leg·i·ble (LEJ·uh·bul) *adj.* clear enough to read: *She writes a legible hand.* — **leg·i·bly** *adv.* — **leg·i·bil·i·ty** (-BIL·uh·tee) *n.*

le·gion (LEE·jun) *n.* **1** an army, esp. a unit of 3 000 to 6 000 soldiers in ancient Rome. **2** a large number: *Tax evaders – their name is legion.* **3** usually **Legion,** a society, as of ex-servicemen: *Royal Canadian Legion.*

le·gion·naire (lee·juh·NAIR) *n.* a member of a Legion.

leg·is·late (LEJ·is·late) *v.* **-lates, -lat·ed, -lat·ing 1** make laws: *The government can only legislate on what it can control.* **2** bring about something by legislating: *No one can legislate quality of life; to legislate equal pay for work of equal value; to legislate strikers back to work.* — **leg·is·la·tor** *n.*

leg·is·la·tion (lej·is·LAY·shun) *n.* the making of laws or statutes: *to adopt, enact, introduce, pass legislation to ban smoking.*

leg·is·la·tive (LEJ·is·luh·tiv) *adj.* having to do with legislation: *a legislative body, decree, measure; legislative authority, reforms.*

leg·is·la·ture (LEJ·is·luh·chur) *n.* a lawmaking body such as the House of Commons.

le·git (luh·JIT) *adj. Slang.* legitimate: *He has switched from nightclub circuits to legit theatre; He's gone legit.* — *n.: strictly **on the legit*** (= within the law).

le·git·i·mate (luh·JIT·uh·mit) *adj.* rightful according to law or other standard: *a legitimate candidate, claim, conclusion, heir, purpose; a legitimate movie star, play; **Legitimate theatre** is drama of literary merit, not musical comedies, motion pictures, etc.* — **le·git·i·ma·cy** (-muh·see) *n.*

le·git·i·mize (luh·JIT·uh·mize) *v.* **-miz·es, -mized, -miz·ing** make or declare to be legitimate.

leg·man *n.* **-men** one engaged in work that involves much moving about, or **leg·work,** esp. an on-the-scene reporter or an assistant on routine duties outside the office.

lei·sure (LEE·zhur, LEZH·ur) *n.* time that one may spend for rest and recreation: *Do it at your leisure* (= convenience). — *adj.: leisure hours, time; the **leisure class** (of people not working for a living); a **leisure suit** (of shirtlike jacket and trousers for casual wear); leisure wear.*

lei·sure·ly (LEZH·ur·lee) *adj.* unhurried: *He works at a leisurely pace; a leisurely meal; adv.: We drove leisurely* (= unhurriedly) *around town.*

lem·ming *n.* a mouselike arctic animal noted for periodic migrations during which large numbers starve to death or get killed.

lem·on (LEM·un) *n.* **1** a pale-yellow, oval-shaped citrus fruit. **2** *Slang.* a person or thing that turns sour or disagreeable, esp. a bad buy such as a defective car: *a **lemon law** requiring full refund or free repairs.*

lem·on·ade (lem·uh·NADE) *n.* a drink made of water, sugar, and lemon juice.

lend *v.* **lends, lent, lend·ing 1** give money, goods, or services temporarily: *to lend someone $5 000 at 10% interest for one year; Please lend him your car for an hour; **Lend me an ear** (= Listen to me); to **lend a hand** (= to help); a subject that **lends itself to** (= is suitable for) dramatic treatment.* **2** give or impart: *Her presence lends distinction to the proceedings.*

length *n.* how long or extended something is: *the length and width of a room; throughout the length and* *breadth of the land; The room is 10 m in length; She described what happened* **at great length** (= in detail or fully); *He will* **go to great lengths** (= make a great effort) *to help a friend; Our horse won the race by a length* (= horse's length); *a length of rope (of a specific length); a full-length movie (not a short one); People you don't want to get involved with should be kept at* **arm's length** (= at some distance); *At length* (= Finally), *somebody spoke up.*

length·en *v.* make or become longer.

length·wise *adj. & adv.* in the direction of the length. Also **length·ways.**

length·y *adj.* **length·i·er, -i·est** very long, often too long: *a lengthy essay, lecture, speech.* — **length·i·ly** *adv.*

le·ni·ent (LEE·nee·unt, LEEN·yunt) *adj.* **1** mild: *a lenient climate.* **2** merciful: *a lenient judge; lenient rules.* — **le·ni·ence** or **le·ni·en·cy** *n.*

lens (LENZ) *n.* **1** a piece of glass or other transparent body that focusses or spreads light rays, as in the eye or in a camera, microscope, or telescope: *concave and convex lenses; Contact lenses are corrective lenses for the eyes.* **2** any focussing device for sound waves, electrons, etc.

lent *pt. & pp.* of LEND.

leop·ard (LEP·urd) *n.* a large fierce cat of Asia and Africa valued for its black-spotted skin: *a young leopard* (= cub); *"A leopard cannot change its spots."*

le·o·tard (LEE·uh·tard) *n.* usually **leotards**, *pl.* a tight-fitting, one-piece garment, as worn by acrobats; also, tights.

lep·er (LEP·ur) *n.* one who has leprosy; also, an outcast.

lep·re·chaun (LEP·ruh·cawn) *n.* a fairy of Irish folklore.

lep·ro·sy (LEP·ruh·see) *n.* a chronic infectious and ulcerous disease of the skin and nerves that causes disfigurement. — **lep·rous** (-rus) *adj.*

les·bi·an (LEZ·bee·un) *n. & adj.* a female homosexual. — **les·bi·an·ism** *n.*

le·sion (LEE·zhun) *n.* injury to tissue, as an ulcer, tumour, or abscess: *an open lesion.*

less *adj.* a comparative of LITTLE; not as much or as many; smaller, fewer, or lower in rank, importance, quality, etc.: *She's no less a person than the president; He uses little salt and less sugar; Grandma is less than pleased with the rising cost of food; Coffee used to cost 10 cents or less; 10 items or less (Informal for fewer).*
— *adv.* not as much or as often: *to sleep less and work longer.*
— *prep.* minus: *$10 000 less deductions; two years less a day.*
— *n.* a smaller amount: *a little less of it.*
— *adj. suffix* [freely added to nouns] not having or involving: *endless, painless, useless.*

les·see (les·EE) *n.* See LEASE.

less·en (LES·un) *v.* make or become less.

less·er *adj.* a comparative of LITTLE; smaller or less important: *He was found guilty on a lesser charge of manslaughter; the lesser panda* (= not the giant panda, but the red one).

les·son (LES·un) *n.* **1** a learning exercise or something learned: *to take driving lessons* (= instruction); *In our school,* **lessons** *begin at 9 a.m.; a lesson in French; The accident will be a lesson* (= warning) *to him; That should teach him a lesson* (= make sure he doesn't do it again); *an object lesson* (= practical illustration of a principle). **2** a passage from the Bible for reading at a church service.

les·sor (LES·or) *n.* See LEASE.

lest *conj.* for fear that: *He was cautious lest he be misunderstood; Lest we forget; He was afraid lest he should miss the bus.*

-let *n. suffix.* **1** small person or thing: *booklet, piglet, starlet.* **2** small article of attire: *anklet, bracelet, wristlet.*

let *v.* **lets,** *pt. & pp.* **let, let·ting** allow to go, have, pass, etc.: *to let the cat out; We can't let him (come) in; Let us* (= I propose that we) *pray; Surgeons used to let blood (run out) as a cure; a house* **to let** (= for rent); *Please let* (= leave) *it alone; He doesn't have the training,* **let alone** (= not to mention) *experience for the job; He feels badly* **let down** (= disappointed) *by friends; Only friends were* **let in on** (= told) *the secret; As a first offender, she was* **let off** (= allowed to leave) *with a warning; He likes to* **let on** (*Informal for* pretend) *that he has a rich uncle.*
— **let out 1** release or make known. **2** rent: *to let out the basement to boarders.* **3** make larger: *to let out a couple of inches at the waist of the pants.*
— **let up** *Informal.* stop or pause: *The housing shortage will not let up for another year.*
— *n.* in a racket game, an interference with play.
— **without let or hindrance** without obstacles.

let·down *n.* a slowing up; also, a disappointment: *the letdown after the buildup for the Olympics.*

le·thal (LEE·thul, "th" as in "thin") *adj.* capable of causing death: *a lethal* (= deadly) *dose; a lethal injection (given to one condemned to death); rifles, pistols, and such lethal weapons.* — **le·thal·ly** *adv.*

leth·ar·gy (LETH·ur·jee) *n.* a dull, sluggish, or tired state. — **le·thar·gic** (luh·THAR·gic) *adj.*

let's let us.

let·ter (LET·ur) *n.* **1** a character of the alphabet, as A, B, C, etc.: *in block letters; a capital or upper-case letter; lower-case, small letters; follow orders* **to the letter** (= precisely); *He observes* **the letter of the law** (= its literal meaning) *but not its spirit.* **2** a written communication: *the art of writing letters; a business, chain, dead, express, fan, form, love, open, poison-pen letter; Our letters must have crossed in the mail;* **letter quality** *printing that resembles typewriting.* **3** letters [takes sing. or pl. v.] literature; also, learning: *Letters in Canada; a man, woman of letters* (= an author or a literary scholar); *Doctor of Letters.*
— *v.* mark with or inscribe in letters: *to letter a poster.*
— **let·ter·er** *n.*

letter carrier *n.* one who delivers mail.

lettered *adj.* **1** marked with letters: *a lettered design; Streets are either numbered or lettered, like 6th and K streets; a boldly lettered T-shirt.* **2** literate; also, learned.

let·ter·head (LET·ur·hed) *n.* writing paper printed with one's name and address; also, such name and address.

lettering (LET·ur·ing) *n.* the art of making drawn, printed, or stamped letters; also, such letters.

letter-perfect (let·ur·PUR·fict) *adj.* correct in every detail.

let·tuce (LET·is) *n.* the large, crisp, green leaves of a plant much used in salads: *a head of lettuce; leaf lettuce.*

let·up *n. Informal.* pause or slackening: *a letup in the rain.*

lev·ee (LEV·ee) *n.* 1 a wall of banked-up earth and sandbags put up along a river's bank to contain floods. 2 a formal reception, as by a sovereign, governor general, mayor, etc.: *a New Year's levee.*

lev·el (LEV·ul) *adj.* equal in height everywhere; horizontal: *Adjust the legs to make the table level; The flood waters were level with the second floor; a level* (= not heaped) *teaspoonful; He always keeps a level* (= sensible) *head; a level* (*Informal* for steady) *voice; a level-headed man; a level crossing* (of road and railway at the same level); *adv.*: *We'll do our level best* (= very best).
—*n.* 1 something that is level: *a parking level; Did we park on this level?* 2 a height or depth: *We can see best at eye level; Basements are below the ground level; the oil level in a car engine; a lake above sea level; The water rose to a level of three metres; a high level of achievement; a clerk at a low level; In 1988, an income of $20 000 a year was below the poverty level* or *line for a family of four; Water finds its own level* (= reaches the same height at all points if allowed); *at the federal, local, municipal, national levels; the highest levels of government.* 3 an instrument used to determine if a plane is horizontal.
— **on the level** of a person or conduct, blameless or genuine.
—*v.* **-els, -elled** or **-eled, -el·ling** or **-el·ing** make horizontal or on the same level: *a town levelled by an earthquake; words levelled* (= directed) *at his critics; Prices are expected to rise and then level off* (= stay the same); *Come on now, level with* (= be honest) *me.*
— **lev·el·ler** or **lev·el·er** *n.*

lev·er (LEV·ur, LEE·vur) *n.* 1 a device such as a crowbar for exerting force. 2 a means of exerting power or moral force: *He used his position as a lever to get votes.*

lev·er·age (LEV·ur·ij) *n.* 1 means of applying force: *The longer the crowbar the greater the leverage.* 2 advantage, effectiveness, or influence: *Teachers have much leverage with the principal.*

leveraged buyout *n.* the buying out of a company using borrowed money.

lev·i·tate (LEV·uh·tate) *v.* **-tates, -tat·ed, -tat·ing** rise and float in the air: *a magnetically levitated transportation system.* — **lev·i·ta·tion** (-TAY·shun) *n.*

lev·i·ty (LEV·uh·tee) *n.* **-ties** lack of proper seriousness; frivolity.

lev·y (LEV·ee) *v.* **lev·ies, lev·ied, lev·y·ing** 1 raise taxes, armies, etc. by legal authority. 2 seize property in satisfaction of a claim. 3 wage: *to levy war on* or *against a nation.*
—*n., pl.* **lev·ies** 1 a fine or tax that is imposed on a person or thing. 2 enlistment for military service or the men enlisted.

lewd (LOOD) *adj.* indecent or obscene.
— **lewd·ly** *adv.;* **lewd·ness** *n.*

lex·i·cal (LEX·uh·cul) *adj.* having to do with word meaning rather than grammar. — **lex·i·cal·ly** *adv.*

lex·i·cog·ra·phy (lex·uh·COG·ruh·fee) *n.* the work or art of compiling dictionaries. — **lex·i·cog·ra·pher** *n.*

lex·i·con (LEX·uh·cun) *n.* 1 the vocabulary of a language. 2 a dictionary, esp. of a classical language.

li·a·bil·i·ty (lye·uh·BIL·uh·tee) *n.* **-ties** the condition of being liable: *No one would accept* or *admit liability* (= responsibility) *for the accident; to acknowledge, assume, take on a liability; a limited, not full liability* (= obligation); *One's sex or colour should be neither a liability* (= disadvantage) *nor an asset in job hunting; Heavy liabilities* (= debts) *forced him into bankruptcy.*

li·a·ble (LYE·uh·bul) *adj.* subject to a responsibility or risk: *a carrier that is not liable to anyone for damage to luggage; If you play with fire, you are liable to get burned; Everyone is liable to make mistakes now and then.*

li·aise (lee·AIZ) *v.* **-as·es, -ased, -as·ing** to have liaison with someone.

li·ai·son (lee·AY·zon, LEE·uh·zon) *n.* 1 communication between different parts of an army, of civilian bodies, etc. for cooperation. 2 illicit sexual relationship.

li·ar (LYE·ur) *n.* [offensive in direct speech] one who tells lies.

lib *n.* [short form] liberation.

li·ba·tion (lye·BAY·shun) *n.* 1 a ceremonial pouring out of wine, oil, etc. as an offering to a god; also, the liquid poured out thus. 2 *Informal.* a drink or drinking that intoxicates.

lib·ber *n. Informal.* [sometimes offensive] a liberationist, esp. a feminist: *a women's libber.*

li·bel (LYE·bul) *n.* 1 the hurting of someone's good name by publishing something written, printed, drawn, etc. unjustly. 2 material that libels.
—*v.* **li·bels, li·belled** or **li·beled, -bel·ling** or **-bel·ing** defame someone by a libel.
— **li·bel·ler** or **li·bel·er** *n.*
— **li·bel·lous** or **li·bel·ous** *adj.*

lib·er·al (LIB·uh·rul) *adj.* 1 free or broad-minded; not narrow, strict, or prejudiced: *He's quite liberal in his interpretation of the Bible.* 2 generous: *a liberal donation, tipper; He's very liberal with other people's money; a liberal* (= plentiful) *supply of provisions.*
—*n.* 1 one who is in favour of progress and reform. 2 **Liberal** a member of a Liberal Party, as in Canada and Britain. — **lib·er·al·ism** *n.*
— **lib·er·al·i·ty** (-RAL·uh·tee) *n.*

liberal arts *n. pl.* languages, literature, philosophy, history, and such subjects of cultural interest and value.
— **liberal education** *n.*

lib·er·al·ize (LIB·uh·ruh·lize) *v.* -iz·es, -ized, -iz·ing
make or become liberal or more liberal: *the agitation
for liberalized abortion laws.*
— **lib·er·al·i·za·tion** (-luh·ZAY·shun) *n.*

lib·er·al·ly (LIB·uh·ruh·lee) *adv.* generously.

lib·er·ate (LIB·uh·rate) *v.* -ates, -at·ed, -at·ing set free,
as from slavery, confinement, dictatorship, enemy
occupation, etc. — **lib·er·a·tor** *n.*
— **lib·er·a·tion** (-RAY·shun) *n.;* **lib·er·a·tion·ist** *n.*

lib·er·tar·i·an (lib·ur·TAIR·ee·un) *n.* one who believes in
freedom, sometimes absolute freedom, in thought and
action: *a civil libertarian* (= one who advocates civil
liberties).

lib·er·ty (LIB·ur·tee) *n.* -ties freedom from restraints
such as slavery: *liberty of action, thought, etc.; She
doesn't let boys take liberties* (= be too familiar) *with
her on dates; May I take the liberty of telling you that
it's getting late?*
— **at liberty** free: *to set prisoners at liberty; A
telephone operator is not at liberty to give out unlisted
numbers.*

li·brar·i·an (lye·BRAIR·ee·un) *n.* one in charge of a
library or one trained in library science.

li·brar·y (LYE·brair·ee) *n.* -brar·ies a collection of
books, manuscripts, tapes, etc. or where it is housed: *a
circulating, lending, mobile, public, reference,
research, school library.*

lice *pl.* of LOUSE.

li·cence or **li·cense** (LYE·sunce) *n.* 1 a formal or legal
permission to do something as a member of society, as
driving, marrying, or practising a profession: *Show me
your driver's licence* (= document granting licence to
drive); *poetic licence* (= ignoring rules for the sake of
poetic effects); *to grant, issue, revoke, suspend a licence.*
2 irresponsible use of freedom.
— **li·cense** or **li·cence** *v.* -cens·es or -cenc·es, -censed or
-cenced, -cens·ing or -cenc·ing to grant a licence to
someone: *a licensed medical practitioner; The
pharmacist is licensed to dispense drugs; licensed
establishments, premises, restaurants* (where liquor may
be sold).

li·cen·see (lye·sen·SEE) *n.* one granted a licence.

li·cen·tious (lye·SEN·shus) *adj.* immoral or lewd.
— **li·cen·tious·ly** *adv.;* **li·cen·tious·ness** *n.*

lic·it (LIS·it) *adj.* permitted by law; not forbidden.
— **lic·it·ly** *adv.*

lick *v.* 1 pass the tongue over an object: *She licked her
fingers; licked them clean; flames licking the walls.*
2 *Informal.* beat or thrash; also, conquer: *If you can't
lick them, join them; He got a good licking; She has the
problems licked* (= solved); *a thesis licked into shape*
(*Informal* for put in proper form) *for submission.*
— *n.* a licking: *One lick of that ice-cream cone satisfied
me.*
— **lick and a promise** *Informal.* a hasty performance,
as of washing and cleaning.

lick·e·ty·split (lick·uh·tee·SPLIT) *adv. Informal.* at full-
speed.

lid *n.* 1 a movable cover, as of a pot or box. 2 an eyelid.

3 a curb or check: *tighter measures to put the lid on
smuggling.* — **lid·ded** *adj.*

lie (LYE) *n.* 1 a deliberate falsehood, esp. a cowardly
one: *His entire life seemed a lie; Facts give or put the
lie to* (= show to be untrue) *his claims; a barefaced,
brazen, downright, monstrous, outright, whopping lie; a
white lie; a web of lies.* 2 the way in which something
lies; lay: *the lie of the land.*
— *v.* 1 lies, lied, ly·ing utter a lie: *You're lying! Don't
lie to me.* 2 lies, lay, lain, ly·ing of a person or heavy
body, place oneself or be in a horizontal position, as
when tired: *Bathers lie on the beach; Let me lie down
for a while; He lay on the floor; to take something lying
down* (= to be meek or submissive); *He was fired for
lying down on the job* (= for being too lazy). 3 stay or
exist, as specified: *Who lies buried here? The U.S. lies
(to the) south of Canada; Fields lie fallow; Her future
lies in medicine, not law; There's someone lying in wait
for you* (= waiting to surprise you) *around the corner.*

liege (LEEJ) *adj.* 1 of a feudal lord, having a right to
homage and loyal service: *his liege lord, sovereign.* 2 of
a vassal, obliged to give homage and loyal service.
— *n.* lord: *My liege!*

lien (LEEN, LEE·un) *n.* [legal use] a claim on property
because of a debt incurred on it, as when a contractor is
not paid for work done on a house: *a mechanic's lien; to
place a lien on* or *against a property; to have a lien
discharged.*

lieu (LOO) *n.* in lieu of instead of.

lieu·ten·ant (lef·TEN·unt, loo-) *n.* an officer who acts in
place of a higher one; also, a corresponding rank just
below captain: *a first, flight, second lieutenant; a
lieutenant colonel, commander, general.*
— **lieu·ten·an·cy** *n.* -cies.

lieutenant governor *n.* 1 (lef·TEN·unt-) an official of
the Crown in a Canadian province, appointed by the
Governor General. 2 (loo·TEN·unt-) a public official
next in rank to the governor, as in the U.S.

life *n.* lives 1 the state of being alive or active: *Is there
life after death? He ran for dear life; She gave, laid
down, risked, sacrificed her life to save her child; to
claim, ruin, restore, snuff out, take a life; to breathe
new life into a dying project; The missing child stood
there as big* or *large as life* (= in person); *a story that is
true to life* (= as in reality); *a picture painted from
(real) life* (= based on a living subject); *the facts of life*
(about sex and reproduction). 2 one that lives, esp. a
person: *Two lives were lost in the fire; No animal or
plant life is found on the moon; marine life; the life
forms of science fiction; the life cycle* (= life history) *of a
butterfly (from egg to death).* 3 a period of existence: *In
the mid-1980s, the life expectancy of Canadian women
was 79.5 years and of men 71.9 years; The maximum
life span* (= the longest one can be expected to live) *of a
turtle is 123 years; the four-year life of a car lease; the
short shelf life of fresh bread; The murderer got life* (= a
sentence of life in prison). 4 a way or kind of living: *He
led a dog's life; a busy, dull, hectic, happy, hard,
miserable, nomadic, peaceful, solitary, stormy life;
adult, city, civilian, love, married, sex, social life; the
quality of your working life.* 5 biography: *Levy's life of
Napoleon.* 6 liveliness or spirit; also, its source: *Let's put*

some life into the singing; Carlos was the life of the party.

— **for life** as long as one lives: *president for life.*

— **for the life of me** or **her** or **him** [used in negative statements] however hard I try: *I can't figure it out for the life of me.*

— **of one's life** the most important: *He's facing the fight of his life.*

life·belt *n.* a beltlike life preserver.

life·blood *n.* something life-giving, as blood to the body.

life·boat *n.* a boat built for rescue work or one carried on a ship for use if the ship is to be abandoned.

life·buoy *n.* a ring-shaped float thrown to drowning people.

life·guard *n.* a person trained in life-saving, esp. in water.

life insurance *n.* insurance to pay a sum of money to one's heirs in case of death: *to take out life insurance on your spouse.*

life jacket *n.* a life preserver made like a sleeveless jacket.

life·less (LIFE·lis) *adj.* having no life: *Unlike plants and animals, minerals are lifeless; a lifeless body; a quite lifeless performance (without energy or vigour).*

life·like *adj.* exactly like the subject in real life: *a lifelike statue.*

life·line *n.* 1 a rope or line thrown to save a person in water. 2 the only means or route for sending help to one in distress.

life·long *adj.* involving a lifetime: *lifelong friends.*

life preserver *n.* a device in the shape of a belt, jacket, or ring, usually filled with air or cork, to keep a person afloat.

lif·er (LYE·fur) *n. Informal.* 1 one sentenced to life imprisonment. 2 a career member of the military.

life·sav·ing (LIFE·say·ving) *adj.* designed or used for the saving of lives: *a lifesaving apparatus, drug.*

life-size or **life-sized** *adj.* of a painting, statue, etc., of the same size as the subject represented.

life·style *n.* a way of life characteristic of a person or group: *Is the Canadian lifestyle less hectic than the American? the lifestyles of the eighties; an affluent, criminal, grandiose, laid-back, luxurious, ritzy, traditional lifestyle; Lifestyle advertising shows people*

having a good time, as in beer commercials.

life-support system *n.* a system designed to provide oxygen, food, water, and such essentials of life to people in space, under water, etc.

life·time *n.* the entire life of a person or thing: *It will last a lifetime; the chance of a lifetime* (= a rare chance); *a lifetime occupation (that lasts a lifetime).*

life vest *n.* same as LIFE JACKET.

lift *v.* 1 raise or rise to a higher level or position: *He can lift his own weight; a small car with a trunk door that lifts back; a short trip to* **lift your spirits** (= to cheer you up); *He refused* **to lift a finger** (= do anything) *to help us.* 2 remove or withdraw: *to lift a ban, blockade, embargo; The fog will lift at dawn; when the rain lifts* (= stops for a time). 3 *Informal.* steal: *He was caught lifting things from shops; a passage lifted from a copyrighted work.*

— *n.* 1 an act of lifting or its result or extent: *An airfoil creates a lift in reaction to gravity; The victory gave his spirits quite a lift; A lift of 100 kg is beyond me; the haughty lift of her chin; Let's give him a lift* (= ride) *home.* 2 anything that lifts or elevates, as a "chair lift" or "ski lift," an elevator, or a promotion.

lift-off *n.* the vertical blastoff of a space vehicle or missile.

li·ga·tion (lye·GAY·shun) *n.* a tying: *tubal ligation to prevent pregnancy.*

lig·a·ture (LIG·uh·chur) *n.* a binding, something to tie with, as a thread used by a surgeon to tie off a blood vessel, or something tied together, as the letters *ffl* and *ae* combined into single characters.

light (LITE) *n.* 1 that by which we see, including ultraviolet and infrared radiation: *the light of the sun; a bright, dull, faint, harsh, soft, strong light; to read by the light of a lamp; Facts* **come to light** (= become known); *to* **see the light** (= understand the truth). 2 a source or supply of light, as the sun, a lamp, a match or cigarette lighter, a lighthouse or traffic signal, a window, or a famous person or "luminary": *to dim, extinguish, shine, switch on, turn down, turn off, turn on, turn up a light* (= lamp); *a backup, dome, parking light (on an automobile); a pilot light (of a clothes dryer or furnace); a traffic light* (= signal); *to cross against, go through, stop at a red (traffic) light; Lights* (= lamps) *flicker, are off, on, out; Florence Nightingale was a guiding light* (= source of inspiration) *for nurses; the northern and southern* **lights** (= auroras). 3 the quality or condition of being lit or illumined: *the contrasts of light and shade in a picture; the harsh light of reality; the light* (= gleam) *in her eyes.* 4 **lights** *n.pl.* the lungs of sheep, pigs, etc. used as food.

— **in (the) light of** considering.

— **see the light of day** come to be or be made public.

— **shed** or **throw light on a subject** make clear or clarify a subject.

— *adj.* 1 bright or pale in colour: *a light complexion; as light as dawn; a light hallway.* 2 not heavy: *light as a feather;* **Light industries** *produce consumer goods; a light jacket, punishment, snowfall;* ***adv.**: Let's travel light (without too much baggage).* 3 having qualities suggesting little weight; delicate, nimble, cheerful, etc.:

a light beer (with less alcohol); a light body frame; light music; light opera (= operetta); *light (not heavy) sleep; light spirits; a light step; a light wine* (= table wine, with less alcohol). **4** lacking due weight or seriousness: *light of purpose; a bit **light in the head*** (= foolish or crazy; also, dizzy); *Don't **make light of*** (= consider as not serious) *his misbehaviour.*
— *v.* **lights,** *pt. & pp.* **light·ed** or **lit, light·ing 1** cause to give light: *Let's light a candle; streets lit by electricity; Six o'clock is lighting-up time; She lighted up* (= lit a cigarette); *a face lit by joy; Her face lit up with pleasure.* **2** come down from an animal's back, from flight, etc.: *A bird lights on a tree; Her eyes lighted on* (= found) *a face in the crowd.*
— **light into** *Slang.* attack or scold.
— **light out** [*pt. & pp.* **lit out**] *Informal.* leave in a hurry *for* a place.

light·en (LYE·tun) *v.* make or become lighter or more cheerful: *The confession lightened her heart.*

light·er *n.* **1** a person or thing that lights: *a cigarette lighter.* **2** a boat or barge for carrying cargo between ships and shore; **light·er·age** (LYE·tuh·rij) *n.*

light-fingered (LITE·FING·gurd) *adj.* having light fingers; also, thievish.

light-footed (LITE·FOOT·id) *adj.* stepping gracefully.

light-headed (LITE·HED·id) *adj.* silly or frivolous; also, dizzy.

light-hearted (LITE·HAR·tid) *adj.* without cares and worries; happy and gay.

light·house *n.* **-hous·es** (-how·ziz) a tower with a flashing light at the top to warn or guide ships.

light·ly *adv.* **1** with little or less-than-usual weight, amount, force, etc.: *Snow fell lightly outside; We dress lightly in hot weather.* **2** delicately, nimbly, cheerfully, etc.: *He took the bad news lightly; She stepped aside lightly.* **3** without due weight or seriousness: *a matter too serious to be treated lightly; He speaks lightly of his elders.*

light·ning *n.* a flash of light in the sky caused by electrical discharges from clouds: *Thunder and lightning struck the town; forked, heat, sheet lightning; a bolt, flash, stroke of lightning; adj.: a **lightning raid** (quick as lightning); a **lightning rod** (fixed to a roof for grounding electricity); The enemy attacked with lightning speed.*

light pen or **light pencil** *n.* a pen-shaped photoelectric device for using on a cathode-ray-tube screen to activate a computer to change or modify images, as in editing a text.

light·some *adj.* light and elegant; light-hearted; nimble: *a lightsome heart; lightsome steps.*

light-year *n.* a unit of astronomical distance equal to the distance that light travels in one year, approximately 9.5 trillion km (6 trillion miles).

lik·a·ble (LYE·kuh·bul) *adj.* easy to like.
— **lik·a·ble·ness** *n.*

like *prep.* [indicating similarity]: *She swims like a fish; She is like her brother; It's just like* (= characteristic) *her to be generous; I don't feel like (taking) a walk; It looks like (it is going to) rain; citrus fruits like (Informal for such as) oranges and lemons.*
— *adj.* similar: *as like as two peas; Like (magnetic) poles repel; a like amount.*
— **like crazy, like the devil, like hell** or **like mad** furiously: *It works like crazy when you turn it on.*
— **like hell!** *Slang.* certainly not!
— *combining form.* similar to or characteristic of a person or thing: *bell-like, catlike, childlike, milklike.*
— *adv. Informal.* probably: *Like enough it will rain.*
— *conj.* **1** *Informal.* as: *The candy tastes good like it should; It looks like* (= as if) *it's going to rain.* **2** *Slang.* [used expletively]: *He's really, like, hyper, you know.*
— *n.* **1** a similar person or thing: *When shall we see her like again? He prefers boas, chimps, **and the like** to humans; The community had no place for **the likes of** him.* **2** what one likes: *I have my own **likes and dislikes*** (= preferences and aversions).
— *v.* **likes, liked, lik·ing 1** feel well toward a person or thing: *He likes company; I like candy, but not now.* **2** wish to have something: *She'd like a drink; As you like; I wouldn't like you to get wet; I like it as it is.*

like·a·ble *adj.* same as LIKABLE.

like·li·hood (LIKE·lee·hood, short "oo") *n.* probability: *the likelihood of raining; In all likelihood it'll rain tonight; There's every likelihood that it'll rain.*

like·ly (LIKE·lee) *adj.* **-li·er, -li·est** probable: *There's a likely chance of rain tonight; It's likely to* or *likely that it will rain; a likely night for rain; adv.: It'll most* or *very likely rain tonight.*

like-mind·ed (LIKE·MINE·did) *adj.* of the same way of thinking: *like-minded people.*

lik·en (LYE·kun) *v.* consider one as similar *to* another; compare.

like·ness *n.* similarity or resemblance: *She bears no likeness to her mother; This statue is a good likeness* (= representation) *of her.*

like·wise *adv.* **1** in the same way as another. **2** moreover; besides.

liking (LYE·king) *n.* what one likes or prefers: *Everything was not to her liking; She has developed a liking for fish; She has* or *shows a special liking for fresh seafood; Everyone has taken a liking for her.*

li·lac (LYE·luc, -lac, -loc) *n.* **1** a shrub bearing clustered blossoms that are usually light purple. **2** light purple or mauve colour; *adj.: a lilac dress, gown.*

lilt *n.* a lively rhythm.
— *v.* play, sing, or move in a lilt: *in a lilting voice.*

lil·y (LIL·ee) *n.* **lil·ies** a plant with stemless leaves growing from a bulb and flowers with six parts, typically white, as in the **lily of the valley.**

lily-livered (lil·ee·LIV·urd) *adj.* cowardly.

lily-white *adj.* **1** pure white. **2** innocent: *not so lily-white as she claims.* **3** of white people only: *a lily-white community, neighbourhood, organization.*

limb (LIM) *n.* **1** a leg, arm, or wing. **2** something similar, as the branch of a tree.
— **out on a limb** *Informal.* in a dangerous or precarious position.

lim·ber *adj.* supple or nimble: *a lean and limber acrobat.*
— *v.* make limber: *some exercises to help you **limber up.***

lim·bo *n.* **-bos 1** the state of being forgotten or unwanted: *The book is in limbo and may never get published.* **2 Limbo** in Christian theologies, a region of confinement for those barred from Heaven because of not being baptized.

lime *n.* **1** a white calcium compound used in making mortar and cement. **2** a citrus fruit resembling a lemon but greener, smaller, and more acid.

lime·ade (lye·MADE) *n.* a sweet beverage made with lime juice.

lime·light *n.* a spotlight, formerly produced by incandescent lime: *in the limelight of publicity.*

lim·er·ick (LIM·uh·rick) *n.* a rhymed five-line humorous verse, like Edward Lear's: *There was an Old Man with a beard, / Who said, 'It is just as I feared! – / Two owls and a hen, / Four larks and a wren, / Have all built their nests in my beard!*

lime·stone *n.* rock containing calcium that is the chief source of lime.

lim·it *n.* **1** a point in time or space that forms a boundary: *a speed limit for drivers; the timber limit above which trees don't grow; to lower the age limit* (=minimum age) *for voting; Pat is* **the limit** (Slang for as much as one can put up with)! **2 limits** *pl.* boundaries: *within the limits of decency; city limits; The boys' change room is* **off limits** *to* (=not to be entered by) *girls.*
— *v.* set a limit to something: *Please limit your call to five minutes.* — **lim·i·ta·tion** (-uh·TAY·shun) *n.*

limited *adj. & combining form.* having a limit or limits; restricted: *a limited-access highway; a **limited company** (with liability limited to its assets); a limited-stop bus or train service; a limited (not all-out) war; a 200-copy limited edition of a book; a time-limited test.*

lim·o (LIM·oh) *n.* **-os** [short form] limousine.

lim·ou·sine (LIM·uh·zeen) *n.* a chauffeured luxury automobile.

limp *n.* a lameness or a halting way of walking.
— *v.* walk or proceed with or as if with a limp.
— *adj.* droopy or weak: *a limp argument, body, handshake, leaf; a body limp with exhaustion.*

lim·pid *adj.* softly clear or transparent: *a limpid stream; limpid eyes; a limpid prose style.* — **lim·pid·ly** *adv.*

lim·y (LYE·mee) *adj.* **lim·i·er, -i·est 1** of or containing lime: *a limy deposit.* **2** covered with birdlime. **3** sticky.

lin·age (LYE·nij) *n.* **1** the number of lines of print or writing. **2** a rate or charge per line.

linch·pin *n.* **1** a pin that keeps a wheel in place on its axle. **2** a key person or element.

line *n.* **1** a piece of thread or wire considered in its length but not width or thickness; hence, anything resembling it: *a clothes line for drying laundry; an angler's hook and line; a plumb line; the lines on an aging face; a stanza of four lines (of verse); Please form a line* (=queue); *Drop me a line* (=brief letter) *when you get there; The starlet fluffed or forgot her **lines** (=words to speak) in the middle of the play; What's your bottom line, prestige or profit?* **2** a long fine mark: *lines drawn on paper; Sign on the dotted line; a broken, curved, heavy, straight, thin, vertical, wavy line.* **3** something thought of as forming a line: *The (phone) line is busy; It's a party line; communication lines between two cities; the hot line between the superpowers; the gas line leading from tank to engine; power lines (carrying electricity); a supply line; the ceasefire line* (=boundary) *between two warring nations; a county, foul, goal, service, snow, state, tree line; a line* (=row) *of trees along an avenue; the line* (=circle) *of the equator; a noble line* (=family) *of kings; a faulty line of reasoning; to follow the **line of least resistance** (=go the easy way); an artillery's **line of fire;** the front **line of battle;** Battle **lines** are drawn and the fight is about to start.* **4** something organized or laid down, as a plan, policy, business, occupation, etc.: *All party members have to fall in line with the rest; We take a firm, hard line on women's issues; a statement in line with our policies; a policeman killed **in the line of duty** (=while doing his duty); Family members tend to think **along the same lines;** What line* (=business) *are you in? We work on an assembly line; I'm in line* (=It's my turn) *for a raise; to **hold the line** on wage increases* (=keep wages from rising); *Stamp collecting is not (in)* **my line** (=one of my interests); *A store cannot carry every **line of goods** (=type of merchandise); There was no truth in **the official line** (=statement) handed out to the press.*
— **bring into line** cause to agree or conform.
— **down the line** from the top to the bottom in an ordered series: *They try to set a good example all **down the line** from the principal to the janitor.*
— **draw the** or **a line** set a limit.
— **on line** connected for operation: *a printer on line with the computer.*
— **on the line** *Informal.* in a position of high risk: *Your job is on the line.*
— **out of line** against the normal way of being or doing: *Your price is out of line; It's way out of line* (=not compatible) *with what I can afford; He got out of line* (=became rude) *and started swearing.*
— **toe the line** conform.
— *v.* **lines, lined, lin·ing 1** mark with lines: *lined writing paper; a forehead lined with age.* **2** arrange or form a line: *People lined the route of the parade; to line up speakers for a function; Athletes line up for a race; We have to line up behind* (=support) *our leader.* **3** put or serve as a lining in something: *a coat lined with fur; Bookshelves line the library walls; People in power sometimes try to **line their pockets** (=make money illicitly).*

lin·e·age (LIN·ee·ij) *n.* **1** the line of descent from an ancestor. **2** such descendants.

lin·e·al (LIN·ee·ul) *adj.* **1** in a direct line of descent, as from father to son: *a lineal descendant, heir.* **2** hereditary: *a lineal feud, right.*

lin·e·a·ment (LIN·ee·uh·munt) *n.* usually **lineaments,** *pl.* distinctive features of a face.

lin·e·ar (LIN·ee·ur) *adj.* **1** having to do with lines: *a linear, not pictorial form of writing; a linear design,* dimension, series; *a linear equation* (whose graph is a straight line). **2** having to do with length: *A metre is a unit of linear measure; an air cushion vehicle propelled by the magnetic waves of a **linear motor** (that does not rotate).* **3** sequential in structure: *a linear learning pattern, procedure, technique.*

lin·en (LIN·un) *n.* **1** a tough yarn or cloth woven of fibres of flax. **2** sheets, tablecloths, napkins, etc. made of linen: *fine linen; fresh linen; to change the linen* (= bed sheets).

line of credit *n.* the maximum amount that a customer is allowed to borrow from a bank.

line of scrimmage *n.* in football, an imaginary line parallel to the goal lines at the most forward point of the ball when it is on the ground.

line printer *n.* a computer printer that handles data line by line, not character by character, as in a serial printer.

lin·er (LYE·nur) *n.* **1** an airplane or ship belonging to a transportation line. **2** material used as lining.

line score *n.* in baseball, a summary of the hits, runs, and errors made by each team.

line·up *n.* an arrangement or listing of persons, as of suspects for identification or players taking part in a game: *a police lineup (of suspects).*

-ling *n. suffix.* small or dependent: *hireling, princeling, sapling, underling.*

lin·ger (LING·gur) *v.* take time, as if reluctant to leave: *Some people linger at the door with a long good-bye; He lingers over his coffee; Doubts lingered in my mind; a longing **lingering** look.*

lin·ge·rie (lan·zhuh·REE, lahn·zhuh·RAY) *n.* women's underclothing and night clothes.

lin·go (LING·go) *n.* **-goes** *Informal* [sometimes derogatory] **1** speech that sounds foreign or is unintelligible to one. **2** jargon: *to speak the lingo of one's profession.*

lin·gua fran·ca (LING·gwuh·FRANK·uh) *n.* a common language for easy communication between speakers of different languages, as a hybrid mixture or pidgin.

lin·guist (LING·gwist) *n.* **1** a specialist in linguistics. **2** one who speaks many languages; polyglot.

lin·guis·tics (ling·GWIS·tics) *n. pl.* [takes sing. v.] the science of language, including the study of pronunciation, syntax, meaning, derivation, etc. — **lin·guis·tic** *adj.*

lin·ing (LYE·ning) *n.* a covering material of a surface: *the inner lining of a coat; a brake lining; a worn lining; "Every cloud has a silver lining"* (= Every misfortune has a bright side).

link *n.* **1** a connection: *a cuff link; We maintain close links with people back home; no links to the underworld; The present forms a link with the past and the future; the supposed **missing** (evolutionary) **link** between apes and humans.* **2** a connected part: *the links of a chain; sausage links.* **3 links** *pl.* a golf course. — *v.* join or connect: *persons linked with a crime; Spacecrafts link up with each other; A **linking verb** such as "be" or "seem" (as in "Books are good" and "She*

seems OK") links subject and or to or with predicate.*

link·age (LINK·ij) *n.* a linking or a system of links.

link·up *n.* a linking together or rendezvous: *a link-up of space vehicles, military forces.*

lint *n.* **1** a soft fleecy material scraped from linen, formerly used as a dressing for wounds. **2** bits of fluff or fuzz of any material. — **lint·y** *adj.*

lin·tel (LIN·tul) *n.* the horizontal beam or bar over a window or door.

li·on (LYE·un) *n.* **1** a large, strong animal of the cat family whose male has a distinctive flowing mane: *The lion is the king of the beasts; the cub of a lion; a pride* (= group) *of lions.* **2** a person distinguished by bravery, strength, or fame: *a social lion.* — **li·on·ess** *fem.*

lion-hearted (lye·un·HAR·tid) *adj.* very brave or courageous.

li·on·ize (LYE·uh·nize) *v.* **-iz·es, -ized, -iz·ing** treat a person as a hero or celebrity.

lion's share *n.* the biggest portion.

lip *n.* **1** either of two fleshy folds forming the mouth: *the upper and lower lips; to part, pucker, purse one's lips; chapped lips; to lick or smack one's lips with pleasure; His name is **on everyone's lips*** (= He is famous); *My **lips are sealed*** (= I can't talk about it). **2** a liplike part or a lip-shaped edge of an opening: *the lip of a bell, crater, pitcher.* **3** *Slang.* insolent talk: *Don't give me any of your lip.* — *adj.* formed or done with the lips: *a lip consonant such as "b," "m," or "p"; to pay **lip service*** (= service only by words) *to a cause.*

lipped *adj. & combining form.* having a lip as specified: *a lipped pitcher; loose-lipped, mean-lipped, tight-lipped; two-lipped* (= petalled) *blossoms.*

lip·py *adj.* **lip·pi·er, lip·pi·est** *Slang.* insolent. — **lip·pi·ness** *n.*

lip-synch or **lip-sync** (LIP·sink) *v.* synchronize lip movements with previously recorded sound, or speech sounds with lip movements, as in dubbing a motion picture in a different language. — *n.* a lip-synching.

liq·uid (LIK·wid) *n.* a substance that flows readily, as water: *a clear liquid.* — *adj.* **1** being a liquid: *liquid air* (at about -190°C); *liquid bleach, soap; a **liquid crystal*** (= organic substance in semisolid state); *a digital watch with a **liquid crystal display*** (LCD); *liquid oxygen.* **2** flowing like a liquid: *liquid fire from a flame thrower; liquid food; a bird's liquid notes; liquid verse.* 3 clear or bright: *liquid blue; her liquid eyes; the liquid sky.* — **liq·uid·i·ty** (luh·KWID·uh·tee) *n.*

liquid assets *n.pl.* cash on hand and bank deposits, bills receivable, etc. that can be quickly converted to cash.

liq·ui·date (LIK·wuh·date) *v.* **-dates, -dat·ed, -dat·ing** 1 clear off a debt, accounts, mortgages, etc. by paying what is owed. 2 settle the affairs of a bankrupt business by dividing up its assets among the creditors. 3 get rid of someone, often by violent means: *rivals liquidated by a dictator.* — **liq·ui·da·tor** (-day·tur) *n.* — **liq·ui·da·tion** (-DAY·shun) *n.*

liq·uor (LIK·ur) *n.* a distilled alcoholic drink such as whisky or gin: *hard liquor; strong liquor;* **adj.:** *a liquor control board; liquor laws, stores.*

lisp *v.* speak like a child or imperfectly, esp. to substitute "th" for "s" and "z," as in "kithing cuthinth" (kissing cousins). — *n.* a lisping or lisping sound.

lis·some or **lis·som** (LIS·um) *adj.* lithe or nimble in a delicate, esp. feminine way.

list *n.* 1 a series of names, words, figures, etc.: *to compile, draw up, make up a list; a patient on the critical list; a laundry list; mailing list; shopping list; I am at the top of the waiting list; A new computer is high on my list of priorities.* 2 a tilt to one side, as of a leaking ship. — **enter the lists** enter a struggle or contest. — *v.* 1 set forth in a list or series: *Not all numbers are listed in the phone book; the alphabetical* **listing** (=entry) *of words in the dictionary.* 2 to tip or tilt. 3 [old use] to please: *"The wind bloweth where it listeth."*

lis·ten (LIS·un) *v.* try to hear, understand, or follow: *to listen to advice, to a speech, to the radio, to one's teachers; You may* **listen in to** *what is being broadcast, but you had better not* **listen in on** *a private conversation.* — **lis·ten·er** *n.*

list·less (LIST·lis) *adj.* having no energy or enthusiasm.

lit a *pt. & pp.* of LIGHT.

lit·a·ny (LIT·un·ee) *n.* **-nies** a form of prayer consisting of a series of supplications.

lite *adj.* [popular spelling] light: *lite beer, ice cream, mayonnaise, whisky.*

li·ter (LEE·tur) *n.* same as LITRE.

lit·er·a·cy (LIT·uh·ruh·see) *n.* ability to read and write: *functional literacy; a literacy test.*

lit·er·al (LIT·ur·ul) *adj.* 1 following the exact words: *a literal interpretation, translation; the literal* (=not figurative) *meaning.* 2 matter-of-fact, not exaggerated: *a literal account, version; the literal truth.* — **lit·er·al·ly** *adv.*

lit·er·ar·y (LIT·ur·air·ee) *adj.* having to do with literature: *a literary journal, style, treatise; the literary profession; a* **literary agent** (=authors' representative).

lit·er·ate (LIT·ur·it) *n. & adj.* 1 (one) who can read and write: *a barely literate society; one of the few literates among them; computer literate* (=able to use a computer). 2 (one) who is well-read or educated: *a passionately literate artist; a literate public; her witty and literate style; a very literate periodical.*

lit·er·a·ture (LIT·ur·uh·chur) *n.* 1 writings of a period, country, or language having lasting appeal because of subject, style, etc.: *Canadian literature; French literature; medieval literature.* 2 writings on a particular subject: *the literature on classical music; There is a considerable body of literature on UFOs; travel literature.* 3 any printed material such as pamphlets and notices: *pulp* (= cheap) *literature; all the literature that arrives as junk mail.*

lithe (LITHE, "TH" as in "thin") *adj.* **lith·er, lith·est** having a supple, slender, or nimble grace.

lithe·some (LITHE·sum, "TH" as in "the") *adj.* having graceful vigour; lissome: *a lithesome gymnast.*

lit·i·gant (LIT·uh·gunt) *n.* a party to a lawsuit.

lit·i·gate (LIT·uh·gate) *v.* **-gates, -gat·ed, -gat·ing** engage in a lawsuit. — **lit·i·ga·tion** (-GAY·shun) *n.*

li·ti·gious (li·TIJ·us) *adj.* 1 disputable at law. 2 given to engaging in lawsuits; quarrelsome.

lit·mus *n.* a dye that turns red when put into acid and blue in alkalis, used as a chemical indicator: *blue litmus and red litmus paper; a decisive* **litmus test** *of their intent to achieve peace.*

li·tre (LEE·tur) *n.* a metric unit of capacity equal to 1 000 cc.

lit·ter *n.* 1 scattered rubbish; hence, untidiness or disorder: *Keep litter in a litter bag.* 2 the young borne at one birth by an animal: *a litter of kittens, puppies.* 3 a single-passenger vehicle consisting of a couch, often curtained, borne on the shoulders of four men. 4 a stretcherlike device for transporting a sick or injured person. 5 straw, hay, leaves, etc. forming a bedding for animals or used to absorb animal excrement. 6 a layer formed on a forest floor by decaying leaves. — *v.* cover or scatter with litter: *Wood shavings littered the shop floor; hallways littered with paper.*

lit·ter·bug (LIT·ur·bug) *n.* a person who litters parks, highways, etc. — *v.* **-bugs, -bugged, -bug·ging:** *fined $500 for litterbugging.*

lit·tle (LIT·ul) *adj. comp.* **lit·tler, less** or **less·er,** *superl.* **lit·tlest** or **least** 1 small, esp. in an endearing way: *a poor little child; the little finger; a dear little man.* 2 not much or long; short: *Please stay a little while.* 3 small-minded or petty: *the little thoughts of little minds.* — *adv. comp.* **less,** *superl.* **least** 1 slightly; somewhat: *a little tired; He is little known around here.* 2 not at all: *He thinks little of the prices of things he buys; It matters little to him; mighty little; precious little; It evaporated* **little by little** (= gradually); *She* **made little of** (= ignored) *the incident.* — *n.* a small amount, short time or distance, etc.: *Wait a little; Walk a little; Have a little of this pie.*

little theatre or **little theater** *n.* amateur or experimental drama.

lit·ur·gy (LIT·ur·jee) *n.* **-gies** ritual for public worship, as in a Christian church.

— **li·tur·gi·cal** (li·TUR·juh·cul) *adj.*

liv·a·ble (LIV·uh·bul) *adj.* that can be lived, lived in, or lived with: *a livable* (=endurable) *climate, existence; a livable* (=habitable) *house, room; a livable* (=easy to live with) *person.*
— **liv·a·ble·ness** or **liv·a·bil·i·ty** (-BIL·uh·tee) *n.*

live (LIV) *v.* **lives, lived, liv·ing** have life or continue in life: *He's living, not dead; They say we shouldn't live to eat (with eating as the main purpose), but eat to live* (=survive); *He lives* (=subsists) *on mere bread and water; Most parents live* (=exist) *only for their children; You may live long; You may live to (the age of) 100; Many have lived to be 90; Good neighbours live in harmony; They live and let (others) live; Some rules are hard to **live with*** (=tolerate); *Spouses live together (in the same house); to **live by*** (=adhere to) *the rules; The birds live from day to day (with no worries about the future); Some people **live beyond their means*** (=spend more than they earn); *A hero's memory **lives on*** (=continues to exist); *Where do you live* (=reside)?
— **live down** cause to be forgotten: *to live down a scandalous past.*
— **live from hand to mouth** to make a bare living.
— **live it up** *Informal.* spend freely: *He lived it up and went broke.*
— **live up to** act in accordance with something: *to live up to an ideal, expectations, a promise, one's reputation, a responsibility.*
— *adj.* (rhyme: "FIVE") having life or its qualities such as movement, growth, heat, energy, etc.: *a live cigar, coal, issue, lobster, topic; a live audience (of actual people); Don't touch a live wire; a live telecast (not a recorded one); adv.: It is being broadcast live* (=directly, not from tape or film).

live·a·ble (LIV·uh·bul) *adj.* same as LIVABLE.

-lived (LIVED, LIVD) *combining form* having life as specified: *long-lived, short-lived; nine-lived* (-LIVED).

live-in (LIV·in) *adj.* **1** having to do with living where working: *a live-in job, maid.* **2** cohabiting: *a live-in partner, relationship.*

live·li·hood (LIVE·lee·hood) *n.* means of living, esp. money for food, clothing, and shelter.

live·long (LIV·long) *adj.* the whole wearisome length of time: *all the livelong day, night, summer.*

live·ly (LIVE·lee) *adj.* **-li·er, -li·est** full of life: *a lively conversation, imagination, time; lively colours.*
— *adv.* in a lively manner: *Step lively* (=hurry up).
— **live·li·ness** *n.*

liv·en (LYE·vun) *v.* make or become lively: *Let's liven things up a bit.*

liv·er (LIV·ur) *n.* **1** a gland that secretes bile, once considered the seat of emotion. **2** an animal's liver used as food: *braised liver with vegetables.* **3** one who lives as specified: *a clean liver; loose liver.*

liv·ere, live·yere or **liv·ier** (LIV·yur) *n.* same as LIVYER.

liv·er·ied (LIV·uh·reed) *adj.* wearing livery; uniformed, as a chauffeur or other servant.

liv·er·y (LIV·uh·ree) *n.* **-er·ies** a characteristic uniform or garb, as formerly issued to servants, esp. retainers in charge of horses.

lives *pl.* of LIFE.

live·stock *n.* farm animals such as cattle, pigs, sheep, poultry, geese, and rabbits.

live·ware (LYVE·ware) *n. Informal.* computer personnel.

live wire *n.* **1** a wire carrying electric current. **2** *Informal.* an energetic and enterprising person.

liv·id *adj.* **1** blue-grey; black-and-blue. **2** very pale: *livid with cold, illness, rage.*

living *adj.* **1** having life: *a living being; An earthquake hasn't struck here **in living memory*** (=as long as anyone can remember); *a living language, monument; **the living*** (=living people) *and the dead.* **2** having to do with life: *our living conditions, quarters, standards; a **living wage** (sufficient for maintaining a reasonable standard of living).*
— *n.* **1** the way one lives: *Canada has the highest **living standard**, or **standard of living**, after Sweden and the U.S.; a woman of plain living and high thinking.* **2** livelihood: *He begs for a living; to earn, eke out a living; to make a comfortable, honest living.*

living room *n.* a room for relaxing, entertaining, etc. in a home.

living standard See STANDARD OF LIVING.

living will *n.* a written request to be allowed to die rather than be kept alive artificially.

liv·yer (LIV·yur) *n. Cdn.* in Newfoundland, a year-round settler of a coastal region, as distinguished from a seasonal fisherman.

lo (LOH) *interj.* look: *Lo and behold!*

load (LODE) *n.* **1** something carried, as in a cart or on an animal's back (as a pack): *to carry, transport a load; to lessen, lighten a load; That's a load* (=burden) *off my mind; The hydro runs at peak load* (=power) *in extreme heat and cold; a social worker's case load; a student carrying a full load (of courses); a teacher's heavy work load; Lu has loads (Informal for plenty) of experience.* **2** a definite quantity, also a load considered as a unit of weight: *two truckloads of gravel.*
— *v.* **1** put a load on a carrier or into a receptacle: *to load a ship with grain; Grain is loaded into or onto ships; The ships are loaded to (maximum) capacity; A gun or camera is loaded before shooting; Flight 213 is now loading* (=taking on passengers) *at Gate 45; Data from storage is loaded* (=transferred) *into the main memory of a computer for processing.* **2** to burden or weight: *a mind **loaded down** with* (=suffering from) *anxiety.*

loaded *adj.* **1** carrying a load or charge: *Cheaters use loaded dice that fall as desired; a loaded truck; Is the gun loaded? A loaded question, remark, or word has a hidden or allusive meaning.* **2** *Slang.* having a lot of money: *He's loaded with riches.* **3** *Slang.* drunk.

load·star, load·stone same as LODESTAR, LODESTONE.

loaf (LOHF) *n.* **loaves** a mass of baked bread in a handy shape or other food such as meat or fish moulded like bread.
— **loaves and fishes** personal gain or profit.

— *v.* 1 spend time idly. 2 idle *away* time on a job.

loaf·er (LOH·fur) *n.* 1 idler or vagabond. 2 a step-in leather shoe.

loan (LONE) *n.* a lending or something lent, esp. money: *a bank loan; a bank's loan officer; to negotiate, raise, repay* or *pay off, secure, underwrite a loan; the loan of your car for a few days; an inter-library loan; a loan of $100; a temporary loan (which has to be returned); The books are on loan from Joe).* — *v.* lend: *Will you loan me your car for a few days? I can loan you $100 any time.*

loan·er *n.* something on loan, as a replacement car given for temporary use.

loan shark *n. Informal.* one who lends money at illegal interest rates. — **loan-sharking** *n.*

loan·word *n.* a word recently borrowed from a foreign language: *"Beef," "mutton," "veal," and "pork" were originally loanwords from French, like "pizza" and "spaghetti" in modern times from Italian.*

loath (LOHTH, "TH" as in "thin") *adj.* [literary use] strongly unwilling *to* do something.

loathe (LOHTH, "TH" as in "the") *v.* loathes, loathed, loath·ing hate with disgust; abhor. — **loathing** *n.*

loath·some ("th" as in "the") *adj.* disgusting: *a loathsome sight, smell.*

loaves (LOHVZ) *pl.* of LOAF.

lob *v.* lobs, lobbed, lob·bing in games such as tennis, baseball, and soccer, to hit, throw, or kick a ball in a high arc but without much force. — *n.* such a stroke, throw, or kick. — **lob·ber** *n.*

lob·by (LOB·ee) *n.* lob·bies 1 a vestibule or entrance hall of a theatre, apartment building, etc.: *We met in the hotel lobby.* 2 a group that lobbies: *an education lobby; the anti-gun lobby; tobacco lobby.* — *v.* lob·bies, lob·bied, lob·by·ing attempt to influence the decisions of lawmakers, officials, etc., as by talking to legislators outside the room where they deliberate: *to lobby against free trade; to lobby for cleaning up the Great Lakes.* — **lob·by·ist** *n.*

lobe *n.* a rounded, projecting, usually fleshy part, as a division of the lung, brain, or liver, the lower ear, etc.: *Maple leaves have three to seven fingerlike lobes.*

lobed *adj.* divided into lobes: *a stork's lobed feet; the lobed maple leaf.*

lob·stick *n. Cdn.* a tall tree such as a spruce or pine with its lower branches lopped off and left standing as a monument or landmark.

lo·cal (LOH·cul) *adj.* having to do with a particular place or body part: *national and local news; a local anesthetic for pulling a tooth; the local area network formed by office computers wired together to share resources and equipment; a feeder or local-service airline; Regional dialects, customs, etc. lend local colour to writing; a municipality's local option (= legal right) to prohibit liquor.* — *n.* something local, as a bus service, a branch of a library, union, etc.: *a local of a teachers' association; a teachers' local; a union local.* — **lo·cal·ly** *adv.*

lo·cale (loh·CAL) *n.* the setting of a story or scene of an event.

local improvement district *n. Cdn.* a quasi-municipal organization established by a provincial or territorial government in a sparsely populated area.

lo·cal·i·ty (loh·CAL·uh·tee) *n.* -ties 1 a neighbourhood or region. 2 awareness or recognition of where one is: *a good sense of locality.*

lo·cal·ize (LOH·cul·ize) *v.* -iz·es, -ized, -iz·ing limit to a particular area or location: *a localized disease, outbreak, pain; a legend that is difficult to localize* (= determine its origin). — **lo·cal·i·za·tion** (-uh·ZAY·shun) *n.*

lo·cate (LOH·cate) *v.* -cates, -cat·ed, -cat·ing 1 find out the position or location of a person or thing: *to locate a hidden treasure, a place on a map, former friends.* 2 establish in a place: *a news correspondent located in London; a suitable place to locate one's business.* — **lo·ca·tor** (-tur) *n.*

lo·ca·tion (loh·CAY·shun) *n.* 1 where something is: *a good location for a factory; The star was hiding at an undisclosed location.* 2 a locating: *a Hollywood movie shot on location in Spain (where the action is supposed to take place, not in a film studio).*

lock *n.* 1 something that closes, fastens, or fixes so as to stop movement or action: *to keep money under lock and key; a combination, deadbolt, safety, time lock; to pick a lock; A series of locks* (= watertight chambers) *helps ships move from one water level to another through a canal; an air lock* (= blockage) *in a water pipe; a wrestler's arm lock* (= hold); *He moved out of the house lock, stock and barrel* (= leaving nothing). 2 a bunch or tuft: *a lock of cotton, hair, wool.* — *v.* close with or as if with a lock: *Please lock and bolt the door; Cattle lock* (= jam) *horns in a fight; a couple walking with arms locked* (= joined); *wrestlers locked in combat; a pension plan with funds locked in* (so that money cannot be taken from it for a certain length of time); *A missile locks on to its target by radar; Employers lock out strikers* (= close the plant) *to make them agree to their demands; to lock up a convict in jail.*

lock·er *n.* a storage chest, closet, or compartment that can be locked.

locker room *n.* a room with lockers for athletes to change clothes. — **locker-room** *adj.* coarsely funny: *locker-room humour; a locker-room joke.*

lock step *n.* marching one behind another in tight formation: *Canada breaks lock step with the U.S. in many matters.*

lock-up *n. Informal.* a jail, esp. one for temporary custody.

lo·co (LOH·coh) *adj. Slang.* crazy, as cattle after eating the narcotic **lo·co·weed** of western North America.

lo·co·mo·tion (loh·coh·MOH·shun) *n.* motion from place to place.

lo·co·mo·tive (LOH·coh·moh·tiv) *adj.* having or causing locomotion: *a locomotive engine; Plants have no locomotive faculty.*

— *n.* an engine that moves a train: *an electric locomotive; locomotive engineer.*

locoweed See LOCO.

lo·cus (LOH·cus) *n., pl.* **-ci** (-sye) a place, position, or point, esp. one of many forming a set or system: *The family is the locus of affection (where love and trust are systematically practised).*

lo·cu·tion (loh·CUE·shun) *n.* 1 a set phrase or other form of expression: *the unique locutions of Newfoundland outporters.* 2 manner of expression: *His locution is sloppy and riddled with obscenities.*

lode *n.* a vein or stratum of metal ore, formerly one with magnetic properties or a piece of such stone, or **lode·stone.**

lode·star *n.* a guiding star, esp. the North Star which shows the way like a lodestone used as a compass.

lodge (LOJ) *n.* 1 a place for temporary stay, as an inn, a hunter's cottage, rented room, etc.: *a hunting lodge; motor lodge; mountain lodge; ski lodge.* 2 an Indian dwelling such as a wigwam or tepee. 3 a den or lair of a beaver or otter. 4 a branch of a fraternal society: *a Masonic lodge.*
— *v.* **lodg·es, lodged, lodg·ing** 1 to house: *a house that lodges students; He's lodging* (= staying) *at a motel; a bullet lodged* (= stuck) *in a bone; to find a **lodging*** (= accommodation) *for the night; a **lodging*** (= rooming) *house; students' **lodgings*** (= rooms). 2 put or lay formally: *to lodge an appeal, a protest, a complaint with the police against someone.*
— **lodg·er** *n.: a family that takes in lodgers.*

loft *n.* 1 an upper room or place, as an attic, the place in a barn where hay is stored, the gallery of a church where the organ is kept, a pigeon's house, etc. 2 in golf, the slope of the hitting face of a club. 3 a high stroke or the height given to a lofted ball.
— *v.* in golf, bowling, and marbles, to shoot or throw relatively high into the air.

loft·y (LOF·tee) *adj.* **loft·i·er, -i·est** high in an imposing or conspicuous way: *a lofty mountain, spire; a lofty* (= grand) *style of writing; a woman of lofty ideals; a lofty* (= haughty) *manner, sneer.*
— **loft·i·ly** *adv.;* **loft·i·ness** *n.*

log *n.* 1 a felled trunk or large branch of a tree: *a raft of logs; logs of firewood; to sleep like a log* (= soundly); *a log cabin (made of logs).* 2 a block of wood, or "log chip," at the end of a line thrown into water from a ship to determine its speed. 3 a ship's daily record of progress: *to keep a log.* 4 a similar record of an operation or performance, as of an airplane or computer.
— *v.* **logs, logged, log·ging** 1 cut down trees; also, cut trees into logs: *a forest destroyed by logging.* 2 measure speed: *The police logged the speeder at 120 km/h.* 3 travel: *a pilot who has logged a million miles.* 4 check in or out of a computer system: *To use a database, you log in or on by typing in your ID and password; Type in "OFF" to log off (when you have finished).*

-log same as -LOGUE.

lo·gan·ber·ry (LOH·gun·ber·ee) *n.* **-ber·ries** a blackberrylike, purplish-red fruit that grows in clusters on a trailing vine and is used in making **loganberry**

wine, esp. on Vancouver Island.

log·book *n.* a book kept as a log or record of progress.

loge (LOHZH) *n.* 1 a booth, stall, or a box in a theatre or opera house. 2 the forward part of a theatre mezzanine.

log·ger (LOG·ur) *n.* one who cuts down trees and makes them into logs; lumberjack.

log·ger·head (LOG·ur·hed) *n.* [regional] a blockhead.
— **at loggerheads** disputing or arguing *with* someone.

log·ic (LOJ·ic) *n.* the science of reasoning and inference; also, its principles, a particular system of logic, reasoning itself, or a logical result or outcome: *deductive, inductive, symbolic logic; the clear, cold logic of her reasoning; There's little logic in his argument; The logic unit of a computer carries out operations involving AND, OR, and NAND.*
— **log·i·cal** *adj.;* **log·i·cal·ly** *adv.*

lo·gi·cian (loh·JISH·un) *n.* a person skilled in logic.

lo·gis·ti·cal (loh·JIS·tuh·cul) *adj.* having to do with logistics: *to provide logistical aid such as helicopters to the rebel army; logistical capability, equipment, nightmare, problems, support.* Also **lo·gis·tic.**
— **lo·gis·ti·cal·ly** *adv.*
— **lo·gis·ti·cian** (loh·jis·TISH·un) *n.*

lo·gis·tics (loh·JIS·tics) *n. pl.* [takes sing. v.] the science of planning and carrying out operations, esp. military, involving transport of people, equipment, and supplies: *The logistics of the rock group included two moving vans full of crew and equipment; the logistics of an election campaign.*
— *adj.* logistical: *a logistics expert, manager, system; a company providing transportation and logistics support.*

log·jam *n.* 1 obstruction caused by logs jamming a watercourse: *to break* or *break up* or *clear a logjam.* 2 piled-up work, a deadlock, or a similar obstacle to progress.

log·o (LOH·goh, LOG·oh) *n.* **-os** an identifying symbol of an organization, for use in advertising and promotion of its image: *the five-ring Olympic logo.*

log·o·type (LOG·uh·type) *n.* [original form] logo.

log·roll·ing (LOG·roh·ling) *n.* in politics, cooperation between parties, as in a legislature by voting for each other's bills, like pioneers helping to roll logs off each other's clearings.

-logue *combining form.* **1** something spoken or written: *catalogue, dialogue, epilogue, monologue.* **2** specialist: *ideologue; sinologue* (= China specialist).

-logy *combining form.* **1** way of speaking or writing: *analogy, eulogy, tautology.* **2** subject: *biology, geology, zoology.*

loin *n.* **1** the back of the body between the hips and the ribs considered as the seat of strength and generative power: *a child of his loins* (= his natural child). **2** the corresponding part of an animal's body: *a loin (cut) of pork.* — **gird (up) one's loins** prepare for action.

loi·ter *v.* **1** move around aimlessly: *No loitering on these premises; to loiter around the mall.* **2** spend time idly: *He likes to loiter away his leisure hours.*

loll (rhyme: "doll") *v.* **1** move about in a relaxed or lazy manner. **2** droop or hang loosely, as a dog's tongue in hot weather.

lol·li·pop or **lol·ly·pop** (LOLL·ee·pop) *n.* a piece of hard candy stuck on a short stick or handle: *to lick, suck a lollipop.*

lol·ly·gag (LOLL·ee·gag) *v.* -gags, -gagged, -gag·ging *Informal.* loaf or dawdle.

lone *adj.* [literary use, before nouns] solitary or lonesome: *the lone nights; the lone traveller in the desert; An outlaw is a lone wolf.*

lone·ly *adj.* -li·er, -li·est **1** being alone and gloomy: *the lonely hearts column of a newspaper; a lonely widow.* **2** alone and isolated: *a lonely house, tree, village.* — **lone·li·ness** *n.*

lon·er (LOH·nur) *n. Informal.* one who prefers to live or work alone.

lone·some *adj.* **1** feeling lonely: *a lonesome bachelor, orphan.* **2** causing one to feel lonely; solitary: *a lonesome existence, road.* — **lone·some·ly** *adv.*; **lone·some·ness** *n.*

long *adj.* long·er (LONG·gur), long·est (LONG·gist) **1** extending from end to end: *ten metres long and two wide; a book 250 pages long; a long* (= not short) *rope.* **2** longer than it is broad: *a long board, skull.* **3** lasting relatively much in time: *It's been a long stretch without a holiday; a long memory; the long vowels of "food," "feed," and "foe."* **4** little likely to succeed; risky: *a long chance, shot; the long odds of 10 to 1.* — **in the long run** or **over the long haul** as time passes; eventually. — **long on** having plenty of something: *He's long on anecdotes, brains, excuses, kindnesses.* — *adv.* for a long time past or to come: *It happened long ago; long before Columbus; She sat up all night long* (= throughout the night). — **as long as** or **so long as** provided that. — *n.* a long time or something lasting long: *The next bus will be here before long; You won't have long to wait; Is the "o" sound of "dog" a long or a short?* — **the long and short of it** the substance or gist of something that may be condensed. — *v.* have a strong desire; yearn: *The prisoner longs to be free; longs for freedom; a longing, lingering look.*

long distance *n.* a telephone service connecting a relatively great distance, esp. when not "local." — **long-distance** (long·DIS·tunce) *adj.* having to do with a great distance: *a long-distance mover, phone call, runner;* **adv.**: *to call London long-distance.*

lon·gev·i·ty (lon·JEV·uh·tee) *n.* the condition of living for a long time: *Increased longevity results from better health care.*

long-faced *adj.* looking glum or sad.

long-hair *n. Informal.* **1** an intellectual with preference for classical rather than popular music: *long-hair music.* **2** a hippie.

long·hand *n.* regular handwriting, not shorthand.

longing *n.* a desire for something hard to attain. — **long·ing·ly** *adv.*

lon·gi·tude (LON·juh·tude) *n.* distance east or west of the prime meridian, measured in degrees from 0 to 180 in either direction: *The 110-degree longitude forms the border between Alberta and Saskatchewan.*

lon·gi·tu·di·nal (lon·juh·TUE·dun·ul) *adj.* **1** of longitude: *The longitudinal lines run north to south from pole to pole.* **2** lengthwise: *a longitudinal measurement; longitudinal* (= not transverse) *stripes, waves.* — **lon·gi·tu·di·nal·ly** *adv.*

long·johns *n. pl. Informal.* long underwear.

long jump *n.* an athletic jump with distance as the aim.

long-lived (LONG·livd, -lived) *adj.* having a long life or existence.

long-range *adj.* having a long range of time or distance: *a long-range forecast, missile, plan, trend.*

long shot *n. Informal.* a promising person or thing whose success is possible but not likely, as a bet at long odds: *Lili is considered a long shot for the principalship; Our horse is a long shot to win the race.* — **not by a long shot** not at all.

long·stand·ing (LONG·stand·ing) *adj.* that has existed for a long time: *a longstanding complaint, feud, invitation.*

long-suf·fer·ing (LONG·SUF·ur·ing) *adj.* enduring insults, pain, injury, etc. for a long time: *Don't put on that longsuffering look; a longsuffering spouse.*

long-term *adj.* based on a rather long period: *a long-term asset, capital gain, commitment, loan, loss, solution; long-term planning.*

long-winded (long·WIN·did) *adj.* **1** tiresomely long: *a long-winded narrative, report, speech, statement.* **2** not getting out of breath easily: *a long-winded horse, runner.*

loo *n. Slang.* washroom or toilet.

look (short "oo") *v.* **1** direct the eyes in order to see: *If you want to see, look! Look at her; Look at her jumping; "Look before you leap"* (= Be cautious); *She looked him in the face and said No; to look in or into a mirror; to look out the window; to look through a telescope; I look through* (= examine) *the morning paper during breakfast.* **2** face or be turned: *The window looks south;*

*It looks out onto a park; Ladies, **look out for** (=watch) your purses; a church looking on a highway.* **3** appear to be: *She doesn't look her age; He's 70 and looks it; He looks old and wrinkled; You **look like a winner**; It **looks like** (it's going to) rain.* **4** turn one's mind, memory, hopes, etc.: *Parents **look after** (=take care of) their children; Travellers **look ahead** to a safe journey; He **looks down on** (=regards with some contempt) the unemployed; They are looking for jobs; I **look forward to** (=anticipate with pleasure) your birthday party; The police **look into** (=investigate) complaints; We need someone to **look to** (=turn to) for help in trouble; Business is **looking up** (=improving).*
— look up **1** check: *to look up words in a dictionary.* **2** visit: *Do look us up when you are in town.* **3** respect: *Children **look up to** their teachers.*
— **n. 1** a directing of the eyes: *to have, steal, take a look; a baleful, cold, curious, dirty, distant, faraway, furtive, grim, hard, hungry, inviting, knowing, loving, nasty, puzzled, sinister, sullen, vacant, withering look.* **2** appearance: *We can't judge people from their looks; From the look of things, we're in for a storm; I don't like the look of that lawn; His good looks got him the job; mere good looks.* — **look·er** n.

look-alike (LOOK·uh·like) *n.* one that looks like another: *the prince's look-alike* (=double); *a look-alike* (=fake) *pill that could cause heart failure.*

looker-on (look·ur·ON) *n.* **lookers-on** an observer or onlooker.

looking glass *n.* a mirror.

look·it *interj. Informal.* look here!

look·out *n.* **1** a person keeping watch. **2** a watching: *Keep a sharp lookout for intruders; That's your lookout* (=worry); *The police are **on the lookout** for the escaped convicts.* **3** an esp. high place from which to watch: *to watch birds from a lookout; a lookout tower.*

look-see *n. Slang.* a quick visual inspection.

loom (long "oo") *n.* a machine for weaving thread or yarn into cloth.
— **v. 1** weave using a loom. **2** come into view dimly, often threateningly, as in mirages over the horizon: *Unemployment looms large in our view of the future.*

loon (long "oo") *n.* **1** a water bird that looks like a large duck, is a good swimmer and diver, and has a weird cry: *as crazy as a loon.* **2** a stupid or crazy person.

loon·y (LOO·nee) *n.* **loon·ies** *Slang.* **1** a lunatic or crazy person. **2** *Cdn.* the Canadian dollar coin with a loon

bird on one side.
— **adj.** *Slang.* crazy: *He's just a bit eccentric, not quite loony; Don't send him to the **loony bin*** (=insane asylum).

loop (long "oo") *n.* **1** the shape of a curve that crosses itself, as in a written "l." **2** anything in this shape: *Fingerprints have arches, loops, and whorls; a **loop antenna** attached to a TV set; the **loop knot** of a lasso; A belt is passed through loops.* **3** a series of computer instructions that repeat themselves till the desired end is reached.
— **knock** or **throw someone for a loop** *Slang.* startle or shock someone.
— *v.* form a loop: *ridges that loop on the tip of a finger; An aerialist **loops the loop*** (=turns in vertical loops).

loop·hole *n.* **1** an opening in a fortress wall for shooting through or for observation. **2** a means of escape: *a legal loophole in the wording of a contract; to close a loophole; to find tax loopholes.*

loose *adj.* **loos·er, loos·est 1** not tight, compact, or firm: *a loose jacket, soil, tooth, weave.* **2** untied, relaxed, or slack: *a cat that is loose* (=not penned up) *at night; loose change (of coins); a man of loose morals; a reputation ruined by the loose tongue of a loose talker; Lu **let loose*** (=released) *a volley of abuse; A mad dog **broke loose*** (=got away); *Who let or set or turned him loose? The dog is now **on the loose*** (=roaming free); *It's running loose; Don't get uptight, just **hang loose*** (*Slang* for relax).
— *v.* **loos·es, loosed, loos·ing** make loose: *to loose a grip, knot; to loose* (=shoot) *a volley or blast.*
— **loose·ly** *adv.*

loose cannon *n. Informal.* one whose behaviour is unpredictable, like a cannon not secured on deck.

loose-leaf *adj.* allowing the leaves or pages to be rearranged or replaced: *a loose-leaf binder, file, notebook.*

loos·en (LOO·sun) *v.* make or become loose or looser: *Laxatives loosen bowels; Liquor may loosen the tongue; Why not loosen up* (=relax) *a bit?*

loose end *n.* an unfinished thing or condition, as the strands at a rope's end: *He found himself **at loose ends*** (=uncertain what to do) *when suddenly laid off from work.*

loot (long "oo") *n.* **1** goods of value taken away, as during a riot or following a natural disaster; plunder. **2** *Slang.* money or gifts received.
— *v.* sack: *stores looted and burned by vandals.*

lop *v.* **lops, lopped, lop·ping 1** cut off a limb or branch. **2** hang limply; droop; *adj. & combining form: A lop-eared rabbit is born with lop ears.*
— *n.* cut-away or discarded parts, as of trees.

lope *v.* **lopes, loped, lop·ing** move at an easy, bounding gait or stride; also *n.*

lop-sid·ed (lop·SYE·did) *adj.* leaning to one side; unsymmetrical or unbalanced: *a lop-sided pumpkin, smile; a lop-sided attitude; a lop-sided vote of 120 against 7.*

lop·stick *n.* same as LOBSTICK.

lord *n.* **1** one who has power over others: *the feudal lord of the manor; the lord of the jungle.* **2 Lord** [as a title]: *the Lord Mayor of London; the House of Lords* (= British nobles) or **the Lords. 3 Lord** [as a title of reverence]: *Lord Buddha; the Lord God; The Lord* (= God) *knows I didn't do it;* **Lord's Day** (= Sunday); **Lord's Supper** (= Eucharist).
— **lord it (over)** act in an authoritarian way toward someone: *Our new supervisor lords it over us.*

lord·ly *adj.* **-li·er, -li·est** noble; also, haughty.
— *adv.* in a lordly manner.

lord·ship *n.* the rank of a lord; [as a title]: *Your* or *His Lordship.*

Lord·y (LOR·dee) *interj.* expressing surprise.

lore *n.* the traditional knowledge of a people, esp. on a particular subject: *the traditional lore of the gypsies; bird lore; Irish lore; sacred lore.*

lor·ry (LOR·ee) *n.* **lor·ries** *Brit.* a truck.

lose (LOOZ) *v.* **los·es, lost, los·ing 1** cease to have; fail to keep, get, exist, etc.: *to lose one's life in an accident; to lose one's balance, patience, wallet; Mia lost the election to Lu; lost to him by a small margin; Don't lose* (= waste) *time.* **2** cause the loss of a person or thing: *A bad error lost him his job; to play a* **losing** *game (that cannot be won).*
— **be lost on** or **upon** be wasted upon someone: *The advice, humour, kindness was lost on him.*
— **get lost!** *Slang.* go away!
— **lose oneself** become engrossed or occupied: *I can lose myself in a good book.*
— **lose out** fail or be defeated: *Jim lost out; He lost out to his rival; He lost out on the contract.*
— **lost in** absorbed in thought, contemplation, etc.
— **los·er** *n.: a bad, born, good, poor, sore loser.*

loss *n.* a losing, being lost, or a lost person, thing, etc.: *a crash with a great loss of life; losses and gains in business; the heavy losses inflicted on the enemy; an irreparable, irretrievable, light, total loss; to incur, make up, offset, recoup, suffer, sustain losses; He was at* **a loss** *for words (not knowing what to say).*

loss leader *n.* an article put on sale at a loss to attract customers by its low price.

lost *pp.* of LOSE: *a lost book, cause, chance, opportunity; "He who hesitates is lost"; She got lost in the crowd.*

lot *n.* **1** the deciding of something by chance, as in a lottery by picking one out of many bits of paper, wood, etc.: *turns decided by lot; They* **cast** or **drew lots to** *decide who would keep the loot.* **2** fate or fortune: *She decided to* **throw** or **cast her lot with** (= join) *the rebels; It fell to his lot* (= fate) *to raise his brother when they were orphaned.* **3** a plot of land: *an empty* or *vacant lot; parking lot; used-car lot.* **4** a set of persons or things: *goods for auction divided into lots; They're not a bad lot (of people); a happy, miserable, sorry lot.* **5** *Informal.* a great deal or amount: *Thanks a lot; She had to pay* **a lot** *(of money) for the car; quite* **a lot of** *money; We had* **lots** *to eat and drink at the party;* **lots of** *food.*

loth (LOHTH, "TH" as in "thin") same as LOATH.

lo·tion (LOH·shun) *n.* a liquid medicinal or cosmetic preparation to apply to the skin: *an after-shave, body, hand, skin, suntan lotion.*

lot·ter·y (LOT·uh·ree) *n.* **lot·ter·ies** a gambling game in which prizes are awarded to ticket holders by the drawing of lots.

lot·to (LOT·oh) *n.* a game of chance similar to bingo.

lo·tus (LOH·tus) *n.* **1** a water plant and flower sacred to Egyptians, Hindus, and Chinese. **2** in Greek myth, a fruit inducing a state of dreamy languor if eaten, as in the "lotus-eaters" of the "Odyssey."

lotus position *n.* a sitting posture in yoga with legs folded and the arms resting on the knees.

loud ("ou" as in "out") *adj.* **1** having great intensity of sound; not quiet: *to speak in a loud and clear voice; a* **loud·mouthed** (= outspoken and vulgar) *politician.* **2** offensive in manner or taste: *a loud dress; loud colours, people; a rather loud necktie.*
— *adv.* in a loud manner; loudly: *You're talking too loud; I hear you loud and clear.*
— **loud·ly** *adv.;* **loud·ness** *n.*

loud-hailer *n.* same as BULLHORN.

loud·speak·er (LOUD·SPEE·kur) *n.* an electrical sound-amplifying device: *The police warned them over a loudspeaker to stay away from the contaminated area.*

lounge (LOWNJ) *v.* **loung·es, lounged, loung·ing 1** stand, sit, or move about in a relaxed or lazy manner: *She lounges around the pool on sunny days.* **2** pass time thus: *He lounges away his leisure hours on the beach.*
— *n.* **1** a room for relaxing: *the cocktail lounge of a club, hotel,* or *restaurant; a faculty lounge (of a university); the transit lounge and the VIP lounge at an airport.* **2** a couch or sofa.

lour *v.* same as ²LOWER.

louse *n.* **1** *pl.* **lice** a small wingless parasitic insect or pest that lives on the sap of plants, as aphids, or on the blood of animals, as crab lice and body lice. **2** *pl.* **lous·es** *Slang.* someone considered as mean and contemptible.
— *v.* **louse up** *Slang.* spoil or mess something up.

lous·y (LOU·zee, "OU" as in "out") *adj.* **lous·i·er, -i·est 1** infested with lice. **2** *Slang.* contemptible or disgusting: *It's lousy to have to watch the same shows everyday.* **3** *Slang.* oversupplied: *Midas was lousy with riches.*

lout (rhyme: "out") *n.* a clumsy or ill-mannered man.
— **lout·ish** *adj.;* **lout·ish·ness** *n.*

lou·vre or **lou·ver** (LOO·vur) *n.* **1** an arrangement of sloping slats or boards over an opening to regulate light and air. **2** one of these slats or boards.
— **lou·vred** or **lou·vered** (LOO·vurd) *adj.: a louvred door, window.*

lov·a·ble (LUV·uh·bul) *adj.* same as LOVEABLE.

love (LUV) *n.* **1** a strong liking or affection for a thing or person: *Teaching is a labour of love to good teachers; Some won't do it for love or for money; blind, platonic, true, undying, unrequited love; your love of ice cream; the love for* or *of one's family; Please give them our love* (= kind regards); *Ma sends her love; adj.: Hippies were called* **love children** *in the days of lovebeads, love-ins,*

*and flower power; Saint Valentine's Day is the time to be bitten by the **love·bug** and for **love letters;** the love affairs of **lovers** (= unmarried spouses); The love **triangle** (= a third party involved with a couple) is a favourite theme in romances.* **2** the object of such affection: *Come, my love!* **3** a zero score in tennis: *Fifteen love* (= 15 for the serving side, nothing for the receiver).
— **in love** affected by love: *Jack is in love; hopelessly in love with Jill; He has fallen in love with her; He's head over heels in love with her.*
— **make love** show one's love, as by embracing or kissing; pet; also, have sexual intercourse: *to make love to someone;* **love·mak·ing** *n.*
— *v.* **loves, loved, lov·ing 1** feel love toward someone: *He loves his wife and children; loves them dearly, deeply, very much; Lovers often love blindly, passionately; I love her the way she is.* **2** *Informal.* like very much: *Jan just loves ice cream; Lou loves to go on dates; Tim loves watching TV.*
— **love·a·ble** (LUV·uh·bul) *adj.*

love·beads *n.pl.* a necklace of beads worn as a love-and-peace symbol.

love·bird *n.* **1** a small parrot, often kept as a cage bird, remarkable for its affectionate manner toward its mates. **2** *Slang.* one of an openly affectionate pair.

love-crossed *adj.* disappointed in love.

love-in *n.* a gathering for expressing mutual love.

love·knot *n.* a knot tied as a token of love.

love·lorn *adj.* suffering because of unreturned love.

love·ly (LUV·lee) *adj.* **-li·er, -li·est 1** beautiful: *a lovely child, home, sight, story.* **2** *Informal.* delightful: *Isn't he lovely! We had a lovely time at the party.*
— **love·li·ness** *n.*

lov·er (LUV·ur) *n.* one who loves: *a jilted lover* (= sweetheart); *a lover* (= devotee) *of music.*

love seat *n.* a sofa for two persons.

love·sick *adj.* **1** suffering with love. **2** expressing such suffering: *a lovesick poem.* — **love·sick·ness** *n.*

loving *adj.* full of love; affectionate: *your loving sister.*
— **lov·ing·ly** *adv.*

low (LOH) *adj.* **1** near the ground or bottom: *a low bow, flight, level, wall.* **2** not high: *a low grade, neckline, position, price, temperature; the **Low Countries*** (= Belgium, Netherlands, and Luxembourg); *low-level radiation; We're running low on gas.* **3** not great or noble: *low company; a low blow, deed, opinion, thought, trick.*
— *adv.* in a low manner: *to aim, fly low; to speak low* (= quietly).
— **lay low 1** knock down. **2** conquer or kill. **3** *Informal.* remain hidden.
— **lie low** remain hidden.
— *n.* **1** something low, as a gear, pressure, region, etc. **2** the characteristic call of a cow.
— *v.* make such a call: *the lowing herd.*
— **low·ness** *n.*

low beam *n.* beam of headlight switched to show the way immediately in front of the vehicle.

low-born *adj.* of low or humble birth.

low-brow *n. & adj. Informal.* (one) having little interest in intellectual or cultural matters.

low-down *n. Informal.* true and factual information: *Give me the lowdown on Saturday's party.*
— **low-down** *adj. Informal.* mean or contemptible: *a low-down, dirty trick.*

low-end *adj. Informal.* cheap or inexpensive: *a low-end computer; Unauthorized photocopying of books is a type of low-end piracy.*

¹**low·er** (LOH·ur) **1** *adj. & adv. compar.* of LOW: *the lower, middle, and upper voice range; the lower* (= more representative) *house of a legislature; the lower* (= down the river) *St. Lawrence;* **Lower Canada** (= formerly Quebec, lower down the St. Lawrence River than Ontario or Upper Canada); *the lower* (= earlier) *division of a geological period; the lower* (= southerly) *lakes of Erie and Ontario; the lower and upper lips; In Ottawa, the lower town is the historically French section east of the Rideau Canal; The lower town of Quebec City is the part nearest the waterfront; to aim, fly, speak lower.* **2** *v.* make or become lower: *to lower a flag; to lower expenses, one's voice; Do not **lower yourself** (in dignity or self-respect).*

²**low·er** (rhyme: "our") *v.* look dark and threatening, as skies, clouds, faces, etc.: *the **lowering** skies.* Also *n.*

lower case *n.* in printing, small, not capital letters.
— **lower-case** *adj.: upper-case and lower-case letters.*

low-grade *adj.* **1** of inferior grade or quality: *low-grade oil.* **2** low in range: *a low-grade fever.*

low-key *adj.* subdued or restrained in style or intensity: *a low-key approach, campaign, ceremony, response, speech; He is a quiet, charming, low-key personality.* Also **low-keyed.**

low·ly (LOH·lee) *adj.* **-li·er, -li·est 1** humble and meek. **2** low in rank or position: *a lowly occupation; a lowly opinion of oneself; a man of lowly origin.*
— *adv.* in a low manner or voice; also, humbly.
— **low·li·ness** *n.*

low·mind·ed (low·MINE·did) *adj.* low or mean.

low profile *n.* a style or behaviour that is inconspicuous or unobtrusive: *to keep a low profile.*

low-rise *adj.* only a few storeys high: *a low-rise apartment building.*

low-spirited (low·SPEER·uh·tid) *adj.* dejected.

low-tension (LOH·TEN·shun) *adj.* low-voltage.

low tide or **low water** *n.* **1** the level or time when the tide is lowest. **2** the lowest point reached by anything; also **low-water mark.**

loy·al (LOY·ul) *adj.* staunchly faithful: *to be loyal to one's country, employer, friends, king, spouse; a loyal friend, husband, servant, subject, wife.*
— **loy·al·ly** *adv.*

loy·al·ist *n.* one who does not join a popular revolt but supports the government, as the **Loyalists** during the American Revolution and the Spanish Civil War.

loy·al·ty (LOY·ul·tee) *n.* **-ties 1** faithfulness: *an employee's loyalty to the company; to swear loyalty to the Sovereign; unswerving loyalty to one's party.* **2** attachment: *conflicting loyalties; the divided loyalties of a double agent.*

loz·enge (LOZ·inj) *n.* a candy, cough drop, etc., originally diamond-shaped.

LP *n., pl.* **LPs** or **LP's** long-playing record; *Trademark.*

lub·ber (LUB·ur) *n.* **1** a big or clumsy sailor. **2** a landlubber. — **lub·ber·ly** *adj. & adv.*

lube (long "oo") *n.* **1** a lubricating oil. **2** *Informal.* a lubrication: *a lube job.*

lu·bri·cant (LOO·bruh·kunt) *n. & adj.* an oil, grease, etc. that reduces friction between moving parts, as of a machine.

lu·bri·cate (LOO·bruh·cate) *v.* **-cates, -cat·ed, -cat·ing 1** apply a lubricant to machinery. **2** make smooth or slippery. — **lu·bri·ca·tor** (·cay·tur) *n.* — **lu·bri·ca·tion** (·CAY·shun) *n.*

luces *pl.* of LUX.

lu·cid (LOO·sid) *adj.* **1** shining or clear; easy to understand: *a lucid style.* **2** clear-headed: *a will made during a lucid interval; his last lucid words.* — **lu·cid·ly** *adv.* — **lu·cid·i·ty** (loo·SID·uh·tee) *n.*

luck *n.* chance or fortune, esp. good fortune or prosperity: *As luck would have it, we lost the race; We had bad, tough luck; It was pure or sheer luck that they won; I wish we had a bit or stroke of luck; Good luck (to you)! You want to try your luck at setting up in business; Don't **press** or **push your luck** (= Don't depend too much on luck); Your luck may improve, run out, turn; a hard luck story.* — **down on one's luck** unlucky, esp. having no money to spend. — **out of luck** unlucky, esp. being unable to do or get what is desired. — *v.* esp. **luck out** *Informal.* to be lucky.

luck·y *adj.* **luck·i·er, -i·est** fortunate, esp. by mere chance: *a lucky escape; It's lucky that you escaped; You're lucky to be alive; a lucky star, winner.* — **luck·i·ly** *adv.*

lu·cra·tive (LOO·cruh·tiv) *adj.* producing wealth; profitable: *a lucrative business, career.*

lu·cre (LOO·cur) *n.* riches: *the worship of filthy lucre.*

lu·cu·bra·tion (loo·cue·BRAY·shun) *n.* a laborious or elaborate work or composition.

lu·di·crous (LOO·duh·crus) *adj.* laughably incongruous or ridiculous.

luff *v.* sail into the wind. — *n.* the act of turning a ship's bow toward the wind.

lug *v.* **lugs, lugged, lug·ging** pull or tug; carry something heavy: *Don't lug a vacuum cleaner, just plug in our central vacuum.*

lug·gage (LUG·ij) *n.* suitcases and such traveller's baggage: *many pieces of luggage; carry-on or hand luggage; luggage to be checked in.*

lu·gu·bri·ous (loo·GOO·bree·us) *adj.* looking or being sad or mournful in an exaggerated way.

luke·warm *adj.* **1** tepid or barely warm: *water that is lukewarm to the touch.* **2** lacking warmth or enthusiasm: *He seems lukewarm about or to our proposal.*

lull *v.* to calm or become calm: *to lull a person's fears, suspicions; to lull a child to sleep.* — *n.* a period of calm or lessened activity: *a lull in the fighting; a lull in a conversation, storm; a lull in trade.*

lull·a·by (LUL·uh·bye) *n.* **-bies** a song to lull an infant to sleep: *to hum a lullaby; to sing a lullaby to the baby.*

lu·lu (LOO·loo) *n. Slang.* a person or thing that is remarkable in some way: *Our new logo is a lulu!*

lum·ber (LUM·bur) *n.* **1** logs sawn and dressed into boards, planks, etc.: *seasoned lumber.* **2** useless furniture and household articles taking up room. — *v.* **1** cut down trees and saw logs into lumber. **2** move along heavily and noisily, as a bear or elephant.

lum·ber·jack (LUM·bur·jack) *n.* **1** a logger: *a lumberjack's appetite, skills; adj.: a red-and-white checkered lumberjack coat, jacket, shirt.* **2** *Cdn.* same as CANADA JAY.

lum·ber·man (LUM·bur·man) *n.* **-men** a logger or one who deals in lumber.

lu·mi·nar·y (LOO·muh·nair·ee) *n.* **-nar·ies 1** a light-giving body such as the sun or moon. **2** a famous person: *a literary luminary.*

lu·mi·nes·cence (loo·muh·NES·unce) *n.* light without burning or heat, as given off by fireflies and by fluorescence; cold light. — **lu·mi·nes·cent** (·unt) *adj.*

lu·mi·nous (LOO·muh·nus) *adj.* giving off light: *a luminous celestial body; a watch's luminous dial; luminous paints; a luminous (= clear or enlightening) performance.* — **lu·mi·nos·i·ty** (·NOS·uh·tee) *n.*

lump *v.* heap together or make into a heap or heaps. — **lump it** *Informal.* endure it: *"Like it or lump it."* — *n.* **1** a shapeless solid mass: *a lump of coal, sugar; adj.: cube-shaped lump sugar, not grain sugar.* **2** a swelling or bump: *a painful lump on the head; One overcome by emotion feels a lump in the throat.* **3 lumps** *pl.* punishment: *He takes his lumps gracefully when attacked in the press.* — **in the lump** in one mass.

lump·y *adj.* **lump·i·er, -i·est 1** full of lumps: *lumpy porridge.* **2** heavy and clumsy, as the "lumpfish" or "lumpsucker" of Northern waters.

lu·na·cy (LOO·nuh·see) *n.* **-cies 1** great folly: *It's sheer lunacy to go skating during the spring breakup; I have had enough of his lunacies.* **2** madness or insanity.

lu·nar (LOO·nur) *adj.* of the moon: *a lunar day, eclipse, month, probe; A lunar (excursion) module takes astronauts to the moon's surface and back from a commmand module that stays in orbit.*

lu·na·tic (LOO·nuh·tic) *n.* one who is insane or utterly foolish; *adj.: a lunatic idea; a lunatic asylum (for the insane).*

lunatic fringe *n.* an extremist or fanatical section of a movement, society, etc.

lunch *n.* a light meal at midday: *The boss is out for lunch; not a box lunch, picnic lunch, or working lunch but a three-martini business lunch; no free lunch* (= not something for nothing); *We'll discuss it at lunch; I took her out to lunch; We went out to lunch, but her mind was totally out to lunch* (*Slang* for crazy).
— *v.* have a lunch: *We usually lunch at the cafeteria.*

lunch·eon (LUNCH·un) *n. Formal.* lunch: *a business luncheon at the Royal York; I met him at an Empire Club luncheon; an awards luncheon; state luncheon.*

lunch·eon·ette (lunch·uh·NET) *n.* a small restaurant serving light meals.

luncheon meat *n.* ready-to-eat, packaged meat in the shape of a loaf.

lunch·room *n.* **1** a room, as in a school or place of work, in which to eat lunch. **2** a luncheonette.

lung *n.* **1** either of a pair of baglike breathing organs in humans and other vertebrates: *congested lungs; smoking and lung cancer.* **2** a device such as an iron lung.

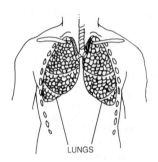

LUNGS

lunge (LUNJ) *n.* a sudden thrust, as with a sword, or a forward leap: *He made a lunge at the burglar.*
— *v.* **lung·es, lunged, lung·ing** make a lunge: *The thief lunged towards him with a knife.*

lunk or **lunk·head** *n. Informal.* a dolt.

lurch *v.* stagger or lean suddenly to one side: *The boat lurched to the right and sank.*
— *n.* a lurching movement to a side or forward: *The leaking boat gave a lurch and hit a ship close by.*
— **leave someone in the lurch** desert a friend or colleague who expects help.

lure *n.* **1** a device such as a bait or decoy used to tempt or entice. **2** an attraction or the power of such attraction: *the lures of Las Vegas.*
— *v.* **lures, lured, lur·ing** tempt or entice with or as with a lure: *She was lured away by false hopes; They lured her into signing the contract.*

lu·rid (LOOR·id) *adj.* **1** shining with a red or fiery light: *a lurid sunset.* **2** gruesome or sensational: *a lurid tale of murder; lurid crimes, details.*

lurk *v.* lie in wait or move about stealthily: *an intruder lurking in the shadows; Doubts still lurked in his mind.*

lus·cious (LUSH·us) *adj.* sweet and delicious; appealing to the senses: *a luscious apple, peach, pear, pie; luscious lips, poetry, scenery.*

lush 1 *adj.* excessively luxuriant in growth: *lush jungles,*

vegetation. **2** *n. Slang.* an excessive drinker; alcoholic.

lust *n.* an intense longing or desire, esp. sexual: *the lust for gold, power; the lusts of the flesh; to arouse, feel, gratify, satisfy one's lust.*
— *v.* to have intense desire: *to lust after* or *for someone.*
— **lust·ful** *adj.*; **lust·ful·ly** *adv.*

lus·tre or **lus·ter** (LUS·tur) *n.* brightness or brilliance of polish, beauty, reputation, etc.: *Lili will add lustre to her new position as president; The new position takes on a new lustre because of Lili.*

lus·trous (LUS·trus) *adj.* glossy or brilliant.

lust·y *adj.* **lust·i·er, -i·est** full of vigour; robust: *a lusty eater, young man; lusty cheers.*
— **lust·i·ly** *adv.*; **lust·i·ness** *n.*

lute *n.* an ancient stringed musical instrument with a flat-topped, pear-shaped body and a distinctive bent-back head. — **lut·ist** (LOO·tist) *n.*

lux *n.* **lux·es** or **lu·ces** (LOO·seez) a unit of illumination equal to one lumen per square metre.

luxe (LOOKS, LUX) *adj.* luxurious: *the luxe look in women's fashions; luxe lace.*

lux·u·ri·ant (lug·ZHOOR·ee·unt) *adj.* **1** rich or abundant in growth, as jungle vegetation: *luxuriant hair.* **2** rich in ornament; florid.
— **lu·xu·ri·ance** *n.*

lux·u·ri·ate (lug·ZHOOR·ee·ate) *v.* **-ates, -at·ed, -at·ing** indulge oneself; revel: *bathers luxuriating in the summer sun.* — **lux·u·ri·a·tion** (-AY·shun) *n.*

lux·u·ri·ous (lug·ZHOOR·ee·us) *adj.* contributing to luxury: *a luxurious existence, hotel; luxurious food, surroundings.*

lux·u·ry (LUK·shuh·ree, LUG·zhuh·ree) *n.* **-ries 1** ease and comfort provided by expensive food, clothes, amusements, etc. beyond the basic necessities: *He lived in luxury all his life; in the lap of luxury; to afford, enjoy the luxury of a heated swimming pool; to wallow in luxury; It would be pure, sheer luxury; adj.: a luxury apartment, hotel; luxury goods.* **2** the use of luxuries or the things themselves: *Cake would be a luxury for people who can't afford bread.*

-ly *suffix.* **1** like the one specified: *knightly, manly, queenly, scholarly.* **2** occurring every specified period: *daily, hourly, yearly.* **3** in the specified manner: *childishly, happily, icily, musically.*

ly·cra (LYE·cruh) *n.* an elastic synthetic textile used for swimsuits; **Lycra** *Trademark.*

lying (LYE·ing) **1** *pres. part.* of LIE. **2** *n. & adj.* the telling of lies or the habit: *Your lying has to stop; a lying tongue.*

lying-in *n.* confinement in childbirth.
— *adj.*: *a lying-in hospital, period.*

lynch (LINCH) *v.* of a mob, to kill an accused person without trial, often by hanging.

ly·on·naise (lye·uh·NAZE) *adj.* prepared with finely sliced fried onions: *lyonnaise potatoes, sauce.*

lyr·ic (LEER·ic) *n.* **1** a short poem with a songlike quality, expressing the poet's deeply felt personal reactions to things, as an elegy, ode, or sonnet. **2 lyrics** *pl.* the words of a song as distinguished from the music. — ***adj.**: a lyric poet; a lyric* (= melodic) *quality; a lyric tenor (with a higher and lighter voice).* — **lyr·i·cism** (-uh·siz·um) *n.*

lyr·i·cal (LEER·uh·cul) *adj.* expressive of emotion; enthusiastic: *It was a humdrum affair, nothing to wax lyrical about.* — **lyr·i·cal·ly** *adv.*

lyr·i·cist (LEER·uh·sist) *n.* **1** a writer of verses for songs. **2** a lyric poet.

lyr·ist *n.* **1** (LIRE·ist) a lyre player. **2** (LEER·ist) a lyricist.

-lysis *combining form.* disintegration or decomposition: *catalysis, electrolysis, paralysis.*

Mm

M or **m** (EM) *n.* **M's** or **m's 1** the 13th letter of the English alphabet. **2** the Roman numeral for 1 000.

Ma or **ma** (MAH) *n. Informal.* mother: *Look, Ma! Our motel is a* ***ma-and-pa*** (= private and independent) *operation, not part of a chain.*

ma'am (MAM) *n. Informal.* [in direct address] madam.

Ma Bell *n.* Bell Canada or a similar telephone company in the U.S.

Mac or **Mack** *n. Slang.* fellow or guy: *Who do you think you are, Mac?*

ma·ca·bre (muh·CAH·bruh, -bur) *adj.* dealing with death, esp. its gruesome aspects: *a macabre story.*

mace *n.* **1** a medieval hand weapon or club with a spiked metal head. **2** a ceremonial, club-shaped staff used, esp. in legislatures, as a symbol of authority. **3** a spice made from the dried outer covering of the aromatic seeds of an East Indian tree.

mac·er·ate (MAS·uh·rate) *v.* **-ates, -at·ed, -at·ing** soften by soaking, as flowers to extract perfume: *Ants make nests with macerated plant tissue.*
— **mac·er·a·tion** (-RAY·shun) *n.*

Mach (MAHK) *n.* the ratio of the speed of an object to the speed of sound: *Mach 2 is twice the speed of sound.* Also **mach.**

ma·che·te (muh·SHET·ee) *n.* a large, heavy knife of Latin America, used for cutting and as a weapon.

mach·i·na·tion (mak·uh·NAY·shun) *n.* a cunning plot or scheme to harm someone.

ma·chine (muh·SHEEN) *n.* **1** a mechanical device or appliance, esp. one with coordinated moving parts to transmit power for a desired end: *A lever is a simple machine; a machine-made, not handmade product; an adding, answering, calculating, composing, computing, copying, duplicating, earth-moving, printing, sewing, slot, vending, voting, washing, X-ray machine; Machines break down, function, run; a* ***machine-readable*** *text that is directly usable by a computer.* **2** a person or group that works like a machine, without thought or will: *the Big Blue Machine; a party machine; propaganda machine; the Nazi war machine.*
— *v.* **-chines, -chined, -chin·ing** process or finish with a machine. — **ma·chin·a·ble** (-nuh·bul) *adj.*

machine gun *n.* an automatic weapon that fires ammunition fed into it from a belt or magazine continuously and rapidly.
— **machine-gun** *v.* **-guns, -gunned, -gun·ning.**
— **machine gunner** *n.*

machine language *n.* a system of signs, characters, or symbols readable by a computer, as one consisting of binary digits.

ma·chin·er·y (muh·SHEE·nuh·ree) *n.* **-ries 1** machines or machine parts collectively: *well-oiled machinery* (= mechanism). **2** the means by which something functions: *We have different machineries for the sales and service functions.*

ma·chin·ist (muh·SHEE·nist) *n.* one skilled in the making and operation of machines or machine tools.

ma·chis·mo (mah·CHEEZ·moh) *n.* strong or aggressive masculinity, as displayed in swearing, fighting, drinking, and such aspects of a macho.

ma·cho (MAH·choh) *adj.* openly and aggressively virile: *a macho actor; macho humour.*
— *n.* a macho man: *Hockey is not just for machos.*

mack·er·el (MAK·ur·ul) *n.* a food fish of the North Atlantic, coloured silvery white below and blue or green with wavy black stripes on its back; *adj.: mackerel clouds; a mackerel sky (marked like a mackerel's back).*

mac·ro (MAC·roh) *adj. & combining form.* large or large-scale: *macrocosm, macroorganism; macroscopic; a macro lens, unit; a* ***macro code*** *(for a computer to carry out several instructions in sequence).*

mac·ro·bi·ot·ics (MAK·roh·bye·OT·ics) *n. pl.* [takes sing. v.] the science of prolonging life, esp. by a diet of unprocessed natural foods.
— **mac·ro·bi·ot·ic** *adj.: a Zen macrobiotic diet of vegetables and cereals; a macrobiotic food cult.*

mac·ro·cosm (MAC·ruh·coz·um) *n.* a large and complex whole, as the universe.
— **mac·ro·cos·mic** (-COS·mic) *adj.*

mad *adj.* **mad·der, mad·dest 1** angry: *He was mad at me because I was late; hopping mad.* **2** crazy or insane: *It's mad to quit school when you're doing so well; stark raving mad; His drinking drives me mad; I'll go mad at this rate; mad with frustration; That dog may be mad* (= have rabies). **3** overly enthusiastic: *She's mad about flying, but not about her flying instructor; He works* **like mad** (*Informal* for furiously) *on the eve of a test.*
— **mad·ly** *adv.;* **mad·ness** *n.*

mad·am (MAD·um) *n.* **1** *pl.* **-ams** a woman who keeps a brothel. **2** *pl.* **mes·dames** (may·DAHM) [used in addressing] a lady.

mad·ame (MAD·um, muh·DAM) *n.* [French title used in addressing a French-speaking married woman, as "Dear Madame," or prefixed like "Mrs."] *pl.* **mesdames** (may·DAHM): *Madame Sauvé.*

mad·cap *n.* a reckless or impulsive person; *adj.: a madcap scheme to raise money.*

mad·den (MAD·un) *v.* make or become mad, esp. irritate.

mad·der (MAD·ur), **mad·dest** (MAD·ist) See MAD.

mad·ding (MAD·ing) *adj.* frenzied; also, maddening: *"far from the madding crowd."*

made *pt.* of MAKE.

ma·de·moi·selle (mad·uh·muh·ZEL) *n. French, pl.* **mes·de·moi·selles** (made·mwah·ZEL) an unmarried, usually young French-speaking woman. [also used like "Miss" as a title]

made-to-measure (MADE·tuh·mezh·ur) *adj.* made to the customer's measurements; custom-tailored.

made-to-order (MADE·tuh·or·dur) *adj.* made according to the customer's requirements.

made-up *adj.* **1** invented: *a made-up excuse, story, word.* **2** finished with makeup: *a made-up clown; made-up with a clown face.*

mad·house *n.* **1** a scene of uproar and confusion. **2** *Informal.* an asylum for the mentally ill.

mad·man *n.* **-men** a lunatic.
— **mad·wom·an** *n.* **-wom·en.**

mad money *n. Informal.* a small amount of money for spending on impulse, for emergencies, etc.

Ma·don·na (muh·DON·uh) *n.* **1** Mary as the mother of Jesus. **2** a picture or statue of her.

mad·ri·gal (MAD·ruh·gul) *n.* a type of short love poem popular in the 16th century.

mael·strom (MAIL·strum) *n.* a violently confused or turbulent condition or situation, like **Maelstrom,** a dangerous whirlpool off the Norwegian coast: *caught up in the maelstrom of war.*

ma·es·tro (MICE·troh, mah·ES·troh) *n.* **-tros** or **-tri** (-tree) **1** a great musical composer, teacher, or performer. **2** a masterly performer in any art.

Ma·fi·a or **ma·fi·a** (MAH·fee·uh) *n.* **1** an underworld organization of criminals, Sicilian in origin. **2 mafia** any dominant group of similar interests or backgrounds: *the Harvard mafia of Kennedy's White House.*

ma·fi·o·so (mah·fee·OH·soh) *n., pl.* **-si** (-see) a member of the Mafia.

mag 1 *n. Slang.* magazine. **2** *adj.* made of "magnesium" alloy: *mag wheels.*

mag·a·zine (mag·uh·ZEEN) *n.* **1** an often illustrated periodical of popular interest carrying a variety of articles: *the weekend magazine section of a newspaper.* **2** a place where a supply is stored, as of film in a camera or cartridges inside a machine gun, or a place for storing military supplies and ammunition: *a gunpowder magazine* (= supply depot).

ma·gen·ta (muh·JEN·tuh) *n.* a purplish red dye.

mag·got (MAG·ut) *n.* the wormlike larva of a two-winged fly. — **mag·got·y** *adj.*

ma·gic (MAJ·ic) *n.* **1** the art of creating illusions by sleight of hand and other tricks: *Magicians perform magic; Caterpillars become butterflies* **as if by magic.** **2** the supposed supernatural power of influencing natural events or of controlling human actions by ritual use of incantations, spells, rites, fetishes, talismans, etc.: *black magic; Witchcraft and sorcery are kinds of magic.* **3** any mysterious power: *the magic of love.*
— *adj.: a magic potion; King Midas's magic touch; a magic trick, wand; a magic* (= wonderful) *moment.*
— **mag·i·cal** *adj.: the magical adventures of Alice in Wonderland; magical events, happenings, powers, stories; the magical touch; the magical million-dollar figure; a magical mystery tour, transformation.*
— **mag·i·cal·ly** *adv.*

ma·gi·cian (muh·JISH·un) *n.* a person who practises magic; sorcerer.

mag·is·te·ri·al (maj·is·TEER·ee·ul) *adj.* **1** having to do with authority. **2** of a magistrate. **3** authoritative or overbearing.

mag·is·trate (MAJ·us·trate) *n.* a government official administering the law, esp. a minor judicial officer, as a justice of the peace.
— **mag·is·tra·cy** (-truh·see) *n.* **-cies.**

mag·lev (MAG·lev) *n.* an engineless train that runs by magnetic levitation which raises the train just above the track and pulls it forward at great speed.

mag·nan·i·mous (mag·NAN·uh·mus) *adj.* noble or generous-spirited, as in forgiving wrongs, not being petty, etc. — **mag·nan·i·mous·ly** *adv.*
— **mag·na·nim·i·ty** (mag·nuh·NIM·uh·tee) *n.*

mag·nate *n.* a person of wealth, position, and influence in business or industry: *an oil magnate; a shipping magnate.*

mag·net (MAG·nit) *n.* an object that attracts, because of the force of a **magnetic field** around it: *A piece of lodestone is a natural magnet; An electrically charged coil of wire is an induced magnet.*
— **mag·net·ic** (mag·NET·ic) *adj.: Iron and nickel are magnetic elements; magnetic recording tape; the magnetic bubbles of a computer's bubble memory; A magnetic needle points to the earth's magnetic poles lying near the geographic poles; a leader with a*

461

magnetic personality (that attracts followers).
— **mag·net·i·cal·ly** *adv.*

mag·net·ism (MAG·nuh·tiz·um) *n.* magnetic force or the power of attraction: *your personal magnetism; a singer who has lost her magnetism.*

mag·net·ize (MAG·nuh·tize) *v.* **-iz·es, -ized, -iz·ing**
1 make or become magnetic so as to attract. 2 to charm or hypnotize: *an audience magnetized by a singer's voice.* — **mag·net·i·za·tion** (-tuh·ZAY·shun) *n.*

mag·nif·i·cent (mag·NIF·uh·sunt) *adj.* impressive because of beauty, richness, or splendour: *a magnificent mansion, palace, tribute, voice; Ottawa's magnificent National Gallery.* — **mag·nif·i·cent·ly** *adv.* — **mag·nif·i·cence** *n.*

mag·ni·fy (MAG·nuh·fye) *v.* **-fies, -fied, -fy·ing** make or make seem larger, as with a lens, or **magnifying glass;** hence, exaggerate: *Don't magnify your problem.*
— **mag·ni·fi·er** (-fye·ur) *n.*
— **mag·ni·fi·ca·tion** (-fuh·CAY·shun) *n.*

mag·ni·tude (MAG·nuh·tude) *n.* greatness of size or strength; degree of importance: *the direction and magnitude of a force; an earthquake of magnitude 7.6 on the Richter scale; The faintest stars are of the sixth magnitude; a problem **of the first magnitude.***

mag·num *n.* a double-size bottle of wine or liquor containing 1.5 L (50 oz.); also, this size.
— *adj.* unusually large: *a magnum cartridge, a .458 magnum rifle.*

magnum o·pus (-OH·pus) *n.* one's greatest work; masterpiece.

ma·hat·ma (mah·HAHT·muh, -HAT·muh) *n.* in India, a great and holy man, as "Mahatma Gandhi."

mah-jong or **mah-jongg** (mah·JONG, -ZHONG) *n.* a game of Chinese origin, played by four people using 144 engraved tiles.

ma·hog·a·ny (muh·HOG·uh·nee) *n.* **-nies** 1 the dark reddish-brown wood of a large tropical American tree of the same name. 2 its colour.
— *adj.: mahogany furniture; a beach boy with a mahogany tan.*

maid *n.* 1 a female servant. 2 a maiden.

maid·en (MAY·dun) *n.* a young unmarried woman.
— *adj.* having to do with a maiden; untried or first-time: *a **maiden** (= unmarried) **aunt;** Ms. Anne Smith uses her **maiden name** (= surname before marriage; i.e. Smith) though married to Mr. Jones; an M.P.'s maiden speech in a legislature; the Titanic's maiden voyage.*
— **maid·en·hood** (short "oo") *n.* — **maid·en·ly** *adj.*

maid-in-waiting (MAID·in·WAY·ting) *n.* **maids-in-waiting** a queen's or princess's female attendant.

maid of honour or **maid of honor** *n.* 1 a woman as a chief bridesmaid. 2 a maid-in-waiting.

maid·serv·ant (MADE·sur·vunt) *n.* [old use] a woman servant; housemaid.

mail *n.* 1 a postal or similar messaging system: *Your cheque is in the mail; I don't mean electronic mail; a reply by return mail (= "within 24 hours"); the origin of the **mails** in Europe.* 2 what is sent through the mail, as letters and parcels: *to address, stamp, and send out mail; to deliver, forward, sort the mail; A bag of mail contains many pieces of mail; certified, domestic, express, fan, first-class, hate, junk, registered, second-class, special-delivery, surface, third-class mail.* 3 a body armour of metal plates, rings, etc.: *chain mail; a coat of mail; a **mailed** (= protected with metal or armour) fist, knight.*
— *adj.: a mail carrier, chute, clerk; mail delivery; a **mail drop** (= place for dropping off mail).*
— *v.* send by mail: *to mail a letter.*

mail·box *n.* 1 a box into which outgoing mail is dropped by the public. 2 a private box for receiving mail.

mail·er *n.* 1 a person or machine that addresses, stamps, or mails. 2 a small container for mailing things, or an advertising leaflet.

mail·man *n.* **-men** a man who delivers mail.

mail order *n.* an order for goods by mail.
— **mail-order** *adj.: a mail-order business, catalogue; a **mail-order house** (= a firm that sells by mail).*

maim *v.* cripple or mutilate.

main *adj.* chief or principal, esp. of a system or connected whole: *the main street of a town; the main course of a meal; a sentence's main and subordinate clauses; a hustler with his eye ever on the **main chance** (= the most advantageous opportunity).*
— *n.* 1 a principal channel, as of water, gas, sewage, or electricity: *The water main burst.* 2 [old use] the ocean: *the western main.* 3 [old use] mainland: *the Spanish main (= South American mainland).*
— **in the main** for the most part.
— **with might and main** with all one's strength.
— **main·ly** *adv.*

main·frame *n.* 1 a computer's central processing unit, not a peripheral such as a printer. 2 a large computer, not a mini or micro.

main·land (MAIN·land, -lund) *n.* the main landmass, as distinguished from outlying islands: *the Chinese mainland.* — **main·land·er** *n.*

main·line *n.* 1 the principal road, route, etc. 2 *Slang.* a large vein.
— *v.* **-lines, -lined, -lin·ing** inject heroin or other narcotic into a large vein.

main·spring *n.* 1 the principal spring of a watch or clock. 2 chief incentive: *Is money the mainspring of your life?*

main·stay *n.* 1 a mainmast's supporting wire or rope. 2 chief support: *The quarterback was the mainstay of the football team.*

main·stream *n.* the principal current; the main direction of flow; the prevailing trend: *in the mainstream of politics; a mainstream candidate, Liberal, Conservative.*
— *v.: the mainstreaming of special students in regular programs.*

Main Street or **main street** *n.* 1 a small town's principal street. 2 the masses, esp. as typifying materialism, mediocrity, provincialism, etc.
— **main·street** *v.* campaign for election along main streets. — **main·street·er** *n.*

462

main·tain (main·TAIN) *v.* **1** keep in existence; keep active or unimpaired: *Police maintain law and order; An automobile has to be maintained in running condition; income sufficient to maintain a family.* **2** argue for something: *He couldn't maintain his innocence in the face of all that evidence; Mimi still maintains that the landing on the moon never took place.*

main·te·nance (MAIN·tun·unce) *n.* **1** a maintaining or support: *health maintenance; preventive maintenance of a car; road maintenance; adj.: a maintenance engineer; maintenance staff.* **2** means of livelihood: *a hobby that provides maintenance; to pay maintenance to one's former spouse and children.*

mai·son·ette (may·zuh·NET) *n.* a duplex apartment or small house.

mai·tre d' (may·tur·DEE) *n., pl.* **mai·tre d's** (·DEEZ) [short form] maître d'hôtel.

maî·tre d'hô·tel (may·truh·doh·TEL) *n., pl.* **maî·tres d'hô·tel** (may·truh·) a headwaiter or chief steward.

ma·jes·tic (muh·JES·tic) *adj.* having majesty or grandeur; stately and lofty in appearance; also **ma·jes·ti·cal. — ma·jes·ti·cal·ly** *adv.*

maj·es·ty (MAJ·is·tee) *n.* **1** lofty grandeur: *the Rocky Mountains in all their majesty.* **2** **Her, His, Your Majesty,** *pl.* **Their, Your Majesties** [title used in speaking of or to a king, queen, emperor, etc.].

ma·jor (MAY·jur) *adj.* relatively greater in size, importance, etc., not minor: *a major disagreement, improvement, poet, portion, subject of study;* [in music] *a major chord* based on a **major scale** (*having half steps after the third and seventh tones); major surgery or operation (requiring general anesthesia).*
— v. of a student, specialize: *She's majoring in history.*
— n. **1** a student majoring in a specified subject or the subject itself: *She's a history major; His major is music.* **2** in the armed forces, a commissioned officer ranking above a captain and below a lieutenant colonel: *A major general ranks above a brigadier general and below a lieutenant general.*

majorette [short form] same as DRUM MAJORETTE.

ma·jor·i·ty (muh·JOR·uh·tee) *n.* **-ties 1** more than half the total number of votes, people, etc.; also, votes or people in excess of a required number: *an absolute, bare, large, narrow, overwhelming, simple, small, working majority; to get, receive, win by a slim majority; in the majority of cases; the silent majority (of people who do not take part in politics); A majority government (with the governing party having a majority in parliament) is more secure than a minority government.* **2** the legal age of responsibility or adulthood: *the age of majority; You attain or reach majority in most places at 18 or 21.* **3** the military rank of a major.

major league *n.* in baseball, either the American League or the National League.
— major-league *adj.: major-league baseball; to play at the major-league level; a major-league (= top-rated) organization, sports stadium; NHL's attempts to develop a major-league image.*

make *v.* **makes, made, mak·ing 1** bring something into being; create, form, shape, or put together: *Did God make the universe? Sam makes dresses; Lou makes a living as a plumber; He died without making a will; Everyone makes mistakes; Poets are born, not made; She makes* (= arranges) *her bed in the morning; "Haste makes waste"; Make peace, not war; What do you **make of** (= How do you interpret) this telegram? Soups made of or out of or with vegetables are not all the same.* **2** cause to be; also, cause oneself to be or become: *Please make sure the door is locked; He's trying to make himself understood; to make someone president; She can make children do their homework; Their work makes her happy; She'll make* (= become) *a good teacher; Don't make him wait; He was made to wait.* **3** attain or reach; achieve: *He had to run to make* (= catch) *the 5 o'clock bus; A story has to be sensational to make the front page; What grade did you make on the test? a challenge that could either make you* (= get you success) *or break you.*
— make away with 1 get rid of or kill. **2** steal.
— make believe pretend or imagine.
— make do manage with something that is not so good: *to make do with fewer clothes; How do you make do on your tiny salary?*
— make for move toward: *When the alarm sounds, make for the exits; Being prepared makes for* (= leads to) *safety.*
— make it succeed: *You have to work hard to really make it.*
— make off run away.
— make off with steal.
— make out 1 see or understand: *It's too faint for me to make out.* **2** (try) to prove: *It is not the cure-all the ads make it out to be.* **3** write or fill out: *Please make this out in duplicate.* **4** *Informal.* succeed: *How are you making out in your new job?*
— make over 1 change or alter. **2** transfer the ownership of something: *The title to the house was made over to his son.*
— make up 1 put together; compose: *an audience made up of students; She's good at making up excuses; It's time to make up your mind* (= decide); *Friends make up* (= become reconciled) *after a fight.* **2** restore or compensate for something lost: *He works longer hours to make up for lost time; to make up a loss; I'll make it up to you for losing your books.* **3** put on cosmetics, stage masks, etc.
— n. the origin of a product: *a bicycle of Canadian make; the year and make* (= brand, as Ford, GM, etc.) *of a car.*
— on the make *Informal.* seeking profit, adventure, etc.

make-believe (MAKE·buh·leev) *n. & adj.* a pretending or imagining: *His exploits are mere make-believe; the make-believe of drama; a make-believe picnic on the moon.*

make-over (MAKE·oh·vur) *n.* a remodelling or beauty treatment: *You see a genuine change in the man, not just an image make-over.*

mak·er (MAY·kur) *n.* one that makes: *a film maker; the maker* (= manufacturer) *of a car; to **meet one's maker** (= to die).*

make·shift *n. & adj.* something temporary or substitute: *a makeshift arrangement, bed of hay, shelter.*

463

make·up or **make-up** *n. & adj.* **1** cosmetics, masks, etc. that are applied on the face: *to apply, put on, remove, wear makeup.* **2** *Informal.* compensation: *a makeup examination for students who were ill.* **3** how something is put together; composition: *the page makeup and design of a newspaper; a makeup editor.*

make-work *n. & adj.* work devised mainly to keep people employed: *a make-work government project.*

making *n.* a being made or becoming: *the making* (= compilation) *of dictionaries; Publicity spoiled our plans while they were still **in the making*** (= being made); *a youngster with the **makings of*** (= potential for becoming) *a soldier; The trouble was not of his own making; His marriage was the making of him* (= cause of his success).

mal·ad·just·ed (mal·uh·JUS·tid) *adj.* not well adjusted to one's environment. — **mal·ad·just·ment** *n.*

mal·a·droit (mal·uh·DROIT) *adj.* not adroit; clumsy or awkward. — **mal·a·droit·ly** *adv.;* **mal·a·droit·ness** *n.*

mal·a·dy (MAL·uh·dee) *n.* **-dies** a bodily disorder, often one that is deep-seated or that may prove fatal.

ma·laise (ma·LAZE) *n.* **1** a disordered condition. **2** a vague feeling of discomfort.

mal·a·prop·ism (MAL·uh·prop·iz·um) *n.* a ludicrous mixing up of similar words, as "We got the R.I.P. treatment" instead of saying "V.I.P. treatment."

ma·lar·i·a (muh·LAIR·ee·uh) *n.* a mosquito-borne parasitic disease characterized by periodic chills and fever. — **ma·lar·i·al** *adj.*

ma·lar·key or **ma·lar·ky** (muh·LAR·kee) *n. Slang.* bunk; nonsense.

mal·con·tent (MAL·cun·tent) *n. & adj.* (one) who is dissatisfied or rebellious.

male *adj.* **1** of the kind in plants, animals, and humans that fertilizes the female for begetting offspring: *A male plant has only flowers with stamens; The stamen and the penis are male reproductive organs.* **2** having to do with males and their qualities: *a male chauvinist; a male* (= projecting) *electrical plug; the male bonding* (= close personal relationships) *among men.*
— *n.* a male person, animal, plant, or flower.
— **male·ness** *n.*

mal·e·dic·tion (mal·uh·DIC·shun) *n.* **1** a curse. **2** slander. — **mal·e·dic·tor·y** *adj.*

mal·e·fac·tor (MAL·uh·fac·tur) *n.* an evildoer or criminal; *fem.* **mal·e·fac·tress.**
— **mal·e·fac·tion** (-FAC·shun) *n.*

ma·lev·o·lent (muh·LEV·uh·lunt) *adj.* wishing others evil; malicious. — **ma·lev·o·lence** (-lunce) *n.*

mal·for·ma·tion (mal·for·MAY·shun) *n.* an abnormal or faulty formation of a body or body part, as a hunched back: *a congenital malformation.* — **mal·formed** *adj.*

mal·func·tion (mal·FUNK·shun) *v.* fail to function properly. — *n.* a malfunctioning.

mal·ice (MAL·is) *n.* desire to harm another: *He bore no malice toward anyone.*

ma·li·cious (muh·LISH·us) *adj.* meant to harm

someone; spiteful: *malicious attacks, behaviour, cruelty, gossips, remarks.* — **ma·li·cious·ly** *adv.*

ma·lign (muh·LINE) *v.* speak evil of someone; slander.
— *adj.* **1** injurious; also, malicious: *a malign doctrine, influence.* **2** cancerous: *a malign tumour.*

ma·lig·nant (muh·LIG·nunt) *adj.* **1** malign: *a malign look, spell.* **2** likely to spread and prove fatal if not checked; not benign: *a malign growth, lump in the breast; malign cholera, hypertension.*
— **ma·lig·nan·cy** (-nun·see) *n.*
— **ma·lig·ni·ty** (-nuh·tee) *n.*

ma·lin·ger (muh·LING·gur) *v.* pretend illness in order to escape duty. — **ma·lin·ger·er** *n.*

mall (MAWL) *n.* **1** a pedestrians-only street lined with shops: *a pedestrial mall.* **2** a covered shopping centre: *West Edmonton Mall.* **3** a broad, parklike walk or promenade, as stretches from the Capitol to the Lincoln Memorial in Washington, D.C. **4** road: *the Mall leading to Buckingham Palace; Toronto's East Mall, West Mall.*

mal·lard (MAL·urd) *n.* a common wild duck.

mal·le·a·ble (MAL·ee·uh·bul) *adj.* **1** of metals, that can be hammered or pressed into thin sheets, as gold, silver, copper, etc., not stiff like cast iron. **2** easily changed, shaped, or trained: *a malleable character; one malleable student in a class of stubborn rebels.*
— **mal·le·a·bil·i·ty** (-BIL·uh·tee) *n.*

mal·let (MAL·it) *n.* a hammer with a wooden head, short-handled for driving a chisel or long-handled for use in polo and other games.

mal·low (MAL·oh) *n.* a herb, shrub, or tree such as the marshmallow with hairy stems and leaves.

mal·nour·ished (mal·NUR·isht) *adj.* poorly nourished.

mal·nu·tri·tion (mal·new·TRISH·un) *n.* a malnourished condition resulting from improper diet.

mal·o·dor·ous (mal·OH·dur·us) *adj.* having a bad odour; stinking.

mal·prac·tice (mal·PRAC·tis) *n.* improper conduct or treatment by a professional, esp. neglect of a patient by a physician.

malt (MAWLT) *n.* barley or other grain that is first soaked and allowed to sprout, then kiln-dried and aged for use in beer-making and distilling: *Dried milk and malt extract powder are mixed in milk to make **malted milk.***

malt liquor *n.* beer, ale, etc. made from malt by fermentation.

mal·treat (mal·TREET) *v.* treat brutally; abuse or hurt.
— **mal·treat·ment** *n.*

ma·ma or **mam·ma** (MAH·muh) *n. Informal.* mother: *He's certainly not a **mamma's boy*** (= sissy).

mam·mal (MAM·ul) *n.* a vertebrate such as a human being, dog, bat, or whale whose females nourish their young with milk from the breast.
— **mam·ma·li·an** (ma·MAY·lee·un) *n. & adj.*

mam·mar·y (MAM·uh·ree) *adj.* having to do with the breasts: *a mammary gland.*

mam·mon (MAM·un) *n.* the greedy pursuit of wealth,

personified as **Mammon.**

mam·moth (MAM·uth) **1** *n.* a huge prehistoric hairy kind of elephant with large curved tusks. **2** *adj.* gigantic or colossal: *a mammoth enterprise, undertaking.*

man *n., pl.* **men 1** an adult human male, in roles such as suitor, husband, servant, follower, or a person with virile qualities: *to live together as man* (= husband) *and wife; all the king's men* (= followers); *He was man enough to apologize; Be a man! Take it like a man! a man of action; a man of the cloth* (= clergyman) *and a man of God, but not a man of the world* (= a worldly man); *a man of letters; a man of his word (who will keep promises); a best man; con* or *confidence man; an advance, enlisted, hatchet, hit, leading, maintenance, marked, organization, right-hand, straight, straw, stunt man.* **2** a member of the human race; a person or individual: *Is man descended from the apes? the Neanderthal man; Man is mortal; a chess man* (= piece); *He's running a one-man show; the* **man in the street** (= the average person); *They fought the invaders* **as one man** or **as a man** (= Everybody fought); *They were wiped out* **to a man** (= All were lost).
— *v.* **mans, manned, man·ning 1** supply with people, usually men, for defence or hard work: *Sailors man a ship.* **2** put courage into oneself: *He manned himself for the ordeal.*
— *combining form.* **1** person, esp. a male: *batsman, chairman, freshman, spokesman.* **2** person: *man-eater, manhandle, manhour, manpower.*

man-about-town (man·uh·bowt·TOWN) *n.*
-men-about-town a man of society who spends much time in clubs, theatres, etc.

man·a·cle (MAN·uh·cul) *n.* usually **manacles** *pl.* handcuffs or fetters: *a prisoner in manacles.*
— *v.* **-cles, -cled, -cling** restrain with or as if with manacles: *Totalitarian regimes manacle the press.*

man·age (MAN·ij) *v.* **-ag·es, -aged, -ag·ing 1** handle or make use of people, resources, etc. efficiently: *someone to manage the sales department; a managing editor; a horse that is difficult to manage* (= control). **2** cope: *Can you manage with just one helper? It's impossible to manage without a pay cheque; He seems to manage well on such a low income; She managed to return* (= succeeded in returning) *the book on time.*
— **man·age·a·ble** (-ij·uh·bul) *adj.;* **man·age·a·bly** *adv.*

man·age·ment (MAN·ij·munt) *n.* a managing, being managed, or a group of managers: *the management of a business; labour and management; senior management* (= managers); *a shop under new management* (= owners).
— **man·age·men·tal** (-MEN·tul) *adj.*

man·ag·er (MAN·ij·ur) *n.* one who manages: *our bank manager; our general, office, sales, service manager; an assistant manager; the branch manager of our bank.*
— **man·a·ge·ri·al** (man·uh·JEER·ee·ul) *adj.: a managerial position, responsibility.*

ma·ña·na (muh·NYAH·nuh) *n. & adv.* [implying the habit of putting things off] tomorrow: *Saying mañana won't get your homework done.*

man·da·rin (MAN·duh·rin) *n.* **1 Mandarin** the dialect of northern China, the most widely spoken form of Chinese. **2** a high military or civil official of or as of the former Chinese empire: *Chinese mandarins; Ottawa mandarins such as deputy ministers.* **3** a tangerine orange.

man·date (MAN·date) *n.* **1** an order or command. **2** authority or commission: *Elected representatives get their mandate from the people; He claims to be carrying out a mandate from Heaven; He doesn't have a clear mandate, though; Britain had a mandate from the League of Nations to administer Iraq which became a* **man·dat·ed** *territory.*

man·da·to·ry (MAN·duh·tor·ee) *adj.* **1** obligatory: *Seat belts were made mandatory long ago; the mandatory metric system; a prisoner free on mandatory supervision; a mandatory drug-testing program, jail sentence, retirement age.* **2** having the nature of a mandate: *a mandatory injunction, order.*

mane *n.* the long and heavy hair around the neck of animals such as lions and horses. — **maned** *adj.*

man-eater *n.* **1** a cannibal. **2** an animal that eats human flesh, as a tiger or shark. — **man-eating** *adj.*

ma·neu·ver (muh·NOO·vur) *n. & v.* same as MANOEUVRE.

man Friday *n.* See FRIDAY.

man·ful *adj.* courageous or resolute as befits a man.
— **man·ful·ly** *adv.*

man·ger (MAIN·jur) *n.* a long box or trough for livestock to eat from, as in a stable.

man·gle (MANG·gul) *v.* **-gles, -gled, -gling 1** tear, hack, or crush so as to mutilate. **2** botch or ruin something.

man·gy (MAIN·jee) *adj.* **-gi·er, -gi·est 1** having the mange: *a mangy dog.* **2** shabby or contemptible.
— **man·gi·ness** *n.*

man·han·dle (MAN·han·dul) *v.* **-dles, -dled, -dling** handle or treat roughly.

man·hole *n.* a covered hole for access to a sewer, ship's tank, etc.: *Open manholes are a threat to pedestrians.*

man·hood (short "oo") *n.* **1** the state of being a man: *to grow to* or *reach manhood.* **2** manly character. **3** men collectively: *the manhood of the nation.*

man-hour *n.* a unit of one hour's work by one person.

man·hunt *n.* an organized hunt for a criminal or fugitive: *to carry out, conduct, organize a manhunt for the escapees.*

ma·ni·a (MAY·nee·uh) *n.* **1** a mental disorder characterized by an uncontrollable urge or excitement: *an arsonist with a mania for setting fire to buildings.* **2** excessive enthusiasm or a craze: *She has a mania for fresh air.*
— **combining form.** mania or craze for specified subject: *kleptomania, megalomania, Trudeaumania.*

ma·ni·ac (MAY·nee·ac) *n. & adj.* **1** (one who is) wildly insane: *a sex maniac.* **2** (one who is) excessively enthusiastic about something: *an exercise maniac; hockey maniacs.*
— **ma·ni·a·cal** (muh·NYE·uh·cul) *adj.: a maniacal rage.*

man·ic *adj.* **1** suffering from mania: *Recurrent bouts of manic depression drove him to suicide.* **2** resembling mania: *a woman of manic energy; The exhibition was a manic maze of display booths and pavilions; manic delight, enthusiasm, intensity, rhythms.*

man·i·cure (MAN·i·cure) *v.* **-cures, -cured, -cur·ing** trim, clean, and polish fingernails: *a well-manicured hand; a manicured lawn (kept like one's hand); the manicured grounds of Memorial Park.*
— *n.* the care of or treatment for the hands, esp. the fingernails. — **man·i·cur·ist** *n.*

man·i·fest (MAN·uh·fest) *adj.* plain and clear to the mind: *facts that are manifest to the view; a manifest error, truth; Some thought territorial expansion was America's **manifest destiny** in the 19th century.*
— *n.* an itemized cargo or passenger list: *a shipping manifest; My name is on the manifest.*
— *v.* display or reveal: *She manifested little interest in the proceedings; Her true feelings began to manifest themselves later; the facts as manifested (= proved) by documents.*
— **man·i·fes·ta·tion** (-TAY·shun) *n.: A dog wags its tail in manifestation of joy; a strike as a manifestation of political support.*
— **man·i·fest·ly** *adv.* clearly: *manifestly absurd, false, unfair.*

man·i·fes·to (man·uh·FES·toh) *n.* **-tos** or **-toes** a public declaration of plans or policies, issued by a government or political party.

man·i·fold (MAN·uh·fold) *adj.* **1** many and various: *the manifold duties and responsibilities of a mayor; The reasons for the decision are manifold.* **2** having many parts or facets: *his manifold wisdom; a manifold personality, plan, program of action.*
— *n.* a pipe fitting with many lateral connections: *an automobile engine's intake manifold; an exhaust manifold.*
— *v.* **1** make manifold. **2** to duplicate, as in making carbon copies.

ma·nip·u·late (muh·NIP·yoo·late) *v.* **-lates, -lat·ed, -lat·ing** handle with skill, dexterity, or craftiness: *He's good at manipulating marionettes; He manipulated the electorate to win the election; The accounts were manipulated in anticipation of the audit.*
— **ma·nip·u·la·tive** (-yuh·luh·tiv) *adj.*
— **ma·nip·u·la·tor** (-lay·tur) *n.*
— **ma·nip·u·la·tion** (-yoo·LAY·shun) *n.*

man·i·tou (MAN·uh·too) *n.* in Algonquian Indian belief, the universal spirit or life force that pervades everything: *The universe is charged with manitou; The Manitou, or Great Spirit, is the omnipotent one.*

man·kind (man·KINED) *n.* **1** the human race; human beings. **2** (MAN·kined) men, as distinguished from women or womankind.

man·ly *adj.* **-li·er, -li·est 1** befitting a man: *manly sports.* **2** as a man should be; courageous, honorable, etc.: *a very manly youngster.* — *adv.* in a manly way.
— **man·li·ness** *n.*

man·made *adj.* made by human beings, not natural: *man-made climatic changes; Traffic, taxation, and such man-made laws; a man-made (= synthetic) fibre, virus.*

man·na (MAN·uh) *n.* **1** in the Old Testament, food dropped from heaven to aid the Israelites in the wilderness. **2** a miraculous supply. **3** spiritual nourishment.

manned (MAND) *adj.* controlled by or carrying human beings: *a manned satellite, spacecraft.*

man·ne·quin (MAN·uh·kin) *n.* **1** a model of the human body, as used to display clothes in shop windows or by artists, tailors, etc. **2** a woman who models clothes for buyers.

man·ner (MAN·ur) *n.* **1** a way of behaving, esp. one characteristic of a person or that is conventional within a group: *an aristocratic, awkward, businesslike, cavalier, charming, courteous, flippant, friendly, gentle, gracious, grand, ingratiating, matter-of-fact, obnoxious, overbearing, pretentious, servile, sheepish, sloppy, statesmanlike, stern, sullen manner; our doctor's fine bedside manner; Hold your fork in this manner (= way); He's a bit of a barbarian, in a manner of speaking (= if I may say so); He speaks French as if to the manner born (= as if French were his mother tongue).* **2 manners** *pl.* social behaviour: *Mind your manners; Children have to learn (good) manners; Bad manners won't be tolerated; the manners and customs of the Saxons.* **3** kind or sort: *All manner of (= every kind of) people were there.*

man·nered (MAN·urd) *adj.* **1** having a certain way of behaving: *Don't be so ill mannered; an ill-mannered clerk; a well-mannered child.* **2** artificial or affected; showing a mannerism: *a mannered style, writer.*

man·ner·ism (MAN·ur·iz·um) *n.* a manner or style that is excessive or peculiar: *Men and women differ in their mannerisms.*

man·ner·ly (MAN·ur·lee) *adj. & adv.* polite or politely.
— **man·ner·li·ness** *n.*

man·ni·kin (MAN·uh·kin) same as MANNEQUIN.

man·nish (MAN·ish) *adj.* suggestive of a man's traits or manners; masculine: *her rather mannish bearing; a mannish style, way.*

ma·noeu·vre (muh·NOO·vur) *n.* **1** a tactical movement, as of the military or of warships: *NATO conducts manoeuvres (= military exercises) in the Atlantic.* **2** a skilful use of people, situations, etc. for private ends, as to achieve or escape something; manipulation or stratagem: *clever, political, tactical manoeuvres.*
— *v.* move skilfully or tactically: *to manoeuvre for*

position in a power struggle; Small cars are easy to manoeuvre into and out of a parking space; He managed to manoeuvre (= force by manoeuvres) the vice-president out of his job. — **ma·noeu·vra·ble** *adj.*

man-of-war *n.,* *pl.* **men-** formerly, a warship.

man·or (MAN·ur) *n.* **1** a mansion on a large estate. **2** formerly, the house of a feudal lord, or "lord of the manor"; also **manor-house.**
— **ma·no·ri·al** (muh·NOR·ee·ul) *adj.*

man·pow·er (MAN·pow·ur, *rhyme:* our) *n.* **1** the power of human strength. **2** the supply of people for work, including the unemployed and the retired seeking work: *Canada's manpower policies.*

man·qué (mahng·KAY) *adj.* [follows its noun] unfulfilled or frustrated: *a poet manqué.*

man·sard (MAN·sard) *n.* **1** a gambrel roof with ridges on four sides instead of two. **2** the storey immediately below it.

manse *n.* a parsonage, esp. a Scottish Presbyterian one.

man·ser·vant (man·SUR·vunt) *n.* **men·ser·vants** a male servant.

man·sion (MAN·shun) *n.* a stately or imposing residence: *the movie star's mansion.*

man-size or **man-sized** *adj.* full-size or large: *a man-size dinner, job, portion (of food).*

man·slaugh·ter (MAN·slaw·tur) *n.* [legal use] the unlawful killing of one human being by another though not with malice as in murder: *a charge of manslaughter in the death of a bicyclist run over by a car.*

man·tel (MAN·tul) *n.* **1** the framework, often with stone or marble facing, around a fireplace. **2** the shelf above a fireplace, or **man·tel·piece.**

man·til·la (man·TIL·uh) *n.* a light scarf worn over the head and shoulders by Spanish and Latin American women.

man·tle (MAN·tul) *n.* anything that covers or envelops, as a loose outer garment, the burning hood of meshwork covering the flame in a gas lamp, the outer body wall of molluscs that secretes the shell material and forms oyster pearls, the part of the earth between crust and core, etc.: *The prophet Elijah cast his mantle (as a symbol of authority and leadership) on Elishah; A mantle of snow covered the mountain; A mantle of darkness descended on the city when the power failed.*
— *v.* **-tles, -tled, -tling 1** cover or be covered, as a pond with scum. **2** flush or blush.

man·tra (MAN·truh) *n.* a Hindu or Buddhist sacred utterance or chant.

man·u·al (MAN·yoo·ul) *adj.* involving use of the hands or requiring physical skill; not automatic: *manual labour; a manual-shift transmission; the **manual alphabet** used by deaf-mutes; **manual training** in arts and crafts.*
— *n.* **1** a handbook: *a car owner's manual; an instruction manual; teacher's manual.* **2** the formal handling routine of a rifle or other weapon; also **manual of arms.** **3** the manual keyboard of an organ.
— **man·u·al·ly** *adv.*

man·u·fac·ture (man·yuh·FAC·chur) *v.* **-tures, -tured, -tur·ing 1** make from raw materials, esp. by use of machines and on a large scale: *hand-made and manufactured goods; Extractive industries like mining supply raw materials to related manufacturing industries; natural and manufactured gases.* **2** invent or make up: *a manufactured excuse.*
— *n.* a product or the act or process of making it: *goods of foreign manufacture.* — **man·u·fac·tur·er** *n.*

ma·nure (mun·YOUR) *n.* animal excrement or dung used as fertilizer: *Spread the manure on your lawn.*
— *v.* **-nures, -nured, -nur·ing** fertilize with manure.

man·u·script (MAN·yuh·script) *n.* something written, not printed: *the typed manuscript of a book; a manuscript submitted for publication; an illuminated medieval manuscript; learned theses lying **in manuscript** (= unpublished).*

man·y (MEN·ee) *adj., comp.* **more,** *superl.* **most** (MOHST) consisting of a large number; numerous: *many cats, men, things; Marc told him to get lost **in so many** (= in those exact) **words.***
— *n. & pron.* a large number of persons or things: *Many of them were absent; A **good many** (= larger number) passed; **Many a** student (= Many students) failed.*

many-sided (MEN·ee·sye·did) *adj.* having many sides, aspects, or possibilities.

map *n.* **1** a representation of a part of the earth on a plane surface showing the more important places, rivers, mountains, seas, etc.: *to read a map; a relief, road, weather map; Our village is not on the map; It was wiped off the map* (= completely destroyed) *by a tornado.* **2** a similar chart of the heavens to show positions of the stars.
— **on the map** well known: *A writeup in a national newspaper put her on the map* (= made her well-known); *The Who's Who entry keeps him on the map.*
— *v.* **maps, mapped, map·ping 1** make a map of a place: *James Vancouver mapped Canada's Pacific coast in the 1790s.* **2** plan: *to **map out** a project, one's time.*
— **map·per** *n.*

ma·ple (MAY·pul) *n.* **1** any of over 100 species of shady trees of temperate regions, bearing double-winged seeds, or "keys," and having leaves that grow opposite each other: *The "sugar maple" yields a sap which is boiled to make **maple syrup** and **maple sugar.*** **2** the hard, light-coloured wood of the maple. **3** the flavour of maple syrup or sugar.

mar *v.* mars, *pt. & pp.* **marred, mar·ring** spoil the beauty of something; damage slightly: *furniture marred by scratches; Nothing could mar her happiness.*

mar·a·thon (MAIR·uh·thon, "th" as in "thin") *n.* **1** a long-distance (52.2 km) foot race, as at the Olympics: *Fitness buffs run marathons; Terry Fox's Marathon of Hope.* **2** an activity requiring great endurance: *a dance marathon to raise money; The marathon session of Parliament ended only in the morning.*

ma·raud (muh·RAWD) *v.* raid and plunder; pillage.
— **ma·raud·er** *n.*

mar·ble (MAR·bul) *n.* **1** a hard limestone rock, cut for use in architecture and carved into sculptures: *The Taj Mahal is built of white marble; a slab of marble for a table top.* **2** a small ball of marble, glass, or stone used in the children's game of "marbles": *a bad loser who picks up his marbles and leaves as soon as he's beaten.*
— *adj.* of or like marble, esp. hard, white, and cold: *a marble floor; marble walls.*
— *v.* **-bles, -bled, -bling** to colour or make like the variegated pattern of marble: *a book's marbled edges; meat with a **marbling** of fat.*

march *v.* **1** to walk in military style: *We could hear the troops marching outside; She marched out of the room as if displeased; At the fire alarm, march (= lead) the children out in single file; He received his **marching orders** (= dismissal) yesterday.* **2** progress steadily: *History marches on.*
— *n.* **1** a marching or its manner or extent: *It's a day's march to the camp; A slow march suits a funeral procession; a death, forced, peace march; The protesters organized a march on Parliament Hill; We'll be on the **march** (= moving along) after breakfast; She stole a **march on** (= outwitted) us by camping out near the box office to buy the first ticket; a **march-past** of troops in review.* **2** a piece of music to accompany a march, as "When Johnny Comes Marching Home": *a funeral, military, wedding march; to play or strike up a march.* **3** a border or frontier (district), as the **Marches** of Wales or Scotland separating it from England.

marchioness See MARQUESS.

Mar·di Gras (MAR·dee·GRAH) *n.* carnival celebration of Shrove Tuesday in the French tradition, as in New Orleans.

ma·re (MAIR·ee) *n., pl.* **-ri·a** (-ee·uh) one of the dark, flat areas of the moon or Mars, once thought to be seas.

mare *n.* a mature female horse, donkey, etc.: *a brood mare (used for breeding).*

mare's nest *n.* **1** a "discovery" that turns out to be deceptive. **2** a mess.

mar·ga·rine (MAR·juh·rin) *n.* a butter substitute made from fats and vegetable oils.

mar·gin (MAR·jin) *n.* an edge or border, as the blank space around the written or printed matter on a page: *a text annotated with notes in the margins; to set a typewriter margin of five spaces; a letter printed out with justified margins; He won the election by a **narrow margin** (= small majority or plurality); a comfortable, handsome, safe, slender, small, wide margin; within the allowed margin of error; a price markup with a large profit margin; a margin of safety.*

— **mar·gin·al** (-ul) *adj.*: *a marginal difference; marginal land (whose yield will barely cover costs); a marginal case, factor; to cut staff by eliminating marginal (= borderline; barely acceptable) staff members.*
— **mar·gin·al·ly** *adv.*

mar·gi·na·li·a (mar·juh·NAY·lee·uh) *n. pl.* notes in the margins.

ma·ri·a·chi (mar·ee·AH·chee) *n.* **-chis 1** an itinerant Mexican band of musicians and singers. **2** their music. **3** a member of the group.

mar·i·jua·na or **mar·i·hua·na** (mair·uh·WAH·nuh) *n.* a drug prepared from the hemp plant, not as strong as hashish, smoked as a narcotic.

ma·ri·na (muh·REE·nuh) *n.* a small harbour for pleasure craft with service and restaurant facilities.

mar·i·nade (mair·uh·NADE) *n.* a spicy solution or sauce to tenderize meat or add flavour to foods.
— *v.* same as MARINATE.

mar·i·nate (MAIR·uh·nate) *v.* **-nates, -nat·ed, -nat·ing** soak in marinade or oil and vinegar: *a marinated leg of lamb; marinated vegetables served as salads.*
— **mar·i·na·tion** (-NAY·shun) *n.*

ma·rine (muh·REEN) *adj.* **1** of the sea: *marine biology, life, stories.* **2** nautical or naval: *marine engineering; marine insurance; a marine propeller.*
— *n.* **1** a soldier specially trained for assault operations by sea and land. **2 Marine** a member of the U.S. Navy's **Marine Corps. 3** the ships of a country collectively: *the merchant marine.*

mar·i·ner (MAIR·uh·nur) *n.* a sailor.

mar·i·o·nette (MAIR·ee·uh·NET) *n.* a puppet controlled by strings or wires held by the puppeteer hidden above the stage.

Mar·i·po·sa lily (MAIR·ee·poh·zuh-) *n.* a lily with narrow leaves and three-petalled cup-shaped flowers: *Stephen Leacock's "Sunshine Sketches of a Little Town" is about a little Canadian town called "Mariposa"; The Mariposa Folk Festival of folk music is held annually in Toronto.*

mar·i·tal (MAIR·uh·tul) *adj.* having to do with marriage; conjugal: *marital bliss, counselling, tax deductions, ties, vows.* — **mar·i·tal·ly** *adv.*

mar·i·time (MAIR·uh·time) *adj.* relating to the sea: *a maritime nation or power with a good navy; maritime laws (of shipping and navigation); Canada's Maritime (= near the sea) Provinces, or the **Maritimes**, are New Brunswick, Nova Scotia, and Prince Edward Island.*
— **Mar·i·tim·er** *n.*

mark *n.* **1** a scratch, spot, trace, etc. made on an object: *Sign at the "X" mark; a punctuation mark such as the comma and period; a question mark; quotation marks; Spots are the distinguishing marks of a leopard; "On your marks, get set, go!" said the starter before firing his pistol; He **made his mark** (= gained recognition) as an inventor.* **2** a target or goal; person or thing aimed at: *to find, hit, miss, overshoot the mark; I don't feel **up to the mark** (= well enough) on Monday mornings; Her replies to questions were all **off the mark** or **wide of the mark**; Drunks are easy marks (= victims) for pickpockets.* **3** indication of some quality: *the marks of*

a gentleman; *to bear the mark of Cain (the murderer); She gets high marks* (=grades) *in history; An M16 rifle is much more sophisticated than a Mark 1 or M1.* **4** a German money unit.
— *v.* carry a mark or other indication: *a face marked by scars; Fireworks marked the end of the celebrations; a promising youth marked* (=destined) *for success;* Mark (=Note) *my words well; items* **marked down** *for quick sale; She's* **marking time** (=waiting) *before springing the surprise on him.* — **mark·er** *n.*

mark·down *n.* a price reduction or its amount.

marked *adj.* easily distinguished: *marked differences of colour; a* **marked man** *with no chance of escape from attack, suspicion, etc.*

mark·ed·ly (MAR·kid·lee) *adv.* plainly or noticeably.

mar·ket (MAR·kit) *n.* **1** a place for buying and selling goods: *a farmer driving to market; an expensive product priced right* **out of the market** *(so nobody can buy it); Excess supply creates a buyer's market with low prices; Publishers put books on the market; There's no market* (=demand) *for air conditioners in the winter; the labour market* (=supply); *the youth market* (=consumer group); *I'm* **in the market** *for* (=interested in buying) *a new car every five years.* **2** a shop or store: *a farmer's, fish, food, fruit, meat, vegetable market.* **3** the activity of buying and selling: *an active, depressed, falling, firm, lively, rising, sluggish, steady market; the black market; bond market; commodities market; futures market; securities market; wheat market.* **4** the stock market: *Speculators play the market; bear* (=falling) *markets and bull* (=rising) *markets; The market opened weak, but closed strong.*
— *v.* sell: *the art of marketing used cars; a talent difficult to market because no one needs it.*
— **mar·ket·a·ble** *adj.;* **mar·ket·er** or **mar·ket·eer** *n.*

mar·ket·place (MAR·kit·place) *n.* **1** where a market is held. **2** the world of business and trade: *the language of the marketplace; competition in the marketplace.*

marking *n.* **1** evaluation: *the marking of essays, projects, tests.* **2** a mark, marks, or their arrangement, as on a bird or animal.

marks·man (MARKS·mun) *n.* **-men** one who is skilled at shooting; **marks·wom·an** *n.* **-wom·en.**
— **marks·man·ship** *n.*

mark·up *n.* the increase in the price of an article from its production cost to its selling price.

mar·ma·lade (MAR·muh·lade) *n.* a clear jelly made of a fruit such as orange and pieces of its rind.

mar·mot (MAR·mut) *n.* a ground-dwelling rodent of the squirrel family: *The woodchuck and groundhog are species of marmot; the hoary marmot of Siberia.*

ma·roon (muh·ROON) *v.* be left stranded and helpless: *people marooned on rooftops by a flood.*
— *n.* **1** a very dark brownish red; *adj.* of this colour. **2** one left marooned like the fleeing black slaves on West Indian islands in the 18th century.

marque (MARK) *n.* a brand or make, as of a luxury or racing car: *the Mercedes marque.*

mar·quee (mar·KEE) *n.* **1** a canopy over an entrance, as

of a theatre or hotel. **2** a large tent.

mar·quess or **mar·quis** (MAR·kwis) *n.* a nobleman ranking below a duke and above an earl or count; **mar·chio·ness** (MAR·shun·nis), *fem.*

mar·riage (MAIR·ij) *n.* **1** the act of taking as husband or wife: *to annul, arrange, break up, consummate, dissolve, enter into, propose a marriage; a common-law, communal, secret, trial marriage; a mixed marriage; a marriage of convenience; to give one's daughter in marriage to someone.* **2** wedding: *the day of the marriage; adj.: the marriage bed, ceremony, night, reception.* **3** married life; wedlock: *a long and happy marriage.* — **mar·riage·a·ble** (-ij·uh·bul) *adj.*

mar·ried (MAIR·eed) *adj.* **1** living together as husband and wife: *I'm single, not married; I may get married some day; adj.: a married couple; a much-married movie star.* **2** having to do with the married state: *married bliss, life;* **married quarters** *for married members of the army.*
— *n.* a married person: *young marrieds; newly marrieds* (=married couples).

mar·row (MAIR·oh) *n.* **1** the soft fatty substance filling the cavities of bones: *a bone marrow transplant; vegetable marrow* (=a summer squash). **2** the best or inmost part: *She felt chilled to the marrow.*

mar·ry (MAIR·ee) *v.* **mar·ries, mar·ried, mar·ry·ing** **1** take as husband or wife: *Lou married Lee; Each has married into a good family.* **2** unite, as in marriage: *The pastor married Lou to Lee; Parents used to* **marry off** *their daughters; to marry urban development with environmental concerns.*

marsh *n.* a tract of low, hence often wet, soft land; swamp or bog. — **marsh·y** *adj.*

mar·shal (MAR·shul) *n.* **1** an official with duties in a public place or at a public event: *a fire marshal* (=head of a fire department); *a parade marshal (in charge of parades, processions, etc.); A U.S. marshal is an officer of the federal court.* **2** an officer in the military or in the police force of a town or village: *The Air Chief Marshal heads the Canadian Air Force; an air marshal; a field marshal in the British army; a provost marshal* (=head of a military police force).
— *v.* **-shals, -shalled** or **-shaled, -shal·ling** or **-shal·ing** usher or present in an orderly fashion: *to marshal arguments, facts, forces; to marshal people into the auditorium.*

marsh gas *n.* same as METHANE.

marsh·mal·low (MARSH·mel·oh, -mal·oh) *n.* **1** a soft spongy candy made from corn syrup, sugar, albumen, and gelatin, originally from the root of the marsh mallow plant: *to roast* or *toast marshmallows.* **2** a person or thing that is soft and sweet: *She started work as a marshmallow and ended up a tough union leader; Some consider Walt Disney movies mere marshmallows because they don't show sex or violence.*

mar·su·pi·al (mar·SOO·pee·ul) *n.* a mammal such as the kangaroo, koala, or opossum that carries its young in a pouch outside the mother's body.

mart *n.* marketplace or centre of trade.

mar·ten (MAR·tun) *n.* **1** a weasellike animal: *the pine marten of the northern coniferous forests.* **2** its soft, thick fur.

mar·tial (MAR·shul) *adj.* of war; warlike: *a martial air; martial arts such as karate and judo; his martial bearing; her martial spirit.* — **mar·tial·ly** *adv.*

martial law *n.* military rule imposed on civilians in a crisis.

Mar·tian (MAR·shun) *n.* a supposed inhabitant of Mars. — *adj.* having to do with Mars: *the Martian landscape, surface; Martian rocks and soils, visitors.*

mar·ti·net (mar·tuh·NET) *n.* a very rigid disciplinarian: *a martinet of an editor.*

mar·ti·ni (mar·TEE·nee) *n.* **-nis** a cocktail made of gin or vodka and dry vermouth: *a dry martini; a three-martini lunch.*

mar·tyr (MAR·tur) *n.* one who suffers much and even submits to death because of his or her beliefs or principles, as the early Christians did for their faith: *a martyr in the cause of freedom; a martyr for the feminist cause; to make martyrs of people* (= make them suffer and become heroes). — *v.* cause to suffer or be killed as a martyr; **mar·tyr·dom** (-dum) *n.*

mar·vel (MAR·vul) *v.* **-vels, -velled** or **-veled, -vel·ling** or **-vel·ing 1** to be filled with astonishment. **2** express wonder at something: *Everyone marvels at her patience.* — *n.* something that causes one to marvel: *a marvel of architectural achievement; Our cook can do marvels with the right ingredients.*

mar·vel·lous or **mar·vel·ous** *adj.* wonderful or splendid. — **mar·vel·lous·ly** or **mar·vel·ous·ly** *adv.* — **mar·vel·lous·ness** or **mar·vel·ous·ness** *n.*

Marx·ism (MARX·iz·um) *n.* a theory of class struggles leading inevitably to a classless society and a "proletarian heaven," as developed by Karl Marx. — **Marx·ist** or **Marx·i·an** *n. & adj.*

mas·ca·ra (mas·CAIR·uh) *n.* cosmetic colouring for the eyelashes. — *v.* **-ras, -raed, -ra·ing:** *Chris arrived heavily mascaraed for the party.*

mas·cot *n.* a person, animal, or thing symbolizing good luck.

mas·cu·line (MASK·yuh·lin) *adj.* referring to or distinctive of the male: *masculine aggressiveness, courage; a masculine voice; the masculine gender of*

"sun" *in French.* — **mas·cu·lin·i·ty** (-LIN·uh·tee) *n.*

mash *n.* a soft, pulpy mass, as of crushed malt or grain in hot water in making beer, whisky, etc. or of bran or meal in water for feeding horses. — *v.* reduce to a mash: *a dish of mashed potatoes; a finger mashed* (= crushed) *by a door.*

mash·er *n. Slang.* a man who frequently makes passes at women.

mask *n.* **1** an artificial likeness of a person's face: *a death mask; Halloween mask; a hypocrite wearing the mask of friendship.* **2** a piece of material worn over part of the face: *Fencers and baseball catchers wear masks; gas mask; oxygen mask; ski mask; surgical mask; a stocking mask worn by a robber.* — *v.* cover or conceal, as with a mask: *She tried to mask her true feelings by smiling; a masked gunman; masked dancers at a masked ball; A painter protects areas not to be painted by using masking tape.* — **mask·er** *n.: a masker taking part in a masquerade.*

mas·kin·onge (MAS·kuh·nonj) *n. Cdn.* a species of large pike found in the Greak Lakes.

mas·och·ism (MAS·uh·kiz·um) *n.* the pleasure or sexual satisfaction derived from one's own pain and suffering. — **mas·och·ist** *n.* — **mas·och·is·tic** (-KIS·tic) *adj.*

ma·son (MAY·sun) *n.* one who builds with stone, clay, brick, or concrete.

ma·son·ry (MAY·sun·ree) *n.* **-ries 1** a structure built by a mason, as stonework or brickwork. **2** a mason's trade or skill.

masque (MASK) *n.* **1** a theatre entertainment of the 1600s having an allegorical theme, with actors wearing masks, and characterized by singing, dancing, and pageantry. **2** a masked ball or masquerade: *a Twelfth Night court masque.*

mas·quer·ade (mas·kuh·RADE) *n.* **1** a party at which masks and fancy costumes are worn. **2** a disguise or false pretence. — *v.* **-ades, -ad·ed, -ad·ing** pose: *A charlatan was caught masquerading as a physician.*

mass *n.* **1** bulk or quantity of matter, esp. large: *An elephant's body has mass.* **2** large size or number; also, the greater part or majority: *The mass of an iceberg is under water; Individuals showed interest, but in the mass* (= as a whole) *people didn't care.* **3** an amount or lump: *a dense mass of smoke; a chimney spewing masses of smoke; The flower beds were masses of colour; a plastic, shapeless, sticky mass of dough; Asia and Europe form one land mass* (= expanse); *a politician's appeal to the masses* (= common people). **4 Mass** or **mass** a celebration of the Eucharist in the Roman Catholic and other churches: *to assist at* or *attend* or *hear Mass; to celebrate, offer, say a Mass for the sick; a Mass for the dead (souls in purgatory); a solemn high Mass on Easter Sunday, not a low* (= ordinary) *Mass; one of Palestrina's Masses* (= musical settings of the Mass). — *adj.* having to do with mass or bulk: *mass* (= large-scale) *buying; a crowd seized with mass hysteria; a mass meeting of citizens.* — *v.* form or gather into a mass: *The troops were massed along the border.*

mas·sa·cre (MAS·uh·cur) *n.* a large-scale, esp. merciless

slaughter of people or animals.
— *v.* **-cres, -cred, -cring** slaughter: *Innocent infants were massacred in the war.*

mas·sage (muh·SAHZH, ·SAHJ) *n.* a rubdown of the body or a part of it by kneading, stroking, etc. to relax muscles or stimulate activity in an organ: *a cardiac massage; a facial massage given in a beauty parlour; a massage treatment.*
— *v.* **mas·sag·es, mas·saged, mas·sag·ing 1** give a massage to someone: *to massage one's body; to massage* (= flatter) *one's ego.* **2** manipulate data, as by a computer.
— **mas·sag·er** or **mas·sag·ist** *n.* Also **mas·seur** (ma·SUR) *n.*, **mas·seuse** (ma·SOOZ), *fem.*

mass-cult *n. Informal.* popular culture as spread through TV and other mass media.

mas·sive (MAS·iv) *adj.* having a large mass; large in quantity, scope, or degree: *a man of massive build; massive rocks; a massive assault, hemorrhage; threat of massive retaliation using atomic weapons; The patient suffered a massive stroke and is in critical condition; a massive* (= impressive) *structure.*

mass media *n. pl.* [usually takes pl. v.] means of communication with the masses, as motion pictures, newspapers, magazines, radio, and TV; also called the **media.**

mass-produce (mas·pruh·DUCE) *v.* **-duc·es, -duced, -duc·ing** produce on a large scale, esp. by use of machinery. — **mass production** *n.*

mass transit *n.* subways and such transportation for the masses.

mast *n.* **1** a long vertical pole or spar supporting a ship's sails, yards, rigging, etc.; also, any supporting post, as of a flagpole, crane, derrick, aerial, or antenna: *Flags are flown at half-mast* (= lowered halfway down the pole) *during mourning.* **2** fallen nuts of forest trees serving as food for swine.

mas·ter (MAS·tur) *n.* **1** a person with power or authority, as the male head of a household, the captain of a merchant ship, a male teacher or tutor, the employer of a servant, etc.: *The taxing master of a court can have your legal bills reduced if found to be excessive; You are your own master when self-employed.* **2 Master** [courtesy title for a boy not old enough to be called "Mister"]: *Master John, son of Mr. Smith.* **3** one who heads an institution or activity: *the Master of Massey College.* **4** the holder of a university degree between bachelor and doctor: *Master of Arts, Education, Science; She's working on her **master's** (degree).* **5** a great artist, musician, or author; also, one who has reached a high level of learning or skill: *the old masters* (= great painters before 1700); *a past master of the art; a master of deceit; apprentices, journeymen, and masters; a chess master; a masters competition in swimming, track and field, etc. for people over a certain age; the Masters tournament for golf masters.* **6** a controlling source or original, as the matrix of a phonograph record or a duplicating stencil or plate.
— *adj.*: *The **master bedroom** is the largest in the house; a master builder, craftsman, hand; a master plumber, not just an apprentice or journeyman; a master* (= main) *switch; the master* (= original) *tape of a motion picture.*

— *v.* become master of or expert in an area: *Can humans master the elements? Kay has mastered calculus.*

mas·ter·ful (MAS·tur·ful) *adj.* **1** domineering, esp. by force of personality: *Lin had become too masterful for Lee to live with.* **2** showing great ability; masterly: *a masterful answer, performance, timing; the masterful Sherlock Holmes.* — **mas·ter·ful·ly** *adv.*

master key *n.* a key that opens many locks.

mas·ter·ly *adj.* expert or skilful: *a masterly command of the language;* **adv.**: *a masterly* (= skilfully) *executed plan.*

mas·ter·mind (MAS·tur·mined) *n.* one who plans and directs an operation or enterprise; *v.*: *a plot masterminded by the deposed king.*

master of ceremonies *n.* **1** one in charge of the formalities of a ceremonial function, as at a church service. **2** one who hosts an entertainment program or banquet, introducing guests, performers, etc.

mas·ter·piece (MAS·tur·peece) *n.* an extraordinary piece of workmanship; one's greatest work: *an enduring masterpiece.*

master plan *n.* an overall or general plan, as of a city.

mas·ter·stroke (MAS·tur·stoke) *n.* a masterly action or its effect: *a masterstroke of genius.*

mas·ter·work (MAS·tur·wurk) *n.* a masterpiece.

mas·ter·y (MAS·tuh·ree) *n.* **-ter·ies** command or control: *her mastery of English; an election giving one party mastery* (= the upper hand) *over another.*

mast·head *n.* **1** the top of a ship's mast. **2** in a newspaper or magazine, the title, address, etc. usually carried at the top of the editorial page. **3** the "flag" or name plate at the top of the front page of a periodical.

mas·ti·cate (MAS·tuh·cate) *v.* **-cates, -cat·ed, -cat·ing** chew food or crush rubber to a pulp.
— **mas·ti·ca·tion** (·CAY·shun) *n.*

mat *n.* **1** a plaited, woven, or felted piece of coarse material or small rug for use on the floor as covering, protective padding, for wiping shoes upon, etc.: *a bath mat; door mat; exercise mat; place mat (for table settings); welcome mat.* **2** a thick tangle or knotted condition: *a mat of messy hair.* **3** a border or background, as for a picture in framing it. **4** a dull surface or finish given to colours, glass, metals, etc.; also **mat, matte. 5** *Informal.* a matrix or printer's mold.
— *v.* **mats, mat·ted, mat·ting 1** make into or cover with a mat: *The hair is all matted; a wall matted with ivy.* **2** put a border or background around a picture, etc. **3** give a dull surface to metals, glass, etc.

mat·a·dor (MAT·uh·dor) *n.* a bullfighter.

match *n.* **1** a person or thing that is like another, hence considered in an equal or opposite role: *A flyweight is no match for a heavyweight; Cy met his match in Sue; Sue is more than his match in* (= is better at) *problem-solving.* **2** a matching, as a contest: *a chess match; football match; to promote, stage a match; a championship, play-off, return match.* **3** a mating, as a marriage: *They're a good match as husband and wife; Jo and Ed will make a perfect match.* **4** a splinter of

wood or a cardboard strip tipped with a substance that will catch fire under friction, as when struck on the specially prepared surface of a "safety match"; to light or *strike a match; The arsonist put* or *set a match to the house; book matches* (= strip of paper matches in a cardboard folder); *a box of matches.*
— *v.* be or get a match for a person or thing: *Red and green don't match; Her beauty is matched by her wit; A blue sock cannot be matched with a red one; She finds herself matched against a world champion; She doesn't* **match up** (= is not equal) *to her rival; a* **matching grant** or **matching funds** *to induce the recipient to come up with half the project's costs.*

match·book *n.* a cardboard folder of safety matches on a strip of paper.

match·less *adj.* without equal; peerless.

match·mak·er (MATCH·may·kur) *n.* **1** one who makes matches for burning. **2** one who arranges marriages or boxing matches. — **match·mak·ing** *n.*

match·wood *n.* pine, aspen, and such wood splintered for making "match sticks."

mate *v.* **mates, mat·ed, mat·ing** join as a pair or couple, esp. in sexual union: *a frog's mating call; Some animals don't mate in captivity; You get a mule if you mate a horse with a donkey; A queen bee mates with a drone; Birds mate in the spring; Spring is the* **mating** *season.*
— *n.* **1** either individual of a matched pair or couple: *a bird crying for its mate; Where is the mate to this sock?* **2** a companion: *He's my apartment mate, not really a roommate; The running mate of the presidential candidate in U.S. elections runs for vice-president.* **3** an assistant or helper. **4** a deck officer of a merchant ship or a naval petty officer.
— *combining form.* companion: *classmate, helpmate, housemate, playmate, roommate, schoolmate.*

ma·te·ri·al (muh·TEER·ee·ul) *n.* basic matter or resource from which other things may be made: *building materials; packing material; padding material; promotional material such as buttons and banners; radioactive material; raw material(s); reading material such as books and papers; paper, pencil, and other writing materials; She's promotable because she's executive material; material* (= cloth) *for dresses; He has enough material to write a book; material for a book.*
— *adj.* **1** physical and tangible, not spiritual or ideal: *the material world; our material comforts, possessions, well-being.* **2** tending to corrupt: *material greed.* **3** having substance or importance: *evidence, facts, testimony, etc. that are material to a case or argument; A bystander was held as a* **material witness** *to the crime.*
— **ma·te·ri·al·ly** *adv.*

ma·te·ri·al·ism (muh·TEER·ee·uh·liz·um) *n.* a theory, doctrine, or tendency that stresses matter and material aspects to the prejudice of the intellectual and the spiritual. — **ma·te·ri·al·ist** *n. & adj.*
— **ma·te·ri·al·is·tic** (-uh·LIS·tic) *adj.*

ma·te·ri·al·ize (muh·TEER·ee·uh·lize) *v.* **-liz·es, -lized, -liz·ing** **1** take physical form or give physical form to something: *A spirit may materialize at a séance.* **2** become real: *Impractical plans don't materialize.*
— **ma·te·ri·al·i·za·tion** (-luh·ZAY·shun) *n.*

ma·te·ri·el or **ma·té·ri·el** (muh·teer·ee·EL) *n.* military or industrial equipment, supplies, etc. as distinguished from manpower.

ma·ter·nal (muh·TUR·nul) *adj.* **1** motherly: *the maternal instinct to protect children.* **2** on or from the mother's side of the family: *a maternal aunt, grandfather, inheritance.* — **ma·ter·nal·ly** *adv.*

ma·ter·ni·ty (muh·TUR·nuh·tee) *n.* pregnancy and motherhood.
— *adj.* having to do with maternity: *maternity benefits, dresses, leave; a hospital's maternity ward; maternity wear (for the pregnant).*

math or **maths** *n.* [short form] mathematics.

math·e·mat·ics (math·uh·MAT·ics) *n.pl.* [takes sing. v.] the science of quantities and their relationships, using numbers, as in arithmetic, symbols, as in algebra, and figures, as in geometry.
— **math·e·mat·i·cal** *adj.;* **math·e·mat·i·cal·ly** *adv.*
— **math·e·ma·ti·cian** (MATH·uh·muh·TISH·un) *n.*

mat·i·nee or **mat·i·née** (mat·un·AY) *n.* an afternoon performance of a play, opera, motion picture, etc.

matri- *combining form.* mother: *matriarch, matricide, matrimony.*

ma·tri·arch (MAY·tree·ark) *n.* a mother who is the head of a family group or tribe.
— **ma·tri·ar·chy** (-kee) *n.* **-chies.**

ma·tri·cide (MAT·ruh·cide, MAY·truh-) *n.* **1** one who kills his or her mother. **2** the crime itself.
— **ma·tri·ci·dal** (-SYE·dul) *adj.*

ma·tric·u·late (muh·TRICK·yuh·late) *v.* **-lates, -lat·ed, -lat·ing** enrol in or be admitted to a college as a student.
— **ma·tric·u·la·tion** (-LAY·shun) *n.*

mat·ri·mo·ny (MAT·ruh·moh·nee) *n.* **-nies 1** marriage, esp. as a sacrament. **2** the married state.
— **mat·ri·mo·ni·al** (-MOH·nee·ul) *adj.*

ma·trix (MAY·trix) *n.,* *pl.* **-tri·ces** (-seez) or **-trix·es** a mould by which something is formed or shaped, as the skin at the base of a fingernail, the rock or groundmass in which crystals are found embedded, a female die for casting types, or a papier-mâché impression for making printing plates.

ma·tron (MAY·trun) *n.* **1** a motherly type of sophisticated or well-to-do woman. **2** a mature woman in a supervisory role, as in a hospital, dormitory, jail, or school. — **ma·tron·ly** *adv.*

matron of honour *n.* a married woman as chief bridesmaid.

matte (MAT) *n.* **1** unrefined metal, as copper, that sinks to the bottom of a smelter. **2** dull surface or finish; mat.
— *adj.* also **matt,** finished with a dull, not shiny surface: *a matte photographic print, projection screen; a semi-matt print.*

mat·ter (MAT·ur) *n.* **1** material or substance that makes up something, esp. physical: *Matter exists in solid, liquid, and gaseous states; the mind's sway over matter* (= material part of the universe). **2** a subject of thought, speech, activity, etc.: *business matters; a matter of common knowledge; a matter of course* (= something

routine or happening regularly); *a matter of life and death; Aging is a matter of time; Owning a home is a matter of time and money; What's the matter?* (= What's wrong?); *to arrange, clear up, complicate, settle, simplify, straighten out matters; to pursue* or *take up a matter; We'll give the matter serious consideration; We will give you our opinion **without mincing matters*** (= candidly); *Going to college is no easy matter; Committing a crime is no laughing matter; a matter of grave importance; to bring matters to a head; Matters came to a head; He's not an expert in matters of constitutional law;* **For that matter** (= concerning that), *he is not even a lawyer; a matter of some urgency; Compatibility is at the heart of the matter.* 3 material or things: *the **front matter** of a book such as the title page, contents page, and preface; foreign matter in one's eye; grey matter* (= brains); *postal matter such as letters and parcels; printed matter; reading matter; organic, solid, vegetable matter; the subject matter of a poem.*
— **as a matter of fact** actually.
— **no matter** of no importance: *I forget who said it, but it's no matter; No matter who asks you, refuse; Assert yourself,* **no matter what** (= whatever happens).
— *v.* have importance; count: *Does it matter who said it? It matters little (to me).*

matter-of-fact (MAT·ur·ov·FACT) *adj.* factual and prosaic: *a matter-of-fact account, report, tone of voice.*

mat·tress (MAT·ris) *n.* 1 a padding of straw, foam rubber, cotton, etc. to sleep on, usually on a bed: *a firm mattress; soft mattress; a spring mattress (supported by coil springs).* 2 an air mattress.

mat·u·ra·tion (mach·oo·RAY·shun) *n.* maturing process.

ma·ture (muh·TYOOR, -CHOOR) *adj.* fully developed or grown: *mature fruits; a mature wine; her mature wisdom.*
— *v.* **-tures, -tured, -tur·ing** become mature: *Some mature faster than others; A wine has to mature to have body; The bond will mature* (= become due for payment) *in 10 years.* — **ma·ture·ly** *adv.*

ma·tu·ri·ty (muh·TYOOR·uh·tee, -CHOOR·uh·tee) *n.* a matured condition: *to reach maturity.*

maud·lin (MAWD·lin) *adj.* sentimental in a tearful or silly way: *a maudlin soap opera; He gets maudlin at family reunions.*

maul *n.* a heavy mallet or hammer for driving stakes, wedges, etc.
— *v.* handle roughly; bruise or mangle: *mauled by a tiger; a new play mauled* (= badly criticized) *by critics.*
— **maul·er** *n.*

maun·der (MAWN·dur) *v.* talk or act in a rambling or confused manner. — **maun·der·er** *n.*

mau·so·le·um (maw·suh·LEE·um, maw·zuh·LEE·um) *n.* **-le·ums** or **-le·a** (-LEE·uh) a magnificent tomb built above ground, as the Taj Mahal or the original Mausoleum of Halicarnassus, Turkey, one of the "seven wonders" of the ancient world.

mauve (MOHV, MAUV) *n.* 1 a delicate shade of purple or violet. 2 such a dye. Also *adj.*

mav·er·ick (MAV·ur·ick) *n. & adj. Informal.* nonconformist, esp. in politics.

ma·ven (MAY·vun) *n. Informal.* expert or connoisseur: *our microwave maven.*

maw *n.* the oral or similar cavity through which a bird, animal, machine, etc. devours something.

mawk·ish *adj.* sentimental in an excessive or insincere style: *a mawkish scene from Dickens.*
— **mawk·ish·ly** *adv.*; **mawk·ish·ness** *n.*

max·i (MAK·see) *n., adj. & combining form, pl.* **max·is** maximum; very long: *She wore a maxicoat over a miniskirt; A dress of maxi length is a maxi; a maxi-taxi* (= very large taxi).

max·im (MAX·im) *n.* a proverb or precept, esp. a practical rule of conduct, as "A stitch in time saves nine."

max·i·mize (MAX·uh·mize) *v.* **-miz·es, -mized, -miz·ing** magnify or increase to the utmost; intensify highly: *to maximize our efforts to achieve an end; to maximize profits with minimum capital; He stayed just long enough on the job to maximize his pension before retiring.*

max·i·mum (MAX·uh·mum) *adj. & n.* (of) the greatest possible or attained quantity, number, value, etc.: *the maximum (speed limit) on a highway; yesterday's maximum temperature; The noise is at its maximum on weekends; a maximum-security prison.*
— **max·i·mal** (-mul) *adj.*

may *auxiliary v., pt.* **might** (MITE) 1 [expressing possibility]: *I may be late; You might have asked yesterday; It may rain tonight; then again, it might not.* 2 [expressing permission]: *You may come in; May I have an apple?* 3 [expressing hope, contingency, etc.]: *He goes to work so that his family may be happy; May you be happy!*

may·be (MAY·bee) *adv.* perhaps: *Maybe I shouldn't have said that; He is maybe about 70 years old.*

May Day *n.* 1 May 1, a spring festival in some countries. 2 Labour Day in socialist countries.

May·day *n.* a distress signal used by ships and aircraft to radio for help.

may·hem (MAY·hem, -hum) *n.* 1 [legal use] a crime of violence that maims a person. 2 violent or willful havoc: *murder and mayhem; the mayhem in our hockey rinks; the mayhem on Children's TV.*

may·n't (MAINT) may not.

may·o (MAY·oh) [short form] mayonnaise.

may·on·naise (MAY·uh·naze) *n.* a thick salad dressing made of egg yolks, oil, and vinegar.

may·or (MAY·ur) *n.* the elected head of a city or borough. — **may·or·al** *adj.*; **may·or·ship** *n.*

may·or·al·ty (MAY·ur·ul·tee) *n.* **-ties** a mayor's term of office or position.

maze *n.* 1 a labyrinth. 2 anything intricate or confusing. — **maz·y** *adj.*

M.C. (EM·see) *n.* same as MASTER OF CEREMONIES.

Mc·Coy (muh·COY) *n.* **the real McCoy** *Slang.* the real or genuine person or thing.

Mc·In·tosh (MAK·in·tosh) *n. Cdn.* a red variety of juicy eating apple. Also **McIntosh Red.**

me (MEE) *pron.* objective case of "I": *Give it to me; people like you and me; the **me** generation of people concerned about their own well-being.*

mead (MEED) *n.* **1** an alcoholic drink made from honey. **2** [old use] meadow.

mead·ow (MED·oh) *n.* a tract of moist, low-lying, level grassland; also **mead·ow·land.** — **mead·ow·y** *adj.*

mea·gre or **mea·ger** (MEE·gur) *adj.* **1** poor or scanty: *a meagre attendance, diet; a meagre fare of bread and soup; a meagre income.* **2** thin, not fleshy or rich: *a meagre face, soil.* — **mea·gre·ly** or **mea·ger·ly** *adv.* — **mea·gre·ness** or **mea·ger·ness** *n.*

meal (MEEL) *n.* **1** food for eating at any time, usually at a **meal·time** such as morning, noon, and evening; breakfast, lunch, dinner, etc.: *to cook, eat, enjoy, fix, have, order, prepare, serve a meal; a heavy, light, skimpy, square, sumptuous meal; Dinner is the main meal of the day.* **2** coarsely ground unbolted grain, esp. corn. **3** any substance ground to powder: *bone meal.*

meal·y (MEE·lee) *adj.* **meal·i·er, -i·est** **1** of, like, or covered with meal. **2** same as MEALY-MOUTHED.

mealy-mouthed *adj.* not speaking plainly or sincerely; given to mincing matters.

mean (MEEN) *v.* **means, meant** (MENT), **mean·ing** **1** signify or refer: *What does "lark" mean? Do you know what it means to be an orphan? "Smoke" means a cigar to him, but to her it means fire.* **2** have in mind, as thought, intention, or purpose: *I didn't mean to hurt you; I mean you no harm; I meant it as a joke; It was meant for everyone; He **means** well (= has good intentions); Your friendship means much (= is of great importance) to us.*
— *adj.* **1** bad by nature or disposition; petty, selfish, hard to manage, etc.: *Backbiting is mean; She's always generous to the poor, never mean (= stingy); I feel mean after saying that.* **2** *Informal.* skilful: *an excellent pitcher who throws a mean curve; He plays a mean banjo (= plays the banjo skilfully); She can run a mean mile (= run a mile easily).* **3** low; humble; poor; common: *the meanest flower of the field; a mean cottage; A Juno Award is **no mean** (= is a fine) tribute to a young singer.* **4** in the middle or halfway between greater and lesser things, opposites, or extremes; average: *the mean annual temperature of a region.*
— *n.* **1** something that is mean or average: *7 is the mean of 3, 5, 9, and 11; the **golden mean** between too much and too little of anything.* **2 means** *n.pl.* [takes sing. or pl. v.] agency or resource by which a purpose is achieved: *by fair means or foul; a means to an end; The end does not justify the means; You run into debt if you live beyond your means (= income); people of moderate means (= wealth); He got through **by means of** cheating; **By all means** (= certainly) let's help her if we can; It's **by no means** (= not at all) the last word on the subject; a **means test** to check how poor you are; the **ways and means** of avoiding a tax.*
— **mean·ly** *adv.*; **mean·ness** *n.*

me·an·der (mee·AN·dur) *n.* a winding course, as of a stream with a series of U-bends.
— *v.* follow a winding course: *a meandering river; Children meander (= wander aimlessly) through the park.*

mean·ie or **mean·y** (MEE·nee) *n.* **mean·ies** *Informal.* one who is mean or petty.

meaning (MEE·ning) *n.* what is meant, as by a word, action, gesture, or other expression: *the meaning of "lexicographer"; a clear, double, figurative, literal meaning; The meaning is obscure; the accepted meaning (= sense) of a word; Lexicographers never lose their meaning (= importance); Childhood experiences often define the meanings (= things of significance) in your life; if you **get my meaning** (Informal for if you understand me).* — **mean·ing·ful** *adj.*

meant *pt. & pp.* of MEAN.

mean·time *n.* **in the meantime** during the time between two happenings; also **mean·while.**

meany same as MEANIE.

mea·sles (MEE·zulz) *n.pl.* [takes sing. or pl. v.] **1** a contagious virus disease characterized by inflammation of the mucous membranes, high fever, and a rash; also called "seven-day measles." **2** a milder disease characterized by a pink rash; also called "German measles" and "three-day measles."

mea·sly (MEEZ·lee) *adj.* **-sli·er, -sli·est** **1** having measles. **2** *Informal.* worthless or contemptible: *a measly little gift.*

meas·ure (MEZH·ur) *n.* **1** the length, weight, area, capacity, etc. of something according to a standard or system: *A hectare is a measure of area; cubic, dry, liquid, metric, square measure; a measure of time such as the minute or hour; a suit that has been **made to measure** (= made to fit the customer); The tailor will take your measure for a suit; The boss may **take your measure** (= judge you) by how you dress; My success is **in a measure** or **in some measure** or **in a large measure** (= to some or to a large degree) due to her; My gratitude to her is **beyond measure** (= without limit).* **2** a measuring instrument: *Use a tape measure.* **3** something measured: *six measures of grain; I'll add $10 to what I owe you **for good measure** (= as extra); She had some measure of success as a lawyer; the full measure of my gratitude.* **4** something measured rhythmically, as a foot of verse, a bar of music, or a dance. **5** a course of action: *to carry out or take measures against crime; coercive, drastic, extreme, harsh, preventive, safety, security, stern, stop-gap, stringent measures.* **6** an act of a legislature; statute: *a measure awaiting a vote in the House of Commons.*
— *v.* **-ures, -ured, -ur·ing** take the measure of a person or thing: *Tailors measure customers; This room measures 10 m by 12 (= is 10 m wide and 12 m long); You can't measure her performance against (= compare her performance with) his; He lost his job because he didn't **measure up** or **measure up to expectations.***
— **measured** *adj.* **1** having been measured: *a measured mile (for checking speed); a measured portion.* **2** regular or rhythmical: *the measured beat of a drum; walking at*

a measured pace; the measured tread of a walk.
3 careful and precise: a measured response.

meas·ure·ment (MEZH·ur·munt) n. a way, act, result, or system of measuring: the measurements of a room; exact measurements; the measurements of a human figure (around the bust or chest, waist, and hips).

meat (MEET) n. 1 animal flesh used as food, esp. the "red meat" of cattle, hogs, and sheep: **Meat and potatoes** are considered basic or essential foods; cooked meats; to carve, cure, cut, fry, roast, slice meat; chopped, kosher, lean, minced, tender, tough meat. 2 food; also, edible part: "One man's meat is another man's poison" (= What is good for one may be harmful to another); to scoop out the meat of a coconut; the meat (= substance or essence) of his argument; Thrillers are **meat and drink** to her (= She gets a lot of satisfaction from reading thrillers).

meat·head n. Slang. a dunce or blockhead.

meat·pack·ing (MEET·pack·ing) n. the industry of slaughtering animals and preparing their meat for sale.

meat·y (MEE·tee) adj. meat·i·er, -i·est 1 having meat or fat: a meaty morsel, texture, wrestler. 2 having substance and content for thought: a meaty essay, letter, speech. — **meat·i·ness** n.

mec·ca (MEC·uh) n. a place one longs to visit, as Mecca in Saudi Arabia, the chief holy city of Moslems.

me·chan·ic (muh·CAN·ic) n. a person skilled in the use of tools and machinery; machinist or repairman: an auto mechanic.
— **mechanics** pl. 1 [takes sing. v.] the physics of forces acting on bodies when at rest and in motion: fluid mechanics; quantum mechanics. 2 [takes pl. v.] practical or functional details: the mechanics of a contract; the mechanics of playing on an instrument; the mechanics of punctuation.

me·chan·i·cal (muh·CAN·uh·cul) adj. having to do with machines or mechanics: a girl with mechanical aptitude; a mechanical dummy who can't change a light bulb; a puppet's mechanical (= machinelike) movements; The longer a crowbar, the greater its **mechanical advantage** (= the amount of work done relative to the force applied); A draftsman's **mechanical drawing** made with instruments shows the exact shape and size of an object to be made; **Mechanical engineering** deals with mechanical power and machinery; A **mechanical pencil** has a supply of lead that may be pushed forward as you write. — **me·chan·i·cal·ly** adv.

mech·a·nism (MEC·uh·niz·um) n. a mechanical part, system, or machinery: the mechanism of a watch; the mechanism of the universe; a defence mechanism for protection against having to face disagreeable situations; an escape mechanism such as daydreaming.
— **mech·a·nis·tic** (-NIS·tic) adj.

mech·a·nize (MEC·uh·nize) v. -niz·es, -nized, -niz·ing 1 do work by machine rather than by hand: The post office has mechanized the sorting of mail. 2 equip with machinery, as an army with armoured vehicles, tanks, etc. — **mech·a·ni·za·tion** (-nuh·ZAY·shun) n.

med·al (MED·ul) n. a metal disk resembling a coin, to commemorate a person or event, given as an award for achievement, or bearing a religious emblem or picture:

a medal struck in honour of a hero; to award, earn, give a medal; the gold, silver, and bronze medals of the Olympics; the Canada Medal for meritorious service beyond the call of duty.
— **med·al·list** or **med·al·ist** (MED·ul·ist) n.

me·dal·lion (muh·DAL·yun) n. 1 a large medal. 2 a medal design, as on a tablet, an architectural panel, or a carpet.

med·dle (MED·ul) v. med·dles, med·dled, med·dling busy oneself or interfere: to meddle in or with other people's affairs. — **med·dler** n.

med·dle·some (MED·ul·sum) adj. having a tendency to meddle: a meddlesome busybody, relative; his meddlesome nature.

me·di·a (MEE·dee·uh) n.pl. 1 [often used as sing.] same as MASS MEDIA: electronic media such as radio and TV; the news media; print media such as newspapers and magazines; The media find [rarely finds] that bad news makes good headlines; the newer media [rarely medias] such as radio and TV; a media relations officer. 2 pl. of MEDIUM.

media event n. an event that has been stage-managed for its publicity value.

me·di·ae·val (mee·dee·EE·vul, med·ee-) same as MEDIEVAL.

me·di·al (MEE·dee·ul) adj. being in the middle: a medial position; the medial, not initial "p" of "principal."

me·di·an (MEE·dee·un) n. a middle or intermediate number, line, etc.: The median (= average of the middle figures) of 1, 3, 5, 7, and 11 is 5; The median of 1, 3, 5, and 7 is 4. — **adj.**: the median income of high school teachers; the **median** or **median strip** separating the opposite lanes of a highway.

me·di·ate (MEE·dee·ate) v. -ates, -at·ed, -at·ing 1 act as a go-between in a dispute: to mediate between the two factions in a dispute. 2 to help settle something by mediating: to mediate a conflict, dispute, issue. 3 to achieve something by mediating: to mediate an agreement, to mediate the release of prisoners.
— **adj.** (-dee·it) with something intervening or in the middle; not direct or immediate: a mediate contact (through a third party). — **me·di·ate·ly** adv.
— **me·di·a·tion** (-AY·shun) n.
— **me·di·a·tor** (-ay·tur) n.; **me·di·a·trix** (-AY·trix) fem.

med·ic n. Informal. a medical student, practitioner, or a member of a medical corps.

Med·i·caid or **med·i·caid** (MED·uh·caid) n. a medical program to help the needy, as in the U.S.

med·i·cal (MED·uh·cul) adj. having to do with medicine: a medical missionary, practitioner.
— **med·i·cal·ly** adv.

Med·i·care or **med·i·care** (MED·uh·care) n. 1 a program of medical and hospital services run by a government. 2 a similar program for people aged 65 and over, as in the U.S.

med·i·cate (MED·uh·cate) v. -cates, -cat·ed, -cat·ing treat with medicine: Physicians are not supposed to *medicate themselves;* **medicated** *cough drops, lotions, shampoos.*

med·i·ca·tion (med·uh·CAY·shun) *n.* medicine as administered: *a patient on medication for a heart condition; She's under medication; to dispense, give, receive, take medication; medication errors.*

me·dic·i·nal (muh·DIS·un·ul) *adj.* having to do with the curing of diseases: *the medicinal properties of herbs.* — **me·dic·i·nal·ly** *adv.*

med·i·cine (MED·uh·sin) *n.* **1** a substance or preparation used in preventing or treating disease: *Take some medicine for your cough; Doctors prescribe medicines* (= drugs); *nonprescription, over-the-counter, patent, proprietary medicines; The punishment proved strong medicine* (= cure); *They* **took their medicine** (*Informal* for accepted their punishment) *cheerfully.* **2** the science or art of treating and preventing diseases: *Doctors practise, study medicine; clinical, folk, holistic, internal, preventive, socialized, veterinary medicine.*

medicine man *n.* a healer who relies on supernatural power, as a witch doctor.

med·i·co (MED·uh·coh) *n.* **-cos** *Informal.* a medical student or practitioner.

me·di·e·val (mee·dee·EE·vul, med·ee·) *adj.* of the Middle Ages: *medieval castles, charm, churches, cities, costume, Europe, heritage, monasteries, studies, times, warfare.*

me·di·o·cre (mee·dee·OH·cur) *adj.* of average or ordinary quality; relatively inferior. — **me·di·oc·ri·ty** (-OC·ruh·tee) *n.* **-ties.**

med·i·tate (MED·uh·tate) *v.* **-tates, -tat·ed, -tat·ing** **1** think with concentration of mind: *to meditate on or upon the quality of our lives.* **2** consider or contemplate an action: *Hamlet meditated revenge.* — **med·i·ta·tion** (-TAY·shun) *n.* — **med·i·ta·tive** (-tay·tiv) *adj.;* **med·i·ta·tive·ly** *adv.*

Med·i·ter·ra·ne·an (MED·uh·tuh·RAY·nee·un) *n. & adj.* the sea enclosed by Europe, Africa, and Asia: *a cruise in the Mediterranean (Sea); the Mediterranean origin of Western civilization; a Mediterranean route.*

me·di·um (MEE·dee·um) *n., pl.* **me·di·a 1** a means of conveying or communicating: *Speech is a medium of communication; Money is a medium of exchange for goods; French is the medium of instruction in French schools; the press as an advertising medium; advertising media such as billboards, direct mail, TV, radio, and periodicals; print and electronic media; local and national media.* **2** *pl.* **mediums** a person through whom spirits communicate with the living: *a spiritualistic medium.* **3** a substance or environment in which something exists or operates: *a culture medium for bacteria; ether as the medium through which light is transmitted; an artist who paints in the oil medium* (= pigment with oil as vehicle). **4** a middle condition or quality: *a happy medium between two extremes; adj.: a man of medium height; a medium income group; a medium radio frequency range (between high and low); a medium-security (not minimum- or maximum-security) prison.*

med·ley (MED·lee) *n.* **-leys 1** mixture of various elements or parts: *a musical medley of marches; a medley relay in swimming (in which team members swim the butterfly, backstroke, breaststroke, and freestyle in that order).* **2** a hodgepodge or jumble.

meed *n.* [poetic use] deserved portion: *meed of praise, victory.*

meek *adj.* **1** patient and submissive, not self-assertive: *the meek and gentle nature of a religious person.* **2** not assertive; spiritless: *I find him too meek and spineless.*

meet *v.* **meets, met, meet·ing 1** come into contact or communication: *We were both at the party but didn't meet; Please meet me at home; Parallel lines never meet; (the corner) where King Street meets Second Avenue; There's more to this than meets the eye* (= This is not so simple as it seems); *We'll meet* (= play against each other) *in the finals; I'd like you to meet* (= be introduced to) *my family; We met all night over the matter; We met them halfway* (= compromised with them); *The Government and the Opposition meet head-on during question period; I have to meet the 8 o'clock flight from New York.* **2** deal with as required: *to meet a challenge, deadline, debt, an enemy, a threat.* — **meet with 1** meet by chance; come across; come upon: *Cab drivers meet with all sorts of people; Her plans met with success* (= were successful); *His idea met with* (= received) *approval; I met with an accident on my way home; met up with an old buddy at the fair.* **2** meet and talk with someone: *We met with the demonstrators; We met face-to-face with their leaders to resolve our differences.* — *n.* a coming together for a competition, the place where it is held, or the people at it: *a swimming meet; track-and-field meets.* — *adj.* [old use] proper or becoming: *It is meet and just that we should do this.*

meeting *n.* a gathering or assembly, esp. to discuss or decide on something: *to adjourn, arrange, break up, call, call off, cancel, conduct, convene, hold, organize, preside over a meeting; a chance, clandestine, closed, open, public, secret meeting between the two; a mass meeting of students; a board, business, cabinet, committee, prayer, staff meeting; She was at the meeting; The chair calls a meeting to order.*

mega- *combining form.* **1** large: *megalomania, megaproject, megavitamins.* **2** one million: *megadeath, megahertz, megaton.*

meg·a·bit (MEG·uh·bit) *n.* one million bits of computer data.

meg·a·bucks (MEG·uh·bucks) *n. pl.* money in millions of dollars.

meg·a·byte (MEG·uh·byte) *n.* one million bytes.

meg·a·death (MEG·uh·deth) *n.* in atomic warfare, a unit of one million deaths.

meg·a·lo·ma·nia (MEG·uh·loh·MAY·nee·uh) *n.* a mental disorder marked by delusions of personal grandeur, power, wealth, etc.; **meg·a·lo·ma·ni·ac** *n. & adj.*

meg·a·lop·o·lis (meg·uh·LOP·uh·lis) *n.* a continuous region of several metropolitan areas, as Hamilton - Burlington - Oakville - Mississauga - Toronto - Oshawa in Ontario.

meg·a·phone (MEG·uh·phone) *n.* a funnel-shaped, hand-held device for making a voice louder, as used by cheerleaders.

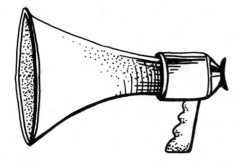

meg·a·ton (MEG·uh·tun) *n.* the explosive power of one million tons of TNT.

meg·a·vi·ta·mins (MEG·uh·vye·tuh·minz) *n. pl.* vitamins in large quantities.

me·gil·lah (muh·GIL·uh, "G" as in "go") *n. Slang.* a boringly detailed account: *the whole megillah.*

meg·ohm *n.* one million ohms.

mel·an·cho·li·a (mel·un·COH·lee·uh) *n.* a mental illness marked by extreme depression. — **mel·an·cho·li·ac** *n. & adj.*

mel·an·chol·ic (mel·un·COL·ic) *adj.* 1 suffering from melancholia. 2 melancholy.

mel·an·chol·y (MEL·un·col·ee) *adj.* gloomy, depressing, or pensive: *a melancholy person, scene, smile, song, thought.* — *n.* a melancholy condition or mood: *afflicted with melancholy.*

mé·lange (may·LAHNZH, -LAHNJ) *n. French.* an incongruous mixture; hodgepodge.

meld *n.* 1 in card games, a scoring card or combination. 2 a mixture or blend. — *v.* announce or show a meld of cards.

me·lee (MAY·lay, may·LAY) *n.* a confused hand-to-hand fight among a number of people.

mel·lif·lu·ous (muh·LIF·loo·us) *adj.* flowing like honey: *mellifluous speech, voices, words.* — **mel·lif·lu·ous·ly** *adv.*

mel·low (MEL·oh) *adj.* soft, sweet, etc., as fruit when it ripens; not sharp, harsh, or strident: *mellow apples, colours; mellow soil that is rich and loamy; the mellow tones of a violin; mellow* (=mature) *wines, wisdom.* — *v.* make or become mellow: *People tend to mellow with age.* — **mel·low·ness** *n.*

me·lod·ic (muh·LOD·ic) *adj.* 1 of or like a melody: *the melodic pattern of a poem; a melodic, not harmonic sequence.* 2 melodious. — **me·lod·i·cal·ly** *adv.*

me·lo·di·ous (muh·LOH·dee·us) *adj.* pleasant-sounding; tuneful. — **me·lo·di·ous·ly** *adv.;* **me·lo·di·ous·ness** *n.*

mel·o·dra·ma (MEL·uh·drah·muh) *n.* drama of a sensational kind with much action and play of emotion. — **mel·o·dra·mat·ic** (-druh·MAT·ic) *adj.*

mel·o·dy (MEL·uh·dee) *n.* **-dies** 1 sweet music. 2 a song or tune: *to hum, play, sing a melody; a haunting melody.* — **mel·o·dist** *n.*

mel·on (MEL·un) *n.* the usually large, juicy fruit of a trailing plant of the gourd family, as the watermelon and cantaloupe.

melt *v.* 1 change or pass from solid to liquid state: *Ice melts to form water; Wax has a low melting point* (=melting temperature). 2 dissolve: *Sugar melts in coffee; Immigration has made America the melting pot or crucible of many cultures.* 3 disappear gradually, as clouds or mist in the sun; blend or merge: *The spy melted into the crowd.* — *n.* melted metal, esp. a quantity melted at one time.

melt·down *n.* 1 the melting of the uranium core of a reactor resulting in release of radioactivity. 2 a devastating change: *the stock-market meltdown* (=crash) *of October 1987.*

mel·ton (MEL·tun) *n.* a short-napped, heavy, smooth, woollen cloth used for overcoats.

melt·wat·er (MELT·waw·tur) *n.* water from melted snow and ice.

mem·ber (MEM·bur) *n.* 1 a limb or similar organ of a plant or animal. 2 a distinct part or unit of a whole: *a member of a family; a Member of Parliament (of Canada); a Member of the Provincial Parliament of Ontario; a Member of the Legislative Assembly (of a province); a Member of the National Assembly of Quebec; an active, card-carrying, charter, corresponding, life, ranking member of our club; the five members of the set of odd numbers less than 10.* — **mem·ber·ship** *n.*

mem·brane *n.* a soft, thin, pliable sheet or layer of tissue covering a body surface or separating spaces, as the eardrum. — **mem·bra·nous** (MEM·bruh·nus) *adj.*

me·men·to (muh·MEN·toh) *n.* **-tos** or **-toes** a souvenir or keepsake.

mem·o (MEM·oh) *n.* **-os** [short form] memorandum.

mem·oir (MEM·wahr, -wor) *n.* 1 a biographical notice or a report based on personal knowledge of a person or subject. 2 **memoirs** *pl.* a wide-ranging first-hand record of events, as of a war, or of recollections, as of one's life. 3 **memoirs** *pl.* the proceedings of a learned society.

mem·o·ra·bil·i·a (mem·uh·ruh·BIL·ee·uh) *n. pl.* 1 things and events worth remembering about a subject. 2 an account of them.

mem·o·ra·ble (MEM·uh·ruh·bul) *adj.* worth remembering; notable. — **mem·o·ra·bly** *adv.*

mem·o·ran·dum (mem·uh·RAN·dum) *n.* **-dums** or **-da** (-duh) 1 a short or informal note, as to help one to remember something. 2 an internal business communication: *an inter-office memorandum about or on leaking secrets to the media.*

me·mo·ri·al (muh·MOR·ee·ul) *adj.* that commemorates an event or person: *a memorial dinner, holiday, service, statue; The Memorial University was built in memory of Newfoundlanders who died in World War I.* — *n.* a memorial statue, publication, holiday, etc.: *the Lincoln Memorial in Washington, D.C.; a war* *memorial; to build, erect, put up, unveil a memorial to the war dead.*

Memorial Day *n.* **1** in Newfoundland, same as CANADA DAY, observed on the Monday nearest July 1. **2** a U.S. holiday in honour of members of the armed forces dead in wars, usually the last Monday in May.

mem·o·rize (MEM·uh·rize) *v.* **-riz·es, -rized, -riz·ing** learn by heart. — **mem·o·ri·za·tion** (-ruh·ZAY·shun) *n.*

mem·o·ry (MEM·uh·ree) *n.* **-ries 1** the capacity to keep something in mind and recall it afterward: *to commit a formula to memory; to recite a poem from memory; to jog someone's memory during a lapse of memory; It slipped my memory* (= I forgot); *She lost her memory as the result of an accident; I have a good memory for faces, a bad memory for names.* **2** what is stored or recalled: *a scene that evokes* or *stirs up memories of the past; walking down **memory lane*** (= recalling the past with nostalgia); *a bitter, blessed, dim, fond, photographic, pleasant, poignant, sacred memory; the coldest winter in living memory* (= that anyone living can remember); *a monument erected **in memory of** war heroes.* **3** a storage and recall system: *a computer memory; random access memory; **read-only memory** (that cannot be manipulated or changed); a **memory bank*** (= data bank).

men *pl.* of MAN.

men·ace (MEN·is) *n.* a threat or danger: *Hoodlums are a menace to society.*
— *v.* be a menace to someone: *Hoodlums menace people in elevators; a **menacing** (= threatening) look.*
— **men·ac·ing·ly** *adv.*

mé·nage or **me·nage** (may·NAHZH, muh-) *n. French.* a household.

me·nag·er·ie (muh·NAJ·uh·ree) *n.* a collection of wild animals, as for a zoo or circus.

mend *v.* of things damaged or needing improvement, to make or become as good as before or as they should be: *Use glue to mend a broken toy; a loafer told to mend his ways or be fired.*
— *n.* a mending or what is mended: *The mend in his coat was showing.*
— **on the mend** improving in health or recovering from an injury.

men·di·cant (MEN·duh·kunt) *adj.* begging alms: *The Franciscans are a mendicant order of friars.*
— *n.* a begging friar.

men·folk or **men·folks** *n.pl. Informal.* men, esp. of a family or other social group.

me·ni·al (MEE·nee·ul) *adj.* domestic and lowly: *a menial task; menial work.*
— *n.* [derogatory] a domestic servant: *the menials of a household.* — **me·ni·al·ly** *adv.*

men·o·pause (MEN·uh·pawz) *n.* the normal cessation of menstruation, occurring in most women between 45 and 50.

men·ses (MEN·seez) *n.pl.* the usually monthly flow of blood from the uterus; period.

men·stru·al (MEN·stroo·ul) *adj.* having to do with menstruation: *the menstrual discharge, flow; menstrual pain.*

men·stru·a·tion (men·stroo·AY·shun) *n.* discharge of the menses.
— **men·stru·ate** (MEN·stroo·ate) *v.* **-ates, -at·ed, -at·ing.**

mens·wear *n.* clothing for men.

-ment *n. suffix.* indicating act, state, result, etc. of a verbal action: *abutment, government, statement; merriment.*

men·tal (MEN·tul) *adj.* **1** of the mind: *mental development, retardation; a man with a **mental age** (= intelligence level) of 12 years.* **2** of mental disorders: *a mental case, hospital, patient; mental health, illness.*
— **men·tal·ly** *adv.*

men·tal·i·ty (men·TAL·uh·tee) *n.* **-ties** mental capacity or attitude.

men·tion (MEN·shun) *v.* refer to or cite: *No one even mentioned it to me; The president mentioned her by name and praised her work; **Don't mention it** (= "You're welcome," in acknowledgment of thanks); The room costs $200 a night, **not to mention** (= not counting) extras.*
— *n.* a reference or citation: *He received only an honourable mention, not a prize; He made no mention of what happened; She winces at the very mention of the incident.*

men·tor (MEN·tur) *n.* a trusted adviser or teacher.

men·u (MEN·yoo) *n., pl.* **-us 1** list of food dishes or the food served, as at a restaurant: *What's on the menu today?* **2** list of choices in using a computer program as shown on the video display: *menu-driven, not command-driven software.*

me·ow (mee·OW) *n.* the cry of a cat; also **me·ou.**

mer·can·tile (MUR·cun·til, -tile, -teel) *adj.* having to do with merchants or trade: *a mercantile economy, firm; mercantile law.*

mer·ce·nar·y (MUR·suh·nair·ee) *n.* **-nar·ies** a soldier or other hired person working mainly for money; hireling: *foreign mercenaries; a mercenary motive.*

mer·cer·ize (MUR·suh·rize) *v.* **-riz·es, -rized, -riz·ing** treat fine cotton chemically for added lustre, strength, and deeper dye.

mer·chan·dise (MUR·chun·dise, -dize) *v.* **-dis·es, -dised, -dis·ing** trade in goods or commmodities, esp. by use of market research, packaging, and promotion methods.
— *n.* goods or commodities: *the lines of merchandise carried by a store; general merchandise as well as specialty items.* — **mer·chan·dis·er** *n.*
Also **mer·chan·dize** *v.;* **mer·chan·diz·er** *n.*

mer·chant (MUR·chunt) *n.* a trader such as a wholesaler, retailer, or shopkeeper.

mer·chant·a·ble (MUR·chun·tuh·bul) *adj.* fit for marketing; marketable.

merciful See MERCY.

mer·cu·ri·al (mur·KYOOR·ee·ul) *adj.* **1** changeable in mood: *a mercurial temperament.* **2** of or containing mercury; also **mer·cur·ic, mer·cur·ous.**
— **mer·cu·ri·al·ly** *adv.*

mer·cu·ry (MURK·yuh·ree) *n.* **1** a heavy, silver-white, normally liquid metallic element used in thermometers, barometers, etc. **2** a column of mercury; hence, temperature: *The mercury dipped* or *fell* or *plunged* or *plummeted to minus 20 degrees Celsius last night.* **3 Mercury** in Roman myths, the swift-footed messenger of the gods.

mer·cy (MUR·see) *n.* **-cies** kindness or compassion shown to someone out of generosity: *justice tempered with mercy; Have mercy on us; It's a mercy* (= blessing) *he wasn't killed in the fire; When the tax evader gets caught, he is* **at the mercy of** (= in the power of) *the government; left* **to the tender mercies** (= at the kind disposal) *of Revenue Canada; The convict threw himself* **at** or **upon the mercy** *of the court.* — **mer·ci·ful** *adj.;* **mer·ci·ful·ly** *adv.*

mercy killing *n.* same as EUTHANASIA.

mere (MEER) *adj.* nothing more or better than: *a mere child; He gets mad at the mere mention of the affair; mere words.*

mere·ly (MEER·lee) *adv.* simply or only: *You don't get money merely by asking for it; An air-conditioned room is not merely cool, but also dust-free.*

mer·est (MEER·ist) *superl. of* MERE; least: *at the merest suspicion of wrongdoing; attention to the merest detail.*

mer·e·tri·cious (mer·uh·TRISH·us) *adj.* alluring or attractive in a deceptive way: *a hooker's meretricious charms.*

merge (MURJ) *v.* **merg·es, merged, merg·ing** combine so as to lose identity or become part of something else: *The colours of the rainbow merge gradually, imperceptibly into one another; A small company may merge with a larger one; Many companies are merged* (= consolidated) *into large corporations.*

merg·er (MUR·jur) *n.* a merging or absorption: *to carry out* or *effect a merger of one company with another.*

me·rid·i·an (muh·RID·ee·un) *n.* **1** an imaginary line drawn from pole to pole passing through a particular point on the globe for measuring its longitude. **2** the highest point; culmination; prime: *in the meridian of his glory.*

me·ringue (muh·RANG) *n.* a dessert topping for pies, puddings, etc., made with egg whites and sugar beaten stiff and baked: *a lemon meringue pie.*

mer·it *n.* real worth; what one has earned: *The picture is a mere copy with no artistic merit; intrinsic merit; Hiring for jobs should be based on merit alone; a question decided on its* **merits;** *the relative merits of law and medicine as careers; the Order of Merit* (= decoration for distinguished service); ***adj.:*** *a Boy Scout wearing a merit badge; merit pay; the* **merit system** *of appointing and promoting people in jobs.* — *v.* earn or deserve: *The award was well merited; an important issue that merits your consideration.*

mer·i·tor·i·ous (mer·uh·TOR·ee·us) *adj.* full of worth or merit: *a meritorious action, deed; meritorious conduct, service.* — **mer·i·tor·i·ous·ly** *adv.*

mer·maid (MUR·maid) *n.* an imaginary sea creature in the shape of a woman's body above the waist and a fish's body from the waist down. — **mer·man** *n.* **-men,** *masc.*

mer·ri·ment (MER·ee·munt) *n.* hilarious fun; gaiety.

mer·ry (MER·ee) *adj.* **mer·ri·er, mer·ri·est** full of fun and laughter: *a merry Christmas party, laugh, tune; We* **make merry** (= have fun) *at a celebration.* — **mer·ri·ly** *adv.;* **mer·ri·ness** *n.*

merry-go-round (MER·ee·goh·round) *n.* **1** an amusement ride with wooden animals such as horses going up and down on a revolving platform. **2** a busy whirl of activities.

mer·ry·mak·ing (MER·ee·may·king) *adj. & n.* (having or full of) fun or merry entertainment. — **mer·ry·mak·er** *n.*

mesdames *pl. of* MADAM or MADAME.

mesdemoiselles *pl. of* MADEMOISELLE.

mesh *n.* **1** one of the openings between the cords or wires of a net, sieve, screen, etc.: *A 60-mesh screen has 60 meshes to the inch.* **2** a woven netlike material: *fine* or *coarse mesh; caught in the* **meshes** (= threads or network) *of a spider's web, of the legal system.* — **in mesh** interlocked. — *v.* engage or interlock, as gears or zippers.

mesh·work *n.* network; meshes.

mes·mer·ism (MEZ·muh·riz·um, MES-) *n.* [former term] hypnotism.

mes·mer·ize (MEZ·muh·rize, MES-) *v.* **-iz·es, -ized, -iz·ing** same as HYPNOTIZE.

mess *n.* **1** an untidy, unpleasant, or confused condition: *What a mess! He made a mess of the job he was given; His office was in a real mess; to clean up* or *sweep up a mess; Use paper towels to mop up the mess.* **2** a group of people, as in the army, who regularly eat together. **3** such eating together or their eating place: *officers' mess; They are at mess now; the mess sergeant in charge of the kitchen.* **4** a portion of food, esp. a dish of something, as of meal or cereal: *a savoury mess; a mess of pottage.* — *v.* **1** make untidy, unpleasant, confused, etc.: *an office messed up by a Christmas party; The sales rep liked to* **mess about** or **around** (= putter around) *in the office instead of getting out to sell, but he did not* **mess with** (*Informal for* treat improperly) *the other employees.* **2** eat together, as in the army: *She was invited to mess with the officers.*

mes·sage (MES·ij) *n.* a communication: *the Queen's Christmas message to the Commonwealth; to convey,*

deliver, garble, scramble, send, transmit a message; a message (= commercial) *from our sponsor; a poem with a message* (= theme or idea).
— **get the message** *Informal.* take the hint or understand what is implied.
— *v.* send as a message or send a message to a place or person: *The captain had messaged "fire on board" before crash-landing; to message someone's voice-mail box; a telecommunications carrier providing voice, data, and messaging services.*

Messeigneurs *pl.* of MONSEIGNEUR.

mes·sen·ger (MES·un·jur) *n.* one who carries a message or goes on a mission or errand.

Mes·si·ah (muh·SYE·uh) *n.* **1** the "deliverer" promised to Israel by the prophets, identified with Jesus by Christians: *to await the Messiah.* **2 messiah** the leader of a cause who promises a bright future: *false messiahs.*

Mes·si·an·ic (mes·ee·AN·ic) *adj.* having to do with a Messiah: *the Messianic age of peace and freedom; the Messianic prophecy, times.*

messieurs *pl.* of MONSIEUR.

Messrs. (MES·urz) *pl.* of MR: *Messrs. T. Jones & Co.; Messrs. Jones, Smith, and McGrath.*

mess·y *adj.* unpleasant or untidy.
— **mess·i·ly** *adv.;* **mess·i·ness** *n.*

met *pt. & pp.* of MEET.

meta- *prefix.* beyond; over; after: *metabolism, metamorphosis, metaphysics.*

me·tab·o·lism (muh·TAB·uh·liz·um) *n.* the process by which a living being transforms food into energy (destructive metabolism or "catabolism") and into living tissue (constructive metabolism or "anabolism"): *the basal metabolism of a body at rest; Running after a meal may disturb or upset your metabolism.*
— **met·a·bol·ic** (met·uh·BOL·ic) *adj.*

met·al (MET·ul) *n.* **1** a mineral substance such as iron, lead, or copper that has a shiny surface, conducts heat and electricity, can be melted, etc.: *base metals; precious metals; sheet metal; Metals corrode, rust; The car was good only for scrap metal after the crash.* **2** an alloy or anything made out of metal. **3** basic material; also, mettle.

me·tal·lic (muh·TAL·ic) *adj.* like metal: *a metallic grey, lustre, sound, voice; a car finished with* **metallic paint** *(that glistens from bits of metal in it).*

met·a·mor·phic (met·uh·MOR·fic) *adj.* that has been changed in appearance and composition by heat, pressure, etc.: *Marble and slate are metamorphic rocks.*
— **met·a·mor·phism** (-fiz·um) *n.*

met·a·mor·phose (met·uh·MOR·foze) *v.* **-phos·es, -phosed, -phos·ing** change in form: *Tadpoles and caterpillars are metamorphosed into frogs and butterflies; rocks metamorphosed by heat.*
— **met·a·mor·phous** (-fus) *adj.*

met·a·mor·pho·sis (met·uh·MOR·fuh·sis) *n., pl.* **-ses** (-seez) a complete change of form, character, etc. as if by magic: *the metamorphosis of a butterfly, frog.*

met·a·phor (MET·uh·fur, -for) *n.* a figure of speech

using words in a meaning different from their literal sense, implying a comparison: *"The dawn of civilization" is a good metaphor; "The dawn and fall of civilizations" is a* **mixed metaphor.**
— **met·a·phor·ic** (met·uh·FOR·ic) or **met·a·phor·i·cal** *adj.;* **met·a·phor·i·cal·ly** *adv.*

met·a·phys·ics (met·uh·FIZ·ics) *n.pl.* [with sing. v.] a division of philosophy that studies fundamental problems of knowledge and reality beyond those of the physical world, as existence, essence, and causality; also called "speculative philosophy."
— **met·a·phys·i·cal** *adj.*

mete (MEET) *v.* **metes, met·ed, met·ing** usually **mete out,** measure out; apportion or allot: *to mete out justice, punishment, rewards.*

me·te·or (MEE·tee·ur) *n.* the streak of light seen as a "shooting star" or "falling star" in the sky when a meteoroid glows on entering the earth's atmosphere.

me·te·or·ic (mee·tee·OR·ic) *adj.* of or like a meteor in swiftness, brilliancy, etc.: *a movie star's meteoric rise to fame; her meteoric career; a meteoric climb, growth, inflation rate.*

me·te·or·ite (MEE·tee·uh·rite) *n.* the part of a meteoroid that does not burn up before reaching the earth.
— **me·te·or·it·ic** (-RIT·ic) *adj.*

me·te·or·oid (MEE·tee·uh·roid) *n.* a chunk of metal or rock falling to earth from space.

me·te·or·ol·o·gy (MEE·tee·uh·ROL·uh·jee) *n.* the study of the atmosphere, esp. weather.
— **me·te·or·ol·o·gist** (-ROL·uh·jist) *n.*
— **me·te·or·o·log·i·cal** (-ruh·LOJ·uh·cul) *adj.*

me·ter (MEE·tur) *n.* **1** a measuring and often recording instrument, as for gas, electricity, distances, parking time, etc. **2** same as METRE.
— *v.* measure: *a seeder with a metering device to meter the spacing; to meter office mail (with a postage meter).*
— **combining form.** measuring device: *odometer, speedometer, thermometer.*

meter maid *n.* a female police employee who issues tickets for parking violations.

meth·am·phet·a·mine (meth·am·FET·uh·meen) *n.* a stimulant amphetamine, also used in weight control; speed *(Slang).*

meth·ane (METH·ane) *n.* a flammable gaseous hydrocarbon formed in marshes and mines by the decomposition of vegetable matter.

meth·a·nol (METH·uh·nol) *n.* a poisonous industrial chemical used as a solvent and in fuels and antifreezes; also called "wood alcohol."

me·thinks (mi·THINKS) *v.* **-thought** [old use] It seems to me.

meth·od (METH·ud) *n.* an orderly way or procedure for doing something: *new teaching methods; the proper method of brushing the teeth; to adopt, employ, use a method; an antiquated, modern, up-to-date method; the deductive, inductive, scientific method; the rhythm method of birth control; There's (a)* **method in his madness** *(= What he's doing is not as crazy as it seems).*
— **me·thod·i·cal** (muh·THOD·uh·cul) *adj.*

— **me·thod·i·cal·ly** *adv.*

meth·od·ol·o·gy (meth·uh·DOL·uh·jee) *n.* **-gies 1** the science of method. **2** a particular system: *the methodology of teaching.*

me·tic·u·lous (muh·TIK·yoo·lus) *adj.* careful, often finicky about minute details: *a meticulous dresser; meticulous in her work.*
— **me·tic·u·lous·ly** *adv.;* **me·tic·u·lous·ness** *n.*

mé·tier (mait·YAY) *n.* a field of work in which one is specially skilled; forte: *Though trained as a teacher, her true métier was journalism.*

Mé·tis (may·TEES, may·TEE, MAY·tee) *n. sing. & pl.* a person of mixed white and native Indian descent; *adj.: a Métis association; The Métis language is composed of Cree, English, and French words; Métis settlements.*

me·tre (MEE·tur) *n.* **1** rhythm in music or verse, based on units such as beats, length or stress of syllables, etc.: *the time signature showing 4/4 metre or common time; the four-line ballad metre.* **2** the basic unit of length in the metric system, equal to 39.37 in. Also **me·ter.**
— **combining form.** metre: *centimetre, kilometre, millimetre.*

met·ric *adj.* having to do with the metre as the basic unit of length: *The decimal metric system of measurement has metre, gram, and litre as basic units; a metric ton of 1 000 kg or 1.1 short tons; metric conversion (to the metric system); Canada started going metric in 1971.*
— **met·ri·cal** (MET·ruh·cul) *adj.* metric: *metrical rhythm; a metrical translation.*

met·ri·cate (MET·ruh·cate) *v.* **-cates, -cat·ed, -cat·ing** change into the metric system.
— **met·ri·ca·tion** (-CAY·shun) *n.*

met·ri·cize (MET·ruh·cize) *v.* **-ciz·es, -cized, -ciz·ing** same as METRICATE.

met·ro or **Met·ro** (MET·roh) *n.* **-ros 1** an underground railway: *Montreal, Paris, Moscow, Washington, etc. have metros; a metro transit system.* **2 Metro** a large city or its administration: *The city of Etobicoke is part of Metro (Toronto); a seat on Metro Council.*

me·trop·o·lis (muh·TROP·uh·lis) *n.* **1** a large, important, or capital city. **2** the centre of a specified activity: *a city once called the crime metropolis* (=capital) *of North America.*

me·tro·pol·i·tan (met·ruh·POL·uh·tun) **1** *adj.* having to do with a large city: *A metropolitan area includes a city and its suburbs; a metropolitan centre, newspaper.* **2** *adj.* having to do with a federation of several municipalities: *a metropolitan region.* **3** *n.* in some Christian churches, the head of an ecclesiastical province, usually an archbishop: *In the Eastern Orthodox Church, a metropolitan ranks above an archbishop and below a patriarch.*

met·tle (MET·ul) *n.* **1** quality of character or temperament. **2** spirit or courage: *to prove* or *show one's mettle.*
— **on one's mettle** ready to do one's best.

met·tle·some (MET·ul·sum) *adj.* high-spirited: *a mettlesome horse.*

mew 1 *n. & v.* same as MEOW. **2** *v.* to cage a hawk, etc.

or shut someone up. **3 mews** *n. pl.* [with sing. v.] an alley or street.

mewl (MYOOL) *n. & v.* a feeble or whining cry: *a mewling baby.*

Mexican standoff *n.* a confrontation that results in an impasse.

mez·za·nine (MEZ·uh·neen) *n.* **1** a middle storey between a building's first floor and second floor. **2** a balcony over the main floor, as of a theatre, esp. its forward part.

mi·aow or **mi·oaw** *n. & v.* same as MEOW.

mi·as·ma (my·AZ·muh) *n.* an evil-smelling vapour, considered infectious, as of swamps.
— **mi·as·mic** or **mi·as·mal** *adj.*

mice *pl.* of MOUSE.

mick·ey (MIK·ee) *n. Cdn. Slang.* a half-bottle of wine or liquor.

Mick·ey Mouse (MICK·ee-) *n. & adj. Slang.* something trivial, petty, or second-rate: *a Mickey Mouse computer system; a Mickey Mouse effort.*

mi·cro (MY·croh) *n.* **-cros** [short form] microcomputer.
— **combining form.** very small: *microcosm, microfilm, microorganism.*

mi·crobe (MY·crobe) *n.* a disease-causing microorganism.
— **mi·cro·bi·al** (my·CROH·bee·ul) or **mi·cro·bic** *adj.*

mi·cro·burst (MY·croh·burst) *n.* same as WIND SHEAR.

mi·cro·chip (MY·croh·chip) *n.* an integrated circuit on a tiny wafer of silicon. Also **mi·cro·cir·cuit** (MY·croh·sur·kit).

mi·cro·com·put·er (MY·croh·cum·PEW·tur) *n.* a computer system built around one or more microprocessors.

mi·cro·cosm (MY·croh·coz·um) *n.* a little world: *the universe in microcosm* (=miniature).
— **mi·cro·cos·mic** (-COZ·mic) *adj.*

mi·cro·e·lec·tron·ics (MY·croh·i·lec·TRON·ics) *n. pl.* [with sing. v.] the electronics of microminiaturized circuits.

mi·cro·fiche (MY·cruh·feesh) *n. sing. & pl., rarely* **-fich·es** *pl.* a card-size sheet of microfilm containing many pages.

mi·cro·film (MY·croh·film) *n.* a film copy of a document, book, etc. in highly reduced size.

mi·cro·form (MY·croh·form) *n.* microfiche, microfilm, or other such method of information storage.

mi·cro·lite (MY·cruh·lite) *n.* a very light aircraft for one person.

mi·crom·e·ter (my·CROM·uh·tur) *n.* an instrument for measuring very small dimensions, used in microscopes, surveyor's instruments, and the *micrometer calliper* which can measure accurately to 0.00254 mm (0.0001 in.).

mi·cro·min·i·a·ture (my·croh·MIN·ee·uh·chur) *adj.* of extremely small electronic circuits: *a microminiature component.* Also **mi·cro·min·i·a·tur·ized** *n.*

mi·cro·or·gan·ism (my·croh·OR·gun·iz·um) *n.* a microscopic animal or vegetable organism such as a bacterium, fungus, or virus.

mi·cro·phone (MY·cruh·fone) *n.* an instrument for changing sound into electrical signals, for transmission as in a telephone or for magnification as in a public-address system.

mi·cro·proc·es·sor (my·croh·PROS·uh·sur) *n.* a data-processing unit built on a tiny silicon chip.

mi·cro·scope (MY·cruh·scope) *n.* an optical instrument for viewing very minute objects.
— **mi·cro·scop·ic** (my·cruh·SCOP·ic) *adj.*
— **mi·cro·scop·i·cal·ly** *adv.*
— **mi·cros·co·py** (my·CROS·cuh·pee) *n.*

mi·cro·sur·ger·y (my·cruh·SUR·juh·ree) *n.* operation on microscopic structures such as blood cells.

mi·cro·wave (MY·cruh·wave) *n.* **1** a radio wave varying between 1 mm and 30 cm in length, as used in radar, TV, and the **microwave oven** for cooking food electronically. **2** a microwave oven.
— *v.* cook in a microwave: *microwaved bacon.*

mid 1 *prep.* [old use] also **'mid**, amid. **2** *adj. & combining form.* middle: *in mid career, ocean, winter; mid-morning; mid-fifties.*

mid·air *n. & adj.* in the air well above the ground: *left suspended in midair; a midair collision of aircraft.*

mid·cult *n.* middle-class culture, only moderately intellectual; middlebrow culture.

mid·day *n. & adj.* the middle of the day; noon: *Is it hottest at midday? a midday meal; the midday heat, sun.*

mid·dle (MID·ul) *adj.* intermediate or in between two extremes of length, duration, size, attitude, etc.: *the middle distance (between foreground and background, as in a picture); Most of the tax is collected from the middle-income group; middle management* (= managers between supervisors and senior administrators); *"Henry" is the middle name (between first name and surname) and "H" the middle initial of John H. Doe; a middle position politically between Right and Left.*
— *n.* a middle point, part, etc.: *the middle of the night, room, street; Pat measures 25 in. (= 63.5 cm) round the middle* (= waist).

middle age *n.* **1** the time of life between youth and old age, usually 40 to 65 years; **middle-aged** *adj.* **2** Middle Ages *pl.* the period of European history between about A.D. 500 and 1500.

Middle America *n.* **1** the American middle class with moderate political views. **2** the Middle West.
— **Middle American** *n. & adj.*

mid·dle·brow (MID·ul·brow, *rhyme:* "how") *adj.* moderately intellectual, neither highbrow nor lowbrow.
— *n.* such a person.

middle class *n.* the social class between the upper class and the lower working class, with an above-average education and standard of living. — **middle-class** *adj.*

Middle East *n.* a large region of northeastern Africa and southwestern Asia, including Iran, Iraq, the Arabian Peninsula, Turkey, Egypt, and the Sudan; Middle Eastern.

mid·dle·man (MID·ul·man) *n.* -men **1** a go-between or intermediary. **2** a trader such as a broker, packer, wholesaler, or retailer who buys from a producer for sale to consumers.

middle-of-the-road *adj.* of moderate views, esp. in politics, avoiding extremes of Right and Left.
— **middle-of-the-roader** *n.*

middle school *n.* a school linking elementary and high school, usually grades 5 to 8.

mid·dling (MID·ling) *adj.* of average size, degree, or quality, often mediocre.

mid·get (MIJ·it) *n.* a person or thing proportionately small of its kind: *a circus featuring midgets.*
— *adj.:* *midget car racing; midget golf (played indoors); a midget submarine.*

mid·i (MID·ee) *n.* a coat, dress, or skirt reaching to the middle of the calf.

mid·land (MID·lund) *n.* the middle or interior of a country.

mid·life crisis *n.* the anxious situation that sometimes results when people realize that they are not young anymore.

mid·night *n. & adj.* of or at the middle of the night; 12 o'clock at night.
— **burn the midnight oil** study or work late at night.

midnight sun *n.* the sun seen above the horizon continuously for six months of the year in the polar regions, as in parts of Norway, the "land of the midnight sun."

mid·point *n.* the middle part or stage of anything having duration or extension.

mid·riff *n.* **1** the middle portion of the human body between chest and waist. **2** a section of a woman's garment that covers or exposes this: *a lace midriff.*

mid·rise *n.* an apartment building that is not a high-rise or walkup.

mid·size *adj.* intermediate in size: *A midsize car is larger than a compact.*

midst *n.* a middle or surrounded position: *a traitor in our midst; I found time to help him in the midst of my other preoccupations.*
— *prep.* [old or poetic use] amidst; also **'midst.**

mid·stream *n.* the middle of a stream.

mid·town *n. & adj.* (in) the middle section of a town between downtown and uptown.

mid·way *n.* an avenue containing amusements, side shows, and concessions at a fair or carnival.
— *adj. & adv.* in the middle: *a midway point; The car broke down midway between home and school.*

Mid·west *n.* the north central region of the U.S. forming the American heartland, bounded by the Rockies, the southern boundaries of Kansas and Missouri, the Ohio River, and the Appalachians.
— **Mid·west·ern** *adj.;* **Mid·west·ern·er** *n.*

mid·wife *n.* **-wives** a woman who helps mothers in childbirth.

mid·wife·ry (MID·wye·fuh·ree, -wif·ree) *n.* the work of a midwife.

mien (MEEN) *n.* one's appearance, bearing, or demeanour as expressive of character or mood: *a man of sorrowful mien.*

miff *v. Informal.* put someone into a peevish fit: *He was miffed by her remarks; He was miffed at her.*

might *pt.* of MAY.
— *n.* overwhelming strength, power, or authority: *a dictator who thinks might is right; She attacked the problem with all her might; He fought* **with might and main** (= with all his strength).

might·y *adj.* **might·i·er, -i·est** extremely strong or great: *the mighty warrior; a mighty blow; How the mighty (people) have fallen!*
— *adv. Informal.* extremely; very: *That's mighty nice of you; It matters mighty little.*
— **might·i·ly** *adv.;* **might·i·ness** *n.*

mi·gnon·ette (min·yuh·NET) *n.* **1** a hardy garden plant with soft-green leaves and tall spikes of fragrant, tiny, yellowish-green flowers. **2** the yellowish-green colour.

mi·graine (MY·grain) *n.* a severe kind of repeatedly occurring headache, usually on one side, sometimes accompanied by nausea and vomiting.

mi·grant (MY·grunt) *adj.* migrating: *a migrant farm labourer, worker.*

mi·grate (MY·grate) *v.* **-grates, -grat·ed, -grat·ing** move to another region or country periodically, as birds and animals to warmer climates in the winter, or permanently, as emigrants and immigrants.
— **mi·gra·tion** (my·GRAY·shun) *n.*

mi·gra·to·ry (MY·gruh·tor·ee) *adj.* migrating: *a migratory bird, habit, pattern.*

mike *n. Informal.* a microphone.

milch (MILK, MILCH) *adj.* of cows and such domestic animals, kept for milking, not for meat or draft.

mild (MILED) *adj.* moderate or agreeable, not severe or harsh: *a mild cheese, cigarette, rebuke, winter.*
— **mild·ly** *adv.;* **mild·ness** *n.*

mil·dew *n.* a minute whitish fungus that forms on plants and materials such as paper, leather, and cloth in damp weather. — *v.* affect or be covered with mildew.

— **mil·dew·y** *adj.*

mile *n.* a unit of length equal to 5 280 ft. (1.609 km).

mile·age (MY·lij) *n.* **1** a per-mile or per-metre travelling allowance, car-rental rate, etc. **2** the number of miles or kilometres travelled, covered, etc.: *the mileage on a car; the mileage figure shown on an odometer; Smaller cars give better mileage; Montreal to Moscow is 4 401 miles on the world air mileage* (= air distance) *chart; a mileage test of fuel consumption; There's not much mileage* (= wear) *left on those tires (which are nearly bald); political mileage* (= advantage or benefit) *from dirty tricks.*

mile·post *n.* a signpost indicating distance from a given point in miles or kilometres.

mil·er (MY·lur) *n.* one who competes in a mile race.

mile·stone *n.* **1** a stone put up as a milepost. **2** a significant stage or event, as during a journey or career.

mi·lieu (meel·YUR, -YOO) *n.* the immediate environment, esp. social.

mil·i·tant (MIL·uh·tunt) *adj.* aggressive or warlike, esp. in fighting for a cause or movement: *a militant attitude, churchman, conservationist; militant trade unionism.*
— *n.* one who is militant. — **mil·i·tant·ly** *adv.*
— **mil·i·tan·cy** *n.*

mil·i·ta·rism (MIL·uh·tuh·riz·um) *n.* the spirit, policy, or condition of being aggressively prepared for war.
— **mil·i·ta·rist** *n.* — **mil·i·ta·ris·tic** (-RIS·tic) *adj.*

mil·i·ta·rize (MIL·uh·tuh·rize) *v.* **-riz·es, -rized, -riz·ing 1** prepare and equip an army, nation, etc. for war. **2** give a military character to a government.

mil·i·tar·y (MIL·uh·tair·ee) **1** *adj.* having to do with soldiers or an army: *a military government, uniform; the military spirit; military law, personnel, police, service, valour.* **2** *n. sing. & pl.,* also **-tar·ies** *pl.* armed forces: *to call in the military; the militaries of various countries.* — **mil·i·tar·i·ly** (-TAIR·uh·lee) *adv.*

mil·i·tate (MIL·uh·tate) *v.* **-tates, -tat·ed, -tat·ing** of facts, evidence, etc., have force or weight *against* [rarely *for*] something or someone.

mi·li·tia (muh·LISH·uh) *n.* **1** an organization of civilians drafted to help their country in an emergency: *to call out the militia.* **2** an organization of part-time members of the army, as the Reserve Force of Canada or the National Guard in the U.S.
— **mi·li·tia·man** (-mun) *n.* **-men.**

milk *n.* **1** the white liquid from the mammary glands of a female mammal; also, this in processed form: *(human) breast milk; condensed, evaporated, fresh, homogenized, pasteurized, skim, whole milk; manufacturers of infant milks* (= formulas); *the milk of human kindness* (= natural sympathy and kindness). **2** a similar liquid, as found in a coconut, the latex of trees and plants, or "milk of magnesia" used as an antacid and laxative.
— *v.* **1** draw milk from a domestic animal: *to milk cows.* **2** draw from a resource capable of yielding something useful: *Some rattlers are milked for venom for use as an antidote; an estate milked dry by litigation; Merchants milk* (= exploit) *the commercial aspect of Christmas.*

milk·maid *n.* a dairymaid or a woman who milks cows.

milk·man *n.* -men a man who sells or delivers milk.

milk·shake *n.* a frothy drink of milk shaken with flavouring and ice cream.

milk·sop *n.* a sissy.

milk tooth *n.* any of the first set of 20 teeth a baby gets that later fall out.

milk·y *adj.* **milk·i·er, -i·est** white like milk or containing or yielding milk: *the milky juice of the lettuce; milky white teeth; rich, milky tea.* — **milk·i·ness** *n.*

mill *n.* **1** a machine that grinds grain, traditionally between two huge, flat stones, one turning against the other, powered by a **mill·wheel** driven by a current of water or a canal called a **mill·race,** or **mill·stream,** often flowing from a **mill·pond,** or **mill·dam. 2** a machine that grinds coffee, pepper, or stones, that presses the juice of sugar cane, apples, etc., or that stamps coins. **3** a factory: *a cotton, flour, lumber, paper, rolling, steel, textile mill.* **4** an establishment with a routine or repetitive operation: *a diploma mill* (= school granting degrees of dubious value); *divorce, photocopying, propaganda mills.* **5** a thousandth part of a dollar, one tenth of a cent, as used in accounting: *A two-mill levy was added to the property tax last year.* — **through the mill** *Informal.* through hard practical training or experience. — *v.* **1** to process using a mill: *Grain is milled into flour or meal; the **milled** (= ridged) edge of a coin; the **milling** (= notches or ridges) given to a coin.* **2** move about in circles or confusion: *Convention crowds milled about in the hotel lobby.*

mil·len·ni·um (mil·EN·ee·um) *n.* **mil·len·ni·ums** or **mil·len·ni·a 1** a thousand-year period. **2 the millenium** the era of peace and happiness prophesied in the Bible (Revelation).

milli- *combining form.* thousandth part: *milliampere, millibar, millimetre.*

mil·li·ner (MIL·uh·nur) *n.* one who makes or deals in millinery.

mil·li·ner·y (MIL·uh·nair·ee) *n.* -ner·ies **1** women's hats. **2** the hat business.

milling machine *n.* a machine with toothed cutters for shaping metal into slots, gears, etc.

mil·lion (MIL·yun) *n.* a thousand thousands; 1 000 000: *The painting was sold for five million dollars; an aircraft costing millions of dollars.* — **mil·lionth** (MIL·yunth) *adj.*

mil·lion·aire (mil·yuh·NAIR) *n.* a very wealthy person, esp. one who has a million or more dollars, pounds, francs, etc.

millpond, millrace, millstream, mill wheel See MILL.

mill·stone *n.* **1** either of two huge, flat, round stones that turn against each other to grind grain into flour. **2** a crushing burden: *The scandal proved a political millstone around the minister's neck.*

mill·wright (MILL·rite) *n.* one who sets up or repairs machinery in a mill or factory.

milque·toast or **Milque·toast** (MILK·tohst) *n.* a very timid person.

mime *n.* **1** acting without speech, using only bodily movements and gestures: *The action of the play is all in mime; The Canadian Mime Theatre.* **2** a mimic or the performance of one. — *v.* **mimes, mimed, mim·ing** act without speech, as in a pantomime.

mim·e·o (MIM·ee·oh) *n.* [short form] mimeograph.

mim·e·o·graph (MIM·ee·uh·graf) *n.* a stencil duplicating machine. — *v.* copy graphic matter using a mimeograph.

mi·met·ic (mi·MET·ic) *adj.* imitative: *the mimetic art; mimetic gestures, movements; A leaf insect's mimetic colouring imitates its surroundings.*

mim·ic *v.* -icks, -icked, -ick·ing **1** resemble or imitate: *A leaf insect mimics its surroundings; A parrot mimics speech.* **2** imitate or ape, esp. for fun. — *n.* one skilled in mimicking.

mim·ic·ry (MIM·ic·ree) *n.* -ries **1** artistic imitation of someone's speech, style, or mannerisms for comic effect: *humour by mimicry.* **2** the imitation of its surroundings by a bird or animal for hiding from its enemies, as by the chameleon or "stick insect."

mi·mo·sa (mi·MOH·suh) *n.* a tree, shrub, or herb of warm climates whose featherlike leaves respond to stimuli by closing and drooping.

min·a·ret (min·uh·RET) *n.* a slender tower, usually attached to a mosque, with a surrounding balcony at the top, from which people are called to prayer.

min·a·to·ry (MIN·uh·tor·ee) *adj.* menacing or threatening.

mince *v.* minc·es, minced, minc·ing **1** chop up into very small pieces: *to mince meat; minced beef.* **2** affect a daintiness of speech or delicacy of manner, as by restraining one's words or walking with shortened, or **mincing,** steps. — **not to mince matters** or **words** to be plain or outspoken.

mince·meat *n.* a mixture of minced meat, beef fat, apples, raisins, currants, spices, etc.: *The Government **made mincemeat of** the Opposition* (= beat them soundly).

mind (MINED) *n.* the faculty by which a person remembers, thinks, understands, reasons, wills, etc.:

What's on your mind? What do you have in mind? Let's keep that in mind (= remember it); *Did it ever cross your mind* (= occur to you) *that you could be wrong? She has* or *is an analytical mind; a clear, closed, inquiring, keen, narrow, one-track, twisted mind; He has a mind of his own* (= is independent in his thinking); *I've half a mind to* (= I am tempted to) *say no to her and give her a bit* or *piece of my mind* (= tell her bluntly what I think).
— **blow one's mind** *Slang.* 1 experience hallucinations, as by use of LSD. 2 be overwhelming, as to surprise or baffle.
— **change one's mind** change one's intention or opinion.
— **make up one's mind** decide; also, decide *to* do something.
— **out of one's mind** mentally ill; crazy.
— **put in mind** remind someone.
— *v.* pay attention to something: *Mind the step (ahead of you); Who's minding* (= looking after) *the store? Mind your own business* (= Don't meddle in other people's affairs); *Do you mind* (= object to) *closing the door? Do you mind? Never mind* (= It does not matter).

mind-bending, mind-blowing or **mind-expanding** *adj.* psychedelic; hallucinogenic.

minded *adj. & combining form.* having a mind as specified: *if you're so minded* (= inclined); *high-minded; narrow-minded.*

mind·ful *adj.* aware or careful: *to be mindful of our duties.*

mind reader *n.* 1 one who seems to guess another's thoughts. 2 one gifted with extrasensory perception.

mind-set *n.* the way one habitually thinks.

mind's eye *n.* imagination: *in one's mind's eye.*

mine *pron.* possessive case of "I": *your children and mine; a friend of mine* (= belonging to me).
— *adj.* [formerly used before a vowel or "h" or after a noun]: *Mine eyes have seen thy salvation; O sister mine!*
— *n.* 1 an excavation for extracting a mineral from the earth: *to close down, open, work a mine; an abandoned mine.* 2 a deposit of such a mineral: *salt mines; an open-pit* (= not underground) *mine for copper, diamonds,* or *phosphates; a strip mine for coal that is near the earth's surface.* 3 an abundant source or supply: *This book is a gold mine of information.* 4 an explosive charge laid under water or ground to blow up an enemy's fortifications, vehicles, or ships: *a land mine; to detect, detonate, disarm a mine; to sweep mines.*
— *v.* mines, mined, min·ing 1 dig something valuable out: *Gold used to be mined here; We're mining* (= digging) *for coal.* 2 blow up using a mine: *The ship sank after being mined; a highway mined by terrorists.*

mine·field *n.* 1 an area in which explosive mines have been laid by the enemy. 2 a potentially dangerous subject or situation: *Reducing the baby bonus proved a political minefield for the government.*

min·er·al (MIN·ur·ul) *n.* a substance such as a metal, a precious stone, salt, coal, petroleum, natural gas, calcium, and sulphur that is mined or quarried from the earth: *Is it animal, vegetable, or mineral? diseases due to mineral deficiencies in the diet; a mineral deposit.*

min·er·al·ize (MIN·ur·uh·lize) *v.* -iz·es, -ized, -iz·ing 1 treat with minerals: *mineralized water (containing minerals).* 2 convert to mineral: *metal mineralized as ore.* — **min·er·al·i·za·tion** (-luh·ZAY·shun) *n.*

mineral oil *n.* any oil of mineral origin, esp. an oily liquid with no colour, taste, or odour that is obtained from petroleum and used as a laxative and in cosmetics.

mineral spring *n.* a spring whose water contains dissolved minerals.

mineral water *n.* water containing mineral salts or gases, sold bottled.

min·gle (MING·gul) *v.* -gles, -gled, -gling mix or blend, esp. without losing identity: *mingled feelings of joy and sorrow; Boys mingle with girls at parties.*

min·gy (MIN·jee) *adj.* -gi·er, -gi·est *Informal.* mean and stingy: *a mingy amount; He's rather mingy about spending money; mingy supplies.*

min·i (MIN·ee) *adj. & combining form.* very small: *a mini coat, dress, tour, van; a supplementary minibudget; minibus, Minicam* or *minicamera, minicomputer, minifloppy (diskette), miniskirt.*
— *n., pl.* min·is 1 a mini dress, coat, etc. 2 a minicomputer.

min·i·a·ture (MIN·ee·uh·chur) *n.* a copy or representation on a much smaller scale than its original, as a painting on ivory or vellum: *a miniature doll house; miniature golf; a miniature* (= tiny bottle) *of whisky; the CN Tower carved in miniature.* — **min·i·a·tur·ist** *n.*
— **min·i·a·tur·ize** (-chuh·rize) *v.* -iz·es, -ized, -iz·ing: *miniaturized electronic components; the miniaturized computer.* — **min·i·a·tur·i·za·tion** (-uh·ZAY·shun) *n.*

min·i·bike (MIN·ee·bike) *n.* a small motorcycle for use on country roads and trails.

min·i·bus (MIN·ee·bus) *n.* a very small bus for 10 to 15 people.

min·i·com·put·er (MIN·ee·cum·PEW·tur) *n.* a small computer designed to do many jobs.

min·i·mal (MIN·uh·mul) *adj.* the smallest or least possible: *a minimal charge; minimal standards, terms.*
— **min·i·mal·ly** *adv.*

min·i·mize (MIN·uh·mize) *v.* -miz·es, -mized, -miz·ing 1 reduce to a minimum: *to minimize a risk.* 2 belittle: *Let's not minimize the importance of education.*

min·i·mum *n.* -mums or -ma the least or lowest amount: *We are cutting expenses to a minimum; to the (absolute) minimum required for survival; There is a minimum (speed) to be maintained on a highway.*
— *adj.* least or lowest: *a low minimum wage; yesterday's minimum temperature; a minimum-security prison.*

min·ion (MIN·yun) *n.* a servile follower; favourite servant.

miniscule [rare spelling] same as MINUSCULE.

min·i·se·ries (MIN·ee·seer·eez) *n.* a TV drama presented in a series of parts spread over many days: *a 12-hour, 8-part miniseries.*

min·i·skirt (MIN·ee·skirt) *n.* a short skirt with the hemline well above the knee: *a min·i·skirt·ed drum majorette.*

min·is·ter (MIN·is·tur) *n.* **1** a high public servant, as a member of a government cabinet, a diplomat ranking below ambassador, etc.: *the **prime minister** of a country; the first ministers of provinces; a **minister without portfolio** (not in charge of any particular government department).* **2** a protestant clergyman.
— *v.* serve: *Nurses minister to (the needs of) the sick and dying; Sam is a **ministering** angel.*
— **min·is·te·ri·al** (-TEER·ee·ul) *adj.*
— **min·is·tra·tion** (-TRAY·shun) *n.*

min·is·try (MIN·is·tree) *n.* **-tries** a minister's office, term, or duties: *a Tory ministry* (= government or cabinet); *the foreign ministry* (= government department); *She was called to the ministry* (= to join the clergy); *the lay ministry* (= religious work carried out by the laity).

mink *n.* a small weasel or its lustrous, deep-brown fur made into a coat, cape, or stole.

mi·nor (MY·nur) *adj.* lesser in importance, rank, size, extent, etc.; not major: *a minor baseball league;* [in music] *a **minor scale** (raised a half tone after the second and fifth notes); a minor operation, repair; a minor subject (of a program of studies); minor surgery.*
— *n.* **1** a person under the age of 18: *A minor may not vote or buy liquor.* **2** a minor or secondary subject of study; *v.: a history major minoring in German.*

mi·nor·i·ty (my·NOR·uh·tee) *n.* **-ties 1** a part, group, or number that is less than half, not a majority: *the Catholic minority of Northern Ireland; Catholics are in a minority there; In a minority of cases, a drug may do more harm than good; Orientals, South Asians, and blacks form visible minorities in a white society; adj.: a minority government (by a party with less than half the seats in a legislature); Jews, blacks, and such minority groups.* **2** the state of being a minor: *You can't vote during your minority.*

min·strel (MIN·strul) *n.* a travelling poet-musician of the Middle Ages: *a wandering minstrel.*

mint *n.* **1** a strongly scented plant such as peppermint or lavender, whose fragrant leaves or oil is used in perfumes, flavouring, medicine, etc.: *a sprig of mint; adj.: mint leaves, sauce, tea.* **2** a place where money is coined.
— **a mint of money** a vast sum of money.
— **in mint condition** of collectibles such as books, stamps, and coins, as good as new.
— *v.* **1** to coin money, medals, etc.: *He literally mints money.* **2** invent or fabricate: *Many trademarks are newly minted words.*

mint·y *adj.* having the flavour of mint.

mi·nus (MY·nus) *prep.* [indicating subtraction or negation]: *3 minus 2 is 1; a temperature of minus five degrees* (= five below zero); *Al returned home minus* (*Informal for* without) *his hat.*
— *n.* the sign (−) indicating subtraction or negation; *adj.: a B minus grade; a minus quantity such as "−2ab"; a minus temperature.*

mi·nus·cule (mi·NUS·cule, MIN·us-) *n.* a small or lowercase letter.
— *adj.* very small: *a minuscule difference, fraction, increment, percentage, script.*

¹**mi·nute** (my·NEWT) *adj.* **-nut·er, -nut·est** very small or insignificant; requiring close scrutiny: *minute details, insects; minute* (= detailed) *instructions.*
— **mi·nute·ly** *adv.;* **mi·nute·ness** *n.*

²**min·ute** (MIN·it) *n.* **1** a 60th part of an hour or of an angular degree; hence, a moment: *Wait a minute* (= a short while); *There were too many applications **at the last minute*** (= close to the deadline); *I want my money back **this minute*** (= right now); *an up-to-the-minute news update; **The minute that** or **The minute*** (= as soon as) *the teacher turns her back, the children start talking; adj.: a clock's minute hand; quick-cooking minute rice.* **2 minutes** *pl.* the official record of the proceedings at a meeting: *The secretary is supposed to keep or take minutes of meetings, then read the minutes to the members who may vote to accept or reject the minutes.*

min·ute·man (MIN·it·man) *n.* **-men** a volunteer of the American Revolutionary War trained to fight "at a minute's notice": *the "Minuteman" ballistic missile.*

minute steak (MIN·it-) *n.* a thin beefsteak for fast frying.

mi·nu·ti·ae (muh·NEW·shee·ee) *n.pl.* minute details; *sing.* **mi·nu·ti·a** (-shee·uh).

minx *n.* a pert or saucy girl; **minx·ish** *adj.*

mir·a·cle (MEER·uh·cul) *n.* **1** an action or event that is beyond human power or understanding, as raising the dead to life: *It's a miracle that she survived the crash; She survived by a miracle; to accomplish, perform, work a miracle; adj.: a **miracle drug** or wonder drug; a miracle worker.* **2** a marvellous person or thing: *She's a miracle of patience.*

mi·rac·u·lous (muh·RAK·yuh·lus) *adj.* surprising and fortunate like a miracle: *his miraculous good fortune; her miraculous recovery from cancer.*
— **mi·rac·u·lous·ly** *adv.*

mi·rage (muh·RAHZH) *n.* **1** an optical illusion of water or phantom images caused by refraction of light in hot air: *The travellers in the desert rushed toward the water hole only to find it was a mirage.* **2** something unattainable or illusory.

mire *n.* **1** a marsh. **2** slush or deep mud: *The wheels got stuck in the mire; He dragged her name through the mire* (= brought her shame) *by publishing his exploits.*
— *v.* **mires, mired, mir·ing 1** soil with mud: *hands all mired from gardening.* **2** get or cause to get stuck or to sink in mud or as if in mud: *Our car got mired (down) in the mudhole; people mired in poverty.*

mir·ror (MEER·ur) *n.* a glass with its back coated with silver so as to reflect images; also, a similar shiny surface: *a full-length mirror; a car's rear-view mirror; side-view mirror; the face as a mirror of character.*
— *v.* reflect, as in a glass: *a building mirrored in a reflecting pool; The election results mirrored the mood of the nation.*

mirth *n.* gaiety and fun, esp. with laughter: *His costume provoked mirth.*

mis- *prefix.* [with negative sense]: *mislead, mismanage, misshapen.*

mis·ad·ven·ture (mis·ud·VEN·chur) *n.* mishap or

misfortune: *The case was ruled death by misadventure* (= accident), *not homicide.*

mis·al·li·ance (mis·uh·LYE·unce) *n.* unsuitable alliance, esp. in marriage.

mis·al·lo·ca·tion (MIS·al·uh·CAY·shun) *n.* improper allocation of funds, resources, etc.

mis·an·thrope (MIS·un·thrope) *n.* one who mistrusts or hates everyone. — **mis·an·throp·ic** (·THROP·ic) *adj.* — **mis·an·thro·pist** (mis·AN·thruh·pist) *n.* — **mis·an·thro·py** (·pee) *n.*

mis·ap·ply (mis·uh·PLY) *v.* -ap·plies, -ap·plied, -ap·ply·ing apply funds or resources illegally or wastefully. — **mis·ap·pli·ca·tion** (MIS·ap·luh·CAY·shun) *n.*

mis·ap·pro·pri·ate (mis·uh·PROH·pree·ate) *v.* -ates, -at·ed, -at·ing take funds, etc. wrongly or dishonestly. — **mis·ap·pro·pri·a·tion** (·AY·shun) *n.*

mis·be·got·ten (mis·bi·GOT·un) *adj.* illegitimate or bastard.

mis·be·have (mis·bi·HAIV) *v.* -haves, -haved, -hav·ing behave badly: *He got drunk at the party and misbehaved.* — **mis·be·hav·iour** or **mis·be·hav·ior** *n.*

mis·brand *v.* brand or label misleadingly.

mis·cal·cu·late (mis·CAL·kyuh·late) *v.* -lates, -lat·ed, -lat·ing wrongly calculate or estimate a result or outcome. — **mis·cal·cu·la·tion** (·LAY·shun) *n.*

mis·car·riage (mis·CAIR·ij) *n.* failure of an intended or proper result: *Mary had a miscarriage* (= "spontaneous abortion" or expulsion of an embryo or fetus from the uterus); *The jury was fixed and the trial was a gross miscarriage of justice; The freight was not delivered because of miscarriage* (= failure to arrive). — **mis·car·ry** (mis·CAIR·ee) *v.* -car·ries, -car·ried, -car·ry·ing.

mis·cast (mis·CAST) *v.* -casts, -cast, -cast·ing cast in an unsuitable role: *Mimi was miscast as the cowardly lion.*

mis·cel·la·neous (mis·uh·LAY·nee·us) *adj.* 1 of varied or mixed items though similar: *a miscellaneous collection; miscellaneous comments, matters, news.* 2 many-sided: *a miscellaneous talent, writer.*

mis·cel·la·ny (MIS·uh·lay·nee) *n.* -nies a miscellaneous collection, esp. a literary one.

mis·chance *n.* a piece of bad luck.

mis·chief (MIS·chif) *n.* harm or injury caused by irresponsible behaviour: *to cause, do, make mischief; Lou is always up to some mischief or other; Lee can't stay out of mischief; It's hard to keep him out of mischief; He's always getting into mischief; a prankster charged with public mischief for pulling the fire alarm; Her eyes are full of mischief* (= playful teasing). — **mis·chie·vous** (MIS·chuh·vus) *adj.*: *a mischievous child, gossip, look, rumour.* — **mis·chie·vous·ly** *adv.*

mis·con·ceive (mis·cun·SEEV) *v.* -ceives, -ceived, -ceiv·ing 1 plan or think out badly: *a wholly misconceived approach, attempt, method, plan, policy.* 2 misinterpret. — **mis·con·cep·tion** (·SEP·shun) *n.*

mis·con·duct (mis·CON·duct) *n.* 1 improper behaviour, esp. adultery. 2 mismanagement, esp. in public office: *gross, professional misconduct.* 3 a penalty in hockey: *The referee handed out* or *gave out 20 minor penalties, 16 majors, two misconducts, and five game misconducts* (= suspensions for the remainder of the game).

mis·con·strue (mis·cun·STROO) *v.* -strues, -stru·ing, -stru·ing misinterpret or misconceive. — **mis·con·struc·tion** (·STRUC·shun) *n.*

mis·cre·ant (MIS·cree·unt) *n.* one who is villainous or depraved.

mis·cue (mis·CUE) *v.* -cues, -cued, -cu·ing give a performer a wrong cue. — *n.* an error, esp. by a player in baseball, football, etc.

mis·deal (mis·DEEL) *v.* -deals, -dealt (·DELT) , -deal·ing deal playing cards wrongly. — *n.* such a deal.

mis·deed (mis·DEED) *n.* a wrong or wicked deed; crime.

mis·de·mean·our or **mis·de·mean·or** (mis·di·MEE·nur) *n.* 1 a violation such as a traffic offence or assault that is less serious than a felony. 2 a misdeed.

mis·di·rect (mis·duh·RECT) *v.* direct wrongly. — **mis·di·rec·tion** (·REC·shun) *n.*

mi·ser (MY·zur) *n.* a stingy person who hoards money, loving it for its own sake. — **mi·ser·ly** *adj.*; **mi·ser·li·ness** *n.*

mis·er·a·ble (MIZ·uh·ruh·bul) *adj.* wretched, poor, or unhappy: *the miserable life of the poor; miserable slums, weather; a miserable failure; a miserable* (= unfriendly) *fellow; You can't get a coffee with a miserable 50 cents.* — **mis·er·a·bly** *adv.*

mis·er·y (MIZ·uh·ree) *n.* -er·ies a cause or condition of being miserable: *a life of misery; the miseries of war; to alleviate, cause, relieve misery; He lived in misery all his life; abject, sheer, untold misery.*

mis·fire *v.* -fires, -fired, -fir·ing fail to fire or to achieve the intended effect: *His plans misfired.* — *n.* a misfiring: *the misfire in a badly tuned automobile engine.*

mis·fit *n.* 1 one not well adjusted socially or in a job. 2 a badly fitted garment. — *v.* -fits, -fit·ted, -fit·ting fit badly: *a boy misfitted in his older brother's clothes.*

mis·for·tune (mis·FOR·chun) *n.* a piece of bad luck: *to have* or *suffer a misfortune; She had the misfortune to get hurt in an accident.*

mis·giv·ing (mis·GIV·ing) *n.* usually **misgivings** *pl.* feelings of doubt or lack of confidence: *We had misgivings about hiring him; misgivings that he might prove undependable.*

mis·guide (mis·GIDE, "G" as in "go") *v.* mislead, esp. into wrongdoing.

mis·guid·ed (mis·GUY·did) *adj.* mistaken; in error: *He's very misguided in his aims though well-meaning; a misguided genius.* — **mis·guid·ed·ly** *adv.*

mis·han·dle (mis·HAN·dul) *v.* -dles, -dled, -dling treat or manage badly.

mis·hap *n.* an unlucky, usually minor accident.

mis·hear (mis-HEER) *v.* -hears, -heard (-HURD), -hear·ing hear incorrectly.

mish·mash *n.* a hodgepodge.

mis·in·form (mis-in-FORM) *v.* give someone false or misleading information: *I'm afraid you're grossly misinformed about what's going on at the office.* — **mis·in·for·ma·tion** (MIS-in-fur-MAY-shun) *n.*

mis·in·ter·pret (mis-in-TUR-prit) *v.* understand or interpret incorrectly. — **mis·in·ter·pre·ta·tion** (-pruh-TAY-shun) *n.*

mis·judge (mis-JUJ) *v.* -judg·es, -judged, -judg·ing judge wrongly or unjustly. — **mis·judg·ment** or **mis·judge·ment** *n.*

mis·la·bel (mis-LAY-bul) *v.* -bels, -belled or -beled, -bel·ling or -bel·ing label incorrectly or falsely.

mis·lay (mis-LAY) *v.* -lays, -laid, -lay·ing misplace or lose something.

mis·lead (mis-LEED) *v.* -leads, -led, -lead·ing to lead someone to go, think, or act in error or badly: *We are misled by bad advice, by illegible writing, by a candid manner; misled about the whole business.* — **mis·lead·ing** *adj.*: *It's misleading to give only the good news; misleading advertising.*

mis·man·age (mis-MAN-ij) *v.* -ag·es, -aged, -ag·ing manage badly or dishonestly. — **mis·man·age·ment** *n.*

mis·match (mis-MATCH) *v.* match badly: *a mismatched pair of socks; They are a mismatched pair (of spouses).* — *n.*: *The boxers were an obvious mismatch.*

mis·no·mer (mis-NOH-mur) *n.* a wrongly given name: *It's a misnomer to call a whale a fish because it is a mammal; a misnomer to call this stuff food.*

mis·place (mis-PLACE) *v.* -plac·es, -placed, -plac·ing put in a wrong place: *A misplaced key is often lost; Only after being jilted did he realize that his affections had been misplaced* (= bestowed on the wrong person).

mis·print (MIS-print) *n.* a printing error. — *v.* (mis-PRINT) print incorrectly.

mis·pro·nounce (mis-pruh-NOUNCE) *v.* -nounc·es, -nounced, -nounc·ing pronounce incorrectly. — **mis·pro·nun·ci·a·tion** (MIS-pruh-nun-see-AY-shun) *n.*

mis·quote (mis-QUOTE) *v.* -quotes, -quot·ed, -quot·ing quote incorrectly. — **mis·quo·ta·tion** (-kwuh-TAY-shun) *n.*

mis·read (mis-REED) *n.* -reads, -read (-RED), -read·ing read wrongly; hence, misunderstand.

mis·rep·re·sent (MIS-rep-ri-SENT) *v.* represent incorrectly or falsely. — **mis·rep·re·sen·ta·tion** (-sen-TAY-shun) *n.*

mis·rule (mis-ROOL) *n.* 1 bad government. 2 disorder or anarchy. — *v.* -rules, -ruled, -ruling govern badly.

miss *v.* 1 fail to attain, get, hit a person or thing: *She missed the target; to miss an aim, appointment, bus, joke, meeting, opportunity, point; to miss* (= fail to notice) *someone in a crowd; You can't miss it* (= It's so obvious); *a missing* (= misfiring) *engine; I just missed* (= escaped) *being hit by the ball; People living in the country are **missing out** on what is going on in town.* 2 notice the absence of a person or thing: *When did you first miss the child?* 3 feel the absence of a person or thing: *I'll miss you when you're gone; You'll be sorely missed; I'll miss working with you; I seem to be missing my wallet.* — *n., pl.* **miss·es** 1 a missing: *Is it a hit or a miss? a clean miss; near miss; strikes, spares, and misses in bowling.* 2 a usually young unmarried woman or girl: *May we have the check, Miss?* 3 **Miss** [title used before an unmarried girl's or woman's name]: *Miss (Mary) Jones* [or rarely] *Miss Mary; Miss Canada* (= winner of a beauty contest of young Canadian women).

mis·shap·en (mis-SHAY-pun) *adj.* deformed: *a misshapen limb.*

mis·sile (MIS-ul) *n.* something directed at a target, esp. a weapon such as a stone, spear, bullet, rocket, etc.: *to fire, intercept, launch a missile; a ballistic, cruise, guided, nuclear, strategic, tactical missile.*

missing *adj.* not where someone or something should be: *Our cat has gone missing; When everyone had taken their seats, one child was missing; soldiers **missing in action*** (= unaccounted for after a war).

mis·sion (MISH-un) *n.* the sending of people on an assignment; also, the people thus sent or their assigned task: *a combat mission; dangerous mission; diplomatic mission to China; He was on a goodwill mission; a rescue mission; a search-and-destroy mission; an Apollo space mission (of exploration); Japanese pilots flew suicide missions (with little chance of survival) during the war; a trade mission to Italy; a pilot who has flown numerous (bombing) missions over Vietnam; to accomplish, carry out, perform, undertake a mission; a mission (to preach the Gospel) to the Indies; to collect money for the **missions*** (= organizations for spreading Christianity); *her lifelong mission* (= calling or vocation) *of caring for the sick.*

mis·sion·ar·y (MISH-uh-nair-ee) *n.* -ar·ies a person on a religious mission. — *adj.*: *a missionary priest, society; Mother Teresa's missionary zeal.*

mission control *n.* the command centre on the ground for space flights.

mis·sion·er (MISH-un-ur) *n.* a missionary.

mis·sis (MIS-uz) *n. Informal.* [written "Mrs." when used as title] one's wife; also, the mistress of a household: *Mrs. Smith; Is the missis home?*

mis·sive (MIS-iv) *n.* an epistle or long letter sent to someone.

mis·spell (mis-SPEL) *v.* -spells, *pt. & pp.* -spelled or -spelt, -spell·ing spell incorrectly. — **mis·spell·ing** *n.*

mis·sus same as MISSIS.

mist *n.* 1 a fog that is not too thick to see through nor so thin as a haze: *a mist* (= fine spray) *of perfume.* 2 something that dims or blurs vision: *a historian who got lost in the mists of antiquity.* — *v.* make or become misty, as eyes with tears.

mis·take (mis-TAKE) *n.* an error of observation, judgment, expression, action, etc.; misunderstanding: *Our mistake, Sir! She opened his letter **by mistake**; to correct, excuse, forgive, make, rectify a mistake; a bad,*

glaring, foolish, slight mistake; It was a mistake to take on that assignment.
— **make no mistake (about it)** You may be sure.
— *v.* **-takes, -took, -tak·en, -tak·ing** make a mistake or take wrongly: *I mistook her words; Twins are often mistaken for each other.*
— **mis·tak·a·ble** (-kuh·bul) *adj.*

mis·tak·en (mis·TAY·cun) *adj.* wrong: *He could be mistaken; a mistaken notion; He was mistaken about what she said; quite mistaken in finding fault with her.*
— **mis·ta·ken·ly** *adv.*

mis·ter *n.* **1** the full form of MR. **2** *Informal.* sir: *Hey, mister! Mr. Coffee, Donut* (= the product or service personified).

mis·tle·toe (MIS·ul·toh) *n.* a parasitic evergreen plant associated with Christmastime: *the Christmas tradition of kissing under the mistletoe.*

mistook *pt.* of MISTAKE.

mis·treat (mis·TREET) *v.* ill-treat. — **mis·treat·ment** *n.*

mis·tress (MIS·tris) *n.* **1** a woman in a ruling or controlling position, as the female head of a household or a teacher or expert, esp. in a special subject: *our dancing mistress; Britain used to be the mistress of the seas; "a mistress in her own house, though a daughter in her mother's."* **2** a woman who regularly has sex with a man she is not married to. **3 Mistress** [old use] Mrs.; Miss.

mis·tri·al (MIS·try·ul) *n.* a judgment that a trial is of no legal effect: *The judge declared a mistrial as the jurors could not agree on a verdict.*

mis·trust (mis·TRUST) *n.* a lack of trust or confidence: *The smooth-talking politician arouses mistrust; I have a deep, profound mistrust of strangers.*
— *v.* feel mistrust toward: *I mistrust my ability to edit my own writing; I mistrust myself as my own editor.*
— **mis·trust·ful** *adj.*; **mis·trust·ful·ly** *adv.*

mist·y *adj.* **mist·i·er, -i·est** covered with mist: *misty air, hills; a misty morning; eyes misty with tears; a misty* (= blurred) *memory, view.*
— **mist·i·ly** *adv.*; **mist·i·ness** *n.*

mis·un·der·stand (MIS·un·dur·STAND) *v.* **-stands, -stood, -stand·ing** fail to understand a message, person, etc. correctly.

mis·un·der·stand·ing (MIS·un·dur·STAN·ding) *n.* a failure to understand properly; hence, a quarrel or falling out.

mis·use (mis·YOOZ) *v.* **-us·es, -used, -us·ing** use a thing or treat a person improperly.
— *n.* (-YOOSE): *a misuse of authority, words.*

mite *n.* **1** a tiny, insectlike, usually parasitic creature that sucks the blood of animals, juice of plants, or torments human beings: *a bird mite; grain mite; itch mite.* **2** a tiny amount, small coin, or very small creature.
— *adv.* *Informal.* a little: *His joke is wearing a mite thin.*

mi·ter same as MITRE.

mit·i·gate (MIT·uh·gate) *v.* **-gates, -gat·ed, -gat·ing** make or become mild or less harsh: *to mitigate one's anger; to mitigate the cold; to mitigate a disaster; to mitigate pain.* — **mit·i·ga·tion** (-GAY·shun) *n.*

mi·tral (MY·trul) *adj.* resembling a mitre: *the mitral valve of the heart.*

mi·tre or **mi·ter** (MY·tur) *n.* **1** the tall, pointed ceremonial headdress of ecclesiastics of the rank of bishop and higher, that is joined in two folding halves facing front and back. **2** a corner joint of two bevelled or rabbeted pieces fitting together in a right angle: *A* **mitre box** *(device) is used as a guide for sawing wood at the proper angle for making a* **mitre joint.**
— *v.* **-tres** or **-ters, -tred** or **-tered, -tring** or **-ter·ing** join in a mitre: *two boards mitred together.*

mitt *n.* **1** a protective covering for the hand but without fingers: *a (baseball) catcher's mitt; an oven mitt.* **2** mitten.

mit·ten (MIT·un) *n.* a glove that covers the four fingers together and the thumb separately.

mix *v.* **mix·es,** *pt. & pp.* **mixed** or **mixt, mix·ing** combine so as to associate together: *Oil and water don't mix; Please mix me a drink; to mix ingredients for a cake; a visit mixing business with pleasure; a sociable woman who mixes well with people of all ages.*
— **mix up 1** confuse: *She got Tim mixed up with his twin brother Tom.* **2** involve: *He was mixed up in a scandal; Better not get mixed up with that crowd.*
— *n.* something mixed or for mixing: *a cake mix; cement mix; pancake mix; soup mix; gin with her favourite mix (such as tonic).*

mixed *adj.* of different kinds: *mixed company (of men and women); a mixed group (of men and women); The movie received mixed* (= good and bad) *reviews; a* **mixed bag** *(of assorted items); a* **mixed drink** (= alcoholic drink with several ingredients); *something of doubtful value received with* **mixed feelings** *(such as joy and regret); a* **mixed marriage** *(between persons of different religions or races); a* **mixed media** *presentation (using film, photographs, slides, tapes, etc.); a* **mixed metaphor** *(with clashing comparisons).*

mixed-up *adj.* confused: *a mixed-up youth.*

mix·er *n.* one that mixes: *an electric food mixer; She's too shy to be a good mixer (in society).*

mix·ture (MIX·chur) *n.* a mixing, being mixed, or something mixed: *Sand and sugar form a mixture, not a compound; a **freezing mixture** of salt and crushed ice.*

mix-up *n.* a confusion or a confused state: *There's been a mix-up; a mix-up about the seats; a mix-up over who sits where; a mix-up in the seating arrangements.*

mne·mon·ic (ni·MON·ic) *adj.* of or meant to help the memory: *jingles, rhymes, and such mnemonic devices.*

moan (MONE) *n.* a low and mournful sound: *the moans of the injured and dying.*
— *v.* say with or utter in a moan: *a patient moaning with pain; "Oh no," she moaned, when she heard the news.*

moat (MOTE) *n.* a deep and wide ditch, usually water-filled, as around a fortress wall or zoo display area.

mob *n.* **1** a disorderly or riotous crowd: *to control, disperse, inflame, stir up, subdue a mob; an angry mob of demonstrators.* **2** the common people or masses: *the tastes of the mob; **adj.**: mob orators, reactions, rule, violence.* **3** *Informal.* a criminal group or gang: *a mob of gangsters; the Mob (= the Mafia).*
— *v.* **mobs, mobbed, mob·bing** crowd around a person or into a place, as a mob: *a movie star mobbed by autograph hunters; shoppers mobbing sales counters.*

mo·bile (MOH·bul, -beel) **1** *adj.* moving or movable: *a mobile library; a **mobile lounge** for carrying passengers between terminal and aircraft; a mobile (= changeable in expression) face; the upwardly mobile middle class.* **2** (-beel) *n.* a delicately balanced, usually suspended decoration or art object made of pieces of metal or plastic attached to wires and rods so as to move in currents of air.
— *combining form.* something moving: *artmobile (= art exhibit in a trailer), bloodmobile, bookmobile, popemobile (= security vehicle for the pope), snowmobile.* — **mo·bil·i·ty** (moh·BIL·uh·tee) *n.*

mobile home *n.* a large trailer used as a home.

mo·bi·lize (MOH·buh·lize) *v.* **-liz·es, -lized, -liz·ing** **1** put into motion or active use. **2** organize or get ready, as troops for war. — **mo·bi·li·za·tion** (-luh·ZAY·shun) *n.*

mob·ster (MOB·stur) *n.* a member of a criminal group or mob; gangster.

moc·ca·sin (MOC·uh·sin) *n.* **1** a heelless sandal or slipper of soft leather, originally used by North American Indians. **2** a water moccasin.

mo·cha (MOH·cuh) *n.* a fine variety of coffee, originally shipped from Mocha, Yemen.
— *adj.* flavoured with coffee or coffee and chocolate: *mocha cakes, ice cream, puddings.*

mock *v.* make fun of or ridicule, esp. by imitating or caricaturing: *a mocking gesture; The bully mocked him, mocked his accent, and jeered at him.*
— *adj.* pseudo or imitation: *a mock battle, parliament, turtle soup.* — **mock·er·y** *n.*

mock·he·ro·ic (mock·hi·ROH·ic) *adj.* imitative of heroic style or character, as "Don Quixote" or Pope's poem "The Rape of the Lock."

mock-up *n.* an accurately built model, usually full-size, for studying, testing, or display, as of an airplane.

mod *n.* one who is bold and unconventional in dress and behaviour: *A mod wears mod clothes.*

mode *n.* a method, manner, or style, esp. one that is usual, customary, or current: *the mode of life of the Inuit; Dad is dressed in the latest mode (= style); the major and minor modes (= scales or keys) in music.*

mod·el (MOD·ul) *n.* **1** one that is to be imitated or copied: *a wax model for a marble statue; an artist's model; She's a model (= perfect example) of decorum; a role model for her children; adj.: a model farm, hospital (for viewing by potential buyers); his model (= exemplary) behaviour; a model (= excellent) husband, pupil, teacher, wife.* **2** one made in the same pattern as others: *the make and model (= particular design, as Chevrolet, Mustang, or Corolla) of your car; a Model T Ford; a new model of computer; an airplane model (= a small representation); a scale model.* **3** a person who displays clothes by wearing them: *a fashion model.*
— *v.* **-els, -elled** or **-eled, -el·ling** or **-el·ing** **1** follow as a model: *a university modelled after Oxford; She models herself on (= admires and imitates) her mother.* **2** work as a fashion model: *She models hats at fashion shows; also models for customers; She models (= does modelling) at $200 an hour.* **3** make models: *He models in clay.*

mo·dem (MOH·dem) *n.* a "modulator-demodulator" device for converting computer data for transmission or reception via telephone lines.

mod·er·ate (MOD·uh·rit) *adj.* within proper bounds, esp. not excessive: *She is moderate in her ambitions, demands, expenditures; a man of moderate habits; a moderate drinker.*
— *n.: a political moderate, more liberal than conservative.*
— *v.* (-rate) **-ates, -at·ed, -at·ing** **1** make or become less excessive: *She exercises a moderating influence on her husband.* **2** act as moderator: *Who's moderating the panel discussion?*
— **mod·er·ate·ly** *adv.;* **mod·er·a·tion** (-RAY·shun) *n.*

mod·er·a·tor (MOD·uh·ray·tur) *n.* one who presides: *the moderator of an examination, meeting, panel discussion.*

mod·ern (MOD·urn) *adj.* **1** recent or current: *Modern English since about 1500; The computer is a modern invention; The New World was settled by Europeans in modern times.* **2** up-to-date: *modern architecture, fashions, views.*
— *n.* one who is modern: *ancients and moderns.*
— **mod·ern·ly** *adv.*
— **mod·ern·ness** or **mod·er·ni·ty** (-DUR·nuh·tee) *n.*

mod·ern·ize (MOD·ur·nize) *v.* **-iz·es, -ized, -iz·ing** make or become modern; **mod·ern·iz·er** *n.*
— **mod·ern·i·za·tion** (-nuh·ZAY·shun) *n.*

mod·est (MOD·ist) *adj.* proper in one's behaviour or appearance, being unassuming, shy, decent, etc.: *a modest sales pitch, not loud or vulgar; He's modest about his qualifications; quite modest in his claims; a modest little cottage; a modest demand; A bikini is not modest enough to wear to church;* **mod·est·ly** *adj.*

mod·es·ty (MOD·is·tee) *n.* the quality of being properly humble, shy, decent, etc.: *the false modesty of keeping* *piano legs covered; the **modesty panel** of a desk for hiding the legs of a woman seated behind it.*

mod·i·cum (MOD·uh·cum) *n.* a small amount: *a modicum of manners, taste, truth, wine.*

mod·i·fy (MOD·uh·fye) *v.* **-fies, -fied, -fy·ing** change or alter, esp. to limit or moderate: *to modify a behaviour, demand, method, one's tone of voice; In "too little," "too" modifies "little."*
— **mod·i·fi·er** *n.;* **mod·i·fi·ca·tion** (-fuh·CAY·shun) *n.*

mod·ish (MOH·dish) *adj.* overly fashionable or stylish: *too modish for my tastes.*
— **mod·ish·ly** *adv.;* **mod·ish·ness** *n.*

mod·u·lar (MOJ·uh·lur) *adj.* having to do with modules; standardized: *a modular telephone cable, cord, coupler, jack; modular equipment; modular house construction; a modular system.* — **mod·u·lar·i·ty** (-LAIR·uh·tee) *n.*

mod·u·late (MOJ·uh·late) *v.* **-lates, -lat·ed, -lat·ing** regulate or adjust, as the tone or pitch of one's voice in speaking, from one key to another in a musical composition, the frequency or amplitude of video and audio signals in broadcasting, etc. — **mod·u·la·tion** (-LAY·shun) *n.;* **mod·u·la·tor** (-lay·tur) *n.*

mod·ule (MOJ·ool) *n.* **1** a structural unit or component with a specific function in a larger unit or system: *building modules; the astronauts in a command module; a lunar excursion module; a learning module (= unit); a spacecraft's service module; work modules making up an office; problem-solving in action modules responding to specific needs.* **2** a standard size or measure: *toothpaste in six metric modules from 25 to 150 ml.*

mo·dus o·pe·ran·di (MOH·dus·op·uh·RAN·dye, -dee) *n. Latin.* mode of operation or procedure.

modus vi·ven·di (MOH·dus·vi·VEN·dye, -dee) *n. Latin.* mode of living or coexisting.

mo·gul (MOH·gul) *n.* **1** magnate: *a movie mogul.* **2** a bump on a ski run.

mo·hair (MOH·hair) *n.* a fabric made of the hair of the Angora goat, usually blended with wool.

moi·e·ty (MOY·uh·tee) *n.* **-ties** a portion, esp. half *of something.*

moist *adj.* moderately wet: *skin that is moist with perspiration;* **moist·ly** *adv.;* **moist·ness** *n.*

mois·ten (MOY·sun) *v.* make or become moist: *Don't wet the stamp, just moisten it before sticking.*

mois·ture (MOIS·chur) *n.* a liquid that causes moistness, esp. water vapour, as in the air.

mois·tur·ize (MOIS·chuh·rize) *v.* **-iz·es, -ized, -iz·ing** make skin, air, etc. moist, as a cosmetic cream does.

mo·lar (MOH·lur) *n.* a tooth adapted for grinding: *The four wisdom teeth are the rearmost of the three molars on each side of the jaws; an impacted molar (tooth); We have 12 molar teeth in all.*

mo·las·ses (muh·LAS·iz) *n.* a thick, sticky, brown syrup obtained as a by-product during the refining of cane sugar.

mold, moldboard, molder, molding, moldy See MOULD, etc.

mole *n.* **1** a congenital, usually dark protuberance on the skin. **2** a small furry burrowing animal that lives underground; also, the pocket gopher of the Canadian prairies. **3** a tunnelling machine. **4** a spy lying in wait to act as a double-agent: *a mole planted by the Soviets in the CIA.* **5** a breakwater, esp. one formed of large stones, earth, or masonry.

mol·e·cule (MOL·uh·cule) *n.* a small particle, esp. the smallest particle of a chemical element or compound, composed of atoms.
— **mo·lec·u·lar** (muh·LEK·yuh·lur) *adj.*

mole·hill *n.* a small mound of earth thrown up by a mole.

mole·skin *n.* **1** the skin of the mole used as fur. **2** a cotton fabric used for work clothes.

mo·lest (muh·LEST) *v.* annoy a weaker person such as a child, esp. sexually; **mo·les·ta·tion** (moh·les·TAY·shun) *n.* — **mo·lest·er** *n.: a child molester.*

moll (MOL) *n. Slang.* a gangster's mistress or girl friend.

mol·li·fy (MOL·uh·fye) *v.* **-fies, -fied, -fy·ing** calm or soothe a person or his or her feelings.

mol·lusc or **mol·lusk** (MOL·usk) *n.* a soft-bodied, shell-enclosed creature such as a snail, oyster, or octopus.

mol·ly·cod·dle (MOL·ee·cod·ul) *v.* **-cod·dles, -cod·dled, -cod·dling** to pamper or fuss over.
— *n.* a boy used to being pampered.

Mo·lo·tov cocktail (MOL·uh·tof·) *n.* a crude hand grenade made of a bottle of gasoline and a wick.

molt *n. & v.* same as MOULT.

mol·ten (MOLE·tun) *adj.* melted: *molten lava, metal.*

mom *n. Informal.* mother.

mom-and-pop *adj. Informal.* of businesses, small and independent; ma-and-pa: *a mom-and-pop store.*

mo·ment (MOH·munt) *n.* **1** a short space of time; instant: *I'll be with you in a moment; Let's forget it for the moment (= now); She got up and protested on the spur of the moment (= without deliberation); the **moment of truth** (= crisis point); a crucial, opportune, rash moment; the psychological moment (= best time) for popping the question.* **2** weight or importance: *a matter of great moment.*

mo·men·tar·i·ly (MOH·mun·tair·ee·lee) *adv.* **1** for a moment: *He was lost for words momentarily.* **2** from moment to moment: *We are expecting the flight to take off momentarily.* **3** in a moment: *He'll see you momentarily.* — **mo·men·tar·i·ness** *n.*

mo·men·tar·y (MOH·mun·tair·ee) *adj.* lasting only a moment.

mo·men·to (moh·MEN·toh) *n.* **-toes** [substandard form] See MEMENTO.

mo·men·tous (moh·MEN·tus) *adj.* of great moment or weight: *a momentous announcement, decision, occasion; of momentous significance.*

mo·men·tum (moh·MEN·tum) *n.* **-tums** or **-ta** the force of a moving body; impetus: *A stone gains* or *gathers momentum as it rolls downhill.*

mom·my (MOM·ee) *n.* **mom·mies** [child's word] mother.

mon·arch (MON·urk) *n.* **1** a supreme ruler such as a king, queen, emperor, or sultan: *A constitutional monarch cannot be an absolute monarch.* **2** an orange-and-black migratory butterfly.
— **mo·nar·chic** (muh·NAR·kic) or **mo·nar·chi·cal** (-kuh·cul) *adj.*

mon·arch·y (MON·ur·kee) *n.* **-arch·ies** a country ruled by a monarch, usually with limited power, as in the U.K.: *to establish, overthrow, set up a monarchy.*
— **mon·arch·ist** *n.*

mon·as·ter·y (MON·uh·stair·ee) *n.* **-ter·ies** a place where a community of monks or nuns lives an ascetic, or **mo·nas·tic** (muh·NAS·tic), life.

mo·nas·ti·cism (muh·NAS·tuh·siz·um) *n.* the condition or system of living a monastic life.

Mon·day (MUN·dee, -day) *n.* the day following Sunday, usually the first working day of the week: *We love weekends and hate Mondays.*

M-1 (EM·wun) *n.* the basic money supply of an economy, consisting of cash and bank deposits.

mon·e·tar·y (MON·uh·tair·ee) *adj.* having to do with money, esp. coinage or currency: *a monetary policy, system, unit, value;* **mon·e·tar·ism** *n.*

mon·ey (MUN·ee) *n.* **mon·eys** or **mon·ies 1** an authorized medium of exchange, esp. coins or paper notes: *to change, circulate, coin, counterfeit money.* **2** wealth or property: *to bank, borrow, deposit, earn, invest, launder, lend, make, put up, raise, refund, save, squander, tie up, withdraw money; We put money into* (= invest in) *Canada Savings Bonds; They sink money into speculative ventures; a man of money; the moneys* (= sums of money) *owed by you; conscience, earnest, easy, hush, mad, marked, pin, pocket, prize, seed money; She wouldn't do it for love or for money; He's out of money at the end of a month.*
— **in the money** *Slang.* **1** rich or prosperous. **2** among the top prizewinners of a race or contest.
— **money talks** *Slang.* You can accomplish things with money.
— **on the money** *Slang.* exactly as expected or desired: *He made a firm pass right on the money.*

mon·ey·bags (MUN·ee·bags) *n.pl. Informal.* a rich and avaricious person.

mon·eyed (MUN·eed) *adj.* rich and wealthy.

mon·ey·lend·er (MUN·ee·len·dur) *n.* one who lends money at interest.

mon·ey·mak·er *n.* (MUN·ee·may·kur) *n.* **1** one skilled in acquiring wealth. **2** a profit-making scheme or product.
— **mon·ey·mak·ing** *n. & adj.*

money order *n.* a document issued at a post office or bank ordering payment of a specified amount on the purchaser's behalf to another person.

-monger *combining form.* [derogatory] dealer in what is specified: *fishmonger, peacemonger, rumourmonger, scandalmonger, warmonger.*

Mon·gol·ism (MONG·guh·liz·um) *n.* same as DOWN'S SYNDROME.

mon·grel (MUNG·grul, MONG-) *n.* a dog of no recognizable breed.
— **adj.** mixed in origin or character: *a mongrel dialect.*

monied same as MONEYED.

monies a *pl.* of MONEY.

mon·i·ker or **mon·ick·er** (MON·uh·kur) *n. Slang.* a nickname: *Eire, the Emerald Isle, Erin, and Irish Free State are monikers for the Republic of Ireland.*

mo·nism (MOH·niz·um, MON·uh-) *n.* the metaphysical doctrine of the oneness of reality, as opposed to dualism, pluralism, etc.; **mo·nist** *n.*
— **mo·nis·tic** (moh·NIS·tic) *adj.*

mo·ni·tion (moh·NISH·un) *n.* admonition; also, an intimation or warning of danger.

mon·i·tor (MON·uh·tur) *v.* to watch or check on the performance of a person or operation: *His movements were monitored closely by the police; a monitoring station listening to broadcasts.*
— **n. 1** a student helping a teacher in class. **2** an output device for receiving audio or video signals: *a tape recorder with a telephone monitor; video monitor; TV monitor; a heart monitor in an operating room.* **3** software for monitoring a system.
— **mon·i·tor·y** *adj.*

monk (MUNK) *n.* a male religious living in a monastery: *Benedictines, Carthusians, and such Christian monks; a Buddhist monk.* — **monk·ish** *adj.*

mon·key (MUNK·ee) *n.* **-keys** a small long-tailed ape or primate: *a horde of monkeys; to make a monkey out of* (*Informal* for to fool) *someone.*
— **v. Informal.** fool or tamper: *He doesn't like cooks monkeying with his favourite dish.*

monkey business *n. Informal.* tricky or mischievous behaviour.

mon·key·shines (MUNK·ee·shines) *n.pl. Slang.* clownish jokes or pranks.

monkey wrench *n.* a wrench with a jaw that is adjustable to various sizes of nuts.
— **throw a monkey wrench into something** disrupt or obstruct the functioning of something going smoothly.

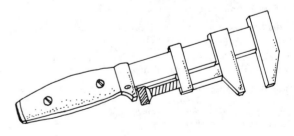

mon·o (MON·oh) *n.* [short form] **1** mononucleosis. **2** a monophonic phonograph record.

mono- *combining form.* one or single: *monochrome, monogamy, monograph.*

mon·o·chro·mat·ic (MON·uh·croh·MAT·ic) *adj.* of one colour; consisting of a single wavelength.

mon·o·chrome (MON·uh·crome) *n. & adj.* a painting, print, etc. in a single colour or shades of one colour: *a monochrome* (= black and white) *TV signal.*

mon·o·cle (MON·uh·cul) *n.* an eyeglass for one eye.

mo·nog·a·my (muh·NOG·uh·mee) *n.* marriage with one person at a time.
— **mo·nog·a·mist** *n.*; **mo·nog·a·mous** (-uh·mus) *adj.*

mon·o·gram (MON·uh·gram) *n.* a design combining the initials of a name.
— *v.* **-grams, -grammed, -gram·ming** print a monogram on something: *monogrammed jewellery, linen, stationery.*

mon·o·graph (MON·uh·graf) *n.* **1** a scholarly work treating a single subject exhaustively. **2** a single volume, not a series. **3** a booklet explaining a single commercial product such as a drug.

mon·o·lin·gual (mon·uh·LING·gwul) *adj.* limited to one language: *a monolingual population.*

mon·o·lith (MON·uh·lith) *n.* **1** a single massive block of stone, as a monument or column. **2** a person or thing that is massive and unyielding.
— **mon·o·lith·ic** (-LITH·ic) *adj.*: *a monolithic column, monument (of one stone), society (that is massive and rigid); integrated circuit (on a single silicon chip).*

mon·o·logue or **mon·o·log** (MON·uh·log) *n.* **1** a long speech by one person of a group: *to recite a monologue.* **2** a soliloquy or other dramatic piece involving one actor.

mon·o·nu·cle·o·sis (MON·uh·new·clee·OH·sis) *n.* a blood disease of young people caused by an abnormality of single-nucleus blood cells; also called "glandular fever" and "kissing disease."

mon·o·phon·ic (mon·uh·FON·ic) *adj.* having to do with sound reproduction using a single channel: *a monophonic, not a stereophonic system.*

mo·nop·o·list (muh·NOP·uh·list) *n.* one who has a monopoly or favours monopoly; **mo·nop·o·lis·tic** (-LIS·tic) *adj.*

mo·nop·o·lize (muh·NOP·uh·lize) *v.* **-liz·es, -lized, -liz·ing** have, get, or keep something exclusively: *to monopolize a conversation.*

mo·nop·o·ly (muh·NOP·uh·lee) *n.* **-lies 1** exclusive marketing control of a commodity or service, as most public utilities: *Canada Post has* or *holds a monopoly on* or *over mail.* **2** a company enjoying such absence of competition: *Is Bell Canada a telephone monopoly? Hydros are government monopolies; Governments try to break up monopolies.*

mon·o·rail (MON·uh·rail) *n.* a single rail or a vehicle travelling on one, with the cars either suspended from the rail or balanced on top of it.

mon·o·syl·la·ble (MON·uh·sil·uh·bul) *n.* a word of one syllable. — **mon·o·syl·lab·ic** (-suh·LAB·ic) *adj.*

mon·o·tone (MON·uh·tone) *n.* sameness of tone of utterance, style of writing, etc.: *He reads in a dull monotone.*

mo·not·o·nous (muh·NOT·uh·nus) *adj.* tiresome because of unvarying tone or style: *a monotonous routine; It's monotonous to eat the same lunch every day.*
— **mo·not·o·ny** *n.*: *VCRs break* or *relieve the monotony of TV watching.*

Mon·sei·gneur (mon·sen·YUR) *n., pl.* **Mes·sei·gneurs** (may·sen·YUR) a French title of honour given to persons of high rank.

mon·sieur (muh·SYUR) *n.* **mes·sieurs** (MES·urz) **1** a gentleman. **2 Monsieur** French title equivalent to "Mr." or "Sir."

Mon·si·gnor (mon·SEEN·yur) *n.* **-gnors** or **-gno·ri** (mone·see·NYOR·ee) a title given to certain dignitaries of the Roman Catholic Church.

mon·soon (mon·SOON) *n.* a seasonal wind blowing over the Indian Ocean, esp. in the summer, accompanied by heavy rains.

mon·ster (MON·stur) *n.* **1** a huge, ugly, or wicked creature such as a dragon. **2** a grossly malformed birth.
— *adj.* huge: *the demolition of small bungalows for building* **monster homes** *in old neighbourhoods; a monster rally.*

mon·strous (MON·strus) *adj.* like a monster; also, wicked: *a monstrous crime; It's monstrous to abuse children; It's monstrous that criminals go unpunished.*
— **mon·strous·ly** *adv.*
— **mon·stros·i·ty** (mon·STROS·uh·tee) *n.* **-ties.**

mon·tage (mon·TAHZH) *n.* in photography, motion pictures, etc., a combining or blending of many distinct pictures for a special effect.

month (MUNTH) *n.* one of the 12 divisions of the year, from 28 to 31 days long, January through December: *The lunar month of about 29½ days is the period of one revolution of the moon around the earth.*

month·ly (MUNTH·lee) *adj. & adv.* every month; once a month. — *n., pl.* **-lies** a monthly publication.

mon·u·ment (MON·yuh·munt) *n.* a tablet, statue, pillar, building, etc. put up in commemoration of a person or event: *The pyramids of Egypt are ancient monuments; The book is a monument to its author's creative genius; A place of historic or scenic interest in the U.S. may be set apart as a national monument for public use.*

mon·u·men·tal (mon·yuh·MEN·tul) *adj.* of or like a monument: *an event of monumental significance; his monumental* (= colossal) *ignorance;* **mon·u·men·tal·ly** *adv.*

moo *v. & n.* **moos, mooed, moo·ing** (make) the sound of the call of a cow.

mooch (long "oo") *v. Slang.* get money, food, etc. by begging; sponge or cadge; **mooch·er** *n.*

mood (long "oo") *n.* **1** a grammatical aspect of the action of a verb: *"He is going"* is in the indicative mood (= aspect of action as a fact); *"I suggest that he go"* is in the subjunctive mood (= aspect of action as a possibility); *"Please go" is in the imperative mood* (= aspect of action as a command). **2** a state of mind; feeling or attitude: *an angry, festive, holiday, genial, jovial, joyful, melancholy, pensive, sullen mood; Talk to him when he is in a good mood; in the mood to listen to you; in no mood for playing games; Don't approach him when he is in a mood* or *in one of his moods* (= when he is in a bad mood); *He is a man of moods* (= uncertain temper); *Could drugs modify one's moods? There is a mood of optimism in the country.*

mood·y *adj.* **mood·i·er, -i·est** gloomy or sullen.
— **mood·i·ly** *adv.;* **mood·i·ness** *n.*

moon (long "oo") *n.* **1** often **Moon,** a heavenly body that is the earth's natural satellite, taking about 29½ days for a full circle, from one "new moon" to the next, during which period it waxes from "crescent" to "full moon" and then wanes: *the harvest moon* (= full moon nearest the September equinox); *The moon comes out when the sun goes down.* **2** any satellite of a planet: *the moons of Jupiter.*
— *v.* **1** spend time or wander *about* or *around* idly. **2** *Slang.* show one's bare buttocks as a prank or gesture of contempt.

moon·beam *n.* a ray of moonlight.

Moon·ie (MOO·nee) *n.* **Moon·ies** a member of a religious cult founded by Sun Myung Moon.

moon·light *n.* the light of the moon: *to walk by moonlight; to go swimming in the moonlight.*
— *v. Informal.* work at a job, as at night, in addition to a regular one; **moon·light·er** *n.*

moon·lit *adj.* lighted by the moon: *a moonlit night.*

moon·shine *n.* **1** moonlight. **2** foolish notions; empty talk. **3** *Informal.* illegally made alcoholic liquor.

moon·shot *n.* the launching of a spacecraft toward the moon.

moon·space *n.* a view of the moon's surface.

moon·stone *n.* a whitish variety of feldspar cut and used as a gem.

moon·struck *adj.* dazed, dreamy, or mentally unbalanced.

moon·walk *n.* an astronaut's walk on the moon.

Moor *n.* a northwest African, esp. a member of the people that conquered Spain in the 8th century A.D.
— **Moor·ish** *adj.*

moor *n.* a tract of marshy wasteland, usually heather-covered; heath; also **moor·land.**
— *v.* secure a ship, boat, etc. in place by fastening it by rope or chain to a pier or to the shore or by anchors.

mooring *n.* also **moorings** *pl.* **1** the place to which a craft is moored. **2** the anchors or chains by which something is secured in place. **3** a person's ties or attachments, as of religion or society, that are a source of security.

moose *n.* a North American elk with flattened antlers, the largest member of the deer family: *a bull* (= male) *moose; calf* (= young) *moose; cow* (= female) *moose; a moose pasture* (*Cdn. Slang* for a worthless mining claim).

moose·bird *n.* same as CANADA JAY.

moose·milk *n. Cdn.* in the North, a mixed drink of rum and milk.

moot *adj.* debatable: *a moot point, question; a dismissal made moot* (= of no consequence) *by resignation; a moot court* (= mock court for law students to practise in).
— *v.* raise for discussion: *The Bigfoot, as is mooted, may not be a myth after all.*

mop *n.* **1** an implement for wiping floors, usually a handle with a bundle of rags or a sponge at the end: *a dry mop; dust mop; wet mop.* **2** a thick head of unruly hair.
— *v.* **mops, mopped, mop·ping** wipe: *a handkerchief to mop your brow; to mop the floor clean.*
— **mop up 1** wipe up: *to mop up a spill.* **2** dispose of remaining members of a group: *to mop up the remnants of a defeated army; mopping up operations.*

mope *v.* **mopes, moped, mop·ing** be gloomy or in low spirits.
— *n.* **1** a gloomy person. **2 mopes** *pl.* low spirits.
— **mop·ish** (MOH·pish) or **mop·y** or **mop·ey** (MOH·pee) *adj.* — **mop·i·ness** *n.*

mo·ped (MOH·ped) *n.* a light motorcycle that can be pedalled.

mop·pet (MOP·it) *n. Informal.* a little child.

mor·al (MOR·ul) *adj.* **1** having to do with accepted standards of good conduct: *our moral behaviour; moral law; to lead a moral life; moral philosophy* (= ethics); *a moral tale; You sound very moral* (= virtuous); *Infants are not moral beings* (= They don't know right from wrong); *a moral* (= well-behaved) *man, person, woman.* **2** based on what one thinks is right and wrong: *a moral duty, question, responsibility, sense; the moral courage* or *fibre to stand up to a bully; a bully's moral cowardice; the moral indignation of the public towards injustices; to exert moral pressure on someone to get something done; Though I can't contribute to your cause, you have my moral support; We lost the election but won a moral victory* (because we deserved to win). **3** based on high probability: *That a mother loves her child is a moral though not an absolute certainty.*
— *n.* **1** a moral lesson: *The story has a moral to it.* **2 morals** *pl.* moral principles, esp. in regard to sex: *a man of good morals; to corrupt the morals of youth; to protect* or *safeguard the morals of society; adj.: a morals charge, conviction, offence.* — **mor·al·ly** *adv.*

mo·rale (muh·RAL) *n.* mental or moral condition in regard to discipline and confidence: *The good news helped to boost* or *lift* or *raise his morale; The morale of an army, team, etc. may be high, low; A leader's bad example may destroy* or *undermine morale.*

mor·al·ist (MOR·uh·list) *n.* **1** an expert in morals. **2** one who favours or is concerned with regulating morals, as through censorship.— **mor·al·is·tic** (-LIS·tic) *adj.*

mo·ral·i·ty (muh·RAL·uh·tee) *n.* **-ties 1** moral quality, system, instruction, etc.: *standards of morality; Christian, Hindu, Moslem, private, public morality; a medieval morality play.* **2** goodness or rightness: *the morality of killing animals for meat.*

morality squad *n.* a police division concerned with

gaming and prostitution.

mor·al·ize (MOR·uh·lize) *v.* -liz·es, -lized, -liz·ing [derogatory] think, talk, or write about morals: *to moralize about* or *on* or *over* or *upon sin and punishment.* — **mor·al·i·za·tion** (-luh·ZAY·shun) *n.*

mo·rass (muh·RAS) *n.* a swamp or marsh; hence, a messy situation: *A dictionary user should not get bogged down in a morass of meanings.*

mor·a·to·ri·um (mor·uh·TOR·ee·um) *n.* -ri·ums or -ri·a an official delay or suspension, as on legal action to collect a debt, testing of nuclear weapons, etc.: *to declare a moratorium; lift a moratorium on the sale of foreign cars; the 1967 moratorium on capital punishment.*

mor·bid *adj.* diseased or sickly; gruesome: *a morbid curiosity, growth, interest in death; the morbid details of a crime;* **mor·bid·ly** *adv.* — **mor·bid·i·ty** (-BID·uh·tee) or **mor·bid·ness** *n.*

mor·dant (MOR·dunt) *adj.* incisive; caustic; pungent: *mordant criticism, wit.* — *n.* 1 a chemical that fixes colours. 2 an etching agent. — **mor·dant·ly** *adv.* — **mor·dan·cy** *n.*

more *comp.* of MANY or MUCH. — *adj.* a greater or additional amount, number, or part: *We need more food; a few more donuts; a little more coffee.* — *adv.: I couldn't agree with you more; I shall be* **more than** (= quite) *happy to help you; He doesn't write to me any more; People are eating out* **more and more** (= in larger numbers); *The baby is* **more or less** (= almost) *asleep;* **What's more** (= in addition), *it is past midnight.* — *n. & pron.: the more the merrier; Some more, please; a few more of the donuts you sold us yesterday; Many were killed, more were wounded.*

more·o·ver (mor·OH·vur) *adv.* besides; in addition.

mo·res (MOR·aiz, -eez) *n. pl.* the traditional morally binding rules and customs of a society: *our social manners and mores; "One wife or husband at a time" is part of our sexual mores.*

morgue (MORG) *n.* 1 a place where unidentified bodies are kept temporarily, as of victims of accidents or violent deaths. 2 a newspaper reference library stocking obituaries, news clippings, etc.

mor·i·bund (MOR·uh·bund) *adj.* in the process of dying out: *a moribund civilization, custom; Are monarchies moribund?*

morn *n.* [poetic use] morning.

morn·ing *n.* the period from dawn to noon, esp. the beginning of a day: *Good morning (to you)! from morning till noon; from morning to night; on a wintry morning; the morning of January 31; a drinking bout and a hangover the morning after; a* **morning-after** *headache following a binge.*

mo·ron (MOR·on) *n.* 1 a foolish or stupid person. 2 formerly, a classification of a mentally retarded person with an I.Q. between 50 and 75. — **mo·ron·ic** (muh·RON·ic) *adj.*

mo·rose (muh·ROSE) *adj.* glum and unsociable; gloomy. — **mo·rose·ly** *adv.;* **mo·rose·ness** *n.*

mor·row (MOR·oh) *n.* [poetic use] morning; also, the next day.

Morse code *n.* an alphabet of dots and dashes for use in telegraphy: *a message in Morse code.*

mor·sel (MOR·sul) *n.* 1 a mouthful or small portion of food. 2 a piece or amount: *a choice morsel* (= something tasty or pleasing); *a dainty morsel.*

mor·tal (MOR·tul) *adj.* having to do with death: *a mortal* (= fatal) *blow, injury, wound; mere mortal man; locked in a mortal combat; one's mortal* (= deadly or hated) *enemy; They live in mortal* (= intense) *danger, fear of being killed; a mortal threat, torment; a* **mortal sin** *(that causes spiritual death); They did mortal* (= great) *damage; our mortal* (= human) *limitations; to* **shuffle off this mortal coil** (= to die). — *n.* a human being: *They are mere mortals; She is no ordinary mortal.* — **mor·tal·ly** *adv.*

mor·tal·i·ty (mor·TAL·uh·tee) *n.* death, esp. its rate in proportion to population: *infant mortality; A* **mortality table** *shows life expectancy.*

mor·tar (MOR·tur) *n.* 1 a bowl of porcelain or other hard material for pounding substances to a powder using a pestle. 2 a short-range cannon that fires shells (dropped down its muzzle) in a high arc, as over a hill or fortification. 3 a hardening mixture of lime, cement, etc. for use between bricks or stones in building.

mor·tar·board (MOR·tur.bord) *n.* 1 a square board used by masons to hold and work mortar. 2 an academic cap with a square board on top from which a tassel hangs.

mort·gage (MORT·gij) *n.* 1 a pledging of property as security for the payment of a loan or debt to the lender, or **mort·ga·gee** (mor·guh·JEE): *to take out a mortgage on one's home; to give, hold, pay off a mortgage.* 2 the deed by which this is conveyed by the owner of the property, or **mort·ga·ger** or **mort·ga·gor** (MOR·guh·jur). — *v.* -gag·es, -gaged, -gag·ing transfer one's rights by or as if by a mortgage: *to mortgage one's house, happiness, future.*

mor·ti·cian (mor·TISH·un) *n.* an undertaker.

mor·ti·fy (MOR·tuh·fye) *v.* -fies, -fied, -fy·ing 1 punish one's body: *Saints mortify their bodies, desires, etc. by fasting and penance; to mortify the flesh.* 2 be punished: *She felt deeply mortified* (= embarrassed) *by her child's behaviour in public; a* **mortifying** *defeat, experience, failure, mistake.* — **mor·ti·fi·ca·tion** (-fuh·CAY·shun) *n.*

mor·tise (MOR·tis) *n.* a hole or notch in one part of a joint of a piece of wood into which the tenon of the other part fits. — *v.* -tis·es, -tised, -tis·ing join with a mortise: *beams mortised, not nailed together.* Also **mor·tice.**

mor·tu·ar·y (MOR·choo·air·ee) *n.* -ar·ies a place where dead bodies are kept before burial or cremation; funeral home; *adj.: a mortuary chapel, service.*

mo·sa·ic (moh·ZAY·ic) 1 *n.* a picture or design made with small coloured pieces of stone, glass, etc. inlaid on a surface such as a floor, ceiling, or wall: *Canada is a mosaic of many cultures; **adj.:** a mosaic design, floor, pavement.* **2 Mosaic** *adj.* having to do with Moses: *The mosaic law includes the Ten Commandments.*

Mo·ses (MOH·ziz) *n.* the lawgiver of the Israelites who led them out of slavery in Egypt: *Holy Moses!*

mo·sey (MOH·see) *v.* -seys, -seyed, -sey·ing *Slang.* move *along* at a leisurely pace.

Mos·lem (MOZ·lum) *n.* a follower of the religion founded by Mohammed.

mosque (MOSK) *n.* an Islamic place of public worship.

mos·qui·to (mus·KEE·toh) *n.* -tos or -toes a two-winged, blood-sucking insect that is often a carrier of disease germs, as of malaria and yellow fever.

moss *n.* a tiny green plant that grows in cushionlike clusters on damp banks, rocks, and trees. — **moss·y** *adj.*

moss·back *n.* **1** an old turtle with algae growing on its back. **2** *Slang.* an old fogey; very conservative person.

moss bag *n. Cdn.* among the Indians, a bag lined with dry moss for carrying babies in, attached to a board strapped to the mother's back.

most (MOHST) *superl.* of MANY & MUCH.
— *n. & pron.* the greatest amount, degree, or number: *Boys form most of the group; a group that is noisier than most; a car that gives only 10 km to the litre **at (the) most** (= as a maximum).*
— *adj. & adv.:* *a most interesting subject; Most people like dogs; She loves children most; as most (Informal for almost) anyone will tell you; The show was good **for the most part** (= almost completely); the hostess with the mostest (Informal for the most charming hostess).*
— *suffix* [forming superlative]: *foremost, topmost, uppermost.*

most·ly *adv.* mainly; usually: *It snows mostly in January.*

mot (MOH) *n.* mots (MOZE) a witty saying.

mote *n.* a speck of dust.

mo·tel (moh·TEL) *n.* a roadside establishment providing furnished rooms and parking spaces for travellers.

moth *n.* an insect that resembles a butterfly but is less brightly coloured, that flies mostly at night, and whose larvae eat wool, fur, etc.

moth·ball *n.* a small ball of camphor or similar material used to keep moths away from clothing: *The new project has been put **in** or into **mothballs** (= shelved or stored*

away).

moth-eaten *adj.* out-of-date: *a moth-eaten idea.*

moth·er (MUTH·ur, "TH" as in "the") *n.* **1** a female parent: *an expectant, foster, step, surrogate, welfare, working mother; the **mother superior** (= head) of a convent.* **2** a source or origin of anything; **adj.:** *the **mother church** (of all the Christian churches); your **mother country** (= country of birth); the **mother house** (= headquarters or original convent) of the nuns; the **mother lode** (= rich source, as in mining); his **mother tongue** (= first-learned and still-understood language).*
— *v.* produce, nourish, or protect, as a mother does: *Mothering comes naturally to most women;* **adj.:** *the mothering instinct; her mothering period, role.*
— **moth·er·hood** *n.:* *Education is like motherhood; No one attacks **motherhood and apple pie** (as they stand for basic North American values);* **adj.:** *a motherhood issue, proposal, statement.*
— **moth·er·ly** *adj.:* *motherly care, fondness, image; a motherly woman.* — **moth·er·li·ness** *n.*

mother-in-law *n.* mothers-in-law the mother of one's spouse.

moth·er·land (MUTH·ur·land) *n.* one's native or ancestral country.

mo·tif (moh·TEEF) *n.* in art, literature, and music, a dominant theme, main feature, or recurring pattern: *Love is the leading motif of romances.*

mo·tion (MOH·shun) *n.* **1** a moving: *Newton's laws of motion; the line of motion of a skier; Who set the universe in motion? Do not get off a train when it is **in motion**.* **2** a formal proposal made in a meeting, legislature, or court of law: *a motion for adjournment; to accept, defeat, make, second, vote down, vote on, withdraw a motion; A motion carries or is passed.* **3** gesture: *I saw Tim **go through the motions of** (= routinely or half-heartedly) brushing his teeth.*
— *v.* gesture: *The chairman motioned us to be seated.*

mo·tion·less *adj.* without moving: *He sat there motionless.*

motion picture *n.* **1** a series of contiguous pictures giving the impression of movement when projected; moving picture. **2** a story in this form. Also **movie** or **moving picture.**

mo·ti·vate (MOH·tuh·vate) *v.* -vates, -vat·ed, -vat·ing provide with or influence as a motive; impel: *What motivates students to complete high school?*
— **mo·ti·va·tion** (-VAY·shun) *n.*
— **mo·ti·va·tion·al** (-VAY·shuh·nul) *adj.:* *motivational analysis, drives, experts, research.*

mo·tive (MOH·tiv) **1** *n.* the cause of an action: *Revenge was the motive for the murder; to establish, find a motive; to question someone's motives; altruistic, base, honourable, noble, selfish, ulterior motives; people acting from the highest motives; the profit motive of corporations; an underlying motive for the kidnapping; Did he have some motive to commit the crime?* **2** *n.* a basic melody or motif, as the first four notes of Beethoven's "Fifth Symphony." **3** *adj.* moving: *the **motive power** of steam.* — *suffix.:* *automotive, electromotive, locomotive.*

mot·ley (MOT·lee) *adj.* 1 many-coloured, as a clown's garment: *a motley dress.* 2 varied in character: *a motley collection, crowd.*

mo·to·cross (MOH·tuh·cros) *n.* a cross-country motorcycle race.

mo·tor (MOH·tur) *n.* one that gives motion, esp. an engine: *a lawnmower powered by an electric motor; a gas motor; the outboard motor of a boat; A motor runs, stalls, works; to start, turn off a motor; **adj.:** The brain's motor area controls neurons that impart motor impulses to muscles; a motor vehicle running on an internal combustion engine.*
— *v.* go or convey by automobile.

mo·tor·bike (MOH·tur·bike) *n. Informal.* same as MOTORCYCLE.

mo·tor·cade (MOH·tur·cade) *n.* a procession of motor vehicles.

motor court *n.* a motel.

mo·tor·cy·cle (MOH·tur·sye·cul) *n.* a heavier and larger type of bicycle powered by an internal combustion engine. — *v.* -cles, -cled, -cling travel by motorcycle. — **mo·tor·cy·clist** *n.*

motor home *n.* an automotive recreational vehicle built on a truck chassis and having living facilities.

motor hotel or **motor inn** *n.* a hotel with parking facilities for guests.

mo·tor·ist (MOH·tur·ist) *n.* a traveller by automobile.

mo·tor·ize (MOH·tuh·rize) *v.* -iz·es, -ized, -iz·ing 1 equip with a motor: *No motorized vehicles are allowed in the park.* 2 equip with motor vehicles: *a motorized regiment.* — **mo·tor·i·za·tion** (-ruh·ZAY·shun) *n.*

motor lodge *n.* same as MOTOR HOTEL.

mo·tor·man (MOH·tur·mun) *n.* -men a driver of an electric train or streetcar.

motor scooter *n.* a scooterlike vehicle with an engine mounted over the rear wheel and the driver seated with feet on a floorboard.

motor vehicle *n.* an automotive vehicle such as an automobile, bus, truck, etc. for use on roadways.

mot·tle (MOT·ul) *v.* **mot·tles, mot·tled, mot·tling** mark with blotches or streaks of different colours: *a mottled finish, leaf, skin.*

mot·to (MOT·oh) *n.* -tos or -toes a rule of conduct, usually a brief expression such as "Be prepared," put on a coat of arms or badge.

mould or **mold** (MOLD) *n.* 1 a frame, matrix, hollow, etc. that gives form or shape to what is put in it. 2 the shape or form or what is formed in a mould, as a jelly or pudding: *monotonous characters cast in the same mould; a jello mould; plaster mould.* 3 a greenish or whitish fungous growth, as seen on bread, cheese, etc.: *Books gather mould in a wet basement.* 4 crumbly rich soil: *a planter filled with leaf mould.*
— *v.* 1 form or shape: *a figure moulded out of clay; a character moulded by experience.* 2 become covered with mould: *cheese starting to mould.*

mould·board or **mold·board** *n.* a type of plough that lifts and turns the soil away from the furrow as it tills.

mould·er or **mold·er** 1 *n.* one that moulds or shapes something. 2 *v.* crumble or decay, esp. by turning into dust: *the mouldering ruins of an ancient temple.*

moulding or **molding** *n.* 1 the act or process of moulding. 2 a continuous moulded surface or strip for decoration or finish, as on buildings or on the side of an automobile's body.

mould·y or **mold·y** *adj.* **mould·i·er** or **mold·i·er, -i·est** 1 mould-covered. 2 stale or musty. — **mould·i·ness** or **mold·i·ness** *n.*

moult or **molt** (MOLT) *v.* of a bird, insect, snake, etc., shed its feathers, skin, shell, or similar worn-out body covering. — *n.* this act or process.

mound (rhyme: "round") *n.* 1 a bank of earth or stones: *a burial mound.* 2 a knoll. — *v.* heap up as a mound.

mount (rhyme: "count") *v.* 1 climb on or toward the top of a thing or animal: *to mount a horse, ladder, platform; the mounting (= rising) cost of living; Police came **mounted** (on horseback); the mounted police.* 2 place or fix in proper position: *to mount a specimen on a slide, stamps in an album, gems in gold, guns on a gun carriage.*
— *n.* 1 [used in names] mountain: *Mount Everest; Mt. Logan.* 2 an animal or machine on which one is mounted. 3 a place to mount something on, as a backing or support: *a cardboard mount for a picture; an engine mount; the vacuum mount of a pencil sharpener; the mount (= bastion) of a castle.*

moun·tain (MOUN·tun) *n.* a very high hill or mass of land, often rising to a peak; also, the peak: *to climb, scale a mountain; the Matterhorn mountain; the height or elevation of a mountain; Everest, the world's highest mountain, is in the Himalayan **Mountains** (= a mountain formation); a chain or range of mountains; rugged, snow-covered, volcanic mountains; mountains (= huge heaps) of garbage; a mountain of work awaiting a vacationer; Let us not **make a mountain out of a molehill** (= magnify small difficulties).*

moun·tain·eer (moun·tuh·NEER) *n.* 1 one who lives in the mountains. 2 a skilled climber of mountains. — *v.* climb mountains as a sport.

moun·tain·ous (MOUN·tun·us) *adj.* 1 full of mountains. 2 huge like a mountain.

Mount·ie or **Mount·y** (MOUN·tee) *n.* **Mount·ies** *Cdn. Informal.* a member of the Royal Canadian Mounted Police.

mounting *n.* a backing or support, as for a picture; mount.

mourn (MORN) *v.* feel or express sorrow or grief for a dead person: *to mourn a death, loss; mourning for or over a dear one.*

mourn·ful *adj.* sorrowful. — **mourn·ful·ly** *adv.;* **mourn·ful·ness** *n.*

mourning *n.* the expression of grief at someone's death, the usually black clothes worn as a sign of it, or the period of such expression: *A nation goes into mourning when its head of state dies; The government declares or*

*proclaims a period of mourning; national mourning;
The country was in mourning for a month.*

mouse *n., pl.* **mice 1** a small gnawing animal with soft fur and pointed snout, esp. the "house mouse" found worldwide and used in laboratories: *Cats catch mice; as quiet as a mouse; a field mouse; white mice.* **2** a timid person. **3** a hand-held, button-operated device attached to a microcomputer for manipulating the cursor on its monitor and selecting routine operations without using the keyboard. **4** *Slang.* a black eye.
— *v.* (MOUZE) **mous·es, moused, mous·ing** hunt for mice, as a cat does. — **mous·er** *n.*

mouse·trap *n.* a trap for catching mice: *Make **a better mousetrap** and the world will beat a path to your door* (= Inventors are in great demand).

mousey same as MOUSY.

mousse (MOOSE) *n.* **1** a light, moulded, chilled dessert made with gelatin and whipped cream: *banana, coffee, maple mousse.* **2** a hairstyling foam.

mous·tache (mus·TASH, MUS·tash) same as MUSTACHE.

mous·y or **mous·ey** (MOU·see, -zee) *adj.* **mous·i·er, -i·est** like a mouse; timid or stealthy. — **mous·i·ness** *n.*

mouth *n.* **1** an opening through which food is taken into the body, and in which speech sounds are made: *to cram or stuff one's mouth with cake; It makes your mouth water* (= tempts you); *a big mouth* (= gossip); *Study the subject before you **shoot your mouth off*** (Slang for before you talk as if you know all about it). **2** any opening or entrance resembling a mouth, as of a cave, jar, or of a river where it empties into a larger body of water.
— **down in** or **at the mouth** *Informal.* in low spirits.
— *v.* ("TH" as in "the") **1** utter words in an affected manner; declaim. **2** form words with the mouth silently.

mouthed *adj. & combining form.* having a mouth or one as specified: *a mouthed shell; foulmouthed, loudmouthed, openmouthed.*

mouth·ful *n.* **-fuls 1** a small quantity, as will fill a mouth. **2** *Informal.* a hard-to-pronounce word or a string of words. **3** *Informal.* an appropriate or significant remark: *You said a mouthful.*

mouth·piece *n.* **1** a part or structure that serves as a mouth, as of a water pipe, or that is placed at or near a person's mouth, as of a musical instrument that is blown into, of a tobacco pipe, or of a telephone. **2** a person or periodical that speaks for another: *a press attaché who serves* or *acts as a mouthpiece for his country.*

mouth·wash *n.* a liquid preparation for rinsing the mouth.

mouth·wa·ter·ing (MOUTH·waw·tur·ing) *adj.* very appetizing or tasty.

mov·a·ble (MOO·vuh·bul) **1** *adj.* that can be moved from place to place, as furniture. **2** movables *n.pl.* personal property.

move (MOOV, long "OO") *v.* **moves, moved, mov·ing 1** change place or position: *Stand still without moving; Who moved this desk? People move from inner cities to suburbs; Our office is moving to Vancouver; We're moving our warehouse to a small town; He moved out of the old neighbourhood when he got a new job; Our new neighbours move in on Monday; Luxury goods are difficult to move* (= sell) *in hard times; She moved up through the ranks to become vice-president.* **2** act or operate: *A door moves on hinges; a story that moves* (= stirs) *people to tears; Everyone was profoundly* or *deeply moved by the story; to move* (= be active) *in academic circles; Purgatives move* (= evacuate) *bowels.* **3** go or come; proceed: *A train going at 120 km/h is moving fast; Police try to keep the crowds moving; Let's move on; People started moving toward the exits; a **moving violation*** (= traffic violation while the vehicle is in motion, as not stopping at a stop sign). **4** apply formally or propose: *The lawyer moved for a new trial; She moved that a new trial be held.*
— **move in 1** close in: *The police surrounded the place and then moved in on the kidnappers; Hunters move in for the kill.* **2** start living with someone: *His mother-in-law wanted to move in with them.*
— **move over** to make room for someone more important.
— *n.* a changing of place or position: *He dared not make a move for fear of being shot; One false move and you are a dead duck; the moves of a chess game; a brilliant move that ended the game; wrong moves; a clever, decisive, smart move; We made a move from Vancouver to Halifax; a move to the east; A warning is given as a first move* (= step or action) *before firing someone; Orders keep three waiters constantly **on the move*** (= moving). — **move·a·ble** same as MOVABLE.

move·ment (MOOV·munt) *n.* **1** the motion of a person or thing in a particular manner or direction: *the movement of the earth around the sun; troop movements along a border; a sonata in three movements* (= parts); *a 17-jewel watch movement* (= mechanism); *to have a bowel movement* (= emptying of stool). **2** organized effort to reach a goal: *a civil-rights movement; a labour, peace, political movement; the movement for reform; a movement against smoking in the workplace; to launch, oppose, support, suppress a movement.*

mover and shaker *n.* a person of power and influence.

mov·ie (MOO·vee) *n.* **1** a motion picture: *to make a home movie; adj.: a movie camera, projector.* **2** a motion-picture theatre: *a drive-in movie.*
— **the movies** *pl.* **1** a movie showing: *We go to the movies on weekends.* **2** the moving-picture industry: *She hopes to get into the movies and become a star.*

mow 1 (rhyme: "how") *n.* a haymow; hayloft. **2** (MOH) *v.* **mows,** *pt.* **mowed,** *pp.* **mowed** or **mown** (MONE), **mow·ing** cut down grass, grain, an army, etc.: *to mow a lawn; The troops were mercilessly **mowed down*** (= killed) *by the enemy.*
— **mow·er** (MOH·ur) *n.: to work a hand mower; to operate a lawn mower; a power mower; a rider mower.*

mox·ie (MOX·ee) *n. Slang.* pluck or guts and know-how.

Mr. (MIS·tur), *pl.* **Messrs.** (MES·urz) [prefixed title used with a man's surname or title]: *Mr. T. Jones; Mr. Jones; Mr. Chairman.*

Mrs. (MIS·iz), *pl.* **Mmes.** (may·DAHM) [prefixed title for a married woman who has taken her husband's surname]: *Mrs. (Mary) Jones, née Chan.*

Ms. (MIZ), *pl.* **Ms·es** (MIZ·uz) [prefixed title used with a woman's surname]: *Ms. (Mary) Jones.*

much *adj. & n. comp.* **more,** *superl.* **most** (in) a great amount, degree, quantity, etc.: *He spent much time on the project;* **How much** *profit did she make? The results didn't amount to much; She doesn't have much of a chance; We have much to learn from older and wiser people; He tends to* **make much** *of the little he does; A dollar a week is* **not much** *of a contribution.*
— *adv.: Prices are much higher than two years ago; Wages are much (=nearly) the same as last year;* **How much** *will you pay?*

muck *n.* **1** farmyard manure. **2** dirt or filth. **3** dark soil rich in decaying matter.
— **muck about** or **around with** *Informal.* be involved with a person or thing in a careless manner.
— **muck up** *Informal.* make a mess of something.
— **muck·y** *adj.*

muck·rak·er (MUCK·ray·kur) *n.* a journalist who searches for and writes sensationally about corruption in government, big business, etc.
— **muck·rake** *v.* **-rakes, -raked, -rak·ing.**

mu·cous (MEW·cus) *adj.* **1** secreting mucus, as the **mucous membrane** lining body cavities. **2** slimy.

mu·cus (MEW·cus) *n.* a thick, slimy fluid produced by the inner lining of the nose, vagina, windpipe, etc. for lubrication and protection.

mud *n.* **1** soft, sticky, wet earth: *a layer of mud; Mud cakes as it dries; Mud oozes, squishes: to spatter someone with mud.* **2** an abusive, malicious attack: *to sling* or *throw mud at someone.*

mud·dle (MUD·ul) *n.* a mess or disorder: *He found it difficult to get out of the muddle he was in; He made a muddle of the project.*
— *v.* **mud·dles, mud·dled, mud·dling** confuse or make confused: *to muddle an issue, plan, task; Liquor tends to muddle one's thinking; Some children put off doing their homework but at the last moment* **muddle through** *somehow (instead of doing it in an organized manner).* — **mud·dler** *n.*

mud·dle·head·ed (mud·ul·HED·id) *adj.* confused; bungling; inept: *a muddleheaded manager, policy; muddleheaded thinking.*

mud·dy (MUD·ee) *adj.* **mud·di·er, mud·di·est** containing or covered with mud: *muddy shoes, water; muddy (=murky or confused) thinking.*
— *v.* **mud·dies, mud·died, mud·dy·ing 1** make or become covered with mud: *to muddy one's clothes.* **2** make cloudy or confused: *muddied reasoning.*
— **mud·di·ness** *n.*

mud·guard *n.* **1** a covering over a vehicle's wheel for protection from mud thrown up by it; fender. **2** same as SPLASHGUARD.

mud room *n.* a room near an entrance where street shoes may be left so as not to track mud into the house.

mud·sling·ing (MUD·sling·ing) *n.* slanderous attack against an opponent. — **mud·sling·er** *n.*

muff *n.* **1** a short, tubelike covering of fur or other warm material into which the hands are inserted to keep them warm. **2** a bungling or awkward handling.
— *v.* bungle or miss a catch, esp. in baseball.

muf·fin *n.* a small round cake of wheat flour or corn meal.

muf·fle (MUF·ul) *v.* **muf·fles, muf·fled, muf·fling** cover closely so as to keep warm or to deaden a sound: *She was muffled in a scarf; muffled voices.*

muf·fler (MUF·lur) *n.* something that muffles, as a scarf or the silencing device attached to an automobile engine.

mug *n.* **1** a cylindrical metal or earthenware cup with a handle, formerly often decorated with a grotesque face: *a drinking mug; shaving mug.* **2** *Slang.* face or mouth.
— *v.* **mugs, mugged, mug·ging 1** *Slang.* make faces, as a ham actor. **2** *Slang.* make a mug shot of a person's face. **3** attack a person to rob. — **mug·ger** *n.*

mug·gy (MUG·ee) *adj.* **mug·gi·er, mug·gi·est** hot and humid: *a muggy day; muggy weather.*
— **mug·gi·ness** *n.*

mug shot *n.* a police photograph of a prisoner's face.

muk·luk (MUCK·luck) *n.* a boot in the style of a usually knee-high Inuit boot made of the skin of seal or reindeer.

mu·lat·to (muh·LAT·oh) *n.* **-lat·toes** a person of mixed white and black descent, esp. one born of a white and a black parent.

mulch *n.* loose vegetable material such as straw, leaves, and wood chips spread around plants to reduce evaporation, enrich the soil, etc.
— *v.* spread mulch on or around: *to mulch the ground, an orchard, a tree.*

mulct *n.* a fine or penalty.
— *v.* get by fraud or extortion: *clients mulcted of their savings.*

mule *n.* **1** the usually sterile hybrid offspring of a jackass and a horse: *stubborn as a mule.* **2** *Informal.* one who is stubborn. **3** a backless slipper for women.
— **mul·ish** *adj.;* **mul·ish·ly** *adv.;* **mul·ish·ness** *n.*

mu·le·teer (mew·luh·TEER) *n.* a mule driver; also **mule skinner** *Informal.*

mull *v.* **1** ponder *over* a problem, proposal, etc. **2** make a warm, sweetened spiced drink of wine, cider, or other beverage: *mulled ale.*

multi- *combining form.* many: *multicoloured, multi-event, multilingual, multimillionaire, multi-user.*

mul·ti·cul·tur·al (mul·tee·CUL·chur·ul) *adj.* having to do with many cultures: *a multicultural program; Canada is a multicultural society.* Also **mul·ti·eth·nic** (-ETH·nic).

mul·ti·far·i·ous (mul·tuh·FAIR·ee·us) *adj.* diverse or varied: *multifarious activities, duties, problems.*

mul·ti·lin·gual (mul·tuh·LING·gwul) *adj.* using many languages.

mul·ti·me·di·a (mul·tee·MEE·dee·uh) *adj.* using several communications media: *a multimedia kit, presentation.*

mul·ti·na·tion·al (mul·tee·NASH·uh·nul) *adj.* with branches in more than two countries: *a multinational corporation, labour union.*

mul·ti·ple (MUL·tuh·pul) *n.* a number obtained by multiplying a whole number by itself two or more times. — *adj.* having many parts: *a **multiple-choice** question with several answers to choose from.*

mul·ti·pli·ca·tion (mul·tuh·pluh·CAY·shun) *n.* 1 a multiplying or increase. 2 a short method of adding equal numbers many times, in an operation indicated by a **multiplication sign** (×).

mul·ti·plic·i·ty (mul·tuh·PLIS·uh·tee) *n.* a great number or variety: *a multiplicity of interests.*

mul·ti·ply (MUL·tuh·ply) *v.* -plies, -plied, -ply·ing 1 increase in number: *Rabbits multiply fast.* 2 find the mathematical product of two numbers: *2 multiplied by 3 is 6.*

mul·ti·pur·pose (mul·tuh·PUR·pus) *adj.* serving several purposes: *a multipurpose fabric, kit.*

mul·ti·ra·cial (mul·tuh·RAY·shul) *adj.* of several races: *a multiracial society.*

mul·ti·stage (mul·tuh·STAGE) *adj.* having several stages: *a multistage pump, rocket.*

mul·ti·tude (MUL·tuh·tude) *n.* a large number, esp. of people.

mul·ti·tu·di·nous (mul·tuh·TUE·dun·us) *adj.* very numerous.

mul·ti·vi·ta·min (mul·tuh·VYE·tuh·min) *adj.* containing all the vitamins essential to health: *a multivitamin tablet.*

mum *adj. & interj.* silent: *Let's keep mum about this; Mum's the word* (= Don't talk)! — *v.* same as MUMMER.

mum·ble (MUM·bul) *v.* -bles, -bled, -bling speak in a low, indistinct mutter, as because of embarrassment; **mum·bler** *n.*

mum·bo jum·bo (mum·boh·JUM·boh) *n.* 1 meaningless or ritualistic talk: *the mumbojumbo of witchcraft.* 2 a fetish or idol.

mum·mer (MUM·ur) *n.* a person who wears a fancy costume or a mask, as at a festival or in a pantomime. — *v.* perform or go visiting as a group of mummers: *Newfoundlanders go mummering during Christmas.*

mum·mer·ies (MUM·uh·reez) *n.pl.* a dumb show or other performance by mummers.

mum·mi·fy (MUM·uh·fye) *v.* -fies, -fied, -fy·ing make into or like a mummy: *a mummified custom.* — **mum·mi·fi·ca·tion** (-fuh·CAY·shun) *n.*

mum·my (MUM·ee) *n.* **mum·mies** a dead body embalmed for burial and preservation, as in ancient Egypt.

mumps *n. sing. & pl.* a contagious virus disease of the salivary glands characterized by painful swelling of the sides of the face and neck: *to come down with the mumps.*

munch *v.* chew vigorously or with a crunching sound.

mun·dane (MUN·dane) *adj.* commonplace or everyday: *mundane activities, affairs; our mundane existence.*

mu·nic·i·pal (mew·NIS·uh·pul) *adj.* having to do with a municipality: *a municipal council, district, government, library, police.*

mu·nic·i·pal·i·ty (mew·NIS·uh·PAL·uh·tee) *n.* -ties a locally self-governing, usually incorporated city, town, or borough.

mu·nif·i·cent (mew·NIF·uh·sunt) *adj.* generous or lavish in a princely way: *a munificent gift, person.* — **mu·nif·i·cence** *n.*

mu·ni·tion (mew·NISH·un) 1 *adj.* having to do with military supplies: *a munition plant.* 2 **munitions** *n.pl.* military supplies such as guns, bombs, and equipment.

mu·ral (MYOOR·ul) *n.* a large-size painting or decoration done on a wall: *a mural painting.* — **mu·ral·ist** *n.*

mur·der (MUR·dur) *n.* 1 the crime of killing a person, esp. on purpose: *a cold-blooded, grisly, mass, ritual, vicious, wanton, premeditated murder; serial murders by a serial killer; Capital murder used to carry the death penalty.* 2 *Informal.* something hard or unpleasant, as a job, the weather, etc.: *Paperwork can be murder; It is murder on one's creativity.* — *v.* commit murder on a person or thing: *He was brutally murdered; to murder* (= botch or mangle) *a song, the English language.* — **mur·der·er** *n., fem.* **mur·der·ess.**

mur·der·ous (MUR·dur·us) *adj.* having to do with murder: *a murderous blow; murderous hate, heat, intent.* — **mur·der·ous·ly** *adv.*

murk·y (MUR·kee) *adj.* **mur·ki·er, -ki·est** dark and gloomy, as because of a vapour or mist: *the murky, smoke-filled air; murky* (= muddled) *logic.*

mur·mur *n.* a soft, low, continuous but indistinct sound or voice, as of a grumbling person, the flow of a stream, distant voices, or a diseased heart valve. — *v.* utter in a murmur: *to murmur a prayer; to murmur one's thanks; to murmur* (= complain) *about poor wages.* — **mur·mur·er** *n.*

mus·cle (MUS·ul) *n.* 1 a fibrous body tissue distributed in bands and bundles, esp. as organs, helping in work and movement: *the biceps, heart, stomach muscles; to contract, flex, tense, move, pull, strain, wrench a muscle; to develop one's muscles.* 2 physical strength or power: *a he-man with more muscle than brains; those high-powered muscle cars with animal names; a bit of muscle-flexing* (= show of force). — *v.* **mus·cles, mus·cled, mus·cling** force by or as if by using muscles: *He jumped the queue and muscled his way in; Criminals tried to **muscle in** on his business* (= get a share of it by force). — **muscled** *adj. & combining form:* *hard-muscled, well-muscled; heavily muscled mercenaries.*

muscle-bound (MUS·ul·bound) *adj.* rigid or stiff, as muscles from too much exercise: *the muscle-bound figure of Serena Schwarz.*

mus·cu·lar (MUSK·yuh·lur) *adj.* having to do with muscles: *a muscular activity, arm; a man of a muscular build* (having good muscles); *muscular power, strain,* *strength.* — **mus·cu·lar·i·ty** (-LAIR·uh·tee) *n.*

muse (MYOOZ) *n.* **1** the source of inspiration, esp. of a poet. **2 the Muses** *pl.* in Greek and Roman myths, nine goddesses of the arts and sciences.
— *v.* **mus·es, mused, mus·ing** ponder or reflect meditatively: *a poet musing on* or *about* or *over* or *upon her past.*

mu·se·um (mew·ZEE·um) *n.* a place where objects of cultural and scientific value are stored and exhibited: *an art, science, wax museum.*

mush *n.* **1** a soft, thick, pulpy mass like corn meal boiled in water. **2** *Informal.* weak sentimentality. **3** *n. & v.* travel over snow with a dog sled.
— *interj.* a shout urging sled dogs forward.
— **mush·y** *adj.* **mush·i·er, -i·est.**

mush·room *n.* a usually umbrellalike, rapidly-sprouting, fleshy fungus: *the mushroom* (= umbrella-shaped) *cloud following a nuclear blast; the mushroom* (= fast) *growth of a boom town.*
— *v.* grow like mushrooms: *the mushrooming of fast-food outlets.*

mu·sic (MEW·zic) *n.* **1** a rhythmic sound or sequence of sounds that is pleasing to the ear: *a poem set to music; background, chamber, country, folk, modern, organ, rock, soul music; The news was music* (= pleasing) *to my ears.* **2** the art of making such sounds systematically, using the voice or instruments: *lessons in music.* **3** written music: *to compose* or *write, perform, play, read music; a piece of music.*
— **face the music** *Informal.* face the consequences, as of one's actions.

mu·si·cal (MEW·zuh·cul) *adj.* having to do with music: *a musical instrument; a musical ear (that is sensitive to music); a musical family (of members who are skilled in music); a musical* (= melodious) *voice.*
— *n.* a play or motion picture having a sentimental or humorous theme worked out with much singing and dancing, as "My Fair Lady." Also **musical comedy.**
— **mu·si·cal·ly** *adv.*

musical chairs *n. pl.* [with sing. v.] **1** a game in which the players move around a row of chairs numbering one less than the number of players and sit down on them when the music stops, leaving one player out of the game, and so on till there are only two players and one chair left: *to play musical chairs.* **2** a situation in which there is much changing of seats.

mu·si·cale (mew·zuh·CAL) *n.* a party featuring a musical program.

mu·si·cian (mew·ZISH·un) *n.* one skilled in music, esp. as a composer or performer. — **mu·si·cian·ly** *adj.*

musk *n.* a strong-smelling substance from a gland of the **musk deer** and other animals that is used in making perfume. — **musk·y** *adj.*

mus·keg *n. Cdn.* **1** a mossy bog or swamp of the Far North. **2** a region of muskegs, as in northern Alberta.

mus·kel·lunge (MUS·kuh·lunj) *n. sing. & pl.* a prized North American game and food fish, the largest of the pike family.

mus·ket (MUS·kit) *n.* a heavy muzzle-loading shoulder firearm of former times.

— **mus·ket·eer** (mus·kuh·TEER) *n.*

mus·kie (MUS·kee) *n. Cdn. Informal.* same as MUSKELLUNGE.

musk ox *n. Cdn.* a shaggy-haired wild ox of the Arctic that gives off a musky smell.

Mus·lim (MUZ·lum) *n.* same as MOSLEM.

mus·lin (MUZ·lin) *n.* **1** a closely woven cloth used for sheets. **2** in Britain, a sheer cotton fabric, originally made in Iraq and India.

muss *n.* a rumpled or disordered condition.
— *v.* put into a muss: *wrinkle-free, hard-to-muss clothes.* — **muss·y** *adj.*

must *auxiliary v., pres. & past* **1** [expressing obligation]: *I must go now; You must not be late.* **2** [expressing possibility, certainty, etc.]: *You must be tired; This book must be Lin's.*
— *n.* **1** *Informal.* something necessary: *A black tie is a must; adj.: a must book, item of clothing.* **2** the fermenting juice of grapes; new wine.

mus·tache (mus·TASH, MUS·tash) *n.* hair growing on a man's upper lip: *to grow, trim a mustache; a "handlebar" mustache.*

mus·tang *n.* a small, hardy horse of southwestern U.S.

mus·tard (MUS·turd) *n.* a pungent condiment in paste or powder form prepared from the seed of a plant used also in plasters and poultices.

mustard gas *n.* a poison gas with a mustardlike odour, used in chemical warfare.

mus·ter *v.* **1** of troops, assemble: *They mustered behind the barricades.* **2** collect soldiers, resources, etc.: *He tried to muster all the support he could from the voters; to **muster up** courage.*
— **muster in** (or **out**) enlist in (or discharge from) the military.
— *n.* an assembly.
— **pass muster** be up to the required standard.

must·n't (MUS·unt) must not.

mus·ty (MUS·tee) *adj.* **-ti·er, -ti·est 1** stale or mouldy, as from dampness or lack of fresh air: *musty air; a musty odour; This water has a musty and metallic taste.* **2** antiquated: *musty customs, ideas.*
— **mus·ti·ly** *adv.;* **mus·ti·ness** *n.*

mu·ta·ble (MEW·tuh·bul) *adj.* changeable by nature; also, fickle. — **mu·ta·bly** (-blee) *adv.*
— **mu·ta·bil·i·ty** (-BIL·uh·tee) *n.*

mu·ta·tion (mew·TAY·shun) *n.* gene change caused by radiations, chemicals, etc. resulting in the appearance of new characteristics that are transmitted to offspring.

mute *adj.* dumb or silent: *deaf and mute; He was mute with astonishment; the mute "b" of "tomb."*
— *n.* 1 a dumb person. 2 a silencing device, as on a musical instrument.
— *v.* **mutes, mut·ed, mut·ing** muffle or soften the sound of a voice, violin string, etc.: *The Opposition muted its criticism of the new legislation while giving it a second look.* — **mute·ly** *adv.;* **mute·ness** *n.*

mu·ti·late (MEW·tuh·late) *v.* **-lates, -lat·ed, -lat·ing** deprive a person, literary work, song, etc. of an essential part, as by maiming or crippling.
— **mu·ti·la·tor** (-lay·tur) *n.*
— **mu·ti·la·tion** (-LAY·shun) *n.*

mu·ti·ny (MEW·tuh·nee) *n.* **-nies** a rebellion, esp. by soldiers or sailors against their officers: *to crush, put down, quell, stir up a mutiny; when a mutiny breaks out.*
— *v.* **-nies, -nied, -ny·ing** rebel: *The army mutinied against the junta.* — **mu·ti·nous** (-nus) *adj.*
— **mu·ti·neer** (mew·tuh·NEER) *n.*

mutt *n. Slang.* 1 a mongrel dog. 2 a despised person.

mut·ter *v.* speak words, curses, etc. in a low and indistinct voice, as if angry or dissatisfied.
— *n.* what is muttered; grumble.

mut·ton (MUT·tun) *n.* the flesh of mature sheep used as food. — **mut·ton·y** *adj.*

mut·ton·chops (MUT·un·chops) *n. pl.* sideburns that are narrow at the top and broad and rounded at the bottom.

mu·tu·al (MEW·choo·ul) *adj.* relating to or shared by each other: *the mutual affection between spouses; Marc and Luc are mutual enemies; Mia is their mutual friend* (= friend of both); *the concepts of nuclear deterrence and "mutual assured destruction" (in case of a nuclear war).* — **mu·tu·al·ly** *adv.*
— **mu·tu·al·i·ty** (-AL·uh·tee) *n.*

muz·zle (MUZ·ul) *n.* 1 the mouth of an animal such as a dog, horse, or cow that is at the end of the projecting part of the head. 2 the mouth of the barrel of a gun or pistol: *a muzzle-loading firearm.* 3 a cover made of straps or wires put around an animal's muzzle.
— *v.* **muz·zles, muz·zled, muz·zling** put a muzzle on an animal; hence, restrain a person, newspaper, etc. from speaking out; gag.

my *adj.* possessive case of "I": *My dear fellows, this is my date!*— *interj.: Oh, my!*

my·o·pi·a (my·OH·pee·uh) *n.* nearsightedness or shortsightedness. — **my·op·ic** (my·OP·ic) *adj.*

myr·i·ad (MEER·ee·ud) *n. & adj.* an indefinitely large number: *the myriad voices chanting slogans; Myriads of voices joined in the chant.*

my·self (my·SELF) *pron.* reflexive or emphatic of "I" or "ME": *I speak only for myself; I fell on the ice and hurt myself; I'm not myself* (= as well as usual) *today.*

mys·ter·y (MIS·tuh·ree) *n.* **-ter·ies** something hidden from human knowledge or hard to understand or explain: *the mystery of three persons in one God; the mysteries of the universe; Her disappearance has remained a mystery; an unsolved mystery; Her whereabouts are a mystery to us; to clear up, fathom, unravel a mystery; a mystery or **mystery novel*** (= detective story); *the air of mystery* (= secrecy) *surrounding the baby's birth; The mystery deepens as people start talking; a project shrouded in mystery; the mysteries* (= rites) *of the Christian religion; to go on a **mystery tour** (without knowing in advance where you are going).*
— **mys·te·ri·ous** (mis·TEER·ee·us) *adj.*
— **mys·te·ri·ous·ly** *adv.;* **mys·te·ri·ous·ness** *n.*

mys·tic (MIS·tic) *n.* one who seeks to learn about God and supernatural things through intuition rather than by use of reason.
— *adj.* 1 of mystics or mysticism: *a mystic experience, influence.* 2 mysterious or occult: *the mystic arts; mystic rites and ceremonies.* Also **mys·ti·cal.**
— **mys·ti·cal·ly** *adv.*

mys·ti·fy (MIS·tuh·fye) *v.* **-fies, -fied, -fy·ing** puzzle or perplex: *Children's questions sometimes mystify adults; the mystified look on her face.*
— **mys·ti·fi·ca·tion** (-fuh·CAY·shun) *n.*

mys·tique (mis·TEEK) *n.* the air of mystery about a person or thing: *the feminine mystique of the Mona Lisa; the mystique* (= impressive professionalism) *of bullfighting.*

myth (MITH) *n.* 1 a primitive, often supernatural story current among a people that seeks to explain something in nature, as stories of creation of the universe. 2 such stories collectively; mythology: *Greek myth and legend.* 3 a false belief; also, a person or thing considered as imagined or invented: *the myth of male superiority; My uncle's fabulous wealth proved to be a mere myth; to debunk, dispel, explode a myth.*
— **myth·i·cal** *adj.: The unicorn is a mythical animal.*

my·thol·o·gy (mi·THOL·uh·jee) *n.* **-gies** 1 the study of myths. 2 a group of myths. — **my·thol·o·gist** *n.*
— **myth·o·log·i·cal** (mith·uh·LOJ·uh·cul) *adj.*

Nn

N or **n** (EN) *n.* **N's** or **n's** the 14th letter of the English alphabet.
— **'n'** and: *kiss 'n' ride; park 'n' fly; rock 'n' roll; show 'n' tell.*

nab *v.* **nabs, nabbed, nab·bing** *Informal.* seize quickly, esp. arrest a person: *The police nabbed the thief before he could escape.*

na·dir (NAY·dur) *n.* the lowest point; opposite of ZENITH: *His hopes were at a nadir; Their decadence reached a nadir just before the fall.*

nag *v.* **nags, nagged, nag·ging** **1** find fault with or worry continually: *Stop nagging me; It's no use nagging at me all day.* **2** annoy or vex: *to be nagged by doubts, suspicions; a nagging backache.*
— *n.* **1** one who nags; scold. **2** an old or worn-out horse.

na·if (nah·EEF) *n.* one who is naive.

nail *n.* **1** the thorny growth at the ends of fingers and toes: *to cut* or *pare one's nails; to bite, file, manicure, polish one's nails.* **2** a pointed metal spike with a broadened head that is hit with a hammer to drive it into pieces of wood or other material for fastening them: *hard as nails* (= having no feeling); *to hit the nail on the head* (= say it exactly right).
— *v.* fasten or secure, as with a nail: *a sign nailed to a wall; Let's nail down the offer with a small deposit.*

na·ive or **na·ïve** (nah·EEV) *adj.* **1** simple or unsophisticated; hence, foolishly simple: *a naive attitude, creature, outlook, person, philosophy, remark; his naive ignorance, judgment.* **2** not previously experimented with; untutored: *a naive informant, rat, subject.* — **na·ive·ly** or **na·ïve·ly** *adv.*

na·ive·té or **na·ïve·té** (nah·eev·TAY, -EEV·tay) *n.* artlessness; also, a naive action or remark. Also **na·ive·ty** (nah·EEV·tee) *n.* **-ties.**

na·ked (NAY·kid) *adj.* unclothed; hence, uncovered or plain; bare: *a body lying naked; stark naked; the naked sword (out of its sheath); the naked truth.*
— **na·ked·ly** *adv.;* **na·ked·ness** *n.*

naked eye *n.* the eye unaided by a magnifying glass, microscope, or telescope: *invisible to the naked eye.*

nam·a·ble (NAY·muh·bul) *adj.* same as NAMEABLE.

name *n.* **1** word or words by which a person, animal, place, or thing is called or known: *your name and address; an assumed, brand, code, common, family, fancy, first, given, legal, maiden, married, middle, pet,* proper, stage, trade name; *I know him only by name (not personally); The booking was made in my name; Joe registered under an assumed name; She called him names* (= bad names). **2** reputation or fame: *He earned a good name as a journalist; made a name for himself in the community; A scandal gives one a bad name; It besmirches* or *smears one's name; She had to go to court to clear her name; the greatest name* (= person) *in boxing; to drop names* (= boast of one's connections); *a name-brand* (= well-known) *soap.*
— **in name only** not in reality; without power or influence: *the boss in name only.*
— **in the name of 1** by the authority of God, the king, the law, etc. **2** on behalf of someone: *He claims to speak in the name of the moral majority.*
— *v.* **names, named, nam·ing** give a name to someone or call by name: *a baby named for* or *after his father; a general accusation without naming any offenders; Can you name the signs of the zodiac? Lin was named to the chair; Lin was named (as the) chairperson; You name* (= mention) *it, we've got it.* — **name·a·ble** *adj.*

name-calling *n.* the calling of bad names: *to engage in* or *resort to name-calling when arguments fail.*

name-dropping *n.* the mentioning of important persons or places in a familiar way in order to impress others.
— **name-dropper** *n.*

name·less *adj.* without a name for various reasons: *a nameless ancestor, crime, feeling, infant; My detractors shall remain nameless for the present.*
— **name·less·ly** *adv.*

name·ly *adv.* that is to say; viz.

name of the game *n.* *Informal.* the essential thing; a goal or the means of attaining it: *The name of the game is profitability..*

name·plate *n.* a plate, plaque, etc. bearing a person's name.

name·sake *n.* one with the same name as another, esp. if named after that other person.

NAND (NAND) *n.* in computer logic, the operator that is the opposite of "and": *The NAND gate* (= device or circuit) *performs NAND operations; The NAND output of statements A and B is true if either A or B is false, and false if both A and B are true.*

nan·ny (NAN·ee) *n.* **nan·nies** *Brit.* a child's domestic nurse.

nanny goat *n.* a female goat.

nano- (NAN·oh) *combining form.* billionth: *nanogram, nanometre, nanosecond.*

nap 1 *n. & v.* **naps, napped, nap·ping** (have) a brief, light sleep: *Have* or *take a nap when you feel tired; to* **catch one napping** (= catch one off guard). **2** *n.* a soft or downy surface, as of fur, velvet, etc.

nape *n.* the back of the neck.

nap·kin *n.* **1** a small towel or piece of cloth or paper used for wiping the lips, etc. while eating: *He always eats with the napkin tucked under his chin.* **2** a sanitary pad or napkin.

nap·py *n.* **nap·pies** *Informal.* a diaper.

narc or **nark** *n. Slang.* a police agent enforcing narcotic laws.

nar·cis·sism (NAR·suh·siz·um) *n.* preoccupation with one's own beauty. — **nar·cis·sist** *n. & adj.* — **nar·cis·sis·tic** (-SIS·tic) *adj.*

nar·cot·ic (nar·COT·ic) *n.* a drug such as opium, codeine, or heroin that deadens pain and causes stupor: *a charge of trafficking in narcotics.* — *adj.: a narcotic addict, effect.* — **nar·co·tism** *n.*

nark 1 *v. & n. Brit. Slang.* (turn) spy or informer for police. **2** same as NARC.

nar·rate (NAIR·ate) *v.* **nar·rates, nar·rat·ed, nar·rat·ing** relate or tell a story, adventures, experiences, etc. — **nar·ra·tion** (nair·AY·shun) *n.* — **nar·ra·tor** (NAIR·ay·tur, nuh·RAY·tur) *n.*

nar·ra·tive (NAIR·uh·tiv) *n. & adj.* a story or tale that recounts events: *a fast-paced narrative; long narrative;* *adj.: a narrative poem; his narrative prose style.*

nar·row (NAIR·oh) *adj.* limited or small in width: *a narrow margin, street; a narrow* (= not liberal) *viewpoint; a narrow* (= limited) *circle of friends; a narrow* (= close) *escape, majority; narrow* (= close) *scrutiny; "Meat" means animal flesh in its narrowest sense.* — *v.* make or become narrower: *You see people narrowing their eyes in bright light; The road narrows round the curve; to* **narrow down** *the choice of candidates to a few.* — *n.* something narrow, esp. **narrows** *pl.* a narrow passage, as a strait or mountain pass. — **nar·row·ly** *adv.;* **nar·row·ness** *n.*

nar·row·cast (NAIR·oh·cast) *v.* televise by cable, not broadcast.

narrow-minded (NAIR·oh·MINE·did) *adj.* limited in outlook, not broad-minded. — **narrow-mindedness** *n.*

nar·y (NAIR·ee) *adj.* **nary a** or **an** not one: *with nary a cent in his pocket.*

na·sal (NAY·zul) *adj.* having to do with the nose: *a nasal bone, sound, voice; A cold could block your nasal passages.* — *n.:* "M," "n," and "ng" are nasals (= sounds produced through the nose); *the nasals* (= nasal bones) *forming the bridge of the nose.* — **na·sal·ly** *adv.*

na·sal·ize (NAY·zuh·lize) *v.* **-iz·es, -ized, -iz·ing** utter or speak nasally: *the nasalized vowels of the French "un bon vin."* — **na·sal·i·za·tion** (-luh·ZAY·shun) *n.*

nas·cent (NAY·sunt, NAS·unt) *adj.* being born or formed; beginning to develop: *a nascent gas; a nascent intellectual; hydrogen in a nascent state during a chemical reaction; nascent tumours.*

nas·ty (NAS·tee) *adj.* **-ti·er, -ti·est** disgusting or offensive to good taste; also, very unpleasant: *a nasty feeling, job, remark, smell, temper, wound; nasty behaviour, weather.* — **nas·ti·ly** *adv.;* **nas·ti·ness** *n.*

na·tal (NAY·tul) *adj.* of or from birth: *a natal day* (= birthday); *the natal hour; the* **natal death rate** (= rate of deaths at birth). — **na·tal·i·ty** (nuh·TAL·uh·tee) *n.* **-ties.**

na·ta·to·ri·um (nay·tuh·TOR·ee·um) *n.* **-ri·ums** or **-ri·a** (-ree·uh) an indoor swimming facility.

na·tion (NAY·shun) *n.* a people with a common history and culture, usually living under one government in a country of their own and using the same language: *a newly independent African nation; the Jewish nation; a member nation of the United Nations; a favoured, friendly, peace-loving, sovereign nation; two warring nations; It snowed across the nation* (= all over the country) *yesterday; the* **Six Nations** (= tribes) *federation of Iroquois.* — **na·tion·hood** *n.*

na·tion·al (NASH·un·ul) *adj.* having to do with a nation: *a national academy, anthem, disaster, disgrace, emergency, flag, food, forest, government, holiday, monument, park; the national character, income; the* **national debt** (= what a nation owes other countries); *national defence, health and welfare, revenue, unity; the National Hockey League of Canada; June 24, the feast of St. Jean Baptiste, is a* **national holiday** (= public holiday) *in Quebec; the Quebec* **National Assembly** (= provincial legislature). — *n.* a citizen or subject: *an Israeli who was a U.S. national; foreign nationals granted Canadian citizenship.* — **na·tion·al·ly** *adv.*

na·tion·al·ism (NASH·uh·nuh·liz·um) *n.* devotion to one's country, esp. in protecting its independence: *rampant nationalism; the cash-register nationalism that encourages foreign imports at the expense of home industry.* — **na·tion·al·ist** *n. & adj.* — **na·tion·al·is·tic** (-LIS·tic) *adj.*

na·tion·al·i·ty (nash·uh·NAL·uh·tee) *n.* **-ties 1** ethnic origin: *Soviet citizens belong to many nationalities.* **2** national origin: *Gypsies of various nationalities.*

na·tion·al·ize (NASH·un·uh·lize) *v.* **-iz·es, -ized, -iz·ing** make national, esp. take an industry, institution, land, etc. under national control. — **na·tion·al·i·za·tion** (-luh·ZAY·shun) *n.*

na·tion·wide *adj.* existing throughout the nation; national: *a nationwide alert; on nationwide television.*

na·tive (NAY·tiv) *adj.* **1** inborn, not acquired: *one's native abilities, instincts, qualities, talents.* **2** having to do with birth or place of origin: *native African customs; a* **Native American** (= American Indian); **Native Canadian** (= Canadian Indian or Inuit); *a* **native Indian** (= Canadian Indian, not one from India); *my native land* (= land of birth); *her native language, tongue* (= mother tongue); *the* **native peoples** (= Indians and Inuit) *of Canada; the native rights of the Inuit;*

native silver (in its natural state); *John Turner, born in London, was hailed as a* **native son** *of B.C.; native tribes; The panda is native to China; a* **native-born** *Canadian of British parents; Some tourists* **go native** (= take on the ways and customs of the natives).
— *n.* a person, animal, or plant that belongs to a specified region by origin or birth: *The koala is an Australian native; Joe is a native of Moose Jaw; natives and foreigners.*

native speaker *n.* 1 one who speaks a language that is his or her mother tongue: *an educated native speaker; Even native speakers make language errors.* 2 one who is a proficient user of a language: *The book should have been translated into French by a native speaker of the language; Jacques uses English with native-speaker ability* (= with proficiency).

na·tiv·ism (NAY·tuh·viz·um) *n.* a self-protective attitude or policy typical of natives toward immigrants and foreigners.

na·tiv·i·ty (nuh·TIV·uh·tee) *n.* -ties 1 birth: *population shown by nativity; your country of nativity.* 2 the **Nativity** the birth of Christ; also, Christmas: *Feast of the Nativity.*

NATO (NAY·toh) *n.* the North Atlantic Treaty Organization which is composed of U.S.A., Canada, Iceland, Norway, Turkey, and all the European Economic Community members except Ireland.

nat·ter (NAT·ur) *v. Informal.* chatter idly *away* or grumble *about* something.

nat·ty (NAT·ee) *adj.* **nat·ti·er, nat·ti·est** of dress or appearance, neat and trim: *a natty dresser; a natty leisure suit.* — **nat·ti·ly** *adv.*

nat·u·ral (NACH·uh·rul) *adj.* 1 having to do with nature: *the natural beauty of the countryside; storms, earthquakes, and such natural phenomena; the natural mother of Liz (who gave birth to Liz); a natural language like English (not artificial like Esperanto or a computer language such as Fortran); a natural* (= illegitimate) *son of the king; water, minerals, land, forests, and such* **natural resources.** 2 having to do with the innate character or nature of a person or thing; not artificial or formal: *You look more natural without makeup; her natural gifts, voice; a natural note* (= in music, a note without a sharp or flat). 3 containing no additives or preservatives; processed very little: *natural fibre, flavour, foods.*
— *n.* one naturally suited for a job, role, etc.; also, the thing itself: *He's a natural to play the part of the wizard; Acting is a natural for him.* — **nat·u·ral·ness** *n.*

natural childbirth *n.* delivery by a mother emotionally and physically trained to bear the pain without the help of an anesthetic.

natural gas *n.* a hydrocarbon gas formed in the earth from organic matter, much used as fuel.

natural history *n.* the nontechnical, popular study of the animals, plants, minerals, and other things in nature.

nat·u·ral·ism (NACH·uh·rul·iz·um) *n.* the use of what is natural and realistic, instead of the unscientific and the supernatural, in art, fiction, drama, etc..

nat·u·ral·ist (NACH·uh·rul·ist) *n.* 1 one who studies

natural history. 2 an advocate of naturalism.
— **nat·u·ral·is·tic** (-ruh·LIS·tic) *adj.*

nat·u·ral·ize (NACH·uh·ruh·lize) *v.* **-iz·es, -ized, -iz·ing** make or become native or like a native: *native-born Canadians and naturalized Canadians* (= immigrants who have become Canadian citizens); *"Spaghetti" is a naturalized Italian word; The African violet was naturalized long ago.*
— **nat·u·ral·i·za·tion** (-luh·ZAY·shun) *n.*

nat·u·ral·ly (NACH·uh·ruh·lee) *adv.* 1 by nature: *naturally curly hair; the naturally unsuspecting child.* 2 in a natural, not artificial manner: *He can't talk naturally when on stage.* 3 as might be expected: *Naturally, he'll be upset by the bad news.*

natural science *n.* a science dealing with nature, as biology, chemistry, geology, or physics, as distinguished from the humanities and social sciences.
— **natural scientist** *n.*

na·ture (NAY·chur) *n.* 1 the world of animals, plants, minerals, forces such as instincts, and phenomena such as wind and rain that are not made by humans: *Everyone loves nature; We try to harness the forces of nature; the back-to-nature philosophy of people tired of city life; Mother Nature* (= nature as a person); *Nudists socialize in a state of nature; freaks of nature; the calls of nature (to urinate and defecate).* 2 real quality or character: *It is the dog's nature to bark; It's not in his nature to attack children; It's human nature to make mistakes; It's all in the nature of things* (= things as they are); *Helping others is second nature to Sam; Tim's true nature comes out when he has to deal with people; Let's appeal to their better natures; Lee is not lazy* **by nature;** *Digging for artifacts is a pursuit of a scholarly nature* (= kind).

nature study *n.* the study of the life and phenomena in nature at the elementary level.

nature trail *n.* a path laid out in a natural environment for the study of animals, plants, etc.

na·tur·ist (NAY·chur·ist) *n.* a nudist.

naught (NAWT) *n.* nothing; zero: *All our efforts came to* or *went for naught; It was all for naught.*

naugh·ty (NAW·tee) *adj.* **-ti·er, -ti·est** 1 disobedient or mischievous: *a naughty child.* 2 off-colour: *a naughty joke.* — **naugh·ti·ly** *adv.;* **naugh·ti·ness** *n.*

nau·sea (NAW·zhuh, -zee·uh) *n.* 1 sickness of the stomach that makes one want to vomit. 2 loathing or disgust.

nau·se·ate (NAW·see·ate, -zee·ate, -shee·ate, -zhee·ate) *v.* **-ates, -at·ed, -at·ing** make one want to vomit: *The very mention of snails nauseates her; She feels* **nauseated;** *a very* **nauseating** *experience, sensation.*
— **nau·se·a·tion** (-AY·shun) *n.*

nau·seous (NAW·shus, -zee·us) *adj.* 1 feeling or causing nausea; nauseated or queasy: *These days, she feels nauseous in the mornings.* 2 disgusting or loathesome; nauseating: *foods that are nauseous to some.*

nau·ti·cal (NAW·tuh·cul) *adj.* having to do with sailors, ships, or navigation: *a nautical college, uniform; "amidships," "fo'c'sle," and such nautical terms; The* **nautical mile** (= distance unit of 6 076 ft. / 1 852 m), or *"sea mile,"* is used in air and sea navigation.

na·val (NAY·vul) *adj.* having to do with a navy: *a naval academy, base, battle, cadet, installation, officer, power, vessel.*

na·vel (NAY·vul) *n.* a depression in the centre of the belly where the umbilical cord was attached at birth: *the navel-fixed gaze of a self-satisfied person in contemplation.*

nav·i·ga·ble (NAV·uh·guh·bul) *adj.* that can be navigated: *a navigable river (that is wide and deep enough for craft); navigable waters; a navigable* (=steerable) *balloon.* — **nav·i·ga·bly** *adv.* — **nav·i·ga·bil·i·ty** (-BIL·uh·tee) *n.*

nav·i·gate (NAV·uh·gate) *v.* -gates, -gat·ed, -gat·ing 1 steer, guide, or manage a ship, plane, etc. through the sea, air, etc. 2 make one's way past or through something: *We had a difficult time navigating the snowbound schoolyard.* 3 get through a river, sea, etc. in a craft: *to navigate the Niagara River.* 4 *Informal.* move or walk steadily: *He finds it difficult to navigate after a couple of drinks.*

nav·i·ga·tion (nav·uh·GAY·shun) *n.* 1 the science of guiding a craft on its course through water, air, or space. 2 a navigating.

nav·i·ga·tor (NAV·uh·gay·tur) *n.* 1 one who navigates. 2 an explorer of the seas.

na·vy (NAY·vee) *n.* -vies 1 a nation's warships collectively or the whole naval establishment including yards, offices, and personnel. 2 [short form] navy blue.

navy blue *n.* a dark purplish blue.

nay *adv.* 1 not only that but also: *She's poor, nay, destitute!* 2 [old use] no; opposite of AYE. — *n.* a negative vote or voter: *"The nays have it"* (=The negative side has won).

nay·say·er (NAY·say·ur) *n.* a person with a negative or pessimistic attitude.

N-bomb (EN·bom) *n.* same as NEUTRON BOMB.

NDP·er (EN·DEE·PEE·ur) *n.* **NDP·ers** *Informal.* a member of the New Democratic Party of Canada.

Ne·an·der·thal (nee·AN·dur·thawl) *n. & adj.* 1 a primitive human of the Stone Age. 2 **neanderthal** one who is backward or primitive: *the neanderthals who set fire to our forests; a neanderthal male chauvinist; her neanderthal mentality; their neanderthal views on computers.*

near (NEER) *adj.* close in distance, relationship, feelings, time, etc.: *Her house is near, not far from here; in the near distance, near future; a near friend, relative; Holidays are near* (=coming soon); *Near beer has less than 0.5 percent alcohol; a move to abolish the sales tax on near foods such as candies and soft drinks; A near miss is almost a hit; near silk; the nearest* (=most direct) *route; adv.: Holidays are drawing near; We came near to scoring a goal; The water is near (Informal for nearly) frozen.* — **near at hand** close by in time or place: *Peace seemed near at hand; Keep your calculator near at hand.* — *v.* approach: *We are nearing the end of our journey.* — **near·ness** *n.*

near·by (NEER·bye, neer·BYE) *adv. & adj.* close by: *She lives nearby; in a nearby town.*

Near East *n.* the countries of southwestern Asia and northeastern Africa; also, the Middle East. — **Near Eastern** *adj.*

near·ly (NEER·lee) *adv.* closely: *We are nearly related; It's nearly* (=almost) *noon.*

near·sight·ed (NEER·sye·tid) *adj.* not able to see far because of defective eyesight.

neat (NEET) *adj.* 1 clean and orderly: *a neat drawing; He writes a neat hand; She's quite neat in all her homework; a neat and tidy kitchen; a neat mind looking for nice distinctions.* 2 *Informal.* pleasing: *That's really neat! a neat dress, haircut; a neat* (=net) *profit of $100 000.* 3 undiluted: *neat brandy; He takes his brandy neat; Two glasses of port and one neat whisky, please.* — **neat·ly** *adv.*; **neat·ness** *n.*

'neath (NEETH, "TH" as in "thin") [poetical] beneath.

neb·bish (NEB·ish) *n. Slang.* a pitifully inept or dull person.

neb·u·la (NEB·yuh·luh) *n.* -las or -lae (-lee) a cloudlike hazy patch seen in the sky at night. — **neb·u·lar** (-lur) *adj.: the nebular hypothesis of the origin of the solar system.*

neb·u·lous (NEB·yuh·lus) *adj.* 1 cloudy or hazy: *a nebulous liquid, state.* 2 confused or vague: *a nebulous concept, idea, notion.* — **neb·u·los·i·ty** (-LOS·uh·tee) *n.* -ties.

nec·es·sar·y (NES·uh·sair·ee) *adj.* needed or required in a pressing manner though not essential: *Food, shelter, and clothing are necessary to or for our existence; It's necessary to eat or that we eat in order to live; the necessary repairs for a car after a collision; the necessary* (=logical) *consequence of an action; Visits to the dentist are a necessary* (=unavoidable) *evil; It's necessary that we visit the dentist regularly.* — *n.* -es·sar·ies something that is necessary: *Children have a right to the necessaries of life such as food, shelter, clothing, medical care, and routine education.* — **nec·es·sar·i·ly** (-SAIR·uh·lee) *adv.*

ne·ces·si·tate (nuh·SES·uh·tate) *v.* -tates, -tat·ed, -tat·ing make necessary: *Crime necessitates punishment; A jail term necessitates living away from home.*

ne·ces·si·ty (nuh·SES·uh·tee) *n.* -ties an urgent or pressing need or thing needed: *Food is a necessity; a dire* necessity; *He managed to survive with the bare, daily necessities of life; Most people go to work out of necessity; She was forced to go on welfare by family necessity* (= poverty); *I must,* **of necessity,** (= forced by circumstances) *limit my speech to five minutes because I've a plane to catch.*

neck *n.* **1** the narrow, slender part connecting the head to the rest of the body: *to crane one's neck for a better view; to* **break one's neck** (= try too hard) *on a job; He* **risked his neck** (= risked his life) *by going down Niagara Falls in a barrel; He was saved* **by a neck** (= narrowly); *You'll* **get it in the neck** (*Slang for* be severely dealt with) *if you ignore warnings.* **2** anything resembling a neck, as a narrow strip of land, the narrowest part of a bottle, violin, tooth, etc.
— **breathe down someone's neck** *Informal.* get too close to someone, as if to use power or influence.
— **in one's neck of the woods** *Slang.* in one's part of the country.
— **neck and neck** running equal, as two horses in a race.
— **stick one's neck out** act too boldly or foolishly.
— **up to one's neck** deeply involved: *I'm up to my neck in work; He's up to his neck in debt.*
— *v. Slang.* kiss passionately: *No necking is allowed in the library.*

neck·er·chief (NEK·ur·chuf, -cheef) *n.* -**chiefs** or -**chieves** (-cheevz) a handkerchieflike piece of cloth worn about the neck.

neck·lace (NECK·lis) *n.* an ornamental chain or string of jewels, beads, etc. worn around the neck.

neck·line *n.* the line formed by the edge of a garment around, esp. at the front of the neck: *a high, low, lowcut, plunging neckline.*

neck·tie *n.* a strip of cloth worn around the neck under a collar, tied at the front of the neck with its loose ends hanging down.

neck·wear *n.* neckties, scarves, etc. collectively.

nec·tar (NEC·tur) *n.* **1** the drink of the gods of Greek myth. **2** a sweet or delicious drink, as the liquid that bees gather from flowers.

nec·tar·ine (nec·tuh·REEN) *n.* a variety of peach with a smooth skin.

née or **nee** (NAY, NEE) *adj.* [used before a married woman's maiden name] born as: *Mary Jones, née Smith* (= born as Miss Mary Smith).

need *n.* a lack of something useful, desired, or required; also, the thing lacked: *She's badly in need of vitamins; There's no need for junk food; no need for you to lose weight; the urgent need to put out a fire; men's daily needs such as toiletries; a nun's simple needs; Our needs come before our wants; to create, feel, fill, meet, minister to, obviate, satisfy a need; Sewers are a crying need in this town; a desperate, dire, material, pressing need; The poor live in constant need; "A friend in need (who helps when one is in trouble) is a friend indeed"; There's no need* (= You are not required) *to apologize; She is prepared to sacrifice her life for her child,* **if need be** (= if the need arises).
— *v.* have need of a person or thing: *People desperately need jobs; A crossing guard is badly, sorely needed at* the school; *Everyone needs to work; Need I say more? The unemployed need* (= are required) *to look for jobs; She need not have hurried since she missed the flight anyhow; He didn't need to hurry to catch the flight since he was much too early; Yvette need not hurry since her flight has been cancelled.*
— **needs** *adv.* [used with "must"] necessarily: *She* **needs must** *go back to get her hat when everyone else is ready to leave!*

need·ful *n. & adj.* what is required or necessary.

nee·dle (NEE·dul) *n.* **1** a slender, pointed piece of steel with a hole at the thicker end through which a thread is passed for sewing: *to look for* **a needle in a haystack** (= something impossible to find). **2** a similar instrument for carrying a thread for knitting, hooking, etc. **3** anything resembling a needle, as the pointer of a gauge or meter, the vibrating pin in the pickup mechanism of a phonograph, the pointed leaf of a pine, or the injecting end of a surgical syringe: *a hypodermic needle.* **4** *Informal.* an injection of a drug: *my weekly needle for allergies.*
— *v.* -**dles,** -**dled,** -**dling** tease or annoy someone with gibes, provocative comments, etc.

nee·dle·leaf (NEE·dul·leef) *adj.* of a tree, having needlelike or scalelike leaves: *Conifers such as pines, firs, and spruces are needleleaf trees.*

need·less *adj.* unnecessary.
— **need·less·ly** *adv.;* **need·less·ness** *n.*

need·n't (NEED·unt) need not.

need·y *adj.* **need·i·er,** -**i·est** in need; poor or destitute.
— **need·i·ness** *n.*

ne'er (NAIR) [poetic] never.

ne'er-do-well (NAIR·doo·wel) *n. & adj.* (one who is) worthless or irresponsible.

ne·far·i·ous (ni·FAIR·ee·us) *adj.* extremely wicked or villainous: *nefarious activities, deeds; a nefarious scheme.* — **ne·far·i·ous·ly** *adv.;* **ne·far·i·ous·ness** *n.*

neg·a·tive (NEG·uh·tiv) *adj.* **1** saying "no"; opposite: *the negative side of a debate; The* **negative option** *of either returning unsolicited merchandise or keeping it and paying for it is a dubious practice.* **2** against or on the other side of something considered positive: *negative film* (with reversed image); *a negative TB test;* — **3** has a **negative sign** before it; *the negative electrode of a battery.*
— *n.* something negative, as a word, vote, or reply, a minus sign or quantity, a film or photographic image, a battery terminal to which current flows, etc.: *He replied* **in the negative** (= said "no"); *"I didn't do nothing" is a double negative which should read "I didn't do anything."*
— *v.* -**tives,** -**tived,** -**tiv·ing 1** vote against or deny. **2** disprove.
— **neg·a·tive·ly** *adv.* — **neg·a·tiv·ism** (-iz·um) n.

negative income tax *n.* a subsidy paid by government to the poor to guarantee a minimum income.

neg·lect (nig·LECT) *v.* give too little attention or care to a person or thing: *Do not neglect your health or your duties; She neglected* (= omitted) *to write home; a* **neglected** (= uncared-for) *child.*

— n. a neglecting or failure to look after a person or thing: *a vacant house in a state of neglect; parental neglect of children; child neglect* (= neglect of a child); *fired for neglect of duty; the policy of **benign neglect** as a tactic for avoiding an issue or not doing justice to a cause.* **— neg·lect·ful** *adj.*

neg·li·gee (neg·luh·ZHAY) *n.* **1** a woman's light and loose-fitting dressing gown. **2** careless or informal attire.

neg·li·gent (NEG·luh·junt) *adj.* habitually or extremely careless: *fired for being grossly negligent in his duty.* **— neg·li·gence** *n.*: *contributory, criminal, gross, willful negligence.* **— neg·li·gent·ly** *adv.*

neg·li·gi·ble (NEG·luh·juh·bul) *adj.* that can be neglected; trifling or unimportant: *a negligible amount, error.*

ne·go·ti·a·ble (ni·GOH·shee·uh·bul, -shuh·bul) *adj.* that may be negotiated: *a negotiable claim, contract (that may be discussed and modified); Our offer is not negotiable* (= cannot be modified or made better); *The road is not negotiable* (= passable) *during the flood; A cheque, money order, or draft that is negotiable* (= can be exchanged for money) *is called a **negotiable instrument.***

ne·go·ti·ate (ni·GOH·shee·ate) *v.* **-ates, -at·ed, -at·ing 1** discuss and arrange: *Labour negotiates with management about* or *over wages, for raises and better working conditions; to negotiate an agreement, loan, sale, settlement, treaty; While both sides negotiated, the strike dragged on.* **2** sell, transfer, or assign something negotiable, as a cheque, funds, etc. **3** successfully go past, over, etc.: *to negotiate a curve, fence.* **— ne·go·ti·a·tion** (-shee·AY·shun) *n.* usually **negotiations** *pl.*: *diplomatic, high-level, peace, round-the-clock negotiations; to break off, conduct, enter into negotiations.* **— ne·go·ti·a·tor** (-shee·ay·tur) *n.*

ne·gri·tude (NEG·ruh·tude, NEE·gruh-) *n.* the fact of being a Negro, esp. the value of black or African culture; also **Ne·gro·ness** (NEE·groh·nus) *n.*

Ne·gro (NEE·groh) *n.* **-groes** [mainly historical use; less favoured than "black" or "African" in current English] a member of the Negroid group or black race of mankind: *There were negro (baseball) leagues before blacks were allowed to play in the major leagues.*

Ne·groid (NEE·groid) *n. & adj.* a race of mankind native to Africa, distinguished by dark skin, kinky hair, and broad lips and nose.

neigh (NAY) *v. & n.* the characteristic cry of a horse.

neigh·bour or **neigh·bor** (NAY·bur) *n.* one living near another: *our next-door neighbour; good neighbours; Love thy neighbour* (= fellow humans). **— v.** live or be situated nearby: *New York State neighbours the Ontario border; The U.S. neighbours on* or *upon Canada; It's our **neighbouring** country.*

neigh·bour·hood or **neigh·bor·hood** (NAY·bur·hood, short "oo") *n.* a particular region, place, or district with the people living there: *a high-income neighbourhood; poor neighbourhoods; a protected neighbourhood; Ask your friendly neighbourhood banker for a loan.* **— in the neighbourhood of** *Informal.* near: *We used to*

live in the neighbourhood of the church; The job pays in the neighbourhood of (= approximately) $50 000 a year.

neigh·bour·ly or **neigh·bor·ly** (NAY·bur·lee) *adj.* like good neighbours; friendly: *neighbourly friendliness, relations; The neighbourly thing to do is to report prowlers to the police.* **— neigh·bour·li·ness** or **neigh·bor·li·ness** *n.*

nei·ther (NEE·thur, NYE-, "th" as in "the") *adj., pron. & conj.* not the one or the other: *The shoe would fit neither foot; would fit neither of the feet; It would fit neither the left foot nor the right.* **— adv.** [used with "no," "not," or other negative in previous clause] also not: *He doesn't smoke; neither do I* or *me neither* (*Informal* for and I don't either).

Nel·lie (NEL·ee) *n.* **1** *Cdn.* a bronze statuette given as an annual award in various categories by the Association of Canadian Television and Radio Artists. **2 nellie** or **Nel·ly,** *pl.* **nel·lies** or **Nel·lies** *Slang.* a weak or effeminate person: *He's a bit on the nellie side; a **nervous Nellie*** (= a worrier); *a **nice Nelly*** (= prude).

nem·e·sis (NEM·uh·sis) *n., pl.* **-ses 1** a fate which the victim deserved; retribution: *to meet one's nemesis.* **2** the punishing agent, like **Nemesis,** the Greek goddess of vengeance: *The parking meter is often the shopper's nemesis.*

neo- *combining form.* new or recent: *neocolonial, neonatal, neo-Nazi.*

ne·ol·o·gism (nee·OL·uh·jiz·um) *n.* a new word or phrase, or a new meaning for an established word. Also **ne·ol·o·gy** (-uh·jee) *n.* **-gies.**

ne·on (NEE·on) *n.* an inert gaseous element found in the air, used in lamps and advertising signs for the bright glow it gives when an electric current is passed through it.

ne·o·na·tal (nee·oh·NAY·tul) *adj.* of the newborn, esp. less than a month old: *neonatal diseases, mortality.*

ne·o·phyte (NEE·uh·fite) *n.* **1** a new convert. **2** a novice or beginner.

neph·ew (NEF·yoo, NEV-) *n.* a son of one's brother, sister, brother-in-law, or sister-in-law.

nep·o·tism (NEP·uh·tiz·um) *n.* favouritism shown to relatives, as in giving jobs.

nerd (NURD) *n. Slang.* one considered as unpleasant or insignificant.

nerve (NURV) *n.* **1** a strand or fibre that carries impulses of sensation and motion between the sense organs and the brain: *sensory nerves; a spinal nerve; The question about her past **hit a (raw) nerve*** (= touched a sensitive point). **2** a vein of a leaf or rib of an insect's wing. **3 nerves** *pl.* nervousness: *She had an attack of nerves; She is a **bundle of nerves*** (= very nervous person); *Some of his puns **get on her nerves*** (= annoy her); *to calm, fray, frazzle, settle one's nerves.* **4** a mental or bodily strength; courage or vigour: *strong, taut, weak **nerves**; She has **nerves** of steel; She likes to **strain every nerve*** (= try her very best) *on the eve of a test; Don't **lose your nerve** and give up at the last moment.* **5** boldness or impudence: *the teenage son's nerve to ask for a Ferrari after totalling a Mustang.* **— v. nerves, nerved, nerv·ing** give strength or courage to do something: *She nerved herself to receive the tragic news.*

nerve centre or **nerve center** *n.* **1** a group of nerve cells controlling a specific function such as respiration or vision. **2** a headquarters or centre of activity.

nerve-racking or **nerve-wracking** *adj.* very trying on one's nerves: *a nerve-racking job, ordeal.*

ner·vous (NUR·vus) *adj.* **1** jumpy or restless: *Gigi feels nervous at the end of the month; She's nervous about the bills waiting to be paid; He's not nervous by nature, but he is a **nervous wreck** before an examination.* **2** animated or vigorous: *the nervous energy that drives her forward.* **3** of the nerves: *nervous excitement.* — **ner·vous·ly** *adv.;* **ner·vous·ness** *n.*

nervous breakdown *n.* a sudden emotional illness accompanied by depression, fatigue, lack of appetite, feelings of inadequacy, etc.

nervous system *n.* the bodily system consisting of the brain, spinal cord, nerves, and nerve endings.

nerv·y (NUR·vee) *adj.* **nerv·i·er, -i·est 1** brash or impudent. **2** showing or requiring courage; bold or courageous. **3** *Brit.* nervous or excitable. — **nerv·i·ly** *adv.;* **nerv·i·ness** *n.*

-ness *n. suffix.* quality or state: *fastness, forgiveness, goodness.*

nest *n.* **1** a cozy place for retiring into, esp. a structure built of twigs or straw in which birds lay and hatch eggs. **2** a place similarly used by insects, fishes, and other animals. **3** a place swarming with something bad; hangout: *a nest of criminals, spies, thieves, vice.* **4** a group of articles, often of gradually varying size, fitting into one another: *a nest of drinking cups, tables.* — *v.* **1** make or form a nest: *Storks nest on roofs and chimneys.* **2** of the members of a series of objects, fit one into the next or another: *stacking chairs and **nesting** tables; a **nested** subroutine (to be carried out within a computer program).*

nest egg *n.* money set aside as a reserve or to start a fund.

nes·tle (NES·ul) *v.* **-tles, -tled, -tling** shelter or settle cozily: *a village nestled in a valley; She nestled down into the chair by the fire; Guy **nestled up** to his mom; Mother nestled (= pressed) the frightened child in her arms.*

nest·ling (NEST·ling) *n.* a bird too young to leave its nest.

net *n.* **1** a fabric knotted or woven of string, thread, hair, etc. with regularly spaced meshes, esp. something made of such fabric for catching fish, butterflies, etc., for dividing a court in games such as tennis and volleyball, for protection against mosquitoes, to keep hair in place, etc.: *to cast, spread a net for fish; a butterfly net; mosquito net; safety net.* **2** a trap or snare. **3** what is left over after deductions from gross; *adj.: a net amount, price; the net income, profit; Your **net worth** (= assets minus liabilities).* — *v.* **nets, net·ted, net·ting 1** catch in a net or as if in a net: *to net fish.* **2** clear or yield as profit: *We netted $20 000 from the sale.*

neth·er (NETH·ur, "TH" as in "the") *adj.* lower or

under: *The team's success rate places it in the nether regions of NHL statistics; the **nether world** (= Hades or hell).*

neth·er·most (NETH·ur·most) *adj.* lowest.

netting *n.* **1** the making of a net. **2** fishing with a net. **3** net material.

net·tle (NET·ul) *n.* a weed with stinging bristles. — *v.* **net·tles, net·tled, net·tling** irritate or annoy someone.

net·tle·some (NET·ul·sum) *adj.* irritating or annoying.

net·work *n.* **1** mesh or something resembling it, as a system of roads, veins, etc. that cross each other, or a group of radio or television stations that may broadcast the same programs simultaneously: *News is broadcast over the national networks; a computer network of databases, terminals, printers, and such devices; adj.: network operations, television.* **2** an association or club: *a feminist network; old-boy networks.*

net·work·ing (NET·wurk·ing) *n.* **1** the making or using of a computer network. **2** a supportive system of people with the same interests and objectives for sharing services and information.

neu·ral (NEW·rul) *adj.* of a nerve or of the nervous system. — **neu·ral·ly** *adv.*

neu·rol·o·gy (new·ROL·uh·jee) *n.* a branch of medicine dealing with the nervous system and its diseases. — **neu·rol·o·gist** *n.* — **neu·ro·log·i·cal** (new·ruh·LOJ·uh·cul) *adj.*

neu·ro·sis (new·ROH·sis) *n., pl.* **-ses** (-seez) a mental disorder characterized by anxiety, phobias, insecurity, and depression. — **neu·rot·ic** (new·ROT·ic) *n. & adj.*

neu·ter (NEW·tur) *n.* a grammatical form or word, as the pronoun "it": *the neuter gender.* **2** an animal, plant, or insect that is neither masculine nor feminine, or sexless, as a worker bee or a spayed animal. — *v.* spay an animal.

neu·tral (NEW·trul) *n. & adj.* (one) belonging to neither side, as a nation not joining a war: *Switzerland remained neutral in the two world wars; the neutral corners of a boxing ring; Beige is a neutral (= bland or weak) colour; Water is chemically neutral (= neither acid nor alkaline); a car in neutral (gear).* — **neu·tral·ly** *adv.*

neu·tral·ism (NEW·truh·liz·um) *n.* the policy or practice of keeping neutral, esp. in international relations; nonalignment. — **neu·tral·ist** *n. & adj.* — **neu·tral·i·ty** (new·TRAL·uh·tee) *n.*

neu·tral·ize (NEW·truh·lize) *v.* **-iz·es, -ized, -iz·ing** make neutral chemically, politically, in artistic effect, etc. — **neu·tral·i·za·tion** (-luh·ZAY·shun) *n.*

neutron bomb *n.* an atomic bomb that would release radioactive neutrons taking lives but without the blast destructive to property.

nev·er (NEV·ur) *adv.* not ever; at no time; also, not at all: *I've never been to China; Never mind, I'm going there next year; Never mind the expense; A bikini will **never do** for something to wear to church; a gas bar that is **never ever** closed (= open 24 hours and 7 days).*

nev·er·more (NEV·ur·more) *adv.* never again.

never-never land *n.* a never-attainable, imaginary condition or unreal place.

nev·er·the·less (NEV·ur·the·LES) *adv.* however.

new *adj.* **1** now or recently come into being, use, possession, etc.: *a new car; a new hand at car repair; Our new home is only about 25 years old; a new arrival, fashion, idea, look; New Canadians* (= recent immigrants to Canada). **2** seen or known for the first time: *the discovery of the New World; new evidence on an old murder; Greece is new to us.* **3** not yet accustomed: *We are new to Greece; I'm new at driving.* **4** news *pl.* [takes sing. v.] new or recent events, esp. as reported in a newspaper or broadcast on radio or TV: *to announce, break, cover, distort, flash, spread, suppress the news; the latest news; We heard it on the Late News; Please turn on the news (on radio or TV); the nightly news; a bit, item, piece of news; Quintuplets always make news; sensational, startling, welcome news; to hold a news conference* (for the media); *Yesterday's news is today's history.* — **new·ly** *adv.;* **new·ness** *n.*

new blood *n.* new people who bring fresh ideas or vigour into an organization.

new·born *adj.* **1** just born: *a newborn babe.* **2** born anew: *a newborn interest.*
— *n. sing. & pl.* a newborn child: *care of the newborn and the elderly.*

new·com·er (NEW·cum·ur) *n.* a new or recent arrival, often a beginner: *a newcomer to Canada.*

new·fan·gled (NEW·fang·guld) *adj.* [derogatory] newly put together: *newfangled devices, gadgets, ideas, notions.*

new-fashioned (NEW·FASH·und) *adj.* of a new fashion in form or style.

New·fie (NEW·fee) *n. & adj.* [sometimes offensive to Newfoundlanders, esp. when used by outsiders] a person of or from Newfoundland: *the distinctive idiom of the Newfies.*
— *adj.* having to do with Newfoundland: *Newfie entertainment at its best; a Newfie joke; the Newfie sense of humour; the Newfie screech.*

new-found *adj.* newly found: *a new-found ally, friend.*

New·found·land (new·fun·LAND) *n.* same as NEWFOUNDLAND DOG.

Newfoundland dog *n. Cdn.* **1** a big, strong working dog with black or black-and-white coat. **2** a breed of short-haired dog from which the Labrador retriever was bred.

New·found·land·er (new·fun·LAN·dur) *n.* **1** a person of or from Newfoundland. **2** a Newfoundland dog.

new·ly *adv.* recently or freshly: *a newly arrived immigrant; newly formed companies; newly industrialized nations; a newly married couple; a newly paved driveway.*

newly-wed (NEW·lee·wed) *n.* one recently married; bride or bridegroom.

new moon *n.* the beginning of the first phase of the moon when it appears totally dark before waxing from a thin crescent to a half moon.

news See NEW.

news·box *n.* a newspaper-vending box.

news·boy *n.* a boy who distributes newspapers.

news·cast *n.* a radio or TV broadcast of news.
— **news·cast·er** *n.*

news·deal·er (NEWS·dee·lur) *n.* a retailer of newspapers and magazines.

news·hound *n.* a dedicated news reporter.

news·let·ter (NEWS·let·ur) *n.* a bulletin or report periodically issued to a group to keep them informed of happenings in their field of interest.

news·mag·a·zine (NEWS·mag·uh·zeen) *n.* a magazine that summarizes and comments on current events.

news·mak·er (NEWS·may·kur) *n.* a newsworthy person.

news·man *n.* -men **1** a news reporter. **2** a newsdealer.

news·pa·per (NEWS·pay·pur) *n.* a periodical, esp. a daily publication, containing news and comments, features, and advertising.

news·pa·per·man (NEWS·pay·pur·man) *n.* -men a newspaper publisher, editor, reporter, etc.
— **news·pa·per·wom·an** *n.* -wom·en.

new·speak (NEW·speek) *n.* a style of official language meant to deceive the public.

news people *n. pl.* news reporters.

news·per·son (NEWS·pur·sun) *n.* a news reporter.

news·print *n.* **1** paper used for printing newspapers, esp. cheap paper made from wood pulp. **2** old newspapers.

news·reel *n.* a short motion picture of news events, as shown in a movie theatre.

news·stand *n.* a stand at which newspapers, etc. are sold.

news·wor·thy (NEWS·wur·thee, "th" as in "the") *adj.* having interest or importance as news.

news·y (NEW·zee) *adj.* news·i·er, -i·est *Informal.* **1** containing much news: *newsy photos; a newsy report.* **2** being the subject of news: *a newsy design; The Canadian Press chose Flora MacDonald as the newsiest woman of 1976.*

new town *n.* a city planned and built as a small self-contained community away from a large urban area to reduce overcrowding.

new wave *n.* **1** a new movement or trend in art, cinema, cooking, music, etc. **2** a type of rock music of the 1970s; *adj.: the new-wave culture of punk rockers.*

New Year or **New Year's** *n.* the first day or days of a new year.

New Year's Day *n.* January 1.

New Year's Eve *n.* the evening of December 31.

next *adj.* nearest, esp. after a person or thing: *the next house; the house next to ours; We'll see you next week; Who's next (in line)? to catch the next train* (= the train after this train or closest to a specified one); *adv.: The* number 4 comes next after 3; What did she do next? the **next best** (= second best) solution to a problem; She did **next to** (= almost) nothing to help us.

next door adv. very close, esp. in the next house: They live next door; next door to us; **adj.**: our next-door neighbours.

next of kin n. nearest relatives.

nex·us n. 1 a link or connection within a system or situation: There should be no nexus between the government and the judiciary. 2 core or centre: a family that is the nexus of a vast fortune.

Ni·ag·a·ra (nye·AG·ruh) n. a cataract or torrent, like Niagara Falls: a Niagara of facts and figures.

nib n. a point or tip, esp. of a fountain pen.

nib·ble (NIB·ul) v. & n. **nib·bles, nib·bled, nib·bling** (take) a small, gentle, or cautious bite: Fish nibble at bait; The book proposal got only nibbles from publishers, no real bites; Rising prices **nibble away** at the value of the dollar. — **nib·bler** n.

nice adj. **nic·er, nic·est** 1 agreeable; good; proper: a nice boy, girl, man, party, person, time; nice weather; Is Toronto a nicer place to live than New York? 2 requiring care or exactness; subtle or refined: a nice legal distinction, shade of meaning, ear for music. — **nice·ly** adv.; **nice·ness** n.

ni·ce·ty (NYE·suh·tee) n. -ties daintiness; exactness; also, something dainty or refined: the niceties of courteous behaviour; She does everything she touches **to a nicety** (= with exactness).

niche (NICH) n. 1 a recess in a wall, as for a statue or vase. 2 a secure position: He occupies a special niche in the organization; She has carved out a niche for herself in her profession.

nick n. a small or superficial cut or chip: a table top with nicks and scratches; A collision was avoided by braking **in the nick of time** (= just in time). — v.: He nicked himself while shaving.

nick·el (NICK·ul) n. 1 a hard silver-white metallic element used in alloys, as in the Canadian five-cent coin. 2 a five-cent piece.

nickel-and-dime adj. small or small-time: a nickel-and-dime dealer, job. — v. weaken or reduce little by little: a government whose taxation policies nickel-and-dime people to death.

nickel belt n. Cdn. the nickel mining region around Sudbury, Ont.

nick·name n. a familiar name given to a person or place, either a descriptive term, as "Fatty," "Winter playground," etc. or a pet name, as "Lizzie." — v. **-names, -named, -nam·ing**: Anne of Green Gables was nicknamed "Carrots" because of her red hair.

niece (NEECE) n. the daughter of one's brother, sister, brother-in-law, or sister-in-law.

nif·ty (NIF·tee) adj. **-ti·er, -ti·est** Informal. smart or stylish.

nig·gard (NIG·urd) n. a stingy person. — **nig·gard·ly** adj. stingy: a niggardly giver; niggardly

praise; Our teacher is never niggardly in her praise of good students.

nig·ger (NIG·ur) n. 1 [offensive except in black use] a Negro. 2 a member of an underprivileged group of society.

nig·gle (NIG·ul) v. **nig·gles, nig·gled, nig·gling** work fussily; be finicky: Lou tends to niggle about or over trivial things.

niggling adj. of an activity, trifling or petty.

nigh adj. & prep. [old use] near: the nigh horse; The time drew nigh; She was nigh unto death. — **well nigh** nearly or almost: The job is well nigh finished.

night (NITE) n. 1 the period from dusk to dawn when it is dark: a dark, restless, sleepless, starlit, stormy night; a weird sound in the dead of the night; the opening night of a play; a wedding night; The lights went out on the night of October 31; He wished me good night and went to a late night movie; We don't watch movies late **at night;** Some people have to work **nights** (= at night); Vancouver **by night** (= during the night) is more colourful than by day. 2 darkness of night; also, a period of gloom or unhappiness: the dark night of the soul.

night·cap n. 1 a cap worn with nightclothes. 2 Informal. an alcoholic drink taken at bedtime: to have a nightcap. 3 Informal. the second game of a doubleheader.

night clothes n.pl. clothes such as pajamas for wearing while in bed.

night·club n. a place of nighttime entertainment that serves food and liquor with music and dancing.

night·dress n. same as NIGHTGOWN.

night·fall (NITE·fall) n. the coming of night; dusk: The stars appear at nightfall.

night·gown (rhyme: "down") n. a loose, light garment that a woman or girl wears in bed.

night·ie (NYE·tee) n. Informal. a nightgown.

night life n. pleasure-seeking activity at night, esp. in nightclubs.

night·ly (NITE·lee) adv. & adj. 1 at or by night: a bird that is seen nightly; his nightly journey. 2 every night: our nightly walk; the nightly news.

night·mare n. 1 a distressing dream. 2 a frightening experience. — **night·mar·ish** (NITE·mair·ish) adj.

night owl n. Informal. one who stays up at night.

night·shift n. 1 the people assigned to work during the night, as in a factory. 2 the period: to work (on) the nightshift.

night·spot n. Informal. nightclub.

night·stand n. a small bedside table; also **night table.**

night·stick n. a policeman's club.

night·walk·er (NITE·waw·kur) n. one who goes out at night as a thief, prostitute, etc.

night·wear n. same as NIGHTCLOTHES.

ni·hil·ism (NYE·uh·liz·um) *n.* in politics, philosophy, etc., the rejection of all traditional and existing beliefs, practices, institutions, etc. — **ni·hil·ist** *n. & adj.* — **ni·hil·is·tic** (-LIS·tic) *adj.*

-nik *n. suffix.* one devoted to what is specified: *beatnik, computernik, no-goodnik, peacenik; sputnik* (= travel companion).

nil *n.* nothing.

nim·ble (NIM·bul) *adj.* light and quick: *a young dancer's nimble feet; the nimble fingers of a piano player; a nimble mind, wit.* — **nim·ble·ness** *n.* — **nim·bly** *adv.*

nin·com·poop (NING·cum·poop) *n.* a foolish or silly person.

nine *n., adj. & pron.* one more than eight; the number 9 or IX. — **ninth** (NINETH) *n. & adj.*

nine-to-five or **9 to 5** *adj.* from 9 a.m. to 5 p.m.: *a nine-to-five job, operation, routine; the nine-to-five grind, rat race.* — **nine-to-fiv·er** *n.*

nine·ty (NINE·tee) *n., adj. & pron.* **-ties 1** nine times 10; 90 or XC. **2 the nineties** numbers, years, etc. from 90 through 99. — **nine·ti·eth** (-tee·ith) *n. & adj.*

nin·ny (NIN·ee) *n.* **nin·nies** fool.

ninth See NINE.

nip *v.* **nips, nipped, nip·ping 1** to pinch or bite, as a crab with its claws: *A gardener nips off shoots to check growth; a dog nipping at a stranger's pants.* **2** blight or destroy, as by frost: *Trouble was brewing, but the principal nipped it in the bud by effective action.* **2** drink liquor in nips or sips. **4** *Informal.* enter quickly: *The child was hurt while nipping in and out of traffic handing out flyers.* — *n.* **1** a pinch or bite; also, a bit. **2** a biting cold: *the nip of a wintry night.* **3** pungent flavour or tang, as of cheese. **4** a sip of liquor: *a nip of sherry.* — **nip and tuck** *Informal.* neck and neck; closely matched.

nip·per (NIP·ur) *n.* **1** one that nips, as the claw of a crab. **2** *Informal.* a little boy: *a cute little nipper with rosy cheeks.* **3 nippers** *pl.* pliers, pincers, etc.

nip·ple (NIP·ee) *n.* **1** a small projection on a breast or udder through which milk is drawn; teat. **2** a teatlike part, as on a nursing bottle.

nip·py (NIP·ee) *adj.* **nip·pi·er, nip·pi·est** sharp or biting: *nippy cheese, fall weather.*

nit *n.* the egg or young of a louse or similar insect.

nite *n.* [popular spelling] same as NIGHT.

nit-picking (NIT·pick·ing) *n. & adj.* fault-finding in a petty manner. — **nit-picker** *n.*

ni·tro·gen (NYE·truh·jun) *n.* a colourless, odourless gas that makes up four fifths of the atmosphere. — **ni·trog·e·nous** (nye·TROJ·uh·nus) *adj.*

nit·ty-grit·ty (NIT·ee·GRIT·ee) *n. Slang.* the basic facts of a situation, problem, etc.: *when you get down to the nitty-gritty; the nitty-gritty of details.*

nit·wit *n.* an idiot.

nix *v. Slang.* say "No" to something. — *adv. & interj.* no; stop!

no (NOH) *adv.* [used to deny, refuse, etc.]: *Do you want it, yes or no? No, I don't! That is no small job.* — *adj.:* *That's no* (= not any) *job for me; He works for no pay.* — *n., pl.* **nos** or **noes 1** a refusal or denial: *a flat no.* **2** a negative vote or voter: *The nos (not ayes) have it.*

no·bil·i·ty (noh·BIL·uh·tee) *n.* **-ties 1** the state of being noble or high in social rank. **2** nobles as a class.

no·ble (NOH·bul) *adj.* **no·bler, no·blest 1** high by birth; famous or excellent: *a noble deed, family, gesture, sentiment; a noble* (= lofty) *edifice.* **2** chemically stable; unaffected by oxygen: *helium, neon, and such noble* (= inert) *gases; Gold and silver are noble* (= precious) *metals.* — *n.* a person of noble birth or rank. — **no·ble·ness** *n.* — **no·bly** (-blee) *adj.*

no·ble·man (NOH·bul·mun) *n.* **-men** a peer.

no·bod·y (NOH·bud·ee, -bod·ee) *pron.* no one. — *n., pl.* **-bod·ies** a person of no importance.

nock *n.* a notch, as at either end of a bow where the bowstring is tied or that of the arrow where it fits over the bowstring. — *v.* fit an arrow over the bowstring for shooting.

noc·tur·nal (noc·TUR·nul) *adj.* of or during the night: *A nocturnal animal such as a bat or owl is active at night; nocturnal bedwetting; nocturnal emission* (= "wet dream"). — **noc·tur·nal·ly** *adv.*

nod *v.* **nods, nod·ded, nod·ding** bend the head downward briefly, as in greeting an acquaintance, to indicate agreement, or when sleepy: *She nodded to the class when she entered the room; He nodded assent; I nodded off* (= fell sleep) *in front of the TV; flowers nodding in the wind; "Even Homer sometimes nods"* (= makes mistakes). — *n.* a nodding of the head: *A project gets* or *is given the nod* (to go ahead).

node *n.* **1** a knot or joint, as the points along a stem from which leaves grow. **2** a receiving or transmitting terminal where several branches of a computer network come together. — **nod·al** (NOH·dul) *adj.*

nod·ule (NOJ·ool) *n.* a small knob, lump, or swelling. — **nod·u·lar** (NOJ·uh·lur) *adj.*

No·el or **No·ël** (noh·EL) *n.* **1** Christmas. **2 noel** or **noël** a Christmas song or carol.

no-fault *adj.* involving no fixing of blame: *no-fault auto insurance, divorce, law, plan.*

no-frills *adj.* of a service or product, without nonessential features that add to cost: *a no-frills air fare, government, grocery store, service; the no-frills approach.*

nog *n.* an alcoholic eggnog.

nog·gin (NOG·in) *n.* **1** a small cup or mug of liquor, originally ¼ pint. **2** *Informal.* one's head: *The retort was like a knock on the noggin.*

no-good *n. & adj. Informal.* worthless person or thing.

noise *n.* a harsh, disagreeable, or unwanted sound: *the noise of a city street; Traffic makes* or *produces noise; Walls reduce* or *cut down on the noise; deafening, loud, shrill noises; People can sleep only when the noise abates* or *dies down; animal noises and barbaric behaviour at hockey games; static noise in radio reception; "snow" caused by noise* (= unwanted signals) *in TV equipment; the **noise pollution** of the environment from airports, automobiles, industry, etc.*
— *v.* **nois·es, noised, nois·ing** spread *about* or *abroad,* as a story or report by rumour.
— **noise·less** *adj.;* **noise·less·ly** *adv.*

noise·mak·er (NOIS·may·kur) *n.* a horn or similar device used to make noise at a party.

noi·some (NOY·sum) *adj.* foul-smelling or harmful: *a noisome odour.*

nois·y (NOY·zee) *adj.* **nois·i·er, -i·est** causing noise: *Rock music is loud to some, noisy to others; noisy neighbours; a noisy quarrel.*
— **nois·i·ly** *adv.;* **nois·i·ness** *n.*

no-load *n.* a mutual fund that charges no commission on sales.

no·mad (NOH·mad) *n. & adj.* a member of a people such as Bedouins and Gypsies with no settled home but wandering about from place to place.
— **no·mad·ic** (noh·MAD·ic) *adj.*

no man's land *n.* **1** an area or scope of activity that is indefinite or ambiguous. **2** land separating opposing armies.

nom de plume (nom·duh·PLOOM) *n., pl.* **noms de plume** (nom·duh-) a pen name used by a writer.

no·men·cla·ture (NOH·mun·clay·chur) *n.* a naming system: *the binomial nomenclature used in biology; Some of the nomenclature of baseball such as Blue Jays, Cardinals, and Orioles is for the birds.*

nom·i·nal (NOM·uh·nul) *adj.* in name only; hence, slight or negligible: *a nominal amount, leader.*
— **nom·i·nal·ly** *adv.*

nom·i·nate (NOM·uh·nate) *v.* **-nates, -nat·ed, -nat·ing** name, often appoint, to an office or position: *He was nominated but not elected; to be nominated for the mayoralty; She was nominated as* or *to be the executor of the estate.*
— **nom·i·na·tion** (-NAY·shun) *n.: Mimi's name was put in nomination for mayor; to accept, reject a nomination.* — **nom·i·na·tor** (-nay·tur) *n.*

nom·i·na·tive (NOM·uh·nuh·tiv) *adj.* naming the subject of a verb: *"He" is the nominative case of "him."*
— *n.* a nominative word or its grammatical case: *"He" is in the nominative.*

nom·i·nee (nom·uh·NEE) *n.* a nominated person.

non- [a prefix freely added, usually without a hyphen except before capitalized words, to adjectives and adverbs to mean "not" and to nouns to mean "not a," "opposite of," or "lack of." The basic meaning and pronunciation of such compounds are usually the same as in the base word. The more unusual compounds are entered and explained below].

non·a·chiev·er (non-uh·CHEE·vur) *n.* one who does not succeed as expected, esp. a student who does not get passing grades.

non·age (NON·ij, NOH·nij) *n.* **1** the period of being legally a minor. **2** the period before maturity; immaturity.

non·a·ligned (non-uh·LINED) *adj.* in international politics, neutral: *a nonaligned nation.*
— **non·a·lign·ment** (-LINE·munt) *n.*

no-name *n. & adj.* (a person or thing) that has no name or is undistinguished; generic: *a no-name brand of gasoline; cheap no-name products; He was a no-name before joining the Blue Jays.*

nonce usually **for the nonce,** for the time being.

nonce word *n.* a word made up for the occasion, as "Coca-colonize" or "chocoholic": *Many nonce words gain currency, as "O.K." did.*

non·cha·lant (NON·shuh·lunt, -shuh·LAHNT) *adj.* coolly indifferent; unconcerned. — **non·cha·lant·ly** *adv.*
— **non·cha·lance** (-lunce, -LAHNCE) *n.*

non·com·mis·sioned officer (non-cuh·MISH·und-) *n.* in the armed forces, an enlisted man with the rank of corporal through sergeant major.

non·com·mit·tal (non-cuh·MIT·ul) *adj.* not committing oneself: *"We will see" is his usual noncommittal reply.*

non·con·form·ist (non-cun·FOR·mist) *n.* **1** one who does not conform to prevailing attitudes or behaviour. **2** **Nonconformist** in the 1600s, one who refused to conform to the Church of England.
— **non·con·form·i·ty** (-FOR·muh·tee) *n.*

non·cred·it (non·CRED·it) *adj.* not having academic credit, as toward a degree: *a noncredit course.*

non·dair·y (non·DAIR·ee) *adj.* not made with milk or milk products: *a nondairy coffee creamer.*

non·de·script (NON·duh·script) *adj.* not easily described, being not distinctive.
— *n.* such a person or thing.

non·drink·er (NON·drink·ur) *n.* one who does not use alcoholic beverages.

none (NUN) *pron.* no one: *None of them is* or *are here; She wants none but the best; That was none other than Joe.*
— *adv.* not at all: *Because of new taxes, I'm none the richer for the pay raise; "None so deaf as those who will not hear."*

non·en·ti·ty (non·EN·tuh·tee) *n.* **-ties 1** one, esp. a person, of little importance. **2** something that has no real existence.

none·such (NUN·such) *n. & adj.* a person or thing that is unequalled or unique.

none·the·less (nun·the·LESS) *adj.* nevertheless; however.

non·e·vent (non·i·VENT) *n.* an event that is made too much of, esp. when it does not take place as predicted.

non·fat *adj.* of foods, not fatty.

non·fic·tion (non·FIC·shun) *n.* writings such as history, biography, and essays.

no-no *n. Slang.* something forbidden, esp. as not good for one: *Chewing gum is a no-no in church.*

non·pa·reil (non·puh·REL) *n. & adj.* (person or thing) that is unequalled or peerless.

non·par·ti·san (non·PAR·tuh·zun, -zan) *adj.* not partisan, esp. in regard to political parties.

non·per·son (NON·pur·sun) *n.* one who is considered as not existing or as rejected: *Stalin became a nonperson in the USSR.*

non·plus (NON·plus, non·PLUS) *v.* **-plus·ses** or **-plus·es, -plussed** or **-plused, -plus·sing** or **-plus·ing** perplex or puzzle utterly or hopelessly.

non·pre·scrip·tion (non·pri·SCRIP·shun) *adj.* available without a doctor's prescription: *a nonprescription drug.*

non·prof·it (non·PROF·it) *adj.* not run for profit, as cultural foundations, the Red Cross, etc.: *a nonprofit organization.*

non·pro·lif·er·a·tion (NON·pruh·lif·uh·RAY·shun) *n.* the stoppage of the spread of nuclear weapons.

non·res·i·dent (non·REZ·uh·dunt) *n. & adj.* a person living elsewhere, not where working, going to school, etc.

non·sched·uled (non·SKEJ·ooled) *adj.* not serving a particular route or following a regular timetable: *a nonscheduled airline, charter, flight.*

non·sense *n.* something that makes no sense or is worthless or stupid: *What nonsense to say I stole your purse; He always speaks* or *talks nonsense after a couple of drinks; complete, outright, perfect, pure, sheer, utter nonsense; No one has to put up with* or *tolerate that kind of nonsense;* **adj.:** *a nonsense syllable (without sense associations); the nonsense verses of Jabberwocky.* — **non·sen·si·cal** (non·SEN·suh·cul) *adj.*

non se·qui·tur (non·SEK·wuh·tur) *n.* an inference or observation that does not logically follow from what was said before it.

non-status (non·STAY·tus) *adj. Cdn.* having lost status under the Indian Act: *the Ontario Métis and Non-Status Indian Association.*

non·stick *adj.* not allowing food to stick: *a nonstick coating of Teflon; a nonstick frying pan, surface.*

non·stop *adj. & adv.* that goes without stopping: *a nonstop flight to Paris; In 1986, the "Voyageur" aircraft flew nonstop around the world without refuelling.*

non·sup·port (non·suh·PORT) *n.* failure to provide for one's legal dependent.

non-treaty *adj. Cdn.* not living under the terms of a treaty, as receiving treaty money: *a non-treaty Indian.*

non·un·ion (non·YOON·yun) *adj.* not made by, belonging to, or recognizing a labour union: *a nonunion company, job, worker.*

non·vi·o·lence (non·VYE·uh·lunce) *n.* avoidance of the use of force, as in civil rights movements. — **non·vi·o·lent** *adj.*

noo·dle (NOO·dul) *n.* **1** a flour paste, usually made with egg, in ribbon form. **2** a simpleton. **3** *Slang.* the head.

nook (short "oo") *n.* a secluded corner or spot: *a breakfast nook in the kitchen; a cozy nook in a library; She looked in **every nook and cranny*** (= everywhere).

noon *n. & adj.* 12 o'clock in the daytime; midday: *at high noon on a hot July day.* Also **noon·day, noon·time; noon·tide** [old use].

no one *pron.* nobody; no person.

noose *n.* a loop made in a rope with a slipknot that tightens as the free end is pulled: *They voted against the noose* (= death by hanging). — *v.* **noos·es, noosed, noos·ing** catch or snare in a noose.

no-par *adj.* having no nominal or par value, only a market value: *no-par stocks.*

nope *adv. Informal.* no.

nor 1 *conj.* [used after a negative, esp. "neither" or "not"] and not; and not either: *Neither Joe nor Jan was there; They will not eat, nor will they drink anything.* **2** *n.* in computers, a logical operation or circuit that produces the inverse of an OR output.

Nor·dic (NOR·dic) *adj.* having to do with ski jumping and cross-country skiing: *a Nordic event.*

no-return (NOH·ri·TURN) *adj.* not to be returned for refund of deposit: *a no-return bottle.*

norm *n.* **1** a standard or model for a group to follow: *to establish* or *set a norm for children to follow; the norms of society.* **2** a group's average performance as a measuring standard.

nor·mal (NOR·mul) *adj.* standard or usual: *Frost is normal in wintertime; a man of normal intelligence; It's perfectly normal for adults to cry at times; "Loves her he" is not the normal word order in English.* — *n.* a condition, level, amount, etc. that is normal: *Ten degrees Celsius is above (the) normal for this time of year.* — **nor·mal·ly** *adv.* — **nor·mal·i·ty** (nor·MAL·uh·tee) *n.*

nor·mal·cy (NOR·mul·see) *n.* the condition of being normal: *the return to normalcy after a war.*

nor·mal·ize (NOR·muh·lize) *v.* **-iz·es, -ized, -iz·ing** make normal: *to normalize relations.* — **nor·mal·i·za·tion** (-luh·ZAY·shun) *n.*

norm·a·tive (NOR·muh·tiv) *adj.* setting a norm or standard: *a normative influence, grammar, principle.*

north ("th" as in "thin") *n.* **1** the direction to the left of one facing the east or rising sun, to which a compass

needle points: *The magnetic North Pole lies close to the geographic north or true north; "the True North strong and free"* (= Canada). **2** also **North,** a region in this direction.
— the North 1 the northern part of Canada, esp. the Territories and the adjoining parts of the provinces from Quebec westward. **2** the northern U.S. comprising the states north of Maryland, the Ohio River, and Missouri.
— adj. & adv. 1 toward the north: *Sudbury is north of Toronto; Canadians from the south go up north in the summer; The north magnetic pole is near Bathurst Island, N.W.T.; the North Shore of New Brunswick facing the Gulf of St. Lawrence and Northumberland Strait.* **2** from the north: *a north wind.*

North American *n. & adj.* a person of or from the northern continent of the Western Hemisphere, from Greenland to Panama, also including the West Indies.

north·east·er (north·EES·tur) *n.* a wind or storm from the northeast. **— north·east·er·ly** *adj. & adv.*
— north·east·ern *adj.* **— north·east·ward** (-wurd) *adj. & adv.;* **north·east·wards** (-wurdz) *adv.*

north·er ("th" as in "the") *n.* a strong north wind or storm, esp. a winter wind over Texas and the Gulf of Mexico.

north·er·ly (NOR·thur·lee, "th" as in "the") *adj. & adv.* **1** from the north: *a cold northerly wind.* **2** toward the north: *He was proceeding northerly on Yonge Street when hit; Inuvik, NWT, is Canada's most northerly town.* **— n. 1** a northerly wind. **2** same as NORTHER.

north·ern (NORTH·urn, "TH" as in "the") *adj.* **1** of, from, in, or toward the north. **2 Northern** of the North.
— north·ern·most *adj.*

north·ern·er or **North·ern·er** (NOR·thur·nur) *n.* a person of or from the north of a country: *a Northerner from Sudbury visiting Toronto.*

North Star *n.* a bright star that appears fixed in the sky with other stars rotating around it.

north·ward (NORTH·wurd) *adj. & adv.* toward the north. Also **north·wards** *adv.*

north·west (north·WEST) *n.* **1** a region in or toward the direction midway between north and west. **2 the Northwest** in Canada, the region north and west of the Great Lakes; in the U.S., the region consisting of the states of Washington, Oregon, and Idaho.
— adj. & adv. from, in, or toward the northwest.
— north·west·er·ly *adj. & adv.* **— north·west·ern** *adj.*
— north·west·ward *adj. & adv.;* **north·west·wards** *adv.*

north·west·er (north·WES·tur) *n.* **1** a northwest wind or storm. **2 Northwester** *Cdn.* a native of the Northwest, esp. a fur trader of the North West Company of the early 1800s. **— north·west·er·ly** *adj.*

Northwest Passage *n.* an Arctic route linking the Atlantic and the Pacific through the waters north of the Canadian mainland.

nose (NOZE) *n.* **1** the breathing and smelling organ with two openings forming part of the face just above the mouth: *to blow, pick, wipe one's nose; to follow one's nose* (= go straight forward); *to tweak someone's nose; an aquiline, bloody, bulbous, running* or *runny nose.*

2 the sense of smell: *Dogs have good noses; a reporter's nose for news.* **3** the projecting front part of a ship, plane, etc.
— count noses count those present.
— cut off one's nose to spite one's face take action that harms one's own interests.
— lead by the nose control someone completely.
— on the nose *Slang.* precisely.
— pay through the nose pay too much for a product or service.
— thumb one's nose at to defy someone.
— turn up one's nose at treat with scorn; sneer at someone.
— under one's nose in plain view.
— v. nos·es, nosed, nos·ing 1 smell out. **2** nuzzle. **3** push something off, one's way into, etc. with a forward part, as a bulldozer. **4** search or pry into someone's affairs.
— nose out defeat one's opponent by a narrow margin.

nose dive *n.* **1** a swift downward plunge of an airplane, kite, etc. **2** a sudden drop in price: *Prices went into* or *took a nosedive.*
— v. nose-dive, -dives, -dived, -div·ing.

nose job *n.* a purely cosmetic job like changing the shape of a nose by surgery.

nosey same as NOSY.

nosh *n. Slang.* a snack: *We asked them in for a nosh and a chat.*

no-show *n.* a person who neither cancels nor shows up to claim a passenger reservation.

nos·tal·gia (nos·TAL·juh) *n.* a sentimental yearning for a period or condition that is past. **— nos·tal·gic** *adj.*

nos·y or **nos·ey** (NOH·zee) *adj.* **nos·i·er, -i·est** *Informal.* prying or inquisitive: *to be nosy about what's going on in someone's backyard.*
— nos·i·ly *adv.;* **nos·i·ness** *n.*

not *adv.* [negative in function]: *Black is not white; Tell him not to worry; It may not rain – I hope not; She's not at all* (= certainly not) *my kind of woman.*

no·ta·ble (NOH·tuh·bul) *adj. & n.* noteworthy or distinguished (person): *a notable contribution to science; a notable event; a notable figure.*
— no·ta·bly *adv.;* **no·ta·bil·i·ty** (-BIL·uh·tee) *n.*

no·ta·rize (NOH·tuh·rize) *v.* **-riz·es, -rized, -riz·ing** certify a document, as a lawyer or notary does.

no·ta·ry (NOH·tuh·ree) *n.* **-ries** a person legally authorized to certify documents, take oaths, etc.; also **notary public.**

no·ta·tion (noh·TAY·shun) *n.* **1** a noting down or what is noted down; annotation. **2** a method or system of representing words, quantities, and such technical data using signs and symbols, as in mathematics and music.
— no·ta·tion·al *adj.*

notch *n.* **1** a V-shaped cut on an edge or surface, as on a stick to keep a tally. **2** anything resembling it, as a narrow mountain defile or the angle formed by a coat's collar with the lapel ("notched lapel").
— v. make a notch: *a notched edge; to notch up* (= score) *a gain, victory, win.*

note *n*. **1** what is jotted down, esp. a short letter or memorandum: *to **take notes** during a lecture; to **compare notes** with classmates on a project; to address, deliver, drop, send someone a note; a diplomatic note; protest notes.* **2** observation or notice: *to make a note of the licence plate of a car; a mental note; No one seemed to **take note of** (= pay attention to) her.* **3** a piece of paper money: *a pound note.* **4** a bank note or promissory note: *a demand note; treasury notes; when a note matures.* **5** a musical tone or sound; hence, an expression with a certain signification: *to hit or strike the high notes of a song; the notes of a trumpet; the note of triumph in her voice; a discordant, false, festive, fresh, jarring, optimistic, pessimistic, sour, triumphant note.* **6** distinction: *men of note; a woman of note in public life.*
— *v*. **notes, not·ed, not·ing** make a note of something: *Please note down what I say; I noted how she spells her name; She noted that I am good at spelling; Did you note the colour of her hair?*

note·book *n*. a book to make notes in: *a loose-leaf notebook.*

noted (NOH·tid) *adj*. widely known: *a noted surgeon; noted for heart transplants.*

note·wor·thy (NOTE·wur·thee, "th" as in "the") *adj*. remarkable or impressive: *a noteworthy accomplishment.*

noth·ing (NUTH·ing, "TH" as in "thin") *n*. no thing; not anything; zero: *There's nothing in his pocket; He is good for nothing* (= worthless); *He means nothing* (= is not important) *to me; Something is better than nothing; We've nothing to lose and everything to gain by trying; lovers whispering sweet nothings to each other; a student who is **nothing if not** ambitious* (= who is quite ambitious).
— *adv*. not at all: *That is nothing remarkable; He went ahead nothing daunted by reverses.*
— **nothing doing** *Informal*. definitely not!
— **in nothing flat** *Informal*. in no time at all; very fast.
— **think nothing of** consider as easy to achieve or as unimportant.

no·tice (NOH·tis) *n*. **1** warning or notification: *He was fired with a month's notice in writing; She was put on notice that her work was not satisfactory; He gave us notice to move; We had to leave the place at or on short notice; No more classes until further notice; She **served notice** on her boss that she was quitting.* **2** attention: *facts that escaped his notice; Your costume may attract notice.* **3** a posted sign or published account for drawing attention to something: *to put up a notice on the bulletin board; The new book received scant notice in the papers; newspaper notices of births and deaths.*
— *v*. **-tic·es, -ticed, -tic·ing** see with the mind: *Did you notice her hairdo? Did you notice him getting off the bus? The play was favourably noticed* (= reviewed) *in the press.*

no·tice·a·ble (NOH·tuh·suh·bul) *adj*. easily noticed or worth noticing. — **no·tice·a·bly** *adv*.

no·ti·fy (NOH·tuh·fye) *v*. **-fies, -fied, -fy·ing** inform someone officially or formally: *to notify a customer of the arrival of the goods ordered; Please notify us in writing.* — **no·ti·fi·ca·tion** (-fuh·CAY·shun) *n*.

no·tion (NOH·shun) *n*. **1** a vague idea, intention, or belief; also, a whim or fancy: *We don't have the slightest notion about or of what's on his mind; a foggy, hazy, preconceived, vague, widespread notion; It took ages to dispel the notion that the earth is flat.* **2 notions** *pl*. miscellaneous small articles such as sewing things.

no·to·ri·e·ty (noh·tuh·RYE·uh·tee) *n*. a being notorious; ill fame: *people who gain notoriety as drug dealers; the notoriety surrounding his disappearance.*

no·to·ri·ous (nuh·TOR·ee·us) *adj*. famous in a bad way: *a notorious drug dealer; He's notorious for cheating customers; quite notorious as a cheater.*
— **no·to·ri·ous·ly** *adv*.

not·with·stand·ing (not·with·STAN·ding) *prep*. in spite of: *The party went on, notwithstanding the lateness of the hour.* — *conj.*: *The party went on, notwithstanding the hour was late.* — *adv.*: *The lateness of the hour notwithstanding, the party went on.*

nought (NAWT) same as NAUGHT.

noun *n*. a word that is the name of a person, thing, place, action, etc.: *an abstract noun such as "beauty"; a collective noun such as "class" or "team"; Jones and Ottawa are proper nouns, not common nouns; "Woman" is a feminine noun; masculine nouns; neuter nouns; A mass noun like "sugar" or "paper" is not a countable noun, as "sugar cube" and "paper route" are; "Flying" as in "Flying is fun" is a verbal noun derived from the verb "to fly."*

nour·ish (NUR·ish) *v*. feed and thus help to grow; foster.
— *adj.*: *Milk is **nourishing*** (= has food value).

nour·ish·ment (NUR·ish·munt) *n*. something that nourishes, as food: *Plants draw nourishment from the soil.*

nou·velle cui·sine (noo·VEL·kwi·ZEEN) *n*. *French*. a style of cooking using light ingredients, wholesome foods such as vegetables, and smaller and more flavourful portions presented artistically.

nov·el (NOV·ul) *adj*. new in an unusual or strange way: *Your first snowfall is a novel experience; a novel idea, sensation, suggestion.*
— *n*. a book-length work of prose fiction dealing with human life and experience: *a detective novel; historical novel; mystery novels.*

nov·el·ist (NOV·uh·list) *n*. the author or a novel.

nov·el·ty (NOV·ul·tee) *n*. **-ties 1** novel quality: *The novelty of your first snowfall wears off after some shovelling.* **2** something novel, esp. a small decorative or useful article: *a shop selling novelties and souvenirs.*

nov·ice (NOV·is) *n*. a beginner, or new recruit, esp. in a religious order: *a rank novice at or in window dressing; a novice nun.*

now *adv*. **1** at this instant, time, juncture, etc.: *I want my dinner now; right now; It's too bad I've had to wait until now; I haven't complained up to now; A pizza will be here just now* (= very soon). **2** [used more as an interjection than as an adverb of time]: *Now hear this; Well, now, what do you think? Now, now, don't do that!*
— *conj*. since: *Now that you're 18, you can vote.*
— *n. & adj.* the present time, hour, age, etc.: *From*

now on, we'll try harder; By now she must be home; up-to-date fashions for the now generation.
— **now and again** or **now and then** occasionally; from time to time.

now·a·days (NOW·uh·days) *adv.* in these days; at the present time.

no·way or **no·ways** *adv.* in no way.

no·where *adv.* not anywhere: *She is nowhere to be seen; Our search is getting* or *going nowhere; We're **nowhere near** (= not nearly) the end of our journey;* **n.**: *It came from* or *out of nowhere.*

no-win *adj.* not helping to win: *a no-win situation.*

nox·ious (NOK·shus) *adj.* harmful or injurious to health: *noxious fumes, weeds; noxious influences (that corrupt).*

noz·zle (NOZ·ul) *n.* a vent or spout shaped for controlling the flow of a gas or liquid, as of a bellows or garden hose.

nth (ENTH) *adj.* multiplied an indefinite or "n" number of times. — **to the nth degree** to the utmost.

nu·ance (NOO·ahnce) *n.* a subtle variation of meaning, tone, or colour.

nub *n.* **1** knob or lump. **2** *Informal.* point or gist; also **nub·bin.**

nub·ble (NUB·ul) *n.* a knob or lump.

nub·bly *adj.* **nub·bli·er, nub·bli·est** of a surface, knotted or lumpy.

nub·by (NUB·ee) *adj.* same as NUBBLY.

nu·cle·ar (NEW·clee·ur, NUKE·yuh·lur) *adj.* **1** forming a nucleus or core: *Parents and children form the **nuclear family.*** **2** having to do with the atomic nucleus or nuclear energy: *the nuclear age; nuclear fission, fusion, physics, power, waste, weapon; the **nuclear club** (of nations that have exploded an atomic device); a **nuclear-free** zone (that is free of nuclear weapons and nuclear energy); the **nuclear winter** (of devastation, darkness, and cold) that would result from a nuclear war.* — **n.** *Informal.* nuclear energy.

nu·cle·us (NEW·clee·us) *n., pl.* **-cle·i** (-clee·eye) or **-cle·us·es 1** core or centre of activity, esp. the central part of a plant or animal cell containing genetic material. **2** the positively charged particle at the centre of an atom in which matter and energy are concentrated.

nude *adj.* unclothed or naked, esp. as in art: *a nude model, picture; nude* (= flesh-coloured) *stockings; Some models pose **in the nude** (= naked).* — **n.** the unclothed human figure, as in art: *Picasso's nudes.* — **nu·di·ty** (NEW·duh·tee) *n.*

nudge (NUJ) *n.* a gentle push or jog, as with the elbow. — *v.* **nudg·es, nudged, nudg·ing** give a nudge.

nu·die (NEW·dee) *n. Slang.* a show, magazine, etc. featuring nudes.

nud·ism (NEW·diz·um) *n.* principle or practice of social nudity. — **nud·ist** *n.*

nu·ga·to·ry (NEW·guh·tor·ee) *adj. Formal.* trifling;

hence, invalid or futile in effect: *The rewards of running in a marathon may be nugatory.*

nug·get (NUG·it) *n.* a lump of something precious from the earth: *gold nuggets.*

nui·sance (NEW·sunce) *n.* a troublesome or annoying person, thing, or situation: *Mosquitoes make a nuisance of themselves in the summer; They are a perpetual nuisance in hot climates; A mischief-maker is a public nuisance; He created* or *caused a nuisance by pulling the fire alarm; One who commits a nuisance can be sued for damages; a confounded nuisance; Sales tax and other government levies collected in small amounts directly from consumers are called **nuisance taxes;** To the government they have more than **nuisance value.***

nuke (rhyme: "duke") *n. Slang.* a nuclear weapon or power-generating station.

null *adj.* **1** of no effect, esp. legal; invalid: *a law declared **null and void** by a court.* **2** amounting to nothing; zero or empty: *a null effect, result.*

nul·li·fy (NUL·uh·fye) *v.* **-fies, -fied, -fy·ing** make valueless; declare null and void; annul. — **nul·li·fi·ca·tion** (-fuh·CAY·shun) *n.*

nul·li·ty (NUL·uh·tee) *n.* something that is null: *The court ruled that the discharge of the employee was a nullity; a decree of nullity in a divorce case.*

null set *n.* in math, a set with no members; empty set: *Two-sided polygons belong to a null set.*

numb (NUM) *adj.* insensible or benumbed, as with cold, shock, etc.: *Her left side is numb; He was numb with fear.* — *v.* make numb: *The painkiller numbed the pain; the mind-numbing tedium of the assembly line.* — **numb·ly** *adv.;* **numb·ness** *n.*

num·ber (NUM·bur) *n.* **1** a numeral figure that tells how many, as 1978 or LXX: *cardinal numbers such as 1, 2, 3, etc. and ordinal numbers such as 1st, 2nd, 3rd, etc.; 1, 3, 5, 7, etc. are odd numbers and 2, 4, 6, 8, etc. are even numbers.* **2** amount; quantity; collection; group: *the growing number of deaths on holiday weekends; Their number is large; A good number will go hungry this winter; the total number of 100; a round number such as 1 000; **A number of** others are homeless.* **3** one of a series: *The back number of a magazine is not its current issue; the call number of a library book; The serial number of an automobile is much longer than its licence number; What number did you dial? She has an unlisted (phone) number; a very popular number* (= item, as of a program). **4** in grammar: *"Fish" could be (in the) singular or plural number; "Goes" is the singular number of "go."* — **beyond** or **without number** too many to be counted. — **do a number on** *Slang.* criticize or humiliate someone. — **numbers 1** arithmetic: *Accountants are good at numbers.* **2** a large group: *People like to travel together because there's safety in numbers.* — *v.* **1** give a number instead of a name to something: *a numbered account, corporation.* **2** count: *a numbering machine; to be numbered among the chosen few.* **3** limit the number of something: *A terminally ill patient's days are numbered.* **4** amount to; add up to; total: *The dead numbered 100.*

num·ber·less (NUM·bur·lis) *adj.* countless.

nu·mer·al (NEW·muh·rul) *n.* a symbol or expression denoting a number or numbers: *The Roman numeral LV is 55 in Arabic numerals;* **adj.:** *a numeral system.*

nu·mer·ate (NEW·muh·rate) *v.* -ates, -at·ed, -at·ing count or list; enumerate.
— **nu·mer·a·tion** (-RAY·shun) *n.*

nu·mer·a·tor (NEW·muh·ray·tur) *n.* in a fraction, the number above the line.

nu·mer·ic (new·MER·ic) *adj.* using figures, not letters; numerical: *a numeric code, computer, readout.*

nu·mer·i·cal (new·MER·uh·cul) *adj.* having to do with numbers: *numerical analysis, control, order, quantity, value.* — **nu·mer·i·cal·ly** *adv.*

nu·me·ro u·no (NOO·muh·roh·OO·noh) *n.* Informal. the "number one" or most important member of a group, usually oneself.

nu·mer·ous (NEW·muh·rus) *adj.* consisting of or being many: *numerous books, complaints, gifts; a numerous* (=large) *clientele, progeny.* — **nu·mer·ous·ness** *n.*

num·skull or **numb·skull** *n.* a blockhead or dunce.

nun *n.* a woman living in a convent under religious vows.

nun·ci·o (NUN·shee·oh, -see·oh) *n.* -os a papal ambassador.

nun·ny·bag (NUN·ee·bag) *n.* Cdn. in Newfoundland, a knapsack made of sealskin used by a hunter to carry food and personal equipment.

nup·tial (NUP·shul) **1** *adj.* of a wedding: *a nuptial ceremony, day, Mass, song.* **2 nuptials** *n.pl.* wedding ceremony.

nurse *n.* **1** a person trained to take care of the sick: *a general-duty nurse; a hospital nurse; male nurses; private-duty nurses; visiting nurses such as the Victorian Order of Nurses and the St. Elizabeth Visiting Nurses; A professional nurse is usually a Registered Nurse.* **2** a woman hired to care for another's children; also **nurse·maid.**
— *v.* nurs·es, nursed, nurs·ing **1** suckle: *to nurse a baby; a nursing mother.* **2** take care of patients: *to nurse the sick; to nurse people back to health; the profession of nursing.* **3** take care of something in a protective manner: *He's staying home nursing a cold; It seems healthier to forgive than to nurse a grudge; He has been at the bar nursing the same drink all evening.*

nurse practitioner *n.* a nurse trained to carry out the more routine functions of a physician.

nurs·er·y (NUR·suh·ree) *n.* -er·ies **1** a children's room. **2** a nursery school or daycare centre: *a child in a day nursery.* **3** a place where plants are grown for transplanting, experimentation, etc.

— **nurs·er·y·man** *n.* -men.

nur·ture (NUR·chur) *n.* nourishment or training: *Nurture builds on nature.*
— *v.* -tures, -tured, -tur·ing give nurture to a person or thing: *A greenhouse nurtures plants; a well-nurtured child; a friendship nurtured from childhood.*

nut *n.* **1** a dry, hard fruit with a seed or kernel enclosed in a shell of woody fibre, as the walnut, peanut, or coconut. **2** a small metal block with a threaded hole to screw on to and lock a bolt in place: *nuts and bolts.* **3** *Slang.* an eccentric or crazy person: *It's no use talking to that nut.* **4** *Slang.* a devotee or enthusiast: *an ecological nut; an aircraft nut who builds models in his spare time.*
— **nuts** *adj. slang.* crazy: *He's not only misinformed, he's nuts! He's nuts about skateboarding; Carl is nuts about* (=very fond of) *Claire; He went nuts.*
— *interj.* expressing scorn: *If you won't listen to me, nuts to you!*
— **nuts and bolts** *n.pl.* Informal. basic or essential working features: *Profit-making is the nuts and bolts of most businesses; Nan is a good nuts-and-bolts organizer.*

nut·meg *n.* a spice obtained from the aromatic seed of an East Indian tree; also, the seed.

nu·tri·ent (NEW·tree·unt) *n. & adj.* a substance or ingredient that is nourishing: *A water-based nutrient solution is used instead of soil in hydroponics.*

nu·tri·tion (new·TRISH·un) *n.* **1** the study of the process by which food is assimilated by an organism. **2** nourishment.
— **nu·tri·tion·al** *adj.* — **nu·tri·tion·ist** *n.*

nu·tri·tious (new·TRISH·us) *adj.* having food-value: *Good cooks can prepare attractive and nutritious dishes; Spinach is very nutritious.*

nu·tri·tive (NEW·truh·tiv) *adj.* having to do with nourishment: *Fish is high in nutritive value; nutritive functions, plasma; the nutritive process.*

nut·shell *n.* the shell enclosing a nut.
— **in a nutshell** in a few words; concisely.

nut·ty (NUT·ee) *adj.* nut·ti·er, nut·ti·est **1** nutlike or containing nuts: *a nutty cookie, flavour.* **2** *Slang.* nuts or crazy; also, enthusiastic. — **nut·ti·ness** *n.*

nuz·zle (NUZ·ul) *v.* nuz·zles, nuz·zled, nuz·zling **1** rub or push against with or as if with the nose or snout. **2** snuggle or nestle: *A baby nuzzles up against its mother.*

ny·lon (NYE·lon) *n.* **1** a strong, elastic synthetic product widely used as fibres, sheets, tubes, etc.: *stockings of sheer nylon.* **2 nylons** *pl.* nylon stockings: *a pair of nylons.*

nymph (NIMF) *n.* in Greek and Roman myths, a goddess of nature inhabiting the water, woods, and hills.

O or **o** (OH) *n.* **O's** or **o's 1** the 15th letter of the English alphabet. **2 O** *interj.* [old use] same as OH.

oaf (OHF) *n.* a stupid or awkward fellow. — **oaf·ish** *adj.*

oak (OHK) *n.* a strong and sturdy tree of the beech family that bears nuts called acorns.
— *adj.* also **oak·en,** made of the wood of an oak.

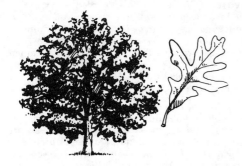

oar (OR) *n.* a broad-bladed implement used in rowing a boat.
— **rest on one's oars** rest after doing some work.
— **oars·man** (ORS·mun) *n.* **-men.**

o·a·sis (oh·AY·sis) *n., pl.* **-ses** (-seez) in a desert, a fertile spot with water and some vegetation.

oat (OHT) *n.* a cereal grass bearing grain used as livestock feed and in making **oatmeal** (= hot cereal), etc. Also **oats** *sing. & pl.* — **oat·en** *adj.*

oath (OHTH) *n.* **1** a solemn promise, often calling on God as witness: *In Canada, M.P.s and senators take* or *swear the oath of allegiance to the Sovereign; A justice administers the **oath of office** to a minister; Witnesses testify **under oath** (to tell the truth).* **2** a swearing or a swearword; curse: *to mutter* or *utter an oath.*

ob·du·rate (OB·dyuh·rut, -duh·rut) *adj.* obstinate or hardhearted: *an obdurate refusal, sinner.*
— **ob·du·rate·ly** *adv.* — **ob·du·ra·cy** (-ruh·see) *n.*

o·be·di·ence (uh·BEE·dee·unce) *n.* the act of obeying or willingness to obey: *The army demands* or *exacts obedience from soldiers; Schools try to instill obedience to rules and regulations; respect and obedience; obedience to a command, to authority; the religious vows of poverty, chastity, and obedience; absolute, blind, enthusiastic, perfect, unquestioning obedience; a puppy trained in obedience; **adj.**: an obedience course,*

lesson, trial.

o·be·di·ent (uh·BEE·dee·unt) *adj.* obeying or submissive: *an obedient child; obedient to its parents.*
— **o·be·di·ent·ly** *adv.*

o·bey (uh·BAY) *v.* **1** carry out: *to obey an order.* **2** be guided by someone: *to obey the authorities, one's conscience, etc.*

ob·fus·cate (OB·fus·cate, ob·FUS·cate) *v.* **-cates, -cat·ed, -cat·ing** confuse or obscure: *drugs that obfuscate the mind; arguments obfuscating the issues.*
— **ob·fus·ca·tion** (-CAY·shun) *n.*

o·bit·u·ar·y (oh·BICH·oo·air·ee) *n.* **-ar·ies** a notice of a person's death or a short biography accompanying it.

ob·ject (OB·jikt) *n.* a person or thing that a feeling, thought, or action is directed toward: *the object of his attentions; an object of derision; an unidentified flying object; In "Joe loves Jan," "Jan" is the grammatical object of the verb; People should not be considered as sex objects; What's the object* (= goal or purpose) *of your research?*
— *v.* (ub·JECT) oppose or disapprove strongly; be opposed: *"I object," shouted the lawyer; People now object to smoking in the workplace.*

ob·jec·tion (ub·JEC·shun) *n.* an expression of or the reason for objecting: *to deal with, make, meet, raise, withdraw an objection; A judge may overrule or sustain an objection raised by a lawyer; We have no objection to your opening the window; I know you wouldn't open the window over our objections.*

ob·jec·tion·a·ble (ub·JEC·shuh·nuh·bul) *adj.* open to objection; unpleasant or disagreeable: *an objectionable report; objectionable language.*

ob·jec·tive (ub·JEC·tiv) *n.* something in the position of object, esp. an intended object or a definite goal: *a great achiever who always aims at clear objectives; The objective of a microscope or telescope is the part closest to the object being viewed.*
— *adj.* **1** having to do with an object: *"Me," "them," "whom," etc. are in the **objective case*** (= they function as objects of verbs). **2** dealing only with facts, not influenced by emotions; not subjective: *an objective analysis, look, report; An **objective test** has a choice of alternatives to be checked and no room for essay-type answers.* — **ob·jec·tive·ly** *adv.*
— **ob·jec·tive·ness** or **ob·jec·tiv·i·ty** (-TIV·uh·tee) *n.*

object lesson *n.* a practical illustration of a principle, esp. one that teaches a lesson.

ob·jec·tor (ub·JEC·tur) *n.* one who objects: *a conscientious objector.*

ob·jet d'art (ob·zhay·DAR) *n.*, *pl.* **ob·jets d'art** (ob·zhay·DAR) *French.* a small object of artistic value.

objet trou·vé (OB·zhay·troo·VAY) *n. French.* a found-art object. See FOUND ART.

ob·late (OB·late) *adj.* flattened at the poles: *The earth is not quite round but a somewhat oblate sphere.*

ob·la·tion (ob·LAY·shun) *n.* a sacrifice or offering to God.

ob·li·gate (OB·luh·gate) *v.* **-gates, -gat·ed, -gat·ing** bind morally or legally: *He did not feel obligated to shop there in spite of gifts received.*

ob·li·ga·tion (ob·luh·GAY·shun) *n.* what one is obliged to do because of an agreement or by one's position, occupation, relationships, etc.: *You are under no obligation to tip our staff; He felt some obligation to pay for the damage; the duties and obligations of a job; to assume, discharge, fulfill, meet an obligation.* — **ob·lig·a·to·ry** (ob·LIG·uh·tor·ee) *adj.*

o·blige (uh·BLIGE) *v.* **o·blig·es, o·bliged, o·blig·ing** bind people by force of law, custom, conscience, etc.: *The law obliges us to drive on the right; She's ready to oblige* (= do a favour) *whenever she can; I'm much* **obliged** by (= grateful for) *your kindness; a very* **obliging** (= accommodating) *neighbour.* — **o·blig·ing·ly** *adv.*

ob·lique (uh·BLEEK) *adj.* **1** slanting, not perpendicular or parallel: *Acute and obtuse angles are oblique angles.* **2** indirect, often underhand: *an oblique accusation, glance, reference.* — **ob·lique·ly** *adv.* — **ob·lique·ness** or **ob·liq·ui·ty** (ub·LIK·wuh·tee) *n.*

ob·lit·er·ate (ub·LIT·uh·rate) *v.* **-ates, -at·ed, -at·ing** destroy all traces of something; wipe out signs, marks, etc. completely. — **ob·lit·er·a·tion** (-RAY·shun) *n.*

ob·liv·ion (ub·LIV·ee·un) *n.* **1** the condition of being forgotten: *People pass* or *sink into oblivion by death, neglect, etc.* **2** forgetfulness or unconsciousness: *The patient sank back into oblivion.*

ob·liv·i·ous (ub·LIV·ee·us) *adj.* forgetful or unaware: *We are oblivious of the passage of time while asleep; to be oblivious of danger.* — **ob·liv·i·ous·ly** *adv.;* **ob·liv·i·ous·ness** *n.*

ob·long (OB·long) *adj.* longer than it is broad; rectangular, not square: *an oblong table.* — *n.* an oblong object or rectangular figure.

ob·lo·quy (OB·luk·wee) *n.* **-quies** shame or disgrace: *The deposed president lived in obloquy till death.*

ob·nox·ious (ub·NOK·shus) *adj.* unbearably offensive or objectionable: *the obnoxious manners of an obnoxious person; He became obnoxious to everyone.* — **ob·nox·ious·ly** *adv;* **ob·nox·ious·ness** *n.*

ob·scene (ob·SEEN) *adj.* immoral or indecent: *obscene dancing, gestures, language, literature, phone calls, prices, profits.* — **ob·scene·ly** *adv.* — **ob·scen·i·ty** (ob·SEN·uh·tee) *n.*

ob·scu·rant·ism (obs·CURE·un·tiz·um) *n.* opposition to progress and enlightenment. — **ob·scu·rant·ist** *n. & adj.*

ob·scure (obs·CURE) *adj.* **1** not clear or distinct; hard to understand: *an obscure corner, meaning; an obscure passage in a book.* **2** little known: *an obscure genius, village.* — *v.* **-scures, -scured, -scur·ing** make dark or hide from view: *Clouds obscure the sun.* — **ob·scure·ly** *adv.* — **ob·scur·i·ty** (-CURE·uh·tee) *n.*

ob·se·quies (OB·suh·kweez) *n.pl.* funeral rites.

ob·se·qui·ous (ob·SEEK·wee·us) *adj.* obedient in a servile or fawning manner. — **ob·se·qui·ous·ly** *adv.;* **ob·se·qui·ous·ness** *n.*

ob·ser·vant (ob·ZUR·vunt) *adj.* mindful of rules, customs, etc.; also, watchful: *He's usually alert and observant while driving; to be observant of what is happening around one.*

ob·ser·va·tion (ob·zur·VAY·shun) *n.* **1** the act or process of examining or studying: *an error of observation; a patient placed* or *kept under close observation.* **2** a remark or comment: *to make a shrewd observation; an astute, keen, penetrating, wise observation.*

ob·serve (ob·ZURV) *v.* **-serves, -served, -serv·ing** **1** abide by or keep: *to observe a custom, holiday, law.* **2** to notice: *changes observed at puberty.* **3** examine or study: *Astronomers observe the stars; to observe everything attentively, carefully, closely.* **4** to comment or remark: *He observed wisely that pride goes before a fall.* — **ob·ser·va·ble** (-uh·bul) *adj.* — **ob·serv·ance** (-unce) *n.* — **ob·ser·ver** *n.*

ob·sess (ob·SES) *v.* occupy one's mind in an unreasonable or unhealthy manner: *Ideas, feelings, and impulses could obsess the mind; Some are obsessed by fear, others with making money; Jean is so obsessed about cleanliness he washes every hour.* — **ob·ses·sion** *n.* — **ob·ses·sion·al** (-SESH·uh·nul) *adj.* — **ob·ses·sive** (-SES·iv) *adj.*

ob·so·les·cence (ob·suh·LES·unce) *n.* the state of being obsolescent or out of date: *Planned obsolescence (for making a product become out of date) is often built into goods.* — **ob·so·les·cent** (ob·suh·LES·unt) *adj.* becoming obsolete or out of date: *an obsolescent custom, mode of travel.*

ob·so·lete (OB·suh·leet, ob·suh·LEET) *adj.* fallen into disuse; outmoded: *an obsolete expression, implement, word; Is the horse-and-buggy obsolete?* — **ob·so·lete·ly** *adv.;* **ob·so·lete·ness** *n.*

ob·sta·cle (OB·stuh·cul) *n.* something that stands in the way of one's progress: *an obstacle to progress; to clear, encounter, overcome, remove, surmount, take an obstacle; a formidable, insurmountable obstacle; the fences, ditches, hurdles, etc. of an* **obstacle course** used in military training.

ob·stet·ric (ob·STET·ric) **1** *adj.* having to do with childbirth: *obstetric forceps; an obstetric nurse, ward;* also **ob·stet·ri·cal. 2 obstetrics** *n.pl.* [takes sing. v.] the branch of medicine concerned with childbirth. — **ob·ste·tri·cian** (ob·stuh·TRISH·un) *n.*

ob·sti·nate (OB·stuh·nit) *adj.* not yielding to reason or remedies: *He remained obstinate in his beliefs till death; He's obstinate about everything he advocates; an*

obstinate fever, habit. — **ob·sti·nate·ly** *adv.*
— **ob·sti·na·cy** (-nuh·see) *n.*

ob·strep·er·ous (ob·STREP·uh·rus) *adj.* noisy or disorderly in an unruly way: *obstreperous behaviour.*

ob·struct (ob·STRUCT) *v.* block movement or activity by placing obstacles in the way: *a pile-up obstructing traffic; Tall buildings obstruct our view.*
— **ob·struc·tion** (ob·STRUC·shun) *n.: an obstruction in the windpipe; The police charged him with obstruction of justice.*

ob·struc·tion·ist (ob·STRUC·shuh·nist) *n.* one that obstructs: *A filibusterer is an obstructionist;* **adj.:** *an obstructionist policy, tactic.* — **ob·struc·tion·ism** *n.*

ob·tain (ub·TAIN) *v.* **1** secure or get through effort, planning, etc.: *how to obtain a licence; evidence obtained by the police; to obtain credit, knowledge.* **2** be prevalent or in use: *superstitious practices still obtaining in some societies.*
— **ob·tain·a·ble** (-uh·bul) *adj.*

ob·trude (ub·TROOD, long "OO") *v.* **-trudes, -trud·ed, -trud·ing** **1** push out: *The bird obtruded its head and looked out.* **2** thrust oneself or one's concerns forward where not wanted: *He never obtruded his ideas on others.* — **ob·tru·sion** (-TROO·zhun) *n.*

ob·tru·sive (ub·TROO·siv) *adj.* pushing or showy: *an obtrusive colour.*
— **ob·tru·sive·ly** *adv.;* **ob·tru·sive·ness** *n.*

ob·tuse (ub·TYOOSE, -TOOSE) *adj.* **1** not acute or sharp: *An obtuse angle is more than 90 degrees.* **2** blunt and insensitive: *He is too obtuse to get the point.*
— **ob·tuse·ly** *adv.;* **ob·tuse·ness** *n.*

ob·verse (OB·vurse) *n.* the front, as the side of a coin or medal with the head or other main design.

ob·vi·ate (OB·vee·ate) *v.* **-ates, -at·ed, -at·ing** remove a difficulty, need, etc. by anticipating it.

ob·vi·ous (OB·vee·us) *adj.* plain to the view: *an obvious truth; It's obvious that they like each other; It's obvious to everyone;* **n.:** *to state the obvious.* — **ob·vi·ous·ly** *adv.*

oc·ca·sion (uh·CAY·zhun) *n.* **1** a particular time, esp. one favourable to an event's taking place: *a propitious occasion; I'd like to take this occasion to thank the principal; I've not yet had an occasion to talk to your parents; I'll do it as the occasion arises; A reunion is a good occasion for making a speech; I've warned you about this on numerous occasions; on the rare occasion of an earthquake.* **2** an event or happening: *The football game was the occasion (though not cause) of the fight; great occasions such as weddings; a festive, gala, fitting, happy, joyful, joyous, memorable, special occasion.*
— **rise to the occasion** meet the challenge.
— **on occasion** now and then.
— *v.* bring about: *Their enmity is well-known, but what occasioned the fight?*

oc·ca·sion·al (uh·CAY·zhuh·nul) *adj.* happening now and then, not regularly: *a forecast of occasional showers; occasional references;* **occasional chairs** *(for auxiliary use);* **occasional music** *(for special occasions).*
— **oc·ca·sion·al·ly** *adv.*

oc·ci·dent (OK·suh·dunt) *n.* the West, esp. the

Occident, Europe and the Americas, as distinguished from the Orient.

oc·ci·den·tal or **Oc·ci·den·tal** (ok·suh·DEN·tul) *adj.* of the West. — *n.* a native of the West.

oc·clude (uh·CLOOD, long "OO") *v.* **oc·cludes, oc·clud·ed, oc·clud·ing** close or block so as to prevent passage: *Clots occlude the blood supply in a coronary artery; the* **occluded front** *formed by cold air overtaking and forcing up a warm air mass; Upper and lower teeth should occlude* (= meet properly). — **oc·clu·sion** (-CLOO·zhun) *n.* — **oc·clu·sive** (-ziv) *adj.*

oc·cult (uh·CULT, OC·ult) *adj.* hidden or concealed from ordinary human knowledge: *Astrology, alchemy, and magic are occult sciences; an occult practice; Fortunetellers claim to know the occult* (= occult matters). — **oc·cult·ism** *n.;* **oc·cult·ist** *n.*

oc·cu·pan·cy (OK·yuh·pun·see) *n.* **-cies** the act or period of occupying a place. — **oc·cu·pant** (-punt) *n.*

oc·cu·pa·tion (ok·yuh·PAY·shun) *n.* **1** an occupying by an enemy: *a territory that is under occupation by a foreign army.* **2** work that one is trained to do or does habitually; profession: *The unemployed man is a cab driver by occupation; A rewarding occupation such as running a free health clinic need not be a profitable occupation.*
— **oc·cu·pa·tion·al** (-shuh·nul) *adj.: The bends is an occupational disease of divers;* **Occupational therapy** *helps overcome handicaps by participation in selected activities.* — **oc·cu·pa·tion·al·ly** *adv.*

oc·cu·py (OK·yuh·pye) *v.* **-pies, -pied, -py·ing** **1** take up or engage: *Matter occupies space; A good book occupies our attention; Hobbies occupy my spare time; The baby-sitter kept the children* **occupied** *and out of trouble.* **2** have possession of a place: *She moved in and occupied the house; an occupied seat; an occupied position that will soon fall vacant.* **3** take possession by force: *when Afghanistan was occupied by the Soviets.*
— **oc·cu·pi·er** *n.*

oc·cur (uh·CUR) *v.* **oc·curs, oc·curred, oc·cur·ring** of an event, thing, etc., happen to be found: *When did his death occur? "The" occurs more frequently than any other word; Did that ever occur to you* (= come to your mind)?
— **oc·cur·rence** (uh·CUR·unce) *n.: a common, daily, regular occurrence.*

o·cean (OH·shun) *n.* **1** one of the great expanses of water around the globe: *the Atlantic, Pacific, Indian, Arctic, and Antarctic oceans.* **2** a great number or quantity: *oceans of funds, time, trouble, words.*

o·cean·go·ing (OH·shun·go·ing) *adj.* **1** naval: *an oceangoing vessel.* **2** maritime: *oceangoing commerce; the oceangoing world.*

o·ce·an·ic (oh·shee·AN·ic) *adj.* having to do with the ocean: *an oceanic climate, current; the oceanic depths; oceanic life; oceanic* (= oceanlike) *vastness of a desert.*

o'·clock (uh·CLOC) *adv.* according to the clock: *8 o'clock in the morning* (= 8 a.m.).

oct-, octa- or **octo-** *combining form.* eight: *octagon, octane, octette, octopus.*

oc·ta·gon (OC·tuh·gun) *n.* an eight-sided plane figure. — **oc·tag·o·nal** (oc·TAG·uh·nul) *adj.*

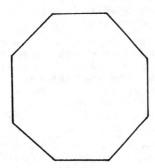

oc·tane (OC·tane) *n.* a petroleum hydrocarbon that gives quality to gasoline: *The higher the* **octane number** or **rating** *of a gasoline, the less the engine knocks.*

oc·tave (OC·tiv, -tave) *n.* **1** an interval of eight full musical tones. **2** the series of tones making up such an interval or the eighth full tone from any given tone. **3** a group of eight verses, festival days, etc.

oc·ta·vo (oc·TAH·voh) *n.* **-vos 1** the page size of 6 in. by 9 in. (15.24 cm by 22.86 cm). **2** a book with octavo pages.

oc·tette or **oc·tet** (oc·TET) *n.* **1** a musical composition or group of singers or players with eight voices or instruments. **2** a set of eight.

oc·u·lar (OC·yuh·lur) *adj.* of the eye or by eyesight; visual. — *n.* the eyepiece lens of a microscope or telescope.

oc·u·list (OC·yuh·list) *n.* [former term] ophthalmologist.

OD (OH·dee) *n.* **OD's** *Slang.* **1** an overdose of a narcotic. **2** one who has taken an OD. — *v.* **OD's, OD'd, OD'ing** take sick or die from an OD: *to OD on drugs.*

odd *adj.* **1** remaining as extra: *an odd stocking without its mate; Keep the odd change after payments; the* **odd man out** *after the others have paired off; hundred-odd* (= 100 plus a few); *He worked at odd* (= casual or occasional) *jobs while seeking employment.* **2** not even: *1, 3, 5, 7, etc. are the odd numbers.* **3** strange or peculiar: *an odd hairstyle; an odd-looking creature.* **4 odds** *pl.* chances: *The odds favour Sam 3 to 1; The* **odds are** *he will win; He's* **by all odds** *the luckiest; They died fighting against heavy odds* (= disadvantages). — **at odds** in disagreement: *two brother at odds with each other.* — **beat the odds** overcome disadvantages. — **odds and ends** miscellaneous things.

odd·ball *n. & adj. Slang.* eccentric.

odds-on *adj.* sure to win: *She's the odds-on favourite to succeed the mayor.*

ode *n.* a ceremoniously lyric poem in an exalted style: *an ode to Napoleon.*

o·di·ous (OH·dee·us) *adj.* hateful in an offensive or disagreeable way: *odious cruelty; an odious epithet.* — **o·di·ous·ly** *adv.;* **o·di·ous·ness** *n.*

o·di·um (OH·dee·um) *n.* widespread hatred of the kind that results in disgrace.

o·dom·e·ter (oh·DOM·uh·tur) *n.* an instrument that records the distance travelled by a vehicle.

o·dor·ous (OH·duh·rus) *adj.* giving forth an odour; fragrant. Also **o·dor·if·er·ous** (-RIF·uh·rus) *adj.*

o·dour or **o·dor** (OH·dur) *n.* what makes anything smell good or bad: *the detection of odours; body odour; to emit, give off, perceive, recognize an odour; a fetid, foul, musty, pleasant, pungent, rank, strong odour; natural and synthetic odours; the odour of scandal; a company* **in bad odour** (= having a bad name) *with the law.* — **o·dour·less** or **o·dor·less** *adj.*

od·ys·sey (OD·uh·see) *n.* **od·ys·seys** a long wandering or journey, as of the Greek hero Odysseus in the ancient epic poem "Odyssey": *Our cruise was a 10-day odyssey one can never forget.*

o'er (OR, OHR) [poetic use] over.

of (ov, uv) *prep.* **1** [indicating origin or cause]: *born of noble blood; He died of hunger; a house of cards; north of* (= from) *Yellowknife.* **2** [indicating a relationship]: *children of God; the works of Shakespeare; love of* (= for) *truth.* **3** having to do with: *words of advice; the Province of Ontario; a house of prayer.* **4** before: *10 minutes of 8* (= 7:50). **5** during: *of a summer evening; of late* (= recently).

off (OF) *adv.* away: *He took his hat off; He went off without a word; Turn off the tap; to pay off a loan; He's way off in his estimate; Taiwan is far off in the east; He saw me off at the airport.* — **off and on** now and then. — *prep.* away from: *His hat is off his head; anchored off the coast; We get off work at 5 p.m.; to get the tops* "off of" [Substandard for off] *bottles; an off-camera interview; a hockey player's off-ice behaviour; an off-the-rack* (= ready-to-wear, not custom-made) *suit.* — *adj.* away: *I'll be off soon; The lights are off* (= not on); *an off* (= unlikely) *chance.* — *interj.* away: *Off with you!*

off-beat *n. Music.* a weakly accented beat. — *adj.* **1** off the regular rhythm. **2** of an unusual kind: *off-beat theatre.*

off-colour or **off-color** (OF·CUL·ur) *adj.* **1** not the right colour. **2** improper or risqué: *an off-colour joke.* **3** not feeling well.

of·fence or **of·fense** (uh·FENCE, AW·fence) *n.* **1** what offends against the law, one's conscience, feelings, etc.: *Speeding is a traffic offence; a capital, criminal, indictable, minor, petty offence; Luc apologized and said the offence was not intended; Strong language is likely to* **give offence** (= to offend); *He's too meek to* **take offence** (= be offended) *at anything.* **2** (OH·fence) attack: *weapons of offence and defence.*

of·fend (uh·FEND) *v.* hurt one's sense of right and wrong; do wrong or displease: *Mom will be offended if you do that; It offends against good manners; It offends good taste.* — **of·fen·der** *n.*

offense same as OFFENCE.

of·fen·sive (uh·FEN·siv) *adj.* **1** unpleasant or insulting: *offensive language; an offensive fellow, smell.* **2** attacking or aggressive: *an offensive army, weapon.* — *n.* attack: *an army on the offensive; a new offensive; to take the offensive; to carry out, launch, mount, undertake an offensive; a peace offensive* (= aggressive move for peace). — **of·fen·sive·ly** *adv.;* **of·fen·sive·ness** *n.*

of·fer (OF·ur) *v.* **1** hold out for acceptance: *Many offered to help her; They offered advice, help, suggestions.* **2** present: *prayers and sacrifices offered to God; The enemy offered little resistance; They didn't even offer* (= attempt) *to defend themselves; Do it if the opportunity offers* (= presents) *itself.* — *n.* an offering or what is offered: *He refused all offers of help; We've received an offer of $200 000 on the house; an offer to purchase; an offer so good that you can't refuse; a job offer; an offer of marriage; to accept, decline, make, reject, spurn, withdraw an offer.*

offering (OF·ur·ing) *n.* an act of presenting or what is presented: *the offering of prayers and sacrifices; the sacrificial lamb as a burnt offering; an offering to the Almighty; a plate to collect church offerings; a school's course offerings.*

of·fer·to·ry (OF·ur·tor·ee) *n.* **1** the offering of bread and wine at a church service, esp. the Mass, and the prayers accompanying this. **2** the taking up of the offerings of the congregation at public worship.

off·hand *adj. & adv.* said or done without preparation: *a speech delivered offhand; offhand remarks.*

off·hour *n.* a period outside of business hours or rush hours.

of·fice (OF·is) *n.* **1** a place from which a service is carried out: *a booking, branch, home, main office; a box office; a lawyer's office; patent office; Sam works at or in a dentist's office; the post office; Our office is open Monday through Friday.* **2** a position of responsibility, esp. public: *The highest office of the nation is that of Governor General; to assume an office; to resign from an office; to hold, run for, seek, take office; A government is in office while in power; A party goes out of office when it loses an election.* **3** prayers: *to recite the divine office; the last offices* (= rites for the dead). — **good offices** *pl.* service: *He got the job through the good offices of a friend.*

office hours *n. pl.* hours of business.

of·fi·cer (OF·uh·sur) *n.* anyone holding a position of authority: *the chief executive officer of a company; personnel officer; police officer; commissioned and warrant officers of the armed forces.*

of·fi·cial (uh·FISH·ul) *adj.* **1** having to do with an office: *an official manner, occasion, position, uniform.* **2** authorized or recognized: *an official announcement; Canada's two official languages; Romansch is a national but not an official language in Switzerland; Is the appointment official? an official record.* — *n.* a person holding office; officer: *public officials; school officials.* — **of·fi·cial·dom** (-dum) *n.* — **of·fi·cial·ism** *n.* — **of·fi·cial·ly** *adv.*

of·fi·ci·ate (uh·FISH·ee·ate) *v.* -ates, -at·ed, -at·ing perform official duties: *to officiate at a ceremeony; to*

officiate as chairperson of the meeting.

of·fi·cious (uh·FISH·us) *adj.* meddlesome, esp. from a position of authority. — **of·fi·cious·ly** *adv.;* **of·fi·cious·ness** *n.*

off·ing *n.* **1** the distant sea as seen from the shore. **2** the immediate future: *Reforms are in the offing* (= impending).

off·ish *adj. Informal.* aloof or reserved in manner.

off·key *adj.* not on the right musical note; not harmonious.

off·limits *adj.* out of bounds: *Bars are off-limits to children.*

off·line *adj. & adv.* not directly connected to a computer; not online: *an off-line printer.*

off·print *n.* a separate print or small edition made from a larger publication, as of a magazine article. — *v.* make an offprint.

off·season (OF·see·zun) *n.* the period outside the regular season; *adj.: a low off-season fare to Florida.*

off·set *n.* **1** a transferring, as printing from an impression made by type on a rubber cylinder instead of directly on paper. **2** make-up or replacement: *an offset arrangement, job.* **3** a bend in a screwdriver to enable it to reach a hidden screwhead. — *v.* (of·SET) -sets, -set, -set·ting balance or compensate for: *higher wages to offset rising prices.*

off·shoot *n.* something proceeding from a main part, as a branch growing from a main stem; derivative.

off·shore *adj. & adv.* **1** away from the shore: *winds blowing offshore; an offshore oil well.* **2** overseas or foreign: *two domestic and three offshore companies; offshore students.*

off·side *adj. & adv.* in hockey, soccer, etc., illegally ahead of the puck, ball, etc.

off·spring *n., pl.* -spring or -springs **1** descendant or progeny: *to produce offspring; numerous offspring.* **2** outcome: *Famine is often the offspring of war.*

off·stage *n.* the part of a stage not visible to the audience. — *adj. & adv.* private or privately; behind the scenes.

off-the-cuff *adj. & adv. Informal.* offhand: *off-the-cuff advice; an off-the-cuff remark, style of humour.*

off-the-record *adj.* confidential.

off-the-wall *adj. Slang.* unusual or unorthodox.

off·track *adj.* away from the race track: *offtrack betting.*

off·white *adj.* greyish or yellowish white.

off·year *n.* **1** a year of reduced activity or production. **2** a year outside of a regular presidential election year in the U.S.

oft *adv.* [poetic] often.

of·ten (OF·un, -tun) *adv.* frequently; also **of·ten·times.**

o·gle (OH·gul) *v.* o·gles, o·gled, o·gling glance with love and desire at someone: *boys and girls ogling each other; Sam ogles at every passing girl.* — *n.* an amorous glance. — **o·gler** *n.*

o·go·po·go (OH·guh·POH·goh) *n. Cdn.* an unidentified sea monster of the Okanagan Lake in B.C.

o·gre (OH·gur) *n.* a man-eating monster of folklore; *fem.* **o·gress** (OH·gris). — **o·gre·ish** *adj.*

oh *interj.* calling someone's attention, expressing surprise, etc.: *Oh John! Oh boy! Oh yes? Oh no!* [with rising and falling tone] *Oh-oh* (= Something wrong)!

o·ho (oh·HOH) *interj.* expressing surprise, taunting, etc.

oil *n.* **1** a greasy or fatty liquid that is lighter than water, obtained from mineral, animal, or vegetable matter: *Oil and water do not mix; A film of oil covered the driveway.* **2** petroleum: *to hit or strike oil; to pump, produce, refine oil; an oil slick on the water; an oil spill from a tanker.* **3** oil colour or oil painting: *to paint in oils; Picasso painted his first oil at age 9.*
— *v.* treat, supply, or lubricate with oil: *well-oiled machinery.*
— *adj.* having to do with oil: *an oil medium, tanker.*

oil·y (OY·lee) *adj.* **oil·i·er, -i·est 1** of or like oil; greasy: *oily cloth, hair, hands, skin.* **2** fawning, esp. in an oily way: *his oily tongue; her oily smile.*

oink *v.* make the noise of a hog.

oint·ment (OINT·munt) *n.* a fatty medicinal or cosmetic preparation to put on the skin.

OK or **o·kay** (oh·KAY, OH·kay) *adj., adv. & interj. Informal.* all right: *Are you OK? Is it OK to smoke here?*
— *n., pl.* **OK's** or **o·kays** approval: *to get the boss's OK; The boss has given his OK to the plan.*
— *v.* **OK's** or **o·kays, OK'd** or **o·kayed, OK'ing** or **o·kay·ing** approve: *He had to OK it first.*

o·ka (OH·kuh) *n. Cdn.* a cheese originally made by Trappist monks in Oka, Quebec.

ol' or **ole** (OLE) *adj. Slang.* old: *good ol' boys back home; Ol' Man River (Mississippi); ol' man winter; Ol' Miss* (= University of Mississippi).

old *adj.* **1** grown in years; not young: *an old lady; She lived to a ripe old age; security in old age.* **2** having existed, been in use, etc. for some time: *old clothes; an old friend; the Old Regime of French rule, as in New France.* **3** advanced in age: *How old is the baby? She's a year old.* **4** former: *a teacher's old students; old school ties; the old-boy network that hinders women and minorities from getting jobs.*
— *n.* the past time: *in days of old.*
— **the old** old persons or things.

old country *n.* an immigrant's original country.

old·en (OLE·dun) *adj.* [poetic] old: *in olden days.*

old-fashioned (OLD·FASH·und) *adj.* **1** old in fashion, ways, tastes, etc.: *an old-fashioned gentleman; a woman of old-fashioned goodness.* **2** out of fashion: *an old-fashioned dress.*

old fogy or **old fogey** *n.* See FOGY.

old guard *n.* the older and more conservative members of a group.

old hat *n. Informal.* something that one is accustomed to: *Your new idea is old hat to me.*

old·ie (OLE·dee) *n. Informal.* an old person or thing, esp. a musical piece: *a golden oldie.*

old·ish *adj.* somewhat old.

old lady *n. Slang.* one's mother or wife.

old-line *adj.* established or conservative.

old maid *n.* **1** a woman who has never married. **2** a prim or fussy person. — **old-maid·ish** *adj.*

old man *n. Slang.* one's father or husband.

old master *n.* **1** a distinguished European painter before 1700. **2** a work by an old master.

old money *n.* inherited wealth.

old school *n.* the conservative or old-fashioned group of society.

old·ster (OLD·stur) *n. Informal.* an old person.

old-time *adj.* of the past; of long standing.

old-tim·er (OLD·TIME·ur) *n. Informal.* a veteran or other old person.

old wives' tale *n.* an old and foolish belief.

Old World *n.* Europe, Asia, and Africa; the Eastern Hemisphere: *Old World charm, hospitality* [used in reference to Western Europe].

ole same as OL'.

ol·fac·to·ry (ole·FAC·tuh·ree) *adj.* of the sense of smell: *olfactory nerves; the olfactory organ* (= nose).

ol·i·gar·chy (OL·uh·gar·kee) *n.* **-chies 1** a state or corporation ruled by a small group. **2** such a group or their government.
— **ol·i·gar·chic** (-kic) or **ol·i·gar·chi·cal** (-kuh·cul) *adj.*

ol·ive (OL·iv) *n.* a Mediterranean evergreen tree with soft grey-green leaves, bearing small, oval fruit that is purple to black when ripe and contains much oil.
— *adj.* yellow to yellow-green.

olive branch *n.* the branch of an olive as a peace emblem: *to extend, hold out, offer the olive branch.*

olive drab *n.* a dark olive cloth, formerly used for army uniforms.

olive green *n.* the colour of unripe olive; yellowish green.

O·lym·pi·ad or **o·lym·pi·ad** (oh·LIM·pee·ad) *n.* **1** the Olympic games. **2** in ancient Greece, a period of four years as between two Olympic games.

O·lym·pi·an (oh·LIM·pee·un) *adj.* **1** of or from

Olympia, a plain in ancient Greece where the ancient Olympic games were held every four years. **2** having to do with Mount Olympus in northern Greece, the supposed home of the gods; hence, lofty: *Olympian heights; decisions handed down from the Olympian detachment of the highest court of the land; two women facing Olympian* (=superior) *odds in a group dominated by 123 men.* — *n.* **1** an Olympic athlete. **2** a god.

O·lym·pic (oh·LIM·pic) *adj.* **1** having to do with the Olympics: *The Olympic games are held every four years; Olympic gold; an Olympic hero, medal.* **2** having to do with Mount Olympus; Olympian.
— **Olympics** *n. pl.* a series of athletic contests held every four years, as in ancient Greece: *The modern international Olympics started in 1876; the summer and winter Olympics; the 1988 Calgary Olympics.* Also **Olympic games.**

om·buds·man (OM·budz·mun, om·BUDZ·mun) *n.* an independent government official investigating citizens' complaints against the government; also, any resident mediator: *a media ombudsman; prison ombudsman; university ombudsman.*

o·me·ga (oh·MEE·guh, -MAY·guh) *n.* the last letter of the Greek alphabet.

om·e·lette or **om·e·let** (OM·lit, -uh·lit) *n.* eggs beaten and cooked in a pan without stirring: *a cheese, Spanish, Western omelette.*

o·men (OH·mun) *n.* something considered as foretelling a future event: *Some people consider a howling dog an omen of death; not a good omen for a journey.*

om·i·nous (OM·uh·nus) *adj.* as if threatening evil: *an ominous sign, sound.* — **om·i·nous·ly** *adv.*

o·mis·sion (oh·MISH·un) *n.* an omitting or thing omitted: *a glaring omission.*

o·mit (oh·MIT) *v.* **o·mits, o·mit·ted, o·mit·ting** **1** fail to include: *to omit a name from a list.* **2** fail to do: *Do not omit to call me when you arrive.*

omni- *combining form.* all: *omnibus, omnipotent, omniscience.*

om·ni·bus (OM·nuh·bus) *n.* **-bus·es** same as BUS.
— *adj.* dealing with many items at once: *an omnibus bill.*

om·nip·o·tent (om·NIP·uh·tunt) *adj.* all-powerful, as God. — **om·nip·o·tence** *adj.*

om·nis·cient (om·NIS·ee·unt, om·NISH·unt) *adj.* knowing all things, as God. — **om·nis·cience** *n.*

om·niv·o·rous (om·NIV·uh·rus) *adj.* eating any sort of food indiscriminately, as a bear: *an omnivorous animal, reader.* — **om·niv·o·rous·ly** *adv.;* **om·niv·o·rous·ness** *n.*

on *prep.* **1** [indicating position implying contact from above or imposition]: *the food on the table; shoes on your feet; pictures on the wall; sitting on a committee (as a member); a tax on profits; He heaped insult on insult; She is on the phone all the time; The police have nothing on* (=no evidence against) *you; The drinks are on me* (=I'm paying for them). **2** toward: *a march on Parliament Hill.* **3** by means of: *seen on TV.*
4 [indicating engaged condition or process]: *a house on fire; cars on sale; men on business; operators on duty.*

5 [indicating time]: *on a clear day; on our departure; on your birthday.* **6** concerning: *a lecture on poetry; books on Milton; bent on mischief.*
— *adv.* **1** [indicating position implying contact from above or imposition]: *Put your coat on.* **2** [indicating the beginning of an activity]: *Turn on the lights.*
3 [indicating continuation of an activity]: *Let's move on; Hold on to the ropes; Go on with your speech! She's well on* (=advanced) *in years; The speech went on and on* (=without stopping).
— **on and off** now and then.
— **on to** *Informal.* aware of: *He seems to be on to something.*
— **and so on** and so forth; et cetera.
— *adj.* in progress or operation: *The movie is on now; The switch was on, not off; Press the on button; You're on* (*Informal for* in the business or competition); *an* **on-again off-again** *friendship.*

on-air *adj.* by means of air waves, not by cable: *on-air radio and TV programs.*

on-camera *adj. & adv.* before a TV or movie camera: *an on-camera interview.*

once (WUNCE) *adv.* at one time; on one occasion: *He visits us once a year; a once* (=formerly) *wealthy man; She was never once* (=ever) *late for work.*
— **once for all** or **once and for all** finally and conclusively.
— **once in a while** now and then.
— **once upon a time** long ago.
— *conj.* as soon as: *You can ask him once he is here.*
— *n.* one time: *Lend me the car just this once.*
— *adj.* former: *T. H. White's "The Once and Future King [Arthur]."*
— **at once** **1** immediately: *Come here at once!*
2 simultaneously: *I can't be in two places at once.*

once-over (WUNCE·oh·vur) *n. Informal.* a quick, evaluating look or action.

on·com·ing (ON·cum·ing) *n. & adj.* approaching: *the oncoming of winter; the oncoming winter; He ran into oncoming traffic.*

one (WUN) *n.* **1** the cardinal number 1: *It's one o'clock now.* **2** something marked one, as a card or bill: *Two fives and three ones make $13.*
— *pron.* a person or thing: *Are you the one who phoned? He is one of us; the ones who are homeless; There's room for only one; One* (=any person) *should watch one's language; Jogging is good for your health, one* (=I, you, we, or people) *would like to think; We are* **at one** (=in agreement) *on this issue; I,* **for one** (=certainly), *am against smoking; family members who love* **one another** (=each other); **One by one** (=One after another) *they came back; We deal with each other* **one on one** (=directly); *a* **one-on-one** *relationship; We are* **one up on** (=We have an advantage over) *the competition with our offer of free tickets instead of discount coupons.*
— *adj.* being a single thing or individual: *one book; two people of one* (=same) *mind; One* (=a certain) *John Smith called.* — **one·ness** *n.*

one-liner (wun·LYE·nur) *n.* a joke or wisecrack in one sentence, as "After she kissed him, he was still a frog."

one-night stand *n.* a one-time performance (as of a play) or experience (as of making love to someone).

one-off (wun·OF) *adj.* occurring only once: *a one-off situation.*

on·er·ous (ON·ur·us) *adj.* burdensome or laborious: *an onerous duty, task.*

one·self (wun·SELF) *pron.* one's own self: *a job difficult to do all by oneself* (= without help).
— **be oneself 1** act naturally. **2** feel well or normal: *I'm not myself today.*

one-shot *adj.* achieved or effective by only one action: *a one-shot affair, approach, answer, deal, lead, remedy, solution, victory.*

one-sided (WUN·SYE·did) *adj.* **1** having one side more prominent or more developed: *a one-sided leaf.* **2** unequal or uneven: *a one-sided game.* **3** prejudiced: *a one-sided decision, umpire.*

one-time *adj.* **1** former: *a one-time professor of McGill.* **2** being or made only once: *a one-time offer.*

one-to-one (wun·tuh·WUN) *adj.* **1** of two sets, matching every element in one with one and only one in the other: *There is no one-to-one correspondence between English letters and their sounds, as of "c" in "cat," "ice," "chat," etc.* **2** direct; one on one: *They fought one-to-one against the enemy; The volunteers worked on a one-to-one basis with the children needing help; a one-to-one dialogue, ratio, relationship.*

one-track *adj. Informal.* thinking about just one thing: *a one-track mind.*

one-up·man·ship (wun·UP·mun·ship) *n.* the art or practice of keeping one step ahead of one's competitor.

one-way *adj.* in one direction only: *a one-way street; one-way traffic; a one-way* (= not return) *ticket home, to New York; a one-way mirror (to hide behind and look through).*

on·go·ing (ON·go·ing) *adj.* moving forward or continuing: *an ongoing business, problem, relationship, research project.*

on-line *adj. & adv.* directly connected to a computer: *an on-line printer; a printer operating on-line.*

on·look·er (ON·look·ur) *n.* one who is looking on.

on·ly (OHN·lee) *adj.* alone of its kind; sole: *the only child of her parents; the only one for me; a club for men only.*
— *adv.* solely: *We've only one pair of hands; I did it only for you; He only got* (= got nothing more than) *a C in the test; I can only walk or run, not fly; He's only* (= just) *a child; I would fly if only I could; I would be only too* (= very) *glad to fly.*
— *conj.* but: *I would fly, only I can't afford it.*

on·rush *n.* a rushing forward. — **on·rush·ing** *adj.*

on·set *n.* a vigorous start or attack: *the onset of a disease, of an enemy, of winter.*

on·shore *adj. & adv.* on or toward the shore; not offshore: *onshore oil; winds blowing onshore.*

on·side *adv.* to the side as support, not offside: *to get more people to come onside and work for them.*

on·slaught (ON·slawt) *n.* a violent attack.

on·to (ON·too) *prep.* **1** to and upon: *thrown onto the ground.* **2** *Informal.* on to; aware of: *Don't let the other guy get onto our plans.*

o·nus (OH·nus) *n.* burden or responsibility: *the onus of proving a charge.*

on·ward (ON·wurd) *adv.* forward; also **on·wards.**
— *adj.:* *the onward march of events; an onward journey.*

oo·dles (OO·dulz) *n. pl. Informal.* a great amount; lots: *toast with oodles of marmalade; There are oodles of things to do.*

ooh and aah *v.* express joy or surprise by sighing: *The children started oohing and aahing when Santa appeared with the gifts;* *n.:* *Santa was greeted with oohs and aahs by the children.*

Ook·pik (long "OO") *Cdn. Trademark.* a sealskin Inuit doll representing an Arctic owl.

Oo·li·chan (OO·luh·cun) *n. Cdn.* a small food fish of the smelt family found along the Pacific coast. Also **oo·la·chan.**

oo·mi·ak same as UMIAK.

oomph (OOMF) *n. Slang.* sex appeal; also, vigour or vitality.

oops same as WHOOPS.

ooze (OOZ) *v.* **ooz·es, oozed, ooz·ing** leak out or seep gradually, as through small holes: *blood oozing from a wound; a broken pot oozing water; Our hostess oozes with* (= is full of) *charm.*
— *n.* **1** something that oozes. **2** mud or slime, esp. the deposit at the bottom of a body of water. **3** a bog or marsh.

oo·zy (OO·zee) *adj.* **-zi·er, -zi·est 1** oozing. **2** slimy.

op or **op art** *n.* abstract painting in geometric patterns creating optical illusions of flickering movement; optical art.

o·pac·i·ty (oh·PAS·uh·tee) *n.* **-ties** a being opaque or something opaque.

o·paque (oh·PAKE) *adj.* **1** impenetrable by light, sound, heat, etc., esp. not transparent or translucent. **2** mentally obtuse; stupid.

op art See OP.

ope *v.* **opes, oped, op·ing** [old use] open.

Op-Ed or **Op-Ed page** *n.* a newspaper page, usually

facing the editorial page, containing special features.

o·pen (OH·pun) *adj.* **1** not closed, covered, confined, clogged, etc.: *an open box, view, wound; Walk in through the open door; We're open for business from 9 to 5; Public parks are open to everyone; the wide open spaces of the countryside; She's quite open* (= straightforward) *with us; in open* (= not frozen) *waters; By publishing it, you're laying yourself open to public criticism.* **2** having holes: *Netting is an open fabric.* **3** public, not secret: *an open challenge, letter, violation.* **4** undecided: *an open question.* **5** receptive, not prejudiced: *an open mind; I'm* **open** *to suggestions.* **6** generous: *He gives to charity with an open hand; We received her with open arms* (= warmly).
— *v.* make or become open: *to open a carton; Open your mouth wide for the dentist; We open* (= start) *our meetings with "O Canada" or by singing "O Canada"; The door of the fridge opens on the left; Schools open after holidays; Children* **open up** (= feel free) *and start talking when you gain their confidence.*
— *n.* **the open 1** open land or water; the outdoors. **2** public knowledge: *Let's bring the dispute out into the open and try to settle it by discussion.* **3** a tournament open to amateurs and professionals: *the Canadian Open (golf tournament).* — **o·pen·er** *n.*
— **o·pen·ly** *adv.;* **o·pen·ness** *n.*

open air *n.* air that is not confined: *out of the house and into the open air.*
— *adj.*: *an open-air* (= outdoor) *theatre.*

open-and-shut case *n. Informal.* an issue that is easily settled, being straightforward or obvious.

open-door policy *n.* a nation's policy of admitting immigrants of all nationalities without bias.

open-ended (OH·pun·EN·did) *adj.* not closed at one end; adaptable in regard to time and such limits: *an open-ended container, contract, mortgage, program, schedule; an open-ended return ticket; open-ended talks.*

open-faced (OH·pun·FAIST) *adj.* **1** candid-looking. **2** without a top slice of bread: *an open-faced sandwich.*

open-handed (OH·pun·HAN·did) *adj.* liberal in giving: *an open-handed policy.*

open house *n.* hospitality that is open to everyone, esp. a social event at an institution for a promotional purpose: *Realtors have* or *hold open houses to attract buyers for their homes.*

open housing *n.* housing without discrimination based on age, race, religion, etc.

opening *n.* **1** a gap or hole; also, a clearing: *an opening in the jungle.* **2** a beginning of operations: *a grand opening of the new building with free coffee and donuts for everyone.* **3** a vacant position or job: *We have an opening for a receptionist.*

open-line (OH·pun·line) *adj.* hot-line or phone-in: *an open-line radio program.*

open-minded (OH·pun·MINE·did) *adj.* free from prejudices; receptive to new ideas.

open-mouthed (OH·pun·mouthed) *adj.* with the mouth open: *an open-mouthed pitcher; He gazed in open-mouthed* (= gaping) *astonishment.*

open shop *n.* a business employing union and nonunion workers, not a closed shop.

op·er·a (OP·ur·uh) *n.* **1** a *pl.* of OPUS. **2** a dramatic composition in which the text is set to music, usually with orchestral accompaniment: *a comic opera; grand opera; light opera.* **3** something similar to an opera: *a soap opera; horse opera* (*Slang* for western).
— **op·er·at·ic** (op·uh·RAT·ic) *adj.*

op·er·a·ble (OP·ur·uh·bul) *adj.* **1** practicable or feasible. **2** that can be surgically operated on: *an operable cancer.*

op·er·ate (OP·uh·rate) *v.* **-rates, -rat·ed, -rat·ing 1** work or run: *He operates a ferry service; It operates day and night; the unfavourable factors operating against us.* **2** perform surgery: *He was operated on for a hernia.*

operating system *n.* a piece of software for routine operations of a computer such as startup, input and output, filing of data, running programs, etc.

op·er·a·tion (op·uh·RAY·shun) *n.* **1** an action or procedure: *the smooth operation of a machine; the operation of a factory, law, plan; a surgical operation to remove a tumour; to have, perform, undergo an operation; major and minor operations; addition, subtraction, and other arithmetical operations; Computers carry out arithmetical, logical, and transfer operations as specified by instructions; The plant is now in operation* (= functioning). **2** a planned and executed mission or project: *military operations; Operation Breadbasket; to conduct, launch an operation; covert, drilling, mopping-up, rescue operations.*

op·er·a·tion·al (op·uh·RAY·shun·ul) *adj.* **1** functioning: *Our computer network is now operational.* **2** having to do with operation: *operational costs, problems, research.*

op·er·a·tive (OP·uh·ruh·tiv) *adj.* **1** effective: *an operative clause.* **2** having to do with a surgical operation: *operative treatment.*
— *n.* an operator, esp. a spy or detective.

op·er·a·tor (OP·uh·ray·tur) *n.* **1** a skilled worker: *a computer, crane, radio, telephone operator.* **2** *Informal.* a skilful user of people and materials for one's own purposes: *a slick* or *smooth operator; a big-time operator.* **3** a mathematical symbol or instruction: *the AND, NAND, OR, and OR ELSE operators of computer logic.*

oph·thal·mic (of·THAL·mic) *adj.* having to do with the eyes: *an ophthalmic dispenser, hospital, vein; ophthalmic drops.*

oph·thal·mol·o·gist (of·thal·MOL·uh·jist) *n.* a physician who is an eye specialist.

o·pine (oh·PINE) *v.* **o·pines, o·pined, o·pin·ing** express the opinion: *The researcher opined that children watch too much TV.*

o·pin·ion (uh·PIN·yun) *n.* a conclusion or judgment that seems true or probable though open to dispute: *a matter of opinion, not a certainty; to air, entertain, express, form, hold, offer, venture, voice an opinion; an opinion about* or *on a subject; a considered, dissenting, expert, informed, lay opinion; He has a good opinion of the applicant; a high opinion of her; a lawyer's professional* *opinion; Get a second opinion from another lawyer; In my humble opinion, I deserve a promotion; He is of the opinion that the death penalty should be restored; an opinion* (= decision) *handed down by a court.*

o·pin·ion·at·ed (uh·pin·yuh·NAY·tid) *adj.* dogmatic in one's opinions.

o·pos·sum (uh·POS·um) *n.* a furry, tree-dwelling North American marsupial that will pretend to be dead if surprised on the ground.

op·po·nent (uh·POH·nunt) *n.* one who opposes, esp. in a formal contest such as a game or election: *a formidable opponent.*

op·por·tune (OP·ur·tune) *adj.* done or happening at a favourable time; timely: *an opportune arrival, moment.* — **op·por·tune·ly** *adv.*

op·por·tun·ism (op·ur·TUE·niz·um) *n.* the taking selfish advantage of opportunities regardless of principles. — **op·por·tu·nist** *n.* — **op·por·tu·nis·tic** (OP·ur·tue·NIS·tic) *adj.*

op·por·tu·ni·ty (op·ur·TUE·nuh·tee) *n.* **-ties** a favourable occasion: *to afford, find, give, have, lose an opportunity; to take the opportunity to do something; a lost, missed opportunity; a job opportunity; an opportunity for mischief; When opportunity knocks* (= offers itself), *seize it; an equal-opportunity employer.*

op·po·sa·ble (uh·POH·zuh·bul) *adj.* that may be opposed or placed against: *the opposable thumb of humans and the great apes.*

op·pose (uh·POZE) *v.* **op·pos·es, op·posed, op·pos·ing** be or place in the way of, against, or in contrast: *We oppose war; We resolutely, vehemently oppose your fighting; We oppose the resolution (that is being debated); You pick up objects by opposing thumb to fingers; Truth is* **opposed to** *falsehood; Humans,* **as opposed to** *beasts, can talk.*

op·po·site (OP·uh·zit) *adj.* set against or contrary to something: *"Truth" and "falsehood" have opposite meanings; They are as diametrically opposite as north and south; the house opposite to ours (across the street).* — *n.: Truth is the opposite of lying; "Truth" and "falsehood" are direct opposites.* — *prep. & adv.: the house opposite ours; the tree standing opposite; An actor plays opposite* (= in a complementary role, e.g. as husband and wife) *an actress or another actor.*

opposite number *n.* a person or thing corresponding to another in a different system or organization; counterpart.

op·po·si·tion (op·uh·ZISH·un) *n.* **1** an act of opposing or the state of being opposed or in contrast: *the opposition to the death penalty; A full moon is in opposition to* (= directly facing) *the sun; to arouse, crush, offer, overcome, put up, run up against, stir up opposition; fierce, stiff, vehement opposition; a bill passed over the opposition of the other parties.* **2** one that opposes: *The Government faces the Opposition during Question Period; an opposition party in parliament.*

op·press (uh·PRES) *v.* **1** keep down in a cruel way: *an oppressed minority; people oppressed by heavy taxes.*

2 weigh down; burden: *minds oppressed with anxiety.* — **op·pres·sion** (-PRESH·un) *n.* — **op·pres·sive** (-PRES·iv) *adj.: the oppressive heat of summer; oppressive laws, taxation.* — **op·pres·sive·ly** *adv.;* **op·pres·sive·ness** *n.* — **op·pres·sor** (-PRES·ur) *n.*

op·pro·bri·ous (uh·PROH·bree·us) *adj.* scornful or abusive: *an opprobrious epithet.* — **op·pro·bri·ous·ly** *adv.*

op·pro·bri·um (uh·PROH·bree·um) *n.* scornful condemnation; infamy: *a term of opprobrium.*

opt *v.* decide in favour of something: *to opt for a course of action; to opt to do something; to opt out of a group; Half the membership* **opted** (= dropped) **out.**

op·tic (OP·tic) *adj.* of the eye or eyesight: *the optic nerve.*

op·ti·cal (OP·tuh·cul) *adj.* having to do with light and vision: *an optical illusion, instrument; an optical* (= visual) *defect such as myopia; an* **optical character reader;** *an* **optical fibre** (= a fibre-optic strand); **optical scanning** *of graphic matter, as coded prices on goods, for computer processing;* **optical storage** *of computer data on compact disks read by laser beams.* — **op·ti·cal·ly** *adv.*

op·ti·cian (op·TISH·un) *n.* one who makes or sells eyeglasses.

op·tics *n. pl.* [takes sing. v.] a branch of physics dealing with light and its properties and phenomena.

op·ti·mism (OP·tuh·miz·um) *n.* the philosophy of looking on the bright side of things or of taking the most hopeful view: *The premier expressed optimism about the future of the province.* — **op·ti·mist** *n.* — **op·ti·mis·tic** (-MIS·tic) *adj.* hopeful: *The politician was cautiously optimistic about or over the future.*

op·ti·mum (OP·tuh·mum) **1** *adj.* best or most favourable for some end: *the optimum temperature for eggs to hatch.* **2** *n.* an amount, degree, condition, etc. that is optimum: *37.7 degrees Celsius is the optimum for hatching eggs.* — **op·ti·mal** (-mul) *adj.;* **op·ti·mal·ly** *adv.*

op·tion (OP·shun) *n.* the right or privilege of choosing: *the option of paying a fine or going to jail; a stock option to buy or sell stocks at a given price within a specified period; A publisher contracts for an option on an author's future work; They may exercise the option to bid on her next novel.*

op·tion·al (OP·shun·ul) *adj.* not required: *Ties are optional but shirts are a must; an optional course of study.* — **op·tion·al·ly** *adv.*

op·tom·e·try (op·TOM·uh·tree) *n.* the testing of eyes for vision and prescribing of glasses to correct defects. — **op·tom·e·trist** *n.*

op·u·lent (OP·yuh·lunt) *adj. Formal.* suggestive of great wealth and luxury: *the opulent court of a prince; opulent surroundings; an opulent* (= abundant) *growth of hair.* — **op·u·lence** *n.*

o·pus (OH·pus) *n., pl.* **op·er·a** or **o·pus·es** a work, esp. a musical composition, its number indicating the order of publication: *Beethoven's Symphony No. 8 in F major,*

Opus 93.

or *conj.* introducing an alternative (e.g. "black" or "white") or equivalent (e.g. "opus, or work").

-or *n. suffix.* 1 one that does as specified: *actor, creator, objector.* 2 an abstract quality or condition: *horror, pallor, terror.*

or·a·cle (OR·uh·cul) *n.* 1 a very wise person or his or her prophetic utterance. 2 in ancient Greece and Rome, an answer, often cryptically worded, given by a god to a crucial question put through a priest concerning the future. 3 such a priest or priestess or a place such as Delphi where oracles were delivered.
— o·rac·u·lar (aw·RAC·yuh·lur) *adj.;* o·rac·u·lar·ly *adv.*

o·ral (OR·ul) *adj.* having to do with the mouth: *Does a mouthwash help oral hygiene? an oral contraceptive* (= the Pill); *an oral* (= spoken) *examination; an* **oral history** *in the form of tape-recorded interviews with people of the time.*
— *n.: He passed his orals* (= oral tests).
— o·ral·ly *adv.*

or·ange (OR·inj) *n.* 1 a round, reddish-yellow, citrus fruit or the tree: *a mandarin orange; navel orange.* 2 a reddish yellow.
— *adj.* 1 of the colour of orange: *a bright orange necktie.* 2 **Orange** Irish-Protestant: *an Orange lodge; the Orange order; Ontario is becoming less and less Orange as immigration increases.*

o·ra·tion (o·RAY·shun) *n.* a rhetorical or ceremonial speech: *to deliver a funeral oration.*

or·a·tor (OR·uh·tur) *n.* an eloquent public speaker.
— or·a·tor·i·cal (·TOR·uh·cul) *adj.*

or·a·to·ry (OR·uh·tor·ee) *n.* **-ries** 1 skill in or the art of public speaking: *campaign oratory; mob oratory.* 2 a small chapel.

orb *n.* a globe, esp. the sun, moon, or other heavenly sphere.

or·bit *n.* a circular path, as of a planet or satellite: *"Sputnik" was the first artificial earth-satellite put into* or *in orbit; a service module in a parking orbit around* or *of* or *round the moon; the orbit* (= range) *of one's ambitions.*
— *v.* move in or put into an orbit: *an orbiting observatory.* — or·bit·al (·tul) *adj.* — or·bit·er *n.*

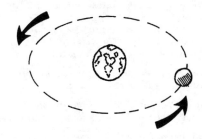

or·chard (OR·churd) *n.* 1 a plot containing fruit trees or nut trees. 2 the trees collectively.
— or·chard·ist or or·chard·man *n.*

or·ches·tra (OR·cuh·struh) *n.* 1 a group of musicians playing together on various stringed, wind, and percussion instruments: *to conduct, direct, lead an orchestra; An orchestra performs; a chamber, philharmonic, symphony, pops orchestra; an orchestra concert.* 2 the space, or **orchestra pit,** between the audience and the stage in a theatre. 3 the whole main floor of a theatre. — or·ches·tral (·KES·trul) *adj.*

or·ches·trate (OR·kis·trate) *v.* **-trates, -trat·ed, -trat·ing** 1 compose or arrange music, as for an orchestra: *to orchestrate a ballet.* 2 organize harmoniously: *a well-orchestrated effort.* — or·ches·tra·tion (·TRAY·shun) *n.*

or·chid (OR·kid) *n.* 1 any of a large family of beautiful flowers with three petals, including a specially shaped "lip," as in the lady-slipper; also, the plant. 2 a pale purple.

or·dain (or·DAIN) *v.* 1 decree or establish, as by a supreme power: *It happened as God had ordained from eternity.* 2 invest with one's office: *to ordain a minister, priest, rabbi; Joe was ordained priest by his bishop.*

or·deal (or·DEEL, OR·deel) *n.* a severe test or experience: *In ancient justice systems, the accused would undergo ordeals by combat, fire, water, etc.; The cross-examination was a trying ordeal.*

or·der (OR·dur) *n.* 1 an authoritative telling of what one wants; command or requisition: *"Go home" is an order, not a request; to carry out, execute, issue, obey, rescind, revoke, take, violate an order; an order to report for duty; a court, gag, restraining order; confined to bed on doctor's orders; marching orders; The sentry is under orders to shoot on sight.* 2 a request for goods or services in return for payment; also, such goods: *to cancel, fill, place, take a customer's order; delivery of an order; two orders of coffee; a money order* (= ordering document) *purchased at a bank.* 3 arrangement according to a system: *words in alphabetical order; events in chronological order; numerical order; arranged according to order of importance; She left the room in good order.* 4 systematic procedure: *a point of order raised in parliament; You're out of order, please withdraw your remark.* 5 harmony with what is considered good: *Governments establish order in society; Police try to maintain law and order; to restore order after a fight.* 6 a rank, grade, or class: *The squirrel, beaver, and rat families belong to the rodent order of the mammal class; Barons are the lowest order of nobles; an intellect of a high order; Brahmins are at the top of the pecking order in Hindu society; An old* (social) *order gives way to a new one.* 7 an organized religious or social group: *the Carmelite Order; a cloistered order; the Loyal Order of Moose.* 8 a form or style: *the Doric, Ionic, and Corinthian orders of Greek architecture.*
— **call to order** order a group or a member to be quiet: *The chair calls a meeting to order.*
— **in order** proper: *Celebrations are in order after a victory.*
— **in order that** so that.
— **in order to** as a means to; so as to.
— **in** (or **out**) **of order** working (or not) working properly, as a machine.
— **on order** ordered but not yet received.
— **on the order of** in the range of: *They got raises on the order of 10%.*

— **the order of the day** what is generally happening or is approved of: *Is vegetarianism becoming the order of the day?*
— **to order** as required by buyer: *a suit made to order.*
— *v.* 1 tell authoritatively; command: *Doctors order patients to bed; just what the doctor ordered; She ordered (food) for the whole family.* 2 arrange according to a system: *to order one's affairs, life.*
— **order about** or **around** tell someone to do this and that in a domineering way.

order-in-council (OR·dur·in·COWN·sul) *n., pl.* **orders-in-council** an order passed by a provincial or federal cabinet.

or·der·ly (OR·dur·lee) *adj.* 1 well-behaved. 2 well-organized.
— *adv.* in a well-organized manner.
— *n., pl.* **-lies** a male attendant, as in a hospital or in the service of an army officer.
— **or·der·li·ness** *n.*

Order of Canada *n. Cdn.* an honour conferred by the Government of Canada on Canadians, in the categories of "Member," "Officer," and "Companion" in ascending order, for outstanding achievements and services to society.

order paper *n.* agenda of a legislature: *Many bills die on the order paper (without being considered).*

or·di·nal (OR·duh·nul) *adj.* expressing order in a series.
— *n.* a number such as 1st, 2nd, 3rd, etc.

or·di·nance (OR·dun·unce) *n.* a law or regulation, esp. one issued by a local authority such as a municipality: *to adopt, apply, enforce an ordinance.*

or·di·nar·y (OR·duh·nair·ee) *adj.* 1 usual or normal: *an ordinary experience; Snow in summer is something out of the ordinary.* 2 common; hence, average or somewhat inferior: *an ordinary dress, poet, wine.*
— **or·di·nar·i·ly** (-NAIR·uh·lee) *adv.*

or·di·na·tion (or·duh·NAY·shun) *n.* an ordaining or being ordained as a priest, minister, or rabbi: *the ordination of women to the priesthood.*

ord·nance (ORD·nunce) *n.* 1 military weapons and ammunition: *naval ordnance.* 2 the tools used in their manufacture and maintenance.

ore *n.* rock or mineral from which gold, silver, iron, sulphur, fluorides, and such deposits may be extracted.

or·gan (OR·gun) *n.* 1 a keyboard musical instrument used esp. in churches for the solemnity and grandeur of its sound effects which are produced by air forced through pipes, as in a "pipe organ," or electrically, as in an "electronic organ." 2 any similar instrument such as a "hand organ" or "mouth organ." 3 a body part with a specific function: *the organs of digestion, locomotion, speech; the reproductive organs of plants and animals; sense, sensory, vital organs.* 4 means of action or communication: *The army is an organ of government; the offical organ (= periodical publication) of a group or party.*

or·gan·ic (or·GAN·ic) *adj.* 1 having to do with a bodily organ: *an organic (= not functional) disorder.* 2 relating to organization into a unit or whole, like that of a living organism: *the organic unity of a literary work; organic

architecture that seems to grow out of its surroundings.* 3 having to do with living things; animal or vegetable: *organic chemistry (of carbon compounds that make up living tissues); organic evolution, fertilizers; organic matter such as peat.* — **or·gan·i·cal·ly** *adv.*

or·gan·ism (OR·guh·niz·um) *n.* a living thing: *harmful, healthy, living organisms; A virus is a microscopic organism.*

or·gan·ist (OR·guh·nist) *n.* an organ player.

or·gan·i·za·tion (or·guh·nuh·ZAY·shun) *n.* 1 an arranging of parts into a whole: *An essay has to have some organization; Your work shows poor organization; Our party needs more organization and muscle.* 2 something organized, esp. a group: *to disband, dissolve, form an organization; business, charitable, nonprofit, philanthropic, professional, religious, student, youth organizations; The United Nations is an international organization;* **adj.**: *An* **organization chart** *shows company officers and departments; an* **organization man** *(dedicated to his company).*
— **or·gan·i·za·tion·al** *adj.*

or·gan·ize (OR·guh·nize) *v.* **-iz·es, -ized, -iz·ing** 1 make or form into a working unit or whole: *to organize a campaign, an essay, one's thoughts; earthworms and such less* **organized** *forms of life.* 2 form into a union or organization: *to organize the workers into a labour union; organized labour.* — **or·gan·iz·er** *n.*

or·gy (OR·jee) *n.* **-gies** 1 unrestrained indulgence in eating, drinking, sex, etc. 2 a party for it: *a drunken orgy.*

o·ri·ent (OR·ee·unt) *n.* 1 **the orient** [poetic use] the east. 2 **the Orient** East Asia, as distinguished from Europe and America.
— *adj.* rising: *the orient sun.*
— *v.* (-ent) place something or oneself in a specific direction: *Businesses are oriented towards profit-making; Employees have to orient themselves accordingly; to orient oneself (= adjust) to a new place.*

O·ri·en·tal (or·ee·EN·tul) *n.* a native of the Orient: *Chinese, Japanese, Koreans, etc. are Orientals.*
— *adj.*: *Oriental arts, cooking, eyes, food, glory, languages, music, pagodas, religions, rugs, silk, splendour, tastes; an oriental-looking bungalow; the difference between the Oriental and Occidental minds.* Also **oriental.**

o·ri·en·tate (OR·ee·en·tate) *v.* **-tates, -tat·ed, -tat·ing** 1 same as ORIENT. 2 to place facing east.
— **o·ri·en·ta·tion** (-TAY·shun) *n.*: *to give recruits an orientation (= introduction) to the new life; the orientation of new members; orientation rites.*

-oriented *combining form.* directed toward: *action-oriented, profit-oriented, sports-oriented.*

o·ri·en·teer·ing (OR·ee·un·TEER·ing) *n.* the sport of navigating through the woods with a map and compass.

or·i·fice (OR·uh·fis) *n.* a mouthlike opening or aperture, as of a tube.

or·i·gin (OR·uh·jin) *n.* 1 how or where something comes into being; beginning: *the origin of the universe; the origin of a river.* 2 ancestry or parentage: *one's land of *origin; a man of humble origin; The word "orgy" is of Greek origin* (= etymology); *"Dab" is of uncertain origin.* **3 origins** *pl.* where something originates; roots: *her aristocratic origins; the origins of civilization.*

o·rig·i·nal (uh·RIJ·uh·nul) *adj.* **1** initial or earliest: *the original inhabitants of the New World; a book translated from the original Latin (text).* **2** new; not copied: *a very original idea; an original work, not a translation; her original* (= inventive) *mind.* — *n.* the very first source or specimen: *a translation that is close to the original; Who was the original of the Mona Lisa?* — **o·rig·i·nal·ly** *adv.*

o·rig·i·nal·i·ty (uh·rij·uh·NAL·uh·tee) *n.* the quality of being original, fresh, or creative.

o·rig·i·nate (uh·RIJ·uh·nate) *v.* **-nates, -nat·ed, -nat·ing** come or bring into being, esp. as new: *Where did the rumour originate? Who originated it? Gossip originates from curiosity; It originates with people talking too much.* — **o·rig·i·na·tor** (-nay·tur) *n.*

or·na·ment (OR·nuh·munt) *n.* something added for greater beauty, as rings, bracelets, Christmas-tree decorations, etc.: *Beauty needs no ornament; a woman who is not just an ornament to her home.* — *v.* (-ment) beautify or embellish: *lace to ornament a dress.* — **or·na·men·ta·tion** (-men·TAY·shun) *n.* — **or·na·men·tal** (-MEN·tul) *adj.*

or·nate (or·NATE) *adj.* much ornamented: *an ornate vase; ornate* (= flowery) *prose.* — **or·nate·ly** *adv.;* **or·nate·ness** *n.*

or·ner·y (OR·nuh·ree) *adj. Informal.* mean or irritable: *an ornery beast, remark.*

or·phan (OR·fun) *n.* a child who has lost its parents: *a war orphan.* — *adj.:* *an orphan child; an orphan home (for orphans).* — *v.:* *Children are orphaned* (= made orphans) *by war, death, fire, etc.* — **or·phan·hood** *n.*

or·phan·age (OR·fuh·nij) *n.* an institution that takes care of orphans.

ortho- *combining form.* straight or correct: *orthodontics, orthodox, orthopedist.*

or·tho·don·tics (or·thuh·DON·tics) *n. pl.* [takes sing. v.] a branch of dentistry dealing with the correction of tooth irregularities, as by use of braces. — **or·tho·don·tic** *adj.* — **or·tho·don·tist** *n.*

or·tho·dox (OR·thuh·dox) *adj.* generally accepted or traditional, esp. in religious doctrine, practices, etc.: *an orthodox Jew; the Eastern Orthodox Church.* — **or·tho·dox·y** *n.*

or·thog·ra·phy (or·THOG·ruh·fee) *n.* **-phies** the study or a system of spelling. — **or·tho·graph·ic** (or·thuh·GRAF·ic) *adj.*

or·tho·pe·dics (or·thuh·PEE·dics) *n. pl.* [takes sing. v.] surgical correction and treatment of deformities, diseases, fractures, etc. of bones and joints. — **or·tho·pe·dic** *adj.* — **or·tho·pe·dist** *n.*

Or·well·i·an (or·WELL·ee·un) *adj.* of society, dehumanized and regimented, as in the novel "1984" by George Orwell.

Os·car (OS·cur) *n.* a statuette awarded annually by the Academy of Motion Picture Arts and Sciences of America to the best stars, directors, producers, etc.

os·cil·late (OS·uh·late) *v.* **-lates, -lat·ed, -lat·ing 1** swing like a pendulum. **2** vary, as an electric current; also, vacillate or waver: *to oscillate between hope and despair.* — **os·cil·la·tor** (-lay·tur) *n.* — **os·cil·la·tion** (-LAY·shun) *n.*

-ose *suffix* **1** *n.* carbohydrate: *cellulose, fructose.* **2** *adj.* full of or fond of something, as specified: *bellicose, jocose, verbose.*

-osis *suffix.* process or condition: *acidosis, metamorphosis, neurosis.*

os·mo·sis (oz·MOH·sis) *n.* the tendency of liquids and gases to pass through a semipermeable membrane or other porous material in order to equalize concentration on both sides: *Plant roots absorb minerals and oxygen enters the blood by osmosis.* — **os·mot·ic** (oz·MOT·ic) *adj.: osmotic pressure.*

os·si·fy (OS·uh·fye) *v.* **-fies, -fied, -fy·ing 1** change into bone, as cartilage in old people. **2** make or become hardened, as in practices, attitudes, etc. — **os·si·fi·ca·tion** (-fuh·CAY·shun) *n.*

os·ten·si·ble (os·TEN·suh·bul) *adj.* professed or seeming: *an ostensible reason, not the real one.* — **os·ten·si·bly** (-suh·blee) *adv.*

os·ten·ta·tion (os·ten·TAY·shun) *n.* a showy or pretentious display of wealth. — **os·ten·ta·tious** (-shus) *adj.*

os·tra·cize (OS·truh·size) *v.* **-ciz·es, -cized, -ciz·ing** banish someone from society, as in ancient Greece. — **os·tra·cism** (-siz·um) *n.*

os·trich *n.* a large, heavy, long-legged, flightless but swift-footed African bird, fabled to hide its head in the sand when frightened.

oth·er (UTH·ur, "TH" as in "the") *pron. & adj.* different person or thing from one already mentioned or implied: *my other car; Any other question? Other than that, I've nothing to say; Some other time, not now; One is Tom, who is the other? Tom, Dick, and others.* — **every other** every second person or thing. — **the other day** or **night** recently. — *adv.* otherwise: *He hasn't called other than* (= except) *to say "no."*

oth·er·wise (UTH·ur·wize) *adv.* **1** differently: *He should be alive today, but Fate willed otherwise; adj.:* *How could it be otherwise? whether living or otherwise* (= not); *conj.:* *Let's hurry, otherwise we may be late.* **2** in other respects: *an otherwise good record (except in math).*

oth·er·world·ly (uth·ur·WURLD·lee) *adj.* having to do with a world to come, as after death, or with things of the mind or imagination: *a man of otherworldly* (= spiritual) *concerns.* — **oth·er·world·li·ness** *n.*

o·ti·ose (OH·shee·oze, OH·tee·ose) *adj.* purposeless or useless: *otiose criticism, remarks.*

oua·na·niche (wah·nuh·NISH) *n. Cdn.* a small salmon native to freshwater lakes in Quebec and Ontario.

ouch *interj.* expressing sudden pain.

ought (AWT) *auxiliary v.* [expressing what is right, desirable, due, etc.]: *You ought to* (=should) *know better; She ought not be kept waiting.*

ought·n't (AWT·unt) ought not.

ounce *n.* 1 a unit of weight equal to 1/16 pound avoirdupois (28.35 g) or 1/12 pound troy (31.10 g). 2 a "fluid ounce" or 1/16 pint (29.57 ml).

our (OWR, AR) *adj.* possessive case of WE: *our books, dog, family.*
— **ours** *pron.*: *None of these is ours; Ours is a poodle.*

our·self (owr·SELF) *pron.* [used by courts, editors, and others using "we" instead of "I"] myself.

our·selves (owr·SELVZ) *pron.* reflexive or emphatic of WE or US: *We ourselves did it; We speak only for ourselves.*

oust (OWST) *v.* drive or force out; expel: *an unruly player ousted from a game.*

oust·er (OWS·tur) *n.* expulsion or eviction.

out *adv.* 1 away from the usual place, condition, etc., esp. away from the centre or inside of something; hence, into the open: *She has gone out; He dropped out of school; to let the dog out; when the moon comes out; an umbrella turned* **inside** *out; He stuck out his tongue; to farm out work; a* **coming-out** (= coming into society) *party.* 2 to completion or exhaustion: *She cried her heart out; fought it out with him; The lights are going out* (=off); *The batter flied out* (=was retired). 3 lacking or short: *I was out $10 after paying the bills; She was a few metres out* (=in error) *in her estimate.*
— **combining form.** 1 do something better than another: *outbid, outdistance, outfox; to out-Ripley Ripley.* 2 outside: *outdoors, outhouse, outlying, outpatient.*
— **out of** 1 away from: *Get out of the way; She was bilked out of her savings; We are out of luck; Such a high raise is out of the question* (=cannot be considered); *He is out of work* (=unemployed). 2 because of: *He cried out of pain.* 3 from: *a statue carved out of wood.*
— **adj.** 1 away: *Fashions are in (style) now and out (of style) later; the Out Islands of the Bahamas; an out tray for papers going out; The jury is still out* (=undecided) *on the case; before the year is out* (=finished); *Lights are out* (=not on). 2 forth or beyond; not inside: *to paint a house inside and out; He is out for a walk; She's out to a meeting; They are out on strike; His calculations are out* (=incorrect) *by $100; The book will be out* (=published) *in the fall.*
— **out for** in search of something: *On a picnic, we're out for fun.*
— **out of it** *Slang.* unaware or uninitiated: *He is so out of it, he doesn't know who the latest hockey stars are.*
— **out to** intent on: *He's out to make money.*
— **v.** be discovered: *Murder will out.*
— **prep.** through or along: *He went out the door; We were driving out Lakeshore Road when the news came out over the radio.*
— **n.** 1 one that is out: *people considered outs in an exclusive society.* 2 exit or excuse: *He was without an out or alibi; She knows all the ins and outs* (=details) *of*

the business.
— **on the outs** *Informal.* at odds: *He's on the outs with his colleagues.*

out·age (OW·tij) *n.* an interruption or suspension, as a power failure.

out-and-out (OUT·un·out) *adj.* utter or complete: *an out-and-out denial, falsehood, radical.*

out·back *n.* back country; hinterland: *Elliot Lake is in the outbacks of Ontario.*

out·bal·ance (out·BAL·unce) *v.* -anc·es, -anced, -anc·ing outweigh.

out·bid (out·BID) *v.* -bids, *pt. & pp.* -bid or -bid·den, -bid·ding make a higher bid than another: *She outbid him for the contract.*

out·board *adj.* outside the hull or body of a boat or other craft: *An outboard motor is fitted to a boat's stern.*
— **n.** an outboard motor or a boat equipped with one.

out·bound *adj.* travelling outward.

out·break *n.* a sudden occurrence or development, as of a war, disease, etc.

out·build·ing (OUT·bil·ding) *n.* a building separate from the main building.

out·burst *n.* a bursting out, as of applause, fury, laughter, joy, etc.: *an angry, sudden, violent outburst.*

out·cast *adj.* cast out from home or society.
— **n.** an outcast person or animal.

out·caste (OUT·cast) *n.* a member of the lowest caste of Hindus; an untouchable.

out·class (out·CLAS) *v.* surpass.

out·come *n.* result or consequence: *the final outcome of the negotiations.*

out·crop *n.* an exposed surface of a rock or stratum.
— **v.** project or appear on the surface.

out·cry *n.* -cries a crying out or scream; hence, an uproar: *a public outcry against the proposed new taxes.*

out·dat·ed (out·DAY·tid) *adj.* out-of-date or obsolete.

out·dis·tance (out·DIS·tunce) *v.* -tanc·es, -tanced, -tanc·ing outstrip.

out·do (out·DOO) *v.* -does, -did, -done, -do·ing do better than others, previously, etc.

out·door *adj.* of the outdoors; open-air: *an outdoor theatre.*

out·doors *n.* open air: *a lover of the great outdoors; as big as all outdoors.*
— **adv.** in or into the open air: *He's gone outdoors; Lee likes to sleep outdoors.*

out·draw (out·DRAW) *v.* -draws, -drew, -draw·ing 1 attract a larger crowd than another person or thing: *The football game outdrew the movie.* 2 draw a gun faster than someone else.

out·er *adj.* 1 farther out: *an outer circle; the* **outer city** (=suburbs). 2 external: *the outer ear; an outer garment.*

out·er·most (OU·tur·most) *adj.* farthest from the centre.

outer space *n.* 1 space immediately beyond the atmosphere. 2 interstellar space.

out·er·wear (OU·tur·ware) *n.* clothes worn on the outside or over other clothes, as gloves, sweaters, jackets, coats, etc.

out·face *v.* -fac·es, -faced, -fac·ing face someone boldly.

out·field *n.* in baseball, the playing area or players beyond the infield. — **out·field·er** *n.*

out·fit *n.* 1 a group such as a business organization or military unit. 2 equipment for an activity. 3 a set of clothes: *a holiday outfit.*
— *v.* -fits, -fit·ted, -fit·ting equip: *He came outfitted for a camping trip; to outfit an expedition;* **out·fit·ter** *n.*

out·flank (out·FLANK) *v.* outmanoeuvre or outwit, as by getting around the flank of enemy troops.

out·flow *n.* a flowing out or what flows out.

out·fox *v.* outwit or outsmart.

out·gen·er·al (out·JEN·ur·ul) *v.* surpass in leadership.

out·go *n.* -goes expenditure.

out·go·ing (OUT·go·ing) *adj.* 1 sociable: *an outgoing woman.* 2 going out: *outgoing mail; the outgoing tide; the outgoing* (= retiring or defeated) *president.*

out·grow (out·GROH) *v.* -grows, -grew, -grown, -grow·ing grow faster than someone, grow too large for clothes, or grow out of early habits, friendships, etc.

out·growth *n.* a growing out; offshoot; hence, a result or development.

out·guess (out·GUESS) *v.* defeat by anticipating; outwit: *She outguessed the others and was first to get in when the doors opened.*

out·house *n.* a small outbuilding, esp. one used as a toilet.

out·ing *n.* a short pleasure trip, ride, walk, etc.: *They went on an outing in the park.*

out·land·ish (out·LAN·dish) *adj.* very strange or bizarre.

out·last (out·LAST) *v.* last longer than something else; outlive.

out·law *n.* a person deprived of legal rights, as a notorious criminal.
— *v.* declare a person to be an outlaw or make something illegal: *Chemical warfare has been outlawed.*

out·law·ry (OUT·law·ree) *n.* the condition of being an outlaw.

out·lay *n.* 1 a spending of money or other resources as an investment: *to make outlays for installing new machinery.* 2 what is spent: *a huge outlay of $10 million.*
— *v.* (out·LAY) -lays, -laid, -lay·ing expend.

out·let *n.* 1 a means of letting something out, as from a container: *an outlet from a lake; an outlet to the sea; to plug a lamp into an electrical outlet; an outlet for one's energies, emotions.* 2 a market or store: *a factory outlet; retail outlet.*

out·line *n.* 1 the shape or main features of a subject: *to draw up* or *make an outline; to draw a map* **in outline;** **the outlines** of a project. 2 a drawing, plan, or summary giving an outline: *the rough outline of a plan; an outline of Canadian literature.*
— *v.* -lines, -lined, -lin·ing give or define in outline: *a skyscraper outlined against the sky; He outlined his proposals for a settlement.*

out·live (out·LIV) *v.* -lives, -lived, -liv·ing live longer than something else; survive: *Cannons have outlived their usefulness.*

out·look *n.* 1 what one sees with the mind, esp. about the future; point of view or prospects: *Gita has a cheerful outlook on life; a bright, dismal, gloomy, healthy, long-range, positive outlook; the outlook for the future.* 2 what one sees on looking out; view: *the outlook from the top of the tower.* 3 a place to look out from; lookout.

out·ly·ing (OUT·lye·ing) *adj.* lying outside the limits or away from the centre: *an outlying district.*

out·ma·noeu·vre (out·muh·NEW·vur) *v.* -vres, -vred, -vring defeat by manoeuvring; outwit.
Also **out·ma·neu·ver.**

out·mod·ed (out·MOH·did) *adj.* out of fashion or out-of-date.

out·num·ber (out·NUM·bur) *v.* exceed in number: *Boys outnumber girls in our school.*

out-of-bounds *adj. & adv.* outside one's limits, as in a game or when straying.

out-of-date *adj.* old-fashioned or obsolete.

out-of-door *adj.* same as OUTDOOR.

out-of-doors *adv.* same as OUTDOORS.

out-of-the-way (OUT·uv·thuh·WAY) *adj.* 1 not commonly known; unusual: *out-of-the-way information; There's nothing out-of-the-way about his manner.* 2 remote or unfrequented: *an out-of-the-way farm, eating place.*

out-of-town·er (OUT·uv·TOWN·ur) *n. Informal.* someone from out of town.

out·pa·tient (out·PAY·shunt) *n.* a patient not staying in the hospital while being treated.

out·per·form (out·pur·FORM) *v.* achieve better results than another: *The new car outperforms the old one.*

out·play (out·PLAY) *v.* play better than another.

out·point (out·POINT) *v.* win more points than someone else.

out·port *n. Cdn.* a coastal fishing village in Newfoundland.

out·post *n.* 1 a base or camp, esp. military, away from the main camp: *the last outposts of a vanishing empire.* 2 the personnel assigned to an outpost. 3 a frontier settlement.

out·pour·ing (out·POR·ing) *n.* a pouring out, esp. an uncontrolled expression: *the outpourings of a tortured soul.*

out·pull (out·PULL) *v.* attract a larger crowd than something else.

out·put *n.* 1 the amount of work done, esp. over a period, as of a machine: *the monthly output of the oil well; to increase* or *step up the output.* 2 a form in which processed information is put out by a computer: *printout, visual display, and other outputs; an output device.*
— *v.* -puts, -put·ted, -put·ting produce as output.

out·rage *n.* 1 a gross violation of the rights or feelings of others: *an outrage against humanity.* 2 extreme offence felt or anger aroused by such a violation: *It's an outrage that such a crime could go unpunished.*
— *v.* -rag·es, -raged, -rag·ing: *a massacre that outraged humanity; He felt outraged by the false report.*

out·ra·geous (out·RAY·jus) *adj.* extremely offensive or shocking: *an outrageous crime, demand, insult; outrageous prices.* — **out·ra·geous·ly** *adv.*

out·rank (out·RANK) *v.* rank higher than another: *An army major outranks a captain.*

out·reach (out·REECH) *v.* reach out; also, overreach.
— *n.* the act of reaching out or its extent: *an outreach program for the disadvantaged.*

out·rid·er (OUT·rye·dur) *n.* 1 an attendant on horseback accompanying a carriage or wagon: *the outriders of a chuckwagon (in chuckwagon racing).* 2 any mounted attendant.

out·rig·ger (OUT·rig·ur) *n.* a boat or canoe equipped with a projecting bracket or framework on either side for supporting the oars or for steadying the craft.

out·right *adj.* complete or utter: *an outright denial, falsehood; an outright and unconditional offer.*
— *adv.*: *She denied the story outright; The fox was run over and killed outright* (= then and there).

out·run (out·RUN) *v.* -runs, -ran, -run·ning 1 run faster than someone else. 2 exceed: *He went broke when he allowed his spending to outrun his income.*

out·sell (out·SEL) *v.* -sells, -sold, -sell·ing sell more than another.

out·set *n.* a setting out; start: *at the outset of her career; From the outset, he has been doing well in his job.*

out·shine (out·SHINE) *v.* -shines, *pt. & pp.* -shone or -shined, -shin·ing shine more brightly than another; hence, surpass.

out·side *n.* an outer side or location: *to wash the outside of a car; a favourable impression from the outside; To people in the North, the rest of Canada is the outside.*
— *adj.* 1 exterior: *a house in need of inside and outside repairs.* 2 remote: *an outside chance, possibility.*
— *adv. & prep.* on or to the outside of something: *She's waiting outside (the door).*
— **at the outside** at the most.
— **outside of** *Informal.* with the exception of: *She wouldn't accept any money outside of expenses.*

out·sid·er (out·SYE·dur) *n.* one from outside a group or region: *Nonresidents are outsiders to Northerners.*

out·size *n.* 1 an unusually large size. 2 an outsize garment. — **out·size** or **out·sized** *adj.*

out·skirts *n. pl.* districts away from the centre, as of a city; outer borders: *Richmond is on the outskirts of Vancouver.*

out·smart (out·SMART) *v.* outdo in smartness or by cunning.

out·spend (out·SPEND) *v.* -spends, -spent, -spend·ing spend more than a limit, another person, etc.

out·spo·ken (out·SPOH·kun) *adj.* open and blunt in speech: *an outspoken critic; He's quite outspoken in his comments.* — **out·spo·ken·ly** *adv.*; **out·spo·ken·ness** *n.*

out·spread (out·SPRED) *adj.* extended: *a bird with its wings outspread; with outspread arms.*

out·stand·ing (out·STAN·ding) *adj.* 1 standing out from the rest; prominent: *an outstanding leader; quite outstanding as a lawyer; She's outstanding in her accomplishments as a lawyer.* 2 unsettled: *debts still outstanding.* — **out·stand·ing·ly** *adv.*

out·sta·tion (OUT·stay·shun) *n.* an outpost in an unsettled area.

out·stay (out·STAY) *v.* stay longer than someone; overstay: *to outstay one's welcome.*

out·stretched (out·STRECHT) *adj.* stretched out; outspread.

out·strip (out·STRIP) *v.* -strips, -stripped, -strip·ping go faster than someone; hence, surpass.

out·vote (out·VOTE) *v.* -votes, -vot·ed, -vot·ing defeat someone in voting.

out·ward (OUT·wurd) *adj.* 1 external: *the outward man; outward appearance, beauty, behaviour.* 2 moving or turned toward the outside: *an outward journey.*
— *adv.* toward the outside: *an outward-bound journey; lines diverging outward from the centre;* also **outwards.**
— **out·ward·ly** *adv.*: *the outwardly respectable hypocrite; the outwardly cautious and inwardly conniving schemer.*

out·wear (out·WARE) *v.* -wears, -wore, -worn, -wear·ing 1 of fabrics, etc., last longer than another fabric in wearing. 2 wear out. 3 become out of date: *outworn furniture, ideas, machinery, metaphors, values.*

out·weigh (out·WAY) *v.* exceed in weight, importance, etc.: *These reasons far outweigh the others.*

out·wit (out·WIT) *v.* -wits, -wit·ted, -wit·ting overcome by superior intelligence or cleverness.

out·work *n.* a small defensive fortification outside the main one.
— *v.* (out·WURK) outdo by working harder, better, etc.

out·worn *adj.* See OUTWEAR.

ova *pl.* of OVUM.

o·val (OH·vul) *n. & adj.* anything egg-shaped or like an ellipse.

Oval Office *n.* the U.S. President's office; hence, the Presidency.

o·va·ry (OH·vuh·ree) *n.* -ries the egg-containing reproductive organ of a female: *A flowering plant's ovary is the seed-producing part.*
— **o·var·i·an** (oh·VAIR·ee·un) *adj.*

o·va·tion (oh·VAY·shun) *n.* enthusiastic applause, with clapping or cheering: *The ballerina got* or *received a standing ovation; a thunderous ovation.*

ov·en (UV·un) *n.* a chamber in a stove or near a fireplace for baking, heating, etc.: *to light, turn off, turn on an oven; a convection oven; microwave oven; self-cleaning oven.*

o·ver (OH·vur) *prep.* **1** above: *a roof over our heads; Who's over you at work?* **2** all through: *We flew over the city; That happened over* (= during) *a long period.* **3** beyond: *Europe lies over the ocean; She is doing over 100 km/h; He leaped over the wall.* **4** about: *to brood over failures.* **5** by means of: *news sent over the airwaves.*
— adv. [indicating an action as carried across or beyond a place or time]: *Hand it over to us; He fell over on his face; Let's talk things over; She's sleeping over at her friend's; Turn over the page; I'm not over* (= very) *tired; Say it over and over* (= again and again) *till you know it by heart.*
— adj. at an end; finished: *The game is over; We are over with it; It's all over between Guy and Gigi; He isn't over borrowing her car.*
— over and out message finished.
— prefix [added without a hyphen to adjectives to mean "too" and to nouns and verbs to mean "too much," as in the following compounds. Compounds whose basic meaning and pronunciation are not the same as in the base word are entered and explained below].

o·ver·act (oh·vur·ACT) *v.* exaggerate in acting a part.

o·ver·age 1 (oh·vur·AGE) *adj.* past the age of usefulness, eligibility, etc. **2** (OH·vur·ij) *n.* surplus or excess.

o·ver·all (OH·vur·all) **1** *adj.* including everything: *overall expenses; an overall operating budget;* **adv.***: It measures two metres overall.* **2 overalls** *n. pl.* loose-fitting trousers with an attached piece to cover the chest, worn by workers to protect their clothes.

o·ver·arm (OH·vur·arm) *adj.* with the arm raised over the shoulder, as in swimming; also, overhand.

o·ver·awe (oh·vur·AW) *v.* -awes, -awed, -aw·ing awe someone into submission; inspire awe in someone.

o·ver·bal·ance (oh·vur·BAL·unce) *v.* -anc·es, -anced, -anc·ing **1** outweigh in amount or value. **2** cause to lose balance and tip over.

o·ver·bear·ing (oh·vur·BAIR·ing) *adj.* domineering or dictatorial.

o·ver·blown (oh·vur·BLONE) *adj.* exaggerated or inflated: *overblown demands, legends, nationalism, praise, tales.*

o·ver·board *adv.* over the side of a ship into the water: *to fall overboard.*
— go overboard *Informal.* act in an overenthusiastic manner: *He is going overboard over* or *about* or *for the new car.*

o·ver·cast (oh·vur·CAST) *adj.* cloudy or dark: *an overcast sky.*

o·ver·charge (oh·vur·CHARJ) *v.* -charg·es, -charged, -charg·ing **1** charge too much. **2** overload with burden or force. **— n.***: an overcharge of $25.*

o·ver·clothes (OH·vur·clothes) *n. pl.* same as OUTERWEAR.

o·ver·cloud (oh·vur·CLOUD) *v.* cloud over or darken.

o·ver·coat (OH·vur·coat) *n.* a usually heavy outer coat worn in cold weather.

o·ver·come (oh·vur·CUM) *v.* -comes, -came, -come, -com·ing conquer or overpower: *She was overcome by fatigue.*

o·ver·do (oh·vur·DOO) *v.* -does, -did, -done, -do·ing do too much or carry to excess: *She overdid* (= overacted) *her part in the play; an overdone* (= overcooked) *steak.*

o·ver·dose (OH·vur·dose) *n.* a larger dose than is safe: *The actress took a fatal* or *lethal overdose of sleeping pills.*
— v. -dos·es, -dosed, -dos·ing: *She overdosed on sleeping pills.*

o·ver·draft (OH·vur·draft) *n.* an overdrawing or the sum overdrawn.

o·ver·draw (oh·vur·DRAW) *v.* -draws, -drew, -drawn, -draw·ing **1** draw from an account more money than there is in it. **2** exaggerate in drawing or portraying.

o·ver·dress (oh·vur·DRES) *v.* dress too elaborately or showily.

o·ver·drive (OH·vur·drive) *n.* in an automobile transmission, a higher gear or forward speed available automatically without strain on the engine when the vehicle is cruising at a certain speed in top gear.

o·ver·due (oh·vur·DUE) *adj.* due some time back; late: *an overdue payment, train; Your payment is past overdue; an overdue baby (who should have been born by now).*

o·ver·es·ti·mate (oh·vur·ES·tuh·mate) *v.* -mates, -mat·ed, -mat·ing set or provide too high an estimate for something.

o·ver·ex·pose (OH·vur·ex·POZE) *v.* -pos·es, -posed, -pos·ing expose a photographic film too long.
— o·ver·ex·po·sure (OH·vur·ex·POH·zhur) *n.*

o·ver·flight (OH·vur·flite) *n.* a flight in an aircraft over a territory.

o·ver·flow (oh·vur·FLOH) *v.* flow over: *A river overflows (its banks) during a flood; The crowd overflowed into the hallways; an overflowing cup; hearts overflowing with happiness.*
— n. 1 a flood. **2** a surplus or excess; **adj.***: an overflow crowd, pipe.*

o·ver·fly (oh·vur·FLY) *v.* -flies, -flew, -fly·ing fly over a place in an airplane.

o·ver·grow (oh·vur·GROH) *v.* -grows, -grew, -grown, -grow·ing **1** grow over: *a garden overgrown with weeds.* **2** outgrow or grow too fast. **— o·ver·growth** *n.*

o·ver·hand (OH·vur·hand) *adv. & adj.* made with the hand raised above the elbow, as in playing tennis; overarm: *an overhand stroke in tennis or handball; an overhand throw.*

o·ver·hang (oh·vur·HANG) *v.* -hangs, -hung, -hang·ing **1** hang or project over. **2** hang over in a gloomy or threatening manner: *the overhanging threat of war.*
— n. (OH·vur·hang) a jutting out: *the overhang of an upper storey over the lower.*

o·ver·haul (oh·vur·HAWL) *v.* examine machines thoroughly and repair as necessary.
— *n.* (OH·vur·hawl) an overhauling: *a major, thorough overhaul of the engine.*

o·ver·head (oh·vur·HED) *adj. & adv.* operating or located above: *cables running overhead; the sun overhead; a garage's overhead door; an overhead projector to throw images above the lecturer; an overhead* (= overhand) *smash.*
— *n.* (OH·vur·hed) business expenses such as rent, maintenance, utilities, etc. covering all operations: *The company's overhead is only about 8% of its earnings.*

o·ver·hear (oh·vur·HEER) *v.* -hears, -heard, -hear·ing hear a speaker or what is spoken without the speaker's being aware of it.

o·ver·joy (oh·vur·JOY) *v.* fill with great joy.
— **o·ver·joyed** *adj.: We're overjoyed to hear about your victory.*

o·ver·kill (OH·vur·kil) *n.* capacity in excess of what is required to achieve an objective, esp. to kill with nuclear power; excessive killing power: *The media blitz was a promotional overkill;* also *v.*

o·ver·land (OH·vur·land) *adj. & adv.* across, by, or on land: *an overland route; They travelled overland to the East.*

o·ver·lap (oh·vur·LAP) *v.* -laps, -lapped, -lap·ping lap or lay over: *roof shingles that overlap (each other).*
— *n.* (OH·vur·lap) an overlapping: *There's an hour's overlap between the day and night shifts.*

o·ver·lay (oh·vur·LAY) *v.* -lays, -laid, -lay·ing place over another; also, cover or finish with something: *a dome overlaid with gold.*
— *n.* (OH·vur·lay) something laid over: *a map with colour overlays showing special features.*

o·ver·lie (oh·vur·LYE) *v.* -lies, -lay, -lain, -ly·ing lie on or over: *The puppy was overlain (and smothered) in sleep by its own mother.*

o·ver·load (OH·vur·lode) *n.* too heavy a load.
— *v.* (oh·vur·LODE): *an overloaded truck; Air-conditioners overloaded the circuit.*

o·ver·look (oh·vur·LOOK) *v.* **1** look over from above; hence, watch or oversee: *a room overlooking* (= giving a view of) *the harbour.* **2** fail to see: *She was not ignored but overlooked in the hurry; a taskmaster who never overlooks* (= ignores or excuses) *our shortcomings.*

o·ver·lord (OH·vur·lord) *n.* one with power over other lords.

o·ver·ly (OH·vur·lee) *adv.* too much; excessively: *I'm not overly excited about the plan.*

o·ver·much (oh·vur·MUCH) *adj., adv. & n.* too much.

o·ver·night (oh·vur·NITE) *adj.* during the night: *an overnight journey, stay, stop, telegram.*
— *adv.: They got ready overnight to start at dawn; a problem difficult to solve overnight* (= quickly).

o·ver·pass (OH·vur·pass) *n.* a crossing at a higher level, as a bridge over a road or railway: *a pedestrian overpass.*

o·ver·play (oh·vur·PLAY) *v.* exaggerate the importance of something or be overoptimistic about an advantage one has: *He lost his bid by overplaying his hand.*

o·ver·pow·er (oh·vur·POW·ur) *v.* conquer by superior power; overwhelm.

o·ver·qual·i·fied (oh·vur·KWOL·uh·fide) *adj.* too highly qualified, esp. for a job.

o·ver·rate (oh·vur·RATE) *v.* -rates, -rat·ed, -rat·ing rate or value too highly.

o·ver·reach (oh·vur·REECH) *v.* **1** outwit, esp. by cunning. **2** be too clever or crafty.

o·ver·re·act (OH·vur·ree·ACT) *v.* react in an excessive or uncalled-for manner, as by an outburst.

o·ver·ride (oh·vur·RIDE) *v.* -rides, -rode, -rid·den, -rid·ing overrule or prevail over something: *The U.S. Congress could override a presidential veto; The Rights Charter may override a law; A constitutional change is required for overriding the Charter; an **overriding** concern, factor, interest, reason.*

o·ver·rule (oh·vur·ROOL) *v.* -rules, -ruled, -rul·ing set aside or decide against something: *His objection was overruled.*

o·ver·run (oh·vur·RUN) *v.* -runs, -ran, -run·ning **1** of enemies, weeds, vermin, etc., run over or occupy a place causing harm: *a lawn overrun with weeds.* **2** go beyond: *to overrun a time limit.*
— *n.* (OH·vur·run) an overrunning: *a cost overrun of 50%.*

o·ver·sea (oh·vur·SEE) *adj. & adv.* beyond the sea; abroad: *oversea communications; an oversea trip.*
— **o·ver·seas** (-SEEZ) *adj. & adv.: He went overseas for higher studies; an overseas assignment, investment, territory.*

o·ver·see (oh·vur·SEE) *v.* -sees, -saw, -seen, -see·ing supervise or manage. — **o·ver·se·er** (OH·vur·see·ur) *n.*

o·ver·shad·ow (oh·vur·SHAD·oh) *v.* be more brilliant than someone else; surpass.

o·ver·shoe (OH·vur·shoo) *n.* a galosh or similar outer shoe.

o·ver·shoot (oh·vur·SHOOT) *v.* -shoots, -shot, -shoot·ing **1** shoot over or beyond a target. **2** go or pass beyond a limit: *The aircraft overshot the runway and ended up in a ditch.*

o·ver·sight (OH·vur·site) *n.* an act of overlooking; failure to notice: *an error due to (an) oversight; We left her name out by or through an oversight.*

o·ver·size or **o·ver·sized** *adj.* larger in size than ordinary.

o·ver·sleep (oh·vur·SLEEP) *v.* -sleeps, -slept, -sleep·ing sleep longer than intended; sleep in.

o·ver·spread (oh·vur·SPRED) *v.* -spreads, -spread, -spread·ing spread over or cover something: *At the mention of the name, a blush overspread his countenance.*

o·ver·state (oh·vur·STATE) *v.* -states, -stat·ed, -stat·ing exaggerate: *to overstate a case.* — **o·ver·state·ment** *n.*

o·ver·stay (oh·vur·STAY) *v.* stay beyond: *to overstay a time limit, one's welcome.*

o·ver·step (oh·vur·STEP) *v.* -steps, -stepped, -step·ping go beyond the limits of something; exceed.

o·ver·stuff (oh·vur·STUF) *v.* stuff with too much of something: *He uses overstuffed upholstery for extra comfort.*

o·vert (OH·vurt, oh·VURT) *adj.* done or manifested openly: *an overt act; overt behaviour, hostility.*
— **o·vert·ly** *adv.*

o·ver·take (oh·vur·TAKE) *v.* -takes, -took, -tak·en, -tak·ing catch up with or pass a moving person or thing: *He was ticketed for overtaking a school bus while its signals were flashing; Fate overtook the Titanic on its maiden voyage.*

over-the-counter (OH·vur·the·COWN·tur) *adj.* sold directly: *over-the-counter drugs (sold without a prescription); over-the-counter trading (of securities not listed on a stock exchange).*

o·ver·throw (oh·vur·THROH) *v.* -throws, -threw, -thrown, -throw·ing defeat or destroy: *charged with plotting to overthrow the government.*
— *n.* (OH·vur·throh) defeat or destruction.

o·ver·time (OH·vur·time) *n.* 1 time in excess of what is standard. 2 the pay for working overtime: *Casual workers get no overtime.*
— *adj. & adv.:* *a game still tied at the end of two overtime periods; fined for overtime parking; He works overtime to double his income.*

o·ver·tone (OH·vur·tone) *n.* 1 in music, a higher tone heard in harmony with a fundamental note that is sounded. 2 a suggestion or implication: *The air was tense with overtones of rebellion; a question with racial overtones.*

o·ver·ture (OH·vur·chur) *n.* 1 a proposal or offer to negotiate: *We made several overtures to the other party for a settlement of the dispute.* 2 a musical composition designed as a prelude or introduction, esp. to an opera: *to compose, perform, play an overture.*

o·ver·turn (oh·vur·TURN) *v.* turn something over; upset: *an overturned truck.*
— *n.* (OH·vur·turn) an overturning.

o·ver·view (OH·vur·view) *n.* a brief survey or summary.

o·ver·ween·ing (oh·vur·WEE·ning) *adj.* conceited or arrogant: *overweening pride, vanity.*

o·ver·weigh (oh·vur·WAY) *v.* 1 outweigh. 2 weigh down or oppress.

o·ver·weight (OH·vur·wait) *n. & adj.* a weight over the standard or normal weight: *He is overweight; suffering from overweight.*

o·ver·whelm (oh·vur·WHELM) *v.* 1 engulf: *a swimmer overwhelmed by the waves.* 2 overcome: *She was overwhelmed by superior forces; overwhelmed with grief at her child's death; overwhelming* (= great) *gratitude, indifference, majority, sorrow, victory.*
— **o·ver·whelm·ing·ly** *adv.*

o·ver·win·ter (oh·vur·WIN·tur) *v.* pass the winter.

o·ver·wrought (oh·vur·RAWT) *adj.* 1 exhausted by too much work or excitement. 2 too elaborate or ornate.

o·vum (OH·vum) *n., pl.* -va (-vuh) an unfertilized egg.

owe (OH) *v.* owes, owed, ow·ing be in debt for something to someone: *I owe you nothing; We owe much to our country; Joe owes* (= bears) *her a grudge; a chronic borrower always owing for something.*
— **owing to** because of; on account of.

owl *n.* a nocturnal bird of prey with large round eyes and tufts of feathers resembling horns or ears on the heads of some species, characterized by its hooting call.
— **owl·ish** *adj.;* **owl·ish·ly** *adv.*

owl·et (OW·lit) *n.* a young or small owl.

own (OHN) *v.* have as one's property or as belonging to one: *I only work here, I don't own the place; a waif whom his parents would not own; He owned* (= admitted) *he had been misled; owned to having lied; She had to own up* (= confess) *to the deed or to doing it.*
— *adj. & pron.:* *to each his own; my own children; your own business.*
— **come into one's own** get what is rightfully one's: *Women have been coming into their own since the 1970s.*
— **hold one's own** defend oneself.
— **of one's own** belonging to oneself: *problems of his own that are not our fault.*
— **on one's own** doing what one wants without help.
— **own·er** *n.* — **own·er·ship** *n.*

ox *n., pl.* **ox·en** (OX·un) 1 a heavy-bodied, long-tailed, cloven-hoofed, cud-chewing animal such as a cow, buffalo, bison, or yak: *the bellowing of oxen; strong as an ox.* 2 a castrated bull used for beef or as a draft animal.

ox·blood (OX·blud) *n.* a deep red colour.

oxen *pl.* of ox.

ox·ford (OX·furd) *n.* 1 a low shoe that is laced over the instep. 2 a cloth of cotton or rayon used for shirts and blouses.

Oxford grey *n.* a dark grey colour.

ox·i·dize (OX·uh·dize) *v.* -diz·es, -dized, -diz·ing combine with oxygen, as metal in rusting or when a substance burns in air. — **ox·i·diz·er** *n.*
— **ox·i·diz·a·ble** (-dye·zuh·bul) *adj.*

ox·y·gen (OX·uh·jun) *n.* a colourless, odourless gaseous element occurring in the atmosphere that is essential to life and for combustion. — **ox·y·gen·ic** (-JEN·ic) *adj.*

ox·y·gen·ate (OX·uh·juh·nate) *v.* -ates, -at·ed, -at·ing treat or combine with oxygen, as in making hydrogen peroxide or in a heart-lung machine. — **ox·y·gen·a·tor** (-nay·tur) *n.* — **ox·y·gen·a·tion** (-NAY·shun) *n.*

oxygen tent *n.* a hood or canopy put over the bed of a patient to provide an extra supply of oxygen.

oys·ter (OIS·tur) *n.* a bivalve marine mollusc valued as food and for the pearls found in certain kinds: *"The world's mine oyster"* (= place for making a profit, like extracting a pearl from an oyster).
— *adj.:* an **oyster bar** *(where oysters are served); an* **oyster bed** *(where oysters breed); oyster farmers, harvests, shells;* **oyster sauce** (= a variety of soy sauce).

oys·ter·ing (OY·stur·ing) *n.* the work of taking oysters from the sea.

o·zone (OH·zone) *n.* a form of oxygen with a sharp odour, formed in air by electric discharges and remaining as a layer in the ozonosphere: *Skin cancer could result from exposure to the sun's ultraviolet rays if the protective ozone layer or shield is depleted by pollution.* — **o·zon·ic** (oh·ZON·ic) *adj.*

o·zon·o·sphere (oh·ZON·us·feer) *n.* a region of the atmosphere up to 48.28 km (38 miles) above the earth in which ozone is found.

Pp

P or **p** (PEE) *n.* **P's** or **p's 1** the 16th letter of the English alphabet. **2** something symbolized by P, as the 16th in a series, or something shaped like the letter. — **mind one's P's and Q's** be very careful about every detail: *Dictionary editors have to mind their P's and Q's.*

pa (PAH, PAW) *n. Informal.* father.

pab·lum *n.* a food, esp. something watered down or simplified: *The book is poor pablum for a 12-year-old;* **Pablum** *Trademark.*

pace *n.* **1** a step in walking: *It's three paces from my desk to the door.* **2** relative speed of movement: *the fast pace of city life; He works at a leisurely pace; a brisk, frantic, slow, sluggish, snail's pace; A change of pace will make you less tense; He's too fast to* **keep pace with;** *an energetic person who* **sets the pace** *(for others to keep up with) at work.* **3** a manner of walking, esp. a horse's ambling gait. — **put someone through his** or **her paces** test or demonstrate someone's abilities. — *v.* **pac·es, paced, pac·ing 1** walk with regular steps: *The anxious parents paced up and down outside the operation theatre; We* **paced off** *the room to measure it (as so many steps long or wide).* **2** lead as a pacer does: *a TV show that always paces the others in popularity ratings.*

pa·ce (PAY·see) *prep. Latin.* without annoyance to someone: *Let me say this pace the competition.*

pace·mak·er (PACE·may·kur) *n.* a tiny electronic device implanted near the heart to regulate its beat.

pac·er (PAY·sur) *n.* **1** one who sets the pace in a race: *a pacer car.* **2** same as PACEMAKER.

pace·set·ter (PACE·set·ur) *n.* **1** a leader. **2** one who sets the pace or speed.

Pa·cif·ic (puh·SIF·ic) **1** *n.* the ocean between Asia and the Americas; also **Pacific Ocean. 2** *adj.* of the Pacific: *the Pacific coast (of North America).* **3 pacific** *adj.* tending to pacify; calm or peaceful; **pa·cif·i·cal·ly** *adv.*

Pacific Rim *n.* the region bordering the Pacific, including Australia, Japan, New Zealand, Philippines, South Korea, and the west coast of North America.

pac·i·fi·er (PAS·uh·fye·ur) *n.* one that pacifies, esp. something for an infant to suck or chew on.

pac·i·fism (PAS·uh·fiz·um) *n.* opposition to war or military action. — **pac·i·fist** *n. & adj.: a pacifist approach to a*

settlement; also **pac·i·fis·tic** (-FIS·tic) *adj.*

pac·i·fy (PAS·uh·fye) *v.* **-fies, -fied, -fy·ing** make peaceful or quiet: *to pacify a country, nation; to keep the people pacified; to pacify a situation; a pacifying influence.* — **pac·i·fi·ca·tion** (-fuh·CAY·shun) *n.*

pack *n.* **1** things wrapped up and tied together as a bundle for carrying, as on one's back: *a back pack; parachute pack.* **2** things considered in sets or groups: *Cigarettes come in packs of 20; beer in 6-packs; a year's pack of salmon (caught in one season).* **3** something compactly put together, as a compress for applying heat, cold, or pressure to a body part: *a cosmetic beauty pack, face pack,* or *mud pack* (= paste); *an undercover police officer wearing a body pack* (= recording device); *an* **ice pack** (= ice bag or pack ice). **4** persons, animals, or things grouped together for a common purpose: *a pack of hunting dogs, thieves, wolves; to run with the pack; a Brownie pack; submarine pack; a pack of lies; to shuffle, cut a pack* (= deck) *of cards.* — *v.* **1** make, put, or crowd into a pack: *Pack everything in two bags; Pack the bags tight; It's time to* **pack up** *and go home; The refugees were* **packed into** *the boats like sardines; We* **pack off** *the kids to school after breakfast; The inept were* **sent packing** (= were dismissed) *from their jobs.* **2** treat so as to make compact or leak-proof: *A plumber packs a pipe joint; A road roller packs the earth; A dentist packs a bleeding gum.* **3** *Informal.* carry in a pack; be loaded with something; also, possess: *He packed a change of clothes in his briefcase; dark clouds packing a storm; I want a word that packs more punch.* **4** arrange with corrupt motives: *to pack a jury (with sympathizers).* — **pack it in** put an end to what one is doing.

pack·age (PAK·ij) *n.* **1** a parcel or bundle: *to deliver, mail, send, wrap a package.* **2** a proposal, plan, offer, etc. containing many items to be accepted as a whole: *a compensation package* (= salary, bonus, etc.); *a software package (of programs for general use by the public);* **adj.:** *a package deal, holiday, tour.* — *v.* **-ag·es, -aged, -ag·ing** put in a package, esp. put together as a unit for presentation or sale: *packaged goods; The* **packaging** (= container) *is sometimes more expensive than the product; a truth-in-packaging law; a candidate packaged by the media.*

pack animal *n.* a load-carrying animal, as a camel, mule, or **pack·mule,** or **pack·horse,** often equipped with a **pack saddle.**

pack·et (PAK·it) *n.* **1** a small parcel, as of mail. **2** a boat plying a regular route carrying passengers, freight, and mail; also **packet boat.**

pack ice *n.* an expanse of masses of broken, piled-up ice; ice pack.

packing *n.* **1** material used to prevent or stop a leakage of water, steam, or air. **2** the processing and packing of food, esp. meat, for wholesale, as is done in a **packing house** or **packing plant.**

pack mule *n.* a load-carrying mule.

pack rat *n.* **1** a North American rodent that carries away small articles and hides them in its nest. **2** one who hoards odd, unnecessary articles.

pack·sack *n.* a travelling bag of sturdy material, strapped to one's back.

pack saddle See PACK ANIMAL.

pack·thread *n.* a strong thread for sewing up bags.

pack·train *n.* a line of pack animals.

pact *n.* a treaty or agreement: *the auto pact between Canada and the U.S.; the free-trade pact; a peace pact; a secret pact between nations; The arms race between the superpowers was like a suicide pact; a pact of friendship.*

pad *n.* **1** a mass of soft material or a cushionlike container: *a heating pad; knee pad; a scouring pad of steel wool or plastic mesh for pots and pans; leg pads and shoulder pads worn for protection while playing; a scratch pad (of paper) for informal notes; an inked stamp pad (for a rubber stamp); a writing pad* (= sheets of paper glued together at one end). **2** a frameless flexible saddle. **3** a water plant's floating leaf. **4** the soft under part of fingers and toes, esp. of the feet of animals. **5** a launch pad. **6** *Slang.* a place to sleep: *a hippie at his pad; crash pad.* **7** *Slang.* a bribe collected by policemen for ignoring illegal activities: *a cop suspected of being on the pad.*
— *v.* **pads, pad·ded, pad·ding** stuff or fill out: *an essay padded with quotations; a heavily padded* (= inflated) *expense account; a well-padded chair; a **padded cell** for violent inmates.*
— **pad about** walk noiselessly: *a child padding about on bare feet.*

padding *n.* material used to pad or fill out.

pad·dle (PAD·ul) *n.* **1** an oar with a broad, flat blade. **2** a similar implement, as a board of a water wheel or the **paddle wheel** of a steamboat, a table tennis racket, or one used in **paddle ball,** a game similar to squash, and in **paddle tennis,** an outdoor game resembling tennis. **3** an instrument used in stirring, mixing, or beating, shaped like a paddle, as a potter's pallet. **4** a handled board formerly used for spanking.
— *v.* **pad·dles, pad·dled, pad·dling:** *Children paddled* (= splashed) *about in the wading pool; At school Jane **paddles her own canoe*** (= manages all by herself).
— **pad·dler** *n.*

pad·dock (PAD·uck) *n.* an enclosure adjoining a stable, for feeding, exercising, or displaying animals, esp. racehorses.

pad·dy (PAD·ee) *n.* **pad·dies 1** rice in the husk, esp.

when standing in the field. **2** a field of rice, often called **paddy-field. 3 Paddy** *Slang.* an Irishman.

paddy wagon *n. Slang.* a patrol wagon.

pad·lock *n.* a lock that can be put on a staple or chain by means of a U-shaped link that snaps shut and stays shut until unlocked; *v.:* *The door was shut and padlocked.*

pa·dre (PAH·dray, -dree) *n.* in Latin countries, a title for a priest; Father.

pae·an (PEE·un) *n.* a song of exultation or triumph: *The media sang paeans to her triumph at the Olympics.*

pa·gan (PAY·gun) *n.* one who has no recognized religion; formerly, not a Christian, Jew, or Muslim. — *adj.:* *pagan beliefs, customs, idols.* — **pa·gan·ism** *n.*

page *n.* **1** one side of a leaf of a book: *the sports page of a newspaper; a book's title page; to tear out a page* (= leaf) *of a book.* **2** an event or series of events: *a glorious page in our life; a page from real life; in the pages of history.* **3** an attendant or messenger, as at a hotel, theatre, or in a legislature.
— *v.* **pag·es, paged, pag·ing 1** arrange into pages; paginate a volume. **2** turn the pages: *to page through a volume.* **3** summon someone using a loudspeaker or similar device. — **pag·er** *n.*

pag·eant (PAJ·unt) *n.* a spectacular show, parade, or procession: *a beauty pageant at which Miss Canada is crowned.*
— **pag·eant·ry** (PAJ·un·tree) *n.:* *the pomp and pageantry of a royal wedding.*

page boy or **page·boy** *n.* **1** a boy who works as a page. **2** a shoulder-length hair style.

pag·i·nate (PAJ·uh·nate) *v.* **-nates, -nat·ed, -nat·ing** arrange a volume into pages.
— **pag·i·na·tion** (-NAY·shun) *n.*

paid *pt. & pp.* of PAY.

pail *n.* **1** a cylindrical vessel, usually with a handle, for liquids; bucket: *a milk pail.* **2** the amount a pail will hold: *two pails of water;* also **pail·ful, -fuls.**

pain *n.* **1** suffering of body or mind: *aches and pains; an acute, dull, excruciating, gnawing, nagging, severe, sharp, shooting, stabbing, throbbing pain; The child cried out in pain; to allay, bear, ease, endure, kill, relieve, soothe, stand, suffer pain; to inflict pain on someone.*
— **pains** *pl.* **1** effort or care: *He went to some pains to satisfy her demands; She took great pains to research her book thoroughly; She spared no pains; He was **at pains** to quiet rumours about his resignation.* **2** physical suffering: *labour pains (of childbirth); the "growing pains" of children.*
— **pain in the neck** *Informal.* nuisance.
— **under** or **on** or **upon pain of** under penalty of something: *He was told to surrender on pain of death.*
— *v.* feel or cause pain: *It pains me to hear you are hurt; I am **pained*** (= distressed) *to hear about the tragedy.* — **pain·ful** *adj.;* **pain·ful·ly** *adv.*
— **pains·tak·ing** *n. & adj.;* **pains·tak·ing·ly** *adv.*

pain·kill·er (PAIN·kil·ur) *n.* something that relieves pain, as a drug. — **pain·kill·ing** *adj.*

paint *v.* **1** apply colour, as with a brush: *to paint a portrait in oil.* **2** make something in colour, as a picture, or **painting. 3** put cosmetics on the face.
— **paint the town red** *Slang.* go on a merrymaking spree.
— *n.* **1** a usually liquid mixture or pigment for coating a surface for decoration or protection: *to apply paint to a surface; to daub paint on something; to scrape paint off a surface; a blob, coat, speck, splash of paint; flat, glossy, grease, latex, war paint.* **2** such a coating: *to apply two coats of paint; "Caution – wet paint!"*
— **paint·er** *n.*

painting *n.* **1** the art of using paints to create pictures: *the painting of a portrait;* **finger painting** *in kindergarten.* **2** such a picture: *the landscape paintings of the Group of Seven; oil and water-colour paintings.*

pair *n.* **1** two persons, animals, or things of the same kind: *four pair* or *pairs of socks; a newly married pair; The skating pairs are next on the program; a pair of oxen; The animals entered Noah's Ark* **in pairs** (= two by two). **2** something with two equal parts: *a pair of pants; to cut with a pair of scissors.*
— **pair off** or **pair up with** form into pairs: *The guests paired off for the dance; The men paired up with the women.*

pais·ley (PAIZ·lee) *n.* a colourful cloth design of curved and swirled figures: *a paisley shawl.* Also **Paisley.**

pa·ja·mas (puh·JAM·uz, -JAH·muz) *n.pl.* a loose-fitting sleeping suit of pants and shirt.
— **pajama** *adj.: pajama bottoms, tops.*

pal·ace (PAL·is) *n.* **1** a large, splendid residence, esp. of a sovereign, archbishop, or other dignitary: *an imperial palace.* **2** a similar building for exhibitions, entertainments, etc.
— *adj.* involving intimacy and influence with persons in power: *palace politics; a palace guard, revolution.*

pal·at·a·ble (PAL·uh·tuh·bul) *adj.* **1** tasty: *Food has to be palatable to the eater.* **2** agreeable: *palatable advice.*

pal·ate (PAL·it) *n.* **1** the sense of taste: *a wine pleasing to the palate; We've delicacies to tickle your palate* (= very tasty delicacies). **2** the roof of the mouth, with the **hard palate** at the front and **soft palate** at the back: *a child with a* **cleft palate** (= split in the roof of the mouth).

pa·la·tial (puh·LAY·shul) *adj.* of or like a palace: *the palatial surroundings of Rideau Hall.*

pa·lav·er (puh·LAV·ur) *n.* extended talk, esp. between

traders.
— *v.* **1** talk profusely. **2** talk flatteringly; cajole.

pale *adj.* **pal·er, pal·est** of the face, bloodless; light or weak: *to go* or *turn pale with fear; a deathly pale colour; a pale blue; a pale* (= poor) *imitation.*
— *v.* **pales, paled, pal·ing** fade: *His accomplishments pale into insignificance when you compare them with hers; They pale before hers; Paola pales at the sight of blood.*
— *n.* **1** a picket or stake. **2** an enclosed area.
— **beyond** or **outside** (or **within**) **the pale** beyond or outside (or within) the limits of the law, of the church, of respectability, etc. — **pale·ly** *adv.;* **pale·ness** *n.*

pale·face *n.* [Indian term] a white person.

Pal·es·tine (PAL·uh·stine) *n.* the land between the Mediterranean and the Jordan River, the birthplace of Judaism and Christianity, and sacred also to Muslims; also called "the Holy Land": *Parts of Palestine belonging to Egypt (Gaza Strip) and Jordan were occupied by Israel in 1967; the Palestine Liberation Organization (of Arabs).*
— **Pal·es·tin·i·an** (-STIN·ee·un) *n. & adj.: Many Palestinians are Palestinian Arabs.*

pal·ette (PAL·it) *n.* **1** an artist's hand-held board for mixing colours. **2** a range of colours: *He paints in a wide palette; A* **palette** or **pallet knife** *is used to mix and apply colours and by printers to spread ink.*

pal·frey (PAWL·free) *n.* [old use] a saddle horse, esp. one for a woman to ride.

pal·i·mo·ny (PAL·uh·moh·nee) *n.* payment awarded by a court to a partner when a couple who have lived together separates.

pal·ing (PAY·ling) *n.* **1** a pale, picket, or stake. **2** a collection of them or a fence made with them.

pal·i·sade (PAL·uh·sade) *n.* **1** a fortification of stakes or pales. **2** one of the stakes used in such a fence. **3** palisades *pl.* a line of cliffs.
— *v.* **-sades, -sad·ed, -sad·ing** surround with or as with a palisade: *Tall cliffs palisade the shore.*

pall (PAWL) *v.* **palls, palled, pall·ing** get boring; cloy: *This show is beginning to pall on me.*
— *n.* a covering, as on a coffin: *Her death cast a pall over* or *on the school reunion* (= made the occasion gloomy); *A pall of smoke hangs over the city.*

pall·bear·er (PAWL·bair·ur) *n.* one who escorts or helps to carry a coffin at a funeral.

pal·let (PAL·it) *n.* **1** a paddlelike wooden tool used by potters for mixing and shaping clay. **2** same as PALETTE. **3** a low, portable platform for storing or moving objects. **4** a makeshift bed or mattress used on the floor.

pal·li·ate (PAL·ee·ate) *v.* **-ates, -at·ed, -at·ing** lessen the severity of a crime, illness, pain, evil, etc.
— **pal·li·a·tion** (-AY·shun) *n.*
— **pal·li·a·tive** (-ay·tiv) *n. & adj.* pale: *a mere palliative and no cure.*

pal·lid (PAL·id) *adj.* pale, as by illness: *a pallid complexion, face.*

pal·lor (PAL·ur) *n.* paleness of the skin due to fear, illness, weakness, etc.

palm (PAHM, POM) *n.* **1** the inner surface of the hand from the wrist to the base of the fingers. **2** a part corresponding to this, as of a glove or the blade of a paddle. **3** a tree without branches but only a trunk and crowns of leaves shaped like a hand. **4** a palm leaf as a symbol of victory.
— **bear** or **carry off the palm** win a personal victory.
— **grease the palm of** to bribe.
— **have an itching palm** *Informal.* be greedy for money.
— *v.* conceal in the palm, as a card; hence, pass off: *The con man **palmed off** a fake diamond on the young lady; He palmed it off as a genuine diamond.*

palm·ist (PAH·mist, PAW-) *n.* one who tells fortunes by reading the lines on a person's palms.

palm·is·try (PAH·mis·tree, PAW-) *n.* the palmist's art.

palm·y (PAH·mee, PAW-) *adj.* **palm·i·er, -i·est** flourishing or prosperous: *the palmy days of one's youth.*

pal·o·mi·no (pal·uh·MEE·noh) *n.* **-nos** a light-coloured horse with white mane and tail.

pal·pa·ble (PAL·puh·bul) *adj.* **1** that can be felt; hence, obvious: *a palpable advantage.* **2** [medical use] that can be examined by palpating: *a palpable lump.*

pal·pa·bly (PAL·puh·blee) *adv.* obviously: *The story is palpably absurd.*

pal·pate (PAL·pate) *v.* **-pates, -pat·ed, -pat·ing** feel with the hand, as in a medical checkup: *Physicians palpate the breasts to check for lumps.*
— **pal·pa·tion** (pal·PAY·shun) *n.*

pal·pi·tate (PAL·puh·tate) *v.* **-tates, -tat·ed, -tat·ing** throb rapidly: *The heart palpitates under exertion or excitement.* — **pal·pi·ta·tion** (-TAY·shun) *n.*

pal·sy (PAWL·zee) *n.* **-sies 1** paralysis or a disorder characterized by trembling, as "Parkinson's disease": *cerebral palsy.* **2** a paralysing influence.
— *v.* **-sies, -sied, -sy·ing** paralyse: *He stood still, palsied by fear; a **palsied** child, limb.*

pal·ter (PAWL·tur) *v.* use trickery; trifle: *a matter too serious to palter with.*

pal·try (PAWL·tree) *adj.* **-tri·er, -tri·est** trifling or contemptibly small: *a paltry amount; paltry concessions, contributions; a paltry 2% raise; a paltry ration of soup and tea; the paltry sum of five dollars.*

pam·pas (PAM·puz) *n.pl.* the vast treeless plains of South America, esp. in Argentina.

pam·per (PAM·pur) *v.* treat with indulgence: *a pampered child; to pamper one's vanity.*

pam·phlet (PAM·flit) *n.* an unbound booklet on a current topic.

pam·phlet·eer (pam·fluh·TEER) *n.* one who issues pamphlets, esp. as propaganda.

pan *n.* **1** a flat, open dish for cooking: *frying pan; pots and pans.* **2** a shallow receptacle, depression, cover, etc.: *the pans (= dishes) of a balance; the brain pan (= part of skull); salt pan (= cavity with deposit of salt); a gold pan (= dish for washing ore).*
— *v.* **pans, panned, pan·ning 1** sift, esp. gravel for gold. **2** *Informal.* criticize harshly: *a movie panned by*

reviewers. **3** turn a movie camera in a sweeping motion for a panoramic view.
— **pan out** *Informal.* of an enterprise, turn out well: *Our plans did not pan out.*

pan- *combining form.* all: *Pan-American, Panarctic, panhuman, pantheism.*

pan·a·ce·a (pan·uh·SEE·uh) *n.* a cure-all remedy: *no panacea for world hunger.*

pa·nache (puh·NASH) *n.* an air of confidence and ease; flamboyance: *He plays Romeo with great panache; She wears new fashions with style and panache.*

pan·cake *n.* a thin batter cake cooked on both sides and served hot.

pan·dem·ic (pan·DEM·ic) *n.* an epidemic spread over a wide area; *adj.: Influenza was pandemic in 1918 – 1919 and killed about 20 million.*

pan·de·mo·ni·um (pan·duh·MOH·nee·um) *n.* wild disorder: *to cause, create, stir up a pandemonium; Pandemonium broke loose, broke out, prevailed, or reigned when the teacher was late for class.*

pan·der (PAN·dur) *n.* a procurer or pimp.
— *v.* act as a pander: *movies that pander to the public's taste for violence.*

Pandora's box (pan·DOR·uz-) *n.* a source of endless trouble, as in the Greek myth of Pandora, the first mortal woman, who caused all earthly ills by opening a box against the advice of the gods.

pane *n.* **1** a division of a window or door framing a sheet of glass. **2** the glass.

pan·e·gyr·ic (pan·uh·JEER·ic) *n.* a formal eulogy or tribute to a person or event.

pan·el (PAN·ul) *n.* **1** a usually rectangular piece, section, or division of a surface such as a ceiling, wall, or door, often at a different level from its surroundings: *a control panel; instrument panel; the panels of a skirt; the panels of an airplane wing.* **2** a number of persons forming a group to discuss or investigate something: *a jury panel; A panel of experts held a **panel discussion** on AIDS.*
— *v.* **pan·els, pan·elled** or **pan·eled, pan·el·ling** or **pan·el·ing** cover with panels: *to panel the walls of a basement with wood **panelling**.*

pan·el·ist (PAN·ul·ist) *n.* a member of a panel of experts or judges.

pang *n.* a sharp, sudden attack of pain: *pangs of hunger, fury, jealousy, remorse; birth pangs; to feel pangs of conscience.*

pan·han·dle (PAN·han·dul) *n.* a strip of territory projecting like the handle of a pan: *the Alaskan panhandle; the Texas panhandle between Oklahoma and New Mexico.*
— *v.* **-dles, -dled, -dling** beg on the street.
— **pan·han·dler** *n.*

pan·ic *n.* a sudden fear, esp. one that spreads, as when a bank fails or a fire breaks out: *to avert, cause, create, prevent panic; He was in a panic over or about the missed flight; We felt panic at the sight of a car coming head-on; We escaped being hit and the panic subsided.*
— **hit** or **press** or **push the panic button** react in a

panicky manner.
— *v.* **-ics, -icked, -ick·ing** feel or cause panic: *Don't panic, it's only a rumour; The passengers panicked at the mention of a bomb.* — **pan·ick·y** *adj.*

pan·jan·drum (pan·JAN·drum) *n.* a pretentious or pompous official.

pan·o·ply (PAN·uh·plee) *n.* **-plies 1** a complete suit of armour. **2** a splendid array: *He was waited on by a full panoply of servants.*

pan·o·ra·ma (pan·uh·RAM·uh) *n.* **1** a view in all directions: *a panorama of the countryside from a hilltop.* **2** an unlimited, comprehensive, or continuous view: *The book depicts the changing panorama of history.*
— **pan·o·ram·ic** *adj.*: *a panoramic view; A Panoramic Camera with a 360-degree view was patented in Elora, Ont., in 1887.*

pant *v.* **1** breathe in gasps, as from exertion; also, gasp: *He rushed in panting for breath; "Water!" he panted* (= said gaspingly). **2** yearn desperately: *a mother panting for the return of her missing child.*
— *n.* a gasp or puff of breath.
— **pants** *n.pl.* **1** *Informal.* trousers: *ski pants;* **adj.** usually **pant**: *a pant leg.* **2** panties.
— **with one's pants down** *Informal.* in an embarrassing position.

pan·ta·loons (PAN·tuh·loons) *n.pl.* men's loose, baggy trousers, as worn in the 19th century.

pant·dress *n.* a dress with a divided skirt.

pan·the·ism (PAN·thee·iz·um) *n.* the belief that God is the same as the forces and manifestations of nature.
— **pan·the·ist** *n.* — **pan·the·is·tic** (-IS·tic) *adj.*

pan·the·on (pan·THEE·un) *n.* **1** a temple dedicated to all the gods. **2** the gods themselves: *a pantheon of national heroes.*

pan·tie or **pan·ty** (PAN·tee) *n.* usually **panties** *pl.* a woman's or child's short underpants.

pan·ti·hose (PAN·tee·hoze) *n.* same as PANTYHOSE.

pan·to·mime (PAN·tuh·mime) *n.* expression using gestures without words, as in the dramatic art form of the same name.
— *v.* **-mimes, -mimed, -mim·ing** use pantomime: *Knowing only English, he had to pantomime his way through China.* — **pan·to·mim·ist** (-mye·mist) *n.*

pan·try (PAN·tree) *n.* **-tries** a room or closet for storing food and table accessories such as china and linens.

pant·suit or **pants suit** *n.* a woman's jacket-and-trouser outfit.

panty See PANTIE.

panty·hose *n. sing. & pl.* a woman's undergarment combining panties and stockings.

pan·ty·waist (PAN·tee·waist) *n.* *Slang.* **1** a child's outfit of shirt and pants buttoned together. **2** a sissy.

pap *n.* **1** soft food, as for infants. **2** anything handed out for consumption that lacks substance or vigour: *The book is mere political pap.*

pa·pa (PAH·puh) *n.* *Informal.* father.

pa·pa·cy (PAY·puh·see) *n.* **-cies 1** a pope's position, authority, or term of office: *the papacy of John Paul II.* **2** popes collectively: *the Italian papacy.* **3** the system of government of the Roman Catholic Church: *The pope is the head of the papacy.*

pa·pal (PAY·pul) *adj.* of the pope: *papal authority; a papal bull; the Papal States; the papal succession.*

pa·pa·raz·zo (pah·puh·RAHT·so) *n., pl.* **-raz·zi** (-RAHT·see) a journalist who doggedly pursues news stories and pictorial subjects.

pa·per (PAY·pur) *n.* **1** a thin, pliable sheet material made of pulp prepared from wood or rags and used for writing, printing, wrapping, covering, etc. **2** a piece or sheet of this: *bond, carbon, filter, litmus, manila, scrap, scratch, tissue, toilet, wax paper; A contract is not a mere scrap of paper; Useless paper is recycled; a plan that looks good* **on paper** (= in theory). **3** something written or printed, as an essay or newspaper: *to deliver, give, present, read a paper to a learned society; Students do, hand in, write papers; a term paper; to get a paper out* (= publish a periodical); *a school paper; You are in today's paper* (= newspaper). **4** document: *a background paper; discussion paper; green paper; white paper; a negotiable paper* (= negotiable instrument).
— **papers** *pl.* **1** documents: *Show your papers to Immigration; citizenship papers; a ship's papers.* **2** students' work: *Teachers correct, grade, mark, read papers.* **3** category of mail: *printed papers such as books, magazines, newspapers, greeting cards with messages of five words or less, etc.*
— *v.* cover with wallpaper: *The statement was designed to* **paper over** (= hide) *the cracks in their administration.* — **pa·per·er** *n.*

pa·per·back (PAY·pur·back) *n.* a book with paper covers.

pa·per·board (PAY·pur·board) *n.* same as CARDBOARD.

paper boy *n.* a newspaper carrier.

paper clip *n.* a wire or plastic clasp for holding papers together.

pa·per·hang·er (PAY·pur·hang·ur) *n.* one who decorates with wallpaper.

paper tiger *n.* a threatening but ineffectual person or thing.

paper-train *v.* train a pet to defecate or urinate only on paper when indoors.

pa·per·weight (PAY·pur·wait) *n.* a weight used to keep papers from being blown away.

pa·per·work (PAY·pur·wurk) *n.* clerical duties incidental to one's main occupation: *I'm trying to catch up on last week's paperwork.*

pa·per·work·er (PAY·pur·wur·kur) *n.* a worker in a paper factory.

pa·per·y (PAY·puh·ree) *adj.* thin like paper.

pa·pier-mâché (PAY·pur·muh·SHAY) *n.* a plastic material made of paper pulp mixed with glue and other additives.

pa·pist (PAY·pist) *n. & adj.* [hostile use] Roman Catholic. — **pa·pist·ry** (-pis·tree) *n.*

Pap test or **Pap smear** *n.* a test for cancer of the vagina using a mucus specimen.

pa·py·rus (puh·PYE·rus) *n.* -rus·es or -ri (-rye) a writing material, document, or scroll of paper made from the pith of an Egyptian reed.

par *n.* **1** standard or common value: *to sell stocks or shares at, above, below par; The Canadian dollar used to be* **on a par with** (=equal to) *the U.S. dollar; His performance has to be* **up to par** (=average) *for him to be confirmed in the job.* **2** in golf, the standard score for a hole or a course.

para- *prefix.* alongside; related; accessory: *paralegal, paramedical, paramilitary, paraprofessional, parapsychology, paratyphoid.*

par·a·ble (PAIR·uh·bul) *n.* a simple story with a moral: *the parable of the prodigal son.*
— **par·a·bol·i·cal** (-BOL·uh·cul) *adj.*

pa·rab·o·la (puh·RAB·uh·luh) *n.* a curve: *A ball thrown at an angle drops to the ground in a parabola.*
— **par·a·bol·ic** (pair·uh·BOL·ic) *adj.*

par·a·chute (PAIR·uh·shoot) *n.* an umbrella-shaped contrivance used for a slow, safe descent from the air to the ground: *Paratroops make parachute jumps; A* **drag parachute** *is used as a brake behind a landing plane.*
— *v.* -chutes, -chut·ed, -chut·ing drop by parachute: *Troops and supplies were parachuted into the jungle.*
— **par·a·chut·ist** *n.*

pa·rade (puh·RAID) *n.* a showy display, esp. an organized public procession: *to hold* or *stage a parade; a May Day parade in Red Square; military parade; New Year's Day parade; ticker-tape parade.*
— *v.* -rades, -rad·ed, -rad·ing go or put on parade: *models parading on a stage; They parade in front of spectators; The prisoners were paraded before a jeering mob; The superrich like to parade* (=display) *their wealth.*

par·a·digm (PAIR·uh·dim, -dime) *n.* **1** a model or pattern: *The "Queen's English" is considered the paradigm of correct usage.* **2** in grammar, a set of the complete inflectional forms of a noun, pronoun, or verb, as "ride, rides, riding, rode, ridden."

par·a·dise (PAIR·uh·dice) *n.* a place of supreme happiness, as heaven or Eden (Paradise): *Niagara Falls is a honeymooners' paradise; an earthly paradise.*

par·a·dox (PAIR·uh·dox) *n.* a seemingly contradictory statement, situation, or person, as a hippie in a three-piece suit.
— **par·a·dox·i·cal** (-DOX·uh·cul) *adj.: "Hasten slowly" sounds paradoxical;* **Paradoxical sleep** *is characterized by rapid eye movements.* — **par·a·dox·i·cal·ly** *adv.*

par·af·fin (PAIR·uh·fin) *n.* **1** a waxy substance made from petroleum and used for candles, waterproofing the inside of milk cartons, etc. **2** *Brit.* kerosene.
— *v.* -af·fins, -af·fined, -af·fin·ing treat with paraffin: *Wax paper is paraffined.*

par·a·graph (PAIR·uh·graf) *n.* **1** a subdivision of a written piece, starting on a new line. **2** a short piece complete in itself, as a news item in a paper.
— *v.* divide into paragraphs: *a neatly paragraphed essay.* — **par·a·graph·ic** (-GRAF·ic) *adj.*

par·al·lax (PAIR·uh·lax) *n.* the apparent difference in position of an object viewed from different directions, as when an extended finger is seen with one eye closed and then with the other.

par·al·lel (PAIR·uh·lel) *adj.* **1** side by side lengthwise but an equal distance apart: *The lines are parallel to each other; Parallel lines never meet; two* **parallel bars** *set horizontally on posts for gymnastic exercises.* **2** simultaneous, not one after another or serial: *a* **parallel printer** *to which the bits of a byte can be transmitted on separate channels at once;* **parallel processing** *of data in which more than one arithmetic operation can be carried out at the same time.*
— *n.* **1** something parallel: *The* **parallels of latitude** *around a globe show distances from the equator; batteries connected* **in parallel** (=negatives together and positives together).* **2** comparison: *a striking parallel; The moon-landing is* **without parallel** (=equal) *in history; The preacher* **drew a parallel** (=made a comparison) *between Easter and spring festivals.*
— *v.* -al·lels, -al·lelled or -al·leled, -al·lel·ling or -al·lel·ing form a parallel with a person or thing: *a creative genius parallelling Shakespeare.*
— **par·al·lel·ism** *n.*

par·a·lyse or **par·a·lyze** (PAIR·uh·lize) *v.* -lys·es or -lyz·es, -lysed or -lyzed, -lys·ing or -lyz·ing cause paralysis in a body: *Paraplegia paralyses the lower body; a city paralysed by a transit strike.*
— **par·a·lys·ing·ly** or **par·a·lyz·ing·ly** *adv.*

pa·ral·y·sis (puh·RAL·uh·sis) *n., pl.* -ses (-seez) **1** the partial or complete loss of sensation and movement in the body or in an organ: *infantile paralysis* (=polio). **2** a state of powerlessness.
— **par·a·lyt·ic** (pair·uh·LIT·ic) *n. & adj.: a paralytic in a wheelchair; a paralytic stroke.*

paralyze same as PARALYSE.

par·a·med·ic (PAIR·uh·med·ic) *n.* an auxiliary medical worker, as a nurse's aide, lab technician, or midwife.
— **par·a·med·i·cal** (-MED·uh·cul) *adj.: Giving injections, taking X rays, etc. are paramedical work.*

pa·ram·e·ter (puh·RAM·uh·tur) *n.* a factor, characteristic, or feature of a system: *Temperature, pressure, and density are the parameters of the atmosphere; to study a problem in all its parameters.*
— **par·a·met·ric** (pair·uh·MET·ric) or **par·a·met·ri·cal** *adj.*

par·a·mil·i·tar·y (pair·uh·MIL·uh·tair·ee) *adj.* auxiliary to a military force: *a paramilitary force; paramilitary training.*

par·a·mount (PAIR·uh·mount) *adj.* supreme or primary: *The privileges of kings used to be paramount over people's rights; a question of paramount importance.*

par·a·mour (PAIR·uh·moor) *n.* an illicit lover, esp. a mistress.

par·a·noi·a (pair·uh·NOY·uh) *n.* a mental disorder characterized by delusions of grandeur, persecution, etc.
— **par·a·noi·ac** (-ac) *n. & adj.*

par·a·noid (PAIR·uh·noid) *n.* a paranoia patient.

— **adj.**: *a paranoid schizophrenic; You don't have to get paranoid* (= scared) *about one anonymous phone call.*

par·a·pet (PAIR·uh·pet) *n.* a low wall or railing at the edge of a balcony, roof, bridge, or atop a rampart.

par·a·pher·na·li·a (pair·uh·fur·NAY·lee·uh) *n. sing.* & *pl.* equipment or gear proper to an activity or office.

par·a·phrase (PAIR·uh·fraze) *n.* a restatement of a text to give the meaning, often in simpler form.
— **v.** -phras·es, -phrased, -phras·ing: *Some poems are difficult to paraphrase.*

par·a·ple·gi·a (pair·uh·PLEE·jee·uh) *n.* paralysis of the lower half of the body. — **par·a·pleg·ic** (-jic) *n.* & *adj.*

par·a·sail·ing (PAIR·uh·say·ling) *n.* the sport of soaring using a parachute.

par·a·site (PAIR·uh·site) *n.* one that exists at another's expense; sponger: *The mistletoe and bacteria are biological parasites; Spongers are parasites of society.*
— **par·a·sit·ic** (-SIT·ic) or **par·a·sit·i·cal** (-SIT·uh·cul) *adj.* — **par·a·sit·ism** (-suh·tiz·um) *n.*

par·a·sit·ize (PAIR·uh·suh·tize) *v.* -iz·es, -ized, -iz·ing live with as a parasite: *Aphids parasitize plants.*

par·a·sol (PAIR·uh·sol) *n.* an umbrella carried as a sunshade.

par·a·troops (PAIR·uh·troops) *n.pl.* soldiers trained to parachute from airplanes. — **par·a·troop·er** *n.*

par·boil *v.* boil partially; precook: *parboiled rice.*

par·cel (PAIR·sul) *n.* **1** a wrapped package or bundle. **2** a collection or group of persons, animals, or things: *a parcel of liars.* **3** a piece or portion: *a parcel of land.*
— **part and parcel** an essential part.
— **v.** -cels, -celled or -celed, -cel·ling or -cel·ing make into a package: *goods parcelled up for shipping; work parcelled out to free-lancers.*

parcel post *n.* a postal service for parcels.

parch *v.* to dry, as by the sun's heat: *parched throats thirsting for a drink; land parched by drought;* **parched** (= roasted) *corn.*

parch·ment (PARCH·munt) *n.* **1** fine writing material made from skins, as vellum, or paper specially processed. **2** a document on such material, as a diploma.

par·don (PAR·dun) *n.* **1** forgiveness: *He begged pardon of her for keeping her waiting.* **2** release from a penalty of law: *a full pardon granted by the Queen.*
— **I beg your pardon** [a polite formula of apology, as for not hearing something said, or, in a more rising tone, a challenge to repeat what was said].
— **v.** forgive: *Pardon me* (= Sorry about not hearing you, offending you, etc.); *We pardon each other's faults; Pardon me for interrupting; Pardon my rudeness.*
— **par·don·a·ble** *adj.*; **par·don·a·bly** *adv.*

pare *v.* pares, pared, par·ing **1** clip or cut the edge or shave the surface of something: *to pare one's nails; a* **paring knife** *to pare an apple with.* **2** reduce: *to pare down a budget; to pare down expenses to a minimum.*

par·ent (PAIR·unt) *n.* **1** a father or mother: *an*

adoptive, foster, loving, natural, permissive, single parent; Children obey their parents. **2** originator or source: *the U.S. parent of a foreign subsidiary; a parent firm.* — **par·ent·hood** *n.*; **par·ent·ing** *n.*

par·ent·age (PAIR·un·tij) *n.* ancestry: *a man of noble parentage.*

par·en·tal (puh·REN·tul) *adj.* having to do with a parent: *parental abductions, authority, consent, control, love, neglect, responsibility.*

parental leave *n.* paid or unpaid leave from work granted to either or both parents of a newborn child.

pa·ren·the·sis (puh·REN·thuh·sis) *n., pl.* -ses (-seez) **1** one of a pair of round brackets ( ) used to enclose words, numbers, or other symbols. **2** a word or clause inserted within a sentence and set off from it by a pair of such brackets, commas, or dashes, i.e. **in** or **within parentheses.** — **par·en·thet·ic** (puh·ren·THET·ic) or **par·en·thet·i·cal** *adj.*

par·en·the·size (puh·REN·thuh·size) *v.* -siz·es, -sized, -siz·ing put something as a parenthesis or in parentheses.

par ex·cel·lence (PAR·ek·suh·LAHNCE) *adj.* preeminent: *a writer par excellence though a poor speaker.*

par·fleche (PAR·flesh, par·FLESH) *n. Cdn.* a piece of raw hide or a bag or pouch made with it, as used by native Indians.

pa·ri·ah (puh·RYE·uh) *n.* an outcast.

pa·ri·e·tal (puh·RYE·uh·tul) *adj.* having to do with walls: *Parietal bones form the sides and roof of the skull; Parietal regulations affect life within college walls, such as dormitory visiting hours.*

parings *n.pl.* what is pared off; leavings or shavings.

pa·ri pas·su (PAIR·ee·PASS·oo) *adj.* & *adv. Latin.* at an equal rate.

par·ish (PAIR·ish) *n.* **1** an administrative division of a diocese, with a priest or minister in charge, or its members collectively: *a parish school.* **2** formerly, in Quebec, New Brunswick, and Prince Edward Island, a subdivision of a county. **3** a county of Louisiana.
— **pa·rish·ion·er** (puh·RISH·uh·nur) *n.*

Pa·ri·sian (puh·RIZH·un) *n.* a person of or from Paris, France; **adj.**: *a Parisian accent; Parisian fashions, French.*

par·i·ty (PAIR·uh·tee) *n.* -ties (-teez) **1** equality, esp. in purchasing power: *parity between prices and incomes; to achieve, attain, establish parity; Firefighters want parity of pay with the police.* **2** the property of being odd or even, as in binary-coded data: *4 and 6 have the same parity; A* **parity check** *determines whether there is an odd or even number of zeros or ones in a set of binary digits.*

park *n.* **1** an area of land set aside for public recreation: *an amusement park; Banff National Park; national historic parks such as the Halifax Citadel; a provincial park; public park; trailer park; theme parks;* **Park rangers** *and* **park wardens** *take care of national and provincial parks.* **2** a commercial area: *a car park* (= parking lot); *a suburban industrial park with offices*

and facilities for parking, recreation, etc.
— *v.* **1** put a vehicle in a place and leave temporarily. **2** *Informal.* put or leave a person or thing somewhere for a time: *No parking of gum under the table; The kids were parked with Grandma.*

par·ka (PAR·kuh) *n.* **1** a hooded fur jacket for winter wear. **2** a similar warm garment of cloth.

park·ade (par·KADE) *n.* an automobile parking facility that is one or more storeys high.

park·ette (par·KET) *n.* a small public park.

parking lot *n.* an area for parking motor vehicles.

parking meter *n.* a coin-operated clock device for regulating the use of a parking space.

parking orbit *n.* an orbit from which a space vehicle may be launched.

par·lance (PAR·lunce) *n.* style of speech: *In common parlance, "inebriated" would be "drunk."*

park·land *n.* **1** wooded land suitable for use as a public park. **2** *Cdn.* in the Prairie Provinces, a belt of rich, lightly-wooded land between the open prairie and the northern forests.

park·way *n.* a broad boulevard or landscaped highway.

par·lay *n.* a bet or series of bets with a previous wager plus winnings as the next bet.
— *v.* bet or risk something in increasing amounts: *She parlayed a small inheritance into a fortune.*

par·ley (PAR·lee) *n.* **-leys** a negotiation for coming to terms with an adversary.
— *v.* negotiate: *Israel refused to parley with the P.L.O.*

par·lia·ment (PAR·luh·munt) *n.* the highest lawmaking body, esp. of Britain and other Commonwealth countries: *A parliament adjourns, convenes, meets; to adjourn, convene, convoke, dissolve a parliament; Candidates stand for parliament (= election); M.P.s sit in parliament; The provincial parliament of Ontario sits at Queen's Park; the Parliament Buildings in Ottawa; A Throne Speech opens a session of Parliament; Parliament is now in session; Parliament rises at the end of a session.*

par·lia·men·tar·i·an (PAR·luh·men·TAIR·ee·un) *n.* an expert in parliamentary procedure.

par·lia·men·ta·ry (par·luh·MEN·tuh·ree) *adj.* having to do with parliaments: *parliamentary language, practice, procedure; the parliamentary system.*

par·lour or **par·lor** (PAR·lur) *n.* **1** a semiprivate room for social conversation: *A sun parlour or porch lets in plenty of sunshine; adj.: a parlour chair, game, piano; a Victorian parlour setting.* **2** a specially designed business establishment: *a beauty, beer, funeral, ice cream, massage, milking, pizza, video parlour.*

parlour car or **parlor car** *n.* a railway car with superior individual accommodation; chair car.

par·lous (PAR·lus) *adj.* perilous or risky: *the parlous state of his campaign; We live in parlous times.*
— *adv.* [old use] extremely: *The night was parlous cold.*

par·mi·gia·na (par·muh·JAH·nuh) or **par·mi·gia·no** (-noh) *adj.* prepared with "Parmesan" cheese: *eggplant*

parmigiana; veal parmigiana.

pa·ro·chi·al (puh·ROH·kee·ul) *adj.* **1** of a parish: *a parochial school.* **2** narrow-minded: *very parochial in her interests.* — **pa·ro·chi·al·ism** *n.;* **pa·ro·chi·al·ly** *adv.*

par·o·dy (PAIR·uh·dee) *n.* **-dies 1** imitation and exaggeration of a person's style for ridiculing: *a parody of Milton.* **2** a poor imitation; travesty: *a mere parody of a court of justice.*
— *v.* **-dies, -died, -dy·ing** make a parody of a person or thing: *Smith likes to parody Shakespeare.*

pa·role (puh·ROLE) *n.* a conditional release from prison before a term is fully served: *a convict on day parole; early parole for good behaviour; to release or free someone on parole; back in prison for violating his parole.*
— *v.* **-roles, -roled, -rol·ing** to free on parole: *Paolo was paroled (from prison) for good conduct.*

pa·rol·ee (puh·roh·LEE) *n.* one who has been paroled.

par·ox·ysm (PAIR·uk·siz·um) *n.* a sudden outburst: *a paroxysm of despair, laughter, rage.*

par·quet (par·KAY) *n.* **1** the part of a theatre's main floor from the orchestra pit to the **parquet circle,** the part beneath the rear balcony. **2** a floor of parquetry.
— *v.* **-quets** (-KAZE) , **-quet·ed** (-KADE) , **-quet·ing** (-KAY·ing) finish with parquetry: *wainscoting parqueted with cedar.*

par·quet·ry (PAR·kit·ree) *n.* **-ries** a mosaic of inlaid wood.

par·rot (PAIR·ut) *n.* **1** one of a family of colourful tropical birds with hooked bills and the ability to mimic speech. **2** one who repeats something without understanding it.
— *v.* repeat without understanding: *The brighter children try to emulate their teachers instead of parroting them.*

par·ry (PAIR·ee) *v.* **par·ries, par·ried, par·ry·ing 1** turn aside a blow, as in fencing. **2** evade adroitly: *He parried reporters' questions with a "No comment."*
— *n., pl.* **par·ries** a parrying or evading: *the thrust and parry of political debates.*

parse *v.* **pars·es, parsed, pars·ing** give a grammatical description of a sentence, phrase, word, etc.: *"Parries" may be parsed as noun, plural of "parry," or verb, singular of "to parry."*

par·si·mo·ny (PAR·suh·moh·nee) *n.* **1** thrift. **2** stinginess or niggardliness.
— **par·si·mo·ni·ous** (-MOH·nee·us) *adj.*

pars·ley (PARS·lee) *n.* a plant whose crinkled leaves are used as a garnish: *Sprinkle with chopped fresh parsley (leaves) before serving.*

par·son (PAR·sun) *n.* a clergyman, usually a Protestant one.

par·son·age (PAR·sun·ij) *n.* a parson's residence.

Parson's table *n.* a rectangular table with straight legs at the corners.

part *n.* 1 a portion or division of something: *Petals are parts of a flower; spare parts for an automobile; The three R's are an essential part of education; an integral part of the system; the major part of the day; Oxygen is a constituent part* (= component) *of water; for **the better part*** (= more than half) *of an hour; a remote part* (= area) *of Africa; the part* (= dividing line) *in your hair; I like the music only **in part*** (= not completely); *Her efforts were wasted **for the most part*** (= mostly). 2 a person's share or role in an activity: *You did your part well; Jane took her mother's part* (= side) *in the family dispute; One of the actors flubbed his part* (= lines) *because he didn't learn or memorize or study his part; A bit part* (= role) *in a movie has little or no speaking; Al played the part of Othello; He acts and looks the part; I didn't **take part*** (= participate) *in the fight, at least not an active part; **For my part*** (= personally), *I like peace and quiet; There was some hesitation **on the part of*** (= by) *John.* 3 **parts** *pl.: a man of parts* (= abilities); *She's travelling in foreign parts* (= regions); *the private parts* (= genitals).
— **in good part** graciously: *He took the criticism in good part.*
— *v.* divide or separate: *The referees parted the fighting teams; They parted as friends; She parts her hair in the middle; We must **part company*** (= leave each other) *in London; He will **part from*** (= leave) *us in a few hours; We **part with** everything we have when we die.*

par·take (par·TAKE) *v.* -takes, -took, -tak·en, -tak·ing take a share or part in something: *The whole town partook in the festival; to partake of a banquet.*
— **par·tak·er** *n.*

par·tial (PAR·shul) *adj.* 1 not total: *a partial eclipse of the moon.* 2 unfairly favouring one side; biassed: *a referee who is partial to one side; He is partial toward his relatives.* — **par·ti·al·i·ty** (-shee·AL·uh·tee) *n.*

par·tial·ly (PAR·shuh·lee) *adv.* to a certain degree: *a student partially dependent on his parents.*

par·ti·ci·pant (par·TIS·uh·punt) *n.* one who takes part in something: *an active participant in sports; a willing participant in the crime.*

par·ti·ci·pate (par·TIS·uh·pate) *v.* -pates, -pat·ed, -pat·ing take part: *to participate in social activities.*
— **par·tic·i·pa·tor** (-pay·tur) *n.*
— **par·ti·ci·pa·tion** (-PAY·shun) *n.*

par·ti·ci·pa·to·ry (par·TIS·uh·puh·tor·ee) *adj.* involving direct or active participation, as of the audience in **participatory theatre.**

par·ti·ci·ple (par·TIS·uh·pul) *n.* a word with characteristics of verb and adjective, as "acting" in "He is acting" and "an acting president."
— **par·ti·cip·ial** (par·tuh·SIP·ee·ul) *adj.*

par·ti·cle (PAR·tuh·cul) *n.* 1 a tiny bit; smallest unit of matter: *dust particles in the air; minute particles; not a particle of evidence against him; protons, electrons, and other atomic particles; Sawdust or wood particles are used to make **particle board.*** 2 an uninflected part of speech or an affix, as "in," "and," "the," "bi-," and "oh."

parti-coloured or **parti-colored** (par·tee·CUL·urd) *adj.* having more than one colour: *a parti-coloured marble; parti-coloured* (= various and diverse) *thoughts about the future.*

par·tic·u·lar (par·TIK·yuh·lur) *adj.* 1 relating to an individual person or thing; specific: *This particular case is an exception to the rule.* 2 special: *a matter of particular concern to me.* 3 exact or careful: *She is very particular about punctuation.*
— *n.* a detail or specific: *Rica's OK in every particular; Flo was fired, but I won't go into particulars; He likes sea food, lobsters **in particular*** (= especially).
— **par·tic·u·lar·i·ty** (-LAIR·uh·tee) *n.*

par·tic·u·lar·ize (par·TIK·yuh·luh·rize) *v.* -iz·es, -ized, -iz·ing specify or give details: *He condemned the whole gang without particularizing about individuals.*

par·tic·u·lar·ly (par·TIK·yuh·lur·lee) *adv.* especially: *Gino is generally good as a student but particularly good at math; not particularly good in reading, though.*

parting *n.* separation: *a tearful parting of friends; They agreed on a **parting of the ways** after 50 years together.*
— *adj.* final: *a dying man's parting words; a parting shot from the getaway car.*

Par·ti Québécois (par·TEE·kay·bek·WAH) *n.* Cdn. a political party of Quebec with separatism as its goal.

par·ti·san (PAR·tuh·zun, -sun) *n.* 1 a strong supporter of a party, esp. a militant. 2 a guerrilla.
— *adj.* favouring one party: *He's too partisan to serve on this committee; partisan politics, propaganda, spirit.*
— **par·ti·san·ship** *n.*

par·ti·tion (par·TISH·un) *n.* division or separation: *a partition between rooms; the partition of Germany and Korea after World War II.*
— *v.: The dining area was partitioned off; India was partitioned into two nations by the British.*

part·ly *adv.* in part: *You're partly right and partly wrong; He's the culprit, but you're partly to blame too.*

part·ner (PART·nur) *n.* one who shares in some activity or business with another or others: *an active partner in my business, not a silent or sleeping partner; a dancing partner; partners in crime.*
— **part·ner·ship** (PART·nur·ship) *n.: to dissolve, form a partnership.*

part of speech *n.* one of the grammatical classes of words, as noun, pronoun, verb, adjective, adverb, preposition, conjunction, or interjection.

partook *pt.* of PARTAKE.

par·tridge (PAR·trij) *n.* any of various plump-bodied game birds such as the quail or grouse.

part-time *adj. & adv.* for less than the usual time: *to work part-time on a part-time job.* — **part-timer** *n.*

part·way *adv.* part of the way; partly: *Partway through the book, Flo fell asleep.*

par·ty (PAR·tee) *n.* **-ties** **1** a group taking part in an organized cause or activity: *a hunting party; ruling party; to establish, dissolve, form a political party; Party politics is not for the common good.* **2** a group on a specific mission: *a boarding, landing, rescue, search party.* **3** a gathering for amusement or celebration: *a birthday, cocktail, dinner, farewell, going-away, pajama, surprise, tea party; to arrange, attend, crash, give, throw a party; The party broke up late at night; Al was the last party animal to leave.* **4** a person: *An innocent party got hit; an aggrieved party; a disinterested third party; Yves would not be a party to* (= participant in) *the deal; the opposite party (in a legal action); the party (Informal for person) who called yesterday.*
— *v.* **-ties, -tied, -ty·ing** hold or attend parties.

party line *n.* **1** a telephone circuit with more than one subscriber. **2** a party's policies and principles: *to deviate from, follow, hew to the party line.*

party spirit *n.* **1** social spirit. **2** narrow loyalty.

party wall *n.* a common wall between two properties.

par·ve·nu (PAR·vuh·new) *n.* one who is new to his wealth and social position; upstart.

pas (PAH) *n., pl.* **pas** (PAHZ) a dance step or a series of steps.

Pasch (PASK) *n.* Passover or Easter.
— **pas·chal** (PAS·cul) *adj.: a paschal candle; the paschal lamb (eaten at Passover); the Paschal Lamb* (= Jesus or a symbolic representation).

pass *v.* **1** get to or cause to get to and past a person or thing: *We passed each other on the street; She passed by my window; Please pass* (= hand) *me the salt; This story passes belief* (= is incredible); *Many years have passed (by) since my graduation.* **2** proceed or depart: *That was a bit insulting, but let it pass; She passed* (= died) *quietly in her sleep.* **3** be or cause to be accepted or approved: *Peg passed the test; The teacher passed her with a C grade; A law is passed; A bill passes (a legislature); The judge passed sentence; The forger tried to pass a bad cheque; Nylon will not pass for silk.*
— **bring to pass** cause to happen or exist: *Space travel has brought to pass many fancies of former ages.*
— **come to pass** happen: *How did this ever come to pass?*
— **pass away** or **on** die: *Grandma passed away last year.*
— **pass off** get accepted: *The shopkeeper passed off a cheap imitation as the real thing.*
— **pass out 1** hand out: *The teacher passed out free tickets for the show.* **2** *Informal.* faint: *He passed out when he heard about the tragedy.*
— **pass over** ignore: *No one was passed over at promotion time.*
— **pass up** refuse or give up: *Who would pass up such an opportunity?*
— *n.* **1** a movement: *A magician makes passes with a wand; a bomber's pass over its target; Cora is annoyed by strangers **making passes at*** (= unwelcome advances to) *her on the street; a forward pass* (= ball thrown

forward) *during play.* **2** a resulting state or condition: *What a pretty pass* (= state of affairs) *we have reached!* **3** something indicating acceptance or allowing progress: *to cancel, issue, revoke a pass; a free pass* (= ticket) *to the games; a convoy advancing through a mountain pass* (= narrow passage); *a pass with honours; a **pass-fail** system instead of grades.*

pass·a·ble (PAS·uh·bul) *adj.* that can be passed: *a bridge that is passable* (= useable) *only in the dry season; a passable* (= adequate) *knowledge of the subject.*
— **pass·a·bly** *adv.: Her French is passably good.*

pass·age (PAS·ij) *n.* a passing: *I forgot the hurt with the passage of time; The bill had a stormy passage in parliament; We were refused passage* (= transit) *without a visa; an underground passage* (= way); *nasal passages* (= channels); *a passage* (= journey) *to Europe by boat; a passage* (= selection or quotation) *from Shakespeare.*

pass·age·way (PAS·ij·way) *n.* a way for passing through: *Hallways and alleys are passageways.*

pass book *n.* same as BANKBOOK.

pas·sé (pas·AY) *adj.* outmoded or oldish.

pas·sen·ger (PAS·un·jur) *n.* one being conveyed in a public or private vehicle: *Buses carry, drop off, leave off, pick up, take on passengers; a transit passenger; the passenger* (= right) *side of a vehicle.*

passer-by (PAS·ur·bye) *n.* **passers-by** a person passing by: *seated atop her car in full view of every passer-by.*

passing *adj.* getting past: *The **passing lane** is not for slow driving; C is the passing* (= satisfactory) *grade; the passing* (= changing) *scene; The hero got only a passing* (= casual) *mention in the press.*
— *n.: The passing* (= death) *of our leader left a void in our hearts; a **passing** bell* (= death bell); *I spoke to her **in passing*** (= briefly) *before boarding my plane.*

pas·sion (PASH·un) *n.* **1** a strong feeling, esp. of love, lust, hate, anger, or enthusiasm: *poetry without passion; Pride is his ruling passion; She has a passion* (= enthusiasm) *for journalism; The child flew into a passion* (= angry outburst); *to arouse, excite, inflame, stir up passion; to curb, gratify, restrain, satisfy one's passion; Passions ran high during the debate.* **2** an object of such feeling: *Journalism was one of her early passions.* **3** **Passion** Christ's sufferings, from after the Last Supper to the Crucifixion: *The Passion is dramatized in **Passion plays; Passion Sunday** ushers in **Passion Week,** the week before Easter.*

pas·sion·ate (PASH·un·it) *adj.* full of passion: *a passionate appeal for help, mercy; a passionate believer, character, embrace, kiss.*
— **pas·sion·ate·ly** *adv.: She's passionately fond of the outdoors.*
— **pas·sion·less** *adj.: a passionless performance of "Hamlet."*

pas·sive (PAS·iv) *adj.* not active but receiving or acted upon: *a passive audience; passive* (= meek) *submission to authority; In **passive euthanasia,** treatment is withheld to allow the patient to die; **passive immunity** (by

injecting a serum containing disease-fighting antibodies); **passive resistance** (= civil disobedience); *a* **passive restraint** *such as an automatic safety belt or airbag for the driver's protection;* **passive smoking** *(by nonsmokers inhaling smoke from smokers).*
— pas·siv·ism *n.;* pas·siv·ist *n.*

passive voice *n.* the verb form used to show that the receiver of the action is the grammatical subject, as in "Ray was seen by Pat."

pass·key (pas·TEEL) *n.* a master key.

pass·port *n.* **1** a government document identifying the bearer's citizenship for purposes of travel abroad: *to issue, lose, revoke a passport; Renew your passport when it expires.* **2** something guaranteeing acceptance or admission: *A university degree is a passport to many careers.*

pass·word *n.* a secret identifying word or phrase, as used to pass through a guarded gate or gain access to a database: *Give the password to the sentry.*

past *adj.* **1** passed by: *Night comes after the day is past; "Ran" is the* **past tense** *of "run."* **2** former: *past achievements; a past president of a society.*
— *n.* former time or life: *memories from the past; the country's glorious past; The politician's past* (= something embarrassing that happened earlier in life) *was revealed during the election campaign; a chequered, dark, murky past; In the past this would not have happened.*
— *prep. & adv.* beyond: *It is 10 minutes past (the hour); A car sped past (us); Miracles are past human understanding.*

pas·ta (PAS·tuh, PAH·stuh) *n.* **1** dough made into spaghetti and such Italian foods. **2** a dish made with pasta.

paste *n.* **1** a sticky or plastic mixture, as of flour and water or like toothpaste. **2** pasta. **3** a soft food prepared by pounding and mixing: *almond paste; anchovy paste; tomato paste.* **4** any soft mixture or substance, as paper adhesives, clay used in pottery, etc. **5** a plastic kind of glass or a gem made with it.
— *v.* pastes, past·ed, past·ing **1** stick: *a wall pasted with posters.* **2** *Slang.* thrash: *The thugs pasted him; They gave him a good* **pasting;** *The Detroit Tigers took a 7-3 pasting from the Minnesota Twins.*

paste·board *n.* a board made of layers of paper pasted together.

paste job *n. Informal.* same as PASTICHE.

pas·tel (pas·TEL) *n.* **1** a chalklike pigment mixed with gum and made into crayons for painting in soft colours. **2** a painting made with such crayons.
— *adj.* soft and delicate in colour effects: *the pure pastel shades of a painting by Degas.*

pas·teur·ized (PAS·chuh·rized) *adj.* sterilized for killing bacteria: *pasteurized milk.*

pas·tiche (pas·TEESH) *n.* a musical or other artistic composition that is a patchwork of borrowings from various sources; potpourri: *The poem is a pastiche of clichés.*

pas·ties (PAS·teez) *pl.* of PASTY.

pas·tille (pas·TEEL) *n.* **1** a medicated lozenge or tablet. **2** a pellet for fumigation or a crayon of pastel. Also **pas·til** (PAS·tul).

pas·time *n.* an activity pursued as a diversion: *Our national pastime is hockey; Flo's favourite pastime is reading.*

past master *n.* an expert or adept *in* or *of* an art, occupation, etc.

pas·tor (PAS·tur) *n.* a minister heading a parish or congregation.

pas·to·ral (PAS·tuh·rul) *adj.* **1** having to do with leadership of a religious group: *a priest's pastoral duties, responsibilities; a bishop's pastoral letter.* **2** of rural life: *Virgil's pastoral poetry; "As You Like It" is pastoral drama; a pastoral scene, setting, theme.*

pas·to·rale (pas·tuh·RAL) *n.* a musical composition with a pastoral theme.

past participle *n.* a verb form or adjective showing completed action, as in "It is *lost*" or "a *lost* hat."

pas·try (PAY·stree) *n.* -tries sweet goods baked from flour paste, as pies, tarts, turnovers, etc.: *light pastry; rich pastry; a Danish pastry.*

pas·ture (PAS·chur) *n.* **1** food for grazing animals. **2** land on which grass and such vegetation grows or is grown; also, a piece of such land; also **pas·ture·land,** **pas·tur·age** (-ij).
— *v.* -tures, -tured, -tur·ing feed on growing grass: *sheep pasturing on a hillside; Farmers pasture livestock.*

pas·ty (PAY·stee) *adj.* -ti·er, -ti·est **1** like paste; sticky and doughy. **2** dull and pale: *a pasty complexion.*
— *n.* (PAS·tee), *pl.* -ties a pie with a meat filling.

pat *n.* **1** a light tap or stroke with a flat surface, as with the palm of the hand: *a pat on the back.* **2** a small flat portion made by or as if by a pat: *a pat of butter for a toast.*
— *v.* pats, pat·ted, pat·ting give a light stroke to a person or animal: *The child patted her cat; Tim patted himself on the back* (= congratulated himself) *and kept up the good work.*
— *adj. & adv.* prompt or promptly: *a resourceful girl with a pat answer for everything; The book was published* **pat on** *schedule.*
— **have** or **have down** or **know something pat** *Informal.* know perfectly, esp. from memory.
— **stand pat** *Informal.* **1** stand firm, without budging. **2** resist change.

patch *n.* **1** a small piece of material that serves to mend, cover, or decorate where it is applied: *a jacket with patches at the elbows; the general with an eye patch over his blind eye; a shoulder patch* (= insignia); *a patch* (= change) *in a computer program to correct or modify it.* **2** something similar to a patch in appearance: *a black dog with a patch of white on its back; a potato or cabbage patch* (= area or plot).
— *v.* **1** put on a patch to mend something: *Sam patched Lou's torn pants; The friends soon* **patched up** (= settled) *their quarrel.* **2** connect with: *Radio hams try to* **patch into** *secret communications.*

patch·work *n.* a piece of work or a design made up of many patches: *a patchwork design, quilt.*

patch·y (PACH·ee) *adj.* **patch·i·er, -i·est 1** having or being in patches; uneven: *patchy colour, fog, sunlight; a patchy lawn.* **2** not uniform; sketchy or incomplete: *patchy evidence.* — **patch·i·ly** *adv.;* **patch·i·ness** *n.*

pâ·té or **pate** (pay·TAY) *n. French.* paste: *pâté of mushrooms; pâté de foie gras* (= liver pâté).

pate *n. Informal.* head or brain: *a bald pate.*

-pated *combining form.* having a head as specified: *addlepated, bald-pated.*

pat·ent (PAT·unt, PAY·tunt) *adj.* **1** (PAY·tunt) plain or evident on inspection: *a patent falsehood; It is patent to everyone.* **2** of a document, open for general inspection: *letters patent.* **3** having to do with patents: *a patent attorney; A patent drug* or *medicine is protected by a trademark;* **Patent leather** *is a glossy black colour.* — *n.* (PAT·unt, PAY·tunt) an exclusive right to an invention or process granted to a person by the government: *to hold, infringe, issue a patent; to take out a patent on a new gadget; A "patent pending" notice, showing that a patent has been applied for, discourages imitators.* — *v.* take out a patent for something new: *A better mousetrap should be patented.* — **pat·ent·a·ble** *adj.*

pat·ent·ly (PAT·unt·lee) *adv.* clearly: *a theory that is patently absurd.*

pat·en·tor (PAT·un·tur) *n.* a government authority that grants patents, as the Canadian Department of Consumer and Corporate Affairs or the U.S. Patent Office.

pa·ter·nal (puh·TUR·nul) *adj.* of, like, or from a father: *paternal affection; a paternal employer, government; one's paternal grandmother.* — **pa·ter·nal·ism** (-nuh·liz·um) *n.* — **pa·ter·nal·is·tic** (-LIS·tic) *adj.*

pa·ter·ni·ty (puh·TUR·nuh·tee) *n.* the state of being a father; *adj.:* Many employers grant **paternity leave** *to new fathers; An unwed mother may bring a **paternity suit** to establish paternity and the father's responsibility; A **paternity test** compares the blood groups of child, mother, and alleged father.*

path *n.* a track or trail: *to beat* or *blaze* or *clear* or *make a path through a forest; A fallen tree blocked our path; an obstacle in our path; a beaten path; bridle paths (for horse riding); mountain paths; progress along predictable paths; the cyclical path* (= orbit) *of a comet; the flight path* (= course or route) *of a satellite; This path goes* or *leads nowhere; Are we on the right path? to stray* or *wander from the path of virtue; on the path to fame, ruin; paths of glory; the path of democracy, war; to lead someone **up the garden path** (by false promises) and **down the primrose path** (in a vain search for pleasure).*

pa·thet·ic (puh·THET·ic) *adj.* causing feelings of pity; pitiful or pitiable: *a futile and pathetic attempt; pathetic efforts; What a pathetic sight! a pathetic story of starving children; It's pathetic that people should be starving.* — **pa·thet·i·cal·ly** *adv.*

path·find·er (PATH·fine·dur) *n.* one who finds a way or route, as through unexplored territory.

path·less *adj.* having no paths: *the pathless desert; a pathless wilderness.*

path·o·log·i·cal (path·uh·LOJ·uh·cul) *adj.* **1** having to do with pathology or diseases: *a pathological analysis, examination, test; pathological evidence; the dumping of pathological waste from hospitals; a pathological condition (caused by a disease).* **2** compulsive: *a pathological aversion, drinker, gambler, liar.*

path·ol·o·gy (path·OL·uh·jee) *n.* **-gies** the study of the origin, nature, and symptoms of diseases, esp. as affecting body tissues. — **path·ol·o·gist** (-jist) *n.*

pa·thos (PAY·thos) *n.* the quality of arousing pity and tenderness: *There was an element* or *touch of pathos in his resignation speech.*

path·way *n.* a path or way leading to a place: *a pathway to success.*

-pathy *combining form.* **1** feeling or emotion: *antipathy, sympathy, telepathy.* **2** disease or treatment: *hydropathy, naturopathy, psychopathy.*

pa·tience (PAY·shunce) *n.* capacity to endure suffering and put up with inconveniences without complaining: *the patience of Job; patience in adversity; the patience to read every word of a boring essay; It taxes or tries your patience; You may lose your patience or run out of patience; I'm out of patience with pranksters; My patience is wearing thin; Dad displays, has, shows patience; endless, great, infinite patience with everyone.*

pa·tient (PAY·shunt) *adj.* having patience: *a patient listener; the patient Griselda; She was patient in suffering; patient with everyone.* — *n.* a person receiving medical care: *to cure, treat a patient; a patient discharged from a hospital.* — **pa·tient·hood** *n.* — **pa·tient·ly** *adv.*

pa·ti·o (PAT·ee·oh) *n.* **-os 1** an open courtyard. **2** an area adjoining a dwelling, used for outdoor lounging, dining, etc.

pat·ois (PAT·wah) *n., pl.* **-ois** (-wahz) a nonstandard variety of a language, as a provincial dialect or the jargon of an occupational class.

patri- *combining form.* father: *patriarch, patricide, patrimony.*

pa·tri·arch (PAY·tree·arc) *n.* **1** the head of a tribe or founder of a family, as Abraham, Isaac, and Jacob in the Bible. **2** any venerable male leader or founder, as Joseph Smith in the Mormon Church. **3** a high-ranking bishop of the Eastern Orthodox Church. — **pa·tri·ar·chal** (pay·tree·AR·cul) *adj.: It is a patriarchal custom for a married woman to take her husband's name.* — **pa·tri·ar·chate** (PAY·tree·ar·kit) *n.* — **pa·tri·ar·chy** (PAY·tree·ar·kee) *n.* **-chies.**

pa·tri·ate (PAY·tree·ate) *v.* **-ates, -at·ed, -at·ing** *Cdn.* to return legislation from a colonial government to the country to which it applies: *Canada's Constitution*

(British North America Act) was patriated in 1982. — **pa·tri·a·tion** (-AY·shun) *n.*

pa·tri·cian (puh·TRISH·un) *n. Formal.* one belonging to a family of high social rank; aristocrat; *adj.: his patrician air; a patrician family.*

pat·ri·cide (PAT·ruh·cide) *n.* 1 the murder of one's father. 2 the murderer. — **pat·ri·ci·dal** (-SYE·dul) *adj.*

pat·ri·mo·ny (PAT·ruh·moh·nee) *n.* -nies a legacy from one's father or ancestors. — **pat·ri·mo·ni·al** (-MOH·nee·ul) *adj.*

pa·tri·ot (PAY·tree·ut) *n.* one who loves his or her country: *an ardent, zealous patriot.* — **pa·tri·ot·ism** (-uh·tiz·um) *n.* — **pa·tri·ot·ic** (-OT·ic) *adj.: the patriotic spirit.*

pa·trol (puh·TROLE) *v.* -trols, -trolled, -troll·ing make a regular circuit of a territory for service, security, etc. — *n.* 1 a patrolling person or body of people: *highway patrol; military patrol; police patrol; school patrol; a Boy Scout or Girl Guide patrol with eight members and a patrol leader; The police are out on patrol in patrol cars.* 2 a group of patrolling ships, planes, etc.: *a (naval) shore patrol.* — **pa·trol·ler** *n.*

pa·trol·man (puh·TROLE·mun) *n.* -men a policeman on patrol duty.

patrol wagon *n.* a small, enclosed police truck for transporting prisoners.

pa·tron (PAY·trun) *n.* 1 a special benefactor, guardian, or protector: *a wealthy patron of the arts; St. George is the patron saint of England.* 2 a regular customer of a shop, library, or other establishment. — **pa·tron·ess** *fem.*

pa·tron·age (PAY·truh·nij, PAT·ruh-) *n.* 1 protection, support, etc. given by a patron. 2 the business brought by a customer: *Thank you for your patronage.* 3 the power to grant favours, esp. political; also, such favours, as appointments, contracts, financial support, etc.: *a patronage appointment.*

pa·tron·ize (PAY·truh·nize, PAT·ruh-) *v.* -iz·es, -ized, -iz·ing 1 be a patron of an establishment: *We don't patronize that store any more.* 2 be condescending toward someone: *Don't patronize me!* — **pa·tron·iz·ing** *adj.: a very patronizing air, attitude.* — **pa·tron·iz·ing·ly** *adv.*

pat·sy (PAT·see) *n.* -sies *Slang.* one who is easily victimized, imposed upon, etc.; an easy victim or scapegoat.

pat·ter (PAT·ur) *n.* 1 quick, light tapping: *the patter of rain on a roof.* 2 the gabble or chatter of a rapidly talking hawker, comedian, or other performer. — *v.* 1 hit or move with light tapping sounds: *rain pattering on the window; The children pattered down the hallway as the bell rang.* 2 to chatter or gabble: *The magician pattered away while we watched.* — **pat·ter·er** *n.*

pat·tern (PAT·urn) *n.* 1 an ideal, model, or guide: *She was a pattern of domestic virtues; a paper pattern for making a dress.* 2 a design with a repeating, predictable arrangement of elements: *a paisley pattern; wallpaper patterns; a series of murders with a pattern to them; a behaviour pattern; group behaviour following a cultural pattern; a winter weather pattern; the holding pattern* (= flight course) *over a busy airport.* — *v.* to model: *Children tend to pattern themselves after or on or upon their parents.*

pat·ty (PAT·ee) *n.* pat·ties a small, flat, disk-shaped form of chopped or minced meat, fish, or other food: *a hamburger patty; A patty shell of baked dough holds a creamed-meat, vegetable, or fruit filling.*

pau·ci·ty (PAW·suh·tee) *n.* smallness or fewness; lack: *a paucity of good speakers; the paucity of evidence in a case.*

paunch *n.* a potbelly. — **paunch·y** *adj.*

pau·per (PAW·pur) *n.* a poor person living on public charity.

pau·per·ize (PAW·puh·rize) *v.* -iz·es, -ized, -iz·ing make poor: *a nation pauperized by drought, corruption, inflation.*

pause (PAWZ) *n.* 1 a partial stop, esp. in reading or speaking: *Commas indicate pauses in a sentence; a pregnant pause during an announcement; a long, awkward pause during the wedding ceremony; a serious matter that should give one pause* (= make one stop and think). 2 a lengthening of a musical note indicated by [⌒] or [⌄] placed over it. — *v.* paus·es, paused, paus·ing make a pause: *Let's pause and catch our breath.*

pave *v.* paves, paved, pav·ing cover or overlay a path, street, or an area with asphalt, concrete, tiles, etc.: *to pave a driveway; The road to ruin is paved* (= full of) *with good intentions; negotiations to pave the way for* (= prepare for) *a peace treaty.* — **pav·er** *n.*

pave·ment (PAVE·munt) *n.* 1 a paved surface, esp. of a street: *to tear up the pavement for laying cables; Pavements buckle during a heat wave; to pound the pavement* (= go about wearily) *looking for a job.* 2 *Brit.* a sidewalk. 3 material used to pave; also **paving.**

pa·vil·ion (puh·VIL·yun) *n.* 1 a tent. 2 a light, tentlike open or temporary structure, as for an exhibit, recreational shelter, or as part of a building complex: *a band pavilion in a park; a hospital's maternity pavilion; the national pavilions at an expo.*

paw *n.* 1 a foot of an animal with claws, distinguished from a hoof. 2 *Informal.* a human hand. — *v.* 1 use the paws to kick, touch, etc. 2 to touch or grasp in a rude manner: *She resented being pawed by the crowd.*

pawn *n.* 1 a chessman of the lowest value. 2 someone under someone else's control: *a helpless pawn.* 3 something given as surety: *The jewels were held in pawn against the payment of the loan.* — *v.* give as surety: *He pawned his guitar for ten dollars.*

pawn·bro·ker (PAWN·broh·kur) *n.* a person who lends money in exchange for personal goods left as security.

pawn·shop *n.* a pawnbroker's place of business.

Pax *n. Latin.* peace, esp. as enforced by a military power: *Pax Romana* (= Roman peace); *Pax Sovietica* (= Soviet peace).

pay *n.* money given for work or service; wages or salary: *equal pay for work of equal value; back, overtime, severance, take-home pay; a writer in the pay of a corporation;* **adj.:** *pay dirt, envelope, telephone, TV.* — *v.* **pays, paid, pay·ing 1** give money or a similar amount in return for a product or service: *I paid $25 000 for the car; He pays rent on his house; She pays handsomely; Employees pay into a pension fund; I pay for purchases by cheque, in cash, out of my own pocket; a pay-as-you-go* (= as the service is received) *system of paying bills or taxes.* **2** be profitable or worthwhile: *It pays to advertise; The business closed because it didn't pay; The job pays $2 000 a week; It pays highly or well.* **3** give something that is due, fair, or proper: *to pay attention to a lecture; to pay compliments; to pay a penalty; to pay a visit to someone; to pay back* (= punish in return) *in the same coin; Jane pays her way* (= pays her expenses) *through college.*
— **pay off 1** pay someone in full: *to pay off a mortgage.* **2** be profitable; bring returns: *Hard work pays off in the long run.* **3** *Informal.* to bribe.
— **pay one's dues** suffer enough, esp. life's hardships.
— **pay out** [*pt.* **payed**] let out a rope or cable gradually.
— **pay the piper** or **fiddler 1** pay for one's pleasure. **2** suffer the consequences of one's action.
— **pay through the nose** pay excessively.
— **pay up** pay fully what is due.
— **pay·er** or **pay·or** *n.*

pay·a·ble (PAY·uh·bul) *adj.* to be paid or due: *accounts payable and receivable; a cheque payable to John Doe; a bill payable at sight; a draft payable on demand.*

pay·back *n.* the recouping of an original investment by the net income received on it.

pay-cable *n.* pay-TV via cable.

pay·cheque or **pay·check** *n.* a cheque in payment of salary or wages: *a weekly paycheque.*

pay·day *n.* the day on which wages are paid.

pay dirt *n.* **1** earth or ore containing enough mineral to make the mining profitable: *to hit pay dirt.* **2** a profitable find or discovery.

pay·ee (pay·EE) *n.* one who receives something paid, or payment.

pay·load *n.* **1** the revenue-producing load in a plane, train, truck, etc. **2** the passengers, instruments, etc. in a spacecraft as distinguished from fuel and other operational loads. **3** a missile's warhead or bomb load.

pay·ment (PAY·munt) *n.* a paying or its amount: *a cash payment; down payment (made initially); a payment for goods; a payment on a loan; to stop payment on a cheque; to suspend payments; $100 in full and final payment* (= settlement) *of a claim.*

pay·off *n.* **1** a paying off of a mortgage, profits, bribe money, etc.; also, what is paid: *Someone made a payoff to the kidnappers; The payoff was $3 million.* **2** what one gets from an investment: *The payoff of laser printers is near-typeset quality.*

pay·o·la (pay·OH·luh) *n. Slang.* bribe.

pay·or (PAY·ur) *n.* one who pays.

pay·out *n.* what is paid out as a winning or dividend.

pay phone or **pay station** *n.* a coin-operated public telephone.

pay·roll *n.* **1** a list of employees and the pay they receive: *to be put on the payroll.* **2** the amount of money needed to pay employees in a given period: *Unable to meet the payroll, the company declared bankruptcy.*

pay-TV *n.* the system of broadcasters selling program packages to viewers on a subscription basis.

pa·zaaz (puh·ZAZ) *n.* same as PIZAZZ.

pea (PEE) *n.* **1** the small, round edible seed borne in the pods of certain vines. **2** any of these vines or a related plant. — **as like as two peas** like twins; exactly alike.

peace (PEECE) *n.* **1** a state of calm and quiet; freedom from war: *The war is over and peace is at hand; to achieve, bring about peace in society; to break, disturb, shatter the peace; a durable, lasting, fragile peace; a breach of the peace; Peace reigned in Jerusalem; Everyone wants to live in peace and quiet; You have peace of mind when at peace with yourself; Hold your peace* (= stay quiet) *when your mother is talking; Christmas is a good time to make (one's) peace with enemies; the U.S. Peace Corps (of volunteers) working in Third World countries; the peace symbol* [☮]; *the Peace Tower of the Centre Block of Canada's Parliament Buildings.* **2** an agreement, esp. between nations, to end a war or not to fight; treaty: *to negotiate a peace with the enemy; the Peace of Paris; The court ordered him to keep the peace* (= obey the laws).

peace·a·ble (PEE·suh·bul) *adj.* peace-loving: *a peaceable man.* — **peace·a·bly** *adv.*

peace·ful (PEECE·ful) *adj.* having peace; free from worry, trouble, violence, etc.: *to lead a peaceful life; peaceful coexistence between the superpowers.* — **peace·ful·ly** *adv.;* **peace·ful·ness** *n.*

peace·keep·ing (PEECE·kee·ping) *adj.* helping to keep the peace: *a Canadian peacekeeping force; peacekeeping operations; the U.N.'s peacekeeping role in the Middle East.*

peace·nik *n.* [disparaging term] a demonstrator for peace.

peace officer *n.* a civil officer such as a police officer, sheriff, or justice of the peace.

peace pipe *n.* a pipe smoked ceremonially by North American Indians at a peace conference.

peace sign *n.* a V-sign made with the fingers of one's palm turned outwards.

peace·time *n.* a period of peace: *in peacetime and wartime;* **adj.:** *peacetime economy; peacetime emergencies such as earthquakes and other natural disasters; peacetime uses of nuclear energy.*

peach (PEECH) *n.* **1** a small, roundish, orange-yellow, fleshy fruit of a low-growing, widely cultivated tree: *a peaches-and-cream* (= healthy and smooth) *complexion.* **2** *Slang.* a highly admired person.

peach·y *adj.* **1** peach-coloured. **2** *Slang.* fine.

pea·cock (PEE·cock) *n.* a large Asiatic bird, the male of the **pea·fowl,** having long greenish blue feathers with tips marked like eyes which it spreads out at the back like a fan in the presence of the female: *proud as a peacock.* — **pea·hen** *fem.*

peak (PEEK) *n.* **1** a pointed top, as of a mountain, a pyramid, or a conical cap; summit: *to scale the peak of Mount Everest.* **2** any tapered end or high point: *the peak of a beard; at the peak of her career; traffic at the peak of the rush hour; Prices reach a peak and then level off; adj.: an engine running at peak efficiency; Summer is the peak season for travel.* **3** the visor of a cap.
— *v.* **1** reach a high: *House prices peak in the spring.* **2** look sickly; waste away: *to peak and pine.*
— **peaked** *adj.* having a peak: *a peaked cap, helmet, lapel, roof.*

peak·ed (PEE·kid) *adj.* pale and wan.

peal (PEEL) *n.* **1** a long, loud sound, esp. of bells; also, any similar sound: *peals of laughter, thunder, trumpets.* **2** a set of tuned bells; carillon; also, changes rung on it.
— *v.* ring or sound loudly: *A carillon pealed forth the victory anthem; the pealing organ.*

pea·nut (PEE·nut) *n.* **1** a tropical vine whose pods ripen underground, yielding seeds, also called "groundnuts" or "goobers," used in preparations such as **peanut butter, peanut oil,** and **peanut brittle,** a candy. **2** *Slang.* a small or insignificant person. **3 peanuts** *pl. Slang.* a trivial sum of money: *No one likes to work for peanuts.*
— *adj.* petty or cheap: *peanut politics; The **peanut gallery** of a theatre has cheap seating.*

pear (PAIR) *n.* a fleshy, sweet, cone-shaped fruit borne by varieties of trees widely cultivated in temperate regions: *a **pear-shaped figure** (that is wide toward the bottom); the **pear-shaped** (= full and resonant) tones of a singer.*

pearl (PURL) *n.* a white or bluish-grey, satiny gem obtained from inside some oyster shells: *a string of pearls; cultured pearls; imitation pearls; "a pearl of great price."*
— **cast pearls before swine** give something valuable to people who cannot appreciate it.
— **pearl·y** *adj.: her pearly white teeth; the **Pearly Gates** (of Heaven).*

pearl grey *n.* bluish grey.

peas·ant (PEZ·unt) *n.* **1** a tiller of the soil; rustic. **2** an uncultured person.

— *adj.: a peasant girl; peasant labour.*

peas·ant·ry (PEZ·un·tree) *n.* peasants as a class: *The peasantry of England led by Wat Tyler revolted in 1381.*

pea soup *n.* **1** a thick soup made with peas as the chief ingredient. **2** *Informal.* a very thick fog; also **pea·soup·er.**

peat (PEET) *n.* partially decayed vegetable matter dug from marshy places and used as fertilizer and, in dried form, as fuel: ***Peat moss** forms soft, spongy peat.*
— **peat·y** *adj.*

peb·ble (PEB·ul) *n.* a small, smoothly worn stone, as found on a beach.
— *v.* **peb·bles, peb·bled, peb·bling 1** cover or finish with pebbles. **2** make to look pebbly: *to pebble leather* (= to give it a grainy surface).

peb·bly (PEB·lee) *adv.* full of or covered with pebbles or little bumps.

pe·can (pi·CAN, -CAHN) *n.* the oval, edible nut of a tree common in southern U.S.

pec·ca·dil·lo (pec·uh·DIL·oh) *n.* **-dil·los** or **-dil·loes** a petty sin or fault.

peck *n.* **1** a unit of dry measure equal to eight quarts: *"a peck of pickled peppers"; a pretty peck of troubles.* **2** a quick jab or stroke with a beak or as if made with a beak, as a light, quick kiss: *a peck on the cheek.*
— *v.* pick, pick at, or pick up, as with a beak: *Using just two fingers, she pecked out the note on an old typewriter; He's just pecking at his food because he's not really hungry.*

pecking order *n.* an order of social dominance or precedence, as in a flock of poultry in which a weaker bird will submit to a stronger one while dominating others weaker than itself: *The No. 2 position in the Cabinet pecking order used to be held by the Finance Minister.*

pec·to·ral (PEC·tuh·rul) *adj.* on the chest or breast: *the pectoral fin of a fish; a bishop wearing a pectoral cross.*

pe·cul·i·ar (pi·CULE·yur) *adj.* **1** particular or special: *an item of peculiar interest to collectors; a custom **peculiar to** certain peoples.* **2** strange or odd: *Peg's peculiar behaviour.* — **pe·cul·iar·ly** *adv.*
— **pe·cu·li·ar·i·ty** (pi·CUE·lee·AIR·uh·tee) *n.*

pe·cu·ni·ar·y (pi·CUE·nee·air·ee) *adj.* having to do with money: *a pecuniary motive.*

ped- *combining form.* **1** foot: *pedicab, pedicure, pedometer.* **2** child: *pedagogue, pediatrician, pedodontist.*

ped·a·gogue (PED·uh·gog) *n.* a teacher of a pedantic or dogmatic kind.

ped·a·go·gy (PED·uh·goh·jee) *n.* the art and science of teaching. — **ped·a·gog·ic** (-GOJ·ic) or **ped·a·gog·i·cal** (-GOJ·uh·cul) *adj.* — **ped·a·gog·i·cal·ly** *adv.*

ped·al (PED·ul) **1** *n.* a lever worked by the foot, as used in an automobile, on musical instruments such as the piano and on machines such as the bicycle and old sewing machines: *the brake pedal; to depress* or *step on the gas pedal.* **2** (also PEE·dul) *adj.* relating to the foot

or to a pedal.
— *v.* ped·als, ped·alled or ped·aled, -al·ling or -al·ing move by pedals: *The bicyclists pedalled uphill; Keep pedalling* (= working the pedals).

ped·a·lo (PED·uh·loh) *n.* a small boat with a paddle wheel turned by pedals.

ped·ant (PED·unt) *n.* one who makes a show of his or her learning, esp. by too much attention to trivial things.
— **pe·dan·tic** (pi·DAN·tic) adj.: *It's pedantic to call a flea "Pulex irritans" or to say "It is I" instead of "It is me" in ordinary speech.*

ped·ant·ry (PED·un·tree) *n.* **-ries** a pedantic manner or an instance of being pedantic: *pedantry parading as scholarship; the pedantries of grammar and pronunciation.*

ped·dle (PED·ul) *v.* ped·dles, ped·dled, ped·dling
1 sell, esp. small articles, from place to place.
2 circulate: *to peddle gossip, lies.*

ped·dler (PED·lur) *n.* a hawker or seller: *a drug peddler; influence peddler; smut peddler; Pimps are peddlers of vice.* Also **ped·lar** (-lur).

pede- or **ped-** *combining form.* foot or feet: *biped, centipede, millipede, quadruped.*

ped·es·tal (PED·us·tul) *n.* the supporting base of a column or statue: *People are beginning to put quality of life on a higher pedestal than material wealth; A pedestal desk has a set of drawers supporting its top on one or both sides; a powder room with a stylish pedestal basin or sink (that is supported by a pedestal).*

pe·des·tri·an (puh·DES·tree·un) *n.* a walker, esp. one out on a street.
— *adj.* 1 having to do with pedestrians: *pedestrian malls, traffic; a pedestrian overpass across a highway.*
2 commonplace: *a pedestrian style of writing.*
— **pe·des·tri·an·ism** *n.*

pe·des·tri·an·ize (puh·DES·tree·uh·nize) *v.* -iz·es, -ized, -iz·ing convert for pedestrian use: *a street pedestrianized into a shopping mall.*

pedi- same as PEDI-.

pe·di·at·ric (pee·dee·AT·ric) 1 adj. relating to pediatrics: *a pediatric hospital ward; pediatric nasal drops.* 2 **pediatrics** *n.pl.* a branch of medicine dealing with the care of children.
— **pe·di·at·ri·cian** (PEE·dee·at·RISH·un) *n.*

ped·i·cab (PED·uh·cab) *n.* a three-wheeled vehicle pedalled like a bicycle, with passengers seated at the back, used as a taxicab in Asian countries.

ped·i·cure (PED·uh·cure) *n.* treatment of the feet and toenails.

ped·i·gree (PED·uh·gree) *n.* 1 ancestry: *a man of noble pedigree; dogs of unknown pedigree; cats with pedigrees.* 2 a list or record, as a family tree, showing ancestry.

pedigreed adj. having a pedigree: *pedigreed cattle, corn, dogs, horses, poultry, wheat.*

ped·i·ment (PED·uh·munt) *n.* a triangular, gablelike structure over a row of columns, a doorway, etc.

pedlar same as PEDDLER.

pedo- See PED-.

pe·do·don·tist (pee·duh·DON·tist) *n.* a dentist specialized in the care of children's teeth.

pe·dom·e·ter (pi·DOM·uh·tur) *n.* an instrument worn for measuring distances walked.

pe·do·phile (PEE·duh·file) *n.* an adult with a sexual desire for young children.

pee *v.* pees, peed, pee·ing [child's word] urinate.

peek *n.* a quick stealthy look; a peeping.
— *v.* take a peek: *to peek at, in, into, through, under something; to peek out from behind the curtains.*

peek·a·boo (PEE·kuh·boo) *n.* a game played with infants by covering one's face, then uncovering it, and saying "Peekaboo!"
— *adj.* see-through: *a peekaboo curtain.*

peel *n.* a skin, rind, or bark that is relatively thin: *a banana peel; lemon peel; orange peel.*
— *v.* to skin: *Boiled potatoes peel easily; We peel a banana to eat it; I'll keep my eyes peeled (Informal for be on the alert) for a job vacancy; An aircraft peels off* (= separates and turns off) *from a flight formation.*

peeling *n.* esp. **peelings** *pl.* parts peeled off: *potato peelings.*

peep *n.* 1 a brief look taken from a hidden position: *the peep of dawn in the eastern sky; a partition with peep-holes for the curious passer-by; The peep show at the circus charges $2 a viewing; A marksman adjusts the peep sight to line up the target and front sight.* 2 the high-pitched cry of young birds, mice, etc.; cheep. 3 a complaining sound: *No one ever hears a peep out of her.*
— *v.* 1 take a peep: *She peeped at her brother through the keyhole; She's always afraid of a peeping Tom* (= voyeur) *under her window.* 2 utter a peep: *The child wouldn't stop peeping; You can hear "peeper" frogs peeping in early spring.*

peep·er (PEE·pur) *n. Slang.* 1 one who peeps.
2 **peepers** *pl.* one's eyes.

peer *v.* 1 look closely, often with narrowed eyes; squint: *She peered at him over her glasses; He peered into her eyes.* 2 appear partly or slowly: *the sun peering through the clouds; The mechanic peered out from under the car.*
— *n.* 1 an equal in rank, value, ability, etc.: *Children learn language from their peers; a peer group; peer pressure; the right to be tried and judged by one's peers; Has there been a peer to Einstein?* 2 a British noble, as a baron, viscount, earl, marquis, and duke (in ascending order).
— **peer·ess** *n. fem.*

peer·age (PEER·ij) *n.* the nobility consisting of peers: *Roy Thomson was raised to the peerage in 1963.*

peer·less (PEER·lis) adj. without equal: *Toscanini was peerless in his time as a conductor.*

peeve (PEEV) *n.* 1 an irritation or grudge: *"Not warm enough" is a pet peeve of hers; He shouldn't take out petty peeves from work on his family.* 2 a bad mood: *You'll rarely find Paola in a peeve.*
— *v.* peeves, peeved, peev·ing irritate or annoy: *Peg is*

easily peeved by loud talkers.

pee·vish *adj.* cross or complaining; also, showing ill temper: *a peevish child, expression, remark; What is Peg so peevish about?*
— **pee·vish·ly** *adv.*; **pee·vish·ness** *n.*

pee·wee *n.* **1** *Informal.* a tiny person or thing: *a peewee baseball league, golf course.* **2** same as PEWEE.

peg *n.* **1** a small, often tapered bolt of wood or metal used to fasten, as a tent to the ground, to plug, as a barrel, to hang things, as on a pegboard, or to tighten, as violin strings: *He's a square peg in a round hole* (= He's badly matched with his position). **2** a degree or step: *In the reshuffle, some were taken down a peg or two* (= humbled); *Pat was moved up a peg to office manager.* **3** in baseball, a hard throw of the ball aimed at putting out a runner.
— *v.* **pegs, pegged, peg·ging 1** fasten, mark, plug, etc. using pegs. **2** work hard: *She pegs away at math all year.* **3** hold at a certain mark or level: *Pay raises are pegged to inflation; Oil was once pegged at $40 a barrel; a pegged* (= fixed) *rate of exchange.*

peg·board *n.* a board with evenly spaced holes into which hooks are inserted for hanging or displaying articles.

peg leg *n.* *Informal.* a wooden leg or a person having one.

peg top *n.* **1** a child's spinning top with a metal peg at its base. **2** **peg tops** *pl.* trousers that are narrow at the ankles; also **peg-top trousers.**

pe·jo·ra·tive (pi·JOR·uh·tiv) *adj.* tending to make worse or lower: *"Silly" got its present meaning by a pejorative change from "blessed" as in the old expression "silly sheep."*
— *n.* a pejorative word, as "egregious" or "knave."
— **pe·jo·ra·tive·ly** *adv.*

pe·koe (PEE·koh) *n.* a high grade of black tea from India and Sri Lanka.

pelf *n.* [contemptuous use] wealth: *the tyranny of pelf and power.*

pel·i·can (PEL·uh·cun) *n.* a large web-footed bird with an elastic pouch under its long bill for scooping up and storing fish, fabled to feed starving young with its own blood.

pel·let (PEL·it) *n.* **1** a tiny, well-packed mass or ball: *a pellet of fertilizer, medication, snow.* **2** a piece of lead shot; small bullet.

— *v.* make into or hit with pellets.
— **pel·let·al** *adj.*

pel·let·ize (PEL·uh·tize) *v.* **-es, -ized, -iz·ing** make into pellets: *pelletized rat poison.*

pell-mell *adv.* in confusion; recklessly: *to rush pell-mell in panic; The early 1980s was a time of pell-mell expansion in the computer industry.*

pel·lu·cid (puh·LOO·sid) *adj.* clear and transparent: *Addison's pellucid prose style.*

pelt *v.* hit continuously; strike repeatedly: *hail pelting a roof; The children pelted each other with mud, snowballs; The angry mob pelted stones at the embassy; Rain pelted down on the crowd.*
— *n.* **1** a pelting: *the pelt of hailstones; The horses ran away at full pelt* (= at full speed). **2** an untanned or undressed skin of a fox, mink, beaver, etc.

pel·vic *adj.* having to do with the pelvis: *The pelvic girdle* or *arch supports a vertebrate's hind limbs; the pelvic fins in fish.*

pel·vis *n.* **-vis·es** or **-ves** (-veez) the basinlike framework of bones of the hip.

pem·bi·na (PEM·buh·nuh, pem·BEE·nuh) *n. Cdn.* a shrub that bears a tart, reddish berry, also called "highbush cranberry."

pem·mi·can (PEM·uh·cun) *n. Cdn.* a concentrated food of dried and powdered meat mixed with fat and fruit.

pen *n.* **1** an instrument for writing with ink or other fluid: *a ball-point, felt-tip, fountain, quill pen; With a stroke of the pen, the country was declared independent.* **2** written expression; writing: *"The pen is mightier than the sword."* **3** an enclosure, esp. one for domestic animals: *a pig pen; submarine pen* (= dock). **4** *Slang.* a penitentiary.
— *v.* **pens, penned, pen·ning** write: *to pen a note; a well-penned letter.*
— *v.* **pens,** *pt. & pp.* **penned** or **pent, pen·ning** confine in or as in a pen: *Don't pen me in; His pent-up fury was unleashed in violence.*

pe·nal (PEE·nul) *adj.* **1** having to do with punishment: *the penal code; a penal colony, institution; penal labour, servitude.* **2** liable to punishment: *a penal offence.*

pe·nal·ize (PEE·nul·ize) *v.* **-iz·es, -ized, -iz·ing** punish: *You may not be penalized if you confess; The poor man was penalized for someone else's crime; The football team was penalized 10 yards.*
— **pe·nal·i·za·tion** (-uh·ZAY·shun) *n.*

pen·al·ty (PEN·ul·tee) *n.* **-ties** punishment: *a penalty for speeding; the death penalty; to impose, pay, rescind a penalty; a light, severe, stiff penalty; ordered to pay the fine on* or *under penalty of going to jail.*
— *adj.: A hockey player is sent to the penalty box (to sit on a bench for two to 12 minutes as penalty); a penalty kick (in soccer); a penalty shot (in hockey).*

pen·ance (PEN·unce) *n.* punishment based on repentance: *For the crimes of his youth, St. Paul did penance for the rest of his life; A sinner receives the sacrament of penance* or *reconciliation from a priest by going to confession, as in the Roman Catholic Church.*

pence a *pl.* of the British PENNY.

pen·chant (PEN·chunt) *n.* a strong inclination: *a writer with a penchant for detail.*

pen·cil (PEN·sul) *n.* **1** a drawing, writing, or marking implement, esp. one with "lead" enclosed in a cylinder of wood: *a lead pencil; mechanical pencil.* **2** a stick of crayon, cosmetic material, etc.: *a cosmetic, eyebrow pencil.*
— *v.* -cils, -cilled or -ciled, -cil·ling or -cil·ing mark with a pencil: *He pencilled some changes on the manuscript.*

pen·dant (PEN·dunt) *n.* a suspended ornament or fixture, as a locket, chandelier, etc.; also **pen·dent.**
— **pendent** or **pendant** *adj.* suspended or hanging: *a balcony pendent over a porch.*

pending *adj.* unsettled: *The case is still pending (in the courts); patent pending* (= applied for).
— *prep.* during: *The museum is closed pending repairs.*

pen·du·lar (PEND·yuh·lur, -juh·lur) *adj.* relating to a pendulum.

pen·du·lous (-lus) *adj.* hanging: *Some birds build pendulous nests.*

pen·du·lum (PEND·yuh·lum, PEN·juh-) *n.* a freely swinging suspended body, as the regulating mechanism of a clock: *a swing of the political pendulum to the Left.*

penes a *pl.* of PENIS.

pen·e·trate (PEN·uh·trate) *v.* -trates, -trat·ing, -trat·ing **1** force a way into and through something: *The wound has penetrated to the bone; a jungle that is too dense to penetrate; to penetrate deep into a forest; a preacher who can penetrate hardened hearts.* **2** see into: *to penetrate a mystery; to penetrate someone's disguise.*
— **pen·e·tra·ble** (-truh·bul) *adj.*
— **penetrating** *adj.*: *a penetrating odour, intellect, study.*

pen·e·tra·tion (pen·uh·TRAY·shun) *n.* a penetrating: *the penetration of a knife through the animal's heart; An ad campaign has to achieve penetration of a market.*

pen·guin (PENG·gwin) *n.* a flightless, web-footed, short-legged sea bird with paddlelike flippers instead of wings.

pen·i·cil·lin (pen·uh·SIL·in) *n.* a powerful antibiotic.

pen·in·su·la (puh·NIN·suh·luh) *n.* a land area almost surrounded by water: *Gaspé Peninsula.*

pen·in·su·lar (puh·NIN·suh·lur) *adj.* having to do with a peninsula: *a peninsular region; Napolean's **Peninsular War** in Spain and Portugal.*

pe·nis (PEE·nis) *n.* -nis·es or -nes (-neez) the erectile male sex organ.

pen·i·tence (PEN·uh·tunce) *n.* the state of being penitent; repentance: *David showed true penitence for his sins.*

pen·i·tent (PEN·uh·tunt) *n.* one who is sorry for having sinned: *a penitent sinner.*
— **pen·i·ten·tial** (pen·uh·TEN·shul) *adj.*: *King David's penitential psalms; a Lenten penitential service.*

pen·i·ten·tia·ry (pen·uh·TEN·shuh·ree) *n.* -ries a prison for serious crimes: *the Kingston Penitentiary; a*

penitentiary offence (punishable by a jail term).

pen·knife *n.* -knives a small pocket knife.

pen·light or **pen·lite** *n.* a small flashlight resembling a fountain pen.

pen·man (PEN·mun) *n.* -men a person skilled in handwriting or calligraphy. — **pen·man·ship** *n.*

pen name *n.* a writer's assumed name; pseudonym: *Charles Dodgson wrote under the pen name of Lewis Carroll.*

pen·nant (PEN·unt) *n.* a long, tapering flag used for signalling, identification, or as a championship emblem: *Who won the Eastern Division (baseball) pennant in 1981?*

pen·ni·less (PEN·ee·lis) *adj.* very poor; destitute.

pen·non (PEN·un) *n.* a banner or pennant.

pen·ny (PEN·ee) *n.* **pen·nies 1** in Canada and the U.S., a cent. **2** a British money unit equal to 1/100 of a pound; *pl.* [collectively] **pence:** *a few pence, tenpence.*
— **cost a pretty penny** cost a good deal of money.
— **pinch pennies** be thrifty or frugal.
— **turn an honest penny** earn a little money honestly.

penny pincher *n. Informal.* a miser.
— **penny-pinching** *n. & adj.*

penny-wise (PEN·ee·WIZE) *adj.* thrifty in minor things: *"penny-wise and pound-foolish."*

pen·ny·worth (PEN·ee·wurth) *n.* a small amount, value, or bargain.

pen pal *n.* a friend with whom one exchanges letters without having met.

pen·sion (PEN·shun) *n.* **1** a regular payment that an employee receives on retirement: *a disability pension; It is hard to live on a fixed pension because of inflation; old-age pension; to award, draw, grant, revoke a pension; adj.: a pension fund; Canada Pension Plan.* **2** (pahn·SYONG) *French.* a boarding house; also, board and lodging.
— *v.* to retire someone: *Some are pensioned off before 65.*
— **pen·sion·a·ble** (-uh·bul) *adj.*: *the pensionable age of 65; a pensionable disability.*

pen·sion·er (PEN·shun·ur) *n.* one receiving a pension.

pen·sive (PEN·siv) *adj.* thoughtful or melancholic: *a pensive mood.*

pent a *pt. & pp.* of PEN.
— *adj.* shut *up* or confined *in* something.

penta- *combining form.* five: *pentagon, pentameter, pentathlon.*

pen·ta·gon (PEN·tuh·gun) *n.* **1** a five-sided figure with five angles. **2** the **Pentagon** a pentagon-shaped building housing the U.S. Department of Defense. **3** the U.S. military establishment.
— **pen·tag·o·nal** (pen·TAG·uh·nul) *adj.*

pen·tath·lon (pen·TATH·lon) *n.* a modern Olympic contest of five events, namely, horseback riding, fencing, pistol shooting, running, and swimming.

Pen·te·cost (PEN·tuh·cost) *n.* a church festival on the seventh Sunday after Easter, celebrating the descent of

the Holy Spirit on Christ's apostles.
— **Pen·te·cos·tal** (-COS·tul) *adj.*: *"Assemblies of God" is a Pentecostal church; Speaking in various tongues is a Pentecostal gift.* — **Pen·te·cos·tal·ism** *n.*

pent·house *n.* an apartment or structure built on the roof of a tall building: *a penthouse suite.*

pent-up *adj.* repressed or bottled up: *pent-up animosity, emotion, frustration, fury.*

pen·u·ry (PEN·yuh·ree) *n.* extreme poverty.
— **pe·nu·ri·ous** (pi·NEW·ree·us) *adj.*: *the penurious years of famine and drought.*

pe·on (PEE·on) *n.* **-ons** or **-on·es** (pay·OH·neez) formerly, a labourer forced to work to pay off a debt.

pe·on·age (PEE·uh·nij) *n.* the Mexican system of employing peons, made illegal in 1917: *a charge of holding 13 workers in peonage.*

peo·ple (PEE·pul) *n.* **1** *pl.* human beings, esp. of a particular place, group, or nation: *"Let my people go," pleaded Moses; a government of the people; the people of Canada; boat people; common, little, old, ordinary, primitive, working, young people; my people* (*Informal* for relatives) *from Parry Sound.* **2** *sing., pl.* **peoples** a race or social group: *a chosen people; the English-speaking peoples; the peoples of Asia; the ant people* (=species; group of creatures).
— **people's 1** socialist or communist: *a people's democracy, republic.* **2** populist or popular: *the People's Bible; a people's party.*
— *v.* **-ples, -pled, -pling** populate: *a planet peopled by apes.*

people meter *n.* a hand-held push-button electronic device hooked up to a computer that measures TV-viewing habits on an individual basis.

people mover *n.* **1** a mass-transport system or vehicle. **2** a horizontal escalator.

people's park *n.* a park without restrictions.

pep *n.* energy or vigour: *Put some pep into your talk.*
— *adj.* morale-raising: *a pep rally, talk.*
— *v.* **peps, pepped, pep·ping** put vigour or life into something: *The coach pepped up their spirits.*

pep·per (PEP·ur) *n.* **1** a pungent condiment obtained by grinding the dried berries, or **pep·per·corns**, of an East Indian vine: *Ordinary pepper is black pepper; White pepper is made from fully ripe berries; There's a dash of pepper in this dish.* **2** capsicum: *green, red, sweet pepper; hot cayenne pepper; chili peppers used in sauces; peppers stuffed with rice.*
— *v.* **1** season with pepper: *a hot peppered sauce.* **2** shower or pelt: *The media peppered the president with questions; They peppered away at him for an hour.*

pep·per·y (PEP·uh·ree) *adj.* **pep·per·i·er, -i·est 1** pungent: *a peppery sauce.* **2** hot-tempered or fiery: *a peppery general, orator.*

pep pill *n. Informal.* a stimulating drug, as an amphetamine.

pep·py (PEP·ee) *adj.* **pep·pi·er, pep·pi·est** having pep: *a peppy veteran who can never sit idle.*

Pé·quiste (pay·KEEST) *n. Cdn.* a member or sympathizer of the Parti Québécois.

per *prep.* **1** for each: *two scoops per child; The price is $2 per (item); a speed of 80 km per (= an) hour.* **2** through: *money sent per bearer of this letter; The order has been filled as per* (*Formal* for according to) *your instructions.*

per·ad·ven·ture (per·ud·VEN·chur) *adv.* [old use] perhaps. — **beyond a peradventure** beyond doubt.

per annum (per·AN·um) *adv.* each year; annually: *an income of $50 000 per annum.*
— *adj.* annual: *a per-annum income of $50 000.*

per cap·i·ta (pur·CAP·uh·tuh) *adv.* per person: *an allowance of $100 per capita.*
— *adj.*: *a per-capita allowance.*

per·cei·va·ble (pur·SEE·vuh·bul) *adj.* that can be perceived: *Ultrasound is not perceivable by the human ear.* — **per·cei·va·bly** (-blee) *adv.*

per·ceive (pur·SEEV) *v.* **-ceives, -ceived, -ceiv·ing** become aware of through the senses, esp. sight, or through the mind: *By the smoke from the chimney, I perceived that the house was occupied; We perceived that lives were in danger unless we acted fast.*

per·cent (pur·SENT) *adj. & adv.* per hundred: *a five percent sales tax.*
— *n.* a hundredth part: *Ten percent of 1 000 is 100.*

per·cent·age (pur·SEN·tij) *n.* **1** a part or portion, esp. of a hundred: *Only a small percentage of pupils were absent.* **2** *Informal.* profit: *There's no percentage in drilling here for oil.*

per·cen·tile (pur·SEN·tile) *n.* a value or range of distribution of a variable within a series of 100 parts: *A score in the 75th percentile is higher than 75% of all the scores.*

per·cep·ti·ble (pur·SEP·tuh·bul) *adj.* capable of being perceived: *Outside the home, the animosity between the two is hardly perceptible; the barely perceptible outline of a flying object; a perceptible change, effect, impact.*
— **per·cep·ti·bly** (-blee) *adv.*
— **per·cep·ti·bil·i·ty** (-BIL·uh·tee) *n.*

per·cep·tion (pur·SEP·shun) *n.* the act or power of perceiving or understanding: *Good perception of depth is important for a pilot; The survivors had no clear perception of what happened in the crash; extrasensory perception; She has a keen perception of scents.*

per·cep·tive (pur·SEP·tiv) *adj.* understanding: *Hearing is a perceptive faculty; a quiet youth with a keen and perceptive mind.* — **per·cep·tive·ly** *adv.*

per·cep·tu·al (pur·SEP·choo·ul) *adj.* having to do with perception: *the perceptual skills of a child; An optical illusion is a perceptual problem.* — **per·cep·tual·ly** *adv.*

perch (PURCH) *n.* **1** a spiny freshwater food fish. **2** a bird's roost. **3** a resting place, esp. a high position. **4** vantage point: *From her perch up in the tree, Eve could see everything around.*
— *v.* place at a height: *a village perched on a mountain height; Children perched on trees to watch the parade.*

per·chance (pur·CHANCE) *adv.* [old use] perhaps.

per·cip·i·ence (pur·SIP·ee·unce) *n.* perception or discernment. — **per·cip·i·ent** (-unt) *adj.* discerning.

per·co·late (PUR·cuh·late) v. -lates, -lat·ed, -lat·ing
pass a liquid or make a liquid pass through a porous
medium; filter or filter through: *to percolate coffee;
ideas that percolate through the student community.*
— **per·co·la·tor** (-lay·tur) n.
— **per·co·la·tion** (-LAY·shun) n.

per·cus·sion (pur·CUSH·un, "USH" as in "rush") n. **1** a
striking or hitting. **2** a section of a band or orchestra
containing instruments such as drums, xylophone, etc.:
a percussion instrument.
— **per·cus·sion·ist** (pur·CUSH·un·ist) n.

per di·em (pur·DEE·um) adj. & adv. by the day: *Supply
teachers are paid so much per diem; a per-diem rate.*
— n., pl. **per diems** a daily allowance.

per·di·tion (pur·DISH·un) n. damnation or hell.

per·dur·a·ble (pur·DEW·ruh·bul) adj. extremely
durable; lasting: *hard and perdurable like granite; the
perdurable author of over 100 books.*
— **per·dur·a·bil·i·ty** (-BIL·uh·tee) n.

per·emp·to·ry (per·EMP·tor·ee) adj. **1** allowing no
appeal or refusal: *A proposed juror may be rejected by a
peremptory challenge (with no reasons given).* **2** abrupt
and dictatorial: *a peremptory manner, order.*
— **per·emp·to·ri·ly** adv.

per·en·ni·al (pur·EN·ee·ul) adj. **1** constantly occurring:
a perennial complaint, conflict, problem. **2** lasting
throughout the year: *a perennial stream (that never
dries up); The iris is a perennial plant; A great book is a
perennial source of inspiration.*
— n. a perennial plant: *hardy perennials such as roses.*
— **per·en·ni·al·ly** adv.

per·e·stroi·ka (per·es·TROY·kuh) n. overhauling and
restructuring of the Soviet economic and political system
started in the 1980s.

per·fect (PUR·fict) adj. flawless; without faults: *No one
is perfect; "Practice makes perfect"; a perfect circle,
stranger; perfect nonsense; perfect weather for a picnic;*
per·fect·ly adv.
— v. (pur·FECT) make perfect: *Practice helps to
perfect a skill.* — **per·fec·ti·ble** adj.
— **per·fect·i·bil·i·ty** (-tuh·BIL·uh·tee) n.: *the
perfectibility of human nature.*

per·fec·tion (pur·FEC·shun) n. the act of making or
state of being perfect: *It takes years to bring an
invention to perfection; to achieve, attain perfection;
Jean does everything **to perfection** (= perfectly).*
— **per·fec·tion·ism** n.

per·fec·tion·ist (pur·FEC·shuh·nist) n. & adj. one who
demands perfection: *Jan is a perfectionist, but
perfectionists are not always popular; the perfectionist
approach.*

per·fi·dy (PUR·fuh·dee) n. -dies (-deez) *Formal.* the
quality or an act of being deceitful or treacherous.
— **per·fid·i·ous** (pur·FID·ee·us) adj.

per·fo·rate (PUR·fuh·rate) v. -rates, -rat·ed, -rat·ing
bore or punch through, esp. make a line of holes, as on
sheets of postage stamps: *An ulcer may perforate
through the stomach wall.* — **per·fo·ra·tor** (-ray·tur) n.
— **per·fo·ra·tion** (-RAY·shun) n.

per·force (pur·FORCE) adv. necessarily: *Much of

science fiction, perforce, is speculative.*

per·form (pur·FORM) v. **1** carry out a task, promise,
function, duty, etc. that requires effort or skill: *A
surgeon performs an operation; Magicians perform
tricks; They perform live on stage; to perform a
ceremony, contract, piece of music, promise; to perform
in the role of "Hamlet"; to perform penance for one's
sins.* **2** put on a show: *a bear that performs; Acrobats
perform on the high wire; the **performing arts** such as
drama, dancing, and music.* **3** behave as expected: *Joe
is highly qualified, but can he perform (on the job)? Our
new car is performing well.* — **per·form·er** n.

per·form·ance (pur·FORM·unce) n. **1** the carrying out
of an action: *Promises are meaningless without
performance; She's very conscientious in the
performance of her duties.* **2** a show: *a beautiful ballet
performance; an evening performance; a benefit,
command, daring, gala, live, repeat performance.*
3 functioning or behaviour: *an engine's poor
performance on the highway.*

per·fume (PUR·fume) n. a pleasant odour; also, a sweet-
smelling fluid preparation: *to dab on or put on
perfume; Ray came in reeking of some cheap perfume.*
— v. (pur·FUME) -fumes, -fumed, -fum·ing put on or
fill with perfume: *a temple perfumed with incense.*
— **per·fum·er** n.

per·func·to·ry (pur·FUNK·tuh·ree) adj. done in a
routine or superficial way just to be finished with it;
casual or indifferent: *He goes about his work in a
perfunctory fashion; a perfunctory inspection, job,
manner, worker.* — **per·func·to·ri·ly** adv.

per·haps (pur·HAPS) adv. possibly or maybe: *Perhaps
I'm mistaken, perhaps not; For perhaps one split-second
I was asleep at the wheel; Perhaps I'm being too careful;
Well, perhaps.*

peri- prefix. around; about; near: *perimeter, perinatal,
peripheral.*

per·il (PER·ul) n. danger or a source of danger: *to avert,
face a peril; the perils of skydiving; Tax evaders live **in
peril of** the law (= risk being caught); Enter at your
peril (= your own risk).*

per·i·lous (PER·uh·lus) adj. dangerous or hazardous: *a
perilous journey, undertaking.* — **per·i·lous·ly** adv.

pe·rim·e·ter (puh·RIM·uh·tur) n. the outer boundary or
border of a figure, area, etc.; also, its length:
*Brampton, Mississauga, and Richmond Hill are on the
perimeter of Metro Toronto.*

per·i·na·tal (per·uh·NAY·tul) adj. around the time of
birth: *Perinatal care of infants lasts from conception to
several months after birth; perinatal medicine,
mortality; a perinatal unit.*

pe·ri·od (PEER·ee·ud) n. **1** a portion of time, esp. one
well marked: *a school day divided into eight periods;
The Cambrian period began 600 million years ago; the
Civil War period; a cooling-off, incubation, question-
and-answer, rest, waiting period.* **2** a punctuation mark
(.) put at the end of a sentence or abbreviation; *interj.*
[used for emphasis]: *Freedom of speech is a question of
freedom, period.* **3** a well-proportioned sentence, esp.
one in which the principal clause is placed at the end.
4 the menses: *to have, miss a period.*

— *adj.* belonging to a specific historical period: *period costumes, furniture; a period play.*

pe·ri·od·ic (peer·ee·OD·ic) *adj.* occurring at regular intervals: *the periodic migration of birds to warmer regions; periodic tides; Engines need periodic tune-ups.*

pe·ri·od·i·cal (peer·ee·OD·uh·cul) *adj.* periodic, esp. published at regular intervals.
— *n.* a weekly, monthly, yearly, etc. publication.
— **pe·ri·od·i·cal·ly** *adv.*

period piece *n.* a work of art or architecture peculiar to a historical period.

pe·riph·er·al (puh·RIF·uh·rul) *adj.* 1 of a periphery; outer or external: *The peripheral nervous system branches out from the central nervous system; peripheral vision (outside the area of direct sight).* 2 incidental: *Having fun working is peripheral to getting the work done.*
— *n.* an external device or unit connected to a computer, as a keyboard, display terminal, or printer.
— **pe·riph·er·al·ly** (-uh·lee) *adv.*

pe·riph·er·y (puh·RIF·uh·ree) *n.* **-er·ies** an outer boundary or surface; outskirts: *Suburbs are on the periphery of a metropolitan city.*

pe·riph·ra·sis (puh·RIF·ruh·sis) *n., pl.* **-ses** (-seez) a roundabout way of speaking; circumlocution.
— **per·i·phras·tic** (per·uh·FRAS·tic) *adj.*

per·i·scope (PER·uh·scope) *n.* an optical instrument that enables one to see above or around an obstacle, used esp. in submarines. — **per·i·scop·ic** (-SCOP·ic) *adj.*

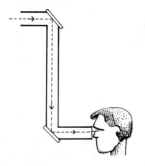

per·ish *v.* be destroyed: *Hundreds perished in the fire; Many perished from famine; "Those who take the sword shall perish by the sword."*
— **perish the thought!** [said of something one does not want to happen].

per·ish·a·ble (PER·ish·uh·bul) *adj.* liable to spoil or decay quickly: *perishable foods.*
— *n.:* *Fruit, vegetables, eggs, etc. are perishables.*
— **per·ish·a·bly** *adv.*

perishing *adv.* very or quite: *It's perishing cold out there; How utterly perishing true!*

per·jure (PUR·jur) *v.* **-jures, -jured, -jur·ing** usually **perjure oneself,** give false evidence or withhold a truth after taking an oath: *perjured* (=false) *evidence, testimony.* — **per·jur·er** *n.*

per·jur·y (PUR·juh·ree) *n.* the act of perjuring oneself or an instance of it: *To lie on the witness stand is to commit perjury.*

perk *n.* [short form] perquisite: *A chauffeur-driven car is one of the perks of the presidency.*
— *v.* 1 [short form] percolate: *freshly perked coffee.* 2 move or behave in a smart, brisk, lively, or pert manner: *The horse perked up an ear at the sound; She's beginning to **perk up*** (=become active) *after her long illness; He came for the interview **perked out** in his Sunday best.*

perk·y (PUR·kee) *adj.* **perk·i·er, -i·est** 1 lively: *a perky little girl; a perky hairdo.* 2 saucy: *They are a brash and perky lot.* — **perk·i·ly** *adv.;* **perk·i·ness** *n.*

perm *n.* Brit. Informal. permanent wave.

per·ma·frost (PUR·muh·frost) *n.* subsoil that is permanently frozen, as in the Arctic.

per·ma·nent (PUR·muh·nunt) *adj.* lasting long or indefinitely, not temporary: *Baby teeth are replaced by 32 permanent teeth; a permanent home, job, resident.*
— **per·ma·nent·ly** *adv.*
— **per·ma·nence** (-nunce) *n.*

permanent or **permanent wave** *n.* a hair wave that lasts through several washings.

permanent press *n.* a fabric treated for wrinkle resistance; durable press.

per·me·a·ble (PUR·mee·uh·bul) *adj.* capable of being permeated; having pores or openings to allow fluids to pass through, as limestone. — **per·me·a·bly** *adv.*
— **per·me·a·bil·i·ty** (-BIL·uh·tee) *n.*

per·me·ate (PUR·mee·ate) *v.* **-ates, -at·ed, -at·ing** 1 pass through or *into* every part of something: *Gases permeate (through) charcoal.* 2 spread through or into a place or thing: *The smell of cooking permeated the house; a philosophy **permeated** with* (=full of) *pragmatism.* — **per·me·a·tion** (-AY·shun) *n.*

per·mis·si·ble (pur·MIS·uh·bul) *adj.* that may be permitted: *permissible evidence; It's not permissible to eat in our library.*
— **per·mis·si·ble·ness** or **per·mis·si·bil·i·ty** (-BIL·uh·tee) *n.*

per·mis·sion (pur·MISH·un) *n.* a permitting or allowing: *The teacher may give* or *grant you permission to leave the classroom.*

per·mis·sive (pur·MIS·iv) *adj.* excessively lenient; indulgent: *permissive child discipline; modern permissive society.*
— **per·mis·sive·ly** *adv.;* **per·mis·sive·ness** *n.*

per·mit (pur·MIT) *v.* **-mits, -mit·ted, -mit·ting** allow to do or exist: *If the weather permits, we'll eat in the patio; Weather permitting, we'll have a picnic; Smoking is not permitted here; An urgent matter **permits** of no delay.*
— *n.* (PUR·mit) permission or licence: *a building permit; fishing permit; work permit; to cancel, give, grant, rescind, revoke a permit.*

per·mu·ta·tion (pur·mew·TAY·shun) *n.* an arrangement of a set of things in a particular order: *CBA is one of the six permutations possible with A, B, and C.*

per·ni·cious (pur·NISH·us) *adj.* severely harmful; deadly: *a pernicious habit, influence.*
— **per·ni·cious·ly** *adv.*

per·nick·e·ty (pur·NIK·uh·tee) *adj.* same as PERSNICKETY.

per·ox·ide (pur·OX·ide) *n.* an oxide containing an unusual proportion of oxygen, esp. "hydrogen peroxide."
— *adj.*: *peroxide blond hair* (= bleached with peroxide).

per·pen·dic·u·lar (pur·pen·DIK·yuh·lur) *adj.* at a 90-degree angle, esp. upright or vertical: *cliffs rising perpendicular to the shore.* — *n.*: *a tower leaning 10 degrees from the perpendicular.*
— **per·pen·dic·u·lar·ly** *adv.*
— **per·pen·dic·u·lar·i·ty** (-LAIR·uh·tee) *n.*

per·pe·trate (PUR·puh·trate) *v.* -trates, -trat·ed, -trat·ing commit, esp. a crime, blunder, or other outrageous act. — **per·pe·tra·tor** *n.*
— **per·pe·tra·tion** (-TRAY·shun) *n.*

per·pet·u·al (pur·PECH·oo·ul) *adj.* continuing indefinitely; ceaseless: *a perpetual nuisance; a land of perpetual sunshine; A **perpetual calendar** can be used for many years; A **perpetual motion** machine is supposed to run for ever.* — **per·pet·u·al·ly** *adv.*

per·pet·u·ate (pur·PECH·oo·ate) *v.* -ates, -at·ed, -at·ing make perpetual: *Superstitions help perpetuate myths; an elixir that claims to perpetuate life.*
— **per·pet·u·a·tor** (-ay·tur) *n.*
— **per·pet·u·a·tion** (-AY·shun) *n.*

per·pet·u·i·ty (pur·puh·TUE·uh·tee) *n.* -ties indefinite duration: *The house was bequeathed to her and her heirs **in perpetuity*** (= for ever).

per·plex (pur·PLEX) *v.* puzzle and worry: *I'm perplexed by* or *about* or *at* or *over her sudden change of mind; He's torn by **perplexing** doubts.*

per·plexed (pur·PLEXT) *adj.* 1 puzzled: *He gave her a perplexed look.* 2 complicated: *a perplexed issue.*

per·plex·i·ty (pur·PLEX·uh·tee) *n.* -ties something that perplexes: *the perplexities of a student's first day in a new school.*

per·qui·site (PURK·wuh·zit) *n.* a bonus, fringe benefit, or a peculiar privilege, esp. one attached to a position or office, as a sales rep's expense account or company car.

per se *adv.* Latin. by or in itself: *Drinking per se, as opposed to drunk driving, is not criminal.*

per·se·cute (PUR·suh·cute) *v.* -cutes, -cut·ed, -cut·ing 1 harass, esp. because of one's beliefs: *She was persecuted for her religious beliefs.* 2 annoy constantly; pester: *The minister felt persecuted by a hostile press.*
— **per·se·cu·tion** (pur·suh·CUE·shun) *n.*: *bloody, political, racial, relentless, religious persecution; to suffer persecution for justice's sake.* — **per·se·cu·tor** *n.*

per·se·vere (pur·suh·VEER) *v.* -veres, -vered, -ver·ing continue doing, esp. something hard; be steadfast: *to persevere in one's efforts to get a gold medal; to persevere at* or *with your studies.*
— **per·se·ver·ance** (-unce) *n.*

Per·sian (PUR·zhun) *n.* 1 a person of or from Persia, the former name of Iran. 2 the chief language of Iran, esp. its ancient and literary forms.
— *adj.*: *the Persian Gulf; Persian carpets, literature; the **Persian cat** with long silky hair.*

per·sist (pur·SIST) *v.* 1 continue being or doing, esp. with a purpose: *She persisted in taking her daily walk despite her illness.* 2 continue to last: *Mountain snows persist till early summer.*
— **per·sis·tence** (-tunce) *n.*: *his quiet persistence in doing things the right way; She shows dogged persistence in her efforts; Only Pat has the persistence to fight to the finish; The continuity of moving pictures is based on persistence of vision.*
— **per·sis·tent** (-tunt) *adj.*: *a persistent cough, questioner; A persistent pesticide or virus takes a long time to get out of a system.* — **per·sis·tent·ly** *adv.*

per·snick·e·ty (pur·SNIK·uh·tee) *adj.* Informal. extremely fussy or fastidious.

per·son (PUR·sun) *n.* 1 a human being: *a displaced person; missing person; stolen by persons unknown; She's a natural person (with nothing artificial about her); A **person-to-person** phone call cannot be dialled directly – it has to be operator-handled; The child found a friend **in the person of** the police officer.* 2 a legal entity having rights and duties: *A company is a legal person.* 3 an individual physically considered: *They threatened him but didn't touch his person; He couldn't find a penny on her person; The president was here **in person*** (= personally). 4 any of the three pronoun categories, as the **first person** (= I, we), **second person** (= you), **third person** (= he, she, it, they).
— *combining form* [as a neutral substitute for "man" and "woman"]: *chairperson, person-hour, personhood, spokesperson.*

per·so·na (pur·SOH·nuh) *n., pl.* -nae (-nee) 1 a character in a play or novel. 2 an author's personality seen through his or her works. 3 *pl.* -nas in psychology, a personality assumed by an individual as a mask.

per·son·a·ble (PUR·suh·nuh·bul) *adj.* pleasing in appearance or personality.
— **per·son·a·bly** (-nuh·blee) *adv.*

per·son·age (PUR·suh·nij) *n.* a person of rank or importance.

per·son·al (PUR·suh·nul) *adj.* having to do with a particular person; private: *a personal and confidential letter; your personal history; a personal assistant, newspaper column; a highly personal remark bordering on slander; a personal* (= live) *appearance by a movie star; **personal hygiene** (of the body); Lack of **personal space**, as in a crowd, makes one tense.*
— **per·son·al·ly** *adv.*

personal computer *n.* a microcomputer, esp. a desk-top one.

personal effects *n. pl.* belongings such as clothing and toiletry.

personal equation *n.* variation in observation or judgment because of one's personality.

per·son·al·i·ty (pur·suh·NAL·uh·tee) *n.* -ties 1 a person's distinctive character; also, a person: *a woman with some personality; a charming, dynamic, forceful, magnetic, multiple, split, strong, weak personality; a TV personality* (= well-known person); *the Soviet **personality cult** of Stalin; Pat and Ray have a **personality problem** (= They can't get along well); Let us not indulge in **personalities*** (= offensive personal

560

remarks).

per·son·al·ize (PUR·sun·ul·ize) v. -liz·es, -lized, -liz·ing make identifiable as one person's: *a personalized greeting card.*

personal property n. [legal use] chattels, not real estate.

persona non gra·ta (-GRAH·tuh) n., pl. **per·so·nae non gra·tae** (pur·SOH·nee·non·GRAH·tee) one who is not acceptable: *A diplomat suspected of being a spy is declared persona non grata by the host country.*

per·son·ate (PUR·suh·nate) v. -ates, -at·ed, -at·ing [legal use] same as IMPERSONATE
— **per·son·a·tion** (-NAY·shun) n.

person-day (PUR·sun·day) n. the duration of a person's average work day.

per·son·i·fy (pur·SON·uh·fye) v. -fies, -fied, -fy·ing make into a person: *the Mississippi personified as "Ol' Man River"; He thinks Bo is beauty personified.*
— **per·son·i·fi·ca·tion** (-fuh·CAY·shun) n.

per·son·nel (pur·suh·NEL) n. employees as a body: *army, enlisted, government, military personnel; The office personnel are on their coffee break; a personnel department.*

per·spec·tive (pur·SPEC·tiv) n. the look of objects as affected by their dimensions and distance from the viewer: *a picture drawn out of perspective; the proper, true, wrong perspective; to see events in the right perspective; a new perspective of history.*
— **per·spec·tive·ly** adv.

per·spi·ca·cious (pur·spuh·CAY·shus) adj. discerning: *a perspicacious analysis of an obscure issue.*
— **per·spi·ca·cious·ly** adv.
— **per·spi·cac·i·ty** (-CAS·uh·tee) n.

per·spi·cu·i·ty (pur·spuh·CUE·uh·tee) n. the quality of being perspicuous or lucid: *the perspicuity of his argument, writing.*

per·spic·u·ous (pur·SPIC·yoo·us) adj. 1 clearly expressed; lucid: *a perspicuous style.* 2 expressing oneself clearly: *a perspicuous writer.*
— **per·spic·u·ous·ly** adv.
— **per·spic·u·ous·ness** n.: *the perspicuousness of her prose.*

per·spire (pur·SPIRE) v. -spires, -spired, -spir·ing to sweat: *We perspire profusely in a sauna.*
— **per·spi·ra·tion** (pur·spuh·RAY·shun) n.

per·suade (pur·SWADE) v. -suades, -suad·ed, -suad·ing move or win over to think or act as desired: *She persuaded him to stop smoking; persuaded him of the need to stop smoking; Are you persuaded (= convinced) that smoking is bad for your lungs?*

per·sua·sion (pur·SWAY·zhun) n. 1 power of persuading: *a convincing speaker with great powers of persuasion; We used friendly persuasion to get him to change his mind.* 2 a group or party with a particular set of beliefs; denomination: *Protestants of all persuasions; a Calvinist of the strictest persuasion; Christians of various persuasions.* — **per·sua·sive** (-ziv) adj.; **per·sua·sive·ly** adv.; **per·sua·sive·ness** n.

pert adj. 1 saucy or flippant: *a pert answer; a pert little girl.* 2 jaunty or lively: *He's feeling pert and refreshed.*

— **pert·ly** adv.; **pert·ness** n.

per·tain (pur·TAIN) v. refer or relate: *evidence that pertains to the mystery; new facts **pertaining** to the case.*

per·ti·na·cious (pur·tuh·NAY·shus) adj. stubbornly clinging to an opinion or course of action: *a pertinacious newshound; a lawyer's pertinacious cross-examination.*
— **per·ti·na·cious·ly** adv.
— **per·ti·nac·i·ty** (-NAS·uh·tee) n.: *a bill-collector's pertinacity in dunning creditors.*

per·ti·nence (PUR·tun·unce) n. relevance.

per·ti·nent (PUR·tun·unt) adj. clearly and directly relevant: *a pertinent question; matters that are not pertinent to the case.*
— **per·ti·nent·ly** adv.: *a question pertinently put at the right moment.*

per·turb (pur·TURB) v. agitate mentally; upset: *He's easily perturbed by or about or over unforeseen events; a **perturbing** revelation.*
— **per·tur·ba·tion** (-tur·BAY·shun) n.

pe·ruse (puh·ROOZ) v. -rus·es, -rused, -rus·ing read or scan, esp. attentively. — **pe·ru·sal** (-zul) n.

per·vade (pur·VADE) v. -vades, -vad·ed, -vad·ing spread through all parts of: *The spirit of camaraderie soon pervaded the camp; an atmosphere **pervaded** with animosity.*
— **per·va·sive** (-VAY·ziv) adj.: *a pervasive influence.*
— **per·va·sive·ly** adv.; **per·va·sive·ness** n.

per·verse (pur·VURSE) adj. contrary to what is desirable, reasonable, or established as normal: *an obstinate and perverse nature; to take a perverse pleasure in doing something wrong-headed; a perverse desire, fascination, thrill.* — **per·verse·ly** adv.
— **per·verse·ness** or **per·ver·si·ty** (-VUR·suh·tee) n. -ties the quality of being perverse; also, something perverse: *the perversities of human nature.*
— **per·ver·sion** (-VUR·zhun) n. a distortion: *The translation seems a perversion of the author's original sense.*

per·vert (pur·VURT) v. turn or cause something normal or desirable to turn to something bad; corrupt or lead astray: *a charge of perverting the course of justice by influencing a trial; a verdict that perverts the ends of justice; the **perverting** influence of TV violence.*
— **n.** (PUR·vurt) a perverted person: *a sexual pervert.*

pes·ky (PES·kee) adj. -ki·er, -ki·est Informal. annoying, as gnats or mosquitoes.

pe·so (PAY·soh) n. -sos the basic money unit of many Latin American countries and the Philippines.

pes·si·mism (PES·uh·miz·um) n. the tendency to expect the worst possible outcome: *the pessimism about or over the future of the environment.* — **pes·si·mist** n.
— **pes·si·mis·tic** (-MIS·tic) adj.; **pes·si·mis·ti·cal·ly** adv.

pest n. 1 a harmful plant or animal, as insects, mice, and weeds: *Snails and larvae are garden pests.* 2 an annoying person; nuisance: *Gossips are pests of society.*

pes·ter (PES·tur) v. annoy or vex: *Rob kept pestering his friend for money; Stop pestering me about the loan; I won't be pestered into lending you any more money.*

pest·hole *n.* a place that helps the spread of disease.

pes·ti·cide (PES·tuh·cide) *n.* a chemical or other agent used against harmful plants and animals.

pes·tif·er·ous (pes·TIF·ur·us) *adj.* 1 disease-causing: *pestiferous germs, vermin.* 2 *Informal.* annoying: *pestiferous telephone solicitations.*

pes·ti·lence (PES·tul·unce) *n.* any fatal epidemic disease, as the plague: *Humanity has survived pestilence, war, and famine.*
— **pes·ti·lent** (-lunt) or **pes·ti·len·tial** (-LEN·shul) *adj.*

pes·tle (PES·ul) *n.* a club-shaped tool used with a mortar for pounding or grinding.

pet *v.* pets, pet·ted, pet·ting 1 fondle or caress: *Children who like to pet and feed animals are welcome at **petting** zoos.* 2 *Informal.* make love by kissing and caressing.
— *n.* 1 a domesticated animal kept for companionship, as a cat, dog, or goldfish: *a household pet.* 2 a young person treated by someone with special care; favourite: *a teacher's pet;* **adj.**: *one's pet peeves; a pet project, rock, theory;* "Bettina" is Beth's **pet name** (= nickname). 3 a peevish mood: *She spent all day in a pet.*
— **pet·tish** *adj.*

pet·al (PET·ul) *n.* one of the separate leaflike parts of a flower's corolla.
— **pet·alled** or **pet·aled** *adj. & combining form: the many-petalled daisy.*

pe·tard (pi·TARD) *n.* an explosive device: *The schemer was **hoist with** or **by his own petard** (= became his own victim, like one blown up by his own bomb).*

pet·cock *n.* a small valve or faucet for draining radiators, boilers, etc.

Pete (PEET) *n.* [short form] Peter.
— **for Pete's sake** [an oath of entreaty]: *For Pete's sake, stop fighting!*

pe·ter (PEE·tur) *v.* esp. in **peter out**, come to an end gradually; be exhausted: *the petering out of one's energies, hopes, provisions.*
— **rob Peter to pay Paul** satisfy one need by creating another, as by using the rent money to make a car payment.

pe·tit (PET·ee) *adj.* [legal use] small or minor; opposed to GRAND, as in **petit jury** (of 12 members), **petit larceny** (= theft of property below a certain value), etc.

pe·tite (puh·TEET) *adj.* of a woman, small and slender in figure.

pe·ti·tion (puh·TISH·un) *n.* 1 a formal request to someone in authority: *to circulate, deny, file, grant, present, reject, withdraw a petition.* 2 a document making such a request: *a petition for retrial.*
— *v.* ask formally: *It's the people's constitutional right to petition the government; 800 citizens petitioned the mayor for a new hospital.* — **pe·ti·tion·er** *n.*

pet·nap·ping or **pet·nap·ing** *n.* stealing of pets, esp. for sale to laboratories for use in experiments.

pet·rel (PET·rul) *n.* a black-and-white sea bird with long wings, esp. the "storm petrel."

Pe·tri dish (pee·tree·DISH) *n.* a small glass dish with a cover used in a biological laboratory: *The first test-tube baby was conceived in a Petri dish.*

pet·ri·fy (PET·ruh·fye) *v.* -fies, -fied, -fy·ing 1 make or become like rock: *The **petrified forests** of Arizona are made up of tree trunks buried in rock millions of years ago.* 2 stun or daze: *He stood motionless, petrified by or with fear.* — **pet·ri·fi·ca·tion** (-fuh·CAY·shun) *n.*

petro- *combining form.* 1 having to do with petroleum: *petrochemical, petrodollars.* 2 having to do with rock: *petroglyph, petrography.*

pet·ro·chem·i·cal (pet·roh·KEM·uh·cul) *n.* a chemical made from crude oil and natural gas and used in plastics, synthetics, fertilizers, etc.
— **pet·ro·chem·is·try** (-KEM·is·tree) *n.*

pet·ro·dol·lars (PET·roh·doll·urz) *n. pl.* excess revenue made by oil-rich countries from increased prices of petroleum.

pet·ro·glyph (PET·roh·glif) *n.* a rock carving: *Study of petroglyphs has shown that a mining site near Trent University was an Indian shrine some time between A.D. 900 and 1400.*

pe·trog·ra·phy (pi·TROG·ruh·fee) *n.* the science of the description and classification of rocks.

pet·rol (PET·rul) *n. Brit.* gasoline.

pe·tro·le·um (puh·TROH·lee·um) *n.* a dark, oily, bituminous liquid found in rock strata, which yields paraffin, gasoline, etc.; crude oil; also called "black gold."

PET scanner *n.* a scanner that shows the functioning of internal organs.

pet·ti·coat (PET·ee·coat) *n.* a woman's underskirt.
— *adj.* female: *petticoat government* (= rule by women).

pet·ti·fog (PET·ee·fog) *v.* -fogs, -fogged, -fog·ging quibble over trifles, esp. in legal matters.
— **pet·ti·fog·ger** *n.*

pet·ty (PET·ee) *adj.* pet·ti·er, pet·ti·est 1 small or unimportant; low in rank: *a petty detail, grievance.* 2 mean or small-minded: *petty partisanship, spite.*
— **pet·ti·ly** *adv.;* **pet·ti·ness** *n.*

petty cash *n.* money for small expenses.

petty jury *n.* same as PETIT JURY.

petty larceny *n.* same as PETIT LARCENY.

petty officer *n.* a naval rank of enlisted personnel varying from **master chief petty officer** down to **petty officer third class** which is just above seaman.

pet·u·lance (PECH·uh·lunce) *n.* petty irritability; peevishness. — **pet·u·lant** (-lunt) *adj.;* **pet·u·lant·ly** *adv.*

pew *n.* a bench with a back, fixed in rows for seating in churches.

pe·wee (PEE·wee) *n.* a small bird related to the flycatcher; also **pee·wee.**

pew·ter (PEW·tur) *n.* 1 a silver-grey alloy of tin used for cooking utensils and tableware. 2 such articles.
— *adj.*: *a pewter craftsman; fine pewter ware.*

pha·lanx (FAY·lanx) *n.* -lanx·es a body of troops in

compact formation.

phan·tasm (FAN·taz·um) *n.* a figment of the imagination; spectre or phantom.
— **phan·tas·mal** (fan·TAZ·mul) or **phan·tas·mic** *adj.*

phan·ta·sy (FAN·tuh·zee) *n.* -sies same as FANTASY.

phan·tom (FAN·tum) *n.* a spectre or ghost.
— *adj.* illusory or ghostlike: *A phantom ship upside down in the sky is a common illusion of sailors.*

phar·i·sa·ic (fair·uh·SAY·ic) or **phar·i·sa·i·cal** (-SAY·uh·cul) *adj.* self-righteous or hypocritical, like the **Pharisees,** an ancient Jewish sect.

phar·ma·ceu·ti·cal (far·muh·SOO·tuh·cul) *adj.* having to do with pharmacy: *a pharmaceutical chemist; pharmaceutical advertising; The Canadian Pharmaceutical Association.* — *n.* a medical drug.

phar·ma·ceu·tics (far·muh·SOO·tics) *n. pl.* [takes sing. v.] the science of preparing and dispensing drugs.

phar·ma·cist (FAR·muh·sist) *n.* one who sells drugs; druggist.

phar·ma·col·o·gy (far·muh·COL·uh·jee) *n.* the science of drugs and their effects, including therapeutics, toxicology, etc. — **phar·ma·col·o·gist** *n.*
— **phar·ma·co·log·ic** (-cuh·LOJ·ic) or **phar·ma·co·log·i·cal** *adj.*

phar·ma·cy (FAR·muh·see) *n.* **1** the profession dealing with the preparation and dispensing of drugs. **2** a drugstore.

phar·yn·gi·tis (fair·in·JYE·tis) *n.* sore throat.

phase (FAZE) *n.* a particular, esp. changing aspect of something; stage of development: *the phases of the moon (as "full moon," "new moon," "first quarter," and "third quarter"); the colour phases of the red fox; the final phase of a war; Windshield wipers have to work in* **phase** (= in a reciprocal relationship).
— **out of phase** not synchronized; out of step: *Drug addicts drift out of phase with the rest of the world.*
— *v.* **phas·es, phased, phas·ing** plan or carry out in stages: *a carefully phased army withdrawal; An addict is phased off a drug; Operations were* **phased down** *in Vietnam long before the U.S. pullout; Innovative changes are* **phased in** *at a plant; An obsolete product line is* **phased out** (= gradually taken off the market).
— **phase-down** *n.* — **phase-out** *n.*

phase-locked *adj.* in precise synchronization *with* something.

phe·nom·e·nal (fuh·NOM·uh·nul) *adj.* extraordinary: *a phenomenal success.* — **phe·nom·e·nal·ly** *adv.*

phe·nom·e·non (fuh·NOM·uh·non) *n.* **1** *pl.* -e·na (-uh·nuh) anything observable or apparent: *natural phenomena such as storms, eclipses, and sunsets.* **2** *pl.* -nons a remarkable person, thing, or event, as a child prodigy: *The Guinness Book of Records is a publishing phenomenon.*

pher·o·mone (FER·uh·mohn) *n.* a scented chemical secretion, usually in the females of species, esp. insects, for eliciting specific responses in others of the species, as to find food or mates.
— **pher·o·mo·nal** (-MOH·nul) *adj.*

phew (FEW) *interj.* expressing impatience, astonishment, etc.

phi·al (FYE·ul) *n.* same as VIAL.

phi·lan·der (fuh·LAN·dur) *v.* of a man, have love affairs in a casual or frivolous manner. — **phi·lan·der·er** *n.*

phi·lan·thro·pist (fuh·LAN·thruh·pist) *n.* one who is generous with gifts of money to help fellow humans, esp. the poor.

phi·lan·thro·py (fuh·LAN·thruh·pee) *n.* -pies **1** the desire to help humanity: *the Canadian Centre for Philanthropy.* **2** a humanitarian effort, gift, or institution, as a charitable foundation.
— **phi·lan·throp·ic** (fil·un·THROP·ic) *adj.*

phi·lat·e·ly (fuh·LAT·uh·lee) *n.* stamp collecting.
— **phi·lat·e·list** (-uh·list) *n.*
— **phil·a·tel·ic** (fil·uh·TEL·ic) *adj.*

-phile *combining form.* one fond of what is specified: *Anglophile, bibliophile, Francophile.*

phil·har·mon·ic (fil·har·MON·ic) *n.* a symphony orchestra or a society sponsoring one.
— *adj.* devoted to music: *a philharmonic society.*

phi·lip·pic (fuh·LIP·ic) *n.* a bitter attack; tirade.

phil·is·tine (FIL·is·teen, fuh·LIS·tun) *n.* an uncultured person who is hostile to the arts, like the biblical **Philistines,** a non-Semitic people at war with the Israelites. — **phil·is·tin·ism** *n.*

phi·lol·o·gy (fuh·LOL·uh·jee) *n.* **1** the study of language. **2** [old use] linguistics, esp. historical.
— **phi·lol·o·gist** (-jist) *n.*
— **phi·lo·log·i·cal** (fil·uh·LOJ·uh·cul) *adj.*

phi·los·o·pher (fuh·LOS·uh·fur) *n.* **1** a student or teacher of philosophy or of a philosophical system. **2** one who seeks truth and wisdom and faces trying situations with calmness.
— **phil·o·soph·ic** (fil·uh·SOF·ic) or **phil·o·soph·i·cal** (-SOF·uh·cul) *adj.*: *a philosophical doubt; the philosophic mind; Jan was philosophical about her defeat* (= accepted it with calmness and courage).

phi·los·o·phize (fuh·LOS·uh·fize) *v.* -phiz·es, -phized, -phiz·ing to see things with calmness and in a rational way: *Jon tried to philosophize about his defeat.*

phi·los·o·phy (fuh·LOS·uh·fee) *n.* **1** the study of the most fundamental nature and principles of things, as causality, space and time, God, etc. **2** learning, esp. in the arts and sciences: *a Doctor of Philosophy in engineering.* **3** *pl.* -phies a system, theory, or the sum total of one's beliefs, esp. as helpful to peace of mind; hence, calmness: *your philosophy of life* (= attitude to life and purpose in life); *to bear sufferings with philosophy; the Epicurean philosophy that right living leads to inner peace.*

phlegm (FLEM) *n.* **1** thick mucus brought up by coughing. **2** apathy; also, not getting too easily excited.
— **phleg·mat·ic** (fleg·MAT·ic) *adj.*: *a phlegmatic temperament; She's too phlegmatic to get easily excited.*

-phobe *combining form.* one who fears or hates, as specified: *Anglophobe, Russophobe, xenophobe.*

pho·bi·a (FOH·bee·uh) *n. & combining form.* an irrational and morbid fear or hatred: *our fears and phobias; agoraphobia, claustrophobia; hydrophobia* (= fear of water). — **pho·bic** *adj.*

phoe·nix (FEE·nix) *n.* a mythical bird, fabled to burn itself after 5 000 years of life, and rise again from its ashes; hence, a symbol of immortality.

-phone *combining form.* sound: *megaphone, telephone, xylophone.*

phone (FONE) *n. & v.* phones, phoned, phon·ing *Informal.* same as TELEPHONE.

phone-in *n.* a TV or radio program in which listeners phone the host to air their views on the topic being discussed; call-in.

pho·net·ic (fuh·NET·ic) **1** *adj.* corresponding to speech sounds: *English spelling is not phonetic; a phonetic pronunciation; phonetic script.* **2 phonetics** *n. pl.* the study of the production and transcription of speech sounds. — **pho·net·i·cal·ly** *adv.*

phoney same as PHONY.

phon·ic (FON·ic) **1** *adj.* having to do with speech sounds, esp. phonics. **2 phonics** *n. pl.* a method of teaching reading using the sound values of letters. — **phon·i·cal·ly** *adv.*

pho·no (FOH·noh) *n.* -nos [short form] phonograph.

pho·no·graph (FOH·nuh·graf) *n.* a machine that reproduces sound as transcribed in a spiral groove on a cylinder or disk, or **phonograph record.**
— **pho·no·graph·ic** (-GRAF·ic) *adj.*
— **pho·no·graph·i·cal·ly** *adv.*

pho·ny or **pho·ney** (FOH·nee) **1** *adj. Informal.* -ni·er, -ni·est not genuine; sham or fake. **2** *n., pl.* -nies or -neys a fake or charlatan: *The new doctor proved to be a phony.* — **pho·ni·ly** *adv.;* **pho·ni·ness** *n.*

phoo·ey (FOO·ee) *interj. Slang.* expressing scorn or disgust: *Phooey to junk food!*

phos·phate (FOS·fate) *n.* a chemical compound occurring naturally as **phosphate rock,** and used in fertilizers, detergents, and soft drinks; also, a similar product.

phos·pho·res·cence (fos·fuh·RES·unce) *n.* **1** the giving of light with little or no burning or heat, as in fireflies. **2** the light thus produced.
— **phos·pho·res·cent** (-unt) *adj.*

pho·tic (FOH·tic) *adj.* having to do with light activity: *The photic driving effect of the lights and sounds of a discotheque makes people feel dizzy; the uppermost photic zone of the ocean that light penetrates.*

pho·to (FOH·toh) **1** *n.* -tos [short form] photograph. **2** *combining form.* light or photographic: *photocopy, photoelectric, telephoto, wirephoto.*

pho·to·cop·i·er (FOH·toh·cop·ee·ur) *n.* a copier for making photocopies.

pho·to·cop·y (FOH·toh·cop·ee) *n.* -cop·ies a copy made with a photocopier.
— *v.* -cop·ies, -copied, -cop·y·ing make a photocopy of something: *Copyrighted materials may not be photocopied.*

pho·to·e·lec·tric (FOH·toh·i·LEC·tric) *adj.* electrically affected by light: *Automatic doors and burglar alarms are operated by photoelectric cells, or electric eyes.*

photo finish *n.* a race finish so close that only a photograph can determine the winner: *It ended in a photofinish.*

pho·to·gen·ic (foh·toh·JEN·ic) *adj.* suitable for being photographed or that looks good in photographs: *a picturesque and photogenic spot; cute and photogenic twins; a photogenic location, setting, show, star.*

pho·to·graph (FOH·tuh·graf) *n.* a picture taken by a camera on light-sensitive film, developed, and printed on paper: *a family photograph; group photograph; to blow up, enlarge, mount, pose for, touch up a photograph.*
— *v.* take a picture of an object: *a bullet photographed in flight; Marc always photographs well* (= looks good in pictures). — **pho·to·graph·ic** (-GRAF·ic) *adj.*
— **pho·to·graph·i·cal·ly** *adv.*
— **pho·tog·ra·pher** (fuh·TOG·ruh·fur) *n.*

pho·tog·ra·phy (fuh·TOG·ruh·fee) *n.* the art or process of taking pictures using cameras: *still photography; trick photography (to create illusions, as of a train about to hit someone).*

photo opportunity *n.* an occasion for the media to take pictures, as of celebrities.

pho·to·play (FOH·toh·play) *n.* a play filmed as a motion picture.

pho·to·sen·si·tive (foh·toh·SEN·suh·tiv) *adj.* sensitive to light.

pho·to·sphere (FOH·tus·feer) *n.* the innermost part of the atmosphere of the sun or of a star.

pho·to·stat (FOH·tus·tat) *n.* a copy made with a photocopier; **Photostat** *Trademark.*

pho·to·syn·the·sis (foh·tuh·SINTH·uh·sis) *n.* a chemical process by which green plants make food by the action of sunlight and give off oxygen.
— **pho·to·syn·thet·ic** (-sin·THET·ic) *adj.*

pho·tot·ro·pism (foh·TOT·ruh·piz·um) *n.* the bending of a plant, usually stalks and leaves, as of the sunflower, toward light or, as some roots do, away from light.
— **pho·to·trop·ic** (foh·toh·TROP·ic) *adj.*

phrase (FRAZE) *n.* **1** a group of words, esp. as a unit within a sentence. **2** a short, pithy expression, as "Peace with honour" or "go the whole hog": *to coin a new phrase; a well-turned phrase; a Czech-English* **phrase book** *for the use of tourists.*
— *v.* phras·es, phrased, phras·ing express in choice words: *a well-phrased toast; inelegant* **phrasing.**

phra·se·ol·o·gy (fray·zee·OL·uh·jee) *n.* -gies style of expression, esp. choice of words.

phys ed (fiz·ED) *n.* [short form] physical education.

phys·ic (FIZ·ic) *n.* a medicine, esp. a laxative.
— *v.* -ics, -icked, -ick·ing treat with medicine.

phys·i·cal (FIZ·uh·cul) *adj.* **1** material: *the physical universe; Ghosts are not physical beings; a university's* **physical plant** (= buildings, equipment, etc.); *a* **physical science** *such as physics, chemistry, or*

astronomy. **2** of the body: *a physical examination; The hockey player got very physical* (= rough); **Physical education** *promotes physical fitness by means of games, gymnastics, etc.; physical medicine;* **physical therapy** (= physiotherapy). **3** having to do with the laws of nature, esp. of matter and energy: *Thawing is a physical change; physical chemistry; To go back in time is a physical impossibility.* **4** of the earth's features: *physical geography.*
— *n.* a physical examination by a doctor: *to do, get, have a physical.* — **phys·i·cal·ly** *adv.*

phy·si·cian (fuh·ZISH·un) *n.* a medical doctor; **phy·si·cian·ly** *adj.*

phys·ics (FIZ·ics) *n. pl.* [with sing. v.] the science of matter and energy and their interactions. — **phys·i·cist** *n.*

phys·i·og·no·my (fiz·ee·OG·nuh·mee) *n.* **-mies** external features, esp. of the face, as indicative of character: *the physiognomy of the moon.*

phys·i·og·ra·phy (fiz·ee·OG·ruh·fee) *n.* geography dealing with the earth's physical features such as land forms and climates. — **phys·i·o·graph·ic** (-ee·uh·GRAF·ic) *adj.*

phys·i·ol·o·gy (fiz·ee·OL·uh·jee) *n.* the branch of biology that deals with the vital functions and processes of living organisms. — **phys·i·ol·o·gist** *n.*

phys·i·o·ther·a·py (FIZ·ee·oh·THER·uh·pee) *n.* the treatment of disease by physical means such as massages, exercise, light, heat, etc.; physical therapy. — **phys·i·o·ther·a·pist** *n.*

phy·sique (fuh·ZEEK) *n.* bodily build: *a man of fine physique; powerful physique.*

pi (PYE) *n.* **1** *pl.* **pis** (PIZE) the 16th letter of the Greek alphabet. **2** *pl.* **pies** (PIZE) mixed-up printing type; also **pie.**
— *v.* **pies, pied, pi·ing** or **pie·ing** mix up: *How did the type get all pied?*

pi·an·ist (pee·AN·ist, PEE·uh·nist) *n.* one who plays the piano.

pi·an·o (pee·AH·noh) **1** *n.* a large percussion instrument with wire strings that are struck by playing on a keyboard or by a mechanical device in a "player piano": *to play the piano; to tune a piano; A piano is either in tune or out of tune; grand piano; upright piano.* **2** *adj. & adv. Music.* soft or softly: *a piano passage.* **3** *n., pl.* **-nos** a passage to be performed softly.

pi·an·o·for·te (pee·AN·oh·fort, -FOR·tee) *n.* same as PIANO.

pi·az·za (pee·AZ·uh) *n.* **1** (*usually* pee·AT·suh) an open public square in Italy. **2** a verandah.

pic *n.* **pics** or **pix** *Informal.* a picture; also, a movie.

pic·a·yune (pik·ee·YOON) *adj.* trivial or petty.

pick *v.* **1** take up, separate, or pull off with the fingers, beak, or a pointed instrument: *Please pick me some flowers; to pick* (= shred) *rags; to pick one's teeth or nose* (*in order to clean it*); *to pick a bone clean; to pick* (= start) *a fight with someone; We have to obey all the laws without* **picking and choosing.** **2** choose or select:

She picked her words carefully as she spoke; to pick (= steal from) *somebody's pocket; A child* **picking at** *her food* (= eating it little by little) *is either ill or not hungry.* **3** dig or pierce: *Rocky soil is hard to pick; a lock that no thief can pick; a watertight alibi you can't pick holes in; She slowly picked her way through the crowd.* **4** pluck the strings of a banjo or guitar; hence, play: *to pick a guitar.*
— **pick off** dispose of someone: *From his ambush, the gunman picked off his victims one by one.*
— **pick on** tease or nag: *Why do you always pick on your kid brother?*
— **pick out 1** select: *Please pick out a red tie for me from the rack.* **2** distinguish or make out: *It's hard to pick her out in the picture.* **3** play on a keyboard: *to pick out "O Canada" on the piano.*
— **pick over** handle: *He picked over the ties for a long time before buying one.*
— **pick up** take or get: *Please pick up the phone and order a pizza; I'll pick up the tab* (= I'll pay); *a suspect picked up by police for questioning; a tie he picked up* (= purchased) *at the store; Where did you pick up* (= learn) *your French? We'll pick up* (= regain) *our trail in the morning; She's slowly picking up* (= recovering) *after the operation; I'll pick you up at noon; It's someone he picked up* (= persuaded to accompany him) *in town; Parents shouldn't have to* **pick up after** (= clean up for) *you as you grow up.*
— **pick up on** *Informal.* become aware of or refer to something: *to pick up on a previous statement.*
— *n.* **1** a picking or choosing; hence, chosen person or thing: *Please take your pick* (= choice); *These apples are the pick* (= the best) *of the crop.* **2** a pickax; also, a tool for breaking: *an ice pick.* **3** a small device for plucking the strings of a musical instrument.

pick·a·back (PICK·uh·back) *adj. & adv.* same as PIGGYBACK.

pick·a·nin·ny *n.* **-nin·nies** [unfavourable term] a black child.

pick·axe or **pick·ax** *n.* a heavy, T-shaped tool for digging.

pick·et (PICK·it) *n.* **1** a pointed stake or pale; one of the posts forming a "picket fence." **2** a person posted as a guard; also, a body of such persons; hence, a striking member of a union stationed outside a place of work, often in a group called a **picket line.**
— *v.* **1** post pickets at a place; also, act as a picket: *to picket a factory.* **2** enclose or secure with a picket: *He picketed* (= tethered) *his horse before going indoors.*
— **pick·et·er** *n.*

pickings *n. pl.* what is picked or gathered; hence, returns or profits: *lean pickings; slim pickings for so much trouble.*

pick·le (PICK·ul) *n.* **1** salt water or vinegar for preserving foods in; hence, an article of food thus preserved; *v.* **-les, -led, -ling:** *to pickle onions.* **2** *Informal.* a predicament: *a sad or fine or pretty or sorry pickle.*

pick·lock *n.* a burglar.

pick-me-up (PICK·mee·up) *n.* a tonic.

pick·pock·et (PICK·pock·it) *n.* one who steals from somebody's pocket.

pick·up *n.* **1** *Informal.* a casual lover. **2** a light truck with an open body. **3** an electronic device for changing vibrations (as from a record player) or sounds and images (as in radio and TV reception) into electrical energy. **4** acceleration: *an engine with good pickup.*

Pick·wick·i·an (pik·WIK·ee·un) *adj.* resembling Samuel Pickwick, a Dickens character: *words used in a Pickwickian sense (to avoid giving offence).*

pick·y *adj.* **pick·i·er, -i·est** choosy or fussy: *Pat's very picky about her clothes.*

pic·nic *n.* **1** an informal meal eaten during an outing; also, such an outing: *to go on a picnic; a picnic shelter for motorists.* **2** *Informal.* a pleasant job or experience: *It's no picnic working in the warehouse.*
— *v.* **-nics, -nicked, -nick·ing** have a picnic.
— **pic·nick·er** *n.*
— **pic·nick·y** *adj.:* *to eat on the lawn in picnicky style.*

pico- *combining form.* one trillionth: *picocurie, picogram, picosecond.*

pic·to·graph (PIC·tuh·graf) *n.* **1** picture writing, as seen in ancient caves. **2** a picture or symbol: *a car and dangling keys is a pictograph for "car rental."*
— **pic·to·graph·ic** (-GRAF·ic) *adj.*
— **pic·tog·ra·phy** (pic·TOG·ruh·fee) *n.*

pic·tor·i·al (pic·TOR·ee·ul) *adj.* having to do with pictures: *a pictorial history of the war.*
— **pic·tor·i·al·ly** *adv.*

pic·ture (PICK·chur) *n.* **1** something drawn, painted, or photographed: *to draw, frame, hang, paint a picture; Let's take a picture* (= photograph); *a motion picture.* **2** any other visual image or an idea: *a clear, gloomy, realistic picture; She looks the picture of health; Get the picture* (*Informal* for the idea)?
— *v.* **pic·tures, pic·tured, pic·tur·ing** make into or form a picture: *Judas is pictured as a villain; I pictured* (= imagined) *myself at my wedding; a **pictured** urn* (decorated with pictures).

Pic·ture·phone (PICK·chur·fone) *Trademark.* a telephone that shows a TV picture of the person one is talking to.

pic·tur·esque (pik·chuh·RESK) *adj.* having a picturelike quality: *a cottage with a picturesque setting in the mountains; a picturesque style of writing.*
— **pic·tur·esque·ly** *adv.;* **pic·tur·esque·ness** *n.*

picture tube *n.* a cathode-ray tube displaying a picture,

as in TV.

picture window *n.* a large window giving a wide view of the outside.

pid·dle (PID·ul) *v.* **pid·dles, pid·dled, pid·dling** trifle or dawdle: *Let's not piddle over petty expenses; It's only a **piddling*** (= trifling) *sum.*

pid·gin (PIJ·in) *n.* a trade jargon used as a bridge between languages, with minimal vocabulary and grammar, as **pidgin English** which has Chinese or South Pacific elements: *The slogan in pidgin English said: "Yumi Bilong Olgeta New Guinea"* (= You and me all together belong to Papua New Guinea).

pie *n.* **1** a baked dish of meat, vegetables, or fruit, usually having a top crust of pastry: *as easy as pie; as American as apple pie; a cherry, lemon meringue, meat, mince pie; a pizza pie; Give me a piece, slice, wedge of pie; Pat has a finger in every pie* (= business); *how to increase your share of the national pie* (= wealth).
2 mixed-up printing type; pi. **3** a parti-coloured bird or animal.
— **pie in the sky** *n.* *Slang.* a vainly hoped-for reward; mere ideal.

pie·bald (PYE·bauld) *adj.* of two colours, esp. black-and-white. — *n.* a piebald horse.

piece (PEECE) *n.* **1** a part, portion, or bit of something: *a piece of chalk, cheese, fruit, paper; a cup broken to pieces; a piece of advice, news.* **2** a single article or amount, often from a larger class or whole: *one piece of luggage; a piece of music; a chess piece; a 50-cent piece; a three-piece suit; cloth sold only by the piece* (= standard length); *a conversation piece* (= subject); *a fowling piece* (= light gun for hunting fowl); *I spoke my piece* (= what I had to say) *and sat down.*
— **go to pieces** break into pieces; also, collapse or break down.
— **of a piece with** in keeping with: *His performance is of a piece with his character.*
— **piece of cake** *Informal.* something very easy.
— **piece of one's mind** *Informal.* a scolding.
— **piece of the action** a share of the benefits or profits.
— *v.* **piec·es, pieced, piec·ing** make into one piece or whole; patch: *to piece a quilt; to **piece out** a personal account by hearsay; odds and ends **pieced together** in one volume.*

pièce de ré·sis·tance (pee·ES·duh·ray·zees·TAHNCE) *n.* the main item or event, esp. a main dish: *The pièce de résistance of the magic show was a woman being sawn in half.*

piece goods *n. pl.* cloth sold by the metre or yard from bolts.

piece·meal *adv.* piece by piece: *to do a job piecemeal; adj.:* *a piecemeal operation.*

piece·work *n.* work based on the amount produced, not the time taken.

pied (PIDE) *adj.* parti-coloured in colour or outfit: *a pied-billed diving bird; the Pied Piper of Hamelin.*

pier (PEER) *n.* **1** a bridgelike structure that juts out, as into the sea for use as a landing place, promenade, or breakwater: *Mobile lounges are cheaper than building finger piers from boarding gates to aircraft.* **2** a pillar or post supporting an arch or bridge, esp. where two spans meet. **3** a section of a wall between windows.

pierce (PEERCE) *v.* **pierc·es, pierced, pierc·ing** go into or through something, esp. at a particular point or with a sharp object: *A nail pierces a tire; a heart pierced with grief; an ear-piercing shriek; a **pierced earring** for use in a pierced ear lobe.* — **pierc·ing·ly** *adv.*

pier glass *n.* a tall mirror set in a wall pier.

pies *pl.* of PI or PIE.

pi·e·ty (PYE·uh·tee) *n.* **-ties** devotion and respect for God and religious things: *Almsgiving is an act of piety; filial piety* (= love and respect shown by children).

pif·fle (PIF·ul) *n. Informal.* trivial talk; also *v.*

pif·fling *adj.* worthless.

pig *n.* **1** a domesticated animal, raised for pork meat, ham, bacon, etc. and thought of as stupid, filthy, and greedy; swine or hog: *Pigs grunt, oink, and squeal; a female pig* (= sow); *male pig* (= boar); *to buy **a pig in a poke*** (*Informal for* something unseen that turns out to be valueless). **2** *Slang.* [offensive] a hated person: *a male chauvinist pig.* **3** a bar into which molten iron is cast; also **pig iron.**
— **pig out** *Slang.* eat too much; gorge oneself: *Peg pigged out on lemon pie.*

pi·geon (PIJ·un) *n.* **1** one of many species of birds of the dove family, usually tame, and often trained as homing and carrier pigeons: *the cooing of pigeons.* **2** one considered easy to dupe, gentle, and timid; hence **pigeon-hearted** or **pigeon-livered** *adj.*

pi·geon·hole (PIJ·un·hole) *n.* a small compartment in a desk or cabinet resembling a pigeon's nesting hole.
— *v.* **-holes, -holed, -hol·ing** classify or shelve: *The collection was pigeonholed and forgotten.*

pig·gish (PIG·ish) *adj.* like a pig: *a piggish manner of eating.* — **pig·gish·ly** *adv.*

pig·gy (PIG·ee) *n.* a little pig.

pig·gy·back (PIG·ee·back) *adj. & adv.* on the back or shoulders: *Dad gave her a piggyback ride; a truck trailer carried piggyback on a railway flatcar; three piggyback commercials during the same break; a spacecraft carrying piggyback capsules.*
— *v.* travel as on someone's back: *I missed the flight but piggybacked home on a charter.*

pig·gy·bank (PIG·ee·bank) *n.* a coin bank in the shape of a piggy.

pig·head·ed (PIG·hed·id) *adj.* stubborn: *too pigheaded to listen to advice.*

pig·let (PIG·lit) *n.* a little pig.

pig·ment (PIG·munt) *n.* a colouring substance, as added to paints, inks, plastics, etc. or as found in plant and animal tissues, esp. in skin and hair.
— *v.* colour: *a deeply pigmented tissue.*
— **pig·men·ta·tion** (-TAY·shun) *n.: Albinos lack pigmentation.*

pig·pen or **pig·sty** *n.* an enclosure for pigs: *The place is filthy as a pigpen.*

pig·skin *n.* **1** leather from the skin of a pig. **2** *Informal.*

a football.

pig·tail *n.* a tight braid of hair worn at the back or side of the the head.

pike *n.* **1** [short form] turnpike: *the first good dictionary to* **come down the pike** (*Slang for* appear) *in a long time.* **2** a wooden shaft with a metal head, once carried by foot soldiers, or **pike·men** (*sing.* **-man**). **3** a freshwater food fish with a long snout, including muskellunge and the walleye; also **pike·perch.**

pik·er (PYE·kur) *n. Slang.* a stingy person; cheapskate.

pike·staff *n.* **-staves 1** the shaft of a pike. **2** a traveller's spiked staff.

pi·laf or **pi·laff** (pi·LAHF) *n.* a flavoured rice dish with meat, fish, etc. boiled together.

pi·las·ter (pi·LAS·tur) *n.* a rectangular column that supports a wall, into which it is set, though partially projecting from it.

pi·lau or **pi·law** (pi·LAW) *n.* same as PILAF.

pile *n.* **1** a heap, as of books, garbage, logs, dishes, etc.: *He made his pile (of money) by the time he was 30.* **2** the raised surface of rugs, fabrics such as velvet, etc.; nap: *a shaggy, smooth, soft, thick pile;* **adj.** *deep-piled carpeting.* **3** a heavy post or beam forming a support or foundation for a dock, bridge, etc. or one driven into the earth with a "pile driver" or "pile engine" (= hammering machine): *to sink a pile.* **4** same as ATOMIC PILE. **5** *pl.* hemorrhoids.
— *v.* **piles, piled, pil·ing** heap or cause to heap: *Five people piled into the back seat; Telegrams piled up on the M.P.'s desk.*

pile-up *n.* a piling up or heap: *a bad pile-up (of vehicles in collision) on a fogbound expressway.*

pil·fer (PIL·fur) *v.* steal or take away in small amounts; filch.

pil·fer·age (PIL·fur·ij) *n.* pilfering or the amount of goods pilfered: *Store losses by pilferage* (= shoplifting) *alone amount to millions of dollars.*

pil·grim *n.* **1** a traveller or wanderer, esp. one going on a pilgrimage to a holy place. **2 Pilgrim** or **Pilgrim Father** one of the English Puritans who first came to America in 1620.

pil·grim·age (PIL·gruh·mij) *n.* a journey to a shrine or sacred place such as Jerusalem or Mecca: *to go on or make a pilgrimage to Mecca.*

pill *n.* **1** a tiny ball, pellet, or capsule of medicine for swallowing whole: *to take a pill; to pop pills* (*Informal for* take narcotics); *sleeping pills.* **2 the Pill** *Informal.* an oral contraceptive: *Peg is on the Pill.*
— **a bitter pill to swallow** something unpleasant to accept or endure.

pil·lage (PIL·ij) *v.* **-ages, -aged, -ag·ing** to loot or plunder.
— *n.* a pillaging or things pillaged; booty or spoils.
— **pil·lag·er** *n.*

pil·lar (PIL·ur) *n.* **1** a vertical, usually cylindrical supporting structure; column: *He was a pillar of strength in times of trouble.* **2** such a pillar set up as a memorial, as the Washington Monument.

— **driven from pillar to post** driven desperately from one resource to another.

pil·lared (PIL·urd) *adj.* having pillars: *the pillared majesty of the Parthenon.*

pill·box *n.* 1 a shallow cylindrical container for pills. 2 a small, low, concrete-and-steel gun emplacement: *to storm a pillbox.*

pill·head *n. Slang.* one addicted to drugs in pill or capsule form.

pil·lion (PIL·yun) *n.* an extra seat behind a horse's saddle or motorcycle seat.

pil·lo·ry (PIL·uh·ree) *n.* **-ries** formerly, a wooden post and framework in which an offender had head and hands locked while exposed to public scorn as punishment.
— *v.* **-ries, -ried, -ry·ing** ridicule publicly: *The play was pilloried by the critics.*

pil·low (PIL·oh) *n.* a cushion to rest the head on while one sleeps: *to fluff up the pillows when making a bed.*
— *v.* rest as if on a pillow: *The child slept, pillowed on her mother's breast.*

pil·low·case (PIL·oh·case) or **pil·low·slip** (PIL·oh·slip) *n.* a removable cover for a pillow.

pillow talk *n.* intimate chatting, as by people in bed.

pil·low·y (PIL·oh·ee) *adj.* soft like a pillow.

pi·lot (PYE·lut) *n.* 1 a person or thing that leads or guides, as the operator of an aircraft, a helmsman of a ship, or an engine sent ahead of a train to see that the line is clear: *the automatic pilot of an airplane.* 2 a sample or the first episode of a proposed TV series.
— *adj.* serving to activate, guide, test, etc.: *a pilot project.*
— *v.* guide or steer: *to pilot a ship through rough seas.*

pilot balloon *n.* a balloon sent up to test the wind's direction and velocity; trial balloon.

pilot film or **pilot tape** *n.* a film or tape of a TV series for advance viewing by sponsors.

pilot lamp or **pilot light** *n.* 1 a flame kept lit for igniting a main burner when needed, as in a home heating furnace. 2 an indicator light.

pi·men·to (pi·MEN·toh) *n.* **-tos** 1 allspice; also, an evergreen tree that yields the spice. 2 a sweet pepper used esp. for stuffing olives; also **pi·mien·to** (pim·YEN·toh) *n.*

pimp *n.* a prostitute's agent; pander.

— *v.* act as a pimp or procurer.

pim·per·nel (PIM·pur·nul) *n.* a small, wild-growing plant of the primrose family with scarlet, white, or blue flowers that close in cloudy weather.

pim·ple (PIM·pul) *n.* a small, inflamed swelling on the skin.
— **pim·pled** or **pimply** *adj.*: *a pimpled face; a pimply shape, teenager.*

pin *n.* 1 a short, stiff piece of wire having a sharp point and tiny head, used in various designs for fastening papers, cloth, etc. together: *the prick of a pin.* 2 a peg of wood or metal similar in shape or function: *bobby pin; bowling pin; cotter pin; hair pin; hat pin; rolling pin; safety pin.* 3 an ornament or badge with a pin or clasp: *a tie pin.* 4 **pins** *pl. Informal.* legs.
— *v.* **pins, pinned, pin·ning** fasten or hold firmly: *Rico is so busy it's hard to **pin him down** to a definite time or place for a meeting; Jane tried to **pin the blame on** someone else; a leader on whom people had **pinned their hopes.***

pin·ball machine *n.* a game machine on which points are scored as a spring-driven ball slides down a board hitting various targets such as pins and bumpers.

pin·cers (PIN·surz) *n. pl.* a tool like the claws of a crab that is used for gripping or nipping things and that is worked like a pair of pliers.

pinch *v.* 1 squeeze between finger and thumb: *She pinched herself to make sure she was awake.* 2 to act or suffer in a tightening or pressing manner: *Tight shoes pinch; I'm pinched for time; the look of faces pinched by famine.* 3 *Slang: Who's pinching* (=stealing) *my pencils? The fellow was pinched* (=arrested) *on a vagrancy charge.*
— **pinch pennies** be stingy: *Pat never pinches pennies when entertaining friends.*
— *n.* a pinching: *a friendly pinch on the cheek; the pinch of poverty; Take tall tales with **a pinch of salt** (=with doubts); a friend who never failed me **in a pinch** (=hardship or emergency).*
— *adj.* having to do with playing as a substitute in baseball: *a pinch hit, homer, runner, single.*

pinch hit *n.* in baseball, a base hit made while pinchhitting.
— **pinch-hit** *v.* **-hits, -hit, -hit·ting** act as a substitute *for* someone, as a **pinch-hitter** who takes a batter's place at a pressing time.

pine *v.* **pines, pined, pin·ing** 1 to long or yearn: *He was pining for or after his absent wife and family; He pined to be reunited with his family.* 2 waste *away* through grief.
— *n.* an evergreen tree with needlelike leaves and cones; also, its wood.

ping *n.* 1 a sharp ringing sound as of a bullet striking metal. 2 the knock in a badly burning engine.
— *v.* make a ping: *an auto engine that pings under load.*

pin·go (PING·goh) *n. Cdn.* a soil-covered mound with a hard core of ice seen here and there on the flat tundra.

ping-pong *n.* 1 same as TABLE-TENNIS: *the ping-pong diplomacy of a Canadian team going to play ping-pong in China.* 2 a table-tennis set; **Ping-Pong** *Trademark.*

— *v.* move or send back and forth: *the ping-ponging of patients from one physician to another.*

pin·head *n.* **1** something tiny or trifling. **2** a stupid person; **pin·head·ed** *adj.*

pin·hold·er (PIN·hole·dur) *n.* a holder for cut flowers that has a pin-studded base.

pin·hole *n.* a minute hole, as if made by a pin.

pin·ion (PIN·yun) *n.* **1** a bird's wing, esp. the outer rear edge having flight-feathers. **2** a small gear whose teeth mesh with a larger wheel or rack: *a rack-and-pinion movement.*
— *v.* **1** hamper or restrain, as by cutting off a bird's pinions. **2** disable a person by holding or binding the arms to the sides of the body.

pink *n.* a pale red colour.
— **in the pink** *Informal.* in the best condition or state: *in the pink of condition, fashion, health, repair.*
— *adj.* **1** of the colour pink: *a pink dress, elephant;* **pink-collar** (= traditionally female) *occupations such as nursing and typing.* **2** with left-wing or Communist leanings. **3** emotionally excited: *Pat was tickled pink at the suggestion.*
— *v.* **1** stab gently; prick. **2** cut with shears to make a zigzag pattern. **3** decorate with a scalloped edge.

pink·ie or **pink·y** (PINK·ee) *n.* **pink·ies** the little finger.

pink·o *n.* [hostile use] a Communist sympathizer.

pink slip *n. Informal.* a notice terminating one's employment: *to get the pink slip.*

pin money *n.* money given or set aside for minor expenses.

pin·na·cle (PIN·uh·cul) *n.* a spire, mountain peak, or other tall, tapering form; also, its highest point: *to reach a pinnacle; at the pinnacle of one's career, glory, power, success.*

pin·point *n.* the point of a pin or something tiny, esp. a spot precisely marked, as with a pin on a map: *pinpont accuracy.*
— *v.* indicate with or as with a pinpoint: *targets pinpointed by radar; an expert who can pinpoint your accent as American or Canadian.*

pin·prick *n.* **1** a prick, as with a pin. **2** a petty annoyance.

pins and needles *n. pl.* a tingling sensation, as in a limb after numbness: *She's been* **on pins and needles** (= anxious) *awaiting her exam results.*

pin·stripe *n.* **1** a very narrow stripe on a fabric. **2** a suit with such stripes, typical of business executives.
— **pin·striped** *adj.*

pin·strip·er (PIN·stry·pur) *n. Informal.* a business executive.

pint ("i" as in "pine") *n.* a unit of volume or capacity equal to 16 oz.; ½ quart; 0.47321 L.

pint-size *adj. Informal.* very small.

pin·up *adj.* designed or suitable for putting up, esp. as a picture for viewing.
— *n.* such a picture: *pinups of movie stars.*

pin·wheel *n.* a paper toy having vanes pinned down in the middle and revolving like a wheel.

pi·o·neer (pye·uh·NEER) *n.* an explorer of a new area: *A wagon train of pioneers headed west; life in a pioneer settlement.*
— *v.* be a pioneer: *The Wright brothers pioneered in aviation; Armstrong and Aldrin pioneered the way to the moon.*

pi·ous (PYE·us) *adj.* **1** showing religious devotion: *a pious act, hope, pilgrim, profession of faith.* **2** showing false piety: *He's a pious fraud; mere pious and empty rhetoric; pious hypocrisy.* — **pi·ous·ly** *adv.*

pip *n.* **1** a dot with a number value, as on dice or dominoes. **2** a small seed, as of the orange or apple. **3** a short, high-pitched signal; also, a blip. **4** a disease of chickens, marked by a crust formed on the tongue. **5** *Slang.* any annoying or depressing disease.

pipe *n.* **1** a tube for conveying water, gas, oil, etc.: *a drain, exhaust, overflow pipe.* **2** a tube with a small bowl at one end for smoking tobacco, etc.: *to puff on a pipe.* **3** a musical tube blown by air, as in a bagpipe or in a pipe organ.
— **pipes** *pl.* **1** bagpipe. **2** *Informal.* organs of respiration or singing.
— *v.* **pipes, piped, pip·ing** **1** play on a pipe. **2** convey by pipes: *to pipe oil from a well into a refinery.*
— **pipe down** *Slang.* stop talking.
— **pipe up** **1** begin to play or sing. **2** *Informal.* speak up.

pipe dream *n. Informal.* a fantasy or vain hope.

pipe·line *n.* **1** a line of connected pipes: *the proposed Mackenzie Valley Pipeline for natural gas.* **2** any channel or process: *a pipeline of information, supplies, etc.; Raises for everyone are* **in the pipeline** (= coming or expected).

pipe of peace *n.* same as PEACE PIPE.

pip·er (PYE·pur) *n.* **pay the piper** See PAY.

pip·ing (PYE·ping) *n.* **1** a system of pipes. **2** pipe music. **3** a pipelike trimming material for edges or seams.
— **piping hot** very hot.

pip·squeak *n.* a person considered as small or insignificant.

pi·quant (PEEK·unt) *adj.* agreeably pungent, lively, vivid, etc.: *a piquant sauce, wit; Carla's piquant charm.*
— **pi·quant·ly** *adv.* — **pi·quan·cy** (-un·see) *n.*

pique (PEEK) *n.* feeling of hurt vanity or pride: *He stomped out of the party in a pique; She said it in a fit of pique.*
— *v.* **piques, piqued, piqu·ing** **1** hurt the pride of someone: *It piqued her not to be invited.* **2** arouse or excite interest, curiosity, etc.: *Her exotic style piques my curiosity.*

pi·ra·cy (PYE·ruh·see) *n.* **-cies** the action of a pirate: *laws against air piracy; piracy on the high seas; literary piracy by infringing copyright; TV piracy via satellite dishes.*

pi·rate (PYE·rit) *n.* **1** a robber of the high seas or a hijacker. **2** one who violates a copyright or patent.
— *v.* **pi·rates, pi·rat·ed, pi·rat·ing** rob or steal: *In some countries, underground publishers pirate textbooks and*

*drive established publishers out of business; a **pirated** tape, textbook.* — **pi·rat·i·cal** (pye·RAT·uh·cul) *adj.*

pir·ou·ette (peer·oo·ET) *n.* a whirling around on the toe or on the ball of the foot, as in ballet. Also *v.* -ettes, -et·ted, -et·ting.

pissed off *Slang.* angry.

pis·tol (PIS·tul) *n.* a small firearm that can be fired with one hand: *an automatic pistol with a magazine of shells.*

pistol-whip (PIS·tul·whip) *v.* -whips, -whipped, -whip·ping beat with the barrel of a pistol.

pis·ton (PIS·tun) *n.* a flat, round device used in pumps and engines, that moves back and forth by the pressure of a fluid inside a cylinder in which it is fitted tightly by **piston rings**, the resulting motion being transmitted by a **piston rod** attached to the piston.

pit *n.* **1** the stone of a fruit: *the pits of almonds, avocadoes, cherries, dates, olives, peaches, plums, prunes.* **2** a hole or cavity in the ground, naturally formed or one dug for burial, mining, trapping, etc.: *"He who digs a pit shall fall into it."* **3** a place or area resembling a pit, as for servicing automobiles, the orchestra's place in front of a stage, a body depression or hollow such as a pock mark, the armpit, or an enclosure for bearbaiting or cockfights, etc.: *the pit of the stomach* (= depression below the breastbone); *It's **the pits** (Slang for* a disgusting situation or place). — *v.* pits, pit·ted, pit·ting **1** remove the pit from a fruit: *to pit cherries; pitted dates.* **2** to place or set: *an unequal contest with one man pitted against three.* **3** to mark with pits or pock marks: *The moon's surface is pitted with craters.*

pit-a-pat (PIT·uh·pat) *n.* a throbbing motion or sound; *adv.: Her heart went pit-a-pat when her name was called.*

pitch *v.* **1** put up; also, set or fix in a particular manner: *to pitch a tent; a voice pitched too low to be heard; hopes pitched too high; The demonstrators fought a **pitched battle** (= a planned and organized fight) with the police.* **2** throw, toss, or hurl: *to pitch hay into a hay rack with a pitchfork; A baseball pitcher pitches the ball to the batter; a boat pitching and rolling in the waves; The heckler was pitched out of the hall.* **3** *Slang.* promote or hype: *The mayor went to Switzerland to pitch his city's bid for the Olympics.* — **pitch in** contribute: *If everyone pitches in, we will finish the work soon.* — **pitch into** join enthusiastically in an activity: *We pitched into the food as soon as we were served.* — **pitch on** choose someone, esp. for something unwelcome: *Jones pitched on me to propose the toast.* — *n.* **1** a pitching or throw: *a bowler's fast pitch; the pitch of a voice* (= its sound quality based on vibrations of the sound waves); *a high-pitched voice that almost sounds shrill; emotion stirred to a fever pitch* (= intensity). **2** *Slang.* sales talk: *A free trip to Florida was included in the sales pitch.* **3** a black, sticky substance made from coal tar or petroleum and used for waterproofing, filling cracks, etc. **4** a court or playing ground for sports such as cricket and horseshoe pitching.

pitch-black *adj.* extremely black or dark; also **pitch-dark**.

pitch·er *n.* **1** one who pitches in a baseball game. **2** a large jug for liquids, with a handle on one side and a lip for pouring on the other.

pitcher plant *n.* a plant that feeds on insects which it traps in its pitcher-shaped leaves: *The pitcher plant is the floral emblem of Newfoundland and Labrador.*

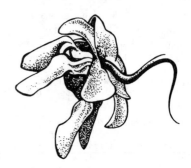

pitch·fork *n.* a large long-handled fork for pitching hay.

pitch·man *n.* -men *Informal.* one who makes a sales pitch.

pit·e·ous (PIT·ee·us) *adj.* deserving or causing pity: *a piteous sight.* — **pit·e·ous·ly** *adv.*

pit·fall *n.* **1** a concealed pit for catching animals or people. **2** any hidden danger: *to avoid a pitfall; the pitfalls of hitchhiking.*

pith·y *adj.* **pith·i·er**, **-i·est** brief and full of meaning: *a pithy maxim, style, utterance.* — **pith·i·ly** *adv.*; **pith·i·ness** *n.*

pit·i·a·ble (PIT·ee·uh·bul) *adj.* arousing regrettable pity: *the pitiable condition of starving children.* — **pit·i·a·ble·ness** *n.*; **pit·i·a·bly** *adv.*

pit·i·ful *adj.* so miserable as to evoke pity: *a pitiful amount, comedy, minority, offer, performance, situation.* — **pit·i·ful·ly** *adv.*; **pit·i·ful·ness** *n.*

pit stop *n.* a stop for fuelling, refreshments, etc., as during an automobile race.

pit·tance (PIT·unce) *n.* a meagre allowance or remuneration: *a mere pittance.*

pit·ter-pat·ter (PIT·ur·pat·ur) *n. & v.* same as PATTER.

pit·y (PIT·ee) *n.* **1** sorrow for another's suffering: *to arouse, feel, show pity; Have or Take pity on a poor beggar; pity for the poor; I gave her my money out of pity; a sense of pity; **For pity's sake**, be kind to animals.* **2** a cause for regret: *What a pity we lost!* — *v.* pit·ies, pit·ied, pit·y·ing feel pity for someone: *We pity the homeless.* — **pit·y·ing·ly** *adv.*

piv·ot (PIV·ut) *n.* **1** a shaft or point on which something turns. **2** a person or thing in a key position, as the **piv·ot·man** or centre in basketball, ice hockey, etc. — *v.* turn: *A ballerina pivots on the tip of her toes; His entire future pivots* (= depends) *on his examination results.* — **piv·ot·al** (-ul) *adj.* central: *a decision of pivotal significance to her career.*

pix a *pl. of* PIC.

pix·el (PIX·ul) *n.* the smallest element of a picture formed on a video display.

pix·ie or **pix·y** (PIX·ee) *n.* **pix·ies** a mischievous fairy; sprite.
— **pix·y·ish** *adj.* resembling a pixy: *her pixyish charm.*

pi·zazz or **piz·zazz** (puh·ZAZ) *n. Slang.* vigour or style: *accessories to give your car a little pizazz.*

piz·za (PEET·suh) *n.* a pie consisting of thinly rolled dough baked with tomato sauce, cheese, meat, vegetables, spices, etc. on it. Also **pizza pie.**

piz·ze·ri·a (peet·suh·REE·uh) *n.* an establishment where pizza is made and sold.

plac·ard (PLAY·card, PLACK·urd) *n.* a notice posted in a public place; poster.
— *v.* **1** announce with placards: *The visit of the circus was placarded in advance.* **2** cover, as with placards: *The walls were placarded with ads.*

pla·cate (pluh·CATE, PLAC·ate) *v.* **-cates, -cat·ed, -cat·ing** soothe or satisfy; appease: *a spoilt child who is hard to placate with gifts.*

place *n.* **1** a definite portion of occupied space, as a city, street, courtyard, building, home, particular spot, etc.: *"No place like home"; "a place for everything and everything in its place"; A church is a place of worship; a meeting place; Let's meet at our place* (= dwelling); *Dad's place is at the head of the table; Who took my place (at the table)? to lay* or *set a place for a guest.* **2** a position, esp. one of rank, office, function, etc.: *a teacher's place in society; A servant had to know his place or he would be **put in his place*** (= rebuked); *A prince and a pauper traded places; to give up a place in line* or *in a queue; The computer network is now **in place*** (= established); *We use a word processor **in place of*** (= instead of) *a typewriter; It's not my place* (= job or duty) *to criticize you, Sir.*
— **go places** *Informal.* start to succeed: *You're going places, boy!*
— **take place** happen.
— *v.* **plac·es, placed, plac·ing** put: *He was placed third in the race; to place an order for books; The orphan child has been placed with foster parents; We place service above sales; The name is familiar, but I can't place* (= identify) *his face; to place* (= present) *the facts before a jury; to place your confidence in your secretary.*

pla·ce·bo (pluh·SEE·boh) *n.* **-bos** or **-boes** a preparation, as sugar pills or coloured water that has no medicinal effect, often given to patients used as a control group in a medical test: *Some arthritic cures have only a **placebo effect.***

place kick *n.* the kicking of a ball held on the ground, as in football.

place value *n.* the value of a digit because of its position in a numeral: *In 22.2, each 2 has a different place value, namely, two tens, two units, and two tenths.*

plac·id (PLAS·id) *adj.* calm and without agitation: *a placid lake; the lake's placid surface; her placid temperament.* — **plac·id·ly** *adv.;* **plac·id·ness** *n.*

pla·gia·rize (PLAY·juh·rize) *v.* **-riz·es, -rized, -riz·ing** use or pass off another's ideas or writings as one's own.
— **pla·gia·rism** *n.;* **pla·gia·rist** *n.*

plague (PLAIG) *n.* an affliction, esp. a deadly epidemic: *the bubonic plague; a plague of locusts; She avoids TV like the plague.*
— *v.* **plagues, plagued, plagu·ing** inflict suffering on someone: *a society plagued by high taxes and rising prices; Stop plaguing* (= annoying) *me for this and that.*

plaid (PLAD) *n.* a pattern of checks or coloured stripes crossing at right angles, as on the woollen scarf worn over the shoulder by Scottish Highlanders; also, this garment. — *adj.:* *a plaid skirt, tie.*

plain *adj.* **1** easy to see, hear, understand, etc.: *It's plain to the view; plain and clear; in plain English, language.* **2** without ornament, colour, seasoning, beauty, etc.: *a plain face; plain fare* (= food); *a police officer in **plain clothes*** (= not in uniform); *the **plain Jane*** (= ordinary) *shopper looking for basic values; a **plain-spoken** young man* (who speaks plainly and frankly). **3** flat: *plain ground.*
— *n.* level land: *a coastal plain; The battle was fought on a plain; the Plains of Abraham in Quebec.*
— *adv.* simply: *just plain bored.*
— **plain·ly** *adv.;* **plain·ness** *n.*

plain sailing *n.* progress that is smooth and easy.

plaint *n.* **1** [poetic use] lamentation. **2** [legal use] complaint.

plain·tiff *n.* one who brings a lawsuit.

plain·tive (PLAIN·tiv) *adj.* mournful: *a plaintive appeal, lament, note, plea, voice; the plaintive lowing of cattle; the plaintive sound of the violin.*
— **plain·tive·ly** *adv.*

plait *n. & v.* braid: *plaited hair.*

plan *n.* a drawing or outline of some action; scheme: *a building plan drawn to scale; a five-year plan; your plans for the summer; a brilliant, elaborate, grandiose, ingenious, well-laid, well-thought-out plan; a contingency, flight, floor, master plan; to pay for appliances on the instalment plan; a health plan* (= health insurance); *pension plan; retirement plan; a plan to cut down on waste; to carry out, concoct, devise, draw up, execute, foil, formulate, frustrate, implement, propose, reject, shelve, thwart, unveil a plan.*
— *v.* **plans, planned, plan·ning** make plans; intend or contemplate: *Are you planning to attend our meeting? I'm planning for my retirement; I'm planning on leaving the company next week.* — **plan·ner** *n.*

pla·nar (PLAY·nur) *adj.* lying in one plane: *a planar surface.*

plane *n.* **1** a flat or level surface; also, a level: *an inclined plane; a high plane of achievement; He kept the discussion on a lofty plane; the supernatural plane.* **2** a carpenter's tool for shaping and smoothing. **3** airplane: *Before boarding his plane, the premier had a **plane-side** chat with the press; a **plane-load** of refugees.*
— *adj.* level or flat: *plane surfaces, figures, geometry.*
— *v.* **planes, planed, plan·ing** make flat and smooth using a plane: *to plane a surface smooth.*
— **plan·er** *n.* — **plane·ness** *n.*

plan·et (PLAN·it) *n.* a heavenly body revolving around the sun whose light it reflects, esp. Mercury, Venus,

Earth, Mars, Jupiter, Saturn, Uranus, Neptune, and Pluto. — **plan·e·tar·y** (-uh·tair·ee) *adj.*

plan·e·tar·i·um (plan·uh·TAIR·ee·um) *n.* **-ums** or **-i·a** (-ee·uh) **1** an optical device for showing the pattern and movement of the planets, sun, moon, and stars projected inside a dome. **2** a building housing this.

plan·gent (PLAN·junt) *adj.* resounding, esp. mournfully: *the plangent sounds of a flute; plangent notes, voices; She sang in a plangent and complaining tone; "pulse of water plangent like a knell."*

plank *n.* **1** a board that is at least 2 in. (5.08 cm) thick and 8 in. (20.32 cm) wide, as used in flooring a stage or platform. **2** an item of a political platform: *A higher minimum wage was one of his campaign planks.* — **walk the plank** be forced to kill oneself, as the crew of a ship captured by pirates made to jump overboard from a plank. — *v.* **1** cover with planks. **2** *Informal.* put down with some force: *She planked down the change and strode out of the room.* **3** cook and serve fish, steak, etc. on a board. — **plank·ing** *n.* a covering of planks or the planks themselves: *new planking for the kitchen floor.*

planned *adj.* organized or regulated: *a planned community; a government-controlled planned economy, not a free one; **planned obsolescence*** (= designing that makes a product useless or out of date after a short time); ***planned parenthood*** (= birth control, esp. as an organized movement).

planning *n.* the act or process of making a plan: *family planning; town planning.*

plant *n.* **1** a living thing that is typically rooted in the ground and nourishes itself with food from air, sunlight, and water; an herb, vine, soft-stemmed shrub, or young tree: *annual, climbing, exotic, perennial, tropical plants.* **2** a machine or machinery used to make a product or provide a service: *a gas plant; power plant.* **3** a factory or building and its equipment: *an automobile plant; heating plant; a college's physical plant; the school plant.* — *v.* **1** put in the ground, as a sapling or seed: *to plant flowers; to plant a field with wheat.* **2** place in a certain way, esp. firmly: *Parents plant good habits in the young early in life; He stood in a threatening attitude with arms akimbo and feet planted wide apart; The boxer planted one on his opponent's left jaw; He was suspected as an undercover agent planted by the enemy; to plant a bomb.*

plan·tain (PLAN·tin) *n.* **1** a kind of banana plant or its fruit. **2** a low-growing herb or weed such as the "broadleaf" and "ribgrass."

plan·tar (PLAN·tur) *adj.* having to do with the sole of the foot: *plantar warts.*

plan·ta·tion (plan·TAY·shun) *n.* **1** a large estate growing a crop such as cotton, rubber, tobacco, sugar cane, or tea with the help of labourers who live on the estate. **2** a colony or settlement.

plant·er *n.* **1** one that plants, as a machine, farmer, or plantation owner. **2** a container for house plants.

plan·ti·grade (PLAN·tuh·grade) *adj.* walking on the sole of the foot: *Bears, apes, and humans are plantigrade animals.*

plaque (PLAK) *n.* **1** a thin, flat piece, as a tablet of wood or metal commemorating some event, an ornamental brooch or badge, etc.: *a memorial plaque; to put up a plaque in honour of the dead hero.* **2** surface coating or deposit: *Dentists remove plaque from teeth.*

plas·ma (PLAZ·muh) *n.* **1** the liquid part of blood, milk, etc. **2** a gas containing equal numbers of positive and negative particles, as in a ***plasma torch*** used in melting and vaporizing solids: *A plasma jet is used in satellites to steer through space.* — **plas·mat·ic** (plaz·MAT·ic) or **plas·mic** (PLAZ·mic) *adj.*

plas·ter (PLAS·tur) *n.* a pasty mixture that hardens on drying, used to coat walls, ceilings, etc.: *to apply plaster to a wall; the crumbling plaster of an old building; a mustard plaster* (= poultice made with mustard); ***plaster of Paris*** *used for statuary, in **plaster casts** holding fractured bones, and to make sheets of board, or **plas·ter·board,** for walls, ceilings, etc.* — *v.* stick with or as if with plaster: *He plasters down his wet hair; a wall plastered with posters.* — **plas·ter·er** *n.*

plas·tic *adj.* **1** having moulding, shaping, or pliable qualities: *Clay, wax, plaster, etc. are plastic substances; sculpture, painting, ceramics, and such **plastic arts;** A **plastic bomb** is a puttylike explosive; plastic bullets (made of plastic) are used in riot control; the plastic* (= easily shaped) *mind of a child; **Plastic surgery** restores deformed or maimed body parts to their original shape.* **2** changeable in form; hence, artificial or insincere: *our plastic culture; his plastic smile.* — *n.* **1** a synthetic, mouldable substance such as nylon or vinyl. **2** same as **plastic money,** credit cards used instead of cash: *They don't take plastic at the post office.*

plat *n.* **1** a plot of land, esp. a building lot. **2** a map or plan indicating such plots.

plate *n.* **1** a flat, shallow circular dish for serving food; also, food so served or dishes and plated utensils collectivley: *a dinner plate; salad plate; vegetable plate; to pass the collection plate (for donations) in church.* **2** a sheet of metal, glass, plastic, etc., as for taking photographs, for printing engraved impressions, etc.: *an automobile licence plate; a printing plate.* **3** a print made with an engraving, esp. a full-page picture in colour: *the plates and illustrations in a book.* **4** a piece of metal or plastic fitted with false teeth; denture: *lower and upper plates.* **5** a protective piece of material such as makes up a ship's steel hull or the horny or bony covering of reptiles and fishes. **6** same as HOME PLATE. **7** any of the large movable pieces making up the earth's crust. — *v.* **plates, plat·ed, plat·ing** **1** cover with plate or with a precious metal: *He ordered the faucets plated with gold; a silver-plated spoon.* **2** make into plates: *a book all plated and ready for printing.*

pla·teau (plat·OH) *n.* **-teaus** or **-teaux** (-TOZE) **1** an elevated flat or level region; tableland: *a high plateau.* **2** a levelling off in a trend; stable period: *House prices reached a plateau* (= levelled off) *in the winter.*

plat·en (PLAT·un) *n.* **1** in a printing press, a plate that presses the paper against the printing surface. **2** the roller of a typewriter.

plate tectonics *n. pl.* the theory that the earth's crust is made up of huge plates, the friction between which causes earthquakes, mountains, volcanoes, etc.

plat·form *n.* **1** an elevated floor, esp. a stage for speakers: *to mount* (= ascend) *a platform; the launching platform* or *pad of a spacecraft.* **2** a statement of principles and policies of a political party or candidate: *to adopt, draft, draw up a platform; a party platform; the planks of a political platform.*

platinum blonde *n.* a woman with silver-white hair.

plat·i·tude (PLAT·uh·tude) *n.* a solemnly made but well-worn or flat statement, as "Whatever will be, will be": *to mouth platitudes;* **plat·i·tu·di·nous** (-TUE·dun·us) *adj.*

pla·ton·ic (pluh·TON·ic) *adj.* purely intellectual or spiritual, with no sexual interest: *platonic friendship, love.* — **pla·ton·i·cal·ly** *adv.*

pla·toon (pluh·TOON) *n.* a military unit usually forming part of a company.

plat·ter (PLAT·ur) *n.* **1** a usually oval dish for serving food: *a serving platter.* **2** a course of a meal: *a salad platter made with cauliflower, broccoli, eggs, and olives.* **3** *Slang.* phonograph record. — **on a platter** as if served; received without effort: *Spoiled children expect everything to be handed to them on a silver platter.*

plau·dit (PLAW·dit) *n.* usually **plaudits** *pl.* an expression of approval; applause: *to earn, receive, win plaudits.*

plau·si·ble (PLAW·zuh·bul) *adj.* believable, esp. as it appears: *It's plausible that life exists on other planets; Her story seems plausible; a plausible argument, candidate, theory.* — **plau·si·bly** (-blee) *adv.* — **plau·si·bil·i·ty** (-BIL·uh·tee) *n.*

play *n.* **1** amusing or recreational activity; sport or fun: *All work and no play makes life dull; Using a computer is child's play* (= an easy task) *to her.* **2** the way such activity is carried on or a stage or act in it: *fair, foul, rough play; A volley ball is* **in play** *till it hits the ground; a subject that brings her writing powers* **into play;** *"The good life depends on the liver" is a* **play on words.** **3** an organized fun activity; a drama or similar performance: *Shakespeare's plays; to perform, produce, put on, rehearse a play; A play closes, opens, runs (in a place).* **4** movement, activity, etc., esp. as being free, light, or quick: *the play of a poet's fancy; There should not be too much play in a steering wheel; the play of moonlight on the lake.* — *v.* **1** do something for fun: *Children like to play all day; to play at* (= have a game of) *teacher and pupil; Canadians playing* (= having a game against) *the Soviet Union; It's dangerous to play* (= do foolish things) *with matches.* **2** work or perform: *to play a trick on someone; The circus plays* (= gives performances in) *southern cities in the winter; to play* (= perform on) *the piano; The officer played* (= directed) *his flashlight under the car; A possum plays* (= pretends to be) *dead; Will you* **play back** (= replay) *the recording for me? The media may* **play down** (= make little of) *or* **play up** (= make much of) *a story; to* **play into the hands of** (= become a victim

of) *someone; Let's* **play it cool** (*Informal* for stay calm); *to* **play off** (= set) *one side against the other; The car dealer* **played on** *or* **upon** (= took advantage of) *his inexperience to sell him a lemon; a student trying to* **play up to** (= gain the favour of) *the teacher.* — **play·er** *n.* — **play·ful** *adj.;* **play·ful·ly** *adv.;* **play·ful·ness** *n.*

play·act·ing (PLAY·ac·ting) *n.* **1** acting on the stage. **2** pretence.

play·back *n.* the replaying of a recording.

play·boy or **play·girl** *n.* one given to pleasure-seeking, esp. sexual.

play-by-play *adj.* detailed: *a play-by-play account of an event.*

play·fel·low (PLAY·fel·oh) *n.* same as PLAYMATE.

play·go·er (PLAY·go·ur) *n.* one who frequents the theatre.

play·house *n.* **1** a theatre. **2** a building for children to play in.

playing card *n.* one of a set of small rectangular cards used in card games.

play·let (PLAY·lut) *n.* a short play.

play·mate *n.* a companion for playing with.

play·off *n.* a contest for breaking a tie or deciding a championship at the end of a tournament.

play·pen *n.* a portable enclosure for an infant to play in.

play·suit *n.* a play outfit consisting of blouse and shorts.

play·thing *n.* a toy.

play·wright *n.* the author of a play.

pla·za (PLAH·zuh, PLAZ·uh) *n.* **1** a public square: *the plazas of Madrid; Rockefeller Plaza.* **2** a commercial area: *a service plaza (for motorists); shopping plaza* (= shopping centre); *toll plaza (containing toll booths).*

plea (PLEE) *n.* **1** an appeal: *a fervent, impassioned, urgent plea; a plea for mercy.* **2** defence, esp. in answer to a charge: *Ignorance of the law is no plea; A defendant enters, makes, puts forward a plea through a lawyer; to* **cop a plea** (*Slang* for plead guilty for avoiding trial on a more serious charge); *a reduced charge as a result of* **plea bargaining** *between prosecuting and defending attorneys.*

plead (PLEED) *v.* **pleads,** *pt. & pp.* **plead·ed** or [*regional use*] **pled, plead·ing 1** argue a case: *Lawyers plead in court.* **2** answer a charge: *How do you plead – guilty or not guilty?* **3** offer as an excuse for something: *to plead insanity when charged with murder.* **4** beg: *He pleaded for more time; She pleaded with her mother to let her watch the late movie.*

plead·er (PLEE·dur) *n.* a person qualified to plead in court.

pleas·ant (PLEZ·unt) *adj.* having a pleasing effect: *We had a pleasant time at the party; a medicine that is pleasant to the taste;* **pleas·ant·ly** *adv.;* **pleas·ant·ness** *n.*

pleas·ant·ry (PLEZ·un·tree) *n.* **-ries 1** joking or fun. **2** a joke or a pleasant remark: *to exchange pleasantries.*

please (PLEEZ) *v.* **pleas·es, pleased, pleas·ing 1** be agreeable to someone: *a salesclerk eager to please* (=satisfy) *customers; We're greatly, highly* **pleased** *to welcome you; His manner was most* **pleasing.** **2** [as a polite formula]: *Please come in;* **If you please,** *I'd like the window closed;* **Yes, please** (= I accept your offer with thanks); [as an order] *Stop please!*
— **pleas·ing·ly** *adv.*

pleas·ur·a·ble (PLEZH·ur·uh·bul) *adj.* enjoyable: *a pleasurable experience.* — **pleas·ur·a·bly** *adv.*

pleas·ure (PLEZH·ur) *n.* **1** the feeling of being pleased; enjoyment: *the pleasure of your company; He took secret pleasure in his rival's defeat; It gives me great pleasure to accept this award; Pastimes afford pleasure; a life of pleasure; to feel, find, take pleasure in sports; She derives no pleasure from watching boxing; to mix business with pleasure on a trip; I do it for pleasure rather than for money; The dying patient couldn't find any pleasure in living.* **2** something that pleases: *to forgo a pleasure; It's a pleasure to introduce the next speaker; a genuine, rare, real pleasure; the pleasures of country living.*

pleat (PLEET) *n.* a fold, as on a skirt or drapes, stitched flat at the top. — *v.: a skirt with pleated ruffles.*

ple·be·ian (pli·BEE·un) *n.* one of the common people, not a patrician.
— *adj.* vulgar or coarse: *plebeian habits, humour, tastes.*

pleb·i·scite (PLEB·uh·site) *n.* a vote by all the people of a nation or section of it to elicit their opinion on a political issue: *to hold a plebiscite on school financing; A plebiscite is less binding on a government than a referendum.*

pled a *pt. & pp.* of PLEAD.

pledge *n.* **1** a promise or vow: *to take a pledge of allegiance to the flag; to honour a pledge; Politicians make campaign pledges; to* **take the pledge** *(not to drink).* **2** a person or thing placed as security or guarantee: *a diamond ring as a pledge of his fidelity.* **3** a member accepted but not yet initiated into a club, fraternity, etc. **4** the state of being held as a pawn or hostage: *Innocent passengers were held* **in pledge** *by the hijackers.*
— *v.* **pledg·es, pledged, pledg·ing 1** give as a pledge: *She pledged her jewellery as security for the loan; He pledged $100 to the Heart Fund.* **2** bind solemnly: *The oath pledged him to secrecy.* **3** promise: *He pledged his support for the cause; to pledge allegiance to the Queen; The students pledged not to smoke, drink, or take drugs.*

ple·na·ry (PLEE·nuh·ree, PLEN·uh·) *adj.* full or complete, esp. in membership: *a plenary session of the council.*

plen·i·tude (PLEN·uh·tude) *n.* fullness or completeness: *a queen appearing in the plenitude of her majesty.*

plen·te·ous (PLEN·tee·us) *adj.* [poetical use] plentiful: *a plenteous harvest.*

plen·ti·ful (PLEN·tee·ful) *adj.* existing in large numbers or amounts: *plentiful goods, harvests, supplies; Natural gas is plentiful in Alberta; Quebec's cheap and plentiful*

electricity. — **plen·ti·ful·ly** *adv.*

plen·ty (PLEN·tee) *n.* a large number or amount: *We get plenty of homework; We've plenty to do on weekends; We live in times of plenty* (= well supplied with life's necessities).
— **in plenty 1** in large supply: *We have apples in plenty.* **2** having an abundance of goods: *They live in plenty.*
— *adj. Informal.* sufficient: *There's plenty food.*
— *adv. Informal.* very: *I got plenty hungry.*

ple·num (PLEE·num) *n.* **-nums** or **-na 1** a full space or enclosure, not a vacuum: *The fan of a heating furnace regulates the warm-air plenum and the cold-air return duct.* **2** a full assembly, esp. of a legislative body: *the plenum of the Soviet Communist Party.*

pleth·o·ra (PLETH·uh·ruh) *n.* an overabundance; fullness to excess: *a plethora of praise.*

plex·i·glas (PLEX·uh·glass) *n.* a light but tough acrylic plastic used in aircraft windows, lenses, helmet shields, etc. **Plexiglas** *Trademark.*

pli·a·ble (PLY·uh·bul) *adj.* **1** easy to bend or twist: *Leather is pliable; a pliable twig.* **2** easy to persuade or influence: *The power brokers thought a novice minister would be pliable to their influence.*
— **pli·a·bil·i·ty** (-BIL·uh·tee) *n.*

pli·ant (PLY·unt) *adj.* willing to comply.
— **pli·an·cy** (-un·see) *n.*

pli·ers (PLY·urz) *n. sing. & pl.* a tool with a pair of jaws for gripping, bending, cutting wires, etc.

plight (PLITE) *n.* **1** an unfortunate condition: *the sad plight of refugees.* **2** [old use] a solemn promise.
— *v.* [old use, as in the marriage formula]: *"Till death do us part ... I plight* (= promise) *thee my troth."*

plod *v.* **plods, plod·ded, plod·ding 1** walk heavily or with effort: *The weary travellers plodded along.* **2** apply oneself steadily to a difficult task: *children plodding away at their chores.* — **plod·der** *n.* — **plod·ding·ly** *adv.*

plop *v.* **plops, plopped, plop·ping** set, drop, or throw down, as a stone into water.
— *n.* a plopping or its sound.

plot *n.* **1** a small piece of ground, esp. a measured area, as on a ground plan: *a garden plot; a plot of land.* **2** a map, chart, or graph: *the plot of a ship's course.* **3** the plan of events in a literary work such as a novel or play: *a plot built around a wedding; The plot thickens as the wedding day draws near.* **4** a secret plan of action to hurt a person, group, or nation: *the Gunpowder Plot; to devise, expose, foil, hatch, thwart a plot; a sinister plot against the government; a diabolic plot to kidnap a child.*
— *v.* **plots, plot·ted, plot·ting 1** to mark, as on a map, graph, or chart: *a subdivision plotted out for new housing; to plot a temperature curve; X and Y coordinates are used to plot the position of a ship.* **2** plan: *to plot the overthrow of a dictator; a well-plotted novel.* — **plot·ter** *n.*

plough or **plow** (rhyme: "how") *n.* **1** a farm implement for turning up the soil in furrows and drawn by animals or a tractor. **2** a snowplough.
— *v.* work, as with a plough: *to plough a field; He ploughs a lonely furrow* (= works all by himself); *Profits are **ploughed back** (= reinvested) into our business; She **ploughs into** (= gets busy with) her work soon after breakfast; a book that is difficult to **plough through** (= laborious to go through) in a week.*
— **plough·a·ble** (-uh·bul) *adj.* — **plough·er** *n.*

plough·man *n.* -men a farm worker.

plough·share *n.* the blade of a plough.

plow See PLOUGH.

ploy *n.* a tactic or device: *a clever ploy to make a fast buck; a marketing ploy.*

pluck *v.* **1** pull off: *to pluck a bird's feathers; to pluck a chicken* (= pull the feathers off the dead bird); *to pluck flowers or fruit from a tree.* **2** pull or tug at something: *a singer plucking away at his guitar; Someone in the crowd plucked at her sleeve; I couldn't **pluck up** (= summon) enough courage to protest.*
— *n.* boldness or courage: *the pluck to try and try again.*
— **pluck·y** *adj.*: *a plucky litte girl who plays hockey on a boys' team; a plucky escape, game, spirit.*

plug *n.* **1** a small piece of wood or metal used to stop up a hole. **2** something similar, as a device with prongs to connect with an electrical outlet or an automobile spark plug: *They didn't have the heart to **pull the plug on** (Informal for* disconnect the life-support system of) *the dying patient.* **3** *Informal.* a favourable bit of publicity, esp. on TV or radio: *a commercial plug.*
— *v.* plugs, plugged, plug·ging **1** stop, as by putting something into a hole: *Wire-tapping was used to plug the leak of top-secret information; An electric kettle is plugged* (= connected by inserting its plug) *into a wall outlet; language students plugged into* (= listening to) *a tape player.* **2** promote: *a bestseller plugged by the networks.*
— **plug away** work laboriously: *She plugs away at her homework till bedtime.*

plug·o·la (plug·OH·luh) *n.* *Slang.* a payola or bribe given for a plug or favourable publicity.

plum *n.* **1** a smooth-skinned, juicy dark-red or yellow fruit with a large stone; also, the tree it grows on. **2** a raisin, as used in plum cakes and puddings. **3** something attractive or desirable: *That job is a real plum; politicians craving for the plums of office; adj.: a plum*

assignment, job, position, role.

plum·age (PLOO·mij) *n.* a bird's feathers.

plumb (PLUM) *n.* a small weight **(plumb bob)** attached to a line **(plumb line)** to measure the depth of water or to test whether a wall is vertical.
— **out of plumb** or **off plumb** not vertical or straight.
— *adj.* **1** vertical: *The post has to be erected plumb.* **2** downright: *a plumb fool; adv.: She's plumb wrong on that point.*
— *v.* to understand fully: *to plumb (the depths of) a mystery.*

plumb·er (PLUM·ur) *n.* one skilled in plumbing: *A plunger is often called a "plumber's friend or helper."*

plumbing (PLUM·ing) *n.* **1** the putting in and repairing of pipes and fixtures for water, gas, sewage, etc. **2** the pipes and fixtures themselves.

plume (PLOOM) *n.* **1** a large feather used as an ornament; also, a tuft of feathers. **2** a feathery part, as of a seed, leaf, or insect: *"Plume hyacinth," "plume moth," and "plume poppy" have plumes.* **3** a formation resembling a feather; trail: *a plume of smoke rising from a chimney or volcano.*
— *v.* plumes, plumed, plum·ing provide with plumes: *a white-plumed bird; A swan plumes* (= preens) *its feathers; The boss **plumes himself on** (= is proud of) his secretary's achievements.*

plum·met (PLUM·it) *n.* a plumb bob or line.
— *v.* plunge: *Stock prices plummeted on Black Monday.*

plum·my (PLUM·ee) *adj.* plum·mi·er, plum·mi·est **1** good and desirable; plum. **2** characterized by an affected upper-class style of speaking: *a plummy accent, enunciation, voice.*

plump *adj.* **1** rounded or chubby: *Paula is pleasantly plump.* **2** direct or blunt: *A plump "no" was her answer.*
— *adv.* heavily or suddenly: *He dropped himself plump into the chair.*
— *v.* **1** make or become plump: *The child is eating well and gradually plumping up; He plumped up the pillows before getting into bed.* **2** let fall or drop: *She plumped her books down on the bed.*
— **plump for** support or champion: *Each teacher seemed to plump for her own pupils.*

plum·y (PLOO·mee) *adj.* plum·i·er, -i·est adorned with plumes; also, feathery.

plun·der (PLUN·dur) *v.* rob, esp. on a large scale, as invaders do; loot or pillage.
— *n.* what is taken in robbery, as bribe, etc.: *a pirate ship loaded with plunder; a price so high it borders on plunder.* — **plun·der·er** *n.*

plunge (PLUNJ) *v.* plung·es, plunged, plung·ing **1** go or send down suddenly into water or as if into water or other deep place: *She plunged her burned hand into the water; He plunged into the pool to save the drowning child; He was plunged in grief by the death of his wife; a **plunging** V-neckline.* **2** *Informal.* to gamble or speculate rashly.
— *n.* an act of plunging: *a plunge in the pool; a plunge into the stock market that left him a pauper; He wants to give up his job to start a business, but hesitates to **take the plunge.***

plung·er (PLUN·jur) *n.* **1** a long-handled suction cup for freeing clogged drains. **2** one who plunges, esp. a rash speculator.

plunk *n.* a metallic or twanging sound, as made by plucking on a stringed musical instrument.
— *v.* fall or drop heavily; plump: *He plunked the change down on the counter and walked out.*

plu·ral (PLOOR·ul) *adj.* being more than one.
— *n.* a word form indicating more than one, as "boys," "boxes," "oxen," "fish," or "women."

plu·ral·ism (PLOOR·uh·liz·um) *n.* the condition of having more than one, as having various ethnic groups with equal rights in the same society.
— **plu·ral·is·tic** (-LIS·tic) *adj.*: *Canada is a pluralistic society.*

plu·ral·i·ty (ploo·RAL·uh·tee) *n.* **-ties 1** in an election, the number of a winner's votes if less than a majority. **2** the excess of such a winner's votes over the nearest rival's.

plu·ral·ize (PLOOR·uh·lize) *v.* **-iz·es, -ized, -iz·ing** make into plural: *"Fish" is pluralized in "Fish swim."*
— **plu·ral·i·za·tion** (-luh·ZAY·shun) *n.*

plus *n.* **plus·es** or **plus·ses 1** the addition sign (+). **2** something added; hence, an advantage: *One of the pluses of our new car is air-conditioning.*
— *prep.* added to something: *Two plus two is four; qualifications plus experience.*
— *adj.* extra: *She got a B plus in math; a plus factor, quantity; on the plus* (= positive) *side.*
— *conj. Informal: He's jobless, plus* (= in addition) *he's in debt.*

plush *n.* a fabric like velvet but with a thicker pile.
— *adj.* soft or luxurious: *plush carpeting; a plush toy; He dines in plush* (= luxurious) *surroundings.*
— **plush·ly** *adv.*

ply *n.* **plies** a layer, fold, or strand of a material such as woven cloth, twisted rope, or plywood: *a tire built with four plies of polyester cord; a two-ply paper towel.*
— *v.* **plies, plied, ply·ing 1** travel regularly: *a ferry plying between Borden, P.E.I., and Cape Tormentine, N.B.; It has been plying the same route for many years.* **2** work at steadily: *to ply a trade; She plied the child with questions to get her to tell the truth; a cutter plying* (= using) *his shears.*

ply·wood *n.* a building material made of sheets of wood glued and pressed together.

pneu·mat·ic (new·MAT·ic) *adj.* having to do with air, esp. air under pressure: *a pneumatic drill, hammer, tire, tool; pneumatic tubes to shoot messages between two points, as in an office or a plant.*

poach *v.* **1** cook egg, fish, or fruit without its shell or skin in a boiling liquid or over steam: *bass poached in cider; pears poached in wine and honey.* **2** take game or fish illegally.

poach·er *n.* **1** one who poaches game or fish. **2** a covered pan or baking dish for poaching food.

pock *n.* **1** an eruption on the skin caused by a disease such as smallpox. **2** a pitlike mark or scar left by it.

pock·et (POCK·it) *n.* **1** a small bag forming part of one's clothing, for carrying money, handkerchief, etc.: *People stood around with hands in their pockets* (= idle); *Don't let someone pick* (= steal from) *your pocket.* **2** a similar hollow or isolated space: *a billiard pocket; an air pocket* (= trapped air); *a pocket* (= small area) *of unemployment.*
— **in someone's pocket** under someone's control.
— **out of pocket** short of cash: *He was out of pocket after paying off the mortgage; petty cash for out-of-pocket* (= incidental) *expenses.*

pock·et·book (POCK·it·book) *n.* **1** a book in a small format. **2** a purse or wallet; hence, financial resources.

pocket money *n.* money given for small personal expenses.

pod *n.* **1** a seed case or shell, as of beans or peas, that splits open when ripe. **2** a cocoon or egg capsule. **3** a container, enclosure, or housing outside a craft for carrying fuel, instruments, etc.: *the engine pod of an aircraft; a rest pod* (= recessed area) *for factory workers to relax in.* **4** a group of animals: *a pod of seals, whales.*
— *v.* **pods, pod·ded, pod·ding** to form pods.

po·di·um (POH·dee·um) *n., pl.* **-di·a 1** a small platform for standing on, as for an orchestra conductor: *The skyscraper stands on a three-storey podium at the corner of King and Bay streets.* **2** a lectern.

po·em (POH·um) *n.* a piece of creative writing in verse form with emotional and imaginative content: *to compose, recite, write a poem.*

po·e·sy (POH·uh·see) *n.* [old use] poetry.

po·et (POH·it) *n.* one who composes poetry.
— **po·et·ess** (-is) *n.* [uncomplimentary use] female poet: *a prairie poetess; the poetess of doom and gloom.*
— **po·et·ic** (poh·ET·ic) or **po·et·i·cal** *adj.*
— **po·et·i·cal·ly** *adv.*

poetic justice *n.* the rewarding of good and punishing of evil as seen in uncaused events: *the poetic justice of a pickpocket being robbed.*

poetic licence *n.* freedom to ignore a rule or convention for the sake of an artistic effect, as in composing poetry.

poet laureate *n.* a nation's official poet.

po·et·ry (POH·uh·tree) *n.* **1** the art of writing poems. **2** poems collectively: *the poetry of Milton.*

po·gey (POH·gee, "g" as in "go") *n. Cdn. Slang.* welfare, unemployment benefits, or charity: *You go on the pogey while looking for a job.*

po·go stick (POH·goh-) *n.* a stilt with handles at the top and springy footrests at the bottom with which a child makes short leaps for moving around.

po·grom (poh·GROM, POH·grum) *n.* an organized massacre, as of Jews in Czarist Russia.

po·gy same as POGEY.

poign·ant (POIN·yunt) *adj.* painful to the mind and feelings: *poignant memories, sights, sorrow, tale.*
— **poign·ant·ly** *adv.* — **poign·an·cy** *n.*

point *n.* **1** a tapering end, as of a pencil; tip: *a sharp point; a hostage taken at the point of* (= using) *a gun; Middle Island in Lake Erie, Ontario, is Canada's most southerly point;* [in place names] *Point Pelee; Hanlan's*

Point. **2** a dot or mark made with a tip: *the decimal point in 1.5* (= one point five); *an exclamation point* [!] **3** a position in time or space: *the point at which the lines meet; a focal, rallying, starting, turning, vantage point; the high and low points of one's career; The patient was at the point of death last night; a terminal case of cancer past the point of no return (like an airplane without enough fuel to return to its starting point); Information from point-of-sale transaction terminals helps to keep store records up to date; Being optimistic or pessimistic depends on your point of view* (= attitude). **4** a mark as a unit or measure: *You score 10 points if you win; the set point of a game (that may decide the set in favour of the player who is leading); the boiling and freezing points* (= degrees of temperature) *of water; N.N.E. is a point of the compass* (= one of 32 directions). **5** a single detail, item, or particular: *Let me answer you point by point; You've raised an interesting point* (= matter); *to argue, concede, emphasize, illustrate, labour, stress, win a point; You've made your point* (= proved your case); *He has good and bad points* (= sides) *as a writer; Sometimes he misses the point* (= the main idea) *altogether; His good looks are beside the point* (= irrelevant); *This essay is a case in point* (= a relevant example); *In point of fact* (= in regard to fact), *only a few attended the meeting.* **6** purpose or urgency: *There's no point in arguing further.*
— *v.* **1** make into a point: *Use a sharpener to point a pencil; a pointed remark that made the listeners uneasy.* **2** show or indicate: *to point out a place on a map; All the symptoms point to stomach ulcers; Errors of grammar and spelling point up the need for remedial English.* **3** aim: *The gun was pointed at his head; It's rude to point at people (with the finger when they are looking).* — **point·ed·ly** *adv.*

point-blank *adj. & adv.* close or closely: *He was gunned down at point-blank range; a point-blank* (= outright) *denial of the charge; She refused him point-blank* (= bluntly).

point·er *n.* **1** one that points, as a rod: *a few pointers* (= hints or advice) *on what to look for in a used car.* **2** a breed of hunting dog that sniffs out game and stays pointing to it.

point·less *adj.* without a point or purpose; meaningless. — **point·less·ly** *adv.;* **point·less·ness** *n.*

point man *n.* leading player; one in the forefront.

point·y *adj.* **point·i·er, -i·est 1** having many points: *a pointy clown's cap.* **2** pointed: *boots with pointy toes; a pointy-headed* (= egghead) *bureaucrat.*

point zero *n.* the place of explosion of an atomic bomb.

poise (POIZ) *n.* **1** self-possession: *a woman of great poise; to keep, lose, maintain one's poise.* **2** the way one carries oneself; carriage: *her graceful poise.*
— *v.* **pois·es, poised, pois·ing** balance or be balanced: *The diver stands poised at the edge of the diving board; to poise* (= brace) *oneself for the dive.*

poi·son (POY·zun) *n.* **1** a substance that causes illness or death in a living organism. **2** anything destructive or harmful, such as certain chemicals, plants, snake bites, and stings of insects.
— *v.* put poison in something: *The drink was poisoned;*

books that poison young minds; She was poisoned (= killed by poisoning).
— *adj.* containing poison: *poison gas, ivy, oak.*
— **poi·son·ous** (-us) *adj.*

poison-pen letter *n.* a malicious, harassing letter, usually by an anonymous writer.

poison pill *n.* a legal provision that would make the takeover of a company too costly for the buyer.

poke *v.* **pokes, poked, pok·ing 1** prod or jab; push: *Someone in the crowd poked her; He poked his head in my door to announce the visitor; to poke around in the bushes for a lost ball; a dawdler poking along* (= proceeding slowly) *with his work; He likes to poke fun at* (= tease) *his sister.* **2** *Informal.* punch.
— *n.* a prod or push: *a friendly poke in the ribs; She took a poke at him (Informal for gave him a punch).*

pok·er (POH·kur) *n.* **1** a metal rod for stirring a fire. **2** a card game in which bets are placed on the value of the cards held.

poker face *n. Informal.* a face without any expression.

pok·ey or **pok·y 1** *adj.* **pok·i·er, -i·est** annoyingly slow. **2** dull, dowdy, or stuffy and cramped.
— **pok·i·ly** *adv.;* **pok·i·ness** *n.*

pol *n.* [short form] politician.

po·lar (POH·lur) *adj.* having to do with the North or South Pole: *a polar ice cap; the polar circles* (= Arctic and Antarctic circles); *the polar lights* (= auroras); *the polar orbit of a spacecraft (passing over the poles); a polar region, route; the large, white-furred polar bear of the Arctic; Falsehood is the polar* (= direct) *opposite of truth.*

po·lar·i·ty (puh·LAIR·uh·tee) *n.* **-ties** the condition of having opposed poles: *A magnet or battery has negative and positive polarity; the political polarity* (= opposition) *between capital and labour.*

po·lar·ize (POH·luh·rize) *v.* **-iz·es, -ized, -iz·ing** give or get polarity: *Polarized sunglasses cut out much reflected light; a camera with a polarizing filter; a community polarized* (= badly divided) *by rivalries.*
— **po·lar·i·za·tion** (-ruh·ZAY·shun) *n.*

pole *n.* **1** a long, slender, and usually rounded piece of wood or metal, as used to push a boat with: *a ski pole; telephone pole; tent pole; a pole lamp (with several lights fixed on a pole reaching from floor to ceiling).* **2** either end of an imaginary rotating axis, as of the earth; hence North Pole, South Pole. **3** either of two opposing forces or principles: *the opposite poles of a magnet; The negative pole* (= terminal) *of one battery is to be connected to the positive pole of the other when using a booster cable; The two sides were poles apart* (= widely separated) *when they started talks.* **4 Pole** a person of or from Poland.

po·lem·ic (puh·LEM·ic) **1** *adj.* having to do with controversy; also **po·lem·i·cal. 2** *n.* a controversy. **3 polemics** *n.pl.* [takes sing. v.] the art of controversy.
— **po·lem·i·cist** (-uh·sist) *n.*

pole·star *n.* the North Star; hence, a guiding principle: *Duty was the polestar of his life.*

po·lice (puh·LEECE) *n.* **1** a department of government that prevents crime, maintains public peace and safety, enforces laws, etc.; also, its members: *to call the police; Ontario Provincial Police; mounted police; plainclothes police; adj.: a police car, officer, outpost, patrol, post.* **2** any similar private organization providing security services: *campus, military, secret, security police.*
— *v.* -lic·es, -liced, -lic·ing **1** guard: *to police a neighbourhood.* **2** keep a military area clean and orderly.
— **po·lice·man** (-mun), -men *n.;* **po·lice·wom·an** *n.* -wom·en.

police officer *n.* a policeman or policewoman.

police state *n.* a state in which social, political, and economic life is repressed, usually by use of secret police.

police town or **village** *n. Cdn.* an Ontario town run by an elected board of trustees

pol·i·cy (POL·uh·see) *n.* -cies **1** a principle, conduct, or plan of action: *"Satisfaction or money back" is the store policy; the foreign policy of peaceful coexistence; to adopt, carry out, formulate, implement, pursue, set, shape a policy; a company policy; Canada's foreign policy.* **2** an insurance contract: *to issue, take out, write up a policy.*

pol·i·cy·hold·er (POL·uh·see·hole·dur) *n.* one to whom an insurance policy has been issued.

po·li·o (POH·lee·oh) *n.* [short form] poliomyelitis.

po·li·o·my·e·li·tis (POH·lee·oh·my·uh·LYE·tis) *n.* an acute viral infection of the central nervous system, which sometimes leads to paralysis.

pol·ish ("ol" as in "doll") *n.* **1** a glossy surface finish, as of glass. **2** a substance used to give this finish: *nail polish; shoe polish.* **3** refinement or culture.
— *v.* give polish to something: *to polish furniture, shoes; highly polished* (= refined) *manners.*
— **polish off** finish: *He polished off his dinner in no time.*
— **polish up** practise and improve: *Better polish up your French before going to Paris.*

Pol·ish (POH·lish) *n.* the language of the Poles.
— *adj.* of or from Poland.

Po·lit·bu·ro (POL·it·byoor·oh) *n.* a Communist party's top policy-making group. Also **politburo.**

po·lite (puh·LITE) *adj.* -lit·er, -lit·est **1** correct and proper in one's behaviour; not rude: *a polite young woman; At least be polite if you can't be friendly; polite applause; polite* (= subtle) *prejudice.* **2** cultured, polished, or elegant: *a man of polite learning; She moves in polite society.* — **po·lite·ly** *adv.;* **po·lite·ness** *n.*

pol·i·tic (POLL·uh·tic, "OLL" as in "doll") *adj.* shrewd and tactful: *She thought it politic not to disagree with the boss.*

po·lit·i·cal (puh·LIT·uh·cul) *adj.* having to do with government or politics: *The Russian athlete sought political asylum in the U.S.; a political office, party; political economy, patronage, science; amnesty for political prisoners.* — **po·lit·i·cal·ly** *adv.*

pol·i·ti·cian (poll·uh·TISH·un) *n.* **1** one who is busy with political affairs, esp. one in political office: *an astute, great, honest, shrewd politician.* **2** an opportunist: *a crooked politician; just a scheming politician, not a statesman.*

po·lit·i·cize (puh·LIT·uh·size) *v.* -ciz·es, -cized, -ciz·ing make political in character: *to politicize the Olympics.*
— **po·lit·i·ci·za·tion** (-suh·ZAY·shun) *n.*

pol·i·tick (POLL·uh·tic) *v.* be busy with political activities.

po·lit·i·co (puh·LIT·uh·coh) *n.* -cos or -coes a party politician.

pol·i·tics (POLL·uh·tics) *n. pl.* **1** [takes sing. v.] the science of government: *Politics is her major.* **2** [takes sing. or pl. v.] political principles or activities, including intrigue or rivalry: *Politics are to blame for the fiasco; Is politics a dirty game? to play, talk politics; office, partisan, party, power politics.*

polka dot *n.* a round dot repeated as a pattern on fabric: *a polka-dot design.*

poll (POLE) *n.* **1** a voting, its results, or the counting of votes: *A heavy poll is expected; The poll was light because of bad weather; a straw poll.* **2** polls *pl.* voting place: *Britain goes to the polls tomorrow; The polls close at 8 p.m.* **3** an opinion survey on a specific issue: *a Gallup poll; Harris poll; a public-opinion poll; to carry out, conduct, take a poll of the student population on the voting age.*
— *v.* **1** vote: *a polling booth.* **2** receive as votes: *The winner polled 60% of the votes.* **3** survey by means of a poll: *A random sample of the population was polled on the issue.* **4** shear or crop wool, horns, head hair, etc.
— **poll·er** *n.*

pol·len (POLL·un, "OLL" as in "doll") *n.* a fine powder produced by flowers for the fertilization of other flowers by the agency of wind, insects, etc.

pollen count or **pollen index** *n.* the estimate of the number of pollen grains in the air for warning hay-fever victims.

pol·li·nate (POLL·uh·nate, "OLL" as in "doll") *v.* -nates, -nat·ed, -nat·ing fertilize a flower by pollen.
— **pol·li·na·tor** (-nay·tur) *n.*
— **poll·i·na·tion** (-NAY·shun) *n.*

pol·li·wog (POLL·ee·wog, "OLL" as in "doll") *n.* a tadpole.

poll·ster (POLE·stur) *n.* one who conducts a poll of public opinion.

poll tax *n.* a uniform per-head tax, not based on income or property; also called "head tax" or "capitation tax."

pol·lu·tant (puh·LOO·tunt) *n.* smoke, noise, wastes, or exhausts that pollute the environment.

pol·lute (puh·LOOT, long "OO") *v.* pol·lutes, pol·lut·ed, pol·lut·ing make unclean; defile, esp. the environment. — **pol·lu·ter** *n.*
— **pol·lu·tion** (-LOO·shun) *n.: air, noise, soil, sound, water pollution; the **pollution index*** (= measure of impurities in the air).

Pol·ly·an·na (poll·ee·AN·uh) *n.* one who sees an optimistic side in even the most tragic events.

po·lo (POH·loh) *n.* a ball game played on horseback

using mallets.

polo shirt *n.* a short-sleeved, knitted pullover of cotton or jersey.

pol·ter·geist (POLE·tur·guyst) *n.* the supposed spirit behind the phenomena of haunted houses such as fire-raising, stone-throwing, china-smashing, and door-slamming.

pol·troon (poll·TROON, "oll" as in "doll") *n.* a contemptible coward.

poly- *combining form.* much or many: *polyandry, polyglot, polygon.*

pol·y·an·dry (POLL·ee·an·dree) *n.* the practice or custom of having more than one male spouse at a time.

pol·y·clin·ic (poll·ee·CLIN·ic) *n.* a hospital with various specialist departments.

pol·y·es·ter (poll·ee·ES·tur) *n.* a synthetic material used in making paints, fibres, films, plastics, etc.

pol·y·eth·yl·ene (poll·ee·ETH·uh·leen) *n.* a plastic used for containers, kitchenware, tubing, etc.

po·lyg·a·mous (puh·LIG·uh·mus) *adj.* **1** that practises polygamy: *a polygamous society, tribe.* **2** having both bisexual and unisexual flowers: *Certain ashes and maples are polygamous.*

po·lyg·a·my (puh·LIG·uh·mee) *n.* marriage with more than one spouse at the same time, esp. having more than one wife. — **po·lyg·a·mist** (-guh·mist) *n.*

pol·y·glot (POLL·ee·glot) *adj.* speaking, writing, or containing several languages: *a polyglot edition, population.* — *n.* a multilingual person or text.

pol·y·gon (POLL·ee·gon, *rhyme:* on) *n.* a closed plane figure, usually one with five or more straight sides. — **po·lyg·o·nal** (puh·LIG·uh·nul) *adj.*

pol·y·graph (POLL·ee·graf) *n.* a lie detector. — *v.: He was arrested, thumb-printed, and polygraphed.*

pol·y·math (POLL·ee·math) *n.* a person of wide-ranging knowledge.

pol·yp (POL·ip) *n.* **1** a simple sea animal such as a coral that has a hollow cylindrical body with one end attached to the sea bottom while the other, equipped with tentacles, acts as its mouth. **2** a tumour projecting from the mucous membrane of the bladder, intestine, nose, or uterus.

po·lyph·o·ny (puh·LIF·uh·nee) *n.* a musical composition of two or more harmonizing melodies; counterpoint. — **pol·y·phon·ic** (poll·ee·FON·ic) *adj.*

pol·y·sty·rene (poll·ee·STY·reen) *n.* a tough, clear plastic used for housewares, toys, electrical insulation, radio cabinets, etc.

pol·y·syl·lab·ic (POLL·ee·suh·LAB·ic) *adj.* of many syllables: *a polysyllabic word.*

pol·y·tech·nic (poll·ee·TEK·nic) *n.* a school providing instruction in many technical subjects.

pol·y·the·ism (poll·ee·THEE·iz·um, "TH" as in "thin") *n.* a religion with more than one god. — **pol·y·the·ist** *n.* — **pol·y·the·is·tic** (POLL·ee·thee·IS·tic) *adj.*

pol·y·un·sat·u·rat·ed (POLL·ee·un·SACH·uh·ray·tid) *adj.* of a fatty acid or vegetable oil, lacking four or more hydrogen atoms: *Margarine and most vegetable oils are sources of polyunsaturated fats.*

pol·y·u·re·thane (poll·ee·YOOR·uh·thane) *n.* a synthetic rubber used in flexible and rigid forms as foams, moulded products, etc.

po·made (poh·MADE, -MAHD) *n.* a scented ointment for the hair. — *v.* -mades, -mad·ed, -mad·ing apply pomade to something: *pomaded hair.*

pom·mel (PUM·ul) *n.* a knoblike projection, as on a sword's hilt or the front end of a saddle.

pomp *n.* a showy display: *a ceremony full of pomp and pageantry; an emperor's life of pomp and circumstance.*

pom-pom *n.* an ornamental tuft or ball of soft material; also **pompon.**

pom·pous (POM·pus) *adj.* showy or pretentious: *a pompous manner, speech, style.* — **pom·pous·ly** *adv.* — **pom·pous·ness** or **pom·pos·i·ty** (pom·POS·uh·tee) *n.*

ponce *n.* *Slang.* same as PIMP.

pon·cho (PON·choh) *n.* -chos **1** a cloak resembling a blanket with a hole through it for the wearer's head. **2** a similar garment, esp. a raincoat.

pond *n.* a body of water smaller than a lake.

pon·der (PON·dur) *v.* weigh mentally; consider deeply: *a philosopher pondering a truth; to ponder on* or *over* or *upon one's future.*

pon·der·a·ble (PON·dur·uh·bul) *adj.* appreciable in regard to weight or importance.

pon·der·ous (PON·dur·us) *adj.* heavy, clumsy, or dull: *an elephant's ponderous gait; a ponderous essay, lecture.*

pone *n.* cornmeal bread in oval loaves, common in southern U.S.

pon·tiff *n.* a bishop, esp. the **Pontiff** or **Supreme Pontiff** (= Pope).

pon·tif·i·cal (pon·TIF·uh·cul) *adj.* **1** papal: *a pontifical institute; pontifical robes.* **2** pompous or dogmatic. **3 pontificals** *n. pl.* a pontiff's ceremonial vestments and insignia.

pon·tif·i·cate (pon·TIF·uh·kit) *n.* a pontiff's office or term of office. — *v.* (-cate) -cates, -cat·ed, -cat·ing **1** officiate as a pontiff. 2 speak pompously: *to pontificate on a subject you know little about.*

pon·y (POH·nee) *n.* **-nies 1** a small horse. **2** a small glass of liqueur. **3** *Informal.* a crib, as notes used by a student to cheat at a test.

pony express *n.* a system of transporting mail by a relay of riders, once used in western U.S.

po·ny·tail (POH·nee·tail) *n.* hair tied behind the head and hanging down like a pony's tail.

pooch *n. Slang.* a dog.

pooh *interj.* indicating impatience or contempt.

pooh-bah *n.* a self-important official with much authority.

pooh-pooh *v.* treat with contempt; dismiss as of no worth.

pool *n.* **1** a small basin or body of water: *an indoor, shallow, stagnant, swimming, wading pool.* **2** a puddle or small collection of liquid: *The accident victim lay in a pool of blood.* **3** a form of billiards, played on a six-pocket **pool table,** often in a **pool hall** or **pool room:** *He was shooting pool all evening.* **4** a group or combination of people or resources for a common purpose: *We formed a car pool (to share the driving to work); a typing pool (of available typists); football pool* (=money for betting); *a gene pool.* **5** a business combine or cartel for controlling a market.
— *v.* put in a common fund: *We pooled our talents to make the show a success.*

poop *n.* **1** a raised deck at the stern of a ship; also **poop deck. 2** *Slang.* excrement: *a **poop scoop** bylaw requiring dog owners to clean up after their pets in public places.* **3** *Slang.* inside information: *a **poop sheet** handed out to journalists.*
— *v. Informal.* be exhausted: *Pat's all **pooped out** at the end of the day.*

poor *adj.* **1** lacking in quality or amount: *a poor essay, job, performance; a poor showing at the polls; poor English; He's poor in spelling.* **2** needy: *one of the poorer Third World countries; the poor people; a poor widow; the rich and **the poor** (people).* **3** needing pity: *a poor orphan.* — **poor·ly** *adv.*

poor·house *n.* formerly, a publicly supported institution for the poor.

poor-mouth *v. Informal.* portray oneself as poor for complaining, excusing oneself, etc.

pop *n.* **1** *Informal.* father. **2** a carbonated drink: *orange pop; soda pop.* **3** **pops** *pl.* pop music: *Boston pops orchestra.* **4 pop** or **Pop** art that uses everyday subjects and techniques based on commercial art; also **pop art** or **Pop art; pop artist** or **pop·ster. 5** a light explosive sound, as a gun shot: *The cork went pop.* **6** in baseball, a short, high fly ball; also **pop fly, pop-up.**
— *adj.* popular in artistic or cultural appeal: *pop art, culture, evangelism, fiction, music, psychology, singer.*
— *v.* **pops, popped, pop·ping** do or make happen lightly, quickly, or with a sound: *You will pop* (=burst) *the balloon if you prick it; He popped* (=dropped) *into her office for a short visit; to **pop the question*** (=propose marriage); *hippies popping* (=putting into their mouths quickly) *pills and blowing marijuana; There's no end to the problems that **pop up*** (=rise

suddenly) *at work.*
— **pop off** *Slang.* **1** die suddenly. **2** talk or write carelessly.

pop·corn *n.* the white kernels of Indian corn puffed out by heating, usually in a **pop·per.**

pope *n.* the head of the Roman Catholic Church.

pop·eyed *adj.* having bulging eyes.

pop fly *n. See* POP.

pop·gun *n.* a toy gun that fires a cork or pellets with a popping sound.

pop·in·jay (POP·un·jay) *n.* a vain person; fop.

pop·lar (POP·lur) *n.* a fast-growing tall tree such as the aspen.

pop·lin *n.* a tightly woven ribbed fabric with a plain weave.

pop-off *n. Slang.* a person who pops off in speech or writing.

pop·py (POP·ee) *n.* **pop·pies** an herb with large, usually red flowers and a milky juice: *Bakery products are sometimes flavoured with **poppy seed.***

poppy·cock *n. Informal.* nonsense.

popster *See* POP.

pop-top *n. & adj.* (a soda or beer container) having a ring for pulling the top open.

pop·u·lace (POP·yuh·lis) *n.* the common people; the masses.

pop·u·lar (POP·yuh·lur) *adj.* of or for the common people, esp. appealing to or liked by them: *a popular government, politician, price; teachers who are popular with students; left-wing parties united in a popular front against fascism; An M.P. is chosen by popular vote.*
— **pop·u·lar·ly** (-lur·lee) *adv.*
— **pop·u·lar·i·ty** (-LAIR·uh·tee) *n.*

pop·u·lar·ize (POP·yuh·luh·rize) *v.* **-iz·es, -ized, -iz·ing** make popular.

pop·u·late (POP·yuh·late) *v.* **-lates, -lat·ed, -lat·ing** inhabit or supply with people to inhabit: *Animal life existed before humans populated the earth; a densely, heavily, sparsely **populated** area.*

pop·u·la·tion (pop·yuh·LAY·shun) *n.* the people or the number of people of a place or group: *the adult male population of Canada; an aging, expanding, growing, rising, shrinking, transient population; the falling population of urban areas; the recent **population explosion** all over the world due to improved living conditions and lower rates of infant mortality.*

pop·u·list (POP·yuh·list) *n.* a member of a political party devoted to helping the common people as against moneyed interests: *a populist image, party.*
— **pop·u·lism.**

pop·u·lous (POP·yuh·lus) *adj.* thickly populated: *The Niagara peninsula is the most populous area of Canada.*
— **pop·u·lous·ness** *n.*

pop-up *n. See* POP.

por·ce·lain (POR·sul·in) *n.* a fine-grained, white, translucent, glazed ceramic ware; china.

porch *n.* **1** a roofed entrance to a building. **2** a verandah: *a glass-covered sun porch.*

por·cu·pine (PORK·yuh·pine) *n.* a large rodent with a covering of long, sharp spines for protection.

pore *n.* a tiny opening on leaves, skin, etc. for the absorption or passage of fluids, as when sweating.
— *v.* **pores, pored, por·ing** study long and intently: *She has been poring over that book all day.*

pork *n.* the meat of a pig or hog, esp. when cured.

pork barrel *n.* public funding of local projects for the political benefit of elected representatives: *pork barrel politics.*

pork·er *n.* a young hog raised for food.

pork·y *adj.* **pork·i·er, -i·est** like pork: *a porky* (= fat) *fellow.*

porn or **por·no** *n. & adj.* [short form] pornography; pornographic: *hard-core porn; nude without being porno; a porn bookstore, movie; porno films, movies, videotapes.*

por·nog·ra·phy (por·NOG·ruh·fee) *n.* writings and pictures meant to arouse sexual desire: *explicit, hard-core, soft-core pornography.*
— **por·no·graph·ic** (-noh·GRAF·ic) *adj.*

po·rous (POR·us) *adj.* full of pores; allowing light, air, etc. to pass through. — **po·rous·ly** *adv.*
— **po·rous·ness** or **po·ros·i·ty** (puh·ROS·uh·tee) *n.*

port *n.* **1** a harbour: *to arrive at, call at a port; clear* (= leave) *a port; to make or reach port; to put into port (and stay there for a time).* **2** a harbour city. **3** a strong, dark-red wine of Portugal. **4** a ship's or aircraft's left side for one facing front. **5** an opening, as in a fortress wall; also, a porthole. **6** one's bearing or carriage.

port·a·ble (POR·tuh·bul) *adj.* easy to carry or move, as a small TV or computer: *a portable pension plan for employees changing jobs or moving to another province.*
— *n.* one that is portable: *classes housed in portables.*
— **port·a·bil·i·ty** (-BIL·uh·tee) *n.*

port·age (POR·tij) *n.* a place or route for carrying boats and provisions overland, as from one river to another; *adj.: a portage path, road, route, track.*
— *v.* **-ag·es, -aged, -ag·ing** carry boats and cargoes at a portage: *They rode the rapids and portaged around the waterfalls.*

por·tal (POR·tul) *n.* an entrance, esp. an imposing one.

por·ta·pak (POR·tuh·pak) *n. Cdn.* a classroom housed in temporary quarters.

por·tend (por·TEND) *v.* be a warning of some future event; bode.

por·tent (POR·tent) *n.* a foreboding or omen.

por·ten·tous (por·TEN·tus) *adj.* **1** ominous or foreboding. **2** arousing awe; amazing; hence, pompous.

por·ter *n.* **1** a servant such as baggage carrier, doorman, or janitor in a hotel, train, etc. **2** a heavy, dark-brown beer.

port·fo·li·o (port·FOH·lee·oh) *n.* **-os 1** a thin, flat case, usually of leather, for papers and documents. **2** the office or department of a cabinet minister: *A minister*

without portfolio has general functions. **3** a list of one's investments such as stocks and bonds.

port·hole *n.* an opening in a ship's or aircraft's side as a window.

por·ti·co (POR·tuh·coh) *n.* **-cos** or **-coes** a porch with a row of columns supporting its roof.
— **por·ti·coed** (-code) *adj.: a porticoed entrance, hotel.*

por·tiere (port·YAIR) *n.* a curtain hung over a doorway.

por·tion (POR·shun) *n.* **1** a shared part of something, as a serving of food, an inheritance, or a dowry. **2** one's lot in life: *Sorrow was her portion all life long.*
— *v.* distribute: *The aged farmer portioned out the land among his children.*

port·ly *adj.* **-li·er, -li·est** fat but stately in bearing: *a portly gentleman.* — **port·li·ness** *n.*

port·man·teau (port·MAN·toh) *n.* **-teaus** or **-teaux** (-toze) a suitcase that opens into two compartments hinged together.

portmanteau word *n.* a word formed by joining two words together, as "motel" (motor + hotel) or "smog" (smoke + fog).

port of call *n.* a port where ships stop for repairs, supplies, cargo, etc.

port of entry *n.* an official port for cargo and people to enter a country.

por·trait (POR·trit, -trait) *n.* **1** a picture or representation, esp. of a person or persons: *to commission, paint, pose for, sit for a portrait; a family portrait.* **2** a graphic or dramatic portrayal: *The book is a portrait of a very controversial figure.*

por·trait·ist (POR·tray·tist) *n.* one who paints portraits.

por·trai·ture (POR·truh·chur) *n.* **1** the art of portraying. **2** a portrait or portraits.

por·tray (por·TRAY) *v.* **1** draw or paint a picture of a person or thing: *An artist portrays a scene; a book that portrays (in words) pioneer life; people portrayed as heroes.* **2** act out or enact: *a character hard to portray on the modern stage.*
— **por·tray·al** (-ul) *n.: Richard Burton's portrayal of Mark Antony.*

pose (POZE) *v.* **pos·es, posed, pos·ing 1** assume or make assume a certain position: *She poses* (= works as a model) *for artists; She can pose for hours; to pose for a photograph; A photographer poses a group for a picture.* **2** affect a posture or attitude; pretend to be someone else: *He gained entry by posing as a detective.* **3** raise a question, esp. a baffling one: *Overpopulation poses many problems; to pose a challenge, danger, question, threat.*
— *n.* a posing: *He assumes the pose of a martyr; to strike a pose; his pose as a pundit; His piety is a mere pose.*

pos·er (POH·zur) *n.* **1** one who poses. **2** something baffling.

po·seur (poh·ZUR) *n.* one who poses for effect.

posh *adj. Informal.* elegant or luxurious: *a posh hotel, job, neighbourhood.*

pos·it (POZ·it) *v.* put forward as a fact; postulate.

po·si·tion (puh·ZISH·un) *n.* **1** a place or location, esp. in relation to other factors: *Troops move into position before a parade; to take a safe position behind a wall; to negotiate from a position of strength; opposing parties manoeuvring for position (of advantage); I'm not in a position to tell you what is going on; a defensive, dominant, embarrassing, impregnable, leading, ludicrous, prominent, vulnerable position; to attack, hold, occupy, regain, storm, surrender, take up a position* (= military site). **2** a posture: *to assume a kneeling position; an awkward, lotus, prone, sitting, squatting, supine position; the fetal position.* **3** an attitude or stand, as on an issue: *to take a firm, radical, strong position on the death penalty; I don't agree with your position; a **position paper** for discussing policy.* **4** a post of employment: *a clerical, government, permanent, teaching, temporary, vacant position; to apply for, find, seek a position.* **5** a high rank: *men and women of position in our company.*
— *v.* to place or post: *Troops are positioned in readiness for action.* — **po·si·tion·al** *adj.*

pos·i·tive (POZ·uh·tiv) *adj.* **1** not negative: *"Yes" is a positive answer; Current flows from a battery's positive terminal; a positive pregnancy test; a positive (photographic) print; 3 is a **positive integer*** (= whole number greater than zero). **2** definite: *He's not just sure but quite positive about it; a positive refusal; We need helpful, positive* (= creative) *criticisms.*
— *n.* something positive.
— **pos·i·tive·ly** *adv.*; **pos·i·tive·ness** *n.*

pos·se (POS·ee) *n.* **1** a body of persons having legal authority: *a posse of constables.* **2** *Cdn.* a group of horses and their riders who perform at stampedes.

pos·sess (puh·ZES) *v.* **1** have as a natural or acquired quality or skill; own: *a beggar who possesses nothing; an orator possessing great powers of persuasion; a woman **possessed of** initiative and enterprise.* **2** gain control over someone; dominate: *What possessed you to behave like that? a woman possessed with fury; an apostle possessed by missionary zeal; to exorcise a **possessed** person* (= one controlled by an evil spirit).
— **pos·ses·sor** *n.*

pos·ses·sion (puh·ZESH·un) *n.* **1** ownership: *to get, take possession of a newly bought house; a will made while in possession of one's senses.* **2** something owned: *Guam is a possession of the U.S.; He gave away his material **possessions** and became a monk.*

pos·ses·sive (puh·ZES·iv) *adj.* having to do with possession: *the possessive instinct; a possessive nature, parent; a **possessive adjective** such as "my," "his," and "your"; "mine" and "theirs" are **possessive pronouns.***
— *n.* the possessive case or a word in the possessive.
— **pos·ses·sive·ly** *adv.*; **pos·ses·sive·ness** *n.*

pos·si·ble (POS·uh·bul) *adj.* that can exist, happen, or be done: *Please apply as soon as possible; It's possible to beat cancer; We'll do anything that is humanly possible.*

pos·si·bly (POS·uh·blee) *adv.* **1** by any chance: *How could you possibly do such a thing?* **2** perhaps: *She's away, possibly out of town.*
— **pos·si·bil·i·ty** (-BIL·uh·tee) *n.* **-ties.**

pos·sum (POS·um) *n. Informal.* a furry, tree-dwelling marsupial that will pretend to be dead if surprised on the ground.
— **play possum** pretend to be asleep or dead.

post- *prefix.* after in time or place: *postgraduate, postlude, post-mortem.*

post (rhyme: "most") *n.* **1** an upright piece of wood or metal supporting or displaying something, as a bedpost, goalpost, lamppost, signpost: *Line up at the starting post.* **2** a place of duty; job: *Stay at your posts; the post of Secretary of State.* **3** station: *a command, listening, observation, trading post.* **4** postal service: *Canada Post; book post; parcel post.* **5** *Brit.* mail: *Please reply by return of post* (= return mail); *My post is full of praise for the new book.*
— *v.* **1** put up or display: *We'll post it on the bulletin board; Obey posted speed limits; The new business is posting sales of $1 million a year.* **2** to place on duty; station: *A sentry is posted at a gate; He has been posted to London.* **3** mail: *a letter posted in London; We'll keep you **posted*** (= informed) *on what happens.*

post·age (POSE·tij) *n.* the charge for mailing something, usually paid by means of **postage stamps** or a **postage meter** that imprints mail and records the charges.

post·al (POSE·tul) *adj.* having to do with the post office: *A **postal card** has a stamp printed on it, unlike a picture **post·card**; the U.S. Postal Service* (= department).

postal code *n. Cdn.* a series of six alternating letters and numbers that identifies a mail delivery area, as L4W 2C3.

post chaise *n.* a four-wheeled closed carriage.

post code *n.* the British postal code.

post·date (post·DATE) *v.* **-dates, -dat·ed, -dat·ing** to date a cheque, letter, etc. later than the actual time of writing it: *a postdated cheque.*

post·er *n.* a placard for posting, as in a public place: *a campaign poster; to put up wall posters.*

pos·te·ri·or (pos·TEER·ee·ur) *n.* the buttocks.
— *adj.* coming after in position or time.

pos·ter·i·ty (pos·TER·uh·tee) *n.* descendants; future generations.

post·grad·u·ate (post·GRAJ·oo·it) *adj.* following a bachelor's degree; graduate: *M.A. and Ph.D. are postgraduate degrees.* — *n.* a postgraduate student.

post·haste *adv.* with all speed.

post·hu·mous (POS·choo·mus) *adj.* after one's death: *a posthumous award received by his widow; her posthumous daughter (born after the father's death).*
— **post·hu·mous·ly** *adv.: a book published posthumously* (= after the author's death).

post·hyp·not·ic (post·hip·NOT·ic) *adj.* made during hypnosis for carrying out afterwards: *a posthypnotic suggestion.*

post·ie (POSE·tee) *n. Informal.* a postal worker, esp. a letter carrier.

post·lude *n.* **1** a concluding piece of music. **2** a final phase.

post·man (POST·mun) *n.* -men a mailman.

post·mark *n.* a mark stamped on mail by the post office to show the place and date of mailing: *a Feb. 29 postmark.* — *v.:* an *envelope postmarked London, Ont.*

post·mas·ter (POST·mas·tur) *n.* a person in charge of a post office: *The Postmaster General heads the postal system in some countries.*

post·mis·tress (POST·mis·tris) *n.* a woman manager of a post office.

post·mor·tem (POST·mor·tum) *n.* **1** the examination of a body after death, as by a coroner, to determine the cause of death: *to carry out* or *conduct a post-mortem on a body;* **adj.:** *a post-mortem examination, finding, report.* **2** an inquiry following an event: *a post-mortem on the failure of a bank.*

post·na·tal (post·NAY·tul) *adj.* following childbirth: *postnatal care.*

post office *n.* **1** a place where mail is received for distribution, stamps are sold, etc.: *A private **post office box** or "lock box" may be rented for receiving mail.* **2** esp. **Post Office,** a government agency in charge of mail.

post·paid *adv. & adj.* with the postage already paid: *We'll send it postpaid for a few dollars; a postpaid* (= stamped) *envelope for reply.*

post·pone (post·PONE) *v.* -pones, -poned, -pon·ing put off or delay: *"Do not postpone till tomorrow what you can do today."*— **post·pone·ment** *n.*

post·script *n.* something written as an afterthought: *He added a postscript to the letter saying "P.S. I love you."*

post time *n.* the time scheduled for the start of a horse race.

pos·tu·late (POS·chuh·late) *v.* -lates, -lat·ed, -lat·ing assume as a basic truth or axiom; hence, require: *Do natural phenomena postulate the existence of the supernatural?*— *n.* a fundamental principle.

pos·ture (POS·chur) *n.* **1** a way of holding the body: *an erect posture; in a reclining posture; exercises to improve the posture.* **2** a state, condition, or attitude: *a holier-than-thou posture; a defensive posture against the enemy.* — *v.* -tures, -tured, -tur·ing assume a posture, esp. for effect. — **pos·tu·ral** (POS·chur·ul) *adj.*

post·war *adj.* after-the-war: *the postwar population increase.*

po·sy (POH·zee) *n.* -sies [old use] **1** same as POESY. **2** a motto in verse. **3** a bouquet.

pot *n.* **1** a round vessel for domestic use: *to scour pots and pans; a chamber pot; a melting pot of many cultures.* **2** *Informal.* in betting, the entire stake; kitty. **3** *Slang.* marijuana. — **go to pot** go to ruin. — *v.* pots, pot·ted, pot·ting put into a pot for keeping or cooking: *a room full of potted plants.*

po·ta·to (puh·TAY·toh) *n.* -toes the round, hard, starchy underground stem of a widely cultivated plant, with thin skin, eaten baked, boiled, mashed, or fried crisp in slices called **potato chips** or in strips called **french fries.**

pot·bel·lied (POT·bel·eed) *adj.* having a rounded body: *a potbellied stove.*

pot·bel·ly (POT·bel·ee) *n.* -bel·lies a protruding belly.

pot·boil·er (POT·boy·lur) *n.* a usually second-rate work, esp. a book written for one's livelihood.

po·tent (POH·tunt) *adj.* powerful or effective: *a potent argument, medicine, ruler; no longer (sexually) potent after his illness.* — **po·tent·ly** *adv.* — **po·ten·cy** (-tun·see) *n.*

po·ten·tate (POH·tun·tate) *n.* a ruler or sovereign.

po·ten·tial (puh·TEN·shul) *adj.* capable of coming into being: *A coiled spring has potential energy; I see in her a potential leader; Our profits are potential rather than actual.* — *n.* what one can become: *a new recruit with great potential for high positions.* — **po·ten·tial·ly** *adv.* — **po·ten·ti·al·i·ty** (-shee·AL·uh·tee) *n.*

po·ten·ti·ate (puh·TEN·shee·ate) *v.* -ates, -at·ed, -at·ing make more powerful: *alcohol potentiated by drugs.* — **po·ten·ti·a·tion** (-AY·shun) *n.*

pot·head *n. Slang.* a habitual marijuana user.

poth·er ("th" as in "thin") *n. & v.* fuss or bother.

pot·hole *n.* a rounded hole or depression, as in a rocky river bed or worn-out road surface.

po·tion (POH·shun) *n.* a drink, esp. one that is medicinal, poisonous, or supposedly magical: *a love potion.*

pot·latch *n. Cdn.* among West Coast Indians, a celebration marked by gift-giving and partying.

pot·luck *n.* food that is available as regular fare: *Surprise visitors are invited to take potluck with the family; We had a potluck supper (party) with the guests bringing their own favourite dishes.*

pot·pour·ri (poh·poo·REE) *n.* a medley of musical or literary pieces.

pot·shot *n.* a random or casual shot with no regard for rules: *The new play seemed an easy target for critics to take potshots at.*

pot·tage (POT·ij) *n.* [old use] a kind of thick soup or stew: *a mess of pottage.*

pot·ter (POT·ur) *v.* same as PUTTER. — *n.* one who makes pottery.

pot·ter·y (POT·uh·ree) *n.* **1** pots, pans, vases, etc. made of clay. **2** the potter's art. **3** *pl.* pot·ter·ies a potter's workshop.

pot·ty (POT·ee) *n.* a child's toilet: *a baby potty with a music box attached.* — **adj.** *Slang.* crazy or eccentric: *a potty aristocrat, comedy; Pat's gone completely potty.*

pouch (POWCH) *n.* **1** a small bag or sack, as for keeping or carrying something: *a diplomatic pouch (for documents or messages); mail pouch; tobacco pouch.* **2** an animal's baglike body part, as a kangaroo's pocket or the one under a pelican's bill. — *v.* put in a pouch: *a pocket gopher pouching nuts*

under a tree; **adj.**: *Marsupials are **pouched** animals (that have a pouch).*
— pouch·y *adj.*: *cheeks pouchy with age.*

poul·tice (POLE·tis) *n.* a warm, pulpy mass, as of mustard, herbs, flour, etc., applied to a body part as a dressing.

poul·try (POLE·tree) *n.* domestic fowls such as chickens, turkeys, ducks, and geese.

pounce *v.* **pounc·es, pounced, pounc·ing** swoop down, as if to seize a person or thing: *He greedily pounces on every opportunity to make some money.*

pound *n.* **1** an enclosure for confining stray dogs, cattle, or for cars impounded by police. **2** a trap for fish, forming part of a "pound net." **3** a pounding or its sound. **4** the basic money unit of the U.K. and certain African and Middle Eastern countries. **5** a unit of weight equal to 16 oz. avoirdupois (0.4536 kg) or 12 oz. troy (0.3732 kg).
— *v.* strike or hit heavily and repeatedly: *Knock once, don't pound on my door; Use a mortar and pestle to pound the medication; His heart was pounding with terror; She **pounded out** the story on her old typewriter; The unemployed **pound the pavement** (= walk the streets) looking for work.*

pound·age (POUND·ij) *n.* **1** the weight in pounds. **2** the per-pound rate of tax, etc. **3** a confining or the fee charged at an animal pound.

pound-foolish (POUND·FOO·lish) *adj.* careless about large sums of money: *"penny-wise and pound-foolish."*

pour (POR) *v.* flow or cause to flow, as a stream, flood, or heavy rain, freely, copiously, or steadily: *Please pour me a glass of water; a child pouring forth his tale of sorrow with tears pouring down his cheeks; Rush-hour crowds pour out of the subway.*

pout (POWT) *v.* show displeasure by pushing out the lips; sulk.
— *n.* a sulk: *She continued in a pout till she had her way.* — pout·er *n.*

pov·er·ty (POV·ur·tee) *n.* the condition of being poor; want or deficiency: *Many people live in poverty all their lives; to eliminate, eradicate, wipe out poverty; abject, dire, grinding poverty; a poverty of talent; The **poverty line** or **poverty level** is the minimum income needed for buying food, shelter, and clothing; the **poverty-stricken** countries of the Third World.*

pow·der (POW·dur) *n.* **1** a dry material of fine particles such as some cosmetics, medicines, etc.: *bleaching, dusting, scouring, talcum powder; a **powder puff** (= pad or ball for applying face powder).* **2** gunpowder: *That fight is not worth **powder and shot**; Watch out and **keep your powder dry** (= stay calm).*
— *v.*: *She **powders** (= puts powder on) her nose; imported **powdered milk** (in powder form).*
— pow·der·y *adj.*

powder keg *n.* a cask containing gunpowder; hence, a potentially explosive situation.

powder room *n.* a women's lavatory.

pow·er *n.* **1** authority or strength: *to assume, exercise, seize, wield power; the government in power; the discretionary powers of a judge; In a minority*

government, a small party may hold the balance of power (= power to upset the government). **2** capability: *your powers of observation; bargaining, earning, purchasing power; supernatural powers.* **3** a person or state having authority and strength: *an economic summit of the seven major powers; a world power; air, fire, military, naval, sea power; The **powers that be** (= the authorities) willed otherwise.* **4** source of energy: *to cut off, turn off, turn on the power; electric, nuclear, solar, water power.*
— *v.* provide with power: *a small car powered by a big engine.*
— *adj.*: *an automobile equipped with power brakes and power steering; a power mower, saw; a party's **power base** (= centre of support) eroded by scandals; The mayor was a **power broker** (= influence peddler) for politicians; a **power line** (= hydro wires) downed by a storm. a **power pack** for converting electricity to the voltage required for an electronic circuit; the **power structure** (= controlling group or system) of a male-dominated society; The vice-president was jobless after a **power struggle** in the company.*
— pow·er·ful *adj.*; pow·er·ful·ly *adv.*

power of attorney *n.* a document authorizing another to act for one in a legal matter.

power plant *n.* **1** the engine and related parts of an automobile, aircraft, or ship. **2** a plant in which electricity is generated; also pow·er·house, power station.

power train *n.* the mechanism by which power is transmitted from an automobile engine to its axle, including the clutch, transmission, and drive shaft.

pow·wow *n.* **1** a get-together of or with North American Indians. **2** *Informal.* any conference.

pox *n.* **1** a disease such as "chicken pox" or "smallpox" that leaves pock marks on the skin: *A pox (= curse) on drug-pushers!* **2** the pox syphilis.

prac·ti·ca·ble (PRAC·tuh·cuh·bul) *adj.* that can be put into practice; feasible: *A trip to the moon may be practicable but is hardly a practical idea for a holiday.*
— prac·ti·ca·bly *adv.*
— prac·ti·ca·bil·i·ty (-BIL·uh·tee) *n.*

prac·ti·cal (PRAC·tuh·cul) *adj.* **1** having to do with practice rather than theory or ideas: *a scheme full of practical difficulties; It's too unwieldy for practical purposes; a practical mind.* **2** engaged in practice or work: *a practical farmer, physicist.* **3** virtual: *Jack is the boss, but Jill is in practical control.* — prac·ti·cal·ly (-tic·lee) *adv.* — prac·ti·cal·i·ty (-CAL·uh·tee) *n.*

practical joke *n.* a trick played on someone for causing embarrassment, as the hotfoot.

practical nurse *n.* a nurse who helps professional nurses with day-to-day tasks of caring for the sick.

prac·tice (PRAC·tis) *n.* **1** a custom: *superstitious practices such as fortune-telling and voodoo.* **2** a habit: *She makes a practice of arriving late; It's a common practice around here.* **3** exercise: *He's out of practice on the violin; target practice; "Practice makes perfect"; a plan that is difficult to **put into practice** (= carry out).* **4** business of a professional nature: *a flourishing law* practice; the practice of accountancy, medicine, nursing; group practice (by many professionals on the same premises); a lucrative private practice. **5** business method: fair-trade, sharp, unethical practices.

prac·tise or **prac·tice** (PRAC·tis) v. -tis·es or -tic·es, -tised or -ticed, -tis·ing or -tic·ing **1** do something habitually: He practises what he preaches. **2** do something customarily: to practise one's religion; He's a practising Jew. **3** do something repeatedly; exercise: She practises the piano daily; to practise charity, economy, patience, singing. **4** do something professionally: to practise accountacy, law, medicine; to practise as a dentist.

practised or **practiced** (PRAC·tist) adj. skilled: He bore it with practised coolness; a practised pickpocket.

prac·ti·tion·er (prac·TISH·uh·nur) n. one who practises a profession such as medicine: a family, general, nurse practitioner.

prag·mat·ic or **prag·mat·i·cal** (prag·MAT·uh·cul) adj. **1** concerned with practical values; matter-of-fact. **2** having to do with pragmatism: pragmatic philosophy.

prag·ma·tism (PRAG·muh·tiz·um) n. the philosophy of judging things by how they work rather than by abstract values of truth and goodness. — **prag·ma·tist** n. & adj.

prai·rie (PRAIR·ee) n. a region of level or rolling land with tall grass but few trees: a house on the windswept prairie; the Canadian **Prairies** or the **Prairie Provinces** of Alberta, Saskatchewan, and Manitoba.

prairie dog n. a large type of ground squirrel.

prairie lily n. Cdn. a wild lily of the prairies that is Saskatchewan's floral emblem.

praise (PRAIZ) v. prais·es, praised, prais·ing **1** worship: the Lord be praised! **2** speak of with admiration: He was praised by some and hated by others; She was highly praised for her courage. — **n.** a praising: The principal's speech was in praise of his teachers; a cook who receives only praises; to bestow, heap, lavish praise on someone; faint, glowing, unstinting praise; She bores me by **singing the praises** of her children all day long; Praise be to God!

praise·wor·thy (PRAIZ·wur·thee, "th" as in "the") adj. worthy of praise: a praiseworthy act; praiseworthy behaviour.

prance v. pranc·es, pranced, pranc·ing **1** raise the forelegs and spring, as a horse does. **2** strut about; swagger: to prance around the stage. Also **n.**

prank n. a mischievous trick played on someone. — **prank·ish** adj. — **prank·ster** n.

prate v. prates, prat·ed, prat·ing talk foolishly and at length. — **prat·er** n.

prat·fall n. Slang. a fall on one's buttocks.

prat·tle (PRAT·ul) v. prat·tles, prat·tled, prat·tling prate; also, babble. — **prat·tler** n.

prawn n. a shellfish that is larger than a shrimp.

pray v. **1** worship God; also, ask for divine favour: She prays before going to bed; They pray (to) God for help; a hopeless case that is past **praying for. 2** ask humbly; entreat: He prayed his dad not to ground him. **3** Formal. please: Pray be careful.

pray·er (PRAY·ur) n. one who prays.

prayer (PRAIR) n. an act of praying: He says his prayers every night; to offer a fervent prayer in a moment of danger; a prayer for the dead; the Lord's Prayer (as taught by Jesus); Columbus knelt down in prayer; The Book of Common Prayer (= Church of England's official liturgy). — **prayer·ful** adj.; **prayer·ful·ly** adv.

pre- prefix. before in time, position, etc.: prearranged, precursor, prefix.

preach (PREECH) v. **1** deliver a sermon: to preach to our congregation. **2** set forth or urge in a moralistic tone, usually in a tiresome way: always preaching (about) social justice; He likes to preach in his classes; Stop preaching at me and start practising. — **preach·er** n. — **preach·y** adj.

pre·am·ble (PREE·am·bul) n. an introduction to a constitution, statute, etc.

pre·car·i·ous (pri·CAIR·ee·us) adj. dependent on chance; uncertain: a precarious existence in a war-torn country; a precarious hold, position.

pre·cau·tion (pri·CAW·shun) n. care taken against danger, failure, etc. or to ensure good results: a fire-safety precaution; elaborate precautions against being robbed. — **pre·cau·tion·ar·y** (-shuh·nair·ee) adj.: a precautionary measure.

pre·cede (pri·SEED) v. -cedes, -ced·ed, -ced·ing be or happen before in time, position, order, etc.: A precedes B in alphabetical order.

prec·e·dence (PRESS·uh·dunce, pri·SEE·dunce) n. higher position, rank, importance, etc.: The Governor General has precedence over the Prime Minister; Emergency cases take precedence over routine ones.

prec·ed·ent (PRESS·uh·dunt) n. a previous case that serves as an example: Judgments cite, create, establish, set precedents; The destruction of Hiroshima and Nagasaki is without precedent in human history. — **adj.** (pri·SEE·dunt) preceding: precedent circumstances.

pre·cept (PREE·sept) n. a rule of behaviour; maxim: to persuade by example rather than by precept; A familiar precept is "Look before you leap."

pre·cep·tor (pree·SEP·tur) n. a teacher or instructor: a preceptor to the prince.

585

pre·cinct (PREE·sinct) *n.* **1** a subdivision or district: *an election precinct; police precinct; voting precinct.* **2 precincts** *pl.* grounds or enclosure: *No smoking within the school precincts.*

pre·cious (PRESH·us) *adj.* **1** of great value: *gold, silver, and such precious metals; a precious gem, stone; precious qualities; a precious* (= beloved) *child.* **2** affected or overstylized: *a model's precious manner.* — *adv.* very: *precious few, little.*

prec·i·pice (PRES·uh·pis) *n.* a steep cliff or vertical rock face.

pre·cip·i·tate (pri·SIP·uh·tate) *v.* -tates, -tat·ed, -tat·ing **1** cause to happen abruptly: *a border incident that precipitated a crisis; It precipitated* (= pushed) *the country into war.* **2** cause to fall, as from the atmosphere, from a solution, etc.: *Salt precipitates as its solution cools.* — *n.* a substance, usually in crystal form, obtained by precipitation. — *adj.* **1** hasty or rash: *to be precipitate in one's actions.* **2** very steep or precipitous: *a precipitate slope.*

pre·cip·i·ta·tion (pri·SIP·uh·TAY·shun) *n.* what falls from the atmosphere: *Rain, snow, and hail are forms of precipitation; a region of heavy precipitation; acid precipitation.*

pre·cip·i·tous (pri·SIP·uh·tus) *adj.* very steep, almost vertical: *a precipitous hillside.*

pré·cis (pray·SEE, PRAY·see) *n.,* *pl.* -cis (-SEEZ, -seez) a summary or concise statement.

pre·cise (pri·SICE) *adj.* correct or exact: *a precise account of the incident; very precise in her utterances; Be precise about facts and figures; He's too prim and precise for my tastes.* — **pre·cise·ly** *adv.*

pre·ci·sion (pri·SIZH·un) *n.* accuracy or exactness: *the precision of a watch; the unerring precision of his aim; A chronometer tells time with the utmost precision; It is a precision instrument.* — **pre·ci·sion·ist** *n.*

pre·clude (pri·CLOOD, long "OO") *v.* to bar or prevent: *The barbed-wire fence precluded all possibility of escape.* — **pre·clu·sion** (-CLOO·zhun) *n.*

pre·co·cious (pri·COH·shus) *adj.* showing early maturity: *a very precocious child.* — **pre·coc·i·ty** (-COS·uh·tee) *n.*

pre·con·ceive (pree·cun·SEEV) *v.* -ceives, -ceived, -ceiv·ing form an idea or opinion beforehand: *our preconceived notions.* — **pre·con·cep·tion** (-SEP·shun) *n.*

pre·cur·sor (pree·CUR·sur) *n.* forerunner: *The drought was a precursor of or to the famine.*

pre·date (pree·DATE) *v.* -dates, -dat·ed, -dat·ing same as ANTEDATE.

pred·a·tor (PRED·uh·tur) *n.* one who plunders or preys on others, as a bird of prey: *Caterpillars are agricultural predators.* — **pred·a·to·ry** (PRED·uh·tor·ee) *adj.*: *Eagles and hawks are predatory birds; predatory instincts.*

pred·e·ces·sor (PRED·uh·ses·ur, PREE·duh-) *n.* one who has gone before someone.

pre·des·tine (pree·DES·tin) *v.* -tines, -tined, -tin·ing fix the future of someone, as by fate: *She was predestined to become great.*

pre·de·ter·mine (pree·di·TUR·min) *v.* -mines, -mined, -min·ing determine beforehand.

pre·dic·a·ment (pri·DIC·uh·munt) *n.* a perplexing or difficult situation.

pred·i·cate (PRED·uh·cate) *v.* -cates, -cat·ed, -cat·ing **1** assert something as characteristic of someone: *to predicate goodness of God.* **2** base an assertion or statement on something: *The company's plans are predicated on improving quality, not on growth.* — *n.* (-kit) what is said of a grammatical or logical subject: *In "She is great," "is great" is the predicate.* — **pred·i·ca·tion** (-CAY·shun) *n.*

pre·dict (pri·DICT) *v.* tell what one believes is going to happen; foretell: *to predict the future; to predict when it will rain.* — **pre·dic·ta·ble** (-tuh·bul) *adj.* — **pre·dic·ta·bly** (-blee) *adv.* — **pre·dic·tion** (-shun) *n.*

pre·di·lec·tion (pree·duh·LEC·shun, pred·uh-) *n.* a special liking: *a predilection for spiced foods.*

pre·dis·pose (pree·dis·POZE) *v.* -pos·es, -posed, -pos·ing incline in advance; be susceptible: *Military life predisposed him to a strict regimen.* — **pre·dis·po·si·tion** (PREE·dis·puh·ZISH·un) *n.*

pre·dom·i·nant (pree·DOM·uh·nunt) *adj.* that predominates. — **pre·dom·i·nant·ly** *adv.* — **pre·dom·i·nance** (-nunce) *n.*

pre·dom·i·nate (pree·DOM·uh·nate) *v.* -nates, -nat·ed, -nat·ing be greater in number, power, influence, etc.: *Reason should predominate over emotion.*

pree·mie (PREE·mee) *n. Informal.* a prematurely born infant.

pre·em·i·nent (pree·EM·uh·nunt) *adj.* outstanding or surpassing: *a surgeon who is preeminent in her specialty.* — **pre·em·i·nent·ly** *adv.* — **pre·em·i·nence** (-nunce) *n.*

pre·empt (pree·EMPT) *v.* **1** acquire or appropriate something before others. **2** in radio and TV, take the place of something: *a news special preempting regular programs.* — **pre·emp·tion** (-shun) *n.*

pre·emp·tive (pree·EMP·tiv) *adj.* preventive or forestalling: *a preemptive air strike on a nuclear facility (to prevent it from making bombs); a preemptive attack, seizure.*

preen *v.* **1** of a bird, clean and smooth its feathers with the beak. **2** dress oneself carefully: *He primps and preens in front of the mirror before going to school.* **3** pride oneself on something: *He preens himself too much on his sharp business deals.*

pre·fab (PREE·fab) *n.* [short form] a prefabricated building.

pre·fab·ri·cate (pree·FAB·ruh·cate) *v.* -cates, -cat·ed, -cat·ing to make in sections that can be easily assembled: *A prefabricated house can be assembled in a few days.* — **pre·fab·ri·ca·tion** (-CAY·shun) *n.*

pref·ace (PREF·is) *n.* a statement at the beginning of a book, speech, etc. — *v.* pref·ac·es, pref·aced, pref·ac·ing begin: *The* speaker prefaced his remarks with a quotation from Shakespeare.

pref·a·to·ry (PREF·uh·tor·ee) adj. being a preface: a prefatory note; prefatory remarks.

pre·fect (PREE·fect) n. 1 an administrative official, as of ancient Rome, the head of a department in France, etc. 2 a student monitor.

pre·fec·ture (PREE·fek·chur) n. a prefect's office, territory, or residence.

pre·fer (pri·FUR) n. -fers, -ferred, -fer·ring 1 like better: She prefers tea to coffee; He prefers to read rather than watch TV; We prefer taking the bus rather than riding to work; **Preferred stock** has priority over common stock in the sharing of dividends and assets. 2 [legal use] bring forward: to prefer a charge against someone; to prefer a claim to something.
— pref·er·a·ble (PREF·ur·uh·bul) adj.
— pref·er·a·bly (-blee) adv. — pref·er·ence (-unce) n.

pref·er·en·tial (pref·uh·REN·shul) adj. showing favour: a preferential shop favouring union members in hiring; a preferential tariff rate for friendly nations; preferential treatment of favourites.

pre·fig·ure (pree·FIG·yur) v. -ures, -ured, -ur·ing be a prototype of a person or thing; foreshadow.

pre·fix (PREE·fix) n. a word element used at the beginning of a word, as "ante-," "dis-," "ex-," or "pre-."
— v. (PREE·fix, pree·FIX) add before: "Ms." may be prefixed to a woman's name.

preg·nant (PREG·nunt) adj. 1 carrying a developing offspring in the uterus: a pregnant woman. 2 filled with or rich in something: "Cocacolonize" is pregnant with meaning; an idea pregnant with possibilities; a pregnant (=significant) pause. — preg·nan·cy (-nun·see) n. -cies.

pre·heat (PREE·heet) v. heat beforehand: Place the TV dinner in an oven preheated to 400° F.

pre·his·tor·ic (pree·his·TOR·ic) adj. of the time before recorded history, i.e. up to 5 000 years ago: Dinosaurs are prehistoric animals; prehistoric art found in caves.

prej·u·dice (PREJ·uh·dis) v. -dic·es, -diced, -dic·ing 1 harm a right, claim, etc.: behaviour that prejudiced his chances of promotion. 2 cause bias in someone: A jury could be prejudiced by news reports of the crime.
— n. bias: popular prejudices; to arouse, eliminate, stir up prejudice against minorities; racial prejudice; sexual prejudice; a statement made **without prejudice** (=without harm to one's existing rights).
— prej·u·di·cial (-DISH·ul) adj.

prel·ate (PREL·it) n. a high-ranking clergyman, as a bishop.

pre·lim (PREE·lim, pri·LIM) n. & adj. Informal. [short form] preliminary.

pre·lim·i·nar·y (pri·LIM·uh·nair·ee) adj. coming before; introductory: a judge's preliminary hearing on a case; a preliminary discussion.
— n., pl. -nar·ies: competitors eliminated in the preliminaries (= rounds of matches before the main event).

prel·ude (PREL·yood, PRAY·lood, long "oo") n. 1 an action or event leading to something major: a ceasefire as a prelude to a peace treaty. 2 in music, an opening movement of an opera or similar work; also, a separate concert work.
— v. -udes, -ud·ed, -ud·ing introduce: the calm that preluded the storm.

pre·mar·i·tal (pree·MAIR·uh·tul) adj. before marriage: premarital counselling, relations, sex.

pre·ma·ture (pree·muh·TYOOR, -CHOOR) adj. before the proper or usual time, as a baby born more than two weeks early: a premature birth, delivery; It's premature to celebrate when we are not sure of victory.
— pre·ma·ture·ly adv.

pre·med (PREE·med) n. & adj. [short form] premedical.

pre·med·i·cal (pree·MED·uh·cul) adj. preparatory to the study of medicine: a premedical course, student.

pre·med·i·tate (pree·MED·uh·tate) v. -tates, -tat·ed, -tat·ing think out or consider beforehand: a premeditated murder; pre·med·i·ta·tion (-TAY·shun) n.

pre·mier (prim·YAIR, PREE·mee·ur) adj. first in rank or importance: the premier dancer of a ballet; a matter of premier importance.
— n. a chief minister, as of a Canadian province.
— pre·mier·ship n.

pre·miere (prim·YAIR, prim·EER) n. 1 the first public performance of a star. 2 the first showing of a movie or play: a world premiere; to stage a premiere.
— v. -mieres, -miered, -mier·ing 1 give a premiere: The new TV sitcom premieres tonight. 2 appear as a star for the first time: The star of the show is premiering in the new sitcom.

prem·ise (PREM·is) n. 1 the logical basis for drawing a conclusion: a major premise; minor premise. 2 **premises** pl. a piece of land with the buildings on it: No picnicking on these premises; office premises (= building or a portion of it).
— v. -is·es, -ised, -is·ing state or imply as a premise.

pre·mi·um (PREE·mee·um) n. 1 an incentive bonus or reward; a gift offered as an inducement to buy a product or service: the premiums offered with breakfast cereals. 2 an extra payment: theatre tickets bought **at a premium** (= high price) at the last moment; tax loopholes that **put a premium** (= unusual value) on dishonesty; 3 the fee paid on an insurance policy.
— adj. of high grade: premium gasoline.

pre·mo·ni·tion (pree·muh·NISH·un) n. forewarning; also, foreboding or presentiment.

pre·na·tal (pree·NAY·tul) adj. before birth: Mothers need prenatal care; prenatal injury to infants.

pre·oc·cu·pa·tion (pree·OK·yuh·PAY·shun) n. the state of being preoccupied or something that preoccupies.

pre·oc·cu·py (pree·OK·yuh·pye) v. -pies, -pied, -py·ing take up the undue attention of someone: a student preoccupied with outside activities.

pre·or·dain (pree·or·DAIN) v. decree beforehand: Events seem to happen as if preordained by providence.

prep adj. [short form] preparatory: a prep school.
— v. preps, prepped, prep·ping prepare a patient for surgery, etc.

pre·pack·age (pree·PAK·ij) v. -ag·es, -aged, -ag·ing package in standard units or grades for sale: *prepackaged foods.*

prep·a·ra·tion (prep·uh·RAY·shun) n. an act of preparing or something prepared: *to pack up in preparation for a trip; to make last-minute preparations for a wedding; a preparation* (= medicine) *for colds.*

pre·par·a·to·ry (pri·PAIR·uh·tor·ee) adj. that prepares: *a countdown preparatory to a takeoff; A **preparatory** school prepares students for college.*

pre·pare (pri·PARE) v. -pares, -pared, -par·ing make or get ready: *Who will prepare dinner? Layoffs prepare the way for automation; to **be prepared** for emergencies; I'm not **prepared** (= willing) to tell you.*
— **pre·pared·ness** (-PAIR·id·nus) n.: *to test our preparedness for war.*

pre·pay (pree·PAY) v. -pays, -paid, -pay·ing pay beforehand: *a prepaid ticket.* — **pre·pay·ment** n.

pre·pon·der·ance (pri·PON·dur·unce) n. the state of being greater than something else in numbers, weight, power, etc.: *the preponderance of women over men in recent censuses.*
— **pre·pon·der·ant** (-runt) adj. dominating: *Was wealth or ambition the preponderant influence on his life?*

prep·o·si·tion (prep·uh·ZISH·un) n. a word such as "on," "above," or "by" used with a noun or pronoun as its object.

pre·pos·sess (pree·puh·ZES) v. influence in a favourable way: *He seemed prepossessed by the leader's zeal; a woman of **prepossessing** charm.*
— **pre·pos·ses·sion** (-ZESH·un) n.

pre·pos·ter·ous (pri·POS·tuh·rus) adj. contrary to reason and common sense; ridiculous: *He was making preposterous demands on my time and patience.*
— **pre·pos·ter·ous·ly** adv.

prep·py or **prep·pie** (PREP·ee) n. **prep·pies** *Informal.* a product of a private school preparing students for university, considered typical in regard to fashion, behaviour, etc.

pre·pro·gram (pree·PROH·gram) v. -grams, -grammed or -gramed, -gram·ming or -gram·ing program in advance: *to preprogram a computer.*

pre·quel (PREEK·wul) n. a movie, play, novel, or other work that portrays the earlier life of the characters of the main work.

pre·req·ui·site (pree·REK·wuh·zit) n. something required beforehand: *Basic courses are prerequisites for or to the more advanced ones.*

pre·rog·a·tive (pri·ROG·uh·tiv) n. a special privilege or right: *a royal prerogative; It's a woman's prerogative to have babies; the Prime Minister's prerogative to appoint senators.*

pres·age (PRES·ij) n. 1 a sign or omen. 2 a presentiment.
— v. (usually pri·SAGE) -ag·es, -aged, -ag·ing predict or forebode.

pres·by·ter·y (PRES·buh·tair·ee) n. -ter·ies 1 a governing body of the Presbyterian church or the United Church of Canada. 2 a parish priest's residence.

pre·school (PREE·school) n. kindergarten or nursery school.
— **adj.** before school-going age: *a daycare centre for preschool children.* — **pre·school·er** n.

pre·sci·ence (PREE·shee·unce, PRESH·ee-) n. foreknowledge. — **pre·sci·ent** adj.

pre·scribe (pri·SCRIBE) v. -scribes, -scribed, -scrib·ing order or direct with authority to use books, medicines, etc. or to follow a course of action: *to prescribe a remedy.*

pre·scrip·tion (pri·SCRIP·shun) n. 1 something prescribed, esp. a doctor's order for a medicine: *Doctors write prescriptions; Pharmacists fill prescriptions; Some drugs are sold by prescription only; You can get it only on a doctor's prescription; a prescription for peace in the Middle East; a prescription drug.* 2 the medicine itself.

pres·ence (PREZ·unce) n. 1 the state of being present: *a contract signed in the presence of witnesses; troops to maintain the U.S. presence in Europe; He makes his presence felt or known by acting foolishly; to act with **presence of mind** (= calmness) in a panicky situation.* 2 one's bearing or personality; an impressive appearance: *a woman of commanding presence.*

pres·ent (PREZ·unt) adj. existing here and now as specified or understood: *All students were present yesterday; In the present case, no action is called for; to keep up with present-day (= current) fashions; The **present tense** of "got" is "get"; "getting" is the **present participle.***
— **n.** 1 the present time: *She's too busy at present; a light meal to satisfy you for the present; "Do" is in the present (tense).* 2 a gift: *birthday, Christmas, wedding presents.* 3 [old use] a document: *Know ye, by these presents, that ….*
— **v.** (pri·ZENT) *Formal.* 1 offer or give: *A lawyer presents arguments in a case; A new diplomat presents his or her credentials; Graduates are presented with diplomas.* 2 introduce: *A visiting dignitary is presented at court; to present a guest to a gathering.*
— **present arms** [military use] salute by holding a weapon vertically with the point down.
— **pre·sen·ta·tion** (pri·zen·TAY·shun) n.

pre·sent·a·ble (pri·ZEN·tuh·bul) adj. respectable in appearance: *Get a haircut and make yourself presentable for the interview.* — **pre·sen·ta·bly** adv.

pre·sen·ti·ment (pri·ZEN·tuh·munt) n. a feeling that something, esp. bad, is about to happen; premonition or foreboding.

pres·ent·ly (PREZ·unt·lee) adv. 1 at present: *They are presently in Europe.* 2 soon: *The bus will be here presently.*

pres·er·va·tion (prez·ur·VAY·shun) n. a preserving or being preserved.

pre·ser·va·tive (pri·ZUR·vuh·tiv) n. & adj. (one) that preserves: *Salt is a food preservative; no preservatives (= chemicals) added; a preservative medium for a photographic solution.*

pre·serve (pri·ZURV) v. -serves, -served, -serv·ing keep or maintain without harm: *May God preserve you*

(from danger)! Fruits may be preserved (from decay) by cooking with sugar; laws to preserve (=keep safe) our natural resources.
— *n.* **1** a fruit preparation: *strawberry preserves.* **2** grounds: *No poaching on private game preserves; wild-life preserves.*
— **pre·serv·er** *n.*: *Wear a life preserver against drowning.*

pre·set (pree-SET) *v.* **-sets, -set, -set·ting** set beforehand: *a long-range missile with a preset guidance system; a credit card with a preset spending limit.*

pre·shrunk (PREE-shrunk) *adj.* of a fabric, shrunk during manufacture to reduce shrinkage in use.

pre·side (pri-ZIDE) *v.* **-sides, -sid·ed, -sid·ing** have authority or control, esp. as chairperson: *Judges preside at trials; to preside over a meeting.*

pres·i·dent (PREZ-uh-dunt) *n.* the chief executive of a republic, company, college, club, etc.
— **pres·i·den·cy** (-dun·see) *n.*

pres·i·den·tial (prez-uh-DEN-shul) *adj.* having to do with a president: *the presidential oath of office; presidential powers.*

pre·sid·i·um (pre-SID-ee-um) *n.* **-i·ums** or **-i·a** (-ee-uh) in communist countries, a permanent executive committee, as the Presidium of the Supreme Soviet.

pre·spot·ter (pree-SPOT-ur) *n.* a dry-cleaning worker who removes certain stains before cleaning.

press *v.* **1** act upon with steady force: *She pressed the picture to her heart; Press the button for help; to press grapes for wine; fresh juice just pressed; Clothes pressed while you wait; Phonograph records, cotton bales, etc. are pressed* (=made by pressing); *Metal is pressed* (=shaped) *into coins; Candidates for election* **press the flesh** *(Informal for shake hands with people) all day.* **2** urge: *She pressed him to stay for dinner; Politicians press the need for reform; an angry public pressing the government for a royal commission; The police decided not to* **press charges** *and dropped the case; Women and children were* **pressed into** *service* (=forced to serve) *at the height of the war; an army* **pressing on** *to victory; He's away on* **pressing** *(=urgent) business.* **3** weigh heavily; oppress: *She is pressed for time; hard pressed for funds; All the work she has to do is beginning to* **press on** *her mind.*
— *n.* **1** a pressing or its result: *She's driven forward by the press of ambition; a fabric that keeps its press; permanent press; He elbowed his way through the press* (=crowd) *of people.* **2** a machine that presses: *a printing press; wine press;* **Morning papers** **go to press** (=are printed) *after midnight; The book is* **in press** (=being printed).* **3** newspapers or journalists: *Her candidacy will be announced to the press at tomorrow's* **press conference;** *a free press; the yellow press.* **4** publicity: *Her performance received a good press; A* **press agent** (=publicity agent) *worked hard to ensure it; a* **press kit** *of promotional materials; The premier's* **press secretary** *is in charge of public relations.*

press box *n.* a space reserved for reporters, esp. at a sports event.

press·man (PRES·mun) *n.* **-men** the operator of a printing press.

press·room *n.* **1** where the presses are installed in a printing plant. **2** a room for journalists.

pres·sure (PRESH-ur) *n.* the action of pressing or the condition of being pressed: *Atmospheric pressure decreases with altitude; barometric, high, low pressure; Hypertension is high blood pressure; He studies under pressure of exams; to exert* or *put pressure on someone; to* **bring pressure to bear** *on someone; to build up, ease, face, relieve, resist pressure; parental, peer, relentless pressure; As time goes, pressure builds up, eases, falls, rises; A* **pressure cooker** *cooks fast with steam under pressure; A* **pressure suit** *keeps the wearer under normal pressure at high altitudes.*
— *v.* **pres·sures, pres·sured, pres·sur·ing** force by applying pressure: *people pressured into signing sales contracts.*

pressure group *n.* a group that exerts pressure on governments and legislatures to further its own interests.

pres·sur·ize (PRESH-ur·ize) *v.* **-iz·es, -ized, -iz·ing** keep under normal pressure in spite of altitude: *the pressurized cabin of an airplane.* — **pres·sur·iz·er** *n.*

pres·tige (pres-TEEZH) *n.* reputation based on outstanding achievement: *to gain prestige by achievements; great, high, low prestige.*
— **pres·ti·gious** (-TIJ·us) *adj.*: *a prestigious award, institution, position, prize, title, university.*

pres·to (PRES-toh) *interj.* behold: *Hey presto! And the rabbit vanished.*

pre·stressed concrete *n.* concrete cast around steel cables held under tension.

pre·sume (pri-ZOOM) *v.* **-sumes, -sumed, -sum·ing** **1** assume: *Everyone is presumed innocent until proven guilty; "Dr. Livingstone, I presume* (=suppose) *?"* **2** venture: *He presumes to advise his parents; a very* **presuming** *(=presumptuous) young man; It would be* **presuming on** *(=making free use of) his generosity to ask for another loan.* — **pre·su·ma·ble** (-muh·bul) *adj.*
— **pre·su·ma·bly** (-blee) *adv.*

pre·sump·tion (pri-ZUMP-shun) *n.* the act of presuming or something presumed or taken for granted: *the presumption of innocence; It's only a presumption, not a proven fact; It was considered presumption* (=nerve) *for women to want to vote.*

pre·sump·tive (pri-ZUMP-tiv) *adj.* presumed: *the heir presumptive; The stolen goods in his car seem presumptive evidence against him.*

pre·sump·tu·ous (pri-SUMP-choo-us) *adj.* arrogant or excessively forward; presuming; **pre·sump·tu·ous·ly** *adv.*

pre·sup·pose (pree-suh-POZE) *v.* **-sup·pos·es, -sup·posed, -sup·pos·ing** **1** assume: *Let's not presuppose anything before looking at the facts.* **2** require as a logical precondition: *A product presupposes a producer.*
— **pre·sup·po·si·tion** (PREE-sup-uh-ZISH-un) *n.*

pre·tax (PREE-tax) *adj.* before tax: *pretax earnings.*

pre·teen (PREE-teen) *n.* a child who is in the 9 – 12 age group: *preteen fashions.*

pre·tence or **pre·tense** (pri-TENSE, PREE-tense) *n.* **1** a pretending: *begging under the pretence of poverty; He*

gained entry by or *on* or *under false pretences; without any pretence* (= attempt) *at truthfulness; a plain-spoken manner free from all pretence* (= phoniness).
2 appearance: *to maintain some pretence of decorum.*

pre·tend (pri·TEND) *v.* **1** make believe: *Let's pretend we are in space; She pretended not to hear.* **2** claim, esp. falsely: *to pretend illness as an excuse; The young Stuarts pretended to the throne of England.*
— **pre·tend·er** *n.*

pretense same as PRETENCE.

pre·ten·sion (pri·TEN·shun) *n.* claim: *a journalist with no pretensions to scholarship.*

pre·ten·tious (pri·TEN·shus) *adj.* **1** making undue claims to excellence or worth: *a pompous and pretentious style of writing.* **2** showy or ostentatious: *Sam is stylish without being pretentious; a pretentious lifestyle, pundit, title.*

pre·ter·nat·u·ral (pree·tur·NACH·uh·rul) *adj.* **1** out of the ordinary: *a man of preternatural strength.* **2** supernatural or psychic: *miracles and such preternatural phenomena.* — **pre·ter·nat·u·ral·ly** *adv.*

pre·test (pree·TEST) *n. & v.* test in advance.

pre·text (PREE·text) *n.* a false purpose or reason; pretence: *espionage under the pretext of missionary work.*

pret·ty (PRIT·ee) *adj.* **pret·ti·er, pret·ti·est**
1 moderately pleasing and attractive to look at: *a pretty girl; not just another pretty face.* **2** *Informal.* considerable in amount: *a pretty mess you're into; The car cost me a pretty sum.*
— *adv.* fairly: *He'll be here pretty soon; Everything went pretty much as we expected.*
— **sitting pretty** in a fairly advantageous position.
— *v.* **pret·ties, pret·tied, pret·ty·ing** *Informal.* make pretty: *We'll pretty up our basement for the party.*
— **pret·ti·ness** *n.*

pre·vail (pri·VAIL) *v.* be stronger, more usual, or more common: *Reason prevailed against* or *over prejudices; The children prevailed on* or *upon* (= succeeded in persuading) *their mother to take them to the movie; Youth tend to follow the prevailing fashions; The **prevailing** (= generally current) westerly winds make flying from west to east faster in the Northern Hemisphere.*

prev·a·lent (PREV·uh·lunt) *adj.* widespread: *a trend prevalent among teenagers.* — **prev·a·lence** (-lunce) *n.*

pre·var·i·cate (pri·VAIR·uh·cate) *v.* **-cates, -cat·ed, -cat·ing** evade the truth by quibbling or a similar tactic.
— **pre·var·i·ca·tor** (-cay·tur) *n.*
— **pre·var·i·ca·tion** (-CAY·shun) *n.*

pre·vent (pri·VENT) *v.* stop from doing or happening; hinder: *measures to prevent disease; No one can prevent our catching cold; Only prompt action can prevent a fire from spreading.*
— **pre·ven·ta·ble** or **pre·ven·ti·ble** *adj.*
— **pre·ven·tion** (-VEN·shun) *n.* the act of preventing: *fire prevention; the prevention of cruelty to animals; "Prevention is better than cure."*

pre·ven·tive (pri·VEN·tiv) *adj.* helping to prevent something: *a habitual criminal held without bail in*

preventive detention; Vaccination is a preventive measure; the field of preventive medicine.
— *n.* a preventive measure or agent, as a drug.

pre·view (PREE·view) *n.* **1** an advance showing or viewing of a play, movie, or TV program: *a sneak preview;* also *v.* **2** foretaste.

pre·vi·ous (PREE·vee·us) *adj.* earlier: *I cannot be at tomorrow's meeting because of a previous engagement; a commitment made **previous to** (= before) your request.* — **pre·vi·ous·ly** *adv.*

pre·war (PREE·wor) *adj.* before the war, esp. World War II: *in prewar days, years; the prewar era; the great prewar Depression (1929 – 39).*

prey (PRAY) *n. sing.* **1** an animal hunted for food. **2** a victim: *an easy prey; He **fell prey to** (= became a victim of) loansharks.*
— *v.* make a prey of someone: *Larger beasts prey on smaller ones; Guilt preyed on* or *upon her mind.*

price *n.* the amount of money to be paid to the seller of something; cost or worth: *to bring, fetch, fix, pay, put, quote, set a price; to bring down, cut, freeze, hold down, mark down, mark up, raise, slash prices; an asking, bargain, exorbitant, going, inflated, reasonable, retail, sale, stiff, wholesale price; prices drop, fall, go down, go up, skyrocket, slump; They would not agree to peace at any price* (= at too heavy a price); *Governments impose price controls to fight inflation; There are anti-trust laws against price-fixing by members of a trade or profession; Prices drop during a price war among retailers.*
— *v.* **pric·es, priced, pric·ing** put a price on something: *It's priced too high for my pocket; Houses have almost priced themselves out of the market.*

price·less *adj.* having great value: *a priceless gem, treasure.*

pric·ey (PRY·see) *adj.* **pric·i·er, -i·est** *Informal.* expensive.

prick *n.* **1** a little mark or puncture made by a sharp point, as of a pin or thorn. **2** a pricking or the sharp pain thus caused: *the pricks of conscience.*
— *v.* give pain or make a small hole, as with a pin or thorn: *A balloon bursts if pricked; Thickly growing seedlings are **pricked out** (= transplanted) uniformly in larger pans.* — **prick up one's ears** listen closely.

prick·le (PRIK·ul) *n.* **1** a thorn or spine. **2** a sharp sensation. — *v.* **-les, -led, -ling** tingle.

prick·ly (PRIK·lee) *adj.* **-li·er, -li·est** having sharp points: *the prickly porcupine; the itchy reddish rash of **prickly heat** or "heat rash"; the **prickly pear** cactus.*

pride *n.* **1** a sense of one's own worth: *to appeal to one's pride; The low marks hurt his pride; great, injured, wounded pride; to pocket* or *swallow one's pride and accept defeat.* **2** pleasure over one's qualities, possessions, or achievements: *We take pride in a job well done.* **3** a source of such esteem: *David was the pride and joy of her old age.* **4** false esteem of oneself or contempt of others: *"Pride goes before a fall."* **5** the best part; prime: *in the days of her pride; Shakespeare's **pride of place** (= highest position) among dramatists.* **6** a group of animals: *a pride of lions, peacocks.*

— *v.* **prides, prid·ed, prid·ing** be proud of something: *He prides himself on his high marks.*
— **pride·ful** *adj.*; **pride·ful·ly** *adv.*

priest (PREEST) *n.* a religious official who performs religious rites and other functions, esp. a member of the clergy ranking next below a bishop: *Pat was ordained priest yesterday.*
— **priest·ess** *n.*: *a priestess of Venus; Phyllis Diller, the High Priestess of Charm.*
— **priest·hood** (short "oo") *n.*
— **priest·ly** *adj.* — **priest·li·ness** *n.*

prig *n.* a rigid and smug observer of morals and manners.

prig·gish (PRIG·ish) *adj.* like a prig: *He's too priggish to dress casually.*

prim *adj.* **prim·mer, prim·mest** overprecise or formal: *a prim and proper fashion.* — **prim·ly** *adv.*; **prim·ness** *n.*

pri·ma·cy (PRY·muh·see) *n.* **-cies** 1 superiority or preeminence. 2 the rank or office of a church primate.

pri·ma don·na (PREE·muh·DON·uh) *n.*, *pl.* **prima donnas** 1 the leading woman singer in an opera. 2 a vain or temperamental person.

pri·ma fa·ci·e (PRY·muh·FAY·shee·ee) *adj. & adv.* [legal use] adequate without further examination: *a prima facie case; prima facie evidence.*

pri·mal (PRY·mul) *adj.* more basic than primitive in time: *The Earth evolved out of primal material; the primal forces of matter and energy; primal elements, fears, struggles; the **primal scream** therapy for relieving tensions.*

pri·ma·ry (PRY·mair·ee) *adj.* first in time, rank, or importance: *Blue, red, and yellow are the **primary colours**; Your 20 primary (= baby or milk) teeth are replaced by 32 permanent ones; A **primary cell**, as used in a flashlight, cannot be recharged; The **primary school** comprises kindergarten through Grade 3.*
— **pri·ma·ri·ly** (pry·MAIR·uh·lee) *adv.*

pri·mate (PRY·mate) *n.* 1 an animal of the highest order such as the human being, ape, or monkey. 2 (*also* PRY·mit) an archbishop.

prime *n.* 1 the earliest or best stage or period: *The year is at its prime in the spring; She died in the prime of youth.* 2 a number that is not composed of other numbers, as 1, 2, 3, 5, 7, 11, or 13; also **prime number**.
— *adj.* first or chief: *The **prime meridian** of 0 degree longitude passes through Greenwich, England; the **prime minister** of a country; the **prime rate** (of interest) charged to a bank's best customers; The evening hours, usually 6 to 11, are called **prime time** on radio and TV.*
— *v.* **primes, primed, prim·ing** make ready or prepare, as a gun with powder for firing, a water pump by pouring in some water, a painting surface with a first coat, a witness with facts, etc.

prim·er *n.* 1 (PRY·mur) one that prepares, as a first coat of paint, a device to set off an explosive charge, etc. 2 (PRIM·ur) a beginner's textbook: *a primer on Chinese cooking.*

pri·me·val (pry·MEE·vul) *adj.* of the earliest times: *the earth's primeval uninhabited condition; primeval forests, jungles.* — **pri·me·val·ly** *adv.*

prim·i·tive (PRIM·uh·tiv) *adj.* 1 of early times; undeveloped: *primitive instincts, living conditions, tribes, weapons.* 2 crude; lacking modern conveniences: *The accommodation at the camp was rather primitive.*
— *n.* 1 a member of an undeveloped civilization: *Some groups of people used to be called primitives.* 2 one not trained or sophisticated: *She's a primitive in her artistic leanings.* — **prim·i·tive·ly** *adv.*; **prim·i·tiv·ism** *n.*

pri·mor·di·al (pry·MOR·dee·ul) *adj.* primeval: *a primordial joy, urge, voice; Did matter originate as a primordial fireball of radiation? the primordial "soup" from which life arose according to some theories; a primordial swamp.* — **pri·mor·di·al·ly** *adv.*

primp *v.* dress or groom oneself in a fussy manner: *She's busy primping her hair; to primp for a photograph.*

prim·rose *n.* an early-flowering ornamental plant with yellowish flowers.
— **primrose path** or **way** path of pleasure or temptation.

prince *n.* 1 a male member of a royal family: *the Prince of Wales; a crown prince; the prince and the pauper.* 2 the ruler of a small country: *a European prince; the Prince of Monaco.* 3 the chief or excellent one: *a prince among men; a prince of peace; a prince of the church* (= cardinal).

prince consort *n.* a reigning queen's husband.

prince·ling *n.* a petty prince.

prince·ly *adj.* **-li·er, -li·est** noble or generous: *in princely style; We paid a princely sum for that house.*

prin·cess (PRIN·sis, -ses) *n.* a female member of a royal family.

prin·ci·pal (PRIN·suh·pul) *adj.* chief: *the principal ally, character, city, clause, ingredient, interest, source; "Take-took-taken" are the **principal parts** of the verb "to take."*
— *n.* the most important one, as the head of a school, a capital sum bearing interest, the chief actor in a play, a main accomplice in a crime, or the main body of an estate. — **prin·ci·pal·ly** *adv.*; **prin·ci·pal·ship** *n.*

prin·ci·pal·i·ty (prin·suh·PAL·uh·tee) *n.* **-ties** a prince's territory, as Monaco or Andorra.

prin·ci·ple (PRIN·suh·pul) *n.* 1 a fundamental truth, law, or rule: *the principles of mathematics; We agree **in principle** (= in fundamentals) but we have to work out the details.* 2 the basis of an action or operation, esp.

behaviour: *the principles of good government; two machines built on the same principle; a basic, guiding, sound principle; to adhere to, apply, lay down a principle; a matter of principle; Men and women of* **principle** (= having principles) *do everything on* **principle** (= according to principles); *a* **high-principled** *woman* (= woman with high standards of moral conduct).

print *n.* 1 a mark made by pressure, as a fingerprint, type impression, design on cloth, etc. 2 a cloth or paper with such marks: *a Japanese colour print.* 3 something printed: *clear, dark, large print; Read the fine print (in small type) before signing; the* **print media** *such as the press; There are millions of copies of the Bible* **in print** (= published and available); *It has never gone* **out of print** (= being no more published). 4 a photograph made from a negative.
— *v.* 1 reproduce letters, words, pictures, etc. mechanically: *Gutenberg started printing from movable type in 1440; words printed in boldface, italics, roman; Please print your name (using printed letters) instead of writing it; a book printed* (= manufactured) *in Canada; Press "P" (on the word processor) to* **print out** *the essay.* 2 stamp: *Patterns are printed on cloth.*
— print·a·ble (-uh·bul) *adj.*

printed circuit *n.* an electronic circuit in which the connections are printed on an insulated base with a conducting material instead of being wired together.

print·er *n.* 1 a machine that prints type: *a computer printer; dot-matrix printer; laser printer; line printer.* 2 a person whose work or business is printing: *an error of the* **printer's devil** (= printer's young helper).

printing *n.* 1 the art or business of producing books, periodicals, etc. with type or plates: *letterpress printing; litho printing; offset printing; a printing press.* 2 a printing or the copies printed at one time; impression: *The first printing was sold out in a week.*

print·out *n.* a computer's printed output.

pri·or (PRY·ur) *adj.* 1 earlier in time: *I am unable to accept your invitation because of a prior engagement (made before you asked); He was in farming* **prior to** (= before) *entering politics.* 2 preceding in importance or rank: *I must give prior consideration to business engagements.*

pri·or·i·ty (pry·OR·uh·tee) *n.* -ties a level, esp. the top level of importance or urgency: *to establish, reexamine, set priorities; Top priority is given for emergency relief; It takes priority over everything else; adj.: priority mail; a priority project.*

prism (PRIZ·um) *n.* a solid with similar, equal, and parallel ends, and sides that are parallelograms.
— pris·mat·ic (priz·MAT·ic) *adj.: prismatic colours* (= colours of the rainbow).

pris·on (PRIZ·un) *n.* a place of confinement, esp. for convicted criminals: *to break out of, escape from, be sent to, be sentenced to, spend time in prison; adj.: a prison sentence, term.*

pris·on·er (PRIZ·un·ur) *n.* a captive: *Over 100 soldiers were taken prisoner; political prisoners.*

prisoner of conscience *n.* a political prisoner.

prisoner of war *n.* one taken prisoner in war.

pris·sy (PRIS·ee) *adj.* **pris·si·er, pris·si·est** *Informal.* prim or prudish. — pris·si·ly *adv.;* pris·si·ness *n.*

pris·tine (PRIS·teen, pris·TEEN) *adj.* unspoiled or uncorrupted: *a painting restored to its pristine beauty; in pristine environments like the Arctic; nature in its pristine state; a white pristine dress.*

prith·ee (PRITH·ee, "TH" as in "the") *interj.* [old use] I pray thee; please.

pri·va·cy (PRY·vuh·see) *n.* the quality or state of being private; secrecy: *in the privacy of my home; data banks as a threat to privacy; the invasion of one's privacy by electronic snooping.*

pri·vate (PRY·vit) *adj.* having to do with one person or group; not public: *private dealings that serve private ends; a private office; a private school that charges fees; to hire a* **private eye** (= investigator or detective); *the* **private enterprise** (= free enterprise) *system of capitalist societies.*
— *n.* 1 a U.S. soldier or marine of the lowest rank: *A* **private first class** *ranks below a corporal.* 2 **privates** *pl.* genitals. — **in private** privately, not openly.

pri·va·teer (pry·vuh·TEER) *n.* 1 formerly, an armed, privately owned ship in the service of a country. 2 a crew member or commander of such a vessel.

private parts *n. pl.* genitals.

pri·va·tion (pry·VAY·shun) *n.* the condition of being deprived of life's ordinary necessities: *the many privations imposed by war.*

pri·va·tize (PRY·vuh·tize) *v.* -iz·es, -ized, -iz·ing make private: *to privatize the post office.*
— pri·va·ti·za·tion (-tuh·ZAY·shun) *n.*

priv·i·lege (PRIV·lij) *n.* a benefit or advantage granted to an individual or attached to a position: *to abuse, enjoy, grant, suspend a privilege; kitchen privileges for boarders; It's a pleasure and a privilege to work with Pat; no special privileges for anyone; the rights and privileges of membership; a question of parliamentary privilege* (= right).

privileged (PRIV·lijd) *adj.* 1 enjoying a privilege: *We are privileged to live in an affluent society; a privileged class of people.* 2 legally protected: *a privileged communication between lawyer and client; A statement about someone that is privileged in parliament could be slanderous if repeated outside.*

priv·y (PRIV·ee) *adj.* [old use] private or secret: *a ruler's* **privy purse** (= private allowance).
— **privy to** *Formal.* privately informed about.
— *n., pl.* **priv·ies** an outhouse, esp. a toilet.

privy council *n.* a formal body of advisors appointed by a sovereign: *The Federal cabinet acts as the Canadian Privy Council.*

prize *n.* something worth competing for or that is offered to a winner in a competition, lottery, etc.: *to award or give, receive, win a prize; a consolation prize; door prize; first prize; the Nobel prize; adj.: prize cattle* (= cattle that have won prizes); *prize money.*

— *v.* priz·es, prized, priz·ing 1 value highly: *Artifacts of pioneer life are much prized now.* 2 estimate the value of something: *to prize a painting.* 3 force open with a lever; pry.

prize·fight *n.* a professional boxing match. — **prize·fight·er** *n.*

prize ring *n.* a square enclosure of ropes for prize fights.

pro- *prefix.* 1 forward in place or time: *prologue, provision.* 2 in place of: *proconsul, pronoun.* 3 favourable to: *pro-choice, pro-life, pro-Canadian.*

pro (PROH) *n.* pros 1 *Informal.* [short form] professional: *a football pro; She drives like a pro.* 2 something in favour: *to weigh the pros and cons of capital punishment.* — **pro and con** *adv. & prep.* for and against: *He spoke at length pro and con; gave arguments pro and con capital punishment;* **adj.:** *the various pro-and-con arguments.*

prob·a·bil·i·ty (prob·uh·BIL·uh·tee) *n.* -ties a being probable or something that is probable: *There is a 25% probability of rain today; Drowning is one of the probabilities of how he died;* **In all probabilty,** *she will win a gold medal.*

prob·a·ble (PROB·uh·bul) *adj.* likely because reasonable or logical: *It's possible to win $5 million dollars in the draw, but only a few are probable winners; the probable cause of death.*

pro·ba·tion (pruh·BAY·shun) *n.* a trial of a person's conduct or worth: *a six months' probation for new employees; A first offender is given a suspended sentence and placed on probation for one year under a* **probation officer.** — **pro·ba·tion·al** *adj.* — **pro·ba·tion·er** *n.* — **pro·ba·tion·ar·y** (-nair·ee) *adj.:* *a probationary appointment, period.*

probe *n.* 1 an investigation: *to conduct, launch a probe; a probe into corruption; a police probe; pollution probe.* 2 an instrument for probing, as a surgeon's slender metal device for exploring a wound or body cavity. 3 same as SPACE PROBE. — *v.* probes, probed, prob·ing investigate: *a committee probing charges of corruption; Scuba divers probe the hull of a sunken ship.*

pro·bi·ty (PROH·buh·tee) *n.* uprightness of morals; honesty.

prob·lem (PROB·lum) *n.* 1 a question put forward for solution: *to do* or *solve a mathematical problem; a simple problem.* 2 a difficult or perplexing situation or person: *to address, cause, pose, tackle, settle, solve a problem; an acute, complicated, difficult, emotional, involved, knotty, perennial, social, thorny problem; a problem child, drinker;* **No problem** (*Informal for* You're welcome).

prob·lem·at·ic (prob·luh·MAT·ic) or **prob·lem·at·i·cal** (-tuh·cul) *adj.* 1 puzzling. 2 not settled; open to question.

pro·ce·dur·al (pruh·SEE·jur·ul) *adj.* having to do with procedure: *The meeting was delayed by procedural problems.*

pro·ce·dure (pruh·SEE·jur) *n.* 1 method of doing something: *legal procedure; parliamentary procedure;* *the procedure to be followed in applying for a passport; established, normal, standard procedure.* 2 a particular form of action: *operations and such medical procedures.*

pro·ceed (pruh·SEED) *v.* go on: *Stop and proceed slowly at 10 km/h; She thanked him and proceeded to untie the parcel; He was unable to proceed with his studies; to proceed* (= take legal action) *against violators; quarrels proceeding* (= arising) *from old enmities.* — **proceedings** *n. pl.* 1 the activities of a society or their record. 2 [legal use] action: *to initiate* or *institute legal proceedings against someone; divorce proceedings.* — **proceeds** (PROH·seedz) *n. pl.* [takes pl. v.] returns or profit: *The proceeds of this concert will go to charity; net proceeds.*

proc·ess (PROH·ses, PROS·es) *n.* -ess·es (-es·iz) 1 a course or series of actions or their method: *a manufacturing process; He was deported by due process of law; the judicial process; mental* or *thought processes.* 2 an outgrowth or projecting part, as the appendix of the intestine. — *adj.* made by or involving a special process: **Process art** *reflects the artist's conceptual process;* **Process cheese** *is blended from several cheeses; the* **process engineer** *of an assembly-line operation.* — *v.* put through methodically: *to process applications, data, food, orders, recruits; word processing.*

pro·ces·sion (pruh·SESH·un) *n.* an orderly, formal movement, esp. of people: *a funeral, graduation, wedding procession.*

pro·ces·sion·al (pruh·SESH·uh·nul) *n.* a hymn book or music for processions.

proc·es·sor (PROH·suh·sur, PROS·uh·sur) *n.* 1 one that processes: *a food processor; word processor.* 2 a computer or its part that operates on data.

pro-choice *adj.* favouring a woman's right to abortion: *a pro-choice advocate, group, supporter; the pro-choice movement; Are they pro-choice or pro-life?*

pro·claim (proh·CLAIM) *v.* 1 announce publicly and officially: *a public holiday proclaimed in honour of a returning hero; to proclaim a country independent; to proclaim a region a disaster area; to proclaim war; to proclaim a law* (= to put it into effect). 2 glorify: *an ad proclaiming the virtues of a new computer.* — **proc·la·ma·tion** (proc·luh·MAY·shun) *n.:* *to issue a royal proclamation; a proclamation of amnesty.*

pro·cliv·i·ty (proh·CLIV·uh·tee) *n.* -ties a natural weakness for or to something: *a proclivity for making rash judgments; a patient with a proclivity to epileptic seizures.*

pro·cras·ti·nate (proh·CRAS·tuh·nate) *v.* -nates, -nat·ed, -nat·ing put off doing things from day to day. — **pro·cras·ti·na·tor** (-nay·tur) *n.* — **pro·cras·ti·na·tion** (-NAY·shun) *n.*

pro·cre·ate (PROH·cree·ate) *v.* -ates, -at·ed, -at·ing beget offspring. — **pro·cre·a·tor** (-ay·tur) *n.* — **pro·cre·a·tion** (-AY·shun) *n.*

Pro·crus·te·an (proh·CRUS·tee·un) *adj.* ruthless in enforcing conformity, like **Procrustes** (-teez) of Greek myth, who stretched his victims to fit his beds.

pro·cure (pruh·CURE) v. -cures, -cured, -cur·ing
1 obtain, esp. by some effort: *to procure votes; to procure* (= bring about) *a miscarriage.* 2 get someone for prostitution.
— **pro·cure·ment** (-munt) n.: *the procurement of military supplies.* — **pro·cur·er** n.

prod v. prods, prod·ded, prod·ding poke; hence, urge: *to prod cattle; prodded into activity by the approaching exams.*
— **n.** 1 a thrust or jab. 2 a pointed instrument: *a cattle prod.* — **prod·der** n.

prod·i·gal (PROD·uh·gul) n. a wastefully extravagant person; *adj.: an inheritance depleted by prodigal spending; the parable of the prodigal son; Nature's prodigal* (= abundant) *resources.*
— **prod·i·gal·ly** (-guh·lee) adv.
— **prod·i·gal·i·ty** (-GAL·uh·tee) n. -ties.

pro·di·gious (pruh·DIJ·ee·us) adj. very great or marvellous: *a prodigious amount, energy, memory, output; a man of prodigious strength.*

prod·i·gy (PROD·uh·jee) n. -gies something amazing or extraordinary, esp. a marvellously talented child: *Mozart was a musical prodigy; a child prodigy.*

pro·duce (pruh·DUCE) v. -duc·es, -duced, -duc·ing
1 bring or put forward: *evidence produced in court; Cows produce* (= give) *milk.* 2 bring into existence in any of various ways: *a method that produces results; Causes produce effects; She produces* (= prepares for public presentation) *the plays she directs; a book printed and produced* (= manufactured) *in Canada.*
— **n.** (PROD·uce) what is produced by a farm, esp. fruits and vegetables.

pro·duc·er (pruh·DEW·sur) n. 1 one who produces commercial goods or services. 2 one who produces movies, plays, or shows.

producer goods n. pl. raw materials, tools, machinery, etc. for the production of consumer goods.

prod·uct (PROD·uct) n. 1 what is produced: *commercial products such as factory goods; milk, cheese, and such dairy products; farm products such as crops and livestock; the gross national product; a finished product; waste products; the **product line*** (= various goods) *of a manufacturer.* 2 result: *an end product; This poem is a product of genius; These children are products of the 1980s; Six is the product of* (= result of multiplying) *2 and 3.*

pro·duc·tion (pruh·DUK·shun) n. the act of producing or something produced: *the production of goods and services; The movie was hailed as a great production* (= show); *a factory's **production line*** (= assembly line).

pro·duc·tive (pruh·DUC·tiv) adj. 1 producing a lot: *a productive worker.* 2 producing good results: *productive labour.* 3 capable of producing: *Suspicion is productive of enmities.* — **pro·duc·tive·ly** adv.
— **pro·duc·tive·ness** or **pro·duc·tiv·i·ty** (prod·uc·TIV·uh·tee) n.

prof n. [short form] professor.

pro·fane (pruh·FANE) adj. not showing the reverence due to sacred things: *a profane man's profane language.*
— **v.** -fanes, -faned, -fan·ing make profane: *temples profaned by marauders.* — **pro·fane·ly** adv.
— **prof·a·na·tion** (prof·uh·NAY·shun) n.

pro·fan·i·ty (pruh·FAN·uh·tee) n. -ties 1 lack of reverence; profaneness. 2 vulgar or irreverent speech or its utterance: *a mouthful of profanities.*

pro·fess (pruh·FES) v. 1 declare one's faith in something; affirm: *He renounced Buddhism and professed (faith in) Islam.* 2 to practise law, medicine, or another profession. 3 claim: *He professes to know nothing of what happened; professes total ignorance; a **professed*** (= acknowledged or self-declared) *communist.*

pro·fess·ed·ly (pruh·FES·id·lee) adv. admittedly: *She's a professedly poor piano player; He's professedly a radical.*

pro·fes·sion (pruh·FESH·un) n. 1 the act of professing: *a profession of faith, loyalty.* 2 a vocation that involves training or skill: *Law, medicine, and divinity used to be called the learned professions; to practise a profession; a nun by calling but a teacher by profession; Cook by name but doctor by profession; a national body's call **to the profession*** (= people practising the profession).

pro·fes·sion·al (pruh·FESH·uh·nul) adj. 1 having to do with a profession: *a professional nurse; a lawyer's professional ethics.* 2 expert: *professional advice; a professional pickpocket; The break-in seems a professional job.* 3 playing for pay: *a professional boxer, not an amateur; a professional hockey player.*
— **n.** 1 one who practises a profession: *Librarians are professionals; real, true professionals; A football professional coaches players.* 2 one who plays for pay: *An Olympic champion may **turn professional** (to play for pay).* — **pro·fes·sion·al·ism** n.
— **pro·fes·sion·al·ly** (-uh·lee) adv.

pro·fes·sor (pruh·FES·ur) n. a teacher in a college or university: *a professor of physics; an emeritus professor; a professor emeritus; an adjunct, assistant, associate, full, visiting professor.* — **pro·fes·sor·ship** n.
— **pro·fes·sor·i·al** (proh·fuh·SOR·ee·ul) adj.

prof·fer (PROF·ur) n. Formal. offer.
— **v.** prof·fers, prof·fered, prof·fer·ing: *a night's lodging proffered in friendship.*

pro·fi·cient (pruh·FISH·unt) adj. skilled: *He's proficient in or at cooking, though not an expert.*
— **pro·fi·cient·ly** adv. — **pro·fi·cien·cy** n.

pro·file (PROH·file) n. 1 the side view of a face: *Luc looks better in profile.* 2 an outline: *a patient's medication profile; a high-profile job (with high exposure to the public); Keep a **low profile** (= do not draw attention to yourself) and avoid talking to the media.* 3 an outline biography: *Kennedy's "Profiles in Courage" contains biographies of U.S. senators.*
— **v.** -files, -filed, -fil·ing show in profile: *The Queen is profiled on Canadian coins.*

prof·it (PROF·it) n. 1 financial gain: *to make a clear, excess, gross, handsome, net, quick profit; to earn, reap, turn a profit on a sale; The sale brought in or yielded a profit; The car was repaired and sold **at a profit**; business **profits**; the **profit and loss** statement at the close of a financial year.* 2 benefit or advantage: *What profit is there in arguing?*
— **v.** benefit: *to profit by or from one's mistakes.*

prof·it·a·ble (PROF·uh·tuh·bul) *adj.* yielding a profit: *a profitable undertaking; It's not profitable* (= beneficial) *to go on pumping money into a failing business.*
— **prof·it·a·bly** (-blee) *adv.*
— **prof·it·a·bil·i·ty** (-BIL·uh·tee) *n.*

prof·i·teer (prof·uh·TEER) *n.* one who makes excessive profits in a time of scarcity.
— *v.* do thus: *the hoarding of wheat for profiteering.*

prof·li·gate (PROF·luh·git, "g" as in "go") *adj.* dissipated or extravagant; *n.* such a person.
— **prof·li·ga·cy** (-guh·see) *n.*

pro for·ma (proh·FOR·muh) *adj. Latin.* for form's sake: *A pro forma invoice is sent as notice, not to ask for payment.*

pro·found (pruh·FOUND) *adj.* deep: *in profound sleep; my profound apologies, sympathy; a profound thinker; a profound bow; profound* (= thoroughgoing) *changes in society.*
— **pro·found·ly** *adv.: profoundly* (= totally) *deaf.*

pro·fun·di·ty (pruh·FUN·duh·tee) *n.* **-ties** depth: *the profundity of a philosopher's thought; Confucian profundities* (= deep thoughts).

pro·fuse (pruh·FUSE, *rhyme:* produce) *adj.* excessively plentiful: *He shed profuse tears; her profuse thanks; He was profuse in his praise.* — **pro·fuse·ly** *adv.*
— **pro·fu·sion** (-FEW·zhun) *n.* excessive amount: *Rain fell in profusion after the long drought.*

pro·gen·i·tor (proh·JEN·uh·tur) *n.* ancestor or begetter.

prog·e·ny (PROJ·uh·nee) *n.* **-nies** offspring.

prog·no·sis (prog·NOH·sis) *n., pl.* **-ses** (-seez) an estimate of the course, duration, and effect of a patient's illness.

prog·nos·tic (prog·NOS·tic) *adj.* predictive: *a prognostic sign, symptom, weather chart.*

prog·nos·ti·cate (prog·NOS·tuh·cate) *v.* **-cates, -cat·ed, -cat·ing** foretell from a sign or symptom.
— **prog·nos·ti·ca·tor** (-cay·tur) *n.*
— **prog·nos·ti·ca·tion** (-CAY·shun) ;

pro·gram or **pro·gramme** (PROH·gram) *n.* **1** a list of items or events, as for a performance: *the program of the evening.* **2** a broadcast item or performance: *a phone-in, radio, TV program.* **3** a plan of doing something step by step: *to draw up a program of studies; to carry out, launch, terminate a program; a building, development, honours, school program; a program in literature; a program to cut spending; What's on our program* (= schedule) *today?* **4 program** a series of instructions for a computer: *a computer program; to boot up, debug, execute, run, write a program; a user-friendly program.*
— *v.* **-grams** or **-grammes, -gramed** or **-grammed, -gram·ing** or **-gram·ming 1** plan a program of something: *to program a ceremony, function.*
2 program instruct: *to program a computer to do tax returns.*
— **pro·gram·a·ble** or **pro·gram·ma·ble** (proh·GRAM·uh·bul) *adj.: a programable calculator.*
— **pro·gram·er** or **pro·gram·mer** *n.*

pro·gress (PROH·gres, PROG·res) *n.* forward movement; advance: *the progress of civilization through the centuries; to hinder, impede, make progress in doing something; our progress toward reaching an agreement; A meeting is in progress* (= going on).
— *v.* (pruh·GRES) **-gress·es, -gressed, -gress·ing** make progress: *How's the patient progressing? to progress toward perfection.*
— **pro·gres·sion** (pruh·GRESH·un) *n.*

pro·gres·sive (pruh·GRES·iv) *adj.* **1** going forward: *a progressive disease, idea, nation.* **2** favouring continual reform, esp. in government: *a progressive party.*
— *n.* one who favours political reform.
— **pro·gres·sive·ly** *adv.*

progressive rock *n.* a modern form of rock music represented by Pink Floyd and other bands of the 1970s and 1980s.

pro·hib·it (pruh·HIB·it) *v.* forbid authoritatively: *Smoking is prohibited here; You are prohibited from smoking here.*

pro·hi·bi·tion (proh·uh·BISH·un) *n.* a prohibiting, esp. of alcoholic liquors, as in Canada between 1916 and 1917: *Prohibition has failed in most countries; a prohibition against smoking.* — **pro·hi·bi·tion·ist** *n.*

pro·hib·i·tive (pruh·HIB·uh·tiv) *adj.* **1** preventing from buying, doing, etc.: *prohibitive legal fees, house prices, tax rates.* **2** too expensive: *Buying a house these days is becoming prohibitive.*
— **prohibitive favourite** *Informal.* a sure bet.
— **pro·hib·i·tive·ly** *adv.*

pro·hib·i·to·ry (pruh·HIB·uh·tor·ee) *adj.* prohibiting: *a prohibitory order against a publication.*

proj·ect (PROH·ject, PROJ·ect) *n.* **1** a proposed or actual undertaking, often on a large scale: *a highway construction project; a Grade 9 science project; Project Overseas of the Canadian Teachers' Federation.* **2** a group of apartments or houses forming a unit, usually built and run with public funds: *a housing project.*
— *v.* (pruh·JECT) **1** propose: *A tax hike is projected for next year.* **2** extend in space or time: *a cape projecting into the sea; to project* (= estimate by extending known information) *population increases of the next decade.*
3 cause to appear on a surface: *pictures projected on a screen; a world map made by mathematically projecting the globe on a flat surface.*

pro·jec·tile (pruh·JEC·tile, -til) *n.* anything thrown or hurled forward, as a missile or rocket: *to launch a projectile.*

pro·jec·tion (pruh·JEC·shun) *n.* **1** a jutting out: *the projections on a surface.* **2** an estimate of something in the future: *to make a projection of population increases.* **3** something thrown on a surface: *the projection of a picture on a screen from a projection booth; the Mercator projection* (= map) *of the globe.* **4** in psychology, the ascribing or attribution of one's own feelings or motives to other persons or things, often as a defence mechanism. — **pro·jec·tion·ist** *n.*

pro·jec·tor (pruh·JEC·tur) *n.* a machine for projecting pictures: *a movie projector; overhead projector; slide projectors.*

pro·le·tar·i·an (proh·luh·TAIR·ee·un) *n.* a member of the proletariat. — *adj.: proletarian art, literature.*

pro·le·tar·i·at (proh·luh·TAIR·ee·ut) *n.* the industrial working class.

pro-life *adj.* opposed to abortions, euthanasia, and such ways of ending life: *a pro-life group; the pro-life movement.* — **pro-lifer** *n.*

pro·lif·er·ate (pruh·LIF·uh·rate) *v.* -ates, -at·ed, -at·ing multiply or grow rapidly, esp. in an uncontrolled manner: *Corals proliferate by budding.*
— **pro·lif·er·a·tion** (-RAY·shun) *n.: the U.N. treaty to prohibit the proliferation of nuclear weapons.*
— **pro·lif·er·ous** (-ur·us) *adj.: a proliferous growth of new tissue.*

pro·lif·ic (pruh·LIF·ic) *adj.* producing much: *a prolific writer; Rabbits and hamsters are prolific* (= fertile) *animals.*

pro·lix (proh·LIX) *adj.* verbose or long-winded.
— **pro·lix·i·ty** (-uh·tee) *n.*

pro·logue or **pro·log** (PROH·log) *n.* 1 an introductory part: *the prologue to a play, poem, novel.* 2 any introductory act or event: *the prologue to the war.*

pro·long (pruh·LONG) *v.* make longer, esp. in time: *Why prolong the agony? a visit prolonged into the night; a prolonged illness, period; prolonged applause, relief, use.* — **pro·lon·ga·tion** (proh·long·GAY·shun) *n.*

prom *n. Informal.* a formal dance held by a school or college class: *the senior prom.*

prom·e·nade (prom·uh·NAHD, -NADE) *n.* 1 a public walk or ride taken for pleasure. 2 a public place for walking, as a ship's "promenade deck."
— *v.* -nades, -nad·ed, -nad·ing 1 walk about, esp. in display: *Prendergast and his dog like to promenade on the beach.* 2 parade someone, as if for display: *The best of the bunch were promenaded on the stage for the benefit of the judges.*

prom·i·nence (PROM·uh·nunce) *n.* a being prominent or something that is prominent: *a paper that gives prominence to sports stories; Churchill came into prominence during World War II; an iceberg first noticed as a prominence on the horizon; Solar prominences erupt as huge arches of gas.*

prom·i·nent (PROM·uh·nunt) *adj.* 1 projecting: *an insect's prominent eyes; a prominent chin, nose.* 2 conspicuous, distinguished, or eminent: *a prominent leader; prominent people; a prominent position in public life.* — **prom·i·nent·ly** *adv.*

pro·mis·cu·ous (pruh·MIS·cue·us) *adj.* disorderly or indiscriminate, esp. in regard to sex: *a promiscuous life; promiscuous behaviour, youth.*
— **pro·mis·cu·ous·ly** *adv.*
— **pro·mis·cu·ous·ness** or **prom·is·cu·i·ty** (prom·is·CUE·uh·tee) *n.*

prom·ise (PROM·is) *n.* 1 word that binds one to do or not do something: *He was sued for breach of promise because he didn't keep* or *fulfil his promise; He broke his promise; broken, empty, solemn promises; a promise to deliver on time.* 2 an expectation of hope or success: *a juvenile poem that shows much promise; the land of promise flowing with milk and honey; great promise but poor performance.*
— *v.* -is·es, -ised, -is·ing make a promise: *I promise you help; I promise to marry you; the* **Promised Land** *of Canaan* (as promised to the Israelites); *An honest politician never promises the moon.*

promising *adj.* likely to give success or good results: *weather that looks promising; a promising start in life.*

prom·is·so·ry (PROM·uh·sor·ee) *adj.* containing a promise to pay back: *a promissory note for $5 000 due for payment in 60 days.*

pro·mo (PROH·moh) *n.* -mos *Informal.* promotional announcement; commercial: *all those promos for junk food.*

pro·mo·ta·ble (pruh·MOH·tuh·bul) *adj.* that can be promoted: *a promotable candidate; The name "Ryan" is more promotable in the French media than "Regan."*

pro·mote (pruh·MOTE) *v.* -motes, -mot·ed, -mot·ing 1 raise in rank: *They promoted her from major to colonel; He was promoted from Grade 1 to Grade 2.* 2 further the popularity of a person or thing: *a new movie well promoted by ads.* 3 help to establish: *to promote peace and understanding.*
— **pro·mot·er** (-MOH·tur) *n.*
— **pro·mo·tion** (-shun) *n.*
— **pro·mo·tion·al** (-shun·ul) *adj.: a promotional ad campaign.*

prompt *v.* 1 make someone do something: *Good examples prompt others to do the same.* 2 cause something to be: *a gift prompted by charity.* 3 remind by supplying cues or lines: *to prompt an actor.*
— *adj.* acting or done quickly: *prompt action to put out a fire; a prompt reply; He's prompt at* or *in answering questions; We expect prompt obedience from students.*
— **prompt·ly** *adv.*
— **prompt·ness** or **promp·ti·tude** (-tuh·tude) *n.*

prom·ul·gate (PROM·ul·gate, proh·MUL·gate) *v.* -gates, -gat·ed, -gat·ing 1 put into force officially: *a regulation promulgated by executive order.* 2 make widespread: *to promulgate ideas, knowledge, policies.*
— **prom·ul·ga·tion** (-GAY·shun) *n.*

prone *adj.* 1 liable or inclined: *Human beings are prone to error; a nervous and accident-prone driver.* 2 *Formal.* (lying) on one's face: *The body was stretched prone on the pavement; the prone glide in swimming.*
— **prone·ly** *adv.;* **pron·ness** *n.*

prong *n.* a pointed end, as a tine of a fork, fang of a tooth, or the tip of an antler.

pronged *adj. & combining form.* branched: *the pronged antlers of the* **pronghorn** *antelope; a two-pronged tuning fork; a three-pronged attack by the invading army.*

pro·noun (PROH·noun) *n.* a word such as "I," "you," "he," "herself," or "anybody" that functions like a noun.
— **pro·nom·i·nal** (proh·NOM·uh·nul) *adj.*

pro·nounce (pruh·NOUNCE) *v.* -nounc·es, -nounced, -nounc·ing 1 declare formally or officially: *The judge pronounced a sentence; Lu was pronounced guilty; Jo was pronounced dead on arrival at the hospital.* 2 give the pronunciation of a word: *"Waskatenau" in Alberta is pronounced* (wuh·SET·nah).

— **pro·nounce·a·ble** (-suh·bul) *adj.*: *"Chomley" is more pronounceable than "Cholmondeley."*
— **pro·nounced** *adj.* marked or decided: *There's a pronounced change in his behaviour.*
— **pro·nounce·ment** (-munt) *n.* a formal declaration.

pron·to (PRON·toh) *adv. Informal.* quickly or promptly.

pro·nun·ci·a·tion (pruh·NUN·see·AY·shun) *n.* the way of saying a word, syllable, or sound of a language.

proof (long "oo") *n.* **1** the act or process of proving; test or trial: *"The proof of the pudding is in the eating"; a photographer's or printer's proof* (= trial print); *the galley proofs and page proofs of a book; to put a new bike* **to the proof** (= try it out). **2** something that establishes truth or correctness; sure evidence: *A postal receipt is proof of delivery; to furnish, produce, provide proof; ample, clear, convincing, positive proof; The burden of proof is on the accuser.* **3** the strength of liquor: *In Canada, 57.1% by volume of alcohol is 100 proof; Liquor sold in Ontario is about 70 proof* (= 40% alcohol by volume); *A* **proof spirit** *is 100 proof.*
— *adj.* **1** of proven value or strength: *a good coat of paint that is* **proof against** *the ravages of the weather.*
— *combining form: a fool-proof plan* (= a plan that is supposed to succeed); *a rust-proof paint (that prevents rust); a water-proof watch (that water cannot enter).* **2** of coins, having a shiny surface and struck for collectors: *a proof coin, set; of proof quality.*

proof·read (PROOF·reed) *v.* **-reads, -read** (-red) , **-read·ing** read something written, typed, or printed for errors. — **proof·read·er** *n.*

prop *n.* **1** a support or stay: *a corn plant's prop roots; The prop of his old age was an only son.* **2** [short form] propeller. **3** [short form] stage property.
— *v.* **props, propped, prop·ping** support something in a certain way: *to prop a door open; a poor defence propped up by shady witnesses.*

prop·a·gan·da (prop·uh·GAN·duh) *n.* ideas or doctrines spread by an interested party to influence others: *political propaganda; war propaganda; to spread propaganda against the opposition; adj.: a propaganda effort; radio and TV as propaganda instruments.*
— **prop·a·gan·dist** *n.*

prop·a·gate (PROP·uh·gate) *v.* **-gates, -gat·ed, -gat·ing** spread, as with seeds or cuttings: *to propagate a breed of animals, a plant; Trees propagate themselves; Insects propagate diseases; to propagate news; a story propagated on the airwaves.*
— **prop·a·ga·tion** (-GAY·shun) *n.*: *sexual propagation of the species; Society for the Propagation of the Faith.*
— **prop·a·ga·tor** (-gay·tur) *n.*: *a malicious propagator of lies.*

pro·pane (PROH·pane) *n.* a flammable gas obtained from petroleum and natural gas for use as a fuel, in refrigeration, etc.

pro·pel (pruh·PEL) *v.* **-pels, -pelled, -pel·ling** drive something forward: *a man propelled by ambition; a jet-propelled aircraft.*
— **pro·pel·lant** or **pro·pel·lent** *n. & adj.: a rocket propellant composed of a fuel and an oxidizer; Liquid hydrogen is the propellent fuel.*

pro·pel·ler (pruh·PEL·ur) *n.* a revolving device for propelling an aircraft, ship, etc.; also **screw propeller.**

pro·pen·si·ty (pruh·PEN·suh·tee) *n.* **-ties** *Formal.* a natural inclination: *a propensity for punning; a propensity to tell fibs; the human propensity to selfishness.*

prop·er *adj.* **1** right, correct, or suitable, as if belonging or related: *Please put everything back in its proper place; proper conduct for a pupil; Suburbs are outside the city proper* (= the main city); *We are experiencing weather* **proper to** (= typical of) *this time of year; Hank received a proper* (*Informal for* thorough and well-deserved) *tongue-lashing from his uncle.* **2** designating one, not many; not common: *a* **proper noun** or **name** *such as "Ottawa" or "the Joneses."* — **prop·er·ly** *adv.*

propertied (PROP·ur·teed) *adj.* owning property: *the propertied classes.*

prop·er·ty (PROP·ur·tee) *n.* **-ties 1** what is owned by one, esp. real estate and movable goods: *a piece of property; Get off my property; This car is not stolen property; Stage properties* (= equipment) *do not include scenery and costumes; a man* **of property** (= wealthy man); *common, joint, personal, public property.* **2** a quality or characteristic: *Density is one of the properties of matter.*

proph·e·cy (PROF·uh·see) *n.* **-cies** a foretelling or something foretold, esp. if divinely inspired: *to make a prophecy about the end of the world; The prophecy did not come true; The prophecy turned out to be false; The prophecy was fulfilled.*

proph·e·sy (PROF·uh·sye) *v.* **-sies, -sied, -sy·ing** predict that something will happen: *Peg prophesied that Gigi would become president.*

proph·et (PROF·it) *n.* one who tells the future, esp. if divinely inspired or claimed to be: *a false prophet; The weatherman is often a poor prophet; to obey the law and the prophets (of the Old Testament).*
— **proph·et·ess** (-is) *fem.*
— **pro·phet·ic** (pruh·FET·ic) *adj.* foretelling: *Jeremiah's prophetic utterances; a gloom that is prophetic of doom.*
— **pro·phet·i·cal·ly** *adv.*

pro·pi·ti·ate (pruh·PISH·ee·ate) *v.* **-ates, -at·ed, -at·ing** win the favour of someone of influence, esp. of someone who could be displeased; appease: *to propitiate the gods.* — **pro·pi·ti·a·tion** (-AY·shun) *n.*
— **pro·pi·ti·a·to·ry** (-uh·tor·ee) *adj.: a propitiatory offering, sacrifice.*

pro·pi·tious (pruh·PISH·us) *adj.* auspicious or favourable: *The weather seems propitious for the trip; Fortune is propitious to us.*

prop·jet *n.* same as TURBOPROP.

prop·man *n.* a person in charge of stage properties; property man.

pro·po·nent (pruh·POH·nunt) *n.* one who proposes or espouses something: *a proponent of free trade.*

pro·por·tion (pruh·POR·shun) *n.* 1 the proper relation of things one to another as of parts to a whole: *Everyone is paid* **in proportion to** *work done; The arms are somewhat* **out of proportion to** *the statue's body; The cost of living has risen out of all proportion to wages.* 2 ratio: *"1/2 : 3/6" is a proportion.* 3 part or share: *your proportion of the work; the proportion of silver in the coin; a disease of epidemic* **proportions** (= dimensions or size).
— *v.* be or make in due proportion: *We have to proportion our expenses to our earnings; Gina has a well-proportioned figure.*

pro·por·tion·al (pruh·POR·shun·nul) *adj.* in due proportion: *The number of seats held by a party may not be proportional to the population that voted for it; proportional representation; a letter printed out with* **proportional spacing** (= "i," "m," etc. occupying spaces in proportion to their size).
— **pro·por·tion·al·ly** *adv. Also* **pro·por·tion·ate** (-nit) *adj.;* **pro·por·tion·ate·ly** *adv.*

pro·pos·al (pruh·POH·zul) *n.* a proposing or something proposed, as an offer or request: *to make a marriage proposal to someone; to accept, adopt, entertain, put forward a proposal; a proposal to reform the tax system; a proposal for reform.*

pro·pose (pruh·POZE) *v.* -pos·es, -posed, -pos·ing 1 put forward for consideration or acceptance: *We propose Jones for mayor; I propose that we accept the report; I proposed (marriage) and she accepted.* 2 plan or intend: *I propose to go abroad in the summer.*

prop·o·si·tion (prop·uh·ZISH·un) *n.* 1 a statement, esp. a resolution at a meeting: *the proposition that sales taxes be abolished.* 2 *Informal.* a proposed deal or something to be dealt with, as a problem or a person: *That's a tough proposition.* 3 *Informal.* a proposal, esp. for sexual intercourse; also *v.*

pro·pound (pruh·POUND) *v.* put forward for consideration: *to propound a doctrine, question, riddle, scheme, theory.*

pro·pri·e·tar·y (pruh·PRY·uh·tair·ee) *adj.* pertaining to ownership: *a proprietary interest, right;* **proprietary medicine** (= patent medicine).

pro·pri·e·tor (pruh·PRY·uh·tur) *n.* an owner, esp. of a business.

pro·pri·e·ty (pruh·PRY·uh·tee) *n.* 1 the quality or condition of being proper or fitting, esp. in regard to behaviour: *the questionable propriety of chewing gum in church.* 2 **-ties** *pl.* standards or requirements of proper behaviour.

pro·pul·sion (pruh·PUL·shun) *n.* a propelling or its force: *jet propulsion; rocket propulsion.*

pro ra·ta (proh·RAY·tuh, -RAT·uh) *adj. & adv.* proportionate or proportionally; prorated: *The money was insufficient to satisfy all claimants, but it was distributed on a pro rata basis; It was shared pro rata by them.*

pro·rate (proh·RATE) *v.* -rates, -rat·ed, -rat·ing divide, distribute, or assess proportionately to other factors such as share or interest of each individual: *Each extra hour is prorated at $10 per half-hour; Part-timers are paid prorated amounts of the full salary.*
— **pro·ra·tion** (-RAY·shun) *n.*

pro·sa·ic (proh·ZAY·ic) *adj.* matter-of-fact or dull: *a prosaic existence, job, occupation.* — **pro·sa·i·cal·ly** *adv.*

pro·scribe (proh·SCRIBE) *v.* -scribes, -scribed, -scrib·ing *Formal.* prohibit a person or practice as dangerous. — **pro·scrip·tion** (proh·SCRIP·shun) *n.*

prose (PROZE) *n.* ordinary language that is not in verse form.

pros·e·cute (PROS·uh·cute) *v.* -cutes, -cut·ed, -cut·ing 1 pursue: *to prosecute a claim, investigation; to prosecute studies.* 2 bring a criminal action against someone: *Trespassers will be prosecuted; Shopkeepers don't prosecute in every case of theft; the* **prosecuting** attorney (= government lawyer) or **pros·e·cu·tor** (-cue·tur) *n.*

pros·e·cu·tion (pros·uh·CUE·shun) *n.* 1 a bringing of a criminal action: *Shoplifters face prosecution for theft.* 2 the prosecuting party, usually the government.

pros·e·lyte (PROS·uh·lite) *n.* a convert from one religion to another.

pros·e·lyt·ize (PROS·uh·luh·tize) *v.* -iz·es, -ized, -iz·ing to convert, esp. by inducements.

pro·sit (PROH·sit) *interj.* [used as a toast] to your health! Also **prost** (rhyme: "most").

pro·sod·ic (pruh·SOD·ic) *adj.* having to do with prosody: *Metre, rhyme, etc. are prosodic features.*

pros·o·dy (PROS·uh·dee) *n.* verse structure or its study.

pros·pect (PROS·pect) *n.* 1 an extensive view or outlook: *a prospect of the countryside from a hilltop.* 2 an expectation of something; also, someone expected: *She seems a good prospect as a client; a job with good* **prospects** (= chances) *for promotion.*
— *v.* search: *to prospect for gold, oil, minerals.*
— **pros·pec·tor** *n.*

pros·pec·tive (pros·PEC·tiv) *adj.* hoped for or expected: *the prospective bride; a prospective candidate for election.* — **pros·pec·tive·ly** *adv.*

pros·pec·tus (pros·PEC·tus) *n.* an outline, esp. of something proposed, giving its main features: *the prospectus of a book in preparation, of a business, of an educational institution.*

pros·per (PROS·pur) *v.* thrive, esp. financially; succeed.

pros·per·i·ty (pros·PER·uh·tee) *n.* a prospering or thriving: *to enjoy prosperity in business; "Prosperity makes friends, adversity tries them."*

pros·per·ous (PROS·pur·us) *adj.* **1** thriving: *a prosperous business.* **2** favourable: *prosperous weather for tomatoes.* — **pros·per·ous·ly** *adv.*

pros·thet·ic (pros·THET·ic) **1** *adj.* being a replacement part: *A denture is a prosthetic device.* **2 prosthetics** *n.pl.* a branch of surgery dealing with artificial body parts.

pros·ti·tute (PROS·tuh·tute) *n.* a person who provides sex for pay.
— *v.* **-tutes, -tut·ed, -tut·ing** sell one's talents for base purposes.
— **pros·ti·tu·tion** (-TUE·shun) *n.: the prostitution* (= selling out) *of literary talent for political propaganda.*

pros·trate (PROS·trate) *v.* **-trates, -trat·ed, -trat·ing** **1** lie stretched out, usually with the face downward: *Worshippers prostrate themselves before the altar.* **2** lay low: *The body lay prostrate.* **3** weaken or exhaust: *prostrated by heat.*
— *adj.* lying flat; also, laid low or overcome: *a widow prostrate with grief.*
— **pros·tra·tion** (pros·TRAY·shun) *n.: nervous prostration* (= breakdown).

pros·y (PROH·see) *adj.* **pros·i·er, -i·est** like prose; also, prosaic or dull.

pro·tag·o·nist (proh·TAG·uh·nist) *n.* **1** the main character in a play or story. **2** champion or leader.

pro·tect (pruh·TECT) *v.* guard against harm, esp. with or as if with a cover or barrier: *Roofs protect us from or against the elements; tariffs to protect industries from foreign competition; The whooping crane is an endangered and therefore protected species (protected from collectors, hunters, etc.).*
— **pro·tec·tion** (-TEK·shun) *n.: to afford, give, provide protection; police protection; the protection of domestic industries, wild life.*
— **pro·tec·tion·ism** (-iz·um) *n.* — **pro·tec·tion·ist** *n.*

protection money *n.* money extorted by racketeers or paid as bribe for protection.

pro·tec·tive (pruh·TEC·tiv) *adj.* protecting or guarding: *Camouflage is protective coloration against the enemy; Parents are protective of their children; a drunk kept in protective custody by the police; protective tariffs.*
— **pro·tec·tive·ly** *adv.* — **pro·tec·tor** (-tur) *n.*

pro·tec·tor·ate (pruh·TEC·tur·it) *n.* a state or territory dependent on another for defence, foreign relations, etc.: *Solomon Islands was a British protectorate till 1978.*

pro·té·gé (PROH·tuh·zhay) *n.* a person to whom one is patron; *fem.* **pro·té·gée** (-zhay).

pro·tein (PROH·teen) *n.* a complex chemical compound occurring as an essential part of all living things: *Milk, eggs, fish, and lean meat have high protein content.*

pro tem (proh·TEM) *adj.* [short form] pro tempore: *a pro tem administration.*

pro tem·po·re (proh·TEM·puh·ree) *adj. & adv. Latin.* temporary or temporarily: *Al was appointed chairman pro tempore.*

pro·test (pruh·TEST, PROH·test) *v.* **1** object to

something: *minorities protesting (against) discrimination in hiring; We protested (to the government) that the new tax was unjust.* **2** declare solemnly: *Joan of Arc died protesting her innocence.*
— *n.* (PROH·test) a protesting: *loud protests from the public; to enter, file, lodge a protest; to register a strong protest with the authorities against interference in internal matters; Everyone resigned in protest; an unjust levy paid under protest* (= unwillingly).
— **pro·tes·ta·tion** (prot·is·TAY·shun) *n.* solemn declaration. — **pro·test·er** or **pro·tes·tor** (-TES·tur) *n.*

Prot·es·tant (PROT·is·tunt) *n.* a Christian not of the Catholic Church or the Eastern Orthodox Church; *adj.: a Protestant denomination; The Protestant (work) ethic considers work as the road to salvation.*
— **Prot·es·tant·ism** (-tun·tiz·um) *n.*

proto- *combining form.* first in time, importance, etc.: *protohistory, protomartyr, prototype.*

pro·to·col (PROH·tuh·col) *n.* **1** a code of etiquette to be observed on state occasions: *She broke or violated protocol by offering her gloved hand to the Queen; a breach of protocol; to observe diplomatic protocol; military protocol.* **2** an initial draft of a document, esp. a treaty: *to draw up a protocol; the 1925 Geneva Protocol outlawing chemical warfare; a protocol agreement.*

pro·to·type (PROH·tuh·type) *n.* the original or first model; archetype.

pro·tract (proh·TRACT) *v.* lengthen or prolong: *a protracted delay.*

pro·trude (pruh·TROOD, long "oo") *v.* **-trudes, -trud·ed, -trud·ing** (cause to) jut or stick out: *to protrude one's tongue; a protruding jaw.*
— **pro·tru·sion** (-TROO·zhun) *n.*

pro·tu·ber·ance (-TUE·bur·unce) *n.* a bulge.
— **pro·tu·ber·ant** (-TUE·bur·unt) *adj.* protruding or bulging.

proud *adj.* **1** feeling, arousing, or showing proper pride or self-esteem: *You may be justly proud of your achievements; Jean is too proud to beg; the proud* (= glorious) *moment of breaking a world record; a mother proud of her many children; a proud* (= spirited) *steed.* **2** having or showing too high an opinion of oneself: *proud as a peacock; proud and arrogant.*
— **do one proud** *Informal.* do one credit; make one feel gratified. — **proud·ly** *adv.*

prove (PROOV) *v.* **proves,** *pt.* **proved,** *pp.* **proved** or **prov·en, prov·ing** **1** demonstrate or show: *Prove that you can lift this weight; Later events proved my suspicions; They proved him guilty; a charge that you cannot prove beyond a reasonable doubt; to prove conclusively; a proven car that has sold well for many years; The new recruit proved herself in three days; "The exception proves the rule" (because every rule has an exception).* **2** turn out: *The new recruit proved to be a good choice; The book proved fascinating.*
— **prov·a·ble** (-vuh·bul) *adj.*
— **prov·a·bil·i·ty** (-vuh·BIL·uh·tee) *n.*

prov·e·nance (PROV·uh·nunce) *n.* place of origin; source.

prov·en·der (PROV·un·dur) *n.* **1** hay, corn, oats, and such dry food for livestock. **2** *Informal.* provisions or food.

pro·ve·ni·ence (proh·VEE·nee·unce) *n.* same as PROVENANCE.

prov·erb (PROV·urb) *n.* a short, wise saying that has been long in use among a people: *As the proverb goes or runs, "Haste makes waste."*

pro·ver·bi·al (pruh·VUR·bee·ul) *adj.* well-known: *Solomon's proverbial wisdom.* — **pro·ver·bi·al·ly** (-uh·lee) *adv.*: *Dogs are proverbially faithful animals.*

pro·vide (pruh·VIDE) *v.* **-vides, -vid·ed, -vid·ing** see to or supply a need or contingency: *Sheep provide us with wool; Rules provide penalties for offences; They provide that offenders be punished; I provide for my family* (= pay for my family's needs); *insurance to provide for old age and to provide against accidents.* — **provided** or **providing** *conj.* on the condition that; if. — **pro·vid·er** *n.*

prov·i·dence (PROV·uh·dunce) *n.* a being provident; prudent management: *Some see the hand of (divine) Providence in everything that happens to them.*

prov·i·dent (PROV·uh·dunt) *adj.* careful about future needs, as by saving money.

prov·i·den·tial (prov·uh·DEN·shul) *adj.* fortunate in happening at exactly the right moment: *It was providential that a doctor happened to be on the plane.* — **prov·i·den·tial·ly** *adv.*

prov·ince (PROV·unce) *n.* **1** an administrative division of a country: *the 10 provinces of Canada; a Maritime province; a Prairie province.* **2** a sphere of activity or interest: *Marriage counselling is outside the province of a divorce lawyer.*

pro·vin·cial (pruh·VIN·shul) *adj.* **1** having to do with a province: *a provincial highway, legislature, park, parliament.* **2** of outlying areas rather than cities; rustic or unsophisticated: *a provincial accent.* **3** narrow: *His concerns remained rather provincial even after travelling abroad.* — **pro·vin·cial·ism** *n.* — **pro·vin·cial·ly** *adv.*

proving ground *n.* a place for the systematic testing of new equipment, theories, etc.

pro·vi·sion (pruh·VIZH·un) *n.* **1** the act of providing or something provided; arrangement: *There is a provision in the will for gifts to charity; The will makes provision for gifts to charities.* **2 provisions** *pl.* food supplies or stocks.

pro·vi·sion·al (pruh·VIZH·uh·nul) *adj.* temporary: *provisional data, figures; a provisional estimate of unemployment in Canada; a provisional government in exile; a provisional plan.* — **pro·vi·sion·al·ly** *adv.*

pro·vi·so (pruh·VYE·soh) *n.* **-sos** or **-soes** a legal stipulation or condition: *She accepted the job with the proviso that no one interfere with her work.*

prov·o·ca·tion (prov·uh·CAY·shun) *n.* a provoking or something that provokes: *The police fired under extreme provocation; There was much provocation for their behaviour; He tends to shout at the slightest provocation; Various provocations were provided or offered to make her fight.*

pro·voc·a·tive (pruh·VOC·uh·tiv) *adj.* tending to arouse a feeling or reaction: *provocative behaviour; highly provocative language; a very provocative costume.*

pro·voke (pruh·VOKE) *v.* **-vokes, -voked, -vok·ing** **1** stir up or excite: *A cool-headed man is not easily provoked; She was provoked into saying things she now regrets.* **2** cause: *artless comments that provoked laughter; a thought-provoking speech.* **3** irritate: *his very **provoking** behaviour.* — **pro·vok·ing·ly** *adv.*

prow (rhyme: "how") *n.* the front part of a ship, boat, aircraft, etc.

prow·ess (PROW·is, "OW" as in "how") *n.* [literary use] personal bravery or extraordinary ability: *his prowess in battle; She demonstrated* or *displayed her great prowess as a skier; her prowess on the slopes.*

prowl (rhyme: "howl") *v.* go about cautiously like a beast of prey: *enemy subs prowling along our coast; troublemakers prowling the streets; Birders prowl for owls.* — *n.* a prowling: *an all-night prowl by birders; There's a bear **on the prowl*** (= prowling) *in this park; The police arrived in a **prowl car*** (= squad car) *when a **prowler*** (= suspected burglar) *was reported in the neighbourhood.*

prox·i·mate (PROX·uh·mit) *adj.* nearest in order, location, or time: *a proximate cause; Our proximate goal is to graduate and get a job, the ultimate goal is happiness.*

prox·im·i·ty (prok·SIM·uh·tee) *n. Formal.* nearness: *a house located in close proximity to a garbage dump; Marriage between first cousins is sometimes forbidden because of proximity of blood.*

prox·y (PROX·ee) *n.* **prox·ies** a substitute for another person with authority to act for the person or a document giving such authority: *Marriage by proxy is not so common as voting by proxy, as at business meetings; The **proxy statement** (sent to stockholders with information on company affairs for soliciting their proxies) showed the chairman of the board holding 18 000 shares.*

prude (PROOD, long "OO") *n.* one who affects excessive modesty in speech and manners. — **prud·ish** *adj.*; **prud·ish·ness** *n.*

pru·dence (PROO·dunce) *n.* the quality of being prudent.

pru·dent (PROO·dunt) *adj.* cautious and circumspect: *a prudent and thrifty housekeeper; Cats don't like prudent mice; a prudent course of action; a prudent investor; to act in a prudent manner; It's prudent to make a will as you get older.* — **pru·dent·ly** *adv.*

pru·den·tial (proo·DEN·shul) *adj.* having to do with being prudent: *Be prudential* (= use prudence) *in buying insurance; a prudential (Formal for advisory) committee with discretionary powers.* — **pru·den·tial·ly** *adv.*

prud·er·y (PROO·duh·ree) *n.* **-er·ies** a being prudish or an instance of it: *Victorian prudery dictated such pruderies as saying "limb" for "leg."*

prune (PROON) *n.* a dried sweet plum; also, a plum suitable for drying.
— *v.* **prunes, pruned, prun·ing 1** cut out superfluous or dying parts from a plant or tree. **2** trim: *a wordy essay that needs pruning.*

pru·ri·ent (PROO·ree·unt) *adj.* having, showing, or causing lustful desires: *literature catering to the prurient interest.* — **pru·ri·ence** (-unce) *n.*

pry *v.* **pries, pried, pry·ing 1** snoop: *No one likes people to pry into their private affairs; Pat is very prying* (= inquisitive). **2** force out with or as if with a lever: *to pry open a lid; to pry information out of someone.*

psalm (SAHM) *n.* a sacred song or poem, especially one from the **Psalms**, a book of the Old Testament, believed to be by King David, the **Psalmist.**

pseu·do (SUE·doh) *adj. & combining form.* counterfeit or sham: *pseudo learning; pseudoscience.*

pseu·do·nym (SUE·duh·nim) *n.* an assumed name: *Sam Clemens wrote under the pseudonym "Mark Twain."*

pshaw (SHAW) *interj.* expressing contempt, disbelief, etc.

psst *interj.* made to attract someone's attention quietly: *Psst! Your slip is showing.*

psych (SIKE) *v. Slang.* **1** get someone excited. **2** get oneself mentally ready: *She took a few moments to get psyched up for the dive.* **3** psychoanalyse; probe someone's mind; hence, intimidate or be intimidated: *We'll psych him out with this story.*

psy·che (SYE·kee) *n.* one's soul or mind.

psy·che·del·ic (sye·cuh·DEL·ic) **1** *adj.* relating to hallucinogenic drugs such as LSD or their abnormal effects on the mind: *a psychedelic experience; psychedelic lights, music.* **2** *n.* a psychedelic drug or its user.

psy·chi·a·try (suh·KYE·uh·tree, sye-) *n.* a branch of medicine dealing with mental and emotional disorders.
— **psy·chi·a·trist** *n.*
— **psy·chi·at·ric** (sye·kee·AT·ric) *adj.*

psy·chic (SYE·kik) *n.* one who is sensitive to forces outside the physical world, as a spiritualistic medium.
— *adj.* spiritualistic: *I don't know what she thinks, I'm not psychic; PCP, a veterinary anesthetic, has been called a psychic energizer; psychic energy, power; a psychic force, healer.*
— **psy·chi·cal** (SYE·cuh·cul) *adj.: psychical research into spiritualism, ESP, and such psychical phenomena.*
— **psy·chi·cal·ly** *adv.*

psy·cho (SYE·coh) **1** *n. & adj.* **-cos** *Informal.* psychopath or psychopathic. **2** *combining form.* mental: *psychoactive, psychology, psychobabble.*

psy·cho·ac·tive (sye·coh·AC·tiv) *adj.* acting on the mind: *a psychoactive drug that can change behaviour.*

psy·cho·an·a·lyse or **psy·cho·an·a·lyze** (sye·coh·AN·uh·lize) *v.* **-lys·es** or **-lyz·es, -lysed** or

-lyzed, -lys·es or **-lyz·ing** treat by psychoanalysis.

psy·cho·a·nal·y·sis (SYE·coh·uh·NAL·uh·sis) *n.* the probing of a person's repressed desires, fears, and anxieties for treating mental and emotional disorders.
— **psy·cho·a·lyst** (sye·coh·AN·uh·list) *n.;*
— **psy·cho·an·a·lyt·ic** (-an·uh·LIT·ic) or **psy·cho·an·a·lyt·i·cal** *adj.*
— **psy·cho·an·a·lyt·i·cal·ly** *adv.*

psy·cho·bab·ble (SYE·coh·bab·ul) *n.* the jargon used by psychologists.

psy·cho·chem·i·cal (sye·coh·KEM·uh·cul) *n.* a psychoactive chemical such as LSD or nerve gas; also *adj.*

psy·cho·dra·ma (sye·coh·DRAH·muh) *n.* a form of group mental therapy in which patients act out problem situations in order to understand and face them.

psy·cho·gen·ic (sye·coh·JEN·ic) *adj.* caused by mental or emotional conflicts; originating in the mind.

psy·chol·o·gy (sye·COL·uh·jee) *n.* **-gies 1** the science of mental processes and behaviour of people and animals: *abnormal, child, clinical, educational psychology.* **2** the way a person or group behaves: *group psychology; mob psychology; Teachers have to use psychology* (*Informal for* understanding of people) *when dealing with students.* — **psy·chol·o·gist** *n.*
— **psy·cho·log·i·cal** (sye·cuh·LOJ·uh·cul) *adj.*

psy·cho·path (SYE·coh·path) *n.* a mentally ill person.
— **psy·cho·path·ic** (-PATH·ic) *adj.*

psy·cho·sis (sye·COH·sis) *n., pl.* **-ses** (-seez) a major mental disorder, either functional, as schizophrenia, or with an organic cause such as brain damage.

psy·cho·so·mat·ic (SYE·cuh·soh·MAT·ic) *adj.* of a physical disorder, involving both the mind and the body, as certain stomach ulcers, high blood pressure, etc.

psy·cho·ther·a·py (sye·coh·THER·uh·pee) *n.* treatment of mental and emotional disorders by psychological rather than physical means. — **psy·cho·ther·a·pist** *n.*

psy·chot·ic (sye·COT·ic) *n. & adj.* (a person) affected by a psychosis.

Ptol·e·ma·ic (tol·uh·MAY·ic) *adj.* having to do with Claudius Ptolemy, an ancient Greek astronomer: *In the Ptolemaic system, the Earth was the centre of the universe.*

pub *n. Brit. Informal.* a licensed tavern or bar.

pu·ber·ty (PEW·bur·tee) *n.* the age at which one is capable of sexual reproduction: *Girls usually reach puberty before boys.*

pu·bic (PEW·bic) *adj.* of the genital region.

pub·lic *adj.* **1** having to do with the people as a whole: *the public interest; public knowledge, morals; a survey of public opinion; a public cause, park, place; a public* (= nonprofit) *broadcasting system.* **2** civic or governmental: *public assistance (to the needy); public domain, health, official, service; a **public defender*** (= lawyer assigned to defend poor people at public expense); *Canada Day, Thanksgiving, and such paid*

public holidays; a charge of **public mischief** (= intentionally misleading a police officer). **3** not private; well-known: *a public figure; his public life.* — *n.* the people or a section of it: *the reading public, travelling public, and other publics; A private company* **goes public** *(and sells shares on the stock exchange); a crime committed* **in public** (= publicly). — **pub·lic·ly** *adv.*

pub·li·ca·tion (pub·luh·CAY·shun) *n.* **1** something published: *an official publication of the government.* **2** the process of publishing, including printing and distribution: *to begin, start, suspend publication.*

pub·li·cist (PUB·luh·sist) *n.* one who publicizes; press agent.

pub·li·ci·ty (pub·LIS·uh·tee) *n.* **1** public notice and the getting of it: *to avoid, gain, give, provide, receive, seek, shun publicity; She launched her campaign in a blaze of publicity; wide publicity.* **2** articles, announcements, etc. used in the process: *Bad publicity doesn't help the box office.*

pub·li·cize (PUB·luh·size) *v.* **-ciz·es, -cized, -ciz·ing** give publicity to a person or thing.

public relations *n. pl.* [takes sing. v.] the promotion of a favourable public image by means of publicity: *Many prefer "public information officer" to public relations officer as a job title.*

public school *n.* in Canada and the U.S., a free school supported by taxes.

public-spirited (pub·lic·SPEER·uh·tid) *adj.* having the good of the public as one's concern.

public television *n.* noncommercial TV for public information and instruction.

pub·lish *v.* make known publicly, esp. print and distribute something written or drawn, as books, art, and music, to the public. — **pub·lish·er** *n.*

puck *n.* **1** the disk used in hockey. **2** a mischievous spirit, like Puck in Shakespeare's "Midsummer Night's Dream." — **puck·ish** *adj.*

puck·er *v.* draw into folds or wrinkles: *the puckered stripes of seersucker; She puckered up* (= contracted the lips) *and blew a kiss our way.*

pud·ding (POOD·ing, short "OO") *n.* a soft, thick, sweet, cooked dessert as "rice pudding" or a baked one, as "plum pudding."

pud·dle (PUD·ul) *n.* **1** a small pool of liquid, usually of muddy water. **2** a pasty mixture of clay and sand for waterproofing; *v.:* *to puddle* (= stop) *up a hole.*

pudg·y (PUJ·ee) *adj.* **pudg·i·er, -i·est** fat or thickset: *pudgy fingers; People on the pudgy side need to go on a diet.*

pueb·lo (PWEB·loh) *n.* **-los 1** an Indian village of southwestern United States, consisting of compactly built, terraced adobe houses. **2** one of these houses.

pu·er·ile (PYOO·uh·rul) *adj.* childish or silly. — **pu·er·il·i·ty** (-RIL·uh·tee) *n.* **-ties:** *name-calling and such puerilities.*

puff *n.* **1** a short, quick blast or draw of air, smoke, or other gas: *puffs of steam from an iron; a puff of breath;*

a statement punctuated by puffs on his pipe. **2** a swelling, as if full of air, or something air-filled or fluffy: *hair done in puffs; cream puffs and such* **puff pastry;** *a powder puff* (= pad or ball). **3** overblown praise: *The review was a puff for the book.* — *v.* **1** move or come in puffs: *smoke puffing out from chimneys; She puffed out the candles one by one; He puffs away at his cigar when thinking hard; She came in huffing and puffing for air.* **2** swell with air: *a trumpeter with his cheeks puffed out; a young hero all puffed up with pride.* **3** praise: *an ad puffing a product to the skies.* — **puf·fer·y** (PUF·uh·ree) *n.*

puf·fy *adj.* **puf·fi·er, puf·fi·est** swollen: *a boxer's face puffy with bruises.* — **puff·i·ness** *n.*

pug *n.* **1** a small dog with a short turned-up nose and a tail curled up over its back. **2** a nose like a pug's. **3** [short form] pugilist or boxer.

pu·gil·ist (PEW·juh·list) *n.* boxer. — **pu·gil·ism** (-liz·um) *n.;* **pu·gil·is·tic** (-LIS·tic) *adj.*

pug·na·cious (pug·NAY·shus) *adj.* fond of fighting: *the pugnacious offspring of a quarrelsome family.* — **pug·na·cious·ly** *adv.* — **pug·nac·i·ty** (-NAS·uh·tee) *n.*

pug-nosed *adj.* having an upturned nose like a pug's.

pule *v.* **pules, puled, pul·ing** cry feebly; whine.

pull *v.* **1** use force to get action in the direction of the force; opposite of PUSH: *Don't pull that door, push it; She pulled my hair; a child pulling at her mother's sleeve; Pull your horse back; Let's pull this sled up the hill; Please pull the drapes (closed) and lock the door; The boat is leaking, pull for* (= row toward) *the shore.* **2** use or suffer force in various ways: *A dentist pulls* (= extracts) *teeth; She's pulling* (= plucking) *weeds in the garden; The cat pulled the paper to shreds; a toy pulled apart by kids; I pulled* (= sprained) *a muscle in my leg; He pulls* (= sucks) *on his pipe while thinking.* **3** move: *She stepped on the gas and pulled ahead of the other cars; Trains pull into the station and pull out of it; The officer asked the speeder to pull over to the curb; A car pulls up at a stoplight; The ball pulled to the left and missed the pins.* — **pull for** support: *Let's pull for the winning team.* — **pull off** accomplish: *That was a neat trick he pulled off.* — **pull oneself together** compose oneself: *He pulls himself together in no time after each defeat.* — **pull through** *Informal.* **1** recover: *All those taken to hospital pulled through within a week.* **2** get through: *Somehow, we managed to pull through the horrendous week.* — **pull up** reprimand: *He was pulled up for being late.* — *n.* a pulling, its force, or what is pulled: *the pull of gravity; It was a hard pull to the top of the hill; a bell pull* (= handle to pull the bell by); *a long pull* (= drink) *at the bottle; You need some pull* (= influence) *to get that job.*

pull date *n.* the date stamped on perishable goods after which they are not to be sold.

pul·let (PULL·it) *n.* a young hen.

pul·ley (PULL·ee) *n.* **pul·leys** a wheel with a grooved rim for driving a belt that transmits power or for running a rope for raising weights.

pull·out *n.* **1** a withdrawal, as of troops. **2** something to be pulled out, as a magazine insert.

pull·o·ver (pull·OH·vur) *n.* a sweater or shirt that is put on by being pulled over the head.

pulp *n.* **1** a soft moist mass, as the juicy part of a fruit, the soft tissue inside a tooth, the ground mixture of pulpwood, rag, etc. from which paper is made, etc. **2** a cheap or sensationalistic book or magazine, printed on inferior paper made from wood pulp. — **pulp·y** *adj.*

pul·pit (POOL·pit, short "OO") *n.* **1** an enclosed raised structure set up in church for preaching from. **2** the clergy or ministry.

pul·sate (PUL·sate) *v.* **-sates, -sat·ed, -sat·ing** beat or throb with a regular rhythm, as the heart or pulse does. — **pul·sa·tion** (pul·SAY·shun) *n.*

pulse *n.* **1** a regular beat, as of the heart pumping blood which is felt in the arteries, esp. at the wrist: *an erratic, irregular, weak pulse.* **2** an indication of life or feeling: *a Gallup poll reflecting the pulse of the nation.* — *v.* **puls·es, pulsed, puls·ing** **1** beat or throb: *Life pulses in our veins.* **2** move as if with a pulse: *Traffic pulses through a city during rush hour.*

pul·ver·ize (PUL·vuh·rize) *v.* **-iz·es, -ized, -iz·ing** reduce to or become powder. — **pul·ver·i·za·tion** (-ruh·ZAY·shun) *n.*

pum·mel (PUM·ul) *v.* **pum·mels, pum·melled** or **pum·meled, pum·mel·ling** or **pum·mel·ing** pound on repeatedly, esp. with the fists.

pump *n.* **1** a machine for forcing fluids in or out of places, esp. by up-and-down action, as of a lever: *a gasoline pump; heat pump; stomach pump; sump pump; a pump-action rifle.* **2** a low-cut slip-on shoe for formal evening wear. — *v.* use a pump or work up and down like a pump: *The flooded basement had to be pumped out; We pumped it dry; to pump up a bicycle tire; a teacher pumping knowledge into pupils; The reporters pumped (Informal for tried to get information out of) Yves, but he would only say "No comment"; a politician kissing babies and pumping (= shaking) hands; The terrorists pumped (= shot) three bullets into him; Lasers are pumped (= excited for energy radiation) by light, radio waves, electricity, etc.*

pump·kin (PUM·kin) *n.* a large, round, orange-yellow, edible gourdlike fruit.

pumpkin head *n.* a dolt.

pump-priming *n.* government expenditure on public works, relief, etc. in order to stimulate business and employment during a recession.

pun *n. & v.* **puns, punned, pun·ning** play on words, as "Mr. Dole is doleful news." — **pun·ner** or **pun·ster** *n.*

punch *v.* **1** strike with the fist: *The bully punched him on the nose; A boxer practises on a suspended punching bag.* **2** cut, stamp, etc. with a quick thrust: *A ticket is inspected and punched; Workers punch in and punch out of a factory by thrusting a timecard into a time clock; Coded data is punched on a punch card in a key-punch machine.* — *n.* **1** a blow or a thrust of the fist: *a boxer's "one-two punch."* **2** a punching device: *a three-hole paper punch.* **3** *Informal.* vigour or force: *a pep talk full of punch; the punch line of a joke designed to get a laugh at the end of a story.* **4** a sweetened drink of juices, wines, liquors, etc. usually mixed in a large **punch bowl** and ladled out, as at a party. — **beat someone to the punch** *Informal.* do something before someone else does it, like hitting a boxing opponent before he hits you. — **pull one's punches** *Informal.* be ineffective on purpose.

punch-drunk *adj.* dazed by blows.

punch·y *adj.* **punch·i·er, -i·est** having vigour or force: *a punchy comment.*

punc·til·i·o (punc·TIL·ee·oh) *n.* **-os** a fine point of conduct or ceremony. — **punc·til·i·ous** (-ee·us) *adj.*: *a diplomat's punctilious attention to protocol.*

punc·tu·al (PUNK·choo·ul) *adj.* on time, esp. habitually: *He's always punctual in arriving at work.* — **punc·tu·al·ly** *adv.* — **punc·tu·al·i·ty** (-AL·uh·tee) *n.*

punc·tu·ate (PUNK·choo·ate) *v.* **-ates, -at·ed, -at·ing** show pauses, emphases, etc., esp. in written language, using **punctuation marks** such as the comma, question mark, and exclamation point: *a speech punctuated (= interrupted) by frequent cheers.* — **punc·tu·a·tion** (-AY·shun) *n.*

punc·ture (PUNK·chur) *n. & v.* **-tures, -tured, -tur·ing** (make) a tiny hole, esp. with or as if with a point: *to repair a punctured tire; punctured pride.*

pun·dit *n.* **1** a learned person. **2** a supposed authority: *the weather pundits of Channel 9.*

pun·gent (PUN·junt) *adj.* **1** sharp to the taste and smell: *Horse radish is pungent.* **2** keen or biting: *pungent satire.* — **pun·gent·ly** *adv.* — **pun·gen·cy** (-see) *n.*

Pu·nic (PYOO·nic) *adj.* of ancient Carthage: *"Punic faith" meant treachery to Romans.*

pun·ish *v.* cause suffering or discomfort, usually for some offence; penalize: *Offenders are punished; Thievery used to be punished by hanging; The boxer continued to punish (= hurt) his fallen opponent; It was a punishing (= exhausting) climb to the top.* — **pun·ish·a·ble** (-uh·bul) *adj.*

pun·ish·ment (PUN·ish·munt) *n.* a punishing: *The punishment should fit the crime; to escape, impose, mete out, suffer punishment; cruel and unusual punishment; capital, corporal, summary punishment; There's a limit to the punishment one can take; A taxicab gets a lot of punishment (Informal for* rough use).

pu·ni·tive (PYOO·nuh·tiv) *adj.* 1 related to punishment: *punitive damages awarded against wilful wrongdoers.* 2 harsh: *punitive action, laws.* — **pu·ni·tive·ly** *adv.*

punk *n.* 1 a slow-burning, spongy preparation of dried fungi or decayed wood used as tinder. 2 *Slang.* a hoodlum; also, an inexperienced youngster, as a child hobo. — *adj. Slang.* of poor quality: *the punkest grub he ever ate.*

punk rock *n.* rock'n'roll of the late 1970s characterized by rowdy costumes, language, and performing style.

punk·y *adj. Slang.* having to do with punks or hoodlums: *a punky hairdo with flashes of colour in it.*

pun·ster (PUN·stur) *n.* one fond of making puns.

punt *n.* 1 a flat-bottomed boat propelled with a long pole. 2 a kick given to a football dropped from one's hands and before it touches the ground. — *v.* 1 travel by, convey by, or propel a punt boat. 2 give a punt kick to a football.

pu·ny (PEW·nee) *adj.* -ni·er, -ni·est inferior in size, strength, or importance; petty. — **pu·ni·ness** *n.*

pup *n.* 1 a young dog, fox, wolf, etc. 2 a young seal, shark, or whale.

pu·pa (PEW·puh) *n., pl.* -pae (-pee) or -pas an insect in its middle stage of development, between larva and adult, when it is encased in a cocoon; **pu·pal** (-pul) *adj.*

pu·pil (PEW·pul) *n.* 1 a young student, esp. one under a teacher's personal supervision; hence, follower. 2 the black, circular portion inside the iris of the eye. — **pu·pil·lar·y** (-puh·lair·ee) *adj.*

pup·pet (PUP·it) *n.* a doll-like, hand-controlled figure of a person or animal used in a **puppet show.** — **pup·pet·ry** (-it·ree) *n.* — **pup·pet·eer** (pup·uh·TEER) *n.*

pup·py (PUP·ee) *n.* **pup·pies** same as PUP.

puppy love *n.* juvenile love for one of the opposite sex.

pup tent *n.* a small, wedge-shaped shelter tent for one or two persons.

pur·blind (PUR·blined) *adj.* 1 partly blind; dimsighted. 2 obtuse.

pur·chase (PUR·chus) *v.* -chas·es, -chased, -chas·ing *Formal.* buy: *to purchase aircraft, computers, real estate, stocks; The* **purchasing power** *of the dollar goes down with rising prices.* — *n.* a purchasing or thing purchased: *to make a purchase; Where are my purchases? major purchases such as a house, car, and appliances.*

pure (PYOOR) *adj.* 1 pur·er, pur·est free from taint, defects, errors, etc.; unmixed: *pure as snow; "the pure in heart"; pure English; a pure breed.* 2 sheer or absolute: *It happened by pure accident; That's pure nonsense; nonsense pure and simple.* 3 abstract or

theoretical: *pure mathematics.* — **pure·ly** *adv.*

pure·blood *n.* an individual of unmixed ancestry; *adj.: a pureblood Indian.* Also **pure-blooded** *adj.*

pure·bred *n.* an animal of unmixed breed: *purebred livestock.*

pur·ga·tion (pur·GAY·shun) *n.* the act of purging: *the purgation of the soul.*

pur·ga·tive (PUR·guh·tiv) *n. & adj.* a purging agent, as a cathartic: *the purgative effect of castor oil.*

pur·ga·to·ry (PUR·guh·tor·ee) *n.* -ries in Roman Catholic theology, a state of temporary punishment that purifies souls for entry into heaven.

purge (PURJ) *v.* **purg·es, purged, purg·ing** clear or cleanse by getting rid of something undesired: *souls purged of sin; a drug that purges the bowels; to purge away dross from metal; a political party purged of undesirable elements.* — *n.* a purging or something that purges: *They conducted or carried out a sweeping purge of the party; Stalin's purges of the 1930s.*

pu·ri·fy (PYOOR·uh·fye) *v.* -fies, -fied, -fy·ing make or become pure: *to purify water for drinking;* **pu·ri·fi·er** *n.* — **pu·ri·fi·ca·tion** (-fuh·CAY·shun) *n.*

pur·ism (PYOOR·iz·um) *n.* 1 the too strict adherence to what is traditionally correct in language matters without regard for the changing nature of vocabulary, usage, etc. 2 an instance of this, as saying "It is I" instead of "It is me" or (core·RECT) for (cuh·RECT). — **pur·ist** *n.* — **pu·ris·tic** (pyoor·IS·tic) *adj.*

pu·ri·tan (PYOOR·uh·tun) *n.* one who is very strict in matters of religion or morals, as the Puritan group of the Church of England in the 16th and 17th centuries. — **pu·ri·tan·ism** or **Pu·ri·tan·ism** *n.* — **pu·ri·tan·i·cal** (-TAN·uh·cul) *adj.*

pu·ri·ty (PYOOR·uh·tee) *n.* the quality or state of being pure; pureness; freedom from dirt, evil, or foreign elements: *the purity of our water; the purity of the Gold Maple Leaf coin; apartheid laws aimed at racial purity; the ideological purity of communist thought; the tonal purity of her voice.*

pur·loin (pur·LOIN) *v. Formal.* steal: *a publisher of purloined manuscripts.*

pur·ple (PUR·pul) *n.* crimson colour, indicative of high rank: *"clothed in purple and fine linen"; a bishop raised* **to the purple** (= created cardinal). — *adj.* 1 bluish red: *He was purple with rage.* 2 ornate or gaudy in style: *He writes a dull prose except for the occasional* **purple patch** *or* **passage.** 3 *Slang.* off-colour: *a purple joke.* — **pur·plish** *adj.*

pur·port (pur·PORT) *v.* intend or mean supposedly: *The offer was purported to be a generous one; The skin cream purports (= claims) to erase wrinkles.* — *n.* (PUR·port) general meaning or intent; gist: *the purport of the message.* — **pur·port·ed·ly** (pur·POR·tid·lee) *adv.*

pur·pose (PUR·pus) *n.* intention, esp. with determination: *the purpose of our visit; to accomplish,*

achieve, fulfil, serve a purpose; A small car will do **for all practical purposes** (= in reality); *He ignored the letter* **on purpose** (= deliberately) *to snub him; remarks quite* **to the purpose** (= pertinent).
— *v.* **-pos·es, -posed, -pos·ing** intend: *She purposed to stay awake but fell asleep.*
— **pur·pose·ful** *adj.*; **pur·pose·ful·ly** *adv.*

pur·pose·ly (PUR·pus·lee) *adv.* on purpose.

purr *n.* the low murmuring sound of a contented cat.
— *v.* **purrs, purred, pur·ring** make a purr.

purse *n.* **1** a small bag, originally one with drawstrings. **2** a woman's handbag: *Beware of pickpockets and purse-snatchers on the street.* **3** amount of money; means: *The fraud artist retired with a poor pension but a well-lined purse; a prize fight with a $1 million purse* (= stake); *He was presented with a gold watch and a purse* (= gift of money); *a* **purse-proud** *man (who is proud of his money) with no education to boast of; Who controls his* **purse-strings** (= finances)?
— *v.* **purs·es, pursed, purs·ing** pucker: *She pursed her lips in disapproval.*

purs·er *n.* an official in charge of money matters on a ship or of cabin service on an airliner.

pur·su·ance (pur·SUE·unce) *n. Formal.* a carrying out: *a letter written* **in pursuance of** *a client's wishes.*
— **pur·su·ant** (-unt) *adj.*: *goods shipped* **pursuant to** (= according to) *a customer's instructions.*

pur·sue (pur·SUE) *v.* **-sues, -sued, -su·ing 1** follow someone in order to catch up: *police pursuing a getaway car; She was pursued by reporters everywhere she went.* **2** have as an aim, esp. to accomplish something: *She's pursuing her studies at the university; She'll pursue a career in politics.* — **pur·su·er** *n.*

pur·suit (pur·SUIT) *n.* **1** a pursuing or chase: *our pursuit of happiness; The police crossed the border* **in hot pursuit** *of the fleeing car.* **2** occupation or hobby: *His many pursuits include fishing.*

pur·vey·or (pur·VAY·ur) *n.* supplier: *Racists are purveyors of hate; The TV networks are purveyors of culture to or for the masses.*

pur·view *n.* range or scope of authority or perception.

pus *n.* a thick, yellow discharge from an infected body part.

push (short "OO") *v.* **1** press against a person or thing so as to move forward: *You pull that door open and push it shut; to push for* (= urge) *a strike, the right to strike; Grandpa is* **pushing** (= close to) *90; Everyone hates being* **pushed around** (= harassed). **2** force one's way: *to push into an overcrowded bus; to push through a crowd.* **3** move: *Let's push on till we reach home; At the sound of the alarm, people pushed towards the exits.* **4** *Informal.* sell or promote the sale of something: *Get the mayor to push the lottery; Pushing drugs is illegal.*
— *n.* a pushing: *She's a self-starter who never needs a push; A good sales rep has push* (= drive) *but is not pushy.* — **push·er** *n.*

push button *n.* a button that is pushed to operate something: *an elevator operated by push buttons;* **adj.**: *a push-button telephone; Robots would control push-button warfare.*

push·cart *n.* a cart that is pushed, as for supermarket shopping.

push·o·ver (PUSH·oh·vur) *n. Informal.* **1** one easy to impose upon: *He's a pushover for a loan any time.* **2** an easy job; cinch.

push-up *n.* an exercise done by raising and lowering the body held stiffly extended in a prone position.

push·y (PUSH·ee, short "OO") *adj.* **push·i·er, -i·est** *Informal.* unpleasantly aggressive.

puss (short "OO") *n.* **puss·es** *Informal.* **1** a cat; also **puss·y, puss·ies.** **2** face: *He socked him in the puss.*

pus·sy (PUSS·ee) *adj.* like or containing pus.

puss·y·cat (POOS·ee·cat, short "OO") *n.* **1** a cat; pussy. **2** an agreeable or quiet-going person: *He has an aggressive style, but is really a pussycat at heart.*

puss·y·foot (POOS·ee·foot) *v. Informal.* be overly cautious and noncommittal: *to pussyfoot around an issue like bilingualism.*

put (POOT, short "OO") *v.* **puts, put, put·ting 1** to place, esp. move something onto a position: *to put food on the table; to put sugar in your coffee.* **2** make someone or something be in a certain way; set: *Children are put to bed; an idea difficult to put into words; to put one's affairs in order; to put words to music; to put someone to shame.* **3** (rhyme: "but") throw: *putting the shot (in shot put).*
— **put across** convey an idea successfully.
— **put down 1** crush: *to put down a revolt.* **2** write down: *You can put me down for a $10 contribution; Put down the main points in your notes.* **3** *Informal.* snub or belittle.
— **put in** *Informal.* **1** contribute: *She puts in a lot of work on holidays.* **2** apply: *He put in for a loan.*
— **put off 1** postpone: *She wanted to put off buying a new car, but I advised her not to put it off.* **2** turn one away: *The high prices of cars put me off.*
— **put on 1** apply: *The work is putting too much strain on my nerves.* **2** *Informal.* tease: *You're putting me on!*
— **put out 1** in baseball, retire a batter or runner. **2** begin a voyage: *We put out to sea in a boat.* **3** offend: *Dina was put out by his bad manners.*
— **put over** pass something off on someone by trickery: *The class put one over on the teacher so she thought it was a Friday.*
— **put paid to** wipe out, like an account stamped "paid."
— **put up**: *a house put up* (= offered) *for sale; Why don't you put up* (= justify yourself or get ready to fight) *or shut up? He put up a good fight* (= fought well); *She'll put you up* (= lodge you) *for the night; Who put him up to* (= made him do) *this? an unsociable character difficult to put up with* (= bear or tolerate).
— **put upon** impose upon.
— *n.* (rhyme: "but") a throw: *shot put.*
— *adj. Informal.* in place: *Stay put till I return.*

pu·ta·tive (PYOO·tuh·tiv) *adj.* supposed: *an orphan child's putative father.*

put·down *n. Informal.* an act or statement that belittles, criticizes, etc.

put-on *n. Informal.* a pretence or hoax.

605

put-out *n.* of a batter or runner in baseball, a being retired.

pu·tre·fy (PYOO·truh·fye) *v.* **-fies, -fied, -fy·ing** be or make putrid or rotten.
— **pu·tre·fac·tion** (-FAC·shun) *n.*

pu·trid (PYOO·trid) *adj.* **1** rotting or decayed: *the putrid smell of putrid meat.* **2** corrupt or foul: *the putrid air of a porn shop.* — **pu·trid·ness** *n.*

putt *v.* strike a golf ball across the putting green to try to drop it into the hole. — **putt·er** *n.*

put·ter (PUT·ur) *v.* busy oneself aimlessly *in* or *around* something: *to putter around the garden.*

put-up *adj. Informal.* prearranged in a sly or crafty manner: *a put-up job.*

puz·zle (PUZ·ul) *v.* **puz·zles, puz·zled, puz·zling** bewilder: *a stranger puzzled by local customs; He's good at puzzling out* (= solving) *conundrums; She puzzled over* (= tried to think of) *a solution all night.*
— *n.* a problem or task that puzzles or is designed to puzzle: *a crossword puzzle; jigsaw puzzle; The disappearance of the child remained a puzzle to the police; The driver was in a puzzle when he reached the crossroads.* — **puz·zle·ment** (-munt) *n.* — **puz·zler** *n.*

pyg·my (PIG·mee) *n.* **-mies** a person or thing of small stature like a **Pygmy**, a Negroid African people of short stature.
— *adj.* dwarfish: *A pygmy antelope is only 25.4 cm (10 in) tall; The pygmy owl is about 17.8 cm (7 in) long.*

py·ja·mas (puh·JAM·uz) *n. pl. Brit.* same as PAJAMAS.

py·lon (PYE·lon, -lun) *n.* **1** a gateway of an ancient Egyptian temple, esp. one consisting of two pyramidal towers. **2** a framework of steel used to support overhead cables. **3** a post, tower, or conical marker for guiding air or road traffic. **4** a supporting structure, as of an airplane engine.

pyr·a·mid (PEER·uh·mid) *n.* **1** a solid figure with a polygon base and sloping sides that meet at the top. **2** any of the huge structures with a square base and triangular sides meeting at the top built in ancient Egypt for royal tombs. **3** any structure or scheme resembling a pyramid, often an inverted pyramid.
— *adj.:* *a pyramid-fire cooking arrangement at a camp; a pyramid telephone system for passing on messages; a **pyramid scheme** for raising money, as by chain letters.*
— *v.* put in the form of a pyramid; hence, increase or raise: *a financial empire built by the pyramiding of subsidiaries within a holding company; Profits may be pyramided by speculative buying or selling of stock.*
— **py·ram·i·dal** (puh·RAM·uh·dul) *adj.:* *a pyramidal army tent.*

pyre *n.* a woodpile for burning a dead body: *a funeral pyre.*

py·ro·tech·nics (pye·roh·TEK·nics) *n. pl.* **1** fireworks. **2** any brilliant display, as of rhetoric or emotion.
— **py·ro·tech·nic** or **py·ro·tech·ni·cal** *adj.*

Pyr·rhic (PEER·ic) *adj.* won at heavy cost, esp. of lives: *a Pyrrhic victory.*

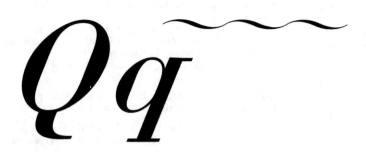

Q or **q** (CUE) *n.* **Q's** or **q's** the 17th letter of the English alphabet.

q.t. or **Q.T.** *Slang.* quiet.
— **on the q.t.** quietly or confidentially.

qua (QUAH, QUAY) *adv.* in the capacity of; as: *Children qua children have a right to be taken care of.*

quack (QUAK) *n.* **1** a duck's cry; also *v.* **2** one who pretends to have medical skills. **3** any charlatan.
— **quack·er·y** *n.* **-er·ies:** *arthritic victims of quackeries.*

quad (QUOD) *n.* [short form] quadrangle or quadruplet.

quad·ran·gle (QUOD·rang·gul) *n.* **1** a flat figure with four sides and four angles. **2** such a four-sided area surrounded by buildings.
— **quad·ran·gu·lar** (quod·RANG·gyuh·lur) *adj.*

quad·rant (QUOD·runt) *n.* **1** one quarter of a circle or its circumference; 90-degree arc. **2** an instrument for measuring angles to determine altitudes.

quad·ren·ni·um (quod·REN·ee·um) *n.* **-ren·ni·ums** or **-ren·ni·a** (-ee·uh) a period of four years.
— **quad·ren·ni·al** (-ee·ul) *adj.*

quad·ri·ple·gi·a (quod·ruh·PLEE·jee·uh) *n.* paralysis from the neck down, affecting all four limbs.
— **quad·ri·ple·gic** (-PLEE·jic, -PLEJ·ic) *n. & adj.*

quad·ru·ped (QUOD·ruh·ped) *adj. & n.* (four-footed) animal.

quad·ru·ple (QUOD·ruh·pul, quod·ROO·pul) *v.* **-ples, -pled, -pling** multiply by four.
— *adj.* **1** multiplied by four: *a quadruple amount; in quadruple time (with four beats per measure).* **2** containing four parts: *a quadruple alliance.*

quad·ru·plet (QUOD·ruh·plit) *n.* **1** one of four born at a single birth. **2** a group of four: *a quadruplet of musical notes.*

quad·ru·pli·cate (quod·ROO·pluh·kit) *adj.* multiplied by four: *Prepare the invoice in quadruplicate* (= in four copies).

quaff (QUOF, QUAF) *v.* drink with zest.
— *n.* drink: *a hearty quaff of ale.*

quag·mire (QUAG·mire) *n.* damp ground that yields underfoot; bog.

quail *n.* a game bird of the grouse and partridge families, esp. the "bobwhite."
— *v.* lose courage and shrink back in fear: *I quail at the thought of going through that ordeal again; The lion quailed under its trainer's whip.*

quaint *adj.* old-fashioned or odd in an interesting or unusual way: *a quaint refrain; his quaint style of writing.*

quake *v.* **quakes, quaked, quak·ing** shake violently, usually from fear or shock: *He quaked with fright; His hands quaked with nervousness; the **quaking** aspen.*
— *n.* a shaking or shivering, esp. an earthquake.
— **quak·y** (QUAY·kee) *adj.*

Quak·er (QUAY·kur) *n.* [not used by members] a member of the religious group called the Society of Friends; Friend.

qual·i·fi·ca·tion (QUOL·uh·fuh·CAY·shun) *n.* **1** a condition: *an answer accepted without qualification.* **2** an accomplishment or skill: *a necessary qualification for the job; a principal with impressive qualifications and experience for her job.*

qual·i·fy (QUOL·uh·fye) *v.* **-fies, -fied, -fy·ing 1** make suitable or competent for an occupation, calling, task, etc.: *Our team has qualified for the finals; a well-qualified applicant.* **2** limit or modify: *Adjectives qualify nouns.* **3** moderate or soften: *to qualify a scolding with a smile.* — **qual·i·fi·er** *n.*

qual·i·ty (QUOL·uh·tee) *n.* **-ties 1** essential nature or characteristic feature: *the qualities of a good student.* **2** worth or excellence: *the fine quality of his singing; fabric of poor quality; a bad movie with few redeeming qualities; a woman of quality; The **quality of life** in a place is measured in terms of crime, pollution, health* *care, living expenses, climate, etc.;* **adj.***: quality control of a manufactured product by sampling and testing; quality ice cream (of high quality); a quality newspaper.*

qualm (QUAHM) *n.* 1 a temporary feeling of sickness or faintness. 2 a feeling of doubt or uneasiness about the rightness of an action: *She had no qualms about letting her child walk home alone.*
— **qualm·ish** *adj.: He felt qualmish as he was about to parachute.*

quan·da·ry (QUON·duh·ree, -dree) *n.* -**ries** a state of uncertainty and hesitation: *She was placed in a quandary as a result of two appointments for the same hour.*

quan·ti·fy (QUON·tuh·fye) *v.* -**fies**, -**fied**, -**fy·ing** determine or indicate the quantity of something: *It's impossible to quantify the value of a good education.*

quan·ti·ty (QUON·tuh·tee) *n.* -**ties** amount or number: *a small quantity of sugar; Stores buy goods* **in quantity** (= in bulk or in large amounts); *Our new teammate is an* **unknown quantity** (= one not yet tried out).

quan·tum (QUON·tum) *n.,* *pl.* -**ta** (-tuh) a specific quantity, esp. one of the quanta, or basic amounts, in which energy is given out or absorbed by a substance, not in continuous waves: *Within an atom, electrons make* **quantum jumps** *or* **leaps** *as they change orbits absorbing or giving off energy; The discovery of the wheel was a quantum leap in human civilization.*

quar·an·tine (QUOR·un·teen) *n.* 1 the detaining of ships, people, animals, etc. in isolation to prevent disease from spreading. 2 the place or time in which they are so held.
— *v.* -**tines**, -**tined**, -**tin·ing** put in quarantine: *a ship quarantined for 40 days at a port of entry.*

quar·rel (QUOR·ul) *n.* 1 an angry dispute: *a bitter, domestic, family quarrel; to pick a quarrel with someone; He had no quarrels with his neighbours.* 2 cause for complaint: *I have no quarrel with the money you are offering me, but I don't like the job.*
— *v.* **quar·rels**, **quar·relled** or **quar·reled**, **quar·rel·ling** or **quar·rel·ing** 1 disagree: *I must quarrel with your decision.* 2 dispute angrily: *to quarrel with a neighbour about* or *over the location of a fence.*

quar·rel·some (QUOR·ul·sum) *adj.* given to quarrelling: *the quarrelsome Donald Duck; a quarrelsome labour union; He is touchy and quarrelsome; Kay is in a quarrelsome mood.*

quar·ry (QUOR·ee) *n.* **quar·ries** 1 an object of pursuit, esp. a hunted animal: *to stalk one's quarry.* 2 a place where rock or limestone is dug from the earth: *an abandoned quarry.*

quart (QUORT) *n.* 1 one fourth of a gallon; two pints or 1.14 litres. 2 a dry measure equalling 1/8 peck.

quar·ter (QUOR·tur) *n.* 1 a fourth part, as of an hour (15 minutes), a year (3 months), a dollar (25 cents or the coin), an animal's carcass (one leg and adjacent parts), etc.: *The time is a quarter to six* (= 5:45); *at a quarter past six* (= 6:15). 2 a region or place; hence, a special district: *the Latin Quarter of Paris.* 3 mercy or compassion: *They give* or *show no quarter to the enemy.*
— **quarters** *pl.* 1 accommodation: *bachelor quarters; married quarters; military quarters; officers' quarters.*

2 source: *news received from reliable quarters.*
— **at close quarters** close together: *Boxers fight at close quarters.*
— *v.* 1 divide into four: *to quarter an apple.* 2 provide with shelter: *Horses are quartered in the stables; soldiers quartered in barracks.* 3 assign troops to a lodging place: *The troops were quartered on the local population.*

quar·ter·back (QUOR·tur·back) *n.* the football player who calls the signals and directs the team's play.

quar·ter·ly (QUOR·tur·lee) *n.* -**lies** a publication issued every three months. — *adj.* & *adv.: a quarterly journal; a report issued quarterly.*

quar·tet or **quar·tette** (quor·TET) *n.* 1 a piece of music for four instruments or people: *to play a string quartet.* 2 the group performing this. 3 any group of four.

quar·to (QUOR·toh) *n.* -**tos** 1 the page size, usually 9 x 12 in. (22.86 x 30.48 cm) resulting from folding one sheet into four leaves. 2 a book printed on such pages.

quartz (QUORTS) *n.* a hard mineral found in rocks and in crystalline form in amethyst: *The* **quartz crystal** *of a radio transmitter or electric clock vibrates with a natural frequency.*

qua·sar (QUAY·sar, -zar) *n.* any of a group of very distant, starlike objects that emit brilliant light and often powerful radio waves.

quash *v.* 1 crush or suppress: *to quash a rebellion.* 2 void legally: *a decision quashed by a higher court.*

qua·si (QUAY·sye, -zye; QUAH·see, -zee) *adj.* & *combining form.* resembling but not quite: *a quasi-humorous situation; to act in a quasi-judicial capacity; a quasi contract.*

quat·rain (KWAH·train) *n.* a stanza of four lines.

qua·ver (QUAY·vur) *v.* tremble or quiver: *His voice quavered with fright.*
— *n.* 1 a trembling or quivering; also, such a sound. 2 in music, an eighth note.

quay (KEE) *n.* wharf.

quea·sy (KWEE·zee) *adj.* -**si·er**, -**si·est** 1 nauseated: *a queasy stomach.* 2 uneasy or troublesome: *a queasy problem; I feel queasy about it.*
— **quea·si·ly** *adv.;* **quea·si·ness** *n.*

Quebec heater *n. Cdn.* a tall stove made in Quebec that heats by burning wood or coal.

Que·beck·er or **Que·bec·er** (kwi·BECK·ur) *n.* a person of or from Quebec, esp. an Anglophone.

Que·be·cois (cay·buh·KWAH) *n. sing.* & *pl. Cdn.* a French-speaking person of or from Quebec.
— *adj.* having to do with Quebec or the Quebecois: *Quebecois cuisine, culture, French, literature, music; a Quebecois flavour; Quebecois designers, poets, singers, writers.*

queen *n.* 1 a female sovereign: *Queen Elizabeth II; She was crowned queen in June 1953; the Queen's accession* or *succession to the throne in 1952.* 2 the wife or widow of a king: *the Queen Mother* or *Queen Mum (Informal).* 3 a woman or object noted for beauty, power, etc.: *a*

beauty queen; movie queen; drag queen (*Slang for* male dressed as a female); *Queen City* (= Toronto, Regina, Victoria, etc.). **4** a mature egg-laying ant, bee, etc. of a colony.
— *v.: The actress likes to* **queen it over** (= act like a queen toward) *her admirers.*
— **queen·ly** *adj.;* **queen·li·ness** *n.*

queen consort *n.* the wife of a reigning king.

queen mother *n.* the mother of a reigning monarch.

Queen's Counsel or **Q.C.** *n. Cdn.* an honorary title conferred by a government on a lawyer in recognition of services.

Queen's English *n.* English usage that is considered as standard or correct.

Queen's Highway *n. Cdn.* a highway maintained by a provincial government.

queen-size *adj.* approximately 60 × 80 in. (1.5 × 2 m): *a queen-size bed; queen-size sheets.*

queer *adj.* unusual or strange, esp. abnormal: *a queer idea; a queer sensation in the stomach.*
— *v. Slang.* spoil: *Doping queered his chances for an Olympic medal.*
— *n. & adj. Slang.* [offensive] homosexual.
— **queer·ly** *adv.;* **queer·ness** *n.*

quell *v.* put an end to; crush: *to quell a rebellion, uprising; to quell one's doubts, fears.*

quench *v.* cool suddenly, esp. something burning: *Steel is tempered by quenching it while red-hot; Water quenches thirst; The outburst quenched his fury.*

quer·u·lous (QUER·uh·lus, -yuh·lus) *adj.* complaining or fretful: *a querulous invalid.* — **quer·u·lous·ly** *adv.*

que·ry (KWEER·ee) *n.* **que·ries 1** question or inquiry. **2** a question mark, esp. one used to express doubt about an item; *v.: The proofreader queried the author's spelling.*

quest *n.* a search or expedition: *the prospector's quest for gold; our quest for happiness.*

ques·tion (KWES·chun) *n.* **1** a sentence or phrase asking for an answer from someone, as "Who is it?": *Send your questions in writing; to address, answer, bring up, field, pose a question; put a question to someone; to* **beg the question** (= take as true something that has to be proved); *a question-and-answer session; The question is* **academic** (= of no value); *a burning, crucial, hypothetical, leading, loaded, moot, rhetorical, relevant, thorny question; a question about or concerning capital punishment; He popped the question (of marriage) after dinner.* **2** doubt: *Age is not* **in question** *for this candidate; There's no question he's of age, but there is some question about his qualifications; His honesty is* **beyond** or **without question;** *The decision was called* **into question.** **3** subject of doubt, discussion, or dispute: *The chairman put the question to the vote; to clear up, resolve a question; It is* **out of the question** (= impossible).
— *v.* **1** ask someone a question or questions: *The reporter questioned the mayor about or on the allegation; Most of those questioned said "no"; The driver was stopped and questioned by the police; She didn't break down under their* **questioning.** **2** ask in a doubting manner: *Mother questioned us about the broken glass; I must question your claim.*
— **ques·tion·er** *n.*

ques·tion·a·ble (QUES·chun·uh·bul) *adj.* that raises questions of truth, goodness, honesty, value, etc.: *a questionable activity, assertion, assumption; questionable ethics; It's questionable whether he can be trusted; a man of questionable reputation.*
— **ques·tion·a·bly** (-blee) *adv.*

question mark *n.* the punctuation mark (?) put at the end of a written question; interrogation mark.

ques·tion·naire (kwes·chuh·NAIR) *n.* a list of questions on a particular subject, as for an opinion survey: *to draw up, fill out, formulate, send out a questionnaire.*

queue (CUE) *n.* **1** a braid of hair which hangs down the back. **2** a line of people waiting in order of arrival: *to form, join, jump the queue; to stand in a queue at a cashier's counter.*
— *v.* **queues, queued, queu·ing** form a line: *Eager fans queued up for tickets.*

quib·ble (QUIB·ul) *v.* **quib·bles, quib·bled, quib·bling** make petty distinctions, esp. in order to evade an issue: *It's no use quibbling with the tax department about or over a small payment.* — **quib·bler** *n.*

quiche (KEESH) *n.* a custard pie filled with cheese and often bacon, mushrooms, etc.

quick *adj.* fast or prompt, esp. in reacting to a stimulus; live and active: *a dog with a quick ear; a quick response to a call; The ambulance was quick to respond to our call; He is quick in math* (= in understanding math); *quick with figures;* **quick bread** *such as muffins and scones (baked quickly using baking powder, not yeast); a* **quick-fix** (*Informal for* fast and superficial) *solution; He's too* **quick-tempered** (= easily angered) *to control himself; a* **quick-witted** *retort (showing a sharp and alert mind).*
— *n.* **the quick 1** a sensitive point: *The child clipped her nails to the quick; Her criticism cut him to the quick* (= hurt his feelings). **2** [old use] living persons: *the quick and the dead.* — **quick·ly** *adv.;* **quick·ness** *n.*

quick·en (KWIK·un) *v.* make or become more active, alive, or fast: *Quicken your pace to catch up with him; The pulse quickens under fear; stories that quicken one's imagination; the quickening* (= movements) *felt in the womb as pregnancy advances.*

quick-freeze *v.* **-freez·es, -froze, -fro·zen, -freez·ing** freeze food rapidly in preparation for long-term storage at low temperatures.

quick·ie (KWIK·ee) *n. & adj. Slang.* (something) done or prepared in a hurry, as a cheap movie: *a quickie* (= wildcat) *strike.*

quick-lunch *n.* a place specializing in quickly prepared food; luncheonette.

quick·sand *n.* soft, wet sand that yields to pressure and sucks down heavy objects on its surface.

quick study *n.* one who is quick at learning or studying something new.

quick-tempered, quick-witted See QUICK.

quid *n.* 1 a piece of chewing tobacco. 2 *Brit. Slang.* a pound sterling; sovereign.

quid pro quo *n.* something expected or given as a return for something else; a consideration.

qui·es·cent (kwy·ES·unt) *adj.* inactive for a time; quiet: *A tourist town that is quiescent though not dormant during the winter.*

qui·et (KWY·ut) *adj.* without noise; calm or peaceful: *a man of quiet disposition; the quiet countryside; a quiet stream; decorated in quiet colours; the quiet diplomacy that characterizes Canada-U.S. relations.*
— *n.* the state of being quiet: *The teacher asked for absolute quiet; neighbours living in peace and quiet; The tragedy shattered the quiet of the neighbourhood.*
— *v.* make quiet: *He quieted the frightened animals; The class quieted down when the teacher arrived.*
— **quiet·ly** *adv.*; **quiet·ness** *n.*

qui·e·tude (KWY·uh·tude) *n.* tranquillity or repose.

qui·e·tus (kwy·EE·tus) *n.* something, esp. death, that ends all activity: *The newspaper story gave the rumours their quietus.*

quill *n.* 1 a stiff, hollow, pointed shaft, as a porcupine's spine or the stem of a goose's feather. 2 the feather itself. 3 an object made from it, as a pen or toothpick.

quilt *n.* a padded blanket or coverlet with its filling kept in place by lines of stitching, often in a pattern: *a crazy quilt pattern; a patchwork quilt.*
— *v:* *a quilted robe; a quilting bee* (= social gathering for making quilts).

quint *n.* [short form] quintuplet.

quin·tal (CAN·tul) *n.* *Cdn.* in Newfoundland, a unit of 112 pounds (about 50.8 kg) used for weighing codfish.

quin·tes·sence (quin·TES·unce) *n.* the purest form or best example: *the Good Samaritan as the quintessence of charity.* — **quin·tes·sen·tial** (-SEN·shul) *adj.*

quin·tet or **quin·tette** (quin·TET) *n.* 1 a piece of music for five voices or instruments. 2 a group of five singers, team of five basketball players, etc.

quin·tu·ple (KWIN·tup·ul, kwin·TUE·pul) *v.* -ples, -pled, -pling multiply or increase by five.
— *n.:* *20 is the quintuple of 4.*
— *adj.* consisting of five: *a quintuple heart bypass operation.*

quin·tu·plet (KWIN·tuh·plit, kwin·TUP·lit) *n.* one of five offspring of a single birth.

quip *n.* a pointed, neatly turned remark or retort.
— *v.* quips, quipped, quip·ping.

quirk *n.* a peculiar characteristic; a turn or twist from what is usual: *the quirks of an eccentric character; by some strange quirk of fate.*
— **quirk·y** *adj.* — **quirk·i·ness** *n.*

quit *v.* quits, *pt. & pp.* quit or quit·ted, quit·ting 1 leave a place or situation; cease doing something; give up: *He quit school; She quit smoking; He quit all claims for damages; The engine suddenly quit on us.* 2 free oneself of a person or thing: *He paid up and quit his debts; She left the party to be quit of his company.*

quit·claim *n.* 1 the formal giving up of a claim or title to a property, right, etc. 2 a document to this effect, or **quitclaim deed.**

quite (KWITE) *adv.* completely: *He's quite wrong; She's quite* (= very) *anxious; Micawber is quite a* (= really a) *character.* — **quite a few** *Informal.* a good number.

quits *adj.* finished: *After one more game, I'll be quits with you* (= on even terms with you); *We'll* **call it quits** (*Informal for* stop or give up) *if it rains.*

quit·ter (QUIT·ur) *n. Informal.* one who gives up without trying hard enough.

quiv·er (QUIV·ur) *n.* 1 a carrying case for arrows. 2 a trembling; quaver: *a quiver of excitement, rage.*
— *v.* tremble: *to quiver with indignation.*

qui vive? (kee·VEEV) *n.* a French sentry's challenge, "Who goes there?": *Be* **on the qui vive** (= watchful) *against pickpockets.*

quix·ot·ic (kwik·SOT·ic) *adj.* like the romantic hero Don Quixote, running into danger trying to do the impossible: *a quixotic adventure, attempt, character, demand, dream, effort, policy, quest.*

quiz *n.* quiz·zes a series of questions, esp. a short test.
— *v.* quiz·zes, quizzed, quiz·zing question: *Father quizzed him about his activities.*

quiz·zi·cal (QUIZ·uh·cul) *adj.* 1 questioning or puzzled: *a quizzical look.* 2 teasing or humorous.

quoin (COIN, QUOIN) *n.* 1 an external angle or corner of a wall. 2 a stone helping to form this; cornerstone.

quoit *n.* a flat metal ring thrown to encircle a peg in the game of quoits *pl.* [takes sing. v.].

quon·dam (QUON·dum) *adj.* that once was; former: *a quondam friend, now archenemy.*

quo·rum (QUOR·um) *n.* the minimum number of a group's members that must be present to transact business legally: *One third of the membership shall constitute* or *make up a quorum.*

quo·ta (QUOH·tuh) *n.* that proportion of a total due from or to a person, group, etc.: *a sales rep's quota of business; to meet a quota; He had exceeded his quota before the end of the year; immigration quotas for ethnic groups; a quota system.*

quo·ta·tion (quoh·TAY·shun) *n.* 1 words repeated exactly: *biblical quotations; a quotation from Shakespeare; a pair of "quotation marks"* [as used here]. 2 current price: *today's stock market quotations.* 3 a stated price: *The contract went to the company that submitted the lowest quotation.*
— **quo·ta·ble** (-tuh·bul) *adj.*

quote *v.* quotes, quot·ed, quot·ing 1 repeat exactly; give words from a source: *to quote a poem; to quote (from) Shakespeare.* 2 present as examples; cite: *I could quote many instances of his bravery.* 3 state the price of goods or services. Also *n.*

quoth (rhyme: "both") *v.* [old use] said.

quo·tient (QUOH·shunt) *n.* the number that results from dividing one quantity by another, as 3 from 21/7: *the intelligence quotient* (= IQ).

Rr

R or **r** (AR) *n.* **R's** or **r's** the 18th letter of the English alphabet.
— **the three R's** reading, writing, and arithmetic, as the basics of education.

rab·bi (RAB·eye) *n.* **rab·bis** the spiritual leader of a Jewish congregation.
— **rab·bin·ic** (ra·BIN·ic) or **rab·bin·i·cal** (-uh·cul) *adj.*

rab·bit (RAB·it) *n.* a small, long-eared, short-tailed burrowing animal with soft fur: *Rabbits breed fast.*

rab·ble (RAB·ul) *n.* a disorderly crowd; mob.

rabble-rouser (RAB·ul·row·zur) *n.* one who tries to arouse a crowd to violent emotions or actions.
— **rabble-rousing** *n. & adj.*

Rab·e·lai·si·an (rab·uh·LAY·zee·un) *adj.* of humour, broad or coarse, in the style of François Rabelais (1494 – 1553), French satirist.

rab·id (RAB·id) *adj.* **1** afflicted with rabies: *a rabid cat, dog, wolf.* **2** violent or fanatical: *a rabid thirst; his rabid zeal; He's rabid about spreading his ideas.*

ra·bies (RAY·beez) *n.* a serious disease which attacks the central nervous system of warm-blooded animals and is transmitted by a bite of an infected animal: *Our dog got rabies and was destroyed.*

race *n.* **1** a major division of humanity: *the human race; the Caucasoid, Mongoloid, and Negroid races.* **2** a plant or animal subspecies: *the canine race.* **3** any group with similar ancestry or characteristics: *a noble race of warriors.* **4** a contest, esp. of speed, to reach a point or achieve an aim: *to run (in) a race; a boat, cross-country, drag, horse, relay race; the 9-to-5 rat race; the arms race between the superpowers; a race against time; a race between the Tories and Grits; the race for mayor; Americans won the race to the moon.* **5** a steady, onward movement on a regular course, as of a river, life, etc.
— *v.* **rac·es, raced, rac·ing 1** compete or engage in a race: *I'll race you to that tree.* **2** run at top speed: *The ambulance raced to the hospital; Don't race the engine when it is cold; With the deadline fast approaching, you are racing against time.* — **rac·er** *n.*

race·course *n.* a course for racing, esp. a usually oval one for racing horses or dogs.

ra·cial (RAY·shul) *adj.* having to do with the human races: *racial backgrounds, bias, conflicts, differences, discrimination, groups, hatred, jokes, minorities,*
segregation. — **ra·cial·ly** *adv.*

racialism, racialistic See RACISM.

racily, raciness See RACY.

racing (RAY·sing) *n.* the sport of holding or engaging in trials of speed: *auto, bicycle, car, dog, harness, horse, sailboat racing.*

ra·cism (RAY·siz·um) *n.* **1** belief in the relative superiority of individual races. **2** discrimination based on this belief: *to stamp out racism; institutionalized racism.* Also **ra·cial·ism** (RAY·shuh·liz·um) *n.*
— **ra·cial·is·tic** (-LIS·tic) *adj.*

ra·cist (RAY·sist) *n.* one who believes in or practises racism: *Hitler was a racist;* *adj.: Apartheid is racist; racist attitudes, bigotry, governments, jokes, overtones, policies.* Also **ra·cial·ist.**

rack *n.* **1** a framework for storing or displaying various items: *a clothes rack; hat rack; a luggage rack over the seats in a bus; It goes on the magazine rack; storage rack; towel rack; a three-tiered **rack car** for transporting automobiles by rail.* **2** a toothed bar that meshes with another toothed structure such as a pinion: *a **rack-and-pinion** railway, steering.* **3** an instrument of torture on which limbs are stretched; hence, any torment: *Martyrs used to die on the rack.* **4** a forequarter or rib cut of meat: *rack of lamb.*
— **rack and ruin** See WRACK.
— **rack one's brains** think hard.
— *v.* torture or torment: *racked by arthritis, doubts, coughing, remorse; He's racked with pain; a racking cough, headache.*
— **rack up** *Informal.* score: *Our team quickly racked up 10 points.*

rack·et (RACK·it) *n.* **1** a long-handled oval frame strung with netting, used in tennis, squash, etc. **2** loud noise, as of revelry: *The party made a terrible racket.* **3** a dishonest scheme or activity, esp. for obtaining money: *to run a blackmail racket.*

rack·et·eer (rack·uh·TEER) *n.* one who runs a racket: *a big-time racketeer; a petty racketeer.*

rac·quet (RACK·it) *n.* a racket used in games.

rac·y (RAY·see) *adj.* **rac·i·er, -i·est 1** having the characteristic flavour, vigour, etc. of something; hence, piquant or spicy: *racy fruit.* **2** suggestive or stimulating to the senses: *Some consider "The Diviners" too racy a book for high school; his racy sense of humour; a racy*

tabloid; clothes that are light, racy, and care-free.
— **rac·i·ly** *adv.;* **rac·i·ness** *n.*

ra·dar (RAY·dar) *n.* "radio detecting and ranging" device for locating faraway objects such as missiles or mountains by reflecting radio waves.

ra·di·al (RAY·dee·ul) *adj.* branching out like rays from a centre: *An amphitheatre has radial seating; A **radial engine** has its cylinders arranged like the spokes of a wheel instead of at an angle as in the V-type; A **radial tire** has its ply cords laid at right angles to the centre line of the thread instead of diagonally as in bias-ply tires.* — **ra·di·al·ly** *adv.*

ra·di·ant (RAY·dee·unt) *adj.* **1** giving off rays, as of light or heat: *Radiant energy is transmitted in waves; radiant heating using hot-water pipes, baseboards, or loops of electric cable.* **2** glowing or happy: *a radiant bride; a face radiant with joy; a necklace radiant with diamonds.* — **ra·di·ance** *n.*

ra·di·ate (RAY·dee·ate) *v.* **-ates, -at·ed, -at·ing** **1** give out rays of something: *The sun radiates energy; a sales rep radiating confidence.* **2** spread out from a centre: *Spokes radiate from a wheel's centre.*

ra·di·a·tion (ray·dee·AY·shun) *n.* emission of rays, esp. X rays: *Radium emits radiation; The Geiger counter is a radiation detector; nuclear radiation; the sun's thermal radiation; the Van Allen **radiation belt** around the earth; **radiation sickness** caused by overexposure to radioactive matter.*

ra·di·a·tor (RAY·dee·ay·tur) *n.* one that radiates, esp. a cooling, heating, or transmission device: *an automobile radiator; heating radiators.*

rad·i·cal (RAD·i·cul) *adj.* **1** basic or fundamental: *a radical error, idea, principle.* **2** affecting the foundation: *a radical change, position, view.* **3** favouring fundamental change of the social structure: *a radical politician, student group; academe's **radical chic** (= trendy associates of radicals).* — *n.* one who is radical. — **rad·i·cal·ism** *n.* — **rad·i·cal·ly** *adv.*

radii a *pl.* of RADIUS.

ra·di·o (RAY·dee·oh) *n.* **-os** **1** the sending and receiving of sound and picture signals using electromagnetic waves without connecting wires, as in broadcasting. **2** a broadcast receiving set or broadcasting as a business, medium, etc.: *Let's turn on the radio for the latest weather; to turn down, turn up, turn off the radio; I listened to the weather on or over my car radio; AM, clock, FM, transistor radios.* — *adj.:* *a radio announcer, engineer, program, wave.* — *v.* **-oes, -oed, -o·ing** communicate with someone or transmit a message by radio.

radio- *combining form.* **1** radio: *radio-frequency, radiotelephone.* **2** radiation: *radiology, radiotherapy.*

ra·di·o·ac·tiv·i·ty (RAY·dee·oh·ac·TIV·uh·tee) *n.* the process by which substances such as radium and uranium give off atomic particles or rays: *a dangerous level of radioactivity.* — **ra·di·o·ac·tive** (-AC·tiv) *adj.*

ra·di·ol·o·gy (ray·dee·OL·uh·jee) *n.* a branch of medicine dealing with the use of radiant energy such as X rays in diagnosis and treatment. — **ra·di·ol·o·gist** *n.*

— **ra·di·o·log·i·cal** (RAY·dee·uh·LOJ·uh·cul) *adj.*

ra·di·us (RAY·dee·us) *n., pl.* **-di·i** (-dee·eye) or **-di·us·es** **1** a straight line from the centre to the outside of a circle or sphere: *the radius of the earth.* **2** the area or distance covered by a radius: *people living within a radius of 20 km from downtown.*

ra·don (RAY·don) *n.* a radioactive gas formed by the natural breakdown of uranium in the earth's crust, as found in the polluted air of tightly sealed homes.

raff·ish (RAF·ish) *adj.* showy; rakish; disreputable: *a playboy's raffish memoirs; the city's raffish district; the raffish hint of gambling.*

raf·fle (RAF·ul) *n.* the casting of lots for prizes: *They held a raffle for the Heart Fund.* — *v.* **raf·fles, raf·fled, raf·fling** hold a raffle or sell off an article by a raffle. — **raf·fler** *n.*

raft *n.* **1** a floating structure of logs or timbers fastened together, or of inflatable plastic, canvas, etc.: *to launch a raft; an inflatable life raft.* **2** *Informal.* collection: *charged with a whole raft of offences.* — *v.* make logs, boards, etc. into a raft, send by raft, or carry on a raft: *We went rafting (= riding by raft) on the Niagara.*

raft·er *n.* one of the sloping beams supporting a roof.

rag *n.* **1** a small, valueless, or torn piece of cloth: *clad in **rags** (= worn-out clothes); the **rags-to-riches** story of a self-made millionaire; to **chew the rag** (Slang for chat); a rag doll; rag paper.* **2** a tune in ragtime. — *v.* **rags, ragged, rag·ging** *Slang.* tease or taunt: *They ragged him about his poor marks.*

rag·a·muf·fin (RAG·uh·muf·in) *n.* a ragged and dirty person, esp. a child.

rag·bag *n.* **1** a bag for rags. **2** a miscellaneous collection.

rage *n.* **1** fury or a fit of fury: *a blind, jealous, sudden, towering, uncontrollable, violent rage; a drunken rage; He flew into a rage; She drove off in a rage.* **2** a fad or vogue: *The rage then was bed-racing; Ray grew up when skateboarding was **all the rage.*** — *v.* **rag·es, raged, rag·ing** **1** be in a rage: *He would rage at or against anyone who opposed him.* **2** go on uncontrollably: *A fire raged out of control; while a storm raged outside.*

rag·ged (RAG·id) *adj.* **1** tattered or torn: *in ragged clothes; a ragged shirt.* **2** shabby or shaggy: *a ragged beard, boy; ragged hair.* **3** uneven or jagged: *a ragged edge; lines printed with a ragged right margin.* — **rag·ged·ly** *adv.;* **rag·ged·ness** *n.*

rag·ged·y (RAG·id·ee) *adj. Slang.* ragged: *a shoeless raggedy kid; a Raggedy Ann doll.*

rag·tag *n.* worthless or disreputable people; riffraff.

rag·time *n.* a strongly rhythmic style of piano playing, a forerunner of jazz.

rah *interj.* hurrah.

rah-rah *adj.* spirited or enthusiastic like cheerleaders: *the rah-rah spirit of the centennial celebration.*

raid *n.* a sudden, hostile attack or invasion: *The U.S. carried out or conducted an air and naval raid against*

Libya; Libya's raid into Chad; a bombing, border, guerrilla, police, retaliatory, suicide raid; a raid on or upon drug traffickers.
— *v.* make a raid on a place: *Police raided the gambling joint; to raid the fridge for snacks.*
— **raid·er** *n.*

rail *n.* 1 either of a pair of parallel connected steel bars forming a track for a train or similar vehicle; hence, a railway: *to travel by rail.* 2 a horizontal bar connecting posts and forming a guard or barrier, as on a fence. 3 a marsh bird such as the coot that has a thin body for slipping through reeds and grasses.
— *v.* fence with rails, or **rail·ing.**

rail·road *n.* same as RAILWAY.
— *v.* 1 send by railway. 2 *Informal.* rush a person, business, etc. through a system without careful consideration: *The bill was railroaded through the legislature; They tried to railroad* (= force) *him off the job.*

rail·way *n.* 1 a track of rails for locomotives and train cars; also, the transportation system. 2 a railway track or a railway for streetcars or other light vehicles.

rai·ment (RAY·munt) *n.* [old use] clothing.

rain *n.* 1 water falling in drops from the sky: *The rain came down in buckets or torrents; acid, driving, freezing, heavy, intermittent, light, pouring, soaking, steady, torrential rain; The rain beats, falls, lets up, patters, pours, starts, stops; Pat's always punctual, come rain or shine* (= whatever the weather); *spring rains* (= seasonal rainfalls of spring). 2 anything resembling rain: *a rain of bullets, kisses, tears.*
— *v.* fall as or like rain: *It's raining outside; It's raining cats and dogs or raining hard; They rained flowers on the returning hero; Tears rained down her cheeks; "It never rains but it pours"* (= Things happen in quick succession); *Polish voters rained on the Communist parade* (= beat the Communists); *The game was rained out* (= postponed because of rain).

rain·bow (RAIN·boh) *n.* an arch of colourful light seen in mist or spray: *the seven colours of the rainbow; A rainbow appears after a rain; a rainbow coalition* (of people of all races).

rain·check *n.* a present offer that is extended for a future occasion, as a ticket from a game stopped by rain or a sales item that is now out of stock: *I'll take a raincheck on that offer.*

rain·fall *n.* 1 a fall of rain: *a region of heavy rainfall.* 2 its amount: *annual, average, light rainfall.*

rain·y (RAY·nee) *adj.* **rain·i·er, -i·est** having to do with rain: *rainy weather; to save for a rainy day* (= future time of need).

raise (RAZE) *v.* **rais·es, raised, rais·ing** 1 move a person or thing to a higher level or position: *to raise the flag; to raise the standard of living; to raise the dead (to life); to raise the Titanic from the bottom of the sea; He never raises his voice (as in excitement); People are raised* (= elevated) *to positions of authority; to raise the people's consciousness.* 2 to bring up: *to raise children, crops, horses, turkeys; a telethon to raise* (= collect) *funds; to raise* (= cause) *a laugh; to raise* (= erect) *a monument; to raise a point* (= bring it up for

discussion). 3 end: *to raise a siege.*
— *n.* an increase: *a 10% raise in wages; The company gave an across-the-board raise to its employees; Some deserved a higher raise (in salary); She got a hefty raise.*

rai·son d'être (ray·zon·DET·ruh) *French.* reason for being what something is.

ra·ja or **ra·jah** (RAH·juh) *n.* a prince of India.

rake *n.* 1 a long-handled tool or machine equipped with prongs for gathering leaves or hay, smoothing the ground, etc. 2 a slant or slope, as of a mast or funnel toward the stern, of a floor from the horizontal, etc. 3 a dissolute man.
— *v.* **rakes, raked, rak·ing** 1 to remove, gather, etc. with or as if with a rake: *to rake leaves off a lawn; Hay is raked into piles; to rake in* (= gather quickly and abundantly) *profits; Why rake up* (= stir up) *long-forgotten enmities?* 2 to slant or slope: *a ship with a short mast raked well forward.*

rake-off *n.* *Slang.* a cut or share of profits.

rak·ish (RAY·kish) *adj.* 1 smart or trim, suggesting speed: *a rakish ship.* 2 jaunty or dashing: *a hat set at a rakish angle.* 3 dissolute: *a rakish life, look.*

ral·ly (RAL·ee) *v.* **ral·lies, ral·lied, ral·ly·ing** 1 come or bring together for a renewed or united effort: *to rally round or to the side of a leader; He rallied his forces for a renewed attack; They rallied to their country's defence; their rallying cry, point.* 2 recover or revive: *Our spirits rallied on hearing the good news; We rally from an illness; The price of gold rallied to the $350 level; The Canadiens rallied with two last-minute goals; Tremblay rallied the Canadiens to a 2-2 tie; The Penguins rallied on goals by Don and Chris; They rallied for a 5-2 victory over the Canucks.*
— *n., pl.* **ral·lies** 1 a rallying, as of the stock market. 2 a coming together of people such as scouts, sports car enthusiasts, or worshippers for a group activity: *to hold, organize a rally; a peace, pep, political rally.*

RAM *n.* the random access memory of a computer: *dynamic and static RAM.*

ram *n.* a male sheep, usually with outward-curving horns.
— *v.* **rams, rammed, ram·ming** butt or strike violently against, down, or into: *Piles are rammed into a river bed; Cars ram into each other in a demolition derby; I can't ram it down his throat if he won't believe me.*

ram·ble (RAM·bul) *v.* **-bles, -bled, -bling** 1 go about in an aimless or leisurely manner: *He likes to ramble in the woods; She rambles the woods; adj.: a rambling* (= spreading irregularly) *house, vine.* 2 wander away, as from a subject while talking: *The lecturer rambled on; He rambled on for an hour about how he got lost.*
— *n.* a roaming or excursion: *a ramble in the woods.*

ram·bler (RAM·blur) *n.* 1 a walker or one who rambles about. 2 one that rambles: *Some roses are ramblers, others are climbers.* 3 a large home with all rooms on one floor.

ram·bunc·tious (ram·BUNK·shus) *adj.* boisterous and unruly: *a crowd of rambunctious students.*

ram·i·fi·ca·tion (ram·uh·fuh·CAY·shun) *n.* 1 a ramifying or branching out: *the ramifications of a system.*

2 [usually in pl.] consequence or outgrowth: *the far-reaching* or *widespread ramifications of a decision; the ramifications of a problem; an intricate plot with many ramifications.*

ram·i·fy (RAM·uh·fye) *v.* **-fies, -fied, -fy·ing** branch out; spread out.

ramp *n.* a sloped means of access to a different level, as at a highway interchange or the staircase used to board a plane: *wheelchair ramps for sidewalks; a steep ramp; to go down, up a ramp; a ramp speed of 20 km/h.*

ram·page (RAM·page) *n.* a spell of reckless or violent behaviour: *The merrymakers went* **on the** or **on a rampage.**
— *v.* (ram·PAGE) **-pag·es, -paged, -pag·ing** rush about wildly or in excitement: *elephants rampaging through a forest; Drunken merrymakers rampaged through the mall breaking store windows.*

ram·pant (RAM·punt) *adj.* unchecked in growth or movement: *Inflation was running rampant at about 25% a year; rampant* (= rank) *vegetation.*

ram·part (RAM·part) *n.* a defensive barrier, esp. one built around a fort with a parapet on top: *The enemy stormed the ramparts.*

ram·pike *n. Cdn.* a tall tree that has no branches, as one that has been burnt in a forest fire.

ram·rod *n.* a rod used to ram a charge into a muzzle-loading firearm.

ram·shack·le (RAM·shack·ul) *adj.* rickety: *a ramshackle dwelling, vehicle.*

ran *pt.* of RUN.

ranch *n.* **1** a large farm for raising cattle, sheep, or horses: *a cattle ranch; a dude ranch for tourists; He works at a ranch but doesn't live on it.* **2** a specialty farm: *a chicken, fruit, mink ranch.* **3** a low-roofed one-storey dwelling; also **ranch house.**
— *v.* manage or work on a ranch. — **ranch·er** *n.*

ranch·er·ie (RANCH·uh·ree) *n. Cdn.* an Indian camp or settlement.

ranch·hand *n. Cdn.* one employed on a cattle ranch.

ran·cid (RAN·cid) *adj.* tasting or smelling like spoiled fat, butter, etc.: *rancid fish.*
— **ran·cid·i·ty** (ran·CID·uh·tee) *n.*

ran·cour or **ran·cor** (RANK·ur) *n.* bitter or spiteful hatred: *to express, feel, show, stir up rancour; He was full of rancour against* or *toward the enemy.*
— **ran·cor·ous** *adj.;* **ran·cor·ous·ly** *adv.*

ran·dom (RAN·dum) *adj.* made or done without a purpose, plan, or aim: *random shots; samples chosen* **at random** *as representative of a large group; to take* or *select a* **random sample.**

random access *n.* access to data in a computer memory in the order desired by user.

ran·dom·ize (RAN·duh·mize) *v.* **-iz·es, -ized, -iz·ing** make at random: *a randomized selection of items.*
— **ran·dom·i·za·tion** (-muh·ZAY·shun) *n.*

ran·dy *adj.* **-di·er, -di·est** lecherous; also, sexually aroused.

rang *pt.* of RING.

range (RAINJ) *v.* **rang·es, ranged, rang·ing 1** vary within an area or distance: *The pay ranges from $30 000 to $50 000; a wide-ranging survey; Buffalo once ranged* (= roamed) *our plains; Radar is a ranging* (= distance-finding) *device.* **2** arrange or classify in groups: *eggs ranged small, medium, and large; The collaborators ranged themselves with* (= joined) *the invaders; They were ranged* (= aligned) *against us.*
— *n.* **1** distance or extent: *a wide range of vision; within range of gunfire; The target seemed out of range; a price, salary range; at close, point-blank range; Let's take a long-range view of the matter.* **2** a grazing area: *a cattle range.* **3** a place for practice: *an artillery, firing, rifle, rocket range; a driving range (for golf).* **4** row or series: *a mountain range.* **5** a cooking stove, usually with oven and storage compartment: *an electric range; gas range.*

rang·er (RAIN·jur) *n.* **1** one who patrols or guards a region: *a forest ranger.* **2** **Ranger** a senior Girl Guide, 16 years or older. **3** *Cdn.* a volunteer military scout in the North. **4** a commando or special police officer: *Texas Rangers.*

rang·y (RAIN·jee) *adj.* **rang·i·er, -i·est 1** able to range about. **2** long-limbed: *rangy cattle or horses; his tall rangy good looks.*

rank *n.* **1** a row, as of a lineup of soldiers: *to form a rank; to break ranks and run; the ranks of the unemployed; to join the ranks* (= army); *a general who came up* or *rose from the ranks (of the enlisted); to close ranks* (= unite) *to meet a challenge.* **2** a position according to grade and seniority, esp. of a military officer: *He holds the rank of colonel; to pull rank on someone* (= to use one's position) *to get an advantage; an official of high rank; cabinet rank.*
— *v.* to rate or be rated: *Canadian actors rank among the best in the world; He ranks as an outstanding poet; He does not rank with Shakespeare; Shakespeare ranks above all dramatists; A major ranks below a colonel; A colonel ranks* (= outranks) *a major.*
— *adj.* **1** coarse and vigorous in growth, as weeds. **2** bad-smelling: *rank tobacco.* **3** complete or utter: *a rank amateur, beginner; rank ingratitude, injustice, nonsense.* — **rank·ly** *adv.;* **rank·ness** *n.*

rank and file *n.* **1** ordinary soldiers. **2** the ordinary membership or people: *the Tory rank and file; The rank and file of the union rejected the offer.*

ranking *adj.* of high rank: *a ranking educator, officer; the ranking* (= highest-ranked) *senator.*

ran·kle (RANK·ul) *v.* **-kles, -kled, -kling** be a source of irritation or soreness: *It rankled her that she was not invited; an insult that still rankles (in her mind).*

ran·sack *v.* **1** search a place thoroughly, as if to plunder. **2** to plunder or pillage.

ran·som (RAN·sum) *n.* a price demanded for freeing a person from captivity: *a child kidnapped and held for ransom; The kidnappers demanded a ransom from the child's family; to exact a ransom; The ransom was not paid.*
— *v.* free by paying a ransom: *The child was rescued by police before being ransomed.*

rant *v.* talk wildly and loudly: *He rants and raves whenever things go wrong; never rants at his wife, though.* — *n.* a noisy or bombastic speech.

rap *n.* 1 a sharp knock: *a rap on the door; He received a **rap on the knuckles*** (= mild punishment or reproof) *from the teacher for being lazy.* 2 *Slang.* legal blame or punishment: *looking for someone to take the rap; He got a bad* or *bum rap* (= was unfairly punished); *jailed on a burglary rap; looked for ways to beat* (= escape) *the rap; a rap sheet.* 3 *Slang.* chat or talk: *a rap session.* 4 *Informal.* the least bit: *I don't give* or *care a rap.* 5 a kind of popular monotone music with a strong beat and rhymes like "The bat hit the cat, and the cat went scat." — *v.* **raps, rapped, rap·ping** 1 tap or knock sharply, as on a door. 2 *Slang.* chat or talk: *He wastes a lot of time rapping on the phone.* — **rap·per** *n.*

ra·pa·cious (ruh·PAY·shus) *adj.* plundering; greedy; grasping: *the rapacious wolf; a rapacious tyrant.* — **ra·pa·cious·ness** or **ra·pac·i·ty** (ruh·PAS·uh·tee) *n.*

rape *n.* 1 a forcing, esp. of a woman, to have sexual intercourse: *to commit rape; attempted, gang, marital, statutory rape; a rape victim.* 2 a plant of the mustard family, the source of rapeseed and rapeseed oil. See also CANOLA. — *v.* **rapes, raped, rap·ing** commit rape; ravish or violate.

rap·id (RAP·id) *adj.* moving at a swift pace; quick: *a rapid pulse, stream; the rapid growth of weeds; rapid-fire questioning; the **rapid eye movement** and rapid breathing and heart rates associated with the dreaming phase of sleep; a **rapid transit** public transportation system using fast trains.* — *n.,* usually **rapids** *pl.* a part of a river with swift currents and rocks beneath the surface: *a shallow boat or raft for riding* or *shooting the rapids of the Niagara.* — **rap·id·ly** *adv.* — **ra·pid·i·ty** (ruh·PID·uh·tee) *n.*

ra·pi·er (RAY·pee·ur) *n.* a narrow-bladed, pointed duelling sword used for thrusting: *the rapier thrust of his wit.*

rap·ist (RAY·pist) *n.* one who commits a rape.

rap·port (ra·POR) *n.* a close relationship implying mutual sympathy and harmony: *to establish a rapport with her colleagues; She works in close rapport with them.*

rap·proche·ment (ra·PROHSH·mahng) *n.* the establishment of cordial relations: *to bring about a rapprochement between the warring factions.*

rap session *n. Slang.* an informal group discussion.

rap sheet *n. Slang.* a police record.

rapt *adj.* absorbed or engrossed in a thinking state or emotion: *He was rapt in thought; They listened with rapt attention.*

rap·ture (RAP·chur) *n.* the state of being rapt in a feeling of bliss: *She spent the night in rapture over her wedding; a rapture of joy.* — **rap·tur·ous** *adj.*

rare *adj.* **rar·er, rar·est** 1 not frequent; without many instances or specimens: *It's rare to see this bird in January; He's a **rare bird** at these meetings; a rare phenomenon.* 2 unusually good: *a rare book, beauty, event, talent.* 3 not dense: *the rare mountain air; the rarer regions of the atmosphere.* 4 of meat, not cooked much: *a rare steak; I like it medium rare.* — **rare·ly** *adv.*

rar·e·fy (RAIR·uh·fye) *v.* **-fies, -fied, -fy·ing** make or become less dense: *a rarefied gas.* — **rar·e·fac·tion** (-FAC·shun) *n.*

rar·ing (RAIR·ing) *adj. Slang.* very eager: *He is raring to go.*

rar·i·ty (RAIR·uh·tee) *n.* **-ties** 1 rareness. 2 an unusual person or thing.

ras·cal (RAS·cul) *n.* 1 a scoundrel; rogue. 2 [used jokingly] a naughty or mischievous person. — **ras·cal·ly** *adv.* — **ras·cal·i·ty** (ras·CAL·uh·tee) *n.*

rash *n.* 1 a skin eruption, often itchy, usually covering an area of the body in spots or patches, as in measles and prickly heat: *a diaper, heat, nettle rash; A rash breaks out; She **broke out in*** (= became covered with) *a rash.* 2 sudden appearance in large numbers: *a rash of accidents on an icy highway.* — *adj.* hasty or thoughtless; precipitate: *a rash action, decision, driver, promise.* — **rash·ly** *adv.;* **rash·ness** *n.*

rash·er *n.* 1 a slice of bacon. 2 a serving of several slices of bacon.

rasp *n.* 1 a coarse file with a surface of points or teeth. 2 the grating sound made as if or when a rasp is used: *a cricket's rasp; the rasp of a saw.* — *v.* utter with a grating sound: *He rasps out his orders; voices that rasp* (= irritate) *one's nerves.* — **rasp·y** *adj.*

rasp·ber·ry (RAZ·ber·ee) *n.* **-ber·ries** 1 a small, round, usually red or purple fruit of a bush of the rose family. 2 *Slang.* a rude noise of disapproval made by sticking out the tongue and blowing strongly: *Ray gave him the raspberry; to blow raspberries.*

rat *n.* 1 a destructive rodent larger than a mouse. 2 *Slang.* a person considered low or mean, as an informer: *a dirty rat!* Also **rat fink.** — *v.* **rats, rat·ted, rat·ting** act in a low way. — **rat on** 1 inform on someone. 2 go back on a promise: *He ratted on his word.* — **smell a rat** suspect something tricky.

rate *n.* a measurement of something variable in relation to something else: *The annual birth rate is about 17 per 1 000 of the population; to fix* or *set the minimum wage rate; an annual, flat, high, hourly, low, moderate, reduced, regular, seasonal, slow, steady rate; an accident, crime, death, discount, divorce, fertility, inflation, metabolic, mortality, pulse, tax rate; Money is loaned at a certain rate of interest; the postal rate for first-class mail; Al is a **first-rate*** (= top-class), *not second-* or *third-rate mind.* — **at any rate** in any case. — *v.* **rates, rat·ed, rat·ing** 1 rank or be ranked: *Al is rated in the top 10% of his class; On a scale of 1 to 10, we would rate him about 2; He's rated among the best students; He rates with the best; He is rated as excellent; is rated very highly.* 2 *Informal.* deserve: *Her work is so good she rates a promotion.* 3 scold or berate.

615

rate·pay·er (RATE·pay·ur) *n.* one who pays taxes to a municipality.

rat·fink *n. Slang.* a mean fellow.

rath·er (RATH·ur, "TH" as in "the") *adv.* 1 more readily, properly, etc.: *He would rather play than work; prefers to play rather than work; prefers playing rather than working; He would rather not work at this hour; I would rather you did your homework than watch TV; He was let go, rather* (=more correctly), *he resigned.* 2 somewhat: *a rather chilly reception.*

rat·i·fy (RAT·uh·fye) *v.* **-fies, -fied, -fy·ing** give formal approval of an agreement, law, treaty, etc., usually by vote. — **rat·i·fi·ca·tion** (-fuh·CAY·shun) *n.*

rating (RAY·ting) *n.* 1 a rank or grade; also, a placement in one. 2 a comparative estimate: *a fuse wire with a 15 amp. rating; a four-star credit rating; an efficiency, high, octane, power rating; a TV show cancelled because of low ratings (as determined by popularity surveys).*

ra·tio (RAY·shee·oh, RAY·shoh) *n.* **-tios** the relation in quantity, amount, or degree between two things or this expressed as the quotient of two numbers; proportion: *The ratio of length to width for the Maple Leaf flag is 2 to 1; The ratio between length and width is 2; Length and width are in the ratio of 2 to 1.*

ra·tion (RASH·un, RAY·shun) *n.* a share or allotment, esp. of food: *a daily, monthly, food, gasoline ration; to issue emergency rations; They were on short **rations*** (=scanty food supply or provisions).
— *v.* distribute as rations: *Food is strictly rationed during a war; Scarce supplies are rationed out to or among the most needy; Each person is rationed* (=limited) *to so much per week; wartime rationing; to end, introduce, terminate rationing.*

ra·tion·al (RASH·uh·nul) *adj.* 1 based on reasoning: *rational behaviour, suggestions; a rational explanation of a mystery.* 2 able to reason: *Humans are rational animals.* 3 sensible: *Let's be rational; the rational thing to do in a situation.* — **ra·tion·al·ly** *adv.*

ra·tion·ale (rash·uh·NAL) *n.* the underlying reasons or rational basis of a belief, custom, phenomenon, etc.: *the rationale of superstitious behaviour; Your rationale* (=explanation) *is not quite convincing.*

ra·tion·al·ism (RASH·uh·nuh·liz·um) *n.* the principle or practice of using reason as the ultimate authority for knowledge, as opposed to faith or sense experience. — **ra·tion·al·ist** *n.;* **ra·tion·al·is·tic** (-LIS·tic) *adj.*

ra·tion·al·ize (RASH·uh·nuh·lize) *v.* **-iz·es, -ized, -iz·ing** 1 treat in a rational manner: *to rationalize a miracle, myth, superstition; attempts to rationalize* (=make rational) *English spelling.* 2 try to justify as a defence mechanism: *He's merely rationalizing; to rationalize an unreasonable behaviour, fear, feeling, prejudice, etc.* — **ra·tion·al·i·za·tion** (-luh·ZAY·shun) *n.*

rat race *n. Slang.* the frantic struggle for survival in a highly competitive environment: *fed up with the 9-to-5 rat race.*

rat·tle (RAT·ul) *n.* 1 a baby's toy that makes noise when shaken; hence, a series of short, sharp sounds. 2 the rattle at the end of a rattlesnake's tail or the warning sound it makes. 3 the gurgling sound made by a dying

person; also called "death rattle."
— *v.* **rat·tles, rat·tled, rat·tling** 1 make the sound of a rattle; hence, talk in an incessant chatter: *He can rattle off* or *away a whole list of names.* 2 *Informal.* disturb one's composure; upset: *It rattled him to hear that his secretary had quit.*

rat·tler (RAT·lur) or **rat·tle·snake** (RAT·ul·snake) *n.* a venomous American snake with a rattle on the end of its tail: *when the rattler strikes.*

rattling *n.* the act of making a sound like a rattle's: *sabre rattling.*
— *adj.* 1 that rattles: *rattling bones, chains, windows.* 2 *Informal.* lively; splendid: *a rattling business;* **adv.:** *a rattling good time.*

rat·trap *n.* 1 a trap for rats. 2 *Informal.* a run-down building.

rau·cous (RAW·cus) *adj.* rough-sounding or rowdy: *raucous parties, voices.* — **rau·cous·ly** *adv.*

raun·chy (RAWN·chee) *adj.* **-chi·er, -chi·est** earthy; lustful; vulgar: *a raunchy magazine; a raunchy TV show; too raunchy for family viewing.* — **raun·chi·ness** *n.*

rav·age (RAV·ij) *v.* **-ag·es, -aged, -ag·ing** cause destruction or devastation: *Floods ravaged the area.* — *n.:* *to repair the ravages of war.*

rave *v.* **raves, raved, rav·ing** 1 talk wildly or furiously, as when delirious: *to rave about* or *at* or *against something; He's **raving mad.*** 2 talk with great, often excessive enthusiasm: *He often raves to his boys about his exploits in the war; a **raving*** (=unusually striking) *beauty.*
— *n. Slang.* enthusiastic praise: *There were raves in the media; adj.: a rave notice, review.*

rav·el (RAV·ul) *v.* **-els, -elled** or **-eled, -el·ling** or **el·ing** 1 tangle or confuse. 2 untwist or unravel.
— *n.* a ravelled part; also **ravelling** or **raveling.**

rav·en (RAY·vun) *n.* a larger-size type of crow with black and lustrous feathers.

ravening (RAV·un·ing) or **rav·en·ous** (-uh·nus) *adj.* 1 very hungry. 2 rapacious: *ravening wolves.* — **rav·en·ous·ly** *adv.*

ra·vine (ruh·VEEN) *n.* a long, narrow, deep depression in the earth's surface, smaller than a valley or canyon.

rav·ish (RAV·ish) 1 transport with joy: *She was ravished with delight.* 2 to rape.
— **ravishing** *adj.* enchanting: *His act is simply*

ravishing; a ravishing beauty, book, show, view of the mountains.

raw *adj.* **1** in the natural state: *raw* (= uncooked) *meat; a raw* (= untrained) *recruit; raw* (= unfinished) *draft; raw* (= unprocessed) *data, fibre, hide, materials, sewage, wool.* **2** rough or harsh: *a raw deal, weather, wind; a raw cut; a raw spot (on the body with the skin removed, as by a wound).*
— **in the raw 1** in a natural state: *to experience life in the raw.* **2** naked: *to go swimming in the raw; to sleep in the raw.*

ray *n.* **1** a thin line of light radiating from a central source such as the sun: *to emit, send forth, send out rays; cathode, cosmic, death, gamma, heat, infrared, light, ultraviolet, X rays; a ray* (= gleam) *of hope.* **2** any similar line or a raylike part, as a petal of the daisy or an arm of the "starfish."

raze *v.* **raz·es, razed, raz·ing** to level or demolish: *The earthquake razed the city, with buildings razed to the ground.*

ra·zor (RAY·zur) *n.* a shaving implement: *a straight razor; to hone or sharpen a razor; a double-edged safety razor; an election won with a **razor-thin** majority.*

razz *v.* tease or ridicule.

raz·zle-daz·zle (RAZ·ul·daz·ul) *v.* **-daz·zles, -daz·zled, -daz·zling** *Slang.* bewilder or deceive with something dazzling or exciting.

razz·ma·tazz (RAZ·muh·taz) *n. Slang.* liveliness or flashiness.

re (RAY, REE) *prep.* regarding: *re your inquiry of March 13th.*

re- *prefix.* [freely added to verbs, using a hyphen to emphasize or distinguish, as in "re-cover"] again or anew: *reactivate, reassurance, re-cover* (= cover again).

reach (REECH) *v.* get to a person, place, or thing: *You can reach me by phone; His fame reaches far and wide; He quickly reached for his coat; Please reach me the hat; She cannot be reached* (= got at or influenced) *by bribes; Reach out* (= extend) *your hand; He tried to reach (toward) the extended hand; Parents try hard to **reach out** to* (= communicate with) *their children because of the generation gap.*
— *n.* a reaching or its extent: *Drugs are kept out of reach* (= extent of reaching) *of children; Tall hockey players have a long reach with their sticks; He lives within easy reach* (= travel) *by subway; Infinity is beyond the reach* (= grasp) *of the human imagination; in the outer reaches* (= limits or extent) *of the atmosphere; the upper reaches of the Nile; the vast reaches of the Sahara.*

re·act (ree·ACT) *v.* **1** act back or in response to someone or something: *If I ask for a raise, how will he react? She reacted with kindness; People react against cruelty; They react strongly; to react to a stimulus; He didn't react to the insult.* **2** act chemically: *Carbon reacts with oxygen to form carbon dioxide.*

re·ac·tion (ree·AC·shun) *n.* **1** a response or acting back: *allergic reaction to smoke; Allergens cause or trigger reactions; the action and reaction of colliding bodies; your reaction to the new tax; The new tax encountered*

or *met with a strong reaction from the public; an adverse or negative reaction; public reaction against the tax; a chain, delayed, favourable, knee-jerk, natural, normal, nuclear, positive, strong, weak reaction; A catalyst speeds up a chemical reaction.* **2** a political or social tendency to return to a former state of affairs.

re·ac·tion·ar·y (ree·AC·shuh·nair·ee) *n. & adj.* **-ar·ies** (one) opposed to progress or reform.

re·ac·ti·vate (ree·AC·tuh·vate) *v.* **-vates, -vat·ed, -vat·ing** make or become active again: *to reactivate a case, disease, fear, program, tendency.*
— **re·ac·ti·va·tion** (-VAY·shun) *n.*

re·ac·tor (ree·AC·tur) *n.* **1** one that reacts, esp. positively in a medical test. **2** a device or vessel in which a chemical process is carried out: *an atomic, nuclear reactor; fission reactor.*

read (REED) *v.* **reads, read** (RED), **read·ing 1** get the meaning, esp. from something written: *Can he read? He reads books, Braille, English; He also reads gestures, minds, thoughts; You can read all* (= get all the information) *about it in the papers; I read* (= hear or understand) *you loud and clear.* **2** say what is written: *Please read aloud; Read to me while I sew; Volunteers read for the sick.* **3** study or learn: *He's reading law; reading for a degree; Better read up on your history before the exam.* **4** show, mean, or be: *The clock reads 10; "Thimk" should read "think"; The memo reads as follows; It reads like a shopping list.*
— *adj.* (RED) informed: *He's well read in medicine.*
— **read between the lines** look for or see a hidden meaning.
— **read something into** see something that is not expressed.
— **read someone out of** expel someone from membership in a political party, etc.
— **read·a·ble** (-duh·bul) *adj.;* **read·a·bly** (-blee) *adv.*
— **read·a·ble·ness** or **read·a·bil·i·ty** (-BIL·uh·tee) *n.*

read·er (REE·dur) *n.* **1** one who reads: *an avid, voracious reader.* **2** a book containing selections for one learning to read: *a basic, elementary reader.* **3** a selection of articles on a given subject: *a history reader.*

read·er·ship (REE·dur·ship) *n.* **1** an audience of readers: *a magazine with a wide readership.* **2** a reader's position or office.

read·i·ly (RED·uh·lee) *adv.* **1** willingly: *They answer readily to requests.* **2** easily: *This is readily available in stores.*
— **read·i·ness** *n.: her readiness to help; A nurse holds herself in readiness for emergencies.*

reading (REE·ding) *n.* **1** the act of one who reads: *Children learn reading and writing; your reading level, skills; a poetry reading session; remedial reading; the final reading* (= consideration) *of a bill in parliament.* **2** reading material: *the assigned reading for a course; light, serious, solid, suggested reading.* **3** what is read, studied, or learned: *a man of wide reading* (= learning); *Take a reading* (= what the meter shows) *every hour; a new reading* (= interpretation) *of the Bible.*

read·out (REED·out) *n.* **1** recorded or displayed data from a computer; also, the process or device used. **2** transmission of data, as from a space vehicle.

read·y (RED·ee) *adj.* **read·i·er, -i·est 1** prepared or willing to do as specified or implied without delay: *Are you ready? We are ready to leave; always ready with an answer; She's ready* (= apt) *to find fault.* **2** immediately available: *Dinner is ready; I need ready cash, money; You have a ready reply for everything; Ambulances are ready for emergencies; The troops moved up with guns* **at the ready** (= state of being ready); **ready-to-wear** (= ready-made) *clothes.*
— *v.* **read·ies, read·ied, read·y·ing** make oneself ready: *They readied themselves for battle.*

ready-made (RED·ee·made) *adj.* **1** made ready for use or sale, not made-to-order: *a ready-made TV dinner, dress.* **2** lacking individuality; commonplace: *a ready-made answer, opinion.*

re·al (REE·ul, REEL) *adj.* existing in fact, not as appears or is supposed to be; genuine; not imaginary: *Is that diamond real or fake? a real experience, not a dream; real* (= immovable) *property, or* **real estate,** *such as land and houses; A concave lens does not have a real focus or form a real image that may be projected on a screen.*
— *adv. Slang.* very: *Her aunt was real nice to us.*
— **for real** *Slang.* serious or seriously: *Practising is over, let's do it now for real.*

re·al·ism (REE·uh·liz·um) *n.* philosophy or action based on things as they are, not as they should be, esp. in the artistic portrayal of life: *The colours lend realism to the scene.*
— **re·al·ist** *n.*: *She's a down-to-earth realist.*
— **re·al·is·tic** (-LIS·tic) *adj.*; **re·al·is·ti·cal·ly** *adv.*

re·al·i·ty (ree·AL·uh·tee) *n.* **-ties 1** the quality of being real: *We have to accept reality, it's no use denying it.* **2** a real person or fact: *the grim, harsh, sober realities of life.* — **in reality** in fact.

re·al·ize (REE·uh·lize) *v.* **-iz·es, -ized, -iz·ing 1** be aware of something: *I didn't realize I was in Mexico; When he fully realized what had happened, it was too late.* **2** make real: *to realize an ambition.* **3** convert into money: *to realize an investment; to realize bonds and stocks; We realized* (= obtained as money) *very little from the sale.* — **re·al·iz·a·ble** (-lye·zuh·bul) *adj.*
— **re·al·i·za·tion** (-luh·ZAY·shun) *n.*

re·al·ly (REE·uh·lee) *adv.* **1** actually: *Are we really late? Not really.* **2** [as intensifier]: *It was really* (= very) *cold last night; I really* (= very much) *love him; You really ought to see this movie; Really?*
— *interj.* indeed: *Well, really!*

realm (RELM) *n.* domain or region: *the realm of fancy, philosophy, science.*

real time *n.* computer system of simultaneous input and processing of data: *Most process-control systems operate in real time;* **adj.**: *Airline bookings must be processed by a real-time system.*

re·al·tor (REE·ul·tur) *n.* an accredited real-estate agent; **Realtor** *Trademark.*

re·al·ty (REE·ul·tee) *n.* **-ties** real estate.

ream (REEM) *n. Informal.* a large quantity: *reams of unpublished poetry.*
— *v.* widen an existing hole or bore using a rotating tool

with a ridge or spiral surface. — **ream·er** *n.*

reap (REEP) *v.* to cut, as with a scythe: *to reap grain; to reap* (= gather) *crops; "You reap* (= harvest) *what you sow."* — **reap·er** *n.*

rear (REER) *v.* **1** to raise: *The animal reared its head; a rearing horse* (rising on its hind legs); *Unemployment rears its ugly head.* **2** bring up: *We reared our children to be good citizens; to rear* (= breed) *livestock.*
— *n.* the back part or position: *in the rear of the house; a car with its engine in the rear; seated in the rear (seat) of the car; The army was attacked from the rear; He got kicked in the rear; In a procession, the most important people* **bring up the rear** (= come last).
— *adj.: a* **rear admiral** (= officer of rank just below vice admiral); *the rear bumper, wheels; the* **rear end** *of the car; a* **rear-ender** (= rear-end collision); *a* **rear-facing** *child seat; the* **rear guard** (= soldiers guarding the rear of an army); *the* **rear-view mirror** *of an automobile.*

rear·most (REER·most) *adj.* farthest at the back; last: *the rearmost car of the train.*

rear·ward (REER·wurd) *adj. & adv.* at or toward the rear. Also **rear·wards** *adv.*

rea·son (REE·zun) *n.* **1** a cause or occasion that explains something: *to cite* or *give reasons; a cogent, compelling, convincing, logical, personal, plausible, sound, strong, underlying, urgent, valid reason; We had every reason to suspect fraud; You can't fire someone without sufficient reason; There's no reason to be concerned; the reasons for and against a course of action; The real reason behind their move was something else; The reason why he did it is not clear; He resigned for personal reasons; for reasons of health; not guilty* **by reason of** (= because of) *insanity; She was fired* **with reason** (= with justification). **2** thinking and judging capacity: *Animals and infants lack reason; He lost his reason in his final days.* **3** logic or good sense: *Please listen to reason; When will you see reason? It* **stands to reason** (= is logical) *that workers be paid; We're prepared to accommodate you* **within reason** (= within reasonable limits).
— *v.* use one's thinking capacity: *our capacity to reason; He's too headstrong to reason with; Let's reason out a solution based on the evidence available; He reasons* (= argues) *that it is too late now.*

rea·son·a·ble (REE·zuh·nuh·bul) *adj.* **1** according to reason: *We are all rational, but not everyone is reasonable; He is always reasonable about paying his dues; It seems only reasonable that we give him more time; The accused was acquitted because the jury didn't think him guilty beyond a reasonable doubt.* **2** moderate or fair: *a reasonable price, demand, excuse; a reasonable house* (that is moderately priced).
— **rea·son·a·bly** *adv.*

reasoning (REE·zun·ing) *n.* the use of reason or an instance of it: *cogent, deductive, faulty, inductive, shrewd, solid, sound reasoning; His reasoning* (= argument) *sounds a bit specious.*

re·as·sure (ree·uh·SURE) *v.* **re·as·sures, re·as·sured, re·as·sur·ing** assure so as to remove the fears of or restore confidence to someone: *She reassured us about or of the health of our child; reassured us he would* *survive; Her words were* **reassuring;** *It's* **reassuring** *that help is available.* — **re·as·sur·ance** (-unce) *n.*

re·bate (REE·bate) *n.* a partial refund of payment: *We got* or *received a tax rebate.*

reb·el *v.* (ri·BEL) **-els, -elled, -el·ling 1** actively resist or fight against authority: *The Métis rebelled; They rebelled against the government.* **2** oppose or feel repelled by something: *Everyone rebels at injustices.* — *n.* (REB·ul) one who rebels: *famous rebels of history;* **adj.:** *a rebel army, soldier, movement.*

re·bel·lion (ri·BEL·yun) *n.* a defiance of authority, esp. armed resistance to one's government: *to foment* or *stir up a rebellion; to crush* or *put down* or *quash* or *quell a rebellion; They were in open rebellion against the government; The rebellion broke out suddenly, but it failed.* — **re·bel·lious** (ri·BEL·yus) *adj.:* *rebellious troops; children who are rebellious by temperament.*

re·birth (REE·birth) *n.* **1** a second birth, as in reincarnation. **2** a revival or renaissance: *the rebirth of learning in Europe.*

re·born (ree·BORN) *adj.* born again.

re·bound (REE·bownd) *n.* a springing back: *The other players were waiting to grab the rebound if he missed; She hit the ball* **on the rebound;** *He married the first woman he met* **on the rebound** (= after being rejected). — *v.* (ree·BOWND) bounce back; also, recover from a setback or frustration.

re·buff (ri·BUF) *v. & n.* snub or repulse: *She offered Omar a ride but was rebuffed; She met with a rebuff; a polite, not sharp rebuff.*

re·buke (ri·BYOOK) *v.* **-bukes, -buked, -buk·ing** blame or reprove sharply: *to be mildly rebuked; sternly rebuked.* — *n.:* *to administer* or *deliver* or *give a rebuke to someone; He drew* or *received a rebuke from his superiors for his tardiness.*

re·but (ri·BUT) *v.* **-buts, -but·ted, -but·ting** refute by use of arguments, evidence, etc., as in court or in a debate.

re·but·tal (ri·BUT·ul) *n.* a rebutting: *to make a rebuttal of the arguments.*

rec (REC) *n.* [short form] recreation.

re·call (ri·CALL) *v.* **1** call back: *an ambassador recalled to Ottawa; defective cars recalled by a manufacturer; We've been recalled (to work) from vacation; recalled after a long layoff; recalled to active duty.* **2** remember: *I don't recall her name but do recognize the face; I can recall her distinctly* or *vividly; I recall seeing her as a young child; cannot recall where I met her; I suddenly recalled I had a dental appointment.* — *n.* (*also* REE-) a recalling: *a retentive memory with almost complete* or *total recall; Nothing is lost beyond recall; the safety recall of defective cars; Return to camp when the recall (signal) sounds.*

re·cant (ri·CANT) *v.* formally withdraw or renounce a belief, opinion, etc.: *He recanted only on his deathbed.* — **re·can·ta·tion** (ri·can·TAY·shun) *n.*

re·cap (REE·cap, ri·CAP) *v.* **-caps, -capped, -cap·ping**

1 retread a worn tire. **2** *Informal.* recapitulate. — *n.* (REE·cap) **1** a recapped tire. **2** a recapitulation.

re·ca·pit·u·late (ree·cuh·PICH·uh·late) *v.* **-lates, -lat·ed, -lat·ing** sum up; repeat main points briefly. — **re·ca·pit·u·la·tion** (-uh·LAY·shun) *n.*

re·cede (ri·SEED) *v.* **-cedes, -ced·ed, -ced·ing** go backward: *The threat has receded; when the tide recedes from the harbour;* **adj.:** *a receding* (= backward-sloping) *chin; the receding* (= moving away from the forehead) *hairline of a balding man.*

re·ceipt (ri·SEET) *n.* **1** an act of receiving something: *We reply immediately on receipt; We acknowledge receipt of letters.* **2** a written confirmation of something received: *to give* or *make out* or *write out a receipt for payments received; Always get receipts; Keep your receipts for tax purposes.* **3 receipts** *pl.* money received: *Each day's receipts are deposited at the bank daily.* — *v.* issue a receipt for something: *to receipt goods; to receipt* (= mark as paid) *a bill or invoice.*

re·ceiv·a·ble (ri·SEE·vuh·bul) *adj.* that may be received or on which payment is to be received: *accounts receivable.* — **receivables** *n.pl.*

re·ceive (ri·SEEV) *v.* **-ceives, -ceived, -ceiv·ing 1** take what is offered or delivered: *to receive a letter, gift, degree; The mind receives ideas; boats receiving loads; He received a crushing blow.* **2** accept: *a widely received opinion.* **3** welcome: *Guests are received at the door; to be received coldly, coolly, favourably, warmly, with open arms; He was received as a returning hero; to receive a convert into the church.*

re·ceiv·er (ri·SEE·vur) *n.* **1** one that receives: *a wireless receiver; a receiver of stolen goods.* **2** the listening end of a telephone line: *to pick up the receiver; hang up* or *put down* or *replace the receiver.* **3** a football player who receives a kickoff or punt. **4** the judicial manager of property in a bankruptcy: *The firm's assets are in the hands of the receiver.* — **re·ceiv·er·ship** *n.:* *A bankrupt firm goes* or *is put into receivership; It has been in receivership since last year.*

receiving line *n.* the host, hostess, and guests of honour standing in a row to greet guests.

re·cent (REE·sunt) *adj.* of a time just passed: *a recent event; a recent acquaintance (made not long ago).* — **re·cent·ly** *adv.* — **re·cen·cy** *n.*

re·cep·tion (ri·SEP·shun) *n.* **1** the receiving of a person or the social function for receiving guests: *to give* or *hold a reception; to host a reception; He got* or *met with a cool reception; He was accorded* or *given an enthusiastic reception; a chilly, cold, cordial, diplomatic, formal, friendly, mixed, official, rousing, warm, wedding reception; We met at the Mayor's reception;* **adj.:** *the reception area, desk.* **2** the quality of the sound in receiving radio or television broadcasts: *We usually have good* or *strong reception; We are experiencing poor* or *weak reception because of the weather.*

re·cep·tion·ist (ri·SEP·shuh·nist) *n.* one employed to receive callers, esp. in an office.

re·cep·tive (ri·SEP·tiv) *adj.* able or ready to receive stimuli, suggestions, etc.: *Our boss is receptive to new ideas.*

re·cess (REE·ses, ree·SES) *n*. **1** an inner place, as a niche or alcove; also, a secluded place: *the innermost recesses of one's heart.* **2** a break in an activity for rest or recreation: *to take a ten-minute recess; the summer recess; Parliament is in recess.*
— *v*. make, take, or put into a recess: *We recess for lunch at noon; The light fixtures are recessed in the ceiling.*

re·ces·sion (ri·SESH·un) *n*. **1** a going backward. **2** a temporary decline in business activity, less severe than a depression: *a business* or *economic recession; Countries go into and come out of recessions.*

re·ces·sion·al (ri·SESH·uh·nul) *n*. a piece of music for the end of a church service.

re·ces·sive (ri·SES·iv) *adj*. receding, esp. of a genetic character or trait that is latent, not dominant.

rec·i·pe (RESS·uh·pee) *n*. **1** a list of ingredients and set of directions for preparing something to eat or drink. **2** a formula or procedure: *a recipe for happiness, peace, success.*

re·cip·i·ent (ruh·SIP·ee·unt) *n*. one who receives: *a worthy recipient of the Nobel prize.*

re·cip·ro·cal (ruh·SIP·ruh·cul) *adj*. involving exchange between two parties or a back-and-forth relationship, as when Tom helps Mary and vice versa: *reciprocal trade agreements between countries; "Each other" is a **reciprocal pronoun***. — **re·cip·ro·cal·ly** *adv*.

re·cip·ro·cate (ruh·SIP·ruh·cate) *v*. **-cates, -cat·ed, -cat·ing** give back in mutual exchange: *to reciprocate a compliment; to reciprocate hospitality, kindness, love; One favour is reciprocated by* or *with another; We would like to reciprocate for your generosity; the reciprocating* (= back-and-forth) *motion of a piston.*
— **re·cip·ro·ca·tion** (-ruh·CAY·shun) *n*.

rec·i·proc·i·ty (ress·uh·PROS·uh·tee) *n*. **-ties** mutual exchange between two parties: *a relationship that began on the basis of reciprocity; It died because of lack of reciprocity between them.*

re·cit·al (ri·SYE·tul) *n*. **1** a reciting of facts; account. **2** a performance, as by a musician or group of dancers: *to give a modern dance recital; piano recital; organ recital; violin recital.*

rec·i·ta·tion (res·uh·TAY·shun) *n*. **1** a reciting, esp. from memory. **2** something that is recited.

re·cite (ri·CITE) *v*. **-cites, -cit·ed, -cit·ing 1** repeat aloud from memory: *to recite a poem, speech, the alphabet to the class.* **2** repeat or enumerate by reading from a text: *The citizens' group recited a litany of complaints.*

reck·less (RECK·lis) *adj*. very careless and unconcerned about consequences; extremely rash: *It was reckless of him to drive while drunk; reckless driving.*

reck·on (RECK·un) *v*. **1** count or compute: *to reckon the per-unit cost; We reckoned* (= depended) *on your helping us.* **2** consider: *He was reckoned peerless in his time; someone to be **reckoned with*** (= taken into consideration). **3** *Informal*. suppose; guess: *I reckon you're right.*

reckoning (RECK·un·ing) *n*. **1** calculation: *the reckoning of a ship's location; By my reckoning we are close to shore; dead reckoning without astronomical observations.* **2** an account or its settlement: *as the day of reckoning drew near.*

re·claim (ri·CLAIM) *v*. get back what was temporarily given up or lost to productive use: *Wasteland is reclaimed by irrigation and drainage; processes to reclaim rubber, metal, etc. from waste; checked baggage to be reclaimed on landing; a reclaimed* (= reformed) *sinner.*
— **re·claim·a·ble** (-muh·bul) *adj.: recycling of reclaimable wastes.*
— **rec·la·ma·tion** (rec·luh·MAY·shun) *n.: land reclamation.*

re·cline (ri·CLINE) *v*. **-clines, -clined, -clin·ing** lean back or lie down: *Recline* (= lay) *your head on the pillow; a **reclining** figure, seat.*

re·clin·er (ri·CLY·nur) *n*. a chair with adjustable back and footrest: *a three-position recliner; a rocker recliner.*

rec·luse (REC·loose, ri·CLOOSE) *n*. one living a secluded or cloistered life, as a hermit or monk: *The old lady was a virtual recluse in her home.*
— **re·clu·sive** (ri·CLOO·siv) *adj*.

rec·og·ni·tion (rec·ug·NISH·un) *n*. **1** a recognizing: *a book burned beyond recognition; The dazed child showed* or *gave no signs of recognition.* **2** favourable notice: *to gain, give, grant, receive recognition; a scientist who has won worldwide recognition; general, official, public, universal, wide recognition; He received recognition for his achievements from the government; an award in recognition of his services to the community.*

re·cog·ni·zance (ri·COG·nuh·zunce) *n*. a legal undertaking entered into before a court: *The accused was released **on his own recognizance*** (= without payment of surety).

rec·og·nize (REC·ug·nize) *v*. **-niz·es, -nized, -niz·ing 1** know from memory; identify: *a face difficult to recognize.* **2** take notice of formally: *Speakers have to be recognized by the chair; He recognized* (= realized) *that his chances were nil; The U.N. recognized* (= accepted) *Communist China in 1971.* **3** take notice of favourably: *His work was recognized only after his death; She is recognized as an authority on the subject; recognized generally, universally, officially, widely; a **recognized** authority on Egypt.*
— **rec·og·niz·a·ble** (-nye·zuh·bul) *adj*.
— **rec·og·niz·a·bly** *adv*.

re·coil (ri·COIL) *v*. spring back in reaction, as at an ugly sight or as a gun does when fired: *She recoils in horror at the sight of blood; recoils from it instinctively; Evil deeds often recoil on* or *upon* (= react against) *the doer.*
— *n*. a recoiling or its distance.

rec·ol·lect (rec·uh·LECT) *v*. remember something forgotten; recall something from the past: *I cannot recollect what happened next; She cannot recollect being taken to the hospital; She only recollects that she was run over by a bicycle.*

rec·ol·lec·tion (rec·uh·LEC·shun) *n*. memory: *I have no recollection of making any promises; hazy, painful, vague, vivid recollections of childhood.*

re·com·bi·nant (ree·COM·buh·nunt) *adj.* combining genes from different sources: *recombinant DNA technology* (= genetic engineering); *recombinant progeny.*

rec·om·mend (rec·uh·MEND) *v.* 1 favour or speak favourably of a person or thing: *I recommend him for admission; I recommend that he be admitted; I recommend your admitting him; He's highly recommended as a scholar; to recommend enthusiastically, strongly; We recommend this book to you.* 2 suggest as a cure: *We've nothing to recommend for a cold.* 3 commend: *He died recommending his soul to God.*

rec·om·men·da·tion (REC·uh·men·DAY·shun) *n.* an act of recommending or something recommended: *We gave him a letter of recommendation; We provided or wrote a recommendation for him; made a recommendation to appoint him to the vacancy; a lukewarm, negative, positive, strong, weak recommendation; They didn't act on or carry out or implement our recommendation; Good grooming is itself a recommendation in a job applicant; recommendations for safe driving.*

rec·om·pense (REC·um·pence) *n.* a compensation or return: *in recompense for his services.*
— *v.* **-pens·es, -pensed, -pens·ing** compensate with money: *He was well recompensed for his services.*

rec·on·cile (REC·un·cile) *v.* **-ciles, -ciled, -cil·ing** 1 restore to harmony: *Soon after each fight they are reconciled; They are reconciled with each other; a story difficult to reconcile* (= make agree) *with the facts.* 2 settle: *to reconcile differences.* 3 resign oneself to something: *She found it hard to reconcile herself to life in a wheelchair; was finally reconciled to her lot.*
— **rec·on·cil·a·ble** (-SYE·luh·bul) *adj.*
— **rec·on·cil·i·a·tion** (-sil·ee·AY·shun) *n.: to bring about* or *effect a reconciliation with his family.*

rec·on·dite (REC·un·dite) *adj. Formal.* abstruse or obscure: *a recondite author, style, subject.*

re·con·di·tion (ree·cun·DISH·un) *v.* repair and put in good condition: *to recondition a used car.*

re·con·nais·sance (ri·CON·uh·sunce) *n.* a military survey to explore or spy for information, esp. about the enemy: *to carry out* or *conduct an aerial reconnaisance.*
— *adj.: a reconnaisance plane, satellite.*

rec·on·noi·tre or **rec·on·noi·ter** (rec·uh·NOY·tur, ree·cuh-) *v.* **-tres** or **-ters, -tred** or **-tered, -tring** or **-ter·ing** make a reconnaissance of a place.

re·con·sid·er (ree·cun·SID·ur) *v.* consider again with a view to changing a decision, view, etc.
— **re·con·sid·er·a·tion** (REE·cun·sid·uh·RAY·shun) *n.*

re·con·sti·tute (ree·CON·stuh·tute) *v.* **-tutes, -tut·ed, -tut·ing** 1 restore powdered milk, frozen juice, etc. to its original consistency by adding water. 2 put together again in a different way: *to reconstitute a cabinet, case, committee, meeting.*

re·con·struct (ree·cun·STRUCT) *v.* rebuild in original form using remaining parts, evidence, etc.: *to reconstruct a city, extinct languages; Plastic surgery reconstructs deformed or maimed body parts.*
— **re·con·struc·tion** (-shun) *n.*

re·cord (ri·CORD) *v.* 1 put or register something heard, felt, seen, etc. on paper, magnetic tape, film, phonograph discs, etc. in a lasting form: *the date as recorded on the birth certificate; The VCR is now recording; It is a recorded, not live broadcast.* 2 show in a lasting form: *A thermometer records temperature; Annual rings record a tree's age.*
— *n.* (REC·urd) 1 the act of recording or being recorded; also, what is recorded, as a document, disc, tape, etc. containing anything written, spoken, sung, etc.: *to keep accurate records of everything; to cut* or *make a long-playing phonograph record; to play a record; to keep a record of the day's events; the wettest day on record* (= officially noted); *You're on record as saying so; Let's set the record straight* (= correct an error or misunderstanding); *It's a matter of public record; In 1982, AIDS became a disease of record* (= having to do with official records) *in Canada; That was a statement made off the record* (= not for putting down or publication). 2 past performance: *a good, clean driving record; a poor safety record; a distinguished record as a public servant; your employment record; a record of convictions; an academic, criminal, police, service record; an excellent, impeccable, mediocre, spotty record.* 3 the highest, lowest, biggest, etc. in regard to something: *1 069 lb. (481.06 kg) was the 1978 record for a man's weight; A record set* or *established today is broken later; Records fall; to equal* or *tie a record held by someone; an unbroken record; a national, Olympic, speed, world record; adj.: a record attendance, height, temperature.*

re·count (ri·COWNT) *v.* 1 narrate; also, enumerate. 2 also **re·count,** count again.
— *n.* (REE·count) the act of counting again.

re·coup (ri·COOP) *v.* get an equivalent for something one has lost: *to recoup one's fortune, health, losses, strength; He needed time to recoup.*

re·course (REE·corse, ree·CORSE) *n.* a seeking of help or protection; also, a source of aid: *to have recourse to legal measures; I was left with no recourse.*

re·cov·er (ri·CUV·ur) *v.* get back or regain: *Police recover stolen property; Work harder to recover lost time; to recover damages (by process of law); to recover* (= gain control of) *a fumbled ball; to recover oneself in a fall; to recover consciousness; to recover from an illness.*

re·cov·er·y (ri·CUV·uh·ree) *n.* **-er·ies** a recovering: *the recovery of stolen vehicles; A quick recovery saved the skidding car; the recovery room where patients are wheeled in from surgery to recover from the effects of anesthesia; to make a rapid, remarkable, slow, speedy recovery; an economic recovery following a recession; the recovery in the bond market; the recovery of the Canadian dollar against the American dollar.*

rec·re·ate (REC·ree·ate) *v.* **-ates, -at·ed, -at·ing** take recreation: *Children prefer to recreate outdoors.*
— **rec·re·a·tive** (-tiv) *adj.: a recreative activity.*

re-create (ree·cree·ATE) *v.* create again: *to re-create the scenes of one's childhood.*

rec·re·a·tion (rec·ree·AY·shun) *n.* means of refreshment after work, as games, picnics, and other leisure-time activities: *He watches birds for recreation; a government department of culture, fitness, and recreation; a parks*

and recreation department; reading and recreation; rest and recreation; **adj.**: recreation ministry, services, therapy; a recreation area, centre, room.
— **rec·re·a·tion·al** (-shun·ul) adj.: recreational facilities; a **recreational vehicle** such as a trailer, camper, or motor home.

re·crim·i·na·tion (ri·CRIM·uh·NAY·shun) n. an act of blaming each other: Why waste time on recriminations when we are both responsible for what happened? mutual recriminations ending in divorce proceedings.

rec room n. recreation room.

re·cruit (ri·CROOT, long "OO") v. enlist new personnel for an army, navy, or other organization: to recruit volunteers from the public.
— **n.** a newly enlisted soldier, sailor, or member of a group: a fresh, green, raw recruit.
— **re·cruit·er** n. — **re·cruit·ment** n.

rec·ti·fy (REC·tuh·fye) v. -fies, -fied, -fy·ing correct by conformity to a standard: to rectify an injustice, mistake, situation; rectified (= purified) spirits; a rectifying device, or **rec·ti·fi·er**, to change alternating current to direct current.
— **rec·ti·fi·ca·tion** (-fuh·CAY·shun) n.

rec·ti·tude (REC·tuh·tude) n. uprightness of character or conduct.

rec·tor (REC·tur) n. 1 a minister or clergyman in charge of a parish. 2 the head of a seminary, college, or school.

rec·to·ry (REC·tuh·ree) n. -ries a rector's residence.

rec·tum (REC·tum) n. the straight final portion of the intestine leading to the anus.

re·cum·bent (ri·CUM·bunt) adj. lying down or reclining: a figure shown in a recumbent position.

re·cu·per·ate (ri·COO·puh·rate) v. -ates, -at·ed, -at·ing regain health or strength: to recuperate from an illness; It takes time to recuperate after a flu attack.
— **re·cu·per·a·tive** (-ray·tiv) adj.
— **re·cu·per·a·tion** (-RAY·shun) n.

re·cur (ri·CUR) v. -curs, -curred, -cur·ring occur again: a recurring nightmare; It keeps recurring (= returning) to him in his dreams; a **recurring decimal** such as 3.33333....
— **re·cur·rent** (-unt) adj.: a recurrent characteristic, headache, theme; recurrent costs, rumours.
— **re·cur·rence** (-unce) n.

re·cy·cle (ree·SYE·cul) v. -cles, -cled, -cling put waste materials through a process or treatment for using again: garbage recycling; recycled paper.
— **re·cy·cla·ble** (-cluh·bul) adj.: We prefer recyclable containers to returnable ones.

red n. 1 the colour of fresh blood: bright, dark, deep, light red; No turn on red allowed at these lights; We are operating $3 million **in the red** (= in debt) this year; The boss will **see red** (= get angry) if he finds out.
— **adj.** red·der, red·dest of the colour red: There are red and white blood cells or corpuscles; He appeared with red (= bloodshot) eyes; The army was on **red alert** (= final stage of warning of an enemy attack) for a couple of hours; There were many **red faces** (= embarrassed people) following the fiasco; the **red meat** of cattle, hogs, and sheep. — **red·dish** adj.

Red n. a communist or an extreme radical.
— **adj.** communist: Some African nations went Red after independence; Red China.

red-blood·ed (RED·blud·id) adj. vigorous or lusty: Every red-blooded Canadian resents being typed as American and vice versa.

red carpet n. an impressive or ceremonial welcome: They rolled out or pulled out the red carpet for the visiting dignitary.
— **red-carpet** adj.: a red-carpet ceremony; He received or was given red-carpet treatment.

red cent n. Informal. even a trifling amount: Don't expect one red cent from the government; Handouts are not worth a red cent; I **don't give a red cent** (= I don't care) for green grapes and avocadoes.

red·coat n. 1 a red-coated British soldier of the American Revolutionary War. 2 Cdn. Informal. a Mountie.

red·den (RED·un) v. make or become red; flush or blush.

re·deem (ri·DEEM) v. get back something or someone in another's possession by paying a price: jewellery redeemed by repaying a loan; The government redeems savings bonds; to redeem (= pay off) a mortgage; the redeeming of slaves; a poor show with few **redeeming** (= saving) features; Christians believe humanity has been redeemed from sin by a **re·deem·er**, or **the Redeemer** Jesus.

re·demp·tion (ri·DEMP·shun) n. a redeeming, being redeemed, or something that redeems: She prayed for his redemption from debt; She left him when she thought he was past or beyond redemption.
— **re·demp·tive** (-tiv) adj.

Red Ensign n. a red flag with the Union Jack at the upper corner, which was Canada's national flag till 1965 and is the official flag of Ontario and Manitoba.

red·eye n. Cdn. a drink of beer with tomato juice.

red-faced adj. embarrassed: He was red-faced with shame.

red-handed (RED·han·did) adj. & adv. in the act of committing a crime: The shoplifter was caught red-handed.

red herring n. something irrelevant used to divert attention from the main issue.

red-hot adj. 1 glowing red with heat: red-hot iron. 2 exciting or sensational: a red-hot campaign, fanatic;

red-hot news, rumours.

re·dis·tri·bu·tion (REE·dis·truh·BEW·shun) *n. Cdn.* a population-based reallocation of the number of seats in the House of Commons for each province and the redrawing of constituency boundaries every ten years.

red-letter day *n.* a memorable or happy occasion.

red light *n.* a warning light or signal, as one requiring traffic to stop: *He didn't stop at a red light; went through* or *ran the red light and was ticketed.*

red·lin·ing (RED·lye·ning) *n.* economic discrimination against a poor neighbourhood, as when a bank refuses mortgages or loans.

red·o·lent (RED·ul·unt) *adj.* smelling or evocative of something: *a kitchen redolent of garlic; a custom redolent of pioneer days; Quebec City is redolent with Old World charm.*

re·dou·ble (ree·DUB·ul) *v.* **-bles, -bled, -bling** increase greatly; intensify: *Her enthusiasm redoubled; She redoubled her efforts to win the scholarship.*

re·doubt·a·ble (ri·DOW·tuh·bul) *adj.* formidable or eminent: *a redoubtable adversary, inventor, warrior.*

re·dound (ri·DOWND) *v.* have a result or reaction: *actions that redound to one's credit.*

re·dress (ri·DRESS) *v.* set right or repair a wrong, grievance, etc.
— *n.* (*also* REE·dress) reparation or the means of finding a remedy: *We sought legal redress when persuasion failed.*

red tape *n.* excessive adherence to rules and regulations, as in government service; bureaucratic routine: *They got caught up* or *involved in red tape; We cut through the red tape and talked to the minister in charge.*

Red Tory *n. Cdn.* a Tory with very liberal views.

re·duce (ri·DUCE, *rhyme:* produce) *v.* **-duc·es, -duced, -duc·ing** make less, lower, smaller, simpler, etc.: *how to reduce expenses, weight; a reducing diet; a family reduced to poverty by unemployment; The heckler was reduced to silence by the retort; The corporal was reduced in rank; was reduced to the rank of private; 3/9 can be reduced to 1/3; Hydrogen acts as a reducing agent in recovering a metal from an ore by removing the oxygen and uniting with it to form water.*
— **re·duc·er** *n.* — **re·duc·i·ble** *adj.*

re·duc·tion (ri·DUC·shun) *n.* a reducing, being reduced, the amount reduced, or a result of reducing: *Employees can buy the same goods at a substantial reduction* (= discount); *the reduction of an argument to absurdity; the reduction of iron ore to metal; The president took a reduction* (= cut) *in salary.*

re·dun·dan·cy (ri·DUN·dun·see) *n.* **1** *pl.* **-cies** an instance of wordiness, as "consenus of opinion." **2** a being redundant. Also **redundance.**

re·dun·dant (ri·DUN·dunt) *adj.* **1** superfluous or unnecessary: *jobs made redundant by automation.* **2** wordy: *redundant expressions such as "exact same"; a redundant style.*

reed *n.* **1** any tall, slender grass plant with a hollow, jointed stem that is often used for musical pipes, arrows, etc.; also, the stem. **2** a thin piece of material used in the mouthpiece of a reed instrument. **3** same as **reed instrument,** a wind instrument such as a clarinet that makes its sound by the vibration of a reed in the mouthpiece.

reef *n.* a ridge of rocks, sand, or coral lying covered near the surface of the water: *The ship struck a reef and sank.* — **reef·y** *adj.*

reef·er (REE·fur) *n.* **1** *Slang.* a marijuana cigarette. **2** *Slang.* a refrigerated van, freight car, etc.

reek *v.* send out a strong, unpleasant smell: *He walked in reeking of alcohol; a department reeking with corruption.*

reel *n.* **1** film, thread, cable, etc. wound on a revolving device such as a roller or spool; also, the device: *rod and reel; The film is in two reels.* **2** a whirling motion. **3** a lively folk dance of the Scottish Highlands.
— *v.* **1** wind on a reel. **2** be or cause to be in a whirl: *The blow sent him reeling; His head was reeling under the blow; Chris came out of the bar and reeled* (= staggered) *down the street.*
— **reel in** pull in a fish using a reeled line.
— **reel off** repeat a list, text, etc. with ease and speed; rattle off.

reeve (REEV) *v.* **reeves,** *pt. & pp.* **reeved** or **rove, reev·ing** pass a rope through a ring or cleat.
— *n. Cdn.* in Ontario and other provinces, the elected head of a rural municipality or of a village council.

ref *n. & v.* **refs, reffed, ref·fing** [short form] referee.

re·fer (ri·FUR) *v.* **-fers, -ferred, -fer·ring 1** direct or send someone or something for information, action, help, etc.: *He referred me to a lawyer; Let's refer the dispute to a judge.* **2** direct one's attention: *He referred to many authorities in the subject; Does this remark refer* (= apply) *to me?*
— **ref·er·a·ble** (REF·uh·ruh·bul, ri·FUR·uh-) *adj.*
— **re·fer·rer** (ri·FUR·ur) *n.*

ref·er·ee (ref·uh·REE) *n.* one who supervises a game, enforcing the rules; umpire: *In many games, as in football and tennis, umpires and referees have different functions.*
— *v.* **-ees, -eed, -ee·ing** act as a referee: *Who's refereeing the basketball game today?*

ref·er·ence (REF·ur·unce) *n.* **1** a referring, being referred, or thing referred to: *There are many references to the Bible in Shakespeare's plays; job applications filed for future reference; a scholarly book with many footnote references; books kept on the desk for easy* or *ready reference; articles alphabetically arranged for ease of reference; Everyone has a personal frame of reference* (= viewpoint) *in terms of which to discuss a subject; an indirect* or *oblique reference; a direct reference;* **with** or **in reference** *to your letter of January 31st; We hire **without reference to** sex, race, or religion.* **2** a source of information on a subject: *May I cite you as a (personal) reference? He showed me excellent references* (= letters of recommendation) *from former employers; They give* or *provide good, positive, satisfactory references.*
— *adj.: a reference book such as a dictionary, atlas, or encyclopedia; a reference librarian, library; a reference mark such as the asterisk.*

ref·er·en·dum (ref·uh·REN·dum) *n.* -dums or -da 1 a reference, as of legislative measures, to the direct vote of the people. 2 such a vote: *to conduct* or *hold a referendum on a subject of national interest; the Quebec referendum of May 20, 1980, on sovereignty-association with the rest of Canada.*

re·fer·ral (ri·FUR·ul) *n.* the act or an instance of referring something to someone: *Our clients come mostly by referral; Specialists receive referrals; a referral made from the President's office to the Dean of Studies; income derived from fees, commissions, and referrals.*

re·fill (ree·FIL) *v.* fill again.
— *n.* (REE·fil) a refilling, as of a drug prescription, or something used to refill, as in a ball-point pen.
— **re·fill·a·ble** (ree·FIL·uh·bul) *adj.: a refillable container.*

re·fine (ri·FINE) *v.* -fines, -fined, -fin·ing 1 make finer or less coarse. 2 purify.
— **refine on** or **upon** improve or improve on a method, notion, invention, etc.

re·fined (ri·FINED) *adj.* 1 made free from impurities: *refined petroleum, sugar.* 2 polished: *refined language; a woman of refined manners, tastes; a refined* (=cultured) *young woman.* 3 subtle: *a refined distinction.*

re·fine·ment (ri·FINE·munt) *n.* 1 fineness of feeling or behaviour: *a man of refinement.* 2 act or result of refining: *Wrought iron is a refinement of pig iron; sarcasm as a refinement of cruelty.*

re·fin·er·y (ri·FYE·nuh·ree) *n.* -er·ies a plant for refining raw materials such as oil or sugar.

re·flect (ri·FLECT) *v.* 1 throw back light, heat, sound, etc.: *Mirrors reflect light, images, one's face; Editorials reflect* (=express) *the views of the paper; Great deeds reflect* (=bring) *credit on their doers; Bad manners often reflect on* (=bring discredit to) *one's parents.* 2 turn one's thoughts back on a subject; seriously consider: *He blurted out nonsense without reflecting; Please reflect (up)on what you said.*

re·flec·tion (ri·FLEC·shun) *n.* 1 a reflecting, being reflected, or something reflected; image: *We see a laterally inverted reflection in a mirror.* 2 thinking or consideration; also, its expression: *quiet, serious, sober reflection; Sorel's reflections on violence; On or after further reflection, he decided not to quit school.* 3 a remark or observation, esp. one casting blame; hence, blame or discredit: *My comments are no reflection on your motives.*
— **re·flec·tive** (-tiv) *adj.* 1 reflecting: *We wear reflective clothing for safety in the dark; Copper foil is used as reflective insulation against heat.* 2 thoughtful: *I found him in a reflective mood.* — **re·flec·tor** (-tur) *n.*

re·flex (REE·flex) *n.* a usually inborn, automatic reaction to a stimulus: *The doctor hit his knee with a hammer to test his reflexes; The mouth watering at the mention of food is a conditioned reflex.*
— *adj.* 1 coming as a reaction: *the reflex speed of a boxer in the ring; You jerk back your hand from a flame by* **reflex action**; *A reflex action works in a* **reflex arc** (=nerve path). 2 reflected back: *A reflex image is used for focussing a "reflex camera."*

re·for·est (ree·FOR·ist) *v.* replant land with trees, as after a fire. — **re·for·est·a·tion** (-is·TAY·shun) *n.*

re·form (REE·form) *v.* form again. — **re·for·ma·tion** *n.*

re·form (ri·FORM) *v.* make or become better, esp. by removing faults: *a reformed criminal, young offender; the Dutch Reformed Church.*
— *n.* an improvement in conditions: *to carry out* or *effect social reforms; an agrarian* or *land reform; spelling reform in English; adj.: a reform bill; a reform group versus the establishment.*
— **re·form·a·tive** (-muh·tiv) *adj.*

ref·or·ma·tion (ref·ur·MAY·shun) *n.* a reforming or being reformed, esp. **the Reformation,** the European religious movement of the 1500s leading to the founding of Protestant churches.

re·form·a·to·ry (ri·FOR·muh·tor·ee) *n.* -ries an institution for young offenders; a correctional training school: *He spent time at* or *in a reformatory.* Also **reform school.**

re·form·er (ri·FOR·mur) *n.* 1 one who works for reform. 2 **Reformer** a leader of the Reformation.

re·fract (ri·FRACT) *v.* subject to refraction; bend: *Water refracts light.*

re·frac·tion (ri·FRAC·shun) *n.* the bending of waves of light, sound, etc. when passing from one medium to another obliquely: *The optometrist does a refraction* (=measuring of the eye's bending of light waves) *before prescribing corrective lenses.*
— **re·frac·tive** (-tiv) *adj.: Water has a lower refractive index* or *index of refraction than glass* (= Water bends light less than glass).

re·frac·to·ry (ri·FRAC·tuh·ree) *adj.* 1 stubbornly resisting control or direction: *a refractory group of people.* 2 able to withstand great heat: *Fireclay is a refractory material.*

re·frain (ri·FRAIN) *n.* a phrase or verse that is repeated at intervals in a poem or song, esp. at the end of a stanza; a chorus or burden: *to sing a refrain.*
— *v.* hold oneself from doing something one is inclined to do: *We refrain from smoking in church.*

re·fresh (ri·FRESH) *v.* 1 make or become fresh again: *a few hints to refresh his memory; We refresh ourselves with a drink, warm bath, etc.; adj.: a refreshing breeze, experience, sleep.* 2 refill: *to refresh supplies, glasses after each drink.*

re·fresh·ment (ri·FRESH·munt) *n.* a refreshing or that which refreshes: *A lemonade is a good refreshment on a warm day; They offer* or *serve light* **refreshments** (=food and drink) *such as coffee and donuts.*

re·frig·er·ant (ri·FRIJ·ur·unt) *adj.* that refrigerates: *A heat pump is a refrigerant device.*
— *n.* a refrigerant fluid such as freon.

re·frig·er·ate (ri·FRIJ·uh·rate) *v.* -ates, -at·ed, -at·ing make or keep food, etc. cold to keep from perishing: *Most food has to be refrigerated for later use.*
— **re·frig·er·a·tion** (ri·FRIJ·uh·RAY·shun) *n.: Perishables are kept under refrigeration.*

re·frig·er·a·tor (ri·FRIJ·uh·ray·tur) *n.* a cabinet or room for keeping food, etc. from perishing: *a frost-free* *refrigerator; Raiding the refrigerator (for snacks) is a North American habit.*

ref·uge (REF·uge, *rhyme:* huge) *n.* a place of shelter or of protection from danger or trouble: *The Salvation Army gives* or *provides refuge to the homeless; a place of refuge for the night; They found* or *took refuge from the storm in a bus shelter; Jasper National Park in Alberta is the largest wildlife refuge in North America; Having nowhere to hide, they sought refuge in flight.*

ref·u·gee (REF·yoo·jee, ref·yoo·JEE) *n.* one who flees from one's country to another for protection: *political refugees; a refugee from persecution.*

re·fund (ri·FUND) *v.* pay back a deposit, an excess payment, the price of an unsatisfactory purchase, etc. — *n.* (REE·fund) a refunding or a refunded amount: *to give* or *pay a refund; They got* or *received a tax refund.* — **re·fund·a·ble** *adj.*

re·fur·bish (ri·FUR·bish) *v.* 1 brighten or polish up. 2 renovate.

re·fus·al (ri·FEW·zul) *n.* 1 a refusing: *We met with a curt, flat, outright, point-blank refusal; an adamant refusal to help.* 2 right or option to acquire something before it is offered to others: *The author gave his publisher first refusal on his next book.*

re·fuse (ri·FYOOZ) *v.* -fus·es , -fused, -fus·ing not do, give, grant, or accept something directly or bluntly: *She refused to change her mind; She refused them permission; refused them outright; refused categorically, completely, point-blank; The horse refused to jump; It refused the carrot; an offer (so good) you can't refuse; She also refused (= rejected) the presidency, advice, gifts.* — *n.* (REF·yoose, -yooze) what is rejected; garbage or trash: *kitchen refuse; paper refuse for recycling; a poor man ready to accept even the refuse of the job market; a refuse dump.*

re·fuse·nik (ri·FUZE·nik) *n. Informal.* a Soviet citizen who has been refused permission to emigrate.

re·fute (ri·FUTE, *rhyme:* CUTE) *v.* -futes, -fut·ed, -fut·ing prove a person or argument to be wrong by use of evidence, reasoning, etc. — **re·fut·a·ble** (-tuh·bul) *adj.* — **ref·u·ta·tion** (ref·yuh·TAY·shun) *n.*

re·gain (ri·GAIN) *v.* get back: *to regain one's confidence, consciousness, footing, health, popularity; territory regained from the enemy; to regain (= get back to) the shore.*

re·gal (REE·gul) *adj.* royal, esp. majestic or splendid as a king or queen: *her regal bearing, dignity, splendour.* — **re·gal·ly** *adv.*

re·gale (ri·GALE) *v.* -gales, -galed, -gal·ing entertain *with* something delightful or delicious. — **re·gale·ment** *n.*

re·gard (ri·GARD) *v.* consider mentally or with the eyes in a specified manner, as with favour or respect: *He regarded her lovingly; The painting is regarded with suspicion; It is regarded as a fake, as of no value; a highly regarded (= esteemed) surgeon.* — *n.* 1 consideration: *Have* or *show some regard for*

safety; He acted without regard to the rights of others; to be held in high, low, some regard (= esteem). 2 **regards** *pl.* good wishes: *Please give him my regards; Convey* or *send my regards to him; with my best regards; with cordial, friendly, kind, kindest, sincere, warmest, personal regards from yours truly.* — **as regards** or **in regard to** or **regarding** or **with regard to** concerning: *As regards* or *in regard to* or *regarding* or *with regard to your application, I have yet to decide; You are all right as regards (= according to) height and weight.* — **re·gard·ful** *adj.* — **re·gard·less** *adj.: He is regardless (= careless) of the rights of others;* **adv.:** *Do it regardless of (= in spite of) costs; Do it regardless (= in spite of costs).*

re·gen·er·ate (ri·JEN·uh·rate) *v.* -ates, -at·ed, -at·ing 1 be reborn spiritually. 2 regrow a part, as plants and lower animals do: *The human body can regenerate hair, nails, etc.* — **re·gen·er·a·tion** (-RAY·shun) *n.*

re·gent (REE·junt) *n.* 1 one who rules a country when the monarch is absent, too young, or ill. 2 a member of a governing body of a school, library, museum, etc. — **re·gen·cy** *n.*

reg·gae (REG·ay) *n.* a popular form of West Indian music blending calypso, blues, and rock'n'roll.

re·gime or **ré·gime** (ruh·ZHEEM, ray-) *n.* 1 a system of government, its rule, or its period: *to establish a democratic regime; The totalitarian puppet regime was overthrown; during the previous regime.* 2 regimen.

reg·i·men (REJ·uh·mun) *n.* 1 a way of living in regard to diet, exercise, sleep, etc.: *He went on a strict regimen to control his weight.* 2 a course of treatment: *a megavitamin regimen.*

reg·i·ment (REJ·uh·munt) *n.* a military unit composed of battalions or squadrons: *an infantry regiment.* — *v.* (-ment) organize, as a school system, in a strict or uniform manner. — **reg·i·men·tal** (-MEN·tul) *adj.* — **reg·i·men·ta·tion** (-men·TAY·shun) *n.*

re·gion (REE·jun) *n.* 1 a usually indefinite area or division with certain common characteristics: *the Hudson Bay region; the Atlantic region; a border, metropolitan, mountainous, outlying, remote, polar, tropical, uninhabited region.* 2 *Cdn.* an area of municipal administration, as in Ontario, covering several cities and townships, which is in charge of land-use planning and services such as police, water, sewerage, and waste disposal. — **re·gion·al** (REE·juh·nul) *adj.: a matter of regional rather than national interest; a regional dialect, expression, flavour; regional geography, government.* — **re·gion·al·ism** *n.* — **re·gion·al·ly** *adv.*

reg·is·ter (REJ·is·tur) *n.* 1 a record: *to keep a case register; a hotel register; a cash register (= recording device).* 2 in computers, a temporary storage device for arithmetic, logic, and other operations: *a buffer register.* 3 a particular compass or range of voice: *A bass sings in a different register from a soprano; "Informal" and "Slang" are different registers (= levels of usage).* 4 a grille over a hole in a wall or floor to regulate the air from a heating or cooling system. — *v.* 1 record: *Births, deaths, etc. are registered at the registry; Guns have to be registered with the police; Her face registered (= showed) no surprise;* **Registered mail**

(which is entered in the records) can be traced; a **registered** home ownership plan, retirement savings plan, trademark. 2 enrol: She registered as a Liberal; She is not registered as a voter; At the college, he registered for four courses; He was registered by the registrar; Many are registered in the course; a **registered** (=licensed) nurse, nursing assistant.

reg·is·trar (REJ·is·trar) n. an official in charge of records.

reg·is·tra·tion (rej·is·TRAY·shun) n. a registering, an entry in a register, the number of those registered, or a certificate of registering, as of an automobile: gun registration; voter registration.

reg·is·try (REJ·is·tree) n. -tries 1 an office of registration. 2 a register book. 3 registration, esp. of a ship: a ship of Liberian registry.

re·gres·sion (ri·GRESH·un) n. the act of going backward: the behaviour regression of an older child acting like an infant; a regression in one's health, skills; a regression made to reread something you have missed; the biological regression (=reversion) to type.

re·gret (ri·GRET) v. -grets, -gret·ted, -gret·ting feel sorrow or dissatisfaction about an action or any unfortunate occurrence: I regret to have to or regret having to say this; He regrets his absence; regrets deeply or very much that he cannot be present.
— n. a feeling or expression of regret: to feel, show regret at or over what happened; She expressed regret(s) for her behaviour, regret at not being able to attend the function; our deep, keen regret; We sent our **regrets** (=a polite note) declining the invitation.
— **re·gret·ful** adj.: I felt regretful (=bad) about the incident. — **re·gret·ful·ly** adv.
— **re·gret·ta·ble** (-tuh·bul) adj.: I felt bad about the whole regrettable incident. — **re·gret·ta·bly** adv.

reg·u·lar (REG·yuh·lur) adj. 1 according to rule or custom; normal; usual: Nine to five are regular business hours; "Fix" is a regular or weak verb with endings "-es," "-ed," and "-ing"; A regular size is not so large as king size; regular and premium (grade) gasoline.
2 habitual or predictable: a regular customer, reader, subscriber; a regular (=likeable) guy; a regular (Informal for thorough) nuisance. 3 even; symmetrical; orderly: a face with regular features; a regular heartbeat; the regular life of a camp. 4 professional or recognized: the regular soldiers of a regular army, not draftees, reserves, or mercenaries; the regular (=religious, not secular) clergy; a regular (=official) nominee of the party.
— n. 1 a regular soldier, clergyman, or player, not a substitute. 2 Informal. a regular contributor, customer, or attender (as at church services).
— **reg·u·lar·ly** adv. — **reg·u·lar·i·ty** (·LAIR·uh·tee) n.

reg·u·lar·ize (REG·yuh·luh·rize) v. -iz·es, -ized, -iz·ing make regular or normal: They regularized their status by becoming landed immigrants; to regularize the spelling and style of a publication.

reg·u·late (REG·yuh·late) v. control or maintain in a controlled state: Signals regulate the flow of traffic; a well-regulated (=well-adjusted) clock, household.
— **reg·u·la·tor** n.

reg·u·la·tion (reg·yuh·LAY·shun) n. 1 control:

unnecessary government regulation; the regulation of traffic during rush hour. 2 a rule for the enforcement of a law: to adopt or enact a regulation; to apply or enforce the traffic regulation that cars would be towed during a snow emergency; to violate a regulation; army, government, military, parking, police, security regulations.
— **adj.** as required by regulations: the regulation size; a regulation uniform.

reg·u·la·to·ry (REG·yuh·luh·tor·ee) adj. that regulates: a regulatory agency, authority, body, gene, measure, move, sign, step, system; a regulatory (=subject to control) product that is dangerous to handle.

re·ha·bil·i·tate (ree·huh·BIL·uh·tate) v. -tates, -tat·ed, -tat·ing restore a criminal, a patient with a severe illness or disability, a run-down neighbourhood, etc. to a good or healthy condition.
— **re·ha·bil·i·ta·tion** (-uh·TAY·shun) n.

re·hash (ree·HASH) v. work up old material in a new form without much improvement.
— **n.** (REE·hash): This lunch is not a rehash of yesterday's leftovers.

re·hears·al (ri·HUR·sul) n. a rehearsing: a wedding rehearsal; a camera rehearsal (before a TV show); a dress (=final) rehearsal.

re·hearse (ri·HURCE) v. -hears·es, -hearsed, -hears·ing practise a play, role, concert, ceremony, etc. for public performance.

reign (RAIN) n. a sovereign's being in power or its period: during the long reign of Queen Victoria.
— v. 1 be the sovereign: She reigned over England for 63 years; A sovereign is said to reign, not rule. 2 prevail: Peace reigned in Jerusalem; a modern office where the computer reigns supreme.

re·im·burse (ree·im·BURCE) v. -burs·es, -bursed, -burs·ing pay a person for money spent: He was reimbursed amply, fully, generously for all his travel expenses; His expenses were reimbursed (=paid).
— **re·im·burse·ment** n.

rein (RAIN) n. 1 one of a pair of long, narrow straps or lines connected to the bridle of an animal for its driver or rider to control it: to draw in or tighten the rein. 2 a check or control: to assume, seize the reins of government; She kept a tight rein on all company expenditure; Unlike reporters, storytellers can **give free** or **full rein** to their imagination.
— v. guide or curb: A rider **reins in** a horse before dismounting; to rein (in) one's passions (=have them under control).

re·in·force (ree·in·FORCE) v. -forc·es, -forced, -forc·ing strengthen: A military force is reinforced with more troops, ships, planes, etc.; In a learning process, a response to a stimulus may be reinforced, as by pairing the taste of a food with a sound or tone as an added stimulus; **Reinforced concrete** is strengthened with metal inside it.
— **re·in·force·ment** n.: to bring up, commit, send **reinforcements** (=military units).

re·in·state (ree·in·STATE) v. -states, -stat·ed, -stat·ing restore to a former position or condition: An unjustly fired cook was reinstated with full pay and seniority in

his former position; was reinstated as cook.
— **re·in·state·ment** *n.*

re·it·er·ate (ree·IT·uh·rate) *v.* -ates, -at·ed, -at·ing repeat a request, warning, belief, etc. insistently: *She reiterated her warning; reiterated that we were heading for bankruptcy.* — **re·it·er·a·tion** (-RAY·shun) *n.*

re·ject (ri·JECT) *v.* 1 refuse to accept, agree to, or submit to something: *to reject an application, claim, offer, plea, protest note, suggestion; She rejected his advances; to reject the Church's authority; to reject help; He was rejected for the army; She rejected the plan completely, flatly, outright, totally.* 2 discard or throw out something or someone: *The underprivileged feel rejected by society; a rejected apple, child, lover.* — **n.** (REE·ject) a rejected person or thing: *Bad apples are discarded as rejects; the rejects and derelicts of society.* — **re·jec·tion** (ri·JEC·shun) *n.: an organism's immunological rejection of a transplanted organ or foreign tissue; a publisher's **rejection slip** sent back with an unsuitable manuscript.*

re·joice (ri·JOICE) *v.* -joic·es, -joiced, -joic·ing be full of great joy: *Let's rejoice; We rejoice to hear you have won; We rejoice in or at or over her win; It rejoices* (= gladdens) *our hearts.* — **re·joic·ing** *n.*

re·join·der (ri·JOIN·dur) *n.* an answer to a reply: *a sharp rejoinder to her reply.*

re·ju·ve·nate (ri·JOO·vuh·nate) *v.* -nates, -nat·ed, -nat·ing make young again or give new vigour to a person or thing: *to rejuvenate a dying organization; to rejuvenate our sagging economy; In 1982, Iacocca helped Chrysler rejuvenate itself and avoid bankruptcy.* — **re·ju·ve·na·tion** (-NAY·shun) *n.*

re·lapse (ri·LAPS) *v.* -laps·es, -lapsed, -laps·ing fall back into a previous condition: *to relapse into a bad habit, coma, former routine; to relapse into error, heresy, obscurity, silence; The patient relapsed when he was sent home from hospital.* — **n.** a relapsing, as a return of symptoms that had disappeared: *to have a relapse; The patient suffered a complete or total relapse; His relapse proved fatal.*

re·late (ri·LATE) *v.* -lates, -lat·ed, -lat·ing 1 tell or narrate an adventure, story, version, etc. 2 connect: *The Smiths are related to the Smythes; related by marriage; "Frail" and "fragile" are related through Latin; Children **relate to** (= form personal ties with) their peers more easily than to elders; We're all interested in what relates (= refers) to ourselves.*

re·la·tion (ri·LAY·shun) *n.* 1 an account or narration. 2 a connection, esp. as a relative: *Bara Yogi is no relation of Mahesh Yogi; They are not close relations; Results should bear some relation to costs; The two had no (sexual) relations though living together; to establish, have or maintain, renew relations with Moscow; to break off or sever relations; to strain relations among or between countries; business, diplomatic, foreign, friendly, labour, public, trade relations; an expert in international relations* (= dealings or affairs). — **in** or **with relation to** concerning: *The memo is in relation to our talks; In relation to* (= compared with) *Ontario, P.E.I. is a small province.* — **re·la·tion·al** *adj.* — **re·la·tion·ship** *n.: The point you raise does not bear*

or have any relationship to what we are discussing; to have a casual, close, intimate, direct, meaningful, warm relationship with someone.

rel·a·tive (REL·uh·tiv) *n.* one related by blood or marriage: *a blood relative; close, distant, near relatives.* — **adj.** related to each other or to something else; comparative: *the relative merits of coffee and pop as beverages; to live in relative comfort (compared with others less rich); "Hot" and "cold" are relative* (= variable from person to person); *Ten times in 2 days is a higher **relative frequency** than 10 times in 3 days.* — **relative to** concerning: *a memo relative to our talks; The cost is nothing relative to* (= compared with) *its importance.* — **rel·a·tive·ly** *adv.*; **rel·a·tive·ness** *n.*

rel·a·tiv·i·ty (rel·uh·TIV·uh·tee) *n.* -ties the quality or condition of being relative: *Einstein's theory of relativity; the relativity of time and space because of motion.*

re·lax (ri·LAX) *v.* make or become less stiff, tense, or severe: *to relax one's muscles; Discipline is relaxed at certain times; Sit back and relax* (= rest); *It's **relaxing** to take a hot shower.*

re·lax·ant (ri·LAX·unt) *n. & adj.* a drug that relaxes muscles: *a muscle relaxant; the relaxant effect of tranquillizers.*

re·lax·a·tion (ree·lak·SAY·shun) *n.* the act of relaxing; hence, rest or recreation: *We play for fun and relaxation.*

re·lay (REE·lay) *n.* a linking of one stage with the next in a continuous operation, as in a relay race: *to run a relay; the relay* (= conveying) *of a puck from one player to another; Volunteers worked in relay, or relays, one relieving the next, to put out the fire.* — **adj.:** *the green postal **relay boxes** for letters awaiting delivery; A **relay race** is a contest among several teams of contestants, each teammate running a part of the distance in sequence with the others; a **relay satellite** for TV and other signals.* — **v.** 1 convey or pass on: *the relaying of messages to remote regions; People were relayed* (= supplied in groups) *to fight the fire.* 2 (ree·LAY) -lays, -laid, -lay·ing lay again.

re·lease (ri·LEECE) *v.* -leas·es, -leased, -leas·ing free or let go from a confined or restricted condition: *Prisoners are released; a priest released from his vows; property released (legally) to a claimant; a statement released for publication on Monday morning.* — **n.** a releasing: *a release of pressure, tension; a feeling of release; release from jail; a statement for immediate release (to the media); a movie awaiting release (to the theatres); He obtained a settlement after signing a release (from further claims).*

rel·e·gate (REL·uh·gate) *v.* -gates, -gat·ed, -gat·ing 1 put away or assign *to* a lower position; hence, cast out or demote. 2 hand over a task or business to be carried out or disposed of. — **rel·e·ga·tion** (-GAY·shun) *n.*

re·lent (ri·LENT) *v.* become less stern or more merciful: *The teacher relented and cancelled the penalty.*

re·lent·less (ri·LENT·lis) *adj.* that does not relent; unyielding: *the lawyer's relentless cross-examination; a relentless door-to-door campaign; her relentless logic; the relentless passage of time.* — **re·lent·less·ly** *adv.*

rel·e·vant (REL·uh·vunt) *adj.* having some bearing on a matter; pertinent: *testimony relevant to a case.*
— **rel·e·vance** (-vunce) *n.*

re·li·a·ble (ri·LYE·uh·bul) *adj.* that may be relied on: *a reliable piece of information; reliable information, news; a reliable product, source, witness.*
— **re·li·a·bly** *adv.* — **re·li·a·bil·i·ty** (-BIL·uh·tee) *n.*

re·li·ance (ri·LYE·unce) *n.* trust or confidence: *He didn't place much reliance on miracle cures.*
— **re·li·ant** (-unt) *adj.*

rel·ic (REL·ic) *n.* something from the past, as an object kept as a souvenir or keepsake, a part of a saint's body venerated as a memorial, or an ancient custom or practice: *the **relics** (= ruins or remains) of ancient Rome.*

re·lief (ri·LEEF) *n.* 1 a removal or lessening of suffering or strain: *to express, feel, find, give, receive, seek relief; great, instant, permanent relief; The medication brought only temporary relief from pain; Comic scenes provide comic relief in Shakespeare's tragedies; a sigh of relief; It's a relief to be home from work; a relief that the day is finished; To my immense relief, the parcel had arrived.* 2 replacement: *working long hours without relief; a relief pitcher.* 3 money, food, clothes, etc. given to the poor: *The family is **on relief** (= receiving public aid).* 4 a figure or design made to stand out from its surface, as "high relief" or "low relief" (= bas relief): *A **relief map** shows the hills, valleys, etc. of a region; The distant hills stood out **in bold** or **sharp relief** against the night sky.*

re·lieve (ri·LEEV) *v.* -lieves, -lieved, -liev·ing 1 remove or lessen suffering, pressure, etc.: *Aspirin relieves pain; measures to relieve misery; I'm relieved or It relieves me to hear you're safe; Anecdotes relieve the monotony of a speech.* 2 replace: *You'll be relieved in a few minutes when the next shift arrives; The ambassador was relieved of his charge and called back home.*

re·liev·er (ri·LEE·vur) or **relief pitcher** *n.* in baseball, a pitcher who relieves another during a game.

re·li·gion (ri·LIJ·un) *n.* 1 the worship of God, gods, or the supernatural; also, a system of worship: *the great religions of the world; the Christian, Jewish, Moslem, pagan religions; Islam is the state religion of Pakistan; Canada is tolerant of all religions; He practises the Hindu religion; Sun worship is not an established or organized religion; At 21 she entered religion (= the life of a religious).* 2 belief in or devotion to such worship: *a man of religion; He suddenly got religion when struck*

by tragedy; *Animals are not capable of religion.*
3 something that is practised with devotion: *She makes a religion of watching hockey on TV.*

re·li·gious (ri·LIJ·us) *adj.* 1 of or devoted to religion. 2 scrupulous or conscientious: *a deeply or profoundly religious person.*
— **n.** *sing. & pl.* a monk, nun, or other member of a religious order.

re·lin·quish (ri·LINK·wish) *v.* give up something one has a claim to or is interested in keeping: *He finally relinquished all hope of getting custody of the child; She relinquished her business interests to her son.*

rel·ish (REL·ish) *n.* 1 olives, pickles, sardines, etc. or a slightly sweet preparation of chopped pickles that gives one a zest for food: *green tomato relish; tart corn relish.* 2 zest or appetite: *Some children have great relish for foods advertised on TV; Ray shows little relish for racy humour.*
— *v.* like the taste of something; enjoy: *He doesn't relish (the prospect of) going on a diet.*

re·luc·tant (ri·LUC·tunt) *adj.* 1 not inclined to do something: *reluctant to answer questions; a reluctant helper.* 2 unwilling: *a reluctant answer; reluctant obedience.* — **re·luc·tant·ly** *adv.*
— **re·luc·tance** (-tunce) *n.*

re·ly (ri·LYE) *v.* -lies, -lied, -ly·ing have confidence that a person or thing will do or be as expected: *He relies on weather forecasts; Rely on your assistants for help or to help, but don't depend on them for everything.*

re·main (ri·MAIN) *v.* continue, keep on, or be left, as when others have departed: *the remaining members of the once popular club; Nothing remained of the house after the fire; She remained a poor woman all her life; We remain standing while the anthem is played; It remains to be seen if he'll do as told; Three remains if you take away 8 from 11.*

re·main·der (ri·MAIN·dur) *n.* 1 what is left: *The remainder of 11 minus 8 is 3, of 21 divided by 3 is zero.* 2 a copy or the copies of a published book for disposal at a very low price after its sales have dropped off.
— *v.* sell as remainder: *The present edition will be remaindered when the revised one is out.*

re·mains (ri·MAINZ) *n.pl.* 1 what is left of something broken up or ruined, as of a destroyed civilization, a dead writer's unpublished works, etc. 2 a dead body: *animal remains; Her mortal remains were laid to rest yesterday.*

re·mand (ri·MAND) *v.* 1 order back, esp. judicially: *an accused remanded in custody* (= kept in prison until the trial). 2 order or commit: *a case remanded to a lower court, to a later date.* — *n.* a remanding.

re·mark (ri·MARK) *n.* a brief comment or casual observation: *to make a biting, casual, caustic, complimentary, cryptic, cutting, derogatory, facetious, flattering, nasty, off-the-cuff, passing, pointed, sarcastic, slanderous, snide, suggestive, trite, trivial, witty remark; She made a remark that it was getting late; a few closing, concluding, opening remarks.*
— *v.* 1 comment *on* or *upon* something: *She remarked to us that it was getting late; No one else remarked on or*

upon the lateness of the hour. **2** observe or point out: *"It's near midnight," she remarked.*

re·mark·a·ble (ri·MAR·kuh·bul) *adj.* worthy of notice; extraordinary: *At 80, he's a remarkable man with a remarkable memory; He's remarkable for his memory; It's remarkable that he remembers so well; It's remarkable how he remembers so well.*
— **re·mark·a·bly** *adv.*

re·me·di·a·ble (ri·MEE·dee·uh·bul) *adj.* that can be remedied: *a remediable defect, weakness.*

re·me·di·al (ri·MEE·dee·ul) *adj.* serving to remedy: *remedial classes, courses, education, English, exercises, measures.*

rem·e·dy (REM·uh·dee) *n.* a cure or treatment for an illness or some other unhealthy condition such as an evil, loss, etc.: *to prescribe, resort to a remedy; to pursue a (legal) remedy; a certain, effective, efficacious, reliable, sure remedy for coughs and colds; a folk remedy for hiccups.*
— *v.* **-dies, -died, -dy·ing** provide or serve as a remedy: *to remedy a situation.*

re·mem·ber (ri·MEM·bur) *v.* **1** keep in mind or recall: *Please remember to phone me; I don't remember (= recall) going there; I didn't remember (= I forgot) to go there; She remembers me as a child; She's doing well, thanks to the rich uncle who remembered her (in his will).* **2** mention someone as sending greetings to another: *Remember me to your friends.*

re·mem·brance (ri·MEM·brunce) *n.* **1** the act of remembering; memory: *our remembrance of the past; To the best of my remembrance no such thing happened; I have many happy remembrances of our life together; prayers offered in remembrance of the dead; We observe* **Remembrance Day** *(= November 11) in honour of those killed in the world wars.* **2** something given or kept as remembrance: *She sends her kind remembrances (= greetings); I keep this book as a remembrance (= memento or keepsake) of the dear one.*

re·mind (ri·MINED) *v.* put in mind; cause to remember: *She reminded him of or about the date; reminded him that it was their anniversary; reminded him to take his pills; She reminds him of his mother, which reminds me – next week is my mother's birthday.* — **re·mind·er** *n.*

rem·i·nisce (rem·uh·NIS) *v.* **-nisc·es, -nisced, -nisc·ing** recall or tell *about* one's past experiences.

rem·i·nis·cence (rem·uh·NIS·unce) *n.* the act of reminiscing; also, an account of usually pleasurable recollections, or **reminiscences** *pl.*
— **rem·i·nis·cent** (-unt) *adj.*: *a song that is reminiscent of the 1950s; Grandpa is becoming more and more reminiscent (= reminiscing) as he gets older.*

re·miss (ri·MIS) *adj.* careless or negligent *in* or *about* performing a task or duty. — **re·miss·ness** *n.*

re·mis·sion (ri·MISH·un) *n.* a remitting: *The medication brought about a complete remission of the disease; The disease is now in remission; the remission of sins in confession.*

re·mit (ri·MIT) *v.* **-mits, -mit·ted, -mit·ting 1** send money as expected or due payment: *Please remit the balance due.* **2** let off or free from punishment, debts, etc.: *the power to remit (= forgive) sins.* **3** lessen efforts, pain, symptoms, etc.
— **re·mit·tance** (-unce) *n.*: *to make, send a remittance; A remittance of $500 is enclosed with the letter.*

rem·nant (REM·nunt) *n.* a small remaining part or piece: *broadloom remnants; the remnants of a defeated army; a* **remnant sale** *(of ends of bolts of cloth, carpet pieces, etc.).*

re·morse (ri·MORSE) *n.* a torturing sense of guilt: *to show, express, feel remorse for or over a crime; a bitter, deep, profound remorse; The killer didn't display a twinge of remorse.* — **re·morse·ful** *adj.*

re·mote (ri·MOTE) *adj.* **-mot·er, -mot·est** far removed in space or time, esp. from a central point: *a remote village in the mountains; in the remote past, future; a remote (= slight) possibility; radio-operated* **remote control** *for garage doors, missiles, planes, toys, etc.*
— **re·mote·ly** *adv.*; **re·mote·ness** *n.*

re·mov·al (ri·MOO·vul) *n.* a removing: *snow removal; furniture removal; his removal from office.*

re·move (ri·MOOVE) *v.* **-moves, -moved, -mov·ing** move or take away: *He removed his hat and coat as he entered the house; to remove stains from clothes; Spots are easily removed by regular cleaning; He was removed from office; He removed himself (= moved away) to Europe to start a new life; I'm his first cousin once* **removed** *(= child of his first cousin).*
— *n.* an interval or degree of distance: *Al lives at a few removes from his old neighbourhood.*
— **re·mov·a·ble** *adj.* — **re·mov·er** *n.*

re·mu·ner·ate (ri·MEW·nuh·rate) *v.* **-ates, -at·ed, -at·ing** pay someone *for* a service or trouble; recompense. — **re·mu·ner·a·tion** (-RAY·shun) *n.*

ren·ais·sance (REN·uh·sahnce) *n.* rebirth or revival: *the* **Renaissance** *of art and literature in Europe from the 14th to the 17th century.*
Also **re·nas·cence** (ri·NAS·unce, -NAY·sunce).

rend *v.* **rends, rent, rend·ing** split or tear apart with violence: *Their shrieks rent the air; a heart-rending scene of families being torn apart; a rent garment.*

ren·der (REN·dur) *v.* **1** give: *to render aid, judgment, services, thanks to God; bills payable when rendered (= presented); a city* **rendered up** *(= surrendered) to the enemy.* **2** cause to be in a specified condition: *people rendered helpless, homeless, speechless (as by fright).* **3** melt: *to render fat for lard; the stench of carcasses from a rendering plant.* **4** interpret artistically by painting, acting, singing, translating, etc.: *It takes a great actor to render Macbeth well; a rendering of the Psalms into Modern English.*

ren·dez·vous (RON·day·voo) *n., pl.* **-vous** (-vooz) **1** a previously agreed-on meeting or the agreement to meet. **2** the meeting place.
— *v.* **-vouses** (-vooz), **-voused** (-vood, long "oo"), **-vous·ing** (-voo·ing) meet or bring together people, ships, spacecraft, etc.

ren·di·tion (ren·DISH·un) *n.* an artistic rendering: *He gave a new rendition (= performance) of "O Canada"; a letter-perfect rendition (= translation) of the Greek original.*

ren·e·gade (REN·uh·gade) *n.* a traitor to one's faith or party; deserter; turncoat.

re·nege (ri·NEG, ri·NIG) *v.* -neges, -neged, -neg·ing 1 go back *on* a promise or commitment. 2 fail to follow suit in a card game in violation of rules.

re·new (ri·NEW) *v.* make new or like new something that has lost its force or effect: *to renew an attack, contract, subscription, supplies; to renew one's efforts, enthusiasm.*
— **re·new·a·ble** (ri·NEW·uh·bul) *adj.: renewable energy; a renewable resource; renewable sources of energy such as wind, sun, tides, and garbage.*
— **re·new·al** (-ul) *n.: urban renewal.*

re·nounce (ri·NOWNCE) *v.* -nounc·es, -nounced, -nounc·ing give up someone or something that one is attached to: *to renounce one's religion, worldly pleasures; She renounced the world and became a religious; renounced all claims to his fortune; She would never renounce her kith and kin.*

ren·o·vate (REN·uh·vate) *v.* -vates, -vat·ed, -vat·ing restore a building, painting, etc. to new condition by cleaning, repairing, etc. — **ren·o·va·tor** (-vay·tur) *n.*
— **ren·o·va·tion** (ren·uh·VAY·shun) *n.: to make renovations in a building; a costly renovation of the old house.*

re·nown (ri·NOWN) *n.* great distinction or fame: *men of great renown; She achieved or attained wide renown as an educator.*

re·nowned (ri·NOWND) *adj.* having renown: *a renowned warrior; He is renowned as a scientist; renowned for his discoveries.*

rent 1 *pt. & pp.* of REND: *a rent garment.* 2 *n.* a torn place in a fabric; split: *a rent in her gown.* 3 *n.* regular payment for the use of a piece of property: *evicted for nonpayment of rent; The landlord just raised the rent on our room; He has more rooms for rent.*
— *v.* give or get the use of something in return for payment: *She rents out rooms to students; We rented the car at the airport; We rented it from Renters Ltd. which rents cars to the public; What does a car rent for nowadays?*

rent·al (REN·tul) *n.* a renting, renting agency, a piece of property rented out, or the payment for it: *a boat, car, film, office rental.*
— *adj.: a rental agreement, car, charge; A rental library charges for books lent.*

rent·als·man (REN·tulz·mun) *n.* -men an ombudsman of landlord-tenant relations.

re·nun·ci·a·tion (ri·NUN·see·AY·shun) *n.* a renouncing or giving up: *the renunciation of an agreement, claim, course of action, hope, policy, right, title.*

re·or·gan·i·za·tion (ree·OR·guh·nuh·ZAY·shun) *n.* an organizing again or anew: *Our company underwent a reorganization.*
— **re·or·gan·ize** (-guh·nize) *v.* -iz·es, -ized, -iz·ing.

rep *n.* [short form] representative: *a sales rep.*

re·pair (ri·PAIR) *v.* 1 restore, esp. something damaged, to good condition. 2 remedy a loss, harm, wrong, etc. 3 betake oneself *to* a place.
— *n.* 1 a repairing or an instance of it: *to do or make the necessary repairs to an old home; extensive, major,*

minor repairs; a body shop for car repairs; The repairs cost a fortune. 2 condition with respect to repairs: *a house kept in (good) repair; The road is closed while under repair; It was in bad repair after years of neglect.*
— **re·pair·a·ble** (ri·PAIR·uh·bul) or **rep·a·ra·ble** (REP·ur·uh·bul) *adj.* — **re·pair·man** (-mun) *n.* -men.

rep·a·ra·tion (rep·uh·RAY·shun) *n.* a making of amends for a wrong: *War reparations are levied on defeated nations.*

rep·ar·tee (rep·ur·TEE) *n.* cleverness or skill in replying wittily: *She's good at repartee.*

re·past (ri·PAST) *n.* meal; food and drink: *a light, meagre repast.*

re·pa·tri·ate (ree·PAY·tree·ate, -PAT·ree·ate) *v.* -ates, -at·ed, -at·ing return a person or thing to the home country: *to repatriate illegal aliens, migrant workers, prisoners of war; Foreign businesses may not repatriate their profits.*
— *n.* (-it) a repatriated person.
— **re·pa·tri·a·tion** (-AY·shun) *n.: the repatriation of Hong Kong from Britain to China in 1997.*

re·pay (ree·PAY) *v.* -pays, -paid, -pay·ing pay back; make a return for something to someone: *to repay a loan, kindness; She became a social worker to repay her debt to society; to repay a creditor, lender; He repaid Jane for her kindness; Love is sometimes repaid with ingratitude.* — **re·pay·a·ble** *adj.*; **re·pay·ment** *n.*

re·peal (ri·PEEL) *v.* cancel or annul, esp. a law.
— *n.* a repealing.

re·peat (ri·PEET) *v.* do or say something again: *He never repeats a mistake; to repeat a formula after someone, as when being sworn in; to repeat a lesson to a class from memory; a tiresome lecturer who tends to repeat himself* (= say again what he said already).
— *n.* 1 a repeating or anything repeated, as a rerun TV program. 2 in music, a passage to be repeated or a symbol indicating this.

repeated (ri·PEE·tid) *adj.* said or done again: *repeated attempts, changes of plan, mistakes, occurrences; a repeated* (= renewed) *failure, pattern, request.*
— **re·peat·ed·ly** *adv.*

re·pel (ri·PEL) *v.* -pels, -pelled, -pel·ling force or drive back: *to repel an attack, enemy, invasion, insinuation; Like (magnetic) poles repel (each other); adj.: It's repelling* (= disgusting) *in appearance, odour; a repelling sight.*

re·pel·lent (ri·PEL·unt) *n. & adj.* (something) that repels: *an insect repellent; a mosquito repellent spray; a water repellent substance, surface; Smoke is repellent to her.* Also **re·pel·lant.**

re·pent (ri·PENT) *v.* feel sorry for something and seek forgiveness, as a sinner: *He repented (of) his past; a foolish decision that he lived to repent* (= regret).
— **re·pent·ance** (-tunce) *n.*; **re·pent·ant** (-tunt) *adj.*

re·per·cus·sion (ree·pur·CUSH·un, *rhyme:* Russian) *n.* a reaction or effect, often far-reaching, of some action or event.

rep·er·toire (REP·urt·war) *n.* the stock of plays, parts, pieces, etc., that musicians, performers, or companies

have at their command.
Also **rep·er·to·ry** (REP·ur·tor·ee) n. -ries.

repertory theatre or **theater** n. a company that has a repertory of prepared plays or operas to put on in rotation during a season.

rep·e·ti·tion (rep·uh·TISH·un) n. a repeating or something repeated.

rep·e·ti·tious (rep·uh·TISH·us) or **re·pet·i·tive** (ri·PET·uh·tiv) adj. tending to repeat; characterized by repetition: *the repetitive nature of rhymes, certain tasks; a speaker's repetitious habit; a repetitious* (= tiresome or boring) *speaker, task.*

re·place (ri·PLACE) v. -plac·es, -placed, -plac·ing 1 take the place of someone or something that is gone or no longer usable: *We replace a burned-out light bulb with a new one; The retired principal was replaced by Ms. Lee; She is now difficult to replace* (= find a good substitute for). 2 put back: *to replace books on a shelf; He was ordered to replace* (= pay for) *the broken china.* — **re·place·a·ble** adj. — **re·place·ment** n.

re·play (ree·PLAY) v. play over or again.
— n. (REE·play) a playing again; repetition: *the instant replay (from videotape) of an action just broadcast.*

re·plen·ish (ri·PLEN·ish) v. to refill: *to replenish glasses, inventories, reserves, supplies; to replenish a wardrobe with new fashions.*

re·plete (ri·PLEET) adj. filled to the maximum: *a book replete with absurdities, errors; a day replete with thrills; Lou fell asleep replete with food and drink.* — **re·ple·tion** (ri·PLEE·shun) n.

rep·li·ca (REP·luh·cuh) n. a duplicate or copy, esp. one made by the original artist.

re·ply (ri·PLY) v. -plies, -plied, -ply·ing answer orally or in writing, esp. in kind or appropriately: *He replied immediately or promptly to her phone call; replied that he would see her the next morning.*
— n.: *to give or make a reply; At first his letter didn't draw or elicit a reply; Then he got or received a curt, gruff, stinging, sullen reply; He sent an immediate, prompt, succinct, terse, witty reply; She waved in reply to his hello.*

re·po (REE·poh) n. *Informal.* [short form] 1 something repossessed. 2 repurchase agreement for securities.
— adj. repossession: *the repo business; Two repo men came to get his car.*

re·port (ri·PORT) v. give information about or an account of what one has seen or done: *a journalist reporting on a disaster from the scene; He **reports back** to the editor; a widely reported story; to report a prowler to the police; She reported him to the police for breaking in; He's reported to be still around; It's reported that he's still around; UFOs were reported seen by the villagers; They reported having seen the UFOs; They reported (their) seeing UFOs; A child has been reported missing; Sorry to report (to you that) I'm ill; My friend has already reported sick; We will not report* (= present ourselves) *for duty at 9 a.m.; Our manager reports* (= answers) *directly to the president.*
— n. 1 a reporting or account: *He will file or give, make, present, submit a report on or about the incident to his boss; He has to draw up or make out, write out,*

write up the report; She has heard but cannot confirm the report that he has resigned; an accurate, annual, biassed, classified, confidential, daily, detailed, exhaustive, favourable, first-hand, interim, minority, newspaper, top-secret, traffic, unconfirmed, weather, written report; a man of good report (= reputation). 2 rumour: *an idle report; as report has it.* 3 a sound, as of a gun or explosion. — **re·port·a·ble** (-tuh·bul) adj.

report card n. a report sent periodically by the school to parents about a pupil's progress.

re·port·ed·ly adv. according to report: *UFO's were reportedly seen by the villagers.*

re·port·er (ri·POR·tur) n. one who reports, esp. news for the media.

re·pose (ri·POZE) v. -pos·es, -posed, -pos·ing 1 put or place trust, confidence, etc. in someone or something. 2 to rest following activity: *He reposed her head on his shoulder; bodies reposing* (= lying at rest) *in their graves undisturbed.*
— n. 1 rest following activity: *The body looked serene in repose; the eternal repose of departed souls.* 2 poise: *her self-assured repose of manner.* — **re·pose·ful** adj.

re·pos·i·to·ry (ri·POZ·uh·tor·ee) n. -ries 1 a storage place or container. 2 a person or institution to which something is entrusted: *He is the repository of her confidences; Books are repositories of knowledge.*

re·pos·sess (ree·puh·ZES) v. take possession of property, as a seller does because of the buyer's default in payments. — **re·pos·ses·sion** (-ZESH·un) n.

rep·re·hen·si·ble (rep·ruh·HEN·suh·bul) adj. blameworthy: *reprehensible behaviour, conduct; a reprehensible deed.*

rep·re·sent (rep·ri·ZENT) v. 1 stand for as a symbol: *Words represent ideas; Let T represent time.* 2 act or speak in place of another: *Lawyers represent their clients.* 3 present: *Satan is always represented as evil; The physician was not licensed as represented to the public; This chart graphically represents the data we have gathered.*

rep·re·sen·ta·tion (REP·ri·zen·TAY·shun) n. 1 a representing or being represented: *"No taxation without representation"; proportional representation; a good representation* (= picture or statue) *of Venus.* 2 representatives as a group. 3 a formal statement of facts or arguments in support of a demand or viewpoint: *in spite of representations made to the government.*

rep·re·sen·ta·tive (rep·ri·ZEN·tuh·tiv) adj. 1 representing: *a representative collection, sample; a painting that is representative of a style.* 2 based on elections: *a representative form of government; a representative assembly, institution.*
— n. 1 one who represents a person or group, as a delegate, sales rep, or agent. 2 **Representative** a member of the lower house of a U.S. state legislature or of Congress.

re·press (ri·PRES) v. 1 keep down, as an undesirable impulse or an unpleasant memory from the conscious mind. 2 put down something developing or seeking an outlet: *She tried to repress her laughter; to repress a rebellion.*
— **re·pres·sion** (ri·PRESH·un) n.: *They live under*

repression.
— **re·pres·sive** (-PRES·iv) *adj.: a repressive measure; under a repressive regime that is repressive of civil rights.*

re·prieve (ri·PREEV) *v.* -prieves, -prieved, -priev·ing give temporary relief from trouble or danger, esp. from death by execution.
— *n.* a reprieving or being reprieved, esp. a temporary suspension of a sentence of death: *He got or received or was given or was granted a last-minute reprieve from execution.*

rep·ri·mand (REP·ruh·mand) *n.* a formal or sharp rebuke, often public, as from one in authority: *The judge administered or issued a reprimand to the offending attorney; a mild reprimand; He received a severe, stern, written reprimand.*
— *v.* give a reprimand to someone.

re·print (ree·PRINT) *v.* to print an edition of a book again.
— *n.* (REE·print): *They have issued a reprint of the 1950 classic.*

re·pris·al (ri·PRY·zul) *n.* an act of retaliation, esp. military or political: *They were threatened with reprisals; The terrorist camps were bombed in reprisal for their attacks on civilians; a reprisal carried out against terrorist attacks.*

re·proach (ri·PROHCH) *v.* find fault with, esp. in a resentful manner: *He was reproached for something he didn't do.*
— *n.* a reproaching, the cause of it, or the resulting discredit or disgrace: *a look of reproach; a term of reproach; the reproaches heaped on her; He earned the reproach of the community; He was thought to be **above** or **beyond reproach*** (= faultless). — **re·proach·ful** *adj.*

rep·ro·bate (REP·ruh·bate) *n.* one who is depraved or very wicked.

rep·ro·ba·tion (rep·ruh·BAY·shun) *n.* censure or condemnation.

re·pro·duce (ree·pruh·DUCE) *v.* -duc·es, -duced, -duc·ing produce copies from an original, sound from a recording, offspring from eggs or by means of spores, etc.— **re·pro·duc·tion** (-DUC·shun) *n.*
— **re·pro·duc·tive** (-DUC·tiv) *adj.*

rep·tile (REP·tile) *n.* a crawling, scaly, cold-blooded vertebrate such as a snake, lizard, crocodile, or turtle: *a creeping or slithering reptile.*
— **rep·til·i·an** (rep·TIL·ee·un) *n. & adj.*

re·pub·lic (ri·PUB·lic) *n.* a state or a form of government headed by an elected president and run by elected representatives, as in France, U.S.A., India, etc.: *Latin American countries used to be called banana republics; Communist states call themselves democratic, people's, or socialist republics.*

re·pub·li·can (ri·PUB·luh·cun) *adj.* 1 having to do with a republic: *a republican government, party, system.* 2 favouring republics: *republican ideas, sympathies.*
— *n.* 1 one who favours a republic. 2 **Republican** a member of the U.S. Republican Party; also *adj.*

re·pu·di·ate (ri·PEW·dee·ate) *v.* -ates, -at·ed, -at·ing disown or reject: *to repudiate a charge, doctrine, friend,*

treaty. — **re·pu·di·a·tion** (-AY·shun) *n.*

re·pug·nance (ri·PUG·nunce) *n.* a strong dislike or aversion: *Kwok feels no repugnance to eating snails; Sam turns away from it in deep repugnance.*

re·pug·nant (ri·PUG·nunt) *adj.* disagreeable or objectionable to one's tastes, ideas, liking, etc.: *Food is repugnant to a sick stomach; We think slavery repugnant.* — **re·pug·nant·ly** *adv.*

re·pulse (ri·PULSE) *v.* -puls·es, -pulsed, -puls·ing repel by force, coldness, discourtesy, etc.; rebuff: *to repulse an attack, attacker, enemy; to repulse an offer of friendship; She is repulsed* (= disgusted) *by creeping things.* — *n.* a repulsing or being repulsed; rejection.

re·pul·sion (ri·PUL·shun) *n.* 1 a being repelled or a repulse: *magnetic attraction and repulsion.* 2 strong aversion or disgust.

re·pul·sive (ri·PUL·siv) *adj.* repelling or disgusting: *a repulsive creature, force, sight; His manners are utterly repulsive to her.*

rep·u·ta·ble (REP·yuh·tuh·bul) *adj.* having a good reputation: *a reputable business, dealer, lawyer.*
— **rep·u·ta·bly** *adv.*

rep·u·ta·tion (rep·yuh·TAY·shun) *n.* a normally good public estimation of character or quality: *a witchhunt that destroyed many reputations; She enjoys a good reputation as a lawyer; an international, local, worldwide reputation; to acquire, establish a reputation; to compromise, guard, live up to, protect, ruin, tarnish one's reputation; a reputation for being sharp; Sam has the reputation of (being) a swindler; He staked his reputation on the outcome of the trial.*

re·pute (ri·PYOOT) *n.* reputation: *He's held in high repute, not in low repute; a lawyer **of repute;** a house of **ill repute*** (= ill fame).

re·put·ed (ri·PEW·tid) *adj.* 1 reputable: *a widely reputed authority.* 2 generally believed: *the reputed father of the orphan; the book's reputed author; He is reputed (to be) the world's richest man.*
— **re·put·ed·ly** *adv.: He's reputedly* (= as generally believed) *the world's richest man.*

re·quest (ri·QUEST) *v.* ask politely or formally: *We request the pleasure of your company; We request a favour of or from the public; We request you not to smoke; We request that you do not smoke.*
— *n.* a requesting, being requested, or something requested: *She filed a request with the authorities; He made a request to her parents; told them he had a request to make of them; They submitted a joint request to the school; considered whether to deny or reject the request; to grant a request; The school agreed to act on the request; a request for more time; a request that they be given more time; a desperate, formal, modest, reasonable, urgent, written request; She's here at your request; a performance repeated **by request;** Refunds are made on or upon request; a request item (for which you have to ask).*

re·quire (ri·QUIRE) *v.* -quires, -quired, -quir·ing demand, as by rule or necessity: *Drivers are required to stop at red lights; It is required by law from or of all drivers; Piano playing requires* (= calls for) *practice; It requires that you (should) practise regularly; This book* *is **required** reading for all students.*

re·quire·ment (ri·QUIRE·munt) *n.* something required or needed: *He has fulfilled, met, satisfied the requirements set or established for the Ph.D. program; admission, entrance, minimum requirements; the requirement that a test of English proficiency be passed.*

req·ui·si·tion (rek·wuh·ZISH·un) *n.* a formal demand for something required, as of military supplies or personnel: *Our only jeep was in constant requisition.*
— *v.* request formally: *Help had to be requisitioned from outside the town.*

re·run (REE·run) *n.* another showing of a motion picture or TV program after the first run: *The local theatre shows only reruns of old movies.*

re·sale (REE·sale) *n.* a selling again of an item to a third party or subsequent buyer.

re·scind (ri·SIND) *v.* annul a law or cancel an agreement, order, permit, etc.

res·cue (RES·cue) *v.* **-cues, -cued, -cu·ing** free or save someone in trouble by quick action: *The child was rescued from the fire.*
— *n.* a rescuing: *to attempt, effect, make, mount a daring, heroic rescue of the hostages from the hands of the terrorists.* — **res·cu·er** *n.*

re·search (REE·surch, ri·SURCH) *n.* a careful search or investigation, esp. an organized scholarly or scientific inquiry: *to conduct or pursue a laborious, original, painstaking, thorough research into the causes of cancer; research in a specific area; a book based on solid market research on buying habits.*
— *v.* do research into a subject: *Scientists are researching the causes of cancer; The essay is well researched.* — **re·search·er** *n.*

re·sem·blance (ri·ZEM·blunce) *n.* similarity, esp. in outward appearance: *The sisters bear a close resemblance to each other; the striking, strong family resemblance between them; a remote resemblance to their cousins.*

re·sem·ble (ri·ZEM·bul) *v.* **-bles, -bled, -bling** be similar to a person or thing in appearance or qualities: *The son closely resembles his mother.*

re·sent (ri·ZENT) *v.* feel or show anger at something offensive or toward an offender: *We strongly resent his jumping the queue; We bitterly resent being left behind.*
— **re·sent·ful** *adj.: We are resentful of queue-jumpers; resentful at or about being left behind.*

re·sent·ment (ri·ZENT·munt) *n.* indignation and ill will resulting from an offence: *The injustice aroused or stirred up resentment in the community; People felt and expressed or voiced their bitter, deep, sullen resentment about it; resentment against authority; resentment toward the police; They harboured a resentment; felt resentment that they were unjustly dealt with.*

res·er·va·tion (rez·ur·VAY·shun) *n.* **1** a reserving or something reserved, as an advance booking of a room at a hotel: *We have reservations for four people; to make, confirm, cancel a reservation.* **2** a tacit or expressed condition: *a mental reservation; our whole-hearted support without reservations.* **3** an Indian reserve.

re·serve (ri·ZURV) *v.* **-serves, -served, -serv·ing** hold back or keep for a particular person, another occasion, later use, etc.: *to reserve a room, seat, table; all rights reserved by the author; He wisely reserved* (= saved) *his energies till the final act.*
— *n.* **1** something reserved, as money or resources kept **in reserve** for later use, public land for forest conservation, a body of trained people **(reservists)**, ships, or aircraft standing by for military service when needed, etc.: *Canada's energy and gold reserves; Alberta's oil reserves; our reserves of capital; bird, game, wildlife reserve; adj.: a reserve first-baseman (in baseball); the reserve forces.* **2** *Cdn.* a tract of land set apart for the exclusive use of a Canadian Indian group: *the Kahnawake Reserve.* **3** the keeping of one's thoughts or feelings to oneself; aloofness: *to display or show reserve in one's dealings; a cool reserve that was hard to break down; He unburdened his mind **without reserve*** (= freely).

re·served (ri·ZURVD) *adj.* **1** set aside: *a reserved seat.* **2** restrained in speech or manner: *He's reserved about his background, reserved toward or with strangers.*
— **re·serv·ed·ly** (-vid·lee) *adv.*

res·er·voir (RES·urv·wahr) *n.* a large supply or store, esp. of water: *a natural or artificial reservoir.*

re·side (ri·ZIDE) *v.* **-sides, -sid·ed, -sid·ing** **1** live, esp. in a settled way: *to reside in the country; to reside at a hotel.* **2** exist; be vested: *In a democracy, power resides in the people.*

res·i·dence (REZ·uh·dunce) *n.* a residing or where one resides; home: *to establish, take up residence in Canada; a poet who is **in residence*** (= living or working on a regular basis) *at a university.*
— **res·i·den·cy** (REZ·uh·dun·see) *n.* **-cies.**

res·i·dent (REZ·uh·dunt) *n.* **1** one who lives in a place: *a Canadian resident; a permanent resident* (= landed immigrant) *in Canada; adj.: a resident Canadian; a resident representative.* **2** a physician in training or on full-time duty at a hospital.
— **res·i·den·tial** (rez·uh·DEN·shul) *adj.: a residential district, hotel, neighbourhood, school.*

re·sid·u·al (ri·ZIJ·oo·ul) *adj.* of or being a residue or remainder: *residual air, estate, product, wastes.*
— *n.* **1** a remainder. **2** in TV, a fee paid to a performer for each rerun of a show or commercial.

res·i·due (REZ·uh·due) *n.* what remains at the end of a process: *the residue of salt left after evaporation of a (salt) solution; the residue of an estate after settlement of claims.*

re·sign (ri·ZINE) *v.* **1** give up a job or position: *He resigned from the board; resigned as chairman; resigned his membership.* **2** be ready to endure: *He had to resign himself to a life on welfare, to living on welfare.*

res·ig·na·tion (rez·ig·NAY·shun) *n.* **1** a resigning or a formal notice of it: *to hand in, offer, submit, tender, withdraw one's resignation.* **2** passive acceptance of suffering or misfortune.

re·signed (ri·ZINED) *adj.* submissive: *He is resigned to his lot in life; She's quite resigned to the life of a widow.*
— **re·sign·ed·ly** (-nid·lee) *adv.*

re·sil·ient (ri·ZIL·yunt) *adj.* springing back to the original form or position, as rubber or a spring:

"Silicone rubber" makes a resilient caulk; a resilient floor tile; a resilient currency (that recovers its exhange value after a fall); a resilient disposition, economy; a sitcom with a resilient cheerfulness about it.
— **re·sil·i·ence** (ri·ZIL·yunce) or **re·sil·i·en·cy** (-yun·see) *n.*

res·in (REZ·in) *n.* an organic substance such as shellac secreted by certain plants, trees, and insects, and much used in paints and varnishes. — **res·in·ous** (-us) *adj.*

re·sist (ri·ZIST) *v.* act against an attack, enemy, temptation, etc. that is trying to overcome one: *I couldn't resist laughing at his jokes.* — **re·sist·er** *n.* — **re·sist·i·ble** *adj.*

re·sist·ance (ri·ZIS·tunce) *n.* **1** a resisting or the power to resist: *to break down, crush, offer, overcome, put down, put up resistance to something; They met with armed, determined, fierce, passive, stiff, strong, stubborn resistance; to take the line* or *course* or *path of* ***least resistance*** (= take the easiest way). **2** the opposition offered by a substance to the passage of electricity. **3** secretly conducted opposition to foreign military occupation, often **Resistance.** — **re·sist·ant** (-tunt) *adj.*

res·o·lute (REZ·uh·loot, long "oo") *adj.* determined or firm in one's purpose.
— **res·o·lute·ly** *adv.*; **res·o·lute·ness** *n.*

res·o·lu·tion (rez·uh·LOO·shun) *n.* **1** determination to achieve an aim; resolve: *She acted with firm resolution; Hamlet lacked resolution.* **2** what is resolved upon: *a New Year's resolution to quit smoking; a resolution* (= statement) *proposed, adopted, passed by the city council.* **3** a solving: *the resolution of a dramatic plot; the resolution of our doubts.* **4** a breaking up or separation: *the resolution of a chemical compound into its elements; the sharp, high resolution of an electron microscope enabling the viewer to distinguish objects.*

re·solve (ri·ZOLV) *v.* **-solves, -solved, -solv·ing** **1** decide or determine: *He resolved to give up smoking; He is firmly resolved never to smoke again; It was resolved that smoking be banned.* **2** solve; break up: *to resolve a mystery; White light is resolved into the colours of the spectrum; the resolving power of a telescope or microscope to provide separate images of closely spaced parts of an object.*
— *n.* resolution: *He made a firm resolve never to smoke.* — **re·solv·a·ble** (-ZOL·vuh·bul) *adj.*

res·o·nance (REZ·uh·nunce) *n.* a resounding quality; an echoing, strengthening, or prolonging of sound, as by a hollow or cavity: *a quartz crystal vibrating in resonance with* (= at the same frequency as) *a generator; the* ***resonance box,*** *or resonator, of a guitar or violin.*

res·o·nant (REZ·uh·nunt) *adj.* having resonance: *A resonant voice depends on one's mouth, throat, and nasal cavities; Vowels are more resonant than consonants.*

res·o·nate (REZ·uh·nate) *v.* **-nates, -nat·ed, -nat·ing** produce resonance; resound. — **res·o·na·tor** *n.*
— **res·o·na·tion** (-NAY·shun) *n.*

re·sort (ri·ZORT) *v.* **1** go often to a place, esp. habitually: *Tourists resort to a beach, shrine, spa.* **2** turn to, as for help: *to resort to force, tears, trickery, violence, war.*

— *n.* a resorting or a place or thing resorted to: *a health, holiday, seaside, summer, winter resort; without resort to force; a drug of last resort; He took to prayer as the* or *as a last resort* (= means of help).

re·sound (ri·ZOUND) *v.* sound loudly; echo or ring.
— **re·sound·ing** *adj.* emphatic or unmistakable: *a resounding failure, success, victory; resounding cheers; a resounding "No"; a resounding 90% vote.*

re·source (REE·sorce, ri·SORCE) *n.* a means or source of help, relief, supply, etc. that may be drawn upon when needed: *a man of resource; the earth's natural resources such as land, water, and minerals; to develop, exploit, tap a country's resources; to pool one's resources; borrowing as a last resource; the financial resources to undertake a project; A* ***resource centre*** *such as a library contains learning resources; a* ***resource person*** *(= general consultant).*

re·source·ful (ri·SORCE·ful) *adj.* good at finding ways and means of solving a problem: *The resourceful boy stuck his finger in a hole in the dike and saved his town from a flood; The resourceful Amish use windmills to pump water.*
— **re·source·ful·ly** *adv.*; **re·source·ful·ness** *n.*

re·spect (ri·SPECT) *v.* have or show esteem for a person or thing: *to respect one's elders; I respect his rights; I respect him as a member; He's a* ***respected*** *member of our club; a suggestion* ***respecting*** *(= concerning) yesterday's announcement.*
— *n.* **1** esteem or proper regard: *He talks of his teacher with respect; pays respect to what she says; She inspires respect; She commands respect from her students; She is held in high respect by them; She has earned, won their respect; Jim lost his respect by behaving badly; He shows little respect for rules; He ought to behave better at least out of respect for his teacher.* **2 respects** *pl.* respectful regards: *I'd like to send her my respects; He's come to pay his respects to her; Please give her my respects.* **3** a point considered: *a great man in many respects; In some respects he's not so great; a memo* ***in*** *or* ***with respect to*** *(= regarding) the raise you asked for.*

re·spect·a·ble (ri·SPEC·tuh·bul) *adj.* **1** worthy of respect: *a respectable family, gentleman; to look respectable; in respectable society.* **2** impressive: *a respectable income, number; an audience of respectable size.* — **re·spect·a·bly** *adv.*
— **re·spect·a·bil·i·ty** (-BIL·uh·tee) *n.*

re·spect·ful (ri·SPECT·ful) *adj.* having or showing respect: *a respectful manner; He's respectful to* or *of his elders.* — **re·spect·ful·ly** *adv.*

re·spect·ive (ri·SPEC·tiv) *adj.* as relates to each individually: *Everyone please get back to your respective seats.*

re·spect·ive·ly (ri·SPEC·tiv·lee) *adv.* in order: *I, II, and III are 1, 2, and 3, respectively.*

res·pi·ra·tion (res·puh·RAY·shun) *n.* breathing by means of lungs or gills in animals and through leaves and buds in plants: *We gave him artificial respiration till help arrived.* — **res·pi·ra·to·ry** (RES·puh·ruh·tor·ee, ris·PYE·ruh-) *adj.*

res·pi·ra·tor (RES·puh·ray·tur) *n.* **1** an artificial breathing device. **2** a mask worn over the nose and mouth to prevent the breathing in of harmful substances.

res·pite (RES·pit) *n.* a temporary relief from an exertion or suffering: *He works without respite from 8 to 12; A coffee break allows* or *gives some respite from work; a brief, temporary respite; The rain brought a respite from the heat.*

re·splend·ent (ri·SPLEN·dunt) *adj.* full of splendour; shining brightly: *He was resplendent with joy; She looked resplendent in glory as carnival queen.*

re·spond (ri·SPOND) *v.* **1** react, as in answer: *to respond to an appeal, call, letter, plea, question, stimulus; We phoned the police and they responded promptly.* **2** show a favourable reaction: *to respond to a medication, to kindness, treatment; The patient did not respond for a couple of hours.*

re·sponse (ri·SPONSE) *n.* a responding, as a reply or any reaction to a stimulus: *At first, our pleas elicited* or *evoked no response; Nothing was heard in response to our calls; The initial response was glib, lukewarm, sullen; She gave a witty response to the heckler's question.*

re·spon·si·bil·i·ty (ri·SPON·suh·BIL·uh·tee) *n.* **-ties** a being responsible or accountable; obligation: *A greater sense of responsibility is required; the responsibility to do a good job; He is old enough to accept, assume, bear, exercise, shoulder, take (on) full responsibility for his actions; to dodge, evade, shirk responsibility; We have to share, if not bear, the responsibility* (= blame) *for what happens around here instead of laying the responsibility at someone else's door; The collective responsibility lies with all of us; The ultimate responsibility for a product is the manufacturer's; an awesome, clear, grave, great, heavy responsibility; the responsibility to inform the next of kin after a body is identified; a terrible responsibility; The terrorists admitted, in fact claimed, responsibility for the explosion; They did it* **on their own responsibility** (= initiative).

re·spon·si·ble (ri·SPON·suh·bul) *adj.* **1** accountable or answerable for an action or happening, often to someone: *We are responsible for our actions, for carrying out our duties; Someone has to be responsible when a fire alarm goes off; Teachers are directly responsible to the principal; The brakes failed and the mechanic was held responsible; a responsible approach, attitude;* **Responsible government** *is answerable to the people; A storm was responsible for* (= was the cause of) *the airplane crash.* **2** having mental and moral qualities; trustworthy: *a very responsible child; responsible adults, citizens, officials; Dogs are more responsible than cats.* **3** involving important duties: *a highly responsible job, position, role.* — **re·spon·si·bly** *adj.*

re·spon·sive (ri·SPON·siv) *adj.* reacting favourably: *to be responsive to a treatment, an appeal.*

rest *n.* **1** a break from activity, as for relaxation; pause: *to have a day of rest from work; to take rest now and then; a well-earned rest; The doctor ordered bed rest; complete rest for body and mind; an explanation to set*
your mind at rest; bodies at rest and in motion; souls gone to their rest (= repose in another world); *Bodies are* **laid to rest** (= buried); *a stool as a rest* (= support) *for the feet; a symbol indicating a half rest* (= interval of silence) *between notes in music; the seaman's rest* (= lodging). **2 the rest** what remains or is left: *the rest of us; We'll do the rest; For the rest, I have nothing to say.* — *v.* **1** stop working; be inactive: *He rests only at night; never rests his horses; The prosecution rests (from presenting evidence in a case).* **2** be at ease; relax: *He wouldn't let me rest till I said "yes"; The patient is resting.* **3** support or be supported; lean: *a pillow to rest your head on; a house resting on a weak foundation.* **4** remain: *Please* **rest assured** *we'll do our best; The decision* **rests with** (= is the responsibility of) *the court.* — **rest·ful** *adj.;* **rest·ful·ly** *adv.*

res·tau·rant (RES·tuh·runt, -rahnt) *n.* a commercial eating place: *He manages, operates, runs a fast-food restaurant; an elegant, first-class restaurant; a licensed restaurant (where liquor is served).*

res·tau·ra·teur (res·tuh·ruh·TUR) *n.* a restaurant operator.

rest home *n.* a nursing home.

res·ti·tu·tion (res·tuh·TUE·shun) *n.* restoration to the owner of the property that he or she was deprived of; the making good of loss or damage: *He offered restitution; to make restitution to her for the broken china.*

res·tive (RES·tiv) *adj.* balky, as a horse; restless or impatient, as if under restraint.

rest·less *adj.* unable to rest; without rest; always busy or moving; impatient: *a restless crowd, night, sleep; the restless waves.*

res·to·ra·tion (res·tuh·RAY·shun) *n.* a restoring or being restored: *restoration of civilian rule; the restoration of a historic site; the restoration of an old painting.*

re·store (ri·STOR) *v.* **-stores, -stored, -stor·ing 1** bring back to its original condition: *to restore a ruined building, damaged painting, health.* **2** return: *to restore books to a shelf, order in class, property to its owner, a job to a fired employee, an employee to his former position.*

re·strain (ri·STRAIN) *v.* keep in check, esp. by use of force or authority: *a leash to restrain a dog from attacking people; restrain your curiosity, temper.*

re·straint (ri·STRAINT) *n.* a restraining, being restrained, or means of restraining; also, control or confinement: *an animal kept* or *put under restraint; to apply restraint; A restraint* (= leash) *is sometimes put on the more difficult cases; She cast off, flung off, shook off all restraint; He sobbed without restraint; the social restraints against smoking; She spoke with restraint, choosing her words carefully; The police displayed, exercised, showed great restraint in dealing with the demonstrators.*

re·strict (ri·STRICT) *v.* confine within limits: *Student activities are restricted to school hours; Restrict your speed to 90 km/h; She restricts herself to a vegetarian diet; a vocabulary restricted to 500 words.* — **re·stric·tion** *n.: to impose, lift, place, put restrictions on wages and prices.*

re·stric·tive (ri·STRIC·tiv) *adj.* confining or limiting: *restrictive clothing; price fixing, monopolies, and such restrictive trade practices.* — **re·strict·ive·ly** *adv.*

rest room *n.* a public lavatory.

re·sult (ri·ZULT) *n.* a final effect or consequence of an action, esp. a desired effect: *We work to achieve, get, produce results; No sure-fire results; The net, overall results are good; Results are evaluated, measured, tabulated; a direct, logical result of the action; It had no lasting results; examination results; All got the same result* (= answer to a problem).
— *v.* have or follow as a result: *Death could result if people drink this; Carelessness results in* (= has as its result) *accidents; Accidents result* (= follow as a result) *from carelessness.*

re·sult·ant (ri·ZUL·tunt) *adj.* resulting: *the resultant effect of more people taking public transport to work.*

re·sume (ri·ZOOM, long "OO") *v.* **-sumes, -sumed, -sum·ing** renew an activity or return to one's seat, etc.: *We will resume work(ing) after lunch; We resume at 2 p.m.* — **re·sump·tion** (ri·ZUMP·shun) *n.*

ré·su·mé or **re·su·me** (REZ·oo·may, rez·oo·MAY) *n.* a summary, esp. of qualifications and employment experience: *the résumé of a book, speech.*

re·sur·gent (ri·SUR·junt) *adj.* tending to rise again.
— **re·sur·gence** *n.: the resurgence of hopes, interest, nationalism, spirits.*

res·ur·rect (rez·uh·RECT) *v.* raise or revive: *Lazarus was resurrected from the dead; to resurrect dead issues, old practices.*

res·ur·rec·tion (rez·uh·REC·shun) *n.* a rising from the dead, as Christ's Resurrection.

re·sus·ci·tate (ri·SUS·uh·tate) *v.* **-tates, -tat·ed, -tat·ing** revive from apparent or near death; bring back to consciousness.
— **re·sus·ci·ta·tion** (-TAY·shun) *n.: to give mouth-to-mouth resuscitation.*

re·tail (REE·tail) *n.* the sale of goods in small quantities to consumers: *Shops buy wholesale and sell at retail.*
— *v.* 1 sell at retail: *the retailing of meat; These radios retail* (= are sold) *at or for $500 each.* 2 retell or relate stories, gossip, slander, etc.
— *adj.: a retail merchant, price, store; the retail trade; adv.: They buy wholesale and sell retail.* — **re·tail·er** *n.*

re·tain (ri·TAIN) *v.* continue to hold or keep, esp. against opposing forces: *insulated so as to retain heat; a good memory that retains everything; to retain a lawyer (so that his services may be available as needed); A retaining wall is put up to hold back a mass of earth, flood waters, or racing cars.*

re·tain·er (ri·TAY·nur) *n.* 1 one that retains: *a retainer for use after braces have been removed from teeth.* 2 a fee to secure the services of a lawyer or other professional: *Put down a retainer and we're in business.* 3 an employee in a wealthy household.

re·tal·i·ate (ri·TAL·ee·ate) *v.* **-ates, -at·ed, -at·ing** return injury or evil, usually in kind: *They retaliated against the guerrillas for their attack on the village; retaliated with bombing of their hide-outs.*
— **re·tal·i·a·tion** (-AY·shun) *n.: in retaliation for their*

attacks; an act of retaliation; massive retaliation against the enemy; swift retaliation.
— **re·tal·i·a·to·ry** (-uh·tor·ee) *adj.*

re·tard (ri·TARD) *v.* slow down; check the progress or movement of something: *to retard development, growth.*
— *n.* (REE·tard) [derogatory] a retarded person.
— **re·tar·da·tion** (ri·tar·DAY·shun) *n.: mental retardation.*

re·tard·ant (ri·TAR·dunt) *n.* a chemical or other substance that slows down a process or resists an action: *a fire retardant; rust retardants.*

retarded *adj.* mentally handicapped: *a child born retarded; the care of the retarded* (= retarded people).

retch *v.* want to vomit: *She retched at the sight.*

re·ten·tion (ri·TEN·shun) *n.* a retaining or retaining capacity.
— **re·ten·tive** (-tiv) *adj.: Al has a very retentive memory.*

ret·i·cent (RET·uh·sunt) *adj.* not speaking freely, esp. from reserve or embarrassment: *She was reticent about what happened.* — **ret·i·cence** *n.*

ret·i·nue (RET·uh·new) *n.* a body of retainers, attendants, or assistants following an important person.

re·tire (ri·TIRE) *v.* **-tires, -tired, -tir·ing** 1 of a person, withdraw from work or activity at the end of the day, a career, etc.: *Employees may retire from service with full pension after 30 years; He retires to his den for study; He retires daily (to bed) at 11 p.m.; takes a hot bath before retiring; to retire from a game such as basketball or cricket by being put out; a **retired** (= no longer in service) teacher leading a retired life.* 2 withdraw: *We'll just retire him to make room for a better worker; to retire bonds, loans, etc. (from circulation); a shy **retiring** (= reserved) man; a **retired** (= secluded) spot.*
— **re·tire·ment** *n.: He went into early retirement at 50; compulsory, forced retirement; Al lives in retirement at Port Hope; He came out of retirement and started a new business.*

re·tort (ri·TORT) *n.* a quick, sharp, or witty reply: *He made an angry retort.*
— *v.: He retorted angrily that he was quitting.*

re·touch (ri·TUCH) *v.* improve a photograph, composition, etc. by slight changes.

re·trace (ri·TRACE) *v.* **-trac·es, -traced, -trac·ing** go back over the way one came, past actions, etc.: *to retrace a route, one's steps.*

re·tract (ri·TRACT) *v.* draw back or withdraw a statement, promise, etc.
— **re·trac·tion** *n.: to issue, make a retraction.*

re·tract·a·ble (ri·TRAC·tuh·bul) *adj.* that can be drawn back: *the retractable roof of Toronto's Skydome; an aircraft's retractable landing gear.*

re·trac·tile (ri·TRAC·tile, -til) *adj.* that has the quality of being drawn back: *a cat's retractile claws.*

re·treat (ri·TREET) *n.* 1 a going back or withdrawal, as from battle: *The retreat was hasty, precipitate, but carried out in good order; a tactical retreat.* 2 a signal for a military retreat: *A retreat is sounded on a bugle or*

drum; The retreat played at dusk ends the working day; They **beat a retreat** (= ran away). **3** a temporary withdrawal from regular occupations for self-improvement: *We went on a weekend retreat; We go into retreat every year.* **4** a place of seclusion; refuge: *a country retreat; mountain retreat.*
— *v.* make a retreat: *The enemy retreated before the advancing armies; They retreated to the mountains; The government retreated from its previous position on wage-and-price controls.*

re·trench (ri·TRENCH) *v.* reduce expenses, staff, etc. for economy; **re·trench·ment** *n.*

ret·ri·bu·tion (ret·ruh·BYOO·shun) *n.* deserved punishment for one's actions: *Divine retribution was visited on the unjust; They were determined to exact retribution from the ruling party.*

re·trieve (ri·TREEV) *v.* **-trieves, -trieved, -triev·ing** regain by making an effort, as a dog, or **retriever,** trained to fetch killed or wounded game: *to retrieve misplaced articles, one's reputation, data from computer storage.*
— **re·triev·a·ble** *adj.* — **re·triev·al** (-vul) *n.*

retro- *combining form.* back or backward: *retroactive, retrofire, retrofit.*

ret·ro·ac·tive (ret·roh·AC·tiv) *adj.* covering a period that is past: *a retroactive law; a decision with retroactive effect; a pay raise retroactive to January 1.*
— **ret·ro·ac·tive·ly** *adv.*

ret·ro·fire (RET·roh·fire) *v.* **-fires, -fired, -fir·ing** fire a retrorocket. — *n.* such firing.

ret·ro·fit (RET·roh·fit) *v.* **-fits, -fit·ted, -fit·ting** modify an aircraft or machinery by fitting it with newly designed parts or equipment: *an oil furnace retrofitted with new devices to increase efficiency.*

ret·ro·grade (RET·ruh·grade) *adj.* tending to take one backward; hence, not progressive: *retrograde ideas, policies, steps.*

ret·ro·rock·et (RET·ruh·rock·it) *n.* on a spacecraft, a small rocket that fires in the direction of flight in order to slow the craft down.

ret·ro·spect (RET·ruh·spect) *n.* a survey of the past.
— **in retrospect** when looking back at what is past.
— **ret·ro·spec·tion** (-SPEC·shun) *n.*
— **ret·ro·spec·tive** (-tiv) *adj.;* **ret·ro·spec·tive·ly** *adv.*

re·turn (ri·TURN) *v.* come, go, give, take, or send back: *We return home each summer; He'll return to work on Monday; We return borrowed books; to return a blow, compliment, visit; A jury returns* (= reports) *a verdict; A candidate is returned* (= elected) *to a legislature or political office; an enterprise that returns* (= yields as profit or earnings) *$10 million annually; to return thanks to God.*
— *n.* a returning or thing returned: *Service will resume on our return to work from holidays; to do one favour* **in return** (= compensation) *for another; to file an income-tax return* (= report); *a joint (tax) return by husband and wife; a business that folded because of poor* **returns** (= yield); *The* **return on** *investment* (= profit) *was just 5%; We wish you* **many happy returns** (= many more days like this); *The election* **returns** (= results) *are not in yet; We've reached the point of no return and it's*

impossible turning back now.
— *adj.:* *a return address, date, journey, match, trip; the return air fare, postage.*
— **re·turn·a·ble** (ri·TUR·nuh·bul) *n. & adj.:* a returnable container.

re·un·ion (ree·YOON·yun) *n.* a uniting again: *a touching reunion of family members separated by war; to hold an annual, class, family reunion; to hope for a reunion after a divorce.*

rev *n. Informal.* a revolution of a motor.
— *v.* **revs, revved, rev·ving** increase the speed of a motor, as by pressing the gas pedal of an automobile: *The company is revving up* (= increasing) *its public relations.*

re·vamp (ree·VAMP) *v.* patch up; hence, reconstruct or revise: *a revamped project; a dissertation revamped into a book; a company trying to revamp its corporate image.*

re·veal (ri·VEEL) *v.* make known or visible something that is hidden: *to reveal a secret; He revealed to us that he was the child's true father; a very* **revealing** *gown (that exposes more of the body than is usual).*

rev·el (REV·ul) *v.* **-els, -elled** or **-eled, -el·ling** or **-el·ing** **1** take part in a revel. **2** take much pleasure in an activity: *a playboy who revels away his nights; a writer who revels in words; children who revel in mischief-making.* — *n.* same as REVELRY.
— **rev·el·ler** or **rev·el·er** *n.*

rev·e·la·tion (rev·uh·LAY·shun) *n.* a revealing or something revealed, esp. something startling and usually pleasing: *He made an astounding, startling, stunning revelation; Her royal roots were a revelation to us; the revelation that her father was of royal blood; the divine revelation made to Moses.*
— **re·vel·a·to·ry** (REV·uh·luh·tor·ee) *adj.*

rev·el·ry (REV·ul·ree) *n.* **-ries** a boisterous merrymaking.

re·venge (ri·VENJ) *v.* **-veng·es, -venged, -veng·ing** avenge a wrong or wronged person in a retaliatory or malicious spirit.
— *n.* a revenging; also, a desire or opportunity for taking vengeance: *Hamlet meant to take revenge on Claudius for his father's murder; He was told to exact, get, have revenge on the murderer; to kill him in revenge for his father's murder; "Revenge is sweet" to the unforgiving.*
— **revenge oneself** or **be revenged** take vengeance *on someone.* — **re·venge·ful** *adj.*

rev·e·nue (REV·uh·new) *n.* **1** income, esp. from an investment: *Sales generate, produce, yield revenue; annual, monthly, yearly revenue.* **2** a government's income from taxes, customs, duties, etc.: *Revenue Canada collects revenue; Federal revenue-sharing with provincial governments; A* **revenue stamp** *is proof of payment of a government tax.*

re·ver·ber·ate (ri·VUR·buh·rate) *v.* **-rates, -rat·ed, -rat·ing** reecho; hence, resound: *The applause reverberated through the hallways.*
— **re·ver·ber·a·tion** (-RAY·shun) *n.*

re·vere (ri·VEER) *v.* **-veres, -vered, -ver·ing** regard usually a person with great respect and love: *a man* *revered for his courage and wisdom.*

rev·er·ence (REV·ur·unce) *n.* love and respect mixed with awe.
— *v.* -enc·es, -enced, -enc·ing regard a person's memory, tomb, and such things with reverence: *a name held in reverence by all mankind; He felt, showed a deep reverence for life.*

rev·er·end (REV·ur·und) *adj.* **1** worthy of being revered. **2** Reverend [used as title for a member of the clergy]: *the Reverend Anne Jones; the Reverend A. Jones; the Reverend Miss Jones; the Reverend Sister Smith; the Reverend Father Smith.*
— *n. Informal.* a member of the clergy, esp. a minister: *He is a reverend; Ask the reverend; Hi, Reverend!*

rev·er·ent (REV·ur·unt) *adj.* feeling or showing reverence. — **rev·er·ent·ly** *adv.*
— **rev·er·en·tial** (rev·uh·REN·shul) *adj.*

rev·er·ie or **rev·er·y** (REV·uh·ree) *n.* -er·ies a pleasant daydream: *Sam reads romances and indulges in reveries.*

re·ver·sal (ri·VUR·sul) *n.* a reversing.

re·verse (ri·VURSE) *n.* **1** the opposite or contrary: *Selling is the reverse of buying.* **2** something that is opposite, esp. in direction: *to put a car in reverse (gear); Watch the rear before you go into* or *shift into reverse; the obverse and the reverse (= back) of a coin; He suffered* or *sustained many financial reverses (= setbacks or misfortunes) before reaching his present position.*
— *adj.: Z, Y, X, W ... is in reverse alphabetical order; the reverse image in a mirror;* **reverse discrimination** *(against members of the majority group).*
— *v.* -vers·es, -versed, -vers·ing turn to the other side or in an opposite direction: *Children learning to write sometimes reverse their letters; to reverse a car (= drive backwards); to reverse (= cancel) a judicial decision; to reverse a policy, trend; to reverse the charges (of a telephone call so that the recipient, not caller, pays).*
— **re·verse·ly** *adv.;* **re·vers·i·ble** (ri·VUR·suh·bul) *adj.*

re·vert (ri·VURT) *v.* **1** go back or return, as offspring to an ancestral type or thoughts to a previous subject or something recalled. **2** of property, go back to a prior owner: *Copyright reverts to the author from the publisher when a book goes out of print.*
— **re·ver·sion** (ri·VUR·zhun) *n.*

re·view (riv·YOO) *n.* **1** a looking at or examination, as of work or events at the end of a period, a higher court's examination of a lower court's decision, or the inspection of troops at a parade: *a comprehensive review of the war; to hold a review of the troops; Your pay is under review; As she lay dying, her whole life passed in review before her.* **2** a critical evaluation of a new book, movie, play, concert, etc.: *to do* or *write a (book) review; The book got* or *received favourable, positive, rave reviews in the media; adj.: a review article; review copies of books for review.* **3** a magazine dealing with current affairs, including also book reviews: *a cultural, financial, literary review.* **4** same as REVUE.
— *v.* to study or examine: *to review a book, decision, movie, parade, situation; He's reviewing (lessons) for the exam; The soldiers marched past the* **reviewing stand.**
— **re·view·er** *n.*

re·vise (ri·VIZE) *v.* -vis·es, -vised, -vis·ing to change, correct, or improve something in a set form: *to revise a*

book, estimate, list, plan, system; the **revised edition** *of a book; the 1881-85* **Revised Version** *of the King James Bible; the 1946-57* **Revised Standard Version** *of the American Standard Version of the Bible.*
— **re·vis·er** or **re·vi·sor** *n.* — **re·vis·ion** (ri·VIZH·un) *n.*

re·viv·al (ri·VYE·vul) *n.* **1** a reviving or being revived; also, a revitalization: *the Revival of Learning (= the Renaissance) in Europe.* **2** a new presentation of a play, fresh publication of a book, etc. **3** an evangelistic meeting for renewal of religious fervour.
— **re·viv·al·ism** *n.;* **re·viv·al·ist** *n.*

re·vive (ri·VIVE) *v.* -vives, -vived, -viv·ing bring back a person, idea, hope, practice, activity, etc. from a lifeless, unconscious, or inactive condition: *Fresh air seemed to revive her spirits; The news story revived old memories; Fears of fresh violence revived (= came back).*

re·voke (ri·VOKE) *v.* -vokes, -voked, -vok·ing cancel a privilege, trust, grant, or licence by withdrawing it.
— **rev·o·ca·tion** (rev·uh·CAY·shun) *n.*

re·volt (ri·VOLT) *n.* an armed uprising: *to incite, stir up a revolt; The peasants' revolt against oppressive conditions was quickly put down; They tried to crush, quell the revolt; the revolt of the American colonies; a rent revolt; tax revolt.*
— *v.* turn away from something: *The colonies revolted against Britain; They revolted (= rebelled); Cannibalism is a practice that revolts (= disgusts) human nature; It's something that human nature revolts (= recoils) against* or *at* or *from.*

revolting *adj.* disgusting: *a revolting crime, habit, practice.*

rev·o·lu·tion (rev·uh·LOO·shun) *n.* **1** the overthrow of something established, esp. a regime; hence, a radical or complete change: *to foment, organize, stir up a revolution; to crush, defeat, put down a revolution; the French Revolution of 1789 – 99; the Industrial Revolution; a cultural, sexual, social revolution; the electronic revolution of the 1980s.* **2** a going round in an orbit: *The annual revolution of the earth around* or *round the sun causes the revolution (= cycle) of the seasons; a motor that makes 5 200 revolutions (= rotations) per minute.*
— **rev·o·lu·tion·ar·y** (-nair·ee) *adj. & n.* -ar·ies.

rev·o·lu·tion·ize (rev·uh·LOO·shuh·nize) *v.* -iz·es, -ized, -iz·ing change completely or radically: *Automation has revolutionized industry.*

re·volve (ri·VOLV) *v.* -volves, -volved, -volv·ing **1** (cause) to move in a circle around a centre or axis: *Satellites revolve around* or *round their planets; a life of leisure revolving around TV; Credit cards operate on the* **revolving credit** *system that automatically renews credit as bills are paid off; A four-leaved* **revolving door** *helps keep out drafts;* **revolving-door medicine** *in which patients are whisked in and out of doctors' offices with a minimum of checking and treatment.* **2** (cause) to turn over in the mind; reflect upon: *She's revolving the pros and cons before deciding.*

re·volv·er (ri·VOL·vur) *n.* a handgun with five to seven cartridges contained in a revolving cylinder: *to aim, level, point a revolver at someone; to cock, draw, fire, load, whip out a revolver; A revolver is fired, goes off, jams, misfires.*

re·vue (ri·VUE, *rhyme:* VIEW) *n.* a variety show consisting of songs, skits, chorus dances, etc.: *to put on, stage a revue.*

re·vul·sion (ri·VUL·shun) *n.* a strong feeling of reaction in disgust or horror: *to express, feel revulsion against, at, toward mass murderers; a feeling of deep, utmost revulsion.*

re·ward (ri·WORED) *n.* something in return for a service, esp. in recognition of merit: *The police offered, paid, posted a reward for information about the wanted man; to claim, reap, receive a due, just, tangible, well-deserved reward; Is virtue its own reward? the intellectual rewards of scholarship.*
— *v.* give a reward to someone: *They rewarded him with a life-time pension; He felt amply rewarded* (= recompensed) *for his time and effort; a **rewarding*** (= satisfying or gratifying) *experience.*

re·write (ree·RITE) *v.* **-writes, -wrote, -writ·ten, -writ·ing** revise, esp. to write a news story reported by telephone in a form fit for publication.
— *n.* (REE·rite) a rewritten story.

rhap·so·dy (RAP·suh·dee) *n.* **-dies 1** a highly enthusiastic expression of feeling, esp. of delight; hence, ecstasy or rapture. **2** a musical composition such as Liszt's Hungarian Rhapsodies.

rhet·o·ric (RET·uh·ric) *n.* **1** the art of effective writing and speaking; hence, skill in this. **2** showy eloquence: *to indulge in, resort to rhetoric; eloquent, impassioned, soothing rhetoric; mere rhetoric.*

rhe·tor·i·cal (ri·TOR·uh·cul) *adj.* having to do with rhetoric: *A **rhetorical question** such as "Is everything satisfactory?" is sometimes asked merely for effect.*

rheu·mat·ic (roo·MAT·ic) *adj.* having to do with rheumatism. — *n.* one who has rheumatism.

rheu·ma·tism (ROO·muh·tiz·um) *n.* any of several diseases affecting the muscles and joints, as rheumatic fever, arthritis, etc.

rhi·no (RYE·noh) *n.* short form of **rhi·noc·er·os** (rye·NOS·ur·us), a huge beast with one or two upward-curving horns on its nose.

rhu·barb (ROO·barb) *n.* **1** a perennial vegetable with reddish, juicy stalks that are used in desserts. **2** *Slang.* a heated argument: *to get into a rhubarb about something.*

rhyme (RIME) *n.* **1** similarity of end sounds between words, as in "beside/decried" and "wall/fall," esp. as used at the ends of lines of verse. **2** verse or poetry, esp. a simple verse composition that rhymes: *a nursery rhyme; He gets mad at people without **rhyme or reason*** (= without sense or logic).
— *v.* **rhymes, rhymed, rhym·ing** make rhyme(s) or put into rhymes: *"Head" doesn't rhyme with "bead"; They don't rhyme.*

rhythm (RITH·um, "TH" as in "the") *n.* a regularly repeated sound forming a pattern suggesting movement, as the tread of marching soldiers, the beating of the heart, the beat of strong and weak syllables in verse, the duration of musical bars, etc.: *We danced to the frenzied, heavy, pulsating, steady, strong rhythm of the music; a children's **rhythm band** of percussion instruments.* — **rhyth·mic** or **rhyth·mi·cal** *adj.*
— **rhyth·mi·cal·ly** *adv.*

rib *n.* **1** one of the 12 pairs of curved bones attached to the backbone and forming the chest cavity enclosing the heart, stomach, and other organs: *to break, fracture a rib; She made the child laugh by poking him **in the ribs.*** **2** anything resembling a rib, as the metal strips supporting an umbrella's cloth, the keel-to-deck timbers of a ship's frame, etc.
— *v.* **ribs, ribbed, rib·bing 1** form or furnish with ribs. **2** *Informal.* tease, like poking in the ribs: *Al took a **ribbing** about it from his friends.*

rib·ald (RIB·uld) *adj.* vulgarly or indecently humorous: *ribald humour, jokes, remarks, tales.* — **rib·ald·ry** *n.*

rib·bon (RIB·un) *n.* a narrow strip or band of material, as used to tie hair or packages, to decorate costumes, or as a badge of honour or mernbership: *to change a typewriter ribbon; His shirt was cut or torn to ribbons* (= tatters); *it hung in ribbons.*

rib cage *n.* the chest cavity.

rice *n.* **1** a cereal grass of warm countries, grown esp. in Asia for food. **2** its grains boiled for food: *converted rice; polished rice; wild rice.*
— *v.* **ric·es, riced, ric·ing** make cooked potatoes, etc. into ricelike grains.

rich *adj.* having more resources, esp. money, property, etc. than is required for normal needs: *a rich banker; Arab nations rich in oil; They **struck it rich** during the 1970s; a rich cake, fuel mixture, soil; rich colours, food, furnishings, tones; That's rich (Informal for very amusing)!*
— **the rich** *n.pl.* wealthy people: *the life of the idle rich.*
— **rich·es** *n.pl.* wealth: *to amass riches; the story of his rise from rags to riches.* — **rich·ly** *adv.;* **rich·ness** *n.*

rick *n.* an outdoor stack of hay, straw, etc.

rick·et·y (RIK·uh·tee) *adj.* feeble or shaky: *a rickety old structure.*

ric·o·chet (RIK·uh·shay) *n.* a glancing rebound or skip from a surface, as a bullet off a wall or a flat stone off a water surface.
— *v.* **-chets, pt. & pp. -cheted** (-shayed) or **-chet·ted** (-shet·id), **-chet·ing** (-shay·ing) or **-chet·ting** (-shet·ing) make a ricochet: *The bullet ricocheted off the windshield.*

rid *v.* **rids, pt. & pp. rid** or **rid·ded, rid·ding** make free of something undesirable: *to rid a dog of fleas; to be rid* *of the nuisance; I tried to **get rid of** it.*

rid·dance (RID·unce) *n.* a ridding: *Good riddance to bad rubbish! It was **good riddance** (= welcome relief) when the noisy party left.*

ridden *pp.* of RIDE.
— **combining form.** dominated by what is specified: *crime-ridden, disease-ridden, guilt-ridden.*

rid·dle (RID·ul) *n.* 1 a puzzling question, often sounding contradictory, and requiring a witty answer, as "What grows bigger the more you take from it?" (A hole): *to solve a riddle; to speak in riddles like a sphinx, like an oracle.* 2 a coarse sieve, as for grading potatoes or sifting coal.
— *v.* **rid·dles, rid·dled, rid·dling** 1 talk in riddles; also, solve: *Riddle me this.* 2 make holes in something: *The car was riddled with bullets; a department **riddled with** (= full of) corruption.* 3 sift with a riddle.

ride *v.* **rides, rode, rid·den** (RID·un), **rid·ing** 1 sit on and manage an animal or vehicle: *to ride a bicycle, horse; a child riding her father piggyback; a mind ridden* (= dominated) *by fears.* 2 travel or be carried by an animal or vehicle: *He rides to work by bus; He has never ridden on* or *in a train; She just rode by; A ship rides the waves; rides at anchor in the harbour; a kite riding the winds; a car that rides* (= runs) *smoothly; The future of the company rides* (= depends) *on this publication; The government decided to **ride out** the storm* (= wait patiently for it to pass); *He's never been known to **ride roughshod over** (= mistreat) his employees.*
— *n.* 1 a riding: *to get, go for, go on, take a ride; to bum, hitch, thumb a ride (Informal for hitchhike); to give someone a ride; a joy ride in a stolen car.* 2 something to ride, as a Ferris wheel: *to go on the rides at a fair.*
— **let ride** *Informal.* let pass or leave undisturbed.
— **take someone for a ride** *Slang.* cheat or victimize someone.

rid·er (RYE·dur) *n.* 1 one who rides. 2 something appended to a contract, bill, etc. as an amendment or addition.
— **rid·er·ship** *n.: Transit ridership* (= number of riders) *is up this year.*

ridge (RIJ) *n.* a long and narrow, usually horizontal line formed by the meeting of two rising surfaces: *the ridge of a mountain range, of an animal's back, of the nose; the ridges on a corded fabric, on ploughed land between furrows, of high pressure on a weather map; the ridge of a roof topped by a **ridge·pole** to which rafters are fastened.*
— *v.* **ridg·es, ridged, ridg·ing** form into or extend in ridges: *The floor of the Atlantic ridges in the middle from north to south.*

rid·i·cule (RID·uh·kyool) *n.* mockery, esp. using words: *The new scheme has drawn* or *incurred the ridicule of the media; Today's cartoon holds it up to ridicule; The editorial heaps* or *pours ridicule on the scheme.*
— *v.* **-cules, -culed, -cul·ing** subject a person or thing to ridicule.

ri·dic·u·lous (ri·DIK·yuh·lus) *adj.* arousing laughter; absurd: *It's ridiculous to spend so much money on the scheme; It's ridiculous that they want $500 million for*

the scheme. — **ri·dic·u·lous·ly** *adv.*

riding (RYE·ding) *n. Cdn.* a constituency or electoral district whose voters elect a member of a legislature.

rife *adj.* widespread: *Rumour is rife that Al is dead; Rumours about his death are running rife* (= out of control); *His hometown is rife with* (= full of) *rumours of his death.*

rif·fle (RIF·ul) *n.* 1 a choppy stretch of water formed by a shoal or reef; also, the ripples caused. 2 a way of shuffling cards by combining the separate decks into one while their edges are bent and rapidly released against each other.
— *v.* **rif·fles, rif·fled, rif·fling** 1 shuffle cards in this manner. 2 leaf rapidly: *to riffle through a book, through files, pages, papers.* 3 make ripples in water, sand, etc.: *See the breeze riffling the water on the lake.*

riff·raff *n.* worthless or disreputable people.

ri·fle (RYE·ful) *v.* **-fles, -fled, -fling** 1 cut spiral grooves in a gun barrel, as of a rifle. 2 search as a robber: *to rifle through office files.*
— *n.* 1 a long-barrelled gun that fires its bullets with a spinning motion: *to aim, fire, handle, level, load, point a rifle; an air rifle; hunting rifle; A rifle fires, goes off, misfires; a rifle range.* 2 a body of riflemen: *the Queen's Rifles.* — **ri·fler** *n.*

ri·fle·man (RYE·ful·mun) *n.* **-men** a soldier armed with a rifle.

rift *n.* a cleft or fissure; hence, a breach of friendship: *to cause a rift among the partners; to heal the rift between the two.* — *v.* split or cleave.

rig *v.* **rigs, rigged, rig·ging** 1 fit out, as a ship, with rigging: *She came to the party rigged out in her best attire.* 2 manipulate dishonestly, as the outcome of a prizefight or election, market prices, etc.
— *n.* 1 the kind and arrangement of a ship's rigging: *the fore-and-aft rig of a schooner.* 2 a large vehicle: *to drive a tractor-trailer rig.* 3 equipment: *an oil-drilling rig.*

rig·a·ma·role (RIG·uh·muh·role) *n.* same as RIGMAROLE.

rigging (RIG·ing) *n.* 1 ropes, chains, etc. supporting a ship's masts, sails, etc. 2 the similar network of ropes and chains controlling theatre scenery.

right *adj.* 1 good, true, correct, just, or proper; not wrong: *You're right; She's right to say "No"; He's right in saying "No"; It's right of you to say "No"; It's not right that they should force you to say "Yes"; the right thing to say; That's just right for me; That's all right; the right clothes to wear.* 2 not left: *He writes with his right hand; the right side; He's politically **Right** (= conservative).* 3 straight, not slanting: *a **right angle** (of 90°); a right (circular) cone.*
— *adv.* 1 well, truly, correctly, justly, or properly: *You guessed right; Everything turned out right in the end.* 2 to the right side: *You face east if you turn right from north.* 3 straight: *Let's do it right now; Come home **right away** or **off** (= immediately); (You're) **right on!** (Informal for quite right).*
— *n.* 1 that which is good, true, correct, etc.: *Infants can't tell right from wrong; She was in the right in saying "No."* 2 that to which one has a just claim: *You are within your rights to say "No"; a bill of rights; our*

social rights and responsibilities; to assert, claim, enjoy, exercise, gain, protect, relinquish, renounce, safeguard, sign away, waive a right; the divine right of kings; a basic, civil, conjugal, exclusive, fundamental, human, inalienable, inherent, legal, natural, sole, voting, women's right; the right to exist, to remain silent; the right to life, liberty, etc. as in the Canadian Charter of Rights and Freedoms. **3** the right side or wing: We drive on the right (of the road); The boxer delivered or threw a stiff right (= blow) to the jaw. **4 right** or **Right** a conservative or reactionary position, person, view, etc.: a party of the right; the extreme, far right in politics. — **by right** or **rights** justly.
— **v. 1** put what is wrong in order: to right a wrong. **2** make straight what is slanting or overturned; also, become straight: The boat righted itself.
— **right·ly** adv.; **right·ness** n.

right·eous (RYE·chus) adj. **1** upright; morally blameless: a righteous person. **2** justifiable: righteous indignation, zeal.

right·ful (RITE·ful) adj. according to just claims; by right: the rightful owner; his rightful rank; a woman's rightful place in society. — **right·ful·ly** adv.

right-hand adj. **1** having to do with the right side: on the driver's right-hand side; the minister's right-hand (= trusted) man. **2** having to do with the right hand: a right-hand blow, glove.

right-handed (RITE·han·did) adj. **1** having a tendency to use the right hand rather than the left: a right-handed pitcher; adv.: He throws right-handed. **2** turning clockwise: a right-handed propeller, screw.
— **right-hand·ed·ly** adv.; **right-hand·ed·ness** n.

right·ist n. & adj. conservative or reactionary.

right-minded adj. morally or intellectually right: a right-minded citizen, employer.

right of way n. **rights of way 1** the right to go first, as of pedestrians at a crossing; precedence: At a pedestrian crossing, people have the right of way over vehicles; Vehicles yield right of way to pedestrians. **2** right to use land owned by another, as to walk through; also, such land or land used by a public utility, railway, or highway: a hydro right of way.

right-to-life(r) n. & adj. same as PRO-LIFE(R).

right wing n. **1** a front-line player or position to the right of centre, as in hockey. **2** the rightist or most conservative group in a party; adj.: right-wing extremism. — **right-wing·er** n.

rig·id (RIJ·id) adj. stiff or strict, not bending or yielding: the rigid frame of a rigid airship; a rigid disciplinarian; He's rigid about rules; rigid economic controls; rigid rules. — **rig·id·ly** adv.
— **rig·id·ness** or **ri·gid·i·ty** (ri·JID·uh·tee) n.

rig·ma·role (RIG·muh·role) n. words or action without sense; something too involved or incoherent.

rig·our or **rig·or** (RIG·ur) n. **1** strictness or exactness: a life of rigour and discipline; the rigour of his logic. **2** severity or harshness: the rigour of military training; the rigours of the Arctic climate. — **rig·or·ous** adj.
— **rig·or·ous·ly** adv.; **rig·or·ous·ness** n.

rile v. **riles, riled, ril·ing** Informal. irritate or anger: It riled him that or He was riled that few turned up for the meeting.

rim n. a circular or curving edge, as the lip of a cup, the spectacle frame around the lenses, or the outer part of a wheel over which a tire is fitted: He was standing on the rim of the canyon when he fell in.
— **v. rims, rimmed, rim·ming 1** form a rim around: horn-rimmed glasses. **2** roll around the rim, as a basketball before dropping into the basket.

rime n. **1** [old use] same as RHYME. **2** hoarfrost; v. **rimes, rimed, rim·ing** cover with rime. — **rim·y** adj.

rind (RINED) n. the thick outer covering or skin of certain fruits such as lemon and melon, of bacon, or of cheese.

¹**ring** n. **1** something curved round like a circle, as the ornamental band worn on a finger: a diamond ring; engagement ring; wedding ring; key ring; to blow smoke rings; piston rings; the rings of Saturn; She can **run rings around** (= far outperform) him; adj.: a **ring binder** (with pages held by metal rings); the **ring finger** (= usually the one next to the little finger). **2** an enclosed area for a circus or prizefight: a three-ring circus; a wrestling ring; He threw his hat into **the ring** (= entered the contest as a candidate). **3** a close group of people working with a selfish or secret aim: a crime, drug, prostitution, sex, smuggling, spy ring.
— **v. rings, ringed, ring·ing 1** encircle: A highway rings the city; The house is ringed (about) with trees. **2** place or put a ring, as in the nose of an animal or around a tree by cutting away bark.

²**ring** v. **rings, rang, ring·ing 1** give forth a clear sound, as a bell: A phone rings; Our phone has been **ringing off the hook** (= constantly) since the want ad appeared; Please ring me at the office; Ring the bell for service; Just ring for service; The story rings true (like a genuine coin) but it doesn't **ring a bell** (= remind me of anything); to **ring down** the curtain on (= conclude) a performance or action; Sales clerks **ring up** (= record and total) customers' purchases (on the cash register). **2** resound; be filled with a sound: a room ringing with laughter; a neighbourhood ringing with a scandal; Her ears were still ringing with the scolding she got; a **ringing** (= strong) endorsement.
— **n.** a sound of or like ringing; also, its characteristic quality: His story has the ring of truth; There's a false, hollow ring to her story; Give me a ring (= phone call) when you're ready.

ring·er n. **1** one that rings. **2** Slang. impostor: a dead ringer (= lookalike) for Jackie.

ring·ette (ring·ET) n. a less aggressive form of hockey played with a straight stick and a rubbery donutlike puck.

ring·side n. a place close to a boxing or circus ring: a ringside seat for a close view of the action.

rink n. a smooth floor or surface prepared for hockey, skating, curling, etc.; also, a building housing it: We met at a rink; Canada's first artificial skating rinks are said to have been built in B.C. in 1911.

rink rat n. Cdn. Slang. a youth who helps at a rink with odd jobs.

rink·y-dink adj. Slang. shoddy or cheap: rinky-dink crime, politics.

rinse (RINCE) v. rins·es, rinsed, rins·ing 1 wash lightly or cleanse thus, as the mouth with water: Rinse the soap out of your hair. 2 to dye or tint hair, fabrics, etc. — n. a rinsing or something used for washing or tinting the hair.

ri·ot (RYE·ut) n. 1 a violent outbreak or disturbance by a group of people: A riot breaks out, erupts; to cause, crush, incite, instigate, put down, quell, spark a riot; communal, food, prison, race riots. 2 something wild or unrestrained: Our garden is a riot of colour in the spring; You're a riot (Informal for extremely funny). — read the riot act give official warning of consequences: The coach read the riot act to the Maple Leafs and they responded with a 3-2 victory. — run riot be wild or unrestrained; also, grow luxuriantly: Weeds run riot in a neglected spot. — v. engage in a riot: The inmates rioted at the penitentiary; They rioted against the warden. — ri·ot·ous (-tus) adj.; ri·ot·ous·ly adv. — ri·ot·ous·ness n.

rip v. rips, ripped, rip·ping 1 tear or split apart quickly, esp. along a joining such as a seam or along the grain of wood, as with a "ripsaw." 2 Informal. rush violently: He came ripping up the street; ripped out with (= uttered) profanities; mercilessly ripped into her (= attacked him verbally). — n. a tear or rent: a rip in his pants. — rip off Informal. 1 steal or rob: Tax evaders rip off the government. 2 exploit: the public ripped off by big business. — rip·per n.

rip cord n. a cord by which a parachute is pulled open during descent.

ripe adj. rip·er, rip·est 1 fully developed or mature: The harvest is ripe; tomatoes ripe for the picking; ripe wine, cheese, wisdom; garbage that is pretty ripe (= smelly). 2 ready for use, action, etc.: The time is ripe for action, change. — ripe·ly adv.; ripe·ness n.

rip·en (RYE·pun) v. make or become ripe: the ripening of fruit, cheese; Their relationship ripened into love.

rip-off n. Informal. an act of theft or exploitation: income-tax rip-offs by corporations; massive rip-off of medical insurance by overbilling; Third World rip-offs by capitalist countries; The show was a clever rip-off designed to plug a new movie; a rip-off artist.

ri·poste (ri·POHST) n. 1 a sharp, quick retort like a fencer's counterattack or thrust following a parry. 2 such a thrust.

rip·ple (RIP·ul) n. a series of little waves, as when still water is disturbed: The wind makes ripples on our swimming pool; She has ripples in her hair; a ripple of laughter. — v. make a ripple: sand rippled by the tide; breeze rippling a field of corn; Laughter rippled through the audience.

rip-roaring (RIP·ror·ing) adj. Informal. boisterous; hilarious.

rise (RIZE) v. ris·es, rose, ris·en (RIZ·un), ris·ing go up or get up, esp. gradually: The sun rises in the east; smoke rising from a chimney; He rises (from bed) at 6 a.m.; the order to **rise and shine** (= get out of bed); rising temperatures, tides; Wages and prices rise; her rising tone of anger; The Fraser River rises (= has its origin) in the Rockies; The rebels rose against the government; The general rose (in his career) from the ranks; the **rising** (= growing) generation; A resourceful person will **rise to** the challenge, to the occasion (= meet it successfully). — n. 1 an upward movement, slope, increase, etc.: You can't see far because of a rise in the road; His meteoric rise to stardom; the rise and fall of the Roman Empire; the sharp rise in prices; Prices are **on the rise** (= increasing). 2 origin or beginning: the rise of the Fraser River in the Rockies; the rise of a storm; the theory of the rise of animals from lower forms of life; the rise of separatism. — **get a rise out of** Slang. get an emotional response or reaction from someone. — **give rise to** originate something unwanted: Unemployment gives rise to poverty and crime.

ris·er (RYE·zur) n. 1 one that rises. 2 the vertical part between two steps.

risk n. 1 the possibility of danger or loss of something: You **run** or **take a risk** by stepping into heavy traffic; You do so at the risk of being killed; a risk to life and limb, to safety; to assume, face, incur risks; a calculated, grave, great, high, low risk; Use the unfinished road **at your own risk** (= without claims for accidents, etc.). 2 a person considered in regard to a risk: She is a security risk; He was rejected for life insurance as a poor risk (= hazard); A healthy person is a good risk (for life insurers). — v. incur or expose to a risk, esp. voluntarily: You risk your life by driving while drunk; risk being killed and killing others.

risk arbitrage n. the buying up of the stocks of firms threatened by takeover in the hope of selling them at the higher price resulting from the takeover.

risk capital n. same as VENTURE CAPITAL.

risk·y adj. risk·i·er, -i·est involving risk: a risky life, undertaking, venture; It's risky to smoke in bed. — risk·i·ness n.

ris·qué (ris·KAY) adj. close to being indecent; off-colour.

rite n. 1 a ceremonial form or act: to administer the last rites to a sick person; to perform a rite; a pagan, religious, solemn rite; initiation, funeral, marriage rites; a Lenten rite (= liturgy); a **rite of passage** (= a ritual marking passage from one status to another, as at marriage or from childhood to adulthood). 2 a church denomination: the Greek Catholic Rite.

rit·u·al (RICH·oo·ul) n. a system of rites or procedure as established for a usually religious ceremony: the Easter ritual; the ritual of voodoo; to go through a ritual for form's sake; She makes a ritual of her Sunday dinners; **adj.**: a ritual dance; ritual laws; the ritual slaughter of kosher chicken. — rit·u·al·ly adv.

ritz·y (RIT·see) adj. ritz·i·er, -i·est Slang. high-class; luxurious; plush: a ritzy hotel.

ri·val (RYE·vul) n. one trying to equal or surpass

another; competitor: *They are rivals in rental cars; rivals for the same business;* **adj.***: a rival company, group.*
— *v.* **-vals, -valled** or **-valed** or **-val·ling** or **-val·ing** equal or excel: *to try harder every day to rival the leader of the market.*

ri·val·ry (RYE·vul·ree) *n.* **-ries** competition between evenly matched opponents: *sibling rivalry; long-standing political rivalries; to stir up rivalry between partners; There is intense, keen, strong rivalry among them; rivalry for the top job.*

rive *v.* **rives,** *pt. & pp.* **rived** or **riv·en** (RIV·un), **riv·ing** split or tear apart violently.

riv·er (RIV·ur) *n.* a natural stream larger than a brook or creek, normally confined within banks, and flowing into a sea, lake, or another river: *to go up, down (the) river; His partner* **sold him down the river** (= betrayed him).

riv·et (RIV·ut) *n.* a metal bolt whose plain end is flattened into another head after being passed through the parts to be joined together.
— *v.* **-ets, -et·ted** or **-et·ed, -et·ting** or **-et·ing** fasten with a rivet: *steel beams rivetted together; a preacher who can rivet your attention for an hour; They stood rivetted to the spot; with all eyes rivetted on her; the most* **rivetting** (= attention-holding) *performer in rock'n'roll.*

roach (ROHCH) *n.* 1 [short form] cockroach. 2 *Slang.* butt of a marijuana cigarette, held with a **roach clip.**

road (RODE) *n.* 1 a usually public path, way, or course for travelling to a destination: *"All roads lead to Rome"; This is the road to take; a back, country, dirt, impassable, main, mountain, paved, rough, service, smooth, straight, toll, winding, wrong road; A travelling sales rep is* **on the road** *much of the time; to get a show on the road* (= touring); *Pat's* **on the road to** (= moving toward) *recovery; Obey the rules of the road; Demonstrators took to the road in large numbers; the royal road to success; Forget about* **one for the road** (= an extra drink); *inventions waiting for us* **down the road** (= in the future). 2 a roadstead, often **roads,** as in "Royal Roads" near Victoria, B.C.

road allowance *n. Cdn.* land set apart by government for a road to go through.

road·block *n.* a barrier placed across a road, as by police at checkpoints; hence, any hindrance: *to establish, run, set up a roadblock; The Government has placed roadblocks in the way of the inquiry commission.*

road hog *n. Informal.* an unmannerly driver, esp. a motorist who drives in the middle of the road.

road·house *n.* an out-of-town restaurant and bar on a main route.

road·side *n.* the side of a road: *to stop on the roadside;* **adj.***: a roadside park, picnic table, restaurant.*

road·stead (ROAD·sted) *n.* a sheltered anchorage for ships near a shore.

road test *n.* 1 the testing of a vehicle for roadworthiness. 2 a test of driving ability.

road·way *n.* 1 a road. 2 the part of a road used by vehicles.

road·wor·thy (RODE·wur·thee, "th" as in "the") *adj.* of vehicles, in good condition. — **road·wor·thi·ness** *n.*

roam (ROME) *v.* go about in a large area without special plan or aim; wander over: *pirates roaming the seas; He roamed about* or *around* or *over* or *through the country after dropping out of school.*

roar (RORE) *n.* a loud, full, and rumbling sound: *the roar of a lion: the roar of a cheering crowd, of an engine, waterfall; the roar of the wind; the roar of thunder, of traffic on a highway; greeted with roars of laughter.*
— *v.* make a roar: *The lion roared; The crowd roared with laughter; The officer roared out his commands.*
— **roaring** *adj. & adv.: Ray came in roaring drunk; The play was a roaring success; We did a roaring trade.*

roast (ROHST) *v.* 1 cook by dry or radiant heat in an oven or over an open fire: *to roast coffee beans, meat, metal ore.* 2 *Informal.* subject a person to ridicule or criticism: *They gave him a good roasting.*
— *n.* 1 roasted meat or meat suitable for roasting: *to make a roast; a chuck, eye, lamb, pork, pot, rib roast;* **adj.***: roast beef, chicken, pig, potatoes.* 2 a picnic at which food is roasted: *corn roast; steer roast.* 3 an event at which a person is ridiculed, usually good-naturedly: *There was a roast for the premier last night.*
— **roasting** *adj. & adv.: It's roasting hot today.*

rob *v.* **robs, robbed, rob·bing** deprive a person or establishment of property, good name, etc. by violence, fraud, or any unjust means: *A swindler robbed the old man of his savings; He robs banks; children caught robbing an orchard; They rob* (= steal) *apples.*
— **rob·ber** *n.: a band* or *gang of robbers.*

rob·ber·y *n.* **rob·ber·ies** theft by violence or any unjust means: *to commit (a) robbery; armed, bank, daylight robbery; highway robbery* (= overcharging of prices).

robe *n.* 1 a long, loose outer garment, as worn wrapped around when lounging or as a bathrobe. 2 a ceremonial garment, as worn by a judge: *a judge dressed in black robes.*
— *v.* clothe with a robe: *Judges are robed in black.*

ro·bot (ROH·bot) *n.* 1 a mechanical person or human automaton. 2 an insensitive, machinelike human being.

ro·bust (roh·BUST, ROH·bust) *adj.* healthy and vigorous in body or mind, not sickly: *a robust young man; his robust* (= vigorous, not delicate) *humour; robust* (= full-bodied) *coffee; robust* (= sturdy) *faith.*
— **ro·bust·ly** *adv.;* **ro·bust·ness** *n.*

rock *n.* 1 the hard, firm, solid part of the earth's crust made up of minerals; also, a large mass of this or a piece: *firm, solid, steady as a rock; He threw a rock* (= stone) *at the crow.* 2 a style of popular music and dance based on blues and country-and-western music, and characterized by heavy rhythms, common melodies, and popular lyrics; rock'n'roll: *hard rock; punk rock;* **adj.***: rock lyrics, music; a rock band, group, hit, quartet, song, video.* 3 a rocking movement.
— **on the rocks** 1 *Informal.* ruined or bankrupt. 2 of a drink, served on ice cubes: *rum on the rocks.*
— *v.* move back and forth upon a base: *to rock a baby to sleep; a building rocked* (= shaken) *by an explosion;*

*waves rocking a boat; Team players should not **rock the boat*** (= try to upset the situation).

rock'n'roll (ROCK·un·role) *n.* same as ROCK, *n.* 2.

rock bottom *n.* the very lowest; ***adj.:*** *a rock-bottom offer; rock-bottom prices.*

rock·er *n.* a chair mounted so as to be rocked by its occupant; also **rocking chair.**
— **off one's rocker** *Slang.* crazy.

rock·et (ROCK·ut) *n.* a spacecraft or projectile powered by a cylinder containing fuel which, when rapidly burned, creates thrust by the force of the escaping gases, as used in shooting fireworks, war missiles, space probes, etc.: *to fire, launch a rocket; a booster rocket.*

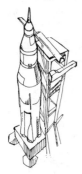

rock·y *adj.* **rock·i·er, -i·est 1** shaky: *a rocky ride.* **2** *Informal.* dizzy or weak: *feeling a bit rocky after the tumble.* **3** full of rocks; consisting of rocks; also, firm or hard as a rock: *a rocky road; rocky soil.*
— **rock·i·ness** *n.*

ro·co·co (ruh·COH·coh) *n.* a highly ornate and elaborate artistic style of the 1700s, more delicate in design than baroque. — ***adj.*** overelaborate or quaint.

rod *n.* **1** a thin, straight stick or bar, as used to fish with, as a measuring unit (16.5 ft. or 5 m), or one carried as a symbol of authority: *a curtain, divining, fishing, lightning, piston, traverse rod; The king ruled the land with a rod of iron; "Spare the rod* (= punishment) *and spoil the child."*

rode *pt.* OF RIDE.

ro·de·o (ROH·dee·oh, roh·DAY·oh) *n.* **-os** an exhibition of or contest in cowboy skills: *to hold, stage a rodeo.*

roe (ROH) *n.* **1** fish eggs or milt: *to spawn roe.* **2** a small, tailless Old World deer whose male, or **roe·buck,** has short, three-tined antlers.

rog·er (ROJ·ur) *interj.* esp. in radio communications, "OK!"

rogue (ROHG) *n.* a scoundrel; rascal.
— **ro·guer·y** (ROH·guh·ree) *n.*
— **ro·guish** (ROH·ghish) *adj.* **1** dishonest. **2** mischievous.

role *n.* **1** an actor's part: *to act out, assume, perform, play, take on a role; cast in the role of Macbeth; to assign roles to players; a leading, supporting, title role.* **2** a part played in real life: *He plays an active role in running the school; She had a key role in organizing the show; Trudeau had to fulfill his role as a father and his*

political role as the nation's leader; the social role of a teacher; the conflict between her roles as breadwinner and as wife; Children often imitate their parents as **role models.** Also **rôle.**

roll (ROLE) *v.* **1** move or cause to move or go forward with a turning motion, as a ball, wheel, or something on wheels: *She rolled me the ball; The years rolled by; Tears rolled down his cheeks; He rolled over and played dead; She rolled up her sleeves and started working; A **rolling stop** won't do for a full stop at a stop sign; **Heads will roll** (= People will be punished); She has learned to **roll with the punches** (= accept adversity without resisting too much); to **start** or **get** or **set the ball rolling** (Informal for make a beginning); He's **rolling it in** (= making money fast); She's **rolling in it** (= very rich).* **2** move or cause to sway from side to side, as a ship tossed by waves; hence, walk with a swagger. **3** have a rising and falling surface: *the rolling country, fields, plain, prairie.* **4** of sounds, have a full or reverberating quality: *the rolling drum, thunder; to roll one's r's* (= utter them with a trill). **5** flatten by using a roller: *We roll dough with a **rolling pin;** to roll a road surface; rolled oats.* **6** *Slang.* rob a drunk, lush, stiff, or other helpless person.
— **roll back** move back, esp. prices to a former level.
— *n.* **1** something rolled up: *a roll of film, money, paper.* **2** a food that is round, rolled, or folded: *cabbage, dinner, jelly, kaiser, sausage rolls.* **3** a list of names: *to call, take the roll; an honour roll of the top students; the roll of honour; Six were **struck off the rolls** (= removed from the list) for misbehaviour.* **4** a rolling movement: *He walks with the roll of a sailor (swaying from side to side).* **5** a rising and falling surface: *the roll of the land.* **6** a rolling sound: *the roll of distant thunder, of drums; the roll* (= long, deep sound) *of his verse.*
— **on a roll** *Informal.* enjoying a series of wins.

roller coaster *n.* an elevated track with ascents, descents, and abrupt turns, carrying passengers in open cars on amusement rides.

rol·lick (ROL·ik) *v.* behave in a carefree, frolicsome manner. — **rol·lick·ing** *adj.*

rolling stock *n.* all the wheeled vehicles of a railway or trucking company.

roll-top *adj.* of a desk, having a sliding top that closes and locks over the desk's working surface.

ro·ly-po·ly (roh·lee·POH·lee) *adj.* of a person or animal, short and plump.

ro·man (ROH·mun) *n.* a type or print that is upright, not italic.

Ro·man candle *n.* a firework that shoots out balls of fire: *The Dow Jones took off like a Roman candle.*

Roman Catholic *n.* & *adj.* (a member) of the Christian church that has the Pope as its head.

ro·mance (roh·MANCE, ROH·mance) *n.* **1** a novel of love and adventure involving characters and events somewhat remote from real life, as of medieval knights; also, this quality or atmosphere: *love and romance; to put romance back into a marriage.* **2** a love story or love affair: *a whirlwind romance; Canadians' romance with the telephone.* **3 Romance** *adj.* having to do with the

languages derived from Latin, as Italian, French, Spanish, and Portuguese.
— *v.* (roh·MANCE) **-manc·es, -manced, -manc·ing** exaggerate, indulge in fancies, or woo someone romantically. — **ro·manc·er** *n.*

ro·man·tic (roh·MAN·tic) *adj.* 1 having to do with romance, esp. love and adventure: *a romantic affair, scene, situation, story.* 2 impractical or visionary: *romantic notions.*
— *n.* a romantic person, or **ro·man·ti·cist.**
— **ro·man·ti·cal·ly** *adv.*

ro·man·ti·cize (roh·MAN·tuh·size) *v.* **-ciz·es, -cized, -ciz·ing** make or be romantic: *a highly romanticized story.*

Ro·me·o (ROH·mee·oh) *n.* an ardent lover, like the hero of Shakespeare's "Romeo and Juliet."

romp *v.* run or jump about in boisterous play: *The Canadian pair romped to easy victories at the Olympics.*
— *n.:* *children out for a romp in the park.*

romp·er *n.* 1 one who romps. 2 usually **rompers** *pl.* a child's playsuit consisting of pants and top.

roof (long "oo") *n.* **roofs** the top covering of a building or a similar part: *the roof of a car; homeless people without a roof over their heads* (= with nowhere to live); *the roof of the mouth* (= palate); *a roof garden* (= garden on a roof).
— *v.* cover with a roof; **roofed** (ROOFT) *adj.*
— **roof·less** *adj.*

roofing *n.* material for roofs; *adj.:* *roofing material, shingles, tiles.*

roof·top *n.* the top of a building: *You don't shout something secret from the rooftops; a rooftop restaurant.*

rook (short "oo") *n.* 1 a chess piece shaped like a castle tower. 2 a bird of the crow family noted for its cunning.
— *v. Slang.* cheat or swindle: *Car owners are being rooked right and left.*

rook·ie (ROOK·ee) *n. Informal.* an inexperienced recruit or a novice; *adj.:* *a rookie constable, M.P., politician.*

room (long or short "oo") *n.* 1 a part of a building set apart by walls or partitions, as for an office or as living quarters; also, the people in it: *He addressed the whole room; We waited in an adjoining room; a banquet, dining, furnished, living, family, guest, locker, men's, reading, rented, rest, spare, storage, utility room; Phone room service* (= food service in a hotel room). 2 space: *plenty of room for four passengers; standing room only; Make room for Daddy; a room to work in; a table that takes up too much room; There's much room* (= scope) *for improvement in your work.*
— *v.* to lodge: *He's rooming at our house; used to room with her;* **room·er** *n.*

room and board *n.* lodging and meals.

rooming house *n.* a house with furnished rooms for rent.

room·y (ROO·mee) *adj.* **room·i·er, -i·est** spacious.
— **room·i·ness** *n.*

roost (long "oo") *n.* a perching place for birds, esp.

domestic fowls: *She* **rules the roost** (*Informal for* is in charge) *here; Al began to regret what he did when the chickens he hatched* **came home to roost** (= when what he did began to backfire).
— *v.* 1 perch on a roost. 2 settle for the night.

roost·er *n.* a male domestic fowl; cock: *Roosters crow; they go "cock-a-doodle-doo."*

root (long "oo") *n.* 1 the usually underground part of a plant that serves as support and draws nourishment from the soil; also, a similar part of a hair, tooth, etc.: *Weeds should be pulled up by the roots; Plants* **strike** or **take root** *in the soil; We have* **struck root** or **roots** (= settled down) *in Canada.* 2 a source or origin: *to get at the root of the matter; The words "root," "wort," and "ramify" have the same root; Blacks have African* **roots;** *adj.:* *the root cause of all this trouble; Potatoes and turnips are* **root crops.**
— *v.* 1 fix or settle, as in the ground: *customs and practices deeply rooted in our culture.* 2 become fixed or begin growing by sending out roots: *Plants root best in the spring.* 3 poke, search, or dig up, as with the snout: *Pigs root for potatoes; They root about or around in the fields; Someone has been rooting around among my papers; We should try to* **root out** (= destroy) *this habit.* 4 *Informal.* cheer: *Let's root for Jane, for the home team.*

rope *n.* a thick, strong cord made of twisted or braided strands of fibre or similar material and traditionally used for ships' rigging, to tether animals, etc.; also, a piece of this for a particular purpose: *a length or piece of rope; a skipping rope; to jump or skip rope; tighten a rope; The rope* (= hanging as punishment) *has been abolished.*
— **give one enough rope** or **plenty of rope** let one act freely and take the consequences.
— **know** or **learn the ropes** *Informal.* know or learn about a job or activity: *to learn the ropes of diplomacy.*
— **on the ropes** in a helpless position, like a boxer about to be knocked out.
— *v.* **ropes, roped, rop·ing** tie, catch, mark off an area, etc. with a rope.
— **rope in** *Informal.* induce someone to do something for another person or cause.

rose (ROZE) *n.* 1 the beautiful, usually fragrant flower of a shrub with a prickly stem; also, the shrub: *Roses are red, violets are blue; a long-stemmed rose; a bouquet of roses; Life is not a* **bed of roses** (= something easy or pleasant); *Everything was* **coming up roses** (= happening as desired) *when tragedy struck.* 2 the flower's commonly reddish colour. 3 *pt.* of RISE.
— *adj.:* *a rose colour, flower; I never promised you a* **rose garden** (= that things would be easy or pleasant); *a rose leaf, window.*

ro·sé (roh·ZAY) *n.* a light pink wine.

rose-coloured (ROZE·cull·urd) *adj.* rosy: *She sees the world through rose-coloured glasses* (= is very optimistic).

ro·sette (roh·ZET) *n.* a rose-shaped ornament, as of ribbon or as used in architecture.

rose water *n.* a watery perfume containing a rose extract.

ros·ter (ROS·tur) *n.* a list, esp. of personnel on duty.

ros·trum (ROS·trum) *n.* -trums or -tra **1** a platform or stage for public speaking: *He mounted the rostrum to address the meeting.* **2** a beaklike part or structure.

ros·y (ROH·zee) *adj.* ros·i·er, -i·est **1** rose-coloured; pinkish red: *rosy cheeks.* **2** optimistic or promising: *a rosy future.* — ros·i·ly *adv.;* ros·i·ness *n.*

rot *v.* rots, rot·ted, rot·ting decompose; decay: *a promising artist rotting in a dead-end job.*
— *n.* **1** decay. **2** a disease of plants and trees, as "potato rot" and "dry rot"; hence, a worsening process: *Stop the rot; Act now before **the rot sets in.*** **3** *Informal.* nonsense: *Don't talk rot.*

ro·ta·ry (ROH·tuh·ree) *adj.* wheellike, circular, or rotating: *a rotary dial phone, not a push-button; a rotary engine, press; the cogwheel emblem of the Rotary Club.* — *n.* -ries a rotary machine or setup.

ro·tate (ROH·tate) *v.* -tates, -tat·ed, -tat·ing **1** turn around a centre or axis, as a wheel or top. **2** (cause to) take turns: *The earth rotates on its axis; to rotate crops, work shifts, etc.*
— ro·ta·tor (-tay·tur) *n.;* ro·ta·to·ry (-tuh·tor·ee) *adj.*
— ro·ta·tion (roh·TAY·shun) *n.*

rote *n.* a repetitive or routine way of doing something: *Math tables are best learned **by rote*** (= memorized by repetition), *by rote learning.*

ro·tis·ser·ie (roh·TIS·uh·ree) *n.* **1** a restaurant or shop featuring roasted meat. **2** a grill with an electrically rotated spit.

ro·tor (ROH·tur) *n.* a rotating part, as of a motor or a generator or the system of blades of a helicopter.

rot·ten (ROT·un) *adj.* spoiled; corrupt; foul-smelling: *a rotten egg, smell; a scheme that is rotten to the core; rotten (Slang for* unpleasant) *weather; rotten ice, rotten snow (that is melting).* — rot·ten·ness *n.*

ro·tun·da (roh·TUN·duh) *n.* **1** a round, usually dome-covered building. **2** the room under the dome, usually a lobby or concourse: *We'll meet in the rotunda.*

rou·é (roo·AY) *n.* a dissolute or dissipated man; rake.

rouge (ROOZH) *n.* **1** a reddish powder used as a cosmetic. **2** a reddish powder used for polishing metal, glass, etc.
— *v.* roug·es, rouged, roug·ing colour with rouge.

rough (RUF) *adj.* not smooth, even, or level: *a rough ride on a rough road; We had a rough time in Russia; rough* (= not gentle) *language, manners; rough* (= stormy) *weather; rough* (= unskilled) *work; rough* (= harsh) *voices; a rough estimate, sketch, translation (that is not exact); a rough* (= general) *idea; a **rough diamond*** (= worthy but crude person).
— *adv.* in a rough manner.
— *n.* **1** a rough or violent person. **2** rough ground, esp. uncleared land along a golf fairway. **3** a rough condition: *to take the rough with the smooth; a diamond **in the rough*** (= not polished).
— *v.* **1** treat roughly; subject a person to roughness: *Al was roughed up by the bigger boys.* **2** do incompletely: *a roughed-in washroom.* **3** sketch roughly: *a roughed-in outline.*
— **rough it** live a rough life: *She's used to roughing it.*

rough·age (RUF·ij) *n.* coarse material, esp. fibrous foodstuff such as bran eaten for bulk.

rough-and-ready (ruf·un·RED·ee) *adj.* effective in a crude way.

rough-and-tumble (ruf·un·TUM·bul) *adj.* rough and disorderly: *our rough-and-tumble existence.*

rough-hew (ruf·HEW) *v.* -hews, *pt. & pp.* -hewed or -hewn, -hew·ing hew stone, timber, etc. without smoothing; hence, give it rough form.

rough·house *v.* -hous·es, -housed, -hous·ing *Informal.* take part in or subject to rough play or fun.

rough·ly (RUF·lee) *adv.* approximately: *It is roughly the same; costly roughly $10 000; We received roughly 500 inquiries; Roughly 25% of the calls were from the U.S.*
— rough·ness *n.*

rough·neck *n.* **1** a coarse or rowdy person. **2** a worker on a drilling rig.

rough·shod *adj.* of horses, with shoes having projecting nail heads.
— **ride roughshod over** treat a person, feelings, etc. roughly.

rou·lette (roo·LET) *n.* a gambling game using a ball rolled over a small revolving wheel (**roulette wheel**) with numbers on it: *People play "parking roulette" by parking illegally, not knowing when they might get a ticket.*

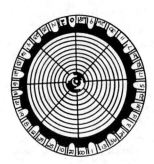

round *adj.* **1** shaped like a circle, ball, or cylinder: *Balls are round; round eyes; a round face, column, table; a round vowel such as "O" (pronounced with rounded lips).* **2** curved or filled out in form or figure: *a round figure; round shoulders; a round dozen; A round figure or number or sum such as 1 000 (instead of 998 or 1 003) is an approximate amount.* **3** vigorous: *She scolded him in round terms; a round scolding; to move at a round pace.*
— *n.* **1** something round, as a ball, a rung of a ladder, a cut of beef below the rump, etc.: *figures sculptured **in the round*** (= not in relief); *a **theatre-in-the-round** (with stage in centre and seats all around).* **2** a course or activity that ends where it begins: *a guard making his rounds; a rumour now going the rounds; the endless round of parties; the earth's yearly round.* **3** something forming a part of the action in a group or sequence, as a section of a boxing match, one shot from a weapon such as a firearm or the ammunition for it, etc.: *Three rounds were fired; a round of applause; He ordered a round of drinks for everyone present; "Three Blind*

Mice" is a round, or musical canon.

— *v.* 1 make or become round: *"O" is said with rounded lips; $2 995.75* **rounds off** *to $3 000; A year abroad* **rounded out** *her studies.* 2 go or turn round: *Slow down to round the corner.*

— **round up** drive or gather together: *A cowboy rounds up cattle; A party whip tries to round up a majority to vote for a bill.*

— *adv. & prep.* 1 in a circular path by a place or person, back to one's position, etc.: *I just saw her going round (the corner); We talked him round to vote for us.* 2 on all sides of a person or place: *We gathered round (the leader); to show visitors round (the displays).* 3 throughout a place or period; around: *In the "rain forests" it rains all round the year, all year round; We spread the news round (the town); He kept watch* **round the clock** (= 24 hours).

— **round·ly** *adv.* severely: *She scolded Lee roundly.*

round·a·bout (ROWN·duh·bowt) *adj.* going round or indirect: *a roundabout course, route, way.*

round·house *n.* 1 a round building for repairing locomotives, with a turntable in the centre. 2 *Informal.* a punch thrown with a wide swing: *John landed a roundhouse right.*

round robin *n.* 1 a petition with signatures in a circle so as not to show who signed first. 2 a letter sent round to a group for comments. 3 a tournament in which each player meets every other in turn; also, a series or round: *a round robin of tax deductions; a round-robin competition.*

round table *n.* a conference of a group of people meeting as equals or without consideration of precedence, as among King Arthur's "Knights of the Round Table."

round-the-clock *adj.* continuing day and night: *a round-the-clock bodyguard, vigil, watch.*

round trip *n.* a trip to and back from a place.
— **round-trip** *adj.*: *a round-trip fare, ticket.*

round·up *n.* 1 a rounding up or gathering of cattle, scattered members of a group, news items for a summary, etc. 2 the people and horses rounding up cattle on a ranch; also, the herd alone.

rouse (ROWZE) *v.* **rous·es, roused, rous·ing** 1 stir, as from sleep; arouse: *He was roused from sleep in the middle of the night.* 2 stir up game from cover or a person to a state of excitement or anger: *She roused the crowd to a fever of excitement; The singer was given a* **rousing** (= enthusiastic) *welcome.*
— **rous·er** *n.*: *a rabble rouser.*

rout (ROWT) *n.* 1 an utter defeat and resulting flight: *The enemy was put to rout; the rout of the enemy forces; Many got trampled in the rout that ensued.* 2 a disorderly crowd.
— *v.* 1 defeat utterly; hence, put to flight: *The enemy forces were completely routed.* 2 dig or scoop out, as pigs root out things from the ground.

route (ROOT, ROWT - rhyme: out) *n.* a regular course or road, as of one making deliveries: *to follow, map out, plan, take a route; a circuitous, devious, direct, roundabout, scenic route; a bus, mail, newspaper, overland, streetcar, trade, truck route.*

— *v.* **routes, rout·ed, rout·ing** send goods, traffic, etc. by a route or arrange the route for it: *We routed the memo to all key personnel.*

rou·tine (roo·TEEN) *n.* a regular series of actions or operations: *our office routine; a daily, dull, ordinary routine; a computer input routine; a comedy dance, routine* (= act or bit).
— *adj.* 1 habitual, not special: *a routine checkup, inquiry.* 2 ordinary or dull: *a routine job.*
— **rou·tine·ly** *adv.*

rou·tin·ize (roo·TEE·nize, ROO·tun·ize) *v.* make routine or regular: *to routinize a process.*

rove (ROHV) a *pt.* of REEVE.
— *v.* **roves, roved, rov·ing** go about or wander over a place, usually with a purpose: *a roving reporter; He has a* **roving eye** (= tendency to admire other women).
— **rov·er** *n.*

¹row (ROH) 1 *n.* a line of persons or things: *a row of seats; seats placed in rows; on death row (awaiting execution); on skid row (as a derelict); She lives on millionaires' row* (= street); *three years* **in a row** (= in succession). 2 *v.* move a boat using oars; hence, carry people or goods in a rowboat: *He went rowing for fun; rowed his family out to Ward's Island.* 3 *n.* a trip in a boat that is rowed.

²row (rhyme: "how") *n.* a noisy quarrel; squabble: *to kick up, make, raise a row; He had a row with the neighbours; a row about or over their noisy parties.*

row·boat (ROH·boat) *n.* a boat that is rowed, not a "sailboat."

row·dy ("ow" as in "how") *n. & adj.* **-di·er, -di·est** (one who is) quarrelsome or disorderly. — **row·dy·ish** *adj.*
— **row·dy·ism** *n.* — **row·di·ness** *n.*

row house (ROH-) *n.* one of a series of connected houses of identical design.

roy·al (ROY·ul) *adj.* 1 having to do with a sovereign, a kingdom, or its government: *the royal couple;* **Royal assent** *has to be given to a piece of legislation for it to become law; the Royal Winter Fair.* 2 regal; majestic or splendid. 3 *Informal.* [used as intensifier]: *a royal pain in the neck.* — **roy·al·ist** *n. & adj.* — **roy·al·ly** *adv.*

roy·al·ty (ROY·ul·tee) *n.* **-ties** 1 royal persons or their rank, quality, etc. 2 a share of receipts from a property or creative work paid to its owner, author, or composer: *Publishers pay royalties on books; Some books continue to bring in royalties long after publication, earning handsome royalties for the author.*

R.S.V.P. or **RSVP** [used with invitations] Please reply.
— *v. Informal.* reply: *Only a few RSVP'd "yes" to the invitation.*

rub *v.* **rubs, rubbed, rub·bing** (cause) to move while pressing against something: *Rub hands (together) to keep warm; An eraser rubs off writing; to rub a surface dry; a tire rubbing against the fender; a hobby of making* **rubbings** *of old coins (by rubbing with a coloured substance on paper placed over them); His shoulder rubbed hers in the crowded elevator; They* **rub elbows** *or* **shoulders** (= associate) *with royalty.*
— **rub down** 1 rub something to polish, clean, etc.: *a good rubbing down with soap and water.* 2 massage.

— **rub it in** irritate someone by repeatedly mentioning something unpleasant: *She's already miserable about losing – don't rub it in anymore.*
— **rub off on** or **onto** of a quality or activity, spread by close contact: *I hope some of her virtues rub off on you.*
— **rub out** erase; also, *Slang.* kill.
— **rub the wrong way** irritate someone.
— *n.* a rubbing; also, something that rubs or irritates: *Give it a good rub; Body rubs* (= massages) *are relaxing; But there's the rub* (= difficulty).

rub·ber (RUB·ur) *n.* 1 one that rubs, esp. an eraser. 2 an elastic substance obtained from the latex of certain trees; also, a similar synthetic product: *crude, foam, sponge rubber.* 3 the rubber tree. 4 **rubbers** *pl.* rubber overshoes.
— *adj.* made of rubber: *rubber balls, bullets, gloves, shoes, tires, trees.* — **rub·ber·y** *adj.*

rubber cheque *n. Informal.* a cheque that is returned because of insufficient funds; an "N.S.F." cheque.

rubber-chicken *adj.* having to do with speaking engagements: *He took to the rubber-chicken circuit after retirement; a rubber-chicken campaign dinner.*

rub·ber·neck *n. Informal.* a gawking sightseer.
— *v.* gawk: *a traffic jam due to drivers rubbernecking at a crash site.*

rubber stamp *n.* 1 a device for stamping dates, signatures, endorsements, etc. 2 *Informal.* one who routinely approves decisions made by others. 3 such approval.
— **rub·ber·stamp** (rub·ur·STAMP) *v.* put a rubber stamp on something: *Does the Senate merely rubberstamp what has been passed in Commons?*

rubbing alcohol *n.* an alcohol-containing liquid for external uses.

rub·bish (RUB·ish) *n.* something worthless or discarded; trash: *garbage and rubbish disposal; a heap, pile of rubbish; He talks rubbish* (= nonsense).

rub·ble (RUB·ul) *n.* a mass of broken stones, bricks, etc.; debris of destroyed buildings: *The town was reduced to rubble by the earthquake.*

rub·down *n.* a massage: *a rubdown parlour.*

rube (long "OO") *n. Slang* [derogatory] a person from the country who does not understand city ways.

Ru·bi·con (ROO·buh·con) *n.* something irrevocable: *Once you cross* or *pass the Rubicon* (= commit yourself to a course of action), *there's no turning back.*

ru·ble (ROO·bul) *n.* the basic money unit of the U.S.S.R.

ru·bric (ROO·bric) *n.* 1 a procedural guide or rule; formula: *A priest has to observe certain rubrics when saying Mass; "And they lived happily ever after" has become a rubric of story-tellers.* 2 the heading of a classification: *Algebra comes under the rubric of mathematics.*

ruck·us *n. Informal.* a row or uproar: *The parents raised a ruckus over their child's low marks.*

rud·der *n.* a hinged piece of wood or metal at the rear end of a boat or aircraft for steering it.

rud·dy (RUD·ee) *adj.* **rud·di·er, rud·di·est** reddish in complexion; healthy-looking.

rude *adj.* **rud·er, rud·est** 1 rough in manner; discourteous: *It's rude to contradict your elders; fired for being rude to customers.* 2 of primitive times; barbarous: *a rude implement; our rude forefathers.* 3 rough in effect: *a rude sketch; a rude awakening, shock.* — **rude·ly** *adv.;* **rude·ness** *n.*

ru·di·ment (ROO·duh·munt) *n.* usually **rudiments** *pl.* basics; elements: *the rudiments of algebra.*

ru·di·men·ta·ry (roo·duh·MEN·tuh·ree) *adj.* undeveloped or beginning: *the rudimentary wings of flightless birds; He has only a rudimentary knowledge of football.*

rue (ROO) *v.* **rues, rued, ru·ing** regret: *He began to rue the day he quit school.* — **rue·ful** *adj.;* **rue·ful·ly** *adv.*

ruff 1 *v.* to trump in a card game. 2 *n.* a trumping. 3 *n.* a stiff, crimped or pleated, frill-like collar once worn by men and women; hence, a similar band of fur or feathers, as around the neck of birds such as the grouse (**ruffed grouse**).

ruf·fi·an (RUF·ee·un) *n. & adj.* (one who is) rough or rowdy: *a gang of ruffians.* — **ruf·fi·an·ly** *adj.*

ruf·fle (RUF·ul) *v.* **ruf·fles, ruf·fled, ruf·fling** 1 make what is smooth and still uneven, rough, or disturbed: *to ruffle feathers, hair, calm waters; to ruffle one's composure, disposition, temper.* 2 shuffle or flip through pages, playing cards, etc.
— *n.* 1 a disturbance; ripple. 2 a strip of material with a frilly edge used as trimming on dresses. 3 the ruff on a bird's neck. 4 a low vibrating drumbeat: *The dignitary was announced with ruffles and flourishes.*

rug *n.* 1 a piece of fabric used as a floor covering: *a scatter rug; throw rug.* 2 a lap robe.
— **pull the rug (out) from under** suddenly withdraw support from a person, project, etc.
— **sweep something under the rug** conceal something one wishes to disregard or forget about.

rug·by (RUG·bee) *n.* a British football game distinguished by continuous play by players wearing little protective gear; also **rug·ger.**
— *adj.:* *rugby football; a rugby field, league, union.*

rug·ged (RUG·id) *adj.* irregular or rough in feature: *a rugged coast, shoreline; rugged ground, terrain; a rugged face with rugged features; the rugged conditions of pioneer life; her rugged individualism.*
— **rug·ged·ly** *adv.;* **rug·ged·ness** *n.*

ruin (ROO·in) *n.* state or cause of complete destruction or damage beyond repair: *the ruin of one's plans; Drinking was his ruin; a city lying in ruins; They sifted through the ancient ruins; a pile of ruins.*
— *v.* come or bring to ruin: *crops ruined by frost; The scandal ruined his career.*
— **ru·in·a·tion** (roo·uh·NAY·shun) *n.*
— **ru·in·ous** (ROO·uh·nus) *adj.;* **ru·in·ous·ly** *adv.*

rule *n.* 1 the way something normally happens or is usually done: *the rules of grammar; "An exception proves the rule"; Snow is the exception rather than the rule at this time of year; As a rule we don't work on Sundays; The golden rule says you should do to others as you would wish them to do to you.* 2 a regulation or a

set of regulations governing life or conduct: *"Drive right" is one of the* **rules of the road;** *Drivers have to observe many* **rules and regulations;** *Everyone has to obey the ground rules of a game; to adopt, apply, break, enforce, rescind, revoke, violate a rule; a firm, general, hard-and-fast, inflexible, strict rule; It's against the rules to drive with the parking lights on; the rule against smoking in elevators; the rules of parliamentary procedure; The monastic rule does not allow talking after hours; We* **bend** *or* **stretch the rules** *a bit in special circumstances; We have made it an invariable rule to pay cash; Everything is done according to rule; No one should be found in violation of the rules.* 3 government: *the rule of law; during the long rule* (= period of government) *of the Liberals; to establish, extend one's rule; British rule over India ended in 1947; benevolent, despotic, foreign, majority, mob, popular rule.* 4 a ruler: *a slide rule.*
— *v.* **rules, ruled, rul·ing** 1 lay down as a rule; make an official decision: *The judge was asked to rule on the matter; She ruled the evidence inadmissible; She ruled against him; ruled him (to be) out of order; We can now* **rule out** (= exclude) *other possibilities.* 2 govern by exerting authority: *Our heads should rule our hearts; He ruled (over) the country with an iron hand.* 3 mark lines on something: *ruled paper.*

rule of thumb *n.* a practical though not precise method for deciding or estimating.

rul·er (ROO·lur) *n.* 1 one who governs; sovereign. 2 a strip of wood, metal, etc. for marking straight lines and measuring short distances.

ruling (ROO·ling) *n.* an official decision, as by a court or umpire: *to give, hand down, make a ruling; a ruling about* or *on the evidence.*
— *adj.* governing or controlling: *the ruling classes, party; one of the ruling families; one's ruling ambition, passion.*

rum *n.* an alcoholic liquor made from molasses.

rum·ble (RUM·bul) *v.* **-bles, -bled, -bling** make a low, heavy rolling sound: *Thunder rumbled in the distance; The truck rumbled* (= moved with a rumbling sound) *down the cobbled street;* **rumblings** (= expressions of dissatisfaction) *about the heavy tax burden; rumblings of discontent.*
— *n.* 1 a rumbling sound; also, a complaining. 2 a street fight, as between teen gangs.

rumble strip *n.* a part of a pavement with slightly raised strips of asphalt for making a rumbling sound when tires go over it.

ru·mi·nant (ROO·muh·nunt) *n.* a cud-chewing animal such as the cow, sheep, camel, or giraffe.
— *adj.* 1 cud-chewing. 2 meditative.

ru·mi·nate (ROO·muh·nate) *v.* **-nates, -nat·ed, -nat·ing** chew the cud; hence, meditate or muse *about* or *on* something.— **ru·mi·na·tion** (-NAY·shun) *n.*

rum·mage (RUM·ij) *v.* **rum·mag·es, rum·maged, rum·mag·ing** 1 search thoroughly *through* a drawer, attic, files, old clothes, etc. by moving things about. 2 find out or turn up something by rummaging.
— *n.* 1 a rummaging. 2 miscellaneous articles, as offered at a **rummage sale,** usually to raise money for charity.

ru·mour or **ru·mor** (ROO·mur) *n.* general talk or a story that is not authentic or verifiable: *to circulate, confirm, deny, dispel, spread rumours; Rumours fly; as rumour has it; There's a rumour that he is broke.*
— *v.* tell or spread by rumour: *It is rumoured that he is broke; He is rumoured to have gone broke.*

rump *n.* 1 buttocks. 2 a corresponding cut of beef: *rump steak.* 3 a remnant, as of a body of people: *A rebel rump of 16 M.P.s broke ranks and voted against the bill.*

rum·ple *v.* **-ples, -pled, -pling** crush a sheet of paper, garment, etc. or tousle hair.
— *n.* a wrinkle or crease.

rum·pus *n. Informal.* a row or uproar: *to raise a rumpus.*

rumpus room *n.* a room set apart in a house for recreational activities, parties, etc.

run *v.* **runs, ran, run·ning** 1 (cause) to move at a pace faster than walking: *He runs for exercise; She is out running her horse.* 2 (cause) to go or move quickly or violently: *He left what he was doing and ran for his life; a ship run aground; She ran her eyes over the page; The car was hit by another running a red light; He was shot trying to run the blockade; He's running* (= contesting the election) *for mayor.* 3 (cause) to go on or keep going: *a train running between Edmonton and Calgary; We need a manager to run the business; An engine left running wastes gas.* 4 exist in a specified way: *"Streets" and "avenues" run at right angles to each other; Prices run high as demand increases; Inflation is running rampant;* [*Informal*] *People run scared as factories close; a talent that runs in his family; Our mail is running 10 to 1 in favour of our plan.* 5 drop stitches or ravel: *a fabric that will not run.* 6 publish: *a story they ran in yesterday's editions.* 7 chase: *to run a rabbit down.* 8 smuggle: *He was charged with running guns into Northern Ireland.*
— **run across** or **into someone** meet someone by chance.
— **run down** 1 decline in strength; deteriorate. 2 hunt down; knock down. 3 speak badly of someone.
— **run in** 1 *Informal.* arrest and put in jail. 2 break in a new car, shoes, a young horse, etc.
— **run out** come to the end of some resource: *Our money ran out; We ran out of* (= had no more) *money.*
— **run short** be lacking in a resource: *He runs short of money toward the end of each month.*
— **run to** extend or amount to the specified limit: *The book runs to 900 pages.*
— **run up** *Informal.* accumulate: *He ran up a huge telephone bill.*
— *n.* 1 a running, its duration, or result: *a 12-hour run; a print run of 10 000 copies; The children have the run* (= free use) *of the house when we are out of town; a dry run* (= trial); *a bombing run* (= a short straight flight for aiming bombs). 2 a trip or route: *a bus on the Montreal-Toronto run.* 3 a series or succession of things: *a run of bad luck; a run (of withdrawals) on a bank.* 4 a track or area: *a dog run; sheep run; ski run.* 5 a ravel, as in stockings.
— **a run for one's money** 1 satisfaction. 2 challenge.
— **in the long run** ultimately.
— **on the run** (while) running or fleeing: *a wanted man on the run, with the police looking for him.*

run·a·round (RUN·uh·round) *n. Informal.* a being referred from place to place in a frustrating manner: *They gave us the runaround at City Hall.*

run·a·way (RUN·uh·way) *n.* one that has run away: *The young runaway was back home for supper.*
— *adj.:* *a runaway* (= fugitive) *slave; a runaway team of horses; runaway inflation (that has got out of hand); a runaway* (= very successful) *bestseller, victory.*

run-down *adj.* not running; declining or deteriorating: *a building in a run-down condition; a run-down factory, neighbourhood, operation; to get run-down* (= exhausted).

run·down *n.* a summary: *a rundown on or of today's main events.*

rung *n.* a crosspiece forming a step of a ladder or one holding together two legs of a chair: *the bottom, lowest, highest, top rung of the ladder.*
— *v.* a *pp.* of RING.

run-in *n. Informal.* encounter or quarrel: *He has frequent run-ins with the police.*

run·ner (RUN·ur) *n.* **1** one who runs, as a racer, messenger, a football player carrying the ball, or a "base runner" in baseball. **2** a piece or strip placed along the length of something, as the blade of a skate. **3** a narrow carpet. **4** a horizontally growing stem that takes root at nodes, forming on it new plants, as the strawberry; also, such a plant.

runner-up *n.* **run·ners-up** a competitor who finishes in second place: *Sam was runner-up in the election, in the race; the runner-up to the champion.*

running *n.* **1** the act or operation of one that runs or manages: *the running of an engine, business, race.* **2** contest: *Some of the candidates who are* **in the running** *for mayor at the start will soon be* **out of the running.**
— *adj.* **1** having to do with movement: *a train's running time between Toronto and Montreal; She made a running leap over the stream; a* **running knot** *(that slides); A ship or aircraft travels with its* **running lights** *on; He came to work in* **running shoes** *(= sneakers).* **2** flowing: *a residential area with* **running water** *(supplied through pipes); a* **running sore** *(discharging pus).* **3** continuous or continuing: *The wire costs $2.50 per running foot; a running commentary, pattern, script.*
— *adv.* continuously: *He hasn't slept for three nights running.*

run·ny (RUN·ee) *adj.* **run·ni·er, run·ni·est 1** thin in consistency: *a runny jam.* **2** flowing, as with mucus: *a runny nose.*

run·off *n.* **1** a final contest between the leading candidates in an election: *a runoff election, vote.* **2** cashing in: *the runoff of Canada Savings Bond holdings.*

run-of-the-mill *adj.* of a product or specimen, commonplace; ordinary: *a run-of-the-mill actor, evening, movie, theme.*

runt *n.* a stunted or undersized plant, animal, or [used derogatorily] person: *the runt of the litter; That grandstanding little runt!*— **runt·y** *adj.*

run-through *n. Informal.* a rehearsal; also, a rundown.

rup·ture (RUP·chur) *n.* **1** a break or tear, as of the spleen, or a weakening of the muscular wall, as in a hernia. **2** a break in relations: *a rupture of diplomatic relations.*
— *v.* cause or suffer a rupture: *An infected appendix may rupture; ruptured relations, unity.*

ru·ral (ROOR·ul) *adj.* having to do with the country, as opposed to the city: *rural (mail) delivery; a rural municipality, scene; a* **rural route** *(= rural mail service).*
— **ru·ral·ism** *n.;* **ru·ral·ly** *adv.*

ruse (ROOZE, ROOSE) *n.* a trick used to mask something, as illness feigned to skip class: *a clever ruse.*

rush *v.* **1** move with great speed or haste: *The doctor rushed to see the patient; rushed to her aid; had her rushed to hospital; She rushed through the sale; rushed headlong into marriage; You're rushing me! the* **rushing** *process of selecting freshmen for fraternities and sororities.* **2** attack with speed and force: *The assailant rushed at his victim with a knife; Commandos had to rush the hijacked plane.*
— *n.* **1** a rushing or rushed activity: *She forgot her hat in the rush; the rush of modern life; the rush to buy lottery tickets; the Klondike gold rush; Drugs give a sudden rush* (= kick) *that makes the heart race and the body quiver.* **2** **rushes** *pl.* the first prints of a movie scene for review by the director: *rushes of the previous day's filming.* **3** a grasslike plant with round stems that grows in marshy places.

rush hour *n.* the time of the heaviest traffic during the day, esp. morning and evening.

Rus·sian (RUSH·un) *n.* a person of or from the Soviet Union; also its official language. Also *adj.*

Russian roulette *n.* the firing of a revolver at one's own head as an act of bravado without knowing if its only cartridge is in the firing chamber: *Hitchhiking is like* **playing Russian roulette with** *(= taking chances on) your life.*

rust *n.* **1** a reddish brown coating formed on exposed metal, esp. iron; also, the colour. **2** a fungus disease of plants, esp. cereals such as wheat, that leaves spores resembling metal rust.
— *v.* become covered with rust; hence, deteriorate.

rus·tic (RUS·tic) *adj.* **1** of the country: *rustic charm, simplicity.* **2** rough, crude, or unpolished: *rustic furniture, humour, manners.*
— *n.* one from the country, esp. an uncouth person.
— **rus·tic·i·ty** (rus·TIS·uh·tee) *n.*

rus·tle (RUS·ul) *n.* the sound of dry leaves, papers, silk, etc. rubbing lightly together.
— *v.* **-tles, -tled, -tling 1** make or move with a rustle. **2** act or move with energy or speed: *to* **rustle up** *(= gather or get ready) a list of items, players for a team, things for a meal.* **3** steal cattle, horses, etc.; **rust·ler** *n.*

rust·proof *adj.* that resists rust.
— *v.* make an automobile safe from rusting.

rust·y (RUS·tee) *adj.* **rust·i·er, -i·est 1** coated with rust or rust-coloured. **2** in need of polishing, as a skill lying unused: *My Greek is a bit rusty.*

rut *n.* **1** a track or furrow, as made by wheels on a road:

deep ruts in the road. **2** a settled, routine, or monotonous way or course of action: *He felt he was in a rut* (= routine job); *longed to get out of the rut and do some travelling.* **3** a period or state of sexual excitement or heat, as of the male deer.
— *v.* **ruts, rut·ted, rut·ting 1** make a rut. **2** be in heat.

ruth·less (ROOTH·lis) *adj.* merciless or cruel: *He is quite ruthless in his criticism.*

— ruth·less·ly *adv.;* ruth·less·ness *n.*

R value *n.* the thermal resistance value of insulation: *To diminish heat loss thorugh the roof of a house, attic insulation to an R value of R30 is recommended.*

rye *n.* **1** a cereal similar to wheat, used to make bread and liquors: *corned beef on rye (bread).* **2** a whisky distilled from rye.

S or **s** *n.* **S's** or **s's 1** the 19th letter of the English alphabet. **2** anything S-shaped.

s 1 [added to make plural form]: *boys, girls, the ABC's.* **2** [added to make the third person singular ending of verbs in the present indicative]: *loves, kills.* **3** [added with apostrophe to make the possessive case of nouns]: *boy's, children's.* **4** [added with apostrophe to make the contracted form of "is," "has," "us," and "does"]: *It's; He's gone; Let's go;* [Informal] *What's it mean?*

Sab·bath (SAB·uth) *n.* a day of rest and worship, as Sunday in Christian practice: *to break, keep the Sabbath.*

Sab·bat·i·cal (suh·BAT·uh·cul) **1** *adj.* having to do with the Sabbath: *Sabbatical observances.* **2 sabbatical** *n.* a year or a shorter period of leave for rest, study, etc. such as may be granted to teachers or professors; also **sabbatical leave.**

sab·o·tage (SAB·uh·tahzh) *n.* damage done to something, esp. property, as a vengeful or subversive act, as by enemy agents or striking workers: *an act of sabotage; adj.: a sabotage mission, plot, squad.* — *v.* **-tag·es, -taged, -tag·ing** commit sabotage on something: *attempts to sabotage a bill; to sabotage the talks.*

sab·o·teur (sab·uh·TUR) *n.* one who sabotages.

sa·bre or **sa·ber** (SAY·bur) *n.* a heavy cavalry sword for cutting and thrusting, usually having a curved blade; also, a fencing foil.

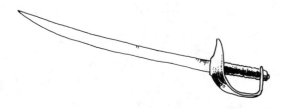

sabre rattling or **saber rattling** *n.* a menacing show of strength, esp. military.

sac *n.* a baglike part of an animal or plant usually containing liquid, as the bladder in humans.

sac·cha·rin (SAC·uh·rin) *n.* a very sweet coal-tar product used as a sugar substitute.

sac·cha·rine (SAC·uh·rin) *adj.* sugary; also, affectedly sweet: *saccharine poetry; a saccharine smile, voice.*

sa·chem (SAY·chum) *n.* the chief of some native Indian tribes: *party sachems of local politics.*

sa·chet (sa·SHAY) *n.* a small sealed bag containing perfume, shampoo, powder, etc. for one-time use: *a sachet of dried yeast, hand lotion, soup mix.*

sack *n.* **1** a large bag of coarse cloth: *Sam got the sack* (Informal for dismissal) *for drinking on the job; a late worker who hits the sack* (Informal for goes to bed) *about midnight.* **2** a dry, white wine popular in the 16th and 17th centuries. — *v. Informal.* **1** fire or dismiss. **2** plunder or pillage: *the sacking of Rome by the barbarians.*

sack·cloth *n.* a coarse cloth for making sacks. — **sackcloth and ashes** the traditional garb of a humble penitent or mourner.

sack·ful *n.* what a sack will hold.

sac·ra·ment (SAC·ruh·munt) *n.* a Christian rite or ceremony considered especially sacred. — **sac·ra·men·tal** (-MEN·tul) *adj.*

sa·cred (SAY·crud) *adj.* **1** set apart or dedicated to someone holy, esp. to the worship of a divine being; holy; inviolable: *a mountain sacred to the Muses; the sacred altar.* **2** worthy of reverence or solemn attention: *the sacred writings of the Bible, Koran, and other holy books; a sacred duty.*

sacred cow *n.* something treated with unquestioning devotion.

sac·ri·fice (SAC·ruh·fice) *n.* an offering or giving up of something valuable for a higher purpose; also, the thing so offered: *a lamb killed as a sacrifice to God; The Aztecs used to offer prisoners as human sacrifices; the sacrifice of one's time and energies in the cause of education; a house sold at a sacrifice* (=loss); *A baseball batter's sacrifice fly* or *sacrifice hit (advances a base runner while the batter is put out).* — *v.* **-fic·es, -ficed, -fic·ing** make a sacrifice; give up something valuable for the sake of something else: *He sacrificed his health in the pursuit of wealth; John (the batter) sacrificed Jack (the base runner) to second base* (=got Jack to second while himself being put out). — **sac·ri·fi·cial** (sac·ruh·FISH·ul) *adj.: a sacrificial* lamb.

sac·ri·lege (SAC·ruh·lij) *n.* a violation of something sacred; gross irreverence.
— **sac·ri·le·gious** (sac·ruh·LIJ·us) *adj.*

sac·ro·sanct (SAC·roh·sanct) *adj.* most sacred; consecrated.

sad *adj.* **sad·der, sad·dest** full of or causing sorrow; not happy. — **sad·ly** *adv.;* **sad·ness** *n.*

sad·den (SAD·un) *v.* make or become sad.

sad·dle (SAD·ul) *n.* **1** the usually padded and curved seat for a rider of a horse, bicycle, etc. **2** something shaped like a saddle, as a cut of lamb, mutton, or venison consisting of the loins and the connecting back portion.
— **in the saddle** in a controlling position.
— *v.* **sad·dles, sad·dled, sad·dling** put a saddle upon an animal or person; hence, burden: *Sam is saddled with a heavy mortgage.* — **sad·dler** *n.*

sad·ism (SAD·iz·um, SAY·diz·um) *n.* the getting of pleasure, esp. sexual, from inflicting pain on another.
— **sad·ist** *n.* — **sad·is·tic** (suh·DIS·tic) *adj.*

sad sack *n. Informal.* a typically inept or stupid person.

sa·fa·ri (suh·FAR·ee) *n.* -**ris 1** a hunting expedition, esp. in Africa. **2** the people and animals in it. **3** a vacation trip to observe animal life: *to go on an East African safari.*

safe *adj.* **saf·er, saf·est** free from danger, harm, risk, etc.: *A locked door is safe; a dark but safe street; The police officer made her feel safe; safe from enemies; Children should be safe in school; quite safe and sound* (= without harm or injury); *a safe* (= not risky) *guess; a safe* (= reliable) *driver, guide; Let's play it safe* (*Informal* for Let's take no risks).
— *n.* a place for keeping something safe, esp. a strongbox or steel container: *to crack a safe; an office safe; a safe-deposit box.* — **safe·ly** *adv.*

safe-conduct (SAFE·con·duct) *n.* permission to pass safely through hostile territory: *He was given safe-conduct through the camp; to issue a safe-conduct (pass).*

safe·guard *n.* protection: *a safeguard against fires; built-in safeguards in the security system.*

safe·keep·ing (SAFE·kee·ping) *n.* a keeping or being kept safe; custody.

safe·ty (SAFE·tee) *n.* -**ties 1** the state of being safe; security: *to assure, not jeopardize her safety; She found safety in flight, in numbers; to live in safety without fear of being attacked; a margin of safety.* **2** a safety device: *to release the safety.* **3** in football, a play worth two points for the defensive team when the ball carrier is downed in his own end zone or steps out of his end zone; also, a defensive back close to his team's goal line.
— *adj.: a safety factor, fuse, helmet, measure, patrol, precaution, rule; safety equipment; a safety-deposit box in a bank vault for storing valuables; shatterproof safety glass; A safety match will strike fire only on a prepared surface; A safety net protects circus performers in case of a fall; A clasplike safety pin has its point held inside a guard; A safety razor has its blade between guards for*

protection; *the safety valve of a steam boiler for release of excessive pressure.*

sag *v.* **sags, sagged, sag·ging** sink or hang down in the middle under weight or pressure, as a stretched rope, horizontal beam, or plank; hence, fall to a lower level: *The roof is sagging; a sagging dollar, economy, morale; sagging prices, spirits, trade; shoulders sagging under the weight of responsibility; Business, confidence, fortunes, prices sag.*
— *n.* a sagging place or condition: *the recent sag in consumer demand.*

sa·ga (SAH·guh) *n.* a long story of heroic deeds, like a medieval Norse historical narrative.

sa·ga·cious (suh·GAY·shus) *adj.* of keen mind and sound practical judgment: *a sagacious decision; Guide dogs are sagacious animals.*
— **sa·gac·i·ty** (-GAS·uh·tee) *n.*

sage *n.* **1** a small shrubby mint whose leaves and stems are used in seasonings; also **sagebrush. 2** an elderly man who is wise and discerning: *One of the seven sages of ancient Greece said "Know thyself."*
— *adj.* wise and discerning: *sage advice.* — **sage·ly** *adv.*

sag·gy (SAG·ee) *adj.* **sag·gi·er, sag·gi·est** having a tendency to sag; sagging: *saggy pants.*

said *pt. & pp.* of SAY.
— *adj.* above-mentioned.

sail *n.* **1** a sheet of cloth spread to catch the wind for power to move a boat. **2** sails collectively; also, a ship. **3** voyage. **4** the arm of a windmill.
— **set sail** begin a voyage.
— *v.* **1** move upon a body of water or be moved forward using sails; also, begin a voyage; set sail: *She sails from Halifax for Europe tomorrow; Naomi James sailed solo around the world; It was smooth or plain sailing* (= trouble-free) *all the way.* **2** manage a sailing vessel. **3** glide smoothly like a ship with outspread sails or under sail: *He sailed through the exams.*
— **sail into** *Informal.* attack or criticize.

sail·board *n.* a surfboard equipped with a sail and rudder. — **sail·board·ing** *n.*

sail·or (SAY·lur) *n.* one who sails, esp. an enlisted person in a navy.

saint *n.* a holy person, esp. one officially recognized by a Christian church. — **saint·hood** *n.*
— **saint·ly** *adj.* -**li·er**, -**li·est.** — **saint·li·ness** *n.*

saith (SETH) [old form] says.

sake *n.* interest or consideration: *For our children's sake, please stop arguing; For the sake of our children, please stop arguing; Please stop arguing, for goodness sake;* [for added force] *For Heaven's sake, please stop arguing; I'm saying this for both our sakes, for your sake and mine; Let's not argue for arguing's sake* (= because we like to argue); *Let's suppose, for argument's sake* (= as a starting point), *that life does exist on Mars.*

sa·laam (suh·LAHM) *n.* an Eastern or Muslim greeting that means "peace" in Arabic.

sal·a·ble (SAY·luh·bul) *adj.* that can be sold; also **sale·a·ble.**

sal·ad (SAL·ud) *n.* a cold dish of green vegetables and fruit: *a fruit salad (of mixed fruits);* **potato salad** (= cooked potato with salad dressing); *a* **tossed salad** *(of greens in an oil dressing); adj.: a salad bowl; a restaurant's self-service* **salad bar;** *the* **salad days** (= naive period) *of one's youth; a* **salad dressing** (= sauce used on a salad).

sal·a·ried (SAL·uh·reed) *adj.* having a salary: *a salaried officer; the salaried staff; a salaried job (that pays a salary, not wages).*

sal·a·ry (SAL·uh·ree) *n.* **-ries** remuneration calculated on a monthly or annual basis and paid regularly, usually for nonmanual services, in contrast to wages: *to earn, negotiate, pay a salary; to raise his salary.*

sale *n.* **1** a selling: *These cars are* **for sale;** *a cash sale (to be paid for at time of sale); a clearance, closeout, discount, fire, garage, going-out-of-business, liquidation, rummage, storewide, warehouse sale; a company with annual* **sales** (= gross receipts) *of $20 million; She works in sales, not promotion (department).* **2** a selling at reduced prices: *spring sale of winter boots; We have a sale on boots; Boots are* **on sale.**
— **sales 1** *adj.: a sales agent, check, director, executive, force, manager, organization, promotion, register, representative, resistance, slip, tax.* **2** *combining form: salesclerk, salesgirl, saleslady, salespeople, salesroom.*
— **saleable** same as SALABLE.

sales·man (SAILZ·mun) *n.* **-men** a man who sells goods or services: *a door-to-door salesman; travelling salesman.* — **sales·girl** *n.* — **sales·la·dy** *n.* **-dies.**
— **sales·wom·an** *n.* **wom·en.** — **sales·man·ship** *n.*

sales·per·son (SAILZ·pur·sun) *n.* a salesman or saleswoman; also **sales representative** or **sales rep** [short form].

sales talk *n.* talk aimed at selling or persuading to buy.

sa·lient (SAIL·yunt) *adj.* prominent: *the salient features of this dictionary; its salient characteristics, points.*
— *n.* an angle, part of a fortification, etc. that points outward; projection: *The Battle of the Bulge is named after a salient; the Rafah salient south of the Gaza Strip.*
— **sa·lience** *n.*

sa·line (SAY·leen, -line) *adj.* of salt; salty: *a saline solution.* — **sa·lin·i·ty** (suh·LIN·uh·tee) *n.*

sa·li·va (suh·LYE·vuh) *n.* the digestive juice produced in the mouth.

sal·low (SAL·oh) *adj.* yellowish or sickly in complexion.

sal·ly (SAL·ee) *v.* **sal·lies, sal·lied, sal·ly·ing** go *forth* or set *out* suddenly (as if) in attack.
— *n.* **1** a sallying forth or sortie: *to make a sally into enemy lines.* **2** a witty remark. **3** an excursion or jaunt.

Sally Ann *n. Informal.* the Salvation Army, a Christian evangelistic and social service organization.

salm·on (SAM·un) *n.* a large food fish that swims back from the ocean to spawn in freshwater streams.

sa·lon (suh·LON) *n.* **1** a reception hall or fashionable gathering place: *a hotel salon.* **2** a business place dealing in goods and services related to women and

fashion: *a beauty salon; couture salon; dress salon; hair-styling salon; net-working salon; shoe salon.*

sa·loon (suh·LOON) *n.* **1** a tavern: *swinging saloon doors.* **2** a large room for a specified social purpose: *a dining saloon.*

sa·loon·keep·er (suh·LOON·kee·pur) *n.* a tavern operator.

salt (SAWLT) *n.* **1** a white, crystalline substance obtained from sea water and mines and widely used as a seasoning and preservative: *common salt.* **2** that which adds piquancy or liveliness to anything. **3** *Informal.* a sailor: *an old salt.* **4 salts** *pl.* a laxative such as "Epsom salts" or a preparation such as "smelling salts" inhaled to relieve faintness, headache, etc.
— **rub salt into** or **pour salt on the wound** make one's pain even worse.
— **salt of the earth** the finest of people.
— **take with a grain** or **pinch of salt** accept with some scepticism.
— **worth one's salt** worth one's pay.
— *v.* season or preserve with salt: *to salt fish, meat; adj.: salt beef, pork.*
— **salt away** lay away safely; put aside or save.

salt chuck *n. Cdn.* in B.C., the ocean and bodies of water connected with it.

salt·wa·ter *adj.* of or living in salty water: *a saltwater lake, fish.*

salt·y *adj.* **salt·i·er, -i·est 1** that tastes of salt: *salty soup.* **2** racy: *salty humour, language.* — **salt·i·ness** *n.*

sa·lu·bri·ous (suh·LOO·bree·us) *adj.* healthful or invigorating: *a salubrious climate; the salubrious mountain air.*

sal·u·tar·y (SAL·yoo·tair·ee) *adj.* healthful or beneficial even if unpleasant: *a salutary exercise, experience, influence, medicine, warning; salutary advice, penance, suffering.*

sal·u·ta·tion (sal·yoo·TAY·shun) *n.* an act or expression of greeting, such as a bow, raising the hat, or "Dear Sir or Madam" at the beginning of a letter.

sa·lute (suh·LOOT) *v.* **-lutes, -lut·ed, -lut·ing** greet, esp. to show honour or respect using a standard gesture such as a bow or a formal act such as raising the right hand or firing a cannon.
— *n.* a saluting act or gesture; greeting: *a 21-gun salute.*

sal·vage (SAL·vij) *n.* **1** the saving of useful property from loss or waste, as ship or cargo from a shipwreck, scrap metal, etc. **2** property salvaged; also, compensation for salvage work.
— *v.* **-vag·es, -vaged, -vag·ing** save property from fire, flood, shipwreck, etc.: *salvaged wastepaper; He escaped with his dignity barely salvaged.*
— **sal·vage·a·ble** (-juh·bul) *adj.*

sal·va·tion (sal·VAY·shun) *n.* **1** the saving of a person from damnation; redemption: *Missionaries preach salvation; sinners seeking salvation from hell; He found salvation in faith and good works.* **2** any saving from a great loss or calamity; also, that which effects it: *The timely arrival of the police proved his salvation (from assault); They found salvation in religion; Her only salvation was in fleeing the fire; Your salvation lies in* *laying off drugs.*

salve (SAV) *v.* salves, salved, salv·ing soothe: *a balm to salve the wound; words to salve her conscience; to salve his ego.*
— *n.* a balm, ointment, or anything that soothes.

sal·vo (SAL·voh) *n.* -vos or -voes simultaneous discharge of guns as a salute or in attack; volley: *to fire a salvo; a salvo of bombs, cheers, insults.*

same *adj. & pron.* (being) the one referred to or implied: *He sleeps in the same bed every day; This is the same lunch as* or *that you ate yesterday* (= same in kind, appearance, amount, etc.); *the same as yesterday's; They are both the same* (= alike); *They are* **one and the same** (= exactly similar); *It's all the same to me;* **All the same** (= In spite of it), *I'm not eating today; Fill in the form and forward same (Nonstandard* for it) *to us.*
— *adv.* in the same manner: *I feel the same (as you).*
— same·ness *n.*

sam·iz·dat (sah·miz·DAHT) *n.* in the U.S.S.R., secret publication and distribution of officially banned writings: *first distributed in samizdat, later published in the West; adj.: samizdat publications, publishing, work.*

sam·ple (SAM·pul) *n.* a part or specimen that shows the quality of a whole: *free samples of a new toothpaste; a random sample of the population; a fair sample* (= instance or specimen) *of his wit.*
— *v.* -ples, -pled, -pling take as a sample; test a part of something.

sam·pler (SAM·plur) *n.* 1 one who samples; also, a collection of samples. 2 a piece of cloth embroidered in various designs for practice or display.

san·a·to·ri·um (san·uh·TOR·ee·um) *n.* -ri·ums or -ri·a (-ree·uh) 1 an establishment for treating a particular group of patients: *a TB sanatorium; a sanatorium for the mentally ill.* 2 a convalescent home.

sanc·ti·fy (SANK·tuh·fye) *v.* -fies, -fied, -fy·ing make holy; consecrate: *a day sanctified by God as the Sabbath; a practice sanctified by custom.*
— sanc·ti·fi·ca·tion (-fuh·CAY·shun) *n.*

sanc·tion (SANK·shun) *n.* 1 official or authoritative approval: *a bill that has received the sanction of Parliament; to give sanction to a bill.* 2 penalty provided by a law for its enforcement: *to apply economic sanctions such as trade boycotts and embargoes, instead of military sanctions, to force a nation to obey international law; trade sanctions imposed by Canada against a hostile nation; to lift sanctions.*
— *v.* approve of officially: *Many churches don't sanction divorce; customs sanctioned by tradition.*

sanc·ti·ty (SANK·tuh·tee) *n.* sacredness: *the sanctity of marriage; the* **sanctities** (= duties, obligations, etc. considered as sacred) *of family life.*

sanc·tu·ar·y (SANK·choo·air·ee) *n.* 1 a consecrated place such as a place of worship, esp. the part of a church containing the altar. 2 a place of refuge or protection: *a bird, wild life sanctuary; to find, offer, provide, seek sanctuary; Hijackers are given sanctuary in certain countries; a sanctuary for political refugees.*

sanc·tum (SANK·tum) *n.* 1 a sacred place: *the inner sanctum of one's conscience.* 2 *Informal.* one's private place of seclusion; den.

sand *n.* loose grains of worn-down rock, finer than gravel but coarser than silt, found in river beds, on seashores, etc.: *the sands* (= sandy tract) *of the desert; to bury* or *hide one's head in the sand* (= to ignore realities).
— *v.* 1 put sand over or into something: *to sand an icy road.* 2 smooth a surface, as of wood, with "sandpaper" or with a "sanding machine."— sand·er *n.*

san·dal (SAN·dul) *n.* a slipper or low shoe with straps joining the sole to the foot: *a pair of sandals; beach sandals.*

sand·bag *n.* a sand-filled bag used for ballast, protection, etc.
— *v.* -bags, -bagged, -bag·ging 1 put sandbags in or around a place for protection. 2 hit someone, as with a sandbag: *The Opposition tried to sandbag the Government into adopting its policies.*

sand·lot *adj.* of sports and games, informal or unorganized: *sandlot baseball.*

sand·wich *n.* two slices of bread with a layer of meat, cheese, jam or other filling between them: *a cheese, club, corned-beef, grilled-cheese, ham, tomato-and-lettuce, tuna sandwich.*
— *v.* to place or crowd in between two other persons or things: *to sandwich a doctor's appointment between meetings.*

sand·y (SAN·dee) *adj.* sand·i·er, -i·est 1 containing or covered with sand. 2 yellowish-red: *sandy hair.*

sane *adj.* san·er, san·est mentally sound; also, sensible.
— sane·ly *adv.*

sang *pt.* of SING.

san·gui·nar·y (SANG·gwuh·nair·ee) *adj.* bloody: *a sanguinary war; a cruel and sanguinary* (= bloodthirsty) *tyrant.*

san·guine (SANG·gwin) *adj.* 1 disposed to be cheerful and confident: *a sanguine temperament; his sanguine hopes.* 2 ruddy: *a sanguine complexion.*

san·i·tar·i·an (san·uh·TAIR·ee·un) *adj.* a sanitation specialist.

san·i·tar·i·um (san·uh·TAIR·ee·um) *n.* -i·ums or -i·a a health resort; also, a sanatorium.

san·i·tar·y (SAN·uh·tair·ee) *adj.* 1 having to do with cleanliness: *the sanitary environment of a hospital; sanitary measures to combat disease; sanitary gloves; the sanitary* (= hospital-clean) *appearance of Dr. Smith's residence; a* **sanitary pad** or **napkin** *worn to absorb the menstrual flow.* 2 having to do with waste disposal: *a sanitary engineer; sanitary fittings; a sanitary landfill site.*

san·i·ta·tion (san·uh·TAY·shun) *n.* aspects of public health that include sewage disposal, water treatment, pollution control, and food processing.

san·i·tize (SAN·uh·tize) *v.* -tiz·es, -tized, -tiz·ing 1 make sanitary. 2 remove objectionable features from a book or other publication.

san·i·ty (SAN·uh·tee) *n*. **1** sound mental health: *to keep, lose, maintain, preserve, retain one's sanity*. **2** soundness of judgment.

sank *pt*. of SINK.

sans (SANZ) *prep*. without: *hockey sans violence*.

San·ta Claus (SAN·tuh·clawz) *n*. the red-suited, white-bearded, jolly old man associated with gift-giving to children at Christmas.

sap *n*. **1** the vital juice that circulates through a plant carrying food and water: *The sap of the sugar maple begins to run in spring when the days are warm and nights cold*. **2** health and vigour. **3** *Slang*. fool. **4** a trench dug for approaching or undermining an enemy's position.
— *v*. **saps, sapped, sap·ping** dig under or undermine; hence, weaken or wear away: *strength sapped by heat*.
— **sap·less** *adj*. lacking in health and vigour.

sap·ling *n*. **1** a young tree. **2** a young person.

sap·phire (SAF·ire) *n*. a bright-blue gem or its colour.
— *adj*.: *Our swimming pool is a sapphire blue; a sapphire necklace, ring*.

sap·py (SAP·ee) *adj*. **sap·pi·er, sap·pi·est 1** full of sap. **2** *Slang*. foolish. — **sap·pi·ness** *n*.

sar·casm (SAR·caz·um) *n*. an ironical and cutting type of humour or remark, often used to ridicule: *biting, keen, piercing, mild sarcasm; His tongue was dripping with sarcasm*. — **sar·cas·tic** (sar·CAS·tic) *adj*.
— **sar·cas·ti·cal·ly** *adv*.

sar·dine (sar·DEEN) *n*. a small herring, usually canned for food or dried and powdered for fish meal: *a bus packed like a can of sardines* (= a very crowded bus).

sar·don·ic (sar·DON·ic) *adj*. scornful or sarcastic: *a sardonic expression; sardonic humour, laughter*.

sarge *n*. *Informal*. sergeant.

sar·to·ri·al (sar·TOR·ee·ul) *adj*. of tailoring, esp. of men's clothes: *sartorial elegance; a sartorial masterpiece; in sartorial splendour*.

sash *n*. **1** a broad strip of cloth worn either as a belt or over one shoulder as a dress accessory or sign of rank. **2** the frame holding the glass in a door or window; also, the sliding frame of a double-hung window (**sash window**).

sa·shay (sa·SHAY) *n*. *Informal*. walk or move in a gliding manner, esp. sideways: *to sashay across a stage*.

Sas·quatch (SAS·kwatch) *n*. *Cdn*. a hairy monster of western Canadian folklore; Bigfoot.

sass·y (SAS·ee) *adj*. **sass·i·er, -i·est** *Informal*. **1** saucy. **2** fresh; lively; stylish.
— *v*. **sass·ies, sass·ied, sass·y·ing** make sassy or stylish: *a little car sassied up with a lot of accessories*.

sat *pt. & pp*. of SIT.

Sa·tan (SAY·tun) *n*. the Devil.

sa·tan·ic (suh·TAN·ic, say-) *adj*. **1** fiendish or evil like Satan: *satanic pride*. **2** referring to Satan worship: *a satanic cult*.

sate *v*. **sates, sat·ed, sat·ing** satisfy a desire or appetite so fully that it dies: *sated with food and drink*.

sat·el·lite (SAT·ul·ite) *n*. **1** a person or thing following another that is larger or more important, as a small planet that revolves around a larger one: *to put an artificial satellite in orbit; to launch a communications satellite; a spy satellite; weather satellites*. **2** one of many nations controlled by a great power: *the former Soviet satellites of Eastern Europe*.
— *adj*.: *the satellite campuses of a university; a satellite city; Kanata is a satellite town of Ottawa*.

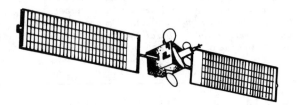

sa·ti·ate (SAY·shee·ate) *v*. **-ates, -at·ed, -at·ing** satisfy a desire or appetite to excess; sate: *satiated with food and drink*. — **sa·ti·a·tion** (-AY·shun) *n*.
— **sa·ti·e·ty** (suh·TYE·uh·tee) *n*.: *filled to satiety with food and drink*.

sat·in (SAT·un) *n*. a smooth and glossy silk or other fabric woven with a lustrous face. — **sat·in·y** *adj*.

sat·ire (SAT·ire) *n*. **1** the use of irony and sarcasm to expose folly and vice, as in cartoons, comedies of manners, and the literature of such writers as Swift and Pope. **2** such a work or works collectively.
— **sat·i·rist** (SAT·uh·rist) *n*.
— **sa·tir·i·cal** (sa·TEER·uh·cal) *adj*.

sat·i·rize (SAT·uh·rize) *v*. **-riz·es, -rized, -riz·ing** attack using satire.

sat·is·fac·tion (sat·is·FAC·shun) *n*. a satisfying or something that satisfies, esp. the discharge of a debt or claim or making up for harm done: *to afford, express, feel, find, give satisfaction; to take satisfaction in doing a good job; deep, quiet satisfaction about a job well done; The work was done to our complete satisfaction; The customer demanded, sought satisfaction* (= compensation); *He got, had, received satisfaction for the loss suffered; "Satisfaction guaranteed or your money back"; Teaching has many satisfactions, job satisfaction being one*.

sat·is·fac·to·ry (sat·is·FAC·tuh·ree) *adj*. satisfying; adequate: *a satisfactory though not outstanding performance*. — **sat·is·fac·to·ri·ly** *adv*.

sat·is·fy (SAT·is·fye) *v*. **-fies, -fied, -fy·ing 1** fulfil: *to satisfy a condition, demand, desire, hope, need; to satisfy her curiosity; to satisfy* (= pay) *a claim for damages; to satisfy the requirements for a Ph.D*. **2** make happy or contented: *a spoiled child who is hard to satisfy* (= please); *a satisfying experience; We're completely, perfectly, thoroughly satisfied with what we bought*. **3** convince: *She satisfied herself that the insult was not intended*.

sat·u·rate (SACH·uh·rate) *v*. **-rates, -rat·ed, -rat·ing**

(cause) to be filled, charged, or soaked to the maximum: *a saturated solution of a substance in water; Air saturated with moisture will condense if cooled; A saturated market (with plentiful supplies) is a buyer's market;* **Saturated fats** *contain the maximum number of hydrogen atoms in their molecules.*
— **sat·u·ra·tion** (-RAY·shun) *n. & adj.* maximum in regard to capacity or limit: *employment saturation in a population or occupation; market saturation of a product; The computer market has reached the saturation point; an evangelist with saturation coverage on Canadian TV; saturation advertising, bombing, level, limit, marketing, strategy.*

Sat·ur·day (SAT·ur·dee, -day) *n.* the last day of the week, following Friday.

Saturday night special *n.* a cheap, dangerous, easily concealed handgun.

sauce *n.* **1** a liquid or soft preparation served with food or as a topping with dessert to add flavour: *barbecue, soy, spaghetti, steak, tomato sauce; Cranberry sauce is stewed fruit.* **2** *Informal.* impudence.
— *v.* **sauc·es, sauced, sauc·ing 1** season; add flavour to a food. **2** *Informal.* be saucy to someone.

sauc·y (SAW·see) *adj.* **sauc·i·er, -i·est** flippant and disrespectful in behaviour.
— **sauc·i·ly** *adv.;* **sauc·i·ness** *n.*

sault (SOO) *n. Cdn.* a rapids or waterfall, as in place names such as Sault Ste. Marie, Ont., and Long Sault, Ont.

sau·na (SAW·nuh) *n.* a steam bath in which water is thrown on hot stones to produce steam; also, the room housing the bath.

saun·ter (SAUN·tur) *n. & v.* walk in a leisurely manner; stroll.

sau·sage (SAW·sij) *n.* chopped and seasoned meat stuffed in a tubular casing; also, one such casing or link: *pancakes and sausages.*

sau·té (soh·TAY) *v.* **-tés, -téed** or **-téd, -té·ing** fry quickly in a little fat: *tomatoes with sautéed zucchini.*
— *n.* sautéed food.

sav·age (SAV·ij) *n.* one who is fierce, brutal, or rough-mannered: *drunken savages; the noble savage.*
— *adj.* utterly uncivilized or brutal: *a savage attack, dog; a savage* (=fierce) *temper.*
— *v.* **-ag·es, -aged, -ag·ing** attack violently or brutally: *a child savaged by an attack dog; a country savaged by fighting; The Government M.P.s ridiculed and savaged the Opposition for its turnabout.*
— **sav·age·ly** *adv.;* **sav·age·ness** *n.*
— **sav·age·ry** (-ij·ree) *n.*

sa·van·na or **sa·van·nah** (suh·VAN·uh) *n.* tropical grassland lying between forests and deserts, as of sub-Saharan Africa, the veldts of South Africa, and the pampas of South America.

sa·vant (suh·VAHNT, SAV·unt) *n.* one who is learned in a particular area: *a literary savant.*

save *v.* **saves, saved, sav·ing** make or keep free from danger, risk, loss, etc.: *The seat belt saved the driver's life; Take a plane to save time; Flying will save us time;*

Read in good light to save your eyes; He's saving money (=putting money aside) *for a vacation; tips to help you save (money); She's trying to save* (=economize) *on travel expenses.*
— *n.* an act, as of a goalkeeper, that prevents an opponent from scoring: *He made a spectacular save.*
— *conj. & prep. Formal.* except(ing): *all save one; I agree with you on everything save that life exists on Mars.* — **sav·er** *n.*

savings *n. pl.* money saved: *to deposit, dip into, withdraw one's savings.*
— *adj.:* a **savings account** in a **savings bank**; a high-interest, fixed-term **savings certificate**; a **savings and loan association** owned and operated by shareholders.

sav·iour or **sav·ior** (SAVE·yur) *n.* one who saves; in Christian religions, Jesus Christ, **the Saviour** or **Savior.**

sa·voir-faire (sav·wahr·FAIR) *n.* tact or ability to get along well in social situations.

sa·vour or **sa·vor** (SAY·vur) *n.* the distinctive taste, smell, or other quality of something: *the savour of soy sauce.*
— *v.* enjoy the savour of something: *She savoured the wine slowly; His style savours* (=smacks) *of arrogance.*

sa·vour·y or **sa·vor·y** (SAY·vuh·ree) *adj.* **-vour·i·er** or **-vor·i·er, -vour·i·est** or **-vor·i·est** pleasing to the smell and taste: *a savoury dish.*

sav·vy (SAV·ee) *n.* shrewd understanding of a subject: *an aide with political savvy; a taxi driver with plenty of practical savvy; a woman with a lot of fashion savvy; marketing savvy.*
— *adj.* shrewd: *He is more savvy than smart; a savvy consumer, merchant.*
— *v.* **sav·vies, sav·vied, sav·vy·ing** know or grasp: *Do you savvy this, young man?*

saw *pt.* of SEE.
— **saw** *n.* **1** a wise saying; maxim. **2** a tool that has a metal blade with teeth on a straight or circular edge for cutting hard substances.
— *v.* **saws,** *pt.* **sawed,** *pp.* **sawed** or **sawn, saw·ing** cut (as if) with a saw with a back-and-forth motion: *a sawed-off shotgun; He sawed the air trying to make gestures.*

saw·bones *n. Slang.* a surgeon.

saw·dust *n.* fine fragments of wood produced in sawing.

saw·horse *n.* a frame with four legs for supporting wood being sawn by hand.

sax·o·phone (SAX·uh·fone) *n.* a wind instrument with a curved body, usually made of brass.

say *v.* **says, said** (SED), **say·ing 1** utter; speak; tell: *Please say what is on your mind; She said a few words in reply; What do you say about that? What can you say for* (=in justification of) *yourself? What do you say (in reply) to that? He's saying his prayers; The clock says* (=shows) *12.* **2** state; declare: *hard to say whether he's telling the truth; It says here, "Take as directed"; He said he would be late; He did not say it in jest; He's said to be a learned man.* **3** [used parenthetically] let us suppose as an example, estimate, etc.: *You would make, say, $200 a day.*

— *n.* expression of one's opinion: *a chance to have her say (on the subject); The boss has the final say* (= power of deciding) *in the matter.*

saying *n.* 1 an act of saying: *It goes without saying you are welcome to join us.* 2 something said, esp. a commonly heard statement: *a common, popular, wise saying; the sayings of Confucius.*

say-so *n. Informal.* a supposedly authoritative assertion or assurance; hence, authority: *It was done on the say-so of the secretary.*

scab *n.* 1 a blood clot on the surface of a wound or the crust formed on a healing wound. 2 a plant disease producing scablike spots. 3 *Slang.* a worker who takes the place of a striker; also, any scoundrel.
— *v.* scabs, scabbed, scab·bing 1 of a wound, become covered with a scab. 2 *Slang.* act as a scab (worker).

scab·bard (SCAB·urd) *n.* a sheath for a sword or dagger.

scab·by *adj.* scab·bi·er, scab·bi·est covered with scabs; hence, low or mean.

scab·rous (SCAB·rus, SCAY·brus) *adj.* 1 rough or scaly: *a scabrous leaf.* 2 scabby; hence, vile; indelicate; obscene.

scads *n.pl. Informal.* a large amount: *scads of money, people, time.*

scaf·fold (SCAF·uld, -oled) *n.* 1 a raised framework, usually of poles and planks, to stand on while working on a building. 2 formerly, a platform from which criminals were hanged. — *v.* furnish with a scaffolding.

scaf·fold·ing (SCAF·ul·ding) *n.* a scaffold for workers; also, the poles, planks, etc. forming it: *to erect, put up, take down scaffolding.*

scal·a·wag (SCAL·uh·wag) *n. Informal.* a rascal, scamp, or reprobate: *the scalawags and carpetbaggers of the Reconstruction period in the U.S.*

scald (SCAWLD) *v.* burn (as if) with a hot liquid or steam. — *n.* a burn caused thus.

scale *n.* 1 a series or sequence forming a classifying and measuring system: *the Celsius and Fahrenheit temperature scales; the Richter scale to measure strength of earthquakes; a salary scale of $50 000 to $60 000; the eight-tone musical scale; How does Chris rate on a scale of one to ten?* 2 relative size or proportion: *a map drawn to scale; a scale of one centimetre to ten kilometres; bribery on a large scale; He threw a party on a grand scale; a scale drawing or model of an airplane (made according to a scale).* 3 any of the thin, flat, horny pieces covering a fish or reptile; also, any layer or piece resembling this. 4 a weighing machine: *Stand on the (bathroom) scale; Let's weigh it on the kitchen scale; a balance with a pair of scales* (= pans, or **scale·pans**); *She tips the scales at* (= weighs) *61 kg.*
— **tip** or **turn the scales** decide or settle an issue: *The speaker's vote tipped the scales in favour of the motion.*
— *v.* scales, scaled, scal·ing 1 climb up as on a ladder. 2 scrape scales from fish or remove in layers or pieces, as bark from trees, tartar from teeth, etc. 3 weigh on a scale.
— **scale up** (or **down**) increase (or reduce) in proportion.

scal·lop (SCOL·up, SCAL-) *n.* 1 a bivalve mollusc with fanlike rounded and ribbed shells; also, a scallop shell. 2 a scallop-shaped decoration, as on the edge of a dress.
— *v.* 1 bake in a casserole with a milk sauce and bread crumbs. 2 decorate or trim with scallops.

scalp *n.* the hair-covered skin and flesh of the head.
— *v.* 1 tear the scalp from the head. 2 *Informal.* buy and sell theatre tickets, stocks, etc. at a high, often illegal profit. — **scalp·er** *n.*

scal·y (SCAY·lee) *adj.* scal·i·er, -i·est having scales.

scam *n. Slang.* a scheme to swindle or defraud.

scamp *n.* a rascal.

scamp·er *v.* run quickly, as small animals or children when scared. — *n.* a playful running or scurrying.

scan *v.* scans, scanned, scan·ning 1 look at closely; go over an object part by part, as a television camera in transmitting a picture or a radar beam in searching an area. 2 go over quickly: *I had time only to scan* (= go quickly over) *the morning's headlines during breakfast.* 3 mark off lines of verse into feet.
— *n.* a scanning. — **scan·ner** *n.*

scan·dal (SCAN·dul) *n.* 1 action or conduct that is shocking and shameful; also, the feeling of general outrage that results from it: *to cause, cover up, create, uncover a scandal; a sensational scandal; When a scandal bursts, erupts; a breath, hint, suggestion of scandal.* 2 slander or evil gossip: *to enjoy, listen to, repeat, spread, talk scandal.*

scan·dal·ize (SCAN·duh·lize) *v.* -liz·es, -lized, -liz·ing outrage the feelings of someone: *The story of corruption scandalized public opinion; He was convicted of contempt for scandalizing the court.*

scan·dal·mon·ger (SCAN·dul·mung·gur, -mong·gur) *n.* one who spreads slander.

scan·dal·ous (SCAN·duh·lus) *adj.* causing scandal: *a scandalous state of affairs; scandalous behaviour.*
— **scan·dal·ous·ly** *adv.*

scant *adj.* falling short of the required size or quantity; barely enough: *spoke with scant regard for truth; paid scant attention to what was said; was scant of breath after the run.*
— *v.* skimp: *a period scanted by historians.*

scant·y *adj.* scant·i·er, -i·est falling short; barely enough: *a scanty bathing suit, breakfast; a region of scanty rainfall.* — **scant·i·ly** *adv.;* **scant·i·ness** *n.*

scape·goat *n.* one made to take the blame for others.

scar *n.* a mark, as of a healed wound or burn: *The experience left many scars; hideous, permanent, psychological scars; She bore, carried the scars all her life.* — *v.* scars, scarred, scar·ring form or leave a scar.

scarce (SCAIRCE) *adj.* scarc·er, scarc·est not easily available: *Water is scarce this summer; a scarce* (= rare) *book; He makes himself scarce* (*Informal* for goes or stays away) *when help is needed.*

scarce·ly *adv.* hardly; almost not: *He's so tired he can scarcely walk; Scarcely had he stood up when he*

collapsed; *He has scarcely any strength left in his legs;*
He scarcely ever walks any more; He could scarcely
(= certainly not) *have come here walking.*
— **scarce·ness** *n.*

scar·ci·ty (SCARE·suh·tee) *n.* **-ties** inadequate supply.

scare *v.* **scares, scared, scar·ing** fill a person or animal
with fear, often so as to put to flight: *She tried to scare*
away the intruder; She was scared out of her wits; scared
stiff; scared to death by the intruder; The experience
scared her into fleeing the city.
— **scare up** *Informal.* get together supplies, etc. to meet
a need.
— *n.* fright: *to get, give someone a scare; to put, throw*
a scare into somebody.

scare·crow *n.* a ragged figure set up in a field to scare
birds away from crops.

scarf *n.* **scarfs** or **scarves 1** a long strip of cloth or a
neckerchief worn for ornament or protection around the
neck, head, waist, etc. **2** a long and narrow table
covering.

scar·let (SCAR·lit) *n. & adj.* (of) a bright red colour, as
of the robes of persons of rank: *A scarlet dress tunic is*
part of a Mountie's formal outfit; **scarlet fever** (= disease
marked by fever and red spots on the skin); *a* **scarlet**
pimpernel (= plant with small, red starlike flowers); *a*
scarlet woman (= prostitute).

scar·y (SCAIR·ee) *adj.* **scar·i·er, -i·est** *Informal.*
frightening or easily frightened. — **scar·i·ly** *adv.*

scat *v.* **scats, scat·ted, scat·ting** *Slang.* **1** go away. **2** in
jazz, sing or speak scat.
— *n.* nonsense sounds or syllables: *a tune with a dash of*
scat; adj.: improvised, no-rule scat singing; scat
syllables; Yodelling is a type of scat vocalizing.
— *interj.* used to drive away an animal.

scath·ing (SCAY·thing, "th" as in "the") *adj.* severe or
harsh: *a scathing attack; scathing criticism, remarks.*
— **scath·ing·ly** *adv.*

scat·ter (SCAT·ur) *v.* go or send in different directions,
as papers by a wind or a flock when driven.

scat·ter·brain (SCAT·ur·brain) *n.* one who cannot
concentrate on a subject. — **scat·ter·brained** *adj.*

scav·enge (SCAV·inj) *v.* **-eng·es, -enged, -eng·ing**
1 search among or gather discarded objects: *a bear*
scavenging for food. **2** feed on rubbish or dead matter,
as do vultures and hyenas. — **scav·eng·er** *n.*

sce·nar·i·o (suh·NAIR·ee·oh) *n.* **-os** a sequence of events
as planned or imagined, esp. a film director's script
containing instructions on camera shots, etc.: *Who*
wrote the scenario? a possible scenario; In a worst-case
scenario, we could be facing death.

scene (SEEN) *n.* **1** the place or stage of an action or
incident: *No one was at the scene of the crime when it*
happened; a reporter on the scene of the accident. **2** a
sphere of activity or way of life: *the disco, drug,*
national, sports scene. **3** an act or episode of a play. **4** a
view, esp. one that has artistic appeal, as a landscape: *a*
scene depicted on canvas; a beautiful, familiar,
gruesome, revolting, tragic scene.
— **behind the scenes** backstage: *The visitor was taken*

behind the scenes; *No one knew what was going on*
behind the scenes (= secretly); **adj.:** *behind-the-scenes*
(= secret) *activity.*
— **make a scene** make an embarrassing display of one's
emotions.

scen·er·y (SEE·nuh·ree) *n.* **-er·ies 1** the features of a
landscape: *We paused to admire the scenery; beautiful,*
majestic, picturesque scenery. **2** the painted screens and
such accessories used on a stage to represent the place of
an action: *to dismantle, move, set up, shift scenery; A*
change of scenery was called for.

sce·nic (SEE·nic) *adj.* **1** having fine scenery: *a scenic*
drive, highway, route. **2** having to do with natural
scenery: *scenic artists, effects.* — **sce·ni·cal·ly** *adv.*

scent (SENT) *n.* **1** a perfume. **2** a smell or the trail left
by a smell: *The hounds picked up and followed the*
scent of the fox; They were thrown off the scent by
water; a faint, not pungent scent (= odour); *a keen scent*
(= sense of smell) *for game.*
— *v.* to smell or suspect: *to scent danger, game, trouble.*
— **scented** *adj.* perfumed: *The air is heavily scented*
with allspice; a scented garden with scented foliage and
fragrant flowers; scented candles, cosmetics, lotions;
mint-scented whipped cream.

scep·ter (SEP·tur) same as SCEPTRE.

scep·tic or **skep·tic** (SKEP·tic) *n.* **1** one who is unwilling
to accept generally held beliefs, esp. religious doctrines.
2 an adherent of scepticism.
— **scep·ti·cal** or **skep·ti·cal** *adj.*
— **scep·ti·cal·ly** or **skep·ti·cal·ly** *adv.*

scep·ti·cism or **skep·ti·cism** (SKEP·tuh·siz·um) *n.*
1 unwillingness to believe anything without absolute
proof: *an air of scepticism; He maintains a healthy*
scepticism about flying saucers. **2** the philosophical
theory that reality is unknowable. **3** religious unbelief.

scep·tre or **scep·ter** (SEP·tur) *n.* the staff carried by a
sovereign as a symbol of power; hence, sovereignty.
— *adj.:* *the sceptred isle* (= Britain).

sched·ule (SKEJ·ool, SHEJ·ool) *n.* a timetable for doing
things according to a plan: *an airline, bus, production,*
publishing, train schedule; to draw up, make up, plan a
schedule; Our flight arrived according to or on
schedule, not ahead of schedule; The train was behind
schedule (= late).
— *v.* **-ules, -uled, -ul·ing** enter in a schedule: *The*
meeting is scheduled to begin at 9 a.m.; It is scheduled
(= planned) *for 9 a.m.; Charter flights are not*
scheduled flights.

sche·mat·ic (skee·MAT·ic) *n.* a scheme or diagram: *the*
schematic of a heating system; the schematics showing
the trajectory of the bullets; adj.: a schematic diagram,
drawing. — **sche·mat·i·cal·ly** *adv.*

scheme (SKEEM) *n.* **1** a plan or systematic
arrangement: *the rhyme scheme of a limerick.* **2** a
project: *a drainage scheme; a grandiose scheme to make*
the desert bloom. **3** an underhand plan or plot: *to*
devise, foil, think up, thwart a scheme; a diabolical,
fantastic, preposterous scheme; a scheme to rig the vote.
— *v.* **schemes, schemed, schem·ing** plot or intrigue: *a*
scheming politician; scheming to get rich quickly.
— **schem·er** *n.*

schism (SIZ·um) *n.* **1** a division or split within a church, as the Great Schism of the 1300s with rival popes: *to cause, create a schism within the church.* **2** the offence of causing religious schism or a resulting sect of such a split. — **schis·mat·ic** (skis·MAT·ic) *n. & adj.*

schiz·o·phre·nia (skit·suh·FREE·nee·uh) *n.* a mental disorder involving a split personality, the emotional side of the patient being disturbed, with consequent aggressive and destructive tendencies. — **schiz·o·phren·ic** (-FREN·ic) *n. & adj.*

schlock (SHLOK) *n. & adj. Slang.* (anything) cheap or trashy: *a schlock movie; schlock shows.*

schmaltz (SHMAHLTS) *n. Slang.* excessive sentimentalism in art, music, etc.

schnook (SHNOOK, short "OO") *n. Slang.* a sucker or dupe.

schol·ar (SCOL·ur) *n.* **1** a learned person: *a distinguished classical scholar; an eminent scholar.* **2** a student: *a history scholar; serious scholars; a Rhodes scholar* (= scholarship holder). — **schol·ar·ly** *adj.: scholarly habits, methods, research; a scholarly pursuit, thesis, treatise, work.*

schol·ar·ship (SCOL·ur·ship) *n.* **1** a grant of money or other aid to help a student: *to apply for, award, establish, found, get, grant, receive, win a scholarship; a scholarship for graduate study; a scholarship to study abroad.* **2** the knowledge or erudition of a learned person; also, a student's level of attainment: *to foster, promote scholarship; solid, sound, thorough scholarship.*

scho·las·tic (scuh·LAS·tic) *adj.* having to do with schools or scholars; also, pedantic.

school (SCOOL) *n.* **1** a place for teaching and learning; hence, education, an educational course or session, or a particular department of instruction: *Children must attend school till they are 16; She goes to school in Winnipeg; goes to a good school; She started school at the age of five; There are accredited, boarding, correspondence, dental, elementary, graduate, high, junior high, primary, nursing, secondary, undergraduate, vocational schools; a school for the handicapped; She left school and went to college; She dropped out of or left or quit school at 16; later finished school and graduated from Queen's; She works at or in a school while her children are still at or in school; He is kept after school when he is late for school.* **2** a group of people who agree in their views, methods, etc.: *an educator of the old school; an avant-garde school of art; a radical school of thought; various schools of opinion on a subject.* **3** a situation or experience having training value: *the school of adversity, hard knocks.* **4** the group of teachers and students: *The whole school assembled in the gym.* **5** a group of the same kind and size of fish or other water animal swimming together. — *v.* **1** teach or train: *Soldiers are schooled to obey; Children should be thoroughly schooled in the basics; well schooled discipline; Your education depends on where you receive your schooling; Many geniuses have had no formal schooling.* **2** swim together, as tuna and sardines.

school board *n.* a local group managing a school system.

school·fel·low (SCOOL·fel·oh) *n.* schoolmate.

school·marm or **school·ma'am** (SCOOL·mahm, -mam) *n. Informal.* **1** a woman schoolteacher. **2** one who is pedantic or priggish.

school·mas·ter (SCOOL·mas·tur) *n.* [old-fashioned] a male schoolteacher; *fem.* **school·mis·tress.**

school·yard *n.* a piece of ground near or around a school; school playground.

school year *n.* the period of the year when school is in session, usually September to June in Canada.

schoon·er (SKOO·nur) *n.* a fore-and-aft-rigged ship with two or more masts.

schuss (SHOOS, short "OO") *n.* a fast run on skis down a steep course. — *v.* make a schuss.

sci·ence (SYE·unce) *n.* **1** systematized knowledge based on observed and tested facts, as distinguished from art; also, a branch of it, as mathematics, logic, and the physical and biological sciences: *to advance, foster, promote science; the sciences* (= natural sciences and mathematics) *as distinguished from the arts; applied, domestic, information, library, linguistic, military, natural, physical, political, social, space science; Linguistics is not an exact science.* **2** a skill or technique: *the science of boxing.*

science fiction *n.* fiction based on imaginative and fantastic applications of science and technology to life on other planets, the future, etc.

sci·en·tif·ic (sye·un·TIF·ic) *adj.* dealing with or based on science. — **sci·en·tif·i·cal·ly** *adv.*

sci·en·tist (SYE·un·tist) *n.* one trained in science, esp. the physical and biological sciences: *a physical scientist; political, social scientists; a Christian Scientist* (= follower of "Christian Science" religion).

sci-fi (SYE·fye) *n.* [short form] science fiction.

scin·til·la (sin·TIL·uh) *n.* spark; a shred or trace: *not one scintilla of evidence; without a scintilla of truth.*

sci·on (SYE·un) *n.* **1** a branch or shoot for grafting. **2** a descendant; offspring.

scis·sor (SIZ·ur) *v.* cut with scissors.

scis·sors (SIZ·urz) *n. sing. & pl.* a cutting instrument for cloth, paper, hair, etc. consisting of two pivoted blades that are squeezed against each other by the action of the hand inserted through two rings at one end of the blades.

scoff *v.* mock or jeer *at* a person or thing that deserves respect. — *n.* a scoffing.

scold *v.* find fault with or rebuke, esp. in an ill-tempered way: *He was scolded for wasting food; scolded about his eating habits.*
— *n.* one who scolds, esp. a woman.
— **scolding** *n.: He was given a good scolding; He got or received a scolding from his mother.*

sconce *n.* a light fixture bracketed to a wall, usually for a candle.

scone (SCONE, SCON) *n.* a quick bread or biscuit baked on a griddle or in an oven.

scoop *n.* **1** a shovellike tool or utensil used to dig or ladle out coal, dirt, flour, grain, ice cream, mashed potatoes, sugar, etc. **2** a scooping or the amount taken up in one scooping: *two scoops of ice cream.*
3 *Informal.* a piece of news published by a paper ahead of its rivals.
— *v.* **1** take up or hollow out with a scoop: *the "stoop and scoop" regulation against pets fouling public places.* **2** *Informal.* beat rival newspapers by publishing a story first.

scoot *v.* be off in a hurry; dart; decamp: *They scooted out of the room before the class was dismissed.*

scoot·er *n.* **1** a child's two-wheeled vehicle consisting of two tandem wheels connected by a footboard, with a steering post connected to the front wheel. **2** a motor scooter.

scope *n.* **1** extent or range of perception or activity: *matters outside the scope of an inquiry; The scope of the human mind is limited; a plan with much scope* (= room or opportunity) *for expansion.* **2** [short form of words ending in -scope, *combining form* meaning "observing instrument"] microscope, stethoscope, telescope.

scorch *v.* burn the outside surface of cloth, vegetation, etc. so as to discolour or damage: *fields scorched by the sun; the scorched earth policy of devastating an area before yielding it to invaders.* — *n.* a superficial burn.

score *n.* **1** a mark, scratch, or notch, as in keeping tally; hence, a record or account, as of points in a game: *to keep the score; We quickly ran up a score of 10 points; a score of 20 to 4 in the deciding game; The score stood (at) 20 to 4 or 20 – 4; We won by a lopsided score; an even score of 4 – 4* (= a tie score); *a (baseball) box score; We paid off or settled some old scores* (= grievances); *I have no regrets on that score* (= account); *It's good to know the score* (= know the favourable and unfavourable facts of a situation) *before sitting down to negotiate.* **2** a set of 20: *She lived three score years and ten* (= 70 years); *three score and ten years; We've seen them scores of* (= many) *times; They came in scores* (= in large numbers). **3** the notation of a musical work containing one or more parts, as for an orchestra: *Who wrote the score?*
— *v.* **scores, scored, scor·ing 1** make or assign as points: *The home team scored 10 points against the visitors; She did most of the scoring for their team; She tried to score (points) off her rival* (= beat him in an argument). **2** keep a record of the number of points.

3 make a mark or line: *The editor scored out the lines to be deleted.* **4** arrange a piece of music in a score: *the art of scoring for an orchestra.* **5** succeed: *It is hard to score with a poorly organized program; She scored high in math but low on the other tests.* — **scor·er** *n.*

score·card *n.* a card for keeping the score in a game.

scorn *v.* regard with contempt: *a know-it-all who scorns advice.*
— *n.* contempt: *an expert who treats lay people with scorn; to express, feel scorn; He heaped scorn on the speaker at the rally.*
— **scorn·ful** *adj.*; **scorn·ful·ly** *adv.*

Scot *n.* a person of or from Scotland.
— **Scots** *n.* & *adj.* same as SCOTTISH.

Scotch 1 *n.* & *adj.* [less preferred form] Scots or Scottish. **2** same as SCOTCH WHISKY.

scotch *v.* **1** wound without killing: *to scotch a snake.* **2** stamp out or crush: *to scotch a rumour, theory.*

scotch tape *n.* an adhesive tape; **Scotch tape,** *Trademark.*
— **scotch-tape** *v.* **-tapes, -taped, -tap·ing:** *to scotch-tape pictures to a wall.*

Scotch whisky *n.* a whisky distilled from barley in Scotland.

scot-free *adj.* unpunished; without loss or injury: *She got off scot-free; He was let off scot-free.*

Scot·tish (SCOT·ish) *n.* & *adj.* of Scotland or its people: *Scottish (English); the Scottish (people); Scottish dialects.*

scoun·drel (SCOWN·drul) *n.* a villain or rascal.
— *adj.* villainous or wicked.

scour *v.* **1** clean or polish pots, pans, etc. by rubbing with something abrasive, as a **scouring pad. 2** dig or wear away by the force of something in motion, as a channel by a stream. **3** search an area, one's memory, etc. by going over quickly and thoroughly.
— *n.* **1** a scouring. **2 scours** *pl.* diarrhea in newborn cattle.

scourge (SCURGE) *n.* **1** a whip. **2** any large-scale punishment or widespread affliction such as a plague or war.
— *v.* **scourg·es, scourged, scourg·ing** punish as with a whip.

scout *v.* **1** to reconnoitre or survey, as a military or police **scout car,** a space vehicle, etc. **2** search for something: *to scout for firewood; to scout around for fresh talent; a scouting expedition.*
— *n.* **1** one sent out to scout: *a talent scout interviewing persons with talent.* **2** a member of the Scouts movement: *a Boy Scout; a Girl Scout from the U.S.*

scowl *n.* an ill-humoured or sullen look or frown with contracted eyebrows.
— *v.* look with a scowl: *He scowled in annoyance; to scowl at someone.* — **scowl·er** *n.*

scrab·ble (SCRAB·ul) *n.* & *v.* **scrab·bles, scrab·bled, scrab·bling** scrape, scramble, or scribble.
— **scrab·bler** *n.*

scrag·gly (SCRAG·lee) *adj.* **scrag·gli·er, scrag·gli·est** irregular or ragged: *a scraggly beard, ear of corn.*

scrag·gy (SCRAG·ee) *adj.* **scrag·gi·er, scrag·gi·est** rugged or scrawny: *scraggy cliffs; a scraggy neck.*

scram *v.* **scrams, scrammed, scram·ming** *Slang.* go away; also *interj.*

scram·ble (SCRAM·bul) *v.* **-bles, -bled, -bling** 1 move forward by climbing, crawling, etc.; struggle: *to scramble up a rock; Football players scramble to get the ball; People scramble for government grants, for a living, for power, seats, wealth.* 2 mix or jumble: *scrambled eggs (that are stirred while frying); a scrambled (= deliberately garbled) radio or TV signal.* — *n.* a scrambling, esp. a disorderly struggle: *Life is a mad, wild scramble; a shanty town that is a scramble of mud and stucco houses.* — **scram·bler** *n.* one that mixes transmission signals; *adj.:* *They use a scrambler phone to avoid wiretaps; Pay-TV operates on a scrambler-descrambler system.*

scrap *n.* 1 a piece or fragment, as of torn paper, leftover meat, or a brief extract from something written or printed; also, discarded metal or trash: *The car was sold for scrap; scrap iron; a scrap book for collecting pictures, clippings, etc.* 2 *Informal.* a fight or struggle: *She put up a good scrap.* — *v.* **scraps, scrapped, scrap·ping** 1 make into scraps; discard as junk: *We scrapped the car when it rusted.* 2 *Informal.* fight or quarrel: *They scrapped over where to sit.*

scrape *v.* **scrapes, scraped, scrap·ing** 1 rub or scratch against or with something rough or sharp: *to scrape paint off with a knife; She fell and scraped her knee; The tire is scraping against the fender.* 2 get by trying very hard: *They scraped together enough money to pay the rent; He scraped through the exam with a bare pass; managed to scrape along on a small income; He scrapes by as a furniture mover; He's not the man to bow and scrape (= to act slavishly) for a favour.* — *n.* 1 a scraping (sound) or a scraped place. 2 a predicament. — **scrap·er** *n.*

scrap·heap *n.* a pile of discarded things.

scrap·per (SCRAP·ur) *n.* fighter: *What a scraper he is!*

scrap·py (SCRAP·ee) *adj.* **scrap·pi·er, scrap·pi·est** 1 made up of fragments; disconnected. 2 *Informal.* quarrelsome; also, tough or gritty. — **scrap·pi·ly** *adv.;* **scrap·pi·ness** *n.*

scratch *v.* 1 mark, cut, or scrape lightly with something sharp or pointed: *furniture scratched by movers; scratches his head when lost for words; The dog scratches at the door when it wants out; The lecturer hasn't even scratched the surface of (= made a start on) the subject; "You scratch my back, I'll scratch yours" (Informal for If you help me, I'll help you).* 2 write or draw hurriedly; also, draw a line through as in striking out a name: *Two candidates were scratched (= withdrawn) from the race.* 3 scrape money together. — *n.* 1 a scratching or a mark or cut made by it: *He came out of the ordeal without a scratch; a scratch test made on the skin for determining a person's allergies.* 2 a line marking the starting point of a race. — **from scratch** from the starting line; from zero or with nothing to build on: *a gadget that he designed from scratch.* — **up to scratch** up to the point of readiness; in acceptable condition: *None of the candidates was up to scratch.* — *adj.* 1 for quick notes: *scratch pad, paper.* 2 hastily put together: *a scratch meal, performance, team.*

scratch·y *adj.* **scratch·i·er, -i·est** that scratches: *scratchy clothes; the scratchy sounds of a scratchy recording; scratchy writing made with a scratchy quill pen; scratchy hair, voices; a scratchy shirt.*

scrawl *v.* write carelessly or hastily. — *n.* such writing: *an illegible scrawl that is hard to decipher.* — **scrawl·er** *n.* — **scrawl·y** *adj.*

scraw·ny (SCRAW·nee) *adj.* **scraw·ni·er, -ni·est** *Informal.* thin and bony: *a turkey's scrawny neck; Ann is lithe without being scrawny; a scrawny teenager.*

scream (SCREEM) *n.* 1 a sharp, shrill cry of pain, fright, etc.: *She heard a bloodcurdling scream outside her window; a loud scream of pain followed by screams of laughter.* 2 *Informal.* a very funny person or thing: *The play is a scream and so is its director!* — *v.* utter a scream: *The child was carried out kicking and screaming; She was screaming her head off; She screamed that she had been lied to; She was not screaming with pain; She screamed and shouted at them; The child screamed blue murder when it couldn't get what it wanted; They screamed for help.*

screech 1 *n. Cdn.* in Newfoundland, a potent dark rum or similar cheap liquor. 2 *n.* a harsh, shrill, piercing sound or cry; shriek. — *v.* 1 make a screech: *the screeching of brakes, of a "screech owl"; The subways screeched to a halt as the strikers walked out; The subway system ground to a screeching halt.* 2 *Cdn.* in Newfoundland, make someone an honorary Newfie by having him or her drink screech: *to screech someone in.* — **screech·y** *adj.*

screen *n.* 1 a covered frame or something similar put up to hide, protect, or separate: *Let's put up a screen here; a painted Japanese screen; a wire mesh screen to keep out flies; a smoke screen against enemy observation.* 2 a projection surface for movies, slides, or other images: *a radar screen; the TV screen; A movie made its debut last week on only 32 screens (= theatres) and made money at a whopping $20 000 a screen; stars of the stage and screen (= the theatre and the movies); A screen test (= filmed audition) is routinely given to all aspirants to movie or TV stardom.* 3 a sieve or other straining device. — *v.* 1 shield to protect or separate: *A row of trees screened (= blocked) our view; a dining area screened (= partitioned) off from the living room; a sheltered life screened (= protected) from unhealthy influences.* 2 show a motion picture on a theatre screen: *to do a screening for a select audience.* 3 sift or separate: *Candidates are carefully screened for sensitive jobs; genetic screening of the newborn for detecting and treating inherited disorders.*

screen·play *n.* the script of a motion picture.

screw *n.* 1 a naillike but spirally threaded metal piece for fastening things by turning a **screw·driv·er** in its

slotted head. **2** any mechanical device working like a screw on an advancing spiral, as a jack for lifting loads, the propeller (**screw propeller**) of a ship or airplane, a corkscrew, thumbscrew, etc.
— **have a screw loose** *Slang.* be crazy.
— **put the screws on** *Informal.* use pressure on someone.
— *v.* **1** twist or turn, as a screw; hence, fasten or tighten: *He screwed the lid on tight; She has her **head screwed on right*** (= She is sensible); *He had to **screw up*** (= gather) *his courage to do it.* **2** twist out of shape; contort one's face. **3** to hurt vindictively: *a hate list of political enemies for screwing.*
— **screw around** *Slang.* **1** to fool around. **2** [vulgar use] be sexually promiscuous.
— **screw up** *Informal.* **1** mess up or mismanage: *to screw up a deal, job, figures, plans: She screwed up the arrangements at the last minute.* **2** make someone nervous: *She got all screwed up waiting for her turn in the dentist's chair.*

screw·ball *n. Slang.* one who is eccentric.

screw·y *adj.* **screw·i·er, -i·est** *Slang.* crazy or eccentric.

scrib·ble (SCRIB·ul) *n.* marks or writing made in a careless or hasty manner: *an illegible scribble.*
— *v.* **scrib·bles, scrib·bled, scrib·bling** make a scribble: *to scribble graffiti on walls.* — **scrib·bler** *n.*

scrim·mage (SCRIM·ij) *n.* **1** a play in football beginning at the "line of scrimmage" when the ball is snapped back. **2** a football team's practice game.
— *v.* **scrim·mag·es, scrim·maged, scrim·mag·ing** take part in a scrimmage or struggle.

scrimp *v.* be sparing or niggardly with food, money, and other resources: *She scrimped to pay for piano lessons; People buy houses by scrimping on luxuries; Some seniors manage by scrimping and saving.*
— **scrim·py** *adj.*

scrip *n.* a receipt or certificate of entitlement to a share of stock, land, money, etc.

script *n.* **1** a handwriting or a type style resembling it. **2** the written text of a motion picture, play, etc.

scrip·tur·al (SCRIP·chuh·rul) *adj.* having to do with sacred writings, esp. the Bible. — **scrip·tur·al·ly** *adv.*

Scrip·ture (SCRIP·chur) *n.* **1** the Bible; also **the Scriptures** *pl.* **2** scripture any sacred book.

scroll (SCROLE) *n.* **1** a roll of paper or parchment usually used for writing on: *the Dead Sea Scrolls written by a Jewish sect.* **2** a scroll-shaped ornamentation as on the head of a violin or, in architecture, the top part of an "Ionic" column.
— *v.* move text up, down, or across a computer screen so as to view a new portion.

Scrooge or **scrooge** (SCROOJ) *n.* a mean and miserly person: *Sam is miserly like Scrooge, but Jan is generous like Santa.*

scrounge (SCROWNJ) *v.* **scroung·es, scrounged, scroung·ing** *Slang.* to go about or to collect by searching, begging, pilfering, etc.: *They had to scrounge around for the firewood; Finally they scrounged it from High Park.* — **scroung·er** *n.*

scrub *n.* **1** small or stunted trees or shrubs; also, land

with such growth. **2** one considered insignificant or inferior. **3** a player not on the regular team.
— *v.* **scrubs, scrubbed, scrub·bing 1** wash or clean utensils, hands, floors, etc. by rubbing hard, usually with a "scrub brush": *to scrub a floor; to scrub the floor clean; to scrub a stain* (= remove it by scrubbing) *off a floor; Keep scrubbing* (= rub hard) *till the stain comes off.* **2** *Informal.* cancel: *Many space missions were scrubbed after the 1986 "Challenger" disaster.*
— *n.* a scrubbing: *A **scrub nurse** assists surgeons in the operating room.*

scrub·by (SCRUB·ee) *adj.* **scrub·bi·er, scrub·bi·est** stunted or covered with scrub: *scrubby growth, land.*

scruff *n.* the back of an animal's neck, esp. the loose skin covering it.

scruf·fy (SCRUF·ee) *adj.* **scruf·fi·er, scruf·fi·est** shabby or grubby: *a scruffy dresser; He works in a scruffy office in the old part of town; The teenagers formed a scruffy grassroots movement for fighting drugs.*
— **scruf·fi·ly** *adv.;* **scruf·fi·ness** *n.*

scrump·tious (SCRUMP·shus) *adj. Informal.* splendid or delicious. — **scrump·tious·ly** *adv.*

scru·ple (SCROO·pul) *n.* a feeling of uneasiness about doing what may not be right or proper: *The fellow has no scruples about drinking and driving; It shows a lack of scruples.*
— *v.* **-ples, -pled, -pling** hesitate to do something; have scruples: *The Film Review Board will not scruple to cut certain passages from a film.*

scru·pu·lous (SCROOP·yuh·lus) *adj.* conscientious; careful about fine points of morality, accuracy, etc.: *We are very scrupulous about giving the devil his due; a scholar's scrupulous attention to detail; a job done with scrupulous care.* — **scru·pu·lous·ly** *adv.*
— **scru·pu·los·i·ty** (·LOS·uh·tee) *n.*

scru·ti·nize (SCROO·tun·ize) *v.* **-niz·es, -nized, -niz·ing** examine carefully with attention to particulars: *to scrutinize the ballots cast.*

scru·ti·ny *n.* **-nies** a careful inspection: *Employees complain of being under constant scrutiny; What is done in public is open to scrutiny by the public; a politician whose record will not bear close scrutiny; the strict scrutiny of the tax auditor.*

scu·ba (SCOO·buh) *n.* underwater breathing equipment, as used by a diver, or **scuba diver.**

scud *v.* **scuds, scud·ded, scud·ding** move fast, as clouds or a boat driven by wind: *clouds scudding across the sky.*
— *n.* a scudding of clouds, etc. driven by wind.

scuff *v.* **1** walk dragging the feet. **2** scratch, scrape, or wear out shoes, floors, etc.
— *n.* **1** a rough or worn spot on a surface. **2** a light, flat, backless house slipper.

scuf·fle (SCUF·ul) *n.* a rough, confused fight at close quarters.
— *v.* **scuf·fles, scuf·fled, scuf·fling** to struggle *with* someone at close quarters.

sculpt *v.* [short form] to sculpture.

sculp·tor (SCULP·tur) *n.* one who produces sculpture.

sculp·ture (SCULP·chur) *n.* **1** the art of carving out or otherwise making three-dimensional works of art. **2** the products of such art collectively or a statue, carving, or other figure carved out, cast, or modelled in clay, wax, etc.
— *v.* **-tures, -tured, -tur·ing 1** carve a sculpture. **2** cover with sculpture or raised design: *a **sculptured** carpet.*

scum *n.* dross or such refuse that rises to the top of a liquid or body of water, as the "green scum" formed by organisms on the surface of a pond: *the scum* (= despicable people) *of society.*
— *v.* **scums, scummed, scum·ming** become covered with or form scum.

scup·per (SCUP·ur) *n.* an opening in the side of a ship at deck level for water to run off.
— *v. Informal.* ruin or destroy: *The support of the media actually scuppered her chances of becoming party leader.*

scur·ril·ous (SCUR·uh·lus) *adj.* foully abusive or jesting: *scurrilous attacks, language, writers.*
— **scur·ril·ous·ly** *adv.*
— **scur·ril·i·ty** (scuh·RIL·uh·tee) *n.* **-ties.**

scur·ry (SCUR·ee) *v.* **scur·ries, scur·ried, scur·ry·ing** scamper: *Some scurried for cover; scurried for safety; Others scurried around like mice.*
— *n.* a scamper or hurrying.

scur·vy (SCUR·vee) *n.* a disease caused by lack of vitamin C in the diet.
— *adj.* **-vi·er, -vi·est** mean or contemptible.
— **scur·vi·ly** *adv.*

scut·tle (SCUT·ul) *n.* **1** a metal pail for carrying and pouring coal. **2** a lidded opening in the hull or deck of a ship. **3** a scamper or scurry.
— *v.* **scut·tles, scut·tled, scut·tling 1** sink a ship by cutting a hole in it. **2** scrap or abandon: *Plans for the picnic were scuttled by the rain; to scuttle an agreement, deal, proposal; to scuttle negotiations.* **3** to scurry or scamper: *Crabs scuttle across the sand.*

scut·tle·butt (SCUT·ul·but) *n.* **1** a ship's drinking fountain. **2** *Informal.* rumour or gossip.

scythe (SITHE, "TH" as in "the") *n.* an L-shaped mowing and reaping implement with a long curved blade and a handle swung by both hands.
— *v.* **scythes, scythed, scyth·ing** cut or work with a scythe.

sea (SEE) *n.* a large body of salt water connected to an ocean; also, the ocean: *the Mediterranean Sea; the landlocked Caspian Sea; The Sea of Galilee is really a freshwater lake; Jim went to sea* (= became a sailor) *at 12; He put out to sea in a junk; The boat drifted out to sea; an invasion by sea and land; a sea of troubles; calm, choppy, heavy, high, open, raging, rough, stormy, turbulent sea(s); blessed with calm seas; a pirate on the high seas; An old salt who has sailed the seven seas* (= travelled the world).
— **at sea** in the ocean: *a sailor buried at sea; He was quite **at sea*** (= bewildered) *when he sat down to take the test.*
— *adj.* of the sea; marine: *the sea air; a sea captain; a **sea change*** (= transformation); *a **sea chest*** (= sailor's storage chest); *a **sea cow*** (= "manatee" or other sea animal); *a **sea dog*** (= veteran sailor); *sea duty; a sea fish, route; sea water.*

sea·board *n.* land bordering the sea: *on the Atlantic seaboard; the eastern seaboard.* Also **sea·coast.**

seal (SEEL) *n.* **1** a sea animal with four flippers that usually lives in coastal waters, esp. in polar regions: *the fur seal; a colony of seals; a bull* (= male) *seal; a cow* (= female) *seal; the bark of a seal; the killing of pup seals* (= baby seals) *for pelt.* **2** a seal's pelt. **3** a stamped design, usually on **sealing wax** made of shellac, etc., that is put on a document to make it official or on a letter, bottle, door, etc. to make it secure; also, the stamp or wax used: *the Great Seal of England; to affix a corporate seal; Contract bids are received **under seal**; a seal of approval; negotiations carried out under a seal of secrecy; a wax seal; Who broke the seal? an Easter seal* (= decorative paper stamp).
— *v.* **1** to hunt seals. **2** close tightly or as if with a seal: *a tightly sealed container, home; to seal an envelope; a sealed jar of preserves; The doors were sealed shut; Sealed bids or tenders are invited for a contract; Police may **seal off** an area under investigation (to prevent anyone entering or escaping).* **3** secure something or make it final or decisive: *His lips were sealed (by the oath of confidentiality); a promise sealed with a kiss; The evidence of the last witness **sealed his fate*** (= made certain he was guilty and would be punished); *to seal* (= make sure of) *one's future, a game, the doom, victory, win; We have a promising new player **signed, sealed, and delivered.***

sea legs *n.pl.* ability to adjust to the rolling of a ship by keeping one's balance, not being seasick, etc.: *to find, get one's sea legs.*

sea level *n.* the average level of the surface of the sea, used as a measuring standard for heights and depths on land: *Toronto is at sea level; Mt. Everest is 29 000 ft. (8.84 km) above sea level; the Dead Sea is 1 300 ft. (400 m) below sea level.*

seam (SEEM) *n.* **1** the line formed by the joining of two edges, esp. of cloth sewn together; also, of boards, as of a boat: *to let out a seam; The plan came apart or fell apart **at the seams*** (= entirely). **2** a layer or bed of coal or other mineral.

— *v.* **1** join together forming a seam. **2** mark with seamlike features such as wrinkles, scars, fissures, etc.
— **seam·less** *n.* without seams; hence, having no breaks or faults of texture or design: *seamless pipes, stockings, tubes; a seamless blend, pattern; Sam returned from Saint-Tropez with a seamless tan.*

sea·man (SEE·mun) *n.* -men a sailor, esp. one in a naval rank below petty officer: *an able, leading, master, ordinary seaman.* — **sea·man·ship** *n.*

seam·y (SEE·mee) *adj.* **seam·i·er, -i·est** sordid or squalid: *the seamy side of life.* — **seam·i·ness** *n.*

sé·ance (SAY·ahnce) *n.* a spiritualist session to communicate with the dead: *Mediums conduct or hold séances; others attend séances; They sit and wait at a séance for spirits to materialize in a bodily shape.*

sear (SEER) *v.* **1** burn the outside tissue so as to harden it, as in branding, cauterizing, or in browning toast. **2** wither or dry up grain, etc.

search (SURCH) *v.* look through or examine a place, person, etc. to find something: *Police searched all the baggage for firearms.*
— *n.* a searching: *the search for a missing child; a careful, exhaustive, fruitless, painstaking, thorough search; a body search; a Canadian's right "to be secure against unreasonable search or seizure"; We are all in search of happiness.* — **search·er** *n.*

searching *adj.* thorough or penetrating: *a searching investigation; The committee asked some searching questions.*

sea·sick *adj.* sick from or as if from the rolling motion of a ship: *She felt seasick; got seasick.* — **sea·sick·ness** *n.*

sea·side *n. & adj.* (of or at) a seashore or seacoast: *a walk by the seaside; a seaside cottage, resort, town, village.*

sea·son (SEE·zun) *n.* **1** one of the four divisions of the year, i.e. spring, summer, autumn, and winter. **2** any special period: *the baseball, dry, fishing, harvest, holiday, hurricane, low, mating, off, planting, rainy, slack, tourist season; The Santa Claus parade ushers in the Christmas season; The shopping season opens with the Santa Claus parade; to close, usher out a season; When does the **open season** on* (= the legal time of year to hunt) *ducks begin? After the budget is presented, it's open season for the Opposition to attack the Government; She wears her hat **in season and out of season*** (= at all times).
— *v.* **1** make food tasty with the use of salt, pepper, spices, etc.: *a highly seasoned sauce; She seasons* (= livens up) *her lectures with humour.* **2** to condition or become conditioned; mature; age: *Seasoned lumber does not warp or shrink; a seasoned air traveller.*
— **sea·son·er** *n.*

sea·son·a·ble (SEE·zun·uh·bul) *adj.* happening or suited to the season, occasion, etc.: *seasonable advice, clothes, gifts; We're having normal, seasonable temperatures.*
— **sea·son·a·bly** *adv.*

sea·son·al (SEE·zun·ul) *adj.* having to do with or dependent on a season: *seasonal blooms, employment, migrations, rates.* — **sea·son·al·ly** *adv.*

seasoning (SEE·zun·ing) *n.* a condiment.

seat (SEET) *n.* **1** a place to sit on: *Please have a seat; Take a seat; Take your seat; We assign seats on a first-come basis; a room with seats for 200; to give up, keep, relinquish one's seat; a box, bucket, driver's, front-row, ringside seat; the seat of one's pants* (= the part on which one sits). **2** where one gets a right to sit: *a reserved seat on a flight; She won a seat in parliament; held her seat for eight years; lost her seat in the last election.* **3** where something is based; centre: *the seat of government; a county seat; Universities are seats of learning.* **4** a dominant or advantageous position: *A small deposit will put you in the driver's seat; in the catbird seat.*
— *v.* cause to sit: *Guests are seated first; Please **be seated;** Please remain seated till the aircraft comes to a stop; This room seats* (= has seats for) *200 people.*

seat belt *n.* a safety belt across the lap and often the chest and shoulder to secure a person, as in an automobile.

seating *n.* sitting accommodation, seats, or their arrangement.

sea·ward (SEE·wurd) *adj.* **1** coming from the sea. **2** toward the sea.
— **sea·ward** or **sea·wards** *adv.* toward the sea.

sea·way *n.* **1** an inland waterway with access from the sea for oceangoing ships: *the St. Lawrence Seaway.* **2** a sea traffic route.

se·cede (si·SEED) *v.* **-cedes, -ced·ed, -ced·ing** of a group, cut itself off as a part *from* a state, religious body, etc.
— **se·ces·sion** (-SESH·un) *n.;* **se·ces·sion·ist** *n.*

se·clude (si·CLOOD) *v.* **-cludes, -clud·ed, -clud·ing** shut oneself off from others: *a secluded area, beach, lake, resort, spot; secluded from public view; the secluded life of a convent.*

se·clu·sion (si·CLOO·zhun) *n.* isolation: *to go into seclusion; Monks used to live in seclusion all their lives.*

sec·ond (SEC·und) *adj.* next after the first: *her second child; He is second in command; Jack placed first in the race, John came in second; He came off **second best;** But he is second* (= inferior) *to none in studies; He'll get a second* (= another) *chance; every second* (= alternate) *year.*
— *adv.: the horse that finished second; November is the second last month.*
— *v.* support: *He was proposed and seconded for election to the office.*
— *n.* **1** a person, thing, or place that is second: *Jill was a close second; Put the car in second (gear); It happened on the second (day of the month); on the second (day) of last April.* **2 seconds** *pl.: The dish was so good she asked for **seconds*** (= a second helping); *a cheap store that sells rejects and **seconds*** (= defective articles). **3** a 60th part of a minute; hence, a moment or instant: *I'll be with you in a second; It happened in a split second; Please wait a second; One second!*
— **sec·ond·er** *n.* — **sec·ond·ly** *adv.*

sec·ond·ar·y (SEC·un·dair·ee) *adj.* that is second, subordinate, or inferior; not primary: *a secondary colour such as orange or green; secondary feathers, sources; The teacher feels that punctuation is secondary* to correct spelling; *There is a secondary accent, or stress, on the third syllable of "secondary"; Elementary school is followed by* **secondary school** *(= high school).* — **sec·ond·ar·i·ly** *adv.*

second-class (SEC·und·class) *adj.* of the second class: *She complained of second-class (=inferior) treatment as a female applicant; Newspapers and periodicals qualify as* **second-class mail** *for reduced postal rates;* — *adv.*: *Magazines are sent second-class; Except when on business, he travels second-class (=economy or tourist accommodation by train, ship, air, etc.).*

second fiddle *n.* subordinate role: *She's tired of playing second fiddle to her boss.*

second-guess (SEC·und·guess) *v. Informal.* use hindsight to criticize someone for something already done.

sec·ond·hand (SEC·und·hand) *adj.* not from the original source: *secondhand information; secondhand (=used or not new) goods from a secondhand dealer; the dangers of nonsmokers inhaling secondhand smoke (from smokers).* — *adv.*: *He got the car secondhand (=in used condition); She gets most of her news* **at secondhand** *(=through someone else).*

second nature *n.* an acquired characteristic or tendency that has become firmly fixed in a person: *Punctuality is second nature to or for or with her.*

second opinion *n.* the opinion of another professional: *Let's get a second opinion before deciding on surgery.*

second-rate (SEC·und·rate) *adj.* of inferior quality; second-class: *a second-rate author, candidate, genius, mind, performance, poet.*

second-string (SEC·und·string) *adj. Informal.* in sports, not of the regular team; reserve or substitute.

second thought or **second thoughts** *n.* reconsideration of a first opinion or judgment: *The Canadian Senate is supposed to provide sober second thought to legislation passed by Commons; I jumped in without giving the matter a second thought; Then I had second thoughts about it; On second thought, I decided not to swim in the cold water.*

second wind *n.* renewal of regular strength, as by regaining one's breath: *She gets or catches her second wind after an afternoon nap.*

se·cre·cy (SEE·cruh·see) *n.* -cies a being secret or kept secret: *Mark it "Confidential" to ensure secrecy; The meeting has to be held in the strictest secrecy; We'll swear everyone to secrecy and meet in secrecy at a remote location.*

se·cret (SEE·crit) *adj.* having to do with concealing or keeping from general knowledge or view: *Let's keep the matter secret from the rest of the family; a secret admirer, door, passage, plot, society; the secret police; the secret service (in charge of government security).* — *n.* something secret or mysterious: *to betray, blurt out, divulge, ferret out, guard, keep, reveal, uncover a secret; She doesn't make a secret of her beliefs; a closely guarded, military, open, state, trade secret; It's a secret*

between us; *Discoveries unlock the secrets of nature; I know the secret (= secret cause) of her many successes; They met* **in secret** *(= secretly or unknown to others) to plan the surprise party.* — **se·cret·ly** *adv.*

sec·re·tar·i·al (sec·ruh·TAIR·ee·ul) *adj.* of a secretary: *a secretarial chair; secretarial duties, jobs.*

sec·re·tar·i·at (sec·ruh·TAIR·ee·ut) *n.* the administrative staff of a government department: *the U.N. Secretariat in New York.*

sec·re·tar·y (SEC·ruh·tair·ee) *n.* -tar·ies 1 an employee who handles the correspondence, keeps records, etc. of a person or organization: *an executive, personal, press secretary; He works as private secretary to or of the mayor.* 2 a company officer with similar duties. 3 the head of a government department, as the Canadian **Secretary of State** for External Affairs: *a defence, foreign, labour secretary.* 4 a writing desk. — **sec·re·tar·y·ship** *n.*

se·crete (si·CREET) *v.* -cretes, -cret·ed, -cret·ing 1 hide in a secret place; cache. 2 discharge, as from a gland; **se·cre·tion** (si·CREE·shun) *n.*

se·cre·tive (SEE·cruh·tiv, si·CREE·tiv) *adj.* tending to conceal rather than communicate; not frank or open: *very secretive about their plans.*

sect *n.* a group following a particular doctrine or leader, often a dissenting group: *a religious sect (= denomination).*

sec·tar·i·an (sec·TAIR·ee·un) *n.* a person devoted to a sect, esp. in a narrow-minded way; *adj.*: *sectarian violence in the Middle East.*

sec·tion (SEC·shun) *n.* 1 a cutting or a cut-off part: *a conical, cross, vertical section; a caesarian section.* 2 a division or part of something larger: *the business, classified, news, sports, travel sections of a newspaper; a city's business, residential sections; the sections of a bookcase (to be assembled); the sections of a chapter, fruit, pie; to play in the brass, percussion, string, or woodwind section of an orchestra; a section of a railway maintained by a group of workers* **(section gang).** — *v.* divide into sections or divide so as to display a section.

sec·tion·al (SEC·shuh·nul) *adj.* 1 having to do with a section: *a sectional drawing, view.* 2 local or regional: *sectional interests, prejudices, quarrels, rivalries.* 3 made up of sections; modular: *a sectional bookcase; sectional furniture.* — **sec·tion·al·ly** *adv.*

sec·tor (SEC·tur) *n.* 1 part of a circle between two radii. 2 area of operation or activity: *in the public and private sectors of industry.*

sec·u·lar (SEC·yuh·lur) *adj.* of the world, not of the church, of a religion, or of religious life: *secular education, society; secular clergy (not belonging to a religious order).*

se·cure (si·CURE) *adj.* protected against danger, harm, risk, fear, worry, etc.; safe: *She feels secure with the doors locked; secure against intruders; a nation secure from attack; feels happy and secure in her beliefs; a secure investment; a secure (= firm) knot.* — *v.* -cures, -cured, -cur·ing make secure: *A door is secured by locking it; Banks secure their loans by* collaterals; *to secure our borders against traffickers; It's good to secure our seats* (= purchase tickets) *before the show is sold out.* — **se·cure·ly** *adv.*

se·cur·i·ty (si·CURE·uh·tee) *n.* **-ties 1** protection or the feeling of being protected or secure: *The Canadian Charter of Rights guarantees the right to life, liberty, and the security of the person; a child brought up in the security of the home; a feeling, sense of security against attack; to compromise, ensure, provide, strengthen, tighten, undermine security; collective, internal, national, personal security; Social Security or social insurance is instituted by government to provide people with social benefits;* **adj.:** *maximum and minimum security prisons; He was refused the job as a security risk; A child clings to its* **security blanket** *as if for protection; the U.N.* **Security Council** *for safeguarding world peace.* **2** something that protects or secures: *His signature is good security for a loan.* **3 securities** *pl.* stocks and bonds: *to issue, register securities; gilt-edged securities; government securities.*

se·dan (si·DAN) *n.* **1** an automobile having an enclosed body with centre posts between front and back windows to support the roof, not a "hardtop." **2** a covered portable chair carried on poles like a litter usually by two men; also **sedan chair.**

se·date (si·DATE) *adj.* calm and composed in manner. — *v.* **-dates, -dat·ed, -dat·ing** give a sedative to someone; **se·da·tion** (si·DAY·shun) *n.* — **se·date·ly** *adv.;* **se·date·ness** *n.*

sed·a·tive (SED·uh·tiv) *n.* a substance such as a barbiturate or bromide that tends to soothe and calm the nerves.

sed·en·tar·y (SED·un·tair·ee) *adj.* involving much sitting: *sedentary habits; a sedentary life, occupation.*

sed·i·ment (SED·uh·munt) *n.* **1** matter settling at the bottom of a liquid; dregs. **2** matter deposited by ice, water (as by a receding flood), wind, etc.

se·di·tion (suh·DISH·un) *n.* **1** the stirring up of discontent or rebellion against a government: *to foment, incite sedition; To advocate the violent overthrow of a Canadian government would be an act of sedition.* **2** such action or speech. — **se·di·tious** *adj.*

se·duce (si·DUCE, *rhyme:* produce) *v.* **-duc·es, -duced, -duc·ing** persuade to do something wrong or unlawful, esp. to have sexual intercourse. — **se·duc·er** *n.* — **se·duc·tion** (si·DUC·shun) *n.* — **se·duc·tive** (-tiv) *adj.*

see *v.* **sees, saw, seen, see·ing 1** be aware of through the eyes: *We can't see anything in the dark; I saw him crossing the street* (= in the middle of the street), *but I can't say I saw him cross the street* (= get to the other side). **2** look at a person or thing: *See this picture; Will you see* (= look and find) *who is at the door?* **3** perceive with the mind: *Do you see what I mean? I see that you're right; I see from the papers that there are no survivors; What do you see in her* (that is so attractive to *you)? He prepared to leave,* **seeing** (= considering) *that it was getting late.* **4** experience or have knowledge of something: *an old house that has seen better times; She would like to see her children settled.* **5** visit: *time to see a lawyer; She doesn't like her boyfriend seeing* (= dating) *other girls.* **6** receive: *The boss will see you now.* **7** make

sure; take care: *Please see that the lights are turned off when you leave; Please see* (= escort) *the last visitor out.* **8** consider: *Can you see him as a future prime minister? Please hire him if you see* (= judge) *fit to do so.*
— **see about** or **after** take care of something: *The boss wants you to see about the invitations.*
— **see eye to eye** agree: *Mom and Dad don't always see eye to eye with each other.*
— **see into** have knowledge of something: *Prophets can see into the future.*
— **see off** say goodbye to someone: *He's gone to the airport to see her off.*
— **see through 1** understand the real nature of a person, scheme, etc.: *It's easy to see right through him.* **2** take care of a person or undertaking till the end of something: *I'll see you through this crisis; I have to see the project through to its completion.*
— **see to** attend to something: *He'll see to the arrangements; His boss will* **see to it that** *the arrangements work.*
— *n.* a bishop's office, authority, or diocese.

seed *n.* **1** the usually grainlike part of a plant from which a new plant will sprout: *to broadcast, plant, sow, spread seeds; Seeds germinate, grow; a bag of lettuce seed, grass seed* (= seeds). **2** source or origin: *tales that sowed seeds of suspicion in her mind.* **3** descendants: *the seed of Abraham.*
— **go** or **run to seed** be finished with flowering and production: *People like to keep working even after retirement lest they go to seed* (= become useless or unproductive).
— *v.* **1** scatter seeds over a field: *to seed a field; a field seeded with wheat; Clouds are seeded with crystals of dry ice and other chemicals to make rain or snow.* **2** remove seeds from fruit such as grapes and dates. **3** to rank a player or team according to ability: *Top-seeded players meet last in a tournament.*
— **seed·er** *n.* — **seed·less** *adj.*

seed·ling *n.* **1** a plant grown from a seed. **2** a young tree smaller than a sapling.

seed money *n.* money for starting an enterprise.

seed·y *adj.* **seed·i·er, -i·est 1** full of seeds. **2** gone to seed. **3** shabby-looking.
— **seed·i·ly** *adv.;* **seed·i·ness** *n.*

seek *v.* **seeks, sought, seek·ing** try to find or get: *to seek advice, fortune, shelter; We seek to please our customers; to seek (after) the truth; a much sought-after speaker.* — **seek·er** *n.: a status seeker.*

seem *v.* appear: *She seems happy; seems like a happy person; What seems to be the problem? We seem to have lost our way; It seems (to me) we have lost our way; It seems a waste of time; his* **seeming** (= apparent) *sincerity.* — **seem·ing·ly** *adv.*

seem·ly *adj.* **-li·er, -li·est** that looks appropriate or proper: *Clothes should be seemly if not attractive; seemly* (= pleasing) *behaviour.* — **seem·li·ness** *n.*

seen *pp.* of SEE.

seep *v.* flow out slowly through cracks of a ceiling, etc. or fine pores, as of sand: *water seeping into a basement.*
— **seep·age** (-ij) *n.*

see·saw *n.* **1** a plank supported in the middle for children to sit on at opposite ends and ride up and down; teeter-totter. **2** an up-and-down or back-and-forth movement, as in warfare or in a game.
— *v.* move up and down or back and forth: *The match was so close, the lead seesawed between the two sides for a long time.*

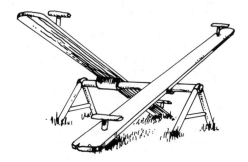

seethe ("th" as in "the") *v.* **seethes, seethed, seeth·ing** be agitated or disturbed, as boiling water: *a nation seething with rebellion; He seethed with fury, resentment.*

seg·ment (SEG·munt) *n.* **1** a natural section or part: *the segments of an orange, earthworm's body, the various segments of the population; a 15-minute segment of a TV program.* **2** a portion of a circle cut off by a plane or that between two parallel planes.
— *v.* (-ment) divide into segments.
— **seg·men·ta·tion** (seg-mun·TAY·shun) *n.*

seg·re·gate (SEG·ruh·gate) *v.* **-gates, -gat·ed, -gat·ing** to separate, esp. as a group and for reasons of race, sex, contagion, etc.: *in racially segregated South Africa; to segregate the boys from the girls; children segregated into academic and nonacademic streams; a segregated area, beach, school.*

seg·re·ga·tion (seg-ruh·GAY·shun) *n.* (policy of) separation of racial groups in housing, education, transportation facilities, etc.: *to maintain, practise segregation; racial, religious, sex segregation.*
— **seg·re·ga·tion·ist** *n.*

sei·gneur or **seign·ior** (seen·YUR) *n.* a feudal lord; nobleman or rich merchant who was granted a tract of land by the king of France, as in early French Canada.

sei·gneur·i·al (seen·YOOR·ee·ul) *adj.* feudal: *The seigneurial system was abolished in Quebec in 1864.*

sei·gneur·y or **seign·ior·y** (SEEN·yuh·ree) *n.* a tract of land owned by a seigneur.

seis·mic (SIZE·mic, SICE-) *adj.* of or caused by an earthquake: *A "tidal wave" is a seismic sea wave.*

seis·mo·graph (SIZE·muh·graf, SICE-) *n.* an instrument that records the duration, intensity, and direction of an earthquake.

seis·mol·o·gy (size·MOL·uh·jee, sice-) *n.* the science of earthquakes.— **seis·mol·o·gist** *n.*
— **seis·mo·log·i·cal** (-muh·LOJ·uh·cul) *adj.*

seize (SEEZ) *v.* **seiz·es, seized, seiz·ing** take hold or possession of a thing or person suddenly and with force: *He seized the food without waiting to be served;*

*contraband seized by customs; the right of police to search and seize; He likes to **seize on** or **upon*** (= understand and use) *every opportunity to plug his candidate; Jan was seized* (= stricken) *with remorse soon after the deed; Some brakes have a tendency to seize* (= stick fast).

sei·zure (SEE·zhur) *n.* a seizing or being seized: *unwarranted search and seizure of goods; to have a cardiac, heart, epileptic, uncontrollable seizure.*

sel·dom (SEL·dum) *adv.* rarely; not often.

se·lect (si·LECT) *v.* choose or pick out of many, using care and discrimination: *to select a jury; She was selected from among many who applied; We selected her to fill the vacancy.*
— *adj.* carefully chosen: *Only a select few were admitted; a select* (= exclusive) *group of friends.*
— **se·lec·tion** (si·LEC·shun) *n.: Make a selection; Take your selection to the cashier; She was happy to play their (musical) selection.*

se·lec·tive (si·LEC·tiv) *adj.* careful in selecting: *She's very selective in her choices; the **selective service** system of military service based on the classification in which each one falls.*

self *n.* **selves** (SELVZ) one's own person: *by his very self* (= by himself); *her former self* (= as she was before); *He appeared quite like his old self; their true selves* (= their true natures); *He puts self* (= his own interests) *above all else; a cheque payable to self* (= oneself).

self- *combining form.* of, by, to, or for oneself or itself: *self-criticism, self-employed, self-respect, self-worth.*

self-assurance (sel·fuh·SHOOR·unce) *n.* confidence in oneself. — **self-assured** *adj.*

self-centred (self·SEN·turd) *adj.* selfish.
— **self-cen·tred·ness** *n.*

self-composed (self·cum·POZED) *adj.* in control of one's emotions; calm and cool.

self-confidence (self·CON·fuh·dunce) *n.* confidence in oneself: *to acquire, display, gain, have, instill, show self-confidence; to restore, not undermine her self-confidence; the self-confidence to stand up for her rights.* — **self-confident** *adj.*

self-conscious (self·CON·shus) *adj.* **1** aware of oneself: *An animal is conscious but never self-conscious.* **2** unduly aware of oneself; ill at ease: *A good actor shouldn't be self-conscious.*

self-contained (self·cun·TAIND) *adj.* **1** complete within itself; independent: *a self-contained classroom, living unit.* **2** showing self-control. **3** reserved: *silent and self-contained.*

self-control (self·cun·TROLE) *n.* control of one's actions, feelings, desires, etc.: *to exercise, lose self-control; She displays admirable, complete, total self-control in public.* — **self-controlled** *adj.*

self-defence (self·di·FENCE) *n.* defence of oneself, one's rights, actions, etc.: *the art of self-defence; She acted in self-defence; It is unfortunate to have to kill in self-defence.*

self-denial (self·di·NYE·ul) *n.* a sacrifice of one's own desires: *Ascetics exercise, practise self-denial.*

self-destruct (self·di·STRUCT) *v.* destroy oneself or itself: *a sticker designed to self-destruct* (= come off in pieces) *if tampered with.*

self-determination (SELF·di·tur·muh·NAY·shun) *n.* freedom to make one's own decisions, esp. of a people to determine for themselves what form of government they shall have: *the right to self-determination; to achieve, give, grant, want self-determination.*

self-fulfilling (self·ful·FIL·ing) *adj.* becoming fulfilled because predicted or expected: *a self-fulfilling prophecy, as when a manager gets a rush job done by telling her employees that she is confident they can finish it by day's end.*
— **self-fulfilment** or **self-fulfillment** *n.: to achieve, attain, seek self-fulfilment.*

self-government (self·GUV·urn·munt) *n.* government by one's own people, esp. elected representatives.
— **self-governing** *adj.*

self-image (self·IM·ij) *n.* conception of one's own worth, identity, etc.

self-interest (self·IN·trist) *n.* the seeking of one's own advantage over the interests of others; selfishness: *Most of us act in our own self-interest; the policy of enlightened self-interest.*

self-ish (SEL·fish) *adj.* caring too much for oneself without regard for the rights of others.
— **self·ish·ly** *adv.*; **self·ish·ness** *n.*

self·less (SELF·lis) *adj.* unselfish.
— **self·less·ly** *adv.*; **self·less·ness** *n.*

self-made (self·MADE) *adj.* who has reached a position largely through personal efforts: *a self-made businesswoman, man, millionaire.*

self-pity (self·PIT·ee) *n.* pity for oneself: *to indulge in self-pity.*

self-respect (self·ri·SPECT) *n.* respect for one's own worth as a person: *He kept his self-respect and ignored the insult.* — **self-respecting** *adj.*

self-righteous (self·RYE·chus) *adj.* convinced that one is more righteous and moral than others.

self·same *adj.* the very same; identical: *the selfsame one I saw yesterday.*

self-sealing (self·SEE·ling) *adj.* sealing by itself: *a self-sealing tire (when punctured); a self-sealing envelope (by pressure).*

self-seeker (self·SEE·kur) *n.* a seeker of one's own advantage; a selfish person. — **self-seeking** *n. & adj.*

self-serve *adj.* self-service: *a self-serve gas station.*

self-service (self·SUR·vis) *n.* the practice of customers serving themselves, as at a gas station, cafeteria, etc. Also *adj.*

self-serving (self·SUR·ving) *adj.* self-seeking; selfish.

self-starter (self·STAR·tur) *n.* **1** an electrical device for starting an internal combustion engine without cranking. **2** *Informal.* a person with initiative.
— **self-starting** *adj.*

self-styled (self·STILED) *adj.* so named by oneself without justification: *a self-styled "president for life."*

self-sufficiency (self·suh·FISH·un·see) *n.* the condition of needing no outside help: *Many countries have achieved* or *attained self-sufficiency in food.*
— **self-sufficient** *adj.*

self-willed (self·WILLED) *adj.* obstinate or stubborn.

sell *v.* **sells, sold, sell·ing** **1** exchange goods, services, etc. for money or other return: *He sells cars; buys wholesale and sells retail; sells them by the dozen; a used car sold as is* (= with no guarantees) *for $200; It was sold at a loss; He doesn't like to sell to family; a store that sells groceries in bulk; He's in jail for selling state secrets to the enemy; Lottery tickets* ***sell like hot cakes*** (= sell quickly and in large quantities); *panic* ***selling*** *of stocks because of falling prices.* **2** (cause to) be sold or accepted: *Snow tires sell best in winter; He is sold on* (= completely persuaded about) *capital punishment; He sold his voters on* (= convinced them about) *capital punishment; Her excuse just wouldn't sell* (= be accepted).
— **sell down the river** *Informal.* betray someone.
— **sell off** get rid of by selling: *They are selling off their winter stock to make room for spring clothes.*
— **sell out** **1** dispose of completely by selling: *We just sold out today's paper; We are sold out of today's paper; We are planning to sell out (the business) to the competition.* **2** *Informal.* betray.
— **sell short** act on the basis of undervaluing something: *My broker advised me to sell Columbus short (because the stock is going to drop in price); You are selling your kids short* (= cheating them) *by neglecting to read aloud to them.*
— *n.* **1** a selling or its method: *a hard sell; soft sell.* **2** *Slang.* hoax.
— **sell·er** *n.: It's a* ***seller's market*** *when goods are scarce and prices high.*

sell-out *n.* **1** a selling out or a show for which all seats are sold: *The fund-raising show was a sellout; A sellout crowd attended the preview.* **2** *Informal.* a betrayal.

selves *pl.* of SELF.

se·man·tics (suh·MAN·tics) *n.pl.* [takes sing. v.] the study of meanings in language. — **se·man·tic** *adj.*

sem·blance (SEM·blunce) *n.* outward appearance or likeness that differs from the reality: *a story without even the semblance of truth; the semblance of legitimacy, order, reality, wealth; a feeble semblance of authority.*

se·men (SEE·mun) *n.* the male reproductive fluid.

se·mes·ter (suh·MES·tur) *n.* one of the two terms into which an academic year is divided.

semi- *combining form.* half; partly; incompletely: *semicentennial, semi-independent, semipermanent.*

sem·i·an·nu·al (sem·ee·AN·yoo·ul) *adj.* **1** occurring every half year. **2** lasting a half year.

sem·i·col·on (SEM·ee·coh·lun) *n.* the punctuation mark [;].

sem·i·con·duc·tor (SEM·ee·cun·DUC·tur) *n.* a material such as silicon that conducts electricity better than an insulator but not as well as a conductor, hence used in electronic devices such as transistors, lasers, and solar batteries.

sem·i·de·tached (SEM·ee·di·TACHT) *n. & adj.* (one) of two dwellings joined side by side, sharing a common wall or garage.

sem·i·fi·nal (sem·ee·FYE·nul) *adj.* next to the last, as in a tournament. — *n.* a semifinal match or round.

sem·i·month·ly (sem·ee·MUNTH·lee) *adj. & adv.* issued twice a month.
— *n.* a semimonthly periodical.

sem·i·nal (SEM·uh·nul) *adj.* 1 of or having to do with seed or semen: *the seminal fluid.* 2 containing the seeds for later development: *a seminal idea; Woodstock was one of the seminal rock events of the 1960s.*
— **sem·i·nal·ly** *adv.*

sem·i·nar (SEM·uh·nar) *n.* a meeting of a group of people doing research or studying under someone's guidance: *Executives attend, conduct, hold seminars on management methods.*

sem·i·per·me·a·ble (sem·ee·PUR·mee·uh·bul) *adj.* of a membrane, allowing the passage of only certain substances: *He has a semipermeable mind.*

sem·i·pre·cious (sem·ee·PRESH·us) *adj.* of a gemstone, as amethyst or turquoise.

sem·i·trail·er (SEM·ee·tray·lur) *n.* a cargo-carrying trailer with wheels at the rear and in the middle supported at the front by a truck tractor.

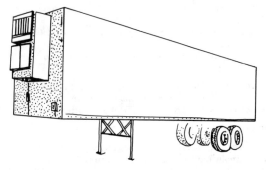

sem·i·vow·el (SEM·ee·vow·ul) *n.* a consonantlike vowel, esp. "w" or "y."

sem·i·week·ly (sem·ee·WEEK·lee) *n. & adj.* (a periodical) published twice a week. Also **adv.**

sen·ate (SEN·it) *n.* 1 the upper branch of a legislature. 2 a legislative or governing council, as of a university: *to convene, convoke, disband, dissolve a senate; A senate adjourns, meets.* — **sen·a·tor** (-uh·tur) *n.*
— **sen·a·to·ri·al** (-uh·TOR·ee·ul) *adj.*

send *v.* **sends, sent, send·ing** 1 cause a person or thing to go without oneself going: *We send children to school; Please send the message to him; Send him the message; Send it by courier; We'll send her on a mission; Send her as our delegate; Send him to get coffee; Send him for* (= to get) *coffee; to send the children to camp; The wind sent the papers flying.* 2 *Slang.* excite or thrill.
— **send for** send a request or messenger for a person or thing: *Please send for the plumber; He likes to send away for* (= order) *everything offered free.*
— **send out:** *to send out invitations; a reporter sent out*

to cover an event; *We **send out for** Chinese food* (= order it delivered) *on busy evenings.*
— **send packing** dismiss without ceremony.
— **send·er** *n.*

send-off *n. Informal.* a farewell in honour of someone leaving a group on a new venture, going on a trip, etc.: *Her students gave her a big send-off.*

send-up *n.* a takeoff: *That TV feature is a send-up of the news media.*

se·nile (SEE·nile) *adj.* relating to weakness of old age, esp. loss of mental powers: *senile condition, deterioriation, psychosis; He is 90 but not at all senile.*
— **se·nil·i·ty** (suh·NIL·uh·tee) *n.*

sen·ior (SEEN·yur) *n.* 1 a student in a graduating class. 2 one who is older or of higher rank: *Airlines offer seniors* (= senior citizens) *special rates.*
— **adj.** older in age, rank, etc.: *He is senior to me by two years; John Smith, Sr.* (= Senior, father of John Smith, Jr.); *a seminar for middle and senior management; the senior partner of the firm.*

senior citizen *n.* an elderly, usually retired person.

senior high school *n.* grades 10, 11, and 12 of high school.

sen·ior·i·ty (seen·YOR·uh·tee) *n.* **-ties** superiority in age; priority because of length of service in a job: *promotion by or according to seniority rather than by merit alone.*

se·ñor (sain·YOR) *n.* **-ño·res** (-YOR·es) *Spanish.* a gentleman; [as a title] Mr. or Sir.

se·ño·ra (sain·YOR·ah) *n. Spanish.* a lady; [as a title] Mrs. or Madam.

se·ño·ri·ta (sain·yuh·REE·tah) *n. Spanish.* a young lady; [as a title] Miss.

sen·sa·tion (sen·SAY·shun) *n.* 1 sense impression, esp. of touch or feeling: *sensations of heat and cold; a sensation of giddiness; a burning, choking, numbing, pleasant sensation.* 2 (cause of) a widespread feeling of excitement: *The announcement caused, created a sensation; She is a great sensation as a singer.*

sen·sa·tion·al (sen·SAY·shuh·nul) *adj.* arousing or meant to arouse general excitement.
— **sen·sa·tion·al·ism** *n.*

sense *n.* 1 a power of feeling or awareness: *the five senses of sight, hearing, smell, taste, and touch, each with a corresponding sense organ such as the eye, ear, etc.; the sixth sense* (= intuition); *a false sense of security.* 2 understanding or appreciation: *your sense of beauty, responsibility; He shows a poor sense of humour; She displays a wry sense of humour; had the good sense to say "Yes"; common sense; horse sense; I wish he had a grain of sense in his head.* 3 a particular meaning: *true in every sense of the word; a figurative, literal, narrow, strict sense of the term; In a sense* (= to a certain extent), *you're right.* 4 **senses** *pl.* normal state of mind: *Have you taken leave of your senses? How can we bring him to his senses? It may be too late when she comes to her senses.*
— **make sense** have meaning: *Your reasons don't make sense; It makes sense to drive within the speed limit; Can you make any sense out of this letter?*
— *v.* **sens·es, sensed, sens·ing** be aware of something;

perceive: *She sensed the danger; sensed right away that something was wrong; A smoke detector can sense (the presence of) smoke; He doesn't seem to have sensed your meaning.* — **sense·less** *adj.*; **sense·less·ly** *adv.*

sen·si·bil·i·ty (sen·suh·BIL·uh·tee) *n.* **-ties 1** ability to sense or perceive. **2** fineness of feelings: *a woman of sense and sensibility; Let's not hurt her **sensibilities** (= sensitive feelings).

sen·si·ble (SEN·suh·bul) *adj.* **1** having good sense; reasonable and practical: *a sensible young woman; Take a sensible stand; It is sensible of her to withdraw; They are sensible* (= appropriate) *shoes for gym wear.* **2** perceiving or aware: *She is sensible of the feelings of others.* **3** that can be perceived: *sensible differences, phenomena; a sensible* (= appreciable) *reduction in price.* — **sen·si·ble·ness** *n.* — **sen·si·bly** *adv.*

sen·si·tive (SEN·suh·tiv) *adj.* **1** able to feel and be affected easily or readily: *a sensitive skin, woman; Lou is sensitive to criticism but not to flattery; a sensitive thermometer; a **sensitive plant** such as the mimosa.* **2** keen or perceptive: *a sensitive and intelligent child; a sensitive soul.* **3** having to do with delicate or secret information: *a sensitive position in government; politically sensitive material; a sensitive issue.* — **sen·si·tive·ly** *adv.*; **sen·si·tive·ness** *n.* — **sen·si·tiv·i·ty** (-TIV·uh·tee) *n.*

sensitivity training See ENCOUNTER.

sen·si·tize (SEN·suh·tize) *v.* **-tiz·es, -tized, -tiz·ing** make or become sensitive: *Children have to be sensitized to the dangers of the street; a sensitized film; sensitized paper.* — **sen·si·ti·za·tion** (-tuh·ZAY·shun) *n.*

sen·sor (SEN·sur) *n.* a sensing device for a physical stimulus such as heat or light: *The burglar tripped a sensor and set off the alarm; sensors planted on the sea floor by spy submarines.*

sen·so·ry (SEN·suh·ree) *adj.* of the senses or sensation: *sensory nerves, organs, perception, stimulation.*

sen·su·al (SEN·shoo·ul) *adj.* having to do with the gratification of the senses: *sensual appetites, enjoyment, life, lips, music, pleasures.* — **sen·su·al·ist** *n.* — **sen·su·al·ly** *adv.* — **sen·su·al·i·ty** (-AL·uh·tee) *n.*

sen·su·ous (SEN·shoo·us) *adj.* having to do with the enjoyment of sense impressions: *sensuous appeal, colours, delight, music, verse.* — **sen·su·ous·ly** *adv.*; **sen·su·ous·ness** *n.*

sent *pt. & pp.* of SEND.

sen·tence (SEN·tunce) *n.* **1** a group of words forming a complete statement, question, or command. **2** a decision, as of a judge, esp. on the punishment for an offence; also, the punishment: *to carry out, commute, execute, impose, pass, pronounce, reduce, serve out, suspend a sentence; He was waiting on death row under sentence of death; a death sentence; a harsh, light, stiff, prison sentence; a suspended sentence* (= a prison term that is not imposed). — *v.* **-tenc·es, -tenced, -tenc·ing** punish judicially: *He was convicted and sentenced to three years in prison.*

sen·ten·tious (sen·TEN·shus) *adj.* wise and moralistic in tone: *a sententious speech, lecturer; the sententious*

voice of Polonius.

sen·tient (SEN·shunt) *adj.* that can feel; conscious: *sentient beings.*

sen·ti·ment (SEN·tuh·munt) *n.* attitude or disposition of mind influenced or refined by feelings, as patriotism (duty influenced by love of country): *Politicians voice patriotic sentiments; the growing sentiment in favour of banning liquor ads; the strong public sentiment against pornography; a speech full of lofty, noble sentiments.*

sen·ti·men·tal (sen·tuh·MEN·tul) *adj.* having to do with sentiment rather than reason: *the sentimental behaviour of a sentimental parent; He is very sentimental about or over his old school; a picture with more sentimental than commercial value.* — **sen·ti·men·tal·ly** *adv.* — **sen·ti·men·tal·ism** *n.*; **sen·ti·men·tal·ist** *n.*

sen·ti·men·tal·i·ty (SEN·tuh·mun·TAL·uh·tee) *n.* **-ties** too much sentiment or its expression: *maudlin, mawkish sentimentality.*

sen·ti·men·tal·ize (sen·tuh·MEN·tul·ize) *v.* **-iz·es, -ized, -iz·ing 1** make sentimental. **2** indulge in sentiment *about* or *over* a person or thing.

sen·ti·nel (SEN·tuh·nul) *n.* a sentry.

sen·try (SEN·tree) *n.* **-tries** a member of a military guard: *The sentry posted at the gate is relieved at night.*

sep·a·ra·ble (SEP·uh·ruh·bul) *adj.* capable of being separated. — **sep·a·ra·bly** *adv.*

sep·a·rate (SEP·uh·rit) *adj.* distinct from another; not together: *Keep them separate (from each other); seated at separate tables; They went their separate ways; the doctrine of separate but equal treatment of minorities in some countries.* — *n.* a blouse, skirt, pants, etc. for wearing in different combinations: *coordinated separates.* — *v.* (-rate) **-rates, -rat·ed, -rat·ing** (cause to) be apart; divide: *War separates families; She was separated from the group and got lost; a wall separating two apartments; The couple separated* (= decided to live apart). — **sep·a·rate·ly** (-rit·lee) *adv.* — **sep·a·ra·tion** (-RAY·shun) *n.*: *the painful separation of a married couple; the separation of church and state.*

separate school *n. Cdn.* a school or school system for children of a particular religious affiliation, often tax-supported, as Roman Catholic schools in Ontario: *a separate-school supporter.*

sep·a·ra·tist (SEP·uh·ruh·tist) *n.* a member of a group that wants to withdraw from a large, esp. political body: *The Quebec separatists want Quebec to withdraw from Confederation; Corsican separatists; Croatian separatists.* — **sep·a·ra·tism** *n.*

sep·a·ra·tor (SEP·uh·ray·tur) *n.* one that separates: *A centrifugal separator is used to separate cream from milk; A metal separator is used in garbage recycling.*

sep·tic *adj.* **1** resulting from or causing poisoning by disease germs: *He died of a septic wound.* **2** having to do with decay: *Sewage decomposes in a **septic tank** by bacterial action.*

se·pul·chral (suh·PUL·crul) *adj.* suggestive of the grave or burial: *sepulchral gloom, voices; a sepulchral* (= hollow and deep) *groan.*

sep·ul·chre or **sep·ul·cher** (SEP·ul·cur) *n.* a tomb.

sep·ul·ture (SEP·ul·chur) *n.* burial.

se·quel (SEEK·wul) *n.* something following or resulting from an earlier happening, as a continuation of a story with the same characters: *the sequels to "Anne of Green Gables."*

se·quence (SEEK·wunce) *n.* **1** an order of succession: *words in alphabetical sequence; Tell us what happened in chronological sequence; the natural sequence of events; The scenes lack sequence* (= continuity of progression). **2** a connected series: *Ace, King, and Queen form a sequence in cards; Any set of terms in a specific order is a mathematical sequence.* **3** an episode: *a movie sequence.*
— **se·quen·tial** (see·KWEN·shul) *adj.*; **se·quen·tial·ly** *adv.*

se·ques·ter (si·KWES·tur) *v.* **1** seclude: *the sequestered life of a convent.* **2** separate or remove: *to sequester oneself from worldly distractions; Jury members are sequestered* (= cut off from family, news, etc.) *during a trial.*

se·ques·tra·tion (seek·wes·TRAY·shun) *n.* **1** separation or isolation: *a life of sequestration.* **2** the temporary placing of a disputed property in the hands of a third party pending a court award.

sera a *pl.* of SERUM.

ser·e·nade (ser·uh·NADE) *n.* music played or sung by a lover under his sweetheart's window.
— *v.* **-nades, -nad·ed, -nad·ing** play or sing a serenade to someone.

ser·en·dip·i·ty (ser·un·DIP·uh·tee) *n.* **-ties 1** the gift for making fortunate discoveries when least expecting them. **2** such discovery: *Dictionary browsing offers the word lover opportunities for serendipity.*
— **ser·en·dip·i·tous** (-tus) *adj.*: *The (exploding star) Supernova 1987A was a serendipitous discovery for the Toronto astronomer Ian Shelton.*

se·rene (suh·REEN) *adj.* **1** calm and clear: *serene skies.* **2** calm and dignified: *a serene life, look, smile.* **3** Serene [used of or to royalty of certain countries]: *His, Her, Your Serene Highness.* — **se·rene·ly** *adv.*
— **se·rene·ness** or **se·ren·i·ty** (suh·REN·uh·tee) *n.*

serf (SURF) *n.* a feudal peasant bound to the soil and to the service of his lord. — **serf·dom** *n.*

ser·geant (SAR·junt) *n.* **1** a noncommissioned military officer ranking above corporal and below warrant officer, as in the Canadian Forces. **2** a police officer ranking above a constable: *In the Ontario Provincial Police, a sergeant ranks above a corporal.*

sergeant-at-arms (SAR·junt·ut·ARMZ) *n.* **sergeants-at-arms** an officer who keeps order in a legislature or court.

se·ri·al (SEER·ee·ul) *adj.* forming a series or succession with others: *serial murders by a **serial killer** (who kills one after another); a **serial novel** (appearing chapter by chapter in a publication); the serial number on a cheque; first **serial rights** (to publish a piece of writing*

first in a periodical); serial transmission of data bit by bit.
— *n.* a serial story or publication: *a TV serial (broadcast one part at a time).* — **se·ri·al·ly** *adv.*

se·ri·al·ize (SEER·ee·uh·lize) *v.* **-iz·es, -ized, -iz·ing** make serial: *to serialize a novel on TV.*
— **se·ri·al·i·za·tion** (-luh·ZAY·shun) *n.*

se·ries (SEER·eez) *n. sing. & pl.* a number of things or events connected with each other: *a series of accidents, lectures, publications; a TV series; an unbroken series.*

se·ri·ous (SEER·ee·us) *adj.* **1** showing or requiring earnestness: *He shows serious interest in his studies; She's serious about her duties; serious attention, consideration.* **2** important or grave: *He told the joke in a serious manner; Murder is a serious crime; a serious matter; serious damage to the car; It's deadly serious; a patient in serious but not critical condition.*
— **se·ri·ous·ly** *adv.*; **se·ri·ous·ness** *n.*

ser·mon (SUR·mun) *n.* **1** a religious or moral talk usually based on Scripture: *Christ's **Sermon on the Mount** contains the Lord's Prayer.* **2** any moralistic talk: *The minister says he doesn't preach sermons but delivers homilies.*
— **ser·mon·ize** *v.* **-iz·es, -ized, -iz·ing**: *Please stop sermonizing and start working.*

ser·pent (SUR·punt) *n.* a big snake, thought of as sly and treacherous.

ser·pen·tine (SUR·pun·teen, -tine) *adj.* like a serpent; twisted, cunning, etc.

ser·rate (SER·ate) *adj.* having a saw-toothed edge, as certain leaves; also **ser·rat·ed.**
— **ser·ra·tion** (suh·RAY·shun) *n.*

ser·ried (SER·eed) *adj.* in close order: *soldiers in serried ranks.*

ser·vant (SUR·vunt) *n.* **1** a person employed in household work: *a domestic, faithful, loyal, trusted servant.* **2** a person in the service of a government: *a civil servant; public servant.*

serve (SURV) *v.* **serves, served, serv·ing 1** carry out duties; function: *People serve as teachers, on juries, at (the) table, under supervisors, with their colleagues; Store clerks serve* (= help) *customers; Soldiers serve* (= work) *in the army; A stick will serve* (= satisfy) *our purpose; It serves to remind them of discipline; His illness served as an excuse.* **2** put a ball or similar thing in play: *It's my turn to serve; He always serves to the weaker opponent.* **3** supply food, needs, etc.: *time to serve lunch; enough food to serve four people; a community well served with health care; Being ticketed for speeding seemed to **serve him right**.* **4** undergo: *She has to serve three years as an apprentice; He has served his term in jail.* **5** present an order, warrant, etc.: *The typist served notice (on her boss) that she was quitting; He was served with a summons to appear in court.*
— *n.* a serving of a ball or similar thing: *an underhand serve; a serve to the backhand.* — **serv·er** *n.*

serv·ice (SUR·vis) *n.* **1** the function or occupation of serving: *He was on active service in World War II; She's in the Federal Service; meritorious, military, public, regular, slow, yeoman service; to introduce, restore*

service; This car will give good service for five years; Our china has seen plenty of service (= been put to much use) *over the years; civil, customer, door-to-door, express, professional service; diplomatic, intelligence, secret service; a medal for distinguished service; I am* **at your service** (= ready to serve or be of use); *He applied to be* **of service** *as a cook; to* **pay lip service** (= give the appearance of agreeing). **2** what is produced by serving, as work, benefit, etc.: *We offer, provide service with a smile; to do, hold, perform, render, suspend a service; an ambulance, answering, burial, bus, dating, delivery, employment, ferry, janitorial, laundry, limousine, news, placement, postal, repair, room, telephone, towing, wire service; to break, lose one's service* (= opening play in a game); *a funeral, marriage, prayer service* (= ceremony); *a bill for services rendered by a professional;* **adj.:** *a service industry; the service sector; a goods-and-services tax.* **3** a set of dishes, spoons, etc. used for serving food: *coffee, dinner, silver, tea service.*
— *v.* **-ic·es, -iced, -ic·ing** do work on something or for someone: *to service a car; A heifer is said to be serviced* (= made to copulate with) *by a bull.*
— *adj.:* *the service area (at a gas station); service centre (for highway travellers); a service charge for processing a cheque; A bank is a* **service company** *(that sells a service, not a product); a service contract; a* **service line** *(from which a ball is served); her service record; a* **service road** (= an access road or a road parallel to an expressway).

serv·ice·a·ble (SUR·vuh·suh·bul) *adj.* useful or durable.

serv·ice·man (SUR·vis·man, -mun) or **serv·ice·wom·an** (SUR·vis·woom·un) *n., pl.* **-men** or **-wom·en 1** a person in military service. **2** one who maintains and repairs machines, appliances, etc.

service module *n.* part of a manned aircraft between the landing module and command module, containing the propulsion, retrofire, and thrust systems.

service station *n.* a facility for supplying gas and repair services to motorists.

servicewoman See SERVICEMAN.

ser·vile (SUR·vile) *adj.* **1** of or like a slave. **2** cringing or submissive. — **ser·vil·i·ty** (sur·VIL·uh·tee) *n.*

serv·ing *n.* a portion or helping of food: *a generous, liberal, second, small serving; a serving of fish.*

ser·vi·tude (SUR·vuh·tude) *n.* bondage or slavery: *a life of servitude* (= forced labour); *penal servitude* (= prison with hard labour).

ses·sion (SESH·un) *n.* the sitting or assembly of a group of people to discuss, deliberate, learn, etc., as of a court, legislature, school, etc., esp. its duration: *a long morning session on safety; during the afternoon session; a briefing, bull, jam, joint, plenary, practice, rap, special, summer, winter, working session; They met in secret sessions; A new session of the Canadian Parliament starts with a Throne Speech; The court is* **in session** *from 10 a.m.* — **ses·sion·al** *adj.*

set *v.* **sets, set, set·ting 1** put or place with a purpose, direction, or in a certain manner or condition: *She set the flowers on the table; He set a match to the dry grass, paper, and kindling; The house was set on fire; styles set in Paris; a ladder set against a wall; Compositors used to*

set type for printing; A manuscript is set in type; a manner that sets everyone at ease; What value do you set on the missing diamond? He loved her from the moment he set his eyes on her; She has her **sights set on** (= She aspires to) *a Ph.D.* **2** assign: *to set a task; She set them to write an essay.* **3** arrange: *to set the table for dinner; Let's set a date for the meeting; to set the stage for a performance; to set a trap for mice; a sonnet set* (= adapted) *to music.* **4** (cause) to be firm or settled in position: *Concrete sets in a mould; to set hair in a perm; The doctor set the broken bone.* **5** go down: *The sun sets in the west.* **6** make (a hen) sit on eggs for hatching; also, sit.
— **set about** or **to** begin: *She set about writing her thesis; As soon as they had been served, the kids set to* (= began eating).
— **set apart** distinguish: *Speech sets humans apart from animals.*
— **set aside 1** put away money, etc. *for* a purpose. **2** reject, as a decision by a higher court.
— **set forth** make known views, plans, etc.
— **set in** of an undesirable condition, begin and continue: *A disease, bad weather, infection, rot sets in.*
— **set off 1** cause something to be suddenly active: *to set off an alarm, bomb, chain reaction, crisis, fireworks, riot; The shooting set off violence in the streets.* **2** begin, as on a journey: *He sets off for work at 8 a.m. every day; They set off on a spending spree.*
— **set on** or **upon** attack: *He was set upon by hoodlums.*
— **set out 1** begin: *to set out for work in the morning; Let's finish what we set out to do.* **2** arrange or spread: *goods set out for viewing; to set out breakfast on the patio.*
— **set sail** leave by ship: *to set sail for Europe.*
— **set up** erect; put up or establish: *a roadblock set up by police; to set up in business; to set up practice as a lawyer; to set up shop; to set up* (= raise) *a cry or shout.*
— *n.* **1** a group or collection of persons or things belonging together: *to belong to the fast, international, jet, smart set; a set of numbers; to lose, play, win a set (of games); a dining-room set (of furniture); a dinner set (of dishes); to break (up), make (up) a set; a carving, chemistry, chess, geometry, tea set; a radio, transistor, TV set* (= assembled equipment). **2** the scenery of a play or motion picture: *to dismantle a set.* **3** the way in which something is formed or forming: *the set of his shoulders; the mind-set of our youth; the set of public opinion on the subject.*
— *adj.* fixed or established: *a set piece (of literature) for recitation; a man of set views; a set time for everything; He is set* (= intent) *on winning; She is dead set against drinking; We are* **all set** (= ready or prepared) *for takeoff, to begin; Get ready, get set, go!*

set·back *n.* a reversal of or check to progress: *to have, receive, suffer a setback; a business, financial, political setback.*

setting *n.* **1** what is set, as eggs that a hen sits on for hatching, the music for a poem or other text, or dishes or silverware for one person at a table: *place settings for 12 guests; to adjust the setting of a thermostat.* **2** what something is set in, as the mounting of a jewel, or the time, place, and surroundings of a play or story: *a natural, romantic, stage setting.*

set·tle (SET·ul) *v.* **set·tles, set·tled, set·tling 1** reach a final decision or agreement *with* a party, *for* something, or *on* a time, place, or plan: *The strikers settled for a 10% raise; an argument that is hard to settle peacefully; We'll try to settle the case out of court; There are accounts to be settled* (= paid) *before leaving; The property was divided and **settled on** or **upon** his children* (= formally given to them). 2 (cause) to take up residence: *Immigrants settle in Canada; The government tries to settle doctors in rural areas; The French settled* (= colonized) *Quebec.* 3 establish oneself or itself: *It takes time to settle into a new job; Marriage helps youth **settle down** (in life); School helped them settle down to study, into a new routine; It was 1 a.m. when they settled down* (= came to rest) *for the night; Some old people are too **settled*** (= established) *in their ways.* 4 (cause) to be in a more stable, composed, or compact state: *A tranquillizer will settle your nerves; Rains help settle (loose) dust; Dust settles* (= comes to rest) *on everything; A new house settles (in its foundation).*

set·tle·ment (SET·ul·munt) *n.* 1 a settling, as an agreement or its terms, bestowal of property on someone, etc.: *to come to, make, negotiate, reach a settlement; a fair, lump-sum, marriage, out-of-court, tentative settlement.* 2 a being settled, as a colony or colonization. 3 a social institution or welfare centre for improvement of living conditions.

set·to (SET·too) *n.* -tos *Informal.* a fight or argument.

set·up *n.* what is set up, as an arrangement, plan, etc.

sev·en (SEV·un) *n., adj. & pron.* one more than six; the number 7 or VII: *seven boys and girls; There are seven of them; They are seven in all.*
— **sev·enth** *n., adj. & adv.*: *the seventh in line; He is seventh; He came seventh.*

seven seas *n.pl.* all the oceans of the world.

seventh heaven *n.* a state of bliss or extreme happiness.

sev·en·ty (SEV·un·tee) *n., adj. & pron., n.pl.* -ties 1 seven times ten; 70 or LXX. 2 **the seventies** the numbers, years, etc. from 70 through 79.
— **sev·en·ti·eth** (-tee·ith) *n. & adj.*

sev·er (SEV·ur) *v.* cut off: *to sever a branch, communication line, connection, rope; a limb that has been severed* (= separated) *from the body.*

sev·er·al (SEV·ur·ul) *adj.* 1 more than two; a few: *several times, people.* 2 different; separate: *They went their several ways; a joint and several liability.*
— *pron.* some: *Several of us were present; I saw several (of the kind mentioned).*

sev·er·al·ly (SEV·ur·uh·lee) *adv.* individually or separately: *Makers are held jointly and severally responsible for a product.*

sev·er·ance (SEV·ur·unce) *n.* a severing or separation: *severance of relations; the **severance pay** given on termination of employment.*

se·vere (suh·VEER) *adj.* -ver·er, -ver·est 1 strict or rigorous: *a severe test of endurance; severe looks, reasoning.* 2 hard to endure: *a severe attack, headache, illness, scolding; severe weather conditions; a severe* (= violent) *storm.* — **se·vere·ly** *adv.*
— **se·ver·i·ty** (suh·VER·uh·tee) *n.* -ties.

sew (SOH) *v.* sews, *pt.* sewed, *pp.* sewn or sewed,

sew·ing 1 fasten with stitches: *to sew pages together to make a book; to sew buttons on a shirt.* 2 make by sewing: *to sew a book, buttonhole, shirt.*
— **sew up** close with stitches: *to sew up a seam, torn shirt, wound; We had the game all **sewed up*** (= made certain) *by the third quarter.* — **sew·er** *n.*

sew·age (SOO·ij) *n.* waste matter carried in sewers and drains: *raw, treated, untreated sewage.*

sew·er (SOO·ur) *n.* a pipe or drain, usually underground, for water and wastes: *a sanitary sewer; storm sewers.*

sew·er·age (SOO·ur·ij) *n.* 1 a sewer system. 2 sewage.

sewing (SOH·ing) *n.* 1 something sewn or to be sewn by hand or with a machine, or **sewing machine.** 2 the occupation.

sex *n.* 1 the male-female distinction: *discrimination based on age and sex; the fair sex* (= women); *members of the opposite sex* (= male or female group). 2 sexual activity, esp. intercourse: *explicit sex in films; illicit sex; premarital sex; all the sex and violence on TV; the joys of sex; Spouses **have sex with** each other; adj.: sex drive, education, functions, organs, test for athletes; people with **sex appeal*** (= sexual attractiveness).
— *v.* to identify the sex of an animal: *to sex chicks, herring.* — **sex·er** *n.*

sex·ism *n.* prejudice or discrimination based on sex, esp. against women.
— **sex·ist** *n. & adj.*: *a sexist attitude, bias, comment, remark; a male-dominated sexist society.*

sex·ploi·ta·tion (sex·ploy·TAY·shun) *n.* exploitation of sex, esp. in movies and commercials.

sex symbol *n.* an entertainer noted for sex appeal.

sex·u·al (SEK·shoo·ul) *adj.* having to do with sex: *sexual behaviour, intercourse, morality, reproduction, revolution; sexual relations* (= intercourse); ***sexual assault*** (= rape, attempted rape, or molestation).
— **sex·u·al·ly** *adv.* — **sex·u·al·i·ty** (-AL·uh·tee) *n.*

sex·y (SEK·see) *adj.* sex·i·er, -i·est *Informal.* sexually stimulating or provocative: *a sexy design, dress, movie; Jan's sexy image.* — **sex·i·ly** *adv.*; **sex·i·ness** *n.*

sh *interj.* hush!

shab·by (SHAB·ee) *adj.* shab·bi·er, shab·bi·est 1 in a much-worn, poor, or run-down condition: *shabby clothes, interiors; a shabby-looking man.* 2 unworthy or mean: *rather shabby treatment.*
— **shab·bi·ly** *adv.*; **shab·bi·ness** *n.*

shack *n.* 1 a small, crude dwelling: *a dilapidated, run-down, tar-papered shack.* 2 room: *a ham operator's basement radio shack.*
— *v.* **shack up** *Informal.* cohabit: *Jack shacks up with Jill.*

shack·le (SHACK·ul) *n.* 1 a manacle or fetter; hence, any restraint: *The slaves threw off their **shackles** and regained freedom.* 2 a fastening or coupling device.
— *v.* shack·les, shack·led, shack·ling restrain with shackles: *a prisoner with his legs shackled; the shackling of press freedom.*

shade *n.* 1 a place that is not in direct light and heat,

esp. of the sun: *to rest in the shade of a tree.* **2** a partly dark condition or relative obscurity: *the lights and shades of a picture; the shades* (= darkness) *of evening; He was* **put in** or **into the shade** (= surpassed) *by his more brilliant brother.* **3** a device to control light, as of a lamp, or to shut out light, as used over a window: *a window shade; to draw, drop, lift, lower, pull down, raise the shades.* **4** gradation of colour: *Maroon is a shade of red; a delicate, dark, light, pale, pastel, soft shade; many shades* (= slight differences) *of meaning; a shade of doubt, fear; One degree Celsius is* **a shade** (= slightly) *above freezing point.* **5 shades** *pl. Informal.* sunglasses: *a movie star hiding behind his shades;* **Shades of** *Chernobyl* (= This reminds one of what happened at Chernobyl)!
— *v.* **shades, shad·ed, shad·ing 1** screen from light: *The hat's wide brim shades her eyes from the sun.* **2** make dark or darker in lighting or colouring: *Shade it a little; The picture needs a little* **shading** (= filling in) *to show darkness.* **3** change little by little, as into a different shade: *The red patches shade off* (= merge) *into pink.*

shad·ow (SHAD·oh) *n.* **1** the shade cast by an object blocking the light: *the shadow of a dog; Shadows fall on the ground; The dog saw its own shadow* (= image) *in the water; to cast, produce, throw a shadow; He walks in her shadow* (= is close to her or under her influence). **2** anything unsubstantial or ghostlike: *Ill health has made him a mere shadow of his former self; his master's shadow* (= follower); *a* **shadow cabinet** (*of opposition members, each studying the work of a real cabinet member*). **3** a shaded area, as in a picture; hence, darkness or gloom: *The death cast a shadow on his life.* **4** slight trace: *beyond the* or *a shadow of a doubt; He likes to shave again in the evening to get rid of the* **five o'clock shadow** (= fresh growth of facial hair).
— *v.* **1** cast a shadow on a person or thing. **2** follow or watch unobserved: *He was being shadowed by the secret police.*
— **shad·ow·y** *adj.* indistinct: *a shadowy figure; the shadowy world of spies.*

shadow-box (SHAD·oh·box) *v.* to box with an imaginary opponent for training or exercise.

shad·y (SHAY·dee) *adj.* **shad·i·er, -i·est 1** in the shade or giving shade. **2** *Informal.* dishonest: *a shady character, deal.*

shaft *n.* **1** a long handle or stem: *the shaft of an arrow, spear.* **2** a dart or similar thrown missile: *shafts of ridicule, wit.* **3** a beam of light: *a shaft of lightning.* **4** a polelike, round, often hollow bar; also, a structure or passage resembling it: *the drive shaft of a car connected to the axles; the shaft of a mine; to bore, sink a shaft; An elevator moves in a shaft.*
— **get the shaft** *Informal.* get unfairly treated.
— *v. Informal.* cheat or trick: *He got shafted in the deal; a politician shafted* (= unfairly dealt with) *by the media.*

shag *n.* **1** cloth, carpet, etc. with long, rough nap. **2** a mass of coarse hair, fibre, or finely shredded tobacco.
— *v.* **shags, shagged, shag·ging** chase after and return a ball when it goes out of play.

shag·gy (SHAG·ee) *adj.* **shag·gi·er, shag·gi·est 1** looking unkempt or needing a shave or haircut.

2 covered with rough coarse fibre or hair: *shaggy eyebrows; a shaggy dog.*

shaggy dog story *n. Informal.* a long story ending in a sudden anticlimax; a dumb joke.

shake *v.* **shakes, shook** (short "oo"), **shak·en, shak·ing 1** (cause to) move jerkily up and down or back and forth: *They shook hands* (= clasped each other's hands in greeting, in congratulation, in agreement); *They shook hands on the deal; Shake the bottle before use; to shake (dust from) a rug; She shook her head* (= said "No"); *swore and shook her fists at him.* **2** (cause to) tremble or totter; hence, waver or weaken: *Earthquakes shake a building; Nothing could shake his faith in his leader; A visibly shaken premier announced the bad news; The news shook* (= upset) *the nation.*
— **shake down 1** get by shaking, as fruit from a tree. **2** *Slang.* extort money from a victim. **3** cause to settle down; hence, get adjusted or accustomed.
— **shake off** get rid of something: *to shake off a sense of dread, a feeling of exhaustion.*
— *n.* a shaking or something shaken: *Give the rug a good shake; She ordered a shake* (= milkshake); *He has got* **the shakes** (= a trembling disease); *I want a fair shake* (*Informal* for fair deal); *He's* **no (great) shakes** (*Informal* for not especially good) *as a journalist.*

shake·down *n.* **1** *Slang.* extortion of money, as by graft. **2** a getting adjusted or accustomed, as of new equipment, of people to a new environment, etc.; *adj.:* *a shakedown* (= test) *cruise, flight.*

shake·out *n.* a reorganization, as in a business or industry, which results in the survival of only the best.

shak·er (SHAY·kur) *n.* **1** one who shakes: *the movers and shakers* (= people who influence events) *in Canada's foreign policy.* **2** a container used for shaking or shaking out something: *a cocktail shaker; a salt shaker; sugar shaker.*

shake·up *n.* a drastic reorganization, esp. of personnel.

shak·y (SHAY·kee) *adj.* **shak·i·er, -i·est** weak, not firm: *a shaky foundation, partnership, table, voice.*
— **shak·i·ly** *adv.*

shall (SHAL) *auxiliary v., pt.* **should** (SHOOD – short "OO" *or* shud) *Formal.* **1** [expressing future time in the first person]: *I shall be away on business; We shall see.* **2** [expressing necessity or obligation]: *You shall not smoke; She shall be your boss; They shall not pass; Should I give up smoking? You should not have done that.*

shal·low (SHAL·oh) *adj.* **1** not deep: *a shallow dish; shallow water.* **2** superficial; lacking depth of mind or character.
— **shallows** *n.pl.* [takes sing. or pl. v.] the shallow part of a body of water.

sha·lom (shah·LOME) *n. & interj.* [used as a Hebrew greeting] peace!

shalt [old form, used with "thou"] shall.

sham *n.* a false or fake person or thing.
— *v.* **shams, shammed, sham·ming** feign or pretend.
— **sham·mer** *n.*

sham·ble *v.* **-bles, -bled, -bling** walk awkwardly; shuffle.

— **n. 1** a shambling gait. **2 shambles** *n.pl.* [takes sing. v.] scene of disorder or destruction: *The room was turned into a shambles; They made a shambles of it; The economy is in (a) shambles.*

shame *n.* a feeling of great dishonour or disgrace; also, a cause of such feeling: *What a shame! Shame on you! You're a shame to your profession; It's a shame to behave or that you behave like that; You've brought shame on or to or upon your family; We felt shame at his behaviour; an awful, bloody, crying, dirty shame; He hung his head in shame; He'll remember this day to his eternal shame; Her cheeks burned with shame.*
— **put to shame 1** make ashamed. **2** surpass.
— **v. shames, shamed, sham·ing** make ashamed; hence, disgrace: *He was shamed into admitting defeat; He was shamed out of his position.*
— **shame·ful** *adj.*; **shame·ful·ly** *adv.*; **shame·ful·ness** *n.*

shame·faced *adj.* **1** bashful. **2** showing shame.
— **shame·fac·ed·ly** (shame·FAY·sid·lee) *adv.*

sham·poo (sham·POO) *n.* **1** a soaplike preparation for washing the hair and scalp. **2** a shampooing.
— **v. -poos, -pooed, -poo·ing 1** use shampoo on the hair or wash the hair of a person with shampoo. **2** clean a rug with liquid soap. — **sham·poo·er** *n.*

shank *n.* **1** part of the human leg between knee and ankle; also, a corresponding part in animals. **2** in a tool, device, etc., a connecting or essential part, usually straight, as a shaft, stem, or handle: *the shank of a fish hook; the shank* (= side) *of a shoe; the shank end* (= early part) *of the afternoon.*

shan't shall not.

shape *n.* outline or form, esp. of something having mass and bulk; configuration: *the shape of an S, a boat, a pear; The god Proteus could appear in* or *assume different shapes; Customers come in all shapes and sizes; In* **no way, shape, or form** (= by no means) *would he join the family business; Ideas* **take shape** *as realities; He keeps* **in shape** (= in good condition) *by lifting weights; exercises to help you* **get into shape;** *She's in good, excellent shape* (= condition) *for a 60-year-old; I'm in no shape to go back to work.*
— **v. shapes, shaped, shap·ing** make in a particular shape: *a statue shaped out of marble; experiences that shape one's character; The employee was told to* **shape up** (= perform satisfactorily) *or ship out.*

shape·ly *adj.* **-li·er, -li·est** having a pleasing shape: *a shapely dress, figure, jacket, leg, model.*

shard *n.* **1** potsherd. **2** any fragment: *The bomb scattered steel shards over a wide area; They endured many* **shards and barbs** (= trials) *on the road to freedom.*

share *n.* **1** a part or portion belonging to or done by one: *your share of the loot; a share of the blame, burden, credit, market, responsibility; Each girl did her share; received a share of the profits; an equal, fair, full, large, lion's, major share; the shares* (of ownership) *held by each stockholder, or* **share·hold·er,** *of a corporation.* **2** a ploughshare.
— **v. shares, shared, shar·ing** use or have something among a group or with others: *three girls sharing a prize; She shared the prize with them; The prize was shared among them; Everyone shared* (= took part) *in*

the celebrations; profit sharing by employees; revenue sharing by the provinces.

shark *n.* **1** a usually large, meat-eating ocean fish with a torpedolike body, reputed to attack humans. **2** one who ruthlessly exploits others: *a card shark; loan sharks.*

sharp *adj.* **1** having a thin cutting edge or fine point: *a sharp knife, pencil; a sharp* (= pointed) *nose; a sharp* (= abrupt) *turn.* **2** pricking or biting: *a sharp taste; sharp words; sharp* (= cold) *weather.* **3** shrill or high-pitched: *a sharp cry of pain; a sharp musical note (half a tone above natural pitch).* **4** having qualities of keenness, quickness, smartness, etc.: *sharp desire, ears; a sharp lawyer; sharp* (= smart) *clothes.* **5** clear-cut: *a sharp contrast; in sharp relief.*
— **n. 1** a musical note or tone raised above its normal pitch by a half tone. **2** the symbol ( ) used to indicate such a note or tone: *a symphony in the key of C sharp.*
— **v.** raise by one half tone; also, sound such a note.
— **adv.** in a sharp manner: *at 8 p.m. sharp; to sing sharp* (= above the correct pitch); *Look sharp* (= watch out)! Also **sharp·ly** *adv.* — **sharp·ness** *n.*

sharp-tongued *adj.* harsh or severely critical in speech.

sharp-witted (SHARP·wit·id) *adj.* having a keen mind and quick tongue.

shat·ter (SHAT·ur) *v.* break into scattering pieces: *Safety glass will not shatter if broken; Her hopes and dreams were shattered; a shattering experience; It was a shattering blow to his pride.*
— **shat·ter·proof** (SHAT·ur·proof) *adj.*

shave *v.* **shaves,** *pt. & pp.* **shaved** or **shav·en, shav·ing 1** remove hair from the face with a razor: *He shaves daily; shaves himself; shaves off his beard; Barbers shave customers; Women shave their legs.* **2** slice ham, etc. thin: *a plane for shaving wood; Wood and pencil* **shavings** (= thin pieces or slices that have been shaved off) *litter the floor.* **3** graze a surface or pass very close to it: *The bullet shaved his leg.*
— **n.** an act or result of shaving: *He has a shave and a shower in the morning; shaves of beef; That was a close shave* (= narrow escape).

she (SHEE) *n. & pron., objective* HER, *possessive* HERS, *pl.* THEY, *objective* THEM, *possessive* THEIR(S) the female human or animal referred to; also, a person or thing thought of as female: *She is their queen; Is the puppy a he or a she? There she* (= the whale) *blows!*

sheaf (SHEEF) *n.* **sheaves** a bundle: *a sheaf of arrows, papers; a sheaf of wheat* (= stalks cut and bound).

shear (SHEER) *v.* **shears,** *pt. & pp.* **sheared** or **shorn, shear·ing 1** strip a sheep of its wool; also, cut off wool: *shorn sheep, wool.* **2** deprive of something: *Samson shorn of his strength; a dictator shorn of his powers.* **3** cut or break by the action of two forces sliding in opposite directions, as causes materials to split into layers: *shearing force, stress; A truck sideswiped the car shearing off the left side doors.*
— *n.* **1** a shearing or a blade of a pair of **shears** (= large scissors): *pinking, pruning, sheep shears; tin shears (for cutting tin).* **2** a shearing force or stress: *a plane crash caused by wind shear.*

sheath (SHEETH, "TH" as in "thin") *n.* **1** a case for the blade of a knife. **2** a similar covering over a cat's claw or the base of a grass's leaf that wraps around its stem. **3** a woman's straight, close-fitting dress.

sheathe (SHEETH, "TH" as in "the") *v.* **sheathes, sheathed, sheath·ing** put into or enclose in a sheath.

she·bang (shuh·BANG) *n. Informal.* business; affair; outfit: *Pat was made head of **the whole shebang.***

she'd (SHEED) she had; she would.

shed *n.* a one-storey structure sometimes open on one side, used for shelter or storage: *a garden, railway, tool, wood shed.*
— *v.* **sheds, shed, shed·ding 1** let drop or fall: *to shed tears; Snakes shed* (= cast off) *their skin; We shed* (= remove and leave) *our coats at the door; a revolution achieved without **shedding blood*** (= killing). **2** give forth; send out: *The sun sheds light; to shed light on* (= clear up) *a mystery; She sheds joy around her.*

sheen *n.* the shiny quality of satin, silk, etc.; soft lustre: *polished to a high sheen; the silky sheen of her hair.*
— **sheen·y** *adj.*

sheep *n. sing. & pl.* **1** an animal related to the goat, raised for its wool, milk, and meat, i.e. mutton and lamb. **2** one considered meek and submissive, like sheep being shorn; hence, a mindless follower, esp. as one of a group.

sheep·ish *adj.* bashful or embarrassed: *a sheepish grin, smile.* — **sheep·ish·ly** *adv.*

sheep·skin *n.* **1** the skin of a sheep. **2** leather or parchment made from it; hence, *Informal.* a diploma.

sheer *v.* swerve or deviate, as a ship from its course: *to sheer away from, sheer off something.*
— *adj.* **1** very thin or transparent: *a sheer fabic such as chiffon; sheer drapes, nylons.* **2** pure or unmixed: *sheer determination, folly, ignorance, luck, nonsense, poppycock.* **3** very steep; precipitous: *sheer cliffs; a sheer rock face.*
— *n.* a sheer fabric, garment, etc.: *voile **sheers*** (= sheer curtains) *for the window.*
— *adv.* directly; also, steeply.

sheet *n.* **1** a broad, thin piece of material or something resembling it: *bed sheets; white as a sheet; to change sheets for a new guest (when making a bed); a sheet of glass, ice, paper, water; a company's balance sheet; The police officer made out a charge sheet; a **scandal sheet*** (= sensational newspaper); *The rain came down **in sheets*** (= as masses of water).

sheeting *n.* material for covering or lining purposes.

sheet lightning *n.* lightning seen in broad flashes from beyond the horizon.

sheet metal *n.* thin-rolled sheets of metal.

sheet music *n.* music printed on unbound sheets of paper.

shelf *n.* **shelves** (SHELVZ) **1** a board attached at a height horizontally to a wall or inside a cabinet for holding things, as books in a bookcase: *to put up shelves; a room with built-in shelves; shelves stocked with books.* **2** a ledge of rocks, esp. one under water: *the continental shelf off the Atlantic coast.*
— **on the shelf** put aside as useless.

shelf life *n.* how long a packaged product will keep if stored.

she'll (SHEEL) she will; she shall.

shell *n.* **1** the hard outer covering of oysters, snails, and other molluscs, insects such as beetles, and of turtles, eggs, seeds, and nuts. **2** a shell-like outer covering, as the framework of a house or ship, a sleeveless pullover blouse, or the case of a pie: *a **shell company** that exists only in name.* **3** a racing rowboat. **4** a hollow artillery projectile; also, a cartridge case for a shotgun or other small arms: *to lob shells into enemy territory; to fire shells at enemy ships.*
— *v.* **1** remove the shell or husk: *to shell nuts.* **2** bombard with artillery shells.
— **shell out** *Informal.* pay or hand out an amount of money, candy, etc.: *We start shelling out candy soon after dusk on Halloween.*

shel·lac (shuh·LAC) *n.* **1** varnish made of refined lac dried into flakes and dissolved in alcohol. **2** lac used in sealing wax and moulded articles.
— *v.* **shel·lacs, shel·lacked, shel·lack·ing 1** varnish with shellac. **2** *Informal.* thrash; also, beat decisively: *to get, give, take a **shellacking*** (= thrashing or defeat).

shell·fish *n.* an oyster, clam, lobster, etc. that is not a true fish.

shell game *n.* a dishonestly played game involving substitution; hence, a cheating or swindle.

shell shock *n.* nervous breakdown resulting from battlefield experiences.

shel·ter (SHEL·tur) *n.* a roof or other cover for protection from the elements or a specific threat: *food, clothing, and shelter; a bomb, bus, fall-out shelter; Get under shelter when bombs start falling; to afford, give, offer, provide shelter; shelter for the homeless; to find, take shelter from the rain; the shelter of a roof, of an umbrella; a tax shelter* (= investment made to get a tax advantage).
— *v.* protect or provide a shelter for a person or thing: *to shelter a child from evil influences; We sheltered* (= found shelter) *under the trees.*
— **sheltered** *adj.* protected: *a sheltered spot; the sheltered life of a convent; a life of sheltered ease; a tax-sheltered investment.*

shelve *v.* **shelves, shelved, shelv·ing 1** put something on a shelf: *Leave the books for the librarian to shelve.* **2** put off or put aside: *The plans were shelved because of lack of funds.* **3** furnish with shelves.

shelves *pl.* of SHELF.

shelving *n.* boards, posts, etc. for putting up shelves.

she·nan·i·gans (shuh·NAN·uh·gunz) *n.pl. Informal.* mischievous, devious, or tricky behaviour; monkey business.

shep·herd (SHEP·urd) *n.* one who tends sheep; *fem.* **shep·herd·ess.**
— *v.* herd or look after as a shepherd: *a teacher shepherding children across a street.*

sher·iff *n.* 1 in Canada, an official who serves summonses, maintains order in the courts, and executes judgments. 2 in the U.S., the chief law-enforcement officer of a county.

sher·ry (SHER·ee) *n.* **sher·ries** a usually yellowish-to-brown fortified wine.

she's (SHEEZ) she is; she has.

shew (SHOW) *n. & v.* **shews,** *pt.* **shewed,** *pp.* **shewed** or **shewn, shew·ing** [old use] same as SHOW.

shib·bo·leth (SHIB·uh·luth) *n.* a custom or usage, esp. in language, narrowly applied as a criterion of membership in a particular class or faction; a test word or password.

shied *pt. & pp.* of SHY.

shield (SHEELD) *n.* a piece of armour held in one hand for protection in battle.
— *v.* protect or defend with or as if with a shield: *She shielded her child from the falling debris; to shield someone against attack; He tried to shield his accomplice by giving false evidence.*

shier, shiest See SHY.

shift *v.* change location, position, or direction in an unstable or restless manner; move: *The wind has shifted to northeast; He kept shifting in his chair nervously; shifted his weight from one leg to the other; We shift into top gear for cruising; He tried to shift (the) blame to his employees; Now you're shifting your ground* (= changing the basis of your reasoning); *He had to* **shift** *for himself* (= take care of himself) *without a home or friends.*
— *n.* 1 change: *a shift in the wind; to bring about a shift in attitudes, policy; a shift of interest, responsibility; Press the* **shift key** *to type capitals.* 2 a group or period in which people work in a relay system: *He works the day shift; Everyone works an eight-hour shift; the graveyard, night, split, swing shift.* 3 a gearshift: *an automatic shift; a manual, standard, stick shift.* 4 a sheathlike but beltless dress; also, a slip: *She stood there in nothing but her shift.*
— **make shift** manage as best one can with available resources.

shift·less *adj.* lazy.

shift·y *adj.* **shift·i·er, -i·est** evasive or tricky: *shifty behaviour, looks.*

shil·ly-shal·ly (SHIL·ee·shal·ee) *v.* **-shal·lies, -shal·lied, -shal·ly·ing** dawdle over a decision.

shim·mer (SHIM·ur) 1 *n.* a wavering or unsteady light; glimmer. 2 *v.* shine with a shimmer: *The lake shimmered in the moonlight.* — **shim·mer·y** *adj.*

shim·my (SHIM·ee) *v.* **shim·mies, shim·mied,**

shim·my·ing 1 shake or wobble, as the front wheels of an automobile that need balancing. 2 dance with shaking movements.
— *n.* 1 a shaking or vibration. 2 a jazz dance of the 1920s.

shin *n.* the front of the leg between the knee and the ankle: *Al barked* or *scraped his shins trying to climb trees.*
— *v.* **shins, shinned, shin·ning** climb *up* a tree trunk, pole, etc. using hands and legs.

shin·dig *n. Informal.* a large and lively social gathering.

shine *v.* **shines, shone** (SHON), **shin·ing** 1 send out or reflect light, as the sun, moon, lights, etc.: *The sun is shining; Shine the lights* (= make the lights shine) *on the dark side of the house.* 2 be brilliant or conspicuous in some respect, at some skill, etc.: *The sun shines on the rich and the poor; He shines at math; a* **shining** *example of self-sacrifice.* 3 [*pt.* usually **shined**] make shiny; polish: *Jon shines shoes.*
— *n.* brightness; brilliance; also, gloss: *Jon will give you a shine* (= will shine your shoes).
— **take a shine to** *Informal.* become fond of someone.

shin·er (SHY·nur) *n. Slang.* a black eye.

shin·gle (SHING·gul) *n.* 1 a flat, thin piece of wood or other material laid in overlapping rows to cover roofs or walls: *a* **shingled** *roof.* 2 *Informal.* a small sign as used by a physician or other professional: *The young lawyer hung out* or *up her shingle and started her practice.* 3 a woman's short haircut tapered at the nape. 4 small well-rounded pebbles or a beach covered with them: *children playing in the shingle;* **shin·gly** *adj.* 5 **shingles** *sing. & pl.* a painful skin disease characterized by blisters: *to develop shingles.*

shin·ny *v.* **shin·nies, shin·nied, shin·ny·ing** same as SHIN.

shin·splints *n.pl.* [takes sing. v.] strain or injury to lower leg muscles from running on hard surfaces.

shin·y (SHY·nee) *adj.* **shin·i·er, -i·est** bright or shining; also, polished: *Put some powder on that shiny nose; a shiny new penny.*

-ship *n. suffix.* state or condition: *authorship, fellowship; readership* (= group of readers); *workmanship* (= skill of a worker).

ship *n.* 1 a large seagoing vessel: *to board, build, christen, launch, load, navigate, refit, sail, scuttle, sink, torpedo, unload a ship; to disembark from a ship; to abandon ship* (when it is sinking); *to raise a sunken ship; to jump ship* (= desert from a ship's crew); *a capital, cruise, hospital, merchant, passenger, sailing, supply ship; The boss runs a tight ship* (= operates efficiently). 2 the officers and crew of a ship. 3 an aircraft or spacecraft: *a lunar ship; the rocket ships of science fiction.*
— **when your ship comes in** or **comes home** when you become rich.
— *v.* **ships, shipped, ship·ping** 1 put on board a ship; hence, transport by sea, rail, road, or air: *We ship goods; Goods are shipped out to distant parts; He was shipped off to boarding schools and summer camps as a child.* 2 take in or install in a ship: *to ship oars, rudder; to ship water* (= be flooded) *in a storm.* 3 go on board a

ship to travel, for service, etc.: *At just 16, Conrad shipped out on a trading ship; Sam has to shape up or ship out* (=leave) . — **ship·per** *n.*

ship·board *adj. & n.* (on) a ship: *It happened on shipboard; a shipboard riot, romance, summit meeting.*

ship·ment (SHIP·munt) *n.* goods shipped or their shipping.

shipping *n.* 1 the ships of a nation, business, etc. collectively: *merchant shipping.* 2 the transportation of goods: *the shipping clerk in a warehouse.*

ship·shape *adj. & adv.* trim and tidy; in good order.

ship·wreck *n.* 1 the loss or destruction of a ship at sea: *the shipwreck of the Titanic; Many sailors have experienced* or *suffered shipwrecks; the shipwreck* (=ruin or failure) *of his hopes and ambitions.* 2 wreckage or a wrecked ship: *the richest shipwreck ever uncovered in Canadian waters.* — *v.* cause or suffer shipwreck: *The Titanic was shipwrecked off Newfoundland; The sailors were shipwrecked and marooned on an island.*

ship·yard *n.* an establishment for the building and repair of ships: *a naval shipyard.*

shirk *v.* avoid doing one's work or duty.

shirt *n.* 1 a garment for the upper part of the body with a front opening, collar, and short or long sleeves, as usually worn by men: *a dress, sport shirt; (a knitted pullover) polo shirt; (a close-fitting) body shirt; a hair shirt worn as penance.* 2 an undershirt. — **lose one's shirt** *Slang.* lose all one's money or property.

shirt·dress *n.* a dress with a shirtwaist.

shirt·ing *n.* cloth for shirts.

shirt·waist *n.* a blouse fashioned like a shirt.

shiv·er (SHIV·ur) 1 *v.* tremble, as from fear or cold: *He was so scared he was shivering in his shoes; Kay was shivering with cold; Some shiver at the very thought of going out in the cold.* 2 *n. & v.* splinter. — *n.* a shivering or shaking: *a chilling story that will send shivers down* or *up and down your spine; It gives you the shivers.* — **shiv·er·y** *adj.*

shlock, shmaltz, shnook same as SCHLOCK, SCHMALTZ, SCHNOOK.

shoal (SHOLE) *n.* 1 a large group: *a shoal* (=school) *of fish.* 2 a shallow place with sand or rocks underneath: *a ship stranded on the shoals.*

shock *n.* 1 a sudden violent shake or jolt, as felt when electric current passes through the body or an earthquake strikes: *The news of his tragic death came as a shock; a shock to everyone in the family; It was a shock to learn of his death; It gave her a shock; She felt, got, had a shock; People expressed shock at the tragedy; a culture, electric, future, mild, profound, rude, severe, terrible shock; adj.: He uses four-letter words for their shock effect; shock treatment, value.* 2 a failure or collapse of the circulatory system resulting from a serious injury or burn; also, a dazed condition brought on by some disaster or personal loss: *She was in shock for several days after the incident; cardiac, insulin, psychic, shell shock.* 3 a thick bushy mass: *a shock of hair.*

4 [short form] shock absorber (as of automobile wheels). — *v.* 1 cause shock to someone: *It shocked him to hear that she had died; He was shocked to hear that she had died.* 2 fill with horror or disgust: *She was shocked into silence.*

shock·er *n.* a person or thing that shocks, esp. a sensational story.

shocking *adj.* causing great surprise, disgust, etc.: *shocking language, news; It was shocking to find out what was going on.*

shock therapy *n.* treatment of severe mental illness using electric current, drugs, etc. to produce convulsions.

shock wave *n.* the blast from an explosion: *The news of the murder sent shock waves through the community.*

shod *pt. & pp.* of SHOE.

shod·dy *n.* shod·dies 1 cloth made of woollen waste. 2 anything of inferior quality though looking good. — *adj.* shod·di·er, shod·di·est inferior: *shoddy merchandise; shoddy* (=shabby) *treatment.* — **shod·di·ly** *adv.;* **shod·di·ness** *n.*

shoe (SHOO) *n.* 1 an outer covering for a foot, usually made of leather: *to break in new shoes; tight shoes; shoes that pinch; basketball, dress, gym, high-heeled, running, sports, tennis, track shoes.* 2 something resembling a shoe in function, position, etc., as a horseshoe, brake shoe, the outer casing of a pneumatic tire, etc. — **fill someone's shoes** take the place vacated by someone. — **the shoe is on the other foot** the situation is reversed. — **where the shoe pinches** where the problem is. — *v.* shoes, *pt. & pp.* shod or shoed, shoe·ing furnish or cover with a shoe: *Blacksmiths shoe horses; shod with steel; well-shod feet.*

shoe·horn *n.* an implement with a curved blade used to ease one's heel into a shoe.

shoe·lace *n.* a length of string or strap for lacing or tying a shoe.

shoe·shine *n.* a cleaning and polishing of a pair of shoes.

shoe·string *n.* 1 shoelace. 2 *Informal.* a small or barely adequate amount of capital: *to operate on a shoestring; adj.: We're on a shoestring budget; a shoestring catch (made just before the ball hits the ground); a shoestring operation.*

shoe tree *n.* a foot-shaped form of wood inserted in a shoe to preserve its shape.

shone *pt.* of SHINE.

shoo *interj.* [used to drive away birds, flies, etc.] go away! — *v.* shoos, shooed, shoo·ing drive away by calling "shoo."

shoo-in *n. Informal.* an easy winner: *a shoo-in for* or *to win the nomination.*

shook *pt.* of SHAKE — **shook up** *Informal.* upset or agitated.

shoot (long "oo") *v.* **shoots, shot, shoot·ing 1** send forth suddenly and swiftly like a bullet, arrow, or other missile: *He shot two rounds; Reporters shoot questions; The flames shot up; cars shooting past spectators; to shoot* (= fire) *a gun; a canoe for shooting* (= passing quickly along) *the rapids of the Niagara; Addicts* **shoot up** (*Slang for* inject) *amphetamines; a* **shooting range** (= an outdoor place for target practice). **2** fire at with or as with a weapon; kill or get by shooting: *The fleeing man was shot at; a robber shot dead; planes shot down; He shot three goals; A camera shoots pictures; Let's shoot* (= aim) *for the top.*
— **shoot from the hip** act hastily.
— *n.* **1** a shooting: *to go on a tiger shoot; He lost the shoot* (= shooting match). **2** something sent forth: *the tender shoots of a fern; bamboo shoots.*

shooting script *n.* a script with scenes arranged in the order required for filming.

shoot·out *n. Informal.* a gunfight.

shop *n.* **1** a small retail store: *a duty-free shop; paint shop.* **2** a place where goods are produced or a service is provided; a workshop or factory: *a barber, beauty, (auto) body, butcher, carpenter's, machine, printing shop; a coffee shop* (= small restaurant); *a union shop (where only workers who will join the union are hired).*
— **talk shop** indulge in or use shoptalk.
— *v.* **shops, shopped, shop·ping** visit stores, as at a mall, or buy from a store: *He's out shopping; shopping for a hat; He shops at Shoppers World Mall; Thanks for shopping Smiths; But first he shops* (= studies) *the ads; a* **shopping bag** *to carry purchases.*
— **shop around** search about *for a bargain, better job,* etc. — **shop·per** *n.*

shop·lift·er (SHOP·lif·tur) *n.* one who steals goods displayed for sale in a store.
— **shop·lift** *v.* — **shop·lift·ing** *n.*

shoppe (SHOP) *n.* [old spelling used in names] shop: *Ye Computer Shoppe.*

shopping *n.* act of shopping: *We do all our shopping on Saturdays; Christmas shopping; comparison shopping (for the best prices).*
— *adj.: a* **shopping-bag lady** (= homeless woman); *shopping centre* or *center with many shops and a parking area; an enclosed* **shopping mall** *with central heating and air-conditioning.*

shopping plaza *n. Cdn.* shopping centre.

shop·talk *n.* **1** discussion of one's business, as with a colleague, esp. using jargon. **2** such jargon.

shop·worn *adj.* **1** of articles displayed for sale, soiled or frayed by having been handled or on display. **2** not fresh or attractive: *a shopworn appearance, cliché, theme.*

shore *n.* **1** land along the edge of a sea, lake, etc.; coast: *a cottage on the shore of a lake; cities along the shores of Lake Ontario; a ship anchored many miles off shore.* **2** a prop or brace to support a structure, esp. on its side.
— *v.* **shores, shored, shor·ing** support or prop: *to shore up a shaky wall; to shore up falling interest rates, the falling dollar.*

shorn a *pp.* of SHEAR.

short *adj.* **1** relatively small in extent or duration; not long or tall: *a short distance, time; a man relatively short in stature; the short vowels of "pat," "pet," "pit," "pot," and "put"; He has a short* (= bad) *memory; You may make some money* **in the short run** (= in a brief period of time). **2** less than sufficient: *Food is in short supply; She is short of breath after the run; We're running* **short of** *supplies; We don't want to be caught short* (= in acute need); *She wants nothing* **short of** (= less than) *what was promised; He cheats his customers with short weight and short change; Being short* (= curt) *didn't help him keep customers.* **3** of pastry and such baked foods, crumbly or flaky. **4** not yet owning securities, goods, etc. sold in advance: *We are short of cotton.*
— **in short order** quickly.
— **get the short end of the stick** *Informal.* receive unfair treatment.
— **make short work of** deal with or dispose of something quickly.
— *adv.: She stopped short* (= abruptly) *in the middle of her speech; He would stop at nothing* **short of** (= except) *murder; to sell cotton short (for future delivery); He cut short his vacation and returned to work; Her performance fell short of expectations.*
— *n.* **1** something short or shortened, as a short form, item, movie, etc.: *"Deli" is short for delicatessen.* **2** a short circuit. **3 shorts** *pl.* short trousers or drawers: *a pair of Bermuda shorts; boxer shorts.*
— **in short** briefly.
— *v.* **1** to shortchange: *The store clerk shorted me.* **2** to short-circuit: *The kettle shorted out with an explosion.*

short·age (SHOR·tij) *n.* a deficiency or its amount: *an acute shortage of water; a food, housing, labour shortage.*

short·change *v.* **-chang·es, -changed, -chang·ing** *Informal.* **1** give less than the correct change. **2** deprive of what is due; cheat.

short circuit *n.* a usually dangerous high flow of electric current between two points bypassing the main circuit.
— **short-circuit** *v.*

short·com·ing (SHORT·cum·ing) *n.* a failing or fault.

short·cut *n.* **1** a way that is shorter than the regular route: *to take a shortcut through the fields.* **2** any way of saving time or effort: *no shortcuts to fame and fortune.*

short·en *v.* **1** make or become shorter: *Please shorten the speech to three minutes; Shorten it by two minutes.* **2** make pastry crisp and flaky by use of shortening.

shortening *n.* butter, lard, etc. added to doughs and batters: *vegetable shortening made from soybean oil.*

short·fall *n.* a falling short or its amount; shortage.

short fuse *n. Informal.* a quick temper.

short·hand *n.* a system of rapid writing using abbreviations and symbols: *The reporter took it down in shorthand; Can you take shorthand?*

short·hand·ed (SHORT·han·did) *adj.* short of helpers.

short list *n.* a list of candidates selected for a position.

short-lived (SHORT·lived, -livd) *adj.* lasting a short time.

short·ly *adv.* **1** in a short time; soon. **2** briefly; in summary. **3** abruptly or curtly. — **short·ness** *n.*

short order *n.* an order for food that can be quickly cooked; also, the food ordered: *We need a **short-order** cook for the lunch counter.*
— **in short order** quickly: *Sometimes it is difficult to get a substitute teacher in short order.*

short-range *adj.* having a short range in distance or time; not long-range.

short shrift *n.* little consideration; curt treatment: *to get short shrift; give somebody short shrift; He made short shrift of* (= quick work of discrediting) *the proposal.*

short·sight·ed (SHORT·sye·tid) *adj.* **1** nearsighted. **2** lacking in foresight.

short-spoken (SHORT·spoh·kun) *adj.* using few words; hence, curt.

short·stop *n.* in baseball, the infielder or the position between second and third base.

short story *n.* a compact work of prose fiction, as published in magazines, with a single plot and a limited number of characters.

short subject *n.* a cartoon, newsreel, or other short item shown before or between feature films.

short-tempered *adj.* quickly angered.

short-term *adj.* having to do with a relatively short period of time; not long-term: *short-term benefits, employment, gains.*

short-winded (SHORT·win·did) *adj.* easily getting out of breath; having difficulty in breathing.

shot *pt. & pp.* of SHOOT.
— *adj.* **1** **shot with** flecked or streaked with something: *a sky shot with patches of cloud; red silk shot with gold thread; an essay **shot through with** (= full of) humour.* **2** *Slang.* worn out or broken, as an automobile part needing replacement: *His health is shot.*
— *n.* **1** a shooting or anything similar, as a scoring attempt in a game, an injection or dose of a drug, a pointed remark, or a random guess: *to fire* or *take a shot at a target; We will have **a shot at it** (= make an attempt to get or accomplish it); a cheap, parting, passing, penalty, pistol, random, rifle, warning shot; a booster shot* (= another injection of a vaccine or antigen); *They were warned not to approach **within shot** (= range) of the rifles.* **2** *Informal.* a person: *a big shot.* **3** a marksman or markswoman: *a bad, crack, good shot.* **4** a solid metal ball, esp. a large one for a cannon; also, smaller lead pellets collectively: *bird shot.* **5** a camera picture or film sequence.
— **call the shots** *Informal.* give orders.
— **shot in the arm** something to stimulate or invigorate.
— **shot in the dark** a wild guess.

shot·gun *n.* a smooth-bore hunting gun that fires lead pellets: *a sawed-off shotgun.*
— *adj.* forced: *a shotgun merger; a **shotgun wedding** or **marriage** forced on the couple by pregnancy.*

shot put *n.* the contest of throwing a heavy metal ball for distance. — **shot-putter** *n.* — **shot-putting** *n.*

should *pt.* of SHALL.

shoul·der (SHOLE·dur) *n.* **1** where the arm is joined to the trunk: *to put one's **shoulder to the wheel** (= work hard); Joe was given the **cold shoulder** (= brush-off) when he offered to help.* **2** a shoulderlike part, esp. the usually unpaved edge of a road: *Spring and fall are shoulder seasons for travel (between high or peak season and low season).* **3** **shoulders** *pl.* the upper part of the back, esp. as bearing burdens: *The responsibility rests on your shoulders; a man with broad shoulders; square shoulders; He shrugged his shoulders in dismay; Ray **rubs shoulders** (= associates) **with** important people.*
— **straight from the shoulder** frankly or directly.
— *v.* push, support, or bear a burden, blame, etc. with or as if with a shoulder or shoulders: *to shoulder a responsibility.*

should·n't should not.

shout *n.* a sudden loud cry or call: *Give me a shout if you need help; shouts of joy, triumph.*
— *v.* utter a shout: *The drowning man shouted for help; No one likes to be shouted at; to **shout down** an opponent* (= make him or her stop talking by continued shouting). — **shout·er** *n.*

shove (SHUV) *v.* **shoves, shoved, shov·ing** push roughly, often to get a person or thing out of one's way.
— **shove around** order about.
— **shove off** *Informal.* leave, as by pushing one's boat away.
— *n.* such a push: *when push comes to shove* (= when things get worse).

shov·el (SHUV·ul) *n.* an implement with a broad, hollowed-out blade and handle for scooping out loose material such as earth, coal, and snow: *Diesel power shovels have replaced steam shovels for digging.*
— *v.* **-els, -elled** or **-eled, -el·ling** or **-el·ing** dig or throw out with a shovel.

shov·el·ful (SHUV·ul·ful, *rhyme:* full) *n.* how much a shovel will hold.

show (SHOH) *v.* **shows,** *pt. & pp.* **shown** (SHOHN) or **showed, show·ing 1** (cause to) be seen: *He showed me a picture; showed me through the building; Your slip is showing; Children like to **show off** (= be watched while doing something they are proud of); He likes to show off (= display) his new car; Half of those who reserved seats failed to **show up** (= arrive); A few showed up late.* **2** explain or demonstrate: *She'll show you how it works; This experiment shows the earth is round.* **3** direct or guide: *The hostess showed us around; showed us to our seats; showed us (to) the door; The party made a good **showing** (= a good impression or performance) at the polls.*
— *n.* **1** a showing: *They voted 112 – 25 in a show of hands.* **2** a display, exhibition, or performance: *a show of strength, temper; to produce, promote, put on, sponsor, stage a show; He's just **putting on a show** (= just pretending); to catch, see, take in a show while in the city; a floor show at a night club; a talent show by children; an air, auto, dog, flower, horse, TV, variety show; The show starts at 8; Let's **get the show on the road** (Informal for get things going); Sam was in charge of the whole show* (= operation); *Good show!* (= Very good!).
— **steal the show** attract the most attention.

show·biz (SHOH·biz) *n. Informal.* show business.

show business *n.* the entertainment industry.

show·case *n.* a glass case for displaying articles in a store or museum: *Expo 86 was the showcase of the nation.*
— *v.: Much young talent was showcased at the school fair.*

show·down *n. Informal.* the bringing out of a dispute into the open in order to force a settlement: *to come to, have, force a showdown with the opposition.*

show·er (rhyme: "our") *n.* **1** a brief fall of rain or anything similar: *a shower of hail, arrows, stones, meteorites; a heavy, light, passing, thunder shower; scattered showers; April showers.* **2** a party for giving gifts to a woman on a special occasion: *a baby, bridal, engagement, wedding shower.* **3** (a bathroom fixture for) an overhead spray of water; also, a wash taken under a shower (**shower bath**): *to take a shower;* **adj.:** *a shower curtain, stall; a* **shower head** (= nozzle).
— *v.* **1** rain briefly. **2** come or send in a shower: *to shower compliments, gifts on or upon someone; He was showered with insults.* **3** take a shower bath: *to shower and shave.* — **show·er·y** *adj.*

show·girl *n.* a woman performer who is more of a decoration than a star: *a slick showgirl.*

show·man (SHOW·mun) *n.* **-men** a man skilled in presenting things in an impressive or dramatic manner; also, a producer of shows. — **show·man·ship** *n.*

shown a *pp.* of SHOW.

show·off *n.* one who vainly displays his or her good points.

show·piece *n.* something considered the best of its kind, as fit for display.

show·place *n.* a place that is proudly shown to tourists.

show·room *n.* a room in which goods are displayed for viewing.

show window *n.* a shop's outside display window.

show·y *adj.* **show·i·er, -i·est** striking or gaudy in appearance. — **show·i·ly** *adv.;* **show·i·ness** *n.*

shrank a *pt.* of SHRINK.

shred *v.* **shreds, shred·ded, shred·ding** cut or tear into narrow strips or fragments: *a paper shredding machine;* **shredded wheat** (*biscuit for use as a breakfast food*).
— *n.* a torn or cut off strip: *His shirt was torn to* **shreds;** *not a shred* (= bit) *of evidence against her.*

shrew (SHROO) *n.* **1** a small aggressive mouselike mammal. **2** a bad-tempered scolding woman.
— **shrew·ish** *adj.*

shrewd (long "OO") *adj.* sharp and clever in practical matters: *a shrewd businessman, guess, observer; shrewd at guessing.* — **shrewd·ly** *adv.;* **shrewd·ness** *n.*

shriek (SHREEK) *n.* a sharp, shrill cry of extreme fear, delight, pain, or other emotion; screech: *shrieks of laughter.*
— *v.* make a shriek: *She shrieked at the sight of blood; The children shrieked with delight, terror.*

shrift *n.* [old use] confession or shriving. See SHORT

SHRIFT.

shrill *adj.* of cries and such sounds, high-pitched and sharp, as of a cricket, whistle, etc.: *A voice gets shrill after some shouting; his shrill* (= insistent but failing) *efforts.* — *v.* utter with or make such a sound.
— **shril·ly** *adv.;* **shrill·ness** *n.*

shrimp *n.* **1** a small shellfish related to crabs and lobsters, valued as sea food. **2** *Informal.* a small insignificant person.

shrine *n.* **1** a place sacred to the memory of a venerated person: *a Shinto shrine; to pray at a shrine.* **2** a tomb or a place in which relics are preserved.

shrink *v.* **shrinks,** *pt.* **shrank** or **shrunk,** *pp.* **shrunk** or **shrunk·en, shrink·ing 1** contract in extent, scope, volume, etc., as fabrics when laundered: *shrinking fortunes, influence, inventory; how to shrink wool* (= make it shrink). **2** draw back instinctively *from something unpleasant or frightening, as a dog from the whip.* — *n. Slang.* a psychiatrist.

shrink·age (SHRINK·ij) *n.* the process of shrinking or its result: *Retail shrinkage from employee thefts, shoplifting, accounting errors, etc. amount to nearly 2% of total sales; shrinkage in employment, of world markets.*

shrinking violet *n.* a shy or timid person.

shrive *v.* **shrives,** *pt.* **shrove** (SHROHV) or **shrived,** *pp.* **shriv·en** or **shrived, shriv·ing** [old use] hear someone's confession, as a priest does.

shriv·el (SHRIV·ul) *v.* **-els, -elled** or **-eled, -el·ling** or **-el·ing** dry up or wither into a wrinkled state, as a leaf or fruit from the heat of the sun: *The crops shrivelled up in the heat wave; shrivelling criticism, remarks.*

shroud *n.* **1** a burial cloth for a dead body. **2** **shrouds** *pl.* the set of ropes supporting a ship's mast.
— *v.* cover or hide: *a kidnapping shrouded in mystery.*

shrub *n.* a woody-stemmed plant smaller than a tree; bush. — **shrub·by** *adj.*

shrub·ber·y (SHRUB·uh·ree) *n.* **1** shrubs collectively: *hiding in the shrubbery.* **2** **shrub·ber·ies** *pl.* a place planted with shrubs.

shrug *v.* **shrugs, shrugged, shrug·ging** raise the shoulders momentarily to show indifference, doubt, etc.: *He shrugged at the idea; He* **shrugged it off** (= dismissed it as unimportant).
— *n.* a shrugging gesture: *He dismissed it with a shrug*

of the shoulders.

shrunk(en) See SHRINK.

shtick n. Slang. 1 a comic routine. 2 a gimmicky thing or quality: his whole artistic shtick.

shuck n. 1 a husk, pod, shell, or similar outer covering. 2 something of little or no value: not worth shucks.
— v. remove the shucks or shell: to shuck corn, peanuts.
— **shucks** interj. expressing impatience or disappointment: Aw, shucks!

shud·der (SHUD·ur) n. a sudden shaking or trembling of the body from horror, disgust, etc.
— v. experience a shudder: I shudder to think what might have happened.

shuf·fle (SHUF·ul) v. shuf·fles, shuf·fled, shuf·fling 1 walk or move in a dragging manner: to shuffle (= drag) one's feet; He shuffled along. 2 mix and rearrange a deck of cards. 3 disarrange papers, etc. usually in search of something.
— n. a shuffling of cards or a shuffling movement, dance, action, etc.

shun v. shuns, shunned, shun·ning avoid a person or thing because of aversion or dislike: a modest man who shuns publicity; Kay shuns society.

shunt v. move or turn off to one side, esp. switch a train from one track to another. — n. a shunting.

shush interj. & v. hush!

shut v. shuts, shut, shut·ting close so as to keep one in or out: Please shut the door; Blinds shut out light; A factory shuts down; It is shut down by a strike; We were **shut in** for several days by the snowstorm; Turn the tap to **shut off** the water; Tall buildings shut off our view.
— **shut up** Informal. [not polite in imperative mood] stop talking.

shut·down n. a shutting down of a factory, usually temporarily.

shut·eye n. Slang. sleep: to catch some shuteye during a break.

shut·in n. one confined indoors by illness.

shut·out n. a preventing of the opposite side from scoring: to score a shutout.

shut·ter n. one that shuts, as a hinged cover for a window or the opening-and-closing device of a camera aperture. — v. furnish with a shutter or shutters.

shut·tle v. shut·tles, shut·tled, shut·tling move back and forth over a course, as the needlelike device carrying threads from side to side in a loom or a vehicle carrying passengers back and forth over a route: The bus shuttles between the city and the suburbs.
— n. something designed to shuttle back and forth: a space shuttle; a shuttle bus service.

shy adj. shy·er or shi·er, shy·est or shi·est reserved or timid in manner; bashful: He feels a bit shy about posing for a picture; We **fight shy of** (= try to avoid) publicity; We are $100 **shy of** (= short of) the target figure.
— v. shies, shied, shy·ing 1 shrink or draw back, esp. suddenly, as a horse startled by something in its way:

The horse shied at the barking dog; Gina shies away from (= avoids) publicity. 2 fling a stone, stick, etc. sideways at a target. — shy·ly adv.; shy·ness n.

Shy·lock n. a hardhearted moneylender.

shy·ster (SHY·stur) n. Informal. a professional, esp. a lawyer, who uses tricky methods.

Si·a·mese twins (sye·uh·MEEZ·) n.pl. twins born joined together.

sib·ling n. a fellow offspring, esp. a brother or sister; adj.: sibling jokes, rivalry.

sic v. sics, sicked, sick·ing incite a dog to attack: She sicked Tiger on(to) the burglar; Sic him, Tiger!

sick adj. suffering from something bodily or mental; ill: You look sick; She's worried sick about her child; sick and tired of (= quite fed up with) eating in restaurants; sick at or to his stomach (= nauseated); sick at heart; a sick (= morbid or macabre) joke; He's sick (= longing) for home; a sick (= migraine) headache; Nurses care for **the sick** (people). — sick·ish adj.

sick bay n. part of a ship or clinic used as a hospital.

sick·en (SICK·un) v. make or become sick: It sickens one to watch the fighting going on in families; The child sickened and died. — sick·en·ing adj.

sick·ie (SICK·ee) n. -ies Informal. one who behaves in a queer or perverted manner.

sick·le (SICK·ul) n. a short-handled tool with a curved blade for mowing grass and grain.

sick·ly adj. -li·er, -li·est 1 having to do with sickness: a sickly complexion. 2 frequently sick: a sickly child.

sick·ness (SICK·nis) n. illness or a particular disease: in sickness and in health; morning, motion sickness (= nausea); radiation sickness; sleeping sickness.

sick·out n. the labour tactic of claiming illness as a group, esp. when unable to strike.

side n. 1 a boundary surface or line, away from the centre, esp. of something considered as not having a front or back: the four sides of a square; Opposition came from all sides; the north, east, south, and west sides of a building; the two sides of a street; the debit and credit sides of a ledger; on a mountain side; the sunny side of a house. 2 the left or right of something having a front, back, etc.: the passenger side of a car; a side of beef (= lengthwise half of the carcass); seated **side by side** (= next to each other); She **split her sides** laughing (= laughed uproariously); the side door of a house. 3 a group or party in relation to another: the opposing sides of a dispute; the losing and winning sides; the sales side (= department) of the business; Referees shouldn't **take sides** (= favour either side). 4 either surface of something flat or considered as having only two sides: the reverse and obverse sides of a coin; the dark side of the moon; the windward side of the island; the seamy side of life; There are two sides to every question; to see the humorous side (= aspect) of an issue.
— **on the side** in addition to the regular or main thing.
— adj.: a side (= not main) street; a side (= not main or central) issue; a side (= not front) view.

— *v.* **sides, sid·ed, sid·ing** take a side: *Dad naturally sides with* (= favours) *Mom in family arguments; Tim usually sides against* (= opposes) *his sister.*

side arm *n.* a sword, pistol, or other weapon worn at the waist.

side·arm *adj. & adv.* of a throw or stroke, not overhand or underhand but made with the arm relatively parallel to the ground.

side·bar *n.* a magazine story or article that throws a sidelight on a main feature.

side·board *n.* a low cabinet that holds dining accessories, its top being used as a side table.

side effect *n.* a usually adverse secondary effect or reaction, esp. of a drug.

sid·ing (SYE·ding) *n.* **1** boards or shingles covering the outside of a frame house. **2** a short railway track branching from a main one.

side·kick *n. Slang.* a pal or partner.

side·light *n.* incidental bit of information that helps to understand a subject or character.

side·line *n.* **1** the side boundary of a playing field or court: *to watch from the sidelines; a player* **on the** **sidelines** (= out of action). **2** a business carried on in addition to one's main business or job.
— *v.* **-lines, -lined, -lin·ing** put out of action, as a player.

side·long *adj. & adv.* directed to one side: *a sidelong glance.*

side·piece *n.* a piece that forms the side of something.

side·split·ting (SIDE·split·ing) *adj.* extremely funny: *a sidesplitting joke, story.*

side·step *v.* **-steps, -stepped, -step·ping 1** step aside. **2** dodge or avoid a blow, responsibility, etc. by stepping aside: *to sidestep an issue.*

side·swipe *v.* **-swipes, -swiped, -swip·ing** give a glancing blow or hit.

side·track *v.* **1** switch a train to a railway siding; *n.* such a siding. **2** distract someone or turn aside from the main issue.

side·ways *adj. & adv.* **1** using a side. **2** with a side forward. Also **side·wise.**

si·dle (SYE·dul) *v.* **-dles, -dled, -dling** move sideways in a shy or furtive manner: *The child sidled up to her mom and whispered in her ear.*

siege (SEEJ) *n.* **1** a surrounding of a place, as a fortress, to force a surrender. **2** the condition of being threatened from or as if from all sides, as by an enemy: *a city under siege; in a state of siege; The siege was lifted after a few days; Help had to be called to raise the siege; Luc has come out of a long siege of cancer; the siege mentality of people considering themselves besieged.*
— **lay siege to** besiege a place.

sieve (SIV) *n.* a utensil with holes for straining out the large particles of a mixture or the solid parts of a liquid.

sift *v.* **1** pass through a sieve: *to sift flour; to sift* (= separate) *fact from fiction.* **2** carefully examine: *to*

sift evidence; to sift through the debris. — **sift·er** *n.*

sigh (SYE) *n.* a long, deep breathing sound, as in relief, sadness, etc.: *to breathe* or *heave a sigh of relief.*
— *v.* make a sigh: *She sighed in pain; a mother sighing* (= yearning) *for her missing child.*

sight (SITE) *n.* **1** the act, power, or range of seeing: *She lost her sight in an accident; We lost sight of the speeding car; He was out of sight in no time; Kay cannot stand the sight of blood; We came within sight of land; an eagle with keen sight.* **2** something seen: *a familiar, horrible, lovely, sorry, ugly sight; to take in* or *see the* (interesting) *sights of a city; He's quite a sight* (= looks odd) *in that hat.* **3** a seeing device: *a telescopic sight; A marksman adjusts his sights; takes a sight* (= aim) *before firing; She has her* **sights** (= aspirations) *set on a Ph.D.* **4** *Slang.* a good deal: *not by a darn sight.*
— **at** or **on sight** as soon as seen: *orders to shoot on sight; love at first sight.*
— **catch sight of** see.
— **know by sight** be able to recognize upon seeing.
— **not by a long sight** probably not; also, not at all.
— **sight unseen** without seeing in advance: *We bought the house sight unseen.*
— *v.* see or take aim, esp. by use of a seeing device.
— **sight·ing** *n.*: *reported UFO sightings.*

sight·ed *adj. & combining form.* having sight as specified: *a sighted firearm* (that has a sight attached); *a sighted* (not blind) *person; clear-sighted, farsighted, shortsighted.*

sight·ly *adj.* **-li·er, -li·est** pleasant-looking.

sight reading *n.* the skill of performing written music, of reading something in a foreign language, etc. without previous preparation.

sight·see·ing (SITE·see·ing) *n.* the visiting of places of interest, as a tourist or other person (**sight·see·er**).

sign (SINE) *n.* **1** a mark, symbol, gesture, etc. that stands for or means something: *a dollar sign; multiplication sign; the* **signs of the zodiac;** *to make the* **sign of the cross;** *the* **sign language** *of deaf-mutes.* **2** a marker bearing a sign: *a "For sale" sign; a "No trespassing" sign; traffic signs; to post, put up, set up a sign; The sign says that the house is sold.* **3** evidence or indication: *Breathing is a sign of life; the body's vital signs; signs of forced entry into a home; an encouraging, sure, telltale, unmistakable sign.*
— *v.* write one's name or signature on a document; hence, agree legally to something: *to sign a contract; Sign on the dotted line; Some authors* **sign away** *their rights in return for small payments.*
— **sign on** or **up 1** enlist: *We signed on 25 volunteers today; Lots of people want to sign up.* **2** start broadcasting: *A TV or radio station* **signs on** *in the morning and* **signs off** *at the end of the day.*
— **sign·er** *n.*

sig·nal (SIG·nul) *n.* **1** a sign with an agreed-on meaning, used to warn, inform, etc.: *red, green, and amber traffic signals; the turn signals of an automobile; smoke signals; "SOS" and "Mayday" are distress signals; to flash, give, pick up, send signals; The attack began on* or *at a signal from the captain.* **2** an electrical or electromagnetic transmission that conveys a message, as in telegraphy, radio, and television.

— *v.* **-nals, -nalled** or **-naled, -nal·ling** or **-nal·ing**
1 give warning, notice, etc. to someone by a signal or signals; hence, communicate: *The Titanic signalled for help to other ships; A siren signals the end of the emergency.*
— *adj.* remarkable or notable: *a signal achievement, defeat, discovery.* — **sig·nal·ly** *adv.*

sig·nal·ize (SIG·nuh·lize) *v.* **-iz·es, -ized, -iz·ing** make remarkable or distinguished: *a year signalized by conquests in space.*

sig·na·ture (SIG·nuh·chur) *n.* **1** an identifying mark, esp. one's name written by oneself: *to affix, forge a signature.* **2** a musical sign placed after the clef to indicate the key or the time, as ¾ **3** in broadcasting, a musical or visual device used to identify a program, performer, etc.

sig·nif·i·cance (sig·NIF·uh·cunce) *n.* what is signified, esp. meaning in regard to its suggestiveness, importance, etc.: *a message that had a special significance for us; an event that was of great significance to his career.*

sig·nif·i·cant (sig·NIF·uh·kunt) *adj.* **1** having a special meaning: *a significant wink; It was significant that his family did not attend the wedding.* **2** important: *the significant events of the war.* — **sig·nif·i·cant·ly** *adv.*
— **sig·ni·fi·ca·tion** (sig·nuh·fuh·CAY·shun) *n.*

sig·ni·fy (SIG·nuh·fye) *v.* **-fies, -fied, -fy·ing 1** be a sign of something; mean: *A nod signifies assent; "sound and fury signifying nothing"; Bells signified the end of the war.* **2** show by means of a sign: *She signfied her willingness* or *that she was willing by nodding.*

si·gnor (seen·YOR) *n., pl.* **-gno·ri** (-YOR·ee) *Italian.* a gentleman; [as a title] Mr.

si·gno·ra (seen·YOR·ah) *n., pl.* **-re** (-ray) *Italian.* a married woman; [as a title] Mrs. or Madam.

si·gno·re (seen·YOR·ay) *n., pl.* **-ri** (-ree) *Italian.* a gentleman; [as a title in direct address] Sir.

si·gno·ri·na (seen·yuh·REE·nuh) *n., pl.* **-ne** (-nay) *Italian.* a young lady; [as a title] Miss.

sign·post *n.* a post having a sign on it.

si·lence (SYE·lunce) *n.* stillness or quiet; hence, absence of any sound or communication: *"Silence gives consent"; Silence reigned throughout the night; to break the silence of the night; to impose, keep, maintain, observe silence; an awkward, complete, eerie, ominous, perfect, stony, stunned, total, utter silence; They were reduced to silence; departed in silence;* **silence money** *(paid to prevent someone from talking).*
— *interj.* Quiet!
— **-lenc·es, -lenced, -lenc·ing 1** make silent: *The teacher silences the class with a stern look; to silence the enemy guns* (= stop them firing). **2** repress: *to silence free speech.*

si·lent (SYE·lunt) *adj.* still; quiet; also, not talkative; not active: *the silent atmosphere of a library; to keep, remain silent during a ceremony; a moment of silent prayer; the silent night; the strong, silent type (of person); the silent* (= not pronounced) *"b" of "bomb" and "n" of "hymn"; the* **silent majority** *of people not actively involved in politics.* — **si·lent·ly** *adv.*

silent partner *n.* one who helps finance a business

without actively helping to run it.

sil·hou·ette (sil·oo·ET) *n.* a solid outline, as of something seen against a light: *a profile in silhouette* (= in solid black on white background or the reverse).
— *v.* **-ettes, -et·ted, -et·ting** show in silhouette: *a building silhouetted against the night sky.*

sil·i·con (SIL·uh·con) *n.* an element found in granite, sand, clay, etc. which is used for making integrated electronic circuits called "silicon chips."

silicon valley *n.* a region with a concentration of high-technology industries, as the Santa Clara valley of California: *The Ottawa area has been called "Silicon Valley North."*

silk *n.* **1** a strong, shiny fibre produced by caterpillars, or **silk·worms**, for cocoons: *They spin silk.* **2** the thread or fabric made from it: *a shirt made of fine silk;* *adj.*: *a silk hat, stocking.* — **silk·en** or **silk·y** *adj.*

silk-stocking *adj.* wealthy or well-dressed: *a silk-stocking crowd, district, society.*

sill *n.* a horizontal supporting part or structure, as at the bottom of a door, window, or outside wall.

sil·ly (SIL·ee) *adj.* **sil·li·er, sil·li·est** lacking in common sense or judgment; stupid or trivial: *Don't be silly; What a silly idea! a silly remark; It sounds silly; behaviour that makes one look silly; the political* **silly season** (= season of little news) *when Parliament is not in session.*
— **sil·ly** or **sil·li·ly** *adv.* — **sil·li·ness** *n.*

silt *n.* fine-grained waterborne sediment, as at the bottom of rivers.
— *v.* obstruct or fill *up* with silt.

sil·ver (SIL·vur) *n.* **1** a white precious metal used for coins, jewellery, and table utensils, esp. spoons and dishes: *a silver platter, spoon.* **2** money or tableware of silver. **3** a lustrous greyish white. — **sil·ver·y** *adj.*

silver lining *n.* the brighter side of an otherwise depressing situation: *"Every cloud has a silver lining."*

silver thaw *n. Cdn.* same as ICE STORM.

sil·ver·ware (SIL·vur·ware) *n.* silver or metal tableware.

Sim·coe Day *n. Cdn.* in Ontario, same as CIVIC HOLIDAY.

sim·i·lar (SIM·uh·lur) *adj.* nearly alike; of the same kind: *Twins are naturally quite similar to each other; Identical twins are strikingly similar; similar in most respects.* — **sim·i·lar·ly** *adv.*

sim·i·lar·i·ty (sim·uh·LAIR·uh·tee) *n.* **-ties** (a point of) likeness: *One bears a striking similarity to the other; the similarity between the twins; the similarities among family members.*

sim·i·le (SIM·uh·lee) *n.* a figure of speech expressing a comparison using "like" or "as"; e.g. "tears flowing like a river."

si·mil·i·tude (suh·MIL·uh·tude) *n.* **1** resemblance. **2** a comparison.

sim·mer (SIM·ur) *v.* **1** keep or remain just below the boiling point: *Turn down the heat to low and let the stew simmer for one hour.* **2** be on the point of breaking out, as with anger, laughter, etc.: *A riot is simmering.*

— **simmer down 1** calm down. **2** get reduced, as by simmering: *the simmering down of the gold market.* — *n.* a simmering: *Slowly bring it to a simmer; Keep it at a low simmer between 54° and 57°C.*

sim·per (SIM·pur) *n.* a silly or affected smile. — *v.* smirk.

sim·ple (SIM·pul) *adj.* **-pler, -plest 1** not complicated; having few parts, frills, etc.: *Oxygen is a simple substance but water is a compound; a simple* (=elementary) *fact of everyday life; in simple* (=plain) *English; simple clothes, food, job, truths;* **simple interest** *based on the principal amount, unlike compound interest; A* **simple sentence** *has one main clause.* **2** of people, unaffected, sincere, or innocent: *a simple child, soul; not so simple* (=inexperienced) *as to believe everything she hears.* **3** common or lowly: *simple peasant folk.*

simple-minded (sim·pul·MINE·did) *adj.* inexperienced or stupid.

sim·ple·ton (SIM·pul·tun) *n.* a fool.

sim·plic·i·ty (sim·PLIS·uh·tee) *n.* **-ties** the state of being simple: *a manner full of simplicity and candour; the simplicity of her costume; The explanation is simplicity itself.*

sim·pli·fy (SIM·pluh·fye) *v.* **-fies, -fied, -fy·ing** make simple or simpler. — **sim·pli·fi·ca·tion** (-fuh·CAY·shun) *n.*

sim·plis·tic (sim·PLIS·tic) *adj.* excessively simple; oversimplified: *a simplistic explanation, theory; a simplistic and almost naive solution.* — **sim·plis·ti·cal·ly** *adv.*

sim·ply (SIM·plee) *adv.* **1** in a simple manner: *Sam came simply dressed.* **2** absolutely: *It's simply wonderful!*

sim·u·late (SIM·yuh·late) *v.* **-lates, -lat·ed, -lat·ing** look or act like having or being something that one is not: *He lay still, simulating death.* — **simulated** *adj.* not real or actual, but pretended or imitated: *a simulated car crash, karate kick, leather, moon landing.* — **sim·u·la·tor** *n.* — **sim·u·la·tion** (-LAY·shun) *n.*

si·mul·cast (SYE·mul·cast) *v.* **-casts**, *pt. & pp.* **-cast** or **-cast·ed, -cast·ing** broadcast simultaneously, as over radio and TV or a U.S. TV show at the same time on a Canadian station. — *n.* such a transmission.

si·mul·ta·ne·ous (sye·mul·TAY·nee·us) *adj.* done or happening at the same time: *events simultaneous with each other.* — **si·mul·ta·ne·ous·ly** *adv.*

sin *n.* **1** an offence against God, as by breaking a religious or moral law: *Murder is a crime and a sin; to commit, expiate a sin; to forgive one's sins; a deadly, mortal, original, unforgivable, unpardonable, venial sin.* **2** something immoral or offensive: *It's a sin to waste food; a sin against society; It's a sin that food is being wasted.* — *v.* **sins, sinned, sin·ning** commit sin: *I have sinned against thee.* — **sin·ner** *n.* — **sin·ful** *adj.;* **sin·ful·ly** *adv.;* **sin·ful·ness** *n.*

since *adv. & prep.* from the time mentioned or implied till now: *They fought once but have been friends ever since; It's 50 years since we opened the store.* — *conj.:* *We've had no trouble since* (=from the time) *we came to this city; He left early since* (=because) *he didn't want to be late.*

sin·cere (sin·SEER) *adj.* **-cer·er, -cer·est** of people or their feelings, desires, etc., without deceit; genuine: *a sincere friend; sincere sympathy.* — **sin·cere·ly** *adv.* — **sin·cer·i·ty** (sin·SER·uh·tee) *n.:* *No one doubts his sincerity; He said it in all sincerity.*

sin·ew (SIN·yoo) *n.* **1** a tendon. **2** muscular power. — **sin·ew·y** *adj.*

sing *v.* **sings**, *pt.* **sang** or **sung**, *pp.* **sung, sing·ing** make pleasant sounds with the voice; utter or tell something musically, in verse, etc.: *to sing a song; He sings to his mother while she sews; sings with joy; Birds sing in the trees; She sang her child to sleep; Parents sing the praises of their children; The poet sings of love; while bullets sang* (=whistled) *past us; He was murdered before he could sing* (Slang for squeal; tell the police). — **sing·er** *n.*

singe (SINJ) *v.* **sing·es, singed, singe·ing 1** scorch or burn superficially. **2** burn hair, feathers, etc. off a body: *to singe a chicken.* — *n.* a slight burn.

sin·gle (SING·gul) *adj.* one only; not combined or associated with another: *He refused without a single reason; a single* (=not double) *bed, room in a hotel; Tom and Jerry in single combat; Bachelors are single men, not married; single women; the single state of bachelorhood; a single* (=spouseless) *father, mother, parent; single* (=without duplicity) *devotion, heart.* — *n.* **1** a single person or thing, as a record with one piece of music on either side, not an album: *A bar patronized by* **singles** (=unmarried people) *is a* **singles bar. 2 singles** *pl.* a match with one player on either side. **3** a baseball hit that allows the batter to reach first base only. — *v.* **-gles, -gled, -gling 1** select someone out of a group: *He was singled out for special treatment.* **2** hit a single baseball hit.

single-breasted (sing·gul·BRES·tid) *adj.* of coats, jackets, etc., not double-breasted.

single file *n.* a line or column of persons or things coming one behind another: *We marched in single file.* — *adv.:* *to march single file.*

single-handed (sing·gul·HAN·did) *adj. & adv.* involving or using only one hand or person: *a single-handed farm operation; She raised her children single-handed.* — **sin·gle-hand·ed·ly** *adv.*

single-minded (sing·gul·MINE·did) *adj.* **1** having only one aim. **2** honest and straightforward; dedicated: *a single-minded husband and father.*

sin·gle·ton (SING·gul·tun) *n.* something occurring alone, esp. a single card of a suit in a player's hand.

single-track (sing·gul·TRACK) *adj.* limited in thinking capacity; one-track: *a single-track mind; a single-track system (that offers no alternatives).*

sin·gly (SING·glee) *adv.* individually; alone.

sing·song *n.* an unvarying speech rhythm or tone.

sin·gu·lar (SING·gyuh·lur) *adj.* **1** standing apart from

others because strange, extraordinary, unique, etc.: *a woman of singular charm.* **2** in grammar, referring to one person: *"Deer" is singular and plural.*
— **n.** the singular number or a singular form: *"Deer" is used in the singular and in the plural.*
— **sin·gu·lar·ly** *adv.*

sin·is·ter (SIN·is·tur) *adj.* suggestive of ill will, threatening evil or danger, etc.: *a sinister appearance, look, motive, plot, smile.*

sink *v.* **sinks,** *pt.* **sank** or **sunk,** *pp.* **sunk, sink·ing** (make) go down or lower, as under water: *to swim or float without sinking; The boat sprang a leak and sank; It sank to the bottom; It was not sunk by torpedoes; The sun sinks in the west; It sinks below the horizon; He sank into the chair, too tired to stand up; Her heart sank when she heard the sad news; an example so telling it sank into our minds.*
— **n. 1** a basin with a drain leading from it: *the bathroom sink; a double sink in the kitchen.* **2** a drain or sewer; hence, a place of filth or corruption. **3** a sunken land area in which water collects.

sink·er *n.* one that sinks or a weight for sinking: *a sinker for a fishing line.*

sinking fund *n.* a fund accumulated for the paying off of a usually public debt.

Si·no- (SYE·noh, SIN·oh) *combining form.* Chinese: *Sino-Soviet, Sino-Tibetan.*

sin·u·ous (SIN·yoo·us) *adj.* **1** of a path or movement, curved or winding; serpentine. **2** devious or crooked.

sip *v.* **sips, sipped, sip·ping** drink little by little from a container.
— **n.** a sipping or a sipped amount: *Take a sip of this syrup.* — **sip·per** *n.*

si·phon (SYE·fun) *n.* a bent-tube device through which a liquid may be drawn up by air pressure and down over a barrier.
— **v.:** *Gasoline was siphoned* (= drawn) *out of the gas tank; business siphoned off by new competitors.*

sir *n.* **1** [a formal term used to address a man, usually in respect, *pl.* "gentlemen"]: *Dear Sir; Your name, sir? Your names, gentlemen? Sir, you're under arrest!* **2** [used for emphasis, sometimes without reference to sex of person being addressed] *No, sir! Yes, sir!* **3** [as a title] *Sir John Smith; Sir John.*

sire *n.* **1** [old use] forefather; [as a title of respect] Lord. **2** the male parent of an animal.
— **v.** **sires, sired, sir·ing** beget: *a racehorse sired from good stock.*

siree same as SIRREE.

si·ren (SYE·run) *n.* **1** a device for producing a wailing sound signal, usually in warning, as on a fire truck or ambulance: *A siren goes off, rings, sounds, wails, is sounded, turned on.* **2** in Greek myth, a sea nymph who would lure sailors to their destruction with her enchanting song; hence, an enchantress: *a Hollywood siren.*

sir·ree or **sir·ee** (suh·REE) *interj.* [meaning "Sir" used after "Yes" or "No" for emphasis]: *Yes sirree!*

sir·up (SEER·up, SUR·up) *n.* same as SYRUP.

sis *n. Informal.* [used as a form of address in speech] sister.

sis·si·fied (SIS·uh·fide) *adj. Informal.* like a sissy.

sis·sy (SIS·ee) *n.* **sis·sies** *Informal.* an effeminate or timid boy or man.

sis·ter (SIS·tur) *n.* **1** a female offspring of the same parents as oneself: *his big, kid, little, older, twin, younger sister.* **2** a half sister, a female fellow-member of a closely knit group, etc. **3** a nun; also, a nurse: *a lay sister (not a religious).* — **sis·ter·hood** *n.*

sister-in-law (SIS·tur·in·law) *n.* **sis·ters-** a sister of one's spouse, wife of one's brother, or wife of one's spouse's brother. — **sis·ter·ly** *adj.*

sit *v.* **sits, sat, sit·ting 1** rest on one's buttocks, as on a chair, in a stable or relaxed condition: *too busy to sit down for meals; to sit still without moving; She sits* (= baby-sits) *for busy parents; He sat* (= seated) *the young rider on the horse.* **2** occupy a place or remain in a position: *a book siting on a shelf; People sit on committees; The court sits* (= is in session) *all day; A hen sits on eggs (to hatch them); We sit* (= pose) *for a portrait; We sit for* (= take) *an exam; The coat doesn't sit well on* (= suit) *you.*
— **sit down** to get busy with something: *to sit down to a long discussion.*
— **sit on** fail to act on something: *They sat on our application for three months and then turned it down.*
— **sit on one's hands** refuse to get involved: *He sat on his hands and watched them lose.*
— **sit on the fence** stay uncommitted or undecided.
— **sit out** take no part in something going on: *He sat out the whole dance.*
— **sit through** stay till the end of something: *We sat through the whole six-hour movie.*
— **sit tight** stay in the same place or position.
— **sit up** be alert or awake: *to sit up late and study; to sit up with a patient; to sit up and take notice* (= become more aware).
— **sit well with** be agreeable to someone: *The decision didn't sit well with him.*
— **sit·ter** *n.:* *a baby sitter; a house sitter.*

sit·com *n. Informal.* situation comedy.

sit-down *n.* a strike or demonstration in which the participants occupy a place till their demands are met; also **sit-down strike.**

site *n.* the location of an activity, structure, etc.: *a camping site; construction site; a **national historic site** such as Cape Spear, Newfoundland, or Quebec City Walls and Gate.*

sit-in *n.* a sit-down in a public place: *to hold, organize, stage a sit-in.*

sitting *n.* a session.

sitting duck *n. Informal.* an easy target or victim: *a sitting duck for muggers.*

sit·u·at·ed (SICH·oo·ay·tid) *adj.* **1** located: *a business situated in the suburbs.* **2** in a specified condition: *financially well situated* (= well off).

sit·u·a·tion (sich·oo·AY·shun) *n.* **1** location or site: *the situation of the house.* **2** state of affairs or condition: *the housing, market, political situation; an awkward, crisis,* *critical, delicate, desperate, embarrassing, emergency, explosive, hopeless, intolerable, life-and-death, no-win, tricky situation; to accept, take stock of a situation.* 3 employment; position: *situations vacant, wanted.*

situation comedy *n.* a light play or comedy, esp. as a radio or TV series, involving a set of characters in various episodes.

sit-up *n.* an exercise involving sitting up and lying back: *to do sit-ups.*

six *n., adj. & pron.* one more than five; the number 6 or VI: *six boys; six of them.*
— **at sixes and sevens** in confusion or disagreement.
— **sixth** *n. & adj.*

six-pack *n.* a package of six cans, bottles, etc.

sixth sense *n.* power of intuition.

six·ty *n., adj. & pron.* **-ties 1** six times ten; 60 or LX. **2 the sixties** *n. pl.* the numbers, years, etc. from 60 through 69. — **six·ti·eth** (-ith) *n. & adj.*

siz·a·ble or **size·a·ble** (SYE·zuh·bul) *adj.* fairly large or bulky: *a sizable amount, impact, fortune, population.*
— **siz·a·bly** or **size·a·bly** *adv.*

size *n.* **1** relative bigness, esp. as measured by length, width, etc.: *hats of all sizes; What size (shoes) do you wear? I wear size* (= classification) *eight shoes; shoes of the right, wrong size; It's a boys' size; a house of enormous, large, small, tremendous size.* **2** a material such as starch, gelatin, or wax added to paper or cloth to impart qualities of smoothness, stiffness, lustre, etc.; also **siz·ing.**
— **size** as in the same size as the original: *It copies size as without reducing or enlarging.*
— *v.* **siz·es, sized, siz·ing 1** arrange in sizes. **2** assess a person, chances, a problem, etc.: *to size up a situation before dealing with it.* **3** treat cloth, paper, walls, etc. with sizing.

-size or **-sized** *combining form.* of a specified size: *bite-size pieces; a large-size kitchen; life-size statue; medium-sized figure; small-sized house.*

sizeable See SIZABLE.

siz·zle (SIZ·ul) *n.* a hissing sound, as of fat in a hot pan: *Some new fashions sell by virtue of their sizzle* (= superficial qualities) *without any steak.*
— *v.* **siz·zles, siz·zled, siz·zling 1** burn or fry with a sizzle. **2** be very hot.

siz·zler (SIZ·lur) *n. Informal.* a hot day.

skate *n.* **1** a shoe fitted with a metal runner for gliding on ice; ice skate; also, the runner: *to sharpen skates.* **2** a roller skate. **3** a flat marine fish with winglike spreading fins on the sides of its body and a slender tail.
— *v.* **skates, skat·ed, skat·ing** move along on skates.
— **skat·er** *n.*

skate·board *n.* a narrow oblong board with rollers at each end for riding on hard surfaces; **skate·board·ing** *n.*

skating (SKAY·ting) *n.* the sport of gliding on skates: *figure, ice, roller, speed skating.*

skein (SKAIN) *n.* a loosely twisted coil of thread or yarn.

skel·e·ton (SKEL·uh·tun) *n.* **1** the framework of bones in an animal's body. **2** any framework, outline, or essential part: *the skeleton of a novel; adj.: a skeleton key designed to open many locks; to manage with a skeleton* (= minimal) *staff.*
— **skeleton in the closet** something secret and embarrassing known only to one's family.
— **skel·e·tal** (-tul) *adj.*

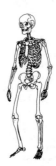

skep·tic, skep·ti·cism same as SCEPTIC, SCEPTICISM.

sketch *n.* **1** a rough outline or drawing: *to make a sketch; a composite sketch of a wanted man prepared by police from descriptions.* **2** a short, light, prose narrative or essay: *a biographical sketch; a brief, thumbnail sketch.*
— *v.* make a sketch or outline of something: *She sketched his life in broad outline.*

sketch·y *adj.* **sketch·i·er, -i·est** hastily done or incomplete like a sketch: *We have only sketchy details of the accident; His notes are too sketchy to be useful.*
— **sketch·i·ly** *adv.*

skew *n.* a slant or twist. — *adj.* having a skew.
— *v.* swerve or slant.

skew·er (SKEW·ur) *n.* a long pin to hold meat or vegetables being roasted or broiled.
— *v.* fasten or pierce with a skewer.

ski (SKEE) *v.* **skis, skied, ski·ing** glide on snow using long, flat runners attached to the shoes and two long poles for support: *the winter sport of skiing; cross-country skiing; downhill skiing; heli-skiing.*
— *n.* a runner used in skiing.
— *adj.: ski areas, boots; a ski bum* (for whom skiing is life); *a ski lift, lodge, pole, resort, slope.*
— **ski·er** *n.*

ski·bob *n.* a bicyclelike vehicle with skis instead of wheels for use on snow-covered slopes.

skid *v.* **skids, skid·ded, skid·ding** slide on a slippery surface, as the wheels of a car, without gripping the road surface: *to skid on ice; to skid on an icy bridge.*
— *n.* **1** a skidding. **2** a runner that enables an aircraft to skid along while landing; also, a sliding wedge used as a braking device. **3** a track for sliding or rolling a heavy object. **4** a low platform or pallet for holding loads.
— **on the skids** *Slang.* headed for failure or ruin.

skid·dy *adj.* **skid·di·er, skid·di·est** slippery.

ski·doo (SKID·oo) *n. Cdn.* a snowmobile; **Skidoo** *Trademark.*

688

skid row n. the slum section of a city frequented by society's derelicts.

skil·ful or **skill·ful** (SKIL·ful) adj. **1** having skill; expert: a skilful writer; skilful at or in acrobatics; skilful with her hands. **2** done with skill: a skilful job.
— **skil·ful·ly** or **skill·ful·ly** adv.
— **skil·ful·ness** or **skill·ful·ness** n.

ski lift n. a cable system for carrying skiers up a slope.

skill n. ability or expertise gained by training and practice: skill in carpentry, diving, languages; typing and such office skills; driving skills; marketable skills; to acquire, hone, master a skill; a man of consummate skill; the skill to manipulate people; She has demonstrated her skill at or in riding; displays technical skill as a mechanic; shows great skill with figures; diplomatic skill; her professional skill as a lawyer; the skill of a magician; The skill-testing question was a mere formality.

skilled adj. having or showing skill: a highly skilled worker; She's skilled at or in acrobatics; He's skilled with his hands; a skilled job (that requires skill).

skill·ful (SKIL·ful) adj. same as SKILFUL.

skim v. **skims, skimmed, skim·ming 1** go lightly over milk and remove cream, over waves, as gulls and such sea birds, over ice, as a skater, or through reading matter, a book, etc. picking up essential facts: to skim off the cream of the crop; to skim the market for a quick profit. **2** send skimming; skip: to skim a flat stone over water. — **skim·mer** (SKIM·ur) n.

skim milk or **skimmed milk** n. milk with the cream removed.

skimming (SKIM·ing) n. **1** what is skimmed off. **2** the practice of evading tax on gambling profits.

skimp v. Informal. scrimp: to skimp on clothes to pay the rent.

skimp·y adj. **skimp·i·er, -i·est** scanty; not ample: a skimpy dress, explanation. — **skimp·i·ly** adv.

skin n. **1** the outer layer of tissue covering a human or animal body; hide or pelt: chapped, oily, rough, smooth, soft skin; Jo has a thin skin (= is very sensitive); Joe has a thick skin (= is not very sensitive); a starving child who is all **skin and bones;** A **skin magazine** features nudes. **2** something resembling skin, as the rind of a fruit, casing of a sausage, etc.: spanking new office towers sporting skins of glass.
— **get under someone's skin** to annoy someone.
— **save one's skin** save oneself; escape unhurt.
— **under the skin** below the surface; at heart.
— v. **skins, skinned, skin·ning 1** remove the skin of something: to skin a banana; She skinned her knee climbing trees; He was skinned alive (= severely punished) for being late. **2** Informal. cheat or swindle.

skin diving n. underwater diving by a swimmer equipped with a scuba or other breathing apparatus.
— **skin-dive** v. **-dives, -dived, -div·ing.**
— **skin diver** n.

skin·flick n. Informal. a pornographic motion picture.

skin·flint n. a mean and stingy person.

skin-graft n. a piece of skin transplanted from another

area.

skin·head n. a young hoodlum.

skinned (SKIND) combining form. having skin of a specified kind: dark-skinned, light-skinned, thick-skinned.

skin·ny adj. **skin·ni·er, skin·ni·est** [unfavourable term] lean or thin-looking. — **skin·ni·ness** n.

skinny-dip (SKIN·ee·dip) n. Informal. a swim in the nude.

skin·tight adj. tight-fitting: skintight jeans.

skip n. **1** a light and quick leap or series of leaps, as a young lamb or child frisking about. **2** captain of a curling team.
— v. **skips, skipped, skip·ping** make a skip: a girl skipping rope (held in the hands and revolved under the feet and over the head); a skipping TV picture; It's fun to skip flat stones on the lake; Al was so good he was allowed to skip (= bypass) a grade; to skip (= not attend) school on flimsy excuses; to skip (= evade) payments on a loan.
— adj.: a **skip account** (= customer who does not pay); **skip tracer** (= bill collector).

skip·per (SKIP·ur) n. a leader, as the master of a ship, captain of an airplane, manager of a basketball team, etc.

skirl n. the shrill sound of bagpipes.

skir·mish (SKUR·mish) n. a minor engagement or encounter, as between two small groups of soldiers.
— v. take part in a skirmish or argument: He skirmished with the police over a parking ticket.

skirt n. **1** a garment that hangs from the waist, esp. a woman's outer garment; also, the bottom part of it: a pleated skirt; to hem a skirt. **2** Slang. a woman or girl: He's no **skirt chaser.**
— v. **1** form, be, or pass along the border or edge of something: a path skirting (along) the lake. **2** avoid something controversial or risky: to skirt the issue; to skirt a charge, problem, question, rule, suggestion.

ski run n. a slope or runway for skiing.

skit n. a short, humorous dramatic sketch: They did a skit on the mayor.

ski touring n. cross-country skiing.

ski tow n. a cable system for pulling skiers up a slope.

skit·ter (SKIT·ur) v. glide or skip lightly: blips skittering across a video screen.

skit·tish (SKIT·ish) adj. **1** excitable or jumpy: a skittish horse. **2** too lively or fickle; capricious: the skittish stock market.

ski·wear (SKEE·ware) n. clothes to wear while skiing.

skulk v. move stealthily; sneak or lurk. — **skulk·er** n.

skull n. **1** the bony case enclosing the brain. **2** head or mind: The point finally penetrated his thick skull.

skunk n. **1** a small furry animal of the weasel family, with black and white markings, noted for the evil-smelling liquid it squirts if molested. **2** Informal. a despised person.

sky *n.* **skies** the usually blue upper region of clouds, heavenly bodies, and celestial phenomena: *a clear, cloudless, cloudy, grey, overcast sky; seen in the skies over Ottawa; a poet lauded* **to the skies** (= excessively).

sky·cap *n.* a porter at an air terminal.

sky·div·ing (SKY·dye·ving) *n.* the sport of jumping from an airplane and executing various manoeuvres during the free fall before opening the parachute.

sky-high *adj. & adv.* very high.

sky·jack *v. Informal.* hijack an aircraft.
— **sky·jack·er** *n.*

sky·lark *n.* the common lark of Europe and Asia noted for the music it showers on the earth as it flies up toward the sky. — *v.* to frolic boisterously.

sky·line *n.* an outline, as of a city's buildings, seen against the sky: *an imposing skyline; the Vancouver skyline.*

sky·lounge *n.* a pickup vehicle for airline passengers that is carried from a city terminal to the airport by helicopter.

sky·rock·et (SKY·rock·it) *n.* a firework rocket.
— *v.* rise or make rise rapidly: *skyrocketing house prices; a star skyrocketed to fame by a movie.*

sky·scrap·er (SKY·scray·pur) *n.* a very tall building.

sky·walk *n.* an elevated walkway: *Glass-enclosed, heated skywalks link downtown buildings.*

sky·ward (SKY·wurd) *adj. & adv.* toward the sky; also **sky·wards** *adv.*

sky·way *n.* **1** an air lane for planes or other air traffic. **2** an elevated highway: *the Burlington Skyway.* **3** a skywalk.

slab *n.* a thick, flat, usually square-cornered piece: *a slab of cheese, ice, concrete, stone, wood.*

slack *adj.* **1** not tight, as the loose end of a rope. **2** careless or dull. **3** slow; not brisk: *at a slack pace; a slack season for travel.*
— *n.* **1** a slack end; inactive condition: *to take up the slack (of a rope); When one family member is unable to work, the others take up the slack.* **2 slacks** *n.pl.* trousers for casual wear: *a pair of slacks.*
— *v.* become slack or inactive: *Don't* **slack off** *as exams approach; She likes to* **slack up** (= relax) *a little before trying harder.* — **slack·er** *n.* — **slack·ness** *n.*

slack·en *v.* to slack.

slain *pp.* of SLAY.

slake *v.* **slakes, slaked, slak·ing** quench or satisfy: *to slake one's thirst, desire for revenge; to slake a fire;* **Slaked lime** *used in mortars and cements is produced by putting water on lime.*

sla·lom (SLAH·lum, SLAL·um) *n.* a skiing race down a zigzag course between poles forming a line of obstacles.

slam *n.* **1** the bang of a violent impact, as of a door pushed shut. **2** [short form] GRAND SLAM or LITTLE SLAM.
— *v.* **slams, slammed, slam·ming** knock or bang: *The sales rep had the door slammed in her face; a pileup of cars that slammed into each other; a book badly* slammed (*Informal* for criticized) *by reviewers.*

slam-bang *adj. & adv.* hurried or headlong: *a slam-bang campaign, decision; a slam-bang style of hockey.*

slam·mer *n. Slang.* jail: *He was sent to the slammer for ten years.*

slan·der (SLAN·dur) *n.* a false statement to harm another's reputation. — *v.* utter a slander.
— **slan·der·er** *n.* — **slan·der·ous** (-us) *adj.*

slang *n.* nonstandard language with a colourful or vigorous quality.
— *v.* use abusive epithets: *M.P.s sometimes slang at each other in Parliament; The debate became a* **slanging match** *between the two parties.*

slan·guage (SLANG·gwij) *n. Informal.* slang language.

slang·y (SLANG·ee) *adj.* having to do with slang: *a slangy style; slangy vocabulary.*

slant *n.* **1** a slope or incline, esp. from the vertical. **2** a particular or personal bias.
— *v.* **1** slope or incline. **2** express with a slant: *slanted news reporting; an editorial slanted against Sunday shopping.* — *adj.* sloping; also **slant·ing.**

slap *n. & v.* **slaps, slapped, slap·ping** hit with a flat surface, esp. the open hand: *a slap in the face; a slap on the wrist* (= mild rebuke); *a hearty slap on the back; to slap paint on a wall; The police stopped the speeder and slapped* (= summarily imposed) *a fine on him.*

slap·dash *adj. & adv.* hurried or haphazardly.

slap-happy (SLAP·hap·ee) *adj. Slang.* giddy or dazed, as from too many blows.

slap·shot *n. Cdn.* in ice hockey, a powerful shot made with a swinging stroke.

slap·stick *n.* comedy characterized by horseplay and broad humour.

slash *n.* **1** a sweeping stroke, as with a knife. **2** a resulting gash or slit. **3** a slanted stroke used in writing, as in "and/or."
— *adj.: a slash mark; a flapless* **slash pocket** *with a slanted opening.*
— *v.* cut, as with a slash: *to slash at someone with a knife; The car was found with its tires slashed; Prices are slashed* (= reduced sharply) *the day after Christmas; to slash* (= cut) *costs, fares, spending; a penalty for slashing* (= swinging the hockey stick at an opponent); *the* **slash and burn** *method of clearing forests.* — **slash·er** *n.*

slat *n.* a narrow strip of material, as of a Venetian blind or the bars of a crib.

slate *n.* **1** a rock that splits in layers and is used for roofing and paving. **2** a slab of slate; also, its bluish-grey colour: *Children write on slates with chalk; We start off with a* **clean slate** (= clean record). **3** a list of candidates, as for an election.

slat·ed (SLAY·tid) *adj.* designated or scheduled: *candidates slated for the presidency; Jane is slated to be the next president; elections slated for the fall.*

slath·er (SLATH·ur, "TH" as in "the") *v. Informal.* pour or spread generously, as jam, paint, etc.: *Our neighbourhood will be slathered with garbage if the* *disposal plan goes through.*

slaugh·ter (SLAW·tur) *n.* massacre; also, butchery: *indiscriminate, mass, needless, relentless, wanton, wholesale slaughter; the slaughter on the highways during the Christmas rush.*
— *v.* commit massacre; also, butcher, as in a slaughterhouse.

slaugh·ter·house (SLAW·tur·house) *n.* an establishment in which animals are killed for food.

slave *n.* 1 a person owned by another: *the liberation of slaves.* 2 a victim of a habit or a person subject to a dominating influence: *a slave to fashion.* 3 one who slaves; *adj.: a slave ant, trader; slave labour.*
— *v.* **slaves, slaved, slav·ing** work like a slave: *to slave over a tiresome task; She slaved away at her thesis for five years.*

slav·er *n.* 1 (SLAY·vur) a slave dealer or his ship. 2 (SLAV·ur) saliva dribbling from the mouth, as of a dog.
— *v.* slobber: *to slaver* (= drool) *over something trivial.*

slav·er·y (SLAY·vuh·ree) *n.* 1 the custom or practice of owning slaves: *to abolish slavery.* 2 the condition of slaves; bondage or drudgery: *to be held in, to live in slavery.*

slav·ish (SLAY·vish) *adj.* of or like slaves; servile.
— **slav·ish·ly** *adv.;* **slav·ish·ness** *n.*

slaw *n.* [short form] coleslaw.

slay *v.* **slays, slew, slain, slay·ing** [literary use] kill violently. — **slay·er** *n.*

sleaze (SLEEZ) *n.* the condition of being sleazy or shabby.

slea·zy (SLEE·zee) *adj.* **-zi·er, -zi·est** 1 squalid or disreputable; cheap; shabby: *a sleazy hotel.* 2 of fabrics, flimsy or thin. — **slea·zi·ly** *adv.;* **slea·zi·ness** *n.*

sled *n.* a vehicle with parallel runners instead of wheels for travelling over snow and ice.
— *v.* **sleds, sled·ded, sled·ding** carry or ride on a sled: *There is some tough sledding* (= riding) *ahead as the exams approach.* — **sled·der** *n.*

sledge *n.* 1 a heavy sled, usually drawn by a horse. 2 a large, heavy hammer, usually swung with both hands; also **sledge·ham·mer** (SLEJ·ham·ur) *n.*
— *v.* 1 carry or draw on a sledge. 2 hit with a sledgehammer.

sleek *adj.* smooth and glossy: *sleek hair; a sleek automobile; a sleek* (= smooth-talking) *sales rep.*
— *v.* slick: *Ballerinas have their heads sleeked into buns.*

sleep *n.* a state of natural unconsciousness that provides periodic rest for mind and body: *We go to sleep at night hoping to get* or *have a good night's sleep; It's no use losing sleep over* (= worrying a lot about) *things we can't do anything about; drugs to induce sleep; a deep, heavy, light, restful, sound sleep; I didn't get enough sleep last night.*
— **put to sleep** 1 to make an animal unconscious. 2 kill mercifully: *The dog was so ill it had to be put to sleep.*
— *v.* 1 be in sleep: *Infants sleep longer than adults; He likes to sleep on* (= take time to consider) *important*

decisions; She never slept (Informal for had sex) with anyone before marrying. 2 to accommodate: *Our motor home sleeps six.*
— **sleep around** *Informal.* be promiscuous: *He stopped sleeping around after getting married.*
— **sleep in** sleep beyond one's waking-up time.
— **sleep off** get over by sleeping: *He sleeps it off if when he has a bad day.*

sleep·er *n.* 1 one that sleeps. 2 also **sleeping car**, a railway car with berths for passengers. 3 a railway tie. 4 *Informal.* a person or thing that suddenly attains fame or success: *a movie sleeper.* 5 an infant's one-piece sleeping garment.

sleeping bag *n.* a bag for sleeping in outdoors.

sleeping pill or **sleeping tablet** *n.* a pill containing a sleep-inducing drug.

sleep·walk·ing (SLEEP·waw·king) *n.* the act or practice of a neurotic person acting as if awake during sleep without remembering it on waking up.

sleep·wear (SLEEP·ware) *n.* night clothes.

sleep·y *adj.* **sleep·i·er, -i·est** 1 inclined to sleep: *a sleepy face, look; sleepy eyes; a sleepy-eyed dog.* 2 quiet or inactive: *a sleepy village.*
— **sleep·i·ly** *adv.;* **sleep·i·ness** *n.*

sleep·y·head (SLEE·pee·hed) *n.* a sleepy person.

sleet *n.* 1 a fall of freezing rain. 2 a glaze or ice formed by freezing rain. — *v.* to shower sleet. — **sleet·y** *adj.*

sleeve *n.* 1 the arm of a garment: *She rolled up her sleeves and got down to work; He wears his heart on his sleeve* (= makes no secret of his feelings). 2 a tubelike part fitting around another part, as in engine bearings. 3 slipcase: *storage sleeves for digital discs, floppies.*
— **up one's sleeve** in secret: *They must be laughing up their sleeves; She seems to have something up her sleeve* (= kept secretly to use later).

sleigh (SLAY) *n. & v.* sled or sledge.

sleight of hand (SLIGHT-) *n.* 1 skill with the hands, as of a magician or juggler. 2 a magician's trick or tricks.

slen·der (SLEN·dur) *adj.* 1 slim and graceful: *a slender beauty, figure.* 2 slight; scanty; meagre: *a slender hope, income; a man of slender means.* — **slen·der·ness** *n.*

slen·der·ize (SLEN·dur·ize) *v.* **-iz·es, -ized, -iz·ing** become or make slender or appear slender.

slept *pt. & pp.* of SLEEP.

sleuth (SLOOTH) *n. & v. Informal.* (act as) a detective.

sleuth·hound *n.* bloodhound.

slew *pt.* of SLAY.
— *n.* 1 *Informal.* a large amount or number; lot: *a whole slew of decisions, fish, offices, people.* 2 a veer or swing. 3 a swampy inlet. 4 *Cdn.* same as SLOUGH, defs. 2 & 3.
— *v.* veer: *The car slewed into a snowbank.*

slice *n.* 1 a thin broad piece cut from bread, meat, cheese, fruits, etc. 2 a share or portion: *a slice of luck, profits; drama as a slice* (= representation) *of life.*
— *v.* **slic·es, sliced, slic·ing** 1 cut (*away, into, off,* or *up*) as a slice or slices: *to slice into the ham; She sliced it*

*thin; the greatest thing since **sliced bread** (Informal for simply the greatest).* **2** hit a ball so that it goes off course or into a backspin. — **slic·er** *n.*

slick *adj.* **1** smooth or slippery, as with oil. **2** facile, clever, or skilful: *slick solutions to a complex problem; a slick excuse, operator, talker; Even the slickest of today's computers can't think like humans.*
— *v.* make smooth or glossy.
— **slick up** smarten; spruce up.
— *n.* an oily spot: *an oil slick on the water.*
— **slick·ly** *adv.;* **slick·ness** *n.*

slick·er *n.* **1** a raincoat, esp. of oilskin. **2** *Informal.* a wily person: *a city slicker.*

slide *v.* **slides, slid, slid·ing** move or cause to move smoothly in contact with a surface: *Sleds slide downhill, slide over snow and ice; The baseball player slid into second base; a sliding door, drawer; Prices slid* (= went down) *2% last month; a matter too urgent to **let slide*** (= drift).
— *n.* **1** a sliding, as of rock, a sliding surface or chute, as on a children's playground, etc. **2** something that is slid into place for use, as a small glass plate containing an object examined under a microscope or a transparency for projection on a screen: *to show slides; to mount slides.*

slide fastener *n.* a zipper.

slid·er (SLY·dur) *n.* **1** a person or thing that slides. **2** in baseball, a slightly curving fast pitch.

sliding scale *n.* a schedule of taxes, fees, wages, etc. that varies to suit changing conditions such as cost of living.

slier, sliest See SLY.

slight *adj.* **1** small; not considerable: *a slight difference, excuse; on the slightest pretext.* **2** small in build: *a slight figure, girl.*
— *v.* treat as insignificant, esp. intentionally: *She felt slighted by his superior manner.*
— *n.* a humiliation or discourtesy.
— **slight·ly** *adv.*

sli·ly (SLY·lee) same as SLYLY.

slim *adj.* **slim·mer, slim·mest** thin or small: *a slim woman; a slim attendance, chance, choice; We made **slim pickings** of the myth* (= destroyed it).
— *v.* **slims, slimmed, slim·ming** make or become slim: *to slim by going on a diet; slimming exercises.*

slime *n.* something sticky and filthy, as soft mud, mould on decaying vegetable matter, or the mucous coating on snails, fish, etc.: *the oozing slime.*
— **slim·y** (SLY·mee) *adj.* **slim·i·er, -i·est.**

slim-jim *n. Slang.* one that is very slim.

sling *n.* **1** a device consisting of a strip of leather for throwing a stone held in its loop. **2** such a fling or throw: *to suffer **the slings and arrows** of outrageous fortune* (= the hard knocks of life). **3** a similar looped device for supporting an arm in a cast, for lifting a load, carrying a rifle, etc.
— *v.* **slings, slung, sling·ing** **1** suspend in or throw as with a sling: *a hammock slung between trees; Her purse was slung over her shoulder; He was accused of **slinging mud at*** (= slandering) *his rivals.* **2** *Slang.* prepare and

serve: *He slings hamburgers at a fast-food outlet; He also knows how to **sling it** or **sling the bull*** (= talk glibly).

sling·shot *n.* **1** a forked stick with an elastic sling attached for shooting stones, etc. **2** such a shot.

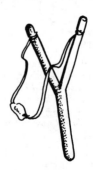

slink *v.* **slinks,** *pt. & pp.* **slunk** or **slinked, slink·ing** go or move *away, by,* etc. in a stealthy manner, as from fear.

slink·y *adj.* **slink·i·er, -i·est** **1** furtive or stealthy. **2** of a woman's clothing, hugging the body; close-fitting: *a slinky evening gown.*

slip *v.* **slips, slipped, slip·ping** **1** (cause) to move smoothly or easily; hence, slide: *She slipped and fell on the ice; He slipped off his coat and shoes; She slipped me a note; Let me slip* (= change) *into something more comfortable; He tried to slip out of the room; Secrets **slip out.*** **2** escape: *Names slip (from) my mind; Don't let a good opportunity slip by; He **let slip** a few epithets in his fury.* **3** decline: *Polls showed his popularity slipping; He's liable to **slip up*** (= err) *in spelling.*
— *n.* **1** a slipping: *a Freudian slip; to make a **slip of the tongue*** (= an unintentional error in speech); *to **give someone the slip*** (= elude someone). **2** something that is slipped on, as a pillowcase, a woman's sleeveless undergarment or petticoat, etc. **3** a docking space for ships between wharves or docks. **4** a piece of paper or something of small size: *a slip of paper; a bank deposit slip; a pink slip* (= notice of being fired); *rejection slip (returned by a publisher with a manuscript); sales slip* (= receipt); *a rose slip* (= cutting) *for planting; a slip of a* (= young or slim) *boy, child, girl.*

slip·case *n.* a protective case or container for a book or phonograph record with one edge open.

slip·cov·er (SLIP·cuv·ur) *n.* a fitted protective cover for a sofa or chair.

slip·knot *n.* a running knot, as of a noose (**slip noose**) or lasso.

slip·page (SLIP·ij) *n.* slipping, as in machinery, or its extent.

slipped disk *n.* rupture or hernia of the disk between two vertebrae causing intense pain in the back and legs.

slip·per *n.* a light loose shoe for indoor wear: *a pair of slippers; ballet slippers; house slippers.*

slip·per·y (SLIP·uh·ree) *adj.* **1** causing slipping: *a wet, slippery road.* **2** slipping away from grasp; hence, unreliable.

slip·shod *adj.* careless in manner or style.

slip-up *n. Informal.* a mistake or mishap.

slit *n.* a straight narrow cut: *a slit in a door for letters.*
— *adj.* having or resembling a long narrow opening: *the slit pupil of a cat's eye; a slit skirt; a slit trench for protection in warfare.*
— *v.* **slits, slit, slit·ting** split open by a slit: *to slit open an envelope.*

slith·er ("th" as in "the") *n.* an unsteady sliding or crawling motion.
— *v.* move along in a slither: *Snakes slither along the ground.* — **slith·er·y** *adj.*

sliv·er (SLIV·ur) *v.* cut or split into long, thin pieces.
— *n.* such a piece; splinter: *almond slivers; a sliver of soap.*

slob *n. Informal.* a slovenly or stupid person.

slob·ber *n.* 1 saliva running from the mouth. 2 excessive sentimentality.
— *v.* 1 wet or smear with slobber. 2 indulge in slobber *over* something. — **slob·ber·y** *adj.*

slob ice *n. Cdn.* slushy ice that clogs movement over water.

sloe-eyed (SLOH·ide) *adj.* having blue-black or almond-shaped eyes.

slog *v.* **slogs, slogged, slog·ging** work hard or toil *at* or *away* at something.
— *n.:* *She earned her Ph.D. after a 10-year slog of night school.*

slo·gan (SLOH·gun) *n.* a catchy phrase or motto used in advertising and promotion, as "Peace with honour" or "Satisfaction or your money back."

slop *n.* 1 something semiliquid or watery, as slush, spilled liquid, gruel, etc. 2 usually **slops** *pl.* liquid waste such as swill or collected urine.
— *v.* **slops, slopped, slop·ping** spill; pass a limit: *He slopped his drink all over the place; Water from the bath slopped over onto the washroom floor.*

slope *n.* an angle made with the horizontal; incline: *the gentle slope of a wheelchair ramp; to coast down a slope; a gradual slope.*
— *v.* **slopes, sloped, slop·ing** make a slope: *a gently, gradually sloping roof.*

slop·py *adj.* **slop·pi·er, slop·pi·est** slovenly: *sloppy habits, work; a sloppy (= messy) eater; sloppy (= muddy) reasoning; sloppy (= slushy and wet) weather.*

sloppy Joe *n.* ground beef prepared with sauce and served on a bun.

slosh *v.* splash through or with slush or muddy water.
— **slosh·y** *adj.*

slot *n.* 1 a small, narrow depression for inserting something, as for coins to operate a SLOT MACHINE. 2 *Informal.* a position in a series or sequence, as on a program: *a story to fill a two-minute slot in the evening news.*
— *v.* **slots, slot·ted, slot·ting** 1 make a slot. 2 *Informal.* to place in a slot: *a marketing wizard who can slot in the right product at the right time.*

sloth (SLAWTH, SLOHTH, "TH" as in "thin") *n.*

laziness in regard to work: *the natural sloth of slave labour.*
— **sloth·ful** *adj.:* *the slothful attitude of workers without incentives; a life of slothful ease.*

slot machine *n.* a machine operated by inserting a coin in its slot, esp. a vending machine or gambling machine.

slouch *n.* 1 a slovenly or incompetent person: *He's no slouch when it comes to cleaning up.* 2 a forward bend or droop of head and shoulders.
— *v.* move, stand, or sit with a slouch. — **slouch·y** *adj.*

slough *n.* 1 (rhyme: "HOW") a place of deep mud; quagmire; hence, a dejected condition: *the slough of despond.* 2 (SLOO) a swamp, esp. a backwater or inlet; slew. 3 (SLOO) in the Prairies, a small body of water formed by rain or melted snow; slew. 4 (SLUF) castoff skin, esp. of a snake; *v.* cast off or discard.

slov·en·ly (SLUV·un·lee) *adj.* **-li·er, -li·est** sloppy or slipshod. — **slov·en·li·ness** *n.*

slow (SLOH) *adj.* taking longer than normal or necessary: *a slow (= not fast) train; He's slow at learning; slow to learn; a slow watch (that falls behind in showing the correct time); a slow fire (slow in burning); a slow (= not lively) party; Business is slow (= slack or sluggish).*
— *adv.* in a slow manner [also **slowly,** used after a verb or with "how"]: *Drive slow(ly); See how slow(ly) she drives; a slow-moving vehicle; Water evaporates slowly; Slowly but surely the end drew near.*
— *v.* make or become slow or slower: *Let's slow down; to slow down an army's advance.*
— **slow·ness** *n.*

slow burn *n. Informal.* controlled but gradually rising anger, esp. as a dramatic device: *to do a slow burn.*

slow·down *n.* a slowing down of a business, operation, etc.: *an economic slowdown; a slowdown in production.*

slow·ly (SLOH·lee) *adv.* See SLOW.

slow motion *n.* motion-picture action shown at slower-than-normal speed: *They showed the action in slow motion.* — **slow-motion** *adj.:* *slow-motion photography.*

slow·poke *n. Informal.* one who moves or does anything slowly.

slow-witted (SLOH·wit·id) *adj.* mentally dull.

sludge *n.* a muddy mixture or slushy deposit, as the sediments resulting from ore refining, sewage treatment, etc. — **sludg·y** *adj.* **sludg·i·er, -i·est.**

slug *n.* 1 a snaillike mollusc without a real shell. 2 a small piece of metal, as a bullet, a disk to use in a slot machine, or a strip of type metal or cast type. 3 a hard blow, esp. with the fist or a bat.
— *v.* **slugs, slugged, slug·ging** hit hard, as with the fist or a bat: *They slugged it out.* — **slug·ger** *n.*

slug·gard (SLUG·urd) *n.* one who is lazy or sluggish.

slug·gish (SLUG·ish) *adj.* slow-moving: *a sluggish mind, stream; sluggish bowels.*

sluice (SLOOSE) *n.* 1 a gate for controlling a flow of water, as of a dam; also **sluice gate.** 2 a channel controlled by a gate, as the **sluice·way** for surplus water from a dam or a trough for washing gold ore of impurities.

— *v.* **sluic·es, sluiced, sluic·ing** **1** let out water, wash gold from ore, send logs, etc. by means of a sluice. **2** wash down with flowing water: *to sluice a driveway.*

slum *n.* an overcrowded, poverty-stricken area, as of a large city: *Most slums have high illness, disease, and crime rates;* **adj.:** *a slum area, landlord; slum clearance, conditions.*
— *v.* **slums, slummed, slum·ming** **1** visit the slums. **2** visit a place inferior to one's usual surroundings: *to go slumming; Bored with high society, she slummed it for a while.*

slum·ber (SLUM·bur) *n.* light sleep; doze: *the peaceful slumber of a newborn babe.*
— *v.* have a light sleep: *a slumbering giant; a slumbering* (= dormant) *volcano.*

slum·lord *n.* the often absentee owner of slum property.

slump *v.* **1** sink or decline suddenly: *She slumped to the ground in a faint.* **2** slouch or droop in posture: *His shoulders slumped under the weight of the pails of water he was carrying.*
— *n.:* *a business, economic, stock-market slump.*

slung *pt. & pp.* of SLING.

slunk *pt. & pp.* of SLINK.

slur *v.* **slurs, slurred, slur·ring** **1** pass hurriedly or carelessly over syllables or sounds in pronouncing: *He tends to slur over* (= minimize) *their mistakes.* **2** to slight or disparage.
— *n.* **1** a slurring. **2** a slighting remark: *to cast a slur on someone's character; an ethnic, racial slur.* **3** slurred musical notes or a line connecting such notes.

slurp *n. Slang.* a sucking noise, as made when sipping.
— *v.* eat or drink with a slurp: *to slurp soup.*

slush *n.* watery mud or partly melted snow.
— **slush·y** *adj.*

slush fund *n.* a fund for corrupt purposes, esp. for bribing public officials.

slut *n.* **1** a slovenly woman. **2** a prostitute.
— **slut·tish** *adj.*

sly *adj.* **sli·er** or **sly·er, sli·est** or **sly·est** crafty or wily: *a sly cat, fox, manoeuvre; a sly* (= furtive) *wink.*
— **on the sly** in a sly manner.
— **sly·ly** or **sli·ly** *adv.;* **sly·ness** *n.*

smack *n. & v.* **1** (have) a slight but distinctive taste, flavour, or suggestion: *His airs smack of superiority; There's a smack of chicory in this coffee.* **2** (make) noise made with lips, as when chewing food, kissing loudly, or with a whip, as when cracking it. **3** *Informal.* slap: *a smack in the face; I'm going to smack you one; She smacked him in the face and vice versa.*
— *adv.* directly: *He fell smack on his face; The place you can't find on the map is* **smack dab** (= right there) *in the centre of the city.*

small (SMAWL) *adj.* **1** relatively not large; of less than the usual size, quantity, importance, etc.: *a small car, child;* REGULAR *and* SMALL *capitals; from small beginnings; a* **small business** *(involving small capital investment and a limited number of employees); Small wonder! "Small world!" he said on meeting me so far*

from home. **2** small in mind: *a small man; a small* (= mean) *nature; One sometimes* **feels small** (= unimportant or shameful) *after saying something nasty.*
— *n.* something small: *the small* (= narrowest part) *of the back.* — **small·ness** *n.*

small arms *n. pl.* firearms that are easy to carry and use, as revolvers, rifles, etc., not artillery.

small fry *n. pl.* offspring or people of little importance.

small hours *n. pl.* 1, 2, 3, etc. a.m.: *in the small hours of the morning; We worked into the small hours of Tuesday night.*

small potatoes *n. pl.* [with sing. or pl. v.] *Slang.* person(s) or thing(s) considered insignificant.

small talk *n.* light conversation; chitchat: *to make small talk at a party.*

small-time *adj. Informal.* minor or mediocre.
— **small-tim·er** *n.*

smart *n. & v.* **1** (cause or feel) sharp pain: *My head is still smarting.* **2** (feel) distress of mind: *I'm still smarting over* or *at* or *under the injustice.*
— *adj.* **1** clever or intelligent: *a smart kid, move, reply, youngster; looking smart and intelligent; a smart* (= stylish) *uniform; the smart* (= fashionable) *set; Don't get smart* (= impudent) *with me.* **2** lively: *a smart pace.* **3** causing sharp pain: *a smart blow.* **4** computer-aided or intelligent: *a* **smart bomb** *(containing a guidance system); a* **smart card** *(that is computer-readable); a* **smart terminal** *(with some data-processing capability, not a "dumb terminal").*
— **smarts** *n. pl.* intelligence: *They've got the smarts and savvy; noted for their smarts; small in size but long on the smarts.* — **smart·ly** *adv.;* **smart·ness** *n.*

smart al·eck or **smart al·ec** (SMART·AL·ick) *n. Informal.* one who is conceited or obnoxious; also *adj.* Also **smart-alecky** *adj.*

smart-ass *n. & adj. Slang.* smart aleck or smart-alecky: *some smart-ass of a lawyer, novelist; a smart-ass answer, lawyer, novelist.*

smart·en *v.* make or become smart or smarter.

smash *v.* **1** break into pieces with violence, as a glass window with a rock. **2** deal a crushing blow to: *to smash an enemy, an uprising.* **3** crash: *The car smashed through the wall and into the living room.*
— *n.* **1** a violent crash or its sound. **2** a crushing blow; ruin. **3** *Informal.* a popular success or great hit; *adj.:* *smash hit, musical.*

smashing *adj.* **1** crushing: *a smashing defeat.* **2** impressive or striking: *The play was a smashing success.*

smash-up *n.* a wreck; disaster.

smat·ter·ing (SMAT·ur·ing) *n.* **1** slight knowledge: *He has (picked up) only a smattering of the language, subject.* **2** a small number or amount: *a big major prize and a smattering of smaller ones.*

smear (SMEER) *v.* spread or daub with anything greasy, sticky, or dirty; hence, mark or stain; soil a reputation: *a wall smeared with paint.*
— *n.* **1** a blotch, mark, or stain; *adj.:* *a smear*

campaign; "Nazi," "Communist," "racist," and such **smear words** used to discredit an opponent. **2** a small sample of a substance for testing medically: *a cervical, vaginal smear; Dr. Jo took a smear of Joe's mouth for a cancer test; Dr. Joe did a Pap smear* (= test) *on her.*
— **smear·y** *adj.*

smell *n.* **1** sense of perception through the nose. **2** the quality so perceived; odour or scent: *Burning rubber gives off an acrid smell; the bad, disagreeable, foul, strong smell of rotten eggs; a faint, slight but persistent smell of tobacco; the rank smell of a rotting carcass; the sweet smell of success.* **3** an act of smelling.
— *v.* **smells,** *pt. & pp.* **smelled** or **smelt, smell·ing** **1** have a particular smell: *A rose smells sweet; What you're cooking smells like bacon and eggs; Your kitchen smells of onions.* **2** stink: *Unwashed children smell (bad).* **3** recognize by or as if by smell: *to smell smoke, trouble, a rat; Don't smell* (= sniff) *it; Police dogs are trained to smell out* (= smell and find) *drugs.*

smell·y *adj.* **smell·i·er, -i·est** having a bad smell.

smelt *n.* a silvery food fish similar to salmon but smaller and with larger scales.
— *v.* **1** melt ore and extract metal. **2** obtain or refine metal by this method.

smelt·er *n.* **1** one who smelts. **2** a furnace for smelting. **3** a smelting works, or **smelt·er·y** *n.* **-er·ies.**

smidg·en (SMIJ·un) *n. Informal.* a small amount: *She brightened a smidgen when she saw us and asked us in; to put up with a smidgen of inconvenience. Also* **smidg·in, smidg·eon.**

smile *n.* a relaxed expression of the face, usually with an upward curving mouth and parted lips, to show amusement, pleasure, etc.; hence, an act of smiling: *She cracked, flashed, hid, repressed a smile; His joke evoked a smile; a beguiling, cheerful, disarming, fixed, forced, happy, intriguing, radiant, sunny, supercilious smile; She was* **all smiles** *when she heard the news.*
— *v.* make a smile: *He smiled at her (in admiration); She was smiling from ear to ear; Fortune smiles on* (= favours) *the brave.*
— **smil·ey** or **smil·y** *adj.: a button with a smiley face* (= happy-face design).

smirk *v. & n.* (put on) an affected or silly smile; simper.

smite *v.* **smites,** *pt.* **smote,** *pp.* **smit·ten** or **smote, smit·ing** **1** [literary] strike or hit with force to injure or kill: *God smote their enemies.* **2** affect or impress strongly: *smitten with* or *by curiosity, (an) illness, love, remorse; You can see he's smitten* (= is in love); *quite smitten with her.*

smith *n.* a worker in metal, esp. a blacksmith.

smith·er·eens (smith·uh·REENZ, "th" as in "the") *n. pl. Informal.* small bits or fragments: *It was broken* or *smashed into smithereens.*

smith·y ("th" as in "the" or as in "thin") *n.* **smith·ies** a smith's workshop.

smock *n.* a loose outer garment worn to protect one's clothes while working.

smog *n.* a mixture of fog and smoke polluting the air.
— **smog·gy** *adj.*

smoke *n.* **1** fumes given off by something burning: *Chimneys belch, emit, give off smoke; smoke pouring, rising from smokestacks eddies, spirals upward; a column, pall, puff, wisp of smoke; People inhale smoke; "Where there's smoke there's fire"; His dream about a windfall* **went up in smoke** (= ended suddenly) *when he woke up; They used to discuss politics in* **smoke-filled rooms.** **2** mist, fog, or anything resembling smoke. **3** a smoking of a cigar, cigarette, etc.: *to have a smoke; He just went out for a smoke.*
— *v.* **smokes, smoked, smok·ing** **1** give off smoke: *a smoking wood stove; The killer was caught red-handed, with the smoking gun in his hand.* **2** use a cigar, cigarette, pipe, etc. for pleasure: *He smokes like a chimney.* **3** treat with smoke, as in curing meat or fish in a smokehouse, in fumigation, blackening glasses, etc.
— **smoke out** force to come out, as snakes from a hole.
— **smok·er** *n.: a chain smoker; heavy smoker.*

smoke detector *n.* a home fire-alarm device that is set off in the presence of smoke.

smoke·house *n.* a room in which ham, bacon, and other salt-cured meats are hung for smoking.

smoke·screen *n.* a thick smoke used to hide troops, ships, etc. from the enemy: *to lay (down) a smokescreen.*

smoke·stack *n.* a tall chimney, as of a factory, or the funnel of a ship, locomotive, etc.

smok·ey (SMOH·kee) *adj.* same as SMOKY.

smoking gun *n.* a conclusive piece of evidence, as smoke from a gun is sure sign of its firing.

smok·y *adj.* **smok·i·er, -i·est** **1** giving off smoke: *a smoky fire.* **2** filled with smoke: *a smoky atmosphere, bar, cafe, club, hall, room; the smoky air of California.* **3** like smoke in appearance, smell, etc.: *a whisky described as raw, strong, and very smoky; a smoky blue-grey colour; meat with a smoky flavour.*
— **smok·i·ness** *n.*

smol·der (SMOLE·dur) See SMOULDER.

smooch (long "oo") *n. & v. Slang.* kiss or pet.
— **smooch·y** *adj.*

smooth ("th" as in "the") *adj.* perfectly even, without roughness; polished: *a smooth surface that is smooth to the touch; smooth as glass, silk; pebbles worn smooth by the waves; smooth sailing on calm seas; a smooth ride; a smooth-bore firearm without grooves in the barrel; a smooth* (= mild-tasting) *wine; a smooth* (= deceptive) *sales pitch; a smooth-tongued flatterer.*
— *v.* make smooth or smoother, easy, or refined: *She stood up to smooth down her ruffled dress.*
— **smooth away** get rid of difficulties.
— **smooth over** reduce differences; make faults, etc. seem less serious.

smooth·ie or **smooth·y** (SMOO·thee, "th" as in "the") *n. Informal.* a suave, often smooth-tongued person: *He was nicknamed "Old Smoothie."*

smor·gas·bord (SMOR·gus·bord) *n.* a buffet luncheon or supper consisting of a variety of foods spread on a table.

smote *pt. & a pp.* of SMITE.

smoth·er (SMUTH·ur, "TH" as in "the") *v.* cover so as to deprive of air: *to smother a fire with ashes; to smother* (= repress) *one's resentment; a child smothered* (= overwhelmed) *with kisses; smothered* (= covered and baked) *chicken; an infant accidentally smothered* (= suffocated) *in bed.*
— *n.* 1 something dense and stifling, as smoke, fog, etc. 2 confusion or welter.

smoul·der or **smol·der** (SMOLE·dur) *v.* 1 burn and smoke without flame: *a smouldering fire.* 2 exist in a suppressed condition: *smouldering hatred, rebellion.*
— *n.* flameless burning.

smudge *n.* 1 a stained or smeared spot. 2 a smoky fire, as from a **smudge pot** or stove used to protect plants from frost or animals from insects.
— *v.* smudg·es, smudged, smudg·ing 1 smear or stain; smudg·y *adj.* 2 protect an orchard with smudge.

smug *adj.* smug·ger, smug·gest self-satisfied or complacent in a superior or secure manner: *a smug look; smug respectability.*

smug·gle (SMUG·ul) *v.* smug·gles, smug·gled, smug·gling bring into or take out of a country illegally or secretly: *Drugs are smuggled across a border, past* or *through customs, into* or *out of a country; to engage in smuggling.* — smug·gler *n.*

smut *n.* obscene talk or writing: *a smut peddler.*
— smut·ty *adj.* smut·ti·er, smut·ti·est.

smutch *n. & v.* soil; stain; grime. — smutch·y *adj.*

snack *v. & n.* (eat) a light meal: *between-meal snacks; party snacks.*

snack bar *n.* a lunch counter serving snacks.

sna·fu (SNAF·oo) *n. Slang.* a state of confusion or disorder.
— *v.* -fues, -fued, -fu·ing throw into confusion: *Airline schedules were snafued when the computer went on the blink.*

snag *n.* 1 an underwater obstacle, as a tree or branch, that is dangerous to boats; also, something sharp or pointed. 2 a hidden or unexpected difficulty: *Our plans hit a snag.*
— *v.* snags, snagged, snag·ging 1 catch using a snag: *Poachers snag fish.* 2 hinder, as if with a snag: *a project snagged by difficulties from the beginning.*
— snag·gy *adj.*

snail *n.* a small, soft-bodied, slow-moving mollusc with a spiral shell on its back for coiling back into if molested.
— **at a snail's pace** very slowly.

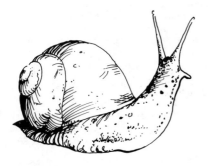

snake *n.* 1 a long, scaly, legless reptile with a forked tongue and tapering tail: *Snakes bite, crawl, strike; a snake in the grass* (= hidden danger or enemy). 2 a sly or deceitful person.
— *v.* snakes, snaked, snak·ing move, wind, or twist like a snake: *to snake one's way through a crowd.*

snake·bird *n.* a swimming bird with a long neck, also called "darter."

snak·y (SNAY·kee) *adj.* snak·i·er, -i·est that looks or moves like a snake: *the snaky eel; a snaky river.*

snap *v.* snaps, snapped, snap·ping 1 make a sudden, sharp sound, as of a dry twig or taut rope breaking or a finger flicked audibly against the thumb: *to snap a whip.* 2 break suddenly: *The rope snapped; Frost can snap tree branches.* 3 make a quick, sharp movement, as an animal snatching food in its jaws: *The fish snapped at the bait; The best bargains were snapped up by those first to arrive; Each one snapped to attention as his name was called; a football snapped back into play from the scrimmage line; She **snaps at** (= speaks sharply to) her child when impatient; Her eyes were snapping* (= flashing) *with fury; tourists snapping pictures* (= taking snapshots).
— **snap out of it** *Informal.* get quickly out of a bad mood or habit.
— *n.* 1 a quick, cracking sound, as of a whip or a sudden bite. 2 a short, sharp utterance. 3 *Informal.* vigour or liveliness. 4 a brief spell of cold weather: *a cold snap.* 5 a fastener or clasp that closes with a click. 6 a thin, crisp cookie: *lemon snaps.* 7 *Informal.* a snapshot. 8 *Slang.* an easy job; cinch: *It was a snap to get* or *getting a ticket to the show.*
— *adj.* 1 quick: *a snap decision, election, judgment, vote.* 2 that fastens with a snapping sound: *a snap fastener* ("press stud"); *snap lock, ring.*

snap·pish (SNAP·ish) *adj.* quick-tempered; irascible: *He tends to be a bit snappish when disturbed during his afternoon nap.*

snap·py *adj.* snap·pi·er, snap·pi·est 1 inclined to be snappish or ill-tempered: *a snappy temperament.* 2 crackling, as a pine fire. 3 smart or lively: *the snappy changing of the guard on Parliament Hill; decorated in bright, snappy colours; a snappy dresser; Make it snappy* (= Move quickly)!

snap·shot *n.* a casual photograph taken with a hand camera.

snare *n.* 1 a trap made with a noose for catching small birds and animals. 2 a pitfall or trap.
— *v.* snares, snared, snar·ing catch as in a snare.

snarl *v. & n.* 1 (make) an angry or threatening growling sound, as a dog with its teeth bared. 2 (utter) sharp, angry words: *The drivers snarled at each other.* 3 tangle; disorder: *a traffic snarl during rush hour.*

snatch *v.* seize or grasp roughly or hastily: *He snatched her purse and ran; a youth snatched from the jaws of death.*
— *n.* 1 a snatching. 2 a short period or small amount: *I caught snatches of the conversation; snatches of a show, of sleep.*

snaz·zy *adj. Slang.* stylish in a showy way: *a line of snazzy clothes for teens; a snazzy outfit, suit, yuppie; fish*

696

with snazzy trimmings.

sneak (SNEEK) *v.* move or act in a stealthy or cowardly manner: *He sneaked away at night; sneaked into the house by a back door; sneaked up on her and gave her a scare; a sneaking* (=secret) *suspicion.*
— *n.* a sneaking or one who sneaks.
— *adj.* stealthy: *a sneak attack, thief.*
— sneak·y *adj.* sneak·i·er, -i·est.

sneak·ers (SNEE·kurz) *n. pl.* sports shoes with soles of soft material; running shoes.

sneak preview *n.* advance showing of a motion picture before its release to test audience reaction.

sneer *v.* show ill-natured contempt by facial expression, words, tone of voice, etc.: *He sneers at anything that is not imported.* — *n.* a sneering or its expression.

sneeze *n.* an involuntary sudden and violent expulsion of air through the nose and mouth to clear the nostrils of something irritating.
— *v.* sneez·es, sneezed, sneez·ing make a sneeze.
— sneeze at *Informal.* scorn or despise: *a respectable offer that is not to be sneezed at.*

snick·er *v. & n.* (utter) a sly, half-suppressed laugh.

snide *adj.* slyly critical: *He made snide references to his opponent's past; a snide aside, remark, suggestion; Jan has a snide* (=mean or spiteful) *side.*

sniff *v.* 1 draw air quickly and audibly through the nose, as to test something by smelling: *He died from sniffing glue for kicks; The dog sniffs at everyone; a police dog trained to sniff out* (=detect) *drugs and explosives.* 2 express scorn by sniffing.
— *n.* a sniffing or its sound; also, a breathing in of something.

snif·fle (SNIF·ul) *v.* snif·fles, snif·fled, snif·fling sniff again and again, as when one has a head cold or is crying.
— *n.* a sniffling sound: *He has the sniffles* (=a head cold with congested nose).

snig·ger (SNIG·ur) *n. & v.* same as SNICKER.

snip *v.* snips, snipped, snip·ping cut off or clip, as hair with scissors, in a short, quick stroke.
— *n.* 1 a snipping or snipped piece. 2 snips *pl.* [with sing. *v.*] hand shears for cutting sheet metal.

snipe *v.* snipes, sniped, snip·ing 1 hunt snipe. 2 shoot at people from a hidden position. 3 make direct verbal attacks *at* people.
— *n.* a long-billed, chunky, black-and-white bird.
— snip·er *n.*

snip·pet (SNIP·it) *n.* a small piece as if snipped from a larger source: *snippets of information, writing.*

snip·py (SNIP·ee) *adj.* snip·pi·er, snip·pi·est *Informal.* snappish or haughty: *a snippy reply.*
— snip·pi·ly *adv.*

snit *n. Informal.* a state of peevish annoyance: *He quit his job in a snit.*

snitch *v. Slang.* 1 pilfer or steal. 2 tattle *on* someone.
— *n. Slang.* an informer or tattletale; also, an act of snitching.

sniv·el (SNIV·ul) *v.* -els, -elled or -eled, -el·ling or

-el·ing cry or whine in a sniffling manner.
— *n.* a snivelling.
— sniv·el·ler or sniv·el·er *n.*

snob *n.* one who cares much for rank and wealth and looks down on people considered socially inferior.
— *adj.: Some luxury cars are sold more for their snob appeal and snob value than for fuel efficiency.*
— snob·bish *adj.;* snob·bish·ly *adv.;* snob·bish·ness *n.*

snob·ber·y (SNOB·uh·ree) *n.* snob·ber·ies a snobbish act or quality.

snood (long "oo") *n.* a net worn by women to hold the hair at the back of the head.

snook (short or long "oo") *n.: to cock a snook at* (=thumb one's nose at) *someone.*

snook·er (short or long "oo") *n.* a game similar to billiards: *to shoot snooker.*
— *v. Slang.* to trick or cheat: *We have been snookered; He was snookered into buying the lemon.*

snoop (long "oo") *v. Informal.* inquire into other people's affairs in a sneaky manner: *to snoop using wiretaps.* — *n.* a snooper.

snoop·y *adj.* snoop·i·er, -i·est prying or nosy.

snoot (long "oo") *n. Informal.* the face, esp. one's nose.

snoot·y (SNOO·tee) *adj.* snoot·i·er, -i·est haughty or snobbish. — snoot·i·ly *adv.;* snoot·i·ness *n.*

snooze *n. Informal.* a nap or doze.
— *v.* snooz·es, snoozed, snooz·ing *Informal.* take a snooze, esp. in the daytime.

snore *n. & v.* snores, snored, snor·ing (make) a rough, hoarse breathing noise while sleeping.

snor·kel (SNOR·kul) *v. & n.* (swim under water using) a curved air tube projecting above the water.

snort *v.* 1 force air suddenly through the nose, as a horse does or as one who shows contempt, anger, etc. 2 inhale and take in: *caught snorting cocaine.*
— *n.* 1 a snorting. 2 *Slang.* a drink of liquor, usually straight and quickly gulped.

snout (rhyme: "out") *n.* a projecting nose and mouth, as of a pig, crocodile, certain beetles and butterflies, etc.

snow (SNOH) *n.* (a falling of) white, feathery crystals of frozen water vapour from the atmosphere: *as white as snow; A blanket of snow covered the landscape; crisp, drifting, driving, heavy, light snow; He shovelled the snow; Children play in the snow.*
— *v.* fall as snow: *It snowed lightly on Christmas Day; It snowed hard, heavily all January.*
— snow in shut in by snow.
— snow under cover with snow or overwhelm, as with accumulated work.

snow·ball *n.* a ball of handpacked snow.
— *v.* 1 throw snowballs at someone. 2 increase rapidly like a rolling mass of snow: *The movement snowballed into a popular revolt.*

snow·bank *n.* a mass of heaped snow; snowdrift.

snow·bird *n.* 1 *Cdn.* a bird that is a common sight in winter, as a "snow bunting" or "junco." 2 a seasonal migrant to the Sunbelt, such as Canadians who winter there.

snow·blow·er (SNOH·bloh·ur) *n.* a machine for clearing snow by blowing it away; also **snow thrower.**

snow·board *n.* a short laminated board used like a surfboard for skiing on snow.
— **snow·board·ing** or **snow·surf·ing** *n.*

snow·bound *adj.* shut in or obstructed by snow: *a snowbound airport, village.*

snow·drift *n.* snow piled up by the wind.

snow·fence *n. Cdn.* a lath-and-wire fence put up to stop snow from drifting across a road.

snow·field *n.* a region or expanse of perennial snow, as at the head of a glacier.

snow·flake *n.* a crystal of falling snow.

snow job *n. Informal.* an effort to persuade mainly by deceptive methods, as by flattery or exaggeration: *He gave her a snow job when he asked her to help with the sales campaign.'*

snow·man *n.* -men a human figure made with packed snow.

snow·mo·bile (SNOH·moh·beel) *n. Cdn.* a motor vehicle with short skis in front for travelling over snow and ice. — **snow·mo·bil·er** *n.;* **snow·mo·bil·ing** *n.*

snow·plough or **snow·plow** (rhyme: "how") *n.* a ploughlike machine for clearing streets, driveways, etc. of snow.

snow·shoe *n.* a light, racketlike wooden frame strung with leather thongs that allows one to walk over snow without sinking.

snow·suit *n.* a warmly lined, usually hooded winter suit for children to wear outdoors.

snow thrower same as SNOWBLOWER.

snow tire *n.* a tire with a heavy tread for extra traction over snow and ice.

snow·y *adj.* snow·i·er, -i·est having to do with snow: *a snowy day, valley; her snowy* (= white as snow) *hair; a snowy TV picture (that looks as if it is snowing).*

snub *v.* snubs, snubbed, snub·bing 1 slight a person; also, treat something with contempt: *Oxford snubbed the Prime Minister by refusing her an honorary degree; to snub an invitation.* 2 check or stop an animal or thing in motion.
— *n.* a slight; scornful treatment: *Some M.P.s found the*

snub disgusting.

snub nose *n.* a short nose with upturned tip: *a nice person with a snub nose and double chin.*
— **snub-nosed** *adj.*

snuck *Regional* or *Informal.* sneaked.

snuff *v.* 1 draw air up the nose; sniff. 2 draw powdered tobacco into the nose. 3 pinch off the burnt wick of a candle to make it burn brighter. 4 put out a candle. 5 destroy or kill someone.
— **snuff out** put an end to something; kill: *Communism failed to snuff out religion in the U.S.S.R.*
— *n.* 1 the charred end of a candlewick. 2 powdered tobacco for snuffing.
— **up to snuff** *Informal.* 1 up to standard. 2 sharp or alert.

snug *adj.* snug·ger, snug·gest 1 warm and sheltered: *a snug cabin, corner; tucked safe and snug in bed.* 2 compact or close-fitting: *The shoe is a snug fit; a snug* (= comfortable) *income; Lee lay snug* (= concealed) *till the danger passed.* — **snug·ly** *adv.*

snug·gle (SNUG·ul) *v.* snug·gles, snug·gled, snug·gling draw closely to someone for cosiness; nestle: *The child snuggled up to her mother.*

snye or **sny** *n. Cdn.* a channel bypassing a rapids; also, a tributary.

so (SOH) *adv.* 1 in the way indicated or implied: *I told you so; He talks so fast no one can follow him; He does it so as to confuse everyone; does it so that everyone is confused.* 2 very (much): *She's so sweet; It hurts so.* 3 likewise: *I live here; so does she.*
— *conj.* with the purpose or result that: *Please be quiet so (that) I can read; I was tired, so (Informal. therefore) I fell asleep.*
— *pron.: a dozen or so* (= approximately that).
— *interj.: So, that's how! So you're back!*
— *adj.: Is that so? She wants everything just so* (= exactly as desired).
— **and so on** or **forth** and the rest.
— **so what?** *Informal.* Even if that's true, what does it matter?

soak (SOKE) *v.* make or become thoroughly wet by keeping or remaining in a liquid: *Soak the clothes before washing; Let them soak in the tub; Water soaks* (= penetrates) *through clothes, soaks into the ground; Towels soak up* (= absorb) *water.*
— *n.* 1 a soaking, being soaked, or a liquid for soaking something in. 2 *Slang.* a drunkard.

so-and-so (SO·un·so) *n.* so-and-sos *Informal.* an unnamed person or thing: *The police officer told Dr. So-and-so she was in violation of section so-and-so of the Highway Traffic Act; She said, "Thank you, so-and-so!"*

soap (SOPE) *n.* 1 a substance made by the action of alkali on fat or fatty acids, used to cleanse by the suds it forms with water: *a bar, cake of soap; liquid soap.* 2 [short form] soap opera.
— **no soap** *Slang.* nothing doing; nothing accomplished.
— *v.* apply soap to a body or part.

soap·box *n.* an improvised platform, as for addressing a crowd in the street.

soap opera *n.* a sentimental daytime serial drama on radio or TV.

soap·y *adj.* **soap·i·er, -i·est 1** covered with or containing soap. **2** smooth or greasy.

soar *v.* rise upward or fly high, as an eagle or glider plane: *soaring ambitions, ideals, prices, skyscrapers.*

sob *v.* **sobs, sobbed, sob·bing 1** weep or cry with short, gasping breaths: *He sobbed his heart out; She sobbed herself to sleep.* **2** utter sobbing: *"I'm sorry," Sam sobbed.*
— *n.* a sobbing or its sound: *Sobs could be heard from the next room; bitter sobs of frustration.*

so·ber (SOH·bur) *adj.* **1** not drunk; also, temperate. **2** serious, tranquil, or sensible: *a sober criticism, estimate, expression; sober clothes in sober* (= quiet, not flashy) *colours.*
— *v.* esp. **sober down** or **sober up,** make or become sober: *a cup of coffee to help you sober up a little.*

so·bri·e·ty (suh·BRY·uh·tee) *n.* the quality or condition of being sober; temperance; seriousness.

so·bri·quet (SOH·bruh·cay) *n.* a fanciful epithet or nickname.

so-called *adj.* so-termed, though inaccurately or unjustifiably: *one of those so-called civilized countries.*

soc·cer (SOK·ur) *n.* the international variety of football, played between teams of 11 players using a round, inflated ball.

so·cia·ble (SOH·shuh·bul) *adj.* **1** liking companionship: *a sociable woman.* **2** marked by friendliness: *a sociable evening, occasion.* — **so·cia·bly** (-blee) *adv.*
— **so·cia·bil·i·ty** (-BIL·uh·tee) *n.*

so·cial (SOH·shul) *adj.* **1** having to do with living and working together: *We are social beings; ants, bees, and such social insects; his social* (= friendly) *nature.*
2 having to do with relationships within human society: *a social club; a **social climber** (who wants to get into higher society); a **social leader** (with a busy social life); social classes, problems, services, studies; the **social disease** (= venereal disease); **social mobility** (between classes, as in a democracy).*
— *n.* a social gathering or party. — **so·cial·ly** *adv.*

social insurance *n.* a government program of aiding those in need because of old age, unemployment, sickness, etc.: *A nine-digit **social insurance number** is given to each Canadian resident.*

so·cial·ism (SOH·shuh·liz·um) *n.* the theory or system of public ownership of the means of production and distribution brought about by nonrevolutionary changes in the social order: *to live under socialism.*
— **so·cial·ist** *n. & adj.*

So·cial·ist (SOH·shuh·list) **1** *n. & adj.* (member) of a socialist political party. **2** *adj.* in Communist theory, leading to the Communist ideal: *a socialist government, republic.* — **so·cial·is·tic** (-LIS·tic) *adj.*

so·cial·ite (SOH·shuh·lite) *n.* a prominent member of fashionable society.

so·cial·ize (SOH·shuh·lize) *v.* **-iz·es, -ized, -iz·ing 1** be or make social: *He was socializing too much at work; the socializing influence of school.* **2** make socialistic; also,

nationalize: *to socialize industry, public services.*
— **so·cial·i·za·tion** (-luh·ZAY·shun) *n.*

socialized medicine *n.* the providing of hospital and medical care for all through public funds.

social science *n.* anthropology, economics, history, political science, psychology, sociology, law, etc. as distinguished from the natural sciences and humanities.
— **social scientist** *n.*

social security or **Social Security** *n.* [U.S. use] same as SOCIAL INSURANCE.

social work *n.* community work involving services such as medical help, family counselling, and aid to the handicapped; also **social service.**
— **social worker** *n.*

so·ci·e·ty (suh·SYE·uh·tee) *n.* **-ties 1** human beings considered as a social group: *Criminals are a threat to society.* **2** an organized group of individuals, as a club or association: *a society established or founded or set up for the prevention of cruelty to animals; to disband or dissolve a society; a historical, humane, learned, literary, mutual-aid, secret society.* **3** a social group with a particular character: *Canadian society; an advanced, affluent, civilized, industrial, pluralistic, primitive society; She moves in high, polite society; leaders of society* (= people in high positions). **4** companionship: *We enjoy her society.*
— *adj.* of high society: *a newspaper's society page; society gossip, women.* — **so·ci·e·tal** (-tul) *adj.*

sock *n.* **1** a short stocking: *a pair of socks; to darn, mend socks.* **2** *Slang.* a hard or vigorous blow: *a sock on the jaw.*
— *v.* punch or hit hard: *Sam socked Pat in the nose.*
— **sock it to someone** *Informal.* act toward or speak very forcefully to someone.
— **socked in** *Informal.* closed, as an airport, or grounded, as planes, by bad weather.

sock·et (SOCK·it) *n.* a hollow part into which something fits or is fitted: *the socket of the eye, of an electric bulb; the ball-and-socket joint of the hip or shoulder.*

sock·o (SOCK·oh) *adj. Slang.* outstanding: *a socko performance, speech.*

sod *n.* the surface layer of earth held together by roots of grass, etc.; also, a piece of this.
— *v.* **sods, sod·ded, sod·ding** cover with sod; turf.

so·da (SOH·duh) *n.* **1** [short form] soda pop or soda water. **2** a carbonated beverage: *club, cream, ice-cream soda; a Scotch and soda* (= club soda). **3** a compound of sodium and carbon: *baking soda; causting soda.*

soda biscuit *n.* a biscuit leavened with baking soda and sour milk or buttermilk.

soda cracker *n.* a light cracker made without sugar or shortening.

soda fountain *n.* a counter at which soft drinks and ice cream are served.

soda pop *n.* a carbonated and sweetened soft drink.

soda water *n.* carbonated water.

sod·den (SOD·un) *adj.* **1** soaked through; drenched; also, stupefied, as if drunk. **2** of baked things, soggy or doughlike: *sodden biscuits, bread.*

so·di·um (SOH·dee·um) *n.* a metallic element that is the chief component of common salt, soda, and other salts and alkalis.

sod turning *n.* the breaking of ground to start a new building.

so·ev·er (soh·EV·ur) *adv. & suffix.* in any way; also, of any kind; at all: *how good soever; whatsoever; whosoever.*

so·fa (SOH·fuh) *n.* a usually upholstered couch or long seat with back and arms.

soft (SOFT, SAWFT) *adj.* 1 not hard or rough to the senses, esp. touch; yielding to pressure; smooth: *soft fur; a soft breeze; Talc is the softest of minerals; a bit soft in the head* (= silly); *soft water (free from minerals).* 2 not sharp, loud, or glaring: *soft colours, music, shadows.* 3 easy and gentle to the feelings: *a soft and luxurious life; a soft job; a soft* (= kind) *heart; She has a soft spot* (= special affection) *for animals; a judge who is soft on* (= lenient towards) *first-time offenders.* 4 opposed to "hard": *a soft drink such as cola or ginger ale; soft drugs like marijuana, amphetamines, and hallucinogens; the soft "c" of "city," "g" of "gem," "ch" of "chip."*
— *adv.* in a soft manner. Also **soft·ly** *adv.*
— **soft·ness** *n.*

soft-boiled *adj.* of eggs, boiled without the yolk becoming hard.

soft·bound or **soft-cover** *adj.* of books, paperback.

soft-core *adj.* of pornography, containing no explicit sex: *a soft-core movie.*

sof·ten (SOF·un) *v.* make or become soft or softer.
— **sof·ten·er** *n.*

soft·heart·ed (SOFT·HAR·tid) *adj.* kind and gentle.

softie See SOFTY.

soft landing *n.* the gentle setting down of a spacecraft without damage to its contents.

soft-line *adj.* conciliatory; accommodating.

soft-pedal (soft·PED·ul) *v.* -als, -alled or -aled, -al·ling or -al·ing *Informal.* play down or tone down, as in playing a piano using the "soft pedal" for reducing volume.

soft sell *n.* a selling method using suggestion or persuasion instead of pressure.

soft soap *n. Informal.* flattery. — **soft-soap** *v.*

soft spot See SOFT.

soft touch *n.* one who is easy to get money out of.

soft·ware *n.* operational directions, procedures, accessory materials, etc. of any system or equipment, esp. the programs used with a computer.

soft water See SOFT.

soft·y *n.* **soft·ies** *Informal.* one who is overly sensitive emotionally or physically; also **soft·ie.**

sog·gy (SOG·ee) *adj.* **sog·gi·er, sog·gi·est** esp. of

ground, soaked or damp; also, sodden: *soggy bread.*
— **sog·gi·ly** *adv.;* **sog·gi·ness** *n.*

soil *n.* 1 the earth's surface or ground, esp. as supporting growth and development: *to cultivate, fertilize, irrigate, till, work the soil; barren, clayey, fertile, poor, sandy soil; a man* or *son of the soil* (= hereditary farmer); *The terrorist was not allowed to set foot on Canadian soil* (= land); *adj.: methods of soil conservation; soil depletion, erosion.* 2 stain or spot; also, foul matter.
— *v.* make or become dirty: *soiled hands, linen; a reputation soiled* (= tainted) *by scandals.*

soi·ree or **soi·rée** (swah·RAY) *n.* an evening party.

so·journ (SOH·jurn) *n.* a temporary stay in a place.
— *v.* (also soh·JURN) stay temporarily: *We used to sojourn abroad in the summer.*

sol·ace (SOL·is) *n.* consolation or relief: *She turned to her friends for solace in her sorrow; Her friends were a solace to her; She also found solace in religion.*

so·lar (SOH·lur) *adj.* having to do with the sun: *solar heat; Our solar day represents one rotation of the earth; solar energy captured by means of a solar battery made up of solar cells in the solar panel of an orbiting satellite; She lives in a solar house that uses solar energy; the sun's solar flares of hydrogen gas; The solar system is composed of the sun and the planets, etc. revolving around it; Solar winds of electrically charged particles flow from the sun into space; The solar year is based on the earth's revolution around the sun.*
— *n.* energy from the sun: *Many people are switching to solar from oil, gas, electricity, etc.*

sold *pt. & pp.* of SELL.

sol·der (SOD·ur) *n.* an alloy used to join metals by melting it with the heat of an electrical device called a **soldering iron.** — *v.* join with solder.

sol·dier (SOLE·jur) *n.* a member of an army, usually not an officer: *an armed, common, seasoned soldier; A soldier defects from, deserts, enlists in, fights in, serves the army; Soldiers go AWOL; a wreath laid at the tomb of the Unknown Soldier* (dead in war); *a soldier of fortune* (= mercenary).
— *v.* work as a soldier: *She soldiered on* (= carried on with determination) *into her seventies.*
— **sol·dier·ly** *adj. & adv.*

sole *n.* 1 the bottom surface of the foot; also, the bottom of a shoe or other footwear. 2 a flat fish of warm seas used as food: *fillet of sole.*
— *v.* **soles, soled, sol·ing** furnish with a sole: *to sole a shoe; rubber-soled slippers.*
— *adj.* one and only: *my sole purpose; the sole survivor; sole* (= exclusive) *publication rights.*

sole·ly *adv.* 1 alone: *He's solely to blame.* 2 exclusively: *It's solely a matter of pride.*

sol·emn (SOL·um) *adj.* 1 serious in an impressive or awe-inspiring way: *a solemn oath, occasion, responsibility; a solemn* (= serious) *face.* 2 formal or ceremonious; religious: *a solemn curse, procession; a Solemn High Mass.* — **sol·emn·ly** *adv.*
— **so·lem·ni·ty** (suh·LEM·nuh·tee) *n.* **-ties.**

so·lic·it (suh·LIS·it) *v.* 1 ask earnestly and respectfully:

to solicit funds for charity; to solicit the membership for donations. 2 entreat or accost for something immoral: *hookers charged with soliciting.*
— **so·lic·i·ta·tion** (-TAY·shun) *n.*

so·lic·i·tor (suh·LIS·uh·tur) *n.* a lawyer in the role of advising clients and preparing cases to be argued by a barrister in court, as in the British tradition: *A Canadian lawyer is usually qualified as both barrister and solicitor.*

so·lic·i·tous (suh·LIS·uh·tus) *adj.* showing care, concern, or solicitude: *a mother solicitous about* or *of her child's welfare.*

so·lic·i·tude (suh·LIS·uh·tude) *n.* 1 care or worry, as about the future: *Yves spoke with sincerity and solicitude.* 2 care in a concerned or protective manner: *parental solicitude for children.*

sol·id *n.* 1 a substance that is not a liquid or gas. 2 a three-dimensional object, as a cube or sphere.
— *adj.* 1 not liquid or gaseous: *solid fuels; It was frozen solid; disposal of solid wastes.* 2 not hollow but filled entirely and uniformly; dense in consistency or texture; hard and firm: *bars of solid gold; a solid structure of solid brick; I waited two solid* (= uninterrupted) *hours; in solid colours, not patterned; "Icebox" is written solid, unlike "ice-skating" and "ice pick."* 3 having qualities of soundness, strength, genuineness, dependability, etc.: *a man of solid build; a solid character, citizen, treatise.* 4 three-dimensional, not flat: *A square is not a solid figure but a cube is; You learn this in* **solid geometry.**
— **sol·id·ly** *adv.;* **sol·id·ness** *n.*
Also **so·lid·i·ty** (suh·LID·uh·tee) *n.*

sol·i·dar·i·ty (sol·uh·DAIR·uh·tee) *n.* unity of purpose, interests, feelings, etc., as of a closely knit group: *to express, feel, show one's solidarity with the striking workers.*

so·lid·i·fy (suh·LID·uh·fye) *v.* **-fies, -fied, -fy·ing** make or become solid, as water by freezing.
— **so·lid·i·fi·ca·tion** (-fuh·CAY·shun) *n.*

so·lil·o·quy (suh·LIL·uk·wee) *n.* **-quies** 1 the act of talking to oneself. 2 a dramatic device or speech in which an actor thinks aloud for the benefit of the audience.

sol·i·taire (SOL·uh·tair) *n.* 1 a card game for one person. 2 a gem set by itself.

sol·i·tar·y (SOL·uh·tair·ee) *adj.* living or existing away from others; alone and isolated: *a prisoner put in solitary confinement; a hermit's solitary life; solitary bees and wasps (that are not social); a solitary* (= lonely) *place.*

sol·i·tude (SOL·uh·tude) *n.* a lonely place or condition; seclusion: *Hermits live in complete, utter solitude; the solitudes of city dwellers; Novelist Hugh MacLennan described the relationship of French- and English-speaking Canada as "the two solitudes."*

so·lo (SOH·loh) *n.* **-los** 1 a musical piece for one voice or instrument: *to perform, play, sing a solo.* 2 any performance by one person.
— *v.* perform a solo.
— *adj. & adv.* alone: *She flew solo; to perform, play, sing solo; a solo dance.*
— **so·lo·ist** *n.*

so long *Informal.* good-bye.

sol·u·ble (SOL·yoo·bul) *adj.* that can be dissolved.
— **sol·u·bly** *adv.*
— **sol·u·bil·i·ty** (-yuh·BIL·uh·tee) *n.*

so·lu·tion (suh·LOO·shun) *n.* 1 (a mixture formed by) the dissolving or dispersion of one substance in another, esp. a solid in a liquid: *a strong solution of salt in water; a weak solution; Salt is (held) in solution in water.* 2 the solving of a problem: *a mystery that defies solution; Is it capable of solution?* 3 the resulting explanation or answer: *to find a satisfactory solution to a problem; the solution of a crime, mystery; no easy, glib, ideal solutions; an ingenious, neat solution.*

solve (SOLV) *v.* **solves, solved, solv·ing** find the answer to a problem, puzzle, mystery, etc.
— **solv·a·ble** *adj.* — **solv·er** *n.*

sol·vent (SOL·vunt) *adj.* 1 dissolving. 2 able to pay all one's debts.
— *n.* a substance such as water or turpentine that can dissolve other substances. — **sol·ven·cy** *n.*

som·bre or **som·ber** (SOM·bur) *adj.* gloomy or melancholy; cheerless: *in a sombre mood; sombre colours, skies, tones.* — **som·bre·ly** or **som·ber·ly** *adv.*

-some 1 *combining form.* body: *centrosome, chromosome.* 2 *adj. suffix.* indicating a condition or quality: *awesome, meddlesome, weirdsome.* 3 *n. suffix.* a group as specified: *foursome, twosome.*

some (SUM) *adj.* of an indefinite number, amount, or quantity: *I had some sleep; It happened some* (= a few) *days back; in some* (= certain) *countries; in some* (= a) *country I can't remember; Consult some (Informal for an unspecified or any) lawyer; That was some (Informal for a remarkable or wonderful) party!*
— *adv.: It happened some* (= about or nearly) *10 days back; I managed to sleep some (Informal for somewhat; a little).*
— *pron.* 1 certain people or things: *Some are good, some are bad.* 2 a few: *I know some of them; some of the boys.*
— **and then some** *Slang.* and a good deal more than that.

some·bod·y (SUM·bod·ee, -bud·ee) *pron.* some person: *He needs somebody to talk to; somebody for support.*
— *n.* a person of importance: *She's somebody around here.*

some·day *adv.* at some future time.

some·how *adv.* by some means.

some·one same as SOMEBODY.

some·place *adv. Informal.* somewhere: *Let's go someplace nice like the zoo.*

som·er·sault (SUM·ur·sault) *v. & n.* (perform) a complete roll of the body with the heels turning over the head: *to do, execute, throw, turn a somersault; She somersaulted through the doorway; The new policy represents a complete somersault* (= reversal) *from the previous position.* Also **sum·mer·sault.**

some·thing *n.* an unspecified thing, amount, or part: *There's something in what she says; She has something for all of us; Heaven is an indefinable, intangible*

something; if you want to make something of the evidence we have; Something unexpected happened today; He's something (= a bit or little) of a jack-of-all-trades; She's something (Informal for a person of importance) in the RCMP.
— **something else** a different or distinctive person or thing.
— *adv.* somewhat: *something like $20 000.*

some·time *adv.* at an unspecified time: *See you sometime tomorrow; It happened sometime back.*
— *adj.* former: *a sometime professor of law.*

some·times *adv.* now and then; occasionally.

some·way *adv.* by some means.

some·what *adv.* to some extent or degree.
— *n.* something: *She's somewhat of a poet.*

some·where *adv.* at some place: *I saw him somewhere; I would place it somewhere in the 1950s; It is somewhere around (= approximately) $100.*

son (SUN) *n.* a male offspring in relation to his parents: *their only son; He was like a son to all of us; a father awaiting the return of his prodigal son; a son of the soil (= hereditary farmer); Diefenbaker is one of Canada's favourite sons.*

so·na·ta (suh·NAH·tuh) *n.* an instrumental composition with several movements contrasting in rhythm but related in thought.

song *n.* 1 a singing or a piece of music for singing; also, a short poem whether set to music or not: *to belt out, compose, hum, play, sing, write a song; They burst into song; a drinking, folk, love, marching, popular, swan, theme song; a hero renowned in song and legend; "The Song of Hiawatha;" the same old song (= complaint); The piano went for a song (= was sold cheaply).* 2 a sound like singing, as of a bird, boiling kettle, etc.
— **song·ster** *n.;* **song·stress** (-stris) *fem.*

song·fest *n.* an informal gathering for singing songs.

son·ic (SON·ic) *adj.* having to do with sound waves: *a sonic depth finder; A supersonic aircraft breaks the* **sonic** or **sound barrier** *of sharply rising aerodynamic drag as it approaches the speed of sound and produces an explosive* **sonic boom.**

son-in-law *n.* **sons-in-law** a daughter's husband.

son·net (SON·it) *n.* a rhymed poem in 14 lines like "Shall I compare thee to a summer's day?": *to compose, write a sonnet to one's beloved.*

son·ny (SUN·ee) *n.* **son·nies** [endearing term] son or boy.

so·no·rous (suh·NOR·us, SON·ur·us – "SON" rhymes with "ON") *adj.* having a full, rich, or impressive sound: *sonorous phrases, voices; a sonorous style.*

soon (long "oo") *adv.* in a short time: *I'll be back soon; He arrived sooner than expected; I'll be there* **as soon as** *possible.*
— **as soon** or **would sooner** rather: *She would as soon die fighting than yield.*
— **sooner or later** sometime; eventually.

soot (short or long "oo") *n.* black, unburned carbon seen as smoke and found sticking to the insides of chimneys.
— **soot·y** *adj.* **soot·i·er, -i·est:** *a sooty chimney; walls made sooty by a fire.*

soothe ("th" as in "the") *v.* **soothes, soothed, sooth·ing** to comfort or relieve: *to soothe a child; to soothe someone's feelings; to soothe pain, a sore throat; a soothing (= pain-lessening) lotion, medicine; soothing (= pleasing) flattery, words.*

sop *v.* **sops, sopped, sop·ping** dip or soak by dipping: *to sop up a spill with a sponge; to sop bread in milk; He came in from the rain* **sopping wet** *(= dripping).*
— *n.* something given to appease, as bread dipped in milk to a child; a concession: *as a sop to his conscience, ego.*

soph·ism (SOF·iz·um) *n.* a clever but logically invalid argument.— **soph·ist** *n.*
— **so·phis·tic** (suh·FIS·tic) or **so·phis·ti·cal** *adj.*

so·phis·ti·cate (suh·FIS·tuh·cate) *v.* **-cates, -cat·ed, -cat·ing** make experienced or cultured by shedding one's natural simplicity.
— *n.* a sophisticated person.
— **sophisticated** *adj.: a sophisticated young woman; She has sophisticated tastes in furniture; sophisticated arguments; modern sophisticated (= highly developed) equipment, techniques, weapons.*
— **so·phis·ti·ca·tion** (-CAY·shun) *n.*

sop·py *adj.* **sop·pi·er, sop·pi·est** soaked or wet through: *his soppy sentimentality.*

so·pra·no (suh·PRAH·no) *n.* **-nos 1** (a singer with) the highest singing voice of women and boys. **2** a singing part for a soprano.
— *adj.: a soprano part, saxophone, voice;* **adv.:** *She sings soprano.*

sor·cer·y (SOR·suh·ree) *n.* **-cer·ies** witchcraft, esp. by use of charms, spells, etc.: *to practise sorcery.*
— **sor·cer·er** *n.;* **sor·cer·ess** *fem.*

sor·did *adj.* dirty or filthy; hence, wretched, base, or mean: *the sordid life of the slums; the sordid details of a crime; a sordid crime, story.*

sore *adj.* **sor·er, sor·est** causing or feeling pain: *a sore leg; a sore throat; I feel sore (= vexed) at being slighted; I am sore (Informal for angry) at him; a sore point of dispute; in sore (= grievous) need.*
— *n.* a sore spot on the body, esp. an infected wound: *a cold sore; an open sore; a running sore.*
— **sore·ly** *adv.;* **sore·ness** *n.*

sore·head *n. Informal.* one who easily becomes angry or disgruntled.

sor·row (SOR·oh) *n.* sadness or grief of a prolonged nature, as from a beloved's death: *to express, feel, show sorrow at or for or over the death of a friend; deep, great, keen, personal, profound sorrow; To her great sorrow, the child died before she could reach the hospital; the joys and sorrows of life.*
— *v.* grieve: *her sorrowing husband; his sorrowing heart; still sorrowing over his dead wife.*
— **sor·row·ful** *adj.*

sor·ry (SOR·ee) *adj.* **sor·ri·er, sor·ri·est 1** feeling sorrow, regret, pity, etc.: *I'm dreadfully, terribly sorry about or for what happened; I am or I feel sorry for my* *sins; I'm sorry to disappoint you;* **I'm sorry** *but I'm going to have to let you go; I am* or *I feel sorry to fire you* or *to have to fire you* or *that I have to fire you; I am* or *I feel sorry* (= pity) *for you.* **2** poor; pitiful: *a sorry excuse, plight, sight, state of affairs; a sorry* (= useless) *mess.*

sort *n.* a group of individuals of the same general kind: *all sorts of cars, people, plans; I never had this sort of trouble; a rushed sort of an existence; He said something of the sort; I don't like his sort (of people).*
— **of sorts** or **of a sort** of mediocre quality.
— **out of sorts** slightly ill or in low spirits.
— **sort of** *Informal.* somewhat; so to speak: *He's sort of disappointed; It was sort of a last hope; It's sort of like being dumped; He just sort of sits and mopes all day; Hopeless? Yes, sort of.*
— *v.* arrange according to kind or character: *Letters are sorted (out) in the post office.*

sor·tie (SOR·tee) *n.* **1** a sally or sudden attack. **2** a combat plane's flight into enemy territory, as for bombing: *to carry out, fly, make a sortie.*

SOS (es·oh·ES) *n.* a distress signal, as used in wireless telegraphy: *to send an SOS.*

so-so *adj. & adv.* fairly or passably (good).

sou·flé (soo·FLAY) *n.* a baked dish made light and puffy by the use of beaten egg whites.

sought *pt. & pp.* of SEEK.

soul (SOLE) *n.* **1** the spiritual part of a person, as distinguished from the body, considered to be immortal and the source of inner strength, inspiration, etc.; hence, essence or spirit: *Missionaries work to save souls; to save souls from damnation, hell, sin; She works* **heart and soul** (= all of herself) *for the cause; She puts* **her heart and soul** *into whatever she does; A living wage is necessary to* **keep one's body and soul together** (= to pay for life's necessities); *After much* **soul-searching** (= self-examination) *they decided not to separate.* **2** a person: *a kindly, kindred, poor, timid soul; Not a soul was in sight.* **3** an emotional and spiritual quality felt to be characteristic of black culture, esp. of black music.
— *adj.* characteristically black in culture: *soul brother* (= a fellow black); *soul food* (= food traditionally popular among the blacks); *soul music* (= jazz based on blues and gospel music); *soul sister.*
— **soul·ful** *adj.;* **soul·ful·ness** *n.*

sound *n.* **1** what is or can be heard: *the sound of fighting, machinery, music, voices; vowel and consonant sounds; We came within sound* (= earshot) *of the guns; to articulate, emit, enunciate, make, produce, pronounce, utter, transmit sounds; Please turn down the sound on the TV; She just turned up the sound on her radio.* **2** a channel wider than a strait, linking two bodies of water or separating an island from the mainland. **3** a narrow coastal inlet, as Howe Sound or Nootka Sound off the B.C. coast.
— *v.* **1** (cause) to make a sound: *Sound your horn; We get up when the alarm sounds.* **2** to seem when heard: *The voice sounds strange; Your plan sounds reasonable; sounds like a good idea to me; It sounds as if they are winning.* **3** measure the depth of something: *to sound the depths of a mystery; a* **sounding** *lead, line, machine; Let's* **sound him out** *on* or *about the new proposal* (= try

to find out his views, feelings, etc.). **4** dive down suddenly, as a whale.
— **sound off** *Informal.* talk freely or loudly, as to complain, boast, etc.
— *adj.* **1** free from defect; good, healthy, or strong: *The building rests on a sound foundation; a will made by one of sound mind; to enjoy sound health; He's sound in mind and body; sound advice, argument, judgment, reasoning, opinions, views.* **2** thorough: *a sound defeat, sleep, thrashing.*
— *adv.* thoroughly: *He is sound asleep.*
— **sound·ly** *adv.: He sleeps soundly at night; She was soundly beaten in the game.* — **sound·ness** *n.*

sound barrier *n.* same as SONIC BARRIER.

sounding board or **sound·board** *n.* **1** a structure or device for increasing or directing sound, as in a violin or piano. **2** someone used for testing out an idea or opinion.

sound·proof *adj.* insulated against sound: *a soundproof ceiling, studio.*

soup (long "oo") *n.* **1** a liquid food made with meat, fish, or vegetables, eaten with a **soup·spoon**: *Make me a bowl* or *cup of soup; a* **soup kitchen** *where the poor are fed.* **2** *Informal.* something thick or heavy, as fog.
— **in the soup** in a hard plight.
— *v.* **soup up** *Slang.* increase the power of something: *a souped up engine; a souped up version of the old disk operating system.*

soup·çon or **soup·con** (soop·SOHNG) *n.* a slight trace or flavour *of* a taste or quality.

sour (rhyme: "our") *adj.* **1** having the sharp, acid taste of fruits such as lemons and avocados. **2** having the acid or rancid taste of foods gone bad: *sour milk.* **3** disagreeable or unpleasant: *sour breath, wine; sour* (= acid) *soil; sour* (= impure) *gasoline; when things begin to go sour; The whole affair, project, proposal turned sour; a sour employee with a sour face.*
— *v.* make or become sour: *Their (mutual) relations soured.*

source (SORCE) *n.* where something rises or originates: *the source of a river; a source of information; an impeccable, original, reliable, reputable, trustworthy, unnamed source; information from a source* (= a person) *close to the premier; light from a remote source; an energy source; a source of trouble; to cite, disclose, indicate, reveal one's sources; to tap a source; A source dries up.*

sour·dough *n. Cdn.* **1** fermented dough used as leaven. **2** a lone prospector or pioneer, as in northwestern Canada and Alaska. **3** an experienced hand or old-timer.

sour grapes *n.* the scorning of something because one does not or cannot have it: *It is just (a case of) sour grapes when he says Cadillacs are no good.*

sour·puss (short "oo") *n. Slang.* a sullen person.

souse (rhyme: "house") *v.* **sous·es, soused, sous·ing** **1** pickle; hence, soak or plunge. **2** *Slang.* make or become drunk.
— *n.* **1** a pickling or soaking, brine for pickling, or pickled pork, fish, etc. **2** *Slang.* a habitual drunkard.

south ("th" as in "thin") *n.* **1** the direction to the right of one facing the rising sun; opposite of north. **2** a region lying in this direction, as **the South,** the southern states of the U.S., south of Pennsylvania, the Ohio River, and Missouri.
— *adj.* in, to, or from the south: *It has been imported from* **south of the border** *(Cdn for* the U.S.).
— *adv.* toward the south: *People go or head south in the winter; The U.S. is directly south of Canada.*

South Asian *n. & adj.* (a person) of or from **South Asia,** the region comprising India, Pakistan, Sri Lanka, and Bangladesh.

Southeast Asian *n. & adj.* (a person) of or from **Southeast Asia,** the region comprising the peninsula east of India and south of China, the Philippines, Malaysia, and western Indonesia.

south·er·ly (SUTH·ur·lee, "TH" as in "the") *adj. & adv.* **1** toward the south: *Canada's most southerly point is Middle Island in Lake Erie.* **2** from the south: *a southerly wind.*

south·ern (SUTH·urn) *adj.* of, from, or toward the south. — **south·ern·er** *n.*

south·paw *n. Slang.* a left-handed person, esp. a baseball pitcher.

south·ward (SOUTH·wurd) *adj. & adv.* toward the south; also **south·wards** *adv.*

sou·ve·nir (soo·vuh·NEER) *n.* an article given, bought, kept, etc. as a reminder of a person, place, or occasion.

sov·er·eign (SOV·run) *n.* **1** a supreme ruler or monarch. **2** a former British gold coin worth one pound.
— *adj.* **1** supreme and independent: *a sovereign power, state; Her will is sovereign in domestic matters.* **2** great in excellence, importance, etc.: *a sovereign remedy; of sovereign importance.*

sov·er·eign·ty (SOV·run·tee) *n.* **-ties 1** supreme and independent authority: *The provinces do not enjoy full sovereignty; Canada's Arctic sovereignty; to claim, establish sovereignty over a disputed territory.* **2** independence: *to violate a nation's sovereignty; to grant sovereignty to a former colony.*

so·vi·et (SOH·vee·et, -it) **1** *n.* in the U.S.S.R., an elected legislative body: *a village soviet; town soviets; the Supreme Soviet of the U.S.S.R.* **2 Soviet** *adj.* of the Soviet Union, the U.S.S.R. **3 the Soviets** *n.pl.* the Soviet Union.

¹**sow** (rhyme: "how") *n.* an adult female swine.

²**sow** (SOH) *v.* **sows,** *pt.* **sowed,** *pp.* **sown** (SONE) or **sowed, sow·ing** to plant seed; hence, spread or scatter: *to sow wheat; to sow a field (with wheat); to sow discord; Reap what you sow; "Sow the wind and reap the whirlwind"* (= Start something that has disastrous consequences). — **sow·er** *n.*

soy sauce or **soy** *n.* a sauce used as a flavouring in Oriental cooking, made from **soy·bean** or **soya bean** seeds.

spa (SPAH) *n.* **1** a mineral spring forming the centre of a health resort; also, such a resort, or "health spa." **2** same as HOT TUB.

space *n.* **1** the boundless expanse or extent which physical objects may occupy: *exploration of space; visitors from (outer) space;* **space-age** (= modern) *technology.* **2** an area or volume limited by objects; room or interval between objects: *a crawl space; parking spaces; storage space; not enough space for a bed; the wide open spaces of the prairies; the spaces between lines; a space-saving measure; to book space* (= accommodation) *in a hotel; some* **breathing space** (= time); *in the space* (= interval) *of an hour; to press the* **space bar** *on a keyboard.*
— *v.* **spac·es, spaced, spac·ing** divide into or separate by spaces: *Please space the lines evenly; Use double* **spacing** *between lines.*

space cadet or **space·out** *n. Slang.* one who is dozy, scatterbrained, or silly; an eccentric.

space·craft *n. sing. & pl.* a vehicle such as a satellite or rocket designed for travel in space: *a manned spacecraft.*

spaced-out *adj. Slang.* **1** under the influence of a narcotic; high. **2** same as SPACEY.

space fiction *n.* fiction dealing with life and travel in outer space.

space·flight *n.* flight into outer space: *an unmanned spaceflight.*

space·man *n.* **-men** a male member of the crew of a spaceship. — **space·wom·an** *n.* **-wom·en.**

space·out *n.* same as SPACE CADET.

space probe *n.* an unmanned spacecraft sent on a probing mission: *to launch a space probe.*

space·ship *n.* a vehicle for travelling in outer space.

space shuttle *n.* a recoverable and reusable space vehicle for linking up with a space station.

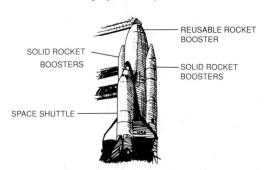

SOLID ROCKET BOOSTERS

REUSABLE ROCKET BOOSTER

SOLID ROCKET BOOSTERS

SPACE SHUTTLE

space station *n.* a manned earth satellite in a fixed orbit used as a centre for space experiments, as a stopping or launching place for spaceships, etc.

space·suit *n.* an astronaut's pressurized garment.

space vehicle *n.* a spacecraft.

space·walk *v. & n.* (engage) in movement outside a spaceship.

space·y or **spac·y** (SPAY·see) *adj. Informal.* out of touch with the real world: *He's described as nutty, spacey, neurotic; a spacey sitcom.*

spa·cious (SPAY·shus) *adj.* large in extent or scope:

spacious accommodation; a spacious life of ease.

spade *n.* **1** a sharp, pointed shovel for turning the soil by pressing its blade into the ground. **2** a black figure (♠) marking a suit of playing cards; also, a card of this suit.
— **call a spade a spade** be frank or forthright.
— **in spades** *Informal.* emphatically or outspokenly: *Everyone loves her in spades; Our hard work is paying off in spades.*

spade·work *n.* the hard preliminary work involved in starting a project.

spa·ghet·ti (spuh·GET·ee) *n.* long, thin strings of pasta.

spaghetti western *n. Informal.* a low-budget western movie made in Italy.

spake [old form] *pt.* of SPEAK: *Thus spake Confucius.*

span *n.* **1** the extent or distance between two linked points such as the ends of a bridge; also, one of its individual parts between pillars or supports: *the span of an arch bridge; a bridge with 10 spans; a child's brief attention span* (= length of concentration); *our life span; memory span.* **2** the maximum distance between the tips of the little finger and the thumb.
— *v.* **spans, spanned, span·ning 1** extend across: *The history of Canada spans several centuries.* **2** measure, as by the span of one's hand.

span·dex *n.* an elastic synthetic fabric used for exercise wear.

span·gle (SPANG·gul) *v.* **-gles, -gled, -gling** decorate (as if) with spangles: *a star-spangled sky.*
— *n.* a small disc of glittering material sewn on fabrics for decoration. — **span·gly** *adj.*

Span·iard (SPAN·yurd) *n.* a person of or from Spain.

Span·ish *adj.* of Spain, its people, or their language.
— *n.* **1** the Spanish language. **2 the Spanish** the people of Spain; Spaniards.

Spanish American *n. & adj.* **1** (an American) of Spanish descent. **2** (a person) of or from **Spanish America**, the parts of Latin America in which Spanish is the chief language.

spank *v.* strike one to be punished on the buttocks with the palm, a slipper, etc.: *to spank a child; to get, give, receive a good spanking.* — *n.* such a blow.

spanking *adj.* **1** rapid or strong: *a spanking breeze.* **2** remarkable: *a spanking tweed jacket.*
— *adv.* very: *The cleaned silver looks spanking new; a spanking good time.*

spar *v.* **spars, sparred, spar·ring 1** make the motions of boxing at someone: *a boxer's sparring partner (with whom he practises).* **2** fight or wrangle *with* someone: *an all-day sparring match between two lawyers; Shawn sparred four rounds with Dan.*
— *n.* a pole supporting a sail, as a mast, boom, or gaff.

spare *v.* **spares, spared, spar·ing 1** relieve someone from having to undergo something: *She spared him some embarrassment; We'll spare you the details; They ate out to spare her the trouble of cooking; I'm alive today because I've been spared (from death) by Providence.* **2** give up or do without something useful or needed: "*Spare the rod and spoil the child*"; *We have*

*time enough and to spare; She spares no expense when helping friends; Can you spare me a dollar? to spare the time for a job; He's very **sparing of** (= restrained in spending) his money and resources.*
— *adj.* **spar·er, spar·est 1** extra; free for use: *spare change, parts, rooms, time, tires.* **2** thin or lean; also, meagre or scanty: *a spare build, diet, figure, meal.*
— *n.* **1** something extra or in reserve, as a spare tire. **2** in bowling, the knocking down of all 10 pins with the first two balls.

spare·ribs *n. pl.* ribs of pork with closely trimmed meat.

sparing *adj.* **1** frugal or careful. **2** scanty or meagre.
— **spar·ing·ly** *adv.*

spark *n.* a particle of fire given off when flint is struck with steel or when electricity jumps across a gap, as in the **spark plug** of an automobile engine: *A short produces a spark; A spark is emitted; Sparks fly from a welder's torch; There's not a spark* (= flash or particle) *of life left in the body.*
— *v.* **1** give off sparks. **2** stir up or stimulate: *The comment sparked a heated discussion; to spark fears, interest, riots, speculation.*

spar·kle (SPAR·kul) *v.* **-kles, -kled, -kling 1** send out sparks. **2** shine or glitter as if giving off sparks: *sparkling gems; a sparkling crystal chandelier, sparkling colours, imagery, sounds; a sparkling career, display, performance; the sparkling white sands of the beach; a **sparkling** (= bubbling) wine.*
— *n.* a sparkling: *the sparkle of light playing on a fountain; the sparkle* (= liveliness) *of her eyes.*

spar·row (SPAIR·oh) *n.* a small, plain-looking, usually brownish bird.

sparse *adj.* **spars·er, spars·est** thinly scattered; not dense: *sparse hair, population, vegetation.*
— **sparse·ly** *adv.*

Spar·tan (SPAR·tun) *adj.* of ancient Sparta or like its people: *the Spartan virtues of frugality, courage, and stern discipline; small and Spartan accommodation.*

spasm (SPAZ·um) *n.* **1** a sudden, involuntary, painful contraction of a muscle or muscles, as a cramp or convulsion. **2** a brief burst of energy or excitement.

spas·mod·ic (spaz·MOD·ic) *adj.* characterized by spasms; happening in brief bursts: *a spasmodic cough; spasmodic efforts; spasmodic periods of joy and despair.*

spat a *pt. & pp.* of SPIT.
— *n.* **1** the young of oysters and other shellfish. **2** usually **spats** *pl.* gaiters covering the instep and ankle. **3** *Informal.* a petty quarrel: *Joe had a spat with his neighbours.*

spate *n.* a large number or outpouring: *a spate of words; a spate of new books; a spate of accidents on an icy expressway; a river **in spate*** (= in flood).

spa·tial (SPAY·shul) *adj.* having to do with space: *The right side of the brain controls our spatial and visual faculties; spatial awareness, concepts, functions, judgment, qualities.* — **spa·tial·ly** *adv.*

spat·ter (SPAT·ur) *v.* to splash liquid in drops or splash a person or thing with mud, etc.
— *n.* a spattering or a spot made by it.

spawn n. eggs or offspring in large numbers, as of fish, frogs, shellfish, etc.
— v. 1 produce spawn. 2 bring forth in great numbers: *computer stores spawned by the electronic revolution.*

spay v. spays, spayed, spay·ing remove the ovaries of an animal.

speak (SPEEK) v. speaks, spoke, spo·ken (SPOH·kun), speak·ing utter or express something using language: *Animals don't speak; She speaks Greek, but speaks in French to her kids; speaks to the class, to the point; speaks with me on business; He was invited to speak* (=make a speech) *at the graduation; to speak bluntly, fluently, frankly, freely, loudly, openly, politely, quietly, rudely, softly; to speak about a subject; to speak from the heart, from experience; to speak ill of someone; to speak well of everyone; Strictly **speaking**, this is against the rules; We had a fight, but we are back **on speaking terms*** (=speaking to each other).
— **so to speak** to use such an expression: *He got his dander up, so to speak.*
— **speak for:** *M.P.s speak for* (=on behalf of) *their constituents; Speak for yourself* (=Don't speak on my behalf)! *They spoke for* (=in support of) *the reintroduction of capital punishment; Our record speaks for itself* (=is proof by itself); *These seats have been **spoken for*** (=reserved); *A Nobel prize **speaks volumes for*** (=is great testimony of) *the winner's achievements.*
— **speak out** speak freely and boldly: *dissidents who **speak out** on human rights; They **speak out against** repression.*
— **speak up** 1 speak louder: *Please speak up, I can't hear you.* 2 be assertive: *We have to speak up in defence of our rights; someone to speak up for the underdog.*

speak·er n. 1 one who speaks: *a fluent speaker; guest speaker; public speaker; I am a native speaker of Tagalog but a better speaker of Spanish.* 2 the head of a deliberative assembly: *the speaker of parliament; Mr. Speaker, Madam Speaker.* 3 a loudspeaker.

spear (SPEER) n. 1 a thrusting or throwing weapon with a long wooden shaft and a pointed head of metal or stone: *to hurl a spear.* 2 a sprout or young shoot of a plant, as of grass.
— v. pierce or stab with or as with a spear: *to spear trout; a hockey player penalized for spearing.*

spear·head n. 1 the pointed head of a spear. 2 the first attacker in an assault or the leader of a movement.
— v. act as the spearhead of an assault, undertaking, etc.

spe·cial (SPESH·ul) adj. of a different or particular kind: *as a special favour; special permission to watch a late movie; a special edition; There's an extra charge for **special delivery** of first-class mail by postal messenger; **special education** for handicapped children; lobbying by a **special-interest group** trying to influence legislation in its favour.*
— n. a special person, train, edition of a newspaper, product on sale, television program, etc.: *a news special.*
— spe·cial·ly adv.

spe·cial·ist (SPESH·ul·ist) n. one specializing in a particular subject or line of work: *to call in, consult a specialist; an ear specialist; a specialist in criminology; a specialist on crime prevention.*

spe·ci·al·i·ty (spesh·ee·AL·uh·tee) n. [Brit. use] same as SPECIALTY.

spe·cial·ize (SPESH·ul·ize) v. concentrate one's work or study in a particular area: *After many years of general studies they specialize (in a specialty) for two years; She's specializing in plastic surgery; has specialized* (=expert) *knowledge of her subject; a restaurant that specializes in seafood; Wings are forelimbs specialized* (=adapted) *for flying.* — spe·cial·i·za·tion (-uh·ZAY·shun) n.

spe·cial·ty (SPESH·ul·tee) n. -ties a special subject, feature, or article: *Greek drama is his specialty; Our specialty is seafood; hardware, jewellery, and such **specialty stores.***

spe·cies (SPEE·sheez) n. sing. & pl. a kind, esp. a biological grouping (under "genus") of varieties of plants and animals or races whose members can interbreed: *The common cat (Felis catus) is genus Felis, species catus; An endangered species may die out, may become extinct; A protected species may survive; the female of **the species*** (=of the human race).

spe·cif·ic (spuh·SIF·ic) adj. of a definite kind: *Please be specific; Give specific reasons; Lions, tigers, and leopards have specific differences (as different species of genus "Panthera"); Give us a few **specifics*** (=specific details or particulars). — spe·cif·i·cal·ly adv.

spec·i·fi·ca·tion (SPES·uh·fuh·CAY·shun) n. 1 something specified. 2 usually **specifications** pl. detailed description of materials, measurements, etc. for a project or undertaking: *to adhere to, meet the specifications; the rigid specifications laid down by government.*

spec·i·fy (SPES·uh·fye) v. -fies, -fied, -fy·ing mention explicitly; also, describe in detail: *The directions specify the dosage; They specify how and when the medicine is to be taken.*

spec·i·men (SPES·uh·mun) n. a sample taken for a close or comparative study: *botanical specimens; a urine specimen; a poor specimen* (=representative) *of humanity.*

spe·cious (SPEE·shus) adj. good, true, correct, etc. in appearance only: *a specious argument, excuse, resemblance.*

speck n. a small mark, spot, or bit: *a speck of dust.*
— v. mark with specks: *a specked apple.*

speck·le (SPEK·ul) n. a small speck.
— **speck·led** (SPEK·uld) adj. marked with speckles, as trout.

spec·ta·cle (SPEC·tuh·cul) n. 1 a sight or display that attracts public attention: *a fine spectacle; He made a spectacle of himself after getting drunk; a movie spectacle (with great scenery, a large cast, etc.).* 2 spectacles pl. eyeglasses.

spec·tac·u·lar (spec·TAK·yuh·lur) adj. impressive or striking in visual impact: *a spectacular performance; a spectacular three-alarm fire.*
— n. a spectacular motion picture or television show: *a three-hour spectacular.*
— spec·tac·u·lar·ly adv.

spec·ta·tor (SPEC·tay·tur) n. one who watches an action without taking part, as at a sports event.

spectator sport *n.* baseball, hockey, racing, etc. as distinguished from hunting or fishing.

spec·tre or **spec·ter** *n.* a ghost or spirit.

spec·trum (SPEC·trum) *n.*, *pl.* **-trums** or **-tra** (-truh) **1** a series of coloured bands representing wavelengths resulting from the diffraction of white light into its constituents. **2** range or array: *people representing a wide spectrum of opinions; immigrants from a broad spectrum of humanity; a broad-spectrum antibiotic.*

spec·u·late (SPEK·yuh·late) *v.* **-lates, -lat·ed, -lat·ing** **1** reflect *upon* or *about* a subject on which there is insufficient evidence; hence, conjecture or guess. **2** trade *in* commodities, gold, land, etc. hoping to profit from future price changes: *to speculate on the stock market.* — **spec·u·la·tion** (-LAY·shun) *n.: to engage, indulge in speculation; idle, wild speculation; speculation in land; a flurry of speculation about the outcome of the vote.* — **spec·u·la·tive** (SPEC·yuh·luh·tiv) *adj.* — **spec·u·la·tor** (-lay·tur) *n.*

speech *n.* **1** the power to speak, the manner of speaking, or a particular language: *freedom of speech; the faculty of speech which humans enjoy; impaired, slurred speech; the speech* (= language) *of the natives; adj.: speech defects, disorders, therapy.* **2** words spoken to an audience: *to ad-lib, deliver, give, improvise, make a speech; an acceptance, after-dinner, campaign, farewell, impromptu, inaugural, keynote, welcoming speech; a speech on* or *about free trade.*

Speech from the Throne See THRONE SPEECH.

speech·less *adj.* dumb or silent; also, unable to speak, as from shock: *She was left speechless; was speechless with astonishment.*

speed *n.* **1** rate of movement: *The car reaches a maximum speed of 120 km/h; going at full speed; a breakneck, cruising, high, lightning, low, top speed; Full speed ahead* (= Go ahead at full speed)*! The sales rep was dispatched with speed* (= swiftness)*; a transmission with four speeds* (= gears)*; a ten-speed bicycle.* **2** *Slang.* a methamphetamine. — *v.* **speeds,** *pt. & pp.* **sped** or **speed·ed, speed·ing** **1** move fast: *The car sped away; a speeding car (going over the speed limit).* **2** cause to move fast: *Use airmail to speed a letter on its way; workers told to **speed up** production.* — **speed·er** *n.* — **speed·ing** *n.*

speed trap *n.* a police watch for drivers who exceed the speed limit.

speed·y *adj.* **speed·i·er, -i·est** **1** swift: *a speedy recovery.* **2** prompt: *a speedy reply.* — **speed·i·ly** *adv.*

spell *n.* **1** an incantation or words used as a charm; also, their influence: *a magic spell; The singer seemed to cast a spell over* or *on her audience; They were under a spell; The spell was broken when the lights went off.* **2** a brief period: *a spell of depression, hot weather, illness; a coughing spell* (= attack). **3** a brief period of work in rotation with others. — *v.* **spells, spelled** or **spelt, spell·ing 1** write or say the letters making up a word: *How is your name spelled? A-N-N-E spells* (= makes up the spelling of) *Anne.* **2** signify or mean: *a series of defeats that spelled disaster for the government.* — **spell out 1** give the letters of a word: *Please spell out your name for me.* **2** explain in detail: *A Speech from the Throne spells out the government's policy for the year ahead.* — **spell·er** *n.*

spell·bind (SPEL·bined) *v.* **-binds, -bound, -bind·ing** hold as if under a spell; also, fascinate: *They listened **spellbound** for two hours; a **spellbinding** orator.*

spelling *n.* the act of spelling or the way a word is spelled: *bad, good, poor spelling; **adj.**: spelling errors, mistakes.*

spelling bee *n.* a spelling contest in which players who make errors are eliminated.

spelt a *pt. & pp.* of SPELL.

spend *v.* **spends, spent, spend·ing 1** use a resource such as money, time, effort, thought, etc.: *to spend money on* or *for the children's education; Children spend time (in) studying.* **2** use up or consume: *The storm has spent itself, has spent its fury.* — **spending** *n.: deficit spending; cuts in government spending; our spending habits.*

spend·thrift *n.* one who spends money wastefully.

spent *adj.* exhausted or used up: *a spent bullet, horse.*

spew *v.* vomit or cast forth.

sphere (SFEER) *n.* **1** a perfectly round solid body; also, a globular body such as a star or planet. **2** formerly, an imagined hollow globe with the earth as its centre and the heavenly bodies revolving around it in fixed concentric shells: *the celestial sphere; the music of the spheres.* **3** the range or domain of an activity or quality: *one's sphere of activity, influence, interest.* — **spher·i·cal** (SFER·uh·cul, SFEER-) *adj.* — **spher·i·cal·ly** *adv.*

sphinx (SFINKS) *n.* **1** a statue with a lion's body and human head, which in Greek mythology was a monster who would strangle every passer-by unable to solve a riddle. **2** an enigmatic or puzzling character.

spice *n.* **1** a food seasoning made from a plant, as pepper, ginger, and mace. **2** something that adds flavour: *"Variety is the spice of life."* — *v.* **spic·es, spiced, spic·ing** season with spice or add zest to something. — **spic·y** *adj.* **spic·i·er, -i·est:** *spicy humour; spicy* (= slightly racy) *stories.*

spick-and-span (SPIC·un·span) *adj.* fresh or spotlessly clean.

spi·der (SPY·dur) *n.* 1 an eight-legged, insectlike creature that spins webs of silk to trap insects. 2 a frying pan. — **spi·der·y** *adj.*

spiel (SPEEL) *n. Slang.* a voluble or glib persuasive talk, as of a circus barker: *a sales spiel.*

spiff·y *adj.* **spiff·i·er, -i·est** *Slang.* smart or stylish: *a spiffy cowboy hat; a spiffy dresser.* — **spiff·i·ly** *adv.*

spig·ot (SPIG·ut) *n.* 1 a faucet. 2 a plug or peg for stopping the vent of a barrel or cask.

spike *n.* 1 a usually large nail or metal point, as those forming the top of an iron fence, the projections on the soles of shoes to prevent slipping, or the fasteners of railway tracks to ties: *the driving of the last spike in laying the transcontinental railway.* 2 a long, pointed cluster of flowers or an ear of grain.
— *v.* **spikes, spiked, spik·ing** 1 connect with spikes, as a rail to a tie. 2 provide with spikes: *spiked hair, shoes, stick.* 3 impale on a spike. 4 prevent or thwart a scheme or attempt: *to spike a rumour.* 5 *Informal.* add alcoholic liquor to a drink.

spill *v.* **spills,** *pt. & pp.* **spilled** or **spilt, spill·ing** 1 let a liquid or a substance in loose particles flow over from a container: *to spill milk, salt; The party was so crowded the guests spilled into the hallways; to spill* (= be guilty of shedding) *blood.* 2 *Informal.* throw off or out: *The horse spilled him.*
— *n.* 1 a spilling or something spilled: *an oil spill; The rider took a nasty spill when the horse bolted.* 2 also **spill·way,** a channel for overflowing water, as from a reservoir.

spilt a *pt. & pp.* of SPILL.

spin *v.* **spins, spun, spin·ning** 1 turn or revolve rapidly, as a top, wheel, etc.: *The car was spinning on the ice; Her head was spinning from the dance.* 2 shape by turning, as on a lathe or wheel: *good at spinning* (= telling) *yarns.* 3 make thread by drawing out and twisting cotton, wool, etc. 4 make something with thread, as a web, or something threadlike from glass, gold, or sugar (i.e. "cotton candy"). 5 move along smoothly and rapidly on a wheeled vehicle.
— *n.* 1 a spinning motion, as of a plane coming down out of control. 2 a ride in an automobile, on a bicycle, etc.: *to go for a spin on Lakeshore Boulevard.*
— **spin·ner** *n.*

spin·ach (SPIN·ich) *n.* a garden vegetable with a thick cluster of leaves rich in vitamins and minerals.

spi·nal (SPY·nul) *adj.* having to do with the backbone composed of bony disks: *the **spinal column*** (= backbone); *the **spinal cord** (of nerve tissue running from the brain through the spinal column); A **spinal tap*** (= extraction of a sample of the spinal fluid for analysis) *is done on a patient suspected of having a spinal disease.*

spin·dle *n.* 1 a short, round, or smooth stick or rod with tapered ends for spinning yarn into thread. 2 anything resembling a spindle in form or function, as a turned wooden piece for a balustrade or the back of a chair.
— **spin·dly** *adj.*

spin doctor *n.* a publicist hired to manipulate the media like a baseball pitcher putting a spin on the ball to control its direction.

spine *n.* 1 a stiff, sharp-pointed, protective growth, as on a cactus or porcupine. 2 the spinal column or anything resembling it, as the hinged back of a book. 3 backbone or courage; **spine·less** *adj.*
— **spin·y** (SPY·nee) *adj.: the spiny lobster.*

spin-off *n.* a benefit, product, etc. derived or resulting from a larger enterprise, as abridged editions of a reference work: *The TV show is a spin-off of the hit movie.*

spi·ral (SPY·rul) *n. & adj.* (a curve or coil) winding in widening circles like the hairspring of a watch or like a screw: *a book with a spiral binding; a spiral* (= circular) *staircase; an inflationary spiral (of rising prices and wages).*

spire *n.* a tapering and pointed structure, as the top of a church steeple, a tapering stalk of grass, or the top part of a sea shell used as a horn.

spir·it (SPEER·it) *n.* 1 an animating principle, as the soul to the body; the moral, religious, or emotional aspect of something: *The spirit is willing though the body is weak; in the spirit of our founder; Our founder will be our guiding, moving spirit; to catch the spirit of the times; the Christmas spirit; a competitive, dauntless, fighting, partisan, rebellious, sporting, team spirit; Obey the letter and spirit of the law; I can't be present, but my wife will be there in body and in spirit; I'll be with you in spirit.* 2 person: *a free, kindred, noble spirit.* 3 disposition or state of mind: *We negotiated in a spirit of good will and cooperation; Let's put some spirit* (= vigour) *into our game; They tried but couldn't break her spirit* (= make her submissive). 4 a bodiless or supernatural being, as God, fairies, ghosts, etc.: *a sorcerer who conjures up spirits; an evil spirit; the Holy Spirit; He composes as the spirit moves him* (= as he feels inspired). 5 **spirits** *pl.* mood or state of mind: *The defeat dampened our spirits somewhat; Our spirits were drooping; We needed something to lift* or *raise our flagging spirits; We were in high spirits on hearing that we had won; low spirits; He's in good spirits* (= cheerful) *though a bit weak; animal spirits* (= overflowing liveliness). 6 usually **spirits** *pl.* a distilled liquid: *spirits of camphor, turpentine; a teetotaller who shuns spirits* (= alcohol).
— *v.* carry a person away secretly: *The captive was spirited away* or *off to a secret location.*
— **spir·it·u·al** (·i·choo·ul) *adj.;* **spir·it·u·al·ly** *adv.*

spir·it·ed (SPEER·uh·tid) *adj.* lively or energetic.

¹spit *n.* 1 small point of land projecting into water. 2 a pointed rod or bar on which meat is roasted over a fire.
— *v.* **spits, spit·ted, spit·ting** pierce with or as if with a spit.

²spit *v.* **spits,** *pt. & pp.* **spit** or **spat, spit·ting** 1 eject saliva from the mouth: *to spit at* or *on something; Never spit into the wind.* 2 throw out something or make a sound like spitting, as a cat when angry or fat when frying: *The child spit out the medicine; guns spitting fire.* — *n.* a spitting or the saliva spat out.

spit and polish *n. Informal.* much or excessive attention to neatness and orderliness, esp. of a superficial kind.

spite *n.* petty ill will with a tendency to annoy or irritate: *Did they do it out of spite?*
— **in spite of** notwithstanding.
— *v.* **spites, spit·ed, spit·ing** show spite toward; annoy

or irritate: *It is foolish "to cut off one's nose to spite one's face."*— **spite·ful** *adj.*

spitting image *n.* a strikingly close resemblance of another person: *She is the spitting image of her dad.*

spit·tle (SPIT·ul) *n.* saliva that is spat out.

splake *n. Cdn.* a hybrid species of speckled trout and lake trout.

splash *v.* dash water, mud, etc. so as to make it scatter in drops: *Try not to splash when painting; passing cars splashing pedestrians; a coat splashed with mud; The children splashed in the pool, then splashed across the flooded street.*
— *n.* a splashing or a spot or noise made by splashing.
— **make a splash** *Informal.* make a sensation; attract much attention.

splash·down *n.* the landing of a spacecraft on water.

splash·y *adj.* splash·i·er, -i·est *Informal.* showy or sensational.

splay·foot *n.* -feet a broad flat foot that is turned outward.

splay·foot·ed (SPLAY·foot·id) *adj.* having splayfeet; hence, clumsy.

spleen *n.* 1 a large glandlike organ lying between the stomach and the diaphragm that acts as a blood filter but was once believed the cause of bad temper: *a ruptured spleen.* 2 spite or ill temper: *He vented his spleen on the first one to cross his path.*

splen·did *adj.* brilliant and impressive: *a splendid palace, victory; a splendid (Informal for excellent) idea.*

splen·dour or **splen·dor** (SPLEN·dur) *n.* brilliance or magnificence: *a pageant full of pomp and splendour; a prince arrayed in regal splendour.*

splice *v.* splic·es, spliced, splic·ing 1 join ropes, wire, etc. without knotting by weaving untwisted ends together. 2 join together pieces of timber, etc. by overlapping. 3 join together different pieces of tape, film, computer data, nerves, or genetic material for a desired effect.
— *n.* a joint made by splicing.

splint *n.* 1 a thin strip of wood or other flexible material for weaving or braiding into baskets, chair seats, etc. 2 a thin strip of wood, a plaster cast, or other device for keeping an injured body part in position while healing; *v.: He used a popsicle stick to splint (= brace or support) her broken finger.*

splin·ter (SPLIN·tur) *n.* a long, thin, sharp piece of broken glass, bone, wood, etc.: *to extract, get out, remove the splinter from a foot; a new party formed by a splinter (= factional) group.*
— *v.* break into splinters.

split *v.* splits, split, split·ting 1 separate lengthwise or along a natural line of division, as along the grain of wood or into layers of slate. 2 cut or divide into parts: *The bag split at the seams; the splitting up of a subdivision into housing lots; He shouldn't have split up with (= separated from) his wife; the splitting of the atom; We'll* **split the difference** *(= compromise by*

agreeing on a middle figure); *Let's not split hairs* (= argue over trivialities); *She was splitting her sides* (= laughing heartily) *at his jokes; Good writers try never to split an infinitive; i.e. try to avoid writing "to never split an infinitive"; a* **splitting** *(= severe) headache.* 3 *Slang.* leave a place.
— *n.* a splitting, crack, division, etc.: *a split in the party ranks; a split between factions.*
— *adj.: a split class of students of different grades; a split (= not unanimous) decision; two scenes shown on TV side by side on a* **split screen; a split shift** *divided into work periods that are far apart.*

split-level (SPLIT·lev·ul) *n. & adj.* (a house) having an intermediate level about half a floor above or below the others built adjacently.

split personality *n.* 1 a personality with conflicting patterns of behaviour. 2 *Informal.* schizophrenia.

splotch *n.* an irregular or blotchy spot or stain.
— *v.* mark with a splotch or splotches; **splotch·y** *adj.*

splurge *n.* a showy or extravagant display: *a splurge following a lottery win.*
— *v.* splurg·es, splurged, splurg·ing *Informal.* make a splurge or spend money extravagantly *on* something expensive.

splut·ter (SPLUT·ur) *v.* make a sputtering sound, esp. speak in an excited and confused manner.
— *n.* a spluttering.

spoil *v.* spoils, *pt. & pp.* spoiled or spoilt, spoil·ing 1 destroy the usefulness or value of a person or thing: *"Too many cooks spoil the soup"; a spoiled (= pampered) child; methods to keep food from spoiling (= beginning to rot); Bad weather spoiled the picnic.* 2 **be spoiling for** *Informal.* be eager for a fight, etc. 3 [old use] rob or plunder.
— *n.* usually **spoils** *pl.* loot or booty: *the spoils of war.*
— **spoil·age** (-ij) *n.*

spoil·er *n.* 1 one that spoils or loots. 2 a plate that acts as an air brake, as on an airplane wing or racing car.

spoil·sport *n.* one who spoils the enjoyment of others.

spoke 1 *n.* any of the radial bars extending from the hub of a wheel to its rim. 2 *pt.* of SPEAK.

spoken 1 *pp.* of SPEAK. 2 *adj.* uttered: *the spoken word.* 3 *combining form* speaking: *loud-spoken, plain-spoken, soft-spoken, sweet-spoken, true-spoken.*

spokes·man (SPOKES·mun) *n.* -men a person expressing the views of another or of a group.
— **spokes·wom·an** *n.* -en. Also **spokes·per·son.**

sponge (SPUNJ) *n.* 1 a water animal with a porous skeleton that resembles a plant in being attached to the bottom of the sea or to other objects. 2 a porous or spongelike mass of rubber, or **sponge rubber,** or other synthetic material used for cleansing, washing, etc. 3 a washing or wiping with a sponge. 4 *Informal.* a parasite; also **spong·er.**
— **throw in** or **toss in the sponge** give up the fight; accept defeat.
— *v.* spong·es, sponged, spong·ing 1 wipe, rub, wash, etc. with a sponge. 2 *Informal.* live at the expense of another: *Since losing his job, Jon has been sponging on his friends; He sponged $50 off me.*

sponge bath *n.* a cleaning of the body using a wet sponge or cloth.

sponge·cake *n.* a light spongy cake made without shortening.

spon·gy *adj.* -gi·er, -gi·est like a sponge; full of holes.

spon·sor (SPON·sur) *n.* an endorser or supporter, as a godparent, the promoter of a legislative proposal, or one paying for a radio or television program by buying commercial advertising. — *v.* act as sponsor for someone: *He sponsored me for the club membership.* — **spon·sor·ship** *n.*

spon·ta·neous (spon·TAY·nee·us) *adj.* caused or happening naturally, without planning or premeditation: *spontaneous laughter; a spontaneous outburst; a spontaneous abortion* (= miscarriage). — **spon·ta·ne·ous·ly** *adv.* — **spon·ta·ne·i·ty** (spon·tuh·NEE·uh·tee) *n.*

spoof (long "oo") *n. Informal.* 1 a hoax or trick. 2 a parody or takeoff. — *v.* ridicule or parody.

spook (long "oo") *n.* 1 *Informal.* a ghost. 2 *Slang.* a spy. — *v.* frighten. — **spook·y** *adj.*

spool *n.* a cylinder or reel on which thread, wire, film, or ribbon is wound.

spoon *n.* 1 a utensil consisting of a shallow bowl at one end of a handle for eating, stirring, etc.: *a dessert, measuring, soup spoon.* 2 something spoon-shaped, as a fishing lure. — *v.* take up with a spoon. — **spoon·ful** *n.* -fuls: *a heaping spoonful, level spoonful.*

spoon·er·ism (SPOO·nur·iz·um) *n.* the interchanging of sounds in running words with comic effect, as in "kinkering congs" for "conquering kings."

spoon·feed *v.* -feeds, -fed, -feed·ing 1 feed with a spoon, as a child. 2 help someone in a way that does not encourage thinking or acting for oneself: *Do the schools spoonfeed students too much?*

spo·rad·ic (spuh·RAD·ic) *adj.* occurring in scattered or isolated instances: *sporadic cases of a disease; sporadic gunfire.* — **spo·rad·i·cal·ly** *adv.*

spore *n.* in algae, fungi, etc., a one-celled body capable of giving rise to a new individual.

sport *n.* 1 a pastime requiring physical exertion and skill, as baseball, bowling, etc.: *sports and games; an amateur, aquatic, competitive, contact, outdoor, spectator, water, winter sport; team sports such as football and hockey.* 2 physical activity: *She is fond of sports; Olympic Games are the greatest events in the world of sport(s); the history of Canadian sport.* 3 fun or amusement: *She only said it for* or *in sport; They like to* **make sport** *of* (= mock) *his accent; cruel sport; He soon became the sport* (= object of fun) *of his class.* 4 *Informal.* a good fellow: *Be a sport! She is a good sport who can take a lot of teasing.* — *v.* 1 play or jest: *She is only sporting.* 2 *Informal.* display: *He came to work sporting a new jacket.* — *adj.* 1 having to do with sports: *a sport(s) car; a sports competition, dictionary, enthusiast, event, model, personality, section, sedan; sports equipment, medicine; the sports world.* 2 for casual wear: *a sport(s) shirt.*

sporting *adj.* having to do with sports: *sporting equipment; the sporting public; a sporting* (= sportsmanlike) *offer; a sporting* (*Informal for* fair) *chance.* — **sport·ing·ly** *adv.*

sports·cast *n.* a broadcast of a sporting event. — **sports·cast·er** *n.*

sports·man (SPORTS·mun) *n.* -men 1 a man who takes part in sports such as hunting and fishing. 2 one who plays fair. — **sports·man·like** *adj.*; **sports·man·ship** *n.* — **sports·wom·an** (SPORTS·wom·an) *n.* -wom·en.

sport·y *adj.* sport·i·er, -i·est *Informal.* 1 good for sports: *a sporty sedan.* 2 flashy or showy: *sporty slacks; a sporty tie; a sporty car with sporty looks.*

spot *n.* 1 a small area or place: *a clear spot in the jungle; the exact spot where he landed; in an isolated, secluded spot; a blind spot that the driver cannot see; some of the high spots* (= high points) *of our visit; He has a soft spot* (= special liking) *for people from his hometown; I found myself in a tight spot* (= difficult situation); *the trouble spots of the world such as Palestine and Northern Ireland.* 2 a small, distinguishable area or mark: *A leopard cannot change its spots; a beauty spot (on the skin); a grease spot* (= stain); *a spot* (= stain) *remover.* — **in a (bad) spot** *Slang.* in trouble. — **on the spot** 1 then and there: *The press got a briefing on the spot; got an on-the-spot briefing; the man on the spot* (= on the actual scene). 2 *Informal.* in a difficult or embarrassing position: *The tax auditor put him on the spot.* — *v.* spots, spot·ted, spot·ting 1 mark or become marked with spots: *a pattern spotted like a giraffe.* 2 to stain: *a page spotted with smudges.* 3 locate; also, see or recognize: *We spotted him in the crowd; He was spotted* (= identified) *as the wanted man.* 4 *Slang.* allow as a handicap or advantage to someone: *an equalizer for the 11 years that Ali was spotting Spinks in age.* — *adj.* happening, done, etc. on the spot: *spot news coverage of a fire; spot transactions; a 30-second spot commercial; Prices are cheaper on the* **spot market** (where commodities are sold for cash on delivery); *spot prices of crude; a* **spot-check** (= random on-the-spot check) *by police.*

spot·light *n.* 1 a bright light thrown on a spot requiring illumination, as on the stage. 2 the focus of public attention: *They turned the spotlight on someone in the audience; He was in the spotlight* (= object of public attention) *for a while.* — *v.* 1 light up with a spotlight. 2 put in public view.

spot·ter *n.* 1 one who removes spots before cleaning clothes. 2 one who locates, identifies, or keeps watch on people, targets, etc.

spot·ty *adj.* spot·ti·er, spot·ti·est spotted; uneven; irregular: *spotty appearance, work; a spotty face (marked by acne).*

spouse *n.* marriage partner, usually one's wife or husband: *a beloved spouse; an unfaithful spouse.*

spout *n.* 1 a jet or stream, as of water, from a pipe, nozzle, or projecting tube, as of a kettle. 2 a projecting part of a pipe, as for rainwater from a roof. — *v.* 1 shoot out, as water from a spout or fountain. 2 *Informal.* utter or speak in a vehement or declamatory manner.

sprain v. stretch or tear the ligaments of a body joint accidentally. — *n.* such an injury.

sprang a *pt.* of SPRING.

sprawl v. lie on one's back with limbs loosely spread out: *bodies sprawled on the beach; the sprawling (= spread-out) city of Toronto; The blow sent him sprawling.*
— *n.* a sprawling or a spread-out condition: *a new land-use plan to halt urban sprawl.*

spray n. 1 (an ornament shaped like) a small cluster of flowers, leaves, or fruit. 2 a mist or jet of tiny drops, as from a breaking wave or a spray gun.
— *v.* apply as a spray: *Insecticide is sprayed on trees; The enemy was sprayed with bullets.*

spray can n. an aerosol container.

spray gun n. a device for applying paints, lacquers, etc. in a spray.

spread (SPRED) v. **spreads, spread, spread·ing** (cause) to cover a large or larger area: *A bird spreads its wings; to spread a rug on the floor; to spread jam on toast; to spread it evenly; The rumour spread quickly; to spread the news; It spread like wildfire; spread to all corners of the nation; to spread seed, contagious diseases; An epidemic spreads unchecked; payments spread over many years; to spread (= arrange) the table for dinner.*
— *n.* a spreading, what is spread, or its expanse or extent: *the spread of an eagle's wings; the spread of civilization; spreads (= covers) for beds, tables, etc.; a tasty sandwich spread; an ad designed as a two-page spread; a centre spread; a 600-acre (243-hectare) spread in Alberta.* — **spread·er** n.

spread-eagle (SPRED·ee·gul) adj. standing or lying spread out like an eagle with outstretched wings and legs.
— *v.* **-gles, -gled, -gling** (make someone) stand or lie in spread-eagle fashion.

spread·sheet n. an accounting worksheet for financial planning or a computer program for this purpose.

spree n. an uninhibited activity or indulgence in something: *to go on a shopping spree; spending spree; the hangover following a weekend spree (= drinking bout).*

sprig n. a small twig or spray: *a sprig of mistletoe.*

spright·ly adv. **-li·er, -li·est** lively or spirited: *a sprightly lad, publication.* — **spright·li·ness** n.

spring v. **springs,** *pt.* **sprang** or **sprung,** *pp.* **sprung, spring·ing** 1 move, esp. rise suddenly and lightly: *to spring out of bed; Weeds spring up on a lawn; He sprang to her defence; He's sprung of or from noble blood.* 2 of a wall, door, etc., give way to pressure and crack, warp, etc. 3 cause to spring: *a trap that is easily sprung; Sue wanted to spring the news on (= make it known suddenly to) her parents; The boat **sprang a leak** and sank; He was sprung from jail (Slang for released) by paying bail.*
— *n.* 1 a springing: *a sudden spring.* 2 an elastic device or quality: *cars with coil springs and leaf springs; the spring of her step.* 3 the growing season that follows

winter: *There's a hint, touch of spring in the air; an early spring; A robin is a harbinger of spring.* 4 a natural stream rising from under the ground: *hot, mineral, thermal, subterranean springs.* 5 source or origin; also, motive.
— *adj.* 1 springing: *a spring device, lock.* 2 of the spring season: *time to do a thorough spring cleaning; spring rains; a spring lamb (born in early spring).* 3 having to do with a spring of water: *fresh spring water.*

spring·board n. a flexible board to jump from with a springing motion, as at a swimming pool: *He used his first job as a springboard to higher positions.*

spring fever n. a feeling of restlessness during the change from the cold of winter to the warmth of spring.

spring·y adj. **spring·i·er, -i·est** elastic or resilient: *a springy mattress, step.*

sprin·kle (SPRINK·ul) v. **-kles, -kled, -kling** fall or scatter in small drops or particles: *to sprinkle salt on food; to sprinkle a lawn (with water); It's sprinkling outside (= raining lightly).*
— *n.* a sprinkling; also, a light rain. — **sprink·ler** n.

sprin·kling n. a small number or quantity.

sprint n. a relatively short race, up to 400 m in track and field; dash.
— *v.* run a sprint. — **sprint·er** n.

sprite n. an elf or fairy.

spritz·er (SPRIT·sur) n. a wine-and-soda drink.

sprout n. 1 a young shoot, as from a seed in the ground. 2 a bud. — *v.* cause or begin to grow; germinate.

spruce (SPROOSE) n. an evergreen tree related to the firs, but with cones hanging downwards.
— *adj.* **spruc·er, spruc·est** neat and smart.
— *v.* **spruc·es, spruced, spruc·ing** make spruce: *He spruced himself up for the party.*

sprung *pp. & a pt.* of SPRING.

spry adj. **spri·er** or **spry·er, spri·est** or **spry·est** esp. of the elderly, vigorous and active.
— **spry·ly** adv.; **spry·ness** n.

spud n. Informal. potato: *P.E.I. is sometimes referred to as "Spud Island."*

spume (long "yoo") n. what is spewed forth, as by force or under pressure: *the spume of whales.*
— *v.* **spumes, spumed, spum·ing:** *The waterfall hits the bottom and spumes upward hundreds of metres in the air.*

spun *pt. & pp.* of SPIN.

spunk n. Informal. pluck or courage: *The children showed lots of spunk in helping to rescue their playmates.* — **spunk·y** adj.

spur n. 1 a pricking device with a sharp point, worn on a rider's heel for urging a horse forward. 2 a stimulus or incentive: *The prize was a spur to greater achievements.* 3 something spurlike, as the small projection on the leg of a rooster, a lateral ridge extending from a mountain, or a railway siding.

— **on the spur of the moment** suddenly and without planning.

— **win one's spurs** gain distinction in one's field: *She has won her spurs as a diplomat.*

— *v.* **spurs, spurred, spur·ring** urge on or incite, as with spurs: *The prize spurred her on to greater efforts; The tragedy stirred the neighbourhood out of its lethargy and spurred them to action.*

spu·ri·ous (SPYOOR·ee·us) *adj.* not genuine or authentic; false: *a spurious allegation, distinction, document, signature; spurious arguments, charges, claims; on spurious grounds.* — **spu·ri·ous·ly** *adv.*

spurn *v.* refuse or reject with disdain: *to spurn a lover, an offer; She spurned his attentions.*

spurt *v.* **1** (cause) to gush out suddenly, as blood from a wound. **2** show a short and sudden burst of energy, as near the finish in a race.
— *n.: Water came out of the tap in spurts; spurts of flame; a spurt of activity in the stock market.*

sput·nik (SPUT·nik) *n.* an earth satellite sent up by the U.S.S.R.

sput·ter (SPUT·ur) *n.* **1** a popping and spitting noise, as of fat when frying. **2** drops or bits of food from the mouth.
— *v.* **1** make a sputtering noise. **2** spit out words or to talk excitedly and with confusion.

spu·tum (SPEW·tum) *n.*, *pl.* **-ta** (-tuh), saliva and mucus that is coughed up.

spy *v.* **spies, spied, spy·ing 1** keep secret watch on a person or search out information for a nation for hostile purposes, as in wartime: *to spy on someone; Al is spying for the enemy.* **2** catch sight of someone: *We spied him breaking into the house from our window.*
— *n.*, *pl.* **spies** one who spies.

spy·glass *n.* a small telescope.

squab·ble (SQUOB·ul) *n.* a petty and noisy quarrel *about* or *over* something.
— *v.* **squab·bles, squab·bled, squab·bling** have a squabble: *neighbours squabbling with each other over a fence; the squabbling going on between the two.*

squad (SQUOD) *n.* **1** the smallest military unit, composed of 10 or 12 soldiers. **2** a small group of people working together: *a demolition, firing, flying, goon, vice squad; an anti-riot squad; a squad appointed to clean up the schoolyard.*

squad car *n.* a police cruiser or patrol car.

squad·ron (SQUOD·run) *n.* **1** an organized military unit, esp. in an air force: *a squadron of bombers, tanks.* **2** any organized multitude: *squadrons of birds, flies; a seven-man squadron of golf players.*

squal·id (SQUOL·id) *adj.* **1** filthy, as from neglect. **2** morally bad; sordid: *a squalid existence; squalid conditions, poverty, slums.*

squall (SQUAWL) *n.* **1** a sudden rise in the wind, esp. at sea, often accompanied by rain, hail, or thunder. **2** a loud, harsh cry or scream.
— *v.* utter a squall. — **squall·y** *adj.*

squal·or (SQUOL·ur) *n.* the state of being squalid; wretchedness; sordidness: *people living in squalor in the slums.*

squan·der (SQUON·dur) *v.* spend wealth, resources, etc. wastefully or extravagantly: *He squandered his heritage on risky ventures.*

square (SQUAIR) *n.* **1** a plane figure with four equal sides and angles. **2** anything in this shape, as a city block, a public place enclosed by streets on all sides, an instrument in the shape of an L or T to make or measure right angles, etc. **3** the product of a quantity multiplied by itself: *49 is the square of 7; 7 is the square root of 49.* **4** *Slang.* an old-fashioned person; one who is not hip: *He's a square.*
— *adj.* **squar·er, squar·est 1** like a square in shape: *a square room; a room 20 m square (= 20 m long on each side); within [square] brackets; square jaws, shoulders.* **2** suggesting evenness, balance, straightness, etc.: *fair and square (= honest) dealings; square (= balanced) accounts; three square (= substantial) meals a day; a square (= straightforward) refusal.* **3** *Slang.* not hip; old-fashioned: *She's square.*
— *v.* **squares, squared, squar·ing** be square, make square, or make into squares: *squared graph paper; Squared timber has rectangular edges; to square (= settle) an account with the bank; performance that does not square (= agree) with promises; 7 squared is 49.*
— **square off** *Informal.* get ready to fight *against* someone, as in boxing.
— **square oneself** *Informal.* make up for a wrong.
— *adv.* in a square shape or manner.
Also **square·ly** *adv.* — **square·ness** *n.*

square one *n.* the starting point, as in games: *right back at or to square one.*

squash (SQUOSH) *v.* **1** squeeze, crush, or beat into a flat mass or pulp. **2** give a crushing blow to something; suppress a riot or silence an adversary. **3** proceed or move by force or with a splashing sound: *They squashed through the crowd.*
— *n.* **1** a squashing fall or its soft, heavy sound. **2** a squashed mass. **3** a gourd of the New World related to pumpkins: *summer squash; winter squash.* **4** a game like handball but played with rackets in a walled court.

squat (SQUOT) *v.* **squats, squat·ted, squat·ting 1** crouch or sit on the heels with bent knees. **2** settle on land without original legal right.
— *n.* a squatting posture.
— *adj.* **squat·ter, squat·test 1** crouching. **2** short and thick in stature, as a toad or puffin; dumpy: *a squat little guy.* Also **squat·ty.**

squat·ter (SQUOT·ur) *n.* one who squats on land: *Sometimes squatters gain title to the lands they occupy; Millions live in squatter settlements (made up of shacks) in developing countries.*

squaw *n.* [disparaging use] a North American Indian woman.

squawk *v.* **1** utter a loud, harsh, complaining cry. **2** *Informal.* protest or complain raucously: *He has nothing to squawk about.*
— *n.* a squawking: *The chickens made loud squawks at the sight of the hawk; squawks (= loud complaints) from the taxpayers.*

squeak (SQUEEK) *v. & n.* (utter) the sharp, high-pitched cry of a mouse or (make) the sound of a door hinge that needs oiling: *She was too choked up even to squeak for help; The bill managed to* **squeak by** or **through** *with a narrow margin; It was a close, narrow squeak* (= escape).
— **squeak·er** *n.*
— **squeak·y** *adj.* squeak·i·er, -i·est: *squeaky floor boards, shoes; "The squeaky wheel gets the grease"* (= You have to make noise to get attention); *a squeaky voice; hair washed* **squeaky-clean;** *a squeaky-clean living room, fairy tale; squeaky-clean gambling that pays for hospitals, etc.; our squeaky-clean image, standards.*

squeal (SQUEEL) *v. & n.* **1** (make) a long squeaking cry or sound, as of a pig when hurt or of faulty brakes: *Children squeal with* or *in delight.* **2** (act as) an informer: *to squeal on someone to the police.*
— **squeal·er** *n.*

squeam·ish (SQUEE·mish) *adj.* **1** prudish or scrupulous: *She is very squeamish about walking in late.* **2** queasy or nauseated: *I felt squeamish at the thought of eating raw fish.*

squeeze *v.* squeez·es, squeezed, squeez·ing **1** press from the sides, as in extracting juice from a fruit, hugging someone, or forcing a way through a crowd: *All the people were squeezed into one room; It was tough to squeeze one's way out of it.* **2** put pressure on a victim or get money, etc. by pressure from someone; hence, oppress.
— *n.* a squeezing or being squeezed: *to put a squeeze* (= restraint) *on bank loans to fight inflation; He found himself in a tight squeeze* (= in difficulty); *a plastic* **squeeze bottle** *for spraying medication; a* **squeeze play** *in baseball, with the batter bunting the ball and the runner scoring from third base.*

squelch *n. Informal.* **1** the act of suppressing or silencing, as with a rebuke, stare, etc. **2** a sucking sound, as made when splashing through mud.
— *v. Informal.* **1** to silence or put down with a squelch. **2** slosh or splash through mud, etc. with a squelch.

squig·gle (SQUIG·ul) *n.* a wavy twist or curve.
— *v.* squig·gles, squig·gled, squig·gling **1** move with or make squiggles. **2** write as a squiggle.
— **squig·gly** (-glee) *adj.*

squint *v.* **1** look with the eyes partly closed; peer: *It's natural to squint when looking at bright lights.* **2** look sideways. **3** be cross-eyed.
— *n.* **1** a peering. **2** a visual problem of cross-eye. **3** a sidelong glance.

squire *v.* squires, squired, squir·ing act as a squire to a woman; escort.
— *n.* **1** a woman's escort. **2** in Britain, a country gentleman, esp. the chief landowner of a district. **3** formerly, a knight's personal attendant or armour bearer.

squirm *v.* **1** wriggle or writhe about, as a worm. **2** do so because of embarrassment: *He squirmed in his chair when the subject was mentioned; Don't let him* **squirm out** *of* (= evade) *that commitment.*
— **squirm·y** *adj.*

squir·rel (SQUR·ul, SQUEER·rul) *n.* a rodent, usually tree-dwelling, related to the chipmunk.
— *v.* squir·rels, squir·relled or squir·reled, squir·rel·ling or squir·rel·ing store something *away* for future use.

squirt *v.* eject a liquid in a thin stream, as through a small pump or syringe.
— *n.* **1** a jet of liquid. **2** a squirting device such as a "water pistol," or **squirt gun.** **3** *Informal.* an impudent youngster.

squish 1 *v.* squash or squeeze: *tiny bungalows squished into postage-stamp lots and sold as detached homes.* **2** *v. & n.* (make) a soft splashing or squashing sound: *The children squished their way through slush.*
— **squish·y** *adj.: a squishy stretch of swamp; a wet squishy day.*

stab *n.* **1** a thrust or a wound made by a thrust with a pointed weapon such as a dagger. **2** a sharp pain as if caused by a stab: *a sudden stab of pain.* **3** *Informal.* attempt: *He made* or *had several stabs at skiing.*
— **stab in the back** a treacherous attack or betrayal.
— *v.* stabs, stabbed, stab·bing pierce or wound someone with or as if with a pointed weapon.
— **stab·ber** *n.*

sta·bil·i·ty (stuh·BIL·uh·tee) *n.* the quality of being stable; firmness; steadiness; permanence.

sta·bi·lize (STAY·buh·lize) *v.* -liz·es, -lized, -liz·ing make stable or steady: *A gyroscope is used to stabilize a ship; to stabilize fluctuating prices; to stabilize an airplane with a horizontal* **sta·bi·liz·er** *in its tail assembly.* — **sta·bi·li·za·tion** (-luh·ZAY·shun) *n.*

sta·ble (STAY·bul) *adj.* -bler, -blest not likely to give way or be overturned: *a stable government; a stable* (= lasting) *chemical compound, design.*
— *n.* **1** a building in which domestic animals are housed and fed. **2** such animals, esp. racehorses, collectively: *a publisher with a good stable of authors.*
— *v.* -bles, -bled, -bling to lodge or be kept in a stable.

stack *n.* **1** a neatly arranged or orderly pile, as a haystack or rifles in a pyramid arrangement. **2** a smokestack.
— **blow one's stack** *Slang.* lose one's temper.
— **stacks** *pl.* the main collection of books in a library.
— *v.* pile or arrange in a stack: *a room stacked with books; Books were stacked against the walls; The jury is stacked* (= so arranged that the outcome of the trial is certain).

— **stack the cards** or **deck** arrange cards so as to cheat: *accused of stacking the cards in favour of his partner; The deck is stacked (against them)* (= They have no chance).

— **stack up** measure up or compare *with* or *to* or *against* a standard: *The two sides stack up fairly evenly; One stacks up well against the other.*

sta·di·um (STAY·dee·um) *n.* a large structure of tiers of seats, often domed, built around a playing field or arena: *a baseball, domed, football, Olympic stadium.*

staff *n., pl.* also **staves** (for 1 & 3). **1** a supporting stick or pole, as used when walking or for hoisting a flag; hence, one that supports or sustains: *Bread is the staff of life; An only son was the staff of her old age.* **2** *pl.* **staffs** a group of workers or officers: *editorial, office, teaching staff; She is on* (= a member of the) *staff; joined the staff today; I work with a skeleton staff; a military chief of staff.* **3** the set of five lines on which music is written.
— *v.* supply with a staff of workers: *to staff an institution.*

staff·er *n.* a member of a staff, as distinguished from casual employees.

stag *n.* an adult male deer.
— *adj.* meant for men to enjoy: *a stag movie, party.*
— **go stag** esp. of men, attend a party unaccompanied by a date.

stage *n.* **1** a step or degree of advance in a process: *the pupa stage of a butterfly; You keep growing till you reach a certain stage; at the beginning, closing, final stages of a campaign; an advanced, critical, crucial stage of an illness; Most skills are learned in easy stages* (= gradually); *to complete a task by easy stages* (= slowly). **2** one of the independently powered sections of a long-range rocket or missile which are jettisoned successively after burning their fuel. **3** a stagecoach. **4** a theatre platform; hence, a scene of action; also, theatre or drama: *a career on the stage* (= in acting); *He'll go* (= appear) *on stage in a few minutes; Bad strike settlements set the stage* (= prepare the way) *for later trouble.*
— *v.* **stag·es, staged, stag·ing** present (as) on a stage: *to stage a play; to stage* (= organize and carry out) *a protest.*

stage·hand *n.* one who helps with the arrangements on a theatre stage.

stage-struck *adj.* having an intense desire to join the acting profession.

stag·ger (STAG·ur) *v.* **1** move unsteadily, as on weak feet, faltering or swaying from side to side: *He staggered into the room; seemed to stagger under the heavy load; staggered to his feet; staggered out of the house; The news dealt a staggering blow to his hopes.* **2** arrange in a zigzag way or alternately: *to plant in staggered rows; Staggered working hours help ease traffic congestion.*

staging (STAY·jing) *n.* the moving forward of personnel or equipment in stages; *adj.: a military staging area; staging facilities for handling boat people; a guerrilla staging ground.*

stag·nant (STAG·nunt) *adj.* not flowing or active as in normal conditions: *stagnant air, water; a stagnant pond; a stagnant* (= sluggish) *market.*

stag·nate *v.* **-nates, -nat·ed, -nat·ing** make or become stagnant. — **stag·na·tion** (stag·NAY·shun) *n.*

stag·y (STAY·jee) *adj.* **stag·i·er, -i·est** theatrical; also, artificial.

staid *adj.* settled or steady in one's behaviour; also, sedate or sober: *the staid banking establishment; the bank building's staid exterior; a staid newspaper like "The Times"; Ontario's staid Tories.*

stain *n.* **1** a colour or spot that soils: *Coffee leaves a stain on cloth; to remove a stubborn stain.* **2** a blemish or dishonour: *a stain on his reputation.* **3** a penetrating dye or pigment, as used to colour wood, glass for ornamental windows of **stained glass,** and substances for examination under a microscope.
— *v.* **1** discolour or soil: *The spill stained the tablecloth.* **2** blemish: *The scandal stained his reputation.* **3** colour or dye: *We stained the wood brown.*

stair *n.* one of a series of steps, or **stairs:** *a flight of stairs; on the top stair; at the foot of the stairs; to climb, come down, fall down, go up, go down the stairs.*

stair·case or **stair·way** *n.* a series of stairs with supporting structure, handrails, etc.: *a winding staircase.*

stair·well *n.* a vertical open space or shaft containing stairs.

stake *n.* **1** a stick or post that is pointed at one end for driving into the ground to mark a boundary, tie a vine to, etc.: *Joan of Arc was burnt at the stake as a heretic.* **2** a share or interest in an undertaking; also, a grubstake. **3** **stakes** *pl.: The stakes are* (= prize is) *high; They've just raised the stakes* (= the risk) *by threatening to execute the hostages.*
— **at stake** at risk: *Lives are at stake.*
— **pull up stakes** *Informal.* leave a place where one is established: *They pulled up stakes and moved to Canada.*
— *v.* **stakes, staked, stak·ing 1** mark with stakes: *Prospectors for gold stake (out) a claim by marking off boundaries.* **2** gamble money, etc.; wager. **3** *Informal.* furnish a person with money or resources; grubstake.
— **stake out** put a place or suspect under surveillance; **stake·out** *n.*

stale *adj.* **stal·er, stal·est** not fresh or new: *stale food, jokes, news; stale* (= flat) *soda; He tried to beat a stale green light but didn't make it through the intersection; A cheque more than six months old may be refused by the bank as stale-dated.*
— *v.* **stales, staled, stal·ing** make or become stale.

stale·mate *n.* a deadlock or standstill: *to break a stalemate; a continuing stalemate.*

stalk (STAWK) *v.* **1** approach or pursue game, a victim, etc. without being seen or heard: *Tigers stalk their prey; Crime stalks the streets of inner cities at night; A dummy stalking horse is sometimes used by hunters to hide behind when stalking game.* **2** walk stiffly, esp. haughtily: *to stalk away or off without saying a word; He stalked out of the house.*
— *n.* **1** a stalking (stride). **2** a connecting part such as the stem of a flower, leaf, or wine glass: *celery stalks;* **stalked** *adj.*

stall (STAWL) *n.* **1** a compartment accommodating one

individual or group, as a stable for an animal, a booth or cubicle at a fair or theatre, a church pew, etc. **2** a stop or standstill, esp. one due to a malfunction; also, the condition of an airplane or wing losing its lift.
— *v.* **1** put or keep in a stall. **2** bring or come to a standstill; stop running or functioning: *The car stalled.* **3** *Informal.* use a delaying tactic or ruse: *to stall off creditors.*

stal·wart (STAWL·wurt) *adj.* strong and sturdy, esp. steadfast in loyalty or staunch in support.
— *n.* a stalwart or loyal supporter.

sta·men (STAY·mun) *n.* the long, slender, threadlike male reproductive organ of flowers.

stam·i·na (STAM·uh·nuh) *n.* vigour or endurance: *You need stamina to run a marathon.*

stam·mer (STAM·ur) *v.* speak haltingly with breaks in or between words; stutter: *He stammered a few words in reply; stammered his thanks.* — *n.* a stammering.

stamp *n.* **1** a small gummed paper label bearing an official design used as a token of payment of postage or revenue; also, any similar seal: *a postage stamp; The post office issues, cancels stamps; We lick, moisten, put, stick stamps on letters; a food stamp; trading stamps.* **2** an official mark or seal of approval, quality, etc.: *The plan received the director's stamp of approval.* **3** any kind or type: *men of that stamp.* **4** a design or message impressed on anything; also, the device used: *a rubber stamp; a date stamp; the stamp (= imprint) of genius in her works.* **5** a stamping, as with one's foot.
— *v.* **1** strike down on something with force, so as to pound or crush: *He stamped the floor in anger; stamped his foot (on the ground) in impatience; He stamped on her toes on the crowded dance floor.* **2** put a stamp on something; imprint: *a self-addressed stamped envelope; events indelibly stamped in his memory; She stamped the bill "Paid"; His accent stamps (= characterizes) him as uneducated.*
— **stamp out** end or put out, as by stamping: *to stamp out a fire, corruption, a rebellion.*

stam·pede (stam·PEED) *n.* **1** a confused, headlong flight, as of a frightened herd of animals: *A scare caused or created the stampede; a stampede (= rush) for the exits; a stampede to buy gold.* **2** a fair featuring a rodeo, as the Calgary Stampede.
— *v.* **-pedes, -ped·ed, -ped·ing** flee, put to flight, or make a rush: *The crowd panicked and stampeded out of the stadium; They were stampeded (= rushed) into selling the house at a loss.*

stamping ground *n. Informal.* a habitual gathering place or favourite haunt.

stance *n.* **1** a way of standing, esp. in regard to position of the feet. **2** posture or attitude.

stanch (STAWNCH, STAHNCH, STANCH) *v.* same as STAUNCH.

stand *v.* **stands, stood, stand·ing 1** be or remain erect or upright on one's feet: *Please sit down, don't stand; You have to stand on a chair to touch the ceiling; He stands six feet (1.83 m); A soldier stands at attention; stands at ease.* **2** (cause) to be in a specified position or condition: *The bookcase stood near the entrance; He*

stands accused of shoplifting; She's standing as a candidate for mayor; He stands (= ranks) first in her class; She stands to get a scholarship if she wins; He stands a good chance of winning. **3** bear or undergo: *He couldn't stand the heat; was ordered to stand trial; Will you stand us (Informal for* bear the expense of buying *us) a drink?*
— **stand by** be near so as to help or be ready for action: *Police and ambulances stood by in case of an emergency.*
— **stand for 1** represent: *The Maple Leaf stands for Canada.* **2** *Informal.* put up with: *She won't stand for such nonsense.* **3** be a candidate for something: *to stand for election, parliament.*
— **stand in 1** act as a stand-in *for* someone. **2** be associated or friendly *with* someone.
— **stand off 1** keep away. **2** put off or stall a creditor, etc.
— **stand on** insist on: *We stand firm on principles; Let's not stand on ceremony.*
— **stand out** be clearly visible or prominent: *White stands out against a dark background; a tall man who stands out in any crowd; She stands out as the best qualified applicant.*
— **stand pat** be steadfast; resist change.
— **stand up 1** rise: *We stand up to greet the teacher; It takes guts to **stand up and be counted** (= assert oneself in the face of opposition) when the going gets tough.* **2** remain intact: *a statement that won't stand up in court; a car that has stood up well through years of hard driving.* **3** *Informal.* ignore an appointment with someone: *John was stood up by his date; Woody Allen and others make a habit of standing up Oscar (= boycotting the awards).*
— **stand up for** support or defend: *to stand up for one's rights.*
— **stand up to 1** defy: *It takes courage to stand up to a bully.* **2** last: *A well-built car will stand up to many years of rough use.*
— *n.* **1** an act of standing: *He took a strong stand against the ban; a resolute stand; She put up a good stand; a one-night stand (= engagement); to take a stand (= position) on an issue.* **2** place of standing: *a taxi stand; bus stand; hot-dog stand; Witnesses **take the stand** in court; shouting from the **stands** (= tiered seats for spectators); a stand (= growth) of trees.*

stand·ard (STAN·durd) *n.* **1** a flag or military banner, esp. of a ruler or leader, as a rallying point. **2** a model or principle of comparison: *a school's admission standards; academic standards; countries still on the gold standard in regard to currency; a low, high standard of living; Dictionaries set the standard for correct use of language; a standard established by usage; to abandon, adhere to, lower, maintain, raise a standard; to apply a double standard for hiring men and women.* **3** an upright support, as of a street lamp.
— *adj.* uniformly accepted: *standard English, procedure; a standard (= recognized) textbook on the subject; Eastern standard time.*

stand·ard·ize (STAN·dur·dize) *v.* **-iz·es, -ized, -iz·ing** make standard or uniform in regard to size, weight, quality, etc.: *to standardize documents, equipment, language and style, products, rules, tests.*
— **stand·ard·i·za·tion** (-duh·ZAY·shun) *n.*

standard of living or **living standard** *n.* the level of use of goods and services to satisfy one's material needs and desires: *Sweden, U.S.A., and Canada have the world's highest living standards.*

stand·by *n.* -bys a person or thing held in reserve for use when needed: *A helicopter is on standby in case of an emergency.* — *adj.: standby credit arrangements with banks; standby duties, power systems.*

stand-in *n.* a substitute person, esp. one taking the place of an actor or actress in routine roles.

standing *n.* 1 an act of standing: *No stopping or standing (by cars is allowed on this portion of the street).* 2 status or rank: *a student in good standing; a woman of high standing (in her profession); His standing among or with the voters is not as good as it used to be; Not everyone is granted standing* (= right to be heard) *at a court hearing.* 3 duration: *a custom, dispute, feud of long standing.* — *adj.* 1 from an upright position: *a standing jump, ovation.* 2 continuing to exist indefinitely: *a standing army, committee, crop, invitation, order, tree; standing* (= stagnant) *water; All seats had been sold and there was **standing room only**; a **standing-room-only** audience, cafeteria, course, crowd, ticket.*

stand·off *n.* 1 a tie or draw. 2 a state of waiting: *The standoff with the terrorists ended when the swat team finally stormed the building.*

stand·off·ish (stand·AW·fish) *adj.* aloof.

stand·point *n.* point of view: *from a practical standpoint; from the standpoint of the consumer.*

stand·still *n.* a complete stop or halt: *The strike brought the city to a complete standstill; Negotiations are at a standstill.*

stand-up *adj.* having to do with standing: *a stand-up comedian, comic, lunch counter.*

stank a *pt.* of STINK.

stan·za (STAN·zuh) *n.* a group of lines of verse forming a division of a poem.

sta·ple (STAY·pul) *n.* 1 the chief marketable commodity or material produced in a place: *Coffee is the staple of their economy; Bread is a staple* (= chief item) *of low-income diets.* 2 a U-shaped piece of wire with sharp ends used to fasten things together. — *adj.* chief: *a nation's staple industries; a staple food, subject of conversation.* — *v.* **sta·ples, sta·pled, sta·pling** fasten using staples: *to staple papers together.* — **sta·pler** *n.*

star *n.* 1 any of the heavenly bodies seen at night as bright points of light, including planets: *a bright, distant, falling, north, shooting star; Stars shine, twinkle.* 2 a favourable configuration of stars; fortune: *He was born under a lucky star; Her star is rising; Our star is setting, waning.* 3 a figure with five or six points, as an asterisk; also, a star-shaped medal or military decoration. 4 a brilliant or leading performer or singer; also, one distinguished in his or her field, as an athlete. — *v.* **stars, starred, star·ring** 1 mark with an asterisk; also, adorn with stars. 2 present an actor, singer, etc. in a leading role or perform in one: *He was starred as a villain; She starred in the lead role.* — *adj.* preeminent: *our star athletes; a star performer.*

— **star·dom** (-dum) *n.*

star·board (STAR·burd, -bord) *n.* the right side of a ship or plane, as one faces forward: *to lean to starboard; the port and starboard sides.*

starch *n.* 1 a white, odourless, tasteless food substance found in potatoes, rice, etc. 2 a form of this used to stiffen cloth or to size paper. — *v.* stiffen with starch.

starch·y *adj.* **starch·i·er, -i·est** having much starch: *rice, spaghetti, and such starchy foods; a starchy* (= stiff or formal) *manner.*

star-crossed *adj.* ill-fated: *a star-crossed journey; star-crossed lovers.*

stare *v.* **stares, stared, star·ing** look long and directly with wide-open eyes, as a child out of curiosity: *She is used to being stared at by strangers; You can't ignore facts that are staring you in the face.* — *n.* an act of staring: *a haughty, icy, rude, vacant stare.* — **star·er** *n.*

stark *adj.* 1 utter; complete: *in stark contrast; stark madness, nonsense, poverty.* 2 stiff in death; also, bare: *a stark landscape.* — *adv.* utterly: *stark naked;* **stark-naked** *adj. & adv.* — **stark·ly** *adv.;* **stark·ness** *n.*

star·let (STAR·lit) *n.* a young actress being promoted as a star.

star·light *n.* the light given by the stars: *They met by starlight under the maples.*

star·lit *adj.* lighted by the stars: *a starlit sky.*

star·ry (STAR·ee) *adj.* **star·ri·er, star·ri·est** lighted by stars; bright.

starry-eyed (STAR·ee·ide) *adj.* dreamy or visionary: *starry-eyed optimism, youth.*

star-spangled (STAR·spang·guld) *adj.* dotted with stars: *a star-spangled sky; the* **Star-Spangled Banner** (= U.S. flag or national anthem).

star-studded (STAR·stud·id) *adj.* filled with stars: *a star-studded sky, uniform; a star-studded cast (of actors).*

start *v.* 1 begin moving or acting, as by taking a first step: *to start on a journey; Let's start moving; It's starting to get late; It's time to start (off) for the airport; Please start the engine; He started (his career) as a low-paid clerk; to start a fire with a match; to start a discussion with someone; to start the ball rolling; to start* (= enter) *a horse in a race; to start* (= loosen) *a bolt, seam.* 2 move suddenly as if surprised or frightened; startle: *He starts at the least sound; to start* (= flush) *game from its hiding place.* — *n.* 1 a beginning; also, a starting point or time: *No one gets a high pay at the start of a career; She would take any job for a start; She made a promising start; From the start she impressed her colleagues as a hard worker; She had a head start* (= advantage) *because of her age; She got off to an early start; to make a fresh start in life after many false starts and failures; a flying, new, running start.* 2 a sudden movement or jerk; also, a spurt of energy: *He works by fits and starts.*

start·er *n.* 1 one who starts: *a slow starter.* 2 **for starters** *Informal.* to begin with.

star·tle (STAR·tul) v. -tles, -tled, -tling surprise or frighten so as to make one move suddenly: *He slammed the door and startled the sleeping child; She's so nervous she startles easily; He was startled at the news; startled to hear that he owes her money; a **startling** discovery.*

start·up n. the beginning of an operation: *the startup of a project; the startup costs of the business.*

starve v. starves, starved, starv·ing (cause to) suffer from continued lack of food: *People are starving around us; Hundreds starved to death during the famine; They were starved by a cruel regime; were starved (= subdued by food shortages) into surrendering; Neglected children starve (= crave) for affection; I'm starving (Informal for hungry).* — star·va·tion (star·VAY·shun) n.

starve·ling n. one that is thin from being ill-fed or starved.

stash v. Informal. hide or store money, supplies, etc. secretly. — n. 1 what is hidden away. 2 a hiding place.

stat n. Informal. a statistic.

state n. 1 a government, nation, or nation's territory: *Canada is a sovereign state; Sue's from **the States** (= U.S.); Louisiana is one of the 50 U.S. states (= units forming the nation); the **city state** of Singapore; a buffer, client, member, police, puppet, secular, welfare state; to establish, found, govern, rule a state; separation of church and state in government policies; affairs of state; adj.: a state banquet, capital, corporation, police, radio, school, secret, trooper, visit; the federal, state, and municipal levels of government; The Queen is Canada's **head of state;** the U.S. **State Department** (of foreign affairs).* 2 a steady condition or mode of existence: *a sad state of affairs; a state of shock; the state of the world; Is happiness a state of mind? solid, liquid, and gaseous states of matter; a building in a good or bad state of repair; A state of emergency was declared during the flood; his poor state of health; A state of war exists between the two countries; a comatose, nervous, unconscious, vegetative, weakened state; The patient is in quite a state (= an excited condition).* 3 rank or station in life: *a humble state; in great state (= dignity); A body **lies in state** (in a public place of honour).* — v. states, stat·ed, stat·ing say formally or carefully: *State your reasons clearly; He stated his views emphatically; as the law states; The judge stated that the case was dismissed; for sale at the stated (= indicated) price, time.*

state·ly adj. -li·er, -li·est majestic; also, haughty. — state·li·ness n.

state·ment (STATE·munt) n. a stating or something stated, as a declaration, assertion, a financial summary, or invoice: *to confirm, deny, issue, make, refute, retract, withdraw a statement; a statement to the effect that he was resigning his position; a brief, short, false, financial, official, public, sweeping, sworn, written statement.*

state of the art n. the highest level of development attained in a field or industry at a given time. — state-of-the-art adj. most advanced: *a state-of-the-art computer; We use state-of-the-art technology.*

states·man (STATES·mun) n. -men a wise, experienced, or skilled leader in public, esp. international affairs: *an elder statesman; a prominent statesman.* — states·man·like adj. — states·man·ship n. — states·wom·an n. -wom·en.

stat·ic (STAT·ic) adj. 1 having to do with rest or equilibrium, not motion; not dynamic: *the static balancing of a wheel; a static existence without progress or change; the static pressure of a column of liquid; static and dynamic RAM.* 2 having to do with static: *the **static** (= present but not flowing) **electricity** on a comb run through one's hair.* — n. 1 an electrical atmospheric disturbance such as interferes with radio or TV reception: *FM radio has little static.* 2 Slang. hostile criticism: *Who needs static?*

sta·tion (STAY·shun) n. 1 an assigned place of duty: *a battle station; Return to your stations.* 2 a stopping place: *a bus station.* 3 a place for a specific use or where a service is provided: *a broadcasting, comfort, filling, fire, gas, police, polling, postal, power, TV station.* 4 social position or rank: *people of all walks and stations in life.* — v. post to a place of duty: *Guards were stationed at all entrances; Canadians stationed overseas; stationed in the Middle East.*

sta·tion·ar·y (STAY·shuh·nair·ee) adj. fixed; not moving; also, unchanging in condition: *a stationary vehicle, weather front.*

sta·tion·er·y (STAY·shuh·nair·ee) n. 1 writing paper and envelopes: *He wrote home on hotel stationery.* 2 writing materials: *a store that sells stationery.*

station wagon n. an automobile with a body extended at the back to allow additional room for passengers and goods, and having a tailgate.

sta·tis·tic (stuh·TIS·tic) n. one of many items making up a set of data: *A drunk driver may end up as a highway statistic.* — sta·tis·ti·cal adj.; sta·tis·ti·cal·ly adv. — stat·is·ti·cian (stat·is·TISH·un) n.

statistics (stuh·TIS·tics) n.pl. 1 [takes sing. v.] the science of gathering and analysing numerical facts or data. 2 such data collectively: *to collect, gather, tabulate statistics; Statistics Canada compiles statistics; Statistics showed that by 1985 each Canadian woman had only 1.7 children; as statistics indicate; the statistics of highway fatalities; vital statistics; to bandy job statistics about without doing anything about unemployment.*

stats [short form] statistical data.

stat·ue (STACH·oo) n. a three-dimensional image of a person or animal that is cast, modelled, or carved: *a statue sculpted out of marble; to unveil a statue; an equestrian statue; a statue cast in bronze.*

stat·u·esque (stach·oo·ESK) adj. like a statue in being well-proportioned or stately: *a statuesque beauty.*

stat·u·ette (stach·oo·ET) n. a small statue: *the Oscar statuettes.*

stat·ure (STACH·ur) n. height reached or eminence attained by a person: *a man short of stature (= not tall); a woman of great moral stature; of imposing stature;*

Margaret Thatcher attained the stature of a world leader.

sta·tus (STAY·tus, STAT·us) *n.* -tus·es state or condition according to some standard: *the (legal) status of a minor; your marital status; people of some status* (= high status); *She has achieved celebrity status; a most-favoured nation status given to a country in a reciprocal trade relationship; Indian women used to lose status under the Indian Act by marrying non-Indian men.* — *adj.: a status seeker; an expensive sports car as a* **status symbol.**

status quo (-KWOH) *n.* the existing state of affairs: *to accept, defend, preserve the status quo; Vested interests like to maintain the status quo.*

stat·ute (STACH·oot) *n.* a law enacted by a legislative body.

staunch (STAWNCH, STAHNCH) *adj.* 1 strong or steadfast: *a staunch defence, friendship, supporter.* 2 watertight: *a staunch ship.* — *v.* stop the flow of blood or of blood from a wound; stanch. — **staunch·ly** *adv.;* **staunch·ness** *n.*

stave *n.* 1 one of the curved strips of wood making up the walls of a barrel or cask. 2 a pole or staff. 3 a musical staff. 4 a stanza. — *v.* **staves,** *pt. & pp.* **staved** or **stove** (STOHV), **stav·ing** make a break or hole in the sides of a cask, boat, etc. — **stave off** prevent or ward off something troublesome.

staves See STAFF.

stay *v.* 1 remain: *Please stay (for) a while; Do stay for supper; Stay off the grass; It's safer to stay away from skid row; Better to stay out of trouble; Stay calm till help arrives; We'll stay home; to stay abreast of current events; to stay ahead of the competition; "Time and tide stay* (= wait) *for no man."* 2 dwell, esp. as a guest for a short while: *Where are you staying? I'm staying the night with Jim; staying at Jim's (house); She's staying at a hotel.* 3 hold back or delay: *to stay an execution; snacks to stay him* (= stay his hunger) *till dinner time; He has little* **staying power** (= endurance or stamina). 4 of a runner, horse, etc., endure or last *to* the end, *for* a period or distance, etc.: *I intend to* **stay the course** (= continue till the end of it). 5 prop or hold up. — **stay put** *Informal.* remain at one's place or where stationed. — *n.* 1 staying or dwelling: *We had a pleasant stay at the hotel.* 2 a holding back or delay: *The court granted a stay of execution pending an appeal.* 3 a prop, brace, or support. 4 a steadying rope or wire, as for a ship's mast; guy.

stead (STED) *n.* 1 **in one's stead** instead of: *He offered himself as a hostage in her stead.* 2 **stand in good stead** be of help when needed: *Your French will stand you in good stead during your trip abroad.*

stead·fast (STED·fast, -fust) *adj.* fixed or unwavering: *her steadfast loyalty; his steadfast gaze.* — **stead·fast·ly** *adv.;* **stead·fast·ness** *n.*

stead·y (STED·ee) *adj.* **stead·i·er, -i·est** stable or regular in movement or behaviour: *a steady heartbeat, job, progress, state, worker; a steady ship (that can stay upright in a rough sea); steady* (= calm) *nerves; steady* (= steadfast) *friendship; one's steady* (= regular) *date.*

— *n., pl.* **stead·ies** *Informal.* one's regular or exclusive date. — *v.* **stead·ies, stead·ied, stead·y·ing** make or become steady. — *adv.* in a steady manner: *Couples* **go steady** (*Informal* for date exclusively) *before getting married.* — **stead·i·ly** *adv.;* **stead·i·ness** *n.*

steak (STAKE) *n.* a fleshy slice of meat, esp. beef, or fish that is broiled or fried like beefsteak: *to broil, grill a steak; a juicy, minute, rump, sirloin, T-bone, tender, tough steak; How do you like your steak (done)? I like it medium, medium-rare, rare, well-done.*

steal (STEEL) *v.* **steals, stole, sto·len** (STOH·lun), **steal·ing** take or get something in a secret, sly, or unexpected manner: *Thieves steal; A starving man may steal food; to steal food from a store; to steal looks, kisses; Sam stole a glance at Paola when she wasn't looking; A baby steals your heart; A runner tries to steal* (= reach) *a base by catching the opposing team off guard; A feeling of shame stole over him; He* **stole** (= sneaked) **out** *of the house when his parents were asleep; Jan* **stole up on** *Gina from behind and said "Boo!" The children's act* **stole the show** (*Informal* for unexpectedly proved the biggest attraction). — *n. Informal.* a stealing or something stolen, esp. an unusual bargain: *At $25 it is a steal!*

stealth (STELTH) *n.* secrecy or furtiveness: *Thieves enter a house* **by stealth** (= secretly or slyly). — **stealth·y** *adj.*

steam (STEEM) *n.* 1 the vapour given off by boiling water. 2 this condensed, as the mist from evaporation inside a heated automobile. 3 (the power of) hot steam under pressure, as used to drive the piston in the cylinder of a **steam engine.** — **let off steam** *Informal.* get rid of excess energy or pent-up feelings. — *v.: a steaming cup of soup (that is so hot it gives off steam); a steamed-up car window (that is foggy because of condensed steam); He is quite* **steamed up** (*Informal* for angry) *over or about my being late; to steam* (= use steam to) *open a sealed envelope.*

steam·er *n.* one that uses steam, as a cooker, cleaning appliance, or a "steamship."

steam·roll·er (STEEM·roh·lur) *n.* a steam-driven roller for road surfaces. — *v.* 1 crush opposition or force legislation *through* a legislature. 2 force one's way *into* a place, as with a steamroller. Also **steam·roll.**

steam·y (STEE·mee) *adj.* **1** having to do with steam. **2** erotic: *a steamy novel.*

steed *n.* [literary] a riding horse.

steel *n.* **1** a hard and tough alloy of iron and carbon. **2** a steel instrument or weapon. **3** steellike hardness and strength. **4** *Cdn.* a railway track or railway line. — *adj.: a steel bar, steel blue, grey.* — *v.* make with or like steel: *He steeled himself* (= prepared himself mentally) *for the ordeal* or *to face the ordeal.* — **steel·y** *adj.*

steel band *n.* a percussion band using steel oil drums of varying pitches.

steel wool *n.* hairlike shavings of steel used in a ball or pad for scouring, smoothing, etc.

steep *v.* **1** (let) soak, as by immersion, esp. for extracting the essence of something. **2** immerse *oneself* in a subject of study. — **steeped in** filled or pervaded with something: *steeped in misery.* — *adj.* **1** sharply sloping: *a steep hill.* **2** *Informal.* excessive or exaggerated: *steep demands, prices.*

steep·en *v.* make or become steep or steeper.

stee·ple (STEE·pul) *n.* **1** a tall tower, usually topped by a spire, on a church building. **2** a spire. — **stee·pled** *adj.*

steer *n.* **1** a young ox, castrated and usually raised for beef: *to rope a steer; a Grade A steer.* **2** *Informal.* direction or tip: *He got a bum steer.* — *v.* **1** direct the course of a vehicle using a wheel, rudder, or other device: *to steer a car; cars equipped with power steering; the steering column of an automobile; the driver at the steering wheel.* **2** direct one's way or follow a course: *Let's steer for home; Don't rock the canoe as we steer the course; She knows how to steer clear of trouble; a steering committee (to prepare the agenda of a session).*

stel·lar (STEL·ur) *adj.* of a star or stars: *stellar light; a stellar distance; the stellar role (of a star player); her stellar* (= excellent) *performance.*

stem *n.* **1** the main part or trunk, as of a tree or plant, from which branches grow: *"Kind" is the stem of the word "unkindness"; wineglasses and such stem·ware (having a stem connecting bowl and base) for serving cold beverages and desserts.* **2** the prow of a ship. — **from stem to stern** from one end to the other; throughout. — *v.* **stems, stemmed, stem·ming 1** derive or develop: *problems stemming from lack of education.* **2** stop or check: *to stem the tide of controversy.*

stench *n.* an offensive odour; stink: *the stench of rotting corpses, rotten eggs, garbage; the stench of hypocrisy.*

sten·cil (STEN·sul) *n.* **1** a sheet of paper, metal, etc. on which designs, letters, etc. are cut for transferring them to a surface by laying the sheet on it and applying ink or colour: *to cut stencils.* **2** a letter or design so made. — *v.* **-cils, -cilled** or **-ciled, -cil·ling** or **-cil·ing:** *He stencilled the address on the cartons.*

step *n.* **1** a lifting of the foot and setting it down in walking, running, dancing, etc.: *Please take a step forward; He retraced his steps to see if he had dropped his key on the way.* **2** the distance, style, sound, or print of a step: *The school is only a few steps* (= short distance) *from my home; It takes years of training to execute* or *perform the difficult steps of ballet; He walks with a mincing step; She walks with a heavy step; I heard steps outside the door; Keep in step when marching together; Try not to fall out of step.* **3** a stair or rung: *Mind the step as you open the door; the steps of a ladder; A flight of steps leads to your room.* **4** a stage or degree in a movement forward or upward: *What's the next step? We're a step closer to a settlement; A major is a step above a captain; The moon-landing was "a giant step for mankind"; a bold, careful, false, historic, positive, risky step.* — **in** or **out of step** in or out of rhythm with someone: *She seemed to be out of step with the feminist movement.* — **step by step** slowly. — **take steps** take the necessary measures. — *v.* **steps, stepped, step·ping 1** put a foot down on something: *He stepped on a nail.* **2** walk: *to step across a street; He stepped aside for his boss to enter first; Please step in (the house) for a minute; She just stepped out for some fresh air; The principal had to step in* (= intervene) *to restore order in the classroom; to step* (= get) *off a train; to step off* (= pace off) *a distance.* — **step down 1** leave one's position in favour of another: *The mayor will be stepping down at the end of her term in January.* **2** reduce: *to step down voltage using a transformer.* — **step on it** *Informal.* go faster, as by pressing the accelerator. — **step up 1** *Informal.* come forward. **2** increase an activity or its pace, intensity, etc.

step- *prefix.* related by remarriage: *stepbrother, stepfather, stepmother, stepparent.*

step·child *n.* child of one's spouse by a former marriage, i.e. a **step·daugh·ter** or **step·son.**

step·lad·der (STEP·lad·ur) *n.* a short ladder with flat steps instead of rungs and hinged to a supporting frame.

step·ping·stone (STEP·ing·stone) *n.* **1** a stone to step on when crossing a stream or when mounting, ascending, etc. **2** a means of advancement: *He used the job as a steppingstone to a better career.*

step-up *n.* a stepping up or increase in amount, intensity, etc.

-ster *n. suffix.* one who does or is associated with something specified: *mobster, punster, trickster.*

ster·e·o (STER·ee·oh, STEER-) *n.* **-os 1** a record player or sound system that uses two or more channels of sound recording and reproduction. **2** a picture or system that gives a three-dimensional view of an object.

ster·e·o·type (STER·ee·uh·type, STEER-) *n.* a fixed or rigid mental impression: *To consider nursing as a woman's job is to perpetuate a stereotype; the "Ugly American" stereotype.* — *v.* **-types, -typed, -typ·ing** make a stereotype of something: *Characters, expressions, etc. that are stereotyped lack originality and objectivity.*

ster·ile (STER·ul) *adj.* **1** unable to bear offspring or fruit, produce crops, seed, results, etc.: *a sterile man, woman; sterile animals, efforts, land, plants.*

2 sterilized: *sterile surgical instruments.*
— **ste·ril·i·ty** (stuh·RIL·uh·tee) *n.*

ster·i·lize (STER·uh·lize) *v.* **-liz·es, -lized, -liz·ing** 1 to make free from living microorganisms: *to sterilize surgical instruments before an operation.* 2 make incapable of reproduction.
— **ster·i·li·za·tion** (-luh·ZAY·shun) *n.*

ster·ling (STUR·ling) *n.* 1 silver that is at least 92.5% pure. 2 British money with the pound as the basic unit.
— *adj.* genuinely excellent: *a woman of sterling character; her sterling qualities; sterling silver.*

stern *adj.* severe or strict in manner or looks: *a stern disciplinarian, face; stern measures; He is stern toward* or *with habitual latecomers.*
— *n.* the rear end of a ship, aircraft, etc.; opposed to BOW. — **stern·ly** *adv.*; **stern·ness** *n.*

ste·ve·dore (STEE·vuh·dor) *n.* a dock worker who loads and unloads ships.

stew *n.* a dish of meat and vegetables made by slow boiling.
— *v.* 1 cook by slow boiling. 2 worry or fret: *He's still stewing over the insult.*

stew·ard (STEW·urd) *n.* 1 one who manages another's estate or finances: *As good stewards of the earth's resources, we should avoid wastage.* 2 a labour union representative: *a shop steward; union steward.* 3 a racetrack official. 4 a man in charge of food service on a ship or airplane or in a club: *a cabin steward.* 5 a male flight attendant. — **stew·ard·ship** *n.*

stew·ard·ess (STEW·ur·dis) *n.* a female flight attendant.

stick *n.* 1 a long and slender twig broken off from a tree. 2 any long, thin piece: *a stick of candy, celery, dynamite, gum.* 3 a specially shaped piece or an implement: *a hockey, swagger, walking stick; They took every **stick** (= piece) of furniture with them when they moved; the carrot and the stick* (= threat of punishment); *a boss who carries a big stick* (= uses coercive tactics). 4 *Informal.* an awkward or boring person.
— **the sticks** *pl. Informal.* the backwoods, far from a city or town: *in the sticks of northern Alberta.*
— *v.* **sticks, stuck, stick·ing** 1 pierce or thrust something into, out, etc.: *ice cream with a spoon stuck in it; Do not stick your head out of* or *through the window; He has a kerchief sticking out* (= protruding) *from his pocket.* 2 be or make something fixed or immovable: *Please stick this stamp on the envelope; Make sure the stamp sticks to it; We were out of gas and got stuck on the road; There is enough evidence to make a charge stick* (= be valid); *People stick* (= cling) *together when in trouble; She was told to **stick around** (Informal for wait) while her car was being serviced; He's known to **stick by** (= remain loyal to) his friends; If you're loyal, the boss will **stick up for** (Informal for defend) you.* 3 *Slang.* cheat or defraud: *He was stuck by phony salesmen; We seem to be stuck* (= saddled) *with this lemon.* 4 hesitate: *a swindler who sticks at nothing.*
— **stick to**: *Please stick to your seats* (= stay seated) *if you don't want to lose them; Let's stick* (= adhere) *to our plans; It's a matter of principle to **stick to our guns** (= be faithful to what we believe in) without giving way.*

stick·er *n.* a gummed label, bur, etc. that sticks: *an air mail sticker; a bumper sticker; the **sticker price** of a new automobile from which discounts are calculated.*

stick·ler (STICK·lur) *n.* one who is strict in the observance of something: *a stickler for correctness, discipline, neatness, precision, protocol, punctuality.*

stick shift *n.* a lever for changing gears, as in an automobile with standard transmission.

stick·up *n. Slang.* an armed robbery; holdup.

stick·y *adj.* **stick·i·er, -i·est** 1 that sticks; adhesive; also, thick or viscous. 2 *Informal.* disagreeable or troublesome: *a sticky problem, valve; sticky* (= hot and humid) *weather.*

stiff *adj.* 1 that resists bending or moving: *stiff joints; a stiff back, leg; a stiff bow (of the back); a stiff* (= hard to stir) *paste; stiff* (= hard to work) *soil.* 2 hard or strong: *a stiff breeze, fine, wind; a stiff drink (that is strong in alcohol); stiff* (= formal) *manners; stiff opposition, penalties, resistance.*
— *adv.*: *He was scared stiff; It is frozen stiff.*
— *n. Slang.* [derogatory use] fellow; bum; drunk: *a working stiff* (= fellow).
— *v. Slang.* cheat someone out of a payment due: *to get stiffed.* — **stiff·ly** *adv.*; **stiff·ness** *n.*

stiff-necked *adj.* stubborn.

sti·fle (STY·ful) *v.* **-fles, -fled, -fling** 1 stop the breath of someone; hence, kill by suffocation. 2 make or become unable to breathe; also, become unconscious: *The firefighters felt stifled by the smoke; the stifling heat of the Sahara.* 3 suppress: *to stifle a cry, yawn; Freedom of speech sometimes gets stifled by restrictions.*

stig·ma (STIG·muh) *n.* **-mas** 1 *pl.* **-ma·ta** (-muh·tuh, stig·MAH·tuh) marks resembling the five wounds of the crucified Christ. 2 a mark of disgrace, as once branded on evil-doers, slaves, etc.: *the stigma once attached to being born illegitimate.*

still *adj.* 1 at rest; motionless: *Stand perfectly still while I sketch you; a **still life** (picture of inanimate objects such as flowers, fruits, pottery, etc.); "Still waters run deep"; a still* (= not bubbling) *wine.* 2 quiet; silent: *Be still; a still night; the still small voice (of conscience).*
— *v.* make quiet or motionless.
— *adv.* 1 without moving: *to sit still (for a portrait).* 2 even to the specified or implied time: *He's still sick; They were still undecided yesterday; He'll still be here tomorrow.* 3 even: *She's tall; her brother is still taller.*
— *n.* 1 a photograph, esp. a frame from a motion picture. 2 stillness: *strange sounds heard in the still of the night.* 3 an apparatus for making alcoholic liquor. 4 a distillery. — **still·ness** *n.*

still·birth *n.* (birth of) a child born dead.

still·born *adj.* born dead.

stilt *n.* 1 one of a pair of poles with supports for the feet at a height, used for walking across water or for amusement. 2 one of a set of piles or posts supporting a building raised above water or swampland.

stilt·ed *adj.* stiffly formal: *a stilted expression (phrase); a* *stilted style.*

stim·u·lant (STIM·yuh·lunt) *n. & adj.* (anything) that stimulates, as caffeine.

stim·u·late (STIM·yuh·late) *v.* -lates, -lat·ed, -lat·ing increase the activity of a person or thing; excite: *to stimulate public interest in the arts; tax refunds to stimulate the economy; Encouraging words stimulate everyone to try harder; a **stimulating** drink, effect, discussion.* — **stim·u·la·tion** (stim·yuh·LAY·shun) *n.*

stim·u·lus (STIM·yuh·lus) *n., pl.* -li (-lye) something that excites one to increased activity: *We respond to stimuli; Lower interest rates are a powerful stimulus to industry.*

sting *v.* stings, stung, sting·ing cause sharp pain, as with the pricking organ of a bee, mosquito, or wasp: *Nettles sting; the stinging taste of ginger; Sam felt stung by the insults; was stung into action by their taunts.* — *n.* a stinging, the wound or pain caused by it, or the stinging organ of an insect or plant. — **sting·er** *n.*

stin·gy (STIN·jee) *adj.* -gi·er, -gi·est miserly; not generous: *too stingy to give to charity; a stingy allowance; Scrooge is stingy with his money.* — **stin·gi·ly** *adv.;* **stin·gi·ness** *n.*

stink (STINK) *v.* stinks, *pt.* stank or stunk, *pp.* stunk, stink·ing give off a bad smell: *A scandal stinks; It stinks of corruption.* — *n.: the stink of rotten fish.*

stink·er *n.* 1 one that stinks. 2 *Informal.* someone or something difficult or disagreeable.

stint *v.* restrict oneself or one's consumption of or expenditure on something: *She never stints on charity.* — *n.* 1 limitation or restraint. 2 a share of work or a brief assignment: *He did or served several stints as a CUSO volunteer.*

sti·pend (STY·pend) *n.* a fixed payment made regularly for services: *She lived on a modest stipend as a chaplain.*

stip·ple *v.* stip·ples, stip·pled, stip·pling paint, engrave, or apply paint, etc. in dots instead of lines: *a stippled ceiling design.*

stip·u·late (STIP·yuh·late) *v.* -lates, -lat·ed, -lat·ing specify as a necessary condition: *The terms stipulated that delivery be made in two years; They stipulated delivery in two years; The contract stipulated for* (= required) *it.* — **stip·u·la·tor** (-lay·tur) *n.* — **stip·u·la·tion** (-LAY·shun) *n.*

stir (STUR) *v.* stirs, stirred, stir·ring move so as to disturb or activate: *A wind stirs the leaves; I noticed someone stirring in the shadows; He stirred the fire into a blaze; to stir* (= mix) *sugar into coffee; The picture stirred memories; a story likely to stir up trouble; His speech stirred them up to mutiny; They stirred themselves to action.* — *n.* a stirring or a state of increased activity, excitement, etc.: *The announcement caused, created a stir in the audience; a big stir over or about who would pay.* — **stir·rer** *n.* — **stirring** *adj.* moving or exciting: *a stirring speech; stirring times.*

stir·rup (STEER·up) *n.* a rider's footrest hanging from the saddle as a loop or ring.

stitch (STICH) *n.* 1 one complete movement of a threaded needle, as in sewing or embroidering: *to make a stitch; to drop* (= lose) *a stitch as in knitting; Basting, running, and hemming stitches are methods of stitching; It took 10 stitches (with a surgical needle) to close the wound; The kids played in the hot African sun with not a stitch* (= least bit of clothing) *on them.* 2 a sharp pain, esp. in the side.
— **in stitches** *Informal.* laughing uncontrollably.
— *v.* make a stitch or series of stitches (in) something.

stock *n.* 1 a collection or supply, as of goods for sale, livestock, or the repertoire of plays with a "stock company": *Ice is not **in stock** at this time; Sorry we are **out of stock** (of ice); We take stock (of our inventory) at the end of each month; to **take stock of** (= evaluate or assess) a situation; rolling stock (= railway vehicles); Puns are the **stock in trade** (= standard equipment) of his humour.* 2 a supporting base: *The barrel of a firearm is fitted into a wooden stock; meat and vegetable juices as stocks for soups and gravies; Rags and wood pulps are stock* (= raw material) *for paper; a book printed on heavy stock* (= paper); *A scion grows best when grafted to a rooted stock* (= stem); *She comes of noble stock* (= family line). 3 invested capital, as of a company, or a part of it owned by a shareholder: *to issue, buy, sell stocks; blue-chip, common, over-the-counter, preferred stocks; She's too level-headed to **take** or **put stock in** (Informal for trust) the rumours going around.* 4 a race or group with a common descent: *They are of Loyalist stock; English is of Indo-European stock.*
— *adj.* 1 available; in common use: *a stock item, size.* 2 commonplace: *a stock answer, joke.* 3 having to do with livestock: *a stock breeder, farm, train.* 4 having to do with stocks: *A stock clerk works in a stock room; a stock* (= shares) *certificate.*
— *v.* 1 keep a supply of something or provide with stock: *We need to stock up on spring goods.* 2 lay in a supply: *We're stocking up for the winter.*

stock car *n.* a standard passenger car modified or rebuilt for racing.

stock exchange *n.* an organized marketplace for the buying and selling of securities.

stock·hold·er *n.* an owner of stock in a company; shareholder.

stocking *n.* a close-fitting knitted covering for the foot and leg.

stock market *n.* 1 a stock exchange: *to gamble, speculate on the stock market.* 2 market activity in securities: *The stock market opened weak on Monday, closed strong on Friday.*

stock·pile *n.* a reserve supply, as of commodities, raw materials, nuclear weapons, etc.
— *v.* -piles, -piled, -pil·ing accumulate a stockpile.

stock·still *adj.* motionless.

stock·y *adj.* stock·i·er, -i·est short but sturdy in build.

stock·yard *n.* a yard for livestock, esp. one connected with a meat-packing operation: *He works at the stockyards.*

stodg·y (STOJ·ee) *adj.* **stodg·i·er, -i·est** dull or heavy: *stodgy food, reading; a stodgy book, newspaper.*

sto·ic (STOH·ic) *n.* one who is stoical.

sto·i·cal (STOH·uh·cul) *adj.* able to endure suffering with calm, being indifferent to pleasure and pain, like the **Stoics** of ancient Greece.
— **sto·i·cal·ly** *adv.* — **sto·i·cism** *n.*

stoke *v.* **stokes, stoked, stok·ing 1** tend and feed something burning: *to stoke a fire, furnace.* **2** work as a stoker.

stok·er (STOH·kur) *n.* **1** one who tends a furnace or boiler. **2** a machine for feeding solid fuel into a furnace.

STOL (STOLE) *n.* an aircraft that requires only a short distance for takeoff and landing: *a STOL aircraft, airport; STOL operations, service.*
— **combining form:** *STOLmobile* (= STOL minibus); *STOLport* (= STOL airport).

stole *pt.* of STEAL.
— *n.* a long scarf worn by women across the shoulders: *a fur stole.*

stolen *pp.* of STEAL.

stom·ach (STUM·uk) *n.* **1** the saclike digestive organ into which food is received from the mouth: *a gruesome sight that could turn your stomach* (= make you feel nauseated); *foods that upset your stomach; It's better to swim on an empty stomach* (= while hungry) *than on a full one; He has no stomach* (= inclination) *for a walk after dinner.* **2** abdomen or belly.
— *v.* **1** relish or swallow. **2** put up with or endure: *He couldn't stomach the insult.*

stomp *v.* stamp heavily with the feet; *n.* a stomping.

stone *n.* **1** (a piece of) hard, solid mineral such as granite or marble: *to throw stones at someone or something; to cast the first stone* (= be the first to accuse someone). **2** something resembling a stone, as a gem, a kidney stone, or the hard seed, or pit, of a fruit such as the cherry or peach. **3** *sing. & pl.* a British unit of weight equal to 14 pounds.
— *v.* **stones, stoned, ston·ing 1** throw stones at a person or thing: *People used to be stoned to death for certain crimes.* **2** remove the stone from a fruit: *stoned prunes.* **3** *Slang.* stop stone-cold; beat: *The Canadiens stoned the Bruins in seven games.*

stone- *combining form.* absolutely or completely: *stone-blind, stone-broke, stone-cold, stone-deaf.*

stoned *adj. Slang.* extremely intoxicated, esp. by a mind-changing drug: *He seemed more stoned than drunk; was stoned on speed.*

stone's throw *n.* a short distance: *He lives only a stone's throw from the school.*

stone·wall *v. Informal.* refuse to answer; refuse to cooperate with someone; obstruct an investigation: *They tried to stonewall the media; But they couldn't stonewall it any longer.*

stone-washed *adj.* of fabrics, faded by removing part of the dye: *the young lady in stone-washed blue jeans.*

ston·y *adj.* **ston·i·er, -i·est 1** full of stones: *a stony field, ground, soil.* **2** like stone; hard or cold: *a stony critic,*

face, heart, silence, stare.
— **ston·i·ly** *adv.;* **ston·i·ness** *n.*

stood *pt.* of STAND.

stooge (STOOJ, long "OO") *n. Informal.* one who serves another's purpose, as an underling: *a stooge of the military regime.*

stook (long "oo") *n.* a stack of sheaves of grain.

stool *n.* **1** a seat without back or arms; also, a footstool. **2** feces.

stool pigeon *n. Slang.* an informer or decoy; also **stool·ie** (-lee), **-ies.**

stoop *v.* **1** bend forward and downward, as the head and shoulders of an aged person. **2** lower or degrade oneself: *Some politicians stoop to dirty tricks.*
— *n.* **1** a stooping carriage or posture. **2** a bending forward. **3** a flight of steps at the entrance to a house.

stoop labour *n.* work involving stooping, as picking strawberries.

stop *v.* **stops, stopped, stop·ping 1** keep from moving or acting: *to stop (the car) at a traffic signal; Stop the thief! Stop him (from) fleeing; He will stop at nothing short of a total victory; He will only stop short of* (= hesitate to commit) *murder; When he saw the police, he stopped dead in his tracks; She stopped to catch her breath; The boxer was stopped* (= knocked out) *in the second round.* **2** bring a movement or action to an end: *Please stop shouting; to stop a leak; Strikes stop work; a cork to stop up* (= close) *a bottle.* **3** press down on a violin string, finger hole of a wind instrument, etc. to produce a desired tone or pitch. **4** stay: *We stopped with friends in London during our tour; They had to stop over in Bombay before flying to Manila.*
— **stop by** or **in** drop in for a visit.
— *n.* **1** a stopping or ending: *They could not bring the train to a stop; The car came to a stop after crashing into the house; came to a dead stop; Drivers have to make a full stop at a stop sign; Learn to make a smooth stop, not a sudden stop; We made a brief stop in London.* **2** a stopping place: *a bus stop; pit stop; truck stop.* **3** a stopping device such as a camera's shutter or a lever or key for changing the pitch or tone of a musical instrument, esp. an organ.
— **pull out all the stops** make a great effort.
— **put a stop to** put an end to something.

stop·gap *n.* a temporary expedient; makeshift.
— *adj.* temporary: *a stopgap arrangement, leader, measure, solution.*

stop·light *n.* **1** a traffic light, esp. when red. **2** a rear light of a vehicle that comes on when the brakes are applied.

stop·o·ver (stop·OH·vur) *n.* a brief stay in the course of a journey: *We made a stopover in Hawaii en route to Tokyo.*

stop·page (STOP·ij) *n.* **1** an act of stopping or the condition of being stopped: *a work stoppage.* **2** a block or obstruction.

stop·per (STOP·ur) *n.* **1** a plug or similar device to close an opening. **2** one that causes a stoppage: *Their act was a show stopper* (= something arresting or rivetting).

stop·watch n. a watch that can be stopped and started as desired for timing races, etc.

stor·age (STOR·ij) n. the storing of goods, as in a warehouse: *We'll put it into storage for the time being; cold storage of perishables; time to take it out of storage; external storage* (= computer memory) *of data.*

store v. stores, stored, stor·ing 1 put aside in a safe place for future use. 2 stock a place *with* something.
— n. 1 a stock or supply of something useful: *a good store of food; Databases are stores of information; It's hard to tell what lies in store* (= in the future) *for us; what the future may have in store* (= have ready) *for us; Children set* or *lay* or *put great store by* (= Children value greatly) *what teachers tell them.* 2 a place where goods are sold: *My dad manages, operates, runs a chain, convenience, department, discount, food, furniture, grocery, hardware, jewellery, liquor, retail, shoe, toy, variety store; Mom minds the store with Dad.* 3 a storehouse. 4 **stores** pl. supplies for the regular needs of an establishment or operation: *military stores; a cache of stores.*

store·front (STOR·frunt) n. 1 the front of a store. 2 a place of business that is easily accessible to the public; **adj.**: *a storefront business, clinic, library, office, operation, service.*

store·house n. 1 a building in which goods are stored. 2 a person or place having a large supply: *a storehouse of information, knowledge.*

sto·rey (STOR·ee) n. **-reys** one of the horizontal divisions of a building; floor level: *on a lower storey; the top storey; an upper storey.* Also **sto·ry, -ries.**

sto·ried (STOR·eed) adj. 1 celebrated in stories or history: *We stayed at the storied Banff Springs Hotel.* 2 ornamented with designs based on history or legend: *a storied urn.* 3 having storeys or floors: *a storied house; a three-storied building.*

stork n. a large wading bird with long legs, neck, and bill, esp. a white one that builds its nest on rooftops and chimneys: *In children's lore, new babies are brought home by the stork.*

storm n. 1 a disturbance of the atmosphere marked by strong winds, rain, snow, or hail: *to ride out, weather a storm; a blinding, dust, severe, violent storm; A storm blows over, brews, gathers, hits, rages, strikes, subsides.* 2 any strong disturbance, or a violent outburst or attack: *The free-trade issue created a storm in Canada; The ad campaign took consumers by storm.*
— v. 1 blow hard. 2 rage or rush violently: *He stormed out of the room in a rage; The demonstrators stormed (their way) into the president's office; They stormed* (= attacked) *the fortress.*

storm door or **storm window** n. an outer door or window as added protection against the weather.

storm·y adj. storm·i·er, -i·est characterized by a storm or similar disturbance: *a stormy meeting, night, scene.*

sto·ry (STOR·ee) n. **-ries** 1 an account or narrative: *to narrate, tell a story; a bedtime, children's, coherent, detective, funny, juicy, love, sob, success story; conflicting stories.* 2 a newspaper report: *a breaking, cover, exclusive, feature, front-page, human-interest story; to carry, edit, kill, rewrite, run a story.* 3 a made-up account: *to concoct, fabricate, invent, make up a story; a cock-and-bull, farfetched, shaggy dog story.* 4 a written story, esp. one with literary qualities: *a short story; a story about love; the story of his adventures.* 5 a story as reflecting truth or falsehood: *to cover up, embellish, embroider, hush up, suppress a story; the inside story; a likely, plausible, true story; the whole story.* 6 the plot of a novel or play. 7 same as STOREY.

sto·ry·book (STOR·ee·book) n. a book of stories, esp. for children.
— adj. fairy-tale or romantic: *a storybook ending, romance, wedding.*

stout (STOWT) adj. 1 strong in resisting strain; having endurance: *a stout rope; a woman of stout heart; They offered stout resistance.* 2 thickset or bulky: *a stout figure, man, woman.*
— n. a dark beer with the flavour of malt and hops.

stove a pt. & pp. of STAVE.
— n. a closed heating or cooking apparatus: *to light, turn on a stove; an electric stove; gas stove, wood stove.*

stove·pipe n. a pipe connecting a stove to a chimney.

stow (STOH) v. pack things closely in a place.
— **stow away** hide on board a ship or aircraft so as to get transport.

stow·a·way (STOH·uh·way) n. one who stows away.

strad·dle (STRAD·ul) v. **strad·dles, strad·dled, strad·dling** 1 stand across a ditch, sit on a fence, animal's back, etc.; also, stand with the legs wide apart. 2 appear to favour both sides of an issue.
— **strad.dler** n.

strafe v. strafes, strafed, straf·ing of aircraft, to attack troops, buildings, etc. on the ground with machine-gun fire while flying low.

strag·gle (STRAG·ul) v. **strag·gles, strag·gled, strag·gling** 1 spread in an irregular manner, as vines. 2 stray from the main group. — **strag.gler** n.
— **strag·gly** (STRAG·lee) adj.: *straggly hair; a straggly beard, plant, vine.*

straight (STRAIT) adj. 1 without curves, bends, angles, etc.: *Draw a straight line; to set the record straight* (= correct); *She set him straight* (= corrected his wrong impressions) *about her past; a straight* (= honest or upright) *citizen; a straight* (= reliable) *tip; straight* (= undiluted) *liquor; a straight A student (who gets all A grades); I like her straight-from-the-shoulder* (= direct)

approach; He votes the straight Democratic ticket (= for candidates of only that party). **2** *Slang.* of people, conservative or conventional; not a drug addict, homosexual, etc.
— *adv.* in a straight manner: *Try to shoot straight* (= accurately); *Go straight* (= directly) *home; a straight* (= upright) *young man; He lives straight* (= directly) *down the road; It went on for ten days straight* (= continuously); *I'll be straight back* (= without delay).
— **straight away** or **off** at once.
— *n.* **1** *Slang.* a square person. **2** something straight, as a straight part of a course.

straight·a·way (STRAIT·uh·way) *n.* a straight or direct course. — *adv.* at once.

straight·en (STRAY·tun) *v.* make or become straight.
— **straighten out** make or become straight in thinking, organization, behaviour, etc.: *A consultant was hired to straighten out the mess.*

straight face *n.* a face showing no sign of emotion, esp. merriment. — **straight-faced** *adj.*

straight·for·ward (strait·FOR·wurd) *adj.* direct; also, candid or frank; also *adv.*

straightjacket, straightlaced same as STRAITJACKET, STRAITLACED.

straight man *n.* one who takes part in a skit by helping the comic with appropriate responses.

straight time *n.* rate of pay for regular working hours, not overtime.

straight·way *adv.* [old use] at once; straightaway.

strain *v.* **1** to stretch or exert to the utmost: *a dog straining at the leash to get away; In poor light you have to strain your eyes to read; Their **strained** relations led to separation; He strained every nerve* (= tried very hard) *to get the best grades.* **2** filter a liquid through a strainer; also, filter out solids.
— *n.* **1** a stretching force or its effect: *Poor posture causes back strain; muscle strain; Stress causes strain* (= deformation) *in materials.* **2** tension: *He quit the job because he couldn't stand the strain; It was a strain on his family life; an emotional, mental, physical strain; Some jobs impose, place, put undue strains on you; Holidays help to ease, relieve the strains of daily life; Some people carry on till they break under the strain.* **3** manner or style: *to speak in a mournful strain.* **4 strains** *pl.* snatches of music or singing. **5** an inherited quality or tendency: *the strain of weakness in his character.* **6** breed or variety: *a good strain of wheat; a virulent strain of bacteria.* — **strain·er** *n.*

strait *n.* **1** a narrow channel connecting two large bodies of water: *Georgia Strait; Strait of Belle Isle.* **2 straits** *pl.* difficulty or need: *financial straits; in desperate, dire straits.* — *adj.* [old use] narrow; hence, strict.

strait·en *v.* make narrow; also, restrict: *He lived in **straitened circumstances** (= in poverty or need) while growing up.*

strait·jack·et (STRAIT·jack·ut) *n.* a jacketlike garment designed to restrain a person physically.
— *v.*: *He was straitjacketed and locked away.*

strait·laced *adj.* severely strict in regard to religion or morals.

strand *n.* **1** one of the threads or wires that are twisted together to make a rope, cable, etc.: *a strand* (= string) *of pearls; the strands of melody in a composition.* **2** the shore or beach of a sea, lake, or river.
— *v.* be or put in a helpless position, as a ship run aground: *The last flight had left and he was stranded in Toronto for the night.*

strange (STRAINJ) *adj.* **strang·er, strang·est** not familiar or accustomed: *The voice sounded strange; strange visitors from space; He felt strange like a fish out of water; a northerner strange to southern ways; Isn't it strange we never heard from him again?*

stran·ger (STRAIN·jur) *n.* a person who is new in a place or unaccustomed to a group or situation: *Children are warned not to talk to strangers; Dogs bark at strangers; a complete, perfect, total stranger; He's no stranger to our culture.*

stran·gle (STRANG·gul) *v.* **-gles, -gled, -gling 1** kill by squeezing the throat: *He was strangled (to death).* **2** choke; also, stifle or suppress.
— **stran·gler** (STRANG·glur) *n.*

stran·gle·hold (STRANG·gul·hold) *n.* a wrestling hold that would choke one's opponent; hence, a deadly grip: *Sam got a stranglehold on the attacker during the struggle; The stranglehold* (= absolute control) *one company had on the market was finally broken.*

strap *n.* a narrow strip of flexible material, as of a belt or wristwatch: *the shoulder strap of a camera, purse, uniform (showing rank); The strap* (= beating with a strap as punishment) *has been abolished in our schools.*
— *v.* **straps, strapped, strap·ping 1** bind with a strap: *The kidnap victim was found strapped to a chair.* **2** punish by beating with a strap: *Pupils used to be strapped for misbehaviour.*

strapped *adj.* **1** having straps. **2** *Informal.* short of something: *strapped for cash, funds.*

strapping *adj.* *Informal.* robust or sturdy: *a strapping young boy, girl; a strapping youth.*

strata a *pl.* of STRATUM.

strat·a·gem (STRAT·uh·jum) *n.* a carefully laid plan or scheme to entrap or outwit an opponent: *a military or political stratagem; He resorted to* or *used a clever, subtle stratagem to get an interview.*

strat·e·gy (STRAT·uh·jee) *n.* **-gies 1** the science or art of planning and directing military operations: *to adopt, apply, plan, pursue, work out a strategy; a global, grand, long-range strategy; It's a matter* or *question of strategy.* **2** the resourceful management of any affair or operation: *the strategy of the game; the strategies* (= methods) *of searching a database.* — **strat·e·gist** *n.*
— **stra·te·gic** (struh·TEE·jic) *adj.*; **stra·te·gi·cal·ly** *adv.*

strat·i·fy (STRAT·uh·fye) *v.* **-fies, -fied, -fy·ing** form into strata or layers: *Coal, flint, and limestone are stratified rocks; the social classes of a stratified, not homogeneous society.*

strat·um (STRAY·tum, STRAT·um) *n.,* *pl.* **-ta** or **-tums** a horizontal or parallel layer, as of stratified rocks: *the* *strata of the atmosphere; cultural and social strata.*

straw *n.* **1** the dried hollow stalks or stems of grains after threshing, used as bedding for animals and to make hats, baskets, etc. **2** one such stem or a similar tube used for sucking up beverages: *to drink through a straw.* **3** something trifling or worthless: *I don't care a straw; "A drowning man will clutch at a straw"; It is only a* **straw in the wind** (= hint of something to come); *The straw that broke the camel's back, as in the fable, was the last straw* (= a final aggravation or burden).
— *adj.: a straw hat; straw* (= yellowish) *colour.*

straw·ber·ry (STRAW·ber·ee) *n.* **-ber·ries** a low-growing vinelike plant with red, pulpy fuit; *adj.: a strawberry farm; strawberry blond* (= reddish blond).

straw boss *n. Informal.* an occasional supervisor with little authority.

straw man *n.* an imaginary opponent.

straw poll or **straw vote** *n.* an unofficial vote to find out a general trend.

stray *v.* wander from the usual or regular path: *The plane strayed into enemy territory; Sheep stray from the fold; The TV evangelist strayed from the path of virtue* (= sinned).
— *adj.: a stray animal, bullet, dog; a stray* (= isolated) *case of smallpox.*
— *n.* a strayed child or domestic animal: *waifs and strays* (= homeless children or animals); *a shelter for strays* (= stray animals).

streak (STREEK) *n.* **1** a long, thin mark such as is made in the sky by a shooting star: *the streak of dawn in the eastern sky; There's a cruel, jealous, mean streak* (= trait) *in his behaviour; a yellow* (= cowardly) *streak; fat and lean streaks* (= layers) *in bacon.* **2** a brief period: *a streak of bad luck; a losing, winning streak; The child was talking a* **blue streak** (= rapid stream of words).
— *v.* **1** have or put streaks in something: *a sky streaked with clouds; She streaks her black hair with orange or purple.* **2** make a streak; move swiftly: *A meteor streaks across the sky; The runners streaked to the finish line.*
— **streak·y** *adj.*

stream (STREEM) *n.* **1** a small river or brook: *a mountain, running, swollen stream.* **2** a flow or unbroken series: *a steady stream of abuse, letters, refugees, tears, visitors; a* **stream-of-consciousness** *narrative that flows continuously and haphazardly; the jet stream (of winds); The assembly plant comes* **on stream** (= into production) *tomorrow.*

— *v.* flow as or like a stream: *eyes streaming with tears; Blood streamed from the wound; People streamed toward the fair; Flags streamed* (= waved) *in the wind.*

stream·er (STREE·mur) *n.* a long, narrow, flowing strip, esp. a pennant or banner.

stream·line *v.* **-lines, -lined, -lin·ing 1** organize an operation for greater speed and efficiency. **2** make streamlined: *Hydroplanes have to be streamlined.*

streamlined *adj.* **1** having a smoothly flowing shape for swift movement through air or water: *a well streamlined vehicle with little drag; the streamlined styling of sports cars.* **2** efficiently organized: *a streamlined office.*

street *n.* **1** a usually paved public road lined with buildings, as in a town or city: *to cross a street; a busy, crowded, quiet street; a cross, dead-end, main, narrow, one-way, through, winding street; They play on* or *in the street; adj.: street clothes, lighting; a street entrance, kid.* **2** the people living or working there.

street·car *n.* a public passenger vehicle moving on rails laid on the streets: *to go by, ride (in), take a streetcar.*

street·wise *adj.* aware of the dangers of the street, esp. in regard to vice and crime.

strength *n.* inherent capacity for action; quality of being strong; power: *The champion weightlifter was a man of great (physical) strength; mere brute strength; He makes a show of strength when he is displeased; She has the strength to lift his weight; great inner strength; strength of character; to build up, develop one's strength; to gain, recoup, save strength; This beer has 5% alcoholic strength; 2% is below strength; We have to bring it up to strength; A movement gathers strength; There's strength in (large) numbers; Our class is at its full, maximum strength of 30 pupils; I would hire him* **on the strength of** *your reference.*

strength·en *v.* make or become strong or stronger.
— **strength·en·er** *n.*

stren·u·ous (STREN·yoo·us) *adj.* demanding much strength or energy: *a strenuous day; strenuous efforts; the strenuous life of an athlete.*

stress *n.* **1** pressure or force that tends to strain or deform the body subjected to it; tension: *mental, physical stress; Most people learn to control stress; He broke under the combined stress of loss of job and family problems; Stomach ulcers, heart attacks, migraine headaches, etc. are stress-related diseases; to undergo a* **stress test** (of the heart and blood vessels) *on a treadmill.* **2** emphasis: *She lays* or *places* or *puts great stress on punctuality; The stress* (= accent) *in "indecision" is on the third syllable.*
— *v.* emphasize: *He stressed each point by thumping the table; stressed that punctuality is important; To an English speaker, the French seem to stress words on the last syllable.*
— **stress·ful** *adj.: a stressful environment, job.*

stretch *v.* draw out or extend: *He stretched a clothesline across the yard; It's not stretched straight; She stretched out a helping hand; He walks around his desk to stretch his limbs; I reached too high and stretched* (= strained) *a muscle; socks that stretch to fit several sizes; a desert stretching to the horizon; to stretch a point, one's*

patience, the truth.
— *n.* **1** a stretching or being stretched. **2** an extent of space or time: *an endless stretch of ocean; the two stretches (backstretch and homestretch) of a racecourse; She can work for hours* **at a stretch** (= without stopping); *That is something unthinkable by any* **stretch of the imagination.**
— *adj.* that stretches easily: *stretch pants, socks; a* **stretch** (= long) *limousine.*
— **stretch·a·ble** (STRETCH·uh·bul) *adj.;* **stretch·y** *adj.*

stretch·er *n.* a device for carrying a sick or dead person flat, usually a light frame with canvas stretched across it. — **stretcher-bearer** *n.*

strew (STROO) *v.* **strewed,** *pt. & pp.* **strewed** or **strewn, strew·ing** scatter or cover by scattering: *a park strewed with litter; a battlefield strewn with bodies.*

strick·en a *pp.* of STRIKE: *a remark ordered stricken from the court record.*
— *adj. & combining form.* afflicted: *to be stricken by* or *with disease, sorrow, trouble; grief-stricken, poverty-stricken; sorrow-stricken.*

strict *adj.* **1** careful in enforcing rules: *a strict parent, teacher; strict in discipline; strict about school attendance; equally strict toward all her students.* **2** carefully observed; exact or precise: *a strict rule; in the strict sense of the term; in the strictest confidence.*

stric·ture (STRIK·chur) *n.* **1** a narrowing or restricting. **2** a restriction or censure: *the loosening of strictures on* or *against Communist artists and writers; liberation from the strictures of Western fashions.*

stride *v.* **strides, strode, strid·den, strid·ing** walk with long steps, as from vigour or enthusiasm: *He confidently strode into the room; Keep your feet dry by striding over the stream.*
— *n.* **1** a long step or the distance covered by it: *The stride of the Sasquatch is estimated at about 1.3 m.* **2** usually **strides** *pl.* progress: *the rapid strides made by the computer industry; great strides in speed and efficiency.*
— **take in stride** deal with something without getting excited or upset: *She has learned to take successes as well as failures in stride.*

stri·dent (STRY·dunt) *adj.* loud in a harsh, grating, or obtrusive manner: *a strident voice; the strident tone of his petition.*

strife *n.* a fighting or quarrel, esp. a struggle between opposing sides: *There's bitter strife between the various factions; communal, domestic, internal, sectarian strife among the population; industrial strife (between labour and management).*

strike *v.* **strikes,** *pt.* **struck,** *pp.* **struck** or **strick·en, strik·ing** hit, esp. aim or deal a blow with the hand or a weapon: *Jim lost his patience and struck the bully; struck him a heavy blow; He struck back at Jim; struck his head against the door; An epidemic strikes a population; He lit a fire by striking a match; The house was struck by lightning; It struck him unconscious; A clock strikes* (= sounds) *the hours; stories that strike terror into young minds; A plant strikes roots as it grows*

in a place; A bright idea struck her; How does her plan strike (= impress) *you? It strikes me as clever; They struck* (= advanced) *across the trackless desert; After some digging, they struck* (= found) *oil; The invaders struck* (= attacked) *without warning; The workers struck* (= went on a strike) *for more pay; They succeeded in striking* (= agreeing on) *a bargain; He often strikes* (= assumes) *the pose of a concerned citizen.*
— **strike it rich** *Informal.* make money, as from a gold mine or oil well.
— **strike off** cross out, as from a list.
— **strike out 1** delete words, as from a record. **2** move forward, as by swimming: *to strike out for* or *toward shore; She decided to quit her job and strike out on her own as a consultant.* **3** in baseball, fail or cause to fail to hit thrice.
— **strike up 1** begin: *to strike up an acquaintance, conversation, friendship.* **2** begin playing: *to strike up a tune; Strike up the band! The band struck up; They struck up "O Canada!"*
— *n.* **1** a striking, esp. an attack: *to carry out an air strike against the enemy; a preemptive strike; the enemy's first-strike capability.* **2** a stoppage of work by employees to force their employer to agree to higher pay or better working conditions: *to avert, break, break up, call, organize, settle, stage a strike; They went (out) on strike; They are on strike; a general, hunger, rent, sit-down, sympathy, wildcat strike.* **3** in baseball, any of four ways in which a failure may be called against a batter: *They have two strikes against them* (= are at a clear disadvantage). **4** in bowling, a knocking down of all the pins with the first ball. **5** a discovery of an oil deposit.

strike·break·er (STRIKE·bray·kur) *n.* one hired to replace a striking worker: *to bring in strikebreakers.*

striking *adj.* **1** that allows a strike: *to come within striking distance.* **2** very impressive: *a striking personality, performance; a woman of striking appearance.*

string *n.* **1** a cord or wire that is thicker than a thread, as for tying up a parcel, working a puppet, or keeping a bow taut: *a string of pearls* (= pearls on a string); *a string* (= series) *of lies.* **2** something resembling a string or cord, as a nerve or the fibre connecting the halves of a bean pod. **3** *Informal.* a condition: *a good offer with no* **strings attached.** **4** group based on ability: *first string; second string.*
— **strings** *pl.* **1** stringed instruments, as of an orchestra, or their players collectively. **2** *Informal.* control or influence: *a man tied to his mother's apron strings* (= still dependent on her); *He knows how to* **pull strings** (= to exert influence).
— *v.* **strings,** *pt. & pp.* **strung** or **stringed, string·ing** arrange in a string or line: *to string beads; to string a racket* (= equip it with strings); *to string words together in sentences; a carcass strung* (= hung) *between two posts; to string* (= put the strings on; also, tune) *a violin; highly strung* (= taut) *nerves; a high-strung* (= easily excited) *person; to string peas and beans* (= clean them of strings); *violins, guitars, and such* **stringed instruments.**

strin·gent (STRIN·junt) *adj.* strictly or severely binding: *stringent regulations; a stringent* (= tight) *market.*
— **strin·gen·cy** *n.*

string·er *n.* **1** a connecting or supporting timber, esp. a horizontal piece. **2** a part-time correspondent for a newspaper.

string·y (STRING·ee) *adj.* **string·i·er, -i·est** having or forming strings; also, sinewy or wiry in build.

strip *v.* **strips, stripped, strip·ping 1** remove what covers a fruit, body, or other surface: *The doctor asked him to strip to the waist; to **strip down** to his underwear; Sam was stripped and searched by the police; to strip old paint off furniture.* **2** deprive of what belongs to one by taking it off completely or forcibly: *Al was stripped of his citizenship; a military general stripped of his powers; a stolen car stripped of its accessories.* **3** damage or break the thread of a screw or teeth of a gear.
— *n.* **1** a long, narrow piece: *strips of cardboard, cloth, land; the median strip of a highway; a landing strip (for airplanes).* **2** a busy thoroughfare along a street: *hotels on the airport strip; a beach-front strip; shopping strip; the action-packed "Strip" of Los Angeles.*

stripe *n.* **1** a long, narrow band of contrasting colour: *A tiger cannot change its stripes; a dark suit with chalk stripes; the **stars and stripes** on the U.S. flag.* **2** usually **stripes** *pl.* a strip of braid or a V-shaped badge worn on the sleeve of a uniform to show the wearer's rank or length of service. **3** sort or type: *Politicians of every stripe were there.*
— *v.* **stripes, striped, strip·ing** mark with stripes: *A candy cane is striped with red; **striped** pants; the **striped** bass, skunk.*

strive *v.* **strives,** *pt.* **strove** (STROHV) or **strived,** *pp.* **striv·en, striv·ing** make great efforts or try hard: *to strive to accomplish something; to strive for an effect.* — **striv·er** *n.*

strode *pt.* of STRIDE.

stroke *v.* **strokes, stroked, strok·ing** pass the hand caressingly over: *to stroke fur, hair, a person, pet.*
— *n.* **1** a stroking: *"Different strokes (= treatments) for different folks."* **2** a striking or blow, esp. one dealt suddenly or sharply: *a stroke of a sword; killed by a stroke of lightning; Age-old customs cannot be changed **at a stroke** (= suddenly); a stroke of luck, misfortune; at the stroke of 12 (o'clock); He had or suffered a stroke* (= apoplexy). **3** an effort, esp. a vigorous or successful one: *a stroke of genius; He didn't do one stroke of work all day.* **4** an action or movement that is repeated rhythmically: *backhand and forehand strokes in tennis; swimming strokes such as the breaststroke and "butterfly" stroke; the strokes of a piston; the up and down strokes of written letters.*

stroll (STROLE) *n.* a leisurely walk: *to go for, take a stroll in the park.*
— *v.* **1** take a stroll along or through a place: *went strolling through the park.* **2** wander: *to stroll the streets; a **strolling** troupe of players.*

strong *adj.* **1** having great power to act or resist; not weak; powerful: *strong muscles, winds; a strong argument, drink, mind, reason, will; strong support.* **2** of a specified number: *Our class is 35 strong.* **3** ill-smelling; foul: *strong breath, cheese, smell.* **4** of a verb, not regular in conjugation, as "sink-sank-sunk."
— **strong·ly** *adv.*

strong-arm *adj. Informal.* using undue force: *the strong-arm approach; a strong-arm man, method; strong-arm police tactics. Also **strong-armed.***
— *v.* use coercion or violence against someone.

strong·hold *n.* **1** a fortress. **2** a place in which a party or cause has strong support: *The Tory candidate won the election in a Liberal stronghold.*

strong·man *n.* **-men** a despot or dictator.

strong-minded (STRONG·mine·did) *adj.* mentally strong or unyielding.

strong·room *n.* a room that is built for keeping valuables safe against fire, burglary, etc. Also **strong room.**

strop *n. & v.* **strops, stropped, strop·ping** (sharpen a razor on) a leather strap.

strove *pt.* of STRIVE.

struck *pt.* or a *pp.* of STRIKE.
— *adj.* affected by a labour strike: *struck businesses, work, workers.*

struc·tur·al (STRUK·chur·ul) *adj.* having to do with structure: *a structural defect, difference; **structural steel** (used in building); **structural unemployment** (caused by the economy).* — **struc·tur·al·ly** *adv.*

struc·ture (STRUK·chur) *n.* **1** anything constructed of parts; building: *a tall structure.* **2** the manner of arrangement of parts in a system: *the structure of society; sentence structure; a power, price, tax, wage structure.*
— *v.* **-tures, -tured, -tur·ing** organize with differentiated parts: *a structured curriculum.*

strug·gle (STRUG·ul) *n.* **1** great effort or exertion: *to wage a struggle against poverty; to carry on a struggle for freedom; the struggle to make a living; the ceaseless, fierce struggle for survival.* **2** strife or conflict: *the class struggle; to put up a struggle; a struggle to the death; a bitter, desperate, frantic, unending, violent struggle.*
— *v.* **strug·gles, strug·gled, strug·gling** make great efforts, as against contending forces: *She struggled to free herself; struggled to her feet; struggled for breath; struggled out of her clothes; struggled bravely through her long illness.*

strum *v.* **strums, strummed, strum·ming** play a guitar, a tune, play *on* the piano, etc. in a casual or unskilful manner.

strung *pt. & pp.* of STRING.
— **strung out 1** *Slang.* addicted to or intoxicated by narcotics: *to be strung out on cocaine.* **2** spread out: *The beds were strung out along the hospital corridors.*

strut *v.* **struts, strut·ted, strut·ting** walk in a jaunty and self-important manner: *to strut like a peacock; a showy actress strutting her stuff* (= showing off) *on the stage.*
— *n.* **1** a strutting walk or gait. **2** a brace or support, as under the rafters of a roof.

stub *n.* a short piece remaining after its main part is used up or broken off: *the stub of a cigarette, pencil, ticket, tooth; the stub* (= stump) *of a tree; the stub of a check (saved as a record).*

— v. stubs, stubbed, stub·bing: *He stubbed his toe* (= hurt it by striking it against something hard); *to stub a cigar* (= put it out by rubbing it on a surface).

stub·ble (STUB·ul) *n.* 1 stumps left projecting from the ground after harvesting. 2 a short, bristly growth, as of hair on the face. — **stub·bly** *adj.*

stub·born (STUB·urn) *adj.* determined not to change one's way; unyielding: *a stubborn child, cough, disposition, resistance, soil (that is hard to work); a stubborn stain.* — **stub·born·ly** *adv.*; **stub·born·ness** *n.*

stub·by (STUB·ee) *adj.* **stub·bi·er, stub·bi·est** 1 short and thick: *stubby fingers; a stubby bottle.* 2 covered with stubs or stumps: *a stubby field.*

stuck *pt.* of STICK.

stuck-up *adj. Informal.* conceited.

stud *n.* 1 a male animal kept for breeding, esp. a stallion, or **stud·horse.** 2 a virile young man: *a stud race-car driver.* 3 one of the upright timbers inside a wall frame to which the boards or panels are nailed. 4 a knoblike head, as used to ornament a leather surface, or a small, two-headed button used on dress shirts: *stud earrings.*
— v. studs, stud·ded, stud·ding decorated or dotted with or as if with studs: *a star-studded sky; a crown studded with diamonds; a studded tire for better traction over snow and ice.*

stu·dent (STEW·dunt) *n.* one who studies a subject or attends a school: *a college, day, excellent, foreign, good, graduate, high-school, outstanding, poor, undergraduate, university student; students of Milton (who study Milton's works).*

studied (STUD·eed) *adj.* deliberate: *his studied politeness; a studied insult; a studied* (= carefully prepared) *reply.*

stu·di·o (STEW·dee·oh) *n.* **-os** 1 an artist's or photographer's workroom: *a dance studio that is really a social club.* 2 a broadcasting room or a place where motion pictures are produced: *a film studio; TV studio.* 3 a more spacious bachelor apartment; also **studio apartment.**

stu·di·ous (STEW·dee·us) *adj.* 1 devoted to study: *studious habits.* 2 diligent: *studious attention, care, efforts.* — **stu·di·ous·ly** *adv.*

stud·y (STUD·ee) *n.* **stud·ies** 1 concentration of the mind on a subject in an effort to learn it; also, any earnest mental effort: *She spends her weekends in study.* 2 a detailed examination of a subject, the subject itself, or a work or treatise discussing it: *She has conducted, done, made a study of the phenomenon; his careful, classic, definitive, detailed, exhaustive, in-depth, scientific study of volcanoes; her published studies of human behaviour; social studies; women's studies; The question is under study.* 3 a room for study. 4 **studies** *pl.* education: *She pursued, completed her studies in Paris; a man of studies.*
— adj.: *a study circle, group; study hall* (= place or time set aside for study in a school); *They walked off the job for a study session with fellow workers.*
— v. stud·ies, stud·ied, stud·y·ing 1 apply one's mind to a subject: *She's studying law; works days and studies nights* (= spends nights in study); *to study for a degree;*

to study diligently, hard; to study under a teacher; to **study up on** (*Informal for* make a close study of) *a subject.* 2 carefully examine or consider: *He's studying the results of the experiment; to study someone's expression, a map.*

stuff *n.* 1 the substance that something is made of or material for making something: *woollen stuff; the right stuff; the same old stuff; the stuff* (= basic qualities) *of genius; the stuff of* (= what makes a) *legend.* 2 *Informal.* thing(s): *What's that stuff you're drinking? Get rid of the stuff; Stuff and nonsense* (= Garbage)! *He knows his stuff* (= what he is supposed to know); *kid stuff* (= something elementary); *heady stuff* (= something exciting).
— v. fill or pack: *A pillow is stuffed with feathers; Feathers are stuffed into pillows; He stuffed himself with cake; That bear is really a stuffed animal; to have a stuffed-up nose (from a cold); a stuffed ballot box (containing fraudulent votes).*

stuffed shirt *n. Slang.* one who is pretentious or pompous.

stuffing *n.* 1 padding used in upholstery. 2 a filling of bread crumbs, seasonings, etc. for roast fowl.

stuff·y *adj.* **stuf·fi·er, stuf·fi·est:** *a stuffy* (= not airy) *room; a stuffy* (= congested) *nose; a stuffy* (= straitlaced) *clergyman; a stuffy* (= dull) *sermon.*

stum·ble *v.* **-bles, -bled, -bling** take a wrong step in walking or running, trip accidentally, or falter because of age or weakness: *We stumbled and fell in the dark; He stumbled through his performance; I stumbled upon* (= happened to find) *what I was looking for.*
— n. 1 a stumbling. 2 a mistake or wrong act.
— stum·bler *n.*

stumbling block *n.* a hindrance or obstacle: *the main stumbling block to progress in the negotiations.*

stump *n.* 1 the part of a tree trunk remaining in the ground after the tree has been felled. 2 something resembling it, as an amputated limb; stub. 3 a political campaigner's speaking platform.
— v. 1 walk stiffly, as if on wooden legs. 2 make political speeches: *to go stumping (the country) for votes; stumping for his favourite candidate.* 3 *Informal.* perplex or confound; floor: *He was stumped by the strange happenings.*

stump·y *adj.* short and thick.

stun *v.* **stuns, stunned, stun·ning** make dizzy, as by a blow: *I was stunned by the news; stunned to learn of her death.*
— adj.: *A stun grenade immobilizes the victim for a few seconds; A stun gun can give a 50 000-volt shock.*

stung *pt. & pp.* of STING.

stunk a *pt. & pp.* of STINK.

stunning *adj.* 1 bewildering: *a stunning announcement, defeat, victory.* 2 strikingly attractive: *a stunning beauty; She looks stunning in that outfit.*
— stun·ning·ly *adv.*

stunt *v.* 1 check growth or development: *factors stunting growth; a stunted tree.* 2 do a stunt.
— *n.* a feat to attract attention or show one's daring, as at a circus: *to do, perform a stunt; a publicity stunt.*
— **stunt man** *n.;* **stunt woman** *n.*

stu·pe·fy (STEW·puh·fye) *v.* -fies, -fied, -fy·ing 1 cause stupor in someone: *stupefied with drink, drugs.* 2 stun: *She was stupefied at the sight of the wreck.*
— **stu·pe·fac·tion** (-FAC·shun) *n.*

stu·pen·dous (stew·PEN·dus) *adj.* astonishing, esp. by immensity or greatness: *a stupendous achievement, marvel.*

stu·pid (STEW·pid) *adj.* showing lack of intelligence; silly: *stupid behaviour; a stupid answer, idea.*
— **stu·pid·ly** *adv.*
— **stu·pid·i·ty** (stew·PID·uh·tee) *n.: the height of stupidity; sheer stupidity.*

stu·por (STEW·pur) *n.* a dazed condition; numbness: *He was in a stupor; fell into a stupor; went into a stupor; was found sleepwalking in a kind of stupor; a drunken stupor; a mindless stupor; a syndrome marked by stupor.* — **stu·por·ous** (-rus) *adj.*

stur·dy (STUR·dee) *adj.* -di·er, -di·est strong and hardy, esp. in build or growth: *a sturdy defender, limb, oak, race; her sturdy common sense.*
— **stur·di·ly** *adv.;* **stur·di·ness** *n.*

stut·ter (STUT·ur) *v.* stammer, esp. by repeating the first sound of a word; also *n.* — **stut·ter·er** *n.*

sty *n.* sties a pen for pigs; hence, any filthy place.

style *n.* 1 a distinctive fashion or mode in one's way of living, esp. dress, indicative of taste or excellence: *a hat that is out of style; She dresses and lives in style; The fellow lacks style.* 2 a distinctive manner of artistic expression or design: *an affected, classic, elegant, flowery, ornate, vigorous style; Shakespeare's style; built in the Byzantine style; Too many rules **cramp one's style*** (*Informal* for limit one's freedom). 3 a formal manner or mode: *the style of addressing clergy; a publisher's house style* (= rules for spelling, punctuation, etc.). 4 a pointed device or structure, as a phonograph needle or an engraving or writing implement.
— *v.* styles, styled, styl·ing 1 make or design according to a style: *clothes styled for comfort; I like the **styling** of his hair* (= way it is styled). 2 call or name: *The ambitious ruler styled himself "emperor."*

styl·ish (STY·lish) *adj.* according to the prevailing fashion; fashionable.

sty·mie (STY·mee) *v.* -mies, -mied, -my·ing block or thwart: *Children taught in metric are stymied by imperial measurements; to stymie attempts, legislation, plans, progress.*

suave (SWAHV) *adj.* polished and gracious in manner or style: *a suave and sophisticated performer; a suave hotel.* — **suave·ly** *adv.;* **suave·ness** *n.*

sub *n.* [short form] submarine; substitute; subordinate.
— *v.* subs, subbed, sub·bing *Informal.* substitute *for* someone.

sub- *prefix.* 1 lower or under; hence, further divided or secondary: *subalpine, subatomic, subcommittee, subcompact, subdivision, subheading, subroutine,* *subspecies.* 2 somewhat; nearly: *subarctic, subtemperate, subtropical.*

sub·con·scious (sub·CON·shus) *adj.* of thoughts and feelings, existing in the mind but not fully recognized.
— *n.* **the subconscious,** the realm of subconscious mental processes. — **sub·con·scious·ly** *adv.*

sub·con·tract (sub·CON·tract) *n.* a contract for carrying out part of a main contract. — *v.: A building contractor subcontracts plumbing, heating, and other installations.*
— **sub·con·trac·tor** *n.*

sub·cul·ture (SUB·cul·chur) *n.* a social group within a larger group exhibiting a culture of its own: *the teen subculture; The prison subculture does not tolerate certain types of criminals.*

sub·due (sub·DEW) *v.* -dues, -dued, -du·ing overpower; hence, bring under control: *The intruder was subdued after a brief struggle; to subdue one's passions.*

subdued *adj.* softened or toned down: *in a subdued light, voice; subdued tones.*

sub·ject (SUB·jict) *n.* 1 a theme or topic of a conversation, study, etc.: *Algebra is his favourite subject; to address, avoid, bring up, broach, cover, deal with, discuss, drop, dwell on, exhaust, pursue, tackle, take up, treat a subject; to take (up) and master a subject; a delicate, ticklish, pleasant, thorny subject; on the subject of literacy; Let's not change the subject; when the subject comes up (for discussion).* 2 a person owing allegiance to a sovereign or ruler: *a British subject; a loyal subject of the Queen.* 3 one undergoing an investigation. 4 one chosen for artistic representation. 5 in grammar, a word or term representing the one about whom something is said, as "Joan" in "Joan loves him," "Joan is here," and "Joan is loved by him."
— *adj.* under another's rule; not independent: *a subject people.*
— **subject to** 1 owing obedience to a person or thing: *You're subject to the laws of your country.* 2 prone or liable to something: *Humans are subject to error.* 3 conditional upon something: *an arrangement subject to approval.*
— *v.* (sub·JECT) bring under a rule or power: *They were never subjected by a foreign power.*
— **subject to** cause to undergo a treatment or experience something: *subjected to foreign domination; subjected to ridicule.*
— **sub·jec·tion** (-JEC·shun) *n.*

sub·jec·tive (sub·JEC·tiv) *adj.* related to the person thinking, not to the object thought of; personal: *a purely subjective opinion.*

subject matter *n.* content, not form or style: *the subject matter of a poem.*

sub·lime (suh·BLIME) *adj.* so elevated or noble as to inspire awe and wonder: *sublime beauty, devotion, heights, virtue.* — **sub·lim·i·ty** (suh·BLIM·uh·tee) *n.*

sub·lim·i·nal (suh·BLIM·uh·nul) *adj.* of stimuli, learning processes, etc., barely perceived: *Toy commercials contain subtle, even subliminal suggestions to buy; subliminal advertising; a subliminal message; the subliminal* (= subconscious) *self.* — **sub·lim·i·nal·ly** *adv.*

sub·ma·rine (sub·muh·REEN) *adj.* underwater: *submarine cables, life, plants, warfare.*
— *n.* a ship designed for underwater operation: *a nuclear submarine; A submarine dives, surfaces.*

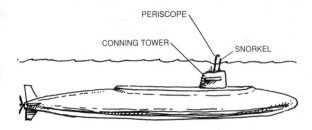

PERISCOPE
CONNING TOWER
SNORKEL

sub·merge (sub·MURJ) *v.* -merg·es, -merged, -merg·ing 1 put or sink under water. 2 sink below a level, as of poverty. — **sub·mer·sion** *n.*

sub·mers·i·ble (sub·MUR·suh·bul) *n. & adj.* (a diving vessel or other vehicle) that can operate under water.

sub·mis·sion (sub·MISH·un) *n.* 1 a submitting or something submitted. 2 obedience: *a life of submission to the monastic rule.* — **sub·mis·sive** (-MIS·iv) *adj.*

sub·mit (sub·MIT) *v.* -mits, -mit·ted, -mit·ting 1 give way or yield *to* a treatment, situation, etc.: *to submit a question to arbitration; never to submit to arbitrary measures.* 2 present as to a higher authority: *to submit a report to the president; I submit* (= claim or affirm) *that you are mistaken.*

sub·or·di·nate (suh·BOR·duh·nit) *n. & adj.* 1 (a person or thing) that is below another in rank: *She is kind to her subordinates.* 2 (one) that is dependent: *"If," "since," "whether,"* etc. start **subordinate clauses** in *complex sentences.*
— *v.* (-nate) -nates, -nat·ed, -nat·ing make subordinate or subservient *to* something.
— **sub·or·di·na·tion** (-NAY·shun) *n.*

sub·poe·na (suh·PEE·nuh) *n.* a legal written order requiring a person to appear or documents to be submitted in court: *to issue a subpoena for a witness to appear in court; A subpoena was served on him.*
— *v.* -naes, -naed, -nae·ing: *The tapes were subpoenaed; were subpoenaed as evidence; to subpoena witnesses to testify.*

sub·scribe (sub·SCRIBE) *v.* -scribes, -scribed, -scrib·ing 1 pay or pledge a sum of money to a cause, fund, etc.: *to subscribe to a charity.* 2 agree to purchase: *to subscribe to a magazine; to subscribe for some shares in the company.* 3 sign one's name at the bottom of a document. 4 give consent or approval: *to subscribe to a measure, opinion; The majority in Iran subscribe to Islam.* — **sub·scrib·er** *n.*

sub·scrip·tion (sub·SCRIP·shun) *n.* a subscribing or the payment made: *to cancel a subscription; renew a subscription before it expires; money collected by public subscription; to raise a subscription for charity.*

sub·se·quent (SUB·sik·wunt) *adj.* coming after: *subsequent developments; subsequent to his arrest.*

— **sub·se·quent·ly** *adv.*

sub·ser·vi·ent (sub·SUR·vee·unt) *adj.* slavishly serving; subordinate *to* someone. — **sub·ser·vi·ence** *n.*

sub·side (sub·SIDE) *v.* -sides, -sid·ed, -sid·ing 1 sink to a lower or more normal level, as receding flood waters, loose earth, etc.: *The flood waters will subside.* 2 of anything agitated or rising, to become tranquil or quiet; abate: *Anger, a fever, noise, a storm subsides.*
— **sub·si·dence** (SUB·sid·unce) *n.*

sub·sid·i·ar·y (sub·SID·ee·air·ee) *adj.* 1 auxiliary or secondary *to* something. 2 allied in a subordinate capacity, as a corporation controlled by a parent or "holding" company.
— *n.: the Canadian subsidiary of a British company.*

sub·si·dize (SUB·suh·dize) *v.* -diz·es, -dized, -diz·ing help with a subsidy: *subsidized meals for employees.*
— **sub·si·di·za·tion** (-duh·ZAY·shun) *n.*

sub·si·dy (SUB·suh·dee) *n.* -dies money or other aid given by a government to farmers, schools, airlines, etc.: *to grant, provide a subsidy for a purpose, to an institution; farm, food, housing subsidies; postal subsidy for publishers.*

sub·sist (sub·SIST) *v.* continue to be or keep alive *on* food or income, *by* some means.

sub·sist·ence (sub·SIS·tunce) *n.* existence; sustenance; livelihood: *a bare, hand-to-mouth subsistence; their only means of subsistence.*
— *adj.: a subsistence diet; the subsistence economy of poor nations; subsistence wages;* **subsistence farming** *that leaves no surpluses for sale.*

sub·stance (SUB·stunce) *n.* 1 what something consists of: *Margarine is a butterlike substance; a controlled substance such as a drug;* **substance abuse** (= drug abuse); *toxic substances; the substance* (= essence) *of what he said; I agree with her* **in substance** (= in its essentials). 2 solid quality; body: *He ate nothing of substance for 10 days; Is there any substance to those charges? a man of substance* (= wealth or property).

sub·stan·dard (sub·STAN·durd) *adj.* below standard: *substandard living conditions; substandard English.*

sub·stan·tial (sub·STAN·shul) *adj.* 1 having substance: *a substantial meal, structure; There's nothing substantial about a dream; a substantial* (= considerable) *improvement.* 2 essential: *two versions in substantial agreement with each other.* — **sub·stan·tial·ly** *adv.*

sub·stan·ti·ate (sub·STAN·shee·ate) *v.* -ates, -at·ed, -at·ing give substance to something; hence, establish by giving evidence: *to substantiate a charge, claim, opinion.* — **sub·stan·ti·a·tion** (-shee·AY·shun) *n.*

sub·stan·tive (SUB·stun·tiv) *adj.* dealing with the substance of something; also, having substance: *We want a substantive discussion, not a symbolic one; a substantive issue, majority, report, study.*

sub·sti·tute (SUB·stuh·tute) *n.* a person or thing that takes the place of another: *a sugar substitute like saccharin; a substitute for sugar; Coffee whiteners are nondairy cream substitutes; a poor substitute; A* **substitute teacher** *fills in when a staff teacher is absent.*
— *v.* -tutes, -tut·ed, -tut·ing replace: *In some*

countries, coffee is substituted with dandelion roots; Margarine substitutes for butter.
— **sub·sti·tu·tion** (-TUE·shun) *n.*

sub·teen (SUB·teen) *n.* a child approaching the age of 13.

sub·ti·tle (SUB·tye·tul) *n.* 1 a secondary or explanatory title, as of a book. 2 printed matter such as translated dialogue shown on a TV or movie screen.
— *v.* -**tles**, -**tled**, -**tling**: *a book subtitled "A true story"; The producer decided on subtitling instead of dubbing the film for English TV.*

sub·tle (SUT·ul) *adj.* -**tler**, -**tlest** 1 difficult to perceive by mind or sense because fine or delicate; not immediately obvious: *a subtle distinction, flavour, hint, joke.* 2 having or showing a keen or clever mind: *a subtle design, observer; a subtle* (= tricky) *scheme.*
— **sub·tle·ty** *n.* — **sub·tly** (SUT·lee) *adv.*

sub·to·tal (SUB·toh·tul) *n.* a total to be added to others for a complete or "grand" total.

sub·tract (sub·TRACT) *v.* take away one number from another. — **sub·trac·tion** *n.*

sub·urb (SUB·urb) *n.* 1 a town, district, or community on the outskirts of a city: *a fashionable suburb.* 2 the suburbs *pl.* a city's residential outskirts.
— **sub·ur·ban** (suh·BUR·bun) *adj.*

sub·ur·ban·ite (suh·BUR·buh·nite) *n.* one living in a suburb.

sub·ur·bi·a (suh·BUR·bee·uh) *n.* suburbs and suburbanites collectively: *offices moving to suburbia.*

sub·vert (sub·VURT) *v.* upset or overthrow something established: *to subvert law, morality, religion.*
— **sub·ver·sion** *n.* — **sub·ver·sive** (-siv) *adj.*

sub·way *n.* 1 an underground railway or its tunnel: *We travel to work by subway.* 2 an underground passage.

suc·ceed (suc·SEED) *v.* 1 come after or follow, as in an office: *to succeed to the throne; Mulroney succeeded Turner as Canada's prime minister.* 2 be successful in one's purpose: *The army succeeded in overthrowing the civilian rulers.*

suc·cess (suc·SES) *n.* 1 wished-for result or outcome, esp. good fortune: *to achieve, attain, enjoy success; meet with success; He had great success in life; a howling, huge, resounding, total, tremendous, unqualified success.* 2 a person or thing that is successful: *The play was a success; a box-office success; a commercial success; a success with the general public.*

suc·cess·ful (suc·SES·ful) *adj.* having success; hence, prosperous or fortunate: *She's highly successful in business; successful at making money.*
— **suc·cess·ful·ly** *adv.*

suc·ces·sion (suc·SESH·un) *n.* 1 the act of succeeding or the right to succeed another: *Queen Elizabeth's succession to the throne.* 2 a coming, one after another, of people or events: *They acquired many companies in quick succession; a succession* (= series) *of calamities; It snowed for five days in succession* (= in a row).

suc·ces·sive (suc·SES·iv) *adj.* coming one after another in series: *It snowed on five successive days.*
— **suc·ces·sive·ly** *adv.*

suc·ces·sor (suc·SES·ur) *n.* one that succeeds another.

suc·cinct (suc·SINCT) *adj.* concise and compact in expression: *a succinct style, summary, writer.*
— **suc·cinct·ly** *adv.*; **suc·cinct·ness** *n.*

suc·cu·lent (SUK·yuh·lunt) *adj.* juicy or fleshy.
— *n.* a fleshy plant adapted for storing water, as cactuses and agaves. — **suc·cu·lence** or **suc·cu·len·cy** *n.*

suc·cumb (suh·CUM) *v.* yield or give way, as from weakness: *to succumb to peer pressure, to temptation; He soon succumbed to his injuries* (= died).

such *adj.* of the kind specified or suggested: *He was such a great poet; He said no such thing; She didn't say any such thing; He did say some such thing; Take such books as you can read in one day; Shakespeare, Milton, and such poets; poets* **such as** *Shakespeare and Milton.*
— *adv.* to that degree: *a woman of such fine manners.*
— *pron.* such a one or ones: *Such was not my intention; A debtor,* **as such**, *owes something to someone; communists, fellow travellers,* **and such** (= such people).
— **such and such** an unspecified thing: *Even if such and such is true, it doesn't prove a thing; Even if such and such a person said it, it wouldn't be true.*

such·like *pron. & adj.* people or things of such a kind: *We sell books, periodicals, films, and suchlike; Television, films, and suchlike media.*

suck *v.* draw in a fluid, esp. a liquid, as by using the lips: *An infant sucks (milk from) its mother's breast; He likes to suck oranges; He sucks on his pipe while thinking; the sucking action of a pump; A vacuum cleaner sucks in dust; Sponges suck up moisture; A tornado could suck your swimming pool dry.*
— *n.* the act of sucking; suction.

suck·er *n.* 1 one that sucks, as a family of fishes with thick lips. 2 a sucking organ, as the roots of a parasitic plant, or a disk-shaped clinging organ, as on the tentacles of an octopus. 3 a lollipop. 4 *Slang.* one who is easily cheated or fooled: *He's a sucker for any sob story; They can't make suckers out of us; v.: We shall not be suckered.*

suck·le (SUCK·ul) *v.* -**les**, -**led**, -**ling** feed at the breast or udder: *Mammals suckle their young.*

suck·ling *n. & adj.* a child or animal that is not yet weaned: *a mere suckling; a suckling infant, pig.*

suc·tion (SUC·shun) *n.* sucking; the process by which a fluid is drawn up, as through a drinking straw, or by which a concave pad or disk sticks to a surface: *a suction pump.*

sud·den (SUD·un) *adj.* happening, met with, done, etc. unexpectedly or hastily: *a sudden death in a car crash; a sudden descent, turn; It came to a sudden stop; a sudden rush of wind; a sudden decision on the eve of the wedding not to get married; a* **sudden death** *overtime play for breaking a tie which ends when one side scores a goal or point.*
— **all of a sudden** suddenly or unexpectedly.
— **sud·den·ly** *adv.*; **sud·den·ness** *n.*

suds (SUDZ) *n. pl.* [takes pl. v.] 1 *Informal.* beer; also, the foam or froth. 2 soapy water; also, the bubbles formed on it.

— *v. Informal.* wash in suds or form suds.
— **suds·y** *adj.*

sue (SOO) *v.* **sues, sued, su·ing 1** take legal action against someone: *He threatened to sue; He sued his doctor; sued for malpractice; sued for one million dollars.* **2** plead or solicit respectfully: *to sue for a favour, for peace.*

suede or **suéde** (SWADE) *n.* soft leather for coats, casual shoes, etc. made by raising a velvety nap on the flesh side of tanned animal hide: *a suede coat, vest; suede shoes.*

suf·fer (SUF·ur) *v.* undergo pain, harm, loss, or anything hard to bear: *We had to suffer much because of the strike; Businesses suffered; They suffered great losses; suffered harm, insults; He's suffering from measles; "Suffer* (= allow) *the little children to come unto me."*— **suf·fer·er** *n.*

suf·fer·ance (SUF·ur·unce) *n.* **1** passive toleration: *He is carrying on at the sufferance of his employer; an unwanted employee kept* **on sufferance** *(instead of being fired).* **2** suffering capacity.

suffering *n.* **1** the bearing of pain, harm, loss, etc.: *a life of suffering.* **2** what is suffered; pain: *the sufferings of the poor; to alleviate, bear, cause, ease, endure, inflict, relieve suffering; great, intense, untold suffering.*

suf·fice (suh·FICE) *v.* **suf·fic·es, suf·ficed, suf·fic·ing 1** be sufficient or enough: *$100 will suffice for expenses; $100 suffices to meet our expenses;* **Suffice it to say,** (= Let it be sufficient to say) *that he is sorry for what happened.* **2** satisfy the appetite of someone.

suf·fi·cient (suh·FISH·unt) *adj.* of a quantity or scope that satisfies needs; enough: *food sufficient for everyone; not sufficient evidence to lay charges; the necessary and sufficient conditions for becoming a Canadian citizen.* — **suf·fi·cient·ly** *adv.* — **suf·fi·cien·cy** *n.*

suf·fix (SUF·ix) *n.* **1** an affix added to the end of a word to form derivatives, as "-ly," "-ness," and "-y." **2** an inflectional ending such as "-ed," "-ing," or "-s."

suf·fo·cate (SUF·uh·cate) *v.* **-cates, -cat·ed, -cat·ing** choke or stifle because of insufficient oxygen or fresh air: *A drowning person suffocates; He was suffocated by carbon monoxide fumes; They found city life quite suffocating.* — **suf·fo·ca·tion** (-CAY·shun) *n.*

suf·frage (SUF·rij) *n.* the right to vote; franchise: *adult suffrage; universal suffrage; women's suffrage; to extend or grant suffrage to the minorities.* — **suf·fra·gist** (-ruh·jist) *n.*

suf·fra·gette (suf·ruh·JET) *n.* a woman advocating women's right to vote: *Nellie McClung was a leader of the suffragette movement in Canada.*

sug·ar (SHOOG·ur, short "OO") *n.* a sweet carbohydrate obtained esp. from the tall tropical grass called **sugar cane** or from **sugar beet** and used as a sweetener of foods: *to produce, refine sugar; a lump of sugar; beet, brown, cane, crude, granulated, lump, table sugar; blood sugar; fruit sugar;* **adj.:** *a sugar bush of sugar maples; a sugar cube.* — **sug·ar·y** *adj.*

sug·ar·coat (shoog·ur·COAT) *v.* cover, esp. something unpleasant, with sugar: *a sugarcoated pill.*

sugaring off *n. Cdn.* **1** the making of maple syrup and

sugar by boiling maple sap. **2** this activity as a social occasion.

sugar maple *n. Cdn.* a maple whose sweet sap is the chief source of maple syrup and maple sugar.

sug·gest (suh·JEST) *v.* **1** put forward an idea or proposal, as for consideration: *She suggests adjourning for the day; He suggests a coffee break; I suggest we have lunch; the various things suggested to us.* **2** bring to mind, as by association of ideas: *the appropriate action suggested by the circumstances; the alternatives that seem to suggest themselves.*

sug·gest·i·ble (suh·JES·tuh·bul) *adj.* easily influenced by suggestion from outside the mind: *Children are suggestible.* — **sug·gest·i·bil·i·ty** (-BIL·uh·tee) *n.*

sug·ges·tion (suh·JES·chun) *n.* **1** a suggesting or what is suggested: *Any suggestions? to act on, adopt, ask for, call for, invite, offer, put forward, reject a suggestion; an appropriate, helpful, preposterous suggestion; a suggestion about what to do next; She made a suggestion that we adjourn for the day; At my suggestion, we adjourned for lunch.* **2** a hint or trace: *a suggestion of scandal, wrongdoing.*

sug·ges·tive (suh·JES·tiv) *adj.* **1** suggesting new things besides what is known: *a suggestive bibliography, commentary, reading list; language that is suggestive* (= indicative) *of prejudice.* **2** suggesting something indecent: *a suggestive dance; suggestive pictures, winks.* — **sug·ges·tive·ly** *adv.;* **sug·ges·tive·ness** *n.*

su·i·cid·al (soo·uh·SYE·dul) *adj.* **1** leading to suicide; disastrous to oneself: *a suicidal action, character; suicidal behaviour, impulses, tendencies; Drunk driving is suicidal.* **2** having an urge to commit suicide: *a suicidal mental patient, person.*

su·i·cide (SOO·uh·cide) *n.* **1** the act of killing oneself intentionally: *to attempt, contemplate, commit suicide.* **2** one who commits suicide. — **adj.:** *The two killed themselves as the result of a suicide pact; the alarming suicide rate among youth.*

suit (SOOT, long "OO") *n.* **1** a set of outer clothes for wearing together, as a jacket and trousers or skirt: *to try on a suit; a bathing, business, custom-made, diving, gym, leisure, sailor, ski, space, sweat, three-piece suit; a child in his birthday suit* (= naked). **2** a suing or legal action: *to bring (a) suit for damages; to file (a) suit against the government; to contest, dismiss, lose, win a suit; a civil, class-action, malpractice suit.* **3** any of the four sets of playing cards: *a trump suit; her strong suit* (= forte or strong point). **4** an entreaty or pleading, as for someone's love; hence, courtship.
— **follow suit 1** play a card of the same suit as the previous player's. **2** follow the previous example: *The children jumped in the pool and the parents followed suit.*
— *v.* be suitable for a person or thing; fit: *a speech that suits the occasion perfectly; She suits her vocabulary to the children's level; Nine o'clock will suit me fine; It suits me to a T; She is* **suited** (= fit) *for the job; quite suited to be a counsellor;* **Suit yourself** (= Do as you please)!

suit·a·ble (SOO·tuh·bul) *adj.* proper or appropriate: *We found the building eminently suitable for the purpose.* — **suit·a·bly** *adv.* — **suit·a·bil·i·ty** (-BIL·uh·tee) *n.*

suite (SWEET) *n.* 1 a set of rooms forming a unit, as in a hotel: *a bridal, executive, luxury, penthouse suite.* 2 a set of matched furniture: *a bedroom suite; a five-piece dining suite; a living-room suite.* 3 in music, a group of instrumental pieces of varying character with related themes, as Tchaikovsky's "Nutcracker Suite." 4 a group attending on an important person; retinue.

suiting (SOO·ting) *n.* fabric for suits.

suit·or (SOO·tur) *n.* 1 a man who courts a woman. 2 one who makes a petition. 3 one who sues.

sulfur See SULPHUR.

sulk *v.* be sulky: *He's still sulking over his defeat.*
— *n.* a sulky spell: *He's usually in a sulk before breakfast; having the sulks* (= sulky mood).

sulk·y *adj.* sulk·i·er, -i·est moody and ill-humoured: *a sulky refusal, scowl, silence.*
— *n., pl.* sulk·ies a light, two-wheeled horse-racing carriage seating one person.
— sulk·i·ly *adv.*; sulk·i·ness *n.*

sul·len (SUL·un) *adj.* gloomy and silent: *a sullen disposition, resentment, silence; sullen looks, skies.*
— sul·len·ly *adv.*; sul·len·ness *n.*

sul·ly (SULL·ee) *v.* sul·lies, sul·lied, sul·ly·ing soil or defile the purity of something: *to sully one's reputation, character.*

sul·phur or **sul·fur** (SULL·fur) *n.* a pale-yellow substance that burns with a stifling odour.
— sul·phur·ic or sul·fur·ic (sul·FEW·ric) *adj.*

sul·tan (SULL·tun) *n.* a Moslem ruler: *the Sultan of Oman.*

sul·try (SULL·tree) *adj.* -tri·er, -tri·est 1 sweltering; hot and moist: *the sultry days of summer; sultry weather.* 2 passionate or sexy: *a sultry glance, siren.*

sum *n.* 1 an amount of money: *to raise a large sum (of money); a nominal, round, substantial, tidy sum; a lump sum as a severance payment.* 2 the total amount or quantity: *The sum of 4, 5, and 6 is 15; the sum* (= height) *of folly, happiness; the sum and substance* (= gist) *of what he said.* 3 an arithmetical problem: *She's good at (doing) sums.*
— in sum in brief.
— *v.* sums, summed, sum·ming esp. sum up summarize: *To sum up or Summing up, I think UFO's don't exist; to sum up arguments, evidence, opinions, the main points of a speech, views; I summed up his behaviour as sheer folly; It could be summed up* (= briefly expressed) *in one word.*

sum·ma·rize (SUM·uh·rize) *v.* -riz·es, -rized, -riz·ing be or make a summary of something: *to summarize an essay; to summarize your arguments.*

sum·ma·ry (SUM·uh·ree) *n.* -ries a brief statement giving the main points: *the summary of a book, speech.*
— *adj.* 1 brief and comprehensive: *a summary account.* 2 carried out without formalities, delays, etc.; prompt: *a summary action, dismissal, proceeding, trial; A summary offence (that is dealt with quickly) is less serious than an indictable offence.*
— sum·mar·i·ly *adv.*

sum·ma·tion (suh·MAY·shun) *n.* a summing up, as of arguments in a trial.

sum·mer (SUM·ur) *n.* the warmest season of the year: *a long hot summer; Schools close for the summer; Swimming pools are open during the summer.*
— *adj.*: *summer camp, clothes, cottage, festival, holidays, resort, school, season, travel.*
— *v.* spend the summer *in* or *at* a place.
— sum·mer·y *adj.*

summersault same as SOMERSAULT.

sum·mer·time (SUM·ur·time) *n.* the summer season.

sum·mit (SUM·it) *n.* 1 the highest point, level, or state: *to reach the summit of a mountain; We stood at the summit admiring the view; the summit of one's achievement, ambition, career.* 2 a meeting of heads of state: *to hold a summit on disarmament; They met at a summit held in Geneva; an economic summit of Western nations.*

sum·mon (SUM·un) *v.* 1 call formally or with authority, as to appear in court. 2 order an assembly to convene: *The relatives were summoned to the dying man's bedside.* 3 call forth by an act of the will: *to summon (up) courage, energy, strength.* — sum·mon·er *n.*

sum·mons (SUM·unz) *n., pl.* sum·mons·es a summoning, esp. to appear in court on a charge: *A traffic summons for careless driving was served on him; to issue a summons to appear in court; a summons for help.* — *v. Informal.* serve a summons on someone.

sump·tu·ous (SUMP·choo·us) *adj.* lavishly provided or richly furnished: *a sumptuous meal; sumptuous clothes.*
— sump·tu·ous·ly *adv.*

sum total *n.* everything added up.

sun *n.* 1 often **Sun,** the bright heavenly body that rises in the east every day shedding light and heat on the earth; also, the light and heat: *The sun rises, sets, shines; the blazing, bright, hot, midday, tropical sun; adj.: a glass-covered sun parlour, sun porch, or sun room.* 2 anything that is a source of light, warmth, glory, etc. 3 any sunlike star with planets orbiting around it.
— from sun to sun from sunrise to sunset.
— a place in the sun a favourable position in life.
— under the sun (anywhere) in the world.
— *v.* suns, sunned, sun·ning to warm or dry oneself in sunlight: *He lay sunning himself by the pool.*

sun·bath *n.* exposure of the body to sunlight or a "sunlamp" giving off ultraviolet rays.
— sun·bathe (SUN·baith, "th" as in "the") *v.* -bathes, -bathed, -bath·ing.

sun·beam (SUN·beem) *n.* a ray or beam of sunlight.

Sun·belt *n.* the southern third of the U.S. as a region of great growth.

sun·burn *n.* a burning of the skin by overexposure to the sun's rays.
— *v.* -burns, *pt. & pp.* -burned or -burnt, -burn·ing cause to get a sunburn.

sun·dae (SUN·dee, -day) *n.* ice cream with a topping of fruits, nuts, syrup, etc.: *strawberry sundaes.*

Sun·day (SUN·dee, -day) *n.* the first day of the week, the Christian day of rest.

sun·der (SUN·dur) *v.* [literary] put asunder; sever; tear apart.

sun·down *n.* sunset: *at sundown.*

sun·dries (SUN·dreez) *n. pl.* sundry things.

sun·dry (SUN·dree) *adj.* miscellaneous: *sundry articles, folk.* — **all and sundry** everyone.

sung *pp. & a pt.* of SING.

sun·glass·es (SUN·glass·iz) *n. pl.* tinted eyeglasses to protect the eyes from the sun.

sunk *pp. & a pt.* of SINK.

sunk·en *adj.* 1 submerged: *sunken ships, treasures.* 2 below the general level: *a sunken living room; sunken* (= hollow) *cheeks; sunken* (= depressed) *spirits.*

sun·light *n.* the light of the sun: *a shaft of sunlight; bright, glaring sunlight.*

sun·lit *adj.* lighted by the sun.

sun·ny (SUN·ee) *adj.* **sun·ni·er, sun·ni·est** 1 full of sunshine: *a sunny day, room, side, sky.* 2 bright or cheerful: *a sunny disposition, smile; the sunny side* (= the more cheerful aspect) *of life.* — **sunny side up** of eggs, served fried on one side only, with the yolk on top.

sun·rise *n.* (the time of) the sun's coming up above the horizon: *to get up at sunrise.*

sun·set *n.* 1 the sun's going down below the horizon, esp. the light and colour accompanying it: *at sunset.* 2 the end of the day marked by the sunset.

sun·shade *n.* 1 a parasol, awning, etc. used as protection against the sun's rays. 2 **sunshades** *pl. Slang.* sunglasses; shades.

sun·shine *n.* 1 the light and heat from the sun: *to lie on the beach soaking up sunshine; the warm sunshine.* 2 cheerfulness. — **sun·shin·y** (-shy·nee) *adj.*

sun·spot *n.* any of the dark spots appearing occasionally on the sun's surface.

sun·stroke *n.* a heatstroke caused by overexposure to the sun or other source of heat, marked by high fever and a dry skin: *to get, have a sunstroke.*

sun·suit *n.* a play outfit consisting of short pants with shoulder straps and bib front.

sun·tan *n.* a tanning of the skin by exposure to the sun or to ultraviolet rays: *He got his suntan in Florida.*

sun·up *n.* the time of sunrise.

sup *v.* **sups, supped, sup·ping** 1 have supper: *We supped on* or *off soup and crackers.* 2 take sips or spoonfuls of a food. — *n.* a sip or mouthful.

su·per (SOO·pur) *adj.* superior in fineness, excellence, sophistication, or quality: *super clothes for super kids; a super secret.* — *adv.* very: *This is super secret; something super special.* — *n. Informal.* a supervisor or superintendent, as of an apartment building.

super- *prefix.* 1 over or above; hence, superior in rank, quality, degree, etc.: *superagency, superhuman,*

superman, superwoman. 2 extra or added; hence, in excess: *superheat, supersize, supersubtle.*

su·perb (soo·PURB) *adj.* of the highest excellence, magnificence, or splendour: *a superb display, performance, view.* — **su·perb·ly** *adv.*

supercede same as SUPERSEDE.

su·per·charge (SOO·pur·charge) *v.* **-charg·es, -charged, -charg·ing** 1 increase the power of an engine as in racing cars. 2 charge excessively: *to be supercharged with emotion, vigour; the supercharged atmosphere of the trial.*

su·per·con·duc·tiv·i·ty (SOO·pur·con·duc·TIV·uh·tee) *n.* absence of electrical resistance in metals such as lead and tin at temperatures near absolute zero.

su·per·du·per (SOO·pur·DOO·pur) *adj. Slang.* excellent.

su·per·fi·cial (soo·pur·FISH·ul) *adj.* 1 of the surface only: *a superficial burn, wound.* 2 shallow: *a superficial education, knowledge, person.* — **su·per·fi·cial·ly** *adv.* — **su·per·fi·ci·al·i·ty** (SOO·pur·fish·ee·AL·uh·tee) *n.*

su·per·flu·ous (soo·PUR·floo·us) *adj.* surplus or unnecessary: *superfluous advice, complements.* — **su·per·flu·i·ty** (soo·pur·FLOO·uh·tee) *n.* **-ties:** *a superfluity of talent.*

su·per·high·way (soo·pur·HIGH·way) *n.* a freeway with four or more lanes.

su·per·hu·man (soo·pur·HEW·mun) *adj.* exceeding normal human power or capacity: *superhuman efforts, strength; a superhuman* (= spiritual) *being.*

su·per·im·pose (SOO·pur·im·POZE) *v.* **-pos·es, -posed, -pos·ing** lay on top of something else, as different scenes blended on a TV screen.

su·per·in·ten·dent (SOO·pur·in·TEN·dunt) *n.* 1 a custodian or director, as of an educational body: *a school superintendent.* 2 a maintenance supervisor of a building: *a building superintendent.*

su·pe·ri·or (suh·PEER·ee·ur) *adj.* higher in excellence, quality, rank, etc.: *her superior ability, performance; He's far superior to anyone else; a Canadian superior* or *supreme court; a superior force; superior in numbers; Grade A eggs are superior to Grade B eggs; She proved herself superior to* (= above) *petty jealousies; his superior* (= haughty) *manners.* — *n.* 1 a person or thing that is superior. 2 the head of a religious community. — **su·pe·ri·or·i·ty** (-OR·uh·tee) *n.*

su·per·jet (SOO·pur·jet) *n.* a supersonic jet airplane.

su·per·la·tive (soo·PUR·luh·tiv) *adj.* of the highest kind or degree: *superlative praise, wisdom; a superlative adjective such as "best," "wisest," or "most beautiful."* — *n.* one that is superlative or of the highest degree: *He speaks in superlatives* (= exaggerated words) *like "amazing," "astounding," "ideal," and "unique."* — **su·per·la·tive·ly** *adv.*

su·per·mar·ket (SOO·pur·mar·kit) *n.* a large, self-service retail store, esp. one of a chain of food stores.

su·per·nat·u·ral (soo·pur·NACH·ur·ul) *adj.* not explainable by the laws of nature; spiritual or divine: *a*

supernatural being such as an angel or devil.
— **su·per·nat·u·ral·ly** *adv.*

su·per·pow·er (SOO·pur-, *rhyme:* our) *n.* any of the two or three most powerful nations, as U.S.A. and U.S.S.R.: *Japan is an industrial superpower.*

su·per·sede (soo·pur·SEED) *v.* -sedes, -sed·ed, -sed·ing succeed or take the place of something, as being better or more modern: *New laws supersede the old; Has New York superseded Paris as the centre of fashion?*

su·per·son·ic (soo·pur·SON·ic) 1 *adj.* faster than sound: *supersonic flight, speed, transport.* 2 **supersonics** *n.pl.* the science of supersonic phenomena, esp. sound waves.

su·per·star (SOO·pur·star) *n.* an exceptionally successful star in sports or entertainment.

su·per·sti·tion (soo·pur·STISH·un) *n.* a belief or practice considered irrational, as knocking on wood for good luck or believing that spilling salt is a bad omen. — **su·per·sti·tious** (-us) *adj.*

su·per·struc·ture (soo·pur·STRUCK·chur) *n.* 1 a structure built on top of another. 2 the part of a building above its foundation.

su·per·vise (SOO·pur·vize) *v.* -vis·es, -vised, -vis·ing direct or oversee people or what they do: *Teachers supervise students; to supervise a ceremony, class, construction, department; to supervise the care of children, sports, the staff.* — **su·per·vi·sion** (-VIZH·un) *n.*: *He was raised under her strict supervision.* — **su·per·vi·sor** (-vye·zur) *n.* — **su·per·vi·so·ry** (-VYE·zuh·ree) *adj.*

su·pine (soo·PINE) *adj.* flat on the back; hence, passive or lazy: *a supine attitude.*

sup·per (SUP·ur) *n.* an evening meal; the last meal of the day.

sup·plant (suh·PLANT) *v.* replace (as if) by use of force or fraud: *a dictator supplanted by the army; Robots supplant workers.*

sup·ple (SUP·ul) *adj.* easily bending or flexing without damage or strain: *a supple vine; supple as leather; a gymnast's supple limbs; a supple mind, prose style.* — **sup·ple·ness** *n.* — **sup·ply** (SUP·lee) *adv.*

sup·ple·ment (SUP·luh·munt) *n.* an addition that makes something better or fuller: *vitamins added as food supplements; vitamin supplements; Annual supplements update an encyclopedia; a newspaper's advertising, literary, Sunday supplements.* — *v.* (sup·luh·MENT) add to something: *Spare-time jobs supplement his income.* — **sup·ple·men·tal** (-MEN·tul) *adj.* — **sup·ple·men·ta·ry** (-MEN·tuh·ree) *n. & adj.*: *Two supplementary angles make up 180 degrees, each being supplementary to the other; a supplementary question; The Speaker allowed the M.P.s to ask a few supplementaries* (= additional questions).

sup·ply (suh·PLY) *v.* sup·plies, sup·plied, sup·ply·ing give or provide: *to supply food to the hungry; to supply them with food; a need that is not hard to supply* (=satisfy); *Lou likes to supply* (=fill in as a substitute) *in place of absent colleagues.* See also SUPPLE. — *n., pl.* **sup·plies** a supplying or a quantity of a needed item supplied: *the economic forces of supply and demand; The Ministry of Supply and Services in Ottawa handles government purchases; to lay in supplies for the winter; an abundant, fresh, liberal, plentiful supply; relief supplies; Water is in short supply during a drought; office supplies such as stationery; Supply lines were cut by the enemy; the **money supply** (=amount of money) in an economy.* — **sup·pli·er** *n.*

supply teacher *n.* a substitute teacher.

sup·port (suh·PORT) *v.* 1 hold up: *stakes to support a tomato plant.* 2 maintain or provide for something: *Oxygen is required to support life; enough income to support a family of four.* 3 back up: *A seconder supports a motion; a charge not supported by evidence; a star and **supporting** actors (in subsidiary roles).* 4 [used with "can," "cannot"] tolerate in existence; bear or endure: *I cannot support this situation any longer.* — *n.* a supporting, one that supports, or a means of support: *The movement lacked support; demonstrations in support of strikers' demands; The breadwinner is the support of a family; to draw, gain, lend, mobilize, pledge, provide, receive, round up, win support; active, liberal, loyal, qualified, popular, solid, strong, unqualified, wholehearted support of the people.* — **sup·port·a·ble** *adj.* — **sup·port·er** *n.*

sup·port·ive (suh·POR·tiv) *adj.* giving support: *supportive evidence; professional and supportive staff; Parents were supportive of teacher's demands; They were supportive during the negotiations.*

sup·pose (suh·POZE) *v.* sup·pos·es, sup·posed, sup·pos·ing assume; take for granted: *Let's suppose there is life on Mars; Who do you suppose this is? Do creatures suppose a creator? **Supposing** (=assuming) there is life on Mars, so what?* — **sup·po·si·tion** (sup·uh·ZISH·un) *n.*

supposed (suh·POZED) *adj.* assumed or taken for granted: *the supposed injustice; Life on Mars is more supposed than real; You're not **supposed** (=allowed) to smoke here.* — **sup·pos·ed·ly** (-POH·zid·lee) *adv.*

sup·press (suh·PRES) *v.* put down by force; keep under; keep back: *to suppress a newspaper, riot, yawn; to suppress freedom of speech, the truth; consciously to suppress desires, memories, thoughts.* — **sup·pres·sion** (suh·PRESH·un) *n.*

sup·pres·sant (suh·PRES·unt) *n.* one that suppresses: *Codeine is a cough suppressant.*

supra- *prefix.* above; beyond: *supranational, supraorbital, supravital.*

su·pra·na·tion·al (soo·pruh·NASH·uh·nul) *adj.* above the level of individual nations: *Multinational corporations wield supranational power; a supranational corporation, organization.*

su·prem·a·cist (suh·PREM·uh·sist) *n.* one who believes in the supremacy of a specified group: *male supremacists; a white supremacist government, organization.*

su·prem·a·cy (suh·PREM·uh·see) *n.* -cies the state of being supreme; supreme authority: *to achieve, establish supremacy; military, naval supremacy; papal supremacy; state supremacy; to gain supremacy over other nations.*

su·preme (suh·PREEM) *adj.* **1** highest in authority or power: *The will of the people should be supreme* or **reign supreme** *in a democracy; NATO's Supreme Allied Commander in Europe; God as **Supreme Being**; a provincial **supreme court**; the **Supreme Court** of Canada; the **Supreme Soviet** of the U.S.S.R.* **2** highest in degree or quality: *supreme courage, effort, happiness; He lives in supreme ignorance of what's going on around him; the supreme moment of his life when he got married; the supreme sacrifice (of one's life).* — **su·preme·ly** *adv.;* **su·preme·ness** *n.*

sur- *prefix.* **1** over or above: *surcharge, surname.* **2** under; beneath: *surreptitious, surrogate.*

sur·charge (SUR·charge) *v.* **-charg·es, -charged, -charg·ing 1** overburden *with* a feeling. **2** charge extra: *The airlines surcharged regular fares to cover rising fuel costs.* **3** overprint with an extra charge: *to surcharge a postage stamp.*
— *n.* **1** an extra charge: *A surcharge is added to the subscription for home delivery; a stamp bearing a surcharge of 10 cents.* **2** an excessive burden *of* grief, etc.

sure (SHOOR) *adj.* **sur·er, sur·est 1** free from doubt: *Are you sure about the time? He is sure the watch is accurate; Please make sure of your facts; Make sure you have them right; She is sure* (= bound) *to succeed.* **2** reliable or unerring: *A smoking pistol is sure evidence of firing; a good sharpshooter with a sure aim; a sure remedy.* — *adv. Informal.* surely.
— **for sure** without doubt: *That's for sure.*
— **sure enough** *Informal.* in fact; certainly.
— **to be sure** surely. — **sure·ness** *n.*

sure-fire *adj. Informal.* sure to succeed; definite: *a sure-fire prospect as a winner; a sure-fire bestseller, success, win, winner; a sure-fire way of making money.*

sure-footed (SHOOR·foot·id) *adj.* not likely to stumble or err.

sure·ly *adv.* certainly: *Surely you have a better idea; Surely!*

sure·ty (SHOOR·uh·tee) *n.* **-ties 1** security or assurance *against* loss, failure, etc. **2** one legally responsible for another's performance according to an agreement or obligation, as guaranteed by a bond.

surf *n.* **1** waves of the sea breaking on the shore. **2** the foam and thundering sound produced.
— *v.* ride the waves on a surfboard in the sport of **surf·ing.** — **surf·er** *n.*

sur·face (SUR·fis) *n.* the outside of anything, as any of the faces of a solid figure, the top of a liquid, etc.: *the smooth surface of ice; the plane surface of a tabletop; the frozen surface of the lake; the rough surface of a stormy sea; below, beneath, under the surface of the ocean; You have only scratched the surface of* (= begun to understand) *the subject; The essay only skims the surface of the topic* (= treats it superficially); *He's gentle* **on the surface** *but can turn violent if provoked.*
— *adj.* **1** of or by the surface: *surface mail (by land or water); surface transit; a surface-to-air missile.* **2** external: *a surface impression; mere surface* (= superficial) *friendships.*
— *v.* **-fac·es, -faced, -fac·ing 1** provide with a smooth surface: *to surface a road.* **2** rise to the surface of the

water, as a submarine.

surf·board *n.* a long, narrow, light-weight board used to ride on in the sport of surfing.

sur·feit (SUR·fit) *n.* **1** an excess of anything good, esp. food or drink. **2** the feeling of nausea resulting from such an excess.
— *v.* feed or fill too much: *surfeited with food, riches.*

surge (SURJ) *v.* **surg·es, surged, surg·ing** move powerfully and suddenly in or like a swelling wave: *the surging flood waters; The crowd surged forward; House prices are surging ahead.*
— *n.* a rushing wave or its onrush: *the surge of the sea; the surge of passion; The surge of power during the storm blew a fuse.*

sur·geon (SUR·jun) *n.* a physician specialized in surgery.

sur·ger·y (SUR·juh·ree) *n.* **-ger·ies 1** the branch of medicine dealing with operations performed on the body to treat disease, injuries, and deformities. **2** a surgeon's work or a place where operations are done.
— **sur·gi·cal** (-cul) *adj.;* **sur·gi·cal·ly** *adv.*

sur·ly (SUR·lee) *adj.* **-li·er, -li·est** ill-tempered or rude.
— **sur·li·ness** *n.*

sur·mise (sur·MIZE) *n. & v.* **-mis·es, -mised, -mis·ing** guess or conjecture.

sur·mount (sur·MOUNT) *v.* **1** be or rise above: *a church spire surmounted by a cross.* **2** get over; hence, overcome difficulties. — **sur·mount·a·ble** (-uh·bul) *adj.*

sur·name (SUR·name) *n.* a person's last name or family name.

sur·pass (sur·PASS) *v.* go beyond or be superior to someone in some quality: *None surpassed Samson in strength; This surpasses* (= defies) *description.*

sur·plus (SUR·plus) *n.* **1** a quantity or amount left over after meeting needs: *farm surpluses of crops and livestock; grain surplus.* **2** excess of assets over debts: *The trade surplus is a surplus of exports over imports; In the 1980s, Canada had an overall surplus in trade with the U.S.*
— *adj.: surplus capacity, electricity, funds, milk; a surplus* (= not deficit) *budget.*

sur·prise (sur·PRIZE) *v.* **-pris·es, -prised, -pris·ing** come upon suddenly and unexpectedly: *He was surprised in the act of stealing; Your behaviour surprises* (= astonishes) *me; They were surprised* (= attacked when off guard) *by enemy troops.*

— **n.** the act or feeling of being surprised: *She sprang a surprise on us; Everyone expressed surprise at the news; It was a complete, total surprise to us; a pleasant surprise to learn that he was getting married; To our surprise, no one had been told; The news was quite a surprise* (= something unexpected); *It **took** us all **by** surprise* (= caught us unprepared).
— **sur·pris·ing·ly** *adv.*

sur·ren·der (suh·REN·dur) *v.* give up a possession or right to something: *The enemy has surrendered; to surrender a fort to the enemy; He refused to surrender (himself) to the police; She surrendered her insurance policy for its cash value.*
— **n.** a surrendering: *an unconditional surrender.*

sur·rep·ti·tious (suh·rep·TISH·us) *adj.* accomplished in a secret or stealthy manner: *surreptitious entry through a window; a surreptitious glance;* **sur·rep·ti·tious·ly** *adv.*

sur·ro·gate (SUR·uh·gate, -git) *n.* **1** a substitute or deputy: *He acts as the surrogate of the prime minister.* **2** a probate court judge.
— **adj.** substitute: *a **surrogate mother** (who acts as mother for a childless couple by carrying their child to term); a surrogate parent.*

sur·round (suh·ROUND) *v.* encircle or cause to be encircled: *Police surrounded the house; He lives surrounded by luxuries; She surrounds herself with admirers.*

sur·round·ings (suh·ROUND·ingz) *n. pl.* things that surround; environment: *He lives in austere surroundings; the elegant surroundings of a mansion.*

sur·tax *n.* an extra tax on something already taxed, as on incomes above a certain level.

sur·veil·lance (sur·VAY·lunce) *n.* close watch kept over someone: *The police have placed him **under surveillance** as a suspect in the murder; to maintain around-the-clock, close, constant, strict surveillance over a suspect.*

sur·vey (sur·VAY) *v.* look over or examine as a whole, as a tract of land using geometrical principles.
— **n.** (SUR·vay) a broad overall study or examination, as in surveying a tract of land, field of study, public opinion on a subject, a situation, etc.: *to conduct, do, make a survey; an aerial, brief, comprehensive, general survey.* — **sur·vey·or** *n.*

sur·vi·val (sur·VYE·vul) *n.* a surviving or something that has survived: *steps to assure the survival of the species; Some customs are survivals from ancient times; the **survival of the fittest** in the process of evolution; adj.: a **survival kit** containing food and emergency equipment.*

sur·vive (sur·VIVE) *v.* **-vives, -vived, -viv·ing** continue in existence after a person or thing; outlive or outlast: *Children normally survive their parents; None survived (the disaster).* — **sur·vi·vor** (-vur) *n.*

sus·cep·ti·ble (suh·SEP·tuh·bul) *adj.* easily acted on or influenced: *Wax is susceptible of impressions; a susceptible young girl; inexperienced youth **susceptible to** the temptations of a big city.*
— **sus·cep·ti·bil·i·ty** (-BIL·uh·tee) *n.* **-ties.**

sus·pect (suh·SPECT) *v.* **1** believe something negative about someone without proof: *She suspects he's cheating; suspects him strongly of cheating; suspects cheating; He is suspected of cheating her; He's suspected as a cheater.* **2** *Informal.* suppose or assume: *She has more brains than he suspected; I suspect you're right.* **3** doubt or distrust: *She suspected the truth of his stories; suspected his truthfulness.*
— **n.** (SUS·pect) one that is suspected, as of a crime: *a prime suspect in the murder case; to arrest, interrogate, question a suspect; a lineup of suspects; **adj.:** His reasons are suspect* (= regarded with suspicion).

sus·pend (suh·SPEND) *v.* **1** hang (as if) from a support: *Chandeliers are suspended from ceilings; There are dust particles suspended in the air.* **2** stop an activity or operation for a time: *Work was suspended in protest; to suspend judgment, payments, rules; a body in **suspended animation** without vital signs, as in drowning, trances, etc.* **3** remove for a while from duties or privileges: *He was suspended (from duty) without pay pending an investigation; He was judged guilty and given a **suspended sentence*** (= prison term that need not be served as long as the criminal behaves).

sus·pen·ders (suh·SPEN·durz) *n. pl.* a pair of shoulder straps to hold up trousers.

sus·pense (suh·SPENCE) *n.* a state of uncertainty or anxiety about an outcome: *a story full of suspense; It keeps you in suspense till the end; Everyone is in suspense over what will happen next;* **sus·pense·ful** *adj.*

sus·pen·sion (suh·SPEN·shun) *n.* **1** an act of suspending, the state of being suspended, or a suspending device: *A **suspension bridge** hangs from cables supported by towers on either end.* **2** a mixture such as milk or smoke in which particles are suspended or dispersed without being dissolved.

sus·pi·cion (suh·SPISH·un) *n.* **1** a suspecting or being suspected: *to arouse, cause, create, sow suspicion in the minds of people; to cast suspicion on his motives; to allay, dispel suspicion; a groundless, lingering, lurking, strong, vague suspicion about his actions; The suspicion seemed to fall on him; Later events confirmed our suspicions; Not everyone is **above suspicion*** (= free of suspicion); *A cloud of suspicion hangs over some; Some people are under suspicion; a mind full of suspicion; One is arrested **on suspicion** of murder.* **2** a slight trace or soupçon: *There's not even the slightest suspicion of dishonesty about her.*

sus·pi·cious (suh·SPISH·us) *adj.* arousing, showing, or feeling suspicion: *He is suspicious about or of people's motives; suspicious behaviour.* — **sus·pi·cious·ly** *adv.*

sus·tain (suh·STAIN) *v.* **1** support actively so as to keep from failing: *The arch is strong enough to sustain any weight; an atmosphere too rare to sustain life; "Objection sustained* (= upheld) *," declared the judge; The driver made a **sustained** (= continuous) effort to stay awake.* **2** suffer or endure: *wounds sustained in battle; He sustained great losses in the fire.*

sus·te·nance (SUS·tuh·nunce) *n.* **1** nourishment or food to sustain life. **2** a means of livelihood.

su·ture (SOO·chur) *n.* a joining together, as by sewing: *the zigzag sutures of the skull bones; Surgical incisions are closed by means of sutures* (= stitches); *The sutures (of gut, silk, or wire) are taken out as the wound heals.*

svelte (SVELT) *adj.* **svelt·er, svelt·est 1** suave.
2 slender or lithe: *slim and svelte; her svelte good looks; He's a svelte 150 pounds (68 kg).*

swab (SWOB) *n.* **1** a cleaning mop. **2** a bit of cotton or other absorbent material at the end of a stick for removing discharged matter from or for applying medicine to a body part. **3** *Slang.* a sailor; gob; also, a lout.
— *v.* **swabs, swabbed, swab·bing** use a swab on something: *to swab the deck of a ship.*

swad·dle (SWOD·ul) *v.* **swad·dles, swad·dled, swad·dling** bind or wrap a newborn baby in long, narrow strips of cloth, or **swaddling clothes.**

swag *n.* **1** a festoon or garland hung in a curve, esp. such a decorative design. **2** *Slang.* loot or stolen goods.

swag·ger (SWAG·ur) *n.* a superior or insolent manner: *the swagger of a conceited fellow; a checked shirt with its frankly male swagger.*
— *v.* walk with a swagger: *He swaggers around like a hotshot.*

swal·low (SWOL·oh) *v.* **1** take from the mouth into the stomach, as food. **2** accept or take in like swallowed food: *so gullible he'll swallow any story; to swallow an insult without protesting; a body swallowed up by (= lost in) the waves.* **3** take back or suppress: *It hurt his pride to swallow his words; He had to swallow his pride and apologize.*
— *n.* **1** a swallowing or the amount swallowed at one time: *He ate the whole thing in one swallow; He took only one swallow of the medicine.* **2** a small, insect-eating bird with powerful wings and a forked tail.

swal·low·tail (SWOL·oh·tail) *n.* a tailcoat.
— **swal·low·tailed** *adj.*

swam *pt.* of SWIM.

swamp (SWOMP) *n.* a tract of low-lying marshy land; *adj.*: *swamp gas, rabbits.*
— *v.* **1** sink in as in a swamp. **2** overwhelm or deluge: *The heavy seas swamped our boat; a switchboard swamped with phone calls; to be swamped by backlogs, debts, homework.* — **swamp·y** *adj.*

swan (SWON, SWAUN) *n.* a graceful, long-necked, usually snow-white water bird related to the geese.

swank (rhyme: "bank") *n. Informal.* dash or style; also, swagger.
— *adj.* stylish in a showy manner; dashing; also **swank·y, swank·i·er, swank·i·est.** — *v.* swagger.

swan song *n.* a person's final speech or performance, like the fabled swan's dying song.

swap (SWOP, SWAUP) *v. & n.* **swaps, swapped, swap·ping** *Informal.* exchange or barter: *They swapped seats so she could have a better view; swapped his orange for her apple; He made a swap for her apple.*
— **swap·per** *n.*

sward (SWORD) *n.* grassy surface; turf.

swarm (SWORM) *n.* **1** a large group of honeybees flying away to form a new colony; also, a settled colony of bees. **2** a large dense crowd or throng: *a swarm of school children.*
— *v.* **1** of bees, migrate in a swarm. **2** fly about or be present in large numbers: *Shoppers swarmed into the store; They swarmed around the movie star; Tourists swarmed through the streets; a place **swarming** with (= full of) mosquitoes.*

swarth·y (SWOR·thee) *adj.* **swarth·i·er, -i·est** dark-complexioned.

swash (SWOSH) *v.* dash or splash water, etc.
— *n.* the sound or action of water washing over something.

swash·buck·ler (SWOSH·buck·lur) *n.* a swaggering soldier or bully. — **swash·buck·ling** *adj.*

swat (SWOT) *n. Informal.* a quick, sharp blow: *a swat team of commandos.*
— *v.* **swats, swat·ted, swat·ting** *Informal.* hit with a swat: *to swat a fly.* — **swat·ter** *n.*

swatch (SWOCH) *n.* a sample piece of cloth: *a swatch book of suitings.*

swath (SWOTH, SWAUTH, "TH" as in "thin") *n.* **1** space cleared by one passage of a mower or cut of a scythe: *The tornado cut a wide swath of destruction through the town.* **2** the row of grass or grain left cut.

swathe (SWAITH, "TH" as in "the") *v.* **swathes, swathed, swath·ing** wrap up in a long strip or bandage: *He came to the door swathed in a bath towel; a lady swathed in fur; The hills were swathed (= enveloped) in mist.*

sway *v.* swing sideways from an upright position: *tall grasses swaying in the wind; They swayed to the rhythm of the music; She would not be swayed (= influenced) by her feelings, by their arguments.*
— *n.* **1** a swaying. **2** control or dominance: *under the sway of Rome; when Rome held sway over Europe.*

swear (SWARE) *v.* **swears, swore, sworn, swear·ing 1** declare, promise, etc. solemnly, calling God to witness; take an oath: *Witnesses swear to tell the truth; They **swear by** or **on** the Bible; She speaks good English and swears by her dictionary (= relies on it); I can **swear to** that (= confirm it); A judge **swears in** public officials (to their offices); They are sworn (= solemnly bound) to secrecy on matters of state security; They swear allegiance to the Crown; She was sworn in as Minister of Education.* **2** curse; utter an oath: *Lu swears at people when angry; Sam never swears.*
— **swear off** renounce or give up: *He decided to swear off smoking as it was affecting his health.*
— **swear out** get an arrest warrant by swearing that what is charged is true.

swear·word (SWARE·wurd) *n.* a word or phrase used in cursing; an oath or obscenity.

sweat (SWET) *n.* **1** moisture formed on the skin, esp. after strenuous exercise; perspiration: *She got her doctorate by the sweat of her brow (= by hard work); All the sweat (= drudgery) you pour into writing a book is lost if it doesn't sell.* **2** anything resembling perspiration, as moisture condensed on a cold surface. **3** a state or spell of sweating induced by fear, anxiety, etc.: *He found the frightened child in a cold sweat; The crew was in a sweat (Informal for impatient) for the plane to take off.*

— **v. sweats**, *pt. & pp.* **sweat** or **sweat·ed**, **sweat·ing** perspire: *You sweat freely in a sauna bath; Cold water pipes sweat on a hot and humid day; Hides, tobacco leaves, etc. are sweated in being processed; She sweat blood* (= worked like a slave) *to write that book; The passengers had to **sweat it out*** (*Informal for* wait anxiously) *until help arrived.*

sweat·er (SWET·ur) *n.* a knitted or crocheted pullover or jacket.

sweat shirt *n.* a loose pullover of heavy cotton jersey.

sweat·shop (SWET·shop) *n.* a place of work characterized by low pay, long hours, etc.

sweat·y (SWET·ee) *adj.* **sweat·i·er**, **-i·est** sweating or causing sweat.

sweep *v.* **sweeps**, **swept**, **sweep·ing** pass swiftly and smoothly over something: *A wind sweeps over a meadow; fingers sweeping the keys of a piano; to sweep* (= clean) *the floor with a broom; Let's sweep the floor clean; Don't sweep it* (= Don't hide the sweepings) *under the rug; Long skirts sweep the ground; She swept out of the room (with dignity); A hurricane swept down on the town; The flood waters swept away the bridge; Excitement swept the nation on election day; The Liberals swept into office; Our team swept the series* (= won every game); *The highway sweeps* (= stretches without a break) *along the coast.*
— *n.* **1** a sweeping: *Give the floor a good sweep; He was arrested during a police sweep of the area; She made a clean sweep* (= capture) *of all the prizes; the sweep of the highway around the hill; a lovely sweep* (= stretch) *of meadow; stars beyond the sweep* (= range) *of our telescopes.* **2** one who cleans chimneys, or "chimney sweep." — **sweep·er** *n.*

sweeping *adj.* **1** covering a wide area: *a sweeping glance; sweeping* (= extensive) *changes, plans, reforms.* **2** having a general effect: *a sweeping victory; a sweeping* (= too general) *generalization, statement.*
— **sweepings** *n.pl.* things swept up from a floor.

sweep·stakes *n. sing. & pl.* a lottery or horse race in which the participants put up the money that is divided as prizes: *to win the sweepstakes.* Also **sweep·stake.**

sweet *adj.* **1** like sugar in taste; hence, agreeable or pleasing: *as sweet as honey; Roses smell sweet; the sweet smell of success; sweet music, praise, smiles, temper; a sweet little child; whispering sweet nothings in her ear.* **2** not sour: *sweet milk, soil; sweet* (= fresh) *butter.*
— *n.* **1** one that is sweet, as a darling. **2** *Brit.* dessert. **3** *Brit.* **sweets** *pl.* sweet things, esp. candy.
— **sweet·ly** *adv.*; **sweet·ness** *n.*

sweet·en *v.* make sweet or pleasant: *a bonus offered to sweeten the pot* (= make the offer more attractive).

sweet·heart *n.* a loved one; darling.

sweetheart deal or **agreement** or **contract** *n.* a secret deal made with the opposite party for selfish reasons, as when a labour leader deals secretly with an employer.

sweet·meat *n.* a candy.

sweet potato *n.* a thick, fleshy, sweet yellow or reddish vegetable that is the root of a climbing plant.

sweet-talk *v. Informal.* flatter or coax; cajole. Also *n.*

sweet tooth *n. Informal.* fondness for sweet foods.

swell *v.* **swells**, *pt.* **swelled**, *pp.* **swelled** or **swol·len** (SWOH·lun), **swell·ing** grow or make bigger than normal in volume, size, etc., as because of pressure from within; (cause to) bulge out: *a swollen ankle; A wind swells the sails; a river swollen by rains; New members have swelled our ranks; He's swelling* (= filled) *with pride.*
— *n.* **1** something swollen, as a rounded hill or a large, rising wave. **2** a swelling sound, as of the organ. **3** a device to control sound volume, as in an organ. **4** *Informal.* a stylish or fashionable person.
— *adj.* **1** *Informal.* stylish; fashionable. **2** *Slang.* excellent: *a swell guy; We had a swell time.*

swelled head *n. Informal.* self-conceit.

swell·head *n.* a conceited person; **swell·head·ed** *adj.*

swelling *n.* **1** a swollen part of the body. **2** a swollen condition or increase in size: *A swelling goes down, subsides.*

swel·ter (SWEL·tur) *v.* be oppressed by heat: *We sweltered for three days in an overheated room; in the **sweltering*** (= oppressively hot) *hotel room.*

swept *pt. & pp.* of SWEEP.

swerve (SWURV) *v.* **swerves**, **swerved**, **swerv·ing** turn aside from the direction of motion or from a course of action: *to swerve from the path of virtue; The jet swerved off the runway when attempting to land; If a car swerves to the right when you apply the brakes, its front end needs aligning.* — *n.* a swerving.

swift *adj.* fast or rapid, esp. in a smooth and easy manner: *a swift pace; a swift-footed messenger; He is swift of foot; He's swift to anger; They were swift to retaliate; a swift flight, reaction, transition.*
— *n.* a swallowlike swift-flying bird.
— **swift·ly** *adv.*; **swift·ness** *n.*

swig *n. Informal.* a deep draft, esp. of liquor: *He took a swig from the flask.*
— *v.* **swigs**, **swigged**, **swig·ging** take deep drafts of a drink: *We ate salted peanuts and swigged Coke at the party.*

swill *n.* kitchen refuse mixed with liquids, as fed to pigs; slops.
— *v.* **1** feed pigs on swill. **2** guzzle or drink greedily.

swim *v.* **swims**, **swam**, **swum**, **swim·ming** **1** move through water using one's limbs, fins, or tail: *Animals swim instinctively; You either sink or swim; She can swim the length of the pool; the sport of **swimming**; They have a portable, above-ground, backyard **swimming pool** besides an in-ground one indoors.* **2** move or be in a condition like swimming: *eyes swimming with tears; He said his head was swimming* (= whirling) *when he fainted.*
— *n.* an act or period of swimming: *to go for a swim; have, take a swim in the river.*
— **in the swim** involved with what is going on around one. — **swim·mer** *n.*

swin·dle (SWIN·dul) *v.* **-dles**, **-dled**, **-dling** cheat a trusting person of money or property: *a naive customer swindled out of his savings.*
— *n.* a swindling; fraudulent scheme. — **swin·dler** *n.*

swine *n. sing. & pl.* **1** a pig. **2** a person considered contemptible or disgusting. — **swin·ish** (SWY-) *adj.*

swing *v.* **swings, swung, swing·ing 1** hang or move to and fro like a pendulum: *People swing their arms while walking; a hammock swung* (= hung) *between trees.* **2** move in a curve with force and freedom: *Tarzan swings from tree to tree; The batter swung his bat at the ball but missed it; The gate swung open; to swing* (*Informal for* successfully conclude) *a business deal, election; Music that swings* (has a lively, relaxed jazz beat). **3** *Slang.* to be free and uninhibited in pursuing pleasure, following the latest in fashions and ways of life.
— *n.* **1** a swinging or its manner or amount: *the swing of a pendulum; There was a swing* (= shift) *to the Right during the last elections.* **2** a swinging blow, gait, rhythm, etc.: *She took a swing* (= aimed a punch) *at him.* **3** activity or progress: *Classes are in full swing* (= fully active) *within days of reopening.* **4** a trip or tour: *a swing through Europe.* **5** jazz music with a happy, relaxed beat and freedom to improvise, as played by big bands in the 1930s and 1940s. **6** *Cdn.* in the North, a train of sleighs or canoes carrying freight; also, a cat-train.

swing·er *n.* **1** one that swings. **2** *Slang.* one who moves with the times and changing fashions. **3** *Slang.* one who is uninhibited in his social life, esp. in sexual behaviour.

swinging *adj.* lively and up to date: *Hull is not dull but swinging with its discos, nightclubs, and restaurants.*

swing shift *n. Informal.* the work shift between the day and night shifts, usually from 4 p.m. to midnight.

swipe *n. Informal.* a strong, sweeping blow.
— *v.* **swipes, swiped, swip·ing 1** hit with a sweeping stroke. **2** *Slang.* pilfer, as by snatching.

swirl *v.* whirl or eddy: *Rumours swirled around Ottawa.*
— *n.* something swirled or swirling; also, a curl or whorl: *the swirl on an ice-cream cone; He resigned amid a swirl of controversy over his private life.* — **swirl·y** *adj.*

swish *v.* (cause) to move with a light hissing or brushing sound, as of a whip cutting the air or of a silk skirt in motion.
— *n.* a swishing movement or sound.
— *adj. Slang.* posh or swanky: *in a swish district of the city.*

switch *n.* **1** a device for controlling a connection: *to flick, throw a switch for turning on the current; Trains change tracks by means of a railway switch consisting of short movable rails; The watchman was asleep at the switch* (= sleeping on the job). **2** change or shift: *We made a last-minute switch in plans.* **3** a slender rod made from a flexible twig to use for whipping. **4** a lash or stroke. **5** a tress of detached or false hair worn as part of a hairdo.
— *v.* **1** turn a light *off* or *on*. **2** shift a train to a different track. **3** shift or change: *to switch plans, positions, topics, hats; We switch to daylight-saving time in April.* **4** strike with or as with a switch; jerk or swing sharply: *A horse switches its tail to drive away flies.*
— **switch·er** *n.*

switch·board *n.* a panel controlling a system of electric circuits, as in a telephone exchange: *He works at the hotel switchboard.*

swiv·el (SWIV·ul) *n.* a coupling device that allows free turning of one part on another, as used in a **swivel chair** with rotating seat.
— *v.* **-els, -elled** or **-eled, -el·ling** or **-el·ing** turn or cause to turn as on a swivel; hence, swing around: *All heads swivelled toward the heckler at the back of the room.*

swob *n. & v.* **swobs, swobbed, swob·bing** same as SWAB.

swol·len a *pp.* of SWELL.
— *adj.* bulging or blown up.

swoon *v.* lose consciousness; faint: *They swooned over the rock singer; Everyone was swooning with ecstasy.* Also *n.*

swoop *n.* a sweeping down or swift descent, as of a hawk seizing its prey: *at one fell swoop* (= at one stroke).
— *v.* **1** make a swift attack: *Commandos swooped down on the hijackers.* **2** seize swiftly: *We swooped her up and rushed to hospital.*

sword (SORD) *n.* a metal weapon consisting of a long blade set in a hilt: *Revenge is a double-edged sword; to draw swords* (= prepare to fight).
— **cross swords** come into conflict *with* someone.
— **put to the sword** kill someone with a sword.

sword of Damocles (-DAM·uh·cleez) *n.* imminent danger, like a sword hung by a hair over the head of Damocles of Greek myth.

sword·play *n.* **1** the art or skill of using a sword. **2** fighting with swords.

swords·man (SORDZ·mun) *n.* **-men 1** one skilled in the use of a sword. **2** one using a sword in fencing, fighting, etc.

swore *pt.* of SWEAR.

sworn *pp.* of SWEAR.
— *adj.* bound by or promised with an oath: *The two are sworn enemies; sworn evidence given by witnesses in court; We are sworn to secrecy on this matter.*

swum *pp.* of SWIM.

swung *pp.* of SWING.

syl·la·ble (SIL·uh·bul) *n.* a part of a word pronounced as an uninterrupted unit, usually consisting of a vowel with or without consonants: *"Syllable" has three syllables in it; He didn't utter a syllable* (= said nothing) *during the whole meeting.*

syl·van (SIL·vun) *adj.* having to do with the woods; wooded: *sylvan glades, surroundings; a sylvan landscape, retreat, setting.*

sym·bol (SIM·bul) *n.* a letter, sign, or object that represents an idea or quality by natural association or by convention, as H (hydrogen), the six-pointed star (Judaism), and the dove (peace): *a religious symbol such as the cross; Our national symbol the maple leaf is also an official emblem; A Cadillac is the status symbol for some.* — **sym·bol·ic** (sim·BOL·ic) or **sym·bol·i·cal** *adj.* — **sym·bol·i·cal·ly** *adv.*

sym·bol·ism (SIM·bul·iz·um) *n.* symbolic representation, symbolic meaning, or a system of symbols.

sym·bol·ize (SIM·bul·ize) *v.* -iz·es, -ized, -iz·ing
represent by symbols or stand as a symbol of something:
*The hammer-and-sickle Soviet emblem symbolizes the
labourer and the farmer.*
— **sym·bol·i·za·tion** (-luh·ZAY·shun) *n.*

sym·me·try (SIM·uh·tree) *n.* -tries correspondence of
opposite parts in regard to size, shape, and position;
also, a pleasing balance of form resulting from this: *The
human body has symmetry; A potato lacks symmetry.*
— **sym·met·ri·cal** (suh·MET·ruh·cul) *adj.*
— **sym·met·ri·cal·ly** *adv.*

sym·pa·thet·ic (sim·puh·THET·ic, "TH" as in "thin")
adj. 1 agreeing or agreeable; in harmony with: *a
sympathetic response, role, shrug, smile; his sympathetic
support; a kind and sympathetic police officer; to be
sympathetic to an idea, to the needs of the poor, to a
reform movement.* 2 of sounds and vibrations, produced
in one body by transmission in the same frequency from
another body: *words that **strike a sympathetic chord** in
the reader.* — **sym·pa·thet·i·cal·ly** *adv.*

sym·pa·thize (SIM·puh·thize) *v.* -thiz·es, -thized,
-thiz·ing feel or show sympathy in feeling or thought: *I
sympathize with you in your suffering; I don't
sympathize (= agree) with your aims;* **sym·pa·thiz·er** *n.*

sym·pa·thy (SIM·puh·thee) *n.* -thies 1 understanding
and sharing of another's feelings; compassion: *Children
turn to their parents for sympathy; to arouse, display,
express, feel, have, show sympathy for a person or
subject; to lavish sympathy on someone; a situation that
commands, captures sympathy; to accept someone's
sympathy; Our deep, great, heartfelt, profound, strong
sympathy goes out to the bereaved family; a gift as a
token of our sympathy; We are doing this out of
sympathy for the cause.* 2 agreement and support: *to be
in sympathy with a person, a person's aims, views, a
plan, proposal, etc.; One union strikes in sympathy with
another; a sympathy strike.*

sym·pho·ny (SIM·fuh·nee) *n.* -nies 1 an elaborate
musical composition for an orchestra, usually in sonata
form. 2 a large orchestra that plays symphonies; also
symphony orchestra. 3 a symphony-orchestra concert.
— **sym·phon·ic** (sim·FON·ic) *adj.*

sym·po·si·um (sim·POH·zee·um) *n.* -si·ums or -si·a
(-see·uh) 1 a conference to discuss a given subject. 2 a
collection of opinions or essays on a subject.

symp·tom (SIMP·tum) *n.* 1 a change in a body organ or
function, as a rash or headache, that indicates a disease:
a patient showing symptoms of the flu. 2 a sign or
indication of a disorder: *Constant fighting is one of the
early symptoms of a marriage breakup.*
— **symp·to·mat·ic** (-tuh·MAT·ic) *adj.*

syn·a·gogue (SIN·uh·gog) *n.* a Jewish congregation or
its place of worship.

sync (SINK) *n. Informal.* synchronization, as of lip
movements with the speech sounds in a movie: *Your
watch seems a couple of minutes **out of sync** with the
local time; to be **in sync** (= in tune) with the times.*
— *v.* synchronize; agree or make agree: *This doesn't
sync (= agree) with what you said a while ago.*
Also **synch.**

syn·chro·nize (SINK·ruh·nize) *v.* -niz·es, -nized,

-niz·ing agree or make agree in time or rate: *Watches
tell the same time when synchronized; In dubbing
movies, voices are synchronized with their lip
movements.* — **syn·chro·ni·za·tion** (-nuh·ZAY·shun) *n.*

syn·chro·nous (SINK·ruh·nus) *adj.* same as
GEOSTATIONARY: *A satellite in a synchronous orbit acts
as a fixed relay station.*

syn·di·cate (SIN·di·cut) *n.* 1 a group of organized
gangsters. 2 an agency selling the same articles,
pictures, etc. to many periodicals. 3 a joint selling
venture or agency, as of the members of a cartel.
— *v.* (-cate) -cates, -cat·ed, -cat·ing form into or sell
through a syndicate: *a syndicated cartoon strip, column,
columnist.* — **syn·di·ca·tor** (-cay·tur) *n.*
— **syn·di·ca·tion** (-CAY·shun) *n.*

syn·drome (SIN·drome, -drum) *n.* the combination or
pattern of a number of symptoms occurring together
that is characteristic of an ailment or abnormality: *a
drug withdrawal syndrome; the sudden infant death
syndrome or "crib death."*

syn·er·gy (SIN·ur·jee) *n.* the combined effect of
different agents working together that is greater than
the sum of their separate effects: *the synergy between
parents and teachers; the corporate synergy developed
by the merger of two companies;* also **syn·er·gism** *n.*
— **syn·er·gis·tic** (-JIS·tic) *adj.: synergistic effects,
growth, relationships.*

syn·fu·el (SIN·few·ul) *n.* a synthetic liquid fuel made
from coal, oil shale, tar sands, etc.

syn·o·nym (SIN·uh·nim) *n.* a word with nearly the same
meaning as another in one or more senses: *"Hit" is a
synonym of "strike."*
— **syn·on·y·mous** (suh·NON·uh·mus) *adj.: "Speed" and
"success" are not synonymous; But some people think
life in the fast lane is synonymous with success.*

syn·op·sis (suh·NOP·sis) *n., pl.* -ses (-seez) a summary
or outline of a story, treatise, etc.: *to give, make,
prepare a synopsis.*

syn·tax (SIN·tax) *n.* the arrangement of words in
phrases, clauses, and sentences.
— **syn·tac·tic** (sin·TAC·tic) or **syn·tac·ti·cal** *adj.*

syn·the·sis (SIN·thuh·sis) *n.* -ses (-seez) the combining
of parts into a whole: *the synthesis of ideas (into a
philosophy), of races (into a nation), of elements (into a
compound): to make a synthesis of modern thought.*
— **syn·the·size** *v.* -siz·es, -sized, -siz·ing.
— **syn·the·siz·er** *n.*

syn·thet·ic (sin·THET·ic) *adj.* 1 having to do with
synthesis; not analytic: *a synthetic mind; synthetic
religions; synthetic chemistry, languages.* 2 having to do
with chemical combination: *synthetic blends, blood,
drugs, dyes, fuels, synthetic crude from oil sands.*
3 artificial, not natural: *synthetic diamonds, fibre,
rubber, turf; a synthetic smile.* — **syn·thet·i·cal·ly** *adv.*

syn·thet·ics (sin·THET·ics) *n.pl.* materials such as
plastics and artificial fibres made by chemical synthesis.

sy·phon (SYE·fun) same as SIPHON.

sy·ringe (suh·RINJ, SEER·inj) *n.* a device consisting of a narrow tube or needle equipped with a rubber bulb or piston for injecting fluids into the body, for cleansing wounds, etc.
— *v.* **-ring·es, -ringed, -ring·ing** inject or cleanse with a syringe.

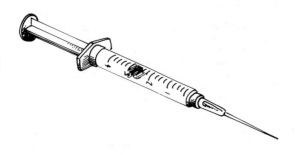

syr·up (SEER·up, SUR·up) *n.* a thick, sugary liquid: *corn syrup; maple syrup; cough syrup* (= medication). — **syr·up·y** *adj.*

sys·tem (SIS·tum) *n.* **1** a related or organized whole composed of many individual parts: *a filing, heating, highway, life-support, public-address, school, sprinkler system; the solar system; the digestive system; Exercise is good for the system* (= body); *Radicals wish to overturn the system* (= social order). **2** a form of organization: *a system of philosophy; a buddy system; the capitalist system; the caste system; a classification system; a computer system for handling a payroll; the decimal system; the immune system; the merit system; a monetary system; the pronunciation system of a dictionary.* **3** a plan or method: *Some work by a system, others without system* (= orderliness).

sys·tem·at·ic (sis·tuh·MAT·ic) or **sys·tem·at·i·cal** (-uh·cul) *adj.* organized, methodical, and thorough. — **sys·tem·at·i·cal·ly** *adv.*

Tt ▼ ▼ ▼ ▼

T or **t** (TEE) *n.* **T's** or **t's** the 20th letter of the English alphabet.
— **to a T** exactly; to perfection: *The nickname suits him to a T.*

tab *n.* **1** a small extension or piece projecting from a garment, filing card, etc. **2** *Informal.* bill or check: *She picked up the tab for the whole group; the tab for entertainment.* **3** tabulator: *to set the tabs for typing or printing in columns.*
— **keep (a) tab on** or **keep tabs on** *Informal.* keep watch on a person or thing.
— *v.* **tabs, tabbed, tab·bing** put a tab on something; also, label or identify.

ta·bas·co (tuh·BAS·coh) *n.* a kind of hot sauce made from red peppers; **Tabasco**, *Trademark.*

tab·by (TAB·ee) *n.* **tab·bies 1** a grey or brown cat with dark stripes. **2** any female domestic cat.

ta·ble (TAY·bul) *n.* **1** a piece of furniture with a flat horizontal top and legs supporting it, esp. one to eat at: *to set the table for dinner; to put food on the table; to clear the table after meals; subjects we don't discuss **at the table** (= while eating); She provides a good table (=fare); at the conference table; a **round table** **conference;** She spoke to the whole table (=group around the table); water table (=level).* **2** a tabulated list: *to compile, draw up a table of data; a metric conversion table; the periodic table (of elements); a **table of contents;** the multiplication tables.* **3** inscribed tablet: *the **tables** of the law.*
— **on the table 1** of a bill, on the agenda. **2** esp. *U.S.,* of a bill, shelved.
— **turn the tables** reverse a situation to an opponent's disadvantage.
— **under the table** secretly and illegally: *money paid under the table (as a bribe).*
— *v.* **-bles, -bled, -bling 1** put on the agenda. **2** esp. *U.S.,* put off consideration of a legislative bill indefinitely.

tab·leau (TAB·loh) *n., pl.* **-leaux** (-loze) or **-leaus 1** a graphic or dramatic picture. **2** a dramatic scene posed by silent actors in costume.

ta·ble·cloth (TAY·bul·cloth) *n.* a covering for a table, as at meals.

table-hop (TAY·bul·hop) *v.* **-hops, -hopped, -hop·ping** leave one's table in a restaurant to chat with friends at other tables.

ta·ble·spoon (TAY·bul·spoon, long "oo") *n.* **1** a large serving spoon or a spoon for eating soup. **2** a tablespoonful: *a heaping, level tablespoon.*

ta·ble·spoon·ful (TAY·bul·spoon·ful) *n.* **-fuls** a measuring unit equal to three teaspoonfuls or ½ fl. oz. (14.2 mL).

tab·let (TAB·lit) *n.* **1** a flat, thin piece of material for writing on, as in ancient times: *clay tablets, stone tablets.* **2** a slab bearing an inscription put at the head of a grave or used as a plaque: *bronze tablets; marble tablets.* **3** a pad of sheets of writing paper glued together at one end. **4** a small, flat cake of medicine, as of aspirin.

table tennis *n.* a tennislike game played on a table with a light, hollow plastic ball.

tab·loid (TAB·loid) *n.* a usually half-size newspaper giving news in condensed form with many pictures and sensational headlines: *a supermarket tabloid.*
— *adj.:* *a tabloid (not broadsheet) newspaper; the tabloid format, style; a tabloid gossip column; sensational tabloid journalism.*

ta·boo (tuh·BOO, tab·OO) *adj.* **1** prohibited because obscene or harmful, as four-letter words. **2** not to be touched because sacred or cursed, as among certain groups: *To Muslims, food is taboo before sunset during Ramadan.*
— *n.* such a prohibition or the custom: *to break, violate a taboo; A taboo is placed on eating before sunset; Eating before sunset during Ramadan is under a rigid taboo.*
— *v.* **-boos, -booed, -boo·ing** prohibit or put under taboo: *Eating before sunset is tabooed.*

tab·u·lar (TAB·yuh·lur) *adj.* **1** having to do with lists or tables: *data in tabular form; tabular computations, value.* **2** flat like a tabletop: *a tabular rock, structure, surface.*

tab·u·late (TAB·yoo·late) *v.* **-lates, -lat·ed, -lat·ing** arrange data in lists or tabular form.
— **tab·u·la·tor** (-lay·tur) *n.*
— **tab·u·la·tion** (-LAY·shun) *n.*

tac·it (TAS·it) *adj.* unspoken; also, implied, not expressed: *tacit approval, understanding.*
— **tac·it·ly** *adv.;* **tac·it·ness** *n.*

tack *n.* **1** a flat-headed, sharp-pointed nail: *carpet tacks; thumb tacks.* **2** a temporary stitch. **3** course of action or policy: *to take a tack to the left; to change*

tack; to try a different tack.
— *v.* **1** fasten with tacks. **2** attach or append to something: *A service charge has been tacked on to the cost of the item.*

tack·le (TACK·ul) *n.* **1** gear or equipment, as a ship's ropes and pulleys: *fishing tackle* (= rod, line, etc.). **2** (method of) tackling an opponent, as in football. **3** in football, an offensive or defensive lineman next to the end.
— *v.* **-les, -led, -ling 1** deal with a person or thing that is challenging or difficult: *to tackle the deficit, an issue, a job, problem, project, question; to tackle the highway during the rush hour.* **2** in football, seize or throw the ball carrier to the ground. **3** lay hold of an opponent: *The police officer tackled the hoodlum to the ground.*
— **tack·ler** *n.*

tack·y (TACK·ee) *adj.* **tack·i·er, -i·est 1** sticky. **2** *Informal.* shabby; gaudy; dowdy. — **tack·i·ness** *n.*

tact *n.* delicate skill in handling people and difficult situations: *She displayed, exercised, showed great tact in dealing with the peddler; He had the tact to avoid mentioning the subject.* — **tact·ful** *adj.*; **tact·ful·ly** *adv.*

tac·tic (TAC·tic) *n.* **1** a skilful move or manoeuvre. **2** usually **tactics** *pl.* methods of gaining advantage: *cheap, delaying, diversionary, pressure, questionable, scare, smear, strong-arm, surprise tactics.* **3 tactics** *pl.* [takes sing. v.] the art or science of conducting a battle.

tac·ti·cal (TAC·tuh·cul) *adj.* **1** well planned: *his tactical moves; her tactical skill.* **2** having to do with tactics or methods: *a tactical error, mistake.* **3** having to do with a shorter distance from a base of operations than in strategy: *A tactical air force provides close support for ground troops; strategic and tactical nuclear weapons.*

tac·tile (TAC·tul, -tile) *adj.* relating to the sense of touch: *a tactile impression, organ, stimulus.*
— **tac·til·i·ty** (tac·TIL·uh·tee) *n.*

tad *n.* *Informal.* **1** a little boy. **2** a little bit: *Things are a tad hectic here.*

taf·fy (TAF·ee) *n.* **taf·fies** a chewy candy prepared from molasses or brown sugar.

tag *n.* **1** a small hanging piece or end: *She was at the tag end* (= very end) *of the procession.* **2** the metal or plastic binding on the end of a shoelace. **3** a small piece of card or leather attached as a label: *a name tag; identification tag; price tag.* **4** an epithet. **5** a quotation or saying used for effect at the end of a speech or story; also **tag line. 6** a game in which one player chases the others and tries to touch one: *to play tag.*
— *v.* **tags, tagged, tag·ging 1** furnish with a tag or label: *His car was tagged* (= ticketed) *and towed away from the no-parking zone.* **2** follow closely; trail: *Jane tagged after the others; She tagged along behind* or *after* or *with her mother.* **3** to touch, as in the game of tag; hence, select or choose. — **tag·ger** *n.*

tail *n.* **1** the backward extension of an animal's body; also, a similar part: *A dog wags its tail; It **turned tail*** (= turned round) *and ran; the tail of an airplane, comet, procession.* **2** *Informal.* one who shadows another, as a detective: *They put a tail on the suspect.* **3 tails** *pl.* the reverse side of a coin; opposite of "heads." **4 tails** *pl.* tailcoat; hence, full dress attire.

— *adj.* at or from the rear: *a tail wind.*
— *v.* **1** furnish with a tail: *the game of tailing the donkey.* **2** *Informal.* follow close behind: *to be tailed by spies.* — **tailed** *adj.* — **tail·less** *adj.*

tail·gate *n.* the gate that opens from the back of a truck, station wagon, etc.
— *v.* **-gates, -gat·ed, -gat·ing** drive too close behind another vehicle.

tail·light *n.* a red warning light at the rear of a vehicle.

tai·lor (TAY·lur) *n.* one who makes or repairs clothes.
— *v.* **1** work as a tailor. **2** make by tailor's work: *a suit tailored to measure; a textbook tailored* (= adapted) *to the needs of the young student.*

tailor-made (TAY·lur·made) *adj.* made esp. for a purpose: *an excuse tailor-made for the occasion.*

tail·spin *n.* **1** spinning motion, as of an airplane coming down out of control: *The bond market went into a tailspin* (= downturn). **2** *Informal.* state of mental confusion.

taint *n.* a trace of corruption or contamination.
— *v.* contaminate; corrupt; spoil: *tainted food, money, reputation; a name tainted by scandal.*

take *v.* **takes, took, tak·en, tak·ing 1** get or seize by force or skill: *They were taken prisoner; Who took the game? We were taken by surprise.* **2** get, obtain, or assume: *She'll take office tomorrow; He's out taking the air; to take the matter lightly, seriously; Don't take anything for granted; I don't take* (= subscribe to) *The Tribune.* **3** get by choice: *You can take it or leave it; Please take a seat* (= sit down). **4** get from a source: *a passage taken from Shakespeare; to take notes of a lecture.* **5** get or receive as offered or due: *He can't take a joke; She's taking a rest; She won't take an insult lying down* (= accept it without protest). **6** understand or feel: *What shall I take this to mean? He took the remark as a compliment; He didn't take notice of her.* **7** do, perform, or execute: *He takes a walk after dinner; She took a swipe at him.* **8** carry or remove: *Where will this road take us? She took the dog for a walk; took the case to the Supreme Court; If you take 4 from 11, the remainder is 7.* **9** have the intended effect: *An inoculation, skin graft, dye, or new publication is said to take; For a fire to take* (= catch), *the kindling has to be dry.*
— **take after** be or act like someone.
— **take a company private** buy out a public company using private funds.
— **take a company public** go public with a company and sell its shares on the stock exchange.
— **take down 1** pull down. **2** write down.
— **take for** consider to be: *What sort of a woman do you take me for?*
— **take in:** *He had to take in boarders to pay off his debts; took in the sights of the town on the last visit; a dress that needs to be taken in* (= reduced) *at the waist; She's too sharp to be easily taken in* (= deceived).
— **take it** *Slang.* endure something hard to bear: *I can't take it any more.*
— **take it out on** *Informal.* make someone else suffer for what one has suffered.
— **take off 1** leave: *An aircraft takes off on a flight; Everyone takes off* (*Informal* for leaves) *for home after school.* **2** *Informal.* mimic: *He takes off celebrities to*

entertain audiences.
— **take on 1** engage or employ. **2** undertake to deal with a person or thing: *to take on an unpleasant job.* **3** acquire a look, appearance, etc.
— **take one's time** be unhurried or slow *doing* something.
— **take over** take charge or control of something.
— **take place** happen or occur.
— **take to 1** go to or resort to something: *Demonstrators take to the streets; Jan took to drink(ing) in frustration.* **2** adapt to an environment; become fond of a person or thing: *The dog seems to take to the cat.*
— **take up 1** begin to do or learn: *to take up a hobby.* **2** fill or occupy a place or time: *a hobby that takes up all my leisure hours.* **3** tighten; make shorter: *to take up the slack (of a rope); to take up a skirt.* **4** accept: *I'm prepared to take you up on that offer.*
— *n.* a taking, what is taken, an amount taken, etc.: *an evening's take at the box office; the many takes* (= filmings) *of a movie scene; He did a double take* (= showed a delayed reaction).
— **on the take** *Slang.* accepting money illicitly.

take-home pay *n.* the money one receives as a pay cheque after taxes, dues, etc. have been deducted.

tak·en (TAY·kun) **1** *pp.* of TAKE: *Is this seat taken* (= reserved)? **2** *adj.* impressed: *The boys were very much taken with the new teacher.*

take-off *n.* **1** a taking off, as in flight. **2** *Informal.* a burlesque or parody: *She's good at doing takeoffs of celebrities.*

take-out *adj.* in ordering food, for consumption away from the premises: *takeout Chinese food, pizza; A takeout restaurant sells takeout food; takeout counter.*
— *n.* takeout food or restaurant: *a fried-chicken takeout.*

take·o·ver (TAKE·oh·vur) *n.* the taking over of power in a government or organization: *a takeover bid.*

taking 1 *adj. Informal.* attractive; captivating: *a taking view.* **2** *n.* seizure: *the taking of the town; It's there for the taking* (= for anyone to take). **3** **takings** *pl.* profits or receipts.

tale *n.* **1** a made-up story, esp. a long one: *to narrate, tell a tale; an exciting, fairy, fanciful, folk, grizzly, harrowing tale; a tall* (= unbelievable) *tale.* **2** falsehood; also, gossip or scandal.
— **tell tales** spread gossip.

tale·bear·er (TALE·bair·ur) *n.* **1** one who spreads gossip. **2** a telltale.

tal·ent (TAL·unt) *n.* **1** a natural ability or aptitude *for* some activity or skill: *to demonstrate, display, show (a) talent for sports; He squandered his natural talents as an artist instead of cultivating and developing them; a woman of considerable, outstanding talent; has the talent to become a maestro.* **2** persons with talent: *to recruit new talent; scouting for talent.*
— *adj.*: *a talent scout, show.*

tal·ent·ed (TAL·un·tid) *adj.* gifted: *She's talented at or in sports; a talented player.*

talk (TAWK) *v.* **1** communicate with spoken words; speak: *Teachers talk to their classes; Parents talk with teachers; He was talking nonsense after a couple of* drinks; *Parrots can talk; No talking allowed in the exam; to talk bluntly, frankly, freely, loudly, openly; to talk on or about a subject;* **Talk about** *punctuality – now see who is late! to talk him into buying* (= persuade him to buy) *the car; to talk him out of* (= dissuade him from) *buying the lemon; to talk oneself hoarse.* **2** tell; relate: *Police know how to make someone talk; Gossips talk behind our backs.* **3** discuss: *Let's talk business; We're talking a million dollars as investment.*
— **money talks** money can get things done.
— **talk back** *Informal.* answer impertinently.
— **talk down** to speak to someone in a superior manner.
— **talk out** discuss openly.
— **talk over 1** discuss something together. **2** persuade someone.
— *n.* **1** a talking; informal conversation or speech: *much talk and little action; She gave her son a little talk about punctuality; blunt, double, heart-to-heart, idle, long, loose, pep, plain, sales, small, straight, sweet talk; There's talk of or about prices coming down; Their divorce is* **the talk of the town** (= subject of gossip). **2** **talks** *pl.* discussions: *peace talks, summit talks in Paris; to break off, conduct, hold talks about a treaty.*
— **talk·er** *n.*: *a fast talker; smooth talker* (= one who talks deceptively).

talk·a·tive (TAW·kuh·tiv) *adj.* fond of talking.

talking head *n. Informal.* a TV personality.

talking-to (TAW·king·too) *n. Informal.* a scolding or lecture.

talk show *n.* a TV or radio show featuring interviews.

talk·y *adj.* talkative.

tall (TAWL) *adj.* **1** of people and things, having great length from top to bottom: *a tall structure; a tall lady; a woman of tall stature; a post three metres tall* (= high); *to stand tall* (= be resolute); *to walk tall* (= be proud). **2** *Informal.* extravagant, exaggerated, or difficult: *a tall price, tale; a* **tall order** (= tough requirement or proposal). — **tall·ness** *n.*

tal·low (TAL·oh) *n.* a hard, white substance obtained by melting animal fat, used chiefly in making candles, soap, etc.

tal·ly (TAL·ee) *n.* **tal·lies 1** formerly, a notched stick as a reckoning device or either half of it split lengthwise for each of the two parties to a deal to keep; hence, a counterpart or duplicate. **2** a score or reckoning or its record: *to make a tally.* **3** a ticket or tag for identification. **4** a group forming a unit in counting; lot.
— *v.* **tal·lies, tal·lied, tal·ly·ing**: *Votes for each side were tallied up* (= reckoned); *two accounts that don't tally* (= correspond or agree); *Your total doesn't tally with mine.*

tal·ly·ho (tal·ee·HOH) **1** *interj.* a huntsman's cry on sighting the fox. **2** *n.* a coach drawn by four horses.

tal·on (TAL·un) *n.* **1** a claw of a bird of prey or animal. **2** a clawlike finger or hand.

tame *adj.* **tam·er, tam·est 1** of animals, domesticated, not wild; made docile. **2** dull or insipid: *a tame ending, show.*
— *v.* **tames, tamed, tam·ing** make tame or docile: *to*

tame a bear, river. — **tame·a·ble** or **tam·a·ble** *adj.*
— **tame·ly** *adv.*; **tame·ness** *n.*

tammy *n.* See TIMMY.

tam-o'-shan·ter (tam-uh-SHAN·tur) *n.* a Scottish cap with a flat crown and a pom-pom in the centre.

tamp *v.* pack earth, tobacco, etc. down by a series of blows or taps.

tam·per (TAM·pur) *v.* interfere with the working of something: *Do not tamper with your watch; The lock has been tampered with; a lawyer accused of tampering with* (= influencing) *a jury.*

tam·pon (TAM·pon) *n.* a plug inserted into a wound or a body cavity to absorb a flow.

tan *n.* a yellowish brown colour, as the skin colour resulting from sunning: *Where did you get your tan?*
— *adj.* **tan·ner, tan·nest** yellowish-brown.
— *v.* **tans, tanned, tan·ning 1** make or become tan. **2** change hide into leather by soaking in dye. **3** *Informal.* whip or thrash.

tan·dem (TAN·dum) *adv.* one behind the other: *riding tandem.*
— *adj.* harnessed or arranged tandem: *a tandem arrangement; a tandem bicycle (with two sets of pedals).*
— *n.* **1** a tandem arrangement or harness: *husband and wife working* **in tandem. 2** a tandem carriage, bicycle, or trailer.

tang *n.* **1** a sharp flavour or odour, as of garlic. **2** the projecting part of a knife or file that is held inside its handle. — **tang·y** *adj.*

tan·gent (TAN·junt) *n.* a line, curve, or surface that touches without cutting.
— **fly** or **go off at a tangent** go away suddenly from one line of thought or action to another.
— **tan·gen·tial** (tan·JEN·shul) *adj.*

tan·ge·rine (tan·juh·REEN) *n.* a delicate, loose-skinned kind of orange with segments that separate easily.

tan·gi·ble (TAN·juh·bul) *adj.* **1** that can be felt by touching: *tangible assets (that can be appraised); an honour without any tangible benefits.* **2** real or definite: *to show tangible improvement; tangible proof.*
— *n.* a material asset or property.
— **tan·gi·bly** (-blee) *adv.*

tan·gle (TAN·gul) *v.* **-gles, -gled, -gling** of threads, hair, etc., twist together or become involved or entangled: *a tangled mass of hair; a tangled web of lies, passions; two hockey players tangling along the boards; The lawyers tangled over the interpretation of the regulations; Don't tangle (Informal for quarrel or fight) with police.*
— *n.* a complicated or confused mass of material or condition: *tangles of hair, vines; a political tangle; a tangle of red tape.*

tan·go (TANG·goh) *n.* **-gos** a ballroom dance characterized by long, gliding steps and intricate poses.
— *v.* **-gos, -goed, -go·ing** dance the tango: *"It takes two to tango."*

tank *n.* **1** a cistern or large container for storing a fluid: *an automobile's gas tank; septic tank; water tank; a think tank* (= group of thinkers); *a railway tank car.* **2** an armoured vehicle moving on endless tracks and equipped with guns. — **tank·ful** *n.*

tank·er *n.* a ship, truck, railway car, or aircraft equipped with a tank for transporting oil, refuelling other planes, etc.

tank top *n.* a sleeveless, collarless top with shoulder straps like those of a one-piece bathing suit (**tank suit**).

tan·ta·lize (TAN·tuh·lize) *v.* **-liz·es, -lized, -liz·ing** torment or tease, as **Tantalus** of Greek myth, punished by continual disappointment whenever he tried to eat or drink what was placed within his reach: *a tantalizing vision of water in the desert.*

tan·ta·mount (TAN·tuh·mount) *adj.* equal in force or effect: *The "friendly warning" was tantamount to a threat.*

tan·trum (TAN·trum) *n.* an outburst of bad temper: *to have, throw a temper tantrum.*

tap *n.* **1** a device for controlling an outflow, as a water faucet or the stopper of a cask: *beer* **on tap** (= ready to be drawn). **2** a fluid drawn out, esp. liquor of a special quality: *spinal tap* (= sample of spinal fluid for diagnosis). **3** a plug-in multiple electrical outlet; also, a wiretap. **4** a tool for cutting an internal screw thread, as of a nut. **5** a light, rapid blow: *a tap on the door.*
— *v.* **taps, tapped, tap·ping 1** draw: *Latex, maple sap, etc. are tapped* (= drawn off) *from trees; to tap* (= draw out the contents of) *a beer barrel; phone lines suspected of being tapped* (= cut in on); *sources of energy waiting to be tapped* (= drawn upon). **2** rap or strike lightly, as on a door or on someone's back for attention: *He tapped out his message in code.* **3** choose someone for a post, membership, etc.: *She was tapped to head the project, for president.* — **tap·per** *n.*

tape *n.* **1** a narrow strip or band of fabric, paper, or light, flexible metal, as for measuring distances, binding or sticking, recording messages in sound or video, etc.: *adhesive, magnetic, masking, measuring, name, ticker tape.* **2** a tape recording: *to make, play, play back a tape.*
— *v.* **tapes, taped, tap·ing** to fasten with or record on tape: *broken pieces taped together; a taped, not live show.*

tape deck *n.* **1** the recording and playback unit of a hi-fi system with separate amplifier and speaker. **2** a tape player.

tape player *n.* a playback machine for tape recordings or cassettes.

ta·per (TAY·pur) *n.* **1** a long wick or slender candle for lighting lamps, fires, etc. **2** a gradual decrease.
— *v.*: *A church spire tapers* (= narrows) *toward the top; Rain will* **taper off** *after midnight.*

tape recorder *n.* a machine that records and plays back sound on magnetic tape.
— **tape-re·cord** (tape·ri·CORD) *v.*; **tape-re·cord·ing** *n.*

tap·es·try (TAP·is·tree) *n.* **-tries** a decorative fabric woven in colourful designs and pictures for use as wall hangings, draperies, etc.

taps *n.pl.* the last bugle call at night signalling "lights out," originally a drum signal: *to play, sound taps; Lights go out at taps.*

tap·ster (TAP·stur) *n.* one who taps and serves liquor in a tavern.

tar *n.* **1** a thick, black, sticky substance obtained from coal, fats, and other organic matter and used in making asphalt, chemicals, etc. **2** *Informal.* sailor.
— *v.* **tars, tarred, tar·ring** cover or smear with tar: *a tarred road; It's not fair to* **tar everyone with the same brush** (= accuse everyone of having the same faults); *a person* **tarred and feathered** (= covered with tar and feathers) *in punishment.*

tar·dy (TAR·dee) *adj.* **tar·di·er, -di·est** slow or late, as because of sluggishness: *tardy progress, reply, students.*
— **tar·di·ly** *adv.*; **tar·di·ness** *n.*

tare *n.* **1** the weight of a container or conveyance; also, allowance made for this when determining the net weight of the goods carried. **2** in the Bible, a weed. **3** a plant used as cattle fodder.
— *v.* **tares, tared, tar·ing** ascertain the tare of a container, etc.

tar·get (TAR·gut) *n.* **1** a mark or other object that is aimed at in shooting; hence, an object of attack: *to aim at, hit, miss, shoot at a target; to finish a project* **on target** (= exactly as intended or planned). **2** a goal or objective: *a target for ridicule;* **adj.**: *the target date for completing a project; the target language into which a translation is made; to conduct target practice.*
— *v.* make a target of a person or thing: *The mob had targeted him as the next victim; a book targeted for spring publication; the show's targeted audience.*

tar·iff (TAIR·if) *n.* **1** a schedule or system of charges, rates, etc., esp. for taxing exports and imports. **2** any such tax, esp. import duty: *to impose, levy, pay a tariff; A* **protective tariff** *is placed on imports to give domestic producers a price advantage.*

tar·mac (TAR·mac) *n.* a paved area, as on an airfield.

tar·nish (TAR·nish) *v.* dull the brightness of polished metal. — *n.* a tarnishing or stain.
— **tar·nish·a·ble** *adj.*

tar·ry (TAIR·ee) *v.* **tar·ries, tar·ried, tar·ry·ing** [literary use] stay temporarily or longer than expected: *He didn't tarry long with us.*
— *adj.* (TAR·ee) **tar·ri·er, tar·ri·est** of or covered with tar.

tar sands *n.pl.* sands containing oil.

tart *adj.* **1** agreeably sour or acid, as certain apples. **2** caustic or sharp: *a tart reply, tongue.*
— *n.* **1** a small, sweet pie with a filling of fruit, jam, or custard. **2** *Informal.* a prostitute.
— *v.* **tart up** decorate or make showy: *a tarted-up version of the same old show.*

tar·tan (TAR·tun) *n.* a plaid woollen cloth, as worn by Scottish clansmen. — *adj.* made of tartan: *a tartan kilt.*

tar·tar (TAR·tur) *n.* **1** a crusty deposit on teeth. **2** a salt deposited as a crust in wine casks, purified into "cream of tartar" for use in medicine and cooking.

task *n.* a piece of usually difficult work assigned to or demanded of someone: *to assign, carry out, do, perform, undertake a task; home tasks* (= homework) *set by teachers; a delicate, difficult, hopeless, monumental, onerous, pleasant, welcome task.*
— **take to task** scold or reprove someone *for* something.

task force *n.* a group, as in the military, organized for a specific operation or inquiry: *the Mayor's Task Force on Multiculturalism.*

task·mas·ter (TASK·mas·tur) *n.* one who sets tasks of a demanding nature.

tas·sel (TAS·ul) *n.* **1** a hanging bunch of loose threads or cords, used as an ornament at the edge of a curtain, cushion, etc. **2** a tassellike tuft of flowers at the top of a cornstalk.
— *v.* **tas·sels, tas·selled** or **tas·seled, tas·sel·ling** or **tas·sel·ing** put on or adorn with tassels.

taste (TAIST) *n.* **1** what is sensed by the organs of the mouth, as sweet, sour, bitter, etc.: *Water has no taste or smell; Freezing spoils the taste of fresh food; a bad, foul, nice, pleasant, sweet taste; The experience left a bitter taste in my mouth.* **2** a small quantity or sample; a tasting: *Take a taste of this jam; an immigrant's first taste* (= experience) *of the Canadian winter.* **3** sense of perception or ability to perceive what is good: *to acquire, cultivate, demonstrate, develop, display, show a sense of taste; a taste for fine furniture; a woman of excellent taste; She has a discriminating taste in ceramics; an elegant, exquisite taste for china; Tastes* (= Likes) *differ; a pun that is not* **in good taste;** *It's* **in bad taste** (= somewhat improper).
— *v.* **tastes, tast·ed, tast·ing 1** have a specified taste: *Sugar tastes sweet.* **2** have or try the taste of something: *He tastes wines for a living; The jailbird tasted* (= experienced) *freedom only briefly.*
— **taste of 1** experience: *a serious accident in which many tasted of death.* **2** have the flavour of something: *It tastes too much of garlic; a reply that tastes of arrogance.*
— **taste·less** *adj.*: *tasteless* (= insipid) *food; tasteless jokes (that are in bad taste).* — **tast·er** *n.*

taste bud *n.* any of the budlike projections on the tongue that act as taste sensors.

taste·ful *adj.* having or showing good artistic taste.
— **taste·ful·ly** *adv.*

tast·y *adj.* **tast·i·er, -i·est** that tastes good: *a tasty and filling meal costing just $5; a tasty and tender cut of* *meat; a wholesome and tasty dish of vegetables; a tasty morsel, recipe, salad, tidbit.* — **tast·i·ness** *n.*

tat·ter (TAT·ur) *n.* **1** a torn strip left loose on a garment. **2** a shred or scrap of paper, etc. **3 tatters** *pl.* torn and ragged clothes.
— *v.* make or become ragged; **tat·tered** *adj.*

tat·tle (TAT·ul) *n.* idle talk; gossip.
— *v.* **tat·tles, tat·tled, tat·tling 1** gossip; tell tales or secrets: *a snitch who tattles on everyone to the authorities.* **2** reveal a secret by tattling. — **tat·tler** *n.*

tat·tle·tale (TAT·ul·tale) *n. Informal.* a telltale or informer.

tat·too (ta·TOO) *n.* **tat·toos 1** a bugle or drum signal calling soldiers, etc. to their quarters at night. **2** a rhythmic rapping or tapping. **3** a coloured design put on the skin by pricking it with inks. **4** a military pageant or display.
— *v.* **tat·tooes, tat·tooed, tat·too·ing** mark the skin or put a design on it in this way: *a tattooed arm, design, sailor, skin.*

tat·ty (TAT·ee) *adj.* **tat·ti·er, tat·ti·est** shabby or worn down: *He works in a tatty old place; Children's books get tatty fast.*

taught *pt. & pp.* of TEACH.

taunt (TAWNT) *v.* jeer at or mock someone repeatedly so as to provoke: *He taunted Jim about his big ears; Jim was taunted into a fight.*
— *n.* such jeering or a taunting remark: *They hurled taunts at him.*

taupe (TOPE) *n.* a brownish grey, as of moleskin.

taut *adj.* **1** tightly stretched: *a taut bow, rope; taut sails.* **2** strained or tense: *taut muscles, nerves; a taut smile.* **3** tidy: *a taut ship.*

tau·tol·o·gy (tau·TOL·uh·jee) *n.* **-gies** the saying of a thing over again without added clarity or force, as in "The infant was lying naked with nothing on."
— **tau·to·log·i·cal** (tau·tuh·LOJ·uh·cul) *adj.*

tav·ern (TAV·urn) *n.* **1** an establishment where alcoholic liquor is served. **2** formerly, an inn.

taw·dry (TAW·dree) *adj.* **-dri·er, -dri·est** cheap and showy: *a tawdry dress, ornament.*

taw·ny (TAW·nee)) *adj.* **-ni·er, -ni·est** brownish-yellow: *the lion's tawny coat; the tawny eagle of Africa; a tawny owl.*

tax *n.* **1** a charge levied on incomes, properties, or businesses by a government: *There's a tax on practically everything we buy or use; taxes such as capital gains; We pay estate, excess-profits, excise, gift, income, nuisance, property, and sales taxes; a goods and services tax; adj.: tax avoidance, evasion; a tax haven in the Bahamas; a* **tax holiday** (= freedom from taxation); *a tax incentive; the tax rate; tax relief; Our annual tax returns should be filed by April 30.* **2** a strain or burden.
— *v.* **1** levy a tax on incomes, purchases, etc. **2** be a strain or put a burden on something: *complaints that tax one's patience.* **3** accuse or charge: *taxed with neglect of duty.* **4** check or evaluate: *The client had his lawyer's bill taxed.*
— **tax·a·ble** *adj.* — **tax·a·tion** (tax·AY·shun) *n.*

tax·i (TAX·ee) *n.* **-is** [short form] taxicab: *to arrive by*

taxi; to hire, take a taxi.
— *v.* **-is** or **-ies, -ied, tax·i·ing** or **tax·y·ing 1** go in a taxicab. **2** of an airplane, move along the ground or on water after landing or in preparation for takeoff.

tax·i·cab (TAX·ee·cab) *n.* a chauffeured automobile for hire, usually equipped with a meter for recording the fare.

tax·pay·er (TAX·pay·ur) *n.* one who pays a tax.

tax shelter *n.* a means of reducing one's income tax, as a financial investment.

T-bar lift *n.* a ski lift consisting of a motor-driven endless cable from which metal bars in the shape of an upside-down "T" are suspended for pulling up two skiers at a time.

T-bone steak *n.* a small beefsteak consisting of a T-shaped bone with some tenderloin.

tea (TEE) *n.* **1** a yellowish-brown, slightly bitter beverage made with the cured leaves of an evergreen Asiatic shrub: *to make a cup of tea; iced, strong, weak tea; adj.: a tea bag, ceremony, party, set; tea time; Modern futurists don't have to read* **tea leaves** *to predict the future.* **2** the plant or the leaves prepared for use. **3** any tealike drink made with plant leaves or roots: *herbal teas.* **4** tea and refreshments served in the afternoon; also, a reception or party. **5** *Brit.* a late-afternoon meal at which tea is drunk: *They have "high tea" on Sundays.*

teach (TEECH) *v.* **teach·es, taught** (TAWT), **teach·ing 1** help to learn: *She teaches art; She teaches us to appreciate art; teaches us how to draw and paint; She could teach you a thing or two; Religions teach that God exists; That will teach you (to do as you are supposed to)!* **2** give lessons to someone: *to teach a class, students; She teaches school; He teaches for a living.*
— **teach·a·ble** *adj.* — **teach·er** *n.*

teaching *n.* **1** a teacher's profession or practice: *to go into teaching as a career; practice teaching; team teaching.* **2** what is taught: *Buddha's* **teachings.**

teaching machine *n.* a device with a corrective "right"-or-"wrong" feedback for use in programmed instruction.

team (TEEM) *n.* **1** a group of workers or players: *to field a team for the game; a combat team; a home, negotiating, opposing, rival, visiting team; Jim didn't make the team* (= didn't get selected). **2** two or more draft animals harnessed to the same plough, wagon, etc.
— *adj.: team play, player, spirit;* **team teaching** *with several teachers for the same group of students.*
— *v.* **1** join individuals together in a team. **2** combine as a team: *Everyone teamed up against him; We teamed up to help him.*

team·mate (TEEM·mate) *n.* a fellow member of one's team.

team·ster *n.* one who hauls loads with a team or truck: *The* **Teamster's Union** *includes workers ranging from truck drivers to public service employees.*

¹tear (TARE) *v.* **tears, tore, torn, tear·ing** pull something apart by force, leaving rough or jagged edges: *She tore the letter open; tore it to pieces; an argument torn to shreds; His shirt tore on a nail; a group torn by factions; I felt torn between conflicting*

*loyalties; She couldn't tear herself away from her family; Demolition crews **tear down** buildings; Critics mercilessly **tore into** (= attacked) him when his book was published; They **tore the book apart** (Informal for criticized it severely).*
— *n.* 1 a tearing. 2 a torn place or rent: *to make, mend a tear; a **tear sheet** of a newspaper ad (containing the ad).*

²**tear** (TEER) *n.* a drop, or **tear·drop**, of the salty liquid shed by the eyes, esp. when one cries: *to break into tears; shed tears; to be **in tears** (= weeping) over something; to weep bitter tears; Tears flow, roll, stream down one's cheeks; Tears well up in one's eyes; Eyes fill with tears.* — **tear·ful** *adj.*; **tear·ful·ly** *adv.*

tear·jerk·er (TEER·jur·kur) *n. Slang.* a highly sentimental play or motion picture.

tea·room *n.* a small restaurant serving tea, coffee, light meals, etc. and sometimes offering fortune-telling by tea-leaf reading.

tease (TEEZ) *v.* **teas·es, teased, teas·ing** 1 worry or annoy by repeated irritating actions or remarks: *She doesn't like to be teased by her playmates; He continued to tease* (= beg) *his parents after being refused.* 2 to card wool, flax, etc. or to comb hair toward the scalp so as to fluff it. — *n.* a teasing or one who teases.

tea·spoon *n.* 1 a small spoon such as is used to stir tea. 2 a teaspoonful: *a heaping teaspoon; level teaspoons.*

tea·spoon·ful (TEE·spoon·ful) *n.* **-fuls** a measuring unit equal to 1/6 fl. oz. (4.7 mL).

teat (TEET) *n.* the nipple on an udder or breast.

tech·ni·cal (TEK·nuh·cul) *adj.* 1 having to do with the practical or skilled aspect of an art or science: *a technical book written in technical language; He gets very technical when discussing his job; a technical expert, institute, journal, school, skill, term, training; technical assistance to developing countries.* 2 in a legal or formal sense: *a technical difference, foul; the **technical knockout** (of a boxer judged too tired to go on fighting).* — **tech·ni·cal·ly** *adv.*

tech·ni·cal·i·ty (tek·nuh·CAL·uh·tee) *n.* **-ties** 1 quality or state of being technical. 2 a technical term, point, detail, etc.: *The case was lost on a legal technicality* (= technical point).

tech·ni·cian (tek·NISH·un) *n.* 1 one skilled in the techniques of a craft or occupation: *a dental, electronic, laboratory, TV technician.* 2 a skilled craftsman: *a superb technician though not an artist.*

tech·nique (tek·NEEK) *n.* 1 the artistic skill or ability required to achieve an effect. 2 a method or manner of execution.

tech·no·crat (TEK·nuh·crat) *n.* a technically trained administrator: *a military technocrat; The Deputy Minister is a hired technocrat, not an elected politician.* — **tech·no·crat·ic** (-CRAT·ic) *adj.*

tech·nol·o·gy (tek·NOL·uh·jee) *n.* **-gies** 1 science as applied to human needs, esp. in industry: *transfer of technology to developing countries.* 2 a technical method or process. — **tech·nol·o·gist** *n.*
— **tech·no·log·i·cal** (tek·nuh·LOJ·uh·cul) *adj.*
— **tech·no·log·i·cal·ly** *adv.*

te·di·ous (TEE·dee·us) *adj.* long and tiresome; wearisome: *a tedious lecturer, lesson, process, trip, wait; tedious work.*

te·di·um (TEE·dee·um) *n.* the condition or quality of being tedious; boredom.

tee *n.* 1 a small peg on which a golf ball is placed for driving. 2 the small area or "teeing ground" from which play is begun at each hole of a golf course.
— *v.* **tees, teed, tee·ing** place a ball on a tee.
— **tee off** begin play.
— **teed off** *Slang.* angry or annoyed *about* or *at* something.

teem *v.* swarm with or be full of living beings: *The river teems with fish.*
— **teeming** *adj.*: *We fished in the teeming river; the teeming jungle; Asia's teeming millions.*

teen *n.* 1 a teenager. 2 **teens** *pl.* the years or numbers from 13 to 19: *She's still in her teens.*
— *adj.* having to do with teen-age: *a teen gang, hit, movie; teen life, shows, troubles; the teen market; my teen years.*

teen-age *adj.* 1 of people in their teens: *a teen-age club.* 2 in one's teens: *a teen-age daughter.* Also **teen-aged.**
— **teen·ag·er** (TEEN·ay·jur) *n.*

tee·ny (TEE·nee) *adj.* **-ni·er, -ni·est** *Informal.* tiny. Also **teen·ny-wee·ny, teen·sy, teen·sy-ween·sy.**

teen·y-bop·per (TEE·nee·bop·ur) *n. Slang.* a young teenager, esp. one following the latest fads.

tee·pee (TEE·pee) *n.* same as TEPEE.

tee shirt *n.* same as T-SHIRT.

tee·ter (TEE·tur) *v.* 1 move unsteadily; waver: *to teeter on the brink of collapse.* 2 teeter-totter; seesaw.

teeter-totter (TEE·tur·TOT·ur) *n. & v.* same as SEESAW.

teeth *pl.* of TOOTH.

teethe (TEETH, "TH" as in "the") *v.* **teethes, teethed, teeth·ing** grow teeth, as an infant.

tee·to·tal·ler or **tee·to·tal·er** (tee·TOH·tul·ur) *n.* one pledged to drink no alcoholic liquor. — **tee·to·tal·ism** *n.*

tef·lon *n.* a tough, heat- and corrosion-resistant plastic used as a nonstick coating on cooking utensils, as an insulator, etc. — **Teflon** *Trademark.*

tele- *combining form.* far or distant: *telebus* (= a dial-a-bus service); *telecast; a telecopier (that sends copies by telephone); television.*

tel·e·cast (TEL·uh·cast) *n. & v.* **-casts,** *pt. & pp.* **-cast** or **-cast·ed, -cast·ing** broadcast by television.
— **tel·e·cast·er** *n.*

tel·e·com·mu·ni·ca·tion (TEL·uh·cuh·mew·nuh·CAY·shun) *n.* communication by radio, telephone, telegraph, etc.

tel·e·com·mute (TEL·uh·cuh·MUTE) *v.* **-mutes, -mut·ed, -mut·ing** work from one's home for another person using a computer and communications equipment.

tel·e·cop·i·er (TEL·uh·cop·ee·ur) or **tel·e·fax** (TEL·uh·fax) *n.* same as FAX.

749

tel·e·gen·ic (tel·uh·JEN·ic) *adj.* of a person, who looks attractive on television.

tel·e·gram *n.* a message sent by telegraph.

tel·e·graph (TEL·uh·graf) *v.* -graphs, -graphed, -graph·ing send a message to a person by telegraph: *She telegraphed him greetings.*
— *n.* a system or apparatus for sending messages by wire or radio using electrical impulses.
— **tel·e·graph·ic** (tel·uh·GRAF·ic) *adj.*
— **te·leg·ra·phy** (tuh·LEG·ruh·fee) *n.*

tel·e·me·ter (TEL·uh·mee·tur) *n.* an apparatus for measuring and transmitting data from a distance, as used in weather balloons and spacecraft.
— **tel·e·met·ric** (-MET·ric) *adj.*
— **te·lem·e·try** (tuh·LEM·uh·tree) *n.*

te·lep·a·thy (tuh·LEP·uh·thee, "th" as in "thin") *n.* communication between persons by thought alone, without sensory means.
— **tel·e·path·ic** (tel·uh·PATH·ic) *adj.*

tel·e·phone (TEL·uh·fone) *v.* -phones, -phoned, -phon·ing speak to someone or communicate a message using the telephone: *to telephone someone; to telephone a message; to telephone the results of the test; He telephoned that he had won.*
— *n.* a system or apparatus for the transmission of speech sounds over wires using electrical impulses: *to answer, dial, disconnect, tap a telephone; She was called to the telephone; talked to him by telephone; had a long talk on or over the telephone; She's on the telephone much of the time.*
— **tel·e·phon·ic** (tel·uh·FON·ic) *adj.*
— **te·leph·o·ny** (tuh·LEF·uh·nee) *n.*

tel·e·pho·to (tel·uh·FOH·toh) *adj.* of a camera or lens, producing a large image of a distant object.

tel·e·play (TEL·i·play) *n.* a play produced for television.

tel·e·print·er (TEL·uh·prin·tur) *n.* teletypewriter.

tel·e·prompt·er (TEL·uh·promp·tur) *n.* an electronic device for giving a speaker on TV a line-by-line view of the script. — **Teleprompter** *Trademark.*

tel·e·scope (TEL·uh·scope) *n.* an instrument for observing distant objects, esp. celestial bodies.
— *v.* -scopes, -scoped, -scop·ing slide into one another like the sections of a collapsible telescope.
— **tel·e·scop·ic** (tel·uh·SCOP·ic) *adj.*

tel·e·text (TEL·uh·text) *n.* the broadcasting of printed information for reception on video terminals.

tel·e·thon (TEL·uh·thon) *n.* a long TV program for a special purpose such as to raise funds for charity.

tel·e·type (TEL·uh·type) *v.* -types, -typed, -typ·ing send a message by teletypewriter.
— *n.* a teletypewriter; **Teletype** *Trademark.*

tel·e·type·writ·er (tel·uh·TYPE·rye·tur) *n.* a form of telegraph in which messages to be sent are typed out and reproduced by means of an automatic typewriter at the receiving end.

tel·e·van·gel·ist (tel·i·VAN·juh·list) *n.* one who preaches the gospel via TV.

tel·e·vise (TEL·uh·vize) *v.* -vis·es, -vised, -vis·ing broadcast by television.

tel·e·vis·ion (tel·uh·VIZH·un) *n.* See TV.

tel·ex (TEL·ux) *n.* a teletypewriter system operated by dialling subscribers' numbers. Also *v.*
— **Telex** *Trademark.*

tell *v.* tells, told, tell·ing 1 make known in words; say or inform: *to tell a story; to tell (them) the truth; Please tell us all about it; Please tell him to start; I'll tell you when to stop; All right, tell me when; It's a secret you're not supposed to tell* (= reveal); *I tell you that it is a secret; You can never tell* (= be certain); *Dead people tell no tales* (= don't reveal secrets); *She's telling her beads* (= counting the beads one by one in prayer); *It's hard to tell the twins apart* (= distinguish them); *hard to tell one (twin) from the other.* 2 have a marked effect: *Every blow tells; High inflation tells heavily on our buying power.*
— **tell off** 1 count off a few from a group for a special task. 2 *Informal.* rebuke or scold.
— **tell on** *Informal.* inform on someone: *She threatened to tell on him for cheating; to tell Dad on him.*

tell·er *n.* 1 one who tells. 2 one who counts votes, money, etc., esp. a bank cashier who receives and pays out money.

telling *adj.* effective; striking: *a telling argument, blow, impression.* — **tell·ing·ly** *adv.*

tell·tale *adj.* revealing: *a telltale blush, sign.*
— *n.* one who informs on others; tattletale.

tel·ly (TEL·ee) *n. Brit. Informal.* television.

te·mer·i·ty (tuh·MER·uh·tee) *n.* rashness or boldness: *the temerity to ask for a raise when his job is in danger.*

tem·per (TEM·pur) *n.* 1 emotional nature or state of mind in regard to anger: *He's in a bad temper; She never loses her temper* (= calmness of mind); *She knows how to control, keep her temper; a calm, even, hot, nasty, quick, ungovernable, violent temper; He broke the vase in a fit of temper; Tempers flare up during arguments; the economic temper of the times; a temper tantrum* (= outburst of bad temper). 2 degree of hardness, strength, and toughness given to a material such as steel or glass by a heating-and-cooling process.
— *v.* 1 soften or mitigate: *to temper justice with mercy.* 2 bring to the proper condition, esp. of toughness: *Clay is tempered by moistening, mixing, kneading, etc.; tempered steel, a sheet of tempered safety glass.*

tem·per·a·ment (TEM·pur·uh·munt) *n.* 1 the nature of a person as shown by behaviour, tendencies, and aspirations: *an artistic temperament; her poetic temperament; his restless temperament.* 2 an excitable or moody nature: *He's a genius, but no one can stand his temperament.*

tem·per·a·men·tal (TEM·pur·uh·MEN·tul) *adj.* having to do with temperament; hence, impulsive or unpredictable: *a temperamental actor, director, elevator, outburst, player, singer; Soufflés can be difficult and temperamental; the temperamental ups and downs of the economy.*

tem·per·ance (TEM·puh·runce) *n.* moderation in indulging the pleasures of the senses, esp. partial or total abstinence from alcoholic liquor.

tem·per·ate (TEM·puh·rit) *adj.* **1** deliberately self-restrained: *temperate language, manners; a temperate reply.* **2** moderate in climate; neither very hot nor very cold: *B.C. has a temperate climate; the temperate Niagara region; the* **Temperate Zones** *lying between the tropics and the polar circles.* **3** moderate in regard to alcoholic drinks.

tem·per·a·ture (TEM·puh·ruh·chur) *n.* **1** degree of heat or cold: *the temperature of boiling water; Keep it at room temperature; Normal body temperature is 37°C (98.6°F); Temperatures drop, fall, go down, go up, rise; The temperature is high, low, normal.* **2** fever: *The patient is having* or *running a temperature; a high temperature; slight temperature; Let's take his temperature.*

tempered (TEM·purd) *adj.* properly conditioned: *tempered clay, glass, steel.*
— **combining form.** having a specified emotional nature: *hot-tempered, quick-tempered, sweet-tempered.*

tem·pest (TEM·pist) *n.* a violent windstorm, often with rain, snow, or hail: *a mere* **tempest in a teapot** (= an uproar about nothing).
— **tem·pes·tu·ous** (tem·PES·choo·us) *adj.*: *a tempestuous affair, career, meeting, romance; tempestuous seas.*

tem·plate (TEM·plit) *n.* **1** a pattern, usually a thin metal plate, from which an exact copy may be traced and cut. **2** any of various guides for cutting tools, or a routing or locating device.

tem·ple (TEM·pul) *n.* **1** a building dedicated to the worship of a god or gods; also, a Christian, Jewish, or Mormon place of worship. **2** either side of the head between forehead and ear. **3** the hinged arm of a spectacle frame.

tem·po (TEM·poh) *n., pl.* **-pi** (-pee) or **-pos 1** in music, speed of movement: *to increase, slow down, step up the tempo.* **2** pace of activity: *the fast tempo of city life.*

tem·po·ral (TEM·puh·rul) *adj.* **1** of earthly life, not eternal or spiritual; secular or worldly: *our temporal affairs.* **2** of the temples of the head: *the temporal bones.*

tem·po·rar·y (TEM·puh·rair·ee) *adj.* lasting only for a time; not permanent: *a temporary appointment, job; temporary quarters.*
— **tem·po·rar·i·ly** (tem·puh·RAIR·uh·lee, TEM·puh·rair·uh·lee) *adv.*

tempt *v.* try to make someone do something attractive but not necessarily good: *Eve tempted Adam to eat the forbidden fruit; When the car stalled yet again, I was tempted to dump it; a very* **tempting** (= attractive) *offer; Daredevils like to tempt* (= risk or defy) *fate.*
— **tempt·er** *n.;* **tempt·ress** (-tris) *fem.*

temp·ta·tion (temp·TAY·shun) *n.* that which tempts or a tempting: *to be exposed to, to face, overcome, resist, succumb to temptation; an irresistible, strong temptation to break the diet.*

ten *n., adj. & pron.* one more than nine; 10 or X.

ten·a·ble (TEN·uh·bul) *adj.* that can be held or defended, as against attack: *a tenable position, theory.*
— **ten·a·bil·i·ty** (-BIL·uh·tee) *n.*

ten·a·cious (tuh·NAY·shus) *adj.* **1** firmly holding, clinging, etc.: *a tenacious glue, grip, memory.* **2** stubborn or resolute: *her tenacious courage; She's very tenacious of her rights; a tenacious sales rep.*
— **te·nac·i·ty** (-NAS·uh·tee) *n.*

ten·an·cy (TEN·un·see) *n.* **-cies** (the period of) occupancy of a tenant.

ten·ant (TEN·unt) *n.* one paying rent for the occupancy and use of land or a building; occupant: *our previous tenant.*
— *v.* occupy as a tenant: *rooms tenanted by students.*

tend *v.* **1** incline or have a tendency: *As we grow old, we tend to forget things; views tending towards the Left; The road tends* (= goes towards) *right from there.* **2** attend to or take care of something: *Shepherds tend sheep; someone to tend the store while I'm away.*

tend·en·cy (TEN·dun·see) *n.* **-cies** a natural inclination or disposition; leaning: *a tendency to fall asleep at the wheel; He suffers from a suicidal tendency; the upward tendency of prices.*

ten·den·tious (ten·DEN·shus) *adj.* one-sided or biassed: *a tendentious report, statement; tendentious writings.*

ten·der (TEN·dur) *n.* **1** a formal offer, proposal, or bid: *The government asks for* or *calls for* or *invites sealed tenders for a contract; A contract is put up for tender; a tender offer to buy up the company shares; Is it legal tender* (= acceptable money) *to offer $10 in pennies?* **2** something that attends to or serves, as a boat or small ship attending a larger vessel to carry supplies and passengers or the car attached to a locomotive to carry a supply of coal and water.
— *v. Formal.* **1** offer or present: *He tendered apologies, thanks; She tendered her resignation; The shareholders tendered their stock (for sale).* **2** propose or bid: *to tender against competitors.*
— *adj.* soft or delicate: *the tender loving care of parents; a tender conscience, heart, subject, tale, wound; Cook the noodles until just tender; tender meat, years; at a tender* (= early) *age.*
— **ten·der·ly** *adv.;* **ten·der·ness** *n.*

ten·der·ize (TEN·duh·rize) *v.* **-iz·es, -ized, -iz·ing** make meat tender by pounding or by using enzymes.
— **ten·der·iz·er** *n.*

ten·der·loin (TEN·dur·loin) *n.* **1** a tender part of a loin of beef or pork. **2 Tenderloin** the district of a city noted for vice and corruption.

ten·don (TEN·dun) *n.* a strong, fibrous band or cord attaching muscles to bones or cartilages: *He pulled a tendon in his foot; An* **Achilles' tendon** *connects the calf muscles to the back of the heel.*

ten·e·ment (TEN·uh·munt) *n.* **1** dwelling house, esp. one divided into units for several families. **2** a living unit or apartment.

tenement house *n.* an overcrowded and run-down dwelling, as in the slums.

ten·et (TEN·it) *n.* a doctrine or belief held in common by a group or profession: *Anglican tenets; the basic tenets of socialism.*

ten·fold *adj. & adv.* ten times.

ten-four *n.* in radio communications, "OK"; "message received."

ten·on (TEN·un) *n.* the projecting end of a piece that fits into a hollow in another to make a mortise joint.

ten·or (TEN·ur) *n.* **1** the general direction or tendency; drift: *the tenor of a conversation; Nothing disturbs the even tenor of her life.* **2** the highest regular adult male voice; also, a part for or a singer with such a voice: *He sings tenor.* **3** an instrument with a tenor range.

tense *n.* the form of a verb showing time: *past, present, and future tenses.*
— *adj.* **tens·er, tens·est 1** stretched tight; taut: *a tense muscle, rope.* **2** showing or feeling nervous tension; hence, anxious: *tense nerves; a tense moment; The atmosphere was tense with expectation.*
— *v.* **tens·es, tensed, tens·ing** make or become tense: *He tensed his muscles as he picked up the weight.*
— **tense·ly** *adv.* — **tense·ness** or **ten·si·ty** *n.*

ten·sile (TEN·sul, -sile) *adj.* of or having to do with tension: *Steel has the highest **tensile strength** (= breaking limit).*

ten·sion (TEN·shun) *n.* **1** a stretched or strained condition; hence, stress: *the tension of a fan belt, violin string.* **2** strain: *Chewing gum is supposed to help relieve (nervous) tension; a hostile meeting in an atmosphere of tension; to alleviate, cause, create, increase, heighten, lessen tension; racial tensions in big cities; There was mounting tension between the U.S. and Russia during the missile crisis; Tension built up, then eased.* **3** gas pressure; also, voltage: *a high-tension wire.*

ten-speed *n.* a bicycle with ten gears.

tent *n.* **1** a light, portable shelter made usually of canvas stretched over supporting poles, as used when camping; also, a tepee or wigwam: *to dismantle, erect, pitch, put up, take down a tent.* **2** a tentlike canopy: *The pneumonia patient was kept in an oxygen tent for several days.*

ten·ta·cle (TEN·tuh·cul) *n.* a slender flexible arm of an animal used for capturing food, as in octopuses, used as feelers, as in molluscs, or for protection, as in the jellyfish.

ten·ta·tive (TEN·tuh·tiv) *adj.* done or made as a trial or first step; provisional: *a tentative acceptance, agreement, plan, proposal, refusal; a tentative (= hesitant) smile.* — **ten·ta·tive·ly** *adv.*

ten·ter·hook *n.*: *He was **on tenterhooks** (= in a state of anxious suspense) waiting for the verdict.*

tenth *adj.* next after the ninth.
— *n.* a tenth person or thing; also a tenth part.

ten·u·ous (TEN·yoo·us) *adj.* extremely thin or fine: *the tenuous spider web; a tenuous distinction, fabric; the tenuous (= rare) mountain air; a tenuous (= flimsy or weak) claim.* — **ten·u·ous·ly** *adv.*; **ten·u·ous·ness** *n.*

ten·ure (TEN·yur) *n.* the act, right, period, or manner of holding an office or position: *during her long tenure in office; to get, grant, receive tenure (= permanence); adj.: a tenured (= permanent) position, professor.*

te·pee (TEE·pee) *n.* the cone-shaped tent used by Plains Indians.

tep·id (TEP·id) *adj.* **1** lukewarm: *tepid water.* **2** lacking fervour or enthusiasm: *He expressed only tepid approval of the plan.* — **te·pid·i·ty** (tuh·PID·uh·tee) *n.*

term *n.* **1** a word or expression with a definite function or precise meaning: *a legal term such as "escrow"; a technical term; There are three algebraic terms in "x² + y² + 2xy."* **2 terms** *pl.* way of expressing oneself; words: *She spoke about him in flattering terms; He described her in glowing terms; They spoke in vague, general terms; "Square circle" is a contradiction in terms; They told him in no uncertain terms (= very clearly) to shape up or ship out.* **3** a set or fixed period: *a four-year term of office; the term of a lease; a school term running from September to December; a baby born **at full term** (= after a full period in the womb); In the short term we may lose money, but we hope to show a profit in the long term.* **4 terms** *pl.* conditions of agreement: *by or under the terms of an agreement, contract, lease, treaty; to negotiate with them on equal terms; They were in no position to dictate terms to us; to state, stipulate terms; He agreed to surrender to us on our own terms; easy, equal, familiar, favourable, intimate terms; We're not on speaking terms (= relations); We had to **come to terms** (= reach an agreement) or someone else would **bring** (= force) us **to terms**; He had to **come to terms with** (= learn to live with) the fact that he was now broke.*
— **in terms of** as regards; concerning.
— *v.* name or call by a term: *Ethelred was termed "the unready."*

ter·mi·nal (TUR·muh·nul) *adj.* **1** having to do with a fixed period or term: *terminal accounts, examinations.* **2** having to do with an end part or final stage: *a terminal bud, outpost; a terminal illness (that ends in death); **terminal leave** granted before retirement.*
— *n.* **1** an end or extremity of a transportation or communication line: *at the keyboard of a computer terminal (where data is typed in); a video display terminal (= screen on which video output is shown); the observation deck of an **air terminal** (where airplanes are boarded and discharged); at a bus, freight, shipping, trucking terminal (= station).* **2** a point of electrical connection: *the positive and negative terminals of a battery.* — **ter·mi·nal·ly** *adv.*

ter·mi·nate (TUR·muh·nate) *v.* **-nates, -nat·ed, -nat·ing** put or come to an end: *to terminate a contract, discussion, employee, job, partnership; to terminate a pregnancy (by abortion); The flight terminates in Toronto.* — **ter·mi·na·tion** (-NAY·shun) *n.*

ter·mi·nol·o·gy (tur·muh·NOL·uh·jee) *n.* **-gies** (a system of) terms used in a branch of study or line of work: *legal, scientific, technical teminology; to codify, establish, standardize a teminology; the basic teminology of grammar.*
— **ter·mi·no·log·i·cal** (-nuh·LOJ·uh·cul) *adj.*

term insurance *n.* life insurance providing protection for a specified period.

ter·mi·nus (TUR·muh·nus) *n., pl.* **-ni** (-nye) or **-nus·es** the final point or place where something terminates: *the terminus of a busline, pipeline, railway.*

ter·mite (TUR·mite) *n.* an antlike social insect that is very destructive to wooden structures.

ter·race (TER·is) *n*. **1** an open courtyard adjoining a house, sometimes overlooking a garden. **2** the flat roof of an Oriental or Spanish house. **3** one of a series of levels bounded by ridges made on sloping land for irrigation and to prevent erosion. **4** a row of houses along a slope above street level.
— **ter·raced** *adj*. made into or using terraces: *a terraced hillside; terraced cultivation.*

terra fir·ma (TER·uh·FUR·muh) *n*. solid ground, as opposed to air or water: *We are glad to be back on terra firma after a troubled voyage.*

ter·rain (tuh·RAIN, TER·ain) *n*. a stretch of land with regard to its natural features or fitness for a use such as warfare: *hilly, mountainous, rough, smooth terrain.*

ter·res·tri·al (tuh·RES·tree·ul) *adj*. **1** of the earth, not celestial: *our terrestrial globe; terrestrial magnetism; a terrestrial rocket guidance system; Mercury, Venus, and Mars are terrestrial planets (like the Earth).* **2** of the ground or land: *sediments of terrestrial origin; terrestrial* (= not aerial or aquatic) *plants.*

ter·ri·ble (TER·uh·bul) *adj*. **1** causing terror or extreme fear: *a terrible crime; a night of terrible* (= extreme) *anxiety.* **2** *Informal.* extremely bad: *a terrible dinner, joke.*
— **ter·ri·bly** *adv. Informal.* extremely: *terribly afraid, sorry.*

ter·ri·fic (tuh·RIF·ic) *adj*. **1** *Informal.* extraordinary; astounding: *a terrific achievement, speed; a terrific* (= magnificent) *view.* **2** causing great fear; terrifying.

ter·ri·fy (TER·uh·fye) *v*. **-fies, -fied, -fy·ing** fill with terror; frighten overwhelmingly: *He was terrified by the thought of what might happen; He's terrified of looking down from the top; terrified that he may lose his balance.*

ter·ri·to·ri·al (ter·uh·TOR·ee·ul) *adj*. having to do with territory or a particular area: *a country's territorial ambitions; territorial government; a nation's rights over its **territorial waters*** (= waters off the coast but not the high seas).

ter·ri·to·ry (TER·uh·tor·ee) *n*. **-ries** an area or region in regard to jurisdiction or control over it: *a mandated, neutral, occupied, trust, unexplored territory; A territory has less self-government than a province or state; India used to be British territory; a territory ceded to China; Most animals defend their territory aggressively; a territory assigned to a sales representative; Religion is outside the territory* (= sphere of activity; province) *of science; For a celebrity, signing autographs **comes** or **goes with the territory*** (= is part of being a celebrity).

ter·ror (TER·ur) *n*. great fear or the cause of it: *The murders struck terror into our hearts; to inspire, resort to, sow terror; a campaign of terror; the Reign of Terror during the French Revolution; People lived in terror of being guillotined; That child is a terror (Informal for is hard to manage); terror tactics used by guerrillas.*

ter·ror·ism (TER·uh·riz·um) *n*. the policy of repressive governments, guerrillas, etc. of using hijackings, killings, kidnappings, etc. as a means to achieve political ends: *an act of terrorism; state terrorism.*
— **ter·ror·ist** *n. & adj.*

ter·ror·ize (TER·uh·rize) *v*. **-iz·es, -ized, -iz·ing** terrify, esp. as a means of coercion: *a people terrorized into submission.*

terse *adj*. **ters·er, ters·est** concise in expression, sometimes witty, often brusque: *a terse "No comment"; a terse announcement, expression, rejection, response, statement, style, writer.*
— **terse·ly** *adv.*; **terse·ness** *n.*

ter·ti·ar·y (TUR·shee·air·ee, -shuh·ree) *adj*. of the third order or rank: *a tertiary colour (obtained by mixing orange, green, and such secondary colours); elementary, secondary, and tertiary* (= university) *education; tertiary or service industries; rocks of the **Tertiary period** of life on the Earth (up to two million years ago); **tertiary recovery** by use of special techniques of extracting oil that is unrecoverable by conventional means.*

test *n*. an examination or trial for comparison with a standard: *a test of intelligence; a blood test for sugar; a driving test; to administer, carry out, conduct, do, fail, give, pass, run, take a test; to put someone to the test; to stand the test of time; an acid test; a demanding, difficult, easy, exhaustive, objective, severe, thorough test; a competency, endurance, litmus, means, nuclear, personality, pregnancy, road test; to run a series of tests on someone; tabulation of tests* (= test results); ***adj.**: a test drive, flight.*
— *v*. **1** put to test: *to test someone for AIDS.* **2** score or rate on tests: *He tested positive; She tested high in intelligence.* — **test·er** *n.*

tes·ta·ment (TES·tuh·munt) *n*. **1** the Old Testament or the New Testament of the Bible. **2** a statement of beliefs. **3** a will disposing of one's property: *my last will and testament.* — **tes·ta·men·ta·ry** (-MEN·tuh·ree) *adj.*

tes·ti·fy (TES·tuh·fye) *v*. **-fies, -fied, -fy·ing** **1** bear witness: *to testify about a case, against the defendant, for the prosecution, to the truth of a statement, under oath; He testified that he was elsewhere at the time of the murder.* **2** serve as evidence of something: *These facts testify to his honesty.*

tes·ti·mo·ni·al (tes·tuh·MOH·nee·ul) *n*. **1** a letter or statement of recommendation or appreciation: *The lives saved are an eloquent testimonial to the efficacy of the drug.* **2** a dinner, gift, or other tribute in honour of someone: *a testimonial dinner.*

tes·ti·mo·ny (TES·tuh·moh·nee) *n*. **-nies** **1** a statement made in court by a witness under oath: *to bear, cite, give, offer, refute testimony; false testimony against the defendant; the testimony about or on behalf of the plaintiff.* **2** evidence or proof: *The honours she has received bear testimony to a life of dedication.*

test tube *n*. a glass container in the shape of a tube closed at one end for use in experiments.

test-tube baby *n*. a baby born from an ovum fertilized in a laboratory vessel and inserted into the uterus of the mother.

tes·ty (TES·tee) *adj*. **-ti·er, -ti·est** quickly angered: *a testy person; a testy* (= irritated) *voice.* — **tes·ti·ly** *adv.*

tête-à-tête (TATE·uh·tate) *n*. a close private talk between two people.
— ***adv. & adj.*** (in) private: *We had dinner tête-à-tête; a*

*tête-à-tête dinner; the S-shaped **tête-à-tête chair** for two people to sit facing each other.*

teth·er (TETH·ur, "TH" as in "the") *n.* a line by which an animal is tied so as to restrict its range of movement. — **at the end of one's tether** at the limit of one's endurance. — *v.* fasten with a tether.

text *n.* **1** the main body of a work or the original words of an author, as distinguished from notes, illustrations, appendices, etc.: *the original text of Shakespeare's plays; a text corrupted by copyists.* **2** a topic or subject: *The preacher chose for his text "Blessed are the meek."* **3** a textbook: *our history text.* — **tex·tu·al** (TEX·choo·ul) *adj.*

text·book *n.* a standard or authoritative book for the study of a subject: *a textbook of physics; a textbook on socialist theory.* — *adj.* standard or typical: *a textbook example of mismanagement.*

tex·tile (TEX·tile) *adj.* **1** having to do with fabrics and fibres: *the textile industry.* **2** woven: *a textile fabric.* — *n.* **1** a cloth or fabric, esp. woven or knit. **2** textile material such as fibre and yarn.

tex·ture (TEX·chur) *n.* a woven, hence surface characteristic, as given by the arrangement and size of threads, esp. as can be seen and felt: *Sackcloth has a coarse, not fine texture; rough, not smooth texture; the granular texture of certain rocks; Brick imparts texture to an interior; the texture (= surface characteristics) of a painting, poem, society.* — **tex·tur·al** *adj.*

tex·tured (TEX·churd) *adj.* having texture: *a textured, not plain surface; **textured vegetable protein** spun from soyabean fibres and made to look like beef, ham, etc.*

T-group *n.* a sensitivity-training group. See ENCOUNTER.

tha·lid·o·mide (thuh·LID·uh·mide) *n.* a drug used in the 1960s that caused deformities of the fetus when taken in early preganancy. — *adj.:* *a thalidomide (= handicapped) baby; a thalidomide family with a thalidomide child.*

than ("TH" as in "the") *conj.* [used to introduce the second term of a comparison]: *Jack is taller than Jill; He would rather fight than argue; Gigi is none other than his wife; She's shorter than him (Informal for than he is).*

thank ("th" as in "thin") *v.* express gratitude to someone: *(I) thank you for your kindness; The neighbours will thank you to (= will be grateful if you) keep your dog quiet; He has only himself to thank (= blame) for his problems.*

thank·ful *adj.* grateful: *We are thankful to her for saving us; thankful (= glad) to be alive.* — **thank·ful·ly** *adv.*

thank·less *adj.* ungrateful; also, unappreciated: *a thankless task.* — **thank·less·ly** *adv.*

thanks *n. pl.* (expression of) gratitude: *Our heartfelt, sincere, warm thanks to everyone for helping us; many thanks; Thanks a lot! If you think you are making me an attractive offer, well, **thanks but no thanks** (= No, thank you)! **Thanks to** (= because of) her seatbelt, she was saved (= She was saved because of her seatbelt, and one is grateful for it).* — *interj.* thank you!

thanks·giv·ing (thanks·GIV·ing) *n.* formal expression of gratitude, esp. to God, as on the annual **Thanksgiving** holiday.

thar ("TH" as in "the") *adv.* [regional] there: *There was gold bullion in that thar ship; Watch them thar handbags.*

that ("TH" as in "the") *pron.* **1** *pl.* **those** (THOZE) a person or thing already mentioned or implied, esp. as farther from the speaker than another, or "this": *Do you like this hat or that? That is my hat; adj.: that man; those men.* **2** [used as a relative pron.] who; whom; which: *the house that Jack built.* — **at that 1** then: *At that, he left the place.* **2** besides: *a good husband and a real friend at that.* — **in that** because: *a good student in that he works hard.* — **that is** in other words: *I'll see you on Friday – tomorrow, that is.* — *conj.:* *He's happy that he's won; That he's bald is obvious; Oh, (I wish) that it were spring!* — *adv.* to that extent: *He's crying, he's that happy.*

that·a·way (THAT·uh·way) *adv.* [regional] in that direction: *She went thataway.*

thatch ("th" as in "thin") *n.* **1** material such as straw or leaves for roofing. **2** a roof covered with thatch. **3** *Informal.* head hair. — *v.* cover as with thatch.

thaw ("th" as in "thin") *v.* **1** of frozen things, become or cause to become warmer so as to melt: *Frozen rivers begin to thaw in warm weather; Leave the turkey out to thaw; Do not refreeze a thawed TV dinner.* **2** of people or their manner, become less cold: *After a while, the crusty old man began to thaw.* — *n.:* *spring thaw; A thaw is forecast; A thaw sets in; the thaw (= softening of relations) between China and the U.S.S.R.; the thaw in international relations.*

the (thuh; *before vowels:* thee) *def. art.* **1** [referring to a certain person or thing]: *the man I met yesterday; He went in the house.* **2** [referring to a unique person or thing]: *She was the greatest; the sun and the moon; the top of your head; the United States; the definite article.* **3** [referring to a whole class or something generalized as representative of a class]: *our neighbours, the Smiths; the grammatical articles; the rich and the poor; the good and the true; in bed with the flu; to play the piano; Our car gives 10 km to the litre.* — *adv.* [used with comparatives] in that degree: *Start early the more surely to catch your flight; the earlier the better (= in what degree earlier, in that degree better).*

the·a·tre or **the·a·ter** (THEE·uh·tur, "TH" as in "thin") *n.* **1** a building or place with rows of seats for viewing a play, motion picture, or other dramatic performance or action: *a lecture theatre; movie, open-air, repertory theatre; a **dinner theatre** (= restaurant showing a play after dinner); a hospital's operating theatre; a **theatre of operations** (= scene of battle) during the war.* **2** drama: *Greek theatre; "Hamlet" is good theatre; the legitimate theatre (= professional drama).* **3** tactical: *theatre nuclear weapons.*

the·at·ri·cal (thee·AT·ruh·cul) *adj.* **1** having to do with the theatre or drama: *a theatrical company, effect.* **2** showy; affected; also, melodramatic: *his theatrical*

behaviour, manner, style.
— theatricals *n. pl.* [takes sing. or pl. v.] **1** amateur performances. **2** dramatics.

the·at·rics (thee·AT·rics) *n. pl.* [takes sing. or pl. v.] **1** the art of the theatre. **2** something done for theatrical effect; histrionics.

thee See THOU.

theft ("th" as in "thin") *n.* stealing or an instance of it: *to commit a theft; to practise theft; petty thefts under $200.*

their (THAIR, "TH" as in "the") *adj. possessive* of THEY of or by them: *their actions, houses.*
— theirs (THAIRZ) *pron.* their one(s): *The child is theirs.*

them ("th" as in "the") *pron.* **1** *objective case* of THEY: *He loves them.* **2** [nonstandard use] those: *them hills; in them houses.*

theme (THEEM, "TH" as in "thin") *n.* **1** a topic or subject: *the dominant theme of her novels; a theme for discussion; a theme* (= short essay) *assigned for an English composition.* **2** a recurrent melody, as elaborated in a composition. **3** a theme song.
— the·mat·ic (thee·MAT·ic, "th" as in "thin") *adj.*
— the·mat·i·cal·ly *adv.*

theme park *n.* an amusement park built around a theme, as Disney World.

theme song *n.* **1** an identifying melody, as one introducing a TV show. **2** a melody repeated throughout a motion picture.

them·selves (them·SELVZ) *pron.* emphatic or reflexive of THEY, THEM: *They themselves did it; They talked among themselves.*

then ("th" as in "the") *adv.* **1** at the same time: *She wasn't born then; the then reigning queen; He paid up then and there.* **2** after that: *I shaved, then I showered; Now it's my turn, then yours; the man, his wife, and then the children.* **3** in that case; therefore: *If we don't pay, then we can't have it;* **but then** (= but on the other hand) *where's the money?*
— n. that time: *By then it was too late; Nothing has happened since then;* **adj.:** *the then queen of England.*

thence ("th" as in "the") *adv.* from there; from then; from that: *a few yards thence; a few months thence; Thence* (= therefore) *it follows that....*

thence·forth *adv.* from then on.
Also **thence·for·ward** or **thence·for·wards.**

the·o·rem (THEE·uh·rum, "TH" as in "thin") *n.* **1** a statement or proposition that can be proved from axioms or postulates: *to formulate, prove, test a theorem.* **2** an established principle.

the·o·ret·i·cal (thee·uh·RET·uh·cul) *adj.* based on theory; hence, not based on fact; not practical. Also **the·o·ret·ic. — the·o·ret·i·cal·ly** *adv.*

the·o·rize (THEE·uh·rize) *v.* **-riz·es, -rized, -riz·ing** form a theory; speculate: *He theorized that the missing child was really hiding.* **— the·o·rist** *n.*

the·o·ry (THEE·uh·ree, THEER·ee) *n.* **-ries 1** the principles of an art or science, as opposed to practice:

He teaches musical theory; Your plan sounds good in theory; to combine theory and practice. **2** a reasoned-out and tested explanation of facts or phenomena: *to advance, advocate, develop, disprove, explode, propose, refute, suggest, test a theory; the theory of evolution; the big-bang, steady-state, and such theories* (= explanations) *of the universe; Is the possibility of life on other planets mere theory* (= speculation)?

ther·a·peu·tic (ther·uh·PEW·tic, "th" as in "thin") **1** *adj.* having to do with curing illness or preserving health: *drugs as therapeutic agents; a therapeutic bath; a therapeutic abortion (for saving the mother); Placebos have no therapeutic value.* **2 therapeutics** *n. pl.* [takes sing. v.] a branch of medicine dealing with the treatment of disease.

ther·a·py (THER·uh·pee) *n.* **-pies** treatment of disease: *group, occupational, physical, shock therapy.*
— ther·a·pist *n.*

there (THAIR, "TH" as in "the") *adv.* **1** at, in, or to that place: *He's there, not here; went there yesterday; She lives over there.* **2** in that matter: *We agree with you there.* **3** [used impersonally with "be," "seem," "appear," etc.]: *There is no time left; There seems to be a way out; There were many reasons.*
— n. that place: *He's in there.*
— interj.: *There, now! I told you so; There, there! Don't cry.*

there·a·bouts (THAIR·uh·bowts) *adv.* near that place, time, amount, etc.: *$2 000 or thereabouts; in Winnipeg or thereabouts.* Also **there·a·bout.**

there·af·ter (thair·AF·tur) *adv.* afterward; after that.

there·at (thair·AT) *adv.* [old use] **1** at that place or time. **2** because of that.

there·by (thair·BY) *adv.* **1** by that means or in that way. **2** by that place or in that connection: *Thereby hangs a tale.*

there·for (thair·FOR) *adv.* for that; for that purpose.

there·fore (THAIR·for) *adv.* for that reason; hence.

there·from (thair·FRUM) *adv.* from that.

there·in (thair·IN) *adv. Formal.* **1** in that place or into that place. **2** in that respect.

there·of (thair·OV) *adv. Formal.* of that or from that.

there·on (thair·ON) *adv.* [old use] **1** on that. **2** thereupon.

there·to (thair·TOO) *adv. Formal.* to that place or thing; also **there·un·to** (thair·UN·too) *adv.*

there·to·fore (thair·tu·FOR) *adv. Formal.* before that time.

there·up·on (thair·uh·PON) *adv.* **1** immediately after that. **2** because of that. **3** [old use] upon that (subject).

there·with (thair·WITH) *adv.* **1** along with that. **2** [old use] then.

there·with·al (THAIR·with·all) *adv.* **1** [old use] besides. **2** with that.

therm(o)- *combining form.* heat; temperature: *thermometer, thermostat.*

ther·mal (THUR·mul, "TH" as in "thin") *adj.* having to do with heat: *thermal air currents, springs; thermal pollution caused by discharge of heated liquids from factories into natural waters; thermal underwear made of specially knit insulating material.*

ther·mom·e·ter (thur·MOM·uh·tur) *n.* an instrument for measuring temperature: *a clinical, meat, oven, rectal thermometer.*
— **ther·mo·met·ric** (thur·moh·MET·ric) *adj.*

ther·mo·nu·cle·ar (thur·moh·NEW·clee·ur) *adj.* having to do with the fusion of atoms at very high temperatures and the release of nuclear energy, as in the hydrogen bomb: *a thermonuclear bomb, reaction, reactor; a thermonuclear war (using thermonuclear weapons).*

ther·mos (THUR·mos) same as VACUUM BOTTLE; Thermos *Trademark.*

ther·mo·stat (THUR·muh·stat) *n.* an automatic device for regulating temperature, as in an automobile, stove, or air conditioner: *We set the thermostat low at night.*

the·sau·rus (thi·SOR·us) *n., pl.* **-ri** (-rye) or **-rus·es** 1 a dictionary of synonyms and antonyms. 2 a treasury or collection of information.

these *pl.* of THIS.

the·sis (THEE·sis, "TH" as in "thin") *n., pl.* **-ses** (-seez) 1 a proposition put forward for exposition and defence: *Martin Luther nailed 95 theses to his church door.* 2 a theory: *to challenge, disprove, put forward, refute a thesis; Chairman Mao's thesis was that political power comes from the barrel of a gun.* 3 a research paper prepared by a candidate for an academic degree; dissertation: *a doctoral or Ph.D. thesis.*

they (THAY, "TH" as in "the") *pron., pl.* of HE, SHE, or IT; *objective* THEM, *possessive* THEIR, THEIRS. 1 the persons, animals, or things previously mentioned or referred to. 2 *Informal.* people in general: *They say prices will come down.*

they'd (THAID) they had; they would.

they'll (THAIL) they will; they shall.

they're (THAIR) they are.

they've (THAVE) they have.

thick ("th" as in "thin") *adj.* 1 with relatively much space between opposite sides or surfaces; not thin: *a thick sheet, slice, wall; thick fingers, rope, skin; a centimetre thick (as measured between opposite surfaces).* 2 crowded or closely set; firm or stiff in consistency; dense: *a thick growth, smoke, soup; The plot is getting thicker; thick (Informal. intimate) friends.* 3 not clear: *thick gloom, voices, weather; a thick (= stupid) head.* 4 *Informal.* too much to endure.
— *adv.* in a thick manner.
— **lay it on thick** *Slang.* praise or blame too much.
— *n.* thickest or hardest part: *in the thick of the battle.*
— **through thick and thin** through good times and bad. — **thick·ly** *adv.;* **thick·ness** *n.*

thick·en (THICK·un) *v.* make or become thick or thicker: *to thicken a gravy.*

thick·et (THICK·it) *n.* a dense growth of shrubs or small trees.

thick·set *adj.* 1 having a thick body; stocky. 2 thickly or closely planted: *a thickset hedge.*

thick-skinned *adj.* 1 having a thick skin. 2 not easily offended by criticism, insults, etc.

thief (THEEF, "TH" as in "thin") *n.* **thieves** (THEEVZ) one who steals something, usually in a secret and nonviolent manner: *a petty thief; sneak thief.*

thieve (THEEV) *v.* **thieves, thieved, thiev·ing** be a thief or steal something. — **thiev·ish** *adj.*

thiev·er·y (THEE·vuh·ree) *n.* **-er·ies** 1 the practice of stealing. 2 a theft.

thigh ("TH" as in "thin") *n.* the part of the leg between the knee and the hip.

thim·ble (THIM·bul, "TH" as in "thin") *n.* a small cap worn on the finger while sewing to protect it when pushing the needle. — **thim·ble·ful** *adj.*

thin *adj.* **thin·ner, thin·nest** 1 with relatively little space between opposite sides or surfaces; not thick: *a thin sheet, wire; a thin wall that is only a few inches thick.* 2 having little flesh or fat; not dense, crowded, or substantial: *a man of thin build; You are getting thin on top (= nearly bald); thin hair, mist, mountain air.* 3 weak; not strong: *thin blood; a thin soup, voice; a thin (= flimsy) disguise, excuse.*
— **on thin ice** on weak ground: *You're skating on thin ice!*
— *v.* **thins, thinned, thin·ning** make or become thin or thinner: *His hair is thinning on top; Use water to thin it down; War and famine thin out a population.*
— **thin·ly** *adv.;* **thin·ness** *n.*

thine ("th" as in "the") *adj. & pron.* [old form, *possessive of* THOU] your or yours: *thine eyes; Thine is the kingdom.*

thing *n.* 1 any object, matter, circumstance, opinion, etc.: *the latest thing in sleepwear; a box containing sewing things; He doesn't know a thing about calculus; She knows a thing or two (= quite a bit); She did the right thing; Do your own thing (Informal for what interests you).* 2 a creature: *a living thing.* 3 a person considered with pity, affection, contempt, etc.: *poor little thing; miserable thing.* 4 *Informal.* an irrational fear or prejudice: *Kay has a thing about cats.*
— **all things considered** everything being taken into account.
— **for one thing** [used to introduce the first of several reasons]: *For one thing, he is always late; for another, he doesn't dress well.*
— **see things** have hallucinations.

thing·a·ma·jig (THING·uh·muh·jig), **thing·um·a·bob** (THING·uh·muh·bob) or **thing·um·bob** (THING·um·bob) *n. Informal.* a thing whose name one cannot recall or does not know: *Where did I put the thingamajig for opening cans? Jack has a new thingamajig for picking lottery numbers.*

think ("TH" as in "thin") *v.* **thinks, thought** (THAWT), **think·ing** use the mind to form images and ideas, to consider things, have opinions, hopes, judgments, etc.: *to think clearly, hard; A good leader thinks ahead; He thinks back to the past when tempted to marry again; He's thinking about or of taking the job; He thinks himself qualified; thinks of (= considers) her with high* regard; *thinks her an able woman; She doesn't think much of* (= have a high opinion of) *him; She thinks that he is too aggressive; He was rebuffed when he thought* (= intended) *to help her; He likes to **think aloud*** (= utter his thoughts) *when alone; She **thought better of*** (= reconsidered) *her refusal and accepted the invitation; She will **think twice*** (= consider carefully) *before making the same mistake; had to **think up*** (= invent) *an excuse for her refusal.* — **think·er** *n.*

think tank *n.* an organization for studying the problems of governments and societies and proposing solutions and policies; also **think factory.**

thin·ner (THIN·ur) *adj. comp.* of THIN.
— *n.* a liquid, esp. a volatile one used to thin paints, etc.

thin-skinned *adj.* 1 having a thin skin. 2 sensitive to criticism, insults, etc.

third ("th" as in "thin") *adj.* next after the second.
— *n.* 1 one that is third. 2 any of three equal parts of something.
— *adv.* in third place; also **third·ly.**

third-class *adj.* 1 of a class of train or ship accommodations that is usually the cheapest: *a third-class ticket.* 2 of a class of mail consisting of identical letters mailed in quantity to thousands of addresses.
— *adv.* by third class.

third degree *n. Informal.* mental or bodily torture as a means of forcing a prisoner to give information.

third-degree burn (THIRD·duh·GREE-) *n.* injury resulting in charred skin and destruction of tissue.

third dimension *n.* the quality of depth or solidity that makes an object or scene seem real.
— **third-dimensional** (third·duh·MEN·shun·nul) *adj.*

third person *n.* a pronoun such as "he," "she," "it," "they," or a verb form such as "goes," "likes," or "wants" (third person singular) that refers to the one or ones spoken of.

third-rate *adj.* lowest-rated; hence, poor or inferior.

Third World *n.* the countries of Asia, Africa, and Latin America that are industrially less developed than other nations.

thirst ("th" as in "thin") *n.* 1 discomfort caused in the mouth and throat by the need to drink. 2 a craving or strong desire.
— *v:* be thirsty or desire ardently: *to thirst for adventure, knowledge, revenge.*

thirst·y *adj.* **thirst·i·er, -i·est** having or causing thirst: *Hot weather makes one thirsty; a land thirsty for rain.*

thir·teen (thur·TEEN, "th" as in "thin") *n., adj. & pron.* three more than ten; 13 or XIII; **thir·teenth** *n. & adj.*

thir·ty (THUR·tee) *adj. & n.* **-ties 1** three times ten; 30 or XXX. 2 **the thirties** *n. pl.* the numbers or years from 30 through 39.
— **thirty and out** the right to retire after 30 years of service with no loss of pension benefits.
— **thir·ti·eth** (-ith) *n. & adj.*

this *pron., pl.* **these** a person or thing that is present or referred to as nearer to the speaker than another, or

"that": *This is my book, that is yours; We chatted about **this and that*** (= many things) *to pass the time.*
— *adj.:* *this book; these books; this* (= coming) *summer; There was once this* (= a certain) *man who had three sons.* — *adv.* to this extent: *this big, far, much.*

thith·er (second "th" as in "the") *adv.* to that place.
— *adj.* on that side.

tho' (THOH, "TH" as in "the") *conj. & adv.* though.

thong ("th" as in "thin") *n.* 1 a narrow strip of leather or plastic, esp. one used as a strap or lace. 2 a type of footwear held on the foot by a thong fitted between the toes.

thorn ("th" as in "thin") *n.* 1 a short, hard, sharp-pointed protective outgrowth on a plant stem, as in the rose. 2 a source of trouble or annoyance: *The critics are a thorn in her flesh; a thorn in her side.* — **thorn·y** *adj.*

thor·ough (THUR·oh, "TH" as in "thin") *adj.* 1 marked by great attention to detail; painstaking: *a thorough scholar, search; very thorough in her work; She has a thorough grasp of her subject.* 2 complete: *He's a thorough scoundrel.*
— **thor·ough·ly** *adv.;* **thor·ough·ness** *n.*

thor·ough·bred (THUR·uh·bred) *n. & adj.* (an animal) of pure stock.

thor·ough·fare (THUR·uh·fare) *n.* a public street open at both ends with free flow of traffic: *a busy thoroughfare.*

thor·ough·go·ing (THUR·uh·go·ing) *adj.* 1 very thorough: *a thoroughgoing disciplinarian.* 2 out-and-out; utter: *a thoroughgoing scoundrel.*

those *pl.* of THAT.

thou ("th" as in "the," *rhyme:* how) *pron.* [old form, *possessive* THY or THINE, *objective* THEE; *pl.* YOU or YE, *possessive* YOUR or YOURS, *objective* YOU or YE] the one spoken to; you.
— *n.* ("th" as in "thin") *Slang.* a thousand dollars.

though (THOH, "TH" as in "the") *conj.* 1 in spite of the fact that; although: *He continues to work though ill; good to take an umbrella though* (= even if) *it may not rain; looks as though* (= as if) *it may rain.* 2 nevertheless: *They get along, though not like friends;* *adv.* however: *They get along – not like friends, though.*

thought *pt.* of THINK.
— *n.* 1 mental consideration of a subject or an expression of it: *He seems lost in thought; He acted without thought; a mother full of thought for her children's future; to abandon, entertain, express, gather, harbour, present, relish a thought; to read someone's thoughts; to sum up one's thoughts; evil, fleeting, happy, passing, refreshing, upsetting thoughts; A thought crosses one's mind, strikes one; to interrupt a train of thought; Perish the thought!* (= It's unthinkable!); *She had no thought* (= intention) *of hurting anyone; a book of thoughts* (= quotations); *Chaucer reflects medieval thought* (= thinking). 2 a little bit: *Be a thought more considerate of others.*

thought·less (THAWT·lis) *adj.* 1 not thinking. 2 not considerate.

thou·sand (THOW·zund, "TH" as in "thin") *n.* ten times 100; 1 000 or M: *three thousand people; thousands* (= a large number) *of people; people in* or *by the thousands.* — **thou·sandth** *n. & adj.*

thrash *v.* beat repeatedly, as in threshing grain with a flail: *In his frustration, he thrashed the mule soundly; children thrashing about in the water; They **thrashed over** the problem* (= discussed it) *for many hours; It took all evening to **thrash out*** (= arrive at) *a solution.*

thread (THRED) *n.* **1** a fine cord made of cotton, flax, etc. spun out and twisted together: *a spool of thread; coarse, heavy, polyester, silk, thin thread.* **2** anything fine and continuous like thread, as the filaments made by a spider or silkworm: *In Greek myth, death occurred when one of the Fates cut the thread of life; Lou's life hangs by a thread* (= Lou is in critical condition). **3** theme: *the thread of an argument, conversation, narrative.* **4** the continous spiral ridge around a screw or inside a nut. **5 threads** *pl. Slang.* clothes. — *v.* **1** pass a thread through a needle, beads, etc. **2** pass through like a thread: *She threaded her way through the crowd; red silk threaded with gold; to thread a roll of film into a camera.* **3** form a screw thread on or in a bolt or nut. **4** form a thread, as syrup of a certain thickness, when dropped from a spoon.

thread·bare *adj.* badly worn out: *a threadbare carpet, suit; threadbare clothes; a threadbare person (in worn-out clothes); a threadbare* (= hackneyed) *argument, excuse, plot.*

thread·y *adj.* **1** stringy. **2** not strong and full: *a thready pulse, voice.*

threat (THRET, "TH" as in "thin") *n.* **1** an expression of one's intention to hurt: *to carry out, constitute, issue, make, pose, utter a threat; a cheap, dire, empty, grave, idle, serious, veiled threat; acting under threat of reprisals.* **2** the possibility or cause of something evil or harmful happening: *a threat of rain; Icy sidewalks are a threat to life and limb; a security threat; Drunk drivers are a threat to public safety.*

threat·en (THRET·un) *v.* **1** utter a threat against someone: *He threatened us with a lawsuit; He threatened to leave her; a **threatening** phone call.* **2** be a threat to a person or thing: *An epidemic threatens a country; Storm clouds threaten* (= are a sign of) *rain; plant and animal species considered **threatened**, endangered, or extinct.*

three ("th" as in "thin") *n., pron. & adj.* one more than two; 3 or III.

3-D (THREE·DEE) *adj.* three-dimensional: *a 3-D movie, picture.*

three·fold *adj.* having three parts or three times as much or as many: *a threefold increase.* — *adv.* three times: *Prices have increased threefold.*

three R's *n.pl.* reading, writing, and arithmetic, as the basics of elementary education.

thresh ("th" as in "thin") *v.* **1** separate grain, as wheat, from the straw by beating. **2** beat out wheat, etc. with a flail or machine; hence, thrash.

thresh·old (THRESH·old, -hold) *n.* **1** the sill of a doorway as the point of entry: *to cross a threshold; A bride is carried over the threshold by the groom.*

2 entrance or starting point: *on the threshold of a career, discovery, new era; A flu outbreak exceeds the epidemic threshold when it accounts for 6% of all reported deaths.* **3** the point at which a stimulus or sensation becomes perceptible: *below the threshold of consciousness; low threshold of pain; A patient's allergy threshold depends on the weather, emotional state, and such conditions.*

threw *pt.* of THROW.

thrice *adv.* three times as many or as much.

thrift *n.* **1** careful management of money or resources; frugality in spending money. **2** in the U.S., a savings-and-loan institution.

thrift shop *n.* a shop selling secondhand clothes and housewares, usually for charity.

thrift·y *adj.* **thrift·i·er, -i·est** economical, esp. in saving; avoiding waste.

thrill *n.* a surge of excited feeling: *the thrill of a discovery; to get, give, have, provide a thrill; The first-time flyer experiences a thrill of joy; It's a thrill to fly; It's a thrill flying; He does it for thrills; for the thrill of it.* — *v.* have or cause a thrill: *We are thrilled to join you on the trip; thrilled with the invitation; The movie thrilled us with its special effects.* — **thrill·er** *n.*

thrilling *adj.* that thrills: *a thrilling experience, motion picture; It was thrilling to watch the acrobats.*

thrive *v.* **thrives,** *pt.* **thrived** or **throve** (THROHV), *pp.* **thrived** or **thriv·en** (THRIV·un), **thriv·ing** prosper or flourish; develop or grow vigorously: *Children thrive on good food and exercise.*

throat *n.* **1** the air-and-food passage inside the neck: *a sore throat from a cold; He cleared his throat to attract her attention; A lump in her throat* (= excess of emotion) *prevented her from speaking; You can't force your ideas down his throat* (= can't force him to accept them). **2** the front part of the neck: *His shirt is open at the throat; Some hockey players go for the throat* (= get violent) *when they are desperate; They're soon **at each other's throats*** (= fighting); *It's like **cutting their own throats*** (= hurting themselves). **3** a narrow passage or part.

throat·y *adj.* **throat·i·er, -i·est** produced in the throat; guttural or husky: *a throaty voice.* — **throat·i·ly** *adv.;* **throat·i·ness** *n.*

throb *v.* **throbs, throbbed, throb·bing** palpitate or pulsate: *the throbbing of the heart; a wound throbbing with pain.* — *n.* a throbbing or strong beat.

throes (THROZE) *n.pl.* pangs or spasms: *the throes of revolution; **in the throes*** (= struggle or agony) *of finishing a task on time.*

throne *n.* **1** a king's or queen's chair of state: *to abdicate, ascend, give up, mount, occupy a throne; a Speech from the Throne; to succeed to the throne.* **2** a similar chair used on ceremonial occasions by a bishop, etc. **3** a sovereign or ruler; hence, sovereignty.

Throne Speech *n.* a statement of government policy and programs for the coming year read to a legislature at its opening session by the representative of the sovereign.

Also **Speech from the Throne.**

throng n. 1 a crowd of people, esp. a moving and jostling one. 2 a multitude.
— v. crowd: *Admirers thronged around the star; Crowds thronged the theatre on opening night.*

throt·tle (THROT·ul) n. a valve regulating the fuel flowing into an engine, as of an automobile, or the mechanism controlling it, as the accelerator pedal.
— **at full throttle** at full speed.
— v. **throt·tles, throt·tled , throt·tling 1** choke or strangle; hence, suppress. 2 reduce the fuel flowing into an engine; hence, lessen speed: *to throttle back* or *down an engine.* — **throt·tler** n.

through (THROO) prep. 1 in at one side of something and out at the other; from beginning to end of a period: *He walked in through the open door; slept through the night; Monday through* (= to and including) *Friday; fined for driving through a red light (without stopping); He's through* (= finished with) *eating.* 2 by reason of something: *He failed through neglect.* 3 by the agency of someone: *I found out through a friend.*
— adv.: *She slept the night through; I read the book through; a train going through* (= nonstop) *to Montreal; He's wet* **through and through** (= completely).
— adj. 1 finished: *Are you through?* 2 involving no stopping: *through flights, traffic, trains; a through bus from Toronto to Winnipeg; a through ticket to Vancouver.*

through·out (throo·OUT) adv. & prep. in every part of something: *He was absent throughout the day.*

through·put n. processing capacity or the amount processed, as by a computer: *Input, throughput, and output are rarely in balance.*

through·way n. an expressway.

throve a pt. of THRIVE.

throw (THROH) v. **throws, threw** (THROO), **thrown** (THRONE), **throw·ing 1** cause to move rapidly or with force, usually through the air: *to throw a ball; A horse throws a rider; He threw himself on the mercy of the judge; was thrown* (= put) *into prison; to throw a switch (by moving a lever to the "on" or "off" position); a discovery that throws light on a subject.* 2 shed, drop, or toss casually or routinely: *to throw off a disguise; Snakes throw their skin; He threw a six (in dice); Domestic animals throw* (= bring forth) *their young.* 3 *Informal.* give: *to throw a party; She threw a punch; He threw the fight* (= gave it up intentionally). 4 to shape or fashion by turning or twisting, as on a potter's wheel or a lathe: *to throw a vase; Thrown silk is stronger than raw silk.*
— **throw a wrench** or **monkey wrench** spoil something going smoothly: *The foreman threw a wrench in the plan* or *a wrench into the works by suddenly switching things around.*
— **throw in** add as a free gift or bargain.
— **throw off 1** give off sparks. 2 get rid of a burden.
— **throw out 1** reject a proposal, expel an intruder or undesirable person, or put out a base runner in baseball. 2 put forth a signal, challenge, etc.
— **throw up 1** give up a job or game. 2 *Informal.* vomit.
— n. a throwing, a distance covered by throwing, or what is thrown over furniture, etc. to cover it, such as a bedspread, blanket, or scarf.

throw·a·way (THROH·uh·way) n. a pamphlet, disposable container, etc. designed to be thrown away after use; **adj.:** *a throwaway item; our* **throwaway society** *(that discards things instead of using them fully and recycling them).*

thru (THROO) *Informal.* through.

thrum v. **thrums, thrummed, thrum·ming** same as STRUM.

thrust v. **thrusts, thrust, thrust·ing** push with force and suddenness: *She thrust the letter into his hand; thrust at him with the sword; He had thrust himself into her presence; She thrust him aside and marched off; an election thrust on an unwilling public.*
— n. the action of thrusting: *the thrust of a sword, an attacking enemy, argument, or speech; the parry and thrust of debate; the supporting thrust of an arch; Jet engines and propellers produce thrust for a plane to overcome drag and move forward; the upward thrust of a rocket in reaction to the flow of exhaust gas.*
— **thrust·er** or **thrus·tor** n.

thru·way (THROO·way) n. *Informal.* throughway or expressway.

thud ("th" as in "thin") n. a dull sound, as of something heavy falling on soft ground.
— v. **thuds, thud·ded, thud·ding** move or hit making a thud.

thug ("th" as in "thin") n. a hoodlum or ruffian.

thumb (THUM, "TH" as in "thin") n. the short, thick opposable digit of the hand.
— **all thumbs** of a person, very clumsy or awkward.
— **turn thumbs down** reject: *The voters turned thumbs down on the government.*
— **under one's thumb** of a person, under one's domination.
— v. turn, handle, soil, etc. with the thumb: *She thumbed through the pages looking for pictures; a well-thumbed book; a hiker trying to* **thumb a ride** (= get a ride by gesturing with the thumb); *She* **thumbed her nose** *at him* (= made a gesture of contempt putting the thumb to the nose).

thumb index n. a set of lettered notches cut in the fore edge of a reference book to help the reader locate its contents.

thumb·nail sketch n. a brief and concise word-picture.

thumb·screw n. a screw that can be turned with the thumb and forefingers.

thumbs up n. approval or encouragement: *to give somebody the thumbs up (sign).*

thumb·tack n. a wide-headed tack that can be pressed into a board with the thumb.

thump ("th" as in "thin") n. 1 a heavy blow with something thick such as a fist. 2 the sound made by such a blow or fall.
— v. strike with a thump or pound: *The speaker thumped the table for attention; She heartily thumped his back in encouragement; His heart was thumping with excitement; a* **thumping** *(Informal for very large or whopping) victory.*

thun·der (THUN·dur, "TH" as in "thin") *n.* 1 the loud sound usually heard after a flash of lightning: *a clap, peal, roll of thunder; Thunder booms, reverberates, roars.* 2 a similar sound, as of a great waterfall or resounding applause.
— *v.* produce thunder or sound like it: *It often thunders when it rains; the thundering Niagara Falls; Cannons thundered in salute; The train thundered past the station.* — **thun·der·ous** (THUN·dur·us) *adj.*

thun·der·bolt (THUN·dur·bolt) *n.* a flash or shaft of lightning with a thunderclap: *a tree struck by a thunderbolt.*

thun·der·clap (THUN·dur·clap) *n.* a loud crash.

thun·der·show·er (THUN·dur·, *rhyme:* our) *n.* a shower with thunder and lightning.

thun·der·storm (THUN·dur·storm) *n.* a rainstorm with thunder and lightning.

thun·der·struck (THUN·dur·struck) *adj.* overcome with astonishment: *The whole town was thunderstruck at the news.*

Thurs·day (THURZ·dee, -day, "TH" as in "thin") *n.* the fifth day of the week, the day after Wednesday.

thus ("th" as in "the") *adv.* in this or that manner; to this or that degree or extent; so; therefore.

thus·ly *adv. Informal.* thus.

thwack ("th" as in "thin") *n. & v.* whack, esp. with something flat or heavy: *the thwack of a ball on gut.*

thwart (THWORT, "TH" as in "thin") *n. & adj.* (a seat) placed across a boat.
— *v.* obstruct, esp. by blocking the way: *The new candidate thwarted her plans; wanted to thwart her in her ambitions.*

thy ("th" as in "the") *adj.* [old form, possessive of THOU] your: *Thy kingdom come.*

thy·self (thy·SELF) *pron.* [old form, reflexive or emphatic of THOU] yourself.

tick 1 *v. & n.* (make) a light, clicking sound, as a clock. 2 *v. Informal.* keep going: *What **makes** the new government **tick** is a mystery to everyone.* 3 *v. & n.* (mark with) a check mark. 4 *n.* a small, blood-sucking, parasitic insect related to mites, some of which transmit diseases such as "tick fever." 5 *n.* the cloth case that is filled to make a mattress or pillow. 6 *n. Informal.* credit or trust.
— **tick off 1** name one by one. 2 *Slang.* anger.

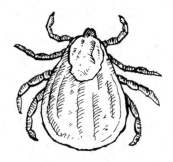

tick·er *n.* 1 *Slang.* the heart. 2 a ticking instrument, esp. a telegraph machine.

tick·et (TICK·it) *n.* 1 a card or piece of paper required for admission, identification, or passage: *theatre tickets for a concert; a ticket to a game; an airplane, bus, train ticket; a round-trip, not one-way ticket to Paris; a complimentary ticket; a season ticket; She bought a lottery ticket; When the lottery was drawn, she held the winning ticket; a claim ticket for a coat left in a checkroom; a price ticket* (= tag)*; a traffic ticket* (= summons) *issued by the police for speeding.* 2 a list of candidates for election; slate: *He's running on the NDP ticket; She was elected on a reform ticket.*
— *v.* tag: *Prices are ticketed on each article; He was ticketed for a parking violation.*

tick·le (TICK·ul) *v.* **-les, -led, -ling** feel or cause a tingling or thrilling sensation in a person, body part, etc. by stroking lightly, as the sole of the foot with a feather: *You have to tickle him to make him laugh; stories that tickle your curiosity.*
— **tickled pink** *adj. Slang.* very pleased.
— *n.* 1 a tickling or the sensation caused. 2 *Cdn.* in Newfoundland, a narrow strait, as between two islands or an island and the mainland; also, a narrow channel leading to a harbour.

tick·lish *adj.* sensitive or delicate: *a ticklish affair that calls for tact; a ticklish problem, situation.*

tid·al (TYE·dul) *adj.* having to do with tides: *a tidal bore in a river; a tidal current, inlet, wave; tidal erosion; a **tidal wave*** (= outburst) *of public indignation.*

tid·bit *n.* a choice morsel of food, gossip, etc.

tide *n.* 1 the rise and fall of ocean waters from the gravitational pull of the moon: *ebb, falling, flood, high, low tide.* 2 the resulting outward and inward flow in estuaries, rivers, etc.: *The tide comes in, ebbs or goes out.* 3 a trend, as of public opinion, events, etc.: *to buck, go against, go with, stem, swim with the tide; the rising tide of discontent; waiting for a turn of the tide (from one condition to its opposite).*
— **combining form.** [old use] season or time: *Christmastide, Eastertide.*
— *v.* **tides, tid·ed, tid·ing** help get through or survive: *Savings tided her over the long illness.*

tidings (TYE·dings) *n. pl.* news: *to bear, bring, receive glad tidings; tidings of great joy; sad tidings.*

ti·dy (TYE·dee) *adj.* **-di·er, -di·est** 1 neat or orderly. 2 *Informal.* relatively large: *a tidy sum of money.*
— *v.* **-dies, -died, -dy·ing** make tidy: *He's tidying up his room.*
— *n., pl.* **-dies** a small protective cover for the back, arms, or headrest of a chair or sofa.
— **tid·i·ly** *adv.;* **tid·i·ness** *n.*

tie (TYE) *v.* **ties, tied, ty·ing** 1 fasten or secure with a string, cord, rope, etc. that can be knotted: *to tie up a parcel; Tie your shoes; She tied* (= made) *a bow in her hair.* 2 connect or link: *two countries tied by common interests; evidence that **ties in with** (= relates to) suspected motives.* 3 restrict or confine: *Road construction ties up traffic; He's **tied down** by family responsibilities; I'm too **tied up** (= busy) to answer phone*

calls. **4** to equal a record or competitor in score: *The home team tied with the visitors for the lead; They tied the game at 12:04 of the first period; The 68-yard return tied the previous record; The last goal tied the score; They are tied for second place with 75 points.*
— *n.* **1** anything that ties or unites, as a cord, necktie, knot, or crosspieces to which railway tracks are fastened: *to cut, sever, strengthen family ties; to establish strong ties; close, intimate, marital ties; ties of friendship; school ties* (= neckties); *old school ties* (= bonds or links); *ties with* or *to foreign companies.* **2** a contest resulting in equality of scores between teams; draw: *The match ended in a tie; a scoreless tie (with zero for both sides); a game played to break a tie.*
— *adj.:* *a tie score; a game played as a **tie-breaker.***

tie-in *n.* a connection with something else, as of a book with a motion picture based on it.

tier (TEER) *n.* one of a series of rows, as of seats in a stadium or balconies in a theatre, arranged one above another.

tie-up *n.* **1** a temporary suspension of work in progress, traffic, etc.: *Production tie-ups forced the factory to close down.* **2** a connection or relation.

tiff *v. & n.* (have) a petty quarrel *with* someone.

ti·ger (TYE·gur) *n.* a large, tawny-coated, black-striped, flesh-eating Asiatic animal of the cat family: *Hockey brings out the tiger* (= aggressiveness) *in him; a paper tiger* (= one that appears strong and aggressive, like a tiger, but is not). — **ti·ger·ish** (TYE·gur·ish) *adj.*

tight *adj.* **1** going around and binding without looseness or slack: *a tight grip, knot; tight* (= tightfitting) *clothes; a tight* (= taut) *rope.* **2** closed firmly against leaks or losses: *a tight roof; a water-tight container; a tight* (= closely fought) *game; a tight schedule (with no spare time); The boss **runs a tight ship** (= operates efficiently); Money is tight* (= not easy to borrow). **3** *Informal.* stingy: *a tight moneylender who is tight with funds.* **4** *Slang.* intoxicated.
— *adv.* closely or firmly: *He decided to **sit tight** on his job and wait for the power struggle to end; sleep tight* (= soundly) . — **tight·ly** *adv.;* **tight·ness** *n.*

tight·en *v.* make or become tight or tighter: *People are expected to tighten their belts in times of scarcity.*

tight·fist·ed (TITE·fis·tid) *adj.* stingy.

tight-lipped *adj.* secretive.

tight·rope *n.* a tightly stretched rope or cable on which acrobats perform: *He walks a tightrope* (= is in a precarious position) *working for that outfit: a tightrope artist.*

tights *n.pl.* a skintight garment for the hips and legs, as worn by acrobats and dancers.

tight·wad *n. Slang.* a stingy person.

ti·gress (TYE·gris) *n.* a female tiger.

tile *n.* **1** a thin slab or piece of baked clay, stone, or synthetic material for covering roofs, floors, and walls. **2** a section of an earthenware drainage or sewage pipe.
— *v.* **tiles, tiled, til·ing** cover with tiles. — **til·er** *n.*

till *prep. & conj.* until.
— *v.* cultivate land by ploughing, sowing, etc.
— *n.* a drawer behind a counter, esp. in a store, in which money is kept: *He was caught **with his hand in the till** (= stealing).*

tilt *v.* **1** (cause) to slope or slant: *a tilting table with uneven legs; Cups, barrels, dump trucks, etc. are tilted to empty them; policies that seem to tilt to the Left; policies tilting* (= inclining) *toward socialism.* **2** charge or attack, as in the medieval lists: *Knights used to tilt on horseback; Don Quixote tilted at windmills mistaking them for giants.*
— *n.* **1** a slope or slant. **2** the medieval contest of knights trying to unhorse each other with lances while charging at speed.
— **(at) full tilt** at full speed.

tilt-top *adj.* of a table, having a top that can be tilted to a vertical position and stored flat against a wall.

tim·ber (TIM·bur) *n.* **1** wood prepared for use, as for building; also, a wooden beam: *a stack of timber; adj.: the timber industry, trade; timber products.* **2** trees bearing wood suitable for use: *the harvesting of timber; standing timber; a timber-cutting licence.*
— *v.* cover, support, or furnish with timbers.
— **tim·bered** (-burd) *adj.:* *a house with timbered walls and thatched roof; half-timbered stone cottages.*

timber limit *n. Cdn.* an area within which timber may be cut by a government licence.

tim·ber·line (TIM·bur·line) *n.* same as TREE LINE.

tim·bre (TAM·bur, TIM-) *n.* the characteristic tone of a voice or instrument, regardless of the pitch or volume of sounds.

time *n.* **1** the continuous period that includes the past, present, and future: *the eternity of time; Time flies, passes; Time will tell which of us is right.* **2** a period of definite duration: *It happened during the time of Queen Victoria; prehistoric time; We spent time waiting to be called; We watched TV to kill time; played cards to pass the time; to find, gain, lose, save, take, waste time; to fritter away one's time; to give equal time on radio or TV to all viewpoints; programs aired during prime time; She finished the job in record time; This hasn't happened in recent times; the travel time between home and office; the running time of a movie; to keep up with the times* (= current happenings); *Take your time* (= Do it slowly); *When we are idle, time drags; Time hangs on our hands; He beat* or *kept time* (= rhythm or rate of movement) *with his feet while she sang; She earns double time* (= rate of pay) *on holidays.* **3** a particular point or occasion for something to be done or to happen: *at the present time; Clocks tell time; Better luck next time; There's a first time for everything; closing, harvest, opening, starting time; It's time to go to bed; to fix, set, specify a time for our meeting; It's high time we met; By the time we got there, it was dark; to **bide one's time** (= wait for one's opportunity).* **4** a period as used or experienced: *We had a good, great, lovely time at the party; had the time of our lives; bad, difficult, hard times of inflation and unemployment; We have no time to waste; free, full, leisure, lost, spare time; We work part-time; "Time is money"* (= is

precious); *The patient is living on borrowed time*
(= living beyond the expected period); *Your time*
(= allotted period) *is up*. 5 a system of measuring time:
*solar time; daylight saving time; Eastern Standard
Time.*
— **against time** trying to finish in a given time.
— **ahead of time** before the due time.
— **at the same time** however.
— **at times** occasionally.
— **do** or **serve time** *Informal*. serve a prison term.
— **for the time being** for a limited period.
— **from time to time** sometimes; occasionally.
— **in time 1** eventually. 2 ahead of the set time: *We
arrived in time for the ceremony.* 3 keeping the right
rhythm or tempo.
— **make time 1** compensate for lost time by going faster
than normal. 2 save time this way.
— **mark time** appear to be active but without making
progress, as when moving the feet up and down without
marching forward.
— **of all time** that there ever has been or will be: *some
of the greatest scientists of all time.*
— **on time 1** at the right time: *We arrived on time.*
2 on credit: *He buys all heavy appliances on time.*
— *v.* **times, timed, tim·ing 1** set the time or speed of
something: *to time one's activities; to time a program.*
2 measure the time or duration of something: *to time a
race, runner, speech.*
— *adj.* having to do with time: *a test with a time limit;
a* **time loan** *that is due at a specified time.*

time bomb *n.* a bomb set to go off at a definite time.

time clock *n.* a clock device for recording employees'
hours of work: *to punch a time clock.*

time-honoured (TIME·on·urd) *adj.* long-existing: *a
time-honoured custom, practice.*

time·less (TIME·lis) *adj.* eternal; also, not affected by
time: *the timeless universe; the timeless beauty of the
Taj Mahal; He saw everything that ever happened to
him in one timeless moment.*

time·ly *adj.* **-li·er, -li·est** happening or done at a suitable
time: *a timely reminder.* — **time·li·ness** *n.*

time·out *n.* a brief suspension of play, as in basketball or
football: *He takes (a) timeout for ten minutes every
hour.*

time·piece *n.* a clock, watch, or other time-measuring
instrument.

tim·er (TYE·mur) *n.* **1** a clock device for indicating the
passage of a period of time: *an egg timer.* 2 an
automatic device for starting and stopping an operation:
We set a timer to turn the lights off and on at night.

times *prep.* multiplied by: *3 times 5 is 15.*

time·serv·er (TIME·sur·vur) *n.* one who servilely seeks to
please those in power or changes his principles to suit
the times. — **time·serv·ing** *n. & adj.*

time-sharing *n.* **1** a system enabling several people to use
the same computer simultaneously in various functions.
2 the sharing of a vacation lodging by several tenants or
owners taking turns using it.

time·ta·ble (TIME·tay·bul) *n.* **1** a schedule of the hours
at which work is started and stopped. 2 a list of times at

which buses, planes, etc. arrive and depart, etc.: *to
follow, make up, upset a timetable.*

time warp *n.* the condition of being in an imaginary
time in a past or future period, as in science fiction.

time·worn *adj.* worn out or hackneyed: *a timeworn
expression, practice.*

time zone *n.* any of the 24 longitudinal divisions of the
world in each of which the same standard time is used
regardless of local time: *There are six time zones from
Newfoundland to British Columbia.*

tim·id (TIM·id) *adj.* **1** cautious and fearful: *a timid
child; Deer are timid by nature.* 2 lacking in the self-
confidence required to assert oneself: *He's too timid to
ask for a raise.* — **tim·id·ly** *adv.*
— **ti·mid·i·ty** (tuh·MID·uh·tee) *n.*

timing (TYE·ming) *n.* **1** regulation of the speed,
duration, etc. of an action: *The timing of your engine
needs adjusting; You should improve your timing; Note
your timing* (= time measurement) *at the end of the run.*
2 choice of the right moment of an action for maximum
effect: *She has a good sense of timing; It's bad timing to
ask for a raise when the boss is in a bad mood.*

Tim·my and Tam·my (TIM·ee, TAM·ee) *n. Cdn.* a
handicapped boy and girl chosen each year by the
Easter Seal Society as the stars of their campaign.

tim·or·ous (TIM·ur·us) *adj.* full of fear and
apprehension: *a timorous glance.*
— **tim·or·ous·ly** *adv.;* **tim·or·ous·ness** *n.*

tin *n.* **1** a light, bluish-white, malleable, corrosion-
resistant metal used in alloys. 2 a container made of tin
plate.
— *v.* **tins, tinned, tin·ning 1** plate with tin. 2 esp.
Brit. to can: *tinned salmon.*

tin can *n.* a packaging container made of tin.

tinc·ture (TINK·chur) *n.* **1** a medication dissolved in
alcohol: *tincture of iodine.* 2 a tinge or trace.
— *v.* **-tures, -tured, -tur·ing** tinge *with* a colour; also,
tint.

tin·der (TIN·dur) *n.* a material that burns easily: *The
long drought left the forest tinder dry.*

tin·der·box (TIN·dur·box) *n.* a potential source of a fire
or flare-up, as a box containing tinder, flint, and steel
formerly used to kindle a fire.

tine *n.* a prong, esp. of a fork.

tinge (TINJ) *n.* a slight colouring, flavour, taste, etc.:
*Ivory gets a yellowish tinge after some time; the tinge of
sadness in her voice.*
— *v.* **ting·es, tinged, tinge·ing** or **ting·ing** modify with
a tinge: *a voice tinged with sadness.*

tin·gle (TIN·gul) *n.* a slight prickling or stinging
sensation, as from cold, excitement, etc.
— *v.* **-gles, -gled, -gling** have or cause a tingle: *a
tingling sensation.*
— **tin·gly** *adj.*

tin·ker (TINK·ur) *n.* **1** one who goes around mending

pots, pans, etc. **2** an unskilled or amateur worker.
— *v.* repair or work in an unskilled way *at* or *with*
something. — **tin·ker·er** *n.*

tin·kle (TINK·ul) *n.* a short, light ringing sound, as of
little bells, esp. a series of such sounds.
— *v.* **-kles, -kled, -kling** make or cause to make a
tinkle.

tin·ny (TIN·ee) *adj.* **tin·ni·er, tin·ni·est 1** like tin in
appearance, value, sound, etc.: *a tinny* (= thin or
metallic) *voice; a tinny* (= not well-made) *car.* **2** of or
containing tin: *a tinny alloy, lode.*
— **tin·ni·ly** *adv.;* **tin·ni·ness** *n.*

tin·sel (TIN·sul) *n.* **1** glittering material used for
decoration in thin sheets, threads, etc., as on Christmas
trees. **2** anything showy, gaudy, and cheap.

tint *n.* a light shade or hue: *Pink is a tint of red.*
— *v.* colour with a tint: *tinted eyeglasses, hair; a
windshield tinted blue.*

ti·ny (TYE·nee) *adj.* **-ni·er, -ni·est** very small; minute.

tip *n.* **1** an end part, esp. a pointed or tapering end: *the
tip of the nose, tongue; the tips of the toes; It was* **on the
tip of my tongue** (= I almost said it); *That's only the* **tip
of the iceberg** (= the least or visible part of the
situation). **2** a light stroke or glancing blow; tap. **3** a
piece of secret information: *an anonymous tip; a hot tip.*
4 a useful hint or suggestion: *a few tips on* or *about
good grooming.* **5** a small gift of money; gratuity: *She
left a handsome tip for the waiter.* **6** a tilt or slope.
— *v.* **tips, tipped, tip·ping 1** have as an end part: *a
cane tipped with brass; a filter-tipped cigarette.* **2** tap:
The ball was tipped into the basket. **3** give a useful hint
to someone: *The police were* **tipped off** *by an
anonymous caller; She was careful not to* **tip her hand**
(*Informal* for reveal her intentions) *by talking loosely.*
4 give a gratuity: *She never forgets to tip the waiter; She
tips generously, liberally.* **5** tilt or slope: *He's in the habit
of tipping his hat to ladies; A boat may tip over if
loaded unevenly; She* **tips the scales at** (= weighs) *40 kg.*

tip-off *n.* a tipping off; warning.

tip·ple (TIP·ul) *v.* **tip·ples, tip·pled, tip·pling** drink
alcoholic liquor habitually and excessively.
— *n.* liquor for tippling: *Vodka is the main tipple in
Russia.* — **tip·pler** *n.*

tip·py toes (TIP·ee-) *n.pl. Informal.* the tips of the toes.

tip·ster (TIP·stur) *n. Informal.* one who supplies secret
information, usually for pay, as about horse races.

tip·sy (TIP·see) *adj.* **-si·er, -si·est** intoxicated; hence,
unsteady. — **tip·si·ly** *adv.;* **tip·si·ness** *n.*

tip·toe (TIP·toe) *v.* **-toes, -toed, -toe·ing** walk on the
tips of one's toes. — *n.* the tip of a toe.
— **on tiptoe** on one's tiptoes; silently; also, eagerly.

tip·top *n.* the highest point.
— *adj. & adv.* **1** at the very top. **2** *Informal.* excellent.

ti·rade (TYE·rade, tuh·RADE) *n.* a long, vehement or
scolding speech; harangue: *He launched into a tirade
against politicians.*

tire *n.* a usually hollow casing of rubber with a grooved
tread, filled with air and fixed to the rim of a wheel for
a smooth ride: *to change, deflate, inflate, mount, slash*

*a tire; to rotate tires for even wear; A tire blows out,
goes flat; We had a flat tire; a radial, snow, spare, steel-
belted, studded, tubeless, whitewall tire.*
— *v.* **tires, tired, tir·ing** make or become weary or
bored: *One tires of watching TV after a few hours; She
tires easily.*
— **tired** *adj.* **1** exhausted or weary: *She's tired from the
climb; dead tired; I'm tired of* (= bored with) *TV.*
2 worn-out: *a tired joke, suit.*

tire·less *adj.* never getting tired; hence, ceaseless: *a
tireless worker; her tireless efforts, energy.*
— **tire·less·ly** *adv.*

tire·some (TIRE·sum) *adj.* that tires or bores: *It's
tiresome watching* or *to watch TV all day.*

'tis (TIZ) it is.

tis·sue (TISH·oo) *n.* **1** the body substance of animals
and plants consisting of cells: *bone, connective,
muscular, nervous, scar tissue.* **2** web or network: *a
tissue of lies; a tissue of twaddle.* **3** a fine, sheer cloth or
gauze. **4** soft absorbent paper: *facial tissue; toilet tissue.*

tissue paper *n.* lightweight paper used for wrapping,
paper napkins, etc.

tit *n.* **1** a nipple or teat. **2** a small bird.

ti·tan (TYE·tun) *n.* a giant, like the **Titans**, the first
gods of Greek myth.

ti·tan·ic (tye·TAN·ic) *adj.* giantlike in size or strength.

tit·bit *n.* same as TIDBIT.

titch *n. Slang.* a tiny amount: *That's a titch silly.*

tit for tat *n.* blow in return for blow; retaliation.

tithe (TITHE, "TH" as in "the") *n.* a tenth part of one's
income, as traditionally given to the church.
— *v.* **tithes, tithed, tith·ing** pay a tithe. — **tith·er** *n.*

tit·il·late (TIT·ul·ate) *v.* **-il·lates, -il·lat·ed, -il·lat·ing**
excite or stimulate, as if by tickling.
— **tit·il·la·tion** (-AY·shun) *n.*

tit·i·vate (TIT·uh·vate) *v.* **-vates, -vat·ed, -vat·ing**
Informal. dress up; spruce up.

ti·tle (TYE·tul) *n.* **1** the name of a literary or artistic
product: *the title of a play; the title page of a book.*
2 titles *pl.* credits, subtitles, etc. appearing on a TV or
motion-picture screen. **3** a name giving a person's rank
or occupation, as Mister, Miss, Lord, Doctor, Supervisor,
etc.: *a job title; The title "Honourable" is bestowed* or
*conferred on senators for life; She renounced her official
titles in protest.* **4** a championship: *the world
heavyweight title; to clinch, hold, lose, win a title; a title
bout.* **5** a legal right to exclusive ownership of property;
also, a deed or other document showing this: *to give,
hold title to a property; to establish clear title.*
— *v.* **-tles, -tled, -tling** give a title to something.

titled *adj.* having a title of rank or nobility.

ti·tle·hold·er (TYE·tul·hole·dur) *n.* the holder of a
championship.

title role *n.* the character in a play or motion picture
after whom the work is named.

tit·ter (TIT·ur) *n. & v.* giggle.

tit·tle (TIT·ul) *n.* a particle or dot: *It was done without raising a tittle of suspicion.*

tittle-tattle (TIT·ul·TAT·ul) *n.* gossip; idle chatter.

tit·u·lar (TICH·uh·lur) *adj.* 1 of or bearing a title: *a titular head, rank, role.* 2 nominal: *a titular bishop (of a nonexistent jurisdiction); the titular position of chairman of the board.*

tiz·zy (TIZ·ee) *n.* **tiz·zies** *Informal.* state of nervous excitement; dither: *We found them in a tizzy; to be thrown into a tizzy.*

to (TOO, tuh) *prep.* 1 [indicating the direction of an action or movement or its result]: *He goes to school; stood with his back to the wall; came to our rescue; was put to sleep; torn to pieces.* 2 [indicating a limit]: *count to 100; It is five minutes to six; She was faithful to the end.* 3 [indicating a relationship]: *a score of 10 to one; He dances to every tune; She's kind to animals; gives to charity; talks to herself.* 4 [used before verbs to indicate the infinitive]: *He likes to sing; Go if you want to (go).*
— *adv.* [indicating the direction of an action or movement toward something implied]: *He came to (= became conscious) soon after fainting; As soon as they were served, they fell to (= started eating); A door swings to (= becomes shut); He was wearing his hat wrong end to (= forward).*
— **to and fro** forward and back; back and forth.

toad (TODE) *n.* a froglike but less aquatic animal.

toad·y (TOH·dee) *n.* **toad·ies** a servile flatterer.
— *v.* **toad·ies, toad·ied, toad·y·ing** be a toady to a superior: *to toady up to someone.*

toast (TOHST) *n.* 1 a slice of bread browned by heat, as in a toaster: *to make toast; a piece or slice of toast.* 2 a drink or an invitation to drink in honour of a person or thing: *He proposed a toast to the champion; Everyone joined him in the toast; She was the **toast of the town** (= celebrity or hero) on her return from the Olympics.*
— *v.* 1 to brown bread by heat or warm one's body before a fire. 2 propose or drink a toast to someone.

toast·er (TOHS·tur) *n.* a small appliance for toasting bread.

toast·mas·ter (TOHST·mas·tur) *n.* one who presides at a banquet introducing speakers, proposing toasts, etc.; *fem.* **toast·mis·tress.**

to·bac·co (tuh·BAC·oh) *n.* **-bac·cos** 1 a plant whose broad leaves are prepared for smoking, chewing, etc.; also, the prepared leaves: *to chew, cure, grow tobacco; a plug of tobacco (for chewing).* 2 products such as cigarettes and snuff prepared from tobacco leaves.

to·bog·gan (tuh·BOG·un) *n.* a small sled without runners whose front end curves upward.
— *v.* 1 coast downhill on a toboggan. 2 decline rapidly in value.

to·day (tuh·DAY) *n. & adv.* 1 (on or for) this day. 2 (at) the present time; (in) this day or age: *Today we know that the earth is not flat; today's youth.*

tod·dle (TOD·ul) *v.* **tod·dles, tod·dled, tod·dling** walk with short uncertain steps, as a young child, or **tod·dler** *n.*

to-do (tuh·DOO) *n.* **-dos** (-DOOZ) fuss or commotion: *She made a big to-do over the missing keys.*

toe (TOH) *n.* 1 one of the five fingerlike parts of the human foot: *She's careful not to **tread on his toes** (= not to offend him).* 2 the forepart of a foot or hoof.
— **on one's toes** *Informal.* alert and ready.
— *v.* **toes, toed, toe·ing** touch or reach with the toes, as the starting line of a race: *Members of a party are expected to **toe the line** (= conform to policy, rules, etc.); Some toe (= turn the toes) in, others toe out when walking.*

toed (TODE) *adj. & combining form.* having toes or toes as specified: *toed stockings, pigeon-toed, three-toed.*

toe dance *n.* a dance performed on the toes, as in ballet.
— **toe-dance** *v.* **-danc·es, -danced, -danc·ing.**
— **toe-danc·er** *n.*

toe·hold *n.* 1 a narrow footing, as on a ledge: *when the union first got a toehold in that factory.* 2 a slight advantage.

toe·nail *n.* the nail of a toe.

tof·fee (TOF·ee, TAW·fee) *n.* **tof·fees** taffy or caramel. Also **tof·fy, tof·fies.**

tog 1 *v.* **togs, togged, tog·ging** *Informal.* clothe or dress: *properly togged in tuxedoes.* 2 **togs** *n.pl.* clothes.

to·geth·er (tuh·GETH·ur, "TH" as in "the") *adv.* 1 in or into one place or group: *Friends like to be together; working together; The two together weigh 90 kg; the man **together with** his wife.* 2 at the same time: *I heard them singing together; Our cat was missing for days together (= continuously).*
— **get** or **put it together** get organized: *He just couldn't get it together even after months on the job.*
— *adj. Slang.* self-possessed; well-integrated: *a young, happy together couple.*

to·geth·er·ness (tuh·GETH·ur·nis) *n.* closeness of relationship.

tog·gle (TOG·ul) *n.* a device that hangs or pulls crosswise, as a T-head crosspiece passed through a loop, or a **toggle bolt** with a winged nut that spreads out crosswise to lock the bolt in position.

toil *n.* 1 work that is long and laborious: *after years of toil and sweat; arduous, unremitting toil.* 2 usually **toils** *pl.* meshes or a netlike trap.
— *v.* labour hard: *Farmers toil in the fields; Serious students toil over their homework; a tractor-trailer toiling (= moving laboriously) up a hill.* — **toil·er** *n.*

toi·let (TOY·lut) *n.* 1 the bowl-shaped plumbing fixture for receiving body wastes: *to flush the toilet.* 2 a washroom equipped with a toilet: *a pay toilet; public toilets.* 3 the process of washing, dressing, and grooming oneself.

toilet paper or **toilet tissue** *n.* soft paper for wiping oneself after using the toilet.

toi·let·ry (TOY·luh·tree) *n.* usually **toi·let·ries** *pl.* articles such as soap and cosmetics used in washing and grooming.

toi·lette (twah·LET, toi·) *n.* **1** toilet or washroom. **2** costume or attire.

toilet training *n.* the training of a child to use the toilet and control bladder and bowel movements.

toilet water *n.* cologne or similar perfumed liquid.

toil·some *adj.* laborious or wearisome.

to·ken (TOH·kun) *n.* **1** a gift, souvenir, or other article that serves as a sign or indication of an inner quality, feeling, etc.: *a gift as a token of our gratitude; offered* **in token of** (= as a sign of) *our gratitude; a tangible token.* **2** a coinlike piece of metal serving as an admission ticket: *A bus token is dropped in a box; a subway token that is inserted into a slot.* — **by the same token** for the same reason. — *adj.* serving as a token; partial; hence, nominal: *a token payment to acknowledge a debt; a token gesture.*

to·ken·ism (TOH·kun·iz·um) *n.* the policy of making merely nominal concessions to a demand, as for racial equality.

told *pt. & pp.* of TELL: *All told* (= altogether), *some 50 were killed and 500 injured in the earthquake.*

tol·er·a·ble (TOL·ur·uh·bul) *adj.* **1** bearable or endurable: *a tolerable burden, pain.* **2** fairly good: *in tolerable health; a tolerable income, meal.*

tol·er·ance (TOL·ur·unce) *n.* **1** the quality of being tolerant: *social tolerance of people with AIDS; to have, show tolerance for people of all racial backgrounds and religions.* **2** resistance to a drug's ill effects: *Different people have different tolerances; Tolerance increases with use.* **3** the allowable variation from a standard dimension, weight, or fineness, as in minting coins.

tol·er·ant (TOL·ur·unt) *adj.* willing to let others live according to their own beliefs, practices, etc.; also, forbearing: *a tolerant and forgiving nature; to be tolerant of opposition.*

tol·er·ate (TOL·uh·rate) *v.* **-ates, -at·ed, -at·ing** **1** put up with or bear a person or thing: *We will not tolerate such behaviour; a character difficult to tolerate* (= work or live with). **2** resist the ill effects of a drug, etc. — **tol·er·a·tion** (·RAY·shun) *n.*

toll (TOLE) *n.* **1** a charge or fee, as for using a bridge or turnpike, making a long-distance telephone call, or **toll call**, etc.: *a toll-free 800 number; to charge, exact, impose a toll; She collects tolls from a booth on the bridge.* **2** loss or damage suffered: *The earthquake took a heavy toll of lives; the frightening death toll on our highways.* **3** a tolling sound. — *v.* **1** ring a bell in slow, measured strokes. **2** announce the hour of day, a death, etc. or summon by tolling: *The bell tolled for those who died in the war.*

toll road *n.* a turnpike.

tom *adj. & combining form.* male: *tomcat, tomcod; tom turkey.*

tom·a·hawk *n.* a light, axlike tool and weapon of North American Indians.

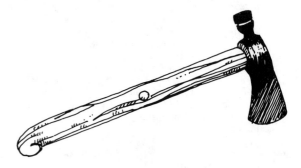

tomb (TOOM) *n.* **1** a burial place for a dead body, as a grave, vault, or other chamber. **2** an above-ground structure such as a cenotaph or mausoleum. — **the tomb** death.

tom·boy *n.* a girl who is boisterous and romps about like a boy. — **tom·boy·ish** *adj.*

tome *n.* a learned or heavy volume: *a scholarly tome.*

tom·fool·er·y (tom·FOO·luh·ree) *n.* **-er·ies** silly or nonsensical behaviour.

to·mor·row (tuh·MOR·oh) *n. & adv.* (on) the day after today.

ton (TUN) *n.* either of two units of weight, "short ton" (2 000 lb. / 907.18 kg) or "long ton" (2 240 lb. / 1 016.05 kg): *The police came down on them* **like a ton of bricks** (= took forceful action).

tone *n.* **1** the sound of a voice or musical instrument, esp. as to its character or quality: *in an angry tone of voice; in angry tones; abusive, apologetic, arrogant, condescending, dulcet, friendly, harsh, imperious, low, patronizing, serious, subdued, sweet, threatening tones; the solemn tones of an organ; the strident tone of his demands; a high moral tone; the dial tone of the telephone.* **2** a musical sound of a particular pitch: *"Doh" and "ray" are a whole tone* (= note or step) *apart; a falling, high, low, rising tone; Chinese, Bantu, and other* **tone languages** *differentiate meaning by pitch of voice.* **3** style or trend: *A keynote speaker sets the tone of the proceedings.* **4** vigour and tension, as of a muscle; also, responsiveness or resilience, as of rubber. **5** the relative lightness or darkness of a colour: *Rose is a tone of red blended with grey; decorated in* **tones** (= shades) *of blue.* — *v.* **tones, toned, ton·ing** give a tone to; also, moderate: *He was too enraged to* **tone down** *his remarks.* — **ton·al** *adj.;* **ton·al·ly** *adv.*

tone-deaf *adj.* unable to distinguish musical tones.

ton·ey (TOH·ney) *adj.* **ton·i·er, -i·est** same as TONY.

tongs *n. pl.* a device for grasping or lifting chunks of coal, sugar, ice, etc., having two arms pivoted or hinged together at one end or in the middle: *a pair of tongs; tongs for curling hair.*

tongue (TUNG) *n.* **1** the fleshy movable structure in the mouth that is used for tasting and speaking: *Children stick out their tongues at each other; He clicked his*

tongue in delight; Flying saucers were on everyone's tongue (= being discussed by everyone) *in the 1950s; Tongues were wagging* (= People were gossiping); *to speak with a forked tongue* (= be deceitful in speech). **2** something similar to a tongue in shape or use, as a strip of land projecting into water, the striking piece inside a bell, or the flap under the lacing of a shoe. **3** the power of speech, a language, or the manner of its use: *his mother tongue; her native tongue; the gift of* **tongues** (= the ability to speak many languages); *So shocked, he couldn't* **find his tongue** (= begin to speak); *Jan has a foul, glib, loose, nasty, sharp tongue* (= manner of speaking).
— **hold one's tongue** be silent.
— **speak in tongues** speak in different languages as a religious phenomenon.
— *v.* **tongues, tongued, tongu·ing 1** lick with the tongue. **2** play a flute or similar musical instrument by using the tongue.

tongued (TUNGD) *adj. & combining form.* having a tongue or tongues as specified: *tongued lightning; red-tongued lilies; a silver-tongued orator.*

tongue-in-cheek *adj. & adv.* ironical(ly) or satirical(ly): *a tongue-in-cheek comment.*

tongue-lashing (TUNG·lash·ing) *n. Informal.* a severe scolding.

tongue-tied *adj.* **1** speechless from embarrassment. **2** unable to speak properly because of shortness of the membrane under the tongue.

tongue twister *n.* a phrase or sentence that is difficult to say fast, as "She sells seashells on the seashore."

ton·ic *n. & adj.* (a drug, medicine, etc.) that is invigorating or bracing: *Take a tonic for your cough;* **Tonic (water),** *as in "gin and tonic," is a carbonated quinine-flavoured mix.*

to·night (tuh·NITE) *adv. & n.* (on) the present or the coming night.

tonne (TUN) *n.* a metric ton of 1 000 kg.

ton·sil (TON·sul) *n.* either of two masses of tissue on the sides at the back of the mouth: *Jim had his tonsils out or removed or taken out.*

ton·sil·li·tis (ton·suh·LYE·tis) *n.* inflammation of the tonsils.

ton·y (TOH·nee) *adj.* **ton·i·er, -i·est** *Informal.* stylish or elegant: *one of the tonier downtown restaurants; a tony crowd; tony clothes, gifts.*

too *adv.* **1** more than enough: *She sleeps too long; He's only too glad to leave.* **2** also: *You too can be rich; I like her too.* **3** *Informal.* very: *I'm not feeling too well.* **4** so; indeed: *"I didn't do it." "You did too."*

took *pt.* of TAKE.

tool *n.* **1** a hand implement such as is used in carpentry, gardening, etc.: *the* **tools of one's** or **of the trade.** **2** a working part of a machine that drills, planes, grinds, etc.; also, such a machine, or "machine tool." **3** one that serves as a means; hence, a stooge or dupe.
— *v.* **1** form or finish an article with a tool. **2** equip a plant with tools or machinery: *to tool up for the new production season.* **3** *Informal.* drive in a leisurely way:

He was tooling around town in his new car.

toot (long "oo") *v.* sound a horn in short blasts.
— *n.* such a blast. — **toot·er** *n.*

tooth (long "oo," "th" as in "thin") *n., pl.* **teeth 1** any of the hard bony structures in the jaws, used for biting, chewing, etc.: *Babies cut teeth* (= have them appear through the gums); *Dentists cap, drill, extract, fill, pull, take out teeth; You brush, clean, clench, floss, gnash, grind, grit, pick your teeth; Teeth ache, chatter, decay, erupt* (= appear), *fall out, rot; abscessed, decayed, discoloured teeth.* **2** a toothlike part of a saw, gear wheel, comb, rake, etc. **3** taste or liking. **4** *pl.* effectiveness: *We need laws with teeth.*
— **fight tooth and nail** fight with all one's strength.
— **long in the tooth** *Informal.* advanced in age.
— **in the teeth of** in the face of or in defiance of something.
— **toothed** *adj.;* **tooth·less** *adj.*

tooth·some *adj.* **1** tasty and tender; delicious: *a toothsome cheesecake.* **2** sexually attractive; delectable.

tooth·y *adj.* **tooth·i·er, -i·est** having or showing prominent teeth: *a toothy grin, smile.* — **tooth·i·ly** *adv.*

too·tle (TOO·tul) *v.* **-tles, -tled, -tling** *Informal.* **1** toot continuously and quietly: *to tootle (on) his whistle, flute.* **2** go in an unhurried manner: *to tootle in for tea; She tootled around the estate; tootled down to the shopping centre.* — *n.* the sound of tootling.

top *n.* **1** a cone-shaped toy for spinning with a string wound around it: *He sleeps like a top* (= soundly). **2** the highest point or upper part: *from the top of the building; from top to bottom; to reach the top of a mountain; climb to the top of the tower; He was at the top of his career when he resigned; the top (surface) of a table; seated at the top* (= head) *of the table; shouted at the top of her voice; The top* (= best) *of the morning to you! a pajama top; a bikini top; His hobby is collecting bottle tops* (= caps); *beet tops (above ground).*
— **blow one's top** *Slang.* lose one's temper.
— **off the top of one's head** *Informal.* making a rough guess.
— **on top of 1** besides: *a bonus on top of his pay.* **2** in control or mastery of: *to be on top of a situation.*
— *v.* **tops, topped, top·ping 1** trim the top of a plant. **2** provide a bottle, box, etc. with a cap or lid. **3** crown or be at the top of something. **4** reach the top of something: *She topped her class last year.* **5** rise above; be or do better than something: *Try to top this act.*
— **top off** complete *with* something as a finishing touch.
— *adj.* highest or foremost: *top man, speed, value; She paid* **top dollar** (*Informal for* maximum amount possible) *for her home; He received* **top billing** (= prominent treatment) *in the media; the* **top dog** (*Slang for* boss) *around here.* — **top·per** *n.*

top brass *n.* high officials or officers.

top-drawer (TOP·draw·ur) *adj. Informal.* of the highest rank or importance.

top-flight *adj. Informal.* of the highest rank; first-rate.

Top 40 *n. & adj.* (of) the best 40, as in the record charts: *a Top-40 hit from the sixties.*

top-heavy (TOP·hev·ee) *adj.* unstable because of being too heavy at the top.

top·ic (TOP·ic) *n.* a theme or subject for an essay, conversation, discussion, etc.: *to bring up a topic; to broach the topic of a raise; Religion and politics are controversial topics; an everyday topic like the weather; the topics of the times* (=matters of current interest).

top·i·cal (TOP·uh·cul) *adj.* **1** having to do with topics. **2** of current or local interest: *a topical discussion, story.* **3** for local, external use on the body surface: *a topical anesthetic, remedy.* — **top·i·cal·ly** *adv.* — **top·i·cal·i·ty** (-CAL·uh·tee) *n.*

top·less *adj.* not wearing a top.

top-level (TOP·lev·ul) *adj.* of the highest level of authority or rank: *a top-level discussion, meeting, official.*

top·mast *n.* the second section of a ship's mast above its deck.

top·most *adj.* highest or uppermost.

top-notch *adj. Informal.* first-rate; excellent.

top·ping (TOP·ing) *n.* something that forms the top or is put on top of something else: *a pie topping.*

top·ple (TOP·ul) *v.* **top·ples, top·pled, top·pling 1** fall *down, over,* etc. being top-heavy: *There is no immediate danger of the Leaning Tower toppling.* **2** overturn or overthrow: *The government was toppled in a coup.*

tops *adj.* topmost: *She's tops in her field; They offered $500 000 tops* (=maximum) *for the house.*

top-secret (TOP·see·crut) *adj.* of the highest secrecy; extremely confidential: *top-secret information.*

top·side *adj. & adv.* on or to a ship's main deck or an upper deck. — *n.* also **topsides** *pl.* the part of a ship above the waterline.

top·sy-tur·vy (top·see·TUR·vee) *adj. & adv.* upside down; hence, in disorder or confusion.

toque (TOKE) *n.* **1** a small, close-fitting, usually brimless hat. **2** same as TUQUE.

tor *n.* a crag or high rocky hill.

torch *n.* **1** a flaming light, as one carried in the hand by a "torchbearer": *to light a torch; Many buildings were put to the torch by the arsonist; Gigi continued to carry the torch for* (*Slang* for to love) *Luc.* **2** a source of enlightenment: *the torch of civilization, learning.* **3** a device such as a blowtorch for shooting a very hot flame: *a welding torch.* **4** *Brit.* flashlight. **5** *Slang.* arsonist.

torch·light *n.* the light of a torch or torches; *adj.: a torchlight procession, rally.*

tore *pt.* of TEAR.

tor·ment (TOR·ment) *n.* **1** great pain or agony. **2** its cause or source; a tormentor. — *v.* (tor·MENT) inflict pain or suffering continuously or by repeated acts: *tormented by annoying questions, jealousy, mosquitoes.* — **tor·men·tor** (-tur) or **tor·ment·er** *n.*

torn *pp.* of TEAR.

tor·na·do (tor·NAY·doh) *n.* **-dos** or **-does** a destructive windstorm or cyclone characterized by a funnel-shaped cloud moving along a narrow path: *A tornado struck our town last summer.*

tor·pe·do (tor·PEE·doh) *n.* **-does** a cigar-shaped, self-propelling underwater missile: *to fire, launch a torpedo; A torpedo hits, misses its target, explodes.* — *v.* **-does** (-doze) , **-doed, -do·ing** attack or destroy with a torpedo.

tor·pid (TOR·pid) *adj.* dormant, sluggish, or inactive, as a hibernating animal.

tor·por (TOR·pur) *n.* the state of being torpid or inactive: *to rouse the nation from its economic torpor.*

tor·rent (TOR·unt) *n.* a swift and violent flow or downpour: *It rained in torrents; a raging torrent; a torrent of abuse, words.* — **tor·ren·tial** (tor·EN·shul) *adj.*

tor·rid (TOR·id) *adj.* **1** parched or scorching: *a torrid climate; the torrid heat of the desert; The **Torrid Zone** extends from the equator to the tropics.* **2** ardent or passionate: *a torrid love scene.*

tor·sion (TOR·shun) *n.* **1** a twisting or being twisted, as when a taut wire or rod fixed at one end is turned left or right. **2** the stress so produced: *Some automobiles have a **torsion bar** suspension instead of coil springs.*

tor·so (TOR·soh) *n.* **-sos** (-soze) or **-si** (-see) the trunk of a human statue or body, esp. as separate from head and limbs.

tor·til·la (tor·TEE·uh) *n.* a round thin cake of unleavened cornmeal, a staple Mexican food.

tor·toise (TOR·tus) *n.* a four-legged animal with its body encased in a hard outer shell; land or freshwater turtle.

tortoise-shell (TOR·tus·shell) *adj.* yellowish brown and mottled, like the shell of a turtle used in making ornamental objects, combs, etc.: *a tortoise-shell cat.*

tor·tu·ous (TOR·choo·us) *adj.* **1** marked by twists and turns: *a tortuous trail.* **2** devious or crooked: *tortuous logic; a tortuous policy.*

tor·ture (TOR·chur) *n.* **1** infliction of severe pain to punish, force a confession, etc.: *a confession made under torture.* **2** severe physical pain or mental agony: *Watching the horror movie was sheer torture.* — *v.* **-tures, -tured, -tur·ing 1** inflict severe pain on someone: *He was tortured by his captors; Lee was tortured with rheumatism.* **2** twist or distort: *language tortured out of its meaning.* — **tor·tur·er** *n.*

To·ry (TOR·ee) *n.* **-ries 1** a member of a conservative party. **2** one who is conservative or reactionary. Also **to·ry.**

toss *v.* **1** throw in a light, easy, or careless manner: *bathers tossing beach balls; She tossed her head (in contempt or indifference).* **2** be restless or agitated: *a ship tossed by the waves; He tossed about in his bed sleeplessly.* **3** flip a coin: *Let's toss up and break the tie; Let's toss for it.* — **toss off 1** produce: *a facile writer who could toss off a story in no time.* **2** consume quickly: *to toss off a drink.* — *n.* a tossing or being tossed: *She won the toss.*

toss-up *n.* **1** a flipping of a coin to decide something. **2** *Informal.* an even chance: *It'a toss-up whether the Grits or Tories will win the election; Many ridings are considered toss-ups.*

tot *n.* a little child.

to·tal (TOH·tul) *n.* a complete amount; sum: *to add up a total; the grand total; sum total.*
— *adj.* whole or complete: *the total amount; a total eclipse, loss; total war* (= all-out, not limited war); *total abstinence, expenses;* **total recall** *(of everything from memory).*
— *v.* **-tals, -talled** or **-taled, -tal·ling** or **-tal·ing 1** add figures. **2** amount to: *The expenses totalled $50 000.* **3** wreck completely: *He totalled his car in the accident.*
— **to·tal·ly** *adv.*

to·tal·i·tar·i·an (toh·TAL·uh·TAIR·ee·un) *adj.* of a government, exercising absolute power over the people, often under a dictator: *a totalitarian government, society.* — *n.* one favouring such a system.
— **to·tal·i·tar·i·an·ism** *n.*

to·tal·i·ty (toh·TAL·uh·tee) *n.* **-ties** a total amount; hence, whole or entirety.

tote *v.* **totes, tot·ed, tot·ing** *Informal.* carry as a load: *to tote baggage for a journey; a gun-toting robber.*
— *n.* **1** a large handbag with pockets and shoulder strap; also **tote bag.** **2** an overshoe: *totes to protect your shoes from slush, salt, and snow.*

to·tem (TOH·tum) *n.* a tribal or family symbol among North American Indians on the west coast in the shape of an animal, bird, or other natural object.

totem pole *n.* **1** a post with a series of totem symbols carved, painted, and placed one on top of another. **2** hierarchy: *Where are you on the totem pole? I'm at the bottom of the totem pole; I'm the low man on the totem pole.*

tot·ter (TOT·ur) *v.* stand or move in an unsteady manner, as if about to fall; stagger.

touch (TUCH) *v.* **1** make physical contact or strike lightly with the hand or some other part of the body: *Things feel hot, cold, rough, hard, etc. when touched; Skyscrapers seem to touch the sky; Teetotallers won't touch* (= use) *liquor; Ships touch (at) many ports; Her talk touched on* or *upon* (= dealt with or referred to) *many questions; a friend whom he can touch* (Slang for ask or solicit) *for a loan now and then.* **2** affect: *She was touched by his sad plight; Here's something that touches*

your interests; a manner touched with envy; flowers and fruits touched (= damaged) *by frost; a* **touching** (= moving) *appeal, moment, scene, story.*
— **touch base with** *Informal.* be in contact with someone.
— **touch down** of an aircraft or spacecraft, to land.
— **touch off** start an action or process suddenly or violently, as an explosive charge with a match.
— **touch on** refer to something: *The book touches on matters of concern to all women.*
— **touch up** improve a painting, literary composition, makeup, etc. by slight changes.
— *n.* **1** a touching or contact: *cold to the touch; Some seed pods burst open at the slightest touch; the magic touch of Midas; He has lost touch* (= contact or acquaintance) *with Latin; is out of touch with Latin; He's a soft touch* (Informal for easy to get money out of). **2** a skilful or artistic stroke: *the deft touches of an artist's brush; There are poetic touches in her writings; a finishing touch.* **3** the sense of feeling or what is felt: *taste and touch; the soft, delicate touch of a baby's skin; typewriter keys with a light touch; a gentle touch; The senator has lost his touch with* (= ability to sense the feelings of) *the masses.* **4** a slight tinge or trace: *a touch of frost in the autumn air; a touch of irony; a touch* (= mild attack) *of the flu.*
— **a touch** a little: *The curry was a touch too spicy for me.*
— **in touch** in contact or communication: *to get, stay in touch; in close touch; Let's keep in touch by letters.*

touch and go *n.* a risky situation: *It was touch and go for a while, but the patient survived.*
— **touch-and-go** (TUCH·un·GO) *adj.* precarious or risky: *a touch-and-go affair, situation.*

touch·down *n.* **1** the moment of landing of an aircraft or spacecraft. **2** in football, a score of six points made by possession of the ball on or past the opponent's goal line; also, such possession.

tou·ché (too·SHAY) *interj.* [as in fencing to acknowledge a hit] score!

touched *adj.* **1** emotionally moved. **2** mentally unbalanced.

touching *adj.* moving; producing sympathy: *a touching appeal.*

touch·stone *n.* a test of genuineness, as by a former method of testing precious metals by rubbing them on a black stone.

touch·tone *n. & adj.* (a telephone) having a set of push buttons instead of a dial, each producing a distinctive tone signal; **Touch-Tone** *Trademark.*

touch·type *v.* **-types, -typed, -typ·ing** type without looking at the keys.

touch·y *adj.* **touch·i·er, -i·est 1** easily offended. **2** risky: *a touchy situation, subject.*
— **touch·i·ly** *adv.;* **touch·i·ness** *n.*

tough (TUF) *adj.* **1** so hard, firm, etc. in texture and consistency as not to be easily torn or broken: *Leather is tough; tough meat, putty.* **2** hard to deal with; stiff: *a*

tough customer, decision, exam, fight, guy, job, opposition; tough (= hard to bear) *luck; It's tough* (= unfortunate) *that you have to live away from family and friends; a tough* (= unruly) *neighbourhood; He's tough* (= difficult) *to work with; a sales rep who talks tough* (= is a hard bargainer); *It's time to* **get tough with** (= take a firm stand against) *traffic violators.*
— *n.* a rough or violent person; ruffian.
— **tough·ly** *adv.;* **tough·ness** *n.*

tough·en (TUF·un) *v.* make or become tough or tougher. — **tough·en·er** *n.*

tour (TOOR, *rhyme:* poor) *n.* **1** a period or shift of work on an assignment or at a specific place: *to do a tour of duty overseas.* **2** a going round visiting or inspecting: *a guided tour of Montreal; a fact-finding tour; a goodwill tour; lecture tour; package tours sold through travel agents; sightseeing tour; study tour; a circus that is always* **on tour** (= touring); *adj.: a tour guide, operator, package.*
— *v.* go on a tour through a place.

tour de force (toor·duh·FORCE) *n.* **tours de force** (toor·duh-) a feat of strength or skill.

tour·ism (TOOR·iz·um) *n.* **1** travelling for pleasure. **2** the industry serving travellers.

tour·ist (TOOR·ist) *n.* one travelling for recreation.
— *adj.: a tourist class, resort, ticket, trap.*

tour·na·ment (TOOR·nuh·munt, TUR-) *n.* **1** a series of athletic contests or games in competition for a championship. **2** formerly, a series of military exercises or contests, esp. between knights, as jousting and tilting. Also **tour·ney** (-nee) , **-neys.**

tou·sle (TOW·zul) *v.* **-sles, -sled, -sling** dishevel hair, etc.; muss.

tout (TOWT) *v. Informal.* **1** publicize or puff: *a highly touted remedy; It's touted as a great boon to humanity.* **2** solicit: *to tout for business, customers, votes.*
— *n.* one who touts.

tow (TOH) *v.* pull along behind, as with a rope or chain: *Illegally parked cars will be towed; towed away to the police pound.*
— *n.* **1** a towing or a vehicle being towed. **2** a boat, barge, or other vehicle that tows. **3** the line used.
— **in tow 1** being towed or following one: *Vito came to call with his family in tow.* **2** in one's care or charge: *She took the child in tow.*

to·ward (TORD, tuh·WORED) *prep.* **1** in the direction of a person or thing: *He turned toward his wife; progress toward peace; He became blind toward* (= approaching or near) *the end of his life.* **2** with respect to: *his attitude toward a settlement; her feelings toward us; contributions toward* (= for) *helping the poor.* Also **towards.**

tow·a·way (TOH·uh·way) *n. & adj.* (the action) of towing away automobiles: *No parking in towaway zones during snow emergencies.*

tow·el (TOW·ul) *n.* an absorbent cloth or paper: *a bath, dish, face, hand, paper towel.*
— **throw in the towel** give up the fight.
— *v.* **-els, -elled** or **-eled, -el·ling** or **-el·ing** wipe or dry with a towel.

tow·er (rhyme: "our") *n.* a structure that is tall relative to its width, rising above its surroundings: *a church tower; fortress tower; observation tower; an airport control tower.*
— *v.* rise high like a tower: *She towers above her peers as a lawyer.*
— **towering** *adj.:* the towering skyscrapers; a towering (= very high) *achievement, ambition;* in a towering (= violent) *rage.*

tower of strength *n.* one looked up to for protection or leadership.

town (rhyme: "down") *n.* **1** a community or settlement larger than a village and smaller than a city: *a boom town; crowded town; ghost town; sleepy town; small town; The whole town is* (= All the people of the town are) *talking about it.* **2** a business and entertainment centre: *to go into town.*
— **go to town** *Slang.* **1** act with energy and enthusiasm. **2** achieve success.
— **on the town** *Informal.* on a spree; having a good time: *out for a night on the town.*
— **paint the town red** *Slang.* go on a wild spree.

town council *n.* the governing body of a muncipality.

town house *n.* one of a continuous row of houses, usually of two or three stories; row house; also **town home.**

town·ie same as TOWNY.

town·ship *n.* **1** a unit of local government; municipality: *the Eastern Townships (of Quebec); The City of Mississauga developed out of "Toronto Township."* **2** a land-survey unit varying in area from province to province.

town·y (TOW·nee, "OW" as in "how") *n.* **town·ies** *Cdn.* esp. in Newfoundland, a person from a town, not from the country.

tow truck *n.* a truck equipped for towing automobiles.

tox·ic *adj.* **1** poisonous: *the toxic effects of certain drugs; toxic fumes, substances, wastes from chemical companies.* **2** of or caused by a toxin: *a toxic illness; the* **toxic shock syndrome** (= a bacterial attack) *resulting from improper tampon use.*
— **tox·ic·i·ty** (tok·SIS·uh·tee) *n.*

tox·in *n.* a poison produced in the human body by bacteria or one secreted by a plant or animal, as snake venom.

toy *n.* **1** an object for a child to play with; a trifle or trinket. **2** anything of small size: *a toy balloon, soldier, train; a* **toy dog** such as a chihuahua, Pekinese, or Pomeranian.
— *v.* **toy with** play idly with something: *He toys with his pencil when lost for a word; to toy with an idea, plan; He was merely toying* (= trifling) *with her affections.*

trace *n.* **1** either of a pair of straps or chains connecting an animal to the vehicle it pulls. **2** a mark or other evidence of an occurrence or presence, as an animal's tracks in the snow: *My cat vanished without a trace.* **3** a barely perceptible or measurable amount: *slight traces of poison; a trace of precipitation; with no trace of remorse; a* **trace element** such as iodine required in minute amounts for proper nutrition.

— **kick over the traces** become unruly; shake off control.

— *v.* **trac·es, traced, trac·ing 1** follow a track or trail *to its origin or originator: to trace criminals, game, the origin of a word; He traces his ancestry back to African forebears; Some phobias may be traced to childhood experiences.* **2** draw an outline. **3** copy an original using transparent paper.

— **trace·a·ble** (TRAY·suh·bul) *adj.* — **trac·er** *n.*

track *n.* **1** the path of something moving or a course to travel over, as the set of parallel rails on which a train moves, a path beaten through a forest, a course laid around a field for running or racing, the path of a hurricane, the groove of a phonograph record, etc.: *He has the **inside track** (= advantageous position) on getting the job; He stopped dead **in his tracks** (= right where he was) when he heard his name called.* **2** the marks left, as the footprints of an animal or ruts made by wheels. **3** the endless belt or tread on which some vehicles such as tanks, bulldozers, and tractors move.

— **keep** (or **lose**) **track of** keep (or fail to be) informed about something: *to keep track of expenses during a trip; He lost track of time and was late getting back.*

— **on** or **off the track** on or off the right course.

— *v.* **1** follow someone's track: *to track an animal; Radio signals help track a satellite from **tracking stations** on the earth.* **2** make tracks on or with something: *to track up a polished floor; to track mud into a house* (= bring it on one's feet or shoes).

— **track down** find: *to track down game; an obscure quotation that is hard to track down* (= find the source of).

track and field *n.* sports events consisting of races, hurdles, etc. around a track and jumps, throws, etc. in the centre of the field. — **track-and-field** *adj.*

track record *n.* a record of achievements in a field of endeavour.

tract *n.* **1** a stretch or extent, esp. of land; a usually large area. **2** a pathway or continuous system of bodily organs with a special function: *The respiratory tract consists of the nose, throat, voice box, air passages, and lungs; digestive tract; intestinal tract.* **3** a pamphlet or small treatise on a religious or political subject.

trac·ta·ble (TRAC·tuh·bul) *adj.* easy to manage or handle: *Be tractable if not docile; a tractable* (= malleable or workable) *metal.*

trac·tion (TRAC·shun) *n.* a drawing, pulling, or being pulled; also, pulling power: *A broken leg is put in **traction** (= pulled by weights over a pulley) to keep the parts in position while healing; They use snow tires for better traction* (= moving without slipping) *over snow and ice; The first tractors, driven by steam, were called **traction engines.***

trac·tor (TRAC·tur) *n.* **1** a powerful vehicle for pulling or pushing farm machines, snow ploughs, etc. **2** the cab-and-engine unit that pulls a freight trailer, or tractor-trailer.

trad *adj. Slang.* traditional: *the mod and the trad in menswear.*

trade *n.* **1** the buying and selling of goods and services; commerce: *to carry on, drum up, engage in, promote,* restrain trade; foreign trade; the illicit trade in drugs; retail trade; the tourist trade (=market); We cater chiefly to the rush-hour trade (= customers or clientele); the carriage trade (= the wealthy). **2** an exchange or swap; also, a bargain: *a fair trade.* **3** a skilled occupation or craft, not a business or profession: *to learn, ply, practise a trade; the book trade; welding trade; rumours circulating **in the trade** (= among people in the trade); a trade school.*

— *v.* **trades, trad·ed, trad·ing 1** buy and sell; do business: *They trade in stocks; no trading with the enemy; There was brisk trading on the commodities exchange; slow, sluggish trading.* **2** swap or exchange: *Let's trade seats; Jim traded his seat for Jan's; People **trade in** their old car (in part payment) when buying a new one;* **trade-in** *n.* **3** be a customer *at* a store, *with* a merchant, etc.

— **trade on** or **upon** use or exploit, usually someone's good nature, to one's own advantage.

trade·mark *n.* **1** a legally registered brand name, slogan, symbol, or device used by a company to identify its product or service. **2** something that is distinctive of a person: *Churchill with his trademark cigar.*

— *v.* register as a trademark: *"Finger-lickin' good" is a trademarked slogan.*

trade name *n.* **1** brand name or trademark. **2** a company's business name.

trade-off *n.* **1** an exchanging of something one owns for another benefit: *Let's do a trade-off.* **2** a balancing of two factors or elements: *Is there a trade-off between unemployment and inflation?* (= Can inflation be reduced at the cost of higher unemployment?).

trade school *n.* a school teaching skilled trades such as carpentry and plumbing.

trades·man (TRADES·mun) *n.* **-men 1** a retailer or shopkeeper: *the tradesman's entrance to a house.* **2** a craftsman.

trades·people *n. pl.* people engaged in trade.

trade union *n.* a worker's union; labour union.

trading post *n.* a store at a frontier or outpost selling supplies, esp. to Indians, in exchange for furs, moccasins, etc.

trading stamp *n.* a stamplike label given as a bonus to retail customers with cash purchases for them to collect and exchange for gifts.

tra·di·tion (truh·DISH·un) *n.* **1** the handing down of beliefs, laws, customs, legends, etc. from generation to generation orally and by practice: *By tradition, the captain of a ship may conduct a wedding ceremony; According to tradition, the Apostle Thomas brought Christianity to India.* **2** a body of such beliefs, etc. or something received by tradition: *Thanksgiving is a North American tradition; a wedding in the Jewish tradition; Some traditions have greater force than customs; to break with, cherish, establish, hand down, maintain, preserve, uphold a tradition; an ancient, cherished, deep-rooted, established, hallowed, popular tradition; tradition and change.*

— **tra·di·tion·al** *adj.;* **tra·di·tion·al·ly** *adv.*

traf·fic *n.* **1** the movement of people and/or vehicles, esp. in a public place such as a street or highway:

*Signals regulate the flow of traffic; Police direct traffic; People block, hold up, obstruct, tie up traffic; one-way, heavy, light, through, vehicular traffic; **adj.**: a **traffic circle** for vehicles to clear an intersection by going round an island (**traffic island**) without stopping for lights; traffic conditions during the rush hour; air traffic controllers; a traffic jam at an intersection; traffic lights; the traffic pattern determined by furniture arrangement in a living area; a traffic sign, ticket, violation.* 2 business done by a transportation or communications company; the volume of passengers, freight, telegrams, etc.: *the traffic manager of a book publisher.* 3 commercial activity; buying and selling: *brisk, lively traffic; no traffic with criminals; the traffic in illicit drugs; Charge the highest price the traffic will bear* (= that buyers will pay).
— *v.* **traf·fics, traf·ficked, traf·fick·ing** carry on trade or traffic, esp. illicitly, as in drugs.

traffic light or **traffic signal** *n.* a set of red, green, and amber lights regulating traffic at an intersection.

trag·e·dy (TRAJ·uh·dee) *n.* **-dies** 1 a serious drama or play with a sad ending. 2 any sad or terrible happening: *A tragedy may strike us anytime.*

trag·ic (TRAJ·ic) *adj.* 1 having to do with tragedy: *a tragic actor, drama, poet, story, writer.* 2 suggestive of tragedy; extremely sad or unfortunate: *a tragic accident, event, loss, mistake, plight.*
— **trag·i·cal·ly** *adv.*

trail *v.* 1 follow closely, as in one's tracks: *police trailing a suspect.* 2 drag, tow, or bring after oneself: *a child trailing a toy truck; the trailing skirt of a wedding gown; The hurt runner began to trail* (= lag behind); *the **trailing** (= rear, not front or "leading") **edge** of an airplane's wing.* 3 move in a casual or aimless manner: *The children trailed behind their mother; smoke trailing from a chimney; creeping plants that trail along the ground and over walls.* 4 become weaker: *The voice on the phone trailed off.*
— *n.* 1 something that trails or is left behind, as a scent, trace, or track: *the vapour trail or exhaust of an aircraft; A trail of blood led to the scene of the murder; The police are on his trail; the trail of misery left by a war.* 2 a route or course: *Pioneers blazed trails through the wilderness by marking trees; to blaze a new trail; an Indian trail; a winding trail; It was time to hit the campaign trail; Ontario's Bruce Trail is a hiking path.*

trail bike *n.* a light motorcycle for rough, cross-country riding.

trail·blaz·er (TRAIL·blay·zur) *n.* a pioneer or explorer.
— **trail·blaz·ing** *n. & adj.*

trail·er *n.* 1 a wheeled vehicle designed to be hauled, either a wagon or closed van carrying cargo, usually pulled by a tractor, or one for recreational travel and camping, equipped as temporary living quarters: *a house trailer; truck trailer.* 2 a mobile home. 3 a creeping plant such as an ivy. 4 a short film consisting of selected scenes from a movie, shown as promotion.

trailer park, trailer camp or **trailer court** *n.* a site equipped with water, electricity, etc. for a community of mobile homes.

trail-skiing *n.* cross-country skiing.

train *n.* 1 a connected series of railway cars pulled by a locomotive: *an electric train; express train; freight train; to board, catch, get off, get on, miss, take a train; We change trains in Kingston for Ottawa; Trains derail; Trains pull in, pull out of a station.* 2 a chain or sequence: *a train of events, thought; A war brings misery in its train; the power train* (= the drive shaft, clutch, transmission, etc.) *of an automobile.* 3 a line or group of people, animals, vehicles, etc. moving along together: *a wagon train; a train* (= caravan) *of camels; a king and his train* (= retinue). 4 a trailing part: *the train of a comet, peacock, wedding gown.*
— *v.* 1 teach, instruct, or practise in order to develop a faculty or skill: *Educators train minds; a trained acrobat; a toilet-trained child; a seal trained to perform; She's training for the Olympics; The **training wheels** on both sides of the rear wheel of a child's bicycle help steady it.* 2 guide or direct physically: *a shrub trained to grow on a trellis; Spotlights were kept trained on the stage.* — **train·er** *n.*

train·ee (tray·NEE) *n.* one being trained.

training *n.* the act of training or being trained: *driver training; in-service training; military training; on-the-job training; a nurse by training; She's in training for the Olympics; a **training school** for young offenders.*

traipse *v.* **traips·es, traipsed, traips·ing** *Informal.* wander or walk about aimlessly: *People traipse through a house that is open for sale.*

trait *n.* a distinguishing feature or quality of a person: *an acquired trait; a character trait; a cultural trait; a personality trait; the characteristic traits of a people.*

trai·tor (TRAY·tur) *n.* one who betrays or is disloyal to his or her faith, country, friends, etc.: *an ally who turned traitor; a traitor to his country.*
— **trai·tor·ous** (-us) *adj.*

tramp *v.* 1 walk with heavy steps. 2 trample. 3 go around on foot, esp. wearily, as in search of a home or work; wander as a tramp.
— *n.* 1 the sound of heavy steps, as of marching soldiers. 2 a hike or march: *a tramp through the woods.* 3 a person without a fixed home, esp. one who lives by doing odd jobs. 4 *Slang.* a streetwalker or prostitute. 5 a cargo ship without regular trade routes or schedules, available for hire as needed: *a tramp steamer.*

tram·ple (TRAM·pul) *v.* **-ples, -pled, -pling** 1 stamp or tread heavily; crush: *a flower bed trampled by a crowd; laws that trample on human rights.* 2 treat ruthlessly: *age-old customs trampled underfoot by tyrants.*
— *n.* a trampling or trampling sound.

tram·po·line (TRAM·puh·leen, -lin) *n.* a structure to bounce on for gymnastic use, consisting of a sturdy sheet or net stretched over a frame.

trance *n.* 1 a partly conscious state without voluntary movement, as in deep hypnosis, or the condition of a spiritualistic medium: *to fall into a trance; go into a trance; Sam was in a trance for several hours.* 2 a trancelike state of absorption. 3 a daze or stupor: *She walked around in a trance looking for her child.*

tran·quil (TRANG·quil) *adj.* 1 peaceful and quiet in a deep or settled way. 2 undisturbed or serene: *a tranquil life, scene.* — **tran·quil·ly** *adv.* — **tran·quil·li·ty** or

tran·quil·i·ty (trang·QUIL·uh·tee) *n.*

tran·quil·liz·er or **tran·quil·iz·er** (TRANK·wuh·lye·zur) *n.* a drug used to relieve anxiety, soothe nervous tension, or reduce high blood pressure.

trans- *prefix.* across; over: *trans-Canada, transnational, transplant, transship, Trans-Siberian Railway.*

trans·act (tran·SACT, -ZACT) *v.* conduct or carry on business with someone.

trans·ac·tion (tran·SAC·shun, -ZAC·shun) *n.* **1** a business deal: *to conduct a transaction; transactions between two parties.* **2** *pl.* a report of the proceedings of a learned society.

trans·at·lan·tic (trans·ut·LAN·tic) *adj.* across or beyond the Atlantic: *a transatlantic cable, flight, nation.*

Trans-Canada Highway *n.* a national road system stretching from St. John's, Nfld., to Victoria, B.C., the world's longest such highway.

tran·scend (tran·SEND) *v.* **1** be above the limits of human powers, experience, etc. **2** surpass: *philanthropy that transcends national boundaries.*
— **tran·scend·ent** *adj.*

trans·con·ti·nen·tal (TRANS·con·tuh·NEN·tul) *adj.* across a continent: *a transcontinental flight, railway.*

tran·scribe (TRANS·cribe) *v.* **-scribes, -scribed, -scrib·ing** make a transcript or transcription of something: *Secretaries transcribe shorthand notes.*

tran·script *n.* a copy, esp. official, of something recorded, as a speech, academic grades, etc.

trans·fer (trans·FUR) *v.* **-fers, -ferred, -fer·ring 1** move someone or convey something from one place or person to another: *a manager transferred from Toronto to Vancouver; A property is transferred from vendor to buyer.* **2** change from one place, position, etc. to another: *Students transfer from school to school; Transfer at the next stop to Route 18.*
— *n.* (TRANS·fur) **1** a transferring, being transferred, or something transferred, as a design or drawing from one surface to another. **2** a ticket allowing a passenger to transfer to another route. **3** a transferring point on a route.— **trans·fer·a·ble** (trans·FUR·uh·bul) *adj.*
— **trans·fer·ence** (-FUR·unce, TRANS·fur·unce) *n.*

trans·fig·ure (trans·FIG·yur) *v.* **-ures, -ured, -ur·ing 1** change the form or appearance. **2** transform so as to glorify or exalt.
— **trans·fig·u·ra·tion** (-yuh·RAY·shun) *n.*

trans·fix (trans·FIX) *v.* **1** pierce through, as with a pointed weapon. **2** hold motionless, as if impaled.

trans·form (trans·FORM) *v.* **1** change the shape, appearance, or nature of a person or thing fundamentally. **2** change from one form to another, as electricity to a different voltage, one mathematical expression to another, or the active to the passive voice.
— **trans·for·ma·tion** (-for·MAY·shun) *n.*

trans·form·er (trans·FOR·mur) *n.* one that transforms, esp. a voltage-changing device: *a step-down transformer; step-up transformer.*

trans·fuse (trans·FUZE) *v.* **-fus·es, -fused, -fus·ing 1** transfer a liquid from one vessel to another, esp. inject blood from one person into the circulatory system of another. **2** infuse or inspire.
— **trans·fu·sion** (-FEW·zhun) *n.: to give a blood transfusion.*

trans·gress (trans·GRES) *v.* **1** go beyond an allowed limit. **2** break a law or command; offend or sin against a person or law.— **trans·gres·sion** (-GRESH·un) *n.*
— **trans·gres·sor** (-GRES·ur) *n.*

tran·ship same as TRANSSHIP.

tran·sient (TRAN·zee·unt) *adj.* short in duration or stay; passing or fleeting: *a transient feeling, tenant.*
— *n.* a temporary lodger, worker, etc.: *a rooming house for transients.* — **tran·sient·ly** *adv.*

trans·it (TRAN·sit) *n.* **1** passage or conveyance: *goods lost in transit between Vancouver and Regina; adj.: a transit lounge, passenger, visa.* **2** a local public transportation system using buses, trains, etc.: *mass transit; public transit; rapid transit.* **3** a surveying instrument with a telescope on a tripod to measure angles.

tran·si·tion (tran·ZISH·un) *n.* a passing from one condition, stage, etc. to another: *a period of transition; to effect a smooth transition of power; a gradual transition to normalcy; in a state of transition.*
— **tran·si·tion·al** *adj.*

tran·si·tive (TRAN·suh·tiv, -zuh·tiv) *adj.* of verbs, having a direct object.
— *n.* a transitive verb such as "give" or "love."
— **tran·si·tive·ly** *adv.*

tran·si·to·ry (TRAN·suh·tor·ee, TRAN·zuh-) *adj.* of things, transient; short-lived, not permanent: *the transitory things of this world; transitory pleasures.*
— **tran·si·to·ri·ly** *adv.;* **tran·si·tor·i·ness** *n.*

trans·late (trans·LATE, tranz-) *v.* **-lates, -lat·ed, -lat·ing** change from one place or condition to another, esp. between languages: *a word that is difficult to translate into another language; a book translated from the original Greek; to translate a philosophy into action.*
— **trans·lat·a·ble** (-LAY·tuh·bul) *adj.*
— **trans·la·tor** (-tur) *n.*

trans·la·tion (trans·LAY·shun, tranz-) *n.* a translating or a translated version: *a close, free, literal, loose translation; I read Homer in translation; the simultaneous translation of a speech into different languages.*

trans·lit·er·ate (trans·LIT·uh·rate, tranz-) *v.* **-ates, -at·ed, -at·ing** write words, letters, etc. in the characters of another language: *The Greek letter "epsilon" is usually transliterated as "e."*

trans·mi·grate (trans·MY·grate, tranz-) *v.* **-grates, -grat·ed, -grat·ing** of the soul, pass from one body after its death into another.— **trans·mi·gra·tion** (trans·my·GRAY·shun, tranz-) *n.*

trans·mis·si·ble (trans·MIS·uh·bul, tranz-) *adj.* capable of being transmitted.

trans·mis·sion (trans·MISH·un, tranz-) *n.* **1** a transmitting or being transmitted by radio or cable: *the transmission of messages, signals.* **2** in a vehicle, the assembly of parts, esp. a set of gears, that transmits power from the engine to the driving wheels.

trans·mit (trans·MIT, tranz-) *v.* **-mits, -mit·ted,**

-mit·ting pass along as an agent or medium: *Germs transmit diseases; to transmit a message by radio; The sun transmits heat and light (through the air).* — trans·mit·tal (-tul) *n.* — trans·mit·ter *n.*

trans·mute (trans-MYOOT, tranz-) *v.* change the nature or substance of a base metal into something different or better. — **trans·mu·ta·tion** (-myoo·TAY·shun) *n.: the supposed transmutation of base metals into gold.*

trans·o·ce·an·ic (TRANS·oh·shee·AN·ic, TRANZ-) *adj.* across or beyond the ocean: *a transoceanic flight; transoceanic transport, travel.*

tran·son·ic or **trans·son·ic** (tran-SON·ic) *adj.* between subsonic and supersonic in speed: *the transonic zone* (= sound barrier).

trans·par·en·cy (tran-SPAIR·un·see) *n.* -cies 1 a transparent quality. 2 something transparent, as a slide for a slide projector: *a set of colour transparencies to use with an overhead projector.*

trans·par·ent (tran-SPAIR·unt) *adj.* that can be seen through, as glass: *a transparent* (= sheer) *fabric; a transparent falsehood; her transparent* (= frank) *sincerity.* — trans·par·ent·ly *adv.*

tran·spire (tran-SPIRE) *v.* -spires, -spired, -spir·ing 1 give off water vapour, as through the pores of a plant's leaves. 2 leak out or become known: *It later transpired that the theft was an inside job.* 3 come about or happen: *No one knows what transpired afterward.* — tran·spi·ra·tion (-spuh·RAY·shun) *n.*

trans·plant (trans-PLANT) *v.* dig up, as a plant, or remove an organ or tissue, people, etc. from one place to implant or resettle in another. — *n.* a transplanting or something transplanted: *a hair transplant to cover a bald spot; corneal, heart, kidney, organ, tissue transplants; A transplant may be rejected by the body.* — trans·plan·ta·tion (-plan·TAY·shun) *n.*

tran·spon·der (tran-SPON·dur) *n.* a radio device that automatically transmits a response signal, as used to identify approaching planes on a radar screen.

trans·port (trans-PORT) *v.* 1 carry or convey, esp. in a vehicle: *to transport goods by truck; Meeting his uncle transported him back to his childhood.* 2 carry away; enrapture: *She was transported with joy on hearing the great news.* — *n.* (TRANS·port) 1 means of transporting: *air transport; road transport.* 2 strong emotion, esp. rapture: *in a transport* or *in transports of joy, rage.*

trans·por·ta·tion (trans·por·TAY·shun) *n.* 1 a transporting or being transported: *sentenced to transportation for life* (= life in a penal colony). 2 a means of transporting or the transporting business: *the task of providing public transportation; the Department of Transportation; the transportation industry.*

trans·pose (trans-POZE) *v.* -pos·es, -posed, -pos·ing 1 change, esp. interchange, the normal position of letters or sounds in a word. 2 change the key of a piece of music, as in playing a composition. — trans·po·si·tion (-puh·ZISH·un) *n.*

trans·ship (trans-SHIP) *v.* -ships, -shipped, -ship·ping transfer from one ship or vehicle to another for further shipment. — **trans·ship·ment** *n.*

trans·verse (trans-VERSE) *adj.* set crosswise: *a transverse beam.* — *n.* (*also* TRANS·verse) a transverse axis, beam, etc.

trap *n.* 1 a device for capturing an animal: *to bait and set a trap for mice.* 2 a device, stratagem, or ambush for catching someone off guard: *He fell into his own trap; a speed trap set up by police to catch speeders; a booby trap; death trap; a tourist trap* (for exploiting unwary tourists by overcharging). 3 a U-shaped bend in a drainpipe to hold water to prevent the return of sewer gas. 4 a light, two-wheeled carriage with springs. 5 in a golf course, a pit filled with sand as a hazard. 6 **traps** *pl.* the percussion devices in a jazz band or orchestra. 7 **traps** *pl. Informal.* belongings. — *v.* traps, trapped, trap·ping 1 trap or snare animals. 2 catch as in a trap. 3 adorn or equip with trappings; caparison. — **trap·per** *n.: an animal trapper; a fur trapper.*

trap·door *n.* an opening in a floor, ceiling, or roof; also, the hinged or sliding door covering it.

tra·peze (tra-PEEZ) *n.* a short bar hung horizontally by two ropes on which an aerialist, or **trapeze artist,** performs in a circus: *on the flying trapeze.*

trappings *n.pl.* ornamental coverings, as of an outfitted horse; hence, accessories or equipment: *all the trappings of high office.*

trash *n.* 1 worthless or discarded stuff; rubbish: *Trash accumulates.* 2 a worthless person; riffraff. — *v. Informal.* 1 vandalize or wreck: *The hockey fans went on a rampage, breaking windows and trashing stores.* 2 discard as trash.

trash·y *adj.* worthless.

trau·ma (TRAW·muh) *n.* -mas or -ma·ta (-muh·tuh) 1 an unpleasant emotional experience such as may cause nervous symptoms. 2 a wound or injury sometimes called "physical trauma". — **trau·mat·ic** (traw·MAT·ic) *adj.*

trav·ail (TRAV·ail, truh·VAIL) *n. & v.* [literary] toil or labour.

trav·el (TRAV·ul) *n.* a journey or trip: *foreign travel; the **travels** of Sindbad; adj.: A **travel** agent makes travel arrangements for clients; a travel plan; the travel time between Ottawa and Halifax.* — *v.* -els, -elled or -eled, -el·ling or -el·ing 1 go from one place to another; journey: *She has travelled widely in Europe; He travels extensively on business; We travel abroad, far and wide; to travel light* (= with minimum luggage); *We travel by air; He travels first-class; to travel across the Sahara; a **travelling** companion, sales rep; Light travels* (= is transmitted) *much faster than sound.* 2 to journey over or through; traverse: *She has travelled Canada from coast to coast.* — **trav·el·ler** or **trav·el·er** *n.: a seasoned air traveller; a fellow traveller* (= Communist sympathizer); *A **traveller's cheque** purchased at a bank may be exchanged for cash when travelling by countersigning it.*

trav·erse (tra·VERSE) *v.* -ers·es, -ersed, -ers·ing 1 travel or move across something extensive, as a desert or sky. 2 move diagonally across a slope, as a skier.

— **n.** (TRAV·urse) something lying or extending across: *the **traverse rod** on which a curtain slides.*

trav·es·ty (TRAV·is·tee) *n.* **-ties** a ridiculous imitation, parody, or burlesque: *Everyone condemned the trial as a travesty of justice.*
— **v.** **-ties, -tied, -ty·ing** make a travesty of something.

tra·vois (truh·VOY, trahv·WAH) *n. Cdn.* an Indian conveyance for goods consisting of two poles with a net or platform across it, drawn by a dog or horse.

trawl *n.* **1** a huge bag-shaped net that is dragged along in the water by a boat, or **trawl·er. 2** a long line called a **trawl line** or "setline" from which short lines with baited hooks are hung.
— **v.** fish or catch cod, shrimp, etc. with a trawl.

tray *n.* a flat open pan with a low rim for holding or carrying food, etc.: *a serving tray; a tea tray.*

treach·er·ous (TRECH·ur·us) *adj.* **1** not to be trusted, as one likely to be disloyal. **2** not reliable, as ice too thin to skate on: *treacherous driving conditions.*
— **treach·er·ous·ly** *adv.*

treach·er·y (TRECH·uh·ree) *n.* **-ries** an act of betrayal.

tread (TRED) *v.* **treads,** *pt.* **trod,** *pp.* **trod·den** (TROD·un) or **trod, tread·ing** step on or walk: *to tread softly; where angels fear to tread; She is careful not to **tread on people's toes** (= offend them); to tread (= crush with the feet) grapes for making wine; to tread out a fire (by stamping on it); a trodden path (formed by walking) through a field.*
— **tread water** *pt.* **tread·ed** keep one's head above water by moving the legs up and down: *Setting up a commission just buys time and treads water.*
— **n. 1** the act, sound, or a way of treading: *the heavy tread of marching soldiers; He walks with a light tread.* **2** a part that treads or is trodden on, as the horizontal part of a step, the grooved surface of a tire, the sole of a shoe, etc.

tread·mill *n.* a machine worked by treading on an endless belt going over wheels: *a monotonous job like being on the treadmill.*

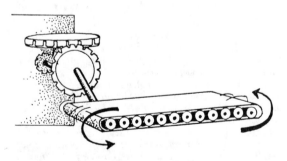

trea·son (TREE·zun) *n.* open disloyalty to one's country, as by joining with or helping an enemy: *an act of treason; charged with high treason for plotting the king's death.*
— **trea·son·a·ble** (-uh·bul) *adj.*: *a treasonable offence.*
— **trea·son·ous** (-us) *adj.*: *It is treasonous to aid the enemies of one's country.*

treas·ure (TREZH·ur) *n.* **1** wealth stored or put away, as money, jewels, etc.: *an expedition to find buried treasure; to raise sunken treasure from the Titanic.* **2** a person or thing of great value: *art treasures; a priceless treasure.*
— **v.** **-ures, -ured, -ur·ing 1** hoard as treasure. **2** value or cherish protectively; *adj.*: *a treasured friendship, gift, memory.*

treas·ur·er (TREZH·ur·ur) *n.* an official in charge of funds, revenues, or finances, as of a treasury.

treasure-trove *n.* **1** treasure found hidden, esp. one of unknown ownership. **2** a valuable discovery.

treas·ur·y (TREZH·uh·ree) *n.* **-ur·ies 1** a place where a treasure or funds are kept. **2** funds. **3** a rich storehouse: *a treasury of information.* **4 Treasury** a government department in charge of financial affairs: *In Canada, the Treasury Board is the finance ministry.*

treat (TREET) *v.* **1** deal with a person or thing: *Sam treats employees fairly; treats even enemies with kindness; to treat someone badly, cruelly, unfairly; He was treated like a son; Doctors treat ailments; They treat patients (for their ailments); a poem that treats (of) the vanity of things; An author treats a subject exhaustively, thoroughly; Don't treat it as a joke; They refuse to treat (= negotiate) with terrorists.* **2** subject to a process: *wood treated with a preservative.* **3** entertain or provide someone with something good: *She treated them to a lunch.*
— **n.** an entertainment, gift, or something special that gives pleasure: *The party was a real treat; It was a treat to listen to her; "Trick or treat!" says the child in Halloween costume.*

trea·tise (TREE·tis) *n.* a book, article, etc. containing a systematic discussion: *He has written a learned treatise on rock music.*

treat·ment (TREET·munt) *n.* **1** a treating of someone or something: *to receive, respond to, undergo treatment for an illness; He's under treatment; brutal, cruel, inhumane treatment of prisoners of war; preferential treatment of friends and relatives; red-carpet treatment of a visiting dignitary.* **2** a medicine or method used in treatment: *There are many treatments for a cold, but no known cure.*

trea·ty (TREE·tee) *n.* **-ties 1** a formal agreement between nations, as for peace, trade, etc.: *to conclude, negotiate, ratify, sign, violate, work out a treaty; a treaty banning or to ban atomic tests in the atmosphere.* **2** a document setting forth the terms of such an agreement.

treaty day *n. Cdn.* the annual meeting for payment of treaty money to Canadian Indians.

treaty Indian *n. Cdn.* a Canadian Indian who receives annual cash payments from the government.

treaty money *n. Cdn.* an annual payment made to Canadian Indians who have signed treaties with the federal government: *In 1965, Indians received treaty money of $4 or $5 a year.*

tre·ble (TREB·ul) *n.* in music, the highest or soprano part that is sung by women or boys and played on instruments such as the violin and clarinet.
— **adj. 1** having to do with the treble; also, high-pitched. **2** triple.
— **v.** **-bles, -bled, -bling** make or become triple.

tree *n.* **1** a large perennial plant with a woody stem and branches starting at a height from the ground: *to climb, cut down, fell, prune, uproot trees.* **2** something treelike: *a clothes tree with hooks and pegs on top for hanging clothes; family tree.*
— *v.* **trees, treed, tree·ing 1** chase a person or animal up a tree. **2** put a shoe in a shoe tree. — **tree·less** *adj.*

treed *adj.* wooded: *a treed lot; a lushly treed valley.*

tree line *n.* the latitude or height above which it is too cold for trees to grow.

trek *v.* **treks, trekked, trek·king 1** travel slowly or laboriously, as by wagon. **2** *Informal.* go on foot: *They trekked across the Sahara; The **trekking industry** caters to mountain climbers.*
— *n.* a journey or migration: *the long trek to freedom; "Star Trek" fans are sometimes called "trekkies."*
— **trek·ker** *n.*

trel·lis (TREL·is) *n.* a lattice framework.
— *v.* support a vine on a trellis.

trem·ble (TREM·bul) *v.* **-bles, -bled, -bling 1** shake, as from fear, cold, etc. **2** quake: *a trembling voice; The ground trembled from the earthquake.*
— *n.* a trembling; also, tremor.

tre·men·dous (tri·MEN·dus) *adj.* **1** awe-inspiring because great or gigantic: *a tremendous achievement.* **2** *Informal.* excellent; very great: *a tremendous party.*
— **tre·men·dous·ly** *adv.*

trem·or (TREM·ur) *n.* **1** a trembling or shaking, as in palsy: *a nervous tremor.* **2** quake: *a low-intensity earth tremor; Her disciplinary action sent tremors through the school system.*

trem·u·lous (TREM·yuh·lus) *adj.* **1** marked by trembling or quivering. **2** fearful.

trench *n.* a long, narrow ditch, as dug for laying pipes or to protect soldiers in warfare: *a slit trench; life in the trenches during World War I.*
— *v.* dig trenches in a place or protect troops with trenches.

trench·ant (TRENCH·unt) *adj.* cutting; clear-cut; effective: *a trenchant policy; her trenchant style, wit.*

trend *n.* **1** a general direction or course, as of events, opinions, fashions, etc.: *a growing, marked, recent trend toward violence on TV; a welcome downward trend in prices.* **2** a current style or vogue: *Designers often create trends; to start a trend; Hollywood often sets the trends for today's youth; Many trends started as fads.*
— *v.* have a trend; tend: *policies trending toward the Right; Incomes trend down during a recession.*

trend·y *adj.* **trend·i·er, -i·est** *Informal.* following the latest fashions; swinging: *a trendy dresser, drug, lifestyle; trendy people, themes; the trendy set; a fashionable but not trendy woman.* — **trend·i·ly** *adv.*

trep·i·da·tion (trep·uh·DAY·shun) *n.* fear or alarm marked by trembling.

tres·pass (TRES·pus, -pass) *v.* intrude unlawfully on another's property or rights; transgress: *The sign said "No Trespassing"; Sorry to trespass on your time.*
— *n.* **1** a trespassing. **2** a moral transgression; sin.
— **tres·pass·er** *n.*

tress *n.* **1** a lock or curl of hair. **2 tresses** *pl.* a woman's or girl's flowing hair.

tres·tle (TRES·ul) *n.* a framework supporting a platform, table top, bridge, etc.

tri- *prefix.* three or third: *triangle, triceps, triennial.*

tri·ad (TRY·ad) *n.* a group or set of three closely related persons or things.

tri·age (tree·AHZH, TREE·ahzh) *n.* a priority system of selecting or sorting, as of wounded in battle to determine order of treatment: *the triage approach for using scarce resources where they will do the most good.*

tri·al (TRY·ul) *n.* **1** a trying or testing: *Wrestling is a trial of strength; a field trial (by actual performance, as on the market); He was hired **on trial** (= on probation) for three months; Animals learn by **trial and error**; the **trial-and-error** method of picking a hat of the right size; adj.: a trial model of a vehicle; a trial run.* **2** the examination of a case in a court of law: *A case is brought to trial (in court); trial by jury; He was ordered to stand trial; was on trial for robbery; got a fair trial; Witnesses testify at a trial; adj.: a trial court, judge, lawyer.* **3** (cause of) hardship or annoyance: *That boy is a trial to his teachers.*

trial balloon *n.* a proposal or announcement made for testing reactions, as a balloon used in weather forecasting: *to send up a trial balloon.*

tri·an·gle (TRY·ang·gul) *n.* **1** a plane figure with three straight sides and angles. **2** anything resembling this, as a percussion instrument made of a steel rod bent into a triangle. — **tri·an·gu·lar** (try·ANG·gyuh·lur) *adj.*

tribe *n.* **1** a group of people with a common way of life, speaking the same language, obeying a chief or elders, and usually of the same ancestry: *the 12 tribes of Israel; an Indian tribe.* **2** a group of people, animals, or plants of the same kind: *the rose tribe; a new tribe of journalists.*
— **trib·al** (TRY·bul) *adj.* — **tribes·man** (-mun) *n.*

trib·u·la·tion (trib·yuh·LAY·shun) *n.* great misery that continues over a period: *to bear, endure the tribulation of a long illness; the trials and tribulations of daily life.*

tri·bu·nal (try·BEW·nul, tri-) *n.* **1** a board appointed to examine and judge a matter of public concern: *a human rights tribunal; police tribunal.* **2** a court of justice; hence, a judgment seat: *the tribunal of public opinion.*

trib·u·tar·y (TRIB·yoo·tair·ee) *adj.* **1** paying tribute; subject: *a tributary state.* **2** contributing to a larger river: *a tributary stream.*
— *n., pl.* **-tar·ies** a tributary state or river.

trib·ute (TRIB·yoot, long "oo") *n.* **1** a payment exacted by a ruler from a subject: *to pay tribute to a conquering nation.* **2** something said or given as a mark of gratitude, respect, etc.: *Speakers paid tribute to the retiring president; They funded an award as a fitting tribute to her memory; a glowing tribute; a floral tribute (= bouquet).*

trice *n.* esp. **in a trice** in an instant.

trick *n.* **1** a skilfully deceptive action such as a prank or fraud: *the "trick (= prank) or treat" greeting of children on Halloween night; to play a dirty trick on someone.*

2 a feat or illusion: *to do a card trick; a hat trick; Magicians perform tricks; People were deceived by a trick of vision; his **bag of tricks** (= expertise). 3 knack: *to learn the tricks* (= devices or expedients) *of the trade.* 4 a peculiar habit or mannerism: *a horse's trick of shying.* 5 a round of play in a card game: *to take the trick.* 6 a shift of duty at the helm of a ship.
— **do** or **turn the trick** achieve the desired result.
— *v.* 1 deceive or cheat: *She was tricked into buying the lemon; was tricked out of her savings.* 2 adorn or deck out: *gaudily tricked out for the occasion.*
— **trick·er·y** (TRICK·uh·ree) *n.* **-er·ies.**

trick·ish *adj.* tricky.

trick·le (TRICK·ul) *v.* **-les, -led, -ling** 1 fall in drops: *Water trickles from a leaking faucet; Do benefits given to big business trickle down* (= get passed on) *to the consumer?* 2 flow or move slowly, as a brook.
— *n.* a small flow: *Highway traffic was reduced to a mere trickle by the accident.*

trick·ster (TRICK·stur) *n.* one who tricks or deceives.

trick·y *adj.* **trick·i·er, -i·est** 1 using tricks; deceptive: *a tricky politician.* 2 intricate; difficult to handle: *a tricky job, situation.* — **trick·i·ly** *adv.*

tri·col·our or **tri·col·or** (TRY·cul·ur) *adj.* having three colours. — *n.* such a flag, as of France.

tri·cot (TREE·coh) *n.* 1 a plain knitted fabric used for underwear and shirts. 2 a pair of knitted tights.

tri·cy·cle (TRY·suh·cul) *n.* a child's three-wheeled vehicle worked by pedals.

tried *pt. & pp.* of TRY.
— *adj.* tested or approved; hence, trustworthy: *a tried and true formula, friendship.*

tri·fle (TRY·ful) *n.* 1 something of small value: *a mere trifle.* 2 a small amount of money.
— **a trifle** to a slight degree: *a trifle annoyed, late.*
— *v.* **-fles, -fled, -fling** talk or act in a frivolous or disrespectful manner: *One does not trifle with sacred things; to trifle away* (= waste) *precious time.*
— **tri·fler** *n.*

trifling (TRY·fling) *adj.* frivolous; trivial: *no trifling matter.*

trig·ger (TRIG·ur) *n.* a lever that is pulled back by the forefinger, or **trigger finger,** to fire a gun: *to pull, release, squeeze the trigger.*
— *v.* set off by or as if by a trigger: *Stimuli trigger responses; a riot triggered by an incident at a soccer game.*

trigger-happy (TRIG·ur·hap·ee) *adj.* 1 too ready to shoot. 2 irresponsible or belligerent, as when shooting without knowing what is going to be hit.

trill *n.* 1 a tremulous or vibrating sound. 2 a warble.
— *v.* sing, speak, or play a musical note with a trill: *the trilled "r" of Spanish.*

tril·lion (TRIL·yun) *n.* 1 a thousand billion (1 followed by 12 zeroes). 2 in the U.K., a billion billion (1 followed by 18 zeros). — **tril·lionth** *n. & adj.*

tril·li·um (TRIL·ee·um) *n.* a wild flower of the lily family having stems bearing three leaves and one three-petalled flower on each: *The white trillium is the floral emblem*

of Ontario.

trim *v.* **trims, trimmed, trim·ming** 1 clip or cut away unwanted parts from a hedge, beard, etc. so as to make it neat and tidy: *to trim the fat from the budget.* 2 decorate a Christmas tree, dress, etc. 3 balance the weight of a vehicle or craft so that it can move forward without tilting; also, balance an aircraft for level flight. 4 adjust the sails of a boat to make full use of the wind. 5 change views or take a position that suits prevailing views, as a politician. 6 *Informal.* defeat; thrash; also, cheat or swindle.
— *adj.* **trim·mer, trim·mest** shapely, well-proportioned, or efficient-looking: *a trim figure, haircut, lawn, ship.*
— *n.* 1 orderly condition: *He found everything in good trim; She's in fighting trim for the race.* 2 what a dress, furniture, automobile, etc. are ornamented with, as lace, handles, chrome, etc. — **trim·ly** *adv.*; **trim·ness** *n.*

tri·mes·ter (try·MES·tur, TRY·mes·tur) *n.* 1 any of the three terms into which an academic year is divided. 2 a three-month period: *during the second trimester (of pregnancy).*

trimming *n.* 1 ornament or decoration. 2 **trimmings** *pl.* trimmed-off parts. 3 **trimmings** *pl.* garnishings and such food accessories: *turkey with all the trimmings.* 4 *Informal.* a beating; also, a fleecing.

trin·i·ty (TRIN·uh·tee) *n.* **-ties** 1 the state or fact of being three; also, a triad. 2 **Trinity** the Christian belief of the union of Father, Son, and Holy Spirit in one Godhead.

trin·ket (TRINK·it) *n.* 1 a cheap ornament or piece of personal jewellery. 2 a trifle or toy.

tri·o (TREE·oh) *n.* **-os** 1 a group of three performing a dance, musical composition, etc. together. 2 a composition for three voices or instruments.

trip *n.* 1 a journey, esp. a short excursion, as for pleasure: *to go on a camping trip; to make, plan, take a trip; Our class went on a field trip to collect butterflies; a business trip; extended trips overseas; a round-the-world trip; a trip through the Maritimes; a trip to the kitchen during a commercial break; a round trip to Europe (and back).* 2 *Slang.* a drug-induced visionary experience or similar deviation: *an acid trip; an ego trip (to please one's vanity); a power trip.* 3 a light, quick stepping. 4 a slip or tumble; also, the action of causing a person to fall by catching his or her foot. 5 a catching device.
— *v.* **trips, tripped, trip·ping** 1 (cause) to stumble or slip up: *He tripped and fell down the stairs; was so sure of his facts, no one could **trip him up** (= catch him making a mistake); He tripped (= stumbled) over a few words of his speech.* 2 move with quick, light steps, as a child. 3 operate or activate a mechanism, esp. by releasing a catching device: *The burglar tripped the alarm and the siren went off.*
— **trip·per** *n.*

tri·par·tite (try·PAR·tite) *adj.* 1 having three parts: *a tripartite leaf.* 2 made between three parties: *a tripartite treaty.*

tripe *n.* 1 the lining of the second and third stomachs of beef animals used as food. 2 *Slang.* talk, writing, etc. considered worthless; trash.

tri·ple (TRIP·ul) *adj.* 1 three times as much, as many, as large, etc.: *a **triple-A** (= top) credit rating; typed with triple-spacing between lines; triple time (with three beats to the measure).* 2 having three parts; threefold: *a triple alliance; the Triple Crown (of horse racing); a **triple jump** (= hop, skip, and jump); a **triple threat** (= a football player good at passing, running, and kicking).*
— *n.* 1 a triple amount, group, etc. 2 a baseball hit that enables the batter to reach third base.
— *v.* **-ples, -pled, -pling** 1 make a threefold increase. 2 in baseball, hit a triple.

tri·plet (TRIP·lit) *n.* 1 one of three born at a single birth: *a set of triplets.* 2 a group of three musical notes or lines of verse.

tri·plex (TRIP·lex) *n.* something that is triple or threefold: *a triplex apartment.*

trip·li·cate (TRIP·luh·kit) *n.* one of three identical copies.— **in triplicate** in three copies.

tri·pod (TRY·pod) *n.* a three-legged stand, stool, etc.: *a camera on a tripod.*

trite *adj.* **trit·er, trit·est** worn out by constant use; hackneyed: *a trite expression, quotation.*
— **trite·ly** *adv.;* **trite·ness** *n.*

tri·umph (TRY·umf) *n.* a glorious or decisive victory or its celebration: *the triumph of good over evil; to score a triumph; Jay returned in triumph from the Olympics.*
— *v.* 1 win or celebrate a triumph *over* an enemy, opposition, etc. 2 succeed or prevail.
— **tri·umph·al** (try·UM·ful) *adj.:* *a triumphal arch, procession, song.*

tri·um·phant (try·UM·funt) *adj.* victorious or rejoicing: *a triumphant army; triumphant fans, shouts.*
— **tri·um·phant·ly** *adv.*

tri·um·vir (try·UM·vur) *n.* **-virs** or **-vir·i** (-vuh·rye) a member of a triumvirate.

tri·um·vi·rate (try·UM·vur·it) *n.* a group of three forming a government, as in ancient Rome.

triv·i·a (TRIV·ee·uh) *n.pl.* little known facts; trifles.

triv·i·al (TRIV·ee·ul) *adj.* insignificant or trifling.
— **triv·i·al·ly** *adv.*

triv·i·al·i·ty (triv·ee·AL·uh·tee) *n.* **-ties** 1 trivial quality. 2 a trifle.

tri-weekly (try·WEEK·lee) *adj. & adv.* 1 thrice a week. 2 every three weeks.

-trix *n. suffix.* feminine of agent nouns ending in "-tor": *aviatrix, executrix.*

trod *pt.* and a *pp.* of TREAD.

trod·den a *pp.* of TREAD.

trog·lo·dyte (TROG·luh·dite) *n.* 1 a cave dweller. 2 an unsocial or brutish person.

troi·ka (TROY·kuh) *n.* 1 a team of three horses; hence, a three-member team, as of administrators: *the classic battlefield troika of infantry, artillery, and armour.* 2 a Russian carriage or sleigh drawn by three horses harnessed abreast.

Tro·jan (TROH·jun) 1 *n. & adj.* (a citizen) of **Troy**, a legendary city of Asia Minor. 2 *n.* one noted for courage and endurance: *She works like a Trojan (= very hard).*

Trojan horse *n.* a person or thing with a hidden destructive or subversive capacity, like a large wooden horse filled with enemy soldiers that the Trojans received as a gift during their war (**Trojan War**) with the Greeks.

troll (TROLE) *n.* 1 in Scandinavian folklore, a dwarfish monster with magical powers. 2 a fishing line with lure or bait used for trolling. 3 a round such as "Three Blind Mice."
— *v.* 1 sing heartily or in a full, rolling voice. 2 draw a fishing line behind a moving boat; also, fish in water in this way: *to troll for bass.*

trol·ley (TROL·ee) *n.* **trol·leys** 1 a pulley (**trolley wheel**) rolling at the end of a pole (**trolley pole**) against an electrified overhead wire that powers a streetcar or bus. 2 a streetcar (**trolley car**) or bus (**trolley bus**) so powered. 3 a wheeled basket or carriage running suspended from an overhead track, as in a store.

troop *n.* 1 a collection of people or animals, esp. an organized unit, as the subdivision of a cavalry regiment, a Boy Scout unit, etc. 2 **troops** *pl.* soldiers: *airborne troops; ground troops; peace-keeping troops stationed in the Middle East.*
— *v.* 1 go *out, off,* etc. as a group: *Children trooped out of the room at the sound of the alarm.* 2 gather *around* someone in a group.

troop·er *n.* a member of a cavalry, mounted police, or state police: *a U.S. state trooper; Lee swears like a trooper (= uses vile language).*

trooping the colour or **colours** *n.* an annual ceremony in which the sovereign receives the flag and inspects the troops.

tro·phy (TROH·fee) *n.* **-phies** 1 something captured in war, displayed as a memorial, or kept as evidence of some exploit, as the mounted head of an animal killed: *a war trophy.* 2 a prize awarded for victory in a contest.

trop·ic *n.* 1 either of the two parallels of latitude, the **Tropic of Cancer** and the **Tropic of Capricorn**, north and south of the equator respectively. 2 **the tropics** or **Tropics** *pl.* the region lying between these latitudes.

trop·i·cal (TROP·uh·cul) *adj.* of the tropics: *tropical fish; the tropical rain forest; a tropical (= very hot) climate.* — **trop·i·cal·ly** *adv.*

trot *n.* 1 the gait of a horse, etc. that is faster than a walk, with the legs moving in diagonal pairs. 2 a person's jogging gait.
— *v.* **trots, trot·ted, trot·ting** ride, go, etc. at a trot or brisk pace.
— **trot out** *Informal.* bring out, as a horse for inspection or approval: *He trotted out the usual excuses for his failure.* — **trot·ter** *n.*

troth (TRAWTH, TROHTH, "TH" as in "thin") *n.* [old use] a word of promise, as to marry, be loyal, etc.; betrothal: *to pledge* or *plight one's troth (= promise to marry).*

trou·ble (TRUB·ul) *n.* 1 worry; difficulty; distress: *a world full of trouble and sorrow; to ask for, avoid, look*

for, steer clear of, stir up trouble; The trouble (=fault) is, you can't have it both ways; Without money, you're **in trouble;** *He's careful not to get into trouble with the police; She knows how to keep herself out of trouble; Trouble is brewing; Jim has heart trouble (=disease).* **2** an instance or cause of pain and worry: *engine trouble; racial troubles; He is a trouble to society; Our troubles are over with death.* **3** inconvenience or exertion: *Walking to work is no trouble to her; She takes the trouble to be on time; went to much trouble to help her neighbours; "No trouble," she said when they thanked her for the service.*
— *v.* **-bles, -bled, -bling** cause trouble to someone; bother: *Bad dreams trouble children; He didn't trouble (himself) to return the book he borrowed; in* **troubled** (=agitated) *waters; May I trouble (=inconvenience) you to return my book?*

trou·ble·shoot·er (TRUB·ul·shoo·tur) *n.* one who can trace a malfunction or other trouble to its source and help to get rid of it.

trou·ble·some (TRUB·ul·sum) *adj.* causing trouble: *troublesome ailments, people.*

trough (TRAWF) *n.* **1** a long, narrow, open container, as for holding water or food for animals, a channel to carry away water from eaves, etc. **2** a low air-pressure area that gives rise to a hurricane.

trounce *v.* **trounc·es, trounced, trounc·ing** **1** thrash or beat. **2** *Informal.* defeat in a game. — **trounc·er** *n.*

troupe (TROOP) *n.* a company or group of actors, singers, etc.
— *v.* **troupes, trouped, troup·ing** travel with a troupe. — **troup·er** *n.*

trou·ser (TROW·zur, "OW" as in "HOW") usually **trousers** *n.pl.* a two-legged outer garment extending from the waist to the ankles, as usually worn by men.
— *adj.*: *a trouser leg, pocket; a* **trouser suit** (=pantsuit).

trous·seau (TROO·soh) *n.* **trous·seaux** (-soze) or **trous·seaus** a bride's personal outfit of clothes, etc.

trout (rhyme: "out") *n.* a freshwater food and game fish related to the salmon.

trove (rhyme: "drove") *n.* [short form] TREASURE-TROVE.

trow (TROH, TROW) *v.* [old use] believe or suppose.

trow·el (TROW·ul, "OW" as in "how") *n.* **1** a hand tool with a broad flat blade for spreading and smoothing plaster or mortar. **2** a similar garden tool but with a curved blade.
— *v.* **-els, -elled** or **-eled, -el·ling** or **-el·ing** spread, smooth, or dig with a trowel.

tru·ant (TROO·unt) *n.* **1** a child who stays away from school without permission: *He played truant and stayed home.* **2** one who shirks his or her duty.
— *adj.* errant; straying: *a truant child.*
— **tru·an·cy** (-un·see) *n.* **-cies.**

truant officer *n.* an official who investigates absences from school.

truce *n.* a temporary ceasing of hostilities by agreement between the fighting parties; cease-fire: *to arrange, violate, work out a truce; The uneasy truce between the*

warring factions didn't last long; to sign a truce (=armistice).

truck *n.* **1** an automotive vehicle for carrying loads, having a rear portion that is either open, as in a "dump truck," pickup, etc., or closed, as in a tractor-and-trailer unit or in a "panel truck": *a delivery truck; fire truck; garbage truck; tow truck; trailer truck.* **2** a swivelling, wheeled frame used at the end of a railway car, locomotive, etc.: *a skateboard truck.* **3** goods for the market, esp. vegetables, as grown on a **truck farm.** **4** small articles; odds and ends. **5** *Informal.* trash. **6** dealings; business: *They would have no truck with radicals.*
— *v.* **1** drive trucks or carry a load on a truck: *"Keep trucking!"* **2** exchange or barter.

trudge *v.* **trudg·es, trudged, trudg·ing** walk wearily *through mud, snow, etc.*
— *n.* a weary walk: *a long trudge of 20 km.*

true (TROO) *adj.* **tru·er, tru·est** **1** agreeing with a norm or standard, esp. ethical; not false: *a true story; He was true to his word; a true humanitarian; the true* (=rightful) *heir; This is like a dream* **come true** (=that has been realized). **2** agreeing with standards of correctness or accuracy: *a statue that is true to life; the true* (=geographic) *north as opposed to magnetic north; "The True North, strong and free"* (=Canada idealized); *Floating ribs are not true ribs.*
— **out of true** not correctly positioned.
— *v.* **trues, trued, tru·ing** make or put in the correct position: *to true up a door frame.*
— *adv.* in a true manner: *a story that rings true; a plant that breeds true to type; That 2 and 2 are 4 holds true under most conditions.*
— *n.* that which is true: *the true, the good, and the beautiful.*

true-blue *adj.* very loyal and staunch: *a true-blue Conservative.*

tru·ism (TROO·iz·um) *n.* a statement that is self-evident and superfluous.

tru·ly (TROO·lee) *adv.* in a true manner; truthfully; faithfully.

trump *n.* a playing card of a suit that ranks higher than others during the play of a hand: *Spades is* or *are* **trumps;** *She has a trump up her sleeve* (=something to be used for advantage when needed); *He always* **comes up trumps** (=He's very helpful).
— *v.* play a trump or take a trick or card with a trump.
— **trump up** bring forward falsely: *arrested on a* **trumped-up** *charge.*

trum·pet (TRUM·pit) *n.* **1** a loud-sounding brass wind instrument with a looped tube and flared bell. **2** a sound like a trumpet's. **3** a trumpetlike hearing aid, or "ear trumpet."
— *v.* **1** blow a trumpet or make a sound like a trumpet's: *the trumpeting* (=loud call) *of the elephant.* **2** proclaim loudly: *Don't trumpet it all over town.*
— **trum·pet·er** *n.*

trun·cate (TRUNK·ate) *v.* **-cates, -cat·ed, -cat·ing** cut off a part, esp. the apex of something; lop: *a truncated pyramid; a truncated quotation, version of the story.*

— *adj.* of a feather or leaf, having a blunt top.
— **trun·ca·tion** (trung·CAY·shun) *n.*

trun·dle (TRUN·dul) *v.* -dles, -dled, -dling roll *along, down,* etc. — **trun·dler** *n.*

trundle bed *n.* a low bed on casters, as for a child, that is rolled under another bed when not in use.

trunk *n.* 1 the main stem, as opposed to branches, of a tree or treelike structure such as a system of nerves or blood vessels. 2 the luggage compartment of a car. 3 **trunks** *pl.* very short trousers worn by men for swimming and athletics. 4 a main transportation or telephone line; also **trunk line**. 5 a human or animal body without head or limbs. 6 the long snout of an elephant. 7 a large reinforced box for a traveller's clothing, etc.: *to pack and ship one's trunks*.

truss *n.* 1 a supporting framework of beams, bars, etc. under a roof or bridge. 2 a support worn to keep in a ruptured groin. 3 a bundle or pack.
— *adj.* reinforced or supported: *a truss beam, bridge, joint*.
— *v.* 1 support a roof, bridge, etc. with a truss. 2 bind or tie a person up so that he or she cannot move. 3 bind the wings or legs of a fowl for cooking.

trust *n.* 1 firm assurance or belief that a person or thing will be as good as hoped or expected: *the implicit trust of children in their parents; absolute, blind trust; God was her sole trust* (= trusted one); *goods sold and bought* **on trust** (= credit); *We take many things around us on trust* (= without proof). 2 something entrusted to a person's care or responsibility: *to fulfil one's trust; not to desert one's trust; He was accused of abusing, betraying a trust; a sacred trust.* 3 the responsibility or obligation resulting from a trust: *A treasurer is in a position of trust; to set up a trust for a child's inheritance; property held* **in trust** *for a minor; a minor put in a guardian's trust* (= care); *People in public office place their holdings in a blind trust (in the charge of someone else) to avoid conflicts of interest.* 4 an illegal business organization that controls other organizations for fixing prices, eliminating competition, etc.; cartel: *to break up a trust.*
— *v.* have trust: *He trusts his employees (to do their duty); I trust* (= hope) *that you're fine; Parents expect children to trust* (= have faith) *in them; Libraries trust* (= rely on) *patrons to return books; Books are trusted* (= entrusted) *to their care; He's very* ***trusting*** (= trustful); *Don't* ***trust to*** (= depend on) *luck to wake up on time to catch your flight.*

trus·tee (trus·TEE) *n.* 1 one to whom property is legally committed in trust. 2 a member of the governing body ("board of trustees") of a school, hospital, etc.
— **trus·tee·ship** *n.*

trust·ful *adj.* full of trust; ready to confide; not suspicious: *Children are trustful; her trustful nature.*
— **trust·ful·ly** *adv.*; **trust·ful·ness** *n.*

trust·wor·thy (TRUST·wur·thee) *adj.* worthy of trust; reliable: *a trustworthy companion, servant, story.*
— **trust·wor·thi·ness** *n.*

trust·y *adj.* **trust·i·er, -i·est** of proven trustworthiness: *a trusty servant, steed, sword.*

truth (TROOTH, "TH" as in "thin") *n.* 1 that which is

true: *to ascertain, establish, find, face, seek, speak, stretch, tell the truth; the absolute, awful, bitter, cold, gospel, plain, unvarnished truth; "Truth will out"* (= The truth will become known some day); *There is some truth in what he says; a grain, kernel of truth; The truth of the matter is that I forgot.* 2 a fact, belief, etc. accepted as true: *a religious truth; the truths of science.*
— **in truth** truly; in fact.

truth·ful *adj.* 1 telling the truth: *a truthful child.* 2 conforming to the facts; true: *a truthful account.*
— **truth·ful·ly** *adv.*; **truth·ful·ness** *n.*

truth serum *n.* a drug used in lie-detector tests.

try *v.* **tries, tried, try·ing** 1 make an effort to do something: *She tried her best; tried hard to succeed but failed; I tried to phone her; I tried phoning many times; I'll try and (Informal for try to) phone her again.* 2 test or put to the proof: *Have you tried this sauce? He was fired for trying the boss's patience; Don't try* (= attempt) *impossible tasks; He was tried (in court) for murder but acquitted; Customers* ***try on*** *suits* (= put them on to check the fit) *before buying.*
— ***try one's hand at*** make an attempt: *She tried her hand at many skills before deciding to become a sculptor.*
— ***try out*** 1 evaluate: *They try out new employees before confirming them; She is trying out* (= auditioning) *for the lead role.* 2 melt down: *Blubber is tried out to extract oil.*
— *n., pl.* **tries** attempt: *Give it a try; It's worth a try; She made a serious try to do better next time.*

trying *adj.* that tries one's patience; hard to endure: *a trying period, person.*

try·out *n. Informal.* a testing of fitness of a candidate or of reaction, as of the audience to a play or show: *They're holding tryouts for the lead role.*

tryst (TRIST, TRY-) *n.* an appointed time, place, or meeting, as between lovers: *He had a tryst with her.*

tsar (TSAR, ZAR) same as CZAR; *fem.* **tsa·ri·na** (tsah·REE·nuh, zah-).

T-shirt *n.* a collarless, short-sleeved, close-fitting pullover shirt, as worn for leisure, sports, or underwear.

tub *n.* 1 a large open container with a wide top, as for washing clothes: *a laundry tub.* 2 a bathtub.

tub·by (TUB·ee) *adj.* **tub·bi·er, tub·bi·est** fat and short like a washtub.

tube *n.* 1 a usually long hollow cylinder, as for conveying fluids; pipe: *the tubes of a boiler; pneumatic tubes worked by air pressure.* 2 a railway tunnel; *Brit.* subway: *to travel by tube.* 3 a container made of a short tube closed at one end: *a test tube; a tube of toothpaste, paint, etc. (with soft metal covering and screw-on cap).* 4 [short form] inner tube; electron tube; vacuum tube: *to watch* ***the tube*** *(Informal for TV); the boob tube (Slang for TV).*
— ***down the tube*** *Informal.* into a state of being lost or finished.
— **tube·less** *adj.*: *A tubeless tire has no inner tube.*

tub·ing (TUE·bing) *n.* a length of tube, material in tube form, or a system of tubes.

tu·bu·lar (TUBE·yuh·lur) *adj.* **1** consisting of or having the form of a tube. **2** made with tubes.

tuck *v.* **1** thrust into a place snugly or compactly: *Children are tucked in bed at night; A shirt is tucked into the trousers; old clothes tucked away in trunks.* **2** make tucks in a garment. **3** pull up in a fold or folds to or as if to shorten: *She tucked up her skirt and waded across the stream.*
— **tuck away** or **into** *Slang.* finish off: *He could tuck away a whole cake before he started dieting.*
— *n.* **1** a fold sewn in a garment, esp. to make it better or to decorate it. **2** a drawing in: *the pelvic tuck* or *tilt exercise routine; A plastic surgeon could give you a tummy tuck to make you slimmer around the waist.*

tuck·er *v. Informal.* tire out or weary: *She got all tuckered out from exercising.*

-tude *n. suffix.* indicating state or condition: *altitude, aptitude, longitude, magnitude, solitude.*

Tues·day (TYOOZ·dee, -day, TOOZ-) *n.* the third day of the week, following Monday.

tuft *n.* a bunch, cluster, clump, etc. that is attached at the base: *a tuft of hair; a rug made of tufts of pile; tufts of grass.*
— *v.* secure or provide with tufts: *A mattress is tufted at intervals to keep its padding in place; a **tufted** carpet.*

tug *v.* **tugs, tugged, tug·ging 1** pull hard *at* something. **2** move by tugging; haul, as with a tugboat.
— *n.* **1** a hard pull: *He gave a tug on her sleeve.* **2** a tugboat: *a seagoing tug.*

tug·boat *n.* a small powerful boat used for towing and pushing ocean liners in and out of harbours, barges along rivers, etc.

tug of war or **tug-of-war** *n.* **1** a contest in which two teams pull at the opposite ends of a rope till one crosses a central line. **2** a power struggle.

tu·i·tion (tue·ISH·un) *n.* **1** instruction, as at a college: *free tuition.* **2** payment for this: *an increase in tuition.*

tu·lip (TUE·lip) *n.* a bulbous herb of the lily family with large, cup-shaped flowers in brilliant colours.

tum·ble (TUM·bul) *v.* **-bles, -bled, -bling 1** fall headlong, esp. head over heels, as in a somersault. **2** move *out* of a place, *into* bed, etc. in a disorderly manner: *clothes tumbling in a dryer.* **3** cause to tumble; upset: *Records were tumbled at the Olympics.*
— *n.* **1** a headlong fall: *Stocks took a tumble yesterday.* **2** confusion or disorder.

tum·ble·down (TUM·bul·down) *adj.* dilapidated; ready to collapse: *a tumbledown house.*

tum·bler (TUM·blur) *n.* **1** one who tumbles, does handsprings, somersaults, etc. **2** a breed of pigeon that does acrobatics in the air. **3** a drinking glass with no stem or handle. **4** a lock mechanism in which levers must be raised to an exact height to move the bolt. **5** a drying machine for clothes.

tum·ble·weed (TUM·bul·weed) *n.* a prickly plant with a round shape that breaks off when dry and is tumbled about by the wind.

tum·my (TUM·ee) *n.* **tum·mies** [child's word] stomach.

tu·mour or **tu·mor** (TUE·mur) *n.* a swelling in a body part from an abnormal growth of tissue, either benign, as a cyst, or malignant, as cancer.
— **tu·mor·ous** (-us) *adj.*

tu·mult (TUE·mult) *n.* a commotion, disturbance, or confusion, as during a storm or battle: *The Speaker's ruling caused a tumult; The House of Commons was in a tumult over the ruling; It was an hour before the tumult subsided.*
— **tu·mul·tu·ous** (tue·MUL·choo·us) *adj.: a tumultuous mob, welcome; tumultuous passions.*
— **tu·mul·tu·ous·ly** *adv.*

tu·na (TUE·nuh) *n.* (the flesh of) a large swift ocean fish of the mackerel family valued as food. Also **tuna fish.**

tun·dra (TUN·druh) *n.* the vast, treeless, swampy plains of the Arctic.

tune (TYOON, TOON) *n.* **1** a melody or air, esp. one that is simple and popular: *to hum, play, sing, strum, whistle a tune; a catchy tune; She's too independent to **dance to your tune** (= comply with your wishes).* **2** the correct musical pitch: *A choir sings in tune; To join a choir, you have to be able to **carry a tune** (= sing with correct pitch); a misfit who is **out of tune** with society; She's **in tune** with the times.*
— **call the tune** be in command.
— **change one's tune** assume a different style or tone of expression.
— **to the tune of** to the extent of a sum of money: *He bilked them to the tune of $2 million.*
— *v.* **tunes, tuned, tun·ing 1** adjust a musical instrument to the proper pitch. **2** put a motor or engine in the best working condition; also **tune up. 3** attune *to* or be in tune *with.*
— **tune in** adjust a radio or TV set for the best reception: *to tune in to a station.*
— **tune out 1** turn off a broadcast or program. **2** turn away from what is happening or ignore a command, etc.
— **tun·er** *n.*

tune·ful *adj.* melodious; pleasant to hear: *tuneful melodies.* — **tune·ful·ly** *adv.*

tune-up or **tune·up** *n.* the checking and adjusting of the parts of an engine to put them in proper working condition: *to do an engine tune-up.*

tu·nic (TUE·nic) *n.* **1** a loose, gownlike, usually belted, knee-length garment, as worn by ancient Greeks and Romans. **2** a jacket-length blouse: *maternity tops in tunic style; a mountie's red tunic.*

tun·nel (TUN·ul) *n.* an underground passageway for a road, sewer, etc.: *to bore, dig a tunnel; to construct a pedestrian tunnel under the street; We drove through a tunnel under the river; a wind tunnel for testing speeds; the light at the end of the tunnel* (= source of hope).
— *v.* **tun·nels, tun·nelled** or **tun·neled, tun·nel·ling** or **tun·nel·ing** make a tunnel *through* a mountain, *under* the sea, etc.: *a cave tunnelled by the action of a river.*
— **tun·nel·ler** or **tun·nel·er** *n.*

tunnel vision *n.* **1** the defect of not having peripheral vision. **2** narrow-mindedness.

tuque (TUKE) *n. Cdn.* **1** a knitted woollen cap with a tapered end hanging by the side when worn. **2** a woollen cap with a round tassel at the top; toque.

tur·ban (TUR·bun) *n.* 1 a man's headdress worn by Muslims and Sikhs, consisting of a scarf wound around the head. 2 a close-fitting brimless hat worn by women.

tur·bid (TUR·bid) *adj.* 1 cloudy or disturbed, as by stirring up sediment: *turbid waters; turbid feelings.* 2 dense or thick: *turbid clouds, smoke.*
— **tur·bid·ly** *adv.*
— **tur·bid·ness** or **tur·bid·i·ty** (tur·BID·uh·tee) *n.*

tur·bine (TUR·bin, -bine) *n.* an engine consisting of a wheel turned by the force of water, steam, or gas.

tur·bo·jet (TUR·boh·jet) *n.* 1 a jet engine with a turbine-driven air compressor. 2 an airplane driven by a turbojet.

tur·bo·prop (TUR·boh·prop) *n.* 1 a turbojet engine with a turbine-driven propeller. 2 an airplane powered by a turboprop.

tur·bo·train (TUR·boh·train) *n.* a high-speed passenger train powered by turbines.

tur·bu·lent (TURB·yuh·lunt) *adj.* causing or marked by a disturbance; tempestuous: *a turbulent sea; a turbulent mob, period of life; turbulent passions.*
— **tur·bu·lent·ly** *adv.* — **tur·bu·lence** *n.*

turf *n.* 1 sod: *artificial or synthetic turf used in a stadium.* 2 peat or a piece of it for fuel. 3 **the turf** horse racing. 4 a track for horse racing. 5 *Slang.* one's territory or domain: *to protect one's turf; on her home turf.* — *v.* cover with turf; sod.
— **turf out** eject or kick out of one's dwelling or other place. — **turf·y** *adj.*

tur·gid (TUR·jid) *adj.* 1 enlarged or bloated, as an organ by excess of blood. 2 disorderly or unrestrained in style: *a turgid narrative.*
— **tur·gid·i·ty** (tur·JID·uh·tee) *n.*

Turk *n.* 1 a person of or from **Turkey,** a west Asian country. 2 **young turk** or **young Turk** one who is impatient for change in an established group that he or she is a member of; radical.

tur·key (TUR·kee) *n.* 1 (the flesh of) a large North American poultry bird: *to carve, raise, roast, stuff turkeys; Turkeys gobble; The male turkey is called a "gobbler," the female a hen.* 2 *Informal.* someone considered stupid; jerk; also, something bad or worthless. 3 See COLD TURKEY.
— **talk turkey** *Informal.* talk bluntly or seriously.

tur·moil (TUR·moil) *n.* a confused or disorderly state: *The nation was in (a) turmoil after the coup.*

turn *v.* 1 (cause) to revolve or rotate: *A wheel turns; to turn a key in a lock; A game turns* (= depends) *on teamwork.* 2 form something by revolving: *a rod turned on a lathe; a well-turned* (= gracefully formed) *ankle, compliment, phrase.* 3 change in position: *to turn the pages of a book; a sight so gruesome it turns your stomach.* 4 change the movement or course of something: *She turned her steps home; He turns the dog out at night.* 5 change direction or trend: *We turned off (from) the highway; We turned into a side street; Turn left at the lights; Let's turn our attention to something else; Friends turned against him* (= became hostile).
6 change nature or condition: *Milk turns sour if not kept cold; He turned traitor after joining the secret service; Can you turn* (= translate) *this into French? Success turned his head* (= unsettled him or made him vain); *Caterpillars turn into butterflies; The leaves turn colour in the fall; Jan turned colour* (= blushed) *at the joke; It is suddenly turning cold.* 7 make: *to turn a profit; to turn* (= perform) *tricks.*
— **turn down** 1 refuse an invitation: *She turned down his offer; She turned him down.* 2 lower: *to turn down the heat, volume.*
— **turn in** 1 hand over or hand in. 2 *Informal.* retire at night.
— **turn loose** set free to go without restraint.
— **turn off** 1 shut off water, gas, electricity, etc. or put out a light. 2 *Informal.* (cause) to lose interest: *Mention of homework turns him off.*
— **turn on** 1 start water, gas, etc. flowing or switch on a light. 2 *Informal.* (cause) to become interested or excited as by taking a narcotic drug: *Some turn on with booze; Computers turn her on.*
— **turn out** 1 turn off: *to turn out the lights; to turn them out* (= drive them out). 2 happen or come to be: *It turned out to be lucky day; Everything turned out well in the end.* 3 appear: *A large crowd turned out to greet her.* 4 produce: *to turn out books, scholars.*
— **turn over** 1 give control or possession of a person or thing: *She turned over her responsibilities to the new recruit; He turned the burglar over to the police.* 2 of an engine, revolve before starting to run: *A cold engine turns over for a while before it starts.* 3 take in as business income: *The company turns over nearly $75 million annually.*
— **turn the trick** achieve the desired result.
— **turn up** 1 raise the volume or intensity of sound, heat, etc. 2 appear or be found; also, happen: *He turned up rather late.*
— *n.* 1 a rotation, as of a wheel. 2 a form or style: *a turn of expression; a roast done **to a turn*** (= just right). 3 a change of direction; also, a bend or curve: *to make a U-turn; a road full of twists and turns; a turn that is difficult to negotiate* or *make; a sharp turn to the left; at the next turn in the road; at the turn of the century* (= around 1899 - 1900); *the turn of the year* (= around Dec. - Jan.). 4 a change in conditions, circumstances, etc.: *a dramatic turn of events; His illness took a turn for the worse.* 5 something done in rotation: *We **take turns*** (= alternate) *with others doing household chores; Wait for your turn; It's your turn to take out the garbage; "One good turn* (= deed) *deserves another"; "Turn and turn about* (= Doing by turns) *is fair play."*
6 natural inclination; bent: *a mechanical turn of mind.*
7 a short walk, ride, or drive: *Let's go for a turn around the block.*

— **at every turn** constantly.
— **by turns** alternately: *He was by turns funny and serious.*
— **in turn** in succession: *when your turn comes.*
— **out of turn** out of proper order.

turn·a·bout (TUR·nuh·bowt) *n.* 1 a reversal of position, policy, allegiance, etc.: *to do a turnabout.* 2 retaliation.

turn·a·round (TUR·nuh·round) *n.* 1 an area in which a vehicle can be turned around. 2 a turnabout or reversal: *December saw a turnaround in the fortunes of the company.* 3 the time needed to complete a process, as in loading, unloading, and servicing a vehicle before it can return to its route: *the turnaround time between billing and getting paid.*

turn·coat *n.* one who deserts his or her political or religious group; renegade: *Kim Philby was a master turncoat who worked as a Soviety spy.*

turn·er *n.* 1 one that turns. 2 one who turns things on a lathe.

turning *n.* 1 the act of one that turns. 2 a bend, as in a road. 3 the use of the lathe.

turning point *n.* a moment of decisive change: *The promotion was a turning point in his career; to reach a turning point in history, in one's life.*

tur·nip *n.* a plant whose roots are used as a vegetable.

turn·key *adj.* of a product or service, delivered so completely finished that starting to use it is as simple as turning a key: *a turnkey program, project, service.*

turn·off *n.* a ramp or road where one turns off from a highway.

turn·out *n.* 1 a gathering of people, as at a function or event: *The show attracted a large turnout; a good, heavy, record turnout; The voter turnout was light, poor, small.* 2 the way one is dressed or something is equipped. 3 a widened place in a road where vehicles can pass; also, a railway siding.

turn·o·ver (TUR·noh·vur) *n.* 1 a turning over or upset; also, in football and basketball, the losing possession of a ball: *The Baltimore Stars forced five Houston turnovers.* 2 a pastry or small pie whose crust has been folded over the filling: *an apple turnover.* 3 rate of replacement, as of employees: *There is a high turnover at fast-food outlets.* 4 the amount of goods sold or business done in a given period.

turn·pike *n.* 1 a highway on which tolls are charged. 2 a tollgate.

turn·stile *n.* a gateway with a rotating device for letting in people one by one or for counting their numbers.

turn·ta·ble (TURN·tay·bul) *n.* a round platform, as for turning locomotives around or playing a phonograph record.

tur·quoise (TUR·kois, -kwois) *n.* a brilliant greenish-blue, mineral or its colour; also *adj.*

tur·ret (TUR·ut) *n.* 1 a towerlike ornamental structure, as at the four corners of a tower. 2 a revolving structure housing guns on a battleship, tank, or airplane. 3 the rotating multiple-sided toolholder of a lathe.

tur·ret·ed (TUR·it·id) *adj.* having turrets.

tur·tle (TUR·tul) *n.* a slow-moving reptile with stumpy, clublike limbs (or flippers in "sea turtles") and a rounded body encased in a protective shell.
— **turn turtle** turn upside down; capsize.

tur·tle·neck (TUR·tul·neck) *n.* a high, close-fitting, turned-down collar or a sweater with one.

tusk *n.* a long, enlarged, pointed tooth projecting on either side of the mouth in the elephant, walrus, boar, etc. — **tusked** *adj.*

tusk·er *n.* a tusked animal, esp. a male elephant.

tus·sle (TUS·ul) *n. & v.* **tus·sles, tus·sled, tus·sling** 1 wrestle or scuffle. 2 struggle.

tu·te·lage (TUE·til·ij) *n.* guardianship or instruction: *Players are **under the tutelage** of their coaches.*

tu·te·lar·y (TUE·tuh·lair·ee) *adj.* guardian: *a tutelary saint, spirit; a guardian's tutelary authority.*

tu·tor (TUE·tur) *n.* a private teacher.
— *v.* act as a tutor to someone: *She tutors him in music.*
— **tu·tor·i·al** (tue·TOR·ee·ul) *n. & adj.: a tutorial* (= course) *in music; a tutorial session.*

tut-tut *interj.* expressing disbelief or disapproval.
— *v.* **-tuts, -tut·ted, -tut·ting:** *"How disgusting," tut-tutted the commentator.*

tu·tu (TOO·too) *n.* a ballerina's short stiff skirt.

tux *n.* [short form] tuxedo.

tux·e·do (tuk·SEE·doh) *n.* **-dos** 1 a man's tailless black jacket. 2 a man's semiformal suit with a tuxedo.

TV *n.* **TV's** or **TVs** 1 the radio transmission of images by converting light signals into electrical signals and back into images on a screen at the receiving end. 2 the TV industry or TV broadcasting: *She is in TV* (= works in the TV industry); *He'll be on TV tonight; prime-time TV.* 3 a television receiving set; TV: *Turn on the TV.* 4 a program or programs received on TV: *We watch TV every night.*
— *adj.: a TV announcer, channel, program, set, show, star, station.* Also **television.**

TV dinner *n.* a frozen dinner packaged in a tray for quick heating and serving.

twad·dle (TWOD·ul) *n.* empty talk or writing.

twain *n., pron. & adj.* [old use] two; pair: *"Never the twain shall meet."*

twang *n.* 1 the sharp, vibrating sound of a plucked string. 2 a sharp, nasal tone of voice: *to speak with a nasal twang.*
— *v.* 1 (cause) to make a twang, as on a stringed instrument. 2 speak with a nasal twang.
— **twang·y** *adj.: a twangy drawl.*

'twas (TWUZ, TWOZ) it was.

tweak (TWEEK) *v.* pinch and twist a nose, ears, etc.
— *n.* a sharp pinch and twist.

tweed *n.* 1 a rough, heavy woollen cloth with a hairy surface, usually woven of fibres in two colours. 2 **tweeds** *pl.* clothes of tweed, esp. a suit.

tweed·y *adj.* **tweed·i·er, -i·est** 1 of or like tweed: *a tweedy coat, style, wool.* 2 informal-looking: *a tweedy* *professor.*

'tween *prep.* [old use] between.

tweet *n. & interj.* the thin chirp of a small bird.
— *v.* utter a tweet.

tweet·er *n.* the speaker or a hi-fi that reproduces only the high-frequency sounds.

tweeze *v.* **tweez·es, tweezed, tweez·ing** *Informal.* pluck with tweezers.

tweez·ers *n.pl.* small pincers for handling tiny objects, esp. for plucking hairs.

twelfth *adj.* following the eleventh; 12th.
— *n.* **1** one that is 12th in order. **2** one of 12 equal parts; 1/12.

twelve (TWELV) *n., adj. & pron.* two more than 10; 12 or XII.

twen·ty (TWEN·tee) *adj. & n.* **-ties 1** two times 10; 20 or XX. **2 the twenties** *n.pl.* the numbers or years from 20 through 29. — **twen·ti·eth** (-uth) *n. & adj.*

twenty-twenty or **20/20 vision** *n.* normal eyesight, i.e. the ability to read characters that a person with normal eyesight can read from 20 feet away; 6/6 vision (in the metric system).

twerp (TWURP) *n. Slang.* an undesirable or ineffectual person.

twice *n.* two times.

twid·dle (TWID·ul) *n.* a twirl or twist.
— *v.* **twid·dles, twid·dled, twid·dling** toy or play with something idly.
— **twiddle one's thumbs** be unoccupied; have nothing to do. — **twid·dler** *n.*

twig *n.* a slender shoot or branch.
— *v.* **twigs, twigged, twig·ging** *Informal.* become aware of or catch on *to* something.

twig·gy (TWIG·ee) *adj.* slender or thin like a twig.

twi·light (TWY·lite) *n.* **1** the faint light of the period just before sunrise or just after sunset. **2** a period of fading light or decline: *in the twilight of his career, life; a drug-induced semiconscious **twilight sleep;** in the **twilight zone** (= grey area) of morality.*

twin *n.* **1** either of two offspring born at the same birth: *a pair of Siamese twins; Ten sets of identical twins were at the party; fraternal twins; One twin may look just like the other.* **2** one of two closely related or similar individuals or things: *The Twins* (= two mountain peaks) *tower over Jasper National Park.*
— *adj.* being a twin: *twin* (= two single) *beds; the twin cities of Kitchener and Waterloo in Ontario; a twin-engine jet; his twin sister.*
— *v.* **twins, twinned, twin·ning 1** bring forth twins. **2** couple or pair: *the **twinning** of a Canadian city with one in a foreign country for cultural exchanges.*

twine *n.* **1** a strong thread or cord made of two or more strands twisted together. **2** an entwining or tangle.
— *v.* **twines, twined, twin·ing 1** twist something together or *into* something. **2** wrap or wind *around* something. **3** meander or extend in a winding manner.

twinge (TWINJ) *n.* a sudden shooting pain: *a twinge of*

toothache; twinges of rheumatism; a twinge of conscience, remorse.
— *v.* **twing·es, twinged, twing·ing** give or feel a twinge.

twi-night (TWY·nite) *adj.* that continues from late afternoon into the evening: *a twi-night doubleheader (in baseball).*

twi-night·er (TWY·nye·tur) *n.* a twi-night doubleheader.

twin·kle (TWINK·ul) *v.* **-kles, -kled, -kling 1** (cause) to shine with a flickering light: *Stars twinkle in the sky.* **2** move quickly and lightly: *the twinkling feet of dancers; Her eyes twinkled with joy; **twinkling** (= sparkling) eyes; vanished in the **twinkling** of an eye (= in an instant).*
— *n.* **1** a gleam or sparkle. **2** a wink or blink.

twirl *v.* spin or whirl with dexterity: *to twirl one's mustache; She can twirl a hula hoop around her hips; a baton-twirling majorette.*
— *n.* curl: *a twirl of hair; a signature with twirls and flourishes.*

twist *v.* **1** to wind or turn, as on an axis: *threads twisted together into a string; a column with a twisted design; She twisted her head to look over her shoulder; to twist* (= break) *off a piece of dough.* **2** bend or force out of shape or position; distort or wrench: *a rope twisted into a knot; bodies twisting about in pain; The road twists and turns on its way up the hill; a twisted* (= sprained) *ankle; He knows how to **twist arms** (= use friendly pressure) to get what he wants; She can twist* (= manipulate) *him around her little finger; a twisted tale of intrigue; words twisted out of their meaning; a car twisted out of shape in a crash.* **3** send a ball spinning in a curved path.
— *n.* **1** bend or curve: *a road with many twists and turns; a board with a slight twist* (= warp). **2** something twisted: *a twist of bread; a twist* (= braid) *of tobacco; a twist of lemon* (= lemon peel for flavouring a drink). **3** distortion or turn: *an unexpected twist in the plans; by an ironic, strange twist of fate; That's a new twist to the story; a queer mental twist* (= kink or quirk). **4** a spin given to a ball in tennis, baseball, bowling, etc. **5** a vigorous dance of the 1950s and 1960s with twisting hip and leg movements: *to do the twist.*

twist·er *n.* one that twists, as a ball sent with a twisting motion, a tornado, or a waterspout.

twit *v.* **twits, twit·ted, twit·ting** taunt or tease a person *with* or *about* a weakness.
— *n. Slang.* an annoyingly silly person: *a pompous twit.*

twitch *n.* **1** a sudden involuntary jerk, as of a facial muscle: *a nervous twitch.* **2** a sharp tug or pull.
— *v.* pull or jerk suddenly or spasmodically: *to twitch a fishing line; twitching fingers; a face that twitches nervously.*

twitch·y *adj.* **1** jerky. **2** nervous or fidgety: *a twitchy face; twitchy fingers; She's a bit twitchy about his behaviour in public.*

twit·ter (TWIT·ur) *v.* **1** chirp or chatter, as birds. **2** titter or giggle. **3** tremble with excitement; flutter.
— *n.* a twittering: *the twitter of swallows; Wedding day found everyone in a twitter* (= excited state).

'twixt *prep.* [old use] between: *"There's many a slip twixt the cup and the lip."*

two (TOO) *n., adj. & pron.* one more than one; 1 or II: *Children can put two and two together* (= see the facts for themselves) *and draw conclusions.*
— **in two** in two parts: *to cut an apple in two.*

two-bit *adj.* cheap: *a two-bit attraction, deal, show.*

two bits *n. Slang.* a quarter of a dollar; 25 cents.

two-edged (too-EJD) *adj.* cutting both ways: *a twoedged sword, argument.*

two-faced (too-FAIST) *adj.* 1 having two faces on the head: *the two-faced god Janus.* 2 deceitful or insincere.

two-fer (TOO-fur) *n. Informal.* a discounted item of which one can buy "two for" the price of one.

two-fisted (too-FIS-tid) *adj. Informal.* vigorous or strong.

two-fold *adj. & adv.* double; doubly.

two-ply *adj.* having two thicknesses, layers, strands, etc.: *a two-ply paper towel, tire, yarn.*

two-some (TOO-sum) *n.* 1 two people. 2 a golf match for two.

two-time *v.* -times, -timed, -tim·ing *Slang.* 1 be unfaithful to one's spouse or partner. 2 double-cross someone.

two-way *adj.* involving two directions or parties: *two-way communication; a two-way radio, street; a two-way race (between two contestants).*

two-way TV *n.* home TV that doubles as a terminal for shopping, banking, requesting data from data banks, sending customer feedback, etc.

ty·coon (tye-COON) *n.* same as MAGNATE: *a tobacco tycoon.*

ty·ee (TYE-ee) *n. Cdn.* an important person, big fish, etc.: *a tyee salmon.*

tying *pres. part.* of TIE.

tyke *n. Informal.* a small child considered as mischievous, helpless, etc.

type *n.* 1 a person or thing considered as belonging to a group or category because of similarity to others: *He's the strong silent type; dramatic characters that are types* (= generalizations) *rather than individuals.* 2 a category, sort, or kind: *a fine type of woman; I don't like this type of novel* (or *Informally,* this type novel); *novels of this type; a plant variety that is true to type* (= to the original). 3 a printing block with raised letters or characters: *Gutenberg printed from movable type; italic and roman type; a complete font of type of the same size and style; A book is first set in type and then printed; small type* (= printed letters).
— *v.* types, typed, typ·ing 1 classify as to type;

typecast: *to type one's blood as A, B, AB, or O; an actor who is always typed as a gangster.* 2 write with a typewriter: *a letter typed by her secretary.*

type·cast *v.* -casts, -cast, -cast·ing cast an actor repeatedly in the same type of role: *an actor typecast in gangster roles; the typecasting of women as sex objects.*

type·face *n.* a design or style of type: *A typeface (as this, Baskerville) includes letters and numerals and comes in roman,* italic, **boldface,** *etc. as well as in different sizes.*

type·script *n.* typewritten matter.

type·set *v.* -sets, -set, -set·ting set book matter in type; compose. — **type·set·ter** *n.*

type·writ·er (TYPE-rye-tur) *n.* a keyboard machine that produces printed characters on paper: *a reporter pounding her typewriter; He does all his writing on a manual typewriter; electronic typewriters.*

ty·phoon (tye-FOON) *n.* a destructive tropical cyclone of the western Pacific.

typ·i·cal (TIP-i-cul) *adj.* having the characteristics of a type or class: *a typical soap opera; Sentimentality is typical* (= characteristic) *of soaps; It is typical of soaps to be sentimental.* — **typ·i·cal·ly** *adv.*

typ·i·fy (TIP-uh-fye) *v.* -fies, -fied, -fy·ing 1 be a type or symbol of something; exemplify: *Solomon typifies wisdom.* 2 characterize: *Wisdom typifies Solomon.* 3 classify into types: *to typify verbs into regular and irregular.*

typ·ist (TYE-pist) *n.* one who uses a typewriter.

ty·po (TYE-poh) *n. Informal.* a typing or typesetting error.

ty·pog·ra·phy (tye-POG-ruh-fee) *n.* 1 the art of printing with type: *Caxton's typography.* 2 the arrangement or appearance of typeset matter: *the typography of a dictionary page.*
— **ty·po·graph·ic** (tye-puh-GRAF-ic) *adj.*

ty·ran·ni·cal (tuh-RAN-i-cul) *adj.* of or like a tyrant; cruel and unjust. — **ty·ran·ni·cal·ly** *adv.*

tyr·an·nize (TEER-uh-nize) *v.* -niz·es, -nized, -niz·ing act or rule as a tyrant or despot; oppress: *the rich tyrannizing (over) the poor;* — **tyr·an·niz·er** *n.*

tyr·an·ny (TEER-uh-nee) *n.* -an·nies 1 a tyrant's rule or authority: *to impose, overthrow a tyranny; a cruel, merciless tyranny.* 2 a cruel and unjust act or use of power: *the tyranny of the majority over the minority.*

ty·rant (TYE-runt) *n.* 1 an absolute ruler or despot: *a cruel, ruthless tyrant.* 2 a cruel or oppressive person in authority: *The boss is not such a tyrant as he used to be.*

ty·ro (TYE-roh) *n.* -ros (-roze) an inexperienced and amateurish beginner in a field of activity.

tzar (TSAR, ZAR) same as CZAR; *fem.* **tza·ri·na** (tsah-REE-nuh, zah-).

Uu

U or **u** (YOO) *n.* **U's** or **u's 1** the 21st letter of the English alphabet. **2 U-** *combining form.* shaped like a U: *a 360° U-turn; the U-tube used in chemistry experiments.* **3** *adj. Informal.* in Britain, upper-class: *U and non-U.*

u·biq·ui·tous (yoo·BIK·wuh·tus) *adj.* seeming to be present or occurring everywhere: *the ubiquitous common crow.* — **u·biq·ui·ty** *n.*

UFO *n.* **UFO's** an unidentified flying object; flying saucer: *the sighting of UFO's.*

ugh (UH, UK) *interj.* expressing disgust or horror.

ug·ly (UG·lee) *adj.* **-li·er, -li·est** hideous or repulsive in appearance: *an ugly toad; an ugly* (= dangerous) *gaping wound; He gave me an ugly* (= ill-natured) *look; an* **ugly duckling** *who could grow into a graceful swan, as in the fairy tale.* — **ug·li·ness** *n.*

uh *interj.* **1** expressing surprise, contempt, or a question. **2** a neutral sound different from any of the regular vowels that is prolonged while thinking or searching for a word.

uh-huh *interj.* indicating that one is receptive to what is being said.

ul·cer (UL·sur) *n.* an open, usually inflamed sore on the skin or on a mucous membrane: *a bleeding ulcer; peptic ulcers.* — **ul·cer·ous** (-us) *adj.*

ul·te·ri·or (ul·TEER·ee·ur) *adj.* **1** lying on the farther side. **2** hidden: *an ulterior motive.*

ul·ti·mate (UL·tuh·mit) *adj.* remotest, beyond which it is impossible to go: *the ultimate origin of the universe; in the ultimate analysis; To many people, God is the Ultimate Reality.* — *n.* an ultimate point, result, fact, etc.; acme: *She enjoyed the ultimate in luxury.* — **ul·ti·mate·ly** *adv.*

ul·ti·ma·tum (ul·tuh·MAY·tum) *n.* **-tums** or **-ta** (-tuh) a final offer or demand threatening consequences if rejected: *to give, issue, receive, withdraw an ultimatum.*

ul·tra (UL·truh) *n.* an extremist. — *adj. & prefix.* going beyond the usual; extreme(ly): *He's too ultra in his views; the ultra Right; ultraconservative; ultrahigh; ultramodern.*

ul·tra·son·ic (ul·truh·SON·ic) **1** *adj.* beyond human hearing range; having to do with ultrasound. **2 ultrasonics** *pl.* [takes sing. v.] the science of ultrasonic sound waves and their applications in science and industry.

ul·tra·sound (UL·truh·sound) *n.* sound of more than 20 000 vibrations per second, too high-pitched for human hearing.

ul·tra·vi·o·let (ul·truh·VYE·uh·lut) *adj.* beyond the violet end of the visible light range: *ultraviolet light, radiation; ultraviolet lamps (yielding radiations of wavelengths between visible light and X rays).*

u·lu (OO·loo) *n. Cdn.* an Inuit woman's knife with a crescent-shaped blade.

um·bil·i·cal (um·BIL·uh·cul) *adj.* of the navel: *The* **umbilical cord** *connects an unborn child to its mother's womb for nutrition and waste removal; it is tied off and cut at birth by the delivering physician or midwife; An "umbilical cord" connects the astronaut to the spaceship during a space walk.*

um·bra (UM·bruh) *n., pl.* **-brae** (-bree) or **-bras** a dark spot or shadow, esp. the darker region of shadow cast by the sun in which a "total eclipse" is experienced. — **um·bral** (-brul) *adj.*

um·brage (UM·brij) *n.* **1 take umbrage at** take offence at something. **2** shady foliage or shade.

um·brel·la (um·BREL·uh) *n.* **1** a circular cover of cloth on a folding frame of hinged ribs sliding on a centre pole, carried for protection against sun or rain. **2** a protective organization, device, etc.: *an air umbrella of military aircraft; The PLO is the umbrella group for Palestinian Arabs.*

u·mi·ak (OO·mee·ak) *n. Cdn.* a large, open Inuit boat made with sealskin stretched over a wooden frame for carrying 10 to 12 people.

ump *n.* [short form] umpire.

um·pire (UM·pire) *n.* a judge in a contest or dispute, esp. in sports such as baseball and hockey, sometimes assisting a referee, as in tennis and volleyball; referee. — *v.* act as umpire: *to umpire a game.*

ump·teen (UMP·teen) *adj. Slang.* innumerable: *I've told you umpteen times.* — **ump·teenth** (ump·TEENTH) *adj.: I'm telling you for the umpteenth time.*

un- a prefix freely added to words, using a hyphen before a capital letter *(un-Canadian),* to mean "not" when added to adjectives, participles, and adverbs *(unable, unsaid, unluckily),* "the opposite of" when added to nouns *(uncertainty, unrest),* and an opposite action when a verb is formed *(uncap, undo).*

un·a·bridged (un·uh·BRIJD) *adj.* **1** not abridged: *the unabridged original novel.* **2** comprehensive: *an unabridged dictionary.*

u·nan·i·mous (yoo·NAN·uh·mus) *adj.* in complete agreement; with the agreement of all: *a unanimous decision.* — **u·nan·i·mous·ly** *adv.* — **u·na·nim·i·ty** (yoo·nuh·NIM·uh·tee) *n.*

un·as·sum·ing (un·uh·SOO·ming) *adj.* not pretentious or forward; modest.

un·at·tached (un·uh·TACHT) *adj.* not attached, esp. in regard to marriage; unmarried or unengaged.

un·a·vail·ing (un·uh·VAY·ling) *adj.* being of no avail; futile. — **un·a·vail·ing·ly** *adv.*

un·a·ware (un·uh·WARE) *adj.* not aware; unawares: *We were caught unaware; We were unaware of the collapse of the bridge; unaware that the bridge had collapsed.* — **unawares** (-WAIRZ) *adv.* **1** by surprise; unexpectedly: *The announcement caught us* or *took us unawares.* **2** unintentionally: *a remark made unawares.*

un·bar (un·BAR) *v.* **-bars, -barred, -bar·ring** **1** unbolt or open a gate, etc. **2** open up a closed channel, field, etc.

un·be·com·ing (un·bi·CUM·ing) *adj.* not appropriate to one's appearance or character: *unbecoming clothes, conduct; conduct unbecoming of* or *to a gentleman.* — **un·be·com·ing·ly** *adv.*

un·be·known (un·bi·NOHN) *adj. Formal.* unknown *to* one; also **un·be·knownst.**

un·be·lief (un·bi·LEEF) *n.* doubt or lack of belief, esp. in something religious. — **un·be·liev·a·ble** (-LEE·vuh·bul) *adj.;* **un·be·liev·a·bly** *adv.* — **un·be·liev·er** (-vur) *n.*

un·bend (un·BEND) *v.* **-bends, -bent, -bend·ing** **1** straighten. **2** relax from formality, tension, etc.: *It's good to unbend a little on weekends.*

un·bend·ing (un·BEN·ding) *adj.* **1** stiff or resolute: *her unbending resolve.* **2** stubborn: *an unbending attitude; He's quite unbending in his attitude.*

un·bid·den (un·BID·un) *adj.* **1** not invited. **2** without being ordered.

un·born (un·BORN) *adj.* not yet born: *an unborn child in the womb; unborn (= future) generations.*

un·bos·om (un·BOOZ·um, long or short "OO") *v.* reveal one's feelings, secrets, thoughts, etc., esp. **unbosom oneself** *to* someone.

un·bri·dled (un·BRY·duld) *adj.* not bridled, esp. uncontrolled: *unbridled anger, enthusiasm, growth, insolence, optimism, power.*

un·bur·den (un·BUR·dun) *v.* **1** to free from a burden. **2** relieve oneself, one's heart, conscience, etc. by confession *to* someone or by disclosing guilt, etc.: *He had no peace of mind till he had unburdened himself to his counsellor.*

un·called-for (un·CAWLD·for) *adj.* not called for; unwarranted: *uncalled-for impertinence, remarks.*

un·can·ny (un·CAN·ee) *adj.* **1** mysterious or weird: *uncanny shapes, sounds; an uncanny feeling of something about to happen.* **2** so remarkable as to seem superhuman: *her uncanny ability to motivate employees; an uncanny instinct for guessing the right answer.*

un·cer·e·mo·ni·ous (UN·ser·uh·MOH·nee·us) *adj.* **1** not ceremonious. **2** abrupt or discourteous: *an unceremonious dismissal, exit, rebuke.*

un·cer·tain (un·SUR·tun) *adj.* **1** not certain or sure: *He felt uncertain about the future; somewhat uncertain as to what might happen; a word of uncertain origin; We told him in no uncertain (= in clear) terms.* **2** changeable or varying: *uncertain health, temper, weather.*

un·cer·tain·ty (un·SUR·tun·tee) *n.* **-ties** **1** an uncertain state: *our uncertainty about the future.* **2** something that is uncertain: *the uncertainties of a hand-to-mouth existence.*

un·char·i·ta·ble (un·CHAIR·uh·tuh·bul) *adj.* harsh or severe, as in judging others: *an uncharitable imputation of motive; It was uncharitable of him to say that.* — **un·char·i·ta·bly** *adv.*

un·chart·ed (un·CHAR·tid) *adj.* **1** of places, not shown on a map. **2** not mapped; unexplored: *uncharted seas.*

un·chris·tian (un·CRIS·chun) *adj.* **1** not Christian. **2** *Informal.* outrageous or unusual: *They charge unchristian prices.*

un·cir·cum·cised (un·SUR·cum·sized) *adj.* **1** not circumcised. **2** [derogatory] non-Jewish; gentile; heathen.

un·cle (UNK·ul) *n.* the brother of one's father or mother; also, one's aunt's husband: *He threw up his hands and **cried Uncle** or **said Uncle** (Informal for admitted defeat).*

Uncle Sam *n. Informal.* the U.S. government or nation, personified as a long-haired man in a tall hat and a costume decorated with stars and stripes.

un·com·fort·a·ble (un·CUM·fur·tuh·bul) *adj.* feeling or causing discomfort: *The baby seems uncomfortable; an uncomfortable chair; an uncomfortable (= uneasy) silence; We felt uncomfortable about her long absence.* — **un·com·fort·a·bly** *adv.*

un·com·mon (un·COM·un) *adj.* **1** rare or unusual: *It is not uncommon to have frost in September.* **2** remarkable or outstanding: *an uncommon*

occurrence; her uncommon generosity.
— **un·com·mon·ly** *adv.*

un·com·pro·mis·ing (UN·com·pruh·MYE·zing) *adj.*
unyielding or inflexible: *an uncompromising attitude; a
woman of uncompromising devotion to duty.*

un·con·cern (un·cun·SURN) *n.* lack of concern, care, or
solicitude, as from selfishness or insensitiveness;
indifference *over a person or thing.*
— **un·con·cerned** (-SURND) *adj.* not concerned,
anxious, or solicitous.

un·con·di·tion·al (un·cun·DISH·un·ul) *adj.* without
conditions attached: *an unconditional offer, rejection,
release, surrender.*

un·con·scion·a·ble (un·CON·shun·uh·bul) *adj.*
1 unreasonable or excessive: *It took an unconscionable
time.* 2 contrary to what the conscience dictates;
unscrupulous: *an unconscionable villain.*
— **un·con·scion·a·bly** *adv.*

un·con·scious (un·CON·shus) *adj.* not conscious or
aware: *He lay bleeding and unconscious; was
unconscious of having offended her; an unconscious
habit, prejudice, tendency.*
— *n.* **the unconscious** the part of the mind containing
thoughts, ideas, feelings, etc. that one is not fully aware
of or that have been repressed.

un·cou·ple (un·CUP·ul) *v.* **-ples, -pled, -pling**
disconnect something coupled together.

un·couth (un·COOTH) *adj.* 1 awkward or clumsy-
looking. 2 unrefined or crude.

un·cov·er (un·CUV·ur) *v.* 1 remove the cover from
something. 2 disclose or expose. 3 bare one's head in
respect.

unc·tion (UNC·shun) *n.* 1 an anointing with oil (as in
church rites) or with ointment (as in medical treatment).
2 the oil or salve used. 3 anything that soothes or
comforts; also, this quality: *She preaches with great
unction.*

un·cut (un·CUT) *adj.* not cut or abridged: *an uncut
version of a movie; a rough, uncut (= not shaped and
polished) diamond.*

un·daunt·ed (un·DAWN·tid) *adj.* not daunted or
disheartened: *undaunted by defeats; undaunted in her
resolve.*

un·der (UN·dur) *prep.* 1 directly below: *Look under the
table; a boulder under the (surface of) water; A shirt is
worn under a jacket; priced under (= less than) $100; 15
is under the voting age.* 2 subject or subordinate to a
person or thing: *a country under a dictatorship; She
testified under oath; I was under a wrong impression;
He's working under a contract; "Beauty" is listed under
(the heading) "B"; She was excused under (= because of)
the circumstances.*
— *adv.* in or to a lower place: *The boat sprang a leak
and went under; to keep wages and prices under
(control); everything priced $100 and under; We are
snowed under by correspondence; Companies* **go under**
*by bankruptcy; The anaesthetic kept her under
(= unconscious) during surgery.*
— *combining form* [meaning "below" as in the
following compounds whose basic meaning and

pronunciation are the same as in the base word in each
case]: *undercook, underdose, undereducated,
underemployed, underpay, underpopulated,
underpriced, underripe, undersized, undersold.*

un·der·a·chieve (UN·dur·uh·CHEEV) *v.* **-chieves,
-chieved, -chiev·ing** do less well in school than expected
for one's level of ability.— **un·der·a·chiev·er** *n.*

un·der·act (un·dur·ACT) *v.* act a dramatic part with less
than the required emphasis; underplay.

un·der·age (un·dur·AGE) *adj.* below the required or full
age.

un·der·arm (un·dur·ARM) 1 *adj.* of the armpit:
underarm wetness. 2 *adj. & adv.* underhand: *an
underarm throw.*

un·der·bel·ly (un·dur·BEL·ee) *n.* 1 the underside of an
animal's body. 2 a weak or vulnerable part.

un·der·bid (un·dur·BID) *v.* **-bids, -bid, -bid·ding** 1 bid
less than what is justified, as by the cards in one's hand.
2 bid lower than another person.

un·der·brush (UN·dur·brush) *n.* low shrubs, small trees,
etc. under the large trees of a forest.

un·der·car·riage (UN·dur·cair·ij) *n.* 1 the supporting
frame or structure of an automobile or other vehicle on
wheels. 2 the landing gear of an airplane.

un·der·charge (un·dur·CHARGE) *v.* **-charg·es,
-charged, -charg·ing** 1 charge a buyer less than the
usual price. 2 load a gun, battery, etc. insufficiently.
— *n.* (UN·dur·charge) such a charge.

un·der·class (UN·dur·class) *n.* the poor and
underprivileged of a society.

un·der·class·man (un·dur·CLASS·mun) *n.* a freshman
or sophomore.

un·der·clothes (UN·dur·clothes) *n. pl.* underwear; also
un·der·cloth·ing (un·dur·CLOH·thing) *n.*

un·der·coat or **un·der·coat·ing** (UN·dur·coh·ting) *n.* 1 a
coating of a tarlike substance given to the underside of
an automobile for protection against rust. 2 a coat of
paint applied to a wall, furniture, etc. before the final
coat.— *v.* apply an undercoat to a vehicle.

un·der·cov·er (UN·dur·cuv·ur) *adj.* (done in) secret, as
spying: *an undercover agent, investigation, officer, unit;
undercover payments, work.*
— *adv.*: *to go, work undercover (= in secret).*

un·der·cur·rent (UN·dur·cur·unt) *n.* a current below the
surface, esp. in an opposite direction, as an undertow:
an undercurrent of resentment.

un·der·cut (un·dur·CUT) *v.* **-cuts, -cut, -cut·ting** 1 cut
away the underpart, as at the bottom of a coal bed for
easy shattering by explosives or on the side of a tree
trunk to make it fall toward a particular side. 2 sell or
work for less than a competitor. 3 hit a ball so as to give
it a backspin, as in tennis, billiards, or golf.

un·der·de·vel·oped (UN·dur·di·VEL·upt) *adj.* of
countries, not advanced industrially and hence poor in
standard of living, education, health care, etc.
Also **developing.**

un·der·dog (UN·dur·dog) *n.* **1** one in a state of subjection. **2** the predicted loser in a contest.

un·der·done (un·dur·DUN) *adj.* not cooked enough.

un·der·es·ti·mate (un·dur·ES·tuh·mate) *v.* -mates, -mat·ed, -mat·ing form too low an estimate of a person's strength, costs of a project, etc. Also *v.*

un·der·foot (un·dur·FOOT) *adj. & adv.* **1** under the foot or feet. **2** in the way of one walking.

un·der·gar·ment (UN·dur·gar·munt) *n.* a piece of underwear.

un·der·go (un·dur·GO) *v.* -goes, -went, -gone (-GON) , -go·ing go through a painful, unpleasant, or dangerous experience.

un·der·grad·u·ate (un·dur·GRAJ·oo·it) *n.* a college student who has not yet received a first degree.

un·der·ground (un·dur·GROUND) *adv. & adj.* **1** beneath the surface of the ground: *Moles live underground; an underground installation, passage; underground testing of atomic bombs.* **2** in or into hiding; away from public knowledge: *She went underground to escape from the police; underground resistance to enemy occupation; dissident publications of the underground press; an avant-garde underground movie.* — *n.* (UN·dur·ground) **1** an underground region or political movement. **2** *Brit.* a subway.

un·der·growth (UN·dur·growth) *n.* same as UNDERBRUSH: *dense, heavy, thick undergrowth; to clear the undergrowth.*

un·der·hand (UN·dur·hand) *adj. & adv.* **1** with the hand swung forward below the level of the elbow or shoulder: *an underhand serve, throw; to pitch a ball underhand.* **2** underhanded or underhandedly.

un·der·hand·ed (un·dur·HAN·did) *adj.* sly or deceitful; not open or honest. — **un·der·hand·ed·ly** *adv.*

un·der·lie (un·dur·LYE) *v.* -lies, -lay, -lain, -ly·ing **1** lie or be situated under. **2** form the basis or foundation of a doctrine, etc.

un·der·line (UN·dur·line, un·dur·LINE) *v.* -lines, -lined, -lin·ing **1** draw a line under something. **2** stress or emphasize. — *n.* (UN·dur·line) a line under a word, passage, etc.

un·der·ling (UN·dur·ling) *n.* a servile follower or subordinate.

un·der·ly·ing (un·dur·LYE·ing) *adj.* **1** lying under: *underlying strata.* **2** basic or fundamental: *underlying motives, principles, reasons.*

un·der·mine (un·dur·MINE) *v.* -mines, -mined, -min·ing **1** dig under or wear away from under something: *to undermine a foundation; flood waters undermining river banks.* **2** weaken or impair gradually, as by insidious means: *rumours that undermine a person's reputation; health undermined (= sapped) by a chronic illness.*

un·der·most (UN·dur·mohst) *adj. & adv.* lowest.

un·der·neath (un·dur·NEETH, "TH" as in "thin") *prep. & adv.* below or beneath, esp. in a hidden place: *He carried a knife underneath his cloak.*

un·der·nour·ished (un·dur·NUR·isht) *adj.* not getting sufficient nourishment.

un·der·pants (UN·dur·pants) *n. pl.* long or short pants worn as underwear.

un·der·pass (UN·dur·pass) *n.* a road passing under a railway or highway.

un·der·pin·ning (UN·dur·pin·ing) *n.* masonry support or prop under a structure. — **underpinnings** *pl.* **1** foundation or basis: *Research data formed the underpinnings of his theory.* **2** *Slang.* a person's legs.

un·der·play (un·dur·PLAY) *v.* **1** underact. **2** play down; treat as not very important.

un·der·priv·i·leged (un·dur·PRIV·uh·lejd) *adj.* not enjoying the rights and privileges of other people, as the poor and minority groups of a society.

un·der·rate (un·dur·RATE) *v.* -rates, -rat·ed, -rat·ing to rate too low; underestimate.

un·der·score (un·dur·SCORE) *n. & v.* -scores, -scored, -scor·ing same as UNDERLINE.

un·der·sea (un·dur·SEE) *adj. & adv.* beneath the surface of the sea; also **un·der·seas** *adv.*

un·der·sell (un·dur·SEL) *v.* -sells, -sold, -sel·ling sell an article at a lower price than a competitor: *We will not be undersold.*

un·der·shirt (UN·dur·shurt) *n.* a vest or similar undergarment worn under a shirt.

un·der·shorts (UN·dur·shorts) *n. pl.* shorts worn by men and boys as underwear.

un·der·shot (UN·dur·shot) *adj.* **1** with the lower jaw projecting beyond the upper jaw or teeth when the mouth is closed. **2** of a water wheel, turned by water flowing underneath.

un·der·side (UN·dur·side) *n.* the lower side or surface, as of a leaf.

un·der·signed (UN·dur·sined) *n.* **the undersigned** the person or persons whose signatures are at the bottom of the document or letter.

un·der·staffed (UN·dur·staft) *adj.* having fewer people on the staff than required.

un·der·stand (un·dur·STAND) *v.* -stands, -stood, -stand·ing **1** get the meaning or significance of something: *Some words are difficult to understand; He tried to make himself understood in French; what people understand by a certain word; Spouses should try to understand each other; Parents understand children; I understand (= sympathize with) how you feel; Please understand (= get the meaning; also, be sympathetic).* **2** learn or infer: *I understand you are ill; I understood her to say she'd be late; When you say "or else," the rest is understood.* — **un·der·stand·a·ble** (-duh·bul) *adj.* — **un·der·stand·a·bly** (-duh·blee) *adv.*

understanding (un·dur·STAN·ding) *n.* **1** (power of) comprehension or knowledge: *a vocabulary within a child's understanding; our limited understanding of the universe.* **2** agreement: *Let's come to an understanding (with each other); to arrive at, reach an understanding*

with the others; a clear, secret, tacit, written understanding; Loans are made on the understanding that they will be paid back. **3** harmony: *to promote understanding between nations; to develop a deeper mutual understanding of each other.*
— *adj.* knowing: *an understanding heart, parent, wink; She's always understanding about her child's problems.*

un·der·state (un·dur·STATE) *v.* **-states, -stat·ed, -stat·ing** state something less than adequately or express in a very restrained manner. — **un·der·state·ment** *n.*

un·der·stud·y (UN·dur·stud·ee) *n.* **-stud·ies** one ready to substitute for another, esp. in a theatrical role.
— *v.* **-stud·ies, -stud·ied, -stud·y·ing** act a role or part as an understudy to someone.

un·der·take (un·dur·TAKE) *v.* **-takes, -took, -tak·en, -tak·ing** take upon oneself a task or *to* do something.

un·der·tak·er (UN·dur·tay·kur) *n.* [a less favoured term] funeral director.

undertaking (UN·dur·tay·king, un·dur·TAY·king) *n.* **1** a task or enterprise. **2** a guarantee.

under-the-counter (UN·dur·the·COWN·tur) *adj. Informal.* of business dealings, secret or illicit: *under-the-counter payments, sales.* Also **under-the-table.**

un·der·things (UN·dur·things) *n.pl. Informal.* women's underwear.

un·der·tone (UN·dur·tone) *n.* **1** a subdued tone of voice or colour: *to speak in an undertone.* **2** an underlying quality: *an undertone of melancholy.*

un·der·tow (UN·dur·toh) *n.* an undercurrent of water moving in the opposite direction of the surface current, as the backward flow of waves breaking on a beach.

un·der·wa·ter (UN·dur·WAW·tur) *adj. & adv.* under the surface of the water: *an underwater demolition team; underwater diving, photography, research.*

un·der·way (un·dur·WAY) *adv.* in progress: *Wedding preparations are already underway; The project will get underway in the new year;* also **under way.**
— *adj.: an underway procedure; underway fuelling.*

un·der·wear (UN·dur·ware) *n.* an article of clothing worn under other clothes, esp. next to the skin, as panties, briefs, shorts, etc.

un·der·world (UN·dur·wurld) *n.* **1** the lower world; Hades. **2** the part of society composed of criminals: *an underworld figure.*

un·der·write (UN·dur·rite) *v.* **-writes, -wrote, -writ·ten, -writ·ing** assume financial liability, as in insuring against loss or risk, in agreeing to buy up unsold stocks and bonds of a particular issue, to finance an enterprise or meet the expenses of educating someone, etc.
— **un·der·writ·er** *n.*

un·dies (UN·deez) *n.pl. Informal.* underthings.

un·do (un·DOO, UN·doo) *v.* **-does, -did, -done, -do·ing** **1** untie a knot, string, parcel, etc. or open or unfasten a button, shirt, etc. **2** annul or cancel the effect of what is done, a magic spell, etc. **3** bring to ruin.
— **un·do·ing** *n.* cause of ruin: *Liquor was his undoing.*

un·done (un·DUN) *pt.* of UNDO: *The knot came undone.* — *adj.* **1** not done; unfinished. **2** ruined.

un·doubt·ed (un·DOW·tid) *adj.* certain beyond a doubt: *a man of undoubted integrity.* — **un·doubt·ed·ly** *adv.*

un·dreamed (un·DREEMD, un·DREMD) or **un·dreamt** (-DREMT) *adj.* never even dreamed *of* or imagined; inconceivable or unimagined: *a discovery that was undreamed of a few years ago; an undreamed-of good fortune.*

un·dress (un·DRESS) *v.* **1** take off one's clothes; disrobe. **2** take the clothes off someone: *to undress a child for bed.*
— *n.* **1** ordinary or informal dress. **2** nakedness: *a state of undress.*

un·due (un·DUE) *adj.* improper or excessive: *with undue haste; undue exploitation of sex; undue importance given to minor things; accused of exerting undue influence in his own favour.*

un·du·late (UN·juh·late) *v.* **-lates, -lat·ed, -lat·ing** have a wavy form or move in waves: *a lake surface undulating in the breeze; undulating wheat fields; the undulating* (= rolling) *prairie.*

un·du·ly (un·DUE·lee) *adv.* improperly or excessively.

un·dy·ing (un·DYE·ing) *adj.* deathless or eternal: *her undying beauty, devotion, fame, gratitude.*

un·earth (un·URTH) *v.* dig up, as from the earth; bring to light, as from a hidden condition: *to unearth fresh evidence, new facts; to unearth a plot.*

un·earth·ly (un·URTH·lee) *adj.* **1** not of this world; hence, strange or weird. **2** *Informal.* preposterous or absurd: *He rang our doorbell at an unearthly hour.*

un·ease (un·EEZ) *n.* lack of ease; disquiet: *a sense of unease.*

un·eas·y (un·EE·zee) *adj.* **-eas·i·er, -eas·i·est** marked by lack of ease in mind or body: *an uneasy laugh, peace, sleep; The child is uneasy in the presence of dogs.*
— **un·eas·i·ness** *n.*

un·em·ployed (un·im·PLOID) *adj.* **1** without a job: *an unemployed worker.* **2** not in use: *unemployed hours, skills, time.*
— **un·em·ploy·ment** (-PLOY·munt) *n.: The Unemployment Insurance Commission makes weekly payments to the unemployed for limited periods.*

un·e·qual (un·EEK·wul) *adj.* **1** not equal in amount, value, etc. **2** not well matched or even. **3** not adequate to a task: *Her health proved unequal to the demands of the job.*

un·e·qualled or **un·e·qualed** (un·EEK·wuld) *adj.* unparalleled; unmatched.

un·err·ing (un·UR·ing) *adj.* making no errors; unfailing or exact: *her unerring aim, blows, precision; She's unerring in her aim.* — **un·err·ing·ly** *adv.*

un·e·ven (un·EE·vun) *adj.* **1** not even, level, or uniform: *an uneven handwriting, performance, surface.* **2** unequal: *an uneven match.* **3** odd: *the uneven numbers 1, 3, 5, etc.* — **un·e·ven·ly** *adv.*

un·ex·cep·tion·a·ble (un·ik·SEP·shun·uh·bul) *adj.* that cannot be found fault with; quite admirable: *unexceptionable behaviour; an unexceptionable record.*
— **un·ex·cep·tion·a·bly** *adv.*

un·ex·cep·tion·al (un·ik·SEP·shun·ul) *adj.* not forming an exception; ordinary: *an unexceptional occurrence.*

un·fail·ing (un·FAY·ling) *adj.* never failing; never coming to an end: *her unfailing courtesy, generosity, patience.*

un·faith·ful (un·FAITH·ful) *adj.* **1** disloyal or adulterous: *an unfaithful spouse.* **2** not true or accurate: *The copy is unfaithful to the original.*

un·fa·mil·iar (un·fuh·MIL·yur) *adj.* **1** not well known: *He is unfamiliar to me.* **2** not acquainted: *I'm unfamiliar with his work.*

un·feel·ing (un·FEE·ling) *adj.* **1** lacking feeling or sensation. **2** cruel or hardhearted. — **un·feel·ing·ly** *adv.*

un·flap·pa·ble (un·FLAP·uh·bul) *adj. Informal.* not easily excited; self-assured.

un·flinch·ing (un·FLINCH·ing) *adj.* resolute; fearless: *her unflinching devotion to the cause of women's rights.*

un·fold (un·FOLD) *v.* open up: *to unfold a newspaper; A bud unfolds into a flower; The plot gets thicker as the story unfolds* (= develops).

un·for·tu·nate (un·FOR·chuh·nit) *adj.* **1** not lucky: *an unfortunate incident.* **2** regrettable: *an unfortunate victim.*
— *n.* one considered to have had bad luck, as an orphan, a homeless person, or social outcast.
— **un·for·tu·nate·ly** *adv.*

un·found·ed (un·FOWN·did) *adj.* baseless; not factual: *an unfounded allegation.*

un·gain·ly (un·GAIN·lee) *adj.* awkward or clumsy.

un·glued (un·GLOOD) *adj.* **come unglued** get upset or go out of control: *Her model husband came unglued.*

un·god·ly (un·GOD·lee) *adv.* **1** sinful or irreligious. **2** *Informal.* outrageous: *to get up at an ungodly hour in the morning.*

un·gov·ern·a·ble (un·GUV·ur·nuh·bul) *adj.* incapable of being restrained or directed; unruly: *an ungovernable temper.*

un·gra·cious (un·GRAY·shus) *adj.* not gracious; rude or unpleasant.

un·guard·ed (un·GAR·did) *adj.* **1** not protected: *an unguarded entrance.* **2** thoughtless or careless: *at an unguarded moment.*

un·hand *v.* remove the hand from or let go of someone.

un·hap·py (un·HAP·ee) *adj.* **un·hap·pi·er, un·hap·pi·est** **1** sorrowful: *an unhappy youth.* **2** unfortunate or inappropriate: *an unhappy choice of words.*
— **un·hap·pi·ly** *adv.;* **un·hap·pi·ness** *n.*

un·health·y (un·HEL·thee, "th" as in "thin") *adj.* **-health·i·er, -i·est** **1** not healthy or healthful: *an unhealthy child, climate, habit.* **2** morally harmful; unwholesome: *an unhealthy atmosphere, influence.*

un·heard (un·HURD) *adj.* **1** not heard: *Are unheard melodies sweeter? That's something unheard of; a hitherto unheard-of phenomenon.* **2** without being given a hearing: *He was condemned unheard.*

un·hinge (un·HINJ) *v.* **-hing·es, -hinged, -hing·ing**

1 remove from the hinges, as a door. **2** dislodge. **3** unsettle; make unstable, esp. mentally: *Her parents' tragic death unhinged her.*

un·ho·ly (un·HOH·lee) *adj.* **-li·er, -li·est** **1** not sacred; also, wicked: *an unholy alliance.* **2** *Informal.* outrageous; unreasonable: *Your room is an unholy mess.*

un·horse (un·HORSE) *v.* **-hors·es, -horsed, -hors·ing** unseat from a horse.

uni- *prefix.* single: *uniform, unilateral, univalve.*

u·ni·corn (YOO·nuh·corn) *n.* a horselike mythical animal with a single horn on its forehead.

u·ni·cy·cle (YOO·nuh·sye·cul) *n.* a vehicle consisting of a wheel and pedals worked by a rider seated on top.

u·ni·form (YOO·nuh·form) *adj.* unvarying in form or character throughout the parts of a substance, series, etc.: *the uniform body temperature of a warm-blooded animal; It's impossible to have uniform* (= same) *laws, standards, taxes, etc. throughout the world.*
— *n.* clothes distinctive of a particular group such as soldiers or nurses. — **u·ni·form·ly** *adv.*
— **u·ni·form·i·ty** (-FOR·muh·tee) *n.*

u·ni·fy (YOO·nuh·fye) *v.* **-fies, -fied, -fy·ing** make or become one or united: *The Canadian Army, Navy, and Air Force were integrated and then unified in 1968.*
— **u·ni·fi·ca·tion** (-fuh·CAY·shun) *n.*

u·ni·lat·er·al (yoo·nuh·LAT·uh·rul) *adj.* involving one side only; one-sided; not bilateral or reciprocal: *unilateral disarmament; the unilateral repudiation of a bilateral agreement.* — **u·ni·lat·er·al·ly** *adv.*

u·ni·lin·gual (yoo·nuh·LING·gwul) *adj.* speaking only one language: *a unilingual civil servant who doesn't speak French; Quebec's unilingual French signs.*

un·im·peach·a·ble (un·im·PEE·chuh·bul) *adj.* that cannot be doubted or questioned: *her unimpeachable authority; his unimpeachable honesty.*

un·in·ter·est·ed (un·IN·tris·tid) *adj.* having or showing no interest; indifferent: *an uninterested listener, onlooker; He's quite uninterested in chess.*

un·ion (YOON·yun) *n.* **1** a joining together or the state of being joined together, usually permanently, as one unit: *matrimonial union; "Union is strength."* **2** a group or whole resulting from joining together: *to break up, dissolve, form a union; a credit union; labour union; student union; the U.S. President's State of* **the Union** (= the U.S.) *message to Congress; adj.: union catalogue* (= library catalogue for several libraries); **union station**

(used by more than one railway). **3** a coupling or similar connecting device.

un·ion·ize (YOON·yuh·nize) *v.* -iz·es, -ized, -iz·ing **1** form a group of workers into a labour union. **2** organize an establishment to conform to the rules of a labour union.

union shop *n.* an establishment in which only members or prospective members of a labour union are hired.

u·nique (yoo·NEEK) *adj.* **1** having no like or equal; one of a kind: *Each of us is unique; The landing on the moon is unique in human history; Bilingualism is not unique to Canada.* **2** *Informal.* unusual or extraordinary: *This is absolutely unique; quite unique; a rather unique achievement.*
— **u·nique·ly** *adv.;* **u·nique·ness** *n.*

u·ni·sex (YOO·nuh·sex) *adj. Informal.* designed to suit both sexes: *unisex clothing; the unisex look (that is not distinguishable as to sex); unisex rates for auto insurance.*

u·ni·son (YOO·nuh·sun) *n.* agreement in pitch or sound: *They spoke in unison (= the same words at the same time); an action taken in unison with other friendly nations.*

u·nit (YOO·nit) *n.* **1** an individual thing or group with specific characteristics, forming part of a complex whole: *The family is the primary social unit; The dollar and pound are basic money units; metric units of weight; a military unit such as the battalion or platoon; to commit a unit to a combat mission; an airborne, armoured, crack, elite, motorized, tactical unit; the pickup unit of a record player; an easy-to-assemble wall unit with shelves, cabinets, etc.* **2** the least whole number; one.

u·ni·tar·y (YOO·nuh·tair·ee) *adj.* characterized by centralization; unified, not divided: *Britain has a unitary system of government, not a federal system like Canada's.*

u·nite (yoo·NITE) *v.* -nites, -nit·ed, -nit·ing join together: *Let's unite; We stand united (against our foes); Jack and Jill were united (in matrimony) by a justice of the peace; Is Canada becoming more and more united? We are united in our aims; a united appeal; a united effort; to offer a united front to the enemy.*

u·nit·ize (YOO·nuh·tize) *v.* -iz·es, -ized, -iz·ing make into one unit: *a unitized body construction.*

unit pricing *n.* labelling of articles with their prices per kilogram, litre, or other standard unit to help shoppers compare prices.

u·ni·ty (YOO·nuh·tee) *n.* -ties **1** the oneness of purpose, spirit, etc. of a complex whole: *artistic unity in variety; the unity of dramatic action or plot; the unity of design achieved by artistic arrangement of lines, shapes, and colours; to bring about national unity; to live together in unity (= harmony).* **2** a quantity or magnitude considered as equal to 1 in calculations.

u·ni·valve (YOO·nuh·valv) *n.* **1** a mollusc with a one-piece shell, as a snail. **2** such a shell.

u·ni·ver·sal (yoo·nuh·VUR·sul) *adj.* **1** relating to all human beings; hence, general: *Death is a universal phenomenon; universal adult suffrage; universal*

approval, conscription, literacy, popularity, rejoicing; a universal problem.* **2** applying to every individual or case within a class or category: *Type O blood is a* **universal donor** *because it is safe for any recipient; Esperanto as a* **universal language;** *a* **universal motor** *for A.C. or D.C. current; The wristlike action of a* **universal joint** *or* **coupling** *lets an automobile ride over bumps without breaking the drive shaft.*
— **u·ni·ver·sal·ly** (-suh·lee) *adj.*
— **u·ni·ver·sal·i·ty** (YOO·nuh·vur·SAL·uh·tee) *n.*

u·ni·ver·sal·ize (yoo·nuh·VUR·suh·lize) *v.* -iz·es, -ized, -iz·ing make universally applicable.

universal product code *n.* a small square of black bars and numbers representing price information imprinted on articles for scanning by automatic checkout systems.

u·ni·verse (YOO·nuh·verse) *n.* all reality; the cosmos; everything in space, esp. the world of human beings: *the origin of the universe.*

u·ni·ver·si·ty (yoo·nuh·VUR·suh·tee) *n.* -ties an educational institution of the highest level for instruction in many branches of study: *She went to university after finishing high school; She later taught at the university.*

un·kempt (un·KEMPT) *adj.* not well cared for; untidy: *his unkempt appearance, hair; an unkempt house, lawn.*

un·known (un·NOHN) *n. & adj.* (one) that is unfamiliar, strange, or unidentified: *a monument dedicated to the unknown soldiers killed in the war; a letter representing an unknown quantity in an algebraic equation; Our new teammate is an* **unknown quanity** *(= one not yet tried out).*

un·law·ful (un·LAW·ful) *adj.* not lawful: *a charge of unlawful assembly brought against three people bent on mischief; unlawful measures; unlawful (= immoral) pleasures.* — **un·law·ful·ly** *adv.*

un·lead·ed (un·LED·id) *adj.* of gasoline, containing no lead-additive.

un·learn (un·LURN) *v.* get rid of or forget something learned, as ideas and habits: *The children had to unlearn many nonstandard expressions they picked up on the playground.*

un·learn·ed *adj.* **1** (un·LUR·nid) lacking learning; ignorant: *an unlearned remark, scholar.* **2** (un·LURND) that has not been learned: *an unlearned habit, lesson.*

un·leash (un·LEESH) *v.* to free from or as if from a leash: *to unleash an animal; He unleashed his fury on an innocent employee.*

un·less (un·LES) *conj.* except when; if not: *You don't get paid unless you work.*

un·let·tered (un·LET·urd) *adj.* not educated, esp. not able to read and write.

un·like (un·LIKE) *adj. & prep.* different from: *The twins are quite unlike; They're unlike each other.*

un·like·ly *adj.* not likely: *an unlikely event; It's unlikely to have taken place; We searched in the most unlikely (= unpromising) places.* — **un·like·li·hood** *n.*

un·list·ed (un·LIS·tid) *adj.* not publicly listed, as a telephone number in a telephone book because confidential: *The operator can't give out an unlisted number.*

un·load (un·LODE) *v.* **1** take or remove a load from one's back, a vehicle, etc. or a charge from a firearm. **2** get rid or dispose of unwanted goods, company stocks, etc. **3** *Informal.* unburden feelings, troubles, etc.: *He unloads on his wife when he has had a bad day at work.*

un·lock (un·LOK) *v.* **1** to open a door, etc. by releasing a lock. **2** release or disclose as if by unlocking: *to unlock nature's mysteries, one's heart, a flood of tears.*

un·make (un·MAKE) *v.* **-makes, -made, -mak·ing** **1** ruin or destroy something made, as a reputation. **2** depose someone from a position, rank, etc.

un·man (un·MAN) *v.* **-mans, -manned, -man·ning** deprive of manly courage; weaken the spirit of someone. **un·man·ly** *adj.*

un·mask (un·MASK) *v.* **1** remove a mask from someone's face. **2** disclose the true nature of a person or thing: *to unmask a crime, thief.*

un·men·tion·a·ble (un·MEN·shun·uh·bul) **1** *adj.* not fit to be referred to in public. **2** **unmentionables** *n.pl.* [jocular] underwear.

un·mit·i·gat·ed (un·MIT·uh·gay·tid) *adj.* not lessened or modified; utter: *unmitigated evil, gall, horror; an unmitigated delight, disaster, failure, liar, scoundrel.*

un·nat·u·ral (un·NACH·ur·ul) *adj.* **1** not natural or normal: *It's unnatural for a mother not to love her children.* **2** morally depraved; perverse: *an unnatural act, offence.*

un·nerve (un·NURV) *v.* **-nerves, -nerved, -nerv·ing** cause to lose one's self-control or power to act.

un·no·ticed (un·NOH·tist) *adj.* not noticed: *Many violations go* or *pass unnoticed because no one gets hurt.*

un·num·bered (un·NUM·burd) *adj.* innumerable; uncounted.

un·or·gan·ized (un·OR·guh·nized) *adj.* not organized into a system, organism, labour union, etc.

un·pack (un·PAK) *v.* **1** remove something from a package: *to unpack a gift.* **2** remove the contents of a trunk, suitcase, etc.: *to unpack after a trip.*

un·par·al·leled (un·PAIR·uh·leld) *adj.* that has no parallel or match: *an event unparalleled in human history.*

un·prec·e·dent·ed (un·PRES·uh·den·tid) *adj.* without precedent; unheard-of.

un·prin·ci·pled (un·PRIN·suh·puld) *adj.* lacking moral principles.

un·print·a·ble (un·PRIN·tuh·bul) *adj.* not fit to be printed, esp. because obscene.

un·pro·fes·sion·al (un·pruh·FESH·un·ul) *adj.* not ethical according to the standards of one's profession.

un·qual·i·fied (un·KWOL·uh·fide) *adj.* **1** not qualified: *an unqualified applicant.* **2** absolute or unrestricted: *unqualified praise; an unqualified privilege, success.*

un·ques·tion·a·ble (un·KWES·chuh·nuh·bul) *adj.* **1** not to be questioned or doubted. **2** beyond doubt.

— **un·ques·tion·a·bly** *adv.*

un·quote (un·QUOTE) [used to end a quotation]: *She said, quote, He is a hero, unquote* (= She said, "He is a hero").

un·rav·el (un·RAV·ul) *v.* **-els, -elled** or **-eled, -el·ling** or **-el·ing** **1** separate the threads of something woven. **2** solve a mystery.

un·read (un·RED) *adj.* **1** not read, as a book. **2** uneducated.

un·real (un·REE·ul) *adj.* not real; imaginary or fanciful.

un·rea·son·ing (un·REE·zun·ing) *adj.* not guided by reason; illogical or irrational.

un·re·mit·ting (un·ri·MIT·ing) *adj.* not ceasing or slackening; incessant. — **un·re·mit·ting·ly** *adv.*

un·re·quit·ed (un·ri·KWY·tid) *adj.* not returned or rewarded: *a story of unrequited love; unrequited efforts, passion.*

un·rest (un·REST) *n.* **1** a state of restlessness. **2** a social condition verging on revolt: *social unrest; to stir up labour unrest; unrest on campuses.*

un·roll (un·ROLE) *v.* **1** open something rolled up; also, become unrolled. **2** display or be displayed: *a scene unrolling before our eyes.*

un·ruf·fled (un·RUF·uld) *adj.* not ruffled; hence, calm and serene.

un·rul·y (un·ROO·lee) *adj.* **-rul·i·er, -rul·i·est** disorderly or disobedient: *an unruly child, crowd.* — **un·rul·i·ness** *n.*

un·sad·dle (un·SAD·ul) *v.* **-sad·dles, -sad·dled, -sad·dling** take the saddle off a horse, etc.

un·sa·vour·y (un·SAY·vuh·ree) *adj.* **1** unpleasant to the taste or smell. **2** morally unpleasant: *an unsavoury character, reputation.*

un·scathed (un·SCATHED) *adj.* uninjured.

un·schooled (un·SCOOLD) *adj.* not educated or trained; hence, not disciplined.

un·scram·ble (un·SCRAM·bul) *v.* **-bles, -bled, -bling** restore to original condition from being scrambled or confused: *You can't unscramble a scrambled egg; to unscramble* (= decode) *a message.*

un·screw *v.* detach or take off by turning or by removing screws: *to unscrew a light bulb, fixture; to unscrew a jar (the jar's top).*

un·scru·pu·lous (un·SCROOP·yuh·lus) *adj.* defying moral principles: *an unscrupulous moneylender.*

un·sea·son·a·ble (un·SEE·zun·uh·bul) *adj.* **1** not usual for the season: *Snow is unseasonable in the summer.* **2** coming at the wrong time: *to arrive at an unseasonable hour.* — **un·sea·son·a·bly** *adv.*

un·seat (un·SEET) *v.* displace from a seat; hence, remove from office.

un·seem·ly (un·SEEM·lee) *adj.* not seemly or becoming: *to leave in unseemly haste.*

un·seen (un·SEEN) *adj.* not seen: *the world of the unseen* (=spirits); *She rented the house sight unseen* (=without seeing it first).

un·set·tle (un·SET·ul) *v.* -set·tles, -set·tled, -set·tling 1 move from a settled position. 2 make or become unstable or disturbed: *an unsettling bit of news.*

un·set·tled *adj.* not settled: *unsettled issues, weather conditions; unsettled* (=unpaid) *debts; unsettled* (=uninhabited) *territory.*

un·sheathe (un·SHEETH, "TH" as in "the") *v.* -sheathes, -sheathed, -sheath·ing draw a sword, etc. from a sheath or as from a sheath.

un·sight·ly (un·SITE·lee) *adj.* not pleasing to the eye; ugly.

un·skil·ful (un·SKIL·ful) *adj.* having no skill or training; awkward or clumsy: *an unskilful manner.*

un·skilled (un·SKILD) *adj.* 1 of persons, not skilled or trained in a line of work: *an unskilled labourer.* 2 of work, not requiring skill: *unskilled labour, occupations.*

un·snarl (un·SNARL) *v.* untangle.

un·sound (un·SOWND) *adj.* not sound: *an unsound argument, structure, undertaking; He's of unsound mind.*

un·spar·ing (un·SPAIR·ing) *adj.* 1 not sparing; liberal: *Our boss is unsparing of praise when we do a good job.* 2 merciless or severe *in* criticism, etc.

un·speak·a·ble (un·SPEE·kuh·bul) *adj.* that cannot be expressed or described: *her unspeakable beauty, joy; unspeakable horrors.* — **un·speak·a·bly** *adv.*

un·sta·ble (un·STAY·bul) *adj.* not stable: *an unstable government, mind, person; an unstable chemical compound, equilibrium, nuclear particle.*

un·stead·y (un·STED·ee) *adj.* not steady or firm: *an unsteady hand, pulse, voice; unsteady market conditions, winds.*

un·stop (un·STOP) *v.* -stops, -stopped, -stop·ping 1 remove the stopper from a bottle, etc. 2 free a pipe, etc. of an obstruction.

un·strung (un·STRUNG) *adj.* 1 in a nervous condition. 2 with the strings of a guitar, rocket, etc. loosened or removed.

un·stuck (un·STUCK) *adj.* loosened or unfastened: *The stamps came unstuck before the letter was mailed; The whole plan came unstuck (Slang for was ruined) when a key player suddenly died.*

un·stud·ied (un·STUD·eed) *adj.* of behaviour, not artificial; natural and spontaneous: *her unstudied modesty.*

un·sung (un·SUNG) *adj.* not celebrated or praised: *an unsung hero.*

un·tan·gle (un·TANG·gul) *v.* -gles, -gled, -gling free from a snarled or entangled condition; disentangle: *to untangle a mess; to untangle knots, mixups.*

un·taught (un·TAWT) *adj.* 1 not educated: *an untaught generation.* 2 naturally acquired or learned: *an untaught skill; untaught wisdom.*

un·think·a·ble (un·THINK·uh·bul) *adj.* that cannot be thought of as possible; unimaginable; inconceivable: *It's unthinkable that he would say such a thing.*

un·think·ing (un·THINK·ing) *adj.* thoughtless or heedless: *He said it in one of those unthinking moments; an unthinking remark.*

un·tie (un·TYE) *v.* -ties, -tied, -ty·ing or -tie·ing to free something tied, knotted, etc. or as from a restraint; unfasten; disentangle.

un·til (un·TIL) *prep. & conj.* up to the time of or when; till: *Please wait until noon; Don't go until you've eaten.*

un·time·ly (un·TIME·lee) *adj.* 1 premature: *an untimely death.* 2 inopportune: *an untimely outburst.*

un·to (UN·too) *prep.* [old use] to or till: *what you do unto others; She was faithful unto death.*

un·told (un·TOLD) *adj.* 1 uncounted; innumerable: *untold thousands of people.* 2 vast or immense: *untold misery, wealth.* 3 not told or revealed: *The story remains untold; an untold tale of intrigue.*

un·touch·a·ble (un·TUCH·uh·bul) *adj.* that cannot or must not be touched. — *n.* a member of the lowest caste of Hindus, formerly shunned by Brahmins; outcaste.

un·to·ward (un·TOH·urd, -TORD) *adj.* 1 unfavourable: *untoward circumstances, happenings; an untoward* (=willful) *child.* 2 improper or unseemly: *an untoward remark.*

un·tu·tored (un·TUE·turd) *adj.* untaught; not educated: *an untutored child; He came to the city untutored in the ways of the world.*

un·used *adj.* 1 (un·YOOZD) not used: *an unused cup.* 2 (un·YOOST) unaccustomed: *She's unused to the Canadian climate.*

un·var·nished (un·VAR·nisht) *adj.* not varnished; hence, plain and simple: *an unvarnished account; the unvarnished truth.*

un·veil (un·VAIL) *v.* 1 reveal or display for the first time: *He unveiled his plans; the unveiling of a statue.* 2 remove one's veil.

un·well (un·WEL) *adj.* sick or ill.

un·whole·some (un·HOLE·sum) *adj.* 1 harmful to body, mind, or morals. 2 not of sound health.

un·wield·y (un·WEEL·dee) *adj.* hard to handle or deal with because of large size, weight, shape, etc.

un·will·ing (un·WIL·ing) *adj.* not willing; reluctant: *She was unwilling to take part in it; an unwilling partner in the crime.* — **un·will·ing·ly** *adv.*; **un·will·ing·ness** *n.*

un·wind (un·WINED) *v.* -winds, -wound, -wind·ing 1 uncoil something wound up, as a ball or spool. 2 untangle. 3 relax: *Weekends are for unwinding.*

un·wise (un·WIZE) *adj.* not wise; imprudent.

un·wit·ting (un·WIT·ing) *adj.* 1 unaware. 2 inadvertent or unintentional. — **un·wit·ting·ly** *adv.*

un·wont·ed (un·WONE·tid, -WUN-, -WAWN-) *adj.* not usual or habitual: *He left the party in unwonted haste.*

un·wor·thy (un·WUR·thee, "th" as in "the") adj. -thi·er, -thi·est not worthy: *unworthy* (= shameful) *conduct; conduct unworthy of* (= unbecoming) *a hero; He was deemed unworthy* (= undeserving) *of an award.*
— **un·wor·thi·ness** n.

un·wrap (un·RAP) v. -wraps, -wrapped, -wrap·ping take off the wrapping.

un·writ·ten (un·RIT·un) adj. **1** not written down: *The letter remained unwritten.* **2** traditional: *Britain's unwritten constitution; the unwritten common law.*

up adv. **1** to a higher position, degree, etc.; not down: *She went up to the top floor; Prices go up; Please speak up* (= louder). **2** to a vertical or active position: *We get up in the morning; Stand up on your feet; He stirs up trouble.* **3** in a steady state without going back or down: *to keep up a practice; That's good, keep it up! He runs so fast it's hard to keep up with* (= stay abreast of) *him.* **4** to the point of completeness or finality: *to tie up a parcel; She ate it all up.* **5** in games, ahead or leading; also, at bat in baseball: *a score of 10 up* (= apiece).
— **up against** *Informal.* faced with: *up against a difficulty, problem.*
— **up there** in heaven.
— **up to 1** till a limit of time or extension: *up to now; He charges up to $100 an hour; I agree with you up to a point* (= to a certain degree); *I've had it up to here* (= up to my neck; as much as I can take). **2** about or planning to do something: *What are you up to?* **3** at the disposition of someone: *The choice is up to you.*
— *prep.* to a higher position, degree, etc.: *to go up the stairs; She rowed her boat up the river; He drove up the street to where we were waiting.*
— *adj.* **1** in a raised or higher position: *Prices are up again; Take the up elevator; What's up* (= happening)? **2** in a steady state; abreast: *Are you up on the latest developments?* **3** ended: *Your time is up.*
— **up and around** or **about** moving around: *She is up and around after her recent illness.*
— **up and doing** busy and active: *He's up and doing by 5 a.m. every day.*
— **up for** offered for: *The house is up for sale.*
— *n.* an upward movement or condition: *the ups and downs of fortune, of his mood; Sales of the new book are on the up and up* (= rising).
— *v.* ups, upped, up·ping raise: *to up prices; He ups and* (*Informal* for gets up and) *walks out of the party.*

up-and-coming (UP·un·CUM·ing) adj. likely to succeed; promising: *one of our up-and-coming politicians.*

up·beat n. **1** in music, an unaccented beat or the upward gesture of the conductor's hand indicating it. **2** an upswing or upturn.
— *adj.* cheerful or optimistic: *in an upbeat mood; upbeat news; The convention ended on an upbeat note.*

up·braid (up·BRAID) v. to reprimand or censure, esp. with justification.

up·bring·ing (up·BRING·ing) n. the bringing up or raising of a child.

up·chuck n. & v. *Slang.* vomit.

up·com·ing (UP·cum·ing) adj. forthcoming; coming soon: *the upcoming elections.*

up·coun·try (UP·cun·tree) n., adj. & adv. of, in, or toward the interior, esp. isolated part of a country or region.

up·date (up·DATE) v. -dates, -dat·ed, -dat·ing bring a book, person, etc. up to date.
— *n.* (UP·date) an updating or something that updates, as a piece of information: *Give me an update on what has been going on.*

up·end (up·END) v. set or stand on end; overturn.

up·front adj. *Informal.* **1** forthright or direct. **2** as an advance or front money: *an upfront payment.*

up·grade n. **1** upward slope. **2** a rise or increase.
— *v.* -grades, -grad·ed, -grad·ing raise to a higher grade or rating: *to upgrade a job, employee.*

up·growth n. upward growth or development.

up·heav·al (up·HEE·vul) n. **1** a heaving up, as of the earth's crust by an earthquake. **2** a sudden or violent change: *social upheavals.*

up·hill adj. **1** going up, as on a hill; **adv.:** *to drive uphill.* **2** tiring or laborious: *an uphill battle, fight, task.*

up·hold (up·HOLED) v. -holds, -held, -hold·ing **1** give moral support to a person, cause, etc. **2** maintain: *to uphold a great principle, tradition; the RCMP motto "Uphold the right."* **3** confirm by higher authority: *The judgment was upheld on appeal.*

up·hol·ster (up·HOLE·stur) v. furnish a chair, seat, etc. with upholstery. — **up·hol·ster·er** n.

up·hol·ster·y (up·HOLE·stuh·ree) n. -ster·ies materials such as fabrics, springs, and padding used to make soft coverings for furniture.

up·keep n. **1** the keeping up or maintaining of a house, garden, dependents, etc. **2** the cost or the state of such maintenance.

up·land (UP·lund, -land) adj. of the higher land of a region, above valleys or plains: *Finland's upland district; upland meadows.*

up·lift n. a lifting up, esp. a movement for social, moral, or spiritual improvement.

up·man·ship (UP·mun·ship) n. same as ONE-UPMANSHIP.

up·most adj. same as UPPERMOST.

up·on (uh·PON) prep. & adv. on: *once upon a time; sat upon his bed.*

up·per (UP·ur) adj. **1** higher in position, rank, etc.: *the upper jaw, lip; the upper house of Parliament* (= Senate); *the upper classes of society; the upper crust* (= the highest group of the upper class) *of society; in the upper-income bracket; the upper St. Lawrence River* (= the region from where it flows down); *Upper Canada* (= Ontario, as the area around the upper St. Lawrence River); *the Upper Great Lakes.* **2** northern: *Buffalo is in upper New York State.* **3** later: *the Upper Cambrian Period.*
— *n.* **1** the part of a shoe or boot above the sole. **2** *Slang.* a stimulant drug such as caffeine, cocaine, or an amphetamine.

upper case n. capital letters.
— **upper-case** adj. in capital letters.

— *v.* -cas·es, -cased, -cas·ing set up in upper case.

up·per·class·man (UP·ur·class·mun) *n.* -men a junior or senior in a high school or college.

upper hand *n.* a position of advantage; mastery: *to gain the upper hand over them.*

up·per·most (UP·ur·most) *adj. & adv.* first or highest in place, authority, etc.

up·pish or **up·pi·ty** *adj. Informal.* haughty or arrogant.

up·raise (up·RAIZ) *v.* -rais·es, -raised, -rais·ing lift up; elevate.

up·rear (up·REER) *v.* 1 lift up or raise. 2 rise or be lifted up.

up·right *adj.* 1 vertically erect. 2 morally straight: *a just and upright man.*
— *n.* 1 something that is upright. 2 an upright or vertical position.
— *adv.* in an upright position. — **up·right·ness** *n.*

upright piano *n.* the commonest type of piano, with strings set up vertically.

up·ris·ing (UP·rye·zing) *n.* a small rebellion or outbreak against a government: *an armed uprising that was put down with an iron hand.*

up·riv·er (UP·riv·ur) *adj. & adv.* toward the source of a river.

up·roar *n.* a noisy disturbance or commotion: *The new taxes caused an uproar; The whole nation was in an uproar till the measures were withdrawn.*

up·roar·i·ous (up·ROR·ee·us) *adj.* noisy or boisterous: *uproarious laughter, welcome; an uproarious (=extremely funny) joke.* — **up·roar·i·ous·ly** *adv.*

up·root (up·ROOT) *v.* remove by or as if by pulling up by the roots: *people uprooted from their ancestral homes.*

up·rush *n.* an upward rush of a liquid or gas.

up·scale *adj.* at the upper end of the social scale; wealthy or superior: *an upscale audience; the upscale market.*

up·set (up·SET) *v.* -sets, -set, -set·ting topple or unsettle from a stable condition: *A flat-bottomed boat does not upset easily; to upset a vase; to upset nerves, plans, schedules; to upset the favoured candidate (in an election); The Jays upset (=defeated) Texas 10 to 9.*
— *adj.* disturbed or worried: *He's a bit upset about or over the small raise he received; He's upset to hear that he can't have the job; emotionally upset; suffering from an upset stomach.*
— *n.* (UP·set) an upsetting, an unexpected defeat, or a disturbance: *a stomach upset; The Jays scored an upset over Texas.*

up·shot *n.* outcome or general effect: *the upshot of the matter.*

up·side *n.* the upper side.
— **upside down** inverted; in(to) confusion or disorder: *hanging upside down from the rafters.*
— **upside-down** (UP·side·DOWN) *adj.* topsy-turvy: *an upside-down cake, image, roller coaster.*

up·stage *adj. & adv.* at or toward the rear of a stage.

— *v.* 1 draw attention to oneself to the disadvantage of someone else. 2 *Informal.* steal the show from someone; snub.

up·stairs *n.* an upper floor: *The upstairs is being renovated.*
— *adj. & adv.* on or to the upper floor: *She is upstairs; He went upstairs; an upstairs window; Instead of being fired, he was kicked upstairs (=promoted) to chairman of the board.*

up·stand·ing (up·STAN·ding) *adj.* upright in carriage or character: *an upstanding citizen.*

up·start *n.* one who has recently acquired wealth or position, hence is haughty or self-assertive.

up·state *adj., adv. & n.* (in, to, or from) the more northern part of a state, away from its principal city: *Buffalo is in upstate New York.*

up·stream *adj. & adv.* 1 against the current of a stream: *It's harder to swim upstream than downstream.* 2 from where the stream is flowing: *The wolf was drinking upstream from the lamb; Exploration is the upstream part of the oil business.*

up·stroke *n.* an upward stroke of a pen, brush, etc.

up·surge (up·SURJ) *n.* a sudden surging up or increase.

up·swing *n.* 1 an upward swinging movement, as of a golf club. 2 upward trend: *Bowling is on the upswing as more professionals participate.*

up·take *n.* a taking up, as by the mind; absorption: *She's quick, not slow, on the uptake (Informal for* in understanding*); the level of oxygen uptake as an indicator of fitness.*

up·tight (up·TITE) *adj. Slang.* tense or nervous *about* something. — **up·tight·ness** *n.*

up-to-date (UP·tuh·date) *adj.* [used before its noun; See DATE for "up to date"] extending to the present time: *a new and up-to-date edition; an up-to-date (=modern) fashion, style.* — **up-to-date.ness** *n.*

up·town *adj., adv. & n.* (in, of, or toward) the upper part of a city or town, away from downtown.

up·turn *n.* an upward turn or improving trend, as after a recession: *a sharp upturn in the economy.*
— *v.* turn up or over; overturn. — **up·turned** *adj.*

up·ward (UP·wurd) *adv. & adj.* in or toward a higher place, position, etc.; up: *The balloons should go upward when they are released; students who are 18 years and upward (=older); aged upward of (=more than) 17; the upward mobility of the middle class.* Also **up·wards** *adv.* — **up·ward·ly** *adv.*

u·ra·ni·um (yoo·RAY·nee·um) *n.* a radioactive element that is the chief source of atomic energy.

ur·ban (UR·bun) *adj.* having to do with a city or cities: *our urban and rural populations; an **urban guerrilla** (=city-based terrorist); the demolition of slums for **urban renewal** and rebuilding; the **urban sprawl** (=city congestion spreading into the suburbs).*

ur·bane (ur·BANE) *adj.* refined or smoothly polite in manner. — **ur·ban·i·ty** (ur·BAN·uh·tee) *n.*

ur·ban·ize (UR·buh·nize) v. -iz·es, -ized, -iz·ing make or become urban or citylike.
— **ur·ban·i·za·tion** (-nuh·ZAY·shun) n.

ur·chin (UR·chin) n. a youngster considered as pert or mischievous: *street urchins.*

urge (URJ) v. **urg·es, urged, urg·ing 1** force or drive forward; spur: *He urged his horses forward with the whip.* **2** ask, plead, or argue earnestly (for something): *She was strongly urged to buy now and pay later; a lawyer urging a claim in court; sterner measures were urged; He did it at the urging of friends.*
— **n. 1** an urging. **2** an impulse or inner drive seeking satisfaction: *to control, feel, satisfy, stifle an urge; an irresistible, natural, sudden urge; an uncontrollable urge to laugh.*

ur·gent (UR·junt) adj. requiring immediate attention: *an urgent message, request; She's in urgent need of help; an urgent* (= insistent) *petitioner.*
— **ur·gen·cy** n.; **ur·gent·ly** adv.

u·ri·nar·y (YOOR·uh·nair·ee) adj. having to do with urine, its secretion into the bladder, or its discharge: *the urinary bladder, system, tract.*

u·ri·nate (YOOR·uh·nate) v. **-nates, -nat·ed, -nat·ing** discharge urine from the body.
— **u·ri·na·tion** (-NAY·shun) n.

u·rine (YOOR·in) n. the yellowish liquid containing waste products that is expelled from the body.

urn n. **1** a footed vase or one with a pedestal, used to hold the ashes of the dead, as in ancient Rome: *a burial urn.* **2** a closed vessel with a spigot for making tea or coffee.

ur·sine (UR·sine) adj. of or like a bear: *a large, indeed, ursine appetite.*

us objective case of WE.

us·a·ble (YOO·zuh·bul) adj. fit for use.
— **us·a·bil·i·ty** (-BIL·uh·tee) n.

us·age (YOO·sij, -zij) n. **1** the act or manner of using; treatment: *subjected to ill usage; damaged by rough usage.* **2** long-established practice: *customs sanctified by usage; Standard English usage is established by good writers and speakers.*

use (YOOZ) v. **us·es, used, us·ing** put into action or service; employ for a purpose: *We use an umbrella when it rains; What's this used for? He uses* (= consumes) *too much sugar; I could use (Informal for would benefit by) some help; The sugar is all used up (= finished).* See also USED.
— **n.** (YOOSE) **1** a using or being used: *the uses of an automobile; No smoking allowed when oxygen is in use* (= being used); *Obsolete words are those that have gone out of use; Computers are being put to use* (= employed) *in all sorts of ways; He makes good use of his time; constant, daily, extensive, external, fair, internal, official, practical, universal, wide use.* **2** purpose, benefit, or advantage of using; usefulness: *It's no use crying over spilled milk; What's the use of crying? There's no use in crying; We have no use for* (= We dislike) *crybabies.* **3** the ability to use: *He lost the use of both eyes in an accident, but regained it later; He gets the use of* (= permission to use) *her car on weekends.* **4** customary practice; habit; usage: *in*

Catholic use; as was the use in their family.
— **use·a·ble** (YOO·zuh·bul), **use·a·bil·i·ty** (-BIL·uh·tee) See USABLE.

used adj. **1** (YOOST): *He's used* (= accustomed) *to walking to school; He used to drive* (= formerly drove) *to school.* **2** (YOOZD): *a used* (= secondhand) *car; an ill-used* (= badly treated) *child.*

use·ful (YOOS·ful) adj. serviceable; helpful.
— **use·ful·ly** adv.; **use·ful·ness** n.

user-friendly (YOO·zur·frend·lee) adj. simple and easy to use for the average person: *a user-friendly computer, program; to make the airport more user-friendly.*

ush·er (USH·ur) n. an official who escorts people to their seats in a church, theatre, etc.
— **v.** go before someone showing the way; conduct or escort: *to usher a patron to her seat; celebrations to usher in* (= start) *the New Year.*

ush·er·ette (ush·uh·RET) n. a female usher.

u·su·al (YOO·zhoo·ul) adj. commonly seen or experienced; ordinary; customary: *Nine to 5 are the usual office hours; She is her usual cheerful self; He appeared cheerful as usual* (= in the usual manner).
— **u·su·al·ly** adv.

u·su·rer (YOO·zhur·ur) n. one who practises usury.

u·su·ri·ous (yoo·ZHOOR·ee·us) adj. excessive: *He lends money at usurious interest rates.*

u·surp (yoo·SURP, -ZURP) v. seize and hold a throne, power, authority, etc. by force or without right.
— **u·surp·er** n.
— **u·sur·pa·tion** (yoo·sur·PAY·shun, yoo·zur-) n.

u·su·ry (YOO·zhuh·ree) n. **1** an excessive rate of interest. **2** the lending of money at such a rate.

u·ten·sil (yoo·TEN·sil) n. an implement or container for domestic use, usually worked by hand: *cooking and eating utensils; kitchen utensils such as pots and pans; writing utensils.*

u·ter·us (YOO·tuh·rus) n., pl. **-ter·i** (-tuh·rye) or **-ter·us·es** the hollow, muscular organ in the pelvis of female mammals in which the young are carried till birth; womb. — **u·ter·ine** (-rin, -rine) adj.

u·til·i·dor (yoo·TIL·uh·dor) n. Cdn. an above-ground system of heating, water, and sewage pipes used in permafrost regions; **Utilidor** *Trademark.*

u·til·i·tar·i·an (yoo·TIL·uh·TAIR·ee·un) adj. having to do with usefulness rather than beauty, truth, etc.

u·til·i·ty (yoo·TIL·uh·tee) n. **-ties 1** a service that is essential to the public, as transportation, communications, electricity, water, gas, garbage disposal, etc.: *a public utility such as sewers; an information utility such as a database.* **2** a company that provides such a service, as a hydro or phone company; also **public utility. 3 utilities** *pl.* company shares issued by a public utility. **4** usefulness.
— **adj.** having various uses: *a utility airport (for small nonjet aircraft); a utility knife, room, table; utility beef (of the lowest grade); a utility player (who can substitute for absent players in various positions); a utility room (for keeping various equipment).*

u·ti·lize (YOO·tul·ize) *v.* **-iz·es, -ized, -iz·ing** put to practical or profitable use: *how to utilize spare time, solar energy; Garbage can be utilized by recycling.* — **u·ti·li·za·tion** (-uh·ZAY·shun) *n.*

ut·most (UT·most) *n. & adj.* the farthest or greatest possible: *a question of the utmost importance; the utmost limit of endurance; That's the utmost we could do.*

U·to·pi·a or **u·to·pi·a** (yoo·TOH·pee·uh) *n.* **1** an imaginary place of ideal social conditions, as in Thomas More's *Utopia.* **2** a perfect society or any visionary scheme. — **U·to·pi·an** or **u·to·pi·an** *adj.*

ut·ter (UT·ur) *adj.* total; absolute: *utter destruction, misery, surprise; This is utter nonsense.*
— *v.* **1** give forth a cry, oath, spell, vocal sound, word, etc. **2** deliver or put counterfeit money, forged notes, etc. into circulation. — **ut·ter·ly** *adv.*

ut·ter·ance (UT·ur·unce) *n.* **1** an act of uttering vocally or what is uttered: *a prophetic utterance.* **2** a manner or style of speaking.

ut·ter·most (UT·ur·most) *n. & adj.* same as UTMOST.

U-turn (YOO·turn) *n.* a 360-degree turn made by a vehicle.

V or **v** (VEE) *n.* **V's** or **v's 1** the 22nd letter of the English alphabet. **2** something shaped like a "V." **3** the Roman numeral for 5.

va·can·cy (VAY·cun·see) *n.* **-cies 1** a vacant or unoccupied state of mind. **2** vacant space or an unoccupied position, as an apartment for rent, office quarters, etc.: *Sorry, no vacancies; The resignation created a vacancy in the firm; a job vacancy; someone to fill a vacancy; time spent daydreaming and staring into vacancy* (= empty space).

va·cant (VAY·kunt) *adj.* not occupied or filled: *a vacant lot; a want ad headed "Situations vacant"; a vacant* (= blank) *mind, stare; She has too much vacant* (= free or idle) *time on her hands since retirement.*
— **va·cant·ly** *adv.*

va·cate (vay·CATE, VAY·cate) *v.* **-cates, -cat·ed, -cat·ing 1** make vacant: *She was ordered to vacate the premises.* **2** cancel or make void: *His conviction was vacated under a new law.*

va·ca·tion (vay·CAY·shun) *v. & n.* (take) a period of rest from work, study, etc.: *He's away on vacation; He's vacationing in the Bahamas.*
— **va·ca·tion·er** or **va·ca·tion·ist** *n.*

vac·ci·nate (VAC·suh·nate) *v.* **-nates, -nat·ed, -nat·ing** inoculate with or administer a vaccine to someone *against* smallpox, etc. — **vac·ci·na·tion** (-NAY·shun) *n.*

vac·cine (vac·SEEN, VAC·seen) *n.* a preparation of bacteria or viruses of a particular disease injected into the body to build up resistance or immunity to the disease.

vac·il·late (VAS·uh·late) *v.* **-il·lates, -il·lat·ed, -il·lat·ing** shift back and forth or waver *in* an opinion or resolution, *between* two positions, etc. in an indecisive manner. — **vac·il·la·tion** (-LAY·shun) *n.*

vac·u·ous (VAC·yoo·us) *adj.* senseless or inane: *a vacuous expression, laugh, mind, remark, stare; the vacuous* (= empty) *life of the idle rich.*
— **vac·u·ous·ly** *adv.;* **vac·u·ous·ness** *n.*

vac·u·um (VAC·yoo·um, VAC·yoom) *n.* **vac·u·ums** or **vac·u·a** (-yoo·uh) an empty space or void without even air in it, usually an enclosed space from which all air has been removed.
— *v.* (VAC·yoom) to clean with a vacuum cleaner.

vacuum bottle or **vacuum flask** or **vacuum jug** *n.* a double-walled bottle with an insulating vacuum between

the walls, which are also heat-reflecting, for keeping liquids hot or cold for up to 24 hours. Also **thermos** or **thermos bottle.**

vacuum cleaner *n.* a machine that cleans floors, carpets, etc. by suction.

vacuum-packed (VAC·yoom·pact) *adj.* packed airtight or in an airtight container.

vag·a·bond (VAG·uh·bond) *n.* a drifter, esp. one who leads a carefree, roaming life; *adj.: a vagabond poet; a vagabond tour of the world; Eurodollars are a pool of vagabond capital shifting from country to country.*
— **vag·a·bond·age** (-ij) *n.*

va·gar·y (vuh·GAIR·ee, VAY·guh·ree) *n.* **-gar·ies** an erratic or unpredictable departure or change from the usual or normal: *the vagaries of fashion, of the market, politics, the weather.*

va·gi·na (vuh·JYE·nuh) *n.* **-nas** or **-nae** (-nee) the canal leading from the genitals to the uterus in female mammals, forming also the opening of the birth canal.
— **vag·i·nal** (VAJ·uh·nul) *adj.*

va·grant (VAY·grunt) *n.* a beggar or similar person who wanders from place to place without a regular occupation, esp. one likely to become a public nuisance.
— *adj.: a vagrant life; vagrant* (= wandering) *melodies, thoughts.* — **va·gran·cy** (-grun·see) *n.* **-cies.**

vague (VAIG) *adj.* **va·guer, va·guest** not clear or distinct: *a vague answer, idea, rumour; He was vague and uncertain about his intentions; She saw the vague outlines of some flying object; I have a vague feeling of something wrong.*

vain *adj.* **1** having or showing too high a regard for one's self; conceited: *He's vain about his good looks.* **2** lacking in value; worthless or empty: *a vain boast; vain pomp, pursuits.* **3** unavailing; useless: *a vain attempt, endeavour.*
— **in vain 1** without success: *All his efforts were in vain.* **2** in a disrespectful manner: *to take God's name in vain.* — **vain·ly** *adv.*

vale *n.* [poetic use] valley.

val·e·dic·tion (val·uh·DIC·shun) *n.* **1** the act of bidding farewell. **2** a farewell utterance.

val·e·dic·tor·i·an (VAL·uh·dic·TOR·ee·un) *n.* a student, usually the highest ranked, who delivers the valedictory at graduation.

val·e·dic·to·ry (val·uh·DIC·tuh·ree) *n. & adj.* -ries (a speech) bidding farewell: *to deliver, give a valedictory; a valedictory address.*

val·en·tine (VAL·un·tine) *n.* 1 a sweetheart chosen on Saint Valentine's Day, February 14, and greeted with a card. 2 the card.

val·et (VAL·it, -ay) *n.* a male servant performing personal services for a man, as a hotel employee who cleans and presses clothes.

val·e·tu·di·nar·i·an (VAL·uh·tue·duh·NAIR·ee·un) *adj.* of weak health or unduly worried about one's state of health. — *n.* such a person.

val·i·ant (VAL·yunt) *adj.* brave or courageous: *a valiant deed, hero.* — **val·i·ant·ly** *adv.*

val·id (VAL·id) *adj.* having the force of law, reason, or evidence: *a valid contract, objection, ticket; a ticket valid for one year.* — **val·id·ly** *adv.* — **va·lid·i·ty** (vuh·LID·uh·tee) *n.*

val·i·date (VAL·uh·date) *v.* -dates, -dat·ed, -dat·ing make or show to be valid: *to validate a claim.* — **val·i·da·tion** (-DAY·shun) *n.*

va·lise (vuh·LEECE) *n.* a bag in which to carry clothes, etc. when travelling.

val·ley (VAL·ee) *n.* **val·leys** 1 a long, narrow depression between hills or mountains, esp. the low land through which a river flows: *down in the valley.* 2 a valleylike dip or channel, as between two slopes of a roof.

val·our or **val·or** (VAL·ur) *n.* courage or bravery, as in battle: *The Cross of Valour is Canada's highest civilian award for bravery; "Discretion is the better part of valour"* (= It is better to be discreet and avoid a dangerous situation than try to be brave). — **val·or·ous** *adj.*

val·u·a·ble (VAL·yoo·uh·bul, -yoo·bul) 1 *adj.* having great value or usefulness: *a valuable contribution, experience, gem, help, lesson, purpose; valuable time; He was chosen the game's most valuable player; It's valuable to cultivate Lee's friendship.* 2 **valuables** *n.pl.* jewellery and such articles of great value.

val·u·a·tion (val·yoo·AY·shun) *n.* 1 a determining of the value of an asset: *Canadian capital gains taxes are based on prices as of Valuation Day fixed at December 31, 1971.* 2 the estimated value or worth.

val·ue (VAL·yoo) *n.* 1 what something is worth in terms of its usefulness or importance: *a story of some news value; the exchange value of the Canadian dollar; the value of education; a keepsake treasured because of its sentimental value; It is of no commercial value; a discovery of great value to humanity; the traditional values* (= ideals, standards, etc.) *of our society; middle-class, moral, spiritual values; Consumers want value* (= adequate return) *for their money; sold at face value; cash, enduring, intrinsic, nominal, nuisance value.* 2 what a symbol or letter is equivalent to: *The value of L as a Roman numeral is 50; ½ and 3/6 have the same value; "x" has the sound value of "ks."* 3 a relative

quality, as the degree of lightness or darkness of a colour, duration of a note or rest in music, etc. — *v.* -ues, -ued, -u·ing 1 think highly of a person or thing: *I value her advice very much; She's a highly valued friend.* 2 estimate; rate: *Most people value health above wealth; His assets are valued at $4 million.*

value-added tax *n.* a government tax on a product or service based on the difference between the producer's sale price and the cost of materials and expenses.

value judgment *n.* a judgment about people or their actions that is based on subjective or personal values.

valve (VALV) *n.* 1 an opening and closing device that controls a flow, as in the heart, in water faucets, and in wind instruments such as the trumpet and French horn for changing musical pitch. 2 a hinged part of the shell of a bivalve mollusc or clam. 3 one of the parts into which a capsule or pod separates on bursting open.

vamp *n.* 1 the upper front covering of a shoe or boot. 2 a patched-up article, as a shoe repaired with a new vamp. 3 a woman who exploits men unscrupulously to get what she wants; adventuress. — *v.* **vamp up** patch up or repair something with pieces of material: *a vamped up excuse; to vamp up a publication* (to make it look like a new one).

vam·pire (VAM·pire) *n.* 1 a ghost of folklore that sucks the blood of sleeping people. 2 one who preys on others, as a blackmailer or adventuress. 3 a bat that sucks the blood of fowl and livestock, and sometimes attacks sleeping people; also **vampire bat.**

van *n.* 1 a large closed truck or wagon for transporting livestock, merchandise, etc.: *a delivery van; moving van.* 2 the vanguard of an advancing army, fleet, etc.

van·dal (VAN·dul) *n.* 1 one who willfully or ignorantly destroys valuable property. 2 **Vandal** a member of a Germanic tribe that sacked Rome in A.D. 455. — **van·dal·ism** *n.*

van·dal·ize (VAN·dul·ize) *v.* -iz·es, -ized, -iz·ing destroy or damage property belonging to others.

vane *n.* 1 a blade of a rotating device as in a turbine or windmill on which the force of water, wind, etc. acts. 2 a weather vane. 3 the feather of an arrow. 4 a plate or strip of metal attached to a rocket or missile to give it stability in flight.

van·guard (VAN·gard) *n.* 1 the front part of an advancing army. 2 the leadership or leading position in a movement.

va·nil·la (vuh·NIL·uh) *n.* 1 a flavouring made from the capsules of a climbing orchid. 2 the capsules or the plant. — *adj.*: *vanilla bean, essence, extract, flavouring, icing; plain vanilla ice cream; a plain-vanilla* (= ordinary) *computer with no bells and whistles.*

van·ish (VAN·ish) *v.* disappear quickly or completely, often mysteriously: *The fairy vanished from sight; vanished into thin air; All their hopes vanished with the death of their only child; Endangered species may vanish from the earth* (= cease to exist) *unless protected.*

vanishing point *n.* a point at which something seems to vanish or cease to exist, as the point on the horizon where parallel lines seem to meet from the perspective of a viewer.

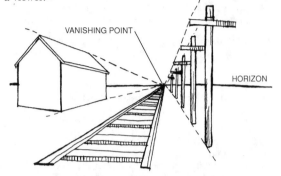

van·i·ty (VAN·uh·tee) *n.* **-ties 1** the quality of being vain; self-conceit: *a compliment that tickles one's vanity.* **2** what one is vain about, as beauty or accomplishments. **3** worthlessness or something considered as of no real value: *the vanity of human wishes.* **4** a mirror and table for a woman to sit at while making up; *adj.: a vanity mirror, sink; a vanity case for cosmetics and toilet articles while travelling.* **5** a storage cabinet fitted under a washroom sink.

vanity plate *n.* an automobile's customized licence plate.

van·ner (VAN·ur) *n.* one who uses a van as a recreational vehicle. — **van·ning** *n.*

van·pool *n.* the sharing of a van by commuters. — **van·pool·ing** *n.*

van·quish (VANK·wish) *v.* defeat utterly; get the mastery of, as in single combat: *a vanquished foe; vanquished fears.*

van·tage (VAN·tij) *n.* a position of strategic advantage or commanding view; also **vantage point.**

vap·id (VAP·id) *adj.* **1** having lost freshness or flavour. **2** flat, dull, or boring: *a vapid conversation; vapid outpourings, prose, speeches.* — **va·pid·i·ty** (va·PID·uh·tee) *n.* **-ties.**

vapor See VAPOUR.

va·por·ish (VAY·pur·ish) *adj.* **1** full of or like vapour. **2** of low spirits or depressing.

va·por·ize (VAY·puh·rize) *v.* **-iz·es, -ized, -iz·ing** change into vapour. — **va·por·iz·er** (-rye·zur) *n.*

va·por·ous (VAY·puh·rus) *adj.* **1** full of or like vapour; foggy or misty. **2** volatile or fanciful.

va·pour or **va·por** (VAY·pur) *n.* **1** the gaseous state of a normally solid or liquid substance. **2** a gas: *Water vapour seen as steam, fog, etc. condenses as dew, rain, and snow; Sulphur vapour condenses as a powder; the vapours* (= fantastic notions) *of a feverish mind.* — *v.* (cause) to rise as vapour; also, give off vapour.

vapourings (VAY·pur·ingz) *n. pl.* boastful talk.

var·i·a (VAIR·ee·uh) *n. pl.* a miscellany.

var·i·a·ble (VAIR·ee·uh·bul) *adj.* likely to vary or change: *variable moods, rates, standards, winds; a curtain rod of variable* (= adjustable) *length; the variable* (= not constant) *value of letters used in algebra; a **variable star** with changing brightness.* — *n.* something variable or changeable: *a random variable.* — **var·i·a·bly** *adv.* — **var·i·a·ble·ness** *n.;* **var·i·a·bil·i·ty** (-BIL·uh·tee) *n.*

var·i·ance (VAIR·ee·unce) *n.* **1** difference or disagreement: *On political questions we find the couple **at variance;** Performance should not be **at variance with** promises.* **2** a deviation or departure: *a variance to a zoning bylaw; He applied for a variance* (= licence) *to set up business in a residential area.*

var·i·ant (VAIR·ee·unt) *n. & adj.* (something) varying from a standard or from others of its kind: *(SHEJ·ool) and (SKEJ·ool) are variant pronunciations of "schedule"; "Humor" is a spelling variant of "humour."*

var·i·a·tion (vair·ee·AY·shun) *n.* a change in form, position, condition, etc.: *temperature variations from the normal; musical variations on a theme by altering the accompaniment, harmonies, etc.; wide variations between individuals, as in complexion, because of genetic differences and environmental factors.*

var·i·col·oured or **var·i·col·ored** (VAIR·i·cul·urd) *adj.* of various colours, as a parrot or marble; variegated in colour.

var·ied (VAIR·eed) *adj.* **1** having variety: *a varied career, style.* **2** of various kinds; diverse: *a man of varied interests, talents.*

var·i·e·gat·ed (VAIR·ee·uh·gay·tid, -ee·gay·tid) *adj.* marked with different colours, spots, etc.: *variegated Easter eggs.* — **var·i·e·ga·tion** (-ee·GAY·shun) *n.*

va·ri·e·tal (vuh·RYE·uh·tul) *n.* a wine made from a particular variety of grape.

va·ri·e·ty (vuh·RYE·uh·tee) *n.* **-ties 1** variation or diversity: *People of different races add* or *lend variety to a population; "Variety is the spice of life"; artistic variety in unity; The store carries a wide variety of goods* (= goods of many different kinds). **2** kind or sort: *many varieties of goods; varieties* (= subspecies) *of roses.* **3** *Brit.* a variety show.

variety meats *n. pl.* nonflesh meats, esp. organs, as tripe.

variety show *n.* an entertainment or show with songs, dances, skits, etc.

variety store *n.* a retail store selling a variety of small items.

var·i·ous (VAIR·ee·us) *adj.* [modifies pl. n.] of different or diverse kinds: *for many and various reasons; as various* (= many) *people have told us.* — **var·i·ous·ly** *adv.*

var·nish (VAR·nish) *n.* **1** a resinous preparation applied to wood, metal, etc. to give a hard glossy surface. **2** such glossy appearance. **3** surface polish or outside show. — *v.* cover with varnish.

var·si·ty (VAR·suh·tee) *n.* **-ties** the main team representing a college, school, or club in a sports competition: *to play on the varsity.*

var·y (VAIR·ee) *v.* **var·ies, var·ied, var·y·ing 1** differ or make different: *People vary in their tastes; Tastes vary* *from person to person; Drivers avoid monotony on the highway by varying their cruising speed.* **2** change or undergo change: *Daytime temperatures vary between 20 and 25 degrees here; They vary from 20 to 25 degrees; Sharpness of vision varies inversely as size of letters read* (= The smaller the letters, the less sharp the vision).

vase (VACE, VAZE) *n.* a decorative rounded vessel of pottery, etc. used esp. to hold flowers.

vas·sal (VAS·ul) *n.* **1** a feudal tenant owing homage and allegiance to his lord. **2** a subordinate or servant.

vas·sal·age (VAS·ul·ij) *n.* **1** a vassal's condition of servitude. **2** the homage and service required of a vassal. **3** the lands held by a vassal.

vast *adj.* very great in extent or range: *the vast Sahara Desert; a vast amount of money.*
— **vast·ly** *adv.*; **vast·ness** *n.*

vat *n.* a large tub, barrel, or similar vessel to hold a liquid, esp. in an industrial process.

Vat·i·can (VAT·uh·cun) *n.* papal headquarters, authority, or government: *an appeal to the Vatican.*

vault *n.* **1** an arched roof or ceiling: *beneath the vault of heaven* (= sky). **2** a chamber or structure with a vault, esp. one underground, usually for a special purpose: *a storage vault for weapons; buried in the family vault; a bank vault for the safekeeping of valuables.* **3** a leap made with the support of the hands or a pole: *a pole vault.*
— *v.* **1** to arch like a vault. **2** cover with or build as a vault: *a vaulted dome.* **3** leap upward or go *over* a barrier, jump *from* or *onto* a horse, etc. supported by the hands or by using a pole: *to vault over a wall; Guy vaulted past Yun in the finals; The Dolphins vaulted from a 7-7 deadlock into a 24-14 lead; a program to vault the business into the major leagues; his vaulting* (= overzealous) *ambition; a vaulting horse* (= gym equipment for vaulting).

vaunt *n. & v.* boast or brag: *his vaunted* (= boasted-about) *popularity.*

veal (VEEL) *n.* a young calf or its flesh used for food.

vec·tor (VEC·tur) *n.* **1** a mathematical quantity or line segment used to represent magnitude and direction, as of a force acting upon the path of a body in motion. **2** the carrier or transmitter of a disease-causing organism or agent, as the mosquito carrying the malarial parasite.

veer *v.* change direction, as under an external force: *The car veered away from the bicyclist; It veered to the left.* — *n.* a change of direction.

veg·e·ta·ble (VEJ·uh·tuh·bul, VEJ·tuh-) *n.* a plant, esp. a plant part, as of the lettuce, beet, or tomato, that is used for food: *They sell fruits and vegetables; garden vegetables; Leafy, green, and yellow vegetables form a basic food group.*
— *adj.* having to do with vegetables: *the vegetable kingdom* (= plants as distinguished from animals and minerals); *a vegetable marrow* (= a summer squash such as zucchini); *vegetable oils; the vegetable existence (without mental activity) of a terminally ill patient on a life-support system.*

veg·e·tar·i·an (vej·uh·TAIR·ee·un) *n.* one who eats no

meat: *a strict vegetarian who does not use fish and dairy products; adj.: a vegetarian diet, restaurant.*
— **veg·e·tar·i·an·ism** *n.*

veg·e·tate (VEJ·uh·tate) *v.* **-tates, -tat·ed, -tat·ing** **1** grow as plants. **2** exist like plants with very little physical or mental activity.

veg·e·ta·tion (vej·uh·TAY·shun) *n.* **1** plant life or growth: *the dense, lush, luxuriant, rank vegetation of the jungle.* **2** the act or state of vegetating.

veg·e·ta·tive (VEJ·uh·tay·tiv) *adj.* having to do with growth: *a vegetative existence; Roots, stems, and leaves are vegetative organs; vegetative processes such as growth and decay.*

veg·gie (VEJ·ee) *n. Informal.* **1** vegetable. **2** a vegetarian.

ve·he·ment (VEE·uh·munt) *adj.* intense in feeling; passionate: *a vehement denial of the charge; vehement desires, utterances; a vehement* (= violent) *wind.*
— **ve·he·ment·ly** *adv.* — **ve·he·mence** *n.*

ve·hi·cle (VEE·uh·cul) *n.* **1** a carriage or conveyance used on land or in space: *a licence to drive* or *operate a motor vehicle; all-terrain, armoured, recreational, re-entry, space vehicles.* **2** a medium: *Language is the vehicle of thought and emotion; The paper serves as a vehicle for propaganda; pigments in vehicles such as oils, resins, latex, etc.; a drug given in an inert vehicle such as syrup.*

ve·hic·u·lar (vi·HIK·yuh·lur) *adj.* having to do with vehicles, esp. motor: *vehicular traffic, tunnels.*

veil (VALE) *n.* a piece of sheer fabric or net used as a curtain, to hide or protect a woman's head or face, etc.: *a bridal veil; a veil of clouds, secrecy.*
— **veiled** *adj.*: *a veiled* (= hidden or implied) *threat; The novel reads like a thinly veiled* (= masked) *biography.*

veiling *n.* a veil or a sheer fabric such as lace or chiffon.

vein (VANE) *n.* **1** a channel carrying blood, sap, etc. or something resembling it: *the veins and arteries of the circulatory system; the network of veins on a leaf; the veins on an insect's wing; a vein* (= seam or lode) *of mineral ore deposited by ground water in rock fissures; the vein* (= streak) *of melancholy running through her poems; adj.: a veined leaf (marked with veins).* **2** mood or manner: *in a lighter vein; in a serious vein.*

vel·cro (VEL·croh) *n.* a nylon fabric used as a fastener made up of two strips pressed tightly together to close and pulled apart to open; **Velcro** *Trademark.*

veldt or **veld** (VELT) *n.* the treeless grasslands of South Africa whose lower regions are often scrub-covered.

vel·lum (VEL·um) *n.* **1** a fine parchment, as used for binding expensive books. **2** a strong paper with a smooth finish imitating vellum, used for diplomas, etc.

ve·loc·i·ty (vuh·LOS·uh·tee) *n.* **-ties** swiftness or speed, esp. of inanimate things: *the velocity of a bullet; at the velocity of light, sound.*

ve·lour or **ve·lours** (vuh·LOOR) *n., pl.* **-lours** (-LOORZ) a velvetlike fabric used for coats, upholstery, etc.

vel·vet (VEL·vut) *n.* **1** a fabric of silk, rayon, etc. with a

soft downy surface: *as smooth as velvet; seductive black velvet.* 2 something resembling velvet, as the furry covering of a deer's growing antlers.
— *adj.* made of, covered with, or suggesting velvet: *the velvet touch of a baby's skin; "an iron hand in a velvet glove"* (= softness masking ruthlessness). — **vel·vet·y** *adj.*

ve·nal (VEE·nul) *adj.* open to bribes or influenced by bribery; corrupt: *venal conduct, politicians, practices.*
— **ve·nal·ly** *adv.*
— **ve·nal·i·ty** (vee·NAL·uh·tee) *n.*

vend *v.* sell, esp. peddle or hawk: *A coin-operated vending machine sells pop and snacks.*

ven·det·ta (ven·DET·uh) *n.* 1 a family feud in which injuries are avenged with violence and bloodshed. 2 any prolonged feud: *to conduct a vendetta against someone.*

ven·dor (VEN·dur) *n.* one that vends; seller: *a news vendor; street vendors.*

ve·neer (vuh·NEER) *n.* a layer of wood, brick, etc. used to cover something inferior: *furniture with an oak veneer; exterior walls of brick veneer; Anyone could see through his thin veneer of urbanity.*
— *v.* cover with a veneer.

ven·er·a·ble (VEN·uh·ruh·bul) *adj.* worthy of deep reverence because of age, dignity, sanctity, etc.

ven·er·ate (VEN·uh·rate) *v.* -ates, -at·ed, -at·ing regard with deep reverence; revere.
— **ven·er·a·tion** (-RAY·shun) *n.*

ve·ne·re·al (vuh·NEER·ee·ul) *adj.* of or transmitted by sexual intercourse: *a venereal disease.*
— **ve·ne·re·al·ly** *adv.*

Ve·ne·tian blind (vuh·NEE·shun·) *n.* a window blind made of slats that can be opened and closed to regulate lighting.

venge·ance (VEN·junce) *n.* punishment in return for a wrong; revenge: *to exact, take, wreak vengeance on or upon someone for something; He vowed vengeance; to seek vengeance for past wrongs; He started dieting* **with a vengeance** (= in a vehement or excessive way).

venge·ful (VENJ·ful) *adj.* seeking vengeance; revengeful; vindictive. — **venge·ful·ly** *adv.*

ve·ni·al (VEE·nee·ul) *adj.* pardonable or excusable: *a venial offence, sin.*

ven·i·son (VEN·uh·sun, -zun) *n.* the flesh of a deer used as food.

ven·om (VEN·um) *n.* 1 the poison of a snake or spider. 2 malice: *to spew or spout venom.*

ven·om·ous (VEN·uh·mus) *adj.* 1 poisonous: *a venomous snake.* 2 spiteful or malicious: *a venomous letter.* — **ven·om·ous·ly** *adv.*

vent *n.* 1 an outlet or opening for a gas to escape through, for air to be drawn in for ventilation, as in an automobile, etc.: *a vent pipe for the escape of sewer gas; He* **gave vent** (= gave free expression) *to his feelings in a letter.* 2 a vertical slit at the edge of a garment: *a jacket with side vents.*
— *v.* 1 discharge or expel: *He vented his anger on everyone he met.* 2 provide with a vent: *Sinks, toilets, etc. are vented through the roof.*

ven·ti·late (VEN·tuh·late) *v.* -lates, -lat·ed, -lat·ing 1 let fresh air into a place: *a well ventilated room.* 2 furnish with a vent, outlet, etc. 3 oxygenate blood in lungs, etc. 4 discuss or examine fully in public: *to ventilate one's grievances; Don't ventilate your family problems in the classroom.* — **ven·ti·la·tion** (-LAY·shun) *n.*

ven·ti·la·tor (VEN·tuh·lay·tur) *n.* 1 an opening or a device such as a fan for ventilating a place. 2 an artificial breathing device; respirator.

ven·tral (VEN·trul) *adj.* of or near the belly; hence, lower. — **ven·tral·ly** *adv.*

ven·tril·o·quism (ven·TRIL·uh·kwiz·um) *n.* the art of talking without moving the lips so that the voice seems to come from a source outside the speaker such as a puppet held in the hand. — **ven·tril·o·quist** *n.*

ven·ture (VEN·chur) *n.* an enterprise or undertaking involving risk but with a chance for profit, as in buying stocks: *a bold, commercial, cooperative, high-risk, joint, speculative venture.*
— **at a venture** taking a risk; without much deliberation.
— *v.* -tures, -tured, -tur·ing expose lives, etc. to risk; dare *to* do something risky or hazardous: *if I may venture a guess, an opinion; He wouldn't venture (to step) outside in the storm.*

venture capital *n.* capital not secured by collateral for investment in enterprises subject to risk; also **risk capital.**

ven·ture·some (VEN·chur·sum) *adj.* 1 of a person, daring: *a venturesome mountaineer.* 2 of a thing or action, hazardous: *a venturesome route up the mountain.*

ven·ue (VEN·yoo) *n.* 1 in law, the locality of the commission of a crime, or the place of jury selection or trial: *The defence lawyer requested a change of venue because of adverse publicity.* 2 the appointed meeting place for a gathering or event: *the venue of the Olympic Games.*

ve·rac·i·ty (vuh·RAS·uh·tee) *n.* 1 habitual truthfulness: *No one doubts her veracity; Her veracity is not in question.* 2 truth or accuracy, as of a report.

ve·ran·da or **ve·ran·dah** (vuh·RAN·duh) *n.* an outside corridor or covered gallery of a building; porch.

verb (VURB) *n.* a part of speech or word expressing action, being, or happening: *active and passive verbs; transitive and intransitive verbs.*

ver·bal (VUR·bul) *adj.* 1 having to do with words: *a verbal distinction; verbal aptitude, imagery; a verbal* (= oral) *assurance, contract; a verbal* (= word-for-word or literal) *translation.* 2 having to do with verbs: *"-ed," "-ing," and such verbal endings; a verbal auxiliary* (= auxiliary verb) *such as "must" or "can."*
— **ver·bal·ly** *adv.*

ver·bal·ize (VUR·buh·lize) *v.* -iz·es, -ized, -iz·ing 1 express in words: *to verbalize an experience, idea.* 2 be verbose or wordy.
— **ver·bal·i·za·tion** (-luh·ZAY·shun) *n.*

ver·ba·tim (vur·BAY·tim) *adj. & adv.* word for word: *The speech was reported verbatim; a verbatim report of the speech.*

ver·bi·age (VUR·bee·ij) *n.* use of too many words; verbosity; wordiness.

ver·bose (vur·BOSE) *adj.* using more words than are necessary: *a verbose speaker, style.* — **ver·bose·ly** *adv.;* **ver·bos·i·ty** (-BOS·uh·tee) *n.*

ver·dant (VUR·dunt) *adj.* green: *verdant grass, meadows; verdant* (=immature) *youth.*

ver·dict (VUR·dict) *n.* a formal decision or finding, as of a jury at the end of a trial: *to arrive at, bring in, reach, return a verdict; a guilty verdict; a verdict of not guilty.*

ver·dure (VUR·jur) *n.* **1** green vegetation. **2** the green colour of growing things.

verge (VURJ) *n.* the brink or extreme edge of something: *on the verge of a cliff, roof; on the verge of bankruptcy, of being exposed, of a breakdown, of tears.* — *v.* **verg·es, verged, verg·ing** be on the verge of something: *His spelling is so poor it verges on illiteracy; He's verging* (= inclining) *toward old age.*

ver·i·fy (VER·uh·fye) *v.* **-fies, -fied, -fy·ing** prove the correctness or truth of something by checking with a standard or authority: *to verify a statement, piece of information; His credentials have been verified; Later events verified* (= confirmed) *his suspicions.* — **ver·i·fi·a·ble** (-FYE·uh·bul) *adj.* — **ver·i·fi·ca·tion** (-fuh·CAY·shun) *n.*

ver·i·ly (VER·uh·lee) *adv.* [old use] truly; in truth.

ver·i·sim·i·li·tude (VER·uh·suh·MIL·uh·tude) *n.* the quality of seeming to be true or real.

ver·i·ta·ble (VER·uh·tuh·bul) *adj.* truly so termed: *a veritable gold mine; a veritable heaven on earth.*

ver·i·ty (VER·uh·tee) *n.* **-ties 1** the quality of being true or real. **2** a fundamental or universal truth: *the eternal verities of all creeds and philosophies.*

ver·mil·ion (vur·MIL·yun) *n.* a bright-red pigment or its colour. — *adj.* bright-red.

ver·min (VUR·mun) *n.* **1** *sing. & pl.* (any of various) insects or small animals that are pests, as fleas, rats, etc.: *a house infested with vermin.* **2** a contemptible person.

ver·mouth (ver·MOOTH) *n.* a white wine flavoured with herbs.

ver·nac·u·lar (vur·NAK·yuh·lur) *n.* **1** the native language of a people or place, esp. its everyday, spoken variety, as distinguished from a literary form: *The Mass is now said in the vernacular* (= local language) *instead of Latin; the salty vernacular* (= spoken style) *of Huck Finn.* **2** the idiom of a group or class: *in the vernacular of the street; the vernacular of baseball, jazz, Texas.* — *adj.* belonging to common speech: *Italian, French, etc. arose as vernacular forms of Latin; "Venus' flytrap" is the vernacular name for "Dionaea muscipula"; the Scottish vernacular* (= dialect) *poet Robert Burns; the vernacular* (= locally rooted) *architecture of Quebec.*

ver·nal (VUR·nul) *adj.* having to do with spring: *vernal flowers, hay fever; The vernal equinox occurs around March 21.* — **ver·nal·ly** *adv.*

ver·sa·tile (VUR·suh·tile, -tul) *adj.* **1** having the skills or aptitude for many different activities: *a versatile genius, mind; She's quite versatile in* or *at foreign languages.* **2** able to turn or swing freely: *an insect's versatile antennae.* — **ver·sa·til·i·ty** (-TIL·uh·tee) *n.*

verse (VURSE) *n.* **1** a line of poetry; also, a stanza or poem. **2** language in verses; poetry: *a story in verse.* **3** a sentence from a chapter of the Bible: *He can cite* or *give* or *quote chapter and verse* (= exact source) *to prove his claim.*

versed (VURST) *adj.* learned or experienced: *a scholar well versed in his specialty.*

ver·sion (VUR·zhun, -shun) *n.* **1** a particular form or variant, esp. an account or description from one point of view: *your version of the incident; the authorized, official, written version; the uncut version of a movie; the movie version of a novel.* **2** a translation of the Bible: *the Authorized Version; the Revised Version.*

ver·sus (VUR·sus) *prep.* against [usually abbreviated to "v." in legal use]: *John Smith v. the Crown; freedom versus* (= contrasted with) *slavery.*

ver·te·bra (VUR·tuh·bruh) *n., pl.* **-brae** (-bray, -bree) or **-bras** one of the segments of the backbone. — **ver·te·bral** (-brul) *adj.*

ver·te·brate (VUR·tuh·brit, -brate) *n. & adj.* (an animal such as a fish, amphibian, bird, reptile, or mammal) that has a backbone.

ver·ti·cal (VUR·tuh·cul) *adj.* upright or erect; perpendicular to the horizontal: *a ski trail with a vertical drop of 800 metres; 800 vertical metres; a vertical-takeoff-and-landing airplane; a library's vertical file of clippings, pamphlets, etc.* — *n.* a vertical line, plane, part, etc. — **ver·ti·cal·ly** *adv.* — **ver·ti·cal·i·ty** (-CAL·uh·tee) *n.*

ver·ti·go (VUR·tuh·go) *n.* **-ti·goes** or **-tig·i·nes** (vur·TIJ·uh·neez) dizziness or giddiness felt when one's sense of balance is disturbed, as in diseases of the inner ear or when looking down from a height.

verve *n.* vigorous energy or enthusiasm; vivacity: *The band performs with verve and zest.*

ver·y (VER·ee) *adj.* **ver·i·er, -i·est 1** [used for emphasis before nouns]: *at that very* (= same) *moment; The very* (= mere) *idea of cannibalism is revolting; as I told you from the very* (= extreme) *beginning; He treated the child as his very own.* **2** [old use] real or genuine: *in very truth; A verier fool was never seen.* — *adv.* [used for emphasis] **1** [before adverbs]: *a very well liked woman; He runs very fast.* **2** [before adjectives that allow degrees of comparison]: *a very great idea; It's very hot outside; That's very true; at the very least* [but "a quite unique event," not "a very unique event"]. **3** [before adjectives with superlative meaning]: *the very first to arrive; your very own child.* **4** [before participles, except participles with clearly verbal meaning]: *a very learned man* [but not "a very learned habit" or "a very liked woman"].

ves·per (VES·pur) **1** *adj.* having to do with the evening or vespers: *the vesper bell.* **2 vespers** or **Vespers** *n. pl.* an evening church service.

ves·sel (VES·ul) *n.* **1** a hollow utensil for holding esp. liquids, as a bowl, barrel, bottle, etc. **2** a ship or large boat: *to charter a vessel; an oceangoing vessel.* **3** a duct or tube of the body: *blood vessels.*

vest *n.* **1** a short sleeveless garment, usually worn under one's suit jacket: *bulletproof vests for police officers.* **2** *Brit.* undershirt.
— *v.* **1** clothe, as in vestments: *a priest vested for Mass.* **2** put authority, rights, etc. in the possession of a person: *by the powers vested in the Crown; to vest someone with authority; the power that vests* (= resides) *in the Crown.*

ves·tal (VES·tul) *adj.* chaste or pure, as a **vestal virgin** (priestess of ancient Rome).
— *n.* **1** a vestal virgin. **2** a chaste woman.

vested interest *n.* **1** an economic, social, or political privilege enjoyed by a group or organization, that may be lost by change. **2** such a group or its selfish concern.

ves·ti·bule (VES·tuh·byool) *n.* a room, hall, or passage serving as an entrance or antechamber.

ves·tige (VES·tij) *n.* a remaining part or remnant of something that is no longer in existence: *The appendix, wisdom teeth, etc. are vestiges from an earlier stage of human history; vestiges of an ancient civilization; the last vestiges of their existence; There's not a vestige* (= least bit) *of truth in his assertion.*

vest·ment (VEST·munt) *n.* a ceremonial outer garment or robe, as worn by the clergy at religious services.

vest-pocket (VEST·pok·it) *adj.* **1** very small: *a vest-pocket dictionary.* **2** secretive: *his vest-pocket conduct in public office.*

vest·ure (VES·chur) *n.* clothing or covering; garments.

vet *n.* [short form] **1** veterinarian; veterinary. **2** veteran.

vet·er·an (VET·ur·un) *n.* **1** a former member of the armed forces, esp. an old soldier, sailor, etc.: *a disabled veteran; war veterans; adj.: veteran benefits, troops.* **2** a person with long experience in an occupation: *a newspaper veteran; TV veteran; adj.: a veteran farmer, journalist, performer, soldier.*

vet·er·i·nar·i·an (VET·ur·uh·NAIR·ee·un) *n.* one who practises a branch of medicine dealing with the treatment of animals.
— **vet·er·i·nar·y** (-nair·ee) *adj.: veterinary medicine.*

ve·to (VEE·toh) *n.* **-toes** (the exercise of) the right to prohibit an act or defeat a move: *the veto exercised by the permanent members of the U.N. Security Council; Parents have veto power over decisions made by children in their care.*
— *v.* **-toes, -toed, -to·ing** forbid or prohibit an action by special right: *The Senate could veto a bill passed by the Commons.*

vex *v.* **1** irritate or annoy in a worrying manner: *They were deeply vexed to hear that their son had lost his job; a vexing bit of news; the vexed* (= much disputed) *question of pay equity.* **2** to plague or afflict: *to be vexed with migraine headaches.*
— **vex·a·tion** (vek·SAY·shun) *n.*
— **vex·a·tious** (-shus) *adj.*

vi·a (VYE·uh, VEE·uh) *prep.* by way of: *a letter sent via*

airmail; to Montreal via Ottawa.

vi·a·ble (VYE·uh·bul) *adj.* **1** capable of surviving, as a fetus outside the womb: *Democracy is not viable under a military regime; a viable economy, industry, operation; to put things on a viable basis.* **2** feasible or practicable: *a viable alternative, decision, option, plan.*
— **vi·a·bly** *adv.* — **vi·a·bil·i·ty** (-BIL·uh·tee) *n.*

vi·a·duct (VYE·uh·duct) *n.* a bridge on tall supports for carrying a railway track or road over another track or road, over a valley, etc.

vi·al (VYE·ul) *n.* a small bottle to hold medicines or other liquids.

via media *n.* a middle way.

vibe *n.* **1** *Slang.* instinctive feeling or reaction; vibration: *bad, good, nice vibes; The vibe is sometimes negative; the vibe of authority.* **2** **vibes** *pl.* [short form] "vibraharp" or "vibraphone," a percussion instrument similar to the xylophone.

vi·brant (VYE·brunt) *adj.* **1** vibrating; hence, resonant. **2** vigorous or energetic: *vibrant colours; a vibrant and expressive style; a vibrant personality.*
— **vi·brant·ly** *adv.* — **vi·bran·cy** *n.*

vi·brate (VYE·brate) *v.* **-brates, -brat·ed, -brat·ing 1** set or be in rapid back-and-forth motion, as a taut string when plucked. **2** oscillate, as a pendulum. **3** respond sympathetically; thrill. **4** resound or echo, as a sound in the ears.

vi·bra·tion (vye·BRAY·shun) *n.* **1** a trembling, as caused by an earthquake or felt in a vehicle because of a wheel that is not properly balanced. **2** oscillation.
3 vibrations *pl.* instinctive reactions or feelings about a person or thing; vibes.

vic·ar (VIC·ur) *n.* **1** a member of the clergy in charge of a parish; minister or parish priest. **2** a deputy or representative of a higher church official, as a vicar apostolic or vicar-general.

vic·ar·age (VIC·ur·ij) *n.* the residence or benefice of a vicar.

vi·car·i·ous (vye·CAIR·ee·us, vi-) *adj.* acting for or as by another: *the vicarious pleasure felt in another's enjoyment; Read travel books for vicarious travel experiences; vicarious* (= delegated) *authority.*
— **vi·car·i·ous·ly** *adv.*

¹vice *n.* **1** a moral fault; immoral habit or tendency: *virtues and vices; drunkenness, gambling, and such vices.* **2** a trick or bad habit of a horse or other domestic animal, as shying. **3** *Brit.* vise.

²vi·ce (VYE·see) *prep.* in the place of someone: *Jones was appointed vice John Smith.*
— **vice-** (VICE) *combining form.* in the place of: *vice-chairman, vice-president, viceregal.*

vice·re·gal (vice·REE·gul) *adj.* of a viceroy: *the viceregal job of Governor General; the viceregal mansion in Ottawa called "Rideau Hall" or "Government House."*

vice ring *n.* a group of people organized for crimes such as prostitution or drug dealing.

vice·roy (VICE·roy) *n.* a ruler representing a sovereign, as in the Spanish and British empires. — **vice·roy·al·ty** *n.*

vice squad *n.* a police squad concerned with crimes relating to prostitution, gambling, pornography, drug-trafficking, etc.

vi·ce ver·sa (VYE·see·VUR·suh, VICE-) *adv.* the other way around: *A equals B and vice versa; Most boys like girls and vice versa.*

vi·cin·i·ty (vuh·SIN·uh·tee) *n.* **-ties** **1** nearness or proximity: *in close, immediate vicinity to the church; His expenses are in the vicinity of $500 a day.* **2** surrounding area: *Vancouver and vicinity.*

vi·cious (VISH·us) *adj.* **1** characterized by vice; wicked: *vicious habits, lies; He gave me a vicious look; a vicious savage; attacked by a vicious* (= unruly) *dog; a vicious* (= severe) *blow.* **2** involving interaction of cause and effect: *the vicious spiral of rising wages and prices.* — **vi·cious·ly** *adv.*; **vi·cious·ness** *n.*

vicious circle *n.* **1** a situation in which the solution of a problem results in a new problem similar to the original one. **2** the fallacy of basing an argument on the very thing to be proved.

vi·cis·si·tudes (vuh·SIS·uh·tudes) *n. pl.* unpredictable and sudden changes usually bringing hardships; ups and downs: *the vicissitudes of life.*

vic·tim (VIC·tum) *n.* one who suffers injury, harm, loss, etc.: *a lamb killed and placed on the altar as the sacrificial victim; the victim of an accident, crime; earthquake, flood, tornado victims; the innocent victim of a crime; the unsuspecting victim of a swindle; In his old age he fell (a) victim to amnesia.*

vic·tim·ize (VIC·tuh·mize) *v.* **-iz·es, -ized, -iz·ing** make a victim of someone. — **vic·tim·iz·er** *n.* — **vic·tim·i·za·tion** (-muh·ZAY·shun) *n.*

victimless crime *n.* a crime such as drug-trafficking, gambling, or prostitution.

vic·tor (VIC·tur) *n.* the winner or conqueror in a battle, struggle, etc.

Victoria Day *n. Cdn.* the birthday of Queen Victoria celebrated as a public holiday on the Monday before May 25.

Vic·to·ri·an (vic·TOR·ee·un) *adj.* of or characteristic of the period of Queen Victoria's reign, often associated with prudery, bigotry, etc. — *n.* a writer of the Victorian period. — **Vic·to·ri·an·ism** *n.*

vic·to·ri·ous (vic·TOR·ee·us) *adj.* **1** conquering: *We emerged victorious in the end; our victorious team.* **2** marked by victory: *a victorious reelection.* — **vic·to·ri·ous·ly** *adv.*

vic·to·ry (VIC·tuh·ree) *n.* **-ries** success in a struggle, esp. in battle or war: *to achieve, gain, score, win a victory in the Olympics; a clear, decisive, glorious, hard-won, hollow, moral, resounding, sweeping, stunning victory over their enemies; to snatch victory from the jaws of defeat.*

vic·tuals (VIT·ulz) *n. pl. Informal* or *Regional.* food supplies; articles of food.

vi·de (VYE·dee) *v. Latin.* please see page, book, etc. referred to.

vid·e·o (VID·ee·oh) *n.* **1** a short film clip with a popular musical recording as the soundtrack: *music videos; rock videos; adj.: a video club, record.* **2** a motion picture sold or rented to the public on a video cassette: *home video; adj.: a video release, rental store, shop.* **3** a recording on videotape: *video art.* **4** television, esp. the picture as distinguished from the sound: *a star of stage and video* (= TV); *adj.: a video amplifier, display, frequency, screen, signal, terminal; video journalism.*

video cassette *n.* a cassette for storing and playback of recordings on film or videotape. — **video cassette recorder** *n.*

vid·e·o·disc (VID·ee·oh·disc) *n.* a disc resembling a phonograph record for storing and playing back pictures and sounds recorded on it. — **videodisc player** *n.*

video display terminal or **monitor** or **unit** *n.* a computer's output device for data and pictures consisting of a TV screen and a keyboard; also **video terminal.**

video game *n.* any game played by manipulating points of light on a TV screen.

vid·e·o·phone (VID·ee·uh·fone) *n.* a telephone that is equipped for users to see each other while talking on the phone.

vid·e·o·tape (VID·ee·uh·tape) *v.* **-tapes, -taped, -tap·ing** record a TV broadcast or motion picture on magnetic tape. — *n.* **1** such a recording; video. **2** the tape itself. — **videotape recorder** *n.*

vid·e·o·tex (VID·ee·uh·tex) *n.* a computer service that supplies subscribers with information displayed on a video terminal or TV screen. Also **vid·e·o·text.**

vie (VYE) *v.* **vies, vied, vy·ing** contend or compete *with* another *for* a position, etc.

view (VYOO) *n.* **1** what is seen by someone looking from a certain position: *Skyscrapers block our view; structures that spoil the view; She asked for a room with a view; The view from the window is superb; You get a magnificent view of the ocean; a beautiful, breathtaking view; He lay there in full view of passers-by; a car's rear-view mirror; as the parade came into view* (= range of sight); *the view* (= picture) *hanging on the wall; an exploded view (showing the components) of a mechanism; a **bird's-eye-view*** (= quick survey) *of Canadian literature; In view of* (= because of) *what you said, I will reconsider the matter; The paintings are **on view*** (= on show). **2** a personal opinion or judgment: *Let's exchange views; Give us your views on the matter; your views on or about capital punishment; It seems wrong from my point of view; His superiors took a dim view of the matter; In their view, there was no basis for the complaint; a woman of conservative, liberal, political, progressive, radical, strong views.* **3** intention or purpose: *He has a pay raise **in view*** (= in mind); *He phoned me **with a view to*** (= for the purpose of) *negotiating a settlement.*

— *v.* consider in a particular manner, from a standpoint, with a feeling, etc.: *She is being viewed as a serious contender for the presidency; prospective buyers viewing* (= inspecting) *a house.*

view·er (VYOO·ur) *n.* one that views, esp. an optical device for looking at slides.

view·point *n.* point of view or attitude.

vig·il (VIJ·ul) *n.* **1** a staying awake; watch: *to keep (a) vigil over a patient needing constant attention; The demonstrators held an all-night vigil outside the embassy.* **2** the eve of a solemn religious festival. **3 vigils** *pl.* devotions or prayers.

vig·i·lance (VIJ·uh·lunce) *n.* watchfulness or alertness, as by vigilantes against danger or trouble: *They exercised great vigilance in preventing infiltration by spies; constant vigilance against the spread of the epidemic; Eternal vigilance is the price of liberty.*

vig·i·lant (VIJ·uh·lunt) *adj.* watchful or alert. — **vig·i·lant·ly** *adv.*

vig·i·lan·te (vij·uh·LAN·tee) *n.* a member of a self-appointed group of citizens enforcing laws, as in pioneer days, usually because of inadequate law-enforcement. — **vig·i·lan·tism** *n.*

vi·gnette (vin·YET) *n.* **1** a short literary sketch, as of a personal experience or incident. **2** a picture or photograph that shades off at the edges without definite borders.

vig·our or **vig·or** (VIG·ur) *n.* **1** strength or vitality: *the vigour of youth; a plant growing with vigour.* **2** effectiveness: *Sam acted with vigour and resolution.* — **vig·or·ous** (-us) *adj.;* **vig·or·ous·ly** *adv.*

vile *adj.* **vil·er, vil·est** disgustingly foul, low, or depraved: *vile habits, language, odours; vile* (= bad) *weather.* — **vile·ly** *adv.;* **vile·ness** *n.*

vil·i·fy (VIL·uh·fye) *v.* **-fies, -fied, -fy·ing** use abusive language about a person. — **vil·i·fi·ca·tion** (-fuh·CAY·shun) *n.*

vil·la (VIL·uh) *n.* a suburban or country residence or estate.

vil·lage (VIL·ij) *n.* a community smaller than a town, esp. one chartered as a municipality: *a farming village; fishing villages along the Newfoundland coast; The whole village* (= all the people of the village) *turned out to greet us; adj.: the village common, green; a village gossip, mentality.* — **vil·lag·er** *n.*

vil·lain (VIL·un) *n.* **1** a wicked person or scoundrel, esp. as a dramatic character in opposition to the hero: *the villain of the piece.* **2** rascal: *an arch villain; the consummate villain;* [used jokingly] *You little villain!* — **vil·lain·ous** (-us) *adj.;* **vil·lain·ous·ly** *adv.*

vil·lain·y (VIL·uh·nee) *n.* **-nies** wickedness or a wicked act.

-ville *suffix* [used in slang coinages to suggest a condition as specified]: *drugsville, dullsville, endsville, weirdsville.*

vim *n.* vitality or energy: *She pursued the matter with vim and vigour.*

vin·ci·ble (VIN·suh·bul) *adj.* conquerable.

vin·di·cate (VIN·duh·cate) *v.* **-cates, -cat·ed, -cat·ing** prove one's innocence under attack or establish a disputed claim, judgment, etc. by evidence, testimony, or a verdict: *We felt vindicated when things turned out as we had predicted.* — **vin·di·ca·tor** *n.* — **vin·di·ca·tion** (-CAY·shun) *n.*

vin·dic·tive (vin·DIC·tiv, VIN·dic-) *adj.* seeking vengeance; unforgiving: *vindictive acts, feelings, people.* — **vin·dic·tive·ly** *adv.;* **vin·dic·tive·ness** *n.*

vine *n.* **1** the grapevine. **2** any plant with a flexible stem, as the cucumber that creeps along the ground or an ivy that climbs trellises, etc.

vin·e·gar (VIN·uh·gur) *n.* a sour liquid used as a seasoning and preservative, made from fruit juices and other liquids containing sugar. — **vin·e·gar·y** *adj.*

vine·yard (VIN·yurd) *n.* a grapevine plantation.

vin·tage (VIN·tij) *n.* **1** a grape harvest, esp. of a particular year or the wine made from it: *a wine label showing vintage; of the vintage of 1955; Chateau Lafitte-Rothschild, vintage 1846.* **2** the make or class, as of an automobile, costume, piano, etc., with reference to its year or age: *an automobile of prewar vintage; an early vintage camera.* — *adj.* **1** superior in quality: *a vintage crop, wine; 1947 and 1955 were vintage years (for wines); Vintage Canadiana.* **2** old or antique: *a vintage typewriter.*

vint·ner (VINT·nur) *n.* a wine maker or wine merchant.

vi·nyl (VYE·nul) *n.* a stiff, flexible plastic material used in making a wide range of products.

vi·o·la (vee·OH·luh) *n.* a stringed instrument of larger size and lower pitch than the violin. — **vi·o·list** *n.*

vi·o·late (VYE·uh·late) *v.* **-lates, -lat·ed, -lat·ing** go against or treat with contempt: *to violate an agreement, the Sabbath, a sanctuary; to violate someone's privacy, rights; to violate* (= rape) *a woman.* — **vi·o·la·tor** *n.*

vi·o·la·tion (vye·uh·LAY·shun) *n.* a violating or being violated, as an infringement, disturbance of the peace, desecration, or rape: *He committed a minor violation; a motorist without any moving violations* (= convictions for nonparking offences) *on his record; Lu was held in violation of the curfew.*

vi·o·lence (VYE·uh·lunce) *n.* (use of) physical force that causes injury, damage, etc.: *to resort to violence; to use violence instead of persuasion; an act of violence against the person; a crime of violence; Violence may break out on a picket line; a strike marred by violence; communal, racial, sporadic violence; the violence of a hurricane; sex and violence in TV shows; the violence* (= distortion) *done to a text by a bad translation.*

vi·o·lent (VYE·uh·lunt) *adj.* involving great, excessive, or unlawful force: *writhing in violent pain; a violent assault; a violent death by murder, suicide, etc.; a violent temper; a violent attack using violent language; colours in violent* (= strong) *contrast.* — **vi·o·lent·ly** *adv.*

vi·o·let (VYE·uh·lut) *n.* **1** a low-growing plant bearing five-petalled, typically bluish-purple flowers in early spring: *shy as a violet; He's not a shrinking violet.* **2** a bluish-purple; also *adj.*

vi·o·lin (vye·uh·LIN) *n.* a four-stringed, high-pitched musical instrument played with a bow. — **vi·o·lin·ist** *n.*

VIP or **V.I.P.** *n.* **VIPs** or **V.I.P.s** a very important person.

vi·per (VYE·pur) *n.* a poisonous snake with fangs.

vi·per·ous (VYE·puh·rus) *adj.* **1** of or like a viper; venomous. **2** spiteful or malicious.

vi·ral (VYE·rul) *adj.* of or caused by a virus: *viral and bacterial diseases, pesticides; viral infections; viral encephalitis; AIDS is a viral disease; viral illnesses such as chickenpox and flu.*

vir·gin (VUR·jin) *n.* one who has never had sexual intercourse, esp. a young woman: *a vestal virgin;* **the Virgin** (= mother of Jesus).
— *adj.* the doctrine of the **virgin birth** *(of Jesus from the Virgin Mary);* the **Virgin Mary,** *mother of Jesus; her virgin modesty; a virgin* (= initial) *effort; a virgin beach, forest, jungle (that has not been invaded by humans); virgin* (= fresh) *snow; Virgin* (= pure) *olive oil has 1% to 3% acidity;* **Extra virgin** *olive oil has less than 1% acidity; virgin* (= uncultivated) *soil, territory; virgin* (= in native form) *silver, sulphur.*

vir·gin·i·ty (vur·JIN·uh·tee) *n.* **-ties 1** the condition of a virgin, esp. maidenhood. **2** celibacy.

vir·gule (VURG·yool) *n.* a diagonal line used as in ⅓, to separate alternatives as in "and/or," to mean *per* as in "km/h," etc.

vir·ile (VEER·ile, VEER·ul) *adj.* manly in being robust, potent, etc. — **vi·ril·i·ty** (vuh·RIL·uh·tee) *n.*

vir·tu·al (VUR·choo·ul) *adj.* being such practically or in effect though not formally: *She was kept in virtual isolation; a virtual impossibility; He's the virtual boss around here; the* **virtual** (= unreal) *image in a mirror; the* **virtual memory** *or* **storage** *of a computer in an external storage device that can be used as an extension of its internal main memory.* — **vir·tu·al·ly** *adv.*

vir·tue (VUR·choo) *n.* **1** a particular moral quality: *the seven virtues; the Christian virtues of faith, hope, and charity and the cardinal virtues of justice, fortitude, prudence, and temperance; virtues and vices.* **2** moral excellence: *She is a paragon of virtue; a* **woman of easy virtue** (= woman of poor morals); *He thought to* **make a virtue of necessity** (= make the best of a bad situation) *by going back to school when he lost his job.* **3** power or efficacy; also, a particular quality or worth: *wonder drugs of dubious virtue; the virtues of exercise; Degrees are conferred* **by virtue of** (= because of) *the authority vested in a university.*

vir·tu·o·so (vur·choo·OH·soh) *n.* **-o·sos** or **-o·si** (-OH·see) an artist with great technical skill. — **vir·tu·os·i·ty** (-OS·uh·tee) *n.*

vir·tu·ous (VUR·choo·us) *adj.* having moral virtue: *Our nuns lead a virtuous life; virtuous* (= chaste) *women.* — **vir·tu·ous·ly** *adv.;* **vir·tu·ous·ness** *n.*

vir·u·lent (VEER·yuh·lunt) *adj.* deadly or dangerous like poison: *a virulent disease, infection; virulent hatred, language.* — **vir·u·lent·ly** *adv.* — **vir·u·lence** *n.*

vi·rus (VYE·rus) *n.* **1** a microorganism that is smaller than bacteria, causing diseases such as influenza, measles, and chickenpox. **2** any poisonous or harmful influence. **3** a computer instruction hidden in a regular program on a disk, designed to destroy other programs and data when the disk is used.

vi·sa (VEE·zuh) *n.* permission granted to enter or stay in a country, as endorsed on a passport: *to cancel, issue, renew, violate a visa; an entry, exit, student, tourist, transit, work visa.*

vis·age (VIZ·ij) *n.* facial appearance or aspect.

vis·aged (VIZ·ijd) *combining form.* faced: *grim-visaged, square-visaged, stern-visaged.*

vis-a-vis (vee·zuh·VEE) *prep.* considered in relation to something: *the great performance of our students vis-a-vis national averages.*
— *adj. & adv.* face-to-face: *They sat vis-a-vis; in a vis-a-vis position.*

vis·cer·a (VIS·uh·ruh) *n. pl.* internal organs, esp. the intestines.

vis·cer·al (VIS·uh·rul) *adj.* **1** of the viscera: *the visceral nervous system.* **2** instinctive or intuitive rather than intellectual; gut: *a visceral impact, quality, reaction.* — **vis·cer·al·ly** *adv.*

vis·cid (VIS·id) *adj.* viscous or sticky: *a viscid secretion; a viscid leaf (covered with something sticky).*

vis·cos·i·ty (vis·COS·uh·tee) *n.* **-ties** viscous quality: *motor oils of high and low viscosities.*

vis·count (VYE·cownt) *n.* a British peer ranking below an earl or count and above a baron; *fem.* **vis·count·ess.**

vis·cous (VIS·cus) *adj.* having a sticky or syrupy quality: *The more viscous a fluid the more slowly it flows, as pitch and molasses.*

vise (VICE) *n.* a device for firmly holding an object being worked on, consisting of parallel jaws closed and opened by a screw with a handle: *to be caught in a vise.*

vis·i·bil·i·ty (viz·uh·BIL·uh·tee) *n.* **-ties** a being visible or its condition, degree, range, etc.: *Visibility increases with height; zero visibility; poor visibility because of fog.*

vis·i·ble (VIZ·uh·bul) *adj.* that can be seen; apparent: *the visible spectrum; plainly visible; a vagrant with no visible means of support; a highly visible* (= conspicuous) *public figure;* **Visible minorities** *stand out from the general white population because of differences of colour, physical features, etc.* — **vis·i·bly** *adv.*

vis·ion (VIZH·un) *n.* **1** power of seeing or perceiving: *Have your vision tested; acute, blurred, double,*

impaired, peripheral, tunnel vision; the field of vision (= sight) of an optical instrument; a woman of great vision (= foresight or imagination); poetic vision.
2 something seen, esp. by the mind or imagination: a vision of heavenly glory; the beatific vision; The vision raised its head and spoke to us; The mystic heard voices and saw visions. — v. see in or as in a vision; envision.

vi·sion·ar·y (VIZH·uh·nair·ee) n. 1 one who sees visions. 2 a dreamer or impractical person.
— **adj.** fanciful and impractical: a visionary idea, scheme.

vis·it (VIZ·it) v. 1 go or come to see for pleasure: to visit Vancouver; to visit the zoo. 2 be a guest or stay with someone: to visit (with) relatives; The boss doesn't like too much visiting (= chatting) on the phone. 3 go or come to see officially or professionally, as a doctor, inspector, supervisor, etc. 4 afflict or inflict: Egypt was visited with plagues; the sufferings God visited on Job. — **n.** 1 a visiting: a flying (= very short) visit. 2 a stay as a guest. — **vis·it·a·ble** (-uh·bul) adj.

vis·i·tant (VIZ·uh·tunt) n. [rare & formal use] a visitor from another world: a ghostly visitant; heavenly visitant; a visitant from Mars.

vis·i·ta·tion (viz·uh·TAY·shun) n. 1 an official or formal visit, as for inspection. 2 reward or punishment sent by God.

visiting nurse n. a nurse whose work is visiting patients in their homes and who takes part in public-health projects.

vis·i·tor (VIZ·uh·tur) n. one who visits on business or for pleasure, as a tourist: a frequent visitor; regular visitor.

vi·sor (VYE·zur) n. a part that shields the face or eyes, as the movable front part of a helmet, a cap's brim, eyeshade, or a shade attached to a windshield for protection from glare; **adj.: a visored** helmet (= helmet with a visor).

vis·ta (VIS·tuh) n. 1 a long narrow view as between rows of trees. 2 an extended or comprehensive mental view or prospect: a discovery that opened up new vistas of knowledge.

vis·u·al (VIZH·oo·ul) adj. having to do with seeing or sight: visual impressions; visual education using **visual aids** such as films, charts, and slides; the **visual arts** of painting, sculpture, ceramics, etc.; 20/20 vision means normal **visual acuity** (= visual sharpness); **visual aphasia** of seeing without understanding words; a **visual binary** (= double) star that appears single to the unaided eye. — **vis·u·al·ly** adv.

vis·u·al·ize (VIZH·oo·uh·lize) v. -iz·es, -ized, -iz·ing form a mental picture of something abstract, forgotten, etc.: I can visualize her as a future prime minister. — **vis·u·al·iz·er** n.
— **vis·u·al·i·za·tion** (-luh·ZAY·shun) n.

vi·ta (VEE·tuh, VYE-) n., pl. **-tae** (VEE·tye, VYE·tee) a brief biography or curriculum vitae.

vi·tal (VYE·tul) adj. 1 having to do with life; important for life: The heart, lungs, liver, brain, etc. are vital organs; a vital (= lively) personality; a vital (= fatal) wound; the lung's **vital** (= inhaling) **capacity;** to check a patient's **vital signs** (= temperature, pulse, blood pressure, and respiration). 2 essential; very important:

one of the most vital issues of our time; Funds are vital to the success of our mission. — **vi·tal·ly** adv.

vi·tal·i·ty (vye·TAL·uh·tee) n. -ties 1 physical vigour; capacity to survive. 2 mental vigour or energy; liveliness.

vi·tal·ize (VYE·tul·ize) v. -iz·es, -ized, -iz·ing give life, vigour, or liveliness to something. — **vi·tal·iz·er** n.

vi·tals (VYE·tulz) n.pl. vital organs, parts, or elements.

vital statistics n.pl. 1 data about births, deaths, fertility, life expectancy, marriages, and divorce. 2 Informal. personal data such as measurements around one's body.

vi·ta·min (VYE·tuh·min) n. a complex organic substance essential to the body's health and growth which is supplied by foods and whose deficiency causes scurvy and other diseases.

vi·ti·ate (VISH·ee·ate) v. -ates, -at·ed, -at·ing make faulty, ineffective, etc.: the original text vitiated (= corrupted) by corrections and changes; A technicality could vitiate (= invalidate) a legal document.
— **vi·ti·a·tion** (-AY·shun) n.

vit·ri·ol (VIT·ree·ul) n. 1 sulphuric acid. 2 sharp or bitter feelings, criticism, etc.: He wrote a scathing letter with pen dipped in vitriol. — **vi·tri·ol·ic** (-OL·ic) adj.

vi·tu·per·ate (vye·TUE·puh·rate, vuh-) v. -ates, -at·ed, -at·ing abuse or revile. — **vi·tu·per·a·tive** (-ruh·tiv).
— **vi·tu·per·a·tion** (-RAY·shun) n.

vi·va·cious (vuh·VAY·shus) adj. lively and buoyant: a vivacious girl, youth.
— **vi·va·cious·ly** adv.; **vi·va·cious·ness** n.
— **vi·vac·i·ty** (-VAS·uh·tee) n.

viva vo·ce (VYE·vuh·VOH·see) adj. & adv. oral(ly): to vote viva voce; a viva voce examination.

viv·id (VIV·id) adj. 1 lively: a vivid description, imagination, personality. 2 brilliant or brightly coloured: painted in vivid colours; The sky was a vivid blue. 3 clear and distinct: a vivid memory, recollection. — **viv·id·ly** adv.; **viv·id·ness** n.

viv·i·fy (VIV·uh·fye) v. -fies, -fied, -fy·ing impart freshness or vitality to something: a vivifying lotion for the skin; to vivify the faded figures of an old painting. — **viv·i·fi·ca·tion** (-fuh·CAY·shun) n.

viv·i·sec·tion (viv·uh·SEC·shun) n. dissection of a living animal for study. — **viv·i·sec·tion·ist** n.
— **viv·i·sect** (VIV·uh·sect) v.

vix·en (VIX·un) n. 1 a female fox. 2 an ill-tempered woman.

viz. namely; that is.

viz·or (VYE·zur) n. same as VISOR.

vo·cab·u·lar·y (vuh·CAB·yuh·lair·ee) n. -lar·ies 1 a list of words, as in a glossary: A dictionary's **vocabulary entries** [shown in boldface in this dictionary] include words, idioms and phrases, derivatives, and inflections. 2 the stock of words used by a person ("active vocabulary") or only understood ("passive vocabulary"): how to develop, enlarge, improve your vocabulary. 3 the word stock of a language, words used in a branch of learning, profession, etc.: the expanding English vocabulary; scientific vocabulary. 4 a set of signs or symbols used in any sort of communication: the vocabulary (= movements) of ballet.

vo·cal (VOH·cul) *adj.* **1** having to do with voice: *the vocal organs of the throat and mouth; Two bands of tissue in the throat called **vocal cords** vibrate to produce sounds; vocal* (= sung, not instrumental) *music.* **2** having voice: *Be vocal* (= outspoken) *about your grievances.*
— *n.* **1** a vocal sound, as a vowel. **2** a vocal solo.
— **vo·cal·ly** *adv.*

vo·cal·ic (voh·CAL·ic) *adj.* having to do with a vowel or vowels.

vo·cal·ist (VOH·cuh·list) *n.* a singer, not an instrumentalist.

vo·cal·ize (VOH·cuh·lize) *v.* **-iz·es, -ized, -iz·ing** use the voice or utter; speak, sing, or shout.
— **vo·cal·i·za·tion** (-luh·ZAY·shun) *n.*

vo·ca·tion (voh·CAY·shun) *n.* **1** the occupation, profession, or trade in which one works: *We think of a career when choosing a vocation.* **2** an occupation one is specially suited or feels called to: *She seems to have missed her vocation – she should have become a lawyer; a vocation to religious life.* — **vo·ca·tion·al** *adj.*

vo·cif·er·ous (vuh·SIF·uh·rus) *adj.* noisy, unrestrained, and vehement: *a vociferous group; They were vociferous in their demands; the silent majority and the vociferous minority (of a population).* — **vo·cif·er·ous·ly** *adv.*

vod·ka (VOD·kuh) *n.* an unflavoured alcoholic liquor distilled from potatoes, rye, barley, etc.

vogue (VOHG) *n.* **1** fashion or popularity at a particular time: *Minis were in vogue in the early 1970s; Fashions come into and go out of vogue.* **2** something that is in fashion: *the latest vogue in swimwear; Minis are becoming the vogue again; when skate-boarding was all the vogue* (= rage); *"input," "interface," "phase out," and such vogue words of the electronic age.* **3** the period of popularity of a vogue. — **vo·guish** *adj.*

voice *n.* **1** a sound communicating thoughts or feelings, esp. of a person speaking, crying, etc.: *The human voice is a highly developed form of the animal cry; She has temporarily lost her voice because of laryngitis; to drop, lower, raise one's voice; She spoke in a clear, firm, gentle, gruff, loud, shaking, subdued, trembling voice; He shouted at the top of his voice; to give voice* (= expression) *to one's frustration; A singer is not in voice* (= proper condition to sing) *till she is well again; Listen to the voice of reason; an inner voice* (= conscience); *the people's voice* (= right to be heard) *in a democracy; a measure approved by the legislators with one voice* (= unanimously). **2** a singer, as in a choir, or the part of a musical composition for one singer or instrument. **3** the active or passive form of a verb.
— *v.* **voic·es, voiced, voic·ing** give expression to in spoken or written form: *He voiced his strong disapproval.*
— **voiced** *combining form.* having voice as specified: *deep-voiced, gravelly-voiced, soft-voiced, sweet-voiced.*

voice box *n.* **1** the voice-producing organ at the top of the windpipe. **2** a voice output device of a computer: *By attaching a voice box to a computer, the blind can hear what they type.*

voice mail *n.* an electronic system of receiving, transmitting, and responding to voice messages, as used in registering students for courses by telephone.

voice-over (VOICE·oh·vur) *n.* a narration or announcement without the speaker being shown, as in TV and motion pictures.

voice·print *n.* a recorded pattern of sound waves characteristic of a person's voice, used like the fingerprint for identification purposes.

void *n.* **1** an empty space. **2** emptiness or a gap: *The death of their only child left a void in their hearts; To fill the void they decided to adopt a child.*
— *adj.* **1** empty or vacant: *void space; language that is void of* (= without) *meaning.* **2** legally invalid: *a contract declared null and void; a void ballot, parking ticket.*
— *v.* **1** make empty or void. **2** empty out or evacuate the bladder. — **void·a·ble** *adj.* — **void·er** *n.*

voi·là (vwah·LAH) *interj. French.* behold! there!

vol·a·tile (VOL·uh·tile, -tul) *adj.* **1** easily changing into vapour at a relatively low temperature, as gasoline or alcohol. **2** easily changeable in condition or mood; fickle: *a volatile crowd; the volatile gasoline market; volatile public opinion; a volatile temper (that is quick to anger).* — **vol·a·til·i·ty** (-TIL·uh·tee) *n.*

vol·can·ic (vol·CAN·ic) *adj.* **1** of or like a volcano: *a volcanic eruption; crystalline volcanic rock formed by cooled lava; volcanic glass formed by rapid cooling of lava.* **2** violent and explosive: *a volcanic temperament.*

vol·ca·no (vol·CAY·noh) *n.* **-nos** or **-noes 1** a funnel-shaped crater spewing lava, ashes, and gases. **2** a cone-shaped mountain with a volcanic crater: *A volcano erupts; an active, dormant, extinct volcano.*

vo·li·tion (vuh·LISH·un) *n.* an act of the will or the power of willing: *She did it of her own volition; He acted on his own volition.* — **vo·li·tion·al** *adj.*

vol·ley (VOL·ee) *n.* **1** the simultaneous discharge of many weapons: *to fire a volley.* **2** a shower of missiles: *a volley of cheers, oaths, questions, shots.* **3** in tennis, etc., a return of the ball before it hits the playing surface: *to hit a ball on the volley.*
— *v.* **vol·leys, vol·leyed, vol·ley·ing 1** discharge or be discharged as in a volley. **2** return a ball in play, before it hits the ground.

vol·ley·ball (VOL·ee·bawl) *n.* a team game played by hitting an inflated ball with the hands back and forth over a high net without letting it touch the ground; also, the ball.

volt *n.* the SI unit of electromotive force.
— **volt·age** (-tij) *n.: to step down, step up (the) voltage.*

volte-face (volt·FAHS) *n.* an about-face in policy, attitude, etc.

vol·u·ble (VOL·yoo·bul) *adj.* talking much and unendingly. — **vol·u·bly** *adv.*
— **vol·u·bil·i·ty** (-BIL·uh·tee) *n.*

vol·ume (VOL·yum) *n.* **1** cubic capacity or the solid content of something three-dimensional: *A two-centimetre cube has a volume of 8 cubic centimetres.* **2** quantity: *volumes of smoke; the daily volume of output; to turn down, turn up the volume* (= sound) *of the radio.* **3** a bound book or one of a series: *a volume of 300 pages; a dictionary in two volumes; a rare volume of Shakespeare's plays; a workbook as a companion volume to the textbook.*
— **speak volumes** be very expressive: *His look of disgust spoke volumes; a small book that speaks volumes for her scholarly attainments.*

vo·lu·mi·nous (vuh·LOO·muh·nus) *adj.* large in content, output, size, etc.: *his voluminous output; a voluminous treatise, writer.* — **vo·lu·mi·nous·ly** *adv.*

vol·un·tar·y (VOL·un·tair·ee) *adj.* done of one's own free will or by choice: *the voluntary contributions and services supporting a voluntary* (= not state-supported) *church or school; Walking, talking, etc. are voluntary actions carried out by use of voluntary* (= will-controlled) *muscles; The company went into voluntary bankruptcy to be free of debts and start afresh.*
— *n.* solo organ music, as played at a church service.
— **vol·un·tar·i·ly** (-TAIR·uh·lee) *adv.*

vol·un·teer (vol·un·TEER) *n.* **1** a person who is in military service of his own free will. **2** one who offers to work for free: *candy stripers, charity collectors, and other volunteers; adj.: a volunteer firefighter, helper.*
— *v.* be an unpaid worker: *to volunteer for the army; Neighbours volunteered to help; She volunteered her services as a language tutor.*

vo·lup·tu·ous (vuh·LUP·choo·us) *adj.* having to do with sensual pleasure: *voluptuous fancies, music; a voluptuous* (= big and sexy) *figure.*

vom·it (VOM·it) *v.* discharge with force from within, as the contents of the stomach through the mouth; throw up: *Do not induce vomiting but call the doctor.*
— *n.* a vomiting or what is vomited: *The patient choked on his own vomit.*

voo·doo (VOO·doo) *n.* **-doos 1** sorcery as practised by some African tribes and some West Indians, including the cult of guardian spirits and the indirect injuring of enemies by sticking pins into images of wax. **2** one who practises voodoo. **3** a charm or fetish used in voodoo.

vo·ra·cious (vuh·RAY·shus) *adj.* devouring or insatiable: *a voracious appetite, reader, shark.*
— **vo·ra·cious·ly** *adv.;* **vo·ra·cious·ness** *n.*
— **vo·rac·i·ty** (vuh·RAS·uh·tee) *n.*

vor·tex (VOR·tex) *n.* **-tex·es** or **-ti·ces** (-tuh·seez) **1** a whirling phenomenon or formation such as a whirlpool, a whirlwind, or the eye of a cyclone. **2** a vortexlike situation or condition: *the vortex of war; drawn into the vortex of the struggle; sucked into the vortex of politics.*

vo·ta·ry (VOH·tuh·ree) *n.* **-ries** a devout worshipper or devoted follower; devotee: *a votary of peace, yoga, Zeus.*

vote *n.* **1** a choice, as between candidates for office, or a formal expression of it, as by ballot: *to put a question to the vote; to take a vote on the question; to influence, swing the vote in our favour.* **2** the right to vote: *Children have no vote; Women got the vote only recently.* **3** a ballot: *to cast a vote; In a tie, the chair casts the deciding vote; He switched his vote at the last moment in favour of the other party; an influential politician who can deliver the votes; It was a close vote; a straw vote; a motion carried by a unanimous vote; elected by a voice vote.* **4** a majority expression of feeling: *a vote of thanks; a **vote of confidence** in a government.* **5** votes collectively: *The rain didn't help to get out the vote; The vote was light, not heavy; the Jewish vote; the Liberal vote; the undecided vote; to count, tally the vote after balloting.*
— *v.* **votes, vot·ed, vot·ing 1** give a vote to someone: *He votes for the Liberals; She voted against the bill;* [U.S. usage] *He votes the Republican ticket.* **2** decide, ratify, etc. by vote: *to vote a candidate to Parliament; to vote by a show of hands; to **vote down** (= defeat) a bill instead of voting it through the legislature; to **vote in** (= elect) a candidate to office; to **vote out** (= defeat) an incumbent mayor; The function was voted* (= judged) *a success.* — **vot·er** *n.*

vo·tive (VOH·tiv) *adj.* having to do with the fulfilment of a vow or thanksgiving for a divine favour: *a votive candle, offering, pilgrimage, prayer, shrine.*

vouch (VOWCH) *v.* give a guarantee or serve as evidence *for* the truth of a statement, someone's qualities, etc.: *She's telling the truth and I can vouch for it.*

vouch·er (VOW·chur) *n.* one that vouches, esp. a document or other piece of evidence of a business transaction, as a cancelled cheque, coupon, etc.

vow *n.* a solemn promise, esp. to God: *to break, make, take, violate a vow; She kept her vows all her life; to renew marriage vows (of fidelity); A nun **takes vows** (usually of poverty, chastity, and obedience).*
— *v.* make a vow: *to vow obedience, revenge, secrecy; He has vowed never to touch alcohol.*

vow·el (VOW·ul) *n.* **1** a vocal sound made with more or less open mouth and no obstruction of breath as in forming consonants: *short and long vowels.* **2** a letter such as "a," "e," "i," "o," and "u" representing such a sound.

voy·age (VOY·ij) *n.* a relatively long journey by water, air, or in space: *to go on a voyage around the world; a voyage of exploration; a voyage to the moon; The Titanic sank on her maiden voyage.*
— *v.* **-ag·es, -aged, -ag·ing** make a voyage: *The Vikings voyaged across the ocean and settled in Newfoundland around A.D. 1000.* — **voy·ag·er** *n.*

voy·a·geur (vwah·yah·ZHUR) *n. Cdn.* a French Canadian boatman, esp. one who worked for a fur-trading company.

voy·eur (vwah·YUR) *n.* one who gets sexual pleasure from secretly watching others undressing or having sex; peeping Tom. — **vo·yeur·ism** *n.*
— **vo·yeur·is·tic** (-yuh·RIS·tic) *adj.*

vroom *n.* the roaring sound of a speeding car.

vul·gar (VUL·gur) *adj.* **1** showing lack of refinement or good taste: *a vulgar expression; vulgar language, manners; vulgar ambition; a vulgar display of wealth.* **2** of the common people or general public: *vulgar errors, superstitions; the vulgar masses.*
— **vul·gar·ly** *adv.*

vul·gar·i·an (vul·GAIR·ee·un) *n.* a vulgar person, esp. one who is rich.

vul·gar·ism (VUL·guh·riz·um) *n.* **1** a coarse or uneducated expression, as "irregardless." **2** vulgarity.

vul·gar·i·ty (vul·GAIR·uh·tee) *n.* **-ties 1** the quality or condition of being vulgar. **2** a vulgar or coarse action, habit, or usage.

vul·gar·ize (VUL·guh·rize) *v.* **-iz·es, -ized, -iz·ing 1** make common, popular, etc. **2** debase or degrade.
— **vul·gar·iz·er** *n.*
— **vul·gar·i·za·tion** (-ruh·ZAY·shun) *n.*

vul·ner·a·ble (VUL·nuh·ruh·bul) *adj.* **1** that can be wounded: *The heel was Achilles' vulnerable spot.* **2** open to attack: *a vulnerable argument, position; when you are young and vulnerable; Politicians are vulnerable to public criticism.* — **vul·ner·a·bly** *adv.*
— **vul·ner·a·bil·i·ty** (-ruh·BIL·uh·tee) *n.*

vul·ture (VUL·chur) *n.* **1** a large, carrion-eating bird of prey of the same family as buzzards and condors. **2** a greedy or ruthless person.

vying *pres. part.* of VIE.

W or **w** (DUB·ul·yoo) *n.* **W's** or **w's** the 23rd letter of the English alphabet.

wab·ble (WOB·ul) *v.* **wab·bles, wab·bled, wab·bling** same as WOBBLE. — **wab·bler** *n.*

wack·o (WACK·oh) *n. & adj. Slang.* (one) who is wacky or eccentric.

wack·y (WACK·ee) *adj.* **wack·i·er, -i·est** *Slang.* eccentric or unconventional in behaviour.

wad (WOD) *n.* a small lump of soft material: *a wad of cotton to plug the ears; a wad of chewing tobacco, of gum; a wad* (= disc) *of felt used in a shotgun cartridge; a wad* (*Slang* for large bundle) *of money.*
— *v.* **wads, wad·ded, wad·ding 1** press or roll up into a wad. **2** to plug with a wad or soft material (**wadding**).

wad·dle (WOD·ul) *v.* **wad·dles, wad·dled, wad·dling** walk with short steps, swaying from side to side, as a duck or penguin. — *n.* such a gait. — **wad·dler** *n.*

wade *v.* **wades, wad·ed, wad·ing 1** walk through a medium such as water, snow, or mud that hinders free movement: *A **wading bird** such as a crane is a shore bird with long legs and bill; A **wading pool** is for children to have fun in.* **2** make one's way *through* dull reading, etc. with difficulty.
— **wade into** attack someone. — *n.* a wading.

wad·er (WAY·dur) *n.* **1** one that wades, as a wading bird. **2 waders** *pl.* a waterproof garment with attached boots, as used by fishermen.

wa·fer (WAY·fur) *n.* **1** a thin, crisp cracker, as used in the Eucharist. **2** an adhesive seal. **3** a disk of silicon carrying an integrated circuit.

waf·fle (WOF·ul) *n.* a batter cake made on a waffle iron.
— *v.* **waf·fles, waf·fled, waf·fling** be vague or indecisive.

waffle iron *n.* a metal utensil with two hinged plates between which a waffle is cooked.

waft (WAFT, WOFT) *v.* move or carry lightly by or as by a breeze or wave: *A delicious aroma wafted in from the kitchen.*
— *n.* **1** an odour or sound thus carried. **2** a slight breeze or wafting movement.

wag *v.* **wags, wagged, wag·ging** shake or swing back and forth, up and down, etc., as a dog's tail: *A scandal makes tongues wag* (= makes people gossip).

— *n.* **1** a wagging. **2** a joker or jester. — **wag·gish** *adj.*

wage *n.* periodic compensation paid for work, esp. manual or physical; also **wag·es** *pl.: to draw, earn, pay a wage; a decent, living, minimum, weekly wage; to freeze wages; Her wages were $500 a week; the minimum wage (rate) fixed by government; "The wages* (= punishment) *of sin is death"; **adj.:** Executives are at a higher wage level; inflationary wage and price increases; the **wage earners** of a family.*
— *v.* **wag·es, waged, wag·ing** carry on a war, battle, campaign, etc. against an adversary: *an aid program to wage war against hunger.*

wag·er (WAY·jur) *n. & v.* bet or gamble: *to lay, make, place a wager; to wager whether a fight will last 15 rounds; She wagered (him) $50 that it won't; to wager money on a horse.*

wag·ger·y (WAG·uh·ree) *n.* **wag·ger·ies** a joke or the act of joking.

wag·on (WAG·un) *n.* **1** a four-wheeled vehicle or cart for hauling loads: *a covered wagon.* **2** a station wagon or truck: *a police paddy wagon or patrol wagon; welcome wagon.*
— **on the wagon** *Slang.* abstaining from alcoholic liquor, formerly "to go on the water wagon."
— **wag·on·er** *n.*

wagon train *n.* a caravan of wagons on a journey.

waif *n.* **1** a homeless or neglected child. **2** a stray animal or something discarded: *waifs and strays.*

wail *n.* a loud and long cry of grief, pain, or hunger.
— *v.* make a wail: *the wailing of an ambulance siren; the **Wailing Wall** of Jerusalem at which Jews pray and seek consolation.*

wain·scot *n.* **1** wood panelling on the interior wall of a room, esp. on its lower part. **2** the lower part of an interior wall finished differently from the top.
— *v.* **-scots, -scot·ted** or **-scot·ed, -scot·ting** or **-scot·ing** line a wall with wood.

waist *n.* **1** the usually narrow part of the abdomen just above the hips: *a slim waist; her wasp waist.* **2** a similar narrowed middle part of a violin. **3** the bodice or blouse of a dress.

waist·line *n.* **1** the line of the waist or the measurement around it, as showing size. **2** the dividing line between the bodice and skirt of a dress, usually at the waist.

wait *v.* **1** stay expecting something; continue in a place

for a time: *Please wait for the next bus; wait till 12; Don't keep the child waiting; a matter so urgent it can't wait; Don't wait up for me; She had to wait (Informal for delay) dinner for him; Join the line and wait your turn.* **2** serve: *Waiters wait at or on tables; Waiters wait table; Store clerks wait on or upon* (= attend to) *customers.*
— *n.* a waiting or its duration: *The long wait seemed like an eternity.*
— **lie in wait for** stay concealed, ready to attack someone.

wait·er *n.* a man or boy who serves customers seated at tables as in a restaurant.

waiting game *n.* the strategy of waiting till one has an advantage over the opposite side or party.

waiting list *n.* a list of people waiting to obtain something: *We were on a waiting list for concert tickets.*

wait·ress (WAIT·ris) *n.* a female waiter.

waive *v.* **waives, waived, waiv·ing 1** give up legally: *to waive a claim, right; He waived custody (of his children) in favour of generous visiting rights.* **2** defer, dispense with, or dismiss: *to waive the formalities, rules; a problem you can't waive away.*

waiv·er *n.* a waiving of a right or claim or a document to that effect: *to sign a waiver.*

wake *v.* **wakes,** *pt.* **woke** or **waked,** *pp.* **waked** or **wo·ken, wak·ing** awaken or rouse: *Please wake me when you wake up; Hibernating animals can wake themselves up; She woke to the sound of sirens; She was quick to wake up to* (= realize) *the danger.*
— *n.* **1** a watch or vigil, as over a dead body before burial: *to hold a wake; An Irish wake is followed by feasting.* **2** the track left in the water by a moving craft: *The war brought famine in its wake* (= following it); *In the wake of the war came famine and disease.*

wake·ful *adj.* **1** sleepless or restless. **2** watchful or alert.
— **wake·ful·ly** *adv.;* **wake·ful·ness** *n.*

wak·en (WAY·kun) *v.* to wake.

walk (WAWK) *v.* **1** go on foot without running: *She walks to school; Don't walk on the grass; The ghost may walk* (= appear) *tonight; a lady walking* (= out with) *her dog; Ray walks (through) the streets exploring the city; He walked* (= accompanied) *his date home; People walked by as if they didn't notice it; The workers walked off the job in a wildcat strike.* **2** conduct oneself: *to walk in peace; Walk in the ways of the Lord; They walked all over us* (*Slang for* treated us badly). **3** in baseball, allow a runner or batter a base after four balls.
— **walk away from** escape unhurt from an accident.
— **walk off** or **away with 1** win easily. **2** steal.
— **walk out** go on strike or quit suddenly.
— **walk out on** *Informal.* desert someone, as a spouse, who is close or has a right to be taken care of.
— **walk the plank** be forced to kill oneself, as the crew of a ship captured by pirates made to jump overboard from a plank.
— *n.* **1** a walking, as for exercise; stroll or hike: *Let's go for a walk; to take a walk around the park; Take a walk* (*Slang for* Go away)! *It's an hour's walk* (= walking distance) *to town.* **2** one's manner of walking: *You can recognize him from his walk.* **3** a place for walking, as a

path laid out in a park: *a scenic walk; a letter carrier's walk* (= route); *a church group that represents people of all walks of life* (= all economic, ethnic, and social groups). **4** in baseball, a going to first base on four balls. — **walk·er** *n.: a tightrope walker.*

walk·a·bout (WAWK·uh·bowt) *n.* a stroll by a public figure for meeting and chatting with people.

walk·a·way (WAWK·uh·way) *n.* an easy victory; walkover.

walk·ie-talk·ie (WAWK·ee·TAWK·ee) *n.* a small, portable radio transmitter-receiver.

walk-in *n.* *Informal.* a sure win.
— *adj.* **1** that may be walked into: *a large walk-in closet, refrigerator, safe.* **2** that may be visited without an appointment: *a walk-in clinic, zoo.*

walking papers *n. pl. Informal.* dismissal from a job or similar position.

walking stick *n.* a stick or cane used in walking.

walk-on *n.* **1** in a dramatic production, a bit part that involves little speaking. **2** an actor playing such a part.

walk-out *n.* **1** a leaving of a meeting or organization as a mark of protest. **2** a work stoppage by employees; strike.

walk-over *n. Informal.* an easy victory.

walk·up *n.* **1** a building without an elevator, usually only a few stories high. **2** an apartment in such a building.

walk·way *n.* a passage for walking.

wall (WAWL) *n.* **1** an upright enclosing, dividing, or protective structure of stone, wood, etc., as of a house: *to build, climb, erect, put up, scale, tear down a wall; a wall lined with bookshelves; a brick, retaining, supporting wall; the wall between two rooms; the Great Wall of China.* **2** a side of a room or hollow structure: *the muscular wall of the stomach; a tire with white walls.*
— **off the wall** *Slang.* unorthodox or off the cuff: *His views are really off the wall.*
— **up the wall** *Slang.* in an extreme or desperate situation: *His behaviour really drives me up the wall* (= drives me crazy).
— **with one's back to the wall** in a desperate situation.
— *v.* to close, cover, or surround with or as if with a wall: *to wall off a part of the house; to wall up an unused fireplace; a walled-in garden.* — **walled** *adj.*

wall·board *n.* a large sheet moulded of wood fibre, plaster and paper, or asbestos and cement for covering walls and ceilings.

wal·let (WOL·ut, WAWL·ut) *n.* a pocketbook for carrying paper money, cards, etc.

wall hanging *n.* a decoration hung on a wall.

wall·flow·er (WALL·flow·er) *n. Informal.* a woman who is too shy or not attractive enough as a dancing partner.

wal·lop (WOL·up) *v. Informal.* to hit very hard: *They were walloped* (= defeated) *in the third round.*
— *n. Informal.* **1** a very hard blow. **2** walloping power; force or vigour: *a small-town weekly that packs the wallop of a national newspaper; the wallop of a hard-hitting editorial.*

— **walloping** *n., adj. & adv.: He got a good walloping; Sam told us a walloping (big) lie.*

wal·low (WOL·oh) *v.* roll oneself about: *Hogs wallow in mud; People wallow* (= indulge excessively) *in luxury, misery, wealth.*
— *n.* a wallowing or a place of mud or dust in which animals wallow.

wall·pa·per (WALL·pay·pur) *n.* coloured decorative paper to put on walls: *to hang wallpaper.*
— *v.* cover or paste with wallpaper.

Wall Street *n.* **1** the financial centre of the U.S. in New York with major banks, the Stock Exchange, etc. **2** U.S. financiers collectively.

wall-to-wall *adj.* extending from one end to the other: *wall-to-wall carpeting, people; a day filled with wall-to-wall appointments.*

wal·rus (WALL·rus, WOL-) *n.* a large seal-like mammal with two tusks growing downward from the mouth: *A* **walrus mustache** *hangs down at the ends.*

waltz (WAULTS) *n.* **1** a gliding ballroom dance in ¾ time. **2** the music for it.
— *v.* **1** dance a waltz: *a couple waltzing at the Moulin Rouge.* **2** move easily, nimbly, or successfully: *She waltzed through customs.*

wam·pum (WOM·pum) *n.* beads of shell often strung together, once used as money by North American Indians.

wan (rhyme: "on") *adj.* **wan·ner, wan·nest** pale or emaciated, as from illness: *a wan expression, look, smile.* — **wan·ly** *adv.;* **wan·ness** *n.*

wand (WOND) *n.* **1** a slender rod, as used by a magician; baton; also, a staff of authority or sceptre: *to wave a magic wand.* **2** a tool or implement: *a wand used in optical scanning of price tags; the cleaning wand (as a vacuum cleaner's) that is moved back and forth over a surface.*

wan·der ("wan-" rhymes with "on") *v.* **1** move about in an aimless manner. **2** stray or meander: *a wandering tribe; to wander from the path of virtue; a mind that wanders from one thing to another; the wandering course of a river; The child wandered away from the group.* — **wan·der·er** *n.*

wan·der·lust (WON·dur·lust) *n.* the urge to travel or wander.

wane *v.* **wanes, waned, wan·ing** **1** become smaller after reaching fullness: *the waxing and waning of the moon.* **2** decline in intensity, power, influence, etc.; become weaker: *His influence over the party has waned over the years.*
— *n.: His influence is* **on the wane** (= is declining).

wan·gle (WANG·gul) *v.* **-gles, -gled, -gling** *Informal.* manage to get by influence, manipulation, persuasion, etc.: *to wangle an invitation out of someone.*

wan·i·gan (WON·uh·gun) *n. Cdn.* a container, cabin, or conveyance of pioneer days, as a storage chest, caboose, van, or houseboat.

want (WAHNT, WAUNT, WUNT) *v.* **1** to desire or wish for something worth having or needed: *He wants a new car very badly; The child did not feel wanted by his classmates; a suspect wanted by police; He's wanted for* murder and robbery; He is on the "most wanted" list; The dog wants out (Informal for wants to get out); She wants out of her contract.* **2** to lack; need; require: *The shirt wants a button; "Waste not, want not"* (= Do not waste, and you won't be lacking in life's necessities); *A contented man* **wants for nothing** (= has everything he needs).
— *n.* desire or need: *Does advertising create wants* (= desires) *or help supply needs? an invention that meets a long-felt want* (= need); *to fill, satisfy, supply a want; to minister to the wants of the poor and needy; to buy a second-rate product* **for want of** (= lacking) *a better one; an unemployed man in want* (= need) *of a job; Welfare is for people* **in want** (= extreme poverty or lack of food, shelter, clothing, etc.).

want ad *n. Informal.* a brief advertisement for an employee, service, goods, etc. wanted by someone.

wanting *adj.* lacking in some essential: *Students found* **wanting in** *math are not promoted.*
— *prep.* lacking: *a shirt wanting a button; a year wanting* (= minus) *a day.*

wan·ton (WAHN·tun, WAUN·tun) *adj.* **1** lacking in restraint; frolicsome: *a wanton child; wanton winds; fruit and flowers in wanton profusion; a wanton* (= loose) *woman; wanton* (= sensual) *thoughts.* **2** unprovoked; unjustified: *a wanton attack, insult; wanton cruelty, damage, disregard, mischief.*
— *n.* a morally loose woman.
— *v.* **1** behave licentiously *with* another. **2** squander.
— **wan·ton·ly** *adv.;* **wan·ton·ness** *n.*

wap·i·ti (WOP·uh·tee) *n.* the North American elk with many-pronged antlers and a whitish rump.

war (WOR) *n.* **1** an open, armed, prolonged conflict, as between nations: *the art of war; the strategy, tactics, and logistics of war; England was at war or in a state of war with France; the war between England and France; to ban, make, outlaw war; to wage war against or with the enemy; to declare war on the enemy; to go to war over a disputed territory; to conduct, end, escalate, fight, lose, win a war; an all-out, atomic, civil, cold, gang, limited, nuclear, price, world war; a war of aggression, attrition, nerves; A war breaks out, rages, spreads; In the end, they lost the war though they won a few battles.* **2** any struggle: *a national program of war on poverty.*
— *adj.: The* **war baby** *boom* (= sudden increase in births after World War II) *put a severe strain on schools; War clouds gather on the horizon; war dead* (= people in

the military killed in war); *a war effort, hero; war hysteria; a war machine* (= military resources for waging a war); *a war memorial* (= monument to war dead).
— *v.* **wars, warred, war·ring** be in conflict; fight: *to war with* or *against neighbours; to war over a tiny piece of land.*

war·ble (WOR·bul) *v.* **-bles, -bled, -bling** sing a song with trills, quavers, etc., as a songbird, esp. a warbler.
— *n.* **1** a warbling song or sound. **2** a painful swelling under an animal's skin, as caused by the larva of a fly called "warble fly."

war·bler (WOR·blur) *n.* a small, active, insect-eating bird.

war chest *n.* a fund to support a political campaign, protracted strike, etc.

war crime *n.* a violation of international rules of warfare, as genocide, inhumane treatment of prisoners, etc.

war cry *n.* a slogan or rallying cry used in fighting for a cause.

-ward or **-wards** *adj. & adv. suffix.* in the direction specified: *backward(s), earthward, homeward, toward(s).*

ward (rhyme: "lord") *v.* usually **ward off 1** turn aside: *to ward off a blow, weapon.* **2** keep away: *to ward off danger, evil, enemies.*
— *n.* **1** an administrative division of a municipality, prison, hospital, etc.: *the children's ward of a hospital; emergency ward; maternity ward.* **2** one under the care of a guardian or law court: *a ward of the Crown.* **3** guardianship or custody.

war dance *n.* a dance formerly performed by North American Indians when preparing for war or celebrating a victory.

war·den (WOR·dun) *n.* **1** an administrative official in charge of a prison ("prison warden"), one enforcing fire regulations ("fire warden") or game laws ("game warden"), one governing a school or hospital in the U.K., etc. **2** *Cdn.* the head of a county council, as in Quebec. **3** a churchwarden.

ward·er *n.* a watchman or guard.

ward heeler *n. Informal.* a hanger-on of a political boss in a ward or riding.

ward·robe *n.* **1** one's collection or stock of clothes: *I needed a whole new wardrobe for my African tour.* **2** a cabinet or closet for clothes.

ward·ship *n.* guardianship.

ware *n.* **1** usually **wares** *pl.* manufactured articles for sale. **2** pottery.
— *combining form.* specified kind of goods: *courseware, firmware, hardware, ironware, lessonware, liveware* (= personnel), *software.*

ware·house *n.* a building or room where goods for sale are stored.
— *v.* **-hous·es, -housed, -hous·ing** store in a warehouse.

war·fare *n.* **1** the waging of a war: *atomic, biological, chemical, conventional, germ, guerrilla, jungle, psychological, trench warfare.* **2** struggle or conflict.

war game *n.* a simulated military exercise for studying tactics.

war·head *n.* the explosive-containing front part of a torpedo or other missile: *a nuclear warhead.*

war·i·ly (WAIR·uh·lee) *adv.* in a wary manner.
— **war·i·ness** *n.*

war·like *adj.* **1** having to do with war: *warlike music, supplies.* **2** bellicose: *a warlike demonstration, people.*

war·lock *n.* a sorcerer or wizard.

war·lord *n.* a military commander-in-chief with supreme power over a region, as in China between 1912 and 1928.

warm (rhyme: "form") *adj.* **1** having or providing comfortable heat; not cold: *a warm fire, room; a warm-air heating system; warm clothing; warm colours such as red, orange, and yellow.* **2** somewhat hot: *He's warm from running; a warm* (= heated) *discussion; a hunting dog on a warm* (= fresh) *scent; pursuing a warm lead; getting warm* (= close to the subject sought); *He quit his job when they made it warm* (*Informal* for unpleasant) *for him.* **3** marked by sympathy and cordiality: *a warm smile, welcome.*
— *v.* make or become warm: *to warm up a room.*
— **warm to 1** become more enthusiastic about a subject, task, etc. as one proceeds with it. **2** become friendly or sympathetic to a person; also **warm toward** or **warm up** to someone.
— **warm up** loosen one's muscles, etc. before a physical activity: *exercises for warming up before jogging.*
— **warm·ish** *adj.;* **warm·ly** *adv.*

warm-blood·ed (WARM·blud·id) *adj.* having a body temperature that does not vary with the environment, as mammals and birds; not cold-blooded.

warmed-over *adj.* **1** of foods, stale but reheated. **2** not fresh or new: *Bits of warmed-over Canadian content were used to Canadianize the publication.*

warm·heart·ed (WARM·har·tid) *adj.* cordial; sympathetic. — **warm·heart·ed·ness** *n.*

war·mon·ger (WOR·mung·gur, -mong·gur) *n.* one who likes to stir up wars.

warmth *n.* the quality or state of being warm.

warm-up *n.* **1** a warming up using exercises before starting a physical activity. **2** the idling of an engine till normal operating efficiency is reached.

warn (WORN) *v.* give advance notice to someone against a danger or penalty: *They warned us of* or *about* or *against the risks of hitchhiking; warned us not to hitchhike; warned us that it is risky to hitchhike; a sign posted to* **warn off** *trespassers.*

warning *adj.* that warns: *a red warning light; warning signal.*
— *n.* something that warns: *The red light serves as a warning to drivers to stop; The accident occurred without warning; Let it be a warning to all of us; to give, issue, send out a warning; a storm warning.*

warp (WORP) *v.* **1** twist or bend out of shape, as a wooden board out of its plane when drying. **2** distort or deform: *Plywood doesn't warp easily; a mind warped by prejudices.*

— **n. 1** a twist or distortion, as in a wooden board because of shrinkage. **2** the lengthwise threads, crossed by the woof or weft, in a woven fabric or in a loom.

war paint n. Slang. cosmetics or makeup.

war·path n. the route taken by a North American Indian group going to war.
— **on the warpath** setting out for battle or in a fighting mood: to go on the warpath against tax hikes; women on the warpath.

war·rant (WOR·unt) n. **1** official or legal authorization; also, justification or reasonable grounds: acted without warrant. **2** a document such as a legal writ authorizing an arrest, search, etc.: The police officer swore out a warrant against her; The court issued a warrant; The warrant was served on the landlady; A warrant is out for her arrest; a bench warrant; He has virtually signed his own death warrant. **3** a voucher for payment. **4** a certificate of appointment issued to a noncommissioned military officer, or **warrant officer.**
— **v. 1** justify: a conclusion that is warranted by the evidence. **2** guarantee or assure: a diamond warranted to be genuine; I'll warrant (you) she'll keep her word.

war·ran·ty (WOR·un·tee) n. **-ties** a guarantee of the quality of a product or service: a one-year warranty on a new car against manufacturing defects; a limited two-year warranty on the power train; a lifetime extended warranty at extra cost; a car that is still under warranty after three years; no implied warranties; Our car broke down the day after the warranty expired or ran out.

war·ren (WOR·un) n. **1** a system of burrows inhabited by rabbits: The basement of the building is a warren of offices; a warren of underground passages. **2** a crowded tenement or slum area.

war·ri·or (WOR·ee·ur) n. a soldier or fighter experienced in battle.

wart (WORT) n. **1** a small, hard growth on the skin, caused by a virus. **2** a similar bulge on a plant.
— **warts and all** exposing even blemishes: The book describes his hero, warts and all; a warts-and-all portrait. — **wart·y** adj.

war·time n. the duration of a war: measures taken in or during wartime; **adj.:** wartime efforts, emergencies, horrors, measures, propaganda, sufferings.

war·y (WAIR·ee) adj. **war·i·er, -i·est** careful or cautious, as if suspicious of danger or trouble: a fox's wary movements; He kept a wary eye for muggers; He was even **wary of** strangers at that time of night.
— **war·i·ly** adv.

was (WOZ, WUZ, wuz) 1st and 3rd person sing. pt. of BE.

wash (WOSH) v. **1** clean with water or other liquid: to wash the dishes after dinner; He shaves and washes (himself) in the morning; to **wash up** (hands and face) before dinner; a stain you can **wash out** (= remove) with soap and water; a fabric that washes (= can be cleaned, esp. without damage) well in cold water; an excuse that won't wash (Informal for is too weak). **2** wet, flow over, or cover with a liquid: a deck washed by waves. **3** move by the force of water: houses washed away by a flood; He was washed overboard during the storm; He likes to **wash down** his meals with cola.

— **washed up** Informal. **1** exhausted: He's all washed up at age 30. **2** finished: After the scandal, she was washed up as a vote getter.
— **n. 1** a washing or being washed: the wash of the waves on the beach; a car wash. **2** what is washed or to be washed, as laundry: the weekly wash; to hang out the wash. **3** a piece of land sometimes covered by the sea. **4** a dry river bed, as in a canyon. **5** a liquid for cleansing, as for the mouth or eyes. **6** a weak or watery liquid; liquid garbage; hogwash. **7** an eddy made in water or air by a moving craft.
— **adj.** washable without damage: a wash dress.

wash·a·ble (WOSH·uh·bul) adj. that may be washed without damage: a washable ink (removable by washing).

wash-and-wear adj. needing little or no ironing after washing; durable-press: a wash-and-wear dress, fabric, shirt.

wash·ba·sin (WOSH·bay·sin) n. a bathroom fixture in which to wash one's face and hands; also **wash·bowl.**

wash·board n. a ridged board on which to scrub dirt out of clothes.

washed-out adj. **1** faded after many washes. **2** Informal. feeling or looking tired.

wash·er n. **1** one that washes, as a washing machine. **2** a flat seal of metal, rubber, or plastic with a hole in it, used with a nut or bolt to ensure tightness, prevent leakage, reduce friction, etc.

washing machine n. a machine for washing clothes.

wash·out n. **1** the washing away of earth by flowing water. **2** Slang. a complete failure: His performance was a washout; a washout punch (= knockout blow).

wash·room n. a room with washing and toilet facilities.

wash·tub n. a tub for soaking and washing clothes; also called "laundry tub."

wash·y adj. **wash·i·er, -i·est 1** of liquids, watery or weak: washy tea. **2** of colours, pale: washy appearance.

was·n't (WUZ·unt, WOZ-) was not.

wasp (WOSP) n. **1** a slender-bodied, winged stinging insect related to bees and ants. **2 WASP** or **Wasp** [usually derogatory] a "white Anglo-Saxon Protestant," as a member of the most privileged class in an English-speaking country; **adj.:** a Wasp community, enclave; the Wasp Establishment; a Wasp preserve; Toronto used to have a Wasp image.

wasp·ish adj. **1** like a wasp. **2 WASPish** or **Waspish** having to do with WASPs: white, Waspish, and Middle American.

wasp waist n. a very slender waist.

wast (WOST, wust) [old form] the form of WERE used with "thou."

wast·age (WAIS·tij) n. **1** loss by use, leakage, decay, etc. **2** the amount thus wasted.

waste v. **wastes, wast·ed, wast·ing 1** spend or be spent uselessly: to waste energy, money, time; You're wasting your breath (= It's useless) trying to persuade him; to waste (= not use) an opportunity; He gets **wasted** (Slang

for intoxicated) *at parties.* **2** wear down gradually: *Tuberculosis is a wasting disease; Starving people waste away.* **3** ravage; lay waste.
— **n. 1** a wasting or something wasted: *a mere waste of time and money; We try to cut down on waste; hazardous, nuclear, radioactive, toxic wastes; body wastes* (= excrement); *Millions of tons of solid waste* (= refuse) *are produced each year in homes, offices, restaurants, etc.* **2** an unused expanse of water, snow-covered land, desert, etc. **3** a gradual wearing down, as of bodily tissue: *the body processes of waste and repair.* **4** a bunch of cotton or wool material used for cleaning, wiping, etc.
— **go to waste** be wasted.
— **lay waste (to)** destroy a place or make it desolate.
— **adj. 1** discarded as useless or unused: *waste matter, water; Solid waste disposal is a municipal job.* **2** desolate; ruined: *waste land.*
— **waste·ful** *adj.: Idling a car is wasteful of gas.*

waste·bas·ket (WAIST·bas·kit) *n.* a basket or other receptacle for waste paper.

waste·land *n.* barren land; hence, unproductive effort.

waste product *n.* a useless by-product of a manufacturing or bodily process.

wast·rel (WAY·strul) *n.* **1** a spendthrift. **2** a good-for-nothing.

watch (WOCH) *v.* **1** follow a person or thing with one's eyes; look at or observe steadily: *to watch a game; a suspect being watched by police; He was beaten up while everyone watched* (= looked on); *He's watching* (= waiting) *for a chance to sneak out.* **2** stay awake or alert: *a mother watching at her sick child's bedside.*
— **watch it** *Informal.* be careful.
— **watch oneself** be careful or discreet.
— **watch out** *Informal.* be on one's guard: *Watch out for pickpockets!*
— **n. 1** a timepiece to carry on one's person, as a wristwatch, stopwatch, etc.: *an analog watch; a digital watch; His watch is fast, hers is slow; Watches keep time, run down, stop.* **2** a state or attitude of attention: *A hurricane watch is one level of preparedness lower than a hurricane warning; to maintain a close, careful watch on people going in and out of the house; Our dog keeps watch over our house; She is* **on watch** (= watching) *all night; She is* **on the watch** *for prowlers.* **3** a guard or his period of duty, as in the navy: *Crew members stand watch for four hours at a time; during the still watches of the night.* **4** formerly, someone on watch duty in a town: *the night watch; Call out the watch!*

watch·dog *n.* **1** a dog kept to guard property. **2** one that guards against theft, waste, etc.: *In Canada, the Auditor General is the watchdog of government spending;* **adj.:** *a watchdog body, committee.*

watch·ful *adj.* keeping careful guard; vigilant.

watch·man (WOCH·mun) *n.* **-men** one who keeps watch over property, esp. at night.

watch·tow·er (WOCH-, *rhyme:* our) *n.* a lookout tower.

watch·word *n.* **1** a guiding principle as embodied in a motto or slogan: *"Merit" should be the watchword for promotions.* **2** a secret password.

wa·ter (WAW·tur, WOT·ur) *n.* **1** the colourless, odourless, tasteless, and transparent liquid that falls as rain and fills lakes, rivers, etc.: *to draw water for a bath; to pour, spill, splash, sprinkle, squirt water; clear, cold, contaminated, distilled, fresh, hard, hot, polluted, soft, stagnant, tepid, warm water.* **2** a waterlike substance such as sap, tears, urine, and saliva: *Infants make* or *pass water whenever necessary; He has water on the knee* (= accumulated fluid following an injury); *water on the brain* (= enlarged condition of the head); *Her water broke* (= bag of fluid holding the fetus ruptured). **3** a waterlike product: *ammonia water; lavender water; mineral water; rose water; soda water; toilet water.* **4** a body of water such as a sea or lake: *People cross the border by water, air, and land; a body found under two feet of water; to feel like a fish out of water; to tread water (to keep afloat); at high and low water* (= tide). **5 waters** *pl.* flowing or moving water: *"Still waters run deep"; The flood waters are receding; International waters lie beyond territorial waters; to take the (mineral) waters* (= to take a water cure) *at a spa; the bag of waters* (= sac holding a fetus). **6** the degree of transparency and brilliance of a precious stone, formerly "first water," "second water," "third water." **7** the wavy, lustrous finish given to silk, linen, metal surfaces, etc.
— **cast one's bread on the waters** do good that does not bring the doer any return.
— **hold one's water** *Slang.* be patient.
— **hold water** of a theory, argument, etc., prove sound; agree with the facts: *Your story won't hold water.*
— **of the first** or **finest** or **purest water** of the highest degree of perfection: *a poet of the finest water; a scoundrel of the first water.*
— **pour** or **throw cold water on** discourage a hope, plan, etc.
— **water under the bridge** something that belongs to the past.
— **v. 1** supply with water: *to water a lawn; to water cattle; a land watered by rivers; watered* (= diluted) *milk, soup, wine; a watered-down* (= weakened) *version of the same argument.* **2** drink or take in water: *cattle watering at a stream; a ship docked for watering.* **3** give out water or a waterlike substance: *Mouths water at the sight of food; Her eyes are watering from the wind.*
— **adj.:** *Ocean birds are water birds; a water heater; water pressure, safety, supply, vapour.*

water ballet *n.* dancelike synchronized swimming.

water bed *n.* a bed with a water-filled mattress.

wa·ter·borne (WAW·tur·born) *adj.* carried by water: *waterborne cargo, diseases.*

water cannon *n.* a device like a fire hose for shooting water at high pressure, used in crowd control.

wa·ter·col·our (WAW·tur·cul·ur) *n.* **1** a pigment that is mixed with water for painting: *to paint in watercolours.* **2** a painting done with watercolours.

water cooler *n.* a machine that dispenses cold drinking water, as used in offices.

wa·ter·course (WAW·tur·course) *n.* **1** a stream, river, or artificial water channel. **2** its bed.

wa·ter·craft (WAW·tur·craft) *n. sing. & pl.* a ship, boat, or similar craft for transport on or in water.

wa·ter·fall (WAW·tur·fall) *n.* a stream flowing down a height; cascade.

wa·ter·fowl (WAW·tur·fowl) *n*. a water bird such as the duck or loon.

wa·ter·front (WAW·tur·frunt) *n*. the section of a city fronting on a body of water; harbour area: *labour trouble on the waterfront (involving stevedores); People gathered along the waterfront.*

water hole *n*. a small pond or pool.

water ice *n*. dessert resembling ice cream but made with fruit juice instead of milk.

watering hole *n*. *Informal*. a place such as a bar, club, or lounge where people gather for drinking and socializing.

watering place *n*. **1** a place at which animals drink from a river, lake, etc. **2** same as WATERING HOLE. **3** a spa with mineral springs.

wa·ter·line (WAW·tur·line) *n*. the varying line along which the water surface touches the side of a ship or boat, depending on the load it is carrying.

wa·ter·logged (WAW·tur·logd) *adj*. filled or soaked with water: *a waterlogged boat; waterlogged fields; waterlogged (= bogged down) in detail.*

Wa·ter·loo (waw·tur·LOO) *n*. a crushing defeat, like the battle fought in 1815 at Waterloo, Belgium, in which Napolean was finally defeated: *to meet one's Waterloo.*

water main *n*. a large pipe carrying water.

wa·ter·mel·on (WAW·tur·mel·un) *n*. a large green melon with a delicious red or yellow pulp.

wa·ter·proof (WAW·tur·proof, long "oo") *adj*. that will not let water through, as coats, hats, etc. treated with rubber.
— *n*. **1** a waterproof material. **2** a raincoat.
— *v*. make waterproof. — **wa·ter·proof·ing** *n*.

wa·ter·shed (WAW·tur·shed) *n*. **1** a dividing ridge between two areas drained by different river systems. **2** a river basin. **3** a turning point: *Retirement marks a watershed in our careers.*
— *adj*. crucial: *a watershed decision, event; 1973 was a watershed year for world economies because of the Arab oil embargo.*

wa·ter·ski (WAW·tur·skee) *v*. **-skis, -skied, -ski·ing** glide over water on boards **(waterskis)** towed by a speedboat.
— *n*. one of a pair of skis that is similar to but wider than a snow ski.

wa·ter·spout (WAW·tur·spowt) *n*. **1** a tornado over the ocean. **2** something that spouts water, as a pipe that drains water from a roof.

water table *n*. the level of underground water, as seen in a well.

wa·ter·tight (WAW·tur·tite) *adj*. **1** so tight as not to let water in or out: *a ship's watertight bulkheads; a watertight rubber suit.* **2** having no loopholes or flaws: *a watertight argument, contract, monopoly, plan; watertight sanctions, security.*

wa·ter·way (WAW·tur·way) *n*. a navigable river, canal, etc.: *inland waterways.*

wa·ter·works (WAW·tur·wurks) *n. pl*. **1** the system of reservoirs, pipes, pumps, etc. for supplying a town with water: *our municipal waterworks.* **2** *Slang*. kidneys and the urinary system.

wa·ter·y (WAW·tuh·ree) *adj*. **1** of, like, or full of water: *watery clouds, eyes, soil; a watery discharge; met a watery grave in the ocean.* **2** diluted; hence, weak: *a watery colour, soup.*

wave *n*. **1** a moving ridge of water, as on the sea, that swells and breaks on the shore: *a high, mountainous, tall wave; the crest of a wave; a destructive tidal wave.* **2** any similar movement: *The invaders attacked in waves; a heat wave; a wave of enthusiasm; A crime wave swept the city.* **3** an up-and-down motion or undulation: *natural waves in hair; a permanent wave; a wave of the flag, hand; Sound travels in waves; light waves; radio transmission in long, medium, and short waves; a brain wave (= sudden inspired idea).*
— **make waves** *Informal*. disturb the existing state of affairs.
— **the wave of the future** a movement or trend that is going to last.
— *v*. **waves, waved, wav·ing** move like a wave: *corn waving (= swaying) in the wind; a field of waving (= undulating) corn; a street lined with people waving (= fluttering) flags; They waved (= motioned with the hand in greeting) to us from the balcony; We waved back at them; All objections were waved aside (= dismissed).*

wave·length *n*. the length of a radio wave from a transmitter: *a husband **on the same wavelength** as (Informal for* in harmony with*) his wife.*

wa·ver (WAY·vur) *v*. **1** hesitate after making a decision or seem to want to go back on it: *Once she makes up her mind, she never wavers; to waver in one's promises, resolution; to waver between two courses of action.* **2** move to and fro; become unsteady: *a wavering flame, voice.* — *n*. a wavering.
— **wa·ver·er** *n*.; **wa·ver·ing·ly** *adv*.

wav·y (WAY·vee) *adj*. **wav·i·er, -i·est** moving in or having waves: *wavy hair, lines, seas.*

wax (rhyme: "axe") *n*. a fatty plastic substance, as made by bees for their cells or as distilled from petroleum and applied to furniture surfaces and floors for protection and polish: *Sealing wax is used to seal letters, jars, bottles, etc.*
— *v*. **1** rub or treat with wax: *a waxed floor.* **2** become or grow as specified: *She waxed eloquent over her child's accomplishments; to wax lyrical, poetic; The moon*

waxes (=grows larger) *from new moon to full moon before waning.*

wax·en (WAX·un) *adj.* 1 made of wax. 2 like wax in smoothness.

wax·y (WAX·ee) *adj.* **wax·i·er, -i·est** like wax, pale yellow, soft and pliable, or shiny. — **wax·i·ness** *n.*

way *n.* 1 a road or route for getting from one place to another: *the way home from school; Do you know the way to the cottage? We lost our way in the woods; It was getting dark when we found our way; the way out of the jungle; Please lead the way* (= go ahead of us); *She went that way* (= in that direction); *our neighbours living across the way* (= street); *She's travelling **down** Mexico **way*** (= to Mexico); *He lives **out our way*** (= in our neighbourhood); *It's a long way* (= distance) *off; quite a **ways** (Nonstandard for distance) from here; to clear, pave, point, prepare, show, smooth the way; to be out of harm's way; to elbow, fight, force, make, muscle, push, squeeze, thread, tunnel, work one's way through a crowd, etc.* or *to a place; Let's get **out of the way** of the bulldozer; Are we **in your way?** Let's **make way** (= room) for the procession to pass; A stream twists* or *wends* or *winds **its way** to its destination; A child worms its way into our hearts; We had a flat tire **on the way to** the airport; I went to Montreal **by way of** Ottawa; Students often **work their way through** college* (= pay their fees by working); *It takes time for freshmen to **know their way** around campus; An apology will **go a long way** (= distance) *toward easing the tension; the **parting of the ways** following graduation; We go **the way of all flesh*** (= We are all mortal). 2 manner or mode of doing something: *"Where there's a will there's a way"; There are easier ways of doing this; the proper* or *right way to use* or *of using your knife and fork; He's so willful he wants his own way all the time; a child with very charming* or *winsome ways; The way she goes about her duties is impressive; She **has a way** (= knows how to deal) *with children; Let's do it the democratic way; You can't **have it both ways** (= choose both alternatives); I may be able to help in a small way; "**No way,**" I said when he asked me for another loan; It's time to **mend your ways** (= improve your behaviour); In some ways (= respects) yours is a better idea; The patient is **in a bad way** (= condition).* 3 **ways** *pl.* structures to support a ship under construction.
— **all the way** without reservations: *He supported her all the way; He would go all the way* (= do the utmost) *for her.*
— **by the way** incidentally.
— **by way of** 1 through: *We went to Edmonton by way of Calgary.* 2 for the purpose of: *He told the story by way of example.*
— **give way** 1 yield: *to give way to someone's demands.* 2 collapse or fail: *The dam gave way.*
— **go out of one's way** make a special effort *to do something.*
— **make way** clear the way *for another person.*
— **out of the way** unusual or strange: *We saw nothing out of the way; adj.: an out-of-the-way experience.*
— **under way** in motion; hence, in progress: *Negotiations will get under way in the fall.*
— **ways and means** *n.pl.* methods and resources for achieving an end, esp. for raising revenue.
— **way to go!** [exclamation of encouragement]

— *adv. Informal.* far: *We are way ahead of the competition; It happened way back in the 1920s; way out in the woods; way* (= long) *after I finished high school.*

way·far·er (WAY·fair·ur) *n.* a traveller, esp. one going on foot. — **way·far·ing** *n. & adj.*

way·lay (way·LAY) *v.* **-lays, -laid, -lay·ing** 1 lie in wait for and attack someone. 2 stop someone on the way unexpectedly.

way-out *adj. Informal.* strange, not following usual custom or style.

-ways *adv. suffix.* in the way specified: *endways, lengthways, sideways.*

way·ward (WAY·wurd) *adj.* 1 willful and disobedient. 2 erratic and freakish.
— **way·ward·ly** *adv.;* **way·ward·ness** *n.*

we (WEE) *pron., pl.* of the first person "I"; *objective* US, *possessive* OUR(S). 1 the first person plural of "I" [representing a group that includes the speaker]: *We* (= you, your mother, and I) *are one family; We* (= the rest of us) *will be here when you come back from school.* 2 a person speaking as the representative of a group: *It gives us* (= the sovereign or the government) *great pleasure to declare this stadium open; I have edited this book according to our* (= of this institution, publisher, editorial board) *house style.* 3 such use: *the royal we; the editorial we.*

weak (WEEK) *adj.* lacking in physical, mental, or moral strength; not strong: *weak arguments, character, health, muscles, resistance; a student who is weak in* or *at math; A **weak verb** is inflected by adding an ending such as "-ed" for past tense and past participle.*

weak·en (WEE·kun) *v.* make or become weak or weaker: *weakened by hunger and thirst.*

weak-kneed (WEEK·need) *adj.* lacking in courage or ability to stand firm and resolute.

weak·ling *n.* one that lacks physical or moral strength.

weak·ly *adj.* **-li·er, -li·est** feeble or weak.
— *adv.:* *in a weak manner.*

weak·ness (WEEK·nis) *n.* 1 lack of strength; hence, a weak point or defect. 2 a fondness or liking that is considered a sign of being weak: *He has a weakness for cigars; Cigars are his weakness* (= weak point).

weal (WEEL) *n.* [old use] well-being; prosperity: *the common weal; the public weal; in **weal and woe*** (= in good times and bad).

wealth (WELTH, "TH" as in "thin") *n.* 1 material goods and resources that have money value; riches: *fabulous wealth; to accumulate, acquire, amass, attain wealth; to flaunt, squander one's wealth; a country's mineral wealth; national wealth; the natural wealth of a region.* 2 abundance: *a wealth of detail, information, imagery, words.*

wealth·y (WELTH·ee) *adj.* **wealth·i·er, -i·est** rich in material resources: *a wealthy family.*

wean (WEEN) *v.* 1 accustom an infant, young animal, etc. to food other than its mother's milk: *A calf is*

weaned from its mother. **2** draw a person away from habits, company, or occupations that are considered bad.
— **weaned on** raised or trained on something: *a generation of students weaned on television.*

weap·on (WEP·un) *n.* **1** any instrument used for fighting, as an arrow, sword, gun, or club: *to brandish, carry, draw, fire, handle, load a weapon; to lay down, throw down one's weapons and surrender; an automatic weapon; a concealed weapon; A restricted weapon needs a police permit; Even a broken beer bottle may constitute an offensive weapon if intended to be used as such; They entered the house with weapons drawn; the ultimate weapon* (= nuclear arms). **2** anything used as a means of defence or attack: *Tears are often a child's best weapon; dirty tricks as political weapons.*

weap·on·ry (WEP·un·ree) *n.* **1** weapons collectively. **2** their design and production.

wear (WARE) *v.* **wears, wore, worn, wear·ing 1** have on one's person or show in one's appearance: *to wear clothes, jewellery, perfume; to wear a beard, smile; She wears her hair short.* **2** make a hole, path, etc. in or on something by constant use: *to wear a hole through a sock; These shoes are worn at the heels; an excuse that has worn thin.* **3** last or endure *well, badly,* etc. as specified. **4** pass or go gradually: *She seemed to age as the years* ***wore on*** *or* ***away;*** *when the effects of the drug* ***wear off.*** **5** tire or exhaust: *a face worn with care; They could not* ***wear down*** *his resistance; They're beginning to* ***wear out*** (= exhaust) *their welcome; Her patience is* ***wearing thin*** (= becoming exhausted).
— *n.* **1** a wearing or being worn: *shoes for summer wear; socks for everyday wear.* **2** clothes: *children's, men's, women's wear; spring, summer, fall, winter wear.* **3** damage from use: *The shoes show wear; The children returned a bit tired, but apparently none* **the worse for wear.** **4** wearing capacity: *There's a lot of wear still left in those shoes.* — **wear·a·ble** *adj.* — **wear·er** *n.*

wear and tear *n.* normal loss or damage from use: *Guarantees do not cover ordinary wear and tear; the wear and tear of our existence.*

wea·ri·some (WEER·ee·sum) *adj.* causing weariness; tiresome.

wea·ry (WEER·ee) *adj.* **-ri·er, -ri·est 1** worn out; exhausted: *feet weary with walking; He's grown weary of city life.* **2** showing tiredness: *a weary sigh.* **3** causing tiredness: *a weary climb.*
— *v.* **-ries, -ried, -ry·ing** make or become weary; tire. — **wea·ri·ly** *adv.;* **wea·ri·ness** *n.*

wea·sel (WEE·zul) *n.* a small, furry, short-legged, flesh-eating animal with an agile and slender body.
— *v.* evade a responsibility or escape from an obligation: *He would like to weasel out of the contract.*

weasel word *n.* an evasive or meaningless expression, like an egg sucked out by a weasel but left outwardly intact.

weath·er (WETH·ur, "TH" as in "the") *n.* the condition of the atmosphere in regard to temperature, precipitation, cloudiness, winds, etc.: *to forecast or predict the weather; atrocious, beastly, beautiful, bleak, clear, cloudy, cold, cool, fair, fine, foul, gloomy, hot,*

humid, inclement, mild, muggy, seasonable, sweltering, unsettled, warm weather; The plane flew into weather (= stormy conditions) over Bermuda; We resumed our journey when the weather cleared up; Wintry weather usually sets in after Christmas.
— **under the weather** *Informal.* out of sorts; ill.
— *adj.*: *a weather balloon, forecast, pattern, report, satellite; on the weather* (= windward) *side.*
— *v.* **1** expose to the action of weather: *Soil results from the* **weathering** (= gradual breaking down) *of rocks.* **2** change in colour or become worn by exposure to the weather. **3** pass through a storm, etc. safely. **4** sail to the windward side of a cape, island, etc.

weather-beaten (WETH·ur·bee·tun) *adj.* seasoned, hardened, worn, etc. by exposure to the weather: *a weather-beaten face, old house, sailor.*

weather bureau *n.* a weather-reporting agency such as the National Weather Service in the U.S.

weath·er·cock (WETH·ur·cock) *n.* **1** a weather vane with the figure of a cock on top. **2** one that is inconstant or changeable.

weather eye *n.* alertness to signs of change, esp. in weather: *The police are* **keeping a weather eye on** *or* **open for** *or* **out for** (= keeping a close watch on) *the escapees.*

weath·er·ize (WETH·ur·ize) *v.* **-iz·es, -ized, -iz·ing** insulate so as to keep out the cold and save heating fuel.

weath·er·man *n.* **-men** one who reports on weather conditions, as in a news broadcast; meteorologist.

weather office *n. Cdn.* the Federal Government's Atmospheric Environment Service which prepares weather forecasts: *the Toronto weather office.*

weath·er·proof (WETH·ur·proof) *adj.* able to withstand exposure to the weather without damage: *a weatherproof finish for the sun deck.*
— *v.* make weatherproof: *to weatherproof a cottage.*

weath·er·strip (WETH·ur·strip) *v.* **-strips, -stripped, -strip·ping** fit or seal with weatherstripping.
— *n.* material such as strips of metal, wood, or felt for sealing the gaps around doors and windows to keep out drafts; also **weath·er·strip·ping.**

weather vane *n.* a device with an arrow on top that turns freely to indicate the direction from which the wind is blowing.

weath·er·wise (WETH·ur·wise) *adj.* skilled in predicting changes in public opinion, spending patterns, weather, etc.

weath·er·worn (WETH·ur·worn) *adj.* weather-beaten.

weave (WEEV) *v.* **weaves,** *pt.* **wove** (WOHV) *or* **weaved,** *pp.* **wo·ven** (WOH·vun) *or* **wove, weav·ing 1** interlace threads, strips, etc. *into* a fabric or an article such as a basket or hat. **2** make a fabric, hat, web, etc. *from* threads, straw, or wicker: *She weaves (cloth) on a loom; to weave a wreath of flowers.* **3** construct a story, poem, musical composition, etc. as if by weaving, *from* strands of plot, melody, etc. or *around* a theme. **4** weave plots, melodies, humour, etc. *into* a story or musical

composition. **5** *pt.* usually **weaved,** make one's way through a place: *He weaved in and out of traffic by changing lanes; She weaved her way though the crowd.*
— *n.* a form or pattern of weaving, as plain or satin.
— **weav·er** *n.*

web *n.* **1** something woven, esp. the network spun by a spider. **2** any network: *He wove an intricate web of lies to cover up his crime; a tangled web of intrigue; a web of deceit; The interdependence of humans, animals, and plants is called the "web of life."* **3** connecting material or tissue, as the membrane joining the toes of swimming birds. **4** a large reel of newsprint, as used on a rotary "web press."
— *v.* **webs, webbed, web·bing 1** join by a web: *Swimming birds have* **webbed** *feet, or* **web·feet.**
2 ensnare or trap, as in a web.

Web·ster's (WEB·sturz) *n.* an American English dictionary. Also **Web·ster.**

we'd (WEED) we had; we should; we would.

wed *v.* **weds,** *pt.* **wed·ded,** *pp.* **wed·ded** or **wed, wed·ding 1** give, take, or join in marriage: *Jean Weds Gigi; They spent the night in* **wedded** (=married) *bliss.* **2** unite closely, firmly, intimately, etc.
— **wedded to** devoted to an occupation, opinion, one's work, etc.

wedding (WED·ing) *n.* **1** a marriage ceremony and festivities: *to attend a wedding; officiate at* or *perform a wedding; a shotgun wedding forced on the couple by the bride's pregnancy.* **2** a marriage anniversary: *diamond wedding* (=60th or 75th year); *golden wedding* (=50th year); *silver wedding* (=25th year).
— *adj.: a wedding anniversary, band, cake, date, day, invitation, ring; Mendelssohn wrote the familiar "Wedding March."*

wedge (WEJ) *n.* **1** a piece of wood, metal, etc. tapering to a thin edge, used for splitting wood, raising weights, etc.: *The dispute drove a wedge between the families.* **2** something wedge-shaped, as a triangular piece of pie.
— *v.* **wedg·es, wedged, wedg·ing:** *to wedge* (=split) *open a log; to wedge a door open* (=keep it open using a block); *to wedge up* (=chock) *a tipping cabinet; to wedge* (=squeeze) *oneself into a car; He was wedged* (=stuck) *between two ladies with parcels on the crowded bus.*

wed·lock (WED·lock) *n.* the state of being married; matrimony: *The couple were joined in wedlock by their pastor; a child born* **out of wedlock** (=illegitimate child).

Wednes·day (WENZ·dee, -day) *n.* the fourth day of the week, following Tuesday.

wee *adj.* **we·er** (WEE·ur), **we·est** (WEE·ist) *Informal.* very small or tiny: *a wee bit bored; in the wee* (=very early) *hours of the morning.*

weed *n.* **1** a plant that is harmful or of no value, esp. when growing in a cultivated field: *a noxious weed.* **2 weeds** *pl.* mourning garments, as of a widow.
— **the weed** *Informal.* tobacco or marijuana.
— *v.* take weeds out of the ground: *to weed a lawn.*
— **weed out** remove: *to weed out troublesome elements; to weed out a herd to improve the breed.*

— **weed·er** *n.;* **weed·y** *adj.*

week *n.* **1** seven successive calendar days, esp. from Sunday through Saturday: *Many workers are paid by the week; Our guests will be here a week from Monday* or *be here Monday* **week;** *They're coming here for a week; They'll be gone in a week; They haven't been here for weeks* or *in weeks.* **2** the working part of the calendar week: *He works a six-day week; During the week, he is too busy to watch TV.*

week·day *n.* any day of the workweek, esp. Monday through Friday: *Most people work (on) weekdays.*

week·end or **week-end** *n.* the period from the close of one working week till the beginning of the next, usually Saturday and Sunday: *Our friends stayed with us over the weekend; We don't work (on) weekends.*
— *v.* spend the weekend: *We weekended with friends at their cabin.*

week·ly *adj.* of or happening once a week: *a weekly pay cheque, publication, visit; adv.: She visits us weekly.*
— *n.,* *pl.* **-lies** a weekly publication.

week·night *n.* a weekday night: *a TV show seen (on) weeknights only.*

wee·nie (WEE·nee) *n. Informal.* a wiener.

wee·ny (WEE·nee) *adj. Informal.* very tiny or small; also **ween·sy.**

weep *v.* **weeps, wept, weep·ing 1** shed tears: *to weep for joy; to weep tears of joy; to weep bitter tears of sorrow; It's no use weeping over* or *about a misfortune; She's weeping* (=mourning) *for her loved ones.* **2** shed or exude drops of water or other liquid: *Cold pipes weep when the weather gets hot.*

weeping willow *n.* a willow characterized by drooping branches.

weep·y *adj.* **weep·i·er, -i·est** *Informal.* inclined to cry easily; tearful.

weft *n.* the threads of a fabric or loom running crosswise to the warp; woof.

weigh (WAY) *v.* **1** measure the weight of something: *Luggage has to be weighed; A cook weighs out the ingredients for a recipe; He weighs* (=has the weight of) *60 kg; Boxers, jockeys, etc. have to* **weigh in** (=have themselves weighed) *before a contest; They must* **weigh in at** (=enter the contest at) *the declared weights; Well-*

wishers weighed in with (=made their presence felt with) *all sorts of suggestions.* 2 bend with or as if with a weight; bear down: *a tree weighed down with fruit; a heart weighed down with grief; lives weighed down by sorrow; His guilty conscience seemed to weigh on* or *upon* (=worry) *him; It weighed him down* (=depressed him).* 3 consider carefully: *He weighs every word before saying anything; She weighed the pros and cons of quitting her job; She weighed the loss of income against being able to care for her children.* 4 have importance or significance; count: *Experience sometimes weighs more with employers than education; A criminal record weighs heavily against a job applicant.*
— **weigh** anchor of a ship, lift the anchor before sailing.
— *n.* **under weigh** [nautical use] progressing or advancing; under way.

weight (WAIT) *n.* 1 how heavy an object is: *His weight is 60 kg; Weight depends on gravitational pull and the mass of an object; Sugar is sold by weight, not volume; to gain* or *put on weight* (=get fatter); *to lose* or *take off weight* (=get slimmer).* 2 a system or unit of weight: *atomic weight; avoirdupois weight; metric weights and measures; molecular weight.* 3 something heavy, as the disks used in "weight-lifting," a "pound," "gram," or other standard piece used in weighing, a quantity weighed out, or an object used to keep papers in place: *a set of weights; to lift weights; a heavy, not light weight.* 4 a burden or load to be supported: *That's a weight off my mind; The animal collapsed under the weight (of its load).* 5 importance or influence: *a man of weight; Public opinion carries considerable weight with politicians; to add, attach, give,* or *lend weight* (=give importance) *to an argument, claim, demand, proposal, rumour, theory.*
— **pull one's weight** do one's share.
— **throw one's weight around** be overbearing or overassertive.
— *v.* put weight on something; hence, burden: *a stick with a weighted tip; a mind weighted down with worries; evidence weighted* (=slanted) *against the defendant.*

weight·y (WAY·tee) *adj.* **weight·i·er, -i·est** very important or serious: *a weighty announcement, argument, decision, speaker; weighty matters of state; a weighty responsibility.* — **weight·i·ly** *adv.*

weir (WEER) *n.* 1 an obstruction erected across a stream or river, as a milldam, for diverting or raising the water. 2 a fence of stakes or brush for catching fish, etc.

weird (WEERD) *adj.* 1 mysterious in an unearthly way: *a weird shriek in the dark.* 2 *Informal.* strange or fantastic: *a weird sense of humour; There's something weird about his attitude.*
— **weird·ly** *adv.;* **weird·ness** *n.*

weird·o (WEER·doh) *n.* **-os** *Slang.* an eccentric person or thing. Also **weird·ie** (-dee).

welch same as WELSH.

wel·come (WEL·cum) *adj.* received with pleasure: *a welcome visitor; a welcome bit of news; a welcome relief from the heat; Contributions are always welcome; We want to make you feel welcome; You're welcome to* (=permitted to) *use our kitchen.*
— **You're welcome** [in response to an expression of

thanks] You are under no obligation.
— *n.* a reception on arrival: *to bid, extend, give someone a welcome; She left early so as not to overstay her welcome* or *not to wear out her welcome; to receive a chilly, cold, cool, cordial, enthusiastic, hearty, rousing, warm welcome from someone.*
— *interj.* you are welcome: *Welcome aboard! Welcome back! Welcome home!*
— *v.* **-comes, -comed, -com·ing** greet or receive someone on arrival: *She was welcomed with a hug; to be welcomed coolly, cordially, enthusiastically, with open arms; He was welcomed to their home; We welcome* (=accept with pleasure) *all credit cards, suggestions.*
— *adj.:* *to put out* or *roll out the welcome mat* (=give a friendly reception); *the welcome wagon (with gifts from the community to which one is being welcomed).*

weld *v.* 1 join pieces of metal by heating to the melting point and fusing, hammering, or pressing together. 2 unite closely or intimately.
— *n.* a welding or welded joint. — **weld·er** *n.*

wel·fare (WEL·fare) *n.* 1 the condition of being healthy, happy, prosperous, etc.: *community, general, public welfare.* 2 the provision of food and such necessities to the needy, as by government programs of public assistance. 3 government aid given to the poor and needy. — **be** or **go on welfare** receive such aid.

we'll (WEEL) we will; we shall.

well *n.* 1 a hole or shaft dug in the ground to get water, oil, gas, etc.: *to bore, dig, drill, sink a well; an oil well; an "artesian" well* (=spring).* 2 a shaft resembling a well, as a "stairwell." 3 a container for holding a liquid, as an "inkwell." 4 source: *He's a well of information.*
— *v.* flow out, rise up, etc. as water from a spring or well: *His eyes welled up with tears on hearing the sad news.*
— *adv.* comp. **bet·ter,** superl. **best** in a good or satisfactory manner: *a job well done; He eats well; Things are going well with him; Shake the bottle well before use; We may well* (=quite likely) *make the deadline; It's well* (=long) *past noon; a well-liked person; well-polished shoes.*
— **as well** in addition: *We are here mainly on business but for some pleasure as well; As well, we would like to do some shopping; We are here on business as well as for pleasure; We thought we might just as well* (=at the same time) *have some fun while we are here.*
— **leave well enough alone** do not try to change what is satisfactory.
— *adj.* good or satisfactory: *All's well that ends well; It's well that he asked my permission; You look well* (=in good health); *He came out of the hospital a well man; a well-baby clinic.*
— *interj.* expressing surprise, agreement, doubt, etc.: *Well, what did I tell you? Well, no!*

well-advised (well·ud·VIZED) *adj.* 1 prudent: *a well-advised decision.* 2 based on good advice: *a well-advised rest.*

well-appointed (well·uh·POIN·tid) *adj.* well equipped or furnished: *a well-appointed office.*

well-balanced (well·BAL·unst) *adj.* 1 properly matched: *a well-balanced ensemble, program, proposal, report,* *team.* **2** healthy: *a well-balanced diet, meal.*

well-being (WELL·bee·ing) *n.* welfare: *our economic well-being; our children's well-being.*

well-born *adj.* born of a good family.

well-bred *adj.* **1** having good manners. **2** of good stock: *a well-bred horse.*

well-connected (wel·cuh·NEC·tid) *adj.* having connections with important people: *a well-connected lawyer.*

well-defined (well·di·FINED) *adj.* clearly distinguishable; distinct: *within well-defined limits; a well-defined outline; a well-defined* (= clearly outlined) *job.*

well-disposed (well·dis·POZED) *adj.* having positive feelings *toward* a person or thing.

well-done *adj.* **1** skilfully performed: *a well-done job.* **2** cooked thoroughly: *a well-done steak.*

well-favoured or **well-favored** *adj.* good-looking; handsome.

well-fed *adj.* plump; fat: *a well-fed cat.*

well-founded *adj.* based on good evidence, judgment, reasoning, etc.: *a well-founded fear, statement, suspicion.*

well-groomed *adj.* neat in appearance: *well-groomed students; a well-groomed lawn; a well-groomed* (= cleaned, curried, etc.) *horse.*

well-grounded (wel·GROUND·id) *adj.* **1** having a good foundation of knowledge *in* a subject. **2** supported by facts: *Her fears were well-grounded; a well-grounded suspicion.*

well-head *n.* the source of an oil well or spring: *the wellhead price of oil charged by the producer.*

well-heeled *adj. Informal.* well-to-do; rich: *a well-heeled patron, publisher, tourist.*

well-informed (wel·in·FORMD) *adj.* having considerable general knowledge *about* something.

well-intentioned (wel·in·TEN·shund) *adj.* having or showing good intentions.

well-knit *adj.* well constructed or joined together: *a well-knit community, group; a play with a well-knit plot; a well-knit* (= sturdily built) *athlete.*

well-known *adj.* **1** famous: *a well-known politician.* **2** familiar: *She is well-known to all of us; a well-known landmark.*

well-mannered (well·MAN·urd) *adj.* having good manners.

well-meaning (well·MEE·ning) *adj.* **1** well-intentioned: *a well-meaning effort, parent.* **2** well-intended though ineffective: *a well-meaning attempt; well-meaning help;* also **well-meant.**

well-nigh *adv.* almost; very nearly.

well-off *adj.* well-to-do; prosperous.

well-ordered (well·OR·durd) *adj.* well-arranged; orderly.

well-preserved (well·pri·ZURVD) *adj.* of an old person, not showing signs of age.

well-read (well·RED) *adj.* having read much: *He's well-read in his subject.*

well-rounded (wel·ROUND·id) *adj.* **1** comprehensive: *a well-rounded program, study.* **2** multi-faceted: *a well-rounded character, education.* **3** shapely: *a well-rounded figure.*

well-spoken (wel·SPOH·kun) *adj.* **1** well-uttered: *a few well-spoken words.* **2** impressive in speech and manner: *a well-spoken young woman.*

well-spring *n.* **1** a spring that is the source of a stream. **2** a never-failing source.

well-thought-of (wel·THOUGHT·ov) *adj.* having a good reputation.

well-timed *adj.* timely; opportune.

well-to-do (wel·tuh·DOO) *adj.* sufficiently rich or prosperous. — **the well-to-do** *n.* [with pl. v.].

well-turned *adj.* gracefully formed or expressed: *a well-turned phrase, well-turned verses.*

well-worn *adj.* **1** much worn: *well-worn shoes.* **2** over-used or trite: *a well-worn saying.*

welsh (WELSH, WELCH) *v. Slang.* evade an obligation, as a bookmaker who fails to pay a bet; cheat: *He would never welsh on a promise.*

welt *n.* **1** a reinforcing strip or border, as used at the joining of a shoe's sole and upper, at the edge of a garment or upholstery, etc. **2** a ridge on the skin. **3** a slash or blow that would raise a welt on the skin. — *v. Informal.* thrash severely.

wel·ter (WEL·tur) *v.* **1** wallow. **2** be soaked *in* something wet such as mud, blood, etc. — *n.* **1** a chaotic rolling or tumbling. **2** a confused mass or jumble *of* data, papers, etc.

wench *n.* **1** [derogatory] a young woman. **2** [old use] a female servant.

wend *v.* go on one's way: *The procession wended slowly along King Street; They wended their way south.*

wen·di·go (WEN·duh·go) *n. Cdn.* a cannibalistic evil spirit of Algonquian myth.

went *pt.* of GO.

wept *pt.* of WEEP.

were (WUR) past second pers. sing., past pl., and past subjunctive of BE: *as if I were a millionaire.* — **as it were** so to speak.

we're (WEER) we are.

weren't (WURNT) were not.

were·wolf (WEER·wolf, WUR-, WAIR-) *n.* **-wolves** (-woolvz) in folklore, a person who changes into a wolf.

wert (WURT) [old form] the form of WERE used with "thou."

west *n.* **1** the direction where the sun sets, opposite of east. **2** a place, region, or country lying west: *Alberta is*

out **West** *for people in the East.*
— the **West 1** western North America: *songs of the Wild West.* **2** in Canada, west of Winnipeg. **3** the countries of Europe and North America as distinguished from Asia. **4** the non-Communist countries of Western Europe and the Americas.
— *adj. & adv.* in or toward the west: *"Go west, young man" (and make your fortune); Drive west 3 000 km to reach B.C.; to* **go west** *(Informal for* to die or expire, like the setting sun); Banff is* **west of** *Calgary.*

west·er·ly (WES·tur·lee) *adj. & adv.* **1** toward the west: *Mirror Creek in the Yukon is Canada's most westerly settlement; We drive westerly.* **2** from the west: *a westerly wind.* — *n., pl.* **-lies** a wind from the west.

west·ern (WES·turn) *adj.* **1** of, toward, or from the west. **2 Western** of the West.
— *n.* a story of the western U.S. featuring cowboy life.
— **west·ern·er** or **West·ern·er** *n.*

west·ern·ize (WES·tur·nize) *v.* **-iz·es, -ized, -iz·ing** give a western character to non-Western societies by introducing cultural elements from the West.

west·ward (WEST·wurd) *adj. & adv.* toward the west. Also **west·wards** *adv.* — **west·ward·ly** *adj. & adv.*

wet *adj.* **wet·ter, wet·test 1** covered or soaked with water or another liquid, not dry: *wet hands; a brow wet with perspiration; a wet sponge; He came out of the pool soaking wet; She came in from the rain dripping wet; wet* (=rainy) *weather; Caution: Wet* (=not yet dry) *Paint.* **2** against prohibition of liquor; permitting alcoholic drinks; not dry: *a wet candidate, county.*
— **all wet** *Slang.* wrong or mistaken.
— **wet behind the ears** *Informal.* immature or naive.
— *n.* **1** that which makes wet; liquid or moisture. **2** rainy weather. **3** one opposed to prohibition.
— *v.* **wets, wet·ted, wet·ting** make or become wet.
— **wet·ter** *n.* — **wet·ly** *adv.;* **wet·ness** *n.*

wet blanket *n.* one who dampens enthusiasm or lessens the gaiety of others.

wet·land *n.* usually **wetlands** *pl.* swamps, marshes, or bogs.

wet nurse *n.* a woman hired to suckle another's infant.

wet suit *n.* a heat-retaining garment of porous material such as foam rubber used by skin divers, etc.

wet·ware *n.* the human brain: *Hardware and software need wetware to make them work.*

we've (WEEV) we have.

whack *n. Informal.* **1** a sharp, resounding blow: *I'll whack you one.* **2** a portion or share.
— **at a** or **one whack** in one attempt.
— **have** or **take a whack at** aim a blow at someone; also, make an attempt at doing something.
— **out of whack** not in proper working order.
— *v. Informal.* strike with a sharp, resounding blow.
— **whack up** divide into shares. — **whack·er** *n.*

whacking *adj. & adv. Informal.* very large; whopping: *It was a whacking great victory; We won with a whacking majority.*

whack·y *adj.* **whack·i·er, -i·est** same as WACKY.

whale *n.* a fishlike but air-breathing, warm-blooded sea mammal that is the largest of animals: *a school* (=group) *of whales; whales of all sizes, including calves* (=young ones), *cows* (=females), *and bulls* (=males).
— **a whale of a** *Informal.* great or impressive: *That was a whale of a party; We had a whale of a good time; She did a whale of a job; It makes a whale of a difference.*
— *v.* **whales, whaled, whal·ing 1** hunt whales. **2** *Informal.* thrash.

whale·bone *n.* a horny, elastic plate attached to the upper jaw of "baleen" whales, used for straining out food and formerly for corset stays.

wham (rhyme: "am") *n. Informal.* a hard impact or solid blow.
— *v.* **whams, whammed, wham·ming** *Informal.* strike with a wham.
— *interj.* a sound imitating a wham.

wham·my (WHAM·ee) *n.* **wham·mies** *Slang.* a jinx; hex; evil: *to put a* or *the whammy on someone; The car dealer was hit with a* **double whammy** *on sales by gasoline shortages and recession.*

wharf (WHORF) *n.* **wharves** or **wharfs** a rectangular structure projecting from the shore along which ships dock for loading and unloading: *Boats are tied up at a wharf; People rushed to the wharves as the ship docked.*

what (WHOT, WHUT) *pron.* **1** [used in questions]: *What is the time? What on earth do you mean? So* **what?** (=If it's so, what follows?). **2** that which: *I heard what you said; Do what you like;* **What's more,** *take your time; She* **has what it takes** (=is quite capable); *She knows* **what's what** (=understands the situation).
— **and** (or **or**) **what have you** *Informal.* and (or other) similar things.
— **what about it?** What do you think about it?
— **what for?** Why? For what purpose?
— **what gives?** *Informal.* What's going on?
— **what's with** what's the matter with: *What's with this guy who won't even say hello to me.*
— *adj.* **1** [used in questions]: *On what date? What time is it?* **2** that or those which: *Get what help you can; She sent me what books she could borrow.* **3** [used in exclamations]: *What an idea! What fools we are!*
— *adv.* **1** In what respect? How much?: *What does it matter?* **2** [used in exclamations]: *What an idea! What woeful neglect!*
— **what with** on account of: *What with inflation and rising prices, poor people are suffering.*

what·ev·er (what·EV·ur) *pron.* **1** no matter what: *He'll get it, whatever the cost.* **2** [used for emphasizing

"what"]: *She'll agree with whatever you say; Whatever is the matter with you? furniture, groceries, stationery,* **or** **whatever** (*Informal for* anything at all).
— **adj. 1** no matter what: *He'll get it at whatever cost to himself.* **2** [used for emphasizing "what"]: *Get any book whatever.*

what·so·ev·er (what·so·EV·ur) *adj. & pron.* [emphatic form] whatever.

wheat (WHEET) *n.* a cereal grass of temperate climates used for bread flour, breakfast foods, pasta, etc.: *to grow, harvest, thresh, winnow wheat; Mills grind wheat into flour; cracked wheat (of coarse particles); whole-wheat flour for making whole-wheat bread.*

whee·dle (WHEE·dul) *v.* **-dles, -dled, -dling 1** use flattery, coaxing, etc. to persuade or influence someone *into* doing something. **2** get something *from* or *out* of someone by flattery, coaxing, cheating, etc.
— **whee·dler** *n.*

wheel (WHEEL) *n.* **1** a circular disk or frame with a central axis on which it rotates: *A wheel spins; The invention of the wheel was a great step forward in civilization; We don't have to **reinvent the wheel*** (= work out something already known). **2** anything shaped or moving like a wheel: *a watch's balance wheel; a Ferris wheel; the potter's wheel; a ratchet wheel; The roulette wheel is a wheel of fortune; an antique spinning wheel; Automobile wheels are aligned, balanced, rotated; front and rear wheels; the steering wheel of an automobile or ship; When you get **behind the wheel*** (= drive a car) *these days, you do so at your own risk.* **3** *Slang.* an influential person; big shot: *the big wheels at city hall.* **4** a bicycle.
— **at the wheel** in control, as a driver or helmsman.
— **wheels** *pl.* **1** moving force or machinery: *the wheels of government; the wheels of progress.* **2** *Slang.* an automobile.
— **wheels within wheels** intricate machinery, motives, influences, etc.
— *v.* **1** move like a wheel: *The vultures wheeled* (= circled) *in the sky ready to swoop down; She wheeled* (= turned) *round to face me; "where the beetle wheels* (= makes in a circle) *his droning flight."* **2** move forward on wheels or in a wheeled vehicle: *She wheeled the typewriter to the side of her desk; The senator in the wheelchair wheeled in to put in an appearance at the final session; He wheeled the barrow up and down the garden; skaters wheeling around on the ice; The courier wheeled slowly down the street looking for the address; a **wheeled** vehicle (that has wheels).*
— **wheel and deal** *Slang.* make deals aggressively or unscrupulously: *She made a spectacular $3 million in a single year of wheeling and dealing in real estate.*

wheel·bar·row (WHEEL·bair·oh) *n.* a small vehicle for moving loads, having a box mounted on a wheel and attached to two shafts that are held in the hands and pushed or pulled.

wheel·base *n.* the distance between the front and rear axles of a motor vehicle.

wheel·chair *n.* a chair mounted on wheels, used by invalids.

wheel·er *n.* one that wheels or has wheels: *a two-wheeler.*

wheeler-dealer (WHEE·lur·DEE·lur) *n. Slang.* a shrewd and aggressive operator in business, politics, etc.

wheel·horse *n. Informal.* a steady and hard worker: *a party wheelhorse with a powerful following.*

wheel·ie (WHEE·lee) *n.* the stunt of balancing a wheeled vehicle on its rear wheel or wheels.

wheeze *v.* **wheez·es, wheezed, wheez·ing** breathe or utter with a whistling sound, as an asthmatic.
— *n.* **1** a wheezing or its sound. **2** an oft-repeated saying or joke: *There's an old wheeze about boxing that you can't hit what you can't catch.*

wheez·y *adj.* **wheez·i·er, -i·est 1** inclined to wheeze. **2** wheezing. — **wheez·i·ness** *n.*

whelp *n.* the cub of a flesh-eating animal such as the dog, wolf, bear, lion, tiger, or leopard.
— *v.* bring forth whelps.

when *adv.* at what time: *When do you wake up?*
— *conj.* **1** at the time that: *Call me when you wake up; He limps when he walks; We had just gone to bed, when I heard a knock on the door.* **2** although; considering that: *He continues to work when he could retire on a fat pension.*
— *pron.* what or which time: *Since when are you a computer expert?*
— *n.* the time, date, or occasion: *the when and where of the happening; the when and how of it.*

whence *adv. & conj.* from what place, source, or cause: *Whence does the need arise? Whence* (= Wherefore) *it follows that the earth is round.*

when·ev·er (when·EV·ur) *adv. & conj.* at whatever time; when.

when·so·ev·er (when·so·EV·ur) *adv. & conj.* [in emphatic uses] whenever.

where (WHAIR) *adv.* in, at, to, or from what place: *Where is the child? Where did he get the money? the hotel where* (= in which) *I stayed; Where* (= in what respect) *did I go wrong?*
— *conj.* in the place in which: *I found it just where I left it; Where there's smoke there's fire; I go where* (= to the place to which) *business takes me; He was born in Ottawa, where* (= in which place) *he went to school.*
— *pron.* what or which place: *He asked us where we are from; Tell us where you are going; That's where you seem to have gone wrong; I know **where you're coming from*** (*Informal for* know what you mean); *That's **where** it's at* (*Informal for* the main or essential question; also, where the action is).
— *n.* the place or scene *of* a happening.

where·a·bouts (WHERE·uh·bowts) *adv. & conj.* about where: *Whereabouts does she live?*
— *n.* the place where a person or thing is: *Her whereabouts is* or *are unknown; the whereabouts of the missing child.* Also [rarely] **where·a·bout.**

where·as (where·AZ) *conj.* **1** [formal use] in view of the fact that; since: *Whereas you have been late Monday through Friday, you are being detained for an hour after school.* **2** while; on the contrary: *I like tea, whereas she likes coffee.*

where·at (where·AT) *adv. & conj.* at or in consequence of which.

where·by (where·BY) *adv. & conj.* by or through which.

where·fore *adv.* for what reason?
— *conj.* for which reason.
— *n.* the reason: *the why and the wherefore of it.*

where·from (where·FROM, -FRUM) *conj.* from which.

where·in (where·IN) *adv.* in what (respect)?
— *conj.* in which; during which; in what way.

where·of (where·OV) *adv. & conj.* of what, which, or whom.

where·on (where·ON) *conj.* on which.

where·so·ev·er (where·so·EV·ur) *conj.* [in emphatic uses] wherever.

where·to (where·TOO) *adv.* to what place?
— *conj.* to which.

where·up·on (where·uh·PON) *conj.* upon which; at which.

wher·ev·er (where·EV·ur) *adv.* [emphatic form] where: *Wherever have you been?*
— *conj.* in, at, or to whatever place: *Stay calm wherever you are.*

where·with·al (WHERE·with·awl) *n.* the necessary money or means: *the wherewithal to finance a project; He lacks the wherewithal for the down payment on a car.*

whet *v.* **whets, whet·ted, whet·ting** 1 sharpen a knife, axe, etc. by rubbing on or with a stone. 2 make keen or stimulate: *to whet one's or the appetite, one's curiosity, interest.* — **whet·ter** *n.*

wheth·er (WHETH·ur, "TH" as in "the") *conj.* 1 [posing a choice between alternatives, expressed by "or" or merely implied]: *It's yours whether you like it or not; Please phone back whether he survived the crash.* 2 if: *It's doubtful whether she will agree.*

whew (HEW) *interj.* expressing relief, surprise, etc.

whey (WHAY) *n.* the liquid part of milk left after the curd separates.

which *pron.* 1 [used in questions to distinguish between several persons or things]: *Which is your dog? Which of them is yours? Which of us is faultless?* 2 [used in subordinate clauses to refer to something already mentioned]: *the car in which he drives to work; The book, which is still being written, will be published next year; I'm hungry, which means it's lunch time.*
— **which is which** which is one and which the other: *Ada and Ida are so much alike it is hard to tell which is which.*
— *adj.: Which dog is yours? "Cats of the World," which book is now being written, may make the author wealthy.*

which·ev·er (which·EV·ur) *pron. & adj.* any of two or more: *Work the day you like, whichever it is; Work whichever day you like.*

which·so·ev·er (which·so·EV·ur) *pron. & adj.* [emphatic form] whichever.

whick·er *n. & v.* neigh; whinny.

whiff *n. Informal.* 1 a slight puff or breath: *a whiff of fresh air; a whiff of smoke.* 2 a slight smell or trace: *a whiff of garlic, scandal; He gets panicky at the first whiff of something burning.*
— *v.* blow or puff lightly.

while *n.* a period of time: *for a little while, short while; a long while ago; The government continued spending* **the while** (= during the time) *its debts grew ever larger.*
— **once in a while** occasionally.
— **worth one's while** worth one's time or effort.
— *conj.* 1 during the time that: *She works while he sleeps.* 2 whereas; although: *She's a Tory, while he's a Grit.*
— *v.* **whiles, whiled, whil·ing** esp. **while away**, spend time in a leisurely way: *to while away the summer.*

whilst (WHY-) *conj.* [rare] while: *He takes people to task for their bad grammar whilst using stilted language himself.*

whim *n.* a sudden fanciful idea or desire: *a childish whim; an idle whim; She acted on a mere whim* (= impulse).

whim·per (WHIM·pur) *v.* 1 cry with whining, broken sounds. 2 utter in this manner. — *n.* a whimpering.

whim·sey (WHIM·zee) *n.* **-seys** same as WHIMSY.

whim·si·cal (WHIM·zuh·cul) *adj.* 1 full of whims; capricious. 2 odd or fanciful: *a whimsical expression, idea, tale.* — **whim·si·cal·ly** *adv.*
— **whim·si·cal·i·ty** (-CAL·uh·tee) *n.*

whim·sy (WHIM·zee) *n.* **-sies** 1 caprice or whim. 2 a fanciful or quaint quality, esp. of humour.

whine *n.* 1 the weak, nasal tone of a complaining child. 2 a complaint or cry made in this tone.
— *v.* **whines, whined, whin·ing** utter with a whine or make a whine: *to whine about the hot weather; He whined something about the room being hot; He whined (to her) that the room was too hot.*
— **whin·er** *n.: Some children are chronic whiners.*

whin·ny (WHIN·ee) *n.* a low and gentle neigh.
— *v.* **whin·nies, whin·nied, whin·ny·ing** make a whinny.

whip *n.* 1 a stick with a lash attached, used as an instrument of punishment or for urging animals forward: *to crack a whip.* 2 a blow using a whip or a whipping or lashing motion. 3 one who drives using a whip, as a coachman, one in charge of a hunting pack, etc. 4 a party official helping the floor leader in a legislature with discipline, attendance during voting, etc. 5 a dessert made by beating egg white with fruit and sugar.
— *v.* **whips, whipped, whip·ping** 1 beat with a whip; lash: *to whip a horse; The poor donkey didn't deserve the whipping; Rain was whipping her face; a rabble-rouser who can whip* (= stir) *any mob into a frenzy.* 2 move suddenly or quickly like the lash of a ship: *Flags whipped in the wind; a wind whipping across the lake; a cold whipping wind; He whipped out his wallet and paid the bill; Then he whipped out of the restaurant.* 3 defeat: *We whipped them in the finals; It was a 9-3 whipping.* 4 wrap or wind a stick, rope, etc. closely with cord for strength or protection. 5 beat cream, etc. until stiff, as in making **whipped cream** topping for desserts using **whipping cream** (= cream containing 32% to 40% butterfat).

— **whip into shape** *Informal.* bring into proper condition by vigorous action: *a teacher who can whip any class of rowdies into shape.*

— **whip up 1** rouse: *to whip up enthusiasm, fury, hatred, interest.* **2** prepare something quickly: *to whip up a milkshake; an entertainer who can whip up a great show in no time at all.*

whip hand *n.* control or advantage: *to have the whip hand over* or *of an opponent.*

whip·lash *n.* **1** the lash of a whip. **2** injury to the neck caused by a severe jolt as in an automobile collision.

whip·per·snap·per (WHIP·ur·snap·ur) *n.* an insignificant but presumptuous person: *a young whippersnapper.*

whipping boy *n.* a scapegoat, like a boy once used to take the punishment for a prince's faults: *Labour is sometimes made the whipping boy for inflation.*

whip·saw *n.* a two-handled or crosscut saw operated by two persons.

— *v.* **1** cut with a whipsaw. **2** *Informal.* cheat or be worsted by the joint action of two people or in two ways at the same time.

whir or **whirr** (WHUR) *n.* a buzzing sound, as of a small machine.

— *v.* **whirs** or **whirrs**, **whirred**, **whir·ring** vibrate, fly, operate, etc. with a whir.

whirl (WHURL) *n.* **1** a rapidly revolving motion, as by the force of wind or water. **2** something that whirls or a condition of dizziness, confusion, etc.: *Her head was in a whirl as she got off the merry-go-round; the social whirl* (= round) *of parties and dances.* **3** an attempt or try: *Give it a whirl and let me know.*

— *v.* swing round and round rapidly and continuously, as leaves caught in the wind or a car gone out of control: *Dancing couples whirled about the room; He whirled her away in his new sports car; Her head whirled* (= She felt dizzy), *and she passed out.*

whirl·i·gig (WHUR·lee·gig) *n.* a whirling or spinning thing, esp. a toy: *A beetle called a "whirligig" whirls on water; the whirligig* (= merry-go-round) *of city life; the whirligig of time* (= changes of fortune brought about by time).

whirl·pool *n.* a spinning mass of water caused by opposing currents or by wind; vortex or eddy: *to be drawn into the whirlpool of political intrigue.*

whirl·wind *n.* a whirling column of air, as seen in deserts.

— *adj. Informal.* fast or hurried: *a whirlwind campaign, romance, tour.*

whirl·y·bird (WHUR·lee·bird) *n. Informal.* a helicopter.

whisk *v.* **1** move or sweep with a light, quick, brushing movement, as with a small bunch of straw, twigs, feathers, etc. used for brushing dust, or lint off clothes: *Security police whisked them through customs and into a waiting van; On being sentenced, he was whisked off to jail.* **2** beat or whip eggs, creams, etc. to a froth using a whisk.

— *n.* **1** a whisking movement. **2** a brush used for whisking dust, etc. off; also **whisk broom.** **3** in African costume, an ornamental bunch of soft, light material

held in the hand for shooing off flies, etc. **4** a kitchen utensil made of looped wires used for whisking eggs, creams, etc.

whisk·er *n.* **1** one of the long, bristly hairs growing above the mouth of a cat, rat, bird, insect, etc. **2** one of the hairs grown on the sides of a man's face. **3 whiskers** *pl.* the beard on a man's face other than the mustache: *to grow whiskers; He had to shave off his whiskers when he joined the police force.* **4** *Informal.* a very tiny amount, degree, distance, or margin: *He won the election by a whisker.*

whisk·ered (WHISK·urd) *adj.* having whiskers: *a whiskered cat, man.*

whis·key (WHIS·kee) *n.* **-keys** same as WHISKY: *Irish whiskey; Bourbon whiskey.*

whis·ky (WHIS·kee) *n.* **-kies** a strong alcoholic liquor distilled from grain and malt, including rye and Scotch: *Canadian whiskies are aged at least three years; Straight whisky is 80% alcohol by volume; There are single-malt whiskies and blended whiskies; He ordered a whisky and soda (drink).* Also **whis·key, -keys.**

whisky-jack *n. Cdn.* a Canada jay.

whis·per (WHIS·pur) *v.* **1** speak or say in a very low voice; hence, tell very privately, as a secret: *He whispered it in her ear; a **whispering campaign** of spreading false rumours, charges, etc. against an opponent.* **2** make a rustling sound, as leaves in the wind.

— *n.* **1** a whispering or something whispered: *The child spoke in whispers.* **2** a rustling sound.

whis·tle (WHIS·ul) *v.* **-tles, -tled, -tling 1** make a shrill, clear sound by forcing breath through pursed lips: *to whistle to* (= call) *a dog; to whistle at someone (in admiration); to whistle for* (= hail) *a cab; She can whistle (the tune of) "O Canada"; a claim that sounds like **whistling in the dark*** (= like something to reassure oneself). **2** make a similar sound, as a bird, wind, steam engine, or with a whistle.

— **whistle for something** *Informal.* expect in vain to get it.

— *n.* **1** a whistling or its sound: *Sam gave a whistle to attract Ray's attention; a shrill whistle; wolf whistle; as clean as a whistle* (= very clean). **2** a device for producing such a sound, as used by police, referees, etc.: *Patients don't like to **blow the whistle on*** (*Informal for* report to the authorities) *doctors who overcharge.* — **whis·tler** *n.*

whistle stop *n.* **1** a brief stop at a small town in a political campaign tour. **2** a small town along a railway route at which a train stops only by request.

whit *n.* the least bit; iota: *The rumours don't worry her one whit; There's not a whit of truth in them.*

white *adj.* **whit·er, whit·est 1** having the colour of fresh snow or milk; light-coloured or pale; not black: *a beautiful white horse; Snow is "white gold" for ski resorts; the white matter of the brain (surrounding the grey matter); a white* (= albino) *mouse; a white* (= snowy) *Christmas; white* (= grey) *hair; a white-haired* (= blond) *youth; the white powder* or *stuff called snow; the white* (= Caucasoid) *race* or *White race; a page with too much white* (= unprinted) *space.* **2** having no colour:

*white blood cells; the incandescent white heat of metals; He turned white with fear, fury; the golden loaves of white enriched bread; Generic **white label** (=no-name) products are cheaper than name brands; **white meat** such as pork, poultry, rabbit, and veal; white (=not green) creme de menthe; white (=pale-coloured) wines such as Chablis.* **3** symbolic of goodness, peace, etc., often "not black": *white as a lily; white (=harmless) lies, magic, witches; waiting for a white knight to come and rescue the company from a corporate raider in a takeover battle; to wave the **white flag** (of truce or surrender); a white (=reactionary) political faction.*
— **n. 1** white colour or pigment. **2** one that is white: *dressed in white (=white clothes); the white (=albumen) of an egg; the white of the eye (around the iris); an uncrowded page with plenty of white (=white space).* **3** a Caucasoid. **4** a member of a reactionary group.

white ant *n.* same as TERMITE.

white-collar (white·COLL·ur) *adj.* clerical or professional; not blue-collar: *a white-collar job, occupation, worker; A **white-collar crime** such as fraud, embezzlement, or tax evasion is committed without use of violence by people in white-collar occupations.*

white elephant *n.* something useless and expensive to maintain, like an albino elephant considered sacred in some Southeast Asian countries.

white feather *n.* esp. **show the white feather** show cowardice.

white flag *n.* **1** a white-coloured flag used to signal a truce or surrender: *to show the white flag.* **2** a token of accepting defeat.

white goods *n.pl.* **1** white household linens. **2** household appliances such as refrigerators, washers, etc. that are usually white-enamelled.

white hope *n.* a person or thing expected to bring glory to a group: *a drug hailed as the great white hope of cancer therapy.*

white-hot *adj.* **1** at white heat. **2** intensely excited, angry, enthusiastic, etc.

whit·en (WHY·tun) *v.* make or become white or whiter. — **whit·en·er** *n.*

white·out *n.* an arctic or winter weather condition in which the snow, either on the ground or blowing, causes poor visibility and makes flying and driving dangerous.

white paper *n.* a document published by a government setting out its policy on a specific subject.

white slave *n.* a female forced to be a prostitute, esp. one sent abroad.

white sound *n.* an electronically produced tone used to mask noises in a work area.

white supremacy *n.* supremacy of the white race.

white·wash *n.* **1** a mixture of lime and water for coating walls, woodwork, etc. **2** a covering up of faults or defects as if by use of whitewash. **3** *Informal.* a defeat that is a shutout.
— *v.* **1** cover or conceal with whitewash. **2** *Informal.* defeat by a shutout.

whith·er (WHITH·ur, "TH" as in "the") *adv.* to what place, result, condition, etc.?
— *conj.* to which place, etc.

whith·er·so·ev·er (WHITH·ur·so·EV·ur) *adv. & conj.* to whatever place.

whit·tle (WHIT·ul) *v.* **whit·tles, whit·tled, whit·tling** **1** pare or cut shavings from wood, etc. with a knife: *to whittle at a stick; to whittle a stick into a handle.* **2** shape or carve an object: *to whittle a handle out of a stick.* **3** reduce: *to whittle down expenses; Inflation whittles away our purchasing power.* — **whit·tler** *n.*

whiz or **whizz** *n.* **whiz·zes** **1** the hissing sound of an arrow, ball, etc. rushing through the air. **2** *Informal.* an expert or skilled person; wizard: *She's a whiz at electronics; a **whiz kid** (=highly intelligent youth).*
— *v.* **whiz·zes, whizzed, whiz·zing** **1** make a whiz. **2** speed past making this sound.

whiz-bang *adj. & n.* first-rate (person or thing): *That's a whiz-bang of an idea; a whiz-bang finance minister who screwed up the economy; He's no whiz-bang as a writer.*

who (HOO) *pron.,* objective WHOM, possessive WHOSE **1** [used in questions about persons]: *Who is the president? Who are these people? Who did you say is coming to dinner? John who?* **2** the person or persons that: *the man who called yesterday; those who smoke; I don't know who (Informal for whom) to trust anymore.*

whoa (WHOH) *interj.* [to a horse, etc.] stop!

who·dun·it (hoo·DUN·it) *n. Informal.* a story, play, etc. dealing with crime detection.

who·ev·er (hoo·EV·ur) *pron.* **1** no matter who; any person who: *Whoever owes money is a debtor.* **2** [emphasizing "who"]: *Whoever is that guy?*

whole (HOLE) *adj.* with no part taken away or left out; entire: *a whole roast pig; herring salted whole; the whole neighbourhood; the whole wide world; He came out alive and whole (=unhurt); **whole blood** (with all its components); a whole (=not half) **brother;** a **whole number** (not a fraction); We don't know **a whole lot** about many things of daily life; to treat the whole person (=the physical, emotional, and other aspects).*
— *n.* complete or entire thing, unit, system, etc.: *the parts of a whole; a complex whole; to constitute, form a whole.*
— **as a whole** as one complete unit, not in parts.
— **on the whole** considering everything; in general.
— **whole·ness** *n.*

whole-hearted (HOLE·har·tid) *adj.* with all one's enthusiasm; not half-hearted.

whole hog *n.* See HOG.

whole-meal *adj.* made of the entire kernel of wheat; whole-wheat: *whole-meal flour.*

whole milk *n.* milk with no butterfat, etc. removed.

whole·sale *n.* the selling of goods in large quantities and at lower prices, usually to retailers.
— *adj.* **1** (selling) in large quantities: *the wholesale price, not retail; a wholesale dealer who supplies retailers.* **2** general; indiscriminate: *wholesale condemnation, criticism, murder, slaughter.*

— *adv.* in a wholesale manner: *Retailers buy wholesale; The plan was rejected wholesale* (= completely).
— *v.* **-sales, -saled, -sal·ing** sell at wholesale.
— **whole·sal·er** *n.*

whole·some *adj.* **1** healthful: *a wholesome climate, environment, food; a wholesome* (= healthy and vigorous) *youth.* **2** beneficial for mind and soul: *wholesome advice, movies, reading material; a wholesome* (= prudent or salutary) *fear of the law.*
— **whole·some·ness** *n.*

whole-wheat *adj.* ground from entire kernels of wheat including the bran, germ, etc.: *whole-wheat flour; whole-wheat bread (made of whole-wheat flour).*

who'll (HOOL) who shall; who will.

whol·ly (HOH·lee, HOLE·lee) *adv.* to the whole extent; entirely; solely.

whom (HOOM, long "OO") *pron.* objective case of WHO: *the man to whom you are married; Whom (Formal for Who) are you married to?*

whom·ev·er (hoo·MEV·ur) *objective case* of WHOEVER.

whomp *v.* usually **whomp up** *Slang.* prepare quickly: *to whomp up some milkshakes.*

whom·so·ev·er (hoom·so·EV·ur) *objective case* of WHOSOEVER.

whoop *n.* **1** an excited long cry or shout: *The crowd let out whoops of joy.* **2** the hoot of an owl, the cry of a crane, etc., as of the **whooping crane.** **3** a long and loud drawing in of the breath following a paroxysm of coughing, as in **whooping cough.**
— *v.* **1** shout or call loudly. **2** hoot as an owl.
— **whoop it up** *Slang.* make merry noisily: *Calgary whooped it up with the 1988 Olympics.*

whoop·ee (WHOO·pee) *interj.* expressing great joy.
— *n. Informal.* noisy fun: *The class was punished for making whoopee when the teacher was late.*

whoop·la (WHOOP·lah) *n.* same as HOOPLA.

whoops (short or long "oo") *interj.* uttered when suddenly realizing one's error or taking a wrong step.

whoosh (short or long "oo") *v. & n.* (make) the loud noise of rushing air.

whop *n. & v.* **whops, whopped, whop·ping** *Informal.* hit or whack.

whop·per (WHOP·ur) *n. Informal.* something huge, as a story, fish, or falsehood.

whopping *adj. & adv. Informal.* extraordinarily huge; colossal; colossally: *a whopping big lie; a whopping* (= impressive) *idea.*

whore (HORE) *n.* a prostitute. — **whor·ish** *adj.*

whorl (WHORL, WHURL) *n.* a whirling or circular shape or formation, as a ring of leaves or flowers around a point on an axis, one of the turns in a univalve shell, or a pattern of circles: *the arches, loops, and whorls of a fingerprint; adj.: the whorled* (= whorl-shaped) *arrangement of the parts of a flower.*

who's (HOOZ) who is; who has.

whose (HOOZ) *pron. possessive case* of WHICH and

WHO: *Whose is this kid? Whose are these kids?*
— *adj.: Whose kid is this? Whose kids are these? a flower whose name I've forgotten.*

who·so (HOO·soh) *pron.* whoever.

who·so·ev·er (HOO·so·EV·ur) *pron.* [emphatic form] whoever.

who's who *n.* **1** a compilation of short biographies: *The Canadian Who's Who; The roster reads like a who's who of the dance world.* **2** the leaders of a group: *The audience was a who's who of oil barons.*

whump *v.* same as WHOMP.

why *adv.* for what reason, cause, or purpose?: *Why do people eat?*
— *conj.: Everyone knows why people eat; The main reason why we eat is to live.*
— *n., pl.* **whys:** *the how and why of our existence;* **the whys and the wherefores** *of marriages breaking up.*
— *interj.* expressing surprise, etc.: *Why, I thought today was a holiday! Why, what happened?*

wick *n.* a piece of cord or tape for drawing up and burning the fuel in an oil lamp, stove, or candle.

wick·ed (WICK·id) *adj.* **1** bad in a willful or immoral way: *a wicked and disobedient child; a wicked witch; a thoroughly wicked old man.* **2** roguish; mischievous: *a wicked joke, look.* **3** *Informal.* skilfully executed or dealt; formidable: *a wicked blow, performance.*

wick·er *n.* **1** a thin, flexible twig or strip of material used for weaving into baskets, furniture, etc. **2** such woven material or objects made with it.

wick·et (WICK·it) *n.* a small gate or opening, as a box-office window, a small door set in a large gate, a wire arch or hoop through which balls are hit in games, etc.

wide *adj.* **wid·er, wid·est 1** having a relatively large measurement from side to side; broad; not narrow: *a wide aperture, doorway, expanse, gap, margin; wide* (= fully open) *eyes; a door two metres wide* (= in width). **2** of great range; extensive: *the whole wide world; a man of wide interests; The shop carries a wide selection of goods.*
— *combining form.* **1** throughout: *citywide, countrywide, nationwide.* **2** broad: *a wide-bodied jet; wide-brimmed, wide-ranging, wide-reaching.*
— *adv.* **1** over a relatively large area or extent; extensively: *He is wide awake; Open your mouth wide; She travels far and wide.* **2** away from the target: *The bullet went wide; It was two feet wide of the mark.*
— **wide·ly** *adv.*

wide-angle (WIDE·ANG·gul) *adj.* having a relatively wide angle of view that takes in a large area of a scene: *a wide-angle lens, shot.*

wide-awake (WIDE·uh·wake) *adj.* **1** fully awake. **2** alert.

wide-eyed *adj.* **1** with wide-open eyes; hence, amazed: *She stared in wide-eyed wonder.* **2** simple or naive: *a wide-eyed admirer; a wide-eyed newspaper article on faith healers.*

wide-mouthed *adj.* having a wide mouth: *a wide-mouthed channel, jar; He stared in wide-mouthed astonishment.*

wid·en (WYE·dun) v. make or become wide or wider; broaden.

wide·spread adj. **1** widely spread out: *The famine is becoming more widespread in Ethiopia.* **2** widely prevalent: *a widespread belief, fear.*

wid·get (WIJ·it) n. an imagined gadget or device: *Suppose you made $100 an hour selling widgets.*

wid·ow (WID·oh) n. a woman after her husband's death but before remarriage: *a war widow.*
— v. cause to become a widow: *a young woman widowed by the war.* — **wid·ow·hood** n.

wid·ow·er (WID·oh·ur) n. a man after his wife's death but before remarriage.

width n. **1** measurement from side to side of something; breadth. **2** a piece of a certain width.

wield (WEELD) v. handle a tool, weapon, etc. skilfully and effectively: *to wield an axe, the pen, a sword; to wield* (= exercise) *influence, power.* — **wield·er** n.

wie·ner (WEE·nur) n. a frankfurter of shorter size; also called "Vienna sausage" or **wie·ner·wurst.**

wife n. **wives 1** a female spouse: *a devoted, estranged, faithful, jealous, unfaithful wife; He had no children by his common-law wife; I'll check with the wife and let you know.* **2** any married woman: *Canadian wives; a Hollywood wife; farm wives; police wives.*
— **wife·hood** n. — **wife·less** adj. — **wife·ly** adj.

wig n. a head covering of false hair: *They sell both wigs and hairpieces.*
— v. **wigs, wigged, wig·ging** Slang. **1** thrill or excite. **2** be thrilled, excited, etc.: *teeny-boppers wigging out over their idols.*
— **wigged out** Slang. out of touch with reality; high: *people wigged out on drugs.*

wigged (WIGD) adj. wearing a wig: *a wigged judge; the wigged look.*

wig·gle (WIG·ul) v. **wig·gles, wig·gled, wig·gling** move with quick, side-to-side movements: *to wiggle one's ears, hips, toes.* — **n.** a wiggling movement.
— **wig·gler** n. — **wig·gly** (WIG·lee) adj.

wig·wag v. **-wags, -wagged, -wag·ging 1** move to and fro; wag. **2** signal a message by waving a flag, light, etc. according to a code.
— **n. 1** the wigwagging of messages. **2** such a message.

wig·wam (WIG·wom) n. a usually dome-shaped dwelling of North American Indians made of a framework of poles covered with bark or woven mats.

wild (WILED) adj. **1** of animals, plants, etc., not tamed or cultivated: *the wild boar of Europe and Asia; wild honey; a wild region; the wild rose.* **2** not civilized or orderly: *wild tribes; the **wild and woolly** (= barbarous) West; wild laughter; a wild* (= erratic) *baseball pitch; a **wild card*** (= playing card with arbitrary rank or value); *a wild guess.* **3** crazy or frantic: *a wild scheme; wild speculations; He was wild with rage; a wild* (= violent) *storm.*
— **adv.:** *weeds growing wild on a lawn; Children shouldn't **run wild** on the streets; They went wild over* (= were very excited about) *their idol.*
— **n.** a wild region or condition: *return to the wild; plants growing in the wild; in the wilds of the Amazon; the call of the wild* (= "Nature").
— **wild·ly** adv.; **wild·ness** n.

wild·cat n. **1** any of the smaller wild animals of the cat family, esp. a bobcat. **2** a fierce fighter. **3** a risky or reckless undertaking, as a gas or oil well drilled in an unproved area.
— **adj.** unauthorized; illegal; illicit: *wildcat operations, stocks, strikes, walkouts.*
— **v. -cats, -cat·ted, -cat·ting** drill for gas or oil in an unproven area. — **wild·cat·ter** n.

wil·der·ness (WIL·dur·nis) n. an uninhabited region without tracks or trails, as a forest or desert.

wild-eyed adj. **1** staring in an angry or deranged manner. **2** irrational or foolish: *wild-eyed notions; She's no wild-eyed radical.*

wild·fire n. a quickly spreading forest fire: *The news spread like wildfire.*

wild·fowl n. **-fowls** or **-fowl** a game bird such as a wild duck or quail.

wild-goose chase n. a foolish or futile pursuit, endeavour, etc.

wild·life n. animals, birds, fishes, etc. in their natural state.
— **adj.:** *wildlife conservation, management; a wildlife preserve, sanctuary.*

wild oat or **wild oats** n. a wild grass resembling oats.
— **sow one's wild oats** esp. of males, be promiscuous in youth.

Wild West n. the western United States of pioneer days: *Lawlessness was such that the Wild West meant just that.*

wile v. **wiles, wiled, wil·ing** lure or entice.
— **wile away** same as WHILE AWAY.
— **wiles** n.pl. sly tricks or arguments used to trap someone: *the wiles of the serpent who tricked Eve; the coquettish wiles of a temptress; "Feminine wiles" is a much-abused term.*

wil·ful same as WILLFUL.

will n. **1** the mental power to make and carry out a decision: *the will to succeed; the will to survive; a terminal patient's will to live; a woman of iron will; They couldn't break her will; an indomitable, inflexible will; a clash of wills; "Where there's a will there's a way."* **2** wish or choice: *elected to carry out the will of the people; a man who imposes his will* (= desire) *on his*

children; *It was done against her will; not of her own free will; He hires and fires **at will** (= as he likes); He has servants to **do his will** (= obey him) round the clock.* **3** a statement of how property is to be disposed of after one's death: *He died without making his will; her last will and testament; to challenge, contest, draw up, execute, make, make out, validate a will.* **4** a feeling or disposition toward another: *She bore him no ill will; a message of good will toward all.*
— *v.* **1** decide or determine: *He wished to live to a ripe old age, but Providence willed otherwise; Willing is more important than mere wishing.* **2** influence by mental power: *She has the psychic power to will someone to turn around.* **3** bequeath a property *to* someone. **4** wish or desire: *Do as you will.* **5** auxiliary *v., pt.* **would** (WOOD) expressing futurity *(The world will end),* willingness or determination *(I will hire her),* capability, habit, or custom *(Boys will be boys; That will be the mailman),* and command *(You will do as I say; That will be all).*

will·ful or **wil·ful** (WIL·ful) *adj.* **1** obstinate or stubborn: *a willful child.* **2** intentional: *willful disobedience, murder.* — **will·ful·ly** or **wil·ful·ly** *adv.* — **will·ful·ness** or **wil·ful·ness** *n.*

wil·lies (WIL·eez) *n.pl. Slang.* jitters: *That kind of talk gives me the willies; to get the willies; suffer from the willies.*

willing *adj.* **1** ready or consenting: *She's willing; She's willing to marry him.* **2** ready and prompt: *willing ears, hands, workers.* **3** voluntary: *willing obedience, sacrifice.* — **will·ing·ly** *adv.* **will·ing·ness** *n.*

will-o'-the-wisp (WIL·uh·thuh·WISP) *n.* **1** a light sometimes seen hovering over marshes, believed to be marsh gas igniting itself; also called "jack-o'-lantern." **2** an elusive and misleading hope or goal: *the will-o'- the-wisp of peace in the Middle East; Love seemed a cruel will-o'-the-wisp that would elude him forever.*

wil·low (WIL·oh) *n.* a tree with long, narrow leaves and slender, pliable branches, often used in weaving baskets; also, its wood.

wil·low·y (WIL·oh·ee, WIL·uh·wee) *adj.* slender or lithe like a willow.

will·pow·er (WIL-, *rhyme:* our) *n.* strength of will or determination; resoluteness: *He overcame his handicap by sheer willpower.*

wil·ly-nil·ly (WIL·ee·NIL·ee) *adj. & adv.* (happening, existing, etc.) whether one wants it or not: *She accepted the nomination willy-nilly; The parties joined together in a willy-nilly coalition.*

wilt *v.* droop or become weak, as a plant from heat or lack of water: *Plants will wilt and die if not watered; His confidence wilted under her severe criticism.*
— *n.* **1** a wilting. **2** a disease caused by fungi, bacteria, or viruses that makes plants wilt and die.

wi·ly (WYE·lee) *adj.* **-li·er, -li·est** full of wiles; sly, as a fox: *the wily coyote; a wily character.* — **wi·li·ness** *n.*

wimp *n. Slang.* a weak and soft person; weakling. — **wimp·y** *adj.*

win *v.* **wins, won** (WUN), **win·ning** succeed in achieving a desired aim by effort, as the result of competition, etc.: *Which team won (the race)? The Blue Jays won easily; They won hands down; We won against considerable odds; to win an audience, a mountain summit, reputation, scholarship, war, wife; He would give anything to win* (= gain) *her favour; You **win a few, lose a few** or **You can't win them all*** (= You cannot always be successful); *Persevering people **win out*** (= succeed) *in the end; It took much persuasion to **win over*** (= get the support of) *the hostile crowd.*
— *n. Informal.* victory or success, esp. in a contest or race: *a lottery win; She chalked up four wins before the day ended.*
— **win·na·ble** (WIN·uh·bul) *adj.: Is a nuclear war winnable?*

wince *v.* **winc·es, winced, winc·ing** shrink back or flinch involuntarily: *He winced in pain; She winces at the thought of the work waiting to be done.*
— *n.* a wincing movement or expression.

¹wind (WINED) *v.* **winds, wound** (WOWND), **wind·ing 1** move or cause to move in a curving or twisting manner: *The river winds (its way) through the plain; a winding* (= spiral) *staircase.* **2** wrap or coil: *A vine winds around its support; He wore a shawl wound around his neck; She can wind him around her little finger* (= knows how to manipulate him); *a body wrapped in a **winding sheet** for burial.* **3** roll into a ball, as yarn, or on a spool or reel, as thread, tape, etc. **4** tighten the spring of a clock or other mechanism for power to operate: *He forgot to wind his old watch; a self-winding (automatic) watch.*
— **wind down 1** come or bring to a gradual conclusion: *The business was so unprofitable they decided to wind it down.* **2** relax; unwind: *He needs his weekends to wind down a little.*
— **wind up 1** make very tense or nervous. **2** of a baseball pitcher, swing the arm to throw the ball. **3** conclude an activity or business: *It happened when the convention was about to wind up; They decided to wind up their operations as soon as possible.* **4** *Informal.* come to an end; end up: *She wound up with less money than in her previous job; He wound up in jail.*
— *n.* a winding or turn. — **wind·er** *n.*

²wind *n.* **1** air in motion, esp. a strong current: *Gale-force winds whipped the waves; a biting, cold, cutting, icy, raw, winter wind; a brisk, fair, favourable, gentle, gusty, heavy, light, stiff, strong wind; the prevailing winds; a blast or gust of wind; A wind blows, falls, howls, picks up, subsides.* **2** a trend or tendency: *Politicians try to find out which way or how the wind is blowing before taking a stand on an issue; They try to test the winds; changing winds* (= trends) *of public opinion; winds of change* (= tendency toward reform). **3** gas from the stomach or bowels. **4** breathing power: *The jogger stopped to recover his wind; He was out of wind; Then he got his second wind* (= renewed energy) *and finished his race; His claims are mere wind* (= empty talk). **5 winds** *pl.* wind instruments of an orchestra, or the players.
— **break wind** expel gas through the anus.
— **get** or **have** or **catch wind of** learn about something, as if by a wind-borne scent.
— **in the wind** about to happen; astir: *A general election is in the wind.*
— **take the wind out of one's sails** take away someone's

advantage by one's own action.
— **the four winds** the four directions or points of the compass: *scattered it to the four winds.*
— *v.* **1** get the scent of something; follow a hunted animal, etc. by scent. **2** put out of breath *by* running, *from* a climb, etc.: *an asthmatic who is easily winded.* **3** *pt.* **wind·ed** or **wound** (WOWND) blow a horn; hence, sound a signal or blast.

wind·bag *n. Informal.* one who talks much but communicates little of importance.

wind·blown (WIND·blone) *adj.* blown by the wind: *windblown hair, trees.*

wind·break *n.* a growth of trees, etc. for breaking the force of the wind.

wind·chill or **wind chill** *n.* an estimate of how cold one feels because of the added effect of a wind blowing at a certain speed; also **windchill factor.**

wind·fall *n.* an unexpected piece of good fortune, esp. financial profit, like ripe fruit blown down by the wind: *He got a sudden windfall in the shape of a lottery win; windfall profits.*

wind instrument *n.* a musical instrument in which air is the vibrating medium, as flutes and trumpets.

wind·mill *n.* a mill or machine moved by the power of the wind acting on a wheel of vanes or sails mounted on top of a tower: *to tilt at windmills* (= fight imaginary opponents).

win·dow (WIN·doh) *n.* **1** an opening in a wall for letting in light and air or for looking through: *The windows of the new house were still covered with plastic; a bay window; He jumped out of an upstairs window; All plans seemed to go out the window; Reading "Ulysses" opened a window on the world of the classics; A **window envelope** has a transparent opening showing the address on an enclosed item.* **2** a framework enclosing sealed or movable panes of glass, etc.: *May I open the window? a double-glazed picture window (that is always shut); Do you wash windows? No, we don't do windows; to roll down, roll up a car window; The rear window is fogged up; a frosted-over window; a stained-glass (church) window; a shop window; We install storm windows well before the start of winter.* **3** a windowpane. **4** a suitable or opportune period or interval: *The launch window for a space shot depends on planetary positions; As the margin of safety disappears, the window of vulnerability gets wider.* **5** any of several portions of a video monitor simultaneously displaying the various functions of a computer.

window dressing *n.* a display that seeks to impress favourably, as of goods in a store window: *The fancy title page of his essay was just window dressing.*
— **window-dress** (WIN·doh·dress) *v.*
— **window dresser** *n.*

win·dow·pane (WIN·doh·pane) *n.* a pane of glass in a window.

window-shop (WIN·doh·shop) *v.* **-shops, -shopped, -shop·ping** look at goods displayed in shop windows without going inside to buy. — **window-shopper** *n.*

wind·pipe *n.* the air passage between the throat and the lungs.

wind·proof *adj.* protecting from the wind: *a windproof jacket.*

wind·row (WIND·roh) *n.* **1** a row of fallen leaves, ridge of ice, etc. formed by wind action. **2** a row of cut hay or grain made for drying: *fish heaped in windrows along the waterfront beaches.*

wind shear *n.* an air disturbance moving in an opposite direction to another, said to cause sudden airplane crashes; microburst.

wind·shield *n.* the screen of glass above the dashboard of an automobile, train, etc.

wind·surf·er (WIND·sur·fur) *n.* **1** same as SAILBOARD. **2** one who rides a sailboard.

wind·surf·ing (WIND·surf·ing) *n.* the sport of riding a sailboard.

wind·swept *adj.* swept by or as if by wind.

wind tunnel *n.* a tunnel with air forced through it at various speeds for testing airplanes, automobiles, missiles, etc.

wind·up (WINED·up) *n.* **1** the close or conclusion of an activity or business. **2** the swinging of a baseball pitcher's arm before the delivery.

wind·ward (WIND·wurd) *n.* the side or direction from which the wind is blowing: *An anchor is cast to windward for safety.*
— *adj. & adv.* on or toward the side from which the wind is blowing; against the wind: *the windward and leeward sides of an island; a windward tide* (= a tide moving against the wind).

wind·y *adj.* **wind·i·er, -i·est 1** having much wind: *a windy day; the windy city (of Chicago); the windy prairies; a windy night; windy weather.* **2** like wind, without substance: *windy* (= empty) *talk; a windy talker (with a tendency to talk a great deal).*
— **wind·i·ly** *adv.;* **wind·i·ness** *n.*

wine *n.* **1** an alcoholic drink made from the fermented juice of grapes: *French, Italian, Portuguese, and such imported wines; domestic wines made in Canada, the U.S., Ireland, etc.; cooking, dessert, sacramental, table wines; dry, red, rosé, sparkling, vintage, white wines; the house wine of a restaurant.* **2** a drink similarly made from the juice of other fruits and plants: *dandelion wine.*
— *v.* **wines, wined, win·ing 1** drink wine. **2** entertain with wine, esp. **wine and dine,** treat someone to food and drink.

wine-coloured (WINE·cul·urd) *adj.* dark purplish-red.

win·er·y (WYE·nuh·ree) *n.* **-ries** a wine-making establishment.

wing *n.* **1** one of the paired organs of flight in birds, bats, insects, etc.: *A bird spreads its wings when flying; The penguin's paddlelike wings were once used for flying.* **2** a structure similar to a bird's wing in function, as the vanes of a windmill, feathers of an arrow, etc.: *the wings of an aircraft; The seeds of the maple, pine, ash, etc. have wings.* **3** a side structure or extension: *He added a new wing to his mansion; the maternity wing of a hospital; an unseen figure shouting from the **wings** (of*

the stage). **4** a section or unit of an organization such as an air force: *A wing is composed of groups, squadrons, and flights* (= two or more aircraft); *A wing commander ranks below group captain and above squadron leader; the Left and Right wings* (= factions) *of a political party.* **5** any of various side positions or players in hockey, football, soccer, etc. **6** means or manner of flight. **7 wings** *pl.* insignia earned by a qualified pilot, navigator, etc. in an air force: *She has earned her wings* (= proved herself competent).
— **clip someone's wings** restrict someone's freedom; bring someone down to size.
— **on the wing** in flight; on the fly.
— **take wing** begin to fly; fly up or away: *His thoughts took wing.*
— **under one's wing** under one's protection.
— **wait in the wings** wait just offstage for an entrance cue; hence, wait in a readily available position.
— *v.* **1** fly: *Canada geese wing (their way) south for the winter.* **2** cause to go fast: *Fear winged his flight.* **3** provide with wings: *an arrow winged with feathers.* **4** to wound in the wing; hence, wound slightly: *He was winged by the bandit's bullet.*
— **wing it** *Slang.* speak off the cuff; extemporize: *When she lost her speech notes, she had to wing it.*

wing chair *n.* a chair with a high back and sidepieces projecting forward.

wing·ding *n. Slang.* an outburst of feeling, esp. a wild party: *It was a wingding of a party; a wingding celebration.*

winged (WINGD, *rarely* WING·id) *adj.* having wings: *Mercury, the winged messenger of the gods; winged* (= significant) *words.*

wing·span *n.* the stretch of an aircraft's wings from wingtip to wingtip.

wing·spread *n.* the distance between the tips of the outspread wings of a bird, insect, etc.

wing·tip *n.* **1** the outer end of a wing. **2** a type of man's shoe with a perforated toe cap that extends in a curved design like wings toward the sides; also **wingtip shoe.**

wing·y *adj. Slang.* intoxicated or high.

wink *v.* **1** close and open one eye as a signal or hint: *Sam winked at me.* **2** flutter the eyes. **3** twinkle or flicker: *stars winking in the sky.*
— **wink at** blink at or ignore violations, irregularities, etc.
— **wink back** or **away tears** repress tears by blinking.
— *n.* a winking or the instant it lasts: *He gave the girl a suggestive wink; She vanished in a wink* (= in an instant); *He didn't sleep a wink; He didn't get a wink of sleep; He has* or *takes forty winks* (= a short nap) *after lunch.*

win·kle (WINK·ul) *v.* pry or extract, as a shellfish ("winkle") from its shell: *Some are good at winkling out figures to support their pet theories.*

winnable See WIN.

win·ner (WIN·ur) *n.* one that wins: *Sam looks like a winner; a likely winner; a sure winner.*

winning (WIN·ing) *n.* the act of one who wins: *the*

winning of the gold medal; The day's winnings (= money won) *totalled $1 000.*
— *adj.* **1** victorious or successful: *the winning champion, horse, team.* **2** attractive or charming: *her winning smile; his winning ways.* — **win·ning·ly** *adv.*

Win·ni·peg couch (WIN·uh·peg-) *n. Cdn.* an old-fashioned couch that opens out into a double bed.

Win·ni·peg·ger (WIN·uh·peg·ur) *n.* a person of or from Winnipeg.

win·now (WIN·oh) *v.* **1** blow the chaff from grain, as with a fanning mill: *to winnow grain.* **2** blow away: *to winnow chaff (from grain); to winnow out the chaff.* **3** sort out; sift: *to winnow out facts from falsehoods.*

win·o (WYE·noh) *n.* **-os** *Informal.* a wine-drinking alcoholic.

win·some (WIN·sum) *adj.* sweet and charming: *a winsome lass; her winsome manner; his winsome smile.*
— **win·some·ly** *adv.;* **win·some·ness** *n.*

win·ter (WIN·tur) *n.* **1** the coldest part of the year; the season following autumn: *a cold, harsh, mild, rough, severe winter; in the dead* (= coldest part) *of winter.* **2** a period of inactivity, decline, or distress: *"the winter of our discontent."*
— *adj.:* *winter carnival; winter sports such as skiing, skating, and bobsledding.*
— *v.* **1** pass the winter *in* a place. **2** feed *on* food or maintain cattle, etc. during the winter.

Winter Games same as WINTER OLYMPICS.

win·ter·ize (WIN·tuh·rize) *v.* **-iz·es, -ized, -iz·ing** to ready an automobile, house, etc. for use in the winter.

win·ter·kill (WIN·tur·kil) *n.* the death of a plant or animal from exposure to winter weather.

Winter Olympics or **Winter Games** *n.* a program of winter sports held every four years prior to the Summer Olympics.

win·ter·time (WIN·tur·time) *n.* the winter season.

winter wheat *n.* wheat that is planted in the fall and harvested in the spring or summer.

win·try (WIN·tree) *adj.* **-tri·er, -tri·est 1** of or like winter. **2** cold, cheerless, etc.: *wintry weather, winds; a wintry smile, welcome.* Also **win·ter·y.**

wipe *v.* **wipes, wiped, wip·ing** clean, dry, etc. by rubbing with a handkerchief, towel, hand, etc.: *He washed and wiped the dishes; wiped them dry; She wiped away her tears; He had to wipe up the mess he made on the floor; She wiped her feet on the mat as she came in; didn't wipe* (= apply) *any dirt on the rug; He used a rag to wipe off the mud from his shoes.*
— **wipe off** or **out** put an end to something: *to wipe off a debt; The whole village was wiped out by the epidemic; It was wiped off the face of the earth.*
— **wiped out** *Slang.* **1** drunk. **2** exhausted.
— *n.* **1** an act of wiping. **2** something to wipe with; wiper. **3** in motion pictures, a special effect by which a new scene displaces another by gradually expanding and occupying the whole frame.

wi·per (WYE·pur) *n.* one that wipes, as a towel or a rubber-edged blade on a handle for wiping a window:

833

We turn on our windshield wipers when it's raining; a wiper blade.

wire *n.* **1** metal drawn out into a slender rod or thread; also, a length of this: *copper wire; He caught his foot on a trip wire and fell on the lawn; She got the car started by crossing* or *jumping wires.* **2** anything made or woven of wire: *barbed wire; chicken wire;* **adj.:** *wire gauze, netting, ropes.* **3** telegraph; also, a telegram or cablegram: *messages by wire; to send a wire; I just received a wire saying everything is OK; Canadian Press news wire* (= wire service). **4** the finish line of a horse race.
— **down to the wire** at or to the last moment: *The election was closely fought down to the wire.*
— **get one's wires crossed** confuse one thing for another; be mistaken.
— **pull wires** *Informal.* exert secret influence as if manipulating puppets.
— **under the wire** barely on time: *His application got in just under the wire.*
— *v.* **wires, wired, wir·ing 1** use or provide with wire or wiring: *broken pieces wired together; a house wired for electricity; The police monitor street conversations using wired undercover officers (wearing recording devices); an undercover officer who is wired for sound; Soon we will be living in* **wired cities** *where activities from shopping to education to voting would be conducted from home computer terminals.* **2** telegraph: *She wired her greetings; They wired back that the wedding had been put off; Students used to wire home for money; They would wire their parents; Parents would wire* (= send by wire) *the money to them.*

wire·drawn *adj.* **1** drawn out into a wire. **2** tenuous or overrefined: *a wiredrawn argument.*

wire·less (WIRE·lis) *adj.* having to do with radio waves: *a wireless operator, set, telegraph.*
— *n.* **1** wireless telegraphy or telephony. **2** *Brit.* radio.

wire·pho·to (WIRE·foh·toh) *n.* a picture sent by wire or radio using electric signals.

wire·pull·ing (WIRE·pull·ing) *n. Informal.* the use of secret influence; **wire·pull·er** *n.*

wire recorder *n.* an early form of recording sound magnetically on steel wire.

wire service *n.* a commercial agency that gathers and distributes news and pictures to subscribing papers using teletypewriter and facsimile machines.

wire·tap *v.* **-taps, -tapped, -tap·ping** tap a telephone line secretly to get information.
— *n.* a wiretapping or wiretap device: *an unauthorized wiretap.*

wiring (WIRE·ing) *n.* a system of wires, as for distributing electricity through a house: *a fire caused by faulty wiring.*

wir·y (WIRE·ee) *adj.* **wir·i·er, -i·est 1** of or like wire: *wiry hair.* **2** lean and strong: *a man of wiry build; a wiry body.* — **wir·i·ness** *n.*

wis·dom (WIZ·dum) *n.* **1** the quality of being wise, having knowledge and judgment, etc.: *in the spirit of wisdom and understanding; She questioned the wisdom of his move; a woman of great wisdom; He had the wisdom to reconsider his move; His action showed wisdom; Solomon in all his wisdom could not have said*

such a thing; *as God in His infinite wisdom has ordained; as conventional wisdom suggests.* **2** wise sayings: *a book containing the wisdom of the ancients.*

wisdom tooth *n.* any of the four teeth, one at the back of each jaw on either side, that usually appear in early adulthood.

wise (WIZE) *adj.* **wis·er, wis·est 1** having or showing good sense, prudence, judgment, etc.: *You did the wise thing; It's wise not to argue with customers; a wise decision, investment, use of resources; a child who is wise beyond her years; He came out of the experience a* **sadder and wiser** *man* (= one who has learned a lot); *What's the use of being* **wise after the event?** **2** learned: *a wise judge, man, saying; wise advice, words.* **3** aware or informed: *He looked wise but wouldn't talk; She seemed* **none the wiser** (= no better informed) *for the experience.*
— **get wise** *Slang.* find out; realize: *It was too late when she got wise to his schemes.*
— **wise to** *Slang.* aware of something: *She was wise to his schemes; Someone's careless remarks* **put her wise to** (= made her aware of) *his plans.*
— *v.* **wises, wised, wis·ing** *Informal.* make or become aware: *They wised her up about what was going on; She wised up before it was too late; She quickly wised up to his plans.*
— *combining form.* **1** in the manner specified: *clockwise, lengthwise, likewise.* **2** with regard to what is specified: *healthwise, saleswise, usagewise.*
— *n.* way or manner: *in no wise; in this wise.*
— **wise·ly** *adv.*

wise·a·cre (WYE·zay·cur) *n.* one who pretends to be wise.

wise·ass *n. & adj.* same as SMART·ASS.

wise·crack *n. Informal.* a clever or flippant remark: *good at making wisecracks about things he knows little about.*
— *v.* make a wisecrack: *She wisecracked that he's trying to do too much – like trying to catch 10 fleas with 10 fingers.*

wise guy *n. Slang.* one who is conceited or pretentious.

wish *v.* **1** like and want to have or do something: *Some wish health, others riches; Do you wish to speak to the manager? Do you wish me to speak to him? Do as you wish.* **2** desire *for* something or to be in some condition: *She had everything she could wish for; She wished she didn't have to go to work; wished herself back home; The child wished she were a bird.* **3** have or express a hope for something: *We wish you good luck, good night; She wishes no one ill; I wish you well in your endeavours; to* **wish upon a star** (= hope for what one wishes as if through a star).
— **wish on** *Informal.* foist or impose on someone: *a job so tough I wouldn't wish it on anyone.*
— *n.* **1** a desire or want; also, an expression of it: *to express, make, realize a wish; a fervent, strong, unfulfilled wish; He got his wish; He granted her every wish; Everything was carried out in accordance with her wishes; a child's* **wish list** *of Christmas gifts.* **2 wishes** *pl.* greetings: *to extend, offer, send one's best wishes for the holidays; good, warm, warmest wishes.*

wish·ful *adj.* longing; desirous: *as though wishful for the* sight of disaster. — **wish·ful·ly** adv.; **wish·ful·ness** n.

wishful thinking n. belief based on hope or desire rather than on reality.

wish·y-wash·y (WISH·ee·WOSH·ee) adj. Informal.
1 weak or watery: a wishy-washy soup, tea. 2 weak or ineffectual: wishy-washy excuses, ideas, people.
— **wish·y-wash·i·ness** n.

wisp n. 1 a small bunch of straw, hay, etc. 2 one that is small or slight: a wisp of hair; wisps of smoke curled from blackened trees; a wisp of a girl, smile.
— **wisp·y** adj.

wist [old form] pt. & pp. of WIT.

wist·ful adj. longing or yearning: a wistful gaze; wistful eyes; in a wistful mood.
— **wist·ful·ly** adv.; **wist·ful·ness** n.

wit n. 1 mental power marked by quickness of perception, esp. to see unusual and amusing relationships between things: He displays or shows a quick wit. 2 **wits** pl. intelligence: "The dog had lost his wits to bite so good a man"; He didn't have the time to collect his wits and react to the situation; His hectic life could drive him **out of his wits** (= make him go crazy); She always **has** or **keeps her wits about her** (= is quick and alert). 3 the ability to say clever and amusing things or their expression; wittiness: "Brevity is the soul of wit"; Shakespeare's wit and humour; He has an acid wit; an earthy, keen, mordant, penetrating, rapierlike, sharp, trenchant wit; Her speeches sparkle with wit and wisdom. 4 a person with such a mind: Bernard Shaw is a famous Irish wit.
— **at one's wit's end** at the end of one's mental resources; at a loss what to do next.
— **live by one's wits** live by clever or crafty means rather than by working.
— v. pres. tense (I, he, she, it) **wot**, pt. & pp. **wist**, **wit·ting** Archaic. know.
— **to wit** that is to say; namely.

witch n. 1 a woman supposed to have supernatural powers, usually evil; sorceress: the burning of witches. 2 any hag or shrew. 3 Informal. a charming or bewitching woman.
— v. bewitch: "the very witching time of night."

witch·craft n. a witch's power or practices; sorcery: to practise witchcraft.

witch doctor n. one who practises tribal medicine using magic.

witch·er·y (WICH·uh·ree) n. -er·ies 1 (an act of) witchcraft. 2 charm or fascination.

witch-hunt n. the searching out and harassing of political opponents, as of persons suspected of witchcraft in former times: to conduct a witch-hunt against a political opponent.

with ("th" as in "the" or "thin") prep. 1 [indicating the relationship of an action to its object]: I agree with you; Bring the book with you; He came with his wife; brother and sister fighting with each other; He fights with (= against) her; to swim with (= in the same direction as) the current. 2 [indicating a person or thing as having something]: a man with a beard; a book with covers; tea with cream and sugar; a lady with a dog; She is **with child** (= pregnant). 3 [indicating the use of something as a means or instrument]: a pen to write with; to shoot with a gun. 4 [indicating the agreement of one action in regard to the time, direction, degree, etc. of another]: Temperature varies with time of day; The day ends with sunset; **With that** (= Then) he got up and left. 5 [indicating cause]: shivering with cold; wet with tears. 6 [indicating the manner of an action]: Handle with care; singing with joy; His said it with good intentions. 7 [indicating association or relationship]: your relations with people; Down with tyrants! Away with it! Let's get on with it. 8 despite; notwithstanding: With all that effort, he achieved very little.
— **with it** Slang. socially or culturally up to date; hip: She's quite with it.

with·al (with·ALL) adv. [old use] 1 besides: Withal, his writing has an archaic quality. 2 [used at the end of a phrase] with: something to feed himself withal.

with·draw (with·DRAW) v. -draws, -drew (-DROO), -drawn, -draw·ing 1 take back: Jan instinctively withdrew her hand from the fire; to withdraw money from a bank account; She asked him to withdraw the remark. 2 remove oneself: The candidate had to withdraw from the election; He withdraws to his den to study in quiet.

with·draw·al (with·DRAW·ul) n. 1 a withdrawing: to make a withdrawal from a bank account; There were mass withdrawals just before the bank collapsed; to carry out, complete, make a troop withdrawal; an orderly, precipitate, strategic, tactical withdrawal. 2 the giving up of a drug that one is addicted to; **adj.**: a patient suffering from withdrawal effects; a withdrawal illness, period, syndrome.

with·drawn (with·DRAWN) adj. 1 retiring or reserved. 2 secluded; isolated.

withe (WITH, WITHE – "TH" as in "the") n. a tough, flexible twig, as of a willow, that is used for tying bundles of firewood, for plaiting, etc.

with·er (WITH·ur, "TH" as in "the") 1 v. dry up, as something growing that loses vitality: Plants wither away in the heat; Our lawn is all withered up; Tea processing starts with the withering of leaves; She withered him with a look; gave him a withering look. 2 **withers** n. pl. the ridge between the shoulder bones of a horse, ox, etc.

with·hold (with·HOLD) v. -holds, -held, -hold·ing 1 hold back; keep back: He tried to withhold his men from attacking the strike-breakers; Employers withhold taxes from pay cheques; The **withholding tax** is collected from employees and sent to Revenue Canada. 2 to keep from giving: to withhold information from the police; to withhold one's consent; to withhold permission.

with·in (with·IN) prep. & adv. to or into the interior; inside: Enquire within; Stay within the house; He remained within call, reach, sight; Try to live within your income or within your means; Return within three days; The school is within a mile of home; Good deeds make you feel good within (= inwardly); a plot to destroy the party **from within** (= from the inside); We haven't had a snowfall like this **within living memory** (= that people still living can recall); *Any demands* **within reason** (= reasonable demands) *will be met.*

with·it *adj. Slang.* up-to-date or modish; hip: *He tries to cultivate a with-it image.*

with·out (with·OUT) *prep. & adv.* **1** lacking; not having: *to go without food and water; He is used to* **going** or **doing without;** *She left without saying good-bye; She is* **without question** (= without doubt) *quite honest; She'll be back* **without fail** (= surely). **2** outside of something: *Guards stood without the palace entrance; The house is well decorated within and without; The house looks new* **from without** (= from the outside).

with·stand (with·STAND) *v.* **-stands, -stood, -stand·ing** stand against; oppose or resist successfully: *to withstand an attack, a Canadian winter, challenges, cold conditions; to withstand the rigours of a long journey; a claim that can withstand scrutiny.*

wit·less (WIT·lis) *adj.* lacking wit or sense; foolish: *a witless observation.*

wit·ness (WIT·nis) *n.* **1** a person who sees something happen and can say so under oath; eyewitness: *the witness of an accident; a witness to the accident; a witness for the prosecution; As a third-party witness, he had attested the deed signed by the two in his presence; The witness took the oath* or was *sworn in; The witness testified (under oath) and then stepped down; The defence couldn't produce one competent, credible, expert, reliable witness; to cross-examine, examine, hear, interrogate, interview, lead, question, swear in, trap a witness; a character, defence, expert, hostile, key, material, prosecution witness.* **2** testimony as given by a witness in court; evidence: *He perjured himself by giving false witness; to* **bear witness** (= give evidence) *against someone.* **3 Witness** a member of the Christian sect called "Jehovah's Witnesses."
— *adj.:* *to go into the* **witness box** *(from where evidence is given in a law court); to take the* **witness stand** *in someone's defence; to put someone on the witness stand.*
— *v.* **1** be a witness of something: *those who witnessed the accident; She witnessed his signing (of the deed).* **2** testify to something: *actions witnessing a guilty mind; Martyrs witness their faith; a properly witnessed* (= attested) *will; He's an obviously rich fellow,* **witness** (= as shown by) *the solid-gold faucets in his home.*

-wit·ted *combining form.* having intelligence as specified: *dim-witted, dull-witted, half-witted, quick-witted, slow-witted.*

wit·ti·cism (WIT·uh·siz·um) *n.* a witty remark.

wit·ting·ly (WIT·ing·lee) *adv.* knowingly or intentionally.

wit·ty *adj.* **wit·ti·er, wit·ti·est** having or showing wit; amusing: *a witty retort, speaker.* — **wit·ti·ly** *adv.*

wiz·ard (WIZ·urd) *n.* **1** a magician or sorcerer. **2** *Informal.* one highly gifted in or skilled *at* an activity: *a financial wizard; a wizard at electronics.*

wiz·ard·ry (WIZ·urd·ree) *n.* magic or sorcery: *by sheer wizardry.*

wiz·ened (WIZ·und) *adj.* withered; shrivelled: *a wizened face; The illness left him a wizened shell of a man.*

wob·ble (WOB·ul) *v.* **wob·bles, wob·bled, wob·bling** **1** to shake from side to side in an unstable manner, as a

table on uneven legs. **2** walk or move unsteadily. **3** waver or vacillate. — *n.* a wobbling movement.

wob·bly (WOB·lee) *adj.* **wob·bli·er, wob·bli·est** shaky or unsteady: *a wobbly table; The wobbly cease-fire never held.*

woe (WOH) *n.* **1** misery or grief of a desperate nature: *a heart full of woe; tales of woe and misery.* **2** a cause of such grief: *poverty, war, and other woes of humanity.*
— *interj.:* *Woe (be) to you! Woe is me* (= Alas)! *Woe betide you* (= You will be punished) *should you fail to deliver!*

woe·be·gone (WOE·bi·gon) *adj.* miserable or dismal in appearance: *a woebegone look.*

woe·ful *adj.* **1** full of woe; wretched: *a woeful expression.* **2** deplorable: *his woeful ignorance; the most woeful washout imaginable; what woeful neglect!*
— **woe·ful·ly** *adv.;* **woe·ful·ness** *n.*

wok *n.* a bowl-shaped pan used in Chinese cooking.

woke, woken See WAKE.

wolf (WOOLF, short "OO") *n.* **wolves** (WOOLVZ) **1** a doglike wild animal with short, upright ears and a long, bushy tail, that hunts game, often in packs: *a pack of howling wolves.* **2** one who is greedy or rapacious. **3** *Slang.* a sexually aggressive male.
— **cry wolf** give a false alarm, like the boy in a fable by Aesop.
— **keep the wolf from the door** keep from starving.
— **wolf in sheep's clothing** one who appears good but has evil intentions.
— *v.* eat greedily: *He wolves down his food.*
— **wolf·ish** *adj.*

wolf whistle *n.* a whistle with a rising-and-falling note given in admiration of a person, performance, etc.

wol·ve·rine (wool·vuh·REEN) *n.* a ferocious, destructive hunting animal of northern regions that resembles a bear and has dark, shaggy hair.

wolves *pl.* of WOLF.

wom·an (WOOM·un, short "OO") *n., pl.* **wom·en** (WIM·un) **1** an adult female human being: *a woman of action, of letters, of refinement, of the world; She received an award as woman of the year; the influx of women into the labour force; an anchor woman; a career woman; a woman who is divorced, married; working women.* **2** the female human being characterized by qualities such as attractiveness to the opposite sex, gentleness, motherliness, etc.: *Women and*

*children (come) first; "O, thou fairest among women";
an attractive, beautiful, grown, handsome, lovely, plain,
single, young woman; a virtuous woman; furious "like a
woman scorned"; the **other woman** (= mistress) in his
life; He was much devoted to **wine, women, and song**
(= a life of pleasure).* **3** feminine nature or qualities;
womanliness: *She is all woman.* **4** women collectively;
womankind: *the place of the modern woman in a male-
dominated society; job discrimination against women
and minorities; The Soviets have a "Women's Day"
corresponding to our "Mother's Day."* **5** a female servant
or attendant: *a queen surrounded by her women; a
cleaning woman; the woman who does the cooking.*
— **adj.**: *a woman doctor* (= female doctor; also,
Informal for gynecologist); *a woman engineer, friend,
priest; woman suffrage* (= women's right to vote); *a
woman worker.*

wom·an·hood (WOOM·un·hood, short "OO") *n.* **1** the
state of being a woman: *when you reach womanhood as
an adult; The job is a challenge to your womanhood*
(= qualities as a woman). **2** women as a group;
womankind: *Equal pay legislation is a challenge to
womanhood; She's a fine example of modern
womanhood.*

wom·an·ish (WOOM·un·ish) *adj.* **1** like a woman.
2 effeminate.

wom·an·ize (WOOM·un·ize) *v.* **-iz·es, -ized, -iz·ing**
Informal. philander.

wom·an·kind (WOOM·un·kind) *n.* women in general.

wom·an·like (WOOM·un·like) *adj.* womanly.

wom·an·ly (WOOM·un·lee) *adj.* being or having the
qualities suitable and becoming in a mature woman: *her
womanly dignity; womanly compassion, modesty.*
— **wom·an·li·ness** *n.*

woman of the world *n.* a woman sophisticated and
experienced in dealing with problems and issues outside
the home.

womb (WOOM) *n.* **1** the uterus. **2** a place of
development or generation: *events in the womb of time.*

women *pl.* of WOMAN.

wom·en·folk (WIM·un·folk) *n.pl. Informal.*
womankind; also **wom·en·folks.**

women's lib *n. Informal.* women's liberation.

women's lib·ber (-lib·ur) *n. Informal.* feminist.

women's liberation *n.* the movement for establishing
women's rights on an equal footing with those of men;
feminism.

won *pt. & pp.* of WIN.

won·der (WUN·dur) *n.* **1** a feeling of surprise and
astonishment aroused by something great or unusual: *to
gaze in wide-eyed wonder.* **2** a person or thing
considered as marvellous: *The pyramids of Egypt are
one of the seven wonders of the ancient world; It's a
wonder* (= miracle) *he survived the crash; a drug that
does or **works wonders** for your system; He was wearing
a seatbelt – **no wonder** (that) he survived; (It's no) **small
wonder** he survived!*
— *v.* **1** feel wonder: *We wonder at or about the marvels
of nature.* **2** be curious about something: *I wonder who*

*he is, what he wants, why he's here, if or whether he's
hungry.*

wonder drug *n.* a drug such as an antibiotic that works
quickly and effectively against disease.

won·der·ful (WUN·dur·ful) *adj.* **1** marvellous or
astonishing: *a wonderful place to visit.* **2** *Informal.*
excellent or admirable: *She's wonderful!*
— **won·der·ful·ly** *adv.*

won·der·land (WUN·dur·land) *n.* **1** a land of wonders,
as in fairy tales. **2** a place of great beauty or tourist
interest: *The Galapagos Islands are a natural
wonderland; Our province is a scenic wonderland; a
winter wonderland; the wonderland of Calgary's
prehistoric park.*

won·der·ment (WUN·dur·munt) *n.* **1** astonishment or
amazement. **2** a thing of wonder.

won·drous (WUN·drus) [literary or old use] *adj.*
wonderful: *He hath done wondrous things.*
— *adv.* wonderfully: *He was wondrous fair, good,
happy, sad.* — **won·drous·ly** *adv.*

wonk·y (WONK·ey) *adj. Slang.* cockeyed: *Fine print
makes her eyes go wonky.*

won't (WOHNT) will not.

wont (WOHNT, WAWNT) *adj.* accustomed: *She was
wont to rise early.*
— *n.* habit or usual practice: *She rose early, as was her
wont.*

wont·ed *adj.* customary; usual; habitual: *in his wonted
style.*

won ton (both "o's" as in "on") *n.* **1** a Chinese dish of
meat-filled noodle casings. **2** a soup containing won ton;
also **won-ton soup.**

woo *v.* **woos, wooed** (WOOD, long "OO"), **woo·ing**
1 court or seek to marry a person. **2** seek to win: *to woo
fame, success, voters, wealth; He spent his life wooing
fortune but ended up a pauper; A store tries to woo
customers away from the competition; The competition
tries to woo them back; to woo over voters to one's side.*

wood (short "oo") *n.* **1** the hard fibrous substance
beneath the bark of a tree or shrub: *to chop, cut, gather
wood; kindling wood; a cord of wood.* **2** lumber or
timber: *hewers of wood and drawers of water.* **3** esp.
woods *pl.* a thick growth of trees, usually smaller than a
forest: *a trail through the woods; There's a thick woods
on the other side of our fence; "The earth [has] its
dower of river, wood, and vale."* **4** something made of
wood, as a cask, golf club, or woodcut.
— **out of the woods** *Informal.* out of a dangerous or
difficult situation.
— *adj.* **1** of wood: *a wood chair; wood chips; wood
carvings, engravings; Cord is a wood measure; wood
pulp, saw, tissue; wood turning* (= shaping wood on a
lathe). **2** found or growing in woods: *a wood duck, rat;
wood sugar* (made from "wood tissue"); *wood trail,
warbler.*

wood·chuck *n.* a squirrel that hibernates in its burrow
in the winter; groundhog.

wood·craft *n.* **1** skill in hunting, trapping, etc. required
for living in the woods. **2** woodworking skill.

wood·cut *n.* **1** an engraving made on a block of wood to print from. **2** a picture or design so printed.

wood·ed (WOOD·id) *adj.* covered with trees: *a wooded area, hill, park, ravine, valley; a house set in a wooded lot.*

wood·en (WOOD·un) *adj.* **1** made of wood: *a wooden chair, figure, horse, leg, shoe.* **2** stiff like wood: *a wooden dialogue, smile; wooden (= clumsy) gestures; a wooden (= lifeless) and insensitive expression.*

wood·en·ware (WOOD·un·wair) *n.* salad bowls, spoons, etc. of wood.

wood·land (WOOD·lund, -land) *n.* land covered with woods; *adj.*: *woodland caribou; the Woodland culture of eastern North America dating from 1000 B.C.; woodland scenery.*

wood·lot *n.* a small area of forest maintained for firewood, timber, etc.

wood·note *n.* the call of a bird in the woods.

wood nymph *n.* a mythical nymph of the forest.

wood·peck·er (WOOD·peck·ur) *n.* a bird noted for its habit of climbing tree trunks, often perching crosswise, and drumming on them with its beak and making holes to search for insects.

wood·pile *n.* a pile of lengths of firewood.

wood·shed *n.* **1** a shed for storing firewood. **2** a place for administering discipline.

woods·man (WOODZ·mun) *n.* **-men 1** one who lives or works in the woods, as a lumberman. **2** one skilled in hunting, trapping, etc.

Wood·stock *n.* a rock-music festival of North American youth held in 1969 in Woodstock, New York: *the Woodstock generation (of believers in love and peace).*

woods·y (WOOD·zee) *adj.* **wood·si·er, -si·est** of or like the woods; sylvan: *a woodsy smell; woodsy surroundings.* **woods·i·ness** *n.*

wood·wind *n.* a wind instrument such as the flute, clarinet, and saxophone, originally made of wood.

wood·work *n.* **1** things made of wood, esp. stairs, doors, mouldings, etc. inside a house. **2** **the woodwork** *Informal.* hiding place: *Drug pushers just disappear into the woodwork.*

wood·work·ing (WOOD·wurk·ing) *n.* the craft of making things from wood, including carpentry, wood carving, etc.

wood·y (WOOD·ee) *adj.* **wood·i·er, -i·est 1** tree-covered; wooded: *a woody hillside, lot, valley.* **2** forming or consisting of wood: *a plant's woody parts; a woody stem, tissue.* **3** like or suggesting wood: *a woody flavour, smell, taste, turnip, vegetable.* **wood·i·ness** *n.*

woo·er (WOO·ur) *n.* one who wooes.

woof (short or long "oo") *n.* same as WEFT.

woof·er (WOOF·ur, short "oo") *n.* a loudspeaker reproducing low-pitched sounds in a hi-fi system.

wool (short "oo") *n.* **1** the soft, warm, curly hair covering the body of sheep, llamas, etc. **2** anything that resembles or feels like wool, as "steel wool." **3** yarn, cloth, or clothing of wool: *pure virgin wool.*

— **pull the wool over someone's eyes** hide the facts from someone: *When politicians try to pull the wool over the public's eyes, voters will eventually recognize the yarn.*

wool·gath·er·ing (WOOL·gath·ur·ing) *n.* daydreaming.

wool·len or **wool·en** (WOOL·un) *adj.* **1** made of wool: *Woollen fabrics are generally softer and bulkier than worsteds.* **2** relating to woollen products: *woollen manufacture.* — *n.* **1** cloth made of wool. **2 woollens** *pl.* woollen fabrics or clothes.

wool·ly (WOOL·ee) *adj.* **wool·li·er, wool·li·est 1** like, consisting of, or covered with wool: *the woolly coat of sheep; woolly clouds; the **woolly bear** caterpillar of the "tiger moth."* **2** indistinct, confused, or hazy: *woolly notions, thinking.* **3** barbarous: *the wild and woolly West.* — *n.* usually **wool·lies** *pl. Informal.* a garment of wool, esp. underwear.
Also **wool·y, wool·i·er, wool·i·est; wool·ies.**

wooz·y (long or short "oo") *adj.* **wooz·i·er, -i·est** *Informal.* dizzy or weak; befuddled: *I'm feeling just a touch woozy; He swayed and staggered while woozy from the anesthetic.* — **wooz·i·ness** *n.*

word (WURD) *n.* **1** a spoken or written unit of language that conveys a meaning and consists of speech sounds: *"The," "of," "and," "a," and "to" are the five most frequent words of English; a coined word like "Kodak"; The reporter tried not to distort their words or quote them out of context; a word that is hard to pronounce; to say, utter, write a word; angry, choice, cross, fighting, harsh, hasty, heated, hollow, hot, sincere words; a four-letter word (= obscenity) that is taboo in polite society; a nonce word like "nowhereness"; a guide word given at the top of this page; a **portmanteau word** like "motel" made up of "motor" and "hotel"; In a word (= briefly), he's lazy; She didn't say he's lazy **in so many words** (= exactly like that); Do you always have to **take the words out of my mouth** (= say exactly what I was going to say)? The essay has been copied **word for word** (= in exactly the same words) from a book.* **2** a unit of information in a computer memory. **3** [used in the sing. without "the"] a message or news: *Any word of the missing child? Someone had to pass word on to her or she wouldn't have learned about it; The boss called and left word that he would be late; **Send word to** (= Inform) his parents.* **4** a talk, esp. a brief one: *May I have a word with you? a word of advice; They had words (= a quarrel or argument).* **5** what is spoken or written as an order, promise, secret code, etc.: *His word is law around here; Give the word (= password) to the sentry; The teacher is in a bad mood – pass the word along; She'll keep her word (= promise); She'll be **as good as her word** (= will keep her promise); He is a **man of his word** (= man who keeps his promise); He has seldom had to **eat his words** (= take back what he said); Neither does he **mince words** (= avoid telling the truth directly and pointedly); You can always **take him at his word** (= depend on what he says).*
— **my word! upon my word!** [expressions of surprise].
— **the last word** See LAST WORD.
— **the Word** the Bible.
— *v.* express in words; phrase: *The memo was strongly*

worded; a politely worded request.

word·age (WUR·dij) *n.* **1** number or quantity of words. **2** verbosity. **3** wording.

word·book (WURD·book) *n.* a word list or dictionary.

wording *n.* the way something is worded; phrasing.

word of honour *n.* a solemn promise.

word of mouth *n.* spoken words: *The news spread by word of mouth before it got into the papers.* — *adj.:* *word-of-mouth* (= oral) *advertising.*

word·play *n.* a play on words, as in punning; verbal wit or repartee, as in "Her model husband came unglued."

word processing *n.* **1** secretarial and editorial work using a computer program. **2** such a program. — **word processor** *n.*

word·y *adj.* **word·i·er, -i·est** using too many words; verbose. — **word·i·ness** *n.*

wore *pt.* of WEAR.

work (WURK) *n.* **1** effort or exertion required to do or produce something: *Digging is hard work; Writing a book is intellectual work; She has been at work on her third novel for a month now; backbreaking, demanding, dirty, easy, good, light, physical, shoddy, slipshod, sloppy, superior work; He didn't do a stroke of work all week; community work; social work; undercover work; to* **go to work on** (= put pressure on) *someone.* **2** employment or occupation, esp. outside the home: *He goes to work; He begins work at 9 a.m. and quits or stops work at 5 p.m.; Sometimes he* **takes time off work** *when he has a dental appointment; He'll be returning to work after the holidays; He is looking for work now that he is* **out of work** (= unemployed); *Please phone me at work* (= the place of employment). **3 works** *pl.* factory: *iron works; gas works.* **4 works** *pl.* the operating parts of a clock. **5** something being worked on or in the process of being produced: *Take your work home; A vise has jaws for holding work.* **6** a product or result of work: *Artists hang their work in art galleries; They exhibit their work; A novel is a literary work; a scholarly work; the collected works of Milton; the complete works of Keats; his published works; Shakespeare's selected works; statues, paintings, poems, and such* **works of art;** *Faith without (good)* **works** *is dead;* **works of mercy** (= charitable acts). **7** operations and structures: *a public works department in charge of highways, dams, bridges, buildings, etc.* **8 the works** *pl. Slang.* everything possible, necessary, available, etc., often **the whole works:** *She ordered a hamburger with the works* (= with ketchup, mustard, tomato slice, onion, pickle, etc.); *Loan sharks threatened to give him the works* (= to use extreme measures) *if he told the police; This Christmas we are having a tree, gifts, carols, turkey dinner, the works.* — **in the works** in preparation. — **make short work of** finish a task, meal, etc. quickly. — *adj.* used at or in work: *the work habit; work clothes, routines, songs; work elephants, horses.* — *combining form:* clockwork, needlework, nightwork. — *v.* **works,** *pt. & pp.* **worked** or **wrought** (RAWT), **work·ing 1** do physical or mental work, esp. outside the home: *She works five days a week; works for a bank; She works occasionally for a charity; Her husband works*

around the house; Students work at their lessons; Some work their way through college; an author working on his book; He's working against the clock (= with a deadline in mind). **2** function or operate as planned, designed, etc.: *a good idea, but will it work? The gadget doesn't work.* **3** cause to work or function: *to work the gears on the machinery; She works herself to death; He worked his head off writing the essay.* **4** get or produce by working: *a drug that works wonders; The storm worked havoc.* **5** control or manage: *Sales representatives work their territories.* **6** get into or cause to get into a new condition gradually: *A screw sometimes works loose; She worked her way up the corporate ladder; worked her way up to the top.* **7** make or shape clay, dough, etc. by kneading, mixing, etc. **8** move or cause to move in an agitated way: *Yeast is used to work beer; You could see his features working with emotion.*
— **work off** get rid of a debt, bad feelings, etc. by working, doing something, etc.
— **work on** or **upon 1** influence or try to persuade someone. **2** continue with an attempt: *The picnic is still up in the air, but we are working on it.*
— **work out 1** solve or accomplish something by resolving difficulties: *to work out the details of a plan; to work out a problem.* **2** develop something: *to work out a new method.* **3** prove effective or successful: *Our plan didn't work out.* **4** have a workout: *Don't argue with him when he is working out.*
— **work up** produce by work or effort: *to work up an appetite for supper; to work up* (= excite) *enthusiasm, feelings; The orator had worked up the mob to a fever pitch before it went on the rampage; She doesn't get worked up* (= upset) *over or about little things; to work up steam; to work up a sweat; to work a business up* (= develop it) *from small beginnings.*

work·a·ble (WUR·kuh·bul) *adj.* that can be worked; hence, feasible or practicable. — **work·a·ble·ness** *n.*

work·a·day (WUR·kuh·day) *adj.* everyday; ordinary: *the workaday world.*

work·a·hol·ic (wur·kuh·HOL·ic) *n.* one who is addicted to the work habit, taking work home, spending weekends at work, etc.

work·bag *n.* a bag for holding working materials such as needlework.

work basket *n.* a basket for holding needlework.

work·bench *n.* a table at which mechanical work such as carpentry is done.

work·book *n.* **1** a book designed to be used with a textbook, containing questions, exercises, etc. **2** a workman's handbook.

work·box *n.* a box for tools and materials used in work.

work·day *n.* **1** the part of the day during which work is done. **2** a day of work, not a holiday.

work·er *n.* **1** one who works: *to dismiss, fire, hire, take on, train workers; Automation makes workers redundant; a blue-collar, efficient, full-time, hard, idle, immigrant, meticulous, migrant, office, part-time, skilled, white-collar worker.* **2** in a colony of ants, bees, wasps, etc., a sexually underdeveloped insect that does the work of providing food, defending the colony, etc.

work ethic *n.* the attitude or belief that work is ennobling: *Employers try to promote the protestant work ethic, but employees like to consider the quality of their working life and devote more time to volunteer work, cultural activities, etc.*

work farm *n.* a farm on which minor offenders serve their terms.

work force *n.* **1** the working part of a population: *A small percentage of the work force is usually unemployed.* **2** a group of workers.

work·horse *n.* **1** a horse that is used for work, as on a farm. **2** one that may be depended on to work hard and long: *Elephants are good workhorses.*

work·house *n.* a house of correction for petty criminals.

working *adj.* that works, is used in working, or is used for working with: *working capital (for running a business); the working classes of society; working clothes; a car in good working condition; the working (= rough) copy or draft of a document; Nine to five are the regular working hours; We have staggered working hours instead of a uniform schedule for everyone; a working hypothesis, model; a working knowledge of a foreign language (sufficient enough for practical purposes); The president holds working lunches to discuss policy; a working majority (sufficient for carrying on work); a working paper (for study and discussion); (a large enough) working sample.*
— *n.* operation or action, as of a machine: *the inner workings of a computer.*

work·ing·man (WUR·king·man) *n.* **-men** a manual or industrial worker. — **work·ing·wom·an** *n.* **-wom·en.**

work·load *n.* the amount of work that a worker has to do in a given period.

work·man (WURK·mun) *n.* **-men 1** a workingman. **2** a skilled craftsman.

work·man·like (WURK·mun·like) *adj.* skilful and satisfactory in execution: *a workmanlike job, performance, publication; The new building was completed on schedule in a workmanlike manner.*
— *adv.* skilfully; well.

work·man·ly (WURK·mun·lee) *adj. & adv.* workmanlike.

work·man·ship (WURK·mun·ship) *n.* the skill or quality of work seen in something finished; craftsmanship.

work·out *n.* **1** an exercise or series of exercises for maintaining physical fitness. **2** a test or trial of performance: *The team will have several workouts before players are eliminated.*

work permit *n.* a permit issued by the government to a nonresident to work temporarily in a country.

work·place *n.* a place where one works for pay: *According to Statistics Canada, a working adult spends less than 40 hours a week in the workplace compared to 50 hours in leisure activities; Workplaces have to be safe and healthy.*

work·sheet *n.* **1** a sheet of paper on which school exercises are to be done. **2** a sheet of paper serving as a work schedule or one on which something is worked out tentatively.

work·shop *n.* **1** an establishment where light manufacturing work is done. **2** a session at which ideas and methods of applying one's knowledge in some field are discussed.

work·sta·tion (WURK·stay·shun) *n.* **1** a work area for one person with equipment such as a computer terminal. **2** such a terminal.

work·ta·ble (WURK·tay·bul) *n.* a table for working at, having drawers, etc. for holding materials and implements.

work·up *n.* a complete diagnostic survey of a patient.

work·week *n.* the portion of a week spent in work: *Many would like a 30-hour, four-day workweek.*

world (WURLD) *n.* **1** the earth as our home: *a trip around the world; the nations of the world; the known world before Columbus's time; We have other worlds to conquer; the people of the Third World; Parents bring children into the world* (= into being). **2** people and their affairs: *a man of the world; Monks lead a life apart from the world; Is the end of the world near?* **3** any domain or sphere of activity: *the world of fashion, letters, the unknown; Do you believe in the next world* (= life after death)? *the world to come (after death); the academic, ancient, animal, financial, literary, medieval, modern, outside, real, scientific world.* **4** the universe; everything: *He looks for all the world* (= very much) *like a jogger* or *as if he's out for a jog; What in the world* (= whatever) *do you mean?* **5** a great deal: *That will do a world of good; You're asking for a world of trouble; There's a world of difference in our views; We're worlds apart* (= very far apart) *on this question.*
— **out of this world** *Informal.* extraordinary; excellent.

world-beater (WURLD·bee·tur) *n. Informal.* one that breaks previous records.

world-class *adj.* of the highest calibre or quality: *a world-class athlete, institution, scholar.*

world·ling *n.* one who is busy with secular or worldly pursuits.

world·ly *adj.* **-li·er, -li·est** of this world; not religious or otherwise: *worldly ambition, knowledge, pleasures, pursuits, wealth; He's too worldly-minded to become a priest.* — **world·li·ness** *n.*

worldly-wise (WURLD·lee·WIZE) *adj.* experienced in the ways of promoting one's worldly interests.

world war *n.* a war involving much of the world, as **World War I** (1914 - 18) or **World War II** (1939 - 45).

world·wide *adv.* throughout the world: *The book has been published worldwide.*
— *adj.* existing worldwide: *He enjoys a worldwide reputation.*

worm (WURM) *n.* **1** a small, slender, soft-bodied, legless, creeping or crawling animal such as an earthworm or a leech: *"The early bird catches the worm"* (= The earlier you are, the more successful you will be); *The worm may be turning – house prices seem to be coming down.* **2** a wormlike larva, mollusc, or other animal. **3** a small, contemptible person; wretch. **4** something wormlike in shape or movement, as the thread of a screw: *The worm of conscience gnawed at his soul.* **5** **worms** *pl.* infection of a body part, esp. the intestine, by parasitic worms.

— *v.* move like a worm or make one's way by creeping or crawling; insinuate: *The guerrillas wormed their way through the bushes; He wormed himself into a position of influence; He wormed (= got by indirect means) many secrets out of her confidantes.* — **worm·y** *adj.*

worm-eaten (WURM·ee·tun) *adj.* 1 burrowed into by worms, as wood. 2 antiquated or worn-out.

worm gear *n.* a gear for transmitting rotary motion, made up of a toothed wheel meshing at right angles with an endless screw on a shaft.

worm·hole *n.* a hole burrowed by a worm in timber, etc.

worm·wood *n.* 1 any of a group of bitter or aromatic plants. 2 something bitter or unpleasant.

worn *pp.* of WEAR.
— *adj.* exhausted or tired: *a face worn with care.*

worn-out *adj.* 1 used up by wear: *worn-out shoes.* 2 tired out: *She is worn-out after 12 hours on the job.*

wor·ri·er (WUR·ee·ur) *n.* one who worries.

wor·ri·ment (WUR·ee·munt) *n.* 1 the state of anxiety or worry. 2 a cause of it.

wor·ri·some (WUR·ee·sum) *n.* 1 causing worry: *Here's some news with worrisome implications; worrisome prospects; Housing costs are becoming as worrisome as soaring food prices.* 2 tending to worry: *Some moms are worrisome by nature.* — **wor·ri·some·ly** *adv.*

wor·ry (WUR·ee) *v.* **wor·ries, wor·ried, wor·ry·ing** bother or trouble physically or mentally in a harassing manner; be uneasy or anxious: *Cats and dogs like to worry their victims into submission; Children tend to worry their loose teeth with the tongue; She's not worried about her losing her job; Parents worry over their children; It worries them when their child is late for lunch; It worries them that she didn't do well in school; Most people worry (= manage to struggle) through life; He's **worried sick** (= very worried) about losing his job.* — **not to worry** don't worry.
— *n., pl.* **wor·ries** 1 trouble or anxiety. 2 a cause of it: *financial worries.*

worry beads *n.pl.* a string of beads that are fingered by a nervous person to avoid fidgeting.

wor·ry·wart (WUR·ee·wort) *n. Informal.* one who worries a lot.

worse (WURSE) *adj. comp.* of BAD & ILL: *His grammar is bad and spelling worse; He is worse than anyone else; I feel worse after taking the medicine.*
— *adv. comp.* of BADLY & ILL: *He was badly shaken by the accident, but others fared worse; They were **worse off**.*
— *n.: Things went from bad to worse; It was a change **for the worse**.*

wors·en (WUR·sun) *v.* make or become worse.

wor·ship (WUR·ship) *n.* 1 great reverence, as for a deity. 2 a religious service or rite: *a day set apart as a day of worship; hero worship; freedom of worship (= religion); the worship of (= extraordinary respect shown to) the almighty dollar.* 3 *Brit.* a title of respect for magistrates, mayors, etc.: *Your or His or Her Worship.*

— *v.* **-ships, -shipped** or **-shiped, -ship·ping** or **-ship·ing** 1 show great reverence, as to a divine being: *Let's worship God.* 2 love or admire very much: *I adore babies and worship mothers; Tony **worships the ground his mom walks on** (= has great love for her).* 3 attend religious services: *Where do you worship?*
— **wor·ship·per** or **wor·ship·er** *n.*

wor·ship·ful (WUR·ship·ful) *adj.* 1 *Brit.* a title of respect for certain officials: *Her Worshipful Mayor Hazel McCallion.* 2 [used in titles of guilds, lodges, etc.]: *the Worshipful Company of Goldsmiths.* 3 full of veneration: *her worshipful eyes.* — **wor·ship·ful·ly** *adv.*

worst (WURST) *adj. superl.* of BAD & ILL: *the worst winter in living memory; a **worst-case** scenario (= how it would be if the worst happened).*
— *adv. superl.* of BADLY and ILL: *She did worst in math.*
— *n.: The worst of the winter was in January, when things were **at their worst**; Be prepared for the worst; You will get only a small fine **at (the) worst**; **If the worst comes to the worst** or **If it comes to the worst** (= If things get too bad) hire a lawyer.*
— *v.* defeat: *"Never dreamed, though right were worsted, wrong would triumph."*

wor·sted (WURS·tid, WOOS-, short "OO") *n.* 1 a smooth, compact woollen fabric made of yarn from long fibres. 2 such a yarn or thread.

wort (WURT) *n.* 1 the mixture of grains and water before it is boiled and fermented into beer, ale, etc. 2 *combining form.* plant: *figwort, liverwort, milkwort.*

worth (WURTH, "TH" as in "thin") *n.* value, as because of intrinsic merit: *Trash is of no worth; a book of some worth; It's well worth the price; Customers want their money's worth; a dollar's worth (= quantity) of nuts; a person's net worth (= assets minus liabilities).*
— *adj.* [used like prep.] 1 having value estimated at an amount: *a painting worth millions; an heiress worth (= having property valued at) $1 billion; money that's not worth the paper it's printed on.* 2 deserving of something: *a book worth reading; not worth your while to complain; Is it worth the trouble?*

worth·while *adj.* worth the time or effort spent; of some value: *a worthwhile occupation, undertaking.*

wor·thy (WUR·thee, "th" as in "the") *adj.* **-thi·er, -thi·est** 1 having value or merit: *a worthy cause, charity.* 2 deserving of something: *a charity that is worthy of your consideration.*
— *n., pl.* **-thies** [sometimes ironical] a person of outstanding merit: *the worthies of City Hall.*
— **worth·i·ly** *adv.*

wot *v. pres.* tense of WIT.

would (WOOD, wud - short "OO") *pt.* of WILL, *v.* 5: *Gigi said she would hire him; She would if she could; They would (= used to) talk for hours about their work; Would (= I wish) that it were possible! if you would (= please) be so good as to lend me some money.*

would-be *adj.* wishing, intended, or pretending to be: *a would-be poet.*

would·n't (WOOD·unt, short "OO") would not.

wouldst (WOODST, short "OO") [old form] the form of WOULD used with "thou."

wound (WOOND, long "OO") *n.* **1** an injury to tissue below the skin: *to inflict a wound on* or *upon someone; to receive a wound; stitch up an open wound; a bullet wound; a gunshot wound; a festering, flesh, gaping, self-inflicted, superficial wound.* **2** injury to one's feelings or good name.
— **lick one's wounds** recover from an injury, loss, defeat, etc.
— *v.* **1** inflict a wound or wounds; hurt or injure: *Jan was fatally* or *mortally wounded in an accident.* **2** (WOWND) *pt. & pp.* of ¹WIND or a *pt. & pp.* of ²WIND, *v.* 3.

wove, woven See WEAVE.

wow *interj.* expressing surprise and admiration.
— *v. Slang.* overwhelm with delight; arouse enthusiasm in someone: *The new rock group wowed their audience.*
— *n. Slang.* **1** a great success; hit: *The singer was a wow in Toronto and New York.* **2** a slow rise and fall of pitch because of faulty sound reproduction: *wow and flutter.*

wrack (RAK) *n.* wreck or destruction, esp. **wrack and ruin;** also **rack and ruin.**
— *v.* torture: *wracked with pain.*

wraith (RAITH, "TH" as in "thin") *n.* an apparition of a dying or dead person; ghost: *The released captives looked like wraiths of their former selves.*

wran·gle (RANG·gul) *v.* **-gles, -gled, -gling 1** argue or quarrel noisily: *He wrangles with his neighbours; He wrangles about their dogs; The neighbours wrangle incessantly over each other's dogs.* **2** in Western Canada and the U.S., to herd or tend cattle, horses, etc. on the range.— *n.* an angry or noisy quarrel or dispute.
— **wran·gler** *n.*

wrap (RAP) *v.* **wraps,** *pt. & pp.* **wrapped** or **wrapt, wrap·ping** cover or enclose by winding or folding around: *paper for wrapping gifts; She wrapped herself in a blanket; He wrapped the shawl around his neck; He sat wrapped in thought; He's too much wrapped up* (=engrossed) *in his studies.*
— **wrap up 1** dress warmly. **2** *Informal.* conclude or settle: *Let's wrap it up and go home.*
— *n.* an outer covering, as a shawl, cloak, or coat: *a freezer wrap; plastic wrap; They kept their plans under wraps* (=secret) *till the last moment.*

wrap·a·round (RAP·uh·round) *n.* **1** a garment or other article shaped so as to curve around a body or follow a contour. **2** in word processing, the automatic shifting of a word that does not fit at the end of one line to the beginning of the next.
— *adj.:* *a wraparound robe, windshield; wraparound sunglasses; a room with a wraparound view; a word processing program with a word wraparound function.*

wrap·per (RAP·ur) *n.* **1** one that wraps, as a woman's dressing gown. **2** that in which something is wrapped, as the dust jacket of a book or the wrapping in which a magazine is mailed: *in a plain brown wrapper;* also **wrap·ping.**

wrap-up *n. Informal.* a summary that concludes a report, statement, etc.: *a wrap-up of the day's news.*

wrath (RATH, RAWTH – "TH" as in "thin") *n.* great anger, as attributed to God, that seeks to punish the wrong-doer: *to incur the wrath of the neighbours; to escape, face, meet, risk someone's wrath.*
— **wrath·ful** *adj.*

wreak (REEK) *v.* to cause or inflict havoc, damage, revenge, vengeance, etc. *on* someone, *among* a group, *in* a place or situation, *with* something, etc.

wreath (REETH, "TH" as in "thin") *n.* **wreaths** (REETHZ) a ring twisted of boughs, flowers, etc.: *to make, place, weave a wreath; a bridal wreath; a floral wreath; a wreath laid at the tomb of the Unknown Soldier; wreaths* (=curls) *of smoke.*

wreathe (REETH, "TH" as in "the") *v.* **wreathes, wreathed, wreath·ing 1** make into a wreath; encircle; adorn: *to wreathe flowers into a garland; happy faces wreathed in* (=covered with) *smiles.* **2** of smoke, etc., coil or circle; spiral upward, etc.

wreck (REK) *v.* ruin or destroy as by a crash or shattering blow: *His leg injury wrecked his chances in the race; a wrecking bar.*
— *n.* **1** a wrecking, being wrecked, or what remains after destruction, as a shipwreck: *Car wrecks are towed off after a highway crash; the total wreck of our hopes.* **2** one who has lost health or money: *He's a nervous wreck.*

wreck·age (REK·ij) *n.* a wrecking or its remains: *The wreckage of the aircraft littered the runway and was strewn over a wide area.*

wreck·er *n.* **1** one that wrecks, as one whose work is tearing down buildings: *Old buildings fall to the wrecker's ball.* **2** one that removes or salvages wrecks.

wrench (RENCH) *n.* **1** a sudden twisting or jerking movement, as sometimes causes back injury. **2** a distortion, as of meaning, or something painful: *Leaving home was a wrench.* **3** a tool for gripping and turning a nut or bolt: *a monkey wrench; pipe wrench; socket wrench.* — **throw a wrench** See THROW.
— *v.* pull with a twisting movement: *She wrenched her hand away from his grip; wrenched the gun out of his hand; He wrenched his ankle while playing tennis; words wrenched out of their context.*

wrest (REST) *v.* to force or wrench something, esp. from another's possession, sometimes with deftness or skill: *He wrested the gun from his attacker's hand; to wrest a living from the harsh environment; usurpers who wrested power from the prince.*
— *n.* a wresting or forcible twist.

wres·tle (RES·ul) *v.* **-tles, -tled, -tling 1** contend or grapple *with* an opponent in hand-to-hand combat, as in the sport of wrestling. **2** struggle *with* a task, problem, temptation, etc.
— *n.* a struggle. — **wres·tler** *n.*

wrestling (RES·ling) *n.* a sport in which two unarmed persons struggle hand to hand, each trying to throw the other to the ground: *arm wrestling; wrist wrestling.*

wretch (RECH) *n.* a miserable, unhappy, or despised person: *a poor wretch.*

wretch·ed (RECH·id) *adj.* utterly poor or miserable: *the*

wretched existence of people in refugee camps; wretched food, slums; He felt wretched when forsaken by friends.
— wretch·ed·ly *adv.;* wretch·ed·ness *n.*

wrig·gle (RIG·ul) *v.* **wrig·gles, wrig·gled, wrig·gling**
1 twist and turn, as a worm does; squirm. **2** move or make one's way by or as if by wriggling: *the wriggling eel; It wriggled away from her grasp; to **wriggle out of** (*=escape by devious means from) *a difficulty.*
— *n.* a wriggling.

wrig·gler (RIG·lur) *n.* the larva of a mosquito.
— **wrig·gly** *adj.*

-wright *combining form.* maker: *playwright, shipwright, wheelwright.*

wring (RING) *v.* **wrings, wrung, wring·ing 1** twist and squeeze with force: *to wring wet clothes; to wring out the water; to wring a bird's neck* (=kill it); *to wring* (=force) *a confession, the truth, a promise, etc. from someone; She wrung her hands (together) in despair; a sad tale that wrung* (=pained) *our hearts.* **2** clasp or squeeze someone's hands in congratulation or friendship. — *n.* a wringing.

wrin·kle (RINK·ul) *n.* **1** a small ridge or crease on a normally smooth surface: *wrinkles on the forehead; wrinkles on an aging skin; to iron the wrinkles out of a newly washed fabric; to press out wrinkles.* **2** a difficulty or problem to be ironed out, as in an agreement. **3** *Informal.* development; gimmick; device: *a new wrinkle in home entertainment; the latest wrinkle in women's fashions.*
— *v.* **-kles, -kled, -kling 1** get wrinkled, as fabrics do: *Synthetics don't wrinkle easily.* **2** make wrinkles in something; crease: *to wrinkle one's forehead, nose.*

wrin·kly *adj.* **-kli·er, -kli·est** wrinkled.

wrist (RIST) *n.* the joint that connects hand and forearm.
— **slap** or **tap on the wrist** *Informal.* a light punishment or rebuke.

wrist·watch *n.* a watch worn on a strap or bracelet about the wrist.

writ (RIT) *n.* something written, esp. a court order: *to file a writ in court; The court issued a writ ordering him to appear in court; to serve a writ on someone; Holy Writ* (=sacred scripture, esp. the Bible).
— *v.* [old use] a *pt. & pp.* of WRITE.

write (RITE) *v.* **writes,** *pt.* **wrote** or [old use] **writ,** *pp.* **writ·ten** (RIT·un) or [old use] **writ, writ·ing 1** make letters so as to form words, using a pen, pencil, etc.: *We learn to read and write; She writes legibly; a pencil that doesn't write well; Please print, don't write your name; Please **write down** what you hear.* **2** communicate by letter: *She writes (to) her parents every month; He thought it too trivial a matter **to write home about.***
3 produce a document, record, literary or artistic work, etc. by writing: *to write books, cheques, music, news reports, plays, stories, wills; to write for a living, for the stage, for the media.* **4** be evident or obvious: *Suspicion was written on his face; Suspicion was **writ large** (=clearly evident) *on his face.*
— **write in 1** add an unlisted candidate's name to a ballot. **2** vote for someone thus.
— **write off** cancel or forget a bad debt, loss, etc.,

depreciate capital expenditures, or ignore a person or thing as of no account.
— **write out** write fully or completely.
— **write up** write an account of a person or thing, as for publication: *His exploits have been written up in the tabloids.*

write-in *n.* a candidate written in by a voter.

write-off *n.* something written off as a loss: *corporate tax cuts through machinery write-offs.*

writ·er (RYE·tur) *n.* one who writes, esp. an author: *a free-lance writer; hack writer; screen writer.*

writer's cramp *n.* a muscle spasm of the hand, as may afflict one who writes for too long.

write-up *n. Informal.* a published report or account *of* a person, event, etc., usually favourable.

writhe (RITHE, "TH" as in "the") *v.* **writhes, writhed, writh·ing 1** twist or turn about: *to writhe in pain.*
2 suffer or squirm in embarrassment or under an insult.

writing (RYE·ting) *n.* **1** the act of one that writes: *the three R's of reading, writing, and arithmetic; Please put it in writing* (=written form); *legible writing; at this writing* (=at the time this is being written). **2** something written, esp. of literary value: *the writings of the ancients; the collected writings of E. J. Pratt; selected writings of Margaret Atwood.* **3** the activity of an author: *He makes a living by writing (as an occupation).*
— **the writing on the wall** signs of what is going to happen: *The writing on the wall was that the company was heading for bankruptcy.*
— *adj.* for writing with or on: *writing implements, materials, paper.*

written *pp.* of WRITE.

wrong (RONG) *adj.* **1** not right, esp. morally: *Cheating is wrong; It's wrong to cheat; I was wrong in doing so; I was wrong to do so.* **2** not just, correct, proper, presentable, desirable, etc.: *wrong spelling; The child came out with shoes on the wrong feet; I was driving the wrong way on a one-way street; There's something wrong with a car that won't start; What's wrong?*
— *n.* what is not right: *Infants don't know right from wrong; He had done much wrong as a dictator; "Two wrongs don't make a right"* (=You don't do one wrong to make up for another, as in taking vengeance); *to redress, right, undo a wrong; a grievous wrong; He soon realized that he was **in the wrong** (=at fault; deserving blame).*
— *adv.* [used after its verb] wrongly: *You guessed it wrong; You did it all wrong.*
— **get someone** or **something wrong** *Informal.* misunderstand: *Don't get me wrong.*
— **go wrong:** *Everything seems to go wrong* (=turn out badly) *on certain days; Where did we go wrong* (=make a mistake)? *Children may go wrong* (=become morally bad) *in bad company.*
— *v.* do wrong to someone; treat unjustly; harm or injure: *They wronged him by firing him without cause.*
— **wrong·do·er** (RONG·doo·ur) *n.*
— **wrong·do·ing** (·ing) *n.*

wrong·ful *adj.* unjust or unlawful: *a wrongful act, arrest, confinement, dismissal, imprisonment.*
— **wrong·ful·ly** *adv.;* **wrong·ful·ness** *n.*

wrong·head·ed (RONG·hed·id) *adj.* **1** stubborn or obstinate in a wrong opinion or judgment; perverse: *wrongheaded youths.* **2** mistaken: *a wrongheaded decision, idea, notion.*

wrong·ly *adv.* [used esp. before a pp.]: *She was wrongly accused; a wrongly spelled word; He was refused, whether rightly or wrongly.*

wrong·o (RONG·oh) *n.* **-os** or **-oes** *Slang.* a bad person or error: *That's a howling wrongo!*

wrote a *pt.* of WRITE.

wrought (RAWT) *v.* a *pt. & pp.* of WORK: *What hath God wrought! to get* **wrought up** (= excited) *over trifles.* — *adj.* formed or shaped, as metals by hammering: *wrought* (= manufactured) *silk.*

wrought iron *n.* iron that has been forged or rolled so as to make it more malleable, tougher, and more durable than cast iron.

wrought-up *adj.* very excited or agitated.

wrung *pt. & pp.* of WRING.

wry (RYE) *adj.* **wri·er, wri·est** twisted; distorted; contorted: *a wry face (showing disgust); wry* (= ironic) *humour; a wry mouth* (= grimace); *a wry smile (of disappointment).* — **wry·ly** *adv.;* **wry·ness** *n.*

wun·der·kind (VOON·dur·kint, short "OO") *n.* child prodigy: *the new wunderkind of Canadian ballet.*

wurst *n.* sausage meat: *Germany consumes several billion pounds of wurst each year.*

X or **x** (EX) *n.* **X's** or **x's 1** the 24th letter of the English alphabet. **2** something resembling an "X." **3** the Roman numeral for 10. **4** an unknown quantity or one whose identity is withheld. **5 X** *n.* a rating used for pornographic motion pictures to which only adults are admitted.
— *v.* **x-es** or **x's,** *pt. & pp.* **x-ed** or **x'd, x-ing** or **x'ing** cross *out* with an x or series of x's.

x-axis *n., pl.* **x-ax·es** (-ax·eez) the horizontal axis on a chart or graph.

xen·o·phobe (ZEN·uh·fobe) *n.* one who fears or hates foreigners.

xen·o·pho·bi·a (zen·uh·FOH·bee·uh) *n.* fear or hatred of foreigners. — **xen·o·pho·bic** (-FOH·bic, -FOB·ic) *adj.*

xer·ic (ZEER·ic) *adj.* deficient in moisture: *a xeric environment, habitat, plant.*

xe·rog·ra·phy (zuh·ROG·ruh·fee) *n.* a dry photographic printing process that uses electrically charged particles fused by heat. — **xe·ro·graph·ic** (zeer·uh·GRAF·ic) *adj.*

xe·rox (ZEER·ox) *v.* **-rox·es, -roxed, -rox·ing** make a photocopy of something: *Please xerox this for me; We are specialists in xeroxing; piles of xeroxed documents.*
— *n.* a photocopy: *A couple of xeroxes will do; A good xerox is preferred to a carbon copy;* **adj.:** *a xerox copy, machine, room.* — **Xerox** Trademark.

Xmas (CHRIS·mus) *n.* [short form] Christmas.

X-rated (EX·ray·tid) *adj.* **1** rated X; pornographic: *an X-rated movie; an X-rated show.* **2** *Informal.* obscene: *an X-rated joke; All X-rated expletives were deleted.*

X ray *n.* an electromagnetic ray of extremely short wavelength, capable of penetrating opaque substances, much used in medical diagnosis and treatment: *a chest X ray; He decided to have an X ray taken of his aching back.*

X-ray *v.* examine or treat with X rays.
— *adj.:* *X-ray astronomy, an X-ray emission, examination; an X-ray laser, photo, star, telescope, tube.*

xy·lo·phone (ZYE·luh·fone) *n.* a percussion instrument consisting of wooden bars that are struck with two small wooden hammers to sound the musical scale.
— **xy·lo·phon·ist** (-foh·nist) *n.*

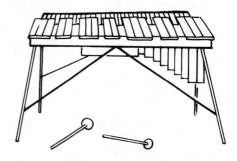

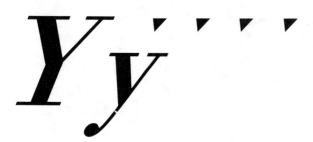

Y or **y** (WYE) *n.* **Y's** or **y's 1** the 25th letter of the English alphabet. **2** anything shaped like a "Y."
— **the Y** [short form] YMCA, YWCA, YMHA, YWHA, or a hostel run by any of them: *We are staying at the Y.*

yacht (YOT) *n.* a small ship used for cruising and racing: *He spends all his weekends on his yacht.*
— *v.* sail a yacht.

ya (YUH) *pron. & adj. Slang.* you or your: *How are ya? How's ya child?*

yachting *n.* the sport of sailing a yacht.

yack *n. & v. Slang.* same as YAK.

ya·hoo (YAH·hoo) *n.* a coarse or uncouth person, like the **Yahoos** of Jonathan Swift's "Gulliver's Travels."

Yah·we or **Yah·weh** (YAH·way) *n.* the Hebrew name of God; Jehovah; also **Yah·ve** or **Yah·veh.**

yak *n.* **1** a long-haired ox of Tibet and Central Asia. **2** *Slang.* idle, endless, or noisy chatter.
— *v.* **yaks, yakked, yak·king** *Slang: truck drivers yakking away on their CB radios.*

yam *n.* a variety of sweet potato.

yam·mer (YAM·ur) *n. & v. Informal.* **1** whimper or whine. **2** loud or voluble chatter: *He yammered away, but no one was listening.* — **yam·mer·er** *n.*

yang *n.* in Chinese thought, the masculine active force or principle of life and being, complementary to YIN.

yank *n. Informal.* a sudden hard jerk; tug.
— *v.* pull with a yank: *A yo-yo is yanked on a string; to yank* (= withdraw) *a child out of school in the middle of the year.*

Yank *n. Slang.* a Yankee, esp. an American soldier of World War I or II.

Yan·kee (YANK·ee) *n.* an American, originally one from New England or northern United States: *George Bush is a Connecticut Yankee from Texas; The room was patriotically decorated in Yankee Doodle red, white, and blue; The Blue Jays beat the (New York) Yankees in 1985.*
— *adj.* having to do with the Yankees: *the Yankee mystique; Yankee aggression, imperialism, industry; Charles Cretors's Yankee ingenuity is to blame for our taste for popcorn during movies.*

Yan·qui (YAHNG·kee) *n.* a U.S. American as distinguished from a Latin American.

yap *n. & v.* **yaps, yapped, yap·ping** *Slang.* bark; yelp; chatter: *What's he yapping about? Teachers don't like too much yapping in class.* — **yap·per** *n.*

yard *n.* **1** a unit of length equal to 3 feet (0.914 m): *Carpeting is usually sold by the square yard.* **2** a slender pole or spear fastened across a mast to support a sail. **3** a piece of ground, as around a house, church, or farm. **4** an enclosed area or pen for poultry, livestock, etc. **5** a place covered with railway tracks where cars are stored, switched, etc.

yard·age (YAR·dij) *n.* **1** length in yards. **2** an extent or distance covered in yards.

yard·arm *n.* either end of a yard supporting a square sail.

yard goods *n. pl.* textiles sold by the yard.

yard·man (YARD·mun) *n.* **-men** a man who works in a railway yard.

yard·mas·ter (YARD·mas·tur) *n.* a person in charge of a railway yard.

yard·stick *n.* **1** a graduated measuring stick one yard in length. **2** a standard of comparison: *We can't apply the same yardstick to children and adults; What yardstick do you use to measure intelligence? Is material prosperity the yardstick of human achievement?*

yarn *n.* **1** a fibre spun into strands for weaving or knitting: *a ball, hank, skein of yarn.* **2** *Informal.* a tall tale or story: *to spin a yarn.*

yar·row (YAIR·oh) *n.* a perennial herb with finely cut aromatic leaves and flat-topped clusters of small white, yellow, or pink flowers.

yaw *n.* a movement about a vertical axis, as when an airplane's nose turns right or left.
— *v.* of a ship, airplane, space vehicle, projectile, etc., turn right or left in its course.

yawl *n.* **1** a small, two-masted, fore-and-aft-rigged ship. **2** a dinghy or rowboat.

yawn *n.* an involuntary taking in of breath with wide-open mouth, usually because of fatigue: *a yawn of utter boredom; a loud yawn; to stifle* or *suppress a yawn; Algebra is a yawn* (= bore) *to Yves.*
— *v.* to open wide, as the mouth during a yawn: *The audience started yawning as the lecturer went on.*
— **yawning** *adj.* wide open: *a yawning gap, hole.*

ye [old form] **1** (YEE) *pron.* you. **2** (*popularly* *pronounced* YEE, *more correctly as* "the") same as THE: *"Ye Olde Candle Shoppe."*

yea (YAY) *adv.* yes; indeed.
— *n.* an affirmative vote or voter; aye: *There were 148 nays and 127 yeas in the 1987 Commons debate on the restoration of capital punishment in Canada.*

yeah (YAH) *adv. Informal.* yes: *Oh, yeah?* (= Is that so?).

year (YEER) *n.* 1 the period of about 365 days that the earth takes to go once around the sun; also called "solar year": *A tragedy like that will not happen in future years; in the years to come; He was sentenced to five years (in jail).* 2 an annual period such as a "calendar year" (January 1 through December 31 in the Gregorian calendar), the usually September-to-June "school *or* academic year," etc.: *Rome was founded in the year 753 B.C.; It happened in the year 1759; an election year; the fiscal year of a corporation; a jubilee year; a leap year; a taxation year running from May 1 to April 30; Who knows what will happen in the year 3000? Last year we had a bad year; a banner, good, lean, memorable, peak, profitable, record year.*
— **years** *pl.* 1 time of life: *the formative years of our childhood; children of tender years; the golden years of retirement.* 2 age: *Grandpa is rather advanced in years; I'm getting along in years.* 3 a long time: *I haven't seen him in years; Years from now, who will remember us?*
— **year after year** or **year in, year out** or **year in and year out** every year.

year·book *n.* an annual publication or reference book reporting on people and events of the preceding year, as of a graduating class, the supplements of an encyclopedia, etc.

year·ling (YEER·ling, YUR·ling) *n.* a one-year-old animal.
— *adj.* one-year-old: *a yearling calf, colt, seal.*

year·long *adj.* lasting through a year: *a yearlong absence, drought, strike, struggle.*

year·ly *adj. & adv.* once a year: *the earth's yearly revolution around the sun; a yearly* (= every year) *trip; She draws a yearly* (= annual) *salary of $100 000; It is paid monthly, not yearly* (= annually).

yearn (YURN) *v.* be filled with longing for someone or something that is missed or desired, pity for someone in trouble, or desire to do or get something: *She yearned to be reunited with her children; yearned for a visit to her homeland.*

yearning *n.* a tender longing: *The runaway expressed a yearning for the joys and comforts of home; an actor's yearning to play Shakespeare; Her yearning became an obsession.*

year-round *adj. & adv.* throughout the year, not seasonal or seasonally: *a year-round complaint; complaints heard year-round; year-round employment; a year-round publication, resort, school.*

yeast (YEEST) *n.* 1 a yellowish, frothy moist substance made up of fungi that cause dough to rise, sugars to ferment, etc., used in baking and brewing. 2 such a fungus. 3 a dried form of yeast sold in powder, granule, or cake form. 4 an agent causing agitation or unrest.

yeast·y (YEEST·ee) *adj.* **yeast·i·er, -i·est** 1 containing yeast. 2 frothy, light, or frivolous: *yeasty comments.* 3 agitated or restless: *a yeasty group, social situation.*

yech (YEK, YUK) *interj.* expressing disgust or rejection. Also **yecch.**

yell *n.* 1 a loud cry or shout expressing anger, fear, joy, etc.: *She let out* or *gave a blood-curdling yell.* 2 a cheer given in unison to encourage teams at school athletic events.
— *v.* utter or say with a yell: *He yelled something to her; He yelled to her to get out of the truck's way; He yelled himself hoarse; The mother yelled at her children; Please don't yell into my right ear.*

yel·low (YEL·oh) *n.* 1 the colour of gold, egg yolk, etc. 2 the yolk of an egg. 3 a yellow pigment, dye, cloth, clothes, etc.
— *adj.* 1 yellow-coloured, as paper by age. 2 *Informal.* cowardly. 3 sensational and vulgar: *yellow journalism.*
— *v.* make or become yellow. — **yel·low·ish** *adj.*

yellow pages *n. pl.* a telephone directory or a section of it, usually printed on yellow paper, containing classified listings and advertisements of businesses, professions, services, etc. Also **Yellow Pages.**

yelp *n.* a short, sharp cry or bark, as of a dog.
— *v.* utter or say with a yelp.

yen *n.* 1 *pl.* **yen** the basic money unit of Japan. 2 a strong desire or urge: *She had a yen to sail around the world; a yen for the sailor's life.*

yeo·man (YOH·mun) *n.* **-men** 1 a petty officer of the U.S. Navy with clerical duties. 2 formerly, a servant in a royal household. 3 a member of a group of small landowners and farmers of medieval England, noted for their patriotism. — **yeo·man·ly** *adj. & adv.*

yeoman of the guard *n.* a ceremonial bodyguard of the British sovereign.

yeo·man·ry (YOH·mun·ree) *n.* yeomen collectively.

yeoman service or **yeoman's service** *n.* good and faithful service.

yep *adv. Slang.* yeah; yes.

yes *adv.* [expressing agreement, confirmation, etc.] aye; yea: *Yes, dinner's ready; Is that you? Yes; She's willing, and yes* (= and what is more), *eager to help.*
— *n., pl.* **yes·es** or **yes·ses** an affirmative reply.

yes-man *n.* **-men** *Informal.* one who agrees with or accepts everything superiors say.

yester- *combining form.* [old use] of yesterday: *yestereve, yestermorn, yesternight, yesteryear.*

yes·ter·day (YES·tur·dee, -day) *n. & adv.* 1 the day before today. 2 the recent past: *our heroes of yesterday; She was not born yesterday; a yesterday's man* (= a man, esp. a politician, whose career is finished).

yes·ter·year (YES·tur·yeer) *n.* the recent past: *Where are the "hot pants" of yesteryear? rock'n'roll favourites from yesteryear; in the yesteryears when more of us could read and write.*

yet *adv.* 1 [in negative and doubtful contexts] up to the specified or implied time: *It's not yet time (to go to bed); She had not yet arrived at midnight; Isn't she*

home yet? Is she home yet? **2** [in affirmative contexts, sometimes with intensive force] still: *She's waiting yet; while there is yet time; This makes things yet more difficult; He may make it yet* (= eventually; someday). **3** nevertheless; however: *strange, yet true.*
— **as yet** up to now: *She hasn't appeared as yet.*
— **conj.**: *It's a strange story, yet it is true.*

Ye·ti (YET·ee) *n.* same as ABOMINABLE SNOWMAN.

yew (YOO) *n.* an evergreen tree or shrub with rich, dark-green leaves and scarlet, berrylike seeds.

yield (YEELD) *v.* **1** give, as from within, in response to one's efforts or by cultivation: *The land yields crops; Trees yield fruit; Mines yield ore; Investments yield profits; ten-year bonds yielding 11%; Nature has been yielding up her secrets in response to our search for knowledge.* **2** give in, give up, give way, etc. *to someone as by right, by persuasion, entreaty, or force of circumstances: Vehicles have to yield right of way to pedestrians at pedestrian crossings; He graciously yielded the floor* (= the right to speak) *to his critic; But he refused to yield* (= grant) *the point (of the argument); She refused to yield* (= submit) *to the blackmailer; wouldn't yield to his demands; It was a question of yielding to temptation or resisting; She yields to no one* (= is as good as anyone) *in her devotion to hockey; an addiction that yields* (= responds) *to treatment;* **3** give way to physical pressure and bend or break.
— **n.** amount or quantity yielded: *This year's yield of wheat has been good; a high yield per hectare; the yields on our stocks; the current yield of your investment.*

yielding *adj.* **1** submissive: *He's very yielding to his superiors.* **2** flexible: *the yielding softness of a carpeted floor.*

yin *n.* in Chinese thought, the female, passive force or principle of life and being, complementary to YANG.

yip *n. & v.* **yips, yipped, yip·ping** *Informal.* yelp.

yip·pee (YIP·ee) *interj.* expressing great joy.
— **n.** *Slang.* a member of a radical group of hippies, the "Youth International Party."

yo·del (YOH·dul) *v.* **-dels, -delled** or **-deled, -del·ling** or **-del·ing** sing with abrupt changes from the normal tone to a high falsetto and back, as practised by the mountain peoples of the Alps.
— **n.** such singing.— **yo·del·ler** or **yo·del·er** *n.*

yo·ga (YOH·guh) *n.* a Hindu school of thought or a system of self-discipline developed by it consisting of physical exercises, control of the senses, and meditation for purifying one's soul: *to practise yoga.*

yo·gi (YOH·ghee) *n.* **-gis** one who practises yoga; also **yo·gin.**

yo·gurt or **yo·ghurt** (YOH·gurt) *n.* a semisolid acid food made by fermenting milk.

yoke *n.* **1** a wooden frame to which a pair of draft animals are harnessed: *to put a yoke on oxen; two yoke* (= pairs) *of oxen.* **2** a yokelike frame fitted to the shoulders of a person carrying a load at either end. **3** bondage or servitude: *to cast* or *throw off the yoke of slavery; India was under a foreign yoke for two centuries; Romania was under the yoke of a dictator.* **4** anything like a yoke in form or function, as the

shoulder-piece of a shirt, blouse, etc., the waist-piece of a skirt supporting gathered parts, or the wheel by which an airplane pilot controls ailerons and elevator. **5** a coupling, clamp, or tie: *the yoke of matrimony.*
— **v.** **yokes, yoked, yok·ing 1** couple with or as with a yoke; join together. **2** harness an animal to a plough, etc.: *to yoke oxen to a cart.*

yo·kel (YOH·kul) *n.* a bumpkin.

yolk (YOKE) *n.* the yellow, inner part of an egg which serves as nourishment for the embryo, or the corresponding part of an ovum or egg cell in mammals.
— **yolked** *adj.*

yon *adj. & adv.* [old use] yonder: *a boat tossed thither and yon by the waves.*

yon·der (YON·dur) *adj.* [literary use] **1** over there, usually within sight: *in yonder hills.* **2** more distant; farther: *the yonder side of the mountains.*
— **adv.**: *Look yonder* (= over there)!

yoo hoo *interj.* used to call attention: *Yoo hoo! Is anybody home?*

yore *n.* time long past: *in days of yore.*
— **adv.** [old use] long ago.

York boat *n. Cdn.* an open-decked freight boat used in the fur trade during the 19th century.

you (YOO) *pron. sing. & pl.* **1** the person or persons spoken to: *How are you, Gigi? How are you boys today?* **2** any person; one: *You feel lost in a jungle; You never know.*

you'd (YOOD, long "OO") you had; you would.

you'll (YOOL) you will; you shall.

young (YUNG) *adj.* **young·er** (YUNG·gur), **young·est** (YUNG·gist) in an early period of one's life; not old: *a young lady; too young to drive; in the morning when the day is still young; How are you, young man? old in years but young* (= not experienced) *in the business; He's 75 years old but young at heart; quite young in spirit and in health; books for the young adult* (= teenager); *a young offender* (= juvenile delinquent).
— **n.** **1** young offspring: *Mammals bring forth their young; a cow that is with young* (= pregnant). **2** young persons: *books for the young; an appeal to young and old* (= everyone).

young blood *n.* **1** young people. **2** youthful energy, vigour, etc.: *a new hiring policy aimed at bringing young blood into the company.*

young·ling *n. & adj.* (one) that is young.

young·ster (YUNG·stur) *n.* **1** a child. **2** a young person.

youn·ker (YUNK·ur) *n.* [rare] a young fellow.

your (YOOR, YOR) *adj.* possessive case of YOU: *your children, country;* [suggesting familiarity] *your average customer;* [in titles] *Your Honour, Lordship, Majesty.*

you're (YOOR) you are.

yours (YOORZ, YORZ) *pron.* **1** one or ones belonging to you: *This book is yours; my books and yours; his, hers, and yours; a book of yours.* **2** [used in complimentary close of letter, before signature]: *Yours sincerely; Sincerely yours;* [informal close] *Yours.*

your·self (yoor·SELF) *pron.* **-selves** (-SELVZ) reflexive or emphatic of YOU(R): *Help yourself; Be yourself; You are old enough to walk by yourself; (You) do it yourself; You don't seem to be yourself* (= as well as usual) *today.*

yours truly *n.* [complimentary phrase used before the signature in business letters] *Informal.* I; me: *Yours truly had to leave; With the compliments of yours truly.*

youth (YOOTH, "TH" as in "thin") *n.* **youths** (YOOTHZ, YOOTHS) **1** the fact, quality, or period of being young, esp. the period between childhood and adulthood: *the vigour of youth; in her youth; in the prime of youth; the promises, thoughtlessness, wantonness of youth; the folly of our youth.* **2** a young person, esp. a male: *a group of youths loitering in the mall.* **3** *pl.* young people: *The youth of the nation are* or *is ready to act.*

youth·ful *adj.* young, esp. having to do with a young person's qualities: *youthful audiences, enthusiasm, pranks, vigour.* — **youth·ful·ly** *adv.;* **youth·ful·ness** *n.*

youth hostel *n.* See HOSTEL.

you've (YOOV, long "OO") you have.

yowl (rhyme: "owl") *n.* a loud, long, complaining cry or howl, as of a dog in pain. — *v.* utter a yowl.

yo-yo (YOH·yoh) *n.* **-yos 1** a toy consisting of a spool with a string wound around it whose free end is held in the hand and manipulated so as to make the spool rise and fall by the unwinding and rewinding of the string. **2** *Slang.* a stupid or gullible person: *The workers were mere yo-yos in the hands of their union leader.* — *adj.* going back and forth or up and down; fluctuating: *the yo-yo phenomenon of weight loss followed by weight gain; the yo-yo syndrome of old people going in and out of hospital with one illness after another.* — *v.* fluctuate; vacillate.

yuk·ky or **yuck·y** (YUCK·ee) *adj.* **yuk·ki·er** or **yuck·i·er, yuk·ki·est** or **yuck·i·est** [child's word] bad-tasting.

Yu·kon·er (YOO·kon·ur) *n.* a person of or from the Yukon Territory.

yule or **Yule** (YOOL, long "OO") *n.* Christmas.

yule log *n.* a large log traditionally used to start the Chrismas Eve fire.

yule·tide or **Yule·tide** *n.* Christmastide: *yuletide greetings.*

yum·my (YUM·ee) *adj.* **yum·mi·er, yum·mi·est** *Informal.* very tasty, delicious, or delightful.

yup *adv. Slang.* yep; yes.

yup·pie (YUP·ee) *n.* a "young urban professional" as a member of a high-spending, trendy social group.

yurt (YOORT) *n.* a domed, tentlike dwelling of Central Asian nomads.

Z or **z** (ZED, ZEE) *n.* **Z's** or **z's** the last letter of the English alphabet.

za·ny (ZAY·nee) *n.* **-nies 1** a clown or buffoon. **2** a silly person.
— *adj.* **-ni·er, -ni·est 1** like a zany; funny. **2** silly or crazy: *a zany scheme.* — **za·ni·ly** *adv.*; **za·ni·ness** *n.*

zap *v.* **zaps, zapped, zap·ping** *Slang.* **1** strike or kill with a sudden blow: *Nonsmokers don't like to get zapped by smoke in airplanes; the idea of using energy rays to zap nuclear missiles; to zap* or *zap out* (= wipe out) *commercials on the TV or video cassette recorder.* **2** zoom or zip.
— *n.* zip; pep; vigour.
— *interj.* expressing swiftness of action, sudden surprise, etc.

zeal (ZEEL) *n.* enthusiastic devotion to a cause and untiring activity in pursuing it: *a missionary's zeal for the salvation of souls; ardent, fervent, excessive, religious zeal; to show* or *display zeal for a cause; In his zeal to outdo his rivals, he overstepped the bounds of discretion.*

zeal·ot (ZEL·ut) *n.* one who is zealous in a fanatic or partisan way: *a religious zealot.*

zeal·ous (ZEL·us) *adj.* full of or characterized by zeal: *zealous efforts, workers; zealous for reform; zealous about* or *in preaching the gospel.*
— **zeal·ous·ly** *adv.*; **zeal·ous·ness** *n.*

ze·bra (ZEE·bruh) *n.* a horselike wild animal of Africa with black and white stripes.

zed *n.* same as zee, the letter Z.

Zeit·geist (ZITE·guyst) *n.* the intellectual and moral climate of an era; the prevailing spirit of the times.

Zen *n.* the Japanese form of Buddhism that stresses enlightenment through intuition.

ze·nith (ZEE·nith) *n.* **1** the point of the sky directly overhead. **2** the highest point: *the zenith of one's career, fortunes, power.*

zeph·yr (ZEF·ur) *n.* **1** a soft breeze; light wind. **2** a yarn, fabric, or garment of soft or light material.

ze·ro (ZEER·oh) *n.* **-ros** or **-roes 1** naught or nothing. **2** the cypher or symbol 0 used to represent it. **3** the beginning or lowest point on a graduated scale, as 0 degree Celsius.
— *adj.* having zero value: *zero gravity; the zero hour.*
— *v.* **-roes, -roed, -ro·ing** adjust to zero point: *to zero in a rifle (at centre of target).*
— **zero in on 1** aim directly at a target, as by adjusting the sights of a firearm: *The armoured division has its artillery zeroed in on the downtown area.* **2** focus on something: *The speaker zeroed in on the premier's credibility.*

zero-base budgeting or **zero-based budgeting** *n.* reassessing of every expenditure from the beginning instead of dealing only with proposed increases.

zero hour *n.* **1** preset time for starting an operation, as when a countdown reaches zero. **2** crucial or critical point. **3** in the SI system, the start of a calendar day: *The day starts at **zero hours** (written 00 h), commuters get up by 06 h, lunch breaks are usually from 12 h to 13 h, and commuters are usually back home by 19 h.*

zero-zero (ZEER·oh·ZEER·oh) *adj.* of weather conditions, with visibility reduced to nil horizontally and vertically.

zest *n.* **1** keen enjoyment; relish; gusto: *He eats with zest; She has lost her zest for life since her husband's death.* **2** a stimulating quality: *Lemon gratings add zest to a dish.* — **zest·ful** *adj.*; **zest·ful·ly** *adv.*
— **zest·ful·ness** *n.*

Zeus (ZOOSE) *n.* the supreme god in ancient Greek mythology.

zig·zag *n.* **1** a series of short, sharp turns from one side to the other. **2** a design or line in a zigzag.
— *adj.* having zigzag form, as "forked" lightning.

— *v.* -zags, -zagged, -zag·ging form or move in a zigzag.

zilch *n. Slang.* zero; nil.

zil·lion (ZIL·yun) *n. Informal.* a very large number: *The odds against finding ancient treasures on the ocean floor are a zillion to one.* — **zil·lionth** (ZIL·yunth) *adj.*

zinc *n.* a bluish-white, rust-resistant metallic element used in alloys and for galvanizing iron and steel.

zing *n. Slang.* **1** a sharp, shrill sound, as of bullets whistling past. **2** liveliness; zest; vigour: *The play lacked zing; The zing has gone out of our aging bureaucracy.* — *v.* make or move with a zing: *a reporter noted for zinging hostile questions at world leaders.*

zing·er *n. Slang.* a punch line or witty retort.

zing·y *adj. Slang.* **zing·i·er**, **-i·est** full of vigour and zest: *The air was alive and zingy; We were watching the zingiest show in town.*

Zi·on·ism (ZYE·uh·niz·um) *n.* the Jewish national movement starting in 1897 that resulted in the establishment of Israel in 1948 and which continues to provide worldwide support for Israel. — **Zi·on·ist** *n. & adj.*

zip *n.* **1** *Informal.* brisk energy; vim; zing: *Can't you put a little more zip into your work?* **2** a zinging sound. **3** *Slang.* zero or a zero score.
— *v.* **zips**, **zipped**, **zip·ping 1** proceed with zip or vigour: *A cleaning crew zips over and wipes graffiti off city property; She zips back and forth between Ottawa and Toronto on her new job; We zip through commercials on the video cassette recorder using the "fast forward" button.* **2** make a zinging sound. **3** work a zipper to fasten something, free someone, etc.: *The dress zips up at the back; Please zip me up; And zip me out later.*

zip code or **Zip Code** *n.* a five-digit number identifying a U.S. postal delivery area, often supplemented by four extra numbers for faster sorting of mail.

Zip gun *n.* an improvised pistol for firing .22 calibre cartridges.

zip·per (ZIP·ur) *n.* a fastener consisting of two interlocking rows of teeth: *to do up a zipper; to undo or unzip a zipper; The zipper got stuck.*
— **zip·pered** *adj.*: *a zippered, not buttoned up, ski jacket.*

zip·py (ZIP·ee) *adj.* **zip·pi·er**, **zip·pi·est** *Informal.* full of energy; brisk; snappy: *There's no zippy sure-fire answer to your problems.*

zo·di·ac (ZOH·dee·ac) *n.* a circular diagram of 12 symbols, or signs, used in astrology to represent portions of the year, from "Aries" (ram) to "Pisces" (fish): *the 12 signs of the zodiac; Money-making is not in my zodiac; I'm a Libra, what's your zodiac sign?*

zom·bie (ZOM·bee) *n.* **-bies 1** in voodoo belief, a corpse reanimated by a supernatural power. **2** this power or spell. **3** *Informal.* a person who behaves as though he is in a trance, dead to the life around him: *The cultists had made a zombie out of their son; a mindless zombie; a citizenry of intellectual zombies; The subway passengers just sat and watched like zombies while the*

assault went on.

zon·al (ZOH·nul) *adj.* having to do with or divided into zones; zoned. — **zon·al·ly** *adv.*

zone *n.* **1** an area or region divided in the form of a belt or band: *the Torrid, Temperate, and Frigid zones of the earth; a time zone.* **2** an area having a special characteristic or restricted use or purpose: *a buffer zone* (= neutal area) *separating two warring nations; a combat zone; a danger zone; the demilitarized* (= neutral) *zone between North and South Korea; a no-parking, postal, residential, towaway zone.*
— *v.* **zones**, **zoned**, **zon·ing** form or divide into zones: *A city is zoned into commercial, residential, and industrial districts; land zoned (as) agricultural; land zoned for agricultural use; agriculturally zoned land; zoning bylaws, permits, restrictions, violations.*

zonk *v. Slang.* stupefy, as by drink: *to be zonked on drugs; He seems completely zonked out; The company was zonked by publicity.*

zoo *n.* **zoos** a place where wild animals are kept for display.

zo·o·log·i·cal (zoh·uh·LOJ·uh·cul) *adj.* having to do with animal life: *The Metro Zoological Society; a zoological garden* (= zoo).

zo·ol·o·gy (zoh·OL·uh·jee) *n.* the scientific study of animals and their relationship to other living things. — **zo·ol·o·gist** *n.*

zoom *v.* **1** move or cause to move with a hum, buzz, or whoosh: *The birds zoomed toward the plaza; The Mirage jet zoomed up and out of sight.* **2** climb upward suddenly: *Her tennis ranking has zoomed from 100 to 10 in a year; Gas prices zoomed after the Arab oil embargo of 1973; The economy didn't zoom for another 10 years.* **3** focus a camera using a zoom lens: *a TV picture that zooms from an entire football field to the helmet of one of the players; The camera zoomed in on the star of the show.*
— *n.* a zooming in on a scene: *There's a zoom telescope at the top of the tower.*
— *interj.* expressing quickness: *Zoom! She was an instant celebrity.*

zoom lens or **zoom·er** *n.* a photographic device for taking quick close-up shots without the need to adjust the focus.

Zou·ave (zoo·AHV) *n.* **1** originally, a member of a French military regiment made up of Algerians wearing a colourful uniform and drilling in a quick, spirited style. **2** a member of any regiment adopting this kind of uniform and drill, as during the U.S. Civil War.

zounds (ZOWNDZ) *interj.* [old use] a mild oath.

zow·ie or **zow·ee** (ZOW·ee, "OW" as in "how") *interj.* expressing enthusiasm, approval, etc.: *Free enterprise is what has made Canada go zowie.*

zuc·chi·ni (zoo·KEE·nee) *n.* a summer squash resembling cucumber.

Zu·lu (ZOO·loo) *n.* a member of a South African people or their language: *a Zulu chief.*

zym- or **zymo-** *combining form.* leavening: *zymase, zymology, zymosis.*

zy·mase (ZYE·mace) *n.* an enzyme present in yeast.

zy·mol·o·gy (zye·MOL·uh·jee) *n.* the science of fermentation.

zy·mo·sis (zye·MOH·sis) *n.* fermentation.

zy·mur·gy (ZYE·mur·jee) *n.* the chemistry of fermentation processes, as in brewing and wine-making.

ZZZ or **zzz** a representation of the sleeping state.